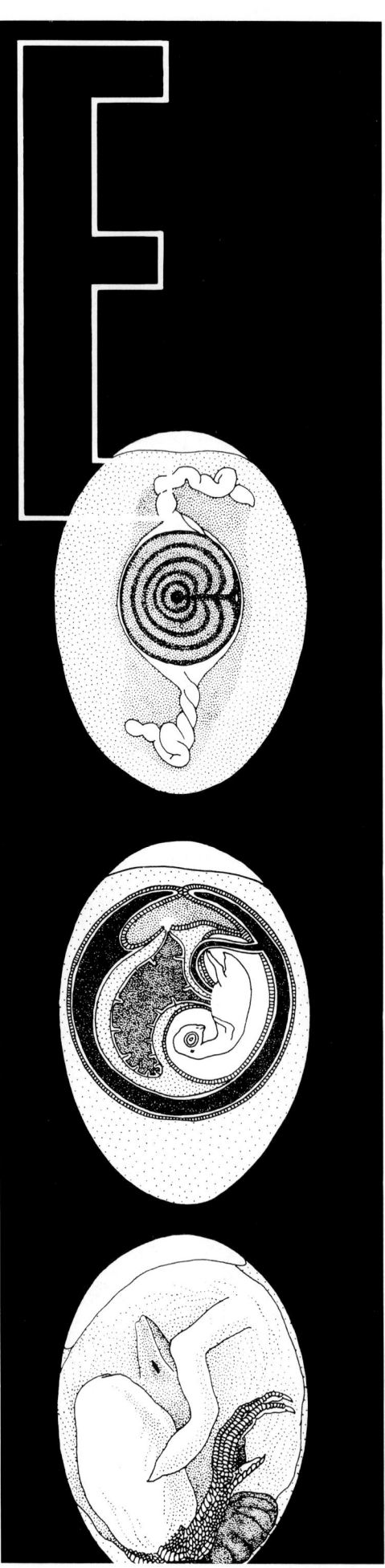

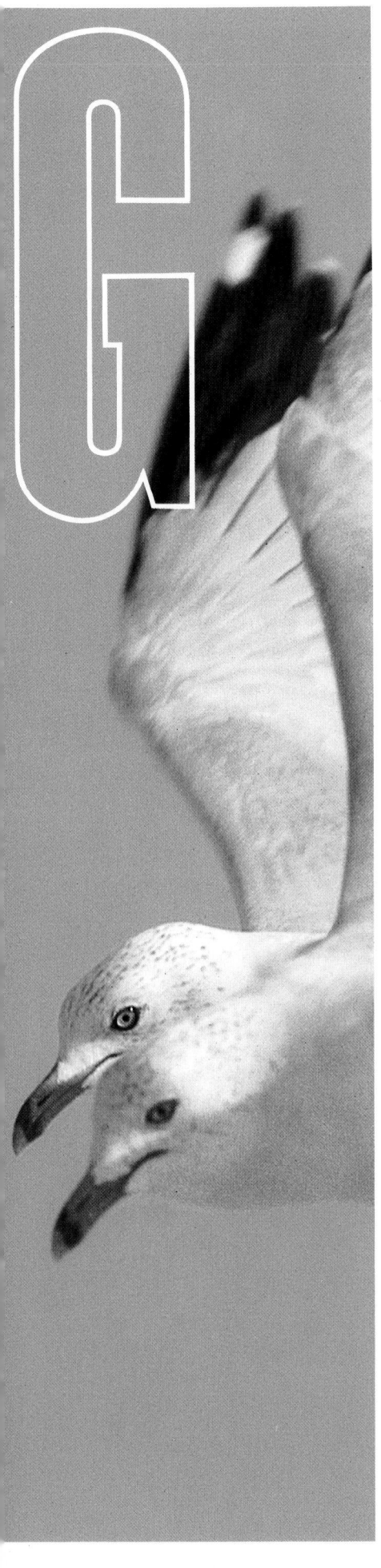

The Audubon Society ENCYCLOPEDIA OF NORTH AMERICAN BIRDS

by John K. Terres

With a foreword by Dean Amadon,
Lamont Curator Emeritus of Birds,
American Museum of Natural History

WINGS BOOKS
NEW YORK
AVENEL, NEW JERSEY

Copyright 1956, 1963, 1974, 1979, 1980 by Alfred A. Knopf, Inc. All rights reserved.

This 1995 edition is published by Wings Books, distributed by Random House Value Publishing, Inc., 40 Engelhard Avenue, Avenel, New Jersey 07001, by arrangement with Alfred A. Knopf, Inc.

Printed and bound in the United States of America

Library of Congress Cataloging-in-Publication Data

Terres, John K.
   The Audubon Society encyclopedia of North American birds/by John K. Terres; with a foreword by Dean Amadon.
      p. cm.
   Includes biographical references and index.

   1. Birds—North America—Encyclopedias. 2. Ornithology—Encyclopedias. I. National Audubon Society. II. Title.
QL681.T43 1991   91-21877
598.297—dc20   CIP
ISBN 0-517-03288-0
12 11 10 9 8 7 6 5 4

CONTENTS

THE NATIONAL AUDUBON SOCIETY

The National Audubon Society is among the oldest and largest private conservation organizations in the world. With 550,000-plus members and over 500 local chapters across the country, the Society works in behalf of our natural heritage through environmental education and conservation action and research. It protects wildlife in more than 70 sanctuaries from coast to coast. It also operates outdoor education centers, ecology workshops, and publishes the prize-winning *Audubon* magazine, *American Birds* magazine, newsletters, films, and other educational materials. For information regarding membership in the Society, write to the National Audubon Society, 950 Third Avenue, New York, New York 10022.

In December 1960, when John Terres resigned his twelve-year editorship of *Audubon* magazine, he told me that he was planning to produce this encyclopedia. I was aware of the gigantic scope of such a project, but then, so was he. Both of us knew that the materials for an encyclopedia of North American birds would have to be extracted from thousands of scientific papers that had been published in journals and technical books in America—some during the latter part of the last century, but most of them during this one.

According to Joel C. Welty, in the preface to his 1975 edition of *The Life of Birds*, in 1864 there were only 2 serial publications devoted exclusively to birds. Today, wrote Welty, there are 250, besides the hundreds of other journals that publish articles about animal behavior, ecology, evolution, physiology, wildlife management, and many other specialized sciences, most of which include some papers about birds—a massive output, which represents more than 570 journals worldwide that publish an average of 4,000 ornithological papers a year, not to mention the many books about birds.

I supposed that John would write some of the articles for his encyclopedia but, as editor, would delegate most of the writing and research to a staff of contributors. He told me that he had given this method considerable thought, but had decided against it. In truth, he said, the contributors would be the many ornithologists who had already published their research, which he would draw upon and cite in his text and bibliography. He hoped that I would not think him lacking in humility, but he, himself, wanted to make a compendium of these research achievements and write them in a nontechnical form that would permit anyone fascinated by birds to benefit from these scientific studies. And he felt that the writing of the entire book by one person would assure it a uniformity of presentation and writing style that would not be possible with a diversity of authors.

At the time, John Terres was certainly no newcomer to nature writing or to translating scientific papers into pleasantly readable prose. He had written articles about birds and other animals, and nature and wildlife conservation in general, for a score of magazines and had written a book about bird-attracting, *Songbirds in Your Garden*, that has become one of the most popular in its field. A lifetime of highly varied field experiences with birds, and his faithful attention to keeping notes and records of his observations for more than thirty years, had helped prepare John for his great undertaking. He had also worked ten years as a field biologist for the U.S. government, specializing in the study of food habits of birds and applied ecology in the wildlife field. Then he had served twelve years as editor of *Audubon* magazine during the critical period of its evolution from the journal *Bird-Lore* to the more broadly oriented *Audubon*.

During these years, John's correspondence and acquaintance with great figures in ornithology and entomology, botany, mammalogy, herpetology, and other natural sciences were extensive and continuous. He was fortunate in having such men as Alexander Wetmore, Secretary of the Smithsonian Institution, W. L. McAtee, a distinguished government biologist, and Francis Harper, a naturalist and scholar of the old school, as his close friends, mentors, and advisors.

When John Terres left *Audubon*, he moved to Chapel Hill, North Carolina. There, while working in the seclusion of a cottage near a 600-acre, semi-wild farm that had become a veritable wildlife reserve, he also had access to the libraries and scholarly facilities of three universities. With him, John took the patience and diligence of the scholar, the vision of this encyclopedia, and the capacity for hard work that the task demanded.

To sustain his devotion to that vision, John Terres knew that he needed an occasional diversion: between long periods of work on the encyclopedia, he took time off to write several other books. One, *From Laurel Hill to Siler's Bog: The Walking Adventures of a Naturalist*, was based upon field observations from his daily walks on the North Carolina farm. It was a proud moment for me at the April 1971 annual meeting of the John Burroughs Memorial Association in New York City, when I presented him with the John Burroughs Medal, awarded by the Association for his distinguished nature writing in this and in others of his books.

While at Chapel Hill, he also wrote the popular and successful *Flashing Wings: The Drama of Bird Flight; Discovery: Great Moments in the Lives of Outstanding Naturalists*, and a revised second edition of *Songbirds in Your Garden*. He also served as editor-in-chief of the twelve-volume *Audubon Nature Encyclopedia* and editor of a thirty-two—volume series of *Living World Books*. But day in and day out, for two decades, his prime task was the writing and research for his encyclopedia of North American birds.

This massive achievement speaks for itself, but perhaps I should say something about the reader-consultor who will enjoy it and profit from its thousands of entries. According to a news release of the U.S. Bureau of Sports Fisheries and Wildlife of 1970, a survey by the Bureau of Outdoor Recreation reported there were at that time more than seven million birders in the U.S., of which, according to an estimate by the Cornell Laboratory of Ornithology, at least three million are seriously interested in the field study of birds.

It is for these millions of birders that this encyclopedia has been written—for those who go outside with binoculars and field guides to identify and list birds, those who enjoy birds by attracting them to the garden, and those who conduct serious scientific studies of birds in the field and laboratory. For I believe that there are few specialists who cannot learn from this vast compendium of up-to-date information about birds. A professional critic who read the manuscript of the encyclopedia in advance of its publication remarked: "I feel as though I have had a cram course (in ornithology)...and feel as prepared for a doctoral exam as I have ever been in my life, on any subject from bird conservation to bird physiology."

This is a fine testimonial to the usefulness of this book for anyone wishing to study it systematically for its ornithology. However, most people will read it at random, with enjoyment of the articles and even with some excitement over much of the subject matter. Anyone browsing through the encyclopedia will be greatly impressed with the scope of its coverage. Nothing, it seems, has been omitted that would be of particular interest to readers, and many subjects have been included that most of us in making such a compilation would have overlooked.

I think I have said enough in this foreword to indicate that I consider John K. Terres's *Audubon Society Encyclopedia of North American Birds* to be one of the outstanding ornithological publications of this or any other time.

Dean Amadon, Lamont Curator Emeritus of Birds, Former Chairman, Department of Ornithology, American Museum of Natural History, New York, New York

ACKNOWLEDGMENTS

I want to make my initial acknowledgments to people whose support I could not have done without. First, I owe a major debt of gratitude to Dr. Dean Amadon, Lamont Curator Emeritus of Birds, American Museum of Natural History, who read and commented upon at least a dozen major articles, some of which I rewrote at his suggestion, and who wrote the foreword to this book; to Eugene Eisenmann, Dr. Wesley Lanyon, John Bull, the late Dr. James P. Chapin and his wife, Ruth Chapin, to Charles O'Brien, and Helen Hays and Mary Lecroy of the Department of Ornithology of the American Museum of Natural History; and to Dr. John C. Pallister of the Department of Entomology for his comments on my articles about the parasites of birds. I thank former librarian Hazel Gay and especially Mildred Bobrovich, Sylvia Diaz, and Paula Perry of the Museum Library Staff for their always gracious cooperation; Dr. Austin L. Rand, Chicago Natural History Museum, for many favors; Dr. Oliver L. Austin, Jr., Florida State Museum, for his constant support and for reading and commenting so helpfully on the migration article. I owe warm thanks to Edwin Way Teale and to Roger Tory Peterson for their kind and helpful suggestions; to Roland C. Clement, Andrew Bihun, Robert Boardman, Robert Arbib, and Susan R. Drennan of the National Audubon Society, all of whom gave me their assistance, encouragement, and support. My special thanks to Les D. Line, Editor of *Audubon*, for his many significant contributions to this encyclopedia. The late Dr. Alexander Wetmore, former Secretary of the Smithsonian Institution, was a great source of inspiration and help in encouraging me throughout the writing of this book and in reading critically the articles on fossil birds and the geological time scale.

I also thank Leon Kelso, Washington, D.C., and Dr. John W. Aldrich, U.S. Fish and Wildlife Service, U.S. Department of the Interior, and especially the late Dr. W. L. McAtee of Chapel Hill, N.C., for many favors; to Dr. Ralph S. Palmer, New York State Museum; and to Dr. Richard H. Pough of New York. Members of the staff of the Laboratory of Ornithology at Cornell University were enormously helpful: the late Dr. Arthur A. Allen and Dr. Elsa Guerdrum Allen, and my friend of many years, Dr. Olin S. Pettingill, Jr., former Director of the Laboratory; my thanks to Dr. William C. Dilger and Dr. Tom J. Cade; also to Dr. William T. Keeton and Dr. Stephen T. Emlen of the Department of Animal Behavior, Cornell University, who were especially helpful with the orientation of birds. I am grateful to Helen Lapham of the Laboratory and her associates there, for suggesting additional useful information and for reading, correcting, and updating the text.

Dr. Douglas A. Lancaster, former Executive Director of the Laboratory of Ornithology at Cornell University, not only suggested specialists in ornithology who were agreeable to reading parts of my manuscript but in the last year worked closely with me on the final manuscript.

My special thanks go to Dr. Charles S. Sibley, Yale University, and I will always be grateful for the kindnesses shown me by the late Dr. Alden H. Miller, University of California at Berkeley, and the late Loye S. Miller.

The following specialists gave me enormous help in reading and commenting on ornithological and related subjects: Dr. Richard C. Banks and Dr. Libero Ajello; Doctors Peter Klopfer, Peter Marler, Nicholas E. Collias, Andrew Meyerriecks, Richard Andrew, John T. Emlen, Lawrence H. Walkinshaw, and George J. Wallace, and the late Margaret Morse Nice; Doctors David W. Johnston, George M. Junkel, and Allen J. Duvall; Doctors Daniel McKinley, Kenneth C. Parkes, Robert Cushman Murphy, and Walter P. Taylor; James Greenway, Donald S. Heintzelman, and Mrs. Charles Smith; John B. Belknap, Henry M. Stevenson, and the late Hobart Van Dusen; Doctors Kenneth P. Able, Frank Bellrose, Sidney Gauthreaux, Jr., S. Dillon Ripley, and Charles E. Jenner; Doctors Charles S. Kendeigh, Herbert H. Friedmann, James P. McGrath, and Paul D. Sturkie; Mrs. Bradley Fisk, T. A. Beckett, III, H. Lewis Batts, Jr., and the late T. Donald Carter, Robert and Elizabeth Teulings, and Dr. William G. Conway, Lee S. Crandall, and Eloise F. Potter; Doctors Heinz Meng, Paul H. Oehser, Robert M. Stabler, E. W. Jameson, Jr., and Alva G. Nye, Jr.; Doctors James L. Gulledge, Donald Borror, and Peter B. Hofslund; Jim Brett and Al Nagy; Dr. Rolf Hartung, the late Robert P. Allen, Harold S. Peters, the late George Dock, Jr., Steve Price, Morlan W. Nelson, Michael Kochert, and Sanford R. Wilbur; Doctors Harold Norton Johnson,

Daniel O. Trainer, Daniel L. Leedy, R. L. Burkhart, and Robert M. Mengel; C. Jerry Wallace, Ray C. Erickson, and Peter Borchelt; Doctors David W. Norton, Warren J. Iliff, and Lawrence Kilham; librarians Edwina Johnson and Florence Blakely, Duke University; librarians Monica de la Salle, the late Nancy Turel, and her assistants Michelle Epstein and Barbara Linton of the National Audubon Society.

At Alfred A. Knopf, my thanks especially to my editor, Angus Cameron, whose help, wise counsel, and constant encouragement have been one of my greatest sources of strength; to his assistant editor, Barbara Bristol, my deepest gratitude for her help and unfailing good cheer and sound advice on problems I shared with her; to the production editing staff headed by Lesley Krauss; to Nancy Clements, production editor; to Peter Mollman, director of production; and to Anthony M. Schulte, executive vice-president, for his direction of the entire project.

I also want to thank Chanticleer Press for their part in producing the book: my gratitude especially to Paul Steiner and Gudrun Buettner for their encouragement; John Farrand, Jr., formerly with the American Museum of Natural History, for his expert guidance with the text and illustrations; Susan Rayfield and Ann Whitman for assembling the photographs, commissioning the artwork, and providing many valuable text suggestions; and Carol Nehring and Lisbeth Budd, who supervised the layout of the book.

My deepest thanks also to those hundreds of authors cited in the bibliography of this book. Without their published researches and observations, and often their stimulating personal letters to me, this book would not have been possible. However, I take full responsibility for all material in the encyclopedia, and any errors that appear in it are my own.

I owe an enormous debt of gratitude to Alice Berea. She was my loyal personal secretary through the final writing and editorial work on this book. I can never repay her for her patience and optimism that carried me through two of the most difficult years of my life.

An especially warm salute to my agent, George F. Scheer. Throughout the years of our involvement with the encyclopedia, he has given me the constant support of a close friend and of a wise and understanding counselor.

And always my gratitude and love to my late wife, Marion Coles Terres, who shared the loneliness of our separation during my years of absence for field work and those long, long hours I spent in research and note-taking in my study.

Les D. Line
Editor, *Audubon* magazine

Susan Rayfield
Senior Editor, Chanticleer Press

Lester L. Short
Chairman and Curator, Department of Ornithology, American Museum of Natural History

Alexander Sprunt, IV
Research Director, National Audubon Society

Robert W. Storer
Curator of Birds, Museum of Zoology; Professor of Biological Sciences, University of Michigan

Glenn E. Walsberg
Assistant Professor of Zoology, Arizona State University

INTRODUCTION

This encyclopedia is a modest attempt to make the fruits of the science of ornithology available to the millions of North Americans who are interested in birds. The popular interest in birds among Americans is as old as our country, older in fact, and even since twenty-one years ago, when the idea of providing an encyclopedia first occurred to me, it has grown enormously. One can scarcely drive a mile in city, suburb, or country without seeing a bird feeder in a backyard or garden that attests, in part, to this widespread involvement of people in the lives and welfare of birds.

And yet, curiously, there is no one-volume book that makes available—from A to Z—some of the vast knowledge that generations of scientists have accumulated about these charming, animated, colorful creatures that touch, illuminate, and influence the lives of so many of us. This lack first came to me forcefully during the twelve years that I edited *Audubon* magazine. Looking back on those years, it seems to me that several times each day, in reading and editing manuscripts for the magazine, I had the need for a comprehensive reference book where I could quickly find specific information about birds beyond my own memory or knowledge and beyond that of many of the authors and readers of the magazine. The answers were scattered among countless, not always accessible, authoritative sources. I began to think of the usefulness a formal encyclopedia would have for the vast number of people interested in birds. I discussed the idea of such a book with fellow ornithologists, librarians, teachers, and many birders, all of whom were enthusiastic and eager for its publication. In 1959, when I began to think about the book in a systematic fashion, I explored the problem with my friend Roger Tory Peterson. Perhaps he, with the perspective of one who himself is the author of many books, had a clearer idea of the tremendous task I would be undertaking. His advice was thoughtful and sensible, cautious and realistic, warning me that I would be devoting a very large part of my life to its research and writing. But he urged me to try, if I thought I could maintain the enthusiasm and energies for it that I would surely require in the years ahead. And, as time passed, and my work on the project expanded, Roger continued to encourage me and to inquire about my progress on a book that we both agreed would meet a very great need.

It may seem presumptuous for one person to have attempted such a large compendium, yet the justification for it lies in that very word—*compendium*. Although the text for the book went through one man's typewriter (my own), the content is the work of hundreds, even thousands, of devoted scientists, naturalists, and scholars whose observations, studies, and discoveries have made this encyclopedia possible.

As author, I think of myself as carrier of this knowledge—from the men and women who created it and built it, to the millions of laymen who may profit by their work and be delighted by their labors. My task was to meet the needs and interests of the general reader and yet command the respect of the scientific community, to make the book readable and useful while at the same time as impeccably authoritative as its sources. To accomplish both of these purposes, I have had to distill the thousands of monographs, research reports, papers, bulletins, articles, and books, in which lay a wealth of facts known only—for the most part—to workers in the science of ornithology, or perhaps to some of those ardent nonprofessionals who pursue birds in an all-consuming hobby.

WHAT TO INCLUDE?

The essential problem in the planning and writing of the book was this: Which ornithological subjects should I include? The limitations of a single volume meant that I could offer only a selection of the almost innumerable subjects and terms used in ornithology. I had to choose those that I believed from personal experience would be of greatest value and interest to readers, just as they are to me, subjects and terms that would introduce birds but would have sufficient depth and breadth of treatment to engage and inform those already knowledgeable about birds.

From the beginning, I depended partly upon my own curiosity, which has always been enormous, to make these choices. Having been the editor of *Audubon* magazine for twelve years, I know that many fundamental questions are asked by people who have a lively, but not necessarily scientific, interest in birds. They may ask questions about bird life—flight, nesting, egg laying, migration—and questions about vital statistics: How fast can birds fly? How high? How long do various birds live? What are the largest birds? The smallest? In order to insure that these beginning birders would find information easily accessible, I had to organize the encyclopedia carefully with these questions in mind and at the same time present the information in such a way as to encourage them to browse through it to enlarge their knowledge of birds and the study of birds.

However, a significant part of the readership I had in mind consists of life-time birders, people who come to the subject with an invaluable accumulation of observations of their own, but who for the most part have very little access to the work of the great bird authorities. Such readers will consult the encyclopedia to read in depth about a particular bird family or species, or to inform themselves about classification, evolution, the workings of the various body systems, the mechanics of flight, molting, and migration. Also, they often want to read further about the behavior they have observed, such as courtship displays, flocking, or territorial defense and hundreds of others subjects.

In choosing the general biological subjects, and some of the more commonly used terms, I reviewed a number of ornithological textbooks to make certain that I had included a wide representation of the subjects and terms that I believe will be useful to my readers. I was guided especially by six very fine works:

Avian Biology, 5 volumes (1971–75), edited by Donald S. Farner
and James R. King. New York: Academic Press.
Biology and Comparative Physiology of Birds, 2 volumes (1960–61),
edited by A. J. Marshall. New York: Academic Press.
Bird Study, by A. J. Berger. New York: John Wiley & Sons, 1976.
Fundamentals of Ornithology, by Josselyn Van Tyne and Andrew J.
Berger. New York: John Wiley & Sons, 1976.
An Introduction to Ornithology, by George J. Wallace. New York:
The Macmillan Company, 1963.
The Life of Birds, by Joel C. Welty. Philadelphia: J. B. Saunders & Co., 1975.

For those who wish to pursue a subject beyond the scope that the encyclopedia covers, I have cited within the text more than 4,000 sources: monographs, technical papers, field guides, general bird books, and texts. All are listed in the bibliography, which spans 300 years of published ornithological literature, from G. A. Borelli's experiments with the gizzards of turkeys (1681) to the latest U.S. Government report on the ten most endangered species in North America (1980).

STYLE

My intention has been to provide a useful and entertaining text that would be instructive and engaging to all readers, and in so doing to pay homage to the naturalists and scientists whose work is the backbone of my own.

Nearly all of the technical information about bird life and biology has been derived from ornithological monographs and scientific works, which are often too specialized for the lay reader. Presenting that information in a clear, readable, and economical form is an act of translation, always a difficult task and freighted with the risk of oversimplification. The author of an encyclopedia must always be certain, in rewriting and digesting data, that he does not misinterpret the original research. To overcome this potential hazard, I sent every major article in the encyclopedia to one or more experts in each subject, including some of the very authors whose papers I have cited. Their generous response and invaluable comments and criticisms not only insured that I did justice to their work, but also brought me up to date on some of the recent developments in their special fields of study.

Much scientific writing, especially on behavior, is based upon observations in the field. Sometimes these are reported in anecdotal notes, much of which I retained where appropriate. These vignettes, I feel, not only are instructive and lively but tell us something about how naturalists and scientists work.

PROGRESS AND RESEARCH

Many theories and information about the study of birds have not changed in recent years, and some have not changed profoundly in the last 100 years. Much of the information about food habits, habitats, breeding biology, and other facts of a bird's life history may be expected to change very little in the years ahead.

However, there are always additions to this knowledge: a bird extends its range, or interbreeds with a closely related species, or takes advantage of some new food source, and new discoveries about birds are made all the time. Improved technology has allowed great advances in various fields, especially in the use of radar for studying bird migration, radiotelemetry for studying the physiology of flying birds, and audiospectrography for analyzing their calls and songs. Ornithologists are gaining greater understanding of bird behavior, general ecology, and population biology. Theories of evolution may be altered by new ways of looking at fossil evidence, and the phylogenetic classification of birds is continually reconsidered and revised. In such an atmosphere of constant research and discovery, *any* encyclopedia will become somewhat out of date. After years of investigation and writing, I have had to accept that one of the limitations of this book is that there are fields in which advances are being made too rapidly to assimilate or record here. I have tried to be vigilant; I have cited the latest editions of the standard sources in the bibliography, and availed myself, when possible, of the most recent published literature, including scientific information published in 1980.

Since 1886, the authoritative American Ornithologists' Union has published five checklists of North American birds (1886, 1895, 1910, 1931, and 1957) showing changes in the scientific and English, or common, names of birds, reflecting new understanding and new relationships. This checklist has been my authority for the names and ranges of North American birds, and the encyclopedia reflects any subsequent changes in names and classification that have been published in two supplements (the 32nd and 33rd supplements, in October 1973 and October 1976, respectively). These supplements were published in *The Auk*, the official journal of the American Ornithologists' Union (A.O.U.). I have also followed the A.O.U.'s definition of the area limits within which North American birds live: North America north of Mexico (the United States, including Alaska and Canada) and including Greenland, Bermuda, and Baja, California.

HOW TO USE THE ENCYCLOPEDIA

The encyclopedia is arranged alphabetically and includes the following categories: biographies of North American birds (and foreign visitors); major articles about bird life and bird biology and its study; definitions of ornithological terms; short biographies of some of the great ornithologists, naturalists, and explorers whose names are associated with North American birds; and about 4,000 cross-references that link related articles and function as an index. The key to the accessibility of the text is this extensive and pervasive system of cross-references. People who are quite knowledgeable about birds, and those who are just beginning to take an interest in them, will approach the encyclopedia in different ways. I kept this in mind when composing the titles of each entry.

THE BIRD BIOGRAPHIES

At the heart of the encyclopedia are the biographies of 847 birds (some 682 nesting) that live part or all of their lives, or have been sighted, in North America. Each bird's biography can be found under the family to which it belongs: the red-winged blackbird is in the *Troupial Family*, but if you do not happen to know or remember its family, look under its stem name, *blackbird*, where you will read: "See in *Troupial Family*." To find the biography of the brown thrasher, if you do not know its family, look under *Thrasher*. The cross-reference there will direct you to the *Mockingbird Family*. There you will find the brown thrasher, alphabetically, between Bendire's thrasher and California thrasher.

Presenting the biography of each bird under its English family name—which often differs, as in the thrasher (there is no "thrasher family")—instantly shows the relationship of birds grouped in a family but with different names. The *Duck Family* has many members with different names: geese, swans, brants, mergansers, scaups, among others; and the *Finch Family* includes sparrows, cardinals, buntings, and juncos. This arrangement also made it possible in each family introduction to discuss its members' common characteristics and thus eliminate repetition in the individual biographies.

The members of a bird family are a closely related group. For each of the 78 families in North America, I have included an introduction that discusses the relationships of the different species within the family. For example, in the introduction to the *Auk Family* you will find: the scientific family name (Alcidae), its pronunciation and derivation; the number of species in the Auk family both worldwide and in North America; the common physical and behavioral characteristics and preferred habitats of members of the family; the order (Charadriiformes) to which the family belongs; and mention of the relatives of members of the Auk Family which you will find by turning to the entry *Charadriiformes*.

Each bird species within the family has its own biography, in which I have given the following information: its English, or common, name; the scientific name, with its pronunciation, derivation, and meaning; and a short physical description; the differences in size or color between the sexes; its characteristic behavior; its calls or songs rendered phonetically; its feeding habits; its nest, eggs, and the length and type of incubation; the first flight of the young, when known; its lifespan; flight speed; incidence of albinism; incidence of hybridism; weight; details of the summer and winter ranges by state and province.

Throughout the text I have included many of the most familiar, alternate, vernacular names of North American birds, such as *Whiskey Jack* (gray jay) or *Snow Bird* (dark-eyed junco), referring the reader to the approved English name within its appropriate family. However, there are many local or folk names (132 for the common flicker; 78 for the ruddy duck) that are gradually falling into disuse as more people become accustomed to using the standardized English names in the authoritative A.O.U. checklist. I have included some of these under Other Names in the bird biographies, for they are colorful and often most appropriate.

THE SYSTEM OF CROSS-REFERENCE

The behavior of birds is one of the most interesting subjects in ornithology. We can postulate here a situation in which you might see an example of bird behavior in the field and want to look it up in the encyclopedia. You have come upon a killdeer flopping pitifully about as though its wing were broken, and you follow it until it flies away, obviously unhurt. You are curious about this "act" and wonder where you might find it discussed in the encyclopedia. If you are quite knowledgeable about birds, you will know that what you have seen is a *distraction display*, which is discussed in detail and illustrated under the entry *Distraction Display*. If you are not familiar with the term, you will perhaps turn to the biography of the killdeer in the *Plover Family*. In the introduction to this family, you will find that this behavior is common to members of the family, and you will be referred to *Distraction Display*. Or you may look under *Behavior*, where you will find, under the subheading Self-Protective Behavior, a general discussion that will again refer you to *Distraction Display*. In the entry *Young and Their Care*, under the subheading Defense of the Young, you will be directed to *Distraction Display*. And you can also find your way there via the cross-reference entries for *Injury-Feigning; Broken-Wing Display;* and *Crippled-Bird Act*. Ideally, the system of cross-references here is like a safety net stretched under a tight-rope walker—wherever you fall you will be caught.

The same principle applies to other entries throughout the encyclopedia. The general treatment under *Diseases* is extensively cross-referenced to more detailed, individual entries such as *Avian Malaria; Avian Tuberculosis; Aspergillosis; Coccidiosis*. If you are seeking an overview of the subject, you will not be overburdened there by the depth and detailed information given under these specific diseases.

In some of the major articles of general interest, I hope you will be drawn as a matter of course to the related, and important, discussions indicated in the cross-references. In the long entry *Food and Feeding Habits*, for example, I have given a summary of the various methods of food-getting and the diverse diets of different birds. Throughout this article, I have recommended to your attention several more detailed discussions under such headings as: *Fishes and Birds, Insects and Birds, Mollusks and Birds*, and *Reptiles and Birds*. In these articles, I discuss primarily the special relationship of birds to these groups of animals in the food chain and the effect that these prey animals may have on the birds themselves.

THE NAMES OF BIRDS

The English, or common, names of all the birds in this encyclopedia are those used by the American Ornithologists' Union in its 1957 Check-list of North American Birds and reflect any subsequent revisions in the 1973 and 1976 supplements. In field guides and other ornithological publications, each bird's English name is given with its scientific name, a system I have followed in the bird biographies. Throughout the encyclopedia, I have generally used the standardized English names when referring to a particular species.

A brief explanation of the function of scientific names is appropriate here. Until the middle of the eighteenth century, when Carl Linnaeus, the great Swedish naturalist, established the practice of applying a two-word Latin name to every plant and animal, there was no standard by which each species could be recognized by one name throughout the civilized world. The thousands of common or vernacular names by which they were known in different countries, and in different languages, were inadequate for international use because the common name of one bird—even in the same language—might sometimes be used for two different birds. The robin of England is not the same bird as our American robin, but for one who depended upon common names alone, this fact might not be apparent.

A widespread bird of prey, called the marsh hawk in America, is called the hen harrier in Great Britain, *Blauwe kuikendief* in Holland, *Kornweihe* in Germany, *Busard Saint-Martin* in France, and *Blå karrök* in Sweden. In the United States and Canada, country people in different places have called the marsh hawk by many other names, among them: rat hawk, rabbit hawk, swamp hawk, and blue harrier. However, the marsh hawk is instantly recognized by naturalists everywhere, no matter what its common name in whatever language, by its scientific name, *Circus cyaneus*.

In the Linnaean system of classification, every bird's name is nearly always Latin in form and derived from Greek or Latin roots. Some are genuine Latin names; others are Latinized forms of Greek words; others have been coined from Latin or Greek words by the scientists who described them; a few have been borrowed from other languages, sometimes in their original form, sometimes Latinized.

The first word is the genus name, the second is the species name. The genus name is always a noun and is always capitalized. It usually refers to the appearance, habitat, food, behavior, or call of the bird, or commemorates an individual naturalist, or makes reference to some legendary association of the bird. The species name is usually an adjective, occasionally a noun, that describes its appearance, calls, habitat, type locality (where first collected) preferred region, status, or resemblance to another bird. A species name, too, may commemorate a naturalist associated with that particular bird.

A genus may include a number of closely related species within a family. For example, the scientific name of the herring gull, *Larus argentatus*, conveys immediately that it is a member of the genus *Larus*, to which most of our gulls belong. The word *Larus* is derived from the Greek for "ravenous seabird." The species name, *argentatus*, refers specifically to the herring gull; the Latin word *argentatus* means "silvered" or "silvery."

Because many species of birds have geographical races—distinct populations that still interbreed where they meet—many birds have a third name, a *subspecies* name. In the encyclopedia I have rarely used the subspecies name; most birds are listed by their genus and species names alone.

The exception to this occurs where a bird has recently been reclassified by the A.O.U. as a subspecies rather than, as formerly thought, a species. For example, in 1973 the A.O.U. classified the Baltimore oriole and the Bullock's oriole as subspecies of the Northern oriole, because the two often hybridize where their ranges overlap in the western plains and prairies. However, in their respective eastern and western ranges, the two birds are quite distinct in appearance and have different songs. Therefore, I have felt it more useful to discuss the birds separately under:

Oriole, Baltimore (northern), *Icterus galbula galbula*
and
Oriole, Bullock's (northern), *Icterus galbula bullockii*
and the entry *Oriole, northern,* will give the reader this explanation and refer to the separate bird biographies.

The use of the encyclopedia should be self-explanatory on all other counts, and will, I hope, satisfy a wide range of interests, needs, and expectations. It is also my hope that the men and women whose research made the encyclopedia possible will feel that I have done justice to the content of their work, and have given a fair sample of its depth and breadth. If I have succeeded in my purpose, then you, as reader and user of this first encyclopedia of North American birds, should find answers to most of the kinds of questions that send us all at times to the columns of an encyclopedia.

ABBREVIATIONS

Ala. — Alabama	Ital. — Italian	Oct. — October
Alta. — Alberta	Jan. — January	Ont. — Ontario
Apr. — April	Kans. — Kansas	Okla. — Oklahoma
Aug. — August	km. — kilometer(s)	Ore. — Oregon
Ariz. — Arizona	Ky. — Kentucky	oz. — ounce(s)
Ark. — Arkansas	La. — Louisiana	Pa. — Pennsylvania
B.C. — British Columbia	Lat. — Latin, Latinized;	Pen. — Peninsula
c. — central	Latitude	pl. — plural
C. — Central	lb. — pound(s)	Prof. — Professor
Centigrade	Long. — Longitude	pron. — pronunciation
Calif. — California	Lt. — Lieutenant	Que. — Quebec
Capt. — Captain	m. — meter(s)	R. — River
cm. — centimeter(s)	Mack. — Mackenzie	R.I. — Rhode Island
Col. — Colonel	Man. — Manitoba	s. / S. — southern
Colo. — Colorado	Mar. — March	
Conn. — Connecticut	Mass. — Massachusetts	Sask. — Saskatchewan
D.C. — District of Columbia	Me. — Maine	S.C. — South Carolina
Dec. — December	Md. — Maryland	S.D. — South Dakota
Del. — Delaware	mi. — mile(s)	Sept. — September
dial. — dialect	Mich. — Michigan	sing. — singular
dim. — diminutive	Minn. — Minnesota	Sp. — Spanish
e. / E. — eastern	Miss. — Mississippi	sq. — square
	mm. — millimeter(s)	Tenn. — Tennessee
ed. — edition	Mo. — Missouri	Terr. — Territory
Eng. — English	Mont. — Montana	Tex. — Texas
F. — Fahrenheit	Mt. — Mount	Va. — Virginia
Feb. — February	Mt(s). — Mountains	vol. — volume(s)
Fla. — Florida	n. / N. — northern	Vt. — Vermont
Fr. — French		w. / W. — western
ft. — foot, feet	N.B. — New Brunswick	
Ft. — Fort	N.C. — North Carolina	Wash. — Washington
Ga. — Georgia	N.D. — North Dakota	Wisc. — Wisconsin
gal. — gallon(s)	ne. — northeastern	W. Va. — West Virginia
Gen. — General	Neb. — Nebraska	Wyo. — Wyoming
Ger. — German	Nev. — Nevada	yd. — yard(s)
gr. — gram(s)	N.H. — New Hampshire	
Gr. — Greek	N.J. — New Jersey	
ha. — hectare(s)	N.M. — New Mexico	
Ill. — Illinois	Nov. — November	
in. — inch(es)	nw. — northwestern	
Ind. — Indiana	N.Y. — New York	
Is. — Island	O. — Ocean	

The Audubon Society
ENCYCLOPEDIA OF NORTH AMERICAN BIRDS

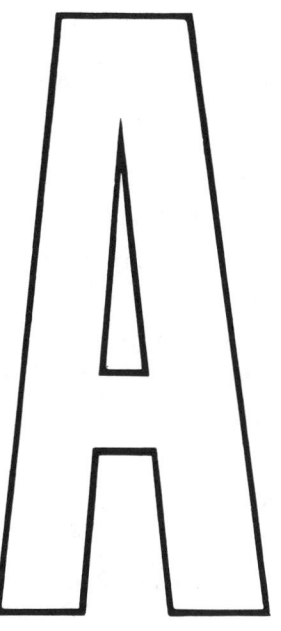

ABDOMEN

or BELLY. That part of the undersurface of a bird's body from the breastbone to the vent or to the opening of the cloaca. *See* Cloaca; *also* Topography.

ABERRANT

(ab-ER-ant). Exceptional, divergent, having marked difference or differences from others of its kind (Van Tyne and Berger, 1959). *See* Albinism; Gynandromorph.

ABERT

(AY-bert), JAMES WILLIAM (1820–97). Born Mt. Holly, N.J.; graduate of West Point (1842), later major in U.S. Army; while on duty in N.M., collected birds for Spencer F. Baird, Smithsonian Institution, Washington, D.C., among them a towhee previously unknown to science. In 1852 Baird named it *Pipilo aberti* in Abert's honor. *See* Names and Naming.

ABMIGRATION

Term proposed in 1931 by A. L. Thomson, British ornithologist, for a kind of migration peculiar to certain male ducks. In winter many ducks in the s. U.S. which breed in north pair on wintering grounds. With return of spring, drakes, or males, instead of flying northward to marsh where they were hatched, accompany female duck to which each is mated. She returns to her home marsh, often in region unfamiliar to male. His migration (with her) termed "abmigration," although such males, after nesting duties are over, sometimes return to marsh where they were hatched (Hochbaum, 1955). *See also* Waterfowl.

ABNORMALITIES

See especially Deformities; *also* Colors of Feathers; Gynandromorph.

ABUNDANCE

See Populations.

ACCENTOR

See Hedge Sparrow Family; *also* Ovenbird in Warbler—American Wood Warbler Family.

ACCIDENTAL

or ACCIDENTAL VISITOR. Term for a bird seen in area far outside its normal and/or seasonal range. Birds may ride with storms and strong winds that carry them to regions strange to them, or may be transported by alighting on ships.

Peterson (1947) describes accidentals as "the rarest of rarities—birds that should not occur in your region at all." According to Peterson, these accidentals are "birds that have occurred less than twenty times in eastern [or western] North America." This definition might be extended to other regions or to even more limited areas. Lowery (1960) defines accidentals as those birds for which there is but one record of their occurrence in a particular state. For a list of accidentals in N. America, see Appendix I in Peterson (1947; 1961). *See also* Casual Visitor; *also* Where Do Birds Live? under Distribution.

ACCIDENTS

Probably most frequent when birds are migrating. Most birds migrate at night, a perilous time (*see* Migration); in flight, they may be struck by aircraft, automobiles, trains, or may dash blindly at night against buildings or other tall structures or may be caught in downdrafts of air and hurled against mountainsides or into oceans or lakes (see Greenhalgh, 1965).

Deathtraps for birds are of many kinds, both natural and man-made: small birds such as chickadees, goldfinches, kinglets, nuthatches are sometimes caught and held in prickly burrs of burdock plants while extracting seeds; ground sparrows and blackbirds are trapped by weed stems and grasses; chipping sparrows, American robins, orioles, barn swallows hang themselves in struggles to free themselves from long hairs or plant fibers used by them in building their nests; hummingbirds, bushtits, house and purple finches get enmeshed in webs of orb-weaving spiders; hole-nesting ducks get entombed in hollow trees and in house chimneys too deep to fly out of; bluebirds get trapped inside "tobacco barns," entered through stovepipe chimneys; small shorebirds get trapped and drowned when clams and oysters snap shut on their feet (*see* Mollusks and Birds); kingfishers are caught and held by the bill by clamped shells of oysters, mussels; ospreys are drowned by diving deep into water and fixing talons into fishes too heavy for them to lift. *See also* Niagara Falls Swan Trap.

Wild ducks, swifts, swallows are killed when colliding in midair with others of their kind; purple martins, screech owls, golden eagles, Baltimore orioles, meadowlarks are electrocuted when perching on electrified wires (*see* Electrocution). Great numbers of small birds are killed by flying each year into utility wires, also into picture windows of private homes; large owls are impaled on TV aerials; hawks, owls, upland game birds, railbirds, wild ducks are killed or injured by flying into barbed-wire fences; pheasants and other ground-nesting birds in hayfields are killed or crippled by having feet or wings cut off by mowing machines; in freak accidents, swallows, flickers, orioles, and a California gull have been struck by golf balls over golf courses. One of the greatest causes of mass destruction from present-day technology has been floating oil on high seas; also dazzling lights of lighthouses, airport ceilometers, and floodlighted buildings; striking TV towers, high bridges, and other tall structures; all of these have accounted for deaths of more birds each year than all other man-made causes except massive spraying of poisons or insecticides over the land (*see* Poisons). See discussion of birds dazzled by lights in James (1956); Herbert (1970); Gochfeld (1973); Cochran and Graber (1958); Avery *et al.* (1976).

In N. America, most reported accidents involving striking tall structures took place at lighthouses along the Atlantic coast, principally before 1930; at tall buildings and bridges between 1930 and 1948; at airport ceilometers between 1948 and 1956; at TV towers since 1956. Television towers now cause the greatest mortality among birds and this is increasing as more and higher towers are built. Deaths of birds at ceilometers (*see* Ceilometer) decreased

Chimney swift

Common nighthawk

ADAPTATIONS TO MAN
As man altered the environment of North America, birds adapted to the changing conditions or declined in numbers. Chimney swifts, which once roosted in hollow trees, now commonly roost in chimneys in large numbers, clinging to the sooty walls in overlapping clusters like shingles and propping themselves with their short, spine-tipped tails. The common nighthawk now may nest on flat city roofs instead of open pastures, exploiting the urban environment.

abruptly after optical filters were installed in them in the 1950s (Terres, 1956a); mortality of birds at lighthouses and tall buildings continues to be reported; its apparent decline in last 50 years is probably real but also must reflect in part a decline in attention paid to it (Nisbet, 1970).

Heaviest casualties at tall structures at night appear to involve songbirds (many migrate at night, whereas ducks, shorebirds, hawks, turkey vultures, woodpeckers, and blue jays, for example, migrate usually by day). *See* Migration. Among songbirds, of 59,032 warblers of 37 species reported killed in U.S. and in e. Canada during autumn migration in 20 years following the early 1950s (at tall structures and at ceilometers, where most casualties are in autumn), 11,236 (19%) were ovenbirds (Taylor, W. K., 1972); there are a few birds, notably the American robin, brown thrasher, common flicker, and white-throated sparrow, that are rarely, if ever, killed at towers. Ganier (1966), in a study of 26 lists of birds killed at TV towers, airport ceilometers, etc., along the midcontinental bird flyway (*see* Waterfowl) between the Mississippi R. and the Appalachian Mtns., concluded that the ovenbird was the most frequently killed warbler, based on 2,513 killed (15.5%) out of a total of 16,118 casualties. It was followed by the Tennessee warbler, red-eyed vireo, and magnolia warbler (about 1,400 each, or 8.8% of the total casualties). Birds that gave evidence of fewer casualties (also seen migrating by day) were the Cape May warbler, black-throated blue warbler, brown thrasher, American robin, mockingbird, and most flycatchers, including kingbirds, also swifts, swallows, chipping sparrow, starling, meadowlark, and blackbirds in general. Those not killed, or absent from the list of casualties, were the orchard oriole, Louisiana waterthrush, white-crowned sparrow, rusty blackbird, and mallard (most ducks migrate by day). See Ganier (1966) for discussion. See Stoddard and Norris (1967) for list of 29,400 birds killed in migration at a Fla. TV tower; see Crawford (1974) for report of an additional 5,550 birds killed at same tower.

According to Boardman (1972), radio and television towers, and the steel cable guy lines that support them, kill an estimated one million birds a year. *See also* Aircraft and Birds; Diseases; Lead Poisoning; Migration; Weather; *also* Deformities.

ACCIPITER
(ak-SIP-ih-ter). Genus name (*see* Genus) given group of "short-winged hawks" in Europe in 1760 (Newton, 1893–96). In America, group includes the goshawk, Cooper's hawk, and sharp-shinned hawk, which are called, collectively, "accipiters" by ornithologists and bird-watchers. *See also* Buteo; Buzzard.

Accipiters, swift in flight, especially on take-off, capture and eat many small birds. *See* Hawk Family. Are often called "blue darters" and "bird hawks." Accipiters are considered by scientists to be only one of many natural checks on populations of small birds (*see* Accidents; Diseases) and by killing and eating them help to keep small birds from becoming too numerous. Even the American robin, much as it is

loved and valued, might be inimical to man's economy if too numerous and able to completely devour crops of cherries and other commercially grown fruit (Sprunt, 1955a). *See* Balance of Nature; Predation.

ACCIPITRIDAE
See Hawk Family; *also* Falconiformes.

ACOUSTIC ORIENTATION
See Echolocation; *also* Ears and Hearing.

ACQUISITION
Ornithological term for a bird skin or bird specimen added to the bird collection of a museum or to a private collection. See Bird Skins; Collections.

ADAMS
EDWARD, M.D. (1824–56). British naval surgeon, explorer, collector of natural history specimens abroad; naturalist and surgeon on two British polar expeditions in mid-19th century that traveled to N. America to discover fate of Sir John Franklin; born Sussex, Eng.; died west coast of Africa; in 1859, G. R. Gray, British zoologist, honored Adams by giving species name of *adamsii* to the then newly described yellow-billed loon from a specimen or specimens collected in "Russian America" (Alaska). See A.O.U. *Check-list* (1957) and Gruson (1972).

ADAPTATIONS TO MANKIND
Changes in birds' environment brought about by man's occupation of land in N. America have been varied. From heavily forested country of little more than 200 years ago, the e. U.S. was heavily cut over, first by settlers carving farmlands from wilderness. With change from virgin forest to open fields, many birds of forest became less numerous; birds of open fields more abundant as favored habitat increased enormously. Horned larks, meadowlarks, blackbirds, bobolinks, bobwhite quail, dickcissels, vesper sparrows, Savannah sparrows, grasshopper sparrows of open fields probably more numerous during latter part of last century and early in this one than ever before, whereas many woodpeckers, grouse, turkeys, and other birds of virgin or mature forest disappeared or retreated into virgin forest or wilderness that remained.

Continental populations of ducks, geese, herons, egrets, bitterns, rails, marsh wrens, and other water and marsh birds shrank considerably because of drought, especially in early 1930s, and because of continual drainage for agricultural use of potholes, marshes, swamps, ponds, and other water areas where these birds live. However, yellowlegs, willets, plovers, sandpipers, sanderlings, curlews (except virtually extinct Eskimo curlew), and other shorebirds increased greatly in population during last 40 years, mainly because of protection from hunting. Egrets, gulls, terns made strong comeback after being almost shot out of existence for their use in the millinery trade. After 1900, with protective laws, sanctuaries, and National Audubon Society's fight to outlaw use of feathers of these birds, they began slow recovery, which reached high point by late 1940s.

Continued increase thereafter of gull populations but slow to rapid decline of egrets, herons, ibises, owing to drainage of swamp rookeries, drought, or drainage of feeding places, especially in Fla.

In East, especially in Northeast, farming of steep, formerly wooded hillsides became unprofitable. Abandoned farms began to revert to forests. After return, first to brushlands, then second-growth forests, many small or medium-sized birds increased enormously. Gray catbirds, chestnut-sided warblers, prairie warblers, yellow-breasted chats, redstarts, American robins, cardinals, song sparrows, goldfinches, indigo buntings, rufous-sided towhees, field sparrows probably more abundant now than ever. Around farm buildings, hedges, orchards, and suburban gardens, many of these birds became more common, along with phoebes, kingbirds, waxwings, swallows, bluebirds, wrens. *See* Bird-attracting; *also* discussion in Clement (1966).

Many of commonest birds now almost semi-domesticated. Robins, chipping sparrows, wrens nest in dooryards, swifts in chimneys; crows and black-crowned night herons live in some city parks, in woods surrounded by built-up suburbs; wood ducks nest in city parks in s. U.S., and in summer 1971, yellow-crowned night herons nested in courtyard of apartment complex in Fort Worth, Tex., and a pair of fulvous tree ducks nested in a children's tree house in Elkhart, Kans. Pileated woodpeckers, once shy forest birds, come to suet feeders in backyards near woods; wood thrushes and blue jays backyard birds within last 60 years. Barn swallows now nest almost nowhere except in buildings, purple martins in gourds or birdhouses in gardens, instead of in hollow trees (*see* Bird-attracting); barn owls almost completely abandoned original nest sites in hollow trees for cupolas of sheds, barn lofts, silos, church steeples of villages, towers of buildings in some large cities.

Peregrine falcons, with normal nesting sites on tall cliffs, nested or wintered on ledges of tall buildings in Toronto, New York, Boston, Philadelphia, Baltimore, Washington, D.C. There they fed on always abundant supply of domestic pigeons and European starlings; however, peregrine disappearing from e. U.S. during 1950s; suspect decline caused by insecticides in tissues of its prey species, and possibly aided often by deadly disease, trichomoniasis. *See* Diseases.

Smallest N. American falcon, the kestrel, or sparrow hawk, also took up abode in large cities, where it nests in crannies in eaves of buildings; feeds itself and young on abundant house sparrows. Nighthawk that nested in open pastures adapted to nesting on flat roofs of buildings of small towns and cities, as did killdeers, least terns, herring gulls; killdeer also nests now on golf courses instead of pastures which many golf courses replaced.

Majority of American birds became more or less adapted to changes in environment through impact of civilization on land. A few species became extinct, others are vanishing, and eagles, hawks, owls, game birds, water birds, and some shorebirds need constant protection. Yet every change of habitat brought by civilization, although reducing numbers of some birds, benefited others. Marsh and swamp dwellers most need help, also certain species such as whooping crane, ivory-billed woodpecker, and California condor, which need large wilderness areas to survive. We should conserve areas for them so that they will be around for generations to come. *See* Rare and Threatened Species; Extinct Birds of North America; Geological Time Scale; *See* Autolycism.

ADAPTIVE CHARACTERS
Term usually applied to feet, bills, wings, tail feathers, and other parts of birds structurally modified though evolution, or said to be *adapted* to bird's use; Convergent Evolution.

ADAPTIVE CONVERGENCE
See Convergent Evolution.

ADAPTIVE RADIATION
Evolutionists' term for the advantages that plants and animals have taken of ecological opportunities to fill unoccupied ecological niches and in the process becoming different (adapted). See Storer, 1971a. Birds on isolated archipelagos of comparatively recent volcanic origin help us to understand how such adaptive radiation is brought about. Darwin's finches of the Galápagos Is. in the Pacific O. west of the S. American continent are an often-cited example of adaptive radiation.

When a small population of a finch-like bird arrived from S. America on the Galápagos, after crossing 600 miles of water (possibly wind-carried in a storm), a dozen islands unoccupied by other landbirds with a series of ecological niches (*see* Ecological Niche) were open to them. Over thousands of years the various islands of the Galápagos Archipelago became colonized by flocks, probably from the original group. Because the finches were terrestrial, the population on one island was effectively isolated from those on other islands. Each population evolved to fill the environmental niches open to it, becoming distinctly different from one another. In time, birds from one island crossed the expanse of water to another island in the archipelago, one already inhabited by another species of finch, and arriving after the resident and new colonizing populations had diverged genetically to become distinct species. The two non-interbreeding populations, now living together, continued to diverge in characters of bill and body size so that competition for food resources became minimal. This scenario was carried out many times, eventually resulting in 14 species radiating from the initial stock of colonizing birds from S. or C. America.

Some retained the original conical, ground finch bill, which evolved into a slightly heavier bill in adapting to gathering and eating seeds; others became tree dwellers with warblerlike bills adapted to eating insects; others, long, down-curved bills adapted to feeding on cactuses; others, parrotlike bills adapted to feeding on fruits; others, a woodpeckerlike bill adapted to chiseling out wood-boring insects from trees. See Lack (1947) for the details of this remarkable story. See another example under Hawaiian Honeycreeper Family.

ADDLED
Term for egg (an addle egg) that is empty or fruitless. Egg that has lost power of development and become rotten. See Eggs and Egg-laying; *also* Fertilization.

ADDUCTOR
One of four sets of muscles with which bird closes its jaws. Interesting differences or modifications of are related to feeding habits. Adductors very powerful in eagles, hawks, owls, also in seed-eating birds that crush seeds before eating them. However, with insectivorous (insect-eating) birds, and pigeons, which merely pick up seeds and swallow them, adductors are relatively weak. Common grackle, which bites open acorns and grain by use of jaws and a sharp keel in roof of mouth, has powerful adductors (Wallace, 1955).

ADULT
Term for a bird that is in its final plumage. (*See also* Immature; Subadult.) Even though a bird in immature or subadult plumage may be a breeding or nesting bird, it is not called adult until it assumes *plumage* of the breeding adult (Van Tyne and Berger, 1959). *Adult* birds change feathers through molting (*see* Molts and Molting), no more than twice a year: before mating and nesting (prenuptial) and after nesting season (postnuptial) (Pettingill, 1956).

ADVENTITIOUS, or ADHERENT, COLOR
Term for a color in feathers caused by a chemical or other matter in bird's environment that discolors or soils plumage (Wing, 1956). In Alberta, Can., usually gray plumage of sandhill cranes becomes reddish brown in spring because of cranes' contact with ferric oxide in muskeg, where they probe with bills. When bill is used to preen plumage, reddish stain is transferred to cranes' feathers (Walkinshaw, 1949a). Rusty color sometimes in white plumage of swans and snow geese is from contact with habitat; however, is not to be confused with stains and dyes put on feathers by bird-banders so as to recognize individuals or certain groups of birds. See Banding. According to important studies of Berthold (1967), rusty coloration in the feathers of birds from contact with subsoils stained with iron oxide is known from more than 120 species.

White breast feathers of woodpeckers sometimes are dark or discolored from rubbing against trunks of trees; house sparrows living in cities often darkened from soot and dirt. Bright-colored plumage of sparrow hawks that alight in burnt-over stubble fields to feed on grasshoppers may get dark from blackened stubble (Wing, 1956). See also Colors of Feathers.

AERIE
The nest of a bird, especially of an eagle, hawk, or other bird of prey, on a cliff or other eminence. Also spelled *aiery* and *ayre*, the Shakespearean English forms of *eyrie*, a hawk's nesting place (Wood and Fyffe, 1943). Falconers (*see* Falconry) more often use the spelling *eyrie*.

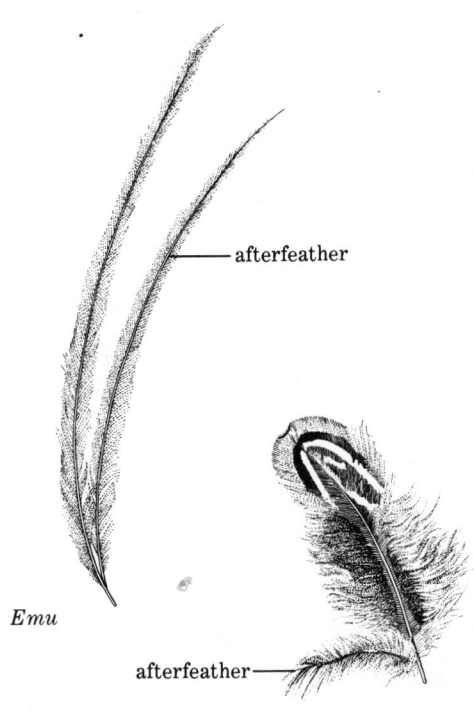

afterfeather

Emu

afterfeather

Ring-necked pheasant

AFTERFEATHER
The afterfeather of an Australian emu is nearly as long as the main part of the feather; the afterfeather of a ring-necked pheasant is smaller but still well-developed.

AERODYNAMICS
See Flight.

AFFINITY
Ornithological term indicating relationship between certain groups of birds believed to have a common ancestor (Van Tyne and Berger, 1959).

AFTERFEATHER
(mistakenly called AFTERSHAFT and HYPORACHIS). Term for a second, accessory feather rising from the inner shaft of a main feather. The afterfeather, which usually grows from the main feathers on the body of a bird, is an ancient type; many primitive birds, now extinct, had afterfeathers (Allen, 1925) but their reduction in size or complete disappearance has not been uniform during the evolution of higher types of birds (Van Tyne and Berger, 1959); afterfeathers are thought to be insulative and to help retain a bird's body heat (Lucas and Stettenheim, 1972).

In the emu and the cassowary, related flightless birds of Australia and New Guinea, the afterfeather is as long or almost as long as the main feather from which it grows; the afterfeather of grouse, pheasants, and quail is well developed and in many herons, hawks, and parrots, it is also long; toucans, woodpeckers, and most songbirds have a lesser one. Ducks, American vultures, and most owls have only a tiny vestigial fringe of feathers representing the afterfeather; it has disappeared in pigeons, hornbills, tropical American woodcreepers, and the S. American ovenbirds (Van Tyne and Berger, 1959). *See* Feather.

AFTERSHAFT
The axis or shaft of an afterfeather.

AGE
One of the factors often troubling to people who are concerned about birds and their welfare (*see* Bird-attracting) is the extreme shortness of the lives of most of them. Enormous hazards face birds (*see* Accidents), some even before they hatch (*see* Hatching; Egg-eating). Yet birds do survive surprisingly well (*see* Nesting Success and Failure under Nests and Nesting) except for those exposed to the dire man-made effects—immediate or long-term—of poisoning or complete destruction of the bird's environment. *See* Poisons.

If a young bird in its first year can survive accidents and diseases (*see* Diseases), migration, winter starvation, and the hunting season (for game species), which takes a heavier toll of immatures than adults, it may live for a surprisingly long time, as shown by banded birds (*see* Banding).

The life span of most small birds in nature is probably no more than 6 months or a year or two (*see* Mortality; Life Expectancy), but some have lived for a remarkably long time: warblers, 5, 6, and some to 8 years; chickadees, 5, 6, 7, and 8 years, and one still alive at 10 years, 10 months; American goldfinches to 6 and 7 years, and one in captivity on Long Is., N.Y., to 13 years. A captive garden warbler, *Sylvia borin,* a small European bird, was reported to have lived for 24 years (Anonymous, 1935).

Among the medium-sized birds, wild cardinals have lived to 10, 11, and 13½ years, and a captive at Atlanta, Ga., to 28½ years; in the wild, rose-breasted grosbeaks to 9 and 10 years, and in captivity, to 15, 17½, and one, a male, to 24 years. A captive robin at Tarrytown, N.Y., lived to 17 years; a pet robin at Redmond, Ore., was still alive and healthy at 17 years. A pet mourning dove at Visalia, Calif., was still alive in Apr. 1972 when 17 years old; a homing pigeon of the U.S. Army lived to 32 years, 8 months, and a captive passenger pigeon to 29 years. *See* under Pigeon Family.

According to their records, most of the captive songbirds had been either orphaned when young or injured in such a way that they could not have survived had they been released. *See* discussion of keeping wild birds and its legality under Legal Protection. Birds in the protection of captivity usually live much longer than those in the wild, exposed to natural and man-made perils, which gives an indication (in captivity) of their real, or potentially real, longevity. *See* under Life Expectancy.

Generally, the larger the bird, the longer its life span. Canada geese in the wild have lived to 18 and 23 years; in captivity to 29, 33, and 42 years; a great egret in the wild to 22 years, 10 months; ospreys, 18–21 years, and one, 32 years; golden eagles in the wild to 30 years; in captivity to 31 and 46 years; a red-shouldered hawk, 19 years, 8 months.

Some of the seabirds are also exceptionally long-lived: herring gulls to 15, 18, and 27 years; two captives to 45 and 49 years; a black-headed gull to 63 years; arctic terns to 23, 27, and 34 years; a sooty tern to 32 years; brown noddies (terns) to 21 and 25 years; a cormorant to 23 years; a Leach's petrel to 24 years; boobies to 22 years; Laysan albatrosses to 18, 21, 34, 39, and 42 years; a frigatebird, 34 years; a brown pelican to 31 years, 5 months. *See* age records of these birds in biographies of each. *See also* Seabird.

Some captive birds reported by Mitchell (1911) apparently lived to a great age: two ravens to 50 and 69 years; two eagle owls to 53 and 68 years; a condor to 52 years; eagles of several species to 56 years, and a pelican to 40 years. Prestwich (1955) reported in England a captive great horned owl, "Lord Thurlow," that had been one of several sent there from N. America; it eventually laid eggs and was believed to be about 100 years old when it died; one of its seven descendants lived to at least 65 years.

At the National Zoological Park, Washington, D.C., a female Siberian, or Asian white, crane, *Grus leucogeranus,* obtained by the zoo on June 26, 1906, died Mar. 22, 1968, after living there 61 years, 8 months, and 26 days (Davis, 1969). *See* ages of other cranes in Crane Family.

According to Johnsgard (1968), some waterfowl have lived for the following number of years: whistling swan, 19 years (captive); greylag goose, 26 years (captive); Egyptian goose, 25 years (captive); green-winged teal, 20 years (in wild); mallard, 20 years (captive) and to 16 years in wild; canvasback, 19 years (captive); European pochard, 20 years (captive) and fertile the entire period (*see* Reproductive Life);

redhead, 16½ years (captive); common gold-eneye, 17 years (in the wild). Kennard (1975), in a summary of ages of banded wild birds, lists a mallard, 29 years, 1 month; a black duck, 19 years, 7 months; a pintail, 26 years, 6 months; and a trumpeter swan still alive in wild at 24 years, 1 month. *See also* Duck Family; Waterfowl.

AGE TERMS FOR YOUNG BIRDS
See descriptions under Nestling; *also* Fledgling; Subadult.

AGGRESSION
See Behavior; *also*, especially, Territory.

AGONISTIC BEHAVIOR
Term of some bird behaviorists for attacking, fleeing, threatening, and submissive behavior. Although involving quite different motor patterns, justifiable to group together according to Hinde (1955) because these behaviors share causal factors and are interrelated in a number of ways. Also often used as synonymous with aggressive behavior. *See* Behavior.

AIGRETTE
See Egret in Heron Family.

AIKEN
CHARLES EDWARD HOWARD (1850–1936). Born Benson, Vt., died Colorado Springs, Colo.; pioneer ornithologist of Colo.; taxidermist, great traveler in West and collector of birds; also entertaining writer. Two of the birds he discovered bear his name—the white-winged junco, *Junco aikeni*, named for him by Robert Ridgway in 1873, and a subspecies of the screech owl, *Otus asio aikeni*, named for him by William Brewster in 1891. *See* Names and Naming. See accounts in Palmer *et al.* (1954) and by Ewan (1950); *also* the A.O.U. *Checklist.*

AILMENTS
See Diseases.

AIR CHAMBER
See Hatching.

AIRCRAFT AND BIRDS
Birds and aircraft have collided since the early days of aviation. The first record of a collision between a bird and an airplane came in 1910 when a pilot flying a plane at Long Beach, Calif., collided with a gull. The bird got immovably wedged between the plane's fin and rudder; the plane crashed and the pilot was killed (Hamel and Turner, 1914).

In the fall of 1911, a pilot, C. Rogers, made the first of a series of successful transcontinental flights between N.Y. and Calif. but was killed in the spring of 1912 when his plane crashed after colliding with a bird (Solman, 1973). Since then, birds and aircraft have continued to compete for air space. Although planes are larger, faster, and stronger, this has not prevented aircraft from being damaged or sometimes destroyed by collisions with birds. See some early history of collisions between birds and aircraft in Terres (1946a; 1946c).

Collisions with birds involving injury or

Potential Life Span of Some North American Birds in the Wild

Species or kind of bird	Years
blackbird, red-winged	4–14½
bluebird, eastern	3–6½
cardinal	4–13½
catbird, gray	4–10
chickadee, black-capped	5–12½
cowbird, brown-headed	5–13¾
creeper, brown	3–5
crow, common	6–14
dove, ground	6
dove, mourning	5–10
dove, rock (domestic pigeon)	6–16+
finch, house	6–10
finch, purple	6–12½
flicker, common (yellow-shafted)	5–12½
flycatcher, great crested	6–11
goldfinch, American	4–8¾
grackle, common	4–16
grosbeak, black-headed	5–6
grosbeak, evening	4–13½
grosbeak, pine	6–8¾
grosbeak, rose-breasted	4–9
*hummingbird, blue-throated	12(?)
hummingbird, ruby-throated	5
jay, blue	5–15
jay, gray	9–10
jay, scrub (Florida)	11
junco, dark-eyed (slate colored)	3–10¾
†kestrel, American (sparrow hawk)	2–4
kingbird, eastern	3–8(?)
martin, purple	4–8
mockingbird	4–12
nuthatch, red-breasted	7½
nuthatch, white-breasted	5–9¾
oriole, northern (Baltimore)	6–8
owl, screech	6–13
phoebe, eastern	8–9
†quail, bobwhite	7–8
†quail, California	4–5
robin, American	4–11½
sparrow, chipping	2–9¾

Species or kind of bird	Years
sparrow, fox	6–9¾
sparrow, house	13⅓
sparrow, song	2½–10⅓
sparrow, tree	6–9
sparrow, white-crowned	7–13⅓
sparrow, white-throated	5½–9½
starling	5–16
swallow, barn	6–8¼
swallow, cliff	4–5
swallow, tree	5–9
tanager, scarlet	3–9
tanager, summer	6
thrasher, brown	4–12¾
thrush, wood	3–8¾
titmouse, plain	5–7
titmouse, tufted	3½–12
towhee, brown	7–10
towhee, rufous-sided	4–12¼
waxwing, cedar	3–7
woodpecker, downy	4–10½
woodpecker, hairy	7–12¾
woodpecker, red-bellied	6½–20½
wren, Carolina	3–6
wren, house	5–7
wren, winter	5¾

(Ages are from official banding records of birds from files of the U.S. Fish and Wildlife Service, Washington, D.C.)

*A male, individually identifiable, regularly dominant over other hummingbirds, appeared in a garden in Ramsay Canyon, Ariz., for 12 years.

†Birds often shot which otherwise might live to at least 10 years.
Note: Hummingbirds, warblers, and other small birds probably live only a year or two but the medium-sized or large birds that live to 3 years may survive for up to 10 years. Two thirds of the young birds that reach flying stage die in their first year; about one fourth of the population dies in the second year. A question mark (?) indicates the higher figure is not definitely known from banding records.

Reprinted with permission from John K. Terres, *Songbirds in Your Garden,* 3rd ed. (New York: Hawthorn Books)

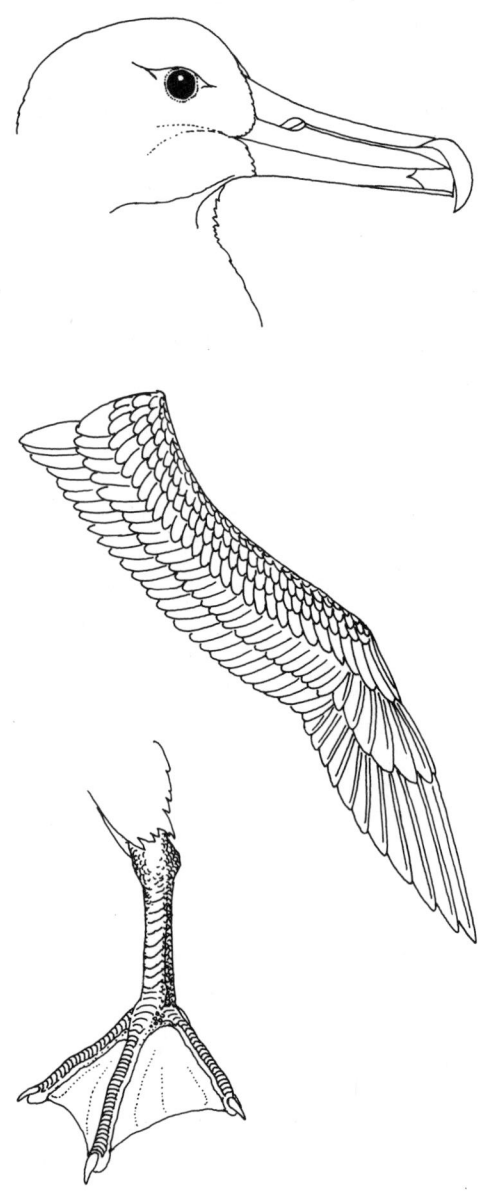

ALBATROSS FAMILY

death of occupants of aircraft increased after 1912, with some reported in World War I and a much larger number in World War II with increasing numbers of planes flown in warfare and afterward, from air bases in both the Atlantic and Pacific (see especially reports of Robbins, 1966a, and Fisher, H.I., 1966) and around the world. The total number of aircraft worldwide that have been damaged or destroyed in collisions with birds may never be known, nor will the total number of birds killed by aircraft. The problem is not the relatively few birds killed by aircraft but the injuries or fatalities to pilots or passengers and the costly damage to planes.

The greatest threat to air travelers occurs in fall and spring when the millions of ducks, geese, swans, and shorebirds migrate up and down the four major continental flyways of the U.S. (see Waterfowl) along with billions of other large and small birds spread across the sky, flying at heights usually up to about 5,000 ft. (see Migration); however, birds that live on or about airports a part of the year and in large winter concentrations are a major continuing potential hazard to aircraft.

The most serious hazards to planes at airports throughout the world are from gulls; in w. Europe, from crows; and a close third in most countries are the threats from flights of shorebirds (see Shorebird). In N. America, those shorebirds that are a threat are primarily the black-bellied plover and some of the sandpipers (Drury, 1966).

Mourning doves and horned larks are often hit by planes in the U.S. because of the abundance of these birds around inland airports; not struck so frequently but still hazardous because of their large size are cranes, swans, and geese; a collision between a snow goose and a jet trainer plane in Tex. caused the death of an astronaut and a nighttime collision between an airplane and a flock of wild swans caused severe damage to the plane but no human casualties (Terres, 1946a).

Possibly the most tragic aircraft-bird accident in the U.S. was that of an Eastern Airlines Electra jet at Logan International Airport, Boston, Mass., on Oct. 4, 1960. In taking off, the plane struck a flock of starlings which clogged its jet engines and caused the plane to crash with a loss of 62 lives among the 72 aboard. Because of the great thrust of jet engines and high speeds of the planes at takeoff and landing, a pilot must concentrate so completely on handling his aircraft that he cannot look for birds on or over the runway and is unable to maneuver to avoid them (Drury, 1966).

Lone birds are sometimes struck high in the air over the U.S. without significant damage to the plane. For example, a Western Airlines plane cruising near Elko, Nev., struck a mallard duck at 21,000 ft.; a plane over Calif. struck and killed a golden-crowned sparrow at 10,000 ft.; two evening grosbeaks were killed by a plane over the Rocky Mtns. in Colo. at 12,500 ft. (see Altitude of Bird Flight); and a small bird struck by a plane at 3,700 ft. was later identified as a catbird by the pilot-ornithologist flying the plane (Terres, 1946a).

Most collisions between aircraft and birds are at low levels and at high speeds on takeoff and landing. The incidence of aircraft strikes on birds, according to Drury (1966), is 1 to 3 collisions per 10,000 takeoffs and landings, and most do no damage to aircraft at all. See the interesting discussion by Drury (1966) of the reasons why birds are attracted to airports, and some biological solutions to the problem. See also the series of papers in *Studies of Bird Hazards to Aircraft*, published by the Canadian Wildlife Service, Report Series No. 14, Ottawa, Canada, 1971.

AIR SAC
See Respiratory System.

ALARM NOTES
Although each species may have one alarm note uttered most frequently, close studies of nesting pairs often show they have others indicating varying degrees of anxiety, alarm, and aggression (Jellis, 1977; *also* Thielke, 1976). Because most birds are preyed upon, they have developed sounds that indicate the presence of a real or potential predator.

Some of the larger oceanic birds (albatrosses, for example) have no alarm sounds; however, most gregarious or social birds utter them, especially those small ones that are preyed upon from both the ground and the sky —the nature of these alarm sounds often discloses to the listener whether the predator is near, in the air (hawk, for example), or on the ground (fox, for example), and it informs the predator that it has been seen.

Many species have alarm notes that are so similar—often of high frequency and drawn out—that one has difficulty telling them apart. For this reason, many woodland birds, for example, respond to the alarm calls of a species not of their own kind; tufted ducks nesting on the outer islands of the Baltic Sea show great dependence on gulls for warnings of danger— the alarm calls of gulls providing signals to the ducks as well as their own kind. *See* Language; Nests and Nesting; *also* Self-protective Behavior under Behavior. Wild mammals (deer, foxes, squirrels) often heed the alarm cries of jays and other birds.

Alarm calls of starlings and of house finches have been recorded, then broadcast to repel starlings from roosts on city buildings and house finches from grape vineyards. See details in Boudreau (1968) and Anderson (1969). *See also* under Starling Family; Control.

ALAUDIDAE
See Lark Family; *also* Passeriformes.

ALBATROSS FAMILY
Diomedeidae (die-oh-me-DEE-ih-dee); according to Gruson (1972), *diomedea* comes from Diomedes, name of a Gr. hero at Troy; according to Gr. mythology, his companions were transformed into birds. The word *albatross* has been traced to *alcatraz*, the name Portuguese navigators gave to seafowl in general; *alcatraz* was later corrupted to *algotross*, then to *albatross*, possibly through influence of Lat. *albus*, white. *See* relatives of albatrosses under Procellariiformes.

Albatrosses are oceanic birds; 13 species in world (Van Tyne and Berger, 1976); most are in southern oceans from about 30° S. Lat. to Antarctic; some in N. Pacific to Bering Sea; a few reach N. Atlantic; family includes albatrosses only; 7 species reported off N. American shores; largest of seabirds (28–53 in. long), capable of long-sustained flight (drink salt water) of months over ocean, alighting only on surface to feed or when becalmed by lack of winds; with long narrow wings inefficient at flapping flight, are masters of gliding on winds of world's oceans (see especially account of Jameson, 1958, of use by albatrosses of dynamic soaring); most of them are migratory and go to land only to breed on remote, uninhabited oceanic islands; nest on ground in large colonies; pairs have elaborate ritualized displays; are monogamous, believed to mate for life (see The Pair Bond under Courtship) or until one or other of pair dies (Palmer, 1962); female lays single egg; from egg to rearing of young takes about 4 or 5 months in the smaller species, but much longer in larger royal and wandering albatrosses, whose young have fledging period of nearly 1 year; therefore larger albatrosses nest only every other year (Matthews, 1964a); young of some albatrosses require 7–9 years to reach breeding age (Rice and Kenyon, 1962b). See Sexual Maturity.

Albatrosses are mainly white or sooty brown; wing tip and edge or entire wings may be black or dark brown; tail and middle of back black in many species; sexes outwardly alike in most species; males significantly larger than females; bill stout and strongly hooked with sheath of horny plates; tubular nostrils and salt-excreting glands present (see Nostrils); nestlings may discharge a stomach oil in defense against intruder (see Regurgitation); also have good sense of smell. (For illustrated details of identification of albatrosses in N. Atlantic, see Warham et al., 1974.)

Legs of albatrosses are rather short, the feet are webbed, the hind toe (hallux) is minute or absent; the wings are long and narrow; tail relatively short; cries are loud and harsh; to take off usually must run on water or on land into wind, or drop off a cliff into the air; feed largely at night on squids, cuttlefishes, and other marine animals, which they catch by descending to surface; some follow ships to feed on garbage. See details in Jameson (1958); Palmer (1962); and Terres (1968a); see especially Murphy (1936).

A great slaughter of albatrosses began in late 19th century when wings were in demand for millinery and body feathers sold for stuffing mattresses and pillows; the largest and best-known albatross rookery was on Laysan Is., 1,000 mi. west of Hawaii; terrible slaughter of albatrosses there led Theodore Roosevelt in 1909 to set aside Laysan and other islands in the Leeward chain as a wildlife reservation (see other details in Austin, 1961).

Almost never kept in captivity; an ill or injured albatross would require a pool of salt (ocean) water on which to rest, swim, and feed; offer meat, shrimp, crab meat, crayfishes or other crustaceans, all finely ground and fed to it on water. Other foods might be offered, as albatrosses feed on ships' garbage, but it should be in small pieces (Walker, 1942).

Black-browed albatross, *Diomedea melanophris* (die-oh-me-DEE-ah mel-an-OH-fris); genus name: *see* family introduction; species name: Lat., from Gr. *melas*, black, and *ophrys*, brow, eyebrow (Jaeger, 1955). (Color ills., pages 39, 40.) Nine records of this species in N. Atlantic off Spitsbergen, Greenland, Norway, and Great Britain (Fisher and Lockley, 1954), and two recent U.S. reports (1972); 31½–37½ in. long; wingspread 7 to 8 ft. (Palmer, 1962); white albatross with *gray-black wings and back;* head, neck, rump, and underparts pure white except broad border of black on underside of wings; named for black line through and over eyes but this mark shared by other species of albatrosses; *bill entirely straw yellow;* glides on stiff, outstretched wings but tends to flap, to turn more sharply, and to bank vertically more than do larger royal and wandering albatrosses (Watson, 1966); most abundant and wide-ranging of the S. Hemisphere species; from Antarctic to Tropic of Capricorn (Murphy, 1936); at sea the most fearless of all albatrosses; closely follows ships and was often caught by European sailors of 19th century on barbless hook baited with fat; said to bray and to grunt in displays ashore; at sea, peevish croaking while feeding (Palmer, 1962).

Feeding Habits: Eats squids, fishes, shrimps, mollusks, smaller seabirds, ships' garbage.
Nest: On oceanic islands in colonies; nest is cuplike bowl of mud and grasses up to foot high.
Eggs: Usually Oct.; 1, dull white, with sprinkling of red spots at larger end.
Incubation: By both sexes; period of incubation 64–79 days (Lockley, 1973); young first takes flight at 116 days after hatching (see Tickell, 1975).
Age: A black-browed albatross that lived on the Faeroes in a colony of gannets from about 1860 to 1894 before it was shot (collected) may have been an escaped pet from a ship (Murphy, 1936); to 1961 was oldest-known living bird but in that year its record longevity of 34 years was exceeded by a European oystercatcher 36 years old, then the oldest-known banded bird in the world (Terres, 1968a; 1975). *See* older birds in biography of Laysan albatross and under Age.
Weights: Up to about 8½ lbs.
Range: In S. Atlantic nests on islands off Tierra del Fuego, Falkland Is., South Georgia, etc., occurs regularly in Falkland and Benguela Currents up to 20° S. Lat.; vagrant in N. Atlantic; reported in West Indies (Watson, 1966); two seen at Buzzards Bay, Mass., June 28, 1972; two seen at sea off Morehead City, N.C., Aug. 19, 1972 (see details in DuMont, 1973).

Black-footed albatross, *Diomedea nigripes* (die-oh-me-DEE-ah NIG-rih-peez); genus name: *see* family introduction; species name: from Lat. *niger*, black, and *pes*, foot. (Color ills., pages 40, 41.) 27–29 in. long; wingspread 6½–7 ft.; only albatross seen regularly off Pacific coast; uniformly dusky bird above and below; at close range, whitish face and pale areas show around tips of wings; light gray under tail; strictly pelagic and seldom seen from shore (Peterson, 1961); sexes alike, but

male averaging slightly larger; at sea, usually silent when alone but in groups may groan during displays on water; squeals or shrieks fighting over food.

Feeding Habits: May follow ships for several hours by day and on moonlit nights to feed on garbage, but main food is fishes, sea urchins, amphipods, squids, caught from ocean's surface at night.
Nest: A shallow scrape in sand in colonies; when sharing nesting island with Laysan albatross, nests on outer edge of colony.
Eggs: On Midway Is., mid-Nov. to early Dec. (Palmer, 1962); 1, dull white, spotted with red-brown.
Incubation: By male and female in turn, 63–68 days; nestling stage about 140 days from hatching; may not breed until 9 years old (Rice and Kenyon, 1962a).
Other Names: Black gooney; gooney bird.
Accidents: On Midway Is., often struck by aircraft.
Age: Records of banded individuals recaptured alive on Midway at ages of about 14–16 years (Palmer, 1962); one trapped and released when 18 years, 8 months, old (Kennard, 1975); two, one 25 years, 7 months, when recaptured on Midway, another at least 27 years old (Clapp, 1976).
Hybrids: Has interbred with Laysan albatross (Fisher, 1972).
Weights: Usually 7–8 lbs.; up to 9 lbs.
Range: Now limited as breeding species to Leeward chain of islands and atolls of Hawaiian archipelago, Marshall Is., Johnston Is. In 1957–58 nesting season, world's population estimated at 300,000; during 1956–57 and 1957–58 breeding seasons, 55,000 nesting pairs in Hawaiian Is. (Rice and Kenyon, 1962b); leaves breeding places mainly in July, ranges over N. Pacific, south to Baja Calif. to Aleutians and Bering Sea; returns to nesting places latter half Oct. to Nov.

Laysan albatross, *Diomedea immutabilis* (die-oh-me-DEE-ah im-mew-TAB-il-iss); genus name: *see* family introduction; species name: Lat., unchangeable or unchanging, in allusion to plumage of immature bird, which is like, or very similar to, that of adult, i.e., unchanged or unchanging; *Laysan* in reference to island of Laysan. (Color ills., page 43.) 31–32 in. long; wingspread to about 6½ ft.; head, neck, and body white to yellowish; uniformly blackish across wings and back; sexes alike, but males average slightly larger; only dark-backed albatross in N. Pacific with white head and white underparts; utters notes higher-pitched and less harsh than those of black-footed albatross, otherwise voice is similar. During 1956–57 and 1957–58 nesting seasons, 280,000 nesting pairs in the Hawaiian Is., about five times more than the black-footed population (Rice and Kenyon, 1962b); probably travel great distances when away from nesting grounds; one banded on nest on Leeward chain of Hawaiian Is., Dec. 3, 1956, recovered 23 days later more than 2,000 mi. away off Hokkaido, Japan (Rice and Kenyon, 1958). *See* Homing; *also* Migration.

ALBATROSS FAMILY
In flight, the albatross may be distinguished by its large size, its long, narrow wings, relatively short tail, and deeply hooked bill. It is an expert glider, soaring on ocean air currents with wings held stiffly, rarely flapping.

Feeding Habits: Eats squids mostly at night when squids come to surface of ocean; not habitually a ship follower (Palmer, 1962).

Nest: A shallow scrape in sand surrounded by low ridge of plant material that each pair in enormous colonies piles around the nest; nests spaced a few feet apart over hundreds of acres; one can walk among these without disturbing the nesting albatrosses. *See* accounts under Tameness. Pairs engage in elaborate "dances" or displays, which are of slower tempo than those of black-footed albatross (Palmer, 1962).

Eggs: Nov.–Dec.; 1, rough surface, dull white to buff, with or without reddish-brown spots at ends; egg is 10% of female's body weight.

Incubation: Shared in turn by both sexes, 62½–68 days; average 65 days (Fisher, 1971); nestling stage about 165 days; young may not breed until 7 years old (Rice and Kenyon, 1962a); see Fisher (1976) for analysis of ages of breeders.

Other Names: Gooney bird; white gooney bird.

Accidents: On Midway often struck by aircraft.

Age: Of 14,420 banded Laysan albatrosses recaptured by Fisher (1975), 23 were 30–34 years old, 18 were 35–39 years old, and 11 were more than 40 years old.

Albinism: Alfred M. Bailey reported several albinos (Palmer, 1962); see also Fisher (1972).

Hybrids: See Black-footed albatross.

Weights: Usually 5–7 lbs.; up to 8 lbs.

Range: Breeding now limited to northwestern islands of Hawaiian chain; does not range as far south as black-footed albatross or as close to land; like black-footed, is pelagic and ranges from Hawaii to Aleutians, Gulf of Alaska; and off coast of Ore. and n. Calif., and rarely to Baja Calif. (*see* Seabird).

Short-tailed albatross, *Diomedea albatrus* (die-oh-me-DEE-ah AL-bah-trus); genus name: *see* family introduction; species name: possibly New Lat., related to *albatus*, whitened (Coues, 1882). (Color ill., page 43.) *Rare;* adult is largest and only white-bodied albatross in N. Pacific; 37 in. long; wingspread 7–7½ ft.; a relatively stout-bodied, white, heavy-billed albatross; adult has blackish primaries, tip of tail black (black-footed albatross is all dark; similar Laysan has black back); immature short-tailed is chocolate brown, paler on chin; bill pinkish, flesh color; larger and darker than immature Laysan albatross with pale bill and feet (Palmer, 1962); not a follower of ships (Tramontano, 1970); very rare, but seems to be increasing slowly; almost wiped out by Japanese plume hunters between 1887 and 1903, when about half a million killed; in 1953, 20 years after last one had been reported, a few appeared to nest again on Torishima, a volcanic islet 400 mi. south of Tokyo (this was formerly the site of largest colony of these birds); in 1957, the islet was declared a Special Reserve by the Japanese government and the short-tailed albatross was designated a Natural National Monument; a census taken in Apr. 1962 showed total of 47 birds (Vincent, 1966; Austin, 1961).

Other Name: Steller's albatross, in honor of G. W. Steller, who discovered the bird.

Range: Near extinction, nests on Torishima; formerly ranged from Japan to China coast, the Japan and Okhotsk Seas, Bering Sea from Komandorskie Is. north to the Diomede Is. and Norton Sound and through N. Pacific from Alaska to Baja Calif.; reported 70 mi. off San Francisco, Feb. 17, 1946; and in Gulf of Alaska, 140 mi. from Cape Spencer, Nov. 25, 1947 (A.O.U. *Check-list,* 1957). One (a subadult) also seen and photographed, May 3, 1970, about 38 mi. west of Westport, Wash. (Wahl, 1970). See Tramontano (1970) for other observations.

Shy albatross. *See* White-capped albatross.

Steller's albatross. *See* Short-tailed albatross.

Wandering albatross, *Diomedea exulans* (die-oh-me-DEE-ah eks-YOU-lans); genus name: *see* family introduction; species name: Lat., banished, exiled; *wandering* in reference to its wide range over southern oceans of the world. (Color ill., page 42.) One grounded 60 mi. north of San Francisco, July 1967, was first N. American record (Paxton, 1968); about same size as royal albatross; 42–48 in. long; wingspread 10–11½ ft.; female noticeably smaller than male; largest wingspread, along with royal albatross, of any living seabird; wings only 9 in. wide (front to back); mainly white bird including underwings, with black wing tips; sometimes dark vermiculations on top of wings; bill pinkish white with yellow tip; immature is blackish brown with white face, throat, underwings, and occasionally white belly; with increasing age, becomes progressively whiter (Watson, 1966); glides on stiff, outstretched wings seldom flapping at all in heavy wind; when accompanying ships, coasts alongside or crisscrosses in ship's wake. (For details of wandering albatrosses' dynamic flight, see Jameson, 1958.) On nesting grounds utters curious gobblings (like turkey), squeals, and cacklings; at sea when competing for food utters harsh croak. Tickell (1968) estimated the world's population at 58,760 birds.

Feeding Habits: Eats fishes, galley refuse; one reported by Murphy (1936) to have eaten a great quantity of the Portuguese man-of-war, a jellyfish; bulk of food is cephalopods, including squids and cuttlefishes.

Nest: In colonies on oceanic islands or islets; arrives from wanderings at sea for courtship Oct.–Dec.; after pairing, nest is built up by pair on base of nest of previous year, using peaty moss and mud; if beginning in new spot, mated pair first scratch with bills a circular trench, push excavated earth and vegetal mold into considerable pile, which they pack down with feet; finished nest is shape of a truncated cone about 3 ft. across at base, up to 18 in. or more high, bowl at top for single egg about 4½ in. across, 1–2 in. deep.

Eggs: South Georgia Is., Dec. 20–late Feb. (Murphy, 1936); 1, white, usually speckled with red-brown at larger end; size range from about 120–144 mm. long (about 4¾–5¾ in.), and 75–86 mm. in diameter (about 3–3½ in.); each freshly laid egg weighs about 429–487 gr., or average about 1 lb. (Murphy, 1936).

Incubation: By both sexes, 75–82 days; one member of pair may incubate as little as 2 days, or up to 38 days, before relief by mate; young have longest nestling life of any bird; may take 9 months (278 days) before it flies (Tickell, 1968); at 50–60 days, before young flies, adults feed it less and less until finally not at all as they begin voluntarily to desert it; young finally takes off on its own; does not begin to breed until 8 or 9 years old; pairs thought to mate for life (*see* Courtship), each pair nests every other year (Pettingill, 1970).

Other Names: Gony (in immature, mottled plumage) or "leopard gony"; Cape sheep.

Age: May have life span of 30–40 years (Lack, 1954); an occasional one may live, theoretically, to 80 years (Tickell, 1968).

Weights: 15–20 lbs.; male up to 26¾ lbs. (Jameson, 1958).

Range: Circumpolar in west-wind belt of S. Hemisphere; ranges mainly from Tropic of Capricorn southward to 70° S. Lat.; nests on Inaccessible Is. (Tristan group), Gough, and other subantarctic islands; and in Antarctic on S. George and other islands; occurs off s. Africa, and regularly crosses Tropic of Capricorn in the Benguela Current; vagrants, especially young birds, have crossed the Equator (Watson, 1966); first N. American record was bird in field overlooking sea, discovered July 11, 1967, by residents of the Sea Ranch, Sonoma, Calif., 60 mi. north of San Francisco; overnight, the wind freshened and on afternoon of July 12, the bird stretched its wings, waddled into the wind, took off over the bluff, and flew out to sea (Paxton, 1968).

White-capped albatross, *Diomedea cauta* (die-oh-me-DEE-ah CAW-tah); genus name: *see* family introduction; species name: Lat., wary, cautious, in allusion, possibly, to behavior. (Color ill., page 42.) Accidental, one record in N. American waters; from Wash., mouth of Quillayute R.; a white albatross with dark mantle; largest of the mollymauks; 36 in. long; wingspread 8 ft.; upper surface of wings gray-brown and paler than in yellow-nosed albatross; forehead white, nape and cheeks gray, brown patch before eyes, underwing white with narrow dark border; bill gray with orange tip and rounded yellow ridge; immature similar but bill entirely gray or olive.

Other Names: Shy albatross; mollymauk.
Range: Nests on islands near New Zealand, ranges north to 25° S. Lat. in S. Indian Ocean and S. Pacific, less commonly in s. Atlantic (Watson, 1966); one record off coast of Wash.

Yellow-nosed albatross, *Diomedea chlororhynchos* (die-oh-me-DEE-ah klo-row-RING-kos); genus name: *see* family introduction; species name: Lat., from Gr. *chloros*, greenish yellow, and *rhynchos*, beak. (Color ill., page 42.) A few stragglers in N. Atlantic waters off Canadian, New England, N.Y. coasts; a small slender albatross; 29½–34 in. long; wingspread 6½–7 ft. (Palmer, 1962); much larger than any gull, with great, long saberlike wings; glides and banks like a shearwater; black back sug-

gests at first appearance a black-backed gull (Peterson, 1947); from below, underwings white with black border, wider than that of white-capped albatross (Watson, 1966); bill of adult slender, black with a narrow orange-yellow ridge, and orange or pink tip; sides of head and neck white or whitish at all ages; usually a dark brow patch mostly in front of eyes; immature has gray neck, pale back and tail, and all-black bill.

Other Names: Molly; mollymauk.
Weights: 4–6 lbs.
Range: Nests, as far as known, only on Tristan da Cunha and Gough Is. (S. Atlantic) and St. Paul Is. (Indian O.); ranges over waters south of Tropic of Capricorn from s. S. Atlantic to se. Australia; ranges north to Tropic of Capricorn off Brazil and to 15° S. Lat. off sw. Africa (Watson, 1966); records in N. America off Atlantic coast, near mouth of Moisie R., Que., Aug. 20, 1885; near Machias Seal Is., mouth of Bay of Fundy, Aug. 1, 1913; Oxford County, Me., female found alive July 23, 1934, died three days later; off Freeport, Long Is., N.Y., photographed May 29, 1960; one reported near Monhegan Is., Me., May 21, 1960 (Palmer, 1962); one reported Buzzards Bay, Mass., May 7, 1971, first record for state (Finch, 1971c).

ALBINISM

The state or quality of being an albino; an albino (from Lat. *albus*, white) bird has white feathers instead of the usual colors of its species (e.g., black or brown), and the white feathers may cover the bird wholly or in part, as there are various degrees of albinism. Some birds such as some swans, geese, herons, egrets, gulls, and others that are normally white are not albinos.

Albinism results from a genetic change that inhibits the formation of an enzyme (tyrosinase) responsible for the synthesis of pigment (melanin).

The various degrees of albinism, classified by two geneticists, Mueller and Hutt (1941), and adopted by Nero (1954) and Pettingill (1956; 1970), are:

(1)*Total Albinism:* The rarest form, in which the bird has a complete absence of melanin (dark coloring pigment) from the eyes, skin, and feathers.

(2)*Incomplete Albinism:* Pigment is completely absent from either eyes, skin, or feathers but not all three.

(3)*Imperfect Albinism:* Pigment formation is partially inhibited (reduced) in eyes, skin, or feathers but pigment is not totally inhibited in any.

(4)*Partial Albinism:* The commonest form; complete or partial albinism within local parts of the body which may involve certain feathers only; it is often symmetrical and each side of the bird may show white feathers in the same pattern. For example, a feral common pigeon, or rock dove, cited by Sage (1962) had an odd white feather or two behind each of its eyes throughout its entire life and molted these annually and new white feathers grew in their place.

A patch of abnormally white feathers on a normally colored bird may also be caused by an

injury, a physiological disorder, or dietary or circulatory deficiencies at the time the feathers are developing (Gross, 1965a). In N.C. in 1944, C. S. Brimley, in discussing albinism in birds caused by injuries, described a male red-winged blackbird that was a partial albino with a large white patch on one side of its breast, covering an old wound where a shot had left a furrow in its flesh. Allan R. Phillips, in 1954, described a great-tailed grackle collected in Mexico that was white on one side of its face. Beneath the white feathers a cyst had developed under the skin around a sliver of some kind embedded in its jaw muscles; a Japanese ornithologist in 1928 wrote of a hen capercaillie which was bitten by a stoat (weasel); after the wound healed, white feathers grew over the affected part. *See* capercaillie in introduction to Grouse Family.

The sudden appearance of white feathers in some birds that are normally dark may be caused by shock. In 1844, a British ornithologist described a captive male blackbird which, after being severely frightened by a cat, molted and became pure white (Sage, 1962). Aging, according to Sage, may cause some birds to become white, perhaps as a person's hair whitens in later life. A British bird-bander (*see* Banding) trapped a male blackbird annually for 2 years and finally, when retrapped at about 5 years old, it had patches of white over most of its plumage. Another became progressively white from 1954 to 1957, when it was pure white. Frazier (1952) reported an American robin which was a normally colored adult male in Apr. 1949, when banded; by June 1951 most of its head feathers were white with white feathers on its throat, nape, breast, lower belly, and undertail coverts. Warne (1926) told of a pet crow which, after 5 years, suddenly grew white feathers in each of its wings, which previously were all-black.

Totally albino birds have all-white feathers, pink or red eyes, and very pale or white feet, legs, and bill. The eyes appear pink because in the absence of color pigment in the irises, the blood in the eyes shows through. *See* Colors of Eyes under Eyes and Eyesight. The rarity of albinism in birds is suggested by records of 30,000 birds banded by Michener and Michener (1936) at Pasadena, Calif., over a 10-year period. Only 17 of the 30,000 birds they handled had albinism in any degree, or only about a half of 1%.

Adult birds that are total albinos are very rarely seen in the wild, especially the small or medium-sized ones. Apparently they are more easily detected in their accustomed environments, such as a forest or in any other dark background where the darker colors of their species render the normally colored birds less conspicuous. In white plumage, they may be selectively eliminated by a predator; falconers, for example, have often noted that their trained predatory birds will single out for attack a white pigeon in a flock, apparently because it is more conspicuous than its darker-colored companions.

Totally albino birds often have weak eyesight, and brittle wing and tail feathers, which may reduce their ability to fly. Keeler and King (*Journal of Comparative Psychology*, 1942) reported that in their studies of abnormally col-

permanent range of the boat-tailed grackle

permanent range of the great-tailed grackle

ALLOPATRIC SPECIES
Once thought to be a single species, the great-tailed grackle and the boat-tailed grackle are now considered two distinct, largely allopatric species. Even in a recently established common nesting ground in Texas, they do not interbreed or do so only very rarely.

ored animals in captivity, faded-feather mutations of the turkey had poor vision, broken or missing feathers, and weak bones. A pair of captive albino collared doves, with little or no color in their irises, had defective vision and they did not fly well.

Albino birds in the wild are often harassed by their own kind. Nero (1954) cited a completely albino female red-winged blackbird in an immense Sept. flock that was chased repeatedly by its companions, yet it always returned to the flock. In Ore., an albino barn swallow was constantly chased by others of its kind, and another near Stone Dam, N.Y., all-white but with dark eyes (incomplete albinism), was chased by other barn swallows whenever it flew. Cherry Kearton (1931), British ornithologist, in his studies of S. African penguins, wrote that three freakish young in a nesting colony (one had an entirely black head, another a white head, the third was a complete albino) were friendless, shunned, and generally abused by their companions.

Brown pigment seems more likely to disappear and to be replaced by albinistic white than red or yellow pigments. There seem to be more records of albinism among blackbirds, crows, hawks, robins, etc., which have in general dark pigment, than among the red or yellow birds such as goldfinches, cardinals, orioles, etc.

Some birds have seasonally alternating white plumage, which is not albinism. White or winter plumage of ptarmigans is normal and acquired each fall by these birds whether it snows or not. In spring, ptarmigans gradually lose their white winter plumage, which is replaced in the molt by the brown summer plumage; apparently these two color changes are adaptive and have evolved in ptarmigans in response to the northern climate and the seasonally alternating environment of snow and bare earth. Ptarmigans are difficult to see on snow when in white winter plumage and equally difficult to see on the ground when in brown summer plumage. *See* discussion under Seasonal Dimorphism in Colors of Feathers.

Up to Apr. 1965, there were records of some degree of albinism in 304 species of N. American birds, represented by 1,847 individuals. Albinism has been reported in all orders, and in 54 families of N. American birds (*see* lists of orders and families under Classification). For records of albinism in individual species, *see* biographies of each. *See also* leucism (paleness of plumage) and melanism (unusually dark plumage) in Abnormal Colors under Colors of Feathers.

According to Gross (1965a), the American robin, with 152 records of albinism (8.22% of all records), and the house sparrow, with 104 records (5.53% of all records), led all other birds in highest incidence of albinism. Among the 1,847 cases of albinism reported by Gross, only 7% were total, or complete, albinos.

ALBUMEN
See Eggs and Egg-laying; *also* Embryo and Its Development.

ALCATRAZ
See Brown booby in Booby Family.

ALCEDINIDAE
See Kingfisher Family.

ALCID
(AL-sid). Seabird of the Auk Family. *See* Auk Family. Ornithologists usually refer to these birds collectively as alcids.

ALCIDAE
See Auk Family.

ALEWIFE BIRD
Name for the common snipe in Mass. from its spring arrival, coinciding with that of the alewife, or branch herring (McAtee, 1955c).

ALEXANDRE
M. M., M.D. Little is known of this "man of mystery" (Palmer, 1928) except that "he practiced in Mexico" (Gruson, 1972) and sent many bird specimens from there to France, where he was honored in 1846 by Bourcier and Musant, who, in naming the black-chinned hummingbird, gave it the species name *alexandri* in his honor, and the type locality (where the first specimen or specimens of this bird were collected) as Sierra Madre (Occidental), Mexico.

ALLANTOIS
(AL-lan-toys). *See* Embryo and Its Development.

ALLEN
ARTHUR A(UGUSTUS) (1885–1964). Born Buffalo, N.Y.; fellow of the American Ornithologists' Union, educator, popular writer and lecturer on birds, explorer, pioneer bird photographer, and research scientist. At Cornell University, Ithaca, N.Y., he became the first teacher in America with the title Professor of Ornithology; was associated there with teaching and research studies in ornithology for more than 50 years; was also a pioneer in studies and recordings of the songs and calls of wild birds; was a co-founder in 1957 of the Cornell Laboratory of Ornithology, which today houses these early sound recordings and many others (*see* Recordings). Author of *The Book of Bird Life* (1930a; 1961), *Stalking Birds with Color Camera* (1951b), and other books. See *American Men of Science* (1960 ed.); also Allen (1962) and Pettingill (1968).

ALLEN
CHARLES A(NDREW) (1841–1930). Allen's hummingbird was named for this collector of birds; in Marin County, Calif., he collected the types of several birds new to science; among his collections was a hummingbird that at the time was also thought to be unnamed and undescribed. In 1877, Henry W. Henshaw described it as a new species and named the bird *Selasphorus alleni* in honor of Charles Andrew Allen, who had sent him the specimen. A prior description of this bird, however, in 1829 by René Primivère Lesson, had been overlooked (*see* law of priority of names under Names and Naming) and the scientific name was later changed from *alleni* to *sasin* in proper defer-

ence to Lesson's earlier name and priority. The English, or popular, name still honors Allen. See Mailliard (1931).

ALLEN

J(OEL) A(SAPH) (1838–1921). "Father of the American Ornithologists' Union," its president for its first 7 years; editor of *The Auk*, its official publication, for 28 years; editor of the eight volumes of its predecessor, *The Bulletin of the Nuttall Ornithological Club;* also edited the first three editions of the Union's *Check-list of North American Birds;* in 1885 appointed Curator of Birds and Mammals at American Museum of Natural History, a post he held to the end of his life (Palmer *et al.,* 1954). For an analysis of Allen's contributions to ornithological progress, see Stresemann (1975).

ALLEN'S RULE

Propounded, or first stated, by J. A. Allen, former Curator of Birds and Mammals, American Museum of Natural History, that in the cold or cool climates of the world, the extensions or extremities of a warm-blooded animal's body—ears and tails of mammals for example—tend to be shorter. This adaptation has evolved, or developed, in response to the cold climate in which some animals live almost perpetually. In a cold environment, an animal with short ears or legs would lose body heat less rapidly than one with long ears and tail. Birds that live in colder parts of the world generally have relatively shorter bills, legs, and wings than their nearest relatives in warmer regions. Such projections lose heat more rapidly than the main bulk of a bird's body.

Welty (1975) citing Huxley (1942) states that a difference of 1% in wing length corresponds to a difference of 2 degrees North Latitude in the common redpoll, *Acanthis flammea;* of just over 1 degree in the Atlantic puffin, *Fratercula arctica,* and a little over 0.5 degrees in winter wrens, *Troglodytes troglodytes.* A study by Johnston and Selander (1971) of the house sparrow in America is one of the best examples of the evolution of geographical changes in a bird that supports Allen's Rule. *See* Ecological Rules; *also* Cline.

ALLIGATORS AND BIRDS

See Reptiles and Birds.

ALLOPATRIC (al-low-PAT-rick) SPECIES

Birds that are closely related but whose geographical ranges do not overlap or overlap only slightly. Some examples are the very similar black phoebe and eastern phoebe; the pygmy nuthatch of the West and the brown-headed nuthatch of the Southeast (see especially Norris, 1958); and the very similar red-bellied woodpecker and golden-fronted woodpecker, each with separate geographic ranges. These two woodpeckers, even though resembling each other closely, do not interbreed where their nesting ranges meet and so retain their species identity.

In some birds that are closely related and strikingly alike and were formerly considered allopatric species because of their geographic separation, where their nesting ranges have expanded so as to meet, instead of retaining their separate identities, they have crossbred, or hybridized. When this hybridization has been general or large-scale, it is apparent that they are not separate but a single species. Examples are the yellow-shafted flicker, the red-shafted flicker, and the gilded flicker, which are now considered one species (the common flicker) because of their ready hybridization where their nesting ranges meet (*see* account under Hybrid). Also the myrtle warbler of the e. U.S. and Audubon's warbler of the w. U.S.; these two also interbreed where their ranges meet; they are now recognized as one species (the yellow-rumped warbler) (American Ornithologists' Union, 1973). Apparently these close relatives of a common ancestor have not been separated long enough to become reproductively isolated from each other. *See* Species.

For examples of similar, closely related species of birds that have achieved reproductive isolation from each other over their largely shared nesting ranges, *see* Sibling Species; Sympatric Species.

ALLOPREENING

(AL-low-preen-ing), or MUTUAL PREENING. Term for the preening of the feathers of one bird by another, usually of the same species and commonly by its mate. This reciprocal preening is usually done by birds that are paired, or associated, as in captivity. *See* discussion under Preening.

ALPINE TUNDRA

See Tundra.

ALPINE ZONE

See Tundra.

ALTITUDE OF BIRD FLIGHT

Ordinarily, the height at which small to medium-sized birds fly during their daily travels is seldom more than 50–100 ft. above the ground; larger birds such as hawks and vultures may soar upward to 1,000 ft. or more. Under special circumstances, certain birds may fly at relatively tremendous heights. The direct sighting (not by radar; *see* Migration) of a bird at one of the greatest heights ever recorded came during the British-sponsored Mt. Everest Expedition of 1921 when a lammergeyer, or bearded vulture, *Gypaetus barbatus,* was seen soaring about its mountain home at 25,000 ft. *See* How High Do Birds Fly? under Flight; *also* Digestion. The lammergeyer is the largest bird of prey in Europe, with a wingspread up to 9 ft. and weight of 14½–18½ lbs. (Brown and Amadon, 1968).

In the Andes, the S. American condor, *Vultur gryphus,* largest bird of prey in the world, with a wingspread to 10 or 10½ ft. and weight up to 25 lbs., has been reported at 19,800 ft. (Meinertzhagen, 1955). *See* Size.

Gilliard (1958) reported alpine choughs, crowlike birds of Eurasia, nesting at great heights in the Alps, with some on Mt. Everest at 27,000 ft., which he believed was "very near the ceiling for birds." Swan (1970) reported an even higher record of bar-headed geese, *Anser indicus,* flying over the Himalayas; a flock was heard calling as they migrated north directly over the summit of Makalu, 27,824 ft. above sea

ALLOPREENING
A pair of green jays engage in mutual preening, concentrating on areas of the body that an individual bird cannot reach with its own bill. The widespread feather maintenance ritual—which at times may become quite violent—is also thought to sublimate aggressive impulses between mated birds.

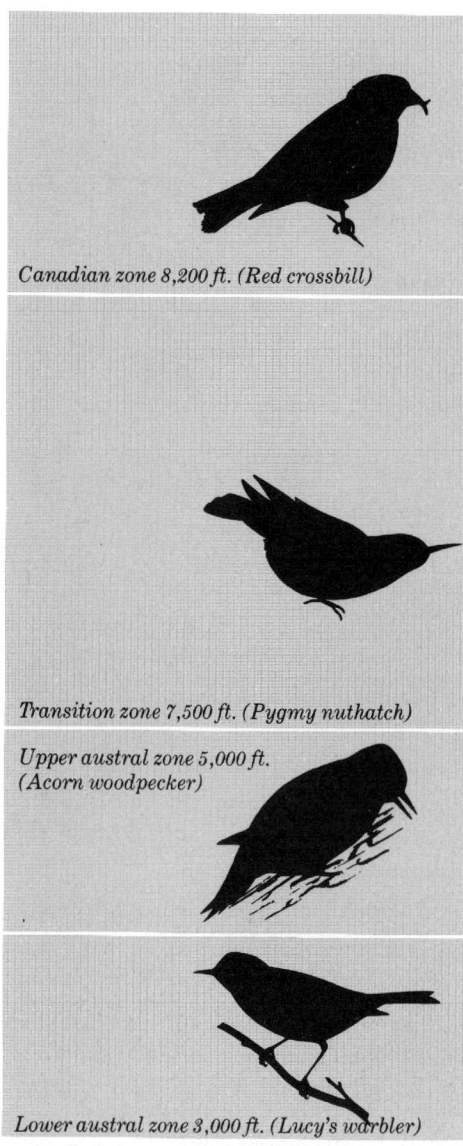

Canadian zone 8,200 ft. (Red crossbill)

Transition zone 7,500 ft. (Pygmy nuthatch)

Upper austral zone 5,000 ft. (Acorn woodpecker)

Lower austral zone 3,000 ft. (Lucy's warbler)

ALTITUDINAL DISTRIBUTION
The changes in the life zones—and the avifauna typical of each—found at different altitudes of a mountain range in the American West correspond to the life zone changes that one would find from subtropical Mexico to Northern Canada.

level. This species is a regular migrant over the crest of the Himalayas.

On Nov. 29, 1973, a Rüppell's griffon—a vulture, *Gyps rueppelli*—collided with a commercial aircraft over Abidjan, Ivory Coast, W. Africa, at an altitude of 37,000 ft. Up to that time, it was the highest altitude ever recorded for a bird in flight. The impact with the vulture (which may have a wingspread of 7–8 ft. and weigh up to about 18 lbs.) damaged one of the aircraft's engines; however, the plane landed safely at Abidjan (Laybourne, 1974). *See* Aircraft and Birds.

Most of the world's greatest altitude records for birds have come from the high Alps and Himalayas, which force birds to fly over them during their spring and autumn migrations. Godwits and curlews—long-winged, swift-flying shorebirds, or wading birds (*see* Sandpiper Family)—have been seen flying past Mt. Everest at 20,000 ft. Meinertzhagen (1955) saw choughs flying at 21,000 ft. above sea level and a wall creeper—a European bird in the same family as the American brown creeper—at 21,000 ft.

Most of the high-altitude records for birds sighted and identified over Europe were much lower: rooks (crowlike birds) over France and Germany up to 7,500 ft.; swifts over Switzerland, Holland, and France up to 4,000 ft. and 9,500 ft. (almost 2 mi.), and some at 11,000 ft. according to James Fisher, British ornithologist; ducks and geese over France at 7,500 ft.; lapwings (*see* Plover Family) at 6,000 ft. and occasionally at 8,500 ft. during their migrations.

An airliner provided the highest altitude recorded for a *positively identified* N. American bird. Late in the afternoon on July 9, 1963, a Western Airlines L-188 Electra, cruising near Elko, Nev., at 21,000 ft., airspeed of 345 knots, struck an object in the air that produced a light thud, according to the pilot. Later, passengers riding in the plane said that it felt like a small explosion. Upon landing, a feather taken from the point of impact on the leading edge of one of the plane's horizontal stabilizers was sent to the U.S. Fish and Wildlife Service for identification. The bird was a mallard (*see* in Duck Family; *also* Aircraft and Birds).

Other positively identified N. American birds either struck by aircraft or sighted from aircraft are chimney swifts near Lufkin, Tex., in Apr. and May at 7,000 and 7,300 ft.; a golden-crowned sparrow between Sacramento and San Bernardino, Calif., at 10,000 ft.; two evening grosbeaks over the Front Range of the Rocky Mtns. near Boulder, Colo., at 12,500 ft.

ADAPTABILITY OF BIRDS TO HIGH ALTITUDES. Ever since reliable records of birds flying at great heights have been available, ornithologists have wondered how birds rise to 18,000 or 20,000 ft. and quickly adapt to an atmosphere where the oxygen is 50% less than at sea level. After ten minutes, men resting and not acclimated at 20,000 ft. are in a state of beginning hypoxic collapse (Armstrong, 1952), and without supplementary oxygen, will fall into a coma and die at 23,000 ft. (Luft, 1965). How then can birds flap strenuously and live at these heights?

To try to answer this question, Vance A. Tucker (1968) at Duke University, in N.C., tested house sparrows in a hypobaric chamber in which he could simulate, and control, conditions of the air at 20,000 ft. Using the sparrows, easily trapped outside his laboratory, Tucker admitted that he was testing a bird that was not flying, and possibly never would fly at that height in nature, but he believed his tests would provide insight into how other birds did it.

At rest, Tucker's house sparrows in the chamber took in oxygen 2.2 times that of house sparrows resting at ground level. They did it by hyperventilating (increasing their respiration) and allowing their body temperatures (*see* Temperature) to drop about 2° C. These adjustments brought more oxygen to the lungs and increased the blood's acceptability of, or affinity with, oxygen. From his tests and estimates, Tucker concluded that a "hypothetical" house sparrow could get adequate oxygen for flight at 20,000 ft. See details in Tucker (1968). *See also* Metabolism; Flight Muscles under Flight.

ESTIMATING THE HEIGHT OF BIRD FLIGHT. Years ago, European ornithologists experimented with methods to help them estimate the height of a flying bird. In 1911, Friedrich Karl Lucanus, a German ornithologist, suspended life-sized facsimiles of certain European birds from a balloon. Knowing the height of the rising balloon, he could tell at what heights the birds were still distinguishable and at what heights they were no longer visible. A European sparrow hawk, about the size of the N. American Cooper's hawk, could be recognized at 800 ft., was a dot in the sky at 1,000 ft., and could not be seen at 2,800 ft., or little more than half a mile up. A rook, a bird much like the common American crow, was distinguishable at 1,000 ft., was a spot at 2,600 ft., and disappeared at 3,300 ft. The fan-shaped tail of a golden eagle could be recognized at 1,500 ft., but was only a dot at 2,000 ft. The life-sized image of the eagle itself was clearly visible as a soaring bird at 3,000 ft., was still recognizable *as a bird* at 5,000 ft., but became a mere dot at 7,750 ft. and disappeared at 8,750 ft. A 3–4 in. N. American hummingbird on a utility wire appears as a dot to the unaided eye when it is 100 ft. away, but a 5–6-in. swallow is clearly recognizable at that distance and becomes a dot at 250 ft.

ALTITUDINAL DISTRIBUTION
A term referring to the change in the animal and plant communities as one moves upward to the tops of the highest mountains. These different plant and animal communities succeed one another in layers, or bands, and are the result of, or response to, the changing altitude and its climate from the base of the mountain to its top, which becomes cooler as one progresses upward. In moving upward—for example, on a peak in the Rocky Mtns., some of which rise to more than 12,000 ft.—a climb of 300 ft. vertically is estimated to bring about climatic changes similar to those one would experience for each degree of latitude that one moves

northward, or about every 67 mi. (Allee *et al.*, 1949). *See* Humboldt's Rule.

While ascending some of the high peaks, one would see the same climatic changes that one would experience traveling northward to the Arctic tundra. The difference is that the changes up the mountain are more abrupt, more dramatic, and more sharply defined (Pettingill, 1956).

ALTITUDINAL MIGRATION
See Some Effects of Weather under Migration.

ALTRICIAL
(al-TRISH-al); from Lat. *altrix*, nurse or wet nurse. Term for young birds that hatch in a helpless condition, most with their eyes closed (see exceptions below), are unable to leave the nest, and are wholly dependent on the parents for food and care. One author (Verheyen, 1948) states that altricials "are born prematurely, like abortions." Examples are the young of robins, cardinals, bluebirds, other songbirds; also the young of some water birds: cormorants, penguins, albatrosses, petrels, herons, storks; and the young of pigeons, owls, hawks, parrots, swifts, woodpeckers. A helpless altricial bird is usually naked at hatching, although the altricial young of herons, hawks, owls are exceptions—they are well-covered with down when hatched, and of these large birds, only the owls have their eyes closed at hatching; hawks and herons hatch with their eyes open.

Precocial (pree-KOH-shal)—from Lat. *praecox*, to ripen beforehand—is the opposite condition, in that the young (called "chicks") are able to move about soon after hatching and drying, and are only partly or not at all dependent on their parents for food and care. They hatch with their eyes open; are down-covered; and leave the nest within a few hours, some within a day or two—gulls and terns, for example. Other examples are the young of quail, grouse, pheasants, domestic chickens, killdeers, cranes, ducks, geese, loons, shorebirds, grebes, and certain others. For a classification at hatching of the stages of development in orders and families of birds, see Nice (1962a). *See* discussion of first coat of feathers worn by young birds under Natal Down; *also* Young and Their Care.

There is an interesting relation between the weight of the yolk of the egg—the more nutritive part—and the condition of the young at hatching. In the young birds that are helpless upon hatching (altricial) and spend a week or two or more of their "childhood" in the nest, the egg yolk is proportionately smaller—only 15–25% of the egg's weight. In the egg of the precocial chick, a bird that is much further developed at hatching, the egg yolk may be 25–50% of the egg's weight (*see* Eggs and Egg-laying). Thus the precocial chick has been much better fed within the egg (*see* Embryo and Its Development) and is prepared to meet life upon hatching without being entirely dependent on the care of the parent birds.

Allen (1925) has pointed out that in tortoise and crocodile eggs (reptiles) the yolk is likewise large—33–50% of the weight of the egg—and the young are able to fend for themselves on hatching. The precocial state corresponds to the reptilian pattern and must have been the primitive one; however, the precocial condition apparently developed quite independently in different classes of birds and at different times. See discussion of this in Nice (1962a).

It may be significant that the helpless chicks of altricial birds are usually hatched in well-constructed nests in trees, where they are fairly safe from attacks of ground-inhabiting animals. Precocial chicks are usually hatched in nests on the ground—quail, grouse, ducks, loons, etc.—so that their ability to run and hide or to swim and to feed themselves is a part of their protection against raccoons, weasels, or other animals that might otherwise be able to devour them in the nest if they were helpless after hatching. *See* Young and Their Care.

Altricial and *precocial* refer to the stages of development of young birds at hatching. *Nidicolous* (nih-DICK-oh-lus)—from Lat. *nidus*, nest, and *colere*, inhabit—is a specific term for young birds that remain in or at the nest and are cared for by the parents; examples are the altricial young of robins, bluebirds, cardinals, woodpeckers, kingfishers, swifts, hummingbirds, cuckoos, parrots, pigeons. *Nidifugous* (nih-DIFF-you-gus)—from Lat. *nidus*, nest, and *fugere*, to flee—refers specifically to young birds that leave the nest rather soon after hatching and drying; examples are the precocial young of loons, grebes, ducks, plovers, quail, turkeys, cranes, and others.

Psilopaedic (SIGH-low-pea-dick)—from Gr. *psilos*, bare, and *paedic*, a mode of hatching, "hatched bare"—is a specific term for a young bird that is naked at hatching, or has only sparse down on its back; a young robin and a catbird are familiar examples, also the young of pelicans, pigeons, parrots. *Ptilopaedic* (TILL-oh-pea-dick)—from Gr. *ptilo*, from *ptilon*, down of birds, and *paedic*, method of hatching, "hatched with down," usually densely over the back and lower parts (Pettingill, 1970). The young of hawks, owls, gulls, quail, plovers, ducks, domestic chickens are good examples. *See also* Fertilization; Embryo and Its Development; Eggs and Egg-laying; Hatching.

ALULA
(AL-you-la). A "bastard wing," or small feathered projection at the bend or joint farthest out on a bird's wing. The alula acts as a wing slot in a bird's flight (*see* Flight), and the number of the alula quills, which are attached to the thumb, or pollex, varies in different birds and may be from two to at least seven (Berger, 1961).

AMBIENS
Muscles that pull the flexor tendons of a bird's legs and are believed to lock it to its perch. *See* under Feet and Legs.

AMBIENT (AM-bih-ent) TEMPERATURE
Term often used in scientific studies of effects of temperature on birds; the temperature of the medium surrounding an object—for example, the air that surrounds the body of a bird.

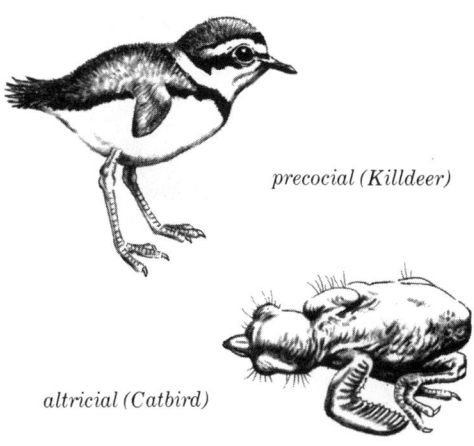

precocial (Killdeer)

altricial (Catbird)

ALTRICIAL
Altricial nestlings, like young catbirds, are born in a helpless condition, often naked with eyes unopened and wholly dependent on the parents for food, warmth, and protection.

Precocial chicks achieve greater maturity within the egg. Like ground-nesting killdeer, they are down-covered and open-eyed at hatching, able to move about soon after, and only partly dependent on the parents.

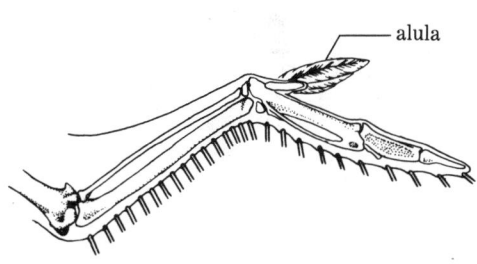

alula

ALULA
The alula is a group of small quill feathers attached to the first digit of a bird's wing. With muscles of its own, it can be moved independently of the other flight feathers.

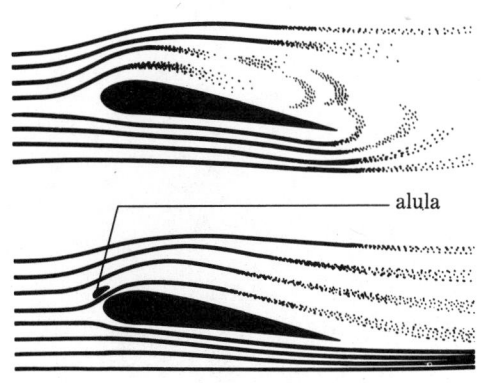

alula

alula

ALULA
Air flows over the curved upper surface of the wing faster than on the underside, creating lower pressure on top and greater pressure below which forces the wing up. This lift is lost if the angle of attack is too steep; the air stream begins to break away, causing turbulence. The alula, which functions as a wing slot, directs rapidly moving air smoothly over the top of the wing and prevents turbulence and stalling.

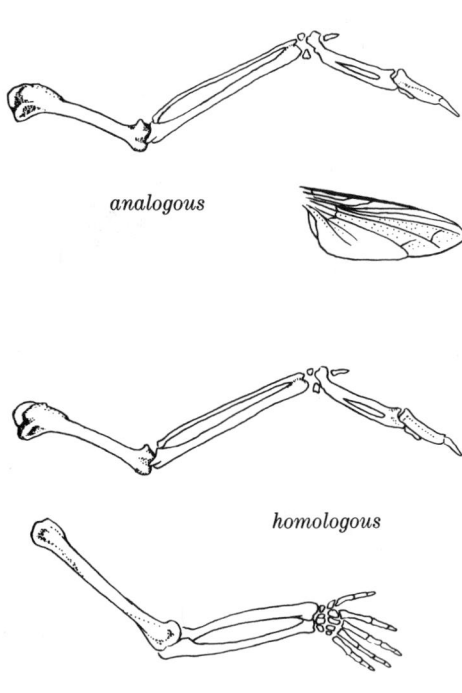

analogous

homologous

ANALOGOUS

Analogous structures are anatomical structures of different origin used by different organisms for the same purpose, such as the wings of birds and insects. Homologous structures have the same origin but need not have the same function, as in the arm of a man and the wing of a bird.

AMBIVALENT BEHAVIOR
See Behavior.

AMERICAN BIRDS
See Ornithological Periodicals.

AMERICAN GOOSANDER
See Merganser, common, in Duck Family.

AMERICAN MERGANSER
See Merganser, common, in Duck Family.

AMERICAN ORNITHOLOGISTS' UNION

A nonprofit educational, membership organization, incorporated Nov. 14, 1888, under the laws of the District of Columbia. Among its purposes are the advancement of ornithological science and the publication of a journal of ornithology. *The Auk* (*see* Ornithological Periodicals) is the official publication issued quarterly each year; the A.O.U. *Check-list of North American Birds*, a large book, is issued irregularly. Besides the *Check-list*, which gives the names and ranges of the birds of N. America, other publications have been *Fifty Years' Progress of American Ornithology* (1933); *Biographies of Members of the American Ornithologists' Union* (1954); and *Recent Studies in Avian Biology* (1955). More recent is Ornithological Monographs, a series of scientific papers each too long for inclusion in *The Auk*, one of which is a book, *The Birds of Kentucky*.

AMERICAN VULTURE FAMILY
See Vulture.

AMERICAN WOOD WARBLER FAMILY
See Warbler.

AMNION
See Embryo and Its Development.

AMPHIBIANS AND BIRDS
Amphibians, especially frogs and toads, are eaten by at least 53 kinds of birds (McAtee, 1932b), by most herons and egrets and other long-legged wading birds, also by some ducks. The common merganser, for example, eats many frogs, and in one study of the belted kingfisher, frogs made up 5% of its food (Cottam and Uhler, 1937). Thirty-four frogs were found by bird food-habits investigators in the stomach of one little blue heron, and the common crow is a voracious eater of frogs; 24 and 29 frogs had been eaten by two crows respectively of a total of 197 crows that had frog remains in their stomachs (McAtee, 1932b).

Among 14 species of birds that ate toads, 16 were common crows; 10, red-tailed hawks; 9, red-shouldered hawks; and 9, broad-winged hawks. Swainson's hawks were seen catching spadefoot toads from surface of water (Sexton and Marion, 1974). Most frequent feeder among birds upon salamanders were common crows, with records of 83 that had fed on them. From 2 ft. away, Coker (1931) in w. N.Y. watched a pair of extraordinarily tame hermit thrushes feed Allegheny mountain salamanders, *Desmognathus ochrophacus*, and red-backed salamanders to their young. Hamilton (1942) reported crows near Ithaca, N.Y., feeding on young (larval) tiger salamanders and the tadpoles of wood frogs in a woodland pool. Terres (1968b) watched belted kingfishers dive into the shallows of a small pond in N.C. to catch the large tadpoles of the bullfrog, *Rana catesbeiana*, and in N.J., Miller (1905) came on a flock of common grackles that were "constantly in motion," feeding on wood frogs, *Rana sylvatica*, which were very numerous that day in the damp Nov. woods. *See* Food and Feeding Habits; Feeding Habits in biography of each bird. *See also* discussions under Esophagus; Crop; Digestion; Young and Their Care.

Frogs sometimes feed on birds. The bullfrog, *Rana catesbeiana*, the largest N. American frog, to 6 or even 8 in. long, has caught and swallowed birds up to size of a woodcock (McAtee, 1932b). A green frog, *Rana clamitans*, caught and swallowed a young phoebe that fluttered from its nest and fell into the Huron R. at Ann Arbor, Mich. (Berger, 1953a). At Winnipeg, Can., Norris-Elye (1944) told of four leopard frogs, *Rana pipiens*, that leaped into the air to catch hummingbirds that hovered at flowers (*see* Hovering Flight under Flight) and a yellow warbler flying close to the ground. *See* Accidents; Mortality; Predation. *See also* Fishes and Birds; Snakes and Birds; Mollusks and Birds.

The amphibians (*amphi*, both; *bios*, life)—the frogs, toads, newts, salamanders, and the limbless, wormlike caecilians (see-SILL-ih-ans)—first dwell in water, then on land. According to Walter and Sayles (1949), they are in many ways intermediate between fishes and reptiles, and bridge one of the greatest gaps in evolution. *See* Evolution. They are cold-blooded (*see* Poikilothermous) vertebrate animals (*see* Vertebrate) of the class Amphibia, of which there are about 2,500 known species in the world (Bogert, 1964).

AMPHIPOD
See Crustaceans and Birds.

ANAL GLANDS
See Skin Glands.

ANALOGOUS
(ah-NAL-oh-gus). According to Moody (1953), "similarity of structure connected with similarity of function is termed *analogy*." For an example of an analogous character, we find that insects resemble birds and bats in that insects have wings just as birds and bats do. However, the wings of a bird are composed of feathers and a skeletal structure of bones; those of a bat have a bony structure covered with a membrane of modified skin. As Moody has pointed out, the wings of insects, although used by them to fly, are really very different from those of birds and bats. Insects are not related to birds and bats, and we may conclude from this example that analogous characters in nature are often superficial, and are not always to be trusted to show true relationships.

For nearly a century, Linnaeus and his followers (*see* Linnaeus) classified birds by purely adaptational characters, or by analogous characters. Birds with webbed feet (swimming birds) were grouped together in one category; hawks and owls, both of which have hooked beaks and taloned feet, were grouped together, and so on. *See* Convergent Evolution.

Eventually ornithologists (specifically, taxonomists) realized that certain obvious characters (webbed feet, for example) are shared by many unrelated birds and are an adaptation to a mode of living. Not only are they subject to rapid changes by selective forces in evolution, but they develop among birds that are entirely unrelated. Analagous characters are useful in distinguishing species and genera of birds, but in dealing with higher categories (families of birds, for example), taxonomists in classifying birds must search for characters in them that remain stable. The classification of animals, then, is based not upon analagous characters but upon *homologous* characters (Mayr *et al.*, 1953).

Homologous (hoh-MOL-oh-gus) is similarity in structure, "similarity of organs, parts, or functions with comparable features in another species or group as a result of a structural pattern derived from a common ancestor" (Mayr *et al.*, 1953). Moody (1953) has defined homology by comparing it with analogy: "Two organs in different [species of] animals are analogous if they are used for the same purpose; two organs in different animals are homologous if they have the same fundamental structure, whether or not they are used for the same purpose."

For example, the wing of a bird is analogous to the wing of a bat because in both it is used in flight; however, in this case it is also homologous because it has the same fundamental structure: it is derived, or modified from, the pentadactyl (five-fingered) limb.

According to the most generally accepted interpretation, homologous structures owe their fundamental similarities to common ancestry. For this reason, the discovery and analysis of homologous structures form one of the most important ways of tracing the evolution and relationships of birds and other animals. See Classification; Phylogenetic Relationship; *also* Origin of Birds and of Bird Flight under Fossil Birds.

ANATID
(AN-ah-tid). Term among ornithologists for a bird that belongs to the family Anatidae—ducks, geese, and swans.

ANATIDAE
See Duck Family.

ANATOMY
Bodily structure; also the scientific study of internal structure as revealed by dissection, contrasted with external form *(morphology)* although the two terms are now often used almost synonymously. *See* Morphology.

Anatomy or anatomical structure of birds includes the study of their bones or skeletal structure (*see* Skeleton), called *osteology;* their nervous system (*see* Nervous System), the study of which is *neurology;* their muscles and muscular system (*see* Muscular System), the study of which is *myology;* their circulatory system (*see* Circulatory System); their organs and tissues of breathing and digestion (*see* Respiratory System; Digestion); voice production structure (*see* Voice and Sound-Making; Songs and Singing); egg-laying (*see* Eggs and Egg-laying); urogenital organs (*see* Urogenital System; Copulation and Copulatory Organs; *also* Fertilization); and so on.

Anatomical structure affords ornithologists important characters used in classification (*see* Classification). Through studies of anatomy, scientists can discover similarities and differences in groups of birds and so try to arrange them in their natural (phylogenetic) relationships. *See* Phylogenetic Relationship; *also* Taxonomy. The study of fossil bones of birds also helps to classify them, based upon their true evolutionary relationships. *See* Fossil Birds.

ANCESTRY
See Evolution; *also* Phylogenetic Relationship.

ANDERSON
MARY VIRGINIA CHILDS. Virginia's warbler named for her; wife of Dr. William Wallace Anderson, assistant surgeon and captain in U.S. Army, who collected birds for Prof. Spencer F. Baird in Tex. and N.M.; in 1858 he collected a warbler new to science at Ft. Burgwyn, N.M.; when he sent the specimen to Baird he requested that it be named for his wife. Baird complied and in 1860 named it *Helminthophaga virginiae* (now *Vermivora virginiae*). See Palmer (1928); Hume (1942). *See also* Names and Naming.

ANDROGEN
See Endocrine Glands; Sexual Dimorphism.

ANHIMIDAE
(an-HIM-ih-dee). The Screamer Family. *See* Anseriformes.

ANHINGA FAMILY
Anhingidae (an-HING-ih-dee); *anhinga* from language of Amazonian Indians. Only two species in world (Van Tyne and Berger, 1959), although some ornithologists divide them into four. One species in Africa and Asia; a single species in W. Hemisphere—s. U.S. to S. America; a southern fish-eating water bird about 3 ft. long, has very long, sharply pointed bill (related similar-appearing cormorants have hook at tip of bill); anhinga has cutting edge on bill (serrated) and nostrils have no outer openings (*see* Nostrils). Has totipalmate swimmer's foot (*see* Feet and Legs), like related cormorants, pelicans, etc. (*see* under Pelecaniformes).

Sometimes anhingas swim with only snake-like head and part of neck above water with body submerged; like grebes, they can control amount of air in their bodies, thus either floating high on water or sinking below surface while stalking prey (*see* Swimming and Diving). Feathers of anhingas, like those of cormorants, despite their other adaptations to water, are wettable, not waterproof, as they are in ducks and geese, for example, which forces them to come to land to dry their wings. See Owre (1967).

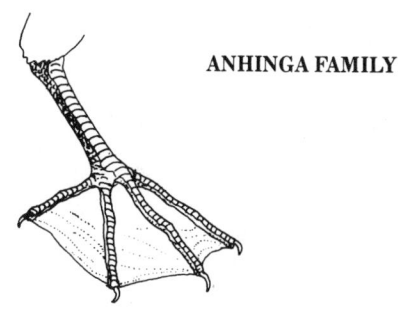

ANHINGA FAMILY

duck

swan

ANSERIFORMES

Anhinga, or snakebird, *Anhinga anhinga* (an-HING-gah); genus and species names: *see* family introduction. (Color ills., page 44.) Frequently seen in Fla.; 32–36 in. long; wingspread to 4 ft. (Palmer, 1962); blackish with *very long thin neck,* small snakelike head, long fanlike tail; *silver* on forewings—all distinguish it from cormorants when perched along freshwater canals, in trees or bushes, marshy sloughs, cypress ponds, lakes, rivers, often perches with wings spread to sun like cormorant; has scarlet to ruby-red eyes; females have pale buffy head, neck, and breast; male has black; immatures overall brown instead of dark; live mainly about quiet or slowly moving and sheltered waters; although move clumsily about on perches, are graceful strong fliers; may spiral to tremendous heights and soar, appearing like dark crosses in sky; long stiff tail fanned appears like that of turkey, thus another name: water turkey; often quarrels; utterance commonest to both sexes: distinct rapid clicking like sound of treadle-operated sewing machine (Palmer, 1962).

Feeding Habits: Dives under from surface or while flying over water, or from perch; spears on bill catfishes, pickerel, mullet, mojarrita, sunfishes, gizzard shad, and bream; also may take goldfishes from outdoor pond; eats aquatic insects, crayfishes, leeches, and spears frogs, water snakes, and young alligators; also takes small terrapins; known to eat hackberries (Palmer, 1962).
Nest: In small groups with herons, egrets; either appropriates nest of common and snowy egret and little blue heron or builds own; of sticks lined with moss and *green cypress foliage.*
Eggs: Fla., Feb.–June; La. and Tex., April–June (Bent, 1922); 1–5, usually 3–5, chalky blue-green.
Incubation: By both sexes, in turn, estimated at 25–28 days; young at hatching, eyes open; both parents feed young regurgitated food; when about two weeks old, if disturbed, young may jump out of nest into water; age when young first fly, unknown (Palmer, 1962; see also Harriott, 1970; Allen, 1961).
Other Names: American darter; black darter; black-bellied darter; darter; snakebird; water turkey; white-bellied darter.
Age: One banded in wild in Miss., found dead Veracruz, Mex., when 9 years, 8 months, old (Kennard, 1975); one lived in National Zoo, Washington, D.C., 16½ years.
Weights:: To 3 lbs.
Range:: Nests from se. Okla. and e. Tex. to e. N.C., south to S. Fla., Cuba, and Argentina; withdraws to Gulf coast, Fla., and s. S.C. in winter; has strayed to Ariz., N.M., Kans., Neb., Mich., Ont., Ohio, Va., Md.; more recently to Cape May, N.J. (see Scott and Cutler, 1972).

ANHINGIDAE
See Anhinga Family.

ANI
See in Cuckoo Family.

ANIMAL KINGDOM
See Aves; Species.

ANIMALS CARRIED BY BIRDS
See Hippoboscid Flies; Lice; Mollusks and Birds; Parasite; Phoresy.

ANISODACTYL
(an-ih-so-DAK-til). *See* Feet and Legs.

ANNA
DUCHESS OF RIVOLI. Anna's hummingbird named for her; wife of Prince Victor Masséna, son of Field Marshal André Masséna, Duc di Rivoli and Prince d'Essling. In 1829, René Primivère Lesson named the hummingbird *Calypte anna* from the type specimen of this bird which was in the bird collections of the Prince. According to John James Audubon, who met her in Paris in Sept. 1828, she was "a beautiful young woman, not more than twenty, extremely graceful and polite." See other details in Palmer (1928).

ANSERIFORMES
(an-ser-ih-FOR-meez); from Lat. *anser,* goose, and *forma,* form; goose-shaped. An order or grouping of birds almost worldwide that resemble each other fundamentally in structure (*see* Order); includes 2 families: (1) S. American birds called screamers, of 3 species, in Screamer Family, Anhimidae—fairly long-legged wading and swimming birds about size of small turkeys—and (2) the 148 species (Johnsgard, 1978), worldwide, of ducks, geese, and swans of the Duck Family, Anatidae.
Among some of characteristics in common: Both families are water birds (*see* Water Bird); their plumages are thick and waterproof; and they have 11 primary (wing) feathers, the first one always small. All ducks, geese, and swans swim; screamers, although they frequent edges of water, swim only occasionally. Among some of their differences: Ducks, geese, and swans are web-footed, and have somewhat flattened lamellate bills (a series of toothlike ridges or sawlike "teeth" along inside edges of bill; *see* Duck Family). Screamers have small, curved, chickenlike bills, scarcely webbed feet; two large sharp spurs on forward edge of wings, and no feather tracts, or apteria. *See* Feather. For further details see Austin (1961) and Van Tyne and Berger (1959). For discussion of how birds are grouped according to relationships, *see* Classification; Phylogenetic Relationship; Morphology; *also* Check-list Order.

ANTAPOSEMATIC
Pertaining to the coloration of a bird or its display used as a threat, or to dominate its rivals, specifically those of its same sex and species (Van Tyne and Berger, 1959). See Colors that Advertise under Colors of Feathers.

ANTEBRACHIUM
(an-tee-BRAY-kih-um). *See* Forearm.

ANTING
Term for the action of birds in putting crushed or live ants among their feathers, supposedly in feather maintenance (*see* Preening) to rid their plumage of lice, mites, and other parasites

which presumably cause them discomfort. Over 200 kinds of birds (all passerines) are known to practice anting, and observations of it extend all over the world (Simmons, 1964a). Twenty-four species of ants are known to be used by birds in their plumage, and at least 40 kinds of substitute materials are rubbed by birds into their feathers, including beetles, mealworms, the flesh of lemons, orange juice, coffee, vinegar, beer, cigarette and cigar butts, hot chocolate, soapsuds, and sumac berries. Most of the substitute materials that they use are acid, and the ants they choose to place in their plumage usually give off formic acid (Chisholm, 1959). Terres (1962a) watched a wood thrush go through anting motions with a land snail.

John James Audubon published the first known reference to this habit in his *Ornithological Biography* (1831), in which he wrote of watching wild turkeys roll in ants' nests "to clear their growing feathers of the loose scales and prevent ticks and other vermin from attacking them, these insects being unable to bear the odor of the earth in which ants have been."

Another American ornithologist, Abbott A. Frazar (1876), wrote an account of anting behavior by his pet crow in which he described it as standing on an anthill and permitting the ants to crawl over it and to "carry away the troublesome vermin."

Chisholm (1959) gave an excellent summary of all that was known up to that time of the strange practice. He wrote that within little more than 20 years at least 200 references to the subject had been made in articles, books, and broadcasts, and some very curious facets of the practice were recorded. "Various writers have referred to it as a puzzle, an enigma, and a mystery, and there have been . . . expressions of astonishment at the actions of the birds in their efforts to anoint the least accessible (ventral) portions of their plumage—efforts that promote ecstasy . . . and often result in behavior . . . 'clownishly beautiful' . . . or the birds wallow or 'bathe' among ants, and while doing so sometimes endure . . . a scarcely bearable irritation." Chisholm wrote further that sometimes the birds rubbed hot cigarette butts on themselves and even "bathed" in flames.

In Melbourne, Australia, a boy in 1935 saw starlings and Indian mynas placing ants beneath their wings—these were sugar ants, *Camponotus consabrinus*—and the birds practiced their anting mostly on humid days. From late 1935 onward, Chisholm discussed the subject in the Melbourne *Argus*, and soon got records of a magpie lark and a gray thrush bathing among ants, and of a Pekin robin and a house sparrow placing ants in their plumage and of an apostle bird placing small beetles beneath its wings. Most of the reports came in late summer and early autumn. One remarkable record from Britain was of "a tame magpie that made a habit of picking up ants, flying to its owner's shoulders, and dipping the ants into the hot ashes of the man's pipe, then applying the mixture to its plumage."

In America, grackles anoint their feathers with chokecherries and the juice from the hulls of English walnuts. Near Lancaster, Pa., a woman watched grackles, over a period of 15 years, come to her English walnut trees, beginning in early June when the walnuts were not yet fully developed. The walnuts grow in clusters at the ends of the branches. The grackles would alight on these and begin to pick holes in the sticky hulls. After a grackle had dug out a good-sized hole, it dipped in its bill, and then thrust its bill through its feathers. The grackles were most active at this during July and they might continue it into Aug. (Groff, 1946).

Grackles in "anting" will even use mothballs in their feathers as a substitute for ants. A woman in Milwaukee, Wisc., put mothballs in her vegetable garden to prevent cottontail rabbits from eating the young green plants, and observed one morning that a flock of grackles were picking up the mothballs in their bills and preening with them, rubbing them under their wings and over the feathers of their bodies.

Holger Poulsen of Denmark (1956) gave the results of his experiments with 152 birds of 24 families and 85 species in which he discovered that 56 species of 15 families anted. He was astonished to find that some birds discarded the insects after anting; that others "bathed" in ants; and that birds discriminated in their use of ant species and that there are different types of anting behavior which are specific as to a species. Poulsen, after concluding that anting in birds is released by "irritating and tactile stimuli on the skin," or by visual stimuli, or even by taste, could only conclude that "this amazing antic, widespread among birds, must have a function, but as yet no satisfactory definite solution can be given."

Even some domesticated cage birds will ant. In Melbourne, a man threw a mass of termites into his aviary and watched in astonishment when a female manakin anted with them. A country resident near Melbourne said he had seen an emu pluck bees from a hive and ruffle them in its feathers.

In America, H. Roy Ivor, a Canadian, reported (1943) anting largely by native N. American birds that he had in partial captivity, though the birds were free to come and go in his aviary. Ivor reported that 20 species in his aviary anted: blue jay, Pekin robin, gray catbird, American robin, wood thrush, hermit thrush, veery, cedar waxwing, bobolink, Baltimore (northern) oriole, cardinal, rose-breasted grosbeak, black-headed grosbeak, indigo bunting, dark-eyed junco, Harris' sparrow, white-crowned sparrow, white-throated sparrow, fox sparrow, and song sparrow. Ten species only ate the ants provided them. These were: common flicker, horned lark, brown thrasher, eastern bluebird, European blackbird, brown-headed cowbird, evening grosbeak, purple finch, greenfinch, and brambling. The ants used by Ivor in his experiments were: *Formica sanguinea*, the warlike blood-red slave-making ant; *Lasius niger*, the small brown garden ant; and *Camponotus pennsylvanicus*, one of the black carpenter ants of the e. U.S. and s. Canada. See details in Creighton (1950).

Some other N. American birds that have been seen to ant in the wild are: scarlet tanagers, summer tanagers, towhees, starlings, cardinals, gray catbirds, American robins, and

ANTAPOSEMATIC
The distinct black cap of the tern is an antaposematic color: when two male terns in the same breeding colony defend their individual territories, they may lower their heads in a threatening display that warns the other not to encroach.

active anting (Blue jay)

passive anting (Common crow)

ANTING
A blue jay, engaged in active anting, places or rubs an ant in its plumage. In passive anting, a common crow bathes in an ant's nest, allowing the insects to crawl through its plumage. The formic acid secreted by ants may help some birds rid themselves of parasites and relieve skin irritation at the time of molt.

others. For other records of wild birds anting, see Brackbill (1948); Groskin (1950); Whitaker (1957); Potter (1970); Hauser (1973).

Simmons (1964a) believed that anting is part of feather care—that it is linked with the chemical properties of ant fluids, of which formic acid and certain other ant secretions are insecticidal and "would certainly kill or discourage ectoparasites"; also, the essential oils could serve to supplement the oil from the preen gland that most birds use in "dressing" their feathers. *See* Parasite; Preening; Bathing.

Potter (1970) reviewed all the theories about the uses of anting to a bird; she concluded that, because the behavior is most intensive in Aug. in N. American birds, when it coincides with heavy and prolonged rainfall (at least in e. U.S.) and with the seasonal molt and new feather growth, it does have possible effectiveness in soothing skin irritation (Whitaker, 1957), and agrees with Simmons' views (1966) that anting is related to feather maintenance. Potter believed that additional studies of anting among wild birds will show that, usually, it is directly related to the emergence of a bird's new feathers. See Potter and Hauser (1974); *also* Smoke Bathing.

ANTIPHONAL SINGING
Term for the alternate singing of a mated pair of birds, "in which both sexes sing either the same or different songs" (Van Tyne and Berger, 1959). It is also called "responsive singing." *See* Songs and Singing.

ANTS AND BIRDS
See Insects and Birds; *also* Anting.

ANUS
See Cloaca.

A.O.U. CHECK-LIST
See American Ornithologists' Union; Checklist; Names and Naming; Ornithological Periodicals.

APAULINA
See Protocalliphora.

APODIDAE
See Swift Family; Apodiformes.

APODIFORMES
(ah-pod-ih-FOR-meez); Lat., from Gr. *apous, apodos,* without feet, and Lat. *forma,* form. An order or grouping of birds that resemble each other fundamentally in structure (*see* Order); includes 3 families of some 389 species (Van Tyne and Berger, 1976): the Swift Family, almost worldwide; the Hummingbird Family, limited to the W. Hemisphere; and the Crested Swift Family of s.e. Asia and the w. Pacific from India to the Solomon Is. The birds of the order, despite the name, are not without feet, but have small inconspicuous ones called by ornithologists "weak."

The two families represented in N. America are the Swift Family, Apodidae, very fast-flying, insect-eaters, and the most aerial of all land birds (*see* Swift Family), and the Hummingbird Family, Trochilidae (*see* Hummingbird Family). The hummingbirds are among the

smallest of birds, fast-flying, and eaters of insects and nectar; they are noted for hovering in flight (*see* Flight), and usually have iridescent plumage. The two groups—swifts and hummingbirds—although different in appearance and action, seem more closely related to each other than to any other bird group. It was thought that they evolved from a common ancestor, but these small, fragile birds are not well represented in fossils; however, the slight remains of swifts from rocks in France of the lower Miocene (*see* Geological Time Scale; also Collins, 1976) show that swifts were well separated from hummingbirds at least 40 million years ago. Recent studies have brought doubt about the close relationships of swifts and hummingbirds. In the future their classification in the same order may be changed (Cohn, 1968). The order Apodiformes appears to be distantly related to the goatsuckers. *See* Caprimulgiformes; *also* Classification; Morphology; Phylogenetic Relationship.

APPETITE
See Digestion; Esophagus; Food and Feeding Habits; Young and Their Care; *also* Behavior.

APTERIA
(sing.: *apterium*). Term for spaces on the skin of a bird that are more or less bare of feathers; however, these spaces may have some down and semiplumes growing from them (*see* Feather). The apteria (literally, "without feathers") are between the feather tracts in which the feathers of most birds grow. Some of the flightless birds, however, such as penguins, ostriches, rheas, cassowaries, emus, and a few others, have feathers rather uniformly distributed over their bodies (Pettingill, 1970).

APTOSOCHROMATISM
(ap-toe-so-CRO-ma-tism). An old term of scientists for the supposed phenomenon that new pigment in a bird's plumage must somehow spread occasionally into old feathers. Scientists now agree that a full-grown feather is not capable of further growth and repair, and that a bird's physiology cannot control the pigment in its feathers (Allen, 1896). *See also* Colors of Feathers; Molts and Molting.

AQUATIC BIRD
See Water Bird.

ARAMIDAE
See Limpkin Family; Gruiformes.

ARBOVIRUS
An arthropod-borne virus, carried between birds and other animals by some of the arthropods (*see* Arthropod)—for example, mosquitoes, certain flies, ticks, and mites. The arbovirus (*see* Virus) is a tiny, intracellular parasite, 20–200 millimicrons in diameter (Scherer, 1963). In nature, blood-sucking animals such as mosquitoes and ticks receive the virus when they bite a bird (or other animal) infected with an arbovirus. These mosquitoes or ticks can then infect the blood of other susceptible animals with the arbovirus when they bite them. Thus, the infected birds, for example, do not spread the virus-caused disease di-

hummingbird

swift

APODIFORMES

rectly; they are reservoirs or carriers of arboviruses which are spread from animal to animal by the bites of these blood-sucking arthropods. *See* Parasite.

Arboviruses are widely distributed in the world and among those that are a major threat to the health of horses and human beings are the encephalitis viruses, which can cause inflammation of the brain and eventual death (Scherer, 1963). *See* Encephalitis Viruses; also discussion of other virus infections under Diseases.

ARCHAEOPTERYX
(ar-kee-OP-ter-icks). *See* special discussion and illustration under Fossil Birds.

ARCTIC ZONE
One of six *life zones* of N. America, each of which is characterized by its plant life and certain birds. Life zones are still relied on by some authorities in mapping locally the ecological distribution of N. American birds. The system has advantages and disadvantages. *See* discussion of biomes and life zones under Distribution. The Arctic Zone corresponds in its plants and birds to the tundra biome. *See* location of the tundra biome and its plants and birdlife under Tundra. See Pettingill (1970; 1972) for details.

ARDEIDAE
See Heron Family.

AREA CENTRALIS
See Eyes and Eyesight.

ARENA BIRD
Term applied to a species in which the males engage in communal courtship displays on traditional "arenas," or leks (*see* Dancing Ground; Lek). Males maintain small courting grounds on the arena, or lek, where they display and which they defend against adjacent males or newcomers—usually younger males attempting to establish their own courting grounds on the arena. Females appear at the arena only to select and copulate with a displaying male; copulation occurs only on the small territory (*see* Territory); females, however, form no pair bonds as do most other birds (*see* The Pair Bond under Courtship); instead, the females leave following one or more matings and nest some distance away from the arena. The male takes no part in selecting the nest site, in building, or in incubating. His role is that of making himself conspicuous and available to females (Gilliard, 1962). *See* Incubation; *also* other male and female associations under Sexual Relationships.

Ten families of birds are known to have species that engage in communal displays on arenas, or leks: some hummingbirds (*see* Hummingbird, Reiffer's, for example, and discussions by Skutch, 1951; Wiley, 1971) the ruff and great snipe, both Eurasian species of the Sandpiper Family; some manakins (Snow, 1964a), a family of small tropical passerines of the New World; some birds of paradise of New Guinea; the brilliant cock-of-the-rock, a large passerine of S. America (*see* Cotinga Family); some bowerbirds of Australia and New Guinea; one

bustard, a gallinaceous bird from Eurasia; the peacocklike argus pheasant of Asia (*see* introduction to Pheasant Family); some N. American and Eurasian grouse; and some weaverbirds, including the paradise whydah of E. Africa. As many as 100 of these birds may dance in an arena, each with his own clearing in the grass, and in its center a tall column of grass which the male tramps and jumps upon as he circles, while spreading his great tail to the females that may come to his bower for copulation (Gilliard, 1958).

One of the most spectacular of the arena birds is the N. American sage grouse (*see* in Grouse Family) of the western sagebrush and grasslands; it is regarded as the classic example of an arena bird in N. America (Scott, 1942; Johnsgard, 1973; Wiley, 1974), partly because its arenas, or leks, are the largest; one big one may be half a mile long and 200 yds. wide with 400 male grouse within it, each about 25–40 ft. apart. The most successful cocks are those that maintain territories near the center of the arena, or lek. These males (less than 10% of the arena birds) copulate with more than 75% of the visiting females. One male was seen copulating with 21 hens in one morning. *See also* Prairie chicken and Sharp-tailed grouse in Grouse Family. *See* comparable behavior of the wild turkey in Turkey Family.

Another example of a remarkable arena bird is the Eurasian ruff, some of which migrate regularly to the N. American continent (*see* in Sandpiper Family; Hogan-Warburg, 1966; van Rhijn, 1973; Shepard, 1975). The males in spring return thousands of miles from their wintering grounds to the ancestral courtship area, or lek—a "hill" of slightly raised ground on wet moors, meadows, and marshy grasslands. According to Tekke (1954), in Holland, several of these courting or fighting areas (leks) have been used by successive generations of ruffs for more than 100 years.

On the small lek, which may be only several yards across and occupied by 2–20 males, each male establishes a "run" (display territory) that may be only 8–16 in. in diameter and 15–25 in. from runs occupied by other males. Each male defends his small territory against wandering males, mostly young ones that try to invade the dance areas as well as neighboring males.

When excited, a male displays to other males by a run, or charge, in which he spreads his feathered ruffs, opens and droops his wings, then, seemingly in a trance, sinks slowly to his belly and drives his bill into the ground (Gilliard, 1958). He remains there a few seconds, quivering his wings, recovers, then returns in a short flight to his small territory to doze (the males' territories are not used for feeding or nesting but only for copulation). Females visit the leks over 4–5 days, making several short visits each day, and then each copulates with a male of her choice.

When the female ruff (reeve) is attracted to a display of the males, she walks into the arena, and as she moves along, males go into vigorous displays. Gilliard (1958) reports that the female selects the male of her choice by biting him; however, females may copulate with more than

ARENA BIRD
In spring, male sage grouse gather in a courtship arena to strut before the females. They display by inflating the yellowish air sacs on their breasts and spreading their long pointed tail feathers. Usually only one dominant male will mate with several hens, but no pair bond is formed. The hens will leave the arena after copulation to build their sparse nests and incubate the eggs without the assistance of the male.

one male at a lek, or with males at more than one lek; males are promiscuous and copulate with as many females as solicit them; the females nest, solitarily, away from the leks, in tall grass, where nests are hidden on the ground. Males remain on the leks from Apr. or May through July or until all females are nesting, then they leave the breeding grounds ahead of the females, which, later, migrate with the young (Pettingill and Lancaster, 1973b). A comparable lek system also occurs in the N. American buff-breasted sandpiper. *See* comparable behavior in biography of the pectoral sandpiper under Sandpiper Family and remarks of Pitelka therein.

In the lek breeding system of the ruff, a small number of males achieve most of the copulations with the females, which prefer those males that are primarily most active and vigorous in their displays and have greater ability to attract the females and to stimulate them to copulate. *See* Copulation and Copulatory Organs. See Pettingill and Lancaster (1973b) and Shepard (1975) for other details; *see also* Ruff in Sandpiper Family, and for a discussion of mating associations, *see* Sexual Relationships.

ARMINJON

VITTORIO (1830–97). Captain and commander of first Italian naval vessel to sail around the world; on this scientific trip, members of his party collected on South Trindade Is., in the S. Atlantic, the bird later described and named in 1868 in Arminjon's honor by Giglio and Salvidori as *Pterodroma arminjoniana*, the South Trinidad (or Trindade) petrel. See details of Arminjon's life in Gruson (1972).

ARTHROPOD

(ARE-throw-pod). A group of invertebrate, joint-legged animals (*see* discussion of invertebrates under Vertebrate) that includes about three fourths of all known species of animals in the world (Buchsbaum, 1938). The major classes of arthropods are: *crustaceans* (crayfishes, lobsters, shrimps, crabs, sowbugs, water fleas, barnacles, etc.); *centipedes; millipedes; arachnids* (spiders, scorpions, ticks, mites); and by far the largest class of all in numbers of species—*insects*. Insects are also the most important of all arthropod foods for birds (*see* Insects and Birds). For discussions of some other of these groups of arthropods and their relationships to birds, *see* Crustaceans and Birds; Spiders and Birds. *See* especially Economic Ornithology; Food and Feeding Habits. For specific food habits of each species, *see* Feeding Habits in each bird biography.

ASPERGILLOSIS

(as-per-jill-OH-sis). A locally common acute or chronic infection usually fatal to birds, caused by a fungus, or mold, *Aspergillus fumigatus*. The fungus grows in damp or wet bird seed and in the hulls or straws and other residues in bird-seed mixtures when they are exposed to dampness and open air, also in bird nesting materials (see O'Meara and Witter, 1971). Pigeon fanciers sometimes become infected. See Christensen (1951).

Birds breathe in the spores of this mold while they are feeding and the fungus lodges in their lungs and air sacs (*see* Respiratory System), eventually causing avian pneumonia and bronchitis. Among the breeders or propagators of game birds the illness is called "brooder pneumonia."

HOSTS AND SYMPTOMS. Cowbirds, house sparrows, juncos, grackles, quail, hawks, the bald eagle (see Coon and Locke, 1968), gulls (see Friend and Trainer, 1969), and other wild birds afflicted show various signs of the illness. O'Meara and Witter (1971) list 48 species of birds, either wild or captive—from pigeons, waterfowl, grouse, and quail to gulls, owls, ravens, crows, and songbirds—reported to be hosts to aspergillosis.

The disease seems to progress through stages; in the beginning, birds afflicted gasp and wheeze, and then begin to mope, or to sit about with their feathers fluffed. Among seed-eating birds, crowded at feeders, the sick ones may continue to feed and to stand feebly in the bird feeder while doing so. One of the last signs of the illness may be severe diarrhea. There seems to be no cure for wild birds suffering from aspergillosis; however, the best remedy for birds at feeding stations is to protect them from it. There are treatments for captive birds, however; for captive cormorants see DeLaRonde and Greichus (1972); the preventive treatment suggested for captive shorebirds by Serventy *et al.* (1962); and suggestions for treating captive birds of prey in Peeters and Jameson (1970).

PREVENTION FOR SEED-EATING BIRDS. Buy only clean bird seed and be sure that the mixture of seeds and grain in the feeders is not allowed to get moldy. If it does, clean out feeder at once, allow it to dry thoroughly before putting feed back in it; in wet or damp weather, put only enough feed in feeders that birds can clean up within a few hours.

Aspergillosis is apparently not spread from one bird to another by bodily contact but from spores of the fungus in the air and from the droppings of a sick bird, which can contaminate the feed or the water in the birdbath. If one has more than one bird feeder or birdbath in the garden, their use should be rotated so as to allow them to be periodically scrubbed and disinfected. Clean and scrub feeders with Lysol or some other disinfectant before putting them back into use. If an increasing number of birds show signs of illness, feeding should be stopped for at least a week or two until all of the afflicted birds have died or have moved elsewhere; this must be done even in cold, severe winter weather if the lives of many healthy birds are to be saved. See cleaning and maintenance of bird feeders in Terres (1968c). These precautions may also help to protect garden birds agains other infectious diseases. *See*, for example, Salmonellosis; *also* Bird-attracting and under Diseases.

ATLANTIC FLYWAY

See Waterfowl.

ATRETIC (ah-TRET-ik) FOLLICLE

Common in birds generally. As a follicle (in this case, a sac, or small bag) containing the ovum, or egg, ripens, it increases to the size of the yolk of the egg to be laid. With an abundance of follicles in birds, many at an early stage become *atretic*—that is, the firm follicle may grow flabby like a deflated balloon. After this, the egg yolk is quickly resorbed and in about 4 or 5 days the follicle has shrunk to a small size. Apparently the follicle and the egg within it do not develop again once the follicle becomes atretic. Atresia of the ovarian follicles at a more developed stage in brant and other geese results in smaller than average numbers of eggs laid, or no nesting at all. This may be an adaptation to the short Arctic nesting season, especially in seasons that are too short for successful nesting (Barry, 1962). *See* Brant in Duck Family; *also* Eggs and Egg-laying.

ATTENTIVE PERIOD

The bouts of time that a parent spends at the nest incubating eggs or feeding and brooding the young. An incubating or brooding bird tends to spend more time on the nest toward evening and in early morning when the weather is cooler; attentive periods are also longer in cool, rainy weather, in hot weather, and as the hatching time of the eggs approaches. In most songbirds, in which the female incubates, time spent on the nest is about 75–80% of the bird's total nesting time. *See* Inattentive Period.

Some songbirds may spend long periods on the nest; for example, a red crossbill sat 14 hours, 36 minutes, on her nest continuously, and then was off the nest (*see* Inattentive Period) for 36 minutes; however, while she was on the nest, the male fed her three times (Wallace, 1955). See other details in Pettingill (1972).

Larger birds have longer attentive and inattentive periods than smaller ones. See Eggs and Egg-laying; Hatching.

ATTRACTING BIRDS

See Bird-attracting.

AUDUBON

JOHN JAMES (1785–1851). Artist, explorer, frontiersman, and ornithologist; possibly the most popular naturalist of America, for whom the Audubon Society was named (*see* National Audubon Society). Audubon gained worldwide fame for *The Birds of America*, in which his 435 life-size, full-color paintings of 489 species of N. American birds were published in elephant folio size (see Fries, 1973) of 39½ by 29½ in., untrimmed pages, beginning in 1827 in London. The serial publication and subsequent reprintings of this great work required 11 years and frequent trips by Audubon to and from America. The New-York Historical Society in New York City owns all but three of Audubon's life-size watercolors from which the plates of the double elephant folio were engraved (Murphy, 1956).

Besides *The Birds of America*, Audubon wrote an *Ornithological Biography*, published originally in five volumes, a 3,000-page series of life histories of all the birds he had illustrated in *The Birds of America*. Audubon also collaborated with the Rev. John Bachman of Charleston, S.C., in writing and illustrating a three-volume work on American mammals,

The Viviparous Quadrupeds of North America (1846–54), two volumes of which were published after Audubon's death. He died Jan. 27, 1851, at his estate in upper New York City. See details of Audubon's life in the definitive biography by Herrick (1917); see also Arthur (1937); Ford (1969); Audubon (1960).

Audubon's name was commemorated in Audubon's warbler, *Dendroica auduboni* (now called yellow-rumped warbler); Audubon's shearwater, *Puffinus ilherminieri;* and three subspecies of birds—a hermit thrush, a caracara, and a black-headed oriole (A.O.U. *Check-list,* 1957).

AUDUBON

A publication. *See* National Audubon Society; Ornithological Periodicals.

AUDUBON BREEDING BIRD CENSUS
See Census.

AUDUBON CHRISTMAS BIRD COUNT
See Christmas Bird Count.

AUDUBON FIELD NOTES
See Ornithological Periodicals.

AUDUBON SOCIETY
See National Audubon Society.

AUGURY

(AW-gew-rih). The ancient art or practice of foretelling events by *auspices* (*see* Auspice) or omens; divination. "Among the ancient Latins this was an important matter, and no enterprise was begun without first making the proper application to the sacred birds [geese in ancient Rome; owls in Greece] to learn of its probable success. Moreover, the credit for the final success, as of a victory or a safe journey, was given not to the commanding general but to the one who made the propitious augury" (Allen, 1925).

In the pre-Christian centuries, the principal and most numerous omens were drawn from birds, on the theory that their actions conveyed the will of the gods. Early in its development there arose certain "wise men" who declared they could understand the language of birds and their actions. This was the origin of the profession of *augury,* "a word that spells 'bird talk' in its root meaning [*see* Folklore], with its later product 'auspices,' or 'bird-viewers.' The *augur* originally was a priest . . . who listened to what the birds said; the *auspex* was another who watched what they did, or examined their entrails to observe anything abnormal that he might construe as an answer to prayer . . . or in the nature of an omen" (Ingersoll, 1923). See detailed article by Harrison (1964).

AUK, THE

A publication. *See* Ornithological Periodicals.

AUK FAMILY

Alcidae (AL-sih-dee); from *alca,* Lat. form of the Scandinavian name for these birds. 22 species of seabirds that live around northern parts of the world (Van Tyne and Berger, 1976); 20 species in N. America, including auklets, the dovekie (called little auk in Great Britain), guillemots, murres, murrelets, puffins, and the razorbill; also an additional one, the great auk, has been extinct since the 19th century; members of the Auk Family, called alcids, frequent salt water and rarely seen elsewhere; most prefer open seas; are small to large (6–30 in. long), ducklike but with short necks and in flight beat their wings in a rapid whir. All have a large head, short tail, and chunky body; are largely black and white, and resemble small penguins; they are skillful divers and swimmers (*see* under Swimming and Diving) and use their short, pointed wings to "fly" underwater, usually steering with their feet, in pursuit of fishes and small marine invertebrates; legs are short and attached toward rear of body; the three toes are webbed (no hind toe, or hallux), and sexes are outwardly alike; some species are migratory but most simply disperse after breeding season over adjacent seas; are highly gregarious, utter moans, barks, whistles (guillemots), hisses; go ashore from sea only to breed; in spring, return in great flocks to cliffs where they were hatched, often to same ledge (Gilliard, 1958); courtship rituals include parading about on water and "water dances," but much courtship takes place on land; they nest in colonies around fringes of Arctic O. and along N. Atlantic and N. Pacific coasts; lay 1–2 eggs.

Alcids are the ecological counterparts of the penguins of the Antarctic; both have dense, waterproof plumage and dive and swim for their food; unlike the flightless penguins, all alcids can fly (only the extinct great auk and several other extinct species were flightless); most alcids except the very smallest molt all flight feathers at one time and are flightless until new feathers develop. (*See* Flightless Birds.)

Alcids are as far apart in their evolution from penguins as in their range; their nearest relatives are shorebirds, terns, and gulls, and all, including the alcids, are in the large order Charadriiformes. Two similar but unrelated families—auks and diving petrels—are remarkable examples of convergence in evolution; each is descended from different ancestors but each group is strikingly similar in appearance and ways of life in different parts of the world. *See* Convergent Evolution; especially, Monophyletic Descent.

All members of Auk Family are protected by law (*see* Legal Protection) and may not be kept in captivity without a permit; however, disabled birds may be kept alive until able to fend for themselves by feeding them small strips of fish (¼–½ in. thick and 2–4 in. long), squids, shellfishes, meat, and shrimp. Dip strips of fish in salt water before feeding and provide a pool in which the birds may swim and dive.

Best time and place to see alcids is in stormy weather, mainly in winter, along coasts, where a few strays may come close to shore.

Auk, great, *Pinguinus impennis* (PIN-gwin-us im-PEN-iss); genus name: New Lat. for penguin, the vernacular name given the bird by early European explorers from two Welsh words, *pen,* head, and *gwyn,* white, or white-headed, in allusion to large oval spot of white on head of great auk; species name: Lat., feath-

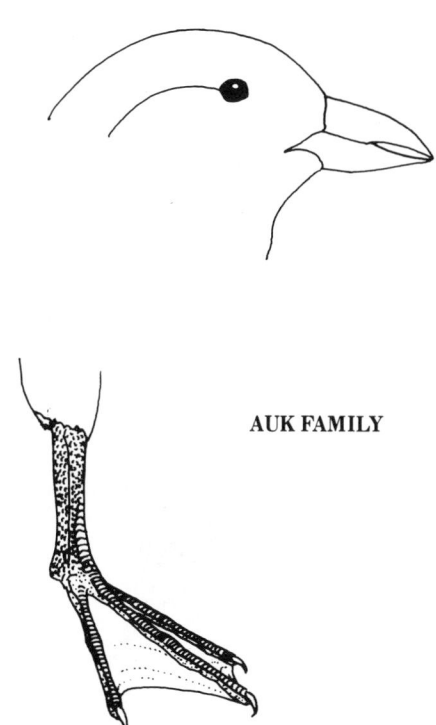

AUK FAMILY

erless, i.e., wingless, from *in*, negative, and *penna*, a feather (Coues, 1882). *Extinct;* lived mostly in waters of n. Europe and of n. N. America; about 30 in. long, stood more than 2 ft. high, was largest member of Auk Family; black above, including head, with large white spot before each eye; white underparts; very small wings, black with white tips on secondaries (shorter than those of the related, living razorbill), one of the few flightless seabirds in N. Hemisphere (*see* Flightless Birds); its short but strong wings were well adapted to swimming underwater (*see* Swimming and Diving) and were powered by the great auk's strong pectoral (breast) muscles attached to the large keel on the sternum, or breastbone; it swam from place to place sometimes for considerable distances in spring and fall migrations, to and from its breeding grounds; was said to have uttered a croak and a gurgling noise (Townsend, 1919); it dived for its food and dived when frightened; was well known to early sailors, who killed great auks for food (fresh meat); the great auk was the original "penguin," a name later given by explorers to the similarly adapted penguins of the S. Hemisphere (Storer, 1964); because the great auk was flightless and helpless on land, it was killed in enormous numbers (population was estimated to be in millions at one time) by sailors and Eskimos for food and by fishermen for bait (Greenway, 1958); greatest known breeding colony on Funk Is., off e. coast of Newfoundland, was extirpated over a period of 56 years (1785–1841); finally destroyed by ravages of commercial hunters who killed the birds with clubs and stripped them of their feathers for use in pillows and mattresses (Gilliard, 1961); the last living specimens of the great auk (a pair) were taken June 3, 1844, on Eldey Rock, island off the s. coast of Iceland (Greenway, 1958).

Feeding Habits: Apparently ate fishes and other marine animals but not definitely known.
Nest: No material but apparently eggs laid on bare rock.
Eggs: Probably May–mid-July; 1, white, conical, spotted with gray, black, and brown; about 5 in. long (Greenway, 1958).
Incubation: Estimated at 44 days.
Other Names: Garefowl; penguin; wobble.
Range: In N. America, nested on Bird Rocks in Gulf of St. Lawrence; Funk Is., Newfoundland; and Leifs Is. and Eric den Røde Is., near Greenland; also on Icelandic islands—the Westman's and Geirfuglasker (destroyed by volcano in 1830), Eldey, and others; in British Isles on St. Kilda, Outer Hebrides, etc. (A.O.U. *Check-list,* 1957); in N. America, wintered from s. Greenland south to Me., Mass., and casually to S.C. and Fla.

Auk, little. *See* Dovekie.

Auk, razor-billed. *See* Razorbill.

Auklet, Cassin's, *Ptychoramphus aleuticus* (tye-koh-RAM-fus ah-lee-OOT-ih-cus); genus name: from Gr. *ptychos,* fold, and *ramphos,* beak; species name: Lat., of the Aleutian Is.; common name: for John Cassin, 19th-century Philadelphia ornithologist. (Color ill., page 45.)

Great auk

AUK FAMILY

One of most abundant and widely distributed small alcids of offshore Pacific coast; chunky, 8–9 in. long; smaller than murrelets, dark gray on back, head, rump, and wings; white belly and dusky breast; small white spot; lower mandible has light spot at base.

Feeding Habits: Eats almost entirely small copepods, amphipods, and other crustaceans or surface-feeding marine invertebrates.
Nest: In colonies but little known about its nesting habits until recently (because by day it keeps hidden about its breeding islands) when Asa Thorensen (1964) studied their nocturnal ways without frightening them in a lighted place around buildings on Farallon Is., Calif.; pairs arrive soon after early Dec. rains and begin to repair old burrows or to dig new ones; males and females take turns digging with sharp claws, often pause to bow to one another or to fight with neighbor and utter *kreek* notes; fighting birds stand face to face, then leap at each other like birds in cockfight; each pair dug at night for 60 days or more until burrow of variable length is finished.
Eggs: Mar.–July; 1, white, tinted with blue or green.
Incubation: By both sexes; at least 37 days; parents stuff dusky chick with shrimps and small fishes carried in gular pouch (see Speich and Manual, 1974); parent arriving with food clicks bill, to which chick in darkness of burrow answers with *chir* note; parents feed young by regurgitation; young first fly when more than 40 days old; breeding season lasts over 8 months in southern part of nesting range; adults incubating fresh egg in same burrow with full-grown young suggests more than one brood annually; adults preyed upon by peregrine falcon and western gulls (*see* Storm-Petrel Family).
Other Names: Aleutian auk; sea quail; wrinkle-nosed auk.
Flight Speed: Timed by Thorensen (1964) at about 45 m.p.h.
Weights: 172.6 gr., or about 6 oz. (Bedard, 1969).
Range: Nests from Sanak Is., Shumagin Is., and Kodiak Is. in Alaska, south on islands and coasts of Pacific to w.-c. Baja Calif., winters on open seas from Vancouver Is. south; accidental in interior Wash. and Ore.

Auklet, crested, *Aethia cristatella* (EE-thee-ah cris-tah-TELL-ah); genus name: Lat., from Gr. *aithuia,* used in writings of Homer and Aristotle for "water bird"; species name: Lat., dim. of *cristatus,* crested (Coues, 1882). (Color ill., page 45.) Common resident in sw. Alaska in Aleutian, Pribilof, and Shumagin Is.; one of most abundant birds in N. Pacific; sexes alike; about 9 in. long; dark, with forward-drooping dark feathered crest; long, thin, white plumes extend backward from in back of each eye; its manner of flight, quail size, color, and crest have suggested local common name of sea quail from fancied resemblance to California quail; in breeding season has an orange bill with orange-colored plate at corner of mouth, bill gives off pungent, citruslike odor; may have some significance in breeding behavior (*see* Smell) in nesting crevices; natives on Aleutian

Is. call this bird cannooskie, or little captain; bill ornaments are shed after nesting season when bill becomes brown; also crest is shorter; immatures have no crest or bill ornaments; on nesting grounds one of noisiest of the auklets, utters loud honk, chirping, and grunting sounds (Bent, 1919).

Feeding Habits: Eats free-swimming amphipod crustaceans found in astonishing abundance in Alaskan waters; enormous food supply for auklets of different species (Bent, 1919); apparently crested auklets can dive deeply, as their remains have been found in stomachs of bottom-feeding codfish caught 200 ft. below surface (Humphrey, 1965). *See* Swimming and Diving; Fishes and Birds.

Nest: In colonies of 10 to 20 pairs or up to thousands, in crevices of cliffs and under boulders along shore, no nesting material, egg laid on bare rock.

Eggs: June–Aug.; 1, white to pale blue, unmarked.

Incubation: Period of and age when young first fly unknown; parents carry food from sea in pouch under tongue; in Sept., when young flying, leave for open ocean.

Other Names: Crested stariki; dusky auklet, snub-nosed auk; snub-nosed auklet.

Weights: Two collected (shot) St. Lawrence Is., Alaska, averaged 289 gr. (Hughes, 1970), or about 10 oz.; 284.5 gr. (Bedard, 1969).

Range: In N. America nests in crevices in cliffs or under boulders along coast from Pribilofs and Aleutians east to Shumagin Is., Alaska, also from Chukotski Pen., Soviet Union, to Diomede Is., Sakhalin, and c. Kuriles in e. Siberia; winters from Bering Sea to c. Japan, accidental in interior Alaska and Iceland.

Auklet, least, *Aethia pusilla* (EE-thee-ah pew-SILL-ah); genus name: *see* Auklet, crested; species name: from Lat. *pusillus*, petty, here used in sense of small (Coues, 1882). (Color ill., page 45.) Locally common in Bering Sea and Aleutians; sparrow-sized, about 6 in. long, smallest member of Auk Family; short, stocky, in summer sooty black above, white throat, dark band across upper breast and sides; white below with spotted sides; white plumes extend back from forehead and eyes; red swollen bill with white tip; in winter throat and underparts all white; bill smaller and gray; white shoulder patch shows as horizontal slash when bird resting on water; millions swarm in June and July on the waters, and in the air, about the rocky beaches of Pribilof Is.; in flight, swirling about observer like small buzzing bees, most abundant on St. George Is. and probably on all of Pribilofs; vibrating their short wings in flight, they fill the air, uttering twitters and squeals; sound at times like small tree frogs piping in spring.

Feeding Habits: Dives in little leaps below surface to catch and eat small amphipod crustaceans.

Nest: No materials, lays eggs on bare rocks or beds of small stones on site chosen in rocky crevice on inaccessible cliffs or under loose boulders on rocky beaches.

Eggs: June–Aug.; 1, pure white.

Incubation: Period of unknown, but while one of the pair incubates, the other feeds all day at sea, returns at dusk to relieve mate; age when young first fly unknown but by end of Aug. young are fully grown and fledged (Bent, 1919).

Other Names: Choochkie (by natives of Alaska and Aleutians); knob-billed auklet; knob-nosed auklet; minute auklet.

Weights: Two collected St. Lawrence Is., Alaska, averaged 96 gr. (Hughes, 1970), or about 3⅓ oz.; 86.3 gr. (Bedard, 1969).

Range: Nests from Chukotski Pen., Soviet Russia, and Diomede Is. in Bering Strait, Cape Lisburne on nw. coast of Alaska, south on islands in Bering Sea, including Pribilofs, to Aleutians and Shumagin Is.; winters at sea off coast of e. Siberia south to islands off n. Japan, and off Aleutians; casual along Arctic coast of Alaska to Point Barrow and to n. Mack.

Auklet, parakeet, *Cyclorrhynchus psittacula* (sye-klow-RING-cus sit-ACK-you-lah); genus name: from Gr. *kyklos*, circle, and *rhynchos*, beak; species name: from Lat. *psittacus*, little parrot, resemblance to bill. (Color ill., page 45.) Summers on coasts of Siberia and on islands of Alaska; about 9–10 in. long; quail size, with rather long neck; sooty black above, including neck and head; white below; has heavy, almost circular, *upturned red bill* (only red-billed auklet south of Alaska—Robbins *et al.*, 1966); in breeding season, has long, thin white plumes that extend from eyes to behind head; in winter with sooty-black back, all-white underparts, upturned duskier bill, white plumes lacking; in flight, like other alcids, rolls from side to side, the trailing feet brake and steer; perhaps least gregarious of all auklets, not nearly as abundant as least auklet of Arctic waters; comparatively solitary, unobtrusive and quiet, but even though usually silent, sometimes utters a trilled whistle, *chu-u-u-ee, chu-u-u-ee-ee*, rising in pitch.

Feeding Habits: Flies out to sea for food every morning and returns to its mate on breeding grounds at night; eats mainly amphipods and other small crustaceans which it finds while swimming on or near surface or catches by diving to rocky bottoms at moderate depths (naturalists' former belief that the peculiar upturned bill was used by this auklet to pry open bivalves was not well founded; see in Bent, 1919).

Nest: In small colonies or a few scattered pairs, in crevices or holes in rocky cliffs; sometimes with crested and least auklets, together with tufted puffins, under loose piles of water-worn boulders on high, rocky islands; no nest material but eggs laid on bare rock or ground or on bed of loose pebbles; a few sometimes nest among fulmars and puffins but eggs in inaccessible places among rocks.

Eggs: June–Aug.; 1, dull white or blue-white without luster.

Incubation: Period of and age when young first fly unknown; by middle of late Aug. most of young can fly and begin to leave nesting islands, gradually all move out to sea; like other auklets, have beneath tongue a pouch or sac in

which they store food or carry it to young (Humphrey, 1965).

Other Names: Baillie brushkie (so called by natives of Arctic); paroquet auklet; pug-nosed auklet.

Weights: 317.6 gr. (Bedard, 1969), or about 11 oz.

Range: Nests from coasts and islands of ne. Siberia south on Komandorskie, St. Lawrence, St. Matthew Is. and Pribilofs in Bering Sea and south to Aleutians and Chirikof Is. southeast of Kodiak Is., Alaska; winters from Bering Sea south to the Kurile Is. and Japan, and to coasts of Wash., Ore., and c. Calif.

Auklet, rhinoceros, *Cerorhinca monocerata* (ser-oh-RING-kah mon-oh-seh-RAY-tah); genus name: from Gr. *keras*, horn, and *rhynchos*, beak, or snout; species name: Lat., from Gr. *monos*, one, and *keras*, horn; one-horned; in reference to the short "horn" at base of bill. (Color ill., page 45.) Common along entire Pacific coast in winter; largest of the auklets and the murrelets; sexes alike; 14–15½ in. long; brownish above; white below with grayish throat and breast; in nesting season of summer, bill orange-brown or yellowish, prominent with an odd little horn at base of bill which gives it name of "rhino" auklet, also white "whiskers" on each side of face, and narrow white plume behind each eye; legs and feet pale yellow; in winter white plumes in adult are shorter and horn is absent; and when resting on water, lack of white throat and its even dark color are distinctive according to Peterson (1961); young very brownish, also lack horn and white plumes; have very dark bills; like Cassin's auklet and murrelets, this species is seldom seen by day in nesting season; flight is rapid and direct, seldom turning; on ocean usually solitary or in small groups (Bent, 1919); usually escapes by diving; silent at sea but very noisy on nesting grounds, barks, growls, utters parrotlike shrieks.

Feeding Habits: Dives in seas for small fishes (sardines) and crustaceans.

Nest: Small accumulation of sticks, grasses, and feathers placed at end of burrow dug by both members of pair 8–20 ft. deep and may be in sloping sides of island, from shoreline to 400–500 ft. up bank; a favored site is in spruce woods, where soil soft and friable (Bent, 1919); pair may refurbish old burrow or dig new one; dig burrow with bill and claws (no indication that horn on bill helps or hinders); banding of mated pairs on Protection Is., Wash., indicates that these auklets maintain same mates each year and same burrow (Richardson, 1961).

Eggs: Apr.–June; 1, white, some may be spotted with gray or lavender.

Incubation: By both sexes, 31–33 days; young just about able to fly at 35–42 days after hatching, when they flutter down to water from burrow (Richardson, 1961); both parents feed young almost exclusively on sand launce, *Ammodytes tobianus*, at Protection Is.; chief cause of mortality there: burying of adults and young in burrows by earth slides caused by people or by grazing sheep.

AUK FAMILY
The black guillemot is a highly specialized, skillful swimmer. It will dive in pursuit of fishes and "fly" underwater with beats of its short, stubby, muscular wings, steering with its powerful legs and webbed feet.

Other Names: Horn-bill auk; unicorn auk.
Weights: 544.1 gr. (spring 1970), or about 1 lb. 3 oz.
Range: Nests on coasts, offshore islets, and islands from se. Alaska to c. Calif. (Farallones), also from s. Sakhalin and s. Kuriles off Russian coast south to Korea and n. Honshu; non-breeding birds seen in summer along Pacific coast of N. America, casually to s. Calif.; winters from southern part of breeding range south off coast to Baja Calif., Korea, and Japan.

Auklet, whiskered, *Aethia pygmaea* (EE-thee-ah pig-MAY-ah); genus name: *see* Auklet, crested; species name: Lat. for a pygmy (Coues, 1882); *whiskered* refers to wispy white plumes on each side of face of adult at all seasons. (Color ill., page 45.) Lives on remote islands of nw. Pacific; least known of the auklets, few ornithologists have seen it (Humphrey, 1965); 7 in. long, a little larger than least auklet, one of handsomest of Auk Family; small, dark, resembles crested auklet but curled black forehead crest longer and thinner, and *has two long white plumes forking from base of bill* besides one from eyes extending backward (three plumes in all); red bill tipped with white and without wattles at base of bill; immature resembles immature crested auklet, but in profile two faint white streaks, one below, the other in front of eyes; like other auklets, leaves nesting colonies after breeding season and spends winter in small flocks on open ocean; also, like least auklet, makes small leaps from surface of water before diving; voice or utterances apparently not yet described.

Feeding Habits: Main food is amphipods (gammarids), snails, and crabs.
Nest: In rock crevices and in holes of steep rocky shores of islets and islands.
Eggs: Apr.–May(?); 1, dull white.
Incubation: Period of and age when young first fly unknown; downy young hatch latter part of June and in July.
Other Names: Red-nosed auk; whiskered auk.
Range: Is resident, and nests locally, in c. Aleutian Is., Alaska, on Komandorskie Is. in Bering Sea, and s. Kuriles north of Japan.

Dovekie, *Alle alle* (AL-ee); genus and species names: Swedish name of the bird; *dovekie* (DUV-kih or DUV-kee), dim. of dove, in reference to small size. (Color ill., page 47.) Nests north of Arctic Circle in millions in vast colonies on sea cliffs of N. America and n. Eurasia; in N. Atlantic probably exceeds thick-billed murres' millions; highly important as food for Arctic foxes, glaucous gulls, gyrfalcons, and Eskimos; has been found in stomachs of white whales (Tuck, 1961); winters off Atlantic coast; sexes alike, 8–9 in. long; black above, white below, with black throat and breast in summer, all white underparts in winter to behind eyes, series of white "slashes" across back from shoulder to shoulder; chubby, short-necked, with very short black bill, black feet and legs; offshore, small flocks fly with quick wingbeats close to waves or rest on sea; sometimes utters harsh squeaks, short, sharp screech, and piping notes; is often killed by floating oil from tankers or found disabled or "oiled" along Atlantic coastal beaches or carried far inland by hurricanes; if found injured, starving, or exhausted, may be offered small strips of fish, squid, meat, or shrimp; should have small pool of water and rocks on which to rest.

Feeding Habits: Dives for food from surface, uses wings to "fly" through water; has been timed in dives lasting average of 33 seconds, maximum of 68 seconds (Bent, 1919); eats almost exclusively minute marine crustaceans, also small fishes from freshwater ponds.
Nest: In colonies, no nest material, eggs laid on bare rock in crevices of talus slopes of High Arctic seacoast.
Eggs: June–July; 1, blue-white, laid well back in crevice.
Incubation: About 24 days; young begin to fly 28 days after hatching; enter water before fully fledged (Bateson, 1961).
Other Names: Alle; ice bird; knotty (from pine knot, which see); little auk; pine knot (from hardiness to cold; "tough as a pine knot"); rotch; sea dove.
Albinism: Two records (Sealy, 1969b).
Weights: Nov., Conn., immature (1), 3¼ oz. (Wetherbee, 1934); Manomet, Mass. (2), 103 and 115.5 gr. (Fisk, 1971b), or about 3¾ oz. and 4 oz.; 166.2 gr. (Johnson, 1935), or about 5⅞ oz.
Range: In N. America, nests along Arctic coasts of Ellesmere Is., Can., and Greenland; winters in ice-free waters south of breeding range to Southampton Is., Ungava Bay, along Gulf of St. Lawrence, offshore of se. Newfoundland, Nova Scotia, Bay of Fundy, south to New England, rare but regular offshore winter visitor to Long Is., N.Y., less commonly off N.J. coast; on Nov. 19, 1932, a tremendous flight along Atlantic coast reached s. Fla. and Cuba (Bull, 1964); has strayed to Point Barrow, Alaska; Kewatin, Man., and Ont., Minn., Wisc., Mich., interior ne. U.S., Fla.

Guillemot, black, *Cepphus grylle* (SEP-fus GRILL-ee); genus name: from Gr. *kepphus*, sea bird; species name: said to be from Gr., meaning "I grunt" (Coues, 1882); common name (GILL-eh-mot): dim. of Fr. *Guillaume*, William. (Color ills., pages 46, 47.) In N. America, lives from Maine north and along Canadian (Labrador) coast; also Arctic coast of Alaska; rare and local within sight of land in winter along N. Atlantic coast south to Long Is., N.Y., and N.J.; small, 12–14 in. long; wingspread about 23 in.; sexes alike, adult *in summer breeding plumage, a ducklike black water bird with red feet, pointed black bill, and extensive white patches on wings;* eyes brown or black, inside of mouth vermilion or coral red (some adults retain black summer plumage into winter); in fall and winter, mostly white; upperparts mottled dark brown; white below; wings black with white patch; black tail; immature, sooty black above with mottled white on back and wings where adult has the white patch; white below; less gregarious than other alcids such as murres; utters a faint, piping whistle, and when disturbed at nest, a hiss; sitting on water, dabs at surface with bill; flight is strong and swift, usually close to water in wide circle, wings beating rapidly, white wing patches flashing, bright red feet trailing behind.

Feeding Habits: On coast of Me. feeds largely on rock eels—small fishes that it finds under loose stones; also eats small mussels and other mollusks, shrimps, small crabs and other crustaceans, and marine worms that it captures from rocky bottom; in diving, flops under surface of water with open wings and uses them regularly in its underwater "flight" (Bent, 1919), as do all alcids.

Nest: At nesting sites, usually only a few pairs, eggs laid in crevices, sometimes in caves of faces of inaccessible sea cliffs or under rocks or loose boulders lower down at foot of talus slopes on headlands of Northeast or on rocky islands.

Eggs: June–July; 1–2, usually 2, dull white, some may be tinted with green or yellow, spotted and blotched with grays and dark brown.

Incubation: About 21–30 days; young first fly about 39–40 days after hatching (Fisher and Lockley, 1954); before leaving nest young exercise their wings considerably; the adults attend the chick's first flight from the rocks; one observer saw a black guillemot parent dangle a live eel before its 40-day-old youngster to entice it off a rocky ledge; upon reaching the water, swimming chick or chicks are convoyed by parents to sea (Fisher and Lockley, 1954).

Other Names: Geylle; Mandt's guillemot; scapular guillemot; sea pigeon; spotted Greenland dove; tysty, or tystie (in British Isles); white guillemot; white-winged guillemot.

Age: One, banded, reported from Great Britain, 13 years, 11 months old (Clapp, 1976).

Albinism: Seven records (Sealy, 1969b).

Weights: According to Belopol'skii (1957), 427.5 gr., or about 15 oz.

Range: Nests in N. America along coasts of Alaska and adjacent Canadian coast, and from Ellesmere Is. and Greenland south to James Bay, and Me.; winters in shallow open waters off nesting places from n. Alaska and east south to R.I., rarely to Long Is., N.Y., casually to N.J.; frequents rocky shores; accidental in e. Pa.; in Eurasia nests in Arctic on Franz Josef Land, Spitsbergen, Iceland, Severnaya Zemlya, Novaya Zemlya, New Siberian Is., Wrangel Is., and n. Europe.

Guillemot, pigeon, *Cepphus columba* (SEP-fus coh-LUM-bah); genus name: *see* Guillemot, black; species name: Lat., dove, or pigeon. (Color ill., page 46.) One of most widespread and frequently seen members of the Auk Family along Pacific coast, where resident south to Santa Barbara, Calif.; resembles black guillemot, except that a wedge-shaped bar of black extends into the prominent white wing patch; 12–14 in. long; so similar to black guillemot that some ornithologists believe that it is a geographic race of that species; like its cousin, the black guillemot, the pigeon guillemot has a "water dance" in spring in which pairs sometimes gather on the water near the nesting colony for a mutual display, calling and showing the red linings of the mouth, and forming lines on the water for a few seconds which suddenly break up when whole party dives with individuals chasing each other below the surface (Fisher and Lockley, 1954); while floating on surface, have nervous habit of frequently dabbing bill into water and of rising from surface

to skitter across it before immediately taking off; like black guillemot, utters low piping whistle.

Feeding Habits: Is good underwater "flier"; dives to feed on bottom-dwelling small fishes, mollusks, crustaceans, and marine worms.

Nest: Solitary or in small colonies up to 50 pairs; along Pacific coast in general; nest site is in crevices or in caves or in talus slopes at foot of cliffs on rocky islands near salt water where eggs are laid on bare rock or on open ledges, also in abandoned burrows of puffins and rabbits and even under railroad ties (Humphrey, 1965); nests in burrows in clay banks in Puget Sound region of Wash., where it digs its own burrows, sometimes in banks 200 ft. above the sea (Bent, 1919); on beach at Mandarte Is., B.C., pairs defended area about 3 ft. in diameter from which they drove away all intruders (Drent, 1965).

Eggs: May–July; 1–2, usually 2, same appearance as eggs of black guillemot.

Incubation: 30–32 days, young fly 29–39 days after hatching (Drent, 1965).

Other Name: Sea pigeon.

Albinism: One record (Sealy, 1969b).

Weights: According to Bedard (1969) and Swartz (1967), 483.8 gr., or about 1 lb. 1 oz.

Range: Nests from Chukotski Pen. at Arctic Circle in Soviet Union to islands in Bering Sea (except Pribilofs) south to Japan, and in N. America from St. Lawrence Is., St. Matthew Is., Hall and Bogoslof Is., e. Aleutians, Shumagin Is., Kodiak, and se. Alaska south to Santa Barbara Is., Calif.; winters from Pribilof and Aleutian Is. to Kamchatka and the Kurile Is. and to s. Calif.

Guillemot, white-winged. *See* Black guillemot.

Murre, Atlantic. *See* Common murre.

Murre, bridled. *See* Common murre.

Murre, Brunnich's. *See* Thick-billed murre.

Murre, California. *See* Common murre.

Murre, common, *Uria aalge* (YOU-rih-ah AHL-geh); genus name: from Gr. *ourein,* to dive; species name: Scandinavian word for the bird; common name (MER): of obscure European origin, may be related to *marrot,* local English dialect, for an auk, guillemot, or puffin. (Color ills., pages 46, 47.) Lives in both N. Atlantic and N. Pacific O.; in N. America, summers along coasts from Greenland south to Newfoundland and along Pacific coast, from Alaska south to c. Calif.; nests in enormous colonies, one of most abundant seabirds in N. Hemisphere (Tuck, 1961); winters on ocean, usually about 5 mi. off Atlantic coast south to Me., and a few south to s. Calif.; sexes outwardly alike; 16–17 in. long; wingspread about 30 in.; the dark-backed murres (common and thick-billed) can be distinguished from all other alcids by the long, dark slender bill, longer than that of any other alcids; common murre in breeding plumage, upperparts including head and neck are rich dark brown, underparts

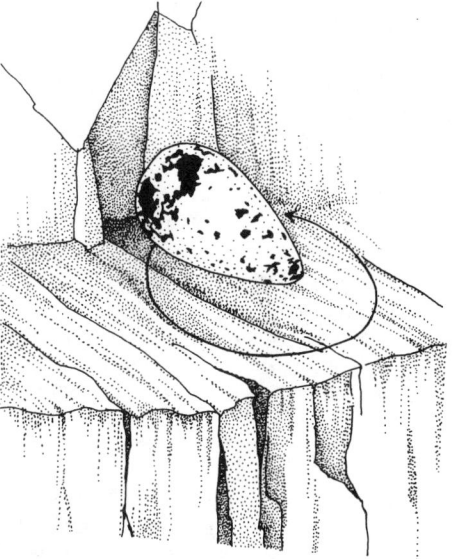

AUK FAMILY
The murre lays its remarkable, pear-shaped (pyriform) egg—without a nest—on bare ledges, often high over the sea. If disturbed, the egg will roll in a small circle around its pointed end; an oval egg might roll straight over the edge.

white; rear edge of wing white; inside of mouth yellow; feet dark; a form called the bridled murre has a narrow white eye-ring and a thin white line from eye back over side of head, once thought to be a distinct species, now recognized as a genetic (inherited) variation or form of the common murre, and known only from populations in N. Atlantic; winter plumage of common murre is similar to that of summer but throat and cheeks white instead of dark brown, and a dark mark running from each eye back over the white cheeks helps distinguish it from the larger thick-billed murre; flight is swift, strong, direct, with steady wingbeats; when traveling long distances flies in flocks high in air; about feeding or breeding grounds flies close to water, frequently turning from side to side; is so heavy-bodied and small-winged that it cannot rise off water without pattering along surface; often forms large rafts on water, and flies in lines; gentle and harmless; utters soft, purring sounds suggestive of its name; also croaks, growls, and moans about nesting colony—also called a loomery; largest nesting colonies in ne. N. America, at Funk Is., Newfoundland, with half a million pairs in 1959 (Tuck, 1961); along Pacific, widely dispersed colonies along coasts of Wash., Ore., and Calif., one of largest and best-known on Farallon Is., Calif., another at Three Arch Rocks, Ore., with estimated 750,000 birds.

Feeding Habits: Flies underwater as other alcids do; congregates on feeding waters and dives from surface; probably best diver among alcids except razorbill; greatest depths of dives unknown but have been caught in trawler nets off Newfoundland 240 ft. deep; frequently stays submerged for 60 seconds (Tuck, 1961); catches in bill small fishes up to 7 in. long and carries them lengthwise with tail hanging out of bill—polar cod, capelin, launces, small Atlantic cod, and herring predominate with some marine worms, amphipods, shrimp, and Arctic squids; close-packed nesting colonies are sustained by almost unlimited food supply in cold seas; excrement of murres, rich in potash, important to growth and abundance of marine life of oceans on which murres live; their colonies are fertilizing factories of northern seas; colonies seem as numerous today as in historical times (Tuck, 1961).

Nest: No materials but occasionally a few pebbles sometimes cemented together by excrement which may keep egg from rolling; in colonies on bare rock ledges or cliff tops of high rocky coasts, usually on steep cliff facing sea (low islands such as Funk are exceptional).

Eggs: Atlantic coast, May–July; Pacific coast, Mar.–July; 1, pure white to shades of blue, green, or brown, spotted or scrawled with brown, lilac, and black; pear shape of egg minimizes rolling.

Incubation: In turn by both sexes, varies from 28 to 34 days owing to microclimate at nest site (Tuck, 1961); chick(s) sometimes protected from prematurely jumping off nest ledge into water by group of adults in colony which stand between chick(s) and sea; chick leaves nest ledge 18–25 days after hatching; leaps off ledge from cliff, some 800–1,500 ft. above water; flutters down or may have only short drop from low rock island nest site; group of adults or a single adult accompanies chicks as they swim to sea, where cared for communally by adults until able to fly, about 39–46 days after hatching (Tuck, 1961). In nesting colony on Farallon Is., Calif., Gress *et al.* (1971) reported a 13% thinning of eggshells of common murres in 1968, attributed to chlorinated hydrocarbon pesticides in the Calif. coastal marine food chain of the common murre, and therefore a possible future threat to their continued reproductive success. See also Coulter and Risebrough (1973).

Other Names: Atlantic murre; California murre; thin-billed murre; foolish guillemot; guillemot (in Great Britain); tinker; tinkershire; willock.

Age: One, banded, reported from U.S., 7 years, 7 months, old (Clapp, 1976).

Albinism: In 1956, a full or complete albino chick and a partial albino discovered; in 1958, three albinistic chicks on Funk Is., at least five in N. American museums, and six shot in coastal waters of Newfoundland; melanism even more rare, three in collections of museums on Pacific coast of U.S., several from w. Greenland, and one shot on Trinity Bay, Newfoundland, winter 1952 (Tuck, 1961).

Flight Speed: Timed from ship at 36 m.p.h. with bursts to 45 m.p.h., actual airspeed once timed at estimated 50–60 m.p.h. (Tuck, 1961).

Weights: One on St. Lawrence Is., Alaska, 1,031 gr. (Hughes, 1970), or about 2 lbs. 4⅓ oz.; one 984.6 gr. (Swartz, 1967), or about 2 lbs. 2¾ oz.

Range: In N. America, nests along coast of s. Greenland, Labrador, and Gulf of St. Lawrence to Newfoundland and Nova Scotia, most southerly limit in e. N. America; in Pacific from Komandorskie Is. and St. Matthew Is. in Bering Sea, and nw. Alaska, south through the Aleutians and Pribilofs to coast of s. B.C., and n. Wash. and Ore. south to Hurricane Point, Calif., which is southern limit of breeding range in w. N. America; also nests in N. Atlantic from coast of Iceland and in n. Europe south to Portugal; in N. Pacific from islands in Bering Sea south to Kuriles, e. Korea, and Japan; winters on ocean off Atlantic coast south to Me., more rarely to Mass., unreported on Long Is., N.Y., until 1936, when live and dead "oiled" birds were washed ashore; unreported south of coastal N. J. (Bull, 1964); however, one picked up alive on Feb. 13, 1973, on beach at Back Bay, Va., was first confirmed record for the state (Scott and Cutler, 1973).

Murre, Pallas, *See* Murre, thick-billed.

Murre, thick-billed, *Uria lomvia* (YOU-rih-ah LOM-vih-ah); genus name: *see* Murre, common; species name: Swedish word for a guillemot, or diving bird; *thick-billed* refers to thicker bill than that of common murre. (Color ill., page 47.) Outwardly similar to common murre but somewhat larger (17–19 in. long); sexes outwardly alike; bill is shorter and thicker than bill of common murre, and in breeding plumage shows a white streak along cutting edge at base of dark upper mandible; other differences: in summer, white of breast makes sharp inverted "V" in black of neck; in winter, black of crown extends well below each eye and has no dark stripe in white of ear coverts as in common murre (Peterson, 1961); may be most abundant seabird in N. Hemisphere, although probably exceeded by dovekie in N. Atlantic and by least auklet in N. Pacific (Tuck, 1961); both the common and thick-billed murres nest at Kodiak Is., Alaska; large colonies of thick-billed nest on Bogoslof Is.; also either the colony at St. George Is. or the one on Walrus Is. in Pribilofs may be the largest nesting colony of murres in the world, with millions nesting; Tuck (1961) estimated world population of murres at 56 million with thick-billed outnumbering the common murre by three to one; in courtship, has group displays on water (*see* under Pigeon guillemot). Feeding habits, voice, nest, eggs, and incubation all very similar to that of common murre (each probably breeds for first time in third summer of life).

Other Names: Brunnich's murre; Brunnich's guillemot (in Great Britain); egg bird; Frank's guillemot; Pallas' murre; polar guillemot; thick-billed guillemot.

Albinism: Four records (Sealy, 1969b), and several of melanism (see Tuck, 1961, for details).

Weights: 964.4 gr. (Swartz, 1967), or 2 lbs. 2 oz.

Range: In N. America, nests from Ellesmere Is. and Greenland south to n. Hudson Bay, n. Que., Labrador, Newfoundland, and St. Mary Is. Bird Rocks in Gulf of St. Lawrence; Ellesmere I. and south in N. Pacific from New Siberian Is. and coast of Siberia to Wrangel Is., south to Kamchatka, the Komandorskie Is., and Kuriles to Japan; from n. Alaska south to Pribilofs, Aleutian and Kodiak Is.; winters in open waters of breeding range from Greenland south into Hudson Bay and on Atlantic coast to Long Is., N.Y., more rarely off coast of N.J., Del., and Md., casually south to S.C. and to Great Lakes and Lake Champlain; accidental inland in Ont., Que., Mich., Iowa, Ind., Ohio, Pa. (Conneaut Lake), Mass., N.H., N.Y., Conn., N.C., S.C.; winters in Pacific from Bering Sea south to Japan and to se. Alaska, casually to n. Yuk. and B.C.

Murre, thin-billed. *See* Common murre.

Murrelet, ancient, *Synthliboramphus antiquus* (sin-thlih-bo-RAM-fus an-TIE-kwus); genus name: Lat., from Gr. *synthlibo*, to press, and *ramphos*, beak, referring to the laterally compressed bill; species name: Lat., old or ancient, in sense of grayish or whitish feathers on head in breeding season; *murrelet:* dim. of murre. (Color ill., page 47.) In summer nests on islands of N. Pacific, in Asia, and from Alaska south to B.C., casually to Wash., in winter along Pacific coast of U.S. to Mexico, but mostly at sea out of sight of land; all murrelets are small, chubby seabirds that appear short-necked; are generally patterned (at least in winter) dark above, white below; in winter plumage, ancient murrelet has yellowish bill and black crown that contrasts with its gray back; and a *white* throat and sides of neck; in summer plumage, when gathered in small groups of 4–6 on bays of Aleutian Is., Alaska, or when swimming in line, one ahead of the other, shows *black* throat and white sides of neck, pale bill, and has jagged *white streak just over each eye,* extending along sides of head; narrow white plumes on shoulders—lacks these in winter plumage; flight is swift, direct, usually close to water and for short distance when drops in again; rapid swimmer, and dives in forward arc-like plunge; uses wings to "fly" underwater (see details of underwater "flight" of this and other members of Auk Family in a chapter, "Flying Under Water," in Terres, 1968a; *also* Swimming and Diving); utters soft, shrill whistles while at sea; low chirps and whistles at breeding colony; lives on open seas in winter and comes to small islands in spring mostly for nesting; active at night, usually inactive around breeding islands during day.

Feeding Habits: Dives for food, which is mainly small marine invertebrates.
Nest: On Aleutian Is., where often shares nesting grounds with Leach's and fork-tailed storm-petrels and Cassin's auklets; sometimes scratches out hollow under large tussocks of matted grass, at other times little or no nest made and eggs laid on bare rocks in rock crevices or in abandoned burrows of Cassin's auklets (Bent, 1919; Sealy, 1975).
Eggs: Alaska, May–July; Queen Charlotte Is., B.C., Apr.–June; 1–2, usually 2, blue milk-white to cream or olive, flecked, blotched, or spotted irregularly with brown and gray.
Incubation: By both sexes, which exchange places nightly; period of and age when young first fly unknown; at night, within 2–3 days after young hatch, parents assemble at water's edge and begin chorus of chirps to call young from burrows or crevices in rocks; young swarm down hillsides to water and swim away with adults, which apparently tend chicks without returning to land, and until chicks can fend for themselves.
Other Names: Black-throated guillemot; black-throated murrelet; gray-headed murrelet; old man.
Weights: 223.6 gr. (Bedard, 1969), or about 8 oz.
Range: In N. America, nests from Aleutian Is. and Kodiak Is., Alaska, to Graham and Langara Is. in Queen Charlotte group, B.C., casually to nw. Wash.; and in Asia, from Komandorskie Is. and Kamchatka to the Kuriles and Korea; winters from Pribilofs to n. Baja Calif.; accidental in interior B.C., Ore., Nev., Idaho, Neb., Minn., Wisc., Ohio, s. Ont., and s. Que.

Murrelet, Craveri's, *Endomychura craveri* (en-doe-my-CUE-rah CRAV-er-eye); genus name: from Gr. *endomychos,* secret, or hidden, and *oura,* tail, in reference to the "secret" short tail; species name: for Frederico Craveri, Italian chemist and naturalist who lived in Mexico in 19th century and collected in Baja Calif. the murrelet named in his honor. Ranges north in fall and winter off Calif. coast to Monterey but so difficult to distinguish from Xantus' murrelet that very rarely reported (see below); small, about 8½ in. long; has no seasonal difference in plumage; is slaty black above, white below, strikingly resembles Xantus' murrelet and believed by some ornithologists to be a subspecies, or race, of that species; in field, both birds look like tiny murres and impossible to distinguish them, but Craveri's has dark underwing linings and is slightly smaller than Xantus'; on nesting islands in Gulf of California, pairs of Craveri's do much chasing near burrows at dawn; active mostly at night, utter harsh notes or chatterings.

Feeding Habits: Probably small marine crustaceans, like Xantus' murrelet.
Nest: In colonies, usually a slight depression in earth at end of crevice in rock on islands.
Eggs: Mar.–July; 1–2, usually 2, vary from white to yellowish, olive, or brown, blotched, spotted, or scrawled with brown (Bent, 1919).
Incubation: By both sexes, 22 days; young take to sea with adults 2 days after hatching (Bent, 1919); age when young first fly unknown.
Weights: 151.1 gr. (Bedard, 1969), or about 5 oz.
Range: Nests on islands in Gulf of California, and off Baja California; after nesting season ranges north off w. Baja Calif. to Monterey, Calif.; according to Small (1974), probably occurs off Calif. coast regularly but difficulty of distinguishing from Xantus' makes its status uncertain.

Murrelet, Kittlitz's, *Brachyramphus brevirostris* (brack-ih-RAM-fus brev-ih-ROS-tris); genus name: from Gr. *brachys,* short, and *ramphos,* beak, for very short bill; species name: from Lat. *brevis,* short, and *rostrum,* bill; *Kittlitz* for F. H. Kittlitz, 19th-century German scientist who accompanied a Russian expedition to Kamchatka (see other details of his biography in Gruson, 1972), named in Kittlitz's honor by Friedrich Brandt, eminent German zoologist. (Color ill., page 47.) In N. America, summers along coasts of Alaska; small, 9 in. long; bill very short; in summer plumage heavily streaked and mottled on head, back, and breast with pale yellowish tan; paler above than other alcids; in winter plumage, crown dark, *entire face is white* even over eyes, which distinguishes it from similar marbled murrelet; and has a complete, or almost complete, dark *neck band;* in summer is locally common near glacial waters on coasts of mainland Alaska; up to 500 have been seen on Glacier Bay, Alaska, apparently center of its abundance (Bent, 1919); flight much swifter than that of other murrelets and appears to be wilder; said to utter a hoarse, long-drawn *squak* note (Peterson, 1961).

Feeding Habits: Little known but said to feed on crustaceans and "slippery sluglike animals" (Bent, 1919).
Nest: Site is on bare rock some distance from sea, above timberline in mountains.
Eggs: May–June; 1, described as olive dotted with dark and light brown; first N. American nesting discovered by Colonel John E. Thayer, who (in Bent, 1919) told of a single egg on bare lava and surrounded by snow, high on Mt. Pavlof, a volcano 8,200 ft. high on sw. side of Alaska Pen., found in June 1913; a Russian, A. A. Kischiuskii (1968), described a "nest" with single egg slightly incubated from which an incubating parent bird was flushed, laid on bare

Craveri's murrelet

AUK FAMILY

gravel of a patch of rock detritus about 18 mi. inland from the Siberian coast at Shelikhov Bay and about 180 mi. from the nearest stream and 5 mi. from the nearest forest.

Other Name: Known in Russia as the short-billed murrelet.

Weights: 237 gr. (Bedard, 1969), or about 8⅓ oz.

Range: In summer, locally, from Point Barrow, Alaska, south to Glacier Bay; winters on adjacent open seas of south part range and from se. Siberia to n. Japan.

Marbled murrelet

AUK FAMILY

Murrelet, marbled, *Brachyramphus marmoratus* (brack-ih-RAM-fus mar-more-AY-tus); genus name: *see* Murrelet, Kittlitz's; species name: Lat., marbled, refers to mottled or irregular spots and streaks or bars of summer plumage. Summers on Alaskan islands and on mainland; south to c. Calif.; sexes much alike; 9–10½ in. long; small, chunky, short neck; bill appears relatively more slender and longer than in other alcids of comparable size; in spring and summer, sooty-brown upperparts, barred with darker reddish brown; heavily barred below, which gives marbled appearance (both the marbled and Kittlitz's murrelets are unusual for their kind in that before breeding season, in late winter and early spring, they molt from the generally black and white all-year plumage of other murrelets to the brown or gray-brown-barred plumage; this protective coloration presumably helps hide these two species from predators while they incubate their eggs in the open, either on bare rocks in mountains on ground or on large limbs of evergreen trees—other murrelets nest hidden in rock crevices, under plant growth, or in burrows in ground); in winter, marbled is dark gray above, spotless white below, with incomplete collar and white cheeks; has strip of white in dark upperparts, between back and wing (scapulars), conspicuous as a white wing patch in flight—"in winter, only alcid *south of Alaska* that has these white scapulars" (Robbins *et al.,* 1966); in summer, seen skimming over surface of water along navigable inside passages or waterways from Puget Sound to Alaska (its summer range includes most of belt of coniferous coastal forest); if on water, sometimes escapes by diving but flight is swift, direct, and strong, usually flies close to surface when on feeding waters but at great height when flying inland; can fly underwater with wingbeats of 2 or 3 per second (Bent, 1919); calls with shrill, exultant *meer-meer-meer-meer* or *keer* both in winter and when flying to and from nesting grounds.

Feeding Habits: Eats small fishes which it gets by diving in tide rips and other places where small fishes swim in schools; also eats mollusks and marine crustaceans.

Nest: Apparently breeds on mountains near coast; first known nest found "in rock slide at 1,900 ft. on Chichagof Is., Alaska, June 13, 1931" (Gabrielson and Lincoln, 1959); first egg known to science of this species taken from oviduct of a female shot on Prince of Wales Archipelago off Melville Sound, Arctic O., May 23, 1897; a stunned bird with brood patch and fragments of egg, but no nest, taken from de-

bris of large hemlock felled on Queen Charlotte Is., B.C., in 1953 (Guiget, 1956); on Aug. 7, 1974, a tree trimmer in Santa Cruz County, Calif., accidentally shook a chick from its nest 140 ft. up in a Douglas fir; nest was on large branch near its junction with trunk; chick had well-developed flight feathers (see details in Stallcup and Greenberg, 1974); see especially Binford *et al.* (1975); in 1978 a nest was found on the ground on an island off the coast of s. Alaska (Simons, 1980); in Russia, A. P. Kuzyakin, noted Russian ecologist, discovered a marbled murrelet on its nest 20 ft. above ground in a larch tree, June 17, 1961, with single slightly incubated egg in taiga inland from City of Okhotsk; he collected egg and nest, which was simply a natural cushion of dendroid lichens to which no nesting material had been added (Kuzyakin, 1963).

Eggs: June; 1, pale green-yellow, evenly marked with small black-brown spots (color as described by Sutton and Semple, 1941, who took egg from oviduct of a female, and color corroborated by Kuzyakin); newly hatched young still unreported to 1974.

Other Name: Long-billed murrelet (in Russia).

Weights: Adult males (37), 196.2–252.5 gr., or about 7–9 oz.; adult females (37), 188.1–269.1 gr., or about 6⅔–9½ oz. See these and other details in Sealy (1975).

Range: In Asia, from Kamchatka to Japan; in N. America, resident from Aleutian and Kodiak Is., Alaska to c. Calif. (Peterson, 1961).

Murrelet, Xantus', *Endomychura hypoleuca* (en-doe-my-CUE-rah high-poe-LEW-kah); genus name: *see* Murrelet, Caveri's; species name: from Gr. *hypo,* under, and *leukos,* white, or somewhat white (Coble, 1954); common name: for John Xantus (ZAN-tus), a Hungarian, early collector of birds in Calif., who collected on Cape San Lucas, Baja Calif., and scientifically described, the murrelet that now bears his name. Summers on islands along coast of Baja Calif. north to c. Calif.; like Craveri's, is most southerly of any alcid; sexes outwardly alike, about 9½–10½ in. long; like Craveri's murrelet, which it strikingly resembles (Craveri's may be a subspecies of Xantus'), shows no seasonal change in plumage; about size and shape of marbled murrelet, but no white mark in wings; like Craveri's, has all-black back, all-white underparts *including white underwing linings* (Craveri's has dark underwing linings); black, slender bill; feet pale bluish (Hoffman, 1927); has habits similar to Craveri's; in flight beats wings very rapidly, capable of great speed; in past when attacked by then more numerous peregrine falcon, would allow itself to be caught rather than take to water (Bent, 1919); active by night during nesting season, when heard uttering shrill, twittering whistles until dawn; by day keeps well out to sea, where usually seen in pairs or family groups; will flush from water but refuses to dive unless wounded.

Feeding Habits: Apparently dives for food and probably eats small crustaceans and other invertebrates of marine waters.

Nest: On islands among crannies of loose boulders; in caves; slight hollows under rocks or beneath dense bushes on hillsides; lays its eggs on ground or on rock.

Eggs: Mar.–July; 1–2, usually 2, blue, green, or some may be chocolate, either almost plain or spotted and blotched with lavender or brown (has been credited with two broods a season).

Incubation: By both sexes, period of not known but may be about 22 days, as given for Craveri's murrelet young; conducted to sea by adults when young about 2–4 days old; age when they first fly unknown (Bent, 1919).

Weights: 155.9 gr. (Bedard, 1969), or about 5½ oz.; one reported at 162.5 gr. (Sanger, 1973).

Range: Nests on Anacapa and Santa Barbara chain of islands off coast of s. Calif. and on Los Coronados, off San Diego, and Todos Santos, San Benito, and Natividad Is. of w. Baja Calif.; winters offshore from Cape San Lucas, Baja Calif., north to c. Calif., casually north to Wash. and one off Vancouver and Queen Charlotte Is., B.C., Oct. 1971 (Sanger, 1973).

Puffin, Atlantic. *See* Common puffin.

Puffin, cinereous. Another name for the greater shearwater in Shearwater Family.

Puffin, common, *Fratercula arctica* (frah-TER-cue-lah ARK-tih-kah); genus name: from Lat. *fraterculus,* little brother, in sense of "little friar," but Coues (1882) suggested name may be humorous (as in common name), from puffiness and shape of bird (possibly combined with its upright posture and coloration); Macleod (1954) believed name is from habit of the bird when rising from the sea of clasping its feet together as though in prayer; species name: Lat., northern, of the Arctic. (Color ill., page 48.) Summers along rocky seacoasts of N. Atlantic from Me. to Greenland and in n. Europe; winters farther at sea and in deeper waters than razorbill and murres; seldom seen within sight of land until Mar.; sexes outwardly alike; 11½–13½ in. long; wingspread 21–24 in.; short, stocky; stands upright on land; upperparts black; cheeks white; white below; has large, parrotlike, triangular-shaped bill which in breeding season is "bright reddish orange at tip half with a yellow-bordered patch of blue at the rear half" (Reilly, 1968); whole inside of mouth and tongue yellow; feet orange-red; after breeding season, sheds some of the horny plates of bill at same time as it molts its feathers in Aug. and Sept. (see details in Bent, 1919, and in Forbush, 1925–29); in winter plumage, same as in summer but face is largely dark, and bill with a different shape, appearing same length but not as high; immature has much smaller blackish bill, but has same body shape and gray cheeks of adults; is most closely related to other puffins and the rhinoceros auklet; gathers in huge, dense rafts in early spring on waters below the cliffs or islands where they will nest, to court: males fight on water, pairs bill and go through courtship ceremonies (see details in Fisher and Lockley, 1954); in large nesting colony on land, either bill-rubbing of pairs or two birds fighting attracts neighbors which crowd around and, by joining ceremony, break it down until it ceases; usually walks erect, agile on foot; is tame and often curious; is attacked and killed by great black-backed gulls and colonies soon disappear from islands invaded by rats, cats, dogs, and foxes; is easily shot for food, and near settled areas soon declines; roosts on rocks and ledges; copulates on water; utters low purring notes in buzzy flight; low grunts or groans in nesting colony; rides water lightly like a duck; paddles skillfully with feet; without favoring wind must run along surface of water to become airborne.

Feeding Habits: Dives from air or surface, swims rapidly underwater using wings like other alcids, catches small fishes, mollusks, and crustaceans, which it swallows underwater, but when feeding young, can carry up to 30 small fishes at one time, crosswise in bill owing to round tongue and slight serrations on interior of upper mandible which help it to hold fishes; as each fish is caught, it is apparently killed by grip of sharp pincers at point of bill (Fisher and Lockley, 1954).

Nest: In colonies, in burrow in loose soil at tops of cliffs or on islands, entrance usually concealed under flat rock, burrow often curving; rarely egg laid in rock crevices; male is said to do most of digging of burrow, 2–4 ft. deep; uses bill as pickax and its webbed feet and sharp claws to dig, and to throw soil backward from burrow; carries grass, seaweed, and feathers into nest burrow; drops them at far end, partway down or at burrow entrance; males remain with same females through nesting season, and because of comparative safety of egg in burrow, both male and female may sit outside during day for 2 or 3 hours with other puffins in colony or parade back and forth with assembly of their neighbors.

Eggs: N. America, June–July; 1 (rarely 2), round, white, some may be spotted with brown.

Incubation: By both sexes but male has only minor part; both have *two* small incubation patches and incubating bird must tuck large egg under one wing and lean body on it to incubate (Fisher and Lockley, 1954); incubation period averages 42 days, newly hatched young fed on very small fishes; Lockley (1953) estimated that one chick ate almost its entire weight in fishes daily and was fed some 2,000 while in its burrow (*see* food requirements of some young of birds under Young and Their Care); about 40 days after chick is hatched, its parents abandon it in security of its burrow and go to sea, where they begin autumn molt and for a short time are flightless; chick stays in burrow fasting for about a week (*see* Fasting) and then flutters off cliff at dusk or at night when safer from attacks of predatory gulls and skuas; paddles vigorously out to sea but cannot fly; dives for its own food and first flies when about 49 days old.

Other Names: Atlantic puffin; bottle-nose; coulterneb; Labrador auk; large-billed puffin; pope; sea parrot; tammy norie.

Age: One banded in Norway, when adult, was recovered where banded 21 years later, an old-age record for the species (Holgersen, 1959); half a million puffins are netted each year for their food and feathers on Iceland and in the Faeroes.

Albinism: Ten records (Sealy, 1969b).

Weights: 490.5 gr. (Belopol'skii, 1957), or about 1 lb. 1⅓ oz.

Xantus' murrelet

AUK FAMILY

Range: In N. America, nests along coasts and on islands from Greenland and n. Labrador south to Newfoundland and Anticosti and Magdalen Is. in Gulf of St. Lawrence, Nova Scotia and sw. N.B. to e. Me., farthest south on Atlantic coast of N. America of any alcid except black guillemot and razorbill; winters in open waters of breeding range south in N. Atlantic rarely to Mass. and Long Is., N.Y. (7 records) and casually on offshore waters to s. N.J. (Bull, 1964); apparently the least migratory of all Atlantic alcids; nests also in n. Eurasia in Arctic O. on Spitsbergen, n. coast of Russia, Novaya Zemlya, Jan Mayen, and Iceland and south to Ireland and nw. coast of France; accidental inland at Ottawa, Can.

Puffin, horned, *Fratercula corniculata* (frah-TER-cue-lah corn-ik-you-LA-tah); genus name: *see* Puffin, common; species name: Lat., horned, in reference to small "horn" of fleshy tissue above eyes. (Color ill., page 49.) N. Pacific coast counterpart of common puffin, to which closely related, but ranges do not overlap; 14½ in. long, somewhat larger than common puffin; similar to it in all plumages; sexes alike, black above, white below; triangular yellow bill of adults red-tipped; white cheeks in summer; small dark fleshy "horn" above each eye (shed after breeding season); feet orange; in winter, cheeks gray, bill darker and much smaller; immature lacks red tip on bill.

Feeding Habits: Dives, often with body rising clear of water before plunging under; "flies" rapidly under surface, with both wings; catches mainly small fishes—sand launces, sticklebacks, smelt, also various kinds of mollusks (Bent, 1919); early in morning, most of those not incubating egg fly to sea; return trips during day with bills full of fish either for incubating mate or for young; at night all return to nesting site; around nesting colony, utter low growling or grunting sounds, and harsh quarreling notes in burrows.
Nest: In burrows dug in earth on top of islands, usually on edge of bluffs, 1–3 ft. long, with an enlarged nest cavity at end; also eggs laid in natural crevices in cliffs and in holes in rock slides, some with scanty bed of grasses, mosses, and feathers (Bent, 1919).
Eggs: June–July; 1, white with faint spots and scrawls.
Incubation: By both sexes; period of and age when young first fly unknown; sometimes shares nesting grounds with tufted puffins although it does not nest as far south as tufted.
Weights: Two averaged 572 gr. (Hughes, 1970), or about 1 lb. 4 oz., each; 619 gr. (Bedard, 1969; Swartz, 1967), or about 1 lb. 5¾ oz.
Range: In N. America, nests on coasts and islands from Cape Lisburne, Alaska, south through the Aleutian Is., along Alaska Pen. east and south to Glacier Bay and Forrester Is., Alaska; in Asia, nests along coast of ne. Siberia to e. coast of Chukotski Pen., south to Kamchatka Pen. and to n. Kurile Is.; winters on open sea throughout breeding range south to B.C., Wash., and Ore., casually to Calif.

Puffin, large-billed. *See* Common puffin.

Puffin, tufted, *Lunda cirrhata* (LUN-dah sir-AY-tah); genus name: from Scandinavian *lunde,* a puffin; species name: from *cirratus,* having curled locks or ringlets, well applied to long breeding plumes of head of this species (Coues, 1882); *tufted* refers to breeding plumes. (Color ills., pages 48, 49.) Largest of all puffins; most southern in its distribution (to s. Calif.), and most bizarre in its breeding plumage; sexes alike; 14½–15½ in. long; unlike common and horned puffins, has an *all-dark body* and white face in breeding plumage; has triangular-shaped red bill, and in summer, especially distinguished by its long, backward-curving, straw-colored plumes; in winter, lacks these and can be distinguished from horned puffin, also of Pacific coast, by its dusky sides (horned has white sides), also, at close range, the dark head shows a light line over each eye; immature is dark-backed and light gray below and has smaller, but distinctive, triangular-shaped bill of its kind, without any red on bill; usually silent but in nesting colony utters soft grunts, growls.

Feeding Habits: Dives and swims underwater to catch and eat mainly saltwater fishes such as smelts (up to 8–10 in. long), sardines, herring, and perch, which it carries, like other puffins, crosswise in its bill; also feeds on various invertebrates.
Nest: In colonies, and like other puffins, digs a burrow in soil on rounded tops of islands or in face of sandy bluffs above beaches, in sandy and stony slopes with murres, or under loose rocks, sometimes lay in crevices in rocks and cliffs, sometimes with crested, least, and parakeet auklets or associated with glaucous and glaucous-winged gulls or among murres and cormorants.
Eggs: Calif. coast, Apr.–July; Wash., May–July; Alaskan coast, June–July; 1, pale blue or dull white, spotted and scrawled with lavender and brown; apparently double-brooded (*see* Single-Brooded under Brooding) in southern part of range (Bent, 1919).
Incubation: By both sexes, but period of and age when young first fly unknown.
Other Names: Old man of the sea; sea parrot, toporkie (among Aleuts).
Breeding in Captivity: Bell (1971) reported the breeding of a pair of tufted puffins at the New York Zoological Gardens in summer of 1970; the young puffin hatched in a nesting burrow on July 26, emerged from burrow on Sept. 15; apparently this was first record of captive breeding for any member of the Auk Family.
Weights: One, 734 gr. (Hughes, 1970), or about 1 lb. 10 oz.; according to Bedard (1969) and Spring (1970), 779.4 gr., or about 1 lb. 11½ oz.
Range: In N. America, nests on shores and offshore islands from Kotzebue Sound, nw. Alaska, to Aleutian Is., Kodiak Is., and Kenai Pen., se. Alaska, to B.C., Wash., Ore., south to Santa Barbara Is. off coast of s. Calif.; in Asia, nests from Kolyuchin Is., East Cape, and Diomede Is. in Bering Strait south to Kamchatka and Komandorskie Is. to Kuriles and Japan; winters on open waters adjacent to breeding range, except in far northern part, and south to n. Baja Calif.; wanders north to Point Barrow,

Alaska, and south to Honshu, Japan, and San Nicolas Is., Calif., accidental in Me.

Razorbill, *Alca torda* (AL-kah TOR-dah); genus name: *see* Auk Family; species name: from Swedish name for this bird; *razorbill:* for the thin upper mandible of bill. (Color ill., page 49.) In summer, along rocky seacoasts of N. Atlantic from Greenland south to N.B., Can.; in winter, off Atlantic coast south to Long Is., N.Y., casually farther south; resembles in miniature the extinct great auk, formerly of same region; 16–18 in. long; wingspread 25–27 in.; sexes outwardly alike; black back, head, and neck; white below; large, deep black bill has knifelike upper mandible, cross-grooved, and hooked at tip; bill has narrow vertical white line near tip; a white line also runs from eyes to base of upper part of bill; eyes dark brown or bluish; feet black; in winter, adults are similar but white of underparts reaches up to bill and sides of neck; immature in first winter, much paler than adult, bill very much smaller, more pointed, and lacks grooves and white vertical lines of adult; in flight, compared with murres, is shorter and thicker-bodied, and shows thicker head and neck; back more arched; on water holds thick bill uptilted and holds rather long tail cocked upward; sometimes seen singly or in twos and threes off rocky coasts; in migration, flies in small groups in single file low over water; utters hoarse croaks and growls on breeding grounds; less colonial than murres and returns to nesting grounds later in spring; some come to land mainly at end of Feb. but paired birds do not settle on rocks until beginning of Apr. and even a month later in Far North; moves farther south in fall and winter than does murre; has a mutual display or "water dance" (*see* Water Dance) as does murre; swim about each other, open mouths to show chrome-yellow interior and utter guttural cries.

Feeding Habits: Can dive to great depths; swims swiftly underwater by beating half-spread wings; has been caught in fishermen's nets 60 ft. below surface; catches fishes, squids, and shrimps with bill, usually close to surface.
Nest: In colonies, usually with murres, on open ledges of cliffs where exposed to sun and wind and to predatory gulls; also nests in fissures of rocks and under boulders and even well inside of puffin burrows (Fisher and Lockley, 1954); no nest materials, eggs laid on bare rock or on small stones.
Eggs: N. America, June–July; Great Britain, May–June; usually 1, blue-white or green-white, some spotted or boldly blotched and scrawled with brown or black.
Incubation: By both sexes (each has two very small and narrow brood patches); period is 34–39 days; at 12–14 days after hatching, young leap, usually at dusk or early evening, from cliffs, sometimes more than 600 ft. high, to sea, where they are guarded by adults against predatory gulls until they can fly, about 2 weeks later (Plumb, 1965).
Age: One, banded, reported from Great Britain, 20 years, 3 months, old (Clapp, 1976).

Other Names: Ice bird; razor-billed auk; sea-crow; tinker.

Albinism: One record (Sealy, 1969b).

Range: In N. America nests on rocky seacoasts in w. Greenland, Labrador, the Gulf of St. Lawrence—Cape Whittle, Anticosti Is., Bonaventure Is., Magdalen Is., Bird Rocks—e. Newfoundland to s. N.B. (Grand Manan) and to e. Me.; winters from Greenland south to offshore New York (often oiled birds are found in winter on beaches of Long Is. and N.J.); rarely to Cape May, N.J., casually to offshore Va. and S.C.; accidental on Lake Ontario in Pa.; one found near Montezuma National Wildlife Refuge in upstate N.Y., Nov. 1972 (Rosche, 1973); in Europe nests from Iceland to British Isles, Scandinavia, and n. Russia.

AUKLET
See in Auk Family.

AURICULARS
(aw-RICK-you-lers). Loose-webbed feathers on the sides of a bird's head and overlying its ear openings. These feathers are also called *ear coverts. See* Feather; Ears and Hearing; Topography.

AUSPICE
(AWS-pis; pl.: *auspices*—AWS-pih-seez); from Lat. *avis,* a bird, and *-spicere,* to look at. "Relates to the ancient custom of divination from flights of birds, or the [uttered] notes of tame birds, or from an examination of the entrails of birds kept by the *augures* [*see* Augury] for the purpose of foretelling the probable outcome of any undertaking" (Allen, 1925); usually favorable as to the future. See Harrison, T. H. (1964).

AUSTRALIAN REGION
See Distribution; Faunal Regions.

AUSTRAL REGION
Term for the geographical area covered by three of the life zones—Transition, Upper Austral, and Lower Austral—of the life zone system, still relied upon by some authorities in mapping locally the ecological distribution of N. American birds. *See* discussion of biomes and life zones under Distribution.

AUSTRORIPARIAN
Term of those zoogeographers who still use the life zone concept in studying the natural distribution of N. American birds, for the eastern humid division of the Lower Austral life zone. *See* Austroriparian under Lower Austral; *see also* Life Zones under Distribution.

AUTECOLOGY
(aw-tee-KOL-ah-jih). The study of the individual, or the members of a species collectively, in relation to the environment (Hanson, Herbert C., 1962). The study of a given organism in relation to its environment. It contrasts with *synecology,* which is the study of groups of organisms in the environment (Welty, 1962). *See also* Ecology.

AUTOLYCISM
(aw-TOL-ih-sizm). Term coined by Col. Richard Meinertzhagen, British ornithologist, for the uses that birds make of man, his buildings, ships, etc., and the practical uses birds make of other birds, mammals, reptiles, and fishes. For details, see Meinertzhagen (1959). Birds may use the skin of reptiles, the hairs of mammals, and many of man's manufactured materials—woolen yarn, cotton, pins, wire, etc.—for nesting materials (*see* Nests and Nesting), man's buildings for nesting within or without, his ships for food and transportation, and so on.

Honey guides of Africa use man and certain wild mammals to gain food that may be inaccessible to them. The honey guide leads native tribesmen and sometimes the powerful ratel, a badgerlike animal that is also fond of honey, to the hives of wild honeybees that are within the cavities of trees. Then, after the natives or the ratel have plundered the hive, the honey guide eats the comb and honey that the ratel leaves behind or that the tribesmen set out as a reward to the bird for its services (see Friedmann, 1955; *see also* Piciformes).

Crows, titmice, and other birds pluck the hair of sheep, goats, deer, squirrels, marmots, and even of man himself, to use in their nests. *See* Some Typical Materials Used in Birds' Nests under Nests and Nesting. The chipping sparrow of N. America, before the decline of farm horses, usually lined its nest with long hairs shed from the horses' tails, which the birds picked up about farmyards and stables.

Seabirds watch each other and fly long distances when they see other seabirds fly down to water to feed; vultures and condors in soaring about watch each other in the sky, and when one glides downward to alight at an animal carcass, others soon arrive. *See* discussions under Smell; Vulture—American Vulture Family. Gulls often alight on the backs of large sea turtles that have surfaced on the water and there rest and preen their feathers as phalaropes do when on the backs of surfaced whales.

In Uganda, Charles S. Pitman (1961) reported many kinds of birds perching and resting on the backs of hippopotamuses that were almost submerged in water—anhingas, reed cormorants, sandpipers, ibises, terns, tree ducks, Egyptian geese, wagtails, pratincoles, and kingfishers.

Also in Africa, the charming and brilliantly colored carmine bee-eater, *Merops nubicus,* which ordinarily darts gracefully out in the air from a tree perch to snap up bees and wasps, has developed an amusing and practical habit. In open country where it has few trees or bushes in which to perch, it rides about or sits quietly on the backs of ostriches, grazing sheep, or even on bustards (*see* in Gruiformes), large, ground-dwelling birds of the grassy plains and savannas of the Old World.

Among N. American birds, the groove-billed ani, cowbirds, snowy egret, the introduced starling, and the more recently self-introduced cattle egret (*see* in Heron Family) walk at the feet of cattle and horses to catch grasshoppers, crickets, flies, and other insects stirred up by the movements of the grazing animals. Some perch on the backs of livestock to pick off flies, ticks, etc. (*see* Symbiosis). Formerly, when great herds of bison roamed the western plains,

AUTOLYCISM
The elf owl of the southwestern deserts nests exclusively in cavities excavated by woodpeckers, such as this hole in a saguaro cactus.

cowbirds attended them for the same benefits they get from domestic cattle today.

Insects, birds, and other animals struck and killed by automobiles on highways are eaten by hawks, owls, vultures, crows, and smaller songbirds (Terres, 1956b), which, in turn, are often killed by other cars. Mockingbirds and house sparrows even glean dead insects from the radiators of parked cars (Holland, 1926a).

Rough-legged hawks follow foxes in the Arctic to prey on mice that foxes frighten from their hiding places; snowy egrets stand in shallows to catch fishes driven toward them by the feeding actions of red-breasted mergansers, and the European robin, *Erithacus rubecula*, seems to have an innate tendency to go to a large animal—horse, wild boar, badger, deer, bear, or a man working in the woods—for the insects it may get from the activities of these animals and man (Lack, 1953). For a related type of behavior, *see* Commensalism.

Birds often profit in food-getting in other ways in watching and following the activities of man. Leopold (1923) cited several examples of hawks and owls that followed moving objects—a hunting dog and an automobile moving through game country—and concluded they did so to prey on such game as the dog or car might stir up.

Meinertzhagen (1959) reported that in Africa marsh harriers, *Circus aeruginosus*, a bird similar to the N. American marsh hawk, followed sportsmen to pick up birds killed or wounded by them; he saw in Kenya up to eight harriers attending a quail-shooting party.

Riding on a train between Nogales, on the Arizona-Sonora border, and Guaymas, Mexico, Karl Kenyon (1942) and Ken Stott watched six individual pigeon hawks, or merlins, at different times approach the train, follow alongside the moving cars, then catch and kill in flight small birds frightened by the locomotive—a remarkable example of hawks following a moving train (it was traveling about 40 m.p.h.) and using its passage to "flush their game."

In Africa, the lanner falcon, *Falco biarmicus*, has the habit of attending trains to stoop at doves, rollers, and other birds frightened from their perches on telegraph poles as the train rushes by. In the early days they attended safaris in the apparent hope of catching prey disturbed by the long line of traveling porters.

Both the American robin and the gray catbird have learned to follow the gardener for the grubs or earthworms he spades or plows up; gulls, crows, and other birds follow the farmer's freshly turned furrows for mice, grubs, and other animals unearthed by the plow; rooks and jackdaws have followed the practice in Britain for centuries (Meinertzhagen, 1959). In N. America, swallows and chimney swifts often follow the farmer cutting his hayfields to catch insects that fly up ahead of his clattering mowing machine, and Mississippi kites circle cattle or horsemen to catch insects stirred up from the grass.

Other than in food-getting, birds profit from the home-making of other animals. Small owls, bluebirds, crested flycatchers, titmice, and other hole-nesting birds (*see* Nests and Nest-

ing) that usually do not dig their own nest cavities, often, and sometimes wholly, rely on those dug by woodpeckers (*see* examples of Thick-billed parrot in Parrot Family and Bufflehead in Duck Family). In some parts of the w. U.S., burrowing owls depend on the work of badgers to provide them with nesting burrows (Fautin, 1946). *See* related subject, Helpers among Birds.

Ducks gain protection by nesting in or near colonies of terns and gulls that fiercely defend their own eggs and young, and thus those of their associates, from depredations of ravens and crows. *See* Egg-eating. Many small birds build their nests in the sides or bottoms of those of large hawks and eagles, thereby gaining protection against attacks of other predatory birds; others gain protection from man and other animals by nesting close to the nests of stinging wasps, ants, and bees. *See* other details under Nests and Nesting; Insects and Birds; Parasite. Meinertzhagen (1959) wrote: "I use the word Autolycism. Autolycus was an Athenian, a hanger-on from interested motives, a picker-up of trifles, a scrounger who was notorious for making use of others. It is a vice often met with in the human race, and its study among animal groups other than birds would be a most fascinating work, for all in some form or other make use of others; in fact, the deeper one probes the more one realizes the dependence of almost every form of life on some other form. . . ." In Greek mythology, Autolycus was a son of Hermes and father of Odysseus' mother, Anticlea. He was famed for his skill in thievery. In Shakespeare's *Winter's Tale*, Autolycus is a rogue, a "snapper-up of unconsidered trifles."

AVES

(AY-veez). Usually class Aves (birds) of the Animal Kingdom, and of the subphylum Vertebrata. The vertebrate animals (*see* Vertebrate), or animals with a backbone, include six classes: *Cyclostomata*, or "cyclostomes" (the jawless and finless lamprey eels and hagfishes); *Pisces* (fishes with jaws, fins, and gills); *Amphibia* (toads, frogs, and salamanders); *Reptilia* (snakes, lizards, turtles, alligators, crocodiles, and the sphenodons of New Zealand); *Aves* (birds); and *Mammalia* (mammals, including man) (Walter and Sayles, 1949). *See* Bird.

AVIAN CHOLERA

An infectious disease in which the tissues of the bird are invaded and destroyed by the bacterium *Pasteurella multocida*. Domestic ducks, geese, chickens, turkeys, and fowls of all kinds are susceptible to the disease, also pigeons, sparrows, and other wild birds that visit poultry yards.

In N. America, avian cholera can be epizootic in wild birds and it attacks largely coots, gulls, ducks, geese, and swans (Herman, 1955), although it has also been reported in birds of prey in zoos and in pheasants and quail in captivity. Short-eared owls, marsh hawks, meadow mice, and a weasel were infected in an outbreak in Calif. in 1958; the bacterium has also been isolated from the common flicker, starling,

common grackle, and American robin (Harshfield, 1959).

In the 1940s and 1950s severe outbreaks of avian cholera caused great mortality among waterfowl and other birds: an estimated 40,000 swans, geese, ducks, coots, and some shorebirds died of avian cholera in the San Francisco Bay area of Calif. in the winter of 1948–49 (Rosen and Bischoff, 1949; 1950); more than 60,000 waterfowl perished at the Muleshoe National Wildlife Refuge in Tex. (Jensen and Williams, 1964) during the winter of 1956–57.

In Jan. 1964, more than 1,100 lesser snow geese and blue geese died of avian cholera at Squaw Creek National Wildlife Refuge, Mo., in one night; in the winter of 1965–66, an outbreak of the disease over thousands of square miles in Calif., from Salton Sea north to Tule Lake near the Ore. border, destroyed more than 70,000 birds. Only two enzootic areas of avian cholera exist in the world—the region of n.c. Calif. and the Muleshoe National Wildlife Refuge in Tex. (Rosen, 1971a). Waterfowl losses from the disease fluctuate, however, and in some years, in Muleshoe Refuge, for example, only a few sick or dead birds are noted (Jensen and Williams, 1964).

Although avian cholera breaks out regularly on the Pacific coast of N. America and elsewhere, it was reported on the Atlantic coast for the first time in June 1963 on Goose Is., Me., where more than 70% of the nesting female common eiders died (no males were found dead because they had apparently moved to their molting grounds; their summer molt usually precedes that of the nesting females—*see* under Duck Family); also, herring and black-backed gulls were found there, dead of the same infection (Gershman *et al.*, 1964).

In Feb. 1970, an outbreak of avian cholera in Md. killed an estimated 88,000 waterfowl. Most were diving, or sea ducks: 2,100 oldsquaws, 18,000 white-winged scoters, 500 common scoters, 2,500 buffleheads, also 900 whistling swans. The disease dissipated in Md. after the remaining waterfowl migrated north (Anonymous, 1970b).

Rosen (1971a) reported 53 species of birds (23 of waterfowl), in which avian cholera has been reported; besides waterfowl, species that are hosts to the disease in the wild include herons, hawks, gulls, grouse, quail, pheasants, coots, cranes, owls, crows, ravens, least sandpiper, phalaropes, and, among songbirds, the Baltimore (northern) oriole and evening grosbeak.

According to Jensen and Williams (1964), the bacteria of avian cholera are in both the nasal and anal excretions of infected birds, and when populations of waterfowl are crowded together, the infected birds can quickly contaminate the environment. See, however, discussion by Rosen (1971a) that mode of transmission of avian cholera among waterfowl is not certainly known; that sick birds are rarely seen during an outbreak of the disease but dead ones may lie about among the living, healthy-appearing waterfowl; the afflicted ones in their last agonies move the head either backward over the shoulder or forward and prostrate on the surface. The few that recover become chronic carriers of the disease—in them it is of slow progress or long duration. See treatment for captive or domestic birds in Rosen (1971a) and Harshfield (1959); Harshfield reported that *Pasteurella multocida* infections have been noted in man, but "usually of localized nature," and the source of the infections was generally not determined.

AVIAN LYMPHOMATOSIS
See Avian Pox.

AVIAN MALARIA
Caused by one-celled animals (protozoa) of the genus *Plasmodium* (plaz-MOE-dih-um) which destroy a bird's red blood corpuscles and can cause its death. Sick captive birds, however, may respond to treatment (Becker, 1959). The sporozoite stage of the *Plasmodium* is introduced into a bird's blood with the bite of a mosquito (the malarias of mammals are carried by *Anopheles* mosquitoes; most of those of birds are carried by culicine—*Culex* and *Aedes*—mosquitoes). According to Becker (1959), more than 30 species of *Plasmodium* had been described from birds of various kinds up to a report by Hewitt (1940); however, most recent authorities believe that there are far fewer (see discussion in Garnham, 1966, for more recent information).

Most, if not all, of the species of the genus *Plasmodium* described from wild birds can infect the canary, which in the past proved extremely valuable as an experimental host in testing the malaricidal properties of various drugs for the treatment of malaria (see Becker, 1959). Stabler (1974) points out that the canary as a test host went largely out of favor with the discovery of *Plasmodium berghei* in an African tree rat in 1948; this species of *Plasmodium* takes readily in the laboratory mouse, which has proved a most valuable form for studies of chemotherapy, immunity, etc.

From observations on canaries and other captive birds and domestic poultry such as ducks and turkeys, the harmful effects from avian malaria are apparently considerable even if the mortality rate is not high. Hewitt (1940) calculated that the mean rate of infection for all birds is about 5%. Passerines (songbirds—*see* Passeriformes) are more susceptible than other birds, but the *Plasmodium* parasites have a wide range of hosts in at least 447 species of birds (Coatney and Roundabush, 1949).

The bird malaria parasites are not in general strongly host specific; for example, *Plasmodium cathemerium* was first described from the blood of the house sparrow, and it resembles *P. relictum* in that it occurs commonly in passerines, according to Becker (1959), but see also Rothschild and Clay (1957).

Other plasmodia infect ruffed grouse, domestic chickens and turkeys, geese, pheasants, partridges, and peacocks. *Plasmodium relictum* infects many species of wild birds—mourning doves (also domestic pigeons), pintails, cinnamon teal, wood ducks, and American coots. Others are frequent in sharp-tailed grouse, Hungarian partridges, prairie chickens, and quail. See details in Becker (1959); *see also* related malarialike blood parasites of the genera *Haemoproteus* and *Leucocytozoon* under Diseases.

AVIAN PASTEURELLOSIS
See Avian Cholera.

AVIAN POX
Sometimes called bird pox, foot pox, fowl pox, and avian diphtheria; caused by one of a series of viruses that are confined to birds. The disease, well known to bird banders (*see* Banding), produces warty protuberances on the feet or head of a bird, and its throat and nasal passages may be infected. It is frequently seen in domestic poultry and captive game birds, but it also involves wild birds, including many species of passeriforms, or songbirds (Herman, 1955).

Musselmann (1928) described bird pox (avian pox) in a chipping sparrow that had deformed feet, swellings, and missing toes; Worth (1956) reported a pox virus in the slate-colored junco. According to Meade (1945), the condition known as "foot disease," bird pox, *epithelioma contagiosum*, is particularly common in chipping sparrows and field sparrows, finches, thrashers, and flickers; it is also known in the blue jay and chimney swift, mockingbird, brown-headed cowbird, common grackle, and red-winged blackbird (Prescott, 1971b), and in Swainson's thrush, gray-cheeked thrush, and brown creeper (Kirmse, 1966).

Avian pox has caused severe mortality in wild wood pigeons in Europe (Lack, 1954), in quail imported into the U.S. from Mexico, and in canaries (Karstad, 1971b). There are at least four viruses of bird pox, or strains of the virus, and each is infectious for a particular host (Cunningham, 1959). Karstad regards all avian pox viruses as strains of *Poxvirus avium*. It occurs naturally among domestic geese, ducks, and guineafowl; pheasants are also susceptible to it. Leibovitz (1969) reported the first record of fowl pox (avian pox) in swans in a young mute swan found dead in Aug. 1964 on the shore of Long Island Sound, N.Y. Karstad (1971b) listed 25 species of N. American birds that are susceptible to pox infections, and according to Kirmse (1967), naturally occurring pox infections have been reported in 60 species of wild birds of 20 families. Most of the infections are usually mild; however, a preponderance of lesions of the eyelids from the infection among such birds as pheasants may cause heavy mortality because the lesions make them unable to see to find food (Karstad, 1971b). A natural outbreak among mourning doves was reported in 1954 (Cunningham, 1959).

Poxvirus avium is transmitted directly by contact between infected and susceptible birds and indirectly from their perches, and through bites of mosquitoes which have fed on the blood of infected birds (Karstad, 1971b).

Kirmse (1966) reported that the pox skin lesions persisted for several months in chipping sparrows, for 81 and 109 days in slate-colored juncos, for 82 days in a captive mourning dove, and for 13 months in a common flicker, after which the lesions on the birds disappeared. Birds that recover from pox infection usually are immune to reinfection with that strain. *See also* Tumors; Diseases; Parasite.

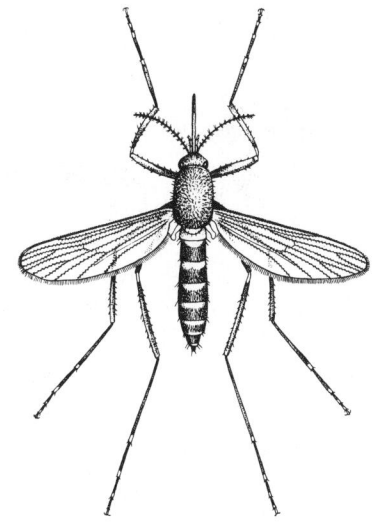

AVIAN MALARIA
One-celled blood parasites (protozoa) of the genus Plasmodium *cause avian malaria. The sporozite stage of* Plasmodium *is transmitted to a bird's blood through the bite of an* Aedes *mosquito.*

AVOCET FAMILY

AVIAN TUBERCULOSIS

Rarely reported in wild birds; a contagious disease known worldwide among domestic chickens; it is dissimilar to tuberculosis in man, which is also dissimilar to that in cattle (Feldman, 1959). Avian tuberculosis is caused by a living bacterial parasite—the tubercle bacillus—*Mycobacterium avium. See* Bacteria. It is most frequent in the North Temperate Zone, is present in most European countries and in the U.S. (Gale, 1971). All species of birds are susceptible to infection from the avian tubercle bacilli (parrots and others of the Parrot Family are highly susceptible) and domesticated birds—ducks, geese, swans, peacocks, and turkeys, for example—are infected more frequently than wild birds. In tuberculous birds, the bacilli attack the liver and spleen more than the lungs, and commonly enter the body through the alimentary tract (Gale, 1971).

Among wild birds, pheasants seem markedly more susceptible, and the disease has also been reported in the house sparrow. Outward signs of the infection vary; in Great Britain, an observer saw a golden eagle die suddenly after alighting (*see also* Diseases), and a hawk from Australia that was severely infected with the disease had normal plumage; however, most birds are emaciated and some develop skin growths around the eyes, on the wing joints, or on the legs.

Feldman (1938) reported avian tuberculosis among N. American birds in the common crow, common raven, barn owl, brown-headed cowbird, and American kestrel or sparrow hawk, and Laskey (1952) reported the death of two American avocets in Calif. from the disease. Snoeyenbos (1966) reported the disease in ruffed grouse, and Yates and Miller (1966) in a starling; it has also been observed in wild waterfowl—trumpeter swan, whistling swan, American wigeon, green-winged teal, pintail, redhead, mallard, and shoveler (Gale, 1971). Houston and Tryphonas (1969) discovered avian tuberculosis in an underweight Swainson's thrush they caught for banding in Sept. 1967 at Saskatoon, Sask.; Mollhoff (1976) reported it in a traffic-killed saw-whet owl on a road south of Hill City, Itasca County, Minn., in Nov. 1974.

Some authorities believe that the tubercle bacilli in wild birds may come from close contact at feeding places with infected poultry; that predatory birds may get it in catching their prey. For example, golden eagles in Scotland that have preyed on wood pigeons infected with tuberculosis have in turn been infected, and gulls in Europe have been infected from the effluence of sewers emptying into rivers where gulls gather in large numbers (Gale, 1971).

AVIFAUNA

(AY-vih-faw-nah). Term for the bird species of an area, often of a continent as a whole. For number of species in N. America, *see* Species; for number in world.

AVOCET (AV-oh-set) FAMILY

Recurvirostridae (ree-cur-vih-ROS-trih-dee); from Lat. *recurvus*, bent (back), and *rostrum*, bill. 7 species around the world (2 in N. America); 11½–20-in.-long wading birds noted for their extremely long legs; includes both the avocets and stilts, of which the stilts have the longest legs in proportion to their body size of any birds, except possibly flamingos; both avocets and stilts have small heads and long, slender bills; they have rather long, pointed wings, fly strongly, and have short, square tails. They utter loud yapping or yelping cries, usually live near water, swim and dive readily (they have slightly webbed to well-webbed feet), and are shorebirds (*see* Shorebird; *also* a discussion of their relatives under Charadriiformes). One might see both avocets and stilts nesting on the Bear River National Wildlife Refuge at Great Salt Lake, Utah.

Both sexes share in nest building, incubating the eggs, and raising the young, which are precocial (*see* under Altricial) and leave the nest shortly after hatching (Kendeigh, 1952b). Apparently the brooding instinct in avocets—in which the chicks are frequently brooded by the parents to keep them dry and warm (*see* Young and Their Care)—is very strong, even in the baby avocets. One of several Old World avocet chicks, *Recurvirostra avocetta*, raised in small indoor aviaries in Germany, when only 2 days old tried to brood its brothers, and when 14 days old adopted two baby water rails, *Rallus aquaticus*, and brooded them for 2 weeks (Frisch, 1959). *See* Helpers among Birds.

Apparently albinism is rare in the family, as Gross (1965a) cites only two records for two species, but does not identify them. Avocets and stilts are both protected by law; however, a crippled or ill bird might be saved by offering it mealworms, small fishes, shrimp, or crabs and a variety of finely ground green plants, all fed to it in water; would need enclosed shallow pool and plenty of ground on which to exercise (Walker, 1942).

Four species of avocets in world: Old World avocet of Eurasia and Africa, the red-necked avocet of Australia, the American avocet, and the Andean avocet—all similar; two species of stilts: the black-necked stilt of the New World, Eurasia, Africa, Australia, and New Zealand, and the banded stilt of interior Australia; a seventh species in Avocet Family is the ibisbill, an avocetlike bird of high elevations of c. Asia (Hall, 1960); see also Austin, 1961; Conder, 1964; and Jehl, 1968b.

Avocet, American, *Recurvirostra americana* (ree-curv-ih-ROS-trah ah-mer-ih-CANE-ah); genus name: from Lat. *recurvus*, bent, and *rostrum*, beak; species name: Lat., of America (Coble, 1954). (Color ills., page 51.) A strikingly handsome long-legged wading bird with long, slender, upcurved bill; probably most graceful of all shorebirds; in summer in Great Basin country and plains of West; sexes outwardly similar but males larger; 17–18½ in. long, including 3¼–3¾-in.-long bill; wingspread 27–38 in.; black and white pattern on back and sides; in spring and summer cinnamon head and neck, grayish at other times, underparts and upper back white; distinctive slender upcurved bill turns up more in females (Harris, V. T., 1972), to 4 in. long; eyes brown-red or carmine; in flight, extends neck slightly forward with long bluish legs trailing behind squared-off tail; alarm call is sharp *plee-eek! plee-eek!* Avocets have courtship and group rituals in which pairs perform an elaborate courtship display; however, see Hamilton (1975). In Old World avocet, similar to American, female observed to crouch with her neck outstretched and lowered so that bill and chin just above water; male preens constantly in apparent excitement and walks from one side of female to other; gradually he gets closer and closer until he brushes female's tail feathers as he passes; finally jumps on her back, copulates, then jumps off but leaves one wing stretched across female's back. Both birds then run a few steps with their bills crossed like swords before they turn away from each other (Conder, 1964).

Feeding Habits: Eats dragonfly nymphs, back swimmers, water boatmen, beetles, flies and their larvae, shrimps and other crustaceans; seeds of marsh and aquatic plants; often feeds in flocks, from 12 to 300 walking slowly, shoulder to shoulder as in drill formation, at each step thrusting bill underwater and sweeping it rapidly from side to side as roseate spoonbill does; the upturned bill along bottom stirs up aquatic insects; bill partly opened to catch food; at times individuals pause to swallow prey; also, in deep water, avocets put head below surface and sometimes upend like surface-feeding ducks; also dive under surface; pick live or dead insects from surface of water (Bent, 1927).

Nest: On sun-baked flats and marshes bordering shallow lakes of West, merely slight hollow lined with a few dry grasses, but when waters rising, pair will build up nest with sticks, weeds, bones, feathers to a foot or more to raise eggs above water.

Eggs: Apr.–June; 3–4, usually 4, olive, spotted with dark brown.

Incubation: By both sexes, 23–25 days (Hamilton, 1975); Old World avocet, 25–26 days (Conder, 1964); downy young, precocial, swim a few hours after hatching; first flights of young estimated at 27 days (Gibson, 1971).

Other Names: Blueshanks; bluestocking; Irish snipe; lawyer; yelper.

Age: One banded bird reported 5 years old; another, 9 years, 7 months, old (Kennard, 1975).

Running Speed: Timed in Utah, 8 m.p.h. (Cottam *et al.*, 1942b).

Weights: About 12 oz. (Pough, 1951).

Range: Lives in and around inland sloughs and saline lakes, also fresh water and saltwater marshes; nests from w. Canada, e.-c. Wash., s.-c. Ore., s. Idaho, n. Mont., c. Alta., s. Sask., and s. Man., south to s. Calif., east to s. Nev., n. Utah, s.-c. Colo., s. N.M., and s. Tex. east to e. N.D., e. S.D., w. Neb., e. Colo. n.-c. Okla.; once nested to s. Mack., w. Minn., Wisc., n. Iowa, and east to Cape May, N.J., where now occasional visitor in fall; agriculture has eliminated avocet from former range, especially in West (Hall, 1960); winters from n.-c. Calif. and s. Tex. south to Baja Calif. and along Pacific coast from Mexico to Guatemala; in recent years, migrants have increasingly visited Atlantic coast from N.J. south to Fla. (Hall, 1960); also winters in se. La. (Lowery, 1960) and fall and spring visitor to Gulf coast of Ala. (Imhof, 1962).

Stilt, black-necked, *Himantopus mexicanus* (high-MAN-to-pus meks-ih-CANE-us); genus name: Lat., from Gr. *himantopos,* thong-foot, or crook-shanked, in reference to stiltlike legs; species name: Lat., of Mexico, based on Mexican specimen, or specimens, of this bird first described in 1760 by Brisson, French systematist and zoologist, who named many N. American birds (Coues, 1884). (Color ill., page 50.) In N. America (also in C. and S. America), in summer, in Far West and Southwest (N.M.) about alkaline lakes, where associated with avocets; most often around fresh water of wet meadows, irrigated or flooded fields; also about brackish ponds of salt marshes and freshwater ponds in back of beaches along Gulf coast and in e. and se. U.S.; 13½–15½ in. long, includes black bill, 2¼–2¾ in. long; bill extremely slender, straight, slightly upcurved and needle-pointed, not flattened or hooked at tip as in avocet; legs pink or red, 8–10 in. long; body slim, black above, white below, including sides of neck, cheeks, and forehead; in flight body appears white, wings black and unpatterned; eyes (irises) carmine or crimson; adult female similar but duller; immature similar to female but duller; very noisy about nesting places; in flight utters sharp *ip-ip-ip* or yelp; some notes resemble those of terns; walks gracefully with long strides that quicken almost to a run; in water, wades to above the "heel" of feet, even belly-deep; can swim (has half-webbed feet) but does so much less than avocet (Hamilton, 1975).

Feeding Habits: Favorite places are shallow, muddy borders of alkaline lakes in West, and most often around fresh water; in East, also about brackish ponds of salt marshes, in wet pastures in Fla., Tex., and other places; very active in feeding, runs about picking up insects on muddy shores or in shallow waters; prefers fresh water more than avocet: eats aquatic bugs, beetles, dragonfly nymphs, caddis flies, mayfly nymphs, flies, billbugs, mosquito larvae, grasshoppers, crayfishes, snails, and a few tiny fishes; also seeds of aquatic and marsh plants (Bent, 1927).

Nest: In small colonies, on ground, sometimes in slight depression in open or partly hidden by plants, in mangrove swamps near ponds or along sandy or gravelly lake shores, on small island or hummock in shallow body of water, and edges of stagnant alkaline or brackish ponds; nest usually lined with weed stalks, twigs, grasses, small bits of shells, fishbones.

Eggs: Apr.–June; usually 4, yellow or buff, irregularly spotted with black or brown.

Incubation: By both parents, incubation period probably about 25 days (Palmer, 1967); young fly about 28 days after hatching; adults very noisy if disturbed at nest; fly to meet intruder; bob up and down by bending knees, strike surface of water with breast to make sharp splashes, also run ashore and practice crippled-bird act (*see* Distraction Display).

Other Names: Daddy longlegs; lawyer; longshanks; stilt; yelper.

Age: One lived in New York Zoological Gardens (Bronx Zoo) to age 19 years, 1 month (Anonymous, 1954).

AVOCET FAMILY
The American avocet bends its long legs to feed in shallow water, sweeping its long, thin, upturned bill from side to side to stir up surface slime, floating seeds, crustaceans, and aquatic insects.

axillars

AXILLARS
The axillars are stiff, long feathers on the underside of the wing, where it joins the body. In the upland sandpiper and certain other shorebirds, the axillars are revealed during displays in which the wings are raised.

Weights: 14½–16 oz. (Palmer, 1967).
Range: Nests from s. Ore., Idaho, s. Sask., n. Utah, s. Colo., e. N.M., Gulf coast of Tex. and s. La., Fla., ne. Baja Calif., locally in Mexico, C. America to Nicaragua, West Indies; Galápagos Is., to coast of Ecuador, probably n. Peru; in e. U.S., north formerly to N.J., now in Del.; first sight records in spring 1962 (Del., Md., Va.); in this century at Little Creek State Wildlife Refuge, Del., first definite nesting records reported spring 1970—nests with eggs and chicks (Holgerson, 1971); apparently first definite nesting records for black-necked stilt north of N.C. since 1810; also nests in S.C., c. and e. Fla., south through West Indies, the Guianas, and n. Brazil; winters from c. Calif., to coast of Sonora, Mexico, Rio Grande Valley, Tex., and nw. coast of Gulf of Mexico east to Mississippi Delta, south locally to southern limits of breeding range in n. S. America; in migration, reported from Sask., N.D., Wisc., N.B., Newfoundland, and Bermuda.

AXILLARS
(AK-sih-lers). The innermost feathers lining the wings; a group of feathers (usually elongate) that grow from the armpit region of birds. They close the space between the spread wings and the body and are sometimes called axillaries (Van Tyne and Berger, 1959). *See* Flight; Topography; Wing.

ALBATROSS FAMILY

Albatrosses are essentially birds of the southern oceans; of the 13 species in this spectacular family, only 3 breed north of the Equator and are the ones usually seen off the Pacific coast of North America. Since they depend on winds from the ocean's waves for their effortless, gliding flight, it is a rare event when albatrosses from the Southern Hemisphere manage to cross the windless doldrums of the Equator and make an appearance in North Atlantic or North Pacific waters. If winds are strong, albatrosses can remain aloft for hours with hardly a stroke of their narrow, tapered wings, which span up to 11½ feet. When descending to the surface to feed, they must spread their wings and run into the wind to regain flying speed. Early mariners considered the behavior of albatrosses to be dumb and gave them such names as gooney bird and mollymauk, the latter derived from a Dutch word meaning "stupid gull."

Black-browed albatross
The most abundant and widespread of Southern Hemisphere species and a persistent ship-follower, the black-browed albatross comes ashore to breed on remote subantarctic islands. The female lays a single egg atop a foot-high mound of mud and grass, then remains on the nest during the entire 2-month incubation period while her mate brings her food. Caring for their young takes several more months; the fledgling albatross makes its first tentative flight at an age of about 150 days.

Black-browed albatross

Black-browed albatross

The most abundant and widespread of Southern Hemisphere species and a persistent ship-follower, the black-browed albatross comes ashore to breed on remote subantarctic islands. The female lays a single egg atop a foot-high mound of mud and grass, then remains on the nest during the entire 2-month incubation period while her mate brings her food. Caring for their young takes several more months; the fledgling albatross makes its first tentative flight at an age of about 150 days.

Black-footed albatross

This sooty-brown bird with a white face breeds on islands and atolls in and near the Hawaiian archipelago in the North Pacific. Both male and female incubate the single egg, laid in a shallow scrape in the coral sand. For the young albatross, the first 9 years of its life, until it reaches breeding age, are spent at sea. This species also follows ships, feeding on garbage; its natural food includes squids, amphipods, and fishes taken at the surface at night.

Black-footed albatross

Black-browed albatross

Black-footed albatross

Black-footed albatross

Laysan albatross
More than a half million Laysan albatrosses congregate during nesting season on the outermost islands of the Hawaiian chain; their vast colonies spread over hundreds of acres. Each nest — a scrape in the sand surrounded by a low heap of vegetation — is spaced a few feet from its nearest neighbors. Albatrosses are believed to mate for life, and their lifespan is among the longest of all birds. Laysan albatrosses banded on Midway Island have been recaptured 40 years later.

Short-tailed albatross
The rarest of its kind, this albatross nests only on the Japanese island of Torishima, 400 miles south of Tokyo. Hundreds of thousands of short-tailed albatrosses were slaughtered by plume hunters, and by the 1930s the species was feared extinct. But a few birds returned to nest in 1953, and the albatross was declared a national monument by the Japanese government.

Wandering albatross
Although they are a mere 9 inches wide, the wings of the wandering albatross may span 11½ feet, the greatest wingspread of any seabird. A volcano-shaped mound, 3 feet wide at the base and 18 inches high, is built to hold the single, large egg, which weighs a pound when newly laid. The young albatross has a longer nestling life than any other bird; 9 months may pass before it makes its first flight, when it has been finally deserted by its parents.

White-capped albatross
The specific name for this bird, cauta, means "wary" — it is also known as the shy albatross; both are misnomers. John Gould, the eminent English ornithologist, named the species in the 1840s, having observed that it seemed to shy away from the vessel on which he was traveling. In truth, the white-capped albatross — recorded only once off the coast of North America — is a regular ship-follower.

Yellow-nosed albatross
Occasionally seen off the North Atlantic coast between Long Island and Quebec, this small albatross has a wingspread of about 7 feet. Its few nesting islands include Tristan da Cunha in the South Atlantic. Albatrosses drink saltwater and eliminate the salt from their bodies with special glands near their tubular nostrils.

Wandering albatross

Yellow-nosed albatross

White-capped albatross

Laysan albatross

Laysan albatross, chick

Short-tailed albatross

ANHINGA FAMILY

Anhinga
This is a bird of several names: anhinga, which comes from the language of the Amazonian Indians; water turkey, because its fanned tail feathers suggest those of a wild turkey; and snakebird, for its snakelike head and neck. Anhingas are usually seen swimming with only their head and neck above the surface or perched in trees with their wings spread to the sun; their feathers are not waterproof and must be dried after each submersion. After spearing a fish with its formidable bill, the anhinga tosses it in the air to position it for swallowing head first.

AUK FAMILY

Cassin's auklet
Abundant on coastal islands from Alaska to Baja California, Cassin's auklet nests in burrows that both male and female dig to a depth of 4 feet. Digging is done at night and may take 2 months. A single egg is laid, but a second brood is sometimes started with a full-grown chick still in the nest.

Crested auklet
This common little seabird of Alaskan waters is decorated with a long, forward-curling crest; thin white plumes that reach backward from each eye; and, in breeding season, orange-red wattles at the base of its bill.

Least auklet
The smallest member of the auk family, this sparrow-size seabird nests by the millions on the Pribilof Islands in the Bering Sea. Least auklets swirl about the beaches like swarms of bees, their twittering calls competing for attention with the raucous noise from fur seals.

Parakeet auklet
While one bird tends the single egg, laid on bare rock or a bed of pebbles, its mate spends the day at sea, feeding on crustaceans caught at or near the surface or diving to the ocean bottom, and returns to its island after dusk. Like other alcids, the parakeet auklet uses its feet in flight to steer and brake.

Rhinoceros auklet
A short horn at the base of its bill explains this auklet's unusual name. Nesting along the Pacific shore from southeast Alaska to Washington, the rhinoceros auklet digs a burrow 8–20 feet long, in which it raises its chick on a diet that largely consists of sand launce, a sardine-size fish.

Whiskered auklet
The "whiskers" of this attractive but little-known resident of northern waters are wispy white plumes on each side of its face. Like other auklets, it departs for the open sea once its chick is fledged.

Anhinga

Anhinga

assin's auklet

Crested auklet

east auklet

Parakeet auklet

Rhinoceros auklet

Whiskered auklet

Dovekie

Uncountable millions of these black-and-white, starling-size seabirds nest north of the Arctic Circle. They are an important food supply for gyrfalcons, gulls, foxes, and polar bears, as well as for native Eskimos, who also use their skins for clothing. So abundant a bird also must have a tremendously abundant food source — minute crustaceans caught on dives that last upwards of one minute. Although great rafts of dovekies occur in North Atlantic waters in winter, they are usually seen by coastal residents only when blown ashore by storms.

Black guillemot

A ducklike bird with bright red feet, the black guillemot does not form great colonies as do many other alcids. Usually only one or a few pairs will occupy any nesting location — a sheer cliff or rocky shore.

Pigeon guillemot

A Pacific coast resident, this may simply be a geographic race of the black guillemot. Both birds have bright red mouth linings that are displayed during mutual "water dances" at breeding time.

Common murre

One of the world's most abundant seabirds, the common murre gathers in enormous nesting colonies on both sides of the continent. Typical is Newfoundland's Funk Island, where a half million pairs breed. Their nests are often crammed together on precipitous ledges, and banding studies have shown that individual birds return to the same spot year after year. The single murre egg is pear-shaped and, if dislodged, will turn in an arc rather than tumble to the sea hundreds of feet below.

Thick-billed murre

Of the world's estimated murre population of 56 million birds, three-quarters belong to this species. Murres are skilled fliers — both above and below the surface. Propelled by their wings, they can dive to depths of 200 feet in pursuit of fish, squid, and other marine life. And their airspeed has been clocked as fast as 50 miles per hour.

Ancient murrelet

Murrelets are small, chubby seabirds of North Pacific waters. The ancient murrelet nests from the Aleutians to Washington, laying 2 eggs in grassy hollows or crevices. From 2–3 days after hatching, the chicks leave their natal island en masse, summoned to water's edge by the persistent chirping of their parents.

Kittlitz's murrelet

Little is known about this species, which frequents glacial waters on Alaska's coast. A few nests have been found on mountainsides above the timberline and miles from the sea.

Black guillemot

Pigeon guillemot

Common murre

Black guillemot

Dovekie

Pigeon guillemot

Thick-billed murre

Kittlitz's murrelet

Common murre

Ancient murrelet

Common puffin

For nearly 6 weeks after their chick hatches, adult common puffins fly out to sea each morning and return to the burrow with bill-loads of up to 30 small fishes. The fishes are caught one at a time as the puffin "flies" underwater with its stubby wings. They are dispatched by sharp pinchers at the point of the bill, shoved to the back of the mouth by the bird's tongue, and held in place by serrations on the upper mandible. A puffin chick will eat its entire weight in fishes daily and consume up to 2,000 fishes before being abandoned by its parents. After a week of fasting, the young bird will leave the burrow at night to avoid attacks by gulls, flutter to the ocean below, and paddle off.

Horned puffin

Except for fleshy horns above its eyes, this resident of Alaskan waters resembles the closely related common puffin of the North Atlantic. At the end of the nesting season, the triangular puffin bill shrinks in size and loses much of its spectacular color, as outer layers are shed.

Tufted puffin

Long, straw-colored plumes that curve backward give this dark puffin a bizarre appearance during the breeding season. Like other puffins, it feeds on small fishes; but it also uses its strong bill to crush the shells of mollusks and sea urchins that abound in the cold waters off its nesting places, from Alaska to southern California.

Razorbill

A smaller version of the extinct great auk that inhabited the same North Atlantic waters, the razorbill has a bright yellow mouth lining that it displays during courtship ceremonies offshore its nesting cliffs. Razorbills are usually found breeding in the company of murres; they may lay their single egg on exposed rock, in fissures, or in former puffin burrows.

Common puffin

Tufted puffin

Horned puffin

Tufted puffin

Razorbill

AVOCET FAMILY

American avocet
This handsome, long-legged shorebird with an upcurved bill is a fixture on sloughs, alkaline lakes, potholes, and marshes from the prairies to the Pacific states. Its distinctive bill, nearly 4 inches long, is thrust underwater and swept from side to side as the bird feeds, stirring up aquatic insects and crustaceans. Avocets often feed in flocks, as many as 100 birds walking shoulder to shoulder in formation. In deeper water, they may dabble like mallards or dive like canvasback ducks.

Black-necked stilt
Among all birds, the 8 to 10-inch legs of the black-necked stilt may be the longest in proportion to body size. Yet the stilt feeds largely in shallow water and on muddy shores, walking gracefully with long strides, picking up aquatic insects, crayfishes, snails, and the seeds of marsh plants. Both parents share incubation duties; 4 eggs is the usual clutch number, and as is typical among shorebirds, the chicks leave their nest shortly after hatching.

BOOBY FAMILY

Gannet
Six-foot wings, splayed tail, webbed feet — all come into play as a gannet brakes for a landing on its North Atlantic nesting cliff. Gannets breed in crowded colonies — one researcher counted 5,000 nests on 22 acres — and an incoming bird faces a phalanx of upturned bills as it flaps toward its tiny piece of turf. Collisions are not uncommon on either landing or takeoff. Gannets mate for life; during the nesting season the pair bond is maintained by complex ceremonies that include presentations of seaweed for the nest mound.

Black-necked stilt

Gannet

American avocet

American avocet

Blue-faced booby

Returning to its nest with a fish, a blue-faced booby is likely to be pursued by a frigatebird, which will even yank at the booby's tail until it disgorges its catch. The lost meal is then seized by the tormentor in mid-air. Blue-faced boobies have been spotted far from land, riding—asleep—on the backs of sea turtles.

Blue-footed booby

Bright blue feet distinguish this Pacific species, which nests from arid islands in the Gulf of California southward to Peru. Like the gannet and other boobies, it plunges from heights of up to 50 feet to capture fish. A hard skull and air sacs under the neck and breast cushion the impact. Fish are not speared with the bill but seized from beneath as the booby returns to the surface.

Brown booby

Like the blue-faced booby, the brown booby is found in all tropical oceans. And like its relatives, it is fond of flying fish. The name "booby" comes from a Spanish word for dunce; sailors considered these birds stupid because they could be caught easily by hand. Brown boobies have been blown as far north as Maine by hurricanes.

Red-footed booby

This species also has feet of a remarkable color. While its relatives prefer to nest on the ground, the red-footed booby builds loose platforms of sticks in the treetops. And in another departure from booby norm, it feeds not by day but at night, ranging far out to sea in quest of flying fish and squid.

BULBUL FAMILY

Red-whiskered bulbul

Bulbuls are forest birds of Africa and Asia, but this species, a popular cage bird in the Orient, became established in Florida after its escape from captivity in 1960. Robin-sized, with bright red patches below each eye, the red-whiskered bulbul feeds largely on the fruits and flowers of a number of exotic plants that also thrive in the semitropical south Florida climate. The population of a few hundred birds is confined to one area near Miami, where they gather in noisy roosts at sundown.

Blue-faced booby

Brown booby

Red-footed booby

Blue-footed booby

Red-whiskered bulbul

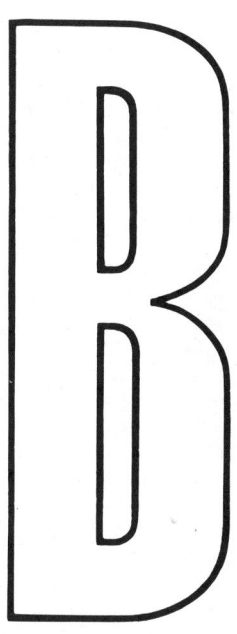

BULBUL FAMILY

Red-whiskered bulbul
Bulbuls are forest birds of Africa and Asia, but this species, a popular cage bird in the Orient, became established in Florida after its escape from captivity in 1960. Robin-sized, with bright red patches below each eye, the red-whiskered bulbul feeds largely on the fruits and flowers of a number of exotic plants that also thrive in the semitropical south Florida climate. The population of a few hundred birds is confined to one area near Miami, where they gather in noisy roosts at sundown.

BABBLER FAMILY
See brief discussion under Wrentit Family.

BACHMAN
REV. JOHN (1790–1874). Naturalist and Lutheran clergyman, for whom John James Audubon named three species of birds: the black oystercatcher *(Haematopus bachmani),* Bachman's sparrow, and Bachman's warbler. Bachman was born in Rhinebeck, N.Y.; his first contact with men of science was at Philadelphia, where he met Alexander Wilson, who introduced him to Baron von Humboldt, the great explorer and naturalist who was visiting the U.S. Bachman taught school in Pa.; an ordained minister in 1814, he was called to St. John's Lutheran Church in Charleston, S.C., in 1815 and was then in the company of a group of naturalists there. His association with Audubon began in mid-Oct. 1831, when Audubon lived with the Bachman family for about a month. See details in Herrick (1917, Vol. II). By 1835, Bachman began to be of indispensable service to Audubon through his collections of southern animals and his studies of their habits. Bachman is best known as the co-author with Audubon of *The Viviparous Quadrupeds of North America*. See *Dictionary of American Biography*.

BACKCROSS
Term in genetics (*see* Genetics) for a cross between a hybrid and either of its parent types (Knight, 1948). Among N. American birds, hybrids are relatively rare; however, some species occasionally hybridize and a noted example is the cross-mating of a blue-winged warbler and a golden-winged warbler in ne. U.S. The product of their crossing is the hybrid known as Brewster's warbler. The Brewster's warbler mates with one of the parent species and they produce at times the rare hybrid the Lawrence's warbler—a backcross. *See* Brewster's warbler and Lawrence's warbler in Warbler—American Wood Warbler Family; *also* discussion under Hybrid.

BACKGROUND ADAPTATION
The agreement between the color and appearance of a bird, or of any other animal, and the general appearance of the environment in which it lives (Knight, 1948). *See* Colors of Feathers.

BACTERIA
(back-TEER-ih-ah; sing.: *bacterium*). Of interest in ornithology because some of them cause diseases in birds (*see* Diseases). They are a large group of unicellular (one-celled) microscopic organisms constituting the class Schizomycetes, widely distributed in the air, water, soil, and the bodies of living animals and plants and dead organic matter. They are classified in a separate kingdom, neither plant nor animal, sometimes called Monera or Protista, and are the smallest living things with self-contained metabolic processes—the smallest are barely visible under an ordinary light microscope and it would require 30 trillion of average size to weigh an ounce (Long, 1966). *See also* Virus.

BADGER-BIRD
See Godwit, marbled, in Sandpiper Family.

BAER
KARL ERNST VON. The Baer's pochard was named for him in 1863; born of a noble Prussian family (Gruson, 1972), he studied medicine at the University of Dorpat; professor of zoology at Königsberg, Prussia, beginning in 1819 (Wynne, 1969); in 1834 went to St. Petersburg (Leningrad) at a time when the Russian government sponsored expeditions to then largely unknown parts of Siberia; Baer served as scientific adviser on several of these expeditions and apparently, on one of these, the duck named for him was collected in the middle Amur R. region. Baer returned to Dorpat in 1864; died there, 1876. See Gruson (1972) for other details.

BAIRD
LUCY HUNTER (1848–1913). Only child of Spencer F. and Mary H. C. Baird, born Carlyle, Pa.; during last decade of her father's life (1877–87) assisted in secretarial work at the Smithsonian Institution and U.S. Fish Commission, Washington, D.C. In 1861, Dr. James G. Cooper, prominent Calif. ornithologist, named a previously unknown American wood warbler Lucy's warbler, in honor of the then 13-year-old Lucy Baird; he discovered the bird near Fort Mojave along the Colorado R. in Ariz. (Palmer *et al.*, 1954).

BAIRD
SPENCER FULLERTON (1823–87). Born Reading, Pa.; as a boy lived at Carlyle, Pa., where he and his brother discovered, then named and described, a bird new to science, the yellow-bellied flycatcher; was secretary of the Smithsonian Institution (1878–87); originator of the U.S. National Museum; organizer of the U.S. Fish Commission; one of the most brilliant, energetic, and influential zoologists of his time; organized the zoological work of the Pacific Railroad Surveys; author of *Catalogue of North American Birds* (1858), *Review of American Birds* (1864–66), *Water Birds* (1884); co-author with Thomas Brewer and Robert Ridgway of *A History of North American Birds* (1874); editor of the various Pacific Railroad Survey reports on zoology and of Dr. James G. Cooper's *Ornithology of California* (1870).

According to Palmer (1928), "Baird did more than any other man of his time to advance the study of ornithology and other branches of zoology." See also "The Bairdian Period" in Coues (1884). Baird described and named several genera and many species of N. American birds (see A.O.U. *Check-list,* 1957). Baird's junco, Baird's sandpiper, and Baird's sparrow honor his name. For nearly 20 years he wrote prolifically about birds; he wrote with great exactness and helped make the definition of local subspecies of birds possible. He was a founder of the "Baird School" of ornithology so ably represented by Elliott Coues, Joel A. Allen, Robert Ridgway, John Cassin, Thomas Brewer, and others. See *Dictionary of American Biography;* see Dall (1915) for his definitive biography; also Mayr (1975).

BANDING

Bird banders stretch fine nets, called mist nets, across openings in woods or shrubs. In these silken mesh traps, smaller birds, such as this warbler, become entangled and are removed, without injury, for banding.

BALANCE

(sense of). *See* Semicircular Canals; Ears and Hearing.

BALANCE OF NATURE

Term for the attainment of animals and plants in nature of a balance or equilibrium with their environment. Nature at times, through parasites, predators, diseases, weather, and other repressing factors, may balance one population of animals against another, or with some factor or factors in the environment, but it is doubtful if anyone knows, or would recognize, when such a "balance" is reached. Certain birds at times reach optimum populations; that is, they become as populous as the best environment for them will allow. Possibly this is the closest approximation that one can get to the popular conception of "the balance of nature." Large predatory birds—eagles, hawks, and owls—kill and devour birds, rodents, and other kinds of animal life, which tends to check their undue, or unhealthy (if too populous for the environment) increase, and small birds, in turn, kill and eat insects and other smaller forms of life, which tends to help keep them within a kind of balance with their environment. *See* Economic Ornithology. Occasionally one species of insect may increase to enormous numbers and is said to "get out of hand," but in time, nature's checks of diseases, weather, other insects, birds, and many other animals that eat insects, tend to bring the species back to normal or below its normal population and the crisis is over until there is another sharp rise in its numbers. The "balance of nature," as conceived by those scientists who accept the term, is a constant, long-time fluctuating of animals and associated plants in which the populations swing upward and downward rather than being balanced evenly. *See* Cycle; Diseases; Predation.

BALDFACE

See Coot, American, in Rail Family.

BALDHEAD

Local name in Fla. for the sandhill crane, in allusion to its head, which is partly unfeathered (McAtee, 1955a).

BALDPATE

See Wigeon, American, In Duck Family.

BALTIMORE-BIRD

See Oriole, northern (Baltimore), Troupial Family.

BANANAQUIT

See in Honeycreeper Family.

BANDING

Term in America for the leg-banding of wild birds (called in Great Britain and Europe, generally, "ringing") in order to trace their times of migration, behavior, routes taken and destinations (*see* flyways under Waterfowl), local movements, population changes, length of life, etc.

On Aug. 16, 1916, Great Britain (on behalf of Canada) and the U.S. signed the Convention for the Protection of Migratory Birds. The treaty was made effective in Canada by the Migratory Bird Convention Act of 1917 and in the U.S. by the Migratory Bird Treaty Act of 1918. These acts gave responsibilities for the protection and welfare of migratory birds to the government of each country. In the U.S. the banding of migratory birds is administered by the Fish and Wildlife Service, Department of the Interior; in Canada by the Canadian Wildlife Service, Department of the Environment. Each agency within its own country issues banding permits to qualified persons at least 18 years old. Each person applying for a permit must be endorsed by other ornithologists or by an experienced bird-bander under whom the applicant may have served an apprenticeship to learn the skills of banding and, especially, identification of birds and accurate record keeping. Except for banding of local or sedentary species for special studies, only migratory birds are banded.

According to Jonkel (1977), about 1.3 million wild N. American birds were banded in Canada and the U.S. in 1976 and more than 35 million since the official banding began in 1920 (see early history of in Lincoln, 1933). In 1976, more than 3,500 persons were authorized by federal and state bird-banding permits (both are required in some states) to band migratory birds in the U.S. These included—besides professional biologists or museum ornithologists, federal and state employees, graduate students and professors/teachers—school custodians, bankers, lawyers, salesmen, organization executives, housewives, clergyman, and other highly qualified amateurs (Duvall, 1966). These persons may band birds all year at their homes or nearby to capture migrant species of birds passing through or to trace the travels and returns of year-round residents which banders may recapture in their backyard wire-cage traps or in mist nets. Some of these migrant birds may be recaptured far to the north, to the south, or to the east or west, by other bird-banders or found by non-banders.

BANDS, BANDING, AND REPORTS. Bands, as well as a Canadian-printed *Bird Banding Manual* and reporting forms, are issued to bird-banders free. The bands are made of aluminum alloys and are the round butt-end or split-ring type. After a wild bird is captured and the bander has taken it carefully in his, or her, hands, either from the wire-cage banding trap or from a mist net stretched across an opening in the woods or garden, or as a young bird in the nest, he places a band around the shank of the bird, just above its toes. After he closes the band, and before releasing the bird, the bander enters in a notebook: the species of bird, serial number of its band, place and date of banding, the bird's age, sex, whether a bird of the year or an adult, and perhaps the color of its eyes, its general condition, stage or condition of its molt, also its weight, and so on. The bander sends his records periodically (at least annually) to the Bird Banding Laboratory at Laurel, Md. There, hundreds of letters may arrive each week from the general public, on whom the government depends for voluntary reporting, or from bird-banders themselves, telling of the recovery or recapture of a banded bird. The letters usually include the band (preferably) taken from the dead bird's leg or simply a report of the bird's band number, along with other details of where it was found, cause of death, etc.

Members of the laboratory staff acknowledge each report, telling the finder where and when the bird was banded. They also send a notice of the bird's recovery to the person who banded it. Besides its own unique serial number, each bird band bears the abbreviated name and address of the U.S. Fish and Wildlife Service—on the outer surface of the larger bands; on the inner surface of the smaller ones. Thus a finder of a band knows where to send it. However, if the banded bird is still alive, perhaps injured but with a chance of surviving, the finder is urged to take down the band number and report it, but if possible, not to take the band from the bird's leg. The finder of the bird is also urged to supply information about where it was found, the town, county, and state, and, if possible, the cause of the bird's death or injury—struck by a car, shot, etc.

Bands range in size from the large one for the legs of swans, flamingos, eagles, pelicans, cranes, gannets, and the great horned owl, to the very small one for tiny birds such as gnatcatchers and kinglets. Even diminutive hummingbirds can be marked with special bands. The *Bird Banding Manual* of the U.S. Fish and Wildlife Service dated 1976 (now issued jointly with the Canadian Wildlife Service), for example, lists band sizes for each species of N. American bird. See also in Lincoln (1947). Waterfowl (*see* Waterfowl) require a different method of capture, with extremely large nets fired with small cannons over flocks of the birds (Glover, 1964), or with large, funnel-shaped traps in waterfowl feeding areas. The birds swim into the traps, unaware of the netting, and eventually into the small end from which they cannot escape. See Lynch (1952) and Cant (1959). For illustrated methods of trapping and banding birds in Europe, see Lockley and Russell (1953). See interesting techniques of banding reported by Marion and Shamis (1977). Interesting details about banding are also given by Anonymous (1960); Duvall (1966); Eyster (1966). For discussion of traps, mist nets, cannon nets, etc., see Pettingill (1970).

RETURN TO NEST SITES AND WINTERING PLACES. One of the useful goals of banding has been to determine the locality-faithfulness (*Ortstreue* of German ornithologists) by banding, also whether birds return to their same nesting and wintering places. Banding has shown that auks, guillemots, herring gulls, and terns usually return to the same colony to nest and often to the same individual territory (*see* Territory); also the same strong attachment to its hatching place or where it has once nested successfully has been shown for many migratory birds—ducks, geese and swans, hawks, eagles, woodpeckers, swifts and swallows, the American robin, flycatchers, jays, starlings, nighthawks, thrushes, wrens, thrashers, sparrows, towhees, buntings, and many other birds. Many birds also return to their same wintering territories, although the site attachment may not be always as strong as the bird's attachment to its nesting place (Welty, 1962). As early as 1915, S. P. Baldwin at Thomasville, Ga., began to record the repeated wintering there of the same white-throated and white-crowned sparrows, chipping sparrows, song sparrows, hermit thrushes, and myrtle (yellow-rumped) warblers. Josselyn Van Tyne was the first field ornithologist to show that some N. American birds (indigo buntings) returned to the same wintering places in the tropics. Northern waterthrushes return to the same wintering places in Trinidad and Venezuela; eight species of migrants—broad-winged hawk, ovenbird and other warblers, summer tanager, and rose-breasted grosbeak—returned in winter to the same places in Panama. See other records especially in Nickell (1968); also in Ely (1973); Woods (1975).

For many records and individual reports of banded birds, ages at recovery, where banded, where recovered, etc., see Lincoln (1936a; 1936b; 1950c); Terres (1964b); Kennard (1975). *See also* in biographies of each species and under Age. An excellent up-to-date source of information is *Bird-Banding: A Journal of Ornithological Investigation*—see source under Ornithological Periodicals. For a history of bird-banding in America, see Lincoln (1933); Wood (1945).

BANK-BIRD
See phalaropes in Phalarope Family.

BANNER-MARKS
See Colors That Advertise under Colors of Feathers.

BAPTORNIS
(bap-TORE-niss); Lat., from Gr. *baptein*, to dip in water, and *ornis*, a bird. Genus name of a flightless, fish-eating, diving bird that lived about 100 million years ago in shallow, warm seas that covered the Great Plains of N. America (*see* Great Plains). The first and still only known species, *Baptornis advenus*, was described in 1877 by Prof. C. O. Marsh of Yale University from a fossilized bone fragment he discovered in the Upper Cretaceous (Niobrara formation) of Kans.; it was in the same chalk formation where, in 1870, Marsh discovered *Hesperornis*. *See* Hesperornis. Apparently *Baptornis* was probably more closely related to grebes of today than to Hesperornis. It was about 18 in. long, not much bigger than a domestic hen, and lived in same waters as the giant, lizardlike, 70-ft.-long pleiosaurs, in an age when the rule of the giant reptiles of the world was coming to an end. *See* discussion under Fossil Birds. The wings of *Baptornis* were mere vestiges, apparently useful to it only in helping it steer through water. Whether or not *Baptornis* had teeth as *Hesperornis* had is unknown because a skull, including jaws, of *Baptornis* has never been found. See Pettingill and Lancaster (1973a) for other details.

BARB; BARBICEL; BARBULE
See Feather.

BARBET
See Piciformes.

BARN OWL
See Owl—Barn Owl Family.

BARREL-MAKER
Local name for the American bittern in Heron Family, from its uttered sounds which resemble resonant pounding. *See* Esophagus.

BARREN-GROUND BIRD
See Rock ptarmigan in Grouse Family.

BARRIER
Term of biogeographers and ecologists for a physical obstruction—a mountain range, water or even grassland, or a forest which certain birds or other animals cannot, or do not, ordinarily cross. It is not only the physical obstruction but its *quality* (a grassland bird may not invade a forest, or a forest bird attempt to penetrate a great open grassland) which may prevent the spread of a species. The barrier may also be one of climate, or one of temperature and rainfall which varies gradually from place to place, and may not physically obstruct the movements of birds or other individual animals, but can prevent their successful establishment if the climate is unfavorable to the breeding of the species (Darlington, 1957). *See* discussion under Distribution; Faunal Regions.

BARROW
SIR JOHN (1764–1848). English traveler, writer, secretary of the Admiralty, chief founder of the Royal Geographical Society, and promoter of Arctic exploration (Palmer, 1928). His principal publications were about Arctic travels (see Palmer) and his name is preserved in Barrow Straits, Cape Barrow, and Point Barrow. Sir John Richardson (in Swainson and Richardson, 1832) named a N. American duck, *Clangula barrowii*, or the Rocky Mountain garrot as he called it, with the words: "The specific appellation is a tribute to Mr. Barrow's varied talents, and his unwearied exertions for the promotion of science." *See* present scientific name under Barrow's goldeneye in Duck Family. Barrow's name is also commemorated in the name of a subspecies of the glaucous gull.

BARTRAM
WILLIAM (1739–1823). N. American traveler and naturalist for whom Alexander Wilson named a N. American bird, *Tringa bartramia*, Bartram's sandpiper (*see* Upland sandpiper in Sandpiper Family). Of the naming of this bird Wilson wrote: "I have honoured it with the name of my very worthy friend near whose Botanic Gardens on the banks of the river Schuylkill [near Philadelphia] I first found it" (Wilson, Vol. VII, 1813).

At Philadelphia, in 1791, Bartram published his *Travels through North and South Carolina, Georgia, East and West Florida, the Cherokee Country, the Extensive Territories of the Muscogulges a Creek Confederacy, and the Country of the Choctaws*. The *Travels*, as Bartram's book was later called, became a classic of American literature; in the 1791 edition, Bartram listed 215 species of N. American birds, the most complete before that of Alexander Wilson, who was inspired by Bartram to produce his *American Ornithology*. See *Dictionary of American Biography;* see especially evaluation of Bartram in Coues (1884); also Cruickshank (1957); Harper (1958). *See also* Names and Naming.

BASKET-BIRD
See Oriole, orchard, in Troupial Family and White-eyed vireo in Vireo Family.

BASTARD WING
See Alula.

BATHING

Among wild birds there are several kinds—the water bath, dust bath, and sun bath. A bird bathes in water to facilitate the oiling and subsequent preening, and secondarily to clean the plumage; in hot weather bathing probably also has a cooling effect. *See* Heat and Birds. Probably most land birds take water baths, although some gallinaceous birds do not; instead, they dust their plumage. The smaller and medium-sized birds—for example, blackbirds, bluebirds, robins, catbirds, blue jays, cardinals, grosbeaks, orioles, thrashers, goldfinches, tanagers, thrushes, warblers, vireos, sparrows, starlings, grackles, cowbirds, cuckoos, flickers and other woodpeckers, etc.—and even the larger birds such as eagles, hawks, crows, and owls, bathe in shallow pools along the edges of streams, in shallow ponds, in pools of rain water and melted snow, in springs, and in any standing water available to them. Grackles and house sparrows have been seen bathing even in water that has accumulated in a hollow in a tree.

Most songbirds and other land birds that have relatively strong feet and pliable wings bathe standing on their feet. They usually wade into the water and choose a depth suitable to them—from about 1 to 3 in. usually. The smaller songbirds bathe rapidly, splashing continuously; hawks and pigeons usually lie partly immersed and motionless between periods of violent splashing. In bathing, most birds duck the head into the water, quickly raise it, then beat the wings, splashing water over the back while depressing and raising the tail in the water (see Slessers, 1970, for details).

Immediately after bathing, a bird usually flies up from the bathing place to a tree or other perch, where it preens its feathers or may spread them to dry in the sunshine. In drying themselves, birds usually shake out their feathers and whir their wings as they begin their preening actions. *See* Preening.

Aerial birds such as swifts and swallows bathe while in flight, splashing repeatedly into the surface of a pond or other waters; flycatchers dive from a perch to the water, then return to the perch, where they vibrate their wet feathers. While bathing in a backyard birdbath, a wet bird cannot fly away quickly and is vulnerable to cats and other predators if the birdbath is at ground level. People who attract birds usually use an elevated birdbath, placed under a bush or limb of a tree, which gives the bird an advantage of height and a chance to fly upward and escape the pounce of a predator. *See* Bird-attracting.

water bathing

BATHING
A grackle dips its head into the water and beats its wings vigorously, spraying the ruffled feathers of its back. It will fly to a less vulnerable perch to shake itself dry and to preen.

LEAF AND DEW BATHING. After a rain, some small birds, warblers particularly, will flutter about on the surfaces of wet leaves of trees and shrubs to take a so-called leaf bath. Even a merlin (formerly called pigeon hawk) was seen one Sept. day taking a leaf bath at Hawk Mountain, Pa., where it was passing southward in its migration.

In dry summers of coastal Calif., when water may be locally scarce, many small birds leaf-bathe—a rufous-crowned sparrow, for example, on wet leaves of a four-foot-tall eucalyptus tree which had been sprayed by a garden hose; two juvenile dark-eyed (Oregon) juncos bathing in wet grass; and a captive white-crowned sparrow "leaf-bathing" on some wet romaine lettuce leaves offered it as food. See in Baptista (1973).

Birds bathe in dew or in condensed fog on the surfaces of leaves or grass. Verbeek (1962) believed that dew bathing is rarely seen in the wild but described it for seven species of small songbirds at Vancouver, B.C., in Aug. 1961. Van Tyne described dew bathing in summer of a Kirtland's warbler, and Berger (1961) mentions dew bathing by captive Traill's flycatchers and yellow-bellied flycatchers which flew through wet grass. Dow (1968), in Tenn. during a drought in June 1966, watched four female and two male cardinals bathing on dew-covered leaves in the crowns of sassafras, red maple, and willow trees and going through the motions of a bird waterbathing. Bathing movements are apparently inborn in birds, as Bond (1942) reported that his four-week-old goshawks went through bathing movements on dry ground on seeing a brood mate splashing water.

Some garden birds—from robins, cardinals, towhees, and thrashers to hummingbirds—will bathe in the spray of a lawn sprinkler. Some stand on the grass under the spray as it swings and flutter their wings and shake out their feathers when the water strikes them. An observer in Tex. watched a ruby-throated hummingbird, while perched on a flower of scarlet sage, take a shower under the lawn sprinkler (Kenesson, 1914); hummingbirds also fly in and out of the moving spray of the sprinkler; the Anna's hummingbird flew back and forth through the fine spray of a garden hose (Stoner, 1947).

RAIN BATHING. This seems to be a special kind of deliberate exposure by a bird of its body and plumage to rain. Most birds take shelter in trees, shrubbery, or buildings during a downpour. However, during a sudden shower in England, Harrison (1961) watched a flock of feral pigeons that, instead of taking shelter, lay on the grass on one side with a wing raised vertically, a posture that many birds assume when sun-bathing. Harrison was told that at Whipsnade Zoo in London many species of parrots rain-bathe and many hang head downward when doing so; he was also told that "larks bathe in the rain by lying down in it with outspread wings." In Canada, Dow (1968) noted rain bathing by a cardinal in s. Ont. During a light shower, a male was singing from a dead elm tree; when the rain increased suddenly the cardinal began bathing movements.

DUST BATHING. Not so widespread among species of birds as is water bathing; it is not a substitute for water bathing, but exact function is not known. A dusting bird usually squats or lies down in a sunny, dusty place—on a dirt road, at the edge of a field or garden, or even in cinders along a railway track (house sparrow). According to Simmons (1964a), dusting is most characteristic of birds living in open, often bare, country, for example larks, quail, and ring-necked pheasants; however, it is frequent in ruffed grouse and wild turkeys; also in some N. American songbirds, such as wrens and wren-tits, and in certain hawks and owls. (Most birds that dust bathe do not water bathe.)

House sparrows, bobwhite quail, and domestic chickens are frequent dust-bathers. Most birds form body-size hollows or craters in the dust and while lying in them peck the soft earth and scrape it loose with the feet. While doing so, to sift dust through the feathers, they roll the body with the body and rump feathers fluffed out and shuffle the wings, flicking dust onto the back; some of the larger birds even toss dust over the back with the bill. After dusting, the bird rises and vigorously shakes earth out of its feathers and then preens or scratches its head (Simmons, 1964a). *See* Preening.

In experiments with captive Japanese quail *(Coturnix),* Healy and Thomas (1973) discovered that dust bathing improved the alignment of the barbs of the feathers (*see* Feather) and reduced dandruff, oil, and moisture in the plumage. It also made the contour feathers dry and fluffy so that the down feathers could fill the space between the contour feathers and the birds' skin. This improved the insulating quality of the plumage. The investigators concluded that dusting and preening also could help to dislodge and discourage some of the fleas, mites, lice, and other parasites that live in the feathers or on the outside of a bird's body (*see* Parasite), but they did not experiment to prove it. See Borchelt (1972); *also* Anting; and discussion of dusting by Potter and Hauser (1974).

SUN BATHING. On sudden exposure to hot sunshine, especially in summer, a wild bird may go into an astonishing performance. A cardinal, towhee, thrasher or other ground-feeding songbird, on emerging from shade into the direct sunlight, on a lawn or sandy driveway, may drop on its belly, raise its crown feathers, droop its wings, and spread its tail feathers like a fan. With its back to the sun, and body feathers fluffed fully, it may lean to one side. Then it flattens itself, with its bill open, gasping for air, with its head turned aside, one eye gazing upward directly into the sun. One's first impression is that the bird is suffering from heat prostration and may be dying.

Some birds may sun for only 2 or 3 minutes at a time—bank and cliff swallows, for example, on a bridge road whose surface was so hot one could not touch it with the hands (Barlow *et al.*, 1963). Cardinals may sun-bathe for fully 15 minutes on one spot on the ground, a ground dove for 15 minutes, and crested flycatchers, tufted titmice, blue jays, catbirds, cardinals, and house sparrows were recorded sun bathing for only 1 to 3 minutes while sunning on a com-

post heap whose surface temperature registered 140° F. (Hauser, 1957). Hauser, who reported sun bathing in 33 species of N. American birds, saw only three—brown thrasher, Carolina wren, and house sparrow—that, while dust-bathing, also practiced sunning. Some birds sun-bathe on relatively cool days when the air temperature is 55–60°.

Hauser discovered that a bird may respond to the hot sun in different degrees of posture: it may simply raise its crown feathers, droop its wings and tail feathers, and then suddenly fly away, or may assume the extreme sunning posture in which it flops its wings forward wildly and gasps for air, then falls flat on the ground, or on a feeding tray, or wherever it happens to be when the hot sunshine suddenly triggers its apparently involuntary response.

Birds also sun-bathe on the branches of trees, on the tops of utility poles (red-bellied and golden-fronted woodpeckers), on tops of walls, on fence posts (starling), on windowsills, atop leafy shrubs, on haystacks, on rooftops, against ivy-clad walls, on garden benches, in flower beds, etc. (Gibb, 1947); most birds, however, usually sun-bathe on the ground (Teager, 1967).

In England, Teager (1967) reported a blackbird, *Turdus merula,* a bird related to our American robin, that, while it lay sun-bathing on top of a garden wall, sang "a few phrases at a time, with long [silent] spells between." One male blackbird spent 26 minutes sunning on the ground in various postures, and Teager noted, as did Hauser (1957), that a bird sunbathing attracts others, which sprawled about in groups of the same or different species; birds often sun-bathe on the same site day after day; Hauser noted 10 to 30 birds of six different species sun-bathing regularly in a pear tree in her garden. Hawks and owls also sun-bathe by facing the sun and holding their wings spread wide.

Sun bathing stimulates birds to preen, while sunning or immediately afterward. *See also* Smoke Bathing.

BENEFITS OF SUN BATHING. Cade (1973) reported sun bathing in more than 170 species of birds and in most avian orders. Some of the suggested functions of sun bathing, in which a bird's feathers are fluffed and both its feathers and parts of its skin are exposed to the light and heat of the sun, have been summarized by Kennedy (1969): heat is absorbed into the skin and body; heat and light cause the parasites of its skin and feathers (ectoparasites—*see* Parasite) to move to the bird's head or under its wings, thus making them easier to remove either by scratching (the head) or by preening of the body feathers; drying of the plumage; stimulation of vitamin D production in the bird's skin, feathers, and oil, or preen, gland, by ultraviolet radiation. *See* oil gland under Skin Glands. Potter and Hauser (1974) reported a strong correlation between the time of molting of the feathers by some N.C. land birds and their frequency of sun bathing; at a time when a bird's skin is irritated by the molt, sunning may give it some skin comfort.

According to Storer *et al.* (1975), only recently has solar radiation, as a source of direct

sun bathing

dust bathing

BATHING

Sun bathing may benefit this cardinal in several ways: heat (energy) is absorbed into the skin and body; production of Vitamin D is stimulated by sunlight; and heat and light may cause ectoparasites to move to the head and beneath wings, where the bird can remove them easily.

A house sparrow, bathing in dust, scratches a hollow in soft, dry earth, and rolls, raising dust through its plumage with energetic flicking of its wings. Dust absorbs excess oil in the feathers and may possibly discourage ectoparasites.

energy to birds through heat absorption, been recognized (Hamilton, 1973; Ohmart and Lasiewski, 1971). In their studies of sun bathing by grebes, Storer *et al.* conclude that it may function primarily, if not wholly, in heat absorption. Energy (heat) from solar radiation can reduce (save) the energy a bird requires from its food, and the energy it uses to obtain food. *See* Metabolism.

BAY DUCKS
See diving ducks in Duck Family.

BAZAAR
Term of Russian ornithologists for an association of nesting seabirds and associated nesting land birds such as ravens, peregrine falcons, gyrfalcons, and, in years of scarcity of lemmings in N. Hemisphere, the snowy owl, all of which take opportunities to scavenge or prey on the seabird colony (Tuck, 1961).

BEACH BIRD
See Piping and Semipalmated plovers in Plover Family; *also* Sanderling in Sandpiper Family.

BEAK
Term commonly used for the bill of a bird of prey. *See* Bill.

BEARD
A unique, bristly appendage growing from the breasts of wild and domestic turkeys. Usually a turkey has only one beard, but as many as five have been counted on a male Rio Grande turkey (*see* in Turkey Family) and the same number on a female domestic turkey.

According to Lucas and Stettenheim (1972), the bristles (*see* Feather) that compose the beard of the turkey are solid, horny filaments (not feathers) that grow directly from the surface of the outer layer of skin and project downward from the middle of the turkey's breast. The castration of young male turkeys does not prevent the growth of a beard; its development therefore is independent of a male hormone; although males more often have the beard, females, especially of domestic turkeys, frequently have them. Of 557 female wild turkeys killed by hunters in Va., only 4, or less than 1%, had beards. The beard of a turkey grows continuously, and if cut off or worn off, will grow again.

In experiments in cutting off the beards of two male turkeys in captivity, the beards grew 130 and 133 mm. (about 5 in.) in one year. A beard 311 mm., or about 12½ in., on a male wild turkey in Va., appears to be about the longest that they grow (Schorger, 1957; see also Lewis, 1973). *See also* Breast Sponge; Sexual Dimorphism.

BECARD
See in Cotinga Family.

BEE BIRD
See Kingbird, eastern, in Flycatcher Family; *also* Summer tanager in Tanager Family.

BEE-EATER
See Autolycism; Coraciiformes.

BEARD
The beard of the wild turkey consists of a tuft of bristly filaments growing from its breast.

BEE MARTIN
See Kingbird, eastern, in Flycatcher Family.

BEETLE-HEAD
See Plover, black-bellied, in Plover Family.

BEHAVIOR
Loosely, anything a bird does; the entire complex of its observable, recordable, or measurable activities, is its behavior (Verplanck, 1957); its flocking, feeding and food-getting, drinking, singing, fighting, and territorial defense, its courting, mating, nesting, and parental behavior; its roosting, self-protective behavior, preening, scratching, dusting, anting, bathing, migrations, and so on. According to Emlen (1955): "Behavior is more than organic expression; it is the means by which an animal maintains its relation with the environment, the vital link between the living organism and the surrounding world in which it evolved and of which it is a part. *Stimulus* and *response* are the basic attributes of environment and organism respectively in this relationship."

Of the function of behavior, Tinbergen (1951a) wrote: "Behaviour helps the animal to maintain itself in a hostile world, as do the functions of its intestines, its kidneys, its blood." And as Dr. Nicholas E. Collias wrote (1962): "The world is also friendly, I think."

Birds are particularly good subjects for studies in animal behavior because most of them are active by day and they are abundant and easily accessible for study in the laboratory or in the field. And just as in other animals, they have stereotyped and relatively inflexible responses, although they also have a marked learning ability (Hinde, 1961). Perhaps bird behaviorists have spent more time studying birds because they are primarily "eye and ear behavers," as man is (Meyerriecks, 1962).

STEREOTYPED PATTERNS. In a bird these may include the way in which it moves its wings in flight; the way it flicks its tail just before takeoff; the postures of the male in courting the female; its call notes and song; all of which are usually similar in all members of a species although they may or may not differ between closely related species (Hinde, 1961).

These species-characteristic movements, thought of as "fixed action patterns," form useful units into which innate behavior may be analyzed. Fixed action patterns play a role in every part of a bird's life—in the food-begging of the young, courtship of the adults and their threat postures, sleeping, hunting, and so on. They are useful to the systematist, for they are often as distinctive and as valuable in classifying birds as a feather pattern or a muscle arrangement (Delacour and Mayr, 1945). C. O. Whitman's studies of pigeons; Oskar Heinroth's work on numerous birds, especially ducks; Johnsgard's (1965) treatise on ducks and geese; Desmond Morris' work on the passerine Family Estrildidae (waxbills, mannikins, grassfinches); and M. Moynihan's studies of gulls, all demonstrate the usefulness of behavior traits in relating or grouping birds (Tinbergen, 1951b).

APPETITIVE AND CONSUMMATORY BEHAVIOR. Some bird behaviorists find it convenient in their early analyses of bird behavior to divide and label the behavior of a species into *appetitive* and *consummatory* behavior. However, "appetitive and consummatory behavior differ only in degree, and many behavior patterns of birds have characteristics of both." A bird guarding its territory or one looking for a place to sleep or food to eat is exhibiting types of appetitive behavior. The final stereotyped act of the bird swallowing food, of striking its rival, or of sleeping is termed consummatory (Hinde, 1961).

SIGN STIMULI, OR RELEASERS. Much bird behavior can be provoked experimentally by offering a stimulus to the bird—by "putting a key in the lock." The sign (the key) that is meaningful to the bird releases, or unlocks, its behavior. For example, Lack (1953), in his studies of the European robin, discovered that stuffed adult robins (with a red breast), when placed in the territory of a pair, were always attacked by the adult robins possessing the territory, but juvenile robins, or immatures, which do not have a red breast, were not attacked. Lack went on to prove that even a bunch of red feathers were threatened by the adult robins more than a whole stuffed juvenile robin.

Other experimenters also have proved that a bird or other animal usually responds selectively and appropriately only to some of the numerous stimuli that an animal receives from its environment. Sign stimuli seem to play an essential role in all bird behavior, and are used by birds in social communication; natural selection can operate in both the bird giving the signal and on the sensitivity of the bird receiving it. The result may be the development and the elaboration of the signals into exaggerated movements and postures of birds, into distinctive colors and other plumage features, and into complex calls, all easily recognized and therefore facilitating social communication (*see* Language). Many of these conspicuous colors, displays, and calls of birds are termed by some bird behaviorists "social releasers" because of their sign stimulus effect on each other in releasing definite responses (Hinde, 1961).

WHAT INFLUENCES BIRD BEHAVIOR? Frequently, a bird's behavior is in conflict between tendencies to engage in two different behaviors, such as fighting and fleeing. It is, of course, impossible for the bird to do both at once; therefore, the conflicting tendencies may cause it to (1) inhibit all but one response and thus to behave properly and fly from danger or attack, or (2) alternate between two responses, or (3) show what has been termed *ambivalent behavior*—the exhibition of behavior that shows elements of both the conflicting behaviors, such as fighting and fleeing. The two behaviors, often elicited by the same object, seem to be incompatible, and the bird may show movements or postures that contain components of both. Threat postures are in this category.

Types of behavior, including courtship, nest building, feeding the young, and so on, are usually integrated in birds to produce functional sequences—a chain of responses in which each response of the bird to certain stimuli, or situations, stimulates the release of the next one. Most of the so-called "appetitive behavior to consummatory act" are of this kind (Hinde, 1961).

FEEDING AND FOOD-GETTING. The selection of food and the development of feeding preferences, as in most behavior, is apparently both inherited and learned. There is a great variety of behavior in food-getting—the drilling of woodpeckers for grubs; the deep diving of loons for fishes; the flower probing of hummingbirds for nectar and insects; the aerial dives of the peregrine falcon for its feathered prey; and so on. "Even within a single family or a genus, there is a strong tendency to develop distinctive food habits, and this has high survival value for birds" (Emlen, 1955). For special types of feeding behavior, *see* foot-paddling and wing-flashing under Food and Feeding Habits.

The correlation between a bird's structure and its feeding behavior is often striking—the hooked beak of a hawk; the long legs of a heron; the barbed tongue of a woodpecker; the shearlike bill of a black skimmer. Many structural specializations of birds are impossible to interpret except in their use in the behavior of the bird.

Some birds have developed cooperative or group feeding that is of benefit to the individual members of the flock (Turner, 1964). Flock feeding has been described for the double-crested cormorant (Bartholomew, 1942); the white pelican (Cottam *et al.*, 1942a); among certain other fish-eating birds, and several ducks observed by John T. Emlen, Jr.; among grain-eating birds in blackbirds (Dawson, 1923); among insect-eaters in swallows (Emlen, 1952); and in mixed flocks of temperate (Morse, 1978) and tropical (Moynihan, 1962) birds.

Some birds also "highjack," or "steal," food (*kleptoparasitism—see* Parasite) from other birds that may be more skilled at obtaining it. Predatory seabirds—jaegers and skuas—will take fishes from gulls, gulls will rob terns (Hatch, J. J., 1970), and bald eagles will rob ospreys; other eagles rob hawks of food, and the larger hawks will rob smaller ones; starlings and house sparrows will take earthworms from robins (*see* Earthworms and Birds); blackbirds rob thrushes of snails; shrikes take insects from smaller birds; and in Africa and India, sunbirds get juices from figs broken open by parrots and bulbuls (Meinertzhagen, 1959). The American wigeon, often locally called "poacher," attends flocks of canvasbacks, redheads, and other diving ducks to feed on the wild celery that these ducks bring to the surface of the water; and hummingbirds and warblers will drink the sweet sap of trees from tiny "wells," or holes, drilled in the bark by sapsuckers. *See* Autolycism; Commensalism.

Other forms of behavior that are associated with food-getting are: (1) *migration*, which allows many birds to escape limited food supplies in winter, and (2) *territorialism*, in which birds defend a limited territory, in which they not only nest but also feed, thus ensuring an adequate food resource for themselves and their

forward posture

facing away

BEHAVIOR
Most territorial disputes between gulls are settled by visual displays of appeasement rather than defensive fighting. A male herring gull may turn its head away from an intruder or may hold its head forward and down in a submissive posture. Both displays seem to inhibit the aggression of the intruding gull.

BEHAVIOR

Starlings flying in a loose formation will suddenly close ranks in an alarm response to the appearance of a falcon. The falcon, unable to strike at a single bird, is deterred from diving into a tight flock where it might be injured.

young. Territorialism is a form of social behavior which probably had its origin in connection with pairing and the reproduction of birds (Emlen, 1955). Fighting and territorial defense by pairs of birds against others of their kind seems to function, at least in part, in forming the sexual bond and in maintaining it (Hinde, 1961).

BREEDING BEHAVIOR. Birds, just as in some fishes, some mammals, and in man himself, have developed pair formation, which may account for our human interest in the home lives of wild birds. Pairing behavior serves for a cooperative sharing of feeding and protecting the young, and the activities of a mated pair can include territory defense, nest building, incubating the eggs, and care and feeding of the young. The relative roles of the male and female in this vary greatly from species to species—from those in which one bird, either the male or female, does all the work, to those in which both share in all activities. Most birds are monogamous; a few are polygynous; a smaller number are polyandrous (Emlen, 1955). *See* Sexual Relationships. A pair of birds may remain paired for life, or only for the duration of the mating attempt, depending on the species (Hinde, 1961). *See* Courtship.

Elaborate courtship displays of some birds, primarily for the retention of the mate, are basically social rather than sexual, but also may stimulate sexual excitement. "Bird display may be regarded as comparable in some respects to certain forms of etiquette, which have as their function the conveyance of meaning and the establishment of a particular social or emotional relationship" (Armstrong, 1942).

Most animals actively select their mates and the choice of a mate is often governed by the chosen mate's behavior, which can be a decisive *isolating mechanism*, or a barrier to the mating in the wild of birds not closely related. *See* Species; Sexual Dimorphism.

According to Tinbergen (1951b), there is enough evidence of this to assure behaviorists that these ethologically isolating mechanisms do exist. Dilger (1956a), in his studies of five species of North American thrushes, discovered that the principal reproductive isolating mechanism that kept these thrushes specifically distinct was the songs of the males. The females responded only to the males of their kind, which prevented mixed pairing.

SELF-PROTECTIVE BEHAVIOR. Flight (one of the most efficient means of escaping enemies), keen vision, and hearing—all help to protect birds; also their concealing colors, or protective coloration, and certain assumed postures, which help them to blend with their backgrounds and to escape detection. Birds also utter warning calls at the appearance of predators—calls which are heeded by their own kind and by certain other species of birds. *See* Alarm Notes; Language. Some birds also give *distraction displays* in or around the nest which may lead predators away from the young and thus effect their protection (Hinde, 1961). *See* Distraction Display; Helpers among Birds; Young and Their Care.

Birds, sometimes of many different species,

BEHAVIOR

A pair of cedar waxwings, or a group in a row on a branch, pass a berry from one to another until one swallows it.

also gather to "mob" or harass a common enemy, such as a hawk, owl, snake, or even man himself. Mobbing is a type of social attack that has been observed in many species—from titmice and kinglets to crows and gulls (Nice, 1943). For example, a snowy owl was mobbed and killed by arctic terns (Meinertzhagen, 1959); a barn owl attacked and killed by herring gulls (Peterson, 1948); an American kestrel forced down into water by a small flock of red-winged blackbirds (Smith and Holland, 1974); ravens routed when attacked by hundreds of black-headed gulls; and an osprey mobbed and killed by frigatebirds in s. Fla. See also Nests and Nesting.

ACTIONS OF BIRDS WHEN ATTACKED BY A PREDATOR. Flocks of starlings, ducks, snow buntings, the extinct passenger pigeon, and certain other flocks of birds "bunch up" or close their ranks when attacked in flight by a hawk. The tightly massed group of birds is thought to offer some protection to them by making it difficult for the hawk to single out a lone bird. See discussion and illustrations in Heppner (1974). A pet passenger pigeon in the late 19th century, kept by a Canadian, H. Howitt, flew to him or to a member of his family whenever it sighted a hawk, apparently to seek protection, or sensing that the hawk would not attack it while it was near its protectors. In the summer of 1874, a wild passenger pigeon, when chased by a peregrine falcon in the Dakotas, sought refuge among men and horses of an expedition to that territory. Domestic pigeons when chased by a trained peregrine falcon have taken refuge at the feet of the falconer or other observers.

Generally, defensive fighting is poorly developed in birds, which depend far more on flight or concealment for self-protection. Fighting is usually between individuals of the same species; is more often bluff; and is usually subordinated to the reproductive instinct (Tinbergen, 1951b). See, however, Territory; Nests and Nesting; also Spurs under Feet and Legs.

Birds may gain protection against the weather by communal roosting in which individual flocks of thousands of crows, or mixed flocks of blackbirds, robins, starlings, and others, sleep close together in roosts at night. See Cold and Birds. "Communal breeding, communal roosting, and communal feeding are, without doubt, a protection and (possibly) engender a sense of security" (Meinertzhagen, 1959).

BEHAVIORAL MIMICRY. Known from a few birds, this is especially characteristic of titmice and chickadees. These birds nest in holes in trees or in bird boxes and when disturbed on the nest, instead of leaving the nesting cavity, may utter hissing sounds and spread their wings and tail feathers or raise the feathers of the head. With bill opened and wings partly spread, the bird may sway slowly back and forth on the nest, after which it leaps upward, hisses, then slaps the sides of the nesting cavity with its wings (Berger, 1961). This is the so-called "snake display," which the titmice and chickadees are thought to have evolved in a behavioral resemblance to a snake within the cavity. Its effect is startling and the explosive

performance might well be effective in discouraging animals, including man, from trying to investigate the nest cavity further.

Apparently the zone-tailed hawk has evolved an entirely different kind of behavioral mimicry, which, instead of protective, mimics the harmless turkey vulture in its flight, and thus may give the hawk an advantage in getting close to and surprising its prey. See details in Willis (1963).

SOCIAL ORDER AMONG BIRDS. Birds are brought together, socially, by the attraction of the same species for each other (Collias, 1962). "Birds of a feather flock together." Their social interactions are largely built on the dominance of one bird over another or over others; subordinance of one to others; or a leader-follower relationship (Emlen, 1955). There is a social hierarchy of dominance and subordinance in regulating social interaction of some bird flocks. An example is the well-known "peck order" or social order of domestic chickens, which has been much studied. T. Schjelderup-Ebbe, a Norwegian psychologist, is credited with discovering the peck order among chickens. See also Courtship.

In any flock, one hen usually dominates all others. She can peck any without being pecked in return, and a second hen can peck all but the top hen, and the rest of the flock is arranged by dominance in a descending hierarchy, ending in a hen which is pecked by all others but can peck no other hen herself. Cockerels, or roosters, do not peck hens but have their own peck order; therefore a breeding flock usually has two hierarchies, one for each sex (Guhl, 1956). The peck-order hierarchy of Schjelderup-Ebbe and of other authors exists in many bird societies but by no means in all. Colonially breeding birds such as herons, cormorants, gannets, and probably many other colonially nesting marine birds have no social hierarchy (Lorenz, 1970a).

Large flocks of wild birds, however, are generally open societies which may show very little of the social interaction and hierarchies which exist in closed societies such as in a flock of domestic chickens, except when temporarily brought together when sharing a particular activity (Emlen, 1955)—for example, in group feeding or in group courtship. See, however, Dominance; also Arena Bird.

THE LEARNING ABILITIES OF BIRDS. Learning by birds, as well as inherited "knowledge" (see Instinct), enters into the behavior of birds— "indeed this learning ability is essential for many aspects of avian economy—their active, wide-ranging life and complex social behavior are possible only by virtue of the modifiability of their behavior. Furthermore, through these facilities they are able actively to explore their environment, and their curiosity enables them both to exploit its resources more fully and to avoid its dangers more successfully" (Hinde, 1961).

For a long time, "the known poor development of any brain structures in birds [see Brain] clearly corresponding to the cerebral cortex of mammals led to the assumption among neurologists that birds are primarily creatures of instinct; also that they had little

ability to learn. This preconceived notion, based on a misconceived view of brain mechanisms, hindered the development of experimental studies of bird learning" (Thorpe, 1956b). Yet it has been discovered that in some contexts birds have a learning ability not exceeded by any animals other than the highest mammals. In coordinating their sense impressions in orientation in homing and migration, they appear supreme in the animal world.

HOW AND WHAT BIRDS LEARN. Birds learn in various ways—for example, by *habituation*. The range of objects to which young birds respond is at first large, but this is later reduced by learning in which they become habituated or "used to" certain situations to which they do *not* respond. For example, the young of some birds, soon after hatching, will follow the first relatively large object they see. The young of the European greylag goose, *Anser anser*, do so, and they soon learn the object's behavior characteristics—whether the object is the parent goose, a man, a boat, or some other moving object. This type of learning, known among bird behaviorists as *imprinting*, does not fit neatly into many categories of learning but seems to be related to habituation. It is confined to a definite, brief period early in the individual bird's life when it is narrowing the range of objects to which it responds (Thorpe, 1956b). For the discovery and history of imprinting, and various views about it, see Lorenz (1937; 1970a); Thorpe (1964b); Hess (1964; 1973); Klopfer (1965).

By habituation, birds learn what to fear and what not to fear. Mourning doves are much hunted in the United States, yet, before and after the hunting season, they may be attracted to bird feeders in the garden (see Bird-attracting), where they may lose much of their fear of man. Anyone who has found robins nesting or wintering in deep woods must have compared their wild behavior with those that nest in the protection of our dooryards and run about tamely over the lawn. Many birds—blue jays, crows, wood thrushes, and others that were woodland species 50 or 60 years ago—now nest in our towns, villages, and city parks. See Adaptations to Mankind.

However, birds seldom lose their fear of wild predators and they learn to recognize the forms of hawks, owls, snakes, and other predatory enemies. Many birds have precise responses to the appearance of the particular kind of predator most dangerous to them, but may become habituated to, or learn to ignore, predators that are not a threat to them, or even predators that are a threat to them, simply by recognizing that they are not in a hunting mood (Thorpe, 1956b).

TRIAL-AND-ERROR LEARNING. Birds also learn by *trial and error*, in which their appetitive motor patterns may adjust to changes in their environment (Hinde, 1961). In nature, certain birds—young doves, for example—must learn to drink water, and even the pecking of domestic chicks improves about 30 hours after hatching with an increase in the skill with which they seize and swallow each grain (Moseley, 1925), or perhaps in learning *what* to peck at. Simple trial-and-error learning is believed to

BERGMANN'S RULE
These two subspecies of the hairy woodpecker illustrate Bergmann's Rule that warm-blooded animals will tend to be larger in cold climates and smaller in warm zones. The larger bird, occurring in Canada, is able to produce and conserve heat more efficiently than a small-bodied bird because it has less heat-losing surface area relative to its greater heat-producing body mass. The relatively greater body surface of the smaller woodpecker of Central America presumably aids in cooling by radiation of heat.

be very important to birds in their nest building, although there is little doubt that the nest-building motions of birds are innate, or unlearned (Thorpe, 1956b). *See* Nests and Nesting.

Nice (1943), in her studies of song sparrows, found that the parents improved their feeding skill of the young as a result of learning. Individual learning by birds is sometimes remarkable. For example, in England, titmice of various species learned to open milk bottles left in the early morning on doorsteps and to reach down into the bottle and drink the milk. Within 30 years the habit had spread among these birds to many parts of England, possibly through those watching and imitating others of their kind (Hinde and Fisher, 1952).

In the laboratory, trial-and-error learning by birds has been studied by presenting them with puzzle boxes and mazes. House sparrows, blue jays, and a woodpecker learned to open doors by pulling a string (Porter, 1904, 1906, 1910), although they apparently did not "understand" the relationship between the string and the door. What the birds did learn was to associate disconnected responses and to perform them in the right order (Thorpe, 1956b).

House sparrows have learned to run through a maze with ability equal to that of a rat; pigeons can readily learn mazes of various types; and in tests of captive European songbirds, they quickly learned to run through a small maze in from 4 to 6 trials.

PLAY. Birds also learn by *playing* and there are now sufficiently numerous documented examples to believe that true play is fairly widespread among birds (Thorpe, 1956b). The play of a captive young turaco included sparring and mock attacks; young gannets in captivity were "as playful and mischievous as a litter of puppies"; young white-necked ravens and silvery-cheeked hornbills and a captive common buzzard (similar to the American red-tailed hawk) were playful, and young European kestrels in the wild, when satiated with hunting, returned to their former breeding territory among sand dunes to play with pine cones, grasses, and roots until the time came for them to start hunting again (Thorpe, 1956b).

Adult crows, ravens, and magpies are playful, house sparrows play with pebbles (*see* in Weaverbird Family), and the marsh hawk and other birds of prey, also grebes, are known to play a cat-and-mouse game with their quarry. Woodpeckers often play (see Kilham, 1974c), and in Iceland, eider ducks were seen riding down the waters of a rapids, then climbing the banks to again launch themselves on the stream, apparently for the delight of the swift ride through the swirling waters (Roberts, 1934). About play in birds, Thorpe (1956b) wrote: "In whatever category the behaviour comes . . . it may be of physiological value in maintaining and perfecting muscular co-ordination and control; in other words, it is an important element in both motor and sensory learning." See also Ficken (1977).

CURIOSITY AND MEMORY. Some birds have much curiosity. House sparrows and crows, which have enormous curiosity, are especially intelligent and adaptable birds (Heinroth and Heinroth, 1958), which helps them in trial-and-error learning. Some birds also have remarkable memories. Crows, jays, nutcrackers, and ravens remember where they hide nuts and other items (*see* Food and Feeding Habits) and domestic hens and pigeons are said to remember their homes after several years of absence (Thorpe, 1956b). Pigeons learn local topography around the home loft, which they use with orientation mechanisms in returning (*see* Homing), and some wild migratory birds return, in part, by memory of known landmarks (*see* Migration), and learn to remember their nesting territories as a recognizable unit. *See* Waterfowl.

Birds also learn by imitation of the behavior and voice of other birds. The call notes of a great many birds seem to be inborn, but there is considerable evidence that many species learn a part or even the whole of their territorial songs from members of their own species. It is claimed that the European song thrush's song is innate, or unlearned, but can be slightly modified by learning, while the skylark's song is wholly learned. *See* Songs and Singing.

A few birds use tools—the tailor bird uses spider's silk as thread while using its bill as a tool for sewing in building its nests. The satin bower bird uses fibrous material with which to "paint" the sticks of its bower with coloring material from berries and charcoal, a Galápagos finch uses a long cactus spine to pick insects out of crannies and crevices, and N. American brown-headed nuthatches in La. have been seen using a small piece of bark to remove another bark scale on a tree trunk in order to forage for insects (Morse, 1968). *See* Tool-using.

BIRDS THAT CAN "COUNT." Of all types of learning behavior, one of the most intriguing is the ability of some birds to "count." Children have often wondered if a bird can count its eggs in the nest and the problem puzzled several naturalists of the 16th and 17th centuries. It is not yet clear whether birds know by perception when they have laid a full clutch of eggs (*see* Clutch), which is controlled biologically (*see* discussion under Eggs and Egg-laying), but scientists in Germany have shown that the jackdaw, raven, parrot, and budgerigar (also squirrels) have a "number sense." Outstanding individuals abstracted the "concept" of identifying by number groups of up to 7 objects of completely different and unfamiliar appearance.

The work of O. Koehler and his pupils in Germany on the ability of animals to count "has proved beyond question the existence of ideation in animals. . . . It suggests that man and animals have a pre-linguistic 'counting' ability of about the same degree but that man's superiority in dealing with numbers lies in his ability to use, as symbols for numbers, words and figures. . . ." (Thorpe, 1956b).

BEHAVIORAL MIMICRY
See Behavior.

BELDING

LYMAN (1829–1917). Belding's yellowthroat was named for him (*see* in Warbler—American Wood Warbler Family) by Robert Ridgway in 1882; called by Fisher (1920) "the Nestor of California ornithologists." Belding became interested in birds about 1876; during next 20 years a prominent collector of birds along with field studies in Calif. and Baja Calif.; in 1881 collected the first eggs of Costa's hummingbird known to science. See Fisher (1920); Palmer *et al.* (1954).

BELL

JOHN G(RAHAM) (1812–89). Friend and associate of Audubon, Baird, Cassin, Giraud, Le Conte, and other early American ornithologists and for whom Audubon named the Bell's vireo in 1844. Bell, a naturalist-taxidermist of New York City, accompanied Audubon on his Missouri R. expedition of 1843; was a pioneer in art of taxidermy; gave lessons to 13-year-old Theodore Roosevelt, later President of U.S. Bell was said to have collected the last Labrador duck known to science on Long Is., N.Y., in 1875 (Bull, 1964); his name was also commemorated in the scientific name of the sage sparrow, *Amphispiza belli*, named for him by John Cassin in 1850. See Palmer *et al.* (1954).

BELLBIRD

See Thrush, wood, in Thrush Family; *also* Cotinga Family.

BENDIRE

CHARLES E(MIL) (1836–97). Major in U.S. Army, for whom Bendire's thrasher was named; one of founders of the American Ornithologists' Union. During his long military career in the Army to remote parts of the Far West, he followed his ornithological work vigorously. His chief and well-known publication, the two-volume *Life Histories of North American Birds,* was taken up, and enlarged upon, and carried to completion in a 21-volume series by Arthur Cleveland Bent and collaborators. Bendire's immense collection of birds' eggs, gathered during his military career, he gave to the U.S. National Museum, where for some years he was Honorary Curator of the Department of Oology (Palmer *et al.,* 1954); see the definitive biography of Bendire by Hume (1942).

BERGMANN'S RULE

"Within a polytypic warm-blooded species, the body size of a subspecies usually increases with decreasing (cooling) mean temperature of its habitat"—Julian Huxley, quoted by Knight (1948).

Although there are exceptions, the sizes of warm-blooded animals are usually larger in colder regions and become increasingly smaller toward the Equator. This tendency has been named Bergmann's Rule. In northern climates, the larger birds—with their body surface smaller in proportion to their body volume, compared to smaller birds—lose less heat, an adaptation to cold that conserves their body heat *and energy.* In warmer climates, small body size in warm-blooded animals gives a greater body surface in relation to body volume, and presumably aids *cooling* of the bodies of smaller birds by radiation of heat (Buchsbaum and Buchsbaum, 1957).

Out of this fact, first proposed by A. Bergmann, a German zoologist, came Bergmann's Rule, named for Bergmann, who published a scientific paper about it in 1847. It is a phenomenon of animals that is of great importance to their distribution and capability of living in cold environments (Allee and Schmidt, 1951). *See* Cold and Birds; Metabolism; Temperature. See also discussion of Bergmann's Rule applied to studies of birds by Behle (1973) and Rand (1961).

BEWICK

(BEW-ick), THOMAS (1753–1828). English artist and wood engraver, friend of John James Audubon for whom Audubon named the Bewick's wren. See Audubon's account (1870). Bewick was author and illustrator of one of the great English picture books of the late 18th century, *A History of British Birds* (Fisher, J., 1966). See Herrick's account (1917); Palmer (1928); Gruson (1972).

BIG CRANKY

See Heron, great blue, in Heron Family.

BIG INDIGO

See Grosbeak, blue, in Finch Family.

BILATERAL SYMMETRY

Term for condition in birds or other animals in which, externally, the right and left sides of the body are counterparts of each other. This is the normal, or usual, condition. *Bilateral asymmetry,* or sides that are unlike each other, is relatively rare in nature. For examples of it in birds, *see* Gynandromorph.

BILL

(Lat., *rostrum*). An "instrument" or "implement" with which a bird scratches itself and can reach almost every part of its body; it preens or cleans its feathers with its bill, caresses its mate with its bill, as pigeons and parrots frequently do; collects nesting material and builds its nest with its bill, which it can also use as a weapon with which to threaten or peck its rivals. Above all, a bird's bill is used by it to get its food and to break up food into sizes it can swallow (Hess, 1951). *See* Swallowing; *also* Digestion; Food and Feeding Habits.

The light, horny bill of a bird and the relatively light jaws and their muscles are comparable in their function to the heavier jaws and teeth of mammals. The bill, however, is a hand and mouth in one. As a "hand," it takes, holds, and carries food or nesting material, and is often used to *feel* with. As part of the mouth, the bill tears, cuts, or crushes according to the substance or material the bird eats. The bill acts as both lips and teeth, neither of which our present-day birds possess. Some parrots use the bill for climbing—the Carolina parakeet was said to hang itself up while sleeping by grasping with its bill the inside of a hollow tree. Woodpeckers use the bill as a chisel to dig out their homes; oystercatchers, as a pry when opening shellfishes.

The bill is in two parts: an upper and a lower

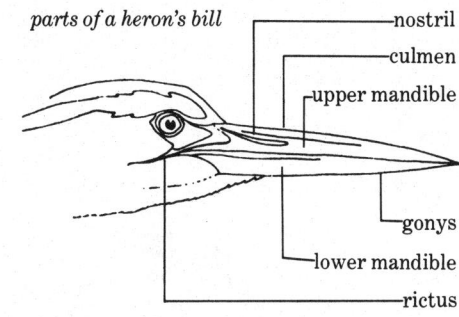

parts of a heron's bill — nostril, culmen, upper mandible, gonys, lower mandible, rictus

BILL

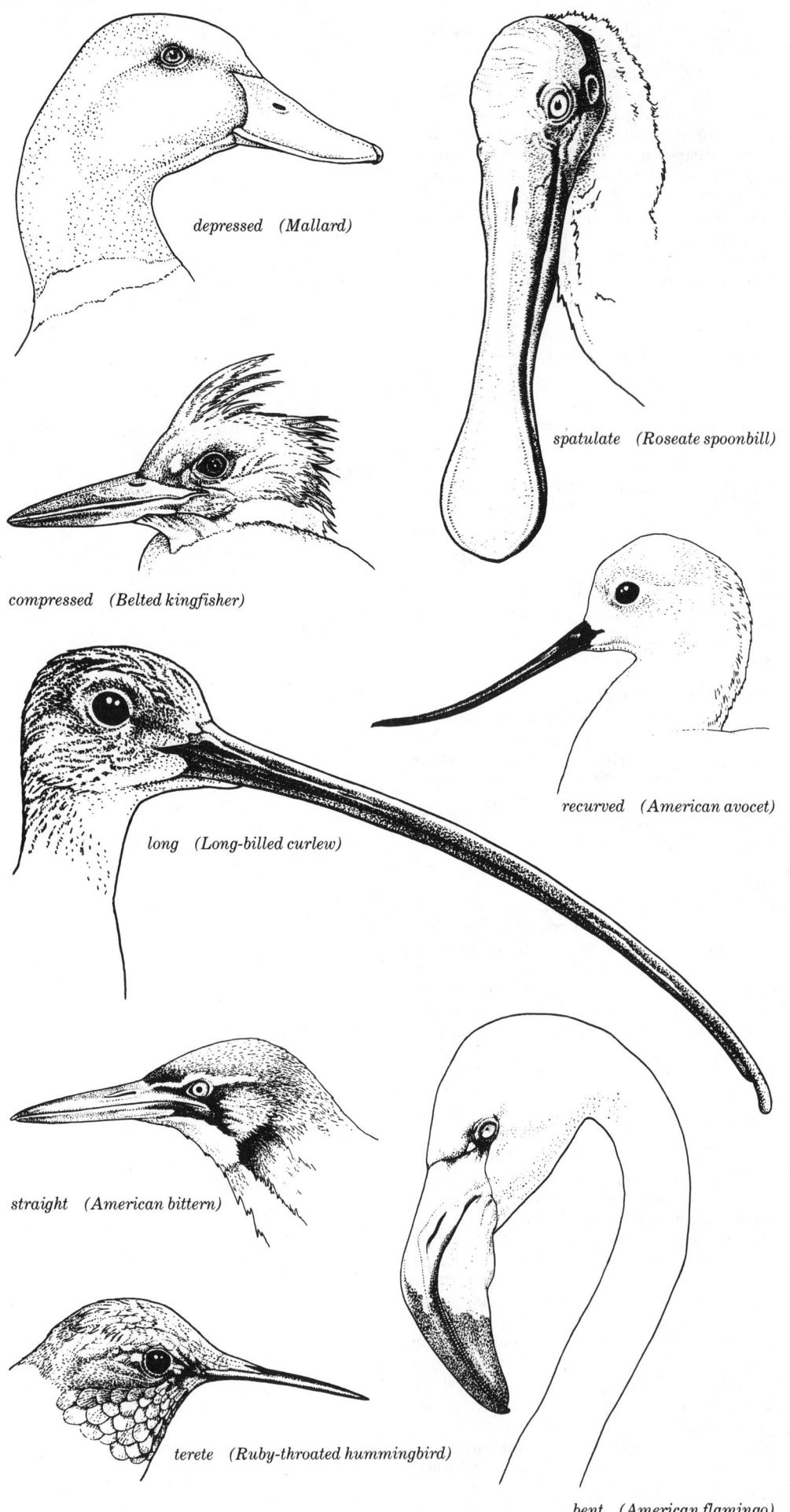

depressed *(Mallard)*

spatulate *(Roseate spoonbill)*

compressed *(Belted kingfisher)*

recurved *(American avocet)*

long *(Long-billed curlew)*

straight *(American bittern)*

terete *(Ruby-throated hummingbird)*

bent *(American flamingo)*

mandible. These lie, as their names indicate, above and below, and are separated by a fissure —the mouth.

SIZE AND SHAPE OF THE BILL. Descriptively, a bill is *long* when notably longer than the head proper, as in the bittern; *short*, when notably shorter, as in a redpoll; *compressed* when higher than wide for a good part of its length, as in a kingfisher; *depressed* when wider than high, as in a duck; *recurved* when curved upward, as in a godwit; *decurved* when curved downward, as in the brown creeper; *terete* (Lat., cylindric) when neither compressed or depressed, but circular as with the round bill of a hummingbird; *bent* when curved upward or downward at an angle, as in a flamingo; *straight* when not out of line with the axis of the head, as in a bittern. See Pettingill (1970) for these and other details. Bills are sometimes abnormal in size, shape, or growth. *See* Deformities.

BILL COVERING. In a great majority of birds, including nearly all perching birds, or song-birds, many walkers, and some waders and swimmers, the covering of the mandibles is wholly hard, horny, or *corneous* (Lat., horn). Probably the softest bill is among the snipes and woodcocks, in which it is thin throughout its length and vascular and sensory at the tip, a true organ of touch, used by snipes and woodcocks to feel for worms when they probe in the mud for them with their bills. *See* Touch. In ducks, the bill is soft but is terminated by a hard, horny *unguis*, or nail. Such a horny tip is on the bills of other water birds with soft bills —pelicans, for example.

Pigeons and doves have modified bills: hard at the tip (the *dertrum*, any specialized tip of the upper mandible—from Gr. *dertron*, beak), but toward, and at, the base of the upper mandible, the horny sheath becomes a soft, tumid texture overarching the nostrils (called the *opercula;* sing.: *operculum*—Lat., a cover or lid); it is much the same in most plovers. The most important feature of this kind is in the bills of parrots and all birds of prey—a *cere* (from Lat. *cera*, wax, because it looks waxy). The cere is a dense membrane saddled on the upper mandible at its base and "so different from the rest of the bill that it might be questioned whether it does not more properly belong to the head than to the bill, were it not for the fact that the nostrils open in it" (Coues, 1884). *See* Nostrils. In parrots, the cere is usually partly feathered; in falcons, some of the curassows, guans, and chachalacas, the pigeons and owls, it is bare and in some of these birds brightly colored (Stettenheim, 1972).

The entire covering of a bird's bill—the two mandibles, or jaws—is called the *rhamphotheca* (ram-foh-THEE-kah—*th* as in *thin*— from Gr. *ramphos*, beak, and *theka*, sheath). The shape of the rhamphotheca is basically that of the underlying bones of the bill but may have local thickenings, such as plates on the bill of the common puffin, knobs on the bills of swans, grooves or ridges on the bills of anis, and other bill projections of birds.

GROWTH OF THE BILL. In most birds, the tip of the bill usually wears down with use, especially among birds that feed on the ground—quail, pheasants, meadowlarks, towhees, sparrows, and finches, for example. The bill grows or renews itself continuously toward the tip, but when the bill is injured and the upper and lower mandibles, for example, are out of line and no longer wear upon one another, the growth of one or both mandibles may be unchecked. If so, the bird with a malformed bill may have great difficulty in eating or cannot eat enough to keep alive; thus it may starve to death. *See* Deformities; Accidents.

COLORS OF THE BILL. In most birds, the bill is black (Pettingill, 1972), but bills may be almost every color; in some birds, as in some toucans, the bill is the most colorful part of the body. The colors of the bill of some birds change with the seasons; starlings and American robins have a yellow bill in the breeding season, a dark brown bill in fall; the reverse is true of the bobolink and house sparrow—their bills are black in the breeding season and yellow or pale brown in fall; the olive-yellow bill of the evening grosbeak becomes bright apple green in the breeding season. See Pettingill (1972). In birds with brightly colored bills, the bill does not attain its full color until the bird is sexually mature. Some birds, such as the puffins in the Auk Family, after the breeding season molt the brightly colored parts of the bill. *See also* Endocrine Glands.

BILLING

Term for the touching or clasping of each other's bills by mated pairs of birds—of frequent occurrence in bird courtship. In puffins, the male approaches the female, and as a prelude to a courtship ceremony, nibbles at her bill; ivory-billed woodpeckers (now extinct, or near extinction) clasp each other's bills; and there is a kind of "kissing," or "nebbing," among birds as various as great crested grebes, herons, hawfinches, black guillemots, pigeons, parakeets, and cedar waxwings. The male waxwing puts his bill in his mate's mouth; and ravens hold each other's bills in a prolonged "kiss" (Armstrong, 1942). The billing of birds has been considered a mark of affection between the mated pairs. It appears to strengthen the pair bond. *See also* Behavior; Courtship; Courtship Feeding.

BILL-WILLIE

See Willet in Sandpiper Family.

BINOCULAR

A prism binocular consists of two small telescopes mounted side by side, each containing prisms, mirrors, and lenses that enable one to see birds and other distant objects "close up," or greatly magnified. The development of the prism binocular permitted (through the use of two prisms in each barrel of the binocular) much larger magnifications than the field glass while retaining the compact size and light weight practical for people to carry about and use. The development of the binocular is largely responsible for the present-day popularity and ease of bird study, and its value is comparable (and complementary) to that of illustrated bird books and field guides, which are of such great help in learning to identify birds. The binocular and the field guide, together, are indispensable to the birder. Many birders use a 7×35 binocular and the 8×40 is popular. See discussion of binoculars and telescopes and their selection and use in McElroy (1974); see also Dock (1948); Barton (1955); Ryan (1971). *See also* Birder; Check-list.

A *field glass* is an optical instrument composed of two simple telescopes brought together. Each telescope barrel has two lenses, one at each end, that together are capable of magnifying objects up to about four or five times. For greater magnification it would be necessary to design the field glass too large and too heavy for easy, practical use. Their field of view is also narrow compared to that of a prism binocular, but the field glass is simple to use and relatively inexpensive, therefore excellent to give to children who are interested in watching birds (Barton, 1955).

The term *field glass* should be used only in reference to a glass without prisms, and the term *binocular* reserved for the prism binocular (Reichert and Reichert, 1951).

Field glasses are useful not only for children but for adults when watching birds at close range—near the house, in the garden, or at the feeding station close by. For watching birds at longer distances, and for greater assurance of seeing marks or colors that help to identify them, a binocular is needed. A field glass of at least 6 power (usually written 6x) or 7 power (7x) is generally adequate.

BINOCULAR VISION
See Eyes and Eyesight.

BINOMIAL, or BINOMINAL, NOMENCLATURE

Term for the system of giving animals and plants two names—a genus name (*see* Genus) and a species name (*see* Species). *See* discussion of this system under Linnaeus; *also* Classification; Taxonomy; Names and Naming.

BIOCHROMES

A term for *pigment* colors of birds or their "true" colors as contrasted with those caused by feather structure (Fox, 1944). *See* Colors of Feathers.

BIOGEOGRAPHY

Term for the geography, or distribution, of animals and plants—the living things of the earth. The animals and plants in various assemblages or communities tend to have similar resemblances and differences, locally, regionally, and on an intercontinental scale. Polar bears live in the Arctic, but grizzlies in w. U.S. and Canada; wild tigers live in Asia, lions in Africa, and wild kangaroos in Australia. These common observations show that communities of living things have a geography of their own, which, because it relates to life, is called *biogeography* (Simpson *et al.*, 1957). *See also* Distribution; Faunal Regions.

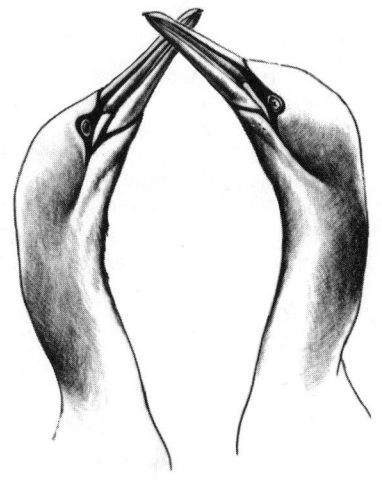

BILLING
A pair of gannets face each other, stretch their necks, raise their bills high, and clatter them together rapidly. This "billing" display, which occurs during courtship and throughout the nesting cycle, appears to reduce the aggression between the two and strengthen the pair bond.

BIOLOGICAL DISCONTINUITIES
See Discontinuities.

BIOLOGICAL SURVEY, U.S.
See Economic Ornithology.

BIOLOGY
The science of life. The knowledge and study of living plants and animals—broadly, zoology, botany, physiology, morphology, genetics, embryology, and allied sciences. In common usage, biology means the study of principles of the origin, development, structure, functions, and distribution of plants and animals and the general phenomena of their lives, growth, and reproduction; "biology" is also used in a narrower sense for *ecology*, or *bionomics*. See definition and scope of in Simpson *et al.* (1957).

BIOME
Term for a major community, such as tundra, coniferous forest, deciduous forest, and grassland, combined with its own community of animal life. Plants play a predominant role in determining what animals live in a region, and green plants are the beginning of all animal food chains (Simpson *et al.*, 1957). *See* Food Chain.

The biome's plant community, or plant formation, has been determined by climate and is called a *climax*—the final and most stable type of plant life possible under the prevailing climate; it is a direct expression of the climate. Climaxes, or major plant formations, are vast and of great permanence unless destroyed by man (Weaver and Clements, 1938). *See* Climax Community.

The dominant plants of each biome give it its form, or characteristic appearance—for example, the coniferous trees of the vast northern coniferous forest; the beach-maple, oak-hickory, or oak-chestnut of the great deciduous forest that once covered most of e. N. America; the grasses of the narrow humid zone of grassland we call prairies; and the dry grassland of our western plains (Buchsbaum and Buchsbaum, 1957).

On land these biomes provide the ecological setting for the birds and other animals adapted to each, which find in them the food, shelter, and other conditions of climate in which they can survive and raise their young. *See*, for example, Habitat Choices of Birds under Distribution.

Many bird species have an attachment for the biome of which they are a part, and those represented in coniferous forest or grassland in one part of the country often live in the same biome in another part of the country, even when they are in widely separated zones of temperature. The distribution of some birds coincides quite closely with the biome of which they are a part, but not all birds are controlled by it. *The value of the biome concept as a part of bird study is that it shows that birds and other animals are not distributed haphazardly over the continent* (Pough, 1949).

The biome concept was developed in N. America by Frederic E. Clements, a plant ecologist, and Victor E. Shelford, an animal ecologist (Clements and Shelford, 1939). It was first applied in detail to the distribution of American birds by Frank A. Pitelka (Pitelka, 1941). Biomes are also called *biotic communities*. *See* discussion under Ecosystem.

Other ideas for dividing N. America into biogeographical areas occupied by certain birds and other animals are the *life zone* concept (*see* Distribution) and the *biotic province*. See critical discussion of the *biome, biotic province,* and *life zone* in Ch. 8 of Amadon (1966b). *See also* Biotic Province.

BIOSPHERE
See Ecosystem.

BIOTA
Collective term for the flora and fauna (plants and animals) of a region.

BIOTIC COMMUNITY
See Biome and especially Ecosystem; *also* Major Biotic Communities under Distribution.

BIOTIC PROVINCE
According to Dice (1943), a biotic province "covers a considerable and continuous geographic area and is characterized by the occurrence of one or more important ecological associations of adjacent provinces. In general, biotic provinces are characterized also by peculiarities of vegetation type, ecological climax, flora, fauna, climate, physiography, and soil."

Dice points out that a biotic province differs from a biome in at least one important way: *a biotic province is never discontinuous* (except on marine islands), whereas a biome is coincident with its plant climaxes, and however far from the main area of the climax, if the climax is the same, it belongs to the same biome. *See* Biome.

Van Tyne and Berger (1959) declare that critics of the biotic province concept claim that these provinces are largely subjective and have never been adequately defined. Alden H. Miller (1951) applied all three major systems—Life Zones, Biomes, and Biotic Provinces—in a study of the distribution of the birds of Calif. and concluded that they are not necessarily mutually exclusive, as the proponents of each system have commonly assumed, and that "each . . . has some, although perhaps not equal, usefulness and expresses certain truths." *See* Life Zones under Distribution.

BIPEDALISM
Term among zoologists for an upright posture in locomotion whereby an animal walks or runs on its two hind feet. Quite a few vertebrates besides man share this upright locomotor posture—for example, many reptiles that lived in the Mesozoic (*see* Geological Time Scale), some living reptiles, birds, and kangaroos. According to Du Brul (1962): "Bipedalism in birds is the consequence of an adaptation for flying." *See* Hopping vs. Walking; Origin of Birds and of Bird Flight in Fossil Birds.

BIRD
A word for which the etymology is unknown, according to Newton (1893–96), but in Old English the word was *brid*, which was originally the name for the young of animals.

Coues (1884) specifically described a bird as a creature whose body is covered with feathers, a kind of skin outgrowth no other animals possess; the blood is hot (a bird is a warm-blooded animal); the heart is perfectly four-chambered; there is but one (the right) aortic arch, which with one pulmonary artery (the left) springs from the heart; the aortic and the pulmonary artery have each three semilunar valves. The lungs are fixed and molded to the cavity of the chest, and some of the air passages run through them to admit air to other parts of the body, as under the skin and in various bones (*see* The Air Sacs under Respiratory System; *also* Circulatory System). Reproduction is oviparous; the eggs are very large, in consequence of the copious yolk and white, have a hard chalky shell, and are hatched outside the body of the parent. There are always four limbs, of which the fore or pectoral pair are strongly distinguished from the hind or pelvic pair, being modified into *wings,* fitted for flying, if at all, by means of feathers. See also Tordoff's definition (1961).

BIRD-ATTRACTING
Term for luring wild birds to one's yard, garden, or larger property for study and enjoyment of them or to help them through difficult times (winter) by providing them with their basic needs of food, shelter, and water. Some of those who attract birds are housewives, teachers, laborers, business executives, lawyers, doctors, government officials, biologists, schoolchildren, etc. According to a report by DeGraaf and Thomas (1974), 43% of households in Amherst, Mass., and 23.8% of households in Boston fed birds. When the relatively low Boston rate was extrapolated for the whole state, in 1972, it was estimated that 419,000 Mass. householders fed birds and spent $3,439,000 doing it. Some birds return to winter bird feeders with remarkable faithfulness. In Ont., Louise de Kiriline Lawrence reported a black-capped chickadee that returned each winter for 9 years, a gray jay for 10, a hairy woodpecker for 16. All were banded birds, so that the individuals were recognizable.

FEEDING BIRDS. Those who attract birds either build or buy bird feeders in which to offer food for birds, or scatter a wild bird seed mixture on the ground, but it is usually preferable to put the bird food in feeding trays or in covered feeders in conspicuous places and near shelter in the garden. Most bird-attractors set up several feeders in the yard, as one may soon be overcrowded with birds, thus preventing the smaller ones from feeding.

Besides wild bird seed mixtures, bird-attractors offer bread, scratch feed (cracked corn), and mixtures of corn bread, suet, and peanut butter as recommended by Dennis (1975) and Terres (1977). Suet (hard beef suet) is put out for birds in special feeders, and the wild bird seed mixtures are either mixed by the bird-attractor or bought in ready mixes sold by many chain grocery stores, by feed stores, and by dealers in bird-attracting supplies. See dealers listed, and illustrated methods of attracting birds, in Terres (1968c; 1977), with a special chapter on feeding hummingbirds. *See also* Hand-taming of Wild Birds under Tameness.

SHELTER. Trees, shrubs, and vines, planted in the yard or garden, provide shelter for birds and places for them to nest. These should also be chosen for their ornamental value as well as their value to birds in offering them fruits or seeds. See planting recommendations and regional lists of trees, shrubs, and vines, and their usefulness to birds, in Terres (1968c; 1977).

WATER. Birds need water to drink and in which to bathe (they bathe and drink in the same water in the garden bath) in summer and in winter. Birdbaths are also sold by dealers in gardening supplies and by those who sell bird-attracting supplies. In summer, water may be more important or necessary to birds than food put out for them, especially in hot, dry parts of the country such as the Southwest and Far West. *See* discussion of this under Heat and Birds; *also* Respiratory System.

BIRDHOUSES. According to Kalmbach and McAtee (1930), there are about 38 species of birds that will nest in bird houses, or nest boxes, although 48 species have been reported doing so. Many of the bluebirds, titmice, chickadees, nuthatches, wrens, tree swallows, all woodpeckers, and certain other birds that nest in the hollows or cavities of trees and dead limbs, will nest in bird houses. Nest boxes for birds must be built to a specified size for each species or the birds for which they are intended may not nest in them. Also, if the entrance hole is large enough for larger birds, such as starlings, to enter, these larger birds will usurp the nest boxes intended for the smaller species. The diameter of the entrance hole to the nest box determines what kinds of birds may enter it. Following is a table of sizes of bird boxes, each of which should be built according to the species of bird one wishes to attract. *See also* Bluebird Trail.

NESTING SHELF or Nest Bracket. A small, roofed wooden platform put up by bird-attractors on the sides of garages or other buildings as nesting places for robins, barn swallows, phoebes, and song sparrows. The shelf has all sides open, or only three, two, or one side open, but should have a sloping roof to keep rain off the nesting bird. The nesting shelf for robins, phoebes, and swallows is usually nailed under the eaves, within 6–15 ft. from the ground. For a song sparrow, it should be placed within 1–3 ft. of the ground (Terres, 1968c; 1977).

Dimensions for Nesting Shelves with One or More Sides Open

Kind of Bird	Size[1]	Depth[2]	Height[3]
Robin	6 × 8	8	6–15
Barn swallow	6 × 6	6	8–12
Song sparrow	6 × 6	6	1–3
Phoebe	6 × 6	6	8–12

1 size of floor (inches)
2 depth inside (inches)
3 height to fasten above ground (feet)

BIRD-ATTRACTING

Kind of birds	Size of floor (in.)	Depth of box (in.)	Height of entrance hole above floor (in.)	Diameter of entrance hole(in.)	Height to fasten above ground (ft.)
bluebird	5x5	8	6	1½	5–10
chickadee	4x4	8–10	6–8	1⅛	6–15
titmouse	4x4	8–10	6–8	1¼	6–15
nuthatch	4x4	8–10	6–8	1¼	12–20
house wren and Bewick's wren	4x4	6–8	4–6	1–1¼	6–10
Carolina wren	4x4	6–8	4–6	1½	6–10
violet-green swallow and tree swallow	5x5	6	1–5	1½	10–15
purple martin*	6x6	6	1	2½	15–20
house finch	6x6	6	4	2	8–12
starling	6x6	16–18	14–16	2	10–25
crested flycatcher	6x6	8–10	6–8	2	8–20
flicker	7x7	16–18	14–16	2½	6–20
golden-fronted woodpecker and red-headed woodpecker	6x6	12–15	9–12	2	12–20
downy woodpecker	4x4	8–10	6–8	1¼	6–20
hairy woodpecker	6x6	12–15	9–12	1½	12–20
screech owl	8x8	12–15	9–12	3	10–30
saw-whet owl	6x6	10–12	8–10	2½	12–20
barn owl	10x18	15–18	4	6	12–18
American kestrel	8x8	12–15	9–12	3	10–30
wood duck	10x18	10–24	12–16	4	10–20
prothonotary warbler	5x5	8	6	1½	5–10

*These are dimensions for one compartment, or a martin house for one pair of birds. It is customary to build martin houses eight compartments at a time, which constitutes a section.

Where to Place Nest Boxes: They should be set on top of posts set in the ground (either on top of the post or on the side), or on the side of a tree, or side of a building.

BIRD-BANDING
See Banding.

BIRD-BANDING
A publication. *See* Ornithological Periodicals.

BIRD CITY
Term for large concentrations of colonially nesting birds. Bird cities are occupied predominantly by gannets, murres, shearwaters, and other seabirds along coasts, usually on rocky islands; also by herons, ibises, egrets, and other water birds that nest together in large rookeries in coastal and inland swamps and marshes. Some of the largest of these bird cities are on the Dry Tortugas in the Gulf of Mexico (sooty terns) off the Fla. coast, the gannet ledges of Bonaventure Is., Gaspé Pen., Canada, the white ibis rookeries of the Fla. Everglades, and the murres of Three Arch Rocks, Ore., and the Aleutian Is., Alaska. Hundreds of thousands of birds nest in these colonies—an estimated 100,000 sooty terns on Dry Tortugas (Sprunt, 1954a), 100,000 to 400,000 white ibises in Fla., and 750,000 murres on Three Arch Rocks. *See* account of enormous nesting colonies of murres in Auk Family.

Unique in N. America at the time was Bird City at Avery Is., La., a private sanctuary owned by the late E. A. McIlhenny. He began it in 1892 with the building of a dam to impound water. Egrets had become scarce and were threatened with extinction owing to a demand for their plumes in the millinery trade. *See* Feather Trade. McIlhenny brought in eight live snowy egrets to his island sanctuary and from these developed an enormous nesting colony, one of the largest heron rookeries on record, which he appropriately called Bird City. See Lowery (1951a); *also* Wildlife Refuges; Sanctuary.

BIRD CLUBS
Groups of people who have organized in order to further their individual knowledge of and interest in birds. One of the attractive functions of bird clubs is the friendships formed between men, women, and young people at the meetings and on the field trips to see birds. One may join the National Audubon Society, a state Audubon Society, or one of the hundreds of branches or affiliates of the National Audubon Society or of state bird societies, all of which are "bird clubs" or natural history clubs. There are excellent advantages in belonging to the national and state groups, but it is the local bird clubs in cities, towns, and villages that are the most numerous and offer more active personal participation and a quick means of learning the local birds. Examples in two large eastern cities are the Linnaean Society of New York, which meets at the American Museum of Natural History, and the Delaware Valley Ornithological Club (DVOC), which holds its meetings in the Philadelphia Academy of Natural Sciences.

Each local club has experienced bird-watchers or professional ornithologists who inspire beginners and teach them how to identify birds and where to look for them, or can help them with sound scientific methods of observation and useful ornithological projects. *See* Checklist; Birder. For instructions in forming a bird club, see Fink (1958), and especially Rickert (1978). For a list of publications of some of the national and local bird organizations, *see* Ornithological Periodicals.

BIRD DAY
A day set aside to teach schoolchildren of America the importance of protecting birds. Bird Day was originated by C. A. Babcock, Superintendent of Schools of Oil City, Pa. The first observance of it was held in the public schools of Oil City in May 1894. Two years later, the U.S. Department of Agriculture issued a circular urging all public schools to observe a special Bird Day in the interest of bird protection. Local schools chose the day and manner of observance of Bird Day, which is similar to exercises held for Arbor Day, and the two programs were frequently combined. Bird Day in some states is (or was) on Apr. 3, the birthday of John Burroughs, in others on Apr. 26, the birthday of John James Audubon. *See* State Birds.

BIRDER
Term usually applied to one who is an amateur in his interest in birds—that is, not professionally employed in work with birds. The terms "birder" and "birding" (both are more active terms than the older British terms "birdwatcher" and "bird-watching") are preferred by Peterson (1966) and others. Birding ranges from simple listing of birds locally each day to the swift travel to far places in N. America to get as large a list as possible for the entire country within a year, to serious studies that may involve many years of banding or observations in the backyard, and other studies in both the laboratory and the field, like those of the professional ornithologist, with whom the amateur birder may often work in special studies.

Many birders participate in the Christmas Bird Count (*see* Christmas Bird Count) and breeding-bird censuses sponsored by the National Audubon Society and U.S. Fish and Wildlife Service cooperatively, others in what is called the Big Day, a spring "roundup," or a bird count similar to that of the Christmas Bird Count but taken usually in May at the height of spring bird migration (see Peterson, 1948; Fischer, 1953). Another birding hobby is bird-attracting (*see* Bird-Attracting), not only for the pleasure of bringing birds into the yard and garden but for studies of their habits and behavior. The big game of bird listing around the country evolved into a competitive and cooperative individual venture in which those who have identified 600 species or more in N. America (*see* geographical definition under North America) within a year are eligible for membership in the "600 Club." The idea for the 600 Club is credited to Stuart Keith, who was the first unofficial secretary of the club. See Keith (1963), and details in Piatt (1973). As of Jan. 1980, headquarters of the 600 Club were 2699 Twiggs Circle, Marietta, Ga. 30067. *See also Birding,* a publication of the American Birding Association, under Ornithological Periodicals.

For most people, birding is a hobby, and an addiction to it is considered incurable and carries with it a lifetime guarantee against boredom (Millar, 1967). For a discussion of birding activities, see Wallace (1963); Fisher (1940; 1951); for methods of identifying birds, see Pet-erson (1949); for etiquette in birding, see Glinski (1976).

According to the Bureau of Sports Fisheries and Wildlife (see Anonymous, 1965b), based on a survey by the Bureau of Outdoor Recreation, there were 8,196,000 birders in the United States, with the definition of bird-watching as "the act of observing birds in their natural surroundings often . . . with binoculars or special equipment." The Cornell Laboratory of Ornithology modified this figure with an estimate of about 3 million people who are seriously interested in field study of birds, for which they buy binoculars, field guides, etc. For an article about equipment required by birders, types of binoculars chosen, cameras and other bird photography equipment and their use, see Cruickshank (1966); for instructions in bird photography specifically, see Cruickshank (1957); Kinne (1962).

BIRD FINDING. This term was coined by birders not only for the action of finding birds but specifically where to find them. For regional places to watch hawks, eagles, and other birds of prey in migration, *see* the end of the introduction to Hawk Family.

Issues of *American Birds* and *Birding* (see Ornithological Periodicals) give information about where to find birds nationally; see also the following books: *The Bird Watcher's America,* by Olin Sewall Pettingill (New York; McGraw-Hill Co., 1965); *A Birdwatcher's Guide to the Eastern United States,* by Alice M. Geffen (Woodbury, N.Y.: Barron's, 1978); *Birdwatcher's Guide to Wildlife Sanctuaries,* by Jessie Kitching (New York: Arco Publishing Co., 1976); *Complete Outfitting and Source Book for Bird Watching,* by Michael Scofield (Marshall, Calif.: The Great Outdoors Trading Company, 1978), which includes a chapter, "Birding Sites," on where to find birds in each of our fifty states; *A Guide to Bird Finding: East of the Mississippi,* by Olin Sewall Pettingill (New York: Oxford University Press, 1951; revised edition, 1977); *A Guide to Bird Finding: West of the Mississippi,* by Olin Sewall Pettingill (New York: Oxford University Press, 1953); *Guide to National Wildlife Refuges,* by Laura and William Riley (Garden City, N.Y.: Anchor Press/Doubleday, 1979); *Roger Tory Peterson's Dozen Birding Hot Spots,* by George H. Harrison (New York: Simon and Schuster, 1976).

BIRD-FLIES
See Hippoboscid Flies.

BIRD HAWK
A common general name for the goshawk, Cooper's hawk, and sharp-shinned hawk, all of which feed to some extent on other birds. The small sharp-shinned hawk is especially a feeder on small songbirds, but it, along with the Cooper's hawk, eats many starlings and may help to be a check on the starling numbers. Rather than being detrimental to the small-bird population, the sharp-shinned hawk merely helps to keep the population of small birds within bounds. *See* Balance of Nature. Predation of the bird hawks is only one factor in limiting the numbers of small birds; diseases

and accidents are considered by biologists to be far more decimating to the small-bird population. *See also* Accipiter; Hawk Family.

BIRDHOUSES
See Bird-attracting.

BIRD LICE
See Lice.

BIRD OF PREY
Name usually applied to any of the carnivorous (meat-eating) birds, such as hawks, eagles, falcons, and owls. *See* Predators.

BIRD OF SATAN
Name in se. U.S. folklore for the blue jay. *See* Folklore of Birds.

BIRD PHOTOGRAPHY
See Birder.

BIRD SANCTUARY
See Sanctuary; *also* Hawk Mountain Sanctuary; Wildlife Refuge.

BIRDS AS "COLLECTORS"
(of other animals). *See* Owl Family; *also* Food and Feeding Habits; Pellet.

BIRDS AS PETS
See Age; Care and Feeding of Abandoned or Injured Birds; *also* Legal Protection.

BIRDS AS WATCHDOGS
See Acuteness of Hearing in Birds under Ears and Hearing.

BIRD SKINS
Truly the skins of birds (including their feathers, feet, skull, and bill) which have been collected (usually shot) by ornithologists and professional collectors of bird skins for universities, museums, or private collections. After shooting the bird, the ornithologist peels the skin from its body in a deft operation, using a scalpel and scissors or a sharp knife. *See* account of speed of skinning under Henshaw, and detailed instructions, "Making Birdskins," in Chapman (1930). For details about methods of collecting and preserving bird skins for further study, see in Pettingill (1970).

Hundreds, or even thousands, of skins of birds are often kept by ornithologists in their private collections (*see* Collections), but the largest numbers have been assembled in our great natural history museums, where the skins are available from the curator for study and comparisons by students in ornithology. *See* Curator.

Anyone who collects birds or wishes to collect them for study (most birds are protected by law either at all times or may be taken only during the hunting season—waterfowl, for example) must have a scientific collector's permit both from the federal government and the government of the state in which one lives.

With modern high-power binoculars or telescopes and with illustrated bird guides, it is no longer necessary to collect a bird simply to identify it; *see*, however, exceptions discussed under Check-list. Birds are collected usually by scientists and students who are making particular studies of certain species, of which there may not be sufficient numbers of study skins available from museums. Some of these studies may be of the molts and plumage variations of a species, or of its geographic races (subspecies) and their evolution, etc. See very useful discussion in Parkes (1963).

BIRD SPECIES
For number of species in N. America and the world, *see* Species.

BIRD STAMPS
See Duck Stamps.

BIRD STUDY
A publication. *See* England under Ornithological Periodicals.

BIRD-WATCHER
See Birder.

BISEXUALITY
See Embryo and Its Development.

BITTERN
See in Heron Family.

BLACKBIRD
See in Troupial Family.

BLACK-BREAST
See Plover, American golden, and Plover, black-bellied, in Plover Family.

BLACKBURNE
ANNA (1726–93). English botanist, whom Johann Gmelin in Linnaeus' *Systema Naturae* (1788) honored with the scientific species name of the Blackburnian warbler, *Motacilla blackburniae* (see American Ornithologists' Union, 1895). It was Thomas Pennant, however, who first gave this bird its English name, Blackburnian warbler, in his *Arctic Zoology*, published in 1785. According to Wystrach (1975), Pennant did so in gratitude to Anna Blackburne for specimens of N. American birds she had sent him. Anna Blackburne maintained a museum of American birds at her home near Warrington, Lancashire, England, and her brother Ashton, living in America, supplied her with birds from N.Y., N.J., and Conn. Pennant used these extensively in compiling his *Arctic Zoology* (Wystrach, 1974). See other details of scientific name changes of this bird in American Ornithologists' Union (1895; 1910); *also* discussion of Pennant in Stresemann (1975).

BLACK HAG
See Shearwater, sooty, in Shearwater Family.

BLACK HAGDON
See Shearwater, sooty, in Shearwater Family.

BLACK-HEAD
See Duck, ring-necked; Scaup, greater; and Scaup, lesser; in Duck Family; *also* Grosbeak, black-headed, in Finch Family.

BLACKHEAD
(enterohepatitis). A disease of domestic poultry and wild game birds caused by a tissue parasite that attacks the liver and caeca of birds; a well-known one is *Histomonas meleagridis*, a flagellate with an amoeba phase that may be harmless or produce mild infection if present in the intestine of chickens, but in turkeys invades the liver and intestinal wall, causing a mortal illness commonly called blackhead.

The parasite does not form a cyst but is transmitted directly when a bird accidentally ingests contaminated feces of infected birds or the eggs of the caecal worm *Heterakis*, which acts as a transport host. For a full discussion of blackhead, see Becker (1959) and in Wehr (1971).

The caecal worm *Heterakis gallinarum* is the best-known of all worms of poultry (Rothschild and Clay, 1957) and is notorious as the carrier of the blackhead disease organism, *Histomonas meleagridis;* the worm is thought to be the probable carrier of blackhead to quail; ruffed grouse succumb to the disease in captivity (Becker, 1959). Blackhead is believed to have been a factor in the decline and eventual extinction of the heath hen (Grange, 1949). *See* Heterakiasis; *also* Diseases. *See* Heath hen in Grouse Family; *also* Extinct Birds of North America.

BLACKIE
See Duck, black, in Duck Family.

BLACKJACK
See Duck, black; Duck, ring-necked; and Scaup, lesser; in Duck Family.

BLACKPOLL
See Blackpoll warbler in Warbler—American Wood Warbler Family.

BLACK-TAIL
See Godwit, Hudsonian, in Sandpiper Family.

BLACK WARRIOR
See Hawk, Harlan's, in Hawk Family.

BLACK WITCH
See Ani in Cuckoo Family.

BLADDER
Birds, except for the ostrich, have no bladders (Sperber, 1960). The ureters open into the cloaca and the urine is normally voided together with, and apparently mixed with, the feces. *See* Cloaca; Digestion.

BLEATER
See Snipe, common, in Sandpiper Family.

BLINDNESS
See Deformities; *also* story of white pelican under Helpers among Birds.

BLOOD
See Circulatory System.

BLOOD QUILL
See Pinfeather.

BLUEBILL

See Duck, ring-necked; Duck, ruddy; Scaup, greater; and Scaup, lesser; in Duck Family.

BLUEBIRD

See in Thrush Family.

BLUEBIRD TRAIL

Term for a series of bluebird houses put up along country roads where these birds are likely to nest (*see* in biographies of bluebirds in Thrush Family). Dr. T. E. Musselman of Quincy, Ill., is thought to be the originator of this idea. Bluebirds had disappeared from his part of the country and he wanted to see them come back. His first experiments were in the spring of 1933 and 1934, when he put up 22 and 50 nest boxes, respectively. During Feb. 1935, he placed 102 bluebird houses along 43 mi. of country road, of which 88, or 86%, were occupied by bluebirds. In his published report about this conservation project (Musselman, 1935), he wrote that "for the first time in twenty years, bluebirds are a common sight along the roads of Adams County, Illinois, and I believe any other enthusiast can duplicate this." For a full account and methods of establishing trails, see Terres (1968c). *See* specifications for bluebird houses in Bird-Attracting.

BLUEBOTTLE FLY

See Protocalliphora; *also* Screwworm.

BLUE DARTER

See Accipiter and under Hawk Family.

BLUE JAY

See in Crow Family.

BLUE JAY, THE

A publication. *See* Canada under Ornithological Periodicals; *also* biography of the blue jay (bird) in Crow Family.

BLUE LIST, THE

List of N. American birds that are of special concern to conservationists; those "which have recently or are currently giving indications of non-cyclical [*see* Cycle] population declines, or range contractions either locally or widespread" (Arbib, 1971).

The birds on the Blue List are not to be confused with the very rare or officially endangered species (*see* Rare and Threatened Species), although some of the birds on the Blue List may be rare and local and others may be rapidly nearing the endangered status. The list excludes those birds already proclaimed to be endangered. See Arbib (1971) for other details; also Arbib (1972; 1973; 1974) and Kibbe (1976).

BLUE METEOR

See Pigeon, passenger, in Pigeon Family.

BLUE PETER

A common name for the American coot, which runs on surface of water before it takes off; also for the common gallinule and purple gallinule in se. U.S.; "Peter" for a bird that can apparently walk on water (when walking on floating plants they appear to be walking on water), seemingly in allusion to St. Peter. *See* details in Storm-Petrel Family.

BLUE POP

See Grosbeak, blue, in Finch Family.

BLUE ROCK

Shortened name, especially in Great Britain, for "blue rock pigeon," the rock dove; also an alternate common name in U.S. for the red-billed pigeon. *See* accounts of these species under Pigeon Family.

BLUESHANKS

See Avocet, American, in Avocet Family.

BLUESTOCKING

See Avocet, American, in Avocet Family.

BLUETHROAT

See in Thrush Family.

BLUE-WING

See Teal, blue-winged, in Duck Family.

BOAT-BILLED HERON FAMILY

See Ciconiiformes.

BOATSWAIN

See Jaeger, parasitic, in Skua Family; *see* reason for name under Bosun Bird.

BOBOLINK

See in Troupial Family.

BOBWHITE,

or BOBWHITE QUAIL.
See in Pheasant Family.

BOG-BULL

Local name for the American bittern in the Heron Family, from its hollow pumping sounds.

BOG HEN

See Bittern, American, in Heron Family.

BOGSUCKER

See Woodcock, American, in Sandpiper Family.

BOG-TROTTER

See Bittern, American, in Heron Family.

BOLUS

A mass or ball of food swallowed by a bird. *See* Digestion.

BOMBYCILLIDAE

See Waxwing Family.

BONAPARTE

CHARLES LUCIEN JULES LAURENT (1803–57). Honored in American ornithology by the English name Bonaparte's gull by George Ord, Philadelphia ornithologist. Born in Paris; his father, Lucien Bonaparte, had been honored with the title Prince of Canino; Charles Lucien, his eldest son, who had been granted the papal title Prince of Musignano, was early in life attracted to natural history, soon specializing in birds. In 1822, when he was only 19, he married his cousin Zenaide, firstborn daughter of Napo-

leon's oldest brother, Joseph, and soon after, when Joseph moved to his large estate at Bordentown, N.J., 25 mi. from Philadelphia, Charles Lucien and his wife followed (Stresemann, 1975). In Philadelphia, Bonaparte began his studies of American birds. During his five years there (1823–28), he became a member of the Academy of Natural Sciences and devoted his attention to continuing Alexander Wilson's work with several volumes; the first (1825) was titled *American Ornithology; or, the Natural History of Birds Inhabiting the United States Not Given by Wilson.* "He was the father of systematic ornithology in America" (Palmer, 1928). In 1828, Charles Lucien went back to Europe, not to return, and continued his distinguished and energetic career. See Stresemann's long and interesting account (1975) of the life and zoological accomplishments of Bonaparte. Bonaparte described and named for science such N. American birds as Cooper's hawk, white-winged scoter, and Swainson's hawk, and also named a number of genera. See A.O.U. *Check-list* (1957), and *Encyclopaedia Britannica* (1969 ed.).

BONES

Of great interest and importance to ornithologists in their studies of birds. The bones reveal something about a bird's evolution and its relationships to other animals; also, since the bones are usually the only parts of birds that are preserved as fossils, they give almost the only clue of the kinds of animals that lived in former times. *See* discussion under Origin of Birds and of Bird Flight under Fossil Birds.

Some of the bones of birds have been especially studied by ornithologists—taxonomists specifically—and their characters (shapes, sizes, placement, arrangement, etc.) have been compared to establish relationships, or to show differences, between groups of birds. For example, the nostrils, or nares (*see* Nostrils), of birds and the nasal cavities are often cited by taxonomists in classifying birds; also the bones of the palate and of the breastbone, or sternum. *See* discussion under Classification. The "unkeeled" or "keeled" condition of the breastbone was for a long time used to define two major groups of birds—the ratite and carinate birds (Van Tyne and Berger, 1959). *See* Carinate; Ratite.

The bones of most birds are porous; many are filled with air, not marrow, and are connected with the respiratory organs. *See* Respiratory System; *also* Swimming and Diving. If air is blown into the upper arm or thighbone of a fresh-killed bird, the air escapes through the bill of the bird and may even produce a musical note in the bird's throat (Hess, 1951). Hunters sometimes blow through the wingbones of turkeys to produce the plaintive note of the hen in luring turkeys close enough for a shot. *See* Turkey Family; *also* Skeleton.

BONXIE

See Skua in Skua Family.

BOOBY FAMILY

Sulidae (SUE-lih-dee); from *sula*, Icelandic for gannet. Includes the similar boobies and gannets—9 species of goose-sized seabirds; the gannets, of 3 species, live in northern and southern temperate waters; the six species of boobies roam the world's warm seas—three are widely distributed: the brown booby, from the "Caribbean and tropical Atlantic westward through the Pacific to n. Australia," and the red-footed booby and blue-faced (masked) booby of the tropical parts of the Atlantic, Pacific, and Indian O.; all three nest on Ascension, an island owned by the British in the S. Atlantic (Thomson, 1964e). Three have more restricted ranges: the little-known Abbott's booby, *Sula abbotti*, of the tropical part of the Indian O.; the blue-footed booby, from Mexico to Peru and the Galápagos Is.; and the Peruvian booby, *Sula variegata*, the S. American "piquero," a guano bird (*see* Guano) of the mountainous coasts of Peru and Chile. One gannet lives in N. American waters; four species of boobies have been seen off N. American coasts.

Gannets and boobies have streamlined, spindle-shaped bodies, generally white in adults, and all have straight, sharp bills; long, wedge-shaped, or pointed, tails; long, pointed wings; and short, strong legs and feet fully webbed (totipalmate). All dive for fishes from spectacular heights over water, then chase their prey under the surface. All have air sacs beneath the skin, just as in their relatives the pelicans, which cushion the impact of their steep dives into water. *See* Swimming and Diving; *also* discussion of relatives of gannets and boobies under Pelecaniformes. Only members of the family that are strongly migratory are the gannets. Albinism is apparently rare, as Gross (1965a) reported only one individual of one species.

The common name *booby* comes from the Spanish *bobo*, a dunce (Murphy, 1936); so named because of their apparent lack of fear, which makes them easy to catch (Gilliard, 1958); they cannot seem to learn that man is an enemy and were long ago called boobies by hungry sailors who caught them after they had landed on sailing ships and made no effort to escape. Boobies have survived, possibly because of their choice of lonely or inaccessible nesting places on islands or cliffs little visited by man (Austin, 1961); they are fond of flying fishes and seem to have learned that ships will disturb them (*see* like behavior of other birds under Commensalism); often accompany vessels and coast back and forth across ship's bow waiting for their prey to leap out of the water.

Both boobies and gannets are protected by federal law (*see* Legal Protection) and may not be kept in captivity without a permit; however, ill or injured birds may be kept alive until able to fend for themselves by feeding them small fishes thrown into water, or pieces of larger fish cut into strips roughly 1 in. across and 2–4 in. long; provide with pools or tanks with a little land to rest on (Walker, 1942).

Booby, blue-faced, *Sula dactylatra* (SUE-lah dack-tih-LAY-trah); genus name; from Icelandic *sula*, the gannet; species name: from Gr. *daktylus*, foot, and Lat. *atra*, black; "black-fingered," or "black-toed." (Color ill., page 52.) Large tropical white seabird with black-bordered wings seen occasionally in Gulf of Mexico off coast of s. Fla. (Dry Tortugas), Tex., and

La., has strayed north along Atlantic coast to Carolinas; 26–34 in. long; wingspread to 5 ft. 8 in. (Palmer, 1962); sexes outwardly alike; white gannetlike bird, largest of the boobies, has *black* pointed tail (gannet has white tail), smaller than gannet; has long, thin neck, large greenish bill; eyes yellow; black feathers on entire rear margin of its white wings (gannet has black outer half of wings); immature is dusky with white belly and white on back; boobies fly directly and rapidly, alternating steady wingbeats with glides over ocean, frequently follow ships, and when feeding, dive vertically from up to 40 ft. above water and submerge 6–10 ft., stay under about 6 seconds; seize fishes in bill, do not stab or spear, and swallow them while underwater; commonly chased by frigatebird, which pursues it and finally grabs booby by tail with its bill, thus forcing booby to disgorge fishes, which frigatebird catches in the air; not social like its relatives the pelicans; generally seen singly or in pairs; sometimes feeds in loose groups; frequently seen far at sea; male utters pathetic whistles, or trumpetings (Murphy, 1936); female, a quacking sound; commonly perches on buoys or pilings; commonly seen far from land riding on backs of sea turtles, where they may sleep with head tucked into back feathers; roosts on land on level ground (Palmer, 1962).

Feeding Habits: Eats flying fishes and small squids; feeds throughout day, returns to roost late afternoon or evening (Palmer, 1962).
Nest: In colonies, loose, scattered groups, on islands, sometimes in trees (Indian O.); present colonies in West Indies thriving; not molested there by man (Palmer, 1962).
Eggs: On Mexican islands, Mar.–May; usually 1, sometimes 2, chalky white.
Incubation: By both adults for about 43 days; age when young first fly 115 days.
Other Names: Masked booby; white booby.
Age: On Howland Is. in Pacific, of four banded there, three were between 22 and 23 years old when recaptured; one was 21 years, 8 months, old; one banded booby was recaptured on her nest when 22 years old (Clapp and Sibley, 1966). *See* Age; Eggs and Egg-laying; and Reproductive Life.
Hybrids: Has crossbred with brown booby; in one pair, the three hybrid young grew to adulthood (Gray, 1958).
Weights: Up to 5 lbs. (Palmer, 1962).
Range: Worldwide in tropical oceans; in S. Atlantic, nests in Greater and Lesser Antilles, on islands off Yucatán and Venezuela, Rocas Reef, Fernando de Noronha, s. coastal Brazil, and on Ascension Is., formerly on Bahamas; also nests on Revilla Gigedo group of islands off w. coast of Mexico; strays to Gulf coast of Tex. and north to the Carolinas.

Booby, blue-footed, *Sula nebouxii* (SUE-lah nee-BOO-ih-eye); genus name: *see* Booby, blue-faced; species name: in honor of Adolphe Simon Nebouxi, French surgeon-naturalist on ship *Vénus* on Pacific cruise, 1836–38 (Gruson, 1972) (Color ill., page 53). Medium-sized booby, casual visitor in late summer and early fall to Salton Sea, Calif., where high count of 48 seen Sept. 6, 1971 (Small, 1974); also sw. U.S.;

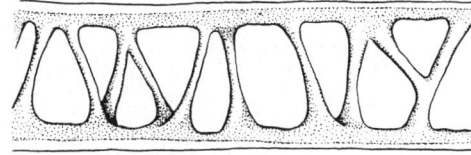

long section of a passerine bone

BONES
The bones of nearly all birds are filled with air rather than marrow. The extensive system of air sacs throughout the skeleton makes the bird lighter and provides internal ventilation, an important adaptation for flight.

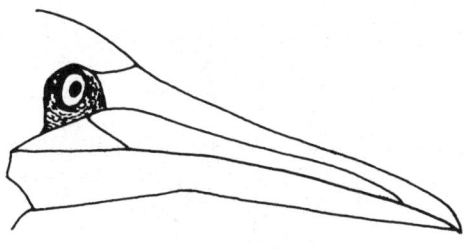

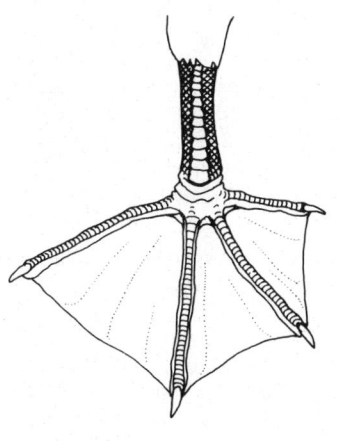

BOOBY FAMILY

ranges along Pacific coast to Galápagos Is. and Peru; 30–33 in. long; sexes outwardly alike; white with whitish head, blackish brown on back, tops of wings and tail; *bill bluish* in adult and feet *bright blue; white patch in upper back and white rump* in adult, distinctive; underwings are dark; adult male utters mild plaintive whistles; female, resonant trumpeting, as does young of both sexes.

Feeding Habits: Feeds almost entirely by diving from air for prey, dives from height of up to 50 ft. into water; occasionally takes flying fish in air; eats largely, if not entirely, fish, but little specific information about this (Palmer, 1962).

Nest: Not strictly in colonies, but often close together on ground; at nesting site is boldest of boobies.

Eggs: Mostly laid Oct.–Apr. on ground, seems to be throughout year on islands in Gulf of Calif.; 2–3, chalky, pale blue-green.

Incubation: By both sexes, 41 days; age when young first fly, 102 days.

Other Name: Camanay.

Age: One banded as juvenile was 17 years, 8 months old when recaptured on island of Oahu, Hawaii; two others were 16½ years old; one at least 17 was incubating an egg when recaptured (Clapp and Sibley, 1966).

Weights: Males (2), 2 lbs. 15 oz. and 3 lbs.; females (2), 3 lbs. 10 oz. and 3 lbs. 14 oz. (Murphy, 1936).

Range: Warm coastal waters, usually not far offshore; accidental in s. Calif. on Salton Sea and Big Bear Lake, San Bernardino County, and off coast of n. Wash.; nests on arid islands in Gulf of Calif., off w. coast of Mexico south, and on islands along coast of Ecuador, n. Peru, and Galápagos Is. Is one of "guano birds."

Booby, Brewster's. Once thought to be a distinct species, now regarded as subspecies of brown booby. *See* Booby, brown.

Booby, brown, *Sula leucogastor* (SUE-lah lew-koh-GAS-ter); genus name: *see* Booby, blue-faced; species name: from Gr. *leukos*, white, and *gaster*, belly; "white-bellied." (Color ill., page 53.) From warm tropical seas of Atlantic, Pacific, and Indian O. ranges north; in N. America, a casual visitor or rare along coast of s. Calif.; a straggler along Gulf coast of U.S. and along Atlantic coast as far as Me.; 26–29 in. long; wingspread 4½–5 ft.; sexes outwardly alike; only booby with entire upperparts (head, neck, back, and tail) dark brown; *white belly sharply marks off brown breast;* eyes (irises) white; eyelids, turquoise blue; bill and feet yellowish; utters loud or subdued quacks, grunts, brays, screeches.

Feeding Habits: Dives into water from 30–50 ft. above surface into ocean, remains under 25–40 seconds (*see* Swimming and Diving), prey is swallowed underwater or on surface; catches mullets, parrot fishes, and flatfishes but chiefly flying fishes and halfbeaks, which are staple diet (Murphy, 1936); usually feeds in daytime, more commonly in coastal waters, occasionally slides along crest of wave like a pelican.

Nest: On ground, bare sand or rock, on level or slope, sometimes prefers tops of cliffs, from which launches into flight.

Eggs: West Indies, fall to spring; 1–3, usually 2, chalky layer over pale bluish or greenish shell.

Incubation: By both sexes, in turn, 40–43 days (Palmer, 1962); young make limited flights about 105 days after hatching.

Other Names: Alcatraz; booby gannet; Catesby's booby; common booby; white-bellied booby; yellow-footed booby; *pájara bobo.*

Hybrids: See biography of blue-faced booby.

Weights: To about 2½ lbs. (Palmer, 1962).

Range: Appears casually in coastal waters of Tex., La., and Fla., Bermuda, se. Calif. (Imperial Dam), and w. Ariz. (Havasu Lake); strays to Mass. (Cape Cod), Long Is., N.Y. (Moriches Inlet and Mecox Bay) following tropical hurricanes; Bull, 1964, and Me.; in S. Atlantic, nests in Bahamas, Greater and Lesser Antilles, s. Gulf of Mexico, C. America; islands off Venezuela, s. coastal Brazil (St. Paul Rocks and Fernando de Noronha); and Cape Verde Is. off w. African coast, Ascension Is., and islets in Gulf of Guinea (Watson, 1966); also off e. coast of Baja Calif. and off w. coast of Mexico.

Booby, masked. *See* Booby, blue-faced.

Booby, red-footed, *Sula sula* (SUE-lah SUE-lah); genus and species names: *see* Booby, blue-faced. (Color ill., page 53.) Wanders to both coasts of Fla., Gulf of Mexico (Watson, 1966); 26–29½ in. long; wingspread 36–40 in.; sexes outwardly similar; smallest booby; has two color phases: (1) all-white with black wing tips and secondaries and (2) all-gray-brown (dark phase), including underwings, but usually with white rump, white tail, white lower belly; in both phases (*see* Phase), a golden cast to the head and much of the body; white tail of dark phase conspicuous at great distance; legs and feet of both phases orange-red; face and bill, light blue; in flight, several flaps and a long soar; when flying low over waves closely resembles Cory's shearwater; is most gregarious of all boobies at sea, frequently circles ships or alights on them, then easily caught because cannot take off from flat deck; utters loud, screeching squawks when disturbed; roosts in colonies and usually returns to islands to sleep (Palmer 1962). *See* Roosting.

Feeding Habits: Often feeds at dusk, especially catches flying fishes and squids (main food) by moonlight, feeds all night usually well out to sea (Murphy, 1936).

Nest: In colonies, usually in treetops, where adults can make good windward takeoff; build loose platform of sticks; male gathers materials, female does most of building; on treeless San Benedicto (Revella Gigedo group off w. coast of Mexico), nests on grass culms, 1–2 ft. high (Palmer, 1962).

Eggs: Belize, Nov.–Apr.; 1, chalky coating covers pale blue-green shell.

Incubation: 42½–46½ days; young fly 91–112 days after hatching.

Other Names: Tree booby; red-faced booby.

Age: One banded wild bird lived to 17 years, 9 months (Kennard, 1975); another 22 years, 10 months (Clapp, 1976).

Range: In N. American waters wanders rarely to Gulf of Mexico to coast of La. (one record, Lowery, 1960; 1974); in S. Atlantic, nests in Greater and Lesser Antilles, islands off C. America and Venezuela, Tobago, Fernando de Noronha, Trindade, s. coast of Brazil, Ascension Is. (Watson, 1966); also on Revilla Gigedo Is. off w. coast Mexico; ranges in Indian O. from Aldabra and Assumption Is. to Bay of Bengal, Java, Bali, Borneo, Malay Pen.; S. China Sea; Pacific to Wake, Hawaiian Is., New Guinea, ne. Australia, etc. (A.O.U. *Checklist*, 1957).

Bobby, white. *See* Booby, blue-faced.

Bobby, white-bellied. *See* Booby, brown.

Bobby, yellow-footed. *See* Booby, brown.

Gannet, or Northern gannet, *Morus bassanus* (MO-rus bass-AY-nus); genus name: Gr., foolish, silly; species name: coined by Carl Linnaeus for Bass Rock at mouth of Firth of Forth, Scotland, nesting place for gannets known since 1447; the one on Bird Rocks, in Gulf of St. Lawrence, known since 1534 (Fisher and Lockley, 1954). (Color ill., page 50.) In N. America, common in summer at nesting cliffs around Gulf of St. Lawrence; in winter, seen over Atlantic coastal waters south to Fla.; sexes outwardly alike; 35–40 in. long; wingspread 5½–6 ft.; adult, largely white with black outer half of wings; bigger than any gull, and gooselike in appearance; white body tapers at both ends; bill long, pale blue; is pointed downward in flight; skin at base of bill, and small gular (throat) patch, bare; head washed with cream, yellowish or buff; white tail is long, wedge-shaped, and pointed; adult soaring above breeding cliffs appears like white cross; adult plumage not attained until 3–4 years old; young in first fall and winter in "pepper and salt" plumage but at distance appears evenly dark; first-year birds are highly migratory and travel much farther south than adults; migrants appear off Atlantic coast from early Sept. into Dec., return north from Mar. into Apr. and May; is bird of coastal waters rather than oceanic, but sometimes seen several hundred miles out at sea; is exclusively marine; and for first 3 years of its life stays at sea all year; in flight, alternates rapid wingbeats (timed at slightly more than three beats per second from ship) with short glides 30–50 ft. above ocean; travels in single file, small flocks; when fishing, each bird alternately dives, slanting downward like a projectile at 60 ft. a second or more; strikes with great splash; floats high when resting on water owing to air-filled cellular tissues under skin of neck and breast which automatically fill with air before gannet dives; usually does not dive from surface (Fisher and Lockley, 1954); like their relatives the cormorants, which also dive for food, gannets have the outer nostril openings closed, or *impervious;* they drink salt water and ingest it with their food, and have salt glands (*see* function under Nostrils); have the totipalmate foot, the so-called "perfect" swimming foot with four toes webbed as do pelicans (*see* other features in common with relatives under Pelecaniformes); can swim rapidly on surface of water; are usually silent at sea but utter guttural croaks around nest; at least 3 years old before start to breed, and usually 5 (Nelson, 1965); up to 1959, six colonies, or gannetries, in N. America, with total of 16,000 breeding pairs (Palmer, 1962), located as follows—*in province of Quebec:* on Bonaventure Is., Gaspé Pen., Bird Rocks (Magdalen Is.), and Anticosti Is. (on Gullcliff Bay); *in Newfoundland:* on Bird Is. off Cape St. Marys (Avon Pen.), Baccalieu Is. (off Avon Pen.), and Funk Is. (see Palmer, 1962, for details and history of some of these colonies in Bent, 1922, and in Fisher and Lockley, 1954; see also Nettleship, 1976); for worldwide gannet population surveys, see Fisher and Vevers (1943; 1944); gannets cling to their nesting sites and never shift from them as cormorants and terns do; some of them doubtlessly occupied for 1,000 years or more.

Feeding Habits: Dives and swims about underwater but not to great depths (possibly no more than 50 ft. deep at most—see details in Fisher and Lockley, 1954); dives in rapid plunges of 50 ft. or more in air into schools of fishes close to surface of oceans and bays; besides mackerel and herring, eats pollack, garfish, haddock, whiting, and gurnard; hard skull structure and cushion of air cells under skin protect gannet on impact with water; while underwater, probably uses both wings and feet to swim; after grasping fish in the pointed bill, rises to swallow it on surface, then flies into air and soars about before next plunge; does not spear fish with bill but grabs it while coming up (Thomson, 1964e).
Nest: In colonies on ledges of cliffs and on flat-topped islands; nest is stack of seaweeds and debris; is highly social nester (Palmer, 1962, cites 5,000 occupied nests on 22 acres of Grassholm Is., Wales); apparently mates for life or until one or other of pair dies; mated pairs maintain pair bond through nesting season by elaborate ceremony at nest.
Eggs: Apr.–May; usually 1, pale blue, chalky.
Incubation: By both sexes, males slightly more than females; 42–44 days; in captivity, 43–45 days; parents feed chick semi-liquid, partly digested fish; about 84–87 days after hatching, in floundering flight reaches sea below nest site (Fisher and Lockley, 1954); still cannot fly or dive but swims out toward open sea; flies when 95–107 days old (Nelson, 1965).
Other Names: Common gannet; Gran Fou; Jan van Gent; northern gannet; solan goose; white gannet.
Accidents: Some choke to death trying to swallow gurnards—fishes with sharp spinous first dorsal fin that gets wedged in gannet's throat; also some killed by diving from air into fisherman's boat containing freshly caught fish; frequently killed by floating oil.
Age: One banded Que., 1922, shot in Newfoundland, 1939, when about 17 years old (Cooke, 1942). *See* ages of other seabirds in Albatross Family. *See also* under Age.
Flight Speed: Timed in Fla., 25 m.p.h. (Longstreet, 1930); 30 m.p.h. (Chapman, 1933); 25–48 m.p.h. (Palmer, 1962).

Weights: Adults 6–7 lbs. (Palmer, 1962).
Range: Nests on offshore islands and on inaccessible sea cliffs from Gaspé Pen., Que., Nova Scotia, and in Newfoundland to Iceland and south to British Isles; also ranges in summer to s. N.B., rarely to Mass.; in winter, rarely from Mass. south, not uncommon off e. coast Fla. and rather common in, at least, e. Gulf of Mexico but scarcely any Tex. records and none for West Indies; accidental in Great Lakes area and at Toronto, Niagara, and Ottawa in St. Lawrence Valley; in Mich., Ind., Ohio, Pa., N.Y., and Vt. (Palmer, 1962).

BOOMING GROUND
See Dancing Ground.

BOOTED
See Tarsus.

BOREAL FOREST
See Coniferous Forest.

BOREAL REGION
Term for the geographical area covered by three of the life zones of the northern part of the N. American continent. From north to south these are the *Arctic, Hudsonian,* and *Canadian,* each ecologically different in its typical plants and animals. The Life Zone System is still used by some authorities in mapping the ecological distribution of N. American birds. *See* Life Zones under Distribution.

BOSUN BIRD
One of common names of the tropic-birds, in reference to shape of projecting middle tail feathers that resemble boatswain's tool, the marlinespike (*see* in Tropic-bird Family); also another name for the jaegers (*see* in Skua Family), for the same reason (McAtee, 1957a).

BOTTERI
SIGNOR MATTEO (1808–77). Well-known Dalmatian botanist and traveler of the 19th century, for whom Philip Lutley Sclater named the Botteri's sparrow from a specimen of the bird collected by Botteri from Orizaba in s. Mexico. Dr. Sclater, a distinguished British ornithologist, named the sparrow for Botteri in 1857 "from a considerable collection of birds formed [by Botteri] in the vicinity of Orizaba ... where he has later been resident in pursuit of his investigations in various branches of natural history" (Sclater, 1857). See other facts in Gruson (1972).

BOTTLE-HEAD
See Plover, black-bellied, in Plover Family.

BOTULISM
(BOT-you-liz'm). A bacterial intoxicant of birds similar to that caused in man by eating spoiled canned foods; wild ducks and pheasants are especially affected (paralyzed) by eating foods containing a toxin (poison) produced by *Clostridium botulinum* type C, an anaerobe that is a natural inhabitant of the soil. It thrives on decaying plants and especially on dead animals; the poison is the end product of the *Clostridium* anaerobes and is the most potent known to man (Rosen, 1971b).

Botulism in birds was originally called "western duck sickness" because it was first reported in ducks from w. U.S. (as early as 1876); it occurs throughout N. America and was subsequently reported in Europe, South Africa, Uruguay, and Australia (Rosen, 1971b). The greatest waterfowl mortality in N. America has been, however, in the w. U.S. and western provinces of Canada, and the incidence of botulism is greatest in warm weather, between late July and mid-Sept., although milder losses may occur in spring while some ice is still on the water (Jensen and Williams, 1964). Incidence of botulism spreads rapidly in waterfowl when fertile soils containing the bacteria are covered by shallow water and warmed by the sun.

Waterfowl mortality has been greatest, in descending order, in the following states and provinces: Calif., Utah, S.D., N.D., Ore., Idaho, Tex., Neb., Sask., Alta., Man., Nev., Ariz., N.M., Minn., Mont., and Kans. In Calif., outbreaks extend from the Salton Sea close to the Mexican border north to Tule Lake and Klamath National Wildlife Refuges on the Ore. border; Utah is close second in botulism losses, which occur mostly among concentrations of ducks about Great Salt Lake (Rosen, 1971b).

BOUNTY
Term for money payments made by local and state governments to hunters and trappers for the feet, scalps, tails, etc. (as proof of killing), of animals such as hawks, owls, crows, and magpies among birds, and wolves, foxes, weasels, gophers, and certain other mammals that have been considered at times to be a threat to agricultural crops or to livestock. *See* discussions under Economic Ornithology; Egg-eating; Food and Feeding Habits; Predation. For some history of the bounty system and its failure economically and biologically, see Allen, D. (1954); Hamilton (1939); and especially Latham (1960). See also Matthiessen (1959). *See* Control; Legal Protection.

BOURCIER
JULES. *See* Hummingbird, Costa's, and Woodstar, Bahama, in Hummingbird Family.

BOWHEAD-BIRD
Name for phalaropes from their association with bowhead whales and eating same food (McAtee, 1923).

BRAIN
A wonderfully complex "switchboard" whose various centers connect with various sets of nerve fibers and control those activities of the bird associated with them (Darling and Darling, 1962). One of functions of brain is in receiving messages from *sense organs*, the receptors of smell, taste, hearing, sight, and touch—the nostrils, mouth, ears, eyes, bill, and skin. From the sense organs, messages (stimuli) from the bird's outside environment are carried by nerve cells (neurons) to the brain. There the "information" is sorted, analyzed, and correlated and the correct responses carried to parts of the body, which respond with the appropriate actions—for example, whether to fight or to fly. *See* discussion

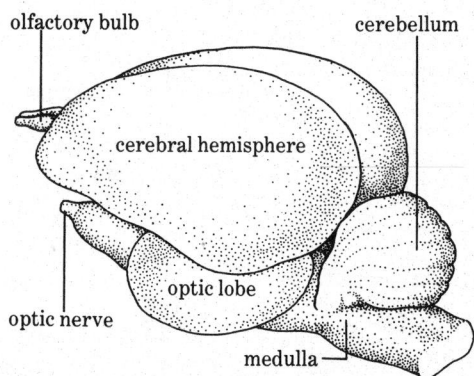

BRAIN
lateral view of the brain of a bird

olfactory bulb
cerebellum
cerebral hemisphere
optic lobe
optic nerve
medulla

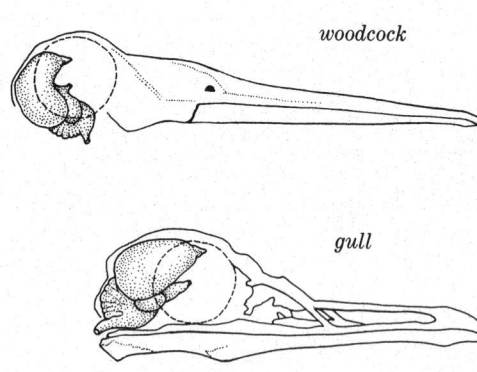

woodcock

gull

BRAIN
In gulls and other birds, the brain fills a relatively small space toward the back of the bird's head. The woodcock exhibits a unique adaptation: the relatively large eye sockets are located high up and back on the head, enabling the woodcock to see above and behind when feeding. To allow for this, the brain has shifted back and down.

under Nervous System; *also* Ears and Hearing; Eyes and Eyesight; Taste; Touch; Smell.

"Despite the slighting expression 'bird brain', birds have a brain proportionately larger than any of the vertebrates except mammals" (Darling and Darling, 1962). Birds' nearest relatives are reptiles—snakes, lizards, turtles, and crocodiles—but the bird brain is ten or more times larger than the brain of a reptile of comparable body weight (Goldby, 1964). Although similar in structure and function to brain of other vertebrates (*see* Vertebrate), the olfactory lobes are relatively small, paralleling the apparently poorly developed sense of smell in most birds (*see* Smell); the optic lobes are large, in keeping with the keen eyesight of birds (*see* Eyes and Eyesight), but are peculiar in being at the sides of the brain instead of in the roof of the midbrain as in reptiles and mammals.

The expansive cerebrum of the bird brain, considerably advanced evolutionarily over the cerebrum of lower vertebrates, is relatively smooth, however, and lacks the folds or fissures of the mammalian brain (Goldby, 1964). The cerebellum, responsible for the precise control of movements of birds, is well developed. The entire brain is restricted to a comparatively small space in the cranium; it is crowded toward the back of the bird's head by the extremely large cavities in the skull that house the eyes (Wallace, 1955). The brain and spinal cord constitute the central nervous system. *See* Nervous System.

In birds, one of the most striking features of the brain is the small extent and rudimentary character of the cortex. "Centers for regulation of excretion or retention of water, for temperature regulation (*see* Temperature), for a general inhibition resulting in sleep, and other functions have been identified with the hypothalamus, which is very important part of the brain of all vertebrates, and associated closely with the pituitary gland" (Goldby, 1964). There are great variations in the sizes of the brain of birds and proportions between its parts, and most of the differences between them are related to each bird's way of life. Weights of the brains of some birds, which may give an indication of the relative size of each, are: ostrich, 42 gr., or about 1½ oz.; white pelican, 18 gr., or about ⅔ oz.; pintail (duck), 5 gr., or about ⅙ oz.; turkey vulture, 9½ gr., or about ⅓ oz.; kestrel, or sparrow hawk, 2½ gr., or about 1/10 oz.; ring-billed gull, 8¾ gr., or about ⅓ oz.; and starling, 1⅞ gr.; house sparrow, 1 gr.; and grackle, 3 gr.—each about 1/10 oz. or less (Wing, 1956). For variation in the weights of brain of the house sparrow, some American thrushes, wood warblers, the bobolink, and rose-breasted grosbeak, see discussion in Graber and Graber (1965). For total weights of birds when known, *see* in each bird biography.

The woodcock is the only bird with an "upside down" brain; it is tilted backward at an angle of 117° from the horizontal, or level, line of its bill, compared with the forward or upward position of the brain in other birds such as the herring gull, semipalmated sandpiper, short-billed dowitcher. Evolution of the brain position in the woodcock allows greater development of eyes to their large size. No bird other

than the woodcock has such relatively large eyes placed so high in the skull and so far to the rear; this suggests that it is easily able to see behind it as well as above when it is feeding (Sheldon, 1971).

The avian brain seems most highly developed in the corvids—the crows, ravens, jays, and magpies—a group of birds that show unusual resourcefulness in coping with their environment, or their world. Parrots, macaws, parakeets, and lories (*see* Parrot Family; Psittaciformes) also have highly developed brains. *See* discussion under Behavior; also Pearson, R. (1972).

BRAMBLING
See in Finch Family.

BRANDT
JOHANN FRIEDRICH (1802–79). Eminent German zoologist who described in 1837 a Pacific coast cormorant whose common name, Brandt's cormorant, honors his name in American ornithology. He studied medicine in Berlin and went to St. Petersburg in 1831, where, later, he became director of the Zoological Museum. See Gruson (1972) for other details. "He published more than 300 papers and described several mammals and birds from western North America and the Northwest Coast" (Palmer, 1928).

BRANT
See in Duck Family.

BRANT-BIRD
See Dunlin; Godwit, marbled; and Turnstone,-ruddy; in Sandpiper Family.

BRASS-EYE
See Goldeneye, common, in Duck Family.

BREASTBONE
or STERNUM. *See* Skeleton.

BREAST SPONGE
Term originated by John James Audubon for a thick mass of fibrous tissue overlying the breast and crop of the males (gobblers) of both wild and domestic turkeys; in spring, just before the breeding season, it becomes so fatty that it may weigh up to 2 lbs. (Schorger, 1966). Breast-sponge fat is a reservoir of energy for the gobblers during the breeding season, when they are so occupied with gobbling and strutting (displaying) before the females (hens) that they eat very little. *See* Fasting; Turkey Family.

BREATHING
See Respiratory System; *also* Heat and Birds.

BREEDING AGE
See Sexual Maturity; Bursa of Fabricius.

BREEDING BIOLOGY
A general and inclusive term for the activities of birds relating to the nesting season. Breeding biology includes courtship, pairing, territorial behavior, nesting, laying of eggs, clutch size, incubation and its duration, role of the male in incubation, hatching of the young, nes-

tling period (length of time young are in the nest), growth of the young, their care by the parent birds, the duration of the breeding period, number of broods raised, physiology and anatomy of breeding, and so on (Davis, 1955). *See* Behavior.

BREEDING BIRD CENSUS
See Census.

BREEDING CYCLE
See stimulus for, under Light; *also* Physiological Preparation under Courtship; Endocrine Glands.

BREEDING POTENTIAL
The theoretical rate at which a species of bird could breed if all eggs hatched and all young grew to maturity (Wing, 1956).

BREEDING RANGE
See Distribution and Range in the biography of each species.

BREEDING SEASON
See Nests and Nesting.

BREEDING STIMULUS
See Courtship; Endocrine Glands.

BREWER
THOMAS M(AYO) (1814–80). Friend of John James Audubon and Thomas Nuttall; Boston physician, ornithologist, political writer, and an editor of the Boston *Atlas*, a leading Whig party paper of his time. Brewer's memory in ornithology is preserved in the Brewer's blackbird, *Quisculas breweri*, named for him by Audubon in 1843, but this scientific name was discarded when it was learned that Wagler in 1829 had already named the bird *Euphagus cyanocephalus* from a specimen of it collected in Mexico; however, the common name Brewer's blackbird was retained; the Brewer's sparrow was named for him by John Cassin in 1856.

Brewer was graduated from Harvard Medical School in 1838; he practiced medicine in Boston for some years before he turned to ornithology, specifically oology; he published the first part of a volume, *North American Oology*, in 1857; the work was not continued because of the great cost of illustrations. He also shared authorship with Spencer F. Baird and Robert Ridgway in *A History of North American Birds*. His collection of bird's eggs, considered one of the best private collections of the time, was left to the Museum of Comparative Zoology, Harvard College (Palmer *et al.*, 1954).

BREWSTER
WILLIAM (1851–1919). A founder and president (1895–98) of the American Ornithologists' Union, also a founder of the Nuttall Ornithological Club of Cambridge, Mass., and its president for more than 40 years. Brewster was a conservationist, field ornithologist, and an excellent and careful writer, author of more than 300 scientific papers. Two of his books, *October Farm* (Harvard University Press, 1936) and the beautifully illustrated *Concord River*

(same publishers, 1937), were composed of selected entry notes and essays from his journals. *See* Brewster's warbler in Warbler—American Wood Warbler Family.

BRISTLE
See Feather.

BRISTLE-TAIL
See Duck, ruddy, in Duck Family.

BRITISH BIRDS
A publication. *See* England under Ornithological Periodicals.

BROADBILL
See Duck, ruddy; Redhead; Scaup, greater; Scaup, lesser; and Shoveler, northern; in Duck Family.

BROKEN-WING DISPLAY
See Distraction Display.

BROOD
The number of birds hatched from a single clutch of eggs. For small, migrant terrestrial species, the number of broods which a species of bird rears in a season is usually correlated in nature with the length of time the species spends in its nesting area, with the time it takes to raise a brood, and with the distance which the species migrates. In Germany, an ornithologist concluded that those species which remain in the nesting area for more than 20–22 weeks (4–5 months) rear more than one brood, and those staying a shorter time usually raise only a single brood. He observed that species which raised but one brood were those that migrated the longest distances. His conclusions appear to apply generally to birds of N. America (Hann, 1953). *See* Clutch; Single-Brooded.

BROODER PNEUMONIA
See Aspergillosis.

BROODING
Provides warmth and shelter (physical protection) for young beyond that furnished by the nest (Emlen, 1955; Skutch, 1976). Many birds utter special call notes when they are broody and show increased belligerence toward any animal that comes near its nest, even potentially dangerous enemies. *See* Young and Their Care.

Broody behavior, which naturally follows egg-laying, can be induced in birds only after a preliminary period of sexual conditioning. The length of the brooding period and the amount of time daily devoted to brooding depends partially on the weather, latitude, degree of development of the young at hatching, and the time it takes the young to develop its own thermoregulation. Brooding behavior does not exist in the megapodes or mound-builders and brush turkeys of Australia (*see* Megapode), or in social parasites such as cowbirds and many cuckoos.

The brooding of young birds when they are small keeps them from getting too cold on cool days; it may also be done to shield them from rain or from direct sunlight on hot days.

Altricial young (*see* Altricial) are not brooded after they leave the nest but precocial young (*see* under Altricial) are brooded for 5 or 6 weeks afterward, depending on the species, or until they grow their juvenal feathers—those succeeding the natal down (*see* Nestling). The precocial young of wild geese and of plovers and other shorebirds are usually brooded on the ground by the parents, and gallinules and possibly other marsh birds (*see* Marsh Bird) may build a new nest or a platform of rushes on which to brood their young. Swans and grebes often take their young ones on their backs and brood them beneath their wings.

SINGLE-BROODED. A species of bird that tries to raise only one brood of young to a stage in which they are independent (on their own) during each breeding season (Berger and Radabaugh, 1968). According to Walkinshaw (1941), however, all single-brooded passerine (songbird) species will apparently re-nest one or more times if the first or a later nest is destroyed before the young are fledged, or leave the nest. The interval between destruction of the first nest and laying of the first egg in a subsequent nest has been determined for several species: prothonotary warbler, 4–7 days (Walkinshaw, 1941); song sparrow, 5 days (usually) to 8 days (Nice, 1937b), 5–7 days (Berger, 1951); American goldfinch, 4–21 days (Stokes, 1950); Kirtland's warbler, 7, 8, 8, and 14 days; average for 12 nests: 6.75 days (Berger and Radabaugh, 1968).

DOUBLE-BROODED. A species of bird that tries to raise to independence two broods of young per nesting season: typically a complete clutch of eggs is found in the subsequent or second nest, but it is not necessary (to fulfill the definition) for female to fledge the young of the second brood to be called double-brooded (Berger and Radabaugh, 1968). *See* related discussions under Eggs and Egg-laying; Nests and Nesting.

BROOD PARASITISM
Term for the regular habit of some birds of laying their eggs in the nests of others. The cowbird, *Molothrus ater*, of N. America is an example of a so-called *obligate parasite* (*see* Parasite) habit of brood parasitism. It builds no nest of its own and lays its eggs in the nests of more than 200 species of N. American birds (Friedmann, 1963). *See* discussion under Cowbird in Troupial Family, and Host to Cowbirds in the biographies of many of the smaller birds victimized.

According to Friedmann (1929), the five birds most frequently parasitized by the cowbird in N.Y. are the red-eyed vireo, American redstart, yellow warbler, chipping sparrow, and song sparrow. The next most parasitized group of five include the ovenbird, common yellow-throat, rufous-sided towhee, indigo bunting, and yellow-breasted chat, followed by the warbling vireo, yellow-throated vireo, chestnut-sided warbler, eastern phoebe, and veery; the wood thrush and field sparrow are next in frequency of being parasitized. Most of the vic-

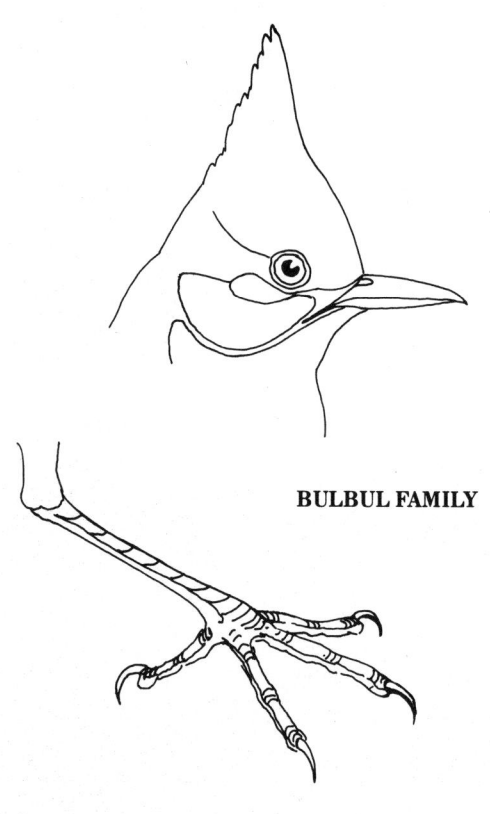

BULBUL FAMILY

tims are in four families—tyrant flycatchers, finches, vireos, and wood warblers.

Birds of five different families in the world are obligate parasites practicing brood parasitism: the black-headed duck (Anatidae) of S. America; several genera of cuckoos (Cuculidae), including the well-known cuckoo, *Cuculus canorus*, of Europe, so much in English literature, whose call is imitated by the "cuckoo clocks" (*see* in Cuckoo Family); the honey guides (Indicatoridae), mostly of Africa and related to the woodpeckers (*see* Piciformes); two genera of the New World cowbirds (Icteridae; *see* in Troupial Family); and in the large family of weaverbirds (Ploceidae), a group called widow weavers, which are brood-parasitic and build no nest (Austin, 1961). *See* related discussions under Obligate Parasite; *also* Dump Nests; Parasite. Lack (1968) cites brood parasitism among 80 or more species of birds. See discussion of worldwide brood parasitism among birds by Southern (1964) and Dorst (1974).

BROOD PATCH
See incubation patch under Incubation.

BROWN-BACK
See Dowitcher, short-billed and Sandpiper, pectoral, in Sandpiper Family.

BRUSH TURKEY
See Megapode.

BUCCAL CAVITY
See Mouth.

BUDGERIGAR
See in Parrot Family.

BUFFALO BIRD
See Cowbird, brown-headed, in Troupial Family and Bunting, lark, in Finch Family.

BUFFLEHEAD
See in Duck Family.

BUGLER
See Swan, trumpeter, in Duck Family.

BUGS
(parasitic). *See* Ectoparasite.

BULBUL (BULL-bull) FAMILY
Pycnonotidae (pick-no-NOT-ih-dee); from Gr. *pychnonotos*, strong-backed (Gruson, 1972). An Old World family of songbirds now represented in N. America by the red-whiskered bulbul in Fla.; members of family are medium-sized, 5½–11¼ in. long; 119 species (Van Tyne and Berger, 1976); live through Africa and s. Asia. Essentially forest birds, many have adapted to living in farming country; are common residents about villages, suburban gardens, orchards, and city parks in their native lands; not striking in colors but move about actively in noisy but musically chattering groups; are inquisitive, somewhat bold; one of their distinguishing characteristics is a patch of hairlike, vaneless feathers on back of nape. Bulbuls are perching birds. *See* Passeriformes.

The red-whiskered bulbul, *Pycnonotus jocosus*, tames easily and is a popular Oriental cage bird; in summer of 1960, at Kendall, Dade County, Fla., in the Miami region, some red-whiskered bulbuls escaped from captivity (see details in Fisk, 1966; Owre, 1973; Carleton and Owre, 1975). The red-whiskered bulbul first reared young in the wild at Kendall in summer of 1961 (Banks and Laybourne, 1968) and it is apparently the first bulbul to become established in N. America. It is a common species from India to China and south through Malaysia; introduced into New South Wales years ago, the red-whiskered bulbul became established in suburbs of Sydney and Melbourne. Bulbuls eat some insects but their main food is berries and fruit (in captivity: fruit, mockingbird food, ground meat, mealworms, canary seed); in their native land bulbuls are somewhat of a nuisance to fruit growers and they damage crops at times; they are not strong fliers and tend to be residents wherever they live, that is, not migratory (Austin, 1961).

Red-whiskered bulbul, *Pycnonotus jocosus* (pick-no-NOW-tus joe-COE-sus); genus name: *see* family introduction; species name: Lat., given to jokes and jesting; apparently in reference to this bird's liveliness and cheerful chatter (Fla. birds that escaped from captivity to become established there are of a race, or subspecies, *Pycnonotus jocosus emeria* [Banks and Laybourne, 1968], the Bengal red-whiskered bulbul, a native of India, e. Pakistan, lower Burma, etc.—see Ali and Ripley, 1971, for details of range in native land); *bulbul* is an ancient Arabic name for a small bird and was used frequently in the poetry of Omar Khayyám (Austin, 1961); *red-whiskered* for the bright red "whisker" patch behind each eye. (Color ill., page 54.) 8 in. long; slightly smaller and slimmer than American robin; sexes so outwardly alike they cannot be distinguished in field; has *black crest*, head black with white cheek patch and white throat; a bright red "whisker" patch slightly behind and below each dark eye; dark back and tail; dark patch sides of breast; white underparts, and a *red crissum* (*see* Crissum) under base of tail; is noisy with various cheery notes; one rollicking phrase sounds like *the rice must be finished off*; also a harsh *lerrr* often uttered for considerable periods toward sunset just before going to roost; one of commonest calls is a lively *pettigrew*, or *kick pettigrew*, or *pleased to MEET you* (Ali and Ripley, 1971); at Kendall, Fla., begins roosting assemblages in July–Aug.; communal roosts in winter are in fig trees, Napier grass, and hedges (Carleton and Owre, 1975).

Feeding Habits: Eats fruits, flowers, nectar, seeds, and some insects, many caught by bulbuls in air from roosts at dusk and daybreak; in Fla., fruit of Brazilian pepper tree, *Schinus terebinthifolius* (see "Ornamental Plantings for Birds" in Terres, 1968c), is very important to the species; also eats fruits of fig trees, jasmines, and drupes and berries of other small fruits of 24 exotic species (Carleton and Owre, 1975).

Nest: Built by both sexes in about 3–4 days (sometimes uses nest of previous year) in crotch of low shrub or small tree, a fairly deep cup of twigs, rootlets, leaves, grasses with bits of paper, bark, plastic, and even snakeskin woven into outer surface.

Eggs: In India, Pakistan, etc., breeding season largely Mar.–July; in Fla., one nest with 3 eggs in Mar. 1964 (Stevenson, 1964); see also Paulson and Stevenson (1962); 2–4, usually 3, pale pink, finely spotted with dark red and purple.

Incubation: By both sexes, 12–14 days; age when young leave nest not reported.

Age: One, banded, reported from Australia, lived in wild to 11 years, 1 month (Clapp, 1976).

Weights: Fla., adults (17), averaged about 27 gr. (Carleton and Owre, 1975), or about 1 oz.

Range: In U.S., range of Fla. birds confined to Kendall, just north of Miami, estimated at 40–50 (Stevenson, 1964); see also Stimson (1962) for early sightings; in winter 1969–70, population estimated at 250 (Owre, 1973).

BULLA

(BULL-ah). Term of waterfowl biologists for the, usually, asymmetrical bony enlargement at the base of the windpipe, or trachea, of a male duck. The bulla is in the syrinx, or vocal organ (*see* Voice and Sound-making) of some male ducks of the subfamily Anatidae, which in N. America includes the shelducks and the introduced S. American Muscovy duck, also the native wood duck, the gadwall, and other surface-feeding, or dabbling, ducks (*see* in Duck Family), and the diving ducks—the pochards (*see* Pochard), eiders, harlequin duck, oldsquaw, scoters, bufflehead, goldeneyes, and mergansers. The male ruddy duck, a primitive diver, lacks a tracheal bulla but has a large tracheal air sac, which he inflates during his courtship display (Johnsgard, 1965).

There is usually a great difference in the voices of the males that have a bulla and the females, which do not (the females have simpler tracheas), and the differences in their voices has been ascribed to the bulla in the male, although there is recent evidence that this may not be true. The bulla varies somewhat in its shape and size in the different species of male ducks that have it. See Fig. 5 in Johnsgard (1968). Presumably, the bony sound chamber (bulla) functions in the same manner as a manufactured whistle—the male duck produces his whistling notes (females of all dabbling ducks, for example, utter loud quacking notes) when air is rapidly passed by the bulla through the male's windpipe, or trachea (Johnsgard, 1968).

Female ducks and males of species that do not have a bulla apparently rely, for their vocal sounds, on the vibrations of the soft tympanic membranes situated between the base of the trachea and the bronchi. See Voice and Sound-making. These thin membranes vibrate readily when air passes across them, and the duck apparently varies the *pitch* of its uttered sounds by using two pairs of opposing muscles to vary the tension on these membranes.

In the geese, and also probably in ducks, the uttered sounds are made both by inhaling and exhaling air—the air sacs in the bird's throat,

or crop area, can frequently be seen to enlarge when a goose or a duck is calling (Johnsgard, 1968). *See* other details of waterfowl in Duck Family.

BULL-BAT

Name for the common nighthawk, from roaring sound made by its wings in aerial courtship dives. *See* Flight.

BULLER

SIR WALTER LAWRY (1838–1906). New Zealand lawyer who became interested in ornithology, was a leading authority on New Zealand birds. During some 40 years he never ceased to collect or to study the birds of New Zealand. One, the New Zealand, or Buller's, shearwater, *Puffinis bulleri*, named for him in 1888, reaches N. American waters off Pacific coast. Buller wrote *History of Birds of New Zealand* (published in 1873), *Manual of Birds of New Zealand* (1882), and other books. He was elected a fellow of the Royal Society (1876) and was knighted in 1886 (Oliver, W.R.B., 1955). See also Palmer (1928) and Gruson (1972) for other details.

BULLFINCH

See in Finch Family.

BULLHEAD

See Scaup, greater, and Scaup, lesser, in Duck Family and Plover, black-bellied, and Plover, American golden, in Plover Family.

BULLNECK

See Canvasback and Duck, ruddy, in Duck Family.

BULLOCK

WILLIAM (1775–?). Born in London, English traveler famous as proprietor of Bullock's Museum in London, which was sold at auction in 1819; a few years later, Bullock became interested in a mine not far from Mexico City; while there, he collected a number of birds previously unknown to science (Palmer, 1928), which he brought back to London in 1823 (Stresemann, 1975). These were named and described by William Swainson. Bullock's name is preserved in the Bullock's oriole, named for him in 1827 by Swainson from a specimen (or specimens) which Bullock had gotten from Real del Monte, Hidalgo, Mexico. *See* in Troupial Family. See also Gruson (1972) for other details about Bullock's travels in the U.S.

BULL-PEEP

One of the larger "peeps." *See* Sanderling and Sandpiper, white-rumped, in Sandpiper Family; *see also* Peep.

BUMBLEFOOT

An affliction of poultry characterized by a swelling, with or without abscess formation, on the ball of the foot; has also been described in the great horned owl (Stoner and Stoner, 1945) and by falconers. Dr. Casey A. Wood (1943) described the hard masses on the feet of captive hawks as "really cystic tumors, often associated with intumescence of the surrounding tissues." *See* Tumors.

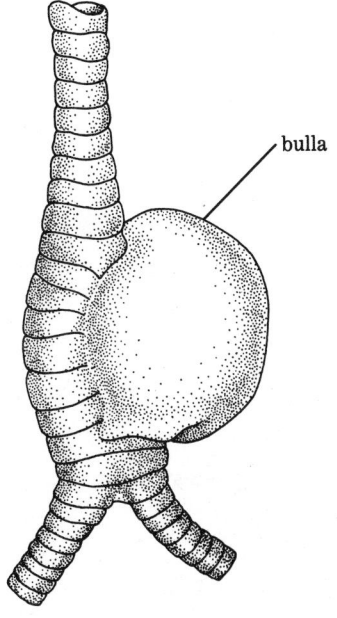

bulla

BULLA
A horny enlargement at the base of the windpipe in the males of many species of ducks, the bulla apparently acts as a sound organ, producing the whistling sounds of these species.

In captive hawks (and owls) these may be caused by hard, unyielding perches of wood or improperly shaped block perches. Waterfowl in captivity, when kept on hard floors, are also very susceptible to bumblefoot. *See also* Diseases. See discussions of what bumblefoot is and experiments in treatments in Swartz (1968) and Hamerstrom (1969a).

BUNTING
See in Finch Family.

BURGOMASTER
See Gull, glaucous, in Gull Family. In allusion to dominating habits.

BURHINIDAE
See Thick-knee Family.

BURNT-LAND BIRD
See Nighthawk, common, in Nightjar Family.

BURROUGHS
JOHN (1837–1921). Naturalist, writer, and one of greatest popularizers of nature study in America; born Apr. 3, 1837, at Roxbury, N.Y., near Catskill Mtns. His first book, of 25, called *Wake Robin*, one of his most popular about birds, was named for a trillium, a wildflower that blooms in spring about time many birds return to Burroughs' home country. In 1878, he built a small cabin in the woods, called Slabsides, on 20 acres along the Hudson R. above Poughkeepsie, N.Y., where he spent almost 25 years of his life. For a warm appraisal of Burroughs as a naturalist and writer, see Sharp (1921); for his definitive biography, see Barrus (1925).

BURSA OF FABRICIUS
(fah-BRISH-ih-us). Named for Johann Christian Fabricius, Danish entomologist; is a glandular sac in the dorsal (upper) wall of the avian cloaca at its junction with the vent (Farner, 1960). It develops in all young birds, in which it remains open and measurably deep, but disappears or becomes closed with age (Wing, 1956). Among the larger game birds—for example, wild turkeys (Mosby and Handley, 1943), pheasants (Gower, 1939), and waterfowl (Hochbaum, 1942)—the age of the bird can be determined with fair accuracy by probing into and measuring the bursa (its stages of involution) during the bird's first year of life; however, with smaller birds the examination must be so precise that it is not recommended (Pettingill, 1956).

According to some authorities, the primary function of the bursa is to produce antibodies in resistance to diseases (Lewis, 1967); it may have a thymuslike (*see* Thymus) function or be the site of white corpuscle manufacture (Welty, 1962).

Weller (1965), in a study of 92 wild-caught great horned owls, measured the depth of the bursa of Fabricius on the assumption that its atrophy would show the approximate age of maturing of each bird. The bursa had disappeared in many of the owls at about 2 years of age and therefore served as a "fair method of determining age." The rate of disappearance also suggested that most individual horned owls do not breed until they are 2 years old, although some yearling females may do so with the bursa still present and of measurable depth. *See* Sexual Maturity.

Weller reported that it is well known that the Canada goose normally breeds first at 3 years of age, although some do when only 2 years old. Elder (1946) noted that the great variation in the bursa regression of individual Canada geese suggested variation in the age of first breeding in this species.

Johnston (1956) demonstrated that in California gulls the bursa normally degenerates at 4 years of age, when the gull's plumage becomes adult. In those that did breed when 3 years old, the bursa was smaller or more degenerated than in those 3-year-olds that did not breed.

BUSHTIT
See in Titmouse Family.

BUSTARD
See Gruiformes; *also* Running Birds.

BUTCHER BIRD
See Shrike Family.

BUTEO
(BEW-tee-oh). English as well as scientific genus name for a group of hawks with similar characteristics that in N. America includes the red-tailed, red-shouldered, broad-winged, and other hawks. *See* Hawk Family; *also* Genus. Among bird-watchers they are called, collectively, buteos. *See also* Accipiter; Buzzard; and Falcon in Falcon Family.

BUTTERBALL
See Bufflehead and Duck, ruddy, in Duck Family.

BUTTER-BILL
See Scoter, black, in Duck Family.

BUTTER-NOSE
See Scoter, black, in Duck Family.

BUTTON-QUAIL
See Gruiformes; *also* polyandry under Sexual Relationships.

BUZZARD
A common alternate name for the black and turkey vultures—black buzzard and turkey buzzard—and for the hawks of the genus *Buteo* (*see* in Hawk Family); for example, broad-winged buzzard for the broad-winged hawk, ferruginous buzzard for the ferruginous hawk, and so on. Early British settlers in America called the turkey vulture a buzzard because of its fancied resemblance in flight to the soaring buteonine hawks of Europe (McAtee, 1955c). Also, in Fla., Spanish buzzard is a local name for the wood stork (*see* Stork Family) because of its soaring flight which rivals that of the turkey vulture.

BUZZARD DAY
A day celebrated around Mar. 15 each year at Hinckley, Ohio, when a flock of turkey vultures, known commonly as "buzzards," return to their nesting ledges overlooking Hinckley Lake. For nesting habits in area of c. Ohio similar to Hinckley area, see Coles (1944). *See also* biography of turkey vulture under Vulture—American Vulture Family.

BUZZARD-HAWK
See Hawk, gray, in Hawk Family.

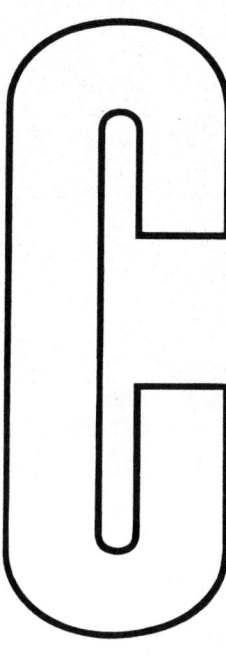

CABANIS

JEAN LOUIS. *See* under Mauri.

CACIQUE

See introduction to Troupial Family.

CAECUM

(SEE-kum; pl.: *caeca*—SEE-kah); from Lat., blind. The usually paired caeca, or "blind guts," so called because they end in culs-de-sac, are pouches, or diverticula (Coues, 1884) at juncture of small and large intestines.

Most birds have two, although in many groups they are not developed sufficiently to become functional in the digestive system. No part of the intestinal tract is so variable as the caeca—there are none in adult kingfishers and parrots, and there is a single caecum in some herons and in grebes (Worden, 1964a); they are lacking or much reduced, though still functional, in some penguins, petrels, hawks, hummingbirds, swifts, falcons, the insectivorous passerines, and woodpeckers. They appear to be most extensively developed in herbivores and in some omnivores, but not in all graminivores (Farner, 1960).

The caeca perform a digestive function in ostriches, rheas, tinamous, and gallinaceous birds —turkeys, quail, pheasants—and many ducks and shorebirds (Van Tyne and Berger, 1959). Their main function seems to be absorption of water and digested proteins and especially microbial decomposition of crude fibrous foods.

The caeca range in size from extraordinarily small in some birds (mere buds on the intestine) to 1 ft. long in geese and swans; in some grouse they are said to be 3 ft. long (Coues, 1884). In domestic fowl they are exceptionally well developed (Worden, 1964a). The length of both the caeca and the small intestine is related to diet—the caeca are longer in birds that browse on buds, leaves, and twigs, such as grouse, than in quail and pheasants that eat seeds.

CAHOW

See Petrel, Bermuda, in Shearwater Family.

CALAMUS

The feather quill from the point of its attachment in the skin of a bird to where the feather vanes begin. The rachis, by contrast (*see* Feather), from which the feather vanes grow, is the central feather shaft, a prolongation of the calamus, or quill.

CALCIUM

(calcium carbonate). A solid mineral occurring in nature as calcite (limestone, marble, etc.); also in plant ashes, bones, and many seashells; it is used in making lime and Portland cement. Calcium salts are in practically all waters and in the bodies of plants and animals.

Biologists have discovered that certain birds, especially ring-necked pheasants (*see* in Pheasant Family), may depend on an adequate amount of calcium in the soil for their survival. Dale (1954) noted a correlation between the availability of calcium and the abundance of pheasants in the major centers of pheasant populations in e. U.S. McCann (1961) asserted that grit (*see* Gizzard) high in calcium and low in magnesium was of pre-eminent importance

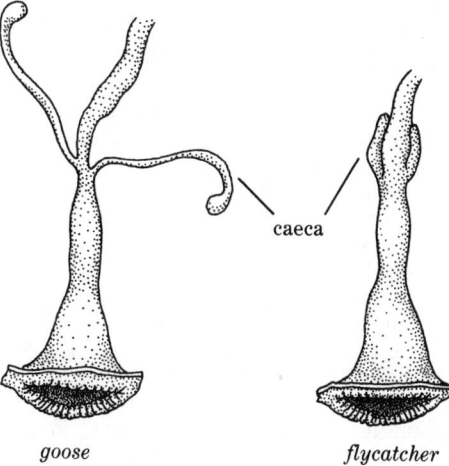

goose   *flycatcher*

CAECUM

The caeca, which perform a digestive function, are paired in most birds and located at the junction of the large and small intestines. The caeca of herbivores such as the goose are larger and more developed than the budlike sacs of insect-eating passerines such as flycatchers.

to wild pheasants in Mich. According to Labiskey *et al.* (1964), the importance of calcium in the reproduction, growth, and other physiological processes of birds is so great that a critical shortage or absence of this mineral could prevent the establishment of self-maintaining pheasant populations. Most biologists who have studied upland game birds such as quail, grouse, and pheasants, which have high calcium demands, believe that their source of calcium is in calcareous grit.

It is thought that there is a mineral deficiency in plant foods of northern finches (*see* Finch Family)—for example, evening grosbeaks and crossbills—which usually live in the Far North and are often avid for salt (*see* Salt) and wood ashes. In attracting birds, many people mix finely crushed oyster and clam shells, which are high in calcium, with the mixed birdseeds they put out for seed-eating birds. *See* Bird-attracting. The crushed shells provide a grit that helps grind seeds in the bird's gizzard and appears to be an important source of calcium and phosphorus; coarse seashore sand also makes good grit for birds (hummingbirds have been seen eating sand—*see* under Hummingbird Family).

Breeders of cage birds, especially of budgerigars (*see* in Parrot Family), recommend grit for them, not only to grind their food but to provide them with minerals, among which calcite, or lime, is highly important. The parathyroid gland in birds produces a hormone that controls calcium and phosphorus metabolism (Berger, 1961). *See* Endocrine Glands; Metabolism.

According to Simkiss (1961), although some calcium for forming the shells of eggs laid by birds comes from the bird's structural bones, there is a special system of bone that is deposited in the marrow cavities of the skeleton under the influence of androgens (male hormones) and estrogens (female hormones); *see* discussion of this under Endocrine Glands.

According to Romanoff and Romanoff (1949), calcium forms 98.2% of the shells of eggs laid by the domestic hen and about 6% of the contents of the egg itself; this calcium comes directly from the daily diet of the hen or from her body reserves of calcium, which are dependent on calcium intake prior to the time when egg-laying begins—the hen stores a reserve of calcium in the cavities of the long bones which can be rapidly recycled by her, or drawn on; the deposition of calcium, according to Höhn (1961), is under the control of estrogens.

The circulatory system carries calcium from the viscera of the bird or from the bones (or from both) to the oviduct, where the calcium is deposited on or in the eggs as calcium carbonate and other calcium salts (*see* Eggs and Egg-laying). About 25% of the body reserves of calcium (about 98% of which is in the bones, or skeleton) can be used in egg formation, and the pre-laying storage of calcium in the body of a domestic hen or in a ring-necked pheasant is sufficient for the laying of about 6 eggs (Labiskey *et al.*, 1964). Simkiss (1961) suggests that the system of calcium storage by birds must be especially important to those living in lime-deficient places or to birds whose foods are deficient in calcium, such as those that eat nectar (hummingbirds, for example).

In some birds, phosphorus as well as calcium is mobilized during egg formation and is closely associated with the calcium complex; as with calcium, reserves of phosphorus must be replenished in the bird's body through its food.

CALICO BIRD
See Turnstone, ruddy, in Sandpiper Family.

CALL-COUNT
See Census.

CALL NOTE
See Language; Songs and Singing.

CAMANAY
See Booby, blue-footed, in Booby Family.

CAMBRIAN PERIOD
See Geological Time Scale.

CAMP ROBBER
See Jay, gray, and Nutcracker, Clark's, in Crow Family.

CAN
See Canvasback in Duck Family.

CANADIAN FIELD-NATURALIST, THE
A publication. *See* Canada under Ornithological Periodicals.

CANADIAN JOURNAL OF ZOOLOGY
See Canada under Ornithological Periodicals.

CANADIAN ZONE
One of six life zones of N. America, each of which is characterized by its plant life and certain birds. Life zones are still relied on by some authorities in mapping locally the ecological distribution of N. American birds. *See* discussion of biomes and life zones under Distribution. The Canadian Zone corresponds in its plants and birds to Coniferous Forest, one of the biomes. *See* location of the Coniferous Forest biome and its plants and birds under Coniferous Forest. See Pettingill (1970; 1972) for details.

CANKER
See trichomoniasis under Diseases.

CANNIBALISM
Term used among ornithologists for eating of a bird by another of its own kind; usually among carnivorous, or meat-eating, birds such as hawks, eagles, owls, also the omnivorous gulls. Among many birds, young hatch usually within a few hours of each other, or at most a day or so apart; this seems to ensure that the young all leave the nest about the same day, which in most species is necessary for survival. This is because most parent birds delay incubation of eggs until most of clutch has been laid (*see* Incubation); however, with raptors (eagles, hawks, and owls) the adult female may lay her eggs at intervals of one, two, or more days and begin incubating with the first egg she lays.

In birds such as the barn owl and short-eared owl, which may lay up to 8, 10, or more eggs in a clutch, there may be a difference of two weeks in age of first owl hatched and last one, therefore a large difference in size. Food supply (wild mice) is fluctuating, in some years enormously abundant, in others very scarce. *See* Cycle. In times of food scarcity, when adult owls are unable to supply their large broods with enough mice and other small animals, the largest owl in the nest may kill and eat some of its younger brothers and sisters. This is true, in fact, of most raptors, even those that produce small egg clutches. *See* Fratricide. Most ornithologists believe this may be natural way of ensuring that a few young in the nest survive, rather than losing the entire brood through starvation (Ingram, 1959). *See* discussion in biography of short-eared owl in Owl—Typical Owl Family.

In a large colony of gulls, the number of chicks successfully fledged may average less than one young for each pair of breeding adults because of cannibalism; great losses may come from parents preying on chicks of their neighbors, especially when chicks wander, or are frightened, into neighboring territories. Probably the amount of such cannibalism depends on the abundance of fish food available for the colony; there is strong evidence that a very young chick which wanders from the nest may not survive, especially among herring and lesser black-backed gulls; when a chick returns home it may even be killed and eaten by its parents, which seem then to consider their own chick to be a stranger. *See* Kronism. A chick may be killed especially if it wanders among burrows or nests of species of birds that parents normally prey upon. Cannibalism in large gull colonies may be effective self-control of some gull populations. *See* Gull Family; Food and Feeding Habits.

CANNON BONE
Term for the three separate bones (metatarsals), one for each front toe, that are fused into a single one which forms the bird's tarsus. *See* Tarsus. The cannon bone is so called because it has a long, gun-barrel shape (Allen, 1925). *See* Feet and Legs.

CANVASBACK
See in Duck Family.

CAPE DRAKE and CAPE RACE
See Red-throated loon in Loon Family.

CAPERCAILLIE
(cap-er-KALE-yih). *See* under Grouse Family.

CAPRIMULGID
(cap-rih-MUL-jid). Shortened name for any member of the Nighthawk Family (Caprimulgidae).

CAPRIMULGIDAE
See Nightjar Family.

CAPRIMULGIFORMES
(kap-rih-mul-jih-FOR-meez); from Lat. *caprimulgus*, a milker of goats (see Folklore), and *forma*, form. An order, or group of birds (*see* Order), that resemble each other fundamentally in structure. According to Van Tyne and

Berger (1959), the order includes 5 families of some 93 species of these nocturnal or crepuscular birds, with long pointed wings, small "weak" feet, insignificant bills, and large gaping mouths. All but one, the S. American oilbird, which eats only fruit (*see* Echolocation), feed mostly on insects—an exception is the N. American chuck-will's-widow, which also eats, occasionally, small birds, which it catches by sweeping them out of the air with the large opened mouth, just as most caprimulgids catch insects as they fly. An exception to this method of feeding is the frogmouths of the Australian region that feed not only on the ground but eat insects and birds; and one species, the tawny frogmouth of Australia, even takes mice. *See* Food and Feeding Habits.

The 5 families of the order are: the Oilbird Family, Steatornithidae, of only 1 species, nonmigratory, which lives locally from c. Peru through Ecuador, Colombia, Venezuela, to French Guiana and Trinidad (*see* account under Echolocation); the Frogmouth Family, Podargidae, of 12 species, of the forested savannas and open woodlands of the Oriental and Australian regions; the Potoo (poh-TOO) Family, Nyctibiidae, of 5 seldom-seen species, a family whose members range from Mexico to s. Brazil and Paraguay, also in Jamaica and Hispaniola (see Gilliard, 1958, and Austin, 1961, for interesting details); the Owlet-Frogmouth Family, Aegothelidae, of 8 species, of the Australian region; and the Nightjar Family, Caprimulgidae, of 67 species, almost worldwide, some migratory, the only family of the order with representatives in N. America north of Mexico. *See* Nightjar Family. *See also* Torpidity; Classification; Morphology.

CAPTIVE BREEDING

(of rare and threatened species). *See* biography of Falcon, peregrine, in Falcon Family; see also in Temple (1977).

CARACARA

See under Falcon Family.

CARBONIFEROUS PERIOD

See Geological Time Scale.

CARDINAL

See in Finch Family.

CARE AND FEEDING OF ABANDONED OR INJURED WILD BIRDS

Most birds are protected by federal and state laws (*see* Legal Protection) and cannot be kept in one's possession. However, under special circumstances they may be kept if one is granted a state or federal permit. Each year, emergencies arise when bird's nests in the backyard or garden are blown out of trees by violent storms and the newly hatched or half-grown birds scattered on the ground. What should one do to help? If the nest and fledglings can be placed securely back in a tree or bush near its original location, it is far better to do so and to let the bird parents go about the exacting job of raising their young, for which they alone are best suited. Or if the nest has been destroyed, the young birds can be placed in a makeshift nest of dried grasses or cut-up newspapers and

these put into a small basket which can be hung from a tree branch where the parents can come to their young and feed them. A young bird found alone is not usually abandoned. The parents may be nearby, hidden in a tree or a bush, waiting for the human intruder to walk away before they continue feeding the young one. If, however, a bird has been deserted by its parents or injured, and it may starve or be threatened by predators, one might take on the job of being a foster parent; that is, if one is prepared to feed a young bird (or birds) at 15-minute intervals for at least 12 hours during each day.

Put the helpless young in a box in a substitute nest, perhaps of grass, lined with soft cloth or tissues so that the birds' feet have something pliable to push against. Keep the birds warm by covering the box with a cloth to protect them from drafts. If the fledglings are old enough to perch, put them in a large cage or, better, give them the freedom of a room in which they can learn to fly.

Young birds should be handled as little as possible and not fed too much at a time. Feed them only during daylight hours, but feedings should be frequent and *regular*, at most every 15 minutes or, at least, every half hour.

FOODS AND FEEDING. Feeding is common sense with a dash of ingenuity. Many people try to feed foundling birds simply on bread, even offering it to meat-eating owls and fish-eating grebes, but each should be offered a food like that eaten by the bird in the wild (*see* recommended food for captives under each bird family in the introduction—for example, to Hawk Family; Finch Family; etc.) or one that approximates or supplements the natural food.

A basic food for every young songbird nestling is equal parts of finely mashed yolk of hard-boiled eggs and finely sifted bread crumbs, *slightly* moistened with milk or cod-liver oil (for some exceptions—birds that are not songbirds—*see* under Pigeon Family; Hummingbird Family). This mixture will agree with blue jays, cardinals, catbirds, robins, orioles, starlings, sparrows, towhees, and other small birds. Good supplementary foods for them are canned dog food, cottage cheese, bits of grapes, cherries, bananas, soft apple pulp, bits of scraped or finely chopped meat, crushed walnuts, and any of the smaller berries. One woman with an orphaned yellow-billed cuckoo got a supply of insects for it each night by attracting insects to a light in her window; using a flashlight, one can stalk earthworms on lawns at night. See, however, the very useful article by Ficken and Dilger (1961).

At first, older fledglings may not eat. To force-feed one, hold the bird by enclosing its body and closed wings in one hand, and use the thumb and index finger of the same hand to gently squeeze the bill at base, at which the bird usually will open its bill. In the other hand, hold a narrow wooden spoon or, better, a small paintbrush to pick up food on the tips of the bristles. If this does not work, use one of the fingers to poke food down the bird's throat (not too much food at once)—in back of the bird's tongue and well down its throat or it may spit out the food. In a short time, the youngster will learn to open its bill for food. Continue feeding

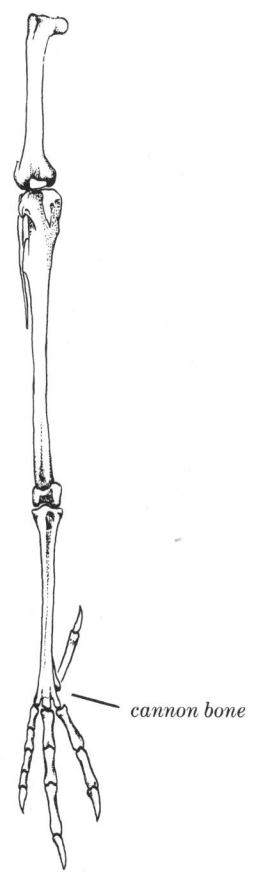

cannon bone

CANNON BONE

nightjar

CAPRIMULGIFORMES

until the bird's crop is full (*see* Crop) and it should be especially full at nightfall before the bird goes to sleep.

Most seed-eaters—cardinals, grosbeaks, sparrows, finches—also need some fine gravel and charcoal, crushed seeds, chopped greens, fruits, mealworms and other insects. Young woodpeckers will eat a mixture of dog food and the basic finely mashed egg yolks, also mealworms and a mixture of Pablum and raw liver chips (Ramp, 1965). Young doves and pigeons should be fed cooked oatmeal (feed it after it cools) to supplement or take the place of "crop milk" fed to it by the parents. *See* Crop. For baby hummingbirds (feed them with an eye dropper) offer the formula given under Hummingbird Family, and after about 10 days one can add to the recommended mixture dried dog food, very finely sifted and thoroughly mixed with the liquid formula. For the methods of feeding, and diets, for young or adult fish-eating birds such as grebes, gulls, terns, cormorants, pelicans, the osprey, kingfishers, murres, auks, mergansers, etc., *see* the recommendations in the introduction to the various families of these birds.

Meating off is a term used in aviculture for changing the food habits of a bird. When a bird is captured and brought into captivity from the wild, there is often the problem; if it is an insect-eating bird, of getting it to eat a mixture of dried foods. This may be tried in several ways. In the New York Zoological Gardens, certain warblers after arrival will not eat readily when newly captured, but will drink water. William G. Conway, the Curator of Birds, says that the trick is to keep the birds warm and dry and to gradually add the dried insect food to their water. "In a little while the warbler is drinking a soup, then a mash, and finally eating our normal moist insectivorous mixture." Another method is used more widely. The insect larvae (caterpillars or grubs) are merely placed on the insectivorous mixture and the bird inadvertently eats some of the mix in eating the insects. The number of insects put on the mix is slowly reduced as the birds learn to eat the mix. "Meating off" should be done cautiously to allow the sensitive species to make the physiological adjustment slowly. "Perhaps the best way is to give the birds a good meal of pure insects in the morning and evening and to do the 'meating off' in between" (Ficken and Dilger, 1961).

Mockingbird food is a special food fed to captive birds that in the wild eat largely fruit and insects. It can be prepared by mixing 5 parts of zwieback, 1 part of crissal (meat meal), ½ part of ant eggs. This preparation will keep indefinitely when stored. As it is used, add to it hard-boiled eggs (the yolks), grated carrots, ground hemp seed, and cod-liver oil (Walker, 1942). Mockingbird food may be fed to flycatchers, larks, chickadees, titmice, nuthatches, wrens, mockingbirds, thrashers, catbirds, vireos, tanagers, robins, thrushes, bluebirds, and woodpeckers.

Young hawks and owls require meat, preferably with the fur or feathers on it, which aids the digestion of raptorial birds. *See* Digestion; Pellet. Feed them freshly trapped rats and mice or poultry and raw beef, sprinkled with cod-liver oil, with which chicken feathers can be mixed. *See* instructions for housing and care under Hawk Family and under Owl.

WATER AND SUNSHINE. Small birds may be killed by forcibly giving them water or milk. In the wild, before they learn to drink, they receive sufficient moisture from their food for their needs. But in captivity they may not. Feed them a little water very carefully with an eye-dropper. When they are old enough to sit on a perch, water may be offered them in a shallow dish. You may also dip their bills into a water cup until they learn to drink by themselves. Young birds must have some sunshine too, but they should be shaded from the heat of the midday sun. Birds, like humans, welcome a cool retreat in hot weather.

WHEN THE BIRD GROWS UP. No matter how attached we may become to the birds we have raised, we must remember that we have been their protectors, not their captors; that wild birds belong to the state. As soon as a bird is strong enough to fly from the floor to the top of a chair, it should be allowed to forage for itself and should be turned loose as soon as it is able to fly and can partially feed itself. If possible, it should be hand-fed in the garden for a few days and food made available to it at all times. If the foundlings are not encouraged to return to a wild, free life, they will learn to depend upon human assistance, which may bring them disaster when they are suddenly thrown upon their own.

HOW TO CARE FOR OLDER BIRDS. When you first get an ill or injured *adult* songbird or a young bird that has learned to fear man, put it in a large cage, or preferably in a large room where it is free to fly. If the bird will not accept some of the wild or natural foods you offer, you may have to force-feed, just as in force-feeding a young bird. You may try to force-feed it on the egg yolk and bread for a few days until it will eat food itself. Meanwhile, any insect-eating bird, such as a warbler, mockingbird, bluebird, and others, should be offered some live mealworms, which one can buy at most pet shops; however, also offer grapes, cherries, and raisins to vary the diet.

If an adult bird will not feed itself, and must be force-fed, it should be fed about three or four times a day. A full-grown bird does not require nearly as much food as a nestling (*see* Food and Feeding Habits), which may eat its own weight in food each day (*see* Young and Their Care). For a well-grown young bird or an adult, put a shallow pan of water—no more than an inch or two deep—on the floor of the room or cage in which the bird is kept. This gives it an opportunity to drink or to bathe whenever it chooses. *See* in the introduction to each family of birds the kinds of food recommended for each. For an account of surgical treatment—how to help wounded or crippled hawks and owls with broken bones—see Mutchler (1972); for care and keeping of owls, *see* under Owl—Barn Owl Family; of hawks under Hawk Family; of falcons under Falcon Family. For suggestions for the temporary care and quarters for injured or ill birds, see also Lake (1958).

CAREERS IN ORNITHOLOGY

According to James *et al.* (1974), in ornithology, unlike many other sciences, those who participate in studies of birds range from amateurs (unpaid workers who study birds scientifically as a hobby) to the professionals who work or teach in colleges and universities or work for federal and state governments or for private conservation organizations or are employed as curators in museums and zoos (*see* Curator). For a detailed discussion of job opportunities in the U.S. and Canada, and of the numbers of those currently employed as working ornithologists, teachers, ecologists, biologists, and so on, with educational requirements for many of these jobs, see the article by James *et al.* The authors of this article represent the views of experts at the time, and their views will probably hold within this century unless there are vast changes in job opportunities not foreseen when the article was written. The authors also include a list of some of the major universities that offer graduate degrees in the biological sciences, and also those that specialize in teaching careers in ornithology; the article includes an appended list of published sources of their information.

CARE OF YOUNG

See Young and Their Care; *also* Care and Feeding of Abandoned or Injured Wild Birds; Helpers among Birds.

CARINA

(kah-RIE-nah). Literally a keel; in ornithology a term for the longitudinal ridge or plate of bone on the underside of a bird's sternum, or breastbone, often called the keel. *See* Bones; Skeleton.

CARINATE

(KAR-ih-nate). Meaning shaped like the keel or prow of a ship. Term used for birds with *keeled* breastbones. The keel of the breastbone separates two masses of muscles in the breast and gives them a strong attachment. *See* Skeleton. *Ratite* birds (the flightless ostrich, rhea, cassowary, emu, and kiwi) lack a keel and have a flat sternum, or breastbone. *See* Flightless Birds.

CARNIVOROUS BIRDS

Include hawks, eagles, kites, falcons, owls. The carnivorous (meat-eating) birds are considered supreme as hunters of living prey but are also known to scavenge, or to feed on the flesh of dead animals. Some other birds, even songbirds, will occasionally eat meat if they have an opportunity, but carnivorous birds are exclusively meat-eaters. *See* Raptors; *also* Food and Feeding Habits; Care and Feeding of Abandoned or Injured Wild Birds.

CAROTENOIDS

(cah-ROT-eh-noids), or LIPOCHROMES. A group of naturally occurring pigments in the feathers and skin—in bill and legs—of birds. These are numerous and diverse in composition and are responsible for most of the bright feather colors—yellows, oranges, and reds—in highly colored species of birds, many of which are tropical.

From results of controlled feeding experiments with yellow canaries, it is clear that birds "depend directly or indirectly upon plant carotenoids in their food for their lipochrome pigments. Practically nothing is known of the process by which ingested plant carotenoids are modified in the body of the bird, or of the factors controlling it. There is no evidence that these pigments can be synthesized by birds, and as far as is known, the basic synthesis of the carotenoids can be performed only by plants" (Rawles, 1960). *See* Colors of Feathers.

Carotenoids were named from the pigment in the root of the cultivated carrot (Van Tyne and Berger, 1959).

CARPENTER BIRD
One of common names of the pileated woodpecker, from its chiseling, with its bill, large holes in sound, dead, or decaying wood.

CARPUS
The wrist, or bend of the wing in birds (Van Tyne and Berger, 1959). There are two carpals, or wristbones. *See* Skeleton; *also* under Flight; Wings.

CARRIER PIGEON
Another name for the homing, or domestic, pigeon. *See* Homing Pigeon; *also* Domestication. The name carrier pigeon is often incorrectly applied to the passenger pigeon. *See* Extinct Birds of North America; Pigeon Family.

CARRION-EATING BIRDS
Seen especially in two families of N. American birds—the New World vultures (Cathartidae) and the caracaras (Falconidae). Ravens, crows, gulls, and some hawks, petrels, and other birds may eat much carrion, but they do not appear to be specialized for this kind of feeding. *See* Scavengers.

CARRYING CAPACITY
Term among biologists and wildlife managers for an important biological principle: that there is a limit to the numbers of any one kind of bird, or other animal, that can be supported by a given area of habitat. *See* Habitat; Ecological Niche; Territory. Among certain species of birds that have been studied in relation to their requirements, and populations in relation to habitat, it is known that an acre of land may support several pairs of song sparrows, but possibly only one pair of bobwhites, whereas it may require a square mile to support a nesting population of three or four pairs of hawks (Berger, 1961). Aldo Leopold (1933) says of carrying capacity that it is "the maximum density of wild game which a particular range is capable of carrying." Allen, D. (1954) says of carrying capacity: "The most important thing about this ability of land or water (or combination thereof) to support a given kind of animal is that it has *strict and measurable limits.*" The carrying capacity of a unit of land may be changed (improved), however, by wildlife management methods. *See* Economic Ornithology.

CARRYING OF EGGS AND OF YOUNG
See Eggs and Egg-Laying; Young and Their Care.

CARUNCLE
(KAR-ung-k'l); dim. of Lat. *caro,* flesh. A small, often brightly colored, naked, fleshy eminence or wrinkled, warty protuberance, for example on the head, upper neck, and to a lesser extent, on the dewlap, or throat wattle, of a turkey; the caruncles of the turkey vary greatly in size; largest are on sides of neck where the bare skin meets the feathered part; they vary in turgidity and color in the turkey according to its emotional state (Lucas and Stettenheim, 1972). *See* under Turkey Family.

Besides both domestic and wild turkeys, vultures and cassowaries are examples of other birds that are carunculated. *See also* Casque; Wattle.

CASQUE
(KASK). A bony growth from the top of the skull, involving chiefly the crown and the forehead of the cassowaries (Lucas and Stettenheim, 1972). *See* Flightless Birds; Running Birds.

CASSIN
JOHN (1813–69). Philadelphia ornithologist. His name is commemorated in two species, Cassin's finch and Cassin's sparrow; also in *Cassinia,* journal of the Delaware Valley Ornithological Club. He was Curator of Birds at the Academy of Natural Sciences beginning in 1842. During his 26 years there he described and named at least 11 species of birds and published *Illustrations of the Birds of California* . . . (1856). He also prepared the ornithological reports of collections made by the Wilkes Exploring Expedition around the world; the Perry Expedition to Japan; the Gillis Astronomical Expedition to Chile; and co-authored, with Spencer F. Baird and George Newbold Lawrence, one of the Pacific Railroad Survey reports. See Stone (1901); Palmer (1928).

CASSINIA
A publication. *See* Ornithological Periodicals.

CASSOWARY
See Flightless Birds; Running Birds.

CAST
or CASTING. *See* Pellet.

CASUAL VISITOR
Term for a species of bird that wanders to and within the borders of a state only at more or less infrequent intervals; arbitrarily, may be defined as birds that have been reported more than once in a state but less than a dozen times (Lowery, 1960). *See also* Lowery's definition of "accidentals" under Accidental, which considers accidentals to be rarer than casual visitors. *See* other ornithological terms for the status of birds in Where Do Birds Live? under Distribution.

CATBIRD
See in Mockingbird Family.

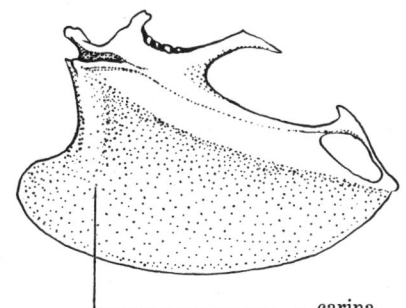

CARINATE
A carinate sternum

carina

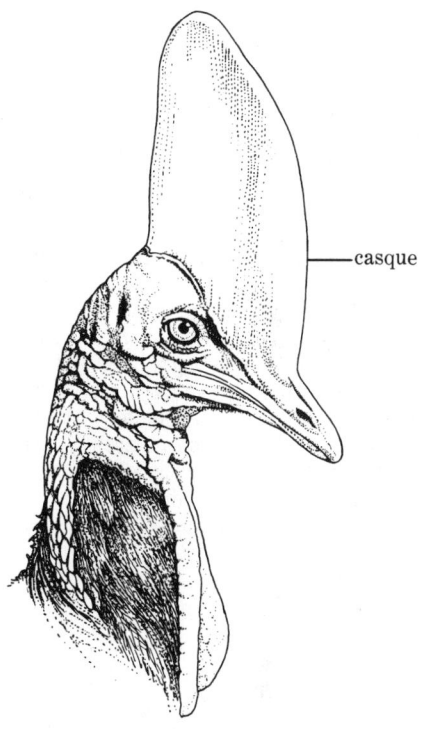

casque

CASQUE
The casque of the flightless cassowaries of Australia and New Guinea is a heavy, bony growth on the forehead and crown.

CATESBY

MARK (1682–1749?). Englishman in early America, "the founder of American ornithology" (Allen, 1951); author and illustrator of 109 N. American birds in his two-volume *Natural History of Carolina, Florida, and the Bahama Islands* (1731–43). It is said that because of the quality of the publication, present-day historians regard him as the first real naturalist in America. See Stevens (1936); also the authoritative biography by Frick and Stearns (1961).

CATHARTIDAE

See Vulture—American Vulture Family.

CAUDAL

Pertaining to the tail.

CEDAR BIRD

See Cedar waxwing in Waxwing Family.

CEILOMETER

(seal-OM-eh-ter). A mechanical device on ground at airports which automatically measures cloud heights for the safety of arriving and departing aircraft. In measuring cloud heights, the ceilometer sends a powerful light beam skyward at night, which, during fall and spring migrations of birds, sometimes fatally attracts them into beam, where, blinded, they fly into each other, against airport buildings, and in darkness beyond may dash themselves into the ground (see Terres, 1956a; Johnston and Haines, 1957; Vosburgh, 1966). Fortunately, fixed-beam ceilometers at airport weather stations are rapidly being replaced by rotating-beam devices, which apparently do not cause disasters among birds (Gauthreaux, 1969). *See* discussion of ceilometers under Accidents; *also* Aircraft and Birds.

CELSIUS

See Centigrade.

CENSUS

(methods of). In order to "manage"—to maintain or to build—populations of song- and game birds and other animals, professional wildlife managers, ornithologists, and birders (*see* Birder) use the census, or a count, of birds and other animals in the wild, within the area to be managed. The game manager needs to know how many pheasants, quail, or grouse are on a certain area at different seasons, and on the basis of his count, can determine whether the bird population is low or high and the factors responsible for it. Quail populations may be low because weeds and brushy cover are scarce or overgrazed by livestock, woodcock and wild ducks may be gone because a marsh or a swamp has been drained, and robins and other songbirds may disappear from a tract which has been heavily sprayed with DDT. Often it is the wildlife census which tells the story of a serious decline, and the census usually precedes the analysis of why certain birds have vanished from an area. After censusing and diagnosing the inadequacy of the tract to produce quail, pheasants, ducks, or songbirds, the game manager can recommend the management measures needed to increase bird populations. *See* Songbird and Game-Bird Management.

Just when the idea of taking a "game census" of wildlife populations began no one seems to know and it is still in an era of change. The wildlife inventory—as vital to wildlife management as an inventory is to merchandising—seems to have begun in the U.S. in the 1920s and 1930s, when it was applied mainly to game species. The winter waterfowl survey, which is an annual inventory made by the U.S. Fish and Wildlife Service, began in 1935 and took the place of more or less desultory observations on waterfowl made prior to that time. Many of the states had made inventories of some kind, but generally these were estimates rather than inventories, or systematic population-trend studies.

The U.S. Fish and Wildlife Service and the Canadian Wildlife Service watch over waterfowl populations on both the breeding and wintering grounds and in the four major waterfowl flyways (*see* flyways and winter censusing under Waterfowl) each year. On the basis of its findings, they regulate the hunting take of waterfowl so as to ensure a continuing supply. They have a national system of wildlife refuges that offer waterfowl feeding and resting places (Terres, 1956c).

Censuses are made in various ways and the methods may depend on the kind of animal censused. With practically every animal, some peculiarity in its makeup or habits lends itself to the methods used for its inventory. For example, it was noted that pheasants are wont to seek dry spots near roads early in the morning, which makes early-morning inventories over properly selected roadways a good and practical way to compare one year's population with that of earlier years. Mourning doves do most of their calling or singing early in the day, just before and just after sunrise, therefore a "call-count" along certain routes gives a year-to-year comparison of the dove population of an area; a count of male sage grouse or of prairie chickens on the booming ground (*see* Dancing Ground), where they are strutting in sight of the concealed hens, gives a good indication of the male birds within a given area. Knowing the ratio of hens to males from earlier counts, the wildlife manager gets a comparative count of them. And so with the sharp-tailed grouse on its dancing ground (*see* Dancing Ground) and the woodcock on its singing ground (*see* Singing Ground). The quail is counted by its whistled calls; the rabbit by live-trapping it at night or by roadside tabulations; squirrels by their leaf nests; and muskrats and beavers by their houses (Terres, 1956c).

Direct counts of a single species can often be made, especially within small or limited areas where the entire population can be counted. *See* in biography of dusky seaside sparrow in Finch Family. By counting the deer tracks entering a yarding area after the first deep snow, the wildlife manager can get a census of deer by direct observation, and he can count the coveys of quail on a farm by working it thoroughly with good dogs (Leopold, 1933). Where the area is too large for complete censusing, sample counts of small sections can be made and the numbers of birds or other animals per unit of area applied to the entire plot. Students of bird populations, especially of songbirds, usually present the results of their censuses as the number of pairs of each species per 100 acres based on counts from a small area typical of the entire tract. Other types of counts or censuses are *block counts*, in tens, one hundreds, or thousands, usually of waterfowl, seabirds, elk, and other animals, made either from the ground or from aircraft; *crowing counts* of pheasants; *drumming counts* of ruffed grouse; and *sign counts* of pellets regurgitated by birds, their tracks at certain seasons, scat (fecal) deposits, and so on, which can be used as an index to populations.

CENSUS OF SONGBIRDS. The first publication of a bird census on a large scale was by Frank L. Burns: "A Sectional Bird Census Taken at Berwyn, Chester County, Pennsylvania, During the Seasons of 1899, 1900, and 1901." The results appeared in *The Wilson Bulletin*, 1901. Burns reported 588 pairs of native birds nesting on 640 acres of Pa. countryside, or less than 1 pair per acre. In the summer of 1907, the University of Illinois made a series of statistical bird counts published by S. A. Forbes in the *American Naturalist* in 1908 (Cooke, 1915b).

During the spring of 1914, the U.S. Biological Survey (now the Fish and Wildlife Service) sent out circulars to many interested persons throughout the country for assistance in making studies of the numbers of nesting birds. The survey recognized that it was important to know the number, distribution, and relative abundance of the breeding birds in the U.S. because of the economic value of birds to agriculture (*see* Economic Ornithology) and the need for formulating regulations for the protection of game- and other birds. The preliminary survey in 1914 proved so satisfactory that the work was repeated the next year on a larger scale. The counts of 1914 and 1915 showed slightly more than 1 pair of birds, or 2 birds, to the acre on farmland north of Md. and east of Kans. The censusing work was continued from 1916 to 1920 with similar results in the counts (Cooke, 1923).

Among birders, the most popular censuses are the breeding bird counts and the Christmas Bird Counts (*see* Christmas Bird Count). The breeding bird counts are made on the principle that in the breeding season the males of most species are in their territories (*see* Territory), where they sing or perform within a limited area. Each male is assumed to represent a breeding pair, although some singing males may not have mates, and some established pairs may be silent at the time of the census. Despite this, the breeding bird census of singing males gives a fairly reliable and comparable index to the summer bird population of an area. See discussion of this method by Sharp (1970), also by Aldrich and Robbins (1970); see also issues of *Audubon Field Notes* and its successor, *American Birds*, listed under Ornithological Periodicals.

In breeding bird censuses sponsored by the National Audubon Society, the census taker selects a sample area of a uniform habitat, say of a prairie, swamp, marsh, second-growth forest, or of climax forest, and counts, usually by the singing-male method, all the birds he can find in the area. The census-taker counts the birds repeatedly and periodically during the breeding season, and by repeating the census year after year, he gets indications of population changes (*see* Populations). When such censuses, taken from over the entire country in all types of bird habitats, are summarized (see Aldrich and Robbins, 1970), they yield information on the total number of breeding pairs of birds of each species.

Peterson (1948) estimated from the breeding bird censuses of the National Audubon Society and from many other sources that the total breeding population of land birds in the U.S. was at that time no less than 5 billion birds and possibly 6 billion. He also wrote that each pair of birds on the average is responsible for about 2 young, so that on a yearly basis, the continental population north of Mexico may be between 12 and 20 billion birds. He concluded: "Inasmuch as there are five continents in the world, the estimate of 100 billion by James Fisher for the global population seems reasonable."

Sample censuses in the wooded hills of much of the Appalachians indicated that the American redstart, the ovenbird (*see* both under Warbler—American Wood Warbler Family), and the red-eyed vireo (*see* Vireo Family) were the three most abundant species, undoubtedly totaling in the high millions (Peterson, 1948).

Concerning Peterson's 1948 estimate that the red-eyed vireo was then one of the three most abundant birds in the deciduous forests of e. N. America, Lawrence (1965) wrote that many observers felt that the time was past for the red-eyed vireo to be so classified and that this vireo now belongs among those "critical" species whose population in a few years had shown a crashlike decline and whose future recovery we can only guess. As proposed by Aldrich and Robbins (1970), only continued censusing of N. American birds can show their yearly fluctuations and relative abundance or scarcity.

Regardless of the type of census or inventory, place, kind of wildlife, or men doing the work, wildlife managers are no longer interested in the total numbers of animals for numbers' sake (except actual countable numbers of rare or threatened species) but for comparison. The total millions of ducks, warblers, or robins are not the important data for determining their welfare. What is important is whether or not the species is holding its own under current conditions, whether its numbers are becoming fewer or increasing. When this is known, the *trend* is evident and proper plans can be effected for their management (Terres, 1956c). *See* Songbird and Game-Bird Management. For experiments that increased songbird populations, see Terres (1977).

CENTIGRADE

(or CELSIUS). Name for temperature scale that expresses temperatures in "degrees centigrade" (abbreviated: ° C.); it is almost universally used in laboratory work (*see* Fahrenheit) and in researches in ornithology. One degree centigrade equals 1.8 degrees Fahrenheit. To convert centigrade readings to the more familiar Fahrenheit thermometer readings, multiply degrees centigrade by 1.8 and add 32.

Example: (37° C. × 1.8) + 32 = 98.6° F.

To convert Fahrenheit temperature readings to centigrade, first *subtract* 32 from degrees Fahrenheit, and then *divide* remainder by 1.8.

Example: (98.6° F. − 32) ÷ 1.8 = 37° C.

See Cold and Birds; Heat and Birds.

CENTIMETER

(SEN-tih-meter). A measure of length in the metric system often used in ornithological papers, reports, journals, and books. One centimeter (cm.) is 0.3937 inches (about two fifths of an inch); 100 centimeters is 1 meter, or 39.37 inches. Measurements of birds in popular books and articles are usually given in inches, and in feet and inches. *See* Millimeter; *also* Dimensions.

CENTRAL FLYWAY

See Waterfowl.

CERE

See Bill; Nostrils.

CEROPHAGY

(see-ROF-ah-jih). The eating of wax. Certain birds, such as the honey guides of Africa and Asia (a small family of picarian, or woodpecker-like, birds related to the barbets, woodpeckers, and toucans), eat beeswax persistently. *See* Autolycism. Many birds that feed on berries swallow the waxy coating of these fruits, perhaps inadvertently. About 30% of the food of the American black-capped chickadee is vegetable matter, largely the seeds of pine and other coniferous trees, and the wax-covered berries of bayberry and poison ivy. Tree swallows and yellow-rumped (myrtle) warblers also eat large amounts of bayberries, especially in winter, although it is not known whether or not they seek bayberries because of their waxy coating (Friedmann, 1955). *See* Food and Feeding Habits; Piciformes.

CERTHIIDAE

See Creeper Family.

CERVICAL SAC

One of a pair of air sacs (*see* The Air Sacs under Respiratory System) just below a bird's vertebral column, between the cervical (neck) vertebrae and the forward margin of the lungs (Salt and Zeuthen, 1960). *See* one of uses of under Voice and Sound-Making.

CESTODES

(SES-toads). Tapeworms of birds; are flattened and ribbon-shaped, usually segmented, worms; as adults, are found mostly in the intestines of their bird hosts (Wehr, 1959). Each species of tapeworm shows some predilection for a particular part of the small intestine, to which it attaches itself with the cuplike suckers or hooks of the tapeworm head. Tapeworms of birds usually require an intermediate host in which to live—for example, a beetle, fly, ant, snail, slug, earthworm, or crustacean—for the larval development of its life cycle. *See* Nematode.

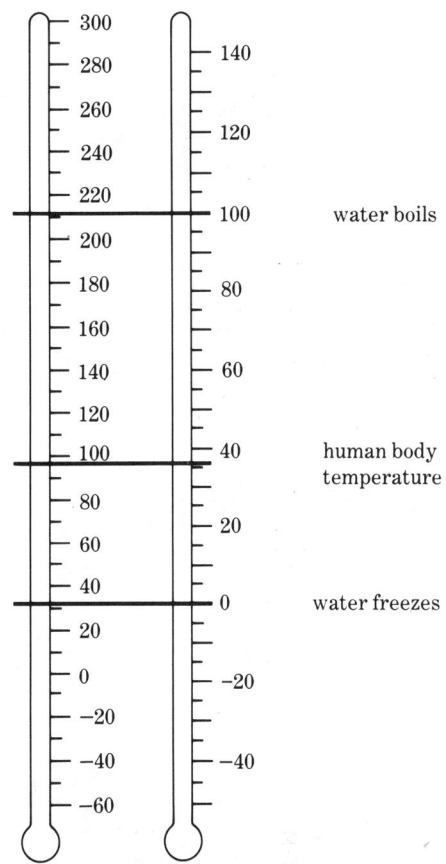

Fahrenheit   Centigrade

*comparison of Fahrenheit and Centigrade
-scales*

CENTIGRADE

*The Centigrade or Celsius scale is
the measure of temperature in the metric
system widely used in ornithological research,
and has a growing general use as well.*

plover

sandpiper

gull

skimmer

auk

CHARADRIIFORMES

CHACHALACA
See under Curassow Family.

CHALAZA
See Embryo and Its Development.

CHALK-LINE
One of the common local names of the green heron, from its habit of excreting a stream of white feces when frightened. *See* in Heron Family.

CHAMAEIDAE
See Wren-tit Family.

CHAM-CHACK
Name from a call note. *See* Woodpecker, red-bellied, in Woodpecker Family.

CHAPARRAL
(chap-ah-RAL). One of the nine biomes (*see* Biome) in N. America north of Mexico used in mapping the ecological distribution of birds. *See* Major Biotic Communities (biomes) under Distribution. The Chaparral is named for dense stands of broad-leaved evergreen shrubs and stunted trees 2–8 ft. high, dominated by chamise and manzanita. This biome is mainly on low hillsides and mountains of sw. Calif.; typical birds are the California thrasher, wren-tit, and gray vireo (Pettingill, 1970; 1972).

CHAPARRAL COCK
See Roadrunner in Cuckoo Family.

CHAPMAN
FRANK M(ICHLER) (1864–1945). Dean of American ornithologists in his time, a pioneer in bird photography, writer, lecturer, Curator of Birds, American Museum of Natural History (1908–42), New York City; author of some 225 articles and 17 books. Chapman's *Autobiography of a Bird Lover* (1933) was followed by *My Tropical Air Castle* and *Camps and Cruises of an Ornithologist.* Most widely used and possibly most important was his *Handbook of Birds of Eastern North America* (1895 and subsequent editions); his museum reports of his studies of birds in S. America were possibly his most important scientific publications (Murphy, 1950); he was also builder of the most extensive ornithological collection in any museum in the world. He was founder, editor, and owner of *Bird-Lore,* a popular bird journal later bought by the National Audubon Society and titled *Audubon Magazine.* See Lemmon (1953) and especially Peterson (1973) for a history of Chapman and his magazine.

CHARADRIIDAE
See Plover Family.

CHARADRIIFORMES
(kar-ad-ree-eh-FOR-meez); from Gr. *charadrios,* a yellowish bird dwelling in clefts (Coble, 1954), and Lat. *forma,* form. A large order of birds worldwide in distribution, including the polar regions; order includes 16 families and 314 species (Van Tyne and Berger, 1976); 11 of the 16 families are represented in N. America; members of this order spend much time in, on, or near water; structural characteristics of this complex assemblage include a tufted oil gland and a small aftershaft (afterfeather) on the body feathers; however, because of the diversity of the group, relatively few of the anatomical characters upon which the orders of birds are distinguished are constant in this group (Goodwin, 1961).

N. American avian taxonomists have divided the order Charadriiformes into three suborders: Charadrii, the Shorebirds; Lari, the Gulls; and Alcae, the Auks (Pettingill, 1970); 7 families of the order are classified in the suborder of Shorebirds—jacanas, oystercatchers, plovers, thick-knees, sandpipers, avocets, and phalaropes; the suborder Lari includes three families—gulls and terns, skuas, and skimmers; the suborder Alcae contains a single family—the auks, murres, and puffins.

See discussion of how birds are grouped according to their relationships under Classification; Morphology. The fossil record of the order goes back about 75 million years to the Cretaceous. *See* Geological Time Scale. *See also* Shorebird.

CHAT
See in Warbler—American Wood Warbler Family.

CHATTERER
See Bohemian waxwing in Waxwing Family.

CHAT, THE
A publication. *See* Ornithological Periodicals.

CHEBEC
Local name for the least flycatcher, from its call note. *See* under Flycatcher—Tyrant Flycatcher Family.

CHECK-LIST
Term for list of the species of birds that professional and advanced amateur ornithologists (*see* Birder) have compiled from their observations within a limited geographical area. Depending on the intensity of observation, it requires several to 10 or more years of observing year-round and identifying the species of birds within an area before a reliable check-list can be prepared.

Although comprehensive lists of the birds of major regions of the world (for example, the A.O.U. *Check-list of North American Birds,* a large bound volume that includes the scientific and common names of each species—*see* Names and Naming—their nesting and wintering ranges, etc.) are maintained in successive editions, the usual field check-lists, which also may be revised from time to time, are local, much simpler, and intended for daily use. They are small, usually pocket size, printed on cardboard or heavy paper, and list the common name of each bird known to occur in the area. Opposite each bird name is a blank space where the observer can make a check mark to indicate that he recorded the species at a particular time and place. There are blank spaces for the name(s) of the observer(s), date of the field trip, period of time in the field, weather, exact locality, and, usually, space for additional notes.

Many observers file these filled-in check-lists for future reference, as they may show the changing distribution or abundance or scarcity of birds from year to year. *See* Distribution. See also suggestions by Short (1970) for an expanded check-list.

Bird-watching, bird-listing, and bird study are usually local; therefore the local list, which tells the watcher what he may expect to see within a limited area, is a valuable guide. In 1961 the National Audubon Society published a long list of available field check-lists of birds for local areas within the U.S. and Canada, and where they could be purchased (Terres, 1961). See especially a state and province list of "bird-finding guides" by Gart (1975).

The A.O.U. *Check-list of North American Birds* is used by most professional and amateur N. American ornithologists as their official guide; the local field check-lists follow it for the sequence in which the local birds are listed. *See* Check-list Order.

In the 5th ed. of the authoritative A.O.U. *Check-list* (1957), the species listed are either (1) monotypic with no recognizable subspecies (for example, the ruby-throated hummingbird) or (2) polytypic, a species that has evolved into two or more subspecies (for example, the Canada goose, a species with 10 recognized races, or subspecies). Local check-lists usually list only the species of each bird, as it usually can be recognized on sight, and do not usually include subspecies, because so many of them cannot be positively identified in the field (through binocular or telescope) by most observers. *See* Species; Subspecies.

Species reaching N. America from other parts of the world, and new to this continent, are accepted by the American Ornithologists' Union and added to the A.O.U. *Check-list* only if proof is offered (1) by a specimen of the bird dead or alive or (2) by a photograph of it that leaves no doubt of its identity or (3) by sight record if the bird is not a species difficult to identify in the field and if it is seen by a number of experienced observers.

CHECK-LIST ORDER
A common term among birders for the sequence, or order, in which birds are listed in the A.O.U. *Check-list of North American Birds*. The order, beginning in N. American birds with the common loon and ending with the N. American McKay's bunting, is phylogenetic, or based on presumed ancestral relationships, from the "lowest" or most primitive birds to the "highest" or most specialized. The Check-List Order is an ascending arrangement that places, progressively, next to, or following, each other orders (with their families, genera and species) believed to be closest to each other in their relationship. *See* Phylogenetic Relationships; Classification.

CHERRY-BIRD
See Cedar waxwing in Waxwing Family and Sparrow, white-throated, in Finch Family.

CHEWING LICE
See Lice; *also* Ectoparasite.

CHEWINK
(chee-WINGK) *See* Towhee, rufous-sided, in Finch Family.

CHICKACOCK
See Gadwall in Duck Family.

CHICKADEE
See in Titmouse Family.

CHICKEN
See Domestication; *see also* Chicken, prairie, in Grouse Family.

CHICKEN-BILL
See Sora in Rail Family.

CHIGGERS
See Ectoparasite.

CHIMNEY-BIRD
See Chimney swift in Swift Family.

CHIMNEY SWEEP
See Chimney swift in Swift Family.

CHIP-COUNTING
A term for estimating the numbers of birds migrating at night by counting and tabulating the call notes of the birds as they fly by overhead. It is considered a wholly unreliable method for determining the total numbers of any species of bird that migrates at night (Berger, 1961). *See* Census.

CHIPPY
See Sparrow, chipping, in Finch Family.

CHLAMYDIOSIS
(klah-mid-ih-OH-sis). A new name suggested by Page (1966, 1968) for an occasionally fatal disease of birds and mammals caused by bacteria of the genus *Chlamydia;* the disease, formerly called psittacosis and ornithosis, was once thought to be caused by a virus. See review and discussion of this by Page (1966, 1968). According to Burkhart and Page (1971), chlamydiosis is a broad term needed to supplant such names as psittacosis ("parrot fever") for a disease passed from psittacine (parrotlike) birds to man, and ornithosis, the same disease carried by birds other than those in the parrot family. See discussion of these older names and their distinctions by Meyer (1959) and by Scheidegger (1960).

According to Meyer (1959), ornithosis (chlamydiosis) has become an occupational disease among breeders of pigeons, poultry farmers, and employees of poultry-processing plants. Fortunately the human mortality rate for the disease has been reduced by use of "the wide spectrum, antimicrobial drugs, especially tetracycline."

There are three ways in which the bacteria are transmitted from birds to man. In order of their importance, they are: (1) from inhalation of the bacteria in the air, (2) by ingestion of bacteria from excreta or nasal discharges of handled sick or latently infected birds, and (3) through contaminated bites of birds which pierce the skin. Transmission between birds may be through the bites of blood-sucking

nest mites and bird lice (Burkhart and Page, 1971).

In serological tests of 34 banders of wild N. American birds (*see* Banding) in Conn., N.Y., N.J., and Pa., 33 tested were negative for ornithosis (chlamydiosis); the single infected bird-bander was a youth with little experience handling birds who might have picked up the disease elsewhere (Worth *et al.,* 1957). The investigators concluded that most species among native wild birds in N. America are not a hazard to man or a reservoir for the disease.

The infection appears in domestic and wild birds and mammals throughout the world (Burkhart and Page, 1971). Of all known hosts for the disease, the feral pigeon, *Columba livia* (*see* in Pigeon Family) is the most common and consistent source of infection; however, although it is a potential reservoir of human infection, there is little evidence to date, according to Burkhart and Page, of transmission of the disease from pigeons to wild birds. Infections have been found worldwide in 139 species of wild birds of 15 orders (*see* Order; Classification). In N. America, these include the willet, sanderling, laughing gull, least tern, common tern, gull-billed tern, royal tern, black skimmer, snowy egret, great egret, glossy ibis, ringed turtle dove, ring-necked pheasant, titmice, and painted bunting. See worldwide list in Burkhart and Page (1971).

Meyer (1959) also includes, in N. America, the northern fulmar, herring gull, black-billed magpie, starling, house sparrow, and the introduced European goldfinch, which has apparently vanished from N. America (*see* in Finch Family). Among cage birds, besides members of the Parrot Family, ricebirds, finches, and canaries have a relatively high susceptibility to chlamydiosis and die, after being afflicted, within a relatively short time.

Signs of acute infection begin with an an exudate from the bird's eyes or nostrils, lack of appetite, and inaction; diarrhea follows, and the feces are gray or rust-colored with blood. As the disease progresses the bird assumes a fixed position with little movement and it shows distress in breathing. In a protracted form of the disease, the symptoms are similar but less pronounced, and death, if it comes, may be delayed while the signs subside and reappear weekly; the bird gradually loses weight and becomes emaciated. See Burkhart and Page (1971) for details of symptoms in pigeons, parrots, ducks, and other groups of birds; it appears little can be done once the infection is established in wild birds, but domesticated or captive birds that are infected can be treated as suggested by Burkhart and Page. If the disease is suspected, however, the local public health authorities should be notified immediately.

Lack (1954) believed that in the wild, in conjunction with food shortages and other adverse environmental conditions, ornithosis (chlamydiosis) might work to reduce populations of wild birds; however, according to Meyer (1959), the infrequency with which epizootics in wild bird populations attract attention, and the infrequency with which humans are infected by the disease from wild birds, may account for our

stork

flamingo

ibis

CICONIIFORMES

heron

lack of knowledge of these infections in the natural environment.

Besides bird-banders, others who catch and handle wild birds may be exposed from time to time to infected birds, especially those with pet parrots, the wildfowlers of the Faeroe Is. who catch fulmars for food (Lack, 1954), and those who catch "muttonbirds" (slender-billed and sooty shearwaters) in the Australian Region, which are also susceptible to the infection (Meyer, 1959).

Chlamydiosis has caused the deaths of wild parrots and parakeets, occasionally hundreds at a time, in Australia and in the Argentine. Consult the U.S. Public Health Bureau for regulations regarding imported wild birds. *See also* Diseases.

CHOANA
(KOH-ah-nah; pl.: *choanae* (KOH-ah-nee). A funnel-like opening. Choanae is the more technical name for the two internal nares which open from the nasal chambers into the roof of the pharynx inside a bird's mouth (Thomson, 1964j). *See* discussion of nares under Nostrils. *See* discussion of pharynx under Mouth.

CHOLERA
See Avian Cholera.

CHORION
See Embryo and Its Development.

CHOW-CHOW
A common name of the yellow-billed cuckoo, imitative of its call.

CHRISTMAS BIRD COUNT
An annual count of late-Dec. birdlife, taken chiefly during Christmas week (usually Dec. 20 to Jan. 1 or 2 inclusive), in which thousands of individuals and groups of American and Canadian birders choose a single day in this period to count all wild birds they see, each within an area 15 mi. in diameter. In the Christmas Bird Count of 1960, 8,928 people participated; they reported 506 species and counted 52,523,850 birds (Scott, 1961). In the 72nd Christmas Bird Count of 1971, 18,798 people participated in 263 counts across the U.S. and Canada; they reported 538 species of birds with an estimated total of 64,584,702 birds. In the 79th Count of 1978, 31,140 people participated (*see American Birds*, July 1979 issue) in 1,269 counts and reported 600 species of birds with an estimated total of 103,403,790 birds.

The birders hunt over plains, marshes, mountains, beaches, and oceans, and travel by foot, on snowshoes, skis, and by sleigh, automobile, horseback, bicycle, canoe, commercial fishing boat, motorboat, marsh buggy, airplane, helicopter, and even by an electric car used by golfers. The count, sponsored by the National Audubon Society and the U.S. Fish and Wildlife Service, is taken in every state, including Alaska and Hawaii, and most provinces of Canada, and may well represent geographically the most widespread ever taken. The results of the count—the names and numbers of each species of bird seen, date of each count, and names of people participating—are published in *American Birds* (formerly titled *Audubon Field*

Notes), issued by the National Audubon Society. For reference to the count and its history, see the article by Robbins (1966b).

CHUCK-WILL'S-WIDOW
See in Nightjar Family.

CHUKAR
also CHUKOR. *See* Chukar, in Pheasant Family.

CHURCH-MARTIN
See Starling in Starling Family.

CHYME
(KIME). *See* Digestion.

CICONIIDAE
See Stork Family.

CICONIIFORMES
(sik-oh-ny-ih-FOR-meez); from Lat. *ciconia*, stork, and *forma*, form; storklike (Coble, 1954). An order or grouping of birds of 112 species (Van Tyne and Berger, 1959) that resemble each other fundamentally in structure (*see* Order); includes 7 families in the world, of which 4 are represented in N. America: Heron Family, Stork Family, Ibis Family, and Flamingo Family (A.O.U. *Check-list*, 1957). Birds in these families are waders that have adapted to living in marshes or shallow waters; a few live on dry uplands. They have long bills and short tails and range in size from the smallest bittern, barely 10 in. high, to the 5-ft.-tall adjutant and saddle-billed storks of Africa; the wings of birds in the Ciconiiformes are long, rounded and broad; the legs very long and feet with four toes (*see* Food and Feeding Habits); the lores (space between the eyes and bill) usually bare of feathers. They are an ancient group, dating back at least 100 million years, to the Cretaceous Period (Austin, 1961). *See* Geological Time Scale.

Other families in the Ciconiiformes in other parts of the world include the Boat-billed Heron Family of 1 species that lives from Mexico south to Peru and s. Brazil; the African Whale-billed Stork Family of 1 species; and the Hammerhead Family of 1 species of sw. Arabia, Africa, and Madagascar. See Van Tyne and Berger (1959) and Austin (1961) for details. *See also* Classification; Morphology; Phylogenetic Relationship.

CINCLIDAE
See Dipper Family.

CIRCULATORY SYSTEM
In birds, composed of the four-chambered heart (*see* Heart), the arteries, veins, and capillaries, and the lymphatic system—a series of nodes and channels. The heart and blood vessels form a closed system of tubes through which the blood is carried to all parts of a bird's body. The circulatory system is run by the heart, which forces blood throughout the vast network of blood vessels. The time required for the blood under normal pressure to make a complete circuit of the body of an adult chicken averages about 6 seconds (Welty, 1962). Main functions of the circulatory system are to carry

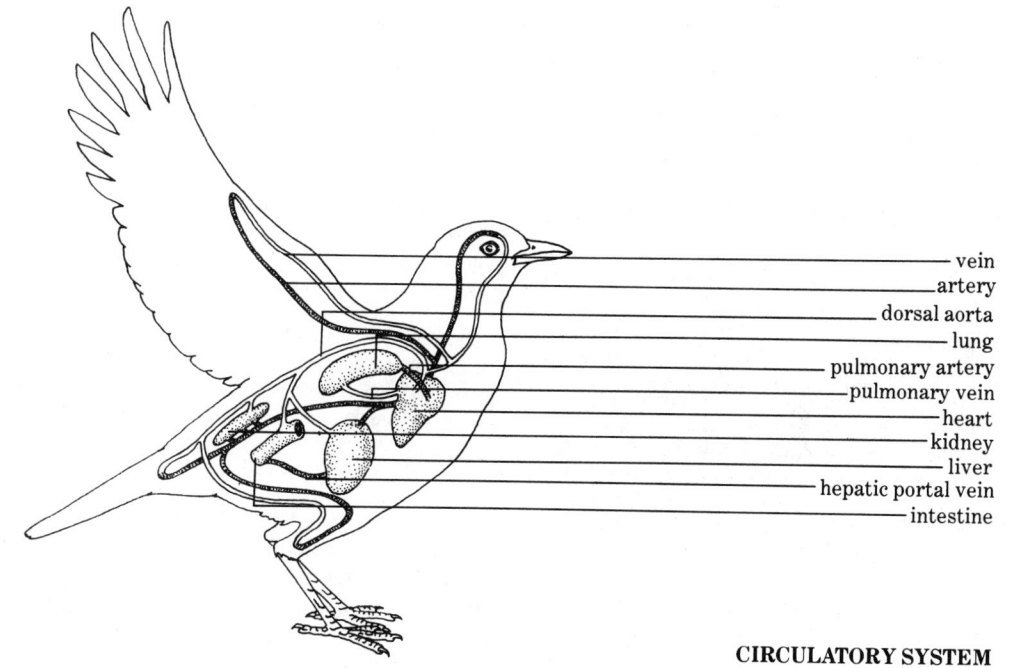

vein
artery
dorsal aorta
lung
pulmonary artery
pulmonary vein
heart
kidney
liver
hepatic portal vein
intestine

CIRCULATORY SYSTEM

digested foods, oxygen, minerals, and hormones to the cells of the body, to carry away carbon dioxide and other metabolic wastes (*see* Respiratory System), to regulate the water content of the tissues, and so on (Welty, 1962). See Simons (1960); Sturkie (1965); and Jones and Johansen (1972) for details. The blood in the circulatory system also plays a main part in controlling and preventing diseases and in regulating and maintaining the body temperatures of birds.

The blood of a bird, as in mammals, consists of a watery fluid (plasma) and the corpuscles, which are carried in the blood. The blood is reported to form about 5–13% of the body weight. There are two main types of corpuscles in the blood of birds—the red cells (erythrocytes) and the white cells (leucocytes). The red cells carry the respiratory pigment, hemoglobin, which forms a loose compound with oxygen (Simons, 1960) and carries the oxygen to the bird's tissues. Red blood cells of birds are larger than those of mammals, and their total number in a bird is influenced by its age, sex, diet, the seasons, and other factors (Sturkie, 1965). Red blood cells of birds are biconvex, oval, nucleated, and range in number from 1.9 million per cc. of blood in a 265 lb. ostrich to more than 6 million per cc. in the blood of a hummingbird weighing about 1/10 oz. and a junco weighing about 3/4 oz. See Table 7.2 in Welty (1962). Usually the more highly evolved flying birds (songbirds, for example) have smaller and more numerous red corpuscles, with richer hemoglobin, than more primitive birds.

Red blood cells are formed mainly in the bone marrow of adult birds, although in passerines (songbirds) they are formed in the spleen and liver (Portmann, 1950a). The leucocytes, or white blood cells, are formed in the early life of a bird in the liver, spleen, kidneys, pancreas, and the bursa of Fabricius (*see* Bursa of Fabricius), but in adult birds are formed mainly in the spleen and caeca (Welty, 1962). The leucocytes help protect the bird's body against diseases, assist in the body's general repairs, and, according to Jones and Johansen (1972), may function in fat metabolism, which is of great importance to a bird during long starvation periods. *See* Fasting.

The plasma is a complex fluid, about 80% water, which carries at times food, hormones, enzymes, antibodies, and waste products. "Most of the carbon dioxide (one of the waste products of metabolism) is carried by the plasma to the lungs, where it is discharged" (Berger, 1961). *See* Respiratory System; *also* Metabolism.

Besides the capillary network of blood vessels, a network of delicate lymph vessels in the tissues of a bird's body, called the lymphatic system, carries the liquid filtered out of the capillary system back into the veins (Simons, 1960). *See also* Digestion.

CLAM-BIRD
See Plover, piping, in Plover Family.

CLAMS AND BIRDS
See Mollusks and Birds.

CLAN
(of birds). *See* Woodpecker, red-cockaded, in Woodpecker Family.

CLAPE
See Flicker, yellow-shafted (common), in Woodpecker Family. Name given it from one of its calls.

CLARK
WILLIAM (1770–1838). Virginian, honored by Alexander Wilson in the English name Clark's crow (now Clark's nutcracker) from specimens and descriptions of this bird along the banks of the Clearwater R. in Idaho, which Wilson obtained from members of the Lewis and Clark expedition. Capt. Clark shared with Meriwether Lewis the command of their famous exploring expedition across the continent (1803–06). *History of the Expedition under the Commands of Captain Lewis and Captain Clark* was first published in 1814.

CLASS
A group of animals or plants of a category above an order and below a phylum. In the Linnaean system of classification, it was the highest category. *See* Aves; Classification.

CLASSIFICATION
In America, ornithologists, specifically *taxonomists* (*see* Taxonomy), have classified or grouped birds in a list that is phylogenetic (*see* Phylogenetic Relationship) or based upon species relationships, beginning with the most primitive, or most ancient, birds—the loons in N. America—to what is considered the most recent, or most highly developed in an evolutionary way, the perching birds—some familiar ones are larks, thrushes, jays, wrens, starlings, wood warblers, and others. Aristotle, the Greek philosopher, was the first to realize that the most practical system of classification of birds and other animals is based on the amount of similarity of characters. Later, morphology, or form, and internal parts became the basis for classification. According to Mayr *et al.* (1953): "The great advantage of this system is that it is based on the sum total of many morphological similarities or differences. Such a system is apt to indicate 'natural affinities' as Linnaeus and even some pre-Linnaean authors contended, and was therefore called the *natural system* in contradistinction to artificial systems based on a single character."

Carl Linnaeus, who established the modern hierarchy, or ranking, of certain categories for birds and other animals, recognized within the animal kingdom only five groupings in a descending order—from the more general to the more specific—*classis* (Class), *ordo* (Order), *genus* (Genus), *species* (Species), and *varietas* (Variety). As our knowledge of animals grew, it became necessary to divide these categories into finer ones. Today the basic hierachy of animals (from the general to the specific) is as follows: Kingdom, Phylum, Class, Order, Family, Genus, and Species (Mayr *et al.* 1953).

Birds are in the Animal *Kingdom, Phylum* Chordata (kor-DATE-ah), *Subphylum* Vertebrata (with a backbone), and *Class* Aves, or Birds.

N. American birds are ranked in twenty *Orders* and the birds of each order resemble each other fundamentally in structure—usually the shape of the bones of the head and their arrangement; the shape of the breastbone; the number or arrangement of the toes of the foot; the number of tail feathers; and so on. However, the size of the birds within an order, their colors, shapes of their wings and bills, all may vary considerably. Yet all birds in an order (*see* Order) are more like each other than those that are classified in another order.

FAMILIES OF BIRDS. Each order of birds has within it one or more *Families*. The family to which a bird belongs may depend on the general shape of its bill, the relative lengths of its wing feathers, the pattern of the scales of its tarsus, and other details. In defining or classifying birds in certain families, variations in a bird's color or color pattern are not important because colors vary widely in most bird families. If several families in an order are more like each other than families in the rest of the order, they may be grouped together in a Superfamily or a Subfamily or the order may be subdivided into Suborders to show this relationship. *See* Family.

GENUS. Each family of birds has at least one *Genus* or a number of *Genera* (plural of *Genus*) in which certain birds are grouped to show close relationships within the family. The distinguishing characters of birds that show they belong in a certain genus are usually the shape of the bill (*see*, however, Convergent Evolution), whether or not the bird has bristles, its distinctive color pattern, its type of nesting habitat—whether forest, grassland, ocean beach or lakeshore, and so on. *See* Genus. We must not be too concerned with names and nomenclature and too little with realities. Dr. Dean Amadon, a taxonomist and student of evolution of birds, wrote (Amadon, 1962): "We are not so much concerned with the technicalities of how to name a genus as with the fact that in evolution, groups of related species have risen (oak trees, viburnums, crows, etc.) and that it is useful to group these in artificial categories called genera. All categories (except species and *some* subspecies) are artificial."

SPECIES. Within each genus there may be from one to many *Species* of birds. All the individuals of a species usually resemble each other about as closely as though they were offspring of the same parents. There is some individual variation, but considerable uniformity runs through a species which distinguishes it from birds of other species. Species cannot always be identified as such on the basis of their form and anatomy, as can orders, families, and genera; *see*, however, discussion of many methods used to determine relationships between birds under Taxonomy. A species has been defined as an interbreeding (or potentially interbreeding) group of birds or other animals that does not *in nature* interbreed significantly with any other group. *See* details under Species; *see also* Hybrid.

SUBSPECIES. In certain geographical regions —deserts, mountains, prairies, and humid forests, for example—groups of a certain species respond so much to variations in climate that they change considerably from other populations of their species in size and color. Though still recognizable as the same species, these geographical varieties, or "races," are known as *Subspecies,* and are able to interbreed with other geographical subspecies of their species, or kind, when their populations meet. Subspecies are separated only geographically, not reproductively.

Should one of these subspecies be isolated long enough, however, from others of its kind (it seems to require thousands of years), it may eventually vary so in habits, courtship, form, and color that it will become reproductively isolated from its former species and become a new species. According to Amadon (1962): "For the evolution of a species, the necessary thing is geographical isolation (partial or complete), whereupon in due time, differences, first racial, eventually specific, will rise. These may be environmental or the result of changing courtship habits (plumes of pheasants, etc.) or just sheer change, as people on different islands come to speak differently. In North America, all species and almost all subspecies have long since been named." *See* What about Discoveries of New Species? under Species. *See also* Subspecies; Names and Naming.

EXTRA CATEGORIES. In most groups of animals, including birds, there has risen an occasional need for an even more precise definition of the taxonomic position than is afforded by the usual grouping of Kingdom, Phylum, Class, Order, Family, Genus, Species, and Subspecies. Thus there is a Subphylum, a Superclass and a Subclass, a Superorder and a Suborder, Superfamily and Subfamily, Tribe and Subgenus.

In current taxonomic practice, the scientific names of tribes, subfamilies, families, and superfamilies have no standardized endings. There are no standardized endings for names of the finer categories above that of Family except in the orders of birds. Note that in the following classification of two living birds, taken from the A.O.U. *Check-list* (5th ed., 1957), certain of the intermediate, finer categories are not always used:

Kingfisher

Class *Aves:* Birds
Subclass *Neornithes:* True Birds
Superorder *Neognathae:* Typical Birds
Order *Coraciiformes*
Suborder *Alcedines*
Superfamily *Alcedinoidea:* Kingfishers
Family *Alcedinidae:* Kingfishers
Subfamily *Cerylinae:* Typical Kingfishers
Genus *Megaceryle*
Subgenus *Streptoceryle*
Species *alcyon:* Belted kingfisher
Subspecies *alcyon*

Robin

Class *Aves:* Birds
Subclass *Neornithes:* True Birds
Superorder *Neognathae:* Typical Birds
Order *Passeriformes*
Suborder *Passeres*

Superfamily: none
Family *Turdidae:* Thrushes, Solitaires, and Bluebirds
Subfamily: none
Genus *Turdus*
Subgenus: none
Species *migratorius:* American robin
Subspecies *migratorius*

For detailed discussions of classification, see especially in Ch. 11 of Berger (1961); Ch. 12 in Van Tyne and Berger (1976); and Ch. 17 in Dorst (1974).

Following are the orders and families of N. American birds as ranked phylogenetically (*see* Phylogenetic Relationship) in the A.O.U. *Check-list of North American Birds* (5th ed., 1957). *Common family names* are those of Van Tyne and Berger (1976); those marked with an asterisk (*) are families of birds of which representatives appeared on the N. American continent (*see* North America) since publication of the 1957 *Check-list* and its supplements. *See* discussion under Family.

Order I. Gaviiformes
  1. Loon Family: Gaviidae
Order II. Podicipediformes
  1. Grebe Family: Podicipedidae
Order III. Procellariiformes
  1. Albatross Family: Diomedeidae
  2. Shearwater Family: Procellariidae
  3. Storm-petrel Family: Hydrobatidae
Order IV. Pelecaniformes
  1. Tropic-bird Family: Phaethontidae
  2. Pelican Family: Pelecanidae
  3. Booby Family: Sulidae
  4. Cormorant Family: Phalacrocoracidae
  5. Anhinga Family: Anhingidae
  6. Frigatebird Family: Fregatidae
Order V. Ciconiiformes
  1. Heron Family: Ardeidae
  2. Stork Family: Ciconiidae
  3. Ibis Family: Threskiornithidae
  4. Flamingo Family: Phoenicopteridae
Order VI. Anseriformes
  1. Duck Family: Anatidae
Order VII. Falconiformes
  1. American Vulture Family: Cathartidae
  2. Hawk Family: Accipitridae
  3. Osprey Family: Pandionidae
  4. Falcon Family: Falconidae
Order VIII. Galliformes
  1. Curassow Family: Cracidae
  2. Grouse Family: Tetraonidae
  3. Pheasant Family: Phasianidae
  4. Turkey Family: Meleagrididae
Order IX. Gruiformes
  1. Crane Family: Gruidae
  2. Limpkin Family: Aramidae
  3. Rail Family: Rallidae
Order X. Charadriiformes
  1. Jacana Family: Jacanidae
  2. Oystercatcher Family: Haematopodidae
  3. Plover Family: Charadriidae
  4. Sandpiper Family: Scolopacidae
  5. Avocet Family: Recurvirostridae
  6. Phalarope Family: Phalaropodidae
 *7. Thick-knee Family: Burhinidae
  8. Skua Family: Stercorariidae
  9. Gull Family: Laridae
  10. Skimmer Family: Rynchopidae
  11. Auk Family: Alcidae

CLASSIFICATION

The taxonomic classification of the common crow

Kingdom	Animalia
Phylum	Chordata
Subphylum	Vertebrata
Class	Aves
Order	Passeriformes
Family	Corvidae (Crow)
Genus	Corvus
Species	brachyrhynchos

The scientific name Corvus brachyrhynchos is a combination of the genus and species names.

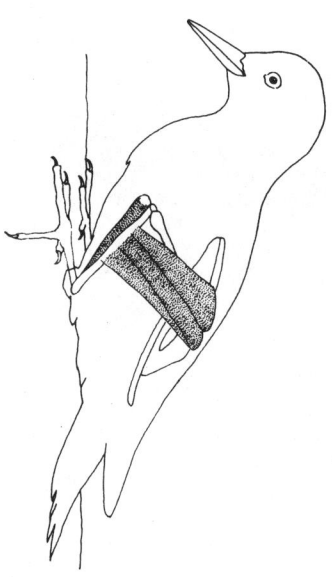

CLIMBING BIRDS
*Powerful muscles hold the legs of the flicker in
position as it clings to the trunk of a tree.*

Order XI. Columbiformes
  1. Pigeon Family: Columbidae
Order XII. Psittaciformes
  1. Parrot Family: Psittacidae
Order XIII. Cuculiformes
  1. Cuckoo Family: Cuculidae
Order XIV. Strigiformes
  1. Barn Owl Family: Tytonidae
  2. Typical Owl Family: Strigidae
Order XV. Caprimulgiformes
  1. Nightjar Family: Caprimulgidae
Order XVI. Apodiformes
  1. Swift Family: Apodidae
  2. Hummingbird Family: Trochilidae
Order XVII. Trogoniformes
  1. Trogon Family: Trogonidae
Order XVIII. Coraciiformes
  1. Kingfisher Family: Alcedinidae
Order XIX. Piciformes
  1. Woodpecker Family: Picidae
Order XX. Passeriformes
  1. Cotinga Family: Cotingidae
  2. Tyrant Flycatcher Family: Tyrannidae
  3. Lark Family: Alaudidae
  4. Swallow Family: Hirundinidae
  5. Crow Family: Corvidae
  6. Titmouse Family: Paridae
  7. Common Nuthatch Family: Sittidae
  8. Creeper Family: Certhiidae
  9. Wren-tit Family: Chamaeidae
*10. Bulbul Family: Pycnonotidae
  11. Dipper Family: Cinclidae
  12. Wren Family: Troglodytidae
  13. Mockingbird Family: Mimidae
  14. Thrush Family: Turdidae
  15. Old World Warbler Family: Sylviidae
*16. Old World Flycatcher Family:
     Muscicapidae
  17. Hedge Sparrow Family: Prunellidae
  18. Pipit Family: Motacillidae
  19. Waxwing Family: Bombycillidae
  20. Silky Flycatcher Family: Ptilogonatidae
  21. Shrike Family: Laniidae
  22. Starling Family: Sturnidae
  23. Vireo Family: Vireonidae
  24. Honeycreeper Family: Coerebidae
  25. American Wood Warbler Family:
     Parulidae
  26. Weaverbird Family: Ploceidae
  27. Troupial Family: Icteridae
  28. Tanager Family: Thraupidae
  29. Finch Family: Fringillidae

CLAVICLE
One of the three bones forming the pectoral
girdle (*see* Skeleton). In most birds, two "collarbones" (the right and left clavicles) fuse just
in front of the breastbone (sternum) to form
the *furcula*, often called the "wishbone" or
"merrythought" (Van Tyne and Berger, 1959).

CLAW
See Claws under Feet And Legs.

CLEPTOPARASITISM
See Kleptoparasitism.

CLIMATE
(effect of on birds). *See* Distribution; *also* discussion under Geological Time Scale; *see also*
Weather.

CLIMAX COMMUNITY
Term for the culminating stage of the development of the plant life of a region. It is a
community of plants that is permanent and is
in entire harmony with a stable habitat but its
equilibrium is dynamic, not static (Weaver and
Clements, 1938). It makes the most efficient
use of all the resources of a community and is
indefinitely self-sustaining; the total community it supports is the ultimate or final stage
of succession for the region unless disturbed
by man or by recurring fires. *See* Subclimax
Community. It is an expression of the climate
of the region and is controlled by climate; it is
therefore called also the *climatic climax*
(Buchsbaum and Buchsbaum, 1957). *See* examples of climax communities and some of the
typical birds associated with each under Tundra; Coniferous Forest; Deciduous Forest;
Grassland; etc. *See* these major biotic communities (biomes) listed under Distribution.
See also Ecosystem.

CLIMBING BIRDS
These are usually divided into two groups: (1)
the woodpeckers (family Picidae), represented
in N. America by some 22 species, the woodcreepers, or woodhewers (family Dendrocolap-
tidae), of the tropical American forests, related
to the tropical American ovenbirds (see discussion by Austin, 1961), and the tree creepers
(family Certhiidae), of which the N. American
brown creeper is an example—all of which use
their tails for support as they climb or rest
against the trunk of a tree; and (2) the nuthatches (family Sittidae), of which there are 4
species in N. America (*see* Nuthatch Family),
and the small, wrenlike piculets (Woodpecker
Family), mostly of the American tropics—all of
which rely completely on their feet as they
climb. *See* Piciformes.

The woodpeckers, woodcreepers, and tree
creepers have some structural characters in
common, probably as a result of evolution in
their climbing habits—for example, the pygostyle and the free caudal vertebrae are much
enlarged and form a strong support for the
attachment of the tail feathers. This is an example of convergent evolution (*see* Convergent
Evolution), in which unrelated birds have developed similar forms or parts of the body because
of similar feeding habits (Storer, 1960a). *See
also* Morphology. See also discussion by Richardson (1942). The chimney swift (*see* Swift
Family) also depends on its spinelike tail feathers to support it when clinging to vertical surfaces.

CLINE
Term of ecologists and taxonomists (*see* Taxonomy) for a gradual geographical change in
the structure, color, pattern, markings, or sizes
of individuals of a species which is widely distributed geographically and is therefore subject to changes influenced by climate and local
environments. The hairy woodpecker, *Dendrocopos villosus*, shows a cline in body size.
The largest forms inhabit the northernmost
parts of the bird's range in Canada and Alaska.
The range extends south through the U.S. into
C. America to w. Panama. The smallest forms
are at the southern part of this woodpecker's

range. These populations exhibit clinal (geographic) variation in their characters, or groups of characters, which may show in a gradual progression in different directions from one part of the species' range to another—east to west, north to south, and so on, depending on the direction or directions in which the changing climate and its impact on the bird or other animal progresses. *See* Ring-Species.

Scientists have noted that the impact of climate (including temperature, humidity, rainfall, snowfall, etc.) tends to produce certain uniform changes in birds and other animals that sometimes can be clinal. These uniform or predictable changes have lent themselves to the following "rules":

Allen's Rule: Within a species, protruding parts such as tails, ears, and bills all tend to be shorter in cold climates, longer in warm climates. *See* Allen's Rule.

Bergmann's Rule: Within a species, the individuals tend to be smaller in warmer climates, larger in colder climates. See Behle (1973); Rand (1961). *See* Bergmann's Rule.

Gloger's Rule: Within a species, colors tend to be darker in moist climates, paler in dry climates. *See* Gloger's Rule.

CLOACA

(kloh-AY-kah); Lat., a sewer. In birds, urine and feces from the digestive tube, and the sperms and eggs from the reproductive organs, all pass out of the body through a common passage, the cloaca. *See* Copulation and Copulatory Organs. The cloaca is incompletely separated into three compartments—a *copropodeum*, into which the large intestine empties; a *urodeum*, into which the ureters and genital ducts empty; and the *proctodeum*, with which the copropodeum and urodeum communicate and which opens to the outside of the body through the vent, or anus, which is the external opening of the digestive tract (Berger, 1961). *See* Digestion; Urogenital System; Kidney.

CLOACAL KISS

See Copulation and Copulatory Organs.

CLUCKING HEN

See Limpkin in Limpkin Family.

CLUTCH

The total number of eggs laid by a female bird for a single nesting. *See also* Brood; and especially Eggs and Egg-laying.

COB

See introduction to Duck Family.

COBBLE

See Red-throated loon in Loon Family.

COCCIDIOSIS

(cock-sid-ih-OH-sis). General term for a protozoan infection among wild and domestic birds. The parasitic protozoa are microscopic animals which grow in the epithelial cells of the digestive tract, usually in the lining of a bird's intestines. The disease got its name from the Coccidia, a subdivision of the great protozoan class

Sporozoa, all of whose representatives are parasitic. There are as many kinds of coccidiosis as there are species of coccidia, each with its own characteristic symptoms (Becker, 1959).

As a group, the coccidioses of chickens cause larger losses than in any other domestic bird. Fortunately the protozoan parasites that cause coccidiosis are usually limited to a single species of bird or other animal, or to a limited group of closely related ones. Many years ago, workers in poultry diseases blamed wild birds, especially house sparrows (*see* in Weaverbird Family), as a source of coccidial infection in poultry flocks, but it was later proved that the coccidia of wild passeriform birds was of a different genus than the one that infects domestic poultry. In general, coccidiosis in any particular bird or mammal is a problem more or less peculiar to it (Becker, 1959).

Of the many known genera of the coccidia only two are of importance as parasites in domestic chickens, turkeys, ducks, and guinea fowl. These are *Eimeria* and *Isospora*. In wild birds these two genera have been reported in pelicans, cormorants, geese, ducks, grouse, pheasants, quail, cranes, coots, plovers, sandpipers, pigeons, doves, hawks, cuckoos, woodpeckers, kingfishers, sparrows, robins, and other songbirds (Becker, 1959). See details in the more recent treatment of coccidia in Todd and Hammond (1971).

Although Stoddard (1931), in his bobwhite quail investigations in Ga., did not find acute coccidiosis in wild quail, he found that losses of captive quail chicks from it could be large and concluded that coccidiosis could be a great hindrance to raising bobwhites in captivity. Birds with acute coccidiosis may show loss of appetite, emaciation, droopiness, and diarrhea, often followed by death. Birds become infected from being crowded together and the coccidia are usually transmitted from bird to bird from food or water contaminated with feces of infected birds. They become infected while they are drinking or feeding through picking up and ingesting the viable sporulated oocysts of the coccidia (Becker, 1959). *See also* Diseases.

COCK

Term for the male of the common barnyard fowl; also much used in British ornithology for the male of songbirds, game birds, and others.

COCKAWEE

See Oldsquaw in Duck Family. Name is phonetic imitation of the bird's cries.

COCK OF THE ROCK

See Arena bird; Cotinga Family.

COCK-TAIL

See Duck, ruddy, in Duck Family. Name from male's habit of often cocking its tail.

COEREBIDAE

See Honeycreeper Family.

COFFIN-CARRIER

See Gull, great black-backed, in Gull Family. From black mantle of adult.

COITUS

(coition). *See* Copulation and Copulatory Organs.

COLD AND BIRDS

Birds have greater resistance to cold than mammals. Heat losses from their bodies are not only diminished by a coat of feathers, which encircles and insulates them with confined air, but the lower legs and feet of birds are tendinous (not with exposed fleshy parts as in mammals); their bills are not of skin but of horn (*see* Bill) and thus give up little heat; body temperatures are higher than those of mammals. See Metabolism; Temperature.

HOW BIRDS ADAPT TO COLD. To keep up their high metabolic rate (heat and energy production), birds eat rich energy foods—seeds, insects, rodents, fruit, and nectar, for example—and have high concentrations of glucose in the blood (about double that of humans), which induces higher metabolism. They have adaptations that conserve heat—some, especially in the North, where seasonal changes are severe, have more feathers in winter than in summer, and smaller birds have more feathers per unit of body weight than larger ones. *See* discussion under Feather.

Exposed skin of birds is minimal; there are no projecting fleshy ears, tails, or legs from which heat may be lost; and many water birds have a thick insulating layer of body fat. When perching, birds may tuck one foot in the belly feathers; ducks on ice often sit with their feet under them, which helps protect them against heat losses from the body; many birds also tuck the horny bill into the feathers during extreme cold, and have air sacs under the skin that may protect them with a layer of insulating air against cold. *See* Respiratory System.

Ducks and geese have a remarkable adaptation that prevents their feet from freezing while they stand on ice; in their feet, the arteries and veins lie against each other, and the cold returning blood of the veins is warmed by the arterial blood, effecting a rapid replacement of lost heat; this adaptation is also present in the bills of some cold-climate birds (Welty, 1975).

Shivering is used by some (perhaps by all) birds (pigeons and chickadees, for example) for short-term adjustment to cold, and is the main way that a bird increases its heat production while the bird is at rest—it converts muscular energy into heat but the used energy must soon be replaced.

Evening grosbeaks and some other northern finches are able to store relatively large amounts of seeds in their well-developed crops (*see* Crop), which seems effective in maintaining high metabolism for them overnight (Dawson and Tordoff, 1959). See also Mugaas and Templeton (1970). Brooks (1968), after many experiments with hoary and common redpolls, discovered they can survive colder temperatures than any other passerine (songbird); they have high rate of energy intake owing in part to a special storage pouch in the esophagus (*see* Esophagus), which they fill with food just before darkness so as to digest the food over-

COLD AND BIRDS
Chickadees can withstand bitter winter cold and adapt to low temperatures by fluffing their feathers, thereby trapping more insulating air.

night, and they select high-calorie foods (birch seeds) over others.

Some birds—swifts, hummingbirds, and the poor-will, for example—become torpid overnight during cool spells by lowering their body temperatures and rate of metabolism, thus conserving their food energy supplies. *See* Torpidity. Mourning doves, in winter during bitter cold and lack of food during storms, do not become torpid but also may use a physiological mechanism "(perhaps lowered body temperatures) to decrease their metabolic expenditures which permits conservation of energy and augments survival" (Ivacic and Labiskey, 1973).

Large birds living in cold climates have an advantage over small ones because of their comparatively small surface areas which lose less heat. *See* discussion under Metabolism; *see also* Bergmann's Rule. Because small birds do not feed at night, many in the North appear to save body heat in extremes of winter by roosting in sheltered places (*see* Roosting) and by reducing their activities (see Kessel, 1976). Chickadees, woodpeckers, and nuthatches sleep in holes in trees; bluebirds pack together with up to a dozen or more sleeping in a bird nesting box (*see* Russian study of huddling, below); evening grosbeaks, cardinals, and crossbills will roost in densely needled branches of coniferous trees; desert horned larks scratch out roosting holes in ground (Trost, 1972). Ptarmigans and ruffed grouse will plunge under loose snow to sleep; snow buntings may stay under snow both night and day through periods of bitter cold; in Alaska, air temperature above snow may be −50° C., but 2 ft. below surface may be a relatively warm −5° C. (*see* equation for converting Centigrade to Fahrenheit, and Fahrenheit to Centigrade, under Centigrade).

In a Russian study of goldcrests *(Regulus regulus)*—small birds related to N. American golden-crowned kinglet—when two huddled together at 0° C., each reduced its heat losses by 23%; huddled in groups of three, each reduced its heat losses by 37% (Gavrilov, 1972).

In n. U.S., winter nights are 14–15 hours long; birds that feed by day must be able to endure the cold for this length of time without food (Kendeigh, 1945b). In tests with house sparrows, Kendeigh discovered that they could go longest without food in summer—for 67½ hours at about 85° F. With a drop in air temperature to about 50° F., there was a rapid decline in the ability of the sparrows to resist starvation. At 5° F., the sparrows could live without food for 15 hours—the length of the winter night; at −20° F., they could live only about 10 hours without food; at −30° F., they lived only about 7 hours.

To survive winter cold, small birds must feed every day, both to replenish energy lost the preceding night and to build a reserve for the night to come (Kendeigh, 1945b), and they must find a sheltered roost. Any difficulty in finding plenty of food and night shelter may be critical for them. *See* Fasting; *also* Food and Feeding Habits; Digestion; Bird-attracting.

HOW MUCH COLD CAN BIRDS ENDURE? As in all animals, there are extremes of cold beyond which some birds cannot endure—the limits vary with the species themselves, age, and health of each, for example. Welty (1962) points out that the European yellowhammer, *Emberiza citrinella,* a finch, many of which spend the winter in the North, can endure temperatures down to −36° C.; however, another member of the Finch Family, the related Ortolan bunting, which migrates south for the winter, can stand only −16° C. *See also* Tree Sparrow in Finch Family for example of a hardy, cold-resistant species.

In many species of birds, if the *body* temperature (*see* Temperature) falls to 21.7° C., it apparently will die; this is its lethal minimum *body* temperature (Benoit, 1950). *See* Heat and Birds.

Some insect-eating birds that migrate may be caught either in spring or in fall in a sudden spell of freezing cold, and will die of exposure, starvation, and weakness because of their inability to get enough food to survive. *See* Disaster Species. In N. America, the Carolina wren, a southern species, which is not migratory, has extended its range far to the north to Canada. With an unusually cold or prolonged winter of heavy snow, it may be so decimated on its northern range that it may not recover its numbers or regain its northward range for several years; however, it is the occasional out-of-season storm or brief but unusual cold spell that overtakes and decimates migrants periodically, and more frequently. Some N. American birds have suffered great losses when flying northward and meeting an unseasonably cold and wet spring—for example, scarlet tanagers, which depend greatly in early spring on spanworms, the caterpillars of the small geometrid moths, and some of the small wood warblers, which may find insects or their larvae killed off or retarded in their emergence by a cold late spring (Terres, 1956d). During one early-Mar. snowstorm on the prairies of the Middle West, millions of Lapland longspurs, migrating northward, died (*see* biography of this bird in Finch Family; see account of the disaster in Roberts, 1932; Terres, 1948); *see also* others under Waterfowl.

In Europe, the European barn swallow has been overtaken and grounded during its southward migration by sudden cold and wintry weather. In the fall of 1931, near Vienna, thousands were overtaken by unusual cold. Chilled and benumbed, the stricken swallows during a driving cold rain were gathered up in great numbers from the countryside by members of the Vienna Animal Protection Society. During two weeks of rescue work, after being fed mealworms, 89,000 of the surviving swallows were shipped by aircraft and by railway express over the Alps to the sunny plains of Italy, where they were released to continue their journey southward.

During a similar catastrophe in Oct. 1974, people in n. Europe picked up an estimated 250,000 tired and hungry barn swallows, which the Swiss Federal Airways, Swissair, and other airlines carried southward. The revived swallows were released and then continued to fly on their way south.

COLD-BLOODED
See Metabolism.

COLIN

(COH-lin). *See* Bobwhite in Pheasant Family.

COLLECTIONS

Collections of once-living birds, or their parts, prepared either for study or for exhibition in natural history museums, usually include those called *mounts* (the "stuffed" bird set up on a foundation in a lifelike pose), study skins (*see* Bird Skins), and fluid-preserved specimens of soft parts, also skeletons of birds and nests and eggs. These research collections form the basis of exact studies of birds relating to many problems in ornithology. *See* Curator. They are used by students in ornithology, and for a discussion of their usefulness, see especially Parkes (1963); see also "Need for Collecting Specimens" in American Ornithologists' Union (1975a).

For locations of research collections of birds in N. America, see report of a survey by Banks *et al.* (1973) that revealed a total of about 4,200,000 bird study skins, 142,150 skeletons, 52,025 fluid-preserved specimens, and 638,840 nests and/or eggs, all in 283 institutions and in private collections in the U.S. and Canada up to 1969. See second report by Clench *et al.* (1976). For general information about ornithological collections and how to prepare a bird skin, see Wallace (1963); for instructions about scientific collecting of birds, see Van Tyne (1952); Pettingill (1970). For a history of early bird collections, see Allen (1925); Peters (1933). Taking, transporting, or possessing migratory game birds and migratory non-game birds or their parts, nests, or eggs for scientific or educational purposes in the U.S. requires a Federal Scientific Collecting Permit (American Ornithologists' Union, 1975a). *See* Legal Protection.

COLOR PHASE

(morph). Some birds have two or more color phases, or color forms, within the same species. The phases can be very different; for example, the white and blue forms of the snow goose, *Chen caerulescens*, were for years thought to be separate species. (*See* discussion below.) When there are only two color phases of a species, the condition is called by biologists *dichromatism* (two colors); when there are more than two, as in the screech owl, it is called *polychromatism* (several or many colors). The difference in color between the two or more phases is independent of age, sex, or season—it is an inherited, year-round, or perennial color.

Many different families of birds show two color phases among their species: the short-tailed hawk, one of the rarest hawks in N. America, is dichromatic, with two distinctly different color forms—a dark and a light phase. The two are so unlike that early American ornithologists believed each to be a separate species (May, 1935). Other hawks that have two color phases—one light, one dark—are the rough-legged, ferruginous, red-tailed, Swainson's, and Harlan's hawks. The reddish egret has a red and a white phase and some petrels, shearwaters, and the northern fulmar and parasitic jaeger have a light and a dark phase; the least bittern has a "normal" and a dark (melanistic) phase (Palmer, 1962), and the great white heron is not a distinct species but a color form of the great blue heron. Furthermore, although there are two extremes, such as gray and red, intermediate forms often occur between them. See Huxley (1955) for an interesting discussion of some of the two or more different, and genetically determined, color forms existing among birds and reasons for their interest to ornithologists.

One of the most interesting examples of two color forms in one species is that of the blue goose and the snow goose. Each of these was thought for years by many ornithologists to be a distinct species until the work of Cooch (1951) and Cooke and Cooch (1968), who found from their genetic studies of these birds that they are one species (conspecific) and that when the two interbred, the blue goose, or blue phase, was dominant over the white. For some details of cross-breeding, *see* Hybrid; see also Cooke and Mirsky (1972). *See* other details of the snow goose and its blue phase under Duck Family.

According to the American Ornithologists' Union (1973), the blue goose is the dark morph, or dark phase, of the snow goose, and "snow goose" remains the common English name. See Lack (1943c, 1947-48) for other kinds of dimorphism in birds.

The gyrfalcon shows polychromatism, with all degrees of intergradation from white to black.

Polymorphism (many forms) is a widespread kind of variation and may involve not only color but structural characters (Simpson *et al.,* 1957). See discussion of polymorphism by Mayr (1942, 1951) and Huxley (1964).

Some color phases are influenced by the climate in which the bird lives. The screech owl is polychromatic, with three color phases in the eastern U.S., but it has mainly two: a red (rufous) phase and a gray phase; an intermediate brown form makes up a small percentage of the population. Van Camp and Henny (1975), in their studies of the screech owl in n. Ohio, discovered that the gray phase population (more abundant than the red phase in the northern part of the screech owl's range) is able to withstand the severe winters better than the red phase. The red phase (more abundant than the gray phase in most of the southern part of the screech owl's range) had significantly higher energy demands (needed more food) in cold, snowy weather than the gray phase. Mosher and Henny (1976), in follow-up studies in the laboratory, concluded that the increased energy needs of the red-phase over the gray-phase birds during extremely cold weather come at a time when deep snow reduces its hunting efficiency, which could lead to greater mortality of the red-phase birds. In December 1951, Ohio had the coldest temperatures and deepest snowfall during the 30-year study of the screech owl there by Van Camp and Henny. Following this period, the red-phase screech owls fell from 23.3% of the screech owl population to 14.7%, suggesting that the gray-phase owls were much better able to survive extreme environmental stress. *See also* Seasonal Dimorphism under Colors of Feathers.

Like the screech owl, the ruffed grouse is polychromatic; the two extremes are gray and

Great white heron

Great blue heron

COLOR PHASE

The great white heron is now considered to be the white phase of the great blue heron, which it resembles in size and form. In its blue phase, this heron is the most widespread in North America; in its white phase, it is found only in Florida and the Caribbean region, although where its range overlaps, intermediates occur.

red, but one phase grades into the other. The gray and red phases of the ruffed grouse show a somewhat similar geographic pattern to that of the screech owl, from north to south, with the gray phase apparently better able to survive the northern winters. See Gullion (1966); Gullion and Marshall (1968).

COLORS OF FEATHERS

Birds are considered the most colorful of all vertebrate animals, and their colors are derived (1) from pigments, or biochromes, (2) from the effects of microscopic feather structure, or schemochromes, and (3) from a combination of both. Biochromes, or pigment colors, are of three types according to their chemical makeup —melanins, carotenoids (*see* Carotenoids), and porphyrins (Van Tyne and Berger, 1959). Heredity plays a dominant role in controlling feather colors; hormones also play a part. *See* Endocrine Glands; Sexual Dimorphism; Gynandromorph.

Melanins, which usually range from soft yellow through red-brown, dark brown, and black (unless modified by feather structure), are the most common bird pigments. Carotenoids are pigments, as in paint, which usually produce yellow, orange, or red. Porphyrins (pyrrolic pigments) are in nitrogenous compounds synthesized by all animals, and are easily detected by their red fluorescence. Two of the porphyrins reported by scientists from bird's feathers are turacoverdin, a green pigment known only in the turacos, or "plantain-eaters," that live in the deep forests of Africa, and turacin, a red pigment known only in these birds. *See* discussion of turacos under Cuculiformes. Another is koproporphyrin, a pink pigment of bustards of the Old World (Fox, 1953).

Schemochrome colors are optical illusions caused by the structure of the feathers of many birds. White feathers, the simplest example of a schemochrome, have no pigments, so that all light falling on them is reflected as white. Many of the colors we see in birds are a result of various rainbow colors of the spectrum, being either reflected or absorbed as light falls on a feather and bounces back to the observer's eyes. Apparently, blue is never the result of blue pigment. For example, the bright blue of the blue jay, bluebirds, and the indigo bunting is not an actual blue, or pigment color, but light waves of blue reflected from a layer of cells which overlies the dark, brownish basal pigment cells in the barbs of the feathers (Gower, 1936). *See* barb under Feather.

The green feathers of a parrot are created in the same way, except that a transparent yellow layer over the blue-producing cells masks, or modifies, the blue and thus produces green.

ABNORMAL COLORS. *Melanism*, not to be considered the opposite of albinism (*see* Albinism), is caused by an excess of dark pigments in feathers, many cases of which are genetically determined (Harrison, J. M., 1964b). It is much less frequent than albinism, even considering that it is more often overlooked (Sage, 1962). Gross (1965b), in his survey of melanism (dark color forms of birds), reported melanism for only 29 species of N. American birds, whereas from the same sources of information he reported albinism in 304 species of N. American birds.

Apparently there are two frequencies of occurrence of melanism—a regularly occurring dark form, as in the N. American rough-legged hawk and short-tailed hawk, and an occasional or even rare dark mutant, such as that in the broad-winged hawk.

Erythrism, term for an excess of reddish-brown pigment in the feathers, is not common in birds; however, it is well known in the screech owl, which has a red form, or red phase. *See* Color Phase. It also occurs with some regularity in the prairie chicken, locally in bobwhite quail and ruffed grouse, and in the least bittern, of which a blackish-chestnut, possibly a melanistic, form, discovered in Fla. by Charles B. Cory, was once considered a distinct species. A reddish color in certain ducks, geese, swans, and cranes, caused by contact with ferric oxide in water or mud of the environment, is not erythrism. *See* Adventitious Color.

Another abnormal color phenomenon of birds is called *schizochroism* (skiz-ZOK-row-ism), a term applied to an abnormally pale, washed-out bird whose paleness results from an absence of one of the pigments normally present in its plumage (Stresemann, 1927–34). Dovekies and murres, among seabirds, and California quail and mourning doves that were described as "dilute" or "pale" mutants were probably examples of schizochroism; also in red-winged blackbirds and house sparrows (Van Tyne and Berger, 1959) of a cinnamon or tan color. McCabe (1970) cited a single fawn-colored wing of a female gray partridge out of a collection of 4,260 wings of this species sent to him by hunters in Wisc. for sex and age determination; he considered this an example of schizochroism. He suggested that schizochroism may be sex-linked in its heredity, as it is among females that sex-linked variants are likely to become apparent. See also *leucism* in Harrison, J. M. (1964b), a condition closely allied to albinism.

Xanthochroism (zan-THOK-row-ism) is an abnormal yellow of the plumage, very rare in the wild, but more common among captive parrots. It is thought to result from the loss of dark pigment (melanin) in the feathers, which allows the yellow carotenoid pigment to dominate over the light-produced and reflected blue. See Harrison (1964b; 1966); Gross (1965b); Pettingill (1970).

Iridescence, or "interference" colors, of feathers are the effect of a thinly laminated structure in the barbules (*see* Feather). This structure interferes with light rays striking the feathers from different angles, thus scattering them and presenting to the observer the brilliant greens, purples, and reds, especially in the plumage of hummingbirds. See Greenewalt (1960) for details of iridescence in hummingbirds' feathers. The wings of many kinds of ducks have a patch of iridescent feathers, called the *speculum;* the plumage of grackles and other birds, including the peacock, is more or less iridescent. Iridescent colors are made more brilliant by underlying pigment colors of the feathers, but are essentially independent of pigments (Van Tyne and Berger, 1959).

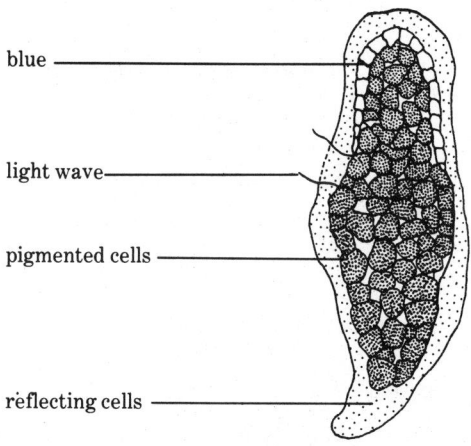

blue —
light wave —
pigmented cells —
reflecting cells —

COLORS OF FEATHERS
In this cross-section of a barb of a blue jay feather, light waves in the blue portion of the spectrum are reflected from a layer of cells that overlie the dark brownish basal pigment cells.

USES OF COLORS TO BIRDS. Colors of feathers help in many ways. Those with dark pigments (black, brown, gray) wear better than white ones, and certain birds, though not all, have dark-colored wing and tail feathers, which are subjected to greater wear (Heinroth and Heinroth, 1958). Colors of birds' feathers may help to promote health and bodily comfort. Dark feathers absorb light and heat rays and conserve energy in cool weather (Serventy, 1971); pale ones, especially of birds that live in deserts, serve, in part, to reflect the light and heat rays, thus insulating the birds' bodies against too much heat and light. The pale feathers also help them to blend with the pale or white desert sand, thus making them less noticeable to predators. See discussion by Serventy (1971) of biological advantages of black color to birds of arid regions.

CRYPTIC, OR CONCEALING, COLORS. Many kinds of birds are cryptically marked in that some match so well the ground, shrubbery, or trees in which they live that, when motionless, they are difficult or impossible to see; this is called *protective coloration.* Owls, whip-poor-wills, woodcock, quail, and ruffed grouse, for example, blend with the trunks of trees or the ground on which some of them crouch for nesting or resting. Among sparrows and marsh birds, the feathers of many are so striped or streaked that when they are motionless they blend with the grasses in which they live; vireos, warblers, goldfinches, etc., that live in thickets or forests of sunlit foliage tend to be yellowish or greenish with black markings. Their colors make them especially difficult to see when they are motionless in times of danger (Wallace, 1955).

A special and much-debated kind of cryptic coloration has been called *obliterative shading,* or *countershading.* Birds such as sandpipers, plovers, sparrows, and others that often feed on the ground have dark-colored backs and white underparts. The principle of countershading, first called to the attention of naturalists by G. H. Thayer (1909), functions as concealing in nature. In such birds, the white of the belly feathers counterbalances the effect of a shadow cast by the bird and it does not stand out from its background in bold relief as would an evenly dark-colored bird (Allen, 1925). The eggs of many ground-nesting birds, especially those of plovers, are protectively colored. *See* Eggs and Egg-laying.

Another type of protective coloration is often called a *ruptive,* or *disruptive,* pattern. In birds so marked, the body color pattern is broken by spots, bands, or is otherwise marked in such a way that the body appears to be cut into unidentifiable pieces. These markings are bold and contrasting, for example, in the killdeer and the semipalmated plover, whose plumage markings make them blend remarkably with their backgrounds of pebbly or stony shores and beaches.

SEASONAL DIMORPHISM. Term for change in the plumage of birds in response to striking seasonal changes in the environment. For example, ptarmigans (*see* Grouse Family), like many other Arctic and so-called high boreal

birds, have a pronounced seasonal dimorphism —a white-feathered one in winter; a brown-pigmented one in summer. Following the winter, or basic, plumage, there are two or three other feather generations from spring to autumn, depending on the sex and species. According to Höst (1942), "the striking manner in which the different plumages blend with the environment has caused ptarmigan to become a classical example of 'seasonal dimorphism' and 'protective coloration.'" *See also* Albinism.

Huxley (1955) points out, however, that the molt of the male rock ptarmigan, *Lagopus mutus,* from white into brown summer plumage, is delayed. This renders the males highly conspicuous during the period when the hens are brooding their eggs of young and appears to be a "deflective" adaptation—it deflects the attacks of predators, such as the golden eagle, away from the brown-colored females to the conspicuous and "biologically less valuable males." *See* Cryptic, or Concealing, Colors above.

Höst discovered in his experiments with willow ptarmigans under laboratory control that light (in nature, length of day) is the main controlling factor in the reproductive cycle and plumage changes in spring and in fall. *See* Light. *See also* Endocrine Glands.

COLORS THAT ADVERTISE. During a bird's life, the colors of its feathers may also serve it as visual signals to birds and other animals of its world. Certain birds have feathers (so-called banner-marks and flash colors) that are conspicuous only when the birds are flying. Thus the suddenly flashing white outer tail feathers of juncos and the white rump patch of a flicker or a meadowlark in flight are thought to serve as a signal to other members of the same species.

Crows, flamingos, and many other flocking birds seem to be without need for cryptic, or concealing, coloration as protection against their enemies. Their conspicuous colors may help individual birds in the flock to correlate their movements with those of the rest of the flock (Van Tyne and Berger, 1959).

Colors of birds that bring the sexes together during the courting and nesting season are called *epigamic.* Colors and markings of birds may enable them to distinguish their sexes and to stimulate members of the opposite sex. *See* Sexual Dimorphism. The brilliant colors of the males of certain species are often used as "threats" to other males of their kind during territorial defense (*see* Territory). These are called *antaposematic colors* (Van Tyne and Berger, 1959). Lack (1953) concluded that the red breast of the European robin is used mainly for this purpose during the breeding season. The brilliant colors of the males may also enhance their plumage displays prior to and during the pairing of birds. *See* Courtship; *also* Behavioral Mimicry under Behavior.

COLOR VISION OF BIRDS
See Eyes and Eyesight.

COLUMBIDAE
See Pigeon Family.

disruptive coloration (Killdeer)

protective coloration (American woodcock)

COLORS OF FEATHERS
Bold, black bands on the white breast of the killdeer break up the form of the bird, creating a pattern that allows it to blend into its background on a pebbly beach.

The "dead leaf" pattern caused by the cryptic markings on the American woodcock makes it difficult to see as it crouches motionless in fallen leaves and under bushes.

winter

summer

seasonal dimorphism (Rock ptarmigan)

COLORS OF FEATHERS
Two distinct plumages of the rock ptarmigan, in winter and summer, reflect the dramatic seasonal change in its environment, and each is remarkable as well for its protective coloration. The length of daylight is the main controlling factor in the plumage changes in the spring and fall.

pigeon

COLUMBIFORMES

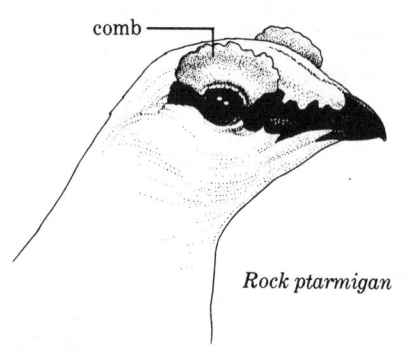

comb

Rock ptarmigan

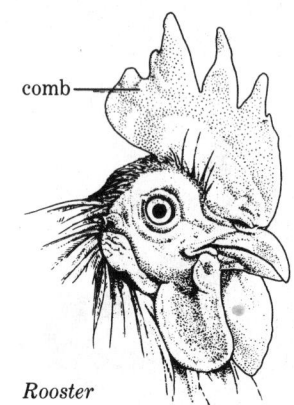

comb

Rooster

COMB
The male rock ptarmigan develops small red combs over its eyes in the spring. The male domestic chicken has a permanent, large, red comb on its crown and forehead.

COLUMBIFORMES

(coh-lum-bih-FOR-meez); from Lat. *columba*, a dove, and *forma*, form; dove-shaped. An order, or group, of 311 or more species of living birds that resemble each other fundamentally in structure (*see* Order); includes 2 living families: the Sandgrouse Family of Europe and Great Britain, Africa, and s. Asia of 16 species (*see* discussion of a new proposed classification of sandgrouse under Swallowing) and the Pigeon Family of 295 or more species, worldwide, with species in N. America. Many ornithologists (specifically, taxonomists) believe that the extinct family Raphidae of 3 species—the dodo and 2 species called solitaires, not to be confused with the N. American Townsend's solitaire, a thrush—should be classified in the Columbiformes.

All living members of the Columbiformes are land birds and share in common compact dense plumage in special feather tracts (*see* Feather), with the feathers set loosely in the skin and easily shed, and a well-developed crop. All feed their young by regurgitation (*see* Regurgitation; *also* Crop), and at least in doves and pigeons have a distinctive way of drinking by sucking up water (*see* discussion under Swallowing; *also* Pigeon Family).

The dodo, a member of the family Raphidae, is a well-known symbol of extinction ("dead as the dodo"). It lived on Mauritius Is., and of the two other similar and closely related extinct solitaires in the family, one lived on Réunion Is., the other on Rodriguez Is. in the Mascarene Is. east of Madagascar, in the Indian O. All were blue-gray, gray-white or white with some yellow or black. They were large, flightless, land-dwelling pigeons, big as a turkey or bigger, weighing up to 50 lbs. They had large heads, heavy hooked bills, fat bodies, short strong legs, short wings, and loose curly tail feathers. Apparently they ate fruit, seeds, berries, and leaves, and the females laid possibly just one egg on the ground. They moved about slowly and clumsily and these flightless birds were thought to be stupid by sailors because they had little or no fear of man. See other details in Austin (1961); Greenway (1958).

The dodo, discovered on Mauritius in 1598, was gone by 1681—it was edible and an easily obtainable food for visiting seamen and explorers. The solitaire on Réunion was extinct by 1746; the one on Rodriguez survived to about 1791 (Fisher, 1970).

There are a few museum specimens of the dodo—one of the best is a mounted bird at Cambridge, Eng. There are also fairly abundant remains of bones, including some complete or nearly complete skeletons, of the dodo and the Rodriguez solitaire. *See* discussion of extinct species under Geological Time Scale. For a discussion of how birds are grouped according to their relationships, *see* Classification; Morphology; Phylogenetic Relationship.

COLUMELLA

(kol-you-MEL-ah). The single earbone of the middle ear of birds; it connects the inner ear with the eardrum (Hann, 1953) and is connected with the pharynx by the pharyngotympanic tube (Berger, 1961). *See* Ears and Hearing.

COMB

A bare, erect, fleshy process on the crown of a bird's head, for example, on that of the domestic chicken; it is larger in the male (rooster) than in the female (hen). See Skin. For details and types of combs in domestic fowl, see in Lucas and Stettenheim (1972). The name "comb" is from its serrated, comblike edge, or margin. Many grouse have a small comb over each eye. *See also* Wattle; Caruncle; Casque.

COMMENSALISM

Term for the actions of birds and other animals while profiting from certain habits of their neighbors, without important effects on those neighbors. Sometimes, in food-getting, they literally "eat at the same table." In commensalism, one of the partners usually gets food, protection, transportation, or a combination of these from the other (Simpson *et al.*, 1957). *See also* discussion under Parasite.

For example, yellow-bellied sapsuckers often drill small holes into the green cambium layer of trunks of trees, then sip sap from the tree as it oozes into the small holes. A sapsucker in Fla. set up a feeding station for other birds when it drilled horizontal rows of holes in the trunk of a sweet gum tree. From a half dozen of these it drank sweet sap; other birds that came to drink were the myrtle (yellow-rumped) warbler, yellow-throated warbler, orange-crowned warbler, ruby-crowned kinglet, red-bellied woodpecker, ruby-throated hummingbird. At Urbana, Ill., a Cape May warbler spent two weeks in a backyard feeding on sap from holes drilled in a willow tree by a sapsucker (Dennis, 1951). In Mich., besides warblers and a ruby-throated hummingbird, Nickell (1965b) saw downy and hairy woodpeckers feeding at sapsucker "wells." At least 35 different kinds of birds associated with sapsucker trees eat either insects or sap, or both (Foster and Tate, 1966).

Hairy and downy woodpeckers often follow, or associate with, the larger pileated woodpecker. After the stronger pileated scales bark off dead trees with its bill in search of insects, the smaller woodpeckers move in to pick up insects the larger bird may have missed or ignored (Bent, 1939). Bluebirds, nuthatches, pine warblers, chickadees, and tufted titmice have been watched catching insects dislodged or uncovered from the bark of trees by the red-cockaded woodpecker (Beckett, 1971b).

In Okeechobee, Fla., a loggerhead shrike in its food storage impaled its prey regularly on twigs of a lemon tree in a side yard. A mockingbird visited the tree several times a day to eat the supply of lizards, frogs, and grasshoppers put there by the shrike (Sprunt, 1954a). After mud-dauber wasps had stored spiders in mud cells they built in an abandoned cabin in Tex., which were to be provender for the young larval wasps, two cañon wrens searched the cells and carried off some of the stored spiders (Martin, 1971). Some hummingbirds pluck small entangled insects from the webs of spiders (Petrides, 1942) but may get caught in the webs and perish. *See* Accidents.

The brown pelican, gannets, gulls, and terns follow porpoises to share in their capture of fishes; ptarmigans follow caribou in winter to benefit from foods the caribou dig up; some herons and the belted kingfisher profit from the feeding of red-breasted and hooded mergansers; and Wilson's phalaropes attend shovelers (ducks) to profit from their feeding. In the British Virgin Is., an observer watched a Bahama duck feed directly in back of a yellowlegs to catch and swallow food stirred up by this shorebird. In Surinam, Haverschmidt (1970b) watched ruddy turnstones stand close to yellow-crowned night herons feeding on crabs to pick up pieces that fell from the bills of the herons. *See* related behavior under Autolycism.

The American wigeon, or baldpate, swims near coots and swans to feed on the aquatic plants that float to the surface after being uprooted by the feeding of these birds. See a review of this type of association by Anderson (1974).

COMMISSURE
The line of closure of the upper and lower parts of the bill—the line along which the upper (maxilla) and lower (mandible) parts of the bill meet when the bill is closed (Berger, 1961).

COMMON NAME
The English, as opposed to the Latin, name of a bird; the popular name as opposed to the scientific name.

COMMUNICATION
See Alarm Notes; Behavior; Courtship; Drumming; Language; Sexual Dimorphism; Waterfowl.

COMPROMISE BEHAVIOR
Term of bird behaviorists for a response of a bird to a situation of two incompatible tendencies. *See* details in What Influences Bird Behavior? under Behavior.

CONCEALING COLORS
See Colors of Feathers.

CONDOR
See under Vulture—American Vulture Family.

CONDOR, THE
A publication. *See* Ornithological Periodicals; *also* Cooper Ornithological Society.

CONES
See Eyes and Eyesight.

CONGENERIC
Term for species of birds that are of, or within, the same genus. *See* Genus.

CONIFEROUS FOREST
One of the nine biomes (*see* Biome) in N. America north of Mexico used in mapping the ecological distribution of birds. *See* Major Biotic Communities (biomes) under Distribution. The Coniferous Forest is in general a dense forest of pines, spruces, firs, hemlocks, etc., which has been divided by Pettingill (1972) into the *Transcontinental Coniferous Forest* (taiga), or *Boreal Forest*, which extends from Alaska and Rocky Mtns. east across Canada to the Atlantic coast, and then branches south on the Appalachians, where it is called the *Eastern Montane* (mountain) *Forest* and the *Western Montane Forest*—the moist coastal coniferous forests along the North Pacific Slope and in the Cascade, Sierra Nevada, and Rocky Mtns. Typical birds of the Western Montane Forest and the Boreal Forest are: goshawk, three-toed woodpeckers, olive-sided flycatcher, gray jay, red-breasted nuthatch, brown creeper, winter wren, hermit and Swainson's thrushes, the kinglets, evening and pine grosbeaks, pine siskin, red crossbill, and others. The Eastern Montane Forest includes at least seven of the birds listed for the Western Montane Forest, but see details in Pettingill (1970 or 1972). *See also* Canadian Zone.

CONSERVATION
See Legal Protection; Census; Sanctuary; Wildlife Refuge; Songbird and Game-Bird Management; Bird-attracting.

CONSPECIFIC
Of the same species. Term applied to the individuals, or to populations, of the same species.

CONTACT CALLS
Term for simple notes of birds that may keep them together by voicings which identify their position to others. The peeping calls of ducklings keep the brood together in dense grasses and sedges and keep the mother duck informed of their location. The young, in turn, follow after the low notes of the mother. Mallard and pintail ducks in evening migration flights northward in spring utter soft chuckling calls that are thought to hold them together in the darkness, and songbirds, migrating at night, especially in fall, have migration calls that are thought to function as a bond to the birds in the darkness (Hochbaum, 1955). *See* Language.

CONTOUR FEATHER
One of the feathers that form the outline or contour of the bird's body. *See* Vaned Feather. Specifically they are the outer feathers of the head, neck, and body and the flight feathers of the wings and tail. Scientists have found considerable variation in the numbers of contour feathers on different kinds of birds. *See* Numbers of Feathers on a Bird under Feather. The contour feathers of most songbirds, except the smallest species, number from 1,500 to 3,000. During the winter, many hardy kinds of birds that remain in the North acquire more feathers as winter approaches. *See* Cold and Birds; Metabolism; Feather; Molts and Molting.

CONTROL
Although most birds, most of the time, are economically useful and aesthetically desirable (Meanley, 1971a), the reduction of a population of certain birds is sometimes called for by private landowners and the public because of crop damage or possible threats to public health. Bird damage control programs are guided or controlled by the federal government and state governments, which are responsible for the legal protection of birds. At certain times and in certain places, there may be concentrated for a short time too many of certain species of

COMMENSALISM
The Cape May warbler is a commensal feeder; it takes insects and sap from the holes, or "wells," drilled by a sapsucker.

Golden eagle

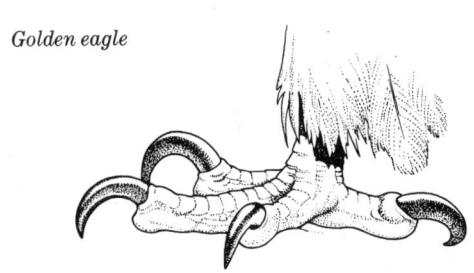

Great horned owl

convergent evolution

CONVERGENT EVOLUTION
Eagles and owls are not closely related, but both have evolved hooked bills and strong talons adapted for preying on other animals. By independently acquiring the same adaptations, these two groups of birds have "converged."

Herring gull

Common tern

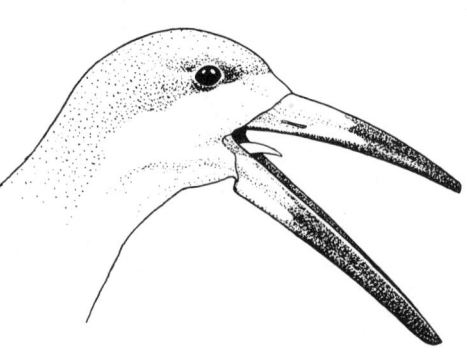

Black skimmer

divergent evolution

The herring gull, common tern, and black skimmer have evolved very different bills, which are adapted to their different methods of feeding. Nevertheless, studies of their anatomy and structure show that these birds are closely related.

birds and these may pose a threat to the best interests of man. *See* discussions under Aircraft and Birds; and especially under Economic Ornithology.

George (1966), in a survey of farmers' complaints, reported seasonal damage, by birds that are often considered economically useful, to at least 63 kinds of farm crops such as grains, small fruits, nuts, melons, and lettuce. Damage to grains such as corn, rice, and wheat is caused mostly by blackbirds, grackles, starlings, and crows. Songbirds, including robins, starlings, and others, have caused the most harm to fruit, especially by eating commercial crops of cherries, grapes, apples, berries, and ornamental holly. Songbirds, including blackbirds, crows, and starlings, have caused more than 80% of the reported bird damage to farm crops.

Most damage by birds is local and transitory, although the rice-growing farmers on the Gulf coast prairies of Tex., La., Ark., and Miss., where an estimated 200 million blackbirds and starlings winter (Meanley, 1971b), or owners of cattle feedlots where blackbirds and starlings gather, may feel that these birds arrive too early on their farms and stay much too long (Parker, 1966). According to the policies of the U.S. Fish and Wildlife Service, as outlined by Parker, methods used against birds in order to control or to minimize damage by them should be humane and carried out in accordance with state and local laws, ordinances, and regulations, and must be co-sponsored by political subdivisions and their elected officials. Permission must be obtained from the owner, occupant, or administrator of tracts of land and water before procedures to limit or control damage by birds are undertaken by the Service. Only methods shall be used that safeguard other desirable birds and other animals, and persons and their property, with the least possible interference to other animals and plants.

The Service prefers that any active control of waterfowl, doves, cranes, and other migratory game birds causing damage because of their concentrations, shall be done through hunting regulations, permits, and special depredation orders. See other details in Parker (1966).

Any methods such as biological control (altering farming practices or changing the habitat, for example) or indirect methods such as the use of frightening devices, herding (chasing with aircraft), etc. (see Williams and Neff, 1966), are preferable to direct killing of flocking birds by shooting or by poisoning (see Dykstra, 1966; Buckley and Cottam, 1966; and especially the article by Cottam, 1966).

Measures aimed at minimizing or controlling damage by birds have, at times, included the massive destruction of roosting blackbirds, starlings, and grackles; sometimes controversial methods have been used in the Southeast. See Graham (1976); Jackson (1976). These may involve the use of surfactants, or wetting agents (see "Animal Damage Control" in Harris, V. T., 1972), because of a threat of histoplasmosis. *See* Histoplasmosis; Diseases. For other discussions of control and methods, see Buchheister (1960); Dykstra (1960); Boudreau (1968); Graham (1971); also a leaflet, *The Blackbird Problem*, by Monroe and Plunkett, issued by the National Audubon Society in 1976.

CONURE
Name for any parrot of the old genus *Conurus*, now *Aratinga*.

CONVERGENT EVOLUTION
Biologists' term for the evolution of structural similarities in birds that are not closely related. Such resemblances result from similarities in life habits, such as feeding. *See* illustrations of bill types under Bill. An example of onetime misconceptions of relationships based on outward appearances of birds (*see* Analogous) was the classifying of all hawks and owls together partly because of similar foot structure. *See* types of feet under Feet and Legs. The hawks and owls are not now considered closely related (*see* exception under Falconiformes) and similarity of their hooked bills and taloned feet is recognized as development from similar habits of these birds in killing and eating their prey. For remarkable examples of convergent evolution and striking similarities between two groups of unrelated birds, *see* introduction to Auk Family.

DIVERGENT EVOLUTION. In contrast to bill similarities of *unrelated* birds (convergent evolution), some closely related ones may have quite different bills as a result of *divergent evolution* (*see* Adaptive Radiation) possibly from different feeding habits. The related gulls, terns, and skimmers have different bills, and to understand their true relationships one would need to study their anatomy, or structure. *See* discussion of this under Morphology; Classification. *See also* Gull Family; Skimmer Family.

COOING GROUND
See Dancing Ground; *also* Chicken, prairie, in Grouse Family; Voice and Sound-making.

COOKACHEEA
Name for the buff-collared nightjar, from its call. *See* in Nightjar Family.

COOLING SYSTEM
See Respiratory System; Temperature; Heat and Birds.

COOPER
JAMES G(RAHAM) (1830–1902). Army surgeon, naturalist, son of William Cooper; became a prominent resident ornithologist of Calif. (Palmer, 1928); was appointed acting assistant surgeon and naturalist, U.S. Army, attached to northern division of Pacific Railroad Survey in Washington Terr.; his best-known ornithological publications were a report of birds collected on the route near the 47th and 49th parallels (jointly with George Suckley) in the Pacific Railroad Surveys and his *Ornithology of California (Land Birds)*, edited by Spencer F. Baird. In recognition of his ornithological work in Calif., the Cooper Ornithological Society bears his name. See details in Hume (1942).

COOPER
WILLIAM (1798?–1864). Father of Dr. James G. Cooper; was honored in 1828 with the naming of the Cooper's hawk for him by Charles Lucien Bonaparte from a specimen (or specimens) collected by Cooper; Cooper also named and described the evening grosbeak in 1825; when he was about 19 years old, he was one of founders of the New York Lyceum of Natural History; later its secretary. He was first American member of the London Zoological Society. See details in Palmer *et al.* (1954); also Fairchild (1887).

COOPERATION AMONG BIRDS
See especially Helpers among Birds; *also* Behavior; Nest-sharing.

COOPER ORNITHOLOGICAL SOCIETY
Originally called the Cooper Ornithological Club; was founded in 1893 and named for Dr. James G. Cooper in honor of his pioneering ornithological work in Calif. *See* Cooper, James G. It is a nonprofit educational and scientific organization incorporated under the laws of Calif. in 1934. Among the purposes of the society are the advancement of ornithological science and the publication of *The Condor*, issued six times (bimonthly) a year. *See* Ornithological Periodicals. Other publications of the society were the occasional ornithological papers issued as the Pacific Coast Avifauna Series, established in 1900; this series has been replaced by *Studies in Avian Biology*. *See* Grinnell.

COOT
See in Rail Family.

COPPERHEAD
See Blackbird, yellow-headed, in Troupial Family.

COPROPODEUM
See Cloaca.

COPULATION AND COPULATORY ORGANS
In birds there is not usually true copulation (by insertion of a penis or copulatory organ), but most males impregnate the females by the "cloacal kiss." This is accomplished when the male bird mounts the female and is able to press his cloaca (or anal opening) against that of the female. The transmission of male sperm into the female cloacal opening follows, and the sperm move up the oviduct, where the eggs are fertilized. *See* Cloaca; Fertilization; Eggs and Egg-laying. There are certain birds, however—for example, ostriches and other ratites, certain ducks, gallinaceous birds, and S. American tinamous—which have well-developed penes, some resembling those of crocodiles (Walter and Sayles, 1949). *See* discussion under Hatching.

Copulation usually follows pair formation, and though there are many variations, most birds have a preliminary period of courtship in selecting mates, followed by other rituals, before copulation actually takes place. Copulation usually is repeated frequently during the breeding season, largely before and during the

COPULATION
In most species of birds the male lacks a penis. Impregnation is achieved when the male mounts the female and presses his cloaca against that of the female. Many terns mate for life and copulate throughout the breeding season, strengthening the pair bond.

egg-laying period of the female. This ensures that the eggs will be fertile, although hens are known to lay fertile eggs three weeks after separation from the rooster. "Copulation may take place on the ground, in water, in bushes and trees, on telephone wires or on fences, in nests or nest boxes, or, in some swifts, in the air." Although copulation fertilizes the eggs, in some species it also helps to maintain the pair bond (*see* Courtship). Pairs of red-bellied woodpeckers and house sparrows, for example, may copulate two months before the eggs are laid (Berger, 1961).

Usually males copulate only with females of their own kind; however, there are many records of crossbreeding in which males or females of different but often closely related species (classified within the same family, for example) copulate and produce hybrid offspring. *See* details under Hybrid; Species.

There is at least one unusual record of copulation between birds belonging to two different orders and therefore more distantly related to each other than birds in the same family (*see* Order; Family). Rea (1973a) reported that in late Dec. 1970, while he and several companions were driving through a coconut grove east of Carabobo, Venezuela, they saw a pair of flycatchers, presumably rusty-margined flycatchers, *Myiozetetes cayenensis*, which are in the Tyrant Flycatcher Family, order Passeriformes, perched on utility wires near a pair of ruddy ground doves, *Columbina talpacoti*, of the Pigeon Family, order Columbiformes. When one of the doves, presumably the male, flew away, one of the flycatchers flew at once to the remaining dove on the wire, thought to be a female, and immediately mounted her. After what appeared to be successful copulation, he flew back to his original position on the wire beside the other flycatcher, assumed to be his mate.

Other observers have seen birds belonging to entirely different families copulate—a flycatcher and a bluebird (Thrush Family), for example, and a male house sparrow (Weaverbird Family) that mounted and copulated repeatedly with a male brown-headed cowbird (Troupial Family). For mating within a single family group—brothers and sisters, etc. ("incest")—and examples of homosexual behavior, *see* discussion under Sexual Relationships.

CORACIIFORMES

(koh-rah-sigh-ih-FOR-meez); Lat. *corax*, raven, and *forma*, form; raven-shaped (Coble, 1954). An order or group of birds (kingfishers, etc.) that resemble each other fundamentally in structure (*see* Order). According to Van Tyne and Berger (1976), the group includes 9 families of 192 species. Birds in the order share in common a striking feature—all have syndactylous toes—that is, two, and sometimes all three, of the forward directed toes are joined along part of their length. *See* Feet and Legs. Most are brightly colored birds, somewhat noisy, many are social in habits, most have relatively large bills; they eat fishes, small mammals, reptiles, amphibians, and insects; some eat fruits and berries. *See* Fishes and Birds. All nest in cavities or crevices; some dig nesting holes in sandy banks, in rotten trees, or in nests

of insects. See Austin (1961) and Gilliard (1958) for details.

Nine families of the order are: the almost worldwide Kingfisher Family of 86 species (3 are N. American—*see* Kingfisher Family); Tody Family of 5 species—tiny birds only 3½–4½ in. long that live in the Greater Antilles; Motmot Family of 8 species that live from Mexico into S. America; Bee-eater Family of 24 species of the temperate and tropical parts of the Old World (*see* interesting habit of bee-eaters in Autolycism); Roller Family of 16 species of Africa, Eurasia, and East Indies; Cuckooroller Family of 1 species of Madagascar and Comores Is.; Hoopoe Family of 1 species of Eurasia; Wood Hoopoe Family of 6 species of c. and s. Africa; Hornbill Family of 45 species of tropical Africa, Asia, Malaysia, and the Philippines (Van Tyne and Berger, 1976). For a discussion of how birds are arranged according to relationships, *see* Classification; Morphology; Phylogenetic Relationship. See *also* Check-list.

CORIUM

See Dermis under Skin.

CORMORANT FAMILY

Phalacrocoracidae (fal-ah-crow-koh-RASS-ih-dee); from Gr. *phalakros*, bald, and *kora*, crow, or raven. The family includes only cormorants; 30 species in world (Van Tyne and Berger, 1959); range around world except in Asia and c. Pacific Is.; 6 in N. America, live along seacoasts, also about large lakes and rivers inland; range in size from a duck to a large goose; long-necked, long- and stout-bodied water birds; dark feather color of N. American species often with green or blue metallic sheen; tail long, stiff, rounded; wings short, rounded; legs short, set far back on body; when perched upright on pilings or rocks, cormorant's back appears hunched; feet are fully (totipalmate) webbed (cormorants related to web-footed pelicans, anhingas, and boobies). *See* Pelecaniformes. Bare patches of skin of face are bright blue, orange, red, or yellow; bill long, thin, sharply hooked at tip; gular sac small; *sexes outwardly very similar;* species nesting in North are migratory; double-crested cormorant is commonest N. American species, limited to N. America, lives along both Pacific and Atlantic coasts; Brandt's cormorant same size as double-crested, is commoner than double-crested on Pacific coast. One of the S. American cormorants, the guanay cormorant, *Phalacrocorax bougainvillii*, has been cited as the most valuable wild bird in the world because of use of its excrement (*see* Guano) as commercial fertilizer from immense deposits on its nesting islands off Peru. See Murphy (1936) and Austin (1961).

Cormorants are gregarious; nest in colonies on rocky islets, ledges of cliffs, or in trees; usually one brood a season, although a few may nest twice each year; parents feed newly hatched young by regurgitation, and using the bill to put partly digested fishes into the young one's bill.

All but the flightless cormorant, isolated long enough on the Galápagos Is. so that its wings have shrunk to the size of a penguin's flippers, are strong fliers and when fishing some species

kingfisher

CORACIIFORMES

often sight prey in the water from the air. They fly to feeding places sometimes singly, in small groups, or in hundreds. The double-crested cormorant gathers in flocks of up to 2,000 on San Francisco Bay. When schools of smelt and other small fishes swim near the surface, the cormorant flock on the water forms a long line to meet them. Some individual cormorants submerge gently, but others, like some ducks, leap forward into the air from the surface and dive below. After catching a fish in the bill, a cormorant usually rises to the surface before swallowing it. The indigestible fishbones and scales it regurgitates later.

Fishing underwater can be dangerous for cormorants; like gulls, loons, and other birds that either float on the surface or dive below, they are sometimes caught and swallowed by large fishes. When swimming underwater, cormorants hold their wings slightly out from their sides and use their webbed feet to propel themselves forward. See Ross (1976) for details. Like loons, grebes, and anhingas, they are heavy-boned and the air sacs are reduced or minimal. By squeezing air out of the plumage and from their bodies to lower their specific gravity, cormorants can sink partly or completely below the surface of the water. Some cormorants have been caught in fishermen's nets 70–100 ft. below the surface. According to Heinroth and Heinroth (1958), as soon as cormorants stop fishing, they go ashore to dry their wings and hold them out to the sun for some time before taking flight (unlike ducks, their feathers are not completely waterproof).

Because of the skill of cormorants in stalking and catching fishes, they have been exploited by man for centuries, especially in Asia. According to Austin (1961), better fishing methods years ago made fishing with cormorants uneconomical in Japan, but it is still practiced by the Japanese imperial household for its cultural interest and as a tourist attraction.

Cormorants, like other large seabirds, are long-lived; albinism is apparently rare. Gross (1965a), in his summary, mentioned four records of albinism among two species of cormorants but did not name them.

Although cormorants feed extensively on fishes, the species they catch are mostly small and of no economic importance—for example, small eels are a favored food of cormorants in bays; also rock cod, carp, and other slow-swimming fishes, and even water snakes; Pacific coast cormorants take smelt, surf fishes, and sardines, yet even where cormorants are abundant, fishes are also abundant. The double-crested cormorant, from a study in Me., eats largely cunners and sculpins (80% of their food) —two fishes that are known to be direct enemies of commercially useful fish (Cottam and Uhler, 1937).

In captivity, feed an ill or injured cormorant small fishes whole, thrown into the water, or pieces of larger fishes cut into strips roughly 1 in. across and 2–4 in. long; provide if possible a pool or tank with some land for the bird to rest upon (Walker, 1942; DeLaRonde and Greichus, 1972). Cormorants are protected by Law. *See* Legal Protection.

Baird's cormorant. *See* Pelagic cormorant.

Brandt's cormorant, *Phalacrocorax penicillatus* (fal-ah-CROW-koh-racks peen-ih-sill-AY-tus); genus name: Lat., from Gr. *phalakros,* bald, and *kora,* crow, or raven; species name: from Lat. *penicillum,* a painter's brush or pencil of hairs (Jaeger, 1955), in reference to long plumes on the neck and back of this species in its breeding plumage; *cormorant* is English corruption of Lat. *corvus marinus* (Coues, 1882)—the cormorant was often called sea-crow in Europe; common name: honors Johann Friedrich von Brandt, German zoologist who gave the bird its scientific name in 1837. (Color ill., page 119.) Common along Pacific coast, Brandt's cormorant is about 35 in. long; wingspread to 49 in. (Palmer, 1962); black, short-tailed, *without a head crest;* adults during breeding season have blue throat patch with buffy band across throat, behind and below pouch; in all flying stages has this buffy band; immatures brownish, paler below but never white; eye irises of adults green (Palmer, 1962); often gather in compact flocks over their feeding grounds on Pacific waters with only head, neck, and part of back above water; utter occasional low grunts.

Feeding Habits: Dives for small saltwater fishes, largely of no commercial value—herring, rock cod, sculpins—also eats crabs and shrimps.
Nest: Male establishes nesting territory on rocky places; brings nest materials to site but loses it to others unless mated; fights fiercely over territory that may be no larger than nest and space to stand by it; both sexes build; dive for marine plants, also use mosses and grasses gathered from land; assembled nest is circular, on top of headland or rocky island, in dense colonies, often nests are so close together one cannot step between them; nests may be used more than one year.
Eggs: Mar.–July; 3–6, commonly 4, pale blue to white (western gull and raven persistently try to get eggs).
Incubation: Both sexes, in turn, but period of unknown (Palmer, 1962); chick at hatching naked, skin black, eyes closed; later covered with grayish down; age at first flight unknown; single-brooded, some first breed at 2 years but most when older (Palmer, 1962).
Other Names: Brown cormorant; penciled cormorant; shag; Townsend's cormorant.
Weights: To about 5½ lbs. (Palmer, 1962); a fat female collected (shot) in June weighed 2,426 gr., or about 5⅓ lbs.
Range: Seen along faces of sea cliffs or outlying pinnacles of rock, strictly marine, never strays inland; nests along Pacific coast from Wash. south to Natividad Is. and Gull Rocks, Baja Calif., also on San Pedro Mártir Is. and Roca Blanca near Isla Partida, Gulf of Calif.; Palmer (1962) reports it may still nest on Guadalupe Is., Mexico; is common breeding bird in Pacific waters of Baja Calif.; is resident near its nesting colonies but ranges in winter to Cape San Lucas, Baja Calif., and widely in Gulf of Calif.; casual in se. Alaska and at Guadalupe, Mexico (A.O.U. *Check-list,* 1957).

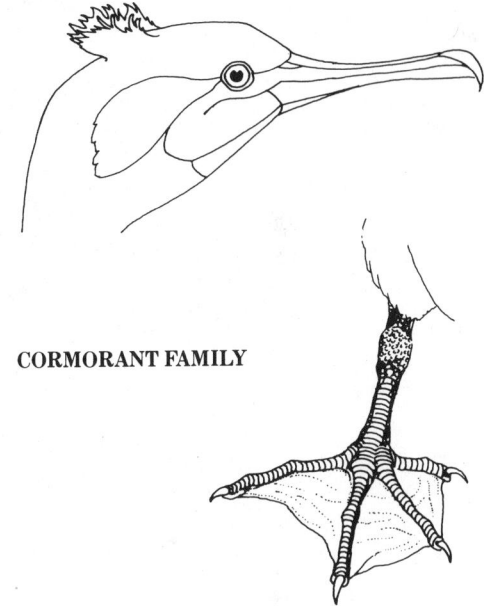

CORMORANT FAMILY

CORMORANT FAMILY
The feathers of the cormorant are inadequately waterproof and become so sodden after it has been fishing underwater that it must hold them open in the sun and breezes to dry.

Double-crested cormorant, *Phalacrocorax auritus* (fal-ah-CROW-koh-racks aw-RI-tus); genus name: *see* Brandt's cormorant; species name: Lat., eared, or crested; *double-crested* refers to rarely seen tufts on crown. (Color ill., page 120.) Like Brandt's cormorant, only in W. Hemisphere, along both Pacific and Atlantic coasts, also only cormorant likely to be seen inland around freshwater lakes and rivers; 29–36 in. long; wingspread about 54 in. (Palmer, 1962); sexes appear essentially alike; large, black (no white flank patches), with long tail; *yellow-orange throat patch;* narrow line around eyes dotted bright blue; eyes light green; double head crest is worn during short period in breeding season, is formed by long, upcurled feathers of crown on each side of head; legs and feet black; immatures have lighter underparts.

Feeding Habits: Dives from surface and swims about in pursuit of prey, generally to depths of 5–25 ft. below surface; stays under usually less than 30 but up to 70 seconds (Palmer, 1962) (*see* Swimming and Diving); catches mainly fishes of no commercial value—in salt and brackish waters: gunnel, sculpins, sand launces, capelin, herring, flounders, tomcod, eels, butterfish, blenny, pollack, sea perch, wrasses, drum, sea catfish, gizzard shad, toadfish, skipjack; in inland fresh waters: yellow perch, bullheads, sticklebacks, crappies, carp, sunfishes (*see* Fishes and Birds); also some salamanders (*see* Amphibians and Birds); some crustaceans such as spider crabs, amphipods, shrimps, and crayfishes; some reptiles, mollusks, and sea worms. See Palmer (1962) for other details. Gress *et al.* (1973) discovered that colonies of double-crested cormorants on Anacapa Is., s. Calif., and on Los Coronados Is., nw. Baja Calif., like those of brown pelicans there were not reproducing young beginning in 1969 through 1971 because of excessive thinning and breaking of eggshells, which decreased in thickness by 34%, attributed to DDT compounds picked up in fish in Pacific O.

Nest: In colonies, built by both sexes on ground (rocks) or in tree, average takes about 4 days to build; old nests often rebuilt, may be used for at least 4 years; in trees, built of sticks and weed stems, lined with leafy twigs and grass; on rocks, often built of seaweeds and trash gathered at water's edge or in diving (Palmer, 1962); some odd objects added—feathers, twigs of evergreen; in salt water, habit of diving for seaweeds for nesting on rocky islands off Labrador coast resulted in remarkable nest materials. Forbush (1925–29) cites account of trading vessel sunk nearby; when fishermen visited cormorant nesting island, found they had decorated their nests with pocketknives, men's pipes, hairpins, and ladies' combs that cormorants had gathered by diving to wreck. *See* Some Man-Made Materials Used by Birds under Nests and Nesting.

Eggs: Mostly Apr.–July; 2–7, sometimes to 9, but usually 3–4, chalky, pale blue, soon nest-stained; single-brooded but may re-lay if nest or eggs destroyed.

Incubation: 24–25 days, by both sexes in turn; chicks naked at hatching, shiny, eyes open in

4–5 days; at 2 weeks, chicks covered with short, thick, black "wool"; both parents feed chicks semi-liquid food; small chicks brooded or shaded during extremes of weather; a captive young attained full immature plumage at 58 days; 3–4 weeks after hatching, young wander from nest, gather in bands that move through entire colony, much sociable visiting, never viciously attacked by other adults; first flight of young usually to water at about 35–42 days after hatching; can dive earlier; at 42 days can take flight from water and accompany adults in fishing or swimming; fully independent of parents at 10 weeks after hatching; some roost in colony, others roost alone or with other young elsewhere (Palmer, 1962). In migration, by day or by night, flocks usually follow coastlines, river valleys, and watercourses; flocks in migration may number up to 10,000 or more but usually 200 or less.

Other Names: Crow-duck; Farallon cormorant (Pacific coast); Florida cormorant (South); lawyer; nigger goose; shag; Taunton turkey (New England); white-crested cormorant.

Age: One banded Que., shot N.C., when 5½ years old; one banded S.D., found dead Hastings, Minn., 8 years, 4 months, later; one lived in National Zoo, Washington, D.C., 13 years; one banded Muscongus Bay, Me., entangled in fisherman's net in same general area 23 years later; also, two records of 17-year-old banded birds (Cadbury, 1966).

Flight Speed: Timed in w. U.S., 22 m.p.h. (Cottam *et al.*, 1942b); in Fla., 20 m.p.h. (Longstreet, 1930); 48 m.p.h. with no wind (Palmer, 1962).

Weights: To more than 6 lbs. (Palmer, 1962); two, 1,787 and 1,929 gr., or about 4 lbs. and 4¼ lbs., sex not noted.

Range: Nests on rocky islands, cliffs facing water, stands of trees near water, lives about almost any waters, salt or fresh, where fishes plentiful; along Pacific coast from the Aleutians to s. Baja Calif., and along Atlantic coast from Newfoundland south to Fla., and to the Bahamas and Cuba; inland, nests from Wash. south to s. Calif. and from c. Alta., c. Sask., e. Man., and Great Lakes region and locally to se. Idaho, n. Utah, ne. Colo., Ariz., N.M., w. Neb., S.D., s. Minn., s. Wisc., n. Mich., south to Iowa, Ill., Ind., Tenn., Tex., s. La.; winters in w. U.S. over most of nesting range except in extreme northern part; inland winters from Tenn. south (A.O.U. *Check-list,* 1957), and from Md. south to Gulf coast but rarely farther north (Bull, 1964). Bull reported very large flocks flying along coast of Long Is., N.Y., in spring and fall, but flocks reported in winter of this species were probably the great cormorant.

European cormorant. *See* Great cormorant.

Great cormorant, *Phalacrocorax carbo* (fal-ah-CROW-koh-racks CARE-boh); genus name: *see* Brandt's cormorant; species name: Lat. *carbo,* coal, charcoal, applied here to bird's uniformly sooty color, as though bird were charred; *great* in allusion to size—it is largest cormorant in N. America. (Color ill., page 121.) Principally a European species; in N. America, only along N. Atlantic coast; called simply "cormorant" in British Isles; 32–40 in. long; wingspread to more than 5 ft. (Palmer, 1962); uniformly blackish, only cormorant with distinct white area around base of bill; also white cheeks; *at close range* shows light yellow chin patch; bill heavier than that of double-crested, is much larger bird; in breeding season, from about Feb. into June, adults have white patch on flanks; eyes turquoise blue. Most cormorants seen in New England in midwinter are this species (*see* Double-crested cormorant); scarce and shy; nests along N. Atlantic coast, total number of breeding birds in N. America in 1940, not including Greenland, was, by count, 2,172 birds (Palmer, 1962); total population in Greenland probably not exceeding 2,000 pairs; apparently this species is a Recent Period (postglacial) immigrant to Greenland. (See Palmer, 1962, for details.) Pough (1951) believes that it occupies niche in environment so close to that already filled by double-crested cormorant that it can make little population advance where double-crested already established.

Feeding Habits: Eats almost entirely fishes— sculpins, haddock, cod, flounders, gurnards, herring; also crustaceans—spider crabs, prawns, shrimps (Palmer, 1962). Dives reported of 71 seconds, usually 20–30 seconds. (See Serventy, 1939.)

Nest: On remote cliffs and rocky islands, in colonies, in Canada, few if any colonies of more than 200 pairs, bulky nests of sticks and debris, lined with finer materials; on ground in N. America on higher parts of cliffs or slopes, on elevated parts of islands, often in close association with double-crested cormorants.

Eggs: Late Apr. to late June; usually 4–5, sometimes 6 (Bent, 1922); larger and more rounded than eggs of double-crested, chalky, faint blue-green soon fades.

Incubation: 29–31 days, by both sexes; both parents feed chicks and both parents in hot weather bring water in gular pouch and crop and pour stream of water over chicks, also pour water into chick's opened bill; eyes of chicks open in 4–5 days; make first flight about 50 days after hatching; subsequently return to the nest regularly; make longer flights and practice fishing but still return to nest at night; completely independent 12–13 weeks after hatching and disappear from colony; first breed at 3–5 years old; single-brooded. See Palmer, 1962, for details.

Other Names: Cormorant; common cormorant; European cormorant; shag.

Age: Ten reached ages of 4 to almost 7 years in Europe.

Flight Speed: Timed in England, 27 and 35 m.p.h. (Roberts, B. B., 1932).

Weights: 5–11 lbs. (Palmer, 1962).

Range: Nests from s. Greenland, sw. Newfoundland, along north shore of Gulf of St. Lawrence, north shore of Anticosti Is., Prince Edward Is., and Nova Scotia; formerly nested to Bay of Fundy and Grand Manan Is.; nonbreeding birds in summer seen west to Grand Manan, N.B., rarely to Muscongus Bay, Me.; winters from breeding grounds south to N.J., rarely farther south (Bull, 1964); casually to S.C. and Ga., has wandered inland to Me., N.Y., Ont., Pa., Vt., and W.Va.; in Old World nests in Iceland, Faeroes, Norway, n. Finland, and n. Kola Pen. south to Mediterranean, c. and s. Europe, and along coasts of Great Britain.

Mexican cormorant. *See* Olivaceous cormorant.

Neotropic cormorant. *See* Olivaceous cormorant.

Olivaceous cormorant, *Phalacrocorax olivaceus* (fal-ah-CROW-koh-racks oll-ih-VAY-see-us); genus name: *see* Brandt's cormorant; species name: Lat., olive-colored; green obscured with neutral tint (Coues, 1882). (Color ill., page 121.) Only cormorant ranging over entire tropical American region of W. Hemisphere; often called neotropic cormorant; reaches U.S. along Gulf coast and in sw. U.S.; sexes outwardly alike; small for a cormorant; 23–29 in. long; wingspread about 40 in. (Palmer, 1962); similar to the double-crested cormorant but smaller, slimmer; a dark cormorant with glossy feathers; in breeding season, its throat patch is edged by a distinct line of white; eyes are green; pouch yellow-brown or darker; young are brown-bodied with pale or whitish underparts. Frequently seen with double-crested cormorants and the anhinga. Unlike other N. American cormorants, it perches on slender twigs and even on wires; "when not swimming, usually in upright stance perched atop dead snags, bushes, or rocks near water, often with wings and tail spread"; while in this spread-eagle pose, does repeated squatting or bouncing movement; when alarmed may escape by flying, more often dives below surface of water (Palmer, 1962).

Feeding Habits: Sometimes fishes in strong surf; sometimes many of them fish cooperatively in swift mountain streams of Mexico; form line across river and beat water with wings, driving fishes ahead, which they dive for and catch (see Bent, 1922, for details); eats, as far as known, mostly freshwater fishes—top minnows, for example—also frogs, tadpoles, and dragonfly nymphs.

Nest: At freshwater lakes, reservoirs, ponds, and on coastal islands; in colonies, in living or dead trees or bushes; 3–20 ft. above water; also on rocks or bare ground when trees or bushes lacking; nest built of sticks and lined with coarse grasses.

Eggs: Tex., Feb.–Oct. (Bent, 1922), nesting reported in 11 months of the year, but along southern border of U.S. concentrated May-Aug. (Palmer, 1962); 2–6 eggs, usually 4, chalky, bluish, soon stained.

Incubation: Period of not known; both sexes feed young; age of young at first flight unknown; much predation in s. Tex. colonies by raccoons, which eat eggs and young; boat-tailed grackles may be even more frequent eaters of the eggs (*see* Egg-eating). See Murphy (1936) for detailed account of this species in S. America.

Other Names: Brazilian cormorant; Mexican cormorant; neotropic cormorant.

Weights: To about 4 lbs. (Palmer, 1962).

Range: Nests from se. La. to s. Tex. and Mexico south to Nicaragua, and, at only locality in N.M., Elephant Butte; also seen on Patagonia Lake, Ariz.; may be limited from ranging farther north in U.S. by competition from double-crested cormorant (Witzeman *et al.*, 1975); nests also in Cuba, Isle of Pines, and Bahamas, and in S. America, from rocky coasts and the Amazon R. to high Andean lakes; winters on coasts of La. and Tex. and through most of its breeding range; accidental in Colo., c. Tex., Kans., and s. Ill.

Pelagic cormorant, *Phalacrocorax pelagicus* (fal-ah-CROW-koh-racks peh-LAJ-ih-cus); genus name: *see* Brandt's cormorant; species name: Gr., pertaining to the sea. (Color ill., page 120.) Small cormorant of Pacific coast; 25–29 in. long; wingspread to 40 in. (Palmer, 1962); black-bodied with metallic gloss; slender neck, small head, and much thinner bill than larger double-crested and Brandt's cormorants; also distinguished from them by conspicuous white patches on flanks in breeding season that show well in flight; facial skin vivid ruby, or magenta, two crests on head; compared with red-faced cormorant, has fully feathered forehead (red-faced forehead is bare, red skin) and has reddish gular pouch (red-faced has bluish pouch); young birds in all seasons darker than other immature cormorants, except red-faced, especially underparts (Palmer, 1962).

Feeding Habits: Sometimes attracted to schools of fishes by actions of gulls and then drive gulls away; dive also into wild seas and surf near boulders, catch chiefly sculpins, herring, tomcod, sand launces, sea poachers, flounders; also crabs, shrimps, crayfishes, amphipods, marine worms; have been caught in fishermen's nets at depth of 180 ft., but Palmer (1962) believes reports of this species going to depths of 480 ft. are highly questionable; flight is more rapid and more graceful than the larger cormorants and can fly from water by using wings only and from an underwater dive.

Nest: In colonies on remote and precipitous cliffs with other cormorants, though not necessarily close by, murres, common eiders, tufted puffins, and glaucous-winged gulls; both sexes build; one gathers material, the other arranges it; nest may be used in successive seasons and added to until 5–6 ft. high, of seaweeds, grasses, rubbish (Palmer, 1962).

Eggs: Usually May–July; 3–7, usually 3–5, chalky, pale bluish.

Incubation: By both sexes; 22 days (Bent, 1922); crows apparently eat the eggs if nest unattended by adults.

Other Name: Baird's cormorant.

Weights: 3½–5½ lbs.; males (9) averaged larger than females (Palmer, 1962).

Range: In N. America, nests on ledges of precipitous rocky inaccessible cliffs along Pacific coast from Aleutians south through B.C. to Los Coronados Is., Baja Calif.; winters at many nesting places except most northerly ones; some migration southward from southern parts of range in loose flocks or individually; in Old World, nests on islands and offshore islets in Bering Sea, Arctic O. off ne. Siberia to Japan.

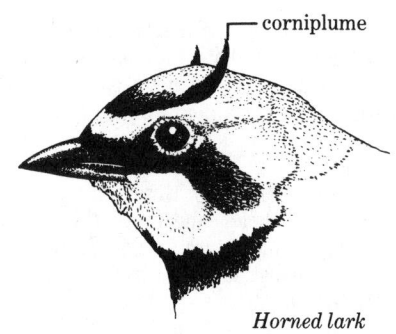

— corniplume

Horned lark

CORNIPLUME
Two small, black tufts of feathers form the corniplume of the horned lark.

CORNIPLUME
Two small, black tufts of feathers form the corniplume of the horned lark.

Red-faced cormorant, *Phalacrocorax urile* (fal-ah-CROW-koh-racks YOU-rile); genus name: *see* Brandt's cormorant; species name: given by Johann F. Gmelin in 1789 in Linnaeus' *Systema Naturae*, possibly a New Lat. place name for the Kurile Is., where, according to Dement'ev *et al.* (1966), the bird formerly occurred in early times. (Color ill., page 121.) In N. America, lives in Aleutians, Pribilofs, and other islands of Alaska; sexes outwardly alike; 31–35 in. long; wingspread to about 48 in.; black cormorant with a blue gular sac and red skin at base of bill; two bronze-colored crests, one over forehead, the other at juncture of crown and nape; large white patch on lower flanks begins to disappear in June.

Feeding Habits: Dives for small fishes, crabs, and shrimps.
Nest: In colonies on broad flat ledges of steep cliffs; large, well built of grasses, seaweeds, sea ferns, sod.
Eggs: Alaska, May–June; 3–4, chalky, pale blue-white.
Incubation: Period estimated at 21 days and young thought to fly when about 60 days old, but not verified (Palmer, 1962).
Weights: To 5¾ lbs., males average larger than females.
Range: Nests from Arctic coast of ne. Siberia and Komandorskie Is. (formerly on Kamchatka and Kurile Is.) east through Pribilof Is., Aleutians to Amak, Shumagin, and Somidi Is.; winters in nesting range and south to Kuriles, casual to St. Michael, Alaska; in winter withstands the severest storms, perched in shelter of cliffs; population has greatly increased in last few decades (Palmer, 1962).

White-crested cormorant. *See* Double-crested cormorant.

CORN CRAKE
See in Rail Family.

CORNIPLUME
A tuft of feathers on the head of a bird (horned lark and great horned owl, for example). It is usually raised like a horn.

CORN-THIEF
See Crow, common, and Jay, blue, in Crow Family.

CORVID
(CORE-vid). Term for any member of the Crow Family.

CORVIDAE
See Crow Family.

CORY
CHARLES B(ARNEY) (1857–1921). A founder and a president of the American Ornithologists' Union; a darkly plumaged least bittern, described by Cory, was once called Cory's least bittern, but later thought to be a melanistic form of that species; his name is commemorated, however, in the English name Cory's shearwater, *Puffinus diomedea*. A native of Boston, Cory moved to Chicago, where he became Curator of Birds in the Field Museum of Natural History, a position he held until his death (Palmer *et al.*, 1954). Cory's first book, *A Naturalist in the Magdalen Islands* (1878), was followed by several others and he became an authority on W. Indian birds. Frank M. Chapman *(Autobiography of a Bird Lover)* wrote that he had never met such a gifted man. See also Gruson (1972).

COSTA
LOUIS MARIE PANTALEON (1806–64). Marquis de Beau-Regard, French collector of hummingbirds for whom Costa's hummingbird was named in 1839 by Bourcier from the type specimen of this bird collected by Adolphe Simon Neboux at Magdalena Bay, Baja Calif., in the autumn of 1837 (Palmer, 1918). According to Palmer (1928), at 15, the Marquis de Beau-Regard had begun a collection of birds and minerals but later gave special attention to hummingbirds. Bourcier named the hummingbird *Calypte costae* in recognition of the Marquis' interest in the Hummingbird Family.

COTINGA FAMILY
Cotingidae (coh-TINGE-ih-dee); from *cotinga* (coh-TING-ah), S. American name of Tupian origin, from the Tupi *coting*, to wash, and *tinga*, white; name applied specifically by Indians of Amazon to the white bellbird, one of few species of tropical birds that are white—few land birds of the world are white except some of those in the Arctic (Austin, 1961). *Cotinga* is name of the typical genus of this tropical American family limited to the New World; they are songbirds, or perching birds (*see* Passeriformes), and most closely related to the tropical American manakins and the Tyrant Flycatchers; about 73 species, 3½–18 in. long (Van Tyne and Berger, 1976); some are among the most spectacularly ornamented birds in the world, only one of which—the small, comparatively modest-appearing rose-throated becard—has ranged north of Mexico into the U.S., first discovered in Ariz. in 1888; later (1937) at Harlingen, Tex. Mostly a tropical family, essentially live in forest trees, are usually seen alone, in pairs, or in small family groups; includes such unusual birds as the two species of cock of the rock—one male bright orange, the other soft red—with flaming fan-shaped crests, and courtship dance system of males displaying together similar to that of N. American sage grouse (*see* Arena Bird); also, the three-wattled bellbird of c. America, the male with three whiplike wattles around its bill, which opens its mouth wide in display; the fruit-eating, crowlike, ornate umbrella birds that live in crowns of forest trees and range from Costa Rica to Brazil have umbrella-like, retractable crests—black feathers in a crown that they spread like a parasol in courtship display—one species with a long, feathered wattle, 13 in. long, that hangs from the chest of a bird that itself is only 18 in. long; besides these and the becards, family includes the tityras; the family ranges from the grossest extremes to birds so small and plain they seem not to belong to same family; however, despite their great differences in sizes and colors, all are united by combination of similar characters of anatomy—odd structure of vocal organs and similarities of legs and feet

(Austin, 1961); some members of family range southward to n. Argentina.

Feather colors may be from dull black to brilliant iridescent ones; from fiery red to delicate blues and purples—one thrush-sized cotinga, an exquisite raspberry red, that lives in Guianas, Venezuela, se. Columbia, e. Ecuador, and n. and c. Brazil, was named the Pompadour cotinga, for the celebrated French courtesan, and not for any character of the bird's own. The first one of its kind to reach Europe had been sent in a shipment of brightly colored bird skins to Madame de Pompadour for her adornment, via a French ship sailing from French Guiana; it was captured by the British, and George Edwards, British naturalist and artist, upon receiving the bird, described and named it in honor of the French woman to whom it had originally been consigned.

In the dull-colored cotingas, both male and female (often gray) are usually of similar color pattern—example is the screaming piha, *Lipaugus vociferans,* of the deep tropical forest, which utters loud cries and has habit of investigating unusual sounds. Some of the gray cotingas have bright spots of color, including the rose-breasted becard that reaches U.S. and is most northerly of all members of the family. See Gilliard (1958) and Austin (1961) for other details of family.

Rose-throated, or Xantus', becard (BEK-ard), *Platypsaris aglaiae* (plah-TIP-sah-ris ah-GLAY-ee); name "becard" from Fr. *bec,* a beak, in reference to thick, slightly crooked bill (Austin, 1961); genus name: from Gr. *platys,* broad, and *psar,* starling; species name: from Gr., name of one of the Greek Graces, associated with beauty (splendor) of plumage (Jaeger, 1955). Mexican and C. American species that reaches U.S. in Ariz., sw. N.M., and s. Tex.; 6½ in. long; resembles a flycatcher; male dark; brown-gray above, including tail; mainly pale gray or dusky below, with patch of rose or rich purple on throat; female with buffy collar, buffy yellow below; upperparts mainly uniform cinnamon or gray-brown, but crown dark gray or blackish; resembles wood pewee but bigger head and shorter tail; first U.S. record, male, June 1888, in Huachuca Mtns., s. Ariz., elevation 7,000 ft.; next record (June 1937), an adult female and young male, seen near Harlingen, Tex.; in April 1943, Davis (1945) discovered nests near Harlingen for first nesting records in U.S.; on June 19, 1947, Phillips (1949) discovered first of two pairs nesting in Santa Cruz drainage, s.-c. Ariz.; in 1948 he discovered four active nests in same area; this species at Colima, Mexico, seen in dense jungle perched quietly on branch just below crown of tree, from which darted into air for insects; in El Salvador, noted in trees, second growth, also in deep swamp, and about edges of clearings, trails, roads; sits motionless for minutes at time on perch, thus easily overlooked in shade of forest (Bent, 1942); local and irregular summer resident along Sonoita Creek, Santa Cruz County, Ariz., also in Guadalupe Mtns., and near Tucson (Phillips *et al.,* 1964); chatters, then utters mournful descending whistle.

Feeding Habits: Eats insects and some wild fruit.
Nest: Large globular or pear-shaped mass, partly pendulous, suspended from twigs at end of drooping branch, about 10–12 in. in diameter, 12–30 in. long, 30–60 ft. above ground, entrance hole on side; entire structure built of long strips of fibrous plant stems, bark, grass, leaves, insect webbing, rootlets, lined (Ariz. nest) with feathers of band-tailed pigeon; female does most of work; large nest reported by Phillips built in week; often builds nest in exact place where nest built previous year, or very close to site.
Eggs: May–June; 2–6, white to cream-white spotted with brown.
Incubation: Period of and age when young first fly unreported.
Host to Cowbirds: Rare, a single record to bronzed cowbird (Friedmann, 1963).
Weights: An adult male (Ariz.) 30.35 gr., or about 1 oz.
Range: In summer in se. Ariz., sw. N.M., also rare and local in summer in lower Rio Grande Valley, where nests occasionally in Hidalgo County, south to Nicaragua and Costa Rica; casual at Rio Grande in winter, accidental at Galveston (Peterson, 1963); a pair built nest in Santa Ana Wildlife Refuge, s. Tex., May 22, 1975; a pair seen there with three young, Aug. 1975; first successful nesting there in more than 15 years (Webster, 1975).

COTINGIDAE
See Cotinga Family.

COTTON-TOP
See Quail, scaled, in Pheasant Family.

COUES
(COWZ), ELLIOTT, M.D. (1842–99). Commemorated in the English name of Coues' flycatcher; was one of the founders of the American Ornithologists' Union and his influence on the progress of scientific ornithology in America was second only to that of Spencer F. Baird, of whom he was a pupil; he was a naturalist, an effective public speaker, and a brilliant and prolific writer whose popularizing of ornithology through his writings was greater than that of any other writer of his time (Palmer *et al.,* 1954).

Coues was commissioned an assistant surgeon in the U.S. Army in 1864 and during his 19 years of military service was stationed at forts in both the East and the West, from which he collected and observed birds, and later wrote reports about them. While at Ft. McHenry, Md., he wrote and illustrated *Key to North American Birds*—"one of the best if not *the* best bird book ever written" (Elliott, 1901; Allen, 1909)—published in five editions from 1872 to 1903; later, *Birds of the Northwest* (1874); *Birds of the Colorado Valley* (1878); and the earlier *Check-list of North American Birds* (1873) with a second edition. Coues died Dec. 25, 1899; he was buried in the National Cemetery, Washington, D.C. See Hume (1942); also Stresemann (1975) and *Encyclopaedia Britannica* (1969 ed.).

Rose-throated becard

COTINGA FAMILY

COURTSHIP
The graceful courtship dance of the whooping crane is performed by both male and female simultaneously. In this sequence, the male bows to its mate, leaps high into the air with wings flapping, and bounds up and down.

COUNTERSHADING
See Uses of Colors to Birds under Colors of Feathers.

"COUNTING"
(by birds). *See* Behavior.

COURLAN
(KOOR-lan). *See* under Limpkin Family.

COURTSHIP
In birds, defined as various kinds of behavior that brings males and females together as mates, or pairs, and leads to coition (Hann, 1953). It is the preliminary ceremonies of both sexes which attract and stimulate them during and after pair formation.

COURTSHIP RITUALS. Courtship often begins aggressively as the need to defend a territory is strongly developed, causing males to attack any interloper, even a potential mate. Courtship itself may involve many rituals, many more than there are species of birds, according to Dr. William C. Dilger of the Laboratory of Ornithology, Cornell University. *See* especially under Waterfowl.

Some of these rituals include singing by birds, both as a means of defending territory against other males of their kind and to advertise to a female the presence of the male; "the flashing of colorful wing and tail patches which supplement the singing; the display by the males of the bright crown patches by such birds as kinglets, the eastern kingbird, and ovenbird; the parading of brilliantly colored tanagers and orioles before the females and rival males; the display of especially brilliant breast feathers of robins and meadowlarks; and elaborate flight songs which males of larks, buntings, and certain other species give while fluttering over prairies, tundra, marsh, and woodlands (the ovenbird) to make themselves conspicuous" (Wallace, 1963). *See* Flight Songs; Courtship Flight under Flight. Usually such performances are by males, but both males and females of some species have courtship flights; the marsh hawk's aerial dips and somersaults are particularly well known.

Most species have courtship displays that involve both sexes.

Many birds do not sing in courtship, but have other means of attracting the attention of females or of rival males. Woodpeckers drum with the bill on dead limbs, and ruffed grouse drum with their wings (*see* Drumming); nighthawks dive down toward their mates, producing a booming sound as the wind rushes through their wing primaries. Prairie chickens and sage grouse gather on their traditional "dancing grounds" and make booming or tooting sounds associated with the inflation of their colorful neck pouches (*see* Arena Bird; Voice and Sound-making), and bitterns boom in the spring marshes (*see* under Esophagus; *also* Language).

Elaborate courtship displays appear to be primarily related to their physiological stimulation and to pairing and retaining mates (Emlen, 1955). *See* Behavior.

PHYSIOLOGICAL PREPARATION. What prepares birds physiologically for pair formation and sexual union? According to Benoit (1956), the male is brought into "breeding condition" by the autonomous activity of the anterior pituitary gland, along with some environmental influence such as daylight, which causes testes to enlarge and completes their maturation. Although the development of the ovary also is under the influence of daylight, other factors are important—depending upon the species—in bringing about the final maturation and ovulation, including an abundant food supply, courtship displays of males, the sight of other conspecifics, the songs or calls of males, and the sight of the nest.

The different roles assumed by the male and female during courtship and pair formation appear to be largely determined by the relative balance between the sex hormones—androgens in the males; estrogens in the females. The behavior that results serves to coordinate their reproductive activities (Van Tyne and Berger, 1959). Once the sexual hormones are put into play, their different actions accentuate the behavioral differences between the two partners of the pair—the male hormones incite a more aggressive role in the males; the female hormones a more submissive role in the females (Benoit, 1956). As courtship progresses, however, the roles often reverse with the males losing their aggressive behavior (showing more courtship), and the females losing their submissive behavior, and often dominating the sequence and rate of courtship displays. It is possible that female sex behavior may also be dependent on male sex hormones which, besides the female sex hormone, are certainly produced in the female gonad (Höhn, 1961).

HOW BIRDS COURT, OR WIN MATES. In choosing mates among birds, the female makes the choice of the mate by *her acceptance* of the male. In familiar N. American territory-holding birds—warblers, thrushes, and songbirds in general—the male, already established in his territory in spring, awaits the arrival of the female. He will then aggressively attack or threaten any bird of his kind that enters his territory, male or female, and usually will drive away an intruding male. The attacked female, however, though she retreats, will remain in or around the area if it is her chosen breeding area. Some of the females of migratory birds on their way farther north will pass on through and some males seem to recognize the transient females and will show no interest in them (Wallace, 1955).

The female will submit to the male's aggressive tactics, and when he modifies them, his courtship of the female begins. Now he will pursue her, running over the ground after her in some species, or pursuing her in courtship flights. The female is not yet attached to the male's territory, as she will be later, and she may wander in and out of the territories of several male birds of her kind before she pairs with a particular one. Meanwhile, the songs of a male may have called her back into his territory, where, usually within a few days, the pair bond between the two is formed.

HOW BIRDS RECOGNIZE THEIR OWN SPECIES AND SEX. Because courtship displays are specific, or peculiar to each species, they may serve, biologically, as *isolating mechanisms* which tend to ensure that only birds of the same species will form pair bonds and copulate (Berger, 1961). To accomplish this, birds must be able to distinguish other members of their species and of their sex. *See* discussion under Species.

Apparently birds do not form mental images of sex or of species, and ornithologists believe that they rely on the interplay of social signals for both sex and species recognition. For example, in a bird in which the sexes are of the same color pattern in their plumage, and "look alike," the recognition of the female by the male may depend on her actions and call notes (social signals). *See* Language.

In Margaret M. Nice's studies of the song sparrow, in which both sexes are outwardly alike, she discovered that the first reaction of a male to another song sparrow intruding into his territory was to fly at the stranger. If the stranger was a male, its first reaction to being aggressively approached was to display, in turn, aggressively (male type behavior), at which the song sparrow in its home territory would fight the stranger by song, display, or actual physical attack in order to drive it away.

If, however, the intruder was a female song sparrow in breeding condition, she gave special call notes and remained in the territory, whereupon the male would court her.

Bright or striking colors of male birds of certain species, and special markings, probably aid them in sex recognition and possibly are used in sex attraction in the elaborate courtship displays of male pheasants, ducks, peacocks, birds of paradise, and certain others. *See* Colors of Feathers; Sexual Dimorphism.

Although sex recognition may be much simpler for birds in which the sexes have strikingly different plumage, in many kinds of birds besides song sparrows, there are only slight outward differences, or none at all. The chief difference between a male flicker and a female is the black-feathered malar stripe, or "mustache," of the males. Many years ago, G. Kingsley Noble, an early student of animal behavior in America, experimented with the sex recognition of flickers. He captured the female of a mated pair in his garden and simulated the black facial markings of the male on the female. When he released her, her mate attacked her vigorously, as though she were indeed a male (Noble, 1936).

William C. Dilger studied five species of N. American thrushes—wood thrush, veery, hermit thrush, Swainson's thrush, and gray-cheeked thrush—in which the males cannot be distinguished outwardly from the females, and discovered that the males and females recognized each other by their behavior. He also concluded that the songs and calls of the males (different in each species) were the primary signs by which females recognized males of their own kind (Dilger, 1956b). *See* Sympatric species.

Wandering albatross

Western grebe

COURTSHIP
The courtship of the wandering albatross is an elaborate and noisy ritual, accompanied by braying, gurgling, preening, and the rattling and touching of bills by male and female. This stance—tails fanned, heads stretched upward, wings opened wide—is the climax of their mutual display.

A male and female western grebe have a spectacular "racing" display: skittering across the water side-by-side with wings held rigid and necks arched—propelled by their feet alone—they gain such speed that their bodies are almost erect.

SEX RECOGNITION OF SOME OTHER BIRDS. Early workers with sex recognition of birds—Craig in 1909 and Whitman in 1919—concluded that doves do not know the sex of a strange individual until they are at close quarters, when they behave differently toward each other. Arthur A. Allen, experimenting with ruffed grouse, concluded that they do not have sex recognition at all, but that, in pair formation, the dominant individual takes the male role and the subordinate bird the female role, irrespective of sex. *See* Homosexual Behavior under Sexual Relationships.

RECOGNITION OF MATES. After the pair bond is formed, sex recognition is a different problem for birds. It is then one of distinguishing the mate, or individual, from others of their kind (Lack, 1940b). Recognition of a mate, either by sight or by calls (or even by the sounds of feet, such as made by a C. American woodhewer when striking against a tree trunk in alighting), has been proved for several species, including herring gull, black-crowned night heron, common (yellow-shafted) flicker, and song sparrow (Berger, 1961). Bobwhite quail can distinguish strangers in a covey; common terns recognize their mates in the air; mated ducks (pintails) identify each other at 300 yds. from the nest; and European robins can do so at 30 yds. The smooth-billed anis distinguish individuals; black-headed gulls know their associates; and the crimson-crowned bishop birds know their neighbors (Armstrong, 1942). Birds recognize each other by the same characteristics by which people get to know their friends—by behavior, by features of the head, and by voice.

DOMINANCE BETWEEN THE SEXES. Birds may exhibit *social* dominance, as in domestic chickens with their so-called peck order (*see* Behavior), and/or sexual dominance during the nesting season. In song sparrows, the male may be sexually dominant when he courts the female by "pouncing" on her, yet in little everyday encounters she dominates him. In a social sense, then, the female song sparrow may dominate the male; however, in studies of the canary, the males normally dominated the females in a social sense but were dominated by the females while they were mated, or in a sexual sense (Lack, 1940b). *See* Dominance.

THE PAIR BOND. According to Lack, there is less known about how birds form pairs than about any other type of their behavior. In becoming paired, most birds develop a pair bond, or an attachment to the mate, the duration of which varies in different species of birds. Also, the time required to form the pair bond will vary from a few hours in the budgerigar to three or four days in some thrushes, or it may require several months in many kinds of ducks, some of which form no pair bond at all.

Lack (1940b) has divided birds into five main groups according to the length of their pair bonds: (1) those in which the sexes meet solely for copulation, as in most grouse (*see* Arena Bird); (2) those that have a pair bond simply for a few days at the time of copulating (the ruby-throated hummingbird is an example); (3) those that form into pairs sometime before copulation but separate soon afterward (ducks); (4) those that remain paired for the raising of the brood or throughout the duration of the breeding season; this is common to the great majority of passerines (perching songbirds), herons, nearly all shorebirds—the sandpipers, plovers, etc.—most seabirds, and in many other groups; the pair bond in these birds is typically formed after the male has established a territory, but in some of these species—auks, gulls, cedar waxwings, and the lesser and Lawrence's goldfinch—each pair bond is formed while they are in winter flocks; (5) those birds that pair for life; swans, geese, cranes, eagles (?), common terns, many parrots, ravens, the roadrunner (see Ohmart, 1973), some species of crows, wren-tits, tufted titmice, white-breasted nuthatches, pigmy nuthatches, and brown creepers may form a permanent pair bond; also albatrosses, some shearwaters and penguins, oystercatchers, herring gulls, cactus wrens, and some house sparrows. See also discussion by Hinde (1964b).

Mating for life usually means only for the lifetime of one of the mated pair. In the wild, if either the male or the female should lose its life during the nesting season, another unmated male or female will usually take its place, sometimes within a few days. However, studies in England of Bewick's swans have not revealed a single case of "divorce" in 8 years, and some bereaved mates have waited as long as 3 years to find a new mate (Scott, 1972). For an interesting article about manifestation of the pair bond, see Erickson (1973).

Bird-banding has revealed some remarkable stories of constancy of mates in birds, some of which, though they may not mate for life, had long attachments for each other. Laskey (1935), at Nashville, Tenn., once had a pair of wild cardinals and a pair of wild mockingbirds in her garden that paired with the same mate for 3 successive years. Shelley (1935b), in N.H., reported a pair of downy woodpeckers that were permanent residents about his home which remained paired during 4 successive years and raised a single brood each year. A pair of welcome swallows, *Hirundo tahitica frontalis*, of New Guinea, were mated for 6 years, during which they nested 13 times on the roof of the Mission and fledged 23 youngsters. Fr. Meyer, the priest who made the study, wrote that during their seventh nesting season together, the female, shortly after she had laid her eggs, was killed by a cat, after which the male acquired a new mate (Nice, 1935b).

A pair of American robins banded by Nice (1933b) at Columbus, Ohio, were mated to each other for 3 successive years, and a pair of Carolina chickadees remained together for at least 1½ years. Two pairs of tree swallows in Conn. and two other pairs in N.H. chose the same mates for 2 successive years (Wetherbee, 1932; Shelley, 1934). A pair of crested flycatchers chose each other for 3 successive years, and a pair of mourning doves (a species which seems strongly attached to its nesting site) mated for 2 successive years (Stewart and Mackey, 1953). Helen Lapham of Cornell University banded a pair of song sparrows in R.I. that remained together for 4 years.

Many ornithologists believe that it is the attachment of both the male and the female to the nesting area that brings some of them together year after year; however, in some of the larger birds, which may remain together throughout the year, the attachment may be to each other rather than to a nest site or territory. McAtee (1924) told a story related to him by Jasper B. White of Waterlily, N.C., who had lived with the waterfowl of Currituck Sound "for an ordinary lifetime." White said that his father had a pair of Canada geese which were mated for 42 years. When the male was accidentally killed, the female died a few months afterward.

W. H. Hudson, the English writer and naturalist, once told (1901) of a pair of wild geese on a wild and lonely plain of S. America that is an example of the powerful attachment geese may have for each other. It was Aug. and the pair, which ordinarily would have been flying in their migration, were walking over the plain. The female, with a broken wing and unable to fly, was being led southward toward the Magellan Is. by her mate. Occasionally the male would rise up screaming and fly ahead, then seeing the female could not follow, he would return and alight in front of her and begin walking ahead as before. Hudson concluded his account by writing: "And in that sad anxious way, they would journey on to the inevitable end when a pair of carrion eagles would spy them from a great distance—the two travelers left far behind their fellows, one flying, the other walking, and the first would be left to continue the journey alone."

COURTSHIP FEEDING

In many different groups of birds, the male feeds the female during their courtship and sometimes during her incubation of the eggs. In most courtship feeding, the female flutters her wings, and opens her mouth to be fed, and in so doing adopts the posture of a young bird begging its parent to be fed. Apparently this stimulates the male to feed her. Doves and pigeons, many hawks and eagles, cardinals, blue jays, magpies, crows, goldfinches, redpolls, American wood warblers, bobwhite quail, tree swallows, Bewick's wren, titmice, chickadees, some species of nuthatches, the brown creeper, bluebirds, Townsend's solitaire, and cedar waxwings are some of the birds that practice courtship feeding (Lack, 1940a).

The male normally places the food he has collected—insects, berries, fishes, or whatever food the species feeds on—directly into the open mouth of the female. In others, notably in some fringillids (redpolls, goldfinches) and gulls, the male regurgitates the food into the female's mouth as he does when feeding the young. In herring gulls and other gulls, the male regurgitates the food on the ground in front of the female and she picks it up in her bill and swallows it. In terns, the courtship feeding, in which the male offers the female a fish, is often followed or preceded by a ceremonial flight. In some birds of prey, notably the marsh hawk, the male passes food to the female while in flight. A. C. Bent (1937) quotes C. L. Broley, a Canadian observer, as follows: "The male flies with the mouse near where the female may be nesting and calls to her; upon which she takes to the air, and, flying 12 to 20 feet over his mate, the male drops the mouse. The female either turns partly over on her back and catches the mouse with her claws, or as on one occasion, just swings her feet out to the side and catches the mouse neatly. I have seen the male carry a mouse 15 minutes awaiting the return of his mate to present it to her."

Males of the yellow-billed cuckoo may feed their mates while copulating with them, and the male bittern regurgitates food into the female's mouth during the act. The male king rail, during courtship of the female, holds a crayfish or fiddler crab in his bill as an offering, which the female takes from him. In Europe, a corncrake (a rail bird similar to the sora, or Carolina rail), after 23 attempts to copulate with a stuffed specimen of its kind, went away and returned with a caterpillar, which he offered to the dummy (Armstrong, 1942). In domestic chickens, the rooster does not present food to the hen but scratches up the ground for her (as a hen does for her chicks), and may even pick up and drop the food with his bill as he calls to her. In the domestic fowl this is called "tidbitting." See examples among gallinaceous birds in Stokes and Williams (1971).

THE FUNCTION OF COURTSHIP FEEDING
Courtship feeding, as distinguished from incubation feeding, has been reported among birds of some 40 families of 16 orders. It seems to be unreported in loons, grebes, petrels, swans, geese and ducks, grouse, auks, woodpeckers, thrashers, starlings, vireos, and weaver finches (Lack, 1940a). Apparently the symbolic gift of food functions as a kind of sexual stimulant (Armstrong, 1942). According to Stokes and Williams (1971), it gets the female to approach the male where he can continue with his courtship; it also keeps the female closer to him, away from other males. In one group, the button-quail, or bustard quail, of the genus *Turnix*, the role of the sexes is reversed and the females feed the males and court them. In many species that practice courtship feeding, the male also feeds the female during her incubation of the eggs.

According to Lack (1940a), the object of courtship feeding is not the food that is passed, but its use as a courtship display. A female herring gull, after returning from the fishing grounds well fed, was seen to beg food from her mate though he had not fed and had remained near the nest during her absence. A European robin, standing on a bird-feeding tray filled with food, begged food of her mate; also, the female American cardinal will often do so at the feeding tray.

Apparently one of the primary functions of courtship feeding is to help maintain the pair bond (*see* Courtship) and is especially important in species of birds in which both the male and the female feed the young, in which it is most common. As far as is known, courtship feeding is not practiced by any other vertebrates (omitting its sporadic practice by human beings) but it is practiced by a group of insects, especially flies of the family Empidae. *See also* Billing.

COURTSHIP FLIGHT
See Courtship; Flight.

COVERTS
The small feathers on top of the wings (wing coverts) and over the tail feathers (upper tail coverts). There are also undertail coverts (*see* Crissum). *See* Topography.

COVEY
Term usually for a group of game birds, especially of quail.

COWBIRD
See in Troupial Family.

CRAB-CATCHER
See Heron, green, in Heron Family.

CRACID
(KRASS-id). Collective term for the members of the family Cracidae—the currasows, guans, and chachalacas.

CRACIDAE
See Curassow Family.

CRAKE
See in Rail Family.

CRANE
Besides members of the Crane Family, some herons are locally, and mistakenly, called cranes because of their superficial resemblance to cranes. For differences, *see* Crane Family; Heron Family.

CRANE FAMILY
Gruidae (GROO-ih-dee); from Lat. *grus*, crane. 15 species, live in tropical and temperate parts of the Old World, and in temperate region of New World; on every continent except S. America (Walkinshaw, 1973); only three species in N. America: the native whooping crane, one of rarest birds in America and in the world, the sandhill crane, and a visitor, the common, or gray, crane of the Old World; cranes are tall, stately birds that live on wide marshlands, wet plains and prairies; 31–60 in. long, with plumage largely brown, gray, or white; long-necked, long-legged with four sharp-clawed toes on each foot, hind toe (hallux) much elevated above the others; bill, long and straight; head, except in young, partly naked of feathers or, in some Old World cranes, adorned with ornamental plumes; wings long and wide, tail short, with 12 rectrices; cranes fly with neck extended forward, feet trailing behind, move wings in slow downbeat but with quick upstroke; sexes outwardly alike but male larger; utter sonorous, trumpetlike notes that can be heard for several miles, produced through specially modified windpipe (trachea) that has been likened to a French horn (*see* Voice and Sound-Making); when migrating by day or night, cranes call frequently, apparently to keep together, but leader of flock does most of calling as they move in V-shaped flocks or in long lines across the sky; often fly at great heights; for example, flock of 80 seen from airplane over English Channel were flying at elevation of

COURTSHIP FEEDING
During courtship, a female tern flutters her wings and opens her mouth to be fed, like a fledgling begging food from a parent. The male places a fish directly into her mouth, a symbolic gift that seems to function as a sexual stimulant.

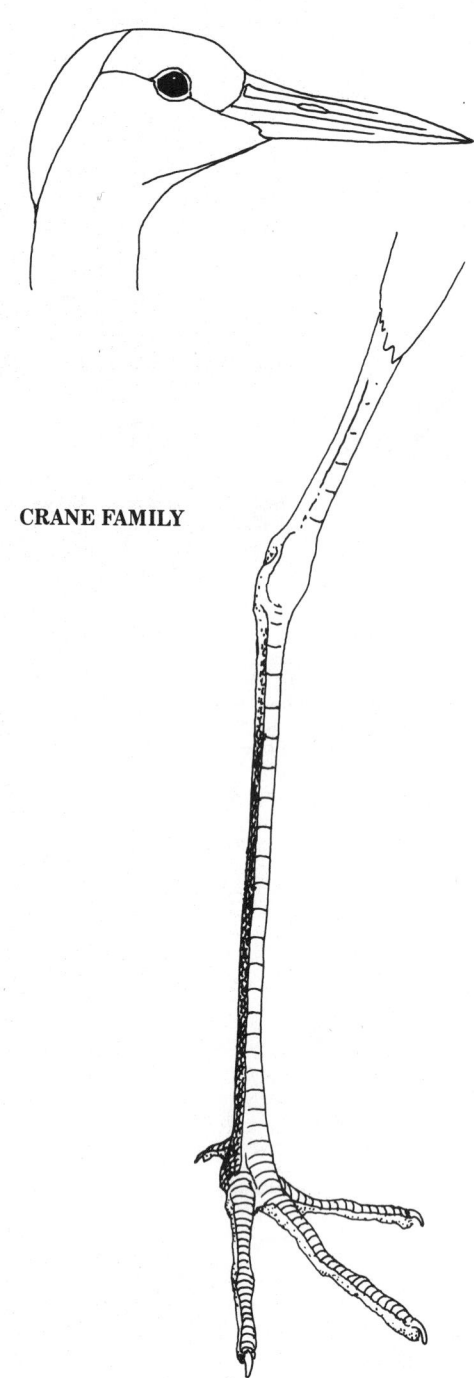

CRANE FAMILY

13,000 ft. (Gilliard, 1958). *See* Altitude of Bird Flight. Cranes are believed to mate for life (Walkinshaw, 1949a); in dramatic and graceful courtship dances, both members of pair leap high into air and bow before each other; some cranes may perform at all seasons of year and immatures may dance almost as often as adults in what is believed sheer exuberance. There is a great deal of variation in the molt of primary and secondary (flight) feathers of cranes. Among some individual sandhill cranes most flight feathers are lost in a few weeks during summer and the bird is flightless while new feathers are growing out. About 60% of the individuals of the same species have an interrupted molt cycle in which 2 or 3 years are required to replace all flight feathers. Birds experiencing the interrupted molt cycle lose 1/3 to 1/2 of their flight feathers each summer and do not become flightless (Lewis, 1979); (see account of N. American cranes in flightless period in summer by Littlefield (1970) and Drewien (1973).

Cranes are apparently a very old group—some fossils date from the Eocene Period 40–60 million years ago—and barely able to maintain their numbers; they have been decreasing with shooting and loss of great marshlands and prairies to human occupation and changed uses of the land; cranes are related to the rails, coots, gallinules, limpkin, sun-grebes, etc. (*see* Gruiformes); most typical of the cranes are 10 species of the genus *Grus*, which includes the N. American whooping and sandhill cranes and the common, or gray, crane, *Grus grus*, of n. Europe and Asia; other genera included in the crane family are one species of *Bugeranus*, the wattled crane of southern Africa; two species of *Anthropoides*, the demoiselle (northern Africa, southern Europe, Asia) and Stanley (southern Africa) cranes; and two species of *Balearica*, the black-crowned and gray-crowned cranes of northern and southern Africa, respectively. For descriptions and ranges of cranes of the world, see Allen (1952); Austin (1961); Gilliard (1958); Junge (1964a); Walkinshaw (1973).

Although cranes are wild and wary, some learn to accept the friendship of man. See remarkable accounts of wild cranes tamed by human patience and kindness in Browne (1937) with a pair of Florida sandhill cranes, and Sieber (1932) with a pair of common, or gray, cranes in Germany; see also remarkable and true story about a whooping crane in Terres (1958); most cranes breed well in captivity (see "My Greater Sandhill Cranes" in Terres, 1958) but are protected by state and federal laws and may not be kept in captivity without a special permit; in trying to help a wounded wild crane, one should beware, for when brought to bay, it may fight desperately; according to Forbush (1925–29), Audubon told of being driven into a river and up to his neck in water to escape an enraged sandhill crane with a broken wing; may strike at one's eyes with its long, strong bill; however, after their capture, most cranes tame easily; to sustain an injured, crippled, or ill one until it can fend for itself, offer it a mixture of grain, chopped or ground leafy greens and vegetables, bread crumbs, grit, and meat; cranes also eat mice, lizards, and insects, and some will take small amounts of fish (Walker, 1942). Albinism apparently rare, as Gross (1965a) reported only two records for one species.

Cranes are long-lived in captivity (*see* Age); some have lived in zoos 20–50 years; a Siberian, or Asiatic white, crane, *Grus leucogeranus*, reported by Davis (1969), lived in the National Zoo, Washington, D.C., for 61 years, 8 months, 26 days—it died Mar. 22, 1968.

Blue crane. *See* Sandhill crane; also another name for the great blue, little blue, and Louisiana herons.

Brown crane. *See* Sandhill crane.

Common, or gray, crane, *Grus grus* (GROOSE); genus and species names: *see* family introduction. A Eurasian species 45 in. long; about size of sandhill crane; has appeared three times in Alta.: in Dec. 1957, Mar. 1958, Sept. 1958 (Godfrey, 1966); first report in Alaska, Apr. 1958, feeding in fields of dairy farm about 2 mi. west of Fairbanks until June 2, then disappeared (Gabrielson and Lincoln, 1959); two reported in Neb., Mar. 31, 1972, each sighted same day about 100 mi. apart in Platte R. valley; gray to brownish, distinguished from sandhill cranes, flock of 30 with which associated, by *black head, black throat, prominent curving white cheek and upper neck patch,* deeper and more extensive black in wings and tail than sandhill cranes; at close range, red skin patch on front of head visible; behavior like that of the lesser sandhill cranes, with which associated (Tremaine, 1972); some of lesser sandhill cranes nest in Siberia; Tremaine suggests that the common cranes, which nest in same area, may have got to N. America by migrating with the lesser sandhill cranes.

Age: Known ages of captives in zoos of Europe, individual birds: 21 years, 10 months, 3 days; 27 years, 11 months, 2 days; 37 years, 4 months, 25 days; 40 years; 42 years, 10 months; and 43 years (Walkinshaw, 1949a).

Range: Nests from Scandinavia, Finland, Livonia, Russia, w. Siberia south to Germany, the Balkans, Asia Minor, and Turkestan; winters in Mediterranean countries and in ne. Africa (Allen, 1952).

Florida crane, or **Florida sandhill crane.** *See* Sandhill crane.

Gray crane. *See* Common crane and Sandhill crane; also another name for the great blue heron.

Lesser sandhill crane. *See* Sandhill crane.

Little blue crane. Another name for the little blue heron.

Little brown crane. *See* Sandhill crane.

Little white crane. Another name for the white-plumaged, immature little blue heron.

Sandhill crane, *Grus canadensis* (GROOSE can-ah-DEN-sis); genus name: *see* family introduction; species name: Lat., of Canada. (Color ills., pages 122, 123.) 34–48 in. long; wingspread 6–7 ft.; long-legged, long-necked, sexes outwardly alike but male larger; adults all-gray with bald red skin on forehead; eyes yellow; immatures have head brown-feathered without red skin patch; the legs, bill, and feet blackish; There are 6 races or subspecies of sandhill crane, and they differ in size and darkness of coloration: 3 races are migratory and 3 are sedentary. The sedentary races have small populations and 2 are threatened with extinction: the Mississippi sandhill crane (*Grus canadensis pulla*) (Aldrich, 1972) of 40–50 individuals found only in Jackson County, Miss. (Valentine, 1979); the Cuban sandhill crane (*G. c. nesiotes*) of w. Cuba and the Isle of Pines thought to number about 200; and the Florida sandhill crane (*G. c. pratensis*) of 4,000–6,000 birds in Fla. and s. Ga. (Lewis, 1977). Most of the remaining Mississippi sandhill cranes now reside inside the Mississippi Sandhill Crane National Wildlife Refuge, which was established in 1974. Another approach to preserving this subspecies is through captive propagation by the U.S. Fish and Wildlife Service: 8 young were produced in 1980, and the captive flock includes 24 subadults and adults; some of the captive birds will be released in suitable wild habitat in the future. The Cuban government has repeatedly rebuffed attempts of U.S. scientists to survey the Cuban cranes and enact conservation measures.

Populations of the 3 migratory races are more secure: the lesser sandhill crane (*G. c. canadensis*) nests in Alaska, Siberia, and n. Canada and winters in Calif., Tex., N.M., and Mexico; the Canadian sandhill crane (*G. c. rowani*) nests in c.-w. Canada and winters in Tex., Okla., e. N.M., and probably Mexico, and numbers about 54,000 (Aldrich, 1979). The lesser and Canadian races are hunted in portions of Canada, the U.S., Russia, and Mexico. More than 400,000 of the latter two races were counted in w. Tex. in Feb. 1980.

The largest race, the greater sandhill crane (*G. c. tabida*), nests in Man., Ont., Mich., Wis., Minn., Mont., Wyo., Idaho, Utah, Nev., Ore., Colo., and n. Calif. The population around the Great Lakes winters in Fla., those of w. Minn. and w. Man. winter on the Tex. coast, and those of the w. U.S. winter in Ariz., Calif., N.M., and Mexico (Lewis, 1977); rust color of some adult sandhill cranes caused by habit of cranes of digging into ground with bill and getting it discolored from soil and water, which often includes ferric oxide (iron); colors transferred to cranes' feathers when preening, or dressing, its plumage, which may become stained yellow to red-brown—brick red in Alta. (Walkinshaw, 1949a). *See* Adventitious Color. From wintering grounds begin migrating northward in high-flying flocks from late Feb. to mid-Mar., arrive on nesting territories on prairie potholes, high mountain meadows, northern forest lakes, and tundra in Apr. and May in groups of 2, 3, or 4 and composites of these sometimes totaling thousands in one flock; the small groups are a pair with young of previous year and the pair soon drive the young away when breeding begins; the Florida sandhill crane remains about shallow ponds, sloughs, and meadows in open

pinewood flats or on Fla.'s Kissimmee prairie; winter flocks begin to break up in Jan. and pairs nest by late Jan., early Feb. (Walkinshaw, 1949a; Sprunt, 1954); during winter, cranes roost together at night, standing in flocks on low damp land or in shallow water; fly from roosting place at dawn to feeding grounds; often dance in spring on roosting grounds in morning and evening (pairs dance also on nesting territory), bounding 6–8 ft. into air with wings half spread, some bowing to others but most bouncing like rubber balls, uttering loud *garooo-a-a-a* calls.

Feeding Habits: On wintering grounds, feed much in newly planted or harvested wheat, corn, and sorghum fields, but in summer feed much in breeding marshes, also fly to neighboring damp meadows, dry hillsides within a mile of nest to feed; may walk great distances when feeding, often probe with bill into ground to dig out roots, tubers; also eat seeds, grain, berries, mice, lemmings, small birds, snakes, lizards, frogs, crayfishes, which they break into small pieces by threshing them on ground, then swallow bit by bit; often feed in pastures, fields, for earthworms, crickets, grasshoppers, beetles.

Nest: Mound of marsh plants, grasses, weeds, whole plants pulled up by roots by cranes, may be 4–5 ft. across in shallow water of ponds or on ground in large marshes, muskeg, and on tundra grasslands.

Eggs: Fla., Jan.–May; Canada, n. U.S., Apr.–May; Alaska, n. Canada, May–July; 1–3, usually 2, olive, spotted with lavender, browns; eggs laid 2–3 days apart, older chick sometimes aggressive toward younger but parents usually keep them separated by walking apart, each followed by one of the chicks; both chicks and adults swim well (Walkinshaw, 1949a; 1965b).

Incubation: By both sexes in turn, 28–30 days; young first fly about 90 days after hatching.

Other Names: Baldhead; blue crane; brown crane; Florida crane; garoo (from trumpetlike call); gray crane; greater sandhill crane; lesser sandhill crane; little brown crane; sandhill whooper; upland crane.

Age: One banded Bitter Lake National Wildlife Refuge, N.M., found dead when 6 years, 1 month, old in Mayno Poligano, Soviet Union (Kennard, 1975); one lived in National Zoo, Washington, D.C., 24 years, 2 months, 18 days; another at Bronx Zoo, New York City, 16 years, 1 month, 1 day (Walkinshaw, 1949a).

Albinism: Two records (Gross, 1965a).

Flight Speed: Timed in Mich., 25–35 m.p.h.

Weights: Adults weigh from 5.7 lb. (2.6 kg., Lewis, 1974) to 14.4 lb. (6.3 kg., Huey, 1959), depending on the subspecies.

Range: See above; formerly more widespread for all races.

Upland crane. *See* Sandhill crane.

White crane. *See* Whooping crane; also local name, misapplied, to the white herons.

Whooping crane, *Grus americana* (GROOSE ah-mer-ih-CANE-ah); genus name: *see* family introduction; species name: Lat., of America. (Color ills., pages 122, 123.) Our larg-

CRANE FAMILY
In flight, cranes move their long, wide wings with a slow downward flap and a rapid upstroke, their legs extending beyond the short tail, and neck outstretched.

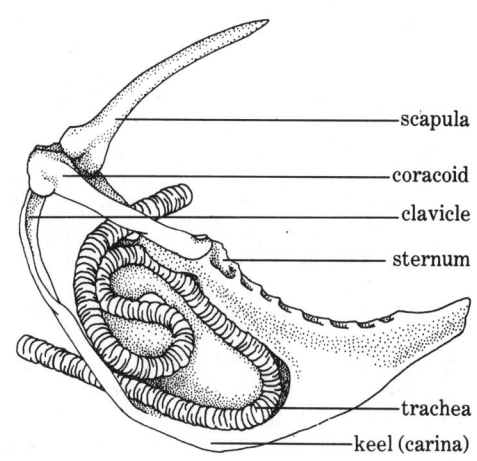

scapula
coracoid
clavicle
sternum
trachea
keel (carina)

trachea of whooping crane

CRANE FAMILY
The trachea or windpipe in the whooping crane reaches a length of five feet, about half of which is looped within the keel of the breastbone. Air passing through the convolutions of the trachea modifies the voice of the whooping crane and accounts for its deep resonant notes, which may carry for two miles.

est crane, adult males average 16 lb. (7.3 kg.), adult females 14 lb. (6.4 kg.); only in New World; tallest bird in N. America (see Size), one of rarest; 49–56 in. long; wingspread about 6½–7½ ft.; largest N. American wading bird, even larger than flamingo, which is almost as tall but less in bulk (Forbush, 1925–29); long-legged, long-necked; sexes outwardly alike except male larger; adults all-white except black wing tips, black mustachial markings on face and bright red bare skin on top of head; white eyes; in its black-and-white flight pattern, might be mistaken for a snow goose or a white pelican, only similar birds that occur over same range; in flight, head and neck extended forward and slightly down, like spear or lance; *long black legs* stretched out behind; slow wingbeat with powerful flick or jerk on upbeat; young birds in first year washed with rust, especially on head and neck; whoopers utter loud, musical *kerloo! ker-lee-oo!* of alarm which can be heard for several miles. Perhaps whooping cranes were never a large population—Allen (1952) estimated that total population in Recent times (see Geological Time Scale), down to years 1860–70 was only about 1,300–1,400 birds—and fossil deposits suggest it first appeared during the Pleistocene, when it was much more wide-ranging; its bone fragments have been found in Calif., Ariz., Idaho, N.D., Kans., Mich., Ill., Ky., Va., and Fla. (Olson, 1972); in Recent times ranged north probably to Arctic coast and south into Mexico, west to Utah, east to Atlantic seaboard in N.J., S.C., possibly to Ga. and Fla. (Allen, 1952). Olson (1972) cites recent Fla. record (mounted specimen) of whooper collected 1927 or 1928. Original, main nesting range in U.S., in prairie marshes from c. Ill. 1,000 mi. northwestward to ne. N.D. and north into Canada, was completely deserted by whooping cranes by 1894, as this region was settled and its nesting sloughs drained and prairies plowed and planted to crops; with disappearance in 1922 of last known nesting pair in Sask., it was gone from all previously known nesting areas in U.S. and Canada (Allen, 1956b); because it is a wild, wary wilderness bird, it could not stand the intrusion of mankind; also changes in habitat brought by uses of the land; only remaining whooping cranes known in N. America by 1930s were: (1) a small flock that wintered (and once nested) in La., which were gone by 1949 (see details in Allen, 1952), and (2) the flock wintering along coast of Tex., which by 1937 had been reduced to about 15 birds; first major effort to protect whooping cranes began in 1937, when U.S. government established the 47,200-acre Aransas National Wildlife Refuge near Austwell, Tex., to give strict protection on their wintering grounds to the largest group of these last birds; also, besides legal protection, great publicity given along migratory route of the white cranes as they flew north each spring from Tex. through Okla., Kans., Neb., S.D., N.D., Mont., Sask., and returned each fall, when sometimes shot by hunters (Allen, 1952); meanwhile, the nesting grounds of this last flock, which had never been found, were finally discovered June 30, 1954, after 10 years of intensive aerial search by biologists of the Canadian Wildlife Service, U.S. Fish and Wildlife Service, and National Audu-

bon Society; it was 2,400 mi. north of the Tex. wintering grounds, in northern part of the 17,300-sq.-mi. Wood Buffalo National Park, Northwest Territories, Canada, near Arctic Circle (see history of search in Allen, 1952, 1956b); by Apr. 1980, census on the Tex. wintering grounds revealed an all-time high, since 1937, of 70 adults and 6 young ready to migrate northward.

The very restricted wintering and nesting habitat of the small wild population leaves them subject to rapid extermination due to a natural disaster, water pollution, or a disease outbreak. To avoid this prospect conservationists began an effort to establish a captive population to preserve the race. Incubation begins as soon as the first egg is laid, thus the second egg, of the normal 2-egg clutch, hatches 1–2 days after the first egg. It is uncommon for more than one chick to be raised to flight age by an adult pair; the cause of chick (colt) death is presumed due to the older chick attacking and driving away the younger, smaller one; thus, one egg of each clutch usually does not benefit the wild population. Canadian and U.S. biologists began, in 1967, removing one egg from each 2-egg clutch and hatching that egg at the Patuxent Wildlife Research Center of the U.S. Fish and Wildlife Service; the disturbed wild pairs did not desert the remaining egg. Egg transfer to Patuxent continued until 1974 and the resultant captive flock of 22 whoopers is now producing eggs. Despite the egg removal the wild flock increased at a faster rate during the period 1967–74 than noted previously.

Begining in 1975 (Drewien and Kuyt, 1979) biologists began a unique experiment directed by Dr. Rod Drewien. The surplus whooper eggs were annually transported to Grays Lake National Wildlife Refuge, Idaho, and substituted for eggs in the nests of wild greater sandhill cranes. The sandhill cranes became foster parents, reared the whoopers, and led them to wintering grounds in N.M. This experiment, designed to create another wild population of whooping cranes, is still in progress. By summer 1980, 7 adult and subadult whoopers had resulted, and 13 eggs were transported from Canada and captive flocks for hatching by foster parent sandhill cranes.

Pairs mate for life (Allen, 1952); begin to dance on their wintering grounds in Dec. and Jan., which apparently keeps pair bond strong; begin migration northward usually from early to middle Apr., not in large flocks as do sandhill cranes, but in pairs or in small family groups—like geese—with young of previous year (see dramatic spring departure in account of Shields and Benham, 1968); reported to reach Sask., Man., in late Apr. to early May, 1,600–1,800-mi. trip in 9–23 days; are nesting in Wood Buffalo Park by May–June; pairs, in courtship, dance near nest site; one of pair begins by lowering head and flapping wings; then leaps stiff-legged 3 ft. into the air with head back, bill pointed skyward, neck arched over its back and flapping its big wings vigorously; its mate runs forward a few steps, pumping its head up and down and flapping its wings, then both leap into the air and bounce up and down as though on pogo sticks but with ponderous dignity; pair

are silent during dance, which ends as suddenly as it begins (Allen, 1952).

Feeding Habits: On wintering grounds in Tex., feeds on brackish-water flats, in pairs or in parties of three, or four, never in large flocks; pairs live within definite territories; eats small fishes in salt-flat ponds, also, especially, blue crabs, shrimps, and other crustaceans; also eats razor clams, snails, amphibians, snakes, acorns, grains, and parts of marsh plants.

Nest: In previous nesting sites on prairies of Minn., Iowa, Sask., nest was built in wet prairie in sloughs, swales, or marshes, usually a flat mound of rushes, sedges, cattails, grasses; nest 4 or 5 ft. across, 8–18 in. above surrounding water, with slight depression in center, where eggs laid; might be in large marshes 3 mi. long, 2 mi. wide; pair very wary when near empty nest, easily alarmed and driven away by human intruder, but defend eggs and young fiercely; at present, in Wood Buffalo National Park, nests built in pothole muskeg region, a bewildering patchwork of irregularly shaped ponds of acre or two to large lakes, nests built in bulrushes of marshy islands in ponds, lakes (Allen, 1956b).

Eggs: May; 1–3, usually 2, cream-buff to olive-buff, usually darker and more heavily marked than eggs of sandhill cranes (Bent, 1926a); average size of 62 eggs, 99.6 × 63.3 mm., or about 4 in. long by 2½ in. in diameter (Allen, 1952); calculated weight of a fresh egg about 212 gr., or about 7½ oz.

Incubation: By both sexes, estimated at 34–35 days (Allen, 1952); female usually incubates at night; male more by day; at hatching, downy chicks quite susceptible to cold and are brooded much by parents; can swim well, fly strongly and with confidence about 100–115 days after hatching; do not attain fully adult plumage until about 25–26 months old, in their third summer (Allen, 1952); believed to reach sexual maturity when 5 years old.

Other Names: Flying sheep (Alta.); garoo; great white crane; whooper.

Losses: One killed Nov. 1965 in migration when it struck high-tension power line near Ludell, Kans; young killed by gray wolf and golden eagle, some shot by hunters, some losses to disease.

Age: One lived in National Zoo, Washington, D.C., for 12 years, 8 months; Josephine, at Audubon Park Zoo, New Orleans, had been in captivity 24 years by 1964; she died Sept. 13, 1965, the day after she had been badly frightened by a helicopter flying over her pen and had battered her body against her pen in terror (McNulty, 1966).

Captives: A long history of; Allen (1952) cites 38 captives from 1864 to 1950s; attempts to breed them in aviaries and zoos unsuccessful; female kept by Lord Lilford, Lilford Hall, Eng., from 1892 to 1930, when she died, at least 40 years old; pair of captive whooping cranes, Crip (male) and Josephine (female), kept in large enclosure at Aransas National Wildlife Refuge, hatched a chick, Rusty, in May 1950, first whooping crane ever hatched in captivity; 4 days after hatching, chick disappeared and never found; in addition to the captive flock

maintained by the U.S. Fish and Wildlife Service, less than a half dozen whooping cranes are kept in other research facilities and zoos.
Flight Speed: 35–45 m.p.h., and can run about as fast as a man (Allen, 1952).
Range: See above.

CRANIAL NERVES
See Nervous System.

CRANKY
or BIG CRANKY. Local name in Carolinas and Fla. for the great blue heron, possibly from its scolding notes when flushed.

CRAVERI
FREDERICO (1815–90). Italian chemist and meteorologist of Turin, Italy, who went to Mexico in 1840 and spent 19 years there as professor of chemistry at the National Museum, Mexico City (Gruson, 1972). While in Mexico, Craveri collected birds for the Turin Academy of Science; he collected (shot) a new and undescribed murrelet in Baja Calif. in June 1845. Twenty years later, Count Salvidori of Turin named it Craveri's murrelet in his honor (Palmer, 1928).

CRAW
See Crop.

CRAZY FLIGHT
(of ruffed grouse). *See* Fall Shuffle.

CRÈCHE
(KRAYSH). Term for the aggregation of the young of certain colonially nesting birds—for example, some penguins, the shelduck, *Tadorna tadorna,* the Sandwich tern, *Sterna sandvicensis,* and flamingos—that gather together a few days after hatching (in flamingos about 2 weeks, or longer, after hatching) where they are fed by the parents. Although it was once thought that the young were fed indiscriminately by many adult birds rather than by their parents alone, Sladen in his observations of the Adélie and chinstrap penguins (1953; 1955), Prévost (1955) studying the emperor penguin, and Brown (1958) in his studies of flamingos, discovered that the parents usually fed their own offspring and not those of others. This apparently ensures that the largest and most aggressive young ones in the crèche do not crowd out the smaller and weaker ones and thus get most of the food (Skutch, 1961). In the flamingos studied by Brown, had each not been fed by its own parents, one of them, with a broken wing, would probably have lost out to those not so handicapped. *See* Flamingo Family.

According to Buckley and Buckley (1970), the chicks of the royal tern also gather in a crèche, to which each parent returns with food; the parent usually recognizes its own chick's call and then feeds it. *See* Tern, royal, in Gull Family; *also* Young and Their Care.

CREEPER FAMILY
Certhiidae (ser-THIGH-ih-dee); Lat., from Gr. *kerthios,* the tree creeper. Small (4¾–7 in. long) tree-dwelling song-, or perching, birds (*see* Passeriformes) of the N. Hemisphere; 6 species in world (Van Tyne and Berger, 1976); 5 of these are the so-called true creepers of the genus *Certhia;* live only in N. Hemisphere; one, the brown creeper, *Certhia familiaris,* is the only representative of Creeper Family in N. America; it is also the only creeper in the British Isles, where it is called tree creeper (Ferguson-Lees, 1964). *See* interesting story of this bird under Sibling Species. Creepers are brown and black above; bill slender; wings and tail long; toes long with sharp, curved, and very long claws; sexes usually outwardly alike; are tree dwellers; creep about on trunks and branches searching for food in bark crevices.

Nearest relatives of the brown creeper are the nuthatches and titmice (Reilly, 1968); the brown creeper ranges south to Nicaragua; its ecological niche southward from C. America is filled by the very similar woodcreepers, of the family Dendrocolcaptidae, whose closest relatives are the tropical American ovenbirds (Austin, 1961). *See* Ovenbird Family.

Creepers are protected by law and may not be kept in captivity; however, to sustain an injured or ill one until it can fend for itself, offer it mealworms, other insects, and ground meat (Walker, 1942). *See* Care and Feeding of Abandoned or Injured Wild Birds. Gross (1965a) could cite no N. American records of albinism for the family.

Black and white creeper. Another name for the black-and-white warbler.

Brown creeper, *Certhia familiaris* (SER-thih-ah fam-ill-ih-AY-ris); genus name: Lat., from Gr. *kerthios,* the tree creeper; species name: from Lat. *familia,* domestic, or common. (Color ill., page 124.) Lives in Eurasia and N. America, in woodlands from Atlantic to Pacific, north to Alaska and s. Canada; small; sexes outwardly alike; 5–5¾ in. long; wingspread 7–8 in.; slender, brown above, speckled and streaked with white; rufous rump and tail; coverts, underparts white, white line over eyes; bill slender, downcurved, pointed; tail long, feathers stiffened at end and pointed, uses tail as prop when climbing; distinctive habit of spiraling *up* tree trunk (does not move down and sideways as nuthatches do) until near top of tree, then fluttering down to base of next tree to repeat, is good identifying character; sometimes takes short hops backward to reinvestigate bark; is generally solitary but will join groups of chickadees and other small birds; summers in mature forests, both hardwoods and conifers (in N.M. in mountains up to 9,000 ft.), and likes densely wooded swamps with dead trees and hanging pieces of loose bark (Tyler, 1948a); utters faint hissing *tss* note, sometimes lengthened, as it climbs up trunk, to *zi-i-i-it,* like sound of small steel chain which, when let fall, tinkles into small heap; sings rarely in migration but on nesting grounds utters high-pitched musical song; flight can be strong and direct, especially in courtship; roosts clinging with sharp claws to trunk of large tree, sometimes by clinging to outside wall of house.

Feeding Habits: Explores trunk and bottoms and sides of branches of trees, and hitches

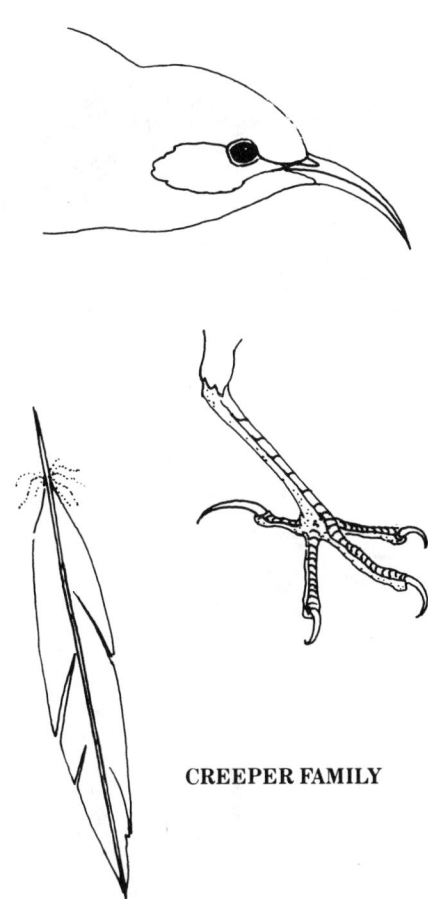

CREEPER FAMILY

California quail

Steller's jay

CREST

The height of the crest of the Steller's jay is an indication of its mood and behavior. The crest is flattened when the jay is foraging, preening, or courting and erected during aggressive displays or territorial defense. The crest of the California quail is a tuft of black plumes arching forward from its crown.

along undersides of limbs with back toward ground searching for insects and larvae; eats weevils, leaf beetles, bugs, aphids, leaf hoppers, scale insects, eggs of katydids, adult ants, sawflies, moths, caterpillars, cocoons of spiders, pupae of codling moths, spiders and pseudoscorpions; takes some vegetable food, largely nuts and seeds; comes to feeding stations for chopped peanuts, peanut butter-cornmeal-suet mixture put in bark of trees for it; tame, in migration known to alight on leg of standing man (Tyler, 1948a).

Nest: Crescent-shaped hammock of mosses, twigs, shredded bark, spiders' cocoons, lined with feathers of grouse, wild ducks, and other birds; built usually under a strip of bark against trunk of dead tree, 5–15 ft. up, sometimes in rotted cavity of tree or in old woodpecker hole.

Eggs: Mar.–July; 4–8, commonly 5–6, white, sparingly dotted with browns.

Incubation: 14–15 days; young leave nest 13–14 days after hatching.

Other Names: American brown creeper; American creeper; California creeper; common creeper; little brown creeper; Mexican creeper; Rocky Mountain creeper; Sierra creeper; tree creeper.

Age: One banded N.H. recaptured when 4½ years old; one (banded) reported from Great Britain lived to 6 years, 9 months old (Clapp, 1976).

Host to Cowbirds: Rare, one record (Friedmann, 1963).

Hybrids: European brown creeper has crossed with European short-toed creeper (Gray, 1958).

Weights: Mich. (3), 8–9.2 gr. (Becker and Stack, 1944), or about ⅓ oz.; autumn, coastal N.J. (177), 6.5–9.8 gr., or about ¼–⅓ oz. (Murray and Jehl, 1964).

Range: In N. America, resident from s.-c. and se. Alaska across s. Canada to Newfoundland; in West, south to s. Calif., through Mexico to Nicaragua; in East, south in Appalachians to e. Tenn. and w. N.C.; some withdrawal or migration south from northern part of breeding range; winters to Gulf coast and Fla.

Pine creeper. Local name for the pine warbler.

Tree creeper. *See* Brown creeper.

CREPUSCULAR

Term for birds that are active at twilight. Whippoor-wills and nighthawks are said to be crepuscular, although they may also be active during the night, when they are said to be nocturnal.

CREST

A tuft of longer feathers of the head that are held erect most of the time by the bird, or are capable of being erected (Van Tyne and Berger, 1959). All birds sometimes raise their crown (top of head) feathers, but only a few N. American land birds have a conspicuous feathered crest on top of the head—the scaled quail, belted kingfisher, pileated woodpecker, ivory-billed woodpecker, blue jay, Steller's jay, phainopepla, cardinal, pyrrhuloxia, and the sev-

CORMORANT FAMILY

Brandt's cormorant
The breeding grounds of Brandt's cormorant, along the Pacific coast from Washington to Baja California, can be so crowded that the territory of a nesting pair is no larger than the nest itself—a circular assemblage of seaweed, moss, and grass—and a narrow space to stand beside it. Three to 6 eggs are laid; the chicks, naked and blind at hatching, are fed partly digested fish regurgitated by the parents. Cormorants feed largely on fish of little commercial value, though in times past they were persecuted by fishermen who blamed the birds for depleting their catches.

Brandt's cormorant

Double-crested cormorant
This widely distributed species, named for 2 tufts of feathers that appear briefly during the breeding season, is found on saltwater shores and on large inland waters across the continent. The feathers of cormorants are not fully waterproof, and the birds are commonly found posed on rocks or pilings, their wet wings spread for drying.

Great cormorant
A familiar bird on European shores, our largest cormorant nests on this side of the Atlantic in small colonies from Newfoundland to Nova Scotia. Its webbed feet propel it underwater on dives that last as long as 71 seconds. In hot weather, great cormorants carry water in their gular pouches to pour over the exposed chicks.

Olivaceous cormorant
A tropical species that reaches the Gulf coast of Louisiana and Texas, the olivaceous cormorant is fond of perching on slender twigs or even overhead utility wires—a feat unique among North American cormorants. It feeds in freshwater lakes and rivers, eating minnows, frogs, and aquatic insects.

Pelagic cormorant
This Pacific species, nesting on precipitous cliffs from the Aleutian Islands to Baja California, has been caught in fishermen's nets at depths of 180 feet and may dive much deeper. Pelagic cormorants will use one nest for several years, piling up seaweed, grass, and miscellaneous ocean rubbish until the mound is 5 to 6 feet high.

Red-faced cormorant
Like others of its family, this bird of wild Arctic shores stays close to its nesting areas during the winter months, finding shelter in cliffside niches during storms that rage over the Bering Sea.

Pelagic cormorant

Double-crested cormorant

Olivaceous cormorant

Red-faced cormorant

Great cormorant

CRANE FAMILY

Sandhill crane

With their long necks extended and long legs trailing behind, migrating sandhill cranes wing across the prairie in spring and fall, announcing their presence with calls that can be heard for miles. The crane's unforgettable trumpeting is produced by a modified windpipe that has been likened to a French horn. The birds call constantly to keep the flock together as they climb to altitudes as high as 13,000 feet, sometimes making spectacular V formations, other times strung out in long lines. Sandhill cranes nest in wetlands from Florida to the Arctic tundra; 2 eggs are laid on a huge mound of marsh plants yanked up by their roots. The 2 chicks hatch 2 or 3 days apart, and the older one is often aggressive to its sibling. The parents keep the youngsters separated by walking apart, each adult followed by one of the chicks.

Whooping crane

The rescue of the whooping crane from the brink of extinction is one of the great success stories in wildlife conservation. The tallest bird in North America, it once nested on prairie wetlands from Illinois to North Dakota, but by the late 1800s it had abandoned its historic homelands because of settlement, drainage, farming, and shooting. By 1937, only 15 birds survived in a remnant flock that wintered on the Texas coast and nested in the Canadian wilderness. Creation of a national wildlife refuge on the Gulf of Mexico and an intensive public education campaign to protect the huge white birds on their migration flights succeeded. By the winter of 1979–80, the Texas flock numbered 76 cranes. Meanwhile, a second wild group has been established at another federal refuge in Idaho. Eggs collected on the whooping crane's nesting grounds in the Northwest Territories, and others laid by captive birds at a government research facility, are hatched under foster parents, sandhill cranes. Adult whoopers are all white except for the black tips of their 7½-foot wings; young birds are washed with rusty brown.

Sandhill crane, chick

Whooping crane

Whooping crane, juvenile

andhill crane

Whooping crane, juvenile, with Sandhill cranes

CREEPER FAMILY

Brown creeper
An inhabitant of mature forests and swampy woodlands, the brown creeper has long toes equipped with sharp, long curving claws that enable it to creep about tree trunks and branches in search of insects and their larvae. Using its tail as a prop, the creeper spirals up the trunk, occasionally hopping backward to investigate a crevice in the bark, or hitches upside down along the undersides of limbs.

CROW FAMILY

Common crow
Probably the best-known bird of rural America, the common crow is often seen along roadsides, scavenging the carcasses of traffic-killed animals. Its diet, however, is utterly opportunistic: it will eat anything handy, from grain and fruit crops to snakes, snails, frogs, insects, earthworms, and eggs and young robbed from the nests of other birds. In fall, crows congregate in roosts that may hold 200,000 birds.

Fish crow
A resident of the Atlantic and Gulf seacoasts, the fish crow persecutes other birds of salt marshes, beaches, and mangrove swamps. It dives at gulls and terns, forcing them to disgorge their catches; and it plunders the nests of shorebirds, rails, wading birds, and even turtles, carrying eggs away in its bill. Skimming a pond, the fish crow can snatch minnows with its feet; and it plucks ticks from the backs of grazing cattle.

Northwestern crow
A beachcomber and scavenger of the Pacific shore, from Alaska to Washington, the northwestern crow carries shellfish aloft, dropping them on rocks to be cracked open.

Common raven
The specific name for the largest member of the crow family, corax, comes from a Greek word meaning "croaker" and aptly describes the common raven's hoarse voice. This is a bird of the wilderness—of high mountains, boreal forests, treeless tundra, rocky seacoasts. A magnificent flier, it is the aerial equal of hawks and falcons. It is the largest passerine, or perching, bird.

White-necked raven
A bird of arid plains and hot desert, the white-necked raven enjoys plunging into whirling "dust devils" and riding their columns to dizzying heights. Trees are scarce in its habitat, and the same nest will be used year after year. The platform of thorny twigs plus an occasional strand of barbed wire is often built on utility poles or windmills.

Brown creeper

Common raven

Common raven

Northwestern crow

Common crow

White-necked raven

Fish crow

Blue jay

A familiar and handsome bird of backyards and mixed woodlands, the blue jay has a bad reputation for robbing the nests of other songbirds. In truth, eggs and nestlings form only a small percentage of its largely vegetarian diet. Blue jays are particularly fond of acorns and beechnuts, which they store in the ground. A raucous bird much of the year, announcing the presence of any intruder in the woods with ear-splitting shrieks, the blue jay becomes silent and secretive during the nesting season. It also has a sweet, musical spring song that few observers hear or recognize.

Gray jay

Woodsmen of northern coniferous forests know this bird as the "camp robber." Incredibly bold, it hangs about the cabins of hunters, trappers, fishermen, and lumberjacks, snatching any loose items whether edible or not and hiding them nearby. Balls of chewed food are stuck in trees with a tacky fluid secreted by glands in the jay's mouth.

Green jay

A resident of Central America and northern South America, the green jay is found in the United States only in south Texas, where it is fairly common along the Rio Grande valley. It lives in dense thickets but wanders about open country in small flocks after the nesting season ends.

Mexican jay

A resident of oak-clad mountainsides from Arizona to the Big Bend country of Texas, the Mexican jay is a gregarious species that lives in noisy flocks the year round. A pair of Mexican jays will help build and defend the nests of their neighbors and even feed their young.

Pinyon jay

Resembling a small, all-blue crow, the pinyon jay roams western mountains in highly organized flocks of hundreds of birds, feasting on the nuts of pinyons and other pines. Feeding flocks will post several sentries to warn of intruders.

Scrub jay

A jay of the arid West (with a separate population in Florida), the scrub jay inhabits dense thickets along watercourses and on mountain slopes. Like its large relative, the crow, it is fond of hoarding bright, shiny objects, from bits of glass or china to pilfered silverware. In Florida, young scrub jays help their parents tend successive broods until they themselves reach breeding age.

Steller's jay

The only crested jay in much of the West, this strikingly colored bird is named for Arctic explorer Georg Wilhelm Steller, who collected the first specimen known to science on the Alaska coast in 1741. Like the blue jay, its counterpart east of the Rocky Mountains, it can mimic the calls of other birds, including hawks and loons.

Blue jay

Gray jay

Green jay

Scrub jay

Pinyon jay

Mexican jay

Steller's jay

Black-billed magpie

Strikingly garbed in black and white, with a streaming tail nearly a foot long, the magpie is instantly identified as it parades about the rangelands of the West, feasting on abundant grasshoppers, digging maggots from carrion, or plucking ticks from the backs of elk and deer. The massive magpie nest, a domed pile of sticks held together by mud and entered through holes in the side, contains 7 to 13 eggs. When nesting ends, magpies move about in small family groups, then form larger flocks at the onset of winter. Old magpie nests never go to waste: they are used for shelter and homes by a variety of birds, including owls, hawks, ducks, herons, doves, and bluebirds.

Yellow-billed magpie

A smaller version of its wide-ranging relative, the yellow-billed magpie is found only in California. It often lives close to houses and becomes quite tame if not molested. Captive birds, in fact, have been known to repeat words picked up from humans. Like other members of the crow family, it is omnivorous. Leftover food may be stored in shallow pits that the bird digs in the ground.

Clark's nutcracker

Discovered on the historic Lewis and Clark expedition to the Pacific Northwest, this bird of the mountains is named in honor of Captain William Clark. A resident of the Rockies and Sierra Nevada from 3,000 to 13,000 feet elevation, Clark's nutcracker feeds on the ground, gleaning pinyon nuts, prying open pine cones with its long bill to reach the seeds. It stores seeds for winter and spring use, digging through snow as deep as 8 inches to reach a cache.

Yellow-billed magpie

Clark's nutcracker

Black-billed magpie

Black-billed magpie, juvenile

Black-billed magpie

CUCKOO FAMILY

Groove-billed ani
Anis are tropical American birds with the remarkable habit of building communal nests. Up to two dozen eggs will be laid in a single nest by several females, who share the duties of incubation and rearing young. Coal-black birds with long tails and parrotlike bills, groove-billed anis nest from the Rio Grande delta of Texas to Peru but may be expanding their range in North America.

Smooth-billed ani
A native of Panama, South America, and the West Indies, the smooth-billed ani was accidentally introduced to south Florida. One colony was established by birds blown across the sea by a hurricane. Largely insect eaters, anis frequent pastureland, gathering insects stirred up by grazing cattle.

Black-billed cuckoo
Old World cuckoos are notorious for laying their eggs in the nests of other birds and leaving the unsuspecting hosts to raise their young. Among North American species, the black-billed and yellow-billed cuckoos are occasionally guilty of brood parasitism, but it is not a regular habit. Secretive birds, cuckoos are heard more often than they are seen. Indeed, a hot summer day in the country would not be complete without the repetitious "cu-cu-cu" of a black-billed cuckoo, uttered while sitting on its nest or on the wing.

Yellow-billed cuckoo
While the black-billed cuckoo frequents the forest edge and wooded riverbottoms, the yellow-billed cuckoo prefers tangled thickets along streams and rural roads. Both species, which sometimes parasitize each other's nests, consume great numbers of caterpillars; 325 tent caterpillars were found in the stomach of one yellow-billed cuckoo. When young cuckoos are about a week old, they leave their nest and scramble about the branches for another 2 weeks until they are able to fly.

Yellow-billed cuckoo

Groove-billed ani

Smooth-billed ani

Black-billed cuckoo

Black-billed cuckoo, fledgling

Yellow-billed cuckoo, nestling

Roadrunner

Though a competent flier, the roadrunner spends much of its life on the ground, dashing about the desert at speeds exceeding 15 miles per hour. This odd, large cuckoo has long legs designed for pursuit of prey, and any small creature is fair game—from centipedes and gophers to scorpions and rattlesnakes. The roadrunner's stick nest, assembled in a thicket or clump of cactus, is lined with anything found loose in the desert—dried manure, snakeskins, feathers, leaves, mesquite pods. Two to 6 young are raised, and the fledgling roadrunners are capable of catching their own food when 3 weeks old. Like many other birds, roadrunners engage in sunbathing. Biologists are at a loss to explain this behavior, but one theory is that the heat absorbed by spreading the wings and tail feathers causes ectoparasites to move about, making it easier to remove them by preening.

Roadrunner

Roadrunner

Roadrunner

Roadrunner

Chachalaca

CURASSOW FAMILY

Chachalaca

Curassows are fowl of the New World tropics, and of the 44 species in the family, only 1 reaches North America. An inhabitant of dry woodland and thickets from Mexico to Costa Rica, the plain chachalaca can be found in the Rio Grande valley at the southern tip of Texas. Its name echoes its cry—a three-syllable "cha-cha-lac" that reverberates through the chaparral at dawn, at dusk, and before thunderstorms, often in synchronized choruses joined by all the birds within hearing. Chachalacas and other curassows are increasingly rare south of the border because of relentless hunting.

eral species of N. American titmice (Berger, 1961), the tufted duck and mergansers.

CRETACEOUS PERIOD
See Geological Time Scale.

CRIPPLED-BIRD ACT
See Distraction Display; *also* under Plover Family; Young and Their Care.

CRISSUM
When the undertail coverts of a bird are of one color (and sometimes they are distinctively and differently colored than the rest of the feathers on the undersurface of a bird) they are collectively called the crissum. Examples are the undertail coverts of the catbird (crissum rusty red); the Colima warbler (bright yellow); the brown towhee (pale rusty), and the Bohemian waxwing (chestnut-red).

CROCKER
See Brant.

CRONISM
See Kronism.

CROP
The crop (often called a craw in chickens) is a dilation or enlargement of the esophagus in the neck region. The crop, where present, serves primarily as a temporary storage organ for food, but also functions in (1) the production of "milk" by pigeons and doves, (2) resonating sounds made during courtship displays of some grouse and other species, and (3) chemical digestion in a few species (hoatzin, owl parrot, domestic pigeon, and domestic fowl). See Farner, 1960, and Ziswiler and Farner, 1972. *See* Digestion; *also* Mouth and discussion of pouches for food-carrying.

Not all birds have a crop; many seed-eating songbirds, some fish-eaters, ducks, geese, and cranes have no true crop, but the elastic wall of the esophagus can be widened by the intake of food for temporary storage; Old World flycatchers, robins, and Old World warblers, which feed on insects, do not have a crop (Heinroth and Heinroth, 1958). N. American swallows, warblers, and other insect-eating birds that feed almost continuously all day have less need for a crop for storing food (Wallace, 1955). The best-known examples of birds with crops are pigeons, gallinaceous birds, parrots, and eagles, hawks, and owls (Heinroth and Heinroth, 1958).

The crop may be rudimentary—a spindle-shaped enlargement of the esophagus in a cormorant or other fish-eating bird that flies long distances to carry food to its young; a "false crop," or a simple diverticulum in the esophagus, of a condor or vulture; or a "true crop" in peafowl (Farner, 1960) or in pheasants, chickens, and other gallinaceous birds.

Apparently the crop is a special adaptation in those birds that need to swallow large amounts of food hurriedly, at a faster rate than the stomach can accommodate it. It is highly developed in the grain-eating or seed-eating birds, such as the turkeys, quail, pheasants, and grouse; also in pigeons and doves. It enables pheasants and grouse, for example, which have

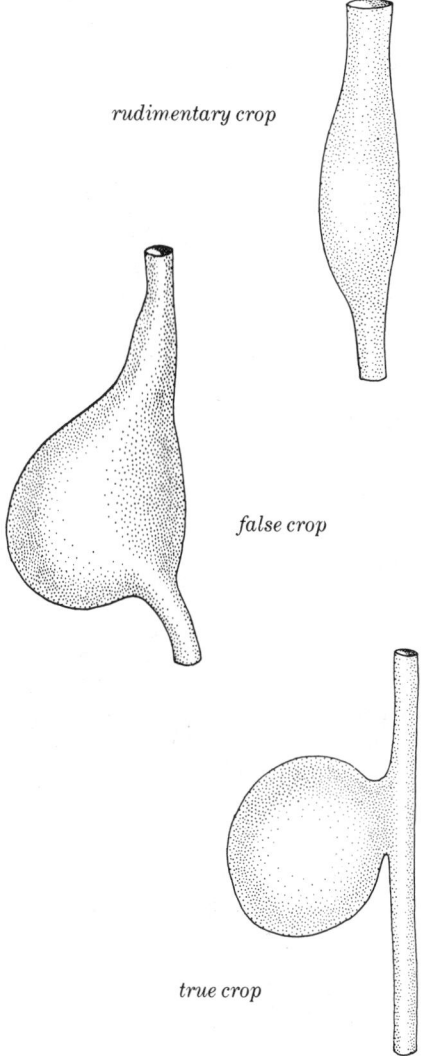

rudimentary crop

false crop

true crop

CROP
The crop functions as a storage organ, holding food that is later digested in the stomach. The crop is highly developed in most seed-eating birds, but in many fish-eaters such as cormorants it is only a rudimentary enlargement of the esophagus. Condors and vultures have a false crop or diverticulum in the esophagus. Most insect-eating birds have no crop at all.

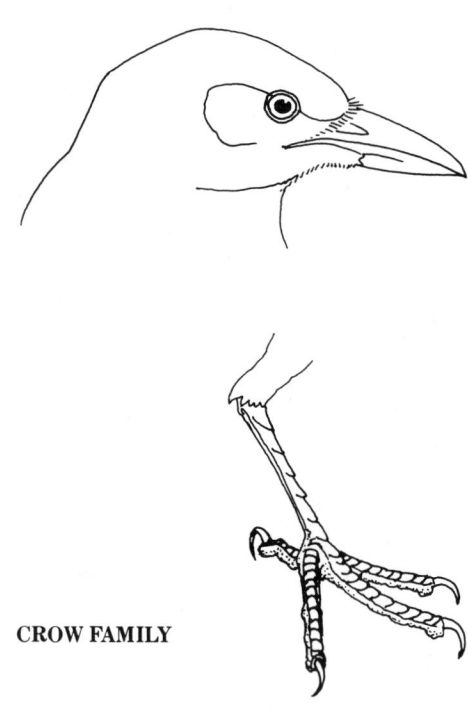

CROW FAMILY

two main feeding periods during the day, to fill the crop and then rest or roost while the food is being assimilated by the stomach; it enables hawks and vultures, which may not find food frequently, and may go for hours or even days without it (*see* Fasting), to gorge themselves on large amounts when they have the opportunity and to be sustained for long periods between feedings (Wallace, 1963).

The capacity of the crop, especially in a big bird such as the wild turkey, may be very large. According to Burget (1957), a large gobbler will eat a pound of food at one meal. During the hunting season, a wild turkey was found to have a pint of food (473 cc.) in its crop (Schorger, 1966); the turkey crop is often crammed with acorns. *See* How Much Will a Bird Eat? under Food and Feeding Habits.

Birds of the Parrot Family, some of the Hawaiian honeycreepers, some members of the Troupial Family (Icteridae), and some members of the Finch Family (Fringillidae) have a crop (Van Tyne and Berger, 1959).

Evening grosbeaks and certain other northern finches that live through winter cold have a crop in which they can store large amounts of sunflower and other seeds before retiring. Dawson and Tordoff (1959) point out that this food supply, which these birds can digest and absorb while roosting, must be of considerable importance in keeping their metabolism (*see* Metabolism) and body temperatures high through a cold winter night. *See* Cold and Birds.

Weymouth, Lasiewski, and Berger (1964) discovered in their studies of the tongues of hummingbirds (*see* Tongue) that the Rivoli's has a well-developed crop and that hummingbirds in the laboratory, while feeding, stored insects and sugar solutions in the crop. Lasiewki suggested that the crop, when filled, might sustain a hummingbird through a cool or cold night without requiring the bird to go into a torpor to conserve its bodily energy until morning. *See* discussion under Torpidity. See Hainesworth and Wolf (1972).

The most specialized crop is that of the doves and pigeons, which is a two-chambered sac that produces a "milk" during the nesting season. This remarkable phenomenon was described as early as 1786 by a British investigator, J. Hunter (Farner, 1960). Witschi (1935) writes: "The crop sacs of pigeons and doves are thin, membranous structures at all stages . . . except during the last eight to ten days of the incubation period. At this time the two lateral pouches of the crop in both sexes increase as much as twenty times in thickness, and during the succeeding three weeks, while the young are being fed, the thickened mucosa is desquamated intermittently in thick layers of caseous 'crop milk.' Formation of crop milk is influenced by exteroceptive stimuli. The cock pigeon with no squabs to feed produces 'milk' if he is able to see adults caring for their young."

Crop milk is rich in fat, 25–30%; lecithin, 5%; protein, 10–15%; but contains no sugar. It apparently has a growth-promoting vitamin, and the proliferation of the crop epithelium and the production of milk is stimulated by prolactin (Farner, 1960). *See* discussion of this under Endocrine Glands.

The adult pigeons regurgitate the crop milk, which the little squab, helpless and blind, gets by sticking its bill into the throats of the adult birds. When the squab is about 5 days old, the parents feed it its first grain, softened and mixed with the milk. The parents go on producing the crop milk for about 18 days. In wild species of doves and pigeons, the young are kept on pure crop milk much longer than the young of the domestic pigeon (Heinroth and Heinroth, 1958).

Another unusual function of the crop is seen in the hoatzin (ho-AT-sin), a S. American tree-climbing bird, which uses its crop to grind or crush masses of thick tropical leaves, largely of arum, on which it feeds. Thus its crop has a gizzardlike function (*see* Gizzard). It is so important to the life economy of the bird that it has become very large in its evolution, apparently usurping the functions of its much-reduced glandular stomach and gizzard (Beebe, 1906). *See* discussion of hoatzin under Galliformes; Cuckoo Family.

Ostriches, which do not have a crop, have a small pocket just behind the base of the tongue in which they store mouthfuls of grass or leaves that they clip off with the bill. When the pocket is full, the ostrich raises its head, and as it swallows, one can see the lump of food slide down its long throat, or esophagus.

CROP MILK
See Crop.

CROSS
A hybrid, or a bird whose parents were of two different species. *See* Hybrid.

CROSSBILL
See in Finch Family.

CROSS-BREED
See Hybrid.

CROW-DUCK
See Coot, American, in Rail Family and Double-crested cormorant in Cormorant Family.

CROW FAMILY
Corvidae (CORE-vih-dee); from Lat. *corvus*, raven. 103 species worldwide except in Antarctica, New Zealand, and some oceanic islands (Van Tyne and Berger, 1976); 18 species in N. America; includes some of largest (ravens) of all songbirds (*see* Passeriformes) and some of most bold, active, noisy, and aggressive of all birds—the ravens, crows, jays, magpies, and Clark's nutcracker in N. America and, for example, choughs, rooks, and jackdaws of Old World. The family is believed to have originated in the north temperate and tropical parts of the Old World, and to have spread from there to present ranges in N. America and other parts of the world; their fossils have been discovered in deposits laid down in Colo. 12 million years ago (Brodkorb, 1978). Nearest relatives of Crow Family are thought to be shrikes, birds-of-paradise of New Guinea, bell-magpies of Australia, drongos of Africa and Asia, and orioles of the Old World. The family has been divided, based on their closeness of relationships, into two groups—the subfamily Cor-

vinae: crows, ravens, rooks, jackdaws, and nutcrackers; and the subfamily Garrulinae: jays, magpies, and choughs (Gilliard, 1958); the name magpie is a contraction of its Middle English name, magot pie.

The crows, as a family, apparently have evolved the highest degree of intelligence among birds. Experiments with captive American crows showed that they can count up to three or four, are keen, wary birds, good at solving puzzles and at performing astonishing feats of memory, and quickly learn to associate various noises and symbols with food (Coburn, 1914); and it has been known to naturalists for years that they have a language of their own (see Chamberlain and Cornwell, 1971; see also Language). Members of the Crow Family can mimic sounds uttered by birds and other animals and, in captivity, the human voice; however, the myth that splitting the tongue allows a crow to talk better is a cruel hoax.

Some members of Crow Family have complex social organizations in flocks; in N. America, among crows and, especially, pinyon jays, Mexican jays, and the scrub jays of Fla. In N. America there are 8 species of jays; their plumage is more colorful than that of crows; the N. American blue jay and Steller's jay are the counterparts of the Old World common jay (Austin, 1961) of Eurasia and North Africa, which has habit of food-storing like nutcrackers.

Magpies occur in w. N. America (2 species), Europe, and Asia, but are absent from S. America and Australia, and reach only extreme nw. Africa and Saudi Arabia; all have bright colors or are black and white with long tails; nutcrackers (1 species in N. America) live mostly in coniferous forests around northern parts of the world and are known for their food-storing habits; for example, the Clark's nutcracker, *Nucifraga columbiana*, depends upon the stored pine seeds from more than one thousand food caches to provide food for itself and its young during the winter and spring. The thick-billed nutcracker, *Nucifraga caryocatactes*, shows remarkable memory for finding these caches in winter even under 18 in. of snow (Swanberg, 1951); of the ravens (2 species in N. America), the common raven, largest-bodied of all songbirds, has spectacular aerobatic flights in which pairs dive to earth like falcons or turn over and over in series of somersaults; sometimes circle for hours like eagles (Bent, 1946); see also Goodwin (1976).

Sexes are outwardly alike in Crow Family, or nearly so; they have 10 primary (wing) feathers; the nostrils are usually concealed by dense tufts of stiff feathers and they have rictal bristles (about mouth). *See* Feathers; see Pettingill (1970) for other characters of Crow Family. Most are strong fliers, usually gregarious (American crows are noted for their enormous flocks in fall and winter); they utter loud, harsh calls, yet some have soft "whisper" songs; some species mate for life—the raven and Florida scrub jay, for example. *See* The Pair Bond under Courtship. Courtship feeding is common and the male continues to feed the female while she is on the nest; usually only the female incubates eggs or broods young; the male helps to feed them.

In captivity, offer a crippled or injured jay, crow, magpie, or other member of the family, various meats, soaked grains, bread, fruit, vegetables, mealworms and other insects, also mice (Walker, 1942).

Crow, American. *See* Crow, common.

Crow, blue. *See* Jay, pinyon.

Crow, carrion. Another name for the black vulture and the turkey vulture.

Crow, Clark's. *See* Nutcracker, Clark's.

Crow, common, *Corvus brachyrhynchos* (CORE-vus brah-kih-RING-koss); genus name: *see* family introduction; species name: from Gr. *brachys*, short, and *rhynchos*, beak; "a short-billed raven." (Color ill., page 125.) From Atlantic to Pacific, Canada to Mexico, common in East, local in West; in Great Basin (Utah, Nev.) restricted mostly to rivers, streams (Richards, 1971); 17–21 in. long; wingspread 33–40 in.; black from end of bill to tip of tail and claws; metallic violet gloss on body; blue-violet and green-blue gloss on wings; adults' eyes, brown; immatures' blue; one of most adaptable of all birds; lives in open and wooded country over almost entire U.S.; usually solitary, pairs nest in tall trees but in Far West in loose colonies in streamside trees on plains and prairies has nested on windmills and even on ground; country altered by man, from forests to cropland, has provided year-round feeding grounds; farm woodlots and scattered trees and windbreaks on former grasslands provide additional nesting places. Because of crow's fondness for corn (mostly waste in fall) and other farm crops, occasional eating of eggs of songbirds and game birds, and often extravagant charges of damage against it, has been shot, poisoned, and roosts bombed by farmers and sportsmen, but still persists by wit, and is economically useful for insect-eating and important ecologically (*see* discussion in Economic Ornithology; also old but thorough scientific appraisal of in Kalmbach, 1920). Migratory in some parts of range, moves southward from n. U.S. and s. Canada to middle and s. U.S. in fall, returns Feb. into May (for example, crows banded in Sask. migrated southward in narrow flyway to winter from N.D. to Tex.), gathers in enormous flocks in fall and winter from few thousands to 200,000 usually near source of food, but flocks may travel up to 50 mi. each day in feeding; flocks often harass (mob) larger hawks and owls (natural enemies) in noisy screaming pursuit; has great versatility of voice, many variations of the common *caw* note (see in Frings and Frings, 1959); Chamberlain and Cornwell (1971) describe 23 calls of crows and their meaning and cite mimicry by crows of whine of dog, human voice, squawk of hen, and others. *See* Mimicry.

Feeding Habits: Eats insects, spiders, millipeds, crustaceans, snails, frogs, salamanders, snakes, eggs and young of birds, earthworms; carries clams, scallops, mussels, sea urchins high in air, then drops them on rocks to crack open and eat contents; scavenges on dead fishes, seals, garbage, traffic-killed animals; also eats corn and other grain crops, wild and cultivated fruit; coughs up in pellet (*see* Pellet) indigestible seeds, bones, etc. (see Gross, 1946a, for food habits details).

Nest: Usually in woods or sometimes in isolated tree, in crotch 18–60 ft. up, sometimes to 100 ft.; sometimes in small tree or bush or in hedge only 6–10 ft. up; on prairies nests on ground rarely or on crossarms of utility poles; well-built nest of branches and twigs, the nest bowl lined with bark, plant fibers, mosses, twine, rags, wool, roots, seaweeds, leaves.

Eggs: Feb.–June; 3–7, usually 4–6, blue-green to olive-green, blotched and spotted with browns and grays; some lay reddish eggs (Gross, 1946a).

Incubation: Possibly by both sexes, 18 days; young first fly when 28–35 days old; make interesting but mischievous pets (see Gross, 1946a; Forbush, 1925–29).

Other Names: American crow; eastern crow; Florida crow; southern crow; western crow; corn-thief.

Age: In Ill., records of banded crows 6 and 7 years old; in Canada, two 8 years old when shot and killed; one banded Man. shot 14 years later in S.D.; in captivity to 20 years or more.

Albinism: Relatively frequent, 58 records (Gross, 1965a); a female shot in Me., pure white, including bill, feet, and claws, eyes pink; three young on wing with normal black parent, one was pure white, two gray, near Dearborn, Mich., spring 1953.

Flight Speed: Small flock, timed in w. U.S., 30 m.p.h. (Cottam *et al.*, 1942b); timed in Wash., individuals, 25–32 m.p.h. (Rathbun, 1934).

Host to Cowbird: Three records, "accidental" (Friedmann, 1963) as crow inappropriate host.

Weights: At winter roost in Ohio, males (30) ranged from 15½ oz. to 1 lb. 6½ oz.; females (45), from 14¾ oz. to 1 lb. 5½ oz. (Hicks and Dalmbach, 1935).

Range: Nests from B.C., s.w. Mack., n. Sask., n. Man., n. Ont., c. Que., and s. Newfoundland, south to n. Baja Calif., c. Ariz., n.-c. N.M., Colo., c. Tex., Gulf coast and s. Fla.

Crow, fish, *Corvus ossifragus* (CORE-vus oss-IF-rah-gus); genus name: *see* family introduction; species name: Lat., bone-breaking. (Color ill., page 125.) Atlantic and Gulf coasts of U.S.; 16–20 in. long; wingspread 30–43 in.; all-black like common crow but slightly smaller, slenderer, more pointed wings, best distinguished from common crow by nasal, falsetto *cah-r, ah-uk,* or *aw-uk,* different from harsh cawing of common crow; inland may feed with common crows but favors coastal marshes, beaches, banks of streams, sometimes inland along rivers in Pa., almost everywhere in Fla., about swamps, rivers, lakes; more sociable and more nearly gregarious at all seasons than common crow (Pough, 1949), seldom seen singly, often nests in small colonies or groups, biggest assemblies are in winter roosts of thousands; flies like common crow but quicker and sails more, a few flaps, then a glide, often hovers on rapidly beating wings as it searches for floating food, often drinks while skimming the water, sometimes catches minnows near surface of water with claws of its feet.

Mexican crow

CROW FAMILY

Feeding Habits: Along seashore, brackish waters of salt marshes, scours shallow waters, mud, or ground for fiddler crabs, shrimps, crayfishes, and carrion, will dive at gulls and terns, forcing them to give up their catches; eats eggs from nests of terns, willets, plovers, clapper rails, also turtles' eggs, unguarded eggs of herons, which it carries off in bill; grubs, ants, grasshoppers, ticks from backs of cattle; hackberries, huckleberries, cedar berries, pokeberries, palmetto, magnolia, holly, dogwood berries, figs, etc. (Bent, 1946).

Nest: Usually in small colonies but in separate trees, sometimes high in crotch of deciduous tree in swamp or along riverbank, or lower in salt-marsh pines, hollies, cedars; of dead sticks, twigs, lined with grapevine bark, pine needles, cattle or horse hair.

Eggs: Apr.–June; 4–5, green or green-blue, with brown spots.

Incubation: 16–18 days, young first fly when 21 days old or more.

Age: One banded La. killed in Ark. when at least 8 years old.

Albinism: A complete or total albino with pink eyes seen in wild near Ardmore, Md., Oct. 1945 by Malcolm Davis.

Weights: 14–15½ oz. (Forbush, 1925–29).

Range: Resident on coasts (although some southward movement in cold winters) from R.I. south along coast to Fla., west to se. Tex., inland along large rivers to sw. Tenn., nw. La., w. Ark., c. Ga., w. S.C., nw. N.C., c. Va., D.C., c. Md., c. Pa., and c. N.Y.

Crow, Jim. Another name for the black vulture.

Crow, John. Another name for the black vulture.

Crow, Mexican, *Corvus imparatus* (CORE-vus im-par-AY-tus); genus name: *see* family introduction; species name: Lat., unready, unprepared, unequipped (Levine *et al.*, 1967). Native Mexican species; 14½–16 in. long; small for a crow, black, resembles the slightly larger fish crow, to which it is thought to be closely related (a subspecies) by some authorities but not by others; first reported in N. America in Aug. 1968 near Brownsville, Tex., by Arvin *et al.* (1975), where three seen feeding on carrion along Texas Highway 4, which is first known occurrence strictly within the U.S. According to Arvin *et al.* (1975), it should be included in the A.O.U. *Check-list* because this crow has moved north across the Rio Grande into the lower Rio Grande valley (in Cameron, Willacy, and Kenedy counties, Tex.), with large flocks on rangeland 8 mi. east of Brownsville in Sept. 1968; by Oct., large flocks roosting near the northern Brownsville limits; later invasions reported but no nesting within Tex. up to 1974 (see details in Arvin *et al.*, 1975). In Mexico this small gregarious crow lives in partly dry brush and in farming country, and according to Peterson and Chalif (1973), from sea level to 3,000 ft. in coastal regions; they state that Mexican crows of the Gulf slope of Mexico utter a low, hoarse *craw* or *khurrr*; those of the Pacific slope a different, higher-pitched, shrill *creow*. For other details see Angell (1978). Some authorities, on the basis of these different voices and separate ranges, consider the western race a separate species, *Corvus sinaloae*.

Other Names: Sinaloa crow; Tamaulipas crow. *Range:* See above.

Crow, northwestern, *Corvus caurinus* (CORE-vus caw-RYE-nus); genus name: *see* family introduction; species name: Lat., of the northwest wind. (Color ill., page 124.) Discovered on nw. coast U.S.; Pacific coast, Alaska to Wash.; smaller than common crow, and with smaller feet; 16–17 in. long; can be distinguished by habitat, which is more like that of fish crow of East, also its *caw* note, which is hoarser and lower-pitched than that of the common crow's; very tame, lives about wooded shores of bays and on beaches with gulls, at low tide on mud flats; lives also about towns and settlements; at home about Indian villages, where walks about like chicken; at times may feed side by side with raven, at others flock may harass it, but raven dominates; nesting pair may drive away bald eagle from their territory; strong attachment between pair; one that had lost part of bill, possibly in trap, was fed by mate, which regurgitated food in front of crippled bird (Bent, 1946). *See* other examples under Helpers among Birds.

Feeding Habits: A beachcomber and scavenger, eats saltwater snails, cockles, amphipods (beach "fleas"), flies aloft and drops mussels and other shellfishes from air to crack open on rocks; eats dead porpoises, refuse thrown away by fishermen; eats eggs of gulls, cormorants, murres, guillemots in seabird colonies; in spring, travels inland to plowed fields, with gulls and Brewer's blackbirds, eats grubs; in summer frequents salmon streams for dead fish, or forages in fields for grasshoppers, in fall eats wild cherries, saskatoon berries, pears, apples.

Nest: Often in small, loose-knit colonies, most often in crotches of low trees or shrubs, 8–20 ft. above ground, sometimes in Douglas firs 70 ft. up; occasionally far back under boulders, or on ground beneath bushes or windfalls near sea; nest like that of common crow: basketlike, of sticks and twigs, lined with cedar bark, dried grasses, deer hair.

Eggs: May–June; 4–5, green-blue, spotted with brown.

Incubation: Period of and age when young first fly unknown; probably same as closely related common crow.

Range: Resident on coasts and islands from s. Alaska (Kodiak, Sitka, Forrester Is.) to w. Wash., wanders inland in Wash. and Ore.

Crow, rain. Another name for the N. American cuckoo.

Crow, Sinaloa. *See* Crow, Mexican.

Crow, storm. Another name for the yellow-billed cuckoo.

Crow, Tamaulipas. *See* Crow, Mexican.

Jay, Arizona. *See* Jay, Mexican.

Jay, black-headed. See Jay, Steller's.

Jay, blue, *Cyanocitta cristata* (sigh-ah-no-SIT-ah kris-TAY-tah); genus name: from Gr. *kyanos*, blue, and *kitta*, chattering bird; species name: from Lat. *cristatus*, crested. (Color ill., page 126.) In Canada, in U.S., largely east of Rocky Mtns.; 11–12½ in. long; wingspread 15¾–17½ in.; upperparts—crest, nape, back, and tail—bright blue; prominent black necklace bordering white face and throat; white underparts, dark eyes; bold, strikingly beautiful American bird; cunning, inquisitive, as intelligent as common crow (Forbush, 1925–29); outstanding character is noisiness, shrieks singly and in chorus at hunter in woods, or other intruders, cats, snakes, owls; lives especially in mixed oak and beech woods, was once bird of wilderness forests; has adapted to living in shade trees of gardens, villages, city and country parks; some remain in same area year-round; others move southward in fall, in flocks of 50–100 or more; return northward in spring usually to same nesting area—see data in Laskey (1958); also migration details in Forbush (1925–29), and summary in Bergstrom (1958); pairs usually solitary in nesting season, when quiet, furtive, but in late summer and fall, when roving about in family groups or small flocks, are especially noisy; most common cry is *jay, jay,* or *jeer, jeer,* much varied, and a high-pitched shriek when discovers enemy such as owl in daytime roost; utters great number of calls, including bell-like *tull-ull,* ringing double note during which jay raises and lowers its head; mostly female utters rapid clicking call; also *teekle* (like word "teacup"), and others; in concealment of evergreen will sing soft, barely audible, sweet, lisping notes; also utters exact imitation of screams of red-shouldered and other hawks; reported to mimic songs or calls of black-capped chickadee, eastern wood pewee, northern (Baltimore) oriole, gray catbird, American goldfinch, and others; pairs are devoted mates. Laskey (1958) banded male in Tenn. that lived more than 8 years; had same mate at least 3 years during lifetime; male feeds mate during courtship and at nest; several known to have fed and guarded old, worn, partly blind jay and led it to water (Forbush, 1925–29). *See* Helpers among Birds.

Feeding Habits: Like its relative the American crow, is omnivorous; eats three times as much vegetable matter—especially acorns, beech nuts, and corn—as animal; feeds much in oak and beech woods; plucks acorns with bill from twigs, may carry one in mouth, one in throat when storing in ground; many of these, uneaten, sprout; habit helps replant forests; also in Fla. eats many palmetto seeds; eats hazelnuts, seeds of sumac, knotweed, sorrel, blackberries, blueberries, currants, wild and cultivated cherries, wild grapes, serviceberries, pokeberries, etc.—see Tyler (1946) for other details; eats insects throughout year; May beetles, fruit-eating beetles, grasshoppers, tent caterpillars and those of gypsy moth, browntail and sphinx moths, eggs of insects, also spiders, myriapods, snails, small fishes, frogs, salamanders, mice, bats; sometimes small birds or their eggs; comes to feeding stations for suet, bread, sunflower seeds (see list in Terres, 1968c; also use of eggshells); can be trained to come to hands for food, especially fond of peanuts; fond of bathing in birdbath, and sun baths.

Nest: False nest of twigs built before actual nest (Hardy, 1961); true nest built in crotch or on branch of many kinds of trees, bushes, vines, in beech and oak woods, in gardens, 5–50 ft. up, usually about 10–15 ft. above ground; both adults break twigs and small branches from trees with bill to make framework of bulky nest, about 7–8 in. in diameter, outer walls include also bark, mosses, lichens, paper, rags, string, wool, leaves, dry grasses, sometimes mud, inner cup lined with fine rootlets.

Eggs: Mar.–July (and into Aug. in Fla.); 3–6, usually 4–5, olive, buff, pale green or dull blue, spotted with browns, grays.

Incubation: Usually by female, 16½–18 days (Laskey, 1958; Tyler, 1946); young leave nest 17–21 days after hatching; adults defend nest and young by dive-bombing and pecking squirrels, cats, sometimes human intruders who come near young.

Other Names: Blue coat; common jay; cornthief; nest robber; jay; jay-bird; northern jay; southern jay.

Age: One banded Long Is., N.Y., recaptured alive when 13 years old at Laurel, Md.; many records of banded blue jays living to 6–9 years; several 10 years; one 11 years, 6 months; one reported (Tyler, 1946) banded wild bird to 15 years (see especially Middleton, 1974).

Albinism: Gross (1965a) reported 22 records; one in Ill. of brood of four was all-white, pink eyes, legs white; a partial albino in Wisc. mated one summer with normally colored jay (Morse, 1963); a melanistic one reported (Prescott, 1971a).

Flight Speed: Timed in New England, 20 m.p.h. (White, 1929).

Host to Cowbirds: Uncommon, an unsuitable host (Friedmann, 1963).

Hybrids: See in biography of Steller's jay.

Weights: In New England (44), average 89.2 gr., or about 3 oz.; fall, coastal N.J. (4), 76.-1–89.1 gr. (Murray and Jehl, 1964), or about 2¾–3 oz.; Fla., adults (100), average 75.5 gr. (Woolfenden, 1973b).

Range: Resident (some migrate from northern parts of range) from n.-c. Alta. east to Newfoundland, southeast of Rocky Mtns. to se. Tex., Gulf states, and s. Fla.

Jay, blue-fronted. See Jay, Steller's.

Jay, brown, *Psilorhinus morio* (sigh-low-RYE-nus MORE-ee-oh); genus name: from Gr. *psilos*, naked, smooth, and *rhinos*, nose (Jaeger, 1955), in this case, bill; "smooth bill"; species name: Lat., a fool, an arrogant person. A Mexican and American species that has entered U.S. in s. Tex.; 14–18 in. long; wingspread 30 in.; large, noisy, gregarious; sooty brown, abdomen pale or cream-white; adult has black bill; young, yellow bill; some with broad white tips on outer tail feathers were formerly considered a separate species (the white-tipped brown jay) but now known to be a color phase of the brown jay (see details in Selander, 1959); first record of brown jay in U.S., a male collected at Brownsville, Tex., Feb. 27, 1897; a set of six eggs taken from first known nesting in U.S. at Brownsville, Apr. 25, 1900; nest of twigs built in small tree in big woods near town, 14 ft. above ground; skin of male and set of eggs in Delaware Museum of Natural History (Hubbard and Niles, 1975); Webster (1972) reported two brown jays seen Apr. 28, 1969, along Rio Grande below Falcon Dam, Tex.; two seen same area June 15, 1972; first photographic record of brown jay in U.S. was taken June 8, 1974: two adults with dark bills, three immatures with yellow bills along Rio Grande 10 mi. west of Roma, Tex. (Shifflett, 1975a). In Mexico, lives in humid lowlands, foothills, second growth, forest borders, open woods; cries similar to those of N. American blue jay, a harsh *thief! thief!* or *jay! jay! jay!* higher-pitched than blue jay's similar call (Peterson and Chalif, 1973).

Nest: In tree or shrub often far out on limb; usually 23–70 ft. up; built of twigs, sticks, lined with vines or other fibrous material.

Eggs: 2–6; usually 3, blue-gray, thickly speckled with brown.

Incubation: By female, 18 days; young leave nest 23–24 days after hatching (Skutch, 1960; 1976). Skutch reported that young broods of previous years (up to 5 helpers per nest) assist adults in feeding the nestlings and guarding them. *See* Helpers among Birds.

Range: Nests from ne. Mexico (Nuevo León and Tamaulipas) south through C. America to nw. Panama; resident throughout range (Selander, 1959).

Jay, Canada. See Jay, gray.

Jay, Gray, or Canada, *Perisoreus canadensis* (per-ih-SO-ree-us can-ah-DEN-sis); genus name: Lat., from Gr. *perisoreyein*, to heap up, in allusion to storing of food; species name: Lat., of Canada. (Color ill., page 126.) In wilderness N. America, across Canada, Alaska, n. U.S. and Rocky Mtns.; 10–13 in. long; wingspread 16–17½ in.; large *gray* bird, smoke gray above, lighter below; forehead and throat white; black patch on back of head; immature, dark, slate-colored; favors coniferous forests, comes about camps of hunters, trappers, fishermen, lumberjacks; very bold, seizes bacon from frying pan, beans and oatmeal from dish, enters tent or cabin to snatch crackers or bread, carries away matches, pencils, plug tobacco, eats soap from dish, pecks candles to pieces, stores food or inedibles in crotches of trees, on branches, between twigs, on squirrel's nest; alights on camper's hand or knee to share his lunch; bites pieces from fresh-caught fish, takes bait from trapper's traps, a gunshot brings it to carcass of fallen deer or moose; alights on bow of moving canoe, looking for food; sound of ax and smoke of campfire brings it close; lonely places are its haunts; does not adapt to settlement; flight is easy, graceful, sails lightly from tree to tree, seldom flaps wings except to rise from ground; has many calls, commonly a loud, hawklike whistle, also *cla, cla, cla, cla, cla* somewhat like cry of sparrow hawk; also said to mimic cries of hawks and songs of small birds; has twittering song

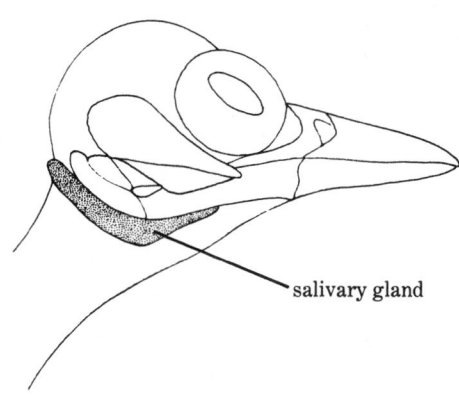

salivary gland

CROW FAMILY

The abnormally large salivary glands of the gray jay secrete a mucous that gives it advantages in food gathering and storage. With its sticky tongue, the jay is able to extract insects and seeds from crevices and can make food particles hold together in a saliva-coated ball that will adhere to the surface of a twig or pine needle, where the jay often hides food.

(Bent, 1946); usually travels in pairs or family groups.

Feeding Habits: Omnivorous, in winter may even feed on lichens, stores much food; in spring, summer, fall, eats grasshoppers, wasps, bees, eggs of tent caterpillars, beetles, and later, berries, mice; probably eats eggs and young of other birds as does blue jay. Bock (1961) discovered mouth glands in gray jay that secrete sticky fluid which coats bolus of food before jay hides it; helps stick food in place (Goodwin, 1976). *See* discussion under Mouth; *also* Tongue.

Nest: Built late winter (Feb.–Mar.), while snow still deep in woods, bulky, of twigs, bark strips, soft plant fibers, mosses, grasses, lined with pine needles, feathers, usually on horizontal branch near trunk or in crotch, 4–30 ft. up, more often 6–8 ft. above ground.

Eggs: Mar.–May; 2–5, usually 3–4, pale gray, pale green, rarely white, spotted with browns, grays.

Incubation: By female, 16–18 days; young fly when about 15 days old.

Other Names: Alaska jay; camp robber; carrion bird; grease bird; meat bird; meat hawk; moose bird; Oregon jay; Rocky Mountain jay; venison bird; Whiskey Jack; Whiskey John.

Age: One banded 1927, Barkerville, B.C., caught and killed 10 years later in rattrap (Cooke, 1937b); one banded as adult recaptured near same place when at least 9 years old.

Range: Resident from n.-c. Alaska, n. Yukon, w. Mack., sw. Keewatin, n. Man., n. Labrador, and Newfoundland, south to n. Calif., c. Ariz., sw. Colo., n. N.M., S.D., n. Minn., n. Wisc., n. Mich., s.-c. Ont. to ne. N.Y., n. New England, N.B., and Nova Scotia; winters in nesting range at lower altitudes and south to s. Ont. and Mass.; in winter casually to c. Minn., se. Wisc., nw. Pa., c. N.Y., nw. Neb.

Jay, gray-breasted. *See* Jay, Mexican.

Jay, green, *Cyanocorax yncas* (sigh-an-oh-COE-rax INK-us); genus name: Lat., from Gr. *kyanos*, blue, and *corax*, raven; species name: first scientific descriptions of the species were based on birds from Peru, land of the Incas. (Color ill., page 127.) Size 10–12 in. long; green body, with yellow outer tail feathers and yellow crissum; blue crown, without crest, black throat; short blue plumes over bill and under eyes; blue-white band across forehead; green jay in s. Tex., lives in densest woods and thickets; outside nesting season, wanders in small flocks in more open country and towns and ranches of lower Rio Grande Valley, where locally common west to Laredo (Robbins *et al.*, 1966); noisy and conspicuous, often tame and bold, called by Mexicans *pájaro verde*—green bird; has great curiosity, human intrusion into live oaks and chaparral draws them out of dense cover; after screaming, cawing, and tooting, return to cover. *See* interesting habit under Smoke Bathing.

Feeding Habits: Eats grasshoppers, crickets, beetles, bugs, also spiders; seeds of grasses, ebony, prickly ash, corn, fruit of palmetto (Bent, 1946).

Nest: Built in densest thickets in fork or outer branches in small trees, 5–15 ft. above ground, bulky, loosely made of fine sticks, thorny twigs, rootlets, lined with mosses, dried grass, leaves.

Eggs: Apr.–June; 3–5, commonly 4, gray-white, green-white, buff, spotted with browns, grays.

Incubation: Period of and age when young first fly unknown.

Other Names: Rio Grande jay.

Age: One banded Santa Ana National Wildlife Refuge, recaptured in same area and released when 9 years, 9 months, old (Kennard, 1975).

Host to Cowbirds: To bronzed cowbird, rare or infrequent (Friedmann, 1963).

Range: Resident from s. Tex. south to n. Honduras and n. S. America.

Jay, long-crested. *See* Jay, Steller's.

Jay, long-tailed. *See* Jay, scrub.

Jay, Mexican, *Aphelocoma ultramarina* (ah-fel-OCK-oh-mah ul-trah-mar-EYE-nah); genus name: from Gr. *apheles*, smooth, and *kome*, hair; "without crest"; species name: in allusion to blue color. (Color ill., page 127.) A Mexican species that ranges north into U.S. in Ariz., N.M., and w. Tex.; large; 11½–13 in. long; wingspread 15 in.; without crest, gray-blue above; light gray below; lacks white throat outlined in blue of similar scrub jay; blackish around eyes; lives all year in oak and oak-pine forests, 2,000–9,000 ft. up, common especially along slopes of Santa Catalina, Huachuca, Santa Rita, and Chiricahua Mtns., s. Ariz., and ranges adjacent to Rio Mimbres, s. N.M., and in Chisos Mtns. of Tex.; gregarious at all seasons, often travels in noisy flocks of 6–20, lives in groups composed largely of close relatives: each group usually has 1–2 nests, and feeding of nestlings by parents assisted by young of previous generations (Brown, 1963; 1970; 1972); flocks with noisy screaming harass hawks, or at discovery of sleeping bobcat or fox, surround and attack snakes on ground; one of calls is rasping *wait-wait-wait*, another is *weenk, weenk, weenk*, or *wheat, wheat, wack, wack wack*, and soft cooing (Bent, 1946); will respond to "squeaking." *See* Sounds That Attract Birds.

Feeding Habits: A staple food is acorns, twists them from twigs, or hops about on ground eating some, hiding others, eats grasshoppers, beetles, weevils, bugs, moths, tent caterpillars, scavenges on dead deer, takes eggs or young of small birds; eats wild fruit, around picnic grounds will come to hands to be fed (Phillips *et al.*, 1964), comes to bird-feeding stations for bread, suet.

Nest: Bulky mass of leafy oak twigs, 6–50 ft. up, usually 15–25 ft., in crotch or on horizontal branch of oak, sometimes in pine, cup of nest is rootlets, lined with dry grasses, horsehair, or cow's hair; in loose colonies.

Eggs: Mar.–July; 3–7, commonly 4–5, gray-green, unmarked.

Incubation: 18 days; young leave nest 24–25 days after hatching (Gross, 1949b).

Other Names: Arizona jay; Couch's jay; gray-breasted jay; ultramarine jay.

Age: One banded Madera, Ariz., recaptured in same area when 4 years, 6 months, old (Kennard, 1975).

Range: Resident c. Ariz., sw. N.M., sw. Tex., south to s. Mexico.

Jay, pinyon, or piñón, *Gymnorhinus cyanocephalus* (jim-no-RYE-nus sigh-an-oh-SEFF-ah-lus); genus name: from Gr. *gymnos*, naked, and *rhis*, nose; "naked nose," in allusion to nostrils being exposed (bare of feathers), which is unusual in Crow Family; species name: from Gr. *kyanos*, blue, and *kephale*, head. (Color ill., page 127.) Discovered by Alexander Philip Maximilian, Prince of Wied, noted German traveler who found the species in Mont. in 1833 (see Palmer, 1928); ranges widely in Rocky Mtn. region and in Sierras and Cascades of Far West; 9–11¾ in. long; dull blue, lighter below, dull white throat streaked with blue, short-tailed; like small blue crow, walks, hops, flies like crow, restless, nomadic outside nesting season, travels in large noisy flocks of hundreds, forages constantly at 3,000–8,000 ft. elevation in foothills and lower mountain ranges where slopes covered with scattered pinyon, pines, and western junipers; migration largely altitudinal; large flights in spring and fall suggest migrations but not truly migratory except in northern part of range; in mass movements during years of poor seed crop, especially of pinyon nuts, flocks may move hundreds of miles (Bent, 1946); nests in small or large scattered colonies of up to 100 birds, from desert up to 9,000 ft. elevation; starts egg-laying in early Feb., in pinyon-juniper woods, also in ponderosa pine forests; has complex social organization, occasionally with helpers at the nest; tightly knit, highly integrated flocks year-round; when not nesting, feeding flock maintains 4–12 sentries posted at some high point, motionless and silent until intruder appears, then sentries give low, rhythmic *krawk-krawk-krawk* warning (Balda and Bateman, 1971); also utter shrill cawing, mewing, chattering jaylike cries; pair begins nest building late Feb. to early Mar., flocks continue to roost together during nest building and feed during day as unit.

Feeding Habits: Sometimes feeds in trees, or forages on ground for pinyon nuts and other pine seeds, grass seeds, also eats grasshoppers, beetles, eggs and young of small birds, fruits, berries, waste grain, comes about ranches for table scraps.

Nest: Bulky, built in pinyons, junipers, and scrub oaks, usually 3–20 ft. up, sometimes to 25, 50, or 85 ft. up in yellow pines, may be three occupied nests in one tree (rarely more than one); built of twigs, shreds of bark, cup built of plant fibers, rootlets, grasses, wool, hair.

Eggs: Usually Feb.–June; 3–6, usually 4–5, blue-white, green-white.

Incubation: About 17 days (Bateman and Balda, 1973); young leave nest when about 21 days old (Bent, 1946).

Other Names: Blue crow; piñon crow; Maximilian's crow; Cassin's jay; Maximilian's jay; piñonero.

Range: Resident from c. Ore., e.-c. Mont., w. S.D., south to n. Baja Calif., c. Nev., c. N.M., and w. Okla., wanders to c. Wash., n. Ida., sw. Sask., throughout Great Basin, Neb., Kans., c. Tex., and n. Mexico.

Jay, San Blas, *Cissilopha sanblasiana* (sis-eh-LOH-fah san-blah-see-AH-na); genus name: from Gr. *kissa*, a magpie, and *lophos*, crest (Jaeger, 1955), for its short frontal erectile crest; species name: Lat. for San Blas, Mexico, where first specimen first collected. Found only on Pacific slope of w.-c. Mex., where it inhabits woodlands, coastal scrub, and mangroves; a medium-sized jay, black on head, nape, and underparts, dark blue on back, wings, and tail; bill black, yellow in immature; the bird is communal, each nest having 3–6 individuals tending it; nest made of sticks and twigs lined with coarse plant fibers; eggs 3 or 4, pinkish buff mottled with darker spots and blotches; food includes lizards, insects taken from ground and trees, also fruit; common call a rapid harsh chatter; sedentary, nonmigratory; only U.S. records date from 1937, 1938, and 1939, when a total of 4 birds were collected near Tucson, Ariz.

Jay, scrub, *Aphelocoma coerulescens* (ah-fel-OCK-oh-mah see-rue-LES-enz); genus name: *see* Jay, Mexican; species name: from Lat. *caeruleus*, blue, turning blue. (Color ill., page 127.) W. U.S. and Fla.; 11–13 in. long; sexes alike; *without crest;* head, wings, tail, blue; narrow white stripe over dark eye patch; center of back, smoky gray; *white throat outlined in blue;* long slender body, long expressive tail; lives in dense shrubbery, from which common name, scrub jäy; in West, from willow-lined streams to dry, wooded, and chaparral-covered slopes of mountains, in pinyon, juniper, and scrub oak thickets, up to 6,000–9,000 ft. in Colo. in summer; resident in Fla. in flat "scrub" country along e. and w. coasts, in thickets of sand pines, shrub oaks, saw palmetto, and rosemary (Sprunt, 1946; see also Woolfenden, 1973b); in West, described as like blue jay: alert, intelligent, bold, quarrelsome, and playful at times (Bent, 1946); in Fla., also bold and becomes very tame (Amadon, 1944) but also secretive, elusive, hidden much in brush but appears in response to "squeaking"; also may come to one's hands or lips for peanuts; like American crow, has habit of hoarding bright, shiny objects—spoons, bits of glass, china—by burying (Sprunt, 1946); also stores acorns and nuts in crevices, shallow pits, or shoved into sand with bill, covers with leaves, stones, in searching

for buried food swings bill from side to side (Amadon, 1944); utters *quay-quay-quay* or *quay-fee?*, also *cheek-cheek-cheek;* sings soft, musical notes or "whisper" songs (by both sexes).

Feeding Habits: Much of time spent hopping about on ground (individuals or small family groups) or in bushes, eats acorns, nuts, pinyons, corn, oats, wild and cultivated fruit, wasps, bees, termites, butterflies, moths, caterpillars of codling moth, cankerworms, cutworms, grasshoppers, crickets, also spiders, scorpions, ticks, mites, mollusks, turtles,

snails, eggs and young of small birds, mice, shrews, lizards, frogs (Bent, 1946); will come to bird-feeding stations for baby chick scratch feed, suet, bread, sunflower seeds.

Nest: Bulky, of sticks, usually with thick-walled cup lined with rootlets, usually built mostly by female, in low tree or bush, 2–12 ft. above ground.

Eggs: Mar.–July; Fla., Feb. into June; 2–7, usually 4–6, ground colors variable, blues, reds, pale green, freckled with dark reds, browns (in Fla., scrub jays are strongly communal in nesting and single-brooded but will lay several clutches if necessary to produce the one brood—Woolfenden, 1973b).

Incubation: By female, male feeds her on nest; she incubates about 16 days (Fla. scrub jay incubates 16–19 days); young leave nest about 18 days after hatching (Bent, 1946); in Fla., young scrub jays, unlike western scrub jays, help their parents feed and care for the young for several years before they become breeders themselves (Woolfenden, 1975). *See* Helpers among Birds.

Other Names: California jay; Florida jay; long-tailed jay; Nicasio jay; Santa Cruz jay; Texas jay; Woodhouse's jay; Xantus' jay (see Bent, 1946, for ranges of these subspecies of scrub jays).

Age: One banded Tampa, Fla., recaptured and released in same area when 11 years, 1 month, old (Kennard, 1975).

Albinism: In Calif., summer 1930, family of four fledged young with very pale feathers, feet, bills, fed by normally colored parents (Michener and Michener, 1936).

Weights: Fla., adults (100), average 80.2 gr. (Woolfenden, 1973b), or about 2¾ oz.

Range: Resident from sw. Wash., Ore., n. Nev. s. Idaho, n. Utah, sw. Wyo., Colo. and c. Tex., south through Mexico, s. Baja Calif., and a disjunct population in s. and c. Fla.

Jay, Steller's, *Cyanocitta stelleri* (sigh-ah-no-SIT-ah STEL-eh-rye); genus name: *see* Jay, blue; species name: for Georg Wilhelm Steller, German zoologist and member of Vitus Bering's Arctic expedition of 1741, who shot, along coast of Alaska, first of species known to science (Bent, 1946). (Color ill., page 127.) From Rocky Mtns. to Pacific coast, Alaskan Pen. south to Mexico; only crested jay in West and west of Rockies, where is counterpart in habits, behavior of eastern blue jay; 12–13½ in. long, darkest N. American jay; crest and front part of body sooty black; rest of body cobalt or purplish; wings and tail ripple-barred with black; common in coniferous forests of West; bold and well known about picnic grounds and campsites but shy in open woods, and difficult to approach (Bent, 1946); ranges to 10,000 or 11,000 ft. elevation in southern Rocky Mtns. among pines, travels in flocks of dozen or more but somewhat less gregarious than other jays; utters low-pitched raucous squawks different from other kinds of jays; calls harsh *waah, waah, shaack, shaack, shaack,* and mellow *klook, klook, klook,* and shrill hawklike cries: *kweesch, kweesch, kweesch,* has sweet soft song somewhat like "whisper song" of robin; female has a rolling click call; is superb at imitating scream of red-tailed hawk (Bent, 1946).

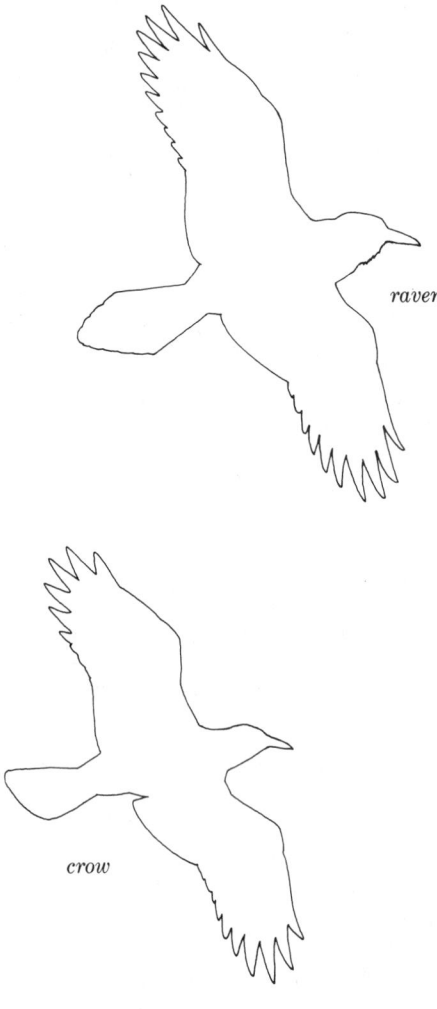

raven

crow

CROW FAMILY

In flight, the raven may be distinguished from a crow—which has a fan-shaped tail—by its wedge-shaped tail and a thicker neck due to fuller throat feathers.

Feeding Habits: Forages much in treetops and on ground, eats many acorns, pine seeds, some wild and cultivated fruit, beetles, wasps, bees, grasshoppers, caterpillars and moths, spiders, sow bugs, frogs, eggs and young of small birds; sometimes attacks and kills snakes; in winter, family groups descend from mountains to lowlands and often invade backyards, where eat scratch feed, and sunflower seeds in bird feeders; plunders stored acorns of acorn woodpeckers; in winter, makes some irruptive flights out into desert in Ariz. (Phillips *et al.*, 1964).

Nest: Bulky foundation of large sticks cemented together with mud; cup lined with rootlets or pine needles; built in crotch of tree or bush or on tree limb, usually in evergreen, 8–15 ft. up, but sometimes to 100 ft. above ground on branches of giant firs (Bent, 1946).

Eggs: Apr.–July; 3–5, usually 4, pale blue, or pale green-blue, sparingly dotted or spotted with browns.

Incubation: Period of and age when young leave nest unknown.

Other Names: Black-headed jay; blue-fronted jay; coast jay; conifer jay; long-crested jay; mountain jay; pine jay.

Age: One at least 5 years old, banded in Colo., retrapped at same place (Cooke, 1937c); many jays especially in w. U.S. short-lived because they are shot; one in Calif. was 7 years old when found dead near place where it had been banded.

Hybrids: Steller's jay with blue jay; first hybrid ever reported: three young hybrids in one family attended by adult Steller's jay, Boulder, Colo., Sept. 1969 (see account of Williams and Wheat, 1971).

Weights: 99 and 121 gr. (Brown, 1973), or 3½–4¼ oz.

Range: Resident s. Alaska, w. and s. B.C., sw. Alta., w. Mont., Wyo., sw. S.D., and w. Neb., south through s. Calif. and Mexico to s. Nicaragua; east to e.-c. Colo., e. N.M., and sw. Tex.

Magpie, American. *See* Magpie, blackbilled.

Magpie, black-billed, *Pica pica* (PIE-kah); genus and species names: Lat., magpie, also refers to black-and-white coloration of the bird (Linsdale, 1946). (Color ills., page 129.) Many allusions to magpies in folklore; black-billed lives west of prairies and north of deserts of N. America to Alaska; also in Eurasia; 17½–22 in. long, including 9½–12-in.-long tail, which is slightly more than half entire length of bird; wingspread 24 in., no other N. American songbirds except scissor-tailed and fork-tailed flycatchers have tails longer than body (*see* ring-necked pheasant in Pheasant Family); large black-and-white bird with long, wedge-shaped, greenish-black streaming tail; white wing patches appear and disappear as wings move in flight, which is usually short, often glides from bush to bush; *black bill* distinguishes it from yellow-billed magpie; lives along streams with tall thickets and scattered trees in open country, also ranges over sagebrush, croplands, pastures; outside of nesting season, usually travels in small family flocks of 6–10 birds but in winter flock may grow to 40 or even 50 (Linsdale, 1946); flock roosts in streamside willows or in trees, some even roost in shed in winter on backs of cattle (members of Lewis and Clark expedition, who first reported this bird in N. America, noted its quickness to take advantage of food supplied by man; it invaded their tents and snatched meat from their dishes); flocks keep up steady chatter, ordinary call is high-pitched *cack, cack, cack,* or *chaeck,* also utters musical whistles; in captivity, pets imitate human speech; some migration from normal range in severe winters and local movements in fall, may ascend to 8,000–10,000 ft. in mountains of Mont., Colo., and N.M.; also wanders eastward in fall and winter, probably in response to scarcity of food (Linsdale, 1946).

Feeding Habits: Much of time spent on ground searching for food; a graceful, sometimes jerky walk, with tail slightly raised and constantly twitched; when in hurry, travels in series of hops; flocks catch grasshoppers in fields, especially in late summer and fall; eats insects throughout year, including flies and their larvae and pupae from carrion, cleans up roadside carcasses of dead animals (Kalmbach, 1927); picks and eats ticks from backs of elk, mule deer, bighorns; eats remains of animals killed by coyotes and other carnivores; sometimes pecks flesh at sores or cuts on backs of horses, cows, sheep; takes some eggs and young of small birds in spring (Linsdale, 1946); also eats mice, snakes, some grain and fruit.

Nest: Built in small scattered colonies along streams or in woods or thickets; bulky large mass of coarse sticks, 2–4 ft. high, base held together with mud, usually roofed with a canopy or dome of thorny twigs with holes in sides for entrances to inner nest cup of rootlets, fine plant stems, and horsehair; in bushes or trees, usually on low horizontal limb, sometimes close to trunk, from few feet up to 25 ft. above ground; nest building said to be part of courtship, in which male brings nest material to female and she arranges it (Austin, 1961); sometimes pair use same nest year after year, is sometimes built close to nests of hawks; abandoned or old nests of magpie used during storms for shelter by robins, bluebirds, and magpies themselves, or by owls as daytime retreats; American kestrels and sharp-shinned hawks nest in them, also ducks, herons, mourning doves, house sparrows, and grackles.

Eggs: Mar.–June; 7–13, usually 7 (Linsdale, 1946), green-gray, blotched with browns.

Incubation: 16–18 days; age when young first fly unknown.

Age: One lived in National Zoo, Washington, D.C., for 11 years, 7 months; a captive in Mont. lived to more than 19 years old (Linsdale, 1937); one, banded, reported from Norway, lived in wild to 14 years, 11 months (Clapp, 1976).

Albinism: Two in brood of which rest were normal, at Littleton, Colo., both "pure white" (Rockwell, 1910).

Flight Speed: Timed in w. U.S., 20–22 m.p.h. (Cottam *et al.*, 1942b).

Weights: In Nev., Ore., Calif., males (10), 169–200 gr., or about 6–7 oz.; females (18),

138.3–180.4 gr., or about 4¾–6⅓ oz. (Linsdale, 1937).

Range: Resident from s. and c. coastal Alaska, s. Yuk., interior B.C., c. Alta., nw. and e.-c. Sask., w. Man., south to e.-c. Calif., w. Nev., s. Idaho, c. and ne. Utah, ne. Ariz. formerly, n. N.M., w. Okla., and w.-c. Kans.; has wandered east of Mississippi R. in U.S. and north and east of normal range in Canada; also lives in Eurasia.

Magpie, yellow-billed, *Pica nuttalli* (PIE-kah NUT-all-eye); genus name: *see* Magpie, black-billed; species name: given by John James Audubon for Thomas Nuttall, English botanist, ornithologist, and early explorer of w. U.S. (Palmer, 1928). (Color ill., page 128.) One of few species of birds limited entirely to Calif.; 16–18 in. long, including 9½–10¼-in.-long tail; wingspread 22 in.; appears almost exactly like black-billed magpie but smaller, with *yellow* bill, small patch of bare yellow skin slightly below and to rear of eyes; usually lives near water, among tall trees bordering streams or in park-like groves either on valley floor or in hills; also open bare ground, cultivated fields, orchards, pastures, and vacant city lots; less timid than black-billed magpie, often lives about houses when not molested, becomes quite tame; some flocking even in nesting time; after nesting season, roost together in trees, thickets. Forages over country by day, sometimes bathes or drinks at cattle troughs, utters *qua-qua, qua-qua-qua,* strikingly similar to notes of acorn woodpeckers, also loud raucous calls, and primitive song as with other members of family; in captivity speaks in phrases picked up from humans; imitates calls of parrots, goats (Linsdale, 1937); buries playthings in sand, nooks, crannies—needles, nails, pins, buttons, money, trinkets, foods; on ground, walks, hops, runs, flight often short, several weak wingbeats followed by several vigorous ones; perches not only in trees but on utility wires.

Feeding Habits: Searches on ground for grasshoppers, ants, bees, wasps, beetles, often flips over with bill wooden chips or cow dung in search (insects are more than half its food); also snatches them out of air in short flights from trees; eats acorns, grain, garbage, refuse from butchered livestock, and fruit of poison oak, coffeeberry, and grapes, when nesting, sometimes takes young of small birds from nests to feed own nestlings; stores acorns, left-over food in trees or in shallow pits it digs in ground; competing for food scrap, two birds may point bills to sky, puff out breasts and throats, walk toward each other, and bump breasts before one gives way, but no blows struck.

Nest: Loose colonies, each pair maintaining own territory with nest nearly always in tall or medium tree, far out among small limbs; bulky, a covered cradle of twigs with entrance or exit holes in two sides; closely resembles clump of mistletoe; 40–60 ft. above ground; colony may begin to build nests long before eggs laid, around mid-Dec. (Linsdale, 1946), and continue into spring; at least one pair of American kestrels takes over a magpie nest in colony.

Eggs: Mar.–June; 5–8, usually 6–7, gray-yellow, pale olive-buff, finely speckled with browns.

Incubation: Assumed to be about 18 days; age at which young first fly unknown.

Albinism: A partial albino reported by Townsend (1883).

Weights: Calif., males (15), 162.5–188.6 gr., or about 5¾–6¾ oz.; females (18), 126–169.6 gr., or about 4½–6 oz. (Linsdale, 1937).

Range: In Calif. only, where limited to area 150 mi. wide and about 500 mi. north and south, west of Sierra Nevada, chiefly in Sacramento and San Joaquin valleys from Shasta County southward to Ventura and Kern counties, and coastal valleys from San Francisco southeast to Ventura County.

Nutcracker, Clark's, *Nucifraga columbiana* (new-SIF-rah-gah co-lum-bih-ANE-ah); genus name: from Lat. *nux, nucis,* nut, and *frangere,* to break; species name: Lat., of the Columbia R.; common name: for Capt. William Clark of Lewis and Clark expedition of 1803–06 to Pacific Northwest and Columbia R., responsible for discovery of the bird (Bent, 1946). (Color ill., page 128.) W. U.S.; 12–13 in. long; its even gray body and conspicuous white patches on black wings and tail suggest a short-tailed mockingbird; walks like a crow, often clings to trunks of trees, pecking like woodpecker with long sharp, black bill; lives in juniper and pine forests of Rockies and Sierras at 3,000–13,000 ft. elevation; noisy, boisterous, at times travels in large flocks, when feeding may be 25–100 on ground or in trees; utters commonly a guttural squawk, *chaar, char-r-r, chur-r-r, kra-a-a,* or *kar-r-ack,* and other cries, some are musical like children's tin trumpets (Bent, 1946); straight flight at times like blue jay's or undulating like woodpecker's, sometimes folds wings and hurtles downward into a canyon, suddenly opens wings to check flight, which makes explosive roar; extremely curious, follows coyotes or passing deer, comes readily to imitation of call of pygmy owl or horned owl; comes about camps for food scraps, may enter tent or cabin, frequents farms and houses looking for kitchen handouts, will come to feeders for scratch feed or sunflower seeds; like gray jay, called camp robber and meat bird.

Feeding Habits: Hops about on ground rather awkwardly, also walks, foraging for insects and fallen nuts; especially fond of pinyon nuts, and seeds of whitebark and Jeffrey pines, eats shells as well as kernels, may carry up to 70 seeds in throat (or in sublingual pouch, Bock *et al.,* 1973); uses bill like crowbar to pry seeds from cones of limber and other pines; eats acorns, juniper berries, stores conifer seeds for winter and spring use (*see* discussion in Birds That Store Food in Food and Feeding Habits); sometimes digs through 8 in. of snow to reach stored food (Bent, 1946); in spring, before seeds ripen, hunts on ground for beetles, ants, grasshoppers, crickets, also launches out in air from tree to catch in bill butterflies and other flying insects; digs grubs from bark by hammering on trunk like woodpecker, eats snails, carrion, sometimes takes eggs and young of small birds.

CROW FAMILY
Nutcrackers are known for their food-storing habits and seem to recover about 70% of their stored seeds. A Clark's nutcracker was observed digging through 8 inches of snow to retrieve a seed cone it had buried.

Nest: Mainly 6,000–8,000 ft. elevation; built by both sexes often in Feb. when snow still on ground, subzero cold, in juniper or pine well out on branch or in bushy top; 11–12 in. in diameter, 8–150 ft. up, of twigs, strips of bark of juniper, lined with grasses, pine needles.

Eggs: Usually Mar.–May; 2–6, usually 2–3, pale green to gray-green, sparingly dotted with browns, grays.

Incubation: By both sexes, often during snowstorms, 17–18 days; young leave nest 24–28 days after hatching; both parents feed young.

Other Names: Camp robber; Clark's crow; meat bird; meat hawk, woodpecker crow.

Age: One banded Crater Lake, Calif., recaptured and released in same area when 17 years, 5 months, old (Kennard, 1975); at time of recapture in Nov. 1969, was oldest reported wild member of Crow Family; one lived in San Diego Zoo for 12 years.

Weights: One collected (shot) in Calif., 146 gr. (Grinnell and Storer, 1924), or about 5 oz.

Range: Resident from c. B.C., sw. Alta., c. and w. Mont., w. and se. Wyo., south in mountains through c. Wash., e. Ore., c. and e. Calif., Nev., to n. Baja Calif., and south in Rocky Mtns. to e. Ariz., w. N.M., and n. Mexico, wanders to c. Alaska, s. Yuk., s. Sask., sw. Man., S.D., w. Neb., Kans., sw. Tex.; accidental in parts of Midwest.

Raven, common, *Corvus corax* (CORE-vus KOH-rax); genus name: *see* family introduction; species name: Lat., from Gr. *korax*, a croaker, the raven. (Color ill., page 124.) E. U.S., Far West, Canada, and Alaska, also in Eurasia; common only in Far North and West; rare and local in Appalachians of East; largest of Crow Family and largest passerine bird; 21½–27 in. long; wingspread 46–56 in., much larger than crow; sexes alike but female smaller; all-black with metallic luster of purple and violet, sometimes green gloss on wings; black bill heavy, arched or curved ("Roman nose"), nostrils large, hidden by bristly tufts of feathers; shaggy throat feathers, resembling beard, show when raven perched; long central tail feathers make tail rounded at end; tail appears wedge-shaped when overhead; flight different from crows, raven alternately flaps and soars; is magnificent flier, can hold position motionless in gale; hovers like American kestrel or rises and circles like large hawk; in courtship flight male flies with wing tips touching female's, dives like peregrine falcon and tumbles over and over in air; pairs mate for life. In Far North, ranges over treeless tundra, seacoast, and banks of rivers; farther south, along Pacific and Atlantic coasts, frequents rocky cliffs, especially near seabird colonies (Me. northward); from Pa. southward lives in Appalachian Mtns., usually above 3,000 ft. elevation (see Hooper *et al.*, 1975); in Far West in Rocky Mtns. and Great Basin west to Calif., both in mountain forests and on plains and deserts; with extermination of bison, on whose carcasses it fed, disappeared from Kans. and Okla. (Bent, 1946); is wilderness bird, sagacious, crafty, resourceful, quick to learn and to profit from experience; over most of range is shy and wary; stays out of range of guns where persecuted, but because of scavenging, frequently caught in baited traps or dies from eating poisoned animal carcasses; outside nesting season, sometimes travels in flight line, morning and evening to and from feeding places; not in flocks but in small groups; when numerous, spends night in communal roosts; in Great Smoky Mtns. groups of 6–14 reported in fall and winter (Stupka, 1963); utters many different notes; common one is loud, deep-toned *croake-croake*, a hoarse *croo-croo*, and *curruk*, given mostly in flight; also a deep-toned bell-like note (Bent, 1946); young in nest caw like crows; in villages of Far North, where a useful scavenger, and about ranches and farmhouses, where not molested, is quite tame.

Feeding Habits: Walks with stately tread, or hops forward or sidewise, largely a scavenger and competes with gulls and vultures in eating dead elk, deer, whales, seals, fishes, also eats frogs, tadpoles, worms, crabs, shellfishes, which it drops from aloft to break on ground or rocks; eats crayfishes, minnows, eggs and young of seabirds, songbirds, herons; in spring, follows plow for insects; eats berries in fall, also mice, lemmings, and young seals caught through cooperation of pair (see Bent, 1946); caches pieces of meat in ground which eats later; in Great Smokies, gleans scraps from picnic sites and eats animals killed along highways.

Nest: In Far North beyond tree limit, nests on cliffs, often near gyrfalcons, usually near coast or along streams, solitary pairs nest in trees, as on wooded islands of coast of Me., and on sea cliffs; in Appalachians both in crotches of coniferous trees, 45–80 ft. up, and on well-shaded cliffs or in rock crevices; large bulky nest, 2–3 ft. across, 4 ft. high, of dead branches broken off by bills of the pair; deep cup in center lined with shreds of bark, hair of deer, moose, muskox, skunk, opossum, bobcat, sheep's wool, mosses, grasses, lichens, seaweeds.

Eggs: Mar.–June; 3–7, usually 4–6, green-gray, light green, spotted or blotched with browns.

Incubation: By female, 18–20 days, male feeds her on nest; both parents feed young and bring water to them in throat (Hauri, 1956); young fly 35–42 days after hatching; one brood a season.

Other Names: American raven; northern raven.

Age: One lived in National Zoo, Washington, D.C., 24 years, 6 months.

Flight Speed: Timed in w. U.S., 35–39 m.p.h. (Cottam *et al.*, 1942b); in Calif., 24 m.p.h.; in Morocco, 28–33 m.p.h.; in Scotland, 32–35 m.p.h. on way to roost (Meinertzhagen, 1955).

Weights: Males (Alaska) average 1,383 gr., or about 3 lbs. 12 oz.; females 1,085 gr., or about 2 lbs. 6 oz. (White and Cade, 1971).

Range: Resident in N. America in Alaska, n. Canada, and Greenland, south through w. U.S. to s. Baja Calif. and Nicaragua; c. and e. N. America to Minn., Wisc., n. Mich., c. Ont., s. Que., and Me. and south in Appalachian Mtns. to nw. Ga.; also in Iceland, n. Europe, Asia, Africa.

Raven, white-necked, *Corvus cryptoleucus* (CORE-vus krip-to-LEW-kus) genus name: *see* family introduction; species name: from Gr. *kryptos*, hidden, and *leukos*, white. (Color ill., page 125.) Sw. U.S. and Mexico; 19–21 in. long; black with purple gloss, smaller than common raven, slightly larger than crow; *white bases of feathers of throat and upper neck hidden unless ruffled or agitated;* against sky may stand out like fluffy boa as male soars, sideslips, wheels, tumbles in courtship flight; distinguished from crow mainly by guttural, lower-pitched voice, more rounded tail in flight, tendency to soar (Bent, 1946); essentially a bird of grassy plains broken only by scattered trees, and desert scrub; perched in tree or bush, isolated courting pairs sit side by side, rubbing bills, bowing and raising wings; on hot summer days, soars high over desert lands, sometimes plunging down into rising "dust devils" (whirlwinds) and riding them to dizzying heights (Ligon, 1961); usually tame or unsuspicious but wary where persecuted, utters hoarse *quark, quark;* outside of nesting season, large flocks may roost together in scrubby brush; moves southward in fall, when flocks may be enormous (Bent, 1946).

Feeding Habits: Scavenges on dead livestock, jackrabbits, and other animals killed on highways; eats rats, field mice, eggs and young of small birds, lizards, spiders, earthworms, snails, scraps of food at camps, beetles, grasshoppers, cutworms, grain sorghum, corn, melons, peanuts, juicy fruit of cactuses.

Nest: Built by female, loose, round mass of thorny twigs, sometimes with barbed wire, 4–40 ft. up in hackberry, cottonwood, sycamore, or in mesquite, ebony, willow, tree yuccas; also in trees about homesteads or stock watering holes, on windmill towers, crossbars of utility poles.

Eggs: April–June; 3–8, usually 5–7, pale green to gray-green, streaked and blotched with lavenders and browns; some unmarked.

Incubation: By both sexes, about 21 days; age when young first fly unknown.

Age: One banded wild bird found dead when 5 years, 8 months, old (Kennard, 1975).

Range: Resident from se. Ariz., s. N.M., ne. Colo., s.-c. Neb., w. Kans., south into Mexico.

CROWING AREA

or CROWING GROUND. Term of American game biologists for the defended territory of a male, or cock, pheasant. See Dancing Ground; Territory.

CROWN

The top of the head of a bird; the area between its forehead (front) and occiput, or back of the head. *See* Topography.

CRUS

Technical name for the "drumstick," or foreleg of a bird; the fleshy section between the knee and heel, just above the scaly "shank," or tarsus (Coues, 1884). *See* Feet and Legs; Topography; Tarsus.

CRUSTACEANS (krus-TAY-shans) AND BIRDS

Many birds eat crustaceans (*see* Arthropod)—for example, shrimps; crabs; water fleas

(Daphnia); wood lice, also called sow bugs and pill bugs; and barnacles; all are important foods for some birds that live in or around water. Fairy "shrimps" of fresh water and brine "shrimps" of salt water—not true shrimps but tiny crustaceans that resemble them—are locally eaten and extensively at times by birds. Ducks—shovelers, lesser scaups, goldeneyes, and green-winged teal—especially eat brine shrimps, as do Wilson's and northern phalaropes, avocets, and black-necked stilts (McAtee, 1932b).

Daphnia, or water "fleas"—tiny crustaceans mostly of fresh water—have been found in numerous stomachs of grebes and wild ducks, with up to 250 in a single bird's stomach. Ostracods—minute crustaceans—which live in or near the bottom of both salt and fresh water, where they crawl or swim actively about feeding on other small animals (Pratt, 1951), have been identified by food-habits investigators from the stomachs largely of 15 species of wild ducks, with up to 1,200 in the stomach of each of two ducks. Barnacles were eaten by 22 species of ducks, gulls, and shorebirds collectively from northern waters of the U.S. and Canada. Amphipods (some live in fresh water, some in salt water—for example, the saltwater sand "fleas" and beach "fleas" of ocean beaches that burrow under sand or live under decaying plant life) have been eaten by more than 80 species of N. American birds. The largest feeders on amphipods are shorebirds, ducks, and other waterfowl, with single birds eating up to 2,500 each (McAtee, 1932b).

From 30 to 40 species of birds eat the familiar sow bugs, pill bugs, or wood lice—small gray, armored animals that live in damp places under boards, logs, and stones (Buchsbaum, 1938). Up to 60 of this land crustacean have been found in the stomach of a single bird; up to 256 of the aquatic kinds were swallowed by another bird. Birds feed abundantly on the true shrimps, with hundreds found in the stomachs of some birds; they also prey upon crayfishes, with 49 the greatest number discovered in the stomach of one bird. In one food-habits study, 794 bird stomachs held crabs of various kinds; some single stomachs held 14 sand crabs or sand bugs; 16 stone crabs; 40 hermit crabs; 36 mud crabs; 16 swimming crabs; 18 edible crabs; 26 shore crabs; 19 fiddler crabs. *See* Food and Feeding Habits and under the individual bird biographies.

CRYING BIRD
See Limpkin Family.

CRYPTIC
That which conceals, or is adapted to conceal. *See* Colors of Feathers.

CRYPTIC SPECIES
See Sibling Species.

CUCKOLD
See Cowbird, brown-headed, in Troupial Family.

CUCKOO FAMILY
Cuculidae (cue-CUE-lih-dee); from Lat. *cuculus,* European cuckoo; name "cuckoo" origi-

nally applied to common cuckoo of Europe from the onomatopoetic call of the male, which frequently utters his name (a song, technically) during the courtship season and even all night.

Birds of the worldwide Cuckoo Family of 127 species (Van Tyne and Berger, 1976), usually live in forested or brushy regions; their closest relatives are the turacos, or touracos, also called plantain-eaters, of Africa. According to Thomson (1964c), 47 species of the so-called true cuckoos of the Old World, including the common cuckoo from which family name derived, get other birds to rear their young by laying their eggs in other birds' nests. *See* discussion of habit in Brood Parasitism, and example of parallel parasitic behavior in cowbirds in Troupial Family.

Of several N. American birds called cuckoos, only the black-billed and yellow-billed are occasionally brood-parasitic. In N. America, the Cuckoo Family includes the anis, cuckoos, and the roadrunner; they are not songbirds, which are in the order Passeriformes, but are structurally different—for example, the feet are zygodactylous, with two toes pointing forward, two backward. For other details of the family, see Thomson (1964c) and Wetmore *et al.* (1964). More recently, Sibley and Ahlquist (1973) have included the S. American hoatzin in the Cuckoo Family (*see* discussion in Cuculiformes); however, such authorities as Delacour and Amadon (1973) continue to class it in the Hoatzin Family (Opisthocomidae) in the order Galliformes.

Ani (AH-nee) is the Spanish and Portuguese name, from Tupian Indian *ani, anu,* for 3 species of tropical American birds; are known only from W. Hemisphere—besides the groove-billed and smooth-billed anis, there is the greater ani, *Crotophaga major,* which lives from c. Panama to S. America.

Anis are wholly black and loosely feathered, some with shining or iridescent plumage; have long, loose-jointed tails, almost as long as the body; sexes are outwardly alike. They are remarkable among members of the Cuckoo Family in being very clannish, with 20 or more occasionally living together in a flock; several pairs build a communal nest; each female lays her eggs in the nest and there may be up to 26 eggs in a single nest, but 10–15 is more usual. The several pairs that live in one nest share incubating the eggs and feeding the young; nesting is irregular, with no definite breeding season; it may be at any time of the year.

Cuckoos in N. America are quiet, shy birds, usually remaining concealed in foliage of trees and shrubs, from which they occasionally call in long, rolling *kuk* or *kow* notes one associates with a hot, humid summer day; they often call while flying, while sitting on the nest, and frequently at night. In many parts of the country they are called rain crows, because their calls are thought to predict rain (*see* Folklore); also kow-kows, from their calls.

Gross (1965a) cites nine reports of albinism in three N. American species in the Cuckoo Family but does not identify the species. Members of the family are protected by law and may not be kept in captivity without a permit; however, ill or injured birds may be kept alive until able to fend for themselves by offering mealworms and other insects, ground meat,

CUCKOO FAMILY

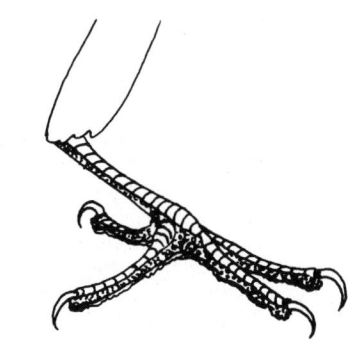

and yolk of hard-boiled eggs. See details in Terres (1968c).

Ani, groove-billed, *Crotophaga sulcirostris* (crow-TOFF-ah-gah sul-sih-ROS-tris); genus name: from Gr. *kroton*, insect or bug, and *phagein*, to eat; species name: from Lat. *sulcus*, furrow or groove, and *rostrum*, beak. (Color ill., page 130.) S. and C. American, nests in U.S. in s. Tex., where first reported by George B. Sennett in 1879; 12–12½ in. long; entirely coal black with loosely jointed tail 6¾ in. long; wingspread 16 in.; wings short, weak in flight, high arched bill with a curved ridge on top (from which gets its scientific species name) that gives it parrotlike appearance; in Mexico lives in open country of many types; however, in Tex., favors bushy pastures, orchards, light second growth, even lawns and clearings about homes, also marshes, moist thickets along rivers, also among scattered cacti and acacias; travels in flocks from few to dozen or more, in tropics excitedly follows army ants for insects and spiders driven from retreats by ants; frequents farm fields and pastures, reported to sometimes alight on backs of cattle to pick and eat ticks from them; often roosts at night in flocks of 30–40 in orange tree; utters note much like flicker, *PLEE-co!* rapidly repeated, by which distinguished from smooth-billed ani, which has different call.

Feeding Habits: Largely insects taken from ground or from shrubs, also eats fruit and berries; forages in pastures near grazing cattle. Rand (1955) reported that in El Salvador, by close watching, discovered that when a groove-billed ani hunted for insects near grazing cow, the animal stirred up so many insects that ani was three times more effective in catching them than when hunting alone. *See* Commensalism.
Nest: Communal, built by 1–3 pairs, usually in thorny shrub or small tree; 6–12 ft. above ground, mass of dead twigs lined with fresh green leaves.
Eggs: 3–4, laid by each female, greenish or bluish with chalky coating.
Incubation: About 14 days. If disturbed, young may leave nest at 6 days after hatching and climb among branches or on ground to hide in grass; climb back into nest at night, where brooded by parents until a week old; make short flights among shrubs 10 days after hatching; young of first brood sometimes feed young of second brood (Bent, 1940).
Other Names: Tick bird; black witch.
Weights: Nicaragua, males (6), 69.5–98.4 gr., or about 2½–3½ oz.; females (3), 72.1–75.2 gr., or about 2½ oz. (Owre, 1977).
Range: Resident from s. Tex. south to n. S. America; casual in La. and Miss., accidental in Minn., Neb., Kans., Okla., Ark., and Fla.

Ani, smooth-billed, *Crotophaga ani* (crow-TOFF-ah-gah AH-nee); genus name: *see* Ani, groove-billed; species name: *see* family introduction. (Color ill., page 130.) Like groove-billed ani, a C. and S. American bird, also from West Indies; nests in U.S. only in Fla.; 12½–13½ in. long; same appearance as groove-billed, but lacks grooves on high ridge of bill; difficult to distinguish from groove-billed except by call—

a whining whistle like notes of wood duck: *quee-ick, quee-ick,* with chuckling notes; originally accidental in Fla.; first reported at Miami Beach, Feb. 1937; first nesting there July 1938 (Sprunt, 1954a); nested at Clewiston, June and Nov. 1946; established a small nesting colony there; believed original members were blown there from native West Indies by tropical hurricane (Merritt, 1951); other records of straying to N.C. and Petty Is., N.J., in Delaware R.

Feeding Habits: Similar to those of groove-billed ani.
Nest: In Fla., bulky, built of sticks, weeds, leaves, and grasses, usually low in vines or small trees. See also Bond (1961) for habits in West Indies.
Eggs: Laid Mar.–Nov., by several females in communal nest; each lays 3–4, pale blue.
Incubation: About 14 days, young probably mature as do those of groove-billed.
Other Names: Black parakeet; black witch; Cuban parrot; death-bird; parrot blackbird; tick bird; voodoo bird.
Weights: Adults (14) in Fla., 77.5–114.2 gr. (Fisk, 1977), or about 2¾–4 oz.; males (9), University of Miami collections, 91.5–124 gr., or about 3¼–4⅓ oz.; females (3), 87.5–104 gr., or about 3–3⅔ oz.
Range: Resident s. Fla. to n. Argentina, and West Indies and Bahama Is.; casual in La.; accidental in N.J., N.C.

Cuckoo, black-billed, *Coccyzus erythropthalmus* (cock-SIGH-zus er-ih-throf-THALL-mus); genus name: from Gr. *kokkyzein*, to call "cuckoo"; species name: from Gr. *erythros*, red, and *ophthalmos*, eye. (Color ills., page 131.) East of Rocky Mtns.; 11–12½ in. long; wingspread 15–16¾ in.; brown above, white below; *bill all-black; narrow red ring around eyes;* no rufous in spread wings; long graduated tail with white spots somewhat indistinct and smaller than in yellow-billed cuckoo; sexes alike; lives in more extensive woodlands than yellow-billed and tends to be more abundant in northern part of range often shared by both species; common call is series of 2–5 *cu-cu-cu,* also utters series of rapid *kuks* all in one pitch without slowed-down *cowk-cowk* at end as in yellow-billed.

Feeding Habits: Like those of yellow-billed cuckoo, primarily caterpillars, especially hairy tent caterpillars and others; beetles, grasshoppers, crickets, small mollusks, fishes, some wild fruits (Bent, 1940).
Nest: Built 2–10 ft. above ground in dense thickets, small trees, of twigs, grasses, lined with leaves of ferns.
Eggs: May–Sept.; 2–5, usually 2–3, blue-green and slightly darker than eggs of yellow-billed; occasionally lays eggs in nest of yellow-billed cuckoo and in nests of gray catbirds, wood thrushes, yellow warblers, and chipping sparrows.
Incubation: By both parents; about 14 days; young at 7–9 days old still under care of parents, climb about branches of nesting tree or shrub for about 2 weeks until able to fly (Bent, 1940).

Other Names: Kow-kow; rain bird; rain crow; rain dove.
Host to Cowbirds: Rarely; 3 records (Friedmann, 1963).
Weights: Fall, coastal N.J. (25), 34.7–40 gr. (Murray and Jehl, 1964), or about 1¼–1½ oz.
Range: Nests east of the Rockies from s. Sask., s. Man., n. Minn., s. Ont., s. Que., N.B., Prince Edward Is., and Nova Scotia, south to se. Wyo., Neb., nw. Ark., e. Kans., e. and c. Tenn., N.C., and S.C., possibly Idaho, and Colo.; winters in nw. S. America.

Cuckoo, black-eared. See Cuckoo, mangrove.

Cuckoo, ground. See Roadrunner.

Cuckoo, mangrove, or Maynard's, *Coccyzus minor* (cock-SIGH-zus MY-nor); genus name: *see* Cuckoo, black-billed; species name: Lat., less, smaller; *mangrove* for its habitat; *Maynard's,* for Charles J. Maynard, American naturalist and collector of birds. In Fla. in summer; 12–13 in. long; brown above, long tail graduated and white-tipped, appears like a yellow-billed cuckoo but is *light pink-brown or yellow-buff below* with *black ear patches;* sexes outwardly alike; lives in low dense thickets near salt water; usually in red and black mangroves of Fla. Keys and w. coast of Fla.; shy and elusive, slips about through mangrove keys like brown shadow; sometimes seen flying rapidly over and across Overseas Highway (Sprunt, 1954a); call is low guttural *gaw-gaw-gaw* or *qua-qua-qua,* somewhat like bark of squirrel.

Feeding Habits: Eats grasshoppers, caterpillars, moths, flies, also spiders, some small fruits and wild berries (Bent, 1940).
Nest: Frail, flat structure of twigs built in dense thicket.
Eggs: Fla., May–July; 2, green-blue.
Incubation: Period of and age when young first fly unknown.
Other Names: Bahama mangrove cuckoo; black-eared cuckoo; rain bird; rain crow; rain dove.
Weights: Females (5), University of Miami collections, 50–75.5 gr. (Fisk, 1977), or about 1¾–2⅔ oz; Fla., males (2), 61.1 and 62 gr. (Owre, 1977).
Range: Resident in West Indies, n. Mexico, s. Fla. (where seen only Mar. to Sept.), south to n. S. America.

Cuckoo, Oriental, *Cuculus saturatus* (cue-CUE-lus sat-you-RAY-tus); genus name: Lat. for European cuckoo; species name: Lat., saturated, full, in allusion to rich, dark color (Coues, 1882). Russian visitor to Alaska across Bering Strait; 13–15 in. long; blue-gray above; gray throat and breast, buffish belly with feathers tipped with black gives barred effect and adds to hawklike appearance; lives in densely wooded *and* open country; is one of parasitic cuckoos of Old World that lays its eggs in nests of small songbirds, especially those of the Asiatic Old World warblers.
Range: Nests from c. Russia east to Kamchatka Pen., south to s. Japan, Formosa, s.

China, Burma; has wandered to Alaska: St. Lawrence Is., Seward Pen., Pribilof Is., and Aleutians.

Cuckoo, yellow-billed, *Coccyzus americanus* (cock-SIGH-zus ah-mer-ih-CANE-us); genus name: *see* Cuckoo, black-billed; species name: Lat., of America. (Color ills., pages 130, 131.) Nests across U.S. and south to Mexican border; range is more southern than black-billed cuckoo but ranges overlap; 11–12½ in. long; wingspread 15½–17 in.; slender, resembles black-billed cuckoo; grayish brown above, white below; distinguished, however, by rufous color on wings, and white spots on *black* undersurface of tail are *larger* and more conspicuous than those of black-billed; also lower mandible is yellow; sexes outwardly alike; lives in dense tangles of undergrowth, seldom in large woods, likes brushy country roadsides, willow thickets by streams and ponds; slips quietly, furtively through thickets or flies swiftly and gracefully, long tail streaming behind, from tree to tree; calls while hidden in thicket, series of *kuks*, ending in slowed *keow-keow-keow*.

Feeding Habits: Eats great numbers of hairy caterpillars; up to 325 found in stomach of one (Bent, 1940); also beetles, grasshoppers, tree crickets, army ants, wasps, flies, and dragonflies, also raspberries, mulberries, grapes and other fruits, small frogs, lizards.
Nest: Built on horizontal limb of small tree or bush, often thorny or evergreen, 2–12 ft. above ground; flimsy, almost flat, of short twigs, lined with a few dry leaves, grasses, mosses, rags, catkins of oaks or willows.
Eggs: In southern part of range, Mar.–Aug.; 1–5, usually 3–4, laid at intervals of 2–3 days (Preble, 1957), pale blue-green.
Incubation: By both sexes, with laying of first egg, hatches after about 14 days; young, as in those of black-billed cuckoo, climb agilely about nesting bush or tree at 7–9 days. Female sometimes lays eggs in nests of black-billed cuckoo, and rarely in nests of other birds (Bent, 1940).
Other Names: Chow-chow; kow-kow; rain bird; rain crow; rain dove; storm crow.
Accidents: In migration at night often strikes TV towers; in Fla., this species struck tower about 10 times more frequently than black-billed (Stoddard and Norris, 1967).
Flight Speed: 22 m.p.h. (Wood, 1933).
Host to Cowbirds: Rarely, 3 records (Friedmann, 1963).
Weights: Male (1), Aug., 57.8 gr. (Baldwin and Kendeigh, 1938), or about 2 oz.; fall, coastal N.J., sex not identified (3), 43.2–57.4 gr., or 1½–2 oz. (Murray and Jehl, 1964).
Range: Nests from s. B.C., N.D., Minn., s. Ont., Que., and N.B. south throughout much of U.S. to Fla. Keys, C. America and s. Baja Calif.; winters in S. America to C. Argentina and Uruguay; has wandered to British Isles, France, Belgium, Denmark, and Italy (Peterson *et al.*, 1954).

Roadrunner, *Geococcyx californianus* (jee-oh-COCK-sicks cal-ih-for-nih-AY-nus); genus name: from Gr. *ge*, earth, and *kokkyks*, cuckoo, a ground cuckoo; species name: Lat., of Califor-

nia; in early days got its common name from habit of running down roads ahead of horse-drawn vehicles. (Color ills., pages 132, 133.) Large, odd ground cuckoo of West and Southwest; state bird of N.M.; 20–24 in. long; slender, strong, heavy black bill nearly as long as shaggy, crested head; patch of bare skin in back of eyes is pale blue, rear half orange-red; pale blue legs long, adapted for running; wings short, rounded, in flight show white crescent patch; body brown above; white below; breast and back heavily streaked; long graduated tail with white-tipped outer tail feathers, occasionally flicks tail; shy, spends most of time on ground; lives in partly arid or dry open places with scattered pinyons, junipers, cactuses, stones, sometimes perches on fence posts or utility poles by highway (Sutton, 1940); runs swiftly (up to 15 m.p.h. or more) through cactus in pursuit of lizards or insects; in spring, at sunrise, male goes to rim of mesa or perches on dead tree or cactus, sings hoarse, throaty *coo, coo, coo, ooh, ooh, ooh*, raising head slightly with each *coo*; has remarkable courtship described by Sutton (1940), Rand (1941), and Whitson (1975); see also general account by Bailey (1945), and especially "The Roadrunner" in Terres (1958); pair bond is apparently permanent, and pair live in their territory year-round (Ohmart, 1973); there are many folk tales about roadrunners and rattlesnakes (Sutton, 1940; Teale, 1965).

Feeding Habits: Eats many insects, especially crickets, large grasshoppers, also cutworms and other caterpillars, beetles, bugs, ants, gophers, mice, cotton rats, birds' eggs and young, lizards, small snakes (including rattlesnakes), scorpions, tarantulas and other spiders, centipedes and millipedes, and various fruits, including prickly pears and seeds; in Calif. garden, also noted eating introduced European snails.
Nest: Usually built in low tree, thicket, or clump of cactus (rarely on ground); about 3–15 ft. up, shallow but compact, about 1 ft. in diameter, foundation of sticks, lined with leaves, grasses, feathers, mesquite pods, snakeskin, roots, and dry pieces of horse or cattle manure.
Eggs: Mar.–July (usually Apr.–May) and, near Tucson, Ariz., also late July–Sept. (Ohmart, 1973), the nesting seasons correlated with food supply; 2–6, commonly 3–5, white, sometimes yellowish.
Incubation: 20 days (Whitson, 1975); age at which young first fly unknown, but when 3 weeks old, catch own food on ground (Sutton, 1940); incubation period reported by Ohmart (1973) is 17–18 days; young fledge 17–19 days after hatching; both parents care for young (*see* Young and Their Care; Kronism).
Other Names: Chaparral cock; churca; correo del camino (roadrunner); cock of the desert; ground cuckoo; lizard bird; paisano (compatriot, or fellow countryman); snake killer.
Age: One lived in National Zoo, Washington, D.C., 5 years, 3 months.
Running Speed: Timed in Ariz., 12 m.p.h.; in Utah, 15 m.p.h. (Cottam *et al.*, 1942b); in Calif., 10 m.p.h. (Hunt, 1920); 15 m.p.h. (Sheldon, 1922); and 20 m.p.h. (Smith, 1924).

Mangrove cuckoo

CUCKOO FAMILY

cuckoo

CUCULIFORMES

Weights: Two averaged 190 gr. (Hughes, 1970), or about 6¾ oz.; 12 adults studied by Lasiewski *et al.* (1971), 269.3–274.2 gr., or about 9½ oz.

Range: Resident from n.-c. Calif., Nev., s. Utah, e. and sw. Kans., c. and e. Okla., w. Ark., and nw. La. south to Baja Calif. and s. Mexico.

CUCKOO-ROLLER FAMILY
See Coraciiformes.

CUCU
See Yellowlegs, greater, and Yellowlegs, lesser, in Sandpiper Family.

CUCULIDAE
See Cuckoo Family.

CUCULIFORMES
(cue-cue-lih-FOR-meez); from Lat. *cuculus*, European cuckoo, and *forma*, form; cuckoo-shaped (Coble, 1954). Order, or group, of birds that resemble each other fundamentally in structure (*see* Order). According to Van Tyne and Berger (1976), Cuculiformes includes two families: the Turaco, or Touraco (too-rah-KOH), Family of 19 species of Africa, and the almost worldwide Cuckoo Family of 127 species with 7 representatives in N. America. *See* Cuckoo Family. The N. American anis and the roadrunner are in the family.

The gorgeously plumaged African turacos (family Musophagidae) appear at first glance to have little in common with the often drably plumaged cuckoos of the Old and New Worlds; however, both are zygodactylous (yoke-toed) (*see* Feet and Legs), both have tender skin and loose plumage and some features in the development of their young that are similar (Wallace, 1961c).

Turacos eat largely plantains and other fruit —they are often called plantain-eaters—and some insects, and most of them live in deep forests. These have strikingly colored green or blue body feathers, with red feathers in the wings (*see* discussion of their unusual pigments under Colors of Feathers; see also Chapin, 1963, for details); they have long tails, crests, and some have bright-colored, short bills; like ospreys and owls can direct the outer toe either backward or forward; climb vines and run squirrel-like over limbs; fly short distances in weak, dipping flight. The young, like those of some of the related cuckoos, after only 10 days in the nest crawl about in nearby branches, where they are fed by the adults. See Austin (1961) and Gilliard (1958) for other details.

Sibley and Ahlquist (1973), after studies of the egg-white protein of the strange S. American hoatzin, *Opisthocomos cristatus* (*see* discussion of use of egg-white protein in determining relationships, under Eggs and Egg-laying), suggested that its correct taxonomic position, or classification, is in the Cuckoo Family (Cuculidae) and in a subfamily Crotophaginae; that its closest relatives are the Guira cuckoo of the Argentine pampas and the anis of the American tropics. *See* biographies of anis in Cuckoo Family. The hoatzin is classified by many ornithologists as belonging in the order Galliformes—among the pheasants, grouse, turkeys, etc. See detailed discussion of life history and classification of the hoatzin by Sick (1964), and especially by Sibley and Ahlquist (1973). Authorities such as Sick (1964) and Delacour and Amadon (1973) continue, however, to place the hoatzin in the family Opisthocomidae, order Galliformes.

The hoatzin is a crested, red-brown bird resembling a chachalaca (*see* chachalaca in Curassow Family) and at certain seasons it has a strong odor (another name for it is stinkbird); it is slenderly built, about 25 in. long; weighs about 810 gr., or 1¾ lbs., and lives in forests along banks of streams in S. America. Besides its strange, prehistoric appearance (it resembles the ancient *Archaeopteryx*—see under Origin of Birds and of Bird Flight in Fossil Birds), the young hoatzin has large claws on the first and second digits of its wings that help it climb through branches; it loses the claws in adulthood but still climbs with its wings, with the help of its feet; both adults and young have a remarkable crop (*see* discussion of it under Crop) for digesting their food, which is almost exclusively leaves, flowers, and fruits of certain marsh plants. It builds its nest in branches over water, often in colonies.

Unlike the Old World cuckoos, N. American members of the Cuckoo Family—black-billed and yellow-billed cuckoos, for example—usually build their own nests and rear their own young; the Old World cuckoos lay their eggs in the nests of other birds and are said to be brood-parasitic. *See* Brood Parasitism; *also* Cowbird in Troupial Family.

For a discussion of how birds are generally grouped, or arranged according to their relationships, *see* Classification; Morphology; Phylogenetic Relationship; *see also* Check-list.

CULMEN
Term for the ridge on the top or upper half (maxilla) of a bird's bill. *See* Bill.

CURASSOW FAMILY
Cracidae (CRASS-ih-dee); Lat., from Gr. *kraks*, head, in reference to the crests and wattles about the heads of many species in the family; according to Delacour and Amadon (1973), the family was named Curassow because first specimens of these birds to reach Europe that were collected for scientists were shipped there from the West Indian island of Curaçao. The Curassow Family is a tropical group known only from the New World; includes 44 species (Delacour and Amadon, 1973) of curassows, guans (pronounced GWAHNS), and chachalacas (only 1 species in entire family, the plain chachalaca, reaches N. America); family is in the order Galliformes, which includes 7 families in the world, 4 of which are represented in N. America; although one species of cracid, the white-winged guan, *Penelope albipennis*, was believed to be extinct, and had been known only from 3 old specimens, it was rediscovered in Peru by John O'Neill in 1979, and its population may number in the hundreds; members of the Curassow Family seem the most primitive of all; medium to large (20–40 in. long); are arboreal; restricted to the tropical mainland of N. and S. America, from s. Tex. (the plain chachalaca) and e. Mexico south

to Peru, n. Argentina, and Uruguay; although plumage never brilliant but usually black or brown, many species have colorful wattles, horns, casques, knobs, or patches of bare skin on the face or throat, and legs and feet of some are brightly colored, with sexes usually colored alike (the bare skin is dull-colored in most chachalacas); some are strikingly crested; all have long tails; wings rather small and rounded, legs and feet are strong, all are fowl-like in appearance with moderate-sized, chickenlike bills; however, the hind toe (hallux), unlike that of other fowl, is situated at same level as the three front toes, which permits them to grasp twigs and branches and to walk along limbs of trees, at which they are adept; on ground, they walk and trot gracefully, and run, although not as rapidly as the more terrestrial pheasants, for example; are mostly vegetarians—"the smaller species eat soft fruits, green shoots and leaves," and blossoms directly from plants; "all cracids roost in trees or vines and during dry season come to pools and streams to drink"; all are highly vocal; "to hear a chorus of chachalacas for first time is unforgettable, so loud and raucous is the effect"; most are social, and tend to gather in small flocks with families or pairs still accompanied by half-grown young; the young cracids are the only gallinaceous birds that are fed directly by the parents; all cracids are nonmigratory (Delacour and Amadon, 1973).

Chachalaca, *Ortalis vetula* (OR-ta-lis VET-you-lah); genus name: from classical Gr. *ortalis*, corresponding to Lat. *pullus*, chick, from resemblance to a fowl; species name: Lat., little old hen, possibly in reference to its loud chattering; also called *plain* chachalaca in reference to its plain colors; *chachalaca* (CHAH-cha-LAH-kah), Spanish from Nahuatl Indian name for the bird, is onomatopoetic of the reverberating choruses of its cries. (Color ill., page 134.) Of the 9 species of chachalacas, only the plain chachalaca reaches N. America, in the lower Rio Grande Valley of s. Tex. (Delacour and Amadon, 1973), locally from near Falcon Dam to Brownsville, formerly ranged upcoast to Raymondville; owing to clearing off of its brushy habitat in s. Tex. for agriculture, it is now largely limited to a few parks and refuges (see Marion, 1974); 20–24 in. long; sexes outwardly alike; a large olive-brown and gray bird with small head, slight crest; long tail has greenish gloss; patch of bare skin on throat is *red;* eyes pale brown; bill, legs, toes, light horn blue; immatures like adults but more brown; lives in dry woodlands and thickets of tall brush or chaparral; primarily a tree dweller but comes to ground frequently, is fond of dust baths; its slender form permits it to thread rapidly through brushy tangles; alarmed group will dash half flying, half hopping, with crests raised high, tails spread wide, the small wings beating laboriously through chaparral; the *chachalaca* cry is its song, given mostly in morning and in evening, especially before thunderstorms, and during the nesting season, although uttered somewhat throughout the year; the cry of individual birds is three-syllabled *cha-cha-lac, cha-cha-lac,* but when a flock joins in the chorus, the word *chachalaca* is clearly enunciated, and when the chorus reaches full strength, "the bass of the old males, soprano of the females, and the scratchy falsetto of the young blend in a strange cacophony" (Sutton, 1951b); male's voice, possibly owing to his looped trachea, is deeper and coarser than female's (Leopold, 1959)—*see* discussion under Voice and Sound-Making; are much hunted as game bird in Mexico and other parts of their tropical range.

Feeding Habits: Eats berries, especially hackberries, also fruit of mesquite, mangoes, junipers, palmettos, persimmons, wild grapes, figs, and green leaves, buds, and shoots of plants, and some insects. See also Marion (1976).

Nest: Small frail structure of sticks, leaves, lined with some green leaves, built in fork in dense bushes and trees 4–20 ft. above ground.

Eggs: Tex., nests early Mar. to Sept.; eggs Mar. 21–Aug. 16; 2–4, usually 3; a "dump nest" in Tex. held 9 eggs, believed product of three or four hens (Delacour and Amadon, 1973); Mexicans often put chachalaca eggs under domestic hens and raise hatched chicks as pets; in U.S., are often kept in zoos and private aviaries.

Incubation: By female, 22–25 days; chicks flutter out of nest and onto surrounding branches when 3–4 days old, are fed regurgitated food directly from bill of parent.

Other Names: Chachalaca; common chachalaca; Mexican chachalaca; plain chachalaca.

Age: A male color-banded in Santa Ana Wildlife Refuge, Tex., sighted there when 8 years, 10 months, old.

Weights: 470–685 gr. (Leopold, 1959), or about 1 lb. 8 oz.; 300–527 gr. (Delacour and Amadon, 1973).

Range: Extreme s. Tex. and e. and s. Mexico; in C. America, south to w. Nicaragua and nw. Costa Rica and Utila Is., Honduras (Delacour and Amadon, 1973).

CURATOR

In ornithology, a term for the custodian or keeper of the bird department of a museum. A curator is generally in charge of the department and his first duties are the care of the bird collections, their proper arrangement and identification, additions to them, and their study (*see* Collections). Each specimen should be labeled, catalogued, and given a serial number before being stored away in dustproof, lightproof, insectproof cases. The system of numbering and storing must have such method that each specimen (*see* Bird Skins), will thereafter always be readily available for examination. The care of the collections, however, is only one of the many duties of a curator in ornithology. The emphasis in a curator's work and the direction of his main activities vary with the type of museum, but in a well-rounded institution his responsibilities fall into three categories: (1) care of a collection, (2) research, and (3) education (Rand, 1962).

CURIOSITY

See Behavior.

CURLEW

See in Sandpiper Family.

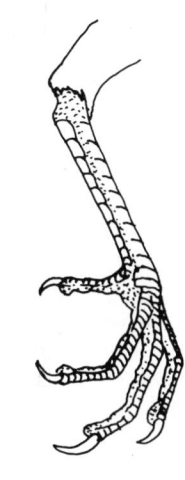

CURASSOW FAMILY

CURLY-TAIL
See Mallard in Duck Family.

CURSORIAL
Said of a bird that is adapted to a running or walking way of life (compared to flying birds); examples are ostriches, the S. American rheas, and the Australian cassowaries and emus.

CUT-WATER
See Black skimmer in Skimmer Family.

CYCLE
A regular periodic fluctuation in populations of some birds and mammals is known as a cycle. Many birds have years of great abundance, which are known as "highs" in the cycle; they also have years of scarcity, known as "lows" in the cycle. Ruffed grouse and other gallinaceous birds seem to have especially violent population changes and the populations can become so low that within a year or two almost all of the birds seem to have disappeared. This is spoken of by game managers and biologists as a *crash* in the population cycle (Leopold, 1933).

"The numbers of various northern birds and mammals fluctuate strongly in 'cycles,' a term applied to population changes in which the successive maxima, or peaks, come at regular intervals" (Lack, 1954). The regularity of the cycles is indicated by the intervals of time between the peaks or "highs" in population. The population peaks themselves tend to be of different heights and the fall and rise in numbers of birds or other animals between these peaks are not symmetrical. Some biologists reserve the term "cycle" for steep fluctuations in numbers but the term is more often used for birds and other animals that have a nearly equal interval between successive peaks (Lack, 1954).

Two main cycles have been demonstrated in N. America, a 3- to 4-year cycle of lemmings and other animals on the Arctic tundra, another 4-year cycle of voles, or meadow mice, and a 9- to 10-year cycle of the varying hare, or snowshoe rabbit. Three groups of animals are affected by these cycles—the dominant rodents themselves; the hawks, owls, shrikes, foxes, lynxes, and other northern animals which prey primarily on the "cyclic" rodents and hares; and the native gallinaceous birds of the same northern regions. Some ornithologists have claimed that the 10-year cycle in Canada affects various other species, including the magpie, introduced pheasant and partridge, and two songbirds—the evening grosbeak and the blue jay (Rowan, 1948, 1950). Although the 4- and 10-year cycles possibly affect various other species of animals, they are certainly known to involve only three groups—the rodents themselves, their predators, and the native gallinaceous birds.

Of the three groups of animals affected by cycles, the fluctuations of the predators seem easiest to explain, as they follow closely those of their prey and their periodic declines are due to food shortages. For example, the snowy owl, which feeds largely on lemmings, which have a 4-year cycle (though it takes hares, voles, and ptarmigan at times), has invaded e. U.S. from the Canadian Arctic regularly about every 4 years (when lemmings and mice are scarce) since 1882. The northern shrike also invades e. N. America about every fourth year (see discussion, however, by Davis, 1974), as does the rough-legged hawk, which feeds its young on voles and lemmings. The American goshawk and the northern horned owl invade s. Canada and n. U.S. from regions farther north about every 10 years, not every 4 years. In Canada the horned owl preys largely on the varying hare, which has a 10-year cycle, and the goshawk on the varying hare and the ruffed grouse, which also has about a 10-year cycle. See discussion by Mueller *et al.* (1977b).

The cycles in gallinaceous birds have been especially studied in the ruffed grouse, which apparently reaches a peak in numbers about every 9 to 11 years, with occasional intervals of 8 to 13 years. However, according to Joseph J. Hickey (1955) in a review paper of the subject, typical population fluctuations of N. American grouse show a 3⅓-year cycle between 55° and 70° N. Lat., and "a frequently reported nine-and-one-half-year cycle at 40 to 50 degrees N. rests upon incomplete indices and short-term censuses . . . there was no complete evidence, at the end of the 1940s, that grouse actually followed the nine-to-ten-year cycles of lynx, mink, and red fox."

As with other cyclic species, the peaks of the ruffed grouse populations do not occur simultaneously throughout its range, and at least twelve different explanations have been published as to the causes of its cyclic fluctuations—cyclic climatic change, possibly aided by sunspots; abnormally cold winters; unusually wet weather; epidemic disease; external parasites; insufficient food in winter; natural predators; scarcity of "buffer" prey (rodents and other animals) for the predators that sometimes feed on ruffed grouse; decrease in the plant cover which protects grouse; hunting; emigration out of areas; and even so-called inbreeding, or close interbreeding, which is sometimes thought to be harmful to game birds (Bump *et al.*, 1947). *See* Inbreeding.

Evidence suggests that the cycles of gallinaceous birds—ruffed grouse, spruce grouse, willow ptarmigan, particularly—parallel those of the cyclic varying hare of the same region. It has been suggested that either the grouse or hares are affected by a common external factor or the numbers of one depend on the other. For the gallinaceous birds, there seems to be no generally accepted view for their cyclic decline (Lack, 1954). *See* Irruption; *also* Populations.

CYGNET
(SIG-net). *See* introduction to Duck Family.

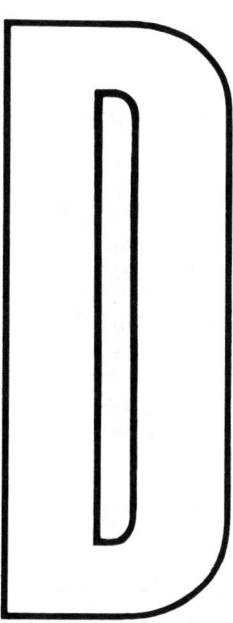

DABCHICK
See Pied-billed grebe in Grebe Family.

DADDY LONGLEGS
See Stilt, black-necked, in Avocet Family.

DAMAGE BY BIRDS
See Economic Ornithology; Control.

DANCING GROUND
An area on the ground on which the males of certain grouse—prairie chicken, sharp-tailed grouse, and sage grouse—gather in the early dawn during the courting season and strut or "dance" in courtship displays before the females. These dances are filled with displays of the plumage of the males; by inflation of air in colorful sacs on the sides of the neck or throat; and booming, cooing, or tooting sounds that carry long distances. *See* Voice and Sound-Making. The dances or group displays of the males, accompanied by some fighting, are among the most colorful and spectacular of any in the animal kingdom (Gilliard, 1958). *See* Arena Bird; Behavior; Census; Courtship.

DARK PHASE
See erythrism and melanism under Colors of Feathers. *See also* Color Phase.

DARTER
See Anhinga in Anhinga Family; *also* Accipiter.

DAW
(Old Low German: *Daha*). Name for the jack or jackdaw of Great Britain, possibly for its fancied cry; smallest and best-known member of the Crow Family in the British Isles (Newton, 1893–96). The name was doubtless applied by early English settlers to a number of American birds that are black and shining—for example, the grackle. *See* Grackle, boat-tailed, in Troupial Family.

DAWSON
WILLIAM LEON (1873–1928). Pioneer bird photographer and member American Ornithologists' Union; author of *Birds of Ohio*; *Birds of Washington* (with J. H. Bowles); and his great work, in four volumes, *Birds of California* (1923). See Palmer (1928); Stone (1928).

DEATH-BIRD
Local name in Fla. for smooth-billed ani (*see* in Cuckoo Family), because of blackness (funereal) of plumage.

DEATHTRAP
See Accidents.

DECIDUOUS FOREST
One of the nine biomes (*see* Biome) in N. America north of Mexico used in mapping the ecological distribution of birds. *See* Major Biotic Communities (biomes) under Distribution. The Deciduous Forest is mostly broad-leaved trees such as beech, basswood, oaks, hickories, maples, and extends over e. U.S. from s. New England and the Appalachians (below the coniferous forests) west to and including the bottomlands along the Mississippi R. and its tributaries. Some of the birds of the Deciduous Forest are: red-shouldered and broad-winged hawks, barred owl, whip-poor-will, red-bellied woodpecker, hairy woodpecker, downy woodpecker, great crested and Acadian flycatchers, eastern wood pewee, Carolina chickadee, tufted titmouse, white-breasted nuthatch, wood thrush, blue-gray gnatcatcher, yellow-throated vireo, and several species of warblers (see details in Pettingill, 1970; 1972).

DECURVED
See Bill.

DEFENSE
See Flight; Self-protective Behavior under Behavior; Colors of Feathers; Distraction Display; Fear; Nests and Nesting; Fighting under Territory; Regurgitation; Young and Their Care.

DEFORMITIES
May be caused by accidents, diseases, or physiological disorders, or possibly may be congenital in some birds. In one intensive study in Ohio, of some 30,000 starlings captured for banding, Hicks (1934) examined 10,000 for afflictions, injuries, or other abnormalities and discovered that 535, or 5.35%, had a physical deformity of some kind. Some 3.14% lacked toenails; 1.82% lacked toes; 0.21% had no feet or legs; 0.83% had broken legs; 0.38% had bill deformities; and 0.46% were blind in one eye. *See* related discussion under Mutation.

Starlings with "club feet" usually had missing toes or toenails and the lower part of the tarsus (foot) swollen into a diseased lump. Four birds had little or no color in their legs, which were red or pink, but the remainder of each bird was normal.

Seven oversize or "giant" birds (normal otherwise) were all males and at least an inch longer overall than average male starlings. Six undersize or "pygmy" birds (five of them were females) were about an inch shorter than the average adult female. One bird not only lacked tail feathers but appeared to have the posterior part of its body shriveled, rounded, and devoid of a tail altogether. (This may have been "rumplessness" reported for domestic fowls.) Another had a "swallow" tail with the two outer pairs of tail feathers about an inch longer than the others. Three starlings had bills that were without pigment (*see* Colors of Feathers) and were semi-transparent; six had the upper mandible (*see* Bill) curved upward and back into an almost complete loop. Five had the upper mandible split into distinctly spreading forks; two others had both mandibles flattened into a small stubby disk. One bill, less than half its normal length, was shaped and proportioned like the bill of a house sparrow; another had the bill so thickened and deepened that it resembled that of a cardinal.

Fourteen starlings had curiously crossed bills of more than twice their normal length; some of these showed definite tendency to spiral and most were somewhat split at the tip. All but one had upper mandible crossing to the left. Brackbill (1969b) reported a white-breasted nuthatch and a brown thrasher with abnormally long upper mandibles that wore down in time and thus "corrected" themselves. For an

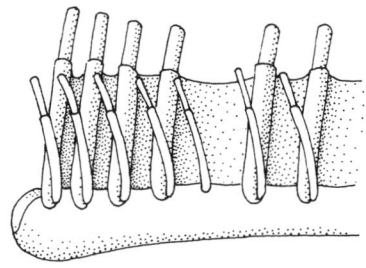

diastataxic

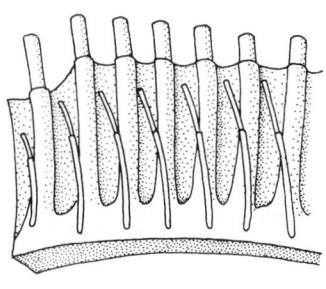

eutaxic

DIASTATAXIC

In gulls, shorebirds, and certain other birds, there is a space between the fourth and fifth secondary feathers of the wing, a condition known as diastataxy. All passerine birds lack this gap and are eutaxic.

illustrated account of an unusual number of odd bill deformities, see Pomeroy (1962).

In a study of some 30,000 passerine birds banded over ten years at Pasadena, Calif., Michener and Michener (1936) discovered that the most common injuries of birds were those of the legs but that an injured leg was not a major handicap to a bird; they get along with almost any degree of leg injury; for example, a California (scrub) jay had its left tarsus broken and the foot had rotated 180° about the tarsus itself, but the jay used this twisted foot as a prop whenever it perched. They reported birds with tumors (*see* Tumors) but very few sick birds. Nickell (1965a), in 33 years of banding 120,000 birds, reported numerous examples of bill, foot, and wing defects in mourning doves, downy woodpeckers, blue jays, American robins, and others that survived these handicaps. Sheldon (1971) reported that the American woodcock is very hardy; many caught in winter on its breeding grounds had survived with missing toes, broken legs that had healed, and had survived migrations even with the loss of a leg. Terres (1960b) told of a screech owl that had survived and was in good condition after the loss of a foot, and a wild ring-necked pheasant that was in good condition after the loss of both feet.

Some of the most bizarre abnormalities of birds are extra wings and extra legs—all congenital, or of the embryonic development of the bird. According to Hutt (1949), these abnormalities of the skeleton are not hereditary; they occur at rare intervals, apparently from accidents in development. Hutt calls the condition of four legs or of four wings *duplicity,* and domestic chicks that occasionally hatch with four legs and four wings do not survive. Some research scientists have attributed such deformities both in domestic chicks and in young wild birds—the common tern, for example—to the effects of chemical pollutants. See Hays and Risebrough (1972).

Johnson (1915) described a green-winged teal, an adult female, shot near Wyoming, Minn., that had four wings, two of which were so-called supernumerary, or abortive. The duck had had no difficulty flying and when it was examined, and the primary or normal wings raised, the supernumerary ones appeared as a "miniature set," springing from the underside of the primary wings at the elbow.

Johnson reported that he could find no previous record of any bird similar to the case he described. He knew of a previous record of a four-winged and four-legged chicken, which also had two tails; a four-footed duck; and three hens and two ducks each with a pair of supernumerary legs appended to an abnormal pelvis; but he knew of no previous record in the scientific literature of a *wild* bird with four wings.

In Feb. 1941, a cock ring-necked pheasant about a year old was found dead on a Conn. game farm. It proved to have two extra wings which were rudimentary feathered stubs, useless to it in flight, but apparently not a hindrance to its flying. Bissonette (1944), who reported the four-winged pheasant, also described a four-legged pheasant chick, about 4 days old. Bissonette suggested that the extra wings of the pheasant may have been an example of abnormalities associated with the high degree of hybridization sometimes occurring in some groups of birds, particularly pheasants among game birds, also doves in laboratory-controlled hybridization.

On July 2, 1961, Robert G. Frankowiak (1962) found near Hickory Corners, Wisc., a mourning dove with three legs. The bird had been dead for some time and the body was badly decomposed. One of the legs was normal, the other had a smaller leg growing from the tibia-tarsal joint; the extra leg had only an inner and outer toe. At Island Beach, N.J., Warburton (1967) reported banding a Baltimore (northern) oriole and a great crested flycatcher, each of which had three legs.

Perhaps rarest of all deformities are birds born blind. Berger and Howard (1968) reported that anophthalmia (without eyes) and microphthalmia (literally small eyes, or the reduction in development of one or both eyes) are fairly common in embryos of domestic fowl—in chickens, caused by a genetic (inherited) factor. In 1839, a fledged domestic pigeon was reported that had no trace of eyes, but up to Berger and Howard's 1968 report, apparently no one had found complete eyelessness in a wild bird.

At Lincoln, Mass., in June 1966, Mrs. Howard, junior author of the report, found an American robin's nest with four eggs; two eggs hatched: one chick was normal, the other had no eyes. When the young were 8 days old, each weighed 51½ gr., a normal weight for their age; 3 days later, the normal robin was still in the nest; the blind one was on the ground but had difficulty maintaining its balance—it repeatedly fell on one side or other but was able to preen its feathers. When caught and examined, the eyeless bird had no suggestion of eyeballs and no well-defined bony orbits, or eye sockets. See also Wallace (1956) and Wetherbee (1958) for reports of an American robin, a common grackle, and a mockingbird with deformed eyes.

DEGLAND

DR. CÔME DAMIEN (1787–1856). Name commemorated in 1850 by Charles Lucien Bonaparte in the species name of the white-winged scoter, *Melanitta deglandi;* was director of the Musée d'Histoire Naturelle in Lille, France. He wrote *Ornithologie Européene* (1849) and several other publications about European birds.

DE LATTRE

ADOLPHE AND HENRY. *See* Hummingbird, Heloise's, in Hummingbird Family.

DEPREDATIONS

Pillaging; "robbing." *See* examples in Feeding and Food-getting under Behavior; *also* kleptoparasitism under Parasite; Economic Ornithology; Predation.

DEPRESSOR MUSCLE

See Flight.

DERMIS

See Skin.

DESCRIBED

Term among ornithologists for a bird that has had a scientific description of it made and usually published in a scientific journal. "The description given at the time of proposal of a name for a new species, genus, or other category is called the *original description*. It has two primary functions. The first . . . is to facilitate subsequent recognition and identification; the second is to make the new name available by fulfilling the requirements of Article 25 of the International Rules of Zoological Nomenclature" (Mayr *et al.*, 1953). *See* Classification; Names and Naming.

DESERTION OF EGGS OR YOUNG
See Nests and Nesting.

DESERTS AND BIRDS
See discussion of some adaptations of birds to deserts under Heat and Birds; Water Requirements; *see also* Distribution. See Serventy (1971); Brown (1968); Austin (1976) for excellent reviews and bibliographies.

DETERMINATE LAYER
See Eggs and Egg-laying.

DE VESEY
See Xantus.

DEVIL-DIVER
See Horned grebe and Pied-billed grebe in Grebe Family.

DEVIL-DOWN-HEAD
See Red-breasted nuthatch and white-breasted nuthatch in Nuthatch Family.

DEW BATHING
See Bathing.

DEWLAP
See Wattle.

DIABLOTIN
See Petrel, black-capped, in Shearwater Family.

DIASTATAXIC
(die-as-ta-TAK-sik). Condition in the wings of certain groups and species of birds in which there is an unusually large space between the 4th and 5th secondary feathers. The wings of the golden eagle, for example, and of all members of the Charadriiformes—shorebirds, gulls, etc.—except the woodcock, are diastataxic. Many of the more primitive birds have this condition in the wings. The opposite condition—that is, without the gap in the secondary wing feathers—is called *eutaxic* (you-TAK-sik). All passerine birds and some other families—such as the bee-eaters, motmots, and trogons—are eutaxic. In a number of other orders and families, both conditions occur, but no bird has ever been recorded with an intermediate condition of the two (Van Tyne and Berger, 1959; see also account by Humphrey and Clark, 1961). *See* Feather.

DIATRYMIFORMES
(die-ah-try-mih-FOR-meez). An order of giant, flightless birds up to 7 ft. tall whose fossilized bones have been discovered in Wyo., N.M., and N.J., also possibly in France and Great Britain (Van Tyne and Berger, 1959). Although resembling an ostrich, they were apparently related to the cranes and rails and lived more than 50 million years ago. *See* discussion under Fossil Birds. *See also* Geological Time Scale. Many ornithologists now classify these ancient birds in a family Diatrymidae rather than in an order. *See* Order; *also* Family.

DÍAZ
AUGUSTÍN (1829–93). Member of the commission appointed in Mexico to negotiate and survey the boundary between the U.S. and Mexico; a military engineer and founder and, until his death, director of the Mexican Geographical and Exploring Commission (Gruson, 1972). Robert Ridgway (1886) named the Mexican duck, *Anas diazi*, in his honor.

DICHROMATIC
Having two color phases, or forms, independent of age or sex. *See* Color Phase.

DICKCISSEL
See in Finch Family.

DIDACTYL
or DIDACTYLOUS. Two-toed, as in the ostrich. *See* Feet and Legs.

DIGESTION
Involves all physical and chemical changes of food before it can be absorbed into the intestines. The entire digestive tract through which food passes, or is treated, "includes bill, mouth, tongue, pharynx, esophagus, crop, proventriculus, gizzard, intestines, caeca, rectum, and cloaca" (Sturkie, 1976).

Food preparation begins with bill (*see* Bill); for example, in seed-cracking by seed-eating birds; flesh-tearing by birds of prey and by vultures and condors. Food may be taken into mouth with tongue in some birds (*see* Tongue), where moistened, or lubricated, by mucus and saliva (*see* discussion under Mouth), then swallowed. *See* Swallowing.

In some species—owls and many seabirds—food such as mice and fishes, for example, is swallowed entire and in those that have a crop (see Crop) food may be stored there until softened, then passed on to the spindle-shaped glandular stomach *(proventriculus)*, which digests the food chemically. It is primarily in the glandular stomach that digestion begins, with gastric juices starting breakdown of food. Within the glandular stomach a peptic enzyme attacks protein foods and is so highly acid that in many carnivorous species—hawks, for example—it dissolves bones. The large lammergeyer, or bearded vulture, which lives in remote mountains from e. Europe to China and eats bone marrow, is said to have a stomach so acid that it can dissolve the whole of a cow's vertebra in one or two days (Heinroth and Heinroth, 1958).

After partly digested food leaves the glandular stomach, it passes into the muscular stomach, or gizzard, which grinds the food, often with aid of grit (coarse sand or pebbles), which serves seed-eating birds as internal teeth and assists in crushing hard seeds, nuts, and grains. *See* details under Gizzard. Indigestible

Diatryma

DIATRYMIFORMES

parts of food—fur, feathers, scales, etc.—are cast up (regurgitated) by many birds in form of pellets. *See* details under Pellet.

After leaving the gizzard, the partly liquid food, now called *chyme* (Worden, 1964a) passes into the short, U-shaped duodenum, which is the first part of the small intestine; the small intestine is the main organ of digestion and absorption of foods (Farner, 1960). *See* Intestine.

The pancreas (*see* Pancreas) lies within the long loop, or two arms, of the duodenum. Secretions from it that pass into the duodenum, along with bile from the liver (*see* Liver), continue the digestion of the chyme (pronounced KIME), possibly aided by juices from the intestinal wall itself. Bile from the liver sometimes shows enzyme activity; acts to neutralize the acid passed into small intestine from the stomach, and to emulsify fats before further digestion. It adds to chyme the bile pigments which are later voided from bird's body (Worden, 1964a).

The long, coiled *ileum*, second part of the small intestine, leads into the large intestine, which is usually called the rectum in birds (Berger, 1961). Digestion continues in ileum with some enzymes probably added by glands in intestinal wall (Worden, 1964a). Once food is digested in the ileum, its products are absorbed by the intestinal lining and passed on into bloodstream, which distributes them through the bird's body. *See* Metabolism.

At the junction of the large and small intestines, a pair of blind tubes—the caeca—branch off. (*See* Caeca.) These tubes are most prominent in birds that eat leaves, buds, grass—plant material with a high cellulose content. Some birds have only a single caecum; in others, such as the shearwaters, the caeca are rudimentary; and the parrots and kingfishers lack them altogether. Caeca have a high bacterial content, which apparently acts upon the cellulose plant material, assisting in its digestion.

The large intestine (rectum) is short and opens into the cloaca. It temporarily holds the food wastes and extracts water from them. No digestion or absorption of food takes place in the large intestine. *See* Cloaca; *see* Urinary System under Urogenital System.

SPEED OF DIGESTION. According to Henderson (1933), young meadowlarks digest grasshoppers in about 3–4 hours; a captive shrike required 3 hours to digest a mouse. A barred owl digested two house sparrows in 1½ hours; a young turkey vulture ate a house snake, or, milk snake, 3½ ft. long, equal to one fifth of its own weight, and completely digested it in 1½ hours, which was learned by dissection. In tests in Mass., black ducks digested and passed blue mussels *(Mytilus edulis)* in 30–40 minutes (Grandy, 1972); mallards passed crayfish *(Cambarus)* in 45 minutes.

In small birds such as song sparrows, food passes through digestive tract, whether insects, grain, or fruit, in an average of 1½ hours (Stevenson, 1933); a cedar waxwing fed watery berries passed them in 16–40 minutes (Nice, 1941a); a thrush fed elderberries excreted the seeds 30 minutes later. In Europe, an investigator found that berries passed through digestive

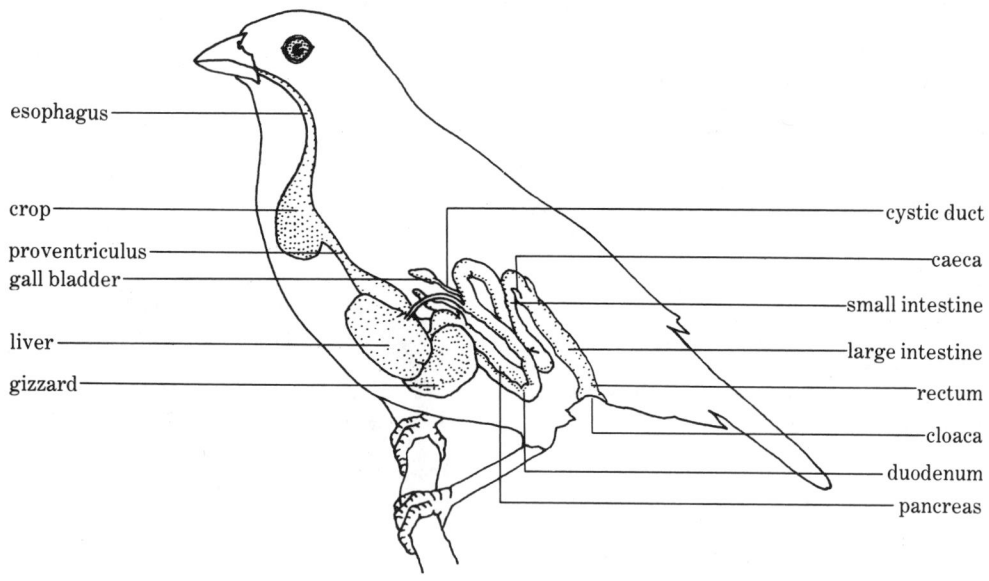

esophagus

crop

proventriculus

gall bladder

liver

gizzard

cystic duct

caeca

small intestine

large intestine

rectum

cloaca

duodenum

pancreas

DIGESTIVE SYSTEM

system of the blackcap, *Sylvia atricapilla*, an Old World warbler (*see* in Warbler—Old World Warbler Family), in 12 minutes, but entire meal of berries required more than 2 hours (Groebbels, 1932).

A domestic hen requires about 2 hours to pass mash through its digestive tract (Worden, 1964b); a goose digested oats in as little as 4 hours, but an entire meal required 17 hours (Groebbels, 1932).

Digestion in birds is rapid in order to maintain the high body temperatures of about 101–112° F.—2 to 14 degrees higher than in mammals, including man's normal 98.6° (Simons, 1960); the smaller ones seem constantly swallowing food at one end and excreting the relatively small amount of wastes at the other. Birds with crops fill both the crop (*see* Crop) *and* the stomach with food about twice a day; insect-eating birds, an average of five to six times daily (Henderson, 1933). Digestion of most birds is not only rapid but highly efficient, especially when they eat foods rich in potential energy such as seeds, fruits, nectar, insects, fishes, and rodents. *See* How Much Will a Bird Eat? under Food and Feeding Habits; *also* Fasting; Metabolism; Pellet; Weight. *See also* Young and Their Care.

DIGITAL FORMULA

A numbering plan for the toes of birds. *See* Feet and Legs.

DIGITIGRADE

Name for the method of standing on the toes, with the heel in the air, as in birds, in contrast to standing with the toes and heel on the ground (plantigrade), as man does. *See* Feet and Legs.

"DILUTE"

(of plumage). *See* Albinism; *also* Colors of Feathers.

DIMENSIONS

Measurements of various parts of a bird taken by ornithologists, and recorded in their studies of birds, usually serve three purposes—to help in systematic studies of differences or similarities between families, genera, species, or subspecies; to compare the sizes of the two sexes and record differences or similarities between them; and to trace the growth of young birds (Pettingill, 1956).

The measurements generally taken are: *Total length:* from tip of bill to end of longest tail feather; with living bird, relaxed and on its back (Palmer, 1962); if of a birdskin (*see* Bird Skins), it is also placed on its back and gently stretched, with commissure of the bill parallel to the ruler. Measurements are usually taken in millimeters, although popular bird books usually give dimensions of birds in inches or feet. Pettingill (1956) recommends, for general use, a ruler about 250 mm. (10 in.) long. For measurements of large birds, its extremities may be marked on a flat surface and then the distance between them measured. *Wingspan,* or *wingspread:* measured distance between tips of outstretched wings of living bird, along the normal curves of the wings, not by flattening them (Palmer, 1962). *Wing length:* measured from

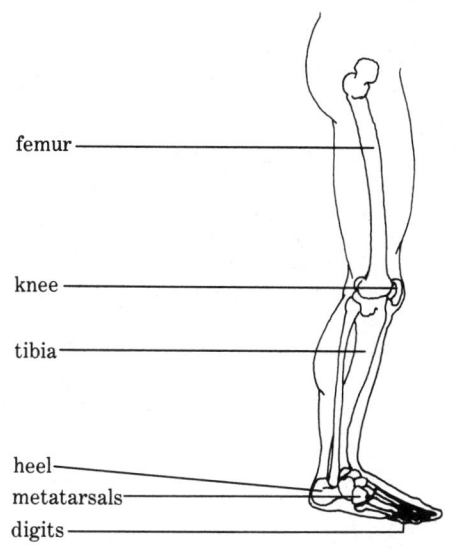
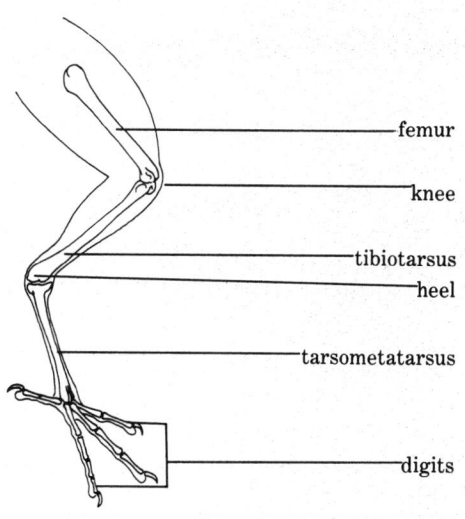

DIGITIGRADE

A bird has a digitigrade stance: its toes are on the ground and its heels in the air. Man's stance is plantigrade: the whole foot—heel and toes—lies flat on the ground.

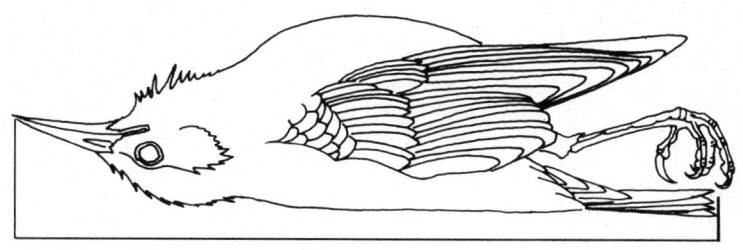

DIMENSIONS

The total length of a bird skin is measured from the tip of the bill to the end of its longest tail feather. Bill length of most birds is measured from the tip of the upper mandible to the point in the center of the forehead where the feathers meet the end of the bill. Bills of eagles, hawks, and falcons are measured from the downcurved upper mandible in a straight line to the center front edge of the cere.

bend of folded wing to tip of longest primary feather. *Tail:* measured from the point between the middle tail feathers, where they emerge from bird's skin, to end of its longest tail feather. *Bill:* measured from tip of upper mandible (*see* Mandible) in straight line to base of feathers where they meet bill in center of bird's forehead—in birds with a cere (*see* Bill; Nostrils), such as falcons, measurement is along a straight line from end of the downcurved upper mandible to front edge of the cere at the center of the bill. *Tarsus:* measured from bend, or heel, of bird's foot—the tarsus (*see* Topography)—to end of last scutellum, or scale, at base of bird's middle toe. *See* Scutellum.

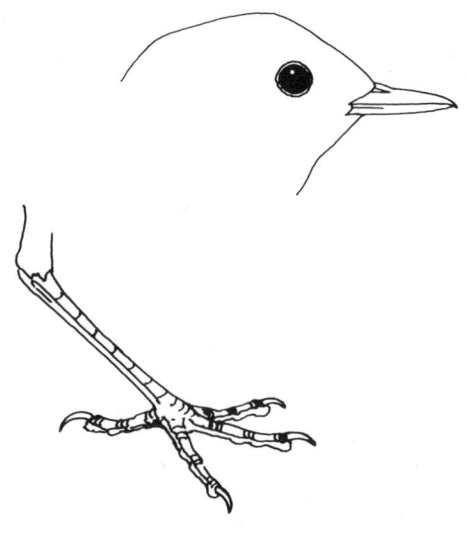

DIPPER FAMILY

DIOMEDEIDAE
See Albatross Family.

DIPHTHERIA
(avian). *See* Avian Pox.

DIPPER
See in Dipper Family; also one of common names of the horned grebe, pied-billed grebe, and ruddy duck.

DIPPER FAMILY
Cinclidae (SINK-lih-dee); Lat., from Gr. *kinklos,* kind of bird. The only truly aquatic songbirds; small, 5½–7½ in. long; 4 species in world (Van Tyne and Berger, 1976); live along mountain streams, 1 species in N. America; another, the white-capped or white-headed dipper, *Cinclus leucocephalus,* in Andes of S. America; 2 others in Europe, Asia; all have similar habits and form (starlinglike in size, shape, and flight); act like wrens, are related to wrens and thrushes with characteristics of both; solitary except at nesting time; each individual or pair remains in territory of half mile to mile of stream's length; have marvelous adaptations to living in or close to water: soft, filmy plumage with thick undercoat of down; large preen gland, which provides oil in keeping feathers waterproof; preen gland is about ten times size of that of any other songbird; has movable flap over nostrils (keeps out water); well-developed nictitating membrane (*see* Nictitating Membrane), used to protect eyes from spray of rapids and waterfalls; has short, stubby wings and tails, and distinct musty body odor (Austin, 1961); strong, rather long legs; toes like those of ordinary perching birds; swims on surface (not very well) by rapidly moving unwebbed feet (Hurrell, 1964); to go below surface, usually wades into stream, also dives from surface, or from boulder; or in flight dives directly below; can fly up from beneath surface and straightaway over water in quail-like buzzing flight; underwater swims strongly by using wings; can "fly" through 20 ft. of water to reach feeding places on bottom (Bent, 1948); can also walk about underwater on stream or pond bed (Hurrell, 1964); probably got name of dipper from habit of bobbing body rapidly up and down, some 40–60 times a minute, while perched along edge of water. Protected by law.

Dipper, *Cinclus mexicanus* (SINK-lus meks-ih-CANE-us); genus name: Lat., from Gr. *kinklos,* kind of bird; species name: Lat., of Mexico. (Color ill., page 199.) Mountain streams of w. N. America; 7–8½ in. long; sexes outwardly alike; body plumage entirely blackish gray; eyes dark, narrow border of short white feathers on upper eyelids; bill black, rather long, slender, slightly hooked, notched at tip; wings short, pointed; tail short, square-tipped; immatures have spotted breasts, suggesting their kinship to thrushes; lives at 2,000–10,000 ft. elevation in Sierras, and in Colo. and N.M. to timberline at 11,500 ft.; does not migrate in fall but moves to lower altitudes if streams freeze and shut off food supply; often perches on snags or boulders in rushing streams; in short, whirring flight, follows stream in all its windings; sings throughout year, clear, bubbling wrenlike song, audible even above roar of rushing torrents (see Muir, 1894); pair drives away other dippers that invade their territory; roost under banks (Bent, 1948).

Feeding Habits: Walks or dives into water, swims below surface and walks about on bottom to catch larvae of caddis flies, stone flies, mayflies, mosquito and midge larvae, aquatic worms, also water bugs, water beetles, and under rocks, stones, takes clams, snails, some trout fry; while swimming on surface picks up floating insects; in winter sometimes takes frozen insects from snow or ice of lakes; may wash food before feeding it to young (*see* Swallowing). For details of food habits, see Bent (1948); Backus (1959); Thut (1970).

Nest: Bulky, by female, 1 ft. in diameter, with side entrance; shaped like oven, sometimes on rock in midstream, more often on ledge of rocky cliff, sometimes under waterfall, on upturned roots of fallen tree near water; on beam under bridge; of green and yellow mosses, fine grasses.

Eggs: Mar.–June; 3–6, usually 4–5, white.

Incubation: By female, 15–17 days; young leave nest when 24–25 days old (Backus, 1959).

Other Names: American dipper; American water ouzel.

Age: Related and similar dipper, *Cinclus cinclus,* of Europe (see Hurrell, 1964), in Switzerland reached ages in wild of 6, 7, and 8 years (Nice, 1966a).

Range: Resident from Aleutian Is. and n.-c. Alaska south in mountains to c. Alta. and sw. S.D., south to s. Calif. and highlands of Mexico to w. Panama.

DIP-TAIL DIVER
See Duck, ruddy, in Duck Family.

DIRECTION FINDING
See Homing; *also* How Do Birds Find Their Way? under Migration.

DIRECTIVE MARKS
The inside mouth linings of young birds are usually brightly colored and in some nestlings (of cuckoos and weaverbirds, for example) there are special areas in the mouth lining that are so colored that they contrast markedly with the rest of the mouth lining. These special colored areas (also sometimes modified in structure) are called *directive*

marks in that they are assumed to direct or coordinate the parent bird's feeding efforts (in addition to the mouth gaping of the young, hungry bird) (Berger, 1961). *See* Gaping; *also* Young and Their Care.

DISASTER SPECIES

Term of bird-watchers for a species that is periodically severely decimated by a cold winter, food shortages, or possibly other causes. The term is applied to birds that are unable to recover, or to bring their populations back to normal, within a single nesting season (James, 1959).

The winter of 1957–58, especially following New Year's Day, was so severe in e. U.S. south to Fla. that Robert J. Newman, writing of it in *Audubon Field Notes* (1959), called it the Year of Disaster, and coined the term "disaster species" for songbirds that were especially decimated by the cold winter and the effects of insecticides. Nesting surveys in the spring and summer of 1958 showed many insectivorous birds to be far below normal numbers. The species hardest hit included the eastern phoebe, house wren, hermit thrush, eastern bluebird, and pine warbler, which, among others, winter mainly in the s. Atlantic and Gulf states. Some of these were also thought to have been affected by the widespread spraying of insecticides for the control of the fire ant in se. U.S. and for gypsy moth control on the nesting grounds of many songbirds in n. U.S. (Bull, 1958).

In analyzing the breeding bird censuses taken in the summer of 1958 on twenty different tracts in e. U.S., Newman (1959) found an overall reduction of 18% in birds, and that within only two of these censused areas was there a rise in the number of singing male birds. *See* Census.

These breeding bird censuses confirmed the earlier observations of birds during spring migration—many insectivorous birds had apparently suffered large losses. Three insectivorous birds that winter in the South led the list of those whose populations were lowest—the eastern bluebird, eastern phoebe, and hermit thrush.

Later, observers of the fall migration of birds in 1958, reported in *Audubon Field Notes* (1959), showed that *all* birds were virtually absent from places in the South that previously had teemed with them in autumn.

Apparently these periodic losses of insectivorous birds that winter in the South are usually, though not always, confined to e. U.S.

Ornithologists have paid particular attention to the effect of occasional hard winters on bird numbers in nw. Europe. In Great Britain, finches and crows suffer very little during a hard winter but the wintering population of the European robin, dunnock, wren, and titmice of the genus *Parus* may be reduced by half; a few species almost exterminated, the long-tailed tit, bearded tit, goldcrest, Dartford warbler, and stonechat (Lack, 1954). Most of these are insect-eating birds; numbers usually return to normal after a few years, though occasionally it may take longer. *See also* Accidents; Waterfowl; Weather.

DISC

or DISK. Term for the circlet of feathers that encircles the eyes of some birds, especially the owls. *See* Owl; *also* Feather.

DISCONTINUITIES

Term of evolutionists for a "bridgeless gap" between species; for example, between five species of N. American thrushes—gray-cheeked, hermit, Swainson's, veery, and wood thrush—all of which resemble each other closely but have, through evolution, become completely separated from each other by "biological discontinuities"—they differ somewhat not only outwardly, in form and markings, but in their behavior and ecological traits. Two or three of them may nest in the same woodland without any signs of interbreeding (Mayr, 1942). Their separation, or species status, is complete. *See* Species; Sympatric Species.

Discontinuities also refer to the distribution of a species. Some species of birds have ranges that are discontinuous: there may be a gap of hundreds or even thousands of miles between one population of its kind and another. An example is the scrub jay with a small population in Fla. widely separated from other scrub jays in sw. U.S. and Mexico. These discontinous populations, shown also in the burrowing owl (*see* biography in Typical Owl Family), the caracara, and the white-tailed kite are also called *disjunct* populations (Pettingill, 1972).

DISEASES

Diseases and parasites are always present and often widespread in wild birds and other animals, and some diseases and parasites exist within or on a bird or other host animal almost indefinitely without killing it (*see* examples under Parasite). The disease organisms may lack virulence or an opportunity to spread when the bird population numbers are low (Grange, 1949), but at other times, under certain ecological conditions, the disease agents may cause sudden detectable illness, followed by death, among vast numbers of them. *See*, for example, under Botulism.

In 1955, Carlton M. Herman, at that time a parasitologist of the U.S. Fish and Wildlife Service, published a review of the diseases of wild birds. Diseases (particular destructive processes in the body) are generally caused by internal animal parasites, bacteria, viruses, and fungi. He pointed out that more was then known about birds' external parasites (ectoparasites), such as lice, mites, and ticks, which suck the blood of birds and thus may transmit diseases to or between them, than was known about the internal disease-causing organisms themselves. Ticks and most other external parasites (see Ectoparasite) can be observed more easily because they do not require a microscope or other specialized equipment and techniques used in the study of the internal parasites (*see* discussion under Parasite). Herman's 1955 review is a useful reference, but more information, especially about viral and bacterial diseases, has been brought up to date in a book by Davis *et al.* (1971). See also the book by Petrak (1969) for diseases of cage and aviary birds.

Some of the blood-sucking parasites are

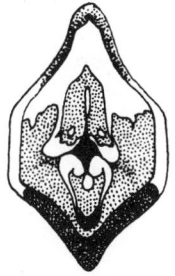

Roadrunner

Black-billed cuckoo

DIRECTIVE MARKS
The mouths of many young birds are brightly colored inside, and many have distinctive patterns that function as targets for the parents in their feeding efforts.

DISC
The facial discs that surround the eyes of owls are believed to collect sound waves, helping the bird to locate prey at night.

known carriers or transmitters of diseases among birds. For example, certain mosquitoes that feed on bird blood transmit encephalitis from bird to bird; others, when blood-sucking, inject the causative agent of bird malaria (*see* Avian Malaria). The biting hippoboscid flies (*see* Hippoboscid Flies) and midges carry the malaria-like *Haemoproteus* blood parasites from bird to bird (*see* Haemoproteus) and the blood-sucking blackflies transmit the malaria-like *Leucocytozoon* infections, especially among waterfowl. *See* discussion of insects, ticks, and mites under Parasite; *see* Ectoparasite; *also* Fleas; Hippoboscid Flies; Lice; Protocalliphora.

INTERNAL PARASITES (ENDOPARASITES). Avian, or bird, malaria is caused by one-celled protozoan animals of the genus *Plasmodium* which destroy the bird's red blood cells; at least 447 species of birds have been found infected with these malarial parasites (Coatney and Roundabush, 1949). *See* Avian Malaria.

Haemoproteus (he-moh-PRO-tee-us), the genus name of a group of protozoan blood parasites (they are related to the *Plasmodium* group) of certain birds that also produce malarialike disease; may occur even more frequently in bird blood than *Plasmodium* (Herman, 1955). Like the *Plasmodium* blood parasites of malaria, they also parasitize the red blood cells (Cook, 1971a). At least one form, or species, of *Haemoproteus* readily kills quail; other forms occur in the blood of domestic pigeons and wild mourning doves; another in the blood of crows and house sparrows; others in wild and domestic turkeys and wild ducks and grouse. See Cook (1971b) for details of each form and their effects on birds.

Another closely related protozoan parasite, *Leucocytozoon* (lew-koh-SIGH-toe-ZO-an), and its forms with life histories similar to *Plasmodium* and *Haemoproteus*, attacks *both* the red and the white corpuscles (Cook, 1971b). Birds are the sole hosts of the *Leucocytozoon* parasites; more than 150 species are known to carry them; among waterfowl the infections occur most frequently in mallards, black ducks, wood ducks, and teal (Fallis and Trainer, 1964).

Leucocytozoon anatis (simondi) has been the cause of large die-offs of young ducks and Canada goose goslings; also a high rate of infection has been noted in black ducks in Canada (Harris, V.T., 1972). Several investigators have shown the relationship of *Leucocytozoon* infection to losses in grouse (Clarke, 1938; Fallis, 1945), and severe losses in turkeys. This blood parasite is carried from bird to bird by the bites of blackflies. Cook (1971b) reported 24 species in the Duck Family (both wild and domestic ducks and geese) in which leucocytozoonosis (lew-koh-SIGH-toe-ZO-oh-NO-sis) occurs commonly throughout the world where *Leucocytozoon simondi* is present and where environmental conditions are suitable for certain blackflies (Simuliidae) and waterfowl. *See* Waterfowl. The significance of *Leucocytozoon* infection in songbirds, hawks, and certain other groups is unknown.

Trichomoniasis (trick-oh-moh-NYE-ah-sis) in birds is caused by *Trichomonas gallinae*, a flagellated protozoan that lives in the throats and in certain viscera—lungs, liver, etc.—of doves and pigeons, and hawks, owls, domestic chickens, and turkeys. It has caused severe losses of wild mourning doves; for example, in Ala. in 1951, an outbreak killed an estimated 25,000 to 30,000. The parasite is passed in "pigeon milk" from infected adults to young when feeding them (see under Crop), and adults may also pick up *Trichomonas gallinae* if they frequent feeding and watering places contaminated by infected pigeons (Kocan, 1969) and through contact between adults during their breeding rituals (*see* under Pigeon Family).

It has been suggested that the parasite *Trichomonas gallinae* may may have been a factor in the extinction of the passenger pigeon (Stabler and Herman, 1951)—this protozoan parasite occurs almost universally in pigeons, which are probably the primary hosts for the disease (Stabler, 1951).

According to Stabler, trichomonads can be transferred from one kind of bird to another—for example, from pigeons to the predatory hawks or falcons which feed on them. Pigeon fanciers call trichomoniasis—the resulting disease—*canker;* falconers call it *frounce*. It is a serious problem for falconers but infected captive falcons, hawks, and pigeons can be treated with Emtryl. See details in Stabler and Kitzmiller (1967) and in Kocan and Herman (1971). *See also* Falconry.

Coccidia are another group of parasitic protozoans that occur frequently in wild birds. Herman (1949) detected coccidiosis in varying intensities among California quail, and Herman *et al.* (1943) noted a relationship between the amount of infection and the kinds of food quail eat seasonally—a lower intensity of infection in summer, when quail were eating seeds, than during the rest of the year, when they were eating green plant foods.

Coccidiosis has also caused serious losses in yearling goldeneye ducks summering in Denmark (Lack, 1954), also in canvasbacks in Miss.; it also affects hawks, pelicans, cormorants, shorebirds, and other groups—Trainer (1974) states that it can and does infect almost every type of bird. *See* Coccidiosis. Blackhead, another disease of poultry and of wild gallinaceous birds, is also a tissue parasite which attacks the liver and caeca; blackhead has also been an important cause of death in wild turkeys. *See* Blackhead.

Wild birds have other internal parasites—tapeworms, flukes, roundworms (*see* Nematode), and spiny-headed (acanthocephaline) worms, all of which have varying effects on the health of birds. A common oviduct fluke, *Prosthogonimus*, of domestic fowl, which also occurs in a wide number of wild birds, may upset egg production, and could be a factor in regulating their populations (Herman, 1955). Most of these parasites (tapeworms, flukes, roundworms, etc.) also require hosts other than birds (intermediate hosts)—insects, snails, caecal worms, crustaceans, etc.—in order to complete their life cycles. *See* discussion of parasites of birds in general under Parasite.

BACTERIAL DISEASES. Bacteria (microscopic organisms) can cause destruction of birds in two ways: (1) by producing toxins and (2) by the destruction of a bird's tissues. Perhaps the best-known bacterial disease of wild birds is botulism (a form of food poisoning), in which the bacterial organism, *Clostridium botulinum* type C, produces a toxin which is highly poisonous to birds. In 1925, an estimated million birds, mostly waterfowl, died of botulism at a lake in Ore.; one to three million at Great Salt Lake, Utah, in 1929; and hundreds of thousands periodically elsewhere (Lack, 1954). *See* losses and reasons for under Botulism.

The famed disease "parrot fever," psittacosis, or ornithosis, now called chlamydiosis, was attributed until recently to a virus but the causative agent is now classified as a bacterium (Burkhart and Page, 1971). *See* Chlamydiosis.

Avian cholera (also called fowl cholera and avian pasteurellosis), unlike botulism, is not caused by bacterial poisoning but by a bacterial infection. This disease has been responsible for widespread and severe destruction of waterfowl in N. America—40,000 in Calif., winter of 1948–49; more than 60,000 in Tex., winter of 1956–57; 88,000 in Md., Feb. 1970. *See* details in Avian Cholera.

FUNGUS DISEASES. Aspergillosis, one of the most frequent of the fungus diseases of birds, is caused by *Aspergillus fumigatus*. The spores of this fungus are widely distributed in nature (see discussion by Christensen, 1951), and ground-feeding birds, including waterfowl, pick them up through contaminated feed and litter. Aspergillosis is also a serious disease of wild birds brought into captivity: it is often fatal to birds of prey kept by falconers (see discussion of it and suggested treatment for hawks in Peeters and Jameson, 1970); it has created some problems in keeping penguins in zoos, and for whooping cranes kept at the Patuxent Wildlife Research Center, U.S. Fish and Wildlife Service, Laurel, Md. *See* preventive methods under Aspergillosis.

Herman (1955) noted that aspergillosis is frequently reported in N. American birds, especially in waterfowl, gulls, and hawks. In one example, it seriously affected 10% of a flock of wood ducks which had been crowded together and had fed on spoiled (moldy) grain (Lack, 1954). Quail and other gallinaceous birds at times die from the disease (Stoddard, 1931). The infection occurs frequently in baby chicks on poultry-raising farms and is referred to as "brooder pneumonia." A bibliography of avian mycosis, or fungus diseases in birds, lists 522 references to fungi in birds (Chute, 1959). *See also* Histoplasmosis.

VIRUS DISEASES. Viruses (*see* Virus) are submicroscopic infectious agents and are capable of rapid multiplication only in living cells.

Encephalitis viruses (arboviruses) may cause infection in man, horses, birds, and reptiles, but outward signs of disease associated with arbovirus infection are not common in native N. American birds (Karstad, 1971a); however, *see* discussion of birds and other animals as reservoirs of the disease under Encephalitis Viruses.

Avian pox, sometimes called bird pox, foot pox, fowl pox, and avian diphtheria, is well known to bird-banders (*see* Banding). It is caused by a virus that is confined to birds. The disease produces warty protuberances on the feet or head of a bird, and the infections are usually mild. *See* details under Avian Pox.

Quail bronchitis, first referred to as "quail disease," an acute, highly contagious respiratory disease of bobwhite quail, is caused by a virus. See details in Du Bose (1971).

Newcastle disease is a virus-caused malady in birds and was first reported in N. America in 1944 (Herman, 1955). It is highly contagious and destructive and chiefly attacks chickens and turkeys, also guinea fowl. In addition, tests show evidence of Newcastle disease in wild Canada geese and mallards in the Mississippi Flyway (*see* flyways under Waterfowl), and there is no effective treatment for the disease. Palmer and Trainer (1971) listed 39 species of birds, worldwide, that have been known to be naturally infected with NDV (Newcastle Disease Virus). The effects of the disease on wild birds are not known, but presumably could be severe. Exotic game birds and others introduced into N. America have been proved to be a means of introducing new strains of the virus into poultry flocks (Herman, 1955). During an outbreak of NDV in Calif. in 1973, the virus was isolated from a number of different wild bird species tested there (Trainer, 1974).

Duck plague, or duck virus enteritis (DVE), is a relatively recent disease of N. American waterfowl. In the winter of 1972–73, at least 43,000 wild ducks and geese at Lake Andes National Wildlife Refuge in N.D. died within a few weeks from duck plague—it was also reported in Wisc. and in Calif. in 1972 and 1973 (Trainer, 1974). The disease has existed for the last 50 years in waterfowl in Europe, especially in the Netherlands; it was first reported in domestic waterfowl in the U.S. in 1967 among some white Peking ducks (*see* Domestication) on a Long Is., N.Y., duck farm.

The outbreak at Lake Andes was the first ever reported of epizootic proportions among wild waterfowl (Anonymous, 1973b), although it had previously been discovered in wild, free-flying waterfowl in 1969 on Long Is. and in c. N.Y., in Pa., and in Md. (Leibovitz, 1971).

Duck plague can be transmitted directly by contact between an infected and a susceptible bird, and indirectly to susceptible birds when they feed on contaminated grounds or waters. The disease is not known to affect people (Anonymous, 1973b) and, according to Leibovitz (1971), is limited to ducks, geese, and swans; all N. American waterfowl are susceptible. *See* Waterfowl. No treatment is known for duck plague, and waterfowl that have recovered from the disease are immune to reinfection (Leibovitz, 1971). For governmental efforts to control, or to limit, spread of the disease, see Anonymous (1973b). For details of these and other diseases of birds, their symptoms and methods of control, see Davis *et al.* (1971) and Biester and Schwarte (1959; 1965). For a discussion of diseases of animals and their relation to man, see especially Hull (1963). *See also* Parasite; Lead Poisoning.

DISPERSAL

Term for the spread of birds away from their original home sites or home ranges which is taking place continually (Pettingill, 1972). Lack (1954) used this term especially for the movements of young birds from their place of hatching. Hickey (1943) included, besides the dispersal of young, which in late summer, after the nesting season, may disperse in every direction —for example, young of herring gulls and black-crowned night herons and the young of little blue herons and the common egret—also the irregular irruptions southward of northern birds such as snowy owls, red crossbills, glaucous and Iceland gulls, goshawks, redpolls, pine and evening grosbeaks, and Bohemian waxwings. *See* discussion of these and others under Irruption; Cycle; Flight Years; *see also* Emigration; Fall Shuffle. *See* especially biography of the evening grosbeak in Finch Family.

Hickey also included another kind of dispersal in which birds are scattered into new regions, far from their regular ranges, by hurricanes—about three or four occur every year in the West Indies from Aug. to Oct. These have sent black-capped petrels of the southern seas and tropical frigatebirds northward; also the yellow-billed tropic-bird to several places in Vt.; greater and Cory's shearwaters inland in Mass.; and the pelagic Wilson's petrels far inland north to Montreal and to Lake Ontario. *See* discussions of some of these under Seabird; *see also* Weather.

A migrating flock of fieldfares (*see* in Thrush Family), carried in a gale in Jan. 1937 from Europe to Greenland, was thus accidentally established in N. America; a colony of the smooth-billed anis was established at Clewiston, Fla., in 1946 after a hurricane had apparently carried them there (*see* in Cuckoo Family); the cattle egret, however, may have established itself by flying across the Atlantic from the Old World (*see* history in its biography in Heron Family; see also evidence by Bowen and Nicholls, 1968). However, of thousands of small N. American birds that have been carried out to sea in migration, and boarded ships that took them to Europe, none became established there. *See* Introduced Birds.

DISPERSAL OF YOUNG. In general, the spread or dispersal of birds has been brought about by the young rather than by the adults (Lack, 1954). Adults, if they survive the winter, usually return to the same nest-site area (*see* examples in The Pair Bond under Courtship; and especially in Return to Nest Sites and Wintering Places under Banding; *also* under Waterfowl). Population pressures promote range expansions by young birds, which have a tendency to strike out in all directions (*postnatal wandering*) to explore their world. This is like a search for new territory to inhabit, and every new generation adds to the competition for food, nest sites, and territory, although daily and annual mortality (*see* Mortality) and hunting seasons on game species take a large toll, and the younger birds that survive must still compete with entrenched older ones. This wanderlust of first-year birds is apparently an adaptive device for finding new or less populated places to inhabit (Welty, 1962). Juveniles of many species of birds gradually leave the nest locality where they were hatched and raised, after becoming independent of the care

range of the snowy owl

DISPERSAL

Snowy owls prey upon lemmings, voles, and hares in the Arctic tundra. The periodic decline of the lemming population drives the snowy owl farther south in irregular migrations, or irruptions, to avoid starvation.

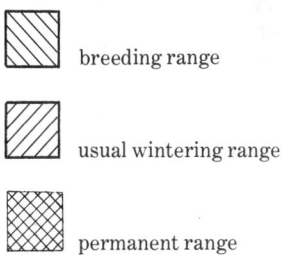

breeding range

usual wintering range

permanent range

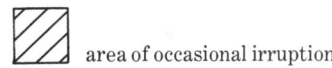

area of occasional irruption

of parent birds. The young often congregate in loose roving bands or in groups of immatures of the same species. This dispersal is often sparked by the parent birds, which may actually drive away the young, as in song sparrows noted by Nice (1943). *See* Young and Their Care; *also* Distribution. *See also* some examples in biographies of the willet and American woodcock in Sandpiper Family; *see also* biography of the Canada goose in Duck Family and discussion under Waterfowl.

DISPERSION

Term for the spread of each species of bird over the suitable habitats within its range (Lack, 1954). Every habitat has a limit to the numbers of birds it may support, but in general, the more variable and lush the plant life, along with potential food and nesting sites, the richer the bird life. *See* Carrying Capacity; Distribution. See especially results of the breeding bird censuses for various types of habitats published in the December issues of *Audubon Field Notes* and *American Birds. See also* Census; Populations.

DISPHARYNX

See Nematode.

DISPLACEMENT ACTIVITY

Occasionally a bird, under the influence of two or more conflicting tendencies, will behave in a manner irrelevant to the situation confronting it. Thus two fighting European titmice may suddenly break off their attacks and peck vigorously at the buds of a tree, and courting ducks may suddenly abandon their courtship tactics and preen their wing feathers (Hinde, 1961). *See* Preening.

This type of inappropriate behavior, also called "substitute activity," is termed by bird behaviorists *displacement activity.* (*See* Types of Behavior under Behavior.) Displacement activities of birds—though they look genuine—are often lacking in some essential: displacement copulation is always abortive; in displacement nest building, the twigs are never worked into the nest; in displacement bathing, the bird never gets wet (Armstrong, 1942). See also Balda and Bateman (1973).

The analyses of the nature of displacement activities are still speculative. "A highly excited bird's actions may be as senseless [futile?] as when a frantic child bangs his head against the wall" (Armstrong, 1942). A captive wren, exasperated because he could not get at his fancied rival (his own image in a mirror) hammered a branch with his bill; a furious oystercatcher attacked a bush; and falcons, angered but fearful of human beings near the nest, will attack and kill other birds passing near the eyrie. *See also* "displacement tapping" of woodpeckers under Drumming.

Displacement activities in bird behavior were recognized and independently analyzed by two European ornithologists, A. Kortlandt and Niko Tinbergen. Of the phenomenon, Tinbergen (1951a) wrote: "An examination of the conditions under which displacement activities usually occur led to the conclusion that, in all known cases, there is a surplus of motivation, the discharge of which through the normal paths is in some way prevented. The most usual situations are: (1) conflict of two strongly activated antagonistic drives; (2) strong motivation of a drive, usually the sexual drive, together with lack of external stimuli required for the release of the consummatory acts belonging to that drive."

DISPLAY

Term for ritualized postures, movements, or vocalizations that usually serve birds in communicating with others; includes threat displays, those of submission, food-begging, pair forming, nest relief, flock integration, etc. (Hinde, 1964a). *See* Courtship; Language; Sexual Dimorphism; Territory; *also* Distraction Display.

DISRUPTIVE PATTERN

See Colors of Feathers.

DISTAL

Farthest from the trunk or midline (center) of the body of a bird; the term is often used when referring to parts of the feet. It is the opposite of *proximal.*

DISTRACTION DISPLAY

Term of behaviorists for a special display by birds in which they often appear to be sick or crippled and cannot fly strongly—"the broken-wing trick," "crippled-bird act," "lure display," or "injury feigning." Its function directs the attention of a predator away from the nest or young and toward the adult bird (Hinde, 1961). It is usually most elaborate in birds that nest in the open on the ground, where nests, eggs, and young are more vulnerable than those of tree-nesting species. See Barash (1975) for a recent discussion of it.

The distraction displays of various birds range from the exact simulation of injury or illness to crude, inappropriate, and even disadvantageous inhibitions of normal movements. Hann (1953) described it: "In the more typical cases the bird moves slowly away from the person, or other animal, spreading and dragging its wings and tail, or tumbling along as if partly helpless. If followed, it keeps out of reach and increases the distance between it and the pursuer as it gets farther from the nest, until finally, when at a considerable distance, it flies away in a perfectly normal manner. In less typical cases the bird may not act as if injured, but may perform quick actions which draw attention from the nest or perhaps from the young while they make good their escape."

Rat run, or *rodent run,* is a type of distraction behavior of certain tundra species, especially in the purple sandpiper, which jumps into view a few feet from the nest, then zigzags away, crouched low and hunched over. The wings are dropped and appear like hind legs, the feathers fluffed and appear like fur, and the bird utters mouselike squeaks (Duffy *et al.,* 1950). *See also* Towhee, green-tailed, in Finch Family. A flaw in the purple sandpiper's display in luring away a human intruder is that, if not pursued, it rushes back and repeats its performance all over, whistling this time for attention; however, this behavior is rather sure to lure away a fox or weasel.

DISTRACTION DISPLAY
A killdeer's simulation of a broken wing draws an intruder away from its nest.

Distraction behavior has been noted in groups of birds from ostriches to sparrows and is especially common in ground-nesting birds, whose young may be either altricial or precocial. *See* Altricial. Konrad Lorenz has called particular attention to the difference between the broken-winged behavior of wild ducks and partridges and the distraction display of small warblers, which, as a rule, act as though they are ill in their displays, rather than injured.

Birds rarely give the distraction display unless they are anxious over an intruder (man or other animal) near the nest and eggs or young. The reaction is most usual when the eggs are well incubated, or when the young are about to leave the nest or have just left the nest.

That fear in a bird is significant in the distraction display has been shown by Lorenz (1935), who found that he could not induce tame or semi-tame birds to give the distraction display. They had become habituated to man. In analyzing the distraction display and its evolution in birds, some bird behaviorists believe that the injured-bird or ill-bird act is formed as a result of conflicting tendencies within the bird itself— its fear reaction to flee from the predator threatening its eggs or young, its aggressive reaction to attack the predator, and possibly its urge to return to the nest to incubate its eggs or brood its young (Hinde, 1961). This is said to result in the bird's floundering action. Other behaviorists, particularly Simmons (1955), a British ornithologist, believe that distraction displays are not expressions of thwarted drives *at present* and are clearly ritualized into a specific action of survival value to the eggs or young of the birds that practice it.

Armstrong (1942) has assembled many examples of the survival value of the distraction display to birds: wild mallards lure away foxes from their nests, and mallards, gadwalls, and blue-winged teals successfully lure dogs from their ducklings. A pintail has been known to lure away coyote; a curlew gave a distraction display that drew a fox away from its nest; and so on.

The red knot, a species of sandpiper, successfully decoys dogs, foxes, and weasels from its chicks, and the Texas nighthawk "injury-feigns" at the approach of a man near its nest and tries to draw him away. The killdeer will fly toward an approaching man or a dog, and display on the ground a short distance ahead of the intruder, but if a horse or a cow approaches its nest, which is on the ground and often in pastures, it changes its tactics. Apparently "knowing" that this type of intruder cannot be *led* away, it flies up into the face of the animal until it turns it away from the nest. The male surfbird (a shorebird) incubates the eggs, and when a mountain sheep *(Ovis)* or a man steps close to its nest, the incubating bird "explodes" into the face of either man or sheep (Dixon, 1927c).

DISTRIBUTION

Birds live in almost every part of the world— from the oceans and highest mountains to tropical swamps and deserts. From their centers of origin, they have evolved and spread out to adapt themselves to almost every available environment.

According to Griscom (1945), 85% of the species and subspecies of birds in the world live in tropical regions; only 15% live in temperate or cold climates. Two thirds of all birds in the tropics live in *humid* rather than arid climates. In S. America, high mountains rising from a tropical base have produced the most varied and concentrated birdlife on earth. In Ecuador and Colombia, in passing from the tropical base of the Andes to the highest peaks, one travels through four climatic belts, or "life zones," each with its own quite different birds and plants. "The resultant wealth of bird-life concentrated in a relatively small total mileage is the greatest in the world. The total distance across Ecuador, as the crow flies, is about 240 miles, but if we took a year on the journey, and stopped in each life zone for a reasonable period of time, we would find a possible total of 1,780 species of birds" (Griscom, 1945).

In the humid American tropics, the annual rainfall is 80–120 in. (200–300 in. a year in Colombia), which is more or less dispersed throughout the year, and produces the dense rain forest where birdlife is so varied. Many tropical birds do not migrate; the nesting season is throughout the year; and there is an abundant and easily procured food supply throughout much of the year. As an example of the wealth of tropical birdlife, there are 1,100 species in the lower third of the Amazon in S. America. In e. Costa Rica, one might see 400 species of birds within an area 10 mi. in diameter, and more species in Panama than in the whole continent of N. America north of Mexico, in spite of the fact that Panama is approximately the size of N.Y. (Griscom, 1945).

WHAT LIMITS BIRDLIFE FARTHER NORTH? As one leaves the tropics and goes northward, the variety of birdlife grows less. Mountain ranges there do not offer the variety of birdlife of those of the tropics because the lowlands on each side, instead of being tropical, are in the temperate zone, including the whole mountain range itself. However, in N. America, where there are fewer species of birds, there may be tremendous numbers. In some of the coastal seabird colonies and in ibis and heron rookeries, often consisting of only one or a few species, there may be hundreds of thousands of birds. *See* Bird City.

In N. America there are only three climates that are markedly different—the arctic, the arid desert, and the mildly temperate. Even the loftiest mountain ranges in N. America cannot produce the factors of isolation such as the mountains of Ecuador, which may have their tops in the alpine zone and bases in a tropical humid zone. According to Griscom (1945), the recent Ice Age and our present rigorous uniform climate accounts for a mere (by comparison with the humid tropics) 650 species of birds, excluding accidentals and foreign visitors on the N. American continent. *See* North America for defined limits.

ZONATION OF BIRDLIFE—SOUTH TO NORTH. The principal zones of birdlife, from the tropics northward, are: (1) the tropics themselves, in which bird species are very numerous; (2) the north temperate zone, in which birds are fewer

in species than in the tropics but may be in tremendous numbers; and (3) the subarctic and arctic zone, in which land birds are very few, but in which there is a unique concentration of breeding of mostly migratory water birds and shorebirds. The boundaries between these zones are not sharp (Darlington, 1957).

HOW DID BIRDS GET WHERE THEY ARE? Although the ranges of N. American birds in summer and in winter, and their migration routes, are now fairly well known, if we ask *why* birds are where they are today, and how they got there, it may be difficult or even impossible to answer with absolute certainty. Or why some birds are restricted to a single island or a particular habitat while others may be worldwide. For example, the two most widespread species of birds in the world are the osprey, which breeds on every continent except S. America, and the barn owl, which breeds on every continent but does not live in *large parts* of several continents.

In any large land mass—continent or island —the bird fauna or *avifauna* is a complex of species that have originated in the region; or have arrived there from adjacent areas or regions at different periods in geological history, including recent centuries. In order to postulate how any avifauna has evolved, it is necessary to learn the area's geological history, investigate its bird species of the past by examining fossil records (see Fossil Birds), and "analyze its present-day avifauna for clues as to where different kinds of birds came from and how they reached their present ranges" (Pettingill, 1956).

The distribution of birds as we know it in the world today has been influenced by time, or past history (geological); by physical barriers that have restricted the movements of birds; by climate and the ecological, or environmental, conditions that birds can tolerate; and by their own mobility, or power of flight. Almost everyone has some idea of both the geographical and ecological distribution of birds—geographically, penguins are associated with the Antarctic, ptarmigans with the Arctic, and hummingbirds (most species) with tropical or subtropical parts of North and South America. Ecologically, or with reference to their chosen habitats (see Habitat), we associate ducks with water, woodpeckers with trees, and bobolinks, meadowlarks, and other so-called "field birds" with fields, prairies, or grassland (Wallace, 1963).

BARRIERS BIRDS CAN'T OR WON'T CROSS. Birds (and dinosaurs) are descendants of thecodont reptiles (see Origin of Birds and of Bird Flight under Fossil Birds) but evolved feathers, warm-bloodedness, and the ability to fly. Feathers and high body temperatures enable birds to stand considerable cold (see Cold and Birds; Metabolism), which, along with flight, has facilitated their dispersal over the world. Northward some birds may reach no absolute limit until they reach the end of land, and seabirds may feed or wander far beyond land (Darlington, 1957). Yet there are physical and ecological barriers that some birds will not, or

winter

breeding

permanent

DISTRIBUTION

Range maps plot the total area in which a species may be found, including its winter range and its breeding and nesting grounds, and make it possible to determine what geographic barriers or climactic factors may affect the distribution of a species. Ornithologists use range maps to record how a bird has extended its range over time, or—as in the case of the endangered peregrine falcon—how a range has been reduced.

North American range of the peregrine falcon

cannot, breach, which accounts for the uneven distribution of birds over the earth.

Seabirds are limited by large bodies of land, and land birds by large bodies of water. A large forest area may be a barrier to the spread of grassland birds (larks, for example), and grassland a barrier to the dispersal of a forest bird (a wood warbler, for example). What serves as a barrier to one kind of bird, however, may be an avenue of travel to another. *See* Barrier.

A mountain range may effectively block further spreading of a bird species that lives on open plains, but it may help to disperse and spread others that are restricted to living in mountains. The dippers of the mountain streams of w. N. America have spread throughout the Rockies, but are believed to have been blocked from reaching the Appalachians of e. U.S. by the formidable broad barrier of the Great Plains (Wallace, 1963).

Wide stretches of water are not barriers to seabirds, which are distributed over the oceans of the world. Some land birds can fly across wide areas of water or over high mountains, but not all birds do. Not only flightless birds but many that can fly are often stopped by moderate stretches of open water. For example, several families of C. and S. American birds—tinamous, cracids, puffbirds, toucans, manakins, and others—will not cross water gaps to get to the West Indies; on the other hand, tiny hummingbirds and wood warblers and the relatively small tyrant flycatchers have crossed the water to spread widely over the islands (Darlington, 1957).

Even large rivers may be a barrier to some birds. The Amazon and its tributaries have broken up the ranges of many S. American forest species, as large rivers and lakes have done elsewhere in the world (Mayr, 1942). Why some land birds habitually cross water barriers and others with equal flying ability do not is difficult to explain.

HISTORY OF NORTH AMERICAN BIRD FAUNA.

Our N. American bird fauna is not stable; it is a temporary assemblage of birds formed in the course of time, some of it recently, by the complex movements of many birds in many directions. It is destined to be partly scattered or destroyed, added to, and re-formed continually (Darlington, 1957). It is one of six main faunal, or zoogeographic, regions of the world that are now generally accepted by zoogeographers: (1) the *Nearctic Region* (the area of the N. American continent, except the tropical part of Mexico and C. America), containing the N. American fauna; (2) the *Neotropical Region* of S. and C. America, including the tropical part of s. Mexico; (3) the *Ethiopian Region*, or Africa (except the northern border and including a part of se. Arabia); (4) the *Oriental Region* (the Indian Region of some of the older zoogeographers) of tropical Asia, with associated continental islands; (5) the *Palearctic Region*, or Eurasia above the tropics and including the northern border of Africa; and (6) the *Australian Region*, which includes Australia, New Guinea, Tasmania, and Polynesia (Darlington, 1957). *See* Faunal Regions.

Darlington (1957) has provided a very interesting summary of the various sources from

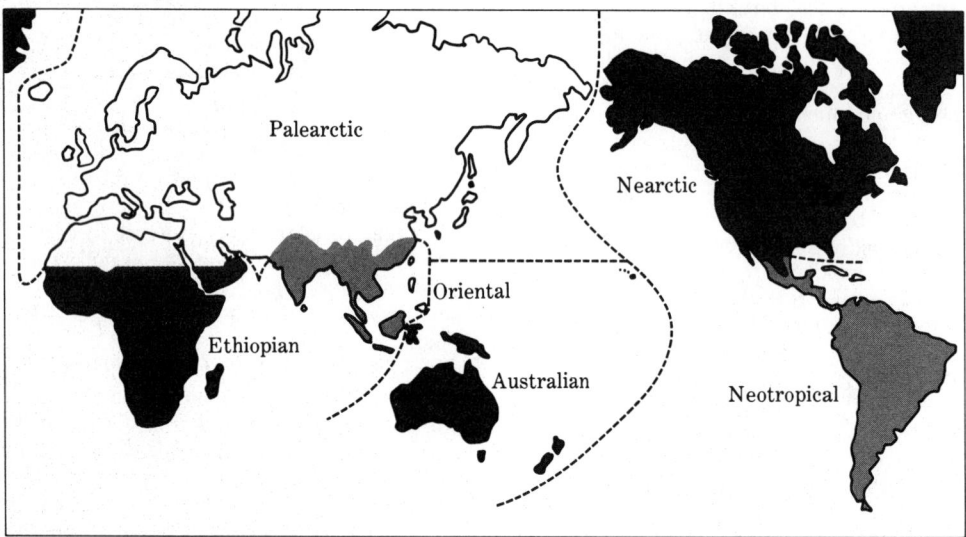

the zoogeographic regions of the world

which some of the birds in our N. American fauna came. The scarlet tanagers and crested flycatchers that spend their summers in the U.S. and Canada originated, not long ago in geologic time, in the rain forests of C. and S. America; our belted kingfishers, possibly in the tropics of the Old World; our eagles and falcons, and some of our hawks, may have come from the Old World rather recently by way of Eurasia; our vultures, probably from tropical America; but our genus *Buteo*, containing our splendid red-tailed hawk, red-shouldered hawk, broad-winged hawk, and others, may be N. American and can be traced back on this continent some 30 million years. *See* Geological Time Scale; Fossil Birds. Yet, since the genus is widespread in Asia and Africa, we cannot be sure it evolved in N. America.

Our barn swallow's ancestors came from Europe and Asia, as did the ancient forebears of our American robin (a thrush); our chickadees and titmice, goldfinches and crossbills, jays and crows, and many other songbirds from Europe and Asia. Tropical America has given us mockingbirds and thrashers; wrens, one of which, the winter wren, has spread across Asia and Europe ,and is now considered the only wren in the Old World; vireos, wood warblers, orioles, blackbirds, cardinals, many American sparrows, and others.

Mayr (1946a) analyzed the N. American bird fauna (*see* Nearctic Region) southward to the edge of the tropical American rain forest. He traced the geological history of N. America—the coastline was not always as it is today—for example, there is good evidence that a land bridge existed intermittently across the Bering Strait, which linked Asia with N. America, and there were oceanic waters over what is now C. America, which intermittently separated N. America from S. America. N. America is now separated from Asia by only a narrow oceanic strait; N. and C. America are now connected by a narrow, 50-mile-wide strip of land, the Isthmus of Panama. See discussion of continental drift theory and early distribution of birds by Vuilleumier (1975).

These separations and connections in geologic time of the N. American faunal area with those of adjoining faunal areas in Asia and S. America required a study of their history, both geologically and climatically, for a full understanding of the faunal history of N. America. From his studies and analyses, Mayr went on to show that the N. American bird fauna has seven "elements" or links with its origin. They are: (1) A *Panboreal Element* of families of birds—loons (Gavidae); auks, murres, and puffins (Alcidae); phalaropes (Phalaropodidae); and many other groups of shorebirds—that are well represented in the northern parts of N. America and the Old World, which possibly originated in the Old World, (2) an *Old World Element* of cranes, pigeons, cuckoos, owls, certain crows and jays, wagtails and pipits, shrikes, and many other songbirds; (3) a *North American Element* of grouse, American quail, turkeys, vireos, wood warblers, wrens, silky flycatchers, and others; (4) a *Pan American Element* of birds of S. American origin, such as hummingbirds, tyrant flycatchers, and blackbirds (Icteridae), which may have "island-

hopped" during the Tertiary from S. to N. America; (5) a *South American Element*, of which a few representatives of some of the well-developed families such as the cotingas have reached the N. American fauna (apparently tinamous, screamers, hoatzins, trumpeters, sun bitterns, antbirds, manakins, and some fringillids such as the cardinals, also originated in S. America); (6) a *Pantropical Element*, composed of birds common to both New and Old World tropics, such as the parrots (Psittacidae) and trogons (Trogonidae) among land birds.

Mayr offers interesting speculation as to where the parent stock of such geographically widely separated New and Old World families originated. He concluded with (7) an *Unanalyzed Element*, composed of most oceanic birds—penguins, boobies and gannets, frigatebirds, gulls and terns, and others—also shorebirds, and freshwater, partly marine birds—grebes, pelicans, cormorants, herons, ducks, geese, swans, and others, whose origin may always remain in doubt.

WHERE DO BIRDS LIVE? The seasons of the year—spring, summer, autumn, and winter—cause a marked shift in the distribution and abundance of many species of N. American birds. *See* Census; Christmas Bird Count; Populations. See especially past issues of *Audubon Field Notes*, now called *American Birds*. These changes in the distribution of birds cause changes in their status. Those that travel from their southern wintering grounds northward in spring to nest, spend the summer, and then migrate southward again in the fall, are called *summer residents*. Those that pass through a region during their northward and southward migrations in spring and fall are termed *transients*. Those that arrive in the U.S. in fall from farther north (after the nesting season), spend the winter, then return northward again in spring, are *winter residents*. Those that do not migrate periodically, and usually remain in the same general area year-round, are *permanent residents*.

The resident or transient status of any species of N. American bird depends, then, on the place and time of the year in which the bird is seen; also on the altitude at which it is seen in high mountains, where many birds may have seasonal altitudinal (up and down) migrations. *See* Altitudinal Distribution; Migration. Because the seasonal status of birds is often local, or at most regional, bird-watchers throughout much of N. America have compiled local checklists, which list not only the species of birds one might see in the area but also the seasonal status of each throughout the year. *See* Check-list; Birder.

RANGES OF BIRDS. The total area in which a bird normally may be seen at different times of the year constitutes its *range*. When a bird species is migratory, such as ducks, geese, swans, cranes, plovers, sandpipers, warblers, tanagers, and hundreds of others, it is usual to divide its range into a *breeding range*, where it nests and raises its young, and a *wintering range*, where it spends the winter. *See* in the biographies of each bird. On the N. American

continent, breeding ranges of migratory birds are usually north of the wintering range. The A.O.U. *Check-list of North American Birds* gives the details of the ranges for each species.

The ranges of most N. American birds, although molded by past history—the changes brought about in the contours of the continent, separation or connection with other land areas, the action of glaciers, and shifts in climate—are not fixed but fluctuating. Wing (1956) has summarized some of the changes or expansions in the ranges of N. American birds. Several have been spreading northward (perhaps temporarily); these include the cardinal, mockingbird, Carolina wren, tufted titmouse, and red-bellied woodpecker. The great black-backed gull has spread *southward* along the Atlantic coast, also the herring gull; and the American robin, song sparrow, chestnut-sided warbler, and house wren have spread south into Ga., apparently because of an increase or spread in cultivation (Odum and Burleigh, 1946; also Odum and Johnston, 1951).

Rainfall, temperature, and humidity may vary gradually from place to place each year, and by producing changes in plant life (habitat) may determine whether a species increases or decreases its range. Also, man's drastic and widespread changes in the environment have caused enormous changes in the species, numbers, and distribution of birds. *See* Adaptations to Mankind.

HABITAT CHOICES OF BIRDS. Within its general range, each species of bird lives within an environment called its habitat. Simpson *et al.* (1957) have compared the communities in which birds and other animals live with the Chinese boxes or wooden eggs (the playthings of children) wherein upon opening one, there is a smaller one within, and a smaller one within that one, and so on. The biggest box is the earth, and the next-smaller one the environment in which large or broad communities of animals live, and there are even environments within environments (microclimates), each with its typical plant and animal life. The refinements of some of these environments for the needs of some birds have been cited by Wing (1956). In one study, an apparently small factor such as the limb density just below the forest crown in certain woodlands limited its use by least flycatchers. (If the habitat, just below the crowns of the trees, was not at least 30% open, few least flycatchers used it.)

MAJOR BIOTIC COMMUNITIES. In N. America north of Mexico, ecologists have described nine *major* biotic communities (called *biomes* by some authorities). Each has its own dominant kind of plant life, for which each community is named, and each is characterized by certain birds confined there or by those birds that show a definite preference for it during the breeding season. Pitelka (1941) has listed these biotic communities with their typical birdlife (see also Pettingill, 1970; 1972). They are: *Tundra; Coniferous Forest* (taiga); *Deciduous Forest; Grassland; Southwestern Oak Woodland; Pinyon-Juniper; Chaparral; Sagebrush;* and *Scrub Desert.* Each of these has been further subdivided and there are *ecotones* where one

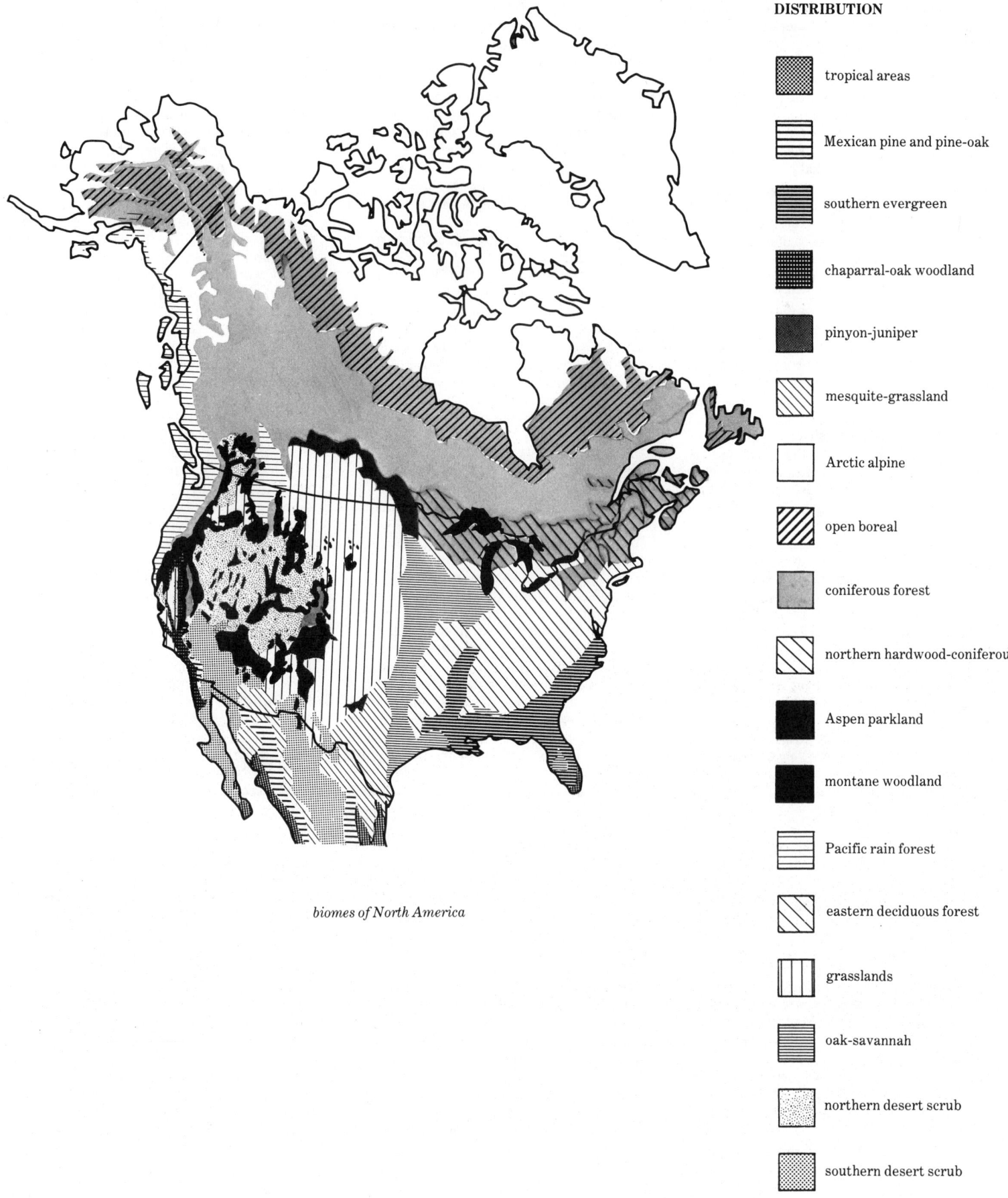

DISTRIBUTION

- tropical areas
- Mexican pine and pine-oak
- southern evergreen
- chaparral-oak woodland
- pinyon-juniper
- mesquite-grassland
- Arctic alpine
- open boreal
- coniferous forest
- northern hardwood-coniferous
- Aspen parkland
- montane woodland
- Pacific rain forest
- eastern deciduous forest
- grasslands
- oak-savannah
- northern desert scrub
- southern desert scrub

biomes of North America

community gives way to another and the plant and animal life is mixed or blended with plants and animals from the adjacent biomes. *See* Ecotone; Ecological Niche.

LIFE ZONES. Many authorities in N. America follow the older concept of life zones instead of biotic communities in mapping the ecological distribution of birds. In each life zone there are certain characteristic species of birds and other animals that are designated as zonal indicators. There are six major life zones, from north to south: the Arctic, Hudsonian, Canadian, Transition, Upper Austral, and Lower Austral. Some of the life zones are further subdivided, longitudinally, on the basis of prevailing moisture and have been given additional names. See discussion by Merriam (1894; 1898) and by Pettingill (1970; 1972).

The limits of these zones of birdlife are based upon certain lines across the continent from east to west or west to east (isothermal lines) which have the same temperature during the same period of the year. In the final analysis, however, life zones are shaped by the control that temperature and humidity have upon plant life and, in turn, the role of certain types of plant life as environments in attracting certain kinds or groups of birds. For a critical and valuable assessment of life zones, biotic provinces, and biomes as ecological systems for classifying the distribution of birds, see Ch. 8 in Amadon (1966b); see also Kendeigh (1954).

According to Pettingill (1970), most ornithologists recognize the inadequacy of life zones in mapping the ecological distribution of birds continent-wide.

DISTRIBUTION OF MARINE BIRDS. The separation of land masses during geologic time had little bearing on the seabird faunas (Mayr, 1946a). According to Serventy (1960), two principal factors govern their distribution: the availability of food and the presence of island or coastal mainland nesting sites. The abundance of food for seabirds in polar seas accounts for the high density of their populations at latitudes where the severity of the climate allows only a comparatively small land bird population.

Mayr (1946a) classified seabirds into three major groups: a southern one (Antarctic), a tropical one (of southern oceans), and a northern one, which is essentially the same as the geographic areas of marine faunas of the marine biologists.

The most distinctive birds of the *Northern Marine Region* are the auks (Alcidae), the only group of family level restricted to the region. The majority of auks live in the N. Pacific, but there has been some slight penetration of the tropics by one—the Craveri's murrelet, which breeds in the Gulf of California. Among the poorly represented petrel group in the Northern Marine Region, the fulmar is the most numerous and widespread. Gulls and terns are well represented, along with four species of skuas and the northern gannet.

Several groups—skuas, albatrosses, and fulmars—live in both northern and southern waters, but not in tropical waters. Past climatic changes may have made this possible; or merely migration and accidental wandering of these birds. Thus, some albatrosses, essentially southern cold-water birds, have established themselves in the N. Pacific. *See* Albatross Family. The fulmar is one of several petrels that have done likewise.

Besides the references cited in this article, there is considerable information about the distribution of N. American birds in back issues of the periodicals *Bird-Lore*, *Audubon Magazine*, and *American Birds* (formerly *Audubon Field Notes*). See also *Conservation of Marine Birds of Northern North America*, U.S. Dept. Interior, Fish and Wildlife Service Wildlife Research Report II, Washington, D.C., 1979.

DIURNAL
Term for birds that are most active in broad daylight. *See* Nocturnal; Crepuscular.

DIVE-DAPPER
See Pied-billed grebe in Grebe Family.

DIVER
See in Loon Family.

DIVERGENT EVOLUTION
See Convergent Evolution.

DIVING
See Swimming and Diving.

DIVING DUCK
See under Duck Family; *also* Swimming and Diving.

DIVING-PETREL FAMILY
See Procellariiformes.

DODO
(DOH-doh). *See* Columbiformes.

DOE-BIRD
See Curlew, Eskimo, in Sandpiper Family.

DOMESTICATION
It might be said that the taming of the young of wild birds is a first step in raising them in captivity; however, the taming of a few individuals of a species does not mean that they can be bred successfully in captivity and then put to economic use by man. Relatively few species have been truly domesticated, perhaps fewer than ten according to Allen (1925).

WHAT IS TRUE DOMESTICATION? Any bird or other animal is said to be domesticable when it can be tamed and will live in or around man's home under his care. However, domestication today implies considerably more. According to William G. Conway (1962), Director of the Bronx Zoo of the New York Zoological Society, it implies bringing about a change in the wild form, usually by human selection of birds and their controlled breeding in captivity. Thus, domestic chickens, ducks, turkeys, certain geese, and other birds have been changed from the original wild bird to one that may be heavier for meat production, a better layer of eggs, or of different form or color for increased beauty, feather production, and so on, all for man's benefit.

The wild jungle fowl, ancestor of the barnyard fowl, the wild mallard and the Muscovy duck, the European greylag goose (progenitor of many varieties of barnyard geese), the swan goose of China (progenitor of the domestic "Chinese goose"), the wild turkey (ancestor of the domesticated turkey), guineafowl, or "guinea hens," and pigeons are some of our commonly known domesticated birds. Each of these has been changed in form or color by selective breeding in captivity. Peafowl have been domesticated more for their beauty than for their economic usefulness.

HISTORY OF SOME DOMESTICATED BIRDS. According to Jull (1927), domestic fowl (chickens), because of their small size, as compared with many other domestic animals, and because of their adaptability to a wide variety of climates, have entered into the interests of more human beings possibly than any other animal. Both the cock and the dog were sacred animals in the religion of Zoroaster, and a verse attributed to Chanakya, written about 300 B.C., says that four things may be learned of a cock: to fight, to get up early, to eat with your family, and to protect your spouse when she gets into trouble. The cock was once regarded as the possessor of many mystic qualities which, in the bird's different parts, gave sterling qualities or protection to the eater. In China the cock was esteemed primarily as an edible bird; in Persia as an object of sacrifice; in India and Greece as a fighter extraordinary; and among many peoples as a creature of great religious significance.

According to Jull (1927), domestication of the cock in China dates as early as 1400 B.C. or possibly earlier; Clark (1948) wrote that the cock was first introduced into China from Burma or adjacent lands some 3,300 years ago, according to Chinese accounts. Zeuner (1963) believed that full domestication took place about 2000 B.C.

DUCKS. The meat of ducks has been esteemed by mankind since the dawn of the human race. Duck bones have been discovered from the Stone Age and in Egyptian monuments along with drawings of ducks dating from 3000 to 1000 B.C. These depicted the wild birds being caught in nets or killed by boomerangs (Jull, 1930). The wild mallard is the ancestor of all breeds of domestic ducks, with the exception of the Muscovy, a wild duck of C. and S. America, which has also been domesticated. According to Phillips (1922), the first attempt at domesticating the mallard was among the Romans during the lifetime of Varro and Columella, when ducks were fattened for food.

The Muscovy, *Cairina moschata* (see in Duck Family), apparently was first domesticated in Brazil and other parts of S. America (Jull, 1930). Delacour (1959) reported that in the 16th century Spanish explorers found that Indians in Colombia and Peru had domesticated the Muscovy, and according to Phillips (1922), it was taken by early European explorers from America to Europe and introduced there about the middle of the 16th century. It has lost favor as a general-utility bird in England and America because it cannot compete with the white Pekin duck, a descendant of the wild mallard developed in China (Phillips, 1922). The Pekin is the "Long Island duckling" of the epicurist.

GEESE. Naturalists agree that the wild European greylag goose, *Anser anser*, is the ancestor of all the barnyard geese of today, except the Chinese goose, which was developed, by selective breeding, from the Asiatic swan goose, *Anser cygnoides*. The swan goose was probably domesticated in China more than 3,000 years ago (Delacour, 1954). Apparently it is not known when the European greylag goose was first domesticated, but Allen (1925) believed it dates from very early times, perhaps in the latter part of the Stone Age. Zeuner (1963) believed there is no doubt that geese were kept by European man from Neolithic times onward.

TURKEYS. The wild turkey, *Meleagris gallapavo*, of N. America and the Mexican table-land, is the only bird of the New World (except the Muscovy duck) that has been truly domesticated—that is, changed in form from the wild bird. According to Schorger (1966), when Francisco Hernández de Córdoba discovered Yucatán, he had opportunities of seeing the wild turkey, which according to Jull (1930) had already been bred in captivity by the natives there. See history of the discovery of the domesticated wild turkey in Mexico in ch. 1 of Schorger (1966). According to Jull, the Mexican turkey was first introduced into Spain in 1519 and from there the domesticated bird spread throughout continental Europe and England, where it was introduced in 1524. *See also* introduction to Turkey Family.

GUINEAFOWL. The widely distributed guineafowl, or "guinea hen," an important domesticated bird throughout the world, is descended from the common guinea hen, *Numida meleagris*, one of seven known species of the family (Numididae), which is restricted to Africa and Madagascar (Gilliard, 1958). Guineafowl are related to pheasants and other fowl-like birds, although males and females, unlike pheasants, have plumage almost alike. According to Jull (1930), it is the only breed of domestic poultry that had its origin in Africa; it was brought by the Portuguese to Europe toward the end of the Middle Ages; however, according to Zeuner (1963), it reached Greece sometime before the 5th century B.C. The Portuguese called it the *pintada*, or painted bird; the English called it "Guinea fowl," or the fowl of Guinea (West Africa). According to Allen (1925), it was carried to the West Indies in the days of the slave trade and even now is found wild on some of these islands, particularly Haiti. See varieties in Palmer, E.L. (1949).

PIGEONS. The rock dove, or common street pigeon, *Columba livia*, was developed in domestication from the wild rock dove of Eurasia and was apparently the first bird to be domesticated. Zeuner (1963) thinks it likely that the Neolithic, or New Stone Age, people bred domestic pigeons, but the earliest proof is in the terra-cotta figurines from the Halafian period in Iraq, dated about 4500 B.C.

In the beginning, man raised pigeons in captivity for their meat and later for their homing and message-carrying abilities. The ancient Romans were said to have used them to carry back to Rome the news of Caesar's conquest of Gaul, and word of Napoleon's defeat at Waterloo reached England by carrier pigeon four days in advance of the news carried there by horse and ship. Homing pigeons kept Alexander the Great's capital informed of the progress of his conquests. They campaigned with Cyrus the Younger, Hannibal, and Scipio, and flew the results of the Olympic games throughout Greece. By the 16th century, there were pigeon postal services that the public could use for a fee (Terres, 1947b).

In World War I, about 5,000 pigeons were used by the American forces; in World War II, they were highly useful in modern warfare and 36,000 American pigeons served overseas, one of which, the most famous, "G.I. Joe," received the Dickin Medal for saving an Allied-occupied Italian village from bombing. The Dickin Medal was an award for animals serving with conspicuous "gallantry" in wartime (Terres, 1947b).

PEAFOWL (PEACOCK AND PEAHEN). Peafowl (*see* introduction to Pheasant Family) live in the wild in se. Asia, and have been raised in captivity since ancient times. For breeding in captivity, see Delacour (1951); see also Delacour (1964).

According to Jull (1930), possibly the first mentions of the "peacock" outside of the Orient were biblical references to this ornamental bird in I Kings 10:22 and II Chronicles 9:21. The Phoenicians brought peafowl from India to the Pharaohs of Egypt. Aristotle stated that Alexander the Great introduced the birds into Greece, and in the 14th century peafowl were in France, Germany, and England. Early Christians adopted the peafowl as a symbol of immortality, and Allen (1925) wrote that King Solomon first imported the peacock into Palestine and that it has always been used as a symbol of pride. See also Palmer, E. L. (1949).

In the wild, peafowl live in groups, usually in dry open forest, and while going to roost, usually in tall trees, they bugle or call loudly as they move gradually upward in their roosts during the afternoon (Gilliard, 1958). On the Palos Verdes Pen., in Calif., peafowl were introduced in the 1920s (Hardy, 1973). The several pairs adapted themselves and the flock became so numerous that one section of the peninsula is called Peacock Canyon. Twelve peafowl were counted there during the Christmas Bird Count of 1966 (Cruickshank, 1967); fifty-three on the Audubon Christmas Bird Count of 1978.

PHEASANTS. According to Zeuner (1963), the pheasant, *Phasianus colchicus*, named after the river Phasis in Greek mythology, was brought from Asia to Greece by the Argonauts in the 1st century A.D.; it reached Italy later than the peacock and from Italy was sent to all parts of the Roman Empire; however, it was never completely domesticated as was the domestic fowl (chicken), and remained a game bird of the rich, who often bred it and raised it with care. (Only in recent times was it thoroughly established in the wild in many parts of Europe and, even more recently, in N. America.)

DOMINANCE

(A term also used in genetics.) Dominance of certain birds over others comes as a result of fighting or aggressive actions. Groups of cage birds, or wild ones living in small groups, have a social, or dominance, hierarchy, called a "peck order" (*see* Social Order among Birds under Behavior), which has at the top the "despot" or alpha bird, which is capable of dominating all others below it in the group hierarchy. Occasionally there are triangular relationships in which A dominates B and B dominates C and C dominates A, but these relationships are usually unstable and commonly end in the straight-line, more normal relationship of A dominating down to the lowest or most dominated (omega) bird, which does not dominate any other bird in the group (Crook, 1964). Among groups of N. American birds studied in the wild, winter flocks of black-capped chickadees (Hamerstrom, 1942; Glase, 1973; Smith, 1976) and mountain chickadees (Dixon, 1965) showed a peck order dominance.

Collias and Taber (1951) reported on flock, or group, dominance among pheasants; Tordoff (1954) among crossbills; Sabine (1959) in juncos; Dilger (1960) in redpolls; Thompson (1960) in house finches.

This kind of group dominance is different from the dominance of a male bird within his nesting or feeding territory over other males of his kind (*see* Territory) or of the male over the female or the female over the male (*see* Dominance Between the Sexes under Courtship).

Bailey and Batt (1974) studied dominance at feeding places between different species of ducks at Delta Marsh, Man., where ducks were feeding on the water close by whistling swans, getting the foods the swans uprooted but did not eat. Canvasbacks and mallards, which did not fight each other, consistently chased away or dominated other ducks that tried to feed. The redhead was second in the feeding hierarchy; pintails were third; and both chased gadwalls, wigeons, and lesser scaups, but, in turn, were chased by the canvasbacks and mallards. Gadwalls were fourth; they chased wigeons and scaups but were dominated by the higher-ranking ducks. Wigeons rarely chased other species. Lesser scaups were sixth and were chased by all higher-ranking ducks. Blue-winged teals were at the bottom of the hierarchy and stayed in a feeding zone farthest from the swans; females of all species were less aggressive than males. The *heaviest* species of ducks were highest in the feeding hierarchy. Evidently the dominance ranking was determined mostly by the body size of each species. See other interesting dominance relationships between ash-throated flycatchers and Cassin's sparrows noted by Austin and Russell (1972); see Leck (1973) on nectar-feeding birds; and Emlen (1973) on warblers. See also Roest (1961). *See* actual fighting between birds under Territory, and dominance between birds at backyard feeding stations in Dennis (1950).

DORSAL

Pertaining to the back; the upper surface of a bird's body. *See* Ventral.

DOTTEREL

See in Plover Family.

DOUBLE-BROODED

See under Brood.

DOUBLE SCRATCH

Term of those who study bird behavior (*see* Behavior). It refers to the scratching action of ground-feeding birds when they jump forward, with both feet, then take a larger jump backward, as they turn over leaves or other debris in seeking food. The "double scratch" is used by such ground-feeding birds as towhees, white-throated and white-crowned sparrows, song sparrows, fox sparrows, the rufous-crowned sparrow, Harris' sparrow, Lincoln's sparrow, tree sparrow, and dark-eyed (slate-colored) junco (Nice, 1943).

According to Clark (1970), the double scratch of these birds, in scraping away leaves or snow when searching for seeds or insects, is apparently inherited (genetic), and birds that do not have the trait—blue jay, house sparrow, and cardinal, for example—do not learn it in spite of opportunities to observe other species using it. Clark did not observe the double scratch in either the field sparrow or the chipping sparrow, but confirmed it in wintering tree sparrows, the rufous-sided towhee, savannah sparrow, slate-colored (dark-eyed) junco, white-throated sparrow, fox sparrow, and song sparrow. See, however, discussion by Hailman (1973).

The single or alternate scratch with either foot is characteristic of domestic chickens and such wild gallinaceous birds as quail, pheasants, and turkeys. *See* Food and Feeding Habits; *see also* a related type of inherited behavior under Head-scratching.

DOUBLE SNIPE

See Snipe, great, in Sandpiper Family.

DOUGH-BIRD

See Curlew, Eskimo, in Sandpiper Family.

DOVE

See in Pigeon Family.

DOVE DISEASE

See trichomoniasis under Diseases.

DOVEKIE

See in Auk Family.

DOWITCHER

See in Sandpiper Family.

DOWNY PLUMAGE

See Feather; Eider Down.

DRAGGING FOOD

See in biography of California condor under Vulture—American Vulture Family; *see also* Food and Feeding Habits; Swimming and Diving; Weight-carrying Capacity.

DRAKE

A male duck.

DREPANIIDAE

See Hawaiian Honeycreeper Family.

DRINKING

See Swallowing.

DRIVER

See Dowitcher, short-billed, in Sandpiper Family.

DROPPINGS

Biologists' term for the excrement of birds. *See* Guano.

DROWNING

Apparently many small land birds are drowned, especially during migration when caught by storms over water and far from land. *See*, for example, in biography of saw-whet owl in Owl—Typical Owl Family; *see also* Accidents; Migration; Weather; Swimming and Diving.

DRUMMING

Woodpeckers and ruffed grouse "drum," or make sounds that resemble the rolling notes of a drum.

According to Lawrence (1967), drumming, or "tattooing" (beating a "tattoo"), of woodpeckers is a loud, rhythmical rapping with the bill on a favored resounding object, such as a dry twig, hollow wood, or metal surface; it corresponds largely to the songs of songbirds (*see* Songs and Singing); it is self-announcing and self-assertive in relation to pairing (establishing the *pair bond—see* Courtship) with the opposite sex and defense of the territory against others of its kind. *See* Territory. Drumming is also used as a direct language communication between woodpeckers of the same species (Lawrence, 1967). *See also* Language.

In his extensive studies of several species of N. American woodpeckers, Kilham discovered that both males and females drum on dead limbs, on the trunks of dead trees, on utility poles, and on other objects that produce a loud reverberation. The yellow-bellied sapsucker, for example, drums not only on wood but on metal (Kilham, 1962a) and the yellow-shafted (common) flicker has been known to drum on the galvanized rain spout of a roof gutter (Terres, 1953), the tin roof of a house, and even on the lid of a garbage can near the back porch of a house (Bent, 1939).

Besides the female yellow-bellied sapsucker, drumming by female woodpeckers has been reported in flickers and downy and hairy woodpeckers. In all four of these species studied in Canada by Lawrence (1967), females drummed at least as often as males, and, at times, even more persistently, especially before pairing with a male had been concluded. All woodpeckers studied by Lawrence, including males and females, had one or several favorite "signaling" posts within their territories—each a spot chosen for its good resonance. A male yellow-bellied sapsucker that Lawrence studied for six years drummed on the handle of a spade that hung from a tree in her yard near a bird-feeding station; for years, a succession of female

DRUMMING
Braced on a log, a male ruffed grouse beats its cupped wings back and forth in the air, producing an extraordinary sound like a muffled heart beat that accelerates to a booming drum roll that can be heard ¼ mile away. At the climax, the wing beats increase to a rate of 20 strokes per second.

hairy woodpeckers drummed on a piece of dry, half-loose bark that hung from the broken-off top of a poplar tree. Lawrence believes that drumming plays a comparatively minor role in the flicker's territorial behavior and that the flicker's "location" call (*see* biography of yellow-shafted flicker in Woodpecker Family) often takes the place of drumming.

TAPPING. Besides the more rapid drumming with their bills, many species of woodpeckers tap at a regular and countable rate during their courtship and while determining the location of the nesting hole (Kilham, 1962a). These pecking sounds usually are not loud, nor always rhythmic, nor always in a definite series; woodpeckers tap the surface of a tree or other object because of various situations which may be related to food, to hole-boring, to a behavioral ritual, or because of a frustrated drive when it may tap in "displacement tapping" (see in Lawrence, 1967; *see also* Displacement Activity; Types of Behavior under Behavior.

Kilham (1959c) believes that mutual tapping (by both members of the pair) of woodpeckers serves to strengthen their pair bond and informs the male whether his choice of an excavation site is acceptable to his mate.

DRUMMING OF THE RUFFED GROUSE. During the first warm days of Mar. and Apr. in woodlands in parts of the U.S. and Canada comes a distant thumping on the soft, warm air—slow and deliberate at first, then accelerating until it ends in a muffled roar. It is the wing-beating, drumming challenge of a male ruffed grouse to other males, and an invitation to a receptive female of his kind. Drumming is part of the courtship performance of the male ruffed grouse, described as early as 1755 in the *Philosophical Transactions of the Royal Society of London* (Bent, 1932).

Drumming is usually performed by a male grouse on a log, on which he stands crosswise, braced backward on his tail, while he brings his cupped wings forward and upward in quick beats. The wing strokes are slow at first, producing a measured thumping, but increase in speed until the sound becomes a rapid *whir*, at which the grouse stops its wing-beating and the sound ends.

For many years, the way in which the bird produced this sound was in dispute. Some held that the grouse struck its wings together behind its back; others that it struck them together in front, or against its breast; and N. American Indians were said to have believed that it beat its wings against the drumming log to produce the sound.

The drumming sound, as first proved by slow-motion pictures by Arthur A. Allen, results from the grouse's cupped wings striking nothing more than the air. According to Bent (1932), the pitch of the sound has been placed between A flat and B flat, and anyone with normal hearing on a quiet day can detect the drumming of a ruffed grouse a quarter of a mile away; however, the drumming that appears to come from far away may actually be close by. According to Allen (1961), the drumming is of such low frequency (40 cycles a second) that it seems no louder to the listener when a grouse

is drumming 200 ft. away than at 600 ft. The low frequency of the sound may account for the fact that great horned owls, which are one of the ruffed grouse's principal natural enemies, very rarely kill a grouse that is drumming on its log (Gullion and Marshall, 1968). Edwards (1943) discovered that the great horned owl's hearing range is from 7,000 cycles to 60 cycles a second; apparently the grouse's drumming sounds, produced at 40 cycles a second, are too low in frequency for the owl to hear them.

Ruffed grouse have been known to drum every month in the year, and during every hour of the day or night, but the really intensive drumming is in early spring. There is a short period, however, in mid-autumn when drumming increases for a few weeks; at other times it is occasional and spasmodic (Edminster, 1947). *See* Grouse, ruffed, in Grouse Family.

THE DRUMMING LOG. In the absence of fallen trees (logs) in the woods, the male grouse will drum while standing on mossy mounds, boulders, stone walls, and similar places that are higher than the woodland floor. The logs selected by the male for his drumming are usually large, and drumming is usually always done on one spot on the log. The same log may be used for many years by succeeding males and the drumming spot becomes quite worn from the feet of the drumming birds.

Logs chosen for drumming by ruffed grouse, in some regions, may be those oriented according to prevailing storm winds, and when the grouse drum, they are capable of controlling the intensity of sound—they sometimes reduce (soften, or lessen) the sound of their drumming when a human observer approaches (Archibald, 1974).

According to Archibald, it has been suggested that the male ruffed grouse answers the drumming sounds of neighboring males by drumming in turn. The male can increase the effect of his drumming on a neighboring male by facing, as much as possible, directly toward the neighbor when drumming, as the sound travels more strongly away from the front of the bird as he fans his wings.

During the spring breeding season, the male roosts at night on the drumming log (*see* Roosting), which is usually inside a woodland, and always near the edge of a clearing, road, or other opening in the woods. Many males use more than one drumming log, but usually have a primary one which they use more than others. Around the drumming log, the grouse establishes his territory, from which he will drive away others of his kind. At such times some male grouse become unusually aggressive and fearless. *See* accounts under Tameness.

DRUMSTICK

The tibiotarsus, or "foreleg," of a bird. *See* Feet and Legs.

DRUNKENNESS

See Poisons.

DUAL SPECIES

See Sibling Species.

DUCK FAMILY

Anatidae (ah-NAT-ih-dee); from Lat. *anas*, a duck. Worldwide, except in polar regions; 148 species (Johnsgard, 1978); includes the ducks, geese, and swans; 64 species in the Duck Family reported for continental N. America, as of 1973; includes the extinct Labrador duck.

Possibly no other group of birds has been more intimately connected with people down through the ages than the waterfowl (ducks, geese, and swans, collectively), called in Great Britain "wildfowl" (Scott, 1964); they were among the first birds domesticated (*see* Domestication); have been hunted for centuries by man for food and for sport, and for pleasure of watching and studying them in the wild or in captivity on ponds of zoological gardens, estates, farms, and in private aviaries; the literature on waterfowl is probably the largest for any group of the world's birds (see long lists of published references in Phillips, 1922–26; Kuroda, 1942; Delacour, 1954–64; Bellrose, 1976; see also in issues of *Wildlife Review* from 1935).

Most waterfowl are classified by U.S. government officials as migratory game birds, hunted each year, subject to federal regulations, with the exception of the mute and trumpeter swans, which are under strict protection at all times, and, periodically, certain geese and ducks whose numbers may, in some years, become too low because of environmental changes or a poor nesting season—for example, canvasbacks, redheads, and brant—or those thought to be too rare to withstand hunting, such as a very rare subspecies of the Mexican duck which reaches northward into N.M., where it is considered an endangered subspecies (Sincock *et al.*, 1964); *see* life history under Mexican duck and discussion of management of waterfowl under Waterfowl; also Legal Protection; Rare and Threatened Species.

Ducks, geese, and swans are outwardly diverse; they are small to large (in N. America, 12–62 in. long) and N. American species range in size from the comparatively tiny masked duck, bufflehead, and the teals of 1 lb. or less, to the 30 lb. or more trumpeter swan, largest of all waterfowl, but have features in common that make all recognized as a related group; they are aquatic, swimming birds (*see* in Swimming and Diving) with the three front toes webbed and the fourth small, somewhat elevated and free; most have comparatively short legs and tails, a rather long neck, and a broad, somewhat flattened lamellate bill with rounded tip; the bill has a soft membranous covering with a "nail," or hooked hard spot, at tip of the upper mandible; the tongue, which in many is typically rectangular, thick, and fleshy, when feeding is raised against the palate to squeeze out water through serrated edges of the bill (Gardner, 1927), which leaves solid foods in mouth (*see* Tongue; Swallowing); the plumage is dense, the feathers usually white, black, or brown, heavily underlain with down; many, particularly some of the ducks, have a crest of head feathers; the wings are narrow and pointed, and many have a colored wing patch called a *speculum;* they are strong and swift fliers; most are gregarious, and feed and migrate in flocks; N. American waterfowl tend to follow north-south flyway patterns (*see* Waterfowl; Migration), with the most dramatic movements in fall, when tremendous numbers in or near the breeding grounds may suddenly take off en masse at onset of winter; the female selects the nesting territory, to which the male partner usually returns with her; they have down-covered young that are precocial—they can swim soon after hatching and some adults of some species swim about with the young on their backs. See Dorst (1962).

Among waterfowl, nest building may be by the female or by both sexes; only rarely does the male do most of work (Johnsgard, 1968); waterfowl do not usually carry nesting materials in the bill but simply reach out from nest-building site and pick up or pluck plant material from around the nest; female usually lays early in morning, in most ducks one egg a day; typical clutches of eight or more eggs are laid in a week or two; most incubating waterfowl pluck down from the lower breast to help keep the eggs warm, and during the egg-laying period, nests of most waterfowl are left unattended while the female is away; before she leaves nest, she usually covers her eggs with down; she does not start to incubate until she lays the last or next-to-last egg in her clutch, thus all young hatch at about the same time; in many waterfowl species, the female remains on nest during the first day after young hatch; at this time the young become ''imprinted'' on their parent and thereafter recognize and follow her (Johnsgard, 1968).

In most ducks, only the female cares for the young; the male normally deserts the female early in her incubation period, then soon begins to molt into his eclipse plumage; during the nesting season or soon afterward, most species in the Duck Family have a complete postnuptial molt; in summer, the males of many species of ducks change by shedding the feathers of their breeding (nuptial) plumage and grow a very different, somber, female-like plumage called the *eclipse* plumage (*see* Eclipse Plumage); the females usually do not start their postnuptial molt until later than the males—after the nesting season is over; at about the height of this molt, both lose all their flight feathers at once and are unable to fly for a few weeks or until the new flight feathers are grown; meanwhile they escape their enemies by swimming away, hiding among marsh plants or by diving below the water's surface (*see* variations and similarities of molt in different groups of birds under Molts and Molting).

Waterfowl are an ancient group that now live on every continent except Antarctica, and on every major island in the world; their oldest fossil remains date back 80 million years (Austin, 1961); their nearest living relatives are the screamers (*see* Anseriformes); some biologists believe that all waterfowl evolved from an ancestor distantly related to some such gallinaceous birds as our chachalacas (*see* Curassow Family); others that they are more nearly related to the flamingos and the storklike birds (Johnsgard, 1968).

There is disagreement among ornithologists about classification of members of the Duck Family, but in general they are divided, based on similarity of anatomy and habits, into 3 sub-families; 2 subfamilies and 7 tribes have representatives in N. America: subfamily Anserinae contains the whistling-ducks (tribe Dendrocygnini) and the swans and geese (tribe Anserini); the subfamily Anatinae includes the dabbling or surface-feeding ducks (tribe Anatini), freshwater diving ducks (tribe Aythyini), sea ducks (tribe Mergini), stifftail ducks (tribe Oxyurini), and perching ducks (tribe Cairinini). *See* Classification. Ducks of all N. American species hybridize freely in captivity. *See* Hybrid.

Swans (Cygninae), 7 species in the world, are 45–62 in. long; largest and most graceful of all waterfowl; males larger than females; 5 that live in N. Hemisphere are pure white: 4 of these occur in N. America.

Swans are much larger than geese and ducks, with long necks which are usually longer than their bodies; male is called a *cob*, female, a *pen*, young one, a *cygnet;* swans cannot spring directly from water into air and fly as freshwater, or dabbling, ducks can. Because of the shortness of their legs, which does not permit a full downstroke of wings over surface of water at start, must run along surface, striking water alternately with each foot, for about 15–20 ft. before able to rise on beating wings into air; in migration, swans often travel at great heights and at great speeds. *See* Aircraft and Birds.

Swans are swift and powerful swimmers and seldom or never dive for their underwater food; however, they can dive if threatened by danger; trumpeter swans, for example, when submerged, are good underwater swimmers (Banko, 1960), and they sleep both on land and on water. Swans have few enemies, other than man, who once shot trumpeter swans almost to extinction for their skins, feathers, and meat, and depleted whistling swans enormously during the 19th century (Banko, 1960). The feather trade in wild N. American birds is now illegal (*see* Feather Trade), but demand was once so great for swan skins that the Hudson's Bay Company sold 108,000 in London between 1823 and 1880; the trumpeter swan, because it nested in fur-trapping country of Canada and n. U.S., was especially vulnerable to exploitation by fur traders and settlers and was almost gone by end of the 19th century (Banko and Mackay, 1964). After the first Migratory Bird Treaty Act of 1918, between the U.S. and Canada, hunting of swans was not permitted until 1962, when a limited season was allowed in Utah on whistling swans (Baldwin *et al.,* 1964); see details in Van Wormer (1972); both trumpeter and whistling swans have died of lead poisoning.

Pairs of adult swans tend to mate for life, and their offspring may require 2, 3, or rarely 4 years to become sexually mature and raise families of their own (Johnsgard, 1965). The beauty and grace of swans have made them subjects of ancient legends, myths, and religious beliefs wherever men have known them (*see* Folklore; Swan Song).

Geese (Anserini) are smaller than swans and have shorter necks, are intermediate in size (21–43 in. long) between swans and ducks; compared with ducks, necks of geese are longer and bodies less flattened; like swans, both sexes are outwardly alike but males larger; some, like

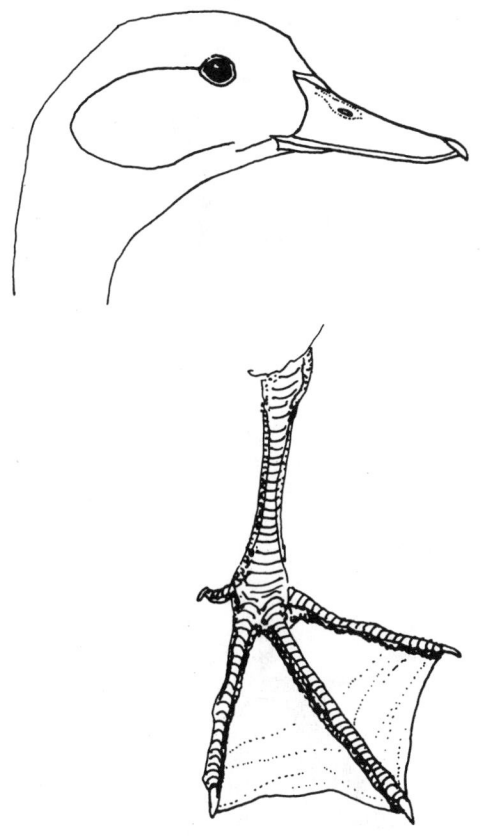

DUCK FAMILY

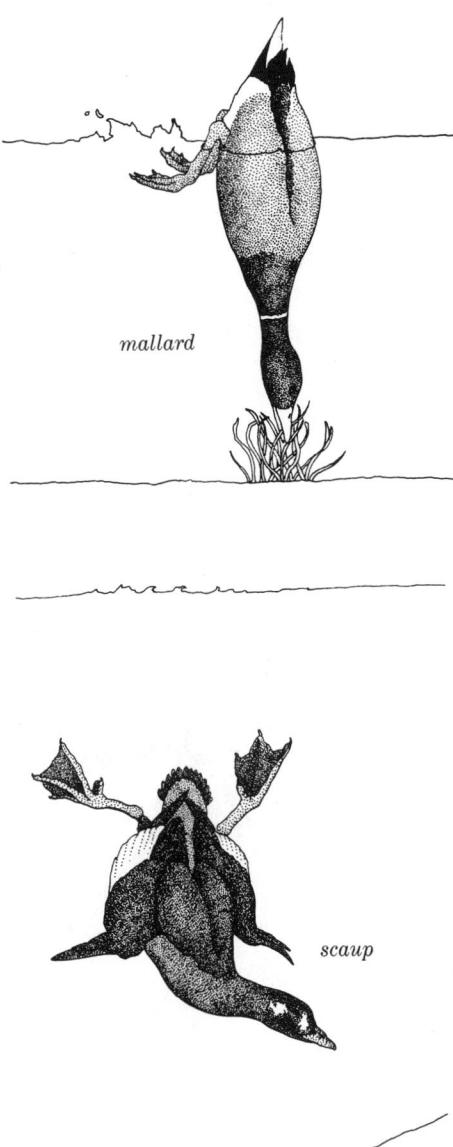

mallard

scaup

DUCK FAMILY
*The mallard, a dabbling duck, usually feeds
in shallow water, tipping up its body to reach
down a foot or two for aquatic plants and seeds.
The scaup, a diving duck, dives for aquatic
insects, plants, and mollusks, often
to depths of 20 feet.*

swans, are white but with dark markings; others dark with white or gray markings; name *goose* was once applied only to female (but now often applied to both sexes); male is the *gander;* young one is a *gosling;* 14 species (Austin, 1961) to 20 (Reilly, 1968) in world; 8 live within limits of N. America—Greenland, Canada, Alaska, continental U.S., Baja Calif., and Bermuda (A.O.U. *Check-list,* 1957); include 1 species of brant, also the barnacle goose and the bean goose, both largely Old World species; the snow goose and its blue color form (*see* Color Phase); Canada goose; emperor goose; Ross' goose; and white-fronted goose.

The circumpolar white-fronted goose is the only one of 5 species of Old World geese, collectively called "gray geese," that has a N. American population (Austin, 1961); most of the gray geese resemble our common barnyard goose, which is a descendant of one of them—the wild greylag goose, *Anser anser,* of n. Europe (*see* Domestication).

Geese differ in other ways from swans in that voice of male is slightly higher-pitched than female's (in swans, male's voice is usually lower-pitched), and almost all geese, including the brant, have feathers of the neck furrowed vertically; in their "threat display" they vibrate these feathers rather than raise them vertically as swans do (Johnsgard, 1965). All geese are noisy and utter loud trumpeting sounds; they are highly social, have strong family bonds, even stronger than those of swans, and strong pair bonds (tend to remain paired for life), and like swans, their offspring may require 2 or more years to become sexually mature. In contrast, most ducks become sexually mature within a year and their pair bonds are less permanent—a female may have several different mates during her lifetime (Johnsgard, 1965).

Geese, like swans and some ducks, have, potentially, long life spans among birds—a captive whistling swan lived to 19 years; a captive Canada goose to 32½ years; a green-winged teal lived in the wild to 20 years; a captive mallard and a captive canvasback to 20 and 19 years respectively; a common goldeneye to 17 years (Johnsgard, 1968).

The legs of geese are farther forward under the body than the legs of ducks and swans, which gives them better balance in traveling on land to graze, as they often do, far from water. In spring they clip with the bill green grasses and blades of sprouting grain in farm fields; in fall and winter, they pick up waste grain and other crop residues (the tongue of a goose or a swan, used by them in feeding to tear up aquatic plants and weeds and grasses, has evolved into a powerful pulling structure).

Geese are wary, and, when feeding, at least one always watches and warns the feeding flock of danger; in flight, each flock has a leader (Delacour, 1954); like swans, they fly in a V or in long lines across the sky (*see* Formation Flying under Flight); in migration they fly usually at 40–60 m.p.h. (Glover, 1964), and some may fly at tremendous heights (*see* Altitude of Bird Flight). The largest N. American goose is the giant Canada goose, to 18 lbs. or more; the smallest is the cackling goose, a race of the Canada goose, averaging 2.8 (females) to 3.4 (males) lbs. (Bellrose, 1976). The Canada goose

is the most numerous of N. American geese, with an estimated population of 2,140,000 (Bellrose, 1976).

The whistling-ducks (tribe Dendrocygnini) include 8 species in the world; 3 reported in N. America; are primarily tropical ducks, intermediate between geese and dabbling ducks (Reilly, 1968); are very gooselike, with long legs, long necks, large webbed feet with sharp claws; dive well for food, also graze on land and usually feed at night; according to Johnsgard (1965), are rather swanlike or gooselike in behavior, and despite being called tree ducks, do not primarily perch, and only rarely nest in holes in trees; they stand erect and walk gracefully and easily; they are gregarious most of the year, they frequent fresh water, and often gather in large numbers but are not true colonial nesters. They utter unducklike whistling notes, high-pitched and shrill, clear or squeaky, resembling the notes of certain songbirds (Delacour, 1954); they also make whistling or whirring sounds with their wings in flight by vibrating the notched or emarginated inner vanes (*see* Feather) of the outer primaries, or flight feathers; in flight, with long necks and long legs extended, they resemble ibises; pairs remain deeply attached and seem to show affection by softly preening feathers of each other's face; their eggs differ from those of other waterfowl in being shorter and rounder (Delacour, 1954).

The surface-feeding, or dabbling, ducks (Anatini) are small to large (11–29 in. long) and best-known group of the Duck Family. Of 39 species in the world (Johnsgard, 1978), 14 occur in N. America (Bellrose, 1976); usually live on fresh water but occasionally on salt or brackish waters in migration; include such ducks as the mallard, black duck, gadwall, pintail, teal, wigeons, shoveler, etc.; most are shorter-legged and shorter-necked than geese and tree ducks; most have a wing speculum (Johnsgard, 1968), and the males have brightly or elaborately patterned plumage and complex courtship displays (*see* Waterfowl); their feet are generally smaller than those of diving ducks, and the hind toe is small with a simple nail, without the flap or lobe of the hind toe of diving ducks and mergansers.

Most dabbling ducks nest in temperate climates, many migrate long distances; only 2 species of waterfowl in N. America are essentially *nonmigratory*—the mottled duck and the Mexican duck (Glover, 1964).

The dabbling ducks, also called dipping ducks, river and pond ducks, and "puddle" ducks, feed in shallow water by tipping up the body and tail and reaching below the surface with bill and neck submerged along edges of lakes, ponds, and small bodies of water; some dive for food more than is generally realized (Johnsgard, 1968); others rarely dive except to escape danger; many, especially shovelers, swim about with bill at surface, dabbling continuously; in rising from water, the dabblers spring upward with strong vertical bound, whereas most of diving ducks and mergansers need a running start along surface before rising into the air.

Dabblers frequently live on small ponds or on lakes bordered by trees or aquatic plants such as cattails, reeds, bulrushes, etc., where open water is limited; they are adapted to living on these often restricted water surfaces because their larger wing areas relative to their body weights (see details and illustrations in Raikow, 1973) permit them to rocket off water or from land into immediate flight within a limited space; also, they can fly more slowly than diving ducks and thus drop with more precision into a smaller area. Because of their short legs and their position toward sides of the body, all dabblers walk with a distinct waddle.

Of all dabbling ducks, only the mallard has been domesticated; however, three others in the family also have been domesticated—the Muscovy duck, greylag goose, and the swan goose, *Anser cygnoides*, ancestor of the domestic "Chinese" goose (Scott, 1964).

The pintail, with wide, circumpolar range, is one of the most numerous duck species in the world, along with the mallard (Johnsgard, 1968).

The small to medium-sized or large diving ducks (13–28 in. long), also called bay, or sea, ducks (Aythyini), include the canvasback, redhead, pochards, ring-necked duck, scaups, tufted duck; 20 species in the world (Johnsgard, 1978), 6 species in N. America (Bellrose, 1976).

Some of the diving ducks, which spend the winter on salt or brackish waters, in summer nest far inland in freshwater habitats (for example, the canvasback, redhead, lesser scaup, ring-necked duck); others (eiders) nest mostly in the Arctic not far from the sea, where they are largely marine, or sea, ducks, as they are in winter. Ducks that spend time on the sea develop enlarged salt (lateral nasal) glands with which, like other marine birds, they eliminate salt from the water they drink.

While some diving ducks winter in relative warmth south to waters of Mexico, the common eider spends the winter on any Arctic waters kept open by currents or tidal rips, even though the air temperature may be −50° F. (Baldwin *et al.*, 1964). Ducks and geese have a remarkable adaptation in the network of arteries and veins in their feet that prevents their feet from freezing while they stand on ice. Warm, outward flowing arterial blood is brought into close proximity with the cooler venous blood returning from the feet. *See* How Birds Adapt to Cold under Cold and Birds.

Diving ducks often dive deeply for their food —the oldsquaw to 180 ft. (*see* Swimming and Diving); diving ducks feed underwater aided in their swimming by large feet and short legs which are farther to rear of their bodies than in dabbling ducks; that is why diving ducks are awkward on land and seldom visit crop fields (Baldwin *et al.*, 1964); in contrast to the dabbling ducks, diving ducks have smaller, more pointed wings, which, aerodynamically, make for swift flight when under way but require them to run or "skitter" across the surface by paddling with their feet and beating their wings over a considerable distance before they become airborne (Raikow, 1973). Thus, unlike the dabbling ducks, they are largely limited to big areas of open water.

Diving ducks are less noisy than the dabbling ducks and males are usually silent except during courtship (Johnsgard, 1965), but sea ducks have a striking variety of calls—male eiders utter various dovelike cooing notes during their courtship displays.

The males of only a few species of diving ducks acquire an eclipse plumage, and none of the American species has a bright-colored speculum; however, courtship displays of some are spectacular, as in the dabblers.

Some of the diving ducks (for example, the redhead) are non-obligate parasites and lay their eggs in the nests of other ducks. At least 21 species of the world's ducks have laid their eggs in the nests of other birds. *See* discussion under Obligate Parasite.

The small (12–18 in. long) so-called stiff-tailed ducks (Oxyurini) include about 9 species in the world; of these, only 2—the ruddy duck and masked duck—are in N. America; they are more aquatic than any other ducks, have dense and shining body plumage somewhat like that of grebes, and act like grebes; can sink slowly below the surface without a ripple or sound; the long, narrow, stiffened tail feathers function as a rudder in their underwater swimming; the short, sturdy legs of the ruddy duck are set so far back on body that it is almost helpless on land; is more skillful underwater than any of the diving ducks or mergansers; dives well but is like no other N. American duck in that male helps female care for the young; is not noisy and female is "voiceless" (Baldwin *et al.*, 1964); the ruddy duck has more colloquial names (about 100) than any other duck (see McAtee, 1923); two names, hickory-head and leatherback, applied to ruddy duck by hunters because its dense feathers thought impervious to gunshot.

Mergansers (Mergini) are small to large (14–28 in. long); 7 known species in world, including the now extinct Auckland Island merganser, *Mergus australis* (see Greenway, 1958); 4 species in N. America, including a foreign visitor, the smew; all are diving, fish-eating ducks, adapted to underwater pursuit of fishes; have streamlined bodies and a long narrow bill with serrations along its edges (backward-projecting "teeth") with which they grasp and hold their slippery prey; swim and dive well but awkward on land; most species are crested; males of 5 species have a partial or complete molt into eclipse plumage in midsummer (Reilly, 1968).

Among 54 families of N. American birds showing albinism, Gross (1965a) lists the Duck Family fourth in highest number of individual records of albinism reported (155) and second among the greatest number of species (35) showing some degree of albinism. *See* Albinism; *also* individual records noted in biographies of some.

Among accidents to ducks on their prairie nesting grounds in Canada and n. U.S., some strike fences, utility wires, power lines, and buildings and are killed; greatest number of accidents are during migration. See accounts of Cornwell and Hochbaum (1971) and by Siegfried (1972). About 500 ducks—mostly redheads, some mallards, and a few scaups, shovelers, and ruddy ducks—were killed at night Oct. 25, 1951, during fog, rain, snow at Hot Springs, S.D., when they tried to alight on glit-

Red-breasted merganser

DUCK FAMILY

With its "saw teeth," the serrated cutting edges of its bill, the red-breasted merganser can grasp and hold small, slippery fishes when feeding underwater.

tering main street; they struck buildings, telephone poles, wires, trees (Schorger, 1952a).

Besides losses of waterfowl from hunting by man and from predators (see especially account of predation and its effects on waterfowl by Errington, 1964), tremendous numbers periodically die from lead poisoning and diseases (see especially Botulism; Lead Poisoning; Avian Cholera; Diseases).

To protect either permanently or temporarily captive waterfowl from dogs and other predators, keep them in a fenced enclosure with water available—a pond, lake, or stream if possible. To prevent them from flying away, the flight feathers of one wing should be clipped, or the wing "pinioned." See methods in Pinion.

Walker (1942) recommends feeding captives a mixture of grains, bread crumbs, chopped green plants and vegetables, with a small amount of ground meat. Geese and swans require more green food than ducks do; mergansers should be offered small live fishes in a pool to catch for themselves or should be offered fish cut into small strips or meat finely ground or sliced. Sea ducks—eiders, scoters, harlequins—not generally kept in captivity, might survive on fish, meat, crab scraps or shrimp, clams, bread crumbs, some soaked grain and green material all ground together. Sea ducks should have large deep pools in which they can dive. See McAtee (1930; 1939) for plantings in the waterfowl aviary and what to feed; for other suggestions for attracting waterfowl, see Addy and MacNamara (1948), and articles in "A Helping Hand" in Linduska and Nelson (1964).

For waterfowl population reports, by species, see series by U.S. Fish and Wildlife Service, Department of the Interior, Washington, D.C.—for example, Waterfowl Status Report, 1972 (see in bibliography); see also periodic news releases of the Service, and Henny et al. (1972).

Brant, Branta bernicla (BRAN-tah BER-nih-klah); genus name: New Lat., from Anglo-Saxon bernan, brennan, to burn (Jaeger, 1955), so named because of charred general dark color of this species; species name: New Lat., meaning barnacle, from legend that these birds hatched from the shells of barnacles (see Barnacle goose). (Color ills., pages 218, 219.) Circumpolar; in N. America, summers in Arctic Canada, ne. Alaska; winters along Atlantic and Pacific coasts; a small to medium-sized goose; a "saltwater cousin of the Canada goose"; 22–26 in. long; wingspread 43½–48 in. (Kortright, 1943); has rather short neck; bill, head, neck, and chest black (chest black to waterline; similar Canada goose's breast shows white above waterline—Peterson, 1947); brant has small white patch on each side of neck, interrupted by parallel striations of the neck feathers, lacks the large white *cheek* patch of the Canada goose (white neck mark is lacking or poorly developed in immature brant); back is dark slaty or brown, underparts white with some gray toward front; white undertail coverts show conspicuously when resting on water; flocks do not usually fly in V like Canada geese but in long wavy lines and have peculiar habit of "balling up" into a large mass, then stringing out in long, undulating "company front"

formation; seldom evidence of a leader (Lincoln, 1950a); flight is swift on long, pointed wings, rapid wingbeat; shy, can swim well but does not dive unless pressed by pursuer; fond of resting on sandy points and bars (Bent, 1925); call is long-drawn, rolling guttural *c-r-r-uk* or *r-r-onk, rr-ronk,* with grunting and hissing that makes babble of sounds; when traveling along coast, usually low over water in lines of 20–50 abreast; have curious aversion to crossing even a narrow strip of land; in winter entire Atlantic coast population concentrates along coast, mostly N.J. to N.C. (Lincoln, 1950a); in Feb. and Mar. begin gradual move northward from wintering places, by Apr. start flight to Arctic nesting grounds, arriving there in late May and early June; see details in Barry (1964); with disappearance of eelgrass along Atlantic coast in 1930s brant went into swift decline, but adaptation to new foods and protection from hunting brought it back; 150,000 to more than 200,000 reported in 1960s; however, by Jan. 1972 down to 73,000 birds (see Chamberlain et al., 1972); according to Reed (1973), by Jan. 1973 at time of federal waterfowl count, had dropped to only about 40,000 because adults produced few young on nesting grounds during two previous years (32,000 reported Oceanville, N.J., Audubon Christmas Bird Count, 1978); recommended closing of hunting season on Atlantic coast brant for at least two years; adults and young start southward in late Aug., early Sept., begin to arrive along Atlantic coast by mid-Oct.

Feeding Habits: Before 1930s, eelgrass made up 80% of winter food but with its disappearance along Atlantic coast, turned to algae—sea lettuce (Ulva) and sea cabbage (Enteromorpha), according to Cottam and Munro (1954); on Arctic nesting grounds eats grasses, algae, mosses, stalks and leaves of Arctic plants; grazes much on land but is true sea goose with salt glands (see Nostrils) that enable it to drink salt water and to eat saltwater plants (Barry, 1964); also eats crustaceans, mollusks, worms, and marine insects (Bent, 1925).

Nest: Nests farther north than any other geese, coasts of Greenland and islets in Canadian Arctic, seldom far from water, often in loose colonies; nest is simple hollow in tundra filled with down, also may use grasses, old feathers, leaves, seaweeds, clumps of driftwood; nest only a bare foot or so above high-tide line on flats, islands, river deltas, and beaches, sometimes on rocks and points at edges of inland lakes (Barry, 1964).

Eggs: June–July; 1–7, usually 3–5, dull white.

Incubation: By female alone, 22–26 days; young follow parents to open water a day or two after hatching; male stays near incubating female (they mate for life), helps defend eggs, and helps raise young.

Other Names: American brant; brant goose; brent goose; burnt goose; clatter goose; common brant; crocker; Eastern brant; light-bellied brant; quink; sea brant; white-bellied brant.

Hybrids: In captivity has crossbred with white-fronted goose, greylag goose, lesser snow goose, emperor goose, and Canada goose (Gray, 1958).

Weights: Males (301) average 3.4 lbs.; females (263) average 3.1 lbs. (Bellrose, 1976).

Range: Nests in High Arctic of e. N. America and Eurasia; in N. America, from Prince Patrick Is., King William Is., and Boothia Pen. to n. Greenland; also Franz Josef Is. and Novaya Zemlya along Arctic coast of Russia; winters in N. America from Cape Cod, Mass., N.Y., N.J. to N.C. on Atlantic coast (occasionally farther north or south, e.g., to Fla.), but most winter in Barnegat Bay area of N.J. (Addy, 1964). For migration corridors, see Bellrose (1976).

Brant, American. *See* Brant.

Brant, Atlantic. *See* Brant.

Brant, bald-headed. *See* Goose, blue.

Brant, black, Branta bernicla nigricans (BRAN-tah BER-nih-klah NIG-rih-kanz); genus and species names: see Brant; subspecies name: Lat., blackish, in reference to this subspecies' dark color. (Color ill., page 218.) Small dark maritime goose of the Pacific coast; darkest of all brant, similar in size, habits, habitat, and breeding biology to the brant, Branta bernicla, of the Atlantic coast, also has similar calls and voice; for years considered a distinct species, but not so classified by the A.O.U. Check-list (1976), which considers it a subspecies; besides black head and neck, *underparts are black;* neck heavily marked with white on sides and in front (Delacour, 1954); immature uniformly dark without white neck markings; white undertail coverts of black brant are conspicuous when it is feeding with rear up and head below surface (see comparison with Canada goose in biography of brant). Because eelgrass die-off was not so severe in Pacific waters the black brant was not so affected by it, and suffered far less than the brant of the Atlantic coast (see discussion and numbers of black brant under Eelgrass). In spring, black brant in May follow their regular migration route northward from wintering along Pacific coast, and then follow shores of Gulf of Alaska to Cold Bay before heading for Arctic nesting grounds; in fall, their southward flight may begin at Point Barrow, Alaska, in middle of Aug.; first fly toward Aleutian chain of islands, then move southward largely offshore along coasts of B.C., Wash., and Ore., and finally reach southern end of fall flight in Baja Calif. (Glover, 1964).

Other Names: China goose; Eskimo goose; sea brant.

Hybrids: Black brant has crossbred with domestic, or greylag, goose, Anser anser, and with Canada goose (Gray, 1958).

Weights: Males (21), 2 lbs. 11 oz. to 3 lbs. 11 oz.; females (14), 2 lbs. 10 oz. to 3 lbs. 10 oz. (Kortright, 1943); Manning et al. (1956) reported an adult male of about 4 lbs. (see also Parmelee et al., 1967).

Range: Nests on coasts of Arctic Alaska south to Nelson Is., east to about 110° Long. in Arctic Canada, usually winters along coasts and bays from sw. B.C. to Baja Calif., and rarely or locally inland in Wash., Ore., s. Idaho, Utah, n. Calif., Nev.; casual in Sask., Wyo., Tex.; accidental occurrence in Mass. (Chatham), N.Y. (Long Is.), N.J. (Egg Harbor), Va. (Cobbs Is.), and Hawaiian Is. (Maui).

Brant, blue. *See* Goose, blue.

Brant, gray. *See* Goose, white-fronted.

Brant, light-bellied. *See* Brant.

Brant, Pacific. *See* Brant, black.

Brant, pied. *See* Goose, white-fronted.

Brant, sea. *See* Brant and Brant, black.

Brant, speckled. *See* Goose, white-fronted.

Brant, tiger. *See* Goose, white-fronted.

Brant, white. *See* Goose, snow.

Brant, white-bellied. *See* Brant.

Brant, white-headed. *See* Goose, blue.

Brant, yellow-legged. *See* Goose, white-fronted.

Bufflehead, *Bucephala albeola* (bue-SEF-ah-lah al-BEE-oh-lah); genus name: from Gr. *boukephalos,* ox-headed or buffalo-headed, in reference to large-headed appearance; species name: Lat., dim. of *albus,* white, in reference to plumage; *bufflehead,* a corruption of buffalo head, from puffiness of the head (Coues, 1882). (Color ill., page 200.) One of smallest ducks and smallest of N. American diving, or sea, ducks; nests only in N. America, largely in forests of n. U.S., nw. Canada, and Alaska (Erskine, 1971a); 13–16 in. long; wingspread 20–24 in.; males larger than females; chunky form, tiny bill; large puffy head of male marked with white patch extending from eyes to crown; body mostly white with black back; in male wing coverts are white; large white wing patches that show in flight; female is gray-brown with small white cheek patch, and whitish underparts; both sexes have a white speculum; bufflehead sometimes mistaken for the larger hooded merganser but white cockade of male hooded is *bordered with black* and sides of body are black; also hooded has spikelike bill; unlike other diving ducks, bufflehead can take off from water without running along surface; buffleheads are usually in motion, flying about, diving frequently; is one of best divers, disappears underwater with suddenness of a grebe, swims underwater with feet only, with wings held to sides, bobs to surface like a cork (Erskine, 1971a); male utters squeaky whistle; female, a harsh quack; are closely related to the goldeneyes; when swimming on surface, bufflehead gives impression of buoyancy; in swift direct flight, beats its short wings rapidly; usually flies low over water except when crossing overland from one pond or bay to another and in migration; although in migration occurs inland on large bodies of fresh water, most buffleheads by early winter reach salt water; is not especially gregarious, groups of more than 50 are rare, usually in singles, twos, or threes (Er-

skine, 1971a); travels northward in Feb., Mar., and Apr.; appears to pair chiefly during spring migration in Apr.; many reach breeding grounds in Canada when waters free of ice; according to Bent (1925), gradual movement southward in fall is mainly inland, from Oct. into Nov. and when generally so fat it is called "butterball"; hunters find it easy to decoy; mostly winters on coastal bays (Pough, 1951).

Feeding Habits: Dives for food often in small groups with one or more on surface to watch for danger; in summer, eats primarily small freshwater aquatic insects—larvae of midges, mayflies, dragonflies, damselflies, caddis flies; also eats water boatmen, shrimplike amphipods, some snails, and small fishes (sculpins, sticklebacks, gobies), and seeds of pondweeds *(Potomogeton)* and naiads *(Najas),* and other water plants, bulrushes, etc.; on salt water, takes shrimp and other small crustaceans and shellfishes, largely snails (see Cottam, 1939; McAtee, 1939).

Nest: Center of abundance in breeding season is about ponds in Canadian woods northwest of Great Plains (Bent, 1925); female normally nests only in flicker holes, not more than 3¼ in. in diameter, and no less than 2¼ in.; adds no nest materials; lays eggs on cavity bottom; favors cavities more than 8 in. deep, 5–20 ft. above ground, often in dead trees, and within about 220 yds. of shores of a lake, pond, or river; a pair nested for 3 years in wooden box put up for them on large tree (Erskine, 1971a).

Eggs: Usually mid-Apr.–May; 6–11, commonly 9, ivory yellow to pale olive-buff.

Incubation: By female, 28–33 days, usually 29–31 days (Erskine, 1971a); young remain in nest 24–36 hours after hatching; are brooded closely by female; young usually leave nest cavity during morning, apparently coaxed out by female, which enters and leaves cavity until young appear at hole and drop to ground; female then leads young away from nest site to nearest lake, pond, or other water; young fly 50–55 days after hatching (Erskine, 1971a).

Other Names: Buffalo-headed duck; buffle-headed duck; bumblebee duck; butter-back; butterball; butter-box; butter duck; conjuring duck; dapper; dipper; dipper-duck; dopper; hell-diver *(see* Grebe Family); little black and white duck; little brown duck; marionette; robin dipper; spirit duck; wool-head.

Age: A male banded as adult at Kent Is., Md., Feb. 18, 1956, shot near Port Huron, Mich., Nov. 10, 1967, when at least 13 years, 5 months; two other males, also banded Kent Is., were shot near there when 12½ years; another when 11 years, 6 months; an adult female caught and banded near Dunkirk, N.Y., recaptured there when she was more than 11½ years old (see other age records in Erskine, 1971a).

Flight Speed: 48 m.p.h. (Cottam *et al.,* 1942b).

Hybrids: Has crossbred with common goldeneye, Barrow's goldeneye, common pochard, greater scaup, tufted duck, velvet scoter, hooded merganser, common merganser, and wood duck (Gray, 1958).

Weights: Males (17), from 13 oz. to 1 lb. 4 oz.; females (14), from 8 oz. to 1 lb. 5 oz. (Kortright, 1943).

Range: Nests from s. coastal and e.-c. Alaska, w. Mack., n. Prairie Provinces of Canada, and n. Ont., south; east of Coast Ranges to nw. Calif., Cascade Mtns. of Ore., and n. Idaho, n. Mont., s. Man., and n.-c. Ont.; winters from Komandorskie Is., Aleutians, Alaska Pen., s. B.C. south to Baja Calif., and Mex., nw. Mont., to Great Lakes, Nova Scotia, Newfoundland, and along Atlantic coast from N.B. and coast of Me., south to n. Fla., Gulf coast west to Tex.

Canvasback, *Aythya valisineria* (AY-thih-ah val-is-ih-NEE-rih-ah); genus name: from Gr. *aithya,* a seabird (Jaeger, 1955); species name: Lat., the scientific name given the bird by Alexander Wilson because of its fondness for the freshwater plant wild celery, *Vallisneria americana* (or *V. spiralis* of some botanists); Wilson misspelled *Vallisneria,* but because of the law of priority in zoological nomenclature, Wilson's misspelled name is retained to this day; *canvasback* has been an American common name for this diving duck since 1800 (Coues, 1882) and refers to the pale gray back and white sides, delicately dotted and lined in a wavelike pattern, resembling canvas fabric (McAtee, 1955b). (Color ill., page 200.) Exclusively N. American, summers in n. and w. U.S., Canada to Alaska, seen in migration and in winter spread widely over U.S., a favorite of hunters and of epicures; 19–24 in. long; wingspread 28–36 in. (largest of the pochards); both sexes noted for a high, sloping forehead that in profile shows a continuous line with the sloping dark bill; male is very white-appearing duck with rust-red neck and head; forebreast shows black to waterline; female is gray-white with slight reddish on head and neck (Peterson, 1961); female resembles redhead but is noticeably lighter-backed and larger; canvasbacks migrate at high altitudes, at great speed, in large V-shaped flocks; the male is generally silent except during certain courtship displays when he peeps, growls, coos, and croaks; female quacks and utters low guttural purring in some displays (see courtship flights and displays in Hochbaum, 1944; Johnsgard, 1965); spring migration begins in Feb. from wintering places on west coast, Gulf of Mexico, and Atlantic coast; well under way in Mar., canvasbacks reach northern breeding grounds in prairie and plains region in Apr.; in fall, a late migrant, sometimes starts in Oct. and in Nov. may arrive on fresh waters of Back Bay, Va., and Currituck Sound, N.C., favorite wintering places (Bent, 1923; see also details in Addy, 1964; Buller, 1964; Chattin, 1964); continental population declines with drainage of breeding marshes and sloughs and with drought. See population counts in Stewart *et al.* (1958) and account of closing of hunting seasons to save low populations in Anonymous (1973a).

Feeding Habits: Extremely wary, in fall and winter gathers in large rafts on coastal bays and broad stretches of inland fresh waters far from shore to feed, sleep, or rest; swims low on water, dives quickly, sometimes in water 20–30 ft. deep, but usually in shallower water 3–12 ft. deep where it eats roots, tubers, and basal parts of bottom plants, one of its main foods, but also eats some mollusks, aquatic insects,

Bahama duck

DUCK FAMILY

and small fishes; however, staple foods are pondweeds and wild celery, also eats seeds of wild rice and other grasses, of sedges, bur reeds, water milfoil, etc., and various parts of water lilies (Cottam, 1939); because canvasbacks strain with bill many of the seeds, especially of wild rice, out of bottom mud, they ingest much lead shot and are especially affected by it (*see* Lead Poisoning).

Nest: Usually built in bulrushes, reeds, or cattails, over shallow water 1–20 yds. from edge of open water, built of bulrushes, reeds, sedges, etc., which female gathers from immediately about nest site; often anchored to surrounding plants or on floating mats of dead plants and built up above high water; lined with down.

Eggs: Usually May–June; 7–12, more often 9–10, gray-green or gray-olive, usually darker than those of redheads and ruddy ducks (Bent, 1923), which may lay their eggs in canvasback's nest.

Incubation: By female, 23–29 days, averages 24 days; young first fly 63–77 days after hatching (Hochbaum, 1944).

Other Names: Bullneck; can; canard cheval; canny; canvas; gray duck; hickory-quaker; horse-duck; red-headed bullneck; sheldrake; whiteback.

Age: A male banded Oakland, Calif., was shot at Sinaloa, Mexico, when it was 14 years, 8 months (Kennard, 1975); one lived to 19 years in captivity (Johnsgard, 1968).

Flight Speed: One timed in Calif., airspeed of 72 m.p.h. (Munson, 1930).

Hybrids: Has crossbred with mallard, lesser scaup, greater scaup, redhead, and ring-necked duck (Gray, 1958).

Weights: One of heaviest of game ducks: males (191) average 2.76 lbs.; females (54) average 2.55 lbs. (Bellrose, 1976); heaviest, in both sexes, up to 3 lbs. 8 oz. (Martin and Nelson, 1952); other reports indicate heaviest male reported was 3 lbs. 12 oz.; heaviest female, shot on lower Potomac R. near Washington, D.C., was 3 lbs. 10 oz. (Anonymous, 1955b).

Range: Nests in freshwater marshes and pothole country (see Addy, 1964) from c. Alaska, c. Yuk., n. Mack., and se. Man. south to n. Calif., w. Nev., n. Utah, n. Colo., Neb., and c. Minn.; winters from s. B.C., nw. Mont., n. Colo., n. Tenn. to e. Great Lakes, Chesapeake Bay, e. Mass., and Que., south to c. Mexico, the Gulf states, and n. Fla.; occasionally to Guatemala and Cuba.

Duck, acorn. *See* Duck, wood.

Duck, American black. *See* Duck, black.

Duck, American tufted. *See* Duck, ringnecked.

Duck, Bahama, *Anas bahamensis* (AY-nas bah-hah-MEN-sis); genus name: Lat., duck; species name: Lat., of, or from, Bahama, from which first specimen of this species described for science (see A.O.U. *Check-list,* 1957). A West Indian and S. American species reported as of casual occurrence in Fla.; one reported Del., Oct. 25, 1967 (Scott and Cutler, 1968); 18–20 in. long; differs from its relative the pintail in its white cheeks and brightly colored red (at base) and blue bill; duller in females (Johnsgard, 1968); narrow green speculum bordered by buff, and its fawn-colored, pointed tail distinguish it; largely coastal but also in interior saltwater ponds and lagoons, on vast tidal flats in the Bahama Is., also in freshwater ponds (see Bond, 1961); frequently a pair or family may be flushed from the salt ponds that are in the center of small mangrove islands (Pough, 1951); food is largely seeds and parts of water plants (see in Bent, 1923).

Other Names: Bahama pintail; white-cheeked pintail.

Hybrids: Has produced hybrids by crossbreeding with the wood duck, pintail, American wigeon, mallard, and others (Gray, 1958).

Weights: About 1½ lbs., females generally the larger (Johnsgard, 1968).

Range: Resident in Bahama Is., Hispaniola, Puerto Rico, Virgin Is., and more northern Lesser Antilles and S. America; casual in Fla. (Cape Canaveral), Wisc., Va., and Cuba. See other details in Delacour (1956).

Duck, black, *Anas rubripes* (AY-nas RUBE-rih-peez); genus name: *see* Duck, Bahama; species name: from Lat. *ruber,* red, and *pes,* foot; *black* in reference to its dark, or dusky, appearance. (Color ill., page 201.) E. N. America (e. Canada and Great Lakes region south to s. Fla.); one of dabbling ducks; sexes similar, uniformly dark brown; paler yellow-brown head and neck finely streaked; purple speculum bordered with black; in flight, overall dark color and white underwing linings distinguish it; feet may be brown to red (Peterson, 1947); bill dull green (female) to bright yellowish (male); male utters low croak; female a loud quack like related female mallard; one of wariest, quickest, most alert of all ducks (Pough, 1951); is the predominant breeding duck in creeks, ponds, freshwater and saltwater marshes, and swamps of north Atlantic coastal belt; a common duck of salt marshes; population reported declining between 1955 and mid-1960s (see articles in Wilder *et al.,* 1968; also Chamberlain *et al.,* 1972); starts into flight with powerful upspring from land or water, rising 8–10 ft. into air before away in swift direct flight; in winter, during day, often in large rafts out on open water along coast, or inland sit on ice of frozen lake or pond; strongly attached to wintering places; may remain as far north as open water for feeding permits; some always winter on New England coast; preferred wintering areas are tidal places and freshwater swamps from N.J. to S.C. in Atlantic Flyway and a few appear in n. Fla. (Addy, 1964); also winters in Mississippi Flyway (*see* flyways under Waterfowl); starts northward in Mar.–Apr. and before mid-June most are in Canada on northernmost part of breeding range (Wright, 1954); in fall, southward migration at peak in early Nov. (Benson and Bellrose, 1964).

Feeding Habits: Usually feeds in shallow waters where it can reach bottom by tipping up tail and probing in mud with bill; eats submerged plants similar to those eaten by mallards—pondweeds, wild celery, and eelgrass—also seeds of sedges, weeds, grasses; in shallow muddy ponds and swamps where black duck summers, eats largely aquatic insects and their larvae, salamanders, small frogs, tadpoles, toads, and even small mammals, also leeches, worms, small freshwater snails; in fall eats wild berries and moves into grain fields to eat wheat, barley, buckwheat, corn; visits woodlands to eat acorns, beechnuts; in winter, along seacoast, resorts mainly to salt marshes to feed at night, returns to open sea or to large lakes or ponds to spend day; in marshes and meadows, eats mostly snails, mussels, periwinkles, and other mollusks, also crustaceans with some vegetable foods (Bent, 1923).

Nest: Breeds in marine and brackish habitat backed by freshwater marshes especially near borders of wooded areas; nest, usually on ground on small island or on high ground near a marsh or open water (Pough, 1951); nest is often grasses and leaves in a depression and lined with down, well hidden in tall grass or under bushes; also nests in meadows or woods a mile or more from water or sometimes directly over water on muskrat house, old stump, in tree crotches or in tree cavities, caves, on or in old duck blinds, sometimes in abandoned nests of hawks or crows, or on ground under protection of beach plum and beach grass (Benson and Bellrose, 1964).

Eggs: Apr.–June; 5–17, usually 9–10 (Reed, 1968), cream-white to green-buff.

Incubation: By female; in Canada, averages 28.8 days; in Md., 26.2 days (Reed, 1968); after hatching, young may have long way to travel, as Wright (1954) reported a black duck leading her brood more than 2 mi. overland from nest to water; age at first flight about 60 days.

Other Names: American black duck; black; black English duck; blackie; blackjack; black mallard; blue-winged duck; brown duck; brown mallard; canard noir; canard noir d'hiver; dusky duck; dusky mallard; English duck; Labrador duck; ledge duck; mallard; marsh duck; nigger duck; old winter duck; outside duck; redleg; red-legged black duck; red-legged duck; red-paddle; sea duck; summer black duck; summer duck; spring black duck; velvet duck; winter black duck.

Age: One banded Long Is., N.Y., caught in muskrat trap 9 years later in Me.; a Mich. black duck lived to 14 years before killed; another, banded Leipsic, Del., picked up injured when 19 years, 7 months, at Norfolk, Va. (Kennard, 1975).

Albinism: Pure-white male, eyes deep reddish, collected (shot) in Berkeley County, S.C.; a pure-white one seen on Cooper R., S.C., with normally colored ones fall of 1930 but not collected to determine degree of albinism (Sprunt, 1931).

Flight Speed: 26 m.p.h. (Wood, 1933).

Hybrids: Gray (1958) lists many crosses, or hybrids, between black duck and other species —pintail, American wigeon, mallard, of which the hybrid offspring were fertile; also has crossed with Muscovy duck.

Weights: Males (346) average 2.76 lbs.; females (224) average 2.45 lbs. (Bellrose, 1976); heaviest to 3 lbs. 5 oz. (Martin and Nelson, 1952).

Range: Nests from c. Canada east to n. Que., n. Labrador, Newfoundland, south to N.D., n. Minn., Wisc., n. Ill., Ind., Ohio, Pa., Md., W.Va.,

e. Va., and sparingly to e. N.C.; winters from southern edge of breeding range south to Gulf coast, Fla., and Bermuda. Casual in Wash., Utah, Mont., Wyo., Colo., Neb., N.D., S.D.

Duck, black-bellied tree. *See* Whistling-duck, black-bellied.

Duck, bleating. *See* Gadwall.

Duck, buffle-headed. *See* Bufflehead.

Duck, bumblebee. *See* Bufflehead and Duck, ruddy.

Duck, burrow. *See* Shelduck.

Duck, Chinese spot-billed. *See* Duck, spot-billed.

Duck, cornfield. *See* Whistling-duck, black-bellied; Whistling-duck, fulvous; and Whistling-duck, West Indian.

Duck, dipper. *See* Bufflehead.

Duck, domestic. *See* Mallard.

Duck, dusky. *See* Duck, black, and Duck, mottled.

Duck, English. *See* Mallard.

Duck, Eskimo. *See* Eider, common.

Duck, fairy. *See* phalaropes in Phalarope Family.

Duck, falcated. *See* Teal, falcated.

Duck, fiddler. *See* Whistling-duck, fulvous.

Duck, fish. *See* Mergansers.

Duck, Florida. *See* Duck, mottled.

Duck, fool. *See* Duck, ruddy.

Duck, French. *See* Mallard.

Duck, fulvous tree. *See* Whistling-duck, fulvous.

Duck, gray. *See* Gadwall.

Duck, Guinea. *See* Common loon in Loon Family.

Duck, harlequin. *Histrionicus histrionicus* (his-trih-OWN-ih-kus); genus and species names: from Lat. *histrio, histrionis,* a stage player; relating to an actor (Jaeger, 1955); name presumably refers to the varied colors of the male that suggests an actor made up to play a role; *harlequin,* from name of a stock character of Italian comedy who wears a mask and parti-colored tights. (Color ill., page 201.) Lives around northern parts of the world; in N. America, breeds from Labrador and Alaska south in Rocky Mtns. to n. Calif. and Wyo., south in winter along coasts to s. Calif., N.J., Md.; small to medium-sized diving duck; fairly

common in West; rare in East except in Far North; most common along coasts of Aleutian Is. and Alaska; 15–21 in. long; wingspread 24–28 in.; male is blue-gray with chestnut sides, a large patch of white before its eyes, small round spot and vertical white line behind the eyes, and odd patches of white on body, wings; has relatively long tail; at distance on water or in flight appears dark—darker and smaller than the similarly shaped goldeneyes; female is uniform brown except for paler belly and three round white spots on head; no white wing patch; in summer, lives on turbulent mountain streams or on ponds and lakes and along rocky Arctic shores; in winter, in heavy surf along rugged rocky coasts with shelves, reefs, and jagged sunken rocks; flies swiftly and directly and usually low over water, often in compact flocks; often swims in close formation, bodies almost touching; male in courtship display utters a mouselike squeaking (Johnsgard, 1965); according to Delacour (1959), male utters low descending whistle, ending in long trill; female croaks harshly; but both sexes usually silent; "the females utter their usual call of *ek-ek-ek-ek,* to which males respond with a low or hoarse *hu,* or *heh-heh*" (Bent, 1925); in spring, move northward to Greenland in Feb. and Mar., arrive Mack., and Yukon in Alaska in May–June; also from wintering places on coasts may migrate short distances to inland mountain streams where many nest, also about pothole, glacial lakes; in fall, move south to wintering places along coasts from Sept. into Nov. (Bent, 1925).

Feeding Habits: Feed by day, usually by themselves, roost on rocks at night (Cottam, 1939); are proficient divers, seem to prefer to feed in rough waters broken by rocks and surf; dive to gravelly bottoms of streams, using feet and wings to swim underwater; walk along bottom against current like a dipper, wings closed, heads held low, poking bills among stones (Michael and Michael, 1922), where they catch and eat nymphs of mayflies, stone flies, and larvae of caddis flies; at sea eat animal life of rocky underwater places; on sandy coasts, feed about sunken wrecks and rock breakwaters (Pough, 1951); eat mostly animal foods (98%), mainly crustaceans (crabs, amphipods, isopods, etc.) and mollusks (barnacles, limpets, snails, chitons, etc., which they dislodge from rocks); also a few small fishes (sculpins), some sea worms, ascidians, bryozoans, etc.—see details in Cottam (1939); will accept bread thrown on water and from a feeding tray, macaroni, cooked potatoes, raisins, etc. (Michael and Michael, 1922).

Nest: In a hollow in ground under bushes and lined with grasses and down or in a hollow tree or cavity among rocks.

Eggs: May–July; 5–10, usually 6–8, cream to buff.

Incubation: By female, 30–32 days (Delacour, 1959); more recent field observations, 28–29 days; age when young first fly estimated at 40 days.

Other Names: Lord-and-lady; mountain duck; painted duck; rock duck; sea mouse; sea pigeon; squealer.

Weights: Females average 1¼ lbs.; males 1½ lbs. (Johnsgard, 1968).

Labrador duck

DUCK FAMILY

Masked duck

Range: Nests south of tundra from Lake Baikal and Lena R., Siberia, east to n. Kamchatka, Komandorskie Is., south to Manchuria, Kuriles; in N. America, from St. Lawrence Is., w.-c. Alaska, s.-c. Baffin Is. to ne. Que., Greenland, Iceland, Aleutian Is., mountains of se. Alaska, B.C., mtns. of Wash. and Ore., western slope of c. Sierra Nevada in Calif., c. Labrador; winters in N. America in Aleutian and Pribilof Is. and Alaska Pen. to c. Calif. (rarely); from se. Labrador, Newfoundland, Nova Scotia, south along Atlantic coast to Long Is., N.Y. (Lake Erie), N.J., and Md., and to Miami area, Fla., for first time, one seen from Nov. 1971 to Mar. 1972 (Stevenson, 1972a).

Duck, horse. *See* Canvasback.

Duck, Labrador, *Camptorhynchus labradorius* (kam-toe-RING-kus lab-rah-DOE-rih-us); genus name: from Gr. *kamptos,* flexible, and *rhynchos,* beak, in reference to soft leathery texture of upper part of bill (maxilla); species name: Lat., of Labrador. *Extinct;* a sea, or diving, duck; was related to the scoters (Scott, 1964); wintered along the Atlantic coast from Nova Scotia to Chesapeake Bay; its breeding range may have centered on Labrador (Johnsgard, 1968), from which it got its name, but its exact breeding grounds are unknown; about 20 in. long; male had white head with narrow black cap, white neck with black necklace, black rump, back, and tail; large white area on black wings; eyes red-hazel to yellow; female completely brown except for extensive white on wings; white line behind eyes, and white throat, also a pure-white speculum; bill like that of male (Greenway, 1958); the black bill unusual in its leathery spoonlike expansion at end of the maxilla (a "flap-edged" bill) with prominent vertical "teeth" (lamellae) in the lower mandible used by it to sift small shellfishes (mussels, clams) from mud or sand shoals (shallows), from which came one of its common names—sand shoal duck (Bent, 1925); according to Audubon, it was shy, difficult to approach; flew swiftly on whistling wings, usually seen in flocks of 7–10; in fall and winter it was shot and appeared in markets of New York, Baltimore, and N.J., probably never abundant or even very common throughout its range; as early as 1844 was rare on its winter range (Bent, 1925); from 1840 to 1860 appeared in fair numbers in New York markets (it was not very good to eat and often rotted before it could be sold); during 20 years (1850–70) it disappeared gradually from its winter range and from the markets (Greenway, 1958); its nest and eggs were unknown to scientists, and only 44 specimens of it exist in museums (Pough, 1951)—see locations of some in Greenway (1958); the last recorded specimen of the Labrador duck was collected (shot) by a Rockland County, N.Y., taxidermist, John G. Bell, along the coast of Long Is., N.Y., in 1875; the last one previous to Bell's bird was shot near Grand Manan Is., N.B., in 1871; a later record of questionable authenticity because of loss of identifiable parts was said to have been shot by a boy on the overflow of the Chemung R., Elmira, N.Y., Dec. 12, 1878. See accounts in Phillips (1922–26), Bent (1925), and Greenway (1958).

Other Names: Pied duck; sand shoal duck; skunk duck.

Duck, long-legged. *See* Whistling-duck, black-bellied; Whistling-duck, fulvous; and Whistling-duck, West Indian.

Duck, long-tailed. *See* Oldsquaw.

Duck, masked. *Oxyura dominica* (OCK-sih-YOU-rah dom-IN-ih-cah); genus name: from Gr. *oxys,* sharp, pointed, and *oura,* tail, referring to pointed tail of this duck; species name: refers to Santo Domingo, early name of the island of Hispaniola, West Indies, where the type specimen of this species was collected (*see* Type Specimen; Names and Naming). Tropical American duck, casual in S. Tex. One of the stiff-tailed ducks, closely related to the ruddy duck; an expert diver; small; 12–14 in. long; wingspread about 20 in.; resembles ruddy duck in form, general color, and behavior but smaller and male has masklike *black face;* buffy underparts; and a *white speculum* (male ruddy duck has white face and solidly dark wings); back is red-brown with black spots; female resembles female ruddy but has white speculum like male of her species (it is usually concealed when swimming on water); also female has two black stripes crossing white sides of face instead of single dark line crossing white cheeks as in female ruddy; immature resembles female with strongly contrasting dark stripes across cheeks and white speculum; this species walks awkwardly because feet are toward rear of body; apparently uses its relatively long tail in swimming underwater and to sweep aside underwater plants, on which it feeds; swims both backward and forward (see details in Delacour, 1959); on surface often swims with stiff tail fanned and tipped forward over back; to fly, first takes shallow dive under water and emerges in flight about a foot ahead of point of submergence; feeds during day; flies about at night; often swims low on water and can sink noiselessly below surface when alarmed; one of most inconspicuous of all ducks; in tropics, lives in dense, rush-grown marshes, and on ponds of fresh and salt water; sometimes seen in coastal mangrove swamps; in Rio Grande delta of Tex., where casual visitor in resacas (former channels of streams) and on ponds; usually seen in pairs or in small groups; in response to loud noise, male utters a distinctive *kuri-kuroo, kuri-kuroo;* female utters lower-pitched hissing sounds and henlike clucking; flies about more than the ruddy duck and especially early in morning or late in evening (Pough, 1951).

Feeding Habits: Eats mostly plant foods—seeds of weeds, grasses, and roots and tubers of plants—also occasionally eats insects and small crustaceans (Cottam, 1939).

Nest: Elaborately built of reeds or other plants in dense cover of marshes not far from water (Austin, 1961); in w. Cuba, built in rice plantations, well covered by growing rice (Bond, 1961).

Eggs: Nov.–Dec.(?); 3–4 (Delacour, 1959), 4–6 (Wetmore, 1965); light buff, smaller and smoother than those of the ruddy duck whose eggs have chalky surface (Bond, 1961); the females of the stiff-tailed ducks lay the largest eggs for their body size of any ducks; male, like male of ruddy duck, assists female in caring for young (Gilliard, 1958).

Incubation: Unrecorded (Delacour, 1959).

Weights: Females average 13 oz. each; males 11.4 oz. (Johnsgard, 1968).

Range: Resident of West Indies, Cuba, Jamaica, Hispaniola, Grand Cayman, and Puerto Rico, in Mexico (locally in Nayarit, Jalisco, Colima, Tamaulipas, and Vera Cruz), south through Guatemala, Costa Rica, south to n. Peru and n. Argentina; a great wanderer to thousands of miles out of its tropical range; in s. Tex. several successful nestings beginning in late 1960s; has strayed to Wis., Vt., Mass., Md., and La.

Duck, Mexican. *Anas diazi* (AY-nas DE-osseye); genus name: *see* Duck, Bahama; species name: given by Robert Ridgway for Augustín Díaz of Mexico, a founder and, until his death in 1893, Director of the Mexican Geographical and Exploring Commission (see Gruson, 1972). (Color ill., page 202.) A Mexican dabbling duck whose northern range extends into N.M. and sw. Tex.; now generally believed to be a subspecies, or race, of the mallard (see, for example, Delacour, 1956) but considered a valid species by Aldrich and Baer (1970); in U.S. never abundant even in frontier days, now rare and endangered (see account by Office of Endangered Species, 1973, listed in bibliography); is one of most difficult ducks to identify because of its resemblance to the mallard and the black duck, but usually seen only with its own kind (Ligon, 1961); 21–26 in. long; wingspread about 33–40 in.; dark brown but not as dark as black duck; both sexes similar and resemble a female mallard, but are more heavily streaked and spotted on the underparts; male's yellow-green bill unmarked; yellow-orange bill of female has dark ridge—bill of female mallard usually mottled (Peterson, 1961); like female mallard, has white-bordered dark blue-violet speculum and female utters mallardlike quacks; is distinguished in flight from mallard by its darker tail; about 500 left in U.S. in 1973; about 15,000 in Mexico; declining because of drainage of wetlands (see Wetmore *et al.*, 1965, and Ligon, 1961, for early history of this duck, and Tomlinson *et al.*, 1973, for later details of its nesting distribution in U.S.); according to Sincock *et al.* (1964), little known of the habits of this duck; most of them usually move southward out of N.M. before the hunting season, but may be heavily hunted in n. Mexico (Ligon, 1961); is wary, and in arid land of its range in U.S. is limited to mud flats, bars, and marshes of river bottomlands; in N.M., along the Rio Grande south of Albuquerque and in the San Simon marshes along the San Simon R.; it lives mostly in cattails, bulrushes, and *Phragmites* interspersed among willows and cottonwoods; it feeds frequently at night in irrigated fields of grain and alfalfa, and the few of its nests that have been discovered were in marshy and grassy places below zone of the mesquite scrub and near open water (Sincock *et al.*, 1964).

Feeding Habits: Eats green shoots of alfalfa and cattails; roots and shoots of grasses, especially panic grasses, also grains—corn and wheat—and seeds of weeds, grasses, aquatic insects, and occasionally small freshwater snails (Huber, 1923).

Nest: In *ciénaga* (marsh) of San Simon in extreme sw. N.M., nests built on ground in clumps of willows and in cattails surrounded by water; another in tall grass on dry ground at base of small tree 20 ft. from a slough; others in moist meadows, built of sedges and grasses, hidden in bulrushes and salt grass (see details in Lindsey, 1946); some hidden by surrounding plants arched over nests.

Eggs: N.M., Apr.–May; 5–13, avg., 9.4; greenish.

Incubation: Not reported but possibly 23–29 days as in mallard; Lindsey (1946) saw a female he disturbed at her nest fly away with an egg in her bill and got strong evidence that two other females he disturbed carried away their eggs from their deserted nests. *See* Birds That Carry Their Eggs under Eggs and Egg-laying.

Other Name: New Mexican duck.

Hybrids: Frequently crossbreeds with the mallard.

Weights: Females from 815 to 990 gr., or about 1 lb. 13 oz. to 2 lbs. 3 oz.; males 960–1060 gr., or about 2–2⅓ lbs. (Leopold, 1959).

Range: In Rio Grande Valley from the Bosque del Apache Refuge, N.M., to sw. Tex. and in the Pecos Valley, N.M., north to Bitter Lake Refuge and in San Simon marshes of Gila R. southward through highlands of Mexico as far as Morelos and Puebla; is commonest in the volcanic cordillera in central uplands of Mexico (Sincock *et al.*, 1964); casual in Neb. and Colo.

Duck, mottled, *Anas fulvigula* (AY-nas ful-VIG-you-lah); genus name: *see* Duck, Bahama; species name: from Lat. *fulvus*, reddish yellow, tawny, or gold-colored, and *gula*, throat; *mottled* refers to plumage. Commonest nesting waterfowl in marshes and coastal prairies of c. and s. Fla., La., Tex., a dabbling duck, thought by some authorities to be another race or subspecies of the mallard, which it closely resembles in appearance, habits, and biology; about 20 in. long; sexes outwardly similar; somewhat darker than female mallard but has paler head and lacks dark blotches on its *yellow* bill (Peterson, 1963); the dark tail and single white line at rear edge of the green-blue speculum helps distinguish it from the mallard; in flight, the white linings of its underwing surfaces show conspicuously as in black duck (Bent, 1923); smaller than black duck and has immaculate buffy throat; in winter, according to Robbins *et al.* (1966), mallards, black ducks, and mottled ducks may be in same marshes but by Jan. mottled ducks are paired, mallards and blacks generally are not; voice similar to mallard's; inconspicuous, usually seen in pairs or in family groups to a dozen, not often in large numbers, but mottled duck bulks fairly large as a duck hunted by sportsmen throughout its range (Sincock *et al.*, 1964); there are two races or subspecies—the Florida mottled duck and the western Gulf mottled duck (see details of ranges of each in Sincock *et al.*, 1964); the Fla. subspecies never leaves the southern part of the state (Baldwin *et al.*, 1964); the total wintering population in U.S. (Central, Mississippi,

Mottled duck

DUCK FAMILY

and Atlantic flyways) in Jan. 1972 estimated at 96,100 (Chamberlain *et al.*, 1972).

Feeding Habits: Reported to eat more animal foods than other puddle ducks—snails and other mollusks, dragonfly nymphs, water bugs, larvae of caddis flies, beetles, etc., and some crayfishes; also eats seeds of grasses and weeds and roots and leaves of grasses (Bent, 1923; see also Beckwith and Hosford, 1957).

Nest: In some years begins to nest in Feb. and season extends through August with peak nesting in May–June; is shy, secretive, and very sensitive to human disturbance (Sincock *et al.*, 1964); nest built on ground under bush or in concealment of clump of grasses on high ground in or near marsh or on island; in Fla., often under palmettos; like black duck, nests in many sites; raccoons, opossums, skunks, grackles, dogs, snakes eat its eggs; ducklings eaten by turtles, alligators, gars and other large fishes, and by swarms of blue crabs when water level is low in coastal marshes; the long nesting season limits numbers of eggs available to predators at any one time; therefore effects of egg-eaters not concentrated as among species with shorter nesting season (Sincock *et al.*, 1964). *See* discussion of adjustments of birds to egg destruction under Egg-Eating; *also* Eggs and Egg-Laying.

Eggs: Fla., Feb.–May; La., Apr.–June; Tex., Apr.–Aug. (Bent, 1923); 8–11, similar to those of black duck, shell smooth to glossy, cream-white to green-white.

Incubation: By female; Bent suggests period of 26–28 days; age when young first fly unknown.

Other Names: Black mallard; dusky duck; Florida duck; summer black duck.

Hybrids: Gray (1958) reported mottled duck hybridizing with shoveler, black duck, and mallard.

Weights: Males average about 2¼ lbs.; females average about same.

Range: Coastal region of s. Tex. and La., peninsular Fla. from Alachua City southward. Casual in Kans. and Colo.

Duck, mountain. *See* Duck, harlequin.

Duck, mud. *See* Coot, American, in Rail Family.

Duck, mule. *See* Shoveler.

Duck, muscovy, *Cairina moschata* (KAY-rye-nah mos-KAY-tah); genus name: given in 1822 by D. D. Fleming but no hint of etymology; name apparently refers to Cairo, Egypt, where this duck was known, but it is native of W. Hemisphere; species name: Lat., having the odor of musk; *Muscovy* (MUS-koh-vih), a corruption of musk, or musky duck, but believed by Sauer (1952) to be a corruption of Muisca, from Muisca Indians of c. Colombia (*see* Domestication). A native Mexican and C. and S. American species; belongs to tribe Cairinini, or Perching Ducks (Johnsgard, 1968); small numbers have been released in Fla., and feral ones are nesting in s. Tex., where they compete in choice of tree cavities for nesting with the black-bellied whistling-duck (Bolen, 1971); a large, black, clumsy duck with short, heavy black legs and large feet armed with sharp claws; sexes outwardly alike but males much larger and heavier; may be twice the weight of females (Delacour, 1959); males 30–35 in. long; females about 25 in. long (Peterson and Chalif, 1973); wild Muscovy is uniformly dark sooty brown or black, the upper parts glossed with green and purple; has conspicuous pure-white wing patches; from bill to yellow-brown eyes, has patch of *bare black skin* (smaller in female) with small knobby, sometimes red caruncles, lacking in female (Delacour, 1959); the domesticated Muscovy, raised for its meat, is heavier, coarser, may be white, speckled, fawn, blue, or gray; the large swollen caruncles in face are red or scarlet (Scott, 1964); eyes may be blue; according to Delacour, wild males are polygamous and do not form pair bonds with females but chase and subdue them to copulate; during the breeding season, males fight each other fiercely with wings and claws; strongest males keep others away from females; Muscovies sometimes gather in small flocks but more often the sexes are separate and alone or members of a flock follow a leader when walking in small groups; a permanent resident of coastal bottomland timber along rivers and streams or of ponds and marshes surrounded by woods; roosts at night on large branches of trees and often rests there in daytime; is usually silent; the hissing of the drake is barely audible and female's quacks are short and weak, usually uttered only when alarmed.

Feeding Habits: Eats small fishes, aquatic insects, some reptiles, termites, small mangrove crabs in brackish or saltwater coves in ne. Venezuela; also eats seeds, mollusks, snails, worms, and aquatic plants; at night goes into grain fields to feed (Phillips, 1922–26).

Nest: Eggs usually laid in bottom of tree cavity, 9–60 ft. up; nest usually has little or no down.

Eggs: Feb.–Mar.; 8–9, white with greenish sheen.

Incubation: In domesticated Muskovies, 35 days; age when young first fly apparently unknown; the downy young swim well and dive easily; resemble young wood ducks.

Other Names: Musk duck; musky duck.

Hybrids: Has hybridized in captivity with the Gambian spur-winged goose, *Plectropterus gambensis*, of Africa, domestic mallard, and other waterfowl (Johnsgard, 1965).

Weights: Males average 6½ lbs.; females 2¾ lbs. (Johnsgard, 1968); in domestic forms, males to 10–11 lbs.; females 5½–8 lbs. (Delacour, 1959, and Palmer, 1949).

Range: In Mexico, on coastal slopes or tropical lowlands from Sinaloa to Chiapas in west; in east, from Nuevo León and Tamaulipas to Yucatán Pen. (where local) (Peterson and Chalif, 1973); Sincock *et al.* (1964) could give no estimate of its numbers in Mexico but in some years not a single one seen in midwinter waterfowl inventories there; disappearance caused not only by man clearing bottomland timber habitat but from hunting; is resident south to Peru in w. S. America; and in east, south to Buenos Aires, Tucumán, and Santa Fe in Argentina (Delacour, 1959).

Muscovy duck

DUCK FAMILY

Duck, musky. *See* Duck, muscovy.

Duck, mussel. *See* Scaup, greater.

Duck, New Mexican. *See* Duck, Mexican.

Duck, North American ruddy. *See* Duck, ruddy.

Duck, painted. *See* Duck, harlequin.

Duck, pied. *See* Duck, Labrador.

Duck, raft. *See* Canvasback, Redhead, and Scaup ducks; name applied to them by hunters because of tendency of these diving ducks to form compact flocks of species of their own kind, or sometimes with other species of ducks that float on the water, seemingly without motion—like a raft (Buller, 1964).

Duck, red-legged black. *See* Duck, black.

Duck, ring-necked, *Aythya collaris* (AY-thih-ah col-AY-ris); genus name: *see* Canvasback; species name: Lat., pertaining to the neck, with collar (Jaeger, 1955), in reference to the brownish ring separating the breast and neck, and discernible only in good light. (Color ill., page 202.) Is one of the pochards (*see* Pochard); more confined to fresh water than other bay, or diving, ducks; summers in interior of n. and ne. U.S. and in Canada, largely in wooded country west of Ont.; winters along Atlantic and Gulf coasts and inland along southern parts of U.S.; rare on Pacific coast of U.S.; 15–18½ in. long; wingspread 24–30 in.; resembles lesser scaup; sexes have different color pattern; both have puffy, triangular-shaped head; male, besides his black head and neck, has *black back* (scaups have gray backs); has conspicuous white "crescent" in front of wings; gray sides; bill black-tipped and ringed twice with white (hunters call this duck the ringbill); brown female has distinct white eye ring and thin white line leading from eye toward back of head; a white ring around bill, indistinct white on face around base of bill; white belly; both sexes have *gray* wing stripe, not white as in scaups, and the outwardly similar tufted duck has no white "crescent" on sides, and has *white* wing stripe; female has no facial markings as in ring-necked duck; ring-neck is especially fond of forested ponds, marshes, swamps, and bogs, especially those with sweet gale and leatherleaf cover; is a good diver and can dive in deep water (to 40 ft., though usually forages in waters less than 5 ft. deep); its feet are large and powerful; it dives with wings tightly closed and swims rapidly below surface by use of feet alone; swims lightly and rapidly on surface; rises readily from the water making whistling sounds with wings as it does; flight is swift and vigorous; flies mostly in small flocks in open formation rather than in tight bunches or in lines (Bent, 1925); usually silent; male utters weak, wheezy whistle; female a harsh *cherr* (Delacour, 1959); winters on fresh or slightly brackish water; concentration of several thousand at one time not uncommon but is generally widely dispersed in marshes and on lakes, ponds, and reservoirs throughout the South (Addy, 1964);

once rare in e. U.S., about 1930 became established as nesting bird in Me. and in Maritime Provinces; now increasing as nesting bird and migrant in neighboring states; estimated total of 159,000 in the four flyways (*see* flyways under Waterfowl) in winter inventory of Jan. 1972 (Chamberlain *et al.*, 1972); moves north in Mar.–Apr., many on nesting grounds by May; migrates southward usually from mid-Sept. into late Nov.

Feeding Habits: Eats mostly plant foods (about 80% of diet): aquatic plants, seeds of sedges, grasses, smartweeds, water lilies, also seeds, rootstocks, tubers, leaves of pondweeds, and muskgrass and other algae; animal foods, especially eaten in summer: aquatic insects, snails and other mollusks, some spiders, water mites, crabs, water fleas, amphipods, annelid worms, etc.; owing to feeding habits of picking up food from muddy bottom is highly susceptible to lead poisoning.

Nest: Bulky structure of marsh plants just above water, in marsh border of pond or slough, floating bog, or muskeg.

Eggs: May–July; 6–14, usually 8–10, green-buff (zeal of nesting red-winged blackbirds in marshes in driving off ravens and crows said to help save eggs of ring-necked and black ducks from being eaten).

Incubation: 25–29 days; young first fly about 49 days after hatching (Mendall, 1958); 49–56 days (Johnsgard, 1968).

Other Names: American tufted duck; bastard broadbill; blackhead; blackjack; bunty; marsh bluebill; moonbill; ringbill; ring-billed blackhead; ring-billed duck; ring-neck; ring-necked scaup.

Age: One lived in National Zoo, Washington, D.C., to 10 years, 10 months; another in wild, lived to 10 years, 5 months (Kennard, 1975).

Albinism: One partial albino reported by E. A. McIlhenny at Avery Is., La.

Hybrids: Some hybrids reported by Gray (1958) of ring-necked duck with green-winged teal, mallard, lesser scaup, redhead, tufted duck, and canvasback; an adult female ring-necked duck × lesser scaup weighing 1 lb. 13 oz. collected (shot) on Missouri R. near Vermillion, S.D., Oct. 1967, from mixed flock of ring-necks and lesser scaups.

Weights: Males and females about same: 1 lb. 3 oz. to 1 lb. 15 oz. (Kortright, 1943); females average about 1½ lbs., males 1¾ lbs. (Johnsgard, 1968).

Range: Nests from s. B.C. and Prairie Provinces of Canada, W. Ont., and s. Que. south to e. Ore., e. Calif. (Lake Tahoe, rarely), White Mountains of Ariz., c. Colo., n. Neb., n. Iowa, nw. Pa. (occasionally), and from Maritime Provinces of Canada south to Me., N.H.; winters inland from s. B.C. south to deltas of the west coast of Mexico and Guatemala; in Nev. (casually), N.M., n. Tex., ne. Ark., s. Ill., and Atlantic coast from Mass. south to Fla. and from interior east-central and southern tier states and Gulf coast of U.S. south to Panama, Bahamas, and Greater Antilles.

Duck, rock. *See* Duck, harlequin.

Duck, ruddy. *Oxyura jamaicensis* (OCK-sih-YOU-rah jah-may-ih-SEN-sis); genus name: *see* Masked duck; species name: Lat., of the island of Jamaica, West Indies, the type locality from which the first specimen of this bird was collected; *ruddy*, for rust-red breeding plumage of the male. (Color ills., page 203.) Along with the cinnamon teal, the only waterfowl to breed in both N. and S. America (Johnsgard, 1968); has breeding range almost as widespread as that of redhead and canvasback—largely the Prairie Provinces of Canada and n.-c. U.S., Utah, Idaho, and Calif., also south to Tex. and sporadically in e. U.S.; small, chubby, one of the stiff-tailed ducks, an expert diver; 14–16 in. long; wingspread 21–24 in.; male larger than female, in summer is rusty red with *conspicuous white cheeks*, bright blue bill, dark cap, underparts white, lightly barred with brown; in winter, male resembles female, is gray with white cheeks (male has no eclipse plumage, molts directly, Aug.–Oct., into winter dress); female similar to winter male but with *horizontal brown streak through white cheeks;* male on water has habit of fanning and cocking tail forward; resembles grebe in flight and in swimming, can sink slowly below surface of water and disappear without leaving ripple, uses tail as rudder when swimming underwater; cannot walk upright on land, dives rather than flies to escape enemies; small rounded wings cannot lift it into air without pattering with large powerful feet for some distance along surface; its jerky flight, recognizable at long distance, is usually close to water; in migration usually flies in fair-sized to large flocks (Bent, 1925); usually silent but male when courting utters continual *chuck-chuck-chuck-chuck-chur-r-r* (see Kortright, 1943, and Johnsgard, 1965, for details of courtship); from winter quarters on large bodies of fresh water or shallow brackish bays, from Atlantic to Pacific coast across c. and s. U.S., moves north in Mar.–Apr.; southward in late Aug. and Sept.; apparently migrates only at night; has declined enormously in past because of tameness and relative ease of shooting, also because of periodic drought in breeding range and drainage; Chamberlain *et al.* (1972) estimated 151,100 in all four (mostly the Pacific and Atlantic) flyways in Jan. 1972 winter survey.

Feeding Habits: Seldom associates with other birds except coots; usually seen singly or in pairs, sometimes 8–12 together (Pough,1951); a diver, gets most of its food on bottom of fresh waters; about 75% plant foods: pondweeds (*Potamogeton* and widgeon grass) and eats large amounts of seeds of sedges, smartweeds, grasses, eats some muskgrass and other algae; also wild celery and other aquatic plants; midge larvae are bulk of its insect food, also eats caddis flies, predacious diving beetles, and others, some shellfishes (especially snails) and some crustaceans (see details in Cottam, 1939).

Nest: In prairie sloughs of Plains states and Canadian provinces, nests wherever it can find bulrushes, *Phragmites*, and cattails for cover; nest is basketlike structure built of surrounding marsh plants, about 8 in. above water and firmly attached to growing reeds of other marsh plants, the growing plants often arched over nest and helping conceal it; also uses old nests of other ducks and of coots, and sometimes builds its own nest on muskrat houses or on floating logs (Pough, 1951).

Eggs: Calif., Apr.–Aug.; N.D., June–July; Colo., May–Aug.; 5–17, usually 6–10, white or cream-white; in southern part of nesting range may raise two broods (Bent, 1925), which is unusual in member of Duck Family; it also lays its eggs in the nests of grebes and of other ducks (*see* discussion under Obligate Parasite); lays relatively enormous eggs for so small a duck (2.45 by 1.79 in.)—a clutch of 14 of its eggs weighs about 3 lbs., or about three times as much as the small female herself; the mallard and canvasback, each three times the size of the ruddy duck, lay substantially smaller eggs (Kortright, 1943). *See,* however, Masked duck.

Incubation: About 23 days (Bull, 1964); young first fly at 42–49 days after hatching (Bellrose, 1976); male, unlike males of most ducks, helps female raise young.

Other Names: Batter-scoot; blackjack; blatherskite; bluebill; booby; booby coot; bristle-tail; broadbill; broad-billed dipper; brown diving teal; bullneck; bumblebee duck; butterball; butter duck; cock-tail; creek coot; dapper; daub duck; deaf duck; dicky; dinky; dipper; dip-tail; dip-tailed diver; diver; dopper; dumb-bird; dumpling duck; dun-bird; dun-diver; fool duck; god-damn; gray teal; hard-head; hard-headed broadbill; heavy-tailed coot; hickory-head; leather-back; light-wood knot; little soldier; mud-dipper; noddy; North American ruddy duck; paddy; paddy-whack; pintail; quill-tailed coot; rook; roody; rudder bird; ruddy diver; saltwater teal; shot-pouch; sleepy brother; sleepy coot; sleepy dick; sleepyhead; spine-tail duck; spoonbill; spoon-billed butterball; sprig-tail; steel-head; stick-tail; stiff-tail; stiff-tailed wigeon; stub-and-twist; tough-head; wire-tail; water partridge; wigeon-coot.

Accidents: 50 (26 males, 24 females) killed or crippled on Man. nesting grounds summer 1971 by striking overhead utility wires near ponds (Siegfried, 1972).

Albinism: A pure-white but incomplete albino shot near La Crosse, Wisc., Oct. 1955; eyes gray-brown; feet and legs bright yellow; bill shell-pink.

Hybrids: Gray (1958) reported ruddy duck × greater scaup hybrids.

Weights: In N. America, males (13) average 1.2 lbs.; females (8) average 1.19 lbs. (Bellrose, 1976).

Range: In N. America, nests from c. B.C. and Prairie Provinces of Canada south to s. Baja Calif., c. Ariz., n. N.M., c. Tex., and to n. Iowa, n. Ill., Ohio, and nw. Pa., se. Me. to e. Mass., s. R.I., c. N.Y. and Long Is., N.Y., and N.J.; very local nester, readily establishes nesting colonies far outside its normal nesting range; since 1940s, increasing and expanding its nesting range in ne. U.S. (Bull, 1964) and into Great Lakes region; winters from s. B.C. south to Baja Calif., s. Nev., c. Ariz., s. N.M., c. Tex., s. La., s. Ill., nw. Pa., and Mass. south to Fla., Bahamas to Guatemala and Costa Rica; casual in Alaska; other subspecies nest in S. America (see Delacour, 1959).

Spot-billed duck

DUCK FAMILY

Duck, sand shoal. *See* Duck, Labrador.

Duck, sea. *See* Eider, common (female).

Duck, sheld. *See* Shelduck.

Duck, shoals. *See* Eider, common, and Eider, king.

Duck, skunk. *See* Duck, Labrador.

Duck, sleepy. *See* Duck, ruddy.

Duck, spine-tail. *See* Duck, ruddy.

Duck, spirit. *See* Bufflehead.

Duck, spoonbill. *See* Shoveler.

Duck, spot-billed, *Anas poecilorhyncha* (AY-nas pee-sil-oh-RING-kah); genus name: *see* Duck, Bahama; species name: from Gr. *poikilos,* variegated, spotted, and *rhynchos,* beak, in reference to the spotted bill of this species. A large, mallardlike Asiatic dabbling duck which Delacour (1956) classifies in three different subspecies, or races; closest to N. America is the Chinese spot-billed duck, *Anas poecilorhyncha zonorhyncha,* which breeds in southern parts of e. Siberia and along Amur R.; also in Mongolia, China, Manchuria, Korea, s. Sakhalin Is. north of Japan in Sea of Okhotsk, the Kurile Is. of Japan; moves south in winter; according to Delacour, much like the American black duck, is partly and moderately migratory; it frequents seacoasts as well as inland waters; the Chinese spot-billed duck, so identified by Gibson (1970), was recorded in N. America for the first time when an adult was seen at Adak Is., Alaska, on Apr. 10, 1970 (it was photographed at close range in color), where it remained until Feb. 15, 1971 (Gibson, 1971); about 24 in. long; sexes are outwardly very similar; in the Chinese spot-billed duck, plumage is buffy gray and black, spotted and laced, and with white patches on wing tertiaries; a blue speculum; and a large yellow spot at the tip of the black bill (Delacour, 1956); buffy face has black streak through eyes and to back of black crown.

Weights: Females average 2¼ lbs.; males 2½ lbs. (Johnsgard, 1968).

Range: See above.

Duck, stiff-tailed. *See* Duck, ruddy, and Duck, masked.

Duck, stock. *See* Mallard.

Duck, surf. *See* Scoter, surf, and Scoter, white-winged.

Duck, swamp. *See* Duck, wood.

Duck, tree. *See* Whistling-duck, black-bellied; Whistling-duck, fulvous; and Whistling-duck, West Indian.

Duck, tufted, *Aythya fuligula* (AY-thih-ah ful-IG-you-lah); genus name: *see* Canvasback; species name: diminutive of Lat. *fuligo,* soot, in reference to the sooty upperparts of the male in breeding plumage; *tufted*, for male's long crest of head feathers (it is the only crested pochard—*see* Pochard). (Color ill., page 202.) A Eurasian diving duck closely related to the scaups (Johnsgard, 1965); most common representative of pochard group in Britain (Scott, 1964); first record of its capture in N. America, a female on St. Paul Is., Alaska, May 9, 1911; was accompanied by a male (Bent, 1923); also reported since from the Aleutian Is., Greenland, and Mass. (A.O.U. *Check-list*, 1957); in winter 1970–71, total of at least 14 seen along Atlantic coast from Iceland south to Long Is., N.Y., and along Pacific coast from Adak Is., Alaska, south to Palo Alto, Calif., led Buckley (1971) to comment: "is colonizing North America . . . along the Atlantic coast from Iceland, and along the Pacific coast from Siberia. Eventual North American breeding is likely"; a male seen at Bayhead, N.J., Feb. 21, 1972 (Scott and Cutler, 1972); one at Chicago, Ill., Dec. 3, 1972, with a flock of greater scaups, remained to Apr. 10, 1973 (Kleen and Bush, 1973); a wild pair reported on pond at Bronx Zoological Gardens, spring 1974; 18–22 in. long; wingspread 30–35 in.; male resembles ring-necked duck with its black head, neck, breast, and upperparts, but has thin *crest on back of head; sides pure white;* and *white wing stripe*—all good field marks (*see* comparison with ring-neck under Ring-necked duck); adult dark brown female has shorter crest than male and *lacks white eye ring* of similar female ring-neck; bill slate blue with narrow black bar near tip; eye iris golden yellow in both sexes; usually frequents open fresh waters of large lakes and reservoirs, even in city parks, seen occasionally on tidal estuaries and bays with saltwater diving ducks and rarely seen at sea except during freezing of fresh waters; early in Mar., large flocks split up into smaller groups, in Britain are paired by end of Mar.; members of pair keep close together during early part of breeding season and become very tame (see courtship behavior in Johnsgard, 1965); from Sept. into Oct., assemble in small companies on large bodies of fresh water; flocks grow larger into Nov.–Dec., when may number thousands (Bent, 1923); male utters soft, repeated whistle; female a harsh *kurr-kurr* (Delacour, 1959); some are migratory, those in temperate climate move about and gather in flocks in winter.

Feeding Habits: An expert diver; eats roots, seeds, and buds of aquatic plants, also skims flies and duckweeds from surface of water; dives for freshwater mussels, snails, aquatic insects, frogs, tadpoles, small fishes (Bent, 1923).

Nest: Built on islands in lakes or on banks of small pools either isolated or in small colonies; a hollow in ground lined with grasses and dark gray down, hidden in reeds or under bushes close to water or in tuft of grass on slopes (Delacour, 1959).

Eggs: May–June; 6–14, usually 8–10, yellow-brown to greenish.

Incubation: By female, 23–28 days; age when young first fly estimated at 45–50 days.

Hybrids: Some of the crosses in captivity noted by Gray (1958) are tufted duck hybridizing with wood duck, pintail, American wigeon, Eurasian wigeon, mallard, lesser scaup, greater scaup, redhead, ring-necked duck, bufflehead, and common goldeneye; Johnsgard (1965) cites hybridizing of tufted duck with greater scaup, common white-eye, and European pochard, hybrids of last two proved fertile.

Weights: Females average 1½ lbs.; males 1¾ lbs. (Johnsgard, 1968).

Range: Nests south of tundra from Iceland, the Faeroes, Scandinavian Pen., Soviet Russia, including Siberia east to Sakhalin, Japan, the Komandorskie Is. south to c. Europe, Syria, nw. Mongolia; winters in British Isles and continental Europe south to Mediterranean and Black seas, in Africa, south to Uganda, s. India, Burma, Vietnam, and c. Philippines; in N. America in winter and in spring, casually along Atlantic and Pacific coasts: accidental in Ill. (Chicago).

Duck, West Indian tree. *See* Whistling-duck, West Indian.

Duck, wood, *Aix sponsa* (AIKS SPON-sah); genus name: from Gr., *aix*, a water bird; species name: Lat., a betrothed, a bride, or "promised one," in reference to its exquisite plumage, as though it were "arrayed for bridal" or a marriage (Coues, 1882); *wood* refers to its preferred habitat. (Color ills., pages 204, 205.) A medium-sized, dabbling freshwater duck, native of N. America, in summer from s. Canada south in U.S. to Tex. and from Atlantic coast to Pacific in suitable habitat; 17–20 in. long; wingspread about 28–30 in.; male in brightly colored breeding plumage considered by many the most beautiful native N. American duck; lives in open woodlands around forested lakes, in swamps, wooded river bottoms, along banks of wooded ponds, and streams, sometimes within city and town parks; male has darkly iridescent head with "slicked-back" crest; eyes orange-red; head striped with white; bill a variegated pattern of red, yellow, black, white; white throat; breast and neck rich burgundy; back dark and iridescent; belly white; dark wings and dark, square tail; female has grayish head with crest, and prominent white ring around dark brown eyes; bill *black;* has white throat; back brown; breast and flanks brownish; brownish underparts streaked with white; male in eclipse plumage of summer resembles female but maintains bright colors of bill and has no white around eyes as has female; underparts are white; in flight, crested head of wood duck held high, with *bill angled downward;* short neck, and contrasting white underparts are good field marks; takes off from water in almost vertical bound; flight is swift and direct; female in flight resembles female (or young) baldpates (American wigeons) but these fly with bill pointed forward, also the tail is *pointed;* on water, wood duck sits high with tail angled upward; on land walks or runs with greater ease than most ducks, and frequently perches in trees; on water, alert for danger, quick to flush when approached; the hen, from water or in flight, utters a loud *hoo-eek* (also attributed to male by some observers) and a sharp *cr-r-ek, cr-r-ek* when alarmed; male's usual call is a sparrowlike *jeeeeee*, high-pitched and rising at end (Hester and Dermid, 1973—see courtship in Delacour, 1959, especially Lorenz, 1971, and Johnsgard, 1965). Many wood ducks court and pair in fall and in winter, when most are on inland waters of s. U.S.; do not usually gather in large flocks and do not closely associate with other waterfowl; family groups often form small flocks of 15–20 in migration; however, in fall and winter, at sunset fly in small flocks from feeding places in surrounding country to pools in swamps or to woodland ponds, where up to 200 or even thousands may enter same roost on water; next morning, at sunrise, depart in small flocks (Hester and Dermid, 1973); an early spring migrant, arrives on northern part of breeding range in Mar.–Apr. after ice has left woodland ponds and timbered sloughs at time when wood ducks in s. U.S. are raising families; in fall moves southward from Oct. to Dec. (Bent, 1923); once threatened with extinction in early 1900s from overshooting, cutting off of forests, drainage of swamps; in 1918, governments of Canada and U.S. closed the hunting season on wood ducks and for following 23 years, until limited hunting allowed in 1941; as result of protection from shooting, a subsequent small bag limit, and increased protection of its habitat, numbers rose steadily until 1960s, when government waterfowl biologists estimated fall population of those years at 2½–3½ million; however, with increasing human population and loss of wood duck habitat, probably cannot maintain this population (see Hester and Dermid, 1973, for details; also Jahn *et al.*, 1966).

Feeding Habits: Feeds in wild rice marshes, in sluggish streams and ponds filled with aquatic plants and insects or along wooded banks; about 90% of food is plant life; is especially fond of tiny floating duckweeds, also called duck's meat, water lentils, and seed "moss"; also eats bald cypress cones and galls, seeds and tubers of sedges, grasses, smartweeds, water chinquapin, pondweeds and their seeds, wild rice, seeds of water lilies, water elm, sometimes wanders deep into woods for acorns, beechnuts, hickory nuts, grapes, and berries; eats more fruits and nuts than any other American duck—a male wood duck shot near Henning, Otter Tail County, Minn., in Oct. 1959, had the unusual number of 56 acorns of bur oak in its throat and crop (Jarosz, 1960); in fall sometimes visits fields in South at dusk and dawn to eat kernels of corn scattered by harvest (Hester and Dermid, 1973); eats many aquatic insects, some minnows, frogs, tadpoles, snails, and small salamanders (Bent, 1923).

Nest: Usually in a natural hollow of the trunk or cavity in large branch of a tree; sometimes near water but may be in hollow of tree a mile or more from water if necessary, also even near a dwelling house or in shade tree of park or village, in a cemetery or near boat docks, also in abandoned nesting or roosting cavity of pileated woodpecker, sometimes, usually fatally, in chimney of house; but usually nests in swamps or along woodland streams, most frequently in cavities of bald cypress, sycamore, silver and red maples, sour gum, oaks, apple, basswood, elms, and sweet gum; may be in cavity 5–50 ft. above ground; hen seems to prefer nesting cavities 30 ft. or more up, above ground or water; average entrance hole about 4½ × 8 in. but prefers smaller openings down to 3½ × 4 in., smallest opening a hen wood duck can enter (Hester and Dermid, 1973; see also Hansen, 1966), and a minimum inside cavity of 5 × 5 in.; cavities less than 50 in. deep are preferred, with average depth of 22 in.; the hen never modifies the cavity and uses only her own down feathers for a nest after she begins laying eggs; will also use man-made nest boxes, preferably set on poles in standing water (see information and illustrations in Hester and Dermid, 1973); recently discovered nesting in s. Tex., an expansion of wood duck's range in a region broadly coincident with the northern nesting range of the black-bellied tree duck (Bolen and Cottam, 1967), both nest in natural cavities in trees, at least two nests were reported in Live Oak County, Tex., in which there were mixed clutches of both wood duck and black-bellied whistling-duck eggs; the female wood duck was found incubating the eggs; apparently hen wood duck dominates hen black-bellied whistling-ducks at the nest site (Bolen, 1971).

Eggs: Fla. and N.C., Feb.–May; elsewhere, usually Apr.–June, sometimes second set of eggs in South (double-brooded)—see details in Hester and Dermid (1973) and Rogers and Hansen (1967); eggs resemble hen's eggs, dull white to brown-white; 9–12, but 20–40 reported from laying of more than one female in same nest (Fuller and Bolen, 1963); 9–14, usually 10–12 (Reilly, 1968).

Incubation: By female, 27–33 days; about half hatch in 30 days (Leopold, 1966); 28–37 days (Hester and Dermid, 1973); at hatching, young have sharp claws and climb to opening of nesting cavity, then leap to ground, regardless of height, in response to calls of female on ground below; she then leads them to nearest water (do not return to nest cavity); young first fly about 63 days after hatching. For incorrect observations of young carried to ground by female, see Bent (1923).

Other Names: Acorn duck; bridal duck; Carolina duck; Carolina wood duck; squealer; summer duck; swamp duck; the bride; tree duck; wood wigeon; woody.

Accidents: Some caught in steel traps set along waterways for muskrats; although females occasionally nest successfully in house chimneys, many more get trapped and die because females cannot get out; according to Stewart, P.A. (1971); can be protected by screening top of chimney.

Flight Speed: Timed in Wisc. flying along river toward roost, 39–55 m.p.h. (Lokemoem, 1967); Stewart measured the flight speed of eight; they averaged 31.2 m.p.h., at which wingbeats were 7.5 per second (see wingbeats per second of other birds in Terres, 1968a).

Hybrids: According to Gray (1958), has crossbred and produced hybrids with 25 species of ducks in captivity but none of its hybrids have proved fertile (Johnsgard, 1965); has crossbred with pintail, shoveler, green-winged teal, cinnamon teal, mallard, gadwall, lesser scaup, redhead, tufted duck, common goldeneye, and others.

Weights: Males (84) average 1.5 lbs.; females (60) average 1.48 lbs. (Bellrose, 1976).

Range: Smaller population of w. N. America nests principally in B.C., Wash., Ore., and Calif. as far south as Santa Barbara; winters north of Los Angeles (is generally absent in the prairie, Rocky Mountain, and Great Basin states), and western population is apparently isolated from that of e. N. America (Hester and Dermid, 1973); larger population of e.-c. N. America nests from s. Man., e. N.D., e. S.D., e. Neb., e. Kans., e. Okla., and n. Minn., s. Ont., s. Que., N.B., Nova Scotia, and Prince Edward Is., south to se. and s. Tex., Gulf coast, s. Fla., and Cuba; eastern population winters from c. Mo., s. Ill., e. Md., Va., to Gulf coast, Fla., and Cuba, casually to Jamaica and Bermuda.

Eider, American. *See* Eider, common.

Eider, common, *Somateria mollissima* (somat-EE-rih-ah mol-LIS-sih-mah); genus name: from Gr. *soma, somatos,* body, and *erion,* wool, or down, referring to the commercially valuable eider down of members of this genus; species name: superlative of Lat. *mollis,* soft; meaning very soft, referring to softness of the down (Coues, 1882); *eider,* from an Icelandic name for the bird. (Color ills., page 207.) Summers along Arctic coasts of n. N. America from Alaska to Newfoundland, and south to Me.; winters south along Pacific coast to Wash.; Atlantic coast to Va., N.C., rarely to Fla., in winter seen in large rafts off Chatham, Mass.; tough and hardy, known to endure temperatures down to −50° F.; the most abundant and most widely distributed eider (Johnsgard, 1968); largest eider, and largest of the sea, or diving, ducks; almost entirely marine; 23–27 in. long; wingspread 35–42 in.; male has *white back and black sides;* considerable white on wings; head white with black cap; two pale green patches on back of head; female light brown, body heavily *barred* with dark browns; at close range, she can be distinguished by sloping (like canvasback) head profile, has long, slender frontal shield which extends much farther above bill than in other eiders; flight of these heavy-bodied sea ducks appears slow and labored but is actually swift and direct; heavy head held low, bill pointed slightly downward; usually in small flocks, fly in Indian file or abreast, often close to shoreline, follow indentations of land but seldom fly over land; in stormy weather, often follow the troughs of the sea and lost to sight between waves; in winter, are usually silent; males utter pigeon-like cooing notes and moans, one a hoarse, grating *kor-er-korkorr-kor;* female voice slightly higher-pitched, utters hoarse quacks (for courtship, see details in Bent, 1925, and in Delacour, 1959); in spring, starts moving northward along New England coast in late Mar. to early Apr.; arrives on northern breeding grounds (males start in advance of females) from late May to early June; in fall, usually appears off coast of New England, Nov. into Dec.; in migration, travel immense distances around land masses such as Alaska and Siberia to reach their breeding or wintering grounds (see Thompson and Person, 1963, and Johnson, 1971, for accounts of eider migrations along

Alaskan coast; see also Gauthier *et al.,* 1976).

Feeding Habits: Seems to prefer feeding in fairly shallow waters around submerged ledges and reefs of rocky shores; an expert diver and if necessary can go down 35–60 ft. (Bent, 1925), uses wings to swim underwater and if alarmed comes out of water flying; feeds mainly by day at low tide; toward evening, flock flies out to sea to spend night; eats virtually 100% animal foods—mussels, clams, and other bivalves, whelks and other gastropods; also starfishes, sea urchins, and other echinoderms; crustaceans such as crabs and amphipods and some fishes (sculpins), and marine worms, etc., all of which give its flesh a strong, fishy flavor; of all foods, the blue mussel, *Mytilus edulis,* which grows in dense beds on rocky or pebbly bottoms, is a favorite and the staple food (185 were found in the gullet and gizzard of a single eider); eiders swallow whole mussels and other shellfishes up to 2 in. long, which are broken into fine pieces in the birds' powerful gizzards. *See* Gizzard. See details of food habits of eiders in Cottam (1939).

Nest: Where not persecuted, nest in colonies, on ground, usually close to salt water, often on islands or rocky headlands, in a depression in ground or in rocks, sometimes among cliff ledges, but often partially or wholly concealed under bushes or among grasses and rushes or under rock overhang, sometimes on tundra or coastal marshes; nest has foundation of matted seaweeds, mosses, sticks, and grasses, the nest profusely lined around, under, and sometimes over the eggs with softly fluffy dull gray down supplied by female (*see* discussion of its uses under Eider Down).

Eggs: Usually May–July; 3–5, pale brown to olive green.

Incubation: By female, about 26–30 days; age when young first fly at least 56 days; as soon as hatched, young are led to water by female.

Other Names: American eider; big sea-duck; black and white coot; canvasback; Dresser's eider; eider duck; Eskimo duck; Isle of Shoals duck; laying duck; looby; northern eider; sea duck (female); squam duck; wamp.

Accidents: Occasionally a mussel closes its shell on the tongue of an eider and the bird is either strangled to death or starves (Cottam, 1939).

Age: One banded wild bird lived to 12 years, 2 months (Kennard, 1975).

Hybrids: Reported, apparently in captivity; crossbreeds with the pintail, mallard, velvet scoter, and king eider; several "presumed natural hybirds between common eider and king eider have been reported" (Gray, 1958); one male hybrid, a cross between common eider and king eider, was shot in 1929 just outside Reykjavik, Iceland (Pettingill, 1959).

Weights: Males (28) average 4.95 lbs.; females (32) average 4.44 lbs. (Bellrose, 1976).

Range: Nests along coasts and offshore islands around northern parts of world; Eurasia; in N. America, from Aleutians and sw. Alaska to Newfoundland, Nova Scotia, and Me., north to Canadian Arctic Is., Greenland; winters along south edge of ice pack and Alaska Pen. south along Pacific coast to B.C., Wash., and lower Mack., and accidentally in interior N. America in Man., Ont., N.D., Kans., Iowa, and south along Atlantic coast to New England and Long Is., N.Y. (winter visitor to Montauk area), rarely to N.J. (Bull, 1964), also casually to N.C. and rarely to Fla., where about five records; one, more recently, to Fla. Keys (Garden Key), Apr. 3, 1967 (see details in Petrovic and King, 1972).

Eider, king, *Somateria spectabilis* (somat-EE-rih-ah speck-TAH-bih-lis); genus name: *see* Eider, common; species name: Lat., conspicuous, spectacular, in reference to its beauty and showiness; *king,* from the male's bright orange knob above bill and pearl-gray crown which may have kingly suggestions (McAtee, 1955c). (Color ill., page 206.) Has more extensive circumpolar distribution than other eiders; in summer on coasts and islands of entire Arctic O., slightly farther north than common eider; enormously abundant in some places in North, especially in migration off Point Barrow, Alaska (see Thompson and Person, 1963, and Johnson, 1971); winters north to limit of open waters; irregular and rare south of Long Is. on east coast and south of Kenai Pen., Alaska, on west coast; in U.S., seen on Great Lakes and south on inland waters as far as Kans. and W.Va.; gregarious, but less sociable than any of its relatives; smaller than common eider; 19–25 in. long; wingspread 35–40 in., male at distance shows *black back and sides; white foreparts;* orange knob or shield on forehead; in flight shows *large white patch* on top of each dark wing and contrasts with *black back* (male common eider has *white back*); crown is pearl gray, cheeks pale green; female is somewhat redder brown than female common eider and with shorter bill, concave, rather than sloping forehead; immatures migrate farther south than adults (Robbins *et al.,* 1966) and appear overall dusky with light brown head; off southern coasts of New England, where an irregular winter visitor, sometimes common, appears in small flocks, prefers outer rock ledges and reefs, sometimes 15 mi. out (Bent, 1925), but on Long Is., N.Y., and N.J. coast, small flocks seen near rock jetties; courting male utters soft, dovelike cooing, *urrr-urrr-URR!;* females, a low *kuck,* or *kwack* (Parmelee *et al.,* 1967); see details of courtship in Delacour (1959) and Johnsgard (1965); in migration, hugs shoreline; in spring moves toward Arctic breeding grounds in Mar.–Apr.; in fall, arrives along Atlantic coast and interior U.S. usually from early Nov. into Dec.

Feeding Habits: Feeds in deeper water, and can remain under longer than any other duck except the oldsquaw (Cottam, 1939); said to have been taken in gill nets at depth of 150 ft. (*see* Swimming and Diving); sometimes descends to 180 ft.; food almost entirely animal (about 95%); dives for mollusks (about 46% of its animal food), mussels may make up almost half the mollusk food; also eats periwinkles, moon shells, whelks, oyster drills, limpets, etc.; crustaceans (second favored group) such as king crabs, cancer crabs, hermit crabs, and amphipods, and, among echinoderms, sand dollars, sea urchins, starfishes, brittle stars, sea cucumbers, etc., also sea anemones, many

aquatic insects such as larvae of caddis flies, and plant foods (about 5% of total diet) such as eelgrass, widgeon grass, and algae.

Nest: Scattered over tundra on mainland well back from coast, not in colonies as with common eider, often far from water.

Eggs: June–July; 4–7, usually 5–6, olive buff.

Incubation: By female, 23–24 days (Parmelee *et al.,* 1967); age when young first fly not reported.

Other Names: Canvasback; cousin; Isle of Shoals duck; king-bird; mongrel drake; passing duck; sea duck; wamp's cousin; warnecootai.

Hybrids: See under Common eider.

Weights: Males (41) average 3.68 lbs.; females (140) average 3.45 lbs. (Bellrose, 1976).

Range: Nests on Arctic coasts and islands from nw. Alaska to Hudson and James bays, and coasts of Greenland and n. Russia east to Novaya Zemlya, along Arctic coasts of Siberia to Chukotski Pen. and north shore of Gulf of Anadyr; winters in Pacific north as far as open water in Bering Sea, south to Kamchatka, Aleutian Is., s. Alaska, to Calif. (casually), occasionally to Great Lakes, and on Atlantic coast from Newfoundland to Mass., more rarely to Long Is., N.Y., N.J., casually to Ga., casually to interior U.S.: Kans., Iowa, Ill., W. Va., Ohio, also in Iceland, British Isles, n. Scandinavia.

Eider, northern. *See* Eider, common.

Eider, Pacific. *See* Eider, spectacled.

Eider, spectacled, *Somateria fischeri* (somat-EE-rih-ah FISH-er-eye); genus name: *see* Eider, Common; species name: given in 1847 in honor of Johann Gotthelf Fischer von Waldheim (1771–1853), doctor and geologist, born in Waldheim, Germany, noted for his work in Russia in natural history (Gruson, 1972); *spectacled,* for the circle of silver-white feathers, framed in black, around each eye, which suggests spectacles. (Color ills., page 206.) Asiatic and N. American diving duck, common along coast of ne. Siberia, but rare in N. America, where it has extremely limited breeding range on Arctic coasts of Alaska; there, unlike the Steller's eider of similar range, it favors shallow, muddy, coastal waters near river deltas and ponds in lowland tundra somewhat near saltwater; wintering concentrations have never been discovered (Johnsgard, 1968); 20–23 in. long; wingspread 35–36½ in.; heavy, clumsy-appearing; male white above, black below, appears like common eider but head mostly pale green and *has large white patch around each eye, surrounded by narrow rim of black (suggests "goggles");* female brown and barred plumage, like that of other eiders, but at close range shows pale suggestion of "goggles" around each eye, and feathers on upper part of bill extend down below nostrils (Peterson, 1961); flies in small compact flocks of rarely more than 50 birds; skims close to surface of ice or of marsh; male utters weak *ah-hoo!* in courtship display (see in Johnsgard, 1965).

Feeding Habits: Frequents brackish pools; during summer subsists on small crustaceans,

grasses, seeds; in winter eats amphipods and other soft-bodied crustaceans, common blue mussels, gastropods, sand dollars, etc.; mollusks (mostly razor clams) are largest volume of its food; also eats moon shells, eats abundantly of larvae of caddis flies and some midge larvae; eats plant foods such as pondweeds, fruits and seeds of crowberry, seeds of sedges, grasses, etc. (see Cottam, 1939).

Nest: Usually 3–4 ft. from water's edge, built of grasses and lined with breast down of female, well concealed in bed of dry grasses near edge of brackish or freshwater pond on tundra or on small island in a pond and on knolls close to water's edge.

Eggs: June–July; 4–9, olive buff to greenish.

Incubation: Period not established but about 24 days; age at which young first fly 50–53 days.

Other Name: Fischer's eider.

Weights: Females 3 lbs. 6 oz. to 3 lbs. 14 oz.; males 3 lbs. 3 oz. to 3 lbs. 12 oz. (Kortright, 1943); females average 3½ lbs.; males 3¾ lbs. (Johnsgard, 1968).

Range: Nests along Arctic seacoast of ne. Siberia from mouth of Lena R. and New Siberian Is. to East Cape, and along nw. coast of Alaska from mouth of Kuskokwim R. and St. Lawrence Is. to Point Barrow; winters off Pribilof and Aleutian Is., and sparingly eastward along the Alaska Pen. to Sanak and Kodiak Is.; casual to Calif.

Eider, Steller's, *Polysticta stelleri* (pol-ih-STICK-tah STEL-er-eye); genus name: Lat., from Gr. *poly,* much, or many, and *stiktos,* punctured, dotted, dappled, spotted; species name: given in 1769 by the German systematic zoologist Peter S. Pallas for the duck's discoverer, Georg M. Steller, German zoologist and traveler who got the first specimens of this bird known to science on the coast of Kamchatka Pen., ne. Russia, near its present center of abundance and not far from its principal breeding grounds in ne. Siberia (Bent, 1925). (Color ill., page 207.) Also nests on Arctic coasts and islands of Alaska; smallest of the eiders, a medium-sized, handsome, oddly marked sea duck; trim, with none of heavy build and clumsy appearance of other eiders; shaped like a mallard, bill stubbier, tail longer; 17–19 in. long; wingspread 28–30 in.; male in breeding plumage has white head, glossy black ring around the eyes, and a green bump (crest) on back of head; black collar with a black line extending down back; white sides with *round black spot* on each side of breast; has *buffy underparts;* unlike other eiders, both sexes have a *purple speculum bordered with white* which distinguishes uniformly dark brown female from other female eiders; she also has tiny rounded crest on back of head; in flight, smaller size and black line of male, extending from neck partway down white back, may be distinguishing mark; flies much swifter than other eiders; in taking off, runs along the water like other diving ducks; wings whistle in flight like a goldeneye's; in winter, seldom wanders south of Aleutian Is., where gathers in large flocks associated with common and king eiders in harbors free of ice; shy at this time (Bent, 1925); male utters low crooning notes; female, harsh growl; in Hooper Bay region of Alaska, is last eider to appear there in spring, by last of May, flying about ponds on tundra (Delacour, 1959). See courtship in Johnsgard (1965).

Feeding Habits: Frequents clear water, shuns muddy shores; in winter at Aleutian Is., flocks feed near sunken ledges and rocky islets, also in shallow, sandy, muddy bay; about 87% of food is animal (Cottam, 1939); especially fond of soft-bodied crustaceans, opens wings when diving; eats amphipods, isopods, and barnacles, also some crabs; among mollusks, eats common blue mussels, razor clams, and others, also moon shells and periwinkles; eats aquatic insects; some small fishes; also annelid worms, sand dollars, etc.; eats some plant foods, especially pondweeds, both seeds and vegetal parts, also eelgrass, some crowberries, and algae, all of which make up about 13% of its food.

Nest: In deep holes in mosses of tundra and lined with down, often between tussocks, generally on or near edge of a pond or on tidewater flats; male remains with female until she has laid her eggs and starts incubating, then moves south (Delacour, 1959).

Eggs: June–July; 6–10, pale yellow to olive green or olive buff.

Incubation: Period of and age when young first fly unknown.

Other Names: Lesser eider duck; also soldier duck (Alaska) from sometime habit of flock in swimming single-file.

Weights: Females 1 lb. 14 oz. to 2 lbs.; males 1 lb. 14 oz. to 2 lbs. 2 oz. (Kortright, 1943).

Range: In N. America, nests along coasts and islands of Arctic Alaska from Hooper Bay to Demarcation Point, and on St. Lawrence Is.; in Siberia from New Siberian Is. east to the Chukotski Pen., south in Bering Sea region to Anadyr Bay; winters in the Pribilof and Aleutian Is. to the Kurile and Komandorskie Is. and off coasts of Kamchatka Pen., Russia, and Scandinavia; the south coast of the Alaska Pen. and the Shumagin Is. to Kodiak and Kenai Pen.; has been taken in Me. and Md.

Gadwall, *Anas strepera* (AY-nas STREP-eh-rah); genus name: *see* Duck, Bahama; species name: from Lat. *streperus,* noisy, apparently in reference to loud calls of the female; *gadwall,* a name of obscure origin, the common English name of this duck since the British ornithologist Francis Willughby used it in 1676 (Newton, 1893–96). (Color ill., page 208.) Dabbling, freshwater duck of temperate zone of both Old and New Worlds; in N. America, uncommon in general, lives primarily in West and Midwest but a separate population nesting in e. N. America and established since 1939 (Anonymous, 1974b); only rarely or locally known in the E. Hemisphere; 19–23 in. long; wingspread 31–36 in.; a slender, gray-brown duck with a *black rump,* which, when it is swimming, contrasts sharply with gray body; has pale brown head and neck; *reddish brown on forewings;* in flight shows white patch of speculum in wings, near body (the only dabbling duck with white speculum); belly white; feet yellow; bill *dark* (the similar black duck is browner with a *yellow* or greenish bill); female gadwall is paler than black duck and usually shows white in wings

when swimming; female utters series of quacks, loud at beginning, then falling in pitch and volume, *kaaak, kaaak-kak-kak-kak* (Peterson, 1961), higher-pitched than similar call of mallard; male utters a single low *quack,* and a shrill whistled call (see courtship in Johnsgard, 1965); walks well on land, flies from water or land by quick spring into air, flight is directly away in straight line; migrates in small flocks of about a dozen birds; from its wintering range, generally in s. U.S. and in Mex., on inland ponds, marshy lakes, sloughs, and swamps, sometimes on brackish pools of Gulf coast, moves northward in spring, usually in Apr.; arrives on northernmost breeding grounds in n. U.S., s. Canada, from late Apr. to early May; in fall, moves southward, usually Sept.–Oct., sometimes later from Nov. into Dec.

Feeding Habits: Eats almost entirely plant foods—mainly stems, leaves, tubers of pondweeds, which it gets by tipping with head below surface or dabbling with bill at edges of marshy ponds, sloughs, sluggish streams, also eats seeds of sedges and grasses; eats algae, duckweeds, etc. (Bent, 1923); one of few dabbling ducks that can, and does, dive for food when necessary; also takes some small fishes, crustaceans, tadpoles, leeches, small mollusks, water beetles, and other insects and their larvae, and worms; often forages, sometimes far from water, in woods for acorns and other mast and in fields for waste grain.

Nest: Built on islands in lakes or in upland meadows, pastures, and on prairies some distance from water; a scooped-out hollow in ground lined with plant materials and down from female's breast, at edges of tall reeds on dry ground, often well concealed under bushes or in grasses that arch over nest.

Eggs: Apr.–July; 7–15, usually 9–11 (sometimes female lesser scaups and American wigeons lay some of their eggs in gadwall's nest); eggs of gadwall, dull cream-white.

Incubation: By female, 26–28 days (Gates, 1962); young first fly 49–63 days after hatching (Johnsgard, 1968).

Other Names: Blarting duck; bleating duck; common gadwall; creek duck; gray duck; gray wigeon; red-wing; speckle-belly.

Age: One banded, Nev., caught and released when 11 years, 5 months, old (Kennard, 1975).

Albinism: A famed albino female, "Goldie," reported from N.D.

Flight Speed: Timed in w. U.S., 29 m.p.h. (Cottam *et al.,* 1942b).

Hybrids: Has crossbred and produced hybrids with wood duck, pintail, American wigeon, shoveler, mallard, and others, presumably in captivity (Gray, 1958); Johnsgard (1965) reported hybrids from gadwall crossbreeding in wild with European wigeon, American wigeon, falcated duck (falcated teal), mallard, pintail, and shoveler.

Weights: Females 1 lb. 5 oz. to 2 lbs. 4 oz.; males 1 lb. 9 oz. to 2 lbs. 8 oz. (Kortright, 1943).

Range: In N. America, nests from s. Alaska, s. B.C., and Prairie Provinces and Que., south through Calif. (mostly west of deserts), Nev., n. Ariz., s. Colo., nw. N.M., n. Tex., sw. Kans., n. Iowa, c. Minn., s. Wisc., to nw. Pa., and in local

breeding colonies along Atlantic coast at N.Y., and Jamaica Bay Refuge; s. N.J. (Egg Island and Brigantine Wildlife Refuge); Del., Md., and N.C., also in Iceland and Eurasia; winters in N. America from s. Alaska to c. Calif. (San Joaquin Valley) but main wintering concentrations in Pacific Flyway in w. Mexico (Chattin, 1964); ne. Colo., n. Ark., s. Ill., W.Va., Long Is., N.Y. (rarely), and Chesapeake Bay, south to n. Fla., U.S. Gulf coast, and mainland Mexico.

Gadwall, common. *See* Gadwall.

Garganey, *Anas querquedula* (AY-nas kwer-KWED-you-lah); genus name: *see* Duck, Bahama; species name: Lat., from Gr. *kerkouris,* a kind of duck (Jaeger, 1955); *garganey* (GAR-gah-nih) from Ital. dial., *garganello,* name for a bird. An Eurasian teal, small dabbling duck about 15 in. long; first record for N. American continent was a male on pond near Cape Hatteras lighthouse, N.C., Mar. 25, 30, and 31, 1957 (Chamberlain, 1957); Houston (1971) reported a Canadian sight record of one seen June 24–26, 1961, at Two Hills, Alta.; Gibson (1970) reported first record for Alaska, a male sighted May 29, 1970, at Kuluk Bay, on water with a flock of 100 common eiders and white-winged scoters, and noted its nearest nesting to N. America as the Kamchatka Pen., ne. Soviet Russia; Houston (1971) reported a male photographed May 23, 1971, in a marsh near St. Ambroise at southern end of Lake Manitoba; it was with a pair of blue-winged teal and the male garganey was charging the male blue-wing; garganey distinguished by large bluish shoulder patches; speculum green; male in breeding plumage has red-brown head and *broad white "eyebrows,"* curving from eyes to nape; female is inconspicuous brown with grayish, rather than blue, wing coverts of other of the "blue-winged ducks," and a distinct dark line from bill through the eyes to nape which distinguishes it from female blue-winged or green-winged teal (Delacour, 1956); has grayer wings and obscure speculum which distinguishes it from green-winged teal (Peterson *et al.,* 1954); male utters distinctive wooden, rattling note (Johnsgard, 1968); *geg . . . geg . . . geg* (see courtship in Delacour, 1956); female quacks; swift and agile in flight; prefers shallow pools and marshes with lots of cover, seldom on salt water; feeding habits and behavior more like a shoveler than a teal; nests in long grasses or in rank plant growth near water (Peterson *et al.,* 1954).

Other Name: Garganey teal.

Hybrids: According to Johnsgard (1965), wild hybrids reported from crossbreeding of garganey with the common teal, pintail, and shoveler; Gray (1958) reported hybrids in captivity from crossbreeding of garganey with wood duck, pintail, northern (common) shoveler, common teal, cinnamon teal, blue-winged teal, European wigeon, mallard, European pochard, and presumed natural hybridizing with American goldeneye.

Weights: Females average 12 oz.; males 1 lb. (Johnsgard, 1968).

Range: Nests in British Isles, and (rarely) Iceland, in Sweden to c. Finland, n. Russia, w. and

e. Siberia to Kamchatka and Komandorskie Is., south to Spain, s. France, c. Italy, Albania, Bulgaria, Crimea, Transcaucasia, to Mongolia, Manchuria; winters in s. Europe, Africa, s. Asia, Philippines to New Guinea; strays to Australia, N. America.

Goldeneye, American. *See* Goldeneye, common.

Goldeneye, Barrow's, *Bucephala islandica* (bue-SEF-ah-lah ice-LAND-ih-kah); genus name: *see* Bufflehead; species name: Latinized directly from the name Iceland, thus meaning Icelandic, not insular (Coues, 1882); common name: honors Sir John Barrow (1764–1848), secretary to the British Admiralty, explorer and geographer, who early in his career traveled to the N. American Arctic (see details in Gruson, 1972); *goldeneye,* from rich yellow color of the irises (EYE-ris-eez). (Color ill., page 208.) In summer, w. Iceland, Greenland, Canada, Alaska, and Rocky Mtns. in U.S., not common even in w. U.S.; diving duck; 16–20 inches long; wingspread 30 in. or more; feathers of crown and nape elongated, making head appear large and bushy on thin neck; black head of male usually has a *white crescent* in front of each eye, not a *round spot* as in similar male common goldeneye but this may be variable in shape and is not always a reliable character; male shows more black on upperparts than common goldeneye; seen on water, black on back (forward of wings) extends almost to waterline; head has purplish gloss, not green as in common goldeneye; head shape distinctive with abrupt forehead and low crown; scapulars have row of white spots; female brown-gray above, whitish below, with a white collar and large white wing markings, similar to female common goldeneye but has shorter and deeper bill, which may become all-yellow in spring and summer (Peterson, 1961); not black with yellow tip as in female goldeneye; however, population in e. N. America has little or no yellow on bill (Johnsgard, 1965); flies close to surface of water before getting up enough speed to rise into air; flight is swift, wings make musical whistle; less gregarious, like common goldeneye, than other diving ducks; shows preference for fresh or brackish waters; in winter may be in large flocks on salt or brackish waters; in summer usually in scattered groups of two, three, or up to a dozen; loves to play in rapids of fast-flowing streams (see in Bent, 1925); utters hoarse croaks; male utters mewing cry and soft grunts during his courtship displays (see Johnsgard, 1965); winters in small numbers in Mont., Wyo., and ne. Utah, but mostly in Gulf of St. Lawrence along Atlantic coast, and n. Pacific coast; only 3 records for Great Lakes; moves to breeding grounds in Apr.; some of those that winter on Pacific coast, into Rocky Mtns.; some of those from Atlantic coast, to Labrador; arrives on breeding grounds by June; in fall, moves southward, Oct. into Nov.

Feeding Habits: Dives and forages in fresh waters of streams, lakes, ponds, for staple foods of aquatic insects, especially nymphs of dragonflies and damselflies; crustaceans, especially crayfishes, and some plant foods such as pondweeds *(Potamogeton);* also takes some small fishes (sculpins); eggs of salmon in streams of West and flesh of salmon that have died after spawning (see Cottam, 1939); in salt water, eats mollusks, especially blue mussels, also periwinkles and other gastropods, some sea urchins, starfishes, and marine worms, etc.
Nest: In wooded country and up to 10,000 ft. elevation in Rockies and other western mountains; like wood duck, hooded merganser, bufflehead, and related common goldeneye, nests in natural cavities of trees and stumps, in abandoned nesting holes of flickers and other woodpeckers, up to 50 ft. or more above ground; prefers cavities in trees close to water but may nest in available tree hollows half a mile from nearest water; in treeless country, nests in rock cavities of cliffs or under rocks, in banks of streams, or in coarse grass among low bushes (Bent, 1925).
Eggs: May–June; 6–15, usually 10–13, pale green to blue-green.
Incubation: By female, about 28 days (Bent, 1925); in captivity, 30 days (Delacour, 1959); 30–34 days (Godfrey, 1966).
Other Names: Rocky Mountain garrot; Rocky Mountain goldeneye.
Hybrids: Reported to have crossbred and produced hybrids only with the common goldeneye.
Weights: Female (1), 1 lb. 10 oz.; male (1), 2 lbs. 14 oz. (Kortright, 1943); females 1⅗ lbs.; males 2⅖ lbs. (Johnsgard, 1968).
Range: Nests in w. N. America from se. Alaska, n. Mack., and nw. B.C., south to e. Wash., sw. Ore. into High Sierras of Calif., also in Colo. Rockies; in e. N. America, ne. Que., n. Labrador, sw. Greenland, and in w. Iceland; winters from s. Alaska south along Pacific coast to c. Calif.; in interior, south, irregularly, from s. B.C. and n. Mont. to Utah, Colo., and along Atlantic coast from Gulf of St. Lawrence south regularly to Mass. and casually to Long Is., N.Y.

Goldeneye, common, *Bucephala clangula* (bue-SEF-ah-lah CLANG-you-lah); genus name: *see* Bufflehead; species name: from Lat. *clangor,* noise; *clangula* is New Lat. diminutive, meaning a small noise, apparently in reference to the whistle of its wings in flight. (Color ill., page 208.) Has a much wider distribution than that of Barrow's goldeneye; a common breeding duck in summer in coniferous forests; in N. America, from ne. N.Y. and Me. north into Alaska, also in Eurasia; one of the diving ducks, has unusually spectacular courtship starting in Feb. on wintering grounds (see details in Bent, 1925, and Johnsgard, 1965); medium-sized duck, 16–20 in. long; wingspread 25–32 in.; differs from similar Barrow's goldeneye in having *green*-glossed head with a *round* white spot between golden eyes and bill; has more extensive white wing patch than Barrow's goldeneye (Johnsgard, 1968); *see* other comparisons and description of female under Barrow's goldeneye; male in flight shows more white than any other duck except common merganser, underparts white and extensive white on back and wings make it appear very white except for dark head; in flight, large round

Garganey

DUCK FAMILY

Barnacle goose

DUCK FAMILY

Bean goose

black head and short, thick neck distinctive; exceedingly swift and strong flier; on nesting grounds very active on wing, circles high in air about lakes or flies up and down streams above treetops, female usually leading male; vibrant whistling of wings can be heard long distance, from which it has common names of whistler and whistle-wing; exceedingly wary and suspicious of man where shot at or persecuted; not noisy, male in courtship utters a harsh, double note, *zeee-zeee* or *zee-zee-at*, resembling call of a nighthawk, and a rattling *rrrrt;* female a low-pitched harsh *quack;* usually migrates in small flocks high in air; winters as far north as open waters inland, also along Pacific coast from s. Calif. north, and Atlantic coast from S.C. north, leaves Mass. coast by May 1 or earlier (Bent, 1925); usually leaves wintering grounds in Feb.–Mar.; arrives most northern nesting grounds in Apr.–May; in fall returns to wintering places along Pacific and Atlantic coasts, and inland, Oct.–Nov.

Feeding Habits: An expert diver, may remain under for 21 seconds (Bent, 1925); can dive to depths of 20 ft. or more in search of shellfishes but usually feeds in water less than 10 ft. deep; swims about underwater by propelling with its feet; during summer and fall, when inland, most of food is insects such as caddis flies and other aquatic insects, also crayfishes and shrimplike crustaceans of fresh water, and seeds, tubers, and vegetative growth of pond-weeds *(Potamogeton),* also wild celery, and seeds of spatterdock; in winter, when many goldeneyes have shifted from the interior to coastal harbors and bays along both Atlantic and Pacific coasts or on ocean just beyond the surf, feeds especially on mud crabs (up to 26 had been eaten by one bird along Pacific coast; remains of 36 in stomach of another along Atlantic coast); also eats saltwater snails (gastropods), mussels, hermit crabs, rock crabs, and others. See Cottam (1939) for details.

Nest: Usually in a large tree cavity, usually close to, or over, water, but some may be a mile from water, in open hollow at top of broken-off trunk, at heights varying from 6 to 60 ft. above ground, in large hardwood trees such as elms, maples, and birches; nest inside may be 5–15 ft. below hole or hollow at which bird enters; occupied cavity may be recognized by one or two pieces of white down clinging to edges of opening; sometimes will nest inside small cavity opening only 3 in. wide, 4½ in. high, and 3 ft. deep, and 6–7 in. across at bottom; nest lined with pure-white down; nesting boxes frequently erected for goldeneyes.

Eggs: May–July; 5–19, commonly 8–12, clear, pale green or gray-green.

Incubation: By female, 28–32 days (Bellrose, 1976); chicks remain in nest for day or two or until strong enough to leap from nesting hole to ground; female clucks and calls to young from water or ground below; chicks beat tiny wings continuously as they descend through air; female then gathers brood and leads them away (see Bent, 1925, and Carter, 1958); young first fly 56–62 days after hatching (Johnsgard, 1968).

Other Names: American goldeneye; brasseye; brass-eyed whistler; bull-head; copper-head; cub-head; cur; European goldeneye; garrot; goldeneyed duck; great-head; iron-head; jingler; merry-wing; spirit duck; whiffler; whistle-duck; whistler; whistle-wing.

Age: One lived to 17 years in wild in Soviet Union (Turcek, 1958).

Flight Speed: Timed in N.Y., 50 m.p.h. (E.P.R., 1913).

Hybrids: Has crossbred in captivity with wood duck, garganey, tufted duck, European pochard, and others; a presumed natural hybrid between common goldeneye and Barrow's goldeneye has been described from N.B., also presumed natural hybrids from mating between common goldeneye and velvet scoter, and with hooded merganser and with common merganser (Gray, 1958). A male goldeneye picked up dying on Westwick Lake, B.C., was intermediate between a common and a Barrow's goldeneye.

Weights: Males (36), 1 lb. 9 oz. to 2 lbs. 14 oz.; females (33), 1 lb. 6 oz. to 2 lbs. 4 oz. (Kortright, 1943); males average 2⅕ lbs.; females 1¾ lbs. (Johnsgard, 1968).

Range: In N. America, nests in coniferous forests from w. and c. Alaska and n. Mack., n. Man., n. Ont., n. Que., e. Lab. south to s. B.C., ne. Wyo., c. Neb., n. Minn., n. Mich., c. Ont., s. Que., ne. N.Y., n. Vt., Me., N.B., and Newfoundland; also c. Europe, sw. and s.-c. Siberia, n. Mongolia, and Kamchatka; in N. America, winters wherever open water, from southern edge of nesting range to Baja Calif. (rarely), and to n. Iowa, c. Wisc., and coasts of Tex., La., Miss., Ala., and Fla.

Goldeneye, European. *See* Goldeneye, common.

Goldeneye, Rocky Mountain. *See* Goldeneye, Barrow's.

Goose, Aleutian Canada. *See* Goose, Canada.

Goose, barnacle, *Branta leucopsis* (BRANtah lew-COP-sis); genus name: *see* Brant; species name: from Gr. *leukos,* white, and *opsis,* appearance, referring to the white face of this species; common name goes back to Middle Ages when Europeans knew nothing of land north of European continent, where the barnacle goose nests; they explained its annual appearance from over the water each fall by the fantasy that these geese hatched from barnacles (*see* Folklore). Primarily an Old World goose that also nests in Greenland, also reported in N. America from Baffin Is. and Labrador to N.C.; a casual visitor along Atlantic coast in fall, when individuals usually accompany flocks of other geese; a close relative of the Canada goose; 23–28 in. long; wingspread 52–56 in.; distinguished by its *entirely white face and forehead,* and black mark, or streak, between eyes and bill (Canada goose has white *cheeks* and does not have black extending over breast as in barnacle goose); similar to brant in habits and appearance, but no white marks on neck; utters short, shrill barks, or yelps; flock in full cry sounds like pack of terriers (Bent, 1925); frequently hisses, with snakelike movements of neck; one of most fearless of all geese;

frequents rivers and marshes in hilly parts of Arctic region.

Feeding Habits: Often seen near seacoasts feeding on mud flats but grazes much on grasses of inland pastures and croplands; also eats sedges, leaves and catkins of alpine willows, and seeds of various plants.

Nest: In scattered colonies; in Greenland, sometimes up to 150 pairs but usually less than 50; nests on rock ledges and hollows of precipitous bluffs and on tops of isolated pinnacles of rock, often far from salt water, also on rocky islands; nest is a hollow in sand or on rock, lined with feathers and down.

Eggs: Greenland, late May to early June; 2–9, usually 4–6; gray-white.

Incubation: By female 24–25 days; goslings hatched on precipitous cliffs some 300 ft. above ground cannot descend; some adults reported to fly down from nesting bluff to shore of nearby lake, carrying young one in bill; others place a young one on back and fly with it to water; others, hatched on gentle slopes, walk down with adults to water (Salomonsen, 1950); age when chicks in wild first fly unknown, but 6–7 weeks in captivity.

Other Name: Bar goose (in Great Britain).

Hybrids: Reported (apparently in captivity) to crossbreed with bar-headed goose, bean goose, blue goose, brent goose (brant), Canada goose, greylag goose, lesser snow goose, swan goose, and white-fronted goose (Gray, 1958).

Weights: Males average 3.69 lbs.; females average 3.30 lbs. (Johnsgard, 1978).

Range: Nests in e. Greenland, Spitsbergen, and Novaya Zemlya; winters in n. Europe south to British Isles; reported in N. America from Baffin Is. to Lab., to N.C.

Goose, bean, *Anser fabalis* (AN-ser fab-AY-lis); genus name: Lat., goose; species name: from Lat. *fabalis,* of or belonging to beans; both the scientific species name and the popular name from habit noticed long ago, when this species arrived in England regularly in fall, of feeding on waste beans left in harvested fields (Bent, 1925). A Eurasian species, it also nests in e. Greenland; accidental visitor to St. Paul Is., and Pribilof Is., Alaska; is one of 5 species of Old World "gray geese" that include the swan goose, bean goose, white-fronted goose, lesser white-fronted goose, and graylag goose (see in Johnsgard, 1965), with similar behavior and typically "gray goose" plumage pattern which lacks distinctive markings; 28–35 in. long; bean goose is browner and generally darker than other "gray geese"; has dark brown head fading to lighter brown on body; the dark wing feathers and tail feathers are edged with white; bill blackish with variable large yellow to pink markings that may at times include the entire bill; also has yellow or pink feet (Johnsgard, 1965); the race that nests in Greenland has pink feet, from which its common name of pink-footed goose (see the various races of the bean goose illustrated in Delacour, 1954); in Arctic N. America, bean goose can be distinguished from white-fronted goose at close range by lack of white area on fore crown and sides of bill, also no black blotches on breast as in white-fronted goose; bean goose is dark-bodied, dark-

winged, utters reedy *ung-unk;* the pink-footed race has a very pale body, very dark neck, pink feet, and utters musical *ung-unk,* higher-pitched than that of other races (subspecies) or an often repeated *wink-wink-wink* (Peterson *et al.,* 1954).

Feeding Habits: Eats all kinds of grains, for which locally called cornfield goose in Britain, harvest goose in France; however, also eats grass and clover (Bent, 1925); according to Pough (1951), in spring, eats new shoots of smartweeds and horsetails, later feeds on new shoots of grasses and sedges, and leaves of Arctic perennials; in winter, frequents both agricultural land and marshes.

Nest: On grassy tussock of tundra or on grassy tussock in partly wooded marshes, or on islets in rivers or swamps, in some places on ledges of cliffs or on talus slopes; nests in colonies but each nest rarely closer than 15 m. (about 45 ft.); nest built of mosses and grasses and lined with down from female's breast.

Eggs: Apr.–June; 4–8, usually 4–5, white.

Incubation: By female, 27–29 days (Delacour, 1954); in smaller, pink-footed subspecies, 25–28 days; young fly about 7–8 weeks after hatching (Johnsgard, 1978).

Age: A male shot out of migrating flock in 1902 lived in a poultry yard in France for 23 years before it died from an accident (Nice, 1935c).

Hybrids: In captivity, reported to crossbreed with barnacle goose, blue goose, domestic or greylag goose, pink-footed goose, snow goose, and white-fronted goose (Gray, 1958).

Weights: 6.06 to 8.70 lbs. for two most common races (Johnsgard, 1978).

Range: Nests in e. Greenland, Iceland, Spitzbergen, n. Norway, Sweden, Finland, and Russia; Kolguev Is. and Novaya Zemlya; Siberia, n. Mongolia and the Altai; winters south to Mediterranean, Black, and Caspian seas, Asia Minor, Persia, Turkestan, China, and Japan; accidental visitor to Alaska (*see* above).

Goose, blue, *Chen caerulescens caerulescens* (KEN see-rue-LES-enz); genus name: Gr., goose; species name: Lat., bluish, in reference to its blue-gray wings; is no longer considered a separate species from the lesser snow goose, but a blue form, or color phase, of the white-plumaged lesser snow goose, which also was formerly thought to be a separate species, *Chen hyperborea hyperborea.* Both forms are now combined under the species name *Chen caerulescens* of the snow goose, a scientific name applicable in its descriptive meaning of bluish only to the blue form; however, the name must stand because of its priority (was published first) over the species name *hyperborea* for the snow goose in the scientific literature—see discussion in A.O.U. *Check-list* (1973). (Color ill., page 225.)

The blue goose is about the same size, and has the same habits, voice, etc., as the snow goose; 25–31 in. long; wingspread 54–60 in.; adults outwardly alike, have dusky gray-brown body *with white head and neck;* white face sometimes stained with rust by ferruginous mud (see Adventitious Color); gray-blue wing coverts, and pink to light purple feet; migrates generally in flocks of its own kind, north and

south from and to Canadian nesting grounds, moving in U-shaped flocks, irregular masses, or oblique lines; seldom in V-formation (Bellrose, 1976); first nest and eggs of the blue goose were discovered by J. Dewey Soper, Canadian ornithologist, on June 26, 1929, on Baffin Is., after a search of some 6 years and 30,000 mi. of Arctic travel (see narrative of in Soper, 1930); center of abundance in nesting season of blue goose is Foxe Basin region of Baffin Is. tundra (*see* details of nest under Snow goose); it intergrades with the white phase lesser snow goose in nesting colonies on the Boas R. delta on Southampton Is., on Cape Henrietta Maria, and at Eskimo Point; farther west, the white form dominates in the important breeding colonies along the Perry R. on Victoria and Banks Is., and in the Wrangel Is. colony of e. Siberia; since the 1950s, the blue phase has increased markedly in some of these colonies and the numbers of the white phase have decreased; often a white phase and a blue phase (mated pair) guard the same nest and tend the same brood (Wellein and Lumsden, 1964); in the large colonies of Southampton and Baffin Is., blue geese were always seen mingling with the white form, and "mixed pairs produced either blue or white chicks, the blue usually predominating"—sometimes intermediate adults are seen with white breasts and dark backs or white head, neck, and breast with dark back (see illustration in Delacour, 1954); in captive flocks, pairs of blue geese "have produced at intervals a small number of white offspring but white ones seldom produce any blue goslings" (Delacour, 1954). *See also* discussion under Color phase.

The white form apparently was the original stock; with the cooling of the climate, the white phase probably evolved from more generalized gray ancestors, according to Delacour; about 1914, the blue goose was relatively rare but by the early 1960s had increased at an annual rate of 2% and was gradually extending its breeding range in Canada westward; in 1930, nesting colonies of the blue goose were limited to Baffin and Southampton Is., but since then have spread southward and westward to other places in the Northwest Territories: Eskimo Point, Perry R., and Banks Is.; the increase has been at expense of the white phase lesser snow goose; according to Cooch (1964b), if the present trend continued until 1975, all nesting colonies of the white phase snow goose in N. America should contain at least 1% of the blue phase and in all colonies around Hudson Bay, 35–95%.

Waterfowl biologists account for the increase of the blue phase over the white to a higher survival rate for the blue phase on the nesting grounds: the white lesser snow geese are more likely to lose their eggs to predators (parasitic jaegers and Arctic foxes) because they nest slightly earlier than the blue form and more of their eggs are devastated at time of the earlier nesting when predators find other foods scarce—during the short Arctic summer the snow geese apparently do not have time to re-nest and raise another brood before onset of fall or winter—also, during migration and on the wintering grounds in the U.S., hunters prefer to shoot the white phase bird (Cooch, 1964b).

Migration of the blue form is generally north-south; from nesting grounds on Baffin and Southampton Is. in n. Canada (migrates in Sept.–Oct., usually arriving in s. U.S. in early Nov.) moves along both eastern and western shores of Hudson Bay to James Bay, then, on what is practically a nonstop flight, the geese arrive on coastal marshes of La.; on northward trip in spring, most move rapidly, generally nonstop in U.S., up Mississippi Valley, usually in Mar., then tend to go westward and fly north through S.D. and se. Man. to the Canadian nesting grounds (Glover, 1964), arriving there by early June (Lincoln, 1950c); may be uncommon to rare, but a regular migrant along Atlantic coast, occasionally fairly common; reported from Me. to Fla. (Bull, 1964); casual in interior N.Y., Ohio, Pa., and W.Va.; strays to Calif., casual in Ore., Utah, Ariz., and N.M. (Peterson, 1961). Feeding habits and nesting like that of lesser snow goose; young, according to Johnsgard (1968), first fly 38–49 days after hatching.

Other Names: Bald-headed brant; blue brant; blue snow goose; blue wavey; blue-winged goose; brant; white-headed brant.

Age: One lived to 9 years, 7 months, in National Zoo, Washington, D.C.

Hybrids: Reported in captivity to crossbreed with domestic or greylag goose, Egyptian goose, pink-footed (bean) goose, and white-fronted goose (Gray, 1958); and in Canada with the small Richardson's Canada goose, *Branta canadensis hutchinsii;* hybrids of this crossbreeding seen not only in Canada but in c. U.S. and along the Gulf coast of U.S. (see details in Prevett and MacInnes, 1973).

Weights: Males (534) average 6.06 lbs.; females (483) average 5.50 lbs. (Bellrose, 1976). For further discussion of the "blue" goose, *see* biography of the snow goose.

Range: See above.

Goose, blue-winged. *See* Goose, blue.

Goose, brant. *See* Brant.

Goose, brent. *See* Brant.

Goose, cackling. *See* Goose, Canada.

Goose, calling. *See* Goose, Canada.

Goose, Canada, *Branta canadensis* (BRAN-tah can-ah-DEN-sis); genus name: *see* Brant; species name: Lat., of Canada. (Color ill., page 220.) Most widely distributed and possibly the best-known generally of all N. American waterfowl; the common "wild goose" of the N. American continent; lives from Atlantic to Pacific coast and from Mexico north to the Arctic coast of Canada; at least 10 or 11 races, or subspecies; all basically alike in color pattern, with long black neck and black head with large white cheek patches which meet under the throat; brown-gray body with pale to dark breast and underparts; black tail with 16–20 tail feathers and white upper and undertail coverts (in flight shows crescent of white feathers just above tail); bill and feet black; varies considerably in size, from 22 in. long in the comparatively tiny cackling Canada goose weighing 3–4 lbs. to

the giant Canada goose up to 48 in. long with a wingspread of 75 in. and weighing up to 24 lbs. (Hanson, 1965); the very large forms utter a deep musical honking—*ah-honk,* or *ka-ronk, ka-lunk*—with a break in middle of the two syllables, the second drawn out and highest in pitch; a flock flying in their typical V formation and calling from a distance sound like a pack of baying hounds (the smaller forms have higher-pitched voices); migrate by day or night, one of earliest migrants in spring; those that have wintered farthest south may start to migrate a month earlier than those that have wintered farther north at or above the frost line; move northward slowly, their advance corresponding closely with the advance of spring, or with the average temperature line (isotherm) of 35° F. (Lincoln, 1950c); Canada geese and other waterfowl only briefly follow landmarks when they parallel their lines of flight, flying, instead, directly over hills and valleys, rivers and lakes, forests and plains, cities and villages; are more likely to use landmarks than other waterfowl because of traditional homing by families and extensive diurnal migration; most waterfowl migrate largely at night (*see* discussion of some caught in storms under Waterfowl, and an aerial disaster under Poisons); many of those wintering in s. U.S. leave in Jan.; arrive in n. U.S. and s. Canada by late Feb. and Mar.; are on northern nesting grounds by late Mar. or mid to late Apr., depending on severity or mildness of spring; however, some may winter far to north in U.S. and s. Canada wherever waters may remain unfrozen; population of the Canada goose in all four U.S. flyways in the Jan. winter waterfowl survey of the U.S. Fish and Wildlife Service was 2,141,000 in 1974 (Bellrose, 1976). *See* flyways and discussion of migration under Waterfowl.

Geese are among the very few birds in which the family does not break up at end of the breeding season; parents and the young raised during the summer have established strong family bonds and stay together almost a year. They migrate together in fall in flocks that contain other family units, and each family stays together on the wintering grounds; the family migrates northward together in spring, with adult pairs usually returning to the nesting territory each pair established in the previous years. Only on the breeding grounds do the young of the previous nesting season, now called yearlings, separate from their parents that are beginning a new nesting season (the young geese do not nest but usually form flocks with other yearlings; yearlings most often move considerable distances (up to several hundred miles) from breeding parents. The closeness of the family system and their semi-colonialism guarantees the return of the Canada geese to traditional breeding sites; it also allows for two different, well-characterized subspecies of the Canada goose to breed in groups not far apart without mixing, and to remain isolated without being geographically separated (Mayr, 1942; Delacour, 1954); in this way, such diverse races as the miniature cackling Canada goose and the giant Canada goose have evolved and, in a practical way, are almost two distinct species (Johnsgard, 1968). *See* How Do Species Begin? and The Speciation

Process under Species. Subadult Canada geese do not normally breed until about 3 years old; some at 2 years. *See* discussion of age determination of sub-adult Canada geese under Bursa of Fabricius. For details of age determination, see in Hanson (1962).

Old belief that a "wise old gander" leads the flock is not always true, although adult male of the family flock starts local flights by vigorous up-and-down tossing of his head and a low guttural "talking" (see behavior patterns in Johnsgard, 1965); at such times it is usually the female that leads the flight, with the male (easily identified by his larger size) bringing up, and guarding, the rear; in spring migration, the females of the already mated pairs lead the male partner in flight (Hanson, 1965) but the leadership at the head of the flock changes from time to time. *See* advantages of formation flights in Formation Flying under Flight.

When taking off from land or water, a Canada goose usually runs for a step or two before leaping into the air and is under way with powerful beating of its wings; occasionally it may spring upward directly into flight from ground or water surface; it alights on water with both webbed feet thrust forward and toes spread; the feet hit water like a pair of skis and at same time that tail feathers touch the water; shortly after the breeding season when the young are about half grown, the adult geese lose their flight and tail feathers in molt; they are flightless for about a month until their new feathers have grown and they are flying again at about time the young start their first flights. See details in Van Wormer (1968).

In the social hierarchy ("peck order") of Canada geese, families dominate mated pairs without families, not tolerating them within the limits of the family flock territory; mated pairs over single adults and yearlings; yearlings over immatures. Nesting pairs of Canada geese hiss in threats directed at other geese, ducks, and especially people or predators near the nest; a gander known to fly directly at person and to strike him hard blows with the wings in defense of its nest (Bent, 1925). Geese communicate with each other through a "language," much as do other birds; Collias and Jahn (1959) discovered that Canada geese utter ten different vocalizations (sounds), each in response to a certain situation confronting them. See summary of these in Van Wormer (1968).

Most geese breed in Arctic and subarctic. Small numbers breed in n. Rocky Mtns. Restocked groups of giant Canada geese breed in scattered areas in Midwest; in winter, Canada geese live throughout much of U.S.; many people privately, and some government agencies, have built farm ponds to attract waterfowl, especially Canada geese (see accounts in Green, 1948, and "A Pond in His Life" in Terres, 1960b, and in Edminster, 1964); many Canada geese nest in the large marshes of w. U.S. and along the coastal plain and inland tundra among ponds, and lakes of n. Canada and Alaska.

Feeding Habits: Feed mostly in early morning and late afternoon, between these feeding times usually rest on open water, open shoreline, sandbars, or mud flats where safe from disturbance; are essentially grazers and with bill crop marsh grasses, fresh blades of sprouting winter wheat in upland fields in spring, also eat bulrushes, glasswort, salt grass, brome grass, clovers, saltbush, cattails, and other plants; reaches head and neck below surface with tail tipped up to feed below surface on roots, tubers, leaves, and seeds of eelgrass, widgeon grass, algae (sea lettuce), and pondweeds; along coasts, some live on tidal flats, where they eat mollusks and small crustaceans; during fall and winter, live on fresh or salt water and feed in shallows and adjacent marshes (lead poisoning from ingesting lead shot is frequent); in fall pick up waste grain; especially fond of corn (see Madson, 1964).

Nest: Usually built on ground near water and on tundra on ridge or other elevated place, on islet in pond, on pond banks, along rivers, on rocky cliffs, on muskrat houses in marshes, on beaver houses, in abandoned nests of ospreys or ravens, owls, herons; also will nest in wire baskets and washtubs filled with straw and put up for them on sunken treetops, atop wooden posts, or on wooden platforms on supports in lakes and ponds (see Yocum, 1956); ground nest is built rather quickly by female of grasses, mosses on foundation of sticks; female first rounds a depression, then with bill sweeps material toward her; the larger Canada goose subspecies build nests about 15–44 in. across with depression in center about 4 in. deep and 10 in. wide where eggs are laid; female lines nest with down from her body.

Eggs: U.S., early Mar.; Arctic N. America, early June; 2–12, usually 5–6, dull white or cream-white.

Incubation: By female, usually with male standing guard nearby; 25–28 days (Van Wormer, 1968); 28–30 days (Bent, 1925); in larger forms, young first fly 63–86 days after hatching; among the smaller subspecies, the cackling goose young fly 42 days after hatching (Johnsgard, 1968); goslings may weigh 3–4 oz. at hatching; within 24 hours, parents lead them from nest to relative safety of open water, or if in tree nest, coax the goslings to leap to ground or water; can dive, swim, and feed themselves while guarded by adults; on water, the gander usually leads, the goslings string out in single file with female bringing up the rear, or this may be reversed; even day-old goslings can dive and swim for 30–40 ft. underwater and they eat almost continuously to attain growth for first southward migration; after 8 weeks each weighs about 7 lbs., or about 24 times its weight at hatching.

Other Names: Bay goose; big gray goose; black-headed goose; calling goose; Canada brant; common wild goose; cravat goose; honker; long-necked goose; reef goose; wild goose.

Age: 12, 18, and 23 years, wild birds banded at Jack Miner Bird Sanctuary at Kingsville, Ont. (Douville and Friley, 1957); Flower (1925) reported two captive Canada geese that lived to 29 years, a third to 33 years; McAtee (1924) learned of a captive pair that were mated for 42 years; another pair for more than 20 years; Leffingwell (1890) reported "as a matter of history" a captive that was killed when it was 80 years old.

Albinism: An almost complete albino described by Murray (1933) and Marquardt (1961) reported a "rare example of incomplete albinism" in one of the smaller subspecies, a Richardson's Canada goose, *B. c. hutchinsonii*, caught alive Oct. 1959 at Salt Plains National Wildlife Refuge, Alfalfa County, Okla.

Flight Speed: Timed in w. U.S., 20–26 m.p.h. (Cottam *et al.*, 1942b); in Wash., 40–55 m.p.h. (Rathbun, 1934).

Hybrids: Crossbreeds in captivity with barnacle goose, blue goose, brant goose, domestic or greylag goose, Egyptian goose, snow goose, swan goose, white-fronted goose, also with Muscovy duck, black swan, mute swan, trumpeter swan, and whistling swan (Gray, 1958); apparently rarely hybridizes with blue goose in wild; only two records in association of 35,000 Canada geese with 10,000 snow and blue geese (Nelson, 1952); however, see Prevett and MacInnes (1973) and *see* in biography of blue goose. Weights (when known) and ranges of the 11 subspecies of the Canada goose recognized by Hansen and Nelson (1964):

1. Aleutian Canada goose, *Branta canadensis leucopareia;* (color ill., page 220) small, about 4½–5½ lbs.; a white ring always present at base of black neck, often broad in front, followed by a dark brown band; on back of neck, sprinkling of white feathers; only about 1,200 remained in Buldir Is., Aleutians, in 1976 (Bellrose, 1976). (See details, Office of Endangered Species, 1973.)

2. Atlantic Canada goose, *Branta canadensis canadensis*, also called common Canada goose, longest-known and best-known of all the subspecies; large; males average 8.8 lbs.; females average 7.6 lbs.(Bellrose,1976); similar to interior Canada goose but whiter on underparts; nests in se. Baffin Is., e. Labrador and Newfoundland, Anticosta Is. and Magdalen Is., occasionally south to Me., and Mass.; winters chiefly from Nova Scotia south to Del., and rare along Atlantic coast to S.C.; wintering population estimated at more than 35,000 (Bellrose, 1976).

3. Cackling Canada goose, *Branta canadensis minima;* (Color ill., page 221) about 22–27 in. long, smallest and darkest of all the Canada geese, scarcely larger than a mallard, weighs 3–4 lbs. (Hansen and Nelson, 1964); some have partial white neck ring near base of black neck (Delacour, 1954); utter a high-pitched *yelk, yelk, a-lick, a-lick,* or *lick, lick, lick* (Peterson, 1961); the rapid "cackle" at end of call has given it name of cackling goose; nests in small district of w. Alaska along Bering Sea, chiefly between Yukon and Kuskokwim rivers; winters mainly in Central Valley, Calif.; some reach nw. Mexico and some have been seen in Hawaii and Japan; casual also in Nev., Wisc., s. Baja Calif.; in autumn, before hunting season, may number about 150,000 (Bellrose, 1976).

4. Dusky Canada goose, *Branta canadensis occidentalis*, formerly called white-cheeked goose; (Color ill., page 221) dark, medium-sized, about 8–10 lbs., darker and smaller than the Vancouver Canada goose, which it resembles in general, "underparts almost uniformly deep brown, white neck ring seldom present" (Delacour, 1954); nests primarily on the Copper R.

delta on s.-c. coast of Alaska; a few scattered across Prince William Sound and Cook Inlet area near Anchorage, Alaska; migrate near coast offshore, pass over se. Alaska, touching on Queen Charlotte and Vancouver Is., but winter in small district of Willamette Valley, Ore., numbers about 20,000 (Hansen and Nelson, 1964).

5. Giant Canada goose, *Branta canadensis maxima*, largest of all races of the Canada goose, records of 14–15 lbs., but many exceptionally large males reported at 17–24 lbs.; males average 12.5 lbs.; females average 11.1 lbs. (Bellrose, 1976); known by large size and long neck, which in proportion to body is longer than in all other subspecies (Hanson, 1965); one reported from Iowa in 1874 had length of 48 in. and wingspread of 75 in.; Hanson measured wingspread of several that were 76½, 76, and 74½ in.; however, most adult males have span of 69–71 in.; one in captive flock in Iowa had spread of 84 in.; a fairly common characteristic is white spot on forehead, quite rare in other subspecies of the Canada goose, also bill is massive, and the white cheek patch has a hook-like extension into the black of the neck; was believed to have become extinct about 1920; original nesting range extended over most of eastern prairie states, parts of the western Great Lakes area, and into s. Canada; was rediscovered in 1960 by Harold C. Hanson, who identified this race wintering as a flock of Canada geese near Rochester, Minn. Others have been identified on national wildlife refuges and game management areas in Minn., S.D., N.D., Mich., and Sask.; largest remnant of the race winters at Rochester, Minn., and some nest between Lake Winnipeg and Lake Manitoba in s.-c. Man. See other details in Hansen and Nelson (1964), and especially in Hanson (1965).

6. Interior Canada goose, *Branta canadensis interior*, fairly large, 32–36 in. long, males average 9.2 lbs.; females average 7.7 lbs. (Bellrose, 1976); similar to Atlantic Canada goose but darker, body "mouse gray with narrow whitish tips to the feathers, less conspicuously barred" (Delacour, 1954); nests in wide zone of forested muskeg around Hudson Bay, from 60th parallel on west side of Hudson Bay south through Man. and Ont. across James Bay through Que. and to Hudson Strait north to s. Baffin Is.; is most abundant of all races of the Canada goose; race numbered about 1,250,000 birds as of 1975 (Bellrose, 1976). See many details about the interior Canada goose in Hanson and Smith (1950).

7. Lesser Canada goose, *Branta canadensis parvipes*, about 26–31 in. long, weigh about 6 lbs, about size of snow goose; a complex group of which true classification not yet fully worked out; size intermediate between the large Canada geese of southern forested and prairie regions and the smallest tundra forms; nest sometimes simply in colonies of Ross' geese, usually inland, in widely scattered groups in open tundra and treeless spaces across Northwest Territories of Canada and e. Alaska between 60th and 70th parallels (see Delacour, 1954, and Hansen and Nelson, 1964, for other details); according to Peterson (1961), abundant in winter in interior valleys of Calif., utters *lo-ank, lo-ank, a-lank, a-lank,* lower-pitched

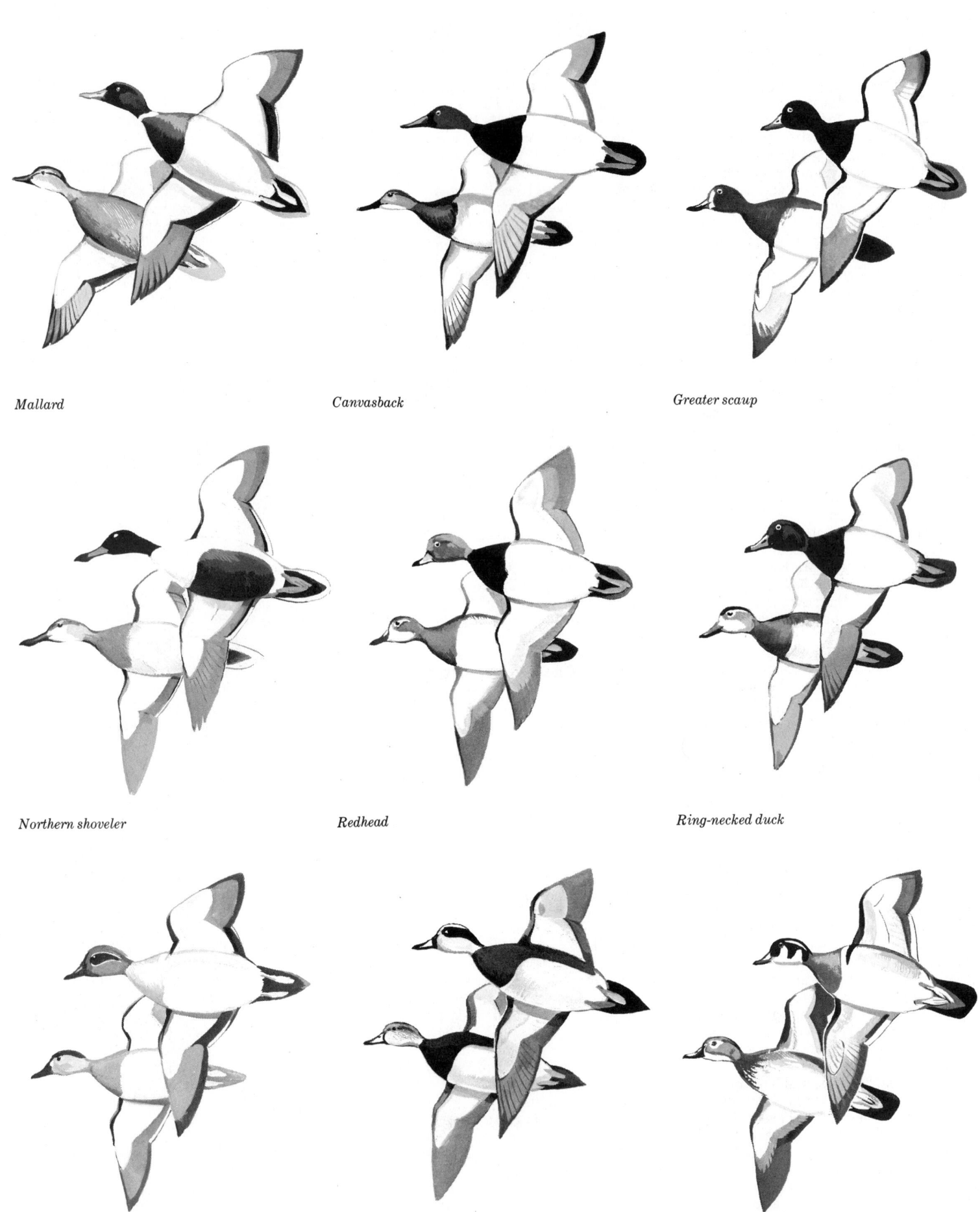

Mallard

Canvasback

Greater scaup

Northern shoveler

Redhead

Ring-necked duck

Green-winged teal

American wigeon

Wood duck

Harlequin duck

Hooded merganser

King eider

Black duck

Oldsquaw

Fulvous whistling-duck

Mottled duck

Common eider

Black scoter

voice than in cackling Canada goose; also winters in Colo., Okla., nw. Tex., La., and Mexico.

8. **Richardson's Canada goose,** *Branta canadensis hutchinsii* (HUTCH-ins-eye); named by Sir John Richardson in 1831 for Dr. Thomas Hutchins, English naturalist and surgeon of the Hudson Bay Company (Palmer, 1928); this small subspecies for a long time was called Hutchins' goose; a very small, light-colored goose, slightly larger than the cackling Canada goose (Delacour, 1954); weighs 3–7 lbs.; nests in Canada on coastal tundra of Southampton Is., sw. Baffin Is., and parts of Melville and Boothia Pen. and Ellesmere Is.; winters in Okla., Tex., and Mexico (Hansen and Nelson, 1964).

9. **Taverner's Canada goose,** *Branta canadensis taverneri* (tah-VER-ner-eye), named by J. Delacour in 1951 for P. A. Taverner, Canadian ornithologist; resembles the lesser Canada goose but generally darker and smaller; however, some may be paler, others as dark as the Aleutian Canada goose, which it resembles closely; nests in w. and n. Alaska distant from the coast; migrates along Pacific coast, most winter in s.-c. Wash. and e. Ore.; some in interior valleys of Calif.; may number up to 100,000 in any year (Hansen and Nelson, 1964).

10. **Vancouver Canada goose,** *Branta canadensis fulva* (FULL-vah); subspecies name means tawny; named for Vancouver Is., B.C., one of breeding places of this subspecies; a big Canada goose, 6–13 lbs.; darker, more fulvous (yellowish), and more uniformly colored above and below than the Taverner's Canada goose, "with very slightly smaller bill and longer legs"; seldom or never has white neck ring; black neck contrasts markedly with brown breast and brown back (Delacour, 1954); nests on coastal se. Alaska from Glacier Bay and southward along the coast to n. Vancouver Is., B.C.; most remain on breeding range, some wander to n. Calif., and 10% or fewer winter in the Willamette Valley of Ore.; population only about 80,000 (Bellrose, 1976).

11. **Western Canada goose,** *Branta canadensis moffitti*; named by John W. Aldrich in 1946 for James Moffitt, Calif. ornithologist (see account of Moffitt's work with Canada geese in Delacour, 1954); also called Moffitt's Canada goose; large, 35–37 in. long, weighs 8–10 lbs., some to 15 lbs., next in size to the giant Canada goose (Hanson, 1965); nests mostly west of Continental Divide in Great Basin north into headwaters of Columbia R.; also in w. Great Plains in Alta., Mont., and Wyo., in ne. Calif., nw. Nev., and s.-c. Ore.; some winter on breeding grounds and Columbia and Snake rivers in e. Wash. and northward in s.-c. Wash., along Snake R. in s. Utah, around Great Salt Lake, and along lower Colorado R., others winter in Sacramento Valley and Imperial Valley of Calif., Ariz., N.M., s. Tex., and n. Mexico; total population estimated at about 115,000 (Hansen and Nelson, 1964); utters a deep, two-syllabled honking, *ka-ronk,* or *ha-lunk, ha-lunk,* slurred upward (Peterson, 1961).

Goose, clatter. *See* Brant, Atlantic.

Goose, cornfield. *See* Goose, bean.

Goose, domestic. Another name for the greylag goose.

Goose, ember. *See* Common loon in Loon Family.

Goose, emperor, *Philacte canagica* (fih-LAK-tee can-ADJ-ih-cah); genus name: from Gr. *philein,* to love, and *akte,* shore; shore-loving; species name: Lat. form of Kanaga (ka-NAH-gah), the island of Kanaga in the Aleutians of Alaska; *emperor* for its handsome color pattern. (Color ill., page 222.) A mostly Alaskan and Siberian species; in winter, somewhat rarely to n. Calif. along Pacific coast; 26–30 in. long; wingspread 48–56½ in.; adult is small blue-gray (ashy) goose *with white head and hind neck* which are usually stained rusty from iron deposits in the water in which it feeds; has *black throat,* body and wings are scalelike black and white; has yellow or orange-colored legs (similar blue goose has pink legs and does not have black throat); immatures not so distinctly marked as adults, "have head and neck dusky and speckled with white" (Peterson, 1961); in flight, emperor goose shows proportionately shorter neck and heavier body than other geese, also short rapid wing strokes; usually flies close to ground, while flying from place to place utters hoarse *kla-ha, kla-ha, kla-ha* and *u-lugh, u-lugh,* unlike notes of any other goose (Bent, 1925); highly social with its own kind; a group on sandbar or mud flat often utter lower-toned, more cackling conversational notes that rise in pitch to welcome new arrivals; much less noisy than the white-fronted and cackling Canada geese; has small heavily loaded (aerodynamically) wings, and a short migration route from coast of Alaska along Aleutian chain (Scott, 1964); population numbers about 150,000 (Bellrose, 1976) but is less known to sportsmen and naturalists than most other American geese (Barry, 1964); summer and winter range is confined to the sparsely settled or uninhabited lands bordering the Bering Sea; it keeps far away from human population centers, even in migration; N. American population leaves wintering range (mostly Aleutian Is.) in late Apr.; arrives breeding grounds (main one is Yukon-Kuskokwim delta) between May 15 and June 1.

Feeding Habits: Is a sea goose, like brant, frequents rocks and reefs, and shoals of salt and brackish lagoons; forages over sandy beaches and mud flats for seaweeds and mussels and other shellfishes (shellfishes give its flesh a disagreeable flavor), in breeding season grazes on marshes above tidal flats, even invades drier tundra to eat crowberries.

Nest: Favors ponds and marshes on flats bordering brant country, which is nearer the sea; however, may nest on flat marshy islands bordering the sea; often chooses to nest in driftwood on line of high tide; pairs are mated on arrival (see Bent, 1925); nest site is depression in ground, lined by female with grasses, feathers and down from her own breast; nest usually near water, sometimes on small island in tundra lake or in marshes; some pairs occasionally nest on tundra with other species of geese.

Eggs: Most clutches completed by second week in June, although dates vary with local climate and weather at beginning of nesting season; 3–8 eggs, white.

Incubation: By female, though male remains nearby, 24 days; about 14–21 days after young hatch, adults molt and are flightless; new flight feathers are grown and adults can fly about time young begin to fly in early Aug.; families usually begin to migrate from nesting grounds for wintering places in Sept.

Other Names: Beach goose; painted goose; white-breasted goose.

Hybrids: In captivity has crossbred and produced hybrids with white-fronted goose, snow goose, and Ross' goose (Johnsgard, 1965).

Weights: Males average 6⅕ lbs.; females 6 lbs. (Johnsgard, 1968).

Range: Nests on sw. coast of Alaska, primarily on Yukon Delta, small numbers on Nunivak Is., Seward Pen.; not known to breed on St. Lawrence Is. in recent years (Bellrose, 1976); also breeds on ne. coast of Siberia; winters mainly in Aleutians and east to Sanak Is., Bristol Bay, west to Kamchatka and Komandorskie Is., casually along Pacific coast, strays south to B.C., Ore., and casual to c. Calif., also occasionally to Hawaii.

Goose, gray. *See* Goose, Canada. "Gray geese" is term applied to 5 Old World species that are related, and resemble each other; 2 of these—the bean goose and the white-fronted goose—reach N. America. *See* Goose, bean, and Goose, white-fronted.

Goose, greylag. One of the Old World "gray geese." *See* brief discussion under Goose, bean.

Goose, Hutchins'. *See* Richardson's Canada goose under Goose, Canada.

Goose, laughing. *See* Goose, white-fronted.

Goose, long-necked. Name for any of the larger subspecies of the Canada goose.

Goose, painted. *See* Goose, emperor.

Goose, pink-footed. *See* Goose, bean.

Goose, Ross', *Chen rossii* (KEN ROSS-ih-eye); genus name: *see* Goose, blue; species name: given in 1861 by John Cassin, Philadelphia ornithologist, for Bernard Rogan Ross, Chief Factor of Hudson's Bay Company, Canada. (Color ill., page 223.) Summers in small part of coastal tundra in Arctic Canada; a relatively rare species; in 1977, population numbered about 106,000 in Central Valley of Calif., where almost the entire population winters; a few seen on coasts of La. and Tex. (Barry, 1964); 21–26 in. long; wingspread 47–54 in.; very small, snow-white goose with black wing tips, similar to the snow goose but considerably smaller, with a pink-red, very short, high bill, bluish at base (bill lacks the black patches of snow goose along bill's cutting edges, called black "lips," or "grinning patches"); "sides of upper mandible, from base to nostrils, corrugated with warty protuberances ('scabby-nosed'), conspicuous in old males but small or absent in females and young birds; legs and feet deep pink" (Delacour, 1954); immatures are paler than similar young snow geese; in flight not as loud and noisy as the snow goose; utters a grunting *kug*, or a weak *kek*, *kek* or *ke-gak*, *ke-gak*, similar to call of cackling Canada goose (Peterson, 1961); following first scientific description in 1861, for 77 years it remained a mysterious migrant that apparently had its breeding grounds somewhere in Canadian Arctic, known from its appearance in fall on Great Slave Lake, then from its flight southwest over the Rockies and Sierras to the Central Valley of Calif., where it was seen frequently with the more abundant snow geese (Ripley, 1965); in June 1938, Angus Gavin discovered the first nest and eggs of this species known to ornithologists on an island in a small lake north of the Arctic Circle, about 12 mi. up the Perry R. from Queen Maud Gulf in Northwest Territories of Canada, and the mystery had been solved (see Gavin, 1947, and other details in Taverner, 1941); in summer of 1960, Barry (1964) counted at least 9,000 Ross' geese along streams and rivers of Arctic that flow into Queen Maud Gulf between Kent Pen. and Sherman Outlet; most were about 100 mi. east of Perry R. where this goose was first discovered nesting; begins northward migration in easy stages in early Mar., passes through e. Ore. in early Apr., and continues into nw. Mont. and along Alta.-Sask. border; among later goose migrants to reach Athabaska Delta and Great Slave Lake in mid-May, usually arrive at Perry R. nesting area in late May; in fall move south in Sept., are among earliest geese to leave the Arctic, usually are headed for Tule Lake, Calif., by mid-Oct. (Barry, 1964).

Feeding Habits: Eats grain and new green growth of grasslands and grain fields.
Nest: Female digs scrape like that of snow geese but smaller and builds up mound in the depression with twigs of willow, birch, grasses, mosses, and lichens, lines it sparsely with down, in loose colonies on remote island-studded lakes and deltas of low tundra country.
Eggs: May–June; 2–6, usually 4–5, white.
Incubation: About 21 days (Barry, 1964); young and adults (after flightless period of adults) are both flying by late Aug.
Other Names: Galoot; horned wavey; little wavey; scabby-nosed wavey, wart-nosed wavey.
Hybrids: Known to crossbreed in captivity with both blue goose and lesser snow goose; hybrids or crosses reported between Ross' goose and domestic greylag goose; also with emperor goose, and cackling Canada goose; in wild, white geese intermediate between Ross' goose and lesser snow goose, studied between 1962 and 1968, were apparently first wild hybrids reported for these species (Trauger *et al.*, 1971).
Weights: Males (47) average 4.0 lbs.; females (32) average 3.56 lbs. (Bellrose, 1976).
Range: Nests on Perry R., ne. Mack., also on Southampton Is.; winters in Sacramento, San Joaquin, and Imperial valleys of Calif.; casual in se. Alaska, B.C., Utah, Nev., Colo., Idaho, Ariz., Tex., and La., one reported Mar. 2, 1968,

at Pea Island National Wildlife Refuge, N.C., first record on or near Atlantic seaboard; other records no closer than La., Okla., Mo., and Ill. (Buckley, 1969). Appears regularly in migration at western end of Lake Athabaska.

Goose, scabby-nosed. *See* Goose, Ross'.

Goose, sea-. Another name for a phalarope.

Goose, short-necked. Name for one of the smaller subspecies *(hutchinsii)* of the Canada goose.

Goose, snow, *Chen caerulescens caerulescens* (KEN see-rue-LES-enz); *see* discussion and meaning of scientific name and its application under Goose, blue. (Color ills., pages 224–25.) The lesser snow goose is the white form of the species that includes the blue goose; it summers in Arctic N. America and ne. Siberia; in N. America, winters along Gulf coast; 25–31 in. long; wingspread about 53–60 in.; sexes outwardly alike, a white goose with black primaries; in autumn, head and breast often stained rusty brown *(see* Adventitious Color); short, high bill, pink to crimson red with cutting edges of both mandibles black (called black "lips" or "grinning patches"); legs and feet deep pink; immatures are dusky with dark bill but general form is recognizable (some snow geese interbreed with blue geese and produce individuals intermediate in color—*see* discussion in biography of blue goose and under Color Phase). migrates north in Mar. and Apr. from main wintering grounds in Calif., Tex., and Mexico, directly north from Calif. and up Mississippi Valley from Gulf coast and straggles up Atlantic coast; reaches breeding grounds in May; migrates south in fall from Aug. into Nov.; in migration flies very high, flock in long extended curved line, sometimes in U-formation; utters shrill falsetto notes and occasional softened *honk* (Bent, 1925); "lesser" snow geese, *Chen caerulescens caerulescens*, including the blue phase, nest in 14 major concentrations between Baffin Is. and Siberia, with a large gap in Alaska (Cooch, 1964b); the breeding range of the "greater" snow goose, *Chen caerulescens atlantica*, a larger subspecies, is generally north of the breeding range of the "lesser" snow goose and its blue form; breeding range of the greater snow goose, which does not to date have a blue form, includes parts of Baffin, Bylot, Devon, and Ellesmere, and Somerset Is. in Canada and w. Greenland; greater snow goose winters in Chesapeake Bay–Currituck Sound area of Md., Va., and N.C., with a major stop and rest point in fall (Sept.–Nov.) at Cape Tourmente, 25 mi. ne. of Que., on the St. Lawrence R. (Cooch, 1964b), where up to 100,000 have been seen; total wintering population within U.S. in all four flyways of blue geese and snow geese in winter survey of Jan. 1972 was 1,854,000; more than 95% were in the Pacific, Central, and Mississippi flyways (Chamberlain *et al.*, 1972).

Feeding Habits: In spring, browses in upland fields of winter wheat and on newly sprouting grasses in pastures; in fall, eats waste grain in stubble fields; on summer breeding grounds,

DUCK FAMILY
The blue goose is now considered to be a color phase of the snow goose, rather than a separate species. Although the white phase was probably the original form, the blue phase is becoming predominant on their common breeding grounds of the Canadian north and northwest.

 blue phase

 white phase

digs out with bill the bulbous roots and soft parts of sedges, rushes, marsh grasses, and aquatic plants.

Nest: In colonies, some in concentrations of 1,200 pairs to the square mile, close to sea on flat tundra of marsh grasses and sedges, in limestone basins, islands of river deltas, and plains, most within 5 mi. of salt water (Cooch, 1964b); nest in a depression filled with mosses and lined with grasses and down from female.

Eggs: June–July; 3–8, usually 4–5, white.

Incubation: By female, but male stands guard close by, 23–25 days; young fly 38–49 days after hatching (Johnsgard, 1968).

Other Names: Common snow goose; common wavey; greater snow goose; lesser snow goose; little wavey; Mexican goose; wavey; white goose.

Age: One lived to 15 years, 11 months, in National Zoo, Washington, D.C.; one banded Tule Lake, Calif., shot at Willows, Calif., when 17 years, 5 months (Kennard, 1975).

Flight Speed: Timed in Calif., more than 50 m.p.h. (Munson, 1930).

Weights: Lesser snow goose: males (534) average 6.06 lbs.; females (483) average 5.50 lbs.; greater snow goose: males (19) average 7.44 lbs.; females (12) average 6.12 lbs. (Bellrose, 1976).

Range: Greater snow goose breeds in a restricted region from Bylot Is. to nw. Greenland and Ellesmere Is.; winters from Va. to S.C., mostly at Pea Is., N.C. The lesser snow goose breeds across the Arctic, except Alaska, from Baffin Is. west to Wrangel Is., Siberia; recent colonies established on west coast of Hudson Bay south to junction of James Bay; winters mostly along Gulf coast from Mississippi R. southwest to Tampico, Mexico; also winters in Central Valley of Calif., Bosque del Apache Natl. Wildlife Refuge in s. N.M., and in n.-c. Mexico; in recent years 100,000–200,000 wintered in Mo., sw. Iowa, Kans., Okla., and e. Neb. See Bellrose (1976) for details.Goose

Goose, tule, *Anser albifrons gambelli.* The common name applied to a western race of the white-fronted goose that winters along the Gulf coast and in c. Calif. A new race (*Anser albifrons elgasi*) has been suggested for the Calif. population. The latter "inhabits marshes overgrown with tules" (bulrushes of the genus *Scirpus*), hence the name tule goose. The goose feeds upon the tubers and rhizomes of tule bulrushes.

Goose, white. *See* Goose, snow.

Goose, white-cheeked. *See* Dusky Canada goose under Goose, Canada.

Goose, white-fronted, *Anser albifrons* (AN-ser AL-bih-frons); genus name: *see* Goose, bean; species name: from Lat. *albus*, white, and *frons*, forehead; *white-fronted*, for white front of face. (Color ill., page 222.) Siberian and N. American species; a bird of West, not often seen east of Mississippi R.; casual along Atlantic coast north to Carolinas; 26–34 in. long; wingspread 53–62 in.; gray-brown goose with pink bill (one of the "gray geese"); *white on front of face* just above bill and the only N.

American goose with *irregular black bars or blotches on its gray underparts* (often called "specklebelly") and only one, except emperor goose, with orange or yellow feet; immatures are dusky brown (without white face) and have pale bill; in flight, white-fronted geese travel in V-shaped flocks, often very high, uttering their peculiar "laughing" notes, and loud and melancholy *wah, wah, wah,* rapidly repeated (Bent, 1925) or a tootling *kah-lah-a-luck* (Peterson, 1961); from wintering grounds in Mexico, in Pacific Flyway, and along Gulf coast, starts north in Mar. with largest flights in Apr.; arrives on breeding grounds in Alaska about mid-May; family groups and non-breeders gather in flocks and leave Alaska in Aug. and Sept.; about 200,000 of population that nests in Alaska (Yukon-Kuskokwim and Bristol Bay districts) winter in Pacific Flyway and Central Valley, Calif., another 70,000 in Central Flyway, about 25,000 in La., most in Laccasine National Wildlife Refuge; another 15,000 along east coast of Mexico and interior highland lakes (Dzubin *et al.*, 1964); according to Jan. 1972 winter survey, 178,300 in three flyways (none reported in Atlantic) within U.S. (Chamberlain *et al.*, 1972). The tule goose (*Anser albifrons gambelli*), a larger and darker race of the white-fronted goose, winters in the Sacramento Valley, Calif.; its breeding grounds remained unknown until 1979, when it was discovered breeding on Cook Inlet near Anchorage, Alaska (Bellrose, pers. commun.).

Feeding Habits: Usually rests on shallow ponds and sloughs in marshes, is primarily a grazer on grasses of marshes, freshly sprouting grain in fields, and fresh growth in burned-over pastures; sometimes feeds heavily on aquatic plants and in grain fields on waste barley, wheat, rice, corn; in Arctic grazes on tundra plants, eats aquatic insects and their larvae, and berries (Pough, 1951).

Nest: Nesting is dispersed on open wet tundra, on hummocks or small hills on borders of shallow marshes, lakes, riverbanks, and islands, deltas, dry knolls, on hillsides near river, ponds, seldom far from water, in loose colonies of 15–20 pairs; female scratches bowl-like depression in ground, lines it with dried grasses, sticks, and her down; male remains near, calls loudly, hisses and flies at other white-fronts that come too near (Dzubin *et al.*, 1964).

Eggs: First sets laid about May 25; 4–7, usually 5–6, cream-colored.

Incubation: By female, 22–28 days, while gander stands guard; young can fly 42–49 days after hatching (Dzubin *et al.*, 1964).

Other Names: American white-fronted goose; gray brant; gray wavey; harlequin brant; laughing goose; marble-belly; pied brant; prairie brant; specklebelly; speckled brant; tiger brant; tule white-fronted goose; yellow-legged brant; yellow-legged goose.

Age: In captivity, a young female in Neb., shot and wounded in 1903 or 1904, lived to at least 46 or 47 years old and laid eggs annually until her death in 1950 (Rankin, 1957); one lived to 20 years, 10 months, in National Zoo, Washington, D.C.

Weights: Males (57) average 6.29 lbs.; females (51) average 5.53 lbs. (Bellrose, 1976).

Range: Nests on Arctic tundra from nw. Siberia east to w. and n. Alaska and ne. Mack., ne. Keewatin and to Greenland; winters mostly west of the Mississippi, from s. B.C., Mont., S. Dak., N.D., and Ill. south to Baja Calif., Tex., La., and to s. Mexico.

Goose, white-headed. *See* Goose, emperor.

Goose, wild. *See* Goose, Canada.

Mallard, *Anas platyrhynchos* (AY-nas plah-tih-RING-koss); genus name: *see* Duck, Bahama; species name: from Gr. *platys*, broad, or flat, and *rhynchos*, beak; *mallard* (MAL-erd), related to maleness, from Old Fr. *maslard*, wild drake, from *masle*, male; *maslard* Anglicized to *mallard*. (Color ills., page 209.) The common wild duck of the temperate regions around the world; the ancestor of all breeds of domestic ducks except the Muscovy, commonly raised in captivity on ponds, lakes of sanctuaries, aviaries; the best-known and possibly the most abundant wild duck throughout most of the N. Hemisphere; is very closely related to the black duck; in N. America, wild population summers from Alaska throughout most of Canada and n. U.S. with most nesting in Prairie Provinces of Canada; medium to large dabbling duck; 20½–28 in. long; wingspread 30–40 in.; larger male: head *glossy green without crest,* narrow *white* collar, chestnut breast; upperparts dark gray, underparts paler, white tail *with center feathers of black, upcurled;* has *yellow* bill, orange-colored feet; female: brown-mottled with white outer tail feathers; *bill orange splotched with black;* feet orange; both male and female have blue speculum *bordered on each side with conspicuous white* which shows in flight (*see also* Mexican duck for comparisons; also, similar but more slender female pintail has white border *only on rear of speculum* (Peterson, 1961); clear white wing linings conspicuous in flight; female has dark cap and a dark stripe through eyes and lacks curled central tail feathers of male; female utters loud *quack, quack-quack, quack, quack-quack* descending the scale (*see* meaning under Waterfowl, and especially in Lorenz, 1971); male utters *raeb-raeb,* double note, and a low *kwek* (see courtship notes in Bent, 1923, and rituals in Johnsgard, 1965); hardy, adaptable, winters as far north as open water, in general avoids salt water, more often seen on any body of shallow fresh water (Pough, 1951); in Greenland and occasionally elsewhere, may be seen on shallow protected marine waters; winters throughout all of U.S. south of Canada, most numerous in winter in Mississippi Valley and Pacific states to s. U.S., very few winter farther south (Glover, 1964); total wintering population in four flyways of U.S. in Jan. 1972 estimated at 8,973,300 birds (Chamberlain *et al.*, 1972); size of breeding population ranged from 5,837,000 in 1965 to a high of 12,690,000 in 1958 (Bellrose, 1976); annual average shooting harvest in excess of 4½ million; are almost always bagged by hunters in greater numbers than other ducks; like other dabbling ducks, can fly up vertically from water or land; arrives on breeding grounds in n. U.S. and Canada Mar. and Apr., may nest in Feb. along Pacific coast

(Bent, 1923); moves southward in fall in Sept. into Nov.

Feeding Habits: Typical river and pond duck; feeds by "tipping up" and reaching below surface with bill in shallows of ponds, sloughs, lakes, streams, and in swamps of interior wherever water about a foot or two deep, although can dive for food in deeper water if necessary; eats seeds of bulrushes (28,700 in one stomach), primrose willow (35,840 seeds in another), which are staples, sedges, etc., and because of habit of picking up seeds from mud bottom often picks up spent lead shot and mortally afflicted with lead poisoning (*see* Lead Poisoning); also eats seeds of wild rice, pondweeds, bur reeds, wigeon grass, coontail, cypress galls, and seeds of water elm, oaks, hackberry, hickory, and other trees of swamps and river bottoms (see details in McAtee, 1939, and Cottam, 1939), on prairies may visit stubble fields to eat waste wheat, oats, barley, corn, in South visits rice fields, also eats freshwater snails and other mollusks, aquatic insects, tadpoles, fishes and fish eggs, and will even scavenge on dead salmon.

Nest: Built usually on ground among dead grasses, reeds, flags at edges of sloughs, lakes, reservoirs, on muskrat houses, in marshes or on dry only slightly marshy ground near water, sometimes far from water on higher ground of prairie among dense stands of *Phragmites*, in lightly grazed pastures, on islands or in bulrushes of swampy creek bottoms, sometimes in alfalfa fields, and even under a pile of brush or under a log, sometimes in hollow in tree, and along Pacific coast, even in fork of large tree (Bent, 1923); some nests are bulky cup of leaves, grasses, lined by female with her down.

Eggs: In Feb. along Pacific coast of Wash., elsewhere may be Mar.–July; 5–14, usually 8–10, light green to white.

Incubation: By female, 26–30 days; as soon as young dry, after hatching, are led by mother to nearest water (see other details in Bent, 1923); young first fly 49–60 days after hatching (Johnsgard, 1968).

Other Names: Common mallard; common wild duck; curly-tail; domestic duck; English duck; French duck; gray duck; gray mallard; greenhead; stock duck.

Age: According to records of U.S. Fish and Wildlife Service, one banded in Mo. shot and killed 14 years later in Sask.; one in Soviet Union lived to 16 years (Turcek, 1958); one banded Lansing, Iowa, found dead when 29 years, 1 month (Kennard, 1975).

Albinism: Pure-white wild one in flock was reported two successive years at Hampton Bay, Long Is., N.Y., in 1950s; a *total* albino shot fall of 1930 in Berkeley County, S.C., another shot there in same year and season (Sprunt, 1931).

Flight Speed: Timed in w. U.S., 40 m.p.h. (Cottam *et al.*, 1942b); in Calif., 60 m.p.h. airspeed, for 10 mi. across Salton Sea (Cooke, 1937a); in Calif., 55 m.p.h. airspeed (Munson, 1930); in England, 58 m.p.h. (Portal, 1922). *See* under Flight.

Hybrids: Gray (1958) reported a long list of waterfowl with which the mallard has crossbred and produced hybrids, especially in captivity, but often crossbreeds with black duck, pin-

tail and other ducks in wild (see also Johnsgard, 1965); the parentage of these hybrids usually distinguishable as hybrids are patchwork of each of the parent species (Pough, 1951).

Weights: Males (1,809) average 2.75 lbs.; females (1,417) average 2.44 lbs. (Bellrose, 1976).

Range: Nests in N. America from Aleutians and Pribilof Is., nw. Alaska, and Canada south to n. Baja Calif., s. N.M., s. Kans., ne. Ark., se. Ill., sw. Ind., s. Ohio, n. and c. W.Va., n. Va., and in Eurasia; winters from c. Alaska, s. Canada, Nova Scotia, n. U.S. south to West Indies, s. Mexico.

Mallard, black. *See* Duck, black, and Duck, mottled.

Mallard, brown. *See* Duck, black, and Duck, mottled.

Mallard, common. *See* Mallard.

Mallard, gray. *See* Mallard.

Mallard, southern. *See* Duck, mottled.

Merganser, American. *See* Merganser, common.

Merganser, common, *Mergus merganser* (MER-gus mer-GAN-ser); genus name: from Lat. *mergus*, a diver; species name: from Lat. *mergus*, from *mergere*, to dip, plunge, and *anser*, goose; *common* because may be seen more often than other members of its genus in N. America and Eurasia. (Color ills., pages 210, 211.) Widespread over N. Hemisphere; summers in Alaska, Canada, n. U.S., and south in mountains to c. Calif., Ariz., N.M.; in n. Midwest and ne. U.S. from Great Lakes to c. N.Y., New England, also in Eurasia; largest of the mergansers, or fish-eating, diving ducks, and largest of all *inland ducks* in N. America; usually seen on fresh water, occasionally on brackish water of bays and inlets; 21–27 in. long; wingspread 34–39 in.; male has long, cylindrical, serrated red bill, long white body, black back, green-black head, with crest not noticeable (similar male goldeneye is chunkier, has puffy head, shorter neck, and white spot in front of each eye); feet red, and tinge of peach color on breast; in flight, very white-appearing, and long slender bill, head and body held in straight line (Peterson, 1947); female has more noticeable crest, and brown-red head and neck which *shows sharp contrast where meets white of throat* (this contrast distinguishes it from similar female red-breasted merganser); she has *large white wing patch* which shows in flight; the male in eclipse plumage resembles the female; on breeding grounds flies low over winding courses of streams or above lakes, seldom rising above treetops (in migration, flies swiftly in small flocks, high in air); to take off, must run along surface beating wings for considerable distance before airborne; male utters harsh croaks and a faint *uig-a*, "reminiscent of the twanging of a guitar string" (Johnsgard, 1965); female a loud harsh *karr, karr;* can swim swiftly on surface and can sink slowly into the water like a grebe; dives quickly with

a forward-curving plunge; many remain in winter north as far as open inland waters of lakes, ponds, rivers, near the breeding grounds, therefore migration is short; arrives on nesting grounds of forested river and lake country of Canada and n. U.S. usually by Mar. and Apr.; moves southward in fall, Nov.–Dec.; usually on brackish or marine waters along coast only when inland bodies of fresh water frozen (Bent, 1923).

Feeding Habits: Expert diver, swims swiftly underwater in pursuit largely of fishes easiest to catch; of its fish food, eats mostly minnows, killifishes, and sticklebacks of no commercial value, also such low-grade commercial species as carp, eels, and suckers (see details in Cottam and Uhler, 1937); also frogs, aquatic salamanders, crayfishes, shrimps, and other small crustaceans (*see* Crustaceans and Birds), snails and other mollusks (*see* Mollusks and Birds), leeches, worms, aquatic insects and their larvae, and the roots and stems of aquatic plants; occasionally visits trout streams when its larger and deeper feeding waters are frozen; by feeding on smaller fishes its effect is to thin population of smaller ones, which makes more food available for larger fishes and indirectly promotes their growth (see Pough, 1951, for a discussion of the relationship of this merganser to fishes and fishermen).

Nest: Often in cavities of trees near water, also on ground, a bulky mass of weeds on ledges under low bushes, on islands in crevices of loose boulders along shores or under dense tangles of bushes on tops of islands, sometimes on floor of old buildings and lighthouses, and in old nests of hawks; nest, in cavities, lined with weeds, grasses, rootlets, and down from female's breast.

Eggs: May–June; 6–17, usually 9–12 (Bent, 1923), buff white or ivory yellow.

Incubation: By female, 28–32 days (Delacour, 1959); young hatched in trees leave nest by leaping to ground (see accounts in Bent, 1923); age when young first fly 60–70 days.

Other Names: American goosander; American merganser; American sheldrake; big sheldrake; break horn; buff-breasted merganser; buff-breasted sheldrake; dun diver; fish-duck; fishing duck; freshwater sheldrake; goosander; greater merganser; morocco-head; pond sheldrake; sawbill; winter sheldrake.

Accidents: A female entered chimney of weekend home in N.H. looking for nesting place, could not get out, starved to death (*see* Accidents).

Hybrids: According to Gray (1958), has crossbred with mallard, goldeneye, hooded merganser, and shelduck, *Tadorna tadorna*, of Eurasia.

Weights: Males (19) average 3.64 lbs.; females (30) average 2.73 lbs. (Bellrose, 1976).

Range: In N. America, nests from Alaska, s. Canada, n. U.S., and south in mountains to c. Calif., Ariz., n. N.M., Great Lakes east to n. New England and N.Y.; also in Iceland, Scotland, c. and n. Europe and through forested part of Russia and Siberia south to n. India, Mongolia; winters in N. America, from breeding range south to Tex., east across Gulf states to S.C. and n. Mexico.

Merganser, hooded, *Lophodytes cucullatus* (low-FOD-ih-teez) or lof-OD-eye-teez kuk-ull-AY-tus); genus name: from Gr. *lophos*, crest, and *dytes*, diver; crested diver; species name: Lat., hooded, for dark feathers of head and neck resembling a hood. (Color ills., pages 210, 211.) Summers in swamps, wooded streams, ponds, and lakes of Alaska, Canada, and parts of U.S. (except Southwest) in suitable habitat, rarely, or locally, breeds to s. U.S.; along coasts seen in ponds of marshes, and on saltwater creeks and inlets; smallest of the N. American mergansers (related smew of Eurasia is smaller; *see also* in Duck Family); 16–19 in. long; wingspread 24–26½ in.; male has *black-bordered fan-shaped white crest*, which he habitually raises and depresses; black head, neck, back, and tail; white breast and underparts; two black vertical bars extend from black back down sides of white breast in front of wings; are good identifying marks (the black-bordered white cockade and dark chestnut sides distinguish it from male bufflehead); male in eclipse plumage resembles female; female distinguished as merganser by her spike-like bill, from other mergansers by her small size, also has loose reddish brown crest, dark head, bill, chest gray; in flight shows white wing patch; flight of this species especially silent, flies very swiftly in direct straight line; usually seen in pairs or in very small flocks; rises from water in full flight without any preliminary motions, and is on wing at once; on water, if suspicious, sinks body until water almost level with its back; dives quickly and is extremely rapid underwater, using wings and feet to "fly" under surface (Bent, 1923); male in sexual display utters rolling, froglike *crrrroooo;* sometimes opens his bill and utters a hollow *pop* (see courtship rituals in Johnsgard, 1965); female utters hoarse *gak;* both species utter low grunts or croaks; some individuals winter over much of summer range; those that winter south of frost line move northward before ice has disappeared, usually Mar.–Apr.; move south in fall, Oct.–Nov.

Feeding Habits: Usually feeds in ponds and other clear quiet waters but when these are frozen feeds in swift-flowing streams; is expert diver, catches and eats small fishes but not nearly so much a fish-eater as common and red-breasted mergansers (Cottam and Uhler, 1937); eats many crayfishes and other crustaceans, many aquatic insects such as caddis fly larvae, dragonfly nymphs, also some frogs, tadpoles, snails and other mollusks, and roots and seeds of aquatic plants and some grain (Bent, 1923).
Nest: In tree cavities, in almost any hole or hollow tree, at any height, if large enough to admit female, even in open hollow top of stump or a fallen log; sometimes a hole in ground, may be far from water; also will nest in bird box (Bent, 1923).
Eggs: Mar. to early June; 6–18, usually 10–12, white, almost round.
Incubation: By female, 29–37 days, young usually leap from nest cavity to ground; age when first fly estimated to be 71 days.
Other Names: Fan-crested duck; hairy-crown; hairyhead; hooded sheldrake; little fish duck; little saw-bill duck; little sheldrake; moss-head;

mud sheldrake; pickax sheldrake; pond sheldrake; round-crested duck; saw-bill diver; spike-bill; summer sheldrake; swamp sheldrake; tadpole; tow-head; tree duck; water pheasant; wood sheldrake.
Hybrids: Has crossbred, and produced hybrids, with redhead, goldeneye, common merganser, red-breasted merganser (Gray, 1958); wild hybrids reported from crossing with common goldeneye (Johnsgard, 1965).
Weights: Males 600–950 gr., or about 1 lb. 5 oz. to 2 lbs. 1 oz.; females 450–675 gr., or about 1 lb. to 1 lb. 8 oz. (Leopold, 1959).
Range: Nests in two separate regions, one east of Great Plains and one in northwest; in east, nests from c. Man. east to Nova Scotia and southeast of Great Plains to Gulf from c. La. to S.C.; in west, nests from n. Calif. through Ore., Wash., n. Idaho, B.C. to panhandle of Alaska (Bellrose, 1976); winters on Pacific coast from B.C. to Baja Calif., on Atlantic coast from N.J. to Fla., and on Gulf coast and south to Mexico (Johnsgard, 1975).

Merganser, red-breasted, *Mergus serrator* (MER-gus ser-AY-tor); genus name: *see* Merganser, common; species name: New Lat., one who saws, a sawyer, in allusion to the backward-pointing serrations on cutting edges of bill—the "saw teeth"; *red-breasted* refers to the reddish-brown, speckled breast. (Color ill., page 211.) Summers north to tree limit in Alaska and Canada south to n.-c. and e. U.S., also in Eurasia; adults measure 16.1–18.6 in. long (Bellrose, 1976); wingspread 31–35 in.; sexes unlike but both have ragged crest, red bill, eyes, feet, and legs; male's rakish, crested, black head glossed with green; has wide white collar above dark red-brown breast; black on back and outer parts of wings; has square white patch on wings; generally dark-bodied appearance (common merganser is whiter); female has head and crest dull red, body gray; has white speculum on wings; differs noticeably from female common merganser in that paler rufous of head merges into pale throat and neck, not abruptly defined as in female common merganser; runs along surface of ground or water for some distance with noisy flapping of wings before airborne, but once on wing, flight is noiseless, and usually close to water; one of swiftest of ducks; also a rapid swimmer and expert diver, often swims with head and neck stretched out in front, with bill skimming surface of water; on land, awkward walker, usually silent; female utters harsh *krrr-krrr* and hoarse croaks; in one of courtship rituals, male utters soft and catlike *yeow* (see in Johnsgard, 1965); most winter on salt water; more gregarious than the common merganser, may appear in flocks of hundreds off beaches just beyond breakers and about inlets, coves, harbors, mouths of rivers, in creeks and channels of salt marshes (Townsend, 1923); along Pacific coast from Alaska to Mexico, others winter on the Great Lakes and appear on inland lakes and rivers during migration; others winter abundantly along Atlantic coast from New England to Gulf coast, from Fla. to Tex., arrive on nesting grounds of Alaska, s. Canada, and e. U.S. Apr. into May; in fall migrates Nov.–Dec.

Feeding Habits: Like the common merganser, eats mostly small fishes—minnows, sticklebacks, and killifishes—and some carp or suckers of little commercial value (Cottam and Uhler, 1937); sometimes flock may string out abreast on water in single file to drive fishes ahead into shallows where more easily caught; also eats more crayfishes and marine crustaceans than does common merganser.
Nest: On ground well-concealed under down-sweeping branches of firs, spruces, or bushes, under log or pile of driftwood, often in grassy borders of freshwater ponds, pools, rivers; also near seacoast and occasionally on shores of ocean or on coastal islands; nest a scooped-out hole or depression lined with feathers and down of female.
Eggs: June–July; 6–16, more often 8–10, green-buff; female is non-obligate parasite and sometimes lays eggs in nests of mallards, gadwalls, and lesser scaups in Wisc. (Pelzl, 1971). See discussion under Obligate Parasite; *also* Dump Nest.
Incubation: By female, 29–35 days; age when young first fly estimated at 59 days.
Other Names: Common saw-bill; fish duck; fuzzyhead; Long Island sheldrake; pheasant; red-breasted goosander; red-breasted sheldrake; saltwater sheldrake; saw-bill; sea robin; shellbird; shelduck; spring sheldrake.
Albinism: A "perfect" albino reported in museum of Philadelphia Academy of Natural Sciences (Townsend, 1883).
Flight Speed: Timed in n. Alaska, chased by airplane, 100 m.p.h. (Thompson, 1961). See under Flight.
Hybrids: Has crossbred with mallard and hooded merganser (Gray, 1958).
Weights: Males about 2 lbs. 6 oz. to 2 lbs. 12 oz.; females about 1 lb. 9¾ oz. to about 2 lbs. (Leopold, 1959); males average 2½ lbs.; females 2 lbs. (Johnsgard, 1968).
Range: Nests in Greenland, Iceland, British Isles, n. Europe and Asia, from Scandinavia to Kamchatka, Aleutian Is., Alaska, east across most of arctic Canada (except n. Keewatin), south to n. B.C., n. Alta., c. Sask., Man., s. Ont., Great Lakes states, n. N.Y., New England, and e. Canada to Newfoundland; winters on coast from se. Alaska to Baja Calif., Gulf coast, Atlantic coast from Gulf of St. Lawrence to Fla., and on Great Lakes.

Oldsquaw, *Clangula hyemalis* (CLANG-you-lah high-eh-MAIL-iss); genus name: dim. of Lat. *clangor*, noise, in reference to its almost continual calls; species name: Lat., pertaining to winter; *oldsquaw*, the general common name for it in allusion to its garrulity, or "talkativeness" (McAtee, 1955b). (Color ills., pages 210, 211.) Main nesting grounds in N. America, from Alaska along Arctic coasts of continent and northern islands of Greenland, where abundant; is one of sea ducks, also nests in Eurasia; only duck species in which male has two distinct bright plumages, one in winter and one in summer each year, *and* an eclipse plumage (see details in Bent, 1925); female also has different plumages in winter and in summer; 15–23 in. long; wingspread 26–31 in.; whether in winter or summer plumage, male can be identified by his long, slender, pointed tail (pintail also has long pointed tail but is a freshwater dabbling duck mostly of inland marshes and ponds, whereas the oldsquaw is a diving duck that prefers salt water); male in winter is a piebald duck but mainly white; with white head and neck with dark patch on cheek; breast, back, and wings, dusky brown; the short bill has bands of black and pink; male in summer has dark head, neck, breast, and back, with *large white cheek patch*, and white sides and belly; female in winter, head and neck whitish with white flanks and undersides; gray patch below and to rear of each eye; female lacks long tail of male in all plumages; in summer she resembles male but has *large dark patch* on white cheek; male in eclipse plumage resembles female; oldsquaws bunch together in irregular flocks; seem continually in motion, fly low over water with many twistings and turnings, alternately showing breast and back, like shorebirds; alight by dropping suddenly on water with great splash, where continually in motion with flock even on calm water, resembling a "white-capped whirlpool" (Reilly, 1968); noisy and garrulous at all seasons, from which many of its given names suggest its notes, such as "south-southerly" and "coween"; utters melodious calls that at times may be heard for a mile, an *ow-ow-owdle-ow* in chorus that resembles baying of hounds (see details of courtship rituals in Bent, 1925; Johnsgard, 1965; and Alison, 1975); when migrating flies high in air in irregular flocks or in Indian file; from wintering grounds on large bodies of water such as Great Lakes and preferred marine waters along Atlantic and Pacific coasts, moves north in Mar.–Apr. mainly along coasts, also overland to northern Arctic coasts of nesting grounds; south in fall, Oct.–Nov.

Feeding Habits: Can dive to great depths in freshwater lakes; taken in fishermen's nets on large lakes at 180–200 ft. below surface (see details in Bent, 1925); however, usually dives in water of moderate depths to beds of common blue mussels and other bivalve and univalve mollusks; staple foods are amphipods, shrimps, crabs, and other crustaceans, also on breeding grounds eats roots, leaves, buds, and seeds of aquatic plants, and some fishes; the young live largely on aquatic insect larvae in tundra pools.

Nest: On Arctic tundra, widely scattered, more often near shores of small freshwater ponds or on small islands in these ponds, usually a depression in sedges, grasses in open but well concealed with thick grasses or under dwarf willows, sometimes near salt water; nest composed of grasses, weed stalks, and bits of female's down that she adds as incubation progresses (Pough, 1951); at Churchill, Man., Evans (1970) found oldsquaw nests were from 3 ft. up to 600 ft. away from water but averaged 6–27 ft.; all in close association with arctic terns, which protected their nests, and those of oldsquaws, by savage attacks on egg-seeking gulls, jaegers, and ravens. *See* Protection of Nests under Nests and Nesting.

Eggs: May–July; 5–11, often 6–8, yellow-buff or cream color.

Incubation: By female, 24 days (Delacour, 1959); 26 days, young fly 35 days after hatching (Alison, 1975).

Other Names: Calloo; cockawee; coween; hound; John Connolly; long-tail; long-tailed duck; old Billy; old granny; old injun; old molly; old wife; quandy; scoldenore; scolder; south-southerly; squeaking duck; swallow-tailed duck; uncle Huldy; winter duck.

Accidents: Tremendous numbers of oldsquaws have been caught and have died in fishermen's nets in the Great Lakes; at Dunkirk, N.Y., in 1890s, fishermen caught 5,000–7,000 oldsquaws in their nets in one haul; on Lake Michigan, during about eight weeks of spring in 1946, one fishermen caught 27,000 oldsquaws! (Schorger, 1947).

Flight Speed: Timed near Toronto, 54, 62, and 73 m.p.h. (Speirs, 1945).

Weights: Males (36) weigh 2.00–2.22 lbs.; females (40) weigh 1.65–1.82 lbs. (Bellrose, 1976).

Range: Nests along Arctic coasts of both hemispheres south to Labrador, s. Hudson Bay, the Aleutian Is. in Alaska, Kamchatka, and s.-c. Norway; winters in N. America from s. Greenland and Bering Strait south along Pacific coast from Aleutians to Wash. and s. Calif., in interior to Great Lakes, Neb., Tex., Ky., and Tenn. and along Atlantic coast to N.C., rarely to Fla. and Gulf coast.

Pintail, *Anas acuta* (AY-nas ack-YOU-tah); genus name: *see* Bahama duck; species name: Lat., pointed, as is tail of this species. (Color ills., pages 212, 213.) In N. America, summers in southern part of tundra region in Arctic Alaska and Hudson Bay, south to Calif., Colo. to Great Lakes region, parts of e. Canada and New England, also in Eurasia; widely distributed throughout N. Hemisphere, an abundant dabbling duck, possibly second only to mallard in abundance; most widely distributed N. American duck, most abundant in west; males, 25–29 in., females 20½–22½ in.; both sexes are slender, with narrow, pointed wings; speculum green-bronze in male, brown in female; male has two long, pointed, middle tail feathers that extend beyond the main, rounded, brown-gray tail; head and upper neck of male rich purple-brown; white of neck of male extends upward in white point along sides of neck; brown-gray on back and flanks, white or yellowish patch at rear of gray flanks; female mottled brown with slender neck, somewhat pointed tail; in flight shows light border on wings along rear of speculum; on water, male sits alertly with slim head and neck raised in swanlike graceful curve, long tail pointed upward at angle; female resembles female mallard but more slender with longer neck and more pointed tail (Peterson, 1947); she is similar to female gadwall but lacks gadwall's white speculum; the oldsquaw, only other N. American duck with long, slender tail, is not a marsh, or freshwater, duck; pintails are fast, graceful fliers; spring upward from water like teal and get off at once; female's quacks (the decrescendo call) not so loud but deeper, hoarser, and more guttural than that of female mallard; male utters a weak, nasal *geeee*, and a mellow, flutelike whistle, *pruh* or *kluk*, when courting (Delacour, 1956; see also courtship rituals in Johnsgard, 1965); from wintering places in U.S., mainly in Pacific states and from inland

ponds and marshes, and from salt bays, brackish marshes, and estuaries along Gulf and Atlantic coasts, moves northward early, beginning in Jan., through Feb. and Mar.; arrives on prairie nesting grounds in n. U.S. and Canada by early Apr., on Alaskan tundra by early May; returns southward early in Aug. and in Sept. (Bent, 1923); see migration pattern in Aldrich *et al.* (1949); each fall more than a million pintails gather at the Sacramento National Wildlife Refuge, Calif., some cross the Pacific 2,000 mi. to winter in Hawaii; occasionally some lose their way; for example, on Nov. 5, 1942, a small flock of almost exhausted pintails landed at Palmyra Is., Hawaii, about 1,000 mi. south and west of Honolulu, and 3,000 mi. west of the American mainland; one was wearing a band that had been put on it Aug. 15, 1942, 82 days earlier, at Bear River Migratory Bird Refuge, Utah, after it had been cured of botulism (Cooke, 1945). *See* Botulism. Estimated total U.S. wintering population in four flyways in Jan. 1972, 5,086,300 (Chamberlain *et al.*, 1972); about 3 million were in Pacific Flyway; about 1½ million in Central Flyway.

Feeding Habits: Like other dabbling ducks, is mostly a shallow-water feeder, with tail tipped straight up above surface of waters of marshes, and paddling with its feet to maintain balance as it reaches below with long neck to feed; almost 90% of food is vegetal, chiefly seeds of sedges, grasses, pondweeds, smartweeds, also eats snails and other mollusks, crabs, crayfishes, minnows, leeches, worms, and aquatic insects (Bent, 1923); because of gathering of seeds from muddy bottoms often ingests spent lead shot and succumbs; in cold weather when marshes frozen, visits upland fields for waste grains or tidal flats to eat marine animals (Pough, 1951).

Nest: A depression or hollow in tundra, often far from water, although most nests near shores of ponds; on prairies, some may nest more than half a mile from water, some in sedge and hay meadows, and lightly grazed pastures or under thickets and brush piles; nest built of sticks, leaves, grasses, mosses, and lined with female's down.

Eggs: Usually May–July; 6–12, usually 6–9; yellow-green or cream-colored.

Incubation: By female, 23–25 days; 22–23 days (Kortright, 1943); young first fly 38–52 days after hatching (Johnsgard, 1968).

Other Names: American pintail; Bahama pintail; common pintail; kite-tail; northern pintail; peak-tail; pheasant-duck; picket-tail; pigeon-tail; sea-pheasant; sharp-tail; spike-tail; spindle-tail; split-tail; sprig; sprig-tail; spring-tail; sprit-tail; female: gray duck; pied gray duck; pied wigeon.

Accidents: Killed in flight on prairie nesting grounds by striking overhead utility wires and barbed-wire fences; and from striking utility wires while migrating (Cornwell and Hochbaum, 1971; Siegfried, 1972).

Age: One lived to 11 years, 10 months, in National Zoo, Washington, D.C., and Cooke (1942) reported one to 13 years old; one banded Oakland, Calif., shot in Calif. when 26 years, 6 months (Kennard, 1975).

Common pochard

DUCK FAMILY

Albinism: "A fine full-plumaged albino male" caught at Avery Is., La., Nov. 1936.

Flight Speed: Timed in w. U.S., 49 m.p.h. (Cottam *et al.*, 1942b); in Ariz., 52 m.p.h. (flock paralleling train) (Grinnell, 1901); and in Calif., 65 m.p.h. airspeed (Munson, 1930).

Hybrids: Crossbreeds with many other species of ducks in captivity (see Gray, 1958); in wild has produced hybrids by crossing with many others and those with common teal and gadwall are known to be fertile.

Weights: Males (390) average 2.26 lbs.; females (166) average 1.91 lbs. (Bellrose, 1976).

Range: In N. America, nests from tundra of arctic Alaska east to n. Mack., s. N.B., w. Greenland south to s. Calif., nw. Nev., n. Ariz., s. Colo., c. Neb., c. Iowa, c. Ill., s. Mich., n. Ohio, and nw. Pa.; in Old World south from Russia and n. Scandinavia to s. Eurasia; winters from se. Alaska, n. Calif., s. Nev., Ariz., N.M., Colo., s. Mo., s. Ill., Ohio, Mass., N.Y., and Chesapeake Bay south throughout Mexico to C. America, Bahamas, Cuba, Jamaica, Hawaii.

Pintail, American. *See* Pintail.

Pintail, Bahama. *See* Duck, Bahama.

Pintail, northern. *See* Pintail.

Pintail, white-cheeked. *See* Duck, Bahama.

Pochard, American. *See* Redhead.

Pochard, Baer's, *Aythya baeri* (AY-thih-ah BAY-er-eye); genus name: *see* Canvasback; species name: given in 1863 in honor of Dr. Karl Ernst von Baer, German embryologist, who served for the Russian government on several early natural history expeditions to Siberia (see Gruson, 1972); *pochard* (POH-cherd or POH-kerd), probably from Old Fr. *pochier* (Fr. *pocher*), to thrust, or place in pocket, "to poach," here in reference to the European pochard, popular as a game bird (Johnsgard, 1968). Baer's, an e. Siberian pochard and diving duck, reported once in N. America (1841) from specimen collected by Titian R. Peale, American artist and naturalist, with locality marked "Oregon," which then included present states of Ore. and Wash. to s. B.C.; 18 in. long; sexes outwardly quite similar but male has white iris, resembles related male redhead (*see* Pochard), but color pattern reversed: has greenish-black head and ruddy breast instead of red head and black breast as in redhead; female has brown head and breast.

Other Name: Baer's white-eye.

Range: Nests in se. Siberia; winters in Burma, China, Korea, and Japan.

Pochard, common, *Aythya ferina* (AY-thih-ah feh-RYE-nah); genus name: *see* Canvasback; species name: Lat., wild, in a state of nature, feral. A Eurasian diving duck reported up to 1957 as "accidental" on St. Paul Is., Pribilof Is., Alaska, but numerous records for Alaska by spring 1971 through spring 1973: a pair at Adak Is., May into June 1971; a male at Adak Is., June 1972; a female on Jones Lake,

DIPPER FAMILY

Dipper

This remarkable bird is a symbol of the untrammeled mountain wilderness, for it lives along (and in!) plunging streams fed by snowmelt, glaciers, and coastal rains. Wading into the torrent or diving from a boulder, the dipper walks about the bottom, where it feeds on the larvae of aquatic insects and on clams, snails, and trout fry. A thick undercoat of down keeps the bird warm in these frigid waters; a preen gland 10 times larger than that of any other songbird provides the oil to waterproof its feathers. Dippers sing year round, their bubbling wrenlike song rising above the roar of waterfalls that often conceal their oven-shaped nests.

Dipper

DUCK FAMILY

Bufflehead
The smallest diving duck in North America nests in old flicker holes in dead trees that are a short overland trek from water. The 8 to 10 ducklings remain in the cavity for 24 to 36 hours after hatching, then jump to the ground at the coaxing of the female and are led to a nearby pond or river. A duck of the north woods, the bufflehead is named for its puffy, buffalo-shaped head.

Canvasback
A favorite of waterfowlers, bird-watchers, epicures, and artists, this handsome diving duck has delicately marked plumage on the back and sides that indeed suggests canvas fabric. A duck of prairie potholes, the canvasback builds its nest over shallow water on floating mats of vegetation or anchored to bulrushes and cattails. Canvasbacks feed on the bottom, straining seeds of wild rice and other grasses from the mud or pulling up the roots of aquatic plants.

Black duck
This sooty brown dabbling duck with the purple speculum on its wing is a familiar sight on both freshwater and saltwater marshes along the Atlantic coast. The black duck's nest, containing as many as 17 eggs, may be built directly over water on a muskrat lodge, in a duck blind, or in a tree crotch, or it may be located as far as 2 miles from shore in distant woods. Black ducks feed on a wide variety of aquatic animal life and vegetation, as well as grain crops and wild nuts.

Harlequin duck
Rushing mountain rivers and storm-tossed coasts are the usual haunts of this stunningly marked waterfowl of the northern wilderness. Though they sometimes nest on quiet tundra ponds and glacial lakes, harlequin ducks prefer turbulent streams, where they dive to the bottom and walk against the current, poking their bills among the stones to catch mayfly and caddis-fly larvae. In winter, flocks of harlequins gather in the heavy surf, feeding about sunken wrecks and breakwaters on barnacles, limpets, chitons, crustaceans, and small fishes.

Bufflehead, immature male

Bufflehead

Canvasback

Black duck

Harlequin duck

Mexican duck

Both male and female Mexican ducks resemble a female mallard, and for years ornithologists have debated whether this rare waterfowl of the Southwest is a separate species or merely a race of its commonplace cousin. Only a few hundred Mexican ducks nest in the United States, and the duck was listed as an endangered species until surveys revealed substantial populations south of the border. Mexican ducks are fond of the green shoots of alfalfa and feed at night on irrigated fields.

Ring-necked duck

"Ringbill" is the name hunters have given this diving duck of forested ponds and bogs, for the two white rings on its bill are far more visible than its brownish collar. A powerful swimmer, the ring-necked duck can forage to depths of 40 feet in search of plant and animal fare.

Ruddy duck

Riding low in the water so that he seems half-submerged, the dapper male ruddy duck normally erects its stiff, fan-shaped tail to an angle of 45 degrees. When courting a female, however, he cocks his tail a full 90 degrees, puffs out his chest, bows, and slaps his bill against his breast. The ruddy is one of our smallest ducks, the female weighing about 1 pound, yet she lays a huge egg—as big as that of a wild turkey. The average clutch is 8 eggs, but female ruddy ducks freely engage in parasitism, depositing their eggs in the nests of other waterfowl. An even stranger habit is the use of a dump nest, where several female ruddies will deposit as many as 60 eggs—and then ignore them.

Tufted duck

This Old World relative of the ring-necked duck is an occasional visitor to North American shores, and some authorities predict it will eventually breed here. Tufted ducks have been reported on the Atlantic coast as far south as Long Island, and on the Pacific coast from Alaska to California. The male closely resembles the ring-necked drake but has a thin crest on the back of its head.

Mexican duck

Ring-necked duck

Tufted duck

Ruddy duck

Ruddy duck

Ruddy duck, female

Wood duck

It is fair to call the elegant wood duck drake the most beautiful duck in North America. Truly birds of the forest, wood ducks nest in hollow trees or pileated woodpecker holes that may be a mile or more from water. They are particularly fond of the nuts of forest trees; the throat and crop of one wood duck contained 56 acorns. The hen, beautiful in her own right, lays 9 to 12 eggs in a cushion of down. Using their sharp claws, the hatchlings climb to the opening of the nest cavity, which may be 50 feet above the ground, then leap out as the female calls nearby.

Wood duck

Wood duck

Wood duck

Wood duck, chicks

Wood duck, female

Common eider

The scientific name for the eider clan, Somateria, means "body wool" and refers to the luxurious gray down with which the hen profusely lines her nest and covers the eggs. The most abundant of eiders and the largest diving duck, the common eider nests in colonies that in some areas, notably Iceland, support a commercial down industry. A bird of wild seacoasts, the common eider feeds on a wide range of marine creatures, from worms to starfish. Mussels in particular are a staple in its diet; they are swallowed whole and the shells ground into bits by the bird's powerful gizzard.

King eider

Nests of this showy sea duck are scattered on tundra shores around the Arctic Ocean. Diving to depths of 180 feet, king eiders feed on mollusks, on such crustaceans as king crabs, and on sea urchins, starfish, and sea anemones.

Spectacled eider

Large circles of silver-white feathers around the eyes of the drake give this Arctic sea duck its name. Faint "goggles" also appear on the hen. A common breeding bird in Siberia, the spectacled eider has a limited nesting range on the northwest coast of Alaska. Unlike other eiders, it frequents shallow, muddy coastal waters and tundra ponds, and its diet includes quantities of plant life and the larvae of freshwater insects.

Steller's eider

The smallest eider, assigned to a separate genus, this oddly marked duck of Alaskan and Siberian shores is trim like a mallard and a swift flier. A male common eider may weigh 4½ pounds, a Steller's eider only 2 pounds. Steller's eider is rarely seen south of the Aleutian Islands, where it winters in large flocks with king and common eiders.

King eider

Spectacled eider, female

Spectacled eider

Common eider

Common eider

Steller's eider

Gadwall

A black rump and white wing patches identify this freshwater dabbler of both Old and New World lakes and marshes. The gadwall's specific name, strepera, means "noisy" and refers to the loud, quacking calls of the female. Its diet is almost totally vegetarian. Gadwalls tip their heads below the surface to eat stems, leaves, and tubers of pondweeds, but will readily dive in deeper water.

Barrow's goldeneye

Mewing and grunting, a Barrow's goldeneye drake courts a mate. Goldeneyes often are called "whistlers" because of the loud, musical sound produced by their wings. They are occasionally killed in midair by both bald and golden eagles.

Common goldeneye

In the spectacular courtship display of the common goldeneye, a drake circles a female, then thrusts his head back almost to the tail while kicking up a great spray of water. Coniferous forests from New York to Alaska and across Eurasia are the summer home of this cavity-nesting diving duck.

Mallard

The world's best-known duck, the mallard breeds across the Northern Hemisphere and has been introduced to Australia and New Zealand. Its North American population alone may exceed 9 million birds. When startled, mallards launch into flight with an almost vertical leap from the surface. The mallard nest is usually built in grass or reeds within a hundred yards of water; the first egg may be laid in a shallow bowl scratched into the moist soil, but a lining of grass and soft down plucked from the female's breast is soon added. Moreover, the body heat of the incubating hen causes rapid growth of adjacent grasses, which she preens into a concealing canopy.

Gadwall

Common goldeneye

Barrow's goldeneye

Mallard, eggs

Mallard, female and male

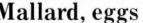

Mallard

Common merganser
Long strings of chicks led by a female common merganser are a familiar sight in summer on northern wilderness lakes. Nine to 12 young is the usual brood, and they are often hatched in hollow trees near the water. The streamlined bodies of mergansers and their long serrated bills are adaptations for underwater pursuit of fish.

Hooded merganser
In courtship, the male hooded merganser erects its fan-shaped white crest, expands its throat, and utters a rolling, froglike croak that can be heard a half-mile away. It may even pursue a potential mate underwater. The smallest merganser in North America, it consumes more crayfish and aquatic insects than it does fish.

Red-breasted merganser
Displaying to a female, a drake red-breasted merganser will "curtsy" by stretching and twisting its neck, then lower the neck and part of its head into the water while mewing like a cat. Unlike other mergansers, this species prefers to nest on the ground rather than in hollow trees.

Oldsquaw
Except for its long pointed tail, an oldsquaw drake seen in summer and again in winter could easily be mistaken for two different birds. For this duck of the Arctic is unique among waterfowl in that it has two distinct and equally beautiful plumages. The champion diver among diving ducks, oldsquaws have been caught in fishnets 240 feet underwater. They are the noisiest of all North American waterfowl the year round; a flock of oldsquaws in full voice resembles a pack of baying hounds.

Common merganser

Hooded merganser, female

Oldsquaw

Common merganser, female

Hooded merganser

Red-breasted merganser

Oldsquaw, winter

Pintail

Poised at the edge of a marsh or springing into flight, the pintail is the epitome of grace and elegance. Our only freshwater duck with a long pointed tail, it is second only to the mallard in abundance. The wintering population in North America has been estimated at 5 million birds; more than 1 million pintails gather in fall at one federal refuge in California. A dabbler, the pintail feeds largely on seeds of aquatic plants gleaned from muddy bottoms.

Redhead

A diving duck of western marshlands, the redhead has been reduced to a fraction of its former abundance by overhunting and by a century of wetlands drainage to benefit wheat growers. Silent most of the year, both male and female redheads become quite vocal during courtship. In winter, redheads congregate in rafts of several thousand birds on ice-free lakes and coastal bays.

Greater scaup

The unusual name for this sea duck apparently comes from a Scottish term, "scalp" or sometimes "scaup," for a bed of shellfish exposed at low tide. Wintering along the coast in rafts of up to 50,000 birds, greater scaup feast on oysters, clams, scallops, mussels, limpets, and barnacles. Diving for food, they can remain underwater for 60 seconds. Greater scaup breed on the tundra of northern Alaska and interior Canada, sometimes in colonies of 50 or more pairs. The white-faced hen commonly lays 9 eggs in a well-concealed nest alongside a pond or lake.

Lesser scaup

"Bluebill" is a commonly used name for both species of scaup, for they are difficult to tell apart in the field. On the water, both drakes appear to be black and white; only in good light can one see the green gloss on the head of the greater scaup, or the purple gloss of the lesser scaup. Lesser scaup are birds of prairie sloughs, and on migration they prefer inland waters. Like other diving ducks, scaup must run along the surface of the water, beating their wings, to become airborne.

Pintail

Greater scaup, chicks

Greater scaup, female

Greater scaup

Pintail, male and female

Lesser scaup

Redhead, male and female

Black scoter

Long strings of scoters skimming the waves are a familiar sight off both Atlantic and Pacific beaches in winter. Smallest of the three species of "sea coots," this Eurasian bird, which nests in North America only on the Alaskan coast, is the most abundant scoter worldwide. Our only all-black duck, the drake is distinguished by a bright orange-yellow knob on its bill.

Surf scoter

An oddly shaped, multi-colored bill and white patches on the forehead and nape identify the surf scoter, a common wintering duck on the Great Lakes as well as on both seacoasts. Scoters consume tremendous quantities of mollusks. Several dozen mussels will be swallowed whole in a single meal, and the stomach of one surf scoter contained 574 periwinkles. Unlike the black and white-winged scoters, the surf scoter nests only in North America; its breeding grounds are the boreal forests of Canada and Alaska.

White-winged scoter

This bird, the largest scoter, is incredibly abundant in winter off the New England coast; 180,000 white-winged scoters were counted on one December day. They dive to 40 feet to feed on shellfish beds. Their powerful gizzards can crush hard-shelled clams that require a hammer blow to break; but occasionally a clam slams shut on the scoter's tongue.

Northern shoveler

This remarkable dabbling duck feeds like a baleen whale, straining pond life from the water with highly developed comblike "teeth" on its huge, spatulate bill. Small groups will swim in circles, stirring up bottom mud rich in minute plant and animal organisms. Or one shoveler will skim the surface with its head half-submerged, capturing larger prey.

Black-bellied whistling-duck

In the family tree of waterfowl, the tropical whistling-ducks rank midway between geese and dabbling ducks. They are gooselike in appearance, with long necks and long legs; they graze grainfields, usually feeding at night. However, their high-pitched whistling calls are typical of neither goose nor duck; and in flight, with necks and legs extended, they suggest a flock of ibises. Nesting colonies of the black-bellied whistling-duck occur in Texas, often around livestock watering areas. When feeding in cornfields, they perch on mature stalks to glean the ears.

Fulvous whistling-duck

"Fulvous" refers to the brownish-yellow color of both sexes. This species nests in freshwater marshes from Florida to California, but wanders as far north as Oregon, Michigan, and Maine in the fall. It feeds on both land and water, and sometimes is blamed for damaging newly planted ricefields.

Black-bellied whistling-duck

Black-bellied whistling-duck

Fulvous whistling-duck

Fulvous whistling-duck

White-winged scoter

Surf scoter

Black scoter

Northern shoveler, female

Northern shoveler

American green-winged teal

Our smallest dabbling duck, the hardy green-winged teal is one of the first waterfowl to move north in spring. Swift fliers, timed at speeds up to 40 miles an hour, they dart about like flocks of shorebirds. The typical diet of aquatic plants and animals is augmented in fall by berries, grapes, and nuts gathered from woods and meadows. And in Alaska, green-winged teal gorge themselves on the rotting carcasses of salmon spent from their spawning runs.

Blue-winged teal

A late arrival on prairie potholes, the blue-winged teal begins its southbound departure early in August; for its migration flights to and from wintering areas in Central and South America may cover several thousand miles. One bird banded in Saskatchewan was shot 6 months later in Peru, 7,000 miles away. And a male blue-winged teal was spotted on South Georgia Island in subantarctic waters! The handsome drake is often seen perched on stumps or boulders in shallow water, preening its nuptial finery.

Cinnamon teal

On marshes west of the Rocky Mountains, up to 100 pairs of cinnamon teals can be found nesting on one square mile of prime habitat. Fully half of the North American population of this colorful little duck nests in Utah, where it is subjected to heavy predation by California gulls. Along with the ruddy duck and the whistling-ducks, this is the only waterfowl to nest in both North and South America.

American wigeon

Better known as the "baldpate," for the white crown on the drake's forehead, this freshwater duck stands apart from other dabblers because of its extensive grazing habits. It is fond of wild celery, a deepwater plant that it poaches from diving birds such as coots, redheads, and canvasbacks.

Eurasian wigeon

This Old World cousin of the baldpate is a regular visitor to North America and may even be nesting on remote islands in the Aleutian chain, where paired birds have been seen during breeding season. Smaller than the native wigeon, it has a russet-red head topped with a gold crown.

Eurasian wigeon

American wigeon

American green-winged teal

Blue-winged teal

Cinnamon teal

Brant

The common name of this little sea goose comes from the German word brand, *meaning "burnt," and refers to its dark feathers. The species name,* bernicla, *is derived from the Norwegian word for "barnacle." According to an ancient legend, these geese hatched from barnacles that cling to driftwood. Birds of the high Arctic, brant breed farther north than any other geese. Their nests, down-filled hollows in the tundra, are usually only a foot or so above the tidal zone and storms often cause heavy losses of eggs. Two races of brant occur in North America. Black brant are dark-bellied birds that nest on the Alaska coast and congregate prior to migration on the vast eelgrass beds of Izembek Bay; 200,000 strong, black brant winter on sheltered lagoons along Baja California. The light-bellied brant that nest in northern Canada and Greenland winter on the Atlantic coast from New Jersey to North Carolina. In the 1930s and 1940s, the Atlantic brant population was decimated when disease destroyed the eelgrass beds that furnished 80 percent of their winter food. Their numbers never regained former levels even though the geese adapted their diet to sea lettuce and sea cabbage. Brant fly in bunches that constantly shift from tight balls to long wavy lines.*

Brant

(Black) brant

Brant

Canada goose

From coast to coast, from the Gulf of Mexico to the Arctic Ocean, the goose we affectionately call the "honker" is known to more Americans than any other species of waterfowl. Cosmopolitan in its choice of habitats, the Canada goose is equally at home on wild tundra ponds and the water hazards of suburban golf courses. And the musical cries from V-shaped flocks of migrants are as familiar a signal of the approach of spring or autumn as budding crocuses or changing leaves. Though Canada geese will occasionally spring into the air like startled puddle ducks, they generally take flight by running a few steps while beating their powerful wings. They land on water like skiers, tail down and webbed feet thrust forward. There are strong family ties among Canada geese. In fall, the adults migrate south with their young of the year, and the family group remains together throughout the winter. In spring, the yearlings follow their parents back to the nesting territory where they were born, then form flocks with other nonbreeding subadults. This habit guarantees inbreeding, which in turn has led to the evolution of about a dozen distinctive races of Canada geese. They range in size from the giant Canada goose, weighing 20 pounds with a wingspread of 70 inches, to the tiny cackling goose, no larger than a mallard duck. The cackling goose, so called because it chatters constantly, is the darkest of all Canada geese; it nests along the Bering Sea and winters in California's Central Valley. The dusky Canada goose, with its large white cheek patches, breeds on Alaska's Copper River delta and winters in the Willamette valley of Oregon. Rarest of the subspecies is the Aleutian Canada goose. Ten years ago, only 300 of these short-necked geese survived on Buldir Island at the far end of the Aleutian chain. Captive breeding, extermination of foxes that were freed on the islands for fur farming, and protection of its wintering areas in California have begun to rebuild the population of this endangered bird.

(Aleutian) Canada goose

Canada goose

(Dusky) Canada goose

(Cackling) Canada goose

Emperor goose

This handsome sea goose is little known beyond Alaskan waters; it nests along the Bering Sea and winters in the Aleutian Islands, though a few birds stray as far south as northern California. Seaweeds and shellfish are mainstays of its diet, but the emperor goose is especially fond of tundra crowberries. Its nest is usually built close to water, often in driftwood and wrack at the high-tide mark. Five or 6 eggs are laid in a depression lined with feathers and down.

Ross' goose

North America's smallest goose was described to science in 1861. There was no secret about its wintering place—in California's Central Valley—but it was not until June 1938, 77 years later, that the nesting territory of Ross' goose was discovered in Canada's Northwest Territories. Snow white with black wing tips, this mallard-sized goose once was considered fairly rare. But its present population is estimated at 70,000, and Ross' geese now winter as far east as Louisiana.

White-fronted goose

Waterfowlers know these birds as "speckle-bellies" for the black bars and blotches on their breasts. And in Europe they are called "laughing geese" because of the high-pitched calls that drift down from migrating flocks. White-fronted geese nest on high Arctic tundra around the pole; but in winter, in North America, they are rarely seen east of the Mississippi River. A Greenland race of white-fronted geese—birds that might be expected to winter on our Atlantic coast—cross the ocean to northwestern Europe.

Emperor goose

White-fronted goose

Ross' goose

Snow goose

Greater snow goose, lesser snow goose, blue goose—the most abundant of all the world's wild geese presents a confusion of names and color phases. Until fairly recently, snow geese and blue geese were considered to be two separate species; one bird was snow white with black wing tips, the other bluish gray with a white head. But white and dark birds nest in mixed colonies, interbreeding is common, and there are many intermediate color forms. So taxonomists ruled that the blue goose was only a color phase of the lesser snow goose, a subspecies that in its white phase is impossible to tell apart from the greater snow goose, a slightly larger eastern race that does not have a blue color phase. To muddle matters even further, the current scientific name for the snow goose is Anser caerulescens, *which means "blue goose"!*

Snow goose

Snow goose

Snow goose, blue phase

Snow goose, blue phase

Mute swan

Brought to these shores from Eurasia to decorate country estates and landscaped parks, the royal swan of England, like the starling, has become a naturalized citizen—and something of a pest, albeit a beautiful one. The feral population exceeds 4,000 birds and is largely concentrated in 3 areas: on the northeast coast from Massachusetts to New Jersey, in Michigan, and on Puget Sound, Washington. The mute swan "explosion" worries wildlife biologists because this huge and belligerent bird may drive native waterfowl from nesting and feeding areas. Usually silent, mute swans are capable of only weak, puppylike barks and menacing hisses. They can be distinguished from native swans by the way they hold their necks in a graceful curve, with orange bills pointed downward.

Trumpeter swan

If the mute swan is aptly named, so too is the world's largest waterfowl. For the deep, far-reaching voice of the trumpeter swan is one of the most soul-stirring sounds of the North American wilderness —especially so since this magnificent bird barely survived extinction in the lower 48 states. While the trachea of a mute swan is virtually straight and capable of producing only modest sounds, that of the trumpeter swan is long and convoluted (the bird's neck is twice the length of its body!). Indeed, at close range the call of a trumpeter is almost deafening. The wingspread of a male trumpeter swan exceeds 8 feet; its weight is more than 30 pounds. Killed by the thousands for food and feathers, the trumpeter was reduced to a mere 66 birds by 1933 except for a large, unmolested (and at that time unknown) population in Alaska. However, the species has made a remarkable comeback under strict protection.

Trumpeter swan

Mute swan

Trumpeter swan

Whistling swan

Contrary to its name, North America's most abundant wild swan does not whistle. Rather, its call has been described as a loud, high-pitched cooing or hooting. Nesting in the remote Arctic, the whistling swan never suffered the human depredations of its much larger cousin, the trumpeter swan. Its population today is estimated at 100,000, and great concentrations of swans are a spectacular sight in winter on such coastal waters as Chesapeake Bay. Apart from its size and voice, the whistling swan can be told from the trumpeter by the yellow lores in front of its eyes. The whistling swan's nest, a large mound of moss and grass, is usually situated on an island in a tundra pond. Four to 5 eggs are laid; the chicks, downy white at hatching, will not fly until they are 11 weeks old.

Whistling swan, cygnet

Whistling swan

Whistling swan

Whistling swan

Whooper swan

Whooper swan

Famous for its loud, bugling call, the whooper swan breeds from Iceland across Eurasia. Most of the eastern population migrates to the Japanese island of Honshu; but several dozen birds regularly cross the Bering Strait to winter in the Aleutian and Pribilof islands, and a few cases of whooper swans nesting in Alaska have been reported. This preening whooper swan can be told from other all-white swans by the large swatch of lemon yellow at the base of its bill. In early times, Icelanders believed that whooper swans possessed supernatural powers and that, after nesting, they flew off to the moon.

Amchitka Is., June 1972; up to 8 seen at Jones Lake, Amchitka Is., May 1973; up to 8 seen Adak Is., May 1973, 1 at Attu Is., and a pair reported on Smew Pond, Adak Is., through mid-June 1973; a female remained at Jones Lake through mid-June 1973; a female at Webster Lake, St. Paul Is., Pribilofs; remarkably similar to canvasback but higher head profile (Johnsgard, 1968) and similar to redhead; 18–23 in. long; male distinguished by his uniformly chestnut-colored head and neck, black breast, pale gray body; similar to male redhead but bill *black* with pale blue-gray ring or band; eyes *red*, not yellow (Peterson *et al.*, 1954); grays of plumage much paler than in redhead; female, brown head and foreparts; blue-gray ring around dark bill (see other details in Delacour, 1959).

Other Names: Curre; dunbird; European pochard; poker.
Range: Nests in Eurasia; winters south to n. Africa, Iran, India, Burma, s. China, and Japan; besides Alaska, has appeared in Azores, Canary Is., Madeira, and Komandorskie Is..

Pochard, European. *See* Pochard, common.

Redhead, *Aythya americana* (AY-thih-ah ah-mer-ih-CANE-ah); genus name: *see* Canvasback; species name: Lat., of America. (Color ill., page 213.) A strictly N. American pochard and diving duck; summers in freshwater marshes of w. U.S. and w. Canada east to w. Pa.; 18–22 in. long; wingspread 29–35 in.; male: gray with *round*, red-brown head and black chest; gray wing stripe (speculum); blue bill with *black tip* (Peterson, 1947); iris yellow instead of red as in the male canvasback and European pochard; female: brownish with pale patch at base of bill; iris brown; has gray wing stripe; redheads fly rapidly during migration in V-shaped flocks like geese, usually "in irregular flocks by themselves, but on water will associate with other species of ducks" (Pough, 1951); especially with lesser scaups; most of year are silent, but very vocal during pairing and courtship; male utters a catlike *meow*, *whee-ough*, or *keyair*, and a rolling purring *rrrrrr*; female, a harsh *squak* (see details of courtship in Bent, 1923; Delacour, 1959; and Johnsgard, 1965); seen in winter in large rafts on lakes and coastal bays, from wintering grounds along Pacific coast east from interior marshes across c. U.S. and from Gulf coast and along Atlantic coast, moves northward mainly in Mar. to nesting grounds concentrated in Bear River marshes of Utah and in other large freshwater marshes in w. U.S.; most important breeding area is still the prairies, where 400,000–500,000 nest; average of 590,000 recorded on Jan. surveys from 1955–74. See Bellrose (1976) for details on populations. Precarious status of redhead in recent years has led to further restrictive hunting regulations, including regional closures.

Feeding Habits: Moves about frequently to feed in mornings and evenings; if necessary, will feed at night; dives in deep water of interior lakes or in shallows of coastal marshes, dives to 10 ft. below surface and sometimes dabbles in shallows with river ducks; in winter, often favors shallow freshwater ponds in back of coastal beaches; food is about 90% vegetal—it feeds less on buds and tubers of aquatic plants than canvasback and more on submerged leaves and stems; eats chiefly pondweeds, widgeon grass, muskgrass and other algae, seeds of sedges, and of grasses such as wild rice and *Panicum*, and of water lilies, coontail, also wild celery, a fall and winter food; skims duckweeds from surface of water; among insects, eats many grasshoppers, and larvae of midges and caddis flies; also takes some mollusks (shellfishes), and small crustaceans in winter from brackish waters (see Cottam, 1939).

Nest: Usually built up out of water on base of matted cattails, reeds, and attached to upright stems of surrounding living plants, commonly in shallows at edge of bays and sloughs in a bulrush or cattail marsh or at edge of water in dense stand of *Phragmites* (Hochbaum, 1944); may be 16 in. across and often has a deep cup; nest built of reeds and blanket of white down (whiter than that of canvasback) from female's breast.

Eggs: Apr.–July; usually 10–16, any more may be laying of more than one female in nest; commonly lays its buff-colored eggs in nests of other ducks; up to 20 eggs of redhead have been found in a canvasback's nest; two or more redheads may lay a similar number in a communal "dump nest."

Incubation: 24–28 days; young first fly 56–73 days after hatching (Johnsgard, 1968).

Other Names: American pochard; fiddler; raft duck; red-headed broadbill; red-headed raft duck.

Age: One banded bird reported to have lived to 12 years.

Albinism: Two partial albinos reported by Townsend (1883); only head and neck parts were white.

Flight Speed: Timed in w. U.S. 31–55 m.p.h. (Cottam *et al.*, 1942b); in Colo., 42 m.p.h.

Hybrids: Crossbreeds in captivity and produces hybrids with many other species of ducks (Gray, 1958); and wild hybrids produced from crosses of redhead with ring-necked duck and greater and lesser scaups (Johnsgard, 1965).

Weights: Males (70), 1 lb. 14 oz. to 3 lbs.; females (26), 1 lb. 6 oz. to 2 lbs. 11 oz. (Kortright, 1943); males average 2½ lbs.; females 2¼ lbs. (Johnsgard, 1968).

Range: Nests from somewhat isolated areas in e. Alaska to w. Canada to nw. Minn. and south to s. Calif. and east to s. Wisc., and nw. Pa.; winters from s. B.C. east to Nev., n. Ark., and s. Ill., e. Ind., e. Mich., N.Y., Conn., and e. Md. to s. Mexico, also to Bahama Is., Cuba, Jamaica.

Scaup, American. *See* Scaup, greater.

Scaup, common. *See* Scaup, greater.

Scaup, greater, *Aythya marila* (AY-thih-ah mah-RYE-lah); genus name: *see* Canvasback; species name: Lat. form of Gr. *marile*, embers of charcoal, black; apparently in reference to the male's dark head, neck, and breast; *scaup* (SKAWP) may be from British term which alludes to ducks that feed on scaups, or scalps—beds of shellfishes (McAtee, 1955c), but the name may also have derived from one of the

DUCK FAMILY

The scaup, a diving duck, has small, pointed wings that are advantageous to underwater swimming. However, its heavy wing-loading requires it to run across the surface of the water to build air speed before taking off. Dabblers, with larger wing areas relative to their body weight, can bound directly from the water into flight.

bird's characteristic calls, rendered *scaup.* (Color ills., page 212.) Is most marine of the pochards and only one that lives in both Old World and New World; sea duck; summers farther north than lesser scaup, mostly in Arctic north of tree limit in Alaska, Canada; 16–20 in. long; wingspread 30–34½ in.; male: solidly dark head and neck, gloss on head, strongly green (similar lesser scaup has head more glossed with purple), bill blue (often called blue-bill by hunters), back and flanks finely barred with gray which appears white at distance; female: brown with white face (around bill), similar to female lesser scaup but best distinction is the *longer,* broad white wing stripe of the greater which extends from its secondaries out over the primary wing feathers; is usually quiet, but a common note is loud *scaup,* also male utters in courtship a soft, fast whistle, *week-week-whew;* female, a low *arrrr* (see courtship patterns in Johnsgard, 1965); is one of "raft ducks" (*see* Raft duck) that may gather in flocks of up to 50,000 on favorable winter feeding grounds on saltwater harbors, bays, estuaries (25,000 seen at Captree, Long Is., N.Y., in Christmas Bird Count, Dec. 1972); is relatively uncommon inland in winter; although possibly as many as 60,000 winter in La. and pass up the Mississippi Valley, most of the population (several hundred thousand) winters on the Atlantic coast between Cape Cod and Chesapeake Bay; these birds migrate through the Great Lakes into interior Canada and Alaska (Bellrose, 1976); arrives nesting grounds usually in Apr.–May; moves southward in fall, usually Oct.–Nov.

Feeding Habits: When food plentiful, often feeds in large flocks, in summer on large freshwater lakes and ponds, in fall usually migrates to salt water; is expert diver, dives to at least 20 ft. deep and can remain underwater seeking food for 50–60 seconds (*see* Swimming and Diving); uses feet to swim underwater, in daily movements travels back and forth with tide and may go to sea if persecuted, then return to feeding waters near shore at night; in summer, more often eats freshwater snails and aquatic insects in shallows, also tadpoles, and small fishes, and such plant foods as seeds of sedges, wild rice, water milfoil, and pondweeds (1,600 seeds in one meal by one scaup), some Atlantic coast birds in winter very partial to muskgrass (total of 332,000 parts of muskgrass taken by one bird in one meal), also sea lettuce, eelgrass, wild celery, widgeon grass (also some salmon and herring eggs and rotted flesh of dead salmon on coast of B.C.), but main food along coasts is mollusks such as oysters (on Pacific coast), clams, scallops, mussels, dog whelks, periwinkles, limpets, oyster drills, etc., also crabs, barnacles, and other crustaceans (Cottam, 1939). *See* Crustaceans and Birds.

Nest: On tundra, built of matted plants concealed in grasses near shores of lakes or ponds; others in marshes and above or in water among rushes, wild rice; sometimes on islands, where may nest in colonies of 50 pairs or more (Bent, 1923).

Eggs: May–July; 8–11, most commonly 9, olive-buff (often lays eggs in nests of other ducks). *See* discussion under Obligate Parasite.

Incubation: By female, 24–28 days; young first fly when about 35–42 days old (Reilly, 1968).

Other Names: American scaup duck; big blackhead; big bluebill; blackhead; black-neck; bluebill; blue-billed wigeon; broadbill; bullhead; common scaup; floating fowl; flock duck; grayback; greater bluebill; green-head; musselduck; raft duck; shuffler; troop-fowl.

Age: A male banded at Willard, N.Y., was shot at Etnier, near Stump Is., in Tenn., when 11 years old; another banded wild greater scaup lived to 13 years.

Hybrids: Crossbreeds and produces hybrids with many other species of ducks in captivity (see Sibley, 1938); wild hybrids reported from crosses of greater scaup with redhead and with tufted duck in Europe; no wild hybrids reported of any crosses of greater with lesser scaup (Johnsgard, 1965).

Weights: Males 1 lb. 5 oz. to 2 lbs. 10 oz.; females 1 lb. 5 oz. to 2 lbs. 15 oz. (Kortright, 1943).

Range: Nests from n. Alaska to c. Que., south to nw. B.C. and se. Mich.; winters from se. Alaska to s. Calif., rarely to Baja Calif., and from e. Great Lakes region and Canadian Maritime Provinces to s. Fla. and Gulf coast; also lives in Eurasia.

Scaup, lesser, *Aythya affinis* (AY-thih-ah aff-EYE-nis); genus name: *see* Canvasback; species name: Lat., adjacent, neighboring, allied, or related to, apparently in reference to the previous species, the greater scaup; *lesser* because smaller than its close relative. (Color ill., page 213.) Breeds most abundantly north of prairies in wetlands of boreal forest in n. Canada and Alaska (Bellrose, 1976); limited to N. America; 15–19 in. long; wingspread about 24–33 in.; male resembles male greater scaup but head usually glossed with purple instead of green, has higher head profile; female resembles female greater, but both sexes of lesser have shorter white wing stripe that shows in flight; also, the blue bill is more spatulate than that of greater scaup; lesser utters *scaup* (skawp) notes; in courtship male utters low short whistle, *whew;* female, a peculiar rattling purr, *kwuh-h-h-h* (Bent, 1923); more inland than greater scaup and prefers smaller lakes, ponds, marshes, although visits salt or brackish water in winter; winters inland and along coasts throughout s. U.S.; large numbers winter in Fla., with 65,000 seen at Cocoa on a Dec. day of 1972 Christmas Bird Count, along La. coast on brackish bays and harbors, one of commonest wintering ducks; migrates northward usually Mar.–Apr., concentrates on lakes, but when stopping to feed, spreads out into marshes, sloughs, shallow ponds; in fall, one of last ducks to leave northern breeding grounds; migrates southward usually Oct.–Nov.

Feeding Habits: Expert diver; swims rapidly underwater by using feet, with wings held tightly closed; confined mostly to fresh water, and most feeding is in depths of 5–6 ft., but, like greater scaup, may also feed in water 15–20 ft. deep; eats similar foods to that of greater scaup; about equally plant and animal foods; eats seeds of pondweeds, widgeon grass, wild rice, sedges, bulrushes; also eats snails and other mollusks, small shrimplike crustaceans, and aquatic insects; along coasts and about larger lakes, with gulls, gathers about sewer outlets to feed (see Cottam, 1939; Munro, 1941); because of feeding in bottom ooze, it frequently ingests spent lead shot and succumbs.

Nest: Well concealed in tall prairie grass, sometimes on islands in small lakes, usually on dry ground, and some may be far from sluggish channel, creek, or prairie slough, in grass-sedge-sow thistle meadow, hay meadow, occasionally in shallows at edges of bays and sloughs among bulrushes; nest is in hollow in ground, profusely lined with female's down and some dried grasses.

Eggs: May–July; 6–15, commonly 9–12, dark olive-buff (Bent, 1923).

Incubation: By female, 22–27 days; young first fly about 49 days after hatching.

Other Names: Blackhead; blackjack; creek broadbill; river bluebill; river broadbill; bullhead.

Accidents: One of chief losses of small young in B.C. is through drowning or suffocation from entanglement of ducklings in weeds or matted layers of filamentous algae on some lakes (Munro, 1941).

Age: One banded wild bird lived to at least 10 years.

Hybrids: Records of hybrids from interbreeding with wood duck, American wigeon, redhead; ring-necked duck (*see* interesting record in biography of ring-necked duck), European pochard, tufted duck, and canvasback (Gray, 1958).

Weights: Males (177) average 1.82 lbs.; females (44) average 1.65 lbs. (Bellrose, 1976).

Range: Nests from c. Alaska to n. Man. south to ne. Colo. and ne. Iowa; winters from s. B.C., southward along Pacific coast to Mexico, n. Ark. to e. Md., s. Ont., N.Y. and Conn. south to n. S. America and West Indies.

Scoter, American. *See* Scoter, black.

Scoter, American velvet. *See* Scoter, white-winged.

Scoter, black, *Melanitta nigra* (mel-ah-NIT-tah NIG-rah); genus name: from Gr. *melos, melanos,* black, and *netta,* duck; species name: from Lat. *niger,* black; *scoter* (SKOH-ter), according to dictionary definition, from dialect words "scote" or "scoot," to hurry off. (Color ill., page 215.) A sea, or diving, duck; in N. America, limited in summer to coasts of Alaska (also lives in Eurasia); rarest and least-known of the 3 species of "sea coots" that breed in N. America; 17–21 in. long; wingspread 30–35 in.; male is only *all-black duck* in N. America, also has bright yellow-orange *knob* on bill, a distinguishing character, from which its names of butter-bill and butter-nose—the similar American coot of the Rail Family; has a *white* bill and white patch under tail; female, dark brown with whitish cheeks and throat and dark cap; females of the other scoters have *two* light spots on each side of head (Peterson, 1961); in flight, both sexes show silvery sheen on undersurfaces of wing primaries; on water, holds head high, bill either horizontal or tipped up,

never down as in other scoters; rises from water more easily than most diving ducks and on feeding grounds does much flying about in small flocks; a very narrow outer primary on each wing produces wing-whistling in flight; are usually silent but in fine calm weather may call much—a plaintive *cour-loo,* the most musical of duck cries (Bent, 1923); male in courtship utters whistle; female's call similar but grating rather than mellow (Johnsgard, 1965); from winter range, mostly on waters along Pacific and Atlantic coasts, some on Great Lakes but rare inland (some non-breeders, as in all scoters, remain on wintering places throughout summer), moves northward in Mar.–May; migratory flocks vary in size and form; some in great irregular masses, others strung out in long straight or curving lines, others in regular V or U shape; usually follows undulations of coastline close to shore, seldom flies overland; in fall, migrates Sept.–Oct.

Feeding Habits: Although able to feed in deep water, seems to prefer to feed in calmer waters of protected coastal bays and sounds where water no more than 25 ft. deep and a bounteous supply of its favorite food, the common blue mussel *(Mytilus edulis)*—one stomach of a black scoter examined held 78 of these abundant mussels; about 65% of its food is mollusks; in feeding over reefs, besides mussels, dives for clams, oysters, scallops (see discussion of relation to commercial shell fisheries in Cottam, 1939), periwinkles, limpets, dog whelks, oyster drills, chitons, and others; also eats such crustaceans as barnacles, shrimps, mud crabs, cancer crabs, hermit crabs, crayfishes, and others, also some fishes and some plant foods such as eelgrass and muskgrass and other algae, will also eat millet seeds, corn, and other grains; in summer, on breeding grounds, eats some aquatic insects and on inland ponds such plants as duckweeds, pondweeds, blue flags, water milfoil, bladderwort, and other aquatics (see details in Cottam, 1939).

Nest: On ground, and when near saltwater and freshwater ponds of Alaska, in depression hidden in standing grasses or under a shrub; also in clefts and hollows about steep banks of lakes, built of coarse grasses lined with feathers and down of female.

Eggs: June–Aug.; 5–8, frequently 8, buff to pink-buff.

Incubation: 27–28 days (Delacour, 1959); age when young first fly estimated at about 46 days.

Other Names: American scoter; black butterbill; black coot; black sea coot; booby; broadbilled coot; butter-bill; butter-billed coot; butter-nose; common scoter; copper-bill; copper-nose; fizzy; hollow-billed coot; pumpkin-blossom coot; sea coot; yellow-bill; yellow-nose; female: brown coot; gray coot; smutty coot.

Weights: Males average 2½ lbs.; females 2¼ lbs.

Range: Nests in w. and s. Alaska and the Aleutian Is., also in Eurasia (more common in Europe than in N. America); winters on Pacific coast from Pribilofs and Aleutians to s. Calif., on Great Lakes, and on Atlantic coast from Newfoundland to S.C., rarely to Fla., irregu-

larly to Wyo., Colo., N.D., Neb., Kans., Iowa, Mo., the Great Lakes, Ky., Tenn., and La.

Scoter, common. *See* Scoter, black.

Scoter, European white-winged. *See* Scoter, velvet.

Scoter, surf, *Melanitta perspicillata* (mel-ah-NIT-ah per-spick-ill-AY-tah); genus name: *see* Scoter, black; species name: Lat., conspicuous, spectacular (Jaeger, 1955), referring to the peculiar and strikingly colored bill (Kortright, 1943); *scoter* and *surf,* from its habit of swimming in, or just beyond, the breaking waves, or ocean surf. (Color ill., page 215.) A diving or sea duck limited to N. America; the most abundant and most widely distributed of the 3 species of scoters breeding in N. America; well known in winter along Atlantic and Pacific coasts and some winter on interior large bodies of water such as the Great Lakes; 17–21 in. long; wingspread 30–36 in.; male all-black but with *white patches*—one on forehead, the other on the nape—bill swollen near base, is orange, red, black, and white; *eyes white,* legs and feet crimson to orange (like other scoters, has no eclipse plumage); female, dusky brown, eyes brown; has two whitish spots on each side of head, similar to female white-winged scoter but lacks her white wing patches; also, her bill, swollen at base, is distinguishing character; when surf scoters flying in flocks well offshore, difficult to distinguish from similar black scoter; flock sizes and formations in flight similar to those of black scoter; also follows coastlines (is thought to be more closely related to white-winged scoter, however); usually silent but occasionally they utter low, guttural croaks; male utters liquid gurgling call in courtship, and a low, clear whistle; less inclined to drift inland to interior lakes than white-winged scoter; in winter, often frequents large ponds just in back of ocean beaches; flocks move along coasts northward in Apr.–May; return southward in Sept.–Oct.

Feeding Habits: Food and feeding habits similar to those of other scoters; it sometimes feeds with flocks of other seafowl in quiet coastal estuaries; often feeds just outside breakers, diving or "scooting" through the foaming crest of a breaking wave; dives to depths of 6–30 ft., and remains under 19–32 seconds; in swimming underwater, uses feet and inner half of its wings, with outer half (primaries, or flight feathers) folded back over tail; feeds during day, especially in morning, and sometimes entire flock dives below surface, all at once (Cottam, 1939); large flocks often in immense rafts, winter within reach of large beds of mussels; like other scoters, feeds more heavily on mollusks throughout year than any other animal foods, especially blue mussels in coastal waters, which make up about 28% of its animal food (one had 212 small ones in its gizzard; another 1,100); also eats many *Macoma* shells—small mollusks of sheltered bays and sounds (34 taken by one scoter in single meal)—rock and razor clams, periwinkles (574 in one surf scoter's stomach); but only small amounts of oysters and scallops; from food-habits investigations of stomach contents, not a serious competitor with shellfish industry (Cottam, 1939); among crustaceans, eats sand and mud crabs and hermit crabs (40 found in stomach of one surf scoter); also eats some fishes (sand launces and killifishes); sea urchins and sand dollars, among echinoderms; some marine worms, and some eelgrass and widgeon grass; in summer, in freshwater ponds and lakes of interior, eats many aquatic insects—larvae of caddis flies, damselflies, dragonflies, beetles, water boatmen, and many others—and plant foods such as pondweeds (*Potamogeton*), wild celery, also muskgrass and other algae, and seeds of sedges and bulrushes (see Cottam, 1939).

Nest: In a hollow or depression in ground of freshwater marsh near lake or pond or, if some distance from water, well concealed under low spreading branches of pines or spruces; in marsh, well built of weeds with cup 6 in. across, hidden in grasses (Bent, 1925).

Eggs: June–July; 5–8, usually 7, buff or pink-buff.

Incubation: Period of and age of first flight of young unknown.

Other Names: baldpate; bay coot; blossom-billed coot; butter-billed coot; goggle-nose; hollow-billed coot; horse-head (coot); Morocco jaw; patch-head (coot); patch-polled coot; pictured-bill; plaster-bill; sea coot; skunk-duck; skunk-head; skunk-top; snuff-taker; speckle-billed coot; spectacle coot; surf duck; surfer; white-head; white scop.

Hybrids: See in biography of velvet scoter.

Weights: Males about 1 lb. 12 oz. to 2 lbs. 10 oz.; females about 1 lb. 8 oz. to 2 lbs. 3 oz. (Leopold, 1959); males average 2¼ lbs.; females 2 lbs. (Johnsgard, 1968).

Range: Nests around freshwater ponds in interior N. America from northern Prairie Provinces of Canada to w. Alaska and Mackenzie Bay and to James Bay and Newfoundland; also c. Labrador; winters along coasts from e. Aleutians to Baja Calif. and Gulf of California, and from Nova Scotia along Atlantic coast to N.C., rarely to Fla. and Gulf coast; also regularly on Great Lakes; rarely and sporadically in s. B.C., Wyo., Neb., Kans., Mo., Ky.

Scoter, velvet, *Melanitta fusca fusca* (mel-ah-NIT-tah FUSS-kah); genus name: *see* Scoter, black; species and subspecies names: from Lat. *fuscus*, dark, dusky, in reference to its plumage color; *velvet* refers to plumage appearance. Listed in A.O.U. *Check-list* (1957) as a casual visitor to N. America (Greenland); 22–23 in. long; a dark sea duck with white wing patches that resembles the white-winged scoter and which Delacour (1959) describes as a form, or subspecies, of the white-winged scoter; however, the male velvet scoter differs from the white-winged in lacking a knob at base of the bill, and in having less white around the eyes and in wings; the female resembles the female white-winged scoter but is generally darker (Reilly, 1968).

Other Name: European white-winged scoter.

Hybrids: According to Gray (1958), velvet scoter has crossed with the common goldeneye and surf scoter; male velvet scoter has been seen paired with a female common eider in the wild with three eggs in nest.

Range: Nests in Eurasia immediately south of tundra in open forested areas; winters off coasts of n. Europe, and on Black and Caspian seas; has strayed to Greenland and Iceland.

Scoter, white-winged, *Melanitta fusca deglandi* (mel-ah-NIT-tah FUSS-kah deg-LAND-eye); genus and species names: *see* Scoter, black; subspecies name: given by Charles Lucien Bonaparte in 1850 for Dr. Côme Damien Degland (1787–1856), French ornithologist (see in Gruson, 1972). (Color ill., page 215.) Summers in interior N. America from N.D. (rarely) and ne. Wash. north through Alaska and east to Hudson Bay, Ungava, and Gulf of St. Lawrence; winters along Pacific and Atlantic coasts, Great Lakes; in winter, probably most abundant scoter along New England coast (Cottam, 1939), and, locally, off Long Is., N.Y., may be enormously abundant at times with 90,000 and 180,000 counted on a Mar. and a Dec. day, respectively, in 1952 (Bull, 1964); largest of the scoters; a diving duck; 19–24 in. long; wingspread 33½–41½ in.; male, black with square white patch on rear of each spread wing; has small white patch around each white eye; bill, orange with black knob at base and on top of upper mandible (male does not molt into eclipse plumage); female, dark brown with whitish eyes and two white patches on each side of head; like male, has square white patch on each wing which distinguishes her in flight from females of the black scoter and surf scoter; immatures resemble females; short-necked, heavy-bodied, flies low over water along coast in long, stringlike lines; in migration, flies high in various irregular formations; like surf scoter, habitually carries bill pointed downward; from wintering grounds, Mar. into May, migrates northward, high overland, to nesting grounds of vast northern area of tundra, prairie ponds, and wooded lake country, stopping on lakes and rivers on way; return in fall begins in Aug. but main flight in Oct. and into Nov.; both males and females utter a whistling note in courtship (see Johnsgard, 1965), and in fall migration, heard to produce in flight, at night, a low, bell-like whistle of 6 or 8 recurring notes, thought to be made by the beating of the wings (Bent, 1925).

Feeding Habits: Dives to 24 or even 40 ft. to get at beds of shellfishes, a favored food, but most feeding and diving in water less than 15 ft. deep; has been timed at 57 seconds below surface; about 90% of adult diet is animal foods, and along Atlantic coast, a favorite is the blue mussel, with one stomach examined containing remains of 40; also takes, at times, oysters, some scallops, and hard- and soft-shell clams (the gullet of one white-wing collected over an oyster bed near Olympia, Wash., contained 10 oysters—see relationship of this bird to commercial shellfish industry discussed by Cottam, 1939—with one shell measuring about 2 in. long); a Va. bird, when shot, had just swallowed four hard-shell clams more than 1 in. across—the strength of the gizzard of the white-wing is astonishing in grinding these hard-shelled mollusks, as it requires a brisk blow of a hammer to break the shell of a hard-shell, or little neck, clam (*see also*, other examples of strength of

gizzard under Gizzard); feeding on shellfishes can be hazardous to scoters when a clam closes on tongues of these birds; they also eat razor clams, *Macoma* shells, surf clams, cockle-shells, dog whelks, moon shells, and, among crustaceans, rock crabs, mud crabs, hermit and spider crabs, amphipods and barnacles; among echinoderms, sand dollars, sea urchins, and starfishes (see other details in Cottam, 1939); on freshwater ponds and lakes on breeding range, eats crayfishes, and small shrimplike crustaceans, aquatic insects, some fishes—minnows sculpins, and gizzard shad—also some plant foods—pondweeds, bur reeds, and other aquatics.

Nest: In hollow scraped in ground, lined with sticks, leaves, and down, usually well hidden under bushes, near slough; or in crevice of loose boulders, often on high ground of islands in lakes.

Eggs: June–Aug.; 6–14, usually 5–17, pink to pale buff.

Incubation: By female, 25–31 days (Delacour, 1959); young probably first fly 63–77 days after hatching (Johnsgard, 1978).

Other Names: American velvet scoter; assemblyman; bell-tongue coot; black surf duck; black white-wing; brant coot; bull coot; eastern white-wing; Lake Huron scoter; May white-wing; pied-wing coot; sea brant; Uncle Sam coot; velvet duck; white-winged surf duck.

Accidents: See above under Feeding Habits.

Hybrids: Reported from crossbreeding of white-winged with surf scoter, and with common goldeneye alleged (Johnsgard, 1965).

Weights: Males about 3 lbs. to 4 lbs.; females about 2 lbs. 3 oz. to about 3 lbs. (Leopold, 1959); males average 3½ lbs; females 2¾ lbs. (Johnsgard, 1968).

Range: Nests from nw. Alaska, Mackenzie delta, and s.-c. B.C., e. Man. (mostly at Churchill), and nw. Ont., south, chiefly east of Rocky Mtns. to nw. Wash., s. Man., and e. N.D., with many non-breeders in summer scattered along Pacific coast; also seen in summer (non-breeders) in n. Ont., James Bay, e. and s. Labrador, and Newfoundland south to Mass.; winters sporadically to s. B.C., Colo., Neb., La., Tenn. (Nashville), and Ala. (Tennessee Valley), on Great Lakes, along Atlantic coast from Gulf of St. Lawrence south to S.C., along Pacific coast from Aleutians to Baja Calif.

Shelduck, *Tadorna tadorna* (tad-OR-nah); genus and species names: Lat., from Fr. *tadorne*, a sheldrake, a kind of duck; *sheld* is old variant of "shield," referring to ornaments or shields, and here referring to broad rust-colored breast band of this species, which suggests a decorative shield (Gruson, 1972). A large Eurasian dabbling duck; gooselike; appears black and white at long distance (Peterson *et al.*, 1954); in N. America, has strayed to Mass. (Ipswich Bay) and Del.; about 24–25 in. long; both sexes outwardly alike (female is smaller) with greenish-black head and neck; prominent *red* bill with (in male) a knob at base of upper mandible; *broad chestnut band across white underparts*, and dark stripe down center of white belly; large white wing patches (forepart of wings) show conspicuously in flight; green speculum, pink legs and feet;

flies much like a goose, walks easily on land, swims well, dabbles and tips up for food, prefers saltwater habitat (see Delacour, 1954, for other details).

Feeding Habits: Eats mollusks, crustaceans, worms, marine weeds, some insects, small fishes.

Nest: In abandoned rabbit burrow, hollows in trees, hay stacks.

Eggs: June; usually 8–15, rounded, cream-white.

Incubation: 24–30 days (Bent, 1923).

Other Names: Burrow duck; common shelduck; sheld-drake.

Weights: 1¾–3½ lbs.

Range: Nests in c. and n.-c. Eurasia; winters south from breeding range to nw. and ne. Africa, c. India, Thailand, and n. Vietnam, also Formosa, Japan, Egypt, has strayed to Mass.; three reported from Bombay Hook National Wildlife Refuge, Del., July 16–17, 1970; very wary, possibly wild ones, but origin "must remain in doubt" (Scott and Cutler, 1970).

Shelduck, common. *See* Shelduck.

Shelduck, ruddy, *Tadorna ferruginea* (tad-OR-nah fer-oo-JIN-ee-ah); genus name: *see* Shelduck; species name: Lat., rusty red, from *ferrugo*, rust, and *ferrum*, iron, in reference to its general rust color. A Eurasian and n. African dabbling duck; in N. America, casual visitor to Greenland; one caught at Barnegat Bay, N.J., Nov. 14, 1916; 25–26 in. long; distinguished by gooselike shape, and overall orange-chestnut color and pale head (head of female almost white); male only has a black neck ring; both have small black bill, black legs and tail; wings have black primaries and secondaries and white forepart of wings conspicuous in flight, also the pale cinnamon body; usually seen in pairs (Peterson *et al.*, 1954).

Other Names: Ruddy sheldrake; sheld-drake.

Weights: Male 3¾ lbs.; female 2¾ lbs. (Johnsgard, 1968).

Range: Nests over wide expanse of c. Asia and to se. Europe, also a population nests in nw. Africa and on Sardinia; winters over much same range as the shelduck (Reilly, 1968).

Shoveler, common. *See* Shoveler, northern.

Shoveler, northern, *Anas clypeata* (AY-nas clip-ee-AY-tah); genus name: *see* Duck, Bahama; species name: from Lat. *clypeatus*, shielded, furnished with a shield, in reference to large spatulate bill of this bird; *shoveler* suggests shape, and use, of bill in feeding. (Color ill., page 215.) A small dabbling duck that lives in temperate zones of both Old and New World; is holarctic, and most widespread of all shovelers of world; is closely related to cinnamon and blue-winged teals and the garganey and has all the habits of this group of worldwide blue-winged ducks (Delacour, 1956); nests in Eurasia and, in N. America, from w. Alaska to Hudson Bay south to s. Calif. and in parts of c. and e. U.S., in freshwater marshes, prairie sloughs, and along slow-flowing muddy creeks; much more abundant in c. and w. than in e. U.S.; 17–20 in. long; wingspread 27–33 in.; out-wardly both sexes distinguished by flat head, long spatulate bill (longer than head), and large pale blue wing patch; on water rides low in front with bill held downward; male sitting on water shows black head glossed with green, white breast, reddish belly and sides, and distinct vertical white patch just before white-margined black tail; has orange-colored legs; sometimes mistaken for mallard by novice duck hunters but mallard has much smaller (and yellow) bill and rufous on *breast,* not on sides as in shoveler (*see* Mallard); male shoveler has an eclipse plumage; female has *large* bill, is mottled brown, with pale blue wing patch, and orange-colored legs; female quacks like female mallard; shoveler is exceedingly active flier and rises quickly from water, mounting straight up into air and darting off in swift if somewhat erratic flight, which is somewhat like that of teals; like them, makes sudden downward plunges out of air; is not shy and shows tendency to return to spot from which flushed; during migrations, flies in small flocks by itself, although in fall often associates with gadwalls, American wigeons, blue-winged teal, and lesser scaups; in mating season, usually seen in pairs with female leading in flight or in trios with female leading two males; is generally silent most of year, but in courtship male utters guttural *woh, woh, woh,* or *took, took, took;* female utters feeble quacks (Bent, 1923) and her decrescendo (quacking) call is a slightly descending *GACK-gack-gack-ga-ga* with last note or two muffled (Johnsgard, 1965); in general, not a hardy bird and a late migrant in spring; although migration is well under way in s. U.S. before end of Mar., does not disappear from wintering marshes of fresh and brackish waters of La. until early May and does not arrive in n. Alaska until about mid-May; in spring migration, in small flocks on ponds and rivers, not usually associating with other species; soon after arrival on breeding grounds, flocks spread out and break up into pairs or groups of three or four (see courtship rituals in Bent, 1923, and in Johnsgard, 1965); one of earliest migrants in fall, with first autumnal frosts, in late Aug. or early Sept., starts drifting southward along with blue-winged teals; large concentrations in winter include 25,000 seen at Bernicia, Calif., on Dec. day during Christmas Bird Count in 1970; is fourth most abundant duck wintering in Pacific Flyway (following more abundant pintail, mallard, and American wigeon), with 487,800 counted in Jan. 1972 winter waterfowl census in Pacific Flyway and total of 950,400 in all four flyways (Chamberlain *et al.*, 1972), but only 20,000 in Atlantic Flyway.

Feeding Habits: Commonly feeds in small groups of three or four that circle about, one following the other as each dabbles in water and mud stirred by feet of duck before it; all surface-feeding ducks have comblike "teeth" along the edges of the upper and lower mandibles (lamellae) but in shoveler they reach their highest development among all ducks, enabling the shoveler to successfully strain out plants and animals such as tiny diatoms, ostracods, and copepods from the surface and muddy bottom; the broad bill, multiplication of straining

Shelduck

DUCK FAMILY

Smew

DUCK FAMILY

lamellae, and elongation of its intestine (*see* Digestion) are all specialized for getting minute organisms; however, while shoveler takes more food from bottom than any other dabbling duck, a relatively small percentage of its diet comes from this source; it is also more of a surface feeder than any other duck (Bent, 1923); it seldom "tips up" to feed by self-immersion but paddles along, quickly skimming the surface with its head half submerged; about 66% of its food is vegetal, about 34% animal, a higher proportion of animal food than taken by most of the dabbling ducks (McAtee, 1922); eats many mollusks, especially freshwater snails, a favorite food; also aquatic insects, especially water boatmen (Corixidae), which swarm about over bottom ooze; also some small fishes (carp) and many tiny freshwater crustaceans; rest of diet mostly seeds of sedges, bulrushes, saw grass, pondweeds, widgeon grass, smartweeds, switch grass, beach grass, waste cultivated rice, algae (muskgrasses), duckweeds, etc.; does no damage to crops of man (McAtee, 1922).

Nest: A grass- and down-lined hollow on high dry ground of prairies often far from water or in moist meadow or near slough or ponds or on islands in lakes, well concealed in tall grasses or under rose bushes scattered among nests of mallards, wigeons, teals, pintails, and lesser scaups.

Eggs: In n.-c. U.S. and s. Canada, May–July; Calif. and Utah, Mar.–July; 6–14, usually 10–12, strikingly like eggs of mallard and pintail, pale olive-buff to green-gray.

Incubation: By female, 22–24 days (Reilly, 1968); 23–25 days (Delacour, 1956); young first fly 39–49 days after hatching (Johnsgard, 1975); when first hatched, bill of young is longer and more spatulate than that of young mallard; about 2 weeks after hatching, the "spoonbill" is distinctive (Bent, 1923); within 24 hours after hatching, young are led to nearest water by female (before young hatch, the males, as in most ducks, gather in small flocks on sloughs and ponds, leaving care of young to their mates).

Other Names: Blue-winged shoveler; broadbill; broady; butter duck; common shoveler; cow-frog (from guttural calls); mud duck; mudshoveler; mule duck; red-breasted shoveler; scooper; shovel-bill; spoonbill; spoon-bill duck; spoon-bill teal; swaddle-bill.

Age: One banded Stillwater, Nev., caught and released when 16 years, 7 months (Kennard, 1975).

Flight Speed: Timed in w. U.S., 25–50 m.p.h. (Cottam *et al.,* 1942b); in Calif., 47–53 m.p.h. (McLean, 1930).

Hybrids: Has crossbred and produced hybrids in captivity with wood duck, pintail, European common teal, cinnamon teal, falcated teal, mottled duck, mallard, gadwall, and Muscovy (Gray, 1958); in wild several times with blue-winged teal (see Childs, 1952; Hall and Harris, 1968; Johnsgard, 1965).

Weights: Males average 1½ lbs.; females 1¼ lbs. (Johnsgard, 1968).

Range: Nests from w. and n. Alaska south to Mack., c. Alta, c. Sask., to Hudson and James bays, and south, east of Coast Ranges, to s. Calif., N.M., Kans., Neb., and w. Great Lakes, occasionally east to w. N.Y. (Montezuma marshes), nw. Pa., and Del. and locally to Ala., ne. N.C., occasionally to Ill., Ind., Wisc., Mich., s. Ont., Ohio, Mo., Tex., also in Eurasia; winters from coast of B.C., se. Wash., south through Baja Calif., to c. Ariz., sw. N.M., and Gulf coast from Tex. to Fla., coast of Ga. and S.C., to mainland of Mexico, Nicaragua, and West Indies; rarely north to Minn., Ill., Me., and Labrador; casual in migration to Hawaii, Gilbert Is., and Bermuda.

Smew, *Mergus albellus* (MER-gus al-BEL-lus); genus name: *see* Merganser, common; species name: Lat., dim. of *albus,* white, meaning whitish; *smew,* possibly from a lost word meaning small; Gruson (1972) suggests *smew* is probably a corruption of Middle Eng. *semawe,* sea smew. Smallest of the mergansers, a European and Asiatic species; first acceptable N. American record (with color photographs) was one in 1960 wintering near Niagara Falls, N.Y., and Ont.; was first seen in Buffalo Harbor, Jan. 17, 1960, and during Feb. on Niagara R. (Speirs and Speirs, 1960); a male subadult seen at Montreal, Feb. 12, 1967 (Carleton, 1967); two females seen on Crater Is., Adak Is., Alaska, Oct. 17–23, 1972, and at least ten Alaskan records, all since 1960; rare in Alaska but apparently regular in c. and w. Aleutians, mainly in fall (Gibson and Byrd, 1973); 14–16 in. long (Johnsgard, 1968); much smaller and more ducklike and shorter-billed than other mergansers; in nuptial plumage, male appears uniformly white at rest on water with conspicuous black eye patch and white crest; in flight, male appears darker than when on water; shows conspicuous black and white in wings; in eclipse plumage, when male resembles female, he has larger white wing patches than female; female smaller, grayer than male, has chocolate or chestnut cap, white cheeks and throat; like other mergansers, both sexes fly with bill, head, neck, and body a horizontal line; immature has brown-white patches in wings; the smew rises easily from the water, and flies in lines or in V formation; usually silent; male has weak whistling notes; female's resemble those of female common merganser (Peterson *et al.,* 1954). Lives on reservoirs, lakes, rivers, sometimes in estuaries and along seacoast.

Feeding Habits: For a merganser, eats relatively few fishes; tends to eat aquatic insects and their larvae as do goldeneyes; the two species often associate in the wild where their ranges overlap (Johnsgard, 1965).

Nest: In hollow trees near water.

Eggs: 6–9.

Incubation: By female, 28 days; in captivity, young can fly 70 days after hatching.

Weights: 1 lb. 2 oz. to 1 lb. 10 oz. (Johnsgard, 1968).

Range: Nests in forested places from Scandinavia across Russia and Siberia to Kamchatka; winters south to coasts of the Mediterranean, Caspian, and Black seas, Asia Minor, Middle East, n. India, China, Korea, Japan.

Swan, black. *See* Cormorants.

Swan, common. *See* Swan, mute.

Swan, domestic. *See* Swan, mute.

Swan, mute, *Cygnus olor* (SIG-nus OL-or); genus name: Lat., a swan; species name: from Lat. *olor*, a swan; *mute* because usually silent but can make sounds (*see* below). (Color ill., page 227.) Large all-white Eurasian "pond" swan, semi-domesticated now feral or naturalized in wild in e. U.S.; Bellrose (1976) reported that Christmas counts in 1972 showed 2,235 birds along Atlantic coast plus 390 in Traverse Bay, Mich.; small numbers occur elsewhere, perhaps as many as 500; introduced into U.S. possibly in middle of 19th century; there is some speculation that it may have first been introduced on the large estates of e. Long Is., N.Y., in Dutchess County on the Hudson R., and elsewhere (see discussion by Phillips, 1928, and by Bull, 1964, and Wood and Gelston, 1972); is resident of waters of well-sheltered bays and open marshes and on many ponds built by damming creeks in general area of Long Is., N.Y., lower Hudson R. valley, and in Grand Traverse County, Mich. (Banko, 1960; Wood and Gelston, 1972), and elsewhere (*see* below under Range); sexes outwardly alike but males larger; 56–62 in. long; wingspread 7 to 8 ft.; distinguished from native N. American swans by *orange-colored bill, black at base, with prominent black knob on forehead;* when swimming holds neck in graceful curve *with bill pointing downward* (the native trumpeter and whistling swans usually carry the bill level and neck erect); male frequently arches secondary wing feathers over its back in aggressive posture; is usually silent but hisses and sometimes utters puppy-like barking notes; sounds not far-reaching because trachea is almost straight, with no long convolutions as in the louder-voiced trumpeter and whistling swans (Taverner, 1947); wingbeats make musical throbbing or humming audible from long way off; usually no mass migration in spring and fall; in winter often moves from icebound freshwater ponds to nearby open salt water, where gathers in flocks of sometimes 100.

Feeding Habits: Similar to those of other swans; adults and cygnets seldom dive; plunge head and neck below surface, or may tip up in deeper waters to pull with bills at aquatic plants, their main food; often attended by American wigeons, which eat plants that float to surface from swans' feeding; because swans usually feed in deeper waters than dabbling ducks, they do not compete with them but make food available to them (Pough, 1951); head and neck of swans sometimes stained brown or rusty from water and mud containing iron.

Nest: Pair usually maintain large territory; often includes entire small lake or pond; only rarely nest together in colony; vigorously defend nests and young from intruders, may attack dogs and even people; can be dangerous to children (Delacour, 1954); nest is large pile of aquatic plants, sticks, reeds, roots gathered by pair of swans on islet in pond or on its banks, and lined with down and feathers.

Eggs: Mar. 30–June 12 (Bull, 1964); average of 4–6; (Wood and Gelston, 1972); gray or blue-green.
Incubation: Usually by female alone, protected by male; 35–38 days, usually 35; young first fly 100–120 days after hatching (Johnsgard, 1968); 115–155 days (Wood and Gelston, 1972); chicks light gray above, remain 1 day in nest; male often takes first-hatched cygnet to water while female continues to incubate rest of eggs; chicks will ride on backs of parents or under their wings.
Other Names: Common swan; domestic swan; in England: swan or wild swan, also tame swan, because of adaptation to presence of people; the mute swan is the "royal swan," an Old World species that has been semi-domesticated in w. Europe for the last 900 to 1,000 years; in England, is subject to special legislation and the Crown granted "royalties" enabling certain noblemen and corporate bodies, such as livery companies of London, to own swans and to mark their bills with registered symbols or "swan marks"; mute swans on Thames R., not so marked, were property of the Crown; annually on the Thames, young mute swans were, and still are, caught for marking in a colorful ceremony called "swan upping" (Scott, 1964).
Age: Have lived 30–40 years in captivity (Kortright, 1943); one reported to have lived to 70 years (Wetmore, 1937b); one lived in National Zoo, Washington, D.C., for 16 years, 9 months; greatest ages for wild mute swans were three banded in Switzerland that were 18, 19, and 19 years old when recovered (Nice, 1966a).
Flight Speed: 50–55 m.p.h. (Wood and Gelston, 1972).
Hybrids: Sibley (1938) lists a cross, or hybrid, of the mute swan and trumpeter swan in captivity; Gray (1958) reported hybridizing of the mute swan with the black swan, Bewick's swan, whistling swan, and whooper swan (see Delacour, 1954, for accounts of swans of world); also with the European greylag or domestic goose, the lesser snow goose, and Canada goose.
Weights: 25–30 lbs. (Kortright, 1943); up to 50 lbs. (Fisher and Peterson, 1964); adult males average 25 lbs.; adult females 21 lbs. (Wood and Gelston, 1972).
Range: Nests in British Isles, n.-c. Europe, and n.-c. Asia; winters south to n. Africa, Near East, nw. India, and Korea; in U.S. wanders along Atlantic coast from e. Mass. south to c. N.J. (first nesting record in Va. at Chincoteague Island National Wildlife Refuge, summer 1972) and reported from R.I., Ohio, w. Pa., and W.Va.

Swan, trumpeter, *Olor buccinator* (OH-lor buck-sih-NAY-tor); genus name: *see* Swan, mute; species name: Lat., a trumpeter, in reference to voice. (Color ills., pages 226, 227.) At one time almost extinct, now recovered (see Status below); limited to W. Hemisphere; during breeding season lives on lakes, ponds, of w. U.S., Canada, and Alaska, sometimes seen in winter along Pacific coast; largest of swans of world, largest N. American waterfowl; 58½–72 in. long (Peterson, 1961); wingspread: female 6 ft., male 8 ft. 2 in. (Banko, 1960; Kortright, 1943); *adults:* sexes outwardly alike (males

larger), entirely white but head and neck usually stained red-brown from feeding in ferrous waters; eyes brown; feet and legs black; likely to be confused with similar whistling swan; however, trumpeter has *solidly black bill* without yellow spot at base; diagnostic for trumpeter is salmon- or flesh-colored stripe at base of black bill, called a "grin line," lacking in whistling swan; most reliable is trumpeter's short, far-reaching *ko-ho*, deep, sonorous, and rasping, like horn of old-fashioned French taxi, uttered most while trumpeter is in flight, often while on ground or on water; *immatures:* gray-brown with yellowish feet and pink bills; mostly white during second year, feet and bill black; first begin to pair during their third year; first breed at about 5 years old (Banko, 1960); most are resident over present breeding range; once bred from n. Alaska and Canada east to Hudson and James bays, south to s. B.C., Neb., Iowa, Mo., and Ind., and wintered along Atlantic seaboard to the Carolinas, in the Mississippi Valley, along Gulf coast, and westward to the Pacific (Banko, 1960).

Feeding Habits: Adults feed mostly in shallow waters, plunging head and neck below surface but in deeper water tips up like mallard and other freshwater ducks to snap off with bill leaves and stems of aquatic plants growing on bottom; uses powerful legs and large webbed, clawed feet on pond or lake bottom, digging holes a foot deep in search of roots and shoots; rarely feeds on land; first food of cygnets is mostly aquatic beetles and crustaceans but eat largely aquatic plants 5 weeks after hatching (Banko, 1960). See excellent chapter on food habits and general life history in Van Wormer (1972).
Nest: Adults begin nesting late Apr., early May; build mass of bulrushes, reeds, grasses, and sedges, hollowed to hold eggs; some nests 5 ft. across; many build nests on muskrat houses surrounded by water, some on beaver lodges, a few along shore; nests of different pairs usually at least a half mile apart; within their territory each pair will drive out other swans but tolerate nesting pairs of ducks and other water birds close by.
Eggs: Apr.–July, one laid every other day; 2–13, usually 4–6 (see size under Eggs and Egg-laying), cream-white, granular (Banko, 1960).
Incubation: Largely or entirely by female; 32–33 days (Banko and Mackay, 1964); 33–37 days (Banko, 1960); 36–40 days (Delacour, 1954); at hatching, downy cygnets either white or gray, weigh 7–7½ oz. each; first week of life most hazardous, when parents may trample young; others in first feeding ventures get entangled in water plants and drown; some die from effects of leeches and other parasites; adults and young both vulnerable to lead poisoning; young first start to fly about 100 days after hatching, or about end of Sept., but may require maximum of 120 days; Rosen (1971a), discussing avian cholera, which causes annual losses among whistling swans that winter on Tule Lake, Calif., suggested that when whistlers migrate north in spring, they may carry the disease to Malheur Lake, Ore., and might precipitate a dangerous epizootic among trum-

peter swans there, and among other waterfowl. *See* Avian Cholera; *also* Diseases.

Status: Strictly protected by law in Alaska, Canada, and the contiguous U.S.; once widespread, but unlimited killing in 19th century for its skin, feathers, and meat caused widespread decline; between 1853 and 1877, the Hudson's Bay Company of Canada sold 17,671 skins of swans (Forbush, 1912), many of which were trumpeters; the skins were for millinery uses, and for powder puffs and down coverings; its eggs were taken and used for food; its young caught or shot for food before they could fly, and adult birds killed at all seasons, at every opportunity (Forbush, 1925–29); by 1900 was almost extinct, and by 1930s, only some 66 lived on widely scattered lakes in the Yellowstone Park region; under strict U.S. government management and protection, a nucleus of trumpeter swans on Red Rock Lakes National Wildlife Refuge in sw. Mont. slowly increased, some of which were caught and transported to start new breeding colonies, mostly in national wildlife refuges in Ore., Nev., Wyo., and elsewhere (see history and remarkable comeback related in Banko, 1960; Banko and Mackay, 1964; and details in Vincent, 1966); in 1968, taken off the rare and endangered list of N. American birds of U.S. Department of the Interior when that organization reported that their successful conservation program had resulted in a total trumpeter swan population in the U.S. of 3,641, and an additional number in Canada and Alaska that made total N. American population of about 4,000–5,000 (Anonymous, 1968b).

Other Names: Bugler; wild swan.

Age: Between 1895 and 1939, the Philadelphia Zoological Gardens had eight trumpeter swans on display, one of which lived for 29 years (Banko, 1960); another, in Canada, lived for 32½ years (Kortright, 1943); one banded in wild, Red Rock Lakes, Mont., caught and released when 24 years, 1 month old (Kennard, 1975).

Flight Speed: Apparently never measured, but Banko, citing the flight speed of a whistling swan chased by an airplane (Weiser, 1933), estimated that the heavier trumpeter swan might fly at 80 m.p.h. with a favoring wind.

Hybrids: Apparently interbreeds only in captivity; Sibley (1938) reported hybridization of captive trumpeter swans with the mute, whooper, and whistling swans and with the Canada goose.

Weights: Males 21–38 lbs.; average of six, 28 lbs. (Kortright, 1943); females 20–25 lbs.

Range: Now nests locally from s. and se. Alaska, w. and se. Alta. (Grande Prairie, Cypress Hills), sw. Sask. (Cypress Hills), to e. Idaho (Island Park area), sw. Mont. (Red Rock Lakes), and nw. Wyo. (Yellowstone National Park); and transplanted with new colonies established or reintroduced into e. Ore., Nev. (Ruby Lake National Wildlife Refuge), nw. Wyo. (National Elk Refuge), Wash. (Turnbull National Wildlife Refuge), and S. D. (Lacreek National Wildlife Refuge) (Anonymous, 1968b); now winters on ice-free fresh waters in se. Alaska, in B.C., sometimes during severe winters in southern parts of Vancouver Is., in nw. Wash., e. Idaho, Mont., and nw. Wyo.; and sighted in Minn. Once strongly migratory, remaining flocks are relatively sedentary except in most northern part of their range (Johnsgard, 1975).

Swan, whistling, *Olor columbianus* (OH-lor koh-lum-bih-AY-nus); genus name: *see* Swan, mute; species name: Lat., the Columbia R., where Lewis and Clark discovered this bird on their expedition to the Rocky Mtns. and Pacific; they gave it the common name of *whistling* from "a kind of whistling sound [which] terminates in a round full note, louder at the end"; however, the authorities cited by Bent (1925) do not mention a whistling sound. (Color ills., pages 228, 229.) Smallest and most widespread N. American swan; summers in Arctic N. America; in winter, especially common along Pacific coast and in interior Calif. and along Atlantic coast on Chesapeake Bay in Md. and on Currituck Sound, N.C.; 47–58 in. long; wingspread 6–7 ft. (Kortright, 1943); *adults:* sexes outwardly alike but male slightly larger; like all-white trumpeter swan but smaller; bill black but usually (not always) with yellow or orange-yellow spot on bare skin of lore in front of eyes near base of bill (*see* comparison under Trumpeter swan); can best be distinguished from trumpeter by its loud, melodious, *high-pitched* call, suggestive of Canada goose call, like distant baying of hounds, but also more like soft, musical laughter, *wow-how-ow*, heavily accented on second syllable (Bent, 1925); also utters long whoops and clarinetlike sounds (its long convoluted windpipe lacks the upward bend of that of trumpeter swan); whistling swan has been authoritatively credited with the so-called swan song after being shot and falling mortally wounded through the air (*see* under Swan Song); to distinguish from mute swan, *see* under Mute swan; *immatures:* brown-gray with mottled pinkish bill, flesh-colored feet; whistler flies with speed and power, long neck stretched straight ahead, black feet back under tail, wings beating slowly and regularly; when traveling great distance, flies in V-shaped wedge, like geese, and for same reason; fly high in migration, sometimes to at least 6,000–8,000 ft., where flocks have been struck by aircraft, resulting in at least two fatal crashes; according to Banko and Mackay (1964), about half of continental total of 70,000–90,000 whistling swans of N. America (estimated at 146,000 within U.S. in winter 1972) winter in e. U.S. in estuaries of Chesapeake Bay and on Currituck Sound; others in coastal states of the Pacific Flyway, largely in Central Valley of Calif., with stopover and largest single concentrations, en route, in Bear River National Wildlife Refuge in n. Utah; the swans often associate on their winter feeding grounds with the wary Canada geese; in flight, they usually flock by themselves and move about largely in family groups of 6–7, but often assemble in large flocks to feed and rest or when moving about in search of such places; migrate northward generally over interior in Mar. and Apr.; are on Arctic nesting grounds by May; some killed en route on misty or foggy nights from alighting on Niagara R. and then being swept over the falls in what has been called the Niagara Falls Swan Trap (see details in Taverner, 1947, and in Fleming, 1908; 1912).

Feeding Habits: Eats largely aquatic plants by plunging head and neck below surface, also eats grasses and sedges; favorite winter foods in Back Bay, Va., Chesapeake Bay, Md., and Currituck Sound, N.C., are wild celery, widgeon grass, eelgrass, and foxtail grasses (see Bent, 1925; Stewart and Manning, 1958; Van Wormer, 1972); also thin-shelled mollusks; its vigorous digging and rooting at bottom seems to stimulate growth of underwater plants, resulting in more food in subsequent years for themselves and for other waterfowl (Pough, 1951). *See* Commensalism.

Nest: Usually a mound of mosses, dried grasses, sedges, 1–2 ft. high, and 2–3 ft. across (Bent, 1925); built on a number of sites—from water's edge to top of low hills half a mile from water but seems to prefer to nest on small islands in shallow tundra pools.

Eggs: Late May to early June; 2–7, usually 4–5, cream or dull white, average about 4.25 × 2.7 in. (see details in Van Wormer, 1972).

Incubation: Mostly, if not entirely, by female (with male standing guard), 35–40 days (Delacour, 1954); average is "probably about 32 days" (Banko and Mackay, 1964); downy chicks, pure white, walk from nest soon after hatching; begin to fly 60–70 days after hatching; adult plumage acquired during second year, when usually pure white and only a few retain some brown feathers.

Other Names: American whistling swan; common swan; swan; wild swan.

Age: One lived for 15 years, 2 months, in National Zoo, Washington, D.C.; Kortright (1943) cited age records of 8, 9, and 19 years, presumably of captive birds.

Flight Speed: Timed in w. U.S., 18–25 m.p.h. (Cottam *et al.*, 1942b); in Pa., 30 m.p.h. (Wood, 1933); in Pa., chased by airplane, a flock reached top airspeed of 50–55 m.p.h. (Weiser, 1933); in Calif., chased by airplane, 45 m.p.h. (Munson, 1930).

Hybrids: No wild ones known but Gray (1958) reported crosses of captive whistling swan with black swan, European greylag goose, and Canada goose; Sibley (1938) reported crossbreeding in captivity of whistling swan with trumpeter swan, and, later, with mute and whooper swans.

Weights: Males 12 lbs. to 18¾ lbs.; females about 10½ lbs to 18 lbs. (Kortright, 1943).

Range: Nests in Arctic N. America, with greatest density (1 pair to square mile) along Arctic coastal strip from west side of Mack. Delta to east side of Anderson Delta; also nests on islets off shores of shallow lakes or flooded tundra, from n. Alaska east to Mack. and Victoria, Baffin, Southampton, and Belcher Is. south to Alaska Pen.; winters along Pacific coast from Aleutians to extreme n. Baja Calif.; rarely in Great Lakes region; and on Atlantic coast rarely from Me., N.J., and Long Is., N.Y., but mainly Chesapeake Bay, Md., to Currituck Sound, N.C., rarely south to Fla. and Gulf coast to La. and Tex., casual in Mex., accidental in Bermuda, Cuba, Puerto Rico, and Siberia.

Swan, whooper, *Olor cygnus* (OH-lor SIG-nus); genus and species names: *see* Swan, mute. (Color ill., page 230.) An all-white Eurasian swan accidental and very rare in N. America—three records up to 1957: two in Alaska (St. Paul and Amchitka Is.) and one in Washington County, Me. (Banko, 1960); about 60 in. long; has black bill, bright lemon color at base (mute swan of Eurasia and ne. U.S. has orange bill with black knob at base); whooper swan utters buglelike *hoo-hoo-hoo*, repeated about ten to a dozen times; noisiest Old World wild swan; while swimming holds neck stiffly erect, or straight, not curved as does mute swan; *immatures:* gray-brown, bill pink with dark tip (see other descriptive and life history details in Bent, 1925; Delacour, 1954; Van Wormer, 1972).

Other Name: Whooping swan.
Range: Nests along seacoasts, tidal waters, lakes, rivers, and tundra of Iceland, n. Eurasia, formerly in s. Greenland, but natives there exterminated it by killing both adults and young during flightless period of late summer; winters south to British Isles, s. Europe, China, Japan, and Korea. Accidental in N. America.

Swan, wild. *See* Swan, trumpeter, and Swan, whistling.

Swan, whooping. *See* Swan, whooper.

Teal, American green-winged, *Anas crecca carolinensis* (AY-nas CREK-ah or CREEK-ah cah-row-lin-EN-sis); genus name: Lat., duck; species name: a Latinized onomatopoetic word to express the *quack* or *creak* note of this duck (Coues, 1882); subspecies name: Lat., of Carolina. (Color ill., page 216.) Once thought to be a full species, *Anas carolinensis,* now considered by American Ornithologists' Union (1973) to be a subspecies of the green-winged teal, *Anas crecca crecca,* of Europe, Siberia, Asia, which lives around world in N. Hemisphere; is typical member of a group that Johnsgard (1965) calls "green-winged" teals, which includes the American and Eurasian green-winged teal, South American teal, Cape teal, and Baikal teal; the N. American subspecies summers in triangular area of N. America from Alaska to nw. Mack., on inland lakes, ponds, rivers, and streams south to s. Calif., east to Newfoundland (Reilly, 1968); is extending its range in e. U.S.; 13–16 in. long; wingspread 20–25 in.; both sexes have bright green speculum; male is small gray duck; brown head with glossy green patch on side of head (shows only in good light), and a *vertical white stripe on each side, in front of wings;* in poor light, only the male's buffy-yellow undertail coverts show conspicuously; in flight, small size and lack of large pale patches on dark wings are diagnostic; female, speckled brown with green speculum; swift bird in flight but, like blue-winged teal, speed overestimated in past (see Bent, 1923); walks gracefully on land and often travels long distances over land in search of food; flies in compact flocks from one pond to another; male utters short, high-pitched, staccato whistle and a lower-pitched trilled note (from distance sounds like piping of spring peepers), and in courtship, a *KRICK-et* note; female a faint *quack* in decrescendo call of about four notes (see courtship rituals in Johnsgard, 1965, and in Bent, 1923); very

hardy, one of earliest migrants in spring; begins to move northward along coastal and inland migration routes from its winter haunts—for example, in lower Mississippi Valley in Feb.—and from wintering places in Ga., S.C., N.C., La., upper Tex. coast, and in Calif. and Mexico; however, in mild winters may remain north even to Nova Scotia and Newfoundland (Addy, 1964, and Moisan, 1967); moves slowly northward in Mar.–Apr.; seldom seen along way in major concentrations; arrives on nesting grounds in n. Alaska in early May; in fall usually moves southward with first cold weather in large flocks, usually by themselves or with blue-winged teals; may linger along way but first snow and ice in North brings main flights in Oct. and Nov. (Bent, 1923); breeding surveys from 1955–74 recorded total average annual population of 2,192,000 green-winged teal in N. America; winter inventories showed average of 1,200,000 birds in U.S. (Bellrose, 1976).

Feeding Habits: In feeding, dabbles with bill in shallow edges of sloughs, ponds, creeks of summer home, probing mud for aquatic insects, small mollusks, crustaceans, tadpoles, and soft parts of aquatic plants and their seeds (is primarily eater of seeds of sedges, smartweeds, pondweeds, and grasses), in fall visits grain fields for waste corn, wheat, oats, barley, buckwheat; also, on wintering rounds in s. U.S. feeds in rice fields and visits brackish marshes for shellfishes and crustaceans; often goes to dry uplands and woods to eat berries, wild grapes, chestnuts, acorns; sometimes feeds in Northwest on eggs of salmon and putrid salmon lying in creeks (Pough, 1951).
Nest: In North, a prairie nester; also prefers wooded potholes and streams more than blue-winged teal; nest is in depression in clump of grass on ground, deeply lined with grasses, weeds, feathers, and down; near or some distance from edges of lakes, sloughs, or on islands, sometimes under clumps of willows or under bushes a quarter of a mile from water; sometimes under a log.
Eggs: May–Aug.; 7–15, usually 8–9, dull white, cream, or pale olive-buff.
Incubation: By female, 21–23 days; age when young first fly estimated at 44 days.
Other Names: Common teal; green-wing; mud teal; red-headed teal; winter teal.
Age: One banded bird lived to 9 years, 7 months (Kennard, 1975).
Flight Speed: Timed in w. U.S., 30–40 m.p.h. (Cottam *et al.,* 1942b).
Hybrids: Johnsgard (1965) cites wild hybrids from crosses with American wigeon, mallard, pintail, garganey, and shoveler.
Weights: Males (113) average 0.71 lbs.; females (79) average 0.68 lbs. (Bellrose, 1976).
Range: Nests in n.-c. Alaska, n. Mack., n. Man., James Bay to se. Que., and Newfoundland south to s. Calif., rarely on lakes of Mogollon Plateau, Ariz., n. N.M., n. Neb., s. Minn., w. Ont., n. Ohio, nw. Pa., w. N.Y., Me., N.B., and Nova Scotia, casually to Mass., and first nesting record for Md., June 5, 1971, on Deal Is. (Scott and Cutler, 1971); winters from s. B.C. through most of U.S. where it finds open waters south to Honduras, Bahamas, most of West Indies, and very rare south of S. Mexico,

Baikal teal

DUCK FAMILY

Gulf coast, and Fla. (Reilly, 1968). Occasionally in winter north to Sitka, Alaska, Lower Great Lakes, and Newfoundland. Casual in Bermuda, Greenland, British Isles, Hawaii, and Japan.

Teal, Baikal, *Anas formosa* (AY-nas for-MOE-sah); genus name: Lat., duck; species name: Lat., finely formed, beautiful; *Baikal* (bye-KAL), for Lake Baikal, Siberia; *teal—see* partial explanation for this word under Blue-winged teal. Small Asiatic dabbling duck that breeds in Siberia and winters south to se. China, Formosa, and Japan; has been collected (shot) in the wild several times in Alaska (Wainwright, King Is., Wales, and St. Lawrence Is.); one record was a mated pair on St. Lawrence Is. but no indication of nesting (see Bailey, 1933, and Gabrielson, 1941); however, reports of it in Calif., Ohio, and Europe were probably escaped captive birds from aviaries of waterfowl fanciers; also, one seen at Tinicum Marsh, Philadelphia, Pa., Jan. 30, 1960, and another seen Cape May Point, N.J., Mar. 19–30, 1961, were considered "escapes"; about 16 in. long; male has slight crest and in breeding plumage head is a variegated pattern of yellow, green, white, and black; female is brownish with a round white patch on side of each cheek at base of bill (see other details in Delacour, 1956).

Other Names: Clucking teal; spectacled teal.
Weights: Males 18 oz. (Johnsgard, 1968).

Teal, blue-winged, *Anas discors* (AY-nas DIS-cors); genus name: Lat., duck; species name: Lat., discordant, inharmonious, possibly in reference to voice; *blue-winged* refers to blue patch on each forewing; *teal,* according to Macleod (1954), from medieval English *tele,* cognate with Dutch *teling,* derived from *telen,* to produce, thus root meaning is the general one of "brood." (Color ill., page 217.) Exclusively a N. American dabbling duck, related to the cinnamon teal, garganey, and shoveler; nests across N. American continent, especially on prairies of c. U.S. and s. Canada; one of smallest ducks (*see* Bufflehead and Masked duck); 14–16 in. long; wingspread 24–31 in.; male in breeding plumage has body color of dull, mottled pink-brown, but has *white crescent on face just in front of eyes,* a large blue patch on each forewing, a white patch on flank, and a black tail (male in eclipse plumage resembles female); male begins molt into eclipse in July, is complete in Aug., when flight feathers also molted (Bent, 1923); eclipse plumage may last into end of year, therefore most males seen in fall "lack the white facial crescent or show it poorly" and resemble females (Peterson, 1961); both sexes have long, bright green speculum; female is mottled brown with *blue patch on each forewing;* the blue-wing springs into air from surface of water and is away, a swift flier in small, compact flocks, but not as fast as credited by early American observers (Bent, 1923); in flight, a group often passes and repasses over a spot as though to be reassured of absence of danger before alighting; when feeding, and at other times, usually silent; male utters a soft, lisping, high-pitched peeping described as *tseeel,* usually when flying; female utters a weak *quack;* in migration usually fly in flocks by themselves but often feed in marshes with other dabbling ducks and with coots, also with shorebirds in shallow lagoons of wintering places in Fla. and La.; fairly large numbers may concentrate in winter in s. U.S., for example, 2,000 seen in Merritt's Island National Wildlife Refuge, Fla., on Christmas Bird Count, Dec. 30, 1970; 4,000 at Freeport, Tex., Dec. 17, 1972, but most (an estimated 95% of total population) winter south of U.S. and migrate north late in spring; many linger in Gulf states through Apr. and even into May, but most arrive on nesting grounds by May; begin return southward in early Aug.–Sept. and continue into Nov., when peak numbers of them in C. and S. America; one banded near Renoun, Sask., shot six months later in marsh near Sullana, Peru, had flown 7,000 mi. from nesting to wintering grounds; another, banded at Delta, Man., was shot in Ecuador on a lake 13,000 ft. above sea level on the slopes of Cotopaxi volcano: it had flown 4,000 mi. from its summer to its winter home.

Feeding Habits: Inclined to be tame and unsuspicious where not persecuted; unlike other surface-feeding, or dabbling, ducks, seldom tips up with feet and tail uppermost but skims water with bill or reaches down with head and neck below surface in shallows of small freshwater ponds, marshes, sluggish creeks, mud flats, grassy sloughs to feed on favorite plant foods (about 70% of diet), such as seeds of sedges, pondweeds, grasses, and smartweeds, especially in fall and in winter, also takes some rice and corn, algae (muskgrasses); leaves of duckweed, and large amounts of mollusks (snails), aquatic insects, and crustaceans (Bent, 1923; Bennett, 1938); rarely visits brackish or saltwater marshes.
Nest: Typical nesting duck of the famed prairie "pothole" country of s. Canada and n.-c. U.S. (see in Leitch, 1964, and Crissey, 1969); nest is concealed in tall grasses usually on dry ground but not far from water, in moist meadows, in dense cattail growth along prairie sloughs, and on islands, occasionally on tussocks of sedges in marsh or on muskrat house; well-built basketlike structure of dead grasses with thick blanket of down (Bent, 1923).
Eggs: May–July; 6–15, mostly 9–11, dull white or cream-white.
Incubation: By female, 23–27 days; young first fly 35–44 days after hatching (Johnsgard, 1968).
Other Names: August teal; blue-wing; summer teal; white-faced teal.
Flight Speed: Bennett (1938) timed speed of the blue-wing with automobile; rarely reaches more than 45 m.p.h.; on one occasion, two paced at 48 m.p.h.; most were seen traveling at 30–40 m.p.h., but with strong tail winds speed would be increased.
Host to Cowbirds: Accidental; one record (Friedmann, 1963) of blue-wing's nest near Delta, Man., in June 1956 held three eggs of the teal, two of a cowbird; another cowbird egg laid about 30 yds. from duck's nest on open ground; apparently cowbird had difficulty finding appropriate host and laid eggs in nest of inappropriate one, and on ground.

Hybrids: Wild hybrids have been reported from crossbreeding of blue-winged with cinnamon teal and with shoveler (duck) and both of these crosses proved fertile in captivity; Gray (1958) reported crosses with American wigeon, mallard, and others.
Weights: Males (35) average 1.02 lbs.; females (129) average 0.83 lbs. (Bellrose, 1976).
Range: Nests from c. B.C. across Prairie Provinces to s. Ont., s. Que., south to e. Wash., e. Ore., e.-c. Calif., Nev., ne. Utah, sw. Colo., to se. Ariz., s. N.M., w.-c. Tex., and La., n. Mo., and Tenn., and e. U.S. to N.C.; winters from s. Calif., Tex., n. Mo., and Tenn. (casually farther north) and Chesapeake Bay area south throughout Mexico, C. America, and in S. America to Peru and n. Brazil.

Teal, bronze-capped. *See* Teal, falcated.

Teal, cinnamon, *Anas cyanoptera* (AY-nas sigh-an-OP-ter-ah); genus name: Lat., duck; species name: from Gr. *kuanos,* blue, and *pteron,* wing; *cinnamon* from general body color. (Color ill., page 217.) A close relative of the blue-winged teal and replaces it in Far West, where common; rare east of Rocky Mtns.; lives in shallow, tule-bordered lakes, freshwater ponds, sluggish creeks, reservoirs, irrigation ditches; occasionally in summer in parts of Tex., Mont., Wyo., Colo., and N.M.; seems to prefer alkaline marshes, not important as a game bird because of early fall migration (Buller, 1964); along with ruddy duck, only waterfowl to breed in both N. and S. America; one of small dabbling ducks; 14–17 in. long; wingspread about 24–26 in.; male, rich cinnamon brown except back and wings, which are blue as in blue-winged teal (both sexes also have green speculum); male in eclipse plumage resembles female; female virtually identical with female blue-wing; male utters low, rattling chatter, *chuk-chuk-chuk;* female a weak quacking much like that of female shoveler; tame, allows close approach; seldom seen in large flocks, mostly in single pairs before nesting season, in fall in small family groups; from wintering grounds in sw. U.S. and south of border, migrates northward in spring in Mar.–Apr.; returns southward Sept.–Oct.

Feeding Habits: About same as blue-winged teal (see details in Bent, 1923).
Nest: On ground, concealed in tall grass or weeds, often on high ground 100 ft. or more from water, in hollow in ground and lined with grasses and down; also in thick beds of cattails or reeds in marsh, above water.
Eggs: Apr.–July; 6–14, usually 9–12, buff pinkish or white.
Incubation: By female, 21–25 days (Bellrose, 1976), age when young first fly estimated at 7 wks.
Other Names: Red-breasted teal; red teal; river teal; silver teal; South American teal.
Flight Speed: Timed in w. U.S., 33–50 m.p.h. (Cottam *et al.,* 1942b); in Calif., 32–59 m.p.h. (McLean, 1930).
Hybrids: Gray (1958) reports hybrids, or crosses, between the cinnamon teal and shoveler, blue-winged teal, mallard, wood duck, and others.

Weights: Males average about 1 lb.; females 13 oz. (Johnsgard, 1968).

Range: Nests from s. B.C., s. Alta., w. Sask., e. Mont., e. Wyo., and w.-c. Neb., south to s. Calif., Baja Calif., N.M., w. Tex., n. Mexico and from s. Peru, Chile, n. Argentina, Paraguay, Uruguay, and se. Brazil to Patagonia and Falkland Is.; winters from c. Calif., c. Nev., and sw. U.S. through C. America to n. S. America; also reported in e. U.S. in w. N.Y., N.C., S.C., Ga., Fla., and in Cuba; reported in Alaska, recent records: a pair May 17, 1972 (Smeaton Bay, Ketchikan area); another pair, May 26, 1973, near Anchorage.

Teal, clucking. *See* Teal, Baikal.

Teal, common. *See* Teal, American green-winged, and Teal, Eurasian green-winged.

Teal, Eurasian green-winged, *Anas crecca crecca* (AY-nas CREK-ah or CREEK-ah); scientific names: *see* Teal, American green-winged. Dabbling duck of Eurasia and Africa, the nominate race (*see* Nominate Subspecies) of the green-winged teal; a rare but regular visitor along Atlantic coast of N. America from Labrador to S.C., also reported from Conn., Ohio, Pa., Calif., Wash., Ore., Nev., and Alaska (according to Buckley, 1971, it breeds in the Aleutians—see numerous records of its occurrence in N. America in *American Birds*); 13–16 in. long; wingspread about 20–25 in.; male is almost exact counterpart of American green-winged teal but has *horizontal* white stripe above the wings, and lacks the vertical white stripe on side of body, just in front of wings, as in the American green-winged teal; female cannot be distinguished from female of the American subspecies (Peterson, 1947).

Other Names: Common teal; European common teal; European teal.

Age: One banded in Soviet Union lived to 20 years (Turcek, 1958).

Teal, European. *See* Teal, Eurasian green-winged.

Teal, falcated, *Anas falcata* (AY-nas fal-KAY-tah); genus name: Lat., duck; species name: Lat., curved, sickle-shaped, in reference to the long, sickle-shaped inner secondary wing feathers (tertials) of the male. An e. Asian dabbling duck; considered by some authorities to be related to the gadwall, and called by Johnsgard (1965) and Delacour (1956) the falcated duck; in N. America first reported at St. George Is., Pribilofs, Apr. 18, 1917 (Bent, 1923), and Attu Is., Aleutians, May 1945 (A.O.U. *Check-list,* 1957); has since been seen in B.C. and Calif. (Peterson, 1961); one in Arlington County, Va., Feb. 1966 (Scott and Cutler, 1967); at Adak Is., Alaska, seven seen between Oct. 15 and Nov. 29, 1970; two females there with mallards and pintails, Feb. 1971 (Gibson, 1971); 18–21 in. long; large-headed, short-tailed, chunky; sexes unlike in breeding season, when male is one of most beautiful of all ducks with brilliant iridescent bronze head, white spot above base of upper mandible, and striking green and bronze nuchal crest (on back of neck); white throat with narrow dark collar, and drooping curved scapulars; body plumage, silver-gray; female, brown, with iridescent green speculum, "mottled and barred with black," resembles a female wigeon but has "short nuchal crest, dark gray bill" (Delacour, 1956); migratory, flies swiftly; on wintering grounds are relatively social, in small to large flocks (Johnsgard, 1978); male utters low-pitched, trilled whistle, somewhat teal-like; female quacks much like a gadwall; in summer lives in marshes, swamps, river valleys, on small lakes, and up into mountains; at other seasons, on salt water as well as fresh; often seen on shallow coastal bays.

Feeding Habits: Eats roots, leaves, seeds of aquatic plants, also eats grains in fields near water.

Nest: In marshy wet ground near river or in wet meadows of mountains, built of grasses, reeds, and lined with down.

Eggs: May–June; 6–10, cream-white.

Incubation: 24–25 days; age when young first fly not reported.

Other Names: Bronze-capped teal; falcated duck.

Hybrids: In captivity, has been crossbred with American wigeon, chestnut or chestnut-breasted teal *(Anas castanea),* northern (common) shoveler, European wigeon (Gray, 1958); wild hybrids have been reported of falcated teal with European wigeon and gadwall (Johnsgard, 1965).

Weights: 1 lb. 3 oz.–1 lb. 8 oz. (Johnsgard, 1978).

Range: Breeds in se. Siberia in May–June; reported in summer in Kamchatka and Komandorskie Is. but no definite breeding records, south to e. Mongolia, Manchuria, Kurile Is., Sakhalin, and n. Japan; winters in Iran, n. Baluchistan, India, Burma, s. and e. China, Korea, and Japan; casual in N. America.

Teal, garganey. *See* Garganey.

Teal, green-winged, *Anas crecca;* genus and species names: *see* Teal, American green-winged. (Color ill., page 216.) General and common scientific names (see American Ornithologists' Union, 1973) for the species representing two closely related subspecies of green-winged teals—American green-winged teal and Eurasian green-winged teal.

Teal, northern green-winged. *See* Teal, American green-winged, and Teal, Eurasian green-winged.

Teal, red. *See* Teal, cinnamon.

Teal, spectacled. *See* Teal, Baikal.

Whistling-duck, black-bellied, *Dendrocygna autumnalis* (den-droh-SIG-nah aw-tum-NAY-liss); genus name: from Gr. *dendron,* tree, and Lat. *cygnus,* a swan, in allusion to swanlike or gooselike appearance, and habit of this long-legged bird of frequently perching in trees; species name: Lat., autumn or belonging to autumn. (Color ills., page 214.) Tropical American species, mainly of Mexico and c.

Falcated teal

DUCK FAMILY

America, a few small nesting colonies in se. Tex. and along lower Rio Grande Valley; in U.S., less common than the fulvous tree duck; water habitat created for it in semi-arid s. Tex. by small reservoirs, cattle tanks, and other man-made water areas (Sincock *et al.,* 1964); 19–21 in. long; a gooselike bird with long pink legs, is cinnamon or chestnut *with black belly and bright pink-red bill;* has broad white area near front of wings which in flight covers whole central part of upper wing surface; female, colors duller; immature has gray bill and legs; lives along banks and shallows of rivers, ponds, and in marshes, swamps, resacas (dried stream beds); does not often alight, or swim, on deep water; goes to woods when disturbed; flies easily about in trees; in flight, flocks utter constantly a peculiar whistle, *pe-che-che-NE* (Bent, 1925), or *wha-CHEW-whe-whe-whew.*

Feeding Habits: Apparently little known; at night often invades cornfields; perches on stalks to eat the grain; prefers to forage while standing in shallow water; eats sorghum grain, seeds of Bermuda grass, smartweeds.

Nest: In cavities of elms, willows, and other trees, 8–30 ft. up, sometimes considerable distance from water; also nests on ground among rushes, weeds, grasses near edge of water (Bent, 1925); does not compete successfully for tree-nesting hollows with wood duck; is dominated at nesting sites by both the hen wood duck and the hen Muscovy duck; Muscovy introduced in wild in se. U.S. (Bolen, 1971).

Eggs: Tex., May–Oct.; 12–16, sometimes fewer; white or cream-white.

Incubation: About 27 days (Delacour, 1954); age of young at first flight, 56–63 days.

Other Names: Autumnal tree duck; black-bellied tree duck; cornfield duck; long-legged duck; red-billed whistling duck; summer duck.

Hybrids: Has crossbred with the fulvous tree duck (Gray, 1958).

Weights: Males (35) average 1.80 lbs.; females (37) 1.85 lbs. (Bellrose, 1976).

Range: Nests from Gulf coast of Tex. and lower Rio Grande Valley south through Mexico and C. America to Ecuador, n. Argentina, and s. Brazil; has strayed to Ariz., Calif., West Indies; migratory in extreme northern part of range, arrives in Tex. in Apr. and May; stays until Dec.; according to Sincock *et al.* (1964), it is establishing small nesting colonies along Tex. coast as far north as Corpus Christi, but is not an important game species in U.S.; in Mexico it is one of the more heavily hunted ducks but seems to be maintaining its numbers. According to Cain (1973), low (cool) temperatures may limit northward extension of its range from its present limit in s. Tex.

Whistling-duck, fulvous, *Dendrocygna bicolor* (den-droh-SIG-nah BYE-color); genus name: *see* Whistling-duck, black-bellied; species name: Lat., two-colored, in reference to its contrasting dark back and light underparts; *fulvous* (brownish yellow, or tawny) refers to its general color; despite old name of *tree duck,* does not ordinarily frequent trees. (Color ills., page 214.) The only waterfowl species that breeds in all hemispheres over a huge and discontinuous range; has five widely separated

populations: one in s. U.S. and Mexico; one in ne. S. America; another in se. S. America; one in e. Africa; one in India (Austin, 1961); a tropical and subtropical species that in W. Hemisphere ranges north from Mexico into the Gulf states and Calif.; along Pacific coast has ranged to Ore. and Vancouver, B.C.; along Atlantic coast to N.B. (Sincock *et al.,* 1964), in U.S. usually frequents La., Tex., and s. Calif. (Baldwin *et al.,* 1964); 18–21 in. long; wingspread about 36 in.; sexes outwardly similar; a long-legged, gooselike bird with long neck, upright carriage; in all plumages has deep tawny head and underparts, with dark back and wings, white rump and white slash marks on sides; in flight, with neck slightly drooped, long legs extending beyond tail, and slow wingbeats, appears like an ibis or heron; in flight utters a thin, almost ploverlike whistle, *k-weeoo,* and weak *kill-dee;* has flat, blue-black bill, webbed grayish feet; lives about freshwater marshes, cultivated lands, especially irrigated lands, and particularly rice fields; more easily approached than many wild waterfowl (Bent, 1925), nonetheless difficult to find, as it congregates among dense bulrushes or far out on marshy ponds; in Apr., part of Mexican population moves north into Tex. and La.; when young are fully grown, flock together in fall at various assembly places; when weather cools, many of the northern-ranging birds move south in Sept.–Oct. into Mexico; therefore few shot by hunters during season in La. and Tex. (Sincock *et al.,* 1964); wanders widely; for years was an accidental visitor on lower Atlantic coast north to N.C.; in 1950s began to appear as fall wanderer in Md., N.J., and N.Y. (see Bull, 1964); on Oct. 28–29, 1960, 6 reported in Brigantine National Wildlife Refuge, N.J.; also 30 in R.I., flock of 21 on Grand Manan Is., N.B., five shot near Frederickton, N.B., in same year; in 1962, eight shot on Lake Erie marshes of Ohio; three near Monroe, Mich.; in 1963, four shot near Merrymeeting Bay, Me. (Mendall and Nelson, 1964), probably the farthest north this tropical duck ever seen in N. America (see discussion by Baird, 1963, of expansion of range and reasons for it); in 1970, flock of eleven (one collected) wintered in Coos Bay marsh, Ore. (Anonymous, 1970c).

Feeding Habits: Mostly feeds at night, walks about on land eating seeds of grasses and weeds; also visits cornfields for waste grain, eats alfalfa and grasses; in rice fields of La. and Tex. sometimes causes damage to newly planted rice (Buller, 1964); also feeds in water by tipping up or simply by lowering head into shallow water.

Nest: In bulrushes, dense beds of cattails, in freshwater marshes or at edge of ponds, swamps, sometimes built on marsh hummock or in rank tall grasses of wet meadows, rarely in tree cavity 4–30 ft. up; nest from simply a grass-lined hollow in ground to handsome nest of grasses or sedges, 6 in. or more high nest (often roofed over) gathered from surrounding vegetation with eggs well above ground or water.

Eggs: U.S., Apr.–Sept.; 10–20, usually 12–14; cream to buff-white, sometimes 30–100 laid by several females in same nest, which is usually abandoned (*see* Dump Nests); also lays eggs in

nests of ruddy duck and redhead (Bent, 1925).

Incubation: By female assisted by male (Gilliard, 1958), 24–26 days; young first fly 55–63 days after hatching (Johnsgard, 1968).

Other Names: Bicolored tree duck; cornfield duck; fulvous tree duck; long-legged duck; Mexican duck; Mexican squealer; Mexican wood duck; squealer; summer duck; tee-kee (from call note); wood duck; Yankee duck; yellow-bellied fiddler duck.

Hybrids: Has crossbred with black-bellied tree duck (Gray, 1958).

Weights: 1½–1¾ lbs. (Johnsgard, 1968).

Range: Eastern Africa, India, Burma, N. and S. America, Mexico; resident in Calif., N.M., Tex., and s. La., nests from c. Calif. and Pacific slope of s. Calif., casually in c. Nev. (Washoe Lake), se. Tex., sw. La., south into s-c. Mexico; greatest numbers in coastal lowlands of Mexico south to Campeche and Oaxaca but is no longer abundant (Sincock *et al.,* 1964); apparently extended its range in U.S. In 1960s, first Fla. breeding record at Lake Okeechobee; since then breeding birds and wintering flocks in other parts of Fla.

Whistling-duck, West Indian, *Dendrocygna arborea* (den-droh-SIG-nah are-BOH-ree-ah); genus name: *see* Whistling-duck, black-bellied; species name: from Lat. *arbor,* tree, from habit of perching, often high in trees; *West Indian,* from its home in West Indies (type locality for the species is the island of Jamaica). Accidental occurrence in Bermuda, where collected once; large, gooselike with long legs; largest of the whistling, or tree, ducks; 19–23 in. long; dark or medium brown with whitish neck and throat, a black band on nape and hind neck, head feathers of occiput (back part of crown) long, form small crest; underparts pale buff, spotted with black; white mottling on flanks; *bill and legs black;* lives in freshwater and saltwater swamps and mangroves, largely nocturnal, often seen flying over swamps at dusk, utters shrill whistled *visisee* (Bond, 1961); feeds mostly at night often on the fruit of the tall royal palms on which it alights; rarely seen swimming on open water; walks easily on land; breeds from June to Oct.; commonly nests among reeds on ground (Delacour, 1954), in a cavity in a tree, or in a cluster of bromeliads high above ground (Bond, 1961).

Eggs: May(?)–Oct.; 10–12, milky white.

Incubation: 30 days.

Other Name: Black-billed tree duck.

Weights: 2½ lbs.

Range: Resident in Bahama Is., Greater Antilles, Virgin Is., Barbuda, and Antigua; accidental in Bermuda.

Wigeon, American, *Anas americana* (AY-nas ah-mer-ih-CANE-ah); genus name: Lat., duck; species name: Lat., of America; *wigeon* (WIDGE-un), apparently from Fr. *vigeon, vingeon, gingeon,* of uncertain origin, possibly from Lat. *vipio, vipionem,* a small crane (see Gruson, 1972). (Color ill., page 216.) Formerly called baldpate. Summers in freshwater marshes, lakes, ponds, from Alaska to Man. and n. U.S. from Wash. and Calif. east to Neb.; medium-sized dabbling duck, somewhat larger than Eurasian wigeon; 18–23 in. long; wingspread about 30–35 in.; male has gray head with *bright white crown* (similar male Eurasian wigeon has *reddish head* and *buff crown*); and large white patches on each *forewing*, conspicuous in flight; male also has band of metallic green on each side of head; sides and back reddish or tan; *pale blue bill has black tip*, is small and compressed and adapted to grazing (Delacour, 1956); female, ruddy brown with gray head and neck (head is paler than that of similar female gadwall), also has white patch on forepart of each wing, not on rear part as in female gadwall (Peterson, 1961); undersurfaces of wings are gray, that of mallard, white; sits buoyantly on water, very wary, when alarmed rises straight up from water with rattling of wings and flies rapidly away; flight is swift, strong, direct; in migration or when flying to and from breeding grounds, flies in small dense flocks, at no great height, flock sometimes turns and wheels rapidly in unison like teal (Pough, 1951); male utters musical, three-noted, throaty whistle, *whew, whew, whew* (middle syllable loudest), on wing or while feeding and swimming; female, a weak guttural *quack;* leaves wintering grounds along coasts, brackish marshes, bays throughout much of U.S. south of northern states, and in lower Mississippi Valley, moves northward in leisurely migration through Mar.–Apr.; arrives nesting grounds in Canada, Alaska, Apr.–May; annual average wintering population from 1955–74 totaled 1,835,000 (Bellrose, 1976).

Feeding Habits: Dabbles with bill in mud or tips up in shallow water and reaches below to eat seeds but mostly leaves, stems, buds of pondweeds, widgeon grass, grasses, sedges (vegetal food about 93% of diet in one study—see in Bent, 1923); is not a diver but very fond of wild celery, a deep-water plant, which it gets from surface after feeding canvasbacks and coots have torn plants loose from bottom, also grazes in fields, digging up young grass and grain plants with bill; visits rice fields in South, also eats some snails, beetles, and crickets.

Nest: Built on islands in freshwater lakes in tall grasses or weeds, always nests on dry land (Baldwin *et al.,* 1964); sometimes at considerable distance (half mile) from water in slight hollow in grassland or in woods under thick spruces or at base of bush or tree, sometimes scarcely concealed, in open; nest well lined with dry grasses, leaves, weed stems, and down from female, which she adds to nest as incubation advances.

Eggs: Arctic America, June–July; in U.S., May–July; 6–12, commonly 9–11, cream-white.

Incubation: By female, 22–24 days (Reilly, 1968); age when young first fly estimated at 45–58 days (Hochbaum, 1944).

Other Names: Bald-crown; bald-head; baldpate; bald wigeon; blue-billed wigeon; California wigeon; green-headed wigeon; poacher; smoking duck; southern wigeon; wheat duck; white belly.

Age: One banded wild bird lived to 9 years, 4 months (Kennard, 1975).

Flight Speed: Timed in w. U.S., 22 m.p.h. (Cottam *et al.,* 1942b).

Hybrids: Wild hybrids reported from crosses of American wigeon with gadwall, green-winged teal, pintail, and common mallard (see also Gray, 1958).

Weights: Males (84) average 1.81 lbs.; females (68) average 1.69 lbs. (Bellrose, 1976).

Range: Nests from coast of Bering Sea through c. Alaska to Yuk. and w. and s. Mack., Man., and Wisc., and rarely in w. Minn., south through interior of B.C., e. Wash., and Ore. to ne. Calif., n. Nev., n. Colo., n. Neb. (formerly east and south to Ind.); recently, and rarely, in Mich., s. Ont., and nw. Pa.; winters from s. Alaska south through Baja Calif., and mainland of Mexico; c. U.S. (Nev., sw. Utah, ne. Colo., s. Ill.) to Gulf states, and from New England south along Atlantic seaboard to Costa Rica and West Indies.

Wigeon, blue-billed. *See* Wigeon, American.

Wigeon, Eurasian, *Anas penelope* (AY-nas pee-NEL-oh-pee); genus name: Lat., duck; species name: in Gr. mythology, Penelope was wife of Ulysses and mother of Telemachus; however, *penelope* may have been written by early ornithologists, mistakenly, for *penelops,* a name used by Linnaeus for a kind of duck (Coues, 1882); *wigeon*—see under American wigeon. (Color ill., page 216.) A Eurasian dabbling duck that has been seen rarely but regularly in N. America for the last 30–40 years but nesting in N. America still not reported up to 1971 (Buckley, 1971); up to 1957 reported on both the Atlantic and Pacific coasts and across interior: from Newfoundland to Fla. and Tex., from Alaska to Baja Calif.; in winter and spring of 1971, many records, some as follows: Halifax, Nova Scotia (1); Ont. (3); Wisc. (1); Cohasset, Mass. (2); Long Is., N.Y. (1); N.J. and Conn. (5); Delaware Valley area of Pa. and N.J. (4); Santee National Wildlife Refuge, S.C. (1); Walkulla Springs, Fla. (1); Adak Is., Alaska (13); and on Seward Pen., first record of a pair, June 28, 1971; 17–21 in. long, wingspread about 32 in., somewhat smaller than American wigeon; male distinguished from American wigeon by reddish head and buff crown, otherwise similar; is a gray wigeon with brownish, rose-colored breast; bill blue-gray; female similar to female American wigeon but head is cinnamon-buff (head of female American is gray); sure distinction of Eurasian species in hand is its underwing dusky axillars ("armpit" feathers), which in American wigeon are white (Peterson, 1947), in flight shows no clear white area on undersurface of wings, although upper surfaces are white as in American wigeon (Peterson, 1947); male utters wild, musical, rolling whistle, *whee-oo,* also a short cheeping note; female utters a throaty croak and a harsh quack when alarmed (Bent, 1923).

Feeding Habits: Similar to those of American wigeon, fond of pondweeds, eelgrass, and other aquatic plants (see Bent, 1923).

Nest: Grass- and down-lined, built in depression on ground, on moorland, marshes, tundra, usually well hidden in tall grasses or other plants, usually near water but often some distance away on moor or meadow.

Eggs: Iceland, May–June; 9–10, usually 7–8, cream-white; indistinguishable from those of American wigeon.

Incubation: In Europe, 24–25 days (Delacour, 1956); age when young first fly 40–45 days.

Other Name: European wigeon.

Weights: Males (84) average 1.81 lbs; females (68) average 1.69 lbs. (Bellrose, 1976).

Range: Nests in Iceland, n. Europe, n. Russia across Siberia to Kamchatka and Komandorskie Is.; winters from British Isles, s. Scandinavia, s. Russia, south to ne. Africa, Mesopotamia, India, Ceylon, Burma, Thailand, Formosa, and Japan.

Wigeon, European. *See* Wigeon, Eurasian.

Wigeon, gray. *See* Gadwall.

DUCK PLAGUE
See under Diseases.

DUCK SICKNESS
See Botulism; Lead Poisoning; *also* Diseases.

DUCK STAMPS
As part of a large national program to help waterfowl, especially ducks whose breeding marshes and potholes had dried up during the "great drought" of the early 1930s, American conservationists and federal authorities originated in 1934 a special Duck Stamp. The Federal Migratory Bird Hunting Stamp Act, passed by Congress March 16, 1934, specified that every duck and goose hunter over 16 years old is required to buy a Duck Stamp in addition to any regular state hunting license fees.

The purpose of the act was "to supplement and support the Migratory Bird Conservation Act by providing funds for acquiring areas for use as migratory bird sanctuaries, refuges, and breeding grounds, for developing and administering such areas for the protection of certain migratory birds, for the enforcement of the Migratory Bird Treaty Act, and regulations thereunder, and for other purposes" (Hon. Lester Johnson, *Congressional Record,* 84th Cong., 1st sess., May 27, 1955). Ira N. Gabrielson, former Director of the U.S. Fish and Wildlife Service, wrote that, according to the Act, "ninety per cent of the money [from Duck Stamps sold] must be used for migratory waterfowl refuges, the remaining ten per cent being available for the administration of the act."

Each year, the Fish and Wildlife Service, U.S. Dept. of the Interior, conducts a public contest open to all artists for the purpose of selecting the new design of some species of waterfowl (ducks, geese, and swans) to illustrate the annual stamp. The competition is the only art contest regularly sponsored by the federal government. The colorful stamps constitute the longest-running annually issued series of stamps in revenue or postage stamp history.

Since 1934, when Duck Stamps first went on sale, more than $176 million in revenue has been collected and used for acquiring 2 million acres of prime waterfowl habitat. By buying the stamps, more than 2.4 million hunters and conservationists provide close to $12 million annually in revenue (Anonymous, 1976). Each year, the Interior Department also encourages non-hunters who also enjoy wildlife through bird-watching, photography, or other wildlife activities to buy a stamp. The stamps are usually for sale in post offices beginning July 1. See also Anonymous (1975b).

DUCK VIRUS ENTERITIS
See under Diseases.

DUETING
Term of some ornithologists for the simultaneous "singing" or uttering of the same sounds together by a mated pair of birds (Van Tyne and Berger, 1959). *See* Songs and Singing.

DUMB-BIRD
A common name for the ruddy duck, because it is generally silent.

DUMMY NEST
Also called cock nest (because male of species builds it), incomplete nest, play nest, and sleeping nest—built by males of house wrens and marsh wrens in N. America, also by the male prothonotary warbler. The function of these extra nests, built in spring by males of species that return to nesting grounds ahead of females (*see* Nests and Nesting), is not fully understood.

Male house wrens will build several round masses of sticks, usually with no lining, in birdhouses, natural cavities in trees, or in abandoned woodpecker holes. After female arrives in his territory he sings a great deal and goes in and out of these nests as though inviting her to adopt one of them for the active nest. Some female house wrens take over one of the nests built by the male and finish it themselves, or may throw out his materials and build a new one.

House wrens and marsh wrens, which are polygamous (*see* Sexual Relationships) may have up to three mates nesting at one time; some of the males remain unmated. The male wrens that are the most zealous builders of extra nests are most successful in attracting females. It is speculated that building of multiple nests is exaggerated courtship, or a method of marking out the male's territory, and of establishing preliminary nest sites. *See* Territory.

After young wrens leave the active nest, or home nest, the male may lead them to one of the dummy nests for an overnight sleeping place. *See* Young and Their Care. The male long-billed marsh wren is known to build up to six nests within his known territory (Welty, 1962).

DUMP NEST
Term of biologists for a nest in which more than one hen bird lays its eggs; for example, several female ring-necked pheasants sometimes lay their eggs by necessity in one of these "dump" nests, lacking one of their own, or on bare ground, because an egg, after development in the oviduct of the female, apparently cannot be arrested and must be laid (*see*, however, discussion under Eggs and Egg-laying). Usually the eggs in dump nests are not incubated. Some dump nests of the redhead (*see*

in Duck Family) have contained from 30 to 87 eggs (Weller, 1959b). *See* discussion under Obligate Parasite.

DUNG HUNTER
See Jaeger, parasitic, in Skua Family.

DUNLIN
See in Sandpiper Family.

DUNNOCK
See in Hedge Sparrow Family.

DUODENUM
(due-oh-DEE-num). *See* described under Intestine and function under Digestion.

DUPLICITY
(of parts). *See* Deformities.

DUST BATHING
See Bathing.

DWIGHT
JONATHAN, JR., M.D. (1858–1929). Fellow, treasurer (1903–20), and past president of the American Ornithologists' Union, noted for his detailed studies and nomenclature of the plumage of birds; author of a notable reference, "Sequence of Plumage and Moults of the Passerine Birds of New York," *Annals of the New York Academy of Sciences*, Vol. XIII, No. 1, 1900. See Fleming (1930).

DYNAMIC SOARING
See Flight.

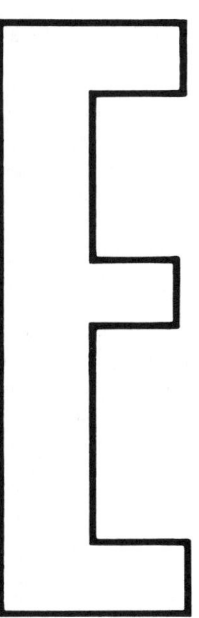

EAGLE
See in Hawk Family.

EARS AND HEARING
Hearing is keen and ranks next to sight in its importance to birds and their survival (Van Tyne and Berger, 1959). The ear openings of most birds are hidden under feathers, and are on the sides of the head; in some birds—Old World vultures and ostriches, for example—no feathers cover the ear openings (Pumphrey, 1964). There is no fleshy and cartilaginous outer ear, or pinna, which catches sound waves as in man and other mammals, but owls have a movable skin fold, most prominent along the front edge of the ears, that reflects sounds that come to the owl from behind (Hess, 1951; Schwartzkopff, 1973).

The feathers that cover the ear openings of birds are called *auriculars* (*see* Topography). These have no barbules (*see* Feather) and do not interfere with a bird's hearing, and in owls may help them to detect sounds. According to Blake (1950), it may be common to see a bird raise its crown feathers when alerted, but raising the auriculars, or ear feathers, is not so well known. Blake saw it twice, once in a rufous-sided towhee, *Pipilo erythrophthalmus,* and once in a hen pheasant, *Phasianus colchicus.* During these observations, each bird had its head turned away from Blake, and when the ear feathers were raised, they appeared as small lateral crests along the sides of the head. "The feathers in front of the ear opening are adapted to minimize turbulence in flight and by this protect the hearing organ itself" (Schwartzkopff, 1973).

THE HEARING OF BIRDS. Birds are highly social and depend on hearing for intersocial communication, or "understanding" of other birds, particularly of their own kind. *See* Language. Hearing also helps them to detect other animals on which they feed, and to be alerted to the dangers that threaten them almost constantly in the places where they live. Thus, hearing strongly influences behavior. *See* Behavior.

Although the hearing acuity of birds has rarely been measured (Emlen, 1955), in some it has been shown to be more acute than in man (Hann, 1953). Owls, parrots, and pheasants have especially acute hearing, and most birds can locate the source of a sound with remarkable accuracy (*see* Sounds That Attract Birds). Pumphrey (1961a) concluded from his survey of the subject that the cochlea of a bird has a *speed of response* about ten times that of the human ear.

Owls, especially the great horned owl, barn owl, and other species of owls that hunt mostly at night, hear especially well. The ear structure of owls is elaborately and asymmetrically developed—that is, the right and left ears are very often differently shaped (Heinroth and Heinroth, 1958), and usually one ear opening is above, and the other below, the horizontal (Payne, 1962; Schwartzkopff, 1973). As early as 1898, W. P. Pycraft, a British ornithologist, suggested that this asymmetrical structure might be helpful to owls in locating their prey.

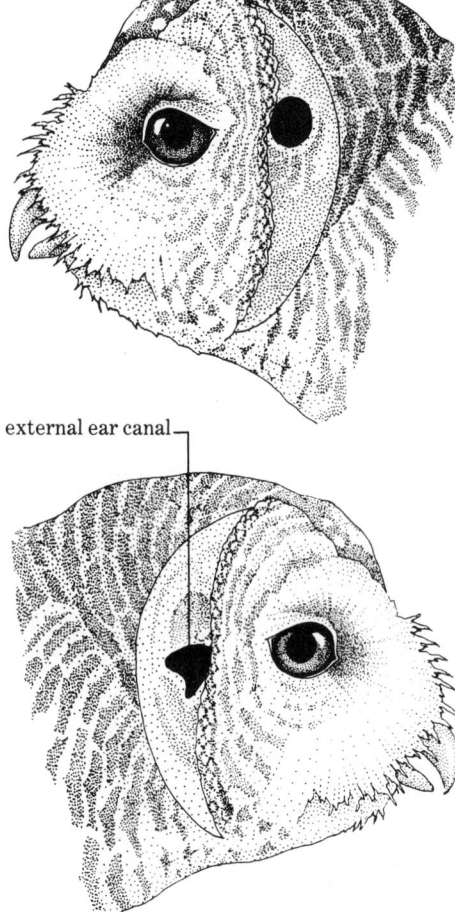

external ear canal

EARS AND HEARING
Owls have acute hearing and many can hunt nocturnally by sound alone. The asymmetrical placement and shape of the external ear canals in many owls are thought to help them determine the exact location of a sound. In front of the ear on each side—beneath the feathered facial discs—is a movable skin fold that reflects and concentrates sound waves coming from behind.

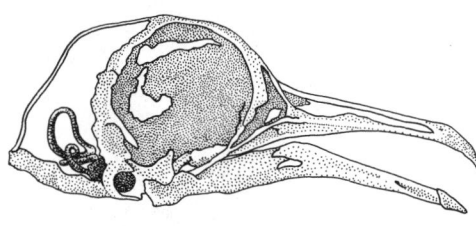

The complex avian inner ear is located in the skull behind the orbit.

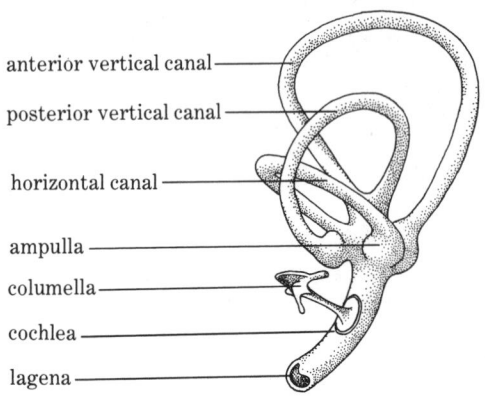

anterior vertical canal —
posterior vertical canal —
horizontal canal —
ampulla —
columella —
cochlea —
lagena —

EARS AND HEARING

Sound waves caught by the external ear strike the ear drum at the end of the external canal and are picked up by the cochlea, which transmits them via a membranous window to the liquids of the inner ear. Inside the chambers of the ampulla, sacculus, and utriculus are hairlike cells that convert vibrations into nerve impulses. Equilibrium is maintained by the semicircular canals.

See, however, account of great horned owl and ruffed grouse under Drumming.

Payne (1962), in his studies of how barn owls locate their prey, was able to verify that a barn owl in complete darkness need only *hear* a mouse rustling in the leaves to locate and strike the animal. Apparently the owl calculates the position of the mouse from the sounds of its movements, and can determine the direction in which the mouse is headed, all of which it does just before it strikes the mouse with its feet and talons. An associate of Payne's was also able to prove in his experiments that the barn owl does not locate its prey by infrared light. *See also* Eyes and Eyesight.

HOW A BIRD HEARS. The ears of birds consist not only of a sensory receiving apparatus within the internal ear but an external ear and a middle ear. Their supplemental functions are primarily to collect and amplify vibrations (sound waves) from the air (Walter and Sayles, 1949).

Sounds picked up by a bird first enter the two small ear openings, one on each side of the head, which in most birds are just below and in back of the eyes. These are the *external auditory canals,* which end at the eardrum, or *tympanic membrane.* Sound waves striking upon the tympanic membrane enter the *middle ear,* an air-filled cavity which extends from the eardrum to the outer bony wall of the *internal ear,* or inner ear. The middle ear connects with the pharynx (*see* Pharynx), or back part of the bird's mouth, through the Eustachian tube (Pumphrey, 1964). *See* Eustachian Tube.

The middle ear houses a single earbone, the partly cartilaginous *columella,* one end of which is attached to the eardrum. The other end of the columella, like the *stapes* in the mammalian ear, is in contact with an oval opening, or window—the *fenestra ovale*—in the wall of the internal ear. The sound vibrations of the eardrum are carried across the middle ear by the columella and stapes to the fenestra ovale, and thence to the cochlea within the internal ear. See Schwartzkopff (1973).

According to Van Tyne and Berger (1959), "the cochlea is the auditory part of the inner ear, a complex structure responsible for the transforming of sound-wave stimuli to nerve impulses, which are conducted to the brain by the cochlea nerve."

"*Corti's organ* is the receptive part of the cochlea; it is much shorter and broader in birds than in mammals" (Pumphrey, 1964). A specialized part of the cochlea is called the *lagena* (lah-JEE-nah). It contains tiny calcium carbonate "ear stones," or *otoliths.* There is no lagena in mammals and evidence of the function of the lagena in birds is still inconclusive. It possibly is responsive to low frequencies of sound (Van Tyne and Berger, 1976). The three semicircular canals by which a bird is able to maintain its equilibrium are also within the internal ear. *See* Semicircular Canals.

ACUTENESS OF HEARING IN BIRDS. During World War I, parrots kept in French fortresses and on the Eiffel Tower gave warning of the approach of airplanes too far away to be seen by human beings. Allen (1925) cites the account

of Dr. Charles Davison, an authority on earthquakes, who said that during World War I, pheasants often were disturbed by air waves from explosions or naval battles inaudible to human ears; however, this has since been attributed, not to hearing, but to a bird's sensitivity to vibrations. *See* Touch. On Jan. 24, 1915, during a naval battle on Dogger Bank, pheasants 216 mi. away from the action "shrieked themselves hoarse" and smaller birds were terrified.

The acuteness of hearing of some domesticated birds has made them valued from time immemorial as "watchdogs." *See* Domestication. The cackling of the sacred geese of Juno's temple, which awakened the sleeping guard, saved Rome from an attack of the Gauls. Geese, tree ducks, and Old World sheldrakes were often kept even by savage tribes as watchdogs; these birds feed much at night and are quick to make an outcry at any unusual sound (Allen, 1925).

WHAT SOUNDS CAN BIRDS HEAR? Birds can hear the sounds made by their own kind and at least some of the sounds made by other species. *See* Language. Scientists have shown, however, by laboratory experiments with captive birds, that there is considerable difference in the ranges of hearing among various species of birds (Schwartzkopff, 1973). Starlings, for example, hear approximately the same high frequencies of sound that a human being does; that is to say, they hear in the higher frequencies up to about 16,000 cycles of sound per second (c.p.s.). Their response to sounds, however, falls off in the lower frequencies at about 1,200 c.p.s. and disappears at about 650 c.p.s.

In tests of the hearing range of a hairy woodpecker, Ramp (1965) discovered that it heard from high frequencies of 18,400 c.p.s. to a low frequency of 34 c.p.s. and that its ability to hear such a wide range of sounds suggested that it can hear the movements of wood-boring insects hidden in the bark or wood of trees and thus locate its prey. *See* in Woodpecker Family.

Man hears as low as about 20 c.p.s. (Brand and Kellogg, 1939). In studies of the songs of starlings in nature, investigators have found that they sing in frequencies of sound no lower than about 100 c.p.s. and that most sounds are produced within the range at which their hearing is most acute.

Brand and Kellogg also discovered that the range of hearing of house, or English, sparrows is about the same as that of starlings; they heard in higher frequencies up to 18,000 c.p.s. and in the lower frequencies to 675 c.p.s., which is a much smaller range of hearing than in man; however, the sounds they make are within the frequencies of sounds that they hear.

Domestic pigeons tested heard up to 7,500 c.p.s., and in the lower frequencies down to 200 c.p.s. The hearing range of the pigeon was about an octave or more lower than that of the starling and the house sparrow. These tests suggested to the investigators that birds hear over a more limited range of sound than do mammals, including man. Man hears about four octaves lower than the pigeon and five octaves lower than the house sparrow and starling.

Hearing Range of Some Birds (cycles per second)

	High	Low	Authority
hairy woodpecker	18,400	34	Ramp (1965)
starling	15,000	650	Brand and Kellogg (1939)
house sparrow	11,500–18,000	675	Brand and Kellogg (1939); Armstrong (1963)
horned lark	7,600	350	Edwards (1943)
pigeon	7,500–12,000	200	Brand and Kellogg (1939); Armstrong (1963)
snow bunting	7,200	400	Edwards (1943)
great horned owl	7,000	60	Edwards (1943)
canvasback (duck)	5,200	190	Edwards (1943)
long-eared owl	18,000	100	Schwartzkopff (1955a)
man	16,000–20,000	20	Schwartzkopff (1955a); Armstrong (1963)

More recent research has shown, however, that pigeons, at least, can detect low frequency sounds (infrasounds), sounds much lower than man can hear. Such infrasounds can originate from weather patterns, geographic features, and ocean waves, and can be detected thousands of kilometers from their source. This discovery has revealed a possible partial explanation for the homing ability of pigeons and possibly the navigational cues of migratory birds. *See* Homing; Migration. See Kreithen and Quine (1979); Kreithen (1978); and Delius and Emmerton (1978).

EAR STONES
See otoliths under Ears and Hearing.

EARTHWORMS AND BIRDS
According to food-habits investigations of birds of N. America (*see* Economic Ornithology), earthworms have been found in the stomachs of 44 species (McAtee, 1932b); the American robin habitually and voraciously feeds upon earthworms, and the American woodcock (*see* in Sandpiper Family) includes earthworms in about 75% of its diet (Sperry, 1940). Sheldon (1971) reported that his captive adult woodcocks each ate an average of 150 gr. (about 5½ oz.) of earthworms during each 24 hours or about equal to their summer body weight (*see* How Much Will a Bird Eat? under Food and Feeding Habits). The common snipe (*see* in Sandpiper Family) includes earthworms in about 11% of its animal food.

Some songbirds, such as starlings and house sparrows, avid for earthworms, will take them from American robins after the robins have pulled them from the ground. For American robin's method of finding earthworms, *see* in its biography in Thrush Family, and for amount of earthworms a robin may eat, *see* Food and Feeding Habits. Even such large birds as gulls

like earthworms. In Calif., Bolander (1932) saw three California gulls and a western gull steal earthworms from robins; they waited until the robins were pulling worms from the ground, then charged to make them release their prey (*see* "stealing" of food from other birds in Feeding and Food-getting under Behavior). Terres (1967) watched cattle egrets eating earthworms on a golf course during a light steady rain at Chapel Hill, N.C.; the egrets not only picked up wet worms from the partly flooded ground but pulled them from their burrows. Gulls flock at airports after rain to eat earthworms near the runways.

In an unusual observation, Reagan (1955), for 6 consecutive Jan. days, watched two red-shouldered hawks at Moorestown, N.J., Friends' School either perch on fence posts or on ground near earthworm burrows at lower end of a wet athletic field, to pick up and eat earthworms as they emerged from ground. One hawk remained in the area for 6 weeks to take advantage of the easily available food supply.

French *et al.* (1957), in studies of nutritional value of earthworms, discovered that in three species all were high in protein and as eaten fresh by birds, contained about 83% moisture, 8–9% protein, 3% carbohydrates, and 1% fat; see also Sheldon (1971) for an interesting report from literature on the ecology and distribution of earthworms in N. America. *See* related discussions under Taste; Touch; Smell.

EASTERN BIRDS
Term for those that in the U.S. usually live *east* of the 100th meridian, a line on standard maps that runs northward from the Mexican border through c. Tex., w. Okla., w. Kans., c. Neb., and through S.D. and N.D. to the Canadian border. The line is an ecological one in that it runs approximately along the eastern edge of the semiarid Great Plains. It is where the tall-grass prairies (east of it) meet the drier short-grass plains to the west. The line is the westward limit of the range of most birds of the humid e. U.S. (Pough, 1949), although the ecological line itself is not a complete barrier, as some eastern birds will go west of it, and some western birds regularly range far to the east of it, in fall and winter to our Atlantic coast. *See* Barrier; Distribution; *also* Western Birds.

EASTERN HEMISPHERE
Synonymous with the Old World. *See* Hemispheres.

EATING HABITS
See Food and Feeding Habits; also in biography of each bird.

EATING OF OWN YOUNG BY PARENTS
See Kronism.

ECDYSIS
(EK-die-sees). Term for the act of molting, or the annual shedding of the feathers of a bird. Endysis (EN-die-sees) is the act of developing a new coat of feathers. *See* Molts and Molting.

ECHOLOCATION
Term for a method of navigating often in darkness used by bats, dolphins, certain birds, some fishes, amphibians, and insects, and by some men. By making sounds which are echoed or bounced back to their ears, certain animals react to these echoed sounds to detect their prey or to avoid obstructions. Insect-eating bats are famous for this navigational ability and on the darkest nights seldom if ever collide with the smallest twig as they fly through the woods (Griffin, 1958).

In 1799, when Alexander von Humboldt began his five-year journey through tropical America, he visited a large cavern at Caripe in what is now Venezuela. There he described in his journals the "guacharo," or oilbird, which he named *Steatornis caripensis*, the oilbird of Caripe. The name oilbird is from the oil obtained by the Venezuelan Indians from the layers of fat in the bodies of the nestlings, which they used for lights (torches), cooking, and nourishment. Humboldt's scientific description of the bird reported it as resembling a goatsucker, related to the nightjars, whip-poor-wills, nighthawks, etc. *See* Nightjar Family. It is classified in a separate family (Steatornithidae) in the order Caprimulgiformes. It is the only nocturnal fruit-eating bird (Snow, 1964b) and the only member of its order that eats fruit (Storer, 1960b).

The oilbird nests in dark caves and at night it comes forth to feed on tropical fruit. Humboldt was impressed by its sharp cries as it flew about in the darkness of the nesting cavern.

In Mar. 1953, Donald R. Griffin, at that time in the Biology Department, Cornell University, and William H. Phelps, Jr., an ornithologist living in Caracas, Venezuela, visited the "Cave of the Guacharos," where Humboldt had made his discovery. They found that the oilbirds did fly in the darkness of the nesting cave, and that while doing so they uttered audible "screeches, clucks, *clicks*, and shrieks" making a real din while flying about. However, when issuing from the cave for their night's hunting for food, they emitted a steady stream of the extremely sharp click notes. Using measuring apparatus that Griffin had previously used to record the high-frequency sounds of bats, they discovered that the click notes of the oilbirds averaged about 7,000 cycles per second, well within the range of human hearing (*see* Ears and Hearing).

In subsequent tests of captive oilbirds flying about in a dark room, when the birds' ears were plugged they flew into the walls of the room, which they had previously avoided when their ears were not plugged. Thus the investigators proved to their satisfaction that the oilbirds depend essentially on sounds they make to guide them in flights through the dark.

The frequencies of sound used by the oilbirds in echolocation are apparently far lower than those used by bats, and, like the insect-eating bats, they use *pulsed* sounds. The oilbirds use echolocation to guide them only when flying in the dark. At other times, when light is available, they apparently use their eyes, which are large and functional (Griffin, 1958). *See also* Histoplasmosis.

The oilbird is not the only bird that flies in the

Cape May warbler

Blackburnian warbler

Black-throated green warbler

Magnolia warbler

ECOLOGICAL NICHE
These four warblers in the same forest may overlap in the physical space they occupy, but their ecological niches are always distinct. The magnolia warbler may feed on insects on the lower trunk and nest less than 15 feet from the ground; the black-throated green warbler feeds on foliage-eating insects close to the trunk and nests in the crotch of lower branches; the Blackburnian warbler may feed among the twigs and needles at treetop, or catch insects on the wing, and nests on a high branch well out from the trunk; the Cape May warbler may feed on sap or insects in the bark and nests close to the top of the tree.

darkness of caves. One species of the swiftlets of the genus *Collocalia* (*see* Nests and Nesting), living in s. India and Ceylon, nests both in well-lighted and in dark caves, which it often shares with night-hunting bats. Griffin, after returning from his visit to the Cave of the Guacharos in Venezuela, was struck by the similarity of the nesting life of these swiftlets to that of the oilbird. From accounts sent to him by ornithologists in the Far East, he learned that certain swiftlets (*Collocalia inexpectata amelis* and *Collocalia troglodytes*, for example) utter continuous twittering notes while flying about in their nesting caves. They did not, however, give the notes continuously while flying in the more lighted parts of the caverns or on the outside. Some ornithologists likened the notes to "clicking" or a sound like the tearing of silk. This suggested to Griffin that they uttered a series of short pulses of sound, similar to the buzzing of an insect-eating bat when approaching obstacles in darkness or flying insects.

Later, two ornithologists in Ceylon experimented with captive swiftlets, *Collocalia brevirostris unicolor*, which nest in caverns. Their investigations added substantial evidence that *Collocalia* guide their flights in dark caves by means of echolocation, and that their audible click notes are strikingly similar to those uttered by oilbirds.

Griffin suggested that other kinds of birds which fly skillfully on dark nights may use echolocation to guide them. Among the birds that may do so, for which there is suggestive evidence, is the common nighthawk, *Chordeiles minor*, of N. America, which utters rasping notes as it swoops downward while hunting insects in the air at night.

ECLIPSE OF SUN

(influence on birds). *See* Light.

ECLIPSE PLUMAGE

Term for the dull, female-like plumage into which many brilliantly colored male ducks molt during the summer; it is a very brief molt, coming at the time that they lose all their flight feathers or *primaries* (*see* under Feather), and cannot fly. While wearing it, they "go into eclipse" for a month or two, are unobtrusive in the dingy female garb, and hide from their enemies in swamps and marshes (Newton, 1893–96). *See* details in introduction to Duck Family; *see also* Molts and Molting.

ECOLOGICAL COMPATIBILITY

Term for two closely related species of birds that can live in the same area yet not compete because the habitats they choose, or are adapted to, are different. *See* Habitat; Ecological Niche. *See* especially Sibling Species; Sympatric Species. "Two species normally cannot co-exist in the same area unless they have sufficiently diverged in their ecological requirements so as not to be severe competitors" (Mayr, 1951).

ECOLOGICAL NICHE

Unlike habitat (*see* Habitat) the ecological niche is the *role* or *function* of a bird species in its give-and-take with its environment—the specific place it occupies in the animal and plant community of which it is a part—the complete natural history of the species. That position is a result of the bird's own structure, physiology, and species behavior. To determine the status (niche) of a bird species, we would need to know its activities—especially its food relations: what *it* eats and what eats *it*, its range of movements, its effect on other members of the community, and so on (Odum, 1953).

The bird species' ecological niche (its performance within the community) is expressed in its activities: whether it hunts for food in trees (red-eyed vireo) or on the ground (ovenbird), whether it is active by day or by night, what types of material it may use to build its nest (whether simply bark, mosses or leaves, grasses or weed stalks), and so on (Pettingill, 1972).

Some birds of related species within the same family occupy separate niches in parts of the same kind of tree. R. H. MacArthur (1958) in his studies of 5 species of N. American wood warblers in the spruce forests of Maine—baybreasted, Blackburnian, black-throated green, Cape May, and myrtle (yellow-rumped) warblers—discovered that each lived in a different zone or part of the spruce tree. All fed on insects and gathered them in different parts of the tree, and each nested in a different part of the tree at various heights above the ground. In their movements, the warblers sometimes overlapped in the physical space they occupied in or about the tree, but their niches did not overlap: each species had its own unique combination of requirements for a nest site, breeding time, area of food-gathering, and feeding behavior that distinguished each within its own ecological niche. Wherever similar species have been examined, differences in niches have been discovered, suggesting that there is usually only one species to a niche. This theory was first clearly demonstrated by G. F. Gause (1934) and is known as *Gause's Rule* or *Gause's Principle. See* Adaptive Radiation; Hawaiian Honeycreeper Family. See Cody (1974).

ECOLOGICAL RELATIONSHIPS OF BIRDS

See discussion under Ecological Niche and Ecosystem, with their cited references.

ECOLOGICAL RULES

See Allen's Rule; Bergmann's Rule; Egg Rule; Gause's Rule; Gloger's Rule; Humboldt's Rule. *See also* discussion of some ecological rules under Cline.

ECOLOGY

(ee-KOL-oh-jih). The study of the interrelationships of animals and plants to one another and to the environment (Hanson, Herbert C., 1962). The branch of biology that deals with the mutual relations between organisms and their environment; bionomics. *See* Ecological Niche; Ecosystem; *also* Autecology.

ECOLOGY

A publication. *See* Ornithological Periodicals.

ECONOMIC ORNITHOLOGY

Scientists and students of *economic ornithology* in America have been largely concerned with analyzing and tabulating what birds eat and how their feeding habits affect the interests of man. The federal government, after 1885, led in this work, especially in studies of the stomach contents of birds to show the value of their feeding habits to farmers by the suppression of insects and rodents destructive to agriculture. See historical reviews by McAtee (1933b); Cameron (1929); Leedy (1961). Government studies of the food habits of songbirds, waterfowl and other game birds were also useful because of the great demand among sportsmen and bird and garden clubs for information on what to plant to attract birds. See Cottam (1939); Martin and Uhler (1939); McAtee (1939; 1940b). *See also* Bird-attracting.

The study of food habits has proved one of the ways to gain understanding of the needs of wildlife. Knowing the foods of birds and mammals and their shelter requirements (habitats), biologists and game managers are able to alter the environment favorably, especially the plant environment, to encourage an increase in numbers or varieties of certain wild birds and other animals (Martin *et al.*, 1951). However, manipulation of plant environments is only one approach to *wildlife management*. See discussion of some wildlife management practices in Ch. 20 by Smith (1974); see also Allen (1954); Burger (1973); Teague (1971); Trefethen (1964). *See* Songbird and Game-Bird Management.

Although food-habits studies have served as a guide to determine whether some birds and mammals may be beneficial or harmful to the interests of man, and to what extent (most present-day biologists prefer to approach such problems, and their solutions, ecologically—see especially Smith, 1974), this has not always been immediately apparent because of the complexity of the relationships of birds and other animals to the animals and plants they eat. A group of federal biologists, experienced in food-habits studies and their history (Martin *et al.*, 1951), wrote that most species of wildlife were labeled, at one time, in their food habits as "good," "bad," or "indifferent" in their relationships to man, his plants, and his livestock.

With increased understanding of the complexity of wildlife food habits—that species may, and often do, change their food habits seasonally and locally—it became evident that few if any species of birds or other wildlife are always good (economically for man), bad (economically destructive), or indifferent (neither good nor bad). Almost always they were somewhere between. For example, gulls that at times feed on New England's wild blueberry crop are at other times valued as scavengers and insect-eaters; mallard ducks, popular in fall with hunters and always of interest to students of wildlife, are not favored by farmers in the Texas panhandle, where, in winter, the mallards feed heavily on the farmers' sorghum crops.

Meadowlarks, praised most of the time for their role in eating insects destructive to farm crops, in early spring may do extensive damage to sprouting corn in the Carolinas. The American robin, regarded with affection and general approval by almost everyone—it is a symbol of spring to many people, has a cheerful song, and eats many insects that feed on forest trees and farm and garden crops (*see* in biography in Thrush Family, and McAtee, 1933a)—may not be liked at all by those whose cherry trees it may plunder (see Beal, 1915). The introduced starling, disliked by many people because of its aggression against native N. American birds, and its large flocks that assemble from fall to spring on city buildings, is one of the principal enemies, among birds, of the Japanese beetle. See Bent (1950). *See also* in Starling Family.

Because of their numbers, large flocks of birds have the potential of doing either great economic good or considerable harm. McAtee (1946), a federal food-habits investigator, cited examples of the damage that could be caused in rice fields and to other grain crops by large flocks of blackbirds and bobolinks. More recently, flocks of millions of grackles, red-winged blackbirds, cowbirds, and starlings in winter in the Southeast have caused concern as a threat to human health and to farm crops (*see* discussion under Control and Histoplasmosis). See also Meanley (1971a) but see also discussion and analysis by Graham (1976) and Jackson (1976).

During the early years of the federal government's investigations of birds' food habits, it gave much attention to studies of the food habits and depredations of ricebirds (bobolinks), blackbirds, house sparrows, and crows. Later, complaints came from farmers about piñon jays that emerged in flocks from the pinyon-juniper hills to feed in nearby fields of grain. White-necked ravens, moving about in flocks, were accused of damaging sorghums, corn, melons, and peanuts. Horned larks, especially in Calif., after the nesting season moved in flocks of old and young down into the farming valleys, where they fed on young vegetables and seed crops. Flocks of western house finches attacked buds, fruit, and even grains, and crowned sparrows were injurious by their feeding on young garden and ornamental plants and buds and blossoms. See Woods (1932).

Large flocks of waterfowl caused damage to rice crops in Calif. and Ark., to lettuce in Wash., corn in Colo., and buckwheat in Mich. To control their depredations, the government recommended various frightening devices (see account of these in Williams and Neff, 1966) and the opening of special seasons in which the birds could be shot (*see* government restrictions and recommendations under Control). Similar treatment of band-tailed pigeons was required because of their depredations on cherry crops of the West. See Neff (1947).

"It is, of course," wrote McAtee (1946), "flocking birds that become obnoxious by roosting where they are not wanted and whose objectionable presence has called for much study as to means of dislodging roosts or destroying the birds. These comprise chiefly starlings, blackbirds, and feral pigeons but sometimes also such desirable species as purple martins and robins." See more recent discussion of crop damage by birds in George (1966); see also Parker (1966).

In all of these examples there were too many birds of one kind in one place, but the remedies, or controls, "should be local and corrective rather than sweeping and vindictive" (McAtee, 1946).

If flocking birds can do great harm by feeding on crops, they can also do great good by gathering to eat insects that attack, in vast numbers, farm crops. Perhaps the most widely publicized example of the role of birds as protectors of crops was that of gulls in the great plague of "crickets" (long-horned grasshoppers, *Anabrus simplex*) that struck the crops of the Mormon settlers in Utah in 1848 and again in 1855. In grateful appreciation to the birds and to divine providence for saving the settlers from almost certain starvation, the Mormons built the beautiful Sea Gull Monument on Temple Square in Salt Lake City at a cost of more than $40,000. See details in Henderson (1933); *see also* Monuments to Birds.

Meadowlarks have given similar aid against the related coulee cricket, *Peranabrus scabricollis*, in Wash.; infestations of cankerworms in Calif. have been wiped out by flocks of Brewer's blackbirds and of climbing cutworms (*Lampra*) by crows. In Man., it was recommended that farm practices be planned with the view of best utilizing the services of birds in destroying white grubs—a remarkable tribute to the utility of birds, including gulls, terns, crows, and blackbirds, which were found to destroy 90% of the white grubs exposed by plowing.

When the Rocky Mountain locust (see Essig, 1942) was so serious an enemy of crops of the early tillers of the Great Plains (1873–76), gregarious birds, especially the yellow-headed and other blackbirds, completely destroyed the pests locally. In recent times, the outbreaks of other grasshoppers in the same region have been suppressed by mass attacks of Franklin's gulls. In N.C., McAtee (1946) found flocks of native sparrows removing "green bugs," or wheat aphids, at the rate of a million a day on a single farm. Among the most effective enemies of the celery leaf-tier, or "leaf-tyer," caterpillars (the adults are called pyraustid moths) and other insect depredators in the commercial celery-growing region of Fla., have been such flocking species as tree swallows, red-winged blackbirds, and bobolinks.

Many such examples, mostly less spectacular, can be cited. McAtee (1920) in an earlier report, listed 70 examples of the local extermination of plagues of insects and other pest animals by birds. In a modern example, woodpeckers were the most important biological factor in the control of Engelmann spruce beetles in the White River National Forest of Colo. See interesting account by Olson (1953). It seems that in natural control, birds, mammals, weather, other insects, parasites, funguses, and diseases, all working together, are usually necessary to reduce the plague populations of an insect effectively. See also Dowden and Mitchell (1966).

The economic role of birds or of other animals in the complex web of life is impossible to evaluate accurately. W. L. McAtee (see record of this man's remarkable career in economic ornithology in Terres, 1963), after a lifetime of study of the food habits of birds, concluded that they play an important part in the *constant suppression*, rather than outright control, of insect pests. They sometimes curb potential outbreaks and on occasion may even avert disaster, but at other times, as in the periodic outbreaks of tent caterpillars, the birds seem ineffective in coping with them. For an early history of economic ornithology in N. America, see McAtee (1933b); for one of the best recent treatises on the subject of interactions between man and birds, see Murton (1971); for references on the feeding habits and economic value of birds, see Weed and Dearborn (1903); Forbush (1907; 1912); and Henderson (1933). *See* Food and Feeding Habits.

ECOSYSTEM

(ECK-oh-SIS-tem). The members of a community of living plants and animals, with their non-living environment of soil, rocks, waters, heat, light, gravity, etc., are inseparably interrelated and interact upon each other. Any natural unit that includes these living and non-living parts all interacting is an *ecosystem*. The ecosystem is the largest functional unit in ecology, since it includes both living communities of animals and plants (biotic communities) and the abiotic (non-living) environment. Each influences the other and both are necessary for maintaining life as we have it on earth.

Ecosystem is a general term used to refer to areas of different size, depending on context. At one extreme it is used synonymously with *biosphere*, the thin outer shell of the earth, including the oceans and the earth's atmosphere. Ecosystem also refers to habitats such as the eastern deciduous forest and the smaller habitats of lakes and ponds (Odum, 1953).

All living plants and animals affect each other directly or indirectly, and collectively are the living, or biotic, environments. No plant or animal in nature can live alone and its life is dependent on the lives of others and on its environment; thus in any given area all the living organisms constitute an association called a *biotic community*—it is a natural, self-sustaining assemblage of plants and animals, interdependent and sharing the same physical environment or habitat. Biotic communities are not all alike—they differ from each other because of variety, or differences as expressed by such different habitats as an oak woods, a sandy beach, a pine forest, a grassy meadow, each of which has its own characteristic assemblage of plants and animals. See details in Buchsbaum and Buchsbaum (1957) and in Smith, R. L. (1966). *See also* Major Biotic Communities under Distribution.

ECOTONE

(ECK-oh-tone). Term of ecologists for the transitional area between two or more adjacent communities. The ecotone, always linear and narrower than the adjacent communities, may be along the edge of a forest where it parallels the edge of a grassy field or between such huge areas as biomes—*tundra, coniferous forest, deciduous forest,* and *grassland,* for example. *See* Major Biotic Communities under Distribution. The biomes are natural areas in which, undisturbed by man, the plant life reaches a stable "climax" which theoretically will maintain itself indefinitely. The transitional areas between any of these biomes are called *ecotones* (Van Tyne and Berger, 1959). *See* Biome.

The ecotone, where one plant community

gives way to another, is an area where there is an overlap in which the plants and animals of the neighboring biomes are intermixed or blended. Besides these, there are plants and animals of the ecotone itself which are often restricted to the ecotone. "The tendency for increased variety and density at community junctions is known as the *edge* effect" (Odum, 1953).

EDGE EFFECT. Aldo Leopold (1933) described "edge" as occurring at places where the types of food and cover which an animal needs come together, or meet, which gives it simultaneous access to more than one kind of environment. In many of his studies of certain game species, Leopold discovered that the edge effect was so impressive that he postulated it as a law of dispersion of game species—that some birds and other animals in particular are "a phenomenon of edge."

Many grouse hunters know by experience that the edges of woods, with grape tangles, haw bushes, and little grassy bays, are the places to look for grouse; quail hunters follow the edge between brushy draws and weedy cornfields; snipe hunters follow the edges of a marsh where it meets a pasture; pheasants often nest in the outer edges of hayfields where they join fencerows; bobwhite quail and Hungarian partridges choose the edges of open roads and trails for nesting; and even wild turkeys show a tendency to nest at the edges of trails. According to Leopold, edge effect seems most important to those species of game birds that have a low cruising radius, or low mobility.

Birds and other animals that spend the most time in these ecotones, or junctional communities, are sometimes called "edge" species (Odum, 1953).

William J. Beecher, in 1937, studied the placement of more than 1,200 wild birds' nests on a tract of 482 acres of upland and marsh near Fox Lake, Ill. (Beecher, 1942). He found that there were more nests, for example, in smaller blocks of cattail marsh than the equivalent acreage of larger ones. That the smaller blocks had more nests was considered a direct function of their much greater amount of edges, or borders. From his studies Beecher concluded that "population density increases directly with increase in number of feet of edge per unit area of the plant society or with the increasing floristic complexity of the environment in terms of communities per unit area."

ECTOPARASITE

A parasite that lives on the outside of a bird's body; some permanently (the feather lice and some mites); others only during a part of their lives (fleas and larvae of the calliphorid flies); and those parasites that alight on a bird temporarily to suck its blood (mosquitoes, midges, and blackflies). All of these suck blood of birds except the feather lice and feather mites that subsist on a bird's feathers and skin.

Some of these ectoparasites are discussed in special articles—fleas under Fleas; louseflies under Hippoboscid Flies; the bluebottle (calliphorid) flies under Protocalliphora; and the chewing lice (Mallophaga) under Lice. Some other ectoparasites—the *ticks, mites,* and *cimicid bugs*—are discussed here. The ticks and mites are arachnids, related to the harvestmen, or "daddy longlegs," and spiders, for example. The cimicid bugs are insects.

TICKS. Harold Peters (1936), a government biologist, reported 198 species of external parasites collected from 255 species of N. American birds east of the Mississippi R. The parasites included lice, hippoboscid flies, mites, and ticks. Ticks were collected from 56 species of birds, and Peters thought it possible that every kind of bird that feeds, or alights, on the ground would carry several kinds of mites and one or more kinds of ticks.

The most widely distributed ectoparasite of Peters' report was the rabbit tick, *Haemaphysalis leporispalustris*, which lives in N. America from Alaska southward. The adults of this tick bite people very rarely (Hubbert *et al.*, 1975), but Peters reported it from 46 species of birds—from grouse, quail, and horned larks to jays, crows, titmice, wrens, mockingbirds, catbirds, thrashers, robins, thrushes, kinglets, starlings, vireos, many wood warblers, meadowlarks, grackles, cowbirds, cardinals, towhees, and many native, mostly ground-dwelling, sparrows. The rabbit tick lives mainly on rabbits and hares, also on dogs, cats, and horses. According to Hubbert *et al.* (1975), the many birds that are hosts to this tick carry it and spread it over a wide area.

The lone star tick, *Amblyomma americanum*, of s.-c. and se. U.S., is also found on birds—bobwhites, the sora (rail), and cardinal (Peters, 1936) and on domestic chickens, and commonly on wild turkeys (Matthysse, 1972). According to Peters (1930), both of these ticks attach themselves by their strong piercing and sucking beaks to the skin at the base of the feathers on top of the bird's head, around its eyes, base of bill, and ear coverts, where the host bird cannot use its bill to get rid of them by preening. *See* Preening.

Ticks are joint-legged, air-breathing arachnids of the superfamily Ixodoidea of the order Acarina, and may attach themselves to a bird either as larvae, nymphs, or adults. There are about 300 species in the world; they are usually brown or red-brown, as they feed entirely on blood, and when fully engorged may be up to one half inch long or more, whereas mites (ticks are really large mites) are so tiny they may be seen in detail only under a microscope or with a high-power hand lens (Rothschild and Clay, 1957).

SOME EFFECTS OF TICKS ON BIRDS. Ticks, by sucking blood, with the head embedded in a bird's skin, can cause blindness and anemia in birds and death by loss of blood (Matthysse, 1972), especially in young birds. Blake, C. H. (1964), at Hillsboro, N.C., in banding birds over many years, found ticks on them, mostly the tick *Ixodes brunneus*, and in winter (Oct.–Apr.) about the heads of 11 species of birds—Carolina wren, mockingbird, hermit thrush, cardinal, purple finch, rufous-sided towhee, slate-colored (dark-eyed) junco, field sparrow, white-crowned and white-throated sparrows, and song sparrow. He found two or three ticks on a bird not uncommonly, and at most, ten.

The ticks had attached themselves close to the eyes of the birds, which had caused a partial closing of the eyelids, but apparently without causing damage to the eyes themselves. See also Worth (1942a). Boyd (1951), however, reported that the tick *Ixodes brunneus* may be so voracious that the bird host may be unable to fly and even dies from its attacks.

In Ark., Ruth Thomas (1941) reported a wild slate-colored (dark-eyed) junco that in Nov. 1936 alighted on her hand, then fluttered to her shoulder, and made its way uncertainly along her arm. The bird was not a tame one (*see* Tameness) but was almost blind from a large tick that had fastened itself below the bird's right eye. In Mar. 1936, she had caught in one of her bird-banding traps another junco that had been almost blinded by a tick just below its left eye. She removed the ticks from both birds by first smearing the tick and infected skin area with olive oil (Vaseline would also do), which kills the tick by plugging its respiratory pores. Then she pulled off the tick slowly with a pair of small tweezers. The olive oil apparently helps heal the area where the tick has been attached to the bird host. See discussion by Thomas (1941).

Williams (1947) found some of the nestlings of prairie falcons, golden eagles, and sparrow hawks (American kestrels) he was banding in Colo. so heavily infested with the tick *Ornithodorus aquilae* that their eyes were almost closed; Webster, H. M. (1944) reported that 65% of young prairie falcons he studied starved during their first month of life through weakness from the blood-sucking of ticks.

Baerg (1944) studied the incidence and effects of the tick *Ixodes baergi* on nestling cliff swallows at a low-placed nesting colony in Ark. and found that these ticks caused only slight damage to the birds. He took as many as 18 ticks from a single nestling swallow that were clustered on its head, chin, forehead, and eyelids. Apparently, however, it is the ground-nesting or ground-dwelling birds that are most infested with ticks, according to Ali (1963) and other authorities. For some other reports of ticks on birds, see Wharton (1931) in S.C., Herman (1938) in Mass., and Snetsinger and Bordner (1966; 1967) in N.J.

SOME BIRDS THAT EAT TICKS. According to McAtee (1911a), the killdeer and upland plover (sandpiper) eat ticks that are disease-carrying and annoying pests of cattle. The black-billed magpie picks off, and eats, ticks from the backs of wild elk, mule deer, and bighorns. The groove-billed and smooth-billed anis eat ticks so frequently that one of their common names is tick bird. Joseph Dixon in Sequoia National Park, Calif., in Mar. 1944, watched a California (scrub) jay alight on the back of a mule deer and hunt for, and pick off, wood ticks from its back.

MITES. These are the smallest of all arthropods and, along with the similar but much larger ticks, belong to the order Acarina. The tiny mites, so small that it is necessary to use a microscope to study their structure, have rounded bodies, eight legs when adult, and the head and thorax are fused together as in spiders and other arachnids. They may be pale-colored or red, are more or less flattened, and have sucking mouth parts. Of the parasitic mites on birds, the best-known group, the red mites (Dermanyssidae), hide and breed in birds' nests and creep out at night to suck blood from their bird hosts (Rothschild and Clay, 1957).

Two common species of this group attack N. American birds. The chicken mite, *Dermanyssus gallinae*, common on poultry, has been taken in e. U.S. from the chimney swift, barn swallow, and house wren, according to Peters (1936). The northern fowl mite, *Liponyssus (Ornithonyssus) sylviarum*, a serious pest of poultry, is even commoner on wild birds. Of 62 species of birds carrying mites, Peters (1936) reported 22 east of the Mississippi R. from which the northern fowl mite has been collected—from the great crested flycatcher and eastern phoebe to swallows, blue jay, common crow, house wren, gray catbird, brown thrasher, American robin, starling, vireos, warblers, and native sparrows.

Both the chicken mite and the northern fowl mite suck the blood of birds, and the northern fowl mite is an especially voracious feeder. It remains on its host most of the time and lives on the skin, on the wings, or near the bird's vent (Boyd, 1951). See descriptions of these mites and their life histories in Matthysse (1972).

Other blood-sucking mites are "chiggers," the larval form of members of the family Trombiculidae. One of these, *Trombicula irritans*, Peters (1936) reported from 9 species of birds, all in the Southeast, from Va. to Fla. and La.

The mites most seen on birds are the feather mites of the family Analgesidae and related groups. These mites are not blood-suckers but spend their lives intimately associated with a bird's feathers, feeding on feathers and the horny layers of a bird's skin. Some members of this family are found exclusively on the wing, or flight, feathers of large birds; the genus *Analges* and its allies contain feather mites that are found on all parts of a bird's plumage except the wing feathers (Rothschild and Clay, 1957). None of the feather mites is a major pest, at least not on poultry (Matthysse, 1972).

Some of the mites (family Analgesidae) are flat, 1 mm. long (about 1/25 in.), and with a captured bird in the hand, may be most easily seen crawling along the barbules of the longer wing feathers (Peters, 1930). *See* barbules under Feather. According to Kelso and Nice (1963), the mouth parts of the feather mites are not strong enough to chew feathers, therefore they eat flaked-off bits of the bird's skin and feather lipid (fatty substances) exuded by the feathers. See also Dubinin (1951).

Skin lesions (scales and crusts) may be caused especially on the legs and feet of birds by tiny itch mites, which are best known as skin parasites of dogs and men. One, the scaly-leg mite of the genus *Knemidocoptes* (family Sarcoptidae), infects not only poultry but also wild birds. Some infestations of these may be severe and can cause depluming of feathers (pulled out by the birds themselves) and mange. See Matthysse (1972) for details.

Carothers *et al.* (1974) reported an outbreak in evening grosbeaks in which the birds developed light-colored scabs or encrustations on their bills and feet. These developed to such a degree in some grosbeaks that parts of their feet broke off and they had difficulty in walking or perching.

OTHER EFFECTS OF MITES ON BIRDS. All red mites (family Dermanyssidae) are true bloodsuckers and when present in large numbers on birds, especially on young ones, may cause them to die of anemia or to bleed to death (Rothschild and Clay, 1957). Allen and Kellogg (1937) wrote that they knew from experience that blood-sucking mites "killed young house wrens, redstarts, Louisiana waterthrushes, phoebes, and other birds." Mites heavily infesting the parent birds may cause them so much nervousness that they cannot properly incubate their eggs, which fail to hatch, or may not be able to properly brood their young.

The chicken mite *(Dermanyssis gallinae)* is a transmitter of fowl cholera from bird to bird, of fowl spirochete, and is a reservoir for the virus of equine encephalitis, as is the northern fowl mite. *See* Diseases; see also Matthysse (1972) for the role of ticks and mites as carriers of diseases of birds and of man, and their control.

Birds eliminate mites and ticks and other ectoparasites from their bodies by preening with the bill, by dust bathing, water bathing, and "anting." *See* Anting; Bathing; Preening. Birds with deformed bills *(see* Deformities) that cannot preen efficiently, or at all, may become heavily infested with ectoparasites. Molting, or loss of feathers in late summer, induces a sharp drop in the number of ectoparasites—mites, for example—on a bird (Boyd, 1951).

CIMICID (SIGH-mih-sid) **BUGS.** These insects of the order Hemiptera, family Cimicidae, resemble their close relatives in the family, the bedbugs, in their habits; however, they live in birds' nests instead of in houses. Very few of the hemipteran bugs are parasitic on birds (Rothschild and Clay, 1957), but in N. America, the Mexican chicken bug, *Haematosiphon inodorus*, of sw. U.S., also known as the poultry bug because it is common in poultry houses, lives in the nests of wild birds.

R. L. Usinger (1947) collected for the first time some of these bugs from the nests of wild birds when he discovered them in nests of the California condor in that state and of the great horned owl in Okla. Since this bug's first scientific description in 1892 by Alfredo Duges, no one up until Dr. Usinger's discovery had published records of it from other than poultry houses (Lee, 1959; see also Lee, 1955a; 1955b). Later, Lee (1955b) found this bug on a new host, the wild turkey, in N.M. and Ariz., and also reported it (1959) from cliffside nests of barn owls in Calif. The bugs were not only in the barn owls' nests but in crevices on the face of the cliff around the nest opening. These small brown bugs suck the blood of their bird hosts while the birds are in the nest, and unlike the bedbugs associated with people, which feed in darkness or subdued light, seem to prefer light.

Platt (1975) reported the effects of the Mexican chicken bug on bird hosts. In May 1974, adult prairie falcons on a cliff in ne. N.M. abandoned their clutch of three eggs because their nest was infested with these bugs. He also reported that two broods of young prairie falcons—four in one nest, three in the other—died from infestations of the bug, also two young red-tailed hawks.

Other cimicid bugs also suck the blood of bird hosts. Baerg (1944) found *Oeciacus vicarius*, the American swallow bug, in the nests of a colony of cliff swallows in Ark.; it also lives in the nests of barn swallows. Another cimicid bug of birds, about which practically nothing is known, or its effects on its bird host, is *Synxenoderus cosmosus*, the parasitic bug of white-throated swifts of w. U.S. A fourth species is *Hesperocimex coloradensis*, reported on the gray-breasted martin in Mexico and on other swallows, and *Cimexopsis nyctalis*, yet another member of the Cimicidae family, on chimney swifts in e. and c. U.S. According to Lee (1959), very little is known about these insects.

EDGE EFFECT AND "EDGE" SPECIES
See Ecotone.

EELGRASS
(Zostera marina). The sudden disappearance of this plant in the 1930s caused a worldwide decline in the brant population *(see* in Duck Family). A submerged marine plant that lives only in salt or brackish waters, it usually grows to a depth of about 10 ft., but far off the s. Calif. coast, to a depth of more than 100 ft. (Cottam and Munro, 1954). Its N. American range is along both the Atlantic and Pacific coasts—from Greenland to the Gulf of Mexico, and from Alaska to Calif. Along the Atlantic coast before the 1930s, eelgrass was the staple winter food of brant, and a valuable food for Canada geese, scaups, and black ducks (waterfowl eat its seeds, leaves, and rootstocks) and scoters, goldeneyes, the oldsquaw, bufflehead, and mallard (McAtee, 1915).

Suddenly, in 1931–32, the vast beds of eelgrass disappeared from waters off the Atlantic coast and from other parts of the world, a disaster described by plant pathologists as the most destructive in the history of plants and their diseases. With the disappearance of the eelgrass, bay bottoms formerly bound by the plant washed and eroded, and the brant went into a rapid decline in numbers around the world (Scott, 1964). See also accounts by Cottam and Addy (1947) and Lincoln (1950a).

Before 1930, eelgrass made up 80% of the winter food in N. America of the Atlantic coast brant *(see* Stenophagous). Without their main food, large wintering flocks along the Atlantic coast wandered from place to place and many died. The federal government imposed a closed season on hunting them, and by 1935, the brant had apparently adjusted to a new diet, and had begun to increase from a low of 22,400 in the early 1930s to a peak of about 265,000 in 1961. Because the eelgrass die-off was not as severe in Pacific waters, the black brant there suffered far less; in the 1960s it numbered about 100,000 to 175,000 birds (Barry, 1964). *See* in Duck Family.

The loss of eelgrass in the decade 1930–40 appeared not only to have decimated the brant but affected their migration, wintering places, and, perhaps most of all, their diet. Formerly most of the brant of the Atlantic coast wintered on Pamlico Sound, N.C.; by 1954, only a small fraction of the population migrated that far south; in many places along the Atlantic coast, flocks were wintering, for example, in bays of s. N.J., where they made sea lettuce, or sea cabbage (*Ulva* and *Enteromorpha*), and other algae their principal foods (Cottam and Munro, 1954). The brant were also seen feeding, or grazing, on the uplands, a habit unheard of on their winter range in former years. At Atlantic City, N.J., brant became a local nuisance on an athletic field and a hazard at an airport where they grazed by the hundreds (Addy, 1964). With their change to a main diet of sea lettuce, the brant lost their appeal as a game bird because the sea lettuce produced a disagreeable taste in their flesh (Barry, 1964).

In time, eelgrass began to recover, and by the mid-1940s colonies of the plant became established in hundreds of places along the Atlantic coast; since the 1950s, in some places, it was comparable to its former abundance.

Many theories about the cause of the abrupt and almost complete loss of eelgrass in 1931 have been suggested, but the losses from what appeared to be a killing disease were attributed mostly to an amoebalike mycetozoan, *Labyrinthula* (Addy, 1964, and Cottam and Munro, 1954).

EGG

See Fertilization; *also* Eggs and Egg-laying.

EGG BIRD

Common name for birds such as gulls, terns, and murres whose eggs were, and still are in some parts of the world, eaten by people. *See* Legal Protection.

EGG-BOUND

See Eggs and Egg-laying.

EGG-BREAKER

See Egg Tooth.

EGG-EATING

A habit of ravens, crows, jays, skuas, and many gulls, which feed, not only themselves but their young, the nourishing contents of the eggs of other birds. Eggs are apparently an important food for many birds and other animals during the spring and summer nesting season, and the bird victims may be compensated for the losses of their eggs by their own perseverance in re-nesting and re-laying. Two European investigators, as reported by Lawrence (1958), discovered that the mean, or average, life expectancy of the chaffinch in the wild is 2½ years. This is unusually long for a passerine, or songbird, and may have evolved as a compensating factor, counterbalancing the heavy losses of its eggs, in its open nests, to crows, jays, and squirrels. The pair repeatedly re-nests after destruction of its eggs until an average of one or two young chaffinches are produced by a pair each season. *See* discussion of adjustment to egg destruction in Eggs and Egg-laying.

Bobwhite quail (*see* in Pheasant Family), a ground-nesting bird, is also a persistent re-nester, even though its clutches of eggs may be repeatedly eaten by such animals as foxes, raccoons, opossums, roving dogs, crows, jays, and snakes. If a pair of bobwhites themselves escape destruction, they will persevere until they raise a brood, even though it is late in the nesting season (Stoddard, 1931). According to Lack (1954), the chief factor affecting the numbers of birds is probably adult mortality, not loss of eggs or young. Some other birds that eat or otherwise destroy eggs of other birds include the house wren (*see* discussion under Territory) and some ducks, turnstones, and oystercatchers, which have been seen eating the eggs and young of terns. The bristle-thighed curlew, ruddy turnstone, golden plover, and possibly the whimbrel also eat eggs of colonially nesting seabirds (Webster, 1941), and American coots in Minn. have been seen eating eggs from nests of Franklin's gulls, red-winged blackbirds, and pied-billed grebes (Burger, 1973). Birds, along with certain mammals and reptiles, are probably the main eaters of birds' eggs. *See* Mammals and Birds; Reptiles and Birds.

A question often asked, "Why don't birds that eat eggs, eat those in their own nests?" has been answered by the Heinroths (1958), who wrote that crows and gulls "consider their own nest taboo and will protect anything in it as long as it looks something like an egg or a young bird." *See* Do Birds Recognize Their Own Eggs? under Eggs and Egg-laying; *see also* Young and Their Care.

Tinbergen (1953a) provides an interesting account of how some birds eat eggs. Herring gulls eat eggs of other herring gulls or of other birds that nest in the open, such as terns, oystercatchers, and eider ducks, if the eggs are unguarded by the parent birds. *See* discussion under Nests and Nesting; *also* Cannibalism. Usually the gull eats the egg on the spot, but sometimes carries it away by holding it between its mandibles, or may swallow it whole and disgorge the whole egg later to eat it or to feed it to its young. Crows, however, first peck a hole in the egg, then thrust the lower mandible into the hole, close the bill, then carry the egg in flight with the hole up so as not to lose a drop of the contents.

Beebe (1906) cited the "ingenious" method of a raven in South Africa in opening an egg in an ostrich's nest. The shells were too tough for the bird to crack with its bill. When the incubating ostrich left the eggs, the raven flew high over the nest and dropped a stone into it. The stone cracked one of the eggs, at which the raven flew down and ate the yolk as it poured from the shell.

Brown and Amadon (1968) give possible credibility to this remarkable habit in the black-breasted buzzard kite, *Hamirostra melanosternon*, of northern and interior Australia. According to aborigines, the bird drops stones on the eggs of emus (and bustards) to break them, but first alights on the ground and advances toward the incubating emu, which it drives from the nest by a threat display with its opened wings. It then flies up and drops a stone or clod of earth into the nest, then descends to eat the contents of the cracked or broken eggs. Brown and Amadon think the story unlike-ly but cite the proved behavior of the Egyptian vulture, *Neophron percnopterus*, which breaks ostrich eggs by hurling stones at them (see Van Lawick-Goodall, 1969), as making the kite story more credible. *See also* Tool-using. *See also* the methods of many birds in cracking open shelled animals under Mollusks and Birds; *see also* Food and Feeding Habits.

EGG RULE

An ecological rule that the average clutch size, or number of eggs in a set (*see* Clutch), laid by passerines, or songbirds and birds in several other orders, tends to increase as one moves north in latitude. In the European robin, *Erithecus rubecula*, for example, the average number of eggs per set increases from 3.5 in the Canary Is. to 6.3 in n. Europe. *See* Eggs and Egg-laying.

EGGS AND EGG-LAYING

Perhaps few natural objects are more interesting than the eggs of birds. They range in size from the smallest—those of the vervain hummingbird, *Mellisuga minima*, of Hispaniola and Jamaica, which are less than ½ in. long—to the largest known—those of some of the extinct elephant birds of Madagascar, whose eggs were 13 in. long and 9½ in. in diameter at their widest part (Van Tyne and Berger, 1959). Each elephant bird egg weighed about 18 lbs. and had a capacity of 2 gals. One of them could hold the contents of 33,000 eggs of the vervain hummingbird (Welty, 1962); of 6 ostrich eggs; or 148 eggs of a domestic hen (Wallace, 1955).

The smallest bird, the bee hummingbird (*Mellisuga helenae*), lays the smallest eggs. The largest egg of any living bird is that of the ostrich—6.8 by 5.4 in. Egg sizes of other large birds are: wandering albatross, about 5.7 by 3.5 in.; mute swan, 4.5 by 2.9 in.; California condor, 4.3 by 2.6 in.; trumpeter swan, 4.3 by 2.8 in.; common loon and white pelican, 3.5 by 2.2 in.; razorbill, 3 by 1.9 in. (Berger, 1961). For the contents of a bird's egg *see* Embryo and Its Development.

Small birds in general lay eggs that are heavier in proportion to their body weight than those of larger birds. For example, a small wren lays an egg that is 13% of its body weight, but an ostrich one that is only 1.7% of its body weight (Welty, 1962).

The kiwis of New Zealand lay very large eggs relative to their size—18–25% of the bird's body weight (Pitman, 1964a).

Some birds that have *precocial* young lay eggs that are relatively larger than the eggs of similar-sized birds with *altricial* young (*see* these terms under Altricial). The precocial eggs contain much more nutritive material and require longer to hatch but the young emerge much more developed. For example, the killdeer (*see* Plover Family), which is about the size of a robin, lays "precocial eggs" that are larger than those of the altricial robin; the eggs of the killdeer require about 26 days to hatch, but the young are able to run about a few minutes after emerging from the egg. On the other hand, the smaller eggs of the robin hatch in only about 13 days, but the young are helpless and in a much more primitive condition at hatching than the precocial young of the kill-

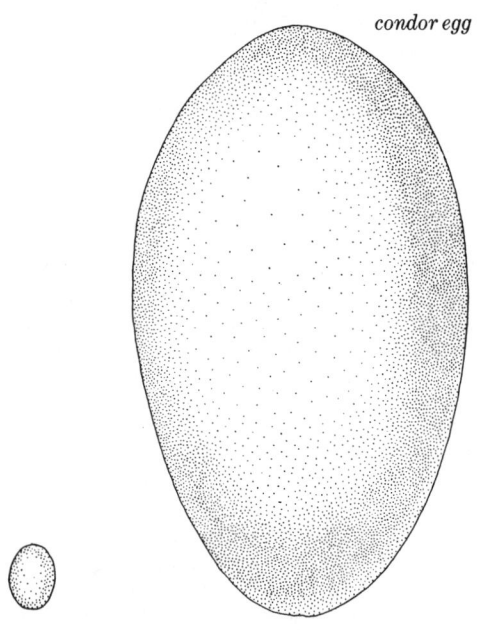

condor egg

hummingbird egg

EGGS AND EGG-LAYING

The California condor, one of the largest flying birds, lays an egg about 4.3 inches by 2.6 inches. A hummingbird's 1/2-inch egg is only about 1/33,000 the size of the largest egg, that of the extinct elephant bird of Madagascar.

deer. The young robins stay in the nest another 10–14 days before they are able to leave and then they flutter about, still under the parents' care. *See* Young and Their Care.

The eggs of birds within each species vary in size as do those of individual birds; occasionally a bird will lay a runt egg, which is considerably smaller than the smallest egg it normally lays. These abnormal eggs usually do not hatch, are probably laid by all species of birds at some time, and have been reported for the eared grebe, Swainson's thrush, yellow-breasted chat, house finch (Berger, 1961), and common tern. For an account of runt, or dwarf, eggs laid by other species and possible causes of them, see Rothstein (1973).

Double-yolked eggs are occasional; triple-yolked eggs very rare. Multiple-yolked eggs are believed to be the result of the simultaneous development and release of two or more ripened ova into the female oviduct from her ovary. If a double-yolked egg is fertilized and successfully hatched, the egg produces fraternal twins (Berger, 1961). According to the New York *Journal-American*, Apr. 7, 1954, when a poultryman of the area watched twin baby chicks hatch from a single egg, it was the first in his 36 years in the business. Berger reported that three American songbirds—a goldfinch, a song sparrow, and a brown thrasher—each laid an egg from which a twin embryo hatched (Berger, 1961). Twins from *single-yolked* eggs are very rare but have been reported from pigeons (Hollander and Levi, 1940).

Either shell-less or soft-shelled eggs are laid frequently by domestic birds, but are little known among wild birds. Berger once found a shell-less egg in the nest of a Traill's flycatcher, and Terres (1936–70) watched a female common grackle expel a shell-less egg from her cloaca onto the grass in Central Park, New York, on May 2, 1955. It appeared to have a normal yolk and egg white.

The Romanoffs, in their studies of eggs, concluded that "the immediate cause of shell-less eggs is either a failure of the glands in the shell-secreting portion of the oviduct, or violent peristalsis, which hurries the egg through this region [of the oviduct] before a shell can be formed. . . . Experiments . . . show that calcium starvation is not necessarily a causative factor in the production of shell-less eggs, as was once thought" (Romanoff and Romanoff, 1949).

The eggshell—the calcified layer that surrounds any normal avian egg—is mostly calcium carbonate, present as calcite, with small amounts of magnesium, sodium, potassium, phosphate, chloride, and citric acid (Tyler, 1964).

The word "egg," as popularly used, includes the ovum and associated materials (yolk, albumen) enclosed with shell membranes and shell. *See* Fertilization.

"Only a small percentage of the oocytes (undeveloped ova) in the ovary of the female bird at hatching time ever mature"(Berger,1961). Each is enclosed in a thin covering tissue called a follicle. Witschi (1956) reported that the ovary of a 13-day-old red-winged blackbird or starling contains about 100,000 oocytes, of which only about 50 will grow and be released from the ovary during the bird's lifetime. There is slow,

microscopic growth of about 100 or more oocytes during winter and early spring in starlings, and though most of them are resorbed by the bird, a series begins to accumulate yolk rapidly. As the amount of yolk increases, the ovarian follicles move toward the surface of the ovary and finally protrude from it (Berger, 1961).

The final growth to form mature ova takes about 4–7 days. Ovulation is the rupture of the mature follicle and the release of the ovum (yolk) into the oviduct, as in mammals. It is fertilized by the male's sperm just after it enters the oviduct. *See* Fertilization. In the domestic hen the egg develops as follows:

As the ripened ovum (egg yolk) bursts from the hen's ovary and passes into the general body cavity, it is gripped by the nearby funnel-like opening of the *infundibulum*, which is the beginning section of the hen's oviduct. The oviduct, through which the egg passes, is a long convoluted tube. It has five sections—infundibulum, magnum, isthmus, uterus, and vagina—each performing a different function (Sturkie, 1965).

The egg, when ejected from the ovary, contains at this stage the ovum plus yolk; it remains in the infundibulum for about 18 minutes, after which it is passed by peristalsis (muscular contraction of the wall of the oviduct) into the *magnum*, which is the longest section of the oviduct and where most of the egg white (albumen) of the egg is formed. After about 3 hours in the magnum, it is passed on, again by peristalsis, from the magnum to the *isthmus*. After about an hour in the isthmus, where the developing egg has received its inner and outer shell membranes, it moves on into the *uterus*. The ovum remains in the uterus for about 20 hours and 40 minutes, during which time it receives its shell, and the pigments that color the shell, which are added during the last 5 hours before the egg is laid.

Finally the completed egg passes quickly through the muscular vagina, which is the part of the oviduct leading from the uterus to the cloaca, from which the egg is expelled into the nest (Sturkie, 1965).

According to Weidmann (1964), some birds may lay an egg after 1–3 minutes of bearing down (contracting the abdominal muscles) and an egg that is ready to be laid can also be held back—a cowbird (which can expel its egg in seconds) is thus able to withhold an egg until its host leaves the nest. Many songbirds postpone laying while quickly building a new nest. Kuerzi (1941) discovered that female tree swallows may suspend egg-laying for up to 7 days during cloudy, cool weather. Some birds, when ready to lay and a nest of their own is not available, may deposit their egg, or the entire clutch, in the nest of another. *See* examples under Dump Nests.

Many species of birds lay early in the morning, the ovenbird and cedar waxwing, for example, even before sunrise; most passerines, or songbirds, lay their eggs shortly after sunrise and many lay an egg each day until the clutch is completed (Davis, 1955; Van Tyne and Berger, 1959). There are many exceptions among birds to early-morning laying—the smooth-billed ani lays its eggs in the afternoon;

many pheasants lay their eggs in the evening; the American coot shortly after midnight (Gullion, 1954); and the ringed plover, *Charadrius hiaticula*, lays its eggs at all hours of the day or even at night. See Stoddard (1931) and Welty (1962) for details about other species; see Skutch (1952) for some tropical American birds.

A bobwhite requires 3–10 minutes at the nest to lay an egg; turkeys and geese are reported to labor at laying an egg for 1–2 hours (Weidmann, 1964). A bird that cannot lay her eggs is said to be *egg-bound*, a condition that may be caused by inflammation or stricture of the oviduct or by a tumor. At times a malformed or oversized egg or a soft-shelled one may be responsible for the condition and may kill the bird. See Weidmann (1964) and Peckham (1972). *See* an example in the biography of the Black-headed gull in Gull Family.

The smaller, more pointed end of the egg (usually protruded first by the domestic hen from her cloaca during laying) may be heavily marked in those eggs of wild birds that have scrawls, spots, splotches, and other color markings on the shell, but if the narrow, or pointed, end is protruded first, as with eggs of some of the Falcon Family, the pointed end will get the heavy markings. The eggs laid by each female are often individually distinctive, which is probably due to heredity (Pitman, 1964a).

Shortly after the egg is laid, an air chamber develops at the blunt end of the egg. It is formed between the two egg membranes that lie against the inside of the shell. Small at first, the air space grows as the embryo develops; its expansion represents the evaporation of water from the egg. Some hours before hatching, the head of the embryo changes position, bringing the bill in contact with the eggshell membrane, which it pierces. At that point the bird begins to breathe the air in the air space (Berger, 1961). *See* Embryo and Its Development; *also* Hatching.

Many birds lay white or nearly white eggs, as do reptiles, and it is thought that originally all birds' eggshells were white—the primitive condition—and that natural selection (*see* Natural Selection) may have later favored colored eggs in birds, owing to the protective coloration and markings of such eggs, which are usually less conspicuous than white ones. *See* especially in Plover Family. This theory has gained support by the fact that certain birds that nest in hollows in trees or in burrows in the ground, where the eggs are usually hidden from the sight of natural enemies that would eat them, lay white eggs. Examples are swifts, some owls, most petrels, parrots, woodpeckers, kingfishers, and certain other birds. According to Allen (1961), wrens, nuthatches, chickadees, crested flycatchers, and bluebirds, all of which build "unnecessary" nests at the bottom of the tree cavities in which they nest (and lay colored eggs), must have recently (in an evolutionary way) developed the hole-nesting habit.

Birds that lay white eggs in open nests—some doves, herons, hummingbirds, owls, and grebes, for example—begin to incubate with the laying of the first egg (Welty, 1962), thus hiding the eggs during the period that the bird is on the nest. Ground-nesting birds that lay white eggs—some ducks, geese, grebes, and many gallinaceous birds—cover their eggs with plants or grasses just before they leave the nest. This hides the conspicuous white eggs from the sight of foxes, skunks, raccoons, crows, snakes, dogs, and other animals that would eat them. No eggs are entirely safe, however, whether white and hidden or of protective colors. Even black bears are a threat (see Dixon, 1927a; DeWeese and Pillmore, 1972; Franzreb and Higgins, 1975), and may gnaw at the nesting holes of woodpeckers to get at the eggs or young. *See* Egg-eating; Mammals and Birds.

White eggs are occasionally laid by birds that ordinarily lay colored eggs. Bluebirds, for example, sometimes lay a clutch of all-white, or so-called albino, eggs (Laskey, 1943a). Birds that lay colored or tinted eggs greatly outnumber birds that lay pure-white eggs—either solid colors of white or off-white marked with various lines, scratches, and scrawls, which are often elaborate (Van Tyne and Berger, 1959). The pigments (porphyrins) responsible for the colors and patterns of eggshells are produced by the breakdown of hemoglobin from ruptured red blood cells. Transformed into bile pigments, these are carried to the uterus by the blood to be deposited in the developing shell (Romanoff and Romanoff, 1949).

Many birds lay eggs that are uniformly colored—some cormorants, starlings, thrushes, and herons lay blue or green-blue eggs; catbirds lay green eggs; ostriches, ivory-colored ones; they are pale green in many ducks, dark green in the emus; olive brown in some bitterns; the tinamous of S. America lay extremely variable-colored very glossy eggs—blue, green, mauve, and purplish pink. In Europe, Cetti's warbler lays eggs that are deep brick red; some birds occasionally lay reddish (erythristic) eggs, then later return to laying normally colored eggs.

There is a strong tendency for birds of allied species to lay similarly colored eggs, which, in addition to other characters of the birds, have been used for identification or to show relationships (Pitman, 1964a). Studies by McCabe and Deutsch (1952) and Sibley (1960) showed that the proteins in egg white differed in structure from group to group, and that those of more closely related birds showed fewer differences than those of more distantly related groups. By the use of electrophoresis, a technique that causes the different proteins to separate and move in a charged field, various taxonomically important information can be determined. See Sibley (1970) and Sibley and Alquist (1972); *see also* hoatzin in Cuculiformes.

When a bird lays an egg, the shape of it, depending on the species, might be oval, round, conical, elliptical, or biconical, with each capable of various shapes, but within species the eggs are alike and within each group of birds the egg shapes usually show resemblances (Pitman, 1964a). The shapes of the eggs necessarily conform somewhat to the limitations of the oviduct (Wallace, 1963), and are probably acquired in the magnum of the oviduct. Diameter and muscular tension on walls of the oviduct probably play a part in the egg's shape; birds with a deep pelvis usually lay round eggs; birds

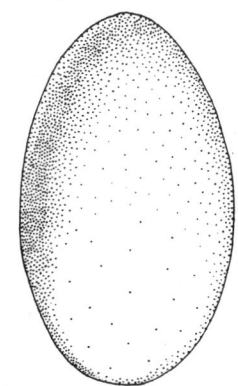

oval (Jacana)

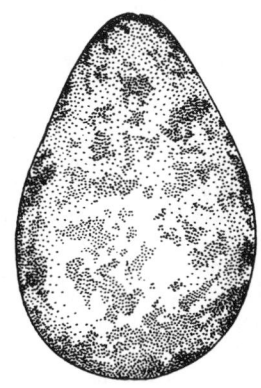

pyriform (Semipalmated sandpiper)

long elliptical (Western grebe)

short elliptical (Rough-legged hawk)

EGGS AND EGG-LAYING

with a dorsoventrally compressed pelvis are inclined to lay elongate eggs (Welty, 1962).

Owls (Strigiformes) lay round eggs, as do kingfishers; swallows and swifts lay elongate ones; auks, murres, and other alcids (*see* Alcids) lay pointed, pear-shaped eggs, which is believed to be an adaptation to the cliff-nesting site: a pear-shaped egg will pivot about its axis rather than roll off the cliff as a round egg would (Wallace,1963). The pear-shaped (pyriform) egg is characteristic of many birds that lay four eggs in a nest—plovers for example. Owing to the shape, they lie with their pointed ends almost meeting in the center of the nest, where they occupy a minimal space and are more easily covered by the relatively small brooding parent. *See* Brooding, *also* Incubation.

Birds lay from 1 to 23 eggs in a clutch (*see* Clutch). Ovulation—the release of the ovum from the ovarian follicle—is caused by the discharge of a hormone (luteinizing hormone) from the anterior pituitary, which secretes more of this hormone into the blood several hours (6–8 in chickens) prior to ovulation. Current evidence indicates that another hormone, arginine vasotocin from the posterior lobe of the pituitary, may be responsible for initiating the uterine contractions that expel the egg from the body (Sturkie, 1976). *See* Fertilization; Endocrine Glands. The number of eggs laid by each species depends upon a variety of factors: food supply, nest site, latitude, and degree of development of the young at hatching (altricial or precocial). Ground-nesting ducks, quail, grouse, pheasants, turkeys, and other game birds, whose eggs and nests are more vulnerable to mammalian predators, lay larger clutches than birds that nest in trees or on inaccessible cliffs and islands.

Lack (1947; 1948) believes that the number of eggs in the clutch of each species has been adjusted by natural selection to the largest number of fledged young (*see* Fledgling) that a pair of birds is capable of producing—that it may be genetically fixed in relation to the food supply available—but Skutch (1949a) found that this did not apply to certain birds in the American tropics.

As a rule (*see* Egg Rule), many birds generally lay fewer eggs in a clutch in the tropics, where the daylight is shorter than in northern latitudes, where more summer food is available during the much longer days (Pitman, 1964a).

Although not a songbird, in the purple gallinule, for example, a bird of the Rail Family, clutches increase from about 3–4 eggs in a set in the tropics to 5–10 eggs in the northern part of its range; for many species of birds, however, such as pigeons and doves, gulls and terns, the number of eggs laid is fixed genetically for a specific number of birds. These determinate layers, as they are called, are not affected by latitudinal distributions, each species laying a fixed number of eggs.

There are seasonal variations in clutch size. Some birds lay more eggs, or have larger clutches, in the first nest of the season; in second or third nests of the season, they may lay a smaller number of eggs (for example, bluebirds). In song sparrows, however, the second clutch is the largest, the third the smallest.

That clutch size in N. America may be correlated with food supply is shown by rough-legged hawks and snowy owls, which lay larger clutches of eggs in years when their main food (lemmings) is plentiful. Barn owls may nest almost continuously during a year when meadow voles (*Microtus*) are at their peak abundance, but lay fewer eggs, or fewer clutches, or even fail to nest when their staple prey is scarce (Wallace, 1963). Other species of hawks and owls also show a food-dependent variation in the size of their clutches.

Certain birds, such as quail, lay smaller clutches in dry years or may not nest at all. *See* Atretic Follicle. Clutch size may vary with the age of the bird—the average clutches may be smaller for birds laying for the first time.

Most birds are *determinate egg-layers;* that is, they lay a certain number of eggs in a clutch and will not lay more even though one or more of their eggs are removed from the nest.

Some determinate layers, for example, are pigeons, doves, plovers and other shorebirds, large birds of prey, gulls and terns, auks and other alcids, and many passerines—crows, black-billed magpies, barn swallows, eastern bluebirds, and tricolored blackbirds (Berger, 1961).

Some birds are *indeterminate layers;* that is, they will continue to lay eggs to replace those removed from the nest. If robbed of its eggs, the common (yellow-shafted) flicker will continue to lay new eggs, or clutches, for a long while, each time replacing those taken from its nesting hole. Bent (1939), an egg collector early in his career, told of taking, in one nesting season, 37 eggs in 49 days from the nest of a flicker. The clutches were laid by the bird in sets of 4, 5, 6, and 7 (the average is 6–8). One of Bent's neighbors, Charles L. Phillips, tried taking one egg each day from a flicker, and leaving one as a "nest" egg, to stimulate the bird to continued laying. He took 71 eggs from the nest in 73 days (Phillips, 1887). The female flicker lays an egg each day; therefore this one rested only two days in the long strain of laying for more than two months. Similar experiments with the laying of ducks, grouse, and other gallinaceous birds, the house wren, and the house sparrow proved that they too are indeterminate layers.

The domestic hen is a good example of a continuous (indeterminate) layer. Although her normal clutch is 11–14, daily removal of the eggs will stimulate her to continue laying. If allowed to lay her normal clutch she will become broody (*see* Brooding) and will begin to incubate her accumulated eggs. Some hens of certain breeds will each lay 300 eggs in a year. An exception was a Black Orpington of New Zealand that laid 361 eggs in 363 days (Romanoff and Romanoff, 1949).

"A single egg in a clutch is laid by most penguins, albatrosses, shearwaters, petrels, gannets, tropic-birds, crab plovers, some auks, potoos, some nightjars, crested swifts, lyrebirds, some sunbirds, and a few others" (Van Tyne and Berger, 1959).

Two eggs are laid in a clutch by loons, boobies, gannets, some penguins, most pigeons and doves, hummingbirds, and many tropical songbirds. A clutch of 3–4 eggs is laid by many plovers, gulls and terns, sandpipers, avocets, and phalaropes; many small songbirds lay clutches of 4–5 eggs; others—wrens, chickadees, titmice, and nuthatches—lay 6–13 eggs in a clutch. Most ducks and gallinaceous birds—quail, pheasants, turkeys, and grouse—lay 6–15 eggs or more, but larger clutches by these birds are usually from the laying of two or three females in the same nest (Van Tyne and Berger, 1959). Herbert L. Stoddard (1931), in his Georgia studies of bobwhite quail, found up to 28 eggs laid by two or three females in a single nest, and up to 40 were reported in one nest. He wrote: "The single eggs occasionally found here and there afield are probably laid by hens whose nests have been destroyed by natural enemies . . . or by hens forced to lay before reaching a nest. . . . An egg cannot be arrested in its development after reaching an advanced state and it must be laid as a matter of course." *See*, however, account (above) of songbirds retaining their eggs; it is possible that gallinaceous birds, also ducks, may not be able to withhold laying—*see* Dump Nest.

Stoddard also reported that where domestic bantam chickens ran at large, they sometimes laid their eggs in the nests of quail, and quail frequently laid their eggs in those of the bantams when the quail became accustomed to coming into farmyards where they were not molested. Of these nests, not one of mixed hatching was reported. In B.C., a man had a broody bantam hen that he discovered one day brooding the eggs of a white-crowned sparrow that had built its nest in his garden (Holdom, 1952). *See* Foster Parents; *also* Young and Their Care.

Cowbirds commonly lay their eggs in the nests of other birds, as this is their life habit (*see* in Troupial Family; *also* Brood Parasitism), but a brown thrasher near South Orange, N.J., laid two fresh eggs in the nest of a wood thrush that contained four eggs of the thrush which had been incubated by the thrush for about a week (Bent, 1948). Brown thrashers have also laid their eggs in the nests of mockingbirds, robins, and cardinals, but this has never been brood parasitism by the thrasher.

An ornithologist in Alta., studying the nesting habits of an island colony of ring-billed gulls, one June day found a freshly laid egg of an American robin in a gull's nest. The robin was not a nesting bird on the island (Munro, 1936).

Two female chipping sparrows laid in one nest, and both were mated to the same male (*see* polygyny under Sexual Relationships). The two females laid a total of 8 eggs, from which 7 young sparrows were raised. Three adult chipping sparrows fed the young birds (Walkinshaw, 1959). *See* other accounts of shared nests under Nests and Nesting. For the number of eggs normally laid in a clutch by each species of N. American bird, see in the biographies of each.

Many birds lay only one clutch of eggs in a season; for example, albatrosses, eagles, hawks, and other birds in which the incubation period is extensive and raising the young to independence requires a long time. Some species may have two or three clutches a season, especially the smaller songbirds. Among the familiar medium and small birds of American gardens, song sparrows, bluebirds and American robins may have two or three; eastern phoebe, house wren, Bewick's wren, and Carolina wren, two, sometimes three; cardinals, gray catbirds, black-capped chickadees, ruby-throated hummingbirds, starlings, barn swallows, tree swallows, and brown thrashers usually two. For suggested reasons for number of eggs laid and broods raised, *see* Brood. *See* related articles of interest under Embryo and Its Development; Nests and Nesting; Young and Their Care. For early ages at which some birds lay, *see* Fertilization; *also* Sexual Maturity.

Some long-lived birds may continue to lay eggs each year to a great age. A captive female herring gull at Morehead City, N.C., laid eggs from 1893 to and including 1934—a span of 42 years (Pearson, 1935). Three captive Canada geese laid annually until their deaths at 29, 29, and 33 years (Flower, 1925). A remarkable record was that of a pair of captive eagle owls, *Bubo bubo*, owned by Mr. Meade-Waldo in England. In 1889, when the male was 53 years old, the female 68, they had bred regularly for 32 years and in that time had raised no less than 93 young (Gurney, 1899). A blue-faced booby recaptured on her nest was still breeding and laying eggs when 22 years old (Clapp and Sibley, 1966). *See* Age; *also* Reproductive Life.

Kaiser, perhaps the oldest-known homing pigeon in history, was still siring young at age 30. *See* Rock dove in Pigeon Family. The average life span of a domestic pigeon, or rock dove, is about 8 years.

After the nest is built (*see* Nests and Nesting), the laying of the eggs which follows is under close control of endocrine glands (*see* Endocrine Glands) and their activity is in turn responsive to environmental influences—length of day, rainfall, temperature, food availability, psychic stimuli, and possibly others. The interval between completing the nest and laying the first egg may be long or short. Some birds begin to lay immediately after finishing the nest (in those that build nests); others wait 2 or 3 days; a few—American goldfinch, for example—may wait a week or more before laying the first egg (Van Tyne and Berger, 1959).

Like the domestic hen, most passerines (songbirds) lay an egg a day until the clutch is completed. *See* Clutch. Usually larger species require a longer interval between laying of eggs. Because the ovum, or egg, will not ordinarily be released into the oviduct until the previously formed egg has been laid, the interval between the laying of each egg depends on the time it takes the oviduct to secrete the layers of albumen, shell membranes, and shell. Cold wet weather may delay the normal pace of egg-laying; also any disturbances (psychic) that upset the hen.

Many songbirds lay early in the morning—purple martin, American robin, cedar waxwing, red-eyed vireo, brown-headed cowbird, American goldfinch, song sparrow (Van Tyne and Berger, 1959); in C. America, the nocturnal pauraque in the Nightjar Family lays after 2 P.M. (Skutch, 1952). Early in their laying period, American coots lay shortly after midnight (Gullion, 1954), and Stoddard (1931) discovered that

bobwhite quail may lay from early morning, progressively later each day, until laying comes late in the evening, at which point a day is skipped and laying resumed early the next morning.

Birds that lay an egg a day, or once every 24 hours, are: most passerines (songbirds), many ducks, some geese, woodpeckers, rollers, small shorebirds, and small grebes; no birds are known to lay successive eggs in less than about 24 hours; birds that lay an egg every 38–48 hours: ostriches, rheas, large grebes, some ducks, swans, herons, bitterns, storks, cranes, bustards, doves, some accipiter hawks, owls, some cuckoos, hummingbirds, swifts, kingfishers. Those that lay an egg every 62 hours: some cuckoos and goatsuckers; at 3-day intervals: emus, cassowaries, and penguins (*Pygoscelis*); those that lay an egg once every 4–5 days: lammergeyer and spotted eagle; once every 5 days: condors and kiwis; every 5–7 days: the booby, *Sula dactylatra*, and some hornbills; those that lay an egg every 4–8 days: some megapodes (*see* Megapode).

DO BIRDS RECOGNIZE THEIR OWN EGGS? *See also* Birds That Can Count under Behavior. In experiments by Noble and Lehrman (1940) with the nesting of the laughing gull on Long Is., N.Y., they discovered it could distinguish its eggs from artificial ones put into its nest that resembled them closely in form and color but could not tell its own eggs from other laughing gulls' eggs that were decidedly different in color tone and markings.

Tinbergen (1953a), in his studies of the nesting behavior of herring gulls, found they were much more attracted to the nesting place, or scrape in the sand, than to their eggs, and would incubate an empty nest while their eggs were laying only a few feet away. They would incubate the eggs of another herring gull and even wooden eggs painted blue or yellow; would incubate rectangular, cylindrical, or prism-shaped eggs, but were very restless trying to sit on wooden eggs with sharp edges, then would desert the nest. This showed, according to Tinbergen, that stimuli of the egg for the gull have to do not so much with color or visual "recognition" of it as an "egg" as with the shape and the *feel* of the egg.

Other egg-recognition tests by investigators of gulls (Kirkman, 1937; Goethe, 1937), of terns (Marples and Marples, 1934; Tinbergen, 1936), and of the black-crowned night heron (Allen and Mangels, 1940) revealed that these species did not recognize their own eggs. See, however, Rothstein (1974) about recognition of cowbirds' eggs by gray catbirds. *See also* Brood Parasitism.

The gray catbird and American robin recognize eggs not their own and will throw from their nests those laid in them by the cowbird. The common murre, which lays on bare rocky cliffs (*see* in Auk Family), has a keen ability to distinguish its eggs from others of its kind. On slanting rock ledges, at times the eggs may roll away from the nest sites. According to Johnson (1941), eggs out of place are ignored by other murres in the colony but are rolled back to the nest site by the owners.

BIRDS THAT CARRY THEIR EGGS. Apparently many species of birds will roll displaced eggs back into the nest, using the bill. This behavior is noticed especially among those birds that nest on the ground, and include gulls, terns, nighthawks, shorebirds, geese, and others. Bent (1929) cites the experience of Walter Hoxie in watching an American oystercatcher carry her eggs from her nest on being disturbed. A clapper rail that accidentally knocked one of its eggs out of the nest picked it up in its bill and replaced it, even from distances up to a foot away (Pettingill, 1938). Hochbaum (1944) reported that local hunting guides at Delta waterfowl marsh in Man. had seen hen mallards carrying eggs in their bills, and Hochbaum himself saw a female shoveler in flight carrying an egg in her bill; she held it between her upper and lower mandibles, near the tip of the bill.

Even birds that nest in trees will carry their eggs. A Florida pileated woodpecker carried away her three eggs, one at a time in her bill, from a hollow tree, the top of which had broken off at the nest-hole site (Truslow, 1970). MacFarlane (1891) cited a remarkable case of a pair of pigeon hawks (merlins) that on being shot at near their nest in a pine tree, apparently carried their eggs to a new site on a muddy bank about 40 yds. away.

Eastern bluebirds (and probably many other birds) pick up in the bill infertile eggs from the nest and carry them some distance away before they drop them (Hartshorne, 1962). *See* sanitary habits under Young and Their Care. Retrieving eggs and putting them back into the nest is, however, another matter. Ground-nesting songbirds (Berger, 1961) and those that build cuplike nests in trees will not attempt to retrieve eggs (Poulsen, 1953), even if one of the eggs is placed only a few inches out of the cup on the nest rim. Grebes, gallinaceous birds, and those hawks, owls, and doves that nest on the ground will, however, attempt to retrieve eggs displaced a short distance from the nest. See interesting experiments in egg retrieval by blue geese and snow geese reported by Prevett and Prevett (1973).

Accounts by John James Audubon and others of the chuck-will's-widow carrying its eggs or young (*see* Young and Their Care) away from the nest have been challenged by Ganier (1964), but on the authority of Wilson (1959) will roll their eggs back into the nest site from up to 6 in. away.

EGG TEMPERATURES

In incubating their eggs (*see* Incubation), birds usually maintain them near a temperature that produces the most rapid development of the embryo and the subsequent hatching of the chicks. This is called the "incubation temperature" and it is the range within which the development of the embryo is possible (Beer, 1964).

According to Witschi (1956), depending on the size of the species of bird, the optimal, or best, temperature for the successful incubation of eggs is 2–4° C. lower (cooler) than the body temperature of the brooding bird. *See* Temperature. At Cleveland, Ohio, Huggins (1941) discovered that the mean temperature of eggs in nests of 37 species of birds—from song sparrow to great blue heron—was 34° C. (93.2°F.), plus or minus 2.38°. (*See* Centigrade for method of converting centigrade temperatures to Fahrenheit). There was little average difference in incubating temperature between eggs laid in nesting boxes (*see* Bird-attracting) by the house wren, purple martin, and tufted titmouse, and those laid by birds in open nests—cuckoos, mourning doves, gray catbirds, American robins, etc.

To get this information, Huggins bored a hole in the eggs and inserted a thermocouple, with wires through the bottom of the nest connecting it to recording instruments in a bird blind, or "hide," from which he made his observations. He sealed the hole in each egg with colodium, which also held the thermocouple in place.

At Anaktuvuk, Alaska, Irving and Krog (1956) reported that 74% of their records of nest temperatures of seven species, during the time the birds were incubating, were between 33° and 37° C. The species they reported on were: pintail (duck), semipalmated sandpiper, yellow wagtail, common redpoll, and tree sparrow. *See also* Eggs and Egg-laying; Embryo and Its Development; Nests and Nesting.

EGG TOOTH
A horny tubercle near the tip of the upper half of bill of a newly hatched bird. *See* Hatching.

EGG-TURNING
See Embryo and Its Development.

EGG WEIGHT
Following are approximate weights of eggs of some N. American birds taken from Wing (1956) and from a more extensive and precise list from Amadon (1943).

Kind of Bird	Egg Weight in Grams
Mute swan	350.0*
Broad-tailed hummingbird	0.5*
Flicker	7.8*
Cowbird	3.2*
Bobwhite (76 eggs averaged)	18.18**
Scaled quail (23 " ")	20.76**
Calif. quail (72 " ")	17.93**
Mountain quail (45 " ")	22.60**
Montezuma quail (22 " ")	19.01**
Gray partridge (35 " ")	26.32**
Common crow (10 " ")	37.95**
Blue jay (10 " ")	11.95**
Gray catbird (10 " ")	7.34**
Cardinal (46 " ")	8.62**
Purple finch (29 " ")	4.19**
American goldfinch (18 " ")	2.72**
Rufous-sided towhee (76 ")	7.55**
Dark-eyed (slate-colored) junco (20 ")	4.47**
Savannah sparrow (57 " ")	3.78**
Vesper sparrow (20 " ")	5.02**
Field sparrow (21 " ")	3.09**
Chipping sparrow (51 " ")	3.01**
Tree sparrow (24 " ")	4.01**
White-throated sparrow (57 " ")	5.38**
Fox sparrow (39 " ")	7.10**
Song sparrow (98 " ")	4.54**
Swamp sparrow (9 " ")	4.41**
Lincoln's sparrow (21 " ")	4.13**
Snow bunting (9 " ")	6.30**

* Wing, 1956; ** Amadon, 1943

EGG-WHITE PROTEIN
See discussion of studies of egg-white proteins and their application in classification of birds under Eggs and Egg-laying; *see also* under Cuckoo Family; Cuculiformes; Galliformes. For accounts of methods of studies of egg-white proteins and their uses in classification, see especially Sibley (1970) and Sibley and Alquist (1972).

EGRET
See in Heron Family.

EIDER
See in Duck Family.

EIDER DOWN
The female common eider (*see* in Duck Family), which nests in colonies around the northern parts of the world, plucks down from her breast with which to line her nest. This is the eider down that is harvested in spring and summer by man, especially in Iceland, where some colonies of this wild sea duck may number up to 10,000 nests (Scott, 1964). Both the eider down and the palatable eggs are a lucrative industry in Iceland, where the eiders are closely protected and encouraged in their nesting. Men who collect the down have learned that each female eider has enough down on her body for about one and one half nests, and so they take part of the down from the eider's nest a few days after the eggs hatch (the best quality) and the second-best quality after the young leave the nest. According to Scott, no artificial substitute has been found and the down from a single nest may be worth about 10 shillings; it requires the down from 35–40 nests to make up a pound. See other details in Austin (1961), and the history of the early destruction of eiders in N. America, and finally the beginning of eider down industry in Canada, under American eider in Kortright (1943).

ELECTROCUTION
Purple martins, screech owls, bald and golden eagles, the Baltimore (northern) oriole and eastern meadowlark, cowbirds, and others have been killed by perching on electrified wires (see especially report by Stewart, 1973, on killing of birds by "electric fences" used on farms). Apparently an electrical circuit is established when a live wire on which a bird is perched is swung by the wind into another live wire. Similarly, an electrical circuit is established when a bird perched on an electrified fence touches the stem (or stems) of any herbaceous plant growing alongside the fence. Eagles have reportedly been killed on wires of high power lines when they spread their wings and touched an adjacent live wire, thus making an electrical circuit, and when a stream of their excreta touched an adjacent wire; purple martins have been electrocuted when they perched on an electrified utility wire and the wind swayed an adjacent live wire into contact with them. *See also* Lightning and Birds under Weather; *also* Accidents; Mortality; see some solutions to the problem in Benton and Dickinson (1966).

ELECTROPHORESIS
A method of analyzing the egg-white and blood-serum proteins of birds to try to determine the closeness of relationship between different kinds of birds. *See* Egg-White Protein.

ELEPHANT BIRD
See Flightless Birds; *see also* size of its eggs under Eggs and Egg-laying.

ELEVATED
Term for the position of a bird's hind toe, or hallux (*see* Hallux), when it is so high on the metatarsus ("leg") that its tip does not reach the ground, as in a rail. *See* in Rail Family. The tracks of such a bird, in sand or in mud, show the impression of only three toes. *See* Incumbent; Feet and Legs.

ELEVATOR MUSCLE
See Flight.

ELLIOTT
DANIEL GIRAUD (1835–1915). A founder and president of the American Ornithologists' Union; wrote many monographs about groups of birds illustrated with his own drawings and color plates; author and illustrator of *Birds of North America* in two volumes (New York, 1866–69) (Chapman, 1917).

EMARGINATE
Term used in reference to a bird's tail as a whole. When the tail is notched at the end, or slightly forked with slight graduations, it is emarginate. Of a remex, one of the flight feathers (remiges), the feather is emarginate if notched or abruptly narrowed or cut away along one edge. If it is gradually cut away along one edge, the feather is said to be *sinuate* (Van Tyne and Berger, 1959). *See* Tail.

EMBERIZID
(em-ber-EYE-zid). Any of certain members of the Finch Family; in the Old World, specifically the fringillines, or buntings, some of which are in the genus *Emberiza* (em-ber-EYE-zah), from which they get their name; like their N. American representatives, they are plainly colored; sexes are usually outwardly alike; all build open cuplike nests, some in bushes or in trees, seldom high up, and some often on the ground (Austin, 1961).

N. American birds called emberizids, or emberizines (em-ber-EYE-zins), are the towhees, largest and most colorful of New World emberizines; the juncos; the circumpolar snow bunting and the rustic bunting; and the many species of streaked sparrows—the fox, Savannah, sharp-tailed, song, tree, vesper, white-crowned, and white-throated sparrows (Vaurie, 1964). Many ornithologists believe that the emberizids should be classified in a separate family—the Emberizidae. *See* Finch Family.

EMBRYO AND ITS DEVELOPMENT
All birds lay eggs, a familiar fact, but remarkable because no other class of vertebrate animals (*see* Vertebrate) are exclusively egg-lay-

ers. *See* Eggs and Egg-laying. Most birds lay their eggs in nests and will defend eggs and young from enemies. *See* Nests and Nesting; Young and Their Care. Birds also incubate their eggs (*see* Incubation), with the exception of a group largely of the Australian region called megapodes, and brood their young, which enables them to raise families even in the cold of the Arctic and Antarctic. *See* Brooding; Cold and Birds; Metabolism.

At the time a bird's egg is laid, the yellowish yolk and white albumen fill the shell completely. The yolk is a mixture of proteins, fats, and carbohydrates, and on top of it lies a tiny blob of protoplasm from which the embryo develops in a fertilized egg. *See* Fertilization. The yolk and protoplasm are enclosed in a transparent bag, the *vitelline membrane*, which keeps the yolk and egg white, of different compositions, from mixing. It also "allows water, salts, some sugars, amino acids, and possibly some proteins to pass from the egg white to the yolk" (Bellairs, 1960). The egg-white proteins are highly specific in birds and may be analyzed to determine relationships and differences between them. *See* details under Eggs and Egg-laying. One of the chief uses of the egg white, which is 88% water and about 10% amino acids and small amounts of minerals, is to keep the developing embryo from drying out; also to help support the yolk and prevent it from collapsing and flattening (Bellairs, 1960).

The shell, with its underlying shell membrane, which protectively encloses the egg, helps to keep it from drying out, and has hundreds of tiny pores which allow gases—oxygen and carbon dioxide—to diffuse in and out, so important to the normal development of the embryo. The two shell membranes are fused together except at the blunt or wide end of the egg, where they separate to form a pocket of air which the chick will breathe just before hatching (Bellairs, 1960). *See* Hatching; Eggs and Egg-laying.

By the time a fertilized egg is laid (*see* Fertilization), the embryo is a small flat disk of cells (blastoderm) lying on the yolk. The embryo may remain in this state for a week or more, although if it is not warmed by this time in an incubator or by an incubating bird, the embryo will eventually die. For it to continue its development, the egg must be kept at a certain temperature. *See* Egg Temperatures. In the domestic hen, the optimum, or most favorable, temperature for the development of the embryo is 38.5° C. (101° F.), which corresponds to her body temperature (Bellairs, 1960). An incubated, fertilized egg of a domestic hen usually hatches in 21 days. *See* incubation periods, when known, in each bird's biography.

The development of the embryo is mainly two processes: (1) An increase in the number of its cells, and when large numbers of them have formed in the embryo, one of the strangest processes of life begins. Groups start to move and take up new positions, and the direction taken and the way in which these cells move is always the same for each particular species of bird or other animal (Bellairs, 1960). (2) A continual change in the structure and arrangement of the cells. Throughout its embryonic life the developing bird must cope with the same problems

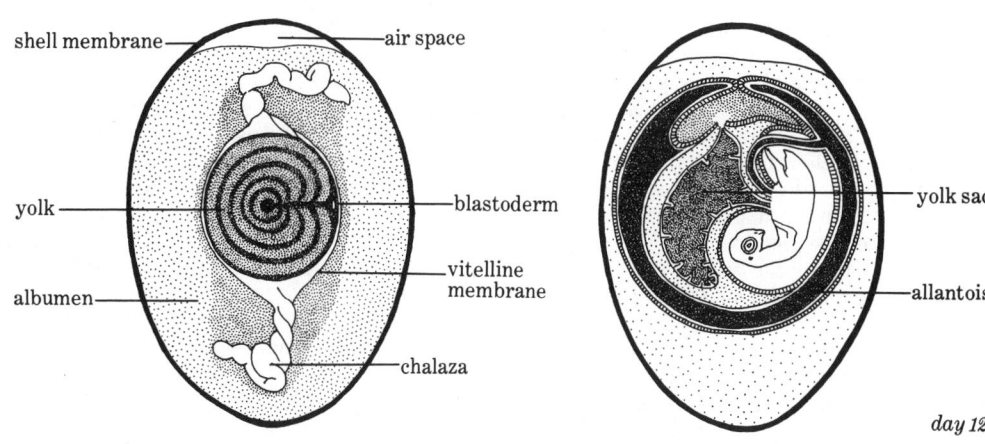

egg of a domestic chicken at the time of laying

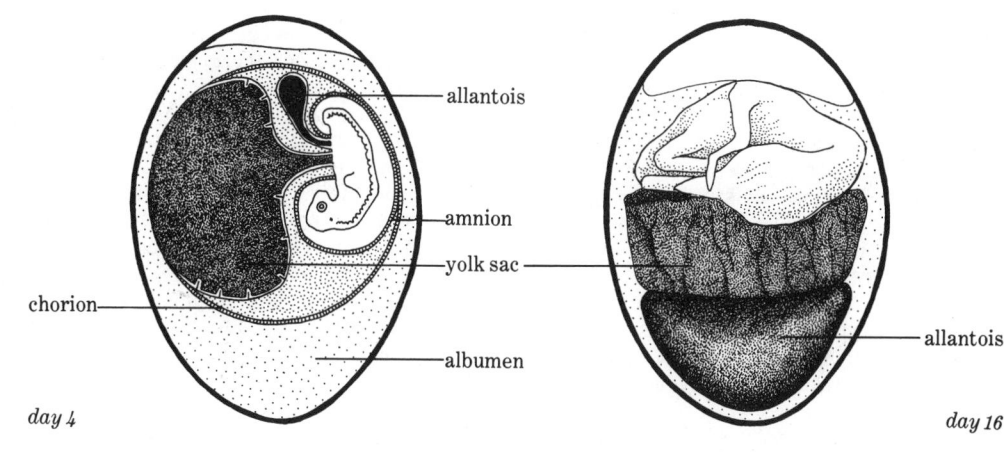

day 4

day 12

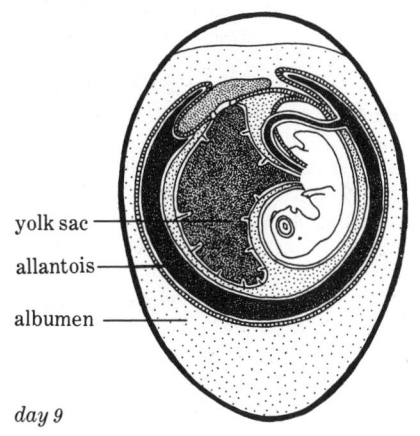

day 9

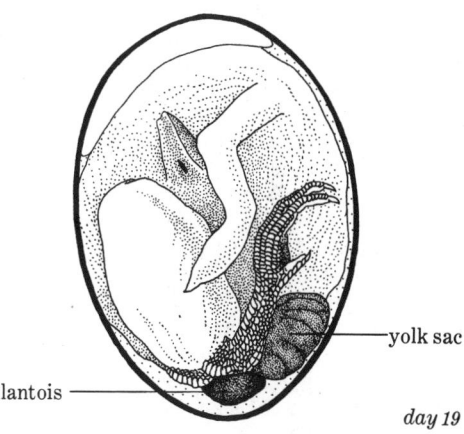

day 16

day 19

EMBRYO AND ITS DEVELOPMENT

The porous shell of a newly laid chicken egg permits the transfer of oxygen and gaseous waste. The yolk, the embryo's source of nutrition, is suspended in the albumen, the embryo's source of amino acids and minerals, and held in place by two chords of albumen called chalazae. The blastoderm, or germinal spot of the embryo, is lighter than the yolk and will always float to the top, close to the source of heat from the incubating parent.

In its fourth day, the embryo is enclosed in the amnion; its large head and eyes have formed, the main blood vessels have developed, and its heart has been beating actively for a full day.

By the ninth day, the albumen and yolk are shrinking noticeably as the embryo withdraws food via tiny vitelline veins in the yolk sac.

By the twelfth day, the extremities are developing and the embryo is capable of convulsive movement.

Down begins to form by the sixteenth day, each feather protected by a sticky film.

After nineteen days, the chick has used all the yolk and albumen except that of the yolk sac attached to its abdomen, and the feet and toes are well-developed. The chick will hatch in two days.

as after it is hatched—the breakdown of food to provide it with energy and to build its tissue proteins. It must have a supply of blood to carry oxygen and food to parts of its body where needed. The wastes must be eliminated or the embryo will be poisoned (Bellairs, 1960).

The embryo develops rapidly with incubation by the parent bird, during which the eggs lose 10–20% of their weight. The rate of evaporation of the eggs, causing the weight loss, increases with continued incubation and rising temperatures (Wallace, 1963).

Within 24 hours the embryo of the domestic chick has the beginnings of its nervous system, digestive tract, and vascular system. Before 36 hours, from beginning of incubation, the heart of the chick embryo begins beating and food comes to it, transported from the yolk by the vitelline veins. Within 48 hours, the eyes, ears, aortic arches, and lobes of the brain are forming (Wallace, 1963). See other interesting details in Bailey and Rinell (1967).

On the third day, the embryo begins to show a transparent sheath around its body—the amnion—a thin enveloping sac. Inside it, the embryonic bird floats in a watery fluid. All birds, reptiles, and mammals are cradled in this embryonic amnion, which acts as a protective cover for the extremely delicate cells and tissues of the rapidly growing young animal. Sealed in its amniotic sac, it cannot breathe or excrete but these functions are served it by an allantois (AL-lan-toys), which is an outgrowth from the rear end of the digestive tract of the embryonic bird.

The allantois is a temporary breathing and excreting organ, filled with a rich network of blood vessels. It grows out into the space between the amnion and the thin inner eggshell membrane, or chorion. Between the chorion and the porous eggshell there is an interchange of gases between the blood of the allantois and the outside world, essential to the breathing of the embryonic bird (Walter and Sayles, 1949).

Food is supplied the chick by a yolk sac, or a second fetal membrane, which is formed by cells that grow downward from the embryo and surround the yolk. The yolk food does not pass directly into the body of the embryo but is carried to it in the blood through the vitelline veins. A day or two before the chick hatches, the remaining yolk sac and its contents will be drawn through the umbilical opening into the bird's body cavity (Berger, 1961), which gives the newly hatched chick an additional or emergency food supply. See Hatching. When the domestic chick embryo in the egg is a week old, and all its important parts created, it is no longer an embryo but is usually called a fetus.

During the incubation of the eggs, the thin disk of protoplasm on the upper surface of the yolk is kept constantly uppermost by its lesser weight when the egg is turned by the parent bird. This turning of the eggs produces the characteristic ropelike twisting within the egg of the chalazae (kah-LAT-see), two dense cords of albumen attached to opposite ends of the yolk. The yolk is centered in the egg "and suspended in the inner layer of thin albumen by the strands of the chalazae." When the egg is turned, the chalazae maintain the embryo's animal pole always up, the heavier vegetal pole

always down, "no matter what the position of the egg in the nest" (Welty, 1962).

The turning of the eggs by the incubating bird apparently helps to keep all of them at more even temperatures; also, it prevents the embryos from sticking to the inside of the eggshells. Birds usually turn their eggs with the bill: a European sparrow hawk about once every 20 minutes; an American redstart about once every 8 minutes. Putnam (1949) reported that a cedar waxwing not uncommonly turned her eggs 12 times in 65 minutes. Holcomb (1969) watched a Traill's flycatcher stand up in the nest to adjust her eggs with her bill about 5 times each hour. Allen (1961) has noted that birds usually turn their eggs when, after a feeding excursion, they have returned to the nest to incubate. From his extensive studies of the nest life of the herring gull, Tinbergen (1953a) concluded that the adults stopped turning the eggs after the eggs were "pipped" by the chicks; that either the movements or the squeaks of the chick inside caused them to treat the pipped egg as a chick. See Hatching.

Sexual differentiation begins in the domestic chick and in songbirds during the fifth day of the embryo's life (Witschi, 1961), and in later stages, hormones circulate within it and cause the development of the sex organs (gonads). See Sexual Dimorphism. The sex of the embryo is determined by sex chromosomes it receives from its mother. She produces two kinds of eggs, or ova, that differ from each other in the number of their sex chromosomes. In the chicken, for example, half of the ova of the female have a male-determining sex; half do not. In the male all sperms are alike and each has a male sex chromosome. Regardless of genetic determination of sex, all embryos start life with essentials for forming all organs of either sex, and whichever one the embryo becomes, male or female, also depends apparently on enzymes produced by the sex chromosome genes (Domm, 1955).

As pointed out by Domm (1955), the embryo is potentially bisexual, which accounts for occasional part, or complete, inversions of the originally determined sex, resulting in what are called intersexes, hermaphrodites, or sex inversions, depending on what organs or tissues are actually present. The sex of vertebrate animals, which is genetically determined, is not fixed and irreversible and all gradations from a typical male to a typical female are possible. See Sex Reversal under Endocrine Glands; Hermaphrodite; Gynandromorph. See Sex Ratio under Hatching.

EMIGRATION

As compared to migration in birds, which is a two-way seasonal movement between the summer and winter home, emigration is a permanent departure from the bird's home or resident area. Many birds that have these eruptive movements, in which they move out of an area permanently, are immigrants, rather than migrants. Chickadees, after being residential for several years, are sometimes struck with a drive that urges them to wander. In wandering about, chickadees appear in habitats unusual for them. During the winters of 1941–42 and 1951–52, according to Kluyver (1961), and

1970–71, there were such emigrations or eruptive movements of chickadees in e. U.S. when many of these birds suddenly appeared south of their home ranges in more northern regions, and local, home-dwelling chickadees emigrated elsewhere.

Such eruptive movements are well known in other northern birds (see Irruption), and also occur in European tits at irregular intervals. Kluyver (1961) says that most of these emigrated birds "never return to their original places." He believes that such movements probably occur after an unusually large production of young during the preceding breeding season or "after unusually cold and cloudy summers. In both cases an acute food shortage might cause the phenomenon." See also Dispersal; Migration.

EMPIDONAX

(em-PID-oh-nax); EMPIDONACES (em-pid-ON-ah-seez), plural. Term for the members of the genus Empidonax, a group of small flycatchers. See in Flycatcher—Tyrant Flycatcher Family.

EMU

See Flightless Birds; Running Birds.

EMU, THE

See Australia under Ornithological Periodicals.

ENCEPHALITIS VIRUSES

(See also Arbovirus.) Cause diseases that include equine (of horses) encephalomyelitis (ensef-ah-low-my-eh-LIE-tis), which also infects man, birds, and reptiles, and was first reported in birds from a ring-necked pheasant in Mass. in 1938. This virus disease, now called eastern encephalitis virus, was also isolated from a pigeon during the 1938 epidemic, which involved both man and horses. There are two antigenically different viruses (see Virus) which cause encephalomyelitis in horses in N. America (Kissling, 1959), and because of their geographic distribution, they are called, respectively, eastern encephalitis virus (EEV) and western encephalitis virus (WEV). See Karstad (1971a) and Kissling (1959) for details. The eastern form ranges in N. America from Wisc. south to Tex. and east to the Atlantic coast, where it is particularly prevalent; the western form until 1953 was thought to be limited in N. America mostly to west of the Mississippi R., but isolations of WEV have since been made from brown-headed cowbirds and house sparrows in N.J. (Scherer, 1963, and Karstad, 1971a).

Besides the eastern and western forms, another in the U.S. is St. Louis encephalitis; in various parts of the world others in this group of arboviruses are Japanese B. encephalitis, Murray Valley encephalitis in Australia, West Nile encephalitis, Venezuelan encephalitis, and possibly others. All of these affect man and apparently occur in birds.

Although eastern encephalitis virus causes a severe and usually fatal disease in man and in horses, there is little evidence that it is harmful to native N. American birds. Clinical disease and death, however, may result among introduced species. Fatal infections of EEV have now been reported in chukar partridges (*see* in Pheasant Family), ring-necked pheasants, domestic white Pekin ducklings (*see* Domestication), and house sparrows. In some parts of N.J. it is considered impractical to try to raise pheasants without prophylactic vaccination of them against EEV (Herman, 1962).

According to Shahan and Schoening (1956), antiencephalitic vaccines have been developed for protection of man, and Long (1966) reported that the onset of the disease is abrupt, fever may be quite high, followed possibly by convulsions and coma. He stated that a satisfactory vaccine had been produced for horses and mules but has not been used for the protection of man to any extent, except among laboratory personnel working with the disease.

In addition to man and horses, some other mammals are susceptible to EEV; for example, natural infections of several species of rodents have been reported. One group of investigators (Thomas *et al.*, 1958) demonstrated the susceptibility of garter snakes to WEV and reptiles in Ga. and Fla. are susceptible to EEV; however, Johnson (1974) suggests that snakes do not seem to act as reservoirs for the arbovirus. Both natural and experimentally induced infections of EEV had been reported in 51 species of wild birds up to 1963 (Stamm, 1963).

EEV is transmitted in nature by several species of mosquitoes, the most important of which is *Culiseta melanura*, a swamp-breeding species of e. U.S. from the Gulf of Mexico to Canada; it is especially fond of the blood of birds (Karstad, 1971a); several other species of mosquitoes, especially of the genus *Aedes*, have been proved biological vectors, or carriers, and transmitters of EEV (*see* method of spread among animals under Arbovirus). Extensive outbreaks of EEV in horses, man, and pheasants have followed hurricanes along the Atlantic coast, which increase the number of surface pools (mosquito breeding places) and often blow large numbers of salt-marsh mosquitoes far inland (Karstad, 1971a). There is also ample evidence that direct transmissions of EEV may occur among penned pheasants during their acts of feather picking and cannibalism. The virus is present in the blood, feather quills, and mouth secretions of infected pheasants (Kissling, 1959).

When EEV successfully invades the central nervous system of infected birds, they become depressed and lethargic, show incoordination and paralysis, and adopt abnormal postures of the head and neck, along with tremors, head retraction, and circling (see Karstad, 1971a, for other details, also for methods of mosquito control). Control of native wild birds that may possibly become infected and serve as reservoirs for the disease and hosts for causing infection among mosquitoes or other blood-sucking arthropods is difficult, impractical, and "could not be defended as sound conservation practice" (Karstad, 1971a).

WEV was first discovered in Calif. in 1930 when it was isolated from the brains of infected horses. According to Karstad (1971a), in 1938 both EEV and WEV were proved to be causes of fatal human encephalitis. A few years later, Cox *et al.* (1941) isolated WEV from a naturally infected prairie chicken in N.D. during a field investigation of encephalitis there in horses and in man.

Several species of mosquitoes are known to serve as vectors of WEV, but the most important one is *Culex tarsalis*, abundant throughout the semiarid regions of w. N. America and the most widespread mosquito in Calif.; it ranges to 9,000 ft. in Utah, and lives as far east as Mich. and Ill. south to w. Fla. and Tex.; the females are fierce biters and readily invade houses (Matheson, 1944). *Culex tarsalis* feeds readily on the blood of both birds and mammals; thus it is able to transmit WEV from wild birds to man and to horses; garter snakes are also considered to be potential overwintering reservoirs of WEV (Thomas and Eklund, 1960).

According to Karstad (1971a), "it is believed that birds are generally unable to carry WEV for long periods of time since they usually have pronounced but brief viremia (virus in the blood) followed by a prompt and enduring antibody response." See Karstad (1971a) for other details of WEV and recommended control—for example, effective vaccines have been developed for the horse and for man. For a splendid history of outbreaks of encephalitis in the U.S. and species of birds and other animals that serve as reservoirs for the arboviruses, see Johnson (1960). *See* other virus infections under Diseases.

ENCEPHALOMYELITIS
See Encephalitis Viruses.

ENDANGERED SPECIES
See Rare and Threatened Species.

ENDEMIC
In ornithological usage, a bird that is restricted to a given region; not found elsewhere (Mayr, 1946a).

ENDOCRINE GLANDS
The endocrine glands in birds include the ovary, testes, adrenals, pituitary, thyroid, pancreas, parathyroid, thymus, ultimobranchial bodies, bursa of Fabricius, pineal, and hypothalamus of the brain (see Assenmacher, 1973; Kobayashi and Wada, 1973; Tixier-Vidal and Follett, 1973). They are ductless, widely scattered in the body of a bird, and secrete chemical substances, hormones (from Gr. *hormon*, to set in motion), which diffuse directly into the bloodstream and are carried all over the body. Hormones exert particular effects on particular tissues and stimulate or regulate the activities of other glands or organs (Höhn, 1961). For comparable "message-carrying," *see* Nervous System.

The pituitary is the "master gland," or "conductor of the orchestra" as one scientist has called it (Marshall, 1964), although there are times when the "conductor" itself is influenced by hormone feedback. For example, the anterior (toward the front) lobe of the pituitary secretes gonadotrophic hormones which activate the gonads, which in turn produce sex hormones that, along with changes at sexual maturity, control, to some degree, the subsequent activity of the anterior lobe of the pituitary itself.

Besides gonadotrophic hormones, the ante-

rior lobe secretes *thyrotropin* (TSH), which stimulates secretions of the thyroid; *adrenocorticotropin*, which stimulates the adrenals; and *prolactin*, which stimulates production of "pigeon's milk" by desquamation (sloughing off cells) in the pigeon's crop. See discussion under Crop. Prolactin also stimulates and regulates broodiness and certain other kinds of parental behavior, and along with estrogen, stimulates full development of the brood patch of incubating birds (Wallace, 1963; Bailey, 1952). *See* Brooding; *also* Incubation Patch under Incubation.

The posterior (toward the rear) lobe of the pituitary produces several hormones that regulate blood pressure, may cause premature laying of eggs, even of soft-shelled ones, and reduce the volume of urine, possibly by increasing resorption of pre-urine in the kidneys (Höhn, 1961). *See* Urinary System under Urogenital System.

The thyroid produces *thyroxin*, which (1) regulates growth, (2) helps maintain a normal rate of metabolism and body temperature (Höhn, 1961), (3) helps to control carbohydrate metabolism, (4) regulates the normal development of feathers and the molt cycle (*see* Feather; *also* Molts and Molting), (5) assists in the normal development of the gonads (in some birds only), and (6) apparently plays a role in the onset of migratory behavior (see Assenmacher, 1973).

The two parathyroid glands, close to the thyroid, secrete *parathormone*, which maintains the calcium and phosphorus levels in the blood and helps in bone formation (Höhn, 1961). *See* Calcium.

The pair of adrenals in birds, generally bright yellow or orange, lie near the cephalic lobe of the kidney, and their secretions and functions are apparently debatable, but norepinephrine and epinephrine, secreted by the medulla, help regulate metabolism and blood pressure. Höhn (1961) speculates that adrenalin may have the same effect upon birds as upon mammals: the sudden increased heart rate and flow of blood, brought on by anger or fear, facilitates violent muscle exercise for fighting or flight.

The pancreas produces the hormones *glucagon* and *insulin*. See Pancreas.

The gonads, besides producing the ova of females and spermatazoa of males, secrete primarily an androgen *(testosterone)*—male hormone—and an estrogen *(estradiol)*—female hormone. Coordinated with other hormones, these control the development of the sex organs (*see* Fertilization), and androgen controls the secondary sexual characters of the male as shown by his plumage, comb, spurs, etc., which strongly influence sexual behavior. *See* discussion of secondary sexual characters under Sexual Dimorphism. See also Assenmacher (1973).

The ultimobranchial bodies are small paired structures lying in the neck just below the thyroid glands. They secrete the hormone *calcitonin*, which apparently is involved in the regulation of calcium metabolism, although its exact role is unclear.

The bursa of Fabricius lies just dorsal (above) the cloaca and opens into it. Although well developed during the birds' embryological

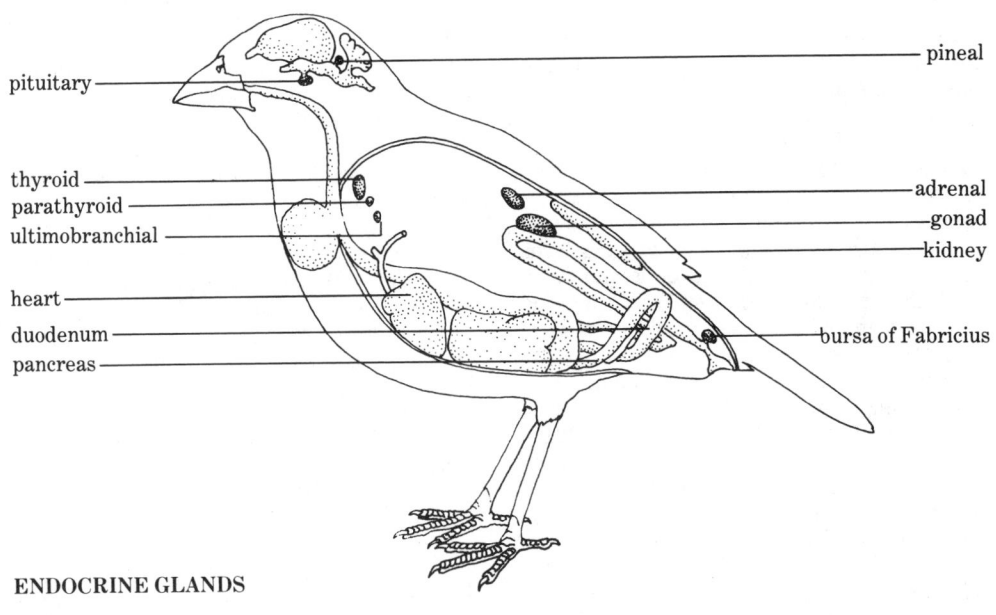

pituitary

pineal

thyroid
parathyroid
ultimobranchial

adrenal
gonad
kidney

heart
duodenum
pancreas

bursa of Fabricius

ENDOCRINE GLANDS

development, it begins to diminish soon after hatching. Its tissues produce secretions that are responsible for the maturation of white blood cells (lymphocytes) which aid in immunological reactions.

The pineal gland, located on the dorsal aspect of the brain, is believed to secrete the hormone *melatonin*. The functions of this gland remain obscure.

SEXUAL REVERSAL. Females of domestic fowls and of certain wild birds may make a dramatic change from females to males when the ovary of the female (*see* Embryo and Its Development) has been destroyed by disease or, experimentally, by ovariectomy. This may induce plumage reversals from female to male and assumption of male behavior. In contrast, according to Rowan (1931), castrated male birds (unless they are treated with androgens) never again exhibit the male traits of singing, fighting to defend territory (*see* Territory), and are permanently "sexless." Females of ostriches, herons, ducks, pheasants, the English robin, and some of the fringillids (*see* Fringillid) have reverted from female to male plumage, and Bergtold (1916b) collected a western form *(montanus)* of the rufous-sided towhee—a female in the plumage of a male—the change of which he ascribed to its diseased and atrophied left ovary. He cited J. Bland-Sutton's book *Evolution and Disease,* published in 1890, in which Bland-Sutton listed females of pheasants, domestic hen, peafowl, partridges, bustard, American (white) pelican, cotinga, bunting, and chaffinch as exhibiting "pseudomasculinity."

In one of the most interesting documented cases of natural sex reversal in history, Crew (1923) reported an Orpington hen which had been a good egg producer and mother of chicks, until she was 3 years old, that began to crow at 3½ years, took on all secondary sexual characters of a rooster (hackle feathers, wattles, etc.), and at 4½ years copulated with a virgin hen and sired two chicks. After its death, an autopsy of the bird showed that it had two functioning testes, but a shriveled left ovary, probably destroyed by a tumor.

In almost all families of birds, the right ovary of the female is vestigial but if the left one is destroyed the vestigial right one may become an ovitestis. At the next molt, deficiency of estrogen, normally produced by the functioning left ovary, and the newly secreted androgens (male hormones) allow plumage reversal to that of the male (Marshall, 1961b). This phenomenon, often resulting in the "crowing hen," has aroused interest or fear in people from the time of Aristotle (Forbes, 1947).

In the house sparrow, and presumably in certain other species, the plumage color is not controlled by hormones, but is genetically fixed. In this species, neither gonadectomy nor experimental injections of hormones can bring about sexual changes; however, the bill color of the house sparrow, African weaver finches of the genus *Euplectes,* the starling, herring gull, and the black-headed gull of Europe, for example, is changed during the breeding season by the action of sex hormones (Witschi, 1961). *See* Sexual Dimorphism; Sex Determination.

Apparently both male and female birds produce androgenic and estrogenic hormones from the gonads (*see* Gonad). Estrogen is responsible for female plumage, and in species of birds subject to a reversal of plumage from female to male, it ordinarily suppresses the action of the male hormone. Androgen becomes active in the female only when her ovary has been removed and estrogen is no longer available. *See,* however, discussion of phalaropes in Phalarope Family; *also* Thymus Gland.

ENDOLYMPH
Term for a fluid in the semicircular canals which helps birds to maintain their equilibrium. *See* Semicircular Canals.

ENDOPARASITES
See Parasite; Diseases.

ENDYSIS
(EN-dih-sis). *See* Ecdysis.

ENEMY
General term for any animal—predator or parasite—which is inimical to a bird's health or threatens its life or its reproduction. The term may be so broad as to include weather—rain, cold, snow, etc.—and other natural elements which cause the deaths of birds, either directly or through food shortages. However, the term is customarily given to its natural enemies such as hawks, owls, shrikes, and other flesh-eating or predatory birds; also to bobcats, foxes, weasels, skunks, certain snakes and turtles, and any other predatory animals that feed directly on birds or their eggs and young. *See* Predation. Parasites are often indirect enemies in their harmful effects on birds. *See* Parasite; *also* Epizootic; Diseases. Any agency that kills a bird, including man, may be called an enemy, although natural enemies, though destructive to individual birds, may be of great benefit to the species itself. *See* Balance of Nature; Accidents; Mortality.

ENERGY NEEDS
or ENERGY REQUIREMENTS. *See* Metabolism.

ENGLISH NAME
See Common Name.

ENTERITIS
See duck plague under Diseases.

ENTEROHEPATITIS
See Blackhead.

ENVIRONMENT
See Ecosystem.

ENZYMES
(pancreatic). *See* Digestion.

EOCENE PERIOD
See Geological Time Scale.

EPIDERMIS
See Skin.

EPIGAMIC DISPLAY
Term of bird behaviorists for a display that synchronizes the mated pair for copulation (Berger, 1961). *See* Copulation and Copulatory Organs. The term is also used more broadly to include all types of display that bring the sexes together and lead to copulation—that is, both gamosematic and epigamic display—and then is said to be synonymous with courtship. *See* Behavior; Courtship Rituals under Courtship; and especially Colors That Advertise under Colors of Feathers.

EPIZOOTIC
(ep-ih-zoh-OT-ick). Term for incidence of a disease that kills widespread populations of birds or other animals, comparable to an *epidemic* in man. Like starvation, it can drastically reduce populations of birds to low numbers; its effects are more dramatic and more effective in temporarily reducing populations of birds and other animals than that of predation, which, in general, exerts a steady pressure or drain on animal populations (Craighead and Craighead, 1966). *See* Predation; Diseases.

EQUILIBRATION
Sense of balance in birds. *See* Semicircular Canals.

ERNE
See Eagle, gray sea, in Hawk Family.

ERUPTIVE MOVEMENTS
See Emigration; Irruption.

ERYTHRISM
(ih-RITH-rizm). *See* Abnormal Colors under Colors of Feathers.

ERYTHROCYTES
See Circulatory System.

ESCAPE
Term for a bird seen in the wild that has escaped from captivity. When these are exotic waterfowl or other foreign species likely to be kept in captivity, and unlike any native N. American bird, they are usually listed as an "escape," though birders know that there is a chance that a foreign bird, far out of its range, or out of its own country, may appear on the N. American continent though there has been no record of it previously. *See* Accidental. Usually the determination of whether the bird is one that has escaped from a zoo or is actually a wild bird recently arrived depends on the experience, knowledge, and judgment of the birder. *See* Birder; *see also* discussion under Checklist.

ESCAPE DISTANCE
Term for the distance at which a bird will fly upon the approach of a man or a predator. According to Hediger (1950), the escape reaction is specific for the bird or other animal according to its sex, age, kind of enemy, and surroundings. He cites authorities for the escape, flight, or flushing distance in the wild at the approach of a man; for example, flamingos, 400 yds.; ostriches, 150 yds.; herring gulls, 15–20 yds.

As one approaches a bird and nears its critical distance, or the closeness of approach it will allow before taking flight, the bird will usually show escape reactions (intention movements—*see* Behavior) by raising the head and stretching the neck, by bobbing the head and moving about nervously, by crouching and slightly raising the wings, etc. Banko (1960) cites a European authority on swans who reported the escape distance of the whooper and mute swans in winter, in shore marshes, as 300 m. (about 900 ft.). Wild trumpeter swans in winter in B.C. have allowed the approach of a man to about 100 yds., but whether on the water and then swimming away to escape or in taking refuge in flight, their escape distance probably averages well over 300 yds.; however, the learned escape distance or inherited escape behavior may be modified by remembered experiences of the bird under various conditions of either constant protection by man or constant persecution (Banko, 1960), by hunting, for example. Precise measurements of a "typical" flushing distance for a species may be difficult to obtain because of some variations from bird to bird and the effects of the specific conditions at the time of measurement.

In upland game birds such as ruffed grouse, escape distance may be affected by the quality or type of protective cover, weather (*see* Weather), time of year (summer contrasted with the hunting season, for example). Many birds show a remarkable reluctance to fly at the close approach of a man in the presence of a perched Cooper's hawk or goshawk, which may influence grouse and quail, for example, to lie low and not to flush from their protective cover. See, however, Stoddard's experiments reported in Stoddard (1961). Some birds, such as wild turkeys and ring-necked pheasants, when approached by a man may run long distances through woods, underbrush, or grass before taking off.

Orr and Sudia (1960) tried, at Lake Itasca, Minn., to determine the escape distance of great blue herons in the area but found the distance to vary from 13 yds. to 166 yds. and concluded that birds should be marked individually to determine their flushing distances. This variation was later found to be caused by the conditioning of some herons on Lake Itasca to the regular presence of fishermen, who often tossed fish on the waters away from the boat, where they were immediately swallowed by great blue herons alighting on the water or carried ashore to be eaten (Longley, 1960). *See* Fear; Tameness.

ESOPHAGUS
(ee-SOF-ah-gus), or GULLET. A muscular membranous tube through which food is conducted by muscular action from a bird's pharynx (the posterior, or rear, part of the mouth) to the stomach. *See* Stomach. The direction of food movement is sometimes reversed in birds, as in hawks, owls, and others that regurgitate (cough up) pellets of indigestible matter (*see* Pellet) and in pigeons and doves, which give out predigested food to their young (Farner, 1960). *See* Young and Their Care. Some unrelated kinds of birds even make sounds from the esophagus by filling it with air from their lungs and then expelling it. During the breeding sea-

son, the male sage grouse can distend the esophagus 25 times more than a non-breeding male can, and the male American bittern has anatomical specializations of the esophagus with which it produces the "pumping" or "booming" sounds in spring (Chapin, 1922). *See* Courtship.

The esophagus has lubricating glands that aid passage of foods, also muscles that help propel the food onward by peristaltic action. In many birds (hawks, for example) the esophagus is enlarged into a crop (*see* Crop), which acts as an expansible storage place for food that the stomach cannot accommodate. An enlarged but less specialized part of the esophagus may also be used for storage by birds that do not have a crop—penguins, petrels, gulls, ducks, geese, owls, woodpeckers, and many passerines, or songbirds (Groebbels, 1932). Many seabirds that swallow fishes too large for immediate digestion go about with the esophagus filled, and the tail of the fish sticking out of the mouth, with no apparent discomfort. *See* Digestion.

In general, the esophagus is larger in diameter and has a greater degree of folding in birds that eat bulky foods—grebes, loons, auks, puffins, petrels, gulls, cormorants, pelicans, storks, herons, coots, hawks, owls, and kingfishers. *See* Food and Feeding Habits. It is smaller in diameter in birds that eat small foods, such as insect-eaters and grain-eating birds (Farner, 1960).

Because of the wide gape of a bird's mouth and the extremely distensible esophagus of some, there are remarkable records of birds that have swallowed relatively large objects. A gull swallowed a 6-in. rib from a seal's carcass; tiny wrens swallow tree toads and lizards half as large as themselves; a captured pelican had a 4-lb. carp in its gular pouch; a great blue heron swallowed a muskrat almost a foot long, exclusive of its tail, and another a water snake 2 ft. long (McAtee, 1927). *See also* Fishes and Birds; Reptiles and Birds; Mammals and Birds. Some birds try to swallow objects too large and choke to death. *See* Swallowing; Digestion.

ESTRILDID

(es-TRIL-did), also ESTRILLID. Common name for any bird of the family Estrildidae native to tropics of the Old World—the waxbills, grass finches, manakins, and Java sparrows. These are popular cage birds which sometimes escape from captivity, the Java sparrow for example. See Immelmann (1966) for habits and ecology of some species; see also Gilliard (1958); Austin (1961).

ESTROGEN

See Endocrine Glands.

ETHIOPIAN REGION

See Distribution; Faunal Regions.

ETHOLOGY

Term used in human sociology for the study of manners, customs, and mores, their growth, decay, and effectiveness, and now used also for the study of animal behavior.

According to Dilger (1962), in the early part of the 20th century ethology sometimes meant simply the study of animal behavior. Shortly after 1935, and the publication of Konrad Lorenz's *Der Kumpan in der Umwelt des Vögels* [*The Companion in the Bird's World*], it began to signify the comparative study and analysis of the instinctive or stereotyped movements of birds and other animals—a more limited approach than that used today. Ethology is now the study of function, biological significance, causation, and evolution of species-typical behavior.

Ethologists study almost any kind of undomesticated animal—from protozoans to man. At the present time they study both innate and learned behavior, and the interrelationship of the two, although some ethologists conclude that all behavior is ultimately the result of learning, or experience. *See* Behavior; Instinct; see also Thorpe (1956b); Tinbergen (1951b); Hinde (1961).

EURASIA

(your-AY-zha). Name given to Europe and Asia as one continent, often used in biographies of birds that have reached N. America from the Old World to indicate their general range there.

EURYPHAGOUS

(you-RIFF-ah-gus); from Gr. *eurys*, wide, broad, and *phagos*, from *phagein*, to eat, particularly a specified kind of food. A term for birds that are ecologically tolerant of a wide variety of foods. The shape of a bird's bill, or beak (*see* Bill), has evolved from, or has become adapted to, the type or types of food that it eats. Some birds—crows and gulls, for example—have simple straight bills with which they eat fishes, birds' eggs, young birds, carrion, frogs, toads, salamanders, seeds, fruits, and many other kinds of foods. Such birds are, in their feeding habits, euryphagous. The ruffed grouse, *Bonasa umbellus*, is another example of a bird that is euryphagous—it eats some 374 kinds of plants (the buds, seeds, leaves, etc.) and 131 kinds of small animals (Edminster, 1947). *See* Monophagous; Stenophagous; Food and Feeding Habits.

EUSTACHIAN TUBE

A canal connecting the middle ear cavity (which is air-filled) with the atmosphere outside the body by way of the throat and mouth. Its function is to equilibrate the air pressure of the middle ear with that of the environment and to serve as a drainage canal (Sturkie, 1954). *See* Ears and Hearing; see also Pumphrey (1961).

EUTAXIC

See Diastataxic.

EVERYBODY'S DARLING

See Sparrow, song, in Finch Family.

EVOLUTION

The theory that the different species of living things have descended, with modifications, from previously living forms, and were not created separately with their present characters (Cain, 1964; 1960). The theory is based upon the belief that all animals and plants came from a few simple organisms, or possibly one; that various living and extinct types of life do not form a straight line in their descent (*see* Monophyletic Descent), but that their descent may be likened to a genealogical tree whose branches show different degrees of divergence from the parental stock; that many branches of the tree have died and are known only from fossil forms. *See* Fossil Birds; Geological Time Scale. While the theory proposes the descent of man from a remote animal ancestor, the once generally accepted public idea that the theory proposed that man descended from anthropoid apes is wrong. The theory of evolution is widely accepted by biologists and all serious students of biology (Cain, 1964a). Its principal proponents were Lamarck, Darwin, and Alfred Russell Wallace. *See* Origin of Birds and of Bird Flight under Fossil Birds; *also* Phylogenetic Relationship. For some references about evolution, see Eiseley (1961); Smith (1958); Moore (1964); Mayr (1963); Brodkorb (1971).

EXCRETA

(eks-KREE-tah). Term for the excrement, or feces, of birds. *See* Droppings.

EXCRETORY SYSTEM

See Urinary System under Urogenital System.

EXPLOITATION

(by birds). *See* Autolycism; Commensalism; *also* Feeding and Food-getting under Behavior; see also Nests and Nesting.

EXTENSOR

Any muscle that extends or straightens a limb or other part of a bird.

EXTINCT BIRDS OF NORTH AMERICA

As used here, those listed are species or well-defined subspecies on the N. American continent or immediately adjacent waters that have ceased to exist within historic, or within civilized man's, times and often under the influence of his actions (*see* number of species that have become extinct worldwide, and largely man-caused, *also* some of those species that became extinct in earlier geological periods, under Geological Time Scale).

In N. America, within 200 years, largely because of the growth of the human population, early market hunting of some species, and destruction of the environment, this continent has compiled the worst record of any comparable land mass in the world for exterminating its birdlife (Greenway, 1958). By contrast, Europe, with a much longer period of occupation, has not lost a single species of bird within historic times. Five birds—the great auk, Labrador duck, heath hen, passenger pigeon, and Carolina parakeet—are gone, never to return; others, for years on the verge of extinction, are, for example, the Eskimo curlew, California condor, Everglade kite, ivory-billed woodpecker (possibly extinct), southern bald eagle, and whooping crane. *See* lists of these and others under Rare and Threatened Species.

For a detailed account of each extinct N. American bird and causes of its demise, *see* Great auk in Auk Family; Labrador duck in Duck Family; Heath hen in Grouse Family; Passenger pigeon in Pigeon Family; Carolina parakeet in Parrot Family. For detailed discussions of extinction of birds and causes, see Greenway (1958); Fisher (1964); and especially Philip (Prince) and Fisher (1970); Udall (1970).

EXTRARENAL EXCRETION

The elimination of salt from the body of a bird by means other than the kidneys and urine. *See* discussion of this, by salt gland, under Nostrils.

EYELASHES

Birds have no true hairs that serve as eyelashes as in man, but they do have modified feathers, either hairlike or featherlike, that serve the purpose. For example, the eyelashes of the ostrich, marsh hawk, and greater roadrunner are "conspicuous bristles [special feathers] that project stiffly outward from a background of bare, often brightly colored skin" (Lucas and Stettenheim, 1972); however, the upper eyelashes of the introduced European starling are "featherlike" bristles. The featherlike bristle has barbules, which give it the plumelike appearance of a contour feather; the hairlike bristle is usually stiff and bare of barbs or barbules except at its base; the rachis tapers from the thicker base to a pointed tip. *See* discussion of barbs, barbules, rachis, and bristle under Feather.

EYELID

Birds have two eyelids, upper and lower, which are folds of skin, one above the eye, and one below. When closing their eyes, birds that are active in daytime draw up the lower lid more (there is little movement of the upper lid), whereas in birds that are active at night—whip-poor-wills and owls, for example—the upper lid is more active. *See* Eyes and Eyesight. Birds also have a *nictitating membrane*, often called the "third eyelid," which can be drawn across the eyes from the lower nasal position upward and rearward to moisten and clean the cornea (Wing, 1956). *See* Nictitating Membrane.

EYES AND EYESIGHT

Birds have a highly developed sense of sight, a generality that is readily apparent to anyone who has observed their behavior (Sillman, 1973). Man's vision is about equal to a bird's, but birds have faster vision, or quickness in picking up details. According to Pumphrey (1961b), a bird with a single glance immediately takes in a picture that a man might accumulate only by laboriously scanning the whole field of vision, piece by piece. Also, a bird's eyes have greater sensitivity for detecting movement than a man's. *See* examples in introduction to Shrike Family.

SIZES OF BIRDS' EYES. Usually the eyes of birds are the largest part of a bird's head, and often weigh more than a bird's brain. Large hawks and owls have eyes which in diameter are comparable to the size of a grown man's. Ostriches, whose eyes are about 2 in. in diameter, have the largest eyes of all birds and supposedly of all land vertebrates (Pettingill, 1956). In looking at a living bird, one sees only a relatively small part of its eyes because the largest part is hidden by the lids and the skull. The eyes are partly protected and supported by

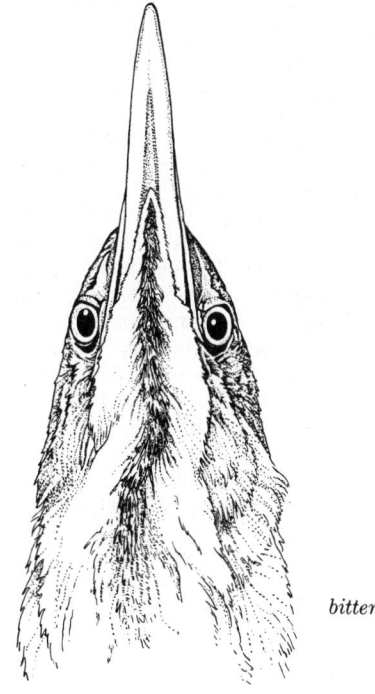

bittern

woodcock

EYES AND EYESIGHT

The bittern usually lives among reeds and often escapes notice by freezing with head pointed skyward. Its eyes are placed low on the head so that the bird can still look forward binocularly while maintaining this pose.

The eyes of the woodcock are located toward the top of its head, enabling it—while it feeds with head down—to see the approach of predators in front, above, and behind it.

owl

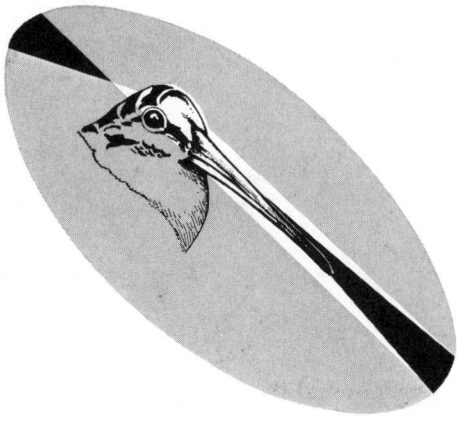

woodcock

The extent of monocular and binocular vision varies greatly in different birds. The owl, whose eyes are located toward the front of its head, has a total frontal field of about 60–70°; however, owls can rotate their heads very rapidly about 270°, which compensates for their less than adequate monocular vision. The woodcock, with eyes near the top of its head, can see binocularly backward and upward and forward and upward. Its monocular field is nearly 180° on each side.

the sclerotic ring, a series of thin bony plates. *See* Skull under Skeleton.

HOW BIRDS USE THEIR EYES. The eyes of birds are fixed in the sockets and generally they cannot "roll" them as a man can in turning his eyes about without moving his head. Birds turn their gaze in different directions by turning the head and neck. An owl can rotate its head on its neck for about 270°, or about three fourths of a full circle, but the story that owls can turn their heads completely around and past a full circle, in one direction, is fiction. Obviously, if it were to do so, it would twist off its head; while watching a person circling it, after an owl has turned its head about three-fourths of the way around its body, it suddenly swivels its head around in the opposite direction, but so swiftly that one cannot see the movement and would believe that it had turned its head all the way around its body.

When a bird holds its head motionless, and is looking or using its eyes, the area that it sees varies greatly among different birds, depending on the placement of the eyes and angle of view. Pigeons, with their eyes lateral (on the sides of the head), have a total view of about 340°; they can see almost everywhere around them except directly in back of the head; their *binocular* (two-eyed) vision—the ability to see straight ahead—is about 24° of their 340° field of view. All birds have both *monocular* (one-eyed) vision—the ability to see independently with each eye—and binocular vision looking straight ahead. Hawks, with their eyes set more forward than in pigeons, ducks, and most songbirds, for example, have a smaller range of monocular (side) vision and cannot see behind them without turning the head; but they have a wider range of binocular vision: about 35–50° in front of them (Wallace, 1963). Owls, with their eyes placed in the front of the head, have a total field of view of about 60–70° in front of them; to increase their breadth of view they turn the head swiftly to look about them. See many technical details about vision in Sillman (1973).

The American woodcock, with its eyes placed toward the top of its head, can see backward and upward, and forward and upward, with binocular vision and laterally almost 180° with each eye.

The American bittern and the least bittern, with their eyes placed low in the head, can see beneath the bill, or downward; they also have forward binocularity. This is an advantage when they "freeze" (become immobile) with the bill pointed skyward to escape detection and when they are stalking prey beneath the surface of the water.

CONES, RODS, AND THE PECTEN. *Cones* and *rods* in the retina at the back of a bird's eye are minute visual cells which act as receptors to form the image that a bird sees. The cones (for their conelike shape) operate in daylight or in bright light and enable a bird to distinguish colors and to receive sharp visual images. The rods (for their rodlike shape) function largely at night or at low light intensities, and are especially rich in the eyes of owls. The *pecten*, a pigmented, conical-shaped body, projects from the retina of the bird's eye into the *vitreous humor* toward the lens. In spite of many theories proposed to explain the function of this unusual structure (Walls, 1942; Sturkie, 1965), the strongest evidence points to the pecten as a structure that provides nutrients to the eye. It may do more, but the "riddle of the pecten remains as yet unsolved" (Sillman, 1973).

Animals that feed on small objects such as seeds and insects must be able to see them sharply and clearly. This is possible only for eyes in which the retina is rich in *cones* and therefore adapted to daytime seeing. Eyes whose retinas are rich in *rods*—those of owls, for example—are better adapted to seeing at night. The only almost pure rod retinas are in nocturnal animals, and the proportion of cones in the retinas of such animals is never high; however, owls have enough cones so that they can see more acutely, or more sharply, by day than by night (Walls, 1942). Walls cites an example of the acuteness of daytime vision in a great horned owl which was picketed in a field by an experimenter; it was discovered that the owl could detect an approaching hawk that was flying so high that it was invisible at the moment to the experimenter and others.

Birds that feed on insects at night (nighthawks and whip-poor-wills, for example) fly rather blindly about and "trawl" for insects by simply holding their mouths open as they fly, though they do have nocturnal vision. Even owls, with so-called night sight, may use sounds made by mice and other animals on which they prey in order to locate them in the dark. *See* Ears and Hearing; *see also* Echolocation.

A reddish pigment, rhodopsin (row-DOP-sin), also called *visual purple*, is largely responsible for the ability of the rods in the eyes of nocturnal animals to "dark-adapt." See discussion by Walls (1942).

VISUAL ACUITY. The resolving power *(visual acuity)* of a bird's eyes is based partly on the large image cast upon its retina and partly on the dense concentration of cones and the high ratio of its optic nerves to its visual cells.

The *area centralis*—a modified region of the retina—provides the greatest visual acuity; it may be round or it may be a horizontal band. The *fovea*—a depression within the area centralis—serves to magnify images; it may be pit-like, troughlike, or absent (Van Tyne and Berger, 1959; Tansley, 1964). All birds that are active by day and most nocturnal birds have at least one sensitive spot, or fovea, on the retina for focusing sharply on an object, and many birds (hawks and eagles, for example) have two. One of these, the *central fovea*, is near the center of the retina and provides sharpened lateral (monocular) views for the bird; the other, the *temporal fovea*, is toward the rear margin of the chamber and functions in looking forward (binocularly), or with both eyes. The central fovea, sometimes called the "search fovea," is used by a bird in picking up objects from the ground or from foliage; the other, the "pursuit fovea," for pursuing flying insects or other moving prey.

The four fovea of hawks and eagles, working together, give them unusual accuracy in per-

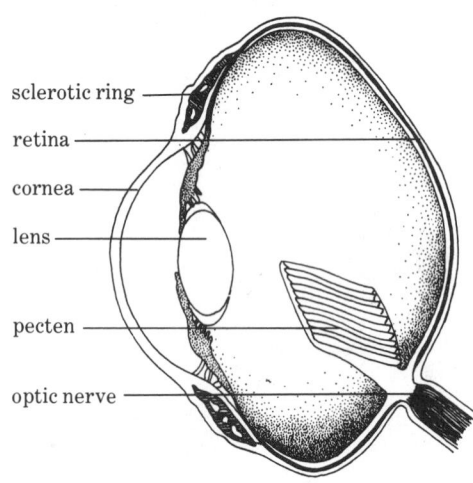

EYES AND EYESIGHT

sclerotic ring

retina

cornea

lens

pecten

optic nerve

ception of objects at a distance; with two fovea in each eye, the retina as a whole is superior to that of most birds (Brown and Amadon, 1968). In the human fovea, there are about 200,000 visual cells to each square millimeter; the house sparrow has about 400,000; the European buzzard, *Buteo buteo*, a hawk much like our N. American red-tailed hawk, has about 1,000,000 visual cells to each square millimeter of the fovea. This number, estimated to be as high for other hawks and eagles, gives them the remarkable resolving power of their eyes in forming distinguishable, unblurred images of small objects (Pettingill, 1970).

Brown and Amadon (1968) point out that it is significant that other kinds of birds (other than hawks and eagles) which have two fovea catch flying insects, which requires good vision. Recent research on the eyesight of birds suggests that, in hawks, color vision may have been sacrificed to some extent in the evolution of their eyesight, resulting in better discrimination of form, distance, and motion.

WHAT COLORS DO BIRDS SEE? The fact seems to be established that there is very little difference between the color vision of birds and of man (Pumphrey, 1948). Sturkie (1965) reported that all birds ordinarily active by day have color vision. Since 1863, when Krause first interpreted the multiplex oil droplet mosaic of birds as a mechanism for discriminating hues, the hue-perceptive capacity of birds has not been doubted (Walls, 1942). For years it was believed that birds were blind to violet and blue, the short-wave end of the spectrum, but later scientific experiments with the vision of domestic chickens proved that they do see blue and violet, though weakly, and the blue-shyness of hens seemed explainable in the fact that for a hen there are no *blue* foods in nature.

The American investigators J. B. Watson and Karl S. Lashley, in 1915 and 1916, working with superlative apparatus, found that domestic chicks could distinguish about the same colors as man, but that they were somewhat more sensitive to the red end of the spectrum. In studies of the color vision of the budgerigar, it showed neither the blue-blindness nor the extrasensitivity to red exhibited by the domestic chicken and other birds. Supposedly this is because the budgerigar lacks the deep red oil droplets present in the retina of the eyes of both the hen and the domestic pigeon (Walls, 1942; see also Sillman, 1973).

FUNCTION OF THE OIL DROPLETS. Although the exact function of the oil droplets (primarily of red, orange, and yellow) in a bird's eyes is uncertain, it has been suggested that they act as filters, "increasing a bird's perception of red, orange, and yellow, but making blues more dull or colorless." The color, amount, and distribution of these oil droplets vary in different species of birds. Pigeons have the yellow droplets concentrated in the lower part of the retina, which is supposed to help them in sky vision by toning down the blue. Kingfishers have a large amount of oil droplets in their eyes, which may offset the glare from the water over which they fly in their search for food (Wallace, 1955). Where the red droplets are numerous, as in songbirds and fowls, these birds are thought to see blue and violet light weakly and unsaturated. Hawks and woodpeckers have few red droplets, parrots perhaps fewer still, or even one in some species. According to Walls (1942), "The primary function of the oil droplets is not to *produce* hue-discrimination; but they do necessarily influence the appearance of colored objects profoundly." However, "none of these suggested roles of the oil droplets has been proven experimentally. It can only be said that the significance of these provocative globules is still open to question"(Sillman, 1973).

COLORS OF BIRDS' EYES. Ordinarily, only the irises of birds' eyes have color; the pigment of the iris epithelium may be the only coloring matter present, but almost always there are stromal pigment cells in the eyes which contain various amounts of the melanins, colored oils, or guanin and related substances which give metallic appearances of silver, of gold, or of colors. Frequently the coloration of the iris is from both pigments and such optical phenomena as interference (with light rays). See Walls (1942); *see also* Colors of Feathers.

In most passerine birds, the irises are dark brown, but they may also be yellow, red, blue, green, and other colors. Most owls and some hawks have yellow eyes and there may be sexual differences in the eye colors of some species. *See* Sex Determination. The colors of the iris in the eyes of some birds change markedly with age. Young crows have blue or blue-gray eyes, which become brown when they are adult; young grackles have brown irises, which become paler with age. Young red-tailed hawks have yellow eyes, which gradually become a rich red-brown after about a year of age, when they begin to molt into their adult plumage.

Slate-colored (dark-eyed) juncos, *Junco hyemalis*, have a change of eye color from gray or gray-brown when they are immature, through brown to a distinctly red-brown when they are adult. The sequence of changes is essentially complete by Dec. 1 of the year of hatching (Blake, 1962). See discussion of changes of eye color, according to age, by Trauger (1974).

In pure albino birds, the irises appear red or pink because of the absence of coloring matter, which allows the color of the blood cells to show. *See* Albinism; *also* Eyelashes; Eyelid; Nictitating Membrane.

EYESHINE
One summer night in 1915, Dr. W. H. Bergtold, a medical doctor and ornithologist of Denver, Colo., was driving his car on a road that led through a particularly dark canyon. Far ahead, in the beam of the car's headlights, he saw "two small glowing pink spots," which disappeared at the approach of his car. Then the pink spots reappeared on the road. Realizing that the pink spots were the reflective eyeshine of a night bird, he stopped, got out, and shot the bird to add it to his bird collection, and to make certain of its identity. It was a poor-will, a western relative of the chuck-will's-widow of e. U.S. (Bergtold, 1916a).

Apparently eyeshine is seen not only in the poor-will but in the chuck-will's-widow and whip-poor-will of the Nightjar Family, but the

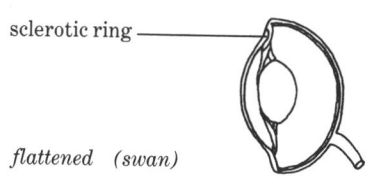

sclerotic ring ——

flattened (swan)

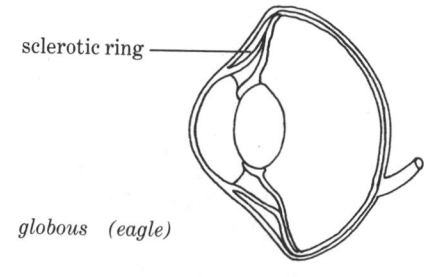

sclerotic ring ——

globous (eagle)

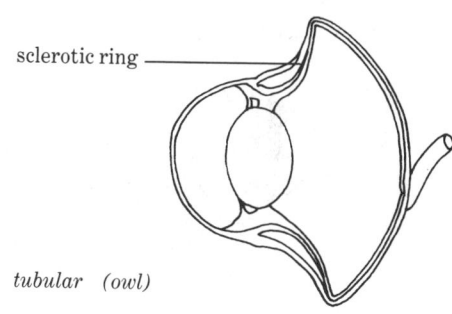

sclerotic ring ——

tubular (owl)

EYES AND EYESIGHT
The shape of the eyeball is determined by the size of the sclerotic ring, a series of thin, boney plates surrounding the cornea. The eyeballs of most birds active in the daytime have a flattened, disclike shape, like those of swans; more tubular-shaped eyes belong to nocturnal birds such as owls and those with the keenest, long-distance sight such as eagles.

eyeshine of the nighthawk, a member of the same family, is not comparable, according to Sutton (1967b).

WHAT CAUSES EYESHINE? According to Walls (1942), when we consider how brightly the eyes of many animals (besides certain night birds, deer and bobcats are examples) reflect the light of our headlights at night, it is apparent that these species must be reflecting light back through their retinas instead of absorbing it. Walls reported that the chorioid coat is a thin, deeply pigmented layer consisting mostly of blood vessels, with connective tissues binding them into a membrane. It lines the eyeball just under the retina toward the back of the eye. Walls says that investigation has borne out the suspicion of a reflective or special mirroring device "located somewhere behind the rod-and-cone layer." It is called the *tapetum lucidum* and exists in deer and other large mammals. Reflections of light from this tapetum will increase the absolute and relative differential between the object looked at and its background, thus increasing the animal's discriminability. However, not all animals which have eyeshine possess a definite tapetum. Walls states that in the ostrich, and possibly in goatsuckers, frogmouths, oilbirds, and some owls, "the light reflex is attributed to the lamina vitrea between pigment epithelium and chorioid, as the lamina is extraordinarily thick in the ostrich. A number of other birds, both nocturnal and diurnal, also show eyeshine, but with no known structural basis for it" (Walls, 1942).

Apparently the sudden shining of a bright light into a bird's or other animal's eyes at night has either a momentarily blinding effect or possibly one of hypnosis, for some birds (the chuck-will's-widow, for example) and some other animals can be approached closely while a light is shining in their eyes and even can be captured. See Sprunt (1940).

EYESPOT

An eye-shaped spot in the feathers of certain birds such as in the tail feathers of the ocellated turkey of Mexico or in the train of a peacock. Also called an ocellus (pl. ocelli). *See* Ocellated.

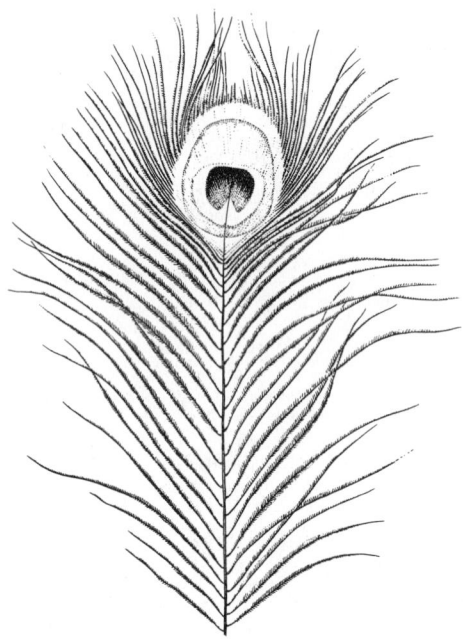

EYESPOT
The tail feathers of the peacock are ocellated: they have spots that resemble eyes.

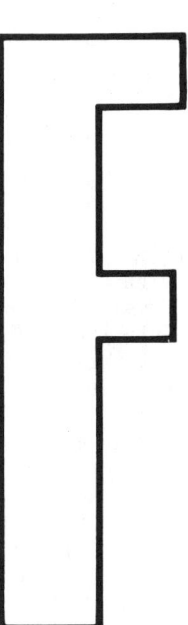

FACIAL DISC
See Disc.

FAHRENHEIT
Name of one type of thermometer in common use; the scale expresses temperatures in "degrees Fahrenheit" (abbreviated °F.); it is commonly used for measuring heat or cold inside or outside of homes in association with weather and in industrial work; the other thermometer in common use is the centigrade, used almost universally for all kinds of laboratory work (Clark *et al.,* 1941); in ornithology it is used usually in researches. *See* simple equation for converting centigrade temperature readings to Fahrenheit, or Fahrenheit to centigrade under Centigrade; *also* Temperature.

FALCATE
or FALCIFORM. Hooked or curved like a sickle or scythe.

FALCON FAMILY
Falconidae (fal-KON-ih-dee); from Lat. *falcon,* a hawk, referring to the hooked (falcate) shape of the claws. 58 species of diurnal birds of prey, almost worldwide except not in Antarctica or on some oceanic islands (Van Tyne and Berger, 1959, 1976); in N. America, 7 living native species (1 extinct) and 1 foreign visitor—the kestrel of Eurasia and Africa; nearest relatives in N. America are hawks, eagles, kites, osprey, vultures (*see* Falconiformes); range in size from relatively tiny, 6½-in.-long falconets, or pygmy falcons, of S. America, Asia, and Africa, to the large peregrine falcon, most prized of all falcons by falconers (*see* Falconry), along with the largest, the 24–25-in. gyrfalcon of the Arctic tundras around the world. Smallest N. American falcon is the 9–12-in. American kestrel; one of rarest N. American falcons has been the disappearing peregrine; in W. Hemisphere, family also includes the tropical American micrasturs (forest falcons), which have general appearance between that of a marsh hawk and that of a goshawk; the primitive forest-dwelling laughing falcon, *Herpetotheres cachinnans,* of tropical lowlands from Mexico south into S. America, noted for loud calling from treetops; and the tropical American, often ground-dwelling caracaras, which live much on carrion. See Brown (1964a) and Brown and Amadon (1968); also Austin (1961).

Members of the Falcon Family resemble those in Hawk Family most in having strongly hooked bill and taloned feet, but differ markedly in certain internal parts (see Friedmann, 1950, and Peeters and Jameson, 1970, for details), and outwardly in that bill of all members of Falcon Family is *conspicuously toothed and notched* (Friedmann, 1950) but faintly so in caracaras. In group called true falcons of genus *Falco* (in N. America, all are in genus *Falco* except caracara), the nostril openings in the cere of bill are circular, with a prominent central bony tubercle (in caracaras, nostrils are slitlike and tubercle concealed); eyes are usually very dark; wings long and pointed, except in caracaras, in which they are long, broad, and rounded. Sexes are usually outwardly alike or very similar; females are larger (*see* Sexual Dimorphism); to ornitholo-

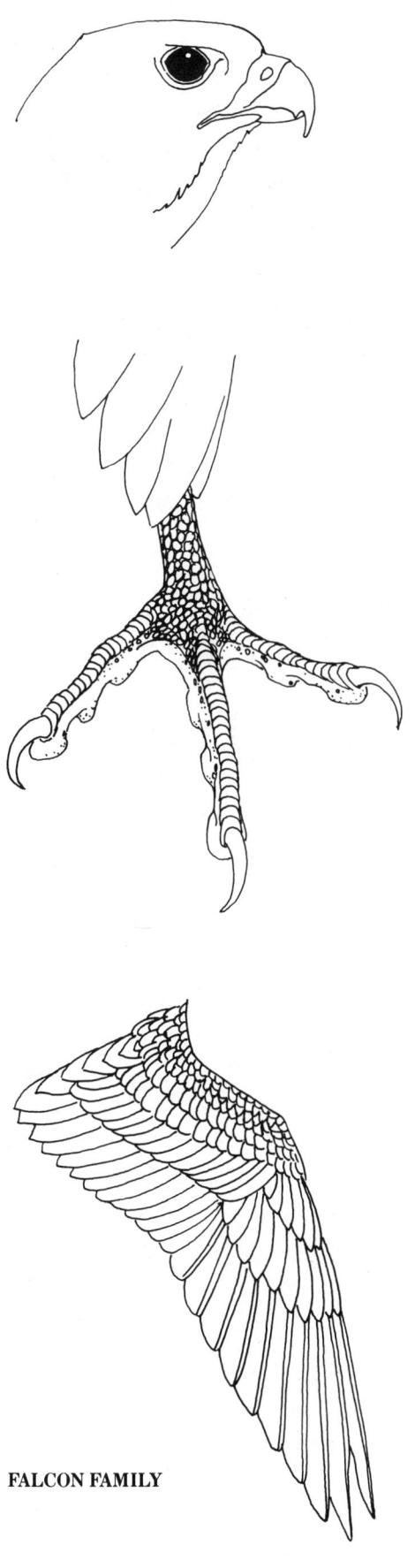

FALCON FAMILY

FALCON FAMILY
*In its spectacularly swift and steep power dive,
the peregrine falcon may reach speeds of 100 to
200 m.p.h. Overtaking a bird in midair, the
peregrine may strike its prey a tremendous,
killing blow with clenched feet or snatch it up
in its talons.*

gists, any of true falcons whether male or female is called a falcon; in falconry terms, the female is the falcon; male is the tiercel, or tercel (based on old belief that every third bird in nest is a male or that male is about one third size of female).

Falcons have bulletlike heads, short necks; the relatively broad, powerful shoulders taper back to the long pointed wings and rather short to medium-long, tapered tail; the feet, especially in peregrine falcon, are relatively large (Audubon called the peregrine the great-footed "hawk"), with long slender toes, and sharply curved talons; falcons are entirely streamlined and all have the so-called high-speed wing (Savile, 1957).

Falcons, like members of the Hawk Family, have extraordinary eyesight; in experiments in Germany, peregrine falcons recognized sitting doves 3,000 ft. away, and a white handkerchief used in "feather play" about 5,100 ft. away (Schmid, 1934). The speed of the peregrine in its power dive, or "stoop" as falconers call it, has been both measured and estimated at 100–275 m.p.h. (see especially Lawson, 1930, and Peterson, 1948; also Brown and Amadon, 1968)—it may be fastest bird in the world; *see*, however, Speed of Flight under Flight.

The peregrine usually hunts from high in the sky over open country while scanning the air and ground below. On sighting its prey, while it is in rapid straightaway flight, it may turn quickly and circle or pause, seemingly motionless in the air. Suddenly it pitches downward, beginning with a few rapid strokes of its wings; then, drawing them partway to its sides, it plunges earthward in a blindingly swift and steep dive. As it overtakes its flying prey—wild duck or crow, for example—and as it passes it, the peregrine suddenly closes and strikes its prey a tremendous blow with its feet. If blow kills quarry, the falcon follows it closely to ground; if prey has shifted in air at last split second and avoided falcon's strike, the falcon will rise above its quarry and stoop at it again —sometimes it may pluck pigeon out of air as it strikes, and carry it away. Small birds, such as swifts, sandpipers, or swallows, it may grasp after overtaking flock in flight or strike them out of air as it passes, turn and pick up prey in its talons before bird falls to ground, or, as it overtakes bird from below, may turn over on back in flight, reach up with feet, and snatch bird out of the air. It then flies to cliff or tree perch, where it plucks feathers of its quarry and bites off pieces of flesh while holding prey under its feet. The smaller pigeon hawk, or merlin, overtakes small birds in flight and catches them in a similar way, but apparently does not stoop at prey from a great height as peregrine does (Bent, 1938).

At times, gyrfalcons hunt 500–1,000 ft. above home in the hilly Arctic country, soaring, flapping, and gliding straight ahead in their searches for their main prey—ptarmigans—occasionally stooping from the heights to strike their prey in flight and to carry it in feet to the ground; sometimes they flap along about 20–60 ft. above earth in attempts to surprise and flush ptarmigans ahead of them; at other times, after gliding along crests of hills and across valleys, alight on rocks, knolls, or small trees to watch

for any movement of ptarmigans on the tundra, much as do goshawks in the Arctic (White and Weeden, 1966).

Some gyrfalcons remain far north throughout the winter; others move far southward, following those ptarmigans that migrate from the north when snow covers their food supplies, or in years when their numbers are unusually high; in irregular or periodic migrations, some gyrfalcons move into U.S.; in winter 1971–72, largest invasion into n. U.S. and Canada in recorded history (Buckley, 1972).

The American kestrel, widespread and smallest N. American falcon, is noted for the lightness and quickness of its flight, during which it may swoop down to pick up small birds, mice and insects from the ground, then carry them off in talons to eat on perch.

Some falcons migrate, especially the peregrine, a powerful long-distance flier. One banded as nestling, Ft. Smith, Northwest Territories, Canada, July 1965, shot and killed six months later, Jan. 1966, territory of Chaco, Argentina, 9,000 mi. from place of banding, a record for the species and high on list of long-distance migration flights of birds (Kuyt, 1967). *See* Migration. Peregrine in migration reported from every major region on earth except Antarctica, has even boarded ships at sea from which to launch attacks at seabirds; in past when more abundant, often seen anywhere from prairies to metropolitan office buildings in large cities of e. U.S., and especially along seacoasts. *See* places of observation, fall migration under Hawk Family.

None of true falcons seem to build their own nest although they may improve on existing ones; they either lay their eggs directly on bare rock ledge, in hollow of a tree, or may appropriate old nests of eagles, hawks, crows (Brown, 1964a). Peregrine is greatly attached to·nest site, which is sometimes called an "ecological magnet" and may be occupied for many successive years and by generations of peregrines (*see* examples of attachment to nest site under Homing). Mates are devoted, but if one member of pair killed, survivor may take new mate and bring to nest site within 36–40 hours (Olendorff, 1971).

The tropical American caracaras of 8 species (Brown and Amadon, 1968)—one of which, the Guadalupe caracara, is extinct—are longlegged vulturelike birds that live only in W. Hemisphere. They are not migratory, and build their own nests; are rather sluggish; spend much time perched or walking on ground but can run swiftly; they associate with vultures at carcasses of dead animals and often rob vultures of food by forcing them to disgorge, much as skuas and jaegers rob gulls. See Feeding and Food-getting under Behavior. Only one species of caracara reaches N. America.

Apparently albinism has rarely been reported in Falcon Family—Gross (1965a) noted only 5 individuals of 4 species.

All members of family are protected by law (*see* Legal Protection) and may not be kept in captivity without a permit from federal and state governments; however, to sustain an ill or injured falcon until it is strong enough to be released, use methods for care described under Hawk Family.

Caracara, *Caracara cheriway* (ker-ah-KAR-ah or kah-rah-KAY-rah CHAIR-ih-way); genus name: of Tupian Indian origin, from the bird's call (Brown and Amadon, 1968); species name: according to Coues (1882), probably a S. American native name. (Color ill., page 295.) National bird of Mexico; reaches northern limits of its range in Fla., Tex., and Ariz., where now local and rare; "rapidly and silently disappearing from . . . Florida" (Kale, 1971); large, long-necked, long-legged, often seen on ground feeding with vultures or perched on fence post; 20–25 in. long; wingspread about 48 in.; adults: sexes alike, distinguished by *black crest;* bare part of face bright red becoming yellow when bird excited; eaglelike bill, white, blue at base; wings, lower back, end of tail, dark; breast and upper part of back cream-white barred with black; lower underparts dark gray; in flight shows *white patches* near tips of dark wings; also has *white breast and white tail* with dark tip which distinguish it from similar black vulture; immatures: like adults but brown instead of black and gray; resident of open or partly open country, either dry or well watered; in c. Fla. in prairie region; occasionally soars like vulture, can fly rapidly with deep wing strokes alternating with short glide, often low over ground, twists and turns like marsh hawk (Bent, 1938); long legs and flat claws enable it to walk or run about searching for food; scratches like domestic chicken for insects; quick to chase any disabled or young bird; when eating small dead mammals or birds, holds them under feet and picks off pieces with bill; usually seen in pairs, strong and aggressive, often called king buzzard because it chases vultures away from dead animal carcass; usually silent but utters, from conspicuous perch in treetop or hillock (apparently during breeding season), *quick-quick-quick-quick-querr;* on last syllable throws head back far over shoulders; name caracara derived from this call (Brown and Amadon, 1968); also gives harsh, grating call of alarm or protest, *trak-trak-trak,* or shrieks; roosts in groves of trees.

Feeding Habits: Besides searching for insects on ground and going with vultures to dead livestock, patrols highways early in morning before vultures are flying to eat animals killed by traffic at night; eats dead or dying fishes, robs pelicans of catches; carries small mud turtles to nest by gripping edge of shell with bill, then tears animal from shell bit by bit to feed young; watches turtles lay eggs then digs them from ground; also catches and eats skunks, prairie dogs, opossums, rats, mice, squirrels, snakes, frogs, lizards, young alligators, crabs, crayfishes, beetles, grasshoppers, worms (Bent, 1938).

Nest: In Fla., usually hidden 15–30 ft. up in thick tops of cabbage palmettos, up to 80 ft. high in solitary pine, sometimes in oak; in Tex., in elm or oak 8–50 ft. up; in Ariz. sometimes in branches of giant cactus; nest is bulky, usually of sticks, twigs, deeply cupped, added to and used year after year.

Eggs: Fla., Dec.–Apr.; Tex., Jan.–June; Mexico, Mar.–Aug.; 2–4, usually 2–3, white to pink-white, usually richly blotched with browns (Bent, 1938).

Incubation: By both sexes, about 28 days; possibly two broods a year; definite age at first flight unknown but said to be 30–60 days after hatching.

Other Names: Audubon's caracara; caracara eagle; common caracara; king buzzard; king of vultures; Mexican eagle; Mexican buzzard.

Age: One lived 13 years in San Diego Zoo (Stott, 1948), another captive reported by Bent (1938) still alive when 12 years old.

Weights: One female, subadult, of the S. American subspecies *P. plancus plancus,* 830.2 gr., or about 1 lb. 13¾ oz.; two others in London Zoo, 3 lbs. 4 oz. and 3 lbs. 5½ oz. (Brown and Amadon, 1968).

Range: Resident, Baja Calif., rare in s. Ariz. (Phillips *et al.,* 1964); s. N.M. (Ligon, 1961) and in s. Tex. Rio Grande delta north along coast to e. Tex. (Peterson, 1963); found separately in c. Fla. and Baja Calif. (*see* under Discontinuities) south through Mexico to s. America, S. America, Cuba, Isle of Pines, and Falkland Is.

Caracara, Audubon's. *See* Caracara.

Caracara, common. *See* Caracara.

Caracara, Guadalupe, *Caracara lutosus* (Ker-ah-KER-ah lew-TOE-sus); genus name: *see* Caracara; species name: Lat., muddy, dirty, possibly in allusion to the darker color of this species; *Extinct;* lived only on Guadalupe Is. off Baja Calif.; was similar to caracara but darker; about 40 specimens preserved; discovered by Dr. Edward Palmer when he visited Guadalupe Is. in 1875; last ones seen alive were collected (shot) by R. H. Beck, Dec. 1, 1900; habits were like those of caracara but nested on rocks and ledges of island; was slaughtered because it attacked and ate young goats of island people. See Greenway (1958) and Brown and Amadon (1968) for details.

Falcon, aplomado, *Falco femoralis* (FAL-koh fem-oh-RAY-liss); genus name: Lat., hawk, referring to the hooked (falcate) shape of the claws; species name: Lat., pertaining to the thigh; *aplomado:* Sp. name in S. America, meaning lead-colored, or leaden. (Color ill., page 297.) Species of Mexico, C. and S. America that reaches northern limits of range in sw. U.S., where almost extinct (Brown and Amadon, 1968); 15–18 in. long; wingspread about 40 in.; plain blue-gray above; has dark underwings; white breast contrasts with black belly; narrowly barred tail longer and wider than in most falcons; black cap; black along sides of head and black "mustache"; a distinctive white line over each eye; thighs and undertail coverts tawny; immatures similar but back brownish; white breast streaked with brown; limited in U.S. to narrow strip along Mexican border east of Calif.; in se. Ariz., where before 1890s fairly common summer resident, since then virtually extinct in state (Phillips *et al.,* 1964); in sw. N.M. has disappeared from most of former range (Ligon, 1961); in Tex. very rare, local in summer in Big Bend country, formerly more widespread (Peterson, 1963); principally on open plains covered with mesquite, cactus, and

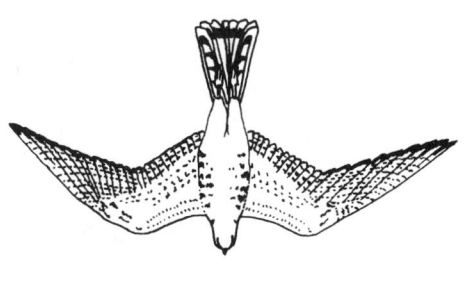

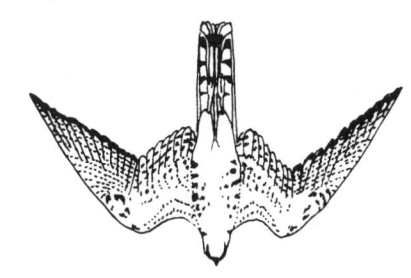

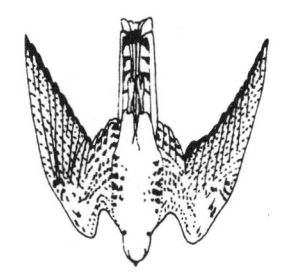

FALCON FAMILY
When a falcon has spotted prey from above, it will turn downward beginning with a few rapid wing beats, then partially fold its wings, decreasing its surface area and air resistance, and plunge toward its prey.

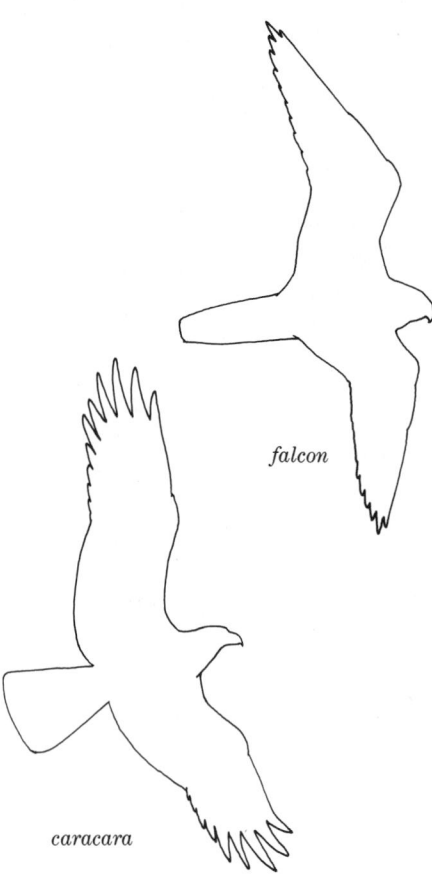

falcon

caracara

FALCON FAMILY
True falcons are stream-lined, with long, pointed wings and tapered tails and fly with rapid wingbeats. Caracaras are large, longer-necked, and their wings are rounder. Their wing strokes are deep, alternating with short glides.

yucca; graceful in flight, not as fast or as dashing as peregrine; frequently alights on bare ground or perches on fence post, utility pole to watch for prey; often hovers like kestrel; hunts in front of prairie fires to catch large grasshoppers in flight, eats them on wing.

Feeding Habits: Often hunts in pairs, eats lizards, snakes, mice, grasshoppers, dragonflies, occasionally parrots, snipe, doves, domestic pigeons.
Nest: Uses old nests of other birds; in Tex., old nests of white-necked raven 8–25 ft. up in mesquite or yucca.
Eggs: Mar.–May; 3–4, white to pink-white, spotted or blotched with browns.
Incubation: Period of and age when young leave nest unknown.
Other Names: American hobby; femoral falcon; orange-chested hobby.
Weights: One male, 8⅓ oz.
Range: See above.

Falcon, Peale's. A very large, dark western form, or subspecies, *Falco peregrinus pealei* (PEAL-eh-eye), of the peregrine falcon. Nests on n. Kurile Is. in Asia; in N. America, from Aleutians, occasionally Pribilofs, south to Queen Charlotte Is.; migrant in winter to Calif. (Brown and Amadon, 1968). Named by Robert Ridgway, Curator of Birds, U.S. National Museum, in Dec. 1873 for Titian R. Peale, Philadelphia artist and taxidermist on Maj. Stephen H. Long's expedition to Rocky Mtns., 1819–20. Brown and Amadon (1968) give weights (of this probably largest N. American peregrine) as: males 1 lb. 12½ oz. to 2 lbs. 5⅓ oz.; females 2 lbs. 11¾ oz. to 3 lbs. 8⅓ oz. *See* Peregrine falcon.

Falcon, peregrine, *Falco peregrinus* (FAL-koh per-eh-GRY-nus); genus name: *see* Falcon, aplomado; species name: Lat., alien, that which comes from foreign parts, wandering. (Color ill., page 297.) Although one of rare and vanishing species, has rivaled osprey and raven as one of most widely distributed birds in world; has reached to ends of earth except Antarctica (Hickey and Anderson, 1969); now largely reduced almost worldwide, and extinct as nesting bird in U.S. west to Pacific coast except for few pairs in s. Rockies (Anonymous, 1973c; Cade *et al.,* 1967); seen in most of U.S. only in winter or in migration; by 1971 almost entire nesting population in N. America limited to Canada, Alaska, and Baja Calif., where also showing effects of pesticides on breeding populations (Cade, 1971); virtually extinct in Calif. by 1970; if rate of decline at that time continued, extinction of peregrine falcon in N. America predicted by Cade and Fyfe (1970) by end of decade, or 1980—see remarkable comeback through captive breeding (Anonymous, 1980b); peregrine is on Threatened Wildlife List (Office of Endangered Species, 1973). Adults of peregrine outwardly similar but female larger; 15–20 in. long; wingspread 43–46 in.; wings long, pointed; barred upperparts dark blue or slate; bill horn color; cere and feet yellow; top of head black, also cheeks and "mustache," which contrast with white throat and sides of neck; underparts white to pink on lower breast,

cross-barred with blackish brown, also on belly, sides; tail long, narrow, blue-gray, rounded, with narrow black bands, broad subterminal bar tipped white, immature similar but upperparts brownish, underparts except throat *streaked* with brown (similar prairie falcon not usually seen east of Plains); in flight, with quick wingbeats resembles flight of domestic pigeon; usually lives in open country around rocky cliffs (in Alaska, bluffs instead of high cliffs) overlooking rivers and lakes inland; oceans and bays along coasts wherever abundance of birds such as gulls, waterfowl, large nesting colonies of seabirds, medium to small songbirds, and especially rock doves (domestic pigeons); nested on Sun Life Building, Montreal (1936–52), where early signs of influence of pesticides on nesting failure noted in N. America (Mosquin, 1970), and on buildings, bridges, water towers in New York (Herbert and Herbert, 1965), Philadelphia (Groskin, 1947, 1952), where pigeons abundant food supply; in fall, northern population usually withdraws southward to winter south of breeding range; some move far south following migration of small birds on which it preys, but appearance in migration irregular; in spring, usually appears on far northern nesting range Mar.–Apr. but may winter within nesting range, especially along Pacific coast; in courtship, pairs roost together on cliff, have cooperative hunting trips, spectacular courtship flights (see in Bent, 1938); during migration a silent bird but in nesting season noisy at nest site, utters repeated long-drawn *witchew, witchew* of recognition of mate, chittering by male during courtship feeding of mate, and long-drawn wail; utters loud harsh alarm notes at human intruder at nest, *cack, cack, cack, cack* with intense angry quality, while diving at great speed or soaring overhead; occasionally attacks humans at nest and in excitement may attack and strike other birds in air nearby—gull, crow, owl, hawk (Brown and Amadon, 1968).

Feeding Habits: Kills and eats domestic pigeons, a favorite, also grebes, auklets, murrelets, terns, petrels, wild ducks, small shearwaters, herons, coots, gallinules, rails, woodcocks, snipes, sandpipers, plovers, upland game birds, marsh hawks and American kestrels, chimney swifts, kingbirds, flickers, jays, crows, blackbirds, orioles, meadowlarks, robins, tanagers, and many other medium to small birds; occasionally takes mammals, beetles, dragonflies, also catches in air monarch butterflies in migration (see in Terres, 1968a), and eats fishes even in captivity (White and Roseneau, 1970); of three commonest, and lethal, diseases of peregrines, especially in juveniles—trichomoniasis, aspergillosus, and coccidiosis—peregrines known to get trichomoniasis (called frounce by falconers) from eating infected doves and pigeons (*see* cure and discussion of under Diseases), but this infection and others not believed to have caused vast decline of peregrine (Stabler, 1969; Trainer, 1974).
Nest: Does not build own nest (Hickey and Anderson, 1969) but throughout world nests mostly on cliffs and in Far North also on bluffs, talus slopes, pinnacles, and on ground (cutbanks); formerly, when nesting in s. U.S., in

hollows of old trees or open tops of cypress, sycamore, cottonwood, 50–90 ft. up; also, in North, in nests of eagles, hawks, ravens, built on cliffs, bluffs, or in trees; on ledges of cliffs, peregrines scrape out shallow hollows in soil, decomposed rocks, gravel, etc., in which to lay their eggs, an evolutionary adaptation that prevents the rounded eggs from rolling off cliff (Hickey and Anderson, 1969); same nest site may be used by peregrines for many years; Hickey (1942) reported 14 eyries in e. N. America occupied by peregrines for more than 50 years each, although not by same pair; in Alaska, Cade *et al.* (1967) knew of four specific cliffs that had a history of occupancy of more than 30 years, two of which had been occupied by pairs of peregrines, in succeeding occupancy, for more than 65 years; among European eyries, several sites have occupancy traced back more than 100 or even 200 years, and more than 350 years on three island sites (Ferguson-Lees, 1957); longest occupancy of a single site (by a female) between 7 and 30 years; closest distance between eyries about a quarter mile (see Olendorff, 1971).

Eggs: Mar.–June; Alaska, July; 2–6, usually 3–4, cream or buff, covered with red-brown markings.

Incubation: 28–29 days for each egg; young fly 35–42 days after hatching (Brown and Amadon, 1968), 30 days (Nelson, 1971); young usually do not breed until 3 years old or in third year after hatching (Nelson, 1972). Peregrine will lay second set of eggs if first set destroyed early in incubation (Beebe, 1967); Bred in captivity (first documented account in world) in Germany by Renz Waller during World War II (Prestwich, 1955; Waller, 1962); Beebe (1967) reported captive pair in Canada laid eggs, 1967, chicks died after hatching; Schramm in state of Wash. bred captive pair in 1968 and 1969 that raised young (Harrell, 1969); in spring 1971, Heinz Meng bred pair of peregrines (Peale's falcons) which raised one young (Hicks, 1971); same pair hatched three young in spring 1972 (Anonymous, 1972a); see also report of Cornell Laboratory of Ornithology summer 1972 (Pettingill and Lancaster, 1972) and other breeding experiments (Olendorff, 1972). From 1972, the breeding program at Cornell Laboratory of Ornithology grew enormously, producing a total of 324 peregrines up to 1978 (20 birds in 1973 but 95 in 1978). Many of these were introduced successfully (by Cornell research teams) in the wild on the East Coast of the U.S. by placing the growing young at potential nesting sites of this species. In 1979, two pairs of the Cornell-bred peregrines set up "housekeeping" at 2 sites although neither pair produced young. More recently, because great horned owls killed many of the young peregrines re-introduced into the wild (there were no parent falcons to protect them), some young peregrines were raised to the flying stage by Cornell research teams on tall city buildings where great horned owls would not be a threat to them. They were especially encouraged to do so because one female from the Cornell project settled by herself at a building in Baltimore in 1978. In 1979, the Cornell research teams gave her some of their young peregrines, which she raised successfully. There are similar programs of breeding and re-introducing peregrines in the wild in Colorado and in Canada (Lapham, 1979). See *The Peregrine Fund Newsletter,* no. 6 (fall 1978), no. 7 (fall 1979), published by Cornell University Laboratory of Ornithology, Ithaca, N.Y. See especially Temple (1977) for captive breeding of threatened species.

Other Names: American peregrine; duck hawk; great-footed hawk; Peale's falcon; rock peregrine; wandering falcon.

Age: Banding records in Europe indicate that young ones often shot and killed in same year they were hatched; of two others banded when young and in same nest in Finland, one killed 7 years, 4 months, later in Germany, the other 15 years, 3 months, after it had been banded and only 160 mi. north of where it had hatched (Nice, 1935a); Hickey and Anderson (1969) cite the famous female peregrine of Sun Life Building, Montreal (Hall, 1970), as at least 18 years old, and three that once nested at eyries along Hudson R., N.Y., were 17, 18, and 20 years old.

Flight Speed: Gliding and flapping, Hawk Mtn., Pa., 28–32 m.p.h. (Broun and Goodwin, 1943); 40 m.p.h. (Cottam *et al.,* 1942b); 40–60 m.p.h., w. Pa. (Terres, 1968a); level or straight flight in England, 62 m.p.h. (Portal, 1922); in stoop at prey, one passed airplane diving at 175 m.p.h. in U.S. (Lawson, 1930).

Hybrids: "Presumed natural hybrids" reported between European peregrine, *Falco peregrinus,* and the Old World lanner falcon, *Falco biarmicus* (Gray, 1958).

Weights: Of N. American subspecies *anatum,* over most of range, males 1 lb. 4¼ oz. to 1 lb. 9¼ oz.; females 1 lb. 14 oz. to 2 lbs. 11 oz. (Brown and Amadon, 1968). *See* weights of larger subspecies of Pacific coast under Peale's falcon; see other weights of peregrines in Beebe (1960); Bond (1936a); Cade (1960).

Range: Nests, or nested (bred), from northern edges of N. America, including Greenland, south to s. S. America, Falkland Is., and from n. Europe, n. Asia south to s. Africa, Madagascar, Australia, Tasmania, Solomon Is., and other islands of w. Oceania; winters (in W. Hemisphere) from sw. Canada south into Baja Calif., Ariz., N.M., Colo., Neb., Mo., s. Great Lakes area east to New England and south through Mexico, c. C. America, and West Indies to n. Chile, c. Argentina, and Uruguay (A.O.U. *Check-list,* 1957). A severe and rapid nesting population decline from 1950 through 1965 paralleled in parts of Europe (Finland, w. Germany, France, British Isles) and in N. America throughout U.S. on a scale that made it, according to Hickey (1969), one of most remarkable recent events in environmental biology. See also Cade *et al.* (1971); Ratcliffe (1963).

Falcon, prairie, *Falco mexicanus* (FAL-koh meks-ih-CANE-us); genus name: *see* Falcon, aplomado; species name: Lat., of Mexico. (Color ills., page 297.) Arid plains, hills, mountains interior w. N. America; adopted as official mascot or representative of flying cadets, U.S. Air Force Academy; 17–20 in. long; wingspread 40–42 in.; similar to peregrine falcon in size and form, with long, pointed wings, long tail; paler, lighter build, clay or sand color; sexes outwardly similar; females larger; adults: upperparts light brown and barred, tawny; bill dark bluish horn, yellow at base; cere and legs yellow; white line over each eye; dark streak below eyes (mustache) extends to white throat; underparts cream-white, heavily streaked with brown spots; tail brown, with buff bars, white tip; immatures: similar but usually buffier, less white below; cere and legs blue-gray; seen from below in flight, distinguished by black patch of "armpit" feathers (axillars) where wings join body; flight is direct, swift; alternates short powerful wingbeats with glide; flies with speed almost equal to peregrine, which it can outfly at higher altitudes because of lighter wing loading (Brown and Amadon, 1968); has been used in falconry but irascible, excitable, difficult to train; around eyrie, attacks and harasses slower-moving eagles, hawks, owls that fly near; alarm note is shrill, cackling *kee, kee, kee,* sometimes utters high-pitched whistling calls (Skinner, 1938); resident over much of range but in Oct. descends from mountains and wanders to live at lower elevations around wind-swept fields of winter wheat where concentrations of horned larks, rosy finches, starlings (see in Enderson, 1964, and White and Roseneau, 1970); can overtake most birds in direct flight but also stoops at them and knocks them out of air with blow of feet or plucks out of air in flight; sometimes hovers like American kestrel over place on ground looking for bird or small mammal prey; arrives at nesting sites in Feb.–Mar., either male or female may arrive first; male in spectacular courtship dives utters loud cries, also struts about on nesting ledge; in best cliff habitat, 23 pairs found nesting along 16 mi.; nests earlier than peregrine falcon and replacing it at eyries especially in Rocky Mtn. region, from which peregrine had disappeared by early 1960s (Enderson, 1969); nesting population of prairie falcon declining in Utah owing to home building near eyries but does not appear to be declining in Colo. where human population high (White, 1969); estimated to be 600 pairs nesting in Colo. and Wyo. (Brown and Amadon, 1968); population declining in w. Canada documented by Fyfe *et al.* (1969), also in agricultural parts of Utah and in Calif. (see p. 542 in Hickey, 1969); some thinning of eggshells of prairie falcons from insecticides cited by Anderson and Hickey (1970); potential hazard from mercury reported in Canada by Fimreite *et al.* (1970) because of high mercury residues in seed-eating horned larks much eaten by prairie falcons. On Threatened Wildlife List (*see* United States Dept. of the Interior, 1973).

Feeding Habits: Eats sparrows, blackbirds, meadowlarks, jays, magpies, mourning doves, quail, horned larks, burrowing owls, snatches from ground mice, ground squirrels, young rabbits, jackrabbits, young prairie dogs, and carries to perch to eat; occasionally hops along ground catching lizards, large grasshoppers.

Nest: Prefers ledges of cliffs with potholes, caves, crevices with protective overhang, mostly in foothills of mountains, in canyons, some high in mountains in Colo. at 10,000 ft.; no nest but slight scrape in loose dirt, gravel, small stones of ledge for eggs, also laid in old nests of cliff-dwelling ravens, red-tailed hawks (Skinner, 1938).

Eggs: Mar.–June throughout much of range in w. U.S., with most laying in Apr.; Tex. and Mexico, Feb.–May (Skinner, 1938); 3–6, usually 4–5, white to pink, heavily marked with brown, purple.

Incubation: Mostly by female, 29–31 days, young leave nest about 40 days after hatching (Brown and Amadon, 1968); 31–33 days, young leave nest when 5–6 weeks old (Reilly, 1968); in captivity, incubation of 35 days for one egg (Enderson, 1971); has been bred successfully in captivity at St. Louis, Mo. (Harrell and Hunter, 1968), and by Enderson (1971); see also successful Canadian experiment by Fyfe reported in Olendorff (1972).

Accidents: Some crippled or killed after striking barbed-wire fences around irrigated fields, when chasing bird prey (Hickey, 1969).

Age: Enderson (1971) had female in captivity 10 years old.

Albinism: An adult female of pair nesting in Colo., May 1931, was cream-white with occasional dark feather, dark eyes, and at least 9 years old (Bailey and Niedrach, 1933).

Flight Speed: "Cruising" at 30 m.p.h. (Cottam *et al.*, 1942b).

Weights: One female weighed 1 lb. 12 oz. (Brown and Amadon, 1968); 2 lbs. (Pough, 1951); a captive female flown in falconry by Austing (1967) ranged from low of 1 lb. 12 oz. to high of 2 lb. 1 oz.

Range: Resident in prairie country, deserts, mountains, canyons from c. B.C., n. Alta., s. Sask., w. N.D., south to Baja Calif., Mexico, s. Ariz. and N.M., n. Tex.; some winter in Mexico but many adults winter over interior N. America to Calgary, Alta.; wanderers reported in Man., Minn., Ill., Iowa, and Ind.

Gyrfalcon, *Falco rusticolus* (FAL-koh russ-TICK-oh-lus); genus name: *see* Falcon, aplomado; species name: from Lat. *rusticola*, living in the country; common name (JER-fall-kon): from Lat. *gyrfalco*, or *girofalco*, said to be Low Lat. corruption of *hierofalco*, or "sacred falcon," for the bird so highly revered by falconers (*see* Falconry) down through the ages (Cade, 1968). (Color ills., page 296.) Lives in Arctic Europe, Asia, Iceland, in Arctic N. America, in Alaska, Canada, Greenland, considered rare over entire range (Cade, 1960); irregularly wanders in fall and winter to s. Canada, n. U.S.; in winter 1970–71, greatest recorded invasion with at least 60 reported (early Sept. to late Mar.) from Nova Scotia to B.C., south to Ore., Wyo., S.D., Ill., s. N.J. (Brigantine National Wildlife Refuge); one to coastal Va.; total of 5 white phase, the others either the dark or the gray phase (Buckley, 1972); magnificent bird of prey, large, swift, majestic; largest of all falcons; sexes outwardly similar but females larger; three color phases, or color forms (*see* Color Phase): *white*, usually with snow-white underparts, white back streaked, spotted, and barred with dark markings; *dark phase*, deep dusky slate gray, slate blue, and brown; and intermediate *gray phase*, gray-brown, spotted and barred with black and white; cere, feet, and legs bright yellow; immatures: cere *slate blue* (Buckley, 1972); body

streaked below instead of barred and spotted; 20–25 in. long; wingspread 48–54 in. (Brown and Amadon, 1968); larger than peregrine falcon, from which the dark or white forms can be distinguished by their generally uniform color above and below and lack of distinct "mustache"; heavily built, powerful falcon with long tail tapering to point; pointed, triangular wings have broad base, wingbeats slower than peregrine; gyrfalcon more apt to fly close to ground; south of nesting range, in winter, preys on ducks, gulls, ptarmigans, rabbits, rats, and other animals of marshes and other open country; noted, when sitting on fence posts, stakes, poles, to perch with body horizontal, appears to lean forward, may alight on rise of ground; in nesting season in Alaska lives mostly in foothill tundra frequently above 2,500 ft. on escarpments away from water, especially in mountains, also on sea cliffs and river bluffs (Cade, 1960); in central Canadian barrens on rocky formations, elevated above surrounding country and called dykes (Fyfe, 1969); dark and intermediate gray phases appear most numerous on N. American continent (Bent, 1938); white phase constitutes the population of n. Greenland, n. Siberia (Dement'ev *et al.*, 1966); total population in Alaska estimated at 200–300 pairs; in Greenland about 855 pairs; total population in N. America probably not more than 5,000 individuals "and may well be less" (Cade, 1960); rare in Canadian Arctic except Anderson R. region; for time being safe from effects of pesticides (see discussion in Cade, 1968); when in competition with peregrine for nesting sites in n. Canada, gyrfalcon is dominant because of larger size and earlier arrival (Mar.–Apr.) on nesting territory; may displace peregrine for better cliff-nesting sites (Fyfe, 1969); sometimes the two species occupy same cliffs together; generally the pair of gyrfalcons are shy about nest; when disturbed, slip away so quietly one may not see them leave the nest; sometimes will return and cackle (Fyfe in Hickey, p. 422, 1969); alarm call much like peregrine's but louder, harsher *hyaik-hyaik-hyaik* or *kyek-kyek-kyek* or *ke-a-ke-a* (Brown and Amadon, 1968).

Feeding Habits: Eats mostly birds, especially Arctic ptarmigans and grouse, also alcids, gulls, jaegers, and from small birds such as snow buntings and shorebirds to ducks and geese, but mostly eats ptarmigans—up to 89% of all food by weight taken in Alaska; some small mammals but nesting not directly affected by numbers of lemmings (Brown and Amadon, 1968).

Nest: Frequently on tall cliff ledge with protective overhang; makes scrape on ledge in which to lay eggs, also lays in old cliff and tree nests of rough-legged hawk and raven; has two or three alternate nesting sites which pair uses in different years (Cade, 1960); in Alaska, has nested on abandoned pile driver, elevated sluice box (White and Roseneau, 1970).

Eggs: Alaska, Apr.–May; 3–8, usually 4, pale, yellow, white or buff, finely spotted with dark red, rarely unmarked pure white (Brown and Amadon, 1968).

Incubation: Mostly by female, 28–29 days; young first fly 46–49 days after hatching.

Other Names: Asiatic gyrfalcon; black gyrfalcon; gray gyrfalcon; Greenland falcon; white gyrfalcon.

Weights: In Alaska, females 2 lbs. 10 oz. to 4 lbs. 6 oz.; males 2 lbs. to 3 lbs. 1 oz. (Cade, 1960).

Range: In N. America, nests in northern part of N. Hemisphere, from n. Alaska, Victoria Is., Ellesmere Is., and n. Greenland south to s. Alaska, n. Mack., Southampton Is., n. Que., and n. Labrador; winters south to mid-Europe, Japan and in N. America in Far North; wanders irregularly south to s. B.C., Mont., s. Man., N.Y., N.J., and Mass.

Kestrel, American, *Falco sparverius* (FAL-koh spar-VER-ih-us); genus name: *see* Falcon, aplomado; species name: Lat., from Fr. *espervier*, sparrow hawk (another name for this bird); misnamed, as sparrows are only small part of its food and it is not a hawk; many ornithologists prefer to call it American kestrel because of its close relationship and resemblance to the Eurasian kestrel of Europe, Asia, and Africa. (Color ill., page 297.) American kestrel is smallest and most common N. American falcon; even smaller than sharp-shinned hawk, which is smallest N. American member of Hawk Family; in summer, north to Alaska and in Canada and in much of U.S. in both summer and winter; 9–12 in. long; wingspread 20–24½ in.; typical falcon shape, short neck, small bulletlike head has black-and-white pattern with dark vertical whiskerlike marks on sides of head; slender, pointed wings; *rufous-red back and tail;* sexes similar but male has *blue-gray wings;* female larger, brown wings; in flight, pointed wings distinguish it from sharp-shinned hawk, which has short, rounded wings; while perched erectly on utility wire or pole along roadside watching for prey on ground, frequently raises and lowers tail; when alarmed utters loud, rapid *klee-klee-klee* or *killy, killy, killy,* thus one of its names, killy hawk; in fall many migrate southward to s. U.S. and into Mexico (Roest, 1957); some remain in pairs in same area all year, but many, alone, defend winter territories against others of kind (Cade, 1955); on nesting range in n. U.S., Canada, Alaska, by Feb. into Mar. (Tyler, 1938); lives along borders of woodlands, open fields, pastures with scattered trees, highways; in Southwest, on arid plains and deserts with giant cactuses, or in wooded canyons, on western plains where trees and shrubs planted and utility lines with poles and wires; perches quietly through middle of day; hunts mostly in morning and late afternoon; flies with rapid wingbeats and short glides over open country or circles about, often stops in midair to hover on rapidly beating wings over certain spot of interest to it on ground; then flaps or glides to new location to hover again; if sees prey, partly folds wings, drops lower, then swoops to ground to grasp mouse or insect in talons and flies to perch to eat; swallows small insects whole, but with large grasshopper or a mouse, bites off pieces while holding it under both feet (Roest, 1957).

Feeding Habits: Eats insects, bats, mice, birds, lizards, small snakes, frogs; in summer, where abundance of grasshoppers, crickets, will make them principal food but in winter, in North, preys mostly on birds, mice; can be kept in captivity indefinitely on diet of fresh meat without drinking water; capacity to live in desert in summer because it is tolerant of great heat; gets moisture from carnivorous diet, which frees it from dependence on drinking water (Bartholomew and Cade, 1956), and stays in shade during intense heat of midday; has been used in falconry and flown at house sparrows.

Nest: Prefers old tree nesting holes of flicker and hollows in trees or cactuses, sometimes in old magpie nests in West; in hole in cliff; within cities and towns where abundant supply of house sparrows, often nests in niches in walls and holes under gables, roosts in same places; also nests in bird boxes built especially for it (see details in Terres, 1968c, and Nagy, 1972b).

Eggs: Fla., mid-Mar. to early June; c. U.S. and East, mid-Apr. to early June; Canada, late May to mid-June; 3–7, usually 4–5, white to cream or pale pink heavily blotched with browns.

Incubation: Mostly by female, 29–30 days (Sherman, 1913); 30–31 days near Bend, Ore. (Roest, 1957); 27–33 days in captivity (Willoughby and Cade, 1964—see also Porter and Wiemeyer, 1972); male calls female from nest hole to feed her; young leave nest 30–31 days after hatching.

Other Names: Grasshopper hawk; killy hawk; house hawk; rusty-crowned falcon; short-winged hawk; sparrow hawk; windhover.

Accidents: One mobbed and killed by blue jays; by a cat; by lightning; flying into a window; hit by car, and by locomotive; man is greatest enemy, most banded birds recovered have been shot.

Age: Out of 558 recoveries of banded birds, only 15 lived to ages 4–6 years (1968 data from U.S. Fish and Wildlife Service files); annual mortality of 57%; life expectancy of a banded American kestrel about 1 year, 3 months (Bond, 1943); 75% of all mortality between Aug. and Nov.; age of captives: in half dozen zoos across U.S. lived from 2 to 3½ years; several lived to 4 years; three to 6 years; one to 7 years; one to 9 years; exception was male kept as house pet that lived to 14 years old, when killed by accident (Roest, 1957); another, in adult plumage when acquired, lived to 14 years in captivity (Schumacher, 1964); a male captive in Canada lived to at least 17 years old.

Flight Speed: Timed in Pa. in migration, Hawk Mtn., 22–36 m.p.h.; in Calif., 22–25 m.p.h. (Wetmore, 1916); in w. U.S., 30–39 m.p.h. (Cottam *et al.,* 1942b).

Weights: Males about 3½–4 oz.; females about 4¼ oz. (Brown and Amadon, 1968).

Range: In N. America, nests from e.-c. Alaska, c. Mack., n. Man., n. Ont., s. Que., Nova Scotia south into Baja Calif., n. Mexico to s. Tex., n. La., n. Miss., and s. Fla., and from Mexico, West Indies south into Tierra del Fuego; winters in N. America over breeding range from s. Canada south to Gulf coast, Fla., and southward.

Kestrel, Eurasian, *Falco tinnunculus* (FAL-koh tin-UN-cue-lus); genus name: *see* Falcon, aplomado; species name: Lat. word for a kind of hawk, or kestrel; common name: from root words in Old Fr. that suggest "creaking"

or "crackling" call (Gruson, 1972). Native of Europe, Asia, and Africa, Canary, Cape Verde, and Azore Is. (Brown and Amadon, 1968); in N. America, first one reported, a female collected at Strawberry Hill near Nantasket, Mass., Sept. 1887 (Cory, 1888); also reported from Greenland; 12½–15½ in. long; wingspread 27–30 in.; much like American kestrel but is larger, lacks black and white head markings of American bird, and *tail and rump are slate or blue-gray* instead of rufous red. A live female picked up exhausted and emaciated Dec. 1959 in village of La Carbet, w. coast of Martinique, French West Indies, had apparently crossed the Atlantic, died very quickly after capture; a female in juvenile plumage captured in mist net, Sept. 23, 1972, at Cape May, N.J., weighed 8 oz., was photographed, banded, and released same day (Clark, 1974). See Pinchon and Vaurie (1961) for other records and details; see life history of Eurasian kestrel in Jourdain (1938).

Age: Of banded wild Eurasian kestrels in Europe, one in Germany lived to 9½ years; oldest in Switzerland reached 16 years, 3 months; greatest cause of death, shooting by man (Johnston, 1965). Has been bred and young raised in aviaries in England and Germany (Prestwich, 1955); Koehler (1969) cited her own successful experiments and others in Europe from 1905 to 1968.

Weights: Males (37), 4 oz. to 8¼ oz.; females (29), 6 oz. to 9¼ oz. (Brown and Amadon, 1968). Eurasian kestrels flown successfully in falconry in Old World especially at starlings; was trained at one time in France to fly at bats.

Merlin, *Falco columbarius* (FAL-koh kohlum-BAY-rih-us); genus name: *see* Falcon, aplomado; species name: Lat., pertaining to doves; former common name of pigeon hawk because it killed pigeons. (Color ill., page 297.) In summer, in n. Europe, n. Asia; in N. America, throughout spruce-fir forests in n. U.S., Canada, Alaska, to limit of trees; small falcon without distinct mustachial stripe; 10–13½ in. long; wingspread 23½–26½ in.; female larger than male; adults: male blue-gray above; white throat; rest of underparts white streaked with brown or black; tail barred with gray, tipped with white; female and immatures: brown above; buffy underparts streaked with dark brown; lives in summer in boreal coniferous zone of n. N. America, in open parkline grasslands, shrubby barrens, bogs; hunts about woods openings, marshes, along edges of lakes, ponds (Forbush, 1925–29); has habit like shrike and gray jay of flying low over ground toward post or stump, then suddenly spreads tail and wings and bounds straight up to perch and alights; watches for prey from top of dead tree, post, boulder; when hunting, often flies low over ground, frequently rising and falling in flight; usually does not stoop at prey, but in swift, veering flight overtakes small birds and plucks them out of air with feet and talons; also dragonflies, which it eats on wing; may fly high but does not soar as American kestrels and peregrines do (Brown and Amadon, 1968); relatively easy to train in falconry to catch small birds (Craighead and Craighead, 1940) but beginning to show harmful effects of pesticides in

e. Canada (Temple, 1972), and in w. Canada, threat to it from mercury in environment (see Fimreite *et al.,* 1970); most merlins winter from Gulf states south to n. S. America; in fall may be seen migrating southward along Atlantic coast, especially at Cape May Point, N.J. (Stone, 1937); also at Hawk Mountain Sanctuary in Pa.; in spring arrives n. U.S. Apr. and May with main migration of small birds on which it preys; males arrive before females, pair return to same general area each year; fearless, often allows close approach to it when perched; fierce in defense of nest, will fly to meet intruder with loud, harsh cackling cries, *ki-ki-ki-ki-kee,* rapidly repeated, resemble alarm calls of American kestrel; known to dive and strike head and hands of person at nest (Craighead and Craighead, 1940); when female solicits food from male, calls *eep-eep-eeep.*

Feeding Habits: Catches and eats petrels, teal, woodcock, snipe, sandpipers, curlews, plovers, quail, pigeons, doves, swifts, flickers, jays, blackbirds, meadowlarks, sparrows, waxwings, swallows, warblers, horned larks, pipits, and many other small birds, also gophers, squirrels, mice, bats, toads, lizards, snakes, dragonflies, butterflies, moths, caterpillars, grasshoppers, crickets, beetles, spiders, crayfishes, scorpions; in winter, on Trinidad, ffrench (1967) noted merlins preying much on wintering flocks of dickcissels (*see* one of its hunting methods under Autolycism).

Nest: In N. America, often uses old tree nests of crows, magpies, hawks, usually 15–35 ft. above ground, which it may reline with bark, feathers, also in natural hollows of trees, or old woodpecker holes, holes in cutbanks, sometimes on bare ledge of cliff with no nest materials and in scraped-out hollow in ground on hummock or small dune, under branches of scraggly bushes or trees.

Eggs: May–June; 2–7, usually 5–6, light buff regularly stippled with chocolate, purple, and brown (Brown and Amadon, 1968).

Incubation: Mostly by female, 28–32 days; young fly about 25–30 days after hatching.

Other Names: American merlin; black pigeon hawk; bullet hawk; eastern pigeon hawk; little blue corporal; pigeon falcon; pigeon hawk; Richardson's pigeon hawk; Suckley's pigeon hawk; western pigeon hawk.

Flight Speed: In Calif., flapping, 30–45 m.p.h. (Bond, 1936b); in Pa., in migration at Hawk Mtn., 28 m.p.h. (Brown and Goodwin, 1943).

Hybrids: In Europe, presumed natural hybrids of the merlin, *F. columbarius aesolon,* and the Eurasian kestrel, *F. tinnunculus* (Gray, 1958).

Weights: E. U.S., males 5–6 oz.; females nearly 8 oz. (Forbush, 1925–29); w. U.S., males about 6 oz.; females 7–9 oz. (Bond, 1936b).

Range: Nests in n. Alaska, n. Yukon, n. Mack., sw. Keewatin, n. Man., n. Ont., n. Que., Newfoundland south to n. Calif., Idaho, n. Mont., n. N.D., n. Minn., Iowa, n. Wisc., n. Mich., s. Ont., n. Ohio, n. N.Y., N.H. (probably), Me., N.B., Nova Scotia; winters south to n. S. America: from Wash., Oreg., Wyo., and Colo., to s. Tex., s. La., Ala., S.C., Ga., Baja Calif., Mexico, and Fla., and West Indies to South America.

falcon

osprey

vulture

hawk

FALCONIFORMES

FALCONIDAE
See Falcon Family.

FALCONIFORMES

(fall-coh-nih-FOR-meez); from Lat. *falco*, a hawk, and *forma*, form; hawk-shaped (Coble, 1954). An order or group of the diurnal birds of prey that resemble each other fundamentally in structure (*see* Order) and include 271 species in the world—the vultures, condors, kites, eagles, hawks, falcons, and the osprey—in 5 families (Van Tyne and Berger, 1959), of which N. America has representatives of 4; *see* Vulture —American Vulture Family; Hawk Family; Falcon Family; Osprey Family. The fifth group is the Secretary-bird Family (Sagittaridae) of Africa of 1 species—a long-legged, cranelike bird that eats mainly snakes, lizards, small mammals, and insects which it catches by stamping them, battering them with its wings, and grasping them in its feet. Although not usually inclined to fly, it soars occasionally like some other hawks. A full-grown male stands about 3 ft. 2 in. tall, wingspread to about 7 ft. (Bannerman, 1964b); its head crest of long plumes suggests an old-fashioned clerk or secretary with long quill pens stuck behind the ears; thus its name.

Falconiformes include the two largest living flying birds—the Andean and California condors (*see* Size). Features generally in common in Falconiformes are hooked bill and the cere (*see* Bill), with a centrally located (in bill) nostril, grasping raptorial foot in which inner toe is shorter than outer; the middle toe is longest and connected to outer by small web; each toe armed with a long, curving claw (Jollie, 1961); also, all Falconiformes are single-brooded (Olendorff, 1971). *See* Brooding. At one time owls were grouped with the hawks, eagles, and falcons (*see* discussion under Convergent Evolution), but were later considered unrelated; however, recent anatomical studies suggest that the owls may be related at least remotely to the falcons (Brown and Amadon, 1968).

There are some marked differences within the order: for example, the New World vultures (American Vulture Family) have weakly raptorial feet, and the heads of the adults are bare of feathers. *See also* discussion under Smell. For a discussion of how birds are grouped according to their relationships, *see* Classification; Morphology; Check-list Order.

FALCONRY

(FALL-kon-rih). Name derived from art of training falcons (*see* Falcon Family) to pursue and capture wild birds, also name for the sport of catching birds and other animals by means of falcons and certain kinds of hawks and eagles (*see* Hawk Family); it is also called *hawking*.

The sport goes back to the remote and unwritten past; little is known of history of earliest falconry except that it began in Near East or Middle East at least 4,000 years ago; falcons appeared in writings, frescoes, and sculptures of early Egyptians and Persians before any mention of use of them in hunting; in ancient Egypt, falcons played an important part in the cult of the dead (Zeuner, 1963); therefore, fal-

cons thought to have been first maintained for religious and ceremonial functions; later, when hunting with falcons began, it seems to have been sport or entertainment limited to nobility and wealthy upper classes; using falcons for food-getting may have originated in Far East (Peeters and Jameson, 1970).

There is some evidence, according to Fisher and Peterson (1964), that trained falcons were flown at prey in China around 2000 B.C.; in Persia, about 1700 B.C. F. E. Zeuner, Professor of Environmental Archaeology, University of London, believed falconry probably reached the Nile around 800 B.C. and spread into Arabia and Syria about 600 B.C.

When travelers Marco Polo and Father Rubruquis explored the little-known regions of Asia during the 14th century, they discovered that falconry was practiced by wandering tribes of Tartars (Goodwin, 1935); the Mongols were rugged hunters and warriors and with them falconry was a sport, apparently without the religious significance it had had in past. According to Goodwin, Marco Polo mentioned a palace at Chang-nor where the Grand Khan, Emperor of Tartary and China, had two court officers of highest rank called Masters of the Chase; Ap. Evans (1960) reported that Kublai Khan kept 200 gyrfalcons and 300 other kinds of hunting hawks and an army of 10,000 beaters for his hawking expeditions.

The Mongols trained hawks or falcons of various kinds, but their most spectacular hunts were with golden eagles (*see* in Hawk Family), which is the most used of all eagles in falconry. The berkut (a Siberian golden eagle) was trained by the Tartars to hunt antelopes, foxes, and wolves (Grossman and Hamlet, 1964), but according to Brown (1970), it is the falconer who kills the 100-lb. wolf, "the eagle only holds it"; flights with golden eagles in pursuit of foxes and wolves are practiced to this day in Outer Mongolia (Peeters and Jameson, 1970).

According to Peeters and Jameson, falconry was well established in Japan in the 4th century A.D., and by the 3rd or 4th century trading caravans from the Near East had carried falconers with trained birds to C. Europe; at least two centuries later, falconry was introduced into the British Isles (Ap. Evans, 1960).

Fisher and Peterson (1964) wrote that falconry in a crude form was known to the ancient Greeks at the time of Aristotle (384–322 B.C.), but penetration of falconry into Europe came slowly; it was mentioned in Rome by Pliny (A.D. 23–79) and by the 7th century it was popular enough in France so that trained hawks had value. Local kings of s. England became enthusiasts—Alfred the Great, who wrote a treatise on the subject, and Welshmen were among earliest in Britain to take up the sport. By the 8th century, there were references to hawking in England (Ap. Evans, 1960), and later, returning Crusaders brought back falconers and trained birds, which gave vast impetus to falconry in Europe (Fuertes, 1920).

According to Fisher and Peterson (1964), from the 8th to the 17th century, falconry was "the rage and fashion of every kingly court in Europe"; among its enthusiasts, besides Alfred the Great, were Ethelbert II, King of Kent; Athelstan, King of Mercia; Howel, the Good

King of Wales; King Edward the Confessor; Harold and William the Conqueror; King Stephen; King Henry II; and others—Thomas à Becket often carried a hawk as a status symbol. The Emperor Frederick II of Germany wrote a splendid treatise, *De Arte Venandi cum Avibus,* on the art of falconry.

From the 14th century on, hawking of the English monarchs became proverbial—Edward I, Edward II, Richard II, Henry VIII, and others. In the so-called Sport of Kings only certain classes could own certain birds: gyrfalcons by royalty only; peregrines by high noblemen; merlins for noblewomen; short-winged hawks —goshawks and European sparrow hawks— for the owners of land and the clergy (Fisher and Peterson, 1964).

Ownership of hawks or falcons became a symbol of power and influence; they appeared on family crests and coats of arms. Falcons were used for handsome gifts—in 1335 the King of Scotland sent King Edward III a single peregrine falcon, and falcons were even given in payment of ransom—a Crusader prince held for ransom by the Saracens was redeemed by payment to his captors of twelve Greenland (white) gyrfalcons (Ap. Evans, 1960). See also Cade (1968) for details.

According to Ap. Evans, by the 13th century, falconry was no longer the prerogative of the King and a few of his nobles; it grew in popularity until it reached its peak in the 16th century, when it was the most widespread and popular sport in England.

By the end of the 17th century, portable firearms which could be readily fired at many birds and other animals took the place of hawking to fill the larder, and, according to Maj. Gen. Anthony Gerald O'Carroll Scott (1964), president of the British Falconers' Club, popularity of the sport declined partly because of Puritan influence during the Civil War and partly because of the enclosure of land in the 17th and 18th centuries.

In latter part of the 18th century, however, the sport was revived in England through efforts of Col. T. Thornton, who with Lord Oxford founded a hawking club about 1775; by 1838 the club came to an end but a number of individual falconers continued the sport. For a comprehensive and detailed history, along with the art and practice of hawking in England and in continental Europe, see especially Ap. Evans (1960), and Peeters and Jameson (1970), whose book, besides its history of the sport, deals largely with falconry and its practice in America. See also Scott (1964) and Fisher and Peterson (1964); see Peterson (1948) for an interesting chapter on American falconry.

According to Nye (1966), an active and enthusiastic falconer, beginning in his youth in Washington, D.C., an interest in falconry began in America early in this century through a small group of falconers in e. U.S. led by Col. R. L. Meredith, along with British-born George G. Goodwin of the American Museum of Natural History.

Col. Meredith, called "Luff" by falconers in America and abroad, is regarded as the father of American falconry. He founded the Falconry Club of America, which for a time published a journal, and from his graduation from the U.S. Military Academy at West Point in 1917 to his death in 1965, he trained and flew falcons with great zeal and high professionalism; he traveled much about the U.S. with his birds and helped many beginning falconers get started in the sport. See Meredith (1934).

Fuertes' excitingly illustrated article in the Dec. 1920 issue of *National Geographic* magazine stimulated many young falconry enthusiasts, especially those in the Washington, D.C., area; many of these and others became the present older generation of American falconers; most of the present-day active ones (being active is a requirement of membership) belong to the relatively recent North American Falconry Association, which publishes a journal.

The first national falconry meet in America was held at Media, Pa., in 1938; the first American books about hawking were Craighead and Craighead (1939) and a "how to do it" falconry book (Russell, 1940); by 1944, an organization called, at that time, the Falconers Association of North America had about 100 members. By 1964, the sport had grown so in popularity that the Secretary of the Interior issued an amendment to the Migratory Bird Treaty Act Regulations, legalizing the use of falcons for hunting of all migratory game birds, including doves and waterfowl; by 1965, falconry was thinly but well established in most states and in Canada (Nye, 1966).

Falconry in America, however, may never become a widespread sport, according to Nye, because of the time required to trap and to train hawks and to give them daily work and care. An increasing scarcity of some birds of prey, especially the peregrine falcon (*see* discussion under Falcon Family) and some of the hawks (*see* in Hawk Family), owing to the increasing population of people in America, consequent disturbance of some birds at their nest sites, destruction of habitat, and effects of deadly pesticides, may limit the numbers of birds of prey available to falconers (see, however, Cade, 1968); also, not all states permit falconry; others require license (see discussion of nationwide survey in Hilton, 1970).

Some falcons and hawks are being bred in small numbers in captivity by ornithologists and falconers in the hope of restocking populations in parts of America from which they have disappeared. *See,* however, in biography of peregrine falcon under Falcon Family. See Harris, V. T., (1972) and issues of *Raptor Research News,* published by Raptor Research Foundation, Inc., Vermillion, S.D., for periodic reports of breeding projects of N. American birds of prey.

FALCONRY
The falcon is held by the falconer by means of jesses, short straps attached to the legs, to which longer leashes may be attached for training. The hood will keep the bird quiet: it will not fly when blind.

FALL SHUFFLE

Term of game biologists for the breakup and dispersal of family groups of game birds, especially ruffed grouse, in the autumn. Strife among the growing young grouse of a family brood increases until some drive away their brothers and sisters, displaying an intolerance to crowding similar to that of the territorial behavior of the adults in spring. According to Edminster (1947), if one of these young birds is continuously chased by other individuals or by family groups of grouse it may meet, before it has settled in a fall territory, it becomes more and more nervous and may end in the so-called *crazy flight*. When in crazy flight, grouse often fly far away from their normal coverts, sometimes into villages or cities, where they fly into buildings or other obstacles and are stunned or killed.

Various fanciful explanations have been offered for crazy flight—falling leaves in autumn cause grouse to become nervous and greatly agitated or the flight is caused by irritation from internal parasites. Edminster (1947) believes that it is "merely an aberration of the fall shuffle—a social phenomenon that likely occurs in most sedentary (non-migratory) species of birds and is well-known in the bobwhite quail."

FALSE CROP

Term for the expansion of the esophagus, especially in the redpoll, in which the "false crop" extends laterally and dorsally around the vertebral column and forms a lesser enlargement on the left side of the column. The enlargement is often filled with seeds that redpolls eat and is therefore a storage place for seeds. *See* Buccal; Crop; Esophagus; *also* Redpoll in Finch Family.

FAMILIES OF NORTH AMERICAN BIRDS

See list under Classification.

FAMILY

Term for a group of related birds that are ranked next below an order in their classification (*see* Classification; Order). Whereas an order of birds may be worldwide in its range, or distribution, a family may be limited to a continent or to neighboring continents (Pettingill, 1956). Each family of birds is composed of at least one genus or a number of genera (plural of genus) in which they have been grouped by taxonomists to show close relationships within the family. Members of the same family show a combination of obvious and similar details—for example, in the shape of the bill, the presence of notches on it, the number of primary (flight) feathers, and the pattern of the scale-like skin that covers the bird's shank, just above its toes. *See* Tarsus. In a family group such as the crows, jays, and magpies, each belong to different genera; nevertheless, they have such similar characters (*see* under Crow Family) that they are united in one family—the Corvidae. See in Storer (1960b) a list of orders and families of birds of the world and the set of external characters that distinguish each.

Like the genus, the family is distinguished by certain characters which have adapted its members to their environment and way of life. For example, the woodpeckers (family Picidae) have feet adapted to clinging to trunks of trees, and bills adapted to probing or drilling into wood or earth for grubs and ants, which constitute a large part of their food. Hummingbirds (family Trochilidae) are usually small, and swift and agile of flight with rapid wingbeats which permit them to hover before flowers in their food-getting; kites, hawks, and eagles (family Accipitridae) are usually strong fliers, active in daylight, with hooked beaks adapted to tearing the flesh of their prey; however, not all similarities or differences, especially in the shape of bills and feet, indicate that birds are, or are not, related. *See* discussion under Convergent Evolution.

"By definition, a family is a monophyletic [*see* Monophyletic Descent] group (i.e., it stems from a single ancestral species), and many families are so well marked that there is not the slightest disagreement among ornithologists about which species should be included in those families.... Other families have not evolved far enough to be sharply demarked and there is considerable disagreement among ornithologists about where the boundary lines should be drawn" (Van Tyne and Berger, 1959). *See* Phylogenetic Relationship.

Ornithologists agree generally that there are about 170 families of birds in the world, each of which may contain anywhere from 1 species to more than 300 (Van Tyne and Berger, 1959). According to the A.O.U. *Check-list* (1957), there were 75 families of N. American birds represented in N. America; however, by 1973, there were about 78 families owing to species new to N. America entering the continent, either by themselves, by escaping from captivity (cage birds), or by man's introduction. See, for example, under Bulbul Family.

The family classification is especially useful because most birds belonging to certain families can be recognized by ornithologists at a glance, and all species in each family occupy a more or less similar niche (*see* Ecological Niche) in their environment (Mayr *et al.*, 1953).

The family names of birds, as in all animal families, always end in *-idae*, which makes the family designation easy to recognize. Mayr *et al.* (1953) cite W. Kirby as first suggesting in 1813 the uniform ending *-idae* to family names of insects as a patronymic appellation "and T. S. Palmer (1928) says that the British ornithologist Nicholas Aylward Vigors introduced into ornithology the uniform termination *-idae* for family names and in 1825 provided a set of such names for families of birds." *See* -Idae.

Family names are Latin plurals and are based on one of the genus names within the family, either the type genus or possibly the oldest or best-known genus of the family. See Mayr *et al.* (1953). For example, the family name Anatidae, or the Swans, Geese, and Ducks, is from *Anas*, the genus containing the domestic duck and its ancestor the mallard. For a list of families of N. American birds, *see* Classification; *see also* discussion under Names and Naming.

FASTEST BIRD

See Speed of Flight under Flight.

FASTING

Some birds can go a long time without food; others will die within a few hours if denied it. The larger predatory hawks, the eagles that kill live prey, and the vultures that eat carrion may be forced at times, because of food scarcity, to go hungry for days. Hatch (1970) had two captive turkey vultures that fasted for 8 and 11 days respectively, without effect on their good health.

In Calif., Fitch *et al.* (1946) followed a young female red-tailed hawk in the wild for 21 full but not consecutive days. For one 5-day period, the hawk apparently caught nothing and made only five kills—a ground squirrel, a cottontail rabbit, a deer mouse, a gopher snake, and an unidentified prey—during the entire 21 days. Her average daily intake of food during this time was less than 100 gr., or about 3 oz. Meanwhile, an adult (captive) of the investigators took 140 gr. of food daily, or about one sixth its own weight. *See* How Much Will a Bird Eat? under Food and Feeding Habits.

Some of the larger species can go a remarkably long time without eating and the longest periods of regular starvation in the wild are during incubation times (Lack, 1954). The female golden pheasant and common eider duck do not eat while incubating their eggs, which may take 3 weeks (Goodwin, 1948; Jourdain, 1939). The male Adélie penguin incubates for at least 40 days before being relieved by the female; the male emperor penguin, in midwinter in the Antarctic, sits on the single egg of his mate for 60 days, the full incubating period, without eating (Stonehouse, 1952). Jordan (1953), experimenting with wild mallard ducks, discovered that they can live without food for little more than 3 weeks in cool air temperature of 57° F. Hen mallards had much greater resistance to starving than drakes.

In Pa., Gerstell (1942), in similar experiments with ring-necked pheasants, discovered that they can live without food for about 2 weeks or more in winter; a wild turkey, 1 week; the gray, or Hungarian, partridge, 4–5 days.

Small birds, because of their small size, have a greater problem maintaining their body temperatures in winter than large ones (see Bergmann's Rule). For example, house sparrows tested by Kendeigh (1945b) could live without food only 15 hours (about the length of a winter night in n. U.S.) if winter cold was −5° F.; for only 10 hours if −20°F. See Cold and Birds. According to Welty (1962), one of the waxbills, a small seed-eating African bird, is said to die, if denied food, only 4–5 hours after its digestive tract is emptied. *See* Digestion; Metabolism.

During unusually cold and stormy winters, birds are often picked up in the wild that are dead or dying of starvation—some of them may weigh only two thirds or even one half their normal weight. *See* Bluebird Trail; Disaster Species. These are usually temporary losses in bird populations which ordinarily return to normal the next year or possibly within a few years (Lack, 1954).

Small birds of three families—hummingbirds, swifts, and poor-wills—in their evolution have developed defense against temporary cold and lack of food by becoming torpid (*see* Torpidity). To survive and to avoid winter cold and unavailability of food, many birds migrate.

FAUNA

The birds and other animals of a continent or of an area. Often used with flora—"fauna and flora"—the animals and plants of an area. *See* Biota; Avifauna.

FAUNAL (ZOOGEOGRAPHIC) REGIONS

Geographically large areas of land or water—continents, islands, and seas—which have typical kinds of animal life peculiar to each. The six now generally accepted by zoogeographers are: *Nearctic Region, Neotropical Region, Ethiopian Region, Oriental Region, Palaearctic Region,* and *Australian Region.* The Nearctic is combined by some zoogeographers with the Palaearctic to form a *Holarctic Region* because of similarities of the faunas in each. *See* accounts of these individually, and alphabetically by name—for example, Australian Region; Ethiopian Region; etc.—but in most detail *see* Nearctic Region, which includes all of N. America. *See also* Distribution.

The faunal regions are not homogeneous assemblages of animals uniformly distributed within each region but vary in composition in different places, and the animals within them enter into complex transitions with adjacent faunas. Nevertheless, in spite of differences, the animals in different parts of one faunal region are in general more related to those of other parts of the same region than to those of other faunal regions.

These regions are delimited by major barriers imposed by climate (air temperature, rainfall, humidity, etc.) or topographical features (mountain ranges, oceans, etc.). *See* Barrier. The change from the Nearctic (N. American) to the Neotropical (largely S. American) across Middle America is gradual, but tends to center along the barrier formed by the change from temperate grassland desert to tropical forests in Mexico. The Sahara and other deserts separate the Palaearctic and Ethiopian regions in Africa. The Himalayas and other mountains are a barrier between the Palaearctic and Oriental in Asia (Simpson *et al.,* 1957). These barriers to the dispersal of animal life or its interchange between faunal regions are not absolute, but they are strong ones. Food supply and plant forms, or types of plants, in the faunal regions powerfully affect the distribution of animals and many are adjusted to them and controlled by them. *See also* biotic community under Ecosystem.

With the wide exploration of the world from the 15th century on, men gathered facts about the distribution of animals of the earth (see Allee and Schmidt, 1951). Zoogeographers of the 19th century divided the world into zoogeographic or faunal regions, each with its own more or less distinctive kinds of animal life, and the six faunal regions now generally accepted were first proposed in 1857 by P. O. Sclater, a British ornithologist, for birds.

Faunal regions are standard patterns or a sort of meter stick by which the distribution of different animals can be measured, described, and compared, their special features determined, and important things about the animals and their histories revealed (Darlington, 1957). Faunal regions help zoologists in different parts of the world to set natural limits to regional studies. *See also* Biogeography; Zoogeography.

FAUNA OF BIRDS' NESTS

See account under Inquilines; *see also* Parasite.

FEAR

Just as in human beings, fear is self-protective. There seems to be a definite age at which young birds first show fear. With the young of those songbirds that usually nest in trees or shrubs and spend considerable time in the nest (*see* Altricial), it begins before they are ready to fly. Nice (1943) wrote that the period beginning when young song sparrows begin to fly "may be the chief time when the young are conditioned by parental behavior with regard to what to fear and what not to fear."

Young song sparrows first try to fly 11 days after hatching; they fly with skill at 17 days; they first utter the "fear note" 19–21 days after hatching (Nice, 1962a). Herrick (1901), writing of young altricial birds, said: "fear comes with a certain maturity of the nervous system, with comparative suddenness, but is usually timed to correspond with the development of the wing-quills and the power of flight."

Herrick pointed out that young belted kingfishers with which he experimented, when fully feathered but unable to fly, showed no fear of him. However, 24–48 hours later, when able to fly, they showed their terror of him and took flight. He wrote: "The late development of [fear] is most opportune, since they are not tempted to leave the security of their [nesting] tunnel in the ground until they can make long excursions and follow their parents to the favorite fishing ground."

According to Herrick, after taking flight, the young of altricial birds are fed by one or both parents for days or even weeks, during which they learn much by imitation of their parents and by individual experience.

Although the young of songbirds that nest in trees and stay in the nest for some 2 weeks or more may not show fear until they are at least a week or more old (Ivor, 1944b), it is different with the precocial young of birds that nest on the ground. Young grouse, quail, killdeers, and others react to predators or possible danger much sooner. Living on the ground for a few weeks before they are able to fly, these downy young birds, which resemble baby chicks, must be born with, or quickly develop the ability to move and to see if they are to escape hawks, owls, weasels, skunks, and many other predatory animals. They usually leave the nest within 24 hours after hatching.

In 3–4 days after hatching, they act like adults—they preen, scratch themselves, and at the approach of danger give the alarm note, run away, and hide. If they are in the open they may squat or "freeze" to avoid detection (Terres, 1960b). *See* precocial under Altricial; *see also* Self-protective Behavior under Behavior; *also* Distraction Display.

FEATHER

Of all animals, only birds grow feathers. These serve mainly as an insulator in retaining body heat, to assist birds in flying, in protective coloration, and in a bird's behavior. *See* Courtship; Sexual Dimorphism. The total feathering is generally waterproof in most birds and protects their tender skin against injuries. Feathers, like the scales on the feet of birds, the claws, and the horny sheath of the bill, are keratinous (mostly protein) outgrowths of the skin. *See* Keratin.

Originally most ornithologists believed that feathers, in their evolution, began as a covering of scales on the bodies of primitive birds, with a few feather filaments (cryptoptiles) scattered between them. As birds became warm-blooded, or homoiothermous, the filaments became of survival value to them as an insulating layer. During the course of evolution, the feathers grew longer and became more numerous.

A second theory held by many ornithologists today is that the first feathers were similar to the contour feathers of birds of today and the down feathers developed later. The development of feathers may have been in response to homoiothermy but they also may have evolved along with the development of flight (Van Tyne and Berger, 1976). See also Parkes (1966).

KINDS OF FEATHERS. Ornithologists generally have classified feathers for their separate uses and location on the body of a bird. Most of the superficial or viewable outer feathers on adult birds are (1) *contour feathers* (*pennae;* sing.: *penna*), which have a stiff shaft (*rachis*) and a complete inner and outer vane, and are moved "by a series of muscles attached to the feather follicle walls" (Rawles, 1960). The contour feathers form the outline of the body of a bird; "typically each has a large firm vane but the base is commonly downy, or *plumulaceous*" (Van Tyne and Berger, 1959), and usually has an afterfeather. *See* Afterfeather. Contour feathers include not only the outer body feathers but those of the wings and tail. The flight feathers of the wings and tail, a type of contour feather, are large, stiff, and modified for flight. *See* Flight. Wing feathers are in general called the *remiges* (rowing feathers), which include the *primaries, secondaries,* and *tertials* (see Tertiary Feather). The long quill feathers of the tail are called *rectrices* (steering feathers). The ear coverts (*auriculars*) are small, modified contour feathers that grow in one to four rows around the external opening of the bird's ear. These appear to screen the ear opening and to improve a bird's hearing ability and are especially well developed in owls and in certain parrots and hawks. *See* Ears and Hearing.

(2) *Semiplumes* combine a large rachis (shaft) with completely downy vanes; structurally, they grade both into contour feathers and into down feathers (Stettenheim, 1972) and grow along the margins of (and within) the contour feather tracts; they are hidden beneath the contour, or body, feathers and are small and white. Semiplumes fill out the contours of the body, insulate it, provide flexibility at constricted places at the base of moving parts—the wings, for example—and, in waterbirds, increase their buoyancy (Van Tyne and Berger, 1959).

(3) *Down* (plumulaceous) *feathers* are small, soft, wholly fluffy feathers, with or without a shaft. In adult birds they are called "definitive downs," or plumules, and commonly have an afterfeather; are usually concealed beneath the contour feathers (see Stettenheim, 1972; Lucas and Stettenheim, 1972). "The main function of the down feathers seems to be insulation of the bird's body; they are especially well developed

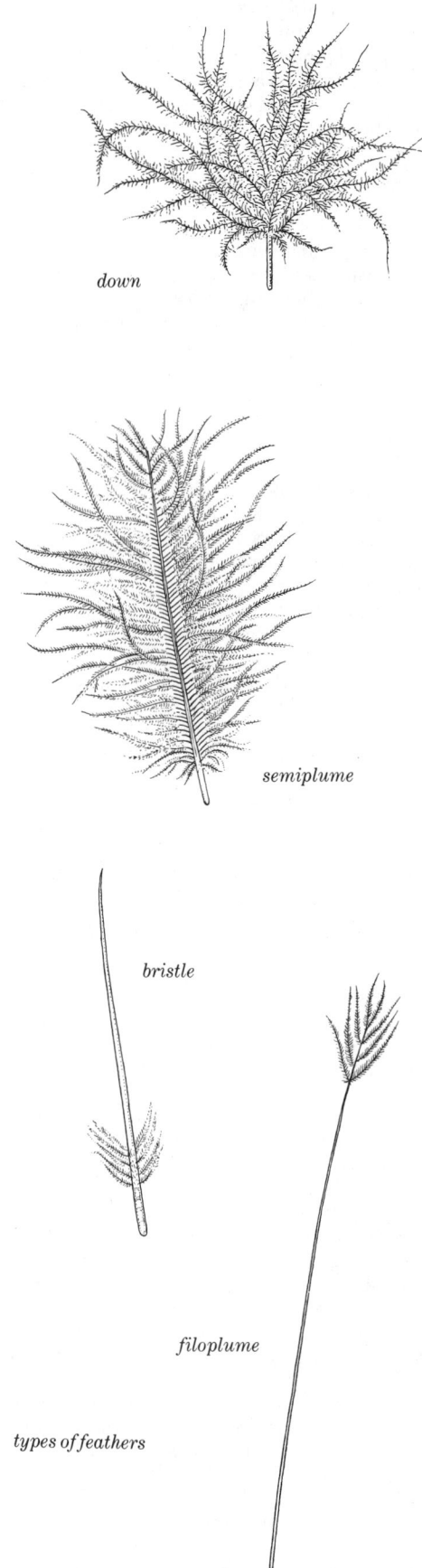

down

semiplume

bristle

filoplume

types of feathers

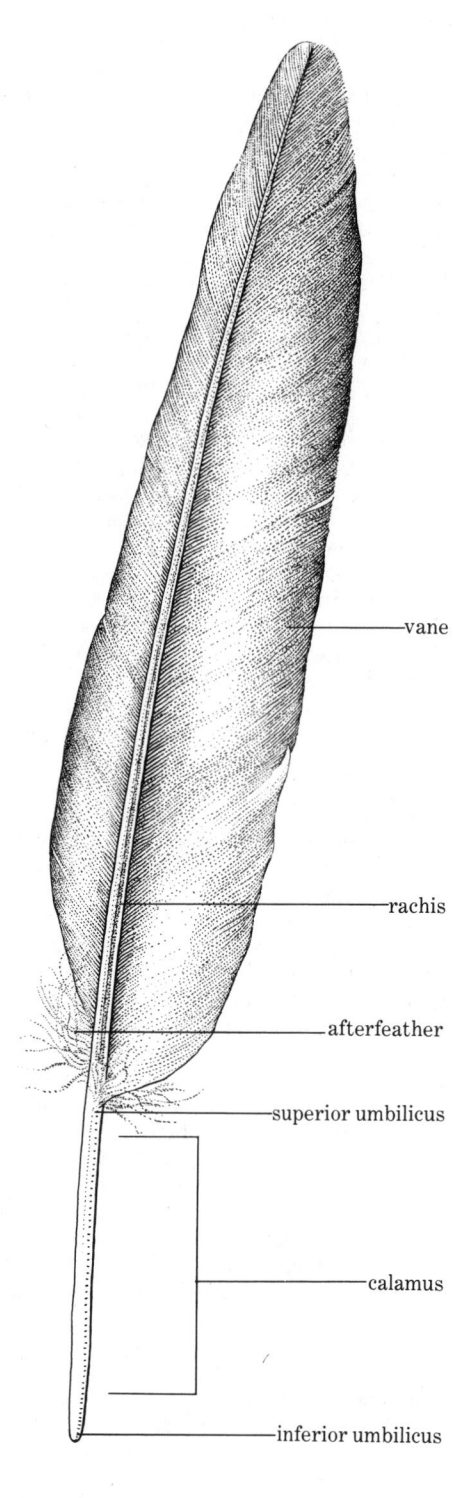

vane

rachis

afterfeather

superior umbilicus

calamus

inferior umbilicus

the parts of a contour feather

FEATHER

in water birds" (Van Tyne and Berger, 1959). Down feathers also provide the natal down covering of newly hatched birds, although many birds hatch naked, or nearly so. *See* Natal Down. *Uropygial down feathers:* Most birds have a uropygial (preen) gland at base of the tail (*see* oil gland under Skin Glands). According to Stettenheim (1972), the papilla of this gland commonly has a tuft of modified down feathers at or near the tip and the tuft aids the bird in transferring the oily secretion from the gland to the bill. See especially Paris (1913) for the nature and arrangement of these feathers of the uropygial gland in many birds.

(4) "*Filoplumes* are specialized, hairlike feathers, sparsely distributed over a bird's body, and are associated with contour feathers. One kind of filoplume has a minute vane at the tip, and grows in groups of two to eight about the base of a contour feather; another type lacks a vane and often extends like a long hair beyond the contour feathers. They are most frequent on the nape and upper back of a bird; can be seen in a fresh specimen of the American robin, and are notably on the nape and back of the hairy-backed bulbul, *Microscelis criniger,* of Malaysia" (Van Tyne and Berger, 1959). Any slight movement or vibration of the contour feathers seems to be transmitted by the filoplumes to pressure and vibration receptors in the skin—these are the Herbst corpuscles, also called lamellar corpuscles (Stettenheim, 1972), or Vater-Pacini corpuscles. *See* Touch. The feathers we singe from a chicken before cooking are filoplumes.

According to Van Tyne and Berger, there are certain other feathers of birds that superficially resemble filoplumes but actually differ in structure; for example, the "bristles" of the bristle-thighed curlew, *Numenius tahitiensis,* "which are true contour feathers with a webbed base, whose outer base has become bare and hairlike."

(5) *Powder (down) feathers* are body feathers so much modified in their evolution that they do not resemble normal feathers at all. They appear as a powdery substance "best seen as paired pectoral and pelvic yellowish patches on the skin of herons and bitterns; probably derived from disintegrating down feathers that persist throughout life" (Wallace, 1955). Van Tyne and Berger state that most bird feathers produce minute particles of powder, but a typical powder feather from an American bittern, for example, may have a *calamus* (feather quill) several centimeters long; in other species of birds, the quill of the powder feather may barely protrude from the skin. The best-developed powder feathers are in the plumage of herons. "They grow continuously from the base of the feather and disintegrate at the tip" (Van Tyne and Berger, 1959). The breakdown of the powder feathers produces a fine waxy powder, which sifts over the rest of the plumage as a soft, whitish bloom. This transforms the coal-black feathers of a swallow-tailed kite into a soft gray; the feathers of a male marsh hawk into a pale gray; and gives a filmy appearance to the feathers of herons. The bloom is easily brushed off and is lost in most museum specimens of bird skins (Allen, 1930a). *See* Bird Skins.

A number of ornithologists who have studied the powder feathers and their possible function (see especially Schüz, 1927) believe that they are used by herons, at least, to remove fish slime and oil from the feathers and to dress their plumage. *See* Preening. Powder down also may protect the feathers from moisture. Most birds have powder feathers but their highest development is in the herons and bitterns, also in the tropical tinamous, mesites, and cuckoo-rollers (Van Tyne and Berger, 1959). For a primitive type of feather, *see* Afterfeather; *see also* Alula.

Bristle. A feather type that grows almost exclusively on the head or neck of a bird; bristles and bristly feathers appear to have developed (evolved) from the contour feathers but they serve birds in ways differing from contour feathers (Stettenheim, 1973). Typical bristles are feathers with a stiff, tapered rachis, without barbs except at the base (the bristles never have barbs at the tip as do the somewhat similar filoplumes).

The tactile rictal bristles (*see* Rictus) surrounding the mouths of birds such as flycatchers, and especially of swallows and whip-poor-wills, which catch insects in their mouths while in swift flight, have been thought to aid them by widening the mouth (gape) and acting as a funnel to help scoop insects out of the air. Apparently such a long-held belief is invalid for flycatchers. Lederer (1972), using high-speed motion pictures of several species of flycatchers, discovered that they caught flies in midair with the tip of the bill, and not farther back in the mouth where the rictal bristles might have helped in their insect captures. Lederer believed that the rictal bristles might serve birds that have them in a sensory function.

Van Tyne and Berger (1959) suggested that the bristles in the marsh hawk, for example, serve it as a sense of touch (*see* Touch); also, owls, for example, which have difficulty seeing objects close to them (Heinroth and Heinroth, 1958), have large facial bristles, and the bristly covering of the nostrils of crows and ravens might serve them as organs of touch (Allen, 1925). Bristles covering the nostrils of woodpeckers may protect them from wood dust when drilling a hole in a tree (Steinbacher, 1964), but may also function as a sense of touch (Lucas and Stettenheim, 1972).

Barn owls are unusual in having bristles on the toes; certain other owls and grouse also have bristlelike feathers on the toes; feathers that resemble bristles grow out of the knee region of the bristle-thighed curlew. The upper and lower eyelids of various birds have bristles called eyelashes. *See* Eyelashes; *also* Topography; Beard.

OTHER SPECIALIZED FEATHERS. Through evolution, some feathers on certain parts of birds have become modified, or changed, so as to be highly ornamental. Functionally, these feathers may serve some kinds of male birds in their plumage displays before the females during courtship or to intimidate rival males. *See* Sexual Dimorphism. For example, peacocks have enormously elongated upper tail coverts which they raise and spread like a magnificent fan when displaying before the female, but

they also do so when alarmed. The spoonbill raises its lovely silver-white crest both for courtship display and to express alarm (Burton, 1954). Ruffed grouse have special ruffs of feathers about the neck, and prairie chickens have pinnae on the neck which they raise in their courtship displays. *See* Courtship.

Among our familiar American birds, the simple elongation of the feathers of the crown, or top of the head, is the commonest example of modified feathers. The tufted titmouse has a "topknot," the blue jay and pileated woodpecker have crests, California quail have ornamental plumes, and some owls—for example, screech and long-eared owls—have two tufts, one on each side of the head, called "horns." These are also present in the horned lark, a songbird (Allen, 1925). Woodpeckers and chimney swifts have specialized spine-tipped tail feathers (rectrices) that help them prop against the vertical surfaces of trees (woodpeckers) and cliffs and hollow trees (swifts).

WHERE FEATHERS GROW. Despite a bird's evenly feathered appearance, the feathers of most of them do not sprout evenly from the body, but develop from special areas of the skin called *feather tracts*, or *pterylae* (sing.: *pteryla*). Contour feathers grow only from the feather tracts; semiplumes grow at the edges of the feather tracts and integrate with the contour feathers. The spaces on the skin between the feather tracts that are more or less bare except for a little down are called *apteria* (sing., *apterium*). The apteria are covered by the overlapping feathers from adjoining pterylae, thus outwardly giving the impression that feathers grow evenly over a bird's body. This distribution of feathers in a pattern over a bird's body is called its *pterylosis* and their study is *pterylography*.

It is probable that, in primitive birds, the feathers grew evenly over the body, much as they do today in a few groups such as ostriches and other ratites (*see* Flightless Birds), penguins, and the screamers (Van Tyne and Berger, 1959), but all other birds have their feathers restricted to definite tracts. To reveal and study these elaborate patterns, of value in tracing the relationships of birds, ornithologists may clip the feathers from the dead bird's body.

NAMED PARTS AND STRUCTURE OF A WING (FLIGHT) FEATHER. Called a *vaned* feather, a flight feather (one of the contour feathers) from the wing of a bird has a central shaft *(rachis)* and an outer and an inner web on each side of it, which, together, constitute the vane. The vane and its shaft make up the flat, expanded part of the feather, one of the wing feathers used in propulsion in flight. *See* Flight. The bare webless end of the rachis nearest the bird's body is called the *calamus*, or *quill*. The calamus is round, semitransparent, and hollow, with a series of delicate partitions within called the *pulp caps*. The tiny opening in the end of the calamus where it is attached to the feather follicle in the bird's skin is the *inferior*, or *lower*, *umbilicus* (pit, or depression). It is through this hole that the feather, while it is growing, gets its nourishment and

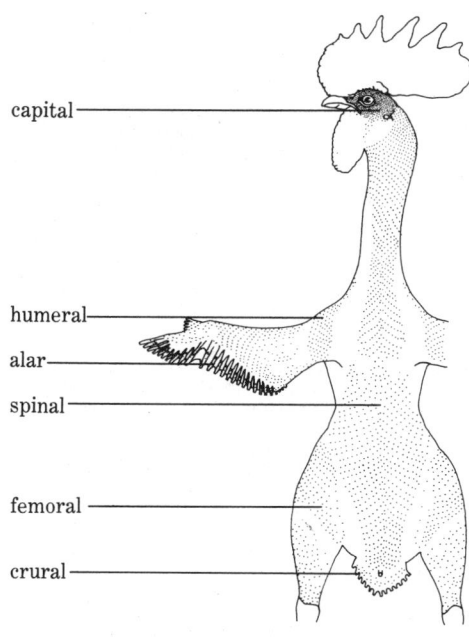

capital
humeral
alar
spinal
femoral
crural

dorsal

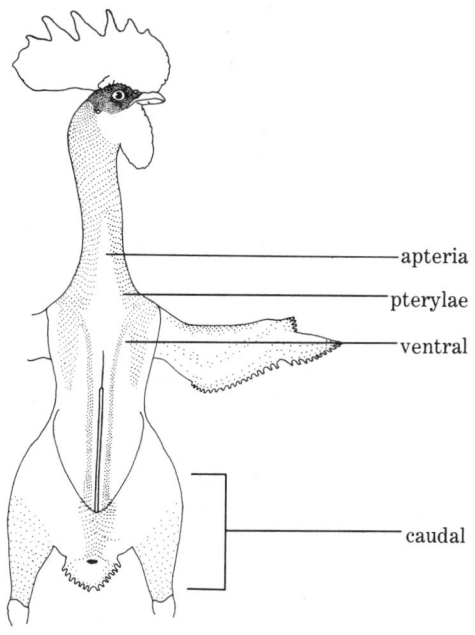

apteria
pterylae
ventral
caudal

ventral

FEATHER
In most modern birds, feathers sprout from tracts in the skin called pterylae, which are surrounded by bare areas known as apteria. Contour feathers grow directly from the pterylae; semiplumes grow from the edges of the tracts; and the overlapping feathers cover the apteria, giving the plumage a smooth uniform appearance.

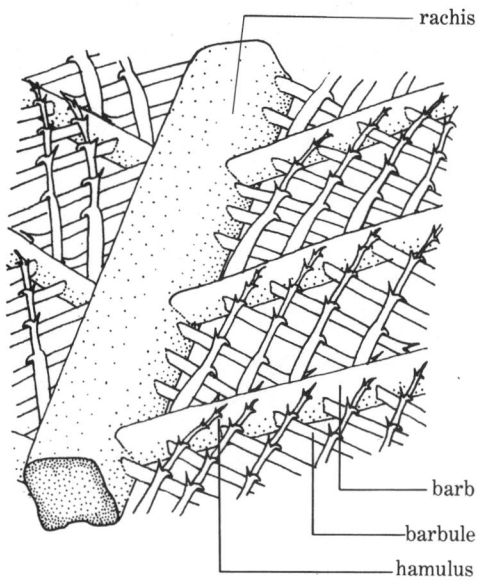

FEATHER

The main shaft of a feather is the rachis, from which slender, toothpicklike barbs grow. A pigeon's primary or flight feather may have 600 pairs of barbs. From each side of the barbs grow barbules, several hundred from each barb. The barbules have rolled edges and tiny hooks, or hamuli, which interlock each barb with an adjacent barb, forming a web.

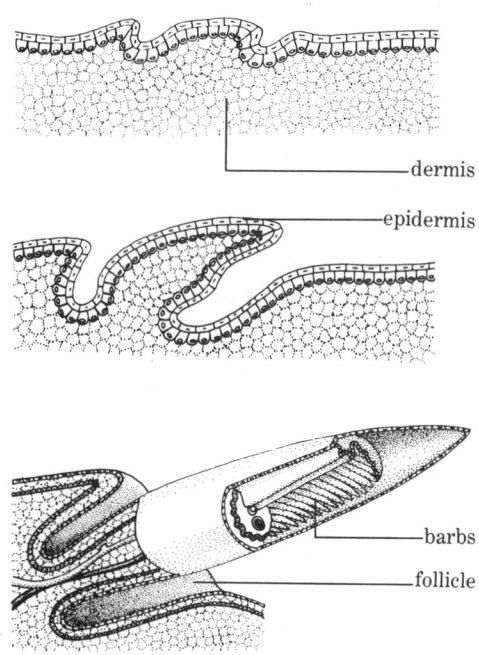

FEATHER

Feathers begin to grow even before a bird hatches from its egg. Starting as a small swelling on the skin, it grows into a cone while its base settles into the skin forming a pit or feather follicle, from which the feather itself emerges.

pigment colors from cells (epidermal and dermal) in the outer layers of the bird's skin.

Above the calamus, the rachis, or main shaft of the feather, is flattened on the inside; it also has a small hole, the *superior*, or *upper, umbilicus*, at the point where the webbed part of the shaft joins the bare calamus. The function of the upper umbilicus is incompletely known. It is from the point of the upper umbilicus, on the shaft, from which grows, in some birds, an afterfeather. *See* Afterfeather.

The webs along the sides of the main feather shaft are formed by slender, toothpicklike branches, called *barbs*. They are closely spaced on each side of the rachis and there are about 600 pairs in a wing primary feather of a domestic pigeon, or rock dove. Each side of a barb gives rise to a series of *barbules*, of which there are several hundred to each barb. The barbules have rolled edges and tiny hooks *(hamuli)* that overlap and interlock each barb with an adjacent barb. This creates a limited, though sliding arrangement of the barbules which makes each feather flat and flexible, yet sufficiently stiff so as to be almost impervious to air and water. See Wallace (1963) and Pettingill (1970) for technical details of the interlocking of these feather parts. The barbs of the webs can easily be pulled apart—for example, in a pigeon's or a chicken's wing feather—and put back in place again by merely pulling the web through one's closed fingers. By preening (*see* Preening) and pulling a feather through its bill, a bird repairs or smooths a disrupted or disarranged feather.

HOW FEATHERS GROW. Feathers are horny (keratin) structures grown by *papillae* (sing.: *papilla*) in the skin of a bird. The papillae, or *feather germs*, are in rows in each of the feather tracts and form a definite pattern. The plumage colors are determined by the hereditary genes in the papillae (*see* Colors of Feathers). "From these papillae successive generations of feathers grow throughout the life of the bird" (Rawles, 1960). The developing feather first appears on the skin of the embryonic bird as a minute pimplelike structure (the papilla). This grows into a cone while its base settles into the skin, forming a pit, or *feather follicle*. After a short period of rapid growth, by hatching time each papilla, within its tubelike feather follicle, is surrounded by the follicle wall with its opening on the surface of the bird's skin. From the papillae, upward and out from the surrounding feather follicles, grow the first downy feathers that appear on the newly hatched bird. Down feathers persist for only a relatively short time and are actually pushed from the feather follicles of the developing young bird by the tips of the succeeding juvenal feathers, to which they remain attached until they rub off.

"Feathers of the juvenal plumage, which replace the down, are more complex, of the contour feather type, and may be easily distinguished from adult feathers by their looser structure and softer texture. Resemblance to adult feathers is in the wing and tail feathers, which are, however, less rigid than those of the adult" (Rawles, 1960).

RATE OF GROWTH. Feathers of the juvenal plumage grow rapidly in many birds. In passerines, or songbirds, for example, "most of this plumage is grown before the young bird leaves the nest and is fully developed in 3 weeks at most" (Rawles, 1960). In others—game birds, birds of prey, waterfowl, and shore birds, for example—it takes much longer for the down of the young bird, or chick, to be replaced; however, the flight feathers of ground-nesting galliform birds grow very rapidly—some quail are able to fly when only a week old. *See* Molts and Molting.

NUMBERS OF FEATHERS ON A BIRD. The flight feathers and their coverts (*see* Flight; Topography) are of a regular arrangement and definite number, according to the species of bird; also, the whole covering of a bird, that is, its contour feathers, are of a definite number according to the species (Van Tyne and Berger, 1959). Wetmore (1936) and Brodkorb (1949) made careful counts of the contour feathers of different species of birds and found there is considerable variation in the numbers between species. Wetmore, making his feather counts near Washington, D.C., found the lowest number of feathers to be 940, on a ruby-throated hummingbird in June. Ammann (1937), who also made careful counts of feathers of birds in Mich., found the largest number of feathers on a bird to be 25,216 on a whistling swan killed in Nov. It is not surprising that larger birds, owing to their larger body size, have more feathers than smaller birds; however, as Staebler (1941) discovered, from many of his studies of smaller birds, they generally have more feathers *per unit of body weight* than larger birds. This is no doubt correlated with the heat-retention needs of smaller birds, which in general have a higher rate of metabolism—hummingbirds and chickadees, for example. *See* Metabolism; Cold and Birds.

Of 74 species of passerines, or songbirds (flycatchers, jays, chickadees, vireos, blackbirds, etc.—*see* the passerines, listed, grouped, and discussed, under Passeriformes), the number of contour feathers ranged from 1,119 in a ruby-crowned kinglet collected in Oct. by Wetmore to 4,607 on an eastern meadowlark taken by Brodkorb in Feb. In 1882, Ernest Thompson Seton counted 4,915 feathers on a Brewer's blackbird; in 1900 Jonathan Dwight recorded 3,235 contour feathers on a bobolink. In most of the feather counts, passerine birds generally, except the smallest species, had contour feathers ranging from 1,500 to 3,000. Birds of the same species in the same area and season generally showed only slight individual differences in the number of their contour feathers, but in those that live in a region where there are marked differences in the seasons, they had different numbers of contour feathers at different times of the year.

For example, Staebler (1941) collected three house sparrows in Mich. during Jan. and Feb. which had respectively 3,546, 3,615, and 3,557 contour feathers, but two in the same area in July had 3,138 and 3,197 respectively. Staebler calculated there were 11.5% fewer feathers on the sparrows in summer than in winter. See lists of birds and numbers of their contour feathers in Wallace (1963) and Pettingill (1970).

FEATHER MUSCLES. A bird can adjust the position or posture of its feathers largely by bands of non-striated muscles in its skin. These "feather muscles" are controlled by the bird's autonomic system and are associated with all types of contour feathers except filoplumes. Typically all of the contour feather follicles, for example, are linked by tiny bunches of feather muscles in the skin. The feathers can be depressed by a depressor muscle, or raised by an erector muscle. Feather muscles not only can raise or lower feathers but can draw them together, twist them, or combine these actions for flight and for courtship and other feather displays of birds before each other. *See* Courtship; Sexual Dimorphism. Other feather muscles appear to aid the bird in spreading and closing the feathers of its wings. For these and other details, see Lucas and Stettenheim (1972); Stettenheim (1972). *See* Feather Wear under Molts and Molting.

FEATHER CARE
See Bathing; Preening; Anting.

FEATHER COMB
Term of ornithologists for a pectinated (meaning "toothed like a comb") claw on the middle toes of the poor-will, whip-poor-will, nighthawk, and others of the worldwide Nightjar Family, Caprimulgidae. Among other N. American birds, the barn owl and the herons and bitterns have the middle claw pectinated. In the caprimulgids, it is the *inner* edge of the middle claw that is pectinated; in the herons, it is the *outer* edge of the middle claw.

According to Brauner (1953), Joseph Grinnell, writing about this comblike structure, called it a "louse comb," in comparing it with a similar formation on the second claw of the hind foot of the American beaver. Some naturalists believe that the "split nail" of the beaver serves as a comb in removing parasites from its fur.

For many years, ornithologists debated the use of the comb-like claw of the birds of the Nightjar Family. Early in the 19th century, some theorized that the claw was used to scratch and straighten the rictal bristles (*see* Feather) that grow about the mouths of these birds; another held that it was used to remove insect parasites (bird lice, etc.) from the feathers of birds. *See* Anting; Preening. One British ornithologist believed that the so-called fern owl, *Caprimulgus europaeus*, a relative of the American nighthawks and whip-poor-wills, used its claw to detach the sharp-hooked feet of beetles (which it captured in flight) from the sides of its mouth.

Alexander Wilson, in his accounts of the nighthawk and whip-poor-will in his *American Ornithology*, described the middle claws of these two species as being pectinated on the inner edge. He believed that the claw was "to serve as a comb to clear the bird of vermin" from the feathers of the heads of the birds because he had found small particles of down on the teeth of the claw-comb.

Brauner (1953) watched the actions of a cap-tive poor-will he raised and verified that it scratched itself with the long middle toe. The comblike middle claw caught and held "fragments of down and feathers." High-speed flash photographs of his bird showed that, in scratching, it turned its foot outward so that the long middle toe and claw with the comb on its inner edge engaged the feathers. Its scratching was limited to its throat, bill, the area about its rictal bristles, the crown and sides of its head, and the nape of its neck. Brauner thought that his bird's scratching also straightened the rictal bristles as suggested by an early-19th-century ornithologist.

Other birds of the world that have the claw of the middle toes pectinated are the frigatebirds (Fregatidae); Boat-billed Heron Family (Cochleariidae); Crab Plover Family (Dromadidae); Pratincole Family (Glareolidae); Barn Owl Family (Tytonidae); and Dipper Family (Cinclidae), which has the middle claw "sometimes slightly pectinated" (Van Tyne and Berger, 1959). *See* Claws under Feet and Legs. *See* Molts and Molting.

FEATHER-EATING
See Gizzard; Pyloric Stomach.

FEATHER FLIES
See Hippoboscid Flies.

FEATHER FOLLICLE
A feather grows from a papilla (*see* Papilla) which is located within a feather follicle—a small depression or cavity in the skin of a bird. Full-grown feathers are lifeless and, much as in cutting our own hair or fingernails, a bird has no feeling when its feathers are cut or trimmed. *See* Feather; *see also* discussion of cutting wing feathers under Pinion.

FEATHER GERMS
See Papilla; *also* Feather.

FEATHER LICE
See Lice.

FEATHER MAINTENANCE
See Anting; Bathing; Preening; Smoke Bathing; and use of oil gland, or preen gland, under Skin Glands.

FEATHER MITES
See Ectoparasites.

FEATHER POCKET
See Swimming and Diving.

FEATHER TRACTS
(pterylae). *See* Feather.

FEATHER TRADE
Term for commercial trade in feathers of wild birds once used in millinery trade, also for stuffing mattresses, pillows, sleeping bags, etc.; *see* some details of slaughter under Albatross Family; Auk Family; Duck Family; Gull Family; Heron Family; Plover Family; Sandpiper Family. See additional details about each species in these families that were exploited in A. C. Bent's *Life Histories of North American Birds;* for especially useful history of feather

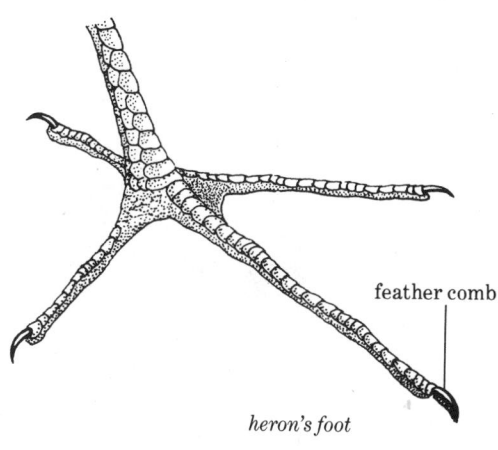

feather comb

heron's foot

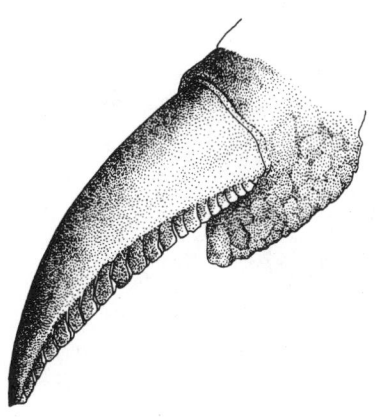

FEATHER COMB
The middle claw of some birds, notably those of the nightjar family and some herons, has pectinations ("teeth") with which the bird scratches itself and which may be useful in removing parasites.

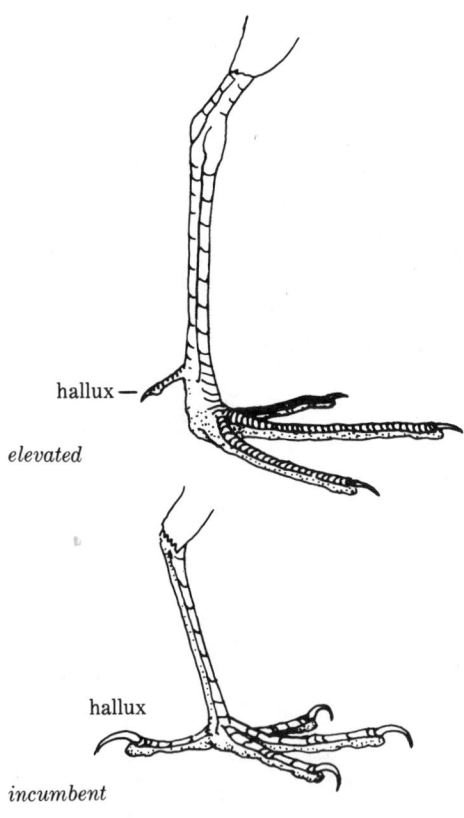

hallux —

elevated

hallux —

incumbent

FEET AND LEGS
In most birds the first toe, or hallux, is turned backwards and grows from the foot at the same level as the other toes, a condition called incumbent. In some birds, especially those that live on the ground such as pheasants, the hallux is elevated and usually does not touch the ground at all.

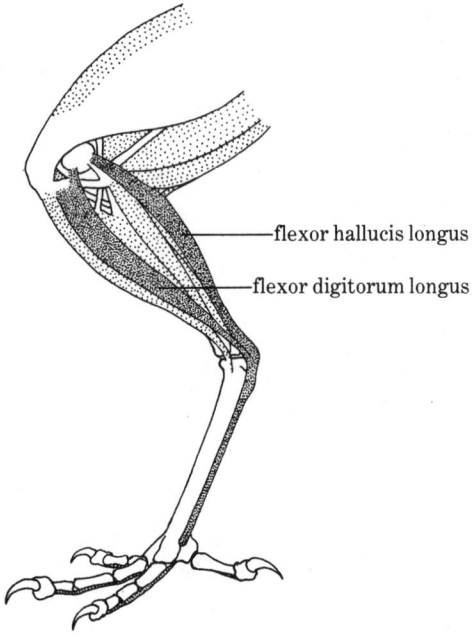

— flexor hallucis longus

— flexor digitorum longus

FEET AND LEGS
When a bird perches, the flexor tendons of its leg tighten, closing the toes and hallux, so that the bird has a tight grasp of its perch even while asleep.

trade, see in Forbush (1912); Graham (1971); Pearson (1937a); and a review and summary by Buchheister and Graham (1973).

FEATHER WEAR
See Molts and Molting.

FECAL (FEE-kal) SAC
While they are in the nest, the young of many species of birds, mainly the songbirds (*see* Passeriformes) and a few orders of birds close to them, void their excrement within a small, whitish, often black-tipped sac, called the *fecal sac;* the parents either eat these or carry them away. *See* discussion under Nests and Nesting; Sanitation; and mainly Young and Their Care.

FEEDING BEHAVIOR
See Autolycism; Behavior; Commensalism; Food and Feeding Habits.

FEEDING BIRDS
See Bird-attracting; Care and Feeding of Abandoned or Injured Wild Birds.

FEET AND LEGS
In using their feet, most birds, except loons and grebes, are remarkable in that they stand, not as man does, on the flat of his foot, but on their toes. *See* Digitigrade. The "instep" of a bird, instead of being short, as in man, is an elongated bone, the *tarsometatarsus,* called simply *tarsus (see* Tarsus), and because it is long and visible, we may call it the bird's leg. As we look at a jay or a thrush hopping, or a starling walking, over the ground, what appears to be its knee, bending *backward* instead of forward as in man, is actually its heel. The bird's true knee joint, hidden from view by feathers, is the next joint above the bird's heel, and it bends forward when the bird squats, just as the knee of man does.

A bird's thigh (femur) is also hidden from sight by feathers that grow over the thigh; consequently its thigh and knee are usually not apparent in the living bird. The long, well-fleshed leg bone (the tibiotarsus, or simply tibia), between a bird's knee and its heel, is the "drumstick," or crus. *See* Crus; Skeleton.

An interesting part of the leg muscles of many kinds of birds, especially the perching birds, is a set of *flexor tendons,* by which it has been thought to lock itself to its perch. Supposedly, as the bird squats on its tree-limb roost, the flexor tendons automatically tighten and cause the bird's toes to grasp firmly around the perch; thus the crouched bird can relax without fear of falling to the ground while it is asleep (*see* Roosting); however, according to Bock's (1965) studies, the toes do not automatically close when the bird's leg is bent. Years ago, in the country, it was the custom of some mothers to give their children the cut-off feet of a chicken after it had been dressed for the pot. Any child who has amused himself by playing with one of these scaly feet will remember pulling on the cut-off ends of the flexor tendons to close the toes in a grasp like that of a human fist.

Birds use their feet or legs in various ways —to run, hop, walk (*see* Hopping and Walking), to swim, perch, to receive impact on alighting, to scratch themselves or to scratch in the ground (*see* Head-scratching; Double Scratch), to grasp prey, to fight, and in some birds to hold or to cover their eggs during incubation or to help turn the eggs (Lucas and Stettenheim, 1972). *See* Incubation; Embryo and Its Development.

NUMBERS OF TOES. Most birds have four toes *(anisodactylous)* and their common arrangement among song or perching birds, for example, is that the first toe (big toe, or hallux) turns backward, the other three forward. The hallux in most birds is a functional toe that grows out backward at the same level as the others—a condition called *incumbent.* In some species, however—the cranes, many rails, and birds in the Pheasant Family, for example, birds which mostly live on, and walk or run on, the ground —the hallux is *elevated* or grows out of the foot above the level of the others and usually does not touch the ground at all.

The usual practice among ornithologists is to identify the toes according to a digital formula by referring to them by the Roman numbers I to IV. The usual numbering pattern for a four-toed bird is: toe I, the hallux; toe II, the inner front toe; toe III, the middle front toe; toe IV, the outer toe (Van Tyne and Berger, 1959).

The ostrich has only two toes, and a few birds have only three—the flightless rheas of S. America, the cassowaries and emus of the Australian Region, some petrels, and most albatrosses. This condition is known as the *tridactyl* foot. Among N. American birds it exists in auks, guillemots, and their relatives in the Auk Family, in all N. American plovers except the black-bellied, in the oystercatchers, sanderlings, and the three-toed woodpeckers.

Swifts and tropical colies have all the toes turned forward, or are capable of turning them forward, a condition called *pamprodactyl;* a less common arrangement is *syndactyl,* in which two toes are fused for part of their length, as in kingfishers and the hornbills (Van Tyne and Berger, 1959).

The specializations of the toes of birds have other names. The condition in which a web of skin connects the three front toes on a duck is called *palmate;* in the cormorants, gannets, and pelicans, which have all four toes connected by webbing, it is called *totipalmate.* There are various degrees of smaller amounts of webbing between the toes in terns, herons, and shorebirds. *See* Shorebird. Grebes, coots, and phalaropes have the surface area of their toes increased by membranous lobes along the sides of the toes; they have the *lobed* foot.

The ruffed grouse has a seasonal specialization of its feet in which, at the approach of winter, a fringe of horny projections grows out along the sides of its toes to serve it as "snowshoes" by distributing its weight over a wider area when walking on snow.

ADAPTATIONS OF THE FEET AND ARRANGEMENT OF THE TOES. The feet of birds, through evolution, have become adapted to serve their various needs, or ways of life. The feet of water birds—ducks, geese, gulls, and others—are either webbed or lobed for swimming (*see* Swimming and Diving); long-toed in some marsh birds, which supports those that walk much over water plants, the jacana for example; the feet and legs are strong in quail, grouse, turkeys, and other gallinaceous birds that scratch in the ground for their food; powerful in hawks and owls that seize their prey with their feet (with a reversible toe in the osprey that captures slippery and agile fishes with its feet); yoke-toed (*zygodactylous*) in cuckoos, parrots, owls, and in woodpeckers (*see also* Climbing Birds), in which toes I and IV are pointed backward, and toes II and III, forward; *heterodactylous* in the trogons, which live in the tropics of both hemispheres and have toes I and II turned backward, and III and IV turned forward; and a condition of birds in the large order of perching birds (*see* Passeriformes) in which the long hind toe (hallux) points backward and helps the bird to secure its foothold on a tree branch or other perch (Berger, 1961).

CLAWS. These are specialized scales forming a horny sheath at the end of each toe and are considered a part of the integumentary system, which includes the skin and all its specializations—the feathers, wattles, spurs, sensory nerve endings, and the oil, or preen, gland (Berger, 1961). The claws grow continuously, and in wild birds are worn down by abrasion from perching on hard surfaces and other uses. Both the claws and the horny fringes (winter snowshoes) on the toes of many kinds of grouse and of the ptarmigans are shed each spring (Lucas and Stettenheim, 1972).

Claws are usually called talons in the birds of prey, and are long and sharp in owls, eagles, and hawks, which seize their prey in their feet, but in some of the carrion-eating birds (vultures, for example), the claws have lost their sharpness and are short and blunt; claws are absent from some albatrosses, possibly a part of the evolutionary process in which the claws may be disappearing in this group (Allen, 1925).

The claws, or nails, of many birds are strong and useful to them in scratching the ground for food, as in domestic hens and other members of the Pheasant Family and in fox sparrows, towhees, and other ground-feeding birds; in others, the strongly curved claws of woodpeckers, nuthatches, and certain others aid them in climbing (*see* Climbing Birds). In grebes, the claws are flattened and incorporated in the foot, used as a paddle; in the tropical jacanas, the nails are very long and slender and function in a way similar to snowshoes in that they support the bird as it runs about over the floating leaves of lilies and other water plants; the exceptionally long hind claws of some horned larks, of longspurs, and some pipits may help to balance them when running over the ground (Harrison, J. G., 1964a).

The pectinate, or combing, claw on the middle toe of the poor-will is used by this bird for scratching the feathers of its head and for straightening the disarranged rictal bristles. *See* Feather Comb; *also* Bristle under Feather. Claws grow in birds from a thickening of the Malpighian layer which forms the "nail bed" out of which the corneous cells grow (Newton, 1893–96).

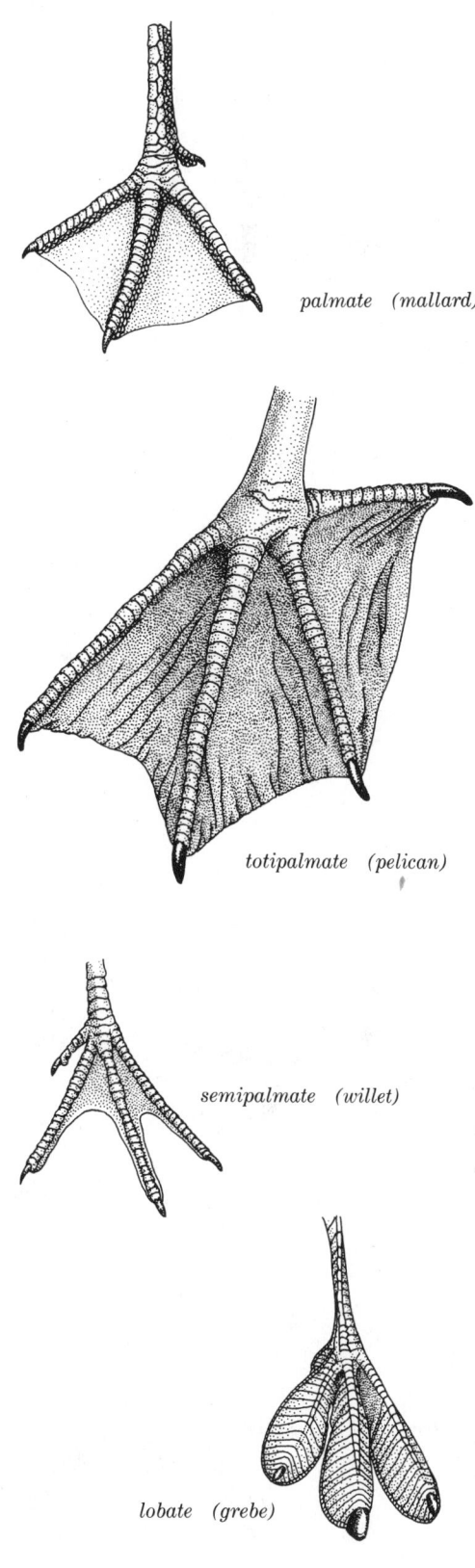

palmate (mallard)

totipalmate (pelican)

semipalmate (willet)

lobate (grebe)

types of feet

FEET AND LEGS

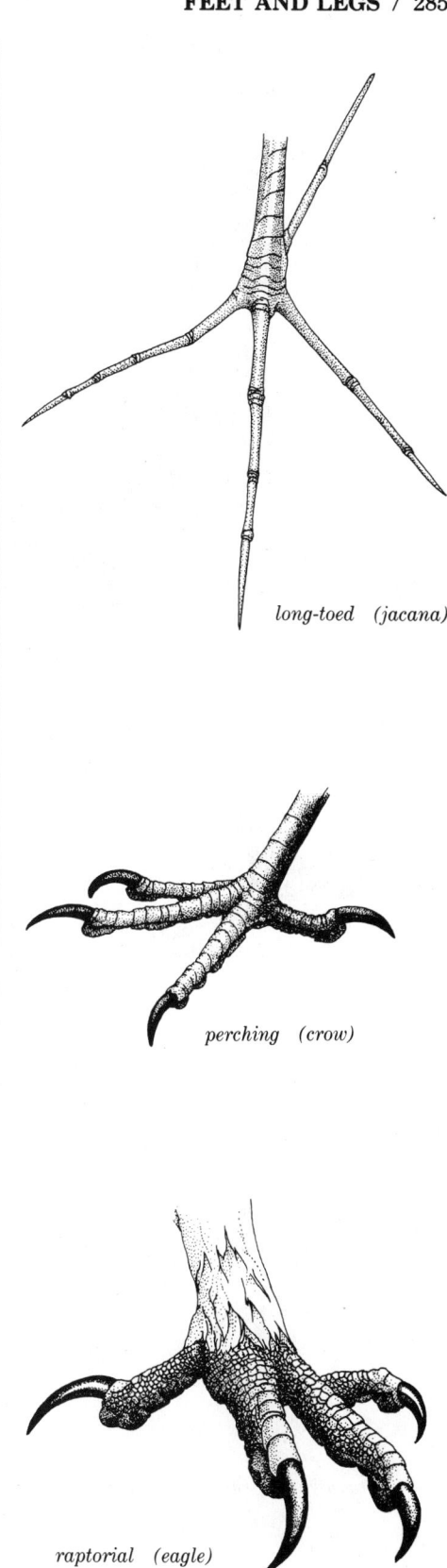

long-toed (jacana)

perching (crow)

raptorial (eagle)

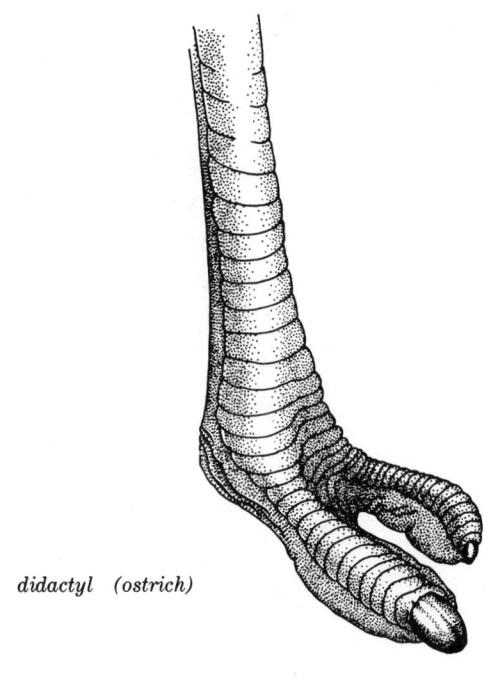

didactyl (ostrich)

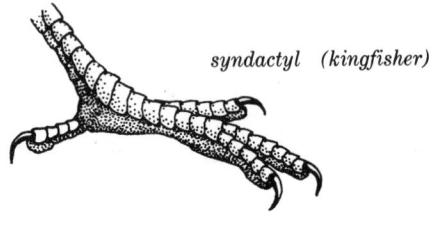

syndactyl (kingfisher)

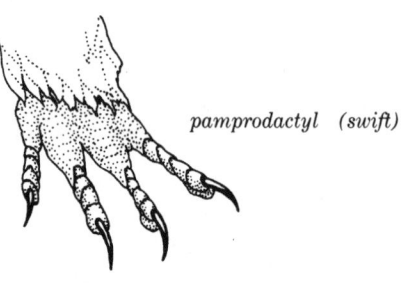

pamprodactyl (swift)

types of toe arrangement

FEET AND LEGS

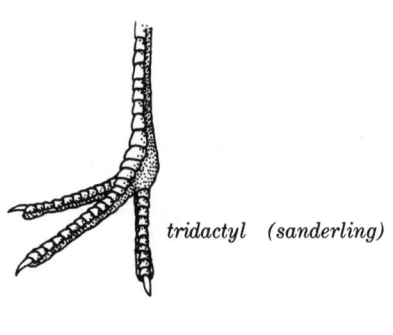

tridactyl (sanderling)

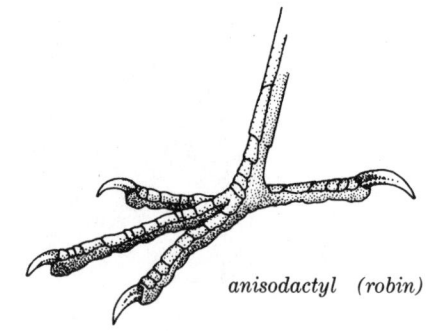

anisodactyl (robin)

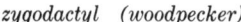

zygodactyl (woodpecker)

heterodactyl (trogon)

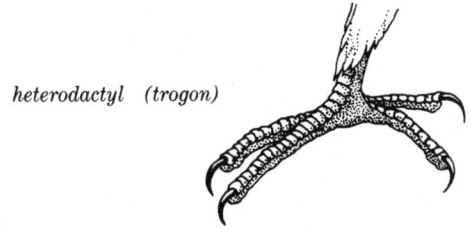

SPURS. These are outgrowths of bone covered with a hard, pointed, horny sheath. They grow from the rear inner side of the bird's leg (tarsus); in wild turkeys, a single spur appears as a button a few inches above the foot during its first year and both sexes of turkeys may have them—some hens have fully developed spurs but this is uncommon (Lewis, 1973); they become sharp with age but rarely grow longer than about 1–1¼ in. long in adult male wild turkeys; dark, smooth and shining, they curve upward to a sharp point; when gobblers fight in spring, they use the spurred legs to strike at a rival; according to reports in past times, occasionally some are killed, but turkeys seldom seriously wound each other. According to Beebe (1936), some pheasants, such as the ocellated and Angus pheasants, have no spurs, but the so-called blood pheasants and all the male peacock pheasants have two or more spurs on each leg; the jungle fowls *(Gallus)* and fireback pheasants are armed with a single spur on each tarsus (*see* Tarsus); it is long, curved, and sharp as a needle, and in the crestless firebacks, even the hens have them; when fighting, during the breeding season, these birds not infrequently kill each other, as do the jungle fowls, which have fighting arenas in open places in the forest (Beebe, 1936).

In the true pheasants *(Phasianus)*, including the common ring-necked pheasant introduced into N. America (*see* in Pheasant Family), the legs of the male are neither very strong nor very long, and each tarsus has a short spur; the male peafowl (peacock) has strong tarsi, each armed with a thick, sharp spur (Delacour, 1951).

TOUGHNESS OF A BIRD'S FEET. Although a bird's feet may occasionally freeze in winter, this seems to be exceptional; apparently the fact that both the tarsus and toes have no fleshy muscles and only tough tendons and a limited supply of nerves and blood makes them far less susceptible to freezing than the fleshy parts of their bodies. The flow of blood to a bird's feet in winter is sluggish, "barely sufficient to maintain feeling" (Wallace, 1955); the feet appear impervious to severe changes in temperature (Zimmer, 1951b), but some birds may suffer severely. Mourning doves, some of which winter in s.-c. Wisc. and s. Mich., may lose several or all of their toes from freezing; those that lost toes or entire feet were still able to walk about on the tarsal stubs and to perch in a tree roost but would have been severely handicapped in scratching in the ground for food (Nickell, 1964b). *See also* Accidents; Deformities.

Norris-Elye (1945) saw a remarkable example of the resistance of the feet of birds to heat; while camping in the Duck Mtns. of Man. in Oct. 1944, he enticed four gray jays (*see* in Crow Family) to come inside his tent for food, where they alighted atop a red-hot stove and stayed on it for periods of up to 8 seconds when the stove was so hot a drop of water on it caused a flash of steam. *See also* Cold and Birds; Heat and Birds.

FEMUR

The large upper legbone of a bird. *See* Skeleton.

FERAL

(FEAR-al). A wild, undomesticated bird; but the term is generally used for a bird or any other animal which has escaped from domestication, or from being reared in captivity, and has returned to its life in the wild. The mute swan of Europe, bred in captivity, particularly in England, for centuries, has been introduced as a "tame" bird into N. America. However, this "pond swan" and its progeny have escaped from the ponds in e. U.S. where they have been introduced and now live on their own as wild, or at least as semi-wild, birds. These wild-breeding mute swans are termed "feral."

FERTILIZATION

The life of a bird begins with the union of two reproductive cells (gametes)—the male sperm cell and the female ovum. The sperm cells (spermatozoa) are produced in the two testes of the male bird; the ova develop in the ovary of the female. The testes and ovary are collectively called the *gonads* (from Gr. *goneuo*, to generate—Jaeger, 1955).

In birds, the gonads are markedly asymmetrical. The left ovary and left oviduct in the female are functional; the right ovary and right oviduct degenerate early in the bird's embryonic development. *See* Embryo and Its Development; *also* Endocrine Glands. Both *testes*, or testicles, of the male are normally present, and both are functional, but the left testis is usually considerably larger than the right one (Tordoff, 1961).

The testes of birds are inside the body cavity, not outside in a bag (scrotum) as in mammals. Both the testes of the male and the ovary of the female are within the belly opposite what corresponds to the "small of the back." They are bound closely to the spine and rest on the floor of the abdomen near the fore end of the kidneys (*see* Urogenital System). The two testes are bean-shaped, are commonly dull, opaque, and whitish, and vary enormously in size depending on the season; when quiescent outside the breeding season each may be only the size of the head of a pin in the house sparrow and may increase to the size of two peas by Apr. (Coues, 1884). The testes of birds may be 400 to 500 times larger in the breeding season than at other times of the year, and may weigh 400 times more at breeding time than in midwinter.

The ovary of the female is single in most species, not paired as are the testes of the male. The reduction in ovaries of female birds from two to one is supposed to be an adaptation for flight by reducing ballast (Welty, 1962); it is also an adaptation that protects the eggs. If a bird had two ovaries and two oviducts, a sudden jarring to the bird's body when alighting might crack the well-developed eggs if they were in oviducts side by side. Some birds of prey—hawks of the genera *Accipiter* and *Circus* and *Falco* (falcons)—have both left and right ovaries, but usually only the left oviduct, which conducts the eggs to the cloaca (*see* Cloaca; Eggs and Egg-laying), develops (Welty, 1962).

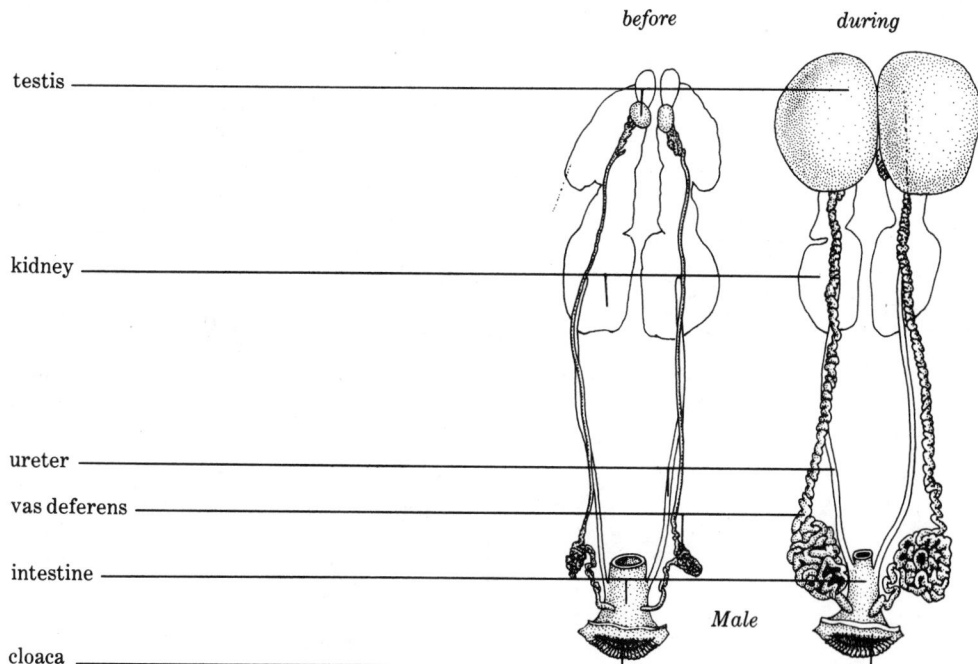

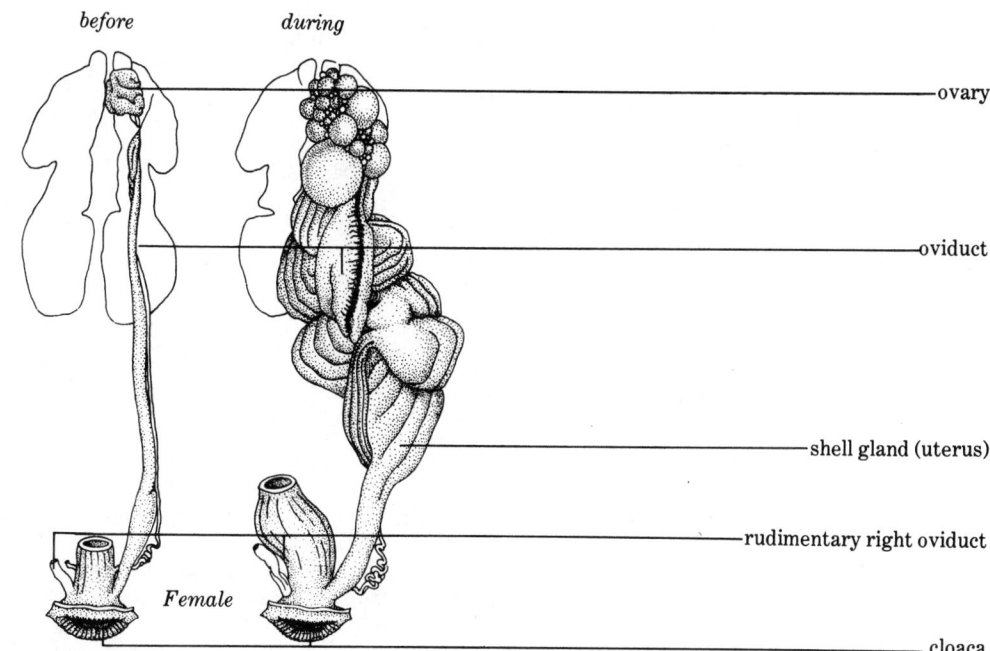

size of the reproductive organs of the house sparrow before and during the breeding season

FERTILIZATION

During the breeding season, the testes of the male house sparrow enlarge from the size of a pin head to the size of a pea. The testes produce sperm, which is passed to the cloacal exit through the vas deferens. If sperm is stored for a time in the lower vas deferens, the cloaca will swell slightly. In most females, only the ovary and oviduct on the left side are functional, and the ovary, which develops to produce ova, shrinks after the eggs are laid. Fertilization occurs in the upper end of the greatly enlarged oviduct when the sperm comes together with the ovum to form a zygote.

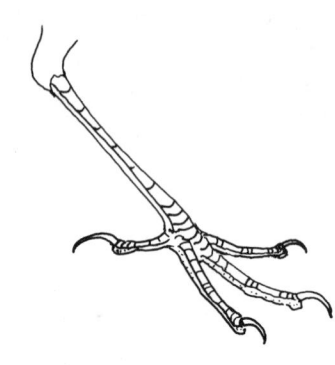

FINCH FAMILY

Each testis of the male is made up of numerous semen-bearing tubules which produce enormous numbers of spermatozoa. The wriggling spermatozoa pass from a testis, pick up semen, and enter into a wavy tube called the *vas deferens*, or sperm duct, situated along the face of the kidney, where the semen accumulates until the bird is ready to fertilize the female.

The sperms are released through the opening of the sperm duct into the cloaca of the male, and from there into the cloaca of the female during copulation. *See* Copulation and Copulatory Organs.

The spermatozoa resemble diminutive tadpoles and swim about in the semen until they reach the ova or die. After copulation by the domestic hen, it may take as little as 26 minutes for the rooster's sperms to swim up the oviduct of the hen and fertilize the eggs at the upper end (Welty, 1962).

The time between copulation and laying of the first fertile egg in the domestic hen averages about 72 hours but may be 19½ hours. The percentage of fertile eggs in domestic chickens is highest 2–3 days after copulation; however, fertile eggs have been laid several months after mating (Welty, 1975).

Primitive birds such as ostriches and ducks have an erectile, grooved penis, which guides the sperms from the cloaca of the male to that of the female during copulation, or "treading" as it is called (Welty, 1962). The more evolutionarily advanced species of birds copulate by engagement of the cloaca (*see* Copulation and Copulatory Organs), when the male stands on the female's back, although some swifts (white-throated) may copulate in flight (Dawson, 1923). During each coition, vast numbers of sperms pass from the male to the female: from the male domestic pigeon, or rock dove, 200 million; the domestic rooster, 4 billion (Stresemann, 1927–34).

Female domestic turkeys may produce eggs that have not been fertilized by a male, yet will develop embryos and will hatch. Called parthenogenesis, this is not yet known in wild birds but is a common method of reproduction among some insects. Schorger (1966) believed that this may indicate that the turkey is low in the scale of avian development. He reported that parthenogenesis produces males only, and cites a parthenogenetic male that was himself capable of siring 37 turkey poults which grew normally. At Beltsville, Md., scientists of the U.S. Department of Agriculture, experimenting with parthenogenesis in domestic turkeys, reported in 1960 that of a hatching of 15 parthenogenetic young, all males, one of these produced semen that fertilized female turkeys, which laid and hatched fertile eggs (Welty, 1962).

Besides producing sperms that pass on hereditary traits of the males to the chicks, the testes produce both the male hormones, or androgens and estrogens, the female hormones (females also produce both androgens and estrogens). Within the tubules of each testis are interstitial cells which are thought to be the source of the male hormones, so influential in fixing the *secondary sex characters* of birds—the outward appearance that in some species shows the differences between males and females; for example, the combs, spurs, body size, songs, and courtship behavior of the males. *See* Sexual Dimorphism.

Male and female birds show sexual differences (dimorphism) internally as well—in their build, or structure, and in function—which are largely due to influences of sex hormones. Primary sexual differences are in the gonads themselves—the ovary of the female, the testes of the male; the sexes of birds of like plumage in male and female (blue jays, for example) can be discovered only by internal examination of the bird after it is captured alive, or when killed for a scientific specimen. Such determinations, of which there are several methods, are called *sexing* of birds. *See* Sex Determination.

All birds do not grow to sexual maturity at the same rate. Usually, smaller species become sexually mature earlier in life than do larger species. Some of the tropical weaverbirds (*see* Weaverbird Family), a group to which our house, or English, sparrow belongs, lay eggs when they are only 8 weeks old; the budgerigar, *Melopsittacus undulatus* (*see* in Parrot Family), at about 12 weeks; button-quail before they are 16 or 17 weeks old (Steinbacher, 1936). *See also* Sexual Maturity.

In the satin bowerbird, *Ptilonorhynchus violaceus*, according to A. J. Marshall's studies (Marshall, 1954), males may take a remarkably long time for a songbird (passerine) to become sexually mature—not until they are 4 or 5 years old; slender-billed shearwaters (*see* in Shearwater Family) when they are 5–7 years old; and in the wandering albatross, not until they are 7–9 years old. *See* Subadult.

Some birds do not mature all of their reproductive processes at the same time (*see* discussion under Bursa of Fabricius) and sexual (reproductive) maturity and attainment by a bird of its adult plumage do not always coincide (Palmer, 1972). Some (birds of prey, for example) may reach sexual maturity while in the immature plumage. There are sight records of peregrine falcons and Cooper's hawks in immature plumage, paired, in the nesting season, with mates in adult plumage. "Herring gulls, while in immature plumage, may pair, build nests, and copulate, but lay no eggs; year-old starlings, bluebirds, and other passerine species begin laying later in the season during their first nesting year, and lay fewer eggs than do older birds of their kind" (Welty, 1975). The testes of year-old male red-winged blackbirds are smaller and develop their maximum size later in the season than do older redwings (Wright and Wright, 1944).

According to Eisner (1960) and Marshall (1954), a rather general chain of development in the breeding behavior of birds in spring is begun and carried through by the increased length of the days (more light), rain, sights and sounds of courtship in other birds of their kind, especially among colonially nesting species such as gulls—all or some of which register in the brain of the bird, which, through the hypothalamus (*see* Endocrine Glands), stimulates the anterior lobe of the pituitary gland into seasonal action. The pituitary, in turn, through hormones, regulates the internal progressive development of behavior responses of birds in the breeding cycle. *See* discussion under Behavior; *see also* Courtship; Nests and Nesting; Eggs and Egg-laying; Embryo and Its Development; Incubation; Brooding; Young and Their Care.

FETUS
See Embryo and Its Development.

FIDDLER
See Redhead and Whistling-duck, fulvous, in Duck Family.

FIELDFARE
See in Thrush Family.

FIELD LARK
See Meadowlark, eastern, in Troupial Family.

FIGHTER
Local name (Fla.) for gray kingbird, but all kingbirds are aggressive. *See* under Flycatcher—Tyrant-Flycatcher Family.

FIGHTING
See Territory; Nests and Nesting; *also* Spurs under Feet and Legs.

FILOPLUMES
(FILL-oh-plooms). Very specialized hairlike, or bristlelike, feathers. The hairlike feathers that we singe from a chicken before cooking are filoplumes—reduced feathers which in their evolutional development lost the web and now consist merely of the slender shaft (Allen, 1925). Filoplumes frequently grow on the underside of a bird or on its wings, beneath its contour feathers. They are sparsely distributed and usually grow at the base and on the dorsal (under) side of a contour feather (Pettingill, 1956). *See* Feather.

FINCH FAMILY
Fringillidae (frin-JILL-ih-dee); from Lat. *fringilla*, small bird, or finch. 436 species of songbirds (Van Tyne and Berger, 1976) in the order Passeriformes (*see* Passeriformes); worldwide except in Antarctica and Oceania, Australia and Madagascar; includes such familiar birds as canary but not house, or English, sparrow; (*see* Weaverbird Family); in N. America, largest family of all families in number of species. It includes about 83 species plus 8 subspecies some of which do not nest in N. America (bullfinch and hawfinch, for example); family includes buntings,* cardinals,* crossbills, dickcissel,* finches, goldfinches, rosy finches, grosbeaks,* juncos,* pyrrhuloxia,* redpolls, siskin, sparrows,* and towhees*: Van Tyne and Berger (1976) have classified the asterisked birds in the Emberizidae, a separate but closely related family, and have included within it the tanagers. In their reclassification, however, they have retained the brambling, bullfinch, crossbills, rosy finches, goldfinches and siskins, grosbeaks, hawfinches and redpolls in the Finch Family. See Van Tyne and Berger (1976) for details. Some of finest N. American songsters are in Finch Family—for example, cardinals and grosbeaks; a few species sing while in flight (flight songs)—for example, black-headed grosbeak and indigo bunting—but most sing from perches; most are strong fliers and most temperate zone species are migratory; many are gregarious when not nesting; migrate in flocks and may spend the winter in flocks (Austin, 1961).

Fringillids nest away from others of their kind (are not colonial nesters) with each pair establishing and male defending a territory; are basically monogamous (have one mate through each nesting); build open cuplike nests in trees, bushes, or on ground; female usually builds the nest, incubates the eggs, and broods young; in most fringillids, male helps care for the young and, in many, the male feeds female while she is incubating. *See* Courtship Feeding.

In general, all fringillids have cone-shaped, strong bills, with the cutting edge angled at the base; bill is adapted to seed-cracking (they are also called, collectively, seed-eaters), but also eat many insects and wild fruit (see Willson, 1971, for favorite seeds of some native N. American members of family). Many ornithologists consider them near the ancestral stock from which the vireos, warblers, icterids, and tanagers have branched (Austin, 1961); they are also related to the weaverbirds, which include the house sparrow and European tree sparrow.

The name brambling, for a Eurasian species that visits N. America, apparently refers to thorny brambles or blackberry bushes, where the bird may occasionally be seen, but its preferred nesting habitat is in trees.

The name bunting (Old Eng. *buntyle*) is of unknown origin; four—the indigo, lazuli, painted, and varied buntings—are brightly colored; their northern relatives, the snow bunting and McKay's bunting, are more nearly related to the longspurs. Crossbills are named for the overlapping tips of the upper and lower mandibles, which they use to pry seeds from the tough cones of some coniferous trees.

The name grosbeak (GROSS-beak) (after Fr. *grosbec*) is from gross, large or thick, and beak. Of five brightly colored N. American grosbeaks, two—the pine and evening—are very hardy and usually live in the North all year or in high mountains of w. U.S.; three, slightly less hardy—the black-headed, rose-breasted, and blue grosbeaks—live farther south.

The pine and evening grosbeaks are noted for their periodic great flights out of the North during years, not of severe winters, but of shortages of their natural foods of seeds and wild fruit. See in Bent (1968) for intervals of flight years, also in James (1958, 1960, 1962); see also recent issues of *American Birds*, published by the National Audubon Society. See also in Forbush (1925–29) and Pearson *et al.* (1936) for history of migration and spread of evening grosbeak and causes; see also Shaub (1963).

Of all members of the family, rosy finches generally nest at highest altitudes—among glaciers or above timberline—in summer; in winter, they descend to lower slopes and valleys where food more accessible or more abundant.

Some members of the Finch Family have special mouth pouches for carrying food; most feed on the ground; all usually have nine primaries (flight feathers) and twelve tail feath-

Evening grosbeak

Red crossbill

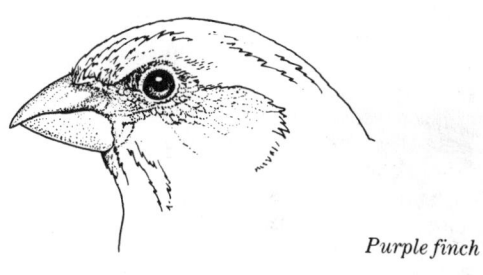

Purple finch

FINCH FAMILY
The bills of finches are adapted for different methods of feeding. The evening grosbeak has a very large, strong bill to crack tough seeds that are a major part of its diet. The red crossbill uses its bill to force apart pine-cone scales and extract the seeds with its tongue. The purple finch's less specialized bill reflects its more diverse feeding habits.

ers. Albinism has been reported in 296 individuals of 42 species, highest frequency of albinism reported for any family of N. American birds (Gross, 1965a).

Members of the Finch Family are protected by law and may not be kept in captivity without a permit; however, ill or injured birds may be kept alive until able to fend for themselves by offering them assorted seeds (wild bird seed mixtures), grain, especially cracked corn, and fruit, lettuce and other greens, ground meat, and mealworms (Walker, 1942).

Brambling, *Fringilla montifringilla* (frin-JILL-ah mont-ih-frin-JILL-ah); genus name: *see* family introduction; species name: Lat., mountain finch. Native to n. Eurasia, visitor to N. America in Alaska, Ore., and e. U.S.; 5¾–6 in. long; male in spring has brilliant black head and back, wings and tail have some white, *orange patch on shoulders, conspicuous white rump;* orange breast, white belly; female has similar color pattern but duller, with olive-brown on head and back, but has white rump; in nesting season in Old World lives in birch and mixed woods, edges or open parts of coniferous forests, also in birch or willow-scrub beyond tree limit (Witherby *et al.*, 1938–41). First N. American record, a male brambling collected (shot) Oct. 1914 on St. Paul Is., Alaska (Kenyon, 1961); in Oct. 1957, Kenyon saw several bramblings on Amchitka Is., Aleutians, later a flock of eight at same place; Jones and Gibson (1975) reported an adult male collected May 26, 1961, on Amchitka Is.; in Dec. 1958, a male at a feeding station near Stanton, N.J., collected and skin deposited Princeton Museum; Banks (1970b) reported another record for N.J. in 1961; also a male at a N.J. feeding station in Apr. 1965; two from w. Mass. seen Feb. to Apr. 1962; one at Tupper Lake, N.Y., Apr. 1962; all these believed by Banks to be wild birds, not escaped from captivity; a male reported at Portland, Ore., winter 1967–68, fed regularly with house finches on sunflower seeds at bird feeding station; status "casual" in ne. U.S.; no nesting in N. America reported to 1970.
Other Names: Bramble finch; mountain finch. See life history of brambling by Congreve and Blair (1968).

Bullfinch, *Pyrrhula pyrrhula* (pie-ROO-lah); genus and species names: Lat., bullfinch, dim. of Pyrrhus, a proper name (Coues, 1882); Lat., from Gr. words meaning fiery red, in allusion to bright color. Resident in n. and c. Eurasia; several records of visiting Alaska; 5¾ in. long; stout-bodied, short-billed; male has striking bright rose-red underparts; white rump; blue-gray above, with black cap, chin, wings, and tail, heavy black bill, one white wing bar (Peterson *et al.*, 1954); female has similar pattern and black cap but pinkish-brown below, gray-brown above. In Old World, lives in or about gardens and hedges. *See* oddity under Gynandromorph.

Bunting, black-throated, *See* Dickcissel.

Bunting, indigo, *Passerina cyanea* (pass-er-EYE-nah sigh-ANE-ee-ah); genus name: from Lat. *passerinus,* pertaining to a sparrow, spar-

rowlike; species name: from Lat. *cyaneus,* dark blue. (Color ill., page 298.) Mostly in e. U.S. and s. Canada; 5¼–5¾ in. long; wing-spread 8–9 in.; adult male in breeding plumage, only small N. American finch to appear blue all over; male in sunshine almost solidly blue, but against sky or in shade may appear black; similarly colored male blue grosbeak is larger, has brown wing bars, noticeably heavier bill; adult female indigo, uniformly brown without *obvious* streaks, wing bars; immatures closely resemble adult female except are more streaked below; lives in summer in weed-grown fields, forest edges, roadsides, hedges, dry brushlands, orchards, open woods of dry uplands, along creeks and rivers with thickets for nesting, highway, power line, and railroad rights-of-way; male usually appears on nesting range in May, strongly defends his territory against other males by singing from trees, utility wires, and other open perches, short series of high-pitched notes, *sweet-sweet, where-where, here-here, see-it, see-it,* suggests rhythm; also delivers a flight song while on wing; sings throughout day into late summer; call note is *tsick* (Taber and Johnston, 1968).

Feeding Habits: Forages in trees, shrubbery, on ground; eats grasshoppers, beetles, weevils, aphids, cicadas, cankerworms, spanworms, flies, mosquitoes; seeds of dandelion, goldenrod, aster, thistle, grasses; small grains, raspberries, elderberries.
Nest: In crotch of saplings, small bushes, weeds, in thickets, raspberry, blackberry patch, canebrakes, only a few feet from ground but sometimes (in trees) 5–15 ft. up; female builds well-woven cup of dried grasses, pieces of dead leaves, bits of snakeskin, strips of bark, Spanish moss, weed stems, facial tissue, lining of cotton, feathers, fine grasses, wool, rootlets, long hairs of cattle, horses.
Eggs: May–Aug.; 3–6, commonly 3–4, blue-white, usually unmarked.
Incubation: 12–13 days; young leave nest 8–10 days after hatching (Taber and Johnston, 1968); usually two broods each year.
Other Names: Blue canary; blue finch; indigo bird; indigo bluebird; indigo finch; indigo painted bunting.
Accidents: Many killed while migrating at night by striking tall city buildings, TV towers.
Age: Blake (1969) had two banded birds at his station, each 6 years old; two banded males, wintering each year at Jamaica, West Indies, at least 8 years old (Downer, 1972).
Flight Speed: Timed in New England, 20 m.p.h. (White, 1929).
Host to Cowbirds: Very frequent, about 200 records (Friedmann, 1963).
Hybrids: Indigo bunting × lazuli bunting; these two hybridize on Great Plains where their ranges meet (Sibley and Short, 1959); see also important discussions by Kroodsma (1975) and Emlen *et al.* (1975); a male hybrid indigo bunting × painted bunting, first documented record of in Apr. 1971, Cape Kennedy, Fla. (Taylor, 1974).
Weights: S.C. (30), averaged about 15 gr. (Beckett, 1971a), or slightly more than ½ oz.; coastal N.J. in fall (5), 12.2–17.3 gr. (Murray and Jehl, 1964), or about ½–⅔ oz.; Homestead,

Fla. (94), 13.1–19.3 gr. (Fisk in Johnston and Downer, 1968).
Range: Nests from sw. S.D., s. Man., n. Minn., w. and s. Ont., s. Que., east to s. N.B., s. Me., south to w. Kans., w. Okla., s-c. and se. Tex., east to n. Fla., sporadically in Colo., sw. Utah, Ariz., and Calif. (in Los Angeles County one mated with lazuli bunting); winters mainly from c. Mexico, West Indies to Panama; also rarely from Gulf coast of U.S. north to N.Y., N.J., Mass. (Taber and Johnston, 1968).

Bunting, lark, *Calamospiza melanocorys* (cal-ah-moh-SPY-zah mel-ah-NOCK-oh-rus); genus name: from Gr. *kalamos,* a reed, and *spiza,* a finch; species name: Lat., from Gr. *melas, melanos,* black, alluding to black color, and *korus,* lark, in reference to its larklike singing in flight. (Color ill., page 299.) Lives on Great Plains east of Rocky Mtns.; state bird of Colo. (see State Bird); 6–7½ in. long; adult male in spring mainly black or dark slate color; like small blackbird but with broad patches of white on wings; often mistaken for bobolink, which has white on *back* as well as on wings; adult female in spring gray-brown and streaked above, almost white below with dusky streaks; white wing patch of female tinged with buff; in fall, all ages, sexes, look alike; resemble adult female; from winter home in Mexico and southern border sw. U.S., flocks move northward in hundreds in migration in early Mar., through Kans. and north to Colo. and s. Canada, the ones at rear of flock fluttering continually to fore, the whole appearing like some enormous wheel rolling over the greening prairies; males in flock with uplifted crowns, fluffed feathers, and singing, court females; with dispersal of flock, still gregarious, males tolerate each other, and pairs often nest only 100 ft. apart (longspurs, horned larks, and mountain plovers are neighbors); strong fliers, males shoot up from ground into air like larks to pour out songs, sometimes a hundred males singing together, or singly from fence posts, a series of rich, warbled trills; call note is soft *hoo-ee* (Baumgarten, 1968).

Feeding Habits: On ground, in summer eats many grasshoppers, caterpillars, weevils, beetles, bugs, ants, bees, seeds of pigweed, knotweed, dandelion, gromwell, smartweed, goosefoot, Russian thistle, waste grains.
Nest: On ground, usually sunken in small depression in grass; loosely built, of grasses, weed stems, rootlets, lined with plant down, hairs, at base of, or in, clump of grasses, weeds, plant debris.
Eggs: May–July; 3–7, usually 4–5, light green-blue, sometimes sprinkled with red-brown spots.
Incubation: Possibly by both sexes, 12 days (Baumgarten, 1968); age when young leave nest unknown.
Other Names: Buffalo bird; prairie bobolink; white-winged blackbird; white-winged bunting.
Host to Cowbirds: Fairly common, locally, but in general infrequent (Friedmann, 1963).
Weights: Male (1), 37.5 gr.; female (1), 36.5 gr. (Easterla, 1970), or about 1⅓ oz.
Range: Nests from s. Alta. east to s. Sask., sw. Mont., se. N.D., sw. Minn., and from w-c.

Mont., and east of Rocky Mtns. to se. N.M., n. Tex., w. Okla., s.-c. and e. Kans., also locally and sporadically in Utah, sw. Colo., Mo. (see Easterla, 1970); winters from s. Calif., Baja Calif., s. Nev., c. Ariz., s. N.M., n.-c. Tex. to s. La., south into Mexico; seen casually east to Pa., N.Y., Mass., south along Atlantic seaboard to Fla. (Baumgarten, 1968).

Bunting, lazuli (LAZZ-you-lie), *Passerina amoena* (pass-er-EYE-nah ah-MEE-nah); genus name: *see* Bunting, indigo; species name: Lat., delightful, charming, dressy (Coues, 1882). (Color ill., page 298.) W. U.S. and w. Canada; close relative of eastern indigo bunting, which it resembles in behavior; 5–5½ in. long; stout, conical bill; adult male has azure-blue head, throat, back, and rump; cinnamon band across breast and sides; white belly, white wing bars; female dull brown, *unstreaked above and below;* two thin white wing bars, gray-blue wings and tail; summers over wide region west of prairies from Canada to Baja Calif., east to Okla. and Dakotas; lives in thicketed swales and draws of prairies, dry bushy hillsides, wooded valleys, in aspens, willows, alders, cottonwoods, wild rose thickets along mountain streams, in sagebrush, open scrublands, and from humid Pacific coast to 10,000 ft. in Sierras, to 8,000 ft. in Rockies of Colo.; in spring, male arrives first on nesting range; from perch in top of oak, pine, willow, or other medium-sized tree, utility wire, or shrub, sings bright, rapid song, *see-see, sweert, sweert, sweert, zee, see, sweet, zeer, see-see;* with spread wings, in courtship, displays colors before newly arrived female, both utter sharp chip call note and defend territory; males are sometimes polygynous (Erickson, 1968).

Feeding Habits: Forages on or near ground or in shrubbery, catches grasshoppers, caterpillars, beetles, bugs, bees, ants; is fond of seeds of wild oats, wild lettuce, canary grass, bluegrass, needlegrass.

Nest: Usually low in thick bushes in crotch of willow, wild rose, currant, chaparral thicket, small pine, manzanita, scrub oaks, vines, stalks of weeds, brake fern, sage; 1½–4 ft., sometimes to 10 ft., above ground; cup of coarsely woven dried grasses, lined with fine grasses or horsehair—John James Audubon reported a nest lined with buffalo (bison) hair.

Eggs: Mar.–July; 3–5, usually 4, pale bluewhite, unspotted.

Incubation: By female, 12 days; young leave nest when 10–15 days old (Erickson, 1968).

Other Name: Lazuli painted finch.

Host to Cowbirds: Uncommon, to brownheaded cowbird; about a dozen records (Friedmann, 1963).

Hybrids: See under Indigo bunting.

Range: Nests from s. B.C. east to s. Sask., c. N.D., ne. S.D., south to se. Calif., nw. Baja Calif., s. Nev., sw. Utah, c. Ariz., n. N.M., w. Okla., east to e. Neb., and w. Kans.; winters from s. Baja Calif., s. Ariz., sw. N.M., into Mexico; accidental in Md.

Bunting, McKay's, *Plectrophenax hyperboreus* (pleck-TROF-eh-nax high-per-BOW-reeus); genus name: from Gr. *plektron,* a clawlike tool for striking the lyre, here referring to the long, straight hind claw of this bird, and *phenax,* cheat (false); the claw only appears like a *plektron;* species name: Lat., from Gr. *hyperboreos,* beyond the north wind; "of the extreme north" (Jaeger, 1955); common name: in honor of Charles L. McKay, U.S. Army Signal Corps, pioneer collector of birds in Alaska for U.S. National Museum. (Color ill., page 299.) Lives on islands in Bering Sea and w. coast Alaska; close relative of snow bunting; about 7 in. long; male in breeding plumage whitest of all N. American songbirds (Gabrielson, 1968); allwhite except dark bill, black tips of wings and tips of central tail feathers (similar male snow bunting in summer has more black on wings, and *black back*); female like female snow bunting in summer except less black on back and scapulars, and more white with pure white head; immatures like young of snow bunting; lives in summer on Arctic tundra of islands in Bering Sea—rolling plateau of bogs with pools of water, wildflowers, mosses, across islands from cliff to cliff; male chases female in courtship, sings loud, flutelike warbling, frequently on wing or from ground.

Feeding Habits: Nothing definite known but "obviously feeds on [seeds of] grasses, sedges, and weed seeds as do other arctic fringillids and . . . insects in summer" (Gabrielson, 1968).

Nest: Few ever seen, built of grasses, on ground, in crevice in rocks and along Arctic beaches in old hollow drift logs.

Eggs: June; 3–5, light green, dotted with pale brown.

Incubation: Period of and age when young leave nest unknown; probably like that of snow bunting.

Other Names: Snowflake; McKay's Snowbunting.

Range: Nests on Hall and St. Matthew Is. in Bering Sea; winters on nesting islands, also Nunivak, and along w. coast Alaska (Gabrielson, 1968).

Bunting, painted, *Passerina ciris* (pass-er-EYE-nah SIGH-ris); genus name: *see* Bunting, indigo; species name: from Gr. ciris, a kind of bird into which Scylla, daughter of Nisus, is fabled to have been changed. (Color ill., page 298.) S. U.S.; 4½–5½ in. long; adult male: no other N. American bird has red underparts and a blue head; greenish back, red-purple rump, underparts scarlet; females and immatures are our only *green,* sparrowlike birds (Sprunt and Chamberlain, 1949); bird of open country, in summer lives in brushy weed-grown fields, hedges, edges of woods, roadside shrubbery, gullies, and thickets along stream banks, also in backyards and gardens of s. U.S.; comes to feeding stations for sunflower seeds, mixed birdseed, scratch feed; also to birdbaths; male sings sweet, musical song, high-pitched, thin, and tinkling; according to Sprunt (1968a), unlike most birds, in which fighting is mostly bluff, males fight fiercely in territorial squabbles, sometimes a combatant loses an eye or is killed; males are polygynous (Parmelee, 1964).

Feeding Habits: Eats mainly seeds of grasses, also spiders, boll weevils, grasshoppers, crickets, wasps, flies, and caterpillars.

Nest: Cup-shaped, built low, usually in thick bush, low tree, or vines, usually 3–6 ft. above ground but up to 10–12 ft.; in Spanish moss, up to 25 ft. or more; nest primarily of dried grasses, weed stalks, and leaves, lined with hairs and dried grasses, occasional bits of dried snakeskin. See also Parmelee (1959) for many details of nesting and behavior.

Eggs: Mar.–July; 3–4, occasionally 5, pale bluewhite, speckled or spotted with brown.

Incubation: By female, 11–12 days; young leave nest when about 12–14 days old; over most of range two broods a year; three or even four (Sprunt, 1968a); some young males do not gain full breeding plumage until their third year.

Other Names: Mexican canary; nonpareil (the incomparable); painted finch; pope.

Age: One banded at Fort Lauderdale, Fla., at least 12 years old; five still coming to feeding station, Homestead, Fla., 8 years after banding (Fisk, 1974b); one in National Zoo, Washington, D.C., lived for 7 years, 10 months.

Host to Cowbirds: Fairly frequent; in some places, commonly to brown-headed cowbird (about 50 records, Okla., Tex., and Miss.), also one record of host to egg of bronzed cowbird (Friedmann, 1963).

Hybrids: See under Indigo bunting.

Weights: S.C. (25), averaged 14.75 gr., or about ½ oz.; range of weights 13–17.2 gr.

Range: Nests from se. N.C., sw. Tenn., s. Mo., e-c. Kans., c. Okla., and s. N.M., to se. Tex., s. La., to c. Fla.; winters south from s. La., c. Fla., Bahamas, and Cuba to Mexico and Panama.

Bunting, rustic, *Emberiza rustica* (em-ber-EYE-zah RUS-tih-cah); genus name: New Lat., from Swiss Ger. *emmeritz,* a bunting; species name: Lat., rustic, rural. Small sparrow of n. Eurasia, has visited Aleutian Is., where several seen in summer 1911 and in Oct. 1951, 1957 (Helminen, 1968); 5–6 in. long; male in breeding season has black crown and cheeks, a conspicuous white line through eyes, white throat and belly, and a *cinnamon breast band,* streaked flanks, conspicuous partly white outer tail feathers on dark tail. See Helminen (1968) for other details. Seen in thickets, undergrowth.

Bunting, snow, *Plectrophenax nivalis* (pleck-TROF-eh-nacks nih-VALE-iss); genus name: *see* Bunting, McKay's; species name: Lat., snowy. (Color ills., page 299.) Summers in Arctic N. America, seen in U.S. in winter; 6–7¼ in. long; wingspread 12–13 in.; in winter, mostly white with tawny cap, touches of cinnamon and black and large white wing patches; overhead in flight appears almost completely white (Peterson, 1947); in winter, often in big flocks that drift over open fields like giant snowflakes, often during snowstorm; a ground-feeding bird attracted to haystacks, barnyards, trash piles along lakeshores and dunes, open beaches of seacoast and salt marshes; even roosts on ground or in snow under shelter of weed or tuft of grass; sometimes a few horned larks and Lapland longspurs in the flocks; during day may perch in groups in trees, roofs of buildings, on utility wires while wintering in U.S.; loves to bathe in snow; can stand temperatures of −40- −58° F. but burrows in snow to keep warm; sometimes killed in great numbers in nesting areas by May–June snowstorms which cover food; by late Mar. start north from U.S., filling air with chorus of double whistles, trills; after flocks break up in spring and summer on nesting grounds, male in breeding plumage has white head, rump, and underparts with black bill, back, tail; central tail feathers black; female similar but black upperparts tinged with brown; male sings broken, twittering warble while fluttering in air, or from rock perch.

Feeding Habits: In early spring eats mostly seeds; in summer and fall, insects, mainly beetles, caterpillars, bugs, crane flies, spiders, seeds, and buds; at seashore eats sand "fleas" (crustaceans) on wet beach.

Nest: Preferably in rocky country, stony beaches, sea cliffs, grassy tundra, on ground; built by female, of mosses, sedges, and earth, usually well hidden in crevice or in mosses, lined with fur of dogs, foxes, lemmings, hares, and feathers of ptarmigans, jaegers, gulls, snowy owls (Parmelee, 1968).

Eggs: May–July; 3–9, usually 4–7, pale blue, gray, or cream-white, streaked with grays and browns.

Incubation: By female, 10–15½ days, depending on her attentiveness (Parmelee, 1968); young leave nest when 10–17 days old, some fly strongly at 13–14 days old; sometimes two broods.

Other Names: Common snow bunting; snow lark; snowbird; snowflake; whitebird; white snowbird.

Age: One, banded Mich., retrapped same place when 6 years old; another, 8 years, 8 months, old (Kennard, 1975).

Flight Speed: Individuals timed at 20 and 26 m.p.h.; flock timed over n. Atlantic from ship at 16.7 m.p.h. (Alexander, 1927).

Hybrids: Sealy (1969a) cites adult male McKay's bunting on St. Lawrence Is., Alaska, mated to a female Snow bunting; also occasional interbreeding of these two species elsewhere where ranges overlap.

Weights: 32–34 gr. (Amadon, 1943), or about 1¼ oz.

Range: Nests farther north than any other land bird; in N. America, on Arctic O. to n. Ellesmere Is. and n. Greenland, south to Pribilof Is., w. Aleutians, Shumagin Is. and sw. Alaska, c. Mack., c. Keewatin, east to n. Que., n.-c. Labrador and s. Greenland; also in n. Europe, and on Jan Mayen, Spitsbergen, Franz Josef Land, and nw. Russia; winters from w.-c. and s. Alaska, nw. B.C., and across s. Canada to Newfoundland, south to nw. Calif., e. Ore., n. Utah, n.-c. N.M., c. Kan., s. Ind., Ohio, Pa., Md., Va., and along Atlantic coast casually to Ga. and Ala. (first record for Fla., St. Johns R., Nov. 1969. Robertson, 1970).

Bunting, varied, *Passerina versicolor* (pass-er-EYE-nah ver-SICK-ul-or); genus name: *see* Bunting, indigo; species name: Lat., variegated, of various colors. (Color ill., page 299.) Mexican bird in sw. U.S. along Mexican border, where replaces lazuli bunting; 4½–5½ in. long; adult male has *red-purple or plum-purple* body that looks black at distance; *bright red nape;* blue crown; lighter blue rump; female plain, unstreaked, gray-brown above; wings and tail faintly glossed with bluish; no wing bars; pale buffy below, throat and belly sometimes whitish; young similar; lives in spring and summer in open country in mesquite-chaparral and associated plants, in streamside thickets; brushy pastures, and in dense vegetation with a few cottonwoods in Chisos Mtns. of Tex. (Wolfe, 1968); in foothill canyons of Ariz. north to Santa Catalina and Baboquivari Mtns.—center of abundance in that state (Phillips *et al.*, 1964); in spring, after male crosses border in Apr.–May into Ariz. and Tex., from conspicuous perch atop bush announces arrival and territorial claim by thin, crisp finch song; is shy and secretive, stays away from human dwellings; when not singing, with female, spends much time on ground close to thickets.

Feeding Habits: No definitive studies of; presumably insects and seeds, like foods of indigo and lazuli buntings (Wolfe, 1968).

Nest: Usually built in crotch of bush, low tree, tangled vine; 1½–5 ft. above ground, cup-shaped nest of dry grasses, plant stems, cotton, cast-off snakeskin, paper, lined with rootlets, hairs, fine grasses.

Eggs: Apr.–July; 3–4, pale blue, unmarked.

Incubation: Probably 12 days; age when young leave nest unknown.

Other Name: Beautiful bunting.

Flight Speed: 28 m.p.h. (Sooter, 1947).

Host to Cowbirds: Two records, to brown-headed cowbird, in Tex. (Friedmann, 1963).

Range: Nests from w. and s. Tex. (and s. Ariz., Phillips *et al.*, 1964), south through c. and e. Mexico, s. Baja Calif.; winters in summer range except extreme northern part.

Canary, blue. *See* Bunting, indigo.

Canary, Mexican. *See* Bunting, painted.

Canary, tarweed. *See* Goldfinch, lesser.

Canary, wild. *See* Goldfinch, American; also another name for the yellow warbler in Warbler—American Wood Warbler Family.

Cardinal, *Cardinalis cardinalis* (car-din-AY-liss); genus and species names: Lat., pertaining to a door hinge, thus that upon which something turns or depends; a "cardinal" principle, important person; the cardinals, important dignitaries of the Roman Catholic Church, wear scarlet robes, and the bird's color is cardinal red. (Color ills., page 300.) Lives mostly in e. U.S. and west to prairies, also in Southwest; state bird of Ill., Ind., Ky., N.C., Ohio, Va., and W.Va.; one of most admired of all N. American songbirds for its brilliant color and songs; 7½–8½ in. long; wingspread 10¼–12 in.; adult male almost entirely red with a red crest which he raises and lowers at will; black patch of feathers surrounds base of large, thick red bill; female olive gray, more brown above; reddish wings, red crest, red bill; young like female but browner and with darker bill; lives year-round in dense thickets along borders of fields, in hedges, edges of woods, thickets of open woods, canebrakes, swamps, stream banks, city and country parks and gardens of suburbs, towns, villages; male sings rich whistled songs every month of year with innumerable variations; phonetically, some rendered as *whoit, whoit, whoit; what cheer, what cheer; wheat, wheat, wheat;* and *pret-ty, pret-ty, pret-ty;* has at least 28 songs; both sexes sing, sometimes together; female's songs like male's but softer; call is sharp *tsip;* male often feeds female in courtship and at nest; both roost in honeysuckle thickets, evergreens, privet hedges; male is strongly territorial; fights other males over territory and mates and own image reflected from windows, hubcaps of cars; practices anting; both sexes bathe (Bent, 1968); come to bird feeders and even to hands for food.

Feeding Habits: Hops about on ground, moves through trees, shrubbery in feeding; eats at least 51 kinds of beetles, cicadas, dragonflies, leafhoppers, aphids, scale insects, ants, sawflies, termites, grasshoppers, crickets, caterpillars, codling moths, cutworms, also spiders, snails, slugs, 33 kinds of wild fruit, 39 of weed seeds (McAtee, 1908); waste corn, oats, rice, blossoms, seeds, and buds of elm trees, drinks maple sap from holes in bark made by sapsuckers (*see* Commensalism); at bird feeding stations likes sunflower seeds, cracked corn, etc. (see in Terres, 1968c).

Nest: Usually built by female, concealed in forks of twigs, sometimes on branch of small tree but usually in dense tangles of thickets or vines, 2–12 ft. (usually 4–5 ft.) above ground; often in young evergreens, rosebushes and honeysuckle, hardwood saplings; bowl-shaped, of weed stems, pliable twigs, strips of bark, grasses, rootlets, leaves, paper.

Eggs: Mar.–Aug.; 2–5, usually 3–4, gray-, buff-, or green-white, speckled and spotted with browns, grays, purple.

Incubation: Usually by female, 12–13 days; young usually leave nest when 10–11 days old; 2–3 or even 4 broods, male cares for first brood while female incubating eggs of next one (Bent, 1968).

Other Names: Cardinal grosbeak; cardinal bird; crested redbird; Kentucky cardinal; redbird; Virginia cardinal; Virginia nightingale, Virginia redbird.

Age: At Nashville, Tenn., one lived to 13½ years; a female, banded Fairfax, Va., trapped and released in same area when 13 years, 8 months, old; one 10 years old at Pittsburgh, Pa.; one lived as house pet, Atlanta, Ga., for 28½ years (1933–61).

Albinism: One with pure-white body, pink bill, red crest, red wings and tail, in Kans. (Capple, 1959); female with white head, eyes dark, rest of body normal, in Pa. (Hartman, 1968).

Flight Speed: Timed in Tex., 26 m.p.h. (Sooter, 1947).

Host to Cowbirds: To brown-headed cowbird, varies in different parts of cardinal's range; sometimes common, or infrequent, about 75 records; also host to bronzed cowbird (5 records) in Tex. (Friedmann, 1963).

Weights: In Mich. (23), 34.6–53.2 gr. (Becker and Stack, 1944), or 1¼–2 oz.; in Ohio (141), average 43.76 gr. (Amadon, 1943), or about 1⅔ oz.

Range: Although adults not truly migratory, young cardinals wander in all directions after grown; few wander far from place of banding; however, one moved 270 air miles from Hartford, Conn., to State College, Pa., one of longest trips on record for this species (Bordner, 1958); has been expanding range steadily northward; resident from se. S.D., c. Minn., w. and s. Ont., N.Y., nw. Vt., e. Mass., south in eastern states and through c. Neb., w. Kans., c. Tex. to n. Mexico, c. La., Gulf coast of Miss., Ala. and s. Fla., also s. Calif., c. Ariz., sw. N.M., south to Baja Calif. and Mexico to Belize; introduced into Hawaii.

Cardinal, Texas. *See* Pyrrhuloxia.

Crossbill, red, or common, *Loxia curvirostra* (LOCK-sih-ah cur-vih-ROS-trah); genus name: Lat., from Gr. *loxos,* crosswise, in reference to crossed mandibles of bill; species name; from Lat. *curvus,* curved, and *rostrum,* bill. (Color ill., page 301.) Coniferous forests of n. U.S. and Canada, from Atlantic to Pacific coasts and in mountains of East and West; 5½–6½ in. long; wingspread 10–10¾ in.; male in breeding plumage brick red, redder on rump, dusky wings (no wing bars) and dark tail; slender mandibles crossed like shears; slender point of upper one curves down; point of lower mandible curves up; female dusky buff-yellow, dark wings (no wing bars) and dusky tail; yellowish rump; immature male resembles adult female but with touches of scarlet on crown, breast, and rump; is not especially shy bird; can be approached with care; while feeding in trees crawls about using bill and feet like small parrot; flight is undulating like woodpecker's or goldfinch's but swifter, more prolonged, and sometimes at considerable height; ordinarily lives in broad nesting range but with population high and/or natural food shortages, makes invasion flights into U.S. (see Baird, 1964, for details). Sometimes flock remains to nest in areas south of usual range; for example, Berkshire Mtns., Mass., Catskills of N.Y., mountains of Pa. and N.C. (Bent, 1968); flock often utters low chattering or twittering while feeding; on nesting grounds in North, flocks break up by mid-Jan. into single pairs; at time of pairing, male comes into song—whistled notes and warbled phrases from tree perch and a flight song in which he rises above female on vibrating wings and circles her in treetop, uttering liquid notes, "an enraptured melody" (Lawrence, 1949).

Feeding Habits: Moves about deliberately in trees while feeding on seeds which it extracts from cones of conifers, using bill to force and hold apart cone scales, while tongue lifts seed out; eats seeds of pines, firs, spruces, hemlock, larch that fall to ground; also eats seeds of birches, alders, willows, poplars, elms, maples, and tender green buds of spruces; also eats caterpillars, aphids, beetles, ants, etc.; is attracted to salt-impregnated soil; sometimes picks mortar from brick walls for calcium; will come to hands for pounded dried mortar (Baynes, 1915).
Nest: Saddled well out on branch or in cluster of needles of pine, cedar, spruce, 5–80 ft. above ground, of twigs, rootlets, strips of bark, lined with fine grasses, mosses, feathers, fur.
Eggs: Various times of year; Jan.–Aug.; 3–5, usually 3–4, pale blue or pale green, spotted with browns, occasional scrawls of black.
Incubation: By female, apparently 12–14 days; young leave nest when about 17 days old; their bills not yet crossed; apparently one brood each season.
Other Name: American crossbill.
Accidents: Attracted to calcium chloride (salt) spread on highways to melt ice and snow, many killed by traffic (Meade, 1942).
Host to Cowbirds: One record (Friedmann, 1963) near London, Ont., Apr. 1909.
Weights: About ¾ oz.
Range: Resident from se. Alaska east to Newfoundland, south in West to n. Baja Calif. and Nicaragua; in East to n. Wisc., Tenn., N.C.; wanders in winter to n. Fla., Gulf coast; also resident in Europe, Russia, Siberia to n. Africa and n. India.

Crossbill, white-winged, *Loxia leucoptera* (LOCK-sih-ah lew-COP-teh-rah); genus name: *see* Crossbill, red; species name: Gr., white wings, alludes to white bars in wings. (Color ill., page 301.) Lives in boreal forests of N. Hemisphere but ranges farther north than red crossbill and usually not as far south; occasionally invades U.S. at times of overpopulation or food shortages (see Baird, 1964; *see also* Irruption); 6–6¾ in. long; adult male wine-red, with dusky tail, *dark wings with two broad white wing bars;* female and young similar to female and young of red crossbill but have white wing bars, which distinguish this species from red crossbill even while in flight; feeding and flocking behavior similar to that of red crossbill; also may nest in Jan.; male sings song like twitter of American goldfinch or of canary, *sweet, sweet, sweet,* from tip-top of spruce or fir, also has flight song; common call note is sharp, metallic *cheet* (Taber, 1968).

Feeding Habits: Eats insects, also seeds of conifers, cottonwood, black alder, birches, beach grass, foxtail grass, ragweed, seeds of sunflower, juniper, crowberry, huckleberry, is attracted to salt-impregnated ground of moose "licks" and salt on surface of highways, which it licks up with tongue and where killed by traffic (Meade, 1942).
Nest: Very similar to red crossbill's; may be built of lichens and spruce twigs, often in spruce trees, 2½–15 ft., or even 70 ft., above ground.
Eggs: Jan.–Apr.; 2–5, usually 3–4, pale blue, green-white, spotted, sometimes scrawled with browns, black.
Incubation: Probably about 12–14 days; age when young leave nest unknown.
Range: Resident n. Alaska, c. Yukon, c. Mack., c. Man., n. Ont., n. Que., Labrador, south to Wash., n. Ore., n. Minn., n. Wisc. s. Ont., n. N.H., N.Y., wanders in winter to Colo. and N.C.; also lives in n. Europe, n. Russia, Siberia.

Dickcissel (DICK-sis-el), *Spiza americana* (SPY-zah ah-mer-ih-CANE-ah); genus name: Gr. *spiza,* finch; species name: Lat., of America; common name: from phonetics of bird's incessant calls on nesting grounds. (Color ill., page 303.) Summers in Midwest, largely between Allegheny Mtns. in East and Rocky Mtns. in West; 6–7 in. long; wingspread 9–11 in.; often associated with meadowlarks, adult male appears, from front, strikingly like small one, often called "little meadowlark"; has yellow breast with black bib; yellow line over eyes; white throat; finchlike bill; female resembles female house sparrow, but has *chestnut* patch at bend of wings; narrow dark streak on side of *white* throat; yellowish breast; young resemble female; in grassland biome most common in summer in tall-grass prairie region (Zimmerman, 1971); also in meadows, pastures, weed patches, grain fields, alfalfa fields; extremely erratic in changing nesting grounds; may be abundant one summer in area, then vanish; arrive next summer in new nesting place; by end of 19th century had disappeared from vast area east of Allegheny Mtns.; reappeared from 1948 on to nest again in N.Y. and in Southeast (Gross, 1968), now appears in winter in Northeast at feeding stations (Gross, 1956) where associates with house sparrows; returns from C. America to s. U.S. in Apr.; arrives nesting grounds in Mo., Ark., Ill., Wisc., Dakotas, Apr.–May; male immediately announces territory by singing repeatedly *dick, dick, dick-cissel* from weed stalk, post, utility wires; sings into late summer; also may sing in winter; when female arrives week or 10 days later, nesting begins; some males are polygynous (Zimmerman, 1966).

Feeding Habits: Ground feeder, eats many kinds weed seeds, waste grain, grasshoppers, crickets, cankerworms, spiders, harvestmen (daddy longlegs).
Nest: Often in trees, hedges; bulky cup of weed stems, grasses, leaves, lined with finer grasses, hairs, rootlets; built by female, 2–14 ft. up, also close to, or on, ground in clumps of tall grass, thistle, etc., in hay, alfalfa, grain fields.
Eggs: Apr.–Aug.; 3–5, usually 4, pale blue, unmarked.
Incubation: By female, 12–13 days; young leave nest when 7–9 days old; two broods a year.
Other Names: Black-throated bunting; Judasbird; little meadowlark.
Accidents: One caught by a foot in tangle of small wires, Iowa, died of starvation (Hodges, 1950); many nests destroyed in hayfields by mowing machines.
Flight Speed: Timed in Tex., 25 m.p.h. (Sooter, 1947).
Host to Cowbirds: Not uncommonly, to brown-headed cowbird, about 55 records from 9 states (Friedmann, 1963).
Weights: Autumn migrants, coastal N.J. (4), 25–29.5 gr. (Murray and Jehl, 1964), or about 1 oz.; in winter in Trinidad, males weighed 30–47 gr., or 1–1¾ oz. (ffrench, 1967).
Range: Nests from e. Mont., nw. N.D., s. Man., nw. and c. Minn., n. Wis., s. Mich., s. Ont., c. N.Y., and Mass., south to c. Colo., w. Okla., Tex., s. La., c. Miss. c. Ala., c. Ga., S.C., to c. Md., in general away from Atlantic coastal plain; winters from c. Mexico to n. S. America, West Indies (Trinidad), where ffrench (1967)

Black rosy finch

FINCH FAMILY

noted flocks roosting in sugarcane or in bamboo; about 66,000 birds in one roost in 1962.

Finch, black rosy, *Leucosticte atrata* (lew-coe-STICK-tee ate-RAY-tah); genus name: from Gr. *leukos,* white, and *stiktos,* punctured, dappled, dotted, in reference to variegated colors of males; species name: Lat., clothed in black, in reference to blackish body of male. Uncommon bird, small, summers high in c. Rockies; about 6 in. long; many ornithologists believe that all three rosy finches are merely geographical representatives of one species; male black rosy finch distinguished from all others by his sooty black breast, head, and back; has light gray patch on back of head, pink wash on belly, flanks, rump, and along bend of folded wings; female generally duller, with less extensive pink, gray crown barely discernible; are very sociable, during most of year are in large flocks which break up only in breeding season; are close-knit, if one chirps and flies, all fly with quick strokes of wings followed by a glide on folded wings which makes undulating flight; in early Apr. have traveled from their wintering grounds on lower mountain slopes and valleys upward to nesting grounds, such as in Wasatch Mtns. of Utah at 11,000 ft. elevation; on bare rocky slopes blown clear of snow by wind, male displays before female in courtship in territory that is unusual among birds in that it centers on female—wherever she moves, her mate goes to drive away other males (males outnumber females 6–1); male does not have true song; he and his mate communicate with call notes: a harsh *chew* or *tsew,* similar to chirping of house sparrow, a low sharp *pert,* and a high piercing *peent* (French, 1968).

Feeding Habits: During nesting season, both sexes of all rosy finches develop a pair of gular sacs (in upper throat) capable of carrying food, as does pine grosbeak; more than 97% of food is seeds of small tundra plants.

Nest: Bulky, hidden among boulders and in rock crevices, site selected by female; one examined potential sites on cliff for 8 days, then began to build next day; she completed it in 3 days; of mosses, grasses, feathers, hair, lined with finer grasses and hair (French, 1968).

Eggs: June–July; 4–5, white, pear-shaped.

Incubation: By female, 12–14 days; young leave nest when about 20 days old (French, 1959); rosy finches start to gather in flocks of several hundreds in high mountains as soon as young independent of parents; remain at high elevations until Oct. and Nov., then move down into valleys and deserts at lower elevations; start using roosts in cave entrances, mine shafts, abandoned cliff swallow nests, piers, outbuildings, barns; in one roost at Roosevelt, e. Utah, flock of 500 roosted in 50-ft.-deep well to escape wind (Scott, 1958).

Hybrids: In Bitterroot Mtns. on Mont.–Idaho border, in broad zone at least 50 mi. long, hybridization or intergradation between black rosy finch and gray-crowned rosy finch. See discussion by French (1968).

Range: Nests in mountains of sw. Mont., c. Idaho, w. Wyo., n. Utah, n. Nev.; winters in valleys of c. Idaho, nw. Wyo., south to Utah,

FALCON FAMILY

Caracara

The national emblem of Mexico, this vulturelike scavenger reaches the northern limits of its range in Florida, Texas, and Arizona, where it is local and rare. No other bird of prey has such a varied diet as the caracara. Walking about on long legs and flat claws, it scratches like a chicken for worms and insects. It catches skunks, prairie dogs, opossums, rats, squirrels, snakes, frogs, crabs, and even young alligators. It carries small turtles to its nest by gripping the edge of the shell with its eaglelike bill, then it tears out the flesh bit by bit to feed its young. Caracaras follow vultures to carrion, often robbing them of their meal by forcing them to disgorge. The call of the caracara is a harsh cackle; when excited, its bright-red face turns yellow.

Caracara

Aplomado falcon

This handsome raptor, fairly common in Central and South America, has virtually disappeared from the border country of Arizona, New Mexico, and Texas, where it once was a regular summer resident. A bird of open plains, the aplomado falcon often hovers like a kestrel, plunging on lizards, snakes, and mice; but small birds and large insects are caught on the wing.

Peregrine falcon

A victim of the indiscriminate use of highly toxic pesticides, this spectacular bird of prey has virtually disappeared as a breeding species from all but its northernmost nesting grounds in North America. But a major and promising effort is underway, using captive breeding and the release of nestlings, to return the peregrine to such former sites as the beaches of New Jersey, the cliffs of the Catskills, and the skyscrapers of New York City.

Prairie falcon

Raised on a diet of ground squirrels, jackrabbits, and a variety of ground-dwelling birds, young prairie falcons are ready to leave their cliffside eyrie when about 6 weeks old. This falcon is not as spectacular a hunter as the peregrine. While prairie falcons occasionally swoop on prey, more often they hover like kestrels, chase birds in low-level flight, or even hop about the ground catching lizards and grasshoppers.

Gyrfalcon

The world's largest falcon hunts the Arctic tundra around the pole. Ptarmigan are the staple of its diet (89 percent of its food by weight in an Alaska study), but the gyrfalcon also pursues the large Arctic hare and in summer raids nesting colonies of dovekies and murres. There are 3 color phases of this magnificent bird of prey—dark, white, and gray.

American kestrel

The smallest falcon in North America is familiar along rural roadsides, where it perches on utility wires, flicking its tail as it watches for prey on the ground. In summer, grasshoppers and crickets form a major part of the kestrel's diet; in winter, it hunts mice and small birds.

Merlin

Coniferous forests across Canada and Alaska are the summer haunt of this small falcon, a nemesis of birds from warblers to teal. The merlin flies low over the ground, overtaking birds and plucking them out of the air with its talons. It is regularly seen during fall migration along Atlantic beaches, following the southward flights of shorebirds and songbirds on which it feeds.

Gyrfalcon, dark phase

Gyrfalcon, white phase

Merlin

Prairie falcon

Aplomado falcon

Prairie falcon

American kestrel

Peregrine falcon

FINCH FAMILY

Indigo bunting
A bird of overgrown fields, brushlands, and roadside thickets throughout the East, the indigo bunting is our only small finch that in bright sunlight appears blue all over. (The blue color is the result of light diffraction through the feathers; there is no blue pigment, and in shade or silhouette the indigo bunting looks solid black.) Its song, often heard in midday heat, is a long series of repeated, high-pitched notes or phrases.

Lark bunting
A larklike flight song gives this inhabitant of the Great Plains its name. Gregarious year round, lark buntings feed and migrate in large flocks and nest in loose colonies where several dozen males may be heard pouring forth their warbled trill at one time.

Lazuli bunting
Like other seed-eating finches, this western counterpart of the indigo bunting augments its diet in summer with a variety of insects.

McKay's bunting
In its breeding plumage, this close relative of the snow bunting is pure white except for the black tips of its wings and central tail feathers. It nests on remote islands in the Bering Sea and winters along Alaska's western coast.

Painted bunting
No other North American songbird could be confused with this gaudy finch of southern thickets. Though secretive and hard to find in its nesting habitat, the painted bunting regularly comes to bird feeders. Males engage in vicious territorial fights in which a combatant may lose an eye—or his life.

Snow bunting
The smart black and white breeding plumage of the snow bunting is known only to residents and visitors on the Arctic tundra. More familiar are the brown and white birds that, in severe winters, descend in great flocks on open fields across the northern tier of states. Hidden beneath a rock or in a clump of moss, the nest is built entirely by the female snow bunting, which lines it with fur from foxes, lemmings, and hares, and feathers of ptarmigans, snowy owls, gulls, and jaegers.

Varied bunting
A secretive bird of dense desert brush on the Mexican borderlands, the varied bunting is a uniformly dark bird whose red-purple colors are visible only in good light conditions.

Indigo bunting

Lazuli bunting

Painted bunting

Snow bunting

Snow bunting, female

Lark bunting

McKay's bunting

Varied bunting

Cardinal

East of the prairies, this is nearly everybody's favorite songbird. The male is as stunningly garbed as a Roman Catholic cardinal in scarlet robes; his mate is attractive in a somewhat subdued plumage. Both are skilled vocalists, and their rich whistled songs—with more than two dozen variations—are heard every month of the year. They regularly nest in suburban gardens, where as many as 4 broods are raised in succession, the male caring for the nestlings while the female incubates the eggs of the next brood.

Red crossbill

Crossbills are named for the overlapping tips of the upper and lower mandibles, which they use to pry seeds from the tough cones of conifers. The bird holds the cone scales apart with its bill, lifting out the seed with its tongue. The red crossbill breeds in evergreen forests across the North from Alaska to Labrador, and southward in pine-clad mountain ranges to North Carolina and Nicaragua. Blessed with a year-round food supply, red crossbills may begin nesting as early as January.

White-winged crossbill

Using both its bill and feet to scramble about pine branches, a feeding crossbill suggests a small parrot. White-winged crossbills range farther north than red crossbills, and only in times of food shortages or overpopulation do they invade the United States in large numbers.

Cardinal, female

Cardinal

White-winged crossbill

Red crossbill

Dickcissel

A flock of migrant dickcissels bursts from a Texas grainfield. With its yellow breast and black bib, the male dickcissel suggests a miniature meadowlark. From April to late summer, it sings its name from a weed stalk, fence post, or utility wire: "dick, dick, dick-cissel." Midwestern grasslands and farmlands are its breeding habitat, and the dickcissel has a special fondness for alfalfa fields. But it is extremely erratic in choosing nesting grounds; it may be abundant in a particular area one summer, then vanish the next.

Brown-capped rosy finch

Rosy finches are birds of alpine meadow, tundra, and snowfield. Chunky and sparrowlike, they feed on the seeds of dwarf tundra plants. In breeding season, both male and female develop a pair of throat pouches in which they carry food to their nestlings. The brown-capped rosy finch summers above 12,000 feet in the central and northern Rocky Mountains. In winter, mixed flocks of rosy finches congregate at roosts in the foothills.

Cassin's finch

This inhabitant of western coniferous forests is closely related to the purple finch and house finch. But the 3 similar birds occupy different habitats. The purple finch is confined to shaded oak canyons at lower elevations; the house finch prefers foothill chaparral and desert. Cassin's finch forages in the treetops or on the ground for conifer seeds; when the ground is snow-covered, it eats tender buds.

Gray-crowned rosy finch

Of the 3 species of rosy finch, the gray-crowned has by far the widest distribution. It breeds from the Brooks Range of Alaska and the Bering Sea islands to the Sierra Nevada of California, hiding its nest among boulders or in rock crevices above timberline. In winter, large flocks of gray-crowned rosy finches wander eastward over the Great Plains.

House finch

In the 1940s, an illegal shipment of house finches destined for the cagebird trade was intercepted in New York City. The birds were released on Long Island and established a small breeding enclave that struggled for several years to survive. Since then, however, a house finch population explosion has spread their numbers up and down the Atlantic seaboard. Indeed, in some areas of the Northeast, house finches now outnumber the pestiferous English sparrow.

Brown-capped rosy finch

Gray-crowned rosy finch

House finch

Cassin's finch

Dickcissel

Purple finch

Described as a "heavy-billed sparrow that has been dipped in raspberry juice," the purple finch is a ravenous guest at bird feeders when seed crops fail in northern coniferous forests. In winter, purple finches travel in undulating flocks, filling the brisk air with their metallic "tick" notes.

American goldfinch

Our familiar "wild canary" begins nesting when most other songbirds have finished raising their young and some species have begun their southward migrations. For the American goldfinch waits on family matters until July or August, when there is an abundance of weed seeds, especially thistle seeds, to nourish the 4 to 6 young. Both adults feed the nestlings, regurgitating partly digested seeds directly into their gaping mouths.

Lawrence's goldfinch

Dry interior valleys in central and southern California, and Baja California, are the habitat of this unpredictable species. An area may be filled with Lawrence's goldfinches one summer and the next year contain none. Access to water is critical, whether the source is a creek, stock tank, or dripping faucet, for the birds are fond of bathing.

Lesser goldfinch

This common goldfinch of the Southwest has 2 races: one with a green back, the other with a black back. The lesser goldfinch raises its young on a diet of unripe dandelion seeds.

Purple finch, female

Purple finch

Lawrence's goldfinch

American goldfinch

Lesser goldfinch

Black-headed grosbeak

"Grosbeak," for anyone not acquainted with these large finches, means exactly what it says: a huge, thick, "gross" beak. A bird of open deciduous woodlands throughout the West, the black-headed grosbeak eats a wide variety of seeds, berries, and insects, and is a tame visitor to bird feeders and campgrounds. The male sometimes delivers his melodious song in flight.

Blue grosbeak

A shed snakeskin decorates the nest of the blue grosbeak, a fairly common bird of southern thickets. Like the smaller indigo bunting, it appears black in poor light. In spring, flocks of male blue grosbeaks arrive from Central America ahead of the females; feeding on plowed fields, they are easily mistaken at a distance for cowbirds.

Evening grosbeak

The arrival of this colorful grosbeak at bird feeders in the northern states is an eagerly awaited but largely unpredictable event. Where large flocks circulated from yard to yard one year, only a few birds—or none—appear the next. Winter movements of evening grosbeaks tend to follow east-west rather than north-south patterns; birds banded in Michigan, for instance, may show up on nesting grounds in the conifer forests of eastern Quebec.

Pine grosbeak

Our largest grosbeak, this tame finch nests in northern forests around the world, moving southward in winter only in times of food scarcity. It is attracted to juniper and cedar trees and to ornamental fruiting shrubs. Like the rosy finches of western mountains, the pine grosbeak has throat pouches for carrying food.

Rose-breasted grosbeak

A familiar voice of springtime in northern deciduous forests, the male rose-breasted grosbeak, to match his handsome garb, has a beautiful song—a long, liquid, robinlike carol. Rose-breasted grosbeaks arrive on their nesting grounds in early May, and several males may fight fiercely for the attention of one female. Both sexes care for the eggs and nestlings, the male often singing while sitting on the nest.

Black-headed grosbeak, female

Black-headed grosbeak

Blue grosbeak

Evening grosbeak, female

Evening grosbeak

Pine grosbeak, female

Pine grosbeak

Rose-breasted grosbeak, female

Rose-breasted grosbeak

Dark-eyed junco

What had been a profusion of juncos suffered harshly at the hands of the American Ornithologists' Union in 1973 when it was ruled that a number of birds long considered to be distinct species were merely geographic races, or subspecies. Four former species, including the slate-colored junco and Oregon junco, were lumped under one banner as the dark-eyed junco, based on evidence that included frequent interbreeding. A common visitor to winter feeders, the slate-colored is the most widespread of all juncos, nesting in northern forests from Alaska to Labrador and wintering throughout the United States. The Oregon junco is an inhabitant of western conifer forests, city parks, and college campuses; its plumage is variable, but many males have black or gray hoods and pink flanks.

Gray-headed junco

An ash-gray head, tawny back, and dark eyes identify this bird of high mountain forests from Idaho to New Mexico. Ranging to timberline, the gray-headed junco builds a nest of coarse grasses at the base of a tree or bush, or under a fallen log or rock.

Yellow-eyed junco

Two North American birds, the Mexican junco and the rare Baird's junco, were among former species now lumped together as the yellow-eyed junco. In Arizona and New Mexico, it is found in coniferous and pine-oak forests above 6,000 feet. Yellow-eyed juncos shuffle mouselike over the ground when feeding, rather than hopping about like other juncos. Very tame, they snatch crumbs from picnic tables at national forest campgrounds.

Dark-eyed (Slate-colored) junco

Dark-eyed (Oregon) junco

Dark-eyed (Slate-colored) junco

Gray-headed junco

Yellow-eyed (Mexican) junco

Chestnut-collared longspur
Ground-dwelling, sparrowlike birds, longspurs are named for the very long claw on the hind toe. The chestnut-collared longspur is an inhabitant of northern prairies, where the male defends his territory with tireless song. The nest is built in a hollow dug in the ground and concealed by tall grass.

Lapland longspur
In winter, immense flocks of Lapland longspurs descend on windswept fields and plains across the northern United States, gleaning weed seeds. Often seen in the company of horned larks and snow buntings, they resemble drab house sparrows, for the male shows only a trace of the glorious breeding plumage that he sports on the Arctic tundra nesting grounds.

McCown's longspur
Arid, short-grass plains are the habitat of this species, which is known to abandon nesting grounds in unusually wet years. Typically a seed eater, it feeds extensively on grasshoppers in summer.

Smith's longspur
One of the least-known North American birds, Smith's longspur nests on the Arctic tundra from Hudson Bay to the Bering Sea coast of Alaska. In winter, small flocks forage over pastures and airports in the Midwest, where they usually remain apart from other longspurs and horned larks.

Pyrrhuloxia
The "gray cardinal" of mesquite shrublands in the Southwest and Mexico has a sharply hooked upper mandible that gives it a parrotlike appearance. Its whistled song is remarkably similar to a cardinal's. In summer, pyrrhuloxias eat great quantities of worms and weevils that damage cotton crops; in winter, they feed on cottonwood catkins and cactus fruits.

Common redpoll
Visits by this little red-capped finch from the tundra are unscheduled; but in some winters, great flocks of common redpolls move south to reap weed seeds in fields across Canada and the northern United States. Tame and unsuspicious, redpolls have been caught in hand at window feeders by bird-banders.

Hoary redpoll
A whitish rump and a stubby bill are the only reliable field marks to distinguish the hoary redpoll, which breeds along the coast of the Arctic Ocean. Its nest is a cup of twigs, grass, and rootlets built on the ground or in the crotch of a dwarf willow or alder.

Chestnut-collared longspur

McCown's longspur

Lapland longspur, female

Smith's longspur

Chestnut-collared longspur, female

Lapland longspur

Common redpoll

Pyrrhuloxia

Hoary redpoll

Pine siskin

In fall and winter, pine siskins forage over northern forests in flocks that may number several thousand birds, feasting on the seeds of conifers, alders, birches, and maples. But they are seen as far south as Florida in years when food shortages trigger southward irruptions.

Baird's sparrow

A little-known bird of northern grasslands, Baird's sparrow was named by Audubon for Spencer F. Baird, a prominent ornithologist who later became Secretary of the Smithsonian Institution. Its main nesting grounds are on the prairies of Saskatchewan and Manitoba.

Black-chinned sparrow

Chaparral and sagebrush on arid mountainsides of the Southwest are the haunt of this uncommon sparrow. A gray head and breast and a pink bill suggest a junco; but the male in breeding season has a black chin patch. Its song is a canarylike trill that carries far down mountain slopes.

Black-throated sparrow

A common bird in the hottest deserts of the West, the black-throated sparrow can live without drinking water during the driest months of the year. The seeds and insects on which it feeds satisfy its needs for moisture.

Brewer's sparrow

On the arid sagebrush flats of the Great Basin, Brewer's sparrow may outnumber all other birds; 47 nesting pairs were counted on one 100-acre tract in eastern Washington. Its name honors Thomas M. Brewer, a Boston physician and ornithologist.

Cassin's sparrow

This ground-dwelling sparrow is most abundant on the short-grass plains of Colorado, Oklahoma, Texas, and New Mexico. The male declares its territory from a singing perch on a cactus, ocotillo, or yucca, launching into a flight song if another male approaches. The species is named for John Cassin, a 19th-century Philadelphia ornithologist.

Chipping sparrow

This tame little sparrow with a rusty cap is a common bird across most of North America. It often nests in gardens, hedges, and dooryard shrubs, lining its nest with horsehair (if available) or the hair of numerous other animals. Its song is a series of chips, sometimes given slowly, other times in a rapid trill.

Black-throated sparrow

Brewer's sparrow

Baird's sparrow

Cassin's sparrow

Black-chinned sparrow

Chipping sparrow

Pine siskin

Clay-colored sparrow
The buzzing song of the clay-colored sparrow is difficult to distinguish from the sounds of insects on the brushy grasslands and prairies of the north-central states and Canada. Young birds leave their bulky nest when 7 to 9 days old.

Field sparrow
Abandoned, overgrown farmland and brushy, cutover woods are the summer habitat of this pink-billed sparrow. The male constantly patrols his nesting territory, declaring possession with a sweet, plaintive song. Field sparrows forage on the ground for insects and seeds.

Fox sparrow
Named for the rufous color of the eastern race, this large sparrow feeds on the ground, vigorously kicking up the leaf litter or snow to uncover seeds and small animal life. Western birds are gray-brown with only a hint of the foxy markings. The fox sparrow is considered to be one of the finest singers in the entire sparrow clan.

Golden-crowned sparrow
An orange-yellow stripe through the crown identifies this close relative of the white-crowned sparrow. A bird of the Pacific coast from Alaska to Baja California, the golden-crowned sparrow nests in alpine meadows and forest clearings, wintering in brushland and chaparral.

Clay-colored sparrow

Golden-crowned sparrow

Field sparrow

Fox sparrow, red race

Fox sparrow, gray race

Grasshopper sparrow

The song of this short-tailed sparrow of the grasslands is so thin and high pitched that it is inaudible, even from a few feet away, to older bird-watchers who have begun to lose the upper register of their hearing. Both male and female sing, often at night. Four to 5 eggs are laid in a domed nest built in a clump of grass or hay.

Harris' sparrow

Audubon named this handsome, large sparrow for Edward Harris, a companion on his Missouri River expedition in 1843. In breeding plumage, both sexes are strikingly marked with a black crown, face, throat, and upper breast. Harris' sparrow nests in scattered patches of stunted timber in northern Canada from the Mackenzie River delta to Hudson Bay.

Henslow's sparrow

John Henslow, for whom this secretive grasslands bird is named, was an English botanist and friend of Audubon. The male is an incessant singer, especially in the rain; but his efforts yield only a brief, insectlike "tis-lick." Henslow's sparrows sometimes nest in loose colonies.

Lark sparrow

Chestnut head markings and a black spot on the breast identify this inhabitant, named for its larklike flight song, of grasslands from the Midwest to the Pacific coast. The male courts a mate by strutting about like a turkey cock, wings trailing and tail spread.

Harris' sparrow

Grasshopper sparrow

Henslow's sparrow

Lark sparrow

Le Conte's sparrow

An inhabitant of prairie wetlands, this secretive bird is almost impossible to flush. It prefers to scurry along in thick cover and flies only a few feet if forced to. Physician-entomologist John Le Conte was honored when Audubon named this species.

Lincoln's sparrow

This bird of northern boglands was first described by Audubon, who named it for Thomas Lincoln, a companion on his Labrador trek of 1833. Often overlooked on migration because of its skulking habits and similarity to the song sparrow, it has a sweet, bubbling song that suggests a house wren or purple finch.

Olive sparrow

Scratching noisily under the thickets for seeds and insects, this drab-colored Central American finch, a year-round resident of south Texas, looks and behaves more like a small towhee than a sparrow.

Rufous-crowned sparrow

This secretive bird of dry, boulder-strewn hillsides in the Southwest and California rarely flies; if flushed, it dives into the grass or behind a rock. Similar in appearance to the chipping sparrow, it has a black "whisker" on each side of the throat.

Sage sparrow

A bird of sagebrush and chaparral from the Great Basin to coastal foothills, the sage sparrow lives mostly on the ground, gleaning insects and seeds as it rushes about under cover. Three or 4 young are raised in a nest that is carefully concealed in sage or a shrub.

Savannah sparrow

Named for the Georgia city where Alexander Wilson found the species in 1811, this sparrow nests over most of North America in a wide range of grassy habitats: sedge bogs; coastal salt marshes; inland meadows, hayfields, prairies; the grass-capped islands of the Aleutian chain. When disturbed, it runs through the grass like a mouse.

Savannah (Ipswich) sparrow

This rare bird nests on Sable Island, a sandy graveyard for ships in the North Atlantic, 100 miles off Nova Scotia. Recently determined to be not a separate species but a geographic race of the Savannah sparrow, it appears ghostly white against the sun-washed dunes.

Seaside sparrow

A resident of coastal marshes from Massachusetts to Texas, the seaside sparrow has relatively large feet that enable it to run over soft ooze. It feeds largely on small animal life that abounds along tidal creeks. One subspecies, the dusky seaside sparrow, is found only near Merritt Island in Florida and appears on the verge of extinction since researchers have been unable to locate a single female of its race.

Le Conte's sparrow

Lincoln's sparrow

Olive sparrow

Savannah sparrow

Seaside sparrow

Sage sparrow

Savannah (Ipswich) sparrow

Rufous-crowned sparrow

Sharp-tailed sparrow
Zigzagging through the grass or over the mud, the sharp-tailed sparrow picks up a wide variety of animal life—from sand fleas and snails to grasshoppers and spiders. This is a bird of freshwater marshes on the northern prairies and salt marshes along the Atlantic coast.

Song sparrow
Our best-known native sparrow is among the first songbirds to herald the approach of spring, with its persistent but pleasing song. Nesting begins as early as February in some locales, and a pair may fledge 3 broods by the end of summer—sometimes re-using the same nest. The song sparrow is a frequent victim of cowbird parasitism.

Swamp sparrow
Declaring its domain, the male swamp sparrow perches on a cattail or willow, spreads its round tail, and sings a musical, one-note trill. A bird of freshwater wetlands, the swamp sparrow often feeds by wading in shallow water, picking up floating insects and seeds.

Tree sparrow
The musical twittering of a flock of tree sparrows is a familiar sound in winter across the northern United States as these birds from the far Arctic descend on weedy fields, roadsides, and feeders. With abundant food, tree sparrows are able to withstand bitter weather as cold as −28 degrees.

Tree sparrow

Song sparrow

Sharp-tailed sparrow

Swamp sparrow

Vesper sparrow

White outer tail feathers that flash as the bird flies across meadows, pastures, and hayfields identify the vesper sparrow, so named because the naturalist John Burroughs believed that it sang most sweetly toward sunset. To defend its territory, the male sings from the highest perch available—a tree, a fence post, or simply a weed. The vesper sparrow nest, hidden on the ground in a slight depression, contains 3 to 5 eggs.

White-crowned sparrow

This handsome sparrow nests or winters over much of the continent but is most abundant in the West. It hops about on the ground to feed, scratching with both feet to uncover seeds and insects. The white-crowned sparrow also eats fruiting capsules of mosses and young garden plants.

White-throated sparrow

Like the wail of a loon or the howl of a wolf, the whistled song of a white-throated sparrow—"Old Sam Peabody, Peabody, Peabody"—is the very essence of the Canadian wilderness where it breeds. The nest, built by the female, is hidden on the ground or in a small balsam fir. A ground feeder, the white-throated sparrow eats mainly seeds and the fruits of various shrubs.

White-crowned sparrow

Vesper sparrow

Vesper sparrow, eggs

White-throated sparrow

Abert's towhee

Towhees are large sparrows that hop about the ground, scratching with both feet to find seeds and insects. The colonial naturalist Mark Catesby coined the name towhee in 1731 after the call of the rufous-sided towhee. Abert's towhee is a secretive but common inhabitant of desert thickets along watercourses in the Colorado River basin. The species was named for an army officer who collected the first specimen, in New Mexico.

Brown towhee

Unlike other towhees, this wary resident of suburban gardens, coastal chaparral, and arid shrublands does not attract attention with noisy, vigorous kicking at the leaf litter, and it rarely emerges from dense, shady cover.

Green-tailed towhee

When alarmed, the green-tailed towhee scurries through the brush like a chipmunk, a tactic to lure predators away from its nest. Widely distributed in the West and Southwest, this species summers in low brush on high plateaus and in mountain forest openings.

Rufous-sided towhee

The eastern and western races of this familiar towhee were once considered separate species. Birds in the West have white-spotted backs, and their song may bear little resemblance to the well-known "drink-your-tea" command of their eastern counterparts. The menu of the rufous-sided towhee includes moths, caterpillars, beetles, woodborers, sow bugs, snails, millipedes, salamanders, lizards, and snakes, as well as a variety of seeds and berries.

FLAMINGO FAMILY

American flamingo

Flamingos may once have nested in the Florida Keys, but today these spectacular pink birds are rare visitors to the United States coast from the Carolinas to Texas. Breeding colonies of American flamingos are found in the Bahamas, West Indies, Yucatán, Galápagos Islands, and South America. Flamingos feed in water of any depth in which they can wade, straining animal life from the bottom ooze with their tongue and unique bill.

Brown towhee

Abert's towhee

Rufous-sided towhee, western race

Green-tailed towhee

Rufous-sided towhee, eastern race

American flamingo

FLAMINGO FAMILY

American flamingo

Flamingos may once have nested in the Florida Keys, but today these spectacular pink birds are rare visitors to the United States coast from the Carolinas to Texas. Breeding colonies of American flamingos are found in the Bahamas, West Indies, Yucatán, Galápagos Islands, and South America. Flamingos feed in water of any depth in which they can wade, straining animal life from the bottom ooze with their tongue and unique bill.

ne. Calif., s. Colo., c. and n. N.M., and n. Ariz.; casual in Ore. and Mont.

Finch, bramble. *See* Brambling.

Finch, brown-capped rosy, *Leucosticte australis* (lew-koe-STICK-tee aus-TRAIL-us); genus name: *see* Finch, black rosy; species name: Lat., southern. (Color ill., page 302.) High mountains of Wyo., Colo., n. N.M.; 5¾–6¼ in. long; like gray-crowned rosy finch but without the distinctive gray markings on head; all rosy finches are chunky, sparrowlike ground birds that appear darker than other ground finches of the region; rosy feathers of brown-capped adult male are bright, especially in midsummer; females are duller and paler than males, less rosy, sometimes show no pink (Packard, 1968); in winter flocks congregate in midafternoon with all three species together in communal roosts, numbering 1,000 birds or more; one such roost at Red Rocks Park, Morrison, Colo., at 6,000 ft. elevation, each bird was occupying hole in cliffs or old mud nests of cliff swallows; occupy foothill roosts until Apr. or May, when move up to nesting grounds and flocks gradually break up; pairs summer on peaks usually above 12,000 ft.; descend altitudinally in fall to lower hills for winter, but rarely below 6,000 ft. elevation; in summer, common bird, especially numerous on lofty meadows of Front Range and Arapahoe Peaks that form eastern chain of Rockies in Colo., one might see groups of brown-capped by climbing almost any suitable peak in Colo. in summer (Packard, 1968); Robbins *et al.* (1966) suggest most easily found on Mt. Evans; habitat, flight, courtship, feeding habits, nesting, etc., similar to that of black rosy finch and gray-crowned. See Packard (1968) for other details.

Range: See above.

Finch, Cassin's, *Carpodacus cassinii* (car-POD-ah-cus cass-IN-ih-eye); genus name: Lat., from Gr. *karpos,* fruit, and *dakos,* biter; species name: for John Cassin, 19th-century Philadelphia ornithologist. (Color ill., page 303.) High mountains of West; 6–6½ in. long; bill large, conspicuous red crown patch, *contrasts sharply with brown neck and brown, streaked back;* rose-red throat, breast, and rump (no streaks on flanks and belly as in house finch); adult female, upperparts gray, streaked with dusky; underparts white with narrower streaks below than in similar female purple finch; summers high in Cascades, Sierras, and other western ranges in cool, semiarid forests of ponderosa, Jeffrey, and lodgepole pines, red firs, and mountain hemlock; locally, range in mountains may overlap that of house finch, which prefers lower, warmer elevations, and purple finch, which is largely confined to moist shaded forests at low or middle altitudes of mountains (Orr, 1968); except in nesting season (May–July), usually in flocks, often with crossbills and evening grosbeaks; after young reared, in family groups in summer; male sings from treetop perch or in flight loud warbled song that combines qualities of songs of house and purple finches, but more varied than either; call note is clear three-syllable *cheep.*

Feeding Habits: Forages either in tops of trees or on ground, eats especially seeds of conifers, also buds, a preferred food especially when snow on ground; in summer eats insects, also berries of cotoneaster, mulberries, and rock salt spread on ground for deer.

Nest: Usually in large conifer, near outer end of limb, 10–80 ft. up, built of fine twigs, weed stems, rootlets, lined with hairs, shredded bark, rootlets.

Eggs: Apr.–July; 3–6, usually 4–5, pale green, blue, speckled and spotted with browns, black.

Incubation: By female, 12–14 (?) days; age when young leave nest unknown; possibly two broods a year (Orr, 1968); after nesting season, Cassin's finches move to lower elevations of mountains; groups as large as 5,000 reported in Dec. (Chapin, 1958).

Other Name: Cassin's purple finch.

Accidents: Late spring and summer snowstorms, hailstorms, are hazard: a female sitting on eggs in Tahoe region was frozen to death during a June snowstorm.

Range: Nests from s. B.C., sw. Alta., Mont., n. Wyo., through e. Wash. and Ore., south into n. Ariz. and Baja Calif., s. Nev. and nc. N.M.; like crossbills, nests wherever an abundance of food, with specific locations changing from year to year (Bailey and Neidrach, 1965); winters from s. B.C., nw. Mont., nw. and c. Wyo., south to coastal and s. Calif., s.-c. Ariz., into highlands of Mexico.

Finch, common rose, *Carpodacus erythrinus grebnitskii* (car-POD-ah-cus ee-rith-RYE-nus greb-NITS-kih-eye); genus name: *see* Finch, Cassin's; species name: Lat., of redness; subspecies name: in 1885 by Leonard Stejneger for N. Grebnitski, then governor of the Komandorskie Is. This Asian subspecies of the common rose finch, called by Dement'ev *et al.* (1970) the eastern common rose finch, was collected in N. America for the first time (an adult male) near Old Kashunuk Village, Clarence Rhodes National Wildlife Refuge, in the Yukon-Kuskokwim Delta of Alaska, June 4, 1972 (Dau and Gibson, 1974). It was feeding alone on a grassy hummock. It has since been found on St. Lawrence Is., St. Paul, Pribilof Is., and on Buldir and Shemya Is. in the w. Aleutians, where it is a casual fall migrant (see Kessel and Gibson, 1978). Peterson *et al.* (1954) call this bird the scarlet grosbeak, and describe it as 5¾ in. long; male with bright rosy-red head, breast, and rump; a bullfinchlike brown bill; dark brown wings; two indistinct white bars, and a white belly; female and immature are nondescript brown above, buffy underparts, and a regularly streaked breast; pale double wing bar somewhat high on the wings, and a forked tail; it flies undulatingly; distinguished from pine grosbeak by much smaller size and indistinct wing bars, and from crossbills by its longer tail and conical bill, the mandibles not crossed; utters a piping *tiu-eek;* in summer lives in thickets and undergrowth near water. Biology not completely known.

Weights: Males (2), about 1 oz. each; females, about ¾ oz. each (see Dement'ev *et al.,* 1970).

Range: This subspecies ranges from e. Siberia north to about the Arctic Circle, to Anadyrland

and Kamchatka in ne. Siberia to n. Sakhalin Is. and in Mongolia and ne. China; it straggles to the Komandorskie Is.; winters south to se. China (see details in Vaurie, 1959, and Dement'ev *et al.*, 1970).

Finch, grass. *See* Sparrow, vesper.

Finch, gray-crowned rosy, *Leucosticte tephrocotis* (lew-koe-STICK-tee tef-ROCK-oh-tiss); genus name: *see* Finch, black rosy; species name: from Gr. *tephros*, ash-colored, and *kotis*, cerebellum, gray-crowned (Coble, 1954). (Color ill., page 302.) From high in mountains of w. N. America east to Great Plains; 5¾–6¾ in. long; male dark brown with pink wash on wings and rump, has light gray patch on back of head, black patch on forehead and fore half of cap; female duller with gray on crown not so obvious as in male; like other rosy finches, usually nests above timberline on highest mountains, around glaciers, melting snow, and bare rocks. Habitat, roosting, flight, nesting, foods, and feeding habits similar to that of black rosy finch and brown-capped. See Bent (1968) for details. Like other rosy finches, has gular pouch for carrying food.

Other Names: Aleutian rosy finch; brown snow-bird; Hepburn's rosy finch; Pribilof rosy finch; Sierra Nevada rosy finch.
Hybrids: See under Black rosy finch.
Weights: Seven weighed at evening roost in Calif. by Mewaldt and Farner (1953) averaged 27.8 gr.; one weighed 32.3 gr., and two, 31.55 gr., or about 1–1¼ oz.; overnight, while roosting, they lost about 2 gr. each.
Range: Nests on rocky islands in Bering Sea, Aleutian Is., c. and ne. Alaska (Brooks Range), c. Yukon, and w. Mack., in mountains south to e.-c. Calif., e. Oreg., and w. Mont.; in winter restless roving flocks at lower elevations swirl about in dense masses over lower mountain slopes and plateaus; many migrate well inland along mountain ranges south to c. Nev., c. Utah, n.w. Neb., and n. N.M.

Finch, house, or Linnet, *Carpodacus mexicanus* (car-POD-ih-kus meks-ih-CANE-us); genus name: *see* Finch, Cassin's; species name: Lat., Mexican. (Color ill., page 302.) W. U.S., Neb., and Okla. to Calif., introduced into e. U.S., had spread by 1971 from Long Is., N.Y., north to n. New England, south to N.C.; 5–5¾ in. long; male has brown upperparts, bright red crown, breast, and rump; brighter red than deeper raspberry or old rose of purple finch; has *striped flanks*, which purple finch lacks; female gray-brown above, whitish and striped below, sparrowlike with heavy convex bill; lives about farms, along highways, about buildings in towns and cities, especially where water available (see Bergtold, 1907), also abundant in bottomlands, scrub growth, canyons, suburbs, and ranches in West; occupies niche in West like that of house, or English, sparrow in East; in Mar. and Apr., when flocks break up, male follows female, flutters wings, sings flowing, variable, warbling song, repeated many times (female also sings); call note is *queet*.

Feeding Habits: About 86% of food is weed seeds, especially of thistle, dandelion, noxious weeds, from old fields, vacant lots; also fruits of cactus, blossoms and buds of wild and cultivated plants, some insects; may do considerable damage in Calif. orchards—peaches, apricots, nectarines, plums, cherries—where abundant; in towns and cities, forages in streets and yards for crumbs, food scraps; sips maple sap from cut branches in spring (Woods, 1968).
Nest: In cavities in trees, buildings, on projections of buildings high up, in bird boxes, in dense outer foliage of trees, shrubs, and in vines, usually about 5–7 ft. above ground, sometimes lower or much higher; in tin cans hanging on posts, in cholla cactus, on ground, in old nests of towhees, orioles, cliff swallows, phoebes, parts of hawks' nests, holes in utility poles, etc., built by female of grasses, plant stems, leaves, rootlets, twigs, hair, string, cotton, wool.
Eggs: Feb.–Aug.; 2–6, usually 4–5, speckled, blue-white.
Incubation: 12–16 days; young are fed dandelion seeds, leave nest 11–19 days after hatching.
Other Names: Burion; crimson-fronted finch; Guadalupe house finch; McGregor's house finch; Mexican house finch; red-head; red-headed linnet.
Accidents: Wings sometimes so ensnared by spider's silk that unable to fly.
Albinism: A complete albino reported Calif. (McClure, 1962).
Age: Banded ones, Calif., lived to 7 and 8 years and one to 9 years; a female banded at Pomona, Calif., trapped and released at Sacramento when 10 years, 10 months, old (Kennard, 1975); one in National Zoo, Washington, D.C., lived to 9 years, 4 months.
Host to Cowbirds: Occasional, 10 records (Friedmann, 1963).
Weights: About 21.0 gr., or about ⅔ oz.
Range: Largely resident from s. B.C. to Idaho, Wyo., w. Neb., south to Okla., Tex., west to Calif., Baja Calif., south into Mexico; in 1940, cage-bird dealers in s. Calif. shipped numbers of house finches (caught illegally in the wild) to New York dealers for sale as "Hollywood finches"; agents of U.S. Fish and Wildlife Service noted the violation of the Migratory Bird Treaty Act, which protects our native songbirds, and stopped the traffic; New York dealers released the birds (Austin, 1961) somewhere on Long Is., and perhaps elsewhere in metropolitan area; first one seen at Jones Beach, Apr. 11, 1941; first nesting in wild at Babylon, Long Is., in May 1943 (see details in Elliott and Arbib, 1953); remarkable spread after 1953 into outlying districts from New York City area (see Bull, 1964); established as nesting bird in roof gardens of New York beginning spring 1971, where nests built in ivy on walls, rose trellises, potted plants on porches, on ledges under eaves, behind shutters, in air conditioners, etc.; Buckley (1971) reported they were well established in Conn., N.H., and Me., at Syracuse, Elmira, and Ithaca, N.Y.; near Lake Erie and Canadian border; southward in Pa., Md., and Va., and had reached N.C. and near S.C. border.

Finch, mountain. *See* Brambling.

Finch, purple, *Carpodacus purpureus* (car-POD-ah-kus purr-PUE-ree-us); genus name: *see* Finch, Cassin's; species name: Lat., purple. (Color ills., page 304.) State bird of N.H.; widespread across northern U.S. and Canada, Atlantic to Pacific; 5½–6¼ in. long; wingspread 9¼–10½ in.; male not purple but appears like a heavy-billed sparrow with a raspberry tinge (Peterson, 1961); suffused largely with rosy red, brightest red is on head and rump but more uniformly red than other red finches; tail is deeply notched; female and immatures brown-gray above, gray-white below, heavily streaked, and broad whitish line over eyes; in summer lives in coniferous forests of Canada and mostly northern states in U.S., about openings in swamps, along streams, also in hillside pastures, Norway spruce trees and other ornamental conifers along country roads, in trees of city parks and suburbs where often at feeding stations; is an erratic migrant southward, like redpolls, crossbills, and siskins, sometimes in great numbers when seed crops of spruces, pines, and other conifers fail (see details in Baird, 1964, and Bagg, 1969); travel in flocks in winter, flight is undulating; as they fly, often utter sharp metallic *tick* or *tuck* note; some males sing while in flocks with several singing in chorus; flowing, rising, and falling warble; in courtship, male dances about female, his wings beating so fast they are blur until he rises into air, all the while chippering softly (Bent, 1968).

Feeding Habits: Mostly a seed-eater, winter and spring; eats seeds of weeds, grasses, elm, white ash, red maple, sycamore, sweet gum, cedar berries, winterberry (a holly), buds of apple, aspen, maple, and birch; late spring, eats beetles, green caterpillars; in summer, blackberries, raspberries, and other wild and cultivated fruit; in fall, eats seeds of tulip poplar, comes to feeding stations for sunflower seeds, hemp, millet. See in Terres (1968c).
Nest: In e. N. America, prefers spruces, firs, pines, cedars, 6–50 ft. above ground, in dense foliage, saddled on branch; in Calif., in both deciduous and coniferous trees, near water, in tall willows, alders, ivy-covered trees, and in mountains, 3,000–5,000 ft. elevation, in ponderosa pines, oaks, redwoods; in Wash., in Douglas firs; built of fine twigs, grasses, mosses, bits of dried snakeskin, string, lined with horsehair, wool.
Eggs: Apr.–July; 3–6, usually 4–5, pale green-blue, speckled with blacks, browns.
Incubation: By female, about 13 days; young leave nest when about 14 days old; apparently two broods a year in Calif., one in e. N. America (Bent, 1968).
Other Names: California purple finch; eastern purple finch; gray linnet (immatures and females); purple linnet; purple grosbeak; red linnet.
Age: Four 7 years old; four 8 years old in Mich.; of thousands banded there, average lived no more than 2 years; one retrapped at Sault Ste. Marie when at least 10 years old; a male banded Hillsborough, N.C., trapped and released in same area when 12 years, 8 months, old (Kennard, 1975).
Albinism: A partial albino in Wisc. resembled a snow bunting; wings and tail black but body

generally white, streaked breast, and yellow wing feathers (Rudy, 1967). See also Bent (1968) for aberrant colors of.

Host to Cowbirds: Uncommon, only 18 records (Friedmann, 1963).

Weights: Adult males (72), in summer and winter, Conn., 20.4–29.98 gr.; females (148), 20–31.29 gr. (Wetherbee, 1934), or about ¾–1 oz.

Range: Nests from n. B.C. across Canada to Newfoundland, south through Wash., Ore., through Calif. in mountains to n. Baja Calif., and south from Canada to n. Ohio, W.Va., ne. Pa., n. N.J., se. N.Y.; winters in West from sw. B.C. south to c. Baja Calif. and mountains of s. Ariz.; in East from s. Canada to se. Tex., Gulf coast, and c. Fla.

Goldfinch, American. *Carduelis tristis* (Car-dyou-EE-liss TRIS-tis); genus name: from Lat. *carduus*, thistle (eats seeds of thistle); species name: Lat., sad, in allusion to its plaintive call (Coues, 1882). (Color ill., page 305.) Coast to coast, and from s. Canada through most of U.S.; state bird of Wash. on Pacific coast, of N.J. on Atlantic, and of Minn. and Iowa in Midwest; 4½–5½ in. long; wingspread 8¾–9 in.; male in spring and summer, bright lemon yellow; only small yellow bird with black wings, black cap and tail (only other bird with similar color pattern is much larger evening grosbeak); female olive yellow, dusky wings with two white wing bars; short, finchlike bill and notched dark tail as in male; both sexes live in mixed flocks most of year which go bounding through air in deeply undulating flight over fields, woods, orchards, roadsides, uttering *per-CHICK-o-ree, per-CHICK-o-ree;* flocks, which often sing in chorus, break up in July and Aug. (in Far West in Apr.), and pairs begin to nest (Tyler, 1968), never far from thistle seed supply (Nickell, 1951); male sings sweet, sprightly, canarylike song; series of twitters, trills with *wee* or *swee* notes interspersed; male often sings in flight; a call note of species is plaintive, questioning *dear-me, see-me?*

Feeding Habits: Flocks eat seeds of birches, alders, conifers, and other trees, seeds of thistles, goldenrod, asters, burdock, dandelion, chicory, etc., also come to seeding heads of garden zinnias, coreopsis, cosmos, lettuce, and others; comes to bird feeders for sunflower seeds and thistle seeds (see in Terres, 1968c); also eats some berries, and insects (Tyler, 1968).

Nest: Female selects nest site in hedge, brushy pasture, border of field, builds nest of woven plant fibers, lined with thistledown, milkweed down, in fork of maple or other hardwood trees, sapling, or bush 1–33 ft. above ground (Nickell, 1951); in Ga. nests sometimes in pine tree 60 ft. up saddled on outer end of one of limbs; may nest also in thistles close to ground; nest so thick-walled it will hold water; young birds left unsheltered by parents in rainstorm have drowned in nest.

Eggs: Calif., begins Apr.; elsewhere, usually June–Sept.; 4–6, commonly 5, very pale blue, unmarked.

Incubation: By female, 12–14 days; young leave nest when 10–16 days old; young raised entirely on seeds, partly digested by adults and regurgitated into mouths of nestlings.

Other Names: Catnip-bird (eats seeds of); common goldfinch; beet-bird (eats seeds of); lettuce-bird; salad-bird (eats leaves of); shiner; thistle-bird; wild canary; willow goldfinch; yellowbird.

Accidents: While feeding on seeds of burdock, sometimes caught by hooked burrs, cannot escape; sometimes caught in webs of orb-weaving garden spiders.

Age: Two banded in Ark., retrapped when 6 and 7 years old; a male banded Storrs, Conn., trapped and released at same place when 8 years, 10 months, old; one lived to 13 years in captivity on Long Is., N.Y. (Elliott, 1954).

Flight Speed: Timed in Mich., 19–39 m.p.h. (Schnell, 1965).

Host to Cowbirds: 53 records (Friedmann, 1963); in most places rare victim of brown-headed cowbird because goldfinch nests at end of egg-laying period of cowbird.

Hybrids: In captivity has crossbred with canary and hybrids raised; also with lesser goldfinch (Gray, 1958).

Weights: Fall, coastal N.J. (6), 11.8–13.3 gr. (Murray and Jehl, 1964), or ⅓–½ oz.

Range: Nests from sw. B.C. east across s. Canada to n. Nova Scotia, south to n. Baja Calif., s. and c. Utah, s. Colo., c. Okla, ne. Tex., and in Midwest and e. U.S. south from s. Canada to n. Miss., c. Ala., c. Ga., and S.C.; winters from n. U.S., se. Canada, south to Ariz., Gulf coast, s. Fla., Baja Calif., and n. Mexico.

Goldfinch, Arkansas. *See* Goldfinch, lesser.

Goldfinch, common. *See* Goldfinch, American.

Goldfinch, dark-backed. *See* Goldfinch, lesser.

Goldfinch, European, *Carduelis carduelis* (car-dyou-EE-liss); genus and species names: *see* Goldfinch, American. Introduced from Europe at Hoboken, N.J., in 1878, from which spread to Central Park, New York, then to Long Is., N.Y., where became established in early 1900s along south shore; increased rapidly around Massapequa, Long Is., during World War II (1940s); by middle 1950s, postwar building boom had destroyed much of its favorite nesting habitat; fewer than 6 birds known in 1955, after which disappeared (Elliott, 1956; 1968a); also established in Bermuda; older introductions, or escaped from captivity, from Mass. to Ont., Mo., and Wisc., to Portland, Ore., and San Francisco, Calif., disappeared (Phillips, 1928); a few recent records, possibly escaped birds (is common in captivity as cage bird), reported: an adult male, Westtown, Pa., Nov. 1961 (Scott and Cutler, 1962), and one at bird feeder, Cleveland, Ohio, Apr. 1966 (Petersen, 1966). Sexes similar; 5–6 in. long; tawny brown, *bright red face and throat; broad yellow band across black wings;* black and white head, white rump, black tail; immatures buffy brown with streaked back and flanks; yellow band across black wings.

Feeding Habits: Like those of American goldfinch, mostly seeds, prefers open country with hedgerows, wastelands, weed-bordered

European goldfinch

FINCH FAMILY

grain fields; on Long Is. mostly independent of feeding stations (Elliott, 1968a).

Nest: In America, mostly in trees, conifers or deciduous, 5–30 ft. above ground; built of grasses, fine roots, plant down.

Eggs: In America, Apr.–July; usually 5, blue-white, spotted and streaked with browns.

Incubation: By female, 12–13 days; young leave nest when 13–14 days old; two broods. Flight undulating like that of American goldfinch.

Other Names: Draw-water; thistle-bird.

Goldfinch, green-backed. *See* Goldfinch, lesser.

Goldfinch, Lawrence's, *Carduelis lawrencei* (Car-dyou-EE-liss LAW-rence-eye); genus name: *see* Goldfinch, American; species name: given in 1850 by John Cassin, Philadelphia ornithologist, for George Newbold Lawrence, of New York. (Color ill., page 304.) Restricted largely to drier interior Calif.; 4–4½ in. long; small, gray-backed; male with black patch that extends from cap to throat, appears from front to be hooded, both summer and winter (Linsdale, 1968b); has small, conical, flesh-colored bill; yellow on breast, rump, and *two yellow wing bars;* underparts white, tail black; female similar but duller and without black "hood"; most irregular or gypsylike of all goldfinches: "A valley in s. Calif. may be filled with the black-chinned gray-bodied birds one summer and the next year contain not one" (Hoffman, 1927); lives in foothills or mountain valleys; particularly from Los Angeles County southward; from Sonoma County along coast of Calif. and from Trinity and Shasta counties inland, nests southward into Baja Calif. (Linsdale, 1968b); kind and amount of seeds produced important to number of goldfinches in area and how long there; need water year-round; drink from creeks until they dry up, then search for water overflow from tanks, wells, dripping faucets; fond of bathing; when not nesting, in flocks; male in spring sings tinkling notes; call note is very different, harsh *kee-yerr.*

Feeding Habits: Largely seeds of weeds; forages for in low-growing herbs, shrubs; in early summer restricted to patches of fiddleneck that furnish most of food when nesting; also eats some insects, visits salt licks, in nesting season (Linsdale, 1968b).

Nest: Often in loose colonies, neat cup of wool, flower heads, fairy grasses, horsehair, feathers, 3–40 ft. above ground, in dense foliage of open oak or pine woods, shrubs of burned-over areas, hedges of Monterey cypresses, junipers, sage.

Eggs: Apr.–July; 3–6, usually 4–5, pale blue, unmarked but sometimes with reddish spots.

Incubation: By female, period of unknown; young leave nest when about 13 days old.

Host to Cowbirds: Two records to brown-headed cowbird (Friedmann, 1963).

Range: Nests in Calif. west of Sierras and in n. Baja Calif.; winters from n.-c. Calif., s. Nev., c. Ariz., sw. and c. and s. N.M., south to n. Baja Calif., n. Mexico, and w. Tex.

Goldfinch, lesser, *Carduelis psaltria* (Car-dyou-EE-liss SALL-trih-ah); genus name: *see* Goldfinch, American; species name: Lat., from Gr., meaning one who plays the lute (Coues, 1882). (Color ill., page 305.) Tex. and Okla. north to Colo., west to Pacific; smallest of all N. American goldfinches; 3¾–4¼ in. long; stout, cone-shaped bill; male dark greenish above, bright yellow below (the so-called green-backed goldfinch); black cap, wings, and tail; in flight patch of pure white shows in middle of each wing, another at base of tail; female greenish above, dull yellow below; adult male of another form, the so-called dark-backed goldfinch, may have solid-black back instead of dark green; was once called Arkansas goldfinch because first one discovered along Arkansas R. in Colo., the dark-backed form apparently more common in eastern part of range, from Colo. south to Tex.; both forms (together called lesser goldfinch) live in or about brushy fields, open woods, farms, gardens, edges of wooded groves, along willow and tree-lined streams, cedar brakes, from lower country to high in mountains; less plentiful along humid Pacific coast, prefers dry foothills but usually where water available and abundance of seed-bearing plants (Linsdale, 1968a); male courts female with courtship feeding, and singing canarylike songs, often in flight; pair may remain together all winter, when they join flocks in search of seeds.

Feeding Habits: Especially fond of seeds of thistle and of other weed seeds that make up about 96% of diet, is attracted to salt-impregnated ground, drinks much water; comes to birdbaths in garden, to overflow pipes, and garden faucets to drink.

Nest: Built by female, neat cup of woven plant fibers, grasses, weed bark, lined with plant down, cotton, a few feathers, saddled on limbs of cottonwoods, willows, sycamores, and other trees and in bushes of dense foliage, 2–30 ft. up or in weeds close to ground.

Eggs: Apr.–Aug.; 3–6, usually 4–5, pale blue-green and pale blue-white, usually unspotted.

Incubation: By female (male feeds her at nest), 12 days; age when young leave nest not definitely known (Linsdale, 1968a).

Other Names: Arkansas goldfinch; Arkansas greenback; dark-backed goldfinch; green-backed goldfinch; tarweed canary.

Host to Cowbirds: Rare, only about 6 or 8 records (Friedmann, 1963).

Range: Resident from sw. Wash., w. Ore., ne. Calif., n. Nev., n. Utah, n. Colo., south to nw. Okla., n.-c. and c. Tex., south through Mexico to n. S. America.

Goldfinch, willow. *See* Goldfinch, American.

Grassquit, black-faced, *Tiaris bicolor* (tie-ARE-iss BIE-color); genus name: from Gr. *tiara,* a Persian headdress worn on great occasions (Jaeger, 1955), apparently in reference to black crown of related species; species name: Lat., two-colored, apparently alludes to black of face and underparts dull green of back; *quit:* a name in English-speaking islands of West Indies for a number of small birds; *grass-*

Black-faced grassquit

FINCH FAMILY

quit applied here probably refers to habitat and food habits. West Indies, except mainland of Cuba, to n. S. America; has wandered to s. Fla.; small; about 4–5 in. long; male, blackish finch with *short* tail, greenish-tinged back, wings and tail; bill short, conical; female gray with lighter, almost olive back (Peterson, 1947, and Bond, 1961); in Bahamas lives mainly about settlements, in gardens, plantations, borders of thickets; common in Nassau, feeds on lawns (seeds of grasses and weeds) or in tall grasses or shrubbery near ground; sometimes small flocks flushed by wayside; does not nest in U.S. (see Bond, 1968, for details of nesting, eggs, etc.); four records in s. Fla.—Sombrero Key; Everglades National Park; Miami; and West Palm Beach (Bond, 1968).

Other Names: Bahama grassquit; Bahama black-faced grassquit.

Grosbeak, black-headed, *Pheucticus melanocephalus* (FEW-tih-cus meh-lan-oh-SEE-fal-us); genus name: Lat., from Gr. *pheucticus,* inclined to avoid, retiring; species name: Gr., black head. (Color ills., page 306.) Eastern foothills of Rocky Mtns. to Pacific; western counterpart (in habits) of closely related rose-breasted grosbeak of e. U.S.; 6–8 in. long; stout, conical, straw-colored bill; male's black head contrasts with brownish-orange underparts; black-and-white tail; white wing patches; female brown with *striped head,* striped back and sides, rusty-brown breast, white wing bar, pale heavy bill; lives about thickets, small trees, along streams, edges of swamps, ponds, edges of open woods (Bent, 1968); males arrive in spring about 6 days before females, male is solitary before arrival of female, begins singing on his arrival, while foraging in trees and shrubs; male sings from perch near female, may suddenly fly up in air and sing (flight, courtship song), resembles rich song of rose-breasted grosbeak, and like that of robin and western tanager but richer, clear whistled notes with trills; both females and males fight to defend territories against other mated pairs.

Feeding Habits: A bird of deciduous and broad-leaved evergreen woods; cracks pine seeds and other seeds in powerful bill, eats cherries, blackberries, raspberries, strawberries, elderberries, mistletoe berries, buds, beetles, scale insects, codling moth caterpillars, cankerworms, grasshoppers, bees, wasps, flies, spiders; comes readily to feeding stations, where very tame; also feeds on ground about campgrounds.
Nest: Built usually in deciduous trees or shrubs, bordering streams, also in gardens, woods, and parks, especially in willows and coast live oaks; built by female, 4–25 ft. above ground, in 3–4 days, usually in dense outer foliage of tree or shrub near an opening; loosely assembled, thin, of rootlets, twigs, other plant materials.
Eggs: Apr.–July; 2–5, usually 3–4, brown-spotted, blue-white or green-white.
Incubation: By both sexes, alternately, 12–13 days, occasionally both sing while on nest; young leave nest when 12 days old (Bent, 1968).
Other Names: Black-head; common grosbeak; Rocky Mountain grosbeak; western grosbeak.

Age: Of three banded in Calif. and recovered there, two, 5 years old, one, more than 6; in captivity has lived to 25 years.
Host to Cowbirds: In only a few places—to brown-headed cowbird in Kans., Neb., Colo., Utah, Mont. (Friedmann, 1963).
Hybrids: Interbreeds with rose-breasted grosbeak where ranges of the two overlap. *See* discussion under Hybrid.
Range: Nests from sw. B.C., east to sw. Sask., ne. Mont., nw. N.D., south through Wash., Ore., and along Pacific coast to n. Baja Calif., c. and se. Ariz., and in N.M. in forested mountains up to 8,000–10,000 ft., and south into Mexico; east to c. Neb., c. Kans., w. Okla.; winters in Mexico; accidental in e. U.S.

Grosbeak, blue, *Guiraca caerulea* (gwee-RAH-kah seh-ROO-lee-ah); genus name: native Mexican name, or S. American, for some bird; species name: Lat., blue. (Color ill., page 306.) Across southern half, or two thirds, of U.S. from Atlantic to Pacific; 6–7½ in. long; male almost entirely deep, rich blue with heavy, conical grosbeak bill; *two rusty-brown wing bars* on each wing; larger than similar indigo bunting, which lacks wing bars; in poor light, male blue grosbeak appears black; female dull brown with buffy wing bars; lives about old fields, overgrown with brambles, young pines, often in damp places, also in mesquite in West, in thickets along roads and streams, edges of woods, in hedges, orchards, gardens, often in willows along irrigation ditches and at base of mountains in N.M.; in Calif., 200–4,000 ft. above sea level; a quiet, peaceable bird but will vigorously defend nesting territory against pairs of own kind; flocks of males arrive in spring in Ala. and S.C. ahead of females; feeding on ground around plowed fields they appear black, easily mistaken for cowbirds; flight is undulating; male, from top of bush, tree, post, utility wire, sings sweet, melodious song, somewhat like that of indigo bunting and purple finch.

Feeding Habits: Hops about, forages much on ground, also in shrubs and trees; eats largely insects—grasshoppers, weevils, May beetles, squash bugs, caterpillars, cutworms, cicadas—also snails, spiders, grain, weed seeds, and wild fruit.
Nest: Built low in pines, willows, alders, sweet gum, mulberries, grape vines, blackberry bushes, young orchard trees, 4–14 ft., usually 2–8 ft., above ground, of grasses, rootlets, weeds, leaves, interwoven with paper and shed snakeskin, lined with thin rootlets or hair.
Eggs: May–Aug.; 2–5, usually 4, light blue, unmarked.
Incubation: By female, about 11 days; young leave nest when about 13 days old (Bent, 1968); commonly two broods in southern part of nesting range.
Other Names: California blue grosbeak; blue pop; big indigo (in South); western blue grosbeak.
Host to Cowbirds: Fairly frequent host to brown-headed cowbird, 30 records; also host to bronzed cowbird in lower Rio Grande Valley, Tex. (Friedmann, 1963).

Hybrids: A presumed hybrid between blue grosbeak and a dickcissel reported by Cockrum (1952).
Weights: N.C. (21), average 28.4 gr. (Teulings and Teulings, 1971), or almost exactly 1 oz.
Range: Nests from c. Calif., s. Nev., Utah, s. Colo. east to c. S.D., and s. N.J., south to Costa Rica; winters from s. Baja Calif. into Mexico, along Pacific coast to C. America; West Indies; south to Costa Rica, rarely in La.

Grosbeak, evening, *Hesperiphona vespertina* (hes-per-ih-FOE-nah ves-per-TINE-ah); genus name: from Gr. *hesperios,* at eventide, and *phone,* voice; species name: Lat., belonging to evening (Coble, 1954); from mistaken belief that this bird sang mainly in the evening. (Color ills., page 307.) Lives in coniferous forest of n. U.S. and across Canada, from Atlantic to Pacific, and in western mountains south to Ariz. and N.M.; 7–8½ in. long, wingspread 13–13¾ in.; large, chunky finch about size of starling; very large *white* (pale green in spring), conical bill; adult male largely dull yellow with black-and-white wings, suggests a large goldfinch; short tail, forked and black; eyes brown; female silver-gray, enough of yellow, black, and white of male to be recognized; undulating flight and large white wing patches distinguish it in air; lives year-round in firs, spruces, and other trees of northern coniferous forest; is highly gregarious, flocks wander about feeding on seeds of spruces, firs, maple trees; when these available stays within its "breeding range"; when these seed crops fail (about every other year) or population of grosbeaks high, large flocks move eastward and southward, deep into U.S., in search of food; evening grosbeaks were unknown east of Great Lakes until 1854, when reported from Toronto; up to winter 1889–90, almost unknown in e. U.S., apparently planting across western plains and in East of box elder or ash-leaved maples (buds and seeds of which are preferred food of evening grosbeaks) lured them eastward; are also extremely fond of sunflower seeds; increasing popularity of bird-attracting using sunflower seeds in e. and s. U.S. also gave grosbeaks large additional winter food supply. See Forbush (1925–29), Pearson *et al.* (1936), and Speirs (1968) for details; for review about more recent invasions, see James (1958 and 1960), Shaub (1963), and for causes, see especially Baird (1964). Evening grosbeaks are gregarious even at nesting time, when small groups seen together; flocks usually roost in pines, spruces; male in courtship feeds female, "dances" in front of her; both sexes may sing a song like that of purple finch, common call is *peet peet kreeck,* etc. (Speirs, 1968).

Feeding Habits: Eats some insects in summer, beetles, spruce budworm, cankerworms; most important food, buds and seeds of maples, conifers, also seeds of chokecherries, cherries, dogwood berries, apples, etc., buds of elm, ash, and other deciduous trees and shrubs; in winter in s. U.S., eats seeds of tulip poplar, maple sap, likes salted sand and gravel; drinks water from birdbath and melted snow.
Nest: In pines, spruces, firs, and other conifers, sometimes in willows, maples, birches, oaks,

mountain ash, 6–70 ft. above ground, usually in dense leaf cluster near end of branch, from sea level in Calif. to 9,000 ft. in Sierra Nevadas; shallow cup built of twigs lined with rootlets. *Eggs:* May–July; 2–5, usually 3–4, blue or blue-green.

Incubation: By female, length unreported in wild, but in captivity, 12–14 days; young leave nest when 13–14 days old (Speirs, 1968).

Other Names: American hawfinch; eastern evening grosbeak; Mexican evening grosbeak; western evening grosbeak.

Accidents: Two killed by airplane over Rocky Mtns., Colo., 1964, first report of plane striking this species (*see* Altitude of Bird Flight); many killed in winter by traffic when attracted to highways for salt spread to melt snow.

Age: Banded birds, Me., Mass., Minn., Vt., were 4–9 years old; one at least 10 years old still alive when recaptured and released; a male banded at Hawk Mtn., Pa., trapped and released at Linwood, N.J., when 13 years, 5 months, old (Savell, 1969); one adult female in aviary in Canada lived to at least 17 years old.

Albinism: 29 reported, partial albinos, up to 1960 (Schaub, 1960); several gynandromorphs reported from e. U.S.; see Laybourne (1967) for summary and description.

Host to Cowbirds: Only one reported, at Saranac, N.Y., July 1949 (Friedmann, 1963).

Weights: Manomet, Mass., in summer (4), 52–63.5 gr. (Fisk, 1971b), or about 2–2⅓ oz.

Range: Nests from n.-c. B.C., ne. Alta., east in narrow belt of coniferous forest across Canada to n. N.B., south to c. Calif., n. Nev., c. Ariz., mountains of N.M., ne. Minn., n. Mich., s. Ont., n. N.Y., s. Vt., and Mass.; winters irregularly and locally in nesting range and south to s. Calif., s. Ariz., w. Tex., Ark., Tenn., and S.C., Ala., Miss., and La., more recently to e. Tex. (Moldenhauer and Bryan, 1970).

Grosbeak, pine, *Pinicola enucleator* (pie-NICK-oh-lah ee-new-klee-AY-tore); genus name: from Lat. *pinus,* pine, and *colere,* to dwell; species name: from Lat. *enucleare,* to take out kernels (Coble, 1954). (Color ills., page 307.) Lives in northern forests of world—n. Europe, Russia, Alaska, Canada, and n. U.S., western mountains; rose, pink, and gray; 8–10 in. long; wingspread 13¾–15 in.; largest of grosbeaks, with dark, heavy, conical bill, slightly forked tail; male varies from rose red to poppy red, has distinctively white wing bars (similar white-winged crossbill, smaller, with much shorter tail); female grayish or brownish; flight is undulating but not so much as that of woodpeckers or goldfinches; can be distinguished in flight from evening grosbeak by long tail; often very tame, some can almost be picked up in hands; not regularly migratory from nesting range, but in some winters moves southward in U.S., not because of severe weather but when shortages of seeds, wild fruit (Forbush, 1925–29; *see* Flight Years; Irruption); usually lives in summer along borders of open places in coniferous woods, adjacent to streams or ponds; also along edges of hayfields, pastures; gregarious; sometimes, when not nesting, in flocks up to 100 birds; during winter visits southward in U.S., flocks favor more open coniferous forests and open hillsides with juniper or cedar trees, which give food (berries) and shelter; also attracted to trees and ornamental fruiting shrubs about homes and gardens; male feeds female in courtship, sings short, clear, musical warble, *tee-tee-tew* notes from tip of hemlock or other tree, like song of purple finch but sweeter, wilder, also sings flight song; a call, two or three mellow whistled notes, sounds like call of yellowlegs, a shorebird.

Feeding Habits: Forages much in trees but comes to ground for seeds; has gular pouches for extra food; eats seeds of maples, birches, larch, pines, firs, spruces, roses, glacier lilies, grasses, hemp, burdock, ragweed, lamb's-quarters, etc.; buds of maples, elms, birches, elder, cottonwoods, alder, pear, poplar, willow; eats fruit of crabapple, mountain ash, especially fond of bittersweet and barberries, rowanberries, snowberries; very fond of sunflower seeds; eats some beechnuts, acorns, also grasshoppers, caterpillars, beetles, flies.

Nest: Often bulky, loose, open, of twigs and roots, lined with grasses, lichens, rabbit's fur; in crotch or on branch of spruce, fir, or shrub; in n. Rocky Mtns., from 2,000 ft. elevation up to timberline; and in mountains in Utah to 10,000 ft.; nest, 6–30 ft. above ground.

Eggs: May–June; 2–6, usually 4, blue-green or gray-green, spotted, speckled with browns, grays.

Incubation: By female, 13–14 (?) days; young leave nest when about 20 days old (Speirs, 1968).

Other Names: American pine grosbeak; California pine grosbeak; Canadian pine grosbeak; pine bullfinch; Rocky Mountain pine grosbeak; mope (in Newfoundland) because it often sits motionless.

Age: One, banded Winnipeg, Canada, found dead at same place when more than 6 years old; a male banded Morris, Conn., found dead on highway when 8 years, 9 months, old (Kennard, 1975).

Range: Often resident year-round, in N. America, from c. Alaska (Cape Prince of Wales, Fairbanks) to Yuk., nw. and c. Mack., n. Man., coastal and ne. B.C., sw. Alta., across Canada to Labrador, Newfoundland, Nova Scotia, south to northern edge of Great Lakes, Ont., n. N.H., c. Me., and south from Wash., Ore., in western mountains to c. Calif., Utah, Ariz., N.M.; winters south to sw. N.M., Ky., and Va.

Grosbeak, rose-breasted, *Pheucticus ludovicianus* (FEW-tih-kus loo-doe-viss-ih-ANE-us); genus name: *see* Grosbeak, black-headed; species name: from Lat. *Ludoviciana,* Louisiana, of or relating to the state (Coues, 1882). (Color ills., page 307.) Eastern counterpart (in habits) of the black-headed grosbeak of the West; summers in ne. U.S. and across s. Canada; 7–8½ in. long; wingspread 12–13 in.; male is black and white with triangle of rose red on breast; white or straw-colored heavy bill; black head, throat, and back, very white underparts, white wing patches and rosy wing linings which show in flight; female dark, buffy brown above, white underparts streaked like a sparrow; pale yellow wing linings, two broad white wingbars; conspicuous white line over brown eyes; in summer, lives in second-growth woods, borders of swamps and streams, dense growths of small trees and shrubs along edges of woods and old pastures; also in gardens and parks of towns and villages; usually arrives in e. U.S. and s. Canada in May; several males may fight fiercely for one female, hovering over her and singing at same time; male sings exquisitely beautiful song, a long, continuous, liquid, robinlike carol; male often sings while on the nest and sometimes at night; female sings similar but softer, shorter song; male also has special "love song" (see Bent, 1968); mates appear affectionate; sometimes touch bills in courtship.

Feeding Habits: Forages much in trees; eats seeds of elms, catalpa, blossoms of hickory and beeches, buds of white ash; beetles, especially Colorado potato beetle, from which one of its common names; Rocky Mountain locusts (grasshoppers), cankerworms, tent caterpillars, tussock moths, gypsy and brown-tailed moths, some fruit, grain, etc.

Nest: Male sometimes selects nest site, may help female build nest, usually in thickets or small trees, low, 5–15 ft. above ground, sometimes 25–50 ft. up in birches, near crotch or fork in branch, often near water, of small sticks, fine twigs, coarse straw, lined with grasses and rootlets, sometimes horsehairs, all loosely woven.

Eggs: May–July; 3–5, usually 4, greenish or bluish, speckled, spotted, blotched with browns.

Incubation: By both sexes, 12–13 days; young leave nest when 9–12 days old; do not fly well until about 15 days old (Bent *et al.,* 1968).

Other Names: Common grosbeak; rose-breast; potato-bug bird; summer grosbeak; throat-cut.

Accidents: Some killed by flying into picture windows; struck by cars while flying across highways.

Age: Banded birds from Ill., Mass., N.H., re-trapped when 4–6 years old; one more than 9 years old; captives (privately owned pets), two to 15 years; one to 17½; a male captive, spring 1928 to fall 1951, died in his 24th year (Bent *et al.,* 1968).

Host to Cowbirds: Frequent, 43 records (Friedmann, 1963).

Hybrids: Interbreeds with black-headed grosbeak where ranges of two overlap. See Bent *et al.*'s references to, 1968; *see* discussion under Hybrid.

Weights: Coastal migrants, autumn, N.J. (13), 38.4–53.9 gr. (Murray and Jehl, 1964), or about 1⅓–2 oz.; summer, Manomet, Mass. (2), 45 and 52 gr. (Fisk, 1971b).

Range: Nests from ne. B.C. across s.-c. Canada to sw. Que., n. N.B., and Nova Scotia and from n. N.D. south to e. Kans., east through c. Mo., to e. Tenn., n. Ga., w. N.C. (in mountains), and north in parts of Atlantic states to se. Pa., se. N.Y., N.J.; winters from s. La. (rarely) south through Mexico to n. S. America.

Grosbeak, scarlet. *See* Finch, common rose.

Grosbeak, western. *See* Grosbeak, black-headed.

Hawfinch, *Coccothraustes coccothraustes* (cock-oh-THROUSE-teez); genus and species names: Lat., from Gr. *kokkos*, grain, and *thrauein*, to shatter (Coble, 1954). Common European grosbeak, strayed once to Pribilof Is., Alaska, Nov. 1911; then four seen at Naval Station, Adak Is., May 31, 1971; one male collected for second definite record of species in N. America (Gibson and MacDonald, 1971); later records, Attu Is., Pribilof Is. (Kessell and Gibson, 1978); nearest nesting is in Kamchatka and e. Siberia across Bering Sea, north to limit of trees; is characteristic bird of northern forest belt of Europe and Asia; 6–7 in. long; has relatively huge bill; gray bull neck, bold blue-black wings with white shoulder patches; short white-tipped tail; tawny crown, black throat and around eyes; chestnut on back, rump, tail; lives in deciduous woods and mixed forests rather than in pure stands of evergreens; locally, sometimes in wooded parks, gardens, orchards; rather shy and quiet except in nesting season; eats mostly seeds, buds of trees, fruit, insects (Austin, 1968a). In Switzerland, greatest ages reported: 6, 7, and 8 years (Nice, 1966a).

Junco, Arizona. *See* Junco, Mexican.

Junco, Baird's (yellow-eyed), *Junco phaeonotus bairdi* (JUNG-koh fee-oh-NO-tus BAIRD-eye); genus name: origin uncertain, perhaps from Lat. *juncus*, rush (color); species name: from Gr. *phaios*, dusky, and *notan*, back; subspecies name: given in 1883 by Robert Ridgway in honor of Prof. Spencer F. Baird, former Secretary of Smithsonian Institution. Resident bird of Victoria Mtns. of Cape Region, Baja Calif.; formerly considered a distinct species; determined by American Ornithologists' Union (1973) to be a subspecies of the species *phaeonotus; see* discussion under Junco, yellow-eyed; 5¼–5¾ in. long; sexes outwardly alike but female smaller; back and scapulars, rump, and sides cinnamon brown, brown extends on breast, sometimes meeting to form breast band; head and hind neck light gray; eyes yellow; upper breast mouse gray; lower breast, belly, and undertail coverts *white* (Banks, 1968a); relatively few ornithologists have seen Baird's junco in its natural habitat; little written about it; very common above 3,000 ft. elevation in oak, pinyon pine, madrone, and cottonwoods in mountain canyons; quite tame, stays in foliage or limbs close to ground, readily responds to "squeaking"; sings warblerlike song, which also resembles that of black-throated sparrow; sometimes forages in small groups at edge of meadows, apparently for seeds or insects; remains in winter in highest part of nesting range.

Nest: Seen building in late May at 6,000 ft. elevation, and in July, either on ground in depression among weeds or in crotch, or leafy extremity of branch, in small pinyon pines 6 ft. above ground; nest built of fine weeds, grasses, lined with horsehair.

Eggs: June (?) and July; 2, white, with small flecks of red-brown.

Weights: Males, adults (2), 16.7 and 17.8 gr.; female 16.7 gr. (Banks, 1968a), or about ⅔ oz.

Junco, Carolina. *See* Junco, slate-colored.

Junco, dark-eyed, *Junco hyemalis;* genus name: *see* Junco, Baird's; species name: *see* Junco, slate-colored; general common, and scientific, name (see American Ornithologists' Union, 1973) for the species representing a group of closely related juncos all characterized by dark eyes and other similarities. (Color ills., pages 308, 309.) Some, however, in different regions of N. America, with variations such as a black hood, white wing bars, or pink sides. *See* biographies of four N. American subspecies of the dark-eyed junco under Junco, Guadalupe; Junco, Oregon; Junco, slate-colored; and Junco, White-winged. Each of these, on most official lists before 1973, had been considered a distinct species (*see* Species) until closer studies of their relationships and frequent crossbreeding by some indicated that each was a geographic representative of a single species.

Junco, gray-headed, *Junco caniceps* (JUNG-koh KAY-nih-ceps); genus name: *see* Junco, Baird's; species name: from Lat. *canus*, hoary, and *caput*, head (Coble, 1954). (Color ill., page 309.) Juncos are in sparrow group of Finch Family; gray-headed lives in coniferous forests of high western mountains; 5½–6 in. long; sexes outwardly alike; gray head, pale gray chest and *sides*, with tawny to rufous back, white belly and tail edges; distinguished by its dark eyes from similar yellow-eyed Mexican junco; gray-headed is one of relatively least-known birds of coniferous forests of s. Rocky Mtns. and Great Basin ranges; lives mostly on mountaintops above 7,000 ft.; in n. Colo., to 8,600 ft. in dense pine and spruce; in ne. Utah, from 7,500 ft. to timberline at 10,000 ft. in Douglas fir, ponderosa pine, blue spruce, aspen, lodgepole pine, Englemann spruce, etc. (Thatcher, 1968); in similar habitat in high ranges of Ariz. and N.M.; in spring starts northward or upward to nesting range in mountains; some arrive Mar.–Apr., when males begin to sing simple trill (song remarkably like that of chipping sparrow) in chosen nesting territories, also utter sharp *tic* note in flight. Some banded as juveniles return to nest within 50 yds. of place where hatched; courtship like that of better-known Oregon and slate-colored (dark-eyed) juncos.

Feeding Habits: Forages mostly on ground and scratches among leaves and snow for weed and grass seeds, green caterpillars, moths; also eats cracked pinyon nuts, and bread crumbs and seed mixtures on ground at bird feeders.

Nest: Usually on ground (sometimes in small tree or vines), at base of tree, bush, weed, grass, in cavity of road bank or stream bank, under fallen log, at timberline may be under rock like that of water pipit; nest built of coarse grasses lined with finer grasses, horsehair, feathers.

Eggs: May–Aug.; 3–5, white or blue-white, speckled with browns.

Incubation: By female, probably 11–12 days (Thatcher, 1968); young leave nest when 11–13 days old.

Other Name: Red-backed junco.

Age: One, banded Cedar Crest, N.M., trapped and released in same area when 8 years, 6 months, old (Kennard, 1975).

Hybrids: Interbreeds freely with Oregon junco where ranges of two meet.

Range: Nests in White Mtns. of Calif., and in mountains from s. Idaho south into Ariz., N.M., and w. Tex.; winters in lower mountains, plains of nesting area south into Ariz., N.M., s. Calif. and into Mexico.

Junco, Guadalupe (dark-eyed), *Junco hyemalis insularis* (JUNG-koh high-eh-MAIL-us in-sue-LAY-rus); genus name: *see* Junco, Baird's; species name: from Lat. *hiemalis*, pertaining to winter; subspecies name: Lat., from *insula*, island. Once considered a full species, *Junco insularis* (see A.O.U. *Check-list*, 1957); resident of Guadalupe Is., about 135 mi. west of Baja Calif. coast; considered by American Ornithologists' Union (1973) to be a subspecies, the island race, or form, of the group of mainland juncos with dark eyes and other similarities. *See* Junco, dark-eyed; see also Howell in Bent *et al.* (1968) for biography of the Guadalupe junco.

Junco, Mexican (yellow-eyed), *Junco-phaeonotus palliatus*—(JUNG-koh fee-oh-NO-tus pal-ih-AY-tus); genus and species names: *see* Junco, Baird's; subspecies name: Lat., cloaked, apparently in allusion to bright rufous back. (Color ill., page 309.) Formerly treated as a distinct species but considered by American Ornithologists' Union (1973) to be a subspecies of a group of related juncos with yellow eyes and other similarities (*see* Yellow-eyed junco); only U.S. junco with yellow eyes; resident of high mountain forests in se. Ariz., sw. N.M., and south into Mexico; sexes outwardly alike; 5½–6½ in. long; a chestnut-backed junco with *bright yellow eyes;* gray above, black lores and uniformly gray-white underparts that distinguish it from Oregon (dark-eyed) junco, which has dark eyes and black head and breast that contrast sharply with its white belly (Blake, E. R., 1953); lives usually from 6,000 ft. up in forest of ponderosa pines, Mexican pinyons, Douglas firs; sometimes descends below forests in bad weather; winters in groups of family size which begin to pair off first week of Apr.; male ascends to treetops to utter song frequently; flares tail, struts around female, sometimes fights intruding male savagely, locking with it bill to bill while female watches; each male has several song patterns and trills, one, three-parted, is *chip chip chip, wheedle, wheedle, wheedle, che che che che che,* all songs have thin sweet quality suggestive of wood warblers (Austin, 1968b).

Feeding Habits: Forages on ground, moves about in strange mouselike fashion, a shuffle or creep, feet move alternately (not hopping as in other juncos) over leaves while picking up food; also runs with long hops to catch insects; scratches through leaf litter to find seeds; very tame around picnic grounds of Forest Service in Ariz. mountains, where takes food crumbs from tables.

Nest: Built by female, usually on ground under bunch of grass, log, bark, flat stone, difficult to find, sometimes in thick shrubbery, under drooping pine limb or young fir; on ground, female scrapes hollow with feet and bill, within it builds outer cup of nest of coarse grasses; inner cup lined with hairs of deer and horses.

Eggs: Apr.–Aug.; 3–5, usually 3–4, gray-white or pale blue-white with spots, speckling of browns, indistinguishable from eggs of gray-headed junco.

Incubation: By female, 15 (?) days, quoted by Austin (1968b); young begin to leave nest when 10 days old.

Other Names: Arizona junco; red-backed junco.

Junco, Oregon (dark-eyed), *Junco hyemalis oreganus* (JUNG-koh or-eh-GAIN-us); genus name: *see* Junco, Baird's; species name: *see* Junco, Guadalupe; subspecies name: Lat., of Oregon. (Color ill., page 308.) Previously thought to be a distinct species; determined by American Ornithologists' Union (1973) to be a subspecies of the dark-eyed junco, *Junco hyemalis;* summers from Alaska and w. Canada south through Calif., east to Idaho and Wyo.; 5–6 in. long; male has hood that may be black, dark gray, or medium gray; back brown or gray; sides may be light ruddy brown, yellowish, or rich pink-cinnamon; belly white; outer tail feathers white; bill flesh-colored; eyes brown; females usually like male but often with paler hood; immatures brown-streaked like sparrow but have hood and adult plumage within 2 or 3 months after hatching (Phelps, 1968); lives in forest edges, especially border between coniferous forests and mountain meadows, along unused woods roads, forest openings along pond or stream, burned-over tracts throughout evergreen forest belt of mountains of Great Basin and from humid forests of Pacific coast to dry forests of interior Calif., and sometimes to timberline in Rocky Mtns.; west of Cascades is city and country dooryard bird, in city parks, college campuses in many parts of West; flocks move northward or upward (in mountains) Feb.–Apr. and break up into pairs on nesting grounds; in flight shows white outer tail feathers; courtship similar to that of gray-headed and other juncos; songs and calls like those of slate-colored junco.

Feeding Habits: Year-round eats weed seeds, in fall and winter also waste grain, in nesting season insects.

Nest: Usually on ground in cup-shaped depression, often near water; built by female and like that of other juncos. See Phelps (1968).

Eggs: Mar.–Aug.; 3–5, usually 4, white to pale blue-white, speckled, spotted, or blotched with browns, grays.

Incubation: By female, probably 11–12 days; young leave nest when 11–14 days old (Weydemeyer, 1971b); two broods each year (Phelps, 1968).

Other Names: Mountain junco; pink-sided junco (once thought to be a separate species, especially common in Yellowstone National Park); Sierra junco; Shufeldt's junco; Thurber's junco.

Accidents: Juncos attracted to warmth of caves in Yellowstone have died there from gases.

Age: One adult, banded at Manor, Calif., picked up dead at same place when 8 years, 4 months, old; may have died of old age.

Albinism: One reported Dayton, Ore., underparts pure white, upperparts cream; head and neck generally black; wings and tail white; one collected (shot) at Witch Creek, Calif., mostly white; a perfect, or complete, albino killed on Sauvies Is. near Portland, Ore. (Phelps, 1968).

Flight Speed: Timed in w. U.S., 26 m.p.h. (Cottam *et al.,* 1942b).

Host to Cowbirds: Rare; three in B.C.; one Berkeley, Calif. (Friedmann, 1963); one near Dishman, Wash. (Friedmann, 1966).

Hybrids: Oregon junco interbreeds with gray-headed junco and possibly with white-winged junco where their ranges overlap (Gray, 1958); also frequently with slate-colored junco (Phelps, 1968).

Weights: Ore., Mar. (6), 18.94–22.62 gr. (Anderson, 1970), or about ¾ oz.

Range: Nests from se. Alaska, c. B.C., w.-c. and s. Alta., and sw. Sask., south from B.C. to w.-c. Calif., mountains of n. Baja Calif., and from s. Idaho, w. Nev., ne. Ore., and nw. Wyo.; winters from se. Alaska, s. B.C., n. Idaho, w. Mont., Wyo., and S.D. south to n. Baja Calif., n. Mexico, and e. Tex.; outside breeding season wanders to Ont., Mass., Md., La., etc.

Junco, pink-sided. *See* Junco, Oregon.

Junco, red-backed. *See* Junco, gray-headed, and Junco, Mexican.

Junco, slate-colored (dark-eyed), *Junco hyemalis hyemalis* (JUNG-koh high-eh-MAIL-us); genus name: *see* Junco, Baird's; species and subspecies names: from Lat., *hiemalis,* pertaining to winter. (Color ills., pages 308, 309.) Formerly considered a distinct species (A.O.U. *Check-list,* 1957) but determined by American Ornithologists' Union (1973) to be a subspecies of a group with dark eyes and other similarities (*see* Dark-eyed junco); this is the nominate subspecies (*see* Nominate Subspecies); most widespread of all juncos, common in winter in e. U.S. and across much of U.S.; 5½–6¼ in. long; wingspread 9½–10 in.; male has sooty-black head, neck, back, and upper breast which sharply contrast with white underparts; has white outer tail feathers that usually show in flight; bill pale pink; eyes brown; female similar color pattern of male but very brown to quite brown where male is sooty (Grant and Quay, 1970); immatures brownish and may be streaked on chest and flanks; slate-colored is common and friendly "sparrow" that nests across N. American continent from Alaska to Labrador and Newfoundland, and from limit of trees in North south into n. U.S. and in Appalachian Mtns. of e. U.S., where it lives year-round in rhododendron thickets and along trails and picnic grounds of upper and lower slopes; summer population in n. U.S., Canada, lives in open woods, edges of coniferous and broad-leaved forests; in clearings, slash piles, edges of roads; in winter moves southward throughout much of U.S. in small flocks that feed in edges of woods, old brushy, weedy fields, hedges, roadsides, city parks, home gardens, often roost on ground under yews, or 3–8 ft. up in Norway spruce thickets, in cedars of old pastures; in Mar. and Apr., flocks that nest in North return to nesting grounds; male proclaims territory by singing from tops of tallest trees; his territorial song is jingling trill; repeated scold note is smacking *tack, tack, tack;* also utters *clink* note that sounds like pebbles struck together.

Feeding Habits: Forages mostly on ground, hops or occasionally runs when chasing a rival or insect; scratches for food in leaves, snow; eats seeds that drop from bird feeders to ground; occasionally eats while perched on feeders; white outer tail feathers often flashed in aggressive display when feeding near other birds; almost half summer food is insects—beetles, weevils, caterpillars, grasshoppers, bugs, ants, wasps, also eats spiders, berries; in winter eats seeds of hemlocks, grasses, small grains, and weed seeds, mostly ragweed, smartweed, pigweed, lamb's-quarters, chickweed, purslane, vetch, sorrels, thistles, broom sedge, crabgrasses; likes seeds of garden plants such as zinnias, cosmos.

Nest: Built by female, usually on ground, edges and openings of coniferous and hardwood forests; male helps gather materials; well hidden in cavity under tree roots, under stumps, brush piles, overhanging bank of stream or road, sometimes in bushes, small trees, ledge beneath gable of house, empty tobacco can, etc.; is deep cup of mosses, twigs, grasses, strips of bark, rootlets, lined with grasses, sedges, hairs.

Eggs: Apr.–Aug.; 3–6, often 4–5, gray or pale blue-white, speckled and spotted with browns, grays.

Incubation: By female, 11–12 days (also reported 12–13 days); young leave nest when 12–13 days old (Tanner, 1958); usually two broods a year.

Other Names: Black chipping bird; black snowbird; blue snowbird; Carolina junco; Cassiar junco; common snowbird; eastern junco; gray snowbird; slate-colored snowbird; snowbird; white-bill.

Age: Fourteen, banded Norristown, Pa., lived 3½–6½ years; one, banded Lenox, Mass., shot at Conway, S.C., when 10 years, 9 months, old (Kennard, 1975).

Albinism: Two partial albinos at Demarest, N.J., winter 1931–32.

Flight Speed: 18 m.p.h. (Wood, 1933).

Host to Cowbirds: Infrequent, 18 records (Friedmann, 1963).

Hybrids: Interbreeds with Oregon junco where ranges overlap; also presumed natural hybrids reported of slate-colored junco with white-throated sparrow (Gray, 1958); see also Short and Simon (1965); abundance of hybrids of slate-colored junco with white-throated sparrow reported by Dickerman (1961).

Weights: Minimum of about 16 gr. to maximum of 26.6 gr., or about ¾–1 oz., reported by Helms and Drury (1960); coastal N.J. in fall (75), 15–20.4 gr. (Murray and Jehl, 1964), or about ½–¾ oz.

Range: Nests from nw. Alaska to Labrador (tree limit) south through Yuk., Mack., to n. B.C., c. prairie provinces of Canada, c. Minn.,

Wisc., c. Mich., s. Ont., N.Y., Conn., and Mass., south in Appalachians to n. Ga.; winters mostly south of northern nesting range, from s. Canada mostly east of Rocky Mtns., south to n. Baja Calif., n. Mexico, s. Tex. and Gulf coast to n. Fla.

Junco, white-winged (dark-eyed), *Junco hyemalis aikeni* (JUNG-koh AY-ken-eye); genus name: *see* Junco, Baird's; species name: *see* Junco, slate-colored; subspecies name: for Charles E. Aiken, pioneering Colo. naturalist, who discovered the bird. Previously thought to be a distinct species, determined by American Ornithologists' Union (1973) to be a subspecies of the dark-eyed junco, *Junco hyemalis*; ranges in mountains of n. Great Plains (S.D. and Wyo.); 6–6¾ in. long; male slate-gray head, neck, chest, back, flanks, distinguished usually by its two white bars in each wing; has large amount of white in tail; female similar to male but paler gray; upperparts, especially back, tinged with light gray-brown; wing bars usually less distinct; immatures resemble female; is one of most numerous and conspicuous birds of pine forests of Black Hills, which are virtually an island surrounded by prairies; white-winged is practically limited to Black Hills and Bear Lodge Mtns. in nesting season, in dry ponderosa forest, where it lives in recently cut-over tracts, brushy clearings; in winter, lives in lower parts of Black Hills or farther south in foothills of Rocky Mtns.; with first warm weather of early Mar., begins moving back to nesting grounds, where each male establishes and defends a territory of a few acres; advertises it with musical trill similar to that of other juncos and much like song of chipping sparrow (Whitney, 1968).

Feeding Habits: No definitive studies made but insects seem to be chief food of adults and young in summer; seeds of grasses and weeds in winter; often appears at bird feeding stations.

Nest: Built on ground under logs, exposed tree roots and rock ledges; in old gallon syrup can and tomato can discarded on floor of pine forest, in and around active sawmills.

Eggs: May–June; 3–4, white or cream-white, speckled and spotted with browns, grays.

Incubation: About 12 days; young leave nest when about 11 days old.

Host to Cowbirds: Two records (Friedmann, 1963).

Hybrids: Interbreeding between white-winged junco and Oregon junco "thought to occur when the ranges of the two species overlap" (Gray, 1958).

Range: Nests from se. Mont. and w. S.D. south to ne. Wyo. and nw. Neb.; winters near nesting grounds, lower parts of Black Hills, and south to sw. Colo.; n-c. N.M., w. Okla., and w. Kans., occasionally to n. Ariz.

Junco, yellow-eyed, *Junco phaeonotus* (JUNG-koh fee-oh-NO-tus); genus name: *see* Junco, Baird's; species name: Gr., for dun-colored (dingy or dull gray-brown) back; general common and scientific name: see American Ornithologists' Union (1973) for the species representing closely related juncos with yellow eyes

and other similarities. (Color ill., page 309.) *See* biographies of the two N. American subspecies under Baird's junco and Mexican junco. Each of these on most official lists before 1973 had been considered a distinct species (*see* Species), until closer studies of their relationships indicated that each was a geographic representative of one species.

Longspur, Alaska. *See* Longspur, Lapland.

Longspur, chestnut-collared, *Calcarius ornatus* (cal-KAY-rih-us or-NAY-tus); genus name: from Lat. *calcar,* spur; species name: Lat., adorned; *longspur,* from the very long nail, or claw, on the hind toe. (Color ills., pages 310, 311.) Ground-inhabiting sparrowlike birds of grasslands of n. U.S. and s. Canada; chestnut-collared is 5½–6½ in. long; male in breeding plumage, black on top of head, *solid-black* (breast to belly) *underparts;* chestnut nape or collar (back of neck); white face and throat with black streak in back of each eye; dark feathers in white tail form a *black triangle;* female dull buffy, streaked like sparrow; *much white in sides of tail,* whitish throat and breast but much variation in her plumage (see Fairfield, 1968); summers on upland northern prairies, often where grass sparse and less than 8 in. tall, from s. Alta. to s. Man., south to Midwest prairies, ranges farther east in the more moist prairies than McCown's longspur of the drier, short-grass plains; after wintering on deserts and plateaus of n. Mexico and plains of sw. U.S., flocks, with other longspurs and horned larks, drift northward through w. Tex., Okla., N.M., and e. Ariz., across Colo. and Kans. to arrive on northern nesting grounds about mid-Apr. (Fairfield, 1968); male defends territory of 1–2 acres by singing many hours from perch atop weed clumps, small shrubs, boulders, fences; song is loud, musical, somewhat similar to quality of song of western meadowlark; also utters flight song while flying upward gradually, wings beating rapidly to peak of flight, then, circling, finally descends with wings beating as rapidly as before; common call note is *til-lup* or *til-lip* (accent on first syllable); male attacks and drives away ground squirrels, gray partridges, meadowlarks, cowbirds, Savannah sparrows if they approach the nest.

Feeding Habits: Eats weed seeds and insects of its prairie environment.

Nest: Built by female, on ground on level or sloping prairie, usually in cup-shaped hollow she digs in ground, often in thicker and taller grasses that offer concealment, sometimes near low moist places, also on grassy knolls, built of dried grasses, the cup lined with hair or feathers when available.

Eggs: May–July; 3–6, usually 3–5, cream-white, spotted, blotched, with small scrawls of dark browns, black (Fairfield, 1968).

Incubation: By female, 11–12½ days; young remain in nest about 10 days (Du Bois, 1935).

Host to Cowbirds: Probably not uncommon, locally (Friedmann, 1963).

Hybrids: Pettingill (Sibley and Pettingill, 1955) collected (shot) a hybrid intermediate between the chestnut-collared and McCown's longspur, two species that normally live in separate habi-

tats of prairie with the McCown's in shorter grass and drier areas.

Weights: About 20 gr. (Fairfield, 1968), or about ¾ oz.

Range: Nests from s. Alta., s. Sask., s. Man., se. to ne. Colo., n-c. Neb., sw. Minn., formerly to w. Kans.; winters from n. Ariz., c. N.M., ne. Colo., and c. Kans., south to Mexico, s. Tex., and n. La.; sometimes wanders out of normal nesting and wintering range (as given in opening paragraphs) to Calif. and east to Atlantic coast, Nova Scotia, south to Mass., N.Y. (four Long Is. records), Md., and south to n. Fla.; adult female shot Aug. 1968 at Stratford, Conn., was first record for state (Bulmer, 1970).

Longspur, Lapland, *Calcarius lapponicus* (cal-KAY-rih-us lap-ON-ih-cus); genus name: *see* Longspur, chestnut-collared; species name: Lat., Lapland. (Color ills., pages 310, 311.) In summer lives over vast expanses of tundra north of tree line, Alaska across Canada, north to Greenland, east to Labrador; also in Siberia, n. Russia, and Lapland, for which named in 18th century; in winter only common longspur east of plains; 6–7 in. long; wingspread 10½–11¾ in.; male in breeding plumage, head and chest deep black, broad white or buffy stripe behind each eye and downward along sides of black throat and chest; upperparts light gray-brown; underparts white; sides streaked with black; tail *black* with white edges; female similar to male but less black throat patch; in winter, when in immense flocks in fields, plains, prairies of n. U.S., south into Mississippi Valley and in w. U.S. to N.M. and Tex.; appears like house, or English, sparrow, but male has *chestnut hind neck,* blackish upper breast patch, white wing bars; usually in flocks often with other longspurs, snow buntings, and horned larks; walks, runs, or takes long hops over fields where weeds project above snow; in smaller flocks in ne. U.S. or even a few or single birds sometimes on sand dunes of coastal beaches with snow buntings, larks, bare windswept pastures, airports; flight is undulating, starts migration northward in Mar., usually arrives on breeding grounds Apr.–June; flocks break up, scattered males take up territories, much fighting between males, male sings courtship songs in flight, less commonly from tussocks, sings tinkling bobolinklike song while floating gently to ground; male carries nest materials in bill in courtship of female.

Feeding Habits: In summer, beetles, weevils, crane flies, mosquitoes, caterpillars, bugs, spiders, seeds of grasses, sedges; in winter, mostly weed seeds.

Nest: In wet or dry hummocky areas of tundra, often among dwarfed trees, built in depression in small hummock of moss, grass, sedge, or base of shrub, built of grasses, mosses, cup lined with hairs of lemmings, caribou, dogs, Arctic hares, feathers of raven, ptarmigan, plant down.

Eggs: May–Aug.; 3–7, usually 4–6, pale green-white to buff-brown, marked with scrawls of black, browns (Williamson in Bent *et al.*, 1968).

Incubation: By female, 12–13 days; 13 days (Jehl and Hussell, 1966); young leave nest when 8–10 days old, fly when about 12 days old.

FINCH FAMILY
The bill of the pyrrhuloxia changes from yellow in summer to gray in winter. It is strong and blunt, with a sharply down-curved upper mandible like that of a parrot.

Other Names: Alaska longspur; common longspur.

Accidents: Sometimes caught in great snowstorms in spring when migrating; on night of Mar. 13–14, 1904, estimated five million died in one storm in Midwest (see Terres, 1948).

Weights: Adults average about 1 oz. (Williamson in Bent *et al.*, 1968).

Range: Nests from Alaskan islands in Bering Sea and coast of n. Alaska south to n. Yuk., nw. Mack., east to n. Man., n. Ont., n. Que., n. Labrador, north to Greenland; winters from s. B.C., Mont., S.D., c. Minn., c. Mich., s. Ont., s. Que., N.B., south to ne. Calif., n. Ariz., n. N.M., n. Tex., s. La., Miss., Ala., w. Tenn., sw. Ohio, e. W.Va., Va., occasionally farther south.

Longspur, McCown's, *Calcarius mccownii* (cal-KAY-rih-us mack-COWN-ih-eye); genus name: *see* Longspur, chestnut-collared; species name: given in 1851 by George Newbold Lawrence in honor of J. P. McCown, a captain in U.S. Army, who discovered the bird on high prairies of w. Tex. (Color ill., page 310.) Summers on dry, short-grass plains, now largely limited in summer to ne. Mont. (last stronghold in U.S.), Sask., and s. Alta., more abundant on nesting grounds in dry years than in wet years (Krause, 1968); lives generally west of summer range of its close relative the chestnut-collared longspur; male in breeding plumage, bill straw yellow; black forehead, white throat, black patch (crescent) on breast, hind neck (nape) *gray,* not chestnut as in other longspurs; tail mostly white *with inverted T shape of black in middle tail feathers;* bend of wings *rusty;* female light buffy brown above, on face and breast; throat white; streaked above and below, black T in all plumages shows conspicuously in white tail in flight; flocks leave wintering grounds in Tex. in Mar. and early Apr., from se. Ariz. in late Feb. and early Mar.; appears in e. and ne. Mont., from mid to late Apr.; male selects territory, begins to sing tinkling song like horned lark from perch on ground or in shrubs or in flight; prefers dry plains dominated by buffalo grass; male and female show unusual attachment for each other, keep close together, usually walk side by side.

Feeding Habits: Walks about over ground, in summer eats mainly weed seeds, also grasshoppers, beetles, moths, caterpillars; drinks water at irrigation reservoirs with horned larks and chestnut-colored longspurs.

Nest: Usually in hollow scraped in ground by pair, female builds nest of dried grasses, lined with fine grasses, wool, horsehair, at base of grass clump, flower stalk, or bush.

Eggs: May–July; 3–6, usually 3–4, white to pink-white or pale green, spotted, lined, scrawled with dark brown.

Incubation: By female, 12 days (Krause, 1968); both parents feed young, which remain in nest until 10 days old; fly when 12 days old; apparently two broods a year (Du Bois, 1935).

Other Names: Black-breasted longspur; ground lark; McCown's bunting; rufous-winged lark bunting.

Host to Cowbirds: Apparently rare or not well known; Friedmann (1963) cites single records for N.D. and Sask.

Hybrids: See under Longspur, chestnut-collared.

Range: Nests from s. Alta., s. Sask., sw. Man., and n-c. N.D., south to se. Wyo., ne. Colo., nw. Neb., and c. N.D.; formerly east to sw. Minn.; winters from c. Ariz., sw. and ne. Colo., w.-c. Kans., and c. Okla., south to s. Tex., and Mexico.

Longspur, Smith's, *Calcarius pictus* (cal-KAY-rih-us PICK-tus); genus name: *see* Longspur, chestnut-collared; species name: Lat., painted, of various colors (Coble, 1954); common name: given by John James Audubon for his friend, Gideon B. Smith, medical doctor of Baltimore, Md. (Color ill., page 310.) One of least-known of N. American birds; nowhere plentiful, elusive (Kemsies, 1968); summers on tundra from Alaskan coast of Bering Sea to Hudson Bay; 5¾–6½ in. long; male in spring breeding plumage has striking black-and-white pied head and face; has broad white wing bar; female and young resemble female and young of Lapland longspur but are *buffier* with *buffy underparts* (Lapland longspur has white underparts); both sexes have slightly slenderer, more pointed bills than other longspurs, and *yellowish* legs; white outer tail feathers; males in winter resemble females; in winter in Midwest (Kans. and Ohio southward) have been seen in flocks of 20–30 scattered through pastures and on airports, where they usually remain apart from other longspurs, wintering sparrows, and horned larks; quite tame, allow close approach, fly up suddenly with low clicking call like sound of winding a cheap watch; swift, erratic flight like zigzag course of common snipe; often drops suddenly to ground but if remains in air, flight becomes undulating; beginning Mar.–Apr., migrate northward in large loose flocks; arrive nesting grounds in n. Alaska late May and June (Kemsies, 1968).

Feeding Habits: Studied only in winter (Ill., Tenn., Ohio, La.), eats seeds of grasses, ragweed, bulrushes, sedges, some wheat, clover, beetles, caterpillars, spiders.

Nest: On ground, usually on hummocks in grassy tundra, raised above wet surroundings, often near trees, sometimes sunk in depressions dug by pair; built of grasses, lined with finer grasses, caribou hair, ptarmigan feathers.

Eggs: June–July; 4–6, usually 4–5, smoky gray, dotted, blotched with browns.

Incubation: By female, 11–12 days (Jehl and Hussell, 1966); age when young leave nest unknown.

Range: Nests from ne. and c. Alaska, n. Yuk., nw. and c. Mack. to s. Keewatin, ne. Man., to Hudson Bay coast of n. Ont.; winters from Kans., c. Iowa, south to Okla., e. Tex., nw. La., nw. Miss., sw. Tenn.; a young female collected in Conn., Mar. 1968, was first record on east coast of N. America in 100 years; second record was one collected on Long Is., N.Y., Sept. 1974 (Kane and Buckley, 1975).

Pyrrhuloxia, *Cardinalis sinuata* (Car-din-Ay-liss sin-you-AY-tah); genus name: *see* Cardinal; species name: Lat., curved (bill). (Color ill., page 311.) Sw. U.S., Baja Calif.; pale relative of the cardinal; 7½–8¼ in. long; slender *gray* cardinal-like bird, with *red-ringed* dark eyes; heavy, parrotlike *yellow* bill; male has red crest, is red, or rose-colored, down center of breast; *gray back*, red on wings and outer tail feathers; female similar to male with gray back, but yellowish breast; tinge of red on crest and wings; similar to female cardinal but *yellow* bill (adult cardinals have pink or red bills); upper mandible sharply downcurved gives parrotlike appearance; lives year-round in thorny thickets, especially edges of mesquite along desert arroyos, remnants of mesquite forests, and in thorny brush at lower, widened mouth of mountain canyons, thickets along streams; comes into dooryards of homes scattered among mesquite, to bird feeding stations, birdbaths; travels in small flocks in winter, which break up late Feb. and early Mar.; males and even females become pugnacious, much chasing, most aggressive males get best territories (Gould, 1961); male proclaims territory by singing much, most frequently in early morning; roughly circular territories 1.3–3.5 acres (*see* Territory); male sings whistled songs from perch on poles, power lines, *queet, queet, queet —queet, queet, queet, quee-u, quee-u*, strikingly like cardinal's songs; apparently only male sings (Anderson, 1968); call note is *squick* or *stick;* flight noisy, undulating like that of cardinal.

Feeding Habits: In winter eats catkins of cottonwoods, bright red fruits of Christmas cactus, seeds of sorghum, grasses, weeds, very fond of mesquite beans; in summer, cotton worms, cotton-boll weevil, caterpillars, grasshoppers.
Nest: Built by female in small twigs of branches of mesquite, thorny bushes, 5–15 ft. up, small, compact, grayish nest of twigs, inner bark, coarse grasses, cup lined with rootlets, thin strips bark, horsehair.
Eggs: Mar.–July; 2–5, usually 3–4, gray-white, green-white, speckled, spotted with browns.
Incubation: By female, 14 days (Gould, 1961); young leave nest when about 10 days old (Anderson, 1968).
Other Names: Bullfinch; bullfinch cardinal; gray cardinal; gray grosbeak; parrot-bill; Texas cardinal.
Flight Speed: Timed in Tex., 20 m.p.h. (Sooter, 1947).
Host to Cowbirds: Six records to brownheaded cowbird; three to bronzed cowbird (Friedmann, 1971).
Range: Resident from c. Baja Calif., s.-c. and se. Ariz., s. N.M., w., c., and se. Tex., south into s. Baja Calif. and c. Mexico.

Redpoll, common, *Carduelis flammea* (cardyou-EE-liss FLAH-me-ah); genus name: *see* Goldfinch, American; species name: Lat., flame; *redpoll*, from red cap. (Color ill., page 311.) Small northern finches that live (in N. America) from southern edge of Arctic tundra south into coniferous forests, from Alaska to Newfoundland; in some winters, unusually large flights from north move south into U.S.; 5–5½ in. long; wingspread 8¼–8¾ in.; red cap, black chin; small, streaked, gray-brown birds with short, conical, sharp-pointed bills; some males, not all, have red breast (Clement, 1968); rump pink;

forked tail, underparts white, mostly streaked; in shape, size, actions, resembles goldfinches and the pine siskin; common redpoll and its close relative the hoary redpoll can survive colder temperatures than any other songbird (*see* Cold and Birds); in winter, immense flocks in Canada and U.S. move about restlessly in undulating flight, wheel about in concert over winter fields, feed clinging to weed tops projecting above snow, or perch in low trees and bushes nearby; from their throats come subdued but constant twitter; tame and unsuspicious; if one stands quietly, some may alight near or on person (Taverner, 1947); individuals come to bird feeders for millet, hemp, sunflower seeds; have been caught in hand at window feeders by bird-banders; winter-bathe in icy waters of brooks or by burrowing into wet snow (Clement, 1968); flocks leave for northern nesting grounds by mid-Mar.; while in flocks males sing juncolike song; are paired by early Apr. in Que., no fighting over territories, pairs sometimes nest close together; a call note is *swee-e-et*, coarser than that of American goldfinch.

Feeding Habits: In trees, eats seeds from cones of birches, alders, seeds of willows, also those of pines, elms, basswood, buds of larch, lilac; on ground, scratches for fallen birch seeds, which may store in crop; eats seeds of many kinds of weeds, grasses; insects in summer and feeds them to young.
Nest: Lives about forest openings, second growth, in swamps of alder, willow, tamarack; built by female on branches of spruce, or in crotch of alder or willow, 3–6 ft. above ground, first a loose platform of small twigs, then loose cup of fine twigs, rootlets, grasses, mosses, lined with thick layer of ptarmigan feathers.
Eggs: Apr.–Aug.; 4–7, usually 4–5; green to blue, spotted or lined with purple to violet-black.
Incubation: By female, 10–11 days; young leave nest about 12 days after hatching (Clement, 1968).
Other Names: Greater redpoll; Holboell's redpoll; lintie; lesser redpoll; little redpoll; mealy redpoll; red-polled linnet.
Age: One, banded, reported from Holland, 7 years, 7 months, old (Clapp, 1976).
Host to Cowbirds: Only one record (Friedmann, 1963), at Castor, Alta.
Hybrids: Presumed natural hybrids between common redpoll and hoary redpoll reported (Gray, 1958).
Weights: 13–14 gr., or about ½ oz.
Range: In N. America, from s. Alaska, n. B.C., east to n. Ont., e. and se. Que., and Newfoundland; winters from southern parts of nesting range in Canada to ne. Calif., n. Nev., ne. Utah, c. Colo., Kans., Iowa, s. Ind., s. Ohio, n. W.Va., e. N.C., and s. S.C.; also nests in n. Eurasia, c. Europe, British Isles.

Redpoll, Coues'. *See* Redpoll, hoary.

Redpoll, greater. *See* Redpoll, common.

Redpoll, hoary, *Carduelis hornemanni* (car-dyou-EE-liss HOR-neh-man-eye); genus name: *see* Redpoll, common; species name: in

honor of the great Danish botanist and professor Jens Wilken Hornemann, given by Carl Peter Holboell. (Color ill., page 311.) Summers in Far North, winters irregularly into n. U.S.; 5¼–5½ in. long; similar to common redpoll but paler, with *whitish* unstreaked rump, which apparently is only reliable field mark; sometimes seen in winter in flocks of common redpolls; Forbush (1925–29) reported it rare in winter in New England; Baldwin (1968) cites its behavior in winter in Alaska and Canada, and at Hawk Mtn., Pa., where four remained in lilac bushes during Mar. snowstorm; did not associate with flock of common redpolls; calls are said to be like those of common redpoll but sharper, higher-pitched.

Feeding Habits: Eats seeds and buds of alder, birch, and willow, seeds of grasses, weeds; in summer, insects and seeds; feeds insects and predigested mash of cotton-grass seeds to young.
Nest: In n. Alaska generally in tundra where scattered low willows and alders along drainage channels of hillsides, often close to water, whereas common redpoll nests in willows of higher tundra farther south; female builds in crotches of bushes 1–7 ft. above ground; also on ground in shelter of rocks or dwarf plants; cup of twigs, coarse grasses, rootlets, cup lined with finer grasses, down of willow and cotton grass, caribou hairs, ptarmigan feathers.
Eggs: June; 3–6, usually 4–5, bluish to green, spotted, speckled with browns.
Incubation: By female, 11–14.4 days (Baldwin, 1968); young leave nest 12–14 days after hatching.
Other Names: Arctic redpoll; Coues' redpoll; Greenland redpoll; Hornemann's redpoll.
Hybrids: See under Common redpoll.
Weights: Adult male (1), Ellesmere Is., Canada, 19.1 gr., or about ⅔ oz.; adult females (2), 17 and 19.4 gr. (Parmalee and MacDonald, 1960).
Range: Arctic regions of N. America, n. Europe, Russia, Siberia, Alaska, across Canada to n. Labrador; winters irregularly (*see* Irruption) south to s. Alaska, s. B.C., e. Mont., S.D., Minn., n. Ill., nw. Ind., n. Ohio, N.J. (Englewood), se. N.Y., Conn., Mass., casual in Md.

Redpoll, Holboell's. *See* Redpoll, common.

Redpoll, Hornemann's. *See* Redpoll, hoary.

Redpoll, lesser. *See* Redpoll, common.

Seedeater, Morrelet. *See* Seedeater, Sharp's.

Seedeater, Sharpe's, or white-collared, *Sporophila torqueola* (spore-OFF-ih-lah tore-QUEE-oh-lah); genus name: Lat., from Gr. *sporos*, seed, and *philos*, loving; species name: from Lat. *torquis*, a necklace, collar (Coues, 1882). Lower Rio Grande Valley of s. Tex., n. N.M.; tiny Mexican finch; 4–4½ in. long; has small, *swollen, stubby bill;* male has black upperparts, wings, and tail, much white in wings; some males have indistinct black band on breast and pale color around neck; buffy underparts; female brown-backed, buffy underparts, two white wing bars; *bill shape* is best clue to identity; lives year-round in open grassy places —pastures, roadsides, weed-grown fields, even in marshes (Bent, 1968); in Tex., males select nesting territories by early Apr., sing much from perches atop bushes; song is loud, clear *sweet sweet sweet cheer cheer cheer*, with variations; when disturbed, call is soft plaintive *che.*

Feeding Habits: Eats seeds, insects.

Nest: Built by female, in crotch of weed, vine, or shrub, 3–5½ ft. up, delicate, cuplike, about 2 in. in diameter, 1½ in. deep; of fine rootlets, plant fibers, grasses, lined with horsehair (Bent, 1968).

Eggs: Mar.–Sept.; 2–3, usually 2, pale blue to gray, speckled or mottled with browns.

Incubation: By female, 13 days; young leave nest when 10–11 days old.

Other Name: Morrelet seedeater.

Host to Cowbirds: Bent et al.(1968) cite a June record in Tex.; Friedmann (1963), "little known."

Range: Resident from w.-c. and n.-c. Mexico, s. Tex., south to Costa Rica.

Siskin, pine, *Carduelis pinus* (car-dyou-EE-liss PINE-us); genus name: *see* Goldfinch, American; species name: Lat., pine; common name: apparently from the siskin of Europe, a yellow-green finch, *Carduelis spinus*, a popular cage bird; *siskin* apparently derived from Danish *sidsken* or Swedish *siska*, a "chirper." (Color ill., page 313.) Wide-ranging across N. America, from Alaska east to Newfoundland and south into U.S.; nests especially wherever high altitude evergreen forests; irregular wanderer, in large flight years (*see* Irruption) some have reached Fla.; 4½–5¼ in. long; sexes alike; small, uniformly dark streaks on gray-brown back and buffy-white underparts, some yellow in wings and in notched tail; bill longer, slimmer than goldfinch's; in fall and winter moves about in groups of a few to flocks of thousands; flocks of 50–200 common; sometimes a few siskins in winter with flocks of goldfinches and redpolls; relatively high and swift flier; flocks compact, fly in long undulating sweeps; forages much in trees for seeds; when flying utters note, *tit-ih-tit;* call notes given in chorus sound like those of goldfinches, redpolls, canaries; utters long buzzy *shreeeee;* by late Jan., males in flocks begin warbled songs, at which flocks break up with much chasing, singing, into smaller groups, then pairs; males feed females (courtship feeding) while still in flocks; males have flight song, also sing from tops of bushes and tallest trees (Palmer, 1968).

Feeding Habits: Forages in trees and on ground for seeds in cones of alder, birches, spruces, pines, also sweet gum, maple seeds, and eucalyptus (in Calif.), flower buds of elms, seeds of thistles and other weeds; also caterpillars, aphids, scale insects, gall insects, grasshoppers; attracted to minerals in clay, ashes, cement, calcium chloride spread on highways to melt ice and snow, salt blocks; drinks nectar from eucalyptus blossoms, sap from tree borings of sapsuckers; bathes and drinks in garden birdbaths; eats mixed seeds from feeders; like

crossbills, so tame some allow very close approach, sometimes settles on person's head and shoulders, in experiments with captives, shows ability to learn (Palmer, 1968).

Nest: Unpredictable where it will nest, especially at edges of or outside normal breeding range; may nest in one area one year, far away the next; usually numerous where food plentiful, often nests in loose colonies with nests rods apart; nest, built by female, is typically in middle height of conifer well out and concealed on needled branch of hemlock, pine, spruce, fir, cedar, redwood, cypress, also in deciduous box elder (N.M. and N.D.), maples and oaks (Ore.), eucalyptus (Calif.), cottonwoods (Mont.); nest is somewhat flat, built of twigs, rootlets, grass, lined with hair, fur, feathers; female sometimes known to dismantle old goldfinch nest and use materials (Palmer, 1968).

Eggs: Apr.–July; 3–5, usually 3–4, pale green-blue, spotted, blotched with lavender or black.

Incubation: By female, 13 days; young leave nest when 15 days old; sometimes two broods a year.

Other Names: American siskin; gray linnet; northern canary bird; pine finch; pine linnet.

Age: Captive in National Zoo, Washington, D.C., lived for 11 years; banded ones, B.C., re-trapped later same place when 3, 6, 7 years old.

Host to Cowbirds: Occasional, 11 records (Friedmann, 1963).

Weights: About 12 gr. (male), or about ½ oz.

Range: Nests from c. and s. Alaska to Yuk., c. and s. Mack., c. Sask., s. Man., n. Ont., and se. Que., s. Labrador, Newfoundland, south to n. Baja Calif., sw. Tex. and into Mexico; and in central and eastern U.S. south to Kans., Io., n. Wisc., s. Ont., N.Y., Conn., and Mass.; winters at lower elevations in mountains, from se. Alaska and s. Canada south to n. Baja Calif., Mexico, s. La., Miss., Fla. (rarely to Miami).

Sparrow, Bachman's, *Aimophila aestivalis* (ay-MOFF-ih-lah es-tih-VAY-liss); genus name: Lat., from Gr. *haima*, blood (referring to reddish or rust color), and *philos*, loving (Coble, 1954); species name: Lat., pertaining to summer; common name: for the Rev. John Bachman, of Charleston, S.C., friend of Audubon, who discovered the bird in S.C. in 1832. Ranges over se. U.S. north to Pa. and Ohio; 5¾ in. long; sexes alike; adults rusty brown, streaked above, yellow at bend of wing, dingy white, *unstreaked*, below; buff on breast; dark bill, noticeably larger than that of small-billed chipping and field sparrows; is best identified by habitat, the only reddish-backed sparrow of overgrown fields and pine woods (Weston, 1968); immatures like adults but streaked below, especially on breast; lives in Southeast (where permanent resident) commonly in dry, open pine or oak woods with undercover grasses, shrubs, scrub palmetto, edges of cultivated fields; farther north (Ohio and W.Va.) summers in abandoned fields grown to goldenrods, asters, grasses, on dry eroded slopes of hill country, almost never in valleys (Weston, 1968); secretive, spends most of time on ground; like Henslow's and Le Conte's sparrows, difficult to see or to flush; in nesting season located by male's ringing song comparable in sweet ethereal quality to hermit thrush's,

quality suggests field sparrow's; sings from pine trees in South; from fences, tall weeds farther north; male also gives flight song; first songs in late Feb. in deep South, and into Aug. in all parts of range; arrives northern part nesting range (W.Va.) in Mar.–Apr. (Weston, 1968).

Feeding Habits: Forages much on ground; eats beetles, weevils, bugs, grasshoppers, crickets, also snails, spiders, millipedes, seeds of pines, grasses, sedges, wood sorrel.

Nest: On ground, as difficult to find as those of grasshopper and Savannah sparrows; in clump of grass, weeds, under saw palmetto, bush, or vine; built by female, of weed stems, grasses, lined with horsehair, corn silk, some nests domed (arched over) with grasses.

Eggs: Apr.–July; 3–5, white.

Incubation: About 12–14 days; young leave nest when about 10 days old (Weston, 1968); incubating bird sits very close; on disturbance, runs from nest uttering snakelike hiss, or flutters about like crippled bird; two broods a year.

Other Name: Pine-woods sparrow.

Host to Cowbirds: Uncommon, a few records from three states—Mo., Ky., and W.Va. (Friedmann, 1963).

Range: Nests from se. Mo., ne. Ill., c. Ind., sw. and n.-c. Ohio, sw. Pa., e. W.Va., w. and c. Md., south to Ga., se. Okla., se. Tex., s.-c. La., s. Miss. s. Ala., c. Fla.; winters north to N.C., se. Okla., ne. Tex., to w.-c. Miss., s.-c. La., c. Ala.

Sparrow, Baird's, *Ammodramus bairdii* (am-ODD-rah-mus BAIRD-ih-eye); genus name: Lat., from Gr. *ammos*, sand, and *dramein*, to run (Coble, 1954); species name: given in 1844 by John James Audubon, who discovered the bird at junction of Missouri and Yellowstone R., for his friend Spencer F. Baird, later secretary of the Smithsonian Institution. (Color ill., page 312.) On grasslands, Mississippi R. to Rockies; 5–5½ in. long; sexes outwardly alike; pale, buffy brown above, streaked, and white below with narrow breast band of fine black streaks, has yellow, or ocher, stripe in middle of crown (Lane, 1968a); starts northward in small groups in late Feb. from grasslands of Ariz., N.M., Tex., arrives main nesting grounds in prairies of Sask., Man., in Apr.–May, where males establish territories of 1–2 acres each in long grass of dry prairie; males then sing much from tuft of grass, low bush, fence post, tinkling syllables with trill, *zip-zip-zip-zr-r-r*, one of most pleasing songs of all "grass sparrows," more musical than insectlike songs of grasshopper, Savannah, Le Conte's, sharp-tailed, and Henslow's sparrows; call note, sharp *chip.*

Feeding Habits: Forages on ground, reluctant to fly, runs like mouse through grass; eats seeds of grasses such as brome, fescue, three-awn, green foxtail; weed seeds: pigweeds, mustards, ragweed, plantain, evening primrose, etc.; also grasshoppers, leafhoppers, caterpillars, moths, spiders.

Nest: Built on ground in drier parts of prairie in tangled grass, sometimes under low shrub, often close together in small community, in slight cavity in ground, of interwoven grasses, weed stems, lined with finer grasses, horsehair.

Eggs: June–Aug.; 3–6, usually 3–5, white, dotted, splotched with lavender, browns.

Incubation: By female, 11–12 days; young leave nest when 8–10 days old, fly when about 13 days old.
Host to Cowbirds: Only 6 records, all from Man. and N.D. (Friedmann, 1963).
Weights: Five killed at TV tower, Kans., Sept., 1965, all in juvenal plumage, 16–18.2 gr. (Rising, 1965a), or about ⅔ oz.
Range: Nests from s. Alta., s. Sask., s. Man., south to nw. Mont., nw. and c. S.D., se. N.D., c. and w. Minn.; winters from se. Ariz., s. N.M., south into Mexico. Accidental in N.Y.

Sparrow, Bell's. *See* Sparrow, sage.

Sparrow, black-chinned, *Spizella atrogularis* (spy-ZELL-ah ay-tro-gew-LAY-riss); genus name: Lat. dim., from Gr. *spiza,* finch; species name: from Lat. *ater, atri,* black, and *gula,* throat (Coble, 1954). (Color ill., page 313.) Tablelands and rugged mountain slopes of sw. U.S. and in Mexico; 5–5½ in. long; has juncolike gray head, breast, and pink bill (male also has black chin patch in nesting season); brown back is streaked, wings brown with white bars; white belly, gray rump; immatures and females have unmarked gray head and breast (without black chin) and contrasting rusty-brown back; lives in dense chaparral and sagebrush or other brushland, on sloping ground and rocky outcrops with scattered pinyons, junipers; in Calif., summer resident in Providence Mtns., 5,000–7,000 ft.; in N.M. on rugged mountain ridges to 6,000–7,000 ft.; are scattered in numbers but in loose local colonies in nesting season; shy, lives under shrub canopy but visits water seepage places and small streams of canyons; male singing from conspicuous perches in top of yuccas, tall chamisal, or rarely in tree, reveals area of nest; canarylike, clear trill carries far down mountain glades, song begins with emphasis, descends gradually (Newman, 1968), *sweet-sweet-sweet-weet-trrrrrrrr,* resembles song of field sparrow.

Feeding Habits: Moves through brush when foraging, may fly near ground through tunnel-like openings under brush or in air over tops of pinyons, junipers, coffeeberry, sage, searching for insects, small seeds.
Nest: Built among twigs of low shrub, a compact cup of dried grasses, weed stems, lined with soft plant fibers, a few feathers, animal hairs, 6 in. to 4 ft. above ground.
Eggs: Apr.–July; 2–5, usually 2–4, pale blue, unmarked or some with few small scattered spots of brown.
Incubation: About 13 days; age when young leave nest unknown.
Other Names: Arizona black-chinned sparrow; California black-chinned sparrow.
Host to Cowbirds: Three records: one in N.M., two in Calif. (Friedmann, 1963).
Weights: About 11.5 gr., or ⅓–½ oz.
Range: Nests from c. Calif., s. Nev., sw. Utah, c. Ariz., s. N. Mex., w. Tex., south to c. Mexico; winters north to s. Calif., s. Ariz., w. Tex.

Sparrow, black-throated, *Amphispiza bilineata* (am-fih-SPY-zah by-lin-eh-AY-tah); genus name: Lat., from Gr. *amphi,* around, and *spiza,* finch, "finch on both sides"; species name: Lat., two-lined, or "two-striped"; refers to stripes on head. (Color ill., page 312.) Great Basin and desert country (cactus, sage, mesquite) of w. U.S.—Calif., Wyo. to Tex. and Mexico; 4¾–5¼ in. long; sexes outwardly similar; *jet-black throat,* gray, *unstreaked* back; *white facial stripes on gray head;* immature has facial stripes but is finely streaked on throat (instead of black throat); no wing bars; black rounded tail with white on outer tail feathers helps distinguish it; dwells in driest, hottest parts of desert uplands, rocky slopes, lives in Death Valley, Calif., along lower Colorado R. and in s. Nev., in places where creosote bushes, cholla cactuses, dwarf juniper, yucca, agave, sagebrush grow (Banks, 1968b); bird at some seasons is apparently independent of water and satisfies its daily intake from its foods (Smyth and Bartholomew, 1966); in deserts of Ariz. north of Tucson, song of male reported as tinkling, canarylike; another observer reported it with syllables *queet! queet! toodle-oodle-oodle-oodle,* with rising inflection on the *"queets";* sings from tops of bushes and from ground; call note is sharp *chip.*

Feeding Habits: Forages on ground for seeds, gravel, and insects.
Nest: Usually builds Apr.–June; extremes, Feb.–Aug. (Banks, 1968b); well concealed, in forking branches of small bushes, thorny shrubs, junipers, a few feet above ground; loosely built cup of grasses, weed stems, lined with plant fibers, rabbit fur, cow hair, wool, porcupine hairs.
Eggs: Apr.–Aug.; 3–4, white, pale blue, unmarked.
Incubation: Period of and age when young leave nest unreported.
Other Names: Black-throat; desert black-throated sparrow; desert sparrow.
Host to Cowbirds: A few records; most from Tex., two from Ariz. (Friedmann, 1963).
Range: Nests from ne. Calif., n. Nev., n. Utah, sw. Wyo., s. and w. Colo., nw. Okla., and n.-c. Tex., south through desert areas to s. Baja Calif., islands Gulf of California, into Mexico; winters from se. Calif., s. Nev., c. Ariz., sw. N.M., south to Baja Calif., islands in Gulf of Calif., and Mexico; has strayed to Wisc., Ill., Ohio, N.J., and Mass.

Sparrow, Botteri's, *Aimophila botterii* (ay-MOFF-ih-lah BOT-er-ih-eye); genus name: *see* Sparrow, Bachman's; species name: given in 1857 for Matteo Botteri, Dalmatian botanist and traveler who discovered the bird near Orizaba, Mexico. Reaches U.S. in extreme s. Tex. and se. Ariz.; 5¼–6¼ in. long; sexes outwardly alike; grayish above with tawny streaks, rusty tinge on wings and tail (much browner tail than that of similar, grayer Cassin's sparrow, which has dusky tail); breast dingy white or buff-white, unstreaked; summers in U.S. in grasslands with scattering of brush or small trees; in Ariz., favors giant sacaton or other tall grasses with mesquite and catclaw; in Tex., likes salt-grass *(Spartina)* habitat with some yucca, prickly pear, and mesquite; in Mexico, prefers open grasslands with live oaks, etc. (see Monson, 1968); arrives Tex. late Apr. to May, in Ariz. latter part of

Botteri's sparrow

FINCH FAMILY

May, disappears by end of Sept.; spends most of time on ground; flushes readily, flies to nearest bush, post, frequently drops back into grass after short flight, often scurries over ground like mouse; male's song, faint, dry, tinkling and rattling, uttered from top of tree, bush, post, never from ground (Monson, 1968); very different from song of similar Cassin's sparrow; usually sings *wit-wit-cheeup-cheeup-cheer, cheer, chee chee che ee e e e*.

Feeding Habits: Known only from a few stomachs in Tex.; largely insects in summer, also seeds of weeds and grasses.
Nest: On ground, in Tex. built mainly in June, said to be built of grasses, but no detailed information because little studied.
Eggs: Laying dates practically lacking; eggs reportedly 2–5, white.
Incubation: Period of and age when young leave nest unreported.
Range: Nests in se. Ariz., s. Tex., south into Mexico; winters probably in Mexico but winter range still vague.

Sparrow, Brewer's, *Spizella breweri* (spy-ZELL-ah BREW-er-eye); genus name: *see* Sparrow, black-chinned; species name: given in 1856 by John Cassin, Philadelphia ornithologist, in honor of Thomas M. Brewer, Boston physician, ornithologist, and friend of John James Audubon. (Color ill., page 312.) Small sparrow closely associated with arid sagebrush country of the Great Basin of w. U.S., and Pacific slopes; ranges from Yuk. south to Mexican border; 5–5¼ in. long; sexes outwardly similar; gray-white stripe over each eye; upperparts brownish, streaked; top of head finely *streaked* (similar chipping sparrow has rufous crown); clear grayish breast, belly white; although closely associated with sagebrush over much of its range, in Yuk. and B.C. lives in balsam-willow habitat, alpine meadows, sometimes nests in higher mountains in sagebrush above timberline; in parts of sagebrush country of Great Basin, may outnumber all other birds; once estimated most abundant sparrow in Death Valley, Calif. (Paine, 1968); is shy, wary, and inconspicuous on nesting range, but, attracted to baby chick scratch feed in Calif. gardens in winter, becomes extraordinarily tame (see Gander in Terres, 1958); male sings usually from end of branch of shrub or tree near nest, as many as 47 pairs on 100 acres in e. Wash.; many males sing in chorus at dawn and at twilight on nesting grounds; a buzzy, long-sustained, cicada-like trill, one of most widespread sounds of sagebrush country.

Feeding Habits: Forages much on ground; in spring and summer eats large numbers of alfalfa weevils; also eats aphids, beet leafhoppers, caterpillars, some beetles; in fall and winter, weed seeds; can exist on diet only of dry seeds; gets daily water or moisture needs from its food (Ohmart and Smith, 1970).
Nest: In sagebrush, cactus, and small shrubs, sometimes in vineyards (Calif.), usually within 4 ft. of ground (rarely on ground); neat compact structure of dried grasses, lined with brown rootlets, horsehair.
Eggs: Apr.–July; usually 3–4, bluish green, speckled, spotted with browns.

Incubation: 13 days (Reilly, 1968); age when young leave nest unreported.
Host to Cowbirds: Three records: Wyo. and N.M. (Friedmann, 1963).
Hybrids: See under Clay-colored sparrow.
Weights: In Ariz., winter and spring, series of 60 live birds, 10–12 gr. (Ohmart and Smith, 1970), or slightly more than ⅓ oz.
Range: Nests from sw. Yuk., nw. B.C., w.-c. Alta., sw. Sask., and sw. N.D., south to s. Calif., s. Nev., c. Ariz., and nw. N.M.; winters from s. Calif., s. Nev., c. Ariz., s. N.M., and c. Tex., south to s. Baja Calif., c. Mexico, and s. Tex.

Sparrow, bush. *See* Sparrow, field, and Sparrow, song.

Sparrow, Canada. *See* Sparrow, tree, and Sparrow, white-throated.

Sparrow, Cape Sable, or seaside, *Ammospiza maritima mirabilis* (am-oh-SPY-zah mih-RAB-ih-liss); genus name: Lat., from Gr. *ammos*, sand, and *spiza*, finch; species name: *see* Sparrow, seaside; subspecies name: Lat., miraculous, wonderful; common name: for Cape Sable, the marshy prairies of Cape Sable, Fla., where it was discovered in 1918. Previously thought to be a distinct species and first new species discovered in N. America in 20th century (*see* Species); however, determined by American Ornithologists' Union (1973) to be an isolated race, or subspecies of the more common seaside sparrow, *Ammospiza maritima;* is on Threatened Wildlife List (Office of Endangered Species, 1973); Cape Sable sparrow is about 6 in. long and is only seaside sparrow in sw. Fla.; streaked, with upperparts more green and underparts more white than in any other seaside sparrow; sexes alike; hind neck and back yellow-olive streaked with fuscous; scapulars edged with white; tail fuscous, edges of wings yellow; white underparts moderately streaked on breast and sides; lives year-round a few miles inland behind sw. coast of Fla. northwest of Cape Sable since devastating hurricane of night of Sept. 2, 1935, which apparently obliterated it from marshes of the cape (Stimson, 1968); however, some adults and young rediscovered in Cape Sable marshes in June 1970 (see Werner, 1971). For long history of destruction of Cape Sable sparrow by hurricanes, drought, fires, drainage, see Stimson (1961; 1968); the bird prefers marshes that vary from salt through brackish to fresh water, with extensive growths of cordgrass (*Spartina*), also of salt grass (*Salicornia*) and saw grass (*Mariscus);* lives in small colonies, in nesting season about 9–10 pairs per sq. mi. marsh (Austin, see in Stimson, 1968); males sing usually from top of grass stem, *churr-buz-z-z*, the last syllable accented and prolonged, or *churr-e-e-e-e*, last part from distance sounds like *ee-e-e-e-e* note of red-winged blackbird; other short calls or alarm notes, *zup-zup-zup*, and high-pitched, twittering *zee-zee-zee;* is shy, secretive, spends most of time concealed on or near ground; in summer, adults and young may be lured from cover by "squeaking" (*see* Sounds That Attract Birds).

Feeding Habits: Eats almost wholly insects: dragonfly nymphs, moths, caterpillars, beetles, bugs, wasps, flies, crickets, grasshoppers; also spiders, some small amphipods and mollusks.
Nest: On ground or waist high, attached to upright marsh grass, built of salt-marsh grasses, lined with finer grasses.
Eggs: Mar.–May; 3–5, green-, gray-, or blue-white, speckled and spotted with reddish browns.
Incubation: Period of and age when young leave nest unreported; probably similar to that of other seaside sparrows.
Range: Resident, sw. Fla., from Ochopee Marshes near Everglades, southeast toward headwaters of Huston R. and mouth of Gum Slough to Shark R. basin; formerly (recently re-established?) on Cape Sable.

Sparrow, Cassin's, *Aimophila cassinii* (ay-MOFF-ih-lah cass-IN-ih-eye); genus name: *see* Sparrow, Bachman's; species name: given in 1852 by Samuel W. Woodhouse in honor of John Cassin, Philadelphia ornithologist. (Color ill., page 313.) Ground-dwelling sparrow most abundant in short-grass plains, w. Tex., Okla., e. N.M., and Colo. (Williams and LeSassier, 1968); 5¼–5¾ in. long; plain grayish sparrow; sexes outwardly alike; head finely streaked with brown, grayish upperparts, either sharply or obscurely marked with black, sandy brown; buffy white underparts unmarked in adults; immatures have streaked breast; prefers dry, open country of sparse short grasses with scattered desert cactus, or mesquite plains with patches of yucca, occasionally in dry foothills or mountain slopes (Davis Mtns. of Tex.), up to 4,000 ft. elevation on mesa surrounding Chisos Mtns.; in N.M. to 5,500 ft. at lower edge of juniper belt; male uses shrubs, yuccas interspersed in its grasslands for singing perches; begins singing late Mar. in s. and w. Tex.; when another male comes near, male in territory launches out from top of bush to sing in flight; exquisitely sweet, haunting song, begins with low soft notes followed by long, loud, high-pitched liquid trill; sings as he floats downward with head up, tail spread; call note is loud *tsip*, also utters a rapid *tzee, tzee, tzee.*

Feeding Habits: In spring and summer, eats caterpillars, beetles; in winter, seeds of weeds, grasses; eats milo sorghum (grain) and ground corn at bird feeding stations; in season, eats flower buds of blackthorn (Williams and LeSassier, 1968); like Brewer's and black-throated sparrows, can exist without drinking water.
Nest: On ground in bunch of grass; foot of small shrub; among grasses under brush heap; often in tangled patch of cactus on ground, but equally above ground low in branches of cactus or other bush; cup-shaped, of weed stems, dead grasses, lined with finer grasses, rootlets, sometimes some horsehair.
Eggs: Apr.–July; 3–5, usually 4, white, unmarked.
Incubation: Period of and age when young first fly unknown.
Host to Cowbirds: Infrequent, records for Tex. only (Friedmann, 1963).
Range: Nests from se. Ariz., sw. N.M., c. Colo., c.-w. Kans., w. Okla., c. and w. Tex, south into

Mexico; winters from sw. Ariz., w. and s.-c. Tex., south into Mexico; has strayed to Island Beach, N.J.

Sparrow, chipping, *Spizella passerina* (spy-ZELL-ah pass-er-EYE-nah); genus name: *see* Sparrow, black-chinned; species name: Lat., pertaining to a sparrow; common name: from its chipping call notes and dry chipping trill. (Color ill., page 313.) Most domestic of all N. American sparrows; common in summer from Alaska and Canada south throughout most of U.S.; 5–5¾ in. long; wingspread 8–9 in.; sexes alike; adults have bright chestnut cap; bill black in spring; a *broad white line over each eye and black streak through it;* light brown or drab above, streaked with black and rusty brown; plain below, unmarked gray or ashen; tail long, slightly forked; young in late summer distinguished by small size, finely streaked below; summers in open grassy woodlands, forest clearings, along shores of lakes and streams, cottonwood groves in prairies, in mountains of Utah, Ariz., 5,000–11,000 ft.; in city and country parks, gardens, orchards, farmyards; migrates to northern part of nesting range in Apr.–May; in South, males singing on territories by late Mar. (Stull, 1968); song is series of *chip* notes, all in one pitch, sometimes given slowly, sometimes so rapidly they run together in trill; sometimes sings at night; one of smallest and tamest of sparrows; comes to porch or yard for bread crumbs, may feed from hands.

Feeding Habits: Eats large amounts of grass seeds (especially crabgrass, pigeon grass), also seeds of clover, ragweed, knotweed, amaranth, wood sorrel, dandelion, etc.; weevils, leaf beetles, leafhoppers, caterpillars, grasshoppers, bugs, ants, also spiders, wasps; pecks at salt blocks.
Nest: Built by female, often on limb of spruce, pine, cedar, arborvitae, also in orchard trees, in vines, from 1 ft. to 40 or even 56 ft. up (Stull, 1968); usually lower than 6 ft.; rarely on ground; built of dead grasses, weed stems, rootlets, cup lined with fine grasses, hairs of humans, dogs, cattle, deer, raccoons, bison, especially fond of using black horsehair.
Eggs: Mar.–Aug.; 3–5, usually 4, pale blue-green, speckled, spotted, blotched, and scrawled with browns, dark blue, black.
Incubation: By female, 11–14 days, depending on air temperatures; male feeds female at nest; young leave nest when 8–12 days old, usually when 9–10 days old (Stull, 1968); sometimes two broods a year.
Other Names: Chip-bird; chippy; hair-bird; hair sparrow; little house sparrow; social sparrow.
Age: In Mich., average age of ten banded birds, 2½ years; of nine banded Me., Man., Wisc., Mass., S.C., four lived to 6 years old, four to 7, one to 9; one banded Beachton, Ga., lived to 9 years, 9 months, old.
Albinism: A "pure-white one" reported by Deane (1880).
Flight Speed: Timed in New England, 15–20 m.p.h. (White, 1935).
Host to Cowbirds: One of commonest victims of brown-headed cowbird, more than 600 records (Friedmann, 1963).

Hybrids: See under Clay-colored sparrow.
Weights: Autumn migration, coastal N.J. (7), 9.7–14 gr. (Murray and Jehl, 1964), or ⅓–½ oz.; in Mich. (19), 10.3–19.7 gr. (Becker and Stack, 1944), or ⅓–¾ oz.
Range: Nests from e.-c. Alaska, c. Yuk., s. Mack., east across Canada to n. Ont., s. Que., sw. Newfoundland, south to n. Baja Calif., c., w., and se. Ariz.; south into Mexico to n. Nicaragua, east along Gulf coast to n. Fla.; winters from c. Calif., s. Nev., c. Ariz., c. N.M., w. Tex., c. Okla. Ark., Tenn., c. Ala., c. and w. Ga., Va., Md. (rarely farther north), southward.

Sparrow, clay-colored, *Spizella pallida* (spy-ZELL-ah PAL-ih-dah); genus name: *see* Sparrow, black-chinned; species name: Lat., pallid, pale. (Color ill., page 314.) A locally common sparrow of midwestern plains and prairies and in mountain valleys of w. Canada (Root, 1968); 5–5½ in. long; sexes alike; paler than chipping sparrow, striped back is smoky gray, has pale, clear breast; white stripe over each eye; has *brown ear patches,* sharply outlined; *pale gray or buff stripe in middle of crown;* prominent *white malar stripe* on each side of throat; two white wing bars; immature like immature chipping sparrow but has buff-brown rump (chipping has gray); summers on brushy grasslands and where fires and lumbering have opened forests; leaves main wintering grounds in Mexico and moves northward in waves of 25–100 (Root, 1968); migrates by day and by night; arrives n. U.S. and Canadian nesting grounds in May; male advertises territory (¼ to 1 acre) by singing insectlike song of short notes, *zee-zee-zee* or *bzzz-bzzz-bzzz,* from low in tree, shrub, weed, fence, or utility wire, singing reaches height in mid-June; one of few Canadian prairie birds that sings into heat of July; call or alarm notes, *tsip* or *chip.*

Feeding Habits: Forages mostly on ground or in low shrubbery; eats many kinds of seeds of grasses, weeds, garden flowers: sweet alyssum, cockscomb, tumbleweed, Bermuda grass, crabgrass, mustard, mesquite, etc.; will eat finely cracked corn, millet, sunflower seeds, bread, at feeders; in summer eats grasshoppers and other insects (Root, 1968).
Nest: Built by female, in shrubby pastures, parklands, edges of fields, poplar-willow bluffs, etc., from ground level to about 4½ ft. up; in tuft of dead grasses at base of wild rose, snowberry, thistle, sweet fern, goldenrod; also in low branch of hawthorn, serviceberry, conifer; cup-shaped, of grasses, fine twigs, weed stems, rootlets, lined with fine grasses, horsehair, deer hair, cattle hair.
Eggs: May–July; 3–5, usually 3–4, pale blue-green, speckled, blotched with browns.
Incubation: Probably by both sexes, alternately, 11–14 days; young leave nest when 7–9 days old; sometimes adults raise two broods (Mich. and Wisc.).
Age: One, banded Wilton, N.D., still alive when 5 years old.
Host to Cowbirds: Frequent (Friedmann, 1963).
Hybrids: Two records of hybrids: one between clay-colored and Brewer's sparrow, another be-

tween clay-colored and chipping sparrow in area in Mich. where both species nest.
Weights: Coastal N.J. in fall (1), 10.9 gr. (Murray and Jehl, 1964), or about ⅓ oz.; adult males (2) killed fall 1954 at Kans. TV tower, 11.6 and 12.2 gr., or about ½ oz., adult female (1), 11.1 gr. (Tordoff and Mengel, 1956).
Range: Nests from ne. B.C., s.-c. Mack., c. Sask., c. Man., w. Ont., and n. Mich., south to sw. Alta., s.-c. Mont., se. Wyo., s.-c. Colo., s. Neb., n. Io., s. Wisc., c. Mich., s. Ont. (sparsely west to B.C. and south to n. Tex.), and recently (June 15, 1971) in w. N.Y. (Allegany County)—see details in Brooks (1971); winters from s. Baja Calif., s. Tex., south into Mexico casually reported in e. U.S. in migration along coast from Fla. north to New England.

Sparrow, desert. *See* Sparrow, black-throated.

Sparrow, dusky seaside, *Ammospiza maritima nigrescens* (am-oh-SPY-zah nih-GRES-enz); genus and species names: *see* Sparrow, Cape Sable; subspecies name: Lat., growing, or turning, black; *dusky* refers to to general dark color. Once considered a distinct species (A.O.U. *Check-list,* 1957) but determined by American Ornithologists' Union (1973) to be a subspecies of its close relative the seaside sparrow, *Ammospiza maritima*—see Trost (1968); one of endangered birds of U.S., largely limited to salt and brackish marshes of Atlantic coast of Fla. within 10-mi. radius of Titusville, Brevard County, has one of most restricted ranges of any N. American bird (Trost, 1968); on list of Threatened Wildlife of United States (see Office of Endangered Species, 1973); 5½–6½ in. long; sexes outwardly alike; upperparts blackish, underparts heavily streaked with black; blackest of seaside sparrows; only one in its range; a few stay in nesting marshes all winter; prefers to nest in damp but not flooded salt marsh with small open ponds; formerly marshes east side of Indian R., where it had ideal habitat (see details in Trost, 1968), but with diking and flooding for mosquito control, population began disappearing; in nesting marshes, males begin to sing from perches atop marsh plants in early Mar., utters song like *toodle-raeeee* or buzzy *cut-azheeeee,* also sings flight song, climbs to 20 ft. in air, flutters back to perch still singing; banding has shown that male returns to same territory in successive years; in nesting season, adults bold, come within 15–20 ft. of human intruder at nest; out of nesting season, shy, concealed in marsh, but Sprunt (1954a) suggests that pausing by marsh and using the "squeak" will often lure birds to grass tops where can be seen (*see* Sounds That Attract Birds). See details of status and threats to in Committee on Rare and Endangered Wildlife Species (1966); Trost (1968); and Sharp (1970). In censuses of this bird in 1977 and 1978, only 24 males were seen; no females, although they are less conspicuous, and no young birds were seen (Lapham, 1979). According to Anonymous (1980b), is possibly most endangered N. American bird; in recent years only a dozen or so counted; not one positively identified as a female, not known if females exist; no nesting observed since 1976.

Dusky seaside sparrow

FINCH FAMILY

Feeding Habits: Eats mostly insects—grasshoppers, crickets, beetles, bugs, horseflies, dragonflies, caterpillars—also spiders and seeds of sedges.

Nest: Small, neat cup of dried grasses in dense patches of pickleweed, bulrushes, or salt hay, 3–20 in. above damp ground.

Eggs: Apr.–July; 2–5, usually 3–4, dull white or pale blue-white, speckled, spotted with browns.

Incubation: By female, 12–13 days; young leave nest when 8–9 days old; apparently two broods a year.

Other Names: Black shore finch; Merritt Island sparrow.

Sparrow, English. Another name for the house sparrow in Weaverbird Family.

Sparrow, Eurasian tree. *See* Sparrow, European tree.

Sparrow, European tree. A member of the Weaverbird Family.

Sparrow, field, *Spizella pusilla* (spy-ZELL-ah pew-SIL-lah); genus name: *see* Sparrow, black-chinned; species name: Lat., very small. (Color ill., page 315.) E. U.S., e. Canada, west to prairies and plains, south to Gulf coast and Fla.; 5¼–6 in. long; wingspread 7¾–8½ in.; sexes alike; adult has *pink bill*, rusty upperparts; rusty cap not so bright as reddish cap of chipping sparrow, and has no central stripe in cap as in similar clay-colored sparrow (Walkinshaw, 1968a); *buff eye-ring* gives it blank expression; sides of head gray with narrow brown streak in back of each eye; two faint bars on each wing; buffy wash on breast and flanks, underparts clear (no streaking); young are finely streaked below; summers in old fields and pastures overgrown with briars, sumac, hawthorn, etc., thicketed fencerows; edges of open, unplowed fields; brushy cut-over woods; rarely nests near houses as do chipping and song sparrows; gentle, rarely aggressive toward other birds; from wintering grounds in s. U.S. moves northward, mostly at night, in Mar.–Apr. in small flocks; male defends territory against other males on nesting grounds by flying from tree to bush in patrol, and singing from bush, tall weed, fence, tree, beginning at dawn, a clear, sweet, plaintive *seea-seea-seea-seea-wee-wee-wee-wee;* sometimes sings on moonlit nights; alarm note is sharp *chip.*

Feeding Habits: Forages much on ground for weevils, beetles, grasshoppers, caterpillars, leafhoppers, ants, flies, wasps, also spiders; picks up grass and weed seeds, some oats at harvesttime.

Nest: On or near ground, in clump of weeds, tuft of grass, or above, from a few inches to about 3 ft. in blackberry, huckleberry, sumac, hawthorn bushes, hickory saplings (Walkinshaw, 1968a); rarely 5–10 ft. up in tree; built by female of coarse dead grasses, leaves interwoven with finer grasses, cup lined with rootlets, hair, some lined entirely with horsehair.

Eggs: Apr.–Sept.; 3–6, usually 3–5, cream, pale-green, or blue-white, speckled, spotted with browns.

Incubation: By female, 10½–17 days, average 11.6 days (Walkinshaw, 1968a); young leave nest when 7–8 days old, at about 12–13 days old can fly short distance; independent of parents when 26–34 days old; some young males sing brief snatches of song by late summer; two or three broods raised a year.

Other Names: Bush sparrow; field bunting; field chippy; ground-bird; huckleberry-bird; rush sparrow; wood sparrow.

Accidents: Many killed by cars on roads; many killed when migrating at night by striking TV towers and cables.

Age: At Nashville, Tenn., of twelve banded, some retrapped when 4, 4½, 5, and 6 years old; one banded Powdermill Nature Reserve, Rector, Pa., trapped and released in same area when 6 years, 11 months old.

Host to Cowbirds: Frequent, more than 125 records (Friedmann, 1963).

Hybrids: Gray (1958) reported a cross between a field sparrow and a vesper sparrow but gave no details.

Weights: Conn., Apr. and Oct., adults (22), 10.6–14.4 gr. (Wetherbee, 1934), or ⅓–½ oz.

Range: Nests from nw. Mont., n. N.D., c. Minn., n. Wisc., n.-c. Mich., s. Ont., sw. Que., and s. Me., south to c. Tex., La., s. Miss., Ala., s. Ga., casually to n. Fla.; winters from Kans., Mo., Ohio, W.Va., s. Pa., and Mass., south to Mexico, s. Tex., Gulf coast, and c. Fla.

Sparrow, five-striped, *Aimophila quinquestriata* (ay-MOFF-ih-lah kwin-kweh-strie-AY-tah); genus name: *see* Sparrow, Bachman's; species name: Lat., five-striped. A gray-brown Mexican sparrow that gets its common and species names from its five white head stripes; occurs casually in se. Ariz.; Phillips *et al.* (1964) report the only known collected specimen of this bird in Ariz. was at west base of the Santa Rita Mtns., June 18, 1957; has since been seen on Sonoita Creek, near Patagonia, Ariz., Jan. 12, 1969; two on June 14, and young ones seen on Aug. 18 and later (Snider, 1969); pair that spent summer near Patagonia brought two young out of nest on Aug. 18, 1969; seen feeding them Aug. 23 (Snider, 1970); 5½ in. long; gray-brown above; resembles a darkened black-throated sparrow or sage sparrow with slaty color over its flanks; its dark cheeks and throat give it strong resemblance to the black-throated sparrow, as does the reddish tinge on its back, but slaty color beneath is obvious when bird held in hands; black blotch on chest; juveniles are unstreaked (Phillips *et al.,* 1964); lives on grassy or brushy, rocky, semi-desert slopes in parts of Mexico; breeds regularly north in Sonora to Imuris region about 45 miles south of Nogales.

Range: Mountains in w. Mexico; ne. Sonora through w. Durango, w. Chihuahua; south, locally, to Jalisco (Peterson and Chalif, 1973). Casual in s.-c. Ariz.

Sparrow, Forbush's. *See* Sparrow, Lincoln's.

Sparrow, fox, *Passerella iliaca* (pass-er-EL-ah eye-lih-AY-cah); genus name: dim. of Lat. *passer,* a sparrow; species name: Lat., relating to flanks (marked) (Coble, 1954); common name:

from reddish or tawny "fox" color of feathers. (Color ills., page 315.) Summers in Alaska, in Canada from Atlantic to Pacific coast, and parts of w. U.S.; 6¼–7½ in. long; wingspread 10½–11¾ in.; sexes appear alike; heavily streaked breast, in e. U.S. has foxy red upperparts (in West, dark brown or gray), bright rufous, or reddish, tail—hermit thrush has similar red tail but has *spotted* breast, not streaked as in fox sparrow, and thinner bill; fox sparrow has dark central breast spot as in smaller song sparrow; lives in dense woodland thickets; during migration often sings during day, moves northward at night in Mar.–Apr.; on nesting grounds dense brushy cover also outstanding requirement, whether thorny tangles of mountain misery (*Ceanothus*) on slopes of Calif. mountains or conifers, alders, willows in Far North (Terrill, 1968); male usually sings from concealed perch in thickets in general area of nest; one of finest, if not best, of singers among sparrows; clear, exultant, melodious, flutelike notes, alarm note is loud *smack*, also utters sharp *chip* and other notes.

Feeding Habits: Forages on ground, scratches, kicking backward with both feet simultaneously so vigorously as to dig hole in ground or snow to humus rich in small animal life; however, essentially vegetarian; eats weed seeds, especially *Polygonum*, blueberries, elderberries, grapes, and other wild fruit; also beetles, crane flies, chinch bugs, spiders, millipedes, minute shellfish; comes to ground beneath feeding stations for wild bird seeds, bread crumbs.
Nest: Built commonly on ground in thickets, on dry ground edge of bog, dry hillsides, also in small spruces, willows along streams, small bushes; composed of twigs, mosses, rootlets, dried grasses, weed stems, chips, shreds of bark, cup lined with grasses, feathers, hairs of caribou, dogs, horses.
Eggs: May–July; 3–5, pale blue or pale green, thickly spotted with browns.
Incubation: Mostly by female, 12–14 days; age when young leave nest unreported.
Other Names: Ferruginous finch; foxy finch; fox-colored sparrow; fox-tail.
Age: One banded when adult in Calif., killed in trap at same place when 6 years old; one banded wild bird, trapped and released same place where banded, when 9 years, 9 months, old (Kennard, 1975).
Host to Cowbirds: Infrequent (Friedmann, 1963).
Weights: Conn. in spring (16), 29.59–47.38 gr. (Wetherbee, 1934), or 1–1¾ oz.; adult female (1) killed in fall at Kans. TV tower, 29.4 gr. (Tordoff and Mengel, 1956), or about 1 oz.
Range: Nests from n. Alaska east to n. Labrador, south to nw. Wash., in mountains to s. Calif., c. Nev., c. Utah, and c. Colo., and to c. Alta., c. Sask., s. Man., c. Ont., s. Que., and Newfoundland; winters along Pacific coast from s. B.C. to n. Baja Calif.; in interior from s. Utah, c. Colo., e. Kans., s. Iowa, s. Wisc., s. Mich., s. Ont., s. N.B., south to s. Ariz., w. and s. Tex., to Gulf coast, and c. Fla.

Sparrow, Gambel's. *See* Sparrow, white-crowned.

Sparrow, golden-crowned, *Zonotrichia atricapilla* (zoe-no-TRICK-ih-ah ay-trih-CAP-ih-lah); genus name: Lat., from Gr. *zone*, girdle, belt (band), and *thrix, trichos*, hair, refers to striped head feathers of birds of this genus; species name: Lat., "black-haired," refers to black border of crown. (Color ill., page 314.) Pacific coast, Alaska to Baja Calif.; 6–7 in. long; sexes outwardly similar; closely resembles white-crowned sparrow, with which it often associates in flocks in winter, but has orange-yellow stripe through center of crown and broad black border along sides of crown, not white line over eyes as in white-crowned; immature golden-crowned resembles female house sparrow but is browner, sometimes with dull yellow on crown (Kelly, 1968); in winter in c. and s. Calif.; usually remains in separate flocks that return same place year after year, in streamside thickets, chaparral broken by openings, and in garden shrubbery; starts north in Apr.; reaches breeding grounds, from Cascades in Wash. north to Alaska, in May; in Alaska summers on local mountains primarily in deep canyons above timberline; alder thickets between timberline and more alpine, heath-covered slopes higher country; male sings continuously in June from low bushes; song is three flutelike notes descending, suggesting words *oh dear me, three blind mice;* to miners laboring along Alaskan gold trails, sounded like *I'm so weary,* for which named it Weary Willie.

Feeding Habits: Forages mostly on ground, in fall eats buds and flowers of such annual garden plants as stocks, primulas, pansies, chrysanthemum, and succulent seedlings in truck gardens, newly sprouted weed seeds; some insects, seeds, wild fruit on nesting grounds.
Nest: Usually on (or close to) ground at base of willow, depression in steep bank; bulky, of fern leaves, stems, sticks, mosses, grasses, cup lined with grasses, moose hair.
Eggs: May–June; usually 3–5, cream to pale blue-white, speckled, spotted with browns.
Incubation: Period of and age when young leave nest unknown.
Other Names: Golden-crown; rain bird (Alaska).
Accidents: Many killed from striking patio and picture windows; also strike lighthouses in northward migration; one killed in migration by airplane at 10,000 ft. over Calif. (Miller, 1957).
Age: One, banded Stanford University campus, recaptured and released when 8 years old; another at least 10 (Stoner, 1969); another, banded Grey Lodge, Calif., trapped and released in same area when 9 years, 6 months, old (Kennard, 1975).
Flight Speed: Timed in Calif., 10.8–20.9 m.p.h. (Pearson, 1961).
Hybrids: In her summary Gray (1958) reported a golden-crowned sparrow crossbred with a white-throated sparrow (a golden-crowned with a white throat), and a golden-crowned with a white-crowned (a male, "presumed natural hybrid").
Range: Nests from w. coastal Alaska, s.-c. Yukon, south to se. Alaska, s. B.C., sw. Alta., and in Cascades to extreme n. Wash.; winters from s. B.C. south, principally in Cascades and

Five-striped sparrow

FINCH FAMILY

Sierras to n. Baja Calif., casually to Ariz., Mexico, east to Utah, Colo., and N.M.

Sparrow, grass. See Sparrow, Savannah, and Sparrow, vesper.

Sparrow, grasshopper, *Ammodramus savannarum* (am-OD-rah-mus sah-van-AY-rum); genus name: *see* Sparrow, Baird's; species name: Lat., of meadows; common name: from song, which is strikingly like stridulations of meadow grasshopper. (Color ill., page 316.) Ranges from Atlantic coast to Calif., s. Canada to s. Fla. and Mexican border; 4½–5¼ in. long; wingspread 8–8½ in.; sexes outwardly similar; only sparrow of grasslands without streaks or markings on breast; short, bristly tail; flat-headed, crown has pale stripe through center; yellow spot between eye and bill; yellow at bend of wings; upperparts streaked, gray-brown; breast and flanks pale buff; immature has streaked breast, resembles adult Henslow's sparrow but not so reddish on wings; flight rapid, fluttering, wrenlike, close to ground; migrating part of population usually leaves southern states and arrives at northern nesting grounds in U.S. and s. Canada Mar.–June; is true grassland bird like meadowlark, usually summers over most of range on meadows, hayfields, pastures, on prairies, in mountains of Pa., W.Va., up to 2,000–4,000 ft.; in Kissimmee prairies of Fla. on burned-over tracts; male lays claim to 1–3-acre territory by singing "grasshopper song" throughout day, accompanied by wing fluttering, from clump of grass, alfalfa stalk, weed, bush, post, utility wire, etc. (Smith, 1968); thin, wiry song, like *pit-tuck zee-ee-e-e-e-e-e-e-e-e;* often sings at night, female also sings; secretive, hops, also runs through grass when disturbed; flies zig-zag for short distance, then drops back into weeds or grass.

Feeding Habits: Eats most insects, especially grasshoppers, also spiders, myriapods, snails, earthworms, waste grain, seeds of weeds, grasses, sedges.
Nest: In loose colonies; on ground at base of clump of grass, alfalfa, clover, etc.; of grasses, lined with grass, rootlets, horsehair, sunk in slight depression in ground, top usually domed with grass at back.
Eggs: Apr.–Aug.; 3–6, commonly 4–5, cream-white, speckled, spotted with browns.
Incubation: By female, 11–12 days; young leave nest when 9 days old (Smith, 1968); commonly 2 broods (Reilly, 1968).
Other Name: Yellow-winged sparrow.
Host to Cowbirds: Seldom, 11 records (Friedmann, 1963).
Hybrids: Hybrid female—grasshopper sparrow with savannah sparrow (Dickerman, 1968).
Weights: Conn., adults (4), 17.53–17.80 gr. (Wetherbee, 1934); adult males (3) killed fall 1954, Kans. TV tower, 16.4–20.6 gr.; adult females (5), 16.8–18.9 gr. (Tordoff and Mengel, 1956), about ⅔–¾ oz.
Range: Nests from n. Calif., e. Wash., se. B.C., east to N.Y., n. Vt., c. N.H., and Me., south to s. Calif., c. Nev., n. Utah, c. Colo., c. Tex., Gulf coast and Fla., and from s. Mex. to n. S. America and some of West Indies; winters from c.

Calif., s. Ariz., Okla., Ark., Tenn., and N.C. to El Salvador.

Sparrow, Harris', *Zonotrichia querula* (zoe-no-TRICK-ih-ah KWER-you-lah); genus name: *see* Sparrow, golden-crowned; species name: Lat., complaining, lamenting (Coble, 1954), with reference to its plaintive song; common name: honors Edward Harris, friend and companion of John James Audubon on his Missouri R. expedition of 1843 (see Audubon, 1870; for history of discovery of this bird, see Baumgartner, 1968a). (Color ill., page 316.) Ranges from Tex., s. Calif., north through tall grass prairies of U.S. to stunted timber and Arctic tundra of n. and c. Canada; 7–7¾ in. long; related to better-known white-crowned and white-throated sparrows; sexes similar, female slightly duller; adults in summer have *black crown, face, throat, and upper breast; pink or light orange-yellow bill;* cheeks, nape, and sides of throat pale gray; back and sides streaked; underparts white; immature similar to adult but brown about head, *white* throat, crown barred with black; blotch of black across breast; on wintering grounds in Okla., lives mostly in shrubbery along creeks and edges of woods; all winter remains in flocks mostly of its own kind; unsuspicious but on nesting grounds in Far North, where lives in scattered patches of stunted timber, is wild, shy, and wary (Baumgartner, 1968a); male's summer song is single whistled, quavering note, repeated up to four or five times; mates may sing to each other; alarm note is loud *weenk.*

Feeding Habits: In U.S., mostly vegetable (92% of food): weed seeds, wild fruit, grain, seeds of grasses; also insects, spiders, snails; at feeding stations attracted to small grains, mixed bird seeds, suet, bread crumbs; kicks and scratches on ground for food, especially among fallen leaves, dry weed stalks.
Nest: On ground at base of dwarf trees, willow shrubs, side of wet mossy hummock, sunken in ground, built of mosses, grasses, weed stalks, rootlets, lined with fine grasses.
Eggs: June–July; 3–5, white or green-white, heavily speckled, spotted with browns (Baumgartner, 1968a).
Incubation: 1 record, 13½ days (Jehl and Russell, 1966).
Other Names: Black-hood; hooded sparrow; mourning sparrow.
Age: One banded on wintering grounds in Iowa returned each year to same place until 8 years old, when disappeared; one banded Kans. lived to 8½ years; one, banded Wisner, Neb., found dead when 9 years, 7 months, old (Kennard, 1975).
Weights: Adults, 28.4–48.8 gr. (Baumgartner, 1968a), or 1–1¾ oz.; first one banded N.J. (two or three sight records for state), Island Beach, 33.7 gr. (Adams, 1970).
Range: Nests n. Canada, from Mackenzie delta to Hudson Bay, south to ne. Sask., n. Man.; winters from s. B.C., s. Idaho, n. Utah, n. Colo., n. Neb., Iowa, south to s. Calif., s. Nev., c. Ariz., s.-c. Tex., n. La., and Tenn.

Sparrow, Henslow's, *Ammodramus henslowii* (am-OD-rah-mus HEN-slow-ih-eye);

genus name: *see* Sparrow, Baird's; species name: given in 1831 by John James Audubon for his friend John Stevens Henslow, professor of botany, Cambridge University, England. (Color ill., page 317.) E. and c. U.S.; meadows and marshy openings in woods; 4¾–5¼ in. long; wingspread 6¾–7½ in.; sexes alike; flat-headed, short-tailed, with pale bill; adults buff or brownish yellow above, head with blackish stripes, hind neck and upper back tinged *greenish;* breast and sides distinctly *streaked* (similar grasshopper sparrow has clear underparts); wings of both adults and young usually *reddish;* summers in weedy prairies, meadows, neglected grassy fields and pastures, often dotted with low shrubs; ground cover usually dense and a foot or two high; prefers low, damp places but also frequents dry upland fields; leaves wintering grounds in se. U.S. Mar.–Apr.; arrives north-central and northeastern states Apr.–May (Graber, 1968); male in full song on arriving in his territory of 1–2 acres; sings by day and at night, incessantly in rain; usually sings from weed or bush, sometimes from ground concealed in grass, a short *tis-lick* or *flee-sic.*

Feeding Habits: Forages on ground, eats especially small black *Nemobius* crickets so abundant in grassy fields, also tree crickets, katydids, beetles, bugs, caterpillars, parasitic wasps, ants, seeds of weeds, grasses, sedges (Graber, 1968).
Nest: Lives in loose colonies, on territories within, but boundaries not always rigidly defended, some males fight each other like tiny roosters; nest well concealed on or near ground, sometimes in depression, usually built at base of thick clump of grass, with bottom 2–3 in. off ground; usually a deep cup of grasses, dead weed parts, lined with finer grasses, sometimes with hair; some nests attached to vertical stems of grasses and herbs, 6–20 in. above ground.
Eggs: May–Aug.; 3–5, cream-white or pale green-white, speckled, spotted with browns.
Incubation: By female, 11 days; young leave nest when 9–10 days old; sometimes raises two broods.
Other Name: Henslow's bunting.
Host to Cowbirds: From locally common (Md.) to occasional (Friedmann, 1963).
Range: Nests from e. S.D., c. Minn., Wisc., Mich., s. Ont., c. N.Y., s. Vt., s. N.H., south to e. Kans., c. Mo., and s. Ill., n. Ky., W. Va., and N.C.; winters on Atlantic coastal plain from S.C. to s.-c. Fla., and from se. Tex. east to Fla.

Sparrow, hooded. See Sparrow, Harris'.

Sparrow, house. A member of the Weaver-bird Family.

Sparrow, Ipswich, *Passerculus sandwichensis princeps* (pass-ER-cue-lus san-witch-EN-sis PRIN-seps); genus name: Lat., little sparrow; species name: *see* Sparrow, savannah; subspecies name: Lat., principal, chief; *Ipswich* (IPS-which) for Ipswich, Mass., where discovered (shot) in 1868 by American ornithologist Charles J. Maynard. (Color ill., page 319.) Formerly regarded as full species, but now considered by American Ornithologists' Union (1973) to be a geographical (island) race, or subspecies, of the Savannah sparrow; only known breeding place was thought to be Sable Is. off Nova Scotia, about 60 mi. south of Cape Breton (Taverner, 1947), where it had previously been reported to have mated with Savannah sparrows (Finch, 1971c); however, Finch reported two females mated in summer 1971 to Savannah sparrows for first known time on mainland of Nova Scotia (see related discussion by Hailman, 1958, and by Elliott, 1968b); is on Threatened Wildlife List (Office of Endangered Species, 1973); 6–6¼ in. long; wingspread 9½–11¼ in.; sexes similar; very pale, sand-colored sparrow, larger than darker and browner Savannah sparrow; Ipswich appears almost ghostly white on dunes, yellow line over each eye prominent in spring but almost white in winter; general breeding range limited to area about 20 mi. long on Sable Is., but main wintering range more than 1,000 mi., although limited to Atlantic coastal strip sometimes only few hundred yards wide (Elliott, 1968b); some winter on Sable Is., but those far down s. Atlantic coast (S.C.) may start north by Apr.; farther north (N.J.) in Mar.; chosen winter habitat is thick beach grass of outermost dunes that provide it needed fresh water in winter (Stobo and McLaren, 1971); males on Sable Is. in spring sing much in early morning and at dusk from top of dune, post, utility pole, *tsip-tsip-tse-e-e-pr-ree-e-ah;* ending sounds much like *tee-arr* of common tern (Forbush, 1925–29).

Feeding Habits: Forages by creeping, running, or walking on sand, grass, or beaches (almost never hops as does Savannah sparrow); on Sable Is. eats beetles year-round and their larvae, caterpillars, ants, bugs, flies, spiders, also eggs and cocoons, snails, also seeds of weeds, berries, and in winter depends much on seeds of beach grass, other grasses, weed seeds, will eat bread crumbs scattered on ground for them in winter.
Nest: In hollow dug in sand, grass, or under shrubs, built of coarse grasses, plant stems, lined with fine grasses, hair.
Eggs: June; 3–5, pale green-white or dingy white, speckled, spotted with browns.
Incubation: Probably about 12 days; young may leave nest when about 14 days old (Elliott, 1968b).
Other Names: Gray bird; Ipswich Savannah sparrow; Maynard's sparrow; pallid sparrow; Sable Island sparrow.
Range: Nests on Sable Is.; winters on coastal dunes, Nova Scotia to s. Ga.

Sparrow, large-billed. *See* Sparrow, Savannah.

Sparrow, lark, *Chondestes grammacus* (con-DESS-teez GRAM-ah-cus); genus name: Lat., from Gr. *chondros,* grain, and *edestes,* eater; species name: line, or lined, alludes to stripes (lines) on crown and back; *lark* refers to its fine song (like lark), uttered in flight. (Color ill., page 317.) In open country, mostly middle, w., and sw. U.S., across s. Canada to B.C., south into Mexico; 5½–6¾ in. long; wingspread

10½–11 in.; sexes outwardly alike; adults striped black, white and chestnut crown; *chestnut ear patches* (just in back of eyes); streaked brown back; single dark spot in center of otherwise unmarked white breast and underparts (young with gray crown, ear patches, similar to adults but have finely streaked breast with no dark central spot); rounded tail with white corners (like towhee's), one of best identifying characters; most ground-dwelling, lives on prairies, treeless plains, abandoned fields, brushy pastures, near farmhouses, along country roads, city parks, edges of towns; in spring on nesting grounds, male courts female by strutting on ground like turkey cock with wings trailing, tail spread, showing white feathers, bubbling fragments of song (Baepler, 1968); frequently fights in air with other males; sings not only from ground, post, tree, utility wire, but also in flight; male sometimes polygynous; one of finest singers among sparrows; song is long, varied series of liquid trills, somewhat like that of indigo bunting.

Feeding Habits: Often feeds on ground in small flocks even in nesting season; walks about or hops, eats mostly seeds of weeds, grasses (about 75% of food); also eats many grasshoppers (more than half its animal food); alfalfa weevils, caterpillars, and other insects.
Nest: Usually on ground in grass at base of small plant or shrub that gives shade during day; sometimes in low cedar, pine, willow, post oak, elm, osage orange, yucca, mesquite, etc., within 3–30 ft. of ground (Newman, 1970); cup-shaped, of grasses, weed stems, twigs, lined with grasses, rootlets.
Eggs: Apr.–July; 3–6, usually 4–5, cream- or gray-white, with scrawls, spots of black, dark brown.
Incubation: By female, about 12 days; young leave nest when able to fly short distances at 9–10 days old (Baepler, 1968).
Other Names: Lark finch; little meadowlark; quail-head; road-bird.
Flight Speed: Timed in Tex., 21–28 m.p.h. (Sooter, 1947).
Host to Cowbirds: Uncommon, to brown-headed cowbird, 30 records (Friedmann, 1963).
Weights: Migrant, coastal N.J. (1), 27.1 gr. (Murray and Jehl, 1966), or about 1 oz.
Range: Nests from w. Ore., c. B.C., c. Idaho, se. Alta., s. Man., nw. and c. Minn., n. Wisc., s. Mich., s. Ont., w. N.Y., c. Pa., south from e. Neb. to s. Tex., La., c. Ala., rarely to w.-c. N.C., and n.-c. Va.; and in West, south to s. Calif., s.-c., Ariz., s. Tex., into Mexico; winters from s. Calif., s. Ariz., c. Tex., s. La., c. and s. Fla. (Keys), and occasionally north along Atlantic coast to Del. and n. N.J.

Sparrow, Le Conte's, *Ammospiza leconteii* (am-oh-SPY-zah lee-KONT-ih-eye); genus name: *see* Sparrow, Cape Sable; common and species names: honor John L. Le Conte, Philadelphia physician, friend of John James Audubon, and distinguished entomologist (Palmer, 1928). (Color ill., page 318.) Summers in prairie marshes of Canada and n.-c. U.S.; 4½–5½ in. long; one of smallest of sparrows; sexes outwardly alike; streaked back and sides; yellow-brown throat and underparts with reddish brown col-

lar; white stripe through dark crown; a bright orange stripe over each eye; bristly (sharp) tail; migrates north in spring (usually Mar.–Apr.) through c. U.S., from wintering grounds in s. and se. U.S.; frequents damp open fields, marshes of dense sedges, grasses; secretive, difficult to flush, prefers to run along ground in thick cover; flies only short distance before dropping back into grass; arrives Minn. and Sask. nesting grounds usually Apr.–May; male sings from grass cover, a grass stem, or in flight; insectlike *z-z-z-buzzzzzz,* for about 1 second, much higher-pitched and shorter than that of Savannah sparrow often heard in same meadows (Walkinshaw, 1968b).

Feeding Habits: Forages on ground for seeds of weeds, grasses, especially in winter; eats insects, spiders, in summer.
Nest: Built on, or about 8 in. above, ground in drier parts of open marsh, beneath tangles of old dead rushes or where grasses, sedges are thickest; extremely difficult to find; Le Conte's first interweaves dead grasses among standing stems, then, within, builds nest, rounded cup of finer grasses, sometimes sunk in ground.
Eggs: May–July; 3–5, usually 4, gray-white, speckled, spotted with browns.
Incubation: By female, about 12–13 days (Walkinshaw, 1968b); age when young leave nest unknown.
Other Name: Le Conte's bunting.
Host to Cowbirds: Possibly fairly common; records from Alta., Sask., Minn.
Hybrids: Murray (1968) reported a Le Conte's sparrow × sharp-tailed sparrow June 1949, Moose R., Ont., near James Bay.
Weights: Immature male (1) killed fall 1954 at Kans. TV tower, 11.2 gr.; immature female (1), 12.2 gr. (Tordoff and Mengel, 1956), or about ⅓–½ oz.
Range: Nests from s. Mack., ne. Alta., east across Canada to n. Ont., south to n.-c. Mont., se. Alta., s. Sask., n. N.D., n. and e. Minn.. ne. Wisc., n. Mich., casually south to se. S.D., ne. Ill., s. Ont.; winters occasionally from s. Mo. and s. Ill., more regularly from w.-c. Kans., c. Okla., nw. Ark. c. Ala., s.-c. Ga., S.C., and south to s. Tex., s. La., s. Miss., Fla., se. Ga.; first record for New England, a female caught Sept. 4, 1971, in a mist net at Manomet, Mass.

Sparrow, Lincoln's, *Melospiza lincolnii* (mel-oh-SPY-zah ling-CONE-ih-eye); genus name: Lat., from Gr. *melos,* song, and *spiza,* finch; species name: given in 1834 by John James Audubon for Thomas Lincoln, young man who accompanied Audubon on his Labrador trip of 1833. (Color ill., page 318.) Summers in Alaska, across Canada from Pacific to Atlantic, in parts of n. U.S. and in mountains of West; 5–6 in. long; adult sexes alike; resembles related song sparrow, but rounded tail shorter; has grayish streak over eye; buffy eye-ring; upperparts gray-brown, streaked with black from crown to rump; *buffy band around breast, finely streaked;* white belly; immature similar but duller streaking; from wintering grounds in C. America, Baja Calif., Fla., Gulf coast, moves north over most of U.S. Apr.–May; secretive, skulks through underbrush especially along watercourses, scrub of cut-over forest, brush along edges of bogs, permanent scrub zone western mountains; male usually sings while hidden in tree, tall grass, shrub, to advertise his 1-acre territory; sweet, gurgling, bubbling quality like house wren or purple finch, sometimes sings in flight, *churr-churr-churr-wee-wee-wee-wah* (Speirs and Speirs, 1968).

Feeding Habits: Scratches in leaves, ground, by kicking back with both feet; eats insects, grain, seeds of weeds, grasses, in migration comes to ground under feeding stations for seeds.

Nest: On ground in shallow depression, well hidden in moss of bog, on ground under shrub, edge of bog, in mountain meadows, sometimes low in alder bush, and to 9,500–11,000 ft. up in mountains in Colo., in grass clump under bushes at edge of road near forest; built by female of dry grasses, lined with hair or feathers.

Eggs: May–July; 3–6, usually 4–5, pale green, green-white, speckled, spotted with browns.

Incubation: By female, about 13½ days (Speirs and Speirs, 1968); young leave nest when 9–10 days old.

Other Names: Lincoln's finch; Lincoln's song sparrow; Tom's finch.

Host to Cowbirds: Rarely reported (Friedmann, 1963).

Weights: In autumn migration, coastal N.J. (5), 15–19.7 gr. (Murray and Jehl, 1964), or about ½–¾ oz.; Mich. (8), 15.2–20.1 gr.

Range: Nests from n. Alaska to e. Labrador, south in mts. to s. Calif., c. Ariz., n. N.M., s. Canada from Alta. to s. Man., s. Ont., Nova Scotia, n. Minn., n. Wisc., n. Mich., n. N.Y., Me.; winters from n. Calif., c. Ariz., Okla., c. Mo., the Gulf states, c. Ga., south to c. Fla. and C. America.

Sparrow, Maynard's. *See* Sparrow, Ipswich.

Sparrow, mourning. *See* Sparrow, Harris'.

Sparrow, Nuttall's. *See* Sparrow, white-crowned.

Sparrow, olive, *Arremonops rufivirgatus* (ah-REE-mon-ops rue-fih-ver-GAY-tus); genus name: Gr. word combining *Arremon*, a genus of C. and S. American sparrows, and *ops*, appearance (of); species name: from Lat. *rufus*, reddish, and *virgatus*, striped; referring to the two dull-brown stripes on crown. (Color ill., page 318.) Mexican species that lives north to s. Tex.; 5½–6 in. long; sexes alike; olive back, prominent *brown eye streak;* brown, striped crown and buffy breast help distinguish it from larger, similar green-tailed towhee; also has white belly feathers; resident (not migratory) in shrubby chaparral, weedy thickets, and undergrowth near forest edges, from sea level to 6,000 ft., locally in Mexico (Blake, E.R., 1953); male sings from low perch in thicket, unmusical series of dry *chip* notes suggestive of song of swamp sparrow.

Feeding Habits: Scratches noisily on ground under thickets for seeds, insects.

Nest: Built in low bush 2–5 ft. above ground; large, of straws, weed stems, twigs, bark,

Olive sparrow

FINCH FAMILY

leaves, lined with finer materials and hairs, domed, in heart of bushes often in cactus.

Eggs: Mar.–Sept.; 2–5, commonly 4–5, white, unspotted.

Incubation: Period of and age when young first fly unknown.

Other Names: Green finch; Texas sparrow.

Host to Cowbirds: A few records of host to brown-headed cowbird; two records of host to bronzed cowbird—all records from Tex. (Friedmann, 1963).

Range: From s. Tex. (Val Verde, Atascosa, and Nueces counties) south into Mexico.

Sparrow, pinewoods. *See* Sparrow, Bachman's.

Sparrow, rock. *See* Sparrow, rufous-crowned.

Sparrow, rufous-crowned, *Aimophila ruficeps* (ay-MOFF-ih-lah ROOF-ih-ceps); genus name: *see* Sparrow, Bachman's; species name: from Lat. *rufus*, red, and *caput*, head. (Color ill., page 319.) Rocky, brushy slopes of w. Great Plains, sw. U.S.; 5–6 in. long; sexes outwardly alike; resembles chipping sparrow; clear unstreaked breast; upperparts with rufous crown and black-striped back; however, chipping sparrow has conspicuous black line through eyes and white line over eyes; rufous-crowned also has black "whisker" mark on each side of throat and an unnotched tail; lives year-round (except in northern part of range) in rocky glades of Great Plains, boulder-strewn grassy hillsides in Tex., brush-covered hills, ravines of mountains in Ariz., bushy, grassy hillsides and coastal scrub of c. Calif.; stays under cover, if flushed quickly dives into grass or behind rocks but can be "squeaked" out; male usually sings from top of rock, bush, or low in small tree; a staccato chittering, which changes in pitch, somewhat like a softened house wren's song (Phillips, 1968b); sprightly, with cadence of lazuli bunting's song (Cogswell, 1968); call is clear, thin, descending notes, *tew-tew-tew.*

Feeding Habits: Forages close to or on ground in grass or under bushes, hops slowly about; eats beetles, crickets, grasshoppers, leafhoppers, olive scale, flies, caterpillars, etc., also seeds of grass, weeds—shifts from seeds to insects in spring; eats baby chick scratch feed on ground at bird feeders, may even enter house to be fed (Cogswell, 1968).

Nest: On or near ground, under rock ledge, in tuft of grass near stream, at foot of sapling, at foot of bank, or built low in branches of cedar tree, sagebrush, about 1–3 ft. above ground; in Calif.; nest cuplike, of twigs, bark strips, grasses, lined with hair of deer, horses, grasses.

Eggs: Mar.–Aug.; 2–5, usually 3–4, white to pale blue-white, unmarked (Phillips, 1968b; Cogswell, 1968).

Incubation: Period of and age when young leave nest unknown.

Other Names: Ashy rufous-crowned sparrow; California rufous-crowned sparrow; rock rufous-crowned sparrow; rock sparrow; Scott's rufous-crowned sparrow.

Range: Largely resident, c. Calif., n.-c. Ariz., sw. N.M., se. Colo., nw. and c. Okla., south discontinuously to s. Baja Calif. and Mexico; east of Rocky Mtns., winters from c. and s. Okla. to n. Tex. and south into Mexico.

Sparrow, rufous-winged, *Aimophila carpalis* (ay-MOFF-ih-lah car-PAY-liss); genus name: *see* Sparrow, Bachman's; species name: Lat., pertaining to last joint of wing, which has rufous shoulder patch. Mexican species, lives in U.S. only in s. Ariz.; although abundant in Mexico, was once thought to be extinct in U.S. but because habitat misunderstood, according to Phillips (1968a); also, according to Phillips, one of last two species of birds to be named and described in U.S. (*see* Species); 5–5½ in. long; sexes outwardly alike; adult, like chipping sparrow, has rufous crown, black-striped gray-brown back, clear unmarked breast, but has brownish bill and *rufous* shoulder patch (not always distinguishable at distance), which help distinguish it from chipping sparrow and similar rufous-crowned sparrow; in fall and winter, does not gather in flocks beyond family size; lives year-round in grass and brushy (preferably dense thorny) habitat in Mexico, and in Ariz. unbroken desert grasslands (see details of habitats in Phillips, 1968a); by mid or late Mar., in years of nesting (does not nest every year, depending on certain ecological conditions), most are paired; male's usual song uttered from perch top of medium-sized cactus or other thorny bush, is much like that of brown towhee; rendered by Phillips (1968a) as *chip burr chee-he-he-he-he-he;* a call note is *tzip* or *seep,* sings in s. Ariz. every month of year (see Anderson, 1965).

Feeding Habits: In summer, when feeds largely in desert hackberry bushes, eats caterpillars, ants, grasshoppers, and other insects; in dry habitat gets water intake from its food (Ohmart, 1969); at other seasons, largely seeds of grasses and weeds which picks up while hopping about on ground.

Nest: Pairs usually delay nesting until immediately after heavy rains, which may be in spring or later in summer; nest is built in bush: desert hackberry, mesquite, palo verde tree, cholla cactus, or other thorny bushes in flat swales, with abundant tall grass; in crotch or fork of branch, about 5–10 ft. above ground, conspicuous, deep cup of dead plant stems, twigs, grasses, leaf blades, lined with fine grasses and horsehair.

Eggs: Apr.–Sept.; 2–5, usually 4, pale blue-white, unmarked (Phillips, 1968a).

Incubation: Period of and age when young leave nest unknown; in fall, small family groups associate with black-throated, chipping, and Brewer's sparrows.

Host to Cowbirds: Little known, a few records to brown-headed cowbird south of Tucson (Friedmann, 1963).

Range: Resident, c. and s. Ariz., Oracle and Tucson region (see Phillips *et al.,* 1964), south into Mexico.

Sparrow, Sable Island. *See* Sparrow, Ipswich.

Sparrow, sage, *Amphispiza belli* (am-fih-SPY-zah BELL-eye); genus name: *see* Sparrow, black-throated; species name: given in 1850 by John Cassin in honor of John G. Bell, naturalist-taxidermist of New York, who accompanied Audubon on his journey up the Missouri R. (Color ill., page 319.) Lives in Great Basin country west of Rockies to Wash., Calif.; 5–6 in. long; sexes alike; upperparts light gray, contrasting with black tail; underparts white with *single dark breast spot;* head dark with *white spot below ear;* when on ground, habit of flicking relatively long tail distinguishes it immediately from lark sparrow, which also has *brown* cheek patches; lives mostly on ground—sand, gravel, alkali hardpan between and under sagebrush or desert scrub; very shy, keeps out of sight, runs under bushes or sometimes when alarmed flies to top of bush; in winter, in flocks of 25–50; some winter on nesting range, those wintering in southern part of breeding range migrate northward, arrive for example Feb.–Mar. in e. Wash., over most of nesting range live in sagebrush of Great Basin, semi-desert scrub of Nev., or in chaparral of Calif. slopes (Miller, 1968); male sings from top of bush, weak, high-pitched, tinkling notes, rendered as *tsit, tsit, TSI-you, tee a-tee,* another as *tweesitity-slip, tweesitity-slip, swer;* alarm note is *tsip.*

Feeding Habits: Gleans over ground, rather than scratches for food; runs about under bushes, now and then stopping to pick up grasshoppers, bugs, beet leafhoppers, beetles, caterpillars, ants, also spiders; eats weed seeds more in winter; on ground at bird-feeding stations eats baby chick scratch feed.

Nest: Sometimes built in depression in ground under bush but more often in sage, *Atriplex,* or other shrub from few inches to 3½ ft. above ground; from desert up to 6,000 ft. elevation in Nev., from coastal slopes to 9,000 ft. in mountains of Calif. (Miller, 1968); cuplike nest about 3 in. across, built in crotch or fork of bush, of twigs, sticks, grasses, bark shreds, lined with dried grasses, weed stalks, wool, seeds, feathers, cow hair, rabbit fur.

Eggs: Mar.–July; 3–5, usually 3–4, pale blue to blue-white, speckled, spotted with browns, lines of black.

Incubation: About 13 days; age when young leave nest unknown; apparently two broods a year (Miller, 1968).

Other Names: Bell's sparrow; gray sage sparrow; northern sage sparrow.

Host to Cowbirds: Very uncommon, a single record from Idaho (Friedmann, 1963).

Weights: Ore. in summer, adult males (26), 16.4–20.2 gr.; females (7), 16.2–19.8 gr. (Moldenhauer and Wiens, 1970), or about ¾ oz.; males averaged about 1 gr. heavier than females.

Range: Nests from c. Wash., s. Idaho, sw. Wyo., nw. Colo., south to s. Baja Calif., s. Nev., n. Ariz., and nw. N.M.; winters from c. Calif., c. Nev., sw. Utah, n. Ariz., c. N.M., south to w. Tex. and c. Baja Calif. and into Mexico.

Sparrow, Savannah, *Passerculus sandwichensis* (pass-ER-cue-lus san-witch-EN-sis); genus name: *see* Sparrow, Ipswich; species

Rufous-winged sparrow

FINCH FAMILY

name: Lat., of place, Sandwich, Unalaska, or Aleutians area, from which came first subspecies, Aleutian Savannah sparrow, to be described; common name: honors Savannah, Ga., where Alexander Wilson discovered the species in 1811. (Color ill., page 319.) Nests over almost entire N. American continent except se. U.S., to Mo. and Md., and in West, south into Mexico; 4½–6 in. long; wingspread 8–9½ in.; sexes outwardly alike; smaller and usually darker than the subspecies *princeps*, called Ipswich sparrow; upperparts dark brown or blackish, streaked above and below; *yellow streak over each eye* in nesting season; some have small spot, like song sparrow, in center of breast, but *tail is shorter, and slightly forked, or notched* (song sparrow's is longer, rounded); legs *pink* or *flesh-colored;* over nesting range prefers marshes or grasslike plant habitat, from sedge bogs of Labrador, salt marshes of northeastern coast, wet meadows and hayfields of U.S. and Canada, to grass-capped islands of Aleutians, short-grass prairies of midwestern Canada, and coastal marshes of Calif. (Baird, 1968a); usually arrives middle and n. U.S. and Canadian nesting grounds Mar.–Apr., on Arctic tundra, Alaska, May–June; along Calif. coast is year-round resident; migrates at night, roosts in groups in grassy fields as at Davis, Calif., but not given to close flocking even in winter; runs like mouse through grass when disturbed or makes short, quick, erratic flight; male on nesting territory sings dreamy, insectlike *tip, tip, tip seeeee saaaay* from rock, low post, tall weed, or bush; call note is *tseep* or *tsip.*

Feeding Habits: Hops about on ground, picks up seeds, sometimes scratches like towhee; besides seeds of weeds, grasses (most of food in fall, winter, spring), eats many insects in summer and other times of year—beetles, grasshoppers, bugs, ants, and other insects, also spiders and snails.
Nest: Usually built by female on ground in natural hollow or one scraped out by the bird; of coarse grasses, mosses, cup lined with hairs, finer grasses, rootlets, well concealed under overarching grasses, vines of old field, meadow, sometimes in hollow of sand dunes, infrequently in loose colonies (Baird, 1968a); at base of bunch of grasses on prairie, in meadows or grassy openings from foothills in Colo. through mountains to 12,000 ft.
Eggs: Mar.–July; 3–6, usually 4–5, green-blue or dingy white, from finely speckled to heavily blotched with browns.
Incubation: By both parents, alternately, 12 days; young leave nest when about 14 days old (Baird, 1968a).
Other Names: Belding's sparrow; field sparrow; grass sparrow; ground-bird; ground sparrow; large-billed sparrow; Savannah bunting.
Age: A banded one in Mich. lived to 7 years.
Flight Speed: Timed in w. U.S., 20–29 m.p.h. (Cottam *et al.,* 1942b); in Calif., 37–42 m.p.h. (McLean, 1930).
Host to Cowbirds: Very infrequent; 28 records scattered over Canada, n. U.S. (Friedmann, 1963).
Hybrids: See under Grasshopper sparrow.
Weights: Fall, coastal N.J. (16), 14.8–19.9 gr. (Murray and Jehl, 1964), or ½–¾ oz.; about

same span of weights at Kans. TV tower (Tordoff and Mengel, 1956).
Range: Resident over large part of nesting range from n. Alaska, n. Yukon, east to Labrador, south, locally, to Guatemala, Mo., Ill., Ind., Ohio, W.Va., w. Md., se. Pa.; winters in s. B.C., s. Nev., s. Utah, c. N.M., Okla., n. Gulf states, and Mass. south to El Salvador.

Sparrow, scarlet. *See* Scarlet tanager in Tanager Family.

Sparrow, seaside, *Ammospiza maritima* (am-oh-SPY-zah mar-IT-ih-mah); genus name: *see* Sparrow, Cape Sable; species name: Lat., maritime, of the sea (Coues, 1882). (Color ill., page 319.) Salt marshes of Atlantic and Gulf coasts; Mass. to Tex.; 5½–6½ in. long; wingspread 8¼–8½ in.; sexes alike; streaked olive-gray upperparts, larger, darker and grayer above than sharp-tailed sparrow, underparts streaked dusky; yellow streak *in front of eyes;* white streak down side of lower jaw; relatively long, pointed bill; tail short, stiff, bristly at tip; lives exclusively in salt and brackish marshes, resident (year-round) except in northern part of range; prefers seaside wet places along channels where cord grass *(Spartina),* black rush, and such shrubs as marsh elder and groundsel bushes provide nesting places; in other parts of range (Fla.) lives where *Salicornia,* salt-marsh grass, and mangroves grow; when not nesting, shy, stays hidden in marsh; relatively large feet adapted for running over soft ooze; when flushed, rises on fluttering wings, flies short distance, then drops out of sight; squeaking (*see* Sounds That Attract Birds) will lure them up out of cover to alight nearby; monogamous male in territory of 1–2 acres (Norris, 1968b) sings from stem of cattail or top of bush, rendered commonly as *tup, tup ZEE-reeeeeeeee* or *oka-CHEE-weeeee* (Woolfenden, 1968); alarm note is *chip, tick,* or *tsip.*

Feeding Habits: Like its relative the sharp-tailed sparrow, eats mostly small animal life: marine insects, noctuid moths, grasshoppers, flies, small crabs, snails, spiders, also seeds of cord grass, glasswort *(Salicornia).*
Nest: In small, loose colonies, built in tussocks of marsh grass, bulrushes, or among stems of marsh elder, 9–11 in. above mud, attached to upright stems of rushes or to 5 ft. up in crotch of groundsel bush or mangrove; a deep cup of coarse grasses, , rushes, lined with finer grasses.
Eggs: Apr.–July; 3–6, commonly 4–5, white to pale green-white, speckled, spotted with browns.
Incubation: By female, about 12 days (Sprunt, 1968b); young leave nest when 9–10 days old (Woolfenden, 1956); one brood a year.
Other Names: Meadow chippy; seaside finch.
Age: Two adults banded N.J. lived to be at least 3 years old, still alive when last seen (Woolfenden, 1958).
Host to Cowbirds: Unusual, or rare, only single record, Martha's Vineyard, Mass. (Friedmann, 1963).
Weights: Fall, coastal N.J. (6), 17.7–23.3 gr. (Murray and Jehl, 1964), or about ⅔–1 oz.

Range: Resident over practically entire range except n. limits in East; with coastal range some hundreds of miles long, and with habitat of *Spartina* or bulrush in northern part of range only few hundred feet wide, owing to housing, industry, and recreational development along Atlantic coast, has lost as high a percentage of habitat during last 25 years as any other N. American species (Vogt, 1970). Mass. south to Fla., Gulf coast to s. Tex.

Sparrow, sharp-tailed, *Ammospiza caudacuta* (am-oh-SPY-zah caud-ah-CUE-tah); genus name: *see* Sparrow, Cape Sable; species name: from Lat. *cauda,* tail, and *acutus,* sharp. (Color ill., page 321.) Summers from B.C. east across Canada, n. U.S., and Atlantic coast south to N.C.; 5–6 in. long; sexes outwardly alike; small marsh sparrow, *rich buff* triangle on side of *face; gray* ear patches; light streaks on gray-brown back; *unstreaked* blackish cap, breast and flanks pale buff, streaked or unstreaked; smaller and browner than seaside sparrow; in flight, short, *pointed* tail distinguishes it from Savannah sparrow with slightly forked tail; immature similar to adult but much more buffy; lives in coastal salt and brackish marshes and inland freshwater marshes; from wintering range in coastal marshes e. and se. U.S. and Gulf coast, migrates north at night, arrives nesting grounds n. Atlantic coast, interior U.S. and Canada, May–June; lives in colonies in wide green salt marshes with narrow, winding tidal creeks; a subspecies, Nelson's sharp-tail, summers exclusively in freshwater sedge marshes along lakes, in wet, boggy swamps, or in short-grass alkaline flats of lakes in S. Canada in tule beds intersected with channels and ponds; sharp-tail is secretive, runs through grass like mouse, but in response to squeaking notes will fly up to perch on stem of marsh grass; male not territorial, promiscuous (Woolfenden, 1956); sings from top of grass or stake, or in flight; song is hissing buzz, *ts-ts-ssssss-tsik, ts-ts-ts-ts-ts-ts-lik* (Hill, 1968).

Feeding Habits: When hunting food, walks and runs rather than hops, zigzag in grass or across mud, picks up food with bill as it goes: ants, beetles, weevils, grasshoppers, caterpillars, moths, leafhoppers, flies; amphipods (sand fleas), spiders, small snails; seeds of grasses, weeds, wild rice.
Nest: On ground in matted bed of rushes, in dense grass or sedges, or 1–3 in. above ground among upright stems; built of coarse dry grasses, bulrushes, and seaweeds, bulky, loosely woven, cup 3–4 in. across, lined with finer material.
Eggs: May–Aug.; 3–7, usually 3–5, green-white, profusely speckled, spotted with browns (Hill, 1968).
Incubation: By female, 11 days; young leaves nest when about 10 days old.
Albinism: Partial albinos reported from Me., Mass., and S.C., a partially melanistic one in Fla. (Hill, 1968).
Age: An adult banded N.J. at least 3 years old when last seen (Woolfenden, 1958).
Host to Cowbirds: Extremely rare, to brown-headed cowbird; one record, Nelson's sharp-

tail, another sharp-tail in Mass. (Friedmann, 1963).

Hybrids: One reported sharp-tailed sparrow × seaside sparrow (Hill, 1968); *see also* under Le Conte's sparrow.

Weights: Fall, coastal N.J. (2), 17.6 and 19.3 gr., or about ¾ oz.; adult males (2) killed fall 1954, Kans. TV tower, 15.2 and 17.1 gr.; adult female (1), 13.3 gr., or about ½ oz.

Range: Nests from ne. B.C. east across c. and s. Canada to N.D., in James Bay area of Canada; along Atlantic coast from s. Que. and Nova Scotia south to N.C.; winters along coast from N.Y. to s. Fla. and west along Gulf coast to Tex.

Sparrow, song, *Melospiza melodia* (mel-oh-SPY-zah mel-ODE-ih-ah); genus name: *see* Sparrow, Lincoln's; species name: Lat., pleasant song. (Color ill., page 320.) Nests from Alaska south to Mexico and across Canada and U.S. from Pacific to Atlantic coasts; 5–7 in. long, wingspread 8¼–9¼ in.; one of best-known of all N. American birds, dwells near people, has persistent and attractive song; abundant, variable (31 forms, or subspecies, nest north of Mexico, show variations from pale desert forms to larger darker birds of Alaskan islands); generally brown above, streaks and stripes on back and face; white breast heavily streaked, with a large central dark breast spot; in short flights, pumps rather long, rounded tail up and down; immature similar to adults, but has buff breast band, finely streaked; likes brushy cover with water nearby, along streams, ponds, shrubby wet meadows, cattail marshes, around mountain lakes, also drier habitat of brushy fencerows along country roads, prairie groves, second-growth woods, shrubbery of yards and gardens, in N.C. mountains to 6,300 ft.; in Rockies up to 6,500 ft., sometimes higher; salt and brackish marshes around San Francisco Bay (Nolan, 1968); winters year-round over many parts of range, but most withdraw from Canada, n. U.S., to winter along coast as far as Fla.; in e. U.S. often winter in loose flocks in marshes, swamps, brushy thickets; migrates at night; in spring moves north to breeding range, from South beginning late Feb.; appears in n. U.S., Canada, Mar.–May; male establishes a territory (usually less than an acre) by fighting and chasing other males, singing from boulders, fences, shrubs, trees, sometimes on wing (female often sings before nesting season begins); song of male is a few long bright notes followed by short notes and trills (first three notes often popularly compared with first three notes of Beethoven's Fifth Symphony); has been rendered by old country people, according to Thoreau: *Maids! maids! maids! hang up your teakettle-ettle-ettle;* call note, *chimp, tchenk, chip,* etc., also a *sst* regarded by Dawson (1923) as flocking or recognition call.

Feeding Habits: In summer, insects are half of food; forages then in grasses, bushes, trees, eats beetles, grasshoppers, cutworms, army worms, ants, wasps, ichneumon flies, winged termites, bugs, leafhoppers, flies, etc., on ground eats seeds of grasses, weeds (about two thirds of yearly diet); also eats some waste grain, wild fruit—blackberries, blueberries,

elderberries, wild cherries, grapes, etc.; scratches on ground; comes to bird feeders for food (see details and food preferences in Terres, 1968c, also garden nest shelf).

Nest: Most are on ground, especially early in nesting season, built by female, hidden among matted clumps of dead grasses, weeds; later, often 2–4 ft. up in small conifer, thorny bush, willows, cattails, cordgrass (in marshes); in pine sapling, and sometimes (in N.C.) out on branch of pine 25 ft. up.

Eggs: Feb.–Aug.; 3–6, pale green to green-white, heavily speckled, spotted, blotched with reddish browns (Nolan, 1968).

Incubation: By female, usually 12–13 days, rarely 14–15 days (Nice, 1968); young leave nest when about 10 days old, usually before they can fly; two, sometimes three, broods raised a year.

Other Names: Bush sparrow; everybody's darling; ground-bird; ground sparrow; hedge sparrow; marsh sparrow; red grassbird; silver tongue; swamp finch.

Albinism: Has been noted (see Nolan, 1968).

Age: In Ohio, average male (banded) lived to 2½ years; several to 7 years; one at least 9½ years old; one banded Longmont, Calif., trapped and released in same area when 10 years, 4 months, old; a captive in National Zoo, Washington, D.C., lived to 9 years, 2 months.

Flight Speed: Timed in w. U.S., 30 m.p.h. (Cottam *et al.,* 1942b); in New England, 17 m.p.h. (White, 1927).

Host to Cowbirds: One of most frequent victims of brown-headed cowbird, more than 900 records; also in Chapultepec Park, Mexico City, 50% of nests parasitized by bronzed cowbird (Friedmann, 1963).

Hybrids: See under White-crowned sparrow.

Weights: Coastal N.J. in fall (115), 16.4–24.4 gr. (Murray and Jehl, 1964), or about ⅔ oz.

Range: Nests from Aleutian Is., Alaska, s. Yukon, s. Mack., n. Sask., east to Newfoundland, south to s.-c. Baja Calif., s. Mexico, n. N.M., n. Kans., n. Ark., s.-e. Tenn., n. Ga., nw. S.C.; winters (migratory forms) from s. Alaska, s. B.C., s.-e. Mont., S.D., s. Minn., s. Wisc., s. Mich., s. Ont., s. Que., c. N.B., and Nova Scotia south to s. Tex., s. Fla., and Mexico. For extraordinary details of life history of song sparrow, see Nice (1937b; 1939; 1943).

Sparrow, swamp, *Melospiza georgiana* (mel-oh-SPY-zah george-ih-AY-nah); genus name: *see* Sparrow, Lincoln's; species name: Lat., of Georgia, because first one of its kind described by scientist came from Ga. (Color ill., page 321.) Close relative of song and Lincoln's sparrows; nests Man. to e. Canada, and from e. U.S. to Great Plains; 5–5¾ in. long; wingspread 7½–8 in.; sexes outwardly alike; dark sparrow with *chestnut cap, white throat,* clear gray breast (similar song sparrow has heavily streaked breast); summers in freshwater marshes, swamps, bogs, wet meadows, alder-grown shores of lakes, slow-moving streams, often where water ankle to waist deep; rarely in coastal brackish meadows (Wetherbee, 1968); outside nesting season, visits upland weed-grown fields, hedges, with other sparrows; in spring moves northward from wintering in s. and e. U.S.; arrives n. U.S. and Canadian nest-

FINCH FAMILY
Defending its territory from the challenge of a rival, the male song sparrow fluffs its feathers, warbling softly, and raises and lowers one or both of its wings.

ing grounds usually Mar.–Apr.; male generally sings from perch on alder, willow, or cattail; while singing spreads somewhat rounded tail noticeably; song is *weet-weet-weet-weet*, somewhat like that of chipping sparrow but louder, more musical; call is *chip* or *cheep* with metallic ring.

Feeding Habits: Does much of feeding wading in shallow water to pick up in bill floating insects—beetles, ants, grasshoppers, crickets; also seeds of sedges, weeds, grasses.

Nest: Often built, usually by female, in cattail stalks, bent-down clumps of stalks of cattails and leaves, 6–24 in. above water; in green tussock of sedge; in c. Mass., builds consistently in bushes (Wetherbee, 1968); to about 6 ft. above water or ground; nests of coarse, dead marsh grasses, inner cup of finer grasses, entrance on side.

Eggs: May–July; 3–6, usually 4–5, pale green to green-white, spotted, blotched, clouded with reddish browns.

Incubation: By female, 12–15 days; young leave nest when 12–13 days old, fluttering away sometimes fall into water, where may be caught and eaten by frogs, fish, turtles; usually two broods a year (Wetherbee, 1968).

Other Name: Swamp song sparrow.

Age: One, banded Plainfield, Vt., trapped and released in same area when 6 years, 4 months, old (Kennard, 1975).

Host to Cowbirds: Uncommon host to brown-headed cowbird; may be frequent locally; cowbirds tend to avoid nests in marshes (Friedmann, 1963).

Weights: Fall, coastal N.J. (10), 14.8–17.8 gr. (Murray and Jehl, 1964), or ½–⅔ oz. Similar weights of three killed Kans. TV tower migrating at night (Tordoff and Mengel, 1956).

Range: Nests from Mack., n. Man., n. Ont., c. Que., and Newfoundland, south to ne. B.C., c. Alta., s. Sask., e. Neb., n. Mo., n. Ill., n. Ind., s. Ohio, s.-c. W.Va., Md., and Del.; winters from e. Neb., Iowa, and s. Wisc., through s. Great Lakes Basin to c. N.Y., and Mass., south to s. Tex., Gulf coast, s. Fla., and c. Mexico.

Sparrow, Texas. *See* Sparrow, olive.

Sparrow, tree, *Spizella arborea* (spy-ZELL-ah are-BOE-ree-ah); genus name: *see* Sparrow, black-chinned; species name: Lat., pertaining to trees (a misnomer for this bird because few spend less time in trees). (Color ill., page 320.) Summers just south of tundra, from Alaska across n. Canada, winters in U.S., Atlantic to Pacific; 5½–6½ in. long; wingspread 8½–9¾ in.; sexes similar; *red-brown cap,* plain gray breast *with brown blotch in middle;* two white bars in each wing; bill: upper mandible dark, lower one yellow; legs dark; wandering winter flocks scattered over often snow-swept weedy fields, marshes, near woods, hedges; flocks vary from 30 to 40 birds of both sexes—usually in small groups of 4–8 that travel and stay together all winter (Baumgartner, 1968b); converse in musical twitter, *teedle eet, teedle eet;* can stand bitter cold to −28° C. (West, 1960); cannot survive such cold without food; in spring, usually leaves wintering grounds in s., c., and e. U.S. for nesting grounds in Mar.–

Apr., most travel 1,500 to 2,000 or even 3,000 mi. (Alaska), flocks broken up on arrival, individuals paired soon afterward; male's territorial defense and courtship display is song (both sexes colored alike), begins with one or two high, sweet, clear notes, followed by warble.

Feeding Habits: Largely on ground, or snow, scratches among dry grasses; eats almost entirely seeds of weeds, grasses; one stomach held 700 seeds of pigeon grass (Beal, 1897), another 982 seeds in crop alone (Baumgartner, 1968b); also eats stone flies, beetles, ants, caterpillars, bugs, grasshoppers, flies, spiders; in summer, outstanding food is seeds of sedges, also eats seeds of wild berries; comes to feeding stations for wild bird seed mixture.

Nest: Among stunted trees, shrubs just south of tundra and along Arctic coasts, on or near ground, in tussocks of grass, mossy hummocks of open tundra; in spruces, dwarf willows, 1–5 ft. up or on ground; built by female, of grasses, plant stems, bark, mosses, lined with ptarmigan feathers, dog hairs, lemming fur.

Eggs: May–July; 3–6, usually 3–5, pale blue or pale green-white, spotted, speckled with browns over entire surface.

Incubation: By female, 12–13 days; young leave nest if undisturbed when 9½ days old, when still unable to fly (Baumgartner, 1968b).

Other Names: Arctic chipper; Canada sparrow; snow chippy; tree bunting; winter chipbird; winter chippy; winter sparrow.

Age: Banded birds reported to 6 years old, 7, and one 8½ years old, another 9 years old when last seen.

Albinism: Very rare; however, complete, or total, albinism reported in two, one at Cape Cod, Mass., another near Chicago, Ill.

Weights: Adults (10), 17.7–19.7 gr. (Baumgartner, 1968b); Conn., adults in spring (48), 17.4–22.38 gr. (Wetherbee, 1934), or about ⅔–¾ oz.; in winter to 25 or 26 gr. (Helms and Drury, 1960).

Range: Nests from n. Alaska to Labrador, south to c. Alaska, n. B.C., n. Sask., and c. Que.; winters from s. B.C., s. Sask., c. Minn., n. Mich., c. Ont., sw. Que., to Nova Scotia, south to n. Calif., c. Nev., c. Ariz., c. N.M., c. Tex., Ark., Tenn., and N.C.

Sparrow, vesper, *Pooecetes gramineus* (poe-ee-SEE-teez gray-MIN-ee-us); genus name: Lat., from Gr. *poa,* grass, and *oiketes,* dweller; species name: Lat., pertaining to grass (fond of); *vesper* from habit of singing toward evening, although sings in nesting season all times of day. (Color ills., pages 322, 323.) Summers e. and n. U.S. west to Calif., s. Canada; 5–6½ in. long; wingspread 10–11 in.; gray-brown and streaked above; dull white below, streaked on throat, breast, sides; *chestnut patch at bend of wing;* white outer tail feathers of notched tail flash as bird flies; lives usually on ground on dry upland fields, close-cropped pastures, meadows with sparse grass cover; flocks in spring, 25–30 or fewer, arrive at nesting grounds in n. U.S., s. Canada, in Mar.–Apr.; male in territory rarely sings from ground; uses highest perch available, often in tree 25 ft. up in woods bordering field (Berger, 1968); where no trees, uses fence, dead weed, shrub;

song plaintive, sweet, two long notes followed by two higher ones, then descending trills; sings brilliantly on calm evenings just after rain; runs ahead on old road or upland pasture; flies only when closely approached, frequently takes dust baths in road ruts, sometimes roosts in ruts at night.

Feeding Habits: Walks or runs over ground; eats beetles, grasshoppers, army worms, cutworms, moths, also large amounts weed seeds, waste grain.

Nest: Usually on ground under dead weed stems in small depression near small patches of bare ground, in alfalfa fields, previous year's cornfields, base of grass tussock or even clod of dirt; also on sand amid beach grass of seashore; openings in sagebrush (e. Calif.); in s. Rockies in meadows at 9,000–12,000 ft. elevation; in Blue Mtns., e. Wash., to 5,000 ft.

Eggs: Apr.–Aug.; 3–6, usually 3–5, cream-white, pale green-white, spotted, blotched, scrawled with browns.

Incubation: By both sexes, usually by female, 11–13 days; young leave nest when 7–12 days old, unable to fly well; two broods a year, sometimes three (Berger, 1968).

Other Names: Bay-winged bunting; bay-winged finch; grass finch; grass sparrow; graybird; ground-bird; pasture-bird.

Age: Three banded Mass., recaptured, released when more than 6 years old.

Flight Speed: Timed in New England, 17 m.p.h. (White, 1927).

Host to Cowbirds: Fairly frequent, about 70 records.

Hybrids: See under Field sparrow.

Weights: Conn., Apr., Oct., adults (20), 22–27.5 gr. (Wetherbee, 1934), or ¾–1 oz.

Range: Nests c. B.C., sw. Mack., e. Sask., s. Man., c. and ne. Ont., s. Que., and Nova Scotia, south to w. Ore., c. Calif., c. Nev., sw. Utah, c. Ariz., c. N.M., Colo., Mo., Tenn., and N.C.; winters from c. Calif., s. Great Basin, Rocky Mtns., c. Tex., Ark., s. Ill., Ky., W.Va., s. Pa., and Conn., south to s. Baja Calif., Gulf coast, c. Fla., and Mexico.

Sparrow, white-crowned, *Zonotrichia leucophrys* (zoe-no-TRICK-ih-ah lew-KOFF-riss); genus name: *see* Sparrow, golden-crowned; species name: Lat., from Gr. *leukos,* white, and *ophrys,* eyebrow. (Color ill., page 322.) Related to Harris', white-throated, and golden-crowned sparrows; abundant in West, nests or winters over parts of N. America from Atlantic to Pacific coasts; 5½–7 in. long; adults, sexes very similar; *high puffy crown strikingly marked with broad black and white stripes;* clear, pearl-gray face, neck, and breast, throat and belly white; brown back, rump, wings, tail; two white wing bars; immature similar but crown striped with red-brown, buff-brown; in se. U.S. winters in flocks of 10–20, in West 30–50 (DeWolfe, 1968); in brushy fencerows, bushes of abandoned farms, shrubbery about homes, university campuses (Berkeley, Calif.); on nesting grounds in North, open stunted tree growth and brush, with grassy openings, dwarf willow thickets along streams or lakes, windswept shrubby places in high mountains of West and along cool Pacific coast;

male sings to advertise territory, fights with other males, song begins with plaintive whistle, like white-throated sparrow's—a sad *more wet wetter chee zee;* call note *tsit* or *pete.*

Feeding Habits: Hops about on ground, vigorously scratches with both feet; eats green capsules of hairy-cap moss, catkins of willows in spring, also flies, mosquitoes, caterpillars, beetles, spiders, but main food is seeds of weeds, grasses, also eats young garden plants—beets, peas; comes to ground under bird feeders for baby chick scratch feed.

Nest: On ground in moss or tussock of grass, under shrub or dwarf tree, or in small conifer, dwarf birch, willow, rarely to 35 ft. up in tree; built by female, bulky cup of twigs, grasses, rootlets, weed stems, lined with fine grasses, hairs of deer, cow, horse, dog, and feathers.

Eggs: Apr.–Aug.; 3–5, pale blue or pale green, spotted with browns, black.

Incubation: By female, 11–16 days; young leave nest when about 10 days old (De Wolfe, 1968).

Other Names: Gambel's sparrow; Nuttall's sparrow; white-crown.

Age: In survey of 226,516 banded (1920–63), of 198 recovered, average age was 1.2 years; oldest bird, immature when banded, lived for 12 years, 9 months (Cortopassi and Mewaldt, 1965); other records to 7, 7½, 8, and one to 13 years, 4 months, old (see Kennard, 1975).

Flight Speed: Timed in Calif., 13.3–19.1 m.p.h. (Pearson, 1961).

Host to Cowbirds: Infrequently, only a few records to brown-headed cowbird (Friedmann, 1963); however, more recent records in Wash., Calif. (Petrinovich and Patterson, 1978).

Hybrids: White-crowned sparrow × song sparrow, collected June 1959, San Juan Is., Wash. (Dickerman, 1961); *see also* under Golden-crowned sparrow.

Homing: In remarkable experiment, of several hundred white-crowns trapped San Jose, Calif., region, shipped to and then released at Patuxent Wildlife Research Center, Md., in Oct. 1962, eight had returned to San Jose one year later.

Weights: 25.2–35.75 gr. (Wetherbee, 1934), or about 1–1¼ oz.; males 22.4–33.2 gr. (Banks, 1964).

Range: Nests from n. Alaska to Labrador, south to s. Calif., Nev., c. Ariz., n. N.M., c. Man., se. Que., and Newfoundland; winters from s. B.C., se. Wash., s. Idaho, Wyo., Kans., Mo., Ky. to w. N.C., south to s. Baja Calif., s. Mexico, Gulf coast, and Cuba.

Sparrow, white-throated, *Zonotrichia albicollis* (zoe-no-TRICK-ih-ah al-bih-COLL-iss); genus name: *see* Sparrow, golden-crowned; species name: from Lat. *albus,* white, and *collum,* neck. (Color ill., page 323.) Summers across Canada to limit of trees, and parts of ne. and n.-c. U.S.; 6–7 in. long; wingspread 8¾–10 in.; adults, sexes similar; conspicuous *white* throat; crown striped narrowly black and white or black, brown, and tan; *yellow spot between eye and bill;* back striped rusty brown; gray-breasted; two white wing bars; immature similar to adult or duller, head stripes brown, dull white on breast, sides, thickly streaked with brown (but age and sex cannot definitely be

determined by plumage—*see* Sex Determination); lives in brush in woodlands, winters mainly in s. and se. U.S., also Calif., in flocks of dozen or more in hedgerows, brushy woods borders, shrubby pastures, brush piles of cut-over woods, cattail marshes, shrubbery of yards, gardens, city parks, residential areas; sometimes sings in winter flocks, individuals often can be lured from ground to branch by whistling a few notes of its easily imitated song, which has given it many of its common names: sweet, quavering, whistled notes; one song often translated as *Old Sam Peabody, Peabody, Peabody,* or *Sow wheat, Peverly, Peverly, Peverly;* female sometimes sings; male sings on nesting grounds usually from coniferous tree; early in season at any time of day or night (Lowther and Falls, 1968); utters several different calls; one is *tseet,* contact note when birds cannot see each other; another, a sharp *chink,* likened to sound of marble cutter's chisel (Chapman, 1900).

Feeding Habits: On ground scratches noisily in leaves; eats mainly weed seeds, also fruits of dogwoods, elder, cedar, spicebush, etc.; comes to bird feeders for mixed bird seeds, scratch grain; also eats ants, beetles, flies, other insects, and buds of oaks, maples, apple.

Nest: Built by female, in wet thickets as well as dry ones, usually on ground at edge of clearing, well concealed under a bush or sometimes in roots of upturned stump, in raspberry bush, and in small balsam fir 3 ft. up; built of coarse grasses, wood chips, twigs, pine needles, lined with grasses, rootlets, deer hair.

Eggs: May–Aug.; 4–6, cream-, blue-, or green-white, heavily marked with reddish browns.

Incubation: By female, 12–14 days; young leave nest 7–12 days after hatching, fly about 2–3 days after leaving nest (Lowther and Falls, 1968); rarely raise more than one brood a year.

Other Names: Canada bird; Canada sparrow; cherry-bird; nightingale; Peabody-bird; peverly-bird; white-throat.

Age: Various ages of banded white-throats: 7, and 8 years old; one to 9 years, 7 months, old (Kennard, 1975)

Albinism: One partial albino seen Newport News, Va., appeared entirely white at distance but with dark wings (Mitchell, 1967).

Host to Cowbirds: Infrequent, but in s. Que., regularly; about 36 total records (Friedmann, 1963).

Hybrids: See under Golden-crowned sparrow; also an "abundance" of hybrids ("crosses") of white-throated sparrow × slate-colored junco (Dickerman, 1961; see Short and Simon, 1965).

Weights: Coastal N.J., fall (341), 19–33.7 gr. (Murray and Jehl, 1964), or ¾–1¼ oz.

Range: Nests from s. Yuk., c. Mack., n. Man., n. Ont., w.-c. and se. Que., s. Labrador, and n. Newfoundland, south to c. B.C., c. Alta., s. Sask., n.-c. N.D., c. Minn., n. Wisc., c. Mich., n. Ohio, n. W.Va., ne. Pa., se. N.Y., nw. Conn., s. N.H., and Mass.; winters from n. Calif., s. Ariz., s. N.M., e. Kans., c. Mo., s. Ill., n. Ky., s. Ohio, n. W.Va., c. N.Y., Conn., and Mass. to s. Tex., Gulf coast, and n. Fla.

Sparrow, Worthen's, *Spizella wortheni* (spy-ZELL-ah WORE-then-eye); genus name:

see Sparrow, black-chinned; species name: in honor of Charles K. Worthen, American naturalist and collector of birds for natural history museums (Palmer, 1954). A Mexican species closely related to the field sparrow; only one ever reported in N. America was collected (shot) June 16, 1884, near Silver City, sw. N.M.; otherwise it is known only from Mexico. See Webster (1968) for details of its life history.

Towhee, Abert's, *Pipilo aberti* (PIP-ih-low AY-bert-eye); genus name: from Lat. *pipo,* to chirp, to peep (Jaeger, 1955); species name: given in 1852 by Spencer F. Baird for Maj. James W. Abert, U.S. Army, who collected (shot) first one known to science in N.M.; common name towhee (TEW-hee or TOE-hee) for the group, from one of common call notes of rufous-sided towhee; towhees, sometimes called towhee buntings, are in a subfamily that includes their close relatives the sparrows. (Color ill., page 324.) Abert's in sw. U.S.; 8–9 in. long; sexes similar; brown, long-tailed bird with *black around base of buffy bill;* underparts *buff-brown;* breast not spotted or streaked as in brown towhee; immature similar to adult; lives year-round near watercourses generally along basin of Colorado R., often in mesquite, cottonwoods, willows, and arrowweed in Ariz. and N.M., also seen about citrus groves, farms, cities, and towns; pairs mated for life (Phillips *et al.,* 1964) (*see* How Birds Court, or Win Mates under Courtship); very shy, difficult to see in thickets of home, but calls frequently with sharp *peep;* male sings succession of rapid notes, *chip, chip, chee-chee-chee.*

Feeding Habits: Scratches on ground in leaves for seeds and insects in shade of bush and in tall arrowweed and saltbush of roadside of desert home (Hoffmann, 1927); no comprehensive study published of food habits (Dawson, 1968).

Nest: Peak of spring nesting in Ariz. follows in 10–14 days after heavy daytime rains in Mar. or Apr. (Marshall, 1963); nest built usually in low bush (willow, mesquite, elderberry, etc.) or in tree, sometimes to 25–30 ft.; bulky, weed stems, dead vines, bark strips, green leaves, deep cup lined with dried grasses, horsehair.

Eggs: Feb.–Sept.; 2–4, usually 3, pale, clay blue, marked with dark brown, black.

Incubation: Period of and age when young leave nest unknown.

Other Name: Gray towhee.

Age: One banded wild bird, shot and killed when 6 years, 7 months, old (Kennard, 1975).

Host to Cowbirds: Occasionally, to brown-headed cowbird; at least nine records in s. Ariz.; at least one in Calif. (Friedmann, 1963).

Range: Resident, usually along river and stream valleys from se. Nev., sw. Utah, sw. N.M., c. Ariz., south along Colorado R. basin to se. Calif., ne. Baja Calif., nw. Mexico, and se. Ariz.

Towhee, brown, *Pipilo fuscus* (PIP-ih-low FUSS-cus); genus name: *see* Towhee, Abert's; species name: Lat., dusky. (Color ill., page 324.) W. and sw. U.S., Ore. to Tex.; 8½–10 in. long; sexes alike; dull, gray-brown bird with fairly long tail; appears like plain large sparrow with short, sparrowlike bill; *cinnamon* or *rusty undertail coverts;* throat and upper breast buff, sometimes with faint dusky streaks; sometimes with rufous cap; permanent resident and ground-dwelling bird from brushy hillsides in Ore., Calif. chaparral and suburban gardens; cholla cactus and pinyon-juniper country of Colo., south to lower mountain canyons of Ariz. and N.M.; in Tex., plateau country of juniper and oak thickets generally in low scrub; not shy around gardens and dooryards but in wild country one of wariest birds, keeps under bushes or near them if in open, keeps on move, hops rapidly over ground; according to Marshall and Johnson (1968), mates "probably" for life (length of life of each member of pair); each pair lives by itself; male stays close to female when feeding on ground and guardedly watches over her; strongly territorial, male is fierce fighter of his own image reflected from window or other shiny surface; a basic note of brown towhee—territorial pronouncement—is repeated, metallic *chip* or *tsip* (Childs, 1968); song of male is elaboration of *chip* note: some sing *chink-chink-ink-ink-ink-ink,* canyon brown towhee sings *chili-chili-chili-chili.*

Feeding Habits: Likes to feed under bushes, fences, old buildings, parked cars, trailers, wagons, within tall grasses (Marshall and Johnson, 1968); comes to feeding stations for birdseed, scratch feed; eats weed seeds, grain, insects; does not scratch as frequently or violently as rufous-sided towhee.
Nest: Bulky, from ground to 35 ft. up in densest part of bush or tree; preferred height 3–12 ft.; bulky, of twigs, grasses, plant stems, lined with strips of bark, leaves, animal hair.
Eggs: Mar.–Sept.; 2–6, usually 3–4, pale blue, pale green, marked with dark brown and black, speckles, spots, scrawls over entire egg.
Incubation: By female, 11 days; young leave nest when 8 days old (Childs, 1968).
Other Names: Brown chippy; California towhee; canyon bunting; canyon towhee; fuscous towhee; Mexicans call it *la viejita* (the little old woman).
Age: Linsdale (1949) reported oldest to 7 years; at Pasadena, Calif., one lived to 8 years; of two others banded Calif., one to 7, one to 9, another was recaptured when at least 10 years old (Stoner, 1969).
Flight Speed: 22 m.p.h. (Pearson, 1961).
Host to Cowbirds: A few records of host to both brown-headed and bronzed cowbirds (Friedmann, 1963).
Range: From sw. Ore., w. and c. Ariz., n. N.M., se. Colo., w. Okla., and w. and c. Tex., south to s. Mexico and Baja Calif.

Towhee, canyon. *See* Towhee, brown.

Towhee, chestnut-crowned. *See* Towhee, green-tailed.

Towhee, gray. *See* Towhee, Abert's.

Towhee, green-tailed, *Pipilo chlorurus* (PIP-ih-low klow-RUE-rus); genus name: *see* Towhee, Abert's; species name: Lat., from Gr. *chloros,* green, and *oura,* tail. (Color ill., page 325.) Smallest of the towhees; 6¼–7 in. long;

sexes similar; *reddish-brown cap, white throat* with 2 vertical stripes are best distinguishing marks; olive-green back, wings, and tail; shows only when bird in strong light; edges of wings and their undersurfaces *bright yellow;* has gray breast and face and white lores and belly; immature has brownish back, no rufous crown; streaked dusky overall; summers in mountains and high plateau country of w. and sw. U.S., Ore. and Mont. to s. Calif. and w. Tex., from low altitude of 2,500 ft., Calif., to 4,350 ft., Colo., to 10,500 ft. in San Francisco Mtns., Ariz.; active, slips in and out of sage and deer brush, curious about people, not always shy, lives in shrubby *Ceanothus,* wild rose, manzanita, chokecherry, mountain mahogany, etc. (Norris, 1968a); avoids forest, prefers brush cover 2–4 ft. high; from winter home in Baja Calif., n. Mexico, southern border U.S., during late Feb. to early May moves northward or up mtns., usually by day, to northern limit of breeding range; has mewing call uttered from low bushes, also nasal *chink;* individual songs of males vary; one phrased *weet-chur-cheeeeeee-churrr* has burr in middle, phrased like rufous-sided towhee's song; when alarmed runs or skulks with tail raised through brush over ground like chipmunk; called "rodent run," which apparently lures predators away from towhee's nest. *See* Distraction Display; Behavior.
Feeding Habits: Scratches under brush like other towhees; eats weed seeds, wild berries, insects; visits feeding stations for bread, birdseed, grain.
Nest: Built from ground level to 28 in. up, at base of sage, or in waxberry, snowbush, cactus; thick-walled, deep-cupped, of twigs, grasses, bark, lined with fine plant stems, rootlets, horsehair.
Eggs: May–July; 2–5, commonly 4, white, profusely spotted, speckled with browns over entire surface.
Incubation: Period of and age when young leave nest unreported.
Other Names: Blanding's finch; chestnut-crowned towhee; green-tailed bunting.
Host to Cowbirds: Only a few records, to brown-headed cowbird (Friedmann, 1963).
Range: Nests from sw. and c. Ore., se. Wash., s. Idaho, sw. Mont., nw., c., and se. Wyo., south through interior mountains to s. Calif., s. Nev., c. Ariz., s. N.M.; winters from s. Calif., s. Ariz., w. and s. Tex., south to s. Baja Calif. and Mex.; in migration to w. Kans., w. Okla., casual east to Mass., N.J., Del., Va., S.C., Ga., Tenn., and La., north to Sask.

Towhee, red-eyed. *See* Towhee, rufous-sided.

Towhee, rufous-sided, *Pipilo erythrophthalmus* (PIP-ih-low er-ih-throf-THALL-mus); genus name: *see* Towhee, Abert's; species name: Lat., from Gr. *erythros,* red, and *ophthalmos,* eye (Coble, 1954). (Color ills., pages 324, 325.) Across N. America from s. Canada south to Mexico; 7–8¾ in. long; wingspread 10–12¼ in.; somewhat resembles robin, but smaller, slenderer; male, *head, throat, and breast black; rusty sides;* white belly; large white spots in outer tips of long, rounded tail;

western races, or subspecies, have two white wing bars and white marks on back; bill black; in most of N. America, eyes red but a race confined to Fla. has white eyes; female, *brown head, throat, and breast* where male is black, otherwise like male; immature dull brown with streaked underparts, has white markings on wings and tail like adults; in e. U.S., lives in dense brush of old pastures, abandoned fields, edges of woods, brushy clearings; in West, in sagebrush, willows, chaparral in woods of forests above desert; not a dooryard bird but sometimes comes to feeding stations for suet, oats, flax seeds (Dickinson, 1968); winters over much of nesting range except northern limits of; arrives on nesting territory, mostly from W.Va. northward, in Mar. and Apr.; males a few days ahead of females; in courtship, male chases female, fans tail, which shows white spots in outer edges; sings from perch in bush or tree, two notes, first one of higher pitch, followed by short trill, variable songs but often in e. U.S. an emphatic *SWEET-bird-chee-e-e-e* or *DRINK-your, teeeeeee;* call notes are *toe-WHEE!, joreee,* and *che-WINK!;* in w. U.S. a buzzy trill; call note *wank!;* apparently some females sing (Dickinson, 1968).

Feeding Habits: Scratches noisily and vigorously under thickets; eats moths, caterpillars, beetles, bugs, wood borers, ants, scale insects, etc.; also spiders, snails, harvestmen, sow bugs, millipedes, small salamanders, lizards, snakes; seeds of weeds, grasses; wild blueberries, bayberries, strawberries, mulberries, holly berries.
Nest: On ground under bush or brush pile, clump of grass, or above ground in vines, trees, bushes, 1–5 ft., rarely 10–18 ft. up; built by female, of grasses, rootlets, twigs, leaves, string, shreds of bark, lined with horse or cattle hair, grasses.
Eggs: Apr.–Aug.; 2–6, usually 3–4, gray, cream-white or green-white, evenly speckled or spotted with browns.
Incubation: Mostly by female, 12–13 days (Dickinson, 1968); young leave nest when 10–12 days old; two broods a year.
Other Names: Bullfinch (Va.); bush-bird; chewink; ground robin; joree; low-ground-Stephen; marsh robin; eastern towhee; red-eyed towhee; spotted towhee; spurred towhee; swamp robin; turkey sparrow; white-eyed towhee.
Age: Many live 4–6 years; one banded bird reported to be 10 years old when last trapped and released; one banded Clemson, S.C., trapped and released in same area when 12 years, 3 months, old (Kennard, 1975).
Albinism: A "perfect" or total albino, Philadelphia (Townsend, 1883); a partial albino, Ga. (Tomkins, 1936); Greenlaw (1973) collected (shot) an unusually reddish (erythristic) rufous-sided towhee in N.J. in June 1968.
Host to Cowbirds: Very frequently to brown-headed cowbird; about 300 records (Friedmann, 1963).
Hybrids: Occasionally hybridizes in Mexico with the collared towhee, *Pipilo ocai* (Blake, E.R., 1953).
Weights: In Calif., Sept.–May, males (116), 33–45.8 gr. (Linsdale and Sumner, 1937); coastal

N.J. in fall (121), 31.4–47.5 gr. (Murray and Jehl, 1964), or about 1–1¾ oz.
Range: Nests from s. B.C. east to sw. Me.; south to Baja Calif., Guatemala, and w. Tex., n. Okla., n. Ark., s.-c. La., east Gulf coast, s. Fla.; often winters north to s. B.C., Utah, Colo., Neb., Iowa, s. Great Lakes, and Mass.

Towhee, spotted. *See* Towhee, rufous-sided.

Towhee, spurred. *See* Towhee, rufous-sided.

Towhee, white-eyed. *See* Towhee, rufous-sided.

FINDING BIRDS
See under Birder.

FIREBIRD
See Oriole, northern (Baltimore), in Troupial Family; *also* Scarlet tanager in Tanager Family.

FIRE-BRAND
See Blackburnian warbler in Warbler—American Wood Warbler Family.

FIRE-TAIL
See Redstart, American, in Warbler—American Wood Warbler Family.

FISCHER,
JOHANN GOTTHELF, VON WALDHEIM (1771–1853). German doctor and geologist, professor of zoology in Moscow in 1804; noted for his work in natural history in Russia (see in Gruson, 1972); his name is commemorated in the species name of the spectacled eider, *Somateria fischeri.*

FISH BIRD
See Ichthyornis; *also* Fossil Birds.

FISH CRANE
Locally common name for some of the herons, especially the yellow-crowned night heron.

FISH DUCK
See Mergansers under Duck Family.

FISHER
A(LBERT) K(ENRICK), M.D. (1856–1948). A founder and past president of the American Ornithologists' Union; about 1885 assisted C. Hart Merriam in founding a branch of economic ornithology in the federal Division of Entomology; author of *The Hawks and Owls of the United States and Their Relation to Agriculture* (1893); in 1891 served as ornithologist on U.S. government expedition to Death Valley and other little-known parts of the Southwest; was also a member of the Harriman Expedition to Alaska in 1899, and the Pinchot South Seas Expedition of 1929 (Chapman, 1951).

FISHES AND BIRDS
Whole families of N. American birds of the so-called lower orders (for example, Loon, Grebe, Cormorant, and Pelican Families) are adapted (*see* Food and Feeding Habits) or specialized in their watery habitats (*see* Habitat), and by the

FISHES AND BIRDS
Gannets dive for fishes from heights of 50 feet or more and pursue schools of mackerel and herring underwater.

nature of their evolution, to prey upon fishes. N. American birds that subsist almost exclusively on them are: western grebe, Caspian tern, royal tern, Sandwich tern, and other terns, black skimmer, anhinga, double-crested cormorant, brown pelican, white pelican, frigatebird, and osprey (McAtee, 1932b).

Birds whose diets are from 50 to 90% fishes are: common loon, red-necked grebe, black guillemot, pigeon guillemot, common murre, thick-billed murre, black-legged kittiwake, glaucous-winged gull, ring-billed gull, gannet, pelagic cormorant, common merganser, red-breasted merganser, bald eagle, and belted kingfisher (McAtee, 1932b).

Fishes are widely preyed upon by fish-eating birds, according to scientific investigators of birds' food habits, but "no important group of North American birds is more widely misunderstood in [their] . . . economic relationships [see Economic Ornithology]. . . . While a few fish-eating birds are known to inflict damage [to young fishes] around fish hatcheries . . . such damage is usually slight and . . . is more than offset by birds consuming large numbers of spawn-eaters [crayfishes, dragonfly nymphs, water bugs, hydras, leeches] and those fishes that are predators of sport and game fishes" (Cottam and Uhler, 1937).

Of 5,000 stomachs of fish-eating birds examined by federal authorities, about 80% of the identifiable remains of fishes came from 10 families well known for their great number of individuals—the catfishes; the suckers, carps, and minnows; the gizzard shads and herrings; the small tooth-carps, killifishes, and top minnows; the sticklebacks; the sculpins (small to medium-sized marine and freshwater fishes); the salmons and trout; the sunfishes and black bass. Thirty-six young catfishes were found in the stomach of a single belted kingfisher; 150 of the small, spiny, 2–4-in. sticklebacks in a great blue heron; 12 young sunfishes in the stomach of a least bittern; 14 in one anhinga; 18 in a little green heron (McAtee, 1932b).

A least bittern and a great blue heron had each eaten 20 of the small to medium-sized yellow perch; a little green heron had eaten 25 darters, small fishes of the perch family, of which the adults range in size from the tiny 1-in. least darter to the 8-in.-long log perch (Schrenkiesen, 1963). Minnows that live widely in fresh, brackish, and salt water had been eaten by 44 species of birds, with up to 50 in the individual stomachs of a belted kingfisher and a hooded merganser (McAtee, 1932b). According to C. J. Henry (1941), the western grebe is almost entirely an eater of minnows.

McAtee and his investigators found 106 young of the common carp in the stomach of one glossy ibis, and reported that 39 species of birds prey on the 2–3-in.-long common killifishes, with a maximum of 526 in the stomach of a little blue heron. Some of the most specialized feeders on the eggs of other fishes are suckers, sculpins, minnows, sticklebacks, killifishes, top minnows, and trout. Some of the passerines, or songbirds, occasionally eat young trout (trout fry)—for example, the robin, Brewer's blackbird, magpies, and spotted sandpiper (Bent, 1926b). The gray catbird and Louisiana waterthrush have also been reported catching small fishes at the water's edge. The dipper, or water ouzel (see in Dipper Family), which lives in and around mountain streams, occasionally eats trout eggs, but of 60 stomachs examined by food-habits investigators, most dippers had eaten small freshwater sculpins, a sucker, and large numbers of aquatic insects, all of which prey on young fishes (Cottam and Uhler, 1937). See also King and Pyle (1966).

Fishes of many sizes and kinds have no greater enemies (see Enemy) than predatory ones—in the oceans: dogfishes and other sharks, swordfish, bluefish, squeteague, conger eel, and the angler fish; in fresh water: catfishes, the burbot, bowfin, gars, sculpins, trout, pikes, and bass (McAtee, 1932b). Three fourths of the food of some of these freshwater predatory fishes is the flesh of their fellow fin-bearers (Forbes, 1890).

FISHES THAT EAT BIRDS. Fishes are often regular eaters of birds wherever birds feed in or around water. In N. America, the angler fish, *Lophius piscatorius*, of the Atlantic coast, from Newfoundland south to Cape Hatteras (Breder, 1948), is sometimes called goosefish because it occasionally feeds on geese. It attacks cormorants, loons, wild ducks, grebes, auks, gulls, guillemots, and other seabirds (see Seabird), and one, when caught, had the remains of seven wild ducks in its stomach (Terres, 1947c). The thresher shark, *Alopius vulpes*, known from all temperate seas, attacks and swallows loons; the 3-ft. monkfish, *Squatina squatina*, a curious skatelike shark (Breder, 1948), catches and eats cormorants that alight on the surface of the water or dive below it in their search for fishes.

Even such large birds as brown pelicans are in danger when floating on the ocean. Sprunt and Chamberlain (1949) reported that E. Milby Burton while off coast of S.C. came on three brown pelicans, one of which could not fly. He caught it and found that one of its wings had been freshly severed close to its body, probably by a shark. Although treated and cared for, it died within 10 days.

On May 7, 1961, an immature tiger shark, *Galeocerdo cuvier*, more than 6 ft. long, was caught in the Gulf of Mexico off Sarasota, Fla. It had in its stomach, besides a blue crab and seven sea catfishes, a leg and feathers of a yellow-billed cuckoo that had apparently fallen into the water in its migration over the Gulf (Saunders and Clark, 1962); in 1966, the remains of a royal tern were reported in the stomach of a tiger shark, also caught in the Gulf of Mexico (Van Velzen, 1971a).

Even the edible cod, *Gadus callarius*, which may grow to 6 ft. or more, will swallow seabirds such as guillemots. One caught off the coast of Newfoundland had in its stomach a ruffed grouse, possibly one that had flown out over the waters during its fall "crazy flight" (Terres, 1947c). See Fall Shuffle; Grouse Family.

A northern pike, *Esox estor*, which according to Schrenkiesen (1963) may grow to 4 ft. and weigh 40 lbs., in the summer of 1956 leaped into the air from the waters of Lake Minnetonka, Minn., and caught in its mouth a black tern, which it dragged beneath the surface. The tern had been dipping into the water to catch small fishes when it became a victim of the larger fish. Kingfishers have also been found in the stomachs of the northern pike, which is a well-known predator of young ducks and other waterfowl in Canada and in Europe. Pike in Canada take enormous numbers of young waterfowl in June and July, when the birds are less than a week old and spend most of their time swimming about in shallow waters (Pitman, 1962c).

In Nov. 1921, a family in Santa Barbara, Calif., were seated by a lotus pool in their yard when a hummingbird (species not identified) flew to the pool and hovered not far above the water. A black bass broke the surface, leaped into the air, and swallowed the hummer.

While fishing on Lake Okeechobee, Fla., a man in a fishing party caught a 3-lb. largemouth black bass, *Micropterus floridanus*, that had in its stomach the remains of a small warbler—a common yellowthroat. Yellowthroats often nest close to water and flutter over the surface to pick up floating insects. See Common yellowthroat in Warbler—American Wood Warbler Family. The same observer saw a bass strike and drag under one downy young of a brood of black-necked stilts which were swimming about when the bass discovered them. He also reported that eight of a brood of twelve domestic ducks had been eaten by bass in the lake during one day (Rand, 1943). See also Accidents; Predation; Food and Feeding Habits; and Feeding Habits in biography of each species. See also Mollusks and Birds.

FISH HAWK
See Osprey in Osprey Family.

FLAMINGO FAMILY
Phoenicopteridae (fee-nih-cop-TER-ih-dee); Lat., from Gr., red-winged; name derived from the fabled phoenix, described as a red bird; the Gr. name *phoinix*, meaning crimson red, was transferred from the phoenix, at some time in early Christian history, to the European, Asian, and African flamingo, *Phoenicopterus antiquorum*, which is red-winged and largest of all flamingos (Allen, 1956a). 6 species in the world (Van Tyne and Berger, 1976); tall, usually pink or pink-white with black flight feathers; long-necked, long-legged, mostly tropical; 36–50 in. long (some stand 6½ ft. high according to Brown, 1964b); 1 species wanders rarely from the Bahamas into N. American region; it is second-largest; 3 others are in S. America—the Chilean flamingo, *Phoenicopterus chilensis;* the Andean flamingo, *Phoenicoparrus andinus;* and the rare James's flamingo, *Phoenicoparrus jamesi;* the lesser flamingo, *Phoeniconaias minor*, in Africa, is smallest in world (Allen, 1956a).

According to Allen, in Jan. 1931 a flock of flamingos, shipped to Miami from Cuba, were released within Hialeah Race Course; they were neither wing-clipped nor pinioned, and next day flew away; they were apparently responsible for many reports in 1930s of wild flamingos in Fla., where they had never been known to breed. In 1937 another flock, this one pinioned, was established at Hialeah; beginning in 1942, they nested there each year and raised about 65 young annually. Flamingos do well in captivity and retain good feather color when fed the proper diet. The Philadelphia Zoo recorded good success in keeping and breeding flamingos with a mixture of "zoo cake" (similar to a high protein poultry feed), ground meat, and carrot juice; should be in small particles mixed together and fed to the flamingo in shallow water so the bird can get it by its feeding method of straining out the food as it pumps water through the bill.

The large downward-bent bill is the most remarkable of any bird in the world; its shape alone serves to identify it and to set the flamingo apart from all other birds; the lower mandible resembles an expanded box and the upper mandible a thin profusely laminated lid that just fits into it; both upper and lower parts of the bill are bent sharply downward just in front of the nostrils; this bent bill is an adaptation for feeding, and designed so that the bent portion is parallel with the bottom of the pond, lake, or flats in which they are feeding. The large fleshy tongue moves rapidly back and forth pumping water out of the bill and sieving out small mollusks, crustaceans, insects, fishes, and vegetable matter which the flamingo eats.

Classification of flamingos has puzzled ornithologists (taxonomists) for many years. Some authorities, according to Palmer (1962), rank the flamingos in a separate order, the Phoenicopteriformes; the American Ornithologists' Union (1957) classified them in the order Ciconiiformes, family Phoenicopteridae. In habits and in their feather lice, they seem closest to the ducks and geese; in some parts of their anatomy, to storks and ibises; however, they honk and babble like geese and the downy young are very gooselike. Finally, studies of their egg-white protein placed them near the herons. The discovery by Feduccia (1976) of a fossil, *Presbyornis*, and studies of it, he believed, contradicted the long-held hypothesis of a relationship of flamingos to the storks and ibises, and show that ancient shorebirds were the basic stock from which both flamingos and ducks arose (see Feduccia, 1978).

American flamingo, *Phoenicopterus ruber* (fee-nih-COP-ter-us RUB-er or RUBE-er); genus name: New Lat., from Gr. *phoinix*, purpled-red, and *pteron*, wing; species name: Lat., red. (Color ill., page 326.) In wild a rare straggler to Fla., populations limited to Yucatán, parts of West Indies and Bahamas, Galápagos Is., and n. S. America (Palmer, 1962); 36–50 in. long; wingspread about 60 in.; sexes outwardly alike, male decidedly larger; birds distinguished by unique bill, long, sinuous neck and long legs that are longer in proportion to body length than that of any other birds (Austin, 1961); gray or light pink to strikingly pink or vermilion, (reddest of all flamingos) but flight feathers of wings black; legs and feet almost entirely pink; eyes yellow; downcurved whitish bill black-tipped; the three front toes are webbed; excellent swimmer; flocks fly with rapid wingbeats, necks extended forward, legs trailing, in long lines; "a cloud of flame-colored pink like the hues of a brilliant sunset" (Scott, 1890); lives on vast mud flats about shallow saltwater bays and lagoons of virtually uninhabited tropical coasts and islands; shy and gregarious, vigilant, difficult to approach, needs isolation to survive; capable of long-sustained flight, travels at night (Palmer, 1962); when flock seen standing long distance away on broad, flat, shimmering waste of marl, are a glowing band of brilliant pink against background of dark green mangroves; flocks talk in low gabbling notes, when alarmed utter deep-voiced honking, one of commonest, *huh-huh-huh*, with strong accent on middle syllable (Chapman, 1905); in flight their notes resemble a chorus of frogs; arrive at nesting areas in flocks, adults in summer; like ducks and geese, molt all their flight feathers at once and become temporarily flightless.

Feeding Habits: Feeds in water of any depth in which it can wade; with head or bill immersed in water, sucks up rich organic bottom ooze, from which tongue and bill filter out, as their main food in the Bahamas, principally algal material plus bacteria, diatoms, etc., along with tiny fishes, probably *Cyprinodon*, all of which are ground up by the bird's powerful stomach muscles (Chapman, 1905; Allen, 1956a). In the s. Caribbean (Bonaire Is.), their principal food consists of the larvae and pupae of the brine fly (*Ephydra* sp.).

Nest: In colonies from hundreds up to 7,000 pairs, on marl or mud flats, from which nests are built by females assisted by males; each nest a cone, usually 6–18 in. high, 17–20 in. in diameter at base with a hollowed top; nests may be 2 ft. apart or closer (Palmer, 1962).

Eggs: Bahamas, Mar.–June; usually 1, rarely 2, chalk white; 20 from Bahamas averaged 91.06 mm. long × 55.48 mm. in girth, or about 3⅔ in. long × 2¼ in. in girth.

Incubation: By both sexes in turn, sits on top of nest mound with legs folded under body, for estimated 28–32 days; at hatching, bill of chick is short and straight, is fed by both parents for 3–4 days on a nutritious red liquid secreted by glands in the digestive tract; later is herded with other chicks into group called a crèche; 40 days after hatching, bill is downcurved like that of adults; can fly about 75–77 days after hatching.

Other Names: Greater flamingo; roseate flamingo; scarlet flamingo; West Indian flamingo; Caribbean flamingo.

Age: A captive lived to 18 years (Allen, R.P., 1954).

Weights: Males to perhaps 8 lbs.; females to 6½ lbs. (Palmer, 1962).

Range: Resident West Indies, n. S. America, Galápagos Is., wandered formerly in large numbers to Fla. but now rarely. Casual in coastal Tex., La., nw. Fla., S.C., N.C., Bermuda, Puerto Rico, and Virgin Is.

Greater flamingo. Common name, originally, for the Old World species *Phoenicopterus antiquorum*, but also the name for the American flamingo by those ornithologists who consider the Old World *antiquorum* and the American *ruber* to be not separate, but merely forms of the same species. See, for example, Palmer's usage (1962).

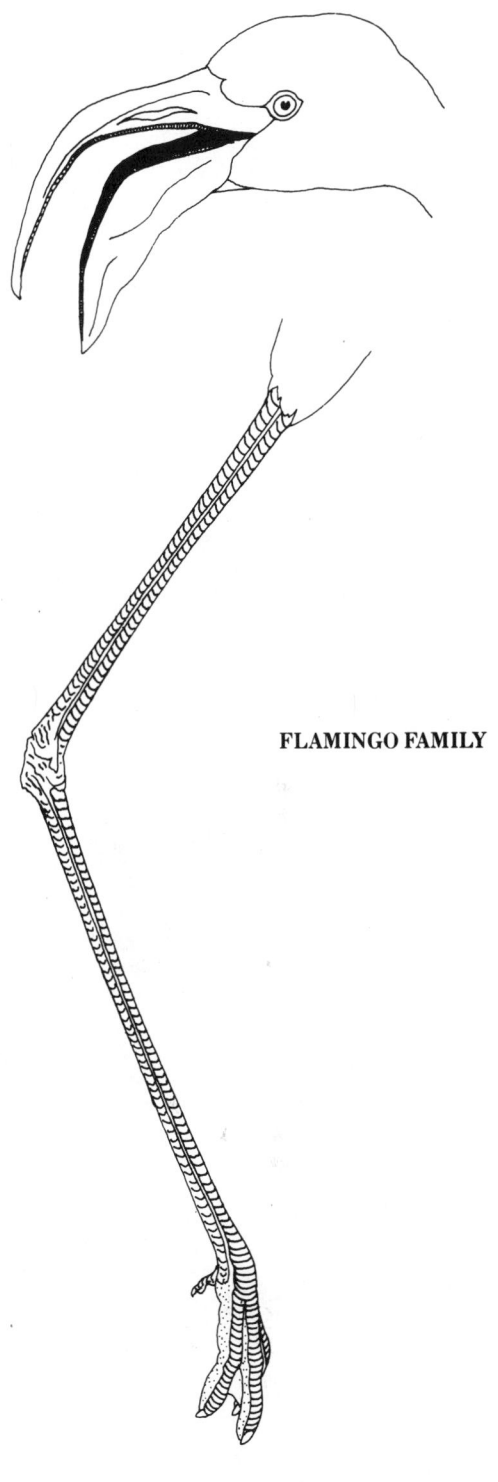

FLAMINGO FAMILY

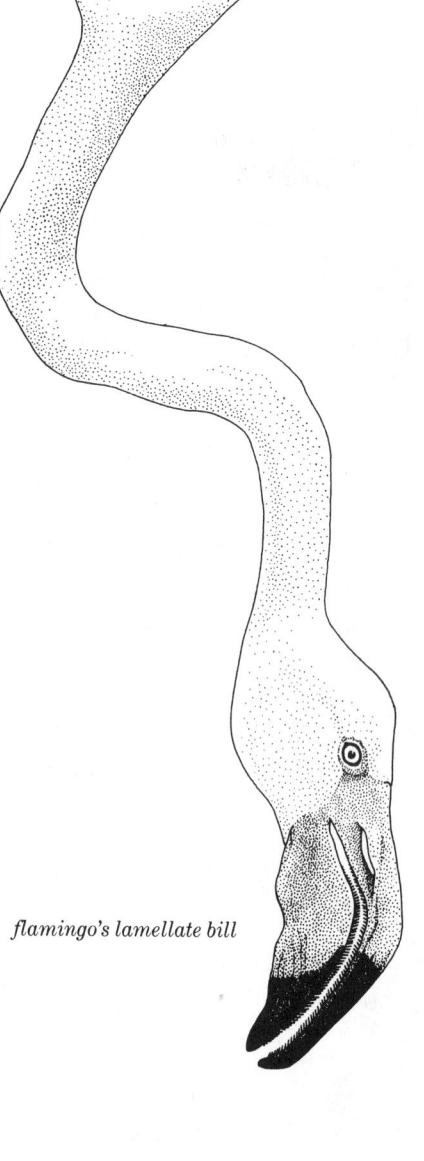

flamingo's lamellate bill

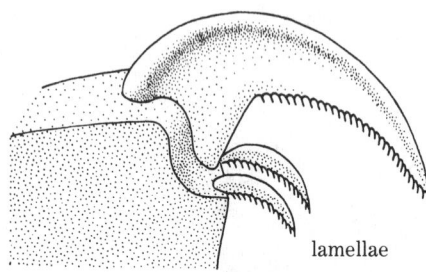

lamellae

FLAMINGO FAMILY
Lamellate bills have transverse, toothlike ridges, which a bird uses as a sieve to filter edible matter from the water.

Roseate flamingo. See American flamingo.

West Indian flamingo. See American flamingo.

FLAPPING
See Flight.

FLASH COLORS
See Colors That Advertise under Colors of Feathers.

FLAT-FLIES
See Hippoboscid Flies.

FLEAS
Very few species of fleas parasitize birds. Of the 1,800 species of fleas in the world (Turner, 1971), only about 100 species have been reported on birds. Rothschild and Clay (1957) reported that only 55 or possibly 60 species of fleas known at that time, live permanently or temporarily on the bodies of birds; of these, 27 had been found on the bodies or in the nests of birds which return to the same nesting sites year after year (*see* Nests and Nesting); 19 species were from ground- or hole-nesting birds, and 9 are known only from islands; many parasitize birds that use mud in their nests, such as swallows.

Fleas are wingless insects of the order Siphonaptera (sigh-fon-AP-ter-ah), and the adults feed exclusively on the blood of living birds and mammals. There are hundreds of species of "mammal fleas," of which such common species known to man are the cat flea, dog flea, rat flea, and human flea. "Bird fleas" are thought to have originated from the mammal fleas, and the bird fleas have not diverged very far from them in the few hundreds of thousands of years of their change-over from mammals to birds as hosts.

Less than one bird in ten harbors fleas, and then usually only one or two are on the bird at a time. If a bird is collected (shot) or captured alive and handled, the fleas, which cannot fly, leap quickly away. In 1910, M. B. Mitzmain, an American naturalist, measured the leap of a flea and found it could jump horizontally about 13 in.

Because relatively few fleas are ever found on the bodies of birds, it is assumed that they spend the greater part of their time in the nest or hiding in debris and visit the bird host only periodically when they are hungry. Fleas often show a preference for certain habitats rather than the bodies of their bird hosts (in the larval state, fleas are not parasitic on birds but live upon organic detritus in nests); for example, the common hen flea, *Ceratophyllus gallinae*, usually lives in the dry elevated nests in hen houses or in nests of sparrows, starlings, and swallows, but the duck flea, *Ceratophyllus garei*, prefers a low swampy habitat (Rothschild and Clay, 1957).

There are about 20 species of bird fleas in N. America; the food of the adult flea is blood; the larvae of fleas sometimes swarm in thousands in one bird nest, where they may live in part upon the nest debris. The wound that the adult bird flea inflicts on its host's skin and flesh is accomplished with its maxillary lacinia (mouth parts)—a pair of tiny sword-shaped blades with rows of upward-projecting teeth on their outer surfaces. On the inner surface of these blades is a gutter or channel down which the flea ejects saliva containing an enzyme which inhibits clotting of the host bird's blood. The few individual fleas that live on the bodies of adult birds and suck their blood are of little harm, but several thousand in a nest filled with young birds can be a serious menace to them. Large numbers constantly draining the blood of nestling birds, especially during spells of cool or cold weather when the parents may have difficulty feeding them enough insects, must be a contributing cause to the deaths of many young birds; however, the effects of fleas on them is difficult to evaluate (see Rothschild, 1965).

According to research reports, fleas do not transmit disease-causing organisms to wild birds. The sticktight flea, *Echidnophaga gallinacea*, however, unlike other bird fleas that merely crawl through a bird's feathers, remains embedded in the skin of the host, usually about the bird's head. In domestic chickens, it can cause weight losses, reduced egg-laying, and even death due to losses of blood. A small amount of pyrethrum or rotenone sifted through a bird's feathers or over its skin will cause most fleas to drop off the infested host (Turner, 1971).

Depending on the flea species, adults lay up to 500 eggs randomly, and usually in small batches on the host. Some eggs stick to the bird host but most drop off into the bottom of the nest or into crevices or onto the floor of the building in which the nest is built.

The greatest enemy of the bird flea is probably its bird host, which in preening its feathers with its bill may capture and destroy fleas. The remains of bird fleas have been found in the crops of birds (*see* Crop), although fleas do not seem to be in the normal diet of any insectivorous bird (*see* Food and Feeding Habits). Remarkably, McAtee (1932b), from examination of the stomach contents of some 80,000 N. American birds, could report only a single record of a flea being eaten.

According to Fox (1940), some fleas of N. American birds are: *Echidnophaga gallinacea*, the sticktight flea of domestic poultry, also found on the Cooper's hawk, blue jay, bobwhite quail; and *Ceratophyllus gallinae*, not only on the domestic hen but on the tree swallow, eastern bluebird, and house sparrow; another flea, *Ceratophyllus celsus*, on the cliff swallow; *Ceratophyllus diffinis*, on the ruffed grouse, eastern bluebird, gray catbird, American robin, ovenbird, veery, and house wren; *Ceratophyllus niger*, on the eastern bluebird; and so on. See Fox (1940) for details; see methods of collecting fleas from birds and for additional groups parasitized by other groups of fleas in Turner (1971); *see also* Parasite; Hippoboscid Flies; Lice; Protocalliphora; Ectoparasite.

FLEDGLING
A young bird that has recently left the nest; is feathered; and still depends on its parent for food. It is a *fledgling* from the time it leaves the nest until it is independent of all parental

care (Berger, 1961). A very few kinds of birds have no fledgling period; the common swift, *Apus apus,* of Europe and Asia is said to be completely independent of the adults when it flies from the nest. *See* Nestling.

FLEXOR TENDONS
See Feet and Legs.

FLICKER
See discussion of name under Flicker, common, in Woodpecker Family.

FLICKER, THE
A publication. *See* Ornithological Periodicals.

FLIES
(parasitic). *See* louse-flies under Hippoboscid Flies; calliphorid flies under Protocalliphora; blackflies (Simuliidae) under Diseases.

FLIGHT
Birds fly by the same aerodynamic principles as an airplane. They use much the same type of equipment—wings for support and steering; propellers to drive them through the air; a tail to help steer and to help brake speed of flight and for control when landing; and wing slots and wing flaps to help take off from the ground or to alight (Storer, J. H., 1952).

Most people, even before they understand the principles of bird flight, are interested in how fast and how high birds can fly. The speed of flight of many birds has been measured by automobile speedometer, by aircraft, and by radar. Ornithologists and other scientists agree that if a wind is blowing, unless one knows the speed of the air mass (wind) with which the bird is being carried, or against which it is flying, there is no way of knowing its true airspeed; however, what interests most of us is how fast a bird gets over the ground regardless of the force or direction of the wind. How fast do birds fly ordinarily? How much faster can they fly when pressed by danger, hunger, or fright?

SPEED OF FLIGHT. According to Col. Richard Meinertzhagen (1955), some birds fly much faster in their courtship flights, others when pursuing their prey, and others when being chased by a predatory bird. In still others— flocks of migrating shorebirds and swallows, for example—each bird may fly faster when in the flock than when flying alone. The colonel's studies also showed that birds have a reserve of speed that, when needed, can carry them a third to twice their normal, or "cruising," speed. The peregrine falcon, for example, may fly in ordinary flight at 40–60 m.p.h. (Terres, 1968a), but is capable of attaining at least 175 m.p.h.—the airspeed of the plane reported by Lawson (1930) when a falcon passed it—in its stoop, or dive, in pursuit of prey. Six racing pigeons (the rock dove, or domestic pigeon, which the peregrine falcon often captures in flight) were timed officially in Great Britain and France at 28, 52, 57, 60, 65, and 82 m.p.h., showing the great variation in flight speed of which this species is capable (Riviere, 1922).

A male red-breasted merganser, pursued by Max C. Thompson (1961) in an airplane in n. Alaska, attained a top airspeed of 80 m.p.h.

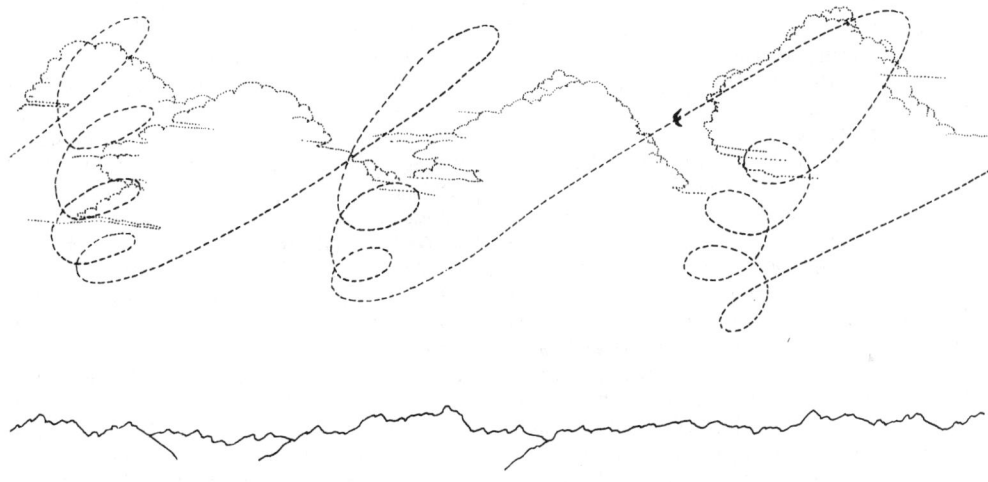

FLIGHT
Static soarers, such as hawks and vultures, can stay aloft without flapping their wings by maneuvering to take advantage of rising currents of warm air called "thermals."

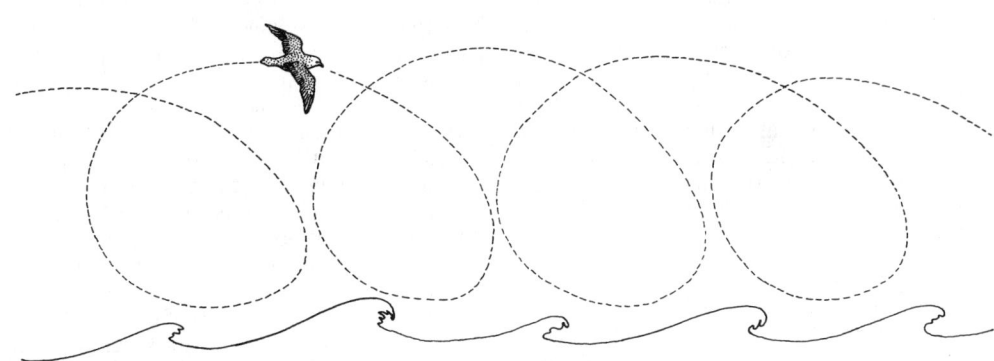

A fulmar dives through the layers of air currents that blow at different velocities, and it builds up speed as it falls through the slower, less resistant air close to the water's surface. At the bottom of its dive, the bird dips one wing and banks sharply. Rising again, boosted by its momentum and by updrafts of air from the waves, it reaches its original height without flapping its wings.

along a river for 1,500 ft. before turning aside. With a wind of 20 m.p.h. assisting the bird, Thompson reported its ground speed as 100 m.p.h. According to Thompson, the previously reported greatest speed for a duck was recorded by an airplane whose pilot pursued a canvasback at 72 m.p.h.

Some of the swiftest fliers among American birds are the small sandpipers of coastal beaches and waters, which, like the falcons, swifts, swallows, hummingbirds, and some ducks, have the so-called high-speed wing. *See* Waterfowl. T. T. McCabe (1942), while piloting his plane over San Francisco Bay, measured the cruising flight speeds of red-backed sandpipers (now called dunlins), godwits, and curlews flying below him at 45 to 55 m.p.h., but one evening, when the red-backed and other sandpipers overtook his plane and flew past him, they were flying, according to McCabe, at not less than 110 m.p.h. and possibly "a great deal more."

Near Richvale, Calif., Donald Dudley McLean (1930) clocked ground speeds of different kinds of birds along a highway with his automobile; a little green heron flew at 34 m.p.h. with no wind blowing, and a barn swallow at 46 m.p.h. A cinnamon teal flew in leisurely flight at 32 m.p.h., but when McLean speeded up to try to overtake the duck it flew at 59 m.p.h. before turning away. Two red-shafted flickers flew at 43 and 44 m.p.h.; a Savannah sparrow at 37 m.p.h., and another, when pressed by McLean, at 42 m.p.h.

Some of the general ranges of the flight speed of birds have been reported by Wetmore (1926):

Crow Family (Corvidae)	31–45 m.p.h.
small perchers (larks, pipits, buntings, etc.)	20–37 m.p.h.
starlings	38–49 m.p.h.
geese	42–45 m.p.h.
ducks	44–59 m.p.h.

One of the modern and accurate ways of measuring the flight speeds of birds is with a radar unit which operates on the same principle as radar used by police to detect speeding of automobile drivers. Using portable radar equipment, which had an error of no more than 1 m.p.h., Gary D. Schnell (1965) reported 1,628 flight-speed records of 17 species of birds in Mich., more speed records than had been reported previously for birds in all history. Birds whose speeds he reported were gulls, terns, swifts, kingbirds, cedar waxwings, red-winged blackbirds, spotted sandpipers, and others. For a more recent list of the flight speeds of 21 species, see Tucker and Schmidt-Koenig, 1977.

Of all flight speeds measured by Schnell, that of the house sparrow was one of the slowest at 16–19 m.p.h. Apparently the minimal speed of birds in order to remain airborne is about 16½ ft. per second, or about 11 m.p.h.

The swiftest straight-forward, wing-beating flight of any bird ever reported was that of two spine-tailed swifts, *Hirundapus caudacutus,* clocked with a stopwatch at 172 and 218 m.p.h. respectively by E. C. Stuart-Baker (1922) in the Cachar Hills of India. *See also,* when known, flight speeds reported in the biographies of each bird.

HOW HIGH DO BIRDS FLY? It is probable that, except during migration, most small to medium-sized birds seldom fly more than 50–100 ft. above their habitat and usually much less, except those swifts, swallows, nighthawks, and certain other birds that virtually live in the air while feeding, and fly at various heights to sweep their flying insect prey out of the air. The European swift, *Apus apus,* sometimes glides about all night and sleeps on the wing high above the earth (Weitnauer, 1956). *See also* Altitude of Bird Flight and Roosting. Ducks, geese, and other water birds may travel up to hundreds of feet above ground or water to move to or from local feeding places in ponds, rivers, etc. Eagles, hawks, and falcons sometimes fly hundreds of feet above the earth to glide or spiral about, looking for mammalian prey on the ground below or to drop down to capture birds that may be traveling through the air below them.

Vultures and condors often soar to great heights, up to thousands of feet, to look about for dead animals on the ground or to watch for other vultures or condors that might be descending to prey they have located. Some of the highest flights ever reported for birds were those of a lammergeyer, or bearded vulture, soaring about its home on Mt. Everest in July at 25,000 ft., and alpine choughs, Eurasian crow-like birds, nesting on Mt. Everest at 27,000 ft., and members of a flock diving and tumbling at each other "in the wildest kind of aerial game" (Gilliard, 1958). Ordinarily it is during migration that the greatest heights of bird flight have been reported. *See* Migration. There is an old record of geese photographed against the sun in India at an estimated 29,000 ft., a record that has been questioned; however, for many high flight records of birds, and especially those of bar-headed geese and a Rüppell's griffon, *see* Altitude of Bird Flight.

THE BIRD'S FLYING EQUIPMENT. The predominant aerodynamic forces—lift and drag—that act on an aircraft in flight also act on a flying bird. During the long evolution of birds (*see* Origin of Birds and of Bird Flight under Fossil Birds), this has influenced the bladelike shape of the wing, the basic lifting surface of either a bird or an airplane. The wing of a bird consists of two functional parts: an inner part nearest the body and moved by the bird's shoulder joint; and the outer part—the "hand" section—which is moved separately by the bird's wrist—the joint at the outer bend of its wing. It is the outer hand section of each wing, with its strong, pliable flight feathers, or primaries (*see* Feather; Topography), that functions as a propeller when the bird beats the air in flapping flight.

The inner part of the wing provides the bird almost exclusively with lift. In flight, whether soaring, gliding, or flapping, the bird holds this part of the wing out rather rigidly from its sides, with a slight tilt upward and forward (the angle of attack) like the rigid wing of an airplane. When held at the proper angle (usually about 3–5° from the horizontal) it supports the bird's weight in the air throughout each wingbeat, but is constantly adjusted by the bird to maintain a steady lifting force (Storer, J. H., 1952).

FLYCATCHER FAMILY

Acadian flycatcher

Flycatchers of the genus Empidonax *(literally translated as "mosquito king") are so similar in size and appearance that a bird-watcher can identify them with certainty only by their calls, habitat, and range. In the case of the Acadian flycatcher, it is the only member of its genus to breed in the southern states. Mature woodlands, especially floodplain forests, are its haunt; perched on a dead twig beneath the canopy, the Acadian flycatcher darts out for beetles, wasps, bees, craneflies, dragonflies, and a host of other passing insects. Prey too large to be swallowed whole will be held in the feet and eaten piece by piece.*

Acadian flycatcher

Alder flycatcher

Dense, damp alder thickets across the north country are the summer home of this Empidonax *flycatcher. Its nest, built close to the ground in the fork of a small shrub, is a loose collection of plant materials.*

Ash-throated flycatcher

This western flycatcher ranges from the broiling desert of Death Valley, below sea level, to open woodland at 9,000 feet in the Sierra Nevada. Though a cavity nester, the ash-throated flycatcher still builds an elaborate nest of weeds, grass, bits of dried dung, animal fur, and the shed skins of snakes and lizards.

Coues' flycatcher

A large Central American relative of the wood pewees, Coues' flycatcher is fairly common in pine-oak forests high on the mountains of Arizona and New Mexico. Its name honors Dr. Eliot Coues, the great 19th-century ornithologist and frontier army surgeon. This flycatcher so vigorously defends its territory against jays, hawks, squirrels, and snakes that other songbirds build their nests close by for protection.

Dusky flycatcher

One of several western Empidonax *flycatchers, this is a bird of chaparral slopes. Three or 4 eggs are laid in a cup of grass and plant fibers woven into the crotch of a small tree.*

Ash-throated flycatcher

Dusky flycatcher

Coues' flycatcher

Alder flycatcher

Gray flycatcher
The blue-gray color of this Empidonax *flycatcher of the Great Basin blends with the sagebrush and juniper of its semiarid habitat.*

Great crested flycatcher
This large, colorful, and noisy bird is the only eastern flycatcher that nests in holes—natural tree cavities, birdhouses, even mailboxes. It aggressively defends its nesting territory against other males, tearing out the feathers of its opponents in fierce aerial combat.

Hammond's flycatcher
Similar in song and appearance to the dusky flycatcher of chaparral hillsides, this species avoids competition for nest sites and food by living higher on the mountains in open coniferous forests.

Kiskadee flycatcher
Named for its loud call, this strikingly colored tropical flycatcher, locally common in the Rio Grande valley of Texas, often behaves like a kingfisher— sitting motionless on a perch over the water, then diving for small fish and tadpoles near the surface. In winter, if insects are scarce, it eats fruit, berries, and seeds.

Least flycatcher
Of all the Empidonax *flycatchers, this is probably the best known; for it frequents village shade trees, city parks, gardens, orchards, and rural roadsides, uttering its song—a vigorous "che-bec!" 50 to 70 times every minute. The young are cared for by both adults for 3 weeks after they leave the nest.*

Kiskadee flycatcher

Least flycatcher

Great crested flycatcher

Hammond's flycatcher

Gray flycatcher

Olive-sided flycatcher
*In summer, boreal and mountain forests
ring with the song of the olive-sided
flycatcher, an emphatic order for "quick,
three beers." This bird of the wilderness
has a special fondness for honeybees.*

Scissor-tailed flycatcher
*Darting over the south-central
grasslands, this remarkable flycatcher
opens and shuts its 9-inch-long tail like a
pair of scissors. It will perch for hours on
a roadside fence post or the limb of an
isolated tree, oblivious to passing
automobiles, dashing out to catch bees
and wasps or dropping to the ground after
grasshoppers and crickets.*

Vermilion flycatcher
*Birders in the arid Southwest have no
difficulty recognizing the male of this
species, which ranges from Utah to South
America. Streamside mesquites, willows,
and cottonwoods are the nesting habitat of
the vermilion flycatcher. The male has a
dramatic courtship flight in which it
hovers like a butterfly, its red crest erect
and breast feathers swollen, then flutters
down to its mate.*

Olive-sided flycatcher

Vermilion flycatcher

Vermilion flycatcher, female

Scissor-tailed flycatcher

Western flycatcher

Yet another member of the confusing Empidonax *clan, the western flycatcher summers in shaded, moist forests from the Rocky Mountains to the Pacific shore. Its nest may be situated in a cliffside niche, among the roots of an upturned tree, in a pile of driftwood, or under the eaves of a building or bridge.*

Wied's crested flycatcher

This Central and South American relative of the great crested flycatcher reaches the American Southwest, where it nests in saguaro cacti, canyon sycamores, and riverside groves of cottonwoods and willows. On several occasions it has been observed catching and eating hummingbirds.

Willow flycatcher

This bird and the almost identical alder flycatcher were considered to be the same species, then called Traill's flycatcher, until research in the 1950s and 1960s showed that there were important differences between the two. The willow flycatcher ranges farther south, and its "fitz-bew" call is easily told from the "fee-bee-o" song of the alder flycatcher.

Yellow-bellied flycatcher

A wash of yellow over the throat and chest and a yellow eye-ring make this the easiest Empidonax *flycatcher to identify. Spruce-fir forests across Canada and the northern United States are its summer home; its nest, a bulky cup of moss, sedges, and rootlets, is usually hidden in a mound of sphagnum.*

Yellow-bellied flycatcher

Wied's crested flycatcher

Western flycatcher

Willow flycatcher

Eastern kingbird

This familiar black and white flycatcher of the open countryside is noted for its fearlessness and audacity. Kingbirds will torment and rout any larger birds that venture over their nesting territory. They will even alight on the backs of hawks and vultures, and have been known to attack low-flying airplanes. Eastern kingbirds raise 3 to 5 young in a bulky nest built far out on a horizontal limb, often of a fruit tree.

Gray kingbird

A common flycatcher on Caribbean islands, the gray kingbird nests in the United States in the coastal regions of Georgia, South Carolina, and Florida. It is regularly seen on utility wires along the highway over the Florida Keys, where it nests in mangrove swamps. In addition to the usual insect prey, the gray kingbird eats lizards and the fruit of tropical trees.

Thick-billed kingbird

A Mexican bird that crosses the United States border into Arizona and New Mexico, the thick-billed kingbird was first discovered in Guadalupe Canyon in 1958. It builds a fragile nest 50 to 60 feet above the ground in streamside sycamores.

Tropical kingbird

Though it nests in the United States only on the Mexican borderlands of Arizona and Texas, this Central and South American species is nonetheless the most common kingbird in the lower Rio Grande valley. In late summer and fall, tropical kingbirds stage a reverse migration along the Pacific coast, wandering as far north as British Columbia.

Western kingbird

This common kingbird of western ranchlands appears more tolerant than others of its kind. In a land where nest sites are scarce, 2 or more pairs will share a single tree. Western kingbirds have even nested in harmony in the same tree with golden eagles.

Thick-billed kingbird

Eastern kingbird

Gray kingbird

Western kingbird

Tropical kingbird

Eastern wood pewee

From its perch high on a dead branch amid the forest gloom, this common inhabitant of eastern woodlands whistles its name, a plaintive "pee-ah-wee!" The lack of an eye-ring distinguishes the wood pewee from the small Empidonax flycatchers that may share its habitat.

Western wood pewee

West of the 100th meridian, the western wood pewee pursues the insect life of open, parklike woodlands. In areas where their ranges overlap, the two pewees are virtually indistinguishable; but the western species has a totally different call, a nasal "pheer" that suggests a nighthawk.

Black phoebe

A year-round resident of the Southwest, the black phoebe is seldom seen far from water: a mountain stream, an irrigation ditch, a livestock watering trough, a marshy pond, a reservoir. It is marked like a junco—slate black except for a white belly—but its behavior is clearly that of a flycatcher. Perched on a low branch or fence, it swoops down to snatch insects close to the ground; occasionally it also takes small fish.

Eastern phoebe

Constantly jerking its tail, the eastern phoebe utters its name as often as 40 times a minute—"fee-bee, fee-bee, fee-bee." This medium-sized flycatcher likes to live near water, and often builds its nest of mud and moss beneath a country bridge. Other favored phoebe nest sites include rock ledges in dark, damp ravines, barn rafters, and the eaves of forest cabins. Two and sometimes 3 broods are raised in a summer. The first bird-banding experiment, by Audubon in 1840, involved tying a silver wire around a phoebe's leg; the bird returned the following year.

Say's phoebe

With its rust-colored belly, this common phoebe of western plains resembles a small robin. Avoiding timbered places, it nests around ranch buildings, on sagebrush-clad bluffs, and on the cliffs of badlands. It constantly darts out from its favored perch to snatch passing insects and sometimes hovers like a kestrel.

Western wood pewee

Eastern wood pewee

Eastern phoebe

Say's phoebe

Black phoebe

FRIGATEBIRD FAMILY

Magnificent frigatebird

Aloft over tropical bays, this relative of pelicans, boobies, and cormorants can be mistaken for no other bird. Sail-like wings with a spread of 7 to 8 feet allow frigatebirds to soar effortlessly over coastal waters; they swoop low over the surface to catch flying fish or harass other seabirds until they give up their catches, which the "man-o'-war-bird" grabs in midair. Not even the osprey is immune to such piratical tactics. The male frigatebird is entirely glossy black; the female can be told by a white breast, and immature birds by their white heads and necks. Commonly seen in the Florida Keys, the magnificent frigatebird was first discovered nesting there in 1969.

"Creative license gone mad" is the way one ornithologist described the enormous scarlet throat sac, or gular pouch, of the male frigatebird. For most of the year the pouch is visible only as a strip of pink skin running down the throat. But for 3 or 4 weeks at the start of the breeding season, it becomes a fantastic flag to attract a mate. With the pouch blown up like a balloon—a process that takes 20 to 30 minutes—the male frigatebird waits on his perch, wings spread, bill pointing up, as he scans the sky for a female. When one appears, the undersides of his wings are turned upward, their silvery surface flashing in the sunlight. Wings trembling, the male throws back his head to expose the full size of the pouch and utters a high, falsetto warble. Males are sometimes seen in flight with their pouches inflated.

Magnificent frigatebird, immature

Magnificent frigatebird

Magnificent frigatebird, immature

Magnificent frigatebird, female

Magnificent frigatebird

If a bird is planning to alight, it raises the angle of attack higher and higher as it descends to the ground, which slows the bird's speed by gradually increasing drag and losing lift. As the bird nears the place at which it will alight, it brings into play a small group of feathers at the front edge of the "wrist" of the wing, which is called, collectively, the alula, or bastard wing. *See* Alula. This is the bird's auxiliary airfoil to help it gain additional lift when alighting (or in taking off). By the time it is within a few inches of the ground, it has raised the angle of attack of its inner wing to about 25°, at which the wings "stall" and the bird touches down lightly, with its feet absorbing the shock as it reaches the surface of the ground (Jack, 1953).

FLAPPING FLIGHT—USING THE "PROPELLERS." In free flight, the bird's powerful breast muscles (the pectorals) sweep the whole wing up and down from the shoulder. The inner part of the wing, although it does not actually need to move for flapping flight, acts as a handle for the propeller (outer part of wing) and gives it greater speed and power.

In the 1860s, Etienne J. Marey, a French scientist who experimented with the way that insects fly, also experimented with studies of the wing movements of crows in flight. He attached bits of white paper to the wing tips of a crow and released the bird so that it could fly against a black background. His photographic images of the white tips of the crow's wings in flight showed that, on the downbeat, the tips swept *forward and downward*, made a loop at the bottom of the downstroke, then, on the upbeat, traveled *upward and backward*, until the wing tips curved again at the high point of the stroke to make the next downbeat. This experiment refuted the previously held theory that in flight birds used their wings as one rows a boat, pushing backward and downward, with the return of the arms and oars forward and upward.

In its normal flapping flight, the wings of a bird sweep through the downbeat fully extended. At the end of the downstroke, the bird flexes its "wrists" to begin the upsweep of the wings. The whole wings then start upward, the hand section first, with the primary, or flight, feathers of the hand section of the wings partially separated like the fingers of a hand, and the inner half of the wings pulling along after the outer hand section, keeping the outer part vertical rather than horizontal as on the downstroke. At the end of the upward sweep of the wings, the hand section, in a sudden powerful burst, flaps *up* and *out* and resumes its position for the next downward sweep of the wings. It is the downstroke that propels the bird forward.

A bird has almost complete control over the hand section of its wings just as a man has over his hands and fingers. The bird can twist its hand (the outer wing primaries) to any position, waggle them about, and can even clap the hands (outer wings) together behind the head and in front of its breast; examples: the domestic pigeon and the ruffed grouse.

The heavier the bird, the faster it must fly to stay aloft. Sir D'Arcy Thompson, an eminent

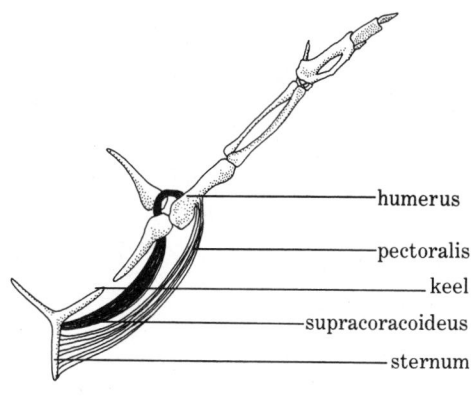

humerus
pectoralis
keel
supracoracoideus
sternum

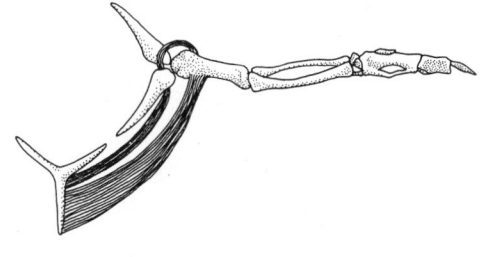

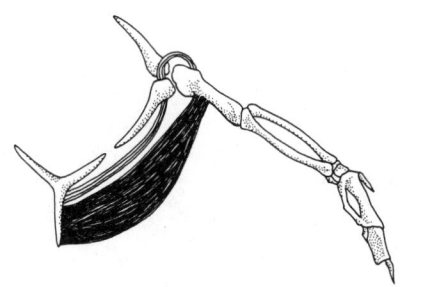

FLIGHT
The two major flight muscles of a bird's wing, the pectoralis and the supracoracoideus, function together smoothly as a pulley system in raising and lowering the wing. The pectoralis, anchored at the sternum and at the humerus, contracts and draws the wing downward; as the pectoralis relaxes, its antagonist contracts, pulling the wing upward.

hovering

FLIGHT

The hummingbird hovers by rotating its shoulder joint and turning its pointed wings completely over on the backstroke and the forestroke, which cut through the air and check the tendency to move forward or backward.

In normal flight, the wings of a bird sweep through the forward downbeat fully extended. To begin the upbeat, the bird flexes its "wrist" and the whole wing starts upward and backward, the "hand" section first, the flight feathers partially separated like fingers. At the end of the upbeat, the hand section flaps up and out and is ready for the next downbeat.

flapping flight

formation flying

Canada geese take advantage of the slipstreams — vortices of disturbed air created off the wing tips of others in the flock — by flying in a V-formation. Each bird thus adds the lift lost by the bird ahead to its own. Geese flying in a V-formation can fly as much as 71% further than they could individually.

British scientist, made a theoretical calculation (using linear dimensions of the house sparrow, which weighs about ⅔ oz., and an ostrich of 250 lbs.) that proved that if an ostrich could fly, it would need to do so at a minimal speed of 100 m.p.h. to stay aloft. The average minimal speed of birds in order to remain airborne is about 16½ ft. per second, or about 11 m.p.h. *See* discussion under Size.

HOW FAST DO BIRDS BEAT THEIR WINGS? Some wingbeat rates measured in a wind tunnel by Greenewalt (1960) were: chickadee, 27 beats per second; mockingbird, 14 per second; male ruby-throated hummingbird, 70 per second, female, 50 per second. Blake (1947), using a fifth-second stopwatch, under normal or unhurried conditions for the birds, measured wing-flapping rates for double-crested cormorant, 2.6 strokes per second; black duck, 2.0 per second; sparrow hawk (American kestrel), 2.4 per second; ring-necked pheasant, 3.2 per second; starling, 4.3 per second; American goldfinch, 4.9 per second; and so on. See also in Terres (1968a; 1975).

GLIDING FLIGHT. Gliding is the simplest and most elementary form of flight and is practiced by all birds except, possibly, hummingbirds. A bird's wings make no propulsive movements in gliding; actually it is coasting "downhill" in relation to the flow of air, the form of flight used by an airplane in landing. A gliding bird coasting downward is simply using its weight to overcome the air resistance to its forward motion. Gliding in still air means a loss of altitude to a bird. To regain it, the bird, if it does not start flapping flight, must find rising currents of air on which to soar aloft again (called static soaring), or use adjacent air currents that are moving at different velocities, a type of flight called *dynamic soaring*, which is especially practiced by albatrosses over the oceans.

SOARING FLIGHT. A soaring bird is one that maintains or even increases its altitude without flapping its wings. The three main requirements of a bird, to soar successfully, are large size, light wing-loading (the weight of the bird in pounds borne by each square foot of its wing surface), and maneuverability, especially the ability to make small or tight circles or to change the direction of flight suddenly to take advantage of changes in the flow of air. The relatively small wing muscles of the soaring birds—vultures, red-tailed, red-shouldered, and broad-winged hawks, for example—show that this type of flight is economical of a bird's energy. Vultures that soar much over land, and albatrosses over oceans, have become so highly adapted to soaring that they use this method of flight almost exclusively.

The "static soarers," which include, besides the buteonine hawks and the vultures, eagles and condors, keep aloft mainly by riding rising currents of warm air called *thermals* or by using *obstruction currents*, which are updrafts of air caused when steady winds strike, and rise over, objects such as mountains, hills, buildings, sand dunes, and even ships at sea and ocean waves, which deflect the wind upward. A dramatic example of the use by migrating birds (*see* Migration) of obstruction currents of air may be seen at Hawk Mountain Sanctuary near Kempton, Pa. See discussion of in Terres (1968a). Ornithologists and birdwatchers in general who travel there each fall to see the autumn migration call the ridge the birds' "glider highway" (Pough, 1935). For other places to see migrating birds of prey in fall, *see* suggestions under Hawk Family; *also* description of soaring flight under Vulture Family.

HOVERING FLIGHT. Many kinds of birds hover, that is, hold themselves in midair by flapping their wings sufficiently to hold their position over one point on ground or water below them. Some kinds of hawks and kingfishers are quite expert at it as they hover in the air to watch for their prey directly below them. By beating its wings up and down and depressing and spreading its tail feathers, with its body held almost vertically, a kingfisher or a kestrel holds its position in the air against the downward pull of gravity. It poises on beating wings until it is ready to dive downward—the kingfisher, with its wings held close to its sides to lessen the air resistance, plunges into the water to seize a minnow in its bill; the kestrel, with folded wings, dives to the ground to seize a grasshopper or mouse in its talons.

Hummingbirds are the most skilled of all at hovering. In their method of hovering before flowers to feed on the nectar and insects within, their wings have become adapted to a helicopterlike flight. The hummingbird's flight method has been likened to the circular whirl of a helicopter's rotor, which allows it to hover or to move ahead, backward, or sidewise at will (Greenewalt, 1960). Although some birds can fly backward a few feet, helped by the wind, the hummingbird is apparently the only one that can do so at will with swiftness, power, and ease. *See* details under Hummingbird Family.

DESIGN OF THE HUMMINGBIRD'S WING. All birds, except hummingbirds, move their wings at the shoulder, elbow, and wrist. *See* Topography. They really fly from the wrist out, on the outer wing with its long flight feathers, but not so the hummingbird. Its entire wing is "hand wing," or propeller, which is why a hummingbird does not soar or glide. It moves its wings completely from its shoulders, which gives the wings their astonishingly free movement and the hummingbird its maneuverability in the air. See details in Terres (1968a).

FLIGHT MUSCLES. The power behind a hummingbird's rapidly beating wings (up to 70 beats a second in a male ruby-throated) is its powerful pectorals, or breast muscles, the "motor" of all flapping birds. The flight muscles of the strongest fliers are about 15–25% of the bird's total weight; the relatively enormous breast muscles of the ruby-throated hummingbird are about 30% of its weight (Greenewalt, 1960).

Flight muscles of birds are of two colors, or two types—the red ones of hummingbirds, ducks, geese, and other swift-flying migrants, and the white flight muscles of the resident quail, grouse, pheasants, and other birds that fly with explosive bursts of speed but over only short distances. The white breast meat of a chicken is a familiar example of the white flight muscles of a domestic bird.

Red flight muscles have more myoglobin and readily oxidized cytochrome than the white ones, and a richer supply of blood capillaries and oxygen—an index of the capacity of the red muscles for sustained flight. *See* Metabolism.

In the wings of all flying birds, a strong *depressor* muscle powers the downbeat, but the *elevator* muscle that raises the wings is relatively weak. Not so in a hummingbird; the elevator muscle that raises its wings so quickly and powerfully is much larger in relation to body size than in other birds.

FORMATION FLYING. When flying, each bird creates behind it a small area of disturbed air, the "slipstream." Any bird flying directly behind another would be caught in this turbulent air and probably canted from its horizontal flight and thrown about in the eddies, thus disrupting its flight. Of the many kinds of birds that fly in flocks (*see* Flocks and Flocking), most of them have probably experienced this; however, some have learned to use the disturbed air to advantage.

As each bird flies, some air is lost over the wing tips, causing a loss to the bird of lift. This circulation of air creates an enlarging spiral wing-tip vortex behind each wing tip, with upswelling air on the outer side of each wing. Wild geese and swans, by flying in formation, use this upswelling air to save their energy when flying. In the V formation of Canada geese, for example, each bird flies, not directly behind the other, but aside or above the bird in front. By so doing each bird rests its inner wing tip in flight on the rising vortex of air from the bird's wing in front of it. By formation flight, a substantial power lost at each bird's wing tip is salvaged and used by others in the flock (Savile, 1957).

In an analysis of bird flight formations, Lissaman and Schollenberger (1970) demonstrate that the power- or energy-saving V flight may give birds that use it 71% more flight distance than the range attainable, say, by a lone bird such as a goose (*see also* Ibis Family). For an interesting review of bird flight formations and alternative theories, see Heppner (1974). More research on this subject is needed.

COURTSHIP AND TERRITORIAL FLIGHT. Some birds have spectacular courtship and territorial flights, usually practiced by the male alone. Sometimes, however, he is joined by the female—for example, in both the red-tailed hawk and the golden eagle, in which the male dives at tremendous speed at the female while both are in flight. As the male reaches his mate, he may reach down with his feet and touch her lightly on the back and both may then touch talons while rolling over and over in the air. The male peregrine (*see* in Falcon Family) has one of the most dashing of all courtship flights, in which he may perform a series of mile-long dives, aerial somersaults, barrel rolls, and "figure eights" at breathtaking speed. These are usually executed by the male over the nesting cliff of the mated pair (Terres, 1968a). *See*

nuptial flight

FLIGHT
In the courtship flight of the bald eagle, the male dives swiftly at the female, touching her lightly on the back; both may then touch feet while rolling over and over in the air.

also Flycatcher, scissor-tailed, in Flycatcher—Tyrant Flycatcher Family.

The male marsh hawk in his spring courtship flights may fly with shrill cries in a series of graceful undulations, like giant U's, over the home-nesting marsh in which the female may be incubating her eggs; some of the owls also have remarkable and noisy courtship flights, surprising in these usually silent-flying birds of the night.

The leading edge of each wing (the outer primary feather) of owls has fine serrations like the cutting edge of a saw. Apparently this ragged edge silences the noise of the vortex of air rushing over the flying owl's wings (Raspet, 1960). But during courtship at least one of the larger owls deliberately makes loud noises with its wings. While soaring about at dusk in its courtship flights, the short-eared owl, after uttering a series of low tooting sounds, suddenly plunges earthward in a shallow dive. This is accompanied by a clapping sound of its wings as it stretches them in back of its body and slaps them together in short strokes. Then it rises into the air to repeat the performance. Some pigeons in courtship practice a loud wing-clapping display, and the chuck-will's-widow, poor-will, and hairy woodpecker clap their wings in flight as a territorial defense or as a courtship display. See discussion of wing-clapping of certain swifts by Collins (1968).

Hummingbirds make sounds with their wings in their courtship flights. The wings of the male woodcock make a musical whistling as he flies about in his evening and early-morning courtship and territorial pronouncement flights, and the male of the common snipe, by spreading his stiff outer tail feathers as he circles over the home swamp, produces a bleating sound as the wind rushes through them. *See* details in biographies of common snipe and American woodcock in Sandpiper Family; *see also* Territory.

In spring, within the range of the ruffed grouse, one can hear the thunder of its wings striking the air in its courtship drumming. *See* Drumming.

The courtship of the male nighthawk, a relative of the whip-poor-will, is an aerial performance as he flies about in the spring and summer dusk. In his plunges earthward, as he reaches the bottom of his dives, his wings make a booming sound that one can imitate by blowing across the mouth of an empty jug, bottle, or jar.

Most charming of all courtship flights are those of the larks, bobolinks, buntings, the ovenbird, and certain other small birds that perform over sunny fields or woodlands in summer and spring. Rising high in the air, they do not flap but float about on trembling wings while uttering bursts of wild sweet notes (Terres, 1968a). *See also* Courtship; Language; Songs and Singing; Territory.

UNITY OF THE FLOCK IN FLIGHT. One of the most spectacular, and possibly the most puzzling, kinds of bird flight is practiced by semi-palmated sandpipers and other shorebirds (*see* Shorebird). When disturbed along beaches, they fly up and dart away over the waters in a closely knit flock, turning and twisting in swift movements in which thirty, forty, fifty or more may fly as one.

Some observers believe that the leading bird in these flocks—the one flying out in front—is the leader and that others follow its every motion and change of direction simultaneously (Nichols, 1931). Some investigators, however, have discovered that the leading bird among sandpipers, pigeons, and other birds that often fly only in groups of their own kind, does not always lead. They have noted that the leadership sometimes seems to sweep through the flock to birds along one edge of it, rather than remaining with the one in front (Allee, 1938). Much work remains to be done on this problem before it is understood. *See also* Do Young Birds "Learn" to Fly? under Young and Their Care.

TIME SPENT IN FLIGHT. Swifts and swallows apparently spend more time in flight than any other land birds. Wing (1956) reported that a man who had banded a N. American chimney swift that had lived for 9 years estimated that during its lifetime it must have flown 1,350,000 mi. This included nine round trips from the U.S. (its summer home) to S. America, where it wintered. *See* Swift Family.

A European (common) swift is estimated to fly at least 560 mi. a day during its nesting season; a small, rather weak-flying European tit, similar to the N. American black-capped chickadee, flies about 62 mi. a day while traveling back and forth to feed its nestlings (Hess, 1951). *See* Young and Their Care. It is probable that the albatrosses spend more time in the air than any other birds. In its wing structure, the wandering albatross is one of the most specialized of any bird that flies. Spanning fully 11 ft. from tip to tip and only about 9 in. from front to back, the narrow wings of these birds are the most superb "sails" of any living creature. As it glides about over the oceans spending most of its life in the air, it is thought at times to even sleep on the wing. For underwater "flight," *see* Swimming and Diving.

FLIGHT
Term often used by sportsmen for a group of birds flying together—for example, "morning flight" and "evening flight" of waterfowl. Ornithologists use the term for "migration flights" of birds and "night flights" when birds are flying to some specific destination, whether from or to night roosts, to feeding grounds, or in stages of the long migration journey.

FLIGHT DISTANCE
or FLUSHING DISTANCE. *See* Escape Distance.

FLIGHT FEATHER
One of the main feathers of the wings, a primary or secondary feather—*see* under Wing Flight—called, collectively, the wing flight feathers. Functionally, a flight feather is also any one of the stiff tail feathers that a bird uses when steering in flight (Van Tyne and Berger, 1959). The wing flight feathers are called, collectively, the *remiges* (REM-ih-jeez); the feathers of the tail, the *rectrices* (rek-TRY-seez). *See* Tail; *also* Topography; Feather.

FLIGHT LANES

See flyways under Waterfowl; *also* Migration.

FLIGHTLESS BIRDS

There are no living species of wild N. American birds that are flightless when fully grown, except for those seasonal periods when some are flightless during the molt. *See* Eclipse Plumage; Molts and Molting. Flightlessness is so unusual in birds that it has been a source of wonder wherever it has been found in the world.

Among some of the familiar flightless birds are the African ostrich (*see* Largest Bird), the emu, the cassowaries and the kiwis of the Australian Region, and the S. American rheas, all of which are ratite birds, so called because they lack a keel on the breastbone (*see* Carinate), and have certain other characters unlike those of flying birds; also the familiar S. Hemisphere penguins, which "fly" so skillfully underwater. All of these birds have wings but lost their power to fly millions of years ago and are believed to have descended from birds that could fly. *See* discussion under Monophyletic Descent.

Many birds that live isolated on oceanic islands, or once lived there and are now extinct (the dodo and the great auk, for example), apparently became flightless in the absence of predators and the consequent gradual disuse of their wings for escape. This is thought to have accounted for the flightlessness of penguins in the Antarctic. Flightless grebes, rails, and cormorants live, or have lived, on oceanic islands. In New Zealand there is even a flightless owl-parrot, or kakapo, and formerly a flightless wren, recently extinct and believed to have been the only flightless passerine bird (Thomson, 1964d), and the weka, a flightless rail.

There is the Falkland flightless steamer duck, and a flightless race, or subspecies, of the brown teal on Auckland Is. A flightless grebe lives on Lake Titicaca (*see* Podicipediformes) and a flightless cormorant on the Galápagos Is. Some of the most spectacular birds in the world were giant flightless birds, long ago extinct but known to primitive man—the elephant bird of Madagascar that stood 9 to 10 ft. tall and is believed to have weighed about 965 lbs. (*see* discussion of its egg under Eggs and Egg-laying) and the New Zealand moas to 13 ft. tall but weighing less—about 520 lbs. *See* Roc; Folklore. *See also* Diatryformes and discussion under Fossil Birds.

FLIGHT MUSCLE

See Flight.

FLIGHT PATTERN

Especially of the large diurnal birds—hawks, eagles, vultures, and kites—the flight patterns are their silhouettes as they soar or fly overhead. These are typical or diagnostic for each species.

Hawks, eagles, and vultures spend much time soaring and flapping overhead and may be identified while on the wing by one who learns the flight pattern, or outline, for each.

FLIGHT SONG

Some species of birds that live in open grasslands, prairies, or tundra, especially Arctic species that live beyond the limit of trees, have flight songs which they give while fluttering high in the air. The European skylark, the horned lark of N. America, and Sprague's pipit often sing at considerable heights (up to at least 800 ft. above the ground). Bobolinks, Cassin's sparrows, and Lapland longspurs habitually sing during flight, usually during the nesting season, and occasionally many other birds do so. The flight song in many species of birds serves as a territorial pronouncement. *See* Territory; Songs and Singing.

FLIGHT YEAR

Term for a year in which northern species of birds, not regularly migratory, move southward in large numbers into the U.S. in fall and winter. The large periodic movements of crossbills, grosbeaks, snowy owls, and other birds from northern regions are called *invasions*, or perhaps more properly *irruptions*. *See* Invasion; Irruption. Flight years of the snowy owl in e. N. America usually come at about 4-year intervals and those of the northern shrike (*see* Shrike Family) are about the same. *See* Cycle. Snowy owl flight years are said by Gross (1947a) to have been 1833, 1837, 1839, 1846, 1853, 1862, 1866, 1876, 1882, 1886, 1889, 1892, 1896, 1901, 1905, 1909, 1912, 1917, 1921, 1926, 1930, 1934, 1937, 1941, 1945, and 1949. According to Hamerstrom (1962), each year some snowy owls move south into the U.S. to winter, but truly big flights are rare.

Some other northern birds with "flight years" are the goshawk, hawk owl, Bohemian waxwing, and red-breasted nuthatch. For some details, *see* Irruption.

FLINTHEAD

Another name for the wood stork in Stork Family, in allusion to the hardness of its head (McAtee, 1955a).

FLOCK

Term often used specifically for a flock of geese, but now used by ornithologists for an aggregation or congregation of birds in general. For example, one may see and record a "flock" of red-winged blackbirds, where the flock consists all of one species, or one may describe and note a "mixed flock" of birds, which may be composed not only of red-winged blackbirds but of grackles, starlings, and possibly other birds which may have joined together on the way to a common roost. In American usage, especially among sportsmen, *covey* is applied specifically to a group of game birds such as quail, whereas *flock* seems to apply to an assemblage of any species of birds.

FLOCKS AND FLOCKING

"Birds of a feather flock together" is an ancient adage and birds of the same kind usually do flock together. However, birds sometimes gather in mixed flocks of different species that may, for example, be drawn to a concentration of food that may be attractive to them all. Most birds gather together for at least part of the year, and few birds live alone, although some

birds of prey are usually solitary. Also, some species of birds which assemble in colonies during the nesting season, including some seabirds, herons, egrets, and others, may be solitary at other times of the year. Weaverbirds, however (which include the house sparrow introduced into N. America), are gregarious at all times (Emlen, 1952).

Flocking is more common outside the nesting season (Hinde, 1973) and individual members of the flock may profit in various ways from collective feeding (*see* examples under Food and Feeding Habits) and, because of the flock's numbers, may be better able to thwart predators, and so on. Common examples are large winter flocks of wild turkeys in the better parts of their range (Schorger, 1966); the enormous flocks of red-winged blackbirds, grackles, cowbirds, and starlings that winter in se. U.S. (*see* Control), and the thousands of ducks, geese, cranes, swallows, and shorebirds that travel and feed in flocks of their kind in migration. And wherever large flocks of birds assemble to feed, some flocks have the potential for doing great economic good; others, harm (*see* discussion under Economic Ornithology).

According to Emlen (1952), the tendency of birds to be drawn to the company of others of their kind (gregariousness) is little understood. Some observers have compared it with hunger—a craving or sensation of discomfort arising from the absence of a physical requirement; another compared it with the appetites of both hunger and sex; and various psychologists have regarded it as a responsiveness to social stimuli which if blocked leads to frustrated actions. Common examples of the attraction of flocks for individuals are straggling starlings hurrying to join the main flock, and small groups of crows in flight that quickly descend to join a flock on the ground.

Hinde (1961) cites an example of a gregarious species, the great tit of Europe, a bird related to our black-capped chickadee, showing a special "appetitive behavior" (*see* Behavior). When separated from the flock, it hops through bushes peering about (presumably looking for its flock companions), frequently uttering the flocking calls of this species. When it rejoins the flock, it resumes feeding quietly, its appetitive behavior ceasing when it is close to others of its kind.

BEHAVIOR OF BIRDS IN A FLOCK. Hinde (1973) noted that among birds which flock there is a strong tendency for "social facilitation"—that is, specific behavior by one member of the flock increases the likelihood that other individuals will behave in the same way. Birds in a flock react sharply to the behavior of their companions; in nesting colonies of terns and other seabirds, when one utters an alarm cry and flies up from the ground, thousands of others behave similarly, and within the colony, the courtship displays and copulation among members will set off the same behavior in others, thus synchronizing the egg-laying and raising of young within the colony. When one in the flock starts to preen, others may be stimulated to preen, and as one goes to sleep, others will start sleeping, and so on (Welty, 1962).

According to Hinde (1973), social facilitation

Gray-spotted flycatcher

OLD WORLD FLYCATCHER FAMILY

in some species is so marked that if a lone domestic hen in a pen is allowed to eat grain until she is satisfied, she will then stop eating, but when another hungry hen is introduced and starts eating, the hen that has eaten her fill will again start eating and may, according to one investigator, eat 34% *more* grain. See Welty (1962) for this and other examples.

Within some winter flocks of wild birds, certain individuals dominate others; for example, in a winter flock of chickadees there is a "peck order" as there is among flocks of domestic chickens. *See* details in Social Order among Birds under Behavior. The dominance hierarchy gives to the flock stability and reduces harmful fighting because each member of the flock knows its position. This reduces competition and saves time and energy for feeding birds which do not have to fight over every bit of food. *See* Dominance; Territory.

Flocks of birds such as shorebirds and pigeons may be so closely integrated that the birds fly only a few inches apart and twist and turn synchronously as they fly about (*see* Unity of the Flock in Flight under Flight). Flocks of Canada geese fly in formation in migration, an apparent advantage to them (*see* Formation Flying under Flight).

SOME ADVANTAGES OF FLOCKING. A flock of birds has many eyes and ears, an advantage for the individual bird, especially in finding food and in sighting predators. A bird in a flock is less likely for this reason to be caught by a hawk. And because of the searching for food by the many members of the flock, new food sources are discovered that a lone bird might have missed.

Of all the actions of the flock, some of the most dramatic are those in which the flock repels or thwarts the aerial attacks of a predator. Flocks of starlings close up their ranks ("ball up") and quickly change direction when attacked by a peregrine falcon. This prevents the falcon from separating a bird from the flock and plucking it out of the air. The falcon, because of its tremendous speed, does not dive *through* the flock, as it might damage itself (Tinbergen, 1953b).

Meyerriecks (1957a), one Nov. day, watched a flock of 25 cedar waxwings closely pursued by a Cooper's hawk, near Southboro, Mass. The hawk, flying slightly in back and above the waxwings, made five separate passes at the flock within 10 minutes. Each time, just as the hawk was about to seize a waxwing, the flock, previously strung out, suddenly bunched together, at which the hawk would veer away. After several more passes at the bunched flock, the hawk gave up and flew away. *See* some other examples in Actions of Birds When Attacked by a Predator under Behavior.

FLORIDA NATURALIST, THE
A publication. *See* Ornithological Periodicals.

FLOWER-PIERCER
See Nectar and Birds.

FLUKES
See Parasite.

FLUSHING BAR
or FLUSHING ROD. A bar attached horizontally to a hay-mowing machine just ahead of the cutting bar of the mower. From the flushing bar are suspended short lengths of chain which drag ahead in the hay or grass and frighten and flush quail, pheasants, and other birds from their nests, thus preventing their destruction. Birds that nest in hayfields, when closely incubating their eggs (*see* Incubation), will sit so tightly on the nest that they will allow the cutting bar of the mowing machine to pass over or under them. Many of these birds are cut to pieces or their legs cut off before they can escape. The flushing bar helps to prevent this.

FLUSHING DISTANCE
See Escape Distance.

FLUSTERER
See Coot, American, in Rail Family.

FLYCATCHER—OLD WORLD FLYCATCHER FAMILY
Muscicapidae (mus-ih-CAP-ih-dee); from Lat. *musca*, fly, and *capere*, to catch. 378 species (Van Tyne and Berger, 1976); throughout Old World; rare, accidental visitor (1 species) to Alaska; have greatest development in Africa and East Indies and Australian Region; most species that nest across Eurasia from tree line southward are migratory; members of family have extended range eastward to Marquesas and Hawaiian Is. (Austin, 1961); are tree-dwelling songbirds, similar in structure to Old World warblers, babblers, and thrushes (Dement'ev *et al.*, 1968); many have rather broad, flat bills, rictal bristles about nostrils, just as in New World tyrant flycatchers, which are thought to help them in catching insects in flight.

Gray-spotted flycatcher, *Muscicapa griseisticta* (muh-SICK-ah-pah gris-ih-STICK-tah); genus name: *see* family introduction; species name: from Lat. *griseus, griseis*, gray, and Gr. *sticta*, dotted, dappled, in reference to spotted plumage. Asiatic species; rare visitor to Alaska, first record, a female collected June 1, 1956, on Amchitka Is., Aleutians; nearest known breeding place, Kamchatka Is., Siberia (Kenyon, 1961); males about 5½ in. long; females slightly smaller; forehead and crown yellow-brown; white eye-ring; upperparts brownish; underparts white with conspicuous gray-brown streaking; throat white, indistinct wing bar; bill and feet black (Dement'ev *et al.*, 1968); usually in second-growth or edges of forest perched upright like N. American flycatchers on some vantage point, from which takes off in short, darting flights after passing insects, which it catches with audible snap of bill.

Other Names: Chinese gray-spotted flycatcher; spotty-breasted flycatcher.

Range: Nests in Siberia, on Kurile Is., Sakhalin, possibly in n. China, Korea; winters in Philippines, Celebes, Moluccas, New Guinea (see Dement'ev *et al.*, 1968, for other details). For other records of this bird's appearance in N. America (Alaska) see Kessel and Gibson (1978).

FLYCATCHER—SILKY FLYCATCHER FAMILY

Not true flycatchers. *See* under Silky Flycatcher Family.

FLYCATCHER—TYRANT FLYCATCHER FAMILY

Tyrannidae (tih-RAN-ih-dee); from Lat. *tyrannus* and Gr. *tyrannos*, monarch, lord, ruler, in allusion to aggressiveness of some members of family. 374 species (Van Tyne and Berger, 1976); only in W. Hemisphere; 35 species (including 1973 arrival of the loggerhead kingbird of the West Indies) reach the U.S.; the family originated in S. America with a secondary radiation, like that of hummingbirds, into N. America (Mayr, 1964b); small-to-medium and large songbirds (3–16 in. long) with 10 primary feathers in each wing; common name of flycatcher from habit of many of catching flying insects out of the air, although they also catch them on foliage and on ground; from perch, where they sit quietly upright, dart out into air to snap up flying insects with audible click of bill, then return to perch; if insect too large to swallow, hold it under feet and bite off pieces with bill; some flycatchers flutter over water to catch insects and even small fishes from shallows (kiskadee flycatcher, for example); some eat berries (Gilliard, 1958). For a summary of foraging methods, see Fitzpatrick (1980).

The family is the most aggressive and most successful, biologically, of the primitive songbirds (Austin, 1961); members range from n. Canada south to Patagonia and to Galápagos and Falkland Is.; all N. American species are migratory; most members of the family are tree dwellers and most species in the American tropics live in lowlands; however, some S. American species in the Andes live at elevations of 12,000 ft. (Gilliard, 1958).

The tyrant flycatchers are related to the tropical American cotingas and manakins; their resemblance in appearance and habits to the Old World flycatchers (see Gilliard, 1958, and Austin, 1961, for discussion of Old World flycatchers) is result of convergent evolution of two different, apparently unrelated groups of birds (*see* Convergent Evolution).

Most of the tyrant flycatchers are plain browns, grays, olive green, yellow; sexes in most, outwardly similar; they have large heads, flattened bills, strongly hooked at tip in N. American species; most have prominent bristles at base of bill; feet and legs are short, weak; most can raise the crown feathers and many have a distinct crest with streak of bright color in center which they use in courtship displays or intimidation of other males.

Some of the most conspicuous members of the family in N. America are the active kingbirds, noted for their audacity; they attack and rout other birds, especially large ones such as crows and hawks, that fly over their territories; the brilliantly red male vermilion flycatcher of sw. U.S. is brightest-colored (red is unusual, blue almost unknown in family); the lovely scissor-tailed flycatcher, with the longest tail feathers of any member of family; the Derby flycatcher, known generally as kiskadee, from its rasping cry that sounds like *kiss-me-dear!*; and the hole-nesting great crested flycatcher of

e. N. America with its fondness for lining its nest with cast-off snakeskin.

Other N. American flycatchers, especially the *Empidonax* (genus name) group, lack conspicuous field marks and may be distinguished with certainty only by their calls; also, the wood pewees, woodland species, that plaintively whistle their name—*pee-ah-wee!*

Gross (1965a), in his summary of albinism among N. American birds, listed 30 individuals of 11 species of flycatchers that showed some form of albinism but did not name the species.

Flycatchers are protected by law and may not be kept in captivity without a permit; they are difficult to keep because of their largely insect-eating habits, but to sustain an ill or injured one until it can be released to fend for itself, offer it mealworms, ground meat, hard-boiled eggs (yolk), and mockingbird food; however, insects are a practical necessity in its diet. Members of family in nature feed much on bees, wasps, and ants (Hymenoptera). *See* Insects and Birds.

Flycatcher, Acadian, *Empidonax virescens* (em-PID-oh-nax vie-RES-enz); genus name: Lat., from Gr. *empis, empidos,* mosquito, and *anax,* "king" (Coble, 1954), apparently in belief that it feeds much on mosquitoes; species name: Lat., greenish; misnamed *Acadian,* as it never reaches Acadia (Nova Scotia). (Color ill., page 359.) Summers in woodlands over most of se. U.S. and Midwest; 5½–6¾ in. long; greenish with pale yellow along sides; conspicuous white eye-ring; two white bars in each wing, identifiable with certainty from similar alder, least, and yellow-bellied flycatchers (usually has whiter throat than yellow-bellied, especially in spring) only by range, habitat, and voice (see Peterson, 1947; also Phillips *et al.*, 1966, for key to identity of this species in hand); lives largely in Southeast in moist mature woodlands, beech woods; deep wooded ravines, often with dry creek bed, wet woods of river swamps and creek bottoms, and in hammocks and cypress bays of South; lives just under canopy of trees, perches in deep shade, often less than 20 ft. from ground, with twitch of tail uttering characteristic abrupt *hick-up!* or *wicky-up!* (Christy, 1942) and *ka-zeep!* and *spit-chee!*, higher note at end; call is soft *peet!*; from winter range in nw. S. America and Costa Rica usually arrives on nesting range in U.S. in Apr.–May.

Feeding Habits: Perches on dead twig under forest canopy, uttering distinctive note; darts out into air for flying insects, especially beetles; also wasps, bees, and ants, which are largest item of its insect food; also houseflies, crane flies, leafhoppers, treehoppers, assassin bugs, tree crickets, and especially moths and caterpillars; also scorpion flies, dragonflies, some spiders, harvestmen, and millipedes, and some wild berries.

Nest: Frail, shallow basket of twigs, fine, dry plant stems, Spanish moss (lichen) and other fibers, bound with spiders' and caterpillars' silk, suspended by rim, like hammock, between horizontal slender forked twigs near end of lower branches of large or small tree, 4–20 ft. above ground or water.

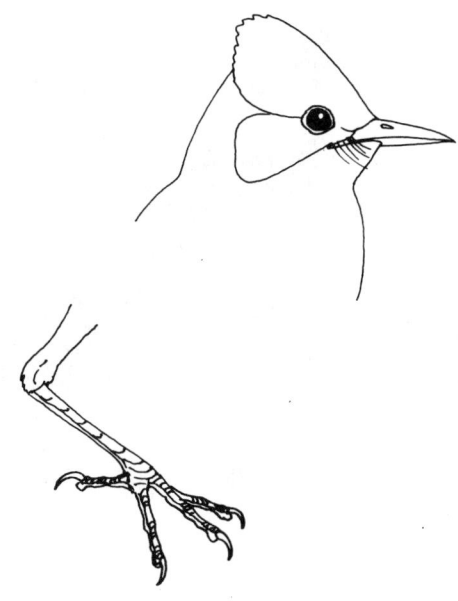

TYRANT FLYCATCHER FAMILY

Beardless flycatcher

TYRANT FLYCATCHER FAMILY

Eggs: Apr.–July; 2–4, usually 3, cream to buff-white, sparingly spotted or dotted with browns.
Incubation: 13–14 days; young leave nest 13–15 days after hatching (Walkinshaw, 1966a).
Other Names: Green-crested flycatcher; green flycatcher; small pewee.
Host to Cowbirds: Uncommon (Friedmann, 1963), although locally frequent, 59 records.
Weights: A male (Wetmore, 1936), in May, 13.7 gr., or about ½ oz., and had 1,554 body (contour) feathers.
Range: Nests from se. S. D., n. Iowa., s. Wisc., s. Mich., s. Ont., ne. Pa., s. N.Y., sw. Conn. (casually from Vt. and Mass.), south through e. Neb., c. Kans., c. Okla., to c. and se. Tex., Gulf coast, and c. Fla., now rarer than formerly or gone from parts of ne. U.S. (a rare migrant on Long Is., N.Y. (Phillips and Lanyon, 1970); winters from Costa Rica to Ecuador and w. Cuba.

Flycatcher, alder, *Empidonax alnorum* (em-PID-oh-nax al-NO-rum); genus name: *see* Flycatcher, Acadian; species name: Lat., of alders; named originally by William Brewster in 1895, who believed it to be a subspecies of the Traill's flycatcher, *Empidonax traillii*, now called the willow flycatcher (see American Ornithologists' Union, 1973). (Color ill., page 361.) A more northern bird than the almost identical willow flycatcher; summers in boreal forest region from ne. U.S. and across Canada to Alaska (Stein, 1958); 5¼–6 in. long; wingspread 7¾–9 in.; brown-olive above (browner-backed than other small *Empidonax* flycatchers, such as Acadian, yellow-bellied, and western *Empidonax* species); larger than least flycatcher and also has greater contrast between its white throat and olive sides; has two white bars in each wing; white eye-ring; a distinctive song or territorial call, *way-bee-o; wee-bee-o;* or, as commonly phrased, *fee-bee-o* (second syllable pitched highest and accented), the only way by which it can be distinguished from its almost identical counterpart, the willow flycatcher (see Stein, 1958 and 1963, for other details), which utters *fitz-bew!* song or *free-beer!* (both syllables about equally high-pitched and accented); see Peterson (1947) for comparisons of alder flycatcher with Acadian, least, and yellow-bellied flycatchers; from winter home in C. and S. America, arrives on N. American nesting grounds generally in May and June; summers usually near water in dense, low, damp thickets of alders, willows, buttonbush, elderberries, red osier, along banks of small streams, shores of ponds, borders of marshes or bogs; during nesting season keeps out of sight in thickets, where it nests; appears occasionally in pursuit of flying insects or perches on twig to give its emphatic song; call is liquid, *pip, pep,* or *peep.*

Feeding Habits: In flight catches many beetles (at least 65 species), aphids, and scale insects, bees, wasps (about 41% of food), also crane flies, robber flies, houseflies, bugs, moths, and caterpillars, grasshoppers, and an occasional dragonfly; also spiders and millipedes, elderberries, blackberries, etc. (Bent, 1942).
Nest: Built 15–33 in. above ground (Stein, 1958) on horizontal branch or in fork of small shrub; nest color brown, comparable to nests of song sparrow and indigo bunting, loosely built of coarse grasses, leaves of cattail, mosses, pine needles, rootlets, bark, twiglets, with only small amounts of cottony material used so much by the similar willow flycatcher (Stein, 1958).
Eggs: May–July; 3–4, white with small spots of brown at large end, sometimes surrounded by larger, more diffuse areas of color.
Incubation: 14 days (Stein, 1958); young leave nest 13–14 days after hatching.
Other Name: Formerly, Traill's flycatcher.
Age: Female banded as adult in Mich. last seen when at least 7 years old (Walkinshaw, 1971).
Albinism: A partial albino, pale lemon-yellow but normal dark olive across shoulders, collected Aug. 1930 in province of Que. (Taverner, 1931); two partial albino young in nest, July 1954, near Dixboro, Mich. (Berger, 1956).
Host to Cowbirds: Occasional, to brown-headed cowbird, but locally a common host (Friedmann, 1963).
Weights: 27 trapped, banded, and released in s. Fla., fall, 11.9–14.9 gr. (Fisk, 1971a), or about ½ oz.
Range: Generally nests north of range of willow flycatcher, nests from c. Alaska, c. Yukon, nw. Mack., ne. Alta., n. Sask., n. Man., n. Ont., Que., and sw. Newfoundland and Nova Scotia, south to c. B.C. (Cariboo Parklands), s. Man., n. and e. Minn., n. Wisc., and Mich., s. Ont., c. N.Y., and New England, and in Appalachian Mtns. to at least w. Md., also possibly at higher elevations in mountains of w. U.S. (Stein, 1963); potential area of overlap (sympatry) of range of alder (formerly called Traill's) and willow flycatchers, according to Stein, is across N. America near U.S.–Canada border; both species have been studied in this area of overlap in N.Y., Ont., Pa., and B.C., also known to overlap in Wisc.; in e. U.S., range of alder flycatcher has been pushed northward in southern parts of its range by the presumably more aggressive willow flycatcher, which is displacing it in c. N.Y., for example (Stein, 1958, 1963); winters from Nicaragua and Costa Rica to Colombia and Ecuador. *See* discussion in Sibling Species.

Flycatcher, Arizona crested. *See* Flycatcher, Weid's crested.

Flycatcher, ash-throated, *Myiarchus cinerascens* (my-ih-ARE-kus sin-er-AS-enz); genus name: Lat., from Gr. *myia,* fly, and *archos,* chief, ruler; species name: Lat., turning ashy (Coble, 1954). (Color ill., page 360.) West and Southwest; 7½–8½ in. long; paler and smaller counterpart of its close relatives the Wied's and great crested flycatchers but with whiter throat and considerably paler undersides; has large, brown "bushy" head and upperparts, conspicuous white throat, two white bars in each wing; *rufous tail* and pale yellow belly (kingbirds have yellow bellies but black or dark brown tails); summers from below sea level in Death Valley, Calif., to 9,000 ft. elevation in Sierra Nevadas, Calif., on low ground along Sacramento R., in sycamores, valley oaks, live oaks; in Ariz., in dense mesquite thickets of creek bottoms, oak groves of hillsides, and shrubbery of canyons leading down from mountains; in open woods and dry brush, and cactus of desert (Bent, 1942); from winter home in s. Ariz., Mexico, C. America, arrives nesting grounds over most of range in U.S. Mar.–May; some of calls are a clear *huit, huit,* and *kabrick,* others resemble those of great crested flycatcher of e. U.S.—*quir-r-r, quirp;* also calls *hip, hip, ha-wheer;* similar Wied's crested flycatcher's call note is loud *bew* (Phillips *et al.,* 1964).

Feeding Habits: Forages over low shrubbery and flies out into air after insects; after aerial sally seldom returns to same perch; eats mostly insects, especially bees, wasps, ants, robber flies (an enemy of honeybees), many bugs, treehoppers, cicadas, caterpillars, moths, grasshoppers, some spiders, also elderberries, mistletoe berries.
Nest: Usually built in natural cavities of mesquite, ash, oak, sycamore, juniper, cottonwood trees, rarely more than 20 ft. above ground, in cavities of old stumps, old woodpecker holes, sometimes in abandoned nests of cactus wren; nest is principally hairs, weed stems, rootlets, grasses, bits of dry cow or horse dung, built on foundation of felted mass of fur of different animals, sometimes dried, shed skins of snakes and small lizards; pair near Colton, Calif., nested on underside of beam of an operating steam shovel and raised family successfully.
Eggs: Mar.–July; 3–7, usually 4–5, pale yellow-white or pink-white, sparingly spotted or lined with browns, purples.
Incubation: About 15 days; young leave nest when 16–17 days old (Bent, 1942).
Weights: One male, in summer, Kans., 28.5 gr. (Rising, 1965a), or about 1 oz.
Range: Nests from sw. Ore. and e. Wash. to s. Idaho, sw. Wyo., Colo., N.M., and n. and c. Tex. to Baja Calif. and Mexico; winters from n. Baja Calif., se. Calif., c. Ariz., south into Mexico, El Salvador, and casually to Costa Rica; has strayed in northern part of range and to B.C., Mont., Kans., Okla., La., and Fla.; one seen Appleton, Me., Sept. 1971; and two collected Md., Nov. 1911 and Nov. 1957; one, R.I., Sept. 1960; one photographed Larchmont, N.Y., Nov. 1970.

Flycatcher, beardless, *Camptostoma imberbe* (cam-TOE-stow-mah or cam-toe-STOW-mah im-BER-bah); genus name: from Gr. *kampto,* to bend (or bent), and *stoma,* mouth, alluding to "the parine [like the titmice] shape of the bill" (Coues, 1903); species name: Lat., beardless; *beardless* refers to suppression in it of the long rictal bristles characteristic of most flycatchers. Mexican and C. American species; in U.S., in Ariz. and Tex.; small, about 4–4½ in. long; wingspread, 7 in.; nondescript, gray-olive above; crown usually darker; two bars in each wing are pale brown and inconspicuous; appears very pale below with no distinct yellow in underparts; distinguished from similar kinglets by the buffy wing bars and lack of distinct eye-ring and no stripes in crown; even smaller than *Empidonax* flycatchers; has tiny dark bill; best distinguished by its thin, high voice, and common call, *pee-yarp* (Phillips *et al.,* 1964) or *pee-yuk;* male sings from tops of tallest trees (Bent, 1942); song is series of three to five clear, descending whistles; in Tex., resident of woodland thickets, mostly in Rio Grande delta, occa-

sionally north to Norias (Peterson, 1963); in Ariz., fairly common summer resident in cottonwoods, heavy mesquite, and in sycamore–live oak–mesquite association, north to Gila R.; winters near Tucson and along lower San Pedro R. (Phillips *et al.,* 1964).

Feeding Habits: In summer catches insects by short flights into air; when perched, flicks tail nervously; in winter, gets much of insect food by gleaning twigs like a vireo or kinglet; also eats small berries.
Nest: Built between bases of stems of palmetto fans, in pendant stems of clump of mistletoe on branch of cottonwood at any height (4½–40 ft.) above ground in Tex., usually near ground in tree or shrub where support for globular nest (about 2–4 in. in diameter) of plant fibers; entrance hole on side leads down into nest chamber.
Eggs: May–July; 2–3, white, finely dotted with browns.
Incubation: Period of and age when young leave nest unreported.
Other Names: Beardless tyrannulet; northern beardless flycatcher.
Range: Nests in s. Ariz. and s. Tex. south to Costa Rica; winters from s. Ariz. southward.

Flycatcher, black-headed. *See* Phoebe, black.

Flycatcher, brown-crested. *See* Flycatcher, Wied's crested.

Flycatcher, buff-breasted, *Empidonax fulvifrons* (em-PID-oh-nax FULL-vih-fronz); genus name: *see* Flycatcher, Acadian; species name: from Lat. *fulvus,* tawny, and *frons,* forehead (Coble, 1954). Mexican and C. American species; in U.S., in Ariz., N.M.; 4½–4¾ in. long; smallest of N. American *Empidonax* flycatchers; brown or gray-brown above; *warmly buffy breast;* two conspicuous gray-buff to white bars in each wing; white eye-ring; call is soft *pit, pit* or *quit-quit;* male calls *chicky-whew;* in Ariz., now a rare summer resident, only *Empidonax* flycatcher that nests in lower parts of southwestern mountains; prefers open stands of pine or streamside deciduous trees, in mixed pine and oak woods, and usually well below altitudes of nesting of more greenish-yellowish western flycatchers; in highlands of n. and w. Mexico, also prefers open trees with bare, weedy, or grassy places beneath (Phillips *et al.,* 1964); in N.M., in summer, uncommon and confined to canyons and foothills adjacent to Mogollon Mtns. and west slope of the Black Range at 6,000–7,000 ft. elevation (Ligon, 1961).

Feeding Habits: Forages much in bushes under trees and from higher up, darts out to snap insects from air or from leaves of trees; eats beetles, bugs, grasshoppers, ants, small bees, wasps (Bent, 1942).
Nest: 2½–3 in. in diameter, deep cup saddled on branch usually against trunk or out on branch of pine, sycamore, oak, often with protective stub of branch above nest, 9–45 ft. above ground; built of plant fibers, grasses, rootlets, bound together with spiders' silk, smoothly lined with fine grasses, rootlets, hair, feathers,

decorated outside with lichens, spiders' cocoons, bits of weeds.
Eggs: May–July; 3–4, cream-white, unmarked.
Incubation: Period of and age when young leave nest apparently not known.
Other Names: Fulvous flycatcher; ruddy flycatcher.
Weights: 6.7–9.5 gr. (Phillips and Lanyon, 1970), or about ¼–⅓ oz.
Range: Nests highlands c. and se. Ariz. and w.-c. N.M., to c. Mexico; winters in Mexico.

Flycatcher, bull-headed. *See* Flycatcher, kiskadee.

Flycatcher, Coues', *Contopus pertinax* (KON-toh-pus PER-tih-nax); genus name: Lat., from Gr. *kontos,* short, and *pous,* foot; species name: Lat., clinging firmly; common name: honors Dr. Elliott Coues (COWS), 19th-century American ornithologist and army surgeon at frontier outposts in U.S. (Color ill., page 361.) A Mexican and C. American species; in U.S., in Ariz. and N.M.; a pewee closely related to western and eastern wood pewees but distinguished from them by larger size, larger head, and lack of distinctive wing bars; 7–7¾ in. long; appears uniformly gray, is dull olive or gray-brown above and below; head with erectile crest; lower mandible yellow (similar olive-sided flycatcher has white streak up middle of breast and white tufts of feathers on rump); common summer resident in se. and c. Ariz., requires tall trees, fairly common in Huachuca Mtns., 7,000–9,000 ft. elevation; in Stoddard Canyon, branch of Ramsay Canyon, lives in tall pines and oaks with undergrowth of bushes on slopes; also summers in sycamore groves along mountain canyons; in N.M., according to Ligon (1961), no nesting records, apparently summers in southwestern part of state north to Zuni Mtns.; call is *pil-pil,* indistinguishable from call of olive-sided flycatcher; its song is lovely, high, thin whistle which carries far, phrased *ho-say, re-ah,* or *ho-say, mah-re-ah,* from which its local name, José Maria (Bent, 1942); arrives on U.S. nesting grounds, Mar. and Apr.; male patrols nesting area, and pair, in defense of nest, immediately attack jay, hawk, squirrel, snake as soon as they appear, thus tanagers, warblers, vireos, and other small birds in area, for protection, are said to build nests close to those of Coues' flycatcher, which tolerates them.

Feeding Habits: From perch on dead branch about midway up in tall pine or other tree, darts out to snap insects from air, then returns to perch; no detailed studies reported of its food habits.
Nest: Deep cup saddled on horizontal fork of branch of pine, spruce, sycamore, maple, oak, 10–40 ft. above ground; built of fine grasses, weed stems, bits of dry leaves, cup 4–5 in. in diameter, decorated on outside with black, gray, or pale-green lichens, bound with spiders' silk.
Eggs: May–July; 3–4, dull white to pale cream, sparingly spotted with browns.
Incubation: Period of and age when young first fly unknown.

Other Names: Coues' pewee; greater pewee; José Maria.
Range: Nests c. and se. Ariz., sw. N.M., into Mexico; winters in Mexico, casually in s. Ariz.; casual in Calif., Colo., and c. Tex.

Flycatcher, crested. *See* Flycatcher, great crested and Crested flycatcher, Wied's.

Flycatcher, derby. *See* Flycatcher, kiskadee.

Flycatcher, dusky, *Empidonax oberholseri* (em-PID-oh-nax o-ber-HOLE-ser-eye); genus name: *see* Flycatcher, Acadian; species name: given by Allan R. Phillips for Harry C. Oberholser, American ornithologist (Phillips, 1939). (Color ill., page 361.) Summers from w. Canada south to Calif. mountains and N.M.; gray-brown above; whitish below, washed with pale yellow; has white eye-ring; two dull-white bars in each wing; is so like Hammond's flycatcher, scarcely distinguishable from it in field; according to Bent (1942), on nesting grounds, dusky prefers chaparral or mixture of chaparral and firs; Hammond's is higher in mountains in taller firs; songs and alarm notes are said to be distinguishably different; Davis (1954) reports that song of dusky is *clip zee whee,* the last note highest; the alarm note of both sexes is *whit,* but female's *tweep* note is like female Hammond's (see Phillips and Lanyon, 1970, for discussion of differences useful to bird banders when these species are in hand); dusky lives in chaparral and brushy cut-over lands and in shrubby openings in forest, but perches in trees to sing (Bent, 1942).

Feeding Habits: Moths and other flying insects caught out of air or caught from beneath leaves.
Nest: Cup built in upright crotch of small tree or shrub, 3–20 ft. above ground, usually 4–7 ft. up; of grasses, plant fibers, inner cup lined with grasses, plant down, feathers.
Eggs: May–July; 3–4, dull white, seldom spotted.
Incubation: 12–15 days; young leave nest when about 18 days old (Bent, 1942).
Other Name: Wright's flycatcher.
Host to Cowbirds: Rare, one record (Friedmann, 1966).
Weights: Female collected (shot) in w. Kans., June, 11.8 gr. (Rising, 1965a), or about ⅓ oz.
Range: S. Yuk., nw. and c. B.C., sw. Alta., sw. Sask., south to s. Calif., s. Nev., sw. Utah, c. Colo., c. Ariz., and n. N.M.; winters from se. Ariz. to s. Mexico.

Flycatcher, dusky-capped. *See* Flycatcher, olivaceous.

Flycatcher, fork-tailed, *Muscivora tyrannus* (mew-SIV-oh-rah tih-RAN-us); genus name: from Lat. *musca,* fly, and *vorare,* to devour; species name: Lat., king (Coble, 1954). Mexican, C. and S. American species; rare in U.S., has strayed north to Me. and e. Canada; large, male 13–16 in. long, female 10–12 in. long; *black crown and white underparts* of adult immediately distinguish it from scissor-tailed flycatcher; entire head black, but crown has large concealed yellow patch; back and scapulars pale gray, darkening on rump; tail black, longer than body and scissorlike; near base of tail, outer tail feathers edged with white; wings dusky brown; immature similar to adult but *sooty brown head,* crown without yellow patch; tail usually shorter than adult's; tail coverts and those of wings edged with cinnamon (Blake, E.R., 1953).

Other Name: Swallow-tailed flycatcher.
Range: In lowlands of se. Mexico, rather uncommon, but may be found locally at all seasons; in C. America, in drier, more open country, according to Skutch, quoted in Bent (1942); ranges from s. Mexico to Argentina and one of a number of birds that nest in southern part of range and migrate northward to winter north of nesting range (Reilly, 1968); at least 17 records in N. America; 10 collected (shot); reported from Miss., Pa., N.J., Mass., and Me. (A.O.U. *Check-list,* 1957); second record for Me., one seen and photographed at Biddleford Pool, Sept. 6–11, 1970; first record for Canada, Sept. 26, 1970, one seen and photographed near Halifax, Nova Scotia; one seen Plum Is., Mass., May 1968 (Finch, 1971c).

Flycatcher, fulvous. *See* Flycatcher, buff-breasted.

Flycatcher, gray, *Empidonax wrightii* (em-PID-oh-nax RIGHT-ih-eye); genus name: *see* Flycatcher, Acadian; species name: given by Spencer F. Baird in 1858 for Charles Wright, 19th-century botanist of Conn., who collected birds in the Southwest. (Color ill., page 363.) Lives mostly in Great Basin of arid parts of West; 5½ in. long; slightly larger, longer-tailed and grayer than Hammond's and dusky flycatchers; is most distinctive of other difficult-to-identify flycatchers in field in West—for example, the dusky, Hammond's, and least flycatchers—for when observed in field, dips its tail gently "like a subdued phoebe instead of jerking it spasmodically like other Empidonaces" (Phillips and Lanyon, 1970); summers in sagebrush plains of semiarid flats overgrown with underbrush and junipers; perches on top of tall sagebrush, from which it darts out for flying insects; when startled, dives from perch, and in flight, keeps hidden among bushes; arrives northern part of nesting grounds in U.S. in Apr.–May; male's song more emphatic than Hammond's and dusky; according to Davis (1954), he sings *tu-wheet* or *pee-ist;* call note of female is *tseet;* alarm note of male is *whit,* of female *prit.*

Feeding Habits: No detailed studies reported on food of adults but apparently eats small insects such as beetles, grasshoppers, moths, wasps, which it feeds to young (Bent, 1942).
Nest: Bulky, deep cup, ragged, rather loosely built, 2–5 ft. above ground in crotch of thornbush, juniper, sage; of dead weed stems, plant down, pieces of juniper and sage bark, grasses, lined with bark, feathers, hairs, wool.
Eggs: May–July; 3–4, white.
Incubation: By female, 14 days; young leave nest 16 days after hatching (Russell and Woodbury, 1941).

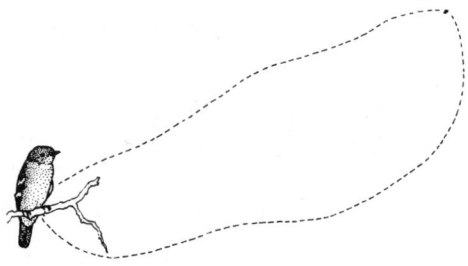

TYRANT FLYCATCHER FAMILY
A flycatcher characteristically darts out from its perch to snap up flying insects, which make up nearly its entire diet, and then returns to the same perch.

Other Name: Wright's flycatcher.

Range: Nests from c. Ore., sw. Idaho, sw. Wyo., ne. Utah, and c. Colo., south to e.-c. Calif., s. Nev., c. Ariz., and w.-c. N.M.; winters from s. Calif., c. Ariz., south to Baja Calif. and s.-c. Mexico; in migration to w. Tex., one collected in Mass., Oct. 1969 (Phillips and Lanyon, 1970).

Flycatcher, great crested, *Myiarchus crinitus* (my-ih-ARE-kus crih-NIGH-tus); genus name: *see* Flycatcher, ash-throated; species name: from Lat. *crinus,* hair, pertaining here to feathers of the head. (Color ill., page 362.) E. U.S. and s. Canada west to prairies; 8–9 in. long; wingspread 12¾–14 in.; olive brown above with head crest; pale gray breast and throat; yellow abdomen; long, *rufous tail; cinnamon color in wings;* white wing bars (see in Phillips and Lanyon, 1970, a key for identifying in the hand the great crested, ash-throated, and Wied's crested flycatchers); crested is largely a woodland bird—the somewhat similar western kingbird, sometimes in e. U.S., perches in open; has *black tail* with white outer tail feathers; from winter range in s. U.S., Mexico, and C. America, arrives over nesting range in U.S. Mar.–May; male establishes large territory in woodland; fights with other males, in aerial combat even striking with claws and tearing out feathers of opponent (Bent, 1942); characteristic call heard when newly arrived is loud musical *wheeeep!* from conspicuous perch in tall tree; lives in farm woodlots, wooded glades, borders of woods, town parks, old orchards, around farms and shade trees.

Feeding Habits: Darts swiftly from perch in tree to snatch dragonflies and other insects out of air, also takes them from or near ground and from crevices of bark; eats at least 52 kinds of beetles, also bees, wasps, sawflies, houseflies, stable flies, mosquitoes, and especially grasshoppers, crickets, katydids, bugs (Hemiptera), large numbers of adult moths and butterflies, caterpillars, cicadas, also spiders, mulberries, pokeberries, blackberries, raspberries, wild black cherries, wild grapes, etc. (Bent, 1942).

Nest: In preferred natural cavities, usually 6–15 ft. up, in trees, also in abandoned holes of woodpeckers, bird boxes; if cavity too deep, the pair fill it with leaves, trash, to within 18 in. of opening, then build cuplike nest about 4 in. in diameter of leaves, grasses, pine needles, mosses, bark fibers, rootlets, feathers of grouse, poultry, cast-off snake skin, also cellophane and onion skins apparently because of shininess comparable to that of snakeskin.

Eggs: Mar.–July; 4–8, usually 5–6, yellow-white to pink-white, blotched, or streaked and lined with browns and purple.

Incubation: 13–15 days; young leave nest about 12–18 days after hatching (Bent, 1942).

Other Names: Crested flycatcher; frate (s. U.S., from call note); great crested yellow-bellied flycatcher; May-bird (s. U.S.); snakeskin bird; wheep.

Age: One, banded St. Paul, Minn., trapped and released in same area when 11 years old (Kennard, 1975).

Host to Cowbirds: Rare (Friedmann, 1963); 5 records.

Weights: At Island Beach, N.J. (20), trapped, banded, 28–42.5 gr. (Murray and Jehl, 1964), or 1–1½ oz.; one near Washington, D.C., in June, 33.8 gr., had 1,570 contour feathers (Wetmore, 1936).

Range: Nests from se. Sask. east to N.B. and n. Me., south to w. Okla., c. Tex., Gulf coast, and s. Fla.; winters from s. Fla., rarely from s. Tex., e. Mexico, south to Colombia; has strayed to Alta., Mont., Wyo., Colo., Ariz., and Nova Scotia.

Flycatcher, green-crested. *See* Flycatcher, Acadian.

Flycatcher, Hammond's, *Empidonax hammondii* (em-PID-oh-nax ham-MOND-ih-eye); genus name: *see* Flycatcher, Acadian; species name: given by John Xantus in 1858 for his friend Dr. William Alexander Hammond, surgeon in U.S. Army. (Color ill., page 363.) Summers in forests high in mountains of West; w. Canada to c. Calif.; 5–5½ in. long; brown-gray above, throat gray; breast dark gray, rest of underparts yellowish, two white wing bars; whitish eye-ring; virtually impossible to distinguish in field from dusky and gray flycatchers but Hammond's may show more olive on back in good light; best told by its calls: male's is sharp *pip* or *chip,* female's *tweep* (Davis, 1954); sharp *pip* is similar to call of pygmy nuthatch (Phillips *et al.,* 1964); male sings over and over from perch in dead fir or other tree, *seput, tsurp, tseep* (Bent, 1942), sometimes sings mellow flight song, *twit-twit-twit;* may be confused with least flycatcher (both call *chebec;* Davis, 1954) but chin and sometimes whole throat of Hammond's is grayish, not distinctly white as in least (see Phillips and Lanyon, 1970); from wintering places in C. America and Mexico, arrives in U.S. on nesting range Mar.–May, summers in open forests of firs, spruces, pines, mainly at higher elevations than other small flycatchers; in mountains of Calif., Colo., 7,500–11,000 ft., but migrates in lower woodlands and thickets.

Feeding Habits: Spends most of time in higher parts of trees, from perch in tree at edge of open place in forest, makes short flights to catch insects, then returns to perch, where flirts tail once or twice; darts swiftly after small aerial prey from exposed perches 18–40 ft. up in foliage of trees; feeds on beetles, moths, flies, bees and wasps, and other aerial insects (Beaver and Baldwin, 1975).

Nest: About 3–4 in. across, cup built in fork of small tree or saddled on horizontal branch of large conifer or deciduous tree; of plant fibers, strips of bark, rootlets, twigs, pine needles, grasses, feathers, lined with dry grasses, mosses, 6–60 ft. above ground (Bent, 1942), usually 25–40 ft. up, many only 10 ft. (Davis, 1954).

Eggs: June–July; 2–4, dull white to cream-white, most unmarked, many with tiny dots of brown.

Incubation: By female, 15 days; young leave nest 17–18 days after hatching (Davis, 1954).

Range: Nests from s. Alaska, s. Yuk., B.C., w.-c. Alta., w. and s.-c. Mont., and nw. Wyo., south to nw. and e.-c. Calif., nw. Nev., Utah, w.

Colo., and n.-c. N.M.; winters from se. Ariz. and ne. Mexico, south to Nicaragua; one collected in Pa., Dec. 1966 (Phillips and Lanyon, 1970).

Flycatcher, kiskadee, *Pitangus sulphuratus* (pih-TANG-us sul-fur-AY-tus); genus name: Lat. form of *pitangua,* the Tupi Indian name (and scientific species name) for the boat-billed flycatcher, *Megarynchus pitangua,* of C. and S. America; species name: Lat., sulphurous, in reference to sulphur-colored underparts; *kiskadee,* from its call. (Color ill., page 362.) Mexican, C. and S. American species; resident in U.S. in lower Rio Grande Valley, Tex.; 9–10½ in. long; big flycatcher, almost size of belted kingfisher and often acts like one (Peterson,1963); large head, face striped with black and white, with a partly concealed yellow crown patch; *conspicuous white throat* and *sulphur,* or *lemon-yellow,* underparts; *rufous on wings and tail;* first discovered in U.S. by George B. Sennett, who shot two in 1879 in the lower Rio Grande Valley of s. Tex.; a locally common resident there, in thickets along streams, in groves and orchards of country and about towns; active and noisy, especially in morning and evening; utters *kis-ka-dee* call; when hunting, uses conspicuous perch and launches out into air for small beetles, wasps, and other flying insects; also eats fishes; sits motionless on perch over water, resembling kingfisher, then dives for tiny fishes and tadpoles near surface; after three plunges becomes water-soaked and must dry plumage in sun before fishing again; in winter when insects scarce, eats fruit, berries.

Nest: Bulky, oval or football shape, up to 14 by 10 in. in size; built of grasses, plant fibers, and other soft materials, with entrance on side; about 10–20 ft. or even 30 ft. up, in mesquite, palm, pine, acacia, or thorny bush (Bent, 1942).

Eggs: Tex., Mar.–June; Mexico, Mar.–July; 2–5, commonly 4, cream-white, sparingly spotted with dark brown.

Incubation: Period of and age when young leave nest unknown.

Other Names: Bull-headed flycatcher; Derby flycatcher; greater kiskadee; kiskadee.

Range: See above.

Flycatcher, least, *Empidonax minimus* (em-PID-oh-nax MIN-ih-mus); genus name: *see* Flycatcher, Acadian; species name: Lat., least. (Color ill., page 362.) Summers across n. U.S. and south in Appalachians, in Canada to Yuk.; 5–5¾ in. long; wingspread 7½–8½ in.; brown-olive above but grayer on back than other *Empidonax* flycatchers, white below, especially throat, with little trace of yellow in plumage (see Phillips *et al.,* 1966, and Phillips and Lanyon, 1970, for details that distinguish bird in hand); dusky gray on sides of breast and flanks; white eye-ring; two white bars in each wing; distinguished by a call, a vigorous *che-bec!* (uttered with jerk of head and twitch of tail), from other small eastern *Empidonax* flycatchers (see Peterson, 1947, for comparisons); ranges west to Wyo. and Mont., east of Rockies, and rare fall migrant in w. Ariz., where might be confused with similar western *Empidonax* flycatchers (Phillips *et al.,* 1964); from winter home in Mexico and C. America, migrates north through U.S. to nesting grounds April–June; summers in open deciduous woodlands, orchards, gardens, shade trees of towns, villages, city parks, along country roads, trees at edges of streams, ponds, partly tree-grown pastures, edges of woods, in Canada in thickets of balsam poplar and quaking aspen, in Appalachians, 1,500–3,300 ft. elevation (Bent, 1942); male defends territory vigorously against other males, utters aggressive call, *weep-weep*, when fighting other flycatchers, gives *che-bec!* note up to 60 times a minute as a territorial display during breeding season (MacQueen,1950); female utters *twit* note, alarm note of both sexes is *tweep;* in 6-year Minn. study, Breckenridge (1956) discovered about 1 pair an acre, and that least flycatcher would not use woodland habitat if too many limbs just under forest canopy—must be at least 30% open; see also MacQueen (1950), who discovered in Mich. that optimum (best) habitat of wood there for least flycatcher had 2.0–2.7 pairs nesting per acre, highest for this species reported in U.S.

Feeding Habits: From bare twig under forest canopy, or from top of fence post, wire, or other perch, darts out to catch passing insect from air, also catches insects by scrambling about bark of trees; eats at least 67 kinds of beetles, many bees, wasps, and especially ants, also gypsy moths, treehoppers, leafhoppers, cankerworms, and takes insects from spiders' webs, eats some dragonflies caught in flight, and eats some spiders, seeds of elderberries, and other small fruits.

Nest: Usually in small hardwood trees, sometimes in conifers, in crotch of horizontal forking branch or in vertical crotch of trunk, also in alders, red osier, shrub willows, 2–60 ft. above ground, usually (in woodlands) 7–35 ft. up (Breckenridge, 1956, and Davis, 1959; Walkinshaw, 1966b); a deep, thin-walled cup, about 2½–3 in. in diameter, of shreds of inner bark of trees, weed stems, grasses, dried blossoms, plant down, spiders' webs, lined with fine grasses, animal hairs, down of thistle, milkweed, etc.

Eggs: May–June; 3–6, usually 4, cream-white, unmarked.

Incubation: By female, 14 days, male may feed female on nest; young leave about 15–16 days after hatching (Davis, 1959); young cared for by both adults up to 20 days after they leave nest; apparently one brood a year.

Other Names: Chebec; sewick.

Age: Two banded Mass., one lived to at least 4 years old, another to 5 years.

Host to Cowbirds: Seldom (Friedmann, 1963); only 19 records.

Weights: Immatures, in summer, Conn. (2), 9.24 gr., or about ⅓ oz. (Wetherbee, 1934).

Range: Nests from sw. Yuk., c. Mack., ne. Alta., n. Sask., c. Man., n. Ont., c. Que., Prince Edward Is., and Nova Scotia; south to ne. B.C., Mont., ne. Wyo., se. S.D., ne. Kans., sw. Mo., c. Ill., s-c. Ind., n. Ohio, w. Pa., W.Va., e. Tenn., and in Appalachians to n. Ga., w. N.C., w. Va., w. Md., and c. N.J.; winters n. Mexico to Panama.

Flycatcher, little. *See* Flycatcher, willow.

Flycatcher, lower California. *See* Flycatcher, Nutting's.

Flycatcher, Mexican. *See* Flycatcher, Wied's crested.

Flycatcher, Nutting's, *Myiarchus nuttingi* (my-ih-ARE-kus NUT-ing-eye); genus name: *see* Flycatcher, ash-throated; species name: given in 1882 by Robert Ridgway, distinguished American ornithologist, for Charles C. Nutting, professor of zoology, University of Iowa, who, while collecting birds in Costa Rica, got the flycatcher that now bears his name. Mexican and C. American species that is "casual" in Baja Calif., and has reached Ariz. (one record); 7 in. long; similar to ash-throated flycatcher but smaller, upperparts usually browner but not readily separable in field from ash-throated (Blake, E. R., 1953), colors also much like those of Wied's crested flycatcher but calls different from both, quite staccato, one a clear, rising whistle; this species in hand differs from both by having bright orange mouth lining; prefers arid, tropical woods to about elevation 5,000 ft., does not hybridize with ash-throated as formerly believed, but is full species (Lanyon, 1961; Phillips *et al.*, 1964).

Other Names: Lower California flycatcher; pale-throated flycatcher.

Flycatcher, olivaceous, *Myiarchus tuberculifer* (my-ih-ARE-kus tyou-ber-CUE-lih-fer); genus name: *see* Flycatcher, ash-throated; species name: from Lat. *tuberculum*, a small tumor, knob, or hump, and *fero*, to bear (Jaeger, 1955); according to Gruson (1972), in allusion to small crest worn by this bird. Mexican, C. and S. American species; reaches U.S. in Ariz., N.M.; small, about size of phoebe; 6½–7 in. long; similar to ash-throated flycatcher—also has yellow belly, but shows little or no rufous in tail, as does ash-throated; smaller and has gray, not white, throat; generally smaller and darker than ash-throated and Wied's; bushy-headed, slender, sits erect, utters distinctive mournful downward-slurred whistle, *peeur* (Peterson,1961); lower-pitched than call of Say's phoebe; imitation of it draws bird near; in hand, can be distinguished by its orange mouth lining (Phillips *et al.*, 1964); in Ariz., summers locally and commonly in dense live oaks, pines, in lower part of mountains, and in streamside vegetation along Santa Cruz R. from Guadalupe Mtns. north to the Graham Mtns., etc.; in N.M., according to Ligon (1961), in San Luis Mtns., also probably in Animas and Peloncillo Mtns.; in Huachuca Mtns. of Ariz., seldom ventures into open, likes dense impenetrable scrub oak thickets of hillsides, though also lives along canyon streams where trees dense enough to provide deep shade; most abundant below 6,000 ft. elevation; arrives there in Apr. (Bent, 1942).

Feeding Habits: While hovering, spends much time picking insects from leaves of deciduous trees and shrubs or needles of pines; stomach of one bird examined yielded 20 different kinds of insects: mayflies, treehoppers, leafhoppers,

spittlebugs, beetles, termites, ant lions, assassin bugs, snipe flies, moths, bees, wasps, etc. (Bent, 1942).

Nest: Built in natural cavities of trees, stumps, or in abandoned woodpecker holes, or in post, large cactus, 4–50 ft. above ground; of grasses, weed stems, dead leaves, straws, strips of bark, lined with fur, fine grasses.

Eggs: Ariz., May–June; Mexico, Apr.–May; 4–5, cream-white, marked with browns, purples.

Incubation: In Guatemala, young left one nest 14 days after hatching (Skutch, 1960).

Other Name: Dusky-capped flycatcher.

Range: Nests in se. Ariz., sw. N.M., south to S. America; winters from Mexico southward; casual in Colo. and Tex.

Flycatcher, olive-sided, *Nuttallornis borealis* (nut-all-OR-nis boh-reh-AY-lis); genus name: given by Robert Ridgway in 1887 for Thomas Nuttall, 19th-century British-American botanist and ornithologist, and from Gr. *ornis,* bird; species name: Lat., northern. (Color ill., page 364.) Summers in forests of Alaska, Canada, n. U.S., and in Appalachians and mountains of West; 7–8 in. long; "bullheaded" with short neck, large bill, short tail, 2 white wing bars, appears sooty as it perches at tip of dead tree or branch; olive above, resembles smaller wood pewee but has narrow strip of white down center of dark breast and belly, and two white patches on lower back (see Phillips and Lanyon, 1966, for other details of bird in hand); from winter range in S. America, arrives on nesting grounds in N. America usually through May; summers in open coniferous forests of tall spruces, firs, balsams, along edges of clearings, shores of wilderness lakes, banks of wooded streams, borders of bogs; in Colo. in mountains 9,000–10,000 ft. elevation; in Baja Calif. to 11,000 ft.; also around sea level in San Francisco Bay region in pine, Monterey cypress, and eucalyptus groves; male from conspicuous perch in tall tree utters distinctive song or territorial call, phrased *look-three-deer!* or *quick-three-beers!* or *whip-whee! wheer!;* alarm call given near nest is *pip-pip-pip;* in Ariz. gives a *pil-pil* call like that of Coues' flycatcher; male defends territory very aggressively, vigorously defends nest against natural enemies and man.

Feeding Habits: From very high, exposed perch darts out to catch flying insects: has special fondness for honeybees of wilderness home, also carpenter ants, click beetles, wood borers, leaf chafers, bark beetles, cicadas, etc. (McAtee, 1926).

Nest: Usually built in conifer, 5–70 ft. above ground, out on branch from main trunk, usually not far from end of horizontal limb in cluster of upright twigs; of grasses, mosses, lichens, straws, rootlets, pine needles on foundation of dead twigs, about 6 in. in diameter.

Eggs: May–July; 3–4, usually 3, cream-white, buff, or pink, lightly spotted with browns, grays.

Incubation: About 14 (?) days; young leave nest about 23 days after hatching (Bent, 1942).

Other Name: Nuttall's pewee.

Host to Cowbirds: Rare, 3 records (Friedmann, 1963).

Weights: Autumn, coastal N.J., migrants (2), 32 and 34.4 gr. (Murray and Jehl, 1964), or about 1 oz.

Range: Nests from n. Alaska, Yuk., s. Mack., ne. Alta., n. Sask., n.-c. Man., n. Ont., c. Que., and c. Newfoundland, south to n. Baja Calif., c. Nev., c. Ariz., n. N.M., c. Sask., s. Man., ne. N.D., c. Minn., n. Wisc., n. Mich., s. Ont., Ohio, and Mass., in mountains of Pa., N.Y., e. W.Va., sw. Va., e. Tenn., and w. N.C.; winters in S. America.

Flycatcher, pale-throated. *See* Flycatcher, Nutting's.

Flycatcher, pewit. *See* Phoebe, eastern.

Flycatcher, ruddy. *See* Flycatcher, buff-breasted.

Flycatcher, scissor-tailed, *Muscivora forficata* (mew-SIV-oh-rah for-fick-AY-tah); genus name: *see* Flycatcher, fork-tailed; species name: from Lat. *forfex, forficis,* scissors (Coble, 1954). (Color ill., page 365.) In summer, in s.-c. U.S. (s. Great Plains), Tex., n. to Kans.; is state bird of Okla.; 11–15 in. long, of which tail feathers may be about 9 in. long, or two thirds of total length; no other N. American songbird, except fork-tailed flycatcher, has such a proportionately long tail (*see* discussion under magpies in Crow Family; *also* Tail); in flight, opens and shuts tail like pair of scissors; perched, it folds or closes "scissors"; resembles similar fork-tailed flycatcher but scissor-tailed has *gray head,* not black; has concealed *scarlet* crown patch; hind neck and back pearl gray, throat, breast white; wings sooty black, touch of scarlet at shoulders; sides and wing linings salmon pink; tail black, outer feathers mainly white; female smaller than male, tail usually shorter; immature resembles adults but tail much shorter, slightly forked; resembles western kingbird but touch of pink on sides instead of yellow (Peterson, 1961); from winter range in s. Tex., Mexico, and C. America, appears in Great Plains Mar.–Apr., on open prairies dotted with trees and along tree-lined country roads, in open chaparral country, about ranches, even in small towns; often seen perched on telephone wires, flagpoles, fences; male in courtship has famous "sky dance," in which he mounts to about 100 ft. in air, plunges back down a fourth of way, then turns sharply up and down in zigzag course, uttering a rolling cackle, like rapid, high-pitched hand-clapping, then rises straight up in air and topples over backward in two or three reverse somersaults, descending like a tumbler pigeon, with all his actions emphasized by the long flowing tail—"an aerial ballet of incomparable grace" (Brandt, 1940); male may repeat his sky dance all through courting period and often until eggs are hatched; is swift flier in direct flight from one tree to another, tail feathers stream out behind and utters sharp, kingbirdlike twittering; also *ka-quee!—ka-quee!*

Feeding Habits: Perches for hours on fence post or limb of isolated tree along road, oblivious of passing cars, darts out into air to catch bees and wasps, or drops to ground to catch grasshoppers, crickets (Orthoptera, about 50% of its yearly food, highest for any flycatcher), also takes bugs (Hemiptera), caterpillars, moths, a few dragonflies, also spiders, some small fruit, berries, and seeds.

Nest: Bulky cup, 7–30 ft. above ground on horizontal limb or in fork of isolated hackberry, mesquite, cedar, elm, live oak, orchard trees, on windmill towers, crossbars of utility poles, etc.; of weed stems, rootlets, cotton, lined with rootlets, horsehair, about 4½–6 in. in diameter.

Eggs: Apr.–July; 4–6, usually 5, white, cream-white, somewhat spotted, blotched with browns.

Incubation: By female, 12–14 days; young leave nest about 14 days after hatching (see Fitch, 1950).

Other Names: Texan bird of paradise; swallow-tailed flycatcher.

Flight Speed: Timed in Tex., 22–25 m.p.h. (Sooter, 1947); in Kans., 18 m.p.h. (Wood, 1923).

Hybrid: A male scissor-tailed flycatcher × western kingbird seen in city of Austin, Tex., Apr. 18–June 22, 1967, defending territory before disappearance (Davis and Webster, 1970), an intergeneric hybrid.

Host to Cowbirds: Rare, about 4 records, all in Tex., to brown-headed cowbird; 2 records of host to bronzed cowbird (Friedmann, 1963).

Range: Nests from e. N.M., w. Okla., se. Colo., Neb., c. and se. Kans., w. Ark., and w. La., south to s. Tex.; winters rather commonly in southern half of Fla. (Oct.–June) and on Keys (Phillips and Lanyon, 1970), and from Mexico to w. Panama; wanders to s. Calif., Ariz., Man., Ont., Que., Vt., south along Atlantic coast from N.B. to Fla., and to Minn., Wisc., Mo., Ind., Ky., Ala.

Flycatcher, sulphur-bellied. *Myiodynastes luteiventris* (my-ih-oh-dih-NAS-teez lew-teh-eye-VEN-triss); genus name: from Gr. *myia,* fly, and *dynastes,* master, ruler (Coble, 1954); species name: from Lat. *luteus,* yellow, and *venter,* belly. Mexican and C. American species; in summer in U.S. in Ariz., where first discovered in Chiricahua Mtns. in 1874; 7½–8½ in. long; *the only conspicuously streaked flycatcher in U.S.;* olive-brown head and back, streaked; *tail rufous,* underparts pale yellow or sulphur color, *boldly streaked with dark brown;* broad black streak through eyes; concealed yellow patch in center of crown; from winter home in w. and c. S. America, arrives in se. Ariz. (where essentially limited) usually in early June, sometimes in late May (Phillips *et al.,* 1964); a fairly common summer resident in watery mountain canyons up to 5,400 ft. where sycamores, oaks, walnuts, Arizona cypress, and pines are common (Ligon, 1971a); not conspicuous despite striking color pattern because it perches, often motionless, in foliage of tallest trees; is noisy, both sexes, often in duet, utter a high, penetrating *kee-ZEE-ick!* like squeaking of a wagon wheel, also a shrill, petulant *P, P, P, pee-yah!* but dawn song is soft liquid *tre-le-re-re, tre-le-re-re.*

Feeding Habits: Darts out from perch in tree, then hovers as it picks insect from leaf, also eats small fruits and berries but no definitive studies of its food habits (Bent, 1942; Ligon, 1971a).

Nest: Usually in tree cavity of sycamore, normally in knothole, 20–50 ft. above ground, occasionally in old flicker hole and even in bird box placed high in tree; often fills hole with large twigs almost to rim of opening, then builds nest proper on this platform but not invariably (Ligon, 1971a); female builds nest, a cup about 3–4 in. in diameter, of petioles of walnut leaves, pine needles.

Eggs: June–Aug., usually June–July; 2–4, white to cream-buff, profusely spotted and blotched with browns, lavender.

Incubation: By female, 15–16 days; chicks open eyes 7 days after hatching; leave nest 16–18 days after hatching, when can fly only short distances (Ligon, 1971a).

Other Name: Arizona sulphur-bellied flycatcher.

Range: Nests from se. Ariz. to Costa Rica; winters in S. America; remarkable as one of few tropical birds that make long migration (Phillips *et al.,* 1964).

Flycatcher, swallow-tailed. *See* Flycatcher, fork-tailed and Flycatcher, scissor-tailed.

Flycatcher, sylvan. *See* Gnatcatcher, blue-gray in Warbler—Old World Warbler Family.

Flycatcher, Traill's, *Empidonax traillii;* named by John James Audubon for his friend Dr. Thomas S. Traill, but common name of Traill's flycatcher changed by American Ornithologists' Union (1973) to willow flycatcher after discovery that Traill's flycatcher was two species, not one. *See* Willow flycatcher and Alder flycatcher; *also* under Sibling Species.

Flycatcher, tyrant. *See* Kingbird, eastern.

Flycatcher, variegated, *Empidonomus varius;* recently recorded in U.S. for first time; found in Maine in 1977 (Abbott and Finch, 1978).

Flycatcher, vermilion, *Pyrocephalus rubinus* (pih-roh-SEF-ah-lus rube-EYE-nus); genus name: Lat., from Gr. *pyr, pyros,* fire, and *kephale,* head (fire-head); species name: Lat., red. (Color ills., pages 364, 365).Mexican, C. and S. American species; in U.S. in semiarid and desert regions of Southwest; sexes *unlike* in colors; 5½–6½ in. long; male, *head and underparts bright red;* upperparts and tail *dark brown;* bill black; often raises red head crest (similar but larger scarlet tanager has *red back*); female, head and back brown; tail black; *breast white, narrowly streaked with dusky;* belly and undertail coverts (crissum) pale salmon or pink; immature, similar to female; in Ariz. not only in summer but some winter there (Phillips *et al.,* 1964); in Tex., in summer; some winter along entire coast (Peterson, 1963); most winter south of Mexican–U.S. boundary (Bent, 1942); are on nesting grounds of mesquite, willow, and cottonwood trees near water, or in roadside shade trees by Apr.; colorful male in courtship flight rises from top of weed or from mesquite tree; uttering ecstatic notes of *pit-a-see! pit-a-see!* or *pu-reet!*, mounts upward vertically in air, red crest erected, breast feathers swollen, tail lifted; with wings vibrating rapidly, hovers in butterflylike flight, then slowly flutters down to female; rather tame, allows close approach of human as it flies from bush or tree perch to top of weed; male is bold, fearless fighter in defense of nest; both sexes have call note, a sharp *peet* or *peent*, given especially by disputing males (Taylor and Hanson, 1970). See Smith (1967, 1970) for displays.

Feeding Habits: No comprehensive studies made but darts into air from perch to catch flying insects, especially bees, or alights on ground to catch grasshopper or small beetles.
Nest: Built in fork of horizontal branch of willow, sycamore, cottonwood, oak, mesquite, hackberry tree, etc., 8–20 ft., sometimes 40–50 ft., above ground, usually near irrigation ditch or stream; flat, about 3 in. in diameter, usually sunken well down into fork, on foundation of twigs, pieces of weeds, fine grasses, rootlets, etc., bound with spiders' silk, lined with finer materials, hairs, feathers.
Eggs: Mar.–July; 2–4, usually 3, white to cream-white, heavily marked with dark browns, lavender.
Incubation: By female, 14–15 days (3 nests, Taylor and Hanson, 1970); young leave nest 14–16 days after hatching (Bent, 1942), probably 2 broods.
Host to Cowbirds: Uncommon, to brown-headed cowbird, records from Tex., Ariz., and Cal.; one record to bronzed cowbird from Mexico (Friedmann, 1963).
Range: Nests from se. Calif. to s. Baja Calif., and s. Nev., sw. Utah, s. and c. Ariz., sw. N.M., and w. and c. Tex., south into s. Baja Calif., and Mexico, and to Guatemala, Honduras, and S. America; has wandered to Colo., Neb., Ont. (Toronto), Ark., nw. Miss., e. Fla.; winters in breeding range and north and east to s. La., s. Miss., and nw. Fla.

Flycatcher, western, *Empidonax difficilis* (em-PID-oh-nax diff-ISS-ih-liss); genus name: *see* Flycatcher, Acadian; species name: Lat., difficult (to observe). (Color ill., page 367.) W. U.S., generally, from Rocky Mtns. to Pacific coast; Alaska to s. Calif. and Tex. (Bent, 1942); 5½–6 in. long; brown-olive above; head more or less *greenish*; throat washed with yellow—the only western *Empidonax* with yellow throat (see Phillips *et al.*, 1964); yellower underparts than similar Hammond's, dusky, and willow flycatchers, but these species have whitish throats; western outwardly similar to eastern yellow-bellied flycatcher (see details of differences when bird in hand in Phillips and Lanyon, 1970); has two dull-white bars in each wing; white eye-ring; call is rising *whee-seet!* or *pee-ist*, and a low *whit;* thin, colorless song, usually heard at daybreak, is *bz-zeek trip seet* (Peterson, 1961); from winter home in Mexico arrives on nesting grounds in U.S. Mar.–May; one of most widespread *Empidonax* species in West; summers in almost any woods, maples and alders along a stream, in moist glades of oak woods, or mixed coniferous and hardwoods of forests of Pacific Coast Ranges but avoids

dense thickets favored by the willow flycatcher; perches on limb under forest canopy in deep shade, from which calls monotonously or darts out to catch passing insect.

Feeding Habits: More than 38% of animal food is Hymenoptera (ants, bees, wasps), also eats many beetles, moths, caterpillars, flies (about 31% of animal food), also some berries and seeds.
Nest: May build among roots of upturned tree, in pile of driftwood, in hole in cliff or under bank of stream, in natural cavity or in woodpecker hole, on top of low stump or in crotch of small tree, usually in forest near low ground and from ground level to 30 ft. up, about summer resorts, under eaves or on beams of unoccupied buildings, under bridges, etc. (Bent, 1942); nest, about 4 in. in diameter, neat cup of mosses, rootlets, grasses, weed stems, strips of tree bark, lined with finer materials of same kind and with hair or feathers.
Eggs: Apr.–July; 3–5, usually 3–4, dull white or cream, spotted or blotched with browns, lavender.
Incubation: 14–15 days (see Davis *et al.*, 1963); young leave nest 14½–17½ days after hatching.
Host to Cowbirds: Occasional, 6 records, all in Calif., to brown-headed cowbird (Friedmann, 1963).
Weights: Adults, in Calif., Apr. and May, males (8), 11.2 gr., females (5), 10.9 gr. (Davis *et al.*, 1963), or about ⅓ oz.
Range: Nests from se. Alaska, s. B.C., w.-c. Mont., n. Wyo., and sw. S.D. south in mountains to Baja Calif., Ariz., N.M., w. Tex., through Mexico, to Honduras; winters in Baja Calif. and Mexico to Honduras.

Flycatcher, Wied's crested, *Myiarchus tyrannulus* (my-ih-ARE-kus tie-RAN-you-lus); genus name: *see* Flycatcher, ash-throated; species name: dim. of Lat. *tyrannus*, monarch, ruler, "little monarch"; common name: for Wied (Prince of Wied-Neuwied, A. P. Maximilian), early-19th-century German natural history collector in N. and S. America. (Color ill., page 367.) Lives in sw. U.S., Nev. to Tex., related to great crested, ash-throated, and olivaceous flycatchers; largest of its genus, or group; 8½–9½ in. long; very similar to great crested flycatcher but has thickened, black bill, and underparts somewhat paler yellow; in Ariz. has a distinctive call, loud *bew*, "exactly the same as the second syllable of call of the Cassin's kingbird" (Phillips *et al.*, 1964); call a sharp *pwit*, and a rolling *purreeet* (Peterson, 1963); one of common notes sounds like *come here, come here*, strongly accented on second syllable (Bent, 1942); summers in saguaro, cottonwood, willow, and sycamore tree association along streams and in desert and in towns north to c. Ariz., wherever trees large enough to provide hole-nesting sites; in Tex. lives about trees near ranches and streamside groves; is loud, active, quarrelsome in defense of nest sites.

Feeding Habits: No definitive studies made but, according to Bent (1942), said to eat largely beetles, other kinds of flying insects, and wild berries; Snider (1971c) noted Wied's crested flycatchers in both Cave Creek and

Ramsay canyons, Ariz., in spring 1971 eating hummingbirds, "probably owing to the lack of insects; a very emaciated one died soon after it was caught by hand . . . May 9; later, July 19, 1971, again saw them catching hummingbirds to eat in Cave Creek Canyon" (Snider, 1971b); a Wied's crested flycatcher killed and ate a rufous hummingbird at Cave Creek Ranch, Portal, Ariz., July 19, 1974 (Gambona, 1977).
Nest: Builds soft nest in holes dug by woodpeckers in trees and fence posts, 5–30 ft. above ground, made of hairs, fur, feathers, usually with large pieces of shed snakeskin.
Eggs: Mar.–July; 3–6, commonly 5, cream-buff, completely marked with elongated blotches, spots, or scrawls, as with an erratic pen, in browns, purple.
Incubation: Period of and age when young leave nest unknown.
Other Names: Arizona crested flycatcher; brown-crested flycatcher; Mexican crested flycatcher; Mexican flycatcher; Wied's flycatcher.
Range: Resident from s. Nev., c. Ariz., sw. N.M., s. Tex., and n.-c. Mexico, south to Costa Rica, the West Indies, and to Paraguay and n. Argentina; has wandered to Calif., Baja Calif., in s. Fla. and Keys, becoming increasingly regular visitor there and presumably winters in small numbers Dec.–Mar. (Phillips and Lanyon, 1970).

Flycatcher, willow, *Empidonax traillii* (em-PID-oh-nax TRAIL-ih-eye); genus name: *see* Flycatcher, Acadian; species name: given in 1831 by John James Audubon for his friend Dr. Thomas Stewart Traill of Edinburgh. (Color ill., page 367.) More southern and western, and lives more in open country, than the almost identical alder flycatcher but distinguished from it in hand by a relatively longer bill, more rounded wings, and less green on back and sides of neck (see details in Stein, 1963); identified in field by its typical song, or call, *fitz-bew!*, both syllables about equally high-pitched and equally accented; in w. U.S., calls *weeps-a-pideea*, or shortened *pi-deea* (see under Little flycatcher in Bent, 1942), utters a single note, *creet!*, and a sharp *whit!;* arrives on nesting grounds in U.S. usually May–June, and, according to Stein (1958), in c. N.Y. region about a week earlier than arrival of alder flycatcher; in w. U.S., its favorite summer haunts are willow-covered islands, shrubbery along watercourses, beaver meadows, borders of mountain parks, where sometimes reaches 8,000 ft. altitude, especially in Calif., Colo., and Utah, also will follow willow- or cottonwood-lined stream out into desert (see account in Bent, 1942, under Little flycatcher).

Feeding Habits: See under Alder flycatcher.
Nest: Gray, comparable in appearance to nest of yellow warbler or of goldfinches; usually in upright fork of shrub but occasionally on horizontal limb, usually higher than nest of alder flycatcher, 1½–9 ft. above ground; nests usually built in area of willows and plants of rose family; those nests built in upright crotches may have silky streamers hanging from bottom of nest, built of shredded bark of milkweeds, cottony tufts of cattail, grasses, silky

materials of aspen and willows, cottony materials often felted together by weather, *regularly lined with fine grasses*, also with feathers.
Eggs: May–July; 3–4, regularly buff (some white), with dark color spots only near end.
Incubation: 12–13 days (Stein, 1963); young leave nest about 13–14 days after hatching.
Other Names: Traill's flycatcher; Little flycatcher.
Age: One, banded Little Falls, Minn., trapped and released in same area when 4 years, 1 month, old (Kennard, 1975).
Range: South and west of range of alder flycatcher through continental U.S. (except in Alaska, nests in most of New England, n. Mich., to Minn., and in some states of extreme Southeast), nests north to plains of Great Lakes into s. Ont., w. and c. N.Y., north into c. B.C. (Cariboo Parklands) and probably in s. Alta. and in Sask. (Stein, 1963). *See* discussion of its overlap (sympatry) in range with that of alder flycatcher under Alder flycatcher. In w. U.S., nests generally from sw. B.C., n. Wash., c. Idaho, and c. Wyo. south to n. Baja Calif., s. N.M., c. Tex., and Durango, Mexico; winters from Nicaragua and Costa Rica to Brazil, Bolivia, and n. Argentina (A.O.U. *Check-list*, 1931). *See also* discussion under Sibling Species.

Flycatcher, Wright's. *See* Flycatcher, dusky and Flycatcher, Gray.

Flycatcher, yellow-bellied, *Empidonax flaviventris* (em-PID-oh-nax flay-ih-VEN-triss); genus name: *see* Flycatcher, Acadian; species name: from Lat. *flavus*, yellow, and *ventris*, pertaining to the belly (Coues, 1882). (Color ill., page 366.) Summers generally in spruce-fir forests in n. U.S. and in Canada; seen in e. U.S. only as migrant; 5–5¾ in. long; similar to other *Empidonax* flycatchers in appearance; greenish back but with definite wash of yellow over *throat and chest;* only eastern *Empidonax* with really yellow throat but similar to western flycatcher (see Phillips and Lanyon, 1970, for details of differences); is usually uniformly yellow from throat to belly; has yellow eye-ring, and two white bars in each wing (see key to the small flycatchers, in hand, in Phillips *et al.*, 1966); possibly best identified by voice, an explosive *pse-ek!* similar to *che-bec!* call of least flycatcher, and an ascending whistled *pur-wee*, resembling a short wood pewee's song; alarm note of male, according to Davis (1954), is *chu-e-E-up;* from winter home in Mexico and C. America, migrates through e. U.S., Apr.–May, mostly silent in migration, hides in wet alder thickets along streams; in summer, lives in understory of forests of spruce, tamarack, fir, paper birch, in wet glades with sphagnum-moss ground cover, in similar habitat in Pocono Mtns., Pa.; difficult to see, keeps well down in thickets, often within a foot of ground but squeaking on back of one's hand may lure it into open (*see* Sounds That Attract Birds).
Feeding Habits: Eats mostly beetles, and especially bees, ants, wasps, some tent caterpillars, moths, leaf rollers, flies, many spiders, and considered by Beal (1912) probably great-

est eater of ants of any of the flycatchers; also may live for several days on mountain ash berries during stormy weather (Bent, 1942).
Nest: Built on or near ground, in side of mossy mound or among roots of upturned tree, usually well hidden in sphagnum moss; a bulky cup of mosses, sedges, rootlets, lined with grasses and pine needles.
Eggs: June–July; 3–5, usually 3–4, white, sparingly dotted with browns.
Incubation: 15 days; young leave the nest about 13 days after hatching (Walkinshaw, 1957b).
Age: One banded bird lived to at least 4 years old.
Host to Cowbirds: Rare, only 3 records, all in Alta. (Friedmann, 1963).
Weights: In Mich. (2), 11.8 and 12 gr. (Becker and Stack, 1944); in fall migration, coastal N.J. (13), 7.19–12.8 gr. (Murray and Jehl, 1964), or ¼–½ oz.
Range: Nests from n. B.C., n. Alta., s. Mack., c. Sask. east across Canada to c. Que., s. Lab., and Newfoundland, south to n. N.D., n. Minn., n. Wisc., s. Ont., ne. Pa., and N.Y. (Adirondack and Catskill Mtns.), s. N.H., and Me.; winters from c. and ne. Mexico south to e. Panama.

Kingbird, Arkansas. *See* Kingbird, western.

Kingbird, Cassin's, *Tyrannus vociferans* (tih-RAN-us voe-SIF-eh-ranz); genus name: Lat., monarch, ruler; species name: from Lat. *vociferari*, to cry out, be clamorous (Coble, 1954); common name: honors John Cassin, 19th-century ornithologist of Philadelphia. Lives in sw. U.S.; 8–9 in. long; upperparts olive gray or slate, with concealed crown patch of red or orange; resembles western kingbird but has more conspicuous white patch between chin and throat *which contrasts sharply with gray of breast and upperparts*, and paler yellow underparts; black, square-tipped tail with slightly white tip, *but no white outer tail feathers* as in western kingbird (similar tropical kingbird has bright yellow breast and belly); best distinguished from western kingbird by coarse, low-pitched call, *che-bew!* or a low nasal *queer*, also an excited *ki-dear, ki-dear, ki-dear*, and *kuh day, kuh day kuhday;* less excitable and active than western kingbird; from winter home in southern part of nesting range in Southwest and Mexico, appears through much of nesting range by Apr.; during nesting season, generally ranges higher in foothills and mountains than western kingbird; in Huachuca Mtns. of Ariz. among large sycamores of lower parts of canyons and sometimes to 7,500 ft., also in open pinyon and juniper hillsides and up into ponderosa pines and along major streams; west of main mountain ranges in s. Calif., summers in open valleys and grasslands of foothills among scattered oaks, cottonwoods, sycamores, where western kingbird also present.
Feeding Habits: From perch in tree, flies out into air to catch beetles, wild bees, wasps, moths, and caterpillars picked from leaves or ground, or from midair while hanging by silken thread, grasshoppers, crickets, bugs, flies, a few dragonflies, and some spiders, also more

vegetable food than any other N. American flycatcher—grapes, small wild berries. See Ohlendorf (1974).
Nest: Built in pine, oak, cottonwood, walnut, hackberry, sycamore, willow, blue gum, etc. (Bent, 1942), almost invariably on branch, near end, 8–40 ft. above ground; bulky, 5–6 in. in diameter, of twigs, rootlets, weeds, strips of inner bark, bits of string, rags, leaves, sides and rim often decorated with feathers, dry flower blossoms, lined with finer materials.
Eggs: Apr.–Aug.; 2–5, usually 3–4, white to cream-white, dotted or spotted with browns.
Incubation: By female, 12–14 days (?); young leave nest about 14 days after hatching (Bent, 1942).
Host to Cowbirds: Very rare, one record, 3 eggs of kingbird, 2 of brown-headed cowbird, Santa Rita Mtns., Ariz., June 1884 (Friedmann, 1963).
Range: Nests from c. Calif., n. Ariz., s. Utah, Colo., e. Wyo., se. Mont., east to sw. Kans., w. Okla., w. Tex., south to nw. Baja Calif. and nw. Mexico; winters from c. Calif. and nw. Mexico, south to s. Baja Calif. and Guatemala, occasionally Tex., has strayed to Ore., Neb., Ont.

Kingbird, Couch's. *See* Kingbird, tropical.

Kingbird, eastern, *Tyrannus tyrannus* (tih-RAN-us); genus and species names: Lat., monarch, ruler. (Color ill., page 368.) Common in summer from Fla. to Canada, west to Tex., Utah, Great Plains, and Pacific Northwest, across Canada to B.C.; 8–9 in. long; wingspread 14–15 in.; black-and-white pattern; *head black*, with concealed crown patch of red; upperparts slate gray; *underparts white; black, fan-shaped tail, broadly tipped with white;* flies with such short, quick beats of wings that they appear to quiver when the bird hovers just above tops of tall grass; conspicuous, noisy, aggressive, utters high-pitched notes with rapid sputtering pattern of telegraph key, *tzi, tzee, tzi, tzee, tzi, tzee;* sometimes sings dawn song from sky, rolling, sharp notes ending like phoebe's song; fearlessly attacks hawks, crows, vultures, diving and sometimes alighting on back of larger bird; has even been known to attack low-flying airplane crossing its territory (Tyler, 1942a; see Ogburn's "The Redoubtable Kingbird," in Terres, 1958); migrates northward in spring, in loose flocks, from winter home in C. and S. America, arrives on nesting grounds from s. U.S. to Canada, Apr.–May; lives in open country about orchards, borders of fields, along highways, in open woods, and in suburbs; perches conspicuously on fence post or utility wires or top of isolated tree.
Feeding Habits: Catches most of insect food by flying from perch to snap them in bill out of air, sometimes alights on ground in plowed field to pluck insects from ground, or dips to scoop them from water without wetting a feather; eats more than 200 kinds of insects and fruit or seeds of 40 kinds of plants (Tyler, 1942a); picks berries from bushes by hovering.
Nest: Usually builds well out on horizontal limb of isolated tree or orchard tree or in low shrubs growing along water's edge, 2–60 ft. above ground, or on stumps or snags above water far

Loggerhead kingbird

TYRANT FLYCATCHER FAMILY

from shore of lake or pond, in hollows of trees near water, in open on fence posts, and in suburbs may nest in rain gutter of house; bulky, about 5½ in. in diameter, outside rough, built of twigs, straw, string, weed stems, feathers, lined with fine grasses, rootlets, horsehair.

Eggs: May–July; 3–5, white to cream- or pink-white, heavily and irregularly marked with small spots, blotches of brown.

Incubation: 12–13 days (?); young leave nest when about 13–14 days old (Tyler, 1942a).

Other Names: Bee bird; bee martin; field martin; tyrant flycatcher.

Age: One banded, Wilton, N.D., trapped and released in same area when 6 years, 11 months old (Kennard, 1975).

Albinism: A "perfect" albino reported in collections of Philadelphia Academy of Natural Sciences (Townsend, 1883); a partial albino, Briggsdale, Colo., Aug. 1927; body snow white, wings, tail lemon yellow, eyes dark as in normal bird (Gordon, 1928).

Flight Speed: Timed in New England, 15–23 m.p.h. (White, 1929, 1935); in Mich., 13–21 m.p.h. (Schnell, 1965).

Host to Cowbirds: Uncommon, only 15 records; pugnacity of kingbird usually repels cowbird (Friedmann, 1963).

Weights: Coastal N.J., in fall migration (26), 34.5–53.5 gr. (Murray and Jehl, 1964), or about 1–2 oz.

Range: Nests from n. B.C., c.-s. Mack., c. Sask., c. Man., n. Ont., s. Que., Nova Scotia, south to w. Wash., Oreg. east of coast ranges, ne. Calif., n. Nev., s. Idaho, n. Utah, Colo., ne. N.M., c. Tex., Gulf coast, and s. Fla.; winters in S. America.

Kingbird, gray, *Tyrannus dominicensis* (tih-RAN-us dom-in-ih-SEN-sis); genus name: *see* Kingbird, eastern; species name: Lat., of Santo Domingo, early name of island of Hispaniola, West Indies, where type specimen collected. (Color ill., page 369.) West Indian, C. and S. American species that reaches N. America in summer in extreme se. U.S., Ala., Fla., to S.C.; 9–9½ in. long; wingspread 14½–16 in.; resembles eastern kingbird but is larger and *upperparts a "ghostly gray";* crown with concealed red patch; dark ear coverts; large, broad bill, flattened at base; all-gray tail with slightly notched tip; in summer often seen perched on utility wires along Overseas Highway of Florida Keys and elsewhere along coast; very noisy, utters chattering cries, one of which is a three-syllabled *pe-CHEER-y;* from winter home in S. America, usually arrives in Fla. in Apr.; in S.C., in May.

Feeding Habits: From exposed perch such as utility wire, darts out into air at passing insects to catch wild bees, wasps, beetles, dragonflies; also takes lizards, cotton worms, army worms from ground or foliage, and eats berries of gumbo-limbo, royal palm, etc. (Sprunt, 1942a).

Nest: Throughout range in Fla. in Keys and along coasts, favors red mangrove trees for nesting, also may nest in pines and other trees, in back of dunes along Fla. and Gulf coast (nests up to 10–15 mi. inland from Fla. coast, largely in towns, according to Phillips and Lanyon, 1970); flimsy nest of coarse twigs, lined with grasses.

Eggs: U.S., Apr.–July; 3–5, usually 3, pink, spotted with browns.

Incubation: Period of and age when young leave nest unknown.

Other Names: Bee bird; fighter; hard-head.

Range: Nests along Gulf coast of Ala. and from S.C. to Ga., Fla., and through the West Indies and islands on coast of C. America and n. S. America; winters from Hispaniola and Puerto Rico south to n. S. America; has wandered north to coast of Mass., Long Is., N.Y., s. N.J., and B.C.

Kingbird, Lichtenstein's. *See* Kingbird, tropical.

Kingbird, loggerhead, *Tyrannus caudifasciatus* (tih-RAN-us caw-dih-fah-sih-AY-tus); genus name: *see* Kingbird, eastern; species name: from Lat. *cauda,* a tail, and *fasciata,* striped. West Indian species first definitely identified in N. America at Islamorada Is. in Fla. Keys, Jan. 31, 1973 (see Woolfenden, 1973a; also Stevenson, 1972a); about 9¼ in. long; according to Bond (1961), resembles gray kingbird but smaller, and back is gray-olive or gray-brown (not a pale or "ghostly" gray) with head uniformly darker, crown patch is yellow (not red), and tail not notched, with white or gray tip; utters a harsh, rolling chatter suggesting that of eastern kingbird; lives more in woods than gray kingbird but also seen in open country. Nest and eggs like that of gray kingbird.

Range: Bahamas, Cuba, Isle of Pines, Cayman Is., Jamaica, Hispaniola, Puerto Rico, and Vieques Is. (Bond, 1961).

Kingbird, olive-backed. *See* Kingbird, tropical.

Kingbird, thick-billed, *Tyrannus crassirostris* (tih-RAN-us crass-ih-ROS-triss); genus name: *see* Kingbird, eastern; species name: from Lat. *crassus,* thick, and *rostrum,* beak. (Color ill., page 368.) Mexican and Guatemalan species discovered in 1958 in U.S. in se. Ariz. and in sw. N.M.; 9 in. long; puffy brown head; dark facial mask; concealed yellow patch in crown; black bill is heavy and thick, throat white, shading to pale gray on breast; belly pale yellow; wings dusky brown (without white bars as in somewhat similar crested flycatchers); upperparts and slightly notched tail, solid dusky brown or dark gray; according to Phillips *et al.* (1964), is Arizona's loudest bird: "its usual calls are a shrill *cut-a-réep* and *kiterréer";* first discovered in Guadalupe Canyon in se. Ariz. and sw. N.M. in June 1958 (see Phillips *et al.,* 1964, and Ligon, 1961); in 1962, another colony discovered along Sonoita Creek near Patagonia, Ariz.; in Guadalupe Canyon, is associated with streamside sycamores.

Feeding Habits: Apparently takes food similar to that of other kingbirds; Phillips *et al.* reported that in its flights in catching food (presumably insects) it quivers its wings and keeps its head feathers erected.

Nest: Dale Zimmerman (see Ligon, 1961) reported two pairs nesting in N.M. part of Guadalupe Canyon, June 1959; both nests in sycamores, 50–60 ft. above ground; thin, frail-appearing, built of slender twigs and grasses; ends of material projecting from rims of nests made them appear bristly and unfinished.
Eggs: 3–4, white, spotted with brown.
Range: Nests in se. Ariz., sw. N.M., and in Mexico; winters in Mexico.

Kingbird, tropical, *Tyrannus melancholicus* (tih-RAN-us mel-an-KOH-lih-cus); genus name: *see* Kingbird, eastern; species name: Lat., melancholy. (Color ill., page 369.) Mexican, C. and S. American species that in summer reaches U.S. in se. Ariz., also in s. Tex., where it is the common kingbird of the lower Rio Grande and winters irregularly (Peterson, 1963); 8–9½ in. long; resembles Cassin's and western kingbirds but *tail is brown* (not black), *without white edges or tip,* and is deeply forked; head gray with dark mask through eyes, has concealed red crown patch; back olive green; throat white; belly *bright yellow;* calls in Tex. are a buzzy *queer* or *chi-queer,* like notes of Cassin's kingbird but higher-pitched, also a *b-re-e-e-e-e-e-r,* with quality of policeman's whistle (Peterson, 1963); sings at dawn a high *pit-it-it-it* and series of thin trills even higher (Skutch, 1960; see also Smith, W. J., 1966); in Ariz. (May–Sept.), nests near Tucson in cottonwoods, also recently elsewhere in Santa Cruz and possibly San Pedro valleys and along Salt R. east of Phoenix; may nest in same row of cottonwoods with western and Cassin's kingbirds (Phillips *et al.,* 1964); in s. Tex., lives in chaparral, where usually hidden in mesquite, ebony, persimmon, retama, and thorny bushes (Bent, 1942); also visits towns and cities.
Feeding Habits: Eats largely insects caught as it flies, often at end of long upward dart, or in evening while it is in swallowlike circling; rarely, catches a number of insects in bill before returning to its perch; at times, swoops downward to snatch grasshopper from low herbage or may alight on ground; often eats berries; rarely, small frogs (Skutch, 1960).
Nest: One on Rio Grande, Tex., was 20 ft. from ground on small lateral branch of an elm not far from ranch house; nest about 6 in. in diameter, of elm twigs, Spanish moss (Bent, 1942); Skutch (1960) described nests in Costa Rica as shallow, bowl-shaped, built by female of dry twigs, rootlets, weed stems, grasses, lined with finer materials, sometimes horsehair, in bush or tree in pasture or beside road, 6–40 ft. up, most below 15 ft.
Eggs: Ariz., May–June; Tex., May; Mexico, Apr.–July; 3–5, usually 2–3, or 3–4, rich buff to cream-pink, blotched and spotted with browns, purples.
Incubation: By female, 15–16 days; young leave nest 18–19 days after hatching (Skutch, 1960).
Other Names: Couch's kingbird; Lichtenstein's kingbird; olive-backed kingbird; West Mexican kingbird.
Host to Cowbirds: 4 records, to bronzed cowbird (Friedmann, 1963).

Range: Besides nesting from Ariz. and Tex. south through parts of Mexico, C. America, and south to Argentina, has wandered to B.C., Wash., and Calif.

Kingbird, western, *Tyrannus verticalis* (tih-RAN-us ver-tih-KALE-iss); genus name: *see* Kingbird, eastern; species name: Lat., pertaining to top of head (the concealed red crown patch). (Color ill., page 369.) Generally in summer from Mississippi R. west to Pacific coast; s. Canada south to n. Mexico; 8–9½ in. long; wingspread 15¼–16½ in.; head and back pale gray; throat white; underparts pale yellow; similar to Cassin's kingbird but the black tail has abruptly white sides—that is, white along edges of outer tail feathers, not white-*tipped* tail as in Cassin's (the similar great crested and Wied's crested flycatchers have white bars in wings and *rufous* tails); has subdued voice for a kingbird, usual call is *kip,* or sharp *whit,* some of its notes like squeaks of grackles, also utters low warbling twitter and harsh metallic *ker-er-ip-ker-er-ip* (Bent, 1942); from winter home in s. Mexico and C. America, arrives on nesting grounds in U.S., late Mar. through May; apparently more social than many other kingbirds, two pairs or more seen nesting in same tree in apparent harmony, and has nested within few yards of occupied nest of Swainson's hawk, and in same tree with golden eagle; however, usually attacks hawks and especially crows and ravens that fly near its nest; lives in open country around ranches and towns, avoids woods but likes timber belts along streams, wanders far out over treeless prairies, using fences or utility wires for perch.
Feeding Habits: Darts out from perch in tree, low bush, fence post, tall weed stalk to catch and eat bees (usually drones, or males), wasps, beetles, moths, drops to ground to catch caterpillars, grasshoppers, crickets, also eats bugs, millipedes, spiders, occasionally tree frogs, fruit of elderberry, hawthorns. See Ohlendorf, 1974.
Nest: Usually in cottonwood, oak, sycamore, willow, or other tree when available; against trunk, in crotch, or more often on horizontal branch, 8–40 ft. above ground, also on bushes, and in absence of trees, on utility poles, water towers, windmills, in barn, church steeple, ledge above kitchen door, rain gutter of house, on grain binder, fence post, etc.; nest is about 6 in. in diameter, of weed stems, twigs, rootlets, string, milkweed down, lined with sheep's wool, cotton, cow hair, chicken feathers, and pieces of dried snakeskin. See Ohlendorf, 1974.
Eggs: Apr.–July; 3–7, usually 4, white, pink, or buff, spotted or blotched with browns.
Incubation: 12–14 days (?); young fly about 14 days after hatching.
Other Name: Arkansas kingbird.
Flight Speed: Timed in Kans., 17 m.p.h. (Wood, 1923).
Age: One killed when 6 years, 11 months, old (Kennard, 1975).
Host to Cowbirds: Rare, apparently one record (Tex.), to brown-headed cowbird (Friedmann, 1963).
Hybrids: One adult male, an intergeneric hybrid—a cross between a scissor-tailed

flycatcher and a western kingbird (Davis and Webster, 1970).
Range: Nests from w. Ore., w. Wash., s. B.C. to s. Man., w. Minn., rarely to s. Wisc., s. Mich., s. Ont., and nw. Ohio, south to n. Baja Calif., s. N.M., n. Mexico, w.-c. Tex., ne. Okla., e.-c. Kans., and rarely n.-c. Mo.; winters in small numbers along Atlantic coast from S.C. to Fla., where winters rather commonly in southern half of state, including Keys (Phillips and Lanyon, 1970); winters chiefly from Mexico to n. Nicaragua; in migration, along Atlantic coast largely in autumn, from Nova Scotia, N.B., south with regular fall records on Long Is., N.Y., along oceanfront perched on wires, fence posts, bushes, usually Sept.–Nov.

Kingbird, west Mexican. *See* Kingbird, tropical.

Kiskadee, greater. *See* Flycatcher, Kiskadee.

Pewee, barn. *See* Phoebe, eastern.

Pewee, bridge. *See* Phoebe, eastern.

Pewee, Coues'. *See* Flycatcher, Coues'.

Pewee, eastern wood, *Contopus virens* (KON-toh-pus VIR-enz); genus name: *see* Flycatcher, Coues'; species name: from Lat. *virere,* to be green. (Color ill., page 370.) Summers from s. Canada south to Fla., west to Dakotas and Tex.; 6–6¾ in. long; upperparts dusky gray-olive, underparts pale yellow-white; wash of olive on sides of breast and on flanks; similar to eastern phoebe but wood pewee has two white bars in each wing, and a *yellow* lower mandible (phoebe's bill is black); can be distinguished from the small *Empidonax* flycatchers by pale line down center of breast and its lack of eye-ring, and while perched, does not usually raise and lower tail (see key to differences when pewee in hand in Phillips *et al.,* 1966); virtually impossible to distinguish in field eastern from western wood pewee (the eastern is only one to be expected regularly east of 100th meridian) at places of overlap in w. Man. and in Neb. (see details in Phillips *et al.*), but songs are different: from perch in deep shade of woods, eastern during day whistles plaintive rising and falling *pee-ah-wee!,* pause, then descending *pee—oh,* and adds phrase, in early-morning and twilight song, with rising inflection, *ah—dih-dee* (Craig, 1943); call note is *chip!,* also utters a squeaky *whee-chuttle-chuttle;* from winter home in C. and S. America, arrives on nesting grounds in e. U.S., Canada, Apr.–May; summers usually in deciduous or mixed deciduous-coniferous woods of country and in tall shade trees of towns, villages, and gardens; likes to sit on high dead branch amid gloom of woods, and when not singing, darts out at passing insects.

Feeding Habits: Eats mostly flies, beetles, bees, wasps, ants, also tussock and gypsy moths, cankerworms, treehoppers, bugs, grasshoppers, also some elderberries, blackberries, pokeberries, etc. (Tyler, 1942c).

breeding range of the eastern wood pewee

breeding range of the western wood pewee

TYRANT FLYCATCHER FAMILY
Although virtually indistinguishable in the field, the eastern wood pewee and the western wood pewee have different ranges and different territorial songs. Even where their breeding ranges overlap slightly, in Western Manitoba and Nebraska, the two species have not been known to interbreed.

Nest: Built on horizontal limb of oak, maple, locust, elm, apple tree, etc., about 15–50 ft. above ground; a thick-walled cup about 3 in. in diameter, usually so well covered with lichens that almost invisible from ground; like knot atop branch; built of weed stems, plant fibers, spider cocoons, string, lined with wool, horsehair, bits of thread, grasses.

Eggs: May–July; 2–4, usually 3, cream to white, irregularly blotched or speckled with browns.

Incubation: 13 days; young leave nest about 15–18 days after hatching.

Other Names: Eastern pewee; pewit or pewee flycatcher.

Age: One, banded at Powdermill Nature Reserve, Rector, Pa., trapped and released in same area when 6 years, 11 months, old (Kennard, 1975).

Albinism: One reported Montclair, N.J., summer 1913, all-white upperparts, lemon yellow and white below, dusky tips to wings; one partially albino male collected University of Wisconsin, Madison, Sept. 1961.

Host to Cowbirds: Fairly regular but not a favorite host of brown-headed cowbird; only 28 records reported over 30 years (Friedmann, 1963).

Weights: Coastal N.J., in fall (10), 11.4–15.4 gr. (Murray and Jehl, 1964), or about ½ oz.

Range: Nests from s. Man., w. and c. Ont., s. Que., n. Me., c. N.B., and n. Nova Scotia, south along edge of Great Plains from e. N.D. to c. and se. Tex, east along Gulf coast to c. Fla.; winters from Costa Rica south into S. America.

Pewee, greater. *See* Flycatcher, Coues'.

Pewee, large-billed wood. *See* Pewee, western wood.

Pewee, Nuttall's. *See* Flycatcher, olive-sided.

Pewee, small. *See* Flycatcher, Acadian.

Pewee, water. *See* Phoebe, eastern.

Pewee, western wood, *Contopus sordidulus* (KON-toh-pus sore-DID-you-lus); genus name: *see* Flycatcher, Coues'; species name: from Lat. *sordidus*, dirty, or soiled, referring to dusky color. (Color ill., page 370.) Summers from Alaska, w.-c. Canada, and in w. U.S. from Pacific coast east to Man., Dakotas, Colo., and w. Tex.; 6–6½ in. long; upperparts quite dark, dusky gray-brown; dark sides of breast divided by a narrow light-colored line down belly, *no white eye-ring as in* Empidonax *flycatchers*, and has two narrow white bars in each wing; dull, dark bill; virtually impossible to distinguish in field from eastern wood pewee (their ranges overlap in w. Man. and in Neb.), but has quite different song or territorial call, a harsh, nasal descending *pee-er* or *pheer* (Phillips *et al.*, 1964); somewhat like call of common nighthawk but weaker; uttered frequently at dusk and after dark (Bent, 1942); from winter range, s. Mexico to Bolivia, reaches nesting range in U.S., Canada, Alaska, Apr.–May; summers in open deciduous and coniferous woods in mountains, from Pacific O. in Calif. to tops of coastal ranges; in large syca- mores, cottonwoods, and other trees along mountain streams 5,000–6,000 ft. elevation in Ariz., also in Puget Sound region of Wash. in cultivated stream valleys, in deciduous trees along borders of lakes, streams, also in cities and in towns.

Feeding Habits: From dead branch at edge of forest, or from shade tree near a house, darts out and seizes flying insect with click of mandibles; almost all of food is insects—bees, wasps, ants (about 40% of its insect food); flies (44%)—horseflies, snipe flies, crane flies, robber flies, etc.; also moths, caterpillars, some dragonflies, mayflies, lacewings, termites, also spiders and a few wild berries.

Nest: Usually built on horizontal branch of aspen, sycamore, ash, birch, eucalyptus, oak, maple, hackberry, etc., 15–75 ft. above ground, occasionally in fork of sapling or bush; larger, more compact, deeper than nest of eastern wood pewee, of plant fibers, fine grasses, gray dead leaves, bud scales, bits of bark, interwoven and held in place with spiders' silk (not usually decorated on outside with lichens as in eastern wood pewee), lined with fine grasses, birds' feathers (Bent, 1942).

Eggs: May–July; 2–4, usually 3, cream-white, spotted and blotched with browns.

Incubation: 12 days (?); age when young leave nest not known.

Other Names: Large-billed wood pewee; western pewee.

Host to Cowbirds: Rare, only 7 records (Friedmann, 1963).

Range: Nests from e.-c. Alaska, s. Yuk., s. Mack., e.-c. Sask., and c. Man. south in mtns. to n. Baja Calif. and Mexico, possibly to Costa Rica, east to the Dakotas, c. and w. Tex.; winters from c. Panama to nw. S. America south to Bolivia; accidental in Alaska and Jamaica.

Phoebe, black, *Sayornis nigricans* (say-OR-nis NIG-rih-kanz); genus name: for Thomas Say, American entomologist, who accompanied Stephen Long on his 19th-century expedition to the Rocky Mtns., during which the phoebe was collected that became the type for the genus *(Sayornis)*, and *ornis*, from a Gr. word meaning bird—"Say's bird"; species name: Lat., blackish. (Color ill., page 371.) Year-round resident in valleys, coastal plains of Southwest; most individuals move south out of U.S. in winter (Verbeek, 1975); 6¼–7 in. long; only *black-breasted* N. American flycatcher (Peterson, 1961); color pattern strikingly like a junco, with sooty black upperparts and breast that contrast sharply with white belly, but thin, flattened bill and erect posture when perched, and habit of lowering, then raising tail slowly, distinguish it; lives about lowland marshy ponds or under sycamores bordering mountain streams, is never far from water—a small backyard pond, watering trough for livestock, or irrigation ditch will attract it; frequently seen about buildings, barnyards, sweeps down over city lawns, lives around reservoirs in mountains; lives only sparingly over drier, interior parts of its range (Bent, 1942); in Ariz., nests commonly along streams and canals of c. and se. parts of state; locally in bottom of Grand Canyon (Phillips *et al.*, 1964); common call is *tsip*, or more prolonged, plaintive *chee*; song is indefinite repetition of two notes, *ti wee*, *ti wee*, each pair with alternating upward or downward inflection.

Feeding Habits: Rarely seeks treetops but perches in shaded lower branches or on fences, stones, other low objects, but seldom on ground, darts out in soft mothlike flight to snap, with click of bill, wild bees, ants, and wasps, beetles, plant lice, flies, moths, and caterpillars, usually swoops downward from perch, so that most of insects taken within few inches of lawn, water, or weed patch below it; sometimes takes small fishes from top of water; Oberlander (1939) discovered that it regurgitates indigestible parts of large insects in small round pellets.

Nest: Mud mixed with fibrous plant materials attached to rough vertical wall of cliff, under eave of building, under bridge, bottom of nest usually not supported as in eastern phoebe and so securely fastened it will break apart rather than give way; sometimes in wells 4–5 ft. below ground surface. See Ohlendorf, 1976.

Eggs: Mar.–Aug.; 3–6, white, usually unmarked but some may be heavily dotted with reds or browns.

Incubation: 15–17 days; young leave nest 20–21 days after hatching.

Other Names: Black-headed flycatcher; western black pewee.

Host to Cowbirds: One record, Solano County, Calif. (Friedmann, 1963).

Range: Resident from Calif., s. Nev., sw. Utah, c. Ariz., s. N.M., and c. Tex., south to Baja Calif., and through Mexico, C. and S. American highlands to n. Argentina; has strayed to Ore. and B.C.

Phoebe, eastern, *Sayornis phoebe* (say-OR-nis FEE-bee); genus name: *see* Phoebe, black; species name: Lat. (pronunciation of name resembles call of the bird), from name in Gr. mythology of a daughter of Gaea. (Color ill., page 371.) In summer, from Atlantic coast of e. U.S. and Canada, west to Rocky Mtns., south to N.M. and se. U.S.; 6¼–7¼ in. long; *black bill;* blackish crown; upperparts olive; no white bars in wings (except in immatures) as in similar wood pewee and other small flycatchers; *throat white;* rest of underparts pale buff-white, pale olive on shoulders and flanks; upright posture and distinctive emphatic call, *fee-bee* or *wheepee,* repeated over and over, distinguish it; most noticeable habit: upon alighting on perch, sweeps tail widely, down, then up, and often toward either side, which gives *wagging* effect (Tyler, 1942b); from winter home in s. U.S. and Mexico, is on nesting grounds in Mar.–Apr.; is one of hardiest N. American flycatchers; likes to be near water, summers in woods with streams and rocky ravines, also about farmyards and along wooded country roads with bridges crossing streams; Tyler (1942b) cited one bridge in New England under which generations of phoebes nested successively for 30 years; at times, remarkably tame; a family marked with silver wire around legs by Audubon in Pa. was first bird-banding experiment in America.

Feeding Habits: Eats many beetles; largest food items are wasps, ants, small wild bees; also eats flies, bugs, grasshoppers, crickets, dragonflies, moths, caterpillars, spiders (airborn), millipedes, ticks, and even hairworms *(Gordius)* from water, and occasionally tiny fishes from shallows.

Nest: In recess on rock ledge of steep wall of ravine or gorge and in caves; now builds extensively on man-made structures, rafters in barns, sheds, or under eaves of houses, on windowsills, doorsills, porch rafters, top of shutters, and especially on girders under bridges or trestles over water; a cup of mud and moss, lined with grasses, hair, feathers, about 4½ in. in diameter; sometimes will build a second nest or even a third, fourth, or fifth one on top of an old nest in subsequent years.

Eggs: Apr.–June; 3–8, commonly 5, white, although a few may be spotted sparingly with brown about large end.

Incubation: 14–17 days (Smith, 1942) but usually 16 days; young leave nest about 15–16 days after hatching; two broods, sometimes three in a season.

Other Names: Barn pewee; bean bird; bridge pewee; dusky flycatcher; pewee; pewit flycatcher; phoebe bird; water pewee.

Age: Two banded in Ind. lived to 9 years old; another wild banded one trapped and released when 8 years, 1 month, old (Kennard, 1975).

Albinism: One cream-colored young among brood of five in nest near Broadway, Va., eyes normal, feet pale (Hostetter, 1934).

Host to Cowbirds: Very commonly, more than 375 records (Friedmann, 1963).

Weights: Coastal N.J., in fall (9), 15.9–20.8 gr. (Murray and Jehl, 1964), or ½–¾ oz.; in Conn., immatures, late summer (38), 15.6–22.5 gr. (Wetherbee, 1934).

Range: Nests from c. Mack., n. Sask., east to s. Que. and N.B., south to ne. B.C., s. Alta., sw. S.D., s.-c. Colo., e. N.M., w. Okla., c. and ne. Tex., Ark., sw. Tenn., ne. Miss., c. Ala., n. Ga., w. S.C., N.C.; winters from Va. south through Atlantic coastal states, then west through Gulf states and south into Mexico; casually farther north as far as Ont. and N.H.,; has strayed to Calif., Baja Calif., in winter to Ariz. and Bermuda.

Phoebe, Say's, *Sayornis saya* (say-OR-nis SAY-yah); genus, species, and common names: for Thomas Say, 19th-century entomologist; *see also* Phoebe, black. (Color ill., page 371.) Summers from Alaska to the Dakotas, south to Tex. and Mexico; generally west of 100th meridian, accidental east of Great Plains; 7–8 in. long; pale gray-buff back contrasts with *black* tail and *rusty underparts,* appears like small robin but has flycatching habits; Peterson (1947) saw an eastern phoebe so stained with Georgia clay it strikingly resembled a Say's; from wintering places in s. Calif., Ariz., N.M., Say's arrives on nesting grounds Feb.–May; lives in open country, at home around ranches, common on sagebrush plains, bluffs, cliffs of badlands, dry barren foothills, and in generally drier country than black phoebe; avoids timbered places, has habits like those of eastern phoebe but even more restless, constantly darting back and forth from perch on small bush,

tall weed, rock, after passing insects, also hovers like a mountain bluebird or American kestrel, when perched rapidly dips and fans tail; not shy around people, sometimes roosts at night in its nest or in niche of wall of old building; call is soft, mournful, descending *phee-eur* or *chu-weer;* fluttering about in air sings rapid *pit-tsee-ar* or *pippety-chee.*

Feeding Habits: Wild bees, wasps, and ants are favored food, also many flies, mostly houseflies, crane flies, and robber flies, also beetles, bugs, moths, butterflies, crickets, grasshoppers, dragonflies, spiders, millipedes, sow bugs; regurgitates hard parts of insects in small pellets; also eats some berries (Bent, 1942).

Nest: Ordinarily no mud used, is flat structure built of weed stems, grasses, mosses, wool, empty cocoons, spiders' silk, hairs; is about 5½ in. in diameter, on rocky shelves, or crevices of cliffs, caves, natural cavities in trees, holes in banks, on rafters under bridges, under roof of cattle shed, inside deserted ranch buildings, in old cliff swallow's nest, etc.

Eggs: Mar.–July; 3–7, usually 4–5, white, although a few may have reddish or brown spots.

Incubation: 12 (?) to 14 days; young leave nest 14–16 days after hatching.

Other Name: Say's pewee.

Host to Cowbirds: Rare, 6 records (Friedmann, 1963).

Range: Nests from Alaska, c. Yuk., w. Mack., c. Alta., s. Sask., and sw. Man., south to c. Mexico; winters from n. Calif., n. Ariz., c. and se. N.M., s. Tex., south to Baja Calif. and s.-c. Mexico; casual in B.C., nw. U.S., Iowa, W. Mo.; has strayed to Wisc., Ill., Ind., N.Y., Conn., Mass., and Que.

Tyrannulet, beardless. *See* Flycatcher, northern beardless.

FLYING SHEEP

Local name in Man. and Alta., Canada, for the whooping crane, from its large size and whiteness (McAtee, 1957a).

FLY-UP-THE-CREEK

Local name for the American bittern and the green heron. *See* in Heron Family.

FLYWAY

See Waterfowl.

FOG AND BIRDS

See Waterfowl; Weather; Migration.

FOLKLORE

Edward A. Armstrong, a British ornithologist and a scholar and student of the folklore of birds, has called the subject a branch of social anthropology dealing with data in which birds play a part, including their local names, their part in proverbs, legends, myths, folktales, rituals, and symbols (see in Armstrong, E. A., 1958; 1964a). He suggests that a knowledge of folklore is indispensable to us as one of the few sources of information about modes of thought and spiritual life in the earliest communities of man. In those earlier times, man was influenced by the flight of birds and their mysterious comings and goings, their disappearance in migrations into the sky, suggesting that they were in touch with, or were, emissaries of powers in the heavens.

Man likened the movements of birds to the departure from earth of the human soul, and he was impressed with the likeness of the dancing and singing of birds to the dancing and singing of men, and that they, too, walked like a man in the upright, bipedal fashion. He saw owls, with their binocular sight, and in the human qualities of their calls, as mysterious and uncanny birds, partly human, and they aroused in him fear and dread. Some black species, such as the raven and the common swift of Europe, were associated with the devil, although some of the plantation Negroes of s. U.S. regarded the blue jay as a bird of Satan (see below). In British and in European folklore in general, the raven was considered a supernatural bird, mostly evil, although like the European cuckoo and some other birds, its actions might foretell good as well as evil. As a bird whose croakings could supposedly predict death or other dire consequences for man, the raven is well known to readers of both European and American literature.

BIRDS THAT SPEAK HUMAN LANGUAGE. According to Ingersoll (1923), when we say, "A little bird told me," we are talking legend, folklore, and superstition all at once. Our Biloxi Indians of the coast of the Gulf of Mexico described in their tales a small bird, the ruby-throated hummingbird, which talked and always told the truth. Both European peasants and N. American Indians of the forests and plains credited all birds with the power of using human language. Conversations with birds, and by birds, were usual in stories told by many blacks of the cotton plantations of the South, where the jaybird (blue jay) was reported *never to be seen on Friday* because on that day he was carrying sticks (and news of the world of men) below to the devil. The blue jay always completed his work for Satan in time to return to earth by Saturday. Then he was unusually gay and noisy, suggesting that he was happy to be a free bird for another week (Barker, 1966).

OTHER AMERICAN SUPERSTITIONS ABOUT BIRDS. In some common superstitions, passed on by country people for generations, it was believed that if a bird flew into the house, it was a forerunner of important news—some said a sign of death if the bird could not get out again. In Ala., some people believed that a bird that came into the house brought good luck, but if a woodpecker tapped on the house, it brought bad news, possibly the death of someone in the family. A whip-poor-will or a screech owl calling or a horned owl hooting was a sign of death or of bad luck, and a crow that croaked three times as it flew over a house portended that someone in the house would die. If a wren built its nest near a house, it brought good fortune, and when you heard the first whip-poor-will of spring, you could be assured that you would be in the same place doing the same thing on the same day of the following year; if you made a wish when you heard the calling of the first whip-poor-will, your wish would come true (Leach, 1949). According to Iroquois Indian leg-

end, wild moccasin flowers *(Cypripedium)*, orchids of N. American woods and swamps, were the whip-poor-will's shoes (Ingersoll, 1923).

A rooster crowing outside of the house announced company, but in Nova Scotia, if a rooster crowed at the wrong time of the night, it was said to announce a death; it was also a general folk belief in the U.S. that it was bad luck to have designs of birds or bird decorations on wedding presents, as the happiness of the wedded couple would all the sooner fly away.

BIRDS AS WEATHER PROPHETS. It was popularly believed, and still is, in the Shetland Is. off n. Scotland, that the red-throated diver (loon), called the "rain-goose," is especially noisy before bad weather. In N. America, the Thompson R. Indians of B.C. believed that the frequent calling of the common loon not only predicted rain but brought it (Armstrong, E. A., 1958).

According to Ingersoll (1923), almost every country has some particular "rain-bird" whose cry is supposed to foretell showers. In England it is the green woodpecker, or yaffle; in some parts of N. America it is the spotted sandpiper; and the name is especially applied to the black-billed and yellow-billed cuckoos, whose frequent calling on hot, sultry days supposedly "calls for rain." On the oceans, the sudden appearance of storm-petrels during windy weather seemed to sailors to presage a storm *(see also* Mother Carey's Chickens), and Alexander Wilson in his *American Ornithology* wrote that when the American osprey circles high in the air with loud cries, then dashes downward, this is almost certain to indicate a change in the weather and that, later, frequently within a few hours, a thunderstorm would appear. In *Weather Lore*, a collection of proverbs and sayings published by Richard Inwards in 1893, the following relate to birds:

If the birds be silent, expect thunder.

If fowls roll in the sand,
Rain is at hand.

If the wild geese gang out to sea,
Good weather there surely will be.

If larks fly high and sing long,
Expect fine weather.

When men-of-war hawks fly high, it is a
sign of a clear sky,
When they fly low, prepare for a blow.

THE THUNDERBIRD. To the Indians of e. U.S. the violent storms of summer were produced by supernatural beings which they spoke of as thundergods; on the prairies and plains of the West, where electrical storms were even more terrifying, American Indians attributed these violent storms to enormous supernatural birds. These "thunderbirds" darkened the rain clouds with their shadows, and caused thunder by flapping their wings, and hurled lightning bolts by opening and closing their eyes or by ripping trees open with their claws. See accounts especially by Ingersoll (1923) and Leach (1949).

SOME FANCIED MEDICINAL PROPERTIES OF BIRDS. In ancient times, people distilled the feet of buzzards (a buteonine hawk of Europe) as a remedy for sciatica, the gall bladder of a crane for palsy, consumption, and blindness, and ground the bills of bitterns into a powder, which if taken before going to bed, supposedly induced sleep (Allen, E. G., 1951). According to John Brickell in his *Natural History of North Carolina*, published in Dublin in 1737, "the dung of the 'goss hawk' is exceeding hot, and being drank fasting in wine, is said to cause conception." Another common belief of country people in the U.S.: that if a man with an aching back, on hearing the call of the whip-poor-will, turned somersaults timed with the bird's calls, his backache would disappear. Among Okefenokee swampers, eating the eggs of mockingbirds would cure stuttering; elsewhere, the bones of a turkey vulture's head hung around the neck "helpeth the headach" and eating the uncooked heart of a kingbird would cure heart disease.

SOME OTHER MISCELLANEOUS MYTHS. That the nests of swifts of the Orient, if made into a soup (*see* Nests and Nesting), have medicinal values and when combined with ginseng are capable of restoring life to a person almost dead; that barnacle geese hatch from ship's barnacles; that American coots (e. N.C.) in summer turn into bullfrogs; that goatsuckers (*see* Nightjar Family) suck the milk of goats; that kingfishers nest on the sea at certain times of the year, at which the gods make the winds behave and the seas calm (the halcyon days); that the cormorant, which launches outward from pile or wharf downward close to the water, does so because it must always get its tail wet before it can fly; that pelicans feed their young on their own heart's blood, which the parents get by puncturing their own breasts with their bills; that cliff swallows return to Capistrano Mission in Calif. on exactly the same date each Mar.; that murres return to Baccalieu Is., Newfoundland, and the osprey arrives on the eastern shore of Md., always on St. Patrick's day; and that a barn frequented by swallows will never be struck by lightning. For a story of legend and fact, *see* Swan Song.

FOLLICLES
(FOL-ih-kls). *See* Atretic Follicles; Eggs and Egg-laying; Feather Follicle.

FOLLOWING HABIT
(of hawks and owls). *See* Commensalism.

FOOD AND FEEDING HABITS
Birds eat animals in almost every phylum of the great divisions of the animal kingdom, from the lowly one-celled protozoans, eaten by wild ducks and probably ingested by them when eating the stems and leaves of aquatic plants, to the hydras, jellyfishes, starfishes, sea urchins, and sea anemones, eaten by ducks, gulls, and members of the Auk Family, and marine worms and leeches eaten by waterfowl and shorebirds, and earthworms eaten by many species of birds (*see* Earthworms and Birds), to the jointed animals (arthropods)—the crustaceans such as crabs, shrimps, crayfishes, sow

bugs, and barnacles (*see* Crustaceans and Birds), and the myriapods—centipedes and millipedes—and the joint-legged insects which were 88% of all animal foods eaten according to the stomach analyses of 80,000 N. American birds reported by McAtee (1932b). *See* Arthropod. Insects are the most numerous class of the arthropods and the most important animal food for many N. American birds. *See* Insects and Birds. Birds also eat the joint-legged arachnids—the scorpions, spiders, and ticks—and almost all kinds of mollusks, with their inner or outer shells, such as slugs, squids, snails, mussels, oysters, and limpets. *See* Mollusks and Birds.

Among the vertebrate animals, birds eat fishes (*see* Fishes and Birds), salamanders, frogs, toads, turtles, lizards, and snakes (*see* Reptiles and Birds), and the small mammals such as shrews, bats, mice, rats, pocket gophers, ground and tree squirrels, rabbits and hares, and skunks (especially by the great horned owl). Some of the larger mammals—porcupines, marmots, and even foxes and the young of deer and antelopes—are occasionally killed and eaten by the golden eagle. *See* Predation; Mammals and Birds.

Some birds also prey upon birds—the predatory eagles, hawks, owls, and shrikes capture and kill smaller birds, and crows, jays, magpies, skuas, jaegers, and gulls eat the eggs and young of other birds, and, like bald eagles and frigatebirds, rob other birds of their prey. *See* Egg-eating; *see also* how birds get food from the efforts or actions of other birds and man under Autolycism; *see* how some birds steal food in Feeding and Food-getting under Behavior.

Among the lower plants, wild ducks sometimes sample filamentous algae—water blooms and pond scums—and brant and some other waterfowl along the Atlantic coast depend much on sea lettuce, a saltwater alga, for food; the tubers and whole plants of freshwater algae called muskgrasses are also important wild duck foods (McAtee, 1939). Grouse eat lichens and ruffed grouse eat the parts of 374 different kinds of plants; swans eat water moss (*Fontinalis*) in considerable quantities (Martin *et al.*, 1951); wild geese graze on grasses, pigeons crop herbs and the leaves of trees, wild turkeys and grouse eat buds of trees and parts of ferns, club mosses, and horsetails, and many birds depend year-round on wild fleshy berries and other fruits of the higher plants, rich in carbohydrates and vitamins; hummingbirds feed much on flower nectar as well as insects (*see* Nectar and Birds), and woodpeckers and many songbirds eat tree sap (*see* Commensalism; Sap-feeding). Many birds depend year-round, and especially from fall into spring, on acorns, beechnuts, and other nuts, rich in fats and proteins, and the dry seeds of ash and maple trees, and elms. Many songbirds and game birds rely heavily on corn, rice, and other grains in crop fields, and eat seeds of weeds and grasses throughout the year. *See* the food eaten by each kind of bird and its method of getting its food under Feeding Habits in the biography of each.

HOW MUCH WILL A BIRD EAT? Birds, with their higher body temperatures and high rates of metabolism (rate of burning up their food to produce energy), eat more food ounce for ounce, in proportion to their weights, than do most other vertebrate animals with the exception of shrews. Large birds, even though they occasionally eat very large amounts of food, usually eat *less* daily in proportion to their body weights than do smaller birds (*see* reasons for under Metabolism).

Among the larger birds, nine golden eagles studied in the wild averaged about 1¼ lbs. of food each in their crops and stomachs each day, or about 15% of their individual weights, and in captivity, a golden eagle will eat 2 lbs. of meat daily (Arnold, 1954). See, however, Brown and Amadon (1968) for a detailed account of the daily intake of food by eagles and other birds of prey. An adult brown pelican eats 4 lbs. of fishes daily, or about 50% of its weight (Austin, 1961); the large black-footed albatross has been called a "feathered pig" because it can swallow half-pound chunks of fresh shark meat in one gulp, and according to Schorger (1966), a large wild turkey will eat a pound of food (acorns, for example) at one meal.

Among some of the smaller birds, Sheldon (1971) reported that his captive woodcocks ate about 5½ oz. each of earthworms during each 24 hours—about equal to this bird's daily summer weight. Captive adult sharp-tailed sandpipers, on a diet of chopped mixed fish and liver, each ate 18 gr. (about ⅔ oz.) of food each day, little stints, 11–15 gr. (about ½ oz.) each, or about 28% and 42–58% of their weights, respectively (Serventy *et al.*, 1962). According to a summary by Wing (1956), some N. American and European birds, in descending order of their sizes (large to small), eat the following percentages of food in relation to their body weights: a domestic goose, weighing 1,800 gr. (about 4 lbs.), eats about 4.4% of its body weight; domestic pigeons, weighing 16–18 oz., eat about 5½–6½% of their body weight; the slightly smaller mourning dove, 11.2% of its weight; and a tiny European blue titmouse, weighing only 11 gr. (less than ½ oz.), eats 30% of its body weight. Nice and Nice (1950) had a captive adult female black-and-white warbler that ate 80% of her weight in grasshoppers daily, and an adult meadowlark, by comparison, weighing about 10 times more than the little warbler, ate about 18% of its weight daily in dog food, puppy meal, and insects.

A bird's daily ration varies with the outdoor temperature and the bird's activity—in cold weather, birds eat more; in warm weather, less. The amount of food eaten by a bird will also depend on its health, age, sex, time of day, and availability and nutritional value of food; however, its daily intake should be enough to maintain its energy or to store energy (body fat) for its daily uses, although some of the larger birds can fast for long periods (*see* Fasting). Others—hummingbirds and the poor-will, for example—can go into a torpor to conserve energy during cold spells and in times of scarcity or unavailability of food. *See* Torpidity.

EXAMPLES OF FOOD EATEN PER MEAL. Some birds may eat a very large number of food items at a meal. Of some duck stomach contents examined by the food-habits division of

Cardinal

cross-section of beak

FOOD AND FEEDING HABITS
The cardinal has a short, heavy, sharp-edged bill and strong, crushing jaw muscles with which it cracks a seed and discards the hard coat. The action of the bill is like that of a nutcracker: the grooved upper mandible holds the seed while the sharp-edged lower mandible moves forward, breaks open, and shucks off the hull.

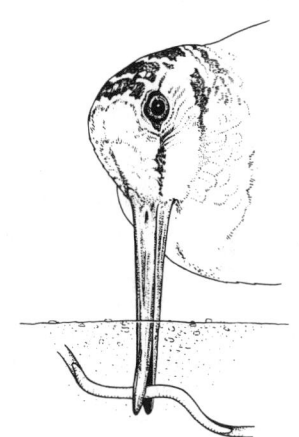

FOOD AND FEEDING HABITS
Probing with its long, delicate bill deep in damp soil, the woodcock can grasp an earthworm with the flexible tip of its upper mandible.

the federal government, the stomach of a mallard shot in La., in Feb., held 28,160 seeds of a bulrush, 8,700 seeds of another sedge, 35,840 seeds of primrose willow, and 2,560 duckweeds —a total of more than 75,000 individual items; another shot in the same area in Dec. had eaten 102,400 seeds of primrose willow. It was estimated that if the seeds from this one bird's stomach had been sown, a foot apart, they would have planted 2½ acres (McAtee, 1918).

A common eider duck examined by the U.S. Biological Survey had eaten 185 blue mussels, *Mytilus edulis*, and another eider stomach held 36 even larger mussels and the fragments of 22 others. A yellow-billed cuckoo had eaten 217 fall webworms; another, 250 tent caterpillars; two flickers had eaten, respectively, 3,000 and 5,000 ants; a nighthawk, 60 grasshoppers; another, 500 mosquitoes; another, 1,000 ants. Nice (1910) had a captive bobwhite quail that ate 568 mosquitoes in two hours; another ate 5,000 plant lice (aphids) in a day; another, 1,000 grasshoppers and 532 other insects in a day and 600–30,000 weed seeds daily.

SOME DANGERS IN FEEDING. Hazards are involved for birds in their food-getting (*see* Deathtraps under Accidents), and even though birds have swallowed some remarkably large objects (*see* under Esophagus), others have choked to death trying to swallow food items too large. In July 1962, six young common terns were found dead in a nesting colony on a sandy island in Moriches Bay, Long Is., N.Y. The young terns were just on the wing and learning to fish for themselves. Each had choked to death on a small but inflated blowfish that was halfway down each bird's throat; in Apr. 1968, a Brandt's cormorant was found dead on a beach near Moss Landing, Calif.; it had choked on a midshipman (fish), *Porichthys notatus*, about 10 in. long, that stuck in its throat; in a similar fatal case, a brown pelican died while trying to swallow a sting ray, *Urotrygon aestrias*, that had embedded its tail spine in the bird's throat. *See also* Reptiles and Birds.

Among songbirds, American robins have been reported by Alexander Wilson, John James Audubon, and others, to have choked to death when trying to swallow the single, large, hard-seeded fruits of the Chinaberry tree, *Melia azedarach*, introduced from Asia in se. U.S. and Calif. *See* Swallowing. Other birds also die from eating natural foods poisonous to them or from natural foods affected by deadly bacteria and funguses or from poisoned grains or insecticides put out by man. *See* Poisons. A golden eagle, after attacking a porcupine, died from the effects of the porcupine's quills in its body. In N.D., in the summer of 1949, a red-tailed hawk died after attacking a weasel and carrying it aloft; the weasel got a death grip on the hawk's throat and forced it to descend to the ground. *See* Mammals and Birds.

FREQUENCY OF FEEDING. Birds usually digest their foods very rapidly (*see* Digestion), and some small birds such as chickadees eat almost constantly, especially during winter in the North (*see* Cold and Birds). Gibb (1958; 1960) discovered that during winter in England, a tit-

mouse in a pine plantation had to catch one average-sized insect every 2½ seconds for 90% of the day in order to gain sufficient energy to meet its bodily needs. Diurnal birds usually feed most heavily early in the morning and late in the afternoon before going to roost (Lack, 1954), but some observers at backyard feeding stations have noted three or four main periods of feeding by medium-sized or small birds— early morning, again sometimes in midmorning, in midafternoon, and in late afternoon; however, birds when not at feeding stations may be pursuing natural foods elsewhere or eating from caches of stored food. Some birds, especially if ill or injured, or if the weather is severely cold or snowy, may be at the feeders almost constantly. *See* Bird-attracting.

BIRDS THAT STORE FOOD. People who feed birds have noted that white-breasted nuthatches, titmice, and other birds which feed on suet, sunflower seeds, and bread, will carry away in the bill small pieces from the bird feeders and hide them in bark crevices or tuck them under leaves or in soft ground; however, other small birds often steal the aboveground stores. Dennis (1957), at his feeding station in Va., noted that in one hour a male white-breasted nuthatch carried away 38 pieces of suet, which it pushed into crevices of bark; however, most of these were later discovered and eaten by a brown creeper, by chickadees, and by other nuthatches. Red-breasted nuthatches extract the seeds of pines from cones and hoard them, and in Russia, Sviridenko (1968) reported that a Eurasian nuthatch, *Sitta europaea*, resembling the N. American white-breasted nuthatch, stores food at all seasons of the year, and at all hours of its waking day. It carries 2 to 4 sunflower seeds in its bill and mouth on each storing strip, and caches them in a tree bark, in mosses clinging to trees, and in soft ground where the density of the unretrieved and sprouting seeds from these stores was 50 per sq. m.

Jays everywhere store food—the blue jay stores acorns and hazelnuts, and sunflower seeds and peanuts, taken from bird feeders, by using the bill to thrust them under leaves or into soft ground; the western Steller's jay similarly buries acorns, and the scrub jay in Calif. has been seen burying pieces of bread and even marbles.

Some birds show a remarkable "place memory" (*see* Curiosity and Memory under Behavior) in returning to and digging up their stores. Eurasian thick-billed nutcrackers, *Nucifraga caryocatactes*, related to the jays, relocate their caches of pine seeds, even when covered by snow, by flying to the spot and digging directly down to them. In a series of experiments, a Russian investigator discovered that these birds, which recover up to 70% of their stored seeds, visually remember the exact places where they bury them (Turcek and Kelso, 1968). See also Swanberg (1951). Cahalane (1944) reported that a Clark's nutcracker in the Rocky Mtns. had dug directly down through 8 in. of snow to recover a seed cone of a Douglas fir that it had apparently stored there. See Bock *et al.* (1973) for details of collecting and carry-

ing food, stored communally, by Clark's nutcrackers.

In Hainault Forest, Essex, England, in the autumn of 1951, 35–40 Eurasian common jays, *Garrulus glandarius*, plucked acorns from oak trees for their winter stores. Individually, they gathered and buried, up to ¾ mi. away, an estimated total of 200,000 acorns, many of which they recovered later by apparently remembering the burial sites (Chettleburgh, 1952). American titmice store sunflower seeds in bark crevices, also under leaves and in grass sod, but may not return to dig up food stored in the ground (Owen and Owen, 1956). In N.C., Terres (personal journals) one Feb. day watched a tufted titmouse store a sunflower seed inside the red flower petals of a camellia bush.

Some of the most energetic hoarders of food are acorn woodpeckers. Dawson (1923) cited an enormous ponderosa pine in Strawberry Canyon in the San Jacinto Mtns., Calif., whose bole from base to crown was studded with an estimated 50,000 acorns, which the woodpeckers had wedged into tightly fitting holes chiseled for the storage of each acorn. This habit is an ancient one in the acorn woodpecker; Miller, R. C. (1950) described acorns, stored by this woodpecker, embedded in tree rings in a redwood tree dating back to 802 A.D.

The Lewis' woodpecker (rarely a pair) stores acorns and commercial nut crops (almonds, for example) for winter use in the dried cracks of utility poles and in the bark of oaks. In the bark of pines, it stores insects which it later feeds to its young; it defends against other woodpeckers its winter caches of nuts and acorns, which it usually eats in the following spring (Bock, 1970). The red-headed woodpecker resembles Lewis' woodpecker in storing acorns, beechnuts, and kernels of corn in the dried cracks of utility poles, fence posts, and standing dead trees in a winter territory that each defends against woodpeckers and other birds; it also stores grasshoppers and other large insects for winter use (Beal, 1911; Bent, 1939), and sometimes seals its winter stores with slivers of damp, rotten wood or bark (MacRoberts, 1975; Kilham, 1958b; 1958c; Bock, 1970; Hay, 1887). Turner (1959) watched three captive choughs, *Pyrrhocorax (Coracia) pyrrhocorax*, a red-billed glossy-black Eurasian member of the Crow Family, after they had eaten some fly pupae, bury others in the cracks between bricks of the floor of their enclosure, then place two or three small stones on top of each cache; later the choughs dug them up and ate them or reburied them elsewhere.

Besides woodpeckers, nuthatches, titmice, and members of the Crow Family, shrikes regularly store food for later use. They make "larders" of insects, mice, small birds, and other foods that they hang on thorns or in crotches of trees and bushes or on the barbs of fences and may return to feed on some of these dried food remains up to 8 months later. *See* Larder; Shrike Family. Caching of parts of the remains of uneaten prey is a well-known habit of the American kestrel, and has also been reported for the peregrine, goshawk, and several owls. (Brown and Amadon, 1968).

OPENING HARD-SHELLED FOODS. Oyster-catchers can open clams and other shellfishes with their bills, but some birds not so adapted use other means. Thrushes crack open snail shells to get at the soft-bodied snail within by picking them up in their bills and hammering them on "anvils" such as rocks; the enormous lammergeyer, or bearded vulture, of the remote mountains of Eurasia, gets nourishment from the bones of animals that have already been picked clean by vultures; it carries the bones to great heights and drops them on rocks to crack them so as to get at the bone marrow (*see also* Digestion); gulls and crows often carry crabs, clams, sea urchins, and other hard-shelled marine animals aloft and drop them on rocks, roads, and hard beaches, and sometimes on softer surfaces in attempts to break them open (Hartley, 1964). Some birds even use tools in their food-getting. *See* Tool-using.

SOME COOPERATIVE AND SOME ODD METH-ODS OF FOOD-GETTING. Some birds practice "flock feeding" to get food more efficiently—cormorants, anhingas, and pelicans join in bands to catch fishes; terns join in loose flocks in hunting for food, with a better chance of locating a school of fishes than a lone bird would have; groups of white pelicans swim abreast or in a semicircle to bring fishes close together or into shallows where they can easily catch them; avocets and black-necked stilts have been seen banding together in cooperative drives on small fishes and aquatic insects by wading in water in compact spearhead or wedge-shaped formations, and 13,000 avocets have been watched in such cooperative feeding efforts (Cottam *et al.*, 1942a). For uses birds make of man and of other birds in feeding, *see also* Autolycism; Commensalism.

Herons of at least 14 species in the world, including the N. American great egret, snowy egret, reddish egret, Louisiana heron, little blue heron, and green heron, practice a peculiar kind of foraging called *foot-stirring, foot-scraping,* or *foot-raking*. The little blue heron, for example, wades slowly forward, stops and extends one leg, with the toes spread, and rakes the watery bottom, after which it peers intently into the raked shallows. Then if a small fish, disturbed by the raking, darts out of hiding, the heron catches it with a quick strike downward of its pointed bill. The snowy egret foot-rakes more than any other N. American heron and for longer periods (Meyerriecks, 1959b; 1971). Sutton (1936) reported that several least bitterns he watched, as they hunted over shallow waters, flicked their wings, which seemed to startle into its view small fishes or aquatic insects that they quickly caught with their bills.

Foot-paddling, or *foot-stirring,* has been repeatedly observed in herring gulls in meadows; this activity brings earthworms to the surface, where the gulls eat them. Several species of gulls also foot-paddle along seashores, usually in shallow pools, apparently to stir within view small aquatic invertebrate animals; lapwings bring earthworms to the surface by quick trembling motions of one foot; northern phalaropes stir up prey animals in the water by "pirouetting" on the surface (Tinbergen,

1951b; 1962). Foot-paddling or foot-trembling in search of food has also been noted in the semipalmated sandpiper and killdeer (Meyerriecks, 1959a; Smith, S. M., 1970).

Perhaps one of the most interesting methods of food-getting, whose motivation by birds that practice it is still not completely understood, is the so-called wing-flashing, used especially by mockingbirds in foraging over grass or ground and even in approaching a piece of string for nesting material (see in Terres, 1960b). Hailman (1960) reviewed the subject and described it: The bird stands with its body at a normal slant upward from the ground. Then it opens both wings simultaneously, showing the white wing patches that seem to "flash" against the mockingbird's gray color, in a series of "hitches," usually one to three, sometimes four to five, or it may raise its opened wings over its head (archangel-like). Hailman concluded that wing-flashing by adult mockingbirds is definitely used by them in foraging, quite possibly to flush insects from the grass or ground, as pointed out by many previous investigators, also in displays against predators (when attacking a blacksnake, for example), and when attacking a dummy screech owl, as shown in experiments by Selander and Hunter (1960). Apparently young mockingbirds do not wing-flash much in foraging but may do so out of fear, suspicion, distrust, or curiosity when confronted by an unfamiliar object. Some tropical American mockingbirds, which do not have the white wing patches, also wing-flash, and the N. American brown thrasher and gray catbird, which also lack white wing patches, were seen to "wing-twitch" or "wing-flash" at the sight of a snake (Michael, 1970). Sutton (1946) had captive roadrunners that "flashed" (opened) their wings or rushed about with their wings spread. This caused certain insects, especially grasshoppers, to move and thus reveal themselves on the ground or in grass.

DRAGGING OR TOWING FOOD. Some of the larger, especially the predatory, birds may seize food in the bill which is too large or too awkward to carry in flight, and will pull or drag it over the ground or across water for remarkable distances. Herring gulls were reported to drag large, dried dead fishes across beach sand 400–450 ft. to water in order to soak the fishes before eating them (Forbush, 1925–29), and in Calif., four condors seized with their bills the carcass of a young 100-lb. grizzly bear, which they dragged over the ground for about 600 ft. An adult bald eagle, in June 1969 on a shallow bay near Vancouver Is., B.C., attacked and killed an immature female arctic loon, which it swam with, by using its wings as paddles, to the nearest shore (Hatler, 1974). Along the coast of Va. where a brant or a duck may be carried off in flight by a bald eagle, the larger Canada goose, which is too heavy to carry, may be towed by an eagle, propelling itself with its wings, along the surface of the water for ½ mi. to land. *See also* accounts in Land Birds That Swim or Alight on Water under Swimming and Diving; *see also* Weight-carrying Capacity.

FOOD AND FEEDING HABITS
The wide, gaping mouth of the pauraque, a nocturnal feeder, enables it to catch large moths, fireflies, and beetles on the wing. As in many other members of the Nightjar Family, its mouth is fringed with rictal bristles, which may serve a sensory function.

FOOD AND FEEDING HABITS
The phalarope rotates on the surface of the water, dabbling with its bill for food stirred up from the bottom by the action of its feet or for insect larvae or plankton on the surface agitated by the spinning motion.

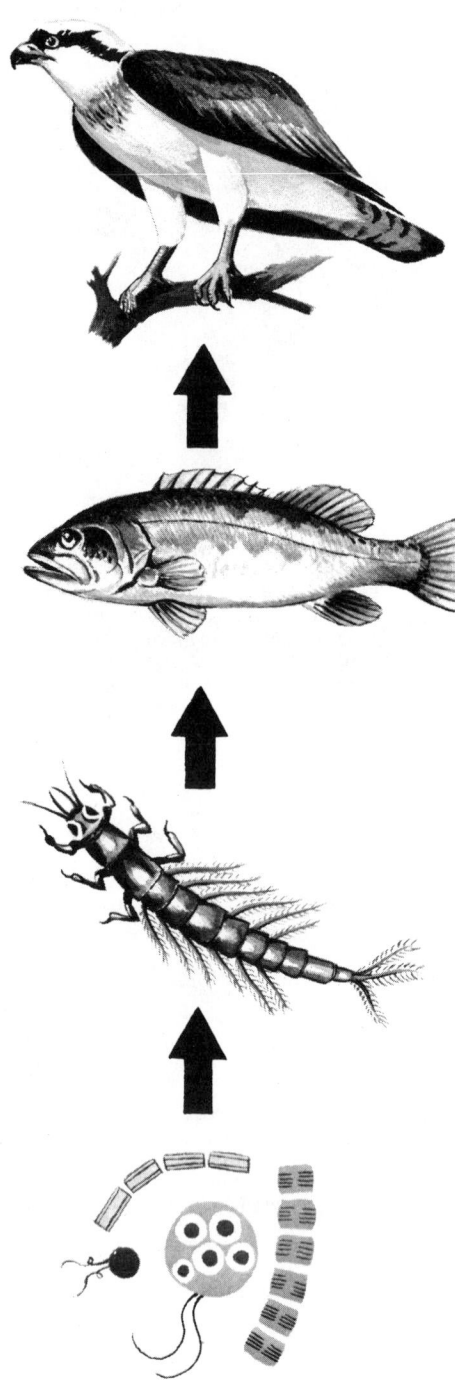

FOOD CHAIN
A simple food chain shows the sequence of "eat-eaten" relationships in a community in and around a pond, from producer to consumers. Aquatic plants manufacture food through photosynthesis; the caddis fly feeds on the plant and plant debris and is itself consumed by the bass. The bass is preyed upon by the osprey. Within each biotic community there are many such food chains, complexly interrelated, forming what is known as a food web.

FOOD-BEGGING
See Language; Young and Their Care; Courtship Feeding.

FOOD CHAIN
All members of the *biotic community* (*see* Ecosystem; Biome) are linked by eat-eaten relationships called *food chains.* In the community, food chains follow a general pattern—"all flesh is grass"—that is, grass, herbs, or other plant food is usually eaten first by an *herbivore* ("grass-eater"); the grass-eater may then be eaten by a small carnivore (meat-eater); the small carnivore may then be eaten by a larger carnivore until we come to a "top" carnivore, such as an eagle among birds, which has no other bird large enough or powerful enough to prey on it. There are also many birds and other animals that eat both plants and animals—these are called *omnivores. See* Omnivorous.

A very simple food chain on land might start with grass: a grasshopper (herbivore) eats grass; a meadowlark eats the grasshopper; a hawk (carnivore) eats the meadowlark. An even simpler one on western grasslands could be: cattle (herbivores) eat grass; man eats cattle. A food-chain sequence in a pond could be: a protozoan (one-celled animal) eats algae (plant); a small aquatic insect eats the protozoan; a larger aquatic insect eats the smaller one; a small bass eats the large aquatic insect; a larger bass eats the smaller one. This might end the sequence in the pond community but it is extended outside to the "land community" when an osprey, or fish hawk, might plunge into the pond to catch and eat the bass, and a bald eagle might chase the osprey and make it give up the fish. *See* in biographies of osprey and bald eagle under Hawk Family.

Most members of a community can, however, eat more than one type of food; for example, the so-called insect-eating birds may eat buds and insects in spring, insects and berries in summer and fall, seeds, berries, and insects in fall and into winter. Such relationships in which a bird or other animal eats several kinds of food, and every kind of food might be eaten by certain animals, are so complicated that they cannot be represented by a simple straight line, or chain. When diagrammed, the total of the food chains in a community, showing their interrelationships, is called a *food web.* See details, many examples, and thorough discussions of food chains in Elton (1936; 1958); Odum (1953); Buchsbaum and Buchsbaum (1957); and Smith, R. L. (1966).

FOOD FORMULAS
See Care and Feeding of Abandoned or Injured Wild Birds; Bird-attracting.

FOOL HEN
See Blue grouse and Spruce grouse in Grouse Family.

FOOT-FREEZING OF BIRDS
See Toughness of a Bird's Feet under Feet and Legs. *See also* Cold and Birds.

FOOT-PADDLING
or FOOT-STIRRING. *See* Food and Feeding Habits.

FOOT POX
A virus disease of birds. *See* Avian Pox.

FORBUSH
EDWARD HOWE (1858–1929). New England ornithologist, writer, lecturer, and conservationist, author of *Birds of Massachusetts and Other New England States*, which Stone (1929) declared "will stand as one of the great classics of ornithology." Forbush was a fellow of the American Ornithologists' Union, president of the Massachusetts Audubon Society, and for a time president of the New England Bird Banding Association and of the Federation of Bird Clubs of New England. He was State Ornithologist of Massachusetts from 1920 to his retirement in 1928 at age 70. Other of his most important books are *Useful Birds and Their Protection* (1907) and *A History of Game Birds, Wild-Fowl and Shorebirds of Massachusetts and Adjacent States* (1920). See Pearson (1930).

FOREIGN BIRDS IN AMERICA
See Introduced Birds.

FOREIGN PUBLICATIONS
See Ornithological Periodicals.

FORM
Term used generally in ornithology for a species or subspecies of bird. *See* Species; Subspecies.

FORMATION FLYING
See Flight.

FORSTER
JOHANN REINHOLD (1729–98). German naturalist and learned pastor who, with his eldest son, George Adam Forster (1754–94), accompanied Cook on his second voyage around the world. Forster was the author of *A Catalogue of Animals of North America* (1771), the first book attempting to cover the N. American fauna. In 1772, Forster published in the *Philosophic Transactions* of the Royal Society of London a valuable account of 58 birds sent there from Hudson Bay, Canada; of these several that Forster described were new to science—white-throated sparrow, blackpoll warbler, boreal chickadee, and Eskimo curlew (Allen, E. G., 1951). Thomas Nuttall (1834), in recognition of Forster's work, named a tern new to science, from the Saskatchewan R., *Sterna forsteri* (Palmer, 1928). See especially Stresemann (1975).

FOSSIL BIRDS
Relatively few complete fossilized skeletons of birds have been discovered in the world, although single bones and fragments have been found. These are usually the larger, denser ends of wing and leg bones or parts of the pectoral girdle—the part of the bony skeleton that supports the wings (*see* Skeleton). Compared with the fossils of other vertebrate animals, the record for birds is incomplete and fragmentary. Because the bones of birds are lightweight and fragile, they are easily and quickly destroyed and rapidly decompose; however, under favorable conditions for their preservation they may

occur in abundance—for example, at Reddick, Fla., and at Rancho La Brea, Calif. (Brodkorb, 1971). *See* La Brea Tar Pits.

Bird fossils have been found mainly in protected places—caves, or under the bottoms of dried-up lakes, in diatomaceous earth strata (fine powdered parts of microscopic marine animals—diatoms), in bogs, rock quarries, tar pits, and kitchen middens—those enormous masses near the seashores of discarded shells, feathers, scales, and bones of animals eaten by primitive men.

The first valid paleospecies (extinct fossil species) of bird was proposed by Koenig in 1825 (Brodkorb, 1971), but the scientific fossil record of all birds began in 1861 with the sensational discovery of a fossil feather in a limestone quarry in Bavaria, Germany. It was followed that year by the first incomplete skeleton of the same kind of bird—*Archaeopteryx*—from another Bavarian quarry, a bird that was estimated to have lived about 140 million years ago. Up to the present it is the world's oldest-known bird. *See* Origin of Birds and of Bird Flight.

The world's second oldest-known was a flamingolike or gooselike bird, *Gallornis straeleni*, as large as an ostrich (Swinton, 1965), that lived about 3 to 15 million years later than *Archaeopteryx* (Van Tyne and Berger, 1976). Its fossil remains were dug up in France in 1931 from rock beds of the early Cretaceous Period of 123 to 136 million years ago.

Dr. Alexander Wetmore (1933), an American paleontologist (pay-lee-on-TOL-oh-jist; one who studies fossils of the geological past), described the fascination of the study of fossil birds when he wrote: "The bits of petrified bone on which our knowledge of fossil birds is based . . . may appear as uninteresting as the most ordinary of dull colored pebbles. . . . Examined in terms of living birds, visualized as sentient active creatures clothed in flesh and feathers, they assume a quite different aspect. . . . When in these fragments we see giant running birds on western plains, chachalacas, tiny parakeets, and limpkins in the forests of ancient Nebraska, or broad-winged condors soaring over . . . Florida we feel the thrill of the little known and realize that we are dealing with facts in a fascinating history. . . ."

There is an enormous gap in the record of fossil birds between the time of *Archaeopteryx* in the Jurassic Period and the next great discoveries, but within 71 million years, by the time of the Cretaceous Period of 65 to 136 million years ago, fossil birds showed that they had evolved into essentially many of the modern forms of aquatic birds we know today (Van Tyne and Berger, 1976). *See* Geological Time Scale for a brief account of the evolution of birds and other animals based upon fossil records of the great geological periods of the world.

SOME FOSSIL BIRDS OF NORTH AMERICA. The first record of a fossil N. American bird was a written account in 1834 of the leg bone (tibia) of a snipelike bird found buried near Arneytown, N.J., in a bed of marl (crumbling material of clay and calcium carbonate, often used for fertilizer) of the Cretaceous Period. In 1870,

Professor O. C. Marsh of Yale University, after studying the fossil, named it *Palaeotringa vetus*. It is the oldest-known fossil bird, in the time of its discovery, from N. America (Wetmore, 1933).

In the 1870s came the first significant American discoveries of fossil birds, mostly by Professor Marsh of Yale; some by his rival the Philadelphia paleontologist Edward Drinker Cope. From N.J. came two extinct rails, one about the size of a king rail of today, a bone fragment thought to have come from a swan, and remains of an extinct wild turkey, taller proportionately than a wild turkey of today; from Md., two seabirds—an extinct shearwater and an extinct gannet; from Idaho, a cormorant which had become fossilized in the Pliocene Period of about 1½ to 10 million years ago; and from N.C., a seabird—a murre—from the older Miocene age.

According to Brodkorb (1971) the Cretaceous avifauna of N.J. includes two fossil cormorants (*Graculavus*), a large pelicaniform (*Laornis*), three rails (*Telmatornis*), and five sandpipers (*Paleotringa*).

In November 1870, Marsh found in Kans. the first fragment of a fossil bird with teeth, *Hesperornis*, perhaps his most remarkable fossil discovery. *See* Hesperornis. His identifications in the early 1870s of three species of this toothed, flightless, loonlike bird from the Cretaceous Period established that toothed birds had existed possibly for another 50 million years or more after *Archaeopteryx*, the first-known bird. In the same formation, Professor Marsh discovered a series of fossils of a small gull-like bird, *Ichthyornis*, also toothed. *See* Ichthyornis; Baptornis.

Marsh made his discoveries in the Niobrara Chalk formation of w. Kans., which in the Cretaceous Period, when it was formed, was the bottom of a vast sea dominated by such creatures as the pterosaurs, or flying reptiles, of which the huge pteranodon, giant of the group, had a wingspread of 25 ft. The remains of this flying reptile were found in the same Niobrara formation. It was the last of the pterosaurs, all of which had disappeared by the end of the Cretaceous, about 65 million years ago. Perhaps these large flying reptiles became extinct because of changes in the environment or competition from the far-ranging, more efficient birds, then becoming evolutionarily modernized (Colbert, 1955). The bones of yet another pterosaur, the largest flying reptile ever known, which lived about 60 million years ago, with an estimated wingspread of 51 ft., was dug up in the early 1970s in Big Bend National Park, as announced in *Science*, March 14, and *The New York Times*, March 12, 1975.

In 1876, Cope, from a fossil bone uncovered in N.M. from the Eocene Period of 40 to 60 million years ago, named the first of a group of strange 7-ft.-tall birds, so far known only from the U.S. He called it *Diatryma giganteum*, and from later studies and discoveries of others of its kind, in the Eocene of Wyo., it was apparently the most awe-inspiring bird to live in N. America. It was flightless and stout-legged, a giant running bird taller than a man. It had a figure like that of a robust ostrich, and a head as large as that of a horse, with an enormous

Archaeopteryx

FOSSIL BIRDS

hooked beak. Although related to the cranes and rails (Howard, 1962b), it was probably predatory and was thought to have disappeared when the predatory mammals of the Oligocene Period of 30 to 40 million years ago displaced it. The diatrymas were the largest and most powerful carnivorous birds known (Storer, 1960a).

Many years later, from the same Eocene of Wyo., another strange fossil bird, a stilt vulture about 20 in. tall, was discovered by Dr. John Clark of the Carnegie Museum. He sent the skeleton and skull to Dr. Alexander Wetmore of the Smithsonian Institution, who named it *Neocathartes grallator*. Its long, stiltlike legs gave it most of its height, and apparently it was a predatory, possibly carrion-eating bird that ran and flew in short flights over the ground. It represented a distinct family of American vultures that long ago disappeared (Howard, 1962b).

Wetmore believes from his studies of fossils that birds reached their maximum abundance during the geological periods of 2 to 60 million years ago, or the so-called Tertiary ages (Wetmore, 1951a). Up to about 1970, about 1,760 species of fossil birds had been identified and named in the world, of which at least 902 of the fossil species are extinct. The remaining 857 found in fossil forms represent kinds of birds still living (Brodkorb, 1971).

One of the early important finds of fossil N. American birds was in Fossil Lake deposits of Ore. in the late 1800s; this was followed by the remarkable discoveries in the sticky asphalt beds of Rancho La Brea (*see* La Brea Tar Pits) in Calif., which have the largest deposits of Pleistocene (within the last million years) birds yet discovered in America. These rich collections initially studied especially by Loye Miller and Hildegarde Howard have greatly broadened our knowledge of the bird life of N. America during the Ice Age.

More than 220 species of fossil birds from 44 places have been discovered in Calif., the most of any state in our country. The Rancho La Brea tar pits have yielded at least 133 species of birds, of which 20, including the passenger pigeon, are now extinct (Howard, 1962a; 1962b). *See* Extinct Birds of North America. From Rancho La Brea came the remains of a giant vulture, *Teratornis merriami*, which lived about 15,000 to 20,000 years ago. It weighed about 40–50 lbs. and had an estimated wingspread of 12 ft. This enormous bird, whose remains have also been found in Fla. and Mexico, was believed to have ranged widely over America during the Ice Age. Later, from Smith Creek Cave in Nev., Hildegarde Howard of the Los Angeles County Museum described an even larger vulturelike bird, *Teratornis incredibilis*, with an estimated wingspread of 5 m., or about 16½ ft., possibly the largest flying bird known.

Although only 2 species of eagles are known today in the U.S.—the golden eagle and the bald eagle—7 species lived in s. Calif. several thousand years ago. The rarest and one of the most interesting of the fossil birds from Rancho La Brea was the Daggett eagle; it was remarkable for having long, slender legs like those of a ground-dwelling, or "walking,"

eagle, such as the secretary-bird of Africa. Another strange bird was the La Brea stork, about 5 ft. tall. An outstanding discovery in Tepusquet Canyon, Santa Barbara County, was the nearly complete skeleton of a gigantic extinct marine bird, like an albatross, that had a potential wingspread of 14–16 ft. and jaws lined with heavy, toothlike projections (Howard, 1962b).

ORIGIN OF BIRDS AND OF BIRD FLIGHT. In 1861, a worker in a limestone quarry at Solnhofen, Bavaria, s. Germany, uncovered the fossilized print of a single bird feather. The discovery, when it was announced Aug. 15, 1861 (Lucas, 1929), caused great excitement among scientists. The impression, 68 mm. long (about 2¾ in.), showing a vane, barbs, and barbules, was distinctly that of a feather, an astonishing new find in a long chain of fossil discoveries in the Bavarian limestone quarries (Swinton, 1965).

The main stone slab with its fossil print was sent to the Museum of the Academy of Sciences, Munich, for study; the impression on the counter slab to the Natural History Museum in Berlin; both are still in these institutions (Swinton, 1965).

Apparently the limestone quarries at Solnhofen had once been the sandy bottom of a shallow sea or lagoon in the Jurassic Period about 150 million years ago. *See* Geological Time Scale. In the 19th century, workers, digging slabs of Solnhofen limestone for use in lithography, had previously uncovered many fossil plants, invertebrate animals, fishes, and reptiles that had died in the old lake and had settled to the bottom, where they had been preserved with its solidification into stone.

A month later (Lucas, 1929), after the discovery of the feather, workmen in the Ottmann limestone quarry at Langenaltheimer Haardt, near Pappenheim, Bavaria, found a fossilized, incomplete skeleton of a reptilelike bird, about the size of a crow, with the clearly marked imprint of feathers attached to the forearm. According to Swinton, the fossil bird caused a sensation among the workers, who had never seen anything like it.

Dr. Friedrich Karl Haberlein, medical officer of the District of Pappenheim, was interested in fossils, and often visited the quarries to see what the workers had discovered. In exchange for fossils he gave them medical services. Haberlein acquired the partial skeleton of the ancient bird and sold it, along with a fine collection of fossils, to the British Museum, which still has it in its collections.

After the discovery of the fossil bird, Hermann von Meyer, who recognized that the first-discovered fossil feather had belonged to the same kind of bird, gave it its scientific name. In 1861, he called it *Archaeopteryx lithographica*, or literally "the ancient-winged creature of the stone for drawing [for lithography]."

Archaeopteryx (ar-kee-OP-ter-icks), up to the present, is the most ancient bird known. It has been theorized that it lived in forests, judging by the position of its big toe (hallux), which was opposite the other three and adapted to gripping a perch. It had feathers arranged precisely as in modern birds (*see* Topography); an

elongate and backwardly directed *pubis*, similar to that of birds of today (*see* Skeleton) and superficially similar to that of dinosaurs; and the fusion of the two clavicles (collarbones) to form the furcula, or "wishbone" (Swinton, 1960). According to Bellairs (1960), it is said that a bird cannot fly if one side of the furcula is broken.

The broad, rounded, galliform wings of *Archaeopteryx* supposedly had six or more primary (flight) feathers (see other estimates in Brodkorb, 1971) attached to the hand and wrist part of the wing, and secondary feathers attached to the forearm; also wing covert feathers just as in modern birds (Swinton, 1965); however, modern birds have nine to twelve primaries, depending on the group to which birds belong.

Among the reptilian features of *Archaeopteryx* (which have not been found in any other bird) was the long, lizardlike tail with its twenty vertebrae, from which feathers grew—not from the base as they do today—and which superficially resembled that of the modern-day chachalaca or the touracos (Brodkorb, 1971); it had an uncomplicated backbone with no fusions of its vertebrae; three unfused fingers with claws on the hand part of the wings, which probably helped it to cling to twigs; no fusions of certain bones of the hand, as in birds; simple ribs; and a simple brain with a small cerebellum (that part which coordinates muscular action). The bill was galliform (chickenlike) and both the upper and lower jaws had vertical, peglike enamel-tipped teeth set in sockets about 5 mm. apart (Brodkorb, 1971).

Archaeopteryx had no hollow bones as modern, or present-day, birds have, and its powers of flight were apparently limited, for it had no powerful flying muscles, indicated by its lack of a keel on its breastbone. (In modern birds this keel is the basis of attachment for the strong flying muscles.) With a small cerebellum (*see* Brain), the bird could not have been expert in maneuvering. It was basically a glider, propelled by weak wings that probably enabled it to rise in flight from branch to branch of its forest home, or from rock to rock.

However, John H. Ostrom (1974), professor of geology at the Peabody Museum of Natural History, Yale University, came to different conclusions about the ability of *Archaeopteryx* to fly. After re-examining the specimens of *Archaeopteryx*, he suggested that its skeleton and the structure of its bones are, in virtually every detail, indistinguishable from those of certain dinosaurs that lived at the same time as *Archaeopteryx*. Although *Archaeopteryx* was a bird, with wings bearing feathers, the wings had not been modified structurally from the skeletal condition characteristic of small theropods (saurischian dinosaurs).

The wings of *Archaeopteryx* differed from those of all modern flying birds in many features necessary to powered flight—unfused manus and metacarpus, unrestricted wrist and elbow joints, unmodified coracoids (*see* Skeleton), and lacking a keeled sternum (breastbone). Thus, concluded Ostrom, the wings of *Archaeopteryx* would appear to have been better adapted to catching prey (predation) than for flight. That *Archaeopteryx* had sharp teeth and other theropod characters seemed to suggest a cursorial (running) predatory way of life.

Ostrom believed that the feathers of *Archaeopteryx* evolved in conjunction with a high level of activity and metabolism, and a need to control or minimize heat loss. "Whatever their initial function, though, if feathers originated as a general body covering, they must have appeared after acquisition [by *Archaeopteryx*] of effective homoiothermy [preserving a uniform body temperature]—which must in turn have preceded *any* flight ability. Accordingly the primordial remiges [flight feathers] must have originated in response to some function other than flight or parachuting."

Ostrom suggested that the bony dinosaur-like structure of the forelimbs and shoulders of *Archaeopteryx* indicated that the enlargement of the contour feathers of the forelimbs or "wings" might well have related to a predatory use of them. He postulated that incipient "wings" of avian ancestors were perfected first as snares to trap insects or other small animals against the ground, or to knock or hold them down until they could be grasped in the hands or teeth. He concluded that *Archaeopteryx* was a ground-dwelling, bipedal, cursorial (running) predator rather like our present-day secretary-bird (*see* Falconiformes).

Compare these recent and controversial studies by Ostrom (1974) with the following conclusions of earlier writers and scientists:

Zoologists have generally agreed that both birds and dinosaurs arose from primitive, unspecialized thecodont (animals with many teeth set in sockets) reptiles of the suborder Pseudosuchia (sue-doh-SUE-kih-ah), from Gr. words meaning "imitation crocodile" (Allen, 1925). These were small carnivorous animals. The origin of birds has largely been arrived at by the researches and deductions of scientists. No fossil evidence exists of all the stages of the remarkable change from reptile to bird; however, evidence of the oldest bird known to man, *Archaeopteryx*, clearly shows its relationship to reptiles (Swinton, 1960). However, no pseudosuchian yet described by paleontologists could be *the* ancestor of birds.

Gerhard Heilmann (1927) reconstructed a hypothetical "proavian" form (before bird) intermediate between certain pseudosuchians *(Euparkeria)*, certain bipedal dinosaurs *(Ornithosochus)*, and the most primitive bird known—*Archaeopteryx*—and this could, theoretically, bridge the gap between the thecodont reptiles and the earliest-known bird (Van Tyne and Berger, 1959). See, however, Brodkorb (1971) for other conclusions; see also Swinton (1960)

Two main theories have been advanced. One is the cursorial (adapted to running or walking) origin of flight, proposed by Williston (1879) and later elaborated on by Baron Francis Nopcsa (1907; 1923), who proposed the development of flight from long-tailed bipedal reptiles that flapped their forelimbs as they ran rapidly over the ground. Baron Nopcsa reasoned that the scales of the forelimbs of these upright reptiles became elongated and their rear or hind margins became frayed, evolving in time into feathers. Baron Nopcsa imagined that there were three stages in the evolution of flight: (1)

parachute, or passive flight, (2) flight by flapping the wings, or flight by force, and (3) soaring, or flight by skill. He thought that the ancient oldest fossil bird, *Archaeopteryx*, was still in the first stage of (2), active flight (Nopcsa, 1907).

However, Gerhard Heilmann (1927), Othniel Charles Marsh (1880), the American paleontologist, who did some of his most brilliant work in ornithology, and Henry Fairfield Osborn (1900), paleontologist and former head of the New York Zoological Society, and many other authorities inclined toward another theory. They believed that the first birds did not run over the ground but were tree dwellers. They thought that the land-dwelling ancestors of birds became tree climbers before there was a great difference between the front and hind limbs, although the bipedal gait of ancestral birds and reptiles had already resulted in some lengthening of the metatarsals. *See* Tarsus. Jumping from branch to branch favored the evolution of the lengthening metatarsals, and of a backward-directed hallux, which enabled these tree-dwelling pre-bird animals to securely grasp branches. The forelimbs, now used for climbing, preserved claws on their digits, remained large, and were not reduced by evolution, as is commonly true of cursorial (ground-running) animals, which, evolutionarily, adopted the bipedal (upright) method of progression.

Each limb therefore became adapted to specialized and different uses (rear limbs for leaping, or hopping; forelimbs for climbing through trees). Heilmann (1927) emphasized the *independence* of the two limbs in contrast with those of the pterosaurs (flying reptiles in no way related to the evolutionary stem of birds) and flying mammals (bats), in which the forelimbs and hind limbs were, and are, connected by a patagial skin fold.

Heilmann also believed that the evolution of feathers, from reptilian scales, preceded warm-bloodedness in birds—that is, *homoiothermism*, or the relatively even body temperature of birds and most mammals, including man. *See* Temperature; Metabolism.

A German paleontologist, Hans Böker (1927), suggested that the original birds flapped their forewings when jumping from branch to branch of trees, but Sir Gaven de Beer (1954) thought it probable that simple gliding preceded flapping because studies of the oldest fossil bird, *Archaeopteryx*, showed that it had no carina (keel on the breastbone for muscle attachment) and therefore its pectoral (flying) muscles must have been weak. *See also* discussion under Monophyletic Descent; Distribution; Classification.

FOSTER PARENTS

Birds that rear the young other than their own; foster parents and young are usually, but not necessarily, the same species. The strong instinct, or drive, of some adult birds during the nesting season to feed or to brood (*see* Brooding) young not their own (*see* Helpers among Birds) may be a carry-over of that drive after loss of their own young. In the examples that follow, these do not include many small birds—vireos, warblers, sparrows, towhees, finches, and flycatchers, for example—that regularly

raise the young of the cowbird, a "social parasite" that deliberately lays its eggs in the nests of other birds, thus getting them to raise its young. *See* this relationship discussed under Brood Parasitism.

In Calif., a pair of American kestrels, making regular trips to a nesting hole in a eucalyptus tree, were discovered to be feeding mice not only to their own four young but to a young screech owl; apparently the female screech owl had laid one egg in the nest hole, and then had been dispossessed by the American kestrels, or the owl may have gotten into the nest of the hawks and laid an egg in their absence (Sumner, 1933). *See* Dump Nest. Near London, Ont., a Canadian ornithologist watched a female flicker carry food into her nesting hole in a dead limb of a tree. When he climbed to investigate, he discovered that the young birds in the nest were starlings, not flickers; he concluded that a female starling, an aggressive competitor of the flicker for nesting holes, had destroyed the flicker's eggs and then had laid a set of her own, which the flicker had adopted and hatched as though they were her own. *See* Do Birds Recognize Their Own Eggs? under Eggs and Egg-laying; *see also* Hatching.

In another highly unusual foster-parent relationship to young, a screech owl adopted a brood of young flickers in a bird nesting box; she not only brooded the young flickers like a setting hen (*see* Brooding) but even brought them a mouse, perhaps intending to feed it to them. All the while the parent flickers were going in and out of the nest box feeding their young; eventually the predatory owl deserted the nest, leaving the baby flickers unharmed (Lyon, 1922).

Not all such relationships may be successful, even when the foods of the foster parents and adopted young are similar. Hartshorne (1962), in an experiment during his studies of bluebirds, once put the eggs of a starling into a bluebird's nest as a substitute for the bluebird's infertile eggs. The female bluebird hatched the young starlings and for a week fed them with great persistence; however, the young starlings were slowly starving. A starling's mouth is so much deeper than a bluebird's that the female, with her shorter bill, could not reach deeply enough into the starlings' throats to release their swallowing reflex (*see* Swallowing); therefore they were not getting enough food. Hartshorne removed the starlings from the nest and hand-fed them to save them. *See* Care and Feeding of Abandoned or Injured Wild Birds; Young and Their Care.

FOVEA

(FO-vee-ah). *See* Eyes and Eyesight.

FOWL

See Chicken in introduction to Pheasant Family; Galliformes; and under Domestication; *see also* Megapode; Waterfowl.

FRANKLIN

SIR JOHN (1786–1847). English navigator and explorer who died in 1847 during an expedition to the Canadian Arctic seeking the Northwest Passage. See details in *Encyclopaedia Britan-*

FREEZING

At the approach of an intruder, a bittern freezes; its cryptic plumage and erect, motionless posture help it blend into its marshy background. The bittern's eyes are set so low on its head that even with its head thrust skyward, it is able to see straight ahead.

nica. Sir John Richardson was surgeon and naturalist to Sir John Franklin on his earlier Arctic expeditions of 1819–22 and 1825–27. In Swainson and Richardson's report (1832) of birds collected on the Franklin expeditions, Richardson named a gull for Sir John Franklin; however, it was later discovered that the gull had been previously named and Richardson's scientific, but not the English, name for the bird was abandoned.

FRATE

or FRATE-BIRD. Local name (s. U.S.) for great crested flycatcher, from bird's call note.

FRATRICIDE

Also *Cainism* (in reference to biblical Cain and Abel). Term of some ornithologists for the killing of a bird by one of its nest mates, frequent among young of birds of prey—eagles, hawks, and owls. *See* account of barn and short-eared owls under Cannibalism. The older nestling of the golden eagle, *Aquila chrysaetus,* will often persistently attack its younger and weaker nest mate, as will the larger young one in nest of the Verreaux's eagle of Africa. In N. America, the bald eagle often has two and sometimes three nestlings, but three eaglets seldom grow up because of the aggressiveness of the oldest bird. Apparently the fighting instinct in the young eagles ceases after the first few weeks, and thereafter, the two or more fledglings, if the younger ones survive, will live amicably together (Ingram, 1959).

Cranes and a few other species of birds that usually lay a clutch of two eggs (*see* Clutch; Eggs and Egg-laying) may also have the brood size reduced through sibling rivalry. Doward (1962), in examining hundreds of nests of brown boobies, and about 100 nests of white boobies (both usually lay two eggs), found only one nest in which two chicks survived—both lived together for 34 days before the smaller one died; Doward also found that the second chick that hatched was weaker than the first, was often outside the nest, and if Doward put the weaker one back in the nest, the older and usually larger chick ejected it; Old World white pelicans lay two eggs several days apart but never seem to raise more than one young because the older chick bullies the younger one until it dies.

With whooping cranes, and sometimes with sandhills, when the first chick hatches, it apparently receives the attention of both parents, and the second egg is abandoned by them, or is destroyed (Miller, R.S., 1973); if the second egg hatches, sibling rivalry through aggression of the older chick may lead to the death of the younger (usually smaller) one—the older chick attacks it and thus kills the younger one, or ejects it from the nest, which may cause it to die of exposure to weather, predators, or starvation. See Miller, R.S. (1973), for a theory about this quick method of reducing brood size by loss or destruction of the second egg or chick, and possible reasons for it. *See also,* especially, Kronism. For protection of eggs and young by adults, *see* Eggs and Egg-Laying; Young and Their Care.

FREEZING

Term of zoologists for a bird or other animal that becomes motionless to escape detection. *See also* Colors of Feathers. Armstrong (1942) cites a young European lapwing that, when surprised crossing a stream, crouched underwater until rescued from imminent peril of drowning. He also describes young terns and young oystercatchers that will squat and "freeze" in the presence of danger until the tide washes over them. The American bittern is well known for its ability to hold an erect, motionless posture, with its bill pointed up, at the approach of a man and even to sway gently from side to side in a motion simulating the swaying of the cattails or reeds of its marshy background.

The rigid vertical position assumed by young cuckoos (freezing) is probably a hiding pose (Bent, 1940). Frederick H. Kennard in a letter to A. C. Bent described a young black-billed cuckoo that first "froze" in a rigid, upright posture often assumed by the American bittern, then suddenly went limp after its capture and "played dead." Screech owls are noted for their "freezing" behavior. An observer reported to Bent that he once came suddenly upon two screech owls sitting side by side on a tree limb. At his approach the owls drew themselves upward, their bodies stretched high, their wings and feathers held close to their bodies. Their upright, long-drawn narrowed figures resembled two long gray, dead stubs projecting from the limb, giving the appearance that they were part of the tree. Catling (1971) reported that the small saw-whet and boreal owls go into freezing postures when disturbed by man. *See* Fear; Behavior.

FREGATIDAE
See Frigatebird Family.

FRIGATEBIRD FAMILY

Fregatidae (freh-GAT-ih-dee); from Ital. *fregata,* a frigate, a war vessel (Coble, 1954), originally a light vessel propelled by sails and oars; name applied to frigatebirds apparently because of similarity to a frigate in their light speedy flight, sail-like wings, and marauding habits. 5 species in world; 1 in N. America; are related to tropic-birds, pelicans, boobies, gannets, cormorants, and anhingas; frigatebirds have 11 primary (flight) feathers in each wing, 12 rectrices (tail feathers); have short legs; the small feet have deeply excavated webs, flexible toes, a pectinate middle toe; have a tufted oil, or preen, gland, and a highly distensible gular pouch in the male (Nelson, J. B., 1975). Frigatebirds live on tropical oceanic islands around the world and over adjacent seas; not migratory like most other seabirds; may stay throughout year in general area of breeding range but may wander after nesting season (see, however, Nelson, 1975). If captured and taken from home area, when released will soon return; Polynesians took young frigatebirds from nest, raised and tamed them, then released them (as modern man uses homing pigeons) to carry messages between islands up to 70–80 mi. apart (Townsend, 1908). The magnificent frigatebird, the only one nesting in N. America, is sometimes seen off coasts of Gulf of Mexico, where a nesting colony was discovered in 1969, and along Atlantic coast north to S.C.

Like hunting falcons, these blackish birds with deeply forked tails, with which they steer in pursuit of prey, and with 7–8-ft.-long pointed wings, soar effortlessly over coastal waters, where they dart down near surface to catch in bill fishes, which they swallow in flight. They also force boobies, pelicans, cormorants, terns, and gulls to give up their catches; for this habit called frigatebird, or man-o'-war-bird; have greatest wing area in proportion to their weight (2–3 lbs.) of any living bird (Van Tyne and Berger, 1959); one of most aerial of all water birds, able to stay aloft even in great cyclonic storms which sometimes carry them far inland in N. America.

Owing to their sail-like wings, wettable plumage, and short, weak legs, frigatebirds are helpless if they alight on water; usually cannot become airborne unless from treetop, rocky crag, or other elevation; however, have been seen to take off from open sands of Dry Tortugas—a group of small islands west of the Fla. coast, north of entrance to Gulf of Mexico (Palmer, 1962).

If necessary to keep an injured or ill one in captivity, most likely to thrive if put in large flight cage with pool of water; can be fed on wing by tossing fishes for bird to catch in midair; may accept fish from hands and may take fish from surface of pool (Walker, 1942).

Magnificent frigatebird, *Fregata magnificens* (freh-GAY-tah mag-NIF-ih-senz); genus name: *see* family introduction; species name: Lat., splendid. (Color ills., pages 372, 373, 374.) Tropical seabird; first confirmed nesting in U.S. discovered Mar. 1969; a colony in Gulf of Mexico at Key West National Wildlife Refuge on Marquesas Keys (Sprunt *et al.*, 1969); 37–41 in. long; wingspread 84–96 in. (7–8 ft.); bill 4 in., straight, hooked at tip, gray; tail long and *deeply forked;* wings long, narrow, pointed, males entirely black with bright red pouch, or gular sac; females larger, without red gular sac and black without gloss of male, sides and breast white; young like female except head and neck entirely white; male while sitting on nest calls to female with hoarse cackles; in courtship male inflates the red gular pouch of throat until it resembles scarlet balloon; sometimes keeps pouch inflated at night or in flight but ceases to after beginning of incubation (Palmer, 1962). When not nesting, still gregarious and gathers in enormous numbers at permanent roosting sites atop trees, mangroves, shrubs, or cliffs on islands or mainland (up to 160 seen in June roosting on abandoned coaling docks on Garden Key, Dry Tortugas—Schnell, 1974); sleeps so soundly that can be caught in hands (Murphy, 1936); for distribution along Gulf Coast of Fla., see Harrington *et al.* (1972). According to Nelson (1975), possibly fewer than 500,000 pairs of this species still exist.

Feeding Habits: Soars about over sea near land using sharp eyesight to locate schools of menhaden, pinfish, sea catfish, weakfish, mullet, or albacores, which it dives upon and catches in its bill from surface; also catches flying fishes, jellyfishes, marine crustaceans, and turtles, and gets some food by robbing other large seabirds of their catches.

Nest: In colonies with pelicans, cormorants, and other members of its own species; as many as 200 pairs may nest on 40 sq. ft. of rock; or 8–9 nests in one tree (Palmer, 1962); builds flimsy, flat nest of twigs, sticks, grasses, and reeds usually in tree or on low mangroves and other coastal bushes or on rocks on ground.

Eggs: Lesser Antilles, mid-Sept. to late Mar. (Diamond, 1973); 1, rarely 2, white.

Incubation: By both sexes, about 50 days (Diamond, 1973), but probably more; young naked at hatching, brooded and fed by regurgitation by both adults; at 140 days old, fully feathered but still unable to fly (Palmer, 1962); young first fly 149–207 days after hatching (Diamond, 1973); may be at least 5–7 years old before first breeding (Nelson, 1975).

Other Names: Frigate pelican; hurricane bird (often seen during or after hurricanes); man-o'-war-bird; rabihorcado.

Age: One lived for 10 years in San Diego Zoo, Calif. (Stott, 1948); a female banded lesser frigatebird, *Fregata minor*, similar in habits, habitats, and biology to the magnificent frigatebird, species that nests on islands in tropical Indian, Pacific, and S. Atlantic O., was caught on her nest in June 1968, incubating her egg on Jarvis Is., south of Equator in c. Pacific. She had been banded as an adult in Aug. 1939, was estimated to be almost 34 years old, and was first age record of a wild frigatebird ever reported (Clapp and Hackman, 1969).

Flight Speed: Measured on Dry Tortugas, Fla., with Doppler radar, summer 1967; recorded speeds of 30–33 m.p.h.; in flat calm, 22.5 m.p.h. (Schnell, 1974).

Weights: 2¼ to about 3 lbs.

Range: Nests on islands of Pacific from Baja Calif. south to Galápagos Is., Ecuador, and occasionally Peru; in Atlantic, from Bahamas south to Brazil and Cape Verde Is.; in U.S., in Gulf of Mexico at Key West National Wildlife Refuge on Marquesas Keys, between Dry Tortugas and Key West, Fla., where colony discovered by Sprunt *et al.* (1969) in Mar., with 54 nestlings counted there Aug. 7, 1969; also nests on offshore islands in s. Gulf of Mexico and in Caribbean Sea and Bahamas, where nestlings seen in Apr.; the species seen straying off coastal Calif. and at Salton Sea and off coast of Tex. to La. and Fla.; casual on Ore. coast; accidental inland in midwestern U.S. and to New England, Que., Newfoundland, and Nova Scotia.

FRIGHTENING DEVICES
(to repel birds). *See* Control.

FRIGHTMOLT
Term for "a partial molt which takes place out of the normal molt period and which is set in motion through fright or fear. . . ." (Juhn, 1957). Juhn says that Heinrich Dathe, a German ornithologist, gives a long list of birds in which frightmolt has been recorded in the *Journal für Ornithologie*, 1955 (96: 5–14). Frightmolt does not seem to have been found in waterfowl or in birds of prey.

In frightmolt, the rectrices (tail feathers) are shed most frequently; next, the smaller feath-

FRIGATEBIRD FAMILY

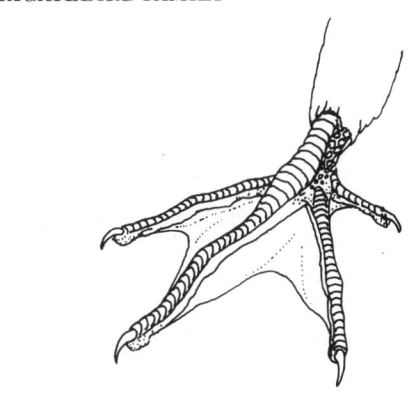

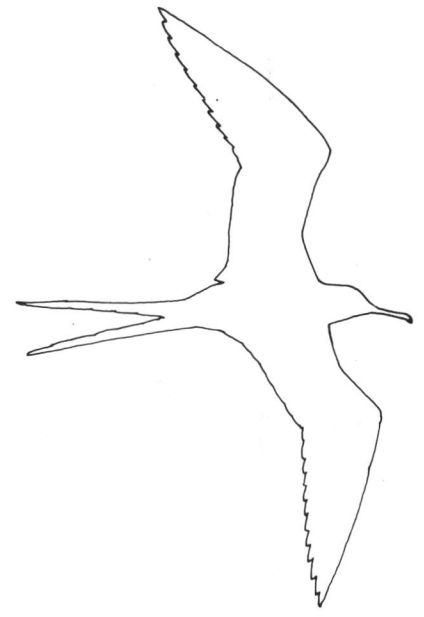

FRIGATEBIRD FAMILY
The magnificent frigatebird has a deeply forked tail and narrow wings that may be 7 to 8 feet across. In soaring flight, each wing appears bent in the middle.

FRONTAL SHIELD
The frontal shield of the American coot, ivory-colored in the adult shown here, is red and blue in the chicks. The sight of the chick's bright shield evidently stimulates the parents to feed it.

ers of the breast and the dorsal tracts; the wing feathers, seldom; and the feathers of the head, never. For the most part, feathers seem to be expelled or dropped; the muscles of the feather follicle seem to become relaxed and the quill is set free to be dropped at the slightest contact or pressure (*see* Feather).

Although Dathe ascribes most of these cases to fear, according to Juhn, Dathe recorded a cockatoo that "frightmolted" with rage. Juhn cites an example of a cardinal that in late spring and early summer had been accustomed to feeding on her terrace. One day, flying toward the place, it struck heavily against a casement window that had been opened farther than usual. The bird fell, stunned, and when Juhn picked it up, it had shed its major tail feathers, which lay close by. Juhn believes that "the entire complex of 'frightmolt' is an interesting question which may involve both nervous and humoral participation."

The passenger pigeon and other members of the Pigeon Family have long been considered "peculiar" for the ease with which their feathers are shed. Audubon wrote that if a passenger pigeon or a mourning dove was taken alive in the hand, the feathers became loosened at the slightest touch, a trait also peculiar to certain upland game birds (Schorger, 1955).

A biologist, M. E. Stempel, writing in the *Iowa Conservationist*, Nov. 1960, has cited what may well be a common example of frightmolt in game birds that are shot at and apparently missed. His interpretation was: "Remember when your companion shot at the quail and the bird flew on, but the feathers streamed out behind. You said, 'Boy, you sure dusted him.' Perhaps you did dust him, but that might also be a demonstration of the oldest trick in animal defense. After all, quail have a lot of feathers, and some of them are sacrificed when the right time comes—just to fool an enemy." *See* Molts and Molting.

FRINGILLIDAE
See Finch Family.

FRINGILLIDS
(frin-JILL-ids). Shortened term for birds of the family Fringillidae. *See* Finch Family.

FROGMOUTH FAMILY
See Caprimulgiformes.

FROGS AND BIRDS
See Amphibians and Birds.

FRONTAL SHIELD
A horny projection extending from the base of the upper mandible (of the bill) onto the forehead, as in coots, gallinules, and the American jacana. *See also* Wattle.

FROST-BIRD
See American golden plover in Plover Family.

FROUNCE
See Trichomoniasis under Diseases.

FRUGIVOROUS
(froo-JIV-o-rus). Feeding on fruit. *See* Food and Feeding Habits.

FULMAR
See in Shearwater Family.

FURCULA
(FUR-cue-lah). The "wishbone" of a bird formed by the fusion of the two bony clavicles; also called the *os furcatum*. *See* Skeleton.

FUSCOUS
(FUSS-cuss). Dusky or somber hue; any of several colors averaging in red-yellow hue; of low saturation and low brilliance. Often used in ornithological textbooks (where applicable) in describing hue of a bird, and in scientific name; *see*, for example, Blackburnian warbler in Warbler—American Wood Warbler Family.

FUSIFORM
Spindle-shaped, or tapering at both ends.

FUTE
See Curlew, Eskimo, in Sandpiper Family.

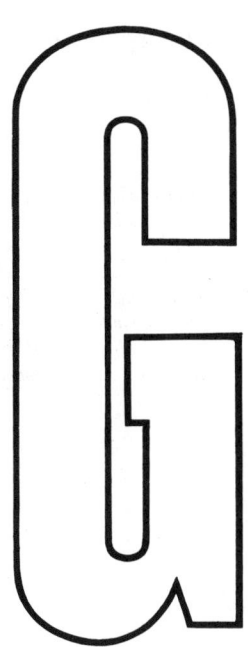

GADFLY PETREL
Name for any one of a group of some 24 species of very closely related petrels around world (Bourne, 1964), several of which have migrated northward from the S. Hemisphere (*see* Hemispheres) into N. American waters. *See* in Shearwater Family.

GADWALL
See in Duck Family.

GAIT
See Hopping and Walking.

GALE-BIRD
Name for the northern phalarope because sometimes blown to coast from sea by high winds and storms.

GALL BLADDER
In most birds, a reservoir for bile. It is attached to the undersurface of the right lobe of the liver, and Van Tyne and Berger (1959) have described the gall bladder in some members of the Woodpecker Family as being very long and tubular, or "intestiniform"—in some birds it is oval or saccular. Not all birds have a gall bladder, and in some *families* the birds have none; however, in no *order* of birds is the gall bladder invariably absent in all species (Fisher, 1955).

Farner (1960) reports that the gall bladder is lacking in many birds—for example, in the ostrich; peregrine falcon; in many parrots, doves, and pigeons, and in at least two species of hummingbirds; in some woodpeckers; and in some passerine, or perching, birds such as the Bohemian waxwing.

Domestic fowl and mallard ducks have a gall bladder and its function gives to those birds that have it an advantage in sending into the intestine a very concentrated bile at the beginning of the digestive period. *See* Digestion. The principal functions of bile in digestion are in neutralizing acid in the chyme and the emulsification of fats.

In birds that have a gall bladder, the right hepatic duct of the liver may have a branch into the gall bladder or may be enlarged locally as a gall bladder (Farner, 1960). *See* Liver.

GALLIFORMES
(gal-ih-FOR-meez); from Lat. *gallus,* a cock, and *forma,* form; cock-shaped (Coble, 1954). An order of chickenlike or fowl-like birds; worldwide, of 256 species of 7 families (Van Tyne and Berger, 1976) that resemble each other fundamentally in structure (*see* Order); includes the megapodes, the chachalacas, guans, and curassows; the peafowl, pheasants, guinea fowl, turkeys, jungle fowl, quails, partridges, ptarmigans, prairie chickens, grouse, and, by many authorities, the hoatzin, but Sibley and Alquist (1973), from their studies of the egg-white protein of the hoatzin, suggest that it is in the Cuckoo Family. *See* explanation and details under Cuculiformes.

In N. America, the Galliformes have representatives in four families—the Curassow Family, Grouse Family, Pheasant Family, and Turkey Family. The other three groups are the odd Megapode Family of 10 species of the Australian and Malaysian region; the Guineafowl

curassow

quail

turkey

grouse

pheasant

GALLIFORMES

Family of 7 species of Africa and Madagascar; and the S. American hoatzin, lone member of the Hoatzin Family (Opisthocomidae).

The Galliformes, known also as game birds, are characteristically a well-defined group: in common, they are basically ground-living birds (terrestrial); they cannot swim but are good runners (*see* Running Birds); the bill is short, culmen downcurved; imperforate nostrils (*see* Imperforate); they have short, rounded wings with 10 bowed, stiff primaries; are capable of swift but short flights (*see* Flight); strong legs, often armed with spurs, and four toes (*see* Feet and Legs) with hard nails well adapted to scratching in the ground for food; also, most have a well-developed caecum, which aids in digesting their food (*see* Caecum). Besides the wild game birds, the Galliformes include the most useful of all domestic birds, the chicken, or barnyard fowl, which is in the Pheasant Family, the guinea fowl (Guineafowl Family), and the domestic turkey (Delacour, 1961c). *See* Domestication.

GALLINACEOUS

(gal-ih-NAY-shus). Resembling the domestic fowls and pheasants; birds such as grouse, pheasants, quail, prairie chickens, and turkeys. *See* Galliformes; *also* Game Bird.

GALLINULE

See in Rail Family.

GAMBEL

WILLIAM (1819?–49). Early field ornithologist in Calif. and first to spend a considerable time there; a protégé of Thomas Nuttall, Gambel crossed the continent in 1841 via the Sante Fe Trail and then from Utah to Calif. via the Mormon Trail; he collected birds in Calif. for several years (Palmer, 1928); during a second trip in 1849, Gambel died of typhoid fever at Rose's Bar on the Feather R., Calif. His name is commemorated in two species of N. American birds —in common and scientific name of the Gambel's quail; in scientific name of the mountain chickadee, *Parus gambeli*. See Gruson (1972) for other details.

GAME BIRD

Any bird considered legal game that may be shot and taken during an open hunting season. Grouse, quail, pheasants, wild turkeys, and other gallinaceous birds (*see* Galliformes) are usually considered game species; also ducks and geese (waterfowl), rails ("railbirds"), gallinules and coots, mourning doves (in some states), white-winged doves, and band-tailed pigeons, also the common snipe and woodcock (shorebirds).

GAME MANAGEMENT

Synonymous with *wildlife management,* the current more widely used term. *See* brief discussion of wildlife management under Economic Ornithology; *see also* Songbird and Game-Bird Management; Census (methods of).

GAMETE

See Fertilization.

GAMIN

See House sparrow in Weaverbird Family.

GANDER

See introduction to Duck Family.

GANNET

See Gannet in Booby Family. Also, local name in Fla. for the wood stork in Stork Family, probably because its white-and-black color pattern resembles that of the true gannet.

GANNET STRIKER

See Tern, Caspian, and Tern, royal, in Gull Family; name alludes to their similarity to the large gannet in the Booby Family in striking the sea when diving for fishes.

GAPE

The mouth opening between the upper (maxilla) part of a bird's bill and the lower (mandible) part when the bill is open (Van Tyne and Berger, 1959). A bird also gapes. *See* Gaping.

GAPEWORM

See Nematode.

GAPING

(GAY-ping). Term of animal behaviorists for the response of young altricial birds (*see* Altricial) to the parents' return to the nest with food. The very young nestlings are still unable to see (their eyes are closed), and their gaping response (opening their mouths widely) is released by various non-visual stimuli: tactile or touch stimuli of the parent birds when a parent alights on the nest; call notes of the adults or sounds or touch of a human observer at the nest will elicit the gaping response (Van Tyne and Berger, 1959). After their eyes have opened, the altricial young no longer stretch their necks vertically but direct their opened mouths toward the head of the parent bird as it perches on or near the nest (Tinbergen, 1951b).

Even after leaving the nest, young birds gape (which elicits the feeding response in the adults—*see* Directive Marks); also, the adult females of many kinds of birds gape when they beg food from their mates. *See* Courtship; Courtship Feeding; *also* Feeding the Young under Young and Their Care.

GAREFOWL

See Auk, great, in Auk Family.

GARGANEY

See in Duck Family.

GAROO

Local name for the sandhill and whooping cranes, imitative of their trumpeting calls.

GARROT

Local name for the Barrow's goldeneye and common goldeneye. *See* in Duck Family.

GAUSE'S RULE

or GAUSE'S PRINCIPLE. First stated by G. F. Gause (1934). It is the theory that two or more species "with identical ecological requirements cannot coexist indefinitely in the same environ-

GREBE FAMILY

Eared grebe

The streamlined bodies and lobed toes of grebes enable them to swim rapidly underwater in pursuit of small fish and crustaceans. The eared grebe nests in colonies in marshes in western North America and in Eurasia. The striped young can sometimes be seen riding on their mothers' backs. In the fall, eared grebes lose their bright plumage and migrate to saltwater, where they feed on marine crustaceans.

Eared grebe

Horned grebe

The horned grebe nests in marshes in the interior of the continent and winters in shallow water on both the Atlantic and the Pacific coasts, where it feeds mainly on small fish. Like all grebes, it builds a floating nest of wet marsh vegetation, and its 3 to 5 chalky white eggs soon become stained with brown. If an intruder approaches a nest, the adult slips quietly away, first pulling up parts of the nest and covering the eggs, so that unless examined closely the nest appears to be empty.

Least grebe

The least grebe is mainly a tropical species, occurring in our area only in southern Texas and occasionally in California. It nests in shallow, weed-choked ponds and feeds almost entirely on aquatic insects. Inhabiting a warm climate, it has no need to migrate; a pair may spend the whole year on a single pond.

Pied-billed grebe

The pied-bill is the most widespread and familiar grebe in the Western Hemisphere, nesting from southern Canada to Argentina. There is hardly a roadside marsh or weedy pond in the United States that does not have a pair of "helldivers." Its stout bill, boldly marked with black and white during the breeding season, enables it to feed on crayfish, one of its favorite foods.

Red-necked grebe

The red-necked grebe is rather scarce in North America, and its range is shrinking as marshes are drained or become polluted. It is easily identified by its stout yellow bill and rather large size.

Western grebe

Also known as the "swan grebe" because of its long, slender neck, this is the largest of all the grebes. At their teeming, noisy breeding colonies on western marshes, pairs engage in a spectacular courtship ritual, rising up and skimming over the surface propelled by their feet alone. The drab gray downy young is unique; all other grebes have boldly striped young.

Red-necked grebe

Horned grebe

Western grebe

Pied-billed grebe

Least grebe

GROUSE FAMILY

Blue grouse

The blue grouse inhabits the dense fir forests of western Canada and the northwestern United States. Unlike many other grouse, males of this species do not gather in groups during the mating season; each male performs its displays alone, fanning its tail and spreading the feathers on the side of its neck to expose the bright yellow or purple skin, and accompanies this performance with a series of loud hooting calls.

Ruffed grouse

Although this famous game bird may be found in many kinds of deciduous and mixed forests in Canada and the northern United States, it is most numerous where birches and poplars grow, for the buds and seeds of these trees are among its favorite foods. In the spring, the drumming of the males—each one standing on a fallen log—may be heard as much as half a mile away. Ruffed grouse populations are subject to periodic "crashes," when the birds virtually disappear from areas where they have been numerous.

Blue grouse

Blue grouse, female

Ruffed grouse

Ruffed grouse

Ruffed grouse, female

Sage grouse

The largest of the American grouse, the sage grouse inhabits the vast sagebrush plains of the interior of the northwestern United States. Each spring males gather in groups and perform courtship displays; females visit these groups for mating and then raise their young without assistance from the males.

Spruce grouse

The spruce grouse is aptly named, for the needles and buds of spruces and other evergreens are a staple food during much of the year. Although it is well known for being very tame—one of its folk names is "fool-hen"—the spruce grouse can be very difficult to find; many bird-watchers have made repeated visits to the coniferous forests of Canada and the northernmost United States, and still have yet to see one.

Sage grouse

Sage grouse

Sage grouse

Spruce grouse

Greater prairie chicken
The greater prairie chicken has not fared well since the coming of European settlers to North America, for the tall-grass prairie it requires has largely been taken over by agriculture. In the steadily shrinking area where these grouse may still be found, the deep booming call of displaying males is a familiar sound in spring.

Lesser prairie chicken
This smaller relative of the greater prairie chicken occupies a more restricted range, inhabiting short-grass prairie with scattered shinnery oaks or sagebrush in Colorado, Kansas, Oklahoma, Texas, and New Mexico. The two prairie chickens are so similar in their behavior and appearance that some authorities consider them a single species.

Sharp-tailed grouse
The sharp-tailed grouse inhabits brushy woodland edges and prairies from Alaska south to Washington and east to the Great Lakes. Since it does not require pure grassland, as does the greater prairie chicken, it is still common in much of its range.

Greater prairie chicken

Greater prairie chicken

Lesser prairie chicken

Sharp-tailed grouse

Rock ptarmigan

Ptarmigans have 3 plumages a year instead of 2, unlike most birds. In summer they are rich reddish brown, in the fall they are grayer, and in winter their white plumage provides effective concealment against the snow. Rock ptarmigans live farther north than willow ptarmigans, often visiting places where the Arctic winds have swept the ground clear of snow, exposing the low tundra willows on whose buds and twigs they feed.

White-tailed ptarmigan

This is the only ptarmigan confined to North America, and the only one with an all-white tail. It inhabits alpine tundra from Alaska south to Washington and New Mexico, with an introduced population in the Sierra Nevada in California. It is like the other ptarmigans in that its principal winter food is the buds and twigs of tundra willows.

Willow ptarmigan

To protect them against the harsh Arctic winter, the feet of ptarmigans are feathered to the tips of their toes. Willow ptarmigans inhabit the tundra from Alaska south to Manitoba and central Quebec. In unusually severe winters, when the snow covers their food, a few willow ptarmigans wander as far south as Minnesota.

Rock ptarmigan, winter

Willow ptarmigan, late spring

White-tailed ptarmigan, winter

White-tailed ptarmigan

White-tailed ptarmigan, female

Willow ptarmigan

Rock ptarmigan

GULL FAMILY

Black-headed gull

This Eurasian gull is a rare but regular visitor to the northeastern United States and the Maritime Provinces of Canada, where it is usually seen feeding with Bonaparte gulls along the coast. In recent years it has been seen so frequently that there are suspicions that it may be nesting somewhere in North America. Although newly fledged young birds have been reported from Newfoundland, no nest has yet been found.

Bonaparte's gull

This small, agile gull nests in the coniferous forests of northwestern Canada and Alaska, and winters along the Atlantic and Pacific coasts, where it feeds on small fish and swimming crustaceans in tidal channels and at the mouths of rivers. Although it gathers to feed on scraps at sewer outlets, it has not increased in numbers as have some of the larger gulls that have taken to scavenging at garbage dumps.

California gull

The California gull nests in large colonies on inland lakes in the western United States and winters along the Pacific coast. It is omnivorous, like other gulls, and during the breeding season it eats many insects. In the late 1840s, when a plague of locusts threatened settlers' crops in Utah, California gulls came to the rescue, and the Mormons showed their appreciation by erecting a statue to the gulls in Salt Lake City.

Bonaparte's gull, immature

Black-headed gull

Bonaparte's gull

California gull

Franklin's gull
This medium-sized, black-headed gull breeds in the prairie marshes of southern Canada and the north-central United States, and winters along the coast from Louisiana and Texas south to Chile. Every spring large flocks of "prairie doves," their breasts tinged with pink, migrate north over the Great Plains. From time to time these migrants pause in their travels, and may be seen following a plow, feeding on insects in the newly turned soil.

Glaucous gull
This large, white-winged gull nests in the Arctic in both hemispheres, placing its 3 heavily blotched eggs in a nest of grass and moss on a coastal cliff. In the winter, the bulk of the population moves out onto the pack ice, but some migrate as far south as the northeast coast of the United States.

Glaucous-winged gull
There are 3 North American gulls without black in their wing tips. Of these so-called white-winged gulls, 2, the glaucous and Iceland gulls, are rare or uncommon visitors to our coasts in winter. However, the glaucous-winged gull is an abundant winter resident along our entire Pacific coast and nests as far south as Oregon, where its breeding range overlaps that of the western gull. Where these 2 species nest together, they occasionally hybridize.

Great black-backed gull
Like the herring gull, the great black-backed gull has extended its breeding range considerably southward in recent decades. While it once nested no farther south than Cape Cod, it now breeds regularly on the Outer Banks of North Carolina. In addition to feeding on dead fish, the eggs and young of other water birds, and garbage, great black-backed gulls occasionally attack birds almost as large as themselves, often working in pairs and stunning the victim with a sudden sharp blow of the bill.

Heermann's gull
This beautiful pearly gray gull with a bright red bill nests on the Pacific coast of Mexico. In early summer, when the breeding season has ended, the birds spread out along the coast, becoming common as far north as Washington and British Columbia and as far south as Guatemala.

Franklin's gull

Franklin's gull

Great black-backed gull

Glaucous-winged gull

Glaucous gull

Heermann's gull

Herring gull

The adaptable herring gull has taken advantage of food available at garbage dumps and has undergone a tremendous population increase in the last few decades, nesting in large colonies in areas where it was formerly only a winter visitor. Although primarily a bird of the seacoast, it is also common on inland waters, especially during migration. Where it has become numerous as a nesting bird, it preys heavily on the eggs and young of terns, causing these smaller and more sensitive birds to decline in number.

Herring gull, nest

Herring gull, egg

Herring gull, chick

Herring gull

Herring gull

Herring gull, first winter

Herring gull, juvenile

Iceland gull
The Iceland gull resembles the glaucous gull but is smaller, with a more delicate bill. Like its larger relative, it is a bird of the Arctic that visits our coasts in the winter. It is primarily a scavenger, feeding at garbage dumps and around fishing piers in settled areas, and on dead fish and seal droppings on the pack ice.

Ivory gull
The ivory gull is a bird of the Arctic ice floes that rarely wanders far enough south to be seen by birders. The plumage of the adult is pure white, while young birds are attractively barred with black. Most of the ivory gulls that reach the Maritime Provinces or New England are birds of the year.

Laughing gull
The attractively hooded laughing gull breeds in salt marshes from Maine to the Caribbean. It is sensitive both to human disturbance and to the depredations of the larger herring and great black-backed gulls, and so has declined in recent years.

Lesser black-backed gull
A dark-backed relative of the herring gull, the lesser black-backed gull has been appearing on the Atlantic coast in steadily increasing numbers since the 1940s. It is not unlikely that it will one day be found nesting in Canada.

Little gull
The little gull appears in small numbers every winter on the Great Lakes and along the northeast coast. For many years it was thought that these birds were vagrants from Europe, where the species normally occurs, but in the early 1960s little gulls were found nesting in small numbers in Canada, raising the possibility that there is a permanent nesting population in the Western Hemisphere.

Mew gull
The mew gull nests on marshes and lakes in the interior of northwestern Canada and Alaska, as well as in Eurasia. In winter, when these inland waters freeze, the birds move to the Pacific coast, where they are common as far south as southern California. The mew gull is smaller and more agile than the glaucous-winged, western, and herring gulls, and is more adept at picking bits of food off the surface of the water. Only rarely does it visit garbage dumps, where its larger relatives feed.

Laughing gull

Lesser black-backed gull

Ivory gull

Iceland gull

Little gull, winter

Mew gull

Ring-billed gull

The ring-billed gull nests in large colonies containing many thousands of pairs on protected islands in lakes in Alaska, much of Canada, and the Rocky Mountains. It winters from southern Canada south to Mexico. Away from the coast it is the most abundant gull in winter.

Sabine's gull

The Sabine's gull is the only one of our gulls that has a forked tail. It nests on the Arctic tundra and spends the winter on the open ocean in tropical latitudes. Since it migrates well offshore, it is seldom seen by birders.

Thayer's gull

For many years no one knew whether this dark-eyed gull was a race of the herring gull, a race of the Iceland gull, or a separate species. It was then found that these birds nest on cliffs within the breeding range of both the herring and the Iceland gulls, and experiments showed that the dark eyes of the Thayer's gull are an important factor in preventing all these birds from interbreeding; Thayer's gull has therefore been given the rank of a full species.

Western gull

Along much of the Pacific coast, this is the only nesting gull. Breeding colonies are located on rocky headlands or offshore islands. The western gull is primarily a bird of the coast, but many move upriver at the end of the breeding season when the salmon are running.

Black-legged kittiwake

This small, oceanic gull nests in large colonies on coastal cliffs in Canada and the American Arctic, as well as in the Old World. Three eggs are placed in a well-made cup of seaweed and moss. Unlike the young of other gulls, young kittiwakes remain in the nest even when an intruder appears; were they to scramble for cover, they would risk falling off the cliff.

Red-legged kittiwake

While the black-legged kittiwake nests on Arctic and cold temperate coasts in both North America and Eurasia, its red-legged cousin breeds only on the Commander Islands, off the coast of Siberia, and in the Pribilofs. It winters on the North Pacific, and is only occasionally seen from land.

Sabine's gull

Thayer's gull

Western gull

Ring-billed gull

Red-legged kittiwake

Black-legged kittiwake

Aleutian tern
This little-known bird breeds in Alaska and winters on the coast of Siberia and Japan. It nests in small colonies or in isolated pairs on tiny coastal islands or on grassy hillsides facing the sea.

Arctic tern
The Arctic tern is famous as a world traveler. At the end of the breeding season it migrates from the Arctic and cold temperate coasts of the Northern Hemisphere all the way to the cold seas off Antarctica. When the birds return to their nesting grounds the following spring, they may have traveled as many as 22,000 miles.

Arctic tern

Arctic tern

Aleutian tern

Arctic tern

Black tern

The marsh-inhabiting black tern has a more buoyant and leisurely flight than other terns, deftly picking aquatic insects off the surface of the water or catching dragonflies in midair. In the fall, most black terns move to saltwater and migrate to their wintering grounds off the coast of South America.

Bridled tern

In recent years it has been found that small numbers of bridled terns occur well off the coast of the Carolinas, in the warm waters of the Gulf Stream. Until these birds were discovered, this tropical species was thought to be only a casual visitor to the United States from its nesting colonies in the West Indies.

Caspian tern

Our largest tern, the Caspian tern nests singly or in small colonies on beaches and sandbars from northern Canada south to the Gulf coast, as well as in Eurasia, Africa, and Australia. Like gulls, these birds often raid colonies of the smaller species of terns, preying on eggs and nestlings.

Black tern

Caspian tern

Bridled tern

Common tern

As its name implies, this is our most abundant tern, nesting both inland and along the coast from southern Canada to the central United States and the Caribbean. The most successful nesting colonies are the large ones, which contain several thousand pairs; smaller colonies seem to be more vulnerable to both human disturbance and the depredations of gulls, which take many eggs and young every year.

Elegant tern

Until 1959, this large, crested tern nested solely on the Pacific coast of Mexico, visiting the United States only after the breeding season and, in small numbers, during the winter. Then a colony was found near San Diego, nesting with a group of Caspian terns.

Forster's tern

While its close relative the common tern nests only occasionally in marshes, the exclusively North American Forster's tern invariably does so, placing its 3 or 4 buff-colored, spotted eggs in a saucerlike nest of grass in prairie marshes from southern Canada to California, and in salt marshes along the Atlantic and Gulf coasts. Like the gull-billed tern, another inhabitant of marshes, it feeds on insects, but it also dives for small fish, as do the common, arctic, and roseate terns.

Gull-billed tern

The short, thick bill of this marsh-nesting tern is evidently an adaptation for eating insects, which form the bulk of its diet during the breeding season. It nests not only in salt marshes on the east coast of the United States and in the West Indies, but also in Eurasia, Africa, and Australia. Like other birds of these salt marshes, its numbers are declining as more and more of its fragile habitat is drained and developed.

Elegant tern

Gull-billed tern

Common tern

Forster's tern

Least tern
This smallest of our terns usually nests singly or in small groups on sandy beaches both along the coast and on large rivers in the interior. It seems less sensitive to disturbance than its larger relatives that generally nest in crowded colonies, its greatest enemy being habitat destruction.

Least tern

Least tern

Least tern, chick

Least tern

Noddy

Noddies are unusual among terns in that they often place their single egg in a compact nest of sticks and seaweed in a bush or tree, rather than in a simple scrape on the ground. Birds of tropical oceans around the world, they nest in American waters only on the Dry Tortugas, off the coast of southern Florida.

Roseate tern

The largest and most flourishing colonies of the roseate tern are in the Indian Ocean. In North America it nests only along the Atlantic coast, where it is a local and declining species, usually occupying marginal habitat around the edges of large colonies of common terns and probably suffering from competition with that species for favorable nesting sites.

Royal tern

The royal tern resembles the Caspian tern but is slightly smaller, with a longer crest and an orange rather than blood-red bill. It nests on sandy beaches from Virginia to Texas and Mexico, and in West Africa. Unlike most of our terns, it usually lays only 1 egg. The royal tern feeds almost entirely on fish.

Sandwich tern

This long-billed, crested tern nests in colonies on sandy beaches and coastal islands from Virginia to the Caribbean and in Europe. Instead of remaining in or near the nest, as do the young of other terns, young sandwich terns gather in a large group called a "creche." Surprising as it may seem, adults bringing food to this jostling throng can pick out their own offspring.

Black noddy

Brown noddy

Roseate tern

Sandwich tern

Royal tern

Sooty tern

Sooty tern
The sooty tern nests on offshore islands in tropical seas, including the Dry Tortugas, off the coast of southern Florida. It spends the bulk of its time feeding far from land and is one of the most aerial of terns, seldom settling on the water, even at night.

ment, because one of them will in all likelihood be more efficient than the others and will eventually outbreed and supplant its competitors" (Dobzhansky, 1957). *See* examples under Ecological Niche.

GAVIIDAE
See Loon Family.

GAVIIFORMES
(gay-vih-ih-FOR-meez); from Lat. *gavia*, sea smew (duck), and *forma*, form; loon-shaped (Coble, 1954). An order, or group, of primitive birds that resemble each other fundamentally in structure (*see* Order); includes only the Loon Family, Gaviidae, of 4 species (Van Tyne and Berger, 1959). Loons nest in summer on islands, lakeshores, edges of ponds around the northern parts of the world; in fall they migrate to temperate regions south of the Arctic or northern breeding grounds. Some take long overland flights of 1,000 mi. or more to the salt waters where they spend the winter. *See* under Loon Family. They are thought to have evolved to much their present form 60–100 million years ago. *See* Eocene Period under Geological Time Scale.

Loons are large water birds, or foot-propelled diving birds, 26–37½ in. long, with straight, sharply pointed bills, with which they catch fishes as they swim rapidly about underwater. *See* Fishes and Birds. They are superbly adapted to life in the water—long-bodied, sleek, and torpedo-shaped, with legs that grow far back on the body and with toes fully webbed. Noted for their swiftness and skill in diving and swimming, they are called, in Great Britain, divers. *See* Swimming and Diving. The body plumage of loons is hard and compact and is strikingly marked in black and white. *See* comparison with the similar but unrelated grebes under Podicipediformes. For a discussion of how birds are grouped according to their relationships, *see* Classification; Morphology; Phylogenetic Relationship.

loon

GAVIIFORMES

GENE
The unit of inheritance within a chromosome. The genes are transmitted from one generation to the next by the gametes (eggs and sperm) and control the development of the individual (Van Tyne and Berger, 1959). *See* Fertilization; Genetics; Eggs and Egg-laying.

GENETIC MOSAIC
See Gynandromorph.

GENETICS
The science of heredity. The name is appropriate, as genetics has proved to be, to a considerable extent, the understanding of *genes,* the ultimate units of *heredity.* Hence genetics is the study of the raw material of organic variation and inheritance: the qualities of organisms which, given reproduction at geometric rates, in a world of limited resources, leads to competition, survival of the fittest *(natural selection),* with consequent adaptation and evolution. *See* Natural Selection. For technical discussion of genetics, see Cain (1964b); Dobzhansky (1957, 1961); Ford (1957); Simpsen *et*

al. (1957); Kalmus and Crump (1948); Welty (1962, 1975).

GENUS

(JEE-nus; pl.: *genera*—JEN-er-ah). A genus is a group of related species descended from a common ancestor. It is a category of classification between family and species; a genus is a group of structurally or phylogenetically related species, or it may be a single very distinct species—a monotypic (one-type) genus. The genus includes one or more species that have a combination of characters shared by no other genus. Genera tend to be separated by greater and by more differences than those which separate species from each other (Mayr, 1942).

The evolutionist sees in the genus a group of species that have descended from a common ancestor—a phylogenetic unit. The collective members of a genus—the species—also occupy a more or less well-defined ecological niche (*see* Ecological Niche), and the genus is thus often a group of species adapted to a particular mode of life. The essential property of a genus is morphological distinctness, usually correlated with a distinct ecological niche. (Mayr *et. al.*, 1953). *See* Genus under Classification.

IDENTIFYING EACH GENUS BY NAME. Each family has usually been divided into several genera in order to show relationships within the family. In the American Wood Warbler Family (Parulidae), there are 17 genera that are represented in N. America, and 40 in the Finch Family (Fringillidae) (A.O.U. *Check-list,* 1957). For convenience, each genus must bear an identifying name. For example, in the Thrush Family (Turdidae), there are 8 genera represented in N. America: (1) *Turdus,* of which the American robins are representatives; (2) *Ixoreus,* the varied thrush; (3) *Hylocichla,* containing the wood thrush; (4) *Catharus,* the hermit thrush, Swainson's thrush, gray-cheeked thrush, and veery; (5) *Sialia,* containing the eastern bluebird, western bluebird, and mountain bluebird; (6) *Oenanthe,* represented by the wheatear; (7) *Luscinia,* of which the European and Asiatic bluethroat and Siberian rubythroat reach Alaska; and (8) *Myadestes,* the solitaires (A.O.U. *Check-list,* 1957; American Ornithologists' Union, 1973).

Thus the genus name is a group name, and the group name is a last name, just as Smith, Brown, and Jones serve as last names for people. All American bluebirds are *Sialia* (sigh-AY-lih-ah), but each has a different first name, or species name. The eastern bluebird's species name is *sialis* (sigh-AY-lis). In a listing of bluebirds by their scientific names, the last name (genus name) is first, the first name (species name) is last, just as people are listed in a telephone directory. The listing for bluebirds would be as follows:

Scientific listing:	*Comparable English-name:*
Sialia sialis	bluebird, eastern
Sialia mexicana	bluebird, western
Sialia currucoides	bluebird, mountain

See Names and Naming.

GEOGRAPHIC BARRIER

See Barrier; Distribution.

GEOGRAPHIC RACE

See Subspecies; *also* Cline.

GEOGRAPHIC VARIATION

(in birds). *See* Subspecies; *also* Cline.

GEOLOGICAL TIME SCALE

Term for a sequence of prehistoric events as shown by the ages of the earth's rocks, in a chronological sequence, from the oldest to the most recent. Careful studies of the disintegration of uranium into lead show that there are rocks in the earth almost 3 billion years old. The first fossils (in abundance) were in the Cambrian Period, beginning more than 600 million years ago; the first vertebrates in the Ordovician Period, more than 425 million years ago; dinosaurs about 200 million years ago; the first fossil birds about 150 million years ago.

Geological factors that shaped the form and composition of the earth's surface—the stages in the emergence of the land from ancient seas, the distribution of land and water throughout the world, the movement of the land masses, the breakdown of rocks into soils, the plants that grow on certain soils—have determined where birds live today (*see* Distribution); have helped shape their evolution; determined their migration routes and their environments and habitats.

Following is a brief survey of a geological time scale, and some of the fossil birds known from each, beginning with the Jurassic Period and the first fossil bird, *Archaeopteryx.* The time scale is based upon Brodkorb (1971).

Jurassic Period (joo-RAS-ik), name from Jura Mtns. of the Alpine region along boundary between France and Switzerland; period from about 136 to 190 million years ago; lasted some 54 million years to beginning of Cretaceous; *Archaeopteryx* appears, first fossil bird. *See* Origin of Birds and of Bird Flight under Fossil Birds. Flying reptiles; first primitive mammals (Welty, 1975); insects abundant, dominance of dinosaurs (Moody, 1953). Seas invade the continents (Swinton, 1965).

Cretaceous Period (kree-TAY-shus), from Lat. *creta,* meaning chalk, in reference to the white cliffs of Dover; from about 65 to 136 million years ago; lasted for 71 million years until beginning of Paleocene; appearance of the second-oldest bird fossil, *Gallornis straelini,* a gooselike fossil discovered in France, which lived about 3 to 25 million years later than *Archaeopteryx* (Brodkorb, 1971); the appearance of another toothed bird, *Hesperornis (Archaeopteryx, Hesperornis* and the gull-like *Ichthyornis* were the only birds known to have possessed teeth; also *Baptornis,* a flightless diver closely resembling the grebes. Other fossil birds of this period resembled cormorants, loons, geese, flamingos, ibises, rails, and sandpipers (Brodkorb, 1971). *See* Baptornis; Hesperornis; Ichthyornis.

Paleocene Period (PAY-lee-oh-seen), meaning "more ancient than Eocene," from about 54 to 65 million years ago; lasted for 15 million years to beginning of Eocene. Very few fossil birds have been found from the Paleo-

cenc, but first evidence of Accipitriformes according to Brodkorb (1971); also representatives of four families: Gaviidae (loons), Phaethontidae (tropic-birds), Cathartidae, and Laridae (gulls and terns).

Eocene Period (EE-oh-seen), meaning "dawn of recent times," from about 38 to 54 million years ago; lasted about 16 million years to beginning of Oligocene; probably period of major evolution in birds, and according to Brodkorb (1971), most, perhaps all the known orders of birds became established by the end of the Eocene. By close, there were 27 families of 14 orders of modern birds known—loons, anhingas, penguins, cormorants, and auks; herons, ibises, flamingos, rails, cranes, painted snipe, and sandpipers; rheas, chachalacas, partridges, grouse, gulls, bustards, and sand grouse; cuckoos, trogons, rollers, hornbills, and shrikelike and titlike forms of early songbirds; also swifts, and the hawks, owls, and American (cathardid) vultures filled some of the niches they fill today (Storer, 1960a); besides these, avocets, ducks, storks, and starlings (Brodkorb, 1971); also the appearance of now extinct genera, the giant flightless *Diatryma (see* Diatrymiformes; Fossil Birds) and its relatives, *Gastornis* and *Remiornis;* the long-legged vultures, *Neocathartes;* and the fossil *Eleutherornis,* which links the carinate and ratite birds (Wetmore, 1955). *See* Monophyletic Descent. Most mammals were small during this period (Moody, 1953) and the Rocky Mtns. formed (Swinton, 1965).

Oligocene Period (OL-ih-go-seen), meaning "a little recent," from about 23 to 38 million years ago; lasted about 15 million years, to Miocene; first appearance of albatrosses, shearwaters, boobies, pheasants, limpkins, plovers, turkeys, parrots, kingfishers, Old World warblers, and sparrows, and rise of modern mammals (Welty, 1962); many gruiform (crane and rail) types, buteonine hawks, and a few genera of modern birds appear (Wallace, 1963).

Miocene Period (MY-oh-seen), meaning "less recent," from about 5 to 23 million years ago; lasted about 18 million years, to Pliocene; majority of modern *families* of birds probably existing (Storer, 1960a). Several modern genera of falcons, the storm-petrels, pelicans, grebes, and thick-knees appear, also some owls; others were doves, crows, thrushes, shrikes, wagtails, and wood warblers (Brodkorb, 1971). Some families of birds becoming extinct (Welty, 1962); the "golden age" of mammals (Russell, 1941).

Pliocene Period (PLY-oh-seen), meaning "more recent," from about 2 to about 5 million years ago; lasted about 3 million years to Pleistocene; mountains formed and climate cooled (Swinton, 1965); bird species probably reached their maximum numbers; our present living birds were having their evolution as genera and species (Wetmore, 1951). Appearance of moas, ostriches, emus, rheas, tinamous, and ospreys, and the first certain woodpeckers, the first larks, swallows, nuthatches, and emberizid sparrows (Brodkorb, 1971).

Pleistocene Period (PLICE-toh-seen), meaning "most recent times," from about 2 million years ago to our present or Recent Period: first, or prehistoric, men (Simpson *et al.,* 1957). All

ERA	EPOCH		

ERA	EPOCH		
CENOZOIC — QUARTERNARY	HOLOCENE	.01	tanagers, frigatebirds
CENOZOIC — QUARTERNARY	PLEISTOCENE	2	phalaropes
CENOZOIC — TERTIARY	PLIOCENE	11	larks
CENOZOIC — TERTIARY	MIOCENE	25	sandpipers
CENOZOIC — TERTIARY	OLIGOCENE	40	plovers, swifts
CENOZOIC — TERTIARY	EOCENE	60	gulls
CENOZOIC — TERTIARY	PALEOCENE	70	loons
MESOZOIC	CRETACEOUS	135	Tyrannosaurus Rex, Hesperornis
MESOZOIC	JURASSIC	180	Archaeopteryx, Stegosaurus
MESOZOIC	TRIASSIC	225	thecodonts
MESOZOIC	PERMIAN	270	Dimetrodon
PALEOZOIC	PENNSYLVANIAN	305	first true reptiles
PALEOZOIC	MISSISSIPPIAN	350	amphibious reptile ancestors
PALEOZOIC	DEVONIAN	400	early amphibians

GEOLOGICAL TIME SCALE

The Devonian period, which began 200 million years into the Paleozoic era, witnessed the development of early amphibians. Archaeopteryx lithographica, the earliest true bird for which a fossil has been discovered, lived during the Jurassic period and still retained many reptilian features. Many birds that evolved as long ago as 70 million years have survived to the present, and others, including the frigatebirds and the tanagers, have been found as fossils from the Holocene epoch, the most recent period of the earth's development.

Numbers given are numbers of years, in millions, since the start of an epoch or period.

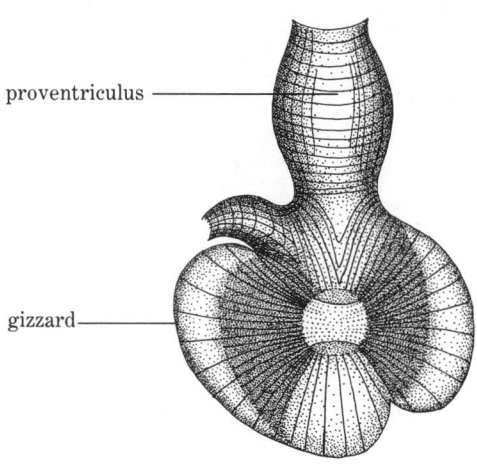

proventriculus

gizzard

GIZZARD

The gizzard—the muscular stomach of birds—has thick, ridged, strong walls whose rhythmic contractions perform the same grinding function of teeth and jaws in mammals. Birds with well-developed gizzards swallow grit to aid the grinding process.

existing species of birds of today thought to have been living in the Pleistocene (Howard, 1950; Wetmore, 1959). Great glaciers periodically covering parts of N. America and Europe; great dispersal of animals and plants owing to Ice Age; widespread extermination of mammals and birds, especially ratites, because of climatic factors (Wallace, 1963).

Recent Period, within the last 10,000 years, more and higher mountains than in past; more volcanoes and earthquakes, within a stage of acute crustal unrest (Russell, 1941). Modern man; birds of today, about 8,650 species remaining in the world. According to Brodkorb (1960), more than 1½ million species of birds lived since the time of the first bird, *Archaeopteryx;* 796 species recognized in N. America (Wetmore, 1959).

More than half of all living birds in the world belong to the order Passeriformes, the songbirds or perching birds (Swinton, 1965), which now dominate in numbers and in species. Worldwide extinction of 78 full species of birds, largely man-caused, from 1680, last year of the dodo, to present (Fisher, 1964); 97 species extinct since the year 1600; 62 species have disappeared in last 150 years (Vincent, 1966); see also Fisher and Peterson, 1964; Philip and Fisher, 1970.

Man dominating; destruction and severe alteration of much of the world environment, with benefits to some birds, but catastrophes for others in drainage of swamps and marshes, real estate developments, etc. (*see* Adaptations to Mankind); polluting of earth, air, and water by human and industrial wastes, with lethal consequences to birds and other kinds of wildlife. *See* Accidents; Poisons. See "Toxic Chemicals and Oil Pollution" in *A New Dictionary of Birds,* ed. by A. L. Thomson (New York: McGraw-Hill Book Co., 1964); also Carson (1962); Graham (1970); Hartung (1971).

GIZZARD

(ventriculus). The muscular part of the stomach of a bird (*see* Digestion). Because of its remarkable power, the gizzard has been of special interest to scientists for 300 years. It has been compared in its function to the grinding teeth and strong jaws of mammals (Farner, 1960). The gizzards of some N. American birds, especially of wood ducks and mallards, crush acorns and hard hickory nuts that they swallow whole (Mabbott, 1920); the strong gizzards of eiders and other diving ducks grind up mussels and other extremely hard shellfishes that they swallow entire (*see* especially White-winged scoter in Duck Family); Schorger (1960) fed wild pecan nuts to turkeys and found they were crushed in the turkey gizzard within an hour; harder-shelled hickory nuts required 30–32 hours.

Borelli (1681) introduced into stomachs of turkeys, through their mouths, glass balls, hollow cubes of lead, and pyramids of wood. By the following day, the glass objects had been pulverized by the gizzards, the lead cubes flattened, the wooden pyramids worn down. Réaumur (1756), French physicist and naturalist, who isolated gastric juices of birds, followed with experiments with turkeys in 1752 and used, besides glass balls, tubes of tin plate that

required 80 lbs. of pressure to bend. These were crushed flat and in part unrolled within 24 hours in the turkey gizzard. Several similar tubes, when squeezed in a vise, required a force of 437 lbs. to flatten them as the gizzards of the turkeys had done (McAtee, 1927). Spallanzani (1787), Italian priest and scholar, discovered in experiments in 1783 that a turkey's gizzard could grind up 12 steel needles in 36 hours and 16 surgical lancets in 16 hours.

The gizzard is shaped like a thick, biconvex lens, with striated muscles arranged usually in bands. The mucous epithelium of the inside of the gizzard (the koilin lining) is very thick and horny; it is yellow, green, or brown because of regurgitated bile pigments that color it (Farner, 1960), is shed regularly in most birds, which is necessary to the food-grinding process (McAtee, 1917), and secretes a fluid that hardens into plates or ridges—the "millstones" for the mechanical grinding of food. The gizzard is also a storage place for food until gastric juices penetrate sufficiently to start acid breakdown of proteins, or until the food passes on into the small intestine (Farner, 1960). *See* Digestion. Lesions comparable to peptic ulcers in man have been reported in the epithelial lining of the gizzards of chickens (Sturkie, 1954).

The grinding action of the gizzard—regular, rotary, rhythmic contractions that in a domestic hen vary from two to three a minute, and can be heard with a stethoscope when coarse food and grit are in the gizzard (Groebbels, 1932)—is aided by the abrasive action of grit (usually coarse sand and pebbles) that birds pick up and swallow. Grit is not necessary to digesting the food but it appears to help. When added to the diets of chickens it increased their digestion of whole grains and seeds by 10% (Titus, 1949), and when swallowed by the chickens, it bypassed the food in the crop (*see* Crop) and went directly to the stomach.

BIRDS THAT USE GRIT. The muscular "grinding" gizzard is best developed in birds that eat plant parts—seeds, grains, leaves, plant roots and stems, grass, twigs, buds, etc. These are mostly the gallinaceous birds: quail, pheasants, turkeys, grouse, etc.; the seed-eating fringillids: finches, sparrows, etc. (*see* Finch Family); ducks and geese; some doves and pigeons (Farner, 1960); in all shorebirds, with possible exception of the painted snipes, the food is ground by particles of grit that birds ingest with their food (Tuck, 1972). Even the chuckwill's-widow, poor-will, and others of the Nightjar Family regularly swallow small stones, which, in their stomachs, apparently help grind up the hard shells of beetles which make up a large part of their diets. See Jenkinson and Mengel (1970) for details. Hummingbirds pick up and swallow sand. *See* Hummingbird Family.

Apparently birds can retain grit in the gizzard and withhold it from leaving the body with their food wastes. Chickens with access to grit, then denied it, still had some in the gizzard after 3 weeks (Browne, 1922), bobwhite quail after 5 months (Nestler, 1946). Even quail chicks will pick up grit during their first 24 hours after hatching, when their food is largely the fragments of small insects (Stoddard,

1931). *See* Hatching; Young and Their Care; Food and Feeding Habits.

CHOICE OF GRIT AND SUBSTITUTES. In Mich., Dalke (1938) reported that the gizzard stones in ring-necked pheasants were bits of quartz, granite, and chert, also very small pieces of limestone which quickly dissolved because of acid in the gizzard. Female pheasants ate more grit during spring and summer, which Dalke correlated with their physiological needs during egg-laying. *See* Eggs and Egg-laying.

In 1939, L. J. McCann reported, after studying the grit requirements of pheasants and other upland game birds, that the second function of grit was to supply them with needed minerals. According to Watmough (1948), nothing is more important in feeding budgerigars than grit, which not only helps grind seeds in the gizzard but also provides minerals for the birds, of which calcium, or lime, is most important. *See* discussion under Calcium. People who attract birds (*see* Bird-attracting) often add grit to the seed mixtures they put out for wild birds, especially when snow covers the natural supply. The usual amount is 5 lbs. of coarse sand or ground oyster or clam shells to each 100 lbs. of grain or feed.

If grit is unavailable, some birds will pick up hard seeds or the pits (stones) of wild fruit and use them as substitutes. Crows will swallow hard seeds for grit (Beer and Tydyman, 1942), and in Neb., Sharp and McClure (1945) reported that pheasants swallowed seeds of wild roses, poison ivy, prickly pear, Virginia creeper, chokecherry, and sand cherry, which appeared in their gizzards but not in their crops. The pheasants had retained the hard seeds as abrasives to help grind their preferred foods of weed seeds and wild fruit because of scarcity of grit, even of coarse sand in the hundreds of miles of Neb. sandhill country. Miscellaneous items in the pheasant gizzards were broken glass, pellets of lead shot, cinders, and coal.

Some remarkable objects, apparently picked up by wild birds to serve as grit, have been recovered from gizzards. In 1911, a local gold rush was started in w. Neb. when small nuggets were recovered from the gizzards of wild ducks shot there (McAtee, 1927). The largest of the nuggets was worth fifty cents, and set the entire community to prospecting. McAtee in his food-habits research once took two lumps of gold worth about a dollar from the stomach of a scaup duck killed in La., which the duck had probably picked up at some distant point during its southward migration. *See* Migration.

Meinertzhagen (1964a) claimed that bright-colored grit is preferred by birds and that the famous ruby mines in Burma originated with the discovery of a ruby in the stomach of a pheasant. He also reported that the type of grit in a migrating bird's gizzard can sometimes reveal the general area from which it came; whooper swans and pink-footed geese shot in Scotland had black lava grit in their gizzards that they had picked up on their nesting grounds in Iceland. *See* Nests and Nesting.

Birds, especially waterfowl—ducks, swans, and geese—while feeding in ponds and marshes often pick up lead pellets from shotgun shells fired during the hunting season. These often kill them from lead poisoning. *See* Lead Poisoning.

Most grebes have the unusual habit of eating their own feathers and of feeding them to their young. The ball of feathers is thought to aid digestion in more than one way (Simmons, 1964b): to protect the walls of the stomachs of grebes against piercing by sharp bones of fishes they eat, and possibly to plug the stomach outlet until the bones are dissolved before passing into the intestines. *See* Intestine; *also* Pyloric Stomach.

OTHER TYPES OF GIZZARDS. In carnivorous, or meat-eating, birds, the gizzard is thin-walled and baglike and is a storage place for indigestible teeth, claws, bones, scales, feathers, and other matter which is later coughed up in a pellet and spat out by hawks, owls, goatsuckers, gulls, terns, herons, swifts, grouse, and by songbirds that feed much on insects, many of which have hard, chitinous shells, or exoskeletons. *See* Pellet; Esophagus; Food and Feeding Habits.

The gizzards of omnivorous birds—crows and gulls, for example—that eat many kinds of foods, and most songbirds that eat insects, show a great variation in their development. Birds that eat fruit—for example, tropical green pigeons and fruit pigeons, toucans, some parrots, hornbills, and others (Barruel, 1954)—have reduced (smaller) gizzards, and a maximum of reduction in tropical fruit-eating tanagers, in which the gizzard is only an insignificant band in the esophagus between the proventriculus (glandular stomach) and the intestine (Farner, 1960). Sutton (1951b) noted that some tropical fruit-eating birds have evolved an almost straight, featureless alimentary tract through which incompletely digested berries pass somewhat continuously.

GLACIAL EPOCH
See Geological Time Scale.

GLAND
See oil gland under Skin Glands; *also* Endocrine Glands; Harderian Glands; Thymus Gland; and mouth glands under Mouth.

GLIDING
See Flight.

GLOGER'S RULE
C. W. L. Gloger, in a book, *The Variation of Birds under the Influence of Climate,* published in 1833, proposed an ecological rule (*see* Ecological Rules), since then known as Gloger's Rule, that the melanins (dark pigments) in the feathers of birds increase in warm, humid parts of its range, making the species darker; in dry or cool climates, however, the lighter reddish or yellow-brown pigments (phaeomelanins) prevail, producing a lighter-colored bird (Mayr, 1942). Some examples of birds that follow this rule and show color variations in synchrony to humidity and heat, or to dryness and heat, are the bobwhite quail, red-tailed hawk, screech owl, hairy woodpecker, horned lark, fox sparrow, and song sparrow (Van Tyne and Berger, 1959). *See* Col-

GLOGER'S RULE
The pigmentation of these two subspecies of the fox sparrow illustrates Gloger's Rule: the bird that inhabits the colder, more humid regions of the American northwest is dark brown; the eastern fox sparrow, living in a warmer climate, is a paler, reddish-brown (fox) color.

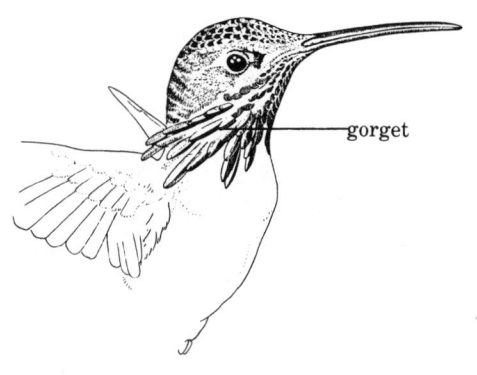

gorget

GORGET
The gorget of the male Costa's hummingbird is brilliant, iridescent purple and includes long feathers that the bird may spread in courtship or aggressive displays.

ors of Feathers; Color Phase; *also* geographic variation under Subspecies.

According to Mayr (1942), F. Frank demonstrated the validity of this rule by a microscopic analysis of the feather pigments of the black-capped chickadee (*see* in Titmouse Family). Mayr himself, and a co-worker, illustrated its effect on the subspecies of Australian warblers. There is a similar effect of climate on the coloration of some insect groups—certain wasps, beetles, and California butterflies, for example.

GLOTTIS
A slitlike opening in the floor of the pharynx, or rear of the mouth. The glottis is the entrance to the larynx and trachea (windpipe) of a bird. The glottis, closed in the act of swallowing (*see* Swallowing; Digestion), is surrounded by a series of cartilages that form the *larynx*. There are no vocal cords in the reduced larynx of birds. Sounds that issue from the mouth and throat of a bird are due to vibrations of membranes in the bird's syrinx (Walter and Sayles, 1949). *See* discussion of syrinx under Voice and Sound-making; *see also* Songs and Singing; Respiratory System.

GNATCATCHER
See in Warbler—Old World Warbler Family.

GOATSUCKER
See in Nightjar Family; *also* Caprimulgiformes; Folklore.

GOBBLER
Common name of a male turkey.

GOD BIRD
See Woodstar, Bahama, in Hummingbird Family.

GODWIT
See in Sandpiper Family.

GOLDENEYE
See in Duck Family.

GOLDFINCH
See in Finch Family.

GONADS
See Fertilization.

GONY
See Wandering albatross in Albatross Family.

GOONEY
or GOONEY BIRD. *See* under Albatross Family.

GOOSANDER
See Mergansers in Duck Family.

GOOSE
See in Duck Family.

GORGET
(GORE-jet). Dim. of "gorge," or throat; a throat patch in hummingbirds, composed of iridescent feather colors; it is variable in size and is sometimes small, equivalent perhaps to a circle ⅜ in. in diameter, and sometimes so large

that the iridescent patch runs well down the chest and around both sides of the neck. See Greenewalt (1960) for details of the structure of iridescent feathers in hummingbirds. *See also* Colors of Feathers.

Apparently the iridescent colors of male hummingbirds are rarely on their backs. In many species they are on the gorget, crown, belly, and tail and tail coverts. These are shown in the male's intimidation display (territorial-defense flights) and in courtship performances of the male hummingbird before the female. *See* discussion under Hummingbird Family; *see also* Courtship.

GOSHAWK
See in Hawk Family.

GOSLING
A young, not full-grown, goose. *See* introduction to Duck Family.

GOURDHEAD
Another name for the wood stork in Stork Family; the shape of its bare head resembles shape of a gourd (McAtee, 1955a).

GRACKLE
See in Troupial Family.

GRADUATED
Term used by ornithologists in reference to a particular outline or structure of the tail feathers of a bird. A graduated tail is one in which the middle feathers are longest; the others (successively outward) are abruptly shorter (Van Tyne and Berger, 1959)—*see* Magpie in Crow Family, for example. *See also* Tail.

GRAM
A unit of weight in the metric system. Bird weights are usually given in grams in scientific reports, papers, and books; in ounces or pounds in popular works. There are 28.3495 grams (gr.) in each ounce avoirdupois; 453.592 grams in a pound.

GRAMNIVOROUS
Said of a bird that eats grass. The snow goose, white-fronted goose, Canada goose, Ross's goose, black duck, mallard, and pintail include some grasses in their food habits; also, the Franklin's gull eats some grass. Grasses they eat are largely the young plants of wheat, barley, oats (cultivated and wild), and rice (Martin *et al.*, 1951). Geese graze or crop grass with their lamellate bills. *See* Lamellate; *also* Anseriformes and under Food and Feeding Habits.

GRANDRY'S CORPUSCLES
See Touch.

GRANIVOROUS
Said of a bird that eats seeds. Although few birds feed exclusively on tree and weed seeds or the kernels of commercial grain crops—corn, wheat, etc.—some are predominantly seed-eaters through much of the year. The fringillids (members of the Finch Family) are largely seed-eaters—for example, cardinals, some of the grosbeaks, buntings, goldfinches,

and other finches, redpolls, crossbills, pine siskins, towhees, sparrows, longspurs, and snow buntings. Some of the icterids—blackbirds, bobolinks, meadowlarks, and cowbirds—are seed-eaters, also the horned lark, English, or house, sparrow, bobwhite quail, pheasants, and other gallinaceous birds. *See* Food and Feeding Habits and under each bird biography.

GRASS-BIRD
See Sandpiper, Baird's, in Sandpiper Family.

GRASSLAND
One of nine major biotic communities of plants and animals in N. America north of Mexico used in mapping the ecological distribution of birds. *See* Distribution. The grassland is primarily of the interior plains or prairies from the forested bottomlands and bluffs along the Mississippi R. and its tributaries west to the Rocky Mtns. and from s.-c. Tex. north into Canada. Some dominant grasses in the eastern part, or the "tall grass" country, are bluestem *(Andropogon)*, Indian grass *(Sorghastrum)*, and switch grass *(Panicum virgatum)*. Dominant grasses of the western part of the grassland on the Great Plains are the "short-grass" type—largely buffalo grass *(Buchloë)* and grama grass *(Bouteloua)*. Some of the typical birds of the grassland are: Swainson's hawk, ferruginous hawk, greater prairie chicken, sharptailed grouse, long-billed curlew, burrowing owl, western meadowlark, lark bunting, and grasshopper sparrow. Birds that are typical in the breeding season in the northern part of the grassland community are: Sprague's pipit, Baird's sparrow, McCown's longspur, and chestnut-collared longspur.

GRASSQUIT
See in Finch Family.

GRAY-BACK
See Dowitcher, short-billed, in Sandpiper Family.

GREASE BIRD
See Jay, gray, in Crow Family.

GREAT BASIN
Area of about 210,000 sq. mi.; arid, elevated region between Sierra Nevadas on west and Wasatch Range or Colorado Plateau of Idaho and Utah on east; Columbia Plateau on north, Rockies on northeast, and Mojave Desert on south; includes most of Nev., parts of Utah, Calif., Idaho, Wyo., and Ore.; includes Great Salt Lake Desert, Carson Sink, Mojave Desert, and Death Valley; rain is sporadic and limited; its rivers have no drainage to ocean; main drainage center is Great Salt Lake *(New Columbia Encyclopedia,* 1975).

GREAT-HEAD
See Goldeneye, common, in Duck Family.

GREAT PLAINS
The smooth, treeless, grassy plains of c. U.S. and c. Canada, extending south from Mackenzie R. delta, in general, through Prairie Provinces of s. Canada to e. Wyo. and Dakotas south to Tex.; it is east of Great Basin (*see* Great Basin); is region traversed by broad, shallow valleys of rivers such as the Missouri, Platte, and Arkansas that rise in Rocky Mtns.; in some parts, especially nw. Neb., has sand hills, buttes, and badlands, (*Webster's Geographical Dictionary,* 1949; *New Columbia Encyclopedia,* 1975).

GREBE FAMILY
Podicipedidae (pod-ih-sih-PED-ih-dee); *see* Podicipediformes. Includes only birds called grebes and dabchicks, a worldwide group of 20 species; 6 species in N. America; they have no known relatives but were once thought related to loons. Grebes are diving and swimming birds that at first glance resemble small ducks, but their slender, pointed bills, never flat, have toothlike or sawlike edges as in ducks. Like coots and phalaropes, unrelated to grebes, they have lobed toes with partial webbing (*see* Feet and Legs and Swimming and Diving), and are said to be one of the most perfectly adapted to water of all birds. Grebes dive and swim rapidly below the surface as they chase aquatic insects and small fishes; they are rather weak fliers, although many are migratory, and at least one species is flightless (*see* Podicipediformes). Albinism is rare (Weller, 1959a).

Grebes do not usually dive as deeply as loons —about 20 ft. below the surface—and usually do not stay underwater as long—ordinarily about 30 seconds while feeding, if undisturbed, although Forbush (1925–29) cites several records of red-necked grebes remaining underwater for 55 seconds. (*See,* however, remarkable performances of horned grebe in its biography.) When apprehensive the pied-billed grebe sinks slowly, expelling air from its body and feathers to lower its specific gravity, then swimming with only the head above water; this occurs rarely in other grebes; when really alarmed, grebes dive so swiftly they have been given the names hell-diver and water witch. A truly frightened bird may swim underwater until it reaches water plants in the shallows at the edges of the pond or lake, and there rest underwater with only its bill and eyes above the surface.

Grebes not only feed, sleep, and court on water but carry their downy chicks about pick-a-back. When alarmed the adults may dive with the young riding on their backs (*see* Young and Their Care). The chicks do not dive well until they are several weeks old and both parents share in carrying them about and in feeding them. Both adults share in nest building, which is a part of a courtship that is usually elaborate and by both sexes.

Grebes have soft, thick, lustrous plumage; the breast feathers were once used in the millinery trade to decorate women's hats, a practice long ago discontinued when grebes were protected by law. Henderson (1933) reported that from 1900 to 1908, in twenty to thirty camps, men about the lakes of s. Ore. were killing and skinning grebes for the feather market, which led President Theodore Roosevelt to set aside Malheur and Klamath lakes as bird reservations. Both sexes of grebes are alike in plumage, but may differ in size.

The incubation periods of grebes are 20–30 days (Austin, 1961) and both sexes incubate

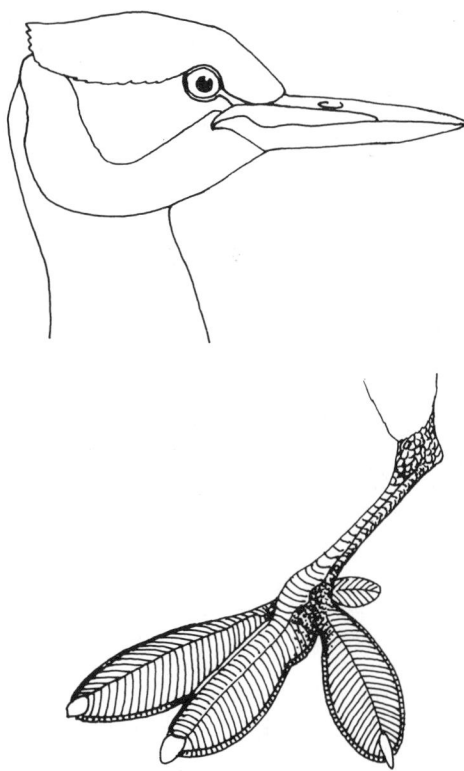

GREBE FAMILY

GREBE FAMILY
In flight, grebes resemble small ducks but have very short tail feathers and steer by extending their feet behind them. Grebes fly with a dip in their slender necks.

about equally (Kendeigh, 1952b). *See* Incubation. Grebes are not noisy birds, but around the nesting marsh one may hear them utter piercing wails, chuckles, croaks, trills, squeaks, and whinnies. Grebes have the singular or possibly unique habit among birds of eating their own body feathers. Even the chicks a few days old have wads of their parents' feathers in their stomachs.

Although relatively weak fliers, grebes that migrate southward from northern nesting grounds fly long distances overland; others that nest farther south fly from inland lakes and ponds to the seacoasts to winter on salt water. Migration is largely at night, especially by moonlight; by day grebes travel close to shore, swimming as they go (Simmons, 1964b).

Grebes have scarcely any tail, with no stiff tail feathers (all have a dip in the neck when flying; mergansers and other ducks fly with neck straight). When they take off from water, they must have a running start of some distance before they are airborne, and when on land, they are clumsy and move with difficulty.

Occasionally grebes are caught on freshwater lakes that freeze late in fall or early winter and many of them starve before they can fly to open waters for their foods of small fishes, water insects, crustaceans, and other small animal life.

One rainy night near Lumberton, N.C., a flock of pied-billed grebes apparently mistook a wet, shining highway for a stream and alighted. Unable to take off from the road, they were killed in great numbers by the heavy automobile traffic (Chamberlain, 1955).

Black-necked grebe. *See* Eared grebe.

Eared grebe, *Podiceps nigricollis* (POD-ih-ceps nig-rih-COL-liss); genus name: from Gr. *pous, podos,* foot, and Lat. *caput,* head (Coble, 1954) (*see* discussion of meaning under Podicipediformes); species name: from Lat. *niger,* dark, or black, and *collum,* neck (called black-necked grebe in British Isles). (Color ill., page 407.) Lives in sw. and w. U.S., also in Eurasia, Africa, and n. S. America; 12½–13½ in long; wingspread 22½ in.; in summer with crested black head, *black neck,* and dark back, and two golden ear tufts; slender black bill appears upturned at tip (Peterson, 1961); eyes scarlet, thin silvery line around pupils; flanks rusty with white patches showing when wings spread; in winter, black above, white to gray below; dark feathers of head and neck broader and less sharply set off, usually a whitish patch just back of each ear; seldom seen in flight except in migration; prefers to escape danger by diving or by merely swimming away, but can rise easily from water and flies swiftly; in courtship utters mellow *poo-eee-chk,* also has rasping, shrill calls; in fall, some migrate in flocks at night southwestward to salt water to winter; others remain inland on large open fresh water in loose flocks in winter; visit salt lakes (e.g., Mono Lake, Calif.) in great number on migration.

Feeding Habits: Dives under, or takes from surface of water, aquatic insects and their larvae, which is bulk of food—damselflies, drag-

onflies, grasshoppers, mayflies; water boatmen (1,300 at one meal); caddis flies, moths, butterflies, beetles, flies, especially midges; also some small fishes, eggs of leeches, crustaceans, mollusks, spiders, mites, centipedes.

Nest: Built in marshy lake shallows, less often on smaller waters, usually by female, in densely populated colonies or sometimes singly, often not concealed; poorly built and floating, contains cattail stalks, rushes, etc. (Bent, 1919).

Eggs: Late Apr. to well into June; 3–9, usually 3–4, rarely 1–6 (Palmer, 1962), dull blue-white or green-white.

Incubation: By both sexes, in turn, 20½–21½ days; age when young first fly unknown; chicks often ride on backs of swimming adults.

Other Names: American eared grebe; black-necked grebe; eared diver.

Albinism: Weller (1959a) reported that Ken Stott saw a white eared grebe in the wild in Calif., but no details whether a partial or complete albino; a partial albino reported from Europe.

Weights: Adults to about 14 oz. (Palmer, 1962).

Range: Nests from c. B.C., nw. Alta., c. Sask., s. Man., c. Minn., nw. Iowa, and to n. Neb., south to s. Tex., n. N.M., c. Ariz., s. Nev., and n. Baja Calif. and Mexico; winters from s. B.C. to n. S. America; sometimes winters in Nev., Utah, N.M., s. Tex.; seen in Wisc. in migration; casual in Miss., Mo., Kans., Ill., Ind., Ohio, Ont., and Tenn.; seen rarely, but regularly, off Atlantic coast, usually in winter and spring, from Mass. south to Long Is., N.Y., and s. N.J.; also very rarely off coast of Va., N.C., and south to s.-c. Fla. (Polk County) and off Pinellas County, in Gulf of Mexico. The eared grebe also nests and winters in Europe, Asia, to c. Africa and in Colombia, S. America.

Holboell's grebe. *See* Red-necked grebe.

Horned grebe, *Podiceps auritus* (POD-ih-seps aw-REE-tus); genus name: *see* Eared grebe; species name: Lat., eared, in allusion to its "horns," or tufts of ear feathers. (Color ill., page 408.) In N. America, mostly in nw. N. America; in winter, along Pacific coast; also along Atlantic coast from Nova Scotia to s. Fla.; 12½–15¼ in. long; wingspread 24 in.; small, ducklike, with small, *straight* black bill tipped with white in summer; in nesting plumage, head is black with conspicuous brown-yellow puffy earlike tufts along side of face which extend from brilliant scarlet eyes to back of neck; fore neck and flanks are reddish; rides high in water; in winter, mostly dark above, white below, with black cap contrasting with *clear white cheeks* and neck; in nesting season, utters weird, loud striking series of croaks and chattering notes followed by several prolonged shrieks (Bent, 1919); also sharp *keark, keark,* or *yark, yark;* flies directly, as do all grebes; when on wing resembles a miniature loon, its neck and legs stretched out to full extent, wings with white patch vibrating very rapidly; in migration usually travels singly or in small flocks.

Feeding Habits: Usually feeds in waters 5–25 ft. deep, eats many small fishes, for which it

dives (*see* Swimming and Diving); can stay under for 1¼–3 minutes, moving 400–500 ft. below surface in one dive (Bent, 1919); eats almost entirely animal food (about 99%); fishes are mostly small ones: carp, darters, anchovies, silversides, perch, gizzard shad, sculpins, sticklebacks, squawfishes; also eats crayfishes, amphipods, prawns, sand shrimps, opossum shrimps; aquatic insects such as water boatmen, back swimmers, water striders, water bugs, diving beetles, water scavenger beetles, larvae of caddis flies, gnats, and mayflies, also land insects such as stinkbugs, ants, wood-boring beetles, weevils, etc.; feathers about 55% of contents of some stomachs (Palmer, 1962); also eats small frogs and tadpoles, salamanders, and leeches.

Nest: Is least wary of all small grebes, usually a solitary nester, sometimes in loose colonies of 4–6 pairs; in quiet waters of small ponds, sloughs, backwaters of rivers, marshes; a mass of plants anchored to reeds or bushes growing in water, or to bottom, usually in shallows but in waters up to several feet deep; built by both sexes, forms a floating nest partly submerged, sometimes not well concealed.

Eggs: Usually Apr.–June; replacement clutches into Aug.; 3–6, usually 4–5, up to 10 in joint laying; dull blue-white to olive-white.

Incubation: By both parents, 24–25 days for individual eggs laid at 2-day intervals; chicks can swim and dive feebly at hatching; fed by both parents, ride on backs and under wings of adults; age at first flight unknown; apparently one brood a year (Palmer, 1962).

Other Names: Devil-diver; dipper; hell-diver; pink-eyed diver; Slavonian grebe (in British Isles); water witch.

Albinism: In Europe, a partial albino reported; there is also one in bird collections of the Denver Museum of Natural History, according to Weller (1959b).

Weights: In spring, males (4), 432, 436, 479, and 485 gr., or 15–17 oz.; maximum to about 1 lb. 2 oz. (Palmer, 1962).

Range: In summer nests on freshwater ponds, marshes with open water, and sheltered parts of lakes and streams, from c. Alaska, n. Yuk., n. Mack., and n. Man. south to s. B.C., probably Nev., e. Idaho, n. S.D., n. Neb., ne. Iowa, and c. and s. Wisc., sporadic in s. Ont., nw. N.Y., sw. N.B., and Gulf of St. Lawrence; seen in summer to e. Me., Mass., Conn., Ill., Mich., and nw. Ont.; nested on Malheur Refuge, Ore., in 1958 (Palmer, 1962); also nests and winters in Europe and Asia; in N. America, winters from Aleutians and s. Alaska along Pacific coast to s. Calif., and along Atlantic coast from Nova Scotia to s. Fla., less commonly from Great Lakes to s. Tex. and N.M., casual in s. Greenland, Newfoundland, Bermuda, Baja Calif., Colo., and Kans.

Least grebe, *Podiceps dominicus* (POD-ih-seps dom-IN-ih-cus); genus name: *see* Eared grebe; species name: Lat., of Santo Domingo, early name of island of Hispaniola, West Indies, where type specimen collected (*see* Type Specimen). (Color ill., page 409.) Smallest grebe, only in W. Hemisphere; in N. America, in s. Tex.; casual in s. Ariz. and s. Calif.; 9–10½ in. long; wingspread 14 in.; small size, *short* neck, and black, straight, slim, pointed, white-tipped bill of this southern border species is distinctive (pied-billed grebe has shorter, chickenlike bill); male can be distinguished from female by heavier, thicker-appearing head and neck and particularly by longer bill; brilliant orange- to gold-colored eyes of both sexes, observable from some distance, is good field mark (Palmer, 1962); in winter, throat is whitish and lacks black contrasting crown; calls with loud trumpetlike *clang* note; trills most frequent call. See Palmer (1962) and Storer (1976).

Feeding Habits: Dives for, or takes from surface of water, largely aquatic beetles and water bugs: predacious diving beetles, water scavenger beetles, crawling water beetles, giant water bugs, water boatmen, back swimmers, also water scorpions, creeping water bugs, chinch bugs, and nymphs of dragonflies and damselflies; feathers in stomachs 6–7% of food volume in Tex. birds (Palmer, 1962); also eats algae, crayfishes, and other crustaceans. See Storer (1976).

Nest: Built by both sexes, make little use of protective cover; build nest of reeds, decayed plants, and mud on inland waters of ponds, lakes, quiet reaches of other waterways, usually anchored to emergent water plants in water 1½–5 or more ft. deep. Males defending territories (35–40 ft. around nest) regularly attack ducks and other least grebes and water turtles.

Eggs: In tropics, every month of year if weather favorable; in s. Tex., Apr.–Aug.; 2–7, usually 4–6, nearly white, pale green or bluish, are soon stained buff by activities of incubating birds.

Incubation: 21 days, by both sexes, in turn; begins with laying of first egg; incubation at night usually by female; both parents regularly carry the young on their backs; chicks can swim and dive almost from hatching, but parents carry them for 3–4 days; age when first fly unknown. Same nest used for successive three to four broods a season.

Other Name: Mexican grebe.

Weights: About 4–5 oz. (Palmer, 1962); males (4), 101.8–136.6 gr., or 3½–4⅞ oz.; females (4), 106.5–127.7 gr., or 3¾–4½ oz.

Range: Lives in or about any body of fresh water, but prefers small intermittent ponds (in Tex.) and roadside ditches; resident from s. Tex., casually s. Ariz., c. Baja Calif. (no recent records, however, Palmer, 1962), West Indies, and southward through Mexico, tropical S. America to n. Argentina; accidental in La.; first sight record in Fla. in 1970 (Robertson, 1971).

Mexican grebe. *See* Least grebe.

Pied-billed grebe, *Podilymbus podiceps* (pod-ih-LIM-bus POD-ih-seps); genus name: from Lat. *podi(ceps),* an abbreviation of *podicipes,* rump foot, and Gr. *(ko)lymbos,* diver (Coues, 1882); species name: *see* Eared grebe. (Color ill., page 409.) The most widespread of American grebes; nests across Canada from B.C. east to Maritime Provinces and south throughout U.S., in suitable habitat, to temperate S. America; the common "hell-diver" of e. U.S. on any sluggish stream or pond and in

marshes; usually rare on salt water; 12–15 in. long; wingspread about 23 in.; small, stocky, short-necked, distinguished by short, blunt bill; in summer, bill encircled by broad black band; upper part of bill downcurved *("chicken-billed"),* is brownest grebe in general, and only one that does not show a sharply defined white wing patch in flight; has white undertail coverts; in winter, no black on throat, chin, and bill; rarely flies, usually escapes by diving with short leap forward or slowly submerges; usually silent except in nesting season, when utters loud, cuckoolike call, *cuck, cuck, cuck, cow-cow-cow, cow-ah-cow-ah,* and other notes (see Bent, 1919); usually the least gregarious (or most solitary) of all N. American grebes, occasionally in close-massed flocks on lakes in migration; usually first of grebes to arrive in spring on northern inland waters, one of last to leave in fall; sometimes in spectacular flights in Sept. and Oct.; in Calif. may reach 20,000 in Salton Sea in Nov.

Feeding Habits: At times one of shyest of the grebes, in winter occasionally dives for shrimps in saltwater bays and estuaries but more often on unfrozen freshwater ponds and in marshes; main food in one study was fishes (24%); crayfishes (a crustacean) (27%); insects (43%); some of fishes were carp, catfishes, eels, roach, sticklebacks, sculpins, silversides, top minnows; insects: nymphs of dragonflies, and damselflies, back swimmers, water boatmen, diving beetles, wasps, bees, ants; feathers about 52% of stomach contents (Palmer, 1962); also eats snails, spiders, frogs, and tadpoles, some seeds and soft parts of aquatic plants (Bent, 1919).

Nest: Built by both sexes, of flags, rushes, sedges, algae, and occasionally mud, entire structure usually attached to grasses, reeds, or bushes growing in water; takes 3–7 days to build (Palmer, 1962); usually in shallows but sometimes on water several feet deep, usually well concealed.

Eggs: Usually early Apr. into late May; in Tex., Mar. to Sept.; 2–10, usually 4–7, initially blue-white or green-white but soon stained brown, usually laid one a day as in other grebes; eggs covered by incubating bird before it leaves nest.

Incubation: Mostly by female, 23 days, but variable (Palmer, 1962); streaked and spotted chicks can swim but crawl up on back of parent or cling to parent's tail and sometimes cling to each other; parents sometimes feed chicks while they ride on parents' backs, and dive with chicks aboard, return to nest frequently with young; two broods a year fairly common.

Other Names: American dabchick; Carolina grebe; dabchick; devil-diver; dive-dapper; dipper; hell-diver; pied-billed dabchick; thick-billed grebe; water witch.

Albinism: Weller (1959a) reported a white pied-billed grebe seen in Colo., no details as to whether a complete or partial albino.

Weights: A male killed at TV tower in Kans., in fall, 394.8 gr., or 14 oz.; females (2), 289.7 and 332.5 gr., or 10 and 11¾ oz.; all fat (Tordoff and Mengel, 1956); range of weights, 9–19 oz. (Palmer, 1962).

Range: Nests mainly along ponds with much emergent water plants and along open waters

in marshes, shores of inlets and bays, from Vancouver Is. and c. B.C., s. Mack., n.-c. Alta., east to c. Sask., n. Man., nw. Ont., s. Que., c. N.B., and Nova Scotia south throughout U.S. where suitable habitat to s. Baja Calif. to S. America, and to Tex., La., and s. Fla.; winters from Vancouver Is. and s. B.C., to c. Ariz. (rarely), Utah, and c. Tex., east and north to line of winter ice in Tenn. and lower Potomac R., rarely to N.Y., s. Ont.; casually in Conn., Mass., and N.B., south to s. Baja Calif., w. Panama, Cuba, and Grenada.

Red-necked grebe, *Podiceps grisegena* (POD-ih-seps gris-eh-JEE-nah); genus name: *see* Eared grebe; species name: from Lat. *griseus,* gray, and *gena,* cheek; formerly called Holboell's grebe (for Carl Peter Holboell, Danish naturalist and governor of South Greenland in 1820s) when named in 1853, but later determined to be an e. Asiatic and N. American subspecies of the red-necked grebe. (Color ill., page 408.) Summers on inland lakes, marshes, and ponds of Alaska, Canada, and n. U.S.; winters along Atlantic and Pacific coasts; second-largest grebe in N. America (western grebe is largest); red-necked is much larger than other grebes in e. U.S.; sexes outwardly similar; 17–22 in. long; wingspread 30–32 in.; in breeding plumage, body, gray above, white below; top of head black, cheeks nearly white, neck dark reddish; bill straight and black, yellowish at base; feather tufts on head fairly prominent; eyes dark brown (Palmer, 1962); in winter, sides of head and throat white; neck and body grayish; carries head level like loon but neck thinner; can be distinguished from loons in flight by *white wing patch, front and rear edges of each wing;* from eared, horned, and western grebes by its stocky build and slightly heavier bill (Robbins *et al.,* 1966); usually silent but in spring migration and in summer, both sexes utter courtship notes that begin with series of loonlike wailings, *ah-ooo, ah-ooo, ah-ooo, ah-ah-ah-ah,* sometimes ends with more staccato chattering trill, heard any time of day or night, often sounds like whinnying of horses; migrates individually or in loose associations, inland by night, coastally, at least partly, by day; in winter often alone, just beyond breakers, on ocean.

Feeding Habits: Dives below surface to feed on or near bottom; catches in bill small fishes: sticklebacks, herring, pilchard, sculpins, top minnows, lake shiners, eels, but fishes are small part of diet in marshes and lakes, where it eats aquatic insects: adults and nymphs of dragonflies and damselflies, water boatmen, whirligig beetles, etc., also land insects: flies, wasps, ants, bees, beetles, etc., and crustaceans: shrimps, prawns, crayfishes, also mollusks, aquatic worms, tadpoles, salamander eggs, and some vegetable matter; also feathers in stomach.

Nest: One of shyest of water birds around nest; usually a solitary nester but sometimes in loose colonies; each pair requires about 10 acres of marsh and pond in woodland, muskeg, on prairie or tundra; one brood, possibly two, rarely (Palmer, 1962); built of marsh grasses, reeds, rushes, and inconspicuous mass usually floating on water 2–3 ft. deep, anchored to upright plants in shallows or to bushes, sometimes built on muskrat house.

Eggs: Early May into June; usually 3–6 (larger clutches of up to 8 laid by more than one female —Palmer, 1962)—*see* Dump Nest. Eggs unmarked, blue-white, soon nest-stained.

Incubation: By both sexes (both have incubation patch), in turn, 22–23 days; downy chicks attended by both parents, have boldly striped heads and necks; parents feed them adult feathers; feed them insect larvae first week after hatching, thereafter small fishes; and sometimes feed chicks while carrying them on back; young still have not flown 72 days after hatching; age at first flight unknown (Palmer, 1962).

Other Names: American red-necked grebe; Holboell's diver; Holboell's grebe.

Accidents: When occasionally winter on large inland lakes into Nov. and Dec., are not uncommonly caught by sudden freeze; without food, starve; are sometimes driven ashore by storms, caught in fishermen's nets.

Albinism: Weller (1959a) reported seeing two juveniles, almost fully grown, accompanied by a normally colored adult; he shot one and found it to be an incomplete albino with brown irises, bill and feet yellow, feathers white; another reported in Europe.

Weights: To about 3 lbs.; summer, Alaska, males (4) 1,002—1,270 gr., female (1), 945 gr., or from about 2 lbs. to 2 lbs. 13 oz.

Range: Nests in watery marshes and marshy lakes from nw. Alaska, c. Yuk. east to nw. Ont., south to ne. Wash., n. Idaho, n. Mont., the Dakotas, and s. Minn., sporadic in s.-c. Wisc., s. Ont., s. Que., and N.H.; has bred at Upper Klamath Lake, Ore., in recent years (Palmer, 1962); winters mainly on salt water along both Pacific and Atlantic coasts, from Pribilof and Aleutian Is., se. Alaska, to c. Calif.; from Maritime Provinces, Canada, south to c. Fla.; also winters more rarely from Great Lakes region inland, south to w. Tenn.; La. had single record; in migration at many inland places in N. America and on James Bay, Canada. Also nests and winters in e. Asia.

San Domingo grebe. *See* Least grebe.

Slavonian grebe. *See* Horned grebe.

Swan grebe. *See* Western grebe.

Thick-billed grebe. *See* Pied-billed grebe.

Western grebe, *Aechmophorus occidentalis* (eek-MOF-oh-rus ock-sih-den-TAY-lis); genus name: from Gr. *aichme,* a spear, and *phoros,* bearing, a "spear-bearer," in reference to sharp pointed bill (Jaeger, 1955); species name: Lat., western. (Color ill., page 408.) Largest N. American grebe, common in w. U.S.; east to Man., Minn.; nests on inland fresh waters; sexes outwardly alike but males larger with relatively larger bills; in this species, sexes differ in bill shape as in bill size; 22–29 in. long; wingspread 30–40 in.; large black-and-white grebe with *long, slender, swanlike neck,* the *slightly upturned* pale yellow bill is much longer and more needlelike than that of other

N. American grebes; back, crown, and back of neck *black;* white below; white cheeks and pure-white neck in front; scarlet eyes; a single white patch in each wing; in any plumage appears as an *all-black-and-white bird* (Peterson, 1947); in flight, drooping head, neck, and feet give broken-back appearance; has a dark and light color phase; preferential mating by dark for dark birds, light for light (see Storer, 1965); utters loud rasping whistle, *c-r-r-ee-er-r-ee,* 1–3 syllables; can be heard when bird is beyond sight of unaided vision; mates apparently use calls often when far apart, perhaps as "location" calls; migration primarily east-west; migrates at night apparently in flocks, in part by day along Pacific coast; in fall first arrivals reach salt water in early Sept.; in mid-Oct., flocks of 1,500 or more may assemble off Vancouver Is., B.C.; in spring, start east in Mar.; leave ocean to fly inland later part of Apr.; noted on nesting grounds in spectacular courtship displays, including the "rushing" display, in which pair moves rapidly across the water side by side, moving feet so rapidly that the erect bodies are completely out of water; necks arched and bill pointed upward during display (Palmer, 1962).

Feeding Habits: On ocean or on inland lakes, eats more fishes than any other grebe, more along coast than interior: carp, lake mullet, chubs, catfishes, perch, bluegills, smelts, herring; also eats mollusks, crabs, marine worms, salamanders, grasshoppers, mayflies, water boatmen, larvae of gnats, ground beetles, water beetles; and stomachs usually contain feathers; also some small stones reported (Palmer, 1962). *See* Pyloric Stomach; Gizzard.

Nest: In colonies of hundreds or even thousands of pairs on some lakes, nests closely spaced, only immediate territory around nest defended by pair; in fairly extensive areas of open water bordered by tules or rushes; built by male and female, of dry or sodden (and some green) plants, sometimes in shallow water, and anchored to, or built up on, submerged roots of bulrushes or other plants, with shallow depression in middle for eggs.

Eggs: Mid-May into June; usually 3–4, pale blue-green or buff, when fresh; may be up to 16 when more than one female lays in nest. *See* Dump Nest; Eggs and Egg-Laying.

Incubation: Both sexes have incubation patch and take turns incubating; female re-lays when nests are destroyed; may or may not cover eggs when leaving nest; incubation period about 23 days (Bent, 1919); soon after hatching, downy gray chicks *(without stripes)* climb among feathers of parents' back; when hatched on dry land, chicks carried overland to water under wings; with young on back, parents dive below surface; chicks begin eating feathers when 3 days old; one swallowed 238, another 331; age at which young first fly or when independent of adults not known (Palmer, 1962).

Other Names: Western dabchick; swan grebe; swan-necked grebe.

Albinism: Apparently the only example of a complete albino grebe—one in collections of Manitoba Natural History Museum—had been killed by hunter; had pink eyes and cream-colored bill and feet (Weller, 1959a).

Weights: From Puget Sound, Wash., 13 in winter ranged from about 1 lb. 12 oz. (a very lean male) to 4 lbs.; average weight, 3 lbs. 4 oz. (Palmer, 1962).

Range: Nests inland from s.-c. B.C., s.-c. Sask., and s.-c. Man., to c. (rarely s.) Calif., w. Nev., n. Utah, w.-c. Wyo., n. N.D., sw. Colo., w. Neb., S.D., sw. Minn.; also nests south to c. Mexico, mostly in mountains; casual in summer from Alaska to Baja Calif.; winters along Pacific coast on salt water and sometimes on inland waters from se. Alaska and B.C. to Baja Calif.; inland locally to Nev., south to Mexico; casual in Yuk., N.M., e. Neb., e. Kans., Okla., Tex., e. Minn., Iowa, Wisc., Ill., Mich., Ind., Ohio, w. Pa., s. Ont., and S.C.; has also wandered east to Mass. and south along Atlantic and Gulf coasts to Tampa Bay, Fla. (Palmer, 1962), and La. and Tex.

GREENBACK
See Plover, American golden, in Plover Family.

GREENHEAD
See Mallard in Duck Family.

GREENLET
Old name for some N. American vireos.

GREENSHANK
See in Sandpiper Family.

GREGARIOUS
Term for those birds that habitually live in flocks or move about in flocks (Van Tyne and Berger, 1959). John T. Emlen, Jr. (1952), in discussing the formation of flocks by birds of the same species (homogeneous flocks), pointed out that flocking, or gregariousness, is little understood despite its conspicuousness and widespread occurrence. Large numbers of a single species—chimney swifts, crows, and starlings —flock together when sleeping, and grackles, red-winged blackbirds, cowbirds, and robins or different species of swallows often gather in very large numbers in mixed (heterogeneous) flocks when roosting. *See* Flocks and Flocking; Roosting; *also* Behavior.

GRIN LINE
Line along the lower mandible—of the trumpeter swan, for example—that gives the bird the appearance of smiling, or of "grinning." *See* Swan in Duck Family.

GRINNELL, JOSEPH
(1877–1939). For 30 years (1908–38) director of the Museum of Vertebrate Zoology, University of California; for 33 years (1906–39), editor of *The Condor,* official publication of the Cooper Ornithological Society; a fellow and past president, American Ornithologists' Union. According to Linsdale (1942), Grinnell was one of the foremost amateur ornithologists of his time in America; he was a tireless field worker, and one of his major accomplishments was his 40 years of study of California birds; he published monographs on the biology of six areas in California and several books, of which *Animal Life in the Yosemite* was the most widely read. See also Palmer (1928).

GRIT

See Gizzard; *also* Digestion; Calcium; Bird-attracting.

GROSBEAK

See in Finch Family.

GROUND-CHAT

See in Warbler—American Wood Warbler Family.

GROUSE FAMILY

Tetraonidae (tet-rah-ON-ih-dee); from Gr. *tetraon*, a grouse; according to some authorities, origin of the name *grouse* is probably from the Fr. *greoche*, *greiche*, or *griais*, meaning a spotted bird. Chickenlike birds, circumpolar; live in N. Hemisphere above about 26° N. Lat.; of 18 species distributed over n. Europe, Asia, and N. America, 10 live in the New World. Of the 10 N. American species, only 2, the rock ptarmigan and willow ptarmigan, also live in the Old World (Sutton, 1965).

Members of the Grouse Family in N. America include 5 species called grouse, 3 called ptarmigans, and 2, prairie chickens. Most live much of their lives on the ground, although some are partly tree-dwelling; are adapted to many environments—forests, prairies, tundra, brushlands, etc. Some others around the world include the red grouse of the moors and peat bogs of the British Isles; the black grouse of n. Europe; another, closely related to it, in Eurasia; the hazel grouse of Europe; the sharp-winged grouse of Siberia; and the turkey-sized 35-in.-long, 8–14-lb. capercaillie of the coniferous forests of n. Europe, largest member of the Grouse Family. See details in Austin (1961); Gilliard (1958); and Hamerstrom and Hamerstrom (1964).

All members of the Grouse Family are fowllike birds with short, curved, strong bills and short, rounded wings; flight is strong and rapid but relatively short. Among N. American species, weight is from about ¾ lb. in the 12–13-in.-long white-tailed ptarmigan to a maximum of some 6–7 lbs. in the 30-in.-long male sage grouse (Johnsgard, 1973).

Grouse, prairie chickens, and ptarmigans differ from other gallinaceous birds such as pheasants, quails, and turkeys (*see* Galliformes) in having the nostrils hidden by feathers. The short hind toe (hallux) is somewhat higher (elevated) than the three front toes and the legs are feathered wholly or in part in most species; also the legs have no spurs. Members of the Grouse Family grow "snowshoes" in fall and early winter, an adaptation to their northern environment. In ptarmigans these are a dense mat of stiff feathers on the toes, and on other grouse, a row of pectinations 2–3 mm. long on each side of the toes. The more southerly Attwater's (a subspecies of the greater prairie chicken) and the lesser prairie chicken have only slightly developed snowshoes or none.

Some grouse move only short distances from summering to wintering places, others farther and are semi-migratory (see Hamerstrom and Hamerstrom, 1964). Males of some species of the Grouse Family are noted for their spectacular social gatherings and their courtship displays and calls (*see* Arena Bird); others such as the spruce grouse and the ruffed grouse are solitary (the ruffed grouse is noted especially for its courtship drumming). Some members of family have bare areas on the sides of the neck that are distensible due to inflation of esophagus during display, and erectile feathers on the head, some on the sides of the neck, and a patch of brightly colored bare skin (comb) over each eye. The sexes may be outwardly alike in their colors and color patterns, or different. Males molt from winter to summer plumage later than females. *See* Sexual Dimorphism. Males are usually larger than females; most males are polygamous, but ptarmigans are relatively monogamous (Johnsgard, 1973). *See* Sexual Relationships. Some grouse are extraordinarily tame in the presence of man (for example, the spruce grouse) and some are individually aggressive, or fearless (ruffed grouse)—*see* Tameness. Adult grouse are primarily grazers and browsers, although many eat waste grains and some fruit and insects.

Prairie chickens of two species—the greater and lesser prairie chickens—are native to the western plains or midcontinental grasslands of N. America. The greater prairie chicken, now uncommon and local, was the common one over the larger area; the rare Attwater's, a subspecies related to the greater prairie chicken, is now limited to s. Tex. Both are on the Threatened Wildlife List (Office of Endangered Species, 1973). The eastern form of the greater prairie chicken, the extinct heath hen, was the nominate subspecies (first named) of the group that includes the greater prairie chicken and Attwater's prairie chicken.

The still-existing smaller and paler species—the lesser prairie chicken—also on the Threatened Wildlife List, is even less common than the greater prairie chicken and lives in a drier environment. Both the lesser and greater prairie chickens can be distinguished in flight from the sharp-tailed grouse of the prairies by their *rounded blackish tails* (the sharp-tailed grouse has a pointed brown tail, edged with white). For a detailed and dramatic description of the courtship display of the greater, lesser, and Attwater's prairie chickens, in which the behavior patterns are virtually alike, see especially Edminster (1954); also Johnsgard (1973).

Prairie chickens are subject to diseases, as are other grouse (*see* Diseases), and, like other grouse, have sharp fluctuations in their populations (Gross, 1932a). *See* Cycle. The disappearance of most prairie chickens has been caused by plowing of much of the native grassland for agriculture; also, use of the land for rice-growing has caused the virtual extinction of the Attwater's prairie chicken, a million of which once lived on 6 million acres of coastal prairies in La. and Tex. (Edminster, 1954). Aerial surveys in 1975 identified total population of about 2,400 birds in 12 Tex. counties.

Ptarmigan (TAR-mih-gan) is from the Gaelic *tarmachan* and the Irish *tarmochan;* according to the *Oxford Universal Dictionary* (1955), the history and origin of the word *ptarmigan* are unknown; the name, first applied in 1599, referred to the European ptarmigan, *Lagopus mutus*, of high altitudes in Scotland, and called in N. America the rock ptarmigan.

GROUSE FAMILY

Ptarmigans are generally ground-dwelling grouse of open tundra or rocky and barren slopes and tops of high mountains; only members of the Grouse Family to have their toes feathered and to have strikingly different plumage in summer and in winter. *See* Colors of Feathers.

Of the three N. American species, two—the rock ptarmigan and willow ptarmigan—live year-round in cold northern regions around the world; of these two, the willow ptarmigan in winter has wandered south into northern U.S., east of the Rockies, from N.D. to Me. (Wetmore, 1937b). The white-tailed ptarmigan, native only to N. America, lives south from Alaska and w. Canada into Wash., and south in the Rockies to N.M. It is an alpine species in the U.S.; a permanent resident of high mountains above timberline most of the year. The white-tailed is the smallest of the ptarmigans, and smallest member of the Grouse Family; the rock ptarmigan is next-largest ptarmigan, and the willow ptarmigan largest of all.

Although walking much, ptarmigans are strong, swift fliers and when startled, rise with an explosive roar and may travel up to a mile before alighting; their claws are long and sharp, adapted to walking over icy slopes, but sometimes ptarmigan may descend rocky slopes by sliding down with the legs forward and the spread tail behind; the nostrils have dense, close feathers that keep out snow in winter. No other bird except the snowy owl is so well clothed and adapted to the Arctic winter (Taverner, 1947).

Ptarmigans fly directly into soft snowbanks to sleep; dozens may roost close together, but none walks to the roosting places because their tracks could be followed by foxes, lynxes, or other predators which might catch ptarmigans in their sleep.

In the Grouse Family, Gross (1965a) reported albinism in 32 individuals of 6 species. Females of grouse, especially the ruffed grouse, are noted for their "crippled-bird act," which leads dogs, foxes, and men away from their chicks. *See* Distraction Display; Young and Their Care.

In captivity, offer any of these birds a mixture of grains, green plant materials, ground meat, and fruit, especially bananas; also mealworms and other insects and mice; supply crushed oyster shells, coarse sand, or fine gravel for grit (*see* discussion of grit under Gizzard); provide dust baths; enclosure for captives should range from cages to yards with moderate-height fences provided that captives are pinioned (*see* Pinion); need ample ground for exercise; also sunshine and fresh water daily.

Chicken, Attwater's prairie. *See* under Chicken, greater prairie.

Chicken, greater prairie, *Tympanuchus cupido* (tim-pan-YEW-cuss cue-PIE-doe); genus and species names: *see* Hen, heath. (Color ills., page 414.) 16½–18 in. long; wingspread 28 in.; generally brown, chickenlike bird, barred on upperparts with dark brown and buff, heavily barred below; has short, rounded, dark tail, black in male, barred in female; both sexes have blackish pinnate feathers on each side of throat, from which often called pinnated grouse; brownish head has slight crest; fleshy, orange-colored eyebrows; feet feathered to toes; toes yellow; bill horn brown; eyes hazel (Edminster, 1954); male has bare yellowish orange "sacs" (enlarged esophagus) on sides of throat called tympani, inflated in courtship; in female, neck sacs very small, orange flesh color lacking, also from eyebrows. In 1970, estimated total hunting kill of all N. American prairie chickens was 85,000, nearly all of which consisted of the greater prairie chicken.

Feeding Habits: In summer, is highly insectivorous May–Oct., especially eats grasshoppers, after which it eats little but plant food: fruit, leaves, flowers, shoots, seeds, grain; is especially fond of rose hips (fruit of wild roses); seeds make up 15% of annual diet: grass, polygonum, weed seeds; in winter, acorns, corn, oats, wheat, rye, sorghum, etc.; eats more grain than any other gallinaceous bird (Gross, 1932a).

Nest: Usually in Apr. or May in pastures, hayfields, woods clearings; a slight hollow in ground among grasses, weeds, or low shrubbery, lined with grasses, well hidden.

Eggs: Late Apr. into early July; 7–17, usually 10–12, olive, spotted with dark brown.

Incubation: Entirely by female, 23–24 days; chicks cared for by female, leave nest, as with many other precocial birds, a few hours after hatching; first flights about 7–14 days after hatching (Schwartz, 1945); one brood a year, may re-nest when first attempt broken up.

Other Names: Pinnated grouse; prairie grouse; prairie hen.

Accidents: Some killed by automobiles along highways; some die from flying into utility wires, fences, and other obstacles.

Albinism: Apparently frequent; one collected (shot) near Missouri R., Iowa, pure white, except minor pale, rust-brown crossbars; another reported in Sac County, Iowa, also pure white (Gross, 1932a).

Flight Speed: Timed in Mich., 42 m.p.h. (Shetter, 1939).

Hybrids: Greater prairie chicken frequently interbreeds, or crosses, with sharp-tailed grouse in Wisc. and Ont. (*see* Hybrid). Presumed hybrids of prairie chickens and pheasants also reported (Gray, 1958).

Weights: Males average a little more than 2 lbs.; largest about 2½ lbs.; females average about 1 lb. 10 oz., some to about 2 lbs. (Edminster, 1954).

Range: Resident, formerly common, on prairies from s. Canada to n. Minn., c. Wisc., northern peninsula of Mich., and s. Ont., south to c. Neb., ne. Colo., Kans., ne. Okla., Mo., s. Ill., and s. Ind., and until recently c. Ohio, Ky., and n.-c. Tenn.; now rare and decreasing in U.S., in eastern part of range limited to parts of Mich., Wisc., and Ill. Attwater's prairie chicken, *Tympanuchus cupido attwateri*, named for Henry P. Attwater, pioneer conservationist in Tex., is rare and threatened and is now limited to se. Tex. and sw. La. About 2,200 left in 1971 (Office of Endangered Species, 1973). The eastern subspecies of the greater prairie chicken, the heath hen, is extinct.

Chicken, lesser prairie, *Tympanuchus pallidicinctus* (tim-pan-YEW-cuss pal-ih-dih-SINK-tus); genus name: *see* Chicken, greater prairie; species name: from Lat. *pallidus*, pale, and *cinctus*, belted, girdled, encircled; probably in allusion to the bars that encircle the body, which are paler than those that encircle the body of the greater prairie chicken. (Color ill., page 415.) 16 in. long; closely resembles the greater prairie chicken but smaller and paler; air sacs of male are dull red, not orange; courtship habits similar to those of greater prairie chicken but booming notes are higher-pitched. See details in Bent (1932); Johnsgard (1973); and Crawford and Bolen (1975); far more than the greater prairie chicken, has suffered substantial population losses recently, and its total fall population is probably under 40,000 birds; now a legal gamebird in only four states (Kan., N.M., Okla., and Tex.), and is probably declining in all of these except N.M.; in 1979 total estimated harvest was about 5,700 birds, mostly from Kan.; there the range of the lesser prairie chicken has been reduced about 55% in past 20 years, while that of the greater prairie chicken has been reduced about 40% in past 36 years.

Feeding Habits: Like those of greater prairie chicken.

Nest: A hollow scooped out of sand by hen and lined with grasses, often at base of sagebrush.

Eggs: Early May to mid-June; 11–13, whitish or buff, sometimes finely spotted with pale brown or olive.

Other Names: Prairie hen; pinnated grouse; prairie grouse.

Accidents: Like those of greater prairie chicken.

Weights: Males about 1 lb. 11 oz. to about 1 lb. 14 oz. (Bent, 1932).

Range: Resident in sandhill and sagebrush country of s. Great Plains; nests from se. Colo., w. Kans., south through w. Okla. to e.-c. N.M., n. Tex.; winters n.-c. Tex., probably also in se. N.M.

Grouse, black. *See* Grouse, spruce.

Grouse, blue, *Dendragapus obscurus* (den-DRAIG-ah-pus ob-SKEW-rus); genus name: from Gr. *dendron*, tree, and *agape*, love, "tree-loving"; species name: Lat., inconspicuous. (Color ills., page 410.) The common grouse of mountains of the West, also called dusky and sooty grouse; 18–21 in. long; male has plain gray or sooty plumage with orange or yellowish "comb" of bare skin above eyes; slightly crested head; both sexes have gray band at end of tail, lacking, however, in those of northern Rockies (Robbins *et al.*, 1966); females dark mottled brown; more uniformly grayish below than spruce grouse. Winter home is in fir forests, summers in deciduous forests of same general range. Usually a solitary species, and though not truly migratory, males in summer sometimes move up to alpine meadows after breeding while females in lowlands are still incubating eggs in July or early Aug.; females and half-grown young follow, so that by end of Sept. all have left nesting grounds; in winter, usually live in upper coniferous forests entirely in trees, except to sometimes roost beneath snow; by Apr., May, or June have descended again to more open woods of breeding grounds, usually on lower slopes and ridges, foothills and valleys (Bent, 1932). Courting males on territories flutter above the ground or make short circular flights (see details in Johnsgard, 1973), then strut in short hurried runs before females, with fanned tail tipped forward, head drawn in and back, wings dragging ground like small turkey gobbler; also take stand on rock, stump, log, or on treetop; inflate purplish-red or yellow air sacs to make hooting or groaning sounds sometimes heard 500 ft. away. In 1970, estimated total annual hunting kill was 370,000 (see Johnsgard, 1973).

Feeding Habits: Feeds in and along edges of aspen groves, coniferous forests, mainly in mountains in U.S.; in summer, moves about eating bearberries, blueberries, serviceberries, strawberries, buffalo berries, also seeks out especially grasshoppers and takes beetles, ants, and caterpillars, flowers and leaves of herbaceous plants, needles of conifers and buds and twigs of trees; at times visits fields for oats and other grains (Bent, 1932).

Nest: In shallow depression in ground at base of tree, near fallen log, or rock, lined with grasses, pine needles, and leaves; in shelter of chokecherry, aspen, cottonwood; sometimes in clearings of woods, under clump of manzanita, and even under scanty sagebrush of open plains. In Mont., Mussehl (1960) found three nests in bunchgrass prairie, 200 yds. to more than 1 mi. from montane forest.

Eggs: Apr.–Aug.; 7–16, usually 7–10, pink-buff, finely dotted with browns.

Incubation: Entirely by female, 26 days; female raises young, which fly some when only a week old.

Other Names: Dusky grouse; fool hen; gray grouse; hooter; pine grouse, pine hen; sooty grouse.

Albinism: One collected (shot) Sept. 1969 above tree line (12,000 ft.) in Colo., very pale gray but with normally colored feet, bill (Braun and Blumberg, 1973).

Hybrids: A presumed cross between a blue grouse and a sharp-tailed grouse taken in B.C., Canada, in 1906; also several presumed hybrids reported from crosses of blue grouse with ring-necked pheasants and one between a blue grouse and a spruce grouse taken in Idaho in 1950 (Gray, 1958).

Weights: In n.-c. Wash., average weights of males, 1,194 gr., or about 2⅔ lbs.; females, 899 gr., or about 2 lbs. (Zwickel *et al.*, 1966); see also Redfield (1973) for comparable summer weights.

Range: Resident from se. Alaska, s. Yuk., sw. Mack., and w. Alta., south in offshore islands of Alaska to Queen Charlotte Is. and Vancouver Is., also w. Wash. and w. Ore., along coast to n. Calif., in mountains to s. Calif., n. Ariz., and w.-c. N.M., Idaho, e. Utah, c. Nev., c. Colo., nw. Wyo.

Grouse, drumming. *See* Grouse, ruffed.

Grouse, dusky. *See* Grouse, blue.

Grouse, Franklin's. *See* Grouse, spruce.

Grouse, pinnated. *See* Prairie chicken and Hen, heath.

Grouse, pin-tailed. *See* Grouse, sharp-tailed.

Grouse, prairie. *See* Grouse, sharp-tailed; Prairie chicken, greater; and Prairie chicken, lesser.

Grouse, ruffed, *Bonasa umbellus* (bon-AY-sah um-BEL-lus); genus name: from Lat. *bonasum*, a kind of buffalo, the aurochs, and Gr. *bonasos*, a wild ox, possibly from similarity of this bird's drumming to bellowing of a bull; however, Jaeger (1955) suggests possibly from Lat. *bonus*, good, and *assum*, a roast; species name: Lat., umbrella, in reference to the feather tufts, or ruffs, of neck. (Color ills., page 411.) State bird of Pa.; resident from Alaska and Canada, across n. U.S. from Calif. to Me. and south to n. Ga.; sexes outwardly similar; a relatively large grouse; 15–19 in. long; wing-spread 22–25 in. (Edminster, 1947); chickenlike bird of brushy woodlands that rises with thunderous roar of wings from almost underfoot; in flight, shows finely barred, rather long, fan-shaped tail with broad black bar near tip; has two color phases: one is reddish, the other gray, which shows much in tail, colors have no relation to sex or age; color varies—along West Coast, birds are usually reddish; those of Rocky Mtns., gray; in e. N. America, both reddish and gray forms (see Edminster, 1947, for details), but reddish grouse more common in southern part of range, gray more common northward. See Gullion and Marshall (1968). Adult male usually larger and heavier than female, both sexes have ruff feathers which form a triangular patch on each side of neck; ruffs are raised to prominence when bird is excited, as are erectile head feathers; in breeding season, male has bright orange-colored comb over eyes, not developed in female; courting males raise crest and ruffs and fan tail on woodland "drumming" logs (*see* Drumming); make these whirring sounds with wings to announce territory, to attract females, and to repel other males; drumming appears to function much as does singing of most birds; males copulate with females at or near drumming logs and, like so many grouse, male is promiscuous; is resident of forests and cut-over woods; winters in same general range but in conifers or in mixed conifers and deciduous woods, where in winter loses its usually solitary nature to roost in dense evergreens with a few others; sometimes plunges into snowbank to escape pursuing goshawk or to roost through storms; both sexes utter short *quit-quit* notes of alarm; female gives loud squeal or whine when surprised with her young; may go into "crippled-bird act" to lead intruder away. Ruffed grouse often called "partridge" by hunters and some country people, and "pheasant" in s. Appalachians, but true partridges are in Pheasant Family; is one of most written-about and most popular of all upland game birds; hunted in more states and provinces in U.S. and Canada than any other grouse, and more shot by hunters each year (about 3,700,000 in 1970). See Johnsgard (1973). Ruffed grouse are noted for their dramatic rise and fall in populations and fall dispersal and, at times, belligerence and fearlessness.

Feeding Habits: Newly hatched chicks eat cutworms, grasshoppers, beetles, ants, wasps, spiders, and caterpillars; adults in summer like to wander in fields and meadows near woods for insects, which form about 30% of their summer food; they also eat almost all kinds of wild berries, apples, plums, wild grapes, and nuts, also seeds of hemlocks, maple trees, and tick trefoil, beggar's-ticks, and many other weed seeds; also blossoms and buds or leaves of poplar, birch, willow, apple, pear, peach, alder, spruce, spicebush, and many, many small herbaceous plants. See Bent (1932) and Edminster (1947) for long lists and details; adults also occasionally eat small garter snakes, red-bellied snakes, frogs, and toads (Hale and Wendt, 1951).

Nest: A slight hollow scraped in leaves and ground in woods by hen, usually at base of a tree, stump, rock, log, or bush; lined with deciduous leaves or conifer needles, twigs, and its molted feathers; usually well concealed.

Eggs: Early Apr. into July; usually 9–12, sometimes 8–14, buffy, sometimes spotted with brown (Bump *et al.*, 1947).

Incubation: By female, 23–24 days; 7 days after hatching, the chicks can fly to a perch a foot above the ground; at 10–12 days, they fly well enough to roost with the mother in trees; by mid-Sept., when chicks are 84 days or more old, the families begin to break up and dispersal of young begins (Johnsgard, 1973).

Other Names: Birch partridge; carpenter bird (from drumming sound); drumming grouse; drumming pheasant; moor fowl; mountain pheasant; partridge; pine hen; ruffed heath-cock; shoulder-knot grouse; tippet; white-flesher; wood grouse; wood hen; woodpile quarker; woods pheasant.

Accidents: Autopsies of grouse by A. A. Allen, Cornell University, showed that one had a fair-sized twig forced down its throat when flying at high speed; another had part of its crop containing acorns torn away and pushed under skin of the lower breast, possibly in flight from striking a tree with terrific force; the crop had healed perfectly. *See* Accidents; Diseases.

Age: Grange (1948) reported an 11-year-old grouse in the wild; Stoll and Davis (1974) reported one 7 years, 7 months, another 7 years, 10 months, old; most are shot or die of predation/or diseases before reaching 10 years.

Albinism: Apparently rare; Deane (1876) reported it and cited a pure-white one shot at West Bridgewater, Mass.; another pure albino was shot near Ballston Spa, N.Y. (Rue, 1973).

Flight Speed: Timed in New England, 22 m.p.h. (White, 1929). According to Rue (1973), its average swiftest flight is about 40 m.p.h.

Hybrids: Interbreeding with domestic chickens reported from W.Va. many years ago, but never confirmed (Gray, 1958).

Weights: 1 lb. to 1 lb. 12 oz. (Edminster, 1947); 17.9–27 oz. (Johnsgard, 1973).

Range: Lives as resident from c. Alaska, c. Yuk., s. Mack., into Sask., c. Man., n. Ont., s. Que., s. Labrador, N.B., and Nova Scotia south to n. Calif., ne. Ore., c. Idaho, c. Utah, nw. Colo., Wyo., w. S.D., Minn. (formerly to e. Neb. and e. Kans.), c. Ark., Ohio, Tenn. (formerly to ne. Ala.), n. Ga., w. S.C., w. N.C., W.Va., ne. Va., and w. Md.; also from Minn., Wisc., Mich., N.Y., New England, Pa., s. N.J., southward to Ky., also a population outside of normal range in Mo., w. Ill., and s. Ind., and also introduced in Newfoundland.

Grouse, sage, *Centrocercus urophasianus* (sen-tro-SER-kus you-row-FAZE-ih-AY-nus); genus name: from Gr. *kentron*, point, and *kerkos*, tail; species name: from Gr. *oura*, tail, and *phasianos*, pheasant. (Color ills., pages 412, 413.) 21–30 in. long; largest of N. American grouse (Edminster, 1954); western as the Stetson hat and sagebrush; gray-brown bird with color pattern that blends with sagebrush of arid plains; male *considerably larger* than female (both sexes can be identified by long, stiff, pointed tail feathers and black belly); male also has white breast and black throat divided by white band lacking in female; in flight, hen rises quickly and dips body alternately from side to side; male rises slowly, keeps steady course without side-dipping (Patterson, 1952); utters deep clucking notes in flight, also cackling; runs over ground much to escape; in courtship most spectacular of all grouse, male struts and inflates air sacs of breast, and spreads pointed tail feathers; same strutting grounds used by generations of grouse; used by 20–70 (rarely several hundred) males. *See* Dancing Ground; Arena Bird. See Patterson (1952), Bent (1932), and Johnsgard (1973) for details. Is permanent resident of sagebrush plains and salt desert scrub on 130 million acres of intermountain country (see threats to its range and environment in Carhart, 1954). In 1970, estimated total annual hunting kill was 250,000 (Johnsgard, 1973).

Feeding Habits: In winter depends entirely on soft evergreen leaves and shoots of plains sagebrush; also for its food and shelter at other seasons; also eats leaves, blossoms, pods, and buds of certain other plains plants; sage grouse's digestive system not adapted to hard seeds and grains (Patterson, 1952). *See* Digestion. Sage grouse also eats insects such as grasshoppers and ants (Bent, 1932); roosts in circle on ground; closely associated with pronghorns, which also depend on sagebrush and associated plants for food.

Nest: Often a shallow depression in ground under small sagebrush; may be sparsely lined with grasses and sage leaves.

Eggs: Mid-Mar. to mid-June; 7–15, usually 7–8 (Johnsgard, 1973), pale green, evenly marked with brown spots and dots.

Incubation: 25–27 days (Patterson, 1952); young fly when about 7–14 days old.

Other Names: Sage chicken; sage cock; sage hen; spiny-tailed pheasant; called "Cock of the Plains" by Lewis and Clark.

Age: One banded female recovered 7 years after banding.

Flight Speed: Timed in w. U.S., 28 m.p.h.; running speed, 2 m.p.h. (Cottam *et al.*, 1942b).

Hybrids: Two sage grouse × sharp-tailed grouse—first record—c. Mont. (Eng, 1971).

Weights: Males weigh twice as much as females: 5 lbs. 8 oz. and maximum of male reported at 6 lbs. 2 oz.; females 2 lbs. 10 oz., maximum to 3 lbs. 3 oz. (Martin and Nelson, 1952).

Range: Locally, premanent resident from c. Wash., e. Ore., s. Idaho, e. Mont., se. Alta., s. Sask., and w. N.D., south to e.-c. Calif., s.-c. Nev., Utah, w. Colo., and e. Wyo., formerly ranged in flocks of thousands when Lewis and Clark wrote of it in 1806, especially at water holes over semiarid plains from s. B.C. south to n. N.M., Ariz., and Okla. (A.O.U. *Check-list*, 1957). According to Edminster (1954), range is much more restricted than previously, owing to livestock grazing and agriculture.

Grouse, sharp-tailed, *Pedioecetes phasianellus* (ped-ih-ee-SEE-teez fay-sih-ay-NELL-us); genus name: Lat., pertaining to level field, from Gr. *pedion*, plain, and *oiketes*, dweller; species name: of Gr. *phasianos*, pheasant, or "little pheasant." (Color ill., page 415.) About size (16–19 in. long) of ruffed grouse but slenderer, with *narrow, pointed* tail which gave it its name; pale, speckled, largely a brushland grouse, usually seen on prairies only in summer; in flight resembles a female ring-necked pheasant except that its pointed tail has white edging, which also distinguishes it in flight from prairie chicken; immatures lack white-edged tail; sexes difficult to distinguish except by behavior in breeding season; adults have small erectile crest on head and yellow-orange bare space (comb) above brown eyes; inflatable esophageal areas or "air sacs," are purple or red-violet area of bare skin in male; no long feathers at sides of throat as in prairie chicken. In spring males gather on dancing grounds; inflate air sacs of throat; utter hollow "booming" or cooing notes, also a chickenlike cackling when flushed; raise and fan tail, rustle and quiver wings in challenge to nearby males and to attract watching females. *See* Arena Bird. Males sometimes get into fights and grip each other fiercely with bill. Hart *et al.* (1950) counted 30–50 different birds in Utah on some 20 open grassy dancing grounds but average was only 12; most dancing grounds used only a few seasons; some may be used year after year if not destroyed by farm plowing or changes by invasion of dense shrubbery. Sharp-tails prefer to walk rather than fly but are strong fliers and occasionally travel 2–3 mi. in a single flight (Edminster, 1954). Roost on ground or under snow in winter; largest flocks in late fall and early winter, usually 10–35 birds but to 50–100 or more; occasionally large mass emigrations of hundreds and even thousands; travel 200–300 mi. when population high and food shortages (see, however, Johnsgard, 1973); a suggested 30-year cycle and a 10-year cycle (see Edminster, 1954, for details); has benefited from cutting and burning of northern spruce forests, which has created large tracts of brushland (Hamerstrom and Hamerstrom, 1951); however, numbers have sharply fluctuated in southern part of range, owing to decrease of its environment (see details in Johnsgard, 1973); in 1970, estimated total annual hunting kill of this bird in N. America was 455,000; in past decade has disappeared from Ore. and N.M. and declined elsewhere.

Feeding Habits: Chicks during first few weeks of life eat mostly insects, also berries; adults eat especially grasshoppers, crickets, beetles, also very fond of rose hips (fruit of wild roses), blueberries, cranberries, snowberries, and others, also eat corn, wheat, and other grains; are great browsers—eat leaves, buds, and flowers of pasqueflowers, dandelions, and buds of willow and birch; leaves of cottonwood, alder, blueberry, etc., flowers of grasses, alder, willow, maple—total food is about 10% insects, about 90% some parts of plants (Bent, 1932).

Nest: Usually on prairie about ½ mi. from a dancing ground, in Apr. or May, on ground, a slight depression, lined with grasses, leaves, some feathers, also may be concealed under bushes or next to stump, sometimes near water or on dry knoll in swamp.

Eggs: Early Apr. into late June; 5–17, usually about 12 (Hamerstrom, 1939a), olive, dark buff, or brown with purple bloom early, some with small dark brown specklings.

Incubation: By female, 23–24 days; after hatching, female leads young away from nest fairly rapidly to open areas where insects and green food abundant (Hamerstrom, 1963); young make first flights 10–14 days after hatching.

Other Names: Blackfoot; brush grouse; northern sharp-tailed grouse; pintailed grouse; prairie grouse; prairie pheasant; sharp-tail; spike-tail; sprig-tailed grouse; white grouse.

Accidents: May fly into tree trunks, electric wires, fences, utility wires, especially telephone wires, most common hazard on plains, and automobiles.

Age: One at least 7½ years old among 93 banded (Ammann, 1957).

Flight Speed: Timed in w. U.S., 28–30 m.p.h. (Cottam *et al.*, 1942b); in Minn., 33 m.p.h. (Anonymous, 1931).

Hybrids: Sharp-tailed grouse and blue grouse; also presumed hybrid between sharp-tailed and heath hen, now extinct; also, frequent wild hybrids between sharp-tailed and greater prairie chicken (Johnsgard, 1973). *See also* in biography of sage grouse.

Weights: Males average 2 lbs. 2 oz.; heaviest males to 2 lbs. 6 oz.; females average 1 lb. 13 oz.; heaviest to 2 lbs. 3 oz. (Martin and Nelson, 1952).

Range: Lives at present from n.-c. Alaska, Yuk., and Yukon R. valley to n. Mack., n. Man., n. Ont., and c. Que., south to e. Wash., Idaho, ne. Utah, Wyo., and Colo., Neb. to e. S.D., ne. Minn., n. Wisc., and n. Mich. (Johnsgard, 1973); formerly Nev., N.M., and Ore.

Grouse, sooty. *See* Grouse, blue.

Grouse, spotted. *See* Grouse, spruce.

Grouse, spruce, *Canachites canadensis* (can-ah-KYE-teez can-ah-DEN-sis); genus name: New Lat., from Gr. *kanachos*, noise, and suffix *-ites*, doer, or maker of (Jaeger, 1955); species name: Lat., of Canada. (Color ill., page 413.) 15–17 in. long; grouse of northern coniferous forests of N. America; male is gray above, black below, white spots along sides, crimson-red comb of bare skin above eyes; red comb-spots lacking in female; she is mottled brownish, rustier than blue grouse, smaller and darker than ruffed grouse, with brown band across end of her blackish tail; a generally silent bird but utters clucking sound when disturbed; usually solitary and small flocks are generally family groups; sometimes called fool hen because remarkably tame and fearless of man; has been locally exterminated by some people who kill the birds "for fun" (see Bent, 1932, and Pough, 1951, for details); male has striking courtship display: with tail partly spread, red combs erect, advertises his territory to other males by whirring of wings and in flight by making sharp wing-cracking or wing-snapping sound by beating wings together (MacDonald, 1968). One study showed that males may have territories of from 3 to 10 or 15 acres; others that territories may be larger; males seldom fight (MacDonald, 1968; see also Ellison, 1971b; 1973). In 1970, estimated total annual hunting kill in N. America was 440,000 (see Johnsgard, 1973).

Feeding Habits: Usually a tree dweller, eats needles and buds of spruce, jack pine, fir, and larch—staple foods; also many kinds of wild berries, seeds of grasses and weeds, mushrooms, herbaceous leaves and fern fronds and a few insects (Bent, 1932; Johnsgard, 1973).

Nest: Well-concealed depression scratched by hen in bare ground or hollowed in moss under low branch of spruce or under bushes; lined with dry grasses, leaves, twigs, and a few feathers. See Ellison (1966–68; 1971; 1973).

Eggs: Early May into early July; 5–10, usually 6–7 (Robinson and Maxwell, 1968); according to Townsend (1932), lays handsomest eggs of any N. American grouse; cinnamon to pink-buff or cream-buff, usually boldly marked with large spots and blotches of rich browns, some thickly and evenly covered with small spots and dots.

Incubation: By female, 23–24 days; young able to flutter from ground at age of 1 week; usually one brood annually (Robinson, 1968–69).

Other Names: Black grouse; Canada grouse; cedar partridge; Franklin's grouse (once thought to be a separate species but now considered a race, or subspecies, of the spruce grouse); fool hen; spotted grouse; spruce partridge; swamp partridge; wood grouse; wood partridge.

Albinism: A female shot near Houlton, Me., had a pure-white tail and white feathers in its wings, giving it a mottled appearance (Deane, 1878).

Hybrids: Spruce grouse × willow ptarmigan —presumed hybrids have been reported; one (a male) shot in Manitoba in 1931; a presumed hybrid between spruce grouse and blue grouse was shot in Idaho in 1950 (Gray, 1958).

Weights: 500–700 gr., or 1 lb. 1 oz. to 1 lb. 9 oz. (Ellison, 1971).

Range: Normally a common bird of northern forests of spruce, fir, cedar, larch, and pines (Robinson, 1969); overall range is transcontinental, largely conforming to the boreal-coniferous forest; from southern end of tundra south from c. Alaska, Yuk., and Mack. east across Canada to Labrador and Cape Breton Is. south to ne. Ore., c. Idaho, w. Mont., nw. Wyo., Man., n. Minn., n. Wisc., Mich., s. Ont., n. N.Y., n. Vt., n. N.H., Me., N.B., and Nova Scotia (A.O.U. *Check-list*, 1957). Introduced and well established in Newfoundland.

Grouse, willow. *See* Ptarmigan, willow.

Hen, heath, *Tympanuchus cupido cupido* (tim-pan-YEW-cuss cue-PIE-do); genus name: Lat., from Gr. *tympanon*, kettle drum, and *echein*, to have (a drum); alluding to booming sound of males uttered in courtship; species name: according to Coues (1882), "named by Linnaeus . . . after the 'blind bow boy' son of Venus, not with any allusion to erotic concerns, but because the little wings on the bird's neck were likened to 'Cupid's wings' " (these tufts of long, erectile, stiff dark feathers are raised like small rounded wings over head of male in his courtship display). Eastern counterpart of the greater prairie chicken of w. U.S.; *extinct;* differences between heath hen and greater prairie chicken not great; same general color but heath hen rustier and had more strongly marked underparts; female was similar to male but smaller and neck tufts very short (Gross, 1932b); 15–18 in. long; wingspread 26½–29 in.; to some extent a forest bird when eastern forests were intact but mostly on brushy scrub oak plains of eastern seaboard; formerly was a resident (nonmigratory) from Mass. (latitude of Boston), possibly from s. N.H. south along Atlantic seaboard through Long Is., N.Y., N.J., e. Pa., Del., Md., and Va. to Potomac R. at Washington, D.C.; limited, after 1835, to island of Martha's Vineyard, Mass., where the last heath hen, a male, was seen on Mar. 11, 1932; on Apr. 1, 1931, it had been trapped and banded (*see* Banding) and at that time was 7 years old and in apparent good health; not one has been seen since (see Greenway, 1958, for details; also Gross, 1928 and 1932b, for historical facts up to time of bird's extinction caused by uncontrolled fires on Martha's Vineyard, shooting by pot hunters and market hunters on mainland; possibly diseases may have been one of the most serious decimating factors in its last decline— see Gross, 1932, and Stone, 1937).

Feeding Habits: Similar to those of the ruffed grouse; in spring, tender shoots of grasses, sorrel, and other plants; in summer and fall, insects, fruit; in winter, acorns, seeds, berries.

Nest: Concealed by low dense shrubs of scrub oak plains, on ground, composed of leaves, grasses, twigs already in place to which it added materials from near nest site.

Eggs: Usually laid May–July; usually 6–10, deep olive-buff, oval, and unspotted.

Incubation: By female, about 24 days.

Other Names: Eastern pinnated grouse; heathcock; hethen.

Weights: About same as ruffed grouse (Forbush, 1925–29).

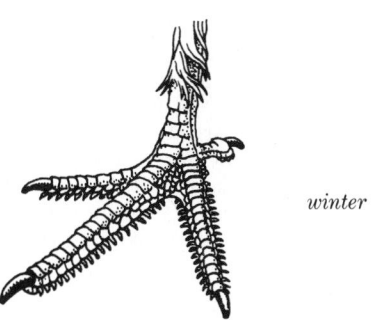

winter

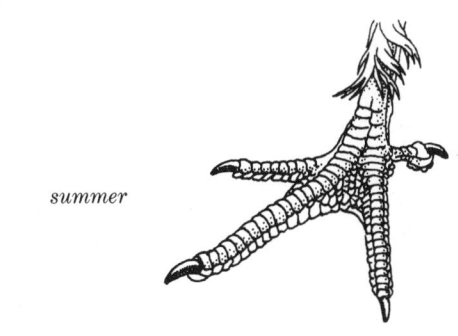

summer

GROUSE FAMILY
Most members of the grouse family live in cold climates, and as an adaptation to snow conditions grow "snow shoes" in the fall. Ptarmigans grow stiff mats of feathers on their toes; other grouse develop pectinations 2–3mm. long on the sides of each toe.

Heath hen

GROUSE FAMILY

Ptarmigan, rock, *Lagopus mutus* (LAG-oh-pus or lah-GO-pus MUTE-us); genus name: Lat., from Gr. *lagos*, hare, and *pous*, foot, "hare-footed," in reference to dense feathers of feet that reach to toes; species name: Lat., silent. (Color ills., pages 416, 417.) Small grouse of Greenland and Arctic N. American continent north of U.S., more Arctic than either the white-tailed or the willow ptarmigan (Taverner, 1947); lives on mountaintops south to c. B.C.; 13–15½ in. long; in summer, brown plumage, much paler and more yellow than larger willow ptarmigan, but females of the two species virtually indistinguishable; black tail in both sexes separates them from white-tailed ptarmigan; in winter, both sexes white, faintly tinged with pink, with black tail; black mark from bill through eyes usually distinguishes male rock ptarmigan from willow ptarmigan; rock ptarmigan prefers higher, more barren hills than willow ptarmigan; males develop small red combs over eyes in spring; on breeding grounds male defends small territory around a hummock on ground where he displays to intimidate other males and to attract hen; both sexes utter whining and clucking sounds (see Bent, 1932; Wetmore, 1937b; MacDonald, 1970). In 1970, estimated total annual hunting kill in N. America of all three ptarmigans was 300,000 (Johnsgard, 1973).

Feeding Habits: In summer, eats insects, spiders, but mostly leaves, buds, and fruit of crowberry, bearberry, whortleberry; terminal leaves and buds of birches and willows; also seeds and mosses; in winter, seeds, buds, and twigs above snow.

Nest: Hen scratches a hollow in open tundra or rocky habitat; lines with grasses, mosses, a few feathers.

Eggs: N. Alaska, May to late July; Arctic Canada, June–July; 6–7 (Pough, 1951); 8–13 (Sutton, 1965); 6–9, sometimes more (Wetmore, 1937b); varies annually (Johnsgard, 1973); buff, strongly marked with black and brown.

Incubation: By female, about 21 days; chicks make short flights at 15–16 days after hatching (MacDonald, 1970).

Other Names: Arctic or white grouse or "partridge"; barren-ground bird; polar grouse; small grouse (all used in Arctic N. America) (Snyder, 1957).

Hybrids: Rock ptarmigan × willow ptarmigan (Gray, 1958); also supposed hybrids occasionally reported—rock ptarmigan × red grouse of Europe but some doubt about authenticity; presumed hybrids of rock ptarmigan × European black grouse reported, also from rock ptarmigan × ring-necked pheasant.

Weights: One female about 1 lb. and two males 1 lb. 1 oz. each (Manning *et al.*, 1956); average of adult males on Ellesmere Is., Canada, 1 lb. 3 oz. to 1 lb. 5 oz. (Parmelee and MacDonald, 1960).

Range: Circumpolar; resident on barest, rockiest uplands and barrens; one of hardiest of all birds; some remain on nesting grounds all winter; others move to lower altitudes from mountains but never seek shelter like willow ptarmigan; in autumn in Far North, some extensive migrations (*see also* Willow ptarmigan) when snow covers food supply of twigs and buds of willows and other Arctic or alpine shrubs (Wetmore, 1937b); a considerable southward movement in winter (Johnsgard, 1973); lives from Arctic O. and its islands south to Eurasia; in N. America, from n. Alaska, nw. Mack., Melville Is., n. Ellesmere Is., n. and s. Greenland, south to Aleutians, Kodiak Is., Alaska, and sw. and c. B.C., S. Mack., Keewatin, n. Que., s. Labrador, and Newfoundland.

Ptarmigan, white-tailed, *Lagopus leucurus* (LAG-oh-pus or lah-GO-pus lew-KUE-rus); genus name: *see* Ptarmigan, rock; species name: Lat., from Gr. *leukos*, white, and *oura*, tail. (Color ills., pages 416, 417.) A truly alpine bird even in Alaska; lives only on highest slopes and ridges of Cascade Mtns. of Wash. and Rocky Mtns.; locally common above timberline; 12–13 in. long; white tail distinguishes it from all other ptarmigans and white wings in summer distinguish it from other grouse. In summer is brown with white tail, belly, and wings; in winter, *all-white* except for black bill and eyes; scarlet comb over eyes of both male and female is prominent in breeding season (Johnsgard, 1973); only ptarmigan known to nest within the U.S. south of Canada (Bent, 1932).

Feeding Habits: Staple winter foods are catkins of alders and buds and twigs of alpine willows, dwarf birches; also eats needles and buds of spruces, pines, and firs; in spring and summer, eats leaves and flowers of herbaceous alpine plants, also buds of willow, some berries, seeds, insects, and some grit.

Nest: A saucerlike depression in short, fine grass of steep slopes or between rocks above timberline; lives at 10,000–14,000 ft. altitude in southern part of its mountain range; female sits on eggs so closely one can almost step on her before she moves; hen difficult to see because of her protective coloration.

Eggs: Mid-June to mid-July; 4–16, usually 3–9 (Mont.), 4–7 (Colo.), pink-buff, finely dotted or blotched with brown (Bent, 1932).

Incubation: Not definitely known but estimated at 22–24 days; chicks leave nest with mother soon after hatching; at 10–21 days can fly 20–150 ft. (Johnsgard, 1973).

Other Names: Mountain quail; Rocky Mountain snow partridge; snow grouse; snow quail; white quail.

Age: 12 of 36 females and 16 of 31 males lived to at least 5 years; estimated maximum longevity about 13–15 years (Choate, 1963).

Weights: 11.4–17.5 oz.; sexes essentially identical in weight.

Range: Resident from c. Alaska, n. Yuk., sw. Mack., south to Kenai Pen.; Vancouver Is., Canada, Cascade Mtns. in Wash., and in Rocky Mtns. from B.C. and Alta. south to n. N.M.; recently released and established in Utah and Ore.

Ptarmigan, willow, *Lagopus lagopus* (LAG-oh-pus or lah-GO-pus); genus and species names: *see* Ptarmigan, rock. (Color ills., pages 416, 417.) State bird of Alaska; circumpolar, common in Arctic from Alaska across Canada to Newfoundland, casual in n. U.S.; 15–17 in. long; larger and with *heavier bill* than rock ptarmigan; in all seasons both sexes may be distinguished from white-tailed ptarmigan by black tail; in summer is brown with white wings (head and breast more reddish or chestnut than rock ptarmigan); females lack the bright red "eyebrows" of adult males; are more gray-brown, more heavily barred on breast and flanks than are males; both sexes utter cackling and other notes; in winter, white with black tail; no black mark from bill to eyes as in rock ptarmigan; in summer, prefers open tundra, and slopes and upper edge of timberline; in winter, in sheltered valleys and willows; winters throughout most of range but has cycles of low and high numbers not yet well understood; is perhaps most migratory (with rock ptarmigan) of all N. American upland game birds (Johnsgard, 1973); in years of greatest numbers flocks make long journeys southward; in spring, on returning to breeding grounds on low tundra, upland valleys, or on or near drift-strewn sea beach, each male selects a bare spot on ground and with swollen red combs begins to strut and call; frequently flies into air, uttering barking notes as he flutters to ground; many fierce battles between males, with feathers plucked, blood flowing; females loiter in cover nearby; after mating with a male, later make nest; unlike other species of ptarmigans, male remains with female throughout incubation period; he hides in thickets close to female while she is on nest; he defends her, flying viciously at gulls, sometimes knocking them over to prevent them from getting at mate's eggs; has even attacked grizzly bear that stumbled over mate's nest, and male will attack persons who catch one of the chicks (Dixon, 1927b). Both parents usually attend young until they are at least 60 days old.

Feeding Habits: In summer, eats tender leaves and flower buds of willows, birches, and alders, also fruits of blueberry, cranberry, crowberry, and kinnikinnick; also insects; in winter, twigs and buds of willow, also catkins and buds of dwarf birches and other trees, and bushes; chicks eat caterpillars, other insects, and spiders.

Nest: Hen scrapes cavity at base of log, bunch of grass, bush, or hummock; lines it with grasses, feathers; nest is on tundra, beaches, or near marshes.

Eggs: May 25–July 10; 5–17, usually 6–7 or may average 10 in Newfoundland (Johnsgard, 1973); yellowish, splotched with brown.

Incubation: By female, 21–22 days; chicks leave nest soon after hatching, make first short, jumping flights at age of 1 week.

Other Names: Alaska ptarmigan, Alexander's ptarmigan, and Allen's ptarmigan (names for subspecies; see Bent, 1932); common ptarmigan; snow grouse; white grouse; willow grouse; willow partridge.

Age: Of 12,000 banded, 4 lived to at least 4 years old (Johnsgard, 1973).

Hybrids: Reports of willow ptarmigan × spruce grouse, and attempted matings between a male willow ptarmigan and a domestic hen; presumed hybrids—willow ptarmigan × rock ptarmigan in Old World. See Gray (1958).

Weights: Males about 1 lb. 2 oz. (Dixon, 1927b); two females, 1 lb. 9 oz. and 1 lb. 8 oz. (Manning *et al.*, 1956); females average slightly lighter than males.

Range: Circumpolar in Europe and Asia; in N. America, from n. Alaska eastward to c. Greenland, south to Alaska Pen., Aleutians, se. Alaska, c. B.C., Alta., Sask., Man., c. Ont., c. Que., and Newfoundland; in winter, occasionally wanders to n. Minn., Wisc., and casually to Mont., N.D., n. N.Y., and Me. (A.O.U. *Checklist,* 1957).

GRUIDAE
See Crane Family.

GRUIFORMES
(groo-ih-FOR-meez); from Lat. *grus,* crane, and *forma,* form (Coble, 1954). A very ancient order of birds (*see* Order) whose fossil history goes back to the Eocene Period. (*See* Geological Time Scale.) The order has sometimes been referred to as "a group of misfits" because it includes such a mixed bag, whose members, however, do not seem to belong anywhere else (Wallace, 1961d). 12 families of birds of 199 species (Van Tyne and Berger, 1976), loosely called "marsh birds" (*see* Marsh Bird), make up the worldwide Gruiformes. It includes, for example, such birds as the mesites or monias, flightless or almost flightless forest birds of Madagascar; the Old World and New World tropical sun-grebes, or finfoots, so called because they dive and swim like grebes and have broad lobes on the toes; the bustards of the grasslands and open plains of Europe, Asia, Africa, and Australia (*see* reference to them in Autolycism); and the family of button-quail (Turnicidae), which Austin (1961) prefers to call "bustard" quail (because they are anatomically like the bustards), which live in the warmer parts of the Old World. They are famed for their classic example of polyandry, with the larger females taking the lead in courtship. *See* polyandry under Sexual Relationships. The order also includes the once thought extinct takahe, or notornis, of New Zealand, and the cranes, rails, gallinules, coots, and limpkins. The only Gruiformes in N. America are represented by the Crane Family, Limpkin Family, and Rail Family. For a discussion of how birds are grouped according to their relationships, *see* Classification; Morphology; Phylogenetic Relationship; Check-list Order.

GRUNTER
See Wilson's phalarope in Phalarope Family.

GUACHARO
(GWAH-chah-ro). Spanish name (meaning "one who cries and laments") for the oilbird, *Steatornis caripensis,* which orients itself in the darkness of its nesting caves by echolocation. *See* Echolocation.

GUAN
See in Curassow Family.

GUANO
(GWAH-no). Spanish name from the Peruvian Quechua *huanu,* or dung, the excrement of seabirds found as large deposits on certain islands off the coast of Peru and on other islands in the southern ocean and off the west coast of Africa. Guano is rich in phosphates, nitrogens, and other materials valuable as fertilizer for plant growth. So-called guano birds—the ones whose excrement provides the fertilizer—are of several species. The camanay, or blue-footed booby, *Sula nebouxii* (*see* in Booby Family), is the only one of the Peruvian guano birds to belong to the avifauna of N. America. The guanay, alcatras, and piquero, respectively the cormorant, pelican, and booby of the Humboldt Current, comprise the great guano-producing triumvirate (Murphy, 1936). *See* also Ornithocoprophilus.

GUILLEMOT
See in Auk Family.

GUINEAFOWL FAMILY
See Galliformes; *also* Domestication.

GUINEA HEN
See Guinea Fowl under Domestication.

GULAR (GEW-lar) FLUTTER
See Heat and Birds.

GULAR (GEW-lar) POUCH
or GULAR SAC. *Gular:* pertaining to the gular, or upper throat next to the chin. This is a skin pouch of the throat, as in pelicans. Nesting pelicans use the gular pouch in panting to lower, or to cool, their body temperatures; also to hold partly digested fishes while the young feed from the pouch. Cormorants, owls, pigeons, pheasants, quail, and certain other birds have a gular pouch, but smaller than that of the pelican. *See* Temperature; Heat and Birds; Young and Their Care. See also discussion of the gular or sublingual pouch and its uses in the Auk Family by Speich and Manuwal (1974), especially Cassin's auklet.

GULL-CHASER
See jaegers in Skua Family.

GULLET
See Esophagus.

GULL FAMILY
Laridae (LAR-ih-dee); from Lat. *larus,* seabird. Includes both gulls and terns of 82 species in world (Van Tyne and Berger, 1959). There are 43 species of gulls in world (Austin, 1961; Gilliard, 1958; Reilly, 1968), and about 39 of terns (Austin, 1961). In N. America, as of 1971, about 25 species of gulls, including two called kittiwakes—*see* in biographies that follow—and 18 of terns, including two called noddies. Gulls and terns are most closely related to the skuas, jaegers, and skimmers—all are grouped by those who classify birds in a suborder Lari (Storer, 1960b) in the order Charadriiformes.

Gulls are medium to large, typically gray-and-white seabirds, usually with black wing tips and a gray mantle (*see* Mantle), known to people throughout the world; their mewing cries are usually associated with the thunder of the surf. Young, or immature, gulls are usually brown with a dark band on the tail (Watson, 1966). *See* Sexual Maturity. Most gulls, rather than being oceanic, live much on or over saltwater seas and bays; some inland around freshwa-

limpkin

rail

crane

GRUIFORMES

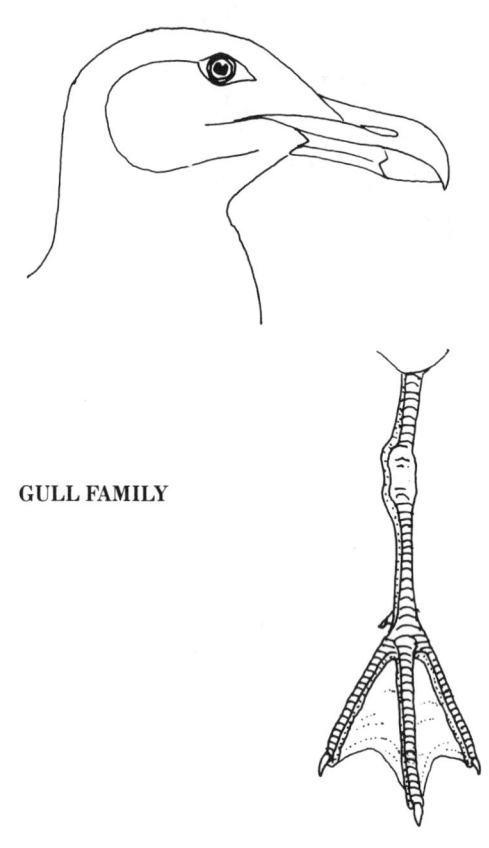

GULL FAMILY

ter lakes, rivers, and marshes, far from the ocean.

One of largest of gulls, the great black-backed of the N. Atlantic coast, is 30 in. long, with a wingspread of 5½ ft.; the herring gull, or "sea gull," most widely distributed gull in N. Hemisphere, is also large, up to 22 in. long, wingspread of about 4½ ft., and is possibly commonest gull along Atlantic coast of N. America; the ring-billed gull, a slightly smaller counterpart of the herring gull, is commonest wintering gull along southern coasts of U.S.; the little gull of Old World, about 11 in. long, is smallest gull in the world, no larger than a pigeon. Along Calif. coast, the western gull is most conspicuous and most abundant seabird there throughout the year (Bent, 1921); the glaucous-winged gull is the characteristic gull of N. Pacific coast from Ore. northward.

Franklin's gull, a small white, black-headed species that nests in large colonies in prairie marshes of s. Canada and n. U.S., is unusual among gulls in that it winters to south of the Equator—to the coasts of Peru and Ecuador. Most pelagic (seagoing) is the cliff-nesting, almost circumpolar black-legged kittiwake, which follows ships, and especially fishing fleets, far out to sea to feed on garbage; the pigeon-sized ivory gull, which nests in the High Arctic of N. America, has the distinction among gulls of being the only one that is pure white (Thomson, 1964g).

Gulls are not strong fliers according to some authorities (Storer, 1948) but depend on long narrow wings mostly for gliding; use updrafts of air from ocean waves, from sides of ships, buildings near water, dunes, cliffs; also rise to great heights on rising currents (thermals) of air over land and sea. See especially Storer (1948) and Terres (1968a).

Over water, gulls circle until they see floating food or fishes at surface, then descend, sometimes hover to pick food up in bill or alight on surface to feed; they can swim well, using webbed feet, but apparently cannot or will not swim underwater; sometimes dive from air or from surface for fishes but prefer to reach below the water for food by immersing head and neck.

Gulls eat almost anything (are omnivorous) and are useful scavengers around harbors and beaches, where they clean up dead fishes, crabs, and other sea animals cast up by tides, and sewage and garbage around cities, but get in trouble around airports when they sometimes collide with planes. See Aircraft and Birds. Most gulls eat young or eggs of other gulls (see Egg-Eating), terns, dovekies, murres, and other small seabirds, and of ducks, cormorants, pelicans, and others that nest in or near the nesting gull colonies; they take food from other birds (see under Behavior) and will eat rabbits, hares, ground squirrels, rats, earthworms, cherries, mice, insects, wheat, and steak bones.

In migration, gulls follow coasts where they can find dead or living sea animals cast up on shores. Herring gulls and possibly others spit up 2-in.-long, loose pellets of harder, indigestible parts of food—fishbones, crabs' claws, for example. Gulls are noted for ingenious ways of getting food—of carrying aloft hard-shelled

clams and tough sea urchins and dropping them on hard surfaces to crack them open. See Mollusks and Birds. Gulls also tread with their feet on sand to bring to surface small animals of watery beaches. See Food and Feeding Habits.

Gulls can drink either salt or fresh water, and eliminate excess salt through a pair of glands located on the top of the skull above the eyes, well developed in most marine birds (see Nostrils); they can walk or run with agility on land and flocks of them follow the plow for unearthed grubs and mice or gather in fields to eat grasshoppers. The California gull has monument erected to it in Salt Lake City for its services to early Mormons in saving their crops from grasshoppers. See account in Economic Ornithology; Monuments to Birds.

Gulls often show little or no fear of man where not molested and will take bread, in flight, almost from one's hands or when tossed in air. A herring gull, recognized by voice, markings, and disposition for 24 years, from fall to spring each year visited area near Brenton's Reef Lightship on Narragansett Bay, where crew tossed it boiled pork and fish.

Gulls are gregarious at all times—roost together in flocks on water or on land (Thomson, 1964g) and breed together in either small or large colonies; on breeding grounds of sea cliffs, sandy islands, marshes, prairies, their harsh calls can be heard—described for herring gull as wailing, chuckling, prolonged screaming, and shorter notes, some buglelike, others squeaking or rattling, or hissing, with great individual variations depending on the gull's mood and circumstances, along with food-begging calls of the young. Gulls have highly evolved rituals besides the calls by which they communicate with each other. See Language. See especially Tinbergen's publications (1953a; 1960).

Most gulls have one brood a year; the chicks are hatched with eyes open and are covered with down; adults feed the very young by regurgitating food and holding it in the tip of the bill for the chick to peck at or by regurgitating it on ground in front of young birds.

Gulls might be confused with related but smaller white and often black-capped or crested terns of coastal beaches, but gulls in flight usually direct the bill straight forward; terns point bill and head downward; gulls usually alight on water to feed, the swallow-shaped terns usually dive into water for their prey.

Gulls at sea might be confused with the unrelated fulmar, but the fulmar has a thicker neck and heavier bill, with tubular nostrils; in flight it glides and banks on stiffly held wings, like a shearwater.

Gulls, also terns, do not have a cere on the bill, as do their relatives the skuas and jaegers—predatory birds of the Skua Family. Gulls are protected by federal law, but to sustain an injured or ill one, offer it fish, mice, fruit, meat, bread, and a pool for bathing (Walker, 1942).

Kittiwake is common name for small graceful gulls: the black-legged kittiwake of the N. Atlantic, the red-legged kittiwake in the Bering Sea; both are N. Hemisphere species that nest on seaward-facing cliffs; range far at sea after nesting season and often follow ships or fishing fleets. According to Austin (1961), some black-legged kittiwakes, banded in Great Britain, and recovered in Labrador and Newfoundland, proved their cross-oceanic wanderings. Black-legged kittiwakes, unlike other gulls that are seldom out of sight of land, range over entire N. Atlantic O.; are most oceanic of all gulls except ivory and Ross' gulls, which range widely over pack ice of Arctic O.; black-legged kittiwakes are probably most numerous of all gulls; nest in enormous colonies. See Fisher and Lockley (1954) for other interesting details; also Coulson (1966), who discovered that 64% of breeding females retain the same mate from previous breeding season.

Terns live along seacoasts and about interior lakes and marshes; are generally smaller than gulls, more slender and more graceful; have sharp-pointed bills, not hooked at tip as in gulls; most have long, pointed wings and deeply forked tails; for this reason often called "sea swallows." Sexes are outwardly alike; most terns are white with black caps; most dive from height in air headfirst into water for live minnows, squids, shrimps. Terns are more selective in their diets (gulls are omnivorous) and in flight seldom soar as gulls do but fly with almost constant beat of wings.

The feet of terns are webbed, and though most terns can alight on water and float buoyantly, they seldom swim because their feet are too small and weak to propel them strongly; calls of terns are harsh and some terns have considerable vocabulary; many pairs, especially coastal species, have a courtship in which both fly swiftly with much wing-fluttering and screaming, others often joining in the chase; at the end of the flight, the male offers a small fish in his bill to the female; male is aggressive in defending the territory. Tinbergen considers that the male tern may carry a fish in flight over the ternery when he is seeking a mate, and there are many variations of the "fish flight." Apparently some or most terns mate for life. Incubation of eggs by terns is by both sexes.

Terns are highly sociable; usually nest in large colonies, but even though nests in colony already prepared, majority may suddenly desert the colony and settle on new area perhaps several miles away; they are most successful in breeding when they can nest close together in large numbers (Fisher and Lockley, 1954); they are vigorous in defending their nesting colonies against gulls, predatory birds, and other animals; will often try to intimidate human intruders. See Nests and Nesting; Young and Their Care.

The downy gray or brown chicks hatch with eyes open but stay in nest for first day or two, during which time the parents brood them against heat of sun (which, if parents kept away from them too long on a hot day, would kill them) and against rain. Both parents feed the young; offer fishes to young which swallow them whole—frequently fishes are longer than chicks themselves—at which chicks gulp uncomfortably with tail of fish hanging from mouths while head being digested in stomach.

Terns are protected by law but to sustain an injured or ill bird, offer it small live fishes. Keep captive within enclosure to keep out dogs, cats, rats, etc., also provide small pool for bathing; also offer some fresh raw meat each day. Provide resting place or it will drown (Fisher and Lockley, 1954).

Natural enemies of terns and their eggs and young are foxes, raccoons, weasels, rats, gulls and other seabirds, also, in tern colonies along open beaches near resorts, people attracted to ternery by screaming birds, and who wander into it (or drive through it), often unknowingly, step on and crush eggs or young, which are difficult to see because of their protective coloration. Another and latest threat to terns has been massive spraying of marshes with insecticides, mainly DDT, for mosquito control. According to Austin (1961), large numbers of terns, some 5 to 12 years old, have been found dead on New England beaches, which autopsies showed had been killed by DDT acquired from minnows. See Hays and Risebrough (1972).

In the last decade of the 19th century and in first decade of present one, plume hunters along the Atlantic coast killed vast numbers of terns for the millinery trade and eggers collected and ate their eggs. The large colonies along the Va. coast of the gull-billed, royal, and least terns were virtually annihilated and similar destruction of terns along the Gulf coast from La. to Fla. and north along Atlantic coast to New England states (Bent, 1921); the smallest N. American tern, the least tern, was killed in incredible numbers—up to 100,000 in a season along east coast of U.S.; from about year 1800, for almost 100 years, feathers of least and roseate terns were in demand—their wings and whole feathered skins were used to decorate women's hats (Fisher and Lockley, 1954).

Noddy is common name for dark tropical terns. In their courtship, noddies have an elaborate head-nodding ceremony, which members of the pair also use in greeting one another at the nesting colony—from this behavior is said to have gotten its common name. The brown noddy is the only N. American tern that nests above ground level (Rand, 1965); noddies are unusual among terns in that they have rounded tails instead of forked, as in other species.

Gull, black-backed. *See* Gull, great black-backed, and Gull, lesser black-backed.

Gull, black-headed, *Larus ridibundus* (LAR-us rid-ih-BUND-us); genus name: Lat., from Gr. word meaning a ravenous seabird; species name: from Lat. *ridere*, to laugh, apparently in allusion to this bird's call. (Color ill., page 418.) A gull of Europe and Asia that sometimes winters in n. and ne. N. America; 14–15 in. long, white gull with bright red bill; brown head, not black; legs and feet red, mantle pale gray; in fall and winter head is white with dark brown spot below the eyes; immatures resemble immature Bonaparte's gulls but are lighter brown, with yellow legs and feet; status has changed in e. N. America since first one was collected, Jan. 27, 1930, at Newburyport, Mass., by Ludlow Griscom; is one of several small hooded gulls whose head is brown rather than black in the breeding plumage; has recently become a wintering bird in some parts of N. America; for example, Erskine (1963) saw 16 near Glace Bay, Nova Scotia, Jan. 15, 1963,

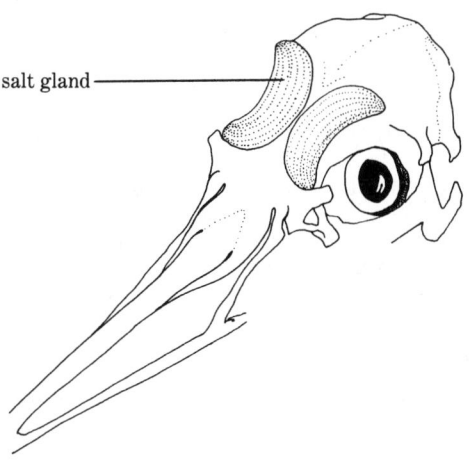

salt gland

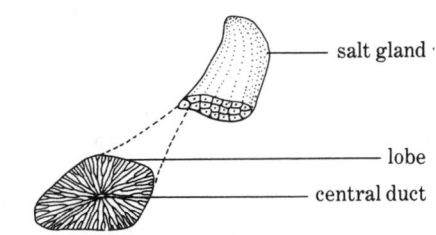

salt gland

lobe

central duct

GULL FAMILY
The presence of a pair of salt glands in gulls and other seabirds enables these birds to drink salt water. Each gland is composed of lobes that have a central duct surrounded by capillaries and thousands of salt-extracting cells. The salt is passed from capillary to cell and flows in a highly concentrated clear fluid through the ducts into the nasal cavities, and is eliminated through the bird's nostrils.

Black-headed gull

GULL FAMILY

merely some of many black-headed gulls now common on the east coast of N. America, and ranging as far south as Fla.

Feeding Habits: Thrives in inland freshwater habitats as well as coastal regions, where it hawks for aerial insects, searches muddy places for worms, or plunges and dips into the water for food. Eats weed seeds and waste grain in fields, grasslands, and marshes; scavenges for food in harbors or sheltered mud flats where sewage discharged.

Nest: Along seacoast or in freshwater marshes, usually in large colonies; nest of loose material, built on ground, sometimes (rarely) in trees, bushes, or on rocks.

Eggs: 3, brown, pale green, or blue, marked with black, brown, and gray.

Incubation: 20–24 days; young estimated to fly first about 40 days after hatching (Fisher and Lockley, 1954).

Age: Greatest ages reached by banded black-headed gulls in Switzerland were 18, 18, 20, and 24 years (Nice, 1966a); in the Netherlands, one reached 30 years (Perdeck and Spreck, 1964); a female banded as chick in English gullery, June 13, 1910, found sitting dead on her nest on May 26, 1930, when 20 years old; had died because she was egg-bound (Robinson, 1938). *See* Eggs and Egg-Laying; Sexual Maturity. A young black-headed gull taken from nest and raised by one of peasants of Faeroes Is. and given its liberty would return to eat from man's hands; was still living 63 years after hatching (Allen, 1925).

Flight Speed: Timed in England, 21–30 m.p.h. (Roberts, B. B., 1932).

Hybrids: Has crossbred with herring gull and others in captivity (Gray, 1958).

Range: Nests in Iceland and n. and c. Eurasia; winters south to n. Africa, s. Asia and Philippines; has strayed to Aleutian Is., Greenland, Labrador, Newfoundland, Mass., and N.Y., Mexico and West Indies; has summered in Nova Scotia and most of coast of e. U.S.

Gull, black-tailed, *Larus crassirostris* (LAR-us crass-ih-ROS-triss); genus name: *see* Gull, black-headed; species name: Lat., thick-billed. Asiatic gull, in N. America accidental at San Diego Bay, Calif., where one collected, Nov. 26, 1954 (Small, 1974); 19 in. long; yellow legs; yellow bill with red tip and black band; gray wings with black primaries, and tail with broad black band almost at tip; immature resembles immature ring-billed gull but tail is almost completely black.

Range: Nests in e. Asia, se. Siberia to China; straggler to N. America.

Gull, black-toed. Another name for the parasitic jaeger in Skua Family.

Gull, Bonaparte's, *Larus philadelphia* (LAR-us): genus name: *see* Gull, black-headed; species name: of the city in Pa. near where type specimen was collected; common name: given by George Ord, Philadelphia scientist, for Charles Lucien Bonaparte, French zoologist, who lived for a time in Philadelphia. (Color ills., pages 418, 419.) In summer, Canada and Alaska; seen in winter along Pacific, Atlantic,

and Gulf coasts; smallest American gull; 12–14 in. long; wingspread about 36 in.; adult in summer has black head, gray mantle, white underparts, white tail, white outer primaries, and red-orange legs; bill small, black; in winter, black head becomes white with conspicuous round black spot behind each eye; utters strident, nasal *cheer*, some notes shrill whistles, ternlike; flight is light and buoyant, more ternlike than gull-like, moves in loose flocks.

Feeding Habits: Largely insects when inland, or fish at surface of lakes and bays; scavenges in harbors and about sewer outlets; also eats crustaceans and marine worms (Bent, 1921).

Nest: Usually solitary or in small groups in spruce-fir forests; often 5–20 ft. up on branch of spruce near or over water ; nest of twigs and sticks lined with mosses, lichens, grasses, saddled on horizontal branch.

Eggs: June–July; 2–3, usually 3, buffy to olive, evenly spotted or blotched with browns.

Incubation: 24 days (Jehl and Hussell, 1966); age when young first fly unknown.

Other Names: Bonaparte's rosy gull; black-headed gull; sea pigeon.

Weights: One, 205 gr. (Hughes, 1970), or about 7¼ oz.

Range: Nests from w. and c. Alaska, s. Yuk., n. and w. Mack., n. Sask., ne. Man., w.-c. Ont., south and west to w.-c. Sask., se. Alta., and c. B.C.; a few may summer in n. U.S.; winters from c. Wash. to s. Baja Calif., from s. Ont., N.Y., and New England south to c. Fla., s.-c. La., and s. Tex., also in Bermuda.

Gull, burgomaster. Name in allusion to dominating habits. *See* Gull, glaucous.

Gull, California. *Larus californicus* (LAR-us cal-ih-FOR-nih-cus); genus name: *see* Gull, black-headed; species name: Lat., of California. (Color ill., page 419.) A gull from w. U.S., slightly smaller than herring gull, which it resembles; state bird of Utah; 21–22 in. long; wingspread about 48–54 in.; yellow bill, lower mandible spotted red and black; has gray mantle, black-tipped wings; green or gray-green legs; first-year (immature) birds are brown.

Feeding Habits: California gull is one of most useful birds to agriculture; on western plains, where it lives in summer, flocks to fields to eat crickets, grasshoppers, cutworms, and mice; also feeds on dead fish and garbage; is commemorated by statue erected to it by Mormons in Salt Lake City. *See* Monuments to Birds.

Nest: Built in colonies, often with ring-billed gulls, on islands in freshwater or alkaline lakes and marshes; nest 14–18 in. across, of rubbish, dead weeds, straw, and feathers built up on bare ground.

Eggs: May–June; usually 3, olive-buff, often boldly marked with striking colors; spotted more or less evenly with small spots of irregular size and shape or with large spots and blotches of gray or darker brown.

Incubation: 23–27 days (Behle and Goates, 1957); age when young first fly unknown; one brood raised each year.

Accidents: One killed in flight when struck by a golf ball (Lincoln, 1931).

Age: Of five banded at Alta., Canada, two found dead at 6 years; one at 7; one at 7½ years; one reported to age 12 years, 2 months (Kennard, 1975); potential longevity probably much greater.

Host to Cowbirds: Accidental (Friedmann, 1963); one record of cowbird's egg in California gull's nest at Stump Lake, N.D., June 1899.

Range: Nests in interior N. America near large lakes from n.-c. Mack., Sask., Man., south to e.-c. N.D., c. Mont., nw. Wyo., e. Idaho, nw. Utah, nw. Nev., ne. Calif., se. Ore., and s. Wash.; a few in summer along Pacific coast from Ore. to s. Calif., B.C., nw. Sask. (see details in Small, 1974); winters from s. Wash., e. Idaho, and southward along Pacific coast around coast of Calif. to Baja Calif., rarely C. America; casual occurrence in sw. Alaska, Ariz., Colo., Kans., s. Tex. and Fla.

Gull, common. See Gull, herring, Gull, Mew, and Gull, ring-billed.

Gull, fork-tailed. See Gull, Sabine's.

Gull, Franklin's, *Larus pipixcan* (LAR-us pip-IX-can); genus name: *see* Gull, black-headed; species name: Aztec word, suggesting Mexico, from which country this species was first described; both the present common name, Franklin's gull, and the old scientific name, *Larus franklini*, were given it by Swainson and Richardson (1832), from a specimen of the gull collected along the Saskatchewan R., Canada, in honor of Sir John Franklin, English explorer of the Arctic; however, it was later discovered that J. G. Wagler, in 1831, had already named the bird *Larus pipixcan*, from one he named and described from Mexico; according to the rules of priority in zoological nomenclature, Wagler's scientific name is the one now used, although the bird still bears the common name Franklin's gull (*see* similar account in biography of Ross' gull). (Color ills., page 420.) Franklin's is a gull of our Great Plains, Prairies, and Great Salt Lake; often called prairie dove, is common gull of summer prairies; winters mostly south of U.S.; 13–15 in. long; wingspread about 36 in.; in summer, *black head* with pale rosy wash on breast; dark mantle; resembles the dark-mantled laughing gull, but Franklin's has black wing tips with white outer edge, and a white band across wings near tips that separates black of tip from gray of inner part of wing; only other gull about prairies resembling Franklin's is ring-billed, which, however, has a *white head* and white spots in the black wing tips (similar laughing gull has dark-blended wing tips); in fall and winter, head of Franklin's is white with dusky patch from eyes to over back of head; immature has dark mantle, white below, and white rump; has dark tail band and touch of dusky on back of head; while feeding utters shrill *kuk-kuk-kuk*, alternated at times with its characteristic *weeh-ah, weeh-ah*, first syllable prolonged and rising; call is higher-pitched than laughing gull's.

Feeding Habits: Eats mostly insects in summer; follows farmer plowing to get unearthed cutworms and grubs; catches dragonflies and other flying insects while in flight; eats grass-

hoppers and crickets; hovers above water of sloughs and small ponds, where it catches aquatic insects, small fishes (Bent, 1921).
Nest: Built of dead marsh plants among reeds of marsh, often floating on water, sometimes attached to standing reeds; nesting colonies of up to 15,000–20,000 reported.
Eggs: May–June; 2–3, usually 3, dull brown or green-brown, spotted or splotched with dark browns.
Incubation: Estimated 18–20 days; age when young first fly unknown (Reilly, 1968).
Other Names: Franklin's rosy gull; prairie dove; prairie pigeon.
Weights: Two averaged 275 gr. (Hughes, 1970), or about 9¾ oz. Another, collected Marysville, Mo., 325 gr., or about 11½ oz., this gull, collected at a sewer lagoon, had swallowed a large prairie vole, *Microtus ochrogaster* (in crop) and an adult western harvest mouse was in its gizzard (see *The Auk*, Feb. 1977, p. 163).
Range: Nests in marshes or along lakeshores from se. Alta., s. Sask., sw. Man., south to e.-c. Ore., nw. Iowa, sw. Minn., Dakotas, nw. Utah; winters in Pacific O. from Guatemala south to Gulf of Panama, Galápagos Is., and Chile, and along n. coast of Gulf of Mexico from Tex. to La.; accidental in Hawaiian Is., and from N.B., Canada, and Mass. south along Atlantic coast to Va., in West Indies and Tristan da Cunha; in Jan. 1968, Peterson and Watson (1971) noted Franklin's gulls all the way to Straits of Magellan, a southern extension of its wintering range of about 1,000 mi.

Gull, frost. *See* Kittiwake, black-legged.

Gull, glaucous, *Larus hyperboreus* (LAR-us high-per-BO-ree-us); genus name: *see* Gull, black-headed; species name: Lat., northern; *glaucous* (GLAW-kus), from Gr. *glaukos*, blue-gray. (Color ill., page 421.) In summer, in N. America, Arctic areas of Canada and Alaska; in winter, along both Atlantic and Pacific coasts, occasionally inland; one of largest of gulls; 26–32 in. long; wingspread 60–66 in.; pale, white-bodied, gray-winged gull with *white* (not dark) wing tips; outstanding characteristics of this gull and of N. Atlantic Iceland gull are their very pale-gray upperparts (mantle) and pure-white wing primaries; glaucous gull is larger than similar Iceland gull but has bright yellow eye-ring (Iceland gull has red eye-ring) and longer, stouter bill; usually silent but utters some wailing notes similar to those of herring gull, also a low chattering croak while gliding (see other details in Bent, 1921).

Feeding Habits: Is to large extent a bird of prey; lives during summer much on young of murres and other alcids, young ducks and young gulls; other fresh foods (it is also scavenger) are fishes and mollusks taken from other seabirds; also eats starfishes, sea urchins, surface-swimming amphipods and crustaceans, and eggs of other seabirds (Bent, 1921). In Arctic, is important predator associated with peak in life cycle of lemmings (Maher, 1970).
Nest: Usually built on narrow ledges of steep cliffs facing the sea; usually near colonies of

murres and other seabirds on which the glaucous gull preys; also on small islets in lakes of the tundra or coastal dunes; built of grasses, mosses, and seaweeds.
Eggs: May–July; 2–3, usually 3, buffy brown or deep olive-buff, irregularly marked with chocolate brown.
Incubation: 27–28 days; age when young first fly unknown; one brood each year.
Other Names: Blue gull; burgomaster gull; harbor gull; ice gull; owl gull; white minister; white-winged gull.
Age: One, banded in Netherlands, 21 years old (Perdeck and Spreck, 1964).
Hybrids: Gray (1958) gives a few records of glaucous gull × lesser black-backed gull; Iceland gull; and great black-backed gull.
Weights: One male, Banks Is., Canada, 5 lbs. (Manning *et al.*, 1956).
Range: In N. America, nests on Arctic coasts and islands from n. Alaska and the Pribilofs and from Greenland south to Hudson Bay, Labrador, and Newfoundland; winters from southern part of breeding range or from edge of open water through Great Lakes region, along Atlantic coast south to Long Is., N.Y., uncommon farther south; casual to Ga. and Fla.; along Pacific coast south to s. Calif., a very rare winter visitor in state (Small, 1974); rare in interior U.S. and Canada: Alta., s. Man., Minn., Wyo., Neb., Utah, Mo., n. Tex., and s. Miss.

Gull, glaucous-winged, *Larus glaucescens* (LAR-us glaw-SES-enz); genus name: *see* Gull, black-headed; species name: Lat. for graying, from Gr. *glaukos*, blue-gray, bluish. (Color ill., page 421.) The most abundant and most widely distributed gull of N. Pacific coast (Bent, 1921); in summer to Alaska; 24–27 in. long; wingspread about 54 in.; adult is *white, pink-footed*, with *pale* gray mantle, and gray at tips of wings marked with small white spots; its flight, behavior, and calls are similar to herring gull's.

Feeding Habits: Omnivorous; scavenges for garbage on docks, dumps, and shores near coastal cities; eats garbage dumped from ships; cleans up wastes of seals slaughtered for their hides on Pribilofs; also forages over ocean a few miles off coast, where eats carrion and fishes; sometimes forces pelicans, cormorants, and sea ducks to give up food; gathers barnacles, mollusks, and sea urchins from shore and drops them on rocks from high in air to crack them open.
Nest: In large colonies, especially in Alaska, also in smaller colonies farther south; nest is mound of dried straw, seaweeds, kelp, sometimes including fishbones and feathers; built among tufts of plant life or in open on rocky ledge.
Eggs: Late May into July; 2–3, usually 3, buff, olive-buff, or olive, marked with various shades of brown.
Incubation: 26–28 days; young first fly about 35–54 days after hatching (Vermeer, 1963); one brood a year.
Age: One, banded state of Wash., 6½ years old; two others: one 8 years, 3 months, old when caught on hook by fisherman; another 9 years, 3 months old; one banded Mittenatch Is., B.C., reached 20 years, 62 days; another on Mandarte Is., 21 years (Campbell, 1968); one banded San Juan Is., Wash., still alive at 22 years, 1 month.
Flight Speed: Timed in state of Wash., 20–28 m.p.h. (Rathbun, 1934).
Hybrids: Interbreeds commonly with the herring gull in Cook Inlet region of Alaska, where nesting areas of the two overlap (Williamson and Peyton, 1963).
Weights: 2½ lbs. (Pough, 1957); also, one 618 gr., or about 1½ lbs.
Range: In summer nests on rocky cliffs among seabird colonies of N. Pacific coast, from Alaska and the islands of St. Lawrence, Pribilofs, and Aleutians, south to nw. Wash.; winters from se. Alaska south along the Pacific coast to s. Baja Calif.; accidental in e. Hawaiian Is.

Gull, gray-winged. *See* Gull, Kumlien's.

Gull, great black-backed, *Larus marinus* (LAR-us mah-RYE-nus); genus name: *see* Gull, black-headed; species name: Lat., marine, of the sea; *great*, for large size. (Color ill., page 421.) In summer and in winter, along N. Atlantic coast of N. America; one of largest of all N. American gulls, comparable in size to more northern glaucous gull; 28–31 in. long; wingspread 60–66 in. (5–5½ ft.); adult is a white gull with black mantle; snow-white head and tail; yellow bill with red spot near tip; pink legs and feet; usually silent except on breeding grounds, where very noisy, uttering loud, harsh cries or ravenlike croaks—a long-drawn scream, *keeaaw*, on lower key than that of herring gull; a short, more quickly uttered *kow, kow, kow*; a hoarse laughing *ha, ha, ha.*

Feeding Habits: Omnivorous and voracious feeder; highly domineering over other gulls on nesting grounds, where it feeds much on eggs, young, and some adults of seabirds; often takes fishes from other seabirds; scavenges on garbage, hunts maritime mud flats for fishes, dead whales, and cormorants washed up by tide.
Nest: Usually built solitary or in small, sometimes large, colonies often with herring gulls on coastal islands on ground or on ledges of cliffs, usually on high place from which it can see all about; nest is of seaweeds, grasses, mosses, and some feathers and sticks, all in a hollow or depression.
Eggs: May–June; 2–3, usually 3, brown or olive, spotted with brown.
Incubation: 26–28 days; young fly first about 42–56 days after hatching (Bannerman, 1962).
Other Names: Black-backed gull; black minister; cobb; coffin-carrier; saddleback; wagell.
Age: One, banded Que., Canada, shot in Newfoundland when 6½ years old; another, banded Gardiners Is., N.Y., still alive when 10 years, 3 months, old; captive lived in National Zoo, Washington, D.C., 17 years, 5 months; one, banded, reported from Finland, lived to 19 years, 11 months (Clapp, 1976).
Hybrids: Gray (1958) reported many crosses in captivity between the great black-backed and the glaucous gull in the Copenhagen and Stockholm zoos; the F_1, or first-generation hybrids, are sometimes fertile, and a few F_2, or second-generation hybrids, have been hatched. Natu-

ral crosses between the great black-backed and the herring gull also reported (Foxall, 1979).
Range: Nests along coast in British Isles, n. France, Iceland, and all of Russia and Scandinavia; in N. America, from c. and s. Greenland south to e. Labrador, se. Que., the Maritime Provinces, and extending range along Atlantic coast from N.J. southward; essentially a coastal species but regularly wanders up large rivers and sometimes on lakes and reservoirs of interior U.S.; winters from e. Labrador and in Great Lakes area south along Atlantic seaboard to Fla. and Bermuda; accidental in Neb., s. Ohio, and W.Va.

Gull, haddock. Local name in Mass. for the black-legged kittiwake.

Gull, harbor. *See* Gull, gláucous and Gull, herring.

Gull, hawk. Another name for the parasitic jaeger in Skua Family.

Gull, Heermann's, *Larus heermanni* (LAR-us HEER-mann-eye); genus name: *see* Gull, black-headed; species name: given in 1852 by John Cassin for Dr. Adolphus Heermann, mid-19th-century field collector of birds and their eggs, especially in Calif. (Color ill., page 421.) A western gull, common along Pacific coast, except in spring when nesting; rare inland; 18–21 in. long; wingspread about 48 in.; darkest of the gulls, only species uniformly dark below (Robbins *et al.*, 1966); easiest of western gulls to identify; adult generally dark gray with *whitish head, red bill,* and *black tail* (Peterson, 1961); utters a whining *whee-ee* (cat-like cry) and oft-repeated *cow-auk, cow-eek* when high in air (Bent, 1921).

Feeding Habits: Eats marine fishes offshore, also shrimp and other crustaceans, also mollusks; scavenges much along shores and beaches with other gulls; at times takes fishes from pelicans and cormorants but is not a great eater of eggs of other birds (see Bent, 1921).
Nest: On rocky islands off coast of Mexico, nests were built on ground between boulders or nestled in bunchgrass; made of sticks, dry grasses, and weeds, sometimes lined with feathers.
Eggs: Apr.–June; 2–3, general ground color, pearl gray with slight cream tinge, spotted and blotched with lavenders, browns, and olive.
Incubation: Period of and age when young first fly unknown.
Other Name: White-headed gull.
Weights: One, 544 gr. (Hughes, 1970), or about 1¼ lbs.
Range: Open marine waters and shores; nests almost entirely on Raza Is., Gulf of Calif., plus a few on islands along the middle of the peninsula off the west coast of Baja Calif.; may range from w. coast of Mexico north to Vancouver Is., B.C.; winters along coast from Ore. to Guatemala; accidental in N.M.

Gull, herring, *Larus argentatus* (LAR-us are-jen-TAY-tus); genus name: *see* Gull, black-headed; species name: Lat., silvered, silvery; *herring* alludes to the fish, which is only part

of its varied diet. (Color ills., pages 422, 423.) The common large "sea gull" of the Atlantic coast (it also winters along the Pacific coast) and along lakes and rivers of interior U.S.; possibly the best-known and most widely studied gull of N. America and Europe (Reilly, 1968); 22–26 in. long; wingspread about 54 in.; adult is white with blue-gray back and mantle; white underparts—look for combination of black wing tips and flesh-colored legs (Peterson, 1947); has yellow bill with red spot near tip of lower mandible; larger than the very similar California gull and ring-billed gull; immatures in first-year plumage are dark brown; in flight, may flap slowly along in calm weather close to water or high in air when usually in loose flocks; in rising, a flock often ascends nearly vertically in a large circle all together in beautiful graceful circling flight (see details in Bent, 1921; see also Appendix I of Terres, 1968, for some technicalities of gull flight); utters loud *kleew kleew,* also a *kak-kak-kak* of alarm, or *kek-kek-kek;* plaintive wailing notes; a loud trumpeting *kyou-kyou-kyou,* squeals, nasal cawing, and mewing cries (see interpretations of calls by Tinbergen, 1953a).

Feeding Habits: Feed on small fish driven to the surface by tuna and other predatory fishes; forages for wastes and sewage along waterfronts of towns, cities, or at dumps; follows ships on ocean for garbage, also fishing boats for wastes thrown overboard; hunts animal carrion, dead fishes, mollusks, crustaceans, marine worms, starfishes, and sea urchins along exposed mud flats and beaches; from aloft, often drops hard shellfishes on ground, roads, boat decks, beaches, or rocks to open them, and in winter, drops mussels on ice (*see* Mollusks and Birds); also eats eggs and young of other seabirds (*see* Egg-Eating; Cannibalism); sometimes ranges far inland to follow plowing of fields for worms and grubs exposed; also eats mice, rats, and other rodents; insects, some wild berries, and marine algae; sometimes takes fishes from other water birds.
Nest: Generally in colonies on ground near sea, lake, or river; often associated with nesting cormorants on rocky or grassy coastal islands; sometimes nests in trees when nests on ground disturbed by man; at Boston, Mass., has even nested on top of buildings; nest, usually in slight hollow in ground, is built up of weeds, grasses, and seaweeds.
Eggs: Me., May–Aug.; Mich., May–June; 2–3, usually 3, ground colors of blues, grays, greens, browns, splotched, spotted, or streaked with browns, blacks, and lavenders.
Incubation: 25–27 days; young first fly at about 42–49 days after hatching; one brood raised a year; young require 3 years of successive annual molts to gain adult plumage.
Other Names: Common gull; harbor gull; lake gull; sea gull; winter gull.
Age: Banded herring gulls in Me., Mass., Mich., Wisc., lived from 4 to 6½, 7, and almost 8 years; another to 15 years, 2 months; one banded by A. O. Gross lived to 27 years; one, banded Holland, 31 years, 11 months, old (Clapp, 1976); another, banded in Me. reportedly lived to about 36 years (Pettingill, 1967) but age was later discovered to be 18 years, not 36 (see Jon-

kel and Pettingill, 1974); another lived in wild to 31 years, 2 months (see Kennard, 1975); two captives at Morehead City, N.C., lived to 45 and 49 years (Pearson, 1935).
Albinism: A total albino, a half-grown young one, pure white, eyes pink, reported at Round Is. in Green Bay, Wisc.; also, two adults reported in spring 1937 in same area (Lyon, 1938) were total albinos with pink eyes; Nickell (1964c) reported two pure albino chicks with pink eyes, one in summer 1962, one in summer 1963, at colony at Rogers City, Mich. Of 7,716 herring gulls banded by Nickell in 7 years, these were the only albinos.
Flight Speed: Timed in Mich., 15–39 m.p.h. in light wind (Schnell, 1965).
Hybrids: Crosses or hybrids of herring gull × lesser black-backed gull in captivity; also reported at times in wild; also herring gull × great black-backed gull in captivity (Gray, 1958); also with black-headed gull; in Cook Inlet region of Alaska, herring gull interbreeds commonly with glaucous-winged gull where their nesting areas overlap (Williamson and Peyton, 1963) and with glaucous gull in Iceland; also in wild with great black-backed gull (Andrle, 1972).
Weights: To about 2½ lbs.
Range: Nests above high water on ground along seacoasts and shores of lakes from Alaska, Mack., Greenland, and on northern islands south to s. B.C., s. Mack., e. Alta., w. Sask., e. Mont., s. Man., n. Minn., c. Wisc., c. Mich., n. Ohio, n. N.Y., and Labrador south to middle Atlantic coast and recently to outer banks of N.C. (Drury and Kadlec, 1974); winters on both coasts from southern limits of nesting range throughout U.S., occasionally as far south as Mexico, Panama, Bermuda, and Barbados.

Gull, ice. Local name (in Me., Mass., where winter visitor) for the glaucous gull.

Gull, Iceland, *Larus glaucoides* (LAR-us glaw-COY-deez); genus name: *see* Gull, black-headed; species name: a combined word formed from Gr. *glaukos* and *eidos,* form, or appearance, meaning like, or resembling, the glaucous gull; *Iceland,* for the Arctic island from which came the specimen, or specimens, of this gull on which its scientific name and description were based. (Color ill., page 425.) An uncommon gull of N. Atlantic coast, rare on Great Lakes; 23–26 in. long; wingspread about 50 in.; smaller than glaucous gull but similar to it in every plumage; *eye-ring is red* (glaucous gull has bright yellow eye-ring); also has proportionately smaller bill than glaucous; smaller than herring gull but differs from it markedly in having *white wing tips* in all plumages (Robbins *et al.*, 1966); in general appearance, adult has white head, tail, breast, a *pale gray mantle,* and a yellow bill; utters calls very similar to those of herring gull, with which it often feeds.

Feeding Habits: Scavengers for refuse around docks, piers, and dumps in winter; often feeds with herring gulls; fishes skillfully; also eats marine crustaceans and some berries (Bent, 1921).

Nest: In colonies on cliffs, sometimes with other species of gulls; nest built of mosses, grasses, and seaweeds.

Eggs: May–July; 2–3, red-brown with chocolate markings.

Incubation: Period of and age when young first fly unknown.

Other Name: White-winged gull.

Hybrids: Crosses of Iceland gull with glaucous gull and with lesser black-backed gull reported (Gray, 1958).

Range: In N. America, nests on cliffs along coast from Ellesmere Is. and Greenland south to Baffin Is., Canada; outside N. America, in Iceland rarely; non-breeding birds reported in summer south to s. Labrador, Mass., and casually to Minn. and Ont.; winters along Atlantic coast from Newfoundland to s. N.J. and Va., seen most frequently at garbage dumps, sewer outlets, and fishing piers; in N.Y. rare to uncommon winter visitor on or near coast; rare inland except around Hudson R. (Bull, 1964); casual in Great Lakes area; accidental in Neb., Minn., Tex., Ga., and Fla.; also winters from Iceland to Faeroes, Norway, and Sweden south to British Isles, n. France, n. Belgium, n. Netherlands, Helgoland, and the Baltic. *See also* Kumlien's gull.

Gull, ivory, *Pagophila eburnea* (pag-OF-ih-lah eh-BURR-nee-ah); genus name: from Gr. *pagos*, ice, or frost, and *philos*, loving, fond of (Jaeger, 1955); species name: Lat., like ivory in whiteness. (Color ill., page 424.) Rarely seen outside of the Arctic; bold, aggressive, one of hardiest gulls in world; lives constantly near snow and ice; reported rarely in winter south of drift ice but occasionally along N. Atlantic coast or Great Lakes; 15–19 in. long; *all-white gull with black legs, feet, and bill,* but black bill yellow-tipped in adult; about pigeon-sized, flight more pigeonlike than that of other gulls.

Feeding Habits: A scavenger, eats garbage, carcasses of dead Arctic animals, occasionally dung of seals, polar bears, whales, and wolves; eats lemming, insects, crustaceans, and mollusks.

Nest: In colonies, often on snow- or ice-covered seaside cliffs but usually in hollow on bare ground; hollow carelessly stacked with mosses, seaweeds, driftwood, feathers, and some lichens.

Eggs: July into early Aug.; 1–2, usually 2, olive-buff, marked with browns (Bent, 1921).

Incubation: About 24–26 days (Bateson and Plowright, 1959).

Other Names: Ice partridge; snow-white gull; white-winged gull.

Range: Nests on northernmost Arctic islands and coasts south to n. Melville Is., n. Baffin Is. (see MacDonald and MacPherson, 1960), n.-c. coasts of Greenland, and in Eurasia in n. Spitsbergen, n. Novaya Zemlya, and n. Severnaya Zemlya; winters over drift ice south casually to Me., more rarely to Mass., Long Is., N.Y., N.J., has strayed to B.C., Colo., Man., Wisc., and Ont.

Gull, jack (meaning small). *See* Kittiwake, black-legged.

Gull, Kumlien's. Once considered a distinct species, *Larus kumlieni* (koom-LEAN-eye); named for Thure Ludwig Theodor Kumlien (KOOM-lean), pioneering Wisc. naturalist; now classified as *Larus glaucoides kumlieni,* the western subspecies, or race, of the Iceland gull, *Larus glaucoides.* 23–24 in. long, wingspread about 50 in.; a white-bodied, *gray-winged* gull with varying amounts of gray in tips of its wings; eyes clear yellow to dark brown with a *reddish-purple eye-ring* (Smith, N. G., 1966). For an account of its fascinating taxonomic history, see Smith, N. G. (1966). Biology—that is, nesting, eggs, young, feeding habits, etc.— much the same as that of the Iceland gull.

Other Names: Gray-winged gull; lesser glaucous-winged gull.

Range: Nesting is limited to the rocky s. and e. coasts of Baffin Is. and nw. Que., where it nests on cliffs, usually in association with glaucous gulls; winters from s. Labrador to middle Atlantic coast, rarely s. U.S.; also on Great Lakes (uncommon).

Gull laughing, *Larus atricilla* (LAR-us ay-trih-SILL-ah); genus name: *see* Gull, black-headed; species name: from Lat. *ater,* black, and *cilla,* tail (name here applies only to black-tailed *immature,* not to white-tailed adults); *laughing,* in reference to its "laughing" or wailing call. (Color ill., page 424.) In summer, common along Atlantic and Gulf coasts; 15–17 in. long; wingspread about 42 in.; adult is a white-bodied, white-tailed gull with dark mantle; in summer has *black head* and white underparts; dark glittering eyes are encircled with white lids; the dark mantle blends into the solidly dark wing tips; entire rear edge of wings has white border (the similar Franklin's gull has white spots in its dark wing tips); in winter, head of laughing gull is white mottled with dusky; in flight utters a hoarse *cheer-ah! cheer-ah!* or *ka-ha, ka-ha,* and a long-drawn *hah-ha-ha-ha—hah-hah-hah,* the last few syllables drawn out in a wail, all sounding like excited laughing, from which its name.

Feeding Habits: Catches small fishes swimming at surface of water; will alight on head of brown pelican and take fishes from its gular pouch; sometimes eats eggs and downy young of terns (*see* Egg-Eating); searches flooded fields for surfacing earthworms; though not excessive scavenger, seeks scraps thrown from boats (Bent, 1921); in flight, is frequently chased vigorously by jaegers and frigatebirds, which force laughing gull to disgorge its food.

Nest: In colonies, usually built on ground of coastal islands or on tufts of grass or reeds in saltwater marshes and along beaches; nest usually large, well built of weeds, sedges, and grasses where eggs usually above tidal waters.

Eggs: La., Tex., Apr.–June; Va., N.J., May–July; 3–4, brown-olive with markings in shades of brown.

Incubation: About 20 days; age when young first fly unknown.

Age: One in National Zoo, Washington, D.C., lived to 19 years, 7 months.

Albinism: On June 4, 1964, at Moore's Beach, Cumberland County, N.J., a partial albino, with white, instead of dark, mantle, collected (shot) from flock feeding on eggs of "horseshoe crab," or king crab (*Limulus*); along shore of Delaware Bay (Frohling, 1967), apparently the first published record of albinism in the laughing gull. A sight observation of a *melanistic* laughing gull at Pensacola, Fla., reported by Weston (1934) was a dark bird with a pale head; it resembled a noddy (tern).

Range: Usually coastal but also along rivers and lakes; nests locally along coast from n. Nova Scotia, Me., and Mass. to Fla., nests on Gulf coast of Mexico from Fla. and La. to Tex., formerly in small numbers on islands at southern end of Salton Sea., Calif.; rarely wanders inland; some birds wander to Belize, Panama, and Trinidad; the only black-headed gull seen in summer in West Indies (Watson, 1966); winters from N.C. south to C. and S. America, Pacific coast of Mexico; accidental in Greenland, N.M., Colo., Neb., S.D., Wisc., and Tenn.

Gull, lesser black-backed, *Larus fuscus* (LAR-us FUSS-cus); genus name: *see* Gull, black-headed; species name: Lat., dusky. (Color ill., page 424.) Eurasian species, rare in ne. U.S.; 20–22 in. long; black to slate-gray mantle; duskily streaked head; like great black-backed gull but smaller and with *yellow,* not pink, feet and legs.

Feeding Habits: Searches in sea, on land and beaches, and in estuaries for small fishes, crustaceans, and mollusks, earthworms, and echinoderms (Bent, 1921). Behavior, calls, eggs, and nesting habits similar to those of herring gull.

Range: Europe and Africa, Persian Gulf; rare winter visitor to ne. U.S.; found south to Fla.; inland records from Hudson Bay, w. N.Y., Colo., Calif.; frequents garbage dumps, sewer outlets, on coastal beaches, tidal flats, and reservoirs, sometimes in plowed fields with herring gulls, great black-backed gulls; hybridizes with herring gull (see remarks by Bull, 1964).

Gull, little, *Larus minutus* (LAR-us mih-NUTE-us); genus name: *see* Gull, black-headed; species name: Lat., small, minute, diminutive. (Color ill., page 425.) *Smallest of all gulls;* a straggler from Europe and now nesting in N. America; 10–11½ in. long; adult in summer, white with gray mantle and jet-black hood; similar to adult Bonaparte's gull, with which it often associates, but is strikingly smaller and black hood of summer is more extensive and has *dark gray to black underwing coverts;* entire rear edge of wings is white; no black at tips of primaries as in Bonaparte's and black-headed gulls; bill, feet, and legs red; ternlike in flight but has somewhat rounded wings; in winter, head becomes white except for black spot behind each eye and dark gray cap from above eyes to back of neck; immature has black terminal tail band; wings white below but blackish V on upper surface of wings distinguishes it from immature Bonaparte's; utters a low *kek-kek-kek* and a repeated *kay-ee* (Peterson *et al.,* 1954).

Feeding Habits: Forages at surface of seas, bays, and estuaries for fishes and crustaceans; eats insects in flight inland; in winter, sometimes seen along Atlantic seaboard (Mass. and in New York City) at sewer outlets of cities.

Nest: In colonies; usually built of grasses and leaves on ground or floating or on emergent islets of plants in inland marshes.

Eggs: N. Europe, May–June; Ont., May–June; usually 3, brown to gray, marked with darker browns, grays.

Incubation: Period of and age when young first fly apparently unknown.

Weights: A male collected in winter in Miss., 4.4 oz., showed slight fat (Davis, W. M., 1971).

Range: Nests in Europe and Asia; wanders occasionally, perhaps regularly, to e. N. America, where first discovered nesting in 1962 in se. Ont. (Bull, 1964); in summer 1970, two pairs of adults with young in black tern colony at Rondeau, Ont. (Goodwin and Rosche, 1971a); an immature female collected (shot) in Stratford, Conn., June 20, 1969, first record for state (Bulmer, 1970); seldom seen beyond Great Lakes and N. Atlantic coastal region: records from Me., Mass., New York City, especially in and around New York City, Long Is., N.J., Maritime Provinces of Canada, Greenland, and Bermuda; has straggled to Ohio, w. Pa., Sask.; one shot in 1958 at Pensacola, Fla.; one collected, Dallas County, Tex., Apr. 1965; two sighted in Calif., one in Nov. 1968, another Dec. 1969 (see Small, 1974). *The first confirmed successful nesting in the U.S.* in n.-c. Wisc. in small marsh at lower Green Bay, Brown County, on June 9, 1975; three nests built up on ground, each with three eggs (Erdmann and Steffen in Tessen, 1975).

Gull, mackerel. A local name in New England for the common tern and roseate tern, from the association of these birds with schools of mackerel.

Gull, mew, *Larus canus* (LAR-us CANE-us); genus name: *see* Gull, black-headed; species name: Lat., hoary or white, this gull's general color; *mew*, from one of its calls. (Color ill., page 425.) Eurasian gull common along Pacific coast of N. America in winter; nests in Alaska and inland Canada, mainly about lakes and sea coasts; small; 16–18 in. long; gray-mantled, white gull with black wing tips; resembles larger ring-billed gull but bill is markedly shorter and *completely* yellow or yellow-green; mantle slightly darker than herring gull's; shows more white in black primary feathers at wing tips than does California or ring-billed gulls (Peterson, 1961); utters a *hiyah, hiyah, hiyah,* higher-pitched than larger herring gull's, and a mewing call, *Queeyou* or *Mee-you,* from which got its common name; immature, first-year birds very dark, brownish.

Feeding Habits: In winter goes to coast, scavenges about harbors; like other gulls, treads in mud flats for worms and other marine animals; very active feeder, rarely plunges below water; descends to surface to catch sand eels and young herring or dips bill into water while hovering; on beaches and rocks of shore picks up crustaceans, mollusks, echinoderms; travels inland from coast in large flocks to follow plow-

man and pick up worms and insect larvae; also feeds about lakes and inland marshes.

Nest: Sometimes solitary but more often in colonies on shores of lakes or sea, never far from water; nest site varies from inland marshes to hills or seaside cliffs, on beaches, or in bushes or trees (in tops of spruces near Alaskan lakes); nest built of seaweeds, grasses, weed stalks, and heather.

Eggs: May–July; usually 3, yellow-brown to green-brown, marked with browns.

Incubation: 22–25 days; young first fly about 30 days after hatching.

Other Names: Common gull; sea mew; short-billed gull.

Age: One, banded in Norway, 13 years old (Holgersen, 1957); one, reported from Denmark, 24 years, 2 months, old (Clapp, 1976).

Range: Nests in n. Europe and British Isles to c. and s. Siberia; in N. America, from n. Alaska south along coast to B.C. and, in interior, ne. Sask. and w. Mack., westward into ne. Alta. and s. Yuk.; in N. America, winters along Pacific coast from se. Alaska south along coast to s. Calif.; accidental in Wyo. and Mass., Baja Calif.

Gull, owl. A local name for the glaucous gull, perhaps because it has white coloration as does the snowy owl, another winter visitor to the U.S.

Gull, ring-billed, *Larus delawarensis* (LAR-us del-ah-war-EN-sis); genus name: *see* Gull, black-headed; species name: Lat., of Delaware; the specimen from which the species was named and described was collected along Delaware R. below Philadelphia, Pa. (Color ill., page 427.) A common gull, especially inland in summer in n. U.S. and s. Canada; strikingly resembles the larger herring gull, from which it can be distinguished by *black ring near tip of bill* (from which its common name) and yellowish or greenish legs; 18–20 in. long; wingspread about 48 in.

Feeding Habits: When inland, lives on small rodents (*see* unusual account under Swallowing), grasshoppers caught in flight, worms, grubs, and other insects picked up in freshly plowed fields; catches fishes and scavenges garbage dumps and along beaches of large bodies of water; occasionally eats eggs of cormorants and other associated nesting species (see Bent, 1921); Broun (1941) watched ring-billed gulls in Fla. hover at crowns of cabbage palmettos to snatch the fruit.

Nest: Usually in colonies on islands or shores of freshwater lakes, associated with terns, cormorants, ducks, and other gulls; nest, about 12 in. across, is made of weeds, grasses, and debris stacked on bare or rocky ground; rarely in low trees.

Eggs: May–June; usually 3, light brown, marked with darker browns, lavender, and gray.

Incubation: About 21 days; young swim at early age when taking to water to escape enemies; age at first flight unknown; most require 3 years to attain adult plumage.

Age: In Mich. study, about 67% of banded ring-bills were 3–5 years old; about 15½% lived to

more than 5; one was 14 years old when found dead in a nesting colony (Southern, 1967); one, banded in Mich., found dead when at least 21 years old.

Albinism: A pure-white, complete albino with pink eyes, legs, and feet and with white bill, reported on beach at Playa del Rey, Calif., Feb. 1959 in company with normally colored ring-billed, western, and Heermann's gulls.

Flight Speed: Timed in Mich., 11–43 m.p.h. with light wind (Schnell, 1965); in N.C., 35 m.p.h. (Cooke, 1937a).

Other Names: Common gull; lake gull.

Weights: Four averaged 488 gr. (Hughes, 1970), or about 1 lb. 1 oz.

Range: Nests in summer from s.-c. Ore., c. Wash., Alta., and n.-c. Sask., s.-c. Man., south to ne. S.D., se. Wyo., s.-c. Colo., s.-c. Idaho, ne. Calif., and in e. N. America from ne. Newfoundland, c. and s. Que., south to Lake Erie, Oneida Lake, N.Y., westward into Ohio, n. Mich., n. Wisc., and ne. Colo.; winters along Pacific coast from Wash. and in interior from Wyo. south to Mexico; also in interior of U.S. and Mexico near large lakes and rivers from Great Lakes to Gulf of Mexico, and along Atlantic seaboard, Gulf of St. Lawrence, to s. Fla. (see details in Southern, 1974b); accidental in Hawaii, Bermuda, Jamaica, Martinique, and Azores.

Gull, Ross', *Rhodostethia rosea* (rod-oh-STEE-thih-ah ROE-zee-ah); genus name: from Gr. *rhodon,* a rose, and *stethos,* breast, in allusion to the bright pink of the breast and underparts of this gull; species name: Lat., rosy, rosy-red; common name: honors James Clark Ross, 19th-century British navigator and explorer of the Arctic, who, in June 1823, on William Edward Parry's second voyage to the Arctic to seek a northwest passage, shot the first specimen of this gull known to science on e. Melville Pen. in the Canadian Arctic (see in Swainson and Richardson, 1832); the old scientific name, *Larus rossii,* also honored Ross (it was so named in 1832 by Swainson and Richardson); however, it was later discovered that in 1824, William MacGillivray, Scottish ornithologist, had already given the bird the species name of *roseus* (now *rosea*), and because of the law of priority of date of publication of scientific names, MacGillivray's name stands (*see* similar example in biography of Franklin's gull; *also* Names and Naming). One of the most beautiful of all gulls, the rarely seen Ross' gull apparently migrates in late summer and fall from its remote nesting grounds in ne. Siberia to Alaska and n. Canada (see story of some of its history in Fisher and Lockley, 1954); first N. American record for U.S. south of Alaska and n. Canada; one seen in adult winter plumage along Merrimack R. at Salisbury along Mass. coast from Dec. 7, 1974, to May 6, 1975 (see details in Miliotus and Buckley, 1975); adult is 13–14 in. long; white with gray mantle, pinkish underparts with rosy tinge strongest on breast (the white *wedge-shaped tail* distinguishes this gull in any plumage); in spring and summer, also has thin black necklace; bill black; feet and legs red; adult has winter plumage similar to that of summer but black necklace has usually been lost in molt and pink on underparts has faded; immature, first-year birds have considerable black on wing coverts and wing tips; a black ear spot; tail tipped with black, except the outermost feathers (Godfrey, 1966); utters a high melodic *a-wo, a-wo, a-wo* and *claw, claw, claw,* and a quarrelsome *miaw, miaw, miaw* (Bent, 1921); flight is ternlike.

Feeding Habits: On Arctic breeding grounds, eats beetles, gnats, and other insects; at sea, possibly marine crustaceans and other animals of the plankton (Bent, 1921; Pough, 1951); small groups often rest on ice or hover along channels of open water of Arctic.

Nest: Usually in colonies, on small low-lying islands in swampy places along rivers of Arctic tundra, often with arctic terns; nest built of dried grasses, sedges, twigs, birch and willow leaves, or even mosses, until nest is about 5–8 in. above wet surface of bogs (Witherby *et al.*, 1938–41).

Eggs: May–June (early June in Kolyma R. delta, Siberia); 2–3, usually 3, deep rich olive-green, spotted with chocolate brown (see also Dement'ev *et al.*, 1969).

Incubation: According to Buturlin (1906), more than 21 days; age when young first fly unknown.

Other Names: Cuneate-tailed gull; Ross' rosy gull; rosy gull; wedge-tailed gull.

Range: Nests in low marshy places among scrub alders in subalpine and wooded parts along lower reaches of rivers in ne. Siberia that empty into Arctic O. (see Buturlin, 1906); also, one nesting record (June 1885) on island in Disko Bay, w.-c. Greenland; in fall, between Sept. 28 and Oct. 22, a main concentration point for Ross' gulls is at Point Barrow, Alaska, with the birds moving northeast (Murdoch, 1885); Barrow has remained a known important flyway for Ross' gulls ever since Murdoch's report; is noted there in Sept. and Oct., always flying eastward; thousands seen migrating there on gray days in Sept. and Oct. (Bailey, 1948); in general, migration mainly in late summer and fall from Asian nesting grounds east to Wrangel and Herald Is. off coast of Alaska to Point Barrow; reported as rare visitor to Canadian Arctic at Boothia Pen. (Felix Harbor), Melville Pen. (Igloolik), Cornwallis Is., and Keewatin (McConnell R.); four seen on e. Baffin Is. by Neal G. Smith (Godfrey, 1966); in migration to w. Greenland and to Spitsbergen and Franz Josef Land (archipelagos in Arctic O.) and Novaya Zemlya, two large islands in Arctic O. off ne. coast of Soviet Russia; casually south in Bering Sea to Bering Is., the Pribilof Is., and St. Michael, a village in w. Alaska on s. coast of Norton Sound; winter range unknown but thought to be at sea on open waters of Arctic region (A.O.U. *Check-list,* 1957); first N. American record south of Alaska and n. Canada, one seen at Newburyport Harbor, Mass. (*see* above); also records for Churchill, Man., Gambell, Alaska, and Chicago (see Balch, *et. al.,* 1979).

Gull, rosy. *See* Gull, Ross'; Gull, Bonaparte's; and Gull, Franklin's.

Gull, Sabine's, *Xema sabini* (ZEE-mah, SAB-in-eye); genus name: New Lat., an arbitrarily invented word; according to Coues (1882), a nonsense word coined by Dr. W. E. Leach of the British Museum (Natural History); species and common names: given by Joseph Sabine for his brother Edward Sabine (SAB-in), British astronomer and physicist. (Color ill., page 426.) Common in summer on breeding grounds along Arctic coasts of N. America; elsewhere alone or in small flocks; 13–14 in. long; wingspread about 36 in.; adult is a white gull with a gray mantle and in summer has a rich, dark gray hood, edged with a fine black line; *only U.S. gull with a well-forked tail* (immature kittiwake has slightly forked tail); jet-black outer primaries of Sabine's gull have *white triangle at hind edge of the wings* in both adult and immature, and is so marked at all seasons; in winter, head is white with some gray at nape; blackish bill is yellow-tipped; feet and legs dark gray to black; in flight, ternlike, flies with continuous wing-beats, seldom glides, dips surface of water for food; never dives into water or drops to surface; occasionally hovers; utters a harsh, grating cry, similar to that of arctic tern but harsher, shorter.

Feeding Habits: Runs on mud flats in manner of plovers to find food and hunts in tundra pools for small fishes, crustaceans, insects, and worms (Bent, 1921). In tropical Atlantic, eats mostly small fishes and crustaceans, also galley scraps (Watson, 1966).

Nest: Often in association with nesting arctic terns; single nest or colonial in hollow in tundra grasses is casually lined with grasses.

Eggs: N. Alaska, May–July; n. Mack., June–July; 2–3, usually 3, brown or green-brown.

Incubation: 23–26 days (Bannerman, 1962).

Other Names: Hawk-tailed gull; fork-tailed gull.

Weights: One male, Banks Is., Canada, 175 gr., or about 6¼ oz.; two females, 155 and 166 gr., or about 5½–6 oz. (Manning *et al.*, 1956).

Range: Nests along Arctic coasts from n. Alaska, n.-c. Mack. and offshore islands, e. Keewatin, Baffin Is., and w. Greenland; also seen in summer in ne. Sask., c. and ne. Man., n. Ont., ne. Que.; reported in migration south in Aug.–Oct. from Alaska to Calif; very rare inland, occasional in the Great Basin, Great Plains, and lower Colorado R., and from Greenland to Me., Mass., and Long. Is., N.Y.; two records, June and Oct., along coast of Va. (Buckley, 1970); ranges south in winter into S. Atlantic O. and south off Pacific coast of Peru. See discussion in Fisher and Lockley (1954).

Gull, sea. *See* Gull, herring.

Gull, short-billed. *See* Gull, mew.

Gull, slaty-backed, *Larus schistisagus* (LAR-us shis-tih-SAH-gus); genus name: *see* Gull, black-headed; species name: Lat., from Gr. for slaty-backed. A rare visitor to Alaska from Pacific coast of Asia; 27 in. long; slaty-black wings and mantle, red-pink legs; similar to great black-backed gull of Atlantic coast but smaller.

Feeding Habits: Eats both dead and living fishes, carrion, berries, small mammals, and mussels obtained at low tide (Bent, 1921).

Ross' gull

GULL FAMILY

tern

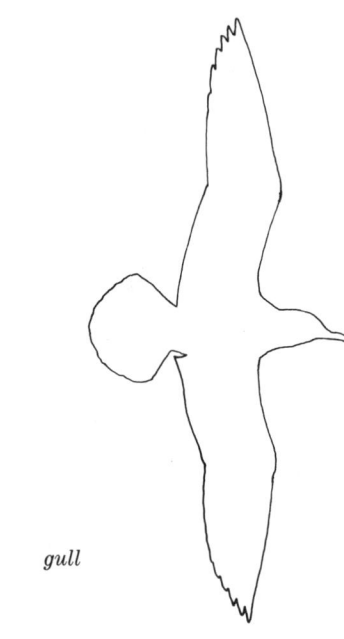

gull

GULL FAMILY
In flight, gulls tend to soar, holding their bills, which are hooked at the tip, straight forward. Terns fly with a near-constant beat of their wings, holding their sharply pointed bills and head downward. Terns are more slender than gulls and have long, pointed wings and deeply forked tails.

Nest: Of seaweeds and grasses, on rocks or small islets near shore; larger colonies when nesting on sandy beaches.
Eggs: Japan, May–June; 3, olive-buff spotted with brown.
Weights: 2½ lbs.
Range: Nests on n. Pacific islands of Asia; recorded in nw. Mack.; casual or accidental in Aleutian and Pribilof Is. and Alaskan coast.

Gull, storm. Another name for the black skimmer in Skimmer Family.

Gull, summer. *See* Gull, laughing and Tern, common.

Gull, Thayer's, *Larus thayeri* (LAR-us THAY-er-eye); genus name: *see* Gull, black-headed; species name: for John E. Thayer of Boston. (Color ill., page 426.) Slightly smaller than the herring gull, of which it was once considered a subspecies, *Larus argentatus thayeri*, until the Canadian Arctic studies of Smith, N. G. (1966), who declared the Thayer's gull to be specifically distinct and reproductively isolated from the herring and other related gulls on its breeding grounds. 22–25 in. long; according to Smith, the adult is a medium-sized, white-bodied, gray-winged gull with varied amounts of black in its wing tips; its eyes, however, are usually dark with mottled-brown irises, and it has a reddish-purple eye-ring. The herring gull has a yellow iris and an orange eye-ring.

Feeding Habits: Same as or similar to those of herring gull.
Eggs: Usually 2–3, similar to herring gull's.
Nest: In colonies on cliffs with Kumlien's and glaucous gulls.
Age: See Herring gull.
Weights: Adult males (4), Ellesmere Is., Canada, 2 lbs. 4½ oz to 2 lbs. 6 oz.; adult females (4), 1 lb. 12¾ oz. to 2 lbs. 2½ oz. (Parmelee and MacDonald, 1960).
Range: Restricted in its nesting to islands of the Canadian Arctic Archipelago, and nw. Greenland (Smith, N. G., 1966), where it nests almost exclusively on cliffs; winters on coasts of w. N. America, from s. B.C. south to s. Calif. and Baja Calif.; migrates off coasts and estuaries of s. Alaska; now considered rare in e. U.S.; records for Great Lakes (Minn., Mich., Ohio, N.Y.), N.D., and east coast south to Fla., Tex.

Gull, tide. Local name in Mass. for the common tern.

Gull, vega. Name for a subspecies of the herring gull.

Gull, wedge-tailed. *See* Gull, Ross'.

Gull, western, *Larus occidentalis* (LAR-us ock-sih-den-TAY-lis); genus name: *see* Gull, black-headed; species name: Lat., western. (Color ill., page 426.) Darkest of all Pacific coast gulls except the smaller Heermann's gull; 24–27 in. long; wingspread about 54 in.; adult is a pink-footed gull with very dark mantle; dark back and wings contrast with white underparts, head, neck, and tail; conspicuous white edge along rear of wings; yellow bill with red spot near tip of lower mandible; in flight along Pacific coast, where there are cliffs, often spirals up on rising currents of warm air until speck in sky; is primarily maritime, seen often along outer coasts of Ore. and Calif.; not often seen inland or beyond reach of tides; most common call is *quock, kuck, kuck, kuck,* uttered very rapidly.

Feeding Habits: At sea follows ships for refuse but catches and eats fishes; also scavenges along beaches for dead fishes, clams, shrimps, worms; catches small mammals; forces pelicans and cormorants to give up their catches of fish; also visits garbage dumps and eats eggs and young of cormorants, murres, and other birds in adjacent nesting colonies; drops sea urchins and mollusks from the air to hard surfaces to break shells and expose soft internal parts.
Nest: On offshore islands, on rocky ledges, or grassy slopes near beaches; nest built of weeds and grasses.
Eggs: May–July; usually 3, buff-olive, spotted with brown.
Incubation: 25–29 days; young fly about 49 days after hatching (Schreiber, 1970).
Age: Reported to 16 years (Kennard, 1975), but potential much greater; *see,* for example, ages of herring gull, in its biography.
Weights: 2½ lbs. (Pough, 1957); according to Hughes (1970), two averaged 1,283 gr., or about 2 lbs. 13 oz.
Range: Nests in colonies from n. Wash. south along Pacific coast to Magdalena Bay on west coast of Baja Calif.; winters from B.C. south through nesting range; accidental in Ariz. and Ill. (A.O.U. *Check-list,* 1957).

Gull, white-winged. *See* Gull, glaucous, Gull, Iceland, and Gull, ivory.

Kittiwake, Atlantic. *See* Kittiwake, black-legged.

Kittiwake, black-legged, *Rissa tridactyla* (RISS-ah try-DACK-tih-lah); genus name: from Icelandic *rita,* the kittiwake; species name: Lat., from Gr. *tridaktulos,* three-fingered, or three-toed (MacLeod, 1954); their shrill but pleasing cries, *kitt-ih-wake!,* have given this species and the red-legged kittiwake their common names. (Color ill., page 427.) In summer, in N. America, from Greenland to Arctic and coastal e. Canada south to Newfoundland; winters offshore along Atlantic coast; 16–18 in. long; wingspread about 36 in.; in summer, adult is all-white with gray mantle; can be distinguished by *black triangular-shaped wing tips with no white spots;* the solid black cuts straight across as if dipped in ink (Peterson, 1961); black legs and feet; has three toes (no hallux, or is rudimentary without claw); bill light yellow tinged with green; eyes dark red-brown; eyelids and inside of mouth orange or red; adults in winter are similar but patch of light gray from crown to back of neck; immatures in first winter can be told by combined dark neck band, short black legs and black wing tips, and very slightly forked, black-tipped tail; flies more swiftly than larger gulls, buoyant, graceful, with more rapid wingbeats; arrive in pairs at breeding cliffs in late Feb. to early Mar. in southern part of range; in Arctic, in Apr. and May (see details of courtship in Fisher and Lockley, 1954).

Feeding Habits: At sea most of time, drinks salt water exclusively (captives refused fresh water); assembles in enormous flocks for scraps thrown into water from ships but is basically an eater of small fishes and small mollusks, crustaceans, and other animals of oceanic plankton that drift with currents; beats wings rapidly but not deeply; usually hovers briefly before settling on surface to pick up food.

Nest: In enormous colonies, usually on high cliffs overlooking the sea; often associated with murres and other seabirds; both sexes build deeply cupped nest of seaweeds, mosses, and grasses, which kittiwakes, like gannets, tear from sides of cliffs and cement together with mud which they carry in bills and then, by treading, mold together (Fisher and Lockley, 1954); in northern waters, where buildings close to nesting cliffs, sometimes nest on building ledges, also in caves.

Eggs: Newfoundland, May–July; usually 2, blue-gray, blue-white, or light shades of buff, pink, and brown, spotted or blotched with gray or dark brown.

Incubation: In a Newfoundland colony (May–June), 23–32 days, by both sexes; young fly about 38–48 days after hatching (Coulson and White, 1958); for an especially detailed discussion of embryos and chicks, see Maunder and Threlfall (1972).

Other Names: Atlantic kittiwake; coddy-noddy; common kittiwake; frost-bird; frost gull and winter gull (in New England, where arrival is at beginning of frosts and real winter); haddock gull; jack gull; kittiwake gull; meterick; pick-me-up; pinny owl, or pinyole; snow gull; tarrock.

Age: One, banded, reported from Denmark, 15 years, 10 months, old (Clapp, 1976).

Weights: 317 gr., or about 11 1/4 oz. (Davis, W. M., 1970).

Range: In N. America, nests on sea cliffs from Greenland south on islands in Hudson Strait, Canada, and along coast of Labrador to Gulf of St. Lawrence (Godbout, Percé Rock, Magdalen Is., Bird Rock) and on Cape St. George and Baccalieu Is., Newfoundland; winters along Atlantic coast and wanders far at sea from Newfoundland and Gulf of St. Lawrence, south to s. N.J. and the Bermudas; rarely to e. Fla.; winters to Baja Calif. in Pacific area, s. N.J. and Bermuda on Atlantic coast; rare inland but records exist for most northern states across country; casual to Gulf coast, w. Va., Ky.; also nests on islands in Arctic O. from Franz Josef Land to Spitsbergen south to Iceland, the Faeroes, British Isles, Channel Is., Brittany (France), Helgoland, and Murmansk coast of n. Russia, and on islands along n. Russian coast—Severnaya Zemlya, Novaya Zemlya, New Siberian Is., Bennett Is., and Wrangel Is.

Kittiwake, common. See Kittiwake, black-legged.

Kittiwake, red-legged, *Rissa brevirostris* (RISS-ah brev-ih-ROS-tris); genus name: *see* Kittiwake, black-legged; species name: from Lat. *brevis*, short, and *rostris*, pertaining to the bill. (Color ill., page 427.) Bird of the Bering Sea and adjacent waters; also in winter along Calif. coast; 14–16 in. long; wing pattern similar to that of black-legged kittiwake, but is smaller bird with *bright red legs*, shorter bill, and dark underwing linings, unlike whitish underwings of black-legged kittiwake; its feeding habits, nest, eggs, voice, and general biology like that of black-legged kittiwake; egg records on Pribilofs, in early July.

Range: Nests on ledges of sea cliffs on the Komandorskie and Pribilof Is. in Bering Sea; winters on adjacent seas; accidental farther south to Ore.; one recent record for Nev.

Noddy, black, *Anous tenuirostris* (AH-nous ten-you-ih-ROS-tris); genus name: from Gr. words meaning mindless, unmindful, in reference to its tameness in allowing people to come near it; species name: Lat., slender-billed. (Color ill., page 436.) A dark tropical wedge-tailed tern; in N. America, seen only at Dry Tortugas, Fla.; about 14 in. long; wingspread about 28 in. (Watson, 1966); similar to the brown noddy but smaller and much blacker with white forehead and relatively longer bill than brown noddy; flight as in brown noddy.

Feeding Habits: As in brown noddy, but usually more pelagic (farther at sea).

Age: A banded one, sex undetermined, recaptured on its nest, Dec. 13, 1972, Sand Is., Midway Atoll, was at least 9 years, 10 months, old (Jobanek, 1976).

Albinism: On Mar. 17, 1968, on Laysan Is., nw. Hawaiian Is., Clapp (1974) saw a strikingly marked albinistic black noddy flying around a large nesting colony. It was an immature female, and was an example of imperfect albinism, or leucism. It had a symmetrical arrangement of whitish spots and white bars in its wings; it was apparently the first record of albinism in this species and was the only albino among 10,000 black noddies observed by Clapp.

Range: Nests on islands off Belize (last reported 1907), and Venezuela, also Fernando de Noronha, St. Paul, Martin Vas, and on Ascension Is., St. Helena, and islets in Gulf of Guinea; since 1960, an annual wanderer to Dry Tortugas Is. off Fla. Keys; to n. S. America and s. Africa; formerly bred in S. Atlantic on Tristan Group (Watson, 1966); also nests and is resident on Hawaiian Is. and tropical islands of Indian and Pacific O. (Reilly, 1968).

Noddy, brown, *Anous stolidus* (AH-no-us STOL-ih-dus); genus name: *see* Noddy, black; species name: Lat., stolid, apathetic, used here in sense of its indifference to man (Coues, 1882). (Color ill., page 436.) About 16 in. long; wingspread about 33 in. (Watson, 1966); the only noddy that nests in N. America (Fla.); lives on warm waters north and south of the Equator in both the Pacific and Atlantic O.; the only *brown* tern except sooty but sooties have forked tail and young sooty, with which brown noddy might be confused, is *completely dark*; brown noddy also has white cap, or crown, black bill,

Black noddy

GULL FAMILY

and a *wedge-shaped or rounded tail;* legs and feet dark brown; call is guttural *kaarrk,* somewhat like a crow's call; flight is strong and swift but erratic like that of nighthawk; has been likened in flight to long-winged, long-tailed dove; beats wings steadily, does not soar as sooty tern does; drinks salt water just as other seabirds do (it has salt-eliminating glands) and does so by skimming surface of ocean with bill; bathes in same way while flying by dipping head and breast in water; sometimes floats on water and swims but more often perches on buoys, floating driftwood, exposed reefs.

Feeding Habits: Seldom or never seen to dive, occasionally alights on water; follows schools of minnows, usually stays 5–10 ft. above water (much lower than sooty tern, with which it associates at sea); when small fishes or squids driven to surface by larger fishes and leap out of water, snatches them up in bill; splashes surface in dives but does not plunge deeply as do black-capped terns; occasionally hovers or feeds on surface like a gull, may also feed at night (Watson, 1966); in nesting season usually feeds near the nesting colony, or singly or in groups.

Nest: On Bird Key, Dry Tortugas, Fla., builds nest in both cactus and bay cedars in bushes to about 12 ft. up; arrives there last week in Apr.; most nests built by both members of pair using dead branches of bay cedar, seaweeds, or combination of these, nest lined with various seashells and corals; nests remain and are re-used from year to year; when new materials added, may grow to large size.

Eggs: West Indies and Fla., Feb. to early July; usually 1, pale pink-buff, spotted with pale lilac to deep red-brown.

Incubation: By both adults, reported to be 35–36 days (Bent, 1921) but this probably in error, as this is much longer than the 21–26 days of incubation of most other terns; each member of pair sits for about 24 hours on its single egg until relieved by its mate during the night; incubating bird is fed by its mate, and while incubating, so tame it will allow itself to be lifted off nest; young leave nest 20 days after hatching and climb about bushes or live on ground, where fed by adults; adults fierce in defense of young and may attack and knock hat off human intruder or strike bare head and draw blood; young believed to first fly about 30 days after hatching; brown noddies have been used in homing experiments by Watson (1908).

Age: One banded Manana Is., Oahu, Hawaii, recaptured there when it was 25 years old; another banded Bush Key, Dry Tortugas, when adult, recaptured 21 years later (Brown and Robertson, 1975).

Weights: In Fla., adults (19), 150–195 gr. (Robertson, 1972), or about 5¼–6⅞ oz.

Range: Breeds on tropical islands throughout the world, including Hawaii, and nests in colonies in bushes on Dry Tortugas, Fla., about 66 statute mi. west of Key West, Fla., also in Bahamas; on islands off coast of Yucatán, Quintana Roo, and Belize, Jamaica, Navassa Is., Hispaniola, Puerto Rico, Virgin Is., St. Martin, Sombrero, Antigua, Redonda, Guadeloupe, Dominica, St. Lucia, St. Vincent, Grenadines, Trindade, Ascension, St. Helena, Tristan da

Cunha, and islands in Gulf of Guinea; also Galápagos Is., and from Tres Marías, w. Mexico, to Cocos Is. in Pacific O. southwest of Costa Rica; casual in s. La., e. Mexico, Indian Key (Daytona Beach), Fla., S.C. (one reported Stone Harbor, N.J., Sept. 1960), and Bermuda; winters on oceans adjacent to nesting places.

Tern, Aleutian, *Sterna aleutica* (STIR-nah ah-LOO-tih-cah); genus name: Lat., stem, from Anglo-Saxon *stearn,* tern (Coble, 1954); species name: Lat., of the Aleutians, but despite its name, never reported from Aleutians until 1962 (Umnak Is.). (Color ill., page 429.) Was first discovered in 1868 on Kodiak Is. in Gulf of Alaska, southeast of Alaska Pen.; 13–15 in. long; wingspread about 32 in.; in breeding plumage is gray with black cap, *white forehead;* deeply forked tail; bill and feet *dark,* sometimes blackish; underparts, including wing linings, lead-colored; the paler arctic tern, only other tern within U.S. range of Aleutian tern, has *red bill* and *red feet,* and lacks white forehead.

Feeding Habits: Little known, probably similar to arctic tern's.

Nest: On ground (Sakhalin in Siberia, St. Michael Is., Alaska, for example, in loose colonies, mixed with those of arctic terns).

Eggs: St. Michael Is., June 23–28; usually 2, clay to olive-buff, blotched with brown; laid directly on matted grass or moss of surface of islands.

Incubation: At least 21 days (Bent, 1921).

Weights: About 4 oz. (Pough, 1957).

Range: Nests on islands in Alaska in Norton Sound, Good News Bay, and near Yakutat, Kodiak Is.; winters in nw. Pacific.

Tern, Anglican (English). *See* Tern, gull-billed.

Tern, Arctic, *Sterna paradisaea* (STIR-nah par-ad-ICE-sih-ah); genus name: *see* Tern, Aleutian; species name: from Lat. *paradisus,* park, later paradise; so named in 1763 by Erik Pontoppidan, Danish historian and Bishop of Bergen, from the original specimen of the gull from Christiansöe Is., Denmark, possibly in reference to the land in which the bird was collected. (Color ills., pages 428, 429.) In summer, nests around northern parts of world; in N. America, from Arctic islands and Alaska south to northern part of Prairie Provinces of Canada, and along Atlantic coast to Me. and Mass.; also Wash. (first Arctic tern colony in contiguous w. U.S. See Manuwal *et al.,* 1979); 14–17 in. long; wingspread 29–33 in.; black-capped white tern with gray mantle; whitish, deeply forked tail; resembles common tern in all seasons, but in spring and summer, *entire bill* of Arctic tern is blood-red (red bill of common tern usually has black tip); can be distinguished from common tern by longer tail, shorter legs, grayer underparts; when Arctic tern perched, its long tail reaches to wing tips; tail of common tern does not extend to wing tips (Robbins *et al.,* 1966); Arctic distinguished especially by tiny feet and legs, so short that when standing it appears to be crouching on ground; walks with mouse-like glide; utters a shrill *kee-kee,* a short *kee-*

kahr of alarm, like common tern but higher-pitched, also utters squeaks and grating calls; one of most famous of all migrant birds (see Rand, 1965); in its extremes of range, migrates from Arctic to Antarctic; from nesting sites of northern summer moves southward each autumn over open sea of Atlantic and Pacific to spend "second summer" near Antarctic Circle; some fly from Arctic nesting grounds down e. Pacific past Americas (common offshore in fall, very rare in spring off Calif.); in fall, some fly from northern nesting grounds eastward across Atlantic and south past Europe and Africa to Antarctic, as first pointed out by Austin (1928); some, in their longest journeys, make a round trip of more than 22,000 mi.—*see* Migration; Seabird; the Arctic tern probably sees more daylight during its lifetime than any other animal; summers in North in Arctic where up to 24 hours of daylight prevail; "winters" in S. Hemisphere where daylight hours greatly exceed those of darkness (Lincoln, 1939).

Feeding Habits: Hovers 30–40 ft. over water on beating wings, suddenly dives, strikes water with splash, often submerging, catches in bill small fish such as capelin, sand launce, or sand eel, also small crustaceans; rises from water, vigorously shakes plumage, then carries prey off in bill; can scream even with fish in mouth without dropping it (Bent, 1921).

Nest: Prefers to nest in colonies of its own kind but also nests with common terns; in Alaska, often with Aleutian terns; nest generally a mere hollow in sand, gravel, or moss, or among rocks on rocky and sandy coastal beaches; in Far North, on islands in lakes, ponds, and in marshes, sometimes on open tundra.

Eggs: June–July; usually 2, sometimes 3, brown or greenish, irregularly marked with dark brown; indistinguishable from eggs of common tern (Bent, 1921).

Incubation: 21–22 days (Witherby *et al.,* 1938–41; Hawksley, 1957); young first fly about 21–28 days after hatching (Fisher and Lockley, 1954).

Other Names: Common tern; crimson-billed tern; long-tailed tern; paradise tern; Pike's tern; Portland tern; sea swallow; short-footed tern.

Age: Two more than 7 years old when retrapped at same place where banded; one trapped alive when 9 years old; according to records of U.S. Fish and Wildlife Service, one found dead at Cape Cod, Mass., at slightly more than 23 years old; one 28 years old reported from Man., Canada; one killed by cat in Germany was 27 years old (Bergstrom, 1952); one trapped alive on its nest at Petit Manan Is., Me., June 19, 1970, was 34 years old, the longest age record of any member of Gull Family up to time; it was rebanded and released (Hatch, 1974).

Hybrids: According to Gray (1958), "presumed hybrids"—crosses between Arctic and common terns—have been reported.

Weights: One adult male and one adult female on Banks Is., Canada, 3½ oz each (Manning *et al.,* 1956); the 34-year-old trapped alive in Me. weighed 119 gr. (4¼ oz.) and appeared in excellent health.

Range: Circumpolar; nests on northern European islands and peninsulas from Iceland to Jan Mayen, Spitsbergen, Franz Josef Land, Novaya Zemlya, to Taimyr Pen. of Soviet Russia, New Siberian Is., Wrangel Is., and Siberian coast south to Bering Strait; in n. and c. British Isles, Netherlands, Denmark, s. Sweden, Estonia, Finland, and in n. Russia; in N. America, on most Arctic islands and coasts from n. Greenland south to Ellesmere Is., n. Alaska, and Aleutian Is., to s. Alaska, s. Yuk., n. Wash., s.-c. Mack., ne. Alta., ne. Man., extreme n. Ont., w.-c. Que., se. Labrador, s. Greenland, Newfoundland, and south along Atlantic coast to Me. and Mass.; winters in S. Hemisphere in subantarctic and antarctic waters of Atlantic, Pacific, and Indian Oceans.

Tern, black, *Chlidonias niger* (klih-DOAN-ih-as NYE-jer); genus name: according to Gruson (1972), a misspelling of *chelidonias,* from Gr. *khelidonias,* swallow; species name: Lat., black. (Color ill., page 430.) Nests in Old World, and in N. America, inland in prairie sloughs, marshes, from Canada south to Ohio, New England; 9–10¼ in. long; in breeding plumage, black-headed, black-bodied, with back, tail, and wings gray; undertail coverts white; has short notched tail, short broad wings; flight erratic and buoyant, somewhat like nighthawk except that this tern hovers frequently (Pough, 1951); immatures and adults in winter have *white head* and underparts; back and wings gray; darkish around eyes, ears, back of neck; dark patch on sides of breast; mottled birds, molting into winter plumage by midsummer, distinguishable by *short tail;* utters a shrill, metallic *kik-kik-kik* in flight but mainly silent in migration, and a prolonged shrill scream, *kreek* or *craik,* when attacking an intruder near its nest; in fall migrates to seacoast, where it may be distinguished from least tern by very plain wings (least has black in its wings).

Feeding Habits: Hovers meadows and grassy marshes and with bill snatches some insects from air; darts down to pick others from tall grasses—dragonflies, moths, grasshoppers, crickets, flies, beetles, and many others; also eats crayfishes and small mollusks, spiders and other invertebrates; at one time, large numbers followed men plowing fields adjacent to prairie marshes, hovering and looking for grubs turned up by plowman; in South, catches moths of cotton bollworm in flight over young cotton plants; when over salt water, in shallow dives catches small fishes, crustaceans, and other marine animals; prefers to pluck food from surface with bill like sooty tern.

Nest: In small, loose colonies, sometimes a hollow in prostrate dead canes of marsh or on floating masses of dead plants; also on muskrat houses; more often a shallow cup of canes or reeds loosely assembled and serving to keep the eggs just above water (Bent, 1921).

Eggs: May to early Aug.; usually 3, olive or buff, heavily marked with brown.

Incubation: 21–22 days (Nice, 1954); young able to leave nest a few days after hatching; closely and vigorously guarded by parents; first fly about 21–28 days after hatching (Fisher and Lockley, 1954; see also Bent, 1921; Cuthbert, 1954).

Other Names: American black tern; sea pigeon; semipalmated tern; short-tailed tern; Surinam tern.

Age: One banded as nestling in Europe lived to 17 years, 2 months (Clapp, 1976).

Flight Speed: Timed in Mich., 9–31 m.p.h. (Schnell, 1965); in w. U.S., 10–23 m.p.h. (Cottam *et al.,* 1942b).

Weights: Three, w. U.S., averaged 60 gr. (Hughes, 1970), or about 2¼ oz.

Range: Nests from e.-c. B.C., ne. Alta., c. Sask., n. Man., and n. Ont., south; formerly nested in n. and ne. Calif. south through Central Valley, now a spring and fall transient and summer visitor in Calif. (see Small, 1974); also nests in n. Nev., n. Utah, Colo., Neb., Mo., Ill., Ky., Ohio, Pa., w. N.Y., nw. Vt., Me., and c. N.B.; also in c. and s. Europe, and sw. Siberia; winters from Panama to Chile, and from Colombia to Surinam, and in Africa to Congo, Angola, and Tanganyika.

Tern, Boys'. *See* Tern, Sandwich.

Tern, bridled, *Sterna anaesthetus* (STIR-nah an-EES-theh-tus); genus name: *see* Tern, Aleutian; species name: from Gr. *anaisthetos,* stolid, "a dullard" (see Gruson, 1972). (Color ill., page 431.) An Asiatic and tropical American species that reaches Atlantic coast of N. America outside its breeding season; 14–15 in. long; wingspread 30 in. (Watson, 1966); black cap, white forehead, gray-brown upperparts with *whitish band across back of neck,* and white line over eyes; paler and smaller than sooty tern with much more white in tail; sooty usually lacks white collar; utters high-pitched crowlike note, unlike that of sooty tern; flight swifter and more graceful and generally a shyer bird than sooty; immatures are heavily barred and streaked on upperparts with dark brown but are much paler than young sooty tern. Sooty and bridled terns are often intimately associated and abundant on tropical islands of the West Indies; the sooty is much more numerous and more widely distributed (Bent, 1921); both are more oceanic than other terns, except noddy.

Feeding Habits: Not well known, probably catches small fishes and squids sometimes by diving; swims on occasion, unlike sooty tern, which shuns immersing in water (Watson, 1966).

Nest: In colonies, often with sooty terns and other seabirds, nests in depression in rocky area or in cavity of rock face or in burrow entrance.

Eggs: Bahama Is., mid–Apr. to late June; 1, white, spotted with brown.

Other Name: Egg bird (throughout Bahamas).

Range: Nests locally on islands in Bahamas, Greater and Lesser Antilles, C. America, Aruba off Venezuela, and elsewhere in nw. Africa, islands in Gulf of Guinea, from Red Sea and Somaliland to Persian Gulf; in Indian O., and in Pacific from Taiwan to New Guinea and Australia; w. C. America and S. America; regular in Gulf Stream north at least to N.C. in summer (Lee and Booth, 1979); occasionally also to Mass., R.I., N.J., and Long Is., N.Y. (Bull, 1964); usually seen after storms; normally remains at sea out of sight of land.

Tern, Cabot's. *See* Tern, Sandwich.

Tern, Caspian, *Hydroprogne caspia* (high-drop-ROG-nee CAS-pih-ah); genus name: from Gr. *hydro,* water, and Lat. Progne, Pandion's daughter, who, according to legend, was turned into a swallow (here in allusion to this bird's swallowlike tail and wings); literally, "water swallow"; species name: Lat., of the Caspian Sea, where specimen was collected from which the species was named by Pallas in 1770. (Color ill., page 430.) Is almost cosmopolitan in range; in N. America, in summer, nests in interior of Canada and of n. U.S., and along southern Atlantic and Gulf coasts of U.S.; 19–23 in. long; wingspread 50–55 in.; almost size of herring gull but differs from it in having black cap, large red bill, and forked tail; largest of terns, similar to royal tern but larger; also, tail of Caspian is forked for only about a quarter of tail length, that of royal, for half the tail length (Pough, 1951); bill is large heavy, *coral red*—bill of similar royal tern more orange; Caspian is a gray tern above, light below, crest at back of head not so prominent as in royal tern; call of Caspian, unlike that of royal tern and different from that of gulls, is hoarse, low-keyed croak, *kaaa,* and a shorter *kow* or *kowk* when angry (Bent, 1921); soars at times like a gull, circling to great heights, but flapping flight and manner of flying, *with bill pointed downward* when fishing, and of hovering are distinctly ternlike, but when migrating, and flying high, points bill forward; is least sociable of all terns and travels singly or in small groups (Pough, 1951).

Feeding Habits: Dives into water for small fishes until completely under surface, but also feeds from surface like a gull; takes largely menhaden, mullet, and suckers (Sprunt, 1954a); occasionally robs other seabirds of their catches; also sometimes eats eggs or young of other terns and of gulls.

Nest: A hollow scrape on sandy island or eggs laid on bare rocky island, nest often lined with grasses, seaweeds, or mosses; also sometimes on floating plants in marsh (Bent, 1921).

Eggs: Tex., Apr.–June; elsewhere, May–July; 1–4, usually 2–3, pale, pink-buff, spotted, sometimes blotched, with dark brown.

Incubation: 20–22 days; young fly about 28–35 days after hatching (see Hayward, 1935).

Other Names: Gannet striker; imperial tern; redbill.

Age: One banded, recaptured when 7 years old; one banded on Lake Michigan and collected as scientific specimen on Lake Erie when 26 years, 2 months, old (Bergstrom, 1952).

Weights: One, w. U.S., 644 gr. (Hughes, 1970), or about 1 lb. 6¾ oz.

Range: In N. America, nests in single pairs, in small groups, or in large colonies near big colonies of other terns and gulls in widely scattered places: on low sandy islands along Atlantic coast from Va. south and on islands in interior lakes and in marshes such as the Klamath region of Ore.; also singly or in groups of few pairs by themselves on islet; locally in interior from c. Mack. and Man. and from e. Wash., e. Ore., to w. Nev., n. Utah, and nw. Wyo., and south through Calif. (interior) in much reduced numbers (Small, 1974) to Baja Calif., in ne. Wisc., Mich., se. Ont., nw. Pa., se. Que., and Newfoundland; on coast of Va., S.C., s. Tex., se. La., and in Pinellas County, Fla. (Woolfenden and Meyerriecks, 1963); winters from c. Calif. south through Baja Calif., along shores of Gulf of Mexico and the Caribbean to Greater Antilles, casually north to N.C. and in West Indies; migrates along both coasts of U.S., less commonly along large rivers of interior; in Old World, breeds in largest concentration especially in sw. Siberia; also in Madagascar, Ceylon (Sri-Lanka), and New Zealand; winters from Mediterranean region to s. Africa, Australia, New Zealand.

Tern, Cayenne. *See* Tern, royal.

Tern, common, *Sterna hirundo* (STIR-nah her-UN-doh); genus name: *see* Tern, Aleutian; species name: Lat., swallow; refers to swallow-like wings and tail; *common* refers to its wide distribution. (Color ill., page 433.) 13–16 in. long; wingspread about 31 in. (Watson, 1966); the tern most often seen along Atlantic coast; coastal and offshore in temperate and tropical waters, generally not far at sea; it is most widely distributed and most common of four terns that closely resemble each other and are sometimes seen together—arctic, common, Forster's, and roseate; common tern has wing tips noticeably darker than in roseate and Forster's; also tail is shorter, and in nesting season, red bill is usually black-tipped (arctic tern in nesting season usually has all-red bill; black bill of roseate is red only at base); breeding plumage of common tern is white with black cap, white rump contrasting with gray mantle, pure-white tail which is dark only along outer edges; immatures and winter adults have only partial black cap—from eye to eye around back of head; bill is dark but red at base; flight is airy, graceful; often utters a somewhat harsh, rolling call, *tee-ar-r-r-r,* also a rapid *tut-tut-tut-tut.*

Feeding Habits: Hovers in air over school of fishes, then suddenly plunges downward like winged arrow into water; seizes with bill small fishes about 3–4 in. long such as sand launces, pipefish, menhaden, alewives; also takes crustaceans and, occasionally, insects; in Mass. often called mackerel gull; along sounds of N.C. is called striker; is attracted to places where mackerel and tuna or other large fishes drive smaller ones to surface, thus often guiding fishermen in placing their nets.

Nest: In colonies, several hundred or up to many thousands assemble in breeding season near extremity of some beach sandspit or on small isolated island of sand and oyster shells, "spoil bank" of dredged sand from bay inlets or channels, or on rocky ledges; pairs scratch a slight depression in soil, smooth and shape it by sitting in the hollow and turning the body; usually line nest with grasses, seashells, or bits of seaweeds.

Eggs: May–Aug.; usually 2–3, olive or brown, spotted.

Incubation: By both parents; 21–26 days (Fisher and Lockley, 1954); 23–27 days (Nisbet, 1976); young fly about 28 days after hatching; adults defend eggs and young fiercely; dive at intruders, may strike, with bill (or with excrement), people, gulls, or other intruders at colony; utter harsh angry cries, *kee-yahrr!*

Other Names: Bass gull; Lake Erie gull; mackerel gull; red-shank; sea swallow; summer gull; Wilson's tern.

Age: One banded bird recovered in England when 25 years old (Bergstrom, 1952); of ten banded in Me., Mass., Mich., and Ohio, two lived to 6 years before they were killed; two were 7, and one, 9; two were 12 years old when they were caught alive and released; one juvenile banded in nest on Long Is., N.Y., June 1969, was caught alive on a trawler off Ivory Coast, w. Africa, Dec. 1969; apparently first transatlantic recovery of a banded N. American common tern (Raynor, 1970).

Flight Speed: Timed in Mich., 21–29 m.p.h.; one at 37 m.p.h.; another at 41 m.p.h. (Schnell, 1965).

Hybrids: According to Gray (1958), "presumed hybrids" of common and arctic terns reported. Hays (1975) trapped five adult terns at Gull Is., N.Y., that appeared to be hybrids of common and roseate terns.

Weights: Average of 80 and 400 adults at Great Gull Is., N.Y., in 1969, 1970, were 121 gr. and 119 gr. respectively (Duffy, 1971), or about 4¼ oz.

Range: In N. America, nests from c. Mack., across Canada to Newfoundland, south to Mont., S.D., ne. Ill., s. Mich., n. Ohio, nw. Pa., and n. N.Y., and from N.B. and Nova Scotia south locally along Atlantic coast to N.C.; se. Tex., Dry Tortugas, Fla., and Bermuda; winters from southern limit of breeding range (on Atlantic coast to S.C.; on Pacific coast casually to s. Calif.) south to n. Ecuador, Brazil; casual in Falkland Is.; in Old World nests in British Isles, n. Europe, and Asia, locally on coasts of Spain, w. and n. Africa, Asia Minor, and Palestine (Reilly, 1968); migrates throughout much of U.S., Mar.–May, Aug.–Dec.; absent as nester from Pacific coast but migrates from s. B.C. south; was almost completely extirpated in early 1900s during height of plumage trade but given full protection in 1913 and recovered again by the 1920s (Bull, 1964).

Tern, crimson-billed. *See* Tern, Arctic.

Tern, elegant, *Thalasseus elegans* (thal-AS-ee-us EL-ee-ganz); genus name: from Gr. *thalassios,* marine, of the sea; species name: Lat., elegant. (Color ill., page 432.) An exquisite tern in form, color, and flight; Mexican species; a regular summer and fall visitor along c. Calif. coast; breeds near San Diego (Small, 1974); 16–17 in. long; bill is deep yellow *without black tip* of Forster's tern; is white with gray mantle and long black crest; strikingly resembles the larger royal tern, with which often seen, but is smaller, has slimmer bill, and black crest is longer; in nesting season, rosy tint on underparts; has different call notes from royal tern—

GULL FAMILY
Hovering with rapid wingbeats, a tern spots a school of fishes just below the water's surface; with a swift, shallow dive it snatches its prey and emerges from the water to swallow it.

a nasal *kareek, karreek,* somewhat like notes of least tern but not as high-pitched.

Feeding Habits: While in Calif., usually on sandy beaches that separate ocean from bays; dives for fishes like other terns; small numbers often sit with other terns well up on beach.

Nest: In colonies, nest hollow is shallow scrape in sand high up on undisturbed beaches.

Eggs: Early Apr. to early May; usually 1, sometimes 2, white to pink-buff, blotched with dark brown or black.

Incubation: Period seems unknown, but possibly around 20 days or more, like other terns of comparable size; age at which young first fly unknown.

Range: Nests on and off both coasts of Baja Calif., and a small nesting colony discovered in c. Calif. in spring 1959 at San Diego Bay with royal terns (Rand, 1965) was first record of breeding of this tern in U.S. and it has bred there intermittently ever since; thousands sometimes reach Monterey County (Small, 1974); nests also in nw. Mexico; winters from Peru to Chile; accidental in Tex., one record, Corpus Christi.

Tern, Forster's, *Sterna forsteri* (STIR-nah FORCE-teh-rye); genus name: *see* Tern, Aleutian; species name: given in 1834 by Thomas Nuttall in honor of Johann R. Forster, German naturalist. (Color ill., page 433.) Common in summer in interior marshes of s. Canada and n. U.S. and along southern Atlantic coast, and Gulf coast, of U.S.; 14–16½ in. long; wingspread 30 in.; outside of nesting season, frequents bays, beaches, ocean; plumage resembles that of common tern; is black-capped with *white breast;* light gray mantle; deeply forked tail is pale gray with *white outer edges* and *dark border along inside of fork;* wing tips *silvery white,* or *frost-gray;* orange-red bill with black tip; orange-red feet; eyes dark brown; in winter, white head lacks black cap but is distinguished by narrow black patch through and back of eyes on side of head; feet yellowish; bill dark; for many years ornithologists did not distinguish this exclusively N. American tern as a separate species in its summer plumage because of its close resemblance to common tern; however, calls are different— a common one of Forster's is *zreep* or *zrurr,* a rasping buzzy note like that of nighthawk; also often utters shrill *pip-pip, pip, pip* or *kit, kit, kit, kit.*

Feeding Habits: Sweeps gracefully through air over marshes to catch in flight emerging adult dragonflies and caddis flies; also swoops to water to pick up dead beetles or other insects floating on surface without wetting a feather (Bent, 1921); also catches and eats Rocky Mountain locusts (grasshoppers), picks up dead frogs and fishes; also dives into water for fishes.

Nest: In loose colonies in saltwater and in freshwater marshes, or solitarily near water of inland lakes; sometimes appropriates nests of grebes or nests on muskrat houses, usually on mats of floating dead canes in marshes or ponds which they line with reeds and grasses, or in a depression in mud, or on sandy places;

they line depression with pieces of shells and grasses.

Eggs: Va., Calif., May–July; n. U.S., s. Canada, June–July; usually 3–4, brown or olive, splotched, or dotted with dark brown or scrawled lines.

Incubation: About 23 days, apparently by both sexes; age at which young first fly unknown (Bent, 1921); young remain in nest for few days until strong enough to run about marsh or swim in water and hide in grass, fed by both parents until able to fly.

Other Names: Havell's tern (so named by Audubon); marsh tern; sea swallow.

Flight Speed: Timed "cruising" in w. U.S., 10 m.p.h. (Cottam *et al.,* 1942b).

Range: Nests most commonly in marshes along coast or inland, from Prairie Provinces of Canada south to se. Calif., s.–c. Idaho, n. Utah, se. Wyo., e. Colo., w. Neb., n. Iowa, to se. Wisc., also along coasts from n. Tamaulipas, Mexico, and se. Tex. to s. La. and north along Atlantic coast to N.J. (a pair nested at Rondeau, Ont., summer 1970, for first breeding of this tern in Ont. in this century—Goodwin and Rosche, 1971a); winters from c. Calif. and Baja Calif. to sw. Mexico; from e. Mexico north and east along shores of Gulf of Mexico to w. Fla. and from Va. south to n. Fla.; migrates widely through c. U.S. from Great Lakes region and New England south.

Tern, gull-billed, *Gelochelidon nilotica* (jell-oh-KELL-ih-don nih-LOW-tih-kah); genus name: from Gr. *gelos,* laughter, and *khelidon,* swallow; "laughing swallow," in reference to its call and swallowlike form; species name: Lat., of the Nile, from which came the specimen in Egypt from which the bird was scientifically named and described. (Color ill., page 432.) An almost cosmopolitan tern, and local in salt marshes, uncommon in U.S. (in s. Calif. and from Long Is., N.Y., and N.J. coast south); 13–15½ in. long; wingspread 33–37 in.; whitest of N. American terns; in summer, white with black cap and nape, gray mantle, but recognized in all plumages by short, thick, black, gull-like bill; very white wings are wide (not narrow as in most terns); stocky body, and slight fork in white tail; legs long and black like feet; distinctive call, dry and rasping *kay-tih-DID* or *kay-DID,* accented on last syllable (Bent, 1921); immatures have white head with fine streaking, as in winter adults, and brown mottled back and brown band at end of tail; once extremely abundant in salt marshes of Atlantic coast from s. N.J. south to Va., but virtually exterminated by early 1900s by those who ate its eggs and by demands of millinery trade, which used plumage to decorate women's hats; has never recovered; only small numbers of scattered pairs still nest on outer beaches associated with other terns (Pough, 1951); was originally a marsh nester like Forster's tern and laughing gull; some still nest in inland marshes and about lakes—for example, at Lake Okeechobee, Fla., and along Indian R.

Feeding Habits: Insects apparently a staple part of diet, caught in air over agricultural fields; swoops to water to pick small animals

from surface; also reported to eat earthworms, spiders, various crustaceans, frogs and toads, and lizards, for which it forages over brushy places in Fla.; also dives occasionally for small fishes; reported to eat small mammals and eggs and young of other birds (Rohwer and Woolfenden, 1968).

Nest: In U.S., discontinuously along marine coasts, either single pairs or in small scattered groups at edges of larger colony of other terns; a depression on sandy, shell-strewn upper beach beyond reach of tides or inland along muddy edges of lakes and rivers, depression sparsely lined with bits of shells, straw, or grasses; sometimes a more substantial nest of weeds and grasses near water or on low marshy islands where eggs may be laid on damp ground or on matted grasses; sometimes on floating reeds in marsh of lake or on old muskrat house.

Eggs: Va., June–July; Tex., May–June; usually 3, pink-buff to yellowish, lightly spotted with dark brown.

Incubation: 22–23 days; young first fly about 28–35 days after hatching (Fisher and Lockley, 1954; see also Bannerman, 1962).

Other Names: Anglican tern; Egyptian tern; marsh tern; Nile tern; Nuttall's tern.

Age: One, banded, reported from Denmark, 15 years, 9 months, old (Clapp, 1976).

Range: In N. America, nests on Salton Sea, Calif., and on coast of Sonora, Mexico; in se. Tex., se. La., s. Miss., w. Fla., and casually in interior Fla., north along Atlantic coast to s. Md., rarely to Del., to s. N.J. and Long Island; very rare and irregular summer and fall visitor to Long Is., N.Y., mostly seen after hurricanes (Bull, 1964) but first nesting in N.Y. discovered June 11, 1975, near Jones Beach, Long Is.; two pairs raised at least two young (Buckley *et al.,* 1975); also nests on Bahamas and Virgin Is.; winters from w. coast of Mexico to Ecuador and from s. Tex., s. La., c. Fla., Caribbean coast of C. America, and n. and ne. S. America to Surinam; accidental or casual on Grand Manan Is., N.B., Ill., Ohio, N.Y., Mass., Me., Bermuda; also lives in British Isles, Eurasia, etc. (see Reilly, 1968).

Tern, Havell's. *See* Tern, Forster's.

Tern, imperial. *See* Tern, Caspian.

Tern, Kentish. *See* Tern, Sandwich.

Tern, least, *Sterna albifrons* (STIR-nah AL-bih-fronz); genus name: *see* Tern, Aleutian; species name: from Lat. *albus,* white, and *frons,* forehead. (Color ills., pages 434, 435.) Smallest of American terns; in N. America, in summer, along Pacific coast from c. Calif. south; interior U.S. from Iowa south; Atlantic coast, from Mass. south; also in Old World; range is very nearly cosmopolitan; 8½–9½ in. long; wingspread about 20 in.; adult is white, black-capped tern with *white forehead;* the yellow bill is black-tipped; legs yellow; in fall, only back of head, and line to each eye, is black; bill dusky to black, *leading edge of wings black* (Watson, 1966); sexes alike, female smaller than male; flight is very light, graceful, buoyant, at times swift; more rapid wingbeats than larger terns; calls very shrill, penetrating: *kip, kip, kip* and *kid-ick, kid-ick, kid-ick,* and harsh, rasping *zr-e-e-e-p!;* while hovering on swiftly beating wings over school of fishes, utters very excited cries.

Feeding Habits: Gets small fishes and crustaceans by skimming surface of water or by hovering, then diving into water; catches prey in its bill; when rising from shallow dive usually swallows prey while in flight or carries to mate or young at nest; called little striker because of plunges into water; occasionally alights on beach to eat its food; eats sand eels, shrimp, and prawns (Bent, 1921).

Nest: Does not always require islands or other isolated places like most terns for breeding but often digs its small unlined scrape in sand on clear beaches of mainland above reach of ordinary tides; solitary or in scattered small colonies; sometimes associated with piping and snowy plovers, common terns, and black skimmers; also nests on rooftops in Fla. (see details in Fisk, 1975).

Eggs: Calif., May–July; usually 2, buff to pale olive-buff, spotted or blotched with dark brown.

Incubation: 20–22 days (Nice, 1954); young fly 28 days after hatching (Fisher and Lockley, 1954; see also Hardy, 1957, and Tomkins, 1959); adults in defense of eggs or young will dive screaming and drop excrement with accuracy on intruder.

Other Names: Little tern (British Isles); little striker; minute tern; sea swallow; silver ternlet.

Age: One, banded at Sunset Beach, Calif., in its first year, caught alive again when 15 years old (Kennard, 1975); one, banded at Cotuit, Mass., reported by Bergstrom (1956) to be 21 years old.

Weights: One in fall, coastal N.J., 31.1 gr. (Murray and Jehl, 1964), or about 1 oz.

Range: Nests locally along flat, open sandy coastal beaches and more rarely inland on sandbars of broad river valleys; in N. America, along Pacific coast from c. Calif. south to s. Baja Calif., and to Peru; inland, along the Colorado, Red, Missouri, and Mississippi river systems north to Neb., Iowa, Mo., Tenn., and Ky., and Ind., Ohio, through w. Kans., c. Okla., ne. Tex., to c. La., also Delaware R. at Tinicum, Philadelphia, Pa. (*Audubon Field Notes,* Oct. 1950, p. 269), and along Atlantic coast from Me. (Morse R., see Hunt, 1975) to Fla., and from coast of e. Mexico and Belize to the Bahamas, Greater and Lesser Antilles, Bermuda, n. Venezuela; winters from Gulf coast and C. America south to Peru and Brazil; in Old World lives from British Isles, s. Sweden, Baltic seacoasts and inland rivers and lakes to Tobolsk, Mesopotamia, n. India, n. Burma, Korea, China, Japan, and Philippines south through the Mediterranean, Black, and Caspian seas to w. Africa, Gaboon, Somaliland, Java, Sumatra, New Guinea, Bismarck Archipelago, and Australia; in the U.S., formerly abundant prior to 1880, its numbers were practically annihilated by professional hunters for the millinery trade, with up to 1,200 birds killed in a day along the Va. coast and as many as 100,000 killed in a season (Bent, 1921); the least tern was fully protected in 1913, and it had come back strongly by the 1920s (Bull, 1964); however,

increasing destruction of its nesting habitats by shore or beach development, and disturbance in its nesting colonies by people walking the beaches, are causing it to decline again. It is especially threatened on the Pacific coast and in the interior U.S. (see Arbib, 1974, for the Blue List of species of N. American birds in 1975).

Tern, little. *See* Tern, least.

Tern, long-tailed. *See* Tern, Arctic.

Tern, marsh. *See* Tern, Forster's and Tern, gull-billed.

Tern, McDougall's. *See* Tern, roseate.

Tern, minute. *See* Tern, least.

Tern, noddy. *See* Noddy, black and Noddy, brown.

Tern, Nuttall's. *See* Tern, gull-billed.

Tern, Pike's. *See* Tern, Arctic.

Tern, roseate, *Sterna dougallii* (STIR-nah dew-GALL-ee-eye); genus name: *see* Tern, Aleutian; species name: given in 1813 by George Montagu for a Dr. McDougall of Scotland (Coues, 1882; see details in Gruson, 1972); *roseate* (ROSE-ih-ate) refers to pinkish breast. (Color ill., page 436.) Widespread in Old World but local over N. American range; nests along Atlantic coast; 14–17 in. long; wingspread about 30 in.; slender, black-capped, white tern; mantle and back pale pearl-gray merging into long, pure-white, deeply forked tail; resembles common and Arctic terns; when perched, roseate's tail, unlike tails of these terns, has long, white outer tail feathers that extend far beyond tips of folded wings; wing tips of roseate are paler, and bill is black with red only at base which varies with age of bird and season (arctic, common, and Forster's terns have reddish bills except in winter); rosy tint on breast seldom visible, but call notes of roseate are high-pitched, rasping *aaak* and soft *chivy;* also has noticeably buoyant flight; iris dark brown; legs and feet vermilion-red or scarlet.

Feeding Habits: Never seen in numbers except over waters near nesting colonies; when bluefish drive small fishes to surface in large schools, the roseates gather in screaming, excited groups; dashing down to cleave water, grasp small fish, then rise into air, shake off salt spray, and hover again before next plunge; food is almost wholly small fishes—sand launces, cunner, mullet, pollock, flounder, and young herring, also some mollusks (Bent, 1921).

Nest: In colonies on sandy place or rocky, pebbly beaches on islands or along shore, often with common terns; usually scrape in ground is concealed in beach grass or in weedy places, sometimes lined with few pieces of dried grass.

Eggs: Mass., June–Aug.; Bahamas and Fla. Keys, late Apr. into June; 1–3, commonly 1–2, pale buff to olive-buff, evenly sprinkled with small spots or dots of brown.

Incubation: By both parents in regular turn, 21 days (Bent, 1921); 23–25 days; young fly about 28 days after hatching (Fisher and Lockley, 1954; see also Bannerman, 1962).

Other Names: Graceful tern; mackerel gull; McDougall's tern.

Age: Of four banded along coast of Mass., two died when 5 years old; two others were trapped and then released when 6 and 7 years old; one, banded Gull Is., N.Y., trapped and released when 9 years old (Kennard, 1975).

Hybrids: See in biography of common tern.

Range: Almost never seen inland; in spring and summer, nests along Atlantic coast, locally, from Nova Scotia south to Va., s. Fla., Yucatán, Bahamas, and West Indies; winters from West Indies to Brazil and casually north to N.C.; accidental in Ind., w. N.Y., Gulf coast of Tex., s. La.; in Old World nests in British Isles, n. France, Tunisia, Denmark, w. Red Sea, e. and s. Africa, Madagascar, Seychelles Is., Ceylon, Malaya, China, Taiwan, New Guinea, Australia, and New Caledonia; winters from Azores and Madeira to s. Africa.

Tern, royal, *Thalasseus maximus* (thal-AS-ee-us MAX-ih-mus); genus name: *see* Tern, elegant; species name: Lat., greatest; *royal* alludes to size. (Color ill., page 437.) Second in size only to Caspian tern; in summer, along both Atlantic and Pacific coasts, and Gulf coast; also in Old World, w. coast Africa; 18–21 in. long; wingspread 42–44 in.; is limited to salt water; wanders inland irregularly; white tern with pale gray mantle; has black head crest *in all plumages;* both adults and young distinguished from similar, larger, black-crested Caspian tern by *white forehead* (royal has solid-black cap only for short time in spring and early summer); and has more deeply forked tail; bill more slender, is orange or orange-yellow (Caspian has bright red bill); adult royal has black legs and feet; in young, light orange or yellow; calls not so loud and raucous as Caspian's, are higher-pitched; note most often heard on nesting grounds is squawk, *quak, kak* or *kowk;* another is lower-pitched and like bleating of sheep; also utters very musical rolling whistle, *tourrrreeee,* like that of upland sandpiper; flies with strong, unremitting flappings; looks like a slim gull in air, much like flight of common tern but less buoyant.

Feeding Habits: Usually flies 40–60 ft. above ocean, bays, or inlets when fishing, hovers, then dives below surface with a splash, takes small fishes up to about 4 in. long in bill; eats young herring, menhaden, silversides, perch, and bluefish, also squid, and reported to eat some mollusks, and shrimps (Bent, 1921); sometimes snatches fish from pouch of brown pelican and in turn may be attacked and forced to give up fish to frigatebird.

Nest: Generally in large, closely packed colonies, a slight depression in sand, often with other kinds of terns on low sandy islands along coast (Pough, 1951); one of largest colonies ever seen in S.C. on coastal Cape Is., of 11,000 nests, was largely destroyed by high water in July 1947 (Sprunt and Chamberlain, 1949); 10,000–12,000 pairs nest at Sprunt Sanctuary, Devereaux Bank, S.C. (Callison, 1975); on Fisherman's Is., Cape Charles, Va., Buckley and Buckley (1970) found colony in which there were average of 6–9 nests per sq. m., or about 1 nest to every 1–1½ sq. ft.; according to Kale *et al.* (1965), royal terns along Ga. coast nest on exposed islets that are free from raccoons and minks but quickly desert these when these predators reach them; they prefer isolated, barren, sparsely vegetated sandspits made by tidal action and storms before the nesting season.

Eggs: N.C., S.C., Miss., May–June; Tex., Apr.–June; usually 1–2, rarely 3–4, white to pale buff or ivory yellow, evenly spotted with small dots and some blotches of dark brown.

Incubation: 20–22 days; young first fly 28–35 days after hatching (Fisher and Lockley, 1954); royal tern is single-brooded (Kale *et al.*, 1965). Chicks of royal tern gather in a crèche (*see* Creche); when parent returns with food, it recognizes its own chick's call and responds; chick answers from crèche, emerges, reaches edge of crèche (of young terns), where parent, after recognizing it, feeds it fish, then departs for more (Buckley and Buckley, 1970); Ashmole and Tovar (1968) discovered two royal terns from U.S. wintering in Peru that were still feeding their young well into late winter and early spring; they believe young royal terns require extraordinarily long time to acquire skills needed to catch fish for themselves.

Other Names: Cayenne tern, so called by John Latham, eminent, early British ornithologist, and by John James Audubon (Audubon also called the very similar Caspian tern the "Cayenne tern," not recognizing these two as distinct species—Bent, 1921); in Va. called gannet and gannet striker; redbill.

Accidents: One found dying Oct. 1962 at Tybee Is., Ga., at edge of surf, had strangled after swallowing a fish—an Atlantic croaker—5½ in. long; this kind of accident rare in this tern (Tomkins, 1963); *see* Accidents; Swallowing; Fishes and Birds.

Age: Sprunt and Chamberlain (1949) reported ages of royal terns banded in S.C. and recovered as 6, 8, 10, and 10 years, 8 months; most of returns (*see* Banding) were from Fla., one from Port Arthur, Tex., and farthest distance traveled, one recovered at Tule Lake, Calif.

Range: Usually seen almost everywhere over southern coasts of U.S., where increasing (Bull, 1964), or over inlets and bays, has very local and discontinuous breeding distribution; nests along coasts, formerly from c. Calif. (first nesting colony discovered there in May–June 1959, San Diego Bay [Rand, 1965], and again in spring 1960, but no breeding records since [Small, 1974]), and Baja Calif. to Tres Marías Is. off w. coast of Mexico; along Gulf coast from s. Tex. to s. La., and Ala. coast in 1958 (Imhof, 1962); along Atlantic coast from Md. to Ga., coast of Yucatán, and the Bahamas locally through West Indies; winters coastally from c. Calif. south to Peru, and from S.C. and Caribbean to Argentina; wanders north to Mass.; in Old World, nests w. Africa.

Tern, Sandwich, *Thalasseus sandvicensis* (thal-AS-ee-us san-vih-SEN-sis); genus name: *see* Tern, elegant; species name: Lat., of Sandwich, Kent, England, where type specimen (*see* Type Specimen) was taken. (Color ill., page

437.) In both Old and New worlds; uncommon and very local in summer along Atlantic and Gulf coasts in N. America; 14–16 in. long; wingspread 34 in.; appears like diminutive royal tern but is only N. American tern with a black bill *tipped with yellow;* summer adults have green-black crown and crest but black crown of courtship period may have white in forehead and in crest by time (or before) eggs are hatched; blue-gray mantle, white on rump, upper tail coverts, and tail; tail deeply forked; feet black; in winter adults have white in crown; forehead of immatures is mostly black, top of head with black markings, mantle spotted with black, and top of wings have black V-shaped markings; bill and feet flesh color or dusky; utters a loud, shrill *kirrick,* less harsh and less grating than that of other large terns (Pough, 1951); young birds have a higher-pitched call; the Sandwich tern rarely visits fresh water; roosts on coastal sandbanks (Watson, 1966).

Feeding Habits: Feeds out at sea more often than smaller terns or among breakers; dives vigorously from considerable heights to disappear underwater; catches in bill small mullets, sand launces, menhaden, anchovies, also shrimps, pelagic worms, and squids.

Nest: In colonies on sandy islands or in small groups, often with royal terns (see Sprunt and Chamberlain, 1949); also with other terns; a shallow scrape or none.

Eggs: Tex., Apr.–June; S.C. (Cape Romain and St. Helena Sound), June; 1–3, usually 1–2, white to seashell pink and cinnamon-buff (Bent, 1921).

Incubation: 21 days (Sprunt and Chamberlain, 1949); 21–24 days; young first fly about 35 days after hatching (Fisher and Lockley, 1954).

Other Names: Boys' tern; Cabot's tern; ducal tern; Kentish tern.

Age: One, banded in Holland, June 1912, killed June 1933 on coast of France 21 years later (Nice, 1935c); one reported in Germany, 23 years, 7 months, old (Clapp, 1976).

Range: Nests along coasts from Va. to S.C., from Tex. to La.; on Cayo Arcas and Alacrán Reef off Yucatán, Mexico, and in Bahamas; winters along Pacific coast from s. Mexico to Panama, from Fla. and the Caribbean to s. Brazil; accidental in s. Ont., Canada, and Calif. (San Diego); according to Bull (1964), not definitely reported along N.Y. coast until one in June 1957 at Mecox Bay, Long Is., probably carried north by Hurricane Audrey; after Hurricane Donna of Sept. 1960, no less than 9 reported on Long Is. beaches; in flight one of swiftest and most skillful fliers among terns and able to outride the severest storms; in Old World nests from British Isles, Denmark, and s. Sweden to nw. Africa, Sardinia, Sicily, and the Black and Caspian seas; winters in the Mediterranean, Red Sea, and Persian Gulf and adjacent seas (Reilly, 1968).

Tern, semipalmated. *See* Tern, black.

Tern, short-footed. *See* Tern, arctic.

Tern, short-tailed. *See* Tern, black.

Tern, sooty, *Sterna fuscata* (STIR-nah fuss-KATE-ah); genus name: *see* Tern, Aleutian; species name: Lat., dusky. (Color ill., page 438.) Wide-ranging seabird in both Pacific and Atlantic; nests in N. America in Gulf of Mexico; 15–17 in. long; wingspread about 34 in.; adult is *only tern with pattern of jet black above, white below* (Peterson, 1947); also has slender, pointed black bill and black legs and feet; eyes dark; head and body entirely sooty black above but has white forehead; deeply forked tail (*see* comparisons under bridled tern); immature is brown-black with dirty-white belly; some white speckling on brown back, lost with wear; immature is only all-dark fork-tailed tern in N. America (Watson, 1966); outside nesting season, strictly pelagic; call note a nasal, clearly enunciated *ker-wacky-wack* (Bent, 1921); flight similar to that of common tern but stronger, steadier wingbeats; occasionally soars high in air and circles while at sea or over nesting colony; other than coming to islands to nest (on Dry Tortugas, Fla., arrives for nesting in Mar.–Apr.; departs late Aug.–Sept.—Sprunt, 1954a), spends most of year over salt water; is thought even to sleep on wing (Rand, 1965); experiments suggest that plumage of sooty tern becomes waterlogged, like that of frigatebird, if in water a few minutes (Watson, 1966); one of most abundant nesting birds of tropical oceans; in 1951, colony on Dry Tortugas (Bush Key) estimated by National Park Service at 100,000 birds (Sprunt, 1954a); Robertson (1969) reported that in 10 years (1959–69), about 130,-000 sooty tern chicks had been banded on Dry Tortugas; up to 1969, 28 of them recovered in w. Africa, all some 3 months to 2 years after banding; other recoveries of sooty terns suggest that juveniles spend July and Aug. in Gulf of Mexico, migrate along s. coast of Caribbean in Sept. and Oct., and cross Atlantic toward coast of w. Africa between Oct. and Dec.; they appear to straggle back to N. American side of Atlantic from time they are 2 years to about their 6th year of age; adults at Dry Tortugas, however, do not migrate far—16 to 18 banded adults were recovered in Gulf of Mexico and Fla. Straits (Robertson, 1969); near Equator, where no marked seasonal changes (Ascension Is., in mid-Atlantic, for example), adults may return to breeding island to nest about every 9–10 months (see Chapin, 1954); youngest age of breeding is 4 years old but most sooties do not breed until 6–8 years; a few not until 10 years old, the longest time to maturity of any member of Gull Family (Harrington, 1974).

Feeding Habits: Hovers, then swoops gracefully to surface of water to pick up in bill small fishes and squids that rise to surface or leap out of water when chased by larger, predatory fishes (Pough, 1951); huge flocks of sooty terns gather to feed on small fishes over schools of tuna, thus an important guide to commercial tuna fishermen (Watson, 1966).

Nest: In dense colonies, a scrape in sand, occasionally lined with leaves from soft plants; or on flat ground, sometimes on ledges of seaside cliffs of tropical islands (Bent, 1921).

Eggs: Fla., Apr.–June; Tex., May; 1–3, usually 1, white to buff, spotted with lavender or red-brown.

Incubation: 26 days; young first fly about 56 days after hatching; average of 57.3 days (Brown, 1976); Crossin and Huber (1970) watched ruddy turnstones harassing sooty terns incubating their eggs in large colony on Eniwetok Atoll, Marshall Is., in Pacific in Jan. 1969; also cited Alexander Wetmore's report to them that ruddy turnstones in 1923 on Laysan Is. made heavy inroads on eggs of sooty tern colony.

Other Names: Egg bird (native people of tropics eat the eggs); wide-awake (on Ascension Is., because birds awake all night calling *wide-awake*).

Age: Of two banded on Howland Is. in Pacific, one recaptured there when 26 years, 7 months, old; another, 26 years, 3 months; two banded and later recaptured on Dry Tortugas, 28 years old (Clapp and Sibley, 1966); another banded Bush Key, Fla., in its first year, was trapped, then released in same area when 32 years, 1 month, old (Kennard, 1975); *see* Homing.

Weights: In Fla., adults (771) weighed 144–234 gr. (Robertson, 1972), or about 5–8¼ oz. See remarkable story of sooty tern, "Jeff," by A. Sprunt, Jr., in Terres (1958).

Range: Nests in Gulf of Mexico from Alacrán Reef off Yucatán to Gulf coast of Fla., and Tex. (where has bred irregularly, but six nests discovered on Pelican Is., May 1967) and coast of La., where a nest was first discovered June 1933 on Curlew Is. in Chandeleur Is., off Mississippi delta, now part of Gulf Island Wildlife Refuge; sooty tern then unreported in La., according to Purrington (1970), for 28 years until two picked up dead after Hurricane Carla in Sept. 1961; in June 1964, another nest discovered on Curlew Is. for second La. nesting record; again nesting in Chandeleurs in 1965 and in 1967, when a small nesting colony of eight nests with eggs and young found on Stake Is., two nests and seven adults there in May 1968; a single nest on Curlew Is., June 1968; all sooty tern nests reported in La. were generally in or near colonies of Sandwich and royal terns (Purrington, 1970); nests on Bahamas, West Indies, and islands in S. Atlantic; nests on oceanic islands, some nearshore islands of Pacific, from Ryukyu, Bonin, Marcus, Wake, and Hawaiian Is. to Revillagigedo, and Tres Marías Is. off w. coast of Mexico to New South Wales, and Lord Howe, Norfolk, and Kermadec Is., Galápagos Archipelago, and San Felix Is., Chile; and on islands in Indian O. south to w. Australia; in N. America, ranges casually and usually after hurricanes along Atlantic coast rarely to Me. and Nova Scotia; occasionally blown inland; regular but rare in Gulf Stream in summer to N.C.

Tern, Trudeau's, *Sterna trudeaui* (STIR-nah TRUE-doe-eye); genus name: *see* Tern, Aleutian; species name: given by John James Audubon in 1838 for his friend James de Bertz Trudeau, who "procured" the bird for Audubon at Great Egg Harbor, N.J. S. American species that was named and described for science only after it had reached N. America; 14 in. long; pale gray tern with white head and upper neck; white head has black patch through eyes; yellow bill has black band; rump white; adults not in breeding plumage and immatures are whiter below; differs from non-breeding Forster's tern only by somewhat shorter tail streamers but ranges of two do not overlap (Watson, 1966); flight like that of common tern; call, a sharp explosive *tik-tik-tik*, somewhat like call of Forster's.

Feeding Habits: Dives in shallow waters for small fishes, apparently prefers freshwater fishes.

Nest: On floating masses of plants in marshes of interior, about shallow lagoons and shallow ponds where it nests.

Eggs: 3–4, olive-yellow brown with darker blotches.

Range: Breeds in interior marshes in n. and c. Chile, se. Brazil to n. Argentina; accidental in s. S. America; questionable record from N.J.

Tern, white-winged black, *Chlidonias leucopterus* (klih-DOAN-ih-as lew-KOP-ter-us); genus name: *see* Tern, black; species name: Gr., white-winged. Eurasian tern, in W. Hemisphere (Wisc., Mass., Barbados—one record there, according to Watson, 1966—and Guam); small; 9½–10 in. long; wingspread about 26 in.; black-bodied with conspicuous white shoulder patch and white tail in summer; underwings in breeding plumage are black; similar to black tern, which is *light gray* beneath wings, and white *beneath* tail; bill and legs of white-winged are red in summer, dark in winter.

Feeding Habits: Eats primarily insects snapped up in bill from surface of water.

Range: Nests from e. Europe and Turkey to se. Siberia; lives in and around inland lakes, rivers, and marshes; winters in Africa, s. Asia, Indonesia, Australia, and New Zealand; accidental in U.S.

Tern, Wilson's. *See* Tern, common.

GULL MONUMENT

See Economic Ornithology; Monuments to Birds.

GYNANDROMORPH

(jih-NAN-dro-morf). Term used in genetics for an animal in which part of the body is genetically female and another part genetically male (Hutt, 1949); it is a sexual mosaic, that is, an individual which appears to be a mixture of male and female tissues caused by an aberration of the genetic mechanism that determines sex in normal individuals. See explanation by Dobzhansky (1961). *Bilateral sexual mosaics* —with male coloring and form on one side, and female on the other—are well known to collectors of butterflies, but it was long thought that gynandromorphism would not show up in the higher vertebrates (birds and mammals) because of the overriding influence of the sex hormones on the expression of *secondary sexual characters* (Hannah-Alava, 1960)—for example, the differences in size and colors between males and females in many species of birds. *See* discussion of secondary sexual characters under Endocrine Glands; Sexual Dimorphism.

According to Hannah-Alava, despite overwhelming evidence in favor of hormonal determination of the secondary sexual characters in vertebrates, reports of gynandromorphs in birds (Witschi, 1961, knew of at least a dozen well-authenticated reports in the scientific literature of lateral gynandromorphs in birds) and mice continue to crop up and various studies have affirmed their genetic basis.

On Nov. 25, 1955, an observer at Pittsfield, Mass., saw an evening grosbeak that was a bilateral gynandromorph. According to Shaub (1960), one half of the bird (a line exactly in the center of its body, lengthwise from head to and including its tail, was the dividing line) was a good bright adult male plumage, the other half was female entirely except that male yellow covered her upper tail coverts. Other than that, the bird's body was entirely divided by the sharp line where its male and female plumages met; *left side* was perfectly *female* in color and markings; *right side* was *male*. The grosbeak mingled with the flock and its companions seemed not to notice its unusual plumage.

Another evening grosbeak—also a bilateral gynandromorph—seen at East Chatham, N.Y., in Jan. 1959, was evenly *male* in color on the *left side* of body, evenly *female* on the *right side*.

A bullfinch (*see* in Finch Family), the skin of which is in collections of the American Museum of Natural History, New York, is another bilateral gynandromorph with male coloring on one side of its body, female on the other.

Apparently an American kestrel (*see* in Falcon Family) reported by Brodkorb (1935) was the first wild gynandromorph reported among N. American birds. It was shot at Grafton, N.D., in 1925 and the skin at the time of Brodkorb's report was in the bird collection of the University of Michigan. After the bird was shot, it was sexed (sex determined by examination of gonads—*see* description of gonads under Fertilization) as a female; it was female size but feathers on left side of breast were male with a few male feathers on right side. Female plumage covered the underwing coverts on both sides of body; head and remainder of body were normal female color pattern.

GYRFALCON

See in Falcon Family.

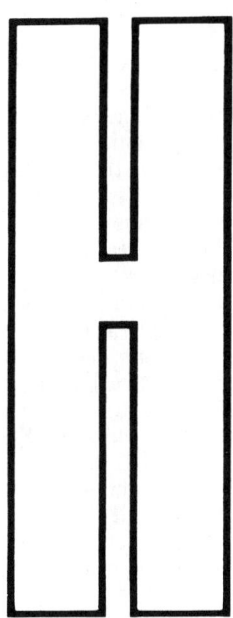

HABITAT

Place where a bird or other animal lives, or where we go to find it (Odum, 1953). Although habitat is often thought of as simply a vegetational type (forest or a grassland, for example), each habitat is the entire environmental complex, both living and non-living. Besides plants, birds, and other animals, each habitat includes the air, water, soil, temperature, humidity, rainfall, sunlight, food, safe places to nest, and so on—all the elements and conditions that satisfy the living requirements of a bird so it can successfully produce offspring in sufficient numbers to perpetuate its kind. *See* Nest and Nesting; Young and Their Care.

For convenience and simplicity in the study of birds, it is customary for ecologists to assign birds to the major kinds of habitats they occupy (*see* Distribution)—for example, forest, grassland, desert, marsh, and so on. However, forests differ, as do grasslands and deserts, therefore birds often select narrow habitat choices within the broad or major habitat in which they live. *See* Ecological Niche.

According to Berger (1961), we know little about the details whereby a bird selects a certain habitat, although Koskimies (1957) believed that *habitat recognition* may be acquired by some young birds while in the nest. Apparently Thorpe (1944) was the first to suggest "locality imprinting" as a phenomenon, whereby a newly hatched bird develops an attachment for the immediate environment and, when it becomes adult, chooses it as its breeding place. See also Hess (1973). A knowledge of the chosen habitats of birds is important to the beginning student in ornithology in seeking them out. See especially McElroy (1974). See Allen, A. A. (1961, Ch. 3) for a discussion of habitats, and Pettingill (1972) for an article about habitat selection. *See also* Distribution; Species.

HABITUATION

See Behavior.

HACKLE FEATHERS

The long slender feathers on the necks of gallinaceous birds, especially of the domestic rooster. *See* Domestication.

HAEMATOPODIDAE

See Oystercatcher Family.

HAEMOPROTEUS

See Internal Parasites under Diseases.

HAG

Local name, signifying witch, for the greater shearwater.

HAGDON

See Shearwater, greater, in Shearwater Family.

HAILSTORMS AND BIRDS

See Hail under Weather.

HAIR-BIRD

See Sparrow, chipping, in Finch Family.

HAIRYHEAD

See Merganser, hooded, in Duck Family.

HALCYON

See Belted kingfisher in Kingfisher Family.

HALF-MOON EYE

One of common names of the white-winged scoter from crescent-shaped white spot behind and below eyes. *See* Scoter, white-winged, in Duck Family.

HALF-SNIPE

See Jacksnipe, European, in Sandpiper Family.

HALLUX

Term for the hind toe of a bird, which in songbirds, or perching birds (*see* Passeriformes), and in most other birds, is the toe that is directed backward. It is the first digit of the foot; usually directed backward, but in the woodpecker genus *Picoides*, or three-toed woodpeckers, the hallux is lacking and toe IV is turned backward. For the digital formula, or numbering system for birds' toes, *see* Feet and Legs.

HAMMERHEAD

Another name for the N. American wood stork. *See also* Flinthead.

HAMMERHEAD FAMILY

See Ciconiiformes.

HAMMOCK-BIRD

See orioles in Troupial Family.

HAMMOND

WILLIAM ALEXANDER, M.D. (1829–1900). Born Annapolis, Md., Surgeon General, U.S. Army (1862–64), for whom Hammond's flycatcher was named in 1858 by his subordinate and friend John Xantus; Hammond did most of his collecting of birds at Ft. Riley, Kans. See Hume (1942); Palmer (1928).

HAND

The part of a bird's wing beyond the bend (wrist or carpus) that bears the primary feathers. *See* Manus; *also* Flight.

HAND-QUILLS

The primary wing feathers, or the quill feathers of the wings. *See* Flight.

HAND-TAMING

See Tameness.

HANGING BIRD

See White-eyed vireo in Vireo Family.

HANG-NEST

See Oriole, northern (Baltimore), and Oriole, orchard, Troupial Family, which is sometimes called Hang-nest Family; *see also* Red-eyed vireo in Vireo Family.

HARCOURT

EDWIN WILLIAM VERNON (1825–91). English traveler and writer, in 1851 described and named the storm-petrel, *Thalassidroma* (now *Oceanodroma*) *castro*, in his *Sketch of*

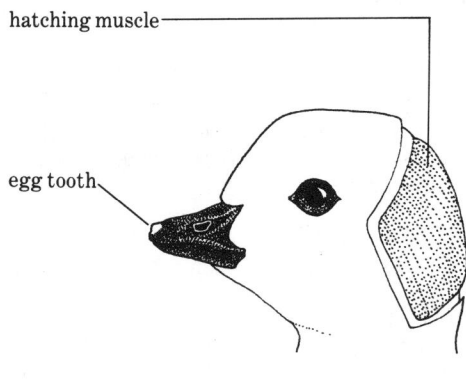

HATCHING
The hatching muscle is used by the emerging chick to help it break out of its shell. It provides the force necessary for the egg tooth, located on the tip of the bill, to penetrate the shell.

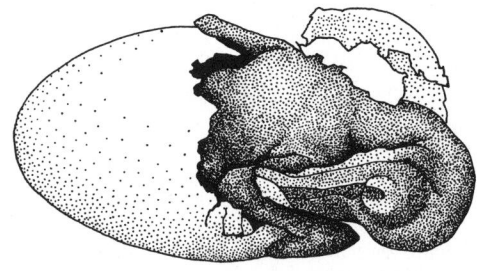

HATCHING
Once the chick has pipped the shell with its egg tooth, the hatching process may take from several hours to several days, depending on the species and individual bird. This brown pelican chick, in the last stages of hatching, has pushed the blunt end of the shell completely open.

Madeira, from birds of this species he saw on the Desertas Is.; the bird thereafter has been commonly called Harcourt's petrel. *See* in Storm-petrel Family.

HARD-BILLED BIRD
Term for a bird that eats seeds—for example, sparrows, grosbeaks, and finches. *See also* Soft-billed Bird.

HARDERIAN GLANDS
The eyes of birds have both lachrymal (LAK-rih-mal) and Harderian (har-DEER-ih-an) glands, which vary in their size and amount of secretion according to the habits of the bird. In water birds such as ducks and geese, the lachrymal glands are small, possibly because these birds do not greatly need secretions for moistening the surface of their eyes; however, Harderian glands may be very large in the eyes of marine birds—for example, cormorants—in which the oily secretions of these glands protect the surfaces of their eyes from the effects of salt water (Pettingill, 1956).

The Harderian glands were named for J. J. Harder (1656–1711), a Swiss anatomist. They are one of the lachrymal glands on the inner side of the orbit of the eyes of many animals that have a nictitating membrane. *See* Nictitating Membrane; Eyes and Eyesight; Gland.

HARLAN
RICHARD, M.D. (1796–1843). Prominent Philadelphia physician and naturalist; author of *Fauna Americana* (1825); good friend to John James Audubon, who named the Harlan's buzzard (hawk) in his honor. See Palmer (1928).

HARMFUL ACTS
(economically). *See* Economic Ornithology; Control.

HARPY
See Harpy eagle in introduction to Hawk Family.

HARRIER
One of names of the marsh hawk and its relatives in Europe, from habit of raiding or harrying its prey. *See* Hawk, marsh, in Hawk Family.

HARRIS
EDWARD (1799–1863). Born and resident at Moorestown, N.J., was friend and patron of scientific men, for whom Audubon named the Harris' hawk and Harris' sparrow; Harris accompanied Audubon on his Missouri R. expedition to the Yellowstone region. See Audubon, M. R. (1960); Herrick (1917); Morris (1902); McDermott (1951).

HARRY-WICKET
See flickers in Woodpecker Family. Name derived from calls.

HATCHING
In the life of a bird, there is no more dramatic or critical time than the few hours during which it breaks out of its shell to become, on emerging, a chick, no longer a fetus dependent on temporary internal organs for food and air. *See* Embryo and Its Development.

For some days before it breaks the shell, the fetus of the domestic chick starts swallowing the amniotic fluid, which provides its tissues, especially the muscles, with a high water content at hatching. Before breaking the shell, it must change, gradually, from getting air from fluid to breathing air with its lungs (Portmann and Stingelin, 1964).

The head of the developing embryo lies near the blunt end of the egg near the *air chamber*, which has been enlarging through constant evaporative loss of water from the egg and contraction of the inner contents of the shell during incubation. *See* Incubation.

To get its first air, the fetus must push its bill through the shell membrane and into the air chamber. If the chamber has developed abnormally, in some place other than at the blunt end of the egg near the head of the chick, the chick may suffocate.

The temperature of the eggs (*see* Egg Temperatures) during incubation is also important to hatching, and may be affected by the brooding behavior of the parents, by the position of each egg in the nest, and even by construction of the nest in either a dry or a damp place (Barth, 1955). *See* Nests and Nesting. Eggs require moisture for hatching. In controlled experiments with the eggs of mallard ducks, best hatching successes were from those dipped in water once a day and incubated at 65% relative humidity. This may explain why ducks nesting in fields far from water have poorer hatchings in dry summers (Welty, 1962). *See also* Atretic Follicles.

The moment that the fetus pierces the air chamber in the egg with its bill, often announced 2 or 3 days before hatching by peeping of baby bobwhite quail, domestic chickens, and other gallinaceous birds, it begins its breathing of air. "The air chamber is rich in carbon dioxide and insufficient for the respiratory needs of the young bird, but the blood supply of the still functioning allantois [*see* Embryo and Its Development] provides it with necessary oxygen" (Portmann and Stingelin, 1964).

With its bill in the air chamber, the fetus-soon-to-become-chick starts partial respiration with its lungs. When it finally pips the shell, rapid drying up of the allantois begins, although the blood vessels of the allantois continue active until the last moment when the chick's navel is closed (Portmann and Stingelin, 1964), and the residues of the allantois and other particles are left in the abandoned eggshell. Just before hatching, the yolk sac, with the remaining yolk, is drawn up into the chick's body by its abdominal muscles.

Immediately after the embryo's bill pierces the air chamber, it stretches its body from a transverse position to lengthwise, which brings its head and the egg tooth atop its bill close to the inner surface of the eggshell, and brings into play the *hatching muscle* on the back of its head.

Most embryonic birds have an egg tooth (see Parkes and Clark, 1964), except ostriches and megapodes, which are apparently large and strong enough at hatching to break out of the shell without one. The shell is always weaker after incubation through loss of mineral substances dissolved out of it, carried by the blood through the embryo's body, and used for the first hardening of its bones (Portmann and Stingelin, 1964).

The egg tooth first appears on the bill of the embryonic domestic chick at age 7 or 8 days. After 10 days, it develops rapidly and reaches its greatest size on the 20th day, just before the chick hatches. It is lost soon after the chick emerges from the shell; however, in Cooper's hawks, red-tailed hawks, and golden eagles it persists for several weeks after hatching (Sumner, 1929); in still others, noticeably passerines, it gradually disappears without apparently falling off (Parkes and Clark, 1964). See also Jehl (1968a); Clark (1961); Sealy (1970).

According to Fisher (1958), the hatching muscle, *musculus complexus*, provides the chick's head with the strong thrust that, with the egg tooth, finally breaks the shell. The egg tooth and hatching muscle develop together; the muscle is somewhat enlarged in the embryos of the domestic chick, house sparrow, and red-winged blackbird when 7 or 8 days old. The hatching muscle of five species of N. American grebes have also been studied and that of Franklin's gull, and its function is believed to be, as in the domestic chick, to help produce the "pip" in the egg that is the first sign of hatching.

Gradually the chick, using its egg tooth, enlarges the hole in the pipped egg and, alternately struggling and resting, turns in the shell until it may have punctured the egg all around, at which the blunt end falls away and the chick emerges. It is still wet from the amniotic fluid but soon dries in the warmth of the nest (Bellairs, 1960).

The time required for young birds to hatch varies among different species. In the domestic chick it may take several hours; in the ovenbird, a warbler, the eggs are pipped 15–20 hours before they hatch. Young wood thrushes require 5–22 hours from first pipping of eggs to hatching; the European wren, *Troglodytes troglodytes*, 2 days; the American coot, 12–76 hours; the royal albatross, 1½–4½ days; and the sooty shearwater, at least 4 days.

Because retention of the yolk sac ensures them food for a short time, newly hatched birds (in songbirds the retained yolk sac is up to 5% of the body weight; in precocial birds, such as a domestic chicken, 25% of the body weight—Portmann and Stingelin, 1964), the chicks of precocial species may live for several days without gathering food; the chicks of altricial birds, for hours before being fed by the parents. *See* Altricial; Young and Their Care.

Once the bird hatches, parental care begins, but sometimes, even before it breaks out of the shell, on hearing it peep, the adult birds may show excitement and even bring food to the nest (Welty, 1962). According to Impekoven (1973), the sounds from the hatching chicks within the eggs help to shift parental behavior from incubating to caring-for-the-young behavior.

SEX RATIO AT HATCHING. In newly hatched birds or those still in the care of the parents, the sex ratio is about equal. In domestic chickens, extensive records showed that males were 49.2% of the newly hatched chicks, with prehatching mortality of males seemingly higher than that of females (Witschi, 1961); in pheasants, males were 53% of the day-old chicks, with a greater proportion of females than males dying just before, during, and after hatching (Latham, 1947); 51.5% of the chicks of ruffed grouse *under 3 months old* were males, with the sex ratio more nearly equal at hatching (Bump *et al.*, 1947).

The proportion of wild ducks hatched in incubators was 51% males in the canvasback, and 53% in the redhead, mallard, and pintail (Hochbaum, 1944). A few records for herring gull chicks showed a nearly equal sex ratio (Goethe, 1937). These approximate sex ratios change when the chicks are growing up and in adulthood, when the birds are subjected to various lethal effects from man and the environment. For example, Sheldon (1971) reported that in the American woodcock the sex ratio of juveniles is about even, 103 males to 100 females, but among adults in Me., 63 males to 100 females, etc. See Sheldon for further details; see also Johnston (1971a) and Welty (1962) for other sex ratios of various species.

HATCHING MUSCLE
See Hatching.

HAWAIIAN HONEYCREEPER FAMILY
Drepanididae (drep-an-EYE-dih-dee); downcurved, from Gr. *drepanon*, a sickle, in reference to sickle-shaped bills of some of the birds in this family. Small to medium-sized birds (about 4–8½ in. long) of the forests and shrubby places of the Hawaiian Is. Of the 22 species in the family, 9 are believed to be extinct, possibly because of their susceptibility to diseases and competition from foreign birds and mammals later introduced by man into the islands and because the most specialized of birds in their habits, such as the native Hawaiian birds, are the most susceptible to extinction, as they are unable to adapt to change. See, however, detailed discussion of causes of extinction in Hawaiian birds in Berger (1972).

The Hawaiian honeycreepers are known only from the Hawaiian Islands. The family is believed by some authorities to have evolved from a single flock of passeriform birds (songbirds), possibly of a single species which apparently came to the islands from the American mainland before any other land birds had arrived (see, however, discussion by Berger, 1972). Fisher and Peterson (1964) suggest that, at an unknown time, bunting-, tanager-, honeycreeper-, or finch-like American birds from thousands of miles across the Pacific colonized these remote volcanic islands. Their evolution into quite different-appearing birds (different species) is believed to have been very rapid. *See* Adaptive Radiation.

It is suggested that when the ancestors of these birds arrived in the islands, they found a rich and diversified tropical habitat but almost no competition there from other birds. This stimulated their invasion of one unoccupied ecological niche after another, leading to differences in their food habits (Amadon, 1950) and gradually to differences in the adaptive shapes

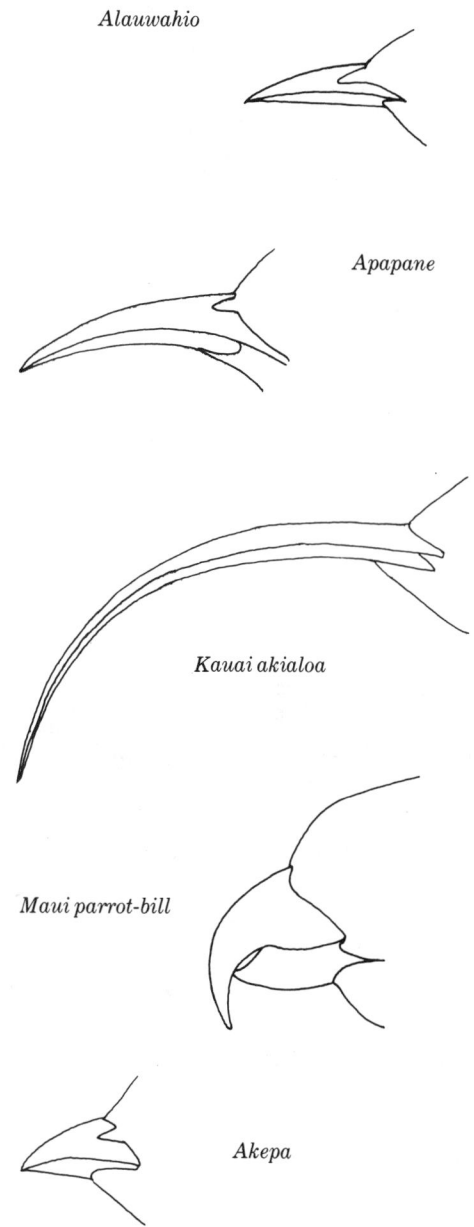

Alauwahio

Apapane

Kauai akialoa

Maui parrot-bill

Akepa

HAWAIIAN HONEYCREEPER FAMILY
Hawaiian honeycreepers are thought to have descended from a single flock of passerine birds that reached the islands from the mainland ages ago and diverged rapidly and widely to fill empty ecological niches. This divergence is graphically illustrated by the variety of bills now found among the honeycreepers that have adapted to different methods of food-gathering.

HAWK FAMILY

and lengths of their bills for obtaining their foods—mainly into those that are long, slender, and downcurved and those that are short and stout, either hooked like a parrot's bill or somewhat heavy and conical like a grosbeak's or finch's bill. The different shapes and lengths of the bills of members of the Hawaiian Honeycreeper Family are examples of *divergent evolution.*

The tongues of the Hawaiian honeycreepers are mostly tubular and are brush-tipped. The various shapes, lengths, and sizes of their bills are adapted either to gathering insects or to taking nectar from variously shaped flowers or to eating seeds or fruit. They nest in spring, Mar.–May; build cuplike nests of twigs and grasses in trees and bushes or in grassy places on the ground; and lay 2–4 white eggs spotted with brown. In the 13 species that still exist, the eggs are incubated by the females, but both sexes feed the young (Baldwin, 1953; Berger, 1972).

HAWFINCH
European bird so called from belief that its chief food is fruit of the hawthorn, *Crataegus oxyacantha* (Newton, 1893–96). *See* in Finch Family.

HAWK FAMILY
Accipitridae (ak-sip-IH-try-dee); from Lat. *accipiter*, a hawk, or bird of prey. 208 species of diurnal birds of prey—eagles, hawks, kites, and Old World vultures—almost worldwide family but not in Antarctic, n. Arctic, or on many oceanic islands (Van Tyne and Berger, 1976); their nearest relatives are the osprey, falcons, American vultures, and condors (*see* Falconiformes); members of family range from 8 to 48 in. long; from small 3–8 oz. sharpshinned hawk to the immense 15–20 lb. harpy eagle of tropical lowland forests from s. Mexico to S. America, possibly largest and strongest eagle in the world (Brown, 1964).

In N. America, there are 26 species in Hawk Family: 4 eagles, 5 kites, and 17 species called hawks. All members of family have bill strongly hooked. The nostrils, small and usually oval-shaped, or slitlike, open in the soft leatherlike skin of part of the upper mandible called the cere, which is often brightly colored (the bill in Hawk Family does not have the notch or tooth as in Falcon Family; see Pettingill, 1970, and Friedmann, 1950, for technical details of family); most members of Hawk Family have broad, rounded wings, except kites, which, like members of Falcon Family, usually have long, narrow, pointed wings.

In Hawk Family, neck is short and strong, head round, feet strong, usually yellow, with sharply curved talons; plumage is mottled, typically blended grays and browns on back, pale or whitish below, often streaked or barred on breast and belly; albinism reported in 48 individuals of 10 species (Gross, 1965a) and melanism in 5 species—broad-winged, ferruginous, Swainson's, red-tailed, and rough-legged hawks—and erythrism (a red phase) in the ferruginous hawk. *See* Colors of Feathers; Albinism; Melanism; Color Phase.

Sexes usually alike outwardly but females larger than males and considerably larger in species most dashing and aggressive in their hunting; for example, in accipiters and some of the eagles (harpy and African crowned), in which female may weigh twice as much as the male (Brown and Amadon, 1968).

Eyes of members of Hawk Family usually yellow, orange, red (goshawk), or brown; paler in young birds, a little deeper in males; fierce appearance, especially of eagles, hawks, accentuated by bony shield over eyes; vision possibly keenest of any living animals (*see* Eyes and Eyesight); eyes so large they move little in sockets; direct their vision by turning head as owls do; have both binocular and monocular vision; use binocular vision in hunting.

Some members of family have spectacular courtship displays (*see* Flight); some eagles reported to fight to death in air over mates or in defense of territory; pairs of eagles thought to mate for life or until one or other of mated pair dies; members of family hunt by day; most migrate between nesting and wintering places, also by day; one can see spectacular fall flights at Hawk Mtn., Pa. (Sept.–Nov.); Derby Hill, N.Y.; Hawk Ridge, Duluth, Minn.; Point Pelee, Ont.; Cape May Point, N.J.; and Cedar Grove, Wisc. See accounts in Allen and Peterson (1936); Stone (1937); Bent (1937); Broun (1949; 1963); Heintzelman (1972); Mueller and Berger (1961); Pettingill (1962); and for observation places in Calif., see Hilton (1971b). *See also* under Birder.

Eagles are actually large hawks; their great size gives them title to term "eagle"; there are 50 species called eagles or hawk-eagles around world (Brown, 1964c); some of largest have wingspreads 6½–8 ft. and generally weigh 8–16 lbs. (the largest native eagle of N. America, the bald eagle, has a 6½–7 ft. wingspread, weighs 8–14 lbs.; the largest eagle to reach N. America, and third-largest in world, the Steller's sea eagle, has wingspread of 7½–8 ft., weighs 11–20 lbs.). See Brown (1970) for comparative sizes of eagles of world—harpy eagle, largest; monkey-eating eagle of Philippines, second-largest; etc.

Despite the enormous size and power of some eagles, according to Bent (1937), Brown (1970), and other authorities, tales of eagles carrying off young children, especially in modern times, are fabrications, perpetuated by lurid journalism. Besides the general aversion of eagles in wild to people, and fear of humans, they are limited in weights they can carry. *See* interesting experiments under Weight-Carrying Capacity. See details in Walker and Walker (1940); Stephen (1950); Arnold (1954). Man is eagles' greatest enemy; among man-made threats to eagles in N. America, at least 300 accidentally killed within 3 years by electrocution when alighting on high-voltage power lines (Anonymous, 1972b).

N. American birds called hawks range in size from the small sharp-shinned, with wingspread of about 2 ft., to the large, almost eagle-sized ferruginous hawk, with wingspread of almost 4½ ft.

Ferruginous, along with Swainson's, redtailed hawk, and other members of the genus *Buteo*, like the eagles, circle much high in air watching ground for mice, ground squirrels, jackrabbits, and other prey, which they swoop down and pounce upon; others, especially the accipiters—sharp-shinned, Cooper's, and goshawk—feed much on birds. With their relatively shorter wings, more rounded than those of the soaring buteos, and with their longer tails, they have greater maneuverability in sharply turning and twisting in flight in pursuit of prey. When hunting, the accipiters dart low and swiftly in and around or through woods, thickets, and hedges, and may snatch a bird out of the air in the talons or surprise and strike one on the ground with their feet. *See* Balance of Nature; Predation. See ecological studies of predation by Craighead and Craighead (1956).

After catching the victim, which eagles and virtually all hawks kill with the grasping feet and talons, they either hold their prey on the ground and eat it or carry it in the talons or in the bill (if it is light enough to be carried) to a perch above the ground. Then, while holding the prey under the feet, with the bill they usually first pluck some of the fur or feathers of their victims, then tear off with the sharply hooked beak pieces of flesh, tendons, and bone, which they swallow; others, such as the buteo hawks, may swallow, whole, small prey such as mice, without plucking.

Kites live in the warmer parts of the world; American kites eat largely insects, reptiles, amphibians, and snails; they are long-winged, long-tailed, graceful fliers; they soar, circle, dip, and glide, resembling large swallows; sometimes they hover, gull-like, wings beating, legs dangling, often they move about lazily over partly open country, sometimes in groups. The 4 species of N. American kites are comparatively gentle, lacking the ferocity of some of the hawks and eagles when they are hungry; they have shorter legs and weaker feet and talons but are well adapted to skillfully catching their small and relatively weak prey. Kites flown by children were so named because of their sudden twisting, diving, or rising in wind like the flight of these birds (Amadon, 1965).

Marsh hawk is only N. American harrier (*see* Harrier); has light, slender body, long wings and tail, and buoyant flight; is one of social hawks, often migrates or roosts in groups; face has owl-like facial discs, and, like owls, often hunts at dusk; circles or glides just over reeds and grasses, drops sharply into marsh, field, or prairie to catch frogs, mice, lizards, small birds.

All members of Hawk Family are protected by federal and state laws (*see* Legal Protection) and may not be kept captive without a permit; however, to sustain an ill or injured bird until it is strong enough to fly and fend for itself, offer it small pieces of fresh, raw, lean beef about twice each day. Keep it in fenced area out of doors if possible, with available shelter from weather. *See* Owl—Barn-Owl Family for similar, more detailed instructions.

All hawks must have, regularly, some freshly killed pigeon, chicken, rabbit, mouse, or sparrow with fur or feathers on them, which is essential to hawk's health. Supply it also at all times with water, fresh daily, in large shallow basin about 3 in. deep (inverted top of a garbage can will suffice) for drinking and bathing. See details of daily care of captive hawks in Peeters and Jameson (1970), and other books

about hawking and falconry. See treatment of broken bones in Mutchler (1972; 1973).

Eagle, American. *See* Eagle, bald.

Eagle, bald, *Haliaeetus leucocephalus* (hal-ih-ay-EE-tus lew-koh-SEFF-ah-lus); genus name: New Lat., from Gr. *haliaetos,* a bird, a sea eagle; species name: from Gr. *leukos,* white, and *kephale,* head. (Color ills., pages 503, 504.) Our national bird; Alaska, Canada, around Great Lakes south to Fla., Baja Calif.; 34–43 in. long; wingspread 6–7½ ft. (Imler and Kalmbach, 1955); adult (sexes alike): snow-white head and tail; body brownish black, the large bill, *eyes,* and feet *bright yellow;* immature: tail, head, and body dark brown, less black than adult, when overhead shows some white on underside of wings; in some the plumage irregularly but extensively blotched with cream or white; bill brownish; eyes pale yellow-gray; feet lemon yellow; tail and head become white when bird 4 or 5 years old (Brown and Amadon, 1968). In gliding or soaring, keeps broad wings flat, not uptilted as in vultures; can be distinguished from similar immature golden eagle by large head, heavier bill, and *unfeathered* legs; not closely related to golden eagle, is one of so-called sea eagles; winters over much of nesting range; seldom seen far from water—seacoasts, large rivers, lakes; magnificent in soaring flight with white head and tail glistening in sunlight or while perched on snag of dead tree; pair often seen together or large numbers concentrated, as along Chilkat R., Alaska, where 3,000–4,000 in mid-Nov. may gather to feed on dead or spent salmon along 10-mi. stretch (Brown and Amadon, 1968), or in winter along Mississippi R. valley; 1,300 reported between s. Minn. and Ark., winter 1961–62, also concentrate in national wildlife refuges, where protected, and especially at large reservoirs from S.Dk. to Okla. (Sprunt and Cunningham, 1962), where open water makes available abundant fish supply; however, population outside se. Alaska, in which estimated 10,000–15,000 (Adolphson and Jonkel, 1969), declining generally over much of range; total winter population in U.S., outside Alaska, only 3,700 (Sprunt and Ligas, 1966); in 1968, only 2,772 counted in the 48 contiguous states (Adolphson and Jonkel, 1969); in mid-January 1979, a much higher count (9,824) in the 48 states by federal, state, and private agencies reflected the participation of many people, not necessarily an increase in the bald eagle population (see Anonymous, 1979a and Lincer *et al.,* 1979); population declining slowly in some parts of country; at catastrophic rate in others (Sprunt, IV, 1969); causes: continued shooting even though bald eagle protected by law and heavy fines (*see* Legal Protection, and especially report by Mulhern *et al.,* 1970), human disturbance at nest sites, loss of nesting trees, and loss of waterside habitat from human occupation, pollution of food, especially by pesticides, and consequent loss of life and of reproduction (Broley, 1950; Sprunt, IV, and Ligas, 1966; 1969; Krantz *et al.,* 1970); population of Fla. bald eagles nests in winter (Nov.–Feb.); many migrate north in spring and summer (for details of early banding, nesting, migrations,

see Broley, 1947, and Howell, 1962; 1968); both sexes utter squealing cackle, almost gull-like; in winter often roost in groups in tall trees, especially along Mississippi R.

Feeding Habits: Feeds largely on fishes, either self-caught or taken from ospreys; also chases and catches injured or shot and crippled waterfowl, during or immediately after hunting season; also muskrats, squirrels, rabbits, etc., eats many traffic-killed animals and other carrion (see Bent, 1937, and Imler and Kalmbach, 1955, for details of food habits).

Nest: Sometimes 7–8 ft. across, 12 ft. deep, built in trees 10–150 ft. above ground; largest of all nests built by single pair of birds (Brown and Amadon, 1968). Sometimes nests on rocky promontory, as along coast of Alaska, or on islands and even on ground; sticks are foundation, with lining of mosses, pine needles, grasses, feathers, or other soft materials.

Eggs: Fla., Nov.–Jan.; farther north, Mar.–Apr. or May; 1–3, usually 2, dull white.

Incubation: In captivity, reported 31–46 days (see Prestwich, 1955, for account of pair breeding at Buffalo, N.Y., zoo in 1909); usually incubation period in wild said to be 35 days but needs confirmation (Brown and Amadon, 1968); after young hatch, so much antagonism between them that frequently weaker one killed by its stronger nest mate or starves (*see* Fraticide); first flight of young 72–75 days after hatching.

Other Names: American eagle; black eagle (young almost completely dark); fishing eagle; gray eagle; Washington eagle; white-headed eagle; white-headed sea eagle.

Accidents: Occasionally caught in steel traps set for furbearers in marshes or along water; many electrocuted each year while perching on, or flying from, wires of high-voltage power lines (see Smith and Murphy, 1972; Laycock, 1973); also nests and young sometimes destroyed by great storms.

Age: One lived captive at Sussex, N.J., for 25 years; another at National Zoo, Washington, D.C., for 30 years, 5 months; captive at West Stephentown, N.Y., still alive at 48 years old in 1968 (Anonymous, 1968a); one banded wild bird, shot in Mexico when 10 years, 5 months, old (Kennard, 1975).

Flight Speed: Gliding and flapping in migration, Pa., 36–44 m.p.h.; in Fla., 35 m.p.h. (Teale, 1951); 30 m.p.h. carrying fish (Cooke, 1937a).

Weights: Male about 8–9 lbs.; female about 10–14 lbs. (Imler and Kalmbach, 1955).

Range: Usually near water, but in migration along mountain ridges (Hawk Mtn., Pa., for example); nests from n. Alaska Mack. Man., se. Que., and Newfoundland south to Baja Calif., Ariz., N.M., s. Tex., Gulf coast and Fla., also in ne. Siberia; accidental in Bermuda and Sweden; winters throughout breeding range. For report of its biology in Alaska, see Sherrod *et al.* (1976).

Eagle, fishing. *See* Eagle, bald, and Osprey.

Eagle, golden, *Aquila chrysaetos* (AK-wih-lah kris-AY-ee-tos); genus name: from Lat. *aquila,* eagle; species name: from Gr. *chrysos,* golden, and *aetos,* eagle. (Color ill., page 505.)

Not closely related to bald eagle (see in Brown and Amadon, 1968); in mountains of Europe, Asia, N. Africa; in N. America, Alaska to Que. and in mountains of e. and especially w. N. America; 33–38 in. long (Pough, 1951); wingspread 6½–7½ ft.; sexes alike but female much larger; adult: dark brown; *eyes dark brown;* powerful bill and claws black; cere and feet yellow; golden feathers on nape inconspicuous at distance; white at base of tail; immature has *broad white tail band with terminal band of black*—called "ringtail" plumage; white at bases of primary feathers of immature are at carpus, or "wrist," of wings and also show in flight. Slow powerful wingbeats often alternate with gliding or soaring; wings long, rounded; legs of golden eagles feathered to toes, similar to immature bald eagle; feathers halfway down tarsus; occasionally has mottled white feathers in tail but not sharply banded tail as in young golden eagle; one of most impressive of all eagles; lifting above hills and plains, soars for hours over some mountain ridge, then rises in spirals until a dark speck in sky; sometimes dives at tremendous speed at prey animal or in play, traveling in its stoop at estimated speed of 150–200 m.p.h. (Brown and Amadon, 1968); generally silent but occasionally yelps or utters mewing cries when soaring in courtship flight, usually alone, but sometimes with mate; one of most convenient places in e. U.S. to see golden eagle in autumn is Hawk Mountain Sanctuary, Kempton, Pa.; most winter south of the main northern nesting grounds in Alaska, Canada, with large concentrations especially in sw. U.S.; golden eagle protected by law; previous to law of Oct. 1962, at least 20,000 killed, 1940–62, mostly from aircraft, in sheep-raising country of w. Tex. and N.M. (Spofford, 1964), because thought by ranchers to prey much on young sheep and goats (see continued destruction, Anonymous, 1971a; 1971c), but McGahan (1966), in Mont. studies in 35 townships where 30,000 sheep raised, found no evidence of eagle predation on sheep or other livestock, but almost 70% of golden eagle food was rabbits, as discovered in studies in West by Craighead *et al.* (1967) and Boeker and Ray (1971). Total golden eagle population of N. America estimated by Spofford in 1964 at 4,000–5,000 pairs, which could not withstand continued large losses; Boeker and Ray in studies (1964–69) found, locally, either increasing populations of golden eagles in w. U.S. or relatively stable population; pesticide residues lower in golden eagle than in bald (Reichel *et al.*, 1969), but see effects on golden eagle in Scotland (Lockie and Ratcliffe, 1964); early in 1971, U.S. Army Engineers announced Eagle Roost Area, Fort Randall Dam, Neb., a registered national landmark, protecting from disturbance more than 280 golden and bald eagles (mostly golden) that concentrate there in winter (Hilton, 1971a); in Aug. 1971, golden eagles and other raptors given 26,225-acre nesting refuge by Bureau of Land Management in sw. Idaho. (*see* Snake River Birds of Prey Natural Area).

Feeding Habits: Food ranges from insects, small mammals, snakes, and turtles, to skunks, prairie dogs, marmots, ground squirrels, to rare extremes of full-grown deer, antelopes, also great horned owls, magpies, domestic pigeons, and cranes (see Arnold, 1954, and Boeker and Ray, 1971); eats carrion but rarely attacks healthy pigs, sheep, deer, or other large mammals (Bent, 1937); usual foods (rabbits, marmots, ground squirrels, sometimes grouse and ptarmigans) far outrank others in volume (Spofford, 1964).

Migration: Most golden eagles in northern part of range (Alaska and Canada) begin to travel south in autumn when food supply on northern range declines; not all eagles migrate; a few stay in Alaska, s. Canada, n. U.S., but inexperienced juveniles (first-year birds) most often migrate and get into trouble—shot or trapped—before reaching winter ranges.

Home Range: In Calif. averaged about 35 sq. mi. for each pair; do not breed every year (see details in Spofford, 1964).

Nest: Some pairs use same nest each year; others use alternate nests in successive years; some apparently nest only every other year in w. U.S. (Boeker and Ray, 1971); most nests built on cliffs, others in pine trees or on earthen mounds; cliffs preferred overlooking grasslands where prey available; in western mountains nest built at elevations of 4,000–10,000 ft. above sea level; nest may be huge if site permits: 8–10 ft. across and 3–4 ft. deep on cliff; bulky, with foundation of sticks, weeds, brush, roots, twigs, lined with soft mosses, lichens, down, and fur; pair often add leafy green branches to nest; other nests may be mere scrape on shelf of cliff with circle of branches surrounding it; each pair has up to 10 nests but only 2 or 3 used in rotation (Brown and Amadon, 1968); same site may be used by succeeding generations of eagles.

Eggs: Calif. to Tex., Feb.–May; Arctic America, May–June; 1–4, commonly 2, dull white, spotted and blotched or freckled with brown or red-brown (Brown and Amadon, 1968; see also Bent, 1937, and interesting report of colors of eggs laid in captivity by Hyndman and Hyndman, 1972).

Incubation: By female but male often takes part; in Scotland, 43–45 days; a record of 43 days in Calif. (Brown and Amadon, 1968); 45 days, Neb. (Mitchell, 1968); young hatch several days apart; older, stronger eaglet will often kill smaller nest mate and adults do nothing to prevent it (Brown and Amadon, 1968); first flight of young at 65–70 days after hatching; after leaving nest, eaglet dependent on its parents for another 30 days or more.

Other Names: American war bird; bird of Jupiter; black eagle; brown eagle; calumet bird; calumet eagle; Canadian eagle; gray eagle; jackrabbit eagle; king of birds; mountain eagle; ringtail; ring-tailed eagle; royal eagle; war bird; white-tailed eagle (Arnold, 1954).

Accidents: In 1935, golden eagle electrocuted in wires of power line near Hugo, Minn., while chasing a hawk; many electrocuted each year while perching on, or flying from, high-voltage power lines; many caught in steel traps set for coyotes and other animals (see Laycock, 1973); many poisoned by ranchers and predatory control men (*see* Poisons).

Age: One lived to 46 years in captivity (Flower, 1938); another reported by Joseph Dixon in Calif. lived in wild at least 30 years; Capt.

Charles Knight, British falconer and lecturer on falconry, had male called "Mr. Ramshaw" that lived to 31 years (Glasier, 1964); one, banded, lived in wild to 10 years, 5 months, before killed (Hilton, 1976).

Flight Speed: Gliding and flapping, 28–32 m.p.h. (Broun and Goodwin, 1943); in Scotland, one chased by peregrines reached 120 m.p.h. (Darling, 1934).

Weights: 9–12½ lbs. (Arnold, 1954); males (7), about 8–10 lbs.; females (4), 9–13 lbs. (Brown and Amadon, 1968); *see also* Weight-Carrying Capacity.

Range: In N. America, nesting range extends from n. Alaska, B.C., Mack., n. Man., southward through mountains to n. Baja Calif., c. Mexico and w. Tex., w. Okla., w. Kans. (formerly), w. Neb., w. S.D., e. Mont., n. Ont.; smaller numbers formerly nested in e. N. America (from Que. southward to mountains of Tenn. and N.C.), have declined steadily and now exist only as scattered pairs; most of nesting habitat now in uplands of n. Canada and w. U.S. (Boeker and Ray, 1971, and see Spofford, 1971). See Alta, "My Friend the Eagle," in Terres (1958).

Eagle, gray. *See* Eagle, white-tailed sea.

Eagle, Mexican. Another name for the caracara in Falcon Family.

Eagle, mountain. *See* Eagle, golden.

Eagle, ring-tailed. *See* Eagle, golden.

Eagle, Steller's sea, *Haliaeetus pelagicus* (hal-ih-ay-EE-tus peh-LAJ-ih-cus); genus name: *see* Eagle, bald; species name: Lat., pertaining to the sea; common name: for Georg Wilhelm Steller, noted 18th-century zoologist and traveler. *The third-largest eagle in the world* (Brown, 1970), largest to reach N. American continent (visitor to Aleutians, Pribilofs, Alaska); magnificent dark brown and white bird with relatively huge, arched, yellow bill; the most impressive in its appearance of all birds of prey; 42–45 in. long; wingspread estimated at 7½, perhaps 8 ft.; combination of immense size, blackish plumage with *white shoulders* and white, *wedge-shaped* tail, big, yellow, highly arched bill, distinguishes adult from all other eagles; immature difficult to distinguish from young gray sea eagle, but large heavy bill is best field character (Brown, 1970).

Feeding Habits: Eats mainly fishes (especially Pacific salmon), also stranded fishes and crabs, mollusks, and carrion; known to kill ptarmigans and birds as large as the 3-ft.-long capercaillie, *Tetrao urogallus*, of Eurasian evergreen forests, largest of the grouse; also young hares, and young seals up to 15–20 lbs.; also kills carnivorous mammals such as sable and arctic fox.

Nest: Huge, may be 8 ft. across, used year after year, built in large trees by preference, more rarely on crags or smaller trees; availability of large trees to some extent determines nesting range; nest built of large branches in treetop, some up to 100 ft. above ground.

Eggs: Apr.–May; 1–3, usually 2, white with slight greenish tinge.

Incubation: 38–45 days; young leave nest when about 70 days old; gets full breeding plumage at about age 4 years but may not breed until later (Brown and Amadon, 1968).

Weights: Males 11–13 lbs.; females 15–20 lbs.

Range: Nests in ne. Siberia—Kamchatka and neighboring coast—along large rivers, never far from sea; casual visitor to Aleutians, Pribilofs, and Kodiak Is., Alaska, records in May, Aug., and Dec.; winters south to Korea and Japan.

Eagle, Washington. *See* Eagle, bald.

Eagle, white-tailed sea, *Haliaeetus albicilla* (hal-ih-ay-EE-tus al-bih-SILL-ah); genus name: *see* Eagle, bald; species name: from Lat. *albus,* white, and *cilla,* tail, white-tailed. The "erne" of crossword puzzles; *fourth-largest eagle in the world;* only a little smaller than Steller's sea eagle (Brown, 1970); mostly lives along seacoasts, valleys of large rivers, inland lakes; casual visitor to Canada; Aleutian Is., Alaska; nests, Greenland; seen off Atlantic coast; 31–40 in. long; wingspread: males 6½–7½ ft., females 6½–8 ft.; adult is huge, gray-brown eagle with a white, wedge-shaped tail; large powerful yellow bill and bare tarsus; immature much darker than adult; has base of tail mottled with white. Spends most of time perched in trees or on crags; utters various barking calls with head thrown up and back: *krick-krick-krick* or *grah-grah-grah* (Brown and Amadon, 1968); males sometimes fight in air over mates.

Feeding Habits: Fishes caught at surface of coastal waters, also those stranded and dying (lumpsuckers, salmon, and pike are favorites); robs gulls, catches murres, coots, ducks, and even swans, also young gulls, fulmars, seals, rabbits, hares, rats, ground squirrels, also eats carrion (Jourdain, 1937).

Nest: Built on rocky ledge when no trees available, even on ground or low hummock; in large trees, usually conifers, often 60 ft. above ground and near water, occupied and added to year after year; nest is often bulky deposit of sticks, grasses, seaweeds, and bones of prey, some are 6 ft. across and 10 ft. deep; pairs have 1 to 11 nests (Brown and Amadon, 1968).

Eggs: Greenland, Apr.–June; 1–3, usually 2, dull white.

Incubation: Estimated at 35–45 days, mostly by female; first flight of young at about 70 days after hatching; no fighting and killing between young as reported for other young eagles.

Other Names: Erne; European sea eagle; gray sea eagle; white-tailed eagle.

Weights: Males 6½–11 lbs.; females 8–14½ lbs. (Brown and Amadon, 1968).

Range: Nests from w. coast Greenland and Iceland to northern parts of Norway, Sweden, Finland, Russia, Siberia, Mongolia, Kamchatka (exterminated from British Isles), and to e. Europe; winters through most of breeding range and southward; casual visitor at Baffin Is., Canada, Unalaska Is., Aleutians; on Nov. 14, 1914, an immature flew aboard Dutch steamship *Arundo* as it passed Nantucket Lightship off Mass., caught and taken to Bronx Zoo, New York; two other sight records of adults seen Newburyport harbor, Mass., 1935 and 1934 (Griscom and Snyder, 1955).

Goshawk, *Accipiter gentilis* (ack-SIP-ih-ter jen-TIE-lis); genus name: Lat., a hawk, bird of prey; species name: Lat., of, or belonging to, the same (noble) clan (Sprunt, 1955a); common name (GOSS-hawk): literally, goose hawk, apparently first applied in Europe. (Color ills., page 506.) Uncommon to rare resident in forests of Canada and n. U.S. and mountains of Far West; also lives in Europe, Asia; handsome, largest of N. American accipiters; considerably larger than a crow; 19–27 in. long; wingspread 40–47 in.; long-tailed, short-winged; female considerably larger than male; adults appear uniformly slate gray; have black crown; blue-gray back, with white underparts mottled with gray; *distinctive white line over each orange-red eye;* immatures closely resemble adults but brown above; white underparts heavily streaked with brown; pronounced light stripe over each yellow eye; normally winters over summer breeding range but irregularly migrates southward in fall when its staple prey of hares, lemmings, and grouse (all cyclic species —*see* Cycle; Irruption) are scarce in North; winter best time in U.S. to see goshawk; numbers reported declining over parts of its northern range (Gauthreaux, 1971a), and thinning of eggshells noted in Calif., presumably because of hard pesticides in environment and in its prey (Anderson and Hickey, 1970). Flight is rapid, steady wingbeats alternated with glide even when flying high; darts in and around woods openings and through tangle of forest limbs; uses long tail and rounded wings to turn sharply or to dodge obstacles; may drop suddenly on prey and kill on ground or in pursuit in air, thrusts long legs and feet forward, strikes victim and drives talons into victim's body, then quickly kills with powerful grip of feet; extremely audacious when hungry, disregards presence of man to seize chicken or wounded game bird and carry off; has even attacked wooden duck decoys and tried to carry away; has attacked barred owl and both died after fight; female is fierce in defense of nest, eggs, and young, often attacks intruding man; utters alarm call like that of Cooper's hawk but harsher, deeper, with gooselike quality, *cac,-cac,cac* or *cuk,cuk,cuk;* female has higher, plaintive call, *kee-a-ah,* like call of red-shouldered hawk; in northern forests prefers mixed hardwoods and conifers; remote stands of big timber.

Feeding Habits: Hares, rabbits, gray squirrels, red squirrels, chipmunks, weasels, ducks, grouse, quail, pheasants, crows, small hawks, owls, woodpeckers, blackbirds, blue jays, grasshoppers, some moth and beetle larvae (Bent, 1937). Meng (1959), in studies of 14 nesting goshawks in Pa. and N.Y., discovered that red squirrels and common crows, which are eaters of grouse eggs, were main foods of goshawks, far exceeding next most frequent items —grackles and blackbirds.

Nest: Male or female builds nest; female, completely dominant partner, mainly incubates

White-tailed sea eagle

HAWK FAMILY

eggs, feeds young, defends nesting territory with little assistance from male (Meng in Berry, 1970); nest is bulky, usually on horizontal branch next to trunk of birch, maple, beech, sometimes in juniper, pine, spruce, fir, about 20–60 ft. up, of sticks and twigs, slightly hollowed in center, lined with bark, fresh twigs of conifers, may be 3–5 ft. across, 2–3 ft. deep (Bent, 1937).

Eggs: Apr.–June; 2–5, usually 3–4, blue-white.
Incubation: By female, 36–38 days, every half hour or so of incubating, she turns the eggs (Brown and Amadon, 1968); after hatching, young are brooded constantly by female for first 8–10 days; young venture out on branches of nest tree when 41–43 days old; first fly about 45 days after hatching.
Age: Captive female used in falconry, or hawking, hatched June 1936, died May 1955, two weeks before 19 years old (Stabler, 1965); one, banded Delta, Ont., shot and killed Smith Falls, Ont., when 6 years, 4 months, old (Kennard, 1975).
Flight Speed: Gliding and flapping in migration, 38 m.p.h. (Broun and Goodwin, 1943).
Weights: Average of 294 shot winter 1936–37 in Pa. for bounty payments: females 1 lb. 8 oz. to 3 lbs. 4 oz.; males 1 lb. 7½ oz. to 2 lbs. 9 oz. (Wood, 1938).
Range: Nests from nw. Alaska, nw. Mack., n. Alta., n. Sask., Ont., Que., Labrador and Newfoundland, south to Calif., Nev., Colo., se. Ariz., n. Minn., Mich., Pa., and w. Md., also through Europe except Great Britain and in Asia; winters from Alaska, B.C., Sask., Ont., Que., Newfoundland and irregularly south to s. Calif., c. Mexico, Tex., Mo., Tenn., Ky., W.Va., and Va.; casual in Fla.

Goshawk, Mexican. *See* Hawk, gray.

Goshawk, northern. *See* Goshawk.

Harrier, northern. *See* Hawk, marsh.

Hawk, American rough-legged. *See* Hawk, rough-legged.

Hawk, bay-winged. *See* Hawk, Harris'.

Hawk, black, *Buteogallus anthricinus* (bew-tee-oh-GAL-lus an-thrah-SIGH-nus); genus name: from Lat. *buteo,* falcon, or hawk, and *gallus,* cock; species name: for the glossy anthracite black of its feathers (Coues, 1882). (Color ill., page 507.) Mexican, C. and S. American species; in summer in Ariz., N.M., and Tex.; occasionally reported other parts of West, and in s. Fla. (Abramson, 1976); adults: sexes outwardly alike; 20–23 in. long; wingspread about 48 in.; large, handsome, chunky black hawk except conspicuous *broad white band across middle of black tail,* which is white-tipped, and white spotting on lower sides of wings at outer bases of primaries (flight feathers); wings exceptionally wide (front to back); cere, legs, and feet bright yellow; immatures: dark back but *head and underparts rich buff* and striped; tail has alternate narrow bands of black and white, about five bands of each (Peterson, 1963); summers regularly in se. and c. Ariz., where arrives mid-Mar. (Phillips *et al.,* 1964);

lives along tree-grown and thicketed creeks, rivers, and arroyos fed by mountain streams (Bent, 1937); very rare visitor and breeder in Tex. locally in lower Rio Grande Valley, nests regularly in sw. N.M. (Ligon, 1961); rather tame and sluggish, often perched in low branches over water watching for prey; at nesting time may soar high in sky, then plunge down toward tree below, suddenly slow dive, and pull up with yellow legs dangling and snap off with feet dead branch of a tree while in full flight; utters three-syllable whistle and prolonged squealing cry like *ka-a-a-ah, ka-a-a-ah.*

Feeding Habits:: Besides perching over water, often stalks around sandbars and mud flats in search of crabs or stranded fishes; frogs, fishes, crabs, and reptiles are main diet, in some places eats exclusively land crabs, also eats small mammals, insects, and, rarely, birds.
Nest: Initially small structure built on branches and smaller twigs, lined with twigs and some green leaves, in palmettos, cypresses, pines, cottonwoods, sycamores, and other trees, 15–100 ft. above ground.
Eggs: Tex. and southward, Feb.–May; N.M., Apr.–June; see Bent (1937) and Ligon (1961); 1–2, rarely 3 in northern part of range; coarse-grained, gray-white with brown markings.
Incubation: Period of and age when young leave nest unreported.
Other Names: Common black hawk; crab hawk; lesser black hawk; Mexican black hawk.
Weights: One female, Campeche, Mexico, 2 lbs. 1 oz. (Brown and Amadon, 1968).
Range: Nests, sometimes resident, c. Ariz., s. N.Mex., locally in s. Tex., south through Mexico and c. America to n. S. America; also summers in s. Utah; occasionally in other parts of western U.S. and s. Fla.; winters in southern part of range and some in more northern parts.

Hawk, broad-winged, *Buteo platypterus* (BEW-tee-oh plah-TIP-teh-rus); genus name: Lat., a kind of falcon or hawk; species name; Lat., from Gr. *platys,* broad, wide, and *pteron,* wing. (Color ill., page 507.) Summers east of Rocky Mtns., Canada to Tex. and Fla.; smallest of N. American buteos, about size of crow; 13½–19 in. long; wingspread 32–39 in.; chunky-appearing; adults: dark brown upperparts; underparts barred with brown-red; wings, underside, silver-white with black tips; tail has conspicuous broad, black and white bands, usually three black and two white, about equally wide; immatures: have dark, more numerous and narrower bands in tail, crowding out white; belly white with dark vertical streaks; when soaring, from below, body and head appear broad, wings long and rounded; in flight, like a red-tailed or red-shouldered hawk but much smaller; eyes red-hazel; rarely a melanistic (sooty brown to black) broadwing seen; several collected (shot) in Man., Minn., and Iowa (Bent, 1937; see also records in Gross, 1965b); some broadwings winter in parts of Fla., and in spring great numbers migrate northward from tropical America in loose flocks up Mississippi Valley, then spread over n. U.S. and Northeast; arrives on U.S. nesting grounds Mar.–Apr. (Bent, 1937); noted for vast Sept. flights southward over hawk observation points in e. U.S.

(Hawk Mtn., Pa., for example, where 21,448 passed over on Sept. 14, 1979); quiet and gentle, tamest of all hawks with high plaintive whistled note like that of wood pewee as it soars over home in extensive hardwood forests of chestnut, oaks, beeches, maples, or mixed coniferous-hardwoods around wilderness lakes, streams, swamps, often sits quietly on low limb in woods, from which watches for prey.

Feeding Habits: Catches and eats frogs, toads (a favorite in spring), snakes, lizards, red squirrels, chipmunks, mice, shrews, rabbits, some small birds, caterpillars of large moths, grasshoppers and crickets, beetles, dragonflies, ants, spiders, crayfishes, earthworms, etc. (Bent, 1937).
Nest: Usually near water in woods, built by both members of pair, slowly, may take 3–5 weeks; about 14–21 in. in diameter, of twigs, and often lichen-lined or with chips of pine or oak bark, and usually green sprays of pine or oak leaves; usually in crotch of deciduous tree, but on branch of pine; 15–50 ft. or more from ground; sometimes uses old crow's nest, hawk's or squirrel's nest.
Eggs: About mid-Apr.–June; 2–3, rarely 4, white, blotched with purple and brown.
Incubation: By both sexes but only female has a brood patch; about 21–25 days; young left nest in one nest record when 41 days old (Bent, 1937); according to Matray (1974), incubation is 28 days or more.
Other Name: Broad-winged buzzard.
Accidents: Some struck and killed by cars when swooping down to highway to catch snakes or insects on road.
Age: One, banded Winnipeg, Man., shot when 7 years, 6 months, old (Kennard, 1975).
Flight Speed: Timed in Pa. in migration, gliding and flapping, 20–40 m.p.h. (Broun and Goodwin, 1943).
Weights: Females (13) averaged 1 lb. 1 oz.; males (14) averaged 14–15 oz. (Brown and Amadon, 1968).
Range: Nests c. Alta. east to Nova Scotia, south to Tex., Gulf coast, Fla., and West Indies; winters, Fla. Keys to Brazil; casual farther north.

Hawk, chestnut-thighed. *See* Hawk, Harris'.

Hawk, chicken. *See* Hawk, Cooper's; Goshawk; and Hawk, sharp-shinned.

Hawk, Cooper's, *Accipiter cooperii* (ak-SIP-ih-ter COOP-er-ih-eye); genus name: *see* Goshawk; species name: in honor of William Cooper, of New York, who shot the bird, or birds, from which Charles Lucien Bonaparte described and named the bird for science in 1828. (Color ill., page 507.) A woodland species, uncommon, lives from s. Canada over much of U.S. south to Fla., Tex.; about size of crow; 14–21 in. long; wingspread 27–36 in.; adults: blue-gray upperparts, top of head blackish; white breast and belly cross-barred with reddish; tail usually *rounded* and crossed by four or more obscure blackish bars; eyes yellow to deep red; immatures: like adults but brown upperparts and white breast and belly *streaked with brown;* like other accipiters, distinguished in flight from buteos and falcons by *short wings* and relatively *long tail* and habit of rapid circling while alternately flapping, then gliding, even during migration (see "The Great Glider Highway," in Terres, 1968a); winters over much of U.S. and appears in northern states in Mar.; on nesting grounds lives both in wilderness forests and in farm woodlots; serious decline reported in 1971 nesting season (Gauthreaux, 1971); eggshells growing thinner as result of pesticides in environment (Anderson and Hickey, 1970); when hunting, dashes through woods in low, swift flight, around trees, through brush, and reaches out in air or on ground to catch in talons surprised birds and other prey; fierce and bold in attacks on farm poultry; is *the* "chicken hawk," not the often-blamed large soaring buteos floating conspicuously over farms looking for mice (see Bent, 1937); often difficult to see as it perches quietly in dense leafy crown of tree, but around nest utters noisy alarm call, *cac, cac, cac* or *cuck, cuck, cuck;* occasionally attacks crows and is mobbed by them and attacked by small kingbird.

Feeding Habits: After catching victim in talons, sometimes flies with prey to water in order to drown it; eats small mammals, flickers, woodpeckers, mourning doves, meadowlarks, robins, quail, blue jays, young pheasants; takes young songbirds out of nest (Nelson, R. W., 1968); occasionally eats fishes and ground squirrels; in 3-year study of food habits of 12 broods nesting near Ithaca, N.Y., Meng (1959) discovered that chipmunks and red squirrels made up 94% of mammals eaten; starling most frequent bird eaten; *see* Accipiter; Balance of Nature.

Nest: Does not tolerate smaller, similar, and competitive sharp-shinned hawk within same woodland; nests in both pine and hardwood groves; in cottonwoods and sycamores along streams in West; on horizontal limb of pine, near trunk, in crotch of hardwood; 10–60 ft. above ground, sometimes in old nest of crow; a platform of sticks and twigs lined with bark.

Eggs: Baja Calif. to Fla., Feb.–June; rest of U.S., Canada, Apr.–June; 3–6, usually 4–5, white to green-white, some spotted with brown.

Incubation: Mostly by female, about 24 days; age when young first fly unreported.

Other Names: Big blue darter; chicken hawk; hen hawk; quail hawk; striker; swift hawk.

Age: One, banded, shot when 7 years, 5 months, old (Kennard, 1975).

Flight Speed: In Pa., gliding and flapping, 21–55 m.p.h. (Broun and Goodwin, 1943); 28 m.p.h. (Cottam *et al.*, 1942b).

Hybrids: A presumed natural hybrid of Cooper's hawk × goshawk reported many years ago (Gray, 1958).

Weights: Females average about 1 lb. 4 oz.; males about 13½ oz. (Brown and Amadon, 1968).

Range: Nests from s. B.C., c. Alta., nw. Mont., Wyo., e. N.D., s. Man., w. Ont., n. Mich., s. Ont., s. Que., Me., n. N.B., and Nova Scotia, south to Baja Calif., Mexico, s.-c. Tex., La., c. Miss., c. Ala., and c. Fla.; winters from Wash., Colo., Neb., Iowa, s. Wis. (rarely), s. Minn., s. Mich.,

s. Ont., N.Y., Vt. (casually), s. Me., and Mass., south through U.S. to Costa Rica.

Hawk, crab. *See* Hawk, black.

Hawk, duck. Another name for the peregrine falcon in Falcon Family.

Hawk, ferruginous, *Buteo regalis* (BEW-tee-oh reg-AY-liss); genus name: *see* Hawk, broad-winged; species name: Lat., kingly, royal; common name (fer-OO-jin-us): reference to rusty color. (Color ills., pages 508, 509.) Hawk of open dry country, Great Plains and Great Basin, of w. U.S., w. Canada; becoming rare; one of largest, most powerful of the buteos; 22½–25 in. long; wingspread 56 in. (May, 1935); adults have three color phases; in more common "light" phase: reddish brown above; white below with red-brown legs, which, in flight, stretched backward, show as *dark V against hawk's white underparts;* white undersides of wings show black at tips of primaries (flight feathers); head usually white; tail is pale or white *without bands;* legs feathered down to toes; rare dark (melanistic) phase (deep clove or rufous brown): resembles dark-phase rough-legged hawk but has pale unbanded tail; a red phase is like the dark phase but more rufous (Brown and Amadon, 1968); in spring moves to northern part of range, but may winter throughout nesting range; does not seem to migrate in flocks; is on northern part of summer range by Mar. to early Apr. on treeless plains, grassy prairies; sits quietly on low tree or fence post or even on ground or knoll watching for prey; often called squirrel hawk because of fondness for ground squirrels; when launching into air from perch, flaps slowly, heavily, but when well under way can fly swiftly in pursuit of jackrabbits; soars in great circles high in sky, sometimes flies only few feet above ground, coursing like rough-legged hawk; harsh alarm cries are *kree-ah* or *kaah, kaah,* like one of notes of herring gull; drives away other predators from its nesting area—red-tailed hawks, great horned owls (Bent, 1937)—and even drives coyotes away from accessible nest on ground on rocks or bluffs (Angell, 1969), but is destroyed by hunters who shoot them as they feed on roadside rodents; these hawks now rare in many parts of their range; see especially White (1969).

Feeding Habits: Swoops down from great height in air to catch prairie dogs (see Ligon, 1961); also very fond of jackrabbits, cottontails, mice, gophers, even attacks stray cats and tries to carry off; sometimes catches bats; eats bull snakes, lizards, occasional grouse and meadowlark; grasshoppers, crickets, and beetles (Bent, 1937).

Nest: Apparently prefers to nest in tall trees when available, in timber belts along streams 6–55 ft. above ground or on ledge of cliff, on cutbank, hillside, rocky pinnacle; nests often used year after year, some are 12–15 ft. high, made of sticks, twigs, old bones, lined with turf, dried grasses, cow or horse dung.

Eggs: Feb.–July; 2–6, usually 3–4, white to blue-white, boldly spotted or blotched with browns.

Incubation: By both sexes, about 28 days (Bent, 1937); young leave nest for first flight (in one study) 44–48 days after hatching (Angell, 1969).

Other Names: Chap-hawk; eagle hawk; ferruginous rough-legged hawk; gopher hawk; squirrel hawk.

Accidents: Occasional severe losses of eggs or young in nests blown out of trees by storms (Hunter and Harrell, 1967c).

Age: One, marked with bell and collar at Clayton, N.M., found dead 20 years later at Strongfield, Sask. (Lloyd, 1937); one, banded Colorado Springs, Colo., caught same place when 17 years, 3 months, old (Kennard, 1975).

Host to Cowbirds: Accidental (Friedmann, 1963), only known record was single egg of brown-headed cowbird in nest with four of hawk's eggs, May 1894.

Flight Speed: Timed at 30–35 m.p.h. (Cottam *et al.*, 1942b).

Range: Nests from e. Wash. and s. Alta., s. Sask., sw. Man., south to e. Ore., Nev., N.M., nw. Tex., and w. Okla.; winters mostly from sw. U.S. to Baja Calif. and c. Mexico; casual in Mont., N.D., w. Minn.

Hawk, Ferruginous rough-legged. *See* Hawk, ferruginous.

Hawk, fish. Another name for the Osprey in Osprey Family.

Hawk, gopher. *See* Hawk, ferruginous, and Hawk, Swainson's.

Hawk, grasshopper. *See* Hawk, Swainson's; also another name for the American kestrel in Falcon Family.

Hawk, gray, *Buteo nitidus* (BEW-tee-oh NIT-ih-dus); genus name: *see* Hawk, broadwinged; species name: Lat., bright, shining. (Color ill., page 509.) Mexican, C. and S. American species; in summer in sw. U.S.; 16–18 in. long; wingspread 32–38 in. (May, 1935); not an accipiter as formerly thought but a small buteo; adults have gray back, gray and white finely barred underparts; *white rump; tail with broad black and white bands* (adult broad-winged hawk has similar banded tail but has *reddish underparts);* immatures: back rusty or sooty brown; pale or buffy underparts streaked with brown, tail with narrow dusky bars (Blake, E. R., 1953); usually arrives in Apr. in Ariz., where apparently limited to Santa Cruz R. above Tucson (Phillips *et al.*, 1964); does not wander widely from rivers and seems to require considerable stands of cottonwoods and willows for nesting and hunting; call is plaintive *cree-ee-ee;* relatively recent nesting record along Gila R. in N.M., where it is rare (see Ligon, 1961).

Feeding Habits: Swift in flight, flies more like an accipiter or falcon, darts to ground to pick up in talons swift-running lizards, in Ariz. especially Clark's spiny lizard; also catches and eats snakes, rabbits, squirrels, mice, quails, young doves, fishes, beetles.

Nest: Small, crow-size, about 20 in. across, often hidden in leaves at top of hackberry, cot-

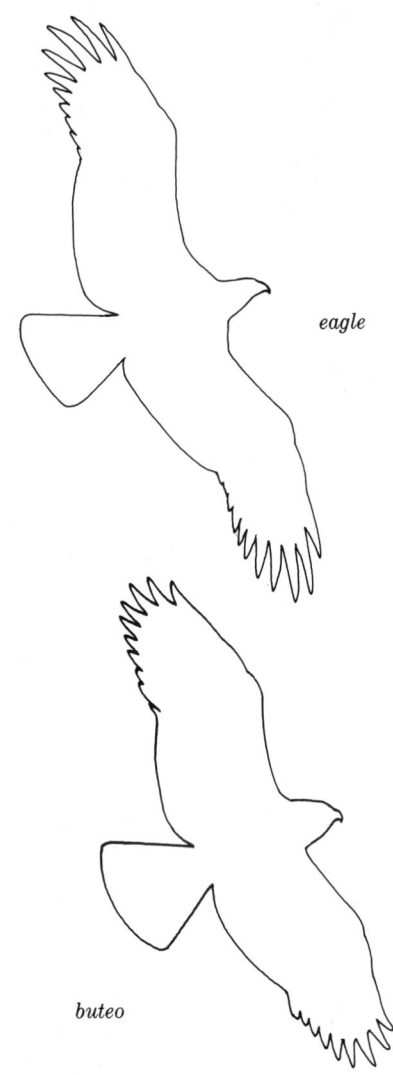

eagle

buteo

HAWK FAMILY

tonwood, or mesquite along large stream, 20–40 ft. up; built of sticks and lined with green-leaved twigs.
Eggs: Mexico and Ariz., Mar.–July; 2–3, usually 2, white to pale blue, most are unmarked (Brown and Amadon, 1968).
Incubation: Period of and age when young first fly unreported.
Other Names: Mexican goshawk; shining buzzard-hawk.
Weights: Males (3), 13–15 oz.; females (3), 1 lb. 4 oz. to 1 lb. 7 oz. (Brown and Amadon, 1968).
Range: S. Ariz., s. N.M., and s. Tex., south to S. America (rare fall and winter visitor to Rio Grande delta, Tex.); winters south of U.S.

Hawk, Harlan's, *Buteo harlani* (BEW-tee-oh HAR-lan-eye); genus name: *see* Hawk, broad-winged; species name: given by John James Audubon, who described this bird for science from a pair shot in La. He named it in 1831 for his friend Dr. Richard Harlan, Philadelphia physician and naturalist. (Color ill., page 512.) Considered a full or distinct species by Bent (1937) and in A.O.U. *Check-list* (1957), but now treated as a subspecies, or geographical form, *Buteo jamaicensis harlani*, of the red-tailed hawk. See Brown and Amadon (1968); Mayr and Short (1970). Harlan's is about size of red-tailed hawk, same form, with broad wings, short tail, but differs markedly in having white or gray tail marbled with dusky near the white tip; there is a dark phase and a light phase. According to Brown and Amadon (1968), the immatures show endless plumage variations.

Other Names: Black warrior; Harlan's buzzard; Harlan's red-tailed hawk.
Range: Harlan's nests from e.-c. Alaska (Yukon Valley) southeasterly to n. Alta. and n. B.C. east of coast ranges; winters from Kans., Ark., s. Mo., south to c. Tex., and La.. Feeding and nesting habits like those of red-tailed hawk. See Bent (1937).

Hawk, Harris', *Parabuteo unicinctus* (par-ah-BEW-tee-oh you-nih-SINK-tus); genus name: Lat., from Gr. *para*, near, and Lat. *buteo*, falcon or hawk; species name: from Lat. *unus*, one, and *cinctus*, girdled, belted, in reference to white "girdle" around base of tail; common name: honors Edward Harris, friend of John James Audubon. (Color ill., page 509.) Mexican, C. and S. American species that reaches U.S. in Southwest; 17½–24 in. long; wingspread about 45 in. (May, 1935); adults are dark, sooty black with flashy white rump and white band across tip of tail; at close range or in good light, shows *chestnut color on shoulders and thighs*, which distinguishes it from other dark or melanistic buteos (Peterson, 1961); immatures: underwing lining is white and chestnut; breast and thighs streaked with russet or brown, rusty shoulders; is similar to red-shouldered hawk but has conspicuous white patch at base of tail; in semi-dry country of mesquite and thorny shrubs of Southwest; lives along watercourses of valleys or draws where hackberry and mesquite (and, in desert, saguaro cactus) offer nesting places; soars in easy spirals high in sky or perches in tip-top of

tallest trees or on utility poles along highways; very tame; when hunting (mostly early morning and evening), flies very swiftly; dashes under low mesquite thickets after rodents; when nest approached by man, utters loud, harsh screams.

Feeding Habits: Besides wood rats, gophers, rabbits, ground squirrels, sometimes pair combine to dash at flock of ducks or herons, often single out and catch one, also takes flickers, Gambel's quail, thrashers, occasionally wrens, mourning doves (Mader, 1975), rails, gallinules, and lizards (Brown and Amadon, 1968). Nesting season in s. Ariz., Feb.–Oct. (Mader, 1975).
Nest: Compact platform of sticks, twigs, weeds, roots, lined with elm shoots, leaves, grasses; built in cactus, mesquite, hackberry, palo verde, ironwood, cottonwood tree, 5–30 ft. up; sometimes a trio (2 males, 1 female) nest together, with extra male helping to feed chicks or bringing food to the nest (Mader, 1979).
Eggs: In U.S., mostly laid Apr. into June; in s. Ariz., most lay eggs early Mar. to mid-Apr.; 2–4, white; sometimes a female lays two clutches in a nesting season (Mader, 1975).
Incubation: By both sexes, 33–36 days (Mader, 1975); in captivity (see White, 1970), in 1968, at Cypress, Calif., two eggs hatched in 33–34 days; young left nest about 54–57 days after hatching (Harrell and Hunter, 1969); in s. Ariz., usually fly about 40 days after hatching.
Other Names: Bay-winged hawk; chestnut-thighed buzzard; Harris' buzzard.
Weights: In Ariz., males (37), 1 lb. 6 oz. to 1 lb. 14 oz.; females (14), 2 lbs. to 2 lbs. 10 oz. (Mader, 1975); for weights in captivity, see White (1970).
Range: Resident from se. Calif., Ariz., N.M., Tex., and casually in La. and Miss., south through Mexico and C. America to c. Chile and Argentina; casual in Iowa, Ohio. See details of range in U.S. in Phillips *et al.* (1964); Ligon (1961); Peterson (1963); Brown and Amadon (1968).

Hawk, hen. *See* Hawk, Cooper's, and Goshawk.

Hawk, hook-bill. *See* Everglade kite.

Hawk, jiddy. Another name for the parasitic and pomarine jaegers in Skua Family.

Hawk, killy. Another name for the American kestrel in Falcon Family. Name derived from call.

Hawk, Krider's. A pale race, or subspecies, of the red-tailed hawk; lives in plains and prairie regions of Midwest; was described and named by Bernard A. Hoopes in 1873 from a pair of these hawks collected (shot) by John Krider in Winnebago County, Iowa, in Sept. 1872 (Bent, 1937). See Krider in Burns (1933); *also* under Hawk, red-tailed.

Hawk, ledge. Another name for the peregrine falcon in Falcon Family.

Hawk, lesser black. *See* Hawk, black.

Hawk, marsh, *Circus cyaneus* (SIR-kus sigh-ANE-ee-us); genus name: Lat., circle, in air; species name: Lat., dark blue. (Color ills., page 510.) A slim, long-tailed, long-legged hawk with owl-like face; ranges over entire U.S., Canada, and north to Alaska; also in Europe, Asia; a harrier (*see* Harrier); sexes unlike in color, but both have *conspicuous white rump patch;* yellow eyes; male, *pale gray;* female, larger, predominantly brown, light buffy below; immatures resemble females, are brown, reddish below; winters over parts of nesting range, but many by mid-Nov. have withdrawn into southern half of nesting range; in one study some of those banded on nesting range in Sask. were later reported scattered from w. Tex. to n. Ga. (Houston, 1968a); arrives on nesting range through U.S. and Canada by Mar.–Apr.; in Alaska by May; in 1971 down in numbers everywhere on nesting range because of diminution of marshlands, influence of pesticides (Gaulthreaux, 1971a; Arbib, 1979); eggshell thinning of up to 20% or more (Anderson and Hickey, 1970); in winter, lives about coastal and river marshes; in summer, around sloughs, wet meadows, marshes, and on prairies, plains; when hunting, usually flies low over ground, 10–30 ft. up, a few wingbeats followed by a short glide with wings held slightly up in V; drops quickly on mouse or small bird in grasses; sometimes perches on ground on stumps of posts; has spectacular courtship flight; some males are polygynous (Hamerstrom, 1969b); roosts on ground, very often communally outside nesting season; both sexes utter various shrill screams, especially *kee-kee-kee; kek, kek, kek;* or flickerlike notes by female when disturbed at nest; repeatedly attacks other hawks that soar over nesting territory, also drives away crows and even eagles; and will dive at man approaching the nest.

Feeding Habits: Eats mainly mice, rats, frogs, small snakes, also lizards, crayfishes, many insects, small birds, and carrion; may hover in front of prairie fire to pick up escaping mice (Bent, 1937).

Nest: Built on ground, mainly by female, commonly near low shrubs, in tall weeds or reeds, sometimes in sphagnum bog; a platform of dry sticks, straws, weed stems, grasses, often on top of low bush above water, or on knoll of dry ground, also on higher shrubby ground but usually near swamp or meadow, margins of sloughs, or even built up in wet places among flags, bulrushes.

Eggs: Mar.–July; 3–9, commonly 5, pale blue when first laid (Hamerstrom, 1969b); dull white later; usually unmarked but some spotted with browns.

Incubation: By female, 31–32 days in N. America; young fly about 30–35 days after hatching (Hamerstrom, 1969a).

Other Names: Blue hawk (male); frog hawk; harrier; hen-harrier; marsh harrier; mouse hawk; northern harrier; white-rumped hawk.

Age: One, banded Hamilton, Kans., at least 10 years old when shot and killed in Tex. (Cooke, 1937c); another, banded while a youngster in Ohio nest, shot and killed when 16 years, 4

months old, at Wallaceburg, Ont., while trying to catch a pheasant (Campbell, 1946); one, banded Imperial Beach, Sask., caught in trap, Scotland, Tex., when 16 years, 5 months, old (Kennard, 1975).

Flight Speed: Timed in migration, flapping and gliding, 24–38 m.p.h. (Broun and Goodwin, 1943).

Weights: Males (7), 12¾ to 13¾ oz.; females (21), 13 oz. to 1 lb. 4 oz. (Brown and Amadon, 1968).

Range: Nests from n. and w. Alaska, nw. Mack., n. Man., n. Ont., c. Que., Labrador, south to n. Baja Calif., s. Ariz., s. N.M., n. Tex., w. Okla., Kans., Mo., s. Ill., s. Ind., Ohio, W. Va., se. Va.; also in n. Europe, Asia; winters from s. B.C., Alta., Sask., w. S.D., Minn., s. Wisc., lower peninsula of Mich., s. Ont., N.Y., and Mass. (casually in Vt. and N.H.), south through Mexico and C. America, to nw. S. America and West Indies.

Hawk, Mexican black. *See* Hawk, black.

Hawk, mosquito. Another name for the common nighthawk in Nightjar Family; also for the Mississippi kite.

Hawk, mouse. *See* Hawk, marsh; Hawk, red-tailed; and Hawk, rough-legged; also another name for the American kestrel in Falcon Family.

Nighthawk. *See* in Nightjar Family.

Hawk, partridge. *See* Goshawk.

Hawk, pigeon. Another name for the merlin in Falcon Family.

Hawk, quail. *See* Hawk, Cooper's.

Hawk, red-bellied. *See* Hawk, red-shouldered.

Hawk, red-shouldered, *Buteo lineatus* (BEW-tee-oh lin-eh-AY-tus); genus name: *see* Hawk, broad-winged; species name: Lat., striped. (Color ills., pages 510, 511.) Resident, e. N. America, s. Canada, to Fla., west to Great Plains; also an isolated population in Calif. and Ore. locally called red-bellied hawk; 17–24 in. long; wingspread 32½–50 in.; adults: brown back; eyes brown; *underparts,* from throat to tail and on thighs, *barred with brown, red, and white;* reddish patch on each shoulder (not always visible); has light patch or translucent "window" at base of primaries (flight feathers) of each wing which show in flight (Peterson, 1961); *narrow white bands on dark tail;* immature: similar to adults, but has underparts heavily *streaked* with brown; little or no reddish shoulder patches; winters over much of nesting range except in n. U.S. and s. Canada; is on northern nesting grounds by Feb.–Mar.; lives in swamps, wooded river bottoms, lowland wet tracts of woods either in remote areas or in thickly settled farming country; even narrow strip of woods along creek provides nesting territory; usually in different area than red-tailed hawk, which prefers upland woods; has strong attachment to nesting territory; in one wood-

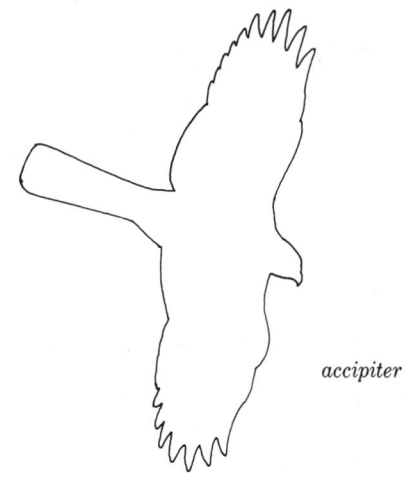

accipiter

kite

HAWK FAMILY
When observed from below, eagles have wedge-shaped tails and long, rounded wings that are flattened in gliding flight; the soaring buteo hawks are chunkier with wider wings; accipiters have longer tails and relatively shorter, rounded wings for greater maneuverability; and kites, the most graceful hawks, have long, narrow, pointed wings and long tails — in the swallow-tail kite, the tail is deeply forked.

land, either same pair or succeeding generations known to occupy same tract each year for 26 consecutive years; another site for 45 years (Bent, 1937); some individuals very tame if not persecuted; pair very noisy in spring, utter loud, rapidly repeated musical *kee-you, kee-you, kee-you, kee-you;* blue jay imitates this call perfectly; red-shouldered reported declining in numbers on nesting range in Midwest, Sask., ne. U.S., and elsewhere (spring 1971); possible reason: eggs laid so thin they break before hatching (Gauthreaux, 1971); see also report by Brown (1971) of losses in winter population in all states except Calif. and W.Va.; in 1979 on threatened species list with continued declining population (see Arbib, 1979); Anderson and Hickey (1970) reported some eggshell thinning, apparently result of pesticides in hawk's prey.

Feeding Habits: Catches and eats mice, shrews, moles, tree squirrels, chipmunks, rabbits, muskrats, opossums, skunks, occasional bird (rails, pheasants, mourning doves, woodcock, screech owls, blackbirds, meadowlarks, American robins), small snakes, lizards, turtles, toads, frogs, salamanders, grasshoppers, crickets, beetles, caterpillars, wasps, katydids, spiders, earthworms, snails, etc. (Bent, 1937); often use old nests as feeding platforms.

Nest: Well built, often deep; 20–60 ft. up, filling crotch of branch or branches against main trunk of hardwood or conifer (in Fla., in palmettos); built of sticks, twigs, bark, mosses, lichens, frequently decorated with green sprigs of evergreen, often uses nests of previous years.

Eggs: Fla., Jan.; Calif., Mar.–Apr.; n. U.S. and Canada, Mar–June; 2–6, commonly 2 (Fla.), 3–4 (n. U.S.), white, blotched with browns.

Incubation: By both sexes, about 28 days; young leave nest when 35–42 days old.

Other Names: Hen hawk; mouse hawk; red-bellied hawk; red-shouldered buzzard; winter hawk.

Accidents: Sometimes caught at water's edge in steel traps set for furbearing animals (Pratt, 1943).

Age: Of 8 banded ne. U.S. and Midwest, one lived to 6 years; three, 8 years; one, 11 years; one, 12 years; one, 18 years; one caught and released in Md. when at least 20 years old (Schmid, 1963).

Albinism: In 1952, Heinz Meng took young albino from nest in N.Y., all-white but with pale blue eyes (Austing, 1964).

Flight Speed: Flapping and gliding in migration, 18–34 m.p.h. (Broun and Goodwin, 1943).

Weights: Males average about 1 lb. 3 oz.; females 1 lb. 8¾ oz. (Brown and Amadon, 1968).

Range: Mainly a resident from n. Calif. to nw. Baja Calif. and from e. Neb., Minn., Wisc., Mich., Ont., and s. Que. south to c. and e.-c. Mexico, the Gulf coast, and s. Fla.; winters in East in e. Kans., Mo., s. Ill., Ind., Ohio, nw. Pa., N.Y., and Mass. (rarely), south to c. Tex. and Mexico, rarely to Gulf coast and Fla., occasionally north to e. Neb., Iowa, c. Ill., s. Mich., s. Ont.; accidental in Scotland; locally common or rare in western U.S. For changing status of this threatened species, see recent issues of *American Birds.*

Hawk, red-tailed, *Buteo jamaicensis* (BEW-tee-oh jah-may-ih-SEN-sis); genus name: see Hawk, broad-winged; species name: Lat., of island of Jamaica, West Indies, from which came first specimen, or specimens, on which scientific name was based. (Color ills., pages 512, 513.) One of best-known, most broadly distributed hawks in N. America; has wider ecological tolerance of habitats than any other N. American hawk (Brown and Amadon, 1968); prefers mixed country of open pastures or fields interspersed with woods, bluffs and streamside trees, in deserts where some trees, in mountain forests of Southwest; lives throughout continent except on tundra or in unbroken forest (Alaska, Canada, U.S.); big, powerful, shares rating with ferruginous hawk as largest N. American buteo; 19–25 in. long; wingspread 46–58 in.; adults: dark brown above; eyes brown; white below with brown streaks on lower neck and *broad band of dark streaking across white belly;* chestnut red on upper side of tail, a character that also distinguished it in its black, or melanistic, phase, which is more characteristic of redtails in West, from other dark-phase buteos (for other color variations of redtail see especially in Brown and Amadon, 1968); see also Harlan's and Krider's hawks; immatures: similar to adults but upperparts somewhat more mottled with white; eyes yellow; breast usually shining white; underparts more streaked and spotted than in adults; tail gray or gray-brown with 6–10 narrow dusky bars; soars much high over woods, fields, utters hoarse, rasping scream with hissing quality in voice, *p-s-s-s,* likened to escaping steam, *kree-e-e-e,* starting high and slurring downward, suggests squeal of pig (Bent, 1937); mainly migratory over northern part of range; most winter farther south but some pairs remain in, or not far from, nesting range; pairs cling to territories year after year; are thought to mate for life or until death of one of pair, at which survivor takes another mate (Austing, 1964); in courtship pair soars about screaming, smaller male may suddenly dive swiftly from great height at female, whereupon she may turn over in air and present her claws to his in mock combat; courtship flights come at any time of year in fair weather; early in nesting season they end with pair swooping to perch in tree and copulation; pairs defend nest by screaming and diving at intruding man but rarely attack in e. U.S.; however, in Calif., female known to dive fiercely at man climbing to nest to rake him with her hind claws (Brown and Amadon, 1968); nests are sometimes pre-empted by earlier-nesting great horned owls; adults fear man, but some young of year may be very tame, therefore easily approached and shot from perches on trees or poles along highways; young are strongly migratory; in Sask., Houston (1967b) discovered that most of banded redtails that scattered south and southeast deep into U.S. had been shot; are also caught in pole traps (steel traps) set by men around game farms and trapped hawks left to die; redtail has been declining steadily since World War II, noted especially in diminishing numbers in Northeast in Hawk Mtn., Pa., fall migration (Spofford, 1969); most numerous in parts of West, but see White (1969); decline caused by persecution by man and elimination of its wild wooded country by increasing human population; some thinning of eggshells also noted, presumably from effects of pesticides in its prey (Anderson and Hickey, 1970); wintering pairs that remain on nesting range noted to roost in thick conifers; may build new nests by Jan., most are on nesting grounds in North by Mar., in Alaska by Apr.–May.

Feeding Habits: May hunt while soaring in sky or hovers along mountain ridge where updrafts hold it aloft; phenomenal eyesight (binocular vision) enables it to see mouse or other prey at great distance; young redtails especially hover about 100 ft. above fields, feed especially on meadow mice; adults sometimes make falconlike stoop at bird or in flight snatch bats out of air; however, main prey is rodents; most often watches for prey from perch in tree or on pole near fields, from which takes off with powerful wingbeats, then glide, in which snatches prey from ground with talons; sometimes hops about in field pouncing on grasshoppers; eats house mice, field mice, rats, red and gray squirrels, gophers, prairie dogs, cottontail rabbits, moles, shrews, chipmunks, muskrats, spermophiles, weasels, skunks, porcupines, may attack wild house cats; catches some waterfowl and domestic poultry, cattle egrets (see Courser, 1971), gallinules, rails, pheasants, grouse, quail, doves, screech owls, kingfishers, woodpeckers, crows, starlings, grackles, meadowlarks, and other small birds; rattlesnakes, copperheads, and other snakes, turtles, toads, lizards, frogs, salamanders, crayfishes, crickets, beetles, spiders, earthworms, carp and catfishes caught at edge of water (Bent, 1937).

Nest: Large, bulky, 2½–3 ft. across, of sticks, twigs, lined with bark, often decorated with some green sprigs of evergreen; built in oaks, pines, and other trees, 15–70 ft. or more up, usually in crotch of branch at trunk, frequently in tallest tree near edge of woods; also, in treeless country, in top of shrub, cactus, or on cliff.

Eggs: Feb.–June; 1–5, commonly 2–3, dull white, sparingly spotted with brown.

Incubation: Mostly by female (male feeds her on nest), about 28–32 days, usually 30; young fly when about 45 days old (Brown and Amadon, 1968).

Other Names: Buzzard; buzzard hawk; eastern redtail; hen hawk; mouse hawk; red hawk; redtail; red-tailed buzzard; western redtail.

Accidents: Has been bitten and killed by rattlesnake after capturing it (Bent, 1937), also by copperheads; also bitten and killed by weasel after weasel caught by redtail was carried aloft.

Age: One, banded as fledgling in Sask., Canada, trapped alive in Kans. when 11 years, 9 months, old (Cooke, 1937c); one, banded Sask., shot in La. at age 14 years; one (immature), banded Oct. 1970 at Cedar Grove, Wisc., killed by car at Athens, Tenn., Mar. 1976, when 16 years, 9 months, old (Mueller *et al.,* 1977a); captive female at New Paltz, N.Y., still alive and laying eggs when 18 years old; captive female at Millbrook, N.Y., lived to 29 years old (Lovejoy, 1970); captive pair in Ohio bred in 1966, of two eggs laid, one hatched; both adults raised the young (Hunter and Harrell, 1967a).

Albinism: Thought to be rare and apparently unreported in w. N. America (Austing, 1964); an albino from Delaware County, Pa., completely white except for russet tail (Townsend, 1883); one pure white reported soaring overhead in Wisc. (Orians and Orians, 1956); Austing (1964) caught an all-white one in Ohio in 1960.

Flight Speed: Flapping and gliding in migration, 20–40 m.p.h. (Broun and Goodwin, 1943); according to Austing (1964), top speed at level flight 35–40 m.p.h., but possibly 120 m.p.h. in aerial dive.

Weights: Males 2 lbs. 4 oz. to 2 lbs. 8 oz.; females 3 lbs. to 3 lbs. 8 oz., but Fla. redtails are smaller (see Brown and Amadon, 1968).

Range: Nests throughout most of N. America, from c. and interior Alaska, c. and e. Canada, south to Panama and West Indies; northern birds winter to Gulf coast and n. Nicaragua.

Hawk, rough-legged, *Buteo lagopus* (BEW-tee-oh lag-OH-pus); genus name: *see* Hawk, broad-winged; species name: Lat., hare's foot, or hare-footed, from resemblance of feathers on legs and feet to a hare's furry foot; also has given it common name. (Color ills., page 513.) Summers north of U.S., from Alaska across Canada, also in Scandinavia, n. Russia, and Siberia; *winters* in U.S.; big hawk of open country with relatively longer wings and longer tail than most buteos; frequently hovers over one spot like American kestrel; 19–24 in. long; wingspread 48–56 in.; two color phases; in dark phase, body is all dark brown above and below, but seen in air from below, usually shows much white at bases of primaries (flight feathers); tail pale, dark at end; in light phase, has brown back and wings but head, neck, underparts, and thighs are white to buffy, streaked and spotted with brown; eyes brown to yellow; *yellow legs feathered to toes; usually has broad band of brown across belly* and on white undersurface of wings; has *conspicuous black patch at wrist, or bend of wings;* tail white, with broad black band at tip (Peterson, 1961); as it wheels in flight, white rump and white at base of tail may be very prominent; moves south into U.S. from northern nesting grounds in great numbers in years of food scarcity (*see* discussion under Cycle; Irruption); often migrates in large flocks; arrives Sept.–Oct., is settled on winter territory Nov.–Mar.; may spiral high in air until only speck in sky; when hunting for mice, alternately flaps and glides close to ground, then pounces on prey; small, weak feet adapted to catching and killing small animals; like marsh hawk, often quarters back and forth over open fields, pastures, and marshes; sometimes watches for prey from low perch atop fence post or in dead tree, atop sagebrush, or stands on small hillock on open prairie watching for rodents, grasshoppers; often hunts at dusk, beating its way in noiseless flight over hunting ground; is tame and unsuspicious, often roosts in groups; mated pairs may remain constant in winter even within flocks (Brown and Amadon,

1968); because of tameness has been shot in enormous numbers in winter in U.S. (see Bent, 1937), where man is greatest enemy; also caught in pole traps; in Utah, migrants killed by cars in great numbers on highways while feeding on traffic-killed jackrabbits (White, 1969); leaves U.S. for northern nesting grounds Mar.–May; arrives generally on nesting grounds, Canada, Alaska, Mar.–Apr.; is usually silent in winter but in spring pair circling in sky utters plaintive whistle, but may screech or squeal loudly on nesting grounds, where Eskimos call it squalling hawk.

Feeding Habits: Catches and eats mostly mice, lemmings, pocket gophers, cutworms and other caterpillars, also occasionally small bird or game bird by short flight from perch; prey usually taken on ground (Brown and Amadon, 1968).

Nest: On nesting range lives on open tundra and mountainsides, not in forests unless plenty of open ground; normally builds nest on rock ledge, usually under overhang, or on low eminence, or on boulder; in southern part of range nests in trees; most nests about 24–30 in. across, built of sticks of dwarf willow and other Arctic plants; nests used for many years, each pair may have several nests used in alternate years.

Eggs: Ordinarily Apr.–June, sometimes July; in years of food scarcity, 2–3; in years of lemming abundance, 5–7; white, blotched or streaked with browns.

Incubation: Usually by female, 28–31 days; young leave nest about 41 days after hatching; may spend 3–6 weeks in Arctic before migrating south for winter (Brown and Amadon, 1968).

Other Names: American rough-legged hawk; black hawk; mouse hawk; rough-leg; rough-legged buzzard; squalling hawk.

Age: One, banded Stockton, Kans., shot at Great Bend, Kans., when 6 years, 9 months, old (Kennard, 1975).

Hybrids: In Europe has crossbred with the buzzard, *Buteo buteo* (Gray, 1958).

Weights: Males (5) averaged 1 lb. 13 oz.; females (7), 2 lbs. 6 oz. (Brown and Amadon, 1968).

Range: Nests from Aleutian Is. and Alaska to Yukon, n. Mack., Victoria Is., sw. Baffin Is., and Labrador, south to Man., se. Que., c. Ont., and Newfoundland; winters from s. B.C., c. Alta., s. Sask., N.D., Minn., Wisc., Mich., s. Ont., s. Que., N.H., and Me., south to c. Calif., Ariz., N.M., Okla., Mo., Tenn., Va.; casual to Tex.; accidental on Pribilof Is., Bermuda.

Hawk, sea. Another name for the jaegers and Skua in Skua Family, and the Osprey in Osprey Family.

Hawk, Sennett's white-tailed. *See* Hawk, white-tailed.

Hawk, sharp-shinned, *Accipiter striatus* (ack-SIP-ih-ter strih-AY-tus); genus name: *see* Goshawk; species name: Lat., striped; *sharp-shinned,* from flattened, thin tarsus, or shank. (Color ills., page 513.) Usually lives in large remote woods throughout most of continent

north to Alaska and Canada; smallest N. American accipiter; 10–14 in. long; wingspread 20–27 in. (May, 1935); sexes outwardly alike, but female much larger than male; body long, slender; wings short and rounded; long slender legs bright yellow; adults: upperparts blue-gray; underparts white, *heavily cross-barred with red-brown,* except throat, which is finely streaked; undertail coverts white, unmarked; eyes scarlet; *tail square at end or slightly forked* (similar Cooper's hawk has *rounded tail*); tail cross-barred with three or four narrow bands of black, narrow white tip; immature: upperparts *brown;* white underparts *streaked* with brown or black; like Cooper's hawk, sometimes seen flying over woodland home just above trees with steady beat of wings, then short glide (usually does not live in same woods with competitive Cooper's); in hunting, fierce, bold; beats low over ground, darting under branches along woods path, across small openings, or through brushy fields or meadows, turns abruptly in flight to drop to ground to grasp small bird or plucks it out of air or from twig and continues on way, bird clutched in its sharp talons; as Pough (1951) points out, older ornithologists years ago called this hawk a "harmful" species because it eats the small "beneficial" songbirds, but ecologists know now that sharp-shin can take some of the surplus of small birds, as they have always done, without harm to regular breeding population; ecologists alarmed in summer 1971 by drastic decline in population of sharp-shin in e. U.S. (Gauthreaux, 1971a); thinning of eggshells by some 8–13% reported (Anderson and Hickey, 1970), apparently result of pesticides in its prey; winters from s. Canada through U.S. and southward; considerable migration in fall and spring; usually on nesting grounds by Apr.–May (Bent, 1937); pair often noisy when human intruder near nest and may even dash down and strike in defense of nest but usually slips away silently; pair utters cackling notes, *kek,-kek,kek* or *kik,kik,kik,* of alarm; call note is plaintive whine.

Feeding Habits: Mostly small birds, from creepers to doves and pigeons, also young chickens; known to attack pileated woodpecker and other birds larger than itself; immatures more likely to attack prey too large to handle (Mueller and Berger, 1970); occasionally eats mice, shrews, bats, frogs, lizards, grasshoppers, moths, butterflies, etc. (Bent, 1937).

Nest: Built of sticks, twigs, lined with strips of bark, is about 2 ft. across in crotch or on branch next to trunk, usually in conifer 10–60 ft. up; usually builds new nest each year; occasionally adapts crow's or squirrel's nest to its use; sometimes builds nest in crevice of rock or in hollow tree.

Eggs: Mar.–July; 3–8, commonly 4–5, white, blotched with browns.

Incubation: By both adults, 34–35 days (Nice, 1954); young first fly about 23 days after hatching (Brown and Amadon, 1968).

Other Names: Bird hawk; bullet hawk; chicken hawk; little blue darter; pigeon hawk; sharp-shin; slate-colored hawk; sparrow hawk.

Age: One, banded Calif., shot there when 6 years old; another, banded Cedar Grove, Wisc., found dead Minneapolis, Minn., when 12 years, 4 months, old (Kennard, 1975).

Flight Speed: Timed in w. U.S., 28 m.p.h. (Cottam *et al.*, 1942b).

Weights: Pa., adult males 3 oz. to 4⅛ oz.; adult females 6 to 8 oz. (Sutton, 1928); Wisc., males (899), trapped and released, averaged 100 gr., or about 3½ oz.; females (1,009), 170 gr., or about 6 oz. (Mueller and Berger, 1970).

Range: Nests from nw. Alaska, Yukon, nw. Mack., n. Sask., c. Man., n. Ont., c. Que., s. Labrador, Newfoundland, south to Calif., Mexico, Tex., La., Tenn., S.C., and Ala. and West Indies; winters from Vancouver Is., s. B.C., w. Mont., Neb., s. Minn. (casually), Ill., s. Mich. (rarely), s. Ont. (casually), N.Y., s. Vt., s. N.H., s. Md., N.B. (casually), and Nova Scotia, south to Panama and the Bahamas.

Hawk, short-tailed, *Buteo brachyurus* (BEW-tee-oh brah-kih-YOU-rus); genus name: *see* Hawk, broad-winged; species name: Lat., from Gr. *brachys*, short, and *oura*, tail (Color ill., page 513.) Mexican and C. and S. American species that reaches U.S. in Fla., where rare and local (Robbins *et al.*, 1966); small, tropical buteo about size of crow; has two color forms —dark and light (*see* Color Phase)—which occur in about equal numbers in Fla. in either sex; light and dark forms interbreed but apparently do not produce intergrades, or offspring of intermediate colors (May, 1935); 15–17 in. long; wingspread about 35 in.; adults, light phase: upperparts black, forehead white near base of bill; immaculate white below, including undersurface of wings; tail white below darkening toward tip, where usually barred dusky; black phase: wholly black above and below, except some white, barred with dusky, on underside of flight feathers (Blake, E.R., 1953); no other small Fla. buteo has either pure-white or jet-black underparts; immature forms—dark or light—similar to adults (Peterson, 1947); in Fla., permanent resident in mangrove and cypress swamps of Everglades National Park, also in Big Cypress Swamp, and along streams and borders of lakes in c. Fla.; most common in mixed woodland-savanna habitats (see Ogden, 1974); might be seen soaring high on rising air currents of midday; often perches in tall trees; at nest screams or utters notes, when disturbed, somewhat like wail of red-shouldered hawk; also high-pitched squeal (Bent, 1937).

Feeding Habits: Little-known, but some small birds (one had eaten a sharp-shinned hawk), lizards, also wasps, grasshoppers (Brown and Amadon, 1968).

Nest: Large for size of bird, bulky, of sticks, twigs, lined with green sprays of cypress, magnolia leaves; 40–100 ft. up, in topmost branches of cypress or other tree, or in top of mangrove.

Eggs: Jan. to early May; 2–3, commonly 2, dull white.

Incubation: Period of and age when young first fly unknown.

Other Names: Little black hawk; short-tailed buzzard.

Weights: Female (1), about 1 lb.; male (1), 1 lb. (Brown and Amadon, 1968).

Range: See above.

Hawk, snail. *See* Kite, Everglade.

Hawk, snake. *See* Kite, swallow-tailed.

Hawk, sparrow. Another name for the American kestrel in Falcon Family.

Hawk, squirrel. *See* Hawk, ferruginous.

Hawk, Swainson's, *Buteo swainsoni* (BEW-tee-oh SWAIN-son-eye); genus name: *see* Hawk, broad-winged; species name: given in 1838 by Charles Lucien Bonaparte for William Swainson, brilliant and versatile English ornithologist of early 19th century (Palmer, 1928). (Color ills., page 514.) Western half of N. America to Alaska; large buteo of western plains near size and shape of red-tailed hawk but wings narrower and slightly more pointed (Peterson, 1947); adults: in light phase, head and entire upperparts dark brown; eyes brown or hazel; *wide chestnut-brown band across chest* contrasts with white throat and pale belly; on underside of wings, white inner half contrasts with dark outer half (flight feathers); tail gray with many narrow bands but wide dark band near end; in dark phase, more or less sooty black all over but tail like that of light phase (similar melanistic redtailed hawk has red tail); in rufous phase, lighter brown below than dark phase, somewhat barred and blotched with rusty brown; there are intermediates between all plumage phases, and immatures similar to adults; migrations most spectacular of any N. American hawk because travels in large, often immense, flocks; route overland from N. America through Mexico and C. America to wintering home in S. America to Argentina; annual trip may be 11,000–17,000 mi. (Pough, 1951); migrates by soaring to tremendous heights on warm rising air, then long, descending glide ahead, then rising on another thermal and glide ahead (see details in Terres, 1968a); arrives U.S. and Canada, Mar.–Apr.; gentle, lives in harmony with other birds, perches on fence post, haycock, or on knoll on ground to watch for rodent prey; because very tame and frequents perches on posts, utility poles along highways to watch for live animals crossing road, or traffic-killed, is shot by those who have prejudice against hawks or shoot at any living target; showing a decrease in Utah, according to White (1969), since 1948 because of shooting by hunters; while perched or in flight, gives a shrill, somewhat plaintive whistle, *kr-e-e-e,* suggestive of cry of broad-winged hawk (Bent, 1937).

Feeding Habits: Flocks sometimes hunt crickets and grasshoppers on ground; groups said to wait at entrance of burrows of ground squirrels, then seize them in talons when they appear; sometimes flocks whirl about in air catching in talons such flying insects as Dobson's flies; are also attracted to swarms of bats; the small population of immature Swainson's hawks that winters in Fla. feeds almost exclusively around freshly plowed fields, where they catch mice and insects (Brown and Amadon, 1968); food is primarily crickets and grasshoppers when available, smaller amounts of mice, ground squirrels, rabbits, lizards, frogs, toads,

and rarely a young game bird; when soaring or in low flight over ground, often has wings slightly raised like marsh hawk or turkey vulture.

Nest: Conspicuous, 3–4 ft. across, often in lone tree on plains, or rather low in giant cactus, also nests in thin timber in big trees (for example, in Yellowstone National Park) up to 100 ft. above ground, occasionally on cutbanks, low cliffs, rocky pinnacles, or on ground, of twigs, weeds, grasses; same nest often repaired and used year after year.

Eggs: Mar.–July; 2–4, usually 2, white, obscurely marked with pale brown, some unmarked.

Incubation: By both sexes, 28 days; young leave nest about 30 days after hatching, said to chase crickets and grasshoppers on ground before learning to catch other prey.

Other Names: Black hawk; brown hawk; grasshopper hawk.

Accidents: Some losses of nest with eggs or young when blown from trees by severe spring or summer storms (Hunter and Harrell, 1967b).

Age: One, banded as fledgling in Tex., captured alive in Okla. when 6 years, 3 months, old; another, banded Laramie, Wyo., shot and killed, Buenos Aires, Argentina, when 9 years, 7 months, old (Kennard, 1975).

Flight Speed: Timed in Kans., 15 m.p.h. (Wood, 1923).

Weights: Females (7) averaged 2 lbs. 5 oz.; males (5), 2 lbs. (Brown and Amadon, 1968).

Range: Nests from c. Alaska, nw. Mack., Sask., Man., w. Minn., south to Baja Calif., n.-c. Mexico, and s.-c. Tex., rarely in Ill. and Mo.; winters in S. America to Argentina; some immatures winter in s. Fla. (Bull, 1964); some straggle in migration to parts of ne. N. America. Declining in numbers in West (see Blue List in Arbib, 1974).

Hawk, swallow-tailed. *See* Kite, swallow-tailed.

Hawk, wasp. *See* Kite, swallow-tailed.

Hawk, white. *See* Kite, white-tailed; also another name for the gyrfalcon in Falcon Family.

Hawk, white-rumped. *See* Hawk, marsh.

Hawk, white-tailed, *Buteo albicaudatus* (BEW-tee-oh al-bih-caud-AY-tus); genus name: *see* Hawk, broad-winged; species name: from Lat. *albus*, white, and *caudatus*, tailed (Coues, 1882). (Color ill., page 515.) Mexican, C. and S. American species that reaches U.S. in Tex., casually in Ariz.; 23–24 in. long; wingspread 48–54 in; adults: slate-gray upperparts including head, with *clear white underparts and a white rump and tail with conspicuous black band near tip;* shoulders *rusty-red;* rump white; wings are held in V when soaring (Robbins *et al.*, 1966); unusually long, narrow wings for a buteo and short tail are good identification characters; immatures: mainly deep sooty brown but, from below, middle underparts of body more or less white and bases of primaries in outer part of wing, and secondaries, are pale, not clear white; tail is pale, mottled with gray (Blake, E. R., 1953), in some, marked with many crossbars, or bands; resident in s. Tex., where lives in coastal prairies, locally from Rio Grande delta to upper coast (Peterson, 1963); in open country where only scattered bushes, yuccas, or large cactuses; perches on bushes, trees, utility wires, or on ground; when disturbed at nest, incubating bird usually leaves silently, then may soar high over intruder, watching; sometimes screams a high-pitched *ke-ke-ke-ke* or *cut-a, cut-a*.

Feeding Habits: Feeds much on abundant rabbits in s. Tex., also eats cotton rats, snakes, lizards, frogs, grasshoppers, cicadas, beetles, occasionally a quail or other bird, and carrion (Brown and Amadon, 1968); may be attracted from 10 mi. away to column of smoke signaling grass fire (Stevenson and Meitzen, 1946), where large numbers of these hawks may gather to prey on rats, rabbits, and other animals fleeing ahead of fire.

Nest: Builds large nest of broken twigs, lined with grasses, also sprays of mesquite; adds to year after year, may be 3 ft. across; on prairies of Tex. nests in sizable bushes, small trees, only 5–15 ft. above ground, like to nest on ridge with view all around.

Eggs: Tex., Mar.–May; 1–3, usually 2, some unmarked white, most spotted with browns, lavender.

Incubation: Period of and age when young leave nest unknown.

Other Names: Prairie hawk; Sennett's white-tailed hawk; white-tailed buzzard.

Range: Resident in s. Tex., casual in Ariz. where it nested in past (see Phillips *et al.*, 1964); south to s. S. America.

Hawk, zone-tailed, *Buteo albonotatus* (BEW-tee-oh albo-no-TAY-tus); genus name: *see* Hawk, broad-winged; species name: from Lat. *albus*, white, and *notatus*, marked with spots or lines. (Color ill., page 515.) Mexican, C. and S. American species that ranges north into sw. U.S.; 18½–21½ in. long; wingspread 47–53 in.; adults: mainly dull black with moderately long tail and somewhat more slender wings than other buteos (Peterson, 1961); two narrow white, or ashy, bands ("zones") in tail, third usually concealed; eyes dark brown; immatures: deep sooty brown, appear black at distance but underparts more or less white-spotted; tail bands narrower; in flight, with wings slightly uptilted in V, strikingly resembles turkey vulture but feathered hawk head, tail bands, and habit of screaming (turkey vultures do not scream) are distinguishing; a summer resident in wooded canyons and tree-lined rivers along middle slopes of desert mountains; rare in U.S. in winter; usually in Ariz. by Apr. (Phillips *et al.*, 1964), nests also in N.M., where rare but has survived especially in Silver City and Capitan Mtn. sections (Ligon, 1961); also in summer in s. Tex. (see Peterson, 1963); flight is lazy and sluggish, tilts body from side to side like vulture; screams at intruder near nest, a peevish whistle suggestive of red-tailed hawk's.

Feeding Habits: Said to be largely lizards, frogs, and small fishes; according to Brown and Amadon (1968), this needs confirmation, as black hawk with these habits has been con-

fused with zone-tailed; known to eat chipmunks, quail, and small birds and to snatch nesting birds in talons while in full flight; glides slowly along while hunting but capable of lightninglike plunges; its mimicry (flight and appearance) of turkey vulture, in which it may not arouse fear in animals as it hunts (Willis, 1963), may be of advantage to zone-tail in its food-getting. *See* Behaviorial Mimicry under Behavior.

Nest: Usually built in large tree in U.S., often in cottonwood along canyon stream, 25–100 ft. above ground in leafy top, rarely in mesquite; coarsely built, bulky, of large sticks, inside decorated with leafy branches.

Eggs: Usually latter half of Apr. in U.S.; 1–3, usually 2, white or blue-white, usually unmarked.

Incubation: Period of and age when young leave nest unreported.

Other Names: Bandtail; band-tailed hawk; zone-tailed buzzard.

Range: Nests from n. Baja Calif., c. Ariz., sw. N.M., and w. Tex., south to northern S. America; winters in most of breeding range but rare in winter in most of Ariz., N.M., and Tex., rarely in s. Calif.

Kite, black-shouldered. *See* Kite, white-tailed.

Kite, blue. *See* Kite, Mississippi.

Kite, Everglade, *Rostrhamus sociabilis* (rostr-HAME-us so-sih-AY-bil-us); genus name from Lat. *rostrum*, beak, and *hamus*, hook; species name: Lat., sociable, gregarious (Coues, 1882). (Color ill., page 516.) Mexican, C. and S. American species that reaches northern edge of range in Fla.; once common all through the Everglades (Bent, 1937), now rare and threatened; 16–18 in. long; wingspread about 45 in.; adult male: *overall dark blue-black* except white patch at base of square tail (Peterson, 1947); eyes red; red at base of extremely hooked, black bill; legs long, bright orange or red; larger female and the immatures: rusty black above; underparts heavily streaked with dark lines on buffy body; dark tail; white line over each eye; kite distinguished from similar marsh hawk in flight by its broad wings and white on tail and at tip, not on rump; rare resident in s. Fla. of freshwater marshes with broad expanses of tall grasses dotted with clumps of small trees and bushes or occasional island of larger trees; some of these kites very tame, often perch in dead tree in or around marsh, sometimes soar to great heights; when hunting, flap slowly with occasional glide, 5–30 ft. above water and marsh grasses, bill pointed downward, watching for freshwater snails; groups of these kites often roost together in leafless, drowned bushes; when courting fly high and repeatedly dive in sudden short dips with wings folded (Bent, 1937); greet each other with harsh call, *kor-ee-ee-a, koree-a* (Lang, 1924); when disturbed by human intruder near nest, utter cackling notes similar to those of osprey, solicitous of nest but not bold enough to attack (Bent, 1937).

Feeding Habits: One of most specialized feeders of all birds; as far as known, eats only snails of genus *Pomacea* (see, however, Sykes and Kale, 1974); this exclusive diet limits Everglade kite to watery marshes where these snails are abundant; in s. Fla., Everglade kite eats *Pomacea paludosa*, the green, or apple, snail, which lays its small white eggs on plant stems a few inches above water; kites said to hunt them most in cool of early morning or late afternoon when snails near surface of water, but Snyder and Snyder (1969) found kites hunting more or less continuously during the day, usually flying with the wind or across it, or watching water from snag perch; on sighting snail, flies to water, in flight grabs snail in either foot and often transfers snail from foot to bill while flying to regular feeding perch; there holds snail in foot against perch, and by method in past much debated by ornithologists, extracts snail's soft body by reaching down and inserting hooked bill between snail's operculum and columella, then frees snail entire from shell by cutting the columellar muscle, after which drops shell and swallows snail whole, or pulls off pieces with bill while holding snail in foot (see Snyder and Snyder, 1969, for this and other interesting details); in s. Fla., Everglade kite now rare but once common early in this century; severely reduced to no more than 20 birds by 1964 (10 counted, 1965) through droughts and man-made canals that drained marshes, thus destroying habitat for snails, the kites' only food, and from shooting of kites by duck hunters from blinds, especially around Lake Okeechobee; in 1966, Everglade kite on list of rare and endangered species of U.S. Fish and Wildlife Service, at which time last of kites principally on Lake Okeechobee and on Loxahatchee National Wildlife Refuge, southwest of Palm Beach (Committee on Rare and Endangered Wildlife Species, 1966); in 1970, entire population in s. Fla. estimated at about 120 (Harris, V. T., 1972), of which 31 seen in summer 1971 at Lake Okeechobee but no nesting because of drought (Kale, 1971); on May 2, 1972, nest with three young discovered in marshes of headwaters of St. Johns R. for first reported nesting there since 1930s (Kale, 1972). See also report of Stieglitz and Thompson (1967). In 1973, 28 nests observed in Fla. and 22 young fledged (Chandler and Anderson, 1974).

Nest: Carelessly built flat structure of sticks, about 1 ft. across, 3–15 ft. above water, either on dense marsh grass or in bushes growing in water, often in colonies of half a dozen pairs or more.

Eggs: Fla., usually Feb.–July; 3–4, occasionally 2, dull white or cream white, boldly and profusely blotched with browns.

Incubation: By both sexes (Haverschmidt, 1970a), about 30 days (Nice, 1954), 26–28 days; young leave nest about 23–28 days after hatching (Chandler and Anderson, 1974).

Other Names: Black hawk; black kite; hookbill hawk; snail hawk; snail kite; sociable marsh hawk.

Weights: For the smaller subspecies *R. sociabilis sociabilis* of Surinam, males (4) weighed 10¾ to 13½ oz.; females (2), 13½ to 14½ oz. (Brown and Amadon, 1968).

Range: S. Fla. and from e. Mexico south throughout C. and S. America to pampas of Uruguay and Argentina; also Cuba, and Isle of Pines.

Kite, fork-tailed. See Kite, swallow-tailed.

Kite, hook-billed, *Chondrohierax uncinatus* (kon-droh-HIGH-er-ax un-sin-AY-tus) genus name: from Gr. *chondros*, composed of cartilage and Gr. *hierakos*, a falcon, or hawk; species name: Lat., hooked, barbed, in reference to the bill. Mexican, C., and S. American and West Indian species that has reached s. Tex; 15–17 in. long; according to Brown and Amadon (1968), a small kite, with large to *very large* sharply and deeply hooked bill, adapted to eating large snails; only one species, has two color forms: a *normal phase*, in which adult male is slate gray all over, darker above, with underparts usually barred with white, and adult female is dark brown above with rufous underparts barred with white; *black phase*, in which sexes alike, entire plumage black, and tail has one broad white bar; mostly a forest bird, usually in dense undergrowth, sometimes in swamps, also in dry tropical upland forest; seen singly or in twos or threes; utters musical oriolelike whistle, also screams and chatters harshly when disturbed (Brown and Amadon, 1968).

Feeding Habits: Eats mostly tree snails and land snails, also some frogs, salamanders, and insects.

Nest: In tropics, in trees of coffee plantations, built of twigs.

Eggs: Brown and Amadon (1968) cite two nesting records of 2 eggs in each nest; round, white, blotched with brown; two downy young in another. On May 1, 1964, R. J. Fleetwood saw a normal phase male and female about 65 miles upstream from the mouth of the Rio Grande where the river forms the southern boundary of the Santa Ana National Wildlife Refuge in s. Tex.; it was first record for this species in the U.S.; both kites were perched in trees, the female with a common land snail, *Bulimulus alternatus*, in her bill; on May 3, Fleetwood returned to the area and found a nest in a black willow tree with three downy young; the nest was on a horizontal limb about 10 feet from the main trunk and 22 feet above the ground, was frail, made entirely of dead twigs and branches of hackberry trees and huisache; about 15 in. across, with saucer-shaped depression about 1½ in. deep. These birds were apparently of the northern subspecies of Mexico, *C. u. aquilonis*, of which the type specimen (*see* Type Specimen) had been collected in Tamaulipas. In the spring of 1978, the hook-billed kite nested again in Santa Ana National Wildlife Refuge—2 downy young reported in the nest (Webster, 1978). See other records in Webster (1979).

Weights: male (6) 247–174 gr.; female (6) 235-300 gr. (Brown and Amadon, 1968).

Range: Through tropical Mexico and C. and S. America to w. Argentina, Paraguay, and se. Brazil.

Kite, Mississippi, *Ictinia mississippiensis* (ick-TIN-ih-ah mis-ih-sip-ih-EN-sis); genus name: Lat., from Gr. *iktinos*, kite; species name: Lat., of Mississippi. (Color ill., page 517.) Uncommon to rare; in summer, from Kans. to S.C., south to Gulf states; 13–17 in. long; wingspread 34–37 in.; adults: slender, falconlike, overall gray except head, which is pale, ashy gray; tail black, without bars; eyes deep red; legs yellow to red; immature: similar to adults but underparts heavily streaked with brown; distinctive black tail of immature has three gray bars; from winter range in Paraguay and Argentina (Brown and Amadon, 1968) migrates in flocks north in spring; pairs appear to be mated on arrival in U.S., Mar.–May; most often seen in flight, smooth, graceful, buoyant, rarely circles in soaring flight; veers deliberately about, coursing slowly over either open prairie or forest hunting for flying insects; gregarious, several sometimes perch in same tree, even when nesting; is social in all activities; does not maintain territories (Fitch, 1963); congregates at roosts in late summer; usually silent, but utters whistled alarm call when intruder near its nest, *kee-e-e*, repeated, also an ospreylike double whistle, *phee-phew*.

Feeding Habits: Mostly insects, and at times entirely eats large insects caught in flight: cicadas, grasshoppers, crickets, dragonflies, beetles; also sometimes small snakes, lizards, frogs; has also been seen chasing bats entering cave in Okla.; sometimes takes insect prey to a perch to eat, but often after catching insects in air with feet, reaches down to pick pieces with bill and eats while in flight; in low flight, flies about cattle, horsemen, to catch insects stirred up from grass.

Nest: In western part of range, builds flat flimsy nest of sticks, lined with fresh green leaves, in fork or on limbs of scattered trees of grasslands or in cottonwoods along creeks; in Southeast, in large pines, oaks, sweet gums of large woods; 12–80 ft. up; in parts of Tex., in mesquite, 4–6 ft. up.

Eggs: Mar.–June; 1–3, usually 2, bluish white.

Incubation: By both sexes, 31–32 days; young leave nest about 34 days after hatching (Brown and Amadon, 1968); one pair in Kans. seen to bring cicadas and plucked chimney swifts to young.

Other Names: Blue kite; Louisiana kite; mosquito hawk.

Weights: Males (11) about 7½–9½ oz.; females (5) about 9¾–12 oz. (Brown and Amadon, 1968).

Range: Nests locally from ne. Kans., Iowa, Tenn., and S.C. south to nw. Fla. and Gulf coast of e. Tex; formerly north to s. Ill. and Ind.; has straggled farther west and north in U.S.; winters from Fla. and s. Tex., south, Mexico and C. America to Argentina; casual or accidental in Colo., Neb., Wisc., Ky., N.J., Pa., N.C.

Kite, snail. See Kite, Everglade.

Kite, swallow-tailed, *Elanoides forficatus* (el-ah-no-EYE-deez or el-ah-NOY-deez for-fick-AY-tus); genus name: Lat., from Gr. *elanos*, kite, and *eidos*, resemblance (to), "kitelike"; species name: New Lat., forked, in reference to tail. (Color ill., page 517.) Largest N. American kite; se. U.S., formerly nested north, from Tex. to Minn. and along coast from Fla. to N.C., now common only in s. Fla. (Brown and Amadon, 1968); 19–25½ in. long; wingspread 45–50 in.; *deeply forked black tail* is 12–15 in. long; forked for more than half its length; adults: strikingly marked with snow-white head, hind neck, and underparts; black above; eyes dark brown to red; bill black; legs blue to blue-gray; immatures: similar to adults but with white tips to many black feathers and narrow black quill streaks on many of the white body feathers; lives in swamps, marshes, along rivers, ponds, lakes, and in open forests; exquisite in perfection and grace of flight as it flies rapidly like giant swallow low over Fla. prairies, its long thin wings cleaving the air like knife blades and forked tail opening and shutting like pair of scissors as it tilts from side to side to change its swift course, then suddenly swoops upward out of prairie or swamp glade and over treetops and is gone; eats on wing, drinks and bathes while skimming surface of lake or pond; is gregarious, when several flying together utter sweet shrill cries, *peat, peat, peat; klee, klee, klee;* or soft whistles (Bent, 1937); a few occasionally winter in Fla., but most of those summering north of Panama apparently winter in S. America (Brown and Amadon, 1968); has disappeared from its former range probably from drainage of marshes, cutting off of swamp forests, and especially from wanton shooting (Pough, 1951); appears in s. Fla. in late Feb. and early Mar. (Sprunt, 1954a).

Feeding Habits: Catches and eats food while in flight; sometimes soars to great heights to catch insects; also sweeps low over fields, prairies to snatch up grasshoppers, crickets, cicadas, small snakes, lizards, frogs; picks dragonflies out of air in talons, also bees, beetles, grasshoppers, and other insects, small birds in nest, and lizards from branches of trees and while in flight, bends head and neck under body to eat prey held in foot.

Nest: Built by both sexes in tops of tall slender trees, 60–100 ft. up, usually in pines or in black mangrove trees in Fla., at edges of woods trails or openings; of dead twigs snapped off trees with feet by pair in flight; nest lined with Spanish moss or beard lichens, which pair may carry long distances; nest 15–20 in. across, pair tolerates other kites near nest but not other hawks, eagles, etc. (Brown and Amadon, 1968). See especially interesting account by Snyder (1974).

Eggs: Fla., mid-Mar. to mid-Apr.; 2–4, most often 2, white or cream-white, boldly and irregularly blotched with browns.

Incubation: Mostly by female; about 28 days; young leave nest 36–42 days after hatching (Snyder, 1974).

Flight Speed: About 40 km. per hour, or about 25 m.p.h., when chasing (or foraging for) aerial prey.

Other Names: Fork-tailed kite; snake hawk; swallow-tail; swallow-tailed hawk; wasp hawk.

Weights: 13¾–14¾ oz.; up to 17½ oz. in a female about to lay eggs (Brown and Amadon, 1968).

Range: Now nests locally from Gulf coast, S.C., Ga., and Fla. south through e. Mexico and C. and S. America; may still stray north in Mississippi and Ohio valleys; has strayed to N. M., Colo., s-c. Canada, New England, Pa., N.Y.,

N.J. (see Bull, 1964; see also Rapp, 1944, for 33 records in ne. U.S.; for two relatively recent records in N.J. and Md., see Scott and Cutler, 1971). For later records see issues of *American Birds.*

Kite, white-tailed, *Elanus leucurus* (EL-an-us lew-CUE-rus); genus name: Lat., from Gr. *elanos,* kite, and *elauno,* to drive (Jaeger, 1955); species name: Lat., from Gr. *leukos,* white, and *oura,* tail. (Color ill., page 517.) Now fairly common (for raptor) resident of Calif.; almost extirpated from U.S. first quarter of present century through persecution (shooting) by man (Eisenmann, 1971); 15–17 in. long; wingspread about 40 in.; most striking feature is its *whiteness;* seen at distance appears wholly white; *falcon shape with long, pointed wings, long tail;* adults: pale gray above, with white head and white tail; black patch on shoulders and in flight also shows black patch on *undersurface* near bend of wings (Peterson, 1947); bill black; eyes orange-rufous; legs buffy yellow; immatures: similar to adults but breast feathers streaked and washed with cinnamon brown; tail pearl gray; when soaring and gliding resembles a gull; often hovers with legs dangling (Bent, 1937); lives in open country about freshwater marshes, moist meadows, alfalfa fields, with scattered clumps of trees used for roosting, nesting; often alone or in pairs, also gregarious with as many as 45 reported roosting in one dead eucalyptus in a marsh; movements and nesting governed by concentrations of field mice (Brown and Amadon, 1968); in U.S., nesting usually Feb.–June; most frequently uttered note as the kites beat slowly about with legs dangling is short, spasmodic whistle, *keep, keep, keep* (Bent, 1937).

Feeding Habits: Male does all of hunting during nesting; surrenders food (mouse, for example) to female perched in tree or she takes from male while he is in slow flight, holding mouse in feet extended below; eat mainly field mice, also wood rats, pocket gophers, ground squirrels, shrews, small birds, small snakes, lizards, frogs, grasshoppers, crickets, beetles, etc.; rather tame and unsuspicious in nesting season, tolerates others of its kind nesting nearby but drives away crows and other hawks.

Nest: Often in oaks and other trees of rolling hills near marsh or in cottonwood or eucalyptus on bank of stream or canal, about 15–60 ft. up, usually in branches near top of tree, of sticks and twigs, lined with grasses, dry stubble, weed stems, rootlets.

Eggs: Feb.–June; 3–6, usually 4–5, white, heavily blotched with rich browns; considered handsomest of all N. American hawks' eggs (Bent, 1937).

Incubation: By female (male roosts at night on perch close by), about 30 days; young leave nest 35–40 days after hatching; pairs sometimes raise second brood (Brown and Amadon, 1968).

Other Names: Black-shouldered kite; white hawk.

Weights: Of a slightly smaller S. American subspecies, males (2), 9 and 10½ oz.; female (1), 10¾ oz. (Brown and Amadon, 1968).

Range: Resident in most Calif. counties except in unsuitable habitat of mountain forest or desert; in 1966, reported as extirpated by hunters as a nesting species in Tex., but recently some increase in s. Tex., and even farther north; farther east, relatively recent sightings reported in 1967 in Fla. and sight records for Ga. and Ala.; in Mexico, now commonly seen along Gulf coast where it has nested in past, and has been seen again in Baja Calif.; increasing in C. America (see detailed report of history and status in Eisenmann, 1971), locally south to Chile and c. Argentina. See recent issues of *American Birds.*

HAWKING
Practice of flying trained falcons and other predatory birds at living prey. *See* Falconry. It is also a term of ornithologists for the action of a bird, such as a swallow or nighthawk, in catching insects out of the air by flying about with the mouth open. *See* Nightjar Family; Swallow Family; Food and Feeding Habits.

HAWK MOUNTAIN SANCTUARY
A 2,000-acre private preserve between Harrisburg and Allentown, Pa., owned and sponsored by the Hawk Mountain Sanctuary Association, Kempton, Pa., founded in 1934 by Rosalie Edge of the Emergency Conservation Committee, New York City. The association is a nonprofit organization devoted to conserving and protecting wildlife within the preserve and especially the predatory birds that have used the migration route over Hawk Mtn. of the Kittatinny Ridge for thousands of years. Its 5,800 members (1976) provide funds through memberships, endowments, contributions, etc., to maintain the wooded sanctuary with its buildings and staff of naturalists who live and work in the sanctuary. During the fall, especially on windy days, following a cold-weather front, impressive numbers of hawks and some eagles migrate past the rocky lookouts on the sanctuary. From 1934 to 1966, observers counted an average of 15,000 hawks each year that passed by the lookouts; from 1967, after a second counting station (lookout) was established, the yearly average rose to a count of 25,000 hawks (Brett, 1976). Previous to 1934 and establishment of the sanctuary, thousands of hawks, many eagles, and other predatory birds of passage along the mountain route had been slaughtered by hunters lying in ambush for the birds along the ridge. See Broun (1949; 1963); Terres (1968a; 1975); Harwood (1973); *see also* introduction to Hawk Family. See annual reports of the Hawk Mountain Sanctuary Association, Kempton, Pa., for yearly counts.

HAWK OWL
See in Owl—Typical Owl Family.

HAY-BIRD
See Sandpiper, pectoral, in Sandpiper Family.

HEAD-SCRATCHING
All birds use a foot to scratch their heads in response to irritations about the face or other parts of the head that they cannot reach with the bill. *See* Preening. They use two methods of head-scratching while standing on one foot and

direct (ovenbird)

indirect (robin)

HEAD-SCRATCHING
A bird scratches its head with one foot while standing on the other foot, and every species characteristically uses one of two approaches to this form of preening: the ovenbird scratches directly, passing its foot below its wing; the robin scratches indirectly, reaching over its drooped wing to its head.

Heart Beat Rate of Various Adult Birds While at Rest

Species	Body Weight (grams)	Heart Rate in (Beats per min.)	Authority
Turkey	8,750	93	Simons (1960)
Brown Pelican	7,500	150	Calder (1968)
Anser sp. (geese)	3,420	113	Calder (1968)
Mallard (duck)	2,670	118	Calder (1968)
Turkey vulture	2,000	132	Calder (1968)
Herring gull	930	218	Calder (1968)
Domestic pigeon	382	166	Calder (1968)
Crow	337	342	Simons (1960)
California quail	138	250	Calder (1968)
Mourning dove	130	135	Calder (1968)
Blue jay	77.1	307	Calder (1968)
Robin	69.5	328	Calder (1968)
Brown thrasher	59.2	303	Calder (1968)
Cardinal	40.0	375	Calder (1968)
Catbird	28.9	427	Calder (1968)
House sparrow	28.0	350	Calder (1968)
Song sparrow	20.0	450	Calder (1968)
Black-capped chickadee	12.0	480	Calder (1968)
House wren	11.0	450	Calder (1968)
Ruby-throated hummingbird	4.0	615	Calder (1968)

Note: Compare these heart beat rates with Breathing Rates and Control of Breathing under Respiratory System.

scratching with the other: (1) the *indirect* method with the foot passed *over* a wing while scratching, and (2) the *direct* method with the foot passed *under* the wing to head-scratch. Some students of bird behavior have used these methods as criteria for establishing relationships between certain groups of birds. For example, as cited by Wallace (1963), an ornithologist pointed out that wrentits in California (family Chamaeidae)—songbirds—used the direct method to head-scratch, which supports their postulated relationship to Old World babblers (family Timaliidae) that also use the direct method.

Usually only one method of head-scratching is characteristic of a species of bird and its family (Simmons, 1964a). As far as it is known, most bird groups scratch directly (under the wing), including the more primitive birds (examples are loons and grebes), whereas the more advanced birds in the evolutionary scale —among N. American birds, for examples, the songbirds, swifts, hummingbirds, nighthawks, and kingfishers—use the indirect method (Simmons, 1964a); an exception is the wrentit pointed out. However, as noted by some other ornithologists, one family of N. American songbirds—the wood warblers—use both methods, and Pettingill (1972) reported that the American robin (a songbird) uses the indirect method of passing the foot over a drooped wing to head-scratch, but the ovenbird (also a songbird) always scratches the head by passing the foot *under* the wing—the direct method.

Usually different groups of birds use one method or the other in head-scratching, but one cannot always depend that all members of a bird family, or even all members of the same species, use the same method (Pettingill, 1972).

HEARING
See Ears and Hearing.

HEART
In birds, just as in man, the heart is four-chambered, but with the right aortic arch (the artery from the heart) still present rather than the left as in mammals (Tordoff, 1961). The four chambers are two atria and two ventricles, and the heart is located within the thoracic cavity, slightly to the left of the middle, and ventral to (below) the lungs (Sturkie, 1954; 1965). The heart is a muscular pump that provides the propelling force for the blood in which the oxygenated blood from the lungs and the blood from other parts of the body containing higher concentrations of carbon dioxide are kept separate. It is divided completely into separate right and left halves, and arteries carry blood away from the heart; veins return blood to it from all parts of the body (Berger, 1961). *See* blood under Circulatory System.

For birds and mammals of comparable body size, the avian heart (1) is about 40% larger, (2) beats at a rate about 35 times less rapid, (3) pumps about the same volume of blood per unit of time (Lasiewski and Calder, 1971). "The relatively high efficiency of a bird's heart apparently is associated with the high respiratory and energy requirements of its flight" (Simons, 1960). *See* Metabolism; Respiratory System.

Odum (1945) demonstrated that heart rate,

or heartbeat, is much higher, or faster, in small birds—from 135 beats per minute in the mourning dove to 615 in the ruby-throated hummingbird; he found that the basal (resting) heart rates of passerine birds (songbirds) varied from 350 to 480 beats per minute, with maximum rates varying from 800 to more than 1,000 beats per minute. Tordoff (1961) reported up to 700 per minute in the house wren compared with 220 per minute for the rock dove, or domestic pigeon. In canaries, the heart beats 1,000 times per minute; in man, 72 beats per minute with two ounces of blood squeezed out at each beat (Walter and Sayles, 1949).

As in mammals, stimulation of the sympathetic nerves in birds accelerates the heartbeat, whereas stimulation of the parasympathetic nerves inhibits or slows the heartbeat (Simons, 1960). Among birds, the relative size of the heart as well as its rate of beating varies inversely with the size of the bird. The smaller birds with higher metabolic rates (*see* Metabolism) usually have the relatively largest and fastest hearts, though larger hearts in some birds may be associated with their permanent residence at high altitudes of mountainous country (Hartman, 1955) or in polar regions. Generally "the best fliers, the fastest runners, the loudest singers have the largest relative heart weights" (Simons, 1960). Hartman (1954), from his studies of the heart and other muscles of hummingbirds, concluded that they have, relatively, the largest hearts of all birds.

HEARTBEAT
See Heart.

HEAT AND BIRDS
In warm weather, a bird gets rid of excess body heat through its respiratory (breathing) system, which collects warm, moist air from its internal overheated tissues and expels it through its lungs. A bird has no sweat glands, and fresh air coursing through its respiratory system reduces its body heat by internal radiation (picking up heat radiated from body cells and the heated blood) and vaporization. According to some investigators, this cooling process at times may be more important to a bird than the taking in of oxygen. A passerine in flight produces about 9 times more heat than when it is resting; a non-passerine about 15 times more heat (Berger and Hart, 1974). *See* the respiratory system of birds described, the breathing rates of birds under different conditions, and breathing control under Respiratory System.

It is fundamental to a bird's existence that it control its body temperature, which during extreme heat or cold may reach lethal limits and result in its death (*see* Temperature; *also* Cold and Birds). In stepping up its breathing rate from ordinary breathing to *panting*, a bird increases the flow of air over the moist surfaces of its mouth, pharynx, bronchi, and possibly its air sacs (King and Farner, 1961). A bird usually begins to pant when the environmental temperature surrounding it reaches 105–107° F. (Miller, 1963). An American robin, for example, running over a lawn under the intense heat rays of the summer sun, while panting with its bill open, is using its cooling (respiratory) system to reduce its body heat. In so doing, it loses

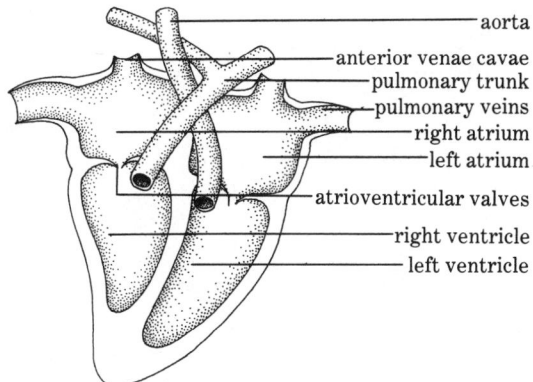

aorta
anterior venae cavae
pulmonary trunk
pulmonary veins
right atrium
left atrium
atrioventricular valves
right ventricle
left ventricle

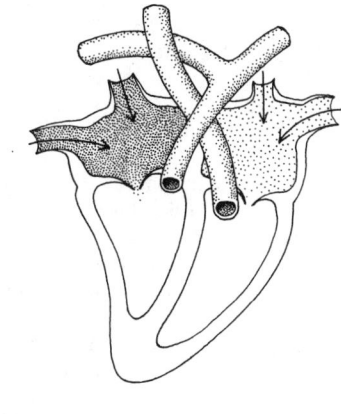

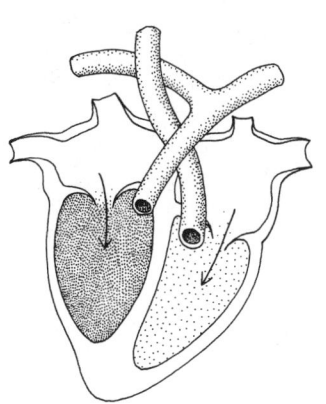

HEART
Oxygen-rich blood from the lungs flows into the left atrium, via the pulmonary veins, to the left ventricle and out through the aorta to the arteries. Venous blood from all other parts of the body comes into the right atrium, via the anterior and posterior venae cavae, to the right ventricle, from which it is pumped through the pulmonary trunk to the lungs to pick up oxygen. The atrioventricular valves on both sides prevent the blood from flowing back into the atria from the ventricles.

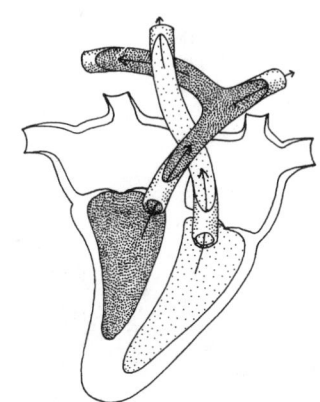

American robin

Turkey vulture

HEAT AND BIRDS

On a hot day, a robin can dissipate about half its metabolic heat production by panting, which releases warm, moist air through its mouth and introduces fresh air into its respiratory system at an accelerated rate.

Some birds, such as vultures, dissipate their body heat by spreading their wings and thus increasing their body surface area.

Mountain accentor

HEDGE SPARROW FAMILY

moisture by evaporation from inside its body, along with some moisture from the skin under its feathers, which it must replace by drinking water. Small birds lose more water from their respiratory tracts, in proportion to their body weights, than do large birds, and available drinking water is important in helping them resist the effects of heat exposure (Bartholomew and Dawson, 1953). In hot, dry climates, survival of many birds depends on available water or, alternatively, succulent plants and insects (Bartholomew and Cade, 1956; see also Moldenhauer and Wiens, 1970). *See* especially the moisture needs of birds under Water Requirements.

In many birds, while at rest, not more than half of their heat production can be dissipated by panting; however, the poor-will is an exception in that it can dissipate 160% of its metabolic heat production (the heat produced when at rest) by panting (Sturkie, 1965). To supplement panting, and to hasten evaporative cooling of the body, some birds—such as owls, great blue herons, cattle egrets, bobwhites, California quail, Gambel's quail, cormorants, anhingas, frigatebirds, nighthawks, poor-wills, roadrunners, pigeons, and doves—flutter, or pulse in and out, the throat skin (gular fluttering), and tropic-birds, boobies, and pelicans flutter the gular pouch under the bill (see Howell and Bartholomew, 1962; Lasiewski, 1972; and Bartholomew *et al.*, 1968, for details).

When all means of evaporative cooling are insufficient to lower body temperatures during the hottest part of the day, birds of hot climates, especially small birds, when temperatures of the environment reach 95–113° F., become less active and find shaded places, where they pant and rest (Salt and Zeuthen, 1960). Most desert birds, unlike mammals, do not retreat into cool underground burrows to escape midday summer heat; however, two observers on the Santa Rita Experimental Range, Pima, Ariz., saw brown towhees and black-throated sparrows use burrows of badgers in which to escape summer heat and thus reduce their water requirements. Bathing, by getting the feet and legs in water, also helps to cool birds (see Bartholomew *et al.*, 1953; Dawson, 1954; Hutchinson, 1954).

Hatch, D.E. (1970), in subjecting five captive turkey vultures to rapidly rising temperatures, discovered that, even before they began panting to lower their internal body heat, they deliberately defecated on their legs. The wet excreta on their bare legs caused their deep body temperatures to drop, or to cool, by 1° C., which they could not accomplish simply by panting. Previously Kahl (1963) had discovered that N. American wood storks and black vultures wet their legs with their combined urine and feces when their environmental temperatures rose, and suggested that the phenomenon be called *urohidrosis*, because of its functional similarity to true perspiring, or sweating. *See* Urohidrosis.

Cormorants have the habit of spreading their wings, usually to dry them after emerging from water, but Curry-Lindahl (1970), a Swedish ornithologist, from his observations of long-tailed cormorants in the African Congo, and Heath (1962), from his experiments with N.

American turkey vultures, suggested that these birds may perch with spread wings for lowering their body temperatures (thermoregulation). The habit has also been seen in the African wood ibis, *Ibis ibis*, and the marabou stork, which, when far from water, assumed spread-wing postures independent of any wetting of the plumage (Clark, 1969).

According to Salt and Zeuthen (1960), in the French Sudan, during the hottest hours in June, July, and Aug., large birds such as the hooded vulture, *Necrosyrtes monachus*, the black, or pariah, kite, *Milvus migrans*, a stork, *Abdimia abdimii*, and a raven, *Corvus scapulatus*, escape the heat during the hottest hours of the day by letting themselves be lifted on rising warm columns of air (*see* Soaring Flight under Flight) to 2,000 or 3,000 ft. above the ground, where they soar about in air 50–60° F. cooler.

HEATH HEN
See in Grouse Family; *also* Extinct Birds of North America.

HEAT REGULATION
See Heat and Birds; Cold and Birds; Temperature.

HECTARE
(HECK-tar). In the metric system, one hectare equals 2.471 acres. Hectares are now used as a unit of measure, instead of acres, in the annual nesting bird censuses conducted by the National Audubon Society and the U.S. Fish and Wildlife Service. See Van Velzen (1971a); *see also* Census.

HEDGE SPARROW FAMILY
Prunellidae (proo-NEL-ih-dee); from Lat. *prunella*, from Fr. *prunelle*, sloe, derived from Lat. *prunum*, plum, in reference to brownish color of birds in this family. Includes about 12 species (Van Tyne and Berger, 1976) of songbirds; only 1, the familiar hedge sparrow, or dunnock, *Prunella modularis*, of the hedges of Britain and Europe, retains the traditional name by which the family is still known.

Most birds of the family live in northern parts of the world, in alpine meadows, brushlands, barrens, forest edges, are 5–7 in. long, have rufous or gray-brown upperparts and streaked or striped underparts; sexes outwardly alike or nearly so; are called accentors (Lat., one who sings with another); only 1, the mountain accentor, *Prunella montanella*, has strayed to N. America.

Most accentors are gregarious, usually ground dwellers, but some perch in trees to sing; on ground, walk or hop; characteristically flick wings and jerk the tail; in size and appearance, resemble sparrows, but their bills are more slender and are pointed; they have the sparrow or fringillid (finchlike) character of having a true crop and a muscular gizzard adapted to a seasonal diet of seeds, but are believed to have affinities with the Thrush Family (Thomson, 1964a).

Accentors sing short, simple songs, highpitched and jingling (Peterson *et al.*, 1954); in summer, eat mostly insects; in winter, seeds and berries; the ovenbird (a N. American wood warbler) has been called the golden-crowned accentor but is not closely related to the accentors; however, both are songbirds, or perching birds, in the order Passeriformes.

Mountain accentor, *Prunella montanella* (proo-NEL-ah mont-ah-NEL-ah); genus name: *see* family introduction; species name: Lat., of the little mountain, the bird's habitat. Asiatic songbird, visitor to Alaska; small; about 6 in. long; somewhat warblerlike, conspicuous black crown and black on sides of face, streak of buff-yellow over eyes; brown above, streaked with black; pale yellow below with irregular black band on breast; quiet, inclined to skulk through low cover, but in nesting season will perch in bush or tree to sing; utters shrill, three-noted call, *til-il-il;* flies short distances in jerky, pipit-like flight (Tucker, 1950b).

Feeding Habits: Insects in summer, with small seeds; almost exclusively seeds in winter.
Nest: Built usually in forks of willow thickets along streams in tundra (Austin, 1961), 1–8 ft. above ground; of twigs and dried grasses, cup lined with mosses, hairs (Tucker, 1950b).
Eggs: June (Dement'ev *et al.,* 1968); 4–6, deep blue.
Incubation: Probably about 12 days.
Other Name: Siberian accentor.
Range: Nests in Siberia in the upper edge of forest zone, from Ural Mtns. to lower Anadyr; winters to n. China, Korea; three stragglers collected in Alaska, one on Nunivak Is., Oct. 3, 1927; another on St. Lawrence Is., Oct. 13, 1936 (Tucker, 1950b); a third on Point Barrow, fall of 1951 (Kessel and Gibson, 1978).

Siberian accentor. *See* Mountain accentor.

HEERMANN
ADOLPHUS LEWIS, M.D. (1827?–65). Born in S.C., for whom John Cassin named the Heermann's gull; was one of the famous medical men attached to the Pacific Railroad Surveys in middle of 19th century; a field collector of birds and their eggs for Spencer F. Baird; was killed near San Antonio, Tex., at age 38 by his own gun when he stumbled and fell while collecting birds. See details in Hume (1942); Stone (1907); Gruson (1972).

HEIGHT OF BIRD FLIGHT
See Altitude of Bird Flight; Flight; Migration.

HELL-DIVER
Local and general name for the common loon, horned grebe, pied-billed grebe, and bufflehead (duck) because when shot at they dive so quickly and often remain underwater so long that early-day hunters drew humorous conclusion that they had dived to hell, or had gone to hell.

HELMET
See Casque.

HELPERS AMONG BIRDS
Birds often assist one another in different ways. Skutch (1961) has listed 130 species, worldwide, that have been seen helping others, and many more have been seen in the role of helper since. He has defined a "helper" as a bird that aids another, other than its mate, in the nesting of an individual, or feeds or otherwise attends a bird of whatever age which is neither its mate nor its dependent offspring. "Helpers may be of almost any age; they may aid other birds . . . including those of distinct [different] species and they assist [them] in various ways."

The most common kind of cooperation is through the alarm cry (*see* Language), which alerts a bird's own species and other birds as well; for example, at the sight of a hawk, cat, or other predator. Sometimes birds of the same or of different species unite to attack a common enemy whether at nests or elsewhere (*see* mobbing in Self-Protective Behavior under Behavior, and Protection of Nests under Nests and Nesting). This is an unintentional kind of help, with each bird defending its own nest and young but thereby helping others nesting nearby (Skutch, 1961).

The next and most commonly noted kind of helpfulness among birds is in feeding others. Survival of the young of most species depends on parental feeding and the urge to feed others is especially strong in birds when they have young in the nest. The feeding "drive" may be prolonged in parent birds for hours or even for days after rearing their own young to independence.

For example, an eastern phoebe whose first brood had become independent began to feed young tree swallows in a nest nearby and continued to feed them for about a week, even though the parent swallows tried to drive her away (Deck, 1945). In England, a European blackbird, a species related to the American robin, after raising her young for three weeks, offered food to any bird that came near her (Lack, 1953). A male cardinal whose nest had been destroyed fed four fledgling American robins for a week and was almost as active in bringing food to the young robins as were the parents. All three adults, the cardinal and the pair of robins, fed the young in harmony (Logan, 1951). *See* Foster Parents.

Often the helper at the nest may be a male whose mate is incubating her eggs. A male eastern bluebird reported by Forbush fed nestling house wrens, which upset the parent wrens, but when the bluebird's mate hatched her eggs, he turned to feeding his own offspring. A male scarlet tanager fed young chipping sparrows until his own nestlings hatched, and a male Oregon (dark-eyed) junco not only fed young Bewick's wrens in a nest nearby but periodically cleaned the nest of the young bird's droppings. *See* Young and Their Care. Some males are so driven to feed their unhatched nestlings that they offer food to the eggs. *See* Hatching.

MALES ADOPTING THE FAMILIES OF OTHER SPECIES. Allen (1961) reported that he knew of a Carolina wren that took over a family of house wrens. The male started by feeding the incubating female house wren, and when her young hatched, he was so busy feeding them that not only did the male house wren leave the brood but the female deserted and left the male Carolina wren in full charge. In a similar performance, a male prothonotary warbler near Ridgway, Ont., fed a female yellow warbler that was incubating her eggs. When her youngsters hatched, the male prothonotary warbler helped to feed them, at which the male yellow warbler deserted his family. For several nesting seasons, this male prothonotary warbler helped raise a yellow warbler family and he even learned to sing the song of the male yellow warbler. And as far as Allen knew, there was not another prothonotary warbler within 50 mi. of this one.

When birds of different species lay eggs in the same nest, the parents of each take turns incubating or may even sit on the eggs side by side. Such odd partners have been a mourning dove and an American robin, a cardinal and a song sparrow, house finches and American robins. *See* account under Nest-sharing. According to Skutch (1961), unless the young of the two cooperating species hatch at about the same time, and are of similar size and feeding habits, it is unlikely that the young of both species will survive.

Some unusual examples of the feeding drive of birds were discussed by Lorenz (1952): a captive raven passed food through the bars of its cage to a wild vulture outside; a cardinal in N.C. reacted to the open mouths of goldfish in a backyard pool and fed them at the water's edge.

Sometimes birds that nest in colonies not only feed their young but care for the adults that cannot gather food for themselves. An old blind white pelican was kept alive on fishes fed it by other members of the colony; an adult brown booby on Enderby Is., in the Pacific, with only one wing, was fed and cared for by its fellows on the Revillagigedo Is. off the west coast of Mexico. Its wing was withered and useless, evidently from its time of hatching; it was fat but had never flown and had been fed all its life by its neighbors. It is believed that these adult helpless birds may have adopted the begging postures of baby birds to induce the adults to feed them. Forbush (1925–29) reported that several adult blue jays fed and guarded an old, partly blind jay and led it to water.

Among the most interesting and appealing of helpers are those young birds hatched earlier in the season that help their parents feed offspring of later broods, hatched during the same year. Skutch (1961) reported 20 species in which the immatures have helped at the nest, and most frequent were the young of the common gallinule; the European barn swallow and house martin; the fairy wrens of Australia; the eastern, western, and mountain bluebirds of N. America; and the golden-masked tanager of C. America.

Although the feeding efforts of some young birds in helping their parents with later broods are often sporadic, Laskey (1939) reported that near Nashville, Tenn., five eastern bluebirds of the same brood, and all less than 2 months old, diligently cared for the four nestlings of the second brood, beginning when the second brood was only 3 days old; they also cleaned the nest of the droppings of the baby birds. Both Laskey (1939) and Nice (1943) cite other records

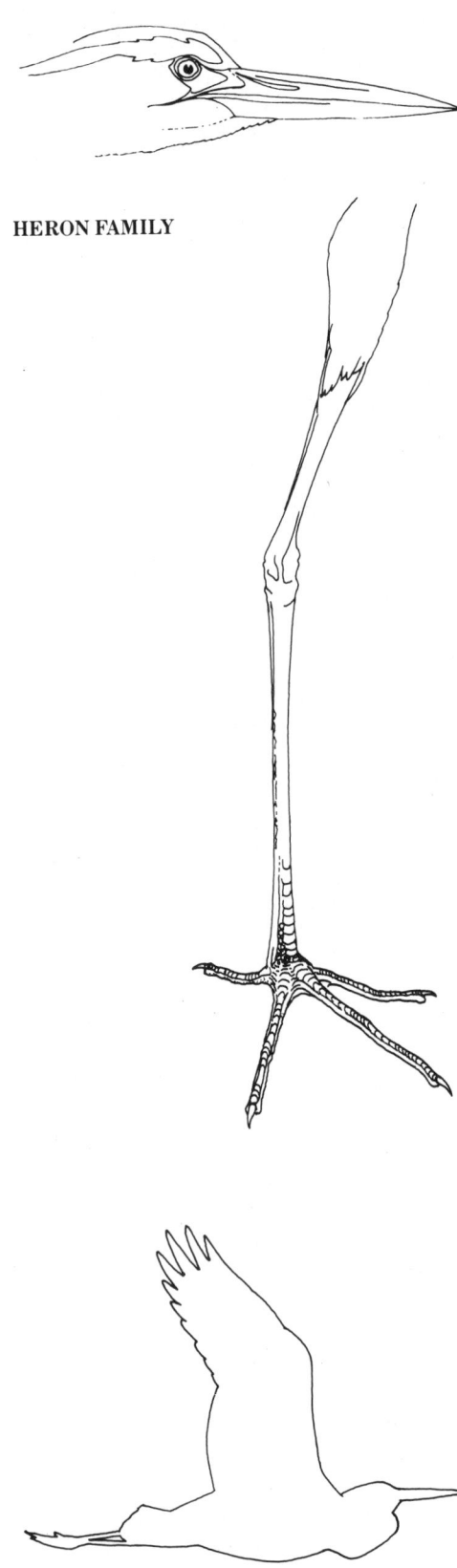

HERON FAMILY

HERON FAMILY
Herons fly with a slow, steady flap of their broad wings. They fold their long necks back in an S-shape, and their legs trail straight behind their short tails.

of young bluebirds feeding younger bluebird siblings.

COOPERATION AT THE NEST BY SOCIAL GROUPS (GROUP BREEDING). The most common example of birds in N. America that are completely mutual helpers is the tropical American communal ani. Several pairs share in every stage of the nest building, incubation of eggs, and rearing of young. Woolfenden (1975) in his studies of scrub jays in Fla. reported that bird helpers at the nest now include about 80 species worldwide in 32 families and these extra helpers cooperate in the breeding activities of the pair at the nest. At Archbold Biological Station, Highlands County, Fla., Woolfenden discovered that the Florida scrub jay helpers participated in defending the territory and nest of the pair (they mobbed predators to drive them away), helped take care of the young by feeding the nestlings and fledglings, and removed fecal sacs from the nest.

Scrub jays do not breed until at least 2 years old. These non-breeders are the birds that help pairs to raise their young before they become breeders themselves. Woolfenden (1973b) reported that Florida jays with helpers produced more young than those without helpers.

The acorn woodpeckers of the Far West, the most social of the woodpeckers of N. America, live year-round in groups of two to ten birds of both sexes and apparently of all ages. All members of each group jointly defend the territory and food supplies, and together incubate the eggs and feed the nestlings which are the offspring of each pair (MacRoberts and MacRoberts, 1972; Ritter, 1938). Bent (1939) reported observations of at least two or three pairs of acorn woodpeckers assisting the original pair in digging the nest hole in a wooden utility pole of a trolley line at Diablo, Calif., and they continued this cooperative behavior, with several different birds working in relays.

The rare red-cockaded woodpecker of the open pine forests of se. U.S. lives in colonies, or "clans," each of which may include three or even five to seven adults in the nesting season. The helpers (adults or young of the previous year and more males than females) may also start digging new roosting cavities which later are used for nesting. In helping feed the young, males of the colony usually dominate, so much so that the female of the original pair may not be seen at the nesting cavity all day. Some helpers do not feed the young directly, but pass food, bill to bill, to other helpers which enter the nesting cavity and feed the young. These non-breeding helpers increase the probability that the mated pair will rear larger broods than if not assisted, especially during inclement weather in years when insects may be less abundant. See Beckett (1971b) for these and other details; see also Ligon (1970a; 1971b); Baker (1971b); Woolfenden and Fitzpatrick (1978). *See also* Behavior; Nests and Nesting.

HEMATOZOAN
(hem-ah-toe-ZO-an), also spelled HEMATO-ZOON. Any parasitic animal living in the blood of other animals. *See,* for example, Haemoproteus under Diseases.

HEMISPHERES
The world's hemispheres (a hemisphere is one of two equal parts into which a sphere is divided by a plane through its center) have been divided by geographers into (1) a Northern and Southern Hemisphere, whose horizontal dividing line is the Equator, and (2) an Eastern and Western Hemisphere, divided by a meridian line (north and south line), such that N. and S. America are in the Western Hemisphere, the other continents chiefly in the Eastern Hemisphere. The term *Old World* is usually used synonymously with *Eastern Hemisphere*, *New World* with *Western Hemisphere*. Birds of the Northern Hemisphere, for example, would be loosely all those that spend most or all of their time north of the Equator; however, the hemispheres are not sharply enough defined for the use of zoogeographers, who use the limitations imposed by climate and other factors, as well as geographic location, to study the distribution of birds and other animals. They call these *faunal regions* of the world, and for an account of them, *see* Faunal Regions. *See also* Distribution; Ecosystem.

HEN-BILL
See Coot, American, in Rail Family.

HEN-HARRIER
See Hawk, marsh, in Hawk Family.

HENSHAW
HENRY WETHERBEE (1850–1930). Born Cambridge, Mass., one of founders of American Ornithologists' Union, and Chief, U.S. Biological Survey (1910–16); ornithologist and all-around naturalist, an easy and graceful writer, and a skilled photographer; was first to discover that the extraordinarily different male and female Williamson's sapsucker (once thought distinct species) were the same species (Bent, 1939); an extremely rapid preparator of bird skins; was able to skin, make up, and label a museum specimen of a bird in less than three minutes (for an account of his extraordinary life, see Nelson, 1932).

HENSLOW
JOHN STEVENS (1796–1861). Professor of botany in the University of Cambridge, England, whom John James Audubon met in 1828, and for whom Audubon named the Henslow's sparrow. See Audubon's account of naming the sparrow (Audubon, J. J., 1870); see Herrick (1917); *see* Names and Naming.

HERBIVOROUS
Term for a bird that eats seeds, buds, or other parts of plants; for example, purple finch, evening grosbeak, and others in the Finch Family. *See* Food Chain. *See*, especially, Food and Feeding Habits; *also* Carnivorous; Frugivorous; Omnivorous.

HERBT'S CORPUSCLES
See Touch.

HERMAPHRODITE
(hur-MAF-roe-dite). An animal having both male and female sex organs. In birds, as in

most vertebrate animals, the ovaries and testes are borne by different individuals; however, there are some hermaphrodites in which the two sexes (Hermes and Aphrodite) are combined in a single individual, a condition not uncommon among invertebrate animals, which by reason of isolation or absence of locomotion need to overcome the difficulties of pairing.

On May 16, 1882, William Brewster shot a green-tailed towhee, *Chlorura chlorura*, at Colorado Springs, Colo., that outwardly resembled a female. However, J. Amory Jeffries, who reported the incident, upon dissecting the bird to determine its sex, discovered that it had "both an ovary and a testicle . . . the one [ovary] on the left side, the other [testicle] on the right side" (Jeffries, 1883). He found the ovary to be normal in position and appearance, presenting the usual resemblance to a bunch of tiny grapes. The testicle was in its usual position on the right side of the bird and it "did not present the slightest resemblance to a modified *right* ovary; the true nature of the gland was undoubted . . . a perfect example of lateral hermaphroditism; the left side being like that of a normal female, and the right very much like that of a normal male." Jeffries could find only three comparable cases in the bird literature—three domestic hens that had been reported on. The first one was a hen with a testicle on the right side and an ovary on the left, much like that of the towhee he had dissected. *See* Fertilization.

Probably the most famous of all hermaphroditic birds was "Beauty, the Thayer Talking Canary," which lived in the Thayer Museum at Lancaster, Mass., until Sept. 15, 1909, when it died at about 10 years old. John E. Thayer, the owner of the bird, sent it after its death to Charles J. Maynard, a Mass. ornithologist, who was making a study of the vocal organs of birds. Upon dissecting it, Maynard discovered on examining its reproductive system that it had both male and female sexual organs. The female ovary was on the left side; a single testicle was on the right side (Maynard, 1928).

Some birds may outwardly resemble both a female and a male of their kind in color pattern, but these also occur rarely. They are called sexual mosaics, or gynandromorphs, by geneticists. A gynandromorph among birds often has the coloring of the male of its kind on one side of its body, the coloring of the female on the other, an example of bilateral asymmetry. *See* Gynandromorph. It is a condition said to be caused by a genetic change in the embryonic cell. *See also* Copulation and Copulatory Organs. For a discussion of these inversions of the originally determined sex, *see* Embryo and Its Development; *also* Sexual Reversal under Endocrine Glands.

HERON FAMILY

Ardeidae (are-DEE-ih-dee); from Lat. *ardea*, heron. Includes the herons, egrets, and bitterns; 63 species worldwide, except in n. N. America and n. Asia, and on some oceanic islands (Van Tyne and Berger, 1976); 11–56 in. long; long-legged, long-necked wading birds, usually associated with water, especially in nesting season; closest relatives are the storks, ibises, and flamingos (*see* Ciconiiformes); wade along shores of ponds, lakes, bays, streams, hunting for frogs, mice, fishes, and other foods, which they usually do not spear with bill but grasp with mandibles, then swallow whole; the undigested parts of food are then regurgitated in pellets. Interestingly, most herons and egrets leave the water to defecate. Their toes are not webbed but almost all can alight on water and take off from it (*see* discussion under Swimming and Diving); 15 species reported in N. America, including 2 foreign visitors—the gray heron and the little egret—and the self-introduced cattle egret of the Old World, now well established in N. and S. America.

In structure, egrets, herons, and bitterns are very similar; however, most egrets are snow white (egrets are actually herons but were given their name from their long plumes—aigrettes—worn during the breeding season); egrets and herons have especially long legs, and, along with the shorter-legged bitterns, fly with their legs straight back and long necks tucked well back on the shoulders in an S shape (the similar long-legged, long-necked cranes, storks, and ibises, for example, fly with their necks extended); egrets and herons often curve the neck while standing, and usually stand straight-legged; when wading to hunt for food, move in slow, stately walk; occasionally dash quickly, changing course in different directions in darting pursuit of fish or other moving prey; sometimes they stir, scrape, or rake bottom with a foot to flush prey into sight, then strike at it with the bill (Meyerriecks, 1959b; 1960; 1971)—*see* Food and Feeding Habits. The lores are bare of feathers; the bill is usually long and spearlike; toes are long and slender, the middle one more or less pectinate; the wings are broad and rounded; the tail short; flight is usually a steady, rather slow flapping. All herons and egrets have 2–3 pairs of powder down patches (*see* Feather); sexes are outwardly alike or nearly so in all species.

Bitterns also differ from egrets and herons in having, besides shorter legs, usually a shorter, heavier body; most bitterns live in the concealment of cattail and sedge marshes, whereas herons usually keep to the more open edges of streams and swamps. Bitterns are experts at concealing themselves by using their cryptic plumage (*see* Colors of Feathers) and upright poses to merge with the brown upright reeds and sedges of the marshes in which they live. *See* Freezing. The American bittern also has an anatomical specialization of the esophagus (*see* Esophagus) for making its booming notes in spring (Chapin, 1922). John James Audubon had a pet least bittern that could compress its 2¼-in.-wide body between two bookends that Audubon reduced gradually to a space of one inch, at which the bittern could still squeeze through.

Members of the Heron Family are protected by law and may not be kept in captivity without a permit (*see* Legal Protection), but to sustain an ill or injured one until it can sustain itself in the wild, offer it fishes, frogs, mice, raw beef or ground beef, and chopped vegetables (Walker, 1942). *Beware of picking up an injured heron, bittern, etc., as in self-defense they strike with the sharp pointed bill, especially at one's eyes.* Gross (1965a) lists 12 individuals of 6 species of family that showed albinism.

Members of the Heron Family, because of their fish-eating habits, have been condemned by some fishermen as competitive with them for game fishes, but detailed studies of food habits of herons and bitterns (see especially in Cottam and Uhler, 1937) show that only a minor part of their food is game fishes (small trout, for example); that most fishes they eat are small, thus exerting a culling or weeding effect in natural waters where small fishes are at times so numerous and crowded they remain stunted (owing to competition for food) instead of growing to game size; and that herons eat far more non-game fishes and various crustaceans and aquatic insects, many of which eat game fishes or their eggs and are competitive with game fishes for natural foods. *See* other details in Fishes and Birds; *also* the fish-eating of mergansers in Duck Family, and of cormorants in Cormorant Family. See in Pough (1951) a clear explanation of the relations of herons to fishes, under Great Blue Heron. For effective methods of protecting fishes in hatcheries from herons and other fish-eating birds, see especially McAtee and Piper (1936).

The beautiful nuptial plumage—long filamentous plumes on the back, lower fore neck, or head, especially of the great egret and snowy egret—was once in such demand by the millinery trade that in 1903 plume hunters were offered $32 an ounce for them—in the great egret, the plumes begin to grow just before the breeding season and are shed soon after the breeding season is over (Bent, 1926a).

The slaughter of adult egrets and herons for their plumes began in Audubon's time (1840) and the devastated birds reached their lowest population in the U.S. in the early 1900s; by 1917, they had started to recover because of strict protection of the remaining rookeries in s. U.S., vigorous education, legislative campaigns to protect them by the National Audubon Society, and cooperation of other conservation organizations. See early history in Pearson (1937a); Bent (1926a); Stone (1937); Graham (1971); Buchheister and Graham (1973); and a brief review of their comeback in e. N. America in Terres (1952). For history of wild bird plumage law that eventually stopped the use of plumes of wild N. American birds in the millinery trade, see Baker (1942; 1951; 1952).

Bittern, American, *Botaurus lentiginosus* (boh-TAW-rus len-tih-jin-NO-sus); genus name: ML, *botaurus*, a bittern; species name: Lat., freckled, in allusion to speckled plumage. (Color ill., page 518.) In summer, over most of U.S., Canada, and adjacent islands except in Far North; 24–34 in. long; wingspread to 50 in.; large, chunky, brown bird, rather common but usually hidden in bogs, marshes, wet meadows, either fresh or salt water; usually solitary, home is among tall marsh plants such as cattails and bulrushes; upperparts streaked with brown and buff; underparts streaked with brown and white; has white throat, pointed bill; eyes yellow; *black stripe, or patch, on each side of neck;* rarely perches in trees like other herons, usually on ground, walks slowly, stealthily; flushes from marsh with wings flopping loosely, feet dangling, utters croak, then flies with rapid wingbeats; in flight, *dark wing tips contrast with overall brown body* (Peterson, 1947); during day, when standing in open, or if senses it is seen, hides by "freezing" motionless, with bill pointed upward and body so contracted it resembles an old stake in marsh (Bent, 1926a); from wintering range, in general over s. U.S. south into C. America, migrants move north, arrive in U.S. in general, s. Canada, in Mar. and first half of Apr., into May; most active at dusk and at night; on warm spring evening in marsh, above twittering flight of swallows, gurgling songs of long-billed marsh wrens from cattails, come bittern's loud guttural notes likened to sound of old-fashioned pump, usually three syllables, middle one sharply accented, *pump-er-lunk* or *pup-er-lunk*, uttered two to seven times, notes carry half mile or more as the bird, after gulping in air, forces it out from its distended esophagus (Chapin, 1922; Bent, 1926a); male has remarkable courtship walk and display of pair of white fanlike ruffs raised over the back and shoulders (see in Bent, 1926a).

Feeding Habits: In marshes, meadows, along edges of shallow ponds, stands motionless, bill level, eyes looking down at water, stretches neck and aims bill with almost imperceptible slowness, then darts bill downward to seize prey; favorite foods are frogs, small eels, catfishes, pickerel, suckers, killifishes, sticklebacks, etc., also garter snakes, water snakes, salamanders, crayfishes, meadow mice, water scorpions, giant water bugs, diving beetles, dragonflies, etc.

Nest: Not in colonies; platform of dead reeds, cattails, cordgrass, sedges, built a few inches above water in cattails, grasses, sedges of wet meadow or marsh; sometimes nest built on ground; apparently female chooses nest site and does all of building.

Eggs: Apr.–July; 2–6, usually 3–5, buff-brown to olive-buff.

Incubation: Apparently by female, about 24 days (Palmer, 1962); young leave nest about 14 days after hatching; age of first flight unknown; apparently one brood a year.

Other Names: Barrel-maker; bog-bull; bog hen; bog-trotter; butterbump; flying fox; Indian hen; Indian pullet; look-up; marsh hen; meadow hen; mire drum; mud hen; poke; pond guinea; scoggin; shitepoke; sky-gazer; stake-bird; stake-driver; sun-gazer; thunder pumper; water-belcher.

Albinism: One shot Salem, Mass., with one secondary feather pure white (Deane, 1878).

Weights: 1 lb. 2 oz. to 2 lbs. (Palmer, 1962).

Range: Nests from c. B.C., s.-c. Mack., across n. Prairie Provinces east to c. Que., Newfoundland, south locally to s. U.S.—n. Tex., La., and Fla., west to Ohio, Tenn., Mo., Kans., Colo., Ariz., and s. Calif.; winters from Canada southward to c. N.M., through Mexico, and from c. Ohio, n. Ga., c. Md., south into C. America, Cuba.

Bittern, Cory's least. First discovered and described as a new species in 1886 by Charles B. Cory of Boston, Mass., from a bird collected (shot) near Lake Okeechobee, Fla.; however,

now regarded not as a species but as a melanistic or erythristic color form of the least bittern. *See* Least bittern. Some 31 of this dark-color form have been collected by ornithologists (1885–1914) from Fla. (7), near Toronto (16), Mass. (1), N.Y. (1), Ohio (1), Ill. (2), Mich. (2), Wisc. (1) (Palmer, 1962).

Bittern, dwarf. *See* Bittern, least.

Bittern, green. *See* Heron, green.

Bittern, least, *Ixobrychus exilis* (icks-oh-BRYE-kus or icks-OBE-rih-kus ex-EYE-liss); genus name: from Gr. *ixos*, mistletoe, but in application to birds, taken to mean reed, and Gr. *brycho, bryko*, to roar or bellow (Jaeger, 1955); species name: Lat., slender, small. (Color ills., page 519.) Smallest member of Heron Family; lives only in W. Hemisphere; in summer, throughout much of U.S. and se. Canada; 11–14¼ in. long; wingspread 16–18 in.; a tiny heron, size of a small rail; has two color phases: in common, normal phase, male has *blackish-green cap and back* and *buff and chestnut wing patches* (which distinguish it from larger, dark-winged green heron); sides of neck yellow-brown; underparts buffy; throat white; head slightly crested; bill slender, dull yellow; eyes yellow; in dark phase, rich brown-red replaces all lighter colors of normal phase and throat is *dark buff* (see Grosvenor and Wetmore, 1937; and *see* under Cory's least bittern); least bittern is a common but very shy bird, usually hidden in tall cattails, sedges of its home in freshwater marshes or in saltwater or brackish marshes near coast in South (Palmer, 1962); slips away by walking or climbing through reeds or even by running through them 2–3 ft. above water, grasping a single reed or several in each foot; when wading in shallow water or walking on land, movements are quick and graceful, its head shooting forward with each step; a weak flier, when flushed barely flutters above reed tops, then drops in marsh again; however, is fair long-distance migrant; from wintering grounds from south of s. Calif., s. Tex., and c. Fla., arrives in s. U.S. usually in Mar., northward to n. U.S., se. Canada through Apr. into May (Bent, 1926a); migrates apparently at night; Stoddard (1962) and Stoddard and Norris (1967) over 11 years reported 14 least bitterns killed at night when striking a Fla. TV tower in fall and spring migration; from summer home in marshes, male advertises his territory with soft song—a series of low dovelike coos, and a *uh-uh-uh-oo-oo-oo-oooah*, similar to one of calls of pied-billed grebe, also an alarm note, *quoh* (Bent, 1926a); when alarmed has hiding posture with body thinned and bill pointed upward similar to hiding pose of American bittern. *See* Freezing.

Feeding Habits: When reaches a fishing spot at edge of water, undulates lower neck back and forth, with head held farther and farther forward, suddenly darts head toward water; captured fish is swallowed headfirst; besides small fishes, eats frogs, tadpoles, salamanders, leeches, slugs, crayfishes, occasionally shrews and mice, and dragonflies, aquatic bugs, etc. (Palmer, 1962).

Nest: Male apparently chooses nest site and builds nest; female brings him materials, usually built in dense growth of cattails, bulrushes, about 8–14 in. above shallow water but close to open water; platform of dried and living plants; ordinarily do not nest in colonies.

Eggs: Fla., mid-Mar. to early July; Calif., mid-Apr. to early July; Ga., Apr.–June; rest of U.S. generally, May–July; 2–7, usually 4–5, pale blue, blue-white or green.

Incubation: Mostly by female, 17–18 days (Weller, 1961); after chicks hatch, adults carry eggshells away from nest and eat small pieces, young fed by regurgitation of food by parents at nest; young assume hiding pose of adults when only 3–4 days old; nestling period about 10–14 days; age at first flight unknown (Palmer, 1962).

Other Names: Dwarf bittern; least heron; little bittern.

Weights: 1½–4 oz. (Palmer, 1962).

Range: Nests generally from c. Ore., Mont., S.D., Minn., n. Mich., s. Ont., N.Y., Me., and N.B., south through Mexico, C. America, Bahamas, Greater Antilles, to most of tropical, subtropical S. America east of Andes; winters Calif., s. Tex., and c. Fla. south to Colombia.

Egret, American. *See* Egret, great.

Egret, blue. *See* Heron, little blue.

Egret, cattle, *Bubulcus ibis* (BUE-bul-kus EYE-bis); genus name: from Lat. *bubulus*, of, or concerning, cattle (Jaeger, 1955); species name: name of sacred Egyptian bird. (Color ill., page 520.) Immigrant from Old World now established in U.S.; 19–21 in. long; wingspread 36–38 in.; usually seen in fields and associated with cattle; all-white heron; yellow or orange-colored bill; eyes yellow; neck shorter and thicker and legs (yellow in non-breeding adults, greenish to black in immatures) shorter than those of other herons; in breeding season, spring to late summer, has orange-buff plumes on crown and nape; white to golden plumes on lower foreneck and mantle; legs coral pink; female similar (Palmer, 1962); formerly limited to largely s. Portugal, Spain, and Africa, rapidly expanding its range; now established on every continent; apparently self-introduced into W. Hemisphere by flight across Atlantic from Africa, first reported in New World in S. America, 1887–82 and 1911–12; first N. American sight record at Clewiston, Fla., 1941 or 1942 (Sprunt, 1955b); first N. American nesting record, Lake Okeechobee, Fla., May 5, 1953 (Sprunt in Grimes, 1953); then spread rapidly and became established as nesting bird from Fla., along Gulf coast locally to Tex., and north locally along Atlantic coast states to Ont., Canada (Palmer, 1962); first nesting records for Conn., Wisc., and Minn., spring and summer 1971; first seen in Idaho in July 1971 and was most numerous heron in Imperial Valley, Calif., in that summer, feeding in flocks in irrigated fields; reached Man., Canada (second record), in June (Gauthreaux, 1971a); for detailed history, with dates of remarkable expansion of its range in entire W. Hemisphere, see Crosby (1972); see also Hubbs (1968).

Feeding Habits: Usually feeds on dry or moist ground near cattle or horses, often perches on cattle; cattle egret attracted to insects, mostly grasshoppers frightened from grass as cattle walk and graze; usually 1–3, sometimes 7 or 8, egrets accompany each cow (Rice, 1954); cattle egret fills environmental niche distinct from other herons in feeding on insects and vertebrate animals usually in fields and pastures away from water (Lancaster, 1970); also takes earthworms (Terres, 1967); in Fla. study by Jenni (1969), cattle egrets showed preference for grasshoppers, crickets, also leopard and cricket frogs, ate spiders regularly, and some toads; see summary by Fogarty and Hetrick (1973).
Nest: Usually with other kinds of herons or in colonies of cattle egrets alone, in various habitats in extensive range: in mangroves in coastal heronries in Fla., in willows at Lake Okeechobee; in coastal N.C., in live oaks and red cedars; in Mo., in pines; at Lake Alice, Fla., most nests were in red maple or in buttonbush (Jenni, 1969); nest built by female of twigs and branches gathered by male, nest 5–12 ft. above floor of heronry, 10–18 in. across, built in 4–7 days (Palmer, 1962).
Eggs: Apr. and May in observations Fla. and S.C. (Palmer, 1962); 2–6, average of about 3½ per clutch (Jenni, 1969), light blue.
Incubation: Average, 22.9 days (Jenni, 1969); 21–24 days (Witherby *et al.*, 1938–41); adults remove eggshells from nest as each chick hatches; only species of heron able to breed in its first year (Kohlar, 1966); usually silent but utters variety of croaking notes in nesting season; young can fly short distances 40 days after hatching, reasonably well at 60 days.
Other Names: Buff-backed heron; cattle heron.
Accidents: Severe windstorms shake young from nest and death by hanging suspended from tree or bush; young falling to floor of heronry often devoured by alligators, which, in turn, keep out such predators as raccoons.
Weights: To about 12 oz. (Palmer, 1962).

Egret, common. *See* Egret, great.

Egret, great, *Casmerodius albus* (kas-mer-ODE-ih-us AL-bus); genus name: combined word from Gr. *kosmos*, ornament, or *kosmetos*, adorned, in reference to the handsome plumage, and *herodios*, a heron; species name: Lat., white. (Color ill., page 520.) In summer, in N. America in U.S. and s. Canada (also lives in Old World); seen along streams, ponds, lakes, rice fields, freshwater and saltwater marshes, mud flats; large heron, all-white at all seasons (no color phases); 37–41 in. long; wingspread to about 55 in.; sexes outwardly similar but males average larger; has *yellow* bill (the smaller snowy egret and immature little blue heron have bills mostly black, and white-phase reddish egret has flesh-colored *black-tipped* bill); no crest or head plumes but beginning in Jan. both sexes have splendid cape (nuptial train) of up to 54 long, flowing white plumes growing from the back which are lost by summer; the shed plumes, soiled and worn, are seldom found (Bent, 1926a); tall, slim-necked, has proportionately longer and broader wings than most other white herons; has slender form, movements in treetops are light and graceful; flight is buoyant; utters a loud, low-pitched, hoarse croak—rapid *cuk, cuk*; unlike some other herons, does not feed at night but after feeding during day, singly or in small groups, at sunset flies in flock after flock to arrive from all directions at a communal roost in trees or shrubbery.

Feeding Habits: Feeds commonly in salt marshes and freshwater ponds and marshes, on fishes, frogs, salamanders, snakes, mainly "water moccasins," crayfishes, mice, cotton rats, aquatic insects, mole crickets, grasshoppers, moths, etc.
Nest: Either singly or in colonies, usually with other herons, ibises, wood storks, cormorants, anhingas, in woods of swamps, mangroves, cypresses, willows near water, nest usually about 20–40 ft. above ground in medium-sized trees, sometimes in bulrushes or in cattails only 1–4 ft. above water; a flimsy platform of sticks and twigs or stems of marsh plants with little or no lining.
Eggs: Fla., Dec.–Jan. and into May or June; La., Feb.; farther north, Apr.–July (see details in Palmer, 1962); 1–6, usually 3–4, or 4–5, pale blue-green.
Incubation: 23–24 days (Bent, 1926a); first flights of young about 42 days after hatching.
Other Names: American egret; angel bird; big plume bird; common egret; great white egret; long white; plume bird; white crane.
Age: One in National Zoo, Washington, D.C., lived to be 8 years, 7 months, old; a hybrid in Tokyo Zoo lived to 10 years; one wild bird, banded in Ohio, shot in Ohio when 22 years, 7 months, old (Kennard, 1975).
Flight Speed: Timed in Calif., 17 m.p.h. (Wood, 1933); in Fla., 18 m.p.h. (Teale, 1951); 17–32 m.p.h. (Palmer, 1962).
Hybrids: None reported in wild; a zoo mating in Tokyo of common egret with Philippine night heron resulted in three young; two of hybrids died within 2 years, the third lived in good health to 10th year (Gray, 1958).
Weights: 32–40 oz. (Palmer, 1962); a female in Fla. in Apr. weighed 917 gr., or about 2 lbs.
Range: Nests from se. U.S. north to Great Lakes and in s. U.S. along Gulf coast from Fla. to Tex., along Atlantic coast north to Me., recently in Canada in sw. Man., sw. Sask, ne. S.D., and in c. Mich., s. Ont., s. Que., and Newfoundland, and in w. U.S. from s. Ore. and c. Idaho, south to Ariz; in winter, from Central Valley of Calif. across the southern tier of states and up the Atlantic coast as far as N.C.

Egret, great white. *See* Egret, great.

Egret, lesser. *See* Egret, snowy.

Egret, little, *Egretta garzetta* (ee-GRET-ah gar-ZET-tah); genus name: from Fr. *aigret*, dim. of heron; species name: Ital. name for the bird. An all-white (exceptionally it is gray) Old World egret—Europe, Asia, Africa, Australia—counterpart of the American snowy egret; two records for W. Hemisphere: a female shot at Flatrock, Conception Bay, Newfoundland, May 8, 1954, and one banded in Spain July 24, 1956, shot 6 months later, Jan. 13, 1957, 4,000 mi. away in Caroni Swamp, Trinidad, West Indies (Palmer, 1962); is 22 in. long, white with black bill and black legs, yellow feet; head with two very long, pointed crest feathers during breeding season; *back plumes straighter than those of similar snowy egret*, and feet never wholly yellow (Reilly, 1968).

Egret, little white. *See* Egret, snowy.

Egret, Louisiana. *See* Heron, Louisiana.

Egret, muffle-jawed. Local name for the reddish egret, probably in reference to its particolored bill (McAtee, 1955c).

Egret, Peale's. Old name for the white color phase of the reddish egret, once thought to be a distinct species. Charles L. Bonaparte (1828) named it *Ardea pealii;* species name in honor of Titian R. Peale, Philadelphia artist and naturalist.

Egret, reddish, *Dichromanassa rufescens* (die-crow-man-AS-ah roof-ESS-enz); genus name: Lat., from Gr. *dichroma*, two-colored, and *anassa*, queen; species name: from Lat. *rufescere*, to become reddish. (Color ill., page 521.) Uncommon to rare; coastal, in N. America, nests in summer in Baja Calif., and along Gulf coast of Tex.; 27–32 in. long; wingspread to about 46 in.; two color phases, a dark and a white; in N. America, more common dark phase has head and neck deep red-brown, often with purple gloss; rest of plumage slate gray (immature of dark phase often wholly gray with uniformly dark gray-black bill; green-black legs); dark phase resembles even darker little blue heron, which has bill pale blue at base whereas adult reddish egret *in both color phases* has stout, flesh-colored bill with blacktip; also has loose-feathered appearance, when feathers fluffed, head and neck appear shaggy (Peterson, 1947); white phase (Peale's egret) resembles great egret; however, two-colored bill of reddish egret distinguishes it from other herons, also characteristic manner when feeding of dashing or lurching about drunkenly; flight is graceful and strong; usually first birds arrive Green Is., Tex., in Mar.; not shy, generally silent but in nesting season utters guttural croaks and, in territory, low clucking, chicken-like notes (Palmer, 1962).

Feeding Habits: One of members of Heron Family that when wading often stirs or rakes bottom with one foot to stir up prey; eats small fishes, frogs, tadpoles, crustaceans.
Nest: In colonies with other herons, egrets, spoonbills, cormorants, in Tex. on dry coastal islands in brushy thickets of yucca and prickly pear, in Fla., mostly in mangroves; nest built on ground or up to 15 ft. above in low bushes or trees (Bent, 1926a); flat platform of sticks, little or no lining, or elaborate nest on ground of grass with deep cup.
Eggs: Fla., Dec.–May; Tex., Apr.–June; 3–7, usually 3–4, pale blue-green (Bent, 1926a).
Incubation: By both sexes; period of and age when young first fly unknown.
Other Names: Muffle-jawed egret; Peale's egret; plume bird.

Age: One wild banded bird lived to 12 years, 3 months.
Flight Speed: One at 20 m.p.h.
Weights: To more than 1 lb.
Range: Nests in Baja Calif., and along Gulf coast of Tex., south to Guatemala, Cuba, Hispaniola, and the Bahamas; winters s. Fla., n. Venezuela; formerly more widespread but early in 20th century was exterminated in Fla. by plumage hunters (Bent, 1926a); breeds commonly now in s. Fla., and regularly in coastal La. in small numbers; has wandered to Calif., Ariz., Colo., Ill., and S.C.

Egret, snowy, *Egretta thula* (ee-GRET-ah THOO-lah); genus name: *see* Egret, little; species name: Chilean name for the bird (Jaeger, 1955). (Color ill., page 521.) Limited to W. Hemisphere; one of daintiest and most exquisite of all marsh birds; smaller than great egret, and handsomest of all herons, especially in breeding season, when spotless white plumage is adorned with waving nuptial plumes; was slaughtered in far greater numbers by plume hunters into early 20th century than its larger relative the great egret, because originally much more numerous and more widely distributed, was less shy, and plumes more in demand than larger stiffer ones of great egret; since its rigid protection has made comeback (see some of early history in Bent, 1926a); now about same general range as great egret and breeds farther north than its original range before its persecution; strays north to Canada and Alaska (see Palmer, 1962); 22–26 in. long; wingspread 38–45 in.; all-white with *black bill, black legs, and bright yellow feet* (larger great egret has *yellow bill* and *black feet*); in breeding season, plumes, in displays, especially recurved ones of back, very conspicuous; in flight, wing strokes quicker than those of great egret; is extremely active, almost as much as reddish egret, moving about with great show of energy, lives around fresh, brackish, and salt water, sometimes in dry fields, where associates with cattle; extremely noisy at start of breeding season in nesting colonies; in e. U.S. winters in marshes along Gulf coast and in Fla., north in small numbers along Atlantic coast to N.J., and spreading northward; western birds usually winter a few hundred miles south, from se. Ore., n. Nev., Utah, and Colo. (Palmer, 1962); arrives on nesting grounds in northern part of range (Long Is., N.Y., and N.J., for example) in Apr.

Feeding Habits: Eats small fishes, frogs, lizards, snakes, shrimps, fiddler crabs, crayfishes, grasshoppers, cutworms, and aquatic insects; more than any other herons that do so, uses one foot to stir bottom of shallows of ponds and marshes to frighten prey into view (Meyerriecks, 1971), also hovers like petrel, then drops to water to catch in bill its victim; also runs swiftly through shallows with wings partly raised chasing prey; seen standing in shallows and catching fishes that merganser drove before them as they fed (Emlen and Ambrose, 1970).
Nest: Built on ground (commonly in w. U.S.) or to 30 ft. high in trees; 5–10 ft. up in trees and shrubs more typical; highly social nester, thou-

sands of pairs in colony, singly or in small colonies with other herons, ibises; many colonies coastal, in Fla. in heavy stands of mangroves; in N.J. from cedars among sand dunes to salt marsh; in Tex. dry islands with nests in prickly pear; in willows and buttonbushes about freshwater lakes, ponds, marshes; in bulrushes at Great Salt Lake and elsewhere in West (Palmer, 1962).
Eggs: Fla., Jan.–July, usually Apr.–May; Tex., Apr.–June; Utah, Apr.–May; 1–6, usually 3–4, or 4–5, pale blue-green.
Incubation: By both sexes, 18 (?) days; young reported to leave nest 20–25 (?) days after hatching (Bent, 1926a); many details of life history of this egret uncertain or poorly known (Palmer, 1962).
Other Names: Brewster's egret (w. U.S.); lesser egret; little egret; little snowy; little white egret; little white heron.
Age: One in National Zoo, Washington, D.C., to age 16 years, 10 months.
Flight Speed: Timed in w. U.S., 30 m.p.h. (Cottam *et al.*, 1942b).
Hybrids: See in biography of little blue heron.
Weights: To about 13 oz. (Palmer, 1962).
Range: Nests in n. Calif., se. Idaho, Colo., c. Okla., Gulf coast, and Me., south locally to Baja Calif., sw. Ariz., s. N.M., Gulf coast, Fla., through Mexico to s. S. America and West Indies; winters from n. Calif., s. Ariz., w. Tex., coastal Tex., Gulf coast, Fla., and S.C. south; wanders north to Wash., Alta., Wisc., s. Mich., N.B., and Newfoundland; accidental in Alaska (Juneau), Canada (Sask.), Tristan Is. in s. Atlantic (Palmer, 1962), and Bermuda Is.

Heron, black-crowned night, *Nycticorax nycticorax* (nick-TICK-oh-racks); genus and species names: Lat., from Gr. *nyktikorax*, night raven. (Color ills., page 523.) Largely but not strictly nocturnal; common around freshwater swamps and tidal marshes from s. Canada south to s. S. America, also in Old World; 23–28 in. long; wingspread to 45 in.; sexes outwardly similar but males average larger; heavy body (chunky), short thick neck, short legs, and heavy bill; adults: head with black cap, short crest, 2–3 narrow white plumes at back of head; eyes scarlet; back black; underparts white; wings and tail gray; legs and feet usually yellow but quite red in the very early part of the nesting season; immature: brown, streaked or spotted with white; at night, black-crowns often seen in sky as dark silhouette—head sunken in line with back, bill pointed ahead, toes barely projecting beyond tail as it flies with steady beats of its broad wings from daytime roosts in trees to feeding places in marshes (sometimes feeds by day); utters loud, guttural *quock* or *quark* as it flies, most often heard at dusk or after dark (similar note of related yellow-crowned night heron is higher-pitched *quak*); some winter in northern part of breeding range but many migrate to s. U.S. or farther south to winter (Houston, 1967a, reported that black-crowns banded in Sask., and later recovered, had moved south and southeast through Tex. into tropical Mexico and to se. U.S.; all had been shot); are in breeding territories in n. U.S., s. Canada, Mar.–May, are commonest near extensive marshes.

Feeding Habits: Expert at still fishing; stands motionless in shallow water, sometimes for long periods, then with quick thrust of bill into water catches small fishes, main food; sometimes flies out over water, alights on surface, can swim well in searching water for food, known to eat algae and other succulent plants, but mostly eats gizzard shad, herring, suckers, minnows, dace, shiners, carp, chubs, catfishes, pickerel, eels (see Palmer, 1962), also frogs, tadpoles, salamanders, garter snakes, queen snakes, Fowler's toads, crayfishes, blue crabs, fiddler crabs, shrimps, squids, clams, mussels, dragonflies and their nymphs; extremely adaptable, eats whatever most plentiful at time and place; may even eat young of colonially nesting birds—young egrets, herons, ibises, chicks of terns (Collins, 1970), young Franklin's gulls, coots, yellow-headed and red-winged blackbirds (Wolford and Boag, 1971); and may feed exclusively on meadow mice when large numbers available (Allen and Mangles, 1940).
Nest: In small to large colonies in almost any habitat: groves of pines, oaks, sassafras, maple, and alders near coastal marshes; groves of spruces on marine islands; hardwood forests; coniferous swamps; cattail marshes on prairies; clumps of tall grass on dry ground (Tex.); in *Phragmites*; apple orchards; in willows and alders; sometimes in tall trees of city parks; nests close together, usually with other heron species; male selects nest site, which may vary from ground to 160 ft. up in tree, nests close together built of coarse twigs, reeds, or branches in foundation, finer materials woven into top and lining, materials gathered by male, nest built by female.
Eggs: Fla., Nov.–Apr.; elsewhere, usually Apr.–May, June, or July (Bent, 1926a; Palmer, 1962); 1–6, usually 3–5, pale blue-green.
Incubation: By both sexes, 24–26 days, but questionable, needs further study; young first fly about 42 days after hatching, when they pursue adults to beg for food.
Other Names: American night heron; night heron; qua-bird; quawk; quok; squawk.
Age: One, banded as fledgling in Mass., spring 1925, found with broken wing 10 years later in Va. (Cooke, 1937c); another, banded in Ohio, was collected (shot) as scientific specimen when 21 years, 1 month, old (Kennard, 1975); one lived in National Zoo, Washington, D.C., to age 16 years, 7 months; of 26,000 banded in U.S. and Canada to 1962, only 933 were recovered; of these, 803, or 86%, were shot or killed in other ways before reaching age of 3 years; of remaining 130, 64 lived from 5 to 10 years, and 11 to more than 10 years; oldest was 17 years, 6 months (Nickell, 1966).
Flight Speed: Timed in w. U.S., 20–35 m.p.h. (Cottam *et al.*, 1942b).
Weights: Adults, Mass., summer: males (3), about 1 lb. 10 oz. to 2 lbs. 4 oz.; females (2), 727 and 884 gr., or about 1 lb. 10 oz. and 2 lbs. (Palmer, 1962).
Range: In W. Hemisphere, nests from nw. Ore., e. Wash., s. Idaho, c. Wyo., ne. Mont., s. Sask., sw. Man., c. Minn., c. Wisc., s. Mich., s. Ont., and s. Que. and ne. N.B., south to s. S. America; in Old World, from s. Europe, se. Asia, and Japan to Africa, Madagascar, Ceylon,

Java, and Philippines, and disperses over much of Europe.

Heron, blue. *See* Heron, great blue, and Heron, little blue.

Heron, buff-backed. *See* Egret, cattle.

Heron, cattle. *See* Egret, cattle.

Heron, European. *See* Heron, gray.

Heron, gray, *Ardea cinerea* (ARE-dee-ah sin-ER-ee-ah); genus name: Lat., heron; species name: Lat., ashen, or ash-colored. Old World counterpart of N. American great blue heron but somewhat smaller and grayer, lacks most of brown or rust of neck and underparts of great blue; has wandered several times to Greenland; 36 in. long.

Other Names: European blue heron; European heron; in British Isles: heron and common heron.

Age: Banded wild ones in Switzerland reported to ages 11, 12, 13 years (Nice, 1966a).

Heron, great blue, *Ardea herodias* (ARE-dee-ah her-ODE-ih-as); genus name: *see* Heron, gray; species name: from Gr. *herodios*, heron; also a proper name. (Color ill., page 523.) Best-known and most widespread of all N. American herons, often called blue crane by country people; along with great white heron, largest heron in N. America; to 4 ft. tall; in summer, nests from se. Alaska and s. Canada south into Mexico, Galápagos Is., West Indies; winters over much of its breeding range; 42–52 in. long; wingspread to 7 ft.; sexes outwardly similar but males average slightly larger; occipital plumes average longer; tall, long-legged, long-necked, with sharply pointed bill; appears gray-blue except for white feathers around head and neck of adults, cinnamon on neck; legs black (see variations in colors in southern part of range under Ward's heron); the great white heron of s. Fla., largest of all white herons, is believed by Mayr (1956) and other authorities to be a white color phase of the great blue heron, with which the great white heron interbreeds freely—see discussion by Meyerriecks (1957b). *See* Color Phase.

Standing motionless and alone along stream or lake, the great blue heron is often only living creature seen in the broad expanse of water and forest; in flight, identified by large size, broad wingspread, head folded back on shoulders (cranes fly with neck extended like a goose), dusky wings beating slowly and majestically, long legs trailing behind, usually silent but in flight may utter honking notes; when startled, low-pitched croaks; lives in both salt-water and freshwater environments; shallow waters and shores of lakes, ponds, streams, bays, marshes, ocean shore, often on tidal flats and sandbars, wary, spends much time both ashore and in shallow water, perches in trees.

Feeding Habits: Fishes by night and by day, most active just before dawn and at dusk; usually stands motionless in shallow water waiting for prey to come within striking distance of sharp, pointed bill; wades into surf to fish; sometimes from perch or while in flight may drop into deep water to strike with bill at schools of fish, usually catches small fishes crosswise in bill, then swallows whole, but spears large fish; often walks about hunting along watercourses, in wet meadows, fields, sometimes far from water, and in suburban ponds, backyard pools; besides small non-game fishes of kind other herons eat, devours frogs, salamanders, lizards, snakes, shrimps, crabs, crayfishes, grasshoppers, dragonflies, and many aquatic insects which prey on young fishes; may rarely kill and swallow rails, phalarope, frequently eats shrews, mice, young rats, ground squirrels, pocket gophers.

Nest: May be built on ground, rock ledges, sea cliffs to tops of tall cypresses, pines, has nested on duck blinds in Tex., in w. U.S. among bulrushes; nests together from groups of few pairs to hundreds, by themselves or frequently with other herons; dozens of nests may be built in top of same tree, in forests of mainland, typically in tallest trees in swamps or on islands, may nest in low shrubs (Palmer, 1962), in Calif. redwoods in upper branches 80–100 ft. up (Pratt, 1970); flat flimsy platforms of sticks 18 in. across well out on tree limb but older nests may be bulky, 3–4 ft. across, repaired and used year after year; lined with twigs, mosses, pine needles, reeds, marsh grasses, mangrove leaves (Fla.).

Eggs: Fla., Nov.–Apr.; elsewhere, Mar.–May (Bent, 1926a; Palmer, 1962); 3–7, usually 4, pale blue-green to pale olive.

Incubation: By both sexes, 25–29 days (Pratt, 1970); about 28 days (Bent, 1926a); incubating bird turns eggs by rolling them with bill average of about once every 2 hours; both parents feed nestlings, when newly hatched, by regurgitating food, usually fish, into mouths of chicks, later into bottom of nest; some young take sustained flights around heronry 60 days after hatching; abandon nest 64–91 days after hatching (Pratt, 1970); at 18 days after hatching, vibrate gular pouches to promote body cooling.

Other Names: Big cranky; blue crane; crane; gray crane; long john; poor joe; Treganza's heron.

Accidents: Some killed by trying to swallow fish too large; one caught a shad about 2 feet long, could not disgorge, and choked to death; some break wing in migration, die of starvation, cold; some strike utility wires and die entangled in them; beware of sharp bill of crippled, wounded heron; one struck a pinewood oar with such force bill protruded through it for 2 in.

Age: One banded wild bird, 21 years old, was oldest of 349 recoveries (Owen, 1959); one lived in National Zoo, Washington, D.C., to age 10 years, 11 months.

Flight Speed: Timed in Calif., 28 m.p.h. (Wetmore, 1916); 23 m.p.h. (Wood, 1933); in w. U.S., 18–36 m.p.h. (Cottam *et al.*, 1942b); 35 m.p.h. (A. A. Allen, 1961).

Hybrids: See Heron, great white.

Weights: 5–8 lbs. (Palmer, 1962).

Range: Nests from se. Alaska and s. Canada to s. Mexico, Cuba, and Jamaica; winters from se. Alaska and c. U.S. to nw. S. America.

Heron, great white. (Color ill., page 522.) Formerly considered a distinct species, *Ardea occidentalis,* now classified by the American Ornithologists' Union (1973) as a white color form and a subspecies, *Ardea herodias occidentalis,* of the great blue heron; most restricted in range of any N. American heron; on rare list of U.S. Fish and Wildlife Service for 1966; is limited mostly to s. Fla. in U.S.; is snow white, about size and form of great blue heron; wingspread 6½–7 ft.; largest white heron in America; yellow bill; *green-yellow legs* distinguish it from smaller, *black-legged* great egret (Peterson, 1947); appears exactly like a white-feathered great blue heron; where its range overlaps that of great blue heron, interbreeds freely with it (see Meyerriecks, 1957b; 1960). Mayr and Short (1970) consider the great white heron "a peripheral Caribbean population of the great blue heron in which the white morph, rare in mainland populations of great blue herons, strongly predominates over the 'normal' blue morph."

In U.S., breeds in Fla. Keys, Fla. Bay, and s. peninsular Fla., north along Atlantic coast to s. Biscayne Bay (Arsenicker Keys) and along Fla. Gulf coast to Cape Romano; disperses regularly (mostly immatures) in summer after nesting season, north to Tampa Bay (Gulf coast) and Cape Kennedy (Atlantic coast); seen in interior Fla. in groups along Tamiami Trail and south to Dry Tortugas; lesser numbers farther north; has wandered north to Miss., S.C., N.C., and Pa.; total population reduced by Sept. 1935 hurricane to about 150; with protection from illegal hunting increased to about 800 by 1941 (Sprunt, 1954a); periodically decimated by hurricanes; about 359 adults killed (40% of population) by Hurricane Donna in 1960 but loss regained by 1963, and from aerial counts, a total of 1,500 adults in Fla. by 1966 (see Committee on Rare and Endangered Wildlife Species, 1966); see also Sanger (1967); lives within U.S. almost entirely within keys and mangroves and shallow marl–turtle grass flats of Fla. Bay and Fla. mainland shore and keys southwest to vicinity of Key West and the Marquesas. Occasionally seen, especially after nesting season, in or around freshwater, as at Lake Okeechobee.

Feeding Habits: Largely eats saltwater fishes of no value to man; also shrimps, crabs, snails; captives of John James Audubon ate young of other herons and domestic fowl, and caught moths. Olson and Johnson (1971) watched a great white heron snatch from ground a black-necked stilt walking near it and swallow it headfirst; occasionally it wet the body of the stilt by dipping it in water in order to swallow it more easily.

Nest: Built in both red and black mangroves, usually in small, scattered groups within interior of Fla. Keys; bulky, large, flat, of sticks; nest may be on ground or up to 10–20 ft. above; breeds throughout year in Fla. Bay but peak in late fall and winter.

Other Names: American great white heron; white crane.

Eggs: In Fla., mostly Dec.–Jan.; 3–5, greenish blue.

Age: One lived in National Zoo, Washington, D.C., to age 6 years.

Range: S. Fla. to Cuba, Isle of Pines, coast of Yucatán.

Heron, green, *Butorides virescens* (bew-tore-EYE-deez vie-RES-enz); genus name: from Lat. *butio,* or *butor,* bittern; species name: Lat., to become green. (Color ill., page 524.) In general most widely distributed of all herons, usually seen about every brook or pond in summer over much of s. U.S. and north over entire e. U.S. to Canada, west to Great Plains, and in Far West and Southwest wherever salt or fresh water; next to least bittern, smallest N. American heron; 18–22 in. long; wingspread to about 26 in.; appears dark and crowlike in flight at distance; flies with slower, more arched wingbeats (Peterson, 1947); close by, appears more blue than green, sometimes mistaken for larger and slimmer little blue heron; has shaggy, green-black cap; chestnut sides of head and most of neck, dark back; eyes yellow to deep orange; bill brown-black; distinguished by its small size, dark underparts, yellow or bright orange legs; immatures, in first-year plumage, heavily streaked below; at home in both saltwater and freshwater marshes; hardly a stream, pond, or other shoreline where may not be found; when perched or when walking about, if it knows it is watched, flicks short tail nervously and raises crest; feeds by day, preferably early morning or late afternoon; may live in small marsh in built-up area; alights commonly in trees, on stumps and dead limbs; roosts on or close to ground; familiar sound is its loudly uttered *skow* or *skeow* while in flight over marsh or creek; from wintering places from Fla. and Mexico southward, migrates northward at night; also by day in n. N. America; both sexes arrive about same time on breeding territory, from late. Mar. in N.C. to late Apr. in Montreal.

Feeding Habits: On muddy margin of pond or sand flats at low tide, may stand motionless watching for small fishes in water, crouched with legs nearly touching ground, head and neck extended straight ahead ("stand and wait"—see Meyerriecks, 1960); appears like bent stick as it waits for small fishes to swim near; rarely misses them in quick strike of pointed bill; also walks stealthily, catlike, putting down each foot with care, then catches prey with strike and grab of bill; eats killifishes, minnows, catfishes, carp, goldfish, bass, eels, frogs, crayfishes, prawns, crickets, katydids, dragonflies, damselflies, water bugs, diving beetles, leeches, also earthworms, small snakes, snails, mice; sometimes dives into water after its prey or leans far out from log or plank over water to catch fish; also wades slowly, stops to extend one leg with toes spread, then rakes or scrapes bottom with backward drag of foot, then peers down into shallows to examine raked area for moving prey (Meyerriecks, 1971).

Nest: May be built away from water in dry woods and orchards or in open marsh away from trees; a structure of reeds and cattails on low tussock or muskrat house; in red mangroves in Fla., even on arched aerial roots only inches above tide; throughout range usually nests singly but sometimes in colonies of 6 pairs or more; nest may be to 30 ft. up but usually 10–15 ft. above ground; in hardwoods, often in conifers; in West, in thickets of willow and wild gooseberry on banks of irrigation ditches; a platform of sticks, some lined with finer twigs, vines, bits of reeds, etc. (Palmer, 1962).

Eggs: Se. U.S., Mar.–July; elsewhere, Apr.–June; 3–6, usually 4–5, pale green or blue-green.

Incubation: By both sexes, 19–21 days; young in first flights 21–23 days after hatching, but still fed by parents.

Other Names: Chalk-line; crab-catcher; fly-up-the-creek; green bittern; little green heron; poke; shitepoke; skeow and skow (because of cries); swamp squaggin.

Flight Speed: Timed in Fla., 25 m.p.h. (Meyerriecks, 1960); in Calif., 34 m.p.h. (McLean, 1930); 22 m.p.h. (Wood, 1933).

Weights: One, Fla., 164.5 gr. (Fisk, 1971c), or about 5¾ oz.; two males, 158 and 191.6 gr., or about 5½ and 6 oz.; one female, 181.5 gr. (Palmer, 1962); about 200 gr., or 7½ oz. (Meyerriecks, 1960).

Range: Nests from sw. Wash., s. Nev., c. Ariz., Tex., Neb., c. Minn., Great Lakes, coastal Me., and N.B., south to Panama and West Indies; winters from coastal Calif., s. Ariz., s. Tex., and Fla. south to Colombia and n. Venezuela; has strayed to Man., Nova Scotia, Newfoundland.

Heron, little blue, *Florida caerulea* (FLAR-ih-dah see-RULE-ee-ah); genus name: for the state; species name: Lat., blue. (Color ills., pages 524, 525.) Nests in summer from c. Okla. to c. Ala. and north along Atlantic coast to Me., south through West Indies to c. Argentina and Peru; a small, dark heron; 25–29 in. long; wingspread to about 41 in.; appears uniformly dark at distance with slender, slightly downcurved bill; sexes outwardly similar; adults: head and neck purple-maroon; rest of plumage slate gray; bill dark gray, outer third black; eyes yellow; legs and feet dark; in mixed group of herons recognized by slow, methodical manner of feeding (Palmer, 1962); immatures: unique among all herons in being snow white in immature plumage with tinge of blue in primaries; bill blue, tipped with black; legs dull green; wears white plumage first summer, fall, and into winter, but starts molting during first Feb. into blue of adult; while in this pied plumage (white blotched with blue) is unlike any other heron; as plumes of little blue heron were not in demand for millinery uses, it suffered less than the white egrets (Bent, 1926a); flight is graceful and strong, wing strokes quicker than that of larger herons, flies with head drawn in on shoulders, legs extended to rear; often associates with Louisiana heron; all through day may be seen walking daintily and actively about on marshes or mud flats; roosts at night in groups in trees and shrubs or breeding heronries; early in morning flies out in detached flocks to feeding grounds; usually silent but occasionally utters low clucking or croaking notes; fighting or quarreling sounds resemble screams of parrots; although often lives about salt or brackish water, is primarily an inland bird and prefers freshwater ponds, lakes, marshes, meadows, marshy shores of streams; spring flights from wintering places in C. America and Mexico, by way of Tex. coast, reach La. coast from late Feb. to early Mar., Ga. by mid-Mar., and N.C. and Va. by early Apr.

Feeding Habits: Does not wade as deeply as some herons, generally hunts prey ashore or in mud or shallow waters, then flies short distance to another spot; has been seen following drove of pigs in Fla. prairie, apparently catching grasshoppers startled by the animals (Howell, 1932). Seldom feeds in salt water; largely eats fishes, frogs, lizards, snakes, turtles, shrimps, fiddler crabs, and crayfishes, also aquatic insects and spiders; when water disappears from swamps and marshes, may live solely on grasshoppers, crickets, beetles, and other insects of grasslands (Palmer, 1962).

Nest: In small or large colonies, usually with other herons, often in dense growth of willows, buttonbush, or swamp privet and red maples; a flimsy platform, or sometimes substantial bulky nest, of sticks, built from a few feet above ground or water to 10–15 ft. up, sometimes to 40 ft. in swamp tree.

Eggs: Fla., late Dec. to June, but usually Apr.; elsewhere (Ark., for example), late Apr.; La., Apr.–May (Bent, 1926a); 3–6, usually 4–5, pale blue-green.

Incubation: By both sexes, 22–24 days; young make first flight when about 30 days old; apparently one brood a year (Palmer, 1962).

Other Names: Blue crane; levee walker (La.); little blue crane; little white crane (applied to immature).

Age: One, banded in Miss., found dead when 7 years, 4 months, old (Kennard, 1975).

Hybrids: Little blue heron × snowy egret; a presumed natural hybrid in Fla. According to Phillips *et al.* (1964), little blue has also hybridized with the Louisiana heron.

Weights: To about 14 oz. (Palmer, 1962).

Range: Nests c. Okla., s.-c. Mo., and Mass., south to Mexico; after nesting season, wide dispersal, especially by the white young, great numbers move northward, but number varies markedly from year to year; has reached Neb., Iowa, Mich., s. Ont., s. Que.; has wandered to Sask., Labrador, and Newfoundland; apparently is extending its winter range, which usually in Mexico, s. Baja Calif., and s. U.S.; first Calif. record reported 1964; another seen near Santa Barbara, reported 1966; also records for Nev., Utah (Hubbs, 1968).

Heron, little green. *See* Heron, green.

Heron, Louisiana, *Hydranassa tricolor* (high-drah-NASS-ah TRI-col-or); genus name: Lat., from Gr. *hydor, hydros,* water, and *anassa,* queen; species name: Lat., three colors, often called tricolored heron. (Color ills., page 527.) Common coastal heron of saltwater shores, Baja Calif., and Gulf and Atlantic coasts of U.S.; 24–26 in. long; wingspread to 36 in.; sexes outwardly similar, males average larger; dark heron, with slate-colored head, neck, and back; long neck and long bill give it generally longer, slimmer appearance than most other herons; white belly and white rump contrast strongly with otherwise dark plumage; in breeding season, has long plumes on head and back, some white (plume hunters did not kill this species, as its plumes were not in demand); front of long neck striped red-brown and white; belly and flanks white; back and wings blue-gray; immatures lack plumes, and gray on neck, which in immature is red-brown; when starting to fly, or on short flights, often flies with neck extended forward in a long S, legs dangling, but when well under way flies with head well back between shoulders, legs straight out behind; much less migratory than little blue heron, and young do not disperse as much after nesting season; winters in s. U.S. to n. S. America, but a few also north along Atlantic coast; arrive on breeding territories in s. U.S. (La., for example) in Mar. but most in Apr., some in May; some remain all year in nesting range; in junglelike islands of tall red and black mangroves in s. Fla., or on willow-grown islands in freshwater marshes, to oyster-reef islands of Tex., tidal marshes of La.; gregarious, noisy, utter harsh croaks, deep groans.

Feeding Habits: Often stands or wades belly-deep in water, does not often feed ashore; when stalking small fishes in shallows, crouches with legs bent almost double, also runs rapidly through shallows, wings partly raised, sometimes stretches one foot far forward and vibrates foot rapidly along bottom to flush prey (Palmer, 1962; *see* Food and Feeding Habits); eats mainly small fishes of no commercial interest to man; also lizards, frogs, tadpoles, salamanders, crayfishes, snails, leeches, worms, spiders, grasshoppers, giant water bugs, dragonflies, water beetles, ground beetles.

Nest: May be built in small or large colonies by themselves or with other herons, on ground or to 20 ft. up in tree, usually 6–15 ft. up; one colony near St. Marks, Fla., nested among tangled rushes; nest of sticks, twigs, in thickets of low trees, bushes.

Eggs: Fla., Mar. to early June; farther north, usually Apr.–May; 3–7, usually 3–4, pale green-blue (Palmer, 1962).

Incubation: 21 days (?); age when young leave nest unreported.

Other Names: Lady-of-the-waters; Louisiana egret; silver-gray heron; scoggin; tricolored heron.

Age: One, banded at Avery Is., La., 1920, retrapped there 1937 when 17 years old.

Hybrids: See under Little blue heron.

Weights: To about 11 oz. (Palmer, 1962).

Range: Resident from c. Baja Calif., Gulf coast of Tex., La., Ala., north along Atlantic coast to N.Y., south along coasts of Mexico and C. America and through Bahamas and Greater Antilles, to Ecuador, Columbia, and Venezuela; wanders north to s. Calif., s. Nev., c. Ariz., Okla., Ark., and N.J.; casual in s. Neb., ne. Mo., c. Ind., c. Pa., coastal N.Y., Mass., and N.B.

Heron, night. *See* Heron, black-crowned night, and Heron, yellow-crowned night.

Heron, snowy. *See* Egret, snowy.

Heron, tricolored. *See* Heron, Louisiana.

Heron, Ward's, *Ardea herodias wardi,* a southern subspecies, or race, of the great blue heron, named by Robert Ridgway in 1882 in honor of Charles W. Ward. Averages paler and larger than other great blue herons; 50–52 in. long; wingspread 77–82 in. (Sprunt, 1954a); nests in se. U.S. from Fla. Keys west along Gulf coast to Tex., north to Kans., Iowa, s. Ill., se. Ind., and S.C.; winters in Fla., s. Ala., to Tex., and south into Mexico. In some Ward's herons, the entire head and crest are pure white. This is the so-called Würdemann's heron, first described in 1858 by Spencer F. Baird as a distinct species and named by him for Gustavus Würdemann of the U.S. Coast and Geodetic Survey; later, ornithologists, on the basis on field studies, concluded that the Würdemann's was not a full species but a hybrid between the Ward's heron and the great white heron. According to Palmer (1962), however, Würdemann's is apparently a white-headed color form, or phase, of the Ward's heron, a form that usually appears only in extreme s. Fla. and usually within the range of the great white heron (Sprunt, 1954a). *See* Heron, great white.

Heron, Würdemann's. *See* under Heron, Ward's.

Heron, yellow-crowned night, *Nyctanassa violacea* (nick-tan-AS-ah vie-oh-LAY-see-ah); genus name: Lat., from Gr. *nyks, nyktos,* night, and *anassa,* queen; species name: Lat., violet-colored. (Color ill., page 526.) In U.S. in summer, nests in lower Mississippi, Ohio, Red, and Arkansas river basins; also along Gulf coast, Tex. to Fla., and Atlantic coast north to Mass.; limited to W. Hemisphere; much less common than black-crowned night heron; sexes outwardly similar; 22–28 in. long; wingspread 40–44 in.; stocky, uniformly gray heron, *adults with distinct black and white face;* crown often suffused with yellow but seldom noticeable in field; also distinguishable from black-crowned by larger head, stout, thick bill, more slender neck, and erect posture; also has higher-pitched *quak* note, often uttered in series (Palmer, 1962); immatures heavily streaked below like immature black-crowned but darker, more slaty, not as brown; have shorter, thicker bill, longer legs, smaller light spots on back (Robbins *et al.,* 1966); in U.S. lives in large cypress swamps of Southeast; also, more usual to find them in lush river swamps, as in S.C., Ga., Fla., Tex.; is more characteristic of mangroves in s. Fla. than black-crowned; hunts at night but also frequently seen feeding by day.

Feeding Habits: Unlike other herons, rarely takes fishes but eats mostly crayfishes and some crabs; eats many land crabs in Fla., also takes mussels, fiddler crabs in coastal marshes; eats some frogs, aquatic insects, snails, small snakes, lizards, leeches, terrapins (Palmer, 1962).

Nest: In small groups to large colonies, sometimes with colonies of black-crowned, little blue, Louisiana, and Ward's herons; sometimes single breeding pairs at edge of nesting range

Ward's heron

HERON FAMILY

HESPERORNIS

or when colonizing new areas; nest built of heavy twigs, lined with finer twigs, rootlets, is well-built heavy structure, usually 15–20 ft. up on larger limbs of mangroves, also high in cypress trees or in low tree or shrub, sometimes on ground.

Eggs: Fla., Mar.–May; La., to June; farther north, Apr.–May; 2–8, usually 3–4, or 4–5, pale blue-green.

Incubation: By both sexes; period of and age when young first fly unknown (Palmer, 1962).

Other Names: Fish crane; Indian hen; quabird; quawk; quok; squawk.

Weights: To at least 23 oz. (Palmer, 1962).

Range: Nests locally from Tex., Okla., se. Kans., Mo., and w. and c. Tenn., rarely from Ill., Ind., and Ohio, and on Atlantic seaboard from Mass. south into e. Mexico, C. America, to Guatemala, Gulf coast of U.S., and through Fla. to Key West; extending range northward; wanders from Tex. north to e. Colo., se. Neb., n. Iowa, se. Wisc., s. Ont., w. N.Y., s. N.H., coastal Me., sw. N.B., Nova Scotia, Newfoundland; winters from s. Tex., s. La., s. Miss., and coastal S.C. south into C. America, West Indies.

HERRICK

FRANCIS HOBART (1858–1940). Born Woodstock, Vt.; professor, Western Reserve University; a fellow, the American Ornithologists' Union; biologist and early American bird photographer; student of bird behavior, author of the first definitive biography of Audubon (*Audubon: The Naturalist*, in two volumes, 1917; single volume, 1937); also wrote a monograph on the American lobster (1895), followed by *The Home Life of Wild Birds* (1901), illustrated with his own photographs. Studies of the nesting of bald eagles at Vermilion, Ohio, resulted in a series of illustrated articles in *The Auk* and a book, *The American Eagle* (1934). See Visscher (1943).

HERRICK

H(AROLD) H. *See* in biography of Lawrence's warbler in Warbler—American Wood Warbler Family.

HERRING-BIRD

See phalaropes in Phalarope Family.

HESPERORNIS

(hes-per-OR-niss); Lat., from Gr. *hesperos,* western, and and *ornis,* a bird. One of the most famous of all fossil birds, discovered by O. C. Marsh, famed because it was a toothed bird like *Archaeopteryx* but lived long after the world's oldest-known bird. *See* discussion under Fossil Birds. See also discussion by Swinton (1965) and evidence that *Hesperornis* was a toothed bird.

Hesperornis is a genus of fossil swimming birds from the Cretaceous Period, first discovered in Kans. In Nov. 1870, Prof. Marsh of Yale University found the first fragment of *Hesperornis* near the Smoky Hill R. in w. Kans. not far from Fort Wallace. Extremely cold weather and hostile Indians prevented further exploration by Marsh at the time, but he returned in July 1871 with a strong escort of soldiers and unearthed the type skeleton of the bird he named *Hesperornis regalis* (Wetmore, 1933).

HAWK FAMILY

Bald eagle

The fierce expression on the face of a bald eagle belies the bird's true nature, for North America's most celebrated bird of prey is primarily an eater of fish and is not above eating any dead fish it finds along the shores of lakes and rivers. Indeed, its fish-eating habits are indirectly the cause of its serious decline in numbers during the last few decades. Pesticides, seeping out of farmlands into rivers, tend to become concentrated in the tissues of fish; when passed along in such large doses to the eagles, the pesticide concentration so drastically interferes with the birds' reproduction that this species now nests in good numbers only in Florida and Alaska, having been all but wiped out everywhere in between.

Bald eagle

Bald eagle
*When the salmon are running in rivers
of the Northwest, bald eagles gather in
large numbers to prey on the tired and
weakened fish. It is sometimes possible
to see several dozen eagles, standing on
sandbars and perched in nearby fir trees.*

Golden eagle
*Despite its great size, the golden eagle is
one of the most graceful of our birds of
prey, soaring for hours over its mountain
habitat with little apparent effort. When it
sights its prey, often a rabbit on a grassy
hillside, it dives at a speed that is said to
reach 150 or 200 miles an hour. Although
most of its food consists of mammals
taken on the ground, golden eagles have
been known to capture flying birds as
large as geese and cranes.*

Bald eagle

Golden eagle

Golden eagle

Goshawk

The largest of the so-called bird hawks, the goshawk is mainly a bird of boreal and mountain forests, where it preys on hares and such birds as grouse. When Cooper's hawk became rare as a result of pesticides, and large areas of deciduous forest no longer supported any large bird hawks, the goshawk began spreading into this unoccupied territory; in parts of the Northeast, it now nests in places where it was unknown as a breeding bird a few decades ago.

Black hawk

The black hawk ranges from the southwestern United States to northern South America. A quiet bird, it spends most of its time perched in a tree watching for its prey, which consists of frogs, crayfish, large insects, and small mammals. Although its sluggish habits make it inconspicuous and hard to find, it is quite tame, and once a bird is discovered it is usually easy to get a good look at it.

Broad-winged hawk

The broad-winged hawk nests in the deciduous forests of the eastern United States and southern Canada, and migrates southward in the fall down the ridges of the Appalachians. In October, when the wind is out of the northwest, thousands may pass a well-known lookout like Hawk Mountain in eastern Pennsylvania in a single day. The birds often travel in a huge wheeling flock, known to hawk watchers as a "kettle."

Cooper's hawk

With its short, rounded wings and long, narrow tail, Cooper's hawk is adept at twisting and darting through the branches of trees in pursuit of small birds, which are its chief prey. During the 1960s and early 1970s, when much attention was paid to the decline of the bald eagle, osprey, and peregrine falcon because of pesticides, the decline of Cooper's hawk received little notice. Because it nests in forests and is easy to confuse with the smaller sharp-shinned hawk, keeping track of changes in its numbers is all but impossible.

Goshawk

Goshawk

Broad-winged hawk

Black hawk

Cooper's hawk

Ferruginous hawk

The ferruginous hawk will nest in trees where available, but in most of the species' breeding range, in the drier parts of the northern Great Plains, nests are built on a low bush, on the ground, or on a ledge. A nest is used year after year and in time becomes as large as that of a golden eagle. As with many of our hawks, the female spends most of her time with the young, and the male brings food both to the young and to his mate.

Gray hawk

This small hawk is found along the Mexican border, where it inhabits scattered groves of trees and river-bottom woodland and feeds mainly on lizards and snakes. Like the red-shouldered hawk, this species is very noisy during the nesting season, when territories and pair bonds are being established.

Harris' hawk

An adaptable predator, Harris' hawk preys on small mammals, birds, and reptiles, and occasionally feeds on carrion. It nests in the southwestern United States but is very local in distribution; large areas of seemingly good habitat are unoccupied. Where the birds are present, however, they are usually easy to find, and their nests are often conspicuous, especially when they are built in tall saguaro cacti.

Ferruginous hawk

Gray hawk

Gray hawk, immature

Harris' hawk

Ferruginous hawk

Ferruginous hawk

Marsh hawk
Instead of watching for its prey from a perch, the marsh hawk hunts by cruising over marshes and grasslands, dropping suddenly on small mammals, birds, snakes, and frogs. It has large ear openings for a hawk, and the ears are surrounded by owl-like disks of feathers; these adaptations probably help the birds to hear mice squeaking and rustling in the grass.

Red-shouldered hawk
During most of the year, red-shouldered hawks are quiet birds, watching for frogs, mice, and large insects in swampy woods and forested riverbanks. But the birds' whereabouts are no secret early in the nesting season, when a pair performs conspicuous circling flights, accompanied by loud screaming, over their territory.

Marsh hawk, female

Marsh hawk

Red-shouldered hawk

Red-shouldered hawk, chick

Red-tailed hawk

The best-known and most widespread of the larger North American raptors, the red-tailed hawk nests from Alaska to Panama. It is mainly a bird of open country and farmland, where it preys on mammals and small birds. Although a typical red-tail has a dark brown back, a white breast streaked with brown, and a bright rufous tail, there is a dark phase in which the bird is wholly dark brown, as well as several gradations between these two extremes.

Red-tailed (Harlan's) hawk

Some of the red-tailed hawks that nest in British Columbia and Alberta, and winter on the southern plains, are dark brown with dull whitish marbling on the tail. For many years these birds were thought to be a separate species, named after a naturalist friend of Audubon's, but since they do not have a distinct breeding range of their own and mate with typical red-tails, they must be considered yet another of the many color variations of the red-tailed hawk.

Rough-legged hawk

The rough-legged hawk is a bird of open country, nesting on the Arctic tundra in Eurasia and North America, and spending the winter on prairies and fields as far south as Virginia and California in the New World. Living in a habitat where there are no trees to perch in, the rough-leg often surveys the ground while hovering, a habit by which it can be identified at great distances. It lives almost entirely on small mammals.

Sharp-shinned hawk

These swift and agile predators feed almost entirely on small birds, which they carefully pluck before eating. They have not been affected by pesticides, unlike their larger relatives the Cooper's hawks, and they are still among our most abundant birds of prey.

Short-tailed hawk

Only a small number of short-tailed hawks live in the cypress swamps and mangroves of southern Florida, separated by hundreds of miles from the rest of the species' range, which extends from Mexico south to Argentina. Thousands of years ago, when tropical forest covered parts of the southeastern United States, this species must have been more widespread, but when the climate grew colder again and tropical conditions withdrew, the short-tailed hawks withdrew too and became stranded in Florida.

Red-tailed (Harlan's) hawk

Red-tailed hawk

Short-tailed hawk

Red-tailed hawk

Sharp-shinned hawk

Sharp-shinned hawk

Rough-legged hawk

Rough-legged hawk

Swainson's hawk
This medium-sized hawk of the open plains is a social bird, gathering into large flocks during migration and feeding in groups on the wintering grounds in Argentina. Swainson's hawk has light and dark color phases, just as the red-tail does; distinguishing between the dark phases of these two species can be very difficult.

White-tailed hawk
This large hawk, unmistakable with its white tail, is a tropical American species that occurs in the United States only in southern Texas, where it nests in isolated trees on the coastal prairie. Although it feeds readily on insects, it will take animals as large as rabbits if these are available. It searches for food by watching from an exposed perch or by hovering.

Zone-tailed hawk
With its narrow wings and tail, this large, swift-flying hawk of the southwestern United States resembles a turkey vulture in outline and sometimes cruises along with its wings slightly uptilted, making the resemblance even stronger. It has recently been suggested that this similarity serves a useful purpose, enabling the bird to approach its prey without evoking fear.

Swainson's hawk

Swainson's hawk, dark phase

Swainson's hawk

Zone-tailed hawk

White-tailed hawk

Everglade kite
Mainly a tropical American species, the everglade kite has a precarious foothold in southern Florida, where it nests in freshwater marshes and feeds entirely on large snails of the genus Pomacea. *Like any specialized bird with a small range, Florida's everglade kites have their ups and downs. A few years ago there were so few left that it seemed certain extinction was only a matter of time, but recently they have staged a comeback, and one year in the late 1970s over 100 young birds were fledged.*

Mississippi kite
Although most small birds recognize hawks and seek cover when one appears, they show no fear of the gentle Mississippi kite, which feeds almost entirely on large insects. Since insect life is scarce in the winter, even in the southern United States where these birds nest, the Mississippi kite is highly migratory, heading south in early fall and wintering in the American tropics.

Swallow-tailed kite
The graceful swallow-tailed kite is the most aerial of our birds of prey, even gathering nesting material while in flight and drinking by skimming over the surface of a pond like a swallow or swift. Although it once nested throughout the southeastern states and north in the Mississippi valley as far as Minnesota, it is very intolerant of civilization; only a few pairs now nest in southern swamplands.

White-tailed kite
No North American bird has responded to protection more dramatically than this delicate bird of southern grasslands and savannas. All but exterminated by the middle of the 20th century and nesting only in southern California and perhaps in southern Texas, the species has now extended its range to include nearly every county in California and re-established itself in Texas, and it appears more and more frequently along the Gulf coast.

Everglade kite

Mississippi kite

Swallow-tailed kite

White-tailed kite

HERON FAMILY

American bittern

This shy heron spends most of its time stalking its prey in dense marshes of cattails and bulrushes, where its brown, streaked plumage makes it difficult to see. In spring, its loud, 3-syllable call, often written "pump-er-lunk," is a characteristic sound in its marshland habitat. The last syllable is the loudest and often carries for as much as half a mile, sounding like someone driving a stake into the ground.

Least bittern

This tiny, marsh-dwelling heron is even more secretive than its larger relative the American bittern. When danger threatens, both species of bitterns freeze, with the neck outstretched and the bill pointed skyward, swaying in imitation of wind-blown cattails. Even nestling least bitterns, still covered with down, adopt this posture when someone approaches the nest.

American bittern

Least bittern

Least bittern, nestlings

Cattle egret
Once confined to the Old World tropics, the cattle egret has undergone an enormous range expansion in this century. After crossing the Atlantic, cattle egrets began nesting in northern South America in the 1930s and colonized North America during the 1950s. At the same time, the species has spread eastward in the Old World to Australia. In all these places the birds usually feed by following cattle and picking up insects disturbed by the grazing animals.

Great egret
The snow-white plumage of the great egret is visible at great distances over open marshland. When a few birds discover a good supply of food, perhaps a large school of minnows feeding in the shallows, other egrets feeding farther away are quick to take notice, and soon dozens of egrets, as well as other species of herons, may be seen feeding in a dense flock. The great egret is one of the most widespread of herons, nesting in tropical and warm temperate areas around the globe.

Reddish egret
Reddish egrets breed in several widely scattered places on the Gulf coast, in the Caribbean, and on the west coast of Mexico. Such a broken and patchy distribution is usually an indication of a species in decline, and indeed the reddish egret seems never to have been an abundant bird, even before its numbers were reduced by plume hunters. The two color phases vary in proportions in different parts of the species' range; in Texas nearly all the birds are dark, while in the Bahamas a majority are white.

Snowy egret
Early in this century, the delicate snowy egret was reduced nearly to extinction in North America by plume hunters who sought the lacy plumes, or aigrettes, for the millinery trade. Now a protected species like all our herons, snowy egrets are again common in the warmer parts of the United States. Snowy egrets often find food by sprinting about in shallow water, causing small fish to dart out from concealment. The bright yellow toes, when raked slowly through the water, are believed to attract fish.

Great egret

Cattle egret

Snowy egret

Reddish egret, dark and white phases

Great blue heron

Although occasionally found feeding in loose flocks, the great blue heron is usually a solitary hunter. As much as two thirds of its diet consists of fish, but it also takes a wide variety of other aquatic animals, as well as land-dwelling rodents and snakes. Moreover, both John James Audubon and Alexander Wilson reported that these birds eat the seeds of water lilies.

Black-crowned night heron

At sunset, when most herons are flying toward their roosting places, the black-crowned night herons are leaving the trees where they have spent the day and scattering over the marshes to feed. By foraging at night, these birds avoid competition with other herons. Probably the most abundant heron in the world, the black-crowned night heron nests on every continent except Australia, where its place is taken by a closely related species.

Great blue heron, white phase

Great blue heron

Black-crowned night heron, immature

Black-crowned night heron

Green heron

The green heron is a shy bird, often skulking like a bittern among the weeds at the edge of a pond or in marshes. Unlike most herons it usually nests singly rather than in colonies; the nest is a shallow platform of sticks in a bush or small tree, usually over water. When surprised, green herons start up from the ground uttering a loud "skeow" and fly off with their orange legs dangling behind them.

Little blue heron

Little blue herons spend the day feeding singly or in small flocks containing both all-dark adults and younger birds with varying amounts of white in their plumage. Nearly pure white when it leaves the nest, a young little blue takes 2 years and several molts to acquire the dark plumage of the adult bird. Older immatures have irregular patches of white feathers, and an observer can quickly learn to recognize each individual by its distinctive, blotchy pattern.

Green heron

Little blue heron

Little blue heron, immature

Little blue heron, nestlings

Louisiana heron
The small, slender Louisiana heron is found from the southern United States to northern South America. Throughout its range it prefers coastal marshes, where it stalks its prey in tidal channels and lagoons, often wading in water so deep that the bird appears to be swimming. Since it has no spectacular plumes, this species was spared by the plume hunters early in this century, and today it is the most abundant heron in the marshes of the southeastern United States.

Yellow-crowned night heron
The elegant yellow-crowned night heron nests in large colonies in the southern states and usually in smaller groups or even isolated pairs in the north. Nests are very hard to find in the dense foliage of trees, and the birds have a habit of slipping quietly away from the colony when an intruder approaches. As a result little is known about the nesting behavior of the species.

Yellow-crowned night heron

Louisiana heron

Louisiana heron

HUMMINGBIRD FAMILY

Allen's hummingbird
Allen's hummingbird is almost entirely confined as a breeding bird to the mountains along the Pacific coast of California. Here, during the nesting season, the males occupy small territories on wooded hillsides, driving away any other bird that encroaches upon this little plot of land. Even large hawks and falcons are no match for these fierce little hummingbirds. When nesting is completed, most Allen's hummingbirds fly nonstop to central Mexico for the winter.

Anna's hummingbird
Anna's hummingbird is most numerous in the Coast ranges of California, where it prefers dry, brush-covered hillsides. In this habitat it is virtually the only nesting hummingbird, and so it does not have to compete with other species for the limited supply of food. Unlike most of our hummingbirds, this species remains in the United States during the winter. The majority stay in California, but a few cross over the mountains to winter in southern Arizona. Anna's hummingbird is named after the Duchess Anna Massena (1806–1896), wife of the Duke of Rivoli, for whom Rivoli's hummingbird was named.

Black-chinned hummingbird
The black-chinned hummingbird is found throughout most of the western United States but is most abundant in the Southwest, where it is perhaps the commonest hummingbird, nesting in backyards and suburban areas as well as in streamside thickets and wooded canyons. The high population of hummingbirds in these habitats imposes a heavy burden on the food supply — nectar and small insects in flowers — and so during the nesting season the males move away from the breeding areas, leaving the available food for the females and growing young.

Blue-throated hummingbird
In the mountain forests along the Mexican border, the blue-throated hummingbird has very exacting habitat requirements. A nesting site must be sheltered from both rain and sunlight, must offer an abundance of flowers for feeding, and must be within a few feet of a stream. Such favored places are scarce in these desert ranges, and once the birds find one they return to it year after year, even building a new nest on top of the previous year's old one.

Allen's hummingbird

Allen's hummingbird

Anna's hummingbird, female

Anna's hummingbird

Black-chinned hummingbird

Blue-throated hummingbird, female

Blue-throated hummingbird

Broad-billed hummingbird

The broad-billed hummingbird is a Mexican species whose range barely enters the United States in southeastern Arizona. These birds are usually found in stands of sycamore and mesquite in the lower reaches of canyons. They also visit gardens and residential areas, but being quiet and retiring birds, they are more easily overlooked than larger and noisier relatives such as the blue-throated and Rivoli's hummingbirds. The broad bill from which the species gets its name is evidently an adaptation for capturing and swallowing insects, which form a larger part of the diet than in most other hummingbirds.

Broad-tailed hummingbird

The broad-tailed hummingbird is a common summer visitor to the mountains of the western United States, nesting in forests of spruce and fir. Here a characteristic sound of mid-summer is the loud, shrill whistle produced by the wings of the male as he darts through the cool coniferous forests. Several mountain wildflowers that bloom in summer depend upon these birds' visits for pollination; among them are columbine, salvia, and the brilliant red Indian paintbrush.

Buff-bellied hummingbird

Once a common nesting species in 4 counties along the Rio Grande in southern Texas, this Mexican hummingbird has largely disappeared north of the border as a result of habitat destruction and the spraying of insecticides. Thickets and tangled vines along the banks of streams and around the edges of ponds are the preferred habitat, but as one recent authority stated, nowadays one must go south into Mexico to be sure of seeing a buff-bellied hummingbird.

Calliope hummingbird

Our smallest hummingbird, the calliope nests in cool mountain forests from southern Canada to Baja California and New Mexico. At the high elevations in which it nests, the night-time temperature often plunges to near freezing. Many hummingbirds, when faced with such cold nights, are able to lower their own body temperature and become torpid in order to conserve energy. But an incubating female calliope hummingbird must maintain a normal body temperature to keep its eggs warm. To make this task easier, the female builds a thick-walled, well-insulated nest and usually places it under an overhanging branch so that little heat is lost to the cold night sky.

Calliope hummingbird, female

Calliope hummingbird

Broad-tailed hummingbird

Broad-tailed hummingbird, female

Broad-billed hummingbird

Buff-bellied hummingbird

Broad-billed hummingbird, female

Costa's hummingbird

Next to the calliope our smallest hummingbird, this species is common in the deserts of the Southwest. As in other hummingbirds, the males take no interest in nesting activities. In fact, many of them leave the breeding grounds in June, when the females are still incubating eggs.

Rivoli's hummingbird

This is the largest North American hummingbird, and its wingbeat is correspondingly slower than that of our smaller species. Rivoli's hummingbird often glides on stiff wings down a hillside, its flight resembling that of a swift. In late summer, the bright-red salvia comes into bloom in the desert mountains; the hummingbirds spend much of their time feeding at these flowers, and soon acquire a conspicuous patch of yellow pollen on the forehead. This hummingbird was named for Prince Francis Victor Massena, Duke of Rivoli (1795–1863), who assembled a large collection of birds, among them many rare hummingbirds.

Ruby-throated hummingbird

From the Atlantic coast to the edge of the Great Plains, the ruby-throated hummingbird is a well-known summer resident and the only member of its family. It feeds on a great variety of flowers, but shows a preference for the color red. A few wildflowers, like trumpetvine and cardinal lobelia, have bright red, tubular flowers, so deep that only the hummingbird can reach their nectar; these plants depend on hummingbirds for pollination. Despite its small size, the ruby-throat is a powerful flier; many fly nonstop across the Gulf of Mexico during migration.

Rufous hummingbird

The breeding range of the rufous hummingbird extends to the coast of southern Alaska, farther north than that of any other hummingbird. At these northern latitudes the nest is built close to the ground where it is sheltered from the wind and cold. In favorable places with plenty of flowers and good nesting sites, several females may nest close together, with small adjoining territories.

Violet-crowned hummingbird

The violet-crowned hummingbird was unknown as a breeding bird in the United States until 1959, when a nesting pair was found in Guadalupe Canyon, Arizona. Since then, the species has spread to a few nearby mountain ranges, but it is still one of our rarest hummingbirds. The violet-crown is unusual among our hummingbirds in that the female wears the same bright colors as the male. The favorite habitat is a grove of sycamores along a stream in a desert canyon.

Costa's hummingbird, female

Costa's hummingbird

Violet-crowned hummingbird

Ruby-throated hummingbird

Rufous hummingbird, female

Rufous hummingbird

Rivoli's hummingbird

White-eared hummingbird

White-eared hummingbird
This Mexican and Central American species is a casual visitor to the mountains of southeastern Arizona and western Texas, where it is most likely to be seen during the summer months. It feeds at tubular flowers like those of salvia. In an experiment in Mexico, small vials of tinted sugar water were hung in an area where several hummingbird species were feeding at a variety of flowers. The white-eared hummingbirds invariably chose vials containing sugar water dyed blue—the same color as the big blue Mexican salvias they were visiting in the surrounding countryside.

It was about 6 ft. long, apparently flightless, and in form and habits much like a loon of today. Marsh dug it from the chalk beds of the Cretaceous in the marine Niobrara formation of what had been an ancient sea (Romer, 1945).

Later, three more species of *Hesperornis* were discovered. Of the four known to paleontologists from N. America, all were from the Upper Cretaceous Period—three found in Kans., one in Mont. Wetmore (1956) classified all species of *Hesperornis* in a superorder, Odontognathae (oh-don-TOG-nah-thee), or New World Toothed Birds. *See* Baptornis; Ichthyornis; Geological Time Scale.

HETERAKIASIS
(het-er-ah-KIE-ah-sis). Name by Wehr (1971) for a disease caused by some of the nematodal (*see* Nematode) worms of the genus *Heterakis* that are internal parasites of wild birds and parasitize the caeca and sometimes the small intestine. *Heterakis gallinarum* is a well-known parasite of domestic chickens and, rarely, of geese and ducks. Its chief significance to birds lies in its role as a carrier of the organism *Histomonas meleagridis*, which causes the disease in birds called blackhead. See Blackhead. The *Heterakis* worms cause gastric disturbances, anorexia, diarrhea, and emaciation in infected birds; they occur in many species of wild birds but infections are usually light and no signs of severe illness have been reported (Wehr, 1971).

HETEROCHROSIS
(het-er-oh-CROW-sis); from Gr. *heteros*, a combining form signifying something other than usual, or different, and *chrosis*, coloring. Term in zoology for abnormal coloration of animals. In ornithology the term is used for color variations in the plumage of birds (Sage, 1962). *See* Abnormal Colors under Colors of Feathers.

HETERODACTYLOUS
(het-er-oh-DAK-tih-lus). Having the toes in pairs with the first and second toes turned backward as in the trogons. *See* zygodactylous under Feet and Legs.

HETEROSEXUAL BEHAVIOR
Showing sexual desire for one of opposite sex is a normal condition in birds; however, *see* aberrations in sexual behavior under Sexual Relationships.

HIBERNATION
State or condition of an animal that is in a deep torpor ("winter sleep"), with its metabolism (*see* Metabolism) and body temperature lowered, its heartbeat slowed, and breathing movements few and irregular (Bourliere, 1964). Some individuals are known to go into a deep torpor during the winter, induced by lack of food in cool or cold weather. *See* discussion under Torpidity.

In early times, when certain birds, such as swallows, disappeared overnight in fall on their migrations, people believed that they had hidden in caves and hollow trees or had buried themselves in the mud of marshes or in the bottoms of ponds and streams to sleep through the winter just as frogs do. The theory of hiber-

nation in birds was first expressed in the 4th century B.C. in the writings of Aristotle, who declared that the kite, swallow, stork, ouzel, turtledove, lark, and many other species became torpid in winter (Wetmore, 1926). *See* Folklore; Migration.

HICKORY-HEAD
Another name for the ruddy duck, called so by hunters because it is said to be tough and difficult to kill. *See* in Duck Family.

HIERARCHY
(HIGH-er-are-kih). In the classification of birds and other animals, a system of ranks, from kingdom to species, which indicates the taxonomic position of the various classification categories (Mayr *et al.*, 1953). *See* Classification.

In bird behavior the term relates to an order of dominance between individual birds. *See* Social Order among Birds under Behavior. *See also* accounts of dominance between sexes under Courtship, and under Dominance.

HIGH-HOLDER
or HIGH-HOLE. British folk names for the green woodpecker from its laughing notes, applied by early British colonists in America to the red-shafted and yellow-shafted flickers (McAtee, 1957a). *See* Flicker, common, in Woodpecker Family.

HIJACKING
See Behavior; *also* Autolycism; Commensalism.

HIND TOE
See Hallux.

HIPPOBOSCID FLIES
(hip-oh-BOS-sid); from a combining form of Gr. *hippos*, horse, and *boskein*, to feed; in reference to an Old World species which sucks the blood of horses. The most highly specialized, or host-attendant, of all flies that parasitize birds (Rothschild and Clay, 1957). The adults live permanently on the bodies of birds and mammals, and both males and females suck blood from their hosts by using their highly specialized mouth parts.

In their choice of a host, the hippoboscid flies are divided into two groups—those that live specifically on birds and those that live on mammals. A bird-fly will not stay permanently on a mammal; nor will a mammal-fly stay long on a bird. Among insects, the female hippoboscid flies are remarkable in that they give birth to a single offspring. After the fertilized egg hatches within the female's body, the larva is nourished for a time by her special "milk glands" until it has achieved its growth and is ready to pupate. Except for two families of small flies parasitic on bats, and the s. African tsetse (TSET-see) flies, to which the hippoboscid flies are related, the female's manner of incubating the young larvae within her body is unknown at present in any other insect (Bequaert, 1953).

Called variously around the world bird-flies, feather-flies, flat-flies, ked-flies, louse-flies, spider-flies, and tick-flies; the depressed, or flattened, thorax, more than any other feature,

Ornithonyia avicularia

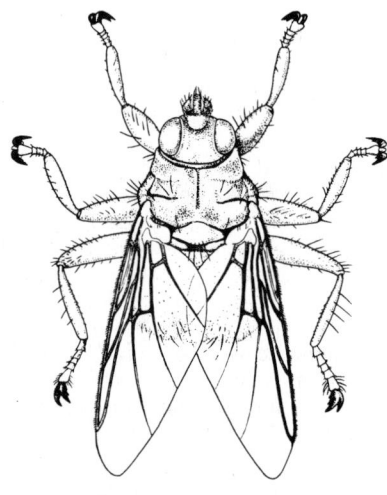

HIPPOBOSCID FLY
Hippoboscid flies are common ectoparasites of birds, living permanently in the plumage and sucking blood with specialized mouth parts. In severe infestations, flies may transmit blood diseases and feather parasites to the host.

gives the hippoboscids their characteristic louselike, or ticklike, appearance.

The bird-flies, of which some 90 species are known to parasitize birds, are large in relation to the body size of a small bird. Any harmful effect of the blood-taking of these flies from their hosts depends on their numbers. True parasitism is strictly a one-sided relation from which only the parasite benefits. *See* Parasite. However, it is necessary for the welfare of the parasite itself that it must not endanger the survival of its host species, or reduce them to the point where future generations of the parasite will no longer have a reasonable chance of reaching the proper host. Bequaert believes that the hippoboscid flies have "solved" this delicate problem of adjustment "to the point of perfection" (Bequaert, 1953). Their low birth rate, for example, results in a generally low density and frequency of their populations, especially in the bird-flies. With many of these, their numbers on a wild bird may be so light that the blood taken from the bird may be negligible.

The numbers of bird-flies found on birds vary considerably; large birds with their larger body size and greater supply of blood are often more heavily infested with hippoboscid flies than smaller ones. Bird-banders in particular (*see* Banding) have reported the numbers and kinds taken from trapped wild birds. At Demarest, N.J., during 1950, B. S. Bowdish found from one to four of a common bird-fly, the finch louse-fly *Ornithomyia fringillina*, on each of 37 songbirds of 13 species—31 had only one fly, 4 had two flies each, and 2 had four. In Ontario, Canada, C. H. D. Clarke took four of these flies from a young evening grosbeak being fed by its mother. *Ornithomyia fringillina* has been found on 104 species of N. American birds, and it seems to prefer some songbirds to others— for example, cowbirds and red-winged blackbirds (Bequaert, 1953).

Besides subsisting on birds' blood, there are other consequences of the bite of a hippoboscid fly. Although the bite itself may not be especially painful or harmful (it may cause a slight bruise or redness and itching), a concentration of blood-sucking bird-flies on the head of a mockingbird in Calif. caused the bird to lose most of its head feathers (Bequaert, 1953). Far more serious to a bird's health may be the effects of certain blood parasites carried by the bird-flies. These are transmitted from the blood of one bird to another by the bites. According to Herman (1955), some of the blood parasites, called *Haemoproteus*, cause a serious malaria-like disease in domestic pigeons and in California quail. *See also* Internal Parasites under Diseases. Herman reported that the hippoboscid flies may also be involved in transmitting other parasitic diseases from bird to bird.

In addition, bird-flies often carry on the outside of their bodies other insect parasites that feed on the feathers of birds. These hitchhikers are *Mallophaga*, the feather-lice of birds, and their method of getting transported by an insect to other bird hosts is called *phoresy*. *See* Phoresy. Each bird-fly usually carries one or two of the bird feather-lice on its body; exceptionally there may be a dozen or more. *See also* Fleas; Lice; Protocalliphora; Ectoparasite.

HISTOPLASMOSIS

(HISS-toh-plaz-MOH-sis). Name for a respiratory disease caused by the airborne spores of a fungus, *Histoplasma capsulatum*, which exists as a saprophyte (lives on dead or decaying organic matter) in the soil. *Histoplasma capsulatum* lives in suitable soil habitats around the world, from about 45° N. Lat. to 45° S. Lat. People breathing air containing the spores of this fungus may become infected, and the most frequent infections in the U.S. are among persons living in humid, rural regions of the Ohio and Mississippi valleys, especially in Ark., Ind., Kans., Ky., Miss., Mo., Ohio, Okla., Tenn., and Tex. (Ajello, 1967).

The fungus does not grow haphazardly in the ground but appears to thrive best on acid soils enriched with the droppings of chickens, grackles, pigeons, and starlings, also in caves in Peru, Venezuela, and Trinidad frequented by oilbirds. Birds are resistant or immune to the infection, and in chickens it was discovered that the fungus is rapidly destroyed in their tissues. Investigators believe that the high body temperature of birds (about 42° C.) prevents the growth of the fungus.

Birds themselves are not carriers of the fungus. According to Dr. Libero Ajello (1975), Director, Mycology Division, Department of Health, Education, and Welfare, Atlanta, Ga., there is no evidence that birds help disseminate the fungus from one site to another, and not all birds' roosts harbor the fungus. Soil enriched with the feces of grackles, red-winged blackbirds, and starlings, for reasons not fully known, give the fungus a competitive growth advantage over the myriads of other soil fungi; poultry farms, with accumulated chicken droppings, are important reservoirs of the fungus; also, sawdust, decayed wood, chicken feathers, and coal dust contaminated with the fungus are sources of infection (Selby, 1975).

Histoplasmosis is not a contagious disease; it is not known to be transmitted from person to person or from birds or other animals to man. Soil containing the fungus, including garden soils, is the primary source of all infections. After the soil inhabited by *Histoplasma capsulatum* dries, the spores of the fungus, scattered by air currents, grow again in suitable soil habitats or infect susceptible persons who happen to inhale the spores (Ajello, 1968).

About 90% of people infected do not show apparent symptoms; the disease is discovered by giving them skin tests with an antigen, histoplasmin, and serological tests; the remaining 10% of infected persons develop what appear to be colds and other viral respiratory ailments, and most clear up spontaneously (Ajello, 1975). Individuals with severe infections will require hospitalization and treatment with a few specific antifungal agents, of which amphotericin B seems the best. See Long (1966). Histoplasmosis, compared with human mortality from other diseases, is basically benign, with an average of about 60 fatal cases yearly in the U.S. over a 10-year period (see Ajello, 1967; 1975). See especially details in Selby (1975).

In Jan. 1975, the Department of the Army filed a *Final Environmental Impact Statement: Blackbird Control on Two Army Installations*, in which it discussed a proposed method for controlling large roosts of black-birds overwintering at Fort Campbell, Ky., Military Reservation, and at Milan, Tenn., Army Ammunition Plant (AAP). The proposed method of control, or reduction, of the black-bird population was application at night by air-craft of an Avian Stressing Agent, PA-14, to the overwintering roosts of an estimated 4 to 5 million birds at Fort Campbell and an additional estimated 7 to 8 million birds roosting at Milan. Each roost, in dense groves of pines, many of which were planted by the Army, averaged an estimated 1 million or more birds. The stress-ing, or wetting, agent, a surfactant, when sprayed on the roosting birds, robs them of their body or feather oils. When the application is accompanied by rain, or followed by a water spray from fire engines used for the purpose, at air temperatures below 45°F., the wet birds go into a coma from shock, after which they freeze to death.

The proposed destruction of the overwinter-ing "blackbirds"—grackles, red-winged black-birds, cowbirds, and starlings—was mainly to eliminate the threat to the personnel of the mili-tary installations and to citizens of the sur-rounding towns or cities. The control program was also proposed because large flocks of birds, entering the roosts in the evening, or leaving them in the morning, were a potential threat to aircraft arriving and departing from a military and a civilian airfield, especially in the Fort Campbell area. See Aircraft and Birds.

On the night of Feb. 19, 1975, the 101st Air-borne Division at Fort Campbell used helicopters to spray the blackbird roosts, with a result-ing "kill" of about 500,000 birds. See one news account of this spray operation by King (1975). The method of control was strongly protested by conservation organizations and by humane societies. Most of the organizations, biologists, and other critics of the control program be-lieved that thinning of the pine plantations (which would have made the roosts unattrac-tive to the birds) might have made the contro-versial spraying program unnecessary. See es-pecially discussions by Graham (1976); Jackson (1976). See a review of the subject, including protest letters and suggestions from individu-als or groups, and replies of the Army to its critics, in *Supplement to the Environmental Impact Statement: Blackbird Control at Two Army Installations*, Aug. 1975, published by the Department of the Army, Washington, D.C. See other methods of control discussed under Control.

HISTORY
(of American ornithology). *See* Ornithology.

HOARDING
See Birds That Store Food under Food and Feeding Habits.

HOATZIN
(hoe-AT-sin). *See* account of especially under Cuculiformes; *see also* Galliformes and under Crop.

HOBBY
See Falcon, aplomado, in Falcon Family.

HOLARCTIC (holl-ARK-tick) REGION
Combines the northern regions of the Old and New Worlds—the Palaearctic (northern Old World) and the Nearctic (northern N. America) regions. *See* Faunal Regions. In 1887, the zoo-geographer A. Heilprin combined these two be-cause of the similarity of their faunas, and called it the Holarctic.

Some of the birds confined in the breeding season to the Holarctic around the northern regions of the world are the common puffin, northern and red phalaropes, northern fulmar, oldsquaw (duck), red-throated loon, snow bun-ting, willow ptarmigan, red crossbill, Bohemian waxwing, and red knot. See Udvardy (1958) for detailed comparisons of the bird life of the Nearctic and Palaearctic regions.

HOLBOELL
CARL PETER (1795–1856). A lieutenant in Danish Royal Navy in 1821; later, while gover-nor of South Greenland, became greatly inter-ested in natural history; named and described several birds (see Palmer, 1928); his name is commemorated in a subspecies of the red-necked grebe, formerly called Holboell's grebe.

HOLE-NESTERS
See Nests and Nesting.

HOME
Has been defined by ornithologists as the place or general area where a bird builds its nest and raises its young. Many N. American birds are sedentary—that is, spend all year within the general breeding or nesting range—cardinal, tufted titmouse, bobwhite quail, pheasant, for example; many others, such as swifts, swal-lows, and a host of other insect-eating birds, migrate and leave the nesting range at the end of summer to winter either in s. U.S. or a coun-try or region south of the U.S.—Mexico, C. and S. America, the West Indies, etc. *See* in the biography of each bird under Range; *also* under Migration. Dorst (1962) calls the breed-ing, or nesting, area "home." *See* Habitat.

A bird's home is different from its *ancestral* home, which is the place or region from which its kind, or race, originated before its gradual dispersal and present-day distribution. *See* Dis-tribution; *also* Homing.

HOME LIFE
See in biography of each bird, especially that of the tufted titmouse in Titmouse Family. *See also* Courtship; Nests and Nesting; Eggs and Egg-laying; Food and Feeding Habits; Young and Their Care.

HOMES FOR BIRDS
See Bird-attracting.

HOMING
Term for the return of a bird either from a relatively short distance (for example, up to 50 or 100 mi. or more) or from a long distance (thousands of miles) to its home, or nesting place. Some authorities make no distinction be-tween homing and migration; usually, how-ever, others see "homing" as applied to local or relatively short returns to the home or nest site; the term "migration" to the generally

longer and *seasonal* exodus and return by those birds that migrate (*see* Migration) and, often (with young birds making their first mi-gration), a journey to an unknown place.

According to Mayr (1937), homing is a return to a known goal. "Homing is a return to a place already familiar" (Rowan, 1931). Domestic, or "homing," pigeons (*see* Rock dove in Pigeon Family), which are not migratory, are best known of all birds that "home"; some have been trained to return to their lofts from a few hundred up to or more than 1,000 mi. by taking them gradually farther and farther away and then releasing them. *See* discussion of recent experiments to discover cues used by pigeons in homing under Migration. See Watson and Lashley (1915) for interesting history of some experiments; also Allen (1925). *See* accounts of the use of pigeons in carrying messages in war-time under Domestication.

Among wild birds, frigatebirds were used for centuries for sending messages from island to island among natives of the South Seas, who knew the frigatebird's homing ability. *See* Frigatebird Family. In ancient times, Romans, who knew of the homing ability of migratory swallows, took adults from the nest, then took them to sports events. There they were color-marked to indicate winners and released to carry the "news" back home.

The modern interest in bird migration led to scientific investigations of the homing of birds in order to try to discover what faculties birds use to find their way back to the nest. Early in this century, Watson and Lashley made some of the first serious experiments in homing with two kinds of seabirds—noddies and sooty terns at their nesting places on the Dry Tortugas off the coast of Fla. (see Watson, 1908; Watson and Lashley, 1915). Two of the sooty terns, carried on a ship north along the Atlantic coast, were released off Cape Hatteras, N.C., about 850 air mi. from the Dry Tortugas; they returned to their nests almost 6 days later; in another ex-periment, five sooty terns and three noddies, also taken by boat from their nesting places, returned from 585 mi. These experiments confirmed the remarkable homing faculties of seabirds. Many of them, including young birds of the year, leave their home islands after the nesting season and scatter during the winter over thousands of miles of open ocean. By the beginning of the next breeding season, they are back on their relatively tiny nesting spots in the wide expanse of the seas. *See also* travels of banded sooty terns in its biography in Gull Family; and account of the remarkable exam-ple of homing from 3,200 statute mi. away of a Manx shearwater in Shearwater Family; *see also* Migration.

Leach's petrel (*see* in Storm-petrel Family), another seabird, finds its way to its nesting place on land through darkness and fog in which vision apparently plays no part (*see also* account under Smell). Each Leach's petrel spends 3–4 days at sea, then returns, regard-less of weather, to relieve its mate incubating the eggs during that time. In homing experi-ments with these birds, Griffin (1940) took Leach's petrels from their nesting burrows near the Bay of Fundy and carried them 65 and up to 710 mi. away. After their release, most of

Bananaquit

HONEYCREEPER FAMILY

HOOD
The black hood of the male hooded warbler contrasts sharply with its yellow face and breast.

them returned to their nests, some from distances of 360 and 470 mi., in a direct line and even over land if necessary; some traveled 65 mi. a day; others 100. Shorebirds too have a strong homing sense: some semipalmated sandpipers, paired and nesting at Barrow, Alaska, were carried by aircraft 400–600 km. away, were released, and returned to their nests after 6–10 days (Norton, 1971). In experiments with the homing flights of herring gulls, taken various distances from a nesting colony near Mt. Desert Is., Me., and released, Williams *et al.* (1974) discovered that they used visual orientation, or a search for familiar landmarks to reach "home."

Many migratory land birds have a strong homing drive—for example, both male and female cowbirds. Manwell (1962) released 738 cowbirds, banded over more than a decade (*see* Banding) near Fayetteville, N.Y., of which 656 returned to the place of banding prior to 1961. Maximum speed of return was 90 mi. in a day; one that had been carried from Fayetteville to Edinboro, Pa., 275 mi. away, and released, returned in 2 days and 3 nights; another returned to Fayetteville from a distance of more than 87 mi. (from Binghamton, N.Y.).

In an unusual experiment, Wimsatt (1940) caught at her eyrie after dark a female peregrine falcon that was incubating eggs on a cliff near Towanda, Pa. Wimsatt took her immediately to Cornell University, Ithaca, N.Y., 60 mi. away. There he banded the bird and broke one of her primary (flight) feathers so as to recognize her in flight. He released her; he reported that she flew directly to the cliff and arrived there on the day she had been released.

John A. Gillespie (1934), in an early American experiment with the homing of a songbird, caught a male rough-winged swallow at its nest in a drain hole in a concrete bridge near Glenolden, Pa., and took it by automobile to Milford, Del., 32½ mi. away. By the time he had returned to the bird's Glenolden nesting place, it had returned home ahead of him and was helping its mate again in feeding five young birds in the nest.

For long-distance returns to their nesting places, some of the albatrosses are probably the greatest "homers" of all. Kenyon and Rice (1958) reported that of 18 Laysan albatrosses nesting on Midway Is. in the Pacific, and carried by aircraft various distances away to check their homing drive, 14 returned to their nests; one that traveled farthest flew 4,120 statute mi. from its release point in the Philippine Is. to its nest on Midway in 32 days; the fastest return, however, was one that was liberated at Whidby Is., Wash., and flew 3,200 mi. back to its nest in about 10 days, at a rate of 317 mi. a day. *See also* some homing records under Waterfowl.

According to Ralph and Mewaldt (1976), most experiments with the homing of birds have dealt with those carried some distance from their breeding sites and released. Few studies have been made of birds taken from their wintering grounds and released to test their homing, or faithfulness of return, to their wintering territories. In their experiments with golden-crowned sparrows and white-crowned sparrows in Calif., with many of these birds carried some distance from their wintering territories, they verified, as discovered by previous experimenters, that far more *adults* returned to their wintering places, after being carried some distance away, than did first-year birds, or subadults. Other investigators found that displaced wintering first-year gulls showed poorer homing ability than did adults; of northern waterthrushes carried 10–65 km. away from their winter homes in Venezuela, only the adults returned, and of white-crowned sparrows displaced from their winter home one year, more of the adults returned. Adult birds on their wintering grounds have had at least one round trip between nesting and wintering places. Apparently they have gotten more acquainted with the topography of the land over which they migrate and have had more experience in learning the cues that a bird uses in migration.

For a discussion of the theories and conclusions about how birds find their way—orientation—*see* Migration.

HOMING PIGEON
Another name for the domestic pigeon, or rock dove (*see* in Pigeon Family). *See also* Homing; Domestication.

HOMOIOTHERMOUS
(ho-MOY-oh-THUR-mus). "Warm-blooded"; having a relatively uniform body temperature, regardless of the temperature outside the body, as in birds and most mammals, including man. *See* Metabolism; *also* related articles under Temperature; Hibernation; Torpidity.

HOMOLOGOUS
(hoh-MOL-oh-gus). *See* under Analogous.

HOMOSEXUAL BEHAVIOR
See Sexual Relationships.

HONEYCREEPER FAMILY
Coerebidae (see-REE-bih-dee); from Brazilian name for a small creeping bird that may be of this family (Coues, 1884). Only in W. Hemisphere; includes a group of New World tropical birds that act much like American wood warblers—they flit about foliage usually singly or in pairs (Austin, 1961); about 36 species; are not migratory, and their food varies from fruit to flower nectar and insects (Skutch, 1954). For a discussion of the feeding habits of some members of this family—the blue honeycreeper, bananaquits, and the slaty flower-piercer—*see* Nectar and Birds.

Members of the family are small songbirds about 4–5 in. long, and are often seen probing the blossoms of shrubs and trees—they have tongues adapted to this kind of feeding (Bond, 1961).

One species reaches N. America—the bananaquit (formerly called the Bahama honeycreeper); has been reported occasionally in s. Fla. The honeycreepers do not have a common origin. Their similarities apparently are the result of convergence of birds belonging to, and derived from, several families: tanagers, wood warblers, and finches.

In captivity, feed fruit—oranges, bananas, apples, with honey—mealworms and other small insects; if flowers made available they will put bills in them to get nectar; orange and pineapple juice in small tubes might be offered them (Walker, 1942).

Bananaquit, *Coereba flaveola* (see-REB-ah flay-vee-OH-lah); from Lat. *flavus*, yellow, and *-olus* (diminutive), small. 4–5 in. long; black-backed with yellow rump; yellow breast band on white underparts and white stripe over eyes; bill curved, sharply pointed; flash of white feathers in wings and end of tail (Robbins *et al.*, 1966); lives in borders of forests, plantations, open areas in country and towns; song is lisping and wheezy.

Feeding Habits: Probes flowers of trees and shrubs for nectar and insects.
Nest: Mass of leaves and fibers with side entrance; built near end of tree limb and up to about 30 ft. from ground; uses nest throughout year as a roost at night.
Eggs: Mar.–May; 3, white with brown spots.
Incubation: 12–13 days; young fly 15–18 days after hatching. See details in Bent (1950) and Skutch (1954).
Other Names: Bahama honeycreeper; see-see; sugar bird.
Range: Casual in se. Fla., resident on Cozumel, Cayman, and Bahama Is.

Honeycreeper, Bahama. *See* Bananaquit.

HONEY GUIDE
See Autolycism; *also* Piciformes. *See also* Nectar and Birds.

HONKER
See Goose, Canada, in Duck Family.

HONORS IN ORNITHOLOGY
See Medals.

HOOD
Term for head part of bird—collectively the head, nape, chin, and breast—in which the feathers are all of one color that contrasts with rest of the plumage. Some, but not all birds, with hood are named for it—for example, hooded oriole, hooded warbler—but male dark-eyed (Oregon) junco, Connecticut warbler, mourning warbler, and others have hoods. *See* Topography for named parts of birds.

HOODLUM
See House sparrow in Weaverbird Family.

HOOPOE (HOO-poo) FAMILY
See Coraciiformes.

HOPPING AND WALKING
Birds in their progression in trees or over the ground either hop or walk. It is generally believed that the first birds dwelt in trees and moved from branch to branch by hopping. *See* Origin of Birds and of Bird Flight; *also* Fossil Birds.

The structure of the feet of *Archaeopteryx*, an ancient bird of the Jurassic Period (*see* Fossil Birds), indicated that it was adapted to perching in trees and possibly to hopping from branch to branch. According to Storer (1960a), it is almost certain that the earliest passerine, or perching, birds were also arboreal (tree dwellers), and probably moved from branch to branch by hopping as most tree-inhabiting songbirds still do. *See* Passeriformes.

Many years ago, William Beebe (1906), American ornithologist, wrote: "No hard and fast rules can be laid down, but it is generally the rule that birds which are especially at home in trees usually hop with both feet simultaneously when on the ground. Ground nesters and feeders . . . the meadowlark, bob-white, and vesper sparrow, usually walk or run."

During the course of evolution, members of many groups of passerine birds became adapted to spending most of their time on the ground. Larks, pipits, and starlings and, among the icterids, blackbirds and meadowlarks evolved a walking gait better suited to life on the ground (Storer, 1960a). Hopping is more tiring to a bird, as with each hop it must raise its entire body weight, whereas in walking, only one leg is swung forward at a time while the other supports the body (Hess, 1951).

Dilger (1956a) found that five kinds of thrushes, all forest inhabitants feeding largely on the forest floor, moved over the ground in "long springing hops." These were the wood thrush, veery, hermit thrush, Swainson's thrush, and the gray-cheeked thrush.

Dilger suggested that the depth of the debris on the ground over which a bird forages has a bearing on the length of a bird's legs. Apparently, length of legs in birds is an adaptation, through evolution, to their feeding habits. Wading birds such as flamingos, herons, egrets, bitterns, cranes, and many of the shorebirds have long legs adapted for walking in various depths of water and over various types of bottom where they feed (Storer, 1960a). *See* Feet and Legs.

SOME BIRDS THAT HOP. Woodpeckers usually hop or "hitch" their way vertically up the trunks of trees; however, flickers sometimes walk or "waddle" over the open ground where they often feed. *See* Insects and Birds.

The yellow-billed cuckoo and black-billed cuckoo, both tree dwellers, hop, but the ground cuckoo, or roadrunner, walks or runs over the ground of the West and Southwest where it dwells.

Flycatchers, jays, titmice, nuthatches, wrens, most thrushes, and most thrashers hop, as do catbirds, vireos, warblers, house sparrows, and many native American sparrows. Orioles hop, but other members of its family may walk, especially those that habitually forage over the ground of lawns, fields, and meadows—for example, cowbirds, grackles, and meadowlarks. Tanagers, cardinals, grosbeaks, finches, and towhees are some other of the passerine birds that hop. See review by Clark (1975).

SOME BIRDS THAT WALK. Most water birds, or swimming birds (*see* discussion in biography of the razorbill in Auk Family), walk when on land —for example, ducks, geese, and swans; also, hawks, eagles, and vultures walk or "waddle" about clumsily when they are on the ground, but they may hop or leap from branch to branch when they are in trees. William C. Dilger in a personal letter to the author wrote: "Some species always walk, some always hop, and some are quite versatile. I have seen song sparrows hopping in a leaf-littered hedgerow then run across a concrete sidewalk to resume hopping in the opposite hedgerow."

Herons, cranes, rails, and limpkins walk, as do oystercatchers, avocets, stilts, and other shorebirds—the plovers, turnstones, and sandpipers. Grouse, quail, turkeys, and pheasants usually walk; gulls, terns, and skimmers walk on the sandy beaches where they spend much of their time. Owls, just as do other large birds of prey, walk when on the ground. Pigeons and doves also walk, and as Dilger (1956a) has pointed out, some of the passerine birds that have adapted to foraging over the open ground walk—crows, starlings, cowbirds, grackles, meadowlarks, pipits, and the true larks such as the horned larks of N. America.

BIRDS THAT RUN. Most of the land birds that walk also can run. Some birds that hop also can run—for example, robins and mockingbirds that hop when in trees often run when on the ground. See Clark (1975) for review. Birds that are primarily adapted to running or walking are called cursorial, of which there seem to be two principal types, according to Storer (1960a): (1) the large running species, such as the ostrich, which may depend on running to escape its enemies (*see* Running Birds); and (2) the smaller running birds, such as the sanderling. The second type is an adaptation common to shorebirds, especially among those that are cryptically colored and may escape predators by running rapidly for a short distance, then "freezing" to escape detection (Storer, 1960a). *See* Freezing; *also* Colors of Feathers. See also Howell (1944).

HORMONES
(effects on birds). *See* Endocrine Glands.

HORNBILL FAMILY
See Coraciiformes.

HORNEMANN
JENS WILKIN (1770–1841). Danish botanist; appointed professor of botany at the University of Copenhagen in 1808 (Wynne, 1969); Holboell in 1843 gave the specific name of *hornemanni* to the hoary redpoll in his honor (American Ornithologists' Union, 1957).

HOST
or HOST SPECIES. A bird or other animal which is said to act as a "host" (at times, more appropriately, "victim") to a parasite or other organism that lives in or on the bird. *See* Parasite. A host may also be broadly interpreted as a bird from whose food-getting another bird profits. *See* Commensalism. A bird is also called a host when it broods the eggs or raises the young of another bird not of its own kind. *See* Foster Parents; Brood Parasitism.

HOUND
So called from chorus of its cries; suggests baying of hounds. *See* Oldsquaw in Duck Family.

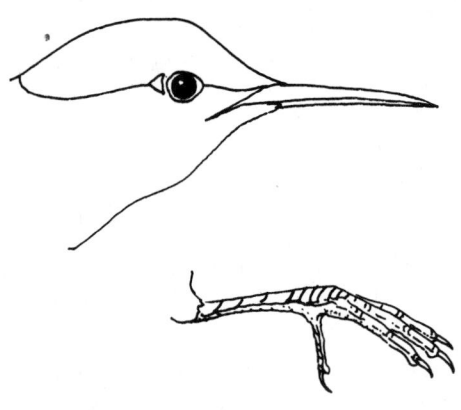

HUMMINGBIRD FAMILY

HOVERING

See Flight; *also* under Hummingbird Family.

HUDSONIAN ZONE

Term for one of the six *life zones* of N. America, each of which is characterized by its plant life and certain birds. Life zones are still relied on by some authorities in mapping, locally, the ecological distribution of N. American birds—the system has advantages and disadvantages. *See* discussion of biomes and life zones under Distribution. According to Pettingill (1970), the Hudsonian Zone corresponds in its plants and birds to an ecotone (*see* Ecotone), or transitional area, between the *Arctic Tundra* (*see* Tundra) and the *Coniferous Forest. See* Tundra–Coniferous Forest Ecotone.

HUMBOLDT'S RULE

In 1850, Alexander von Humboldt pointed out that as one travels from the Equator toward the Poles—either northward or southward—the mean temperature decreases (gets cooler) about one degree of Fahrenheit with each degree of latitude (Humboldt, 1850). This Humboldt's Rule is paralleled by a similar increase (rise) in the mean air temperature with a *loss* of altitude, or in a descent from high mountains to low areas (Chapman, 1933).

In climbing the Andes of S. America, it has been shown that the mean temperature decreases (gets cooler) about one degree Fahrenheit with each (ascent of) three hundred feet. "According to this reckoning, three hundred feet of altitude is the approximate equivalent of sixty-seven miles of latitude. Those birds living in the temperate zone of the Andes at an elevation of twelve thousand feet, although right at the equator, would find the latitudinal equivalent of this elevation some twenty-five hundred miles away either to the north or to the south" (Cutright, 1940). *See* Altitudinal Distribution; Ecological Rules.

HUMERUS

(HUE-mer-us). The upper wing bone (next to the body) of a bird. It is homologous (similar in structure) to the human upper arm, or the humerus. *See* Analagous.

HUMMINGBIRD FAMILY

Trochilidae (troe-KILL-ih-dee); Lat., from Gr. *trochilos;* name applied originally by Herodotus to Egyptian species of plover, also by ancients to some small bird, wren or kinglet, afterward transferred "very curiously" (Coues, 1882) to American hummingbirds; *hummingbird,* from droning of wings in flight. Family ranges from the smallest bird in the world, the 2¼-in.-long Cuban bee hummingbird, *Mellisuga helenae,* with body about the size of a large bee, to the 8½-in-long giant hummingbird, *Patagona gigas,* of S. American Andes (Ridgway, 1891), about size of the purple martin. There are at least 319 species (Van Tyne and Berger, 1976), and in W. Hemisphere only; live in N., C., and S. America and islands of Caribbean. 21 species enter the U.S., of which only 8 penetrate well above Mexican border (7 species nest in Far West) and 4—black-chinned, calliope, ruby-throated, and rufous—nest also in Canada; one, the rufous, champion northern migrant of family, reaches Alaska; ruby-throated is only hummingbird regularly in e. U.S.; calliope is smallest N. American hummingbird and smallest bird in U.S. Several species have also been reported in the U.S. as accidental vagrants from Mexico or West Indies; 2 West Indian species have been reliably reported from s. Fla.—the Bahama woodstar (*see* Woodstar, Bahama) and the Cuban emerald, *Chlorostilbon ricordii;* Cuban emerald has been reported on several occasions in s. Fla., usually during fall or winter; in Tex., five sightings reported of the green violetear, *Colibri thalassinus,* a large highland hummingbird associated with montane forests of Mexico; also two recent but undocumented reports from Tex. of the black-crested coquette, *Paphosia helenae;* the berylline hummingbird, *Amazilia beryllina,* rather similar to the Rieffer's or rufous-tailed hummingbird, reported four times from s. Ariz., and found nesting there in 1976; finally, the plain-capped starthroat, *Heliomaster constantii,* has recently been seen and photographed in Ariz. (Witzeman *et al.,* 1975).

Center of distribution of family is near Equator, in Ecuador and Colombia (Gilliard, 1958); family believed to have originated in S. America with secondary radiation into N. America (Mayr, 1964a); in tropics live from lowest jungle to highest crest of Andes; apparently barrier to crossing from W. Hemisphere to Europe, Asia, and Africa has been thousands of miles of broad Pacific and Atlantic O.; hummingbirds are not songbirds and were thought to be most nearly related, ancestrally, to swifts. However, recent classifiers (taxonomists) have placed the hummingbird family (Trochilidae) in an order of its own, Trochiliformes (Cohn, 1968). *See* Apodiformes.

Besides being largest of non-passerine bird families, and second largest (after the Tyrannidae) of the W. Hemisphere bird families, the rate of discovery of new species in this group is notable; since the last major revision of the family by James Peters in 1945, 11 additional species have been described; there may be as many as 339 valid species in the group; the taxonomy of the family is extraordinarily complex, as a result of the very large number of species, remarkable plumage diversity of the males, and great adaptive variations in bill shape and length among related types.

Almost everything about hummingbirds is unusual—their dazzling iridescent colors surpass those of the birds of paradise of Australia and New Guinea (Austin, 1961); they have slender, pointed bills, straight or curved, adapted especially to probing flowers for nectar; tongues tubular at tip and brush-tipped; with small size (body of ruby-throated hummingbird no larger than end joint of one's thumb) and unique ability among birds to hover and feed at hearts of flowers where they have little competition from other birds; a tiny crop in which they can store food for sustenance overnight; and ability to endure temporary cool weather or cold nights by becoming dormant.

Hummingbirds live in all climates and altitudes of W. Hemisphere; however, most in N. America migrate to escape winter, and in w. N. America, they do not nest in seashore, marsh, and aquatic habitats or in sagebrush and grasslands (Miller, 1951). According to Grant and Grant (1968), there are no hummingbirds in the treeless grassy Great Plains. They do live in tropical jungles, temperate forests, deserts, and, in e. N. America, near seacoast, and in parks, backyards, and gardens throughout N. America—wherever and whenever flowers bloom on which most hummingbirds depend for nectar; many flowers, in turn, depend on hummingbirds for pollination.

Some hummingbirds, especially in West, follow seasonal blooming of flowers up or down mountains; can be attracted to gardens by planting of "hummingbird flowers," and by putting up hummingbird feeders (vials) filled with solution of about one part sugar to four of water. See details of food formulas for hummingbirds and plant lists in Terres (1977).

Hummingbirds are swift in flight with pointed wings that sweep back at their sides like those of speedy aircraft (they have typical "high-speed wing" like that of falcons, swifts, swallows—see Savile, 1950); the ruby-throated hummingbird has been timed out of doors at 50–60 m.p.h., possibly aided by wind, but in experiments by Greenewalt (1960) could fly only about 27 m.p.h. in a wind tunnel; however, Scheithauer (1967), in his aviary, timed the daily courtship chase of a pair of S. American blue-throated sylph hummingbirds, *Aglaiocercus kingi*, at 29.7–47.4 m.p.h.; a pair of C. and S. American violet-bellied hummingbirds, *Damophila julie*, flew at 47–49 m.p.h. in their courtship chases.

In their swift, darting flight, sudden aerial stops and starts, and general elusiveness on the wing, hummingbirds not only hover, fly backward, and shift sideways, but can also fly straight up and down. When hovering, by rotating the shoulder joint (most other birds fly with the "hand" part of the wing—from wrist out) they turn the wings completely over on the backstroke as well as on the forestroke, which permits fore part of the wings to cut the air on the backstroke as well as the forestroke; this checks the tendency to move forward or backward and the bird hangs poised in the air. Hummingbirds are living helicopters. See in Greenewalt (1960).

Because of their small size, speed, and elusiveness, hummingbirds are rarely caught by hawks or other predatory birds; however, William Beebe saw a tropical American bat falcon with a hummingbird in its talons, and Lowery (1938) collected (shot) a pigeon hawk (merlin) that had a ruby-throated hummingbird in its stomach. Sprot (1927) saw a male rufous hummingbird dive at the back of a flying merlin which snatched the hummingbird out of the air. Ernst Mayr saw an American kestrel catch a ruby-throated hummingbird at a bed of zinnias, and Hans Peeters watched a sharp-shinned hawk catch a perched Anna's hummingbird by flying low toward it, screened by bushes, until it was within striking distance (Skutch, 1973). Snider (1971a) reported capture of hummingbirds by Wied's crested flycatcher, and there are two observations of hummingbirds being killed by orioles. Hummingbirds may be caught more often by large frogs, fishes, and tropical spiders. One of greatest hazards to hummingbirds may be picture windows in homes.

Although in larger species males average larger than females, in smaller forms the reverse is true. However, males are more brightly colored in most species, with brilliant iridescent throats, or gorgets. In summer males establish feeding territories from which they chase, very aggressively, not only males and females of their own kind but even bumblebees and hawk moths which come to feed.

Males guard their feeding territories by spectacular, swinging, pendulumlike aerial flights, or intimidation displays (Pitelka, 1942), above flowers guarded; this flight also used in courtship display by male before female when she enters male's territory in breeding condition; apparently in some behavioral way, she makes known to male her sexual readiness; sexes come together only briefly. Polygynous males may mate with more than one female; copulation may be in the air, reported of pair of rufous hummingbirds in flight and of a pair of Anna's hummingbirds (Woods, 1940); of calliope hummingbird, on horizontal perch; of ruby-throated hummingbird, on ground (Tyler, 1940b). Females, which by themselves build the nest and raise the young, establish nesting territories from which they drive out other hummingbirds, including males. For another type of courtship, *see* under Rieffer's hummingbird.

Because of their small size, hummingbirds have the highest metabolism (fastest rate of "burning," or oxidation, of their food, or "fuel") of any warm-blooded vertebrate animal in the world, except possibly shrews, the smallest of the mammals. Hummingbirds must feed (refuel) almost continuously all day to remain alive.

Most N. American hummingbirds migrate long distances and migration requires extra fuel. Hummingbirds have unusually large flight muscles (the pectorals), which have more myoglobin and readily oxidized cytochrome than the relatively "white" muscles of quail and other nonmigratory birds, and a richer supply of blood capillaries and oxygen—an index of the capacity of the red muscles for the long-sustained migration flights. Hummingbirds not only have unusually large flight muscles (22–34 % of total body weight), but also the small pectoral muscles (supracoracoideus) are remarkably large, a reflection of hummingbirds' unique mode of flight and importance of the return wing stroke while hovering.

For example, many ruby-throated hummingbirds, in spring and fall, migrate across 600 mi. of water of the Gulf of Mexico. According to Odum *et al.* (1961), in fall, before migrating, ruby-throats in Fla. and Ga. feed heavily at flowers and add more than 50% to their weight in fat layers (energy reserves) just under the skin. This apparently gives them enough stored fuel (by burning, or oxidizing, body fat) to begin their migration far inland in Fla. and Ga. and to end their flight well into Mexico.

Besides flower nectar (carbohydrate food), hummingbirds get their protein food by eating small beetles, weevils, bugs, flies, gnats, mosquitoes, aphids, leafhoppers, flying ants, parasitic wasps, and spiders and harvestmen (daddy longlegs). Most species get insects and small spiders from flowers, which furnish them in abundance (Wagner, 1946).

Albinism is known (Gross, 1965a) in sixteen individuals of four N. American species. Hybridization reported in at least 9 species of N. American hummingbirds.

Some hummingbirds live to surprising ages. At the New York Zoological Gardens (Bronx Zoo) a green-throated carib from the Lesser Antilles and Virgin Is., an adult when acquired, lived for 10 years, 6 months; a purple-throated carib, to 9 years, 8 months; and in Brazil a captive female planalto hermit (hummingbird), native to S. America, was still alive after 14 years. See Skutch (1973).

Hummingbirds are protected by law and may not be kept in captivity without a permit; however, there may be opportunities to help a sick or injured one until it is well enough to be released. Zoo keepers and aviculturists recommend the following food formula: to 4 oz. of water, add and stir until dissolved 1 level teaspoon of condensed milk, 1½ teaspoonfuls of honey, 2 or 3 drops of Vipenti (vitamin drops), and 1 drop of beef extract, which helps take place of insects in diet of captives. Captive can be given opportunity of catching fruit flies by leaving a bit of banana in cage to attract them. See Walker (1942).

Put food mixture in small vial or vials, with some red nail polish around opening, until bird is used to feeding at container, which can be wired to inside of bird's enclosure. Best and most successful hummingbird feeders can be bought from dealers in bird-attracting supplies. Check with local Audubon Society or see list of dealers in Terres (1977).

Hummingbird, Allen's, *Selasphorus sasin* (seh-LASS-foe-rus SAY-sin); genus name; Lat., from Gr. *selas*, flame, and *phoros*, bearing, in allusion to color of its feathers, especially the gorget; species name: according to Alexander Wetmore (see Choate, 1973), Lesson, in his original description of this hummingbird, named it "sasime" or "sasin" from a French edition of Cook's third voyage, but meaning of the word not known; common name: honors Charles A. Allen, a well-known 19th-century collector of birds in Marin County, Calif. (Color ills., page 528.) Summers along Pacific coast, Ore. to s. Calif., but common only in coastal Calif. (Robbins *et al.*, 1966); 3–3½ in. long; wingspread 4⅓ in.; closely resembles its near relative the rufous hummingbird except back usually metallic green, rufous hummingbird usually has rufous back; in hand, each can be distinguished by differences in the two outer tail feathers (see Stiles, 1972); gorget bright metallic scarlet red (female lacks gorget); has rufous sides, rump, and tail, which distinguish it from other Calif. hummingbirds except migrating rufous; females and young indistinguishable from rufous except in hand; summers in Calif. coastal mountain meadows, moist bottoms of canyons, brushy edges of coniferous forest; according to Cogswell (1957a), the common hummingbird of gardens near coast, also in city gardens from San Francisco to Santa Barbara; male arrives c. Calif. by late Jan., early Feb.; does not sing but in display flight moves rather slowly in back-and-forth flight like arc of giant pendulum, bobbing tail violently to make vibrating sound; some-

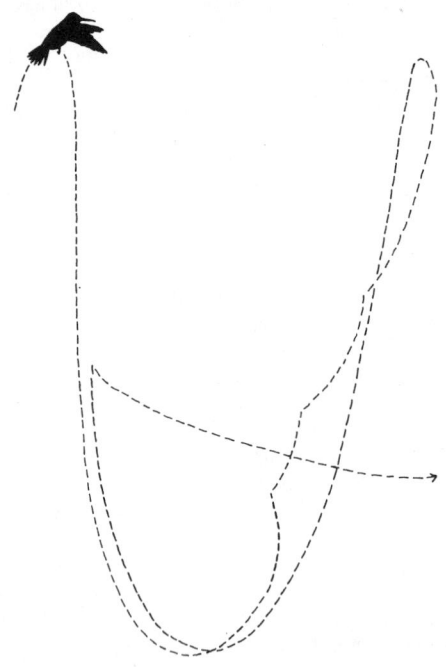

HUMMINGBIRD FAMILY
Hummingbirds can hover, fly straight up or down, backward, and sideways. In the courtship display of the male Allen's hummingbird, the versatility of hummingbird flight is evident.

times poises in front of female to rapidly shuttle back and forth through space of foot or two; utters mouselike squeaks; will attack and rout American kestrel and even large red-tailed hawk.

Feeding Habits: Visits flowers for nectar and insects.

Nest: Built 1–90 ft. above ground, attached to side of twig, limb, or saddled on twigs, stems of weed stalks, in vines or shrubs near water, sometimes in pine trees and even in buildings, usually in dense shade; a deep, thick-walled cup about 2 in. across, of dried weed stems, weed seeds, bits of leaves, and plant down bound with spiders' silk, decorated on outside with lichens, often lined with feathers.

Eggs: Feb.–June; 2, white.

Incubation: 15–17 days (Calder, 1971); young fly about 22 days after hatching; 2 broods a season.

Flight Speed: Timed in controlled experiments in Calif., 18.2–23.8 m.p.h. (Pearson, 1961); wingbeats per second, 35–45, both in hovering and in forward flight (Hagiwara *et al.*, 1968).

Hybrids: Two adult males, Allen's × black-chinned hummingbird, spring 1968, Sacramento County, Calif. (Lynch and Ames, 1970).

Weights: 3.7 gr. (Calder, 1971); males average 3.1 gr., females 3.2 gr.

Range: Nests from sw. Ore., south to sw. Calif., resident population on Santa Barbara Is.; mainland population migrates through Ariz., Baja Calif.; winters in nw. Mexico.

Hummingbird, Anna's, *Calypte anna* (cal-IP-tee AN-na); genus name: Lat., from Gr. *Kalypte*, a proper name, also Gr. *kalyptos*, hidden (Jaeger, 1955), also possibly from Gr. *kalypira*, hood or veil (Coble, 1954), possibly in allusion to violet-colored cap, throat, and long neck feathers; species name: given in 1829 by French naturalist René Primivère Lesson, in honor of Anna, Duchess of Rivoli, wife of Prince Victor Masséna (Palmer, 1928). (Color ills., page 529.) Only hummingbird that nests generally within a single state—Calif.; only one to winter in U.S.; 3½–4 in. long; wingspread about 4¾ in.; bright metallic green above; mostly green below; slightly forked tail noticeable when perched; male has brilliant iridescent red, *both on crown and in throat patch* (gorget); female grayish below, lacks red on forehead but throat usually has a few red feathers, has also heavily spotted throat; either sex distinguished from other hummingbirds by rich green back and wash of green on sides; Anna's is somewhat larger than other Calif. hummingbirds; is common resident west of Sierras in Calif., the common dooryard hummingbird in most of Calif. (Cogswell, 1957b), also common in canyons, foothills, and river bottom woodlands, especially attracted to live oaks; of seven species of hummers in Calif., Anna's is only one to sing —a thin, squeaky warble uttered from a perch or in flight; also, both sexes utter *chick* note or liquid chirp as in feeding they move from flower to flower; after feeding, flies to perch on exposed twig, turning head constantly to one side or other, or preening breast; in Calif., earliest of all Calif. birds to nest, eggs sometimes

laid in late Dec. (Woods, 1940); in courtship flights, male mounts upward till almost lost to sight, then shoots vertically downward at tremendous speed toward female sitting quietly in tree or bush, at bottom of plunge spread tail feathers (or vocalization) produces sharp *peek* sound; this flight used also as intimidation display toward other birds.

Feeding Habits: In winter often gathers to feed at blossoms of eucalyptus trees; tree tobacco, *Nicotiana glauca*, is one of its most valuable nectar sources; also century plant, *Agave americana* (Woods, 1940). Pearson (1954) calculated that a male, in Sept., to meet energy requirements each day, would need nectar from 1,022 blossoms of a bush, *Fuchsia macrostemma*, at which experimental bird did most of its feeding; Anna's also eats many spiders and small insects; apparently depends more on insect food than other N. American hummingbirds (Pitelka, 1942); eats sap from bleeding bark of injured trees, also from holes drilled by sapsuckers; comes to hummingbird feeders for sugar-water solution.

Nest: Tiny lichen-covered cup in bush or small tree, on twig usually in semi-shade, 17 in. to 30 ft. above ground (female may lay eggs while nest of soft plant down is still only a platform, and add walls later); sometimes built on face of cliff, utility wires, etc. (Woods, 1940).

Eggs: Dec.–Aug., but mostly Feb.–mid-May; 2, white.

Incubation: 14–18 days (Calder, 1971); 16–17 days; young first fly 18–21 days after hatching (Woods, 1940); two broods a year. Howell and Dawson (1954), in studies of Anna's, discovered that female while nesting did not go into torpor to conserve energy overnight as male hummingbirds may, but maintained her normal body temperature and egg temperatures—her bodily heat losses were reduced by being at rest and by insulative value of nest. *See* discussion under Torpidity. See Calder (1971). Kelly (1956) reported remarkable faithfulness of a female Anna's to her nest and eggs: she began incubating July 4, 1955, after laying second egg; even though eggs did not hatch, she continued to incubate, and did not give up until 95 days later (Oct. 6); eggs, examined, were infertile.

Albinism: An incomplete albino collected San Rafael, Calif. (Allen, 1878); another, juvenile male, all-white with dark eyes, collected El Cerrito, Calif., 1961 (Banks and Medina, 1963); nestling, completely white with pink eyes, Anaheim, Calif. (Coburn, 1966).

Hybrids: Crosses reported: Anna's × black-chinned hummingbird; Anna's × calliope; and five male hybrids of Anna's × Allen's (Banks and Johnson, 1961).

Weights: 3.4–5.8 gr., or about ⅛–⅕ oz. (Lasiewski, 1963); males average 4.3 gr., females 4.1 gr.

Range: Nests west of higher mountains and deserts of Calif., from c. and n. Calif. south to n. Baja Calif.; winters in nesting range and north to Humboldt Bay and islands off Calif., Baja Calif.; also to s. Ariz. and nw. Mexico into Mexico; accidental in Tex. See also Zimmerman (1973).

Hummingbird, berylline, *Amazilia beryllina* (am-ah-ZILL-ih-ah ber-ih-line-ah); genus name: *see* Hummingbird, buff-bellied; species name: Lat. for the color of beryl, bluish green to sea green. Mexican species that has reached the U.S. border several times since 1967; 4–4½ in. long; wingspread about 5½ in.; sexes nearly alike, *metallic green* above, on the throat, and *over most of the underparts*, the bill mostly blackish, but lower mandible reddish basally, upper wing surface *rufous brown*, and the tail square-tipped and *rufous*; first discovered in U.S. in Ramsay Canyon, Huachuca Mtns., Ariz., in 1967, and seen again in Chiricahuas in 1971; also observed in 1975 in same area (Ramsay Canyon) of Ariz., and finally reported nesting in Chiricahuas in summer of 1976 (Sitzeman *et al.*, 1976).

Hummingbird, black-chinned, *Archilochus alexandri* (are-KILL-oh-kus al-egg-ZANdry); genus name: Lat., from Gr. *archi-*, prefix meaning chief, first in importance, and *lochos*, an ambush, also a company or body of people (Jaeger, 1955); species name: given in 1846 in France by Bourcier and Musant for a medical doctor, M. M. Alexandre, who collected birds in Mexico, among them the bird named in his honor. (Color ill., page 529.) Black-chinned summers from B.C., south along Pacific coast and west to Rocky Mtns., south into Mexico and Tex.; is close relative of ruby-throated hummingbird; 3½–3¾ in. long; male is bright metallic green above, distinguished by black throat and white collar below it (the iridescent blue-violet patch on lower throat shows only in certain light); female green above, entirely white below (Peterson, 1947); white spot behind eyes of both sexes; in summer most abundant in southern part of range, especially in s. Calif., s. Utah, Ariz., and parts of N.M.; in Calif. (Los Angeles County) summer resident from lowlands to summit of mountains, most common in foothills, in July moves to higher slopes following later blooming of flowers at 6,000–8,500 ft. (Bent, 1940); in s. Ariz., Mar.–Sept., the common hummingbird about towns and rivers, usually absent from deserts (see Phillips *et al.*, 1964); in Tex., Mar.–Aug.; courtship or intimidation flights like that of ruby-throated hummingbird; male sings soft, high-pitched warble; when chasing another bird, utters loud, chippering notes.

Feeding Habits: Visits flowers of tree tobacco, scarlet larkspur (*Delphinium cardinale*), chuparosa, paloverdes, etc., for nectar; also eats pollen, insects, for which often darts out like flycatcher from conspicuous perch; comes to feeders for sugar water.
Nest: Round cup of plant down about 1½ in. across, 1 in. high, outside coated with spiders' silk, but unlike ruby-throated nest, has no lichens on outside (Bent, 1940) except in Tex.; saddled on drooping branch or in fork of limb, 4–8 ft. up, frequently over water or dry creek bed. Ross (1970) reported nest at Phoenix, Ariz., built in three days.
Eggs: In Calif., early Apr. to end of Sept., but mostly early May to early June; in Tex., early Apr. to mid-June; 2–3, usually 2, pure white without gloss.

Incubation: By female, 16 days; young leave nest about 20 days after hatching; still fed by female (Ross, 1970); often two, sometimes three broods. See Bené (1947) for many details of life history.
Other Names: Black-chin; black-chinned hummer.
Albinism: A complete albino, "pure white," collected on Turtle Creek, near Kerrville, Tex., July 1913 (Oberholser, 1919).
Hybrids: Two of black-chinned × Allen's weighed 3.2 and 3.3 gr. each. See under Allen's hummingbird. A black-chinned × broad-tailed hummingbird collected, Nev., by Banks and Johnson (1961); two reported crosses between black-chinned and Costa's hummingbirds (Short and Phillips, 1966).
Weights: Males average 3.1 gr., females 3.4 gr.
Range: Nests from sw. B.C. and nw. Mont., south through c. Idaho, w. Colo., Mexico, s.-c. and sw. Tex. to n. Baja Calif. and n. Mexico; winters from n. Baja Calif., se. Calif., and n. Mexico to se. Mexico; accidental in La.

Hummingbird, blue-throated, *Lampornis clemenciae* (lam-POR-nis clem-EN-sih-ee); genus name: from Gr. *lampa*, a lamp, or torch, and *ornis*, bird; literally "torch bird," in allusion to brilliant colors of plumage; species name: given in 1830 by René Primivère Lesson, French naturalist, explorer, and collector of birds, for his wife, Clémence, a painter of flowers and birds. (Color ills., page 529.) Mexican species first discovered in U.S. in Santa Catalina Mtns., Ariz., in May 1884; besides resident in s. Ariz., also in s. N.M. and sw. Tex. (Bent, 1940); 4½–5¼ in. long; largest resident hummer in the U.S., slightly larger than Rivoli's hummingbird; both sexes metallic green above, but male has blue-gray underparts with double white line on face, and a *blue throat* obvious at close range; both sexes have broad blue-black tail *with white spots in outer tail feathers*; frequently fans tail, which shows spots; long black bill slightly downcurved; female evenly gray below, lacks blue throat of male; call note is long, loud *seep* uttered in flight; lives in lush growth of streamsides in lower parts of mountain canyons (in Mexico, lives in mountains to 12,000 ft.); very aggressive against other birds in defense of feeding places, in flight one struck a male Rivoli's hummingbird with such force that it knocked Rivoli's unconscious; flight very swift as it flies directly over or alongside streams.

Feeding Habits: Not only flower nectar and pollen, for which it comes freely to gardens, where it may perch near human observer, but catches beetles, flies, wasps, bugs, also spiders and daddy longlegs.
Nest: Cup of plant down, mosses, about 2½ in. across, 3 in. high (may use same nest for several years, adding to it each time), bound together with spiders' silk. Herbert Brandt (1951) found one nest built almost entirely of webs in which there were "some 15,000 miles of spider and insect thread . . . probably the longest amount of any nest on record." Female bluethroat often builds her nest on stems of flowering plants and ferns along streams, under

eaves of houses, bridges, water towers, and inside buildings.
Eggs: Ariz., May–June; Mexico, Feb.–Sept.; 2, white.
Incubation: Period of and age when young first fly unknown.
Other Names: Blue-throated cacique; blue-throated hummer.
Age: A male, regularly dominant over other hummingbirds, reported to have appeared in garden, Ramsay Canyon, Ariz., for 12 years (Edgerton *et al.*, 1951), but not verifiable because not a banded bird.
Weights: Males average 8.4 gr., females 6.8 gr. (Lyon, 1976).
Range: Resident in mountains of s. Ariz., s. N.M., and sw. Tex. south to s. Mexico.

Hummingbird, broad-billed, *Cynanthus latirostris* (sin-AN-thus lat-ih-ROS-tris); genus name: from Gr. *kyanos*, blue, and *anthos*, bright, in allusion to male's brilliant blue throat feathers; species name: from Lat. *latus*, wide, and *rostrum*, beak; broad-billed. (Color ills., page 531.) Mexican species, also in summer in s. Ariz., sw. N.M., w. Tex.; small; 3¼–4 in. long; wingspread about 5 in.; metallic bronze-green above, distinguished from all other N. American hummingbirds by its broad, red, black-tipped bill (the similar white-eared hummingbird, which occurs in Ariz., also has a red or pink bill but has a *long, broad white stripe* behind each eye—broad-billed has only a tiny white spot behind each eye); male broad-billed has a metallic blue throat, *dark underparts*; female similar to male but has pearl-gray underparts; in Ariz. nests in foothills in arroyos and canyons along stream banks in mesquite-sycamore plant association on or near desert, rarely appears at Tucson in migration, sometimes remains in town; utters chattering notes exactly like those of ruby-crowned kinglet; first record of its appearance in N.M. was Aug. 1893 in Guadalupe Canyon in Peloncillo Range, extreme southwestern part of state; common there in summer 1959 but no nests found (Ligon, 1961).

Feeding Habits: Comes to hummingbird feeders for sugar water; eats flower nectar from red blossoms of ocotillo, paintbrushes (*Castilleja*) and others; eats aphids, leafhoppers, bugs, root gnats, flower flies, ants, parasitic wasps, also spiders and daddy longlegs and pollen grains; female sometimes chases large butterflies from her feeding territory but ignores smaller ones (Bent, 1940).
Nest: Built by female on branch of small tree or stalk of vine or shrub usually 4–7 ft. above ground, of grasses, lined with white plant down, bits of leaves, and bark outside *without lichens* usually in other hummingbirds' nests, very small, inside diameter about ¾ in.
Eggs: Ariz., Apr.–July; Mexico, Jan.–May; 2, white.
Incubation: Period of and age at which young first fly unknown.
Hybrids: A broad-billed hummingbird × Rivoli's collected (shot) in Ariz., 1920 (Short and Phillips, 1966).
Weights: Males average 3.7 gr., one female weighed 3.4 gr.

Range: Nests from n.w. Mexico, sc. Ariz., sw. N.M., to sw. Tex. (one nesting record in Tex. reported 1935—see Bent, 1940), south to s. Mexico; winters in Mexico; accidental in Calif., with five records (Small, 1974); one at San Diego, mid-Nov. 1961 to mid-Mar. 1962; three other birds reported in San Diego County, one fall 1962 and two near Imperial Beach, Nov. 9, 1963; one at Redlands, San Bernardino County, Jan.–mid-Feb. 1964; one at Pacific Grove, Monterey County, Apr. 21, 1969; and one in Jan. at Los Angeles reported in *Los Angeles Times,* Jan. 28, 1976.

Hummingbird, broad-tailed, *Selasphorus platycercus* (seh-LASS-foh-rus plat-ih-SIR-cuss); genus name: *see* Hummingbird, Allen's; species name: Lat., from Gr. *platys,* broad, and *kerkos,* tail; broad-tailed. (Color ills., page 531.) The common nesting hummingbird of the Rocky Mtns. (Idaho, Mont., Wyo. south) but sometimes ranges eastward and westward of mountains (Bent, 1940); 4–4½ in. long; wingspread about 5 in.; back, shining metallic bronze-green; male's throat patch (gorget) bright rose-pink, appears similar to ruby-throated hummingbird; lower neck white, shading to gray on middle underparts; male can best be identified by shrill sound of wings while in display flight; female, green back, underparts pale gray; throat usually minutely speckled with bronze; touch of *rufous on flanks and sides of spread tail* (Peterson, 1961); summers in coniferous forests of Rockies; according to Marshall (1957), male requires deciduous brush such as willow thickets in mountain meadows for his display flights; more often heard than seen in coniferous forest—the shrill sound of wings in display is louder and more rattling (like a cicada) than the buzzing sounds in display flights of rufous and Allen's hummingbirds; the source of the trilling sound of the broad-tailed's wings is unique in N. American hummingbirds: the first two outer primaries are narrowed at their tips (female's are not), which makes slots that produce whistling sound when male dives through air at great speed in display (Edgerton *et al.,* 1951); at Denver, Colo., male usually arrives about mid-May, ahead of female; female nests in mountains at 4,000–11,000 ft. elevation, also in gardens in cities.

Feeding Habits: Eats many tiny insects and small spiders (besides nectar) that it finds in such flowers as penstemon, larkspur, agave, gilia, gooseberry, and on willow catkins; also gleans insects from pine needles, and darts out from perch to snap insects out of air; comes to hummingbird feeders for sugar-water solution; often bathes in shallows on rocks of mountain streams (Bent, 1940).
Nest: Saddled on twig or low horizontal branches of willows, alder, cottonwoods, over stream, or on limbs of pine, fir, spruce, aspen, 4–15 ft. above ground; about 1–2 in. in diameter, of plant down, covered on outside with lichens, bark, or leaves, all bound together with spiders' silk.
Eggs: May–July; 2, white.
Incubation: About 16 days; young fly when about 23 days old (Edgerton *et al.,* 1951).

Flight Speed: Estimated (from high-speed photography by Van Riper) at 18–29 m.p.h. (Stong, 1960).
Hybrids: See under Black-chinned and Costa's hummingbirds.
Weights: Males average 3.2 gr., females 3.6 gr.
Range: Nests from e.-c. Calif. to n. Nev., n. Utah, n. Wyo., Colo., and sw. Tex., and south to Guatemala; winters from c. Mexico south; has wandered in summer to Ore., Idaho, and Mont.

Hummingbird, buff-bellied, *Amazilia yucatanensis* (am-ah-ZILL-ih-ah you-cah-tan-EN-sis); genus name: apparently Latinized from French naturalist Lesson's word, *amazili,* used in plural, *amazilis,* for a group of hummingbirds; meaning of word unknown (Coues, 1882); species name: Lat., of Yucatán, Mexico, the locality where the specimen (or specimens) collected from which it was named and described. (Color ill., page 531.) Mexican species that has extended range north into lower Rio Grande Valley, Tex.; 4–4½ in. long; wingspread about 5½ in.; *sexes alike;* green metallic bronze above; *bright orange or red,* black-tipped bill; throat and upper breast shiny emerald green; lower breast and belly cinnamon-buff; tail cinnamon-rufous or chestnut; first discovered in U.S. near military reservation at Fort Brown, Tex., Aug. 1876; summers in semi-arid coastal scrub in open woods, chaparral thickets, farms and gardens, citrus groves of Rio Grande Valley in s. Tex., and dense thickets and vines near water.

Feeding Habits: Visits flowers for nectar, eats insects.
Nest: Built on small drooping branches or in fork of horizontal twig of small trees or bushes (*Anachuita, Cordia,* ebony, hackberry, sometimes in willow); 3–8 ft. above ground, cuplike nest about 1⅜ in. in diameter, built of plant fibers lined with thistledown, cattle hair, decorated outside with lichens, bits of bark, bound with spiders' silk (Bent, 1940).
Eggs: Tex., Apr.–June; 2, white.
Incubation: Period of and age when young first fly similar to that of other hummingbirds.
Other Names: Fawn-breasted hummingbird; Yucatán hummingbird.
Range: From s. Tex. and in arid lowlands of e. and s. Mexico to Belize; winters in Mexico and Southward.

Hummingbird, bumblebee. *See* Hummingbird, Heloise's.

Hummingbird, calliope, *Stellula calliope* (STELL-you-lah cal-EYE-oh-pee); genus name: Lat., a little star; species name: Lat., from Gr., pleasant, or beautiful (of voice); also Calliope, one of the Muses (Coues, 1882). (Color ills., page 530.) Smallest hummingbird and smallest bird nesting on N. American continent north of Mexico (*see* Size); summers usually in mountains of w. N. America; 2¾–3½ in. long; wingspread about 4¼ in.; metallic green above, white below; straight, black, needlelike bill; male has long, spreading, metallic-purple feathers under chin, overlying white throat, which gives peppermint-candy effect, only hummingbird so marked; female lacks purple-red

throat feathers; throat is speckled, breast white; almost indistinguishable from female rufous hummingbird but does not have rust-colored feathers in center of rump; is much smaller than similar female broad-tailed hummingbird; nests in Cascades, Sierras, and Rockies north into Canada; next to rufous, is second most northerly hummingbird (Calder, 1971); in Sierras nests almost to timberline, 10,000–11,500 ft.; Grant and Grant (1968) reported calliopes in July at 10,000 ft. on Mt. Lassen in the Cascades, and at 11,000 ft. in Sierras, feeding at flowers of penstemon; likes to nest at borders of mountain meadows rimmed by conifers or in canyons and aspen thickets along mountain streams; nesting female, when incubating eggs high in mountains, is often exposed at night to near-freezing cold but she does not become torpid as males may (*see* discussion under Anna's hummingbird), thus able to maintain egg temperatures (Calder, 1971). Nest site (protected from weather) and insulation of nest minimize heat losses of bird and of her eggs at night.

Feeding Habits: Nectar, insects, small spiders.
Nest: Saddled on small dead limbs of pines, or often along branch on cluster of pine cones (which nest strikingly resembles), or in shaded parts of aspen groves on dead, black or gray knots of mistletoe; sometimes in dry canyons or along mountain streams in alders, silver firs, spruces, hemlocks, and other conifers; 2–70 ft. above ground; usually on branch or twig *directly under larger branch or twig* or under foliage, which protects nest from weather; nest cup about 1½ in. outside diameter; of gray or brown plant fibers, mosses, bark scales, lichens, bound with spiders' silk and cocoon fibers; inside lined with plant down; female often builds atop previous year's nest until several nests stacked up, each added perhaps in successive years (Bent, 1940).
Eggs: May–July; 2, white.
Incubation: 15 days (Calder, 1971); young first fly about 20 days after hatching.
Hybrids: A cross between a calliope and a Costa's hummingbird collected in Calif.—first one reported in 1900; a calliope × Anna's hummingbird collected June 1926, Baja Calif. (Banks and Johnson, 1961).
Weights: Males average 2.5 gr., females 2.8 gr., or about 1/10 oz.; for remarkable example of weight-lifting of male *see* under Weight-Carrying Capacity.
Range: Nests from c. B.C. and sw. Alta. south in Rockies to nw. Wyo., Utah, w. Colo., and from Wash., Ore., and Calif., in Cascades and Sierras, south to Baja Calif., east to w. Tex.; migrates southward through mountains often with rufous and Allen's hummingbirds; winters in Mexico; accidental in Sask., casual in sw. Tex.

Hummingbird, Costa's, *Calypte costae* (cal-IP-tee COSS-tee); genus name: *see* Hummingbird, Anna's; species name: given in 1839 by Bourcier in honor of Louis Marie Pantaléon Costa, Marquis de Beau-Regard, in 19th-century France, owner of large collection of hummingbirds (Palmer, 1928). (Color ills., page

532.) Next to calliope, smallest N. American hummingbird (Bent, 1940); s. Great Basin and Southwest, common in southwestern deserts (Robbins *et al.*, 1966); 3–3½ in. long; wingspread 4½ in.; back of both sexes metallic green; male is only N. American hummingbird with purple crown and purple gorget, which has prominent purple streamers down sides of neck; crown and throat appear black until seen in certain lights; females with green back, crown often dull brown; mainly dingy white below; in field, indistinguishable from female black-chinned; summers in dry foothills and lower desert slopes where grow cactuses, yuccas, sagebrush, paloverde, ocotillo; the courtship displays of male, like those of other hummers, are spectacular swoops, dives, and loops near perched female; in dives, sound uttered by male is high, shrill hissing, or shrill whistle, like sound of glancing bullet (Bent, 1940); both sexes utter a soft *chick* note while feeding.

Feeding Habits: Nectar and insects and spiders found in flowers or on plants such as squaw cabbage, wild rose, plum, etc. (Bent, 1940; Bailey, 1902).
Nest: Built on limbs or twigs of oaks, alders, hackberry, willows, etc., in sage, dead yuccas, branching cactuses, paloverde; cup about 1½–2 in. outside diameter, of bits of lichens, weed leaves, buds, strips of bark, willow or yucca down, bound with spiders' silk, usually 1–9 ft. above ground.
Eggs: Feb.–June; 2, white.
Incubation: 15–18 days, young leave nest at 20–23 days; probably one brood raised a year (Pitelka, 1951a).
Accidents: One found helpless, entangled in coarse, heavy spider's web, unable to fly away after released but recovered.
Age: One lived in good health more than 6 years in Bronx Zoo, New York City.
Hybrids: A Costa's hummingbird × broadtailed hummingbird collected June 1932 in Pima County, Ariz. (Banks and Johnson, 1961); *see also* under Hummingbird, black-chinned.
Weights: Males average 3.0 gr., females 3.2 gr.
Range: Nests from c. Calif., s. Nev., and sw. Utah south to Santa Barbara Is., Baja Calif., and offshore islands; s. Ariz., w.-c. Mexico, sw. N.M.; winters from s. Calif. and sw. Ariz. south.

Hummingbird, Cuban emerald, *Chlorostilbon ricordii* (clor-o-STIL-bon rih-CORD-ih-eye); genus name: Gr. *chloros*, green, and *stilbon*, flashing or glittering; species name: after Philippe Ricord (1800–89), French surgeon. West Indian species recorded in Fla. on several occasions; 4–4½ in. long; wingspread about 5½ in.; sexes nearly alike, *metallic bronze-green both above and below*, with a blackish and deeply *forked tail* in males (less so in females), and undertail coverts that are white or mostly white; both sexes with small *white spot* behind eye, females have whitish underparts, becoming greenish on the sides; bill blackish; becoming red toward base of lower mandible; species was first reported in Fla. in fall of 1943, when single bird was seen repeatedly at Miami, and was reported a second time in June 1953 near Cocoa on e. coast; subsequently seen at least

three times, in Naranja in 1961, at Cocoa Beach in October, 1964, and at Hypoluxo Is. in August 1977 (Kale, 1977).

Hummingbird, fawn-breasted. *See* Hummingbird, buff-bellied.

Hummingbird, Heloise's, *Atthis heloisa* (AY-this [*th* as in *thin*] hel-oh-EE-zah); genus name: according to Gruson (1972), *Atthis* is Gr. for Athenian, i.e., Attic; also believed to refer to an Athenian woman, possibly Philomena, who in Gr. mythology was changed into a bird; species name: given the bird by the original French describers, Lesson and De Lattre (1839), possibly for the wife of Adolphe De Lattre, French zoological collector, or for the wife of his brother Henry, both of whom collected birds, including the Heloise's hummingbird, in Mexico in 1838 (Wynne, 1969). Mexican species that strayed one summer into the U.S. in Ramsay Canyon, Huachuca Mtns., s. Ariz.; two females collected there in July 1896; 2¾ in. long; very small, appears in field exactly like calliope hummingbird except that the elongated gorget of the male is not streaked white, but is solid iridescent red-purple; also, tail is rounded, not notched; female much like female calliope but tips of outer tail feathers usually buffy (Peterson and Chalif, 1973). See also details in Blake, E. R. (1953) and in Phillips *et al.* (1964).

Other Names: Bumblebee hummingbird; Morcom's hummingbird.
Weights: Adults average 2.2 gr. (Des Granges, 1979); one of smallest of all hummingbirds, possibly exceeded only by West Indian vervain and bee hummingbirds.
Range: Lives mostly in Mexico, in cloud forest or in pine and pine-oak woods, in mountains of se. Sinaloa, sw. Chihuahua, Nuevo León, south to Oaxaca and Veracruz; accidental in Ariz.

Hummingbird, Lucifer, *Calothorax lucifer* (cal-oh-THO-racks LEW-sih-fer); genus name: Lat., from Gr. *kallos*, beautiful, and *thorax*, breast; species name: Lat., light-bringing, or light-bearing; both words of scientific name refer to glittering plumage (Coues, 1882). Mexican species in U.S. in Ariz., where rare, with two old records, Aug. 1874 (Phillips *et al.*, 1964), recently has reappeared and is irregular in Ariz., and in w. Tex.; recently (1962) discovered nesting in Brewster County, Tex.; 3¾ in. long; both sexes have metallic-green back, but male has dazzling violet-purple to red-purple throat patch (gorget) *without purple on crown* (top of head) as in similar Costa's hummingbird; also has deeply forked tail which Costa's lacks; best field mark for both sexes is slightly decurved bill (Bent, 1940); is common hummingbird of arid slopes of tablelands of e. and c. Mexico at 3,000–18,000 ft. elevation; migratory in northern part of its range (Blake, E.R., 1953); fairly common in Chisos Mtns., w. Tex., in summer, where feeds at agave flowering in June; also hovers around and under spiders' webs to take entangled insects from meshes (Bent, 1940); both sexes very aggressive in defense of nesting or feeding territories; utter loud piercing shriek in attack on larger birds or others of own kind.

Lucifer hummingbird

HUMMINGBIRD FAMILY

Feeding Habits: No definitive studies reported, but observed taking flower nectar, insects, and spiders.

Nest: Built in shrubs 4–6 ft. above ground, cup of soft plant fibers, blossoms, or seeds, bits of lichens, etc., bound with spiders' silk; two nests discovered by the Puliches in dry canyon on cactus-grown slope in Brewster County, Tex., first, July 13, 1962 (first nesting record for U.S.), built about 8 ft. and 6 ft. above ground, and each built on a seed pod of a dead stalk of lechuguilla (agave); of two nests, first held two young about 5 days old; second, discovered Aug. 2, 1962, held two freshly laid eggs (Pulich and Pulich, 1963). Another nest with two eggs discovered in Big Bend National Park, Tex., on May 18, 1968, held two eggs (Nelson, 1970).

Eggs: Mexico (6 records), June–July; U.S. (3 records), May–Aug.; 2, white.

Incubation: 15–16 days; Puliches estimated that young left nest 22–23 days after hatching.

Weights: Adults average 2.9 gr. (Des Granges, 1979).

Range: See above.

Hummingbird, magnificent. *See* Hummingbird, Rivoli's.

Hummingbird, Morcom's. Robert Ridgway (1898) described what he thought was a new species of hummingbird, *Atthis morcomi,* which he named for G. F. Morcom, a collector of birds in rural s. Calif in the 1890s. Later examination of the specimens of this bird proved that it was not a new species but the already described *Atthis heloisa. See* Heloise's hummingbird.

Hummingbird, refulgent. *See* Hummingbird, Rivoli's.

Hummingbird, Rieffer's, *Amazilia tzacatl* (am-ah-ZILL-ih-ah tza-CAT-l); genus name: *see* Hummingbird, buff-bellied; species name: Lat., from Aztec, probably meaning grass (green), according to Coues (1882); the bird was named by Dr. P. De La Lave in 1833 in Mexico; according to Gruson (1972), Tzacatl was name of a high-ranking Toltec warrior; De La Lave named a number of Mexican hummingbirds for historic people of Mexico; apparently little is known about Rieffer, not even his first name, but he made a collection of birds from Colombia in 1840 (Wynne, 1969). Rieffer's hummingbird is a Mexican, C. and S. American species that wandered into U.S. near Brownsville, Tex., in June and July 1876, with a probable sighting in Harris County, 1969; 3½–3¾ in. long; a glittering green hummingbird with bright, chestnut-colored tail (Skutch, 1940a); similar to buff-bellied hummingbird but with grayish (not buffy) belly (Blake, E.R., 1953); tail unnotched; bill rather long, reddish, *tipped* with black; sexes similar; male demonstrates so-called static courtship of some tropical American hummingbirds in that, in breeding season, he establishes himself in one place where he may be found day after day; usually has favorite perch where he rests and calls frequently; among many tropical species, males group in "singing assemblies" of two to many; also frequently alone (Skutch 1940a). See also Skutch (1951) and Wiley (1971).

Other Name: Rufous-tailed hummingbird.

Hybrids: Gray (1958) reported a Rieffer's hummingbird × blue-breasted emerald, *Amazilia amabilis,* also called blue-chested hummingbird (Eisenmann, 1955).

Weights: Males average 5.4 gr., females 4.9 gr.

Range: Nests from s. Tamaulipas south through e. Mexico through C. America to Colombia and w. Venezuela; winters throughout nesting range; accidental in Tex.

Hummingbird, Rivoli's, *Eugenes fulgens* (YOU-jen-eez FULL-jenz); genus name: Lat., from Gr. *eugenes,* well-born; species name: from Lat. *fulgere,* to gleam, glitter (Coues, 1882); common name: given by Lesson, French naturalist, in honor of Victor Masséna, early-19th-century Duke of Rivoli (*see also* Hummingbird, Anna's). (Color ill., page 533.) Mainly a Mexican and C. American species that enters sw. U.S. (first record for U.S. in Pinaleno Mtns., Ariz., Sept. 1873) and in N.M. (first reported in 1892—Phillips *et al.,* 1964, and Ligon, 1961); Rivoli's called by Bent (1940) largest N. American hummingbird, but weights indicate blue-throated is largest—*see* in biography of blue-throated hummingbird; 4½–5 in. long (Blake, E. R., 1953); wingspread about 7 in.; male dark overall, with slightly forked tail; crown *rich violet-blue;* throat patch (gorget) brilliant emerald green (blue-throated has blue throat), which contrasts sharply with glossy black breast and bronze-green back; appears black from distance; female metallic green above, gray below, with gray-white feathers in corners of *square* tail; throat heavily spotted; rather long black bill in both sexes; wingbeats discernible in flight, slower than those of smaller hummingbirds, make soft sound unlike buzz of most hummers; also occasionally sails on set wings like a swift; at times flies quite rapidly (Bent, 1940); is very quarrelsome and often fights with blue-throated and other hummingbirds over feeding territories; utters twittering sound, louder, not so shrill as that of small hummingbirds; call note is sharp *chip,* like that of black phoebe (Phillips *et al.,* 1964); female nests to 10,000 ft. in mountains of Ariz., but usually 5,000–8,500 ft. elevation (Bent, 1940); males and females in same habitats of deciduous woods along streams, in pine or oak woods on mountain slopes and ridges.

Feeding Habits: Visits flowers for nectar, also is considerable feeder on insects and small spiders; snaps insects out of air in flight and hovers at leaves of trees, also pines, to gather them.

Nest: Built on horizontal limb of alder along mountain stream, branch of walnut, pines, maples, sycamores, 20–55 ft. above ground; erect cup about 2¼ in. outside diameter, of silky plant fibers, outside coated with bits of lichens, bound with spiders' silk, inside lined with soft plant down, sometimes fluffy birds' feathers.

Eggs: May–July; 2, white.

Incubation: Period of and age when young leave nest unreported.

Other Names: Magnificent hummingbird; refulgent hummingbird.

Hybrids: See one described under Broad-billed hummingbird.

Weights: Males average 7.7 gr., females 6.4 gr. (Lyon, 1976).

Range: Nests in mountains from s. Ariz., sw. N.M., and w. Tex. (where probably nests), to El Salvador and Nicaragua; winters from n. Mexico south.

Hummingbird, ruby-throated, *Archilochus colubris* (are-KILL-oh-cuss COL-oo-bris); genus name: *see* Hummingbird, black-chinned; species name: derivation and meaning not clear (Coues, 1882); from S. American Indian name *colubri* (Sprunt, 1954a) for these birds (Gruson, 1972); see, however, Choate (1973). (Color ill., page 533.) Closely related to black-chinned, is one of smallest and widest-ranging of N. American hummingbirds; only one that nests east of Mississippi R.; in summer over eastern two thirds of country from s. Canada south to Fla., west to Great Plains; 3–3¾ in. long; wingspread 4–4¾ in.; both sexes metallic green above, gray below; adult male has throat feathers (gorget) that appear black but flash deep fiery red or orange in sunlight, also has slightly forked tail; female has white throat, no fork in tail and with prominent white spots on outer corners; when not seen, ruby-throats can be detected by their rapid, squeaky, chipping notes in flight or by hum of wings; leaves tropical home in late winter and moves northward, keeping pace as season advances with opening of flowers; because of small size, sometimes mistaken for a day-flying hawk moth, which also hovers at flowers; many cross Gulf of Mexico in northward flight; arrive in South in Mar. and early Apr., usually reach Canada by mid-May (Tyler, 1940b); sexes apparently travel apart in migration (males precede females), usually seen singly or at most two or three together, but sometimes up to dozen or more may swarm about a large flowering tree such as horse chestnut (buckeye) or a lilac bush, darting about, probing flowers, chasing each other, uttering bursts of sharp jerky notes; in one of male's courtship flights or intimidation displays (he may have several different ones—see Tyler, 1940b), he swings in wide arc of about 180°, back and forth as though he were hung at end of a swaying wire, facing in toward a vertical axis that runs through center of arc; at bottom of swing, wings make loud buzz. In flight, wings move so rapidly they are blur at bird's sides; in 1936, at Massachusetts Institute of Technology, Dr. Harold E. Edgerton's first high-speed motion pictures of ruby-throated in flight revealed that, when hovering, it beat its wings 55 times (completed strokes) a second, 61 times a second when backing up, and 75 when flying straightaway.

Feeding Habits: Strongly attracted to red; gets flower nectar and insects from many plants; especially attracted to columbines in spring; later to *Salvia,* or scarlet sage; especially to red flowers of trumpet, or coral, honeysuckle, and bee balm *(Monarda);* jewelweed *(Impatiens)* along streamsides; and phlox, petunias, lilies, trumpet creeper *(Campsis radicans),* Siberian pea tree *(Caragana),* and nasturtiums in gardens; sometimes ruby-throat battles with bumblebees over feeding rights to flowers; attacks and chases kingbird, crow, even dives at eagle that flies over territory; eats many insects—from Jan. to Mar. in Costa Rica, depends almost wholly on insects in absence of flowers (Wolf, 1970); eats tree sap (see Sap-Feeding; Commensalism); hovers at spiders' webs and with bill picks out entangled insects; comes to hummingbird feeders in garden or to hands or lips for powdered sugar or sugar water in vials; in N.H. garden, up to 20 visited scattered different feeders at same time; 50 or more in garden within hour (Pettingill, 1937). *Nest:* Usually in open woods, also in dense woods, margins of forests, orchards, saddled on limb or twig of maple, beech, birch, hornbeam, hemlock, etc., about 5–20 ft. above ground, often on down-sloping branch over brook and sheltered overhead by leaves; compactly built of soft down from ferns, milkweed, fireweed, thistles, young oak leaves fastened in place by hummer with her bill, using spiders' silk or web from tent caterpillar's nest; starts with mat on limb about 1 in. long, then builds up sides, decorates outside with bits of lichens, mosses until appears like small knot, about size of walnut or diameter of half-dollar (1–1¼ in.); upper edge of nest very thin and curved inward, which keeps two eggs about size of small beans from rolling out (Allen, 1930b); sometimes built in a day, but usually in a week (Forbush, 1925–29); apparently, if she survives, female returns each year to same place to nest. *Eggs:* Mar.–July; 2, white.

Incubation: 16 days (Nice, 1954); young fly about 20–22 days after hatching; two, occasionally three, broods a season (Bent, 1940).

Other Names: Common hummingbird; ruby-throat.

Accidents: Has been entangled in spiders' webs, stuck on purple flowers of pasture thistle, swept by wind into water in migration and drowned (see Accidents), caught by dragonfly and pinned to ground, snatched out of air by frogs, and three times reported to have been caught at flowers by praying mantis.

Age: A male, banded as juvenile at Oklahoma City, Okla., Aug. 1964, recaptured at same locality 5 years later (Vacin, 1970).

Albinism: Pure-white one with dark eyes photographed at bird feeder, Gardiner, Me. (Johnson, 1953).

Flight Speed: Timed in wind tunnel, maximum about 27 m.p.h. (Greenewalt, 1960); timed along highway in Pa., 45 m.p.h. (Hayes, 1929); and in Va., 55–60 m.p.h. (Allard, 1934).

Host to Cowbird: One record, July 1890, Mass., a single cowbird egg that completely filled the hummer's nest.

Weights: Three (sexes not identified), coastal N.J., in fall, 2.6–4 gr., or about ¹⁄₁₀–¹⁄₇ oz.; in Pa., adult males (32), 2.4–3.6 gr.; females (146), 2.8–4.5 gr.

Range: Nests from c. Alta., east to Nova Scotia, south to Gulf coast and s. Fla., west to e. N.D., e. S.D., c. Neb., c. Kans., s. Okla., and e.-c. Tex.; winters from s. Tex. and n.-c. Mexico, south to Costa Rica; casually to s. Ala., s. Fla., and casual visitor in Alaska, n. Ont., Labrador, Cuba, and Bermuda.

Hummingbird, rufous, *Selasphorus rufus* (seh-LASS-foe-rus ROOF-us); genus name: *see* Hummingbird, Allen's; species name: Lat., reddish. (Color ills., page 533.) Summers farther north than any other hummingbird—to Alaska and s. Yuk.; 3½–4 in. long; wingspread about 4¼ in.; male has reddish brown on back, base of crown, and most of tail (only N. American hummingbird with solidly rufous back), has brilliantly scarlet gorget that shines like burnished gold in certain light; chest white, other underparts pale rufous—only other species like it, Allen's, usually has green back (see Stiles, 1972, for method of distinguishing both sexes of these two look-alikes by their outer tail feathers); female, metallic green above, white below, with pale, rust-colored sides; cannot be distinguished certainly in field from female Allen's; most northern of hummingbirds, exceedingly abundant in low-level route northward in spring, west of Rockies (southbound, follows crest of Rockies and Sierras), in flight from winter home in s. Mexico; males precede females in spring; arrive Calif., late Feb. to early Mar.; Ore., by Mar. 1; Alaska, by mid-Apr.; spring arrival in Ore. coincides with blooming of shrubby crimson-flowered currant *(Ribes sanguineum);* male on breeding grounds in towering courtship flight may be joined by female, with copulation in the air (Bent, 1940); both sexes very aggressive in defense of feeding or nesting territories; not only drive away other hummingbirds but attack blackbirds, thrushes, and even chipmunks; so attracted to red that in camp on Admiralty Is., Alaska, male noted investigating red towel, red fruit box, red label on empty salmon can, and red bandana; in flying, wings make subdued humming, call note is *chewp chewp.*

Feeding Habits: Especially attracted to red flowers—columbines, penstemons, tiger lilies, paintbrushes of alpine meadows, also to white flowers of madrona tree in Ore. for nectar and insects; also tree sap.

Nest: Often built on low branch of conifer in Mont.: firs, larch, spruce, hemlock, etc., although may nest in other trees, shrubs, and vines; in w. Wash. has nested in loose colonies—up to 10 nests in small patch of gorse—but usually on drooping branch of conifer, 5–50 ft. above ground, in low vines or bushes where no trees; sometimes builds new nest on old one of previous year; a cup of cottony plant down, mosses, shreds of bark, about 1½–2 in. outside diameter, decorated on outside with lichens, bound with spiders' silk; also builds in such odd places as on knot of a hanging rope in woodshed; on wires of electric light bulb.

Eggs: May–July; 2, white.

Incubation: Usually by female, but in se. Alaska, a male seen incubating (Bent, 1940); period of not known (13–14 days reported is erroneous); young first fly about 20 days after hatching.

Hybrids: A male rufous × calliope hummingbird collected at Oakland, Calif., May 1896 (Banks and Johnson, 1961).

Weights: Males average 3.2 gr., females 3.4 gr.

Range: Nests from s. Alaska and s. Yuk., e.-c. B.C., sw. Alta., w. Mont., southwest of Cascade Mtns. to nw. Calif., s., Idaho; winters in Mexico;

has wandered to Neb., Okla., Tex., La., S.C., and Fla.

Hummingbird, rufous-tailed. *See* Hummingbird, Rieffer's.

Hummingbird, Salvin's. *See* Hummingbird, violet-crowned.

Hummingbird, violet-crowned, *Amazilia verticalis* (of A.O.U. *Check-list,* 1957) (am-ah-ZILL-ih-ah ver-tih-CAL-iss); genus name: *see* Hummingbird, buff-bellied; species name: Lat., vertical, relating to *vertex,* top or crown of head (Coues, 1882). (Color ill., page 533.) Mexican species that reaches U.S. in Ariz. and N.M.; 3¾–4¼ in. long; bill reddish with black tip; no other N. American hummingbird has *violet crown and gleaming white underparts,* from chin to crissum; female similar but with crown dull green-blue; once considered casual visitor to Huachuca and Chiricahua Mtns. of Ariz., in summer 1959 discovered nesting in Guadalupe Canyon (which straddles border of N.M. and Ariz.) by Seymour Levy and Dale Zimmerman—at least one nest within N.M.; the other on Ariz. side of canyon (Ligon, 1961) and more found in subsequent years; it and black-chinned hummingbird most common ones in Guadalupe Canyon; lives in habitat of streamside plant life in deserts and foothills of mountains.

Feeding Habits: Probably nectar and insects but no definitive studies reported.

Nest: Of cottony plant down, whitish cup, decorated on outside with lichens; nest in N.M. on limb of sycamore about 32 ft. above ground (Ligon, 1961).

Eggs: N.M., July; 2, white.

Incubation: Period of and age when young first fly unreported.

Other Name: Salvin's hummingbird.

Weights: Adults average 5.7 gr. (Des Granges, 1979).

Range: Nests from s. Ariz., s. N.M., south to s. Mexico; apparently winters over most of nesting range.

Hummingbird, white-eared, *Hylocharis leucotis* (high-low-KAH-riss lew-COT-iss); genus name: from Gr. *hyle,* a wood, and *charis,* beauty, delight, grace, charisma; literally "delight of the woods"; species name: Lat., from Gr. *leukos,* white, bright, and *otikos,* of the ear; *white-eared* in reference to white feathered stripe over the ears. (Color ill., page 534.) Mexican and C. American species that in summer has reached s. Ariz.; 3½ in. long; red bill with black tip; only small hummingbird reaching N. America with long white stripe (postocular) from eyes back along sides of head (see details in biography of the broad-billed hummingbird); male appears all-dark except for white stripe on sides of head; purple crown, emerald-green throat (gorget), green underparts, but mostly white; back bronze-green; female without purple crown; underparts white; formerly a rare summer visitor to southeastern mountains of Ariz. north to Santa Catalinas and Chiricahuas, but no authenticated record of occurrence after 1933 until July 4, 1961, since then sporadic; no good evidence that it ever

Xantus' hummingbird

HUMMINGBIRD FAMILY

bred in Ariz. (Phillips *et al.*, 1964). See life habits in Skutch (1940b).
Weights: Males average 3.6 gr., females 3.2 gr. (Lyon, 1976).
Range: Nests in mountains from s. Ariz. southward through highlands of Mexico to El Salvador, Honduras, and Nicaragua; winters Mexico and southward.

Hummingbird, Xantus' (ZAN-tus), *Hylocharis xantusii* (high-low-KAH-riss zan-TUSS-ih-eye); genus name: *see* Hummingbird, white-eared; species name: given by George Newbold Lawrence in honor of John Xantus, 19th-century collector of birds, who collected the then undescribed species in 1859 near Cape San Lucas, Baja Calif. Resident in South District, Baja Calif., also on islands in Gulf of California; small; 3¼–3½ in. long; adult male, upperparts mainly bright metallic bronze-green; throat and chest glittering emerald-green; rest of underparts mainly cinnamon; chestnut tail; has blue-black face; reddish bill with black tip; *white stripe from eyes back along sides of face* (like white-eared, but ranges of two do not overlap); female similar to male but without black on head; no green on throat or breast; has *black* bill; buffy stripe back of eyes; most abundant in mountains south of La Paz, especially on Sierra de la Laguna, where it ranges from high elevations down to lower limits of oaks among foothills, up to 200 seen within hour in Laguna Valley (Bent, 1940); likes mountain canyons, especially those with pools and streams.

Feeding Habits: Little-known, probably insects and nectar.
Nest: Female builds nest hanging from small twigs, or saddled on limbs of trees, 4–12 ft. above ground, often close to running water; built of seeds, plant down, dried flower heads, bound with spiders' silk, covered outside with lichens.
Eggs: Apr.–May in lowlands; July–Aug. in mountains; 2, dull white.
Incubation: Period of and age when young first fly unreported.
Other Name: Black-fronted hummingbird.
Range: See above.

Hummingbird, Yucatán. *See* Hummingbird, buff-bellied.

Woodstar, Bahama, *Calliphlox* (*Philodice* of some authorities) *evelynae* (CAL-ih-flocks ev-eh-LIN-ee); genus name: combined word from Gr. meaning beautiful, or beauty, and *phlox*, a flame (reddish); species name: given by Jules Bourcier, French Consul General to Ecuador (1849–50), a collector of birds, who in his original description in 1847 in the *Proceedings* of the Zoological Society of London, did not identify the person for whom he named it, possibly for his wife (?). The bird is a native of the Bahama Is., where it is *the* common hummingbird and often seen in Nassau, from which the first bird came—an adult male from which the species was described and named; lives about scrubby woods, coppices, and in gardens; wanders to se. Fla.; 3½–3¾ in. long; adult male, mostly green above; throat (gorget) and forehead of some males is red-violet; white upper breast band like a partial collar contrasts with reddish belly and reddish underparts; *deeply forked tail* of male is black and rufous; female has rounded tail and both throat and chest are white (Bond, 1961). Only two living ones, both immature males and reported by competent observers in Fla., have been sighted in U.S. up to 1974 (Owre, 1976). The first one roosted nightly from Aug. 26 to Oct. 13, 1971, alongside a house in Lantana, Fla.; the second, sighted at Homestead, Fla., was there from Apr. 7 to May 15, 1974, and was described by Fisk (1974a) as "bill black and slightly decurved; white spot behind the eye; back, and central rectrices [tail feathers] green; outer rectrices, rufous, with small, black subterminal spots, which, seen from below, formed a black bar [in tail]. Tail very slightly forked . . . a pure white breast band reached to back of nape [hind neck] forming an incomplete collar . . . underparts white with throat slightly buffy, sides of breast and flanks rufous; thighs white, crown grayish, a few green feathertips at bend of the wings." This bird kept to dry scrub with flowering shrubs at Homestead, and perched frequently between periods of feeding at the flowers of half a dozen kinds of tropical plants. *The first record and first specimen* for continental N. America was a dead one discovered by Melvin Finn, who found the dried-up bird with its bill stuck through a window screen of his Miami residence on Jan. 31, 1961 (Owre, 1976). Owre suggests that the Bahama woodstar may be in the beginning of an influx into se. Fla. and, because of its excellent flying abilities and the nearness of the Bahamas to Fla., may even have been wandering into Fla., unnoticed, for a long period of time.

Other Names (in Bahamas): God bird; hummingbird.
Range: Bahama Is., wanders to se. Fla.

HUN
See Partridge, gray, (formerly called Hungarian partridge) in Pheasant Family.

HUNGER TRACES
In captive growing young songbirds, taken just after leaving the nest, only a few days of insufficient feeding will cause the streaks, "fault bars," or hunger traces, which often appear conspicuously in the tail feathers. The streaks appear because the tiny hooks (*see* Feather) which hold together the vane of the feather do not grow properly because of a lack of food, or a lack of the proper kind of food (Heinroth and Heinroth, 1958). *See* Care and Feeding of Abandoned or Injured Wild Birds.

HURRICANES AND BIRDS
See Weather.

HUTCHINS
THOMAS (1730–90). English naturalist and surgeon in service of the Hudson Bay Company from 1775 (Wynne, 1969), but see Allen (1951); after his return to London became secretary of the company and died there June 7, 1790; a keen observer and collector of birds and mammals while in Canada; a small form of the Canada goose, thought at the time to be a distinct spe-

cies, was named *hutchinsii* for him about 40 years after his death by Sir John Richardson (Palmer, 1928).

HUTTON

WILLIAM. Field collector of birds about whom little is known; collected birds about Washington, D.C., in spring 1844, 1845, 1847; visited Calif. 1847–48, where at Monterey he obtained the vireo later described and named for him by John Cassin (Palmer, 1928).

HYBRID

(HIGH-brid). Name often used in a restricted sense for the offspring of the mating of the male of one species with the female of a different species (Gray, 1964), and so used in this item. The mule is the best-known hybrid among domestic animals—the result of crossbreeding of a male donkey (jack) with a female horse (mare).

It is well known that different species, usually closely related—wild ducks, for example—will crossbreed readily in captivity and produce hybrids (see Phillips, 1915; 1922–26) but do not usually do so in nature even where their breeding ranges overlap (Mayr, 1963).

For example, the mallard and pintail ducks are fully interfertile in captivity, or nearly so, but even though they nest side by side in large numbers by ponds, sloughs, or creeks in Europe, Asia, and N. America, very few hybrids are found among them. Species of birds retain their identities in nature, and crossbreeding, or hybridization, is ordinarily prevented by a series of *isolating mechanisms*—two examples are differences in courtship patterns and precise choice of habitat in which to live. *See* details of some of these isolating mechanisms under Species.

Many species of birds, however, do hybridize (crossbreed) in nature; some very rarely; some rather often. One of the most famous hybrid birds in America is Brewster's warbler of ne. U.S. When it was first discovered in the late 19th century by William Brewster, a New England ornithologist, he described it as a species new to science, but later Brewster and others realized that it was a hybrid with some characters of both parental species—the blue-winged warbler and the golden-winged warbler—and it was taken off the official list of species in the American Ornithologists' Union *Check-list of North American Birds*.

Only a small fraction of hybrids will backcross, or breed with either of its parental species (Mayr, 1963), but hybrids of blue-winged and golden-winged warblers do. The Brewster's warbler hybrids actually vary greatly but always lack a dark throat. Rarer is the backcross product or hybrid resembling the blue-winged warbler but with a dark throat patch—the Lawrence's warbler. *See* history of these two hybrids in the biography of the Brewster's and the Lawrence's warblers in Warbler—American Wood Warbler Family. See Gill (1980). The genetics has been explained by Parkes (1951).

According to Ficken and Ficken (1968), species differences in "releasers" (*see* Sign Stimuli, or Releasers, under Behavior) involved in pair formation, the different arrival times in the nesting habitat, and the reduced nesting success of hybrids tend to keep these two species distinct. They suggest that most mixed pairings are at places one species is rarer than the other. However, their area of hybridization has expanded northward (see Short, 1963), and according to Gill (1980), hybridization and northward invasion of the blue-winged warbler may be threatening the continued existence of the golden-winged warbler.

Mayr (1963) explains that the individuals of closely related species that live beyond their solid, or main, range, or at its borders, often have difficulty finding a mate. In the absence of adequate stimuli (its species-courtship behavior, for example) from one of its own kind, a bird is apt to respond to the "lower" stimuli of a bird of a related but different species. For the same reason (because of a lack of a mate of its own species) mismating of birds is commoner in zoos than in nature (see Gray, 1964).

The "Cincinnati warbler," of which the first one known to science was shot near Cincinnati (Madisonville, Ohio) and described in 1880 as a new species (Langdon, 1880), was apparently a hybrid between a blue-winged warbler and a Kentucky warbler (Ridgway, 1880).

Hybrids in nature attract the attention of ornithologists either because the hybrids are different in appearance or because they have songs different from the parental types. Over a dozen hybrids are known between the distinctive white-throated sparrow and dark-eyed junco. The "Sutton's warbler," or "Potomac warbler," of which a male and a female were shot about 18 mi. apart south of Martinsburg, W.Va. (see Brooks, M., 1945), is believed by Mayr (1963) and others to be a hybrid between the northern parula warbler (rare in that area) and a yellow-throated warbler. Mayr believes that pairing of the two species was facilitated by their similar nesting behavior.

There is a relatively high frequency of hybridization in families of birds with no or brief pair bonds (*see* The Pair Bond under Courtship), in which the intimate association of males and females is short (for example, in N. American hummingbirds and grouse). This leaves room for them to err in accepting or in choosing mates; however, the integrity of the parental species is not necessarily broken down even when the hybrids are frequent and fertile, which they rarely are.

Banks and Johnson (1961) discussed 11 hybrid hummingbirds of 7 different parental combinations (*see* these hybrids noted in biographies under Hummingbird Family) and pointed out that hybrids are not very common among birds despite the many references to them, owing to their interest. The distinctive differences in males of the various hummingbird species—in the colors of the gorget, the courtship of each species, including differences in the aerial dives and sounds uttered during their displays before the females—appear to act as isolating mechanisms in the Hummingbird Family.

Prairie chickens and sharp-tailed grouse frequently hybridize in recently cleared areas in Wisc. and in Ont., and the hybrids seem fully fertile. In many populations 5–25% of the birds show every degree of intermediacy between the parental species; however, the hybrid males

Brewster's warbler

Lawrence's warbler

HYBRID

Brewster's warbler is the hybrid offspring of the blue-winged and the golden-winged warblers and has some of the characteristics of each. It very rarely mates with other Brewster's warblers but backcrosses, breeding with one of its parent species. Lawrence's warbler is a rare, recessive hybrid offspring of a Brewster's warbler and a golden-winged warbler.

seem to be less successful in attracting mates (Mayr, 1963). Mallards and black ducks hybridize even more extensively in the eastern states.

Some striking wild hybrids have been reported in N. America—a hybrid between a little blue heron and a snowy egret reported from the north shore of Lake Okeechobee, Fla., by Sprunt (1954b); a cross between a black vulture and a turkey vulture that was caught alive in La. in the 1930s and sent to the National Zoo, Washington, D.C.; and a hybrid between an American coot and a common gallinule that had the red bill of the gallinule but white frontal shield of the coot, along with other mixed characters of both (McIlhenny, 1937).

According to Mayr (1963), by far the most frequent cause of hybridizing is the breakdown, or destruction, of habitat barriers between two species that were formerly separated by their distinctly different habitat preferences. One of the most dramatic examples of this is in the Great Plains of w. N. America.

According to Dillon (1956), the Wisconsin glacial period of about 10,000 years ago, spreading widely from the north to Iowa and S.D., forced birds that usually live in deciduous woodlands to retreat southward to the more temperate southeastern and southwestern parts of the N. American continent.

As the glaciers then receded northward, the climate developed the prairies and grasslands of the Great Plains. These were a broad, essentially uncrossable barrier to birds of forests and brushlands of e. U.S. (the rose-breasted grosbeak, Baltimore oriole, yellow-shafted flicker, indigo bunting, and rufous-sided towhee), also to their counterparts or close relatives of common ancestry in the West (the black-headed grosbeak, Bullock's oriole, red-shafted flicker, lazuli bunting, and spotted towhee). See also discussions about this in Hubbard (1969; 1973b) and in Mengel (1964; 1970).

Although riverine forests always existed coursing through the midcontinent grasslands, the farmers and ranchers settling this part of the country planted trees and shrubs for shade and wind protection. These plantings enhanced the ability of woodland birds of east and west to bridge the gap across the Great Plains. In 1838, the first known hybrid flicker, between the red-shafted of the West and yellow-shafted of the East, was shot by Audubon along the Missouri R.; the first hybrid of the Baltimore oriole and Bullock's oriole in Sask. in 1906; the first hybrid grosbeaks—black-headed and rose-breasted—were discovered in 1920 and 1923 in e. Neb. (see Anderson and Daugherty, 1974); the first hybrid of the indigo bunting and lazuli bunting in 1929; and hybrids of the eastern rufous-sided towhee and the western spotted towhee were more recently studied by Sibley and his co-workers. Following the islands or riverine strips of trees across the Great Plains, the related species and populations from East and West had met and had interbred. Apparently they had not been separated long enough in time to become reproductively isolated. [The American Ornithologists' Union (1973) because of the high frequency of interbreeding between the Baltimore oriole and Bullock's oriole de-

cided they are one species, now called the northern oriole. *See* Troupial Family. The same decision was made for the rufous-sided towhee and its western counterpart, the spotted towhee, now considered one species, called the rufous-sided towhee (*see* Finch Family); and the yellow-shafted flicker, red-shafted flicker, and gilded flicker are all now classified as one species, the common flicker. *See* Woodpecker Family.] *See* discussions under Species; Subspecies. For details of hybridization see papers of Sibley (1950, 1954); Sibley and Short (1959); Sibley and West (1958; 1959); and Short (1965; 1969b).

More recently, Mengel (1963) reported from Anchorage, Ky., a hybrid (presumably a migrant) between a scarlet tanager of the East and a western tanager of the West. He also cited a previous record of one from Minn. as earlier evidence that these formerly allopatric species (*see* Allopatric Species) are descendants of a common ancestor "of the not too distant past."

According to Mayr (1963), these are examples of birds that, even though not reproductively isolated from one another, and hybridizing where parts of their ranges overlap, are still largely allopatric, or live in separate ranges. He suggests calling some of them *semispecies*—birds which show some of the attributes of a species and some of the attributes of subspecies. *See* Species; Subspecies. Short (1969b) defines a semispecies in this way: "I restrict the term semispecies . . . to those forms actually or potentially capable of forming a zone of overlap and hybridization. On basis of suggested evidence for existence of partial isolating mechanisms in situations involving semispecies, I recommend that semispecies be considered taxonomically as species."

Mayr (1963) concludes that hybridism in most groups of animals, including birds, is so exceptional that it justifies a report in the scientific literature when discovered. He estimated that 1 out of 60,000 birds is a hybrid. Mayr and Short (1970) listed 23 situations of hybridization involving more than one or two natural hybrids occurring among no less than 47 species, in addition to 29 cases involving presumed intraspecific hybridization such as that between the flickers and orioles. See additional discussions of hybridism in Huntington (1952); Short (1963; 1965); Sibley (1957; 1961); and West (1962). For records of hybrids, when known, *see* in biography of each bird.

HYBRIDIZATION

In genetics, a term for the production of individual birds or other animals from genetically unlike parents. *See* Heterozygous; *also* Hybrid. In ornithology, in taxonomy specifically, a term for the crossing or crossbreeding between individual birds from different populations, especially between different species (Mayr *et al.,* 1953).

HYDROBATIDAE
See Storm-petrel Family.

HYOID
A bone composed of several parts that is the bony support of the tongue of a bird. *See* Tongue.

HYPOPHYSIS
(high-POF-ih-sis), or PITUITARY GLAND. *See* Endocrine Glands.

HYPOPTILUM
(high-POP-tih-lum). Another name for an afterfeather. *See* Afterfeather.

HYPORACHIS
(high-poh-RAY-kis). The shaft of an afterfeather. *See* Afterfeather.

HYPOTHALAMUS
See What Induces the Molt? under Molts and Molting.

HYPOTHERMIA
(high-poe-THURM-ih-ah). Subnormal, or below normal, temperature of the body as may be exhibited by the poor-will, swifts, hummingbirds, and certain others during cold or stormy weather, when they are likely to become torpid. *See* Torpidity.

IBIS FAMILY

Threskiornithidae (thres-kih-or-NITH-ih-dee); Lat., from Gr. *threskeia,* religious worship (sacred), and *ornis, ornithos,* bird. About 33 species in the world, includes both the ibises and the spoonbills; 5 species in N. America; mostly tropical in Africa, Madagascar, Eurasia, except northern part, Australia, and s. U.S., C. and S. America; medium- to large-sized birds; 19–42 in. long; long-necked, long-legged wading birds; tail short, toes partly webbed with middle toe slightly scalloped; all can swim, usually live about fresh water; in some, face bare of feathers as in storks, related to storks, herons, etc. (*see* relatives of in Ciconiiformes); sexes outwardly alike or nearly so; family is divided into two natural groups—the ibises, with long, thin, strongly downcurved bills with pointed tips, and the spoonbills, with bill broad and flattened at tip (spatulate); all are gregarious, usually nest in colonies in trees, some on ground, travel in flocks, strong fliers; like their close relatives the storks, fly with their heads and necks extended ahead, the long legs trailing behind; spoonbills usually fly with a steady wingbeat; ibises frequently alternate flapping with soaring or gliding and in unison; in flight, ibises and spoonbills fly in diagonal lines across the sky, sometimes in V-shaped flocks with each bird in flock a little to one side of bird ahead (*see* Formation Flying under Flight). Both ibises and spoonbills lack the powder down feathers of the related herons.

The Ibis Family is an ancient group—fossil record goes back some 60 million years to Eocene; their record in human history has been traced back to some 5,000 years ago; ancient Egyptians venerated the Old World sacred ibis, *Threskiornis aethiopica,* as part of their religious and written records; the birds were often mummified and buried in temples with the pharaohs; in Egypt the sacred ibis has been extinct for almost a century (Thomson, 1964h); commonest only in Africa south of the Sahara (Austin, 1961).

Besides species of ibises of N. America, whose biographies follow, others in the W. Hemisphere are the S. American buff-necked ibis, *Thersiticus caudatus;* the green, or Cayenne, ibis, *Mesembrinibis cayennensis,* Panama to n. Argentina; plumbeous ibis, *Harpriprion caerulescens,* c. Brazil and n. Argentina; whispering ibis, *Phimosus infuscatus,* of tropical parts of S. America; and sharp-tailed ibis, *Cercibis oxycerca,* from Orinoco to Río Negro (Thomson, 1964h). One of the most widely distributed in the family is the glossy ibis of both the Old and New worlds; commonest in New World is the white ibis; one of handsomest is the scarlet ibis.

To sustain an ill or injured ibis or spoonbill, offer a wide variety of food—small fishes, meat, ground bread, finely chopped green plants and vegetables. Although these are wading birds, they will take their food from solid surfaces of the protective fenced enclosure (Walker, 1942). To restore or to keep the pink color of roseate spoonbills, captives in the St. Louis Zoo were given a similar diet that included cottage cheese (Allen, 1942). All N. American members of family are protected by law. *See* Legal Protection.

IBIS FAMILY

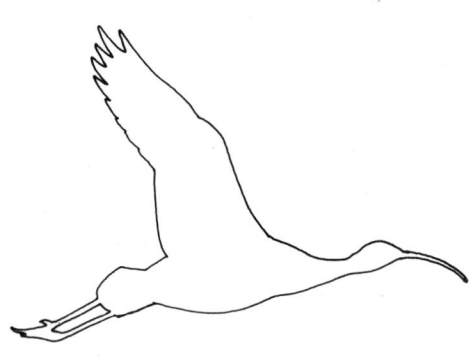

IBIS FAMILY
Ibises fly in diagonal lines or V-formations with their heads and necks extended and long legs trailing, alternately flapping their wings and soaring.

Ibis, eastern glossy. *See* Ibis, glossy.

Ibis, glossy, *Plegadis falcinellus* (PLEA-gah-dis or PLEG-ah-dis fal-sin-EE-lus); genus name: Lat., from Gr. *plegas, plegadis,* scythe, sickle; species name: Lat., a little scythe, small hook, in reference to shape of the bill (Coues, 1882). (Color ill., page 567.) Old World bird of Africa, se. Europe (no longer nests in Spain); sw. Asia, India, Burma, se. Australia; initially an irregularly breeding bird in N. America, in small colonies along Atlantic coast but recently has increased in numbers enormously (a common nesting bird where it was once rare) and ranges inland to great Lakes; Palmer (1962) suggests that this species may be a recent arrival in America from Old World, breeding records for N. America only from 1880s; smallest member of Ibis Family; 19–26 in. long; wingspread to about 38 in.; sexes outwardly alike but males average larger (Palmer, 1962); dark-appearing wading bird of freshwater or saltwater marshes; long downcurved bill; plumage mostly chestnut with metallic gloss but appears black at distance; legs gray or green-black; bare skin at base of bill, slate blue to white; found along Atlantic coast from Me. to Fla.; nests in Fla. from Mar. to May along Shark R., on grassy reefs of Lake Okeechobee, and Palm Beach County (Palmer, 1962); in Fla., usually nests in willows or mixed growths of mangroves, etc., also in willow, gums, swamp maple, and bay of cypress swamps; on N.J. coast, in mixture of holly, red cedar, wild black cherry, sumac, etc.; nested for first time in Conn. at Chimon Is. off Norwalk (Gauthreaux, 1971); withdraws southward to winter; wide dispersal of young after nesting season (*see* Dispersal); according to Palmer (1962), is a "chronic wanderer," has straggled west in U.S. to Mississippi R., also to Panama, Colombia, Bermuda, Iceland; a 1958 census reported a total nesting population in U.S. at only 400 pairs; however, in 1959, more than 1,200 pairs reported in a single colony in S.C. alone at Santee Gun Club.

Feeding Habits: In Fla., much feeding by probing in crayfish holes; eats largely crayfishes, also snakes (95% are water snakes), grasshoppers, cutworms, and other insects.
Nest: In small colonies almost always with herons and other large waders; nest built by both sexes, a platform of sticks on ground in cattail marsh or in trees or bushes, some 10 ft. above water.
Eggs: Mar. to late May; usually 3–4, blue-green.
Incubation: Mostly by female at night, by male during part of day, 21 days; chick feeds on parents' regurgitated food by putting bill in adults' mouth; young fly well and regularly, and can feed themselves 42 days after hatching; probably one brood a year; at nest, adults utter nasal grunting or series of guttural notes.
Other Names: Bay ibis; black curlew; eastern glossy ibis; green ibis; liver; Ord's ibis.
Age: One, banded in wild at Absecon, N.J., trapped and released in Seneca County, N.Y., when 5 years old (Kennard, 1975); one reported in Soviet Union to age of 21 years (Turček, 1958).
Hybrids: Glossy ibis × white-faced glossy ibis frequently in London Zoo (Gray, 1958), but not reported in N. America in wild (Palmer, 1962).
Weights: To about 28 oz. (Palmer, 1962).
Range: See above.

Ibis, scarlet, *Eudocimus ruber* (you-DOSS-ih-mus RUB-er or RUBE-er); genus name: Lat., from Gr. words meaning famous, in good standing, of high repute (Coues, 1882); the ibis of the ancients was a celebrated and sacred bird; species name: Lat., red. S. American species that has strayed north to southern U.S. Palmer (1962) wrote that Fla. birds reported are apparently escapes from zoos; national bird of Trinidad, where completely protected (ffrench and Haverschmidt, 1970); about size of white ibis; 21½–27½ in. long; wingspread about 38 in.; resident about tropical coasts and beaches near mangrove swamps, muddy estuaries, tidal flats, and dense canebrakes; adults outwardly alike, all-scarlet with black wing tips; long, downcurved bill, pink-brown to black; eyes dark brown; immature: upper parts dark brown-gray; underparts white; bill brown-orange; highly gregarious at all seasons, large numbers in roosts; usually silent but flock utters alarm note, a gurgling *gwe, gwe;* when quarreling, rattle bills; nervous and wary, easily driven away from breeding places by human intrusion.

Feeding Habits: In Surinam, eats mainly small crabs and mollusks; in Trinidad, principally fiddler crabs by probing mud often to base of bill; also eats aquatic insects, some fishes, snails, green algae.
Nest: Flimsy, built of dry twigs in forks of branches, sometimes uses old herons' nests; in large colonies, breeds in seasons of heavy rains; in Trinidad and in Surinam, nests and roosts around shallow waters with herons, especially little blue, etc. (ffrench and Haverschmidt, 1970); nests 5–35 ft. up in mangroves.
Eggs: Usually mid-Apr.–May; 2–3, dull olive-green to buff, marked with dark brown.
Incubation: About 23 days; nestlings climb about in trees when 14–21 days old, can fly about 28 days after hatching, but usually not until about 35–42 days old.
Age: One lived in National Zoo, Washington, D.C., to age of 7 years, 7 months.
Hybrids: Female scarlet ibis × male white ibis, both in U.S. and in Great Britain (Gray, 1958), but not considered conspecific with white ibis by ffrench and Haverschmidt (1970).
Weights: Of 20, in Trinidad, males larger than females: males (5) averaged 638 gr., or about 1 lb. 6½ oz., largest male 890 gr., or about 1 lb. 15½ oz.; females (10) averaged 595 gr., or about 1 lb. 5 oz., largest female 855 gr., or about 1 lb. 14 oz. (ffrench and Haverschmidt, 1970). Palmer (1962) reported a male, 935 gr., or about 2 lbs. 1 oz.
Range: Breeding range confined to northern part of S. America—Colombia, Venezuela, Trinidad to Guianas and ne. Brazil; a few isolated records from C. America, s. U.S. (ffrench and Haverschmidt, 1970); accidental in Tex., La., Fla., Jamaica, Honduras, and Costa Rica.

Ibis, white, *Eudocimus albus* (you-DOSS-ih-mus AL-bus); genus name: *see* Ibis, scarlet; species name: Lat., white. (Color ills., pages 568, 569.) Resident of s. U.S.; breeds from Fla. north to N.C., west along Gulf coast of Tex., south along both coasts of Mexico and Baja Calif.; 21½–27½ in. long; wingspread 38 in.; sexes outwardly alike but males average larger than females; size and shape of glossy ibis but adult is snow white with black wing tips, bare pink face; legs and long downcurved bill also pink; these areas red early in breeding season; eyes pale blue; immature: upperparts brown; underparts white; head mottled brown on white; in flight neck outstretched, rapid wingbeats alternate with sailing; in large loose flocks or sometimes in long straggling lines, usually seen not far from coast about saltwater, brackish, or freshwater marshes; in Fla. nests on islands along coast in heavy thickets of red and black mangroves, also in palmettos on Alafia Banks; vast nesting colony head of Shark R., Fla., extends over many acres; when approaching night roost from daytime feeding areas 10–15 mi. away, flocks fly in lines that may extend mile or more; at Duck Rock summer roost in Everglades National Park, 60,000–80,000 poured into mangroves in less than 3 hours (Palmer, 1962); this roost destroyed by hurricane in 1960; utter soft grunting notes, also *croo, croo;* alarm call when taking flight is rather loud *urnk, urnk* or *hunk, hunk, hunk.*

Feeding Habits: In feeding probes mud with slender bill; walks in and out of arching mangrove roots at low tide, or along reedy borders of Fla. prairie ponds, or stand side by side picking up mud crabs and other small animals from grass; utters low nasal grunting while feeding; eats largely crustaceans, also fishes, frogs, small snakes, slugs, snails, aquatic beetles.
Nest: Loosely built platform of sticks, in colonies, in trees, 3–15 ft. above water; also nests in sawgrass and bullrushes in Fla., La., and Mexico.
Eggs: Mar.–mid-May; 3–4, green-white, marked with browns.
Incubation: About 21–23 days; young leave nest 21 days after hatching but do not fly until about 35 days old.
Other Names: Brown curlew; Spanish curlew; stone curlew; white curlew.
Age: One lived in National Zoo, Washington, D.C., to age 18 years, 6 months.
Hybrids: See Scarlet ibis.
Weights: To 2 lbs. (Palmer, 1962).
Range: Resident from c. Baja Calif., Mexico, coastal Tex., S. La., Fla., se. Ga., and N.C., south along both Mexican coasts to n. S. America and to Cuba, Isle of Pines, and West Indies; wanders casually northward, usually in fall to s. Calif., Colo., S.D., Mo., Ill., Va., N.J., Long Is., N.Y., Que., Vt.; compared with glossy ibis, wanders sparingly (Palmer, 1962).

Ibis, white-faced, *Plegadis chihi*; genus name: *see* Ibis, glossy. (Color ill., page 570.) Not considered a full species by some authorities—for example, Palmer (1962), who treats the white-faced ibis (formerly called white-faced glossy ibis) of w. U.S. as a subspecies, *Plegadis falcinellus chihi*, of the glossy ibis of e. U.S.;

both are dark, chestnut-colored, with long, downcurved bill; only during the breeding season can they be distinguished in the field from each other, when white-faced ibis has a narrow border of *white feathers* about the bare facial skin, from top of the bill around the eyes and under the chin; in the glossy ibis, the blue facial skin (at least the edges between the eyes and bill) becomes white at onset of the breeding season (Palmer, 1962), at other times the two birds appear identical (see comparative illustrations in Robbins *et al.*, 1966); however, breeding ranges of the two birds are distinct except, sporadically, in narrow overlap in La., which has not resulted in interbreeding (see Mayr and Short, 1970); white-faced ibis formerly nested from Minn. to Ore. (*see* under Range), now nests in isolated colonies from e.-c. Ore. to Kans., southeast at least to coasts of Tex. and La.; center of greatest abundance seems to be in Utah, Tex., and La. (Ryder, 1967); during summer of 1970, white-faced ibis appeared to be in serious trouble because of pesticides; at least 1,000 adults in colony on island in Lavaca Bay, Tex., produced very few young, and those examined contained lethal concentrations of dieldrin, a chemical much used at the time by rice growers of the area (see Harris, V.T., 1972); some thin-shelled eggs found in colony at Stillwater, Nev., summer 1970, and grave breeding failures, owing to thin-shelled eggs, in colony near Salt Lake City (Gauthreaux and Shugart, 1970).

Feeding Habits: Apparently prefers freshwater marshes, where eats insects, newts, leeches, earthworms, some snails, crustaceans, especially crayfishes, frogs, and fishes; in La., eats crabs and crayfishes (Palmer, 1962).
Nest: In colonies, at times in small groups in heronries; nest usually built in large bed of bulrushes or reeds; a deep cup of dead reeds lined with grasses attached several feet above the water to bulrushes or on floating mats of dead plants (Bent, 1926a).
Eggs: Calif., May–July; Tex., Apr.–June; usually 3–4, greenish-blue.
Incubation: 21–22 days (Bent, 1926a).
Other Names: Black curlew; white-faced glossy ibis.
Age: One lived in San Diego Zoo to age 14 years (Stott, 1948); in wild, oldest banded bird reported was slightly more than 9 years old (Ryder, 1967).
Flight Speed: Timed in w. U.S., 30–33 m.p.h. (Cottam *et al.*, 1942b).
Hybrids: See under Ibis, glossy .
Range: According to A.O.U. *Check-list* (1957), overall nesting range was from c. Calif., e. Ore., n. Utah, Colo., Neb., and Minn. south locally into Mexico, Tex., and sw. La., also Fla., and in e. and s. America (for N. American recent range, see Palmer, 1962, and Ryder, 1967); winters from Calif., se. Ariz. (rarely), s. Tex., sw. La., south into Mexico, C. America, to Costa Rica; wanders casually north to s. B.C., e. Wash., n. Idaho, n. Wyo., N.D., Mich., Ohio, w. N.Y.; reported from Hawaiian Is.

Ibis, white-faced glossy. *See* Ibis, white-faced.

Ibis, wood. Another name for the wood stork; called a wood *ibis* because downcurved bill resembles that of an ibis.

Spoonbill, roseate (ROW-ze-ate), *Ajaia ajaja* (eye-EYE-ah ah-YAH-yah); genus name: old Brazilian name for the bird; species name: Sp., from Tupian, Cariban, or Arawak Indian name for the bird. (Color ill., page 570.) Largest N. American member of Ibis Family; only spoonbill native to W. Hemisphere (Allen, 1942); nests in s. Fla. and along Tex. coast; 30–34 in. long; wingspread to about 52 in.; sexes outwardly alike; adult, bright pink-and-white wading bird with spoonlike bill; neck, breast, and back whitish; tail orange; bright red shoulder pattern on pink wings; head naked of feathers, head skin pale green to golden buff at pairing; eyes ruby red or scarlet; adult is only pink bird likely to be seen within its range in U.S.; spatulate bill distinguishes it from tall, long-legged flamingo and scarlet ibis; immature has head feathers, a largely white bird but bill distinctive; usually in small flocks, frequently associates with other wading birds; in flight, neck is extended straight forward; often glides between wing strokes; flies in bunches, lines, or in wedge-shaped formations; flocks arrive in coastal La. and Tex. late Feb. to early Mar.; nest Apr.–June; after nesting some dispersal before departure for Mexico; part of population remains in Tex. throughout year; late Sept. to early Oct., spoonbills move into e. Fla. Bay, nest there Nov.–Jan. (Palmer, 1962), with a dispersal in late Mar. and Apr. from Cape Sable north along southwest coast to Tampa Bay where few have nested in recent years; in Fla. Bay, nests in mangroves; in Tex., in low bushes along coastal islands and even on treeless spoil banks along Intracoastal Waterway; in La., in Sabine Refuge, nests mainly in willows; Bottle Point Key, Fla. Bay, was original Fla. colony but more important in recent years are other keys in e. and n. Florida Bay. In 1939, only 30 spoonbills remained in Fla., but with strict protection increased to more than 400 by mid-1950s, and to 500–600 nesting pairs in the late 1970's. In Tex. and La., roseate spoonbill is increasing. See also Allen (1942) for complete report of decline and early history of roseate spoonbill.

Feeding Habits: Fla. Bay colonies feed in tidal ponds and sloughs along main chain of keys—Key Largo, Plantation, and Matecumbe, and on the south part of the mainland in Everglades; in Tex., feed in salt, brackish, and fresh waters; in La., mainly in fresh water; each bird swings partly opened bill from side to side through mud and water, *feeling* for small fishes, crustaceans, mollusks, slugs, aquatic insects; when nerve endings along inner lining of bill indicate contact with living animal, spoonbill snaps bill shut, trapping prey (*see* Touch); even in captivity, young spoonbill feeds in same way on killifishes or live shrimp in clear water of basin; feels for them blindly even though able to see them (Allen, 1942).
Nest: Rather bulky, of sticks and twigs, lined with leaves and bark, 5–15 ft. up in densely leaved low tree or bush, in rookeries with her-

Ichthyornis

ICHTHYORNIS

ons, ibises, and other water birds, usually on an island.

Eggs: Fla., laid mostly Nov.; Tex., Apr.; 1–4, usually 2–3, white, spotted with browns.

Incubation: By both sexes, in turn, 23–24 days (one brood a year); chick hatches with bill already spatulate (Palmer, 1962); leaves nest 35–42 days after hatching, but does not perfect flight until 49–56 days old; young not fully adult until in third year.

Age: One lived in National Zoo, Washington, D.C., 10 years, 5 months.

Other Names: Pink curlew; rosy spoonbill.

Weights: To about 3½ lbs. (Palmer, 1962).

Range: Resident, nests in s. Fla. and in La. and coastal Tex., on Gulf coast, nw. Mexico, south to Argentina; also Cuba, Hispaniola, Isle of Pines, and s. Bahamas; winters coast of s. Tex. and S. Fla. southward; has wandered north to Calif., Utah, Colo., Neb., Ind., Ala., Ga., N.C., and Pa.

Spoonbill, white, *Platalea leucorodia* (plah-TAY-lee-ah lew-koh-RODE-ih-ah); genus name: Lat., spoonbill; species name: Lat., from Gr., white rose (Jaeger, 1960). Breeds locally from w. Europe eastward to India; accidental in Greenland; about 34 in. long; white wading bird with spoonlike bill; black legs; black bill with yellow tip; ocher marking on upper breast; in summer has bushy crest; immature birds have black wing tips, pink bills, yellow legs.

IBIS, THE
A publication. *See* England under Ornithological Periodicals.

ICE BIRD
See Dovekie and Razorbill in Auk Family.

ICE STORMS AND BIRDS
See Weather.

ICHTHYORNIS
(ik-thih-OR-nis); Lat., from Gr. *icthys, icthyos,* fish, and *ornis,* a bird. *Ichthyornis,* or "fish bird," is the name of a genus (*see* Genus) of some 7 species of fossil, gull-like flying birds, one of the remarkable discoveries of Professor O. C. Marsh of Yale University. The bones of 6 species were dug from the Niobrara formation of the Upper Cretaceous in Kans. in the 1870s (*see* Geological Time Scale), from which Marsh discovered *Hesperornis. See* Hesperornis. Marsh found the bones of a seventh species of *Ichthyornis* in the Upper Cretaceous near McKinney, Tex. (Wetmore, 1956). Apparently *Ichthyornis* resembled a gull or a tern and was similar to one in size and habits, although some authorities believe it was related to auks; it was a strong-flying bird with a keeled sternum (*see* Carinate) and with well-developed wings. Presumably it lived on fishes, in view of the number of fossil fishbones associated with the discovered fossils of this bird. Both *Ichthyornis* and *Hesperornis* disappeared when the inland seas receded from what is now known as the N. American Great Plains, and they left no known descendants.

For some time, *Ichthyornis* was thought to be a toothed bird, but Gregory (1952), from his investigations, concluded that the toothed jaws

formerly attributed to *Ichthyornis* were actually those of a marine, fish-eating reptile—a mosasaur, or aquatic lizard (Wetmore, 1956); however, Walker (1967), after careful study of the toothed jaws associated with the type specimen of *Ichthyornis dispar* at Peabody Museum, Yale University, stated his belief that until further proof is available, the toothed jaws should be regarded as belonging to *Ichthyornis;* later, Walker found a second partial skeleton of *Ichthyornis* with toothed jaws. See Gingerich (1972), who from his own studies of an additional mandibular fragment of *Ichthyornis dispar* that he found with the bones of the much larger *Hesperornis,* concluded that *both Ichthyornis and Hesperornis* were the last-known surviving birds that had teeth, and not *Hesperornis* alone, as previously believed. *See also* Baptornis; Fossil Birds; Geological Time Scale. *See also* Archaeopteryx under Origin of Birds and of Bird Flight in Fossil Birds.

ICTERID
(IK-ter-id). General term for any of the N. American blackbirds, grackles, orioles, meadowlarks, cowbirds, and the bobolink. Less familiar ones are the tropical troupials, oropendolas, and caciques (ka-SEEKS). All belong to the family Icteridae, or Troupial Family. The name *troupial,* from a S. American oriole that was the first of the group to be described, is used as the family name by Van Tyne and Berger (1959; 1976). *See* Troupial Family.

ICTERIDAE
See Troupial Family.

-IDAE
(ih-dee). Each family of birds (*see* Family) is composed of at least one genus (a group of closely related birds) or a number of genera. Scientists have arranged these genera in separate families, and grouped them to show close relationships within the family. In giving these bird families (usually groups of genera) their scientific names, the Lat. suffix *-idae* is used at the end of the genus name chosen for the family. It (*-idae*) is a feminine plural adjectival suffix, which, when added to the stem of the genus name chosen, designates the scientific family name.

For example, the scientific name of the Pigeon Family is Columbidae. It is a combination of the Lat. name *Columba,* a genus of certain closely related pigeons and doves in the Pigeon Family, and *-idae* (from a Gr. plural meaning "like"), which is substituted for the last syllable of the genitive case of the genus name *Columba*—thus: Columbidae. The genus name chosen for the family may be the chief genus, the earliest known for the family, or the most typical genus of the family. See how scientific family names are chosen in Mayr *et al.* (1953). The family names of birds always end in *-idae,* which makes the family designation easy to recognize. *See* Family; *also* Genus.

IDEATION
See Birds That Can "Count" under Behavior.

-IFORM

(ih-form); plural, IFORMES (ih-FOR-meez), from Lat., *forma*, form or shape; a suffix always used in names of orders of birds, for example, Columbiformes (Col-um-bih-FOR-meez), from Lat. *columba*, dove, and *—iformes* (*forma*); dove-shaped (Coble, 1954). *See* Order.

ILEUM

See Intestine.

ILIUM

One of three paired bones that, with the synsacrum, form the pelvic girdle. *See* Skeleton.

IMMATURE

See Nestling; Subadult.

IMPERFORATE

The nostrils of birds are usually completely separated from each other by a septum, or wall; they are therefore *imperforate;* in those few groups of birds without the nasal septum, in which the nostrils communicate with each other, as in the vultures, they are *perforate.* *See* Nostrils.

IMPERVIOUS

Term for closed nostrils of certain birds such as adult gannets and cormorants. *See* discussion under Nostrils.

IMPRINTING

See How and What Birds Learn under Behavior.

INATTENTIVE PERIOD

Time when an incubating bird is off the nest, when it may feed, bathe (*see* Bathing), preen (*see* Preening), or simply rest. *See* Attentive Period.

INBREEDING

Mating as closely as brothers with sisters, mothers with sons, fathers with daughters. Inbreeding is apparently rare in most species of birds in the wild. *See* some examples under Sexual Relationships.

It has been suggested that close inbreeding among wild game birds could be harmful to them, but according to Stoddard (1931) in his 5 years of study of wild bobwhite quail in Georgia, "it has never been definitely proved that inbreeding alone has been responsible for deterioration in any wild race, either of birds or mammals. . . ." Stoddard discussed conditions among quail in se. U.S. that contributed to a thorough "shuffling" (*see* Fall Shuffle; Dispersal) of the quail before nesting time and concluded that there was little possibility of close inbreeding on normally stocked quail ground. See also discussion of this by Nestler and Nelson (1945) and their experiments with inbreeding of captive quail. See also Allen, D. (1954, p. 296); Crandall (1917, pp. 359–60); and McAtee (1932a).

INCUBATION

The action of a parent bird in sitting on its eggs and applying body heat to them. Nearly all passerine birds and many other small, non-passerine birds lay an egg a day until the clutch is completed. *See* Clutch. Many birds begin to incubate after the last egg in the clutch is laid, although some birds—owls, for example—may start to incubate after laying the first egg in the clutch. *See* Cannibalism.

A bird may sit on its eggs all night after laying them without incubating them, but when incubation begins, a robin, for example, supplies body heat to its eggs through an *incubation patch*. This is a featherless area of bare skin on the underpart, or belly area, of a bird's body which during the breeding season is thickened and develops a rich supply of blood vessels just under the skin. By pressing this bare, warm area—the incubation patch—against the eggs, the bird helps transfer heat to them from its body. When a bird settles on the nest to brood its eggs, it puffs out its breast feathers, and shuffles about until it brings the bare incubation patch, or patches, in contact with the eggs. The periodic development of the incubation patches, according to Bailey (1952), is controlled by hormones. *See* Endocrine Glands.

Bailey studied the incubation patch in 12 families of passerine birds and found no significant variation among them. They have a single large incubation patch coincident in size with the ventral apterium (*see* Apteria). The brood patch forms in several stages: (1) all the down feathers (*see* Feather) of the ventral apterium are molted several days before the bird lays its first egg; (2) after the molting of the down feathers, blood vessels in the skin of the brood patch increase in size and number, and the skin becomes slightly thickened; (3) the incubation patch continues to become vascularized, and the skin swollen; this lasts through the incubation period and through the first part of brooding the young birds after they are hatched; (4) a period of recovery when the swelling and vascularity of the incubation patch subsides and the skin gradually returns to normal. By the time the young are able to fly and feed themselves, the skin of the adult bird's incubation patch has returned to normal, and it becomes refeathered during the fall molt. *See* Molts and Molting. However, if another set of eggs is laid, the cycle is repeated. Bailey found by experiment that the incubation patch can be induced in non-breeding birds by treating them continuously with the hormone estradiol.

NUMBER OF INCUBATION PATCHES IN BIRDS.
Passerines—the perching birds, or songbirds—have a single median incubation patch, as do the birds of prey, grebes, and pigeons. Shorebirds—for example, plovers and sandpipers, also gulls—have a pair of lateral incubation patches and a median posterior one. Gallinaceous birds—pheasants, grouse, turkeys, partridge, quail, etc.—also have three incubation patches, but the median one is between, rather than behind, the other two, with which it becomes more or less confluent.

Some birds, such as all members of the order Pelecaniformes (pelicans, tropicbirds, frigatebirds, cormorants, boobies, gannets, and anhingas) lack an incubation patch. In some species of this group (e.g., gannets), the feet surround the egg and large webs may transfer some heat to the eggs, although in other species (some

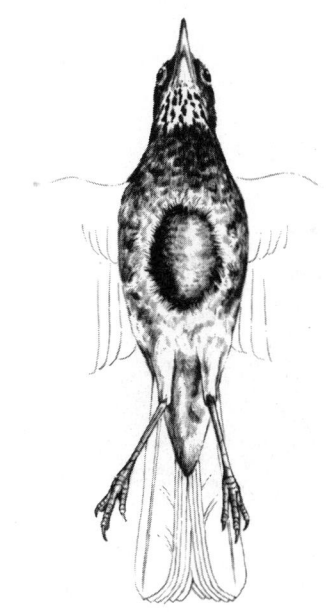

INCUBATION
The robin's single brood patch is typical of passerines. A few days before the eggs are laid, the down feathers drop from the abdomen of the incubating parent, and the bare patch becomes swollen and richly supplied with blood vessels. After the eggs are laid, the bird settles on its nest and brings this warm patch in contact with its eggs, thereby transferring heat to the developing embryo.

boobies and tropicbirds), the feet definitely do not provide the major heat source (see Drent, 1975, for excellent review of incubation). Ducks and geese create an incubation patch by plucking down feathers from their abdomen. The megapodes, or mound builders, of Australia and islands of se. Asia lay their eggs in the earth in decaying vegetation, and allow the heat produced from this to provide warmth for the embryos.

WHICH SEX INCUBATES THE EGGS? In the vast majority of birds, the incubation patches are important to incubation. This is confirmed by the fact that only the sex that has them incubates. Only male phalaropes incubate the eggs and they—not the females—possess incubation patches. In other species in which the male alone incubates, only he has the patches. Only females possess patches if they are the sole caretakers of the eggs. If both sexes incubate, both sexes develop incubation patches.

In most passerines, or songbirds, only the female has the incubation patch, lending some doubt as to the usefulness of the incubating of the males in this group. However, an incubation patch has been discovered during the nesting season in the males of some passerine birds —for example, in the crested flycatcher, Clark's nutcracker, and several Brazilian Tyranni, a suborder of passerine birds that includes the tyrant flycatchers, woodhewers, and their allies.

It is commonly noted that the duller-colored sex is the one that does most of the incubating of eggs and brooding of the young. When the sexes look alike, both may share in the incubation. The duller-colored mate, usually the female, supposedly escapes detection by predators more than her brightly colored mate, with better chances of raising the brood successfully. The brightly colored male, however, often helps to feed the young after hatching and often feeds the incubating female on the nest. In the rose-breasted grosbeak, the brightly colored male shares with his mate the brooding of the eggs. This has aroused skepticism toward the theory that the sex differences in coloration evolved solely because of the protective value of the dull colors of the sitting bird (Kendeigh, 1952b). Van Tyne and Berger (1959), after correspondence with ornithologists in many countries, concluded that of some 160 families or more of living birds of the world, in 54% of the families, incubation is usually by both sexes; in 25%, by the female alone; in 6%, by the male alone; and in 15%, by the male, the female, or both. See discussion by White and Kinney (1974).

In 1950, Swanberg pointed out that it has been known for two centuries that domestic pigeons may sit on the first egg in the nest without applying warmth to it; however, many wild birds begin incubation with the laying of the first egg—loons, grebes, pelicans, herons, storks, eagles, hawks, cranes, many gulls, cuckoos, parrots, owls, swifts, hummingbirds, and a few songbirds, or passerines. See Bateman and Balda (1973). Most passerines, ducks, geese, and gallinaceous birds—quail, turkeys, pheasants, etc.—do not incubate until the last egg in the clutch is laid (Welty, 1962).

INCUBATION
The blue-footed booby incubates its single egg with its webbed feet, which are adapted for rapid circulation of warm blood and are as effective as a brood patch is for other birds.

Nice (1954) states that in nature it is generally possible to determine the incubation period with satisfactory exactness by checking the time from the laying in the nest of the last egg of the clutch to the hatching of the last young. As a rule, this method gives the shortest incubation period, as the development of the embryo in the last egg laid continues without the interruptions to which the earlier-laid eggs are subjected. With grebes and rails, however, the last egg is sometimes neglected, and thus takes longer to hatch than the others. *See* Eggs and Egg-laying. "Normal" incubation may vary a day or more according to season, weather, and attentiveness of the sitting bird (Nice, 1954). *See* Attentive Period; Inattentive Period.

The incubation period varies among different families of birds from a minimum of 11 days in some passerines to about 12 weeks (royal albatross), and during long incubation periods, some birds sit without eating (see Skutch, 1962). The length of the incubation period for each species is apparently a function of inherent rate of development of the embryo, which is genetically fixed. *See* Embryo and Its Development. Tests show that, in general, trying to speed up the incubating period (shortening it) by applying more heat to the eggs experimentally often does not hasten the embryo's development without affecting the embryo adversely. Baldwin and Kendeigh (1932) discovered that the eggs of house wrens show a greater resistance to low (cool) temperatures than high (hot) temperatures. *See* Egg Temperatures. For the incubation periods of various N. American birds, *see* under the biography of each. *See also* Eggs and Egg-laying; Nests and Nesting; Young and Their Care.

INCUBATION PATCH
See Incubation.

INCUBATION PERIOD
See Incubation.

INCUMBENT
Term for position of a bird's hind toe, or hallux. *See* Hallux. The hind toe is said to be incumbent when, as in the meadowlark and robin, it grows out on a level with, or on the same plane as, the other three toes. Tracks of such a bird, in sand or in mud, show the impression of four toes—three pointed forward and the hallux, or hind toe, pointed backward. *See* Elevated; *also* Feet and Legs.

INCURSION
Another term for invasion by birds. *See* Invasion; Irruption.

INDETERMINATE (EGG) LAYER
See Eggs and Egg-laying.

INDIAN HEN
Another common name for the American bittern and night herons in Heron Family; also, as applied in s. U.S. to the ivory-billed and pileated woodpeckers, a wild "hen," or a large bird, with possibly some reference to the pileated's cackling calls.

INDIAN PULLET
See Bittern, American, and Heron, black-crowned night, in Heron Family (McAtee, 1959); *see also* in Limpkin Family.

INDIGO BIRD
See Bunting, indigo, in Finch Family.

INFECTION
See Diseases.

INFUNDIBULUM
(in-fun-DIB-you-lum). *See* Eggs and Egg-laying.

INGLUVIES
See Crop.

INJURIES
See Accidents; Deformities.

INJURY-FEIGNING
See Distraction Display.

INNATE BEHAVIOR
See Instinct.

INQUILINE
An animal that lives in the nests of ants, birds, etc., without doing any particular damage to the host, or giving it any particular benefit (Bates, 1961). For example, snails and a considerable number of species of insects, mites, ticks, spiders, pseudo-scorpions, an occasional centipede, wood louse, or free-living nematode may live in the nest or nests of certain birds without doing the bird harm or benefit. These are *inquilines;* however, other insects and mites, for example, that occupy nests and feed on the blood or feathers of birds are parasites. *See* Ectoparasite; Parasite; see also Rothschild and Clay (1957).

INSECTIVOROUS
Said of birds such as swallows, wrens, warblers, flycatchers, and many others that feed largely on insects.

INSECT PARASITES
(of birds). *See* Fleas; Hippoboscid Flies; Lice; Protocalliphora. *See also* Ectoparasite; Parasite; Diseases.

INSECTS AND BIRDS
The insects, of which there are estimated to be almost one million species in the world, are the most numerous class of arthropods and the most important animal food of birds. In stomach analyses of 80,000 N. American birds reported upon by McAtee (1932b), insects were 88% of all their animal foods. *See* Food and Feeding Habits; *see also* Feeding Habits in the biographies of each bird. Most passerines (songbirds), which make up more than half the species of birds in the world, are predominantly insect-eaters. Even some which as adults are not insect-eaters—for example, the seed-eating passerines such as our native sparrows, grosbeaks, and finches—eat some insects at nesting time and feed them to their young. Following is a very brief survey of some of the insect groups most preyed upon by birds, according to

McAtee (1932b), and some of the birds that eat them.

GRASSHOPPERS, LOCUSTS, AND CRICKETS (ORTHOPTERA). These were nearly 10% of all insects in the stomachs of birds reported by McAtee, and are eaten by all birds except those that are strict vegetarians. When these insects are abundant, birds of all sizes make them their staple food. In McAtee's study, the stomachs of some individual birds, such as crows and meadowlarks, held more than 1,000 grasshoppers; starlings and grackles, more than 1,500. Bluebirds made grasshoppers 22% of their food; the grasshopper sparrow, 23%; meadowlarks, 26%; the western kingbird, 28%; the Franklin's gull, 43%. In an invasion in Neb. by Rocky Mountain locusts, more than 172 species of birds—from hummingbirds to the largest hawks—ate these enormously abundant insects. *See* examples of the suppression of insects by birds under Economic Ornithology; see also Dowden and Mitchell (1966) and Stewart, P. A. (1975).

DRAGONFLIES AND DAMSELFLIES (ODONATA). About 200 species of birds are known to eat Odonata (McAtee, 1932b) and they take nymphs (the aquatic immature forms) as well as the flying adults. From 100 to 125 nymphs were taken from the gullets and gizzards of individual ducks, yellowlegs, and magpies, and birds capture the largest and swiftest adult dragonflies. One of the largest species, *Anax junius*, is commonly eaten by the merlin, or pigeon hawk; up to 28 individuals of this dragonfly were found in a single stomach, and 120 of 128 stomachs of this falcon contained this dragonfly. Purple martins regularly prey on several kinds of dragonflies, from the largest to some of the smaller species.

BUGS, CICADAS, LEAFHOPPERS, APHIDS, SCALE INSECTS, ETC. (HEMIPTERA AND HOMOPTERA). These are much eaten by birds: 39 species in McAtee's report ate chinch bugs, and 3—bobwhite quail, meadowlark, and brown thrasher—had eaten more than 100 at a meal; 87 species of birds had eaten cicadas—from house wrens to nighthawks and crows; 41 species had eaten adult spittlebugs; 136 species had eaten treehoppers (membracids), especially flycatchers, meadowlarks, blackbirds, swallows, house sparrows, vireos, bushtits, and kinglets; 175 species had eaten leafhoppers.

BUTTERFLIES AND MOTHS (LEPIDOPTERA). Birds ate mostly the larvae (caterpillars) of this group, which they consume about equally with grasshoppers, locusts, and crickets. Many birds especially favor cutworms—bobwhite quail, killdeer, the cuckoos, catbird, brown thrasher, robin, and many others—also the small green caterpillars ("loopers" or measuring "worms") of the geometrid moths, so relished by warblers and other small birds.
In McAtee's report, 200–300 stomachs of birds of 8 species held caterpillars—downy woodpecker, blue jay, red-winged and Brewer's blackbirds, warbling vireo, black-capped chickadee, hermit thrush, and eastern bluebird—and caterpillars were in 300–400 stomachs of the red-eyed vireo and American robin. About 75

species, including the tiny chickadees, eat the hairy tent caterpillars; 46 species eat the caterpillars of the gypsy moth; 31 species eat the caterpillars of the brown-tailed moth; some, such as the red-eyed vireo, eat caterpillars of the fall webworm. House sparrows and the American robin eat caterpillars of the tussock moth. *See* records of birds eating large numbers of insects under Food and Feeding Habits.

Birds also eat the adult (imago stage) butterflies and moths; the merlin preys especially on butterflies during its southward migrations, and the peregrine falcon catches and eats in flight monarch butterflies during its migrations. Starlings and the black-billed cuckoo have been seen eating monarch butterflies, although they are distasteful to most birds. Many, especially members of the Nightjar Family, eat large quantities of moths at night; also many owls such as burrowing, screech, saw-whet, elf owl, and flammulated owl eat moths. Forty-five species of birds eat codling moths and their caterpillars (McAtee, 1933b).

BEETLES AND WEEVILS (COLEOPTERA). These may well be among the most favored insect foods of birds owing to their abundance and availability. Some examples are the long-horned beetles, many of which spend their larval (grub) stage in the wood of trees and are eaten by 162 species of birds. Several woodpeckers make them 10–50% of their total food. More than 200 species of birds eat leaf beetles, with 23 species eating the Colorado potato beetle. Weevils, hard-shelled members of the group, are eaten much by birds, with some 20,000 identifications of weevils in birds' stomachs, according to McAtee's 1932 report.

FLIES (DIPTERA). Much eaten by birds, especially the adults of crane flies, midges, and mosquitoes; more than 10,000 records of these insects in birds' stomachs were reported by McAtee; 7 species of swallows made Diptera 13–40% of their total food, and among flycatchers, Diptera constituted 11–44% of their entire subsistence.

MOSQUITOES AND BIRDS. Many birds, especially the smaller, insectivorous ones and the shorebirds, feed upon mosquitoes. Food-habits studies of birds have shown that mosquitoes and their larvae are adequately represented in the stomach contents of birds, but at one time it was difficult to get identifications of flies (mosquitoes are in the Diptera, or Fly Family) found in birds' stomachs and even more so of their larvae. W. L. McAtee, a food-habits investigator for the federal government, from his studies, believed there is no group of birds that habitually avoids Diptera, and reported that he knew of records of 50–500 flies or their larvae taken by a bird at a single meal. Nine species of shorebirds—the northern and Wilson's phalaropes, the stilt, pectoral, Baird's, least, and semipalmated sandpipers, the killdeer, and the semipalmated plover—feed on mosquitoes, and hundreds of mosquito larvae were in several stomachs examined by the federal investigators. Of the food of 28 northern phalaropes from one locality 53% was larvae of the salt-marsh mosquito, *Aedes sollicitans* (McAtee,

INSTINCT
A young Canada goose crouches in response to the presence of a hawk overhead. The experiments of Lorenz and Tinbergen have shown that the gosling reacts instinctively to the sign stimulus of the hawk's short-necked silhouette and its slow, gliding flight.

1911a). Adults and larvae of the biting horse-flies have also been reported from the stomachs of the dowitcher, pectoral sandpiper, Hudsonian godwit, and killdeer.

One of McAtee's correspondents, a reindeer breeder in Alaska, sent him testimony that all small birds living near his camp—yellow-rumped (myrtle), blackpoll, and Wilson's warblers, white-crowned sparrows, and gray-cheeked thrushes—preyed regularly on mosquitoes and fed them extensively to their young. Phalaropes and mallards also feed much on mosquitoes or their larvae, and the arctic warbler feeds mainly on them. *See* discussion of the values of some birds in their feeding habits under Economic Ornithology; *see also* Ectoparasite; Food and Feeding Habits.

ANTS, BEES, AND WASPS (HYMENOPTERA). Ranked high as bird food in McAtee's report and made up a higher percentage of the insect food than beetles, with more than 27,000 records; ants were eaten in greater quantities than bees and wasps. McAtee reported ant-eating by more than 300 species of birds. From 200 to 300 ants had been taken at a meal by some birds; a swallow may get 800 or more; a night-hawk, 1,000; and a woodpecker 2,000 or more. In the gray-cheeked, Swainson's, and hermit thrushes, the veery, and the wood thrush, ants constituted an average of almost 13% of their food. Among 16 species of N. American woodpeckers, ants were 5–85% of their entire diets.

The stomach of one flicker held the remains of more than 5,000 ants; two others had eaten 3,000 each. About 50% of the flicker's entire food is ants (Bent, 1939). The pileated woodpecker is especially fond of the large black carpenter ants *(Camponotus)*, which excavate their galleries in living trees. See interesting records of birds and the species of ants they eat in Bequaert (1922). Many species of swifts and swallows are fond of winged ants and feed on them during the ants' swarming periods. Most songbirds will eat ants; some may do so while anting. *See* Anting.

Flycatchers especially eat wild bees, wasps, and ants, which make up about 35% of the average diet of 17 different N. American species (Beal, 1912). In 13 of these species, Hymenoptera was the largest element of their diet. The eastern kingbird ("bee bird," or "bee martin") has a reputation for catching large numbers of honeybees; however, of 665 stomachs of eastern kingbirds collected in 29 states, only 22 contained a total of 61 honeybees, of which 51 were drones; on the other hand, 19 contained robber flies, which are enemies of honeybees (Henderson, 1933). *See* Economic Ornithology.

In Mo., Rau (1941) told of the destruction of the paper nests of the *Polistes*, or ring wasps, especially by summer tanagers, which fed on the wasp larvae. Tate (1973) noted that yellow-bellied sapsuckers killed and ate wasps and hornets, especially the bald-faced hornets, *Vespula maculata*, that came to feed at this bird's sap "wells."

Judd (1902) reported that most of the wild bees birds ate were small species of the family Andrenidae, mainly *Andrena* and *Halictus.*

Some birds gain protection from predators by nesting near the nests of wasps (*see* Nests and Nesting); however, some small birds, quite rarely, such as the house wren, have died from the sting of a *Polistes* wasp.

The large, introduced Chinese praying mantis has been known to capture and kill a ruby-throated hummingbird at a flower (the bird died of shock from its capture), and a ruby-throat was caught and pinned to the ground by a large dragonfly but was rescued and released by a man who happened to see the event. For accounts of other birds feeding on special groups of animals, *see* Amphibians; Crustaceans; Fishes; Mammals; Mollusks; Reptiles. *See also* Parasite; Ectoparasite; Diseases.

INSECTS IN BIRDS' NESTS
See Inquilines; *see also* Fleas; Protocalliphora; Nests and Nesting.

INSTINCT
David Lack (1953) has defined instinctive behavior in a bird or any other animal as "inherited behaviour . . . not acquired by learning or in any other way during the life of the animal; hence . . . it is characteristic of the species rather than the individual, and all the individuals of a species behave in approximately the same way; that it is mainly stereotyped and unmodifiable except in minor detail; further that it is a complex pattern of behaviour involving the whole animal in a series of co-ordinated actions. The last provision is necessary to distinguish instinct from reflex action. Reflexes such as the knee-jerk or eyeblink have some of the characteristics listed above but involve only very limited portions of the body."

Hochbaum (1955) illustrates instinct at work in the following way: A downy canvasback duckling has just hatched. Soon after its down is dry, it starts life in its environment with a remarkable set of actions with which it is equipped to succeed—it can walk, and the moment it touches water it swims, and, if necessary, it can dive below the surface. It can readily accomplish the complicated process of picking up an object in its bill. All of these actions are not learned by the duckling but are "its inborn heritage." These are examples of its *inborn, innate,* or *instinctive behavior.*

As the duckling grows, there is a *maturation* of other instinctive acts which begin to function (without previous learning) as the time for their use arrives. For example, flight is not learned but is an instinct that will reach maturity when the primary (flight) feathers of the duck's wings are fully grown and it is strong enough, or physically able, to fly. Hochbaum cites ducks that were raised in small pens where they were unable to fly that flew when first cast into the air (*see* Do Young Birds Learn to Fly? under Young and Their Care). Therefore flying ability is as much inherited as the ability to walk but does not mature until the duck's wings have reached their proper stage of development.

During the 15 months that the duck requires to complete its life cycle from hatching to rearing of its own young, other latent, or instinctive, actions come into play as the need for them arises: the hen does not build her nest until she is about a year old, but when her nesting time comes, she builds her first structure with no previous experience and her nest is like those of her ancestors (*see*, however, the need for experience by some birds under Nests and Nesting); also, nesting behavior, courtship displays, and vocal utterances characteristic of pair formation (*see* Waterfowl and in Duck Family) are not fully developed until the bird enters its first reproductive cycle. The *basic actions* by which a duck or any other bird meets its world are inborn, or instinctive, rather than learned; however, each bird's behavior is modified by learning and each individual must learn to adapt to survive in its environment. See Hailman's article (1969), suggesting that instincts may be partly learned. See other examples in Hochbaum (1955); see especially in Tinbergen (1951b); Thorpe (1956b); and Lorenz (1970b) for scientific discussions of instinctive and learned behavior.

Hochbaum has attempted to define, or formulate, instinct, in its more recent usage, as: "An inherited and adapted system of co-ordination within the nervous system as a whole which when activated finds expression in behavior culminating in a fixed action pattern. It is organized on a hierarchical basis, both on the afferent and efferent sides. When charged, it shows evidence of action-specific potential and a readiness for release by an environmental releaser." *See* Nervous System.

INSULATION
See Feather; Cold and Birds; *also* Toughness of a Bird's Feet under Feet and Legs.

INTEGUMENT
A covering, investment, or coat. Vertebrate animals in particular are characterized by a special type of body covering known as the integument. In birds it is the relatively tender and almost glandless skin and its prominent covering of feathers. *See* Feather; Skin. Besides feathers, other derivatives of the skin (integument) are claws, scales, and bills; also the uropygial gland, one of three skin glands of birds. *See* Skin Glands. The uropygial gland is also called oil gland and preen gland. *See* oil gland under Skin Glands and under Preening.

INTEGUMENTARY STRUCTURES
Term for the combs, wattles, and other facial or head decorations of domestic poultry, turkeys, pheasants, and other gallinaceous birds; also the pouches and gular sacs of pelicans, cormorants, and other birds; the spurs on the tarsus of pheasants and the domestic cock; and the spurs on the wings of jacanas and screamers. Like the bills, claws, scales, and feathers of birds, the integumentary structures are derivatives of the epidermis, though some of them have a supply of blood from the underlying dermis. *See* Skin. The integumentary structures usually have a secondary sexual or defensive function, and are regulated by hormones. *See* Endocrine Glands; Sexual Dimorphism; Beard.

INTELLIGENCE
See Learning Ability of Birds under Behavior.

INTENTION MOVEMENTS
Term of bird behaviorists often used for the incomplete movements in certain behavior patterns of a bird. Hinde (1961) says: "Sometimes the bird will make a series of incomplete movements expressing one or other or both of the conflicting tendencies. Thus, a half-tame moorhen *(Gallinula chloropus)* offered food may make incipient pecks toward it, and even swallowing movements, even though it does not dare to approach near enough to take any."

Tinbergen (1951b) in discussing intention movements says that the degree of motivation in a bird determines the degree of sensory stimulation required to release its reaction. "The lowest intensities of response, being no more than a slight indication of what the animal is tending to do, can only be interpreted by an observer who has watched the whole range of intensities. These incomplete movements are called 'intention' movements." *See* Behavior.

INTERBREEDING
See Subspecies.

INTERFERENCE COLORS
See iridescent under Colors of Feathers.

INTERSEX
Term of zoologists for an individual bird or other animal "more or less intermediate in phenotype [outward appearance] between male and female" (Mayr *et al.*, 1953). *See* Hermaphrodite; Gynandromorph.

INTERSPECIFIC
Term used often by ecologists for relationships between birds of *different* species, or kind. A hawk killing and eating a song sparrow is an example of an interspecific relationship. In contrast, competition between two birds of the *same* species, say two song sparrows fighting over territory or over food, is an example of an *intraspecific* relationship. *See* Behavior; Food and Feeding Habits.

INTESTINE
The hind or rearward part of the *digestive tract* (*see* Digestion); it consists of the small intestine and the large intestine. Digestion in birds is mainly accomplished in the small intestine, as it is in other vertebrate animals. *See* Vertebrate.

In most birds that feed on animal life, the small intestine is comparatively short, but is long and extensively looped in birds that are either omnivorous or herbivorous. According to Beebe (1906), the small intestine of the largest vegetarian bird—the ostrich—is 46 ft. long, but only 2 in. long in the nectar- and insect-eating hummingbird. Difference in length of small intestine in these two birds is associated with greater need of intestinal space for digestion, because vegetarian birds require bulkier food than those that feed on animal life. Buffon (1771) reported that intestines of the turkey are nearly four times as long as the distance from tip of its bill to end of its rump. *See* Turkey Family and discussion under Gizzard.

The small intestine consists of the *duodenum* (due-oh-DEE-num)—the initial loop in the first part of the intestine—and the *ileum*, which makes up remainder of intestine. *See*

functions under Digestion. The great length of small intestine of some birds is accommodated internally by three or four loops and folds that run back and forth lengthwise in the body (Allen, 1925). These form a variety of patterns that are characteristic of particular groups of birds and are therefore of value in establishing relationships between birds. This method is little used nowadays because it can be studied only by dissection of bird and there are other more practical methods of determining relationships (Thomson, 1964i). See Classification.

The large intestine is the posterior (rearward) extension of the small intestine.(Farner, 1960); it begins on the level of the intestinal caeca (*see* Caecum) and extends to the cloaca. *See* Cloaca. In most birds it is relatively short and presumably has little function in digestion. *See* Digestion. As Wallace (1955) has pointed out, by the time food passes into the large intestine, digestion has been relatively completed in both those birds that are vegetarian feeders and those that eat animal foods. *See* Food and Feeding Habits.

INTOXICATION
See Poisons.

INTRASPECIFIC
See Interspecific.

INTRODUCED BIRDS
The U.S. has a long record of importations, or introductions, of foreign birds (see Phillips, 1928; Peterson, 1948; Bump and Robbins, 1966; Laycock, 1971), but of some 100 species introduced only a small proportion have become established. For records of some of these, either introduced by man, self-introduced (cattle egret, for example), or escaped from captivity and established, or partly established, in the wild, *see* in the following bird families: Bulbul Family (red-whiskered bulbul); Duck Family (mute swan; Muscovy duck); Heron Family (cattle egret); Lark Family (skylark); Parrot Family (budgerigar, canary-winged parakeet; monk parakeet; orange-fronted parakeet; rose-ringed parakeet); Pheasant Family (ring-necked pheasant; chukar partridge; gray partridge); Pigeon Family (ringed turtle dove; rock dove; spotted dove); Starling Family (common myna; hill myna, starling); Troupial Family (spotted-breasted oriole); Weaverbird Family (European tree sparrow; house sparrow).

INVASION
Term for the periodic southward influx into the U.S. from Canada and Alaska of birds that usually live year-round in the North—grosbeaks, crossbills, and others that irregularly migrate in the N. Hemisphere. Some authorities, however (Cornwallis, 1964), prefer the term *irruption*, and use the term *invasion* for movements of a bird species into new territory in rapid expansion of its range. *See* discussion of "invasions" under Cycle and especially Irruption. *See* discussion of ranges and range expansion under Distribution; *see also* Dispersal.

INVERTEBRATE
See discussion and examples of under Vertebrate.

IOWA BIRD LIFE
A publication. *See* Ornithological Periodicals.

IRIDESCENCE
(ihr-ih-DES-ens). The effect of the changing colors we see so commonly on the black, glossy feathers of grackles, the necks of pigeons, and on hummingbirds is known as iridescence. It is the rainbowlike play of interference colors exhibited in the plumage of certain birds, caused by the scattering of light rays from the special structure of "iridescent feathers," although this effect is produced in different ways in different birds. *See* Colors of Feathers.

IRIS
See Colors of Eyes under Eyes and Eyesight.

IRONHEAD
Another name for the wood stork in Stork Family; *see also* Flinthead.

IRRUPTION
An irregular migration (most migrations of birds are regular—*see* Migration), in N. America, often a spectacular mass movement southward in fall and winter of birds that normally live year-round in parts of Alaska and Canada. According to Cornwallis (1964), some of those best known as flooding southward, periodically, are: pine grosbeaks (eat berries, also seeds of conifers); evening grosbeaks (seeds of conifers and box elder, or ash-leaved maple); purple finches (various seeds); crossbills (seeds of conifers); siskins (seeds of birches and alders); redpolls (seeds of birches); Bohemian waxwings (berries, especially of rowan tree); red-breasted nuthatches (seeds of pines and spruces); black-capped and boreal chickadees (insects and seeds); snowy owls and great gray owls (lemmings, voles, and hares); northern shrikes (voles); goshawks (hares and lemmings); and rough-legged hawks (voles and lemmings). See discussion "The Irruptive Phenomenon" by Baird (1964), and of irruptions of 13 species of northern birds into U.S. (Bagg, 1969). Recently some of the above birds, such as evening grosbeak, have become almost regular in their southward movements.

Generally these birds move southward in fall and early winter in larger numbers than usual when their populations are up, or high, and their natural foods in the North are scarce. For example, the periodic eastward and southward movements of large numbers of evening grosbeaks have been linked with the failure about every 2 years of the seed crop of spruces, pines, and other coniferous trees in the North on which these grosbeaks depend mainly for their food. *See* discussion of this also in biography of evening grosbeak in Finch Family.

Another example of large-scale irregular migration (irruption) of larger than usual numbers of predatory birds of the North is that of the snowy owl and northern shrike (about every 4 years), linked to the low population point in the cycle of lemmings and voles in the North, on which these birds feed. *See* more detailed discussion under Cycle; see also Lack (1954; 1966) and Wynne-Edwards (1962) for detailed and often different conclusions about the causes of high and low populations of birds and other animals. See also Cornwallis (1964) for more details about irruptions. *See* Populations.

According to Alfred O. Gross (1947a), there are records of flight years of the snowy owl into the U.S. at about 4-year intervals that go back to 1833. *See* Flight Year.

ISCHIUM
One of three paired bones that, with the synsacrum, form the pelvic girdle. *See* Skeleton.

ISOLATING MECHANISM
See defined under Species; *also* under Sympatric Species.

ISOTHERM
(EYE-so-thurm); from Gr. *isos*, equal, and *therme*, heat. In physical geography, a line on a map joining or marking points on the earth's surface having the same temperature at a given time; same mean (average) temperature for a given period. The northward movement of certain species of birds in spring corresponds closely with the northward advance of certain average temperature lines (isotherms); for example, the northward movement of Canada geese in spring migration corresponds closely to advancing isotherm 35° F. (Lincoln, 1950c. *See* Migration; *also* Swallow Family.

IVORY-BILL
See Woodpecker, ivory-billed, in Woodpecker Family.

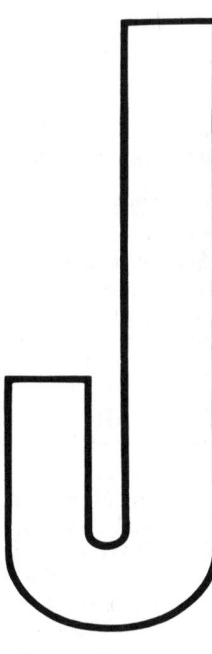

JABIRU
See in Stork Family.

JACAMAR
(JACK-ah-mar). *See* Piciformes.

JACANA FAMILY
Jacanidae (jah-CAN-ih-dee); Brazilian name *jaçana*, from language of Tupi Indians of Amazon region. 8 species; 6½–21 in. long; small to medium-sized birds that resemble members of Rail Family of order Ralliformes, especially the gallinules, but apparently are related most closely to painted snipes (family Rostratulidae) in the order Charadriiformes; live in tropical and semitropical regions of the world; 6 species in Old World; 2 species in New World: northern jacana, *Jacana spinosa*, found in Middle America and the West Indies, rarely to s. Tex., and the wattled jacana, *Jacana jacana*, from n. S. America to Bolivia and Argentina; name *jacana* pronounced by many American ornithologists as jah-KON-ah; by others, YAH-sah-NAH; dictionary pronunciations are ZHA-sah-NAH and JAK-ah-nah; outstanding physical feature of all species is extraordinarily long toes and toenails (nails of some species may be 4 in. long), which enable them to walk over floating water plants of sheltered shallows in freshwater marshes and river swamps, where they hunt for insects, small fishes, and mollusks; above the bill they have a frontal shield similar to that of coots and gallinules, and, like certain plovers, they have a sharp, horny, metacarpal spur at the bend of each wing used in fighting (Gilliard, 1958); plumage colors usually reddish or dark bronze; the frontal shields are red, yellow, or blue; not shy and can be approached closely, but when alarmed, become instantly motionless; the moderately long bill is straight, top of bill curved downward at tip; the wings are rather long; tail short, and they jerk tail with each high, deliberate step; they can run swiftly, are agile swimmers and divers, and submerge to hide, as do the chicks; when alighting, momentarily raise wings, butterflylike, above back; are seldom noisy, but have many grunting, cackling, mewing, whistling calls; may be noisy in breeding season during courtship or when threatening and scolding each other with uplifted wings in territorial disputes; not truly migratory but some seasonal movements; sexes similar in color but female usually larger; according to Pitman (1964b), both sexes may incubate and both take part in nest building; however, Jenni and Collier (1972) discovered that in the northern jacana the female may have one to several mates and each builds his nest, incubates the eggs laid by his female, and cares for the young without any assistance from the female (see details in polyandry under Sexual Relationships); adult parent of the African jacana, *Actophilornis africanus*, has been seen carrying away chicks under its wings when they were threatened by human intruders (see photographs and account in Hopcraft, 1968; *see* Young and Their Care). See other details of Jacana Family around the world in Austin (1961); Gilliard (1958); and Pitman (1964b).

To sustain an ill or injured member of Jacana Family in captivity until able to fend for itself,

JACANA FAMILY

Walker (1942) suggests offering it mealworms, finely ground meat, green plant material, and shrimp.

American jacana. *See* North American Jacana.

Mexican jacana. *See* North American Jacana.

North American Jacana, *Jaçana spinosa* (jah-KON-ah, JAK-ah-nah, or YAH-sah-NAH spin-OH-sah); genus name: *see* family introduction; species name: Lat., having spine, or spur, referring to spur at bend of each wing. (Color ill., page 571.) Has strayed occasionally north from Mexico to Rio Grande delta, Tex., casual elsewhere in state, has bred there (Peterson, 1963); see also records by Fleetwood (1973); also collected once in Fla. at Lake Okeechobee; 8–9 in. long; female larger; adult: ploverlike bill is yellow; forehead has conspicuous yellow, leaflike wattle; head, neck, chest, and upper back *glossy black;* elsewhere, above and below, deep chestnut or maroon; wings have large pale green-yellow patches, underside of wings near bend armed with yellow spur; toes very long; immature: frontal shield, or wattle, much smaller than adult's; broad white stripe over eyes; sides of head and underparts white or blotched; breast sometimes buffy; above, gray-brown, somewhat like a Wilson's phalarope (Peterson, 1963); but has *long toes* and *rounded* wings; jacanas spend much time feeding or playing over surface of lily pads; during courtship, pair raise wings over back and flash the green-yellow wing patches at each other; on freshwater pond in Costa Rica (see Jenni and Collier, 1972), breeding season is Jan.–Oct.; the polygamous female has territory that might include smaller territories of one to four smaller males.

Feeding Habits: In Costa Rican study, Jenni and Collier discovered that adults and young, gleaning floating mat of vegetation, with occasional foraging into adjacent crop fields and lawn, ate almost entirely insects; adults sometimes took small fishes.
Nest: Built by male alone, a few bits of green leaves of cattails or of water lettuce on floating mat of plants, built up just enough to keep eggs from rolling out.
Eggs: Mexico, Apr.–Aug., Costa Rica, Jan.–Oct.; 3–5, usually 4, almost round, brown with fine scrawls of black.
Incubation: By male alone, only male has incubation patches (Jenni and Collier, 1972), 22–24 days (Austin, 1961); as soon as hatched, chicks can run or dive into water and swim below surface; are brooded (*see* Brooding) and attended by male, apparently not fed by him and forage for themselves, are mostly independent of male 28 days after hatching, first flights at 35 days old (Jenni and Collier, 1972).
Other Names: American jacana; Mexican jacana, lily-trotters, and lotus-birds.
Weights: Adult males (16) averaged 86.9 gr.; adult females (12) averaged 145.4 gr.; breeding males averaged about 91 gr., or about 3 oz.; breeding females averaged about 161 gr., or about 5¾ oz. (Jenni and Collier, 1972).

Range: Resident from n.e. and w. Mexico, south to w. Panama; West Indies; rare to s. Tex.; accidental in Fla.

Northern Jacana. *See* Jacana.

Wattled Jacana. *See* Jacana.

JACKDAW
See Grackle, boat-tailed, in Troupial Family.

JACK-PINE WARBLER, THE
A publication. *See* Ornithological Periodicals.

JACKSNIPE
See in Sandpiper Family.

JAEGER
See in Skua Family.

JAY-BIRD
See Jay, blue, in Crow Family.

JENNY WREN
See House wren in Wren Family.

JERFALCON
(JER-fall-kon). A corruption of *Gerfalcon*, and properly *gyrfalcon* (Newton, 1893–96). *See* Gyrfalcon in Falcon Family.

JOHN CROW
See Black vulture under Vulture—American Vulture Family.

JOHN DOWN
See Fulmar, northern, in Shearwater Family.

JONES
LYNDS (1865–1951). Born Jefferson, Ohio, early teacher of ecology; ornithologist with special interest in bird migration; one of founders of the Wilson Ornithological Society; editor of *Wilson Bulletin* for 36 years; its president for 13 years; fellow of the American Ornithologists' Union; a professor of zoology who taught first course in ornithology ever offered in any American college or university, which he established at Oberlin College in 1895 (Kendeigh, 1952a).

JOREE
(joe-REE). *See* Towhee, rufous-sided, in Finch Family.

JOSÉ MARIA
See Flycatcher, Coues', in Flycatcher—Tyrant Flycatcher Family.

JOURNAL OF WILDLIFE MANAGEMENT, THE
See Ornithological Periodicals.

JUDAS-BIRD
Name in S.C. for the dickcissel, because of fancied resemblance of its song to words *Judas Iscariot. See* Dickcissel in Finch Family.

JUGULUM
(JOO-gew-lum). The lower throat of a bird, or that part just above the breast. *See* Topography.

JUNCO
See in Finch Family.

JUNGLE FOWL
See in introduction to Pheasant Family; *also* under Domestication.

JURASSIC
(joo-RAS-ik). A period of geological time in the Mesozoic era. During the Jurassic Period, the sea invaded great areas of w. N. America, Europe, and Asia. The first birds appeared in this era. *See* Geological Time Scale; Fossil Birds.

JUVENAL
(JOO-vee-nal). Term applied in ornithology to the plumage of a young bird that comes in immediately after, or succeeding, its natal down. *See* Natal Down. In birds which have no natal down, the term also applies to the first plumage which succeeds the naked nestling stage, characteristic of some species. The juvenal plumage is the first in the life of a bird that is composed of true contour feathers (Van Tyne and Berger, 1959). *See* Feather; *also* Molts and Molting.

Some passerines, or songbirds—for example, sharp-tailed sparrows and seaside sparrows—wear their juvenal plumage for 2 or 3 months, but most songbirds lose it shortly after leaving the nest by molting all the body feathers into the postjuvenal (prebasic) or first-winter plumage of the so-called immature bird. *See* immature under Nestling.

JUVENILE
See definition under Nestling.

KEEL
See Carina.

KENT
Another name for the ivory-billed woodpecker, derived from one of its call notes.

KENTUCKY WARBLER, THE
A publication. *See* Ornithological Periodicals.

KERATIN
(KER-ah-tin). The parts of a feather (*see* Feather) begin to harden or become hornlike while they are still taking shape in the embryonic feather of an unhatched bird. This is not a result of a mere drying of the feather cells but of the production from the skin of a specific hardening substance, *keratin*, which eventually covers the entire feather. Keratin consists of microscopic fibrils organized into larger filaments which are, in turn, cemented together by an amorphous protein matrix substance. The definitive keratin starts to form in the embryonic feather of a chick of the domestic fowl about the 13th day of its incubation (Lucas and Stettenheim, 1972).

In both the embryonic feathers of a bird and the new feathers regenerated in an adult, keratin is thought to form in the same way that it is formed in the cortical cells of hair and wool, which it resembles structurally (Matoltsy, 1962).

KESTREL
See in Falcon Family.

KICKER SONG
See in biography of Virginia rail in Rail Family.

KIDNEY
See under Urogenital System.

KILLDEE
Another name for the killdeer in the Plover Family, from one of its common cries.

KILLDEER
See in Plover Family.

KILOGRAM
(KILL-oh-gram). Measure of weight used in the metric system. One kilogram equals 1,000 grams, or about 2.2 pounds avoirdupois. Weights of birds may be given in kilograms and/or decimals thereof, in scientific texts. Most American ornithological texts give weights of birds in grams or in equivalent pounds or ounces. *See* gram.

KILOMETER
(KILL-oh-meter). Measure of length in the metric system. Often used in N. American ornithological reports, papers, and other scientific publications, and, usually, in European publications. A kilometer (km.) is 1,000 meters, or 3,-280.8 feet, or almost ⅝ of a *statute mile,* which is 5,280 feet. In popular books and articles about birds, distances are usually expressed in miles or fractions thereof. *See also* Millimeter; Centimeter; Dimensions.

KINGBIRD
General name in allusion to its habit of driving other birds from its nesting territory. *See* in Flycatcher—Tyrant Flycatcher Family.

KING-BIRD, OR KING DUCK
See King eider in Duck Family.

KINGBIRD, THE
A publication. *See* Ornithological Periodicals.

KING-CRAB BIRD
See Ruddy turnstone, in Sandpiper Family. Name from habit of eating eggs of king crab, or horseshoe crab *(Limulus).*

KINGFISHER FAMILY
Alcedinidae (al-see-DIN-ih-dee); from Lat. *alcedo,* kingfisher (Coble, 1954). 86 species worldwide, except in polar regions and on some oceanic islands (Van Tyne and Berger, 1976); small to medium or large land birds; 4–18 in. long; many adapted to catching fishes; most species live in Old World, especially in se. Asia; only 6 species in New World; 3 reach N. America.

Kingfishers are chunky, compact birds with short necks and large heads, in many accentuated by an erectile crest that, when raised, gives them appearance of being startled (Austin,1961); have stumpy tails but some (in New Guinea and Moluccas) with long tails owing to extension of central tail feathers; bills are long, usually sharp-pointed, legs short, feet small and weak, with three toes pointing forward, one backward; characteristic of family is joining together of two front toes (III and IV) for almost their full length—toes II and III are joined basally. For the digital formula, or numbering system of birds' toes, *see* Numbers of Toes under Feet and Legs. When perched, the toe I (hallux) is directed backward.

Most kingfishers are brightly colored—greens, blues, with contrasting patches of dull red, brown, and white; many have bright red or yellow bills and feet; sexes are usually alike or quite similar; they are related to the motmots, bee-eaters, rollers, hoopoes, and hornbills (Austin, 1961). *See* Coraciiformes.

Kingfishers are mainly solitary except when paired in nesting season; have short rounded wings and fly directly and rapidly but usually not far; habitually perch on branch or stump of tree; many eat fishes, amphibians, crustaceans, and aquatic insects, which they catch by diving headlong into the water. These are the so-called true fishers and include all New World species—unlike most *plunging* divers (*see* Swimming and Diving), they are otherwise not aquatic.

The majority of species in the Kingfisher Family that are in the Old World do not fish, and many, such as the forest, or wood, kingfishers, may live far from water and nest in trees or termite mounds. They have broader, more flattened bills and eat mostly insects; however, the distinction in feeding habits is not sharp, as some of the forest kingfishers may occasionally fish, and some of the true fishers may dart from their perches at passing insects.

Two of the most widespread and best known of the fishing kingfishers are the small common kingfisher, *Alcedo atthis,* of the Old World—

KINGFISHER FAMILY

this is *the* kingfisher of Europe and is legendary in Greek mythology (*see* Folklore)—and the belted kingfisher, *Megaceryle alcyon*, of N. America. Others of the family in the New World are the ringed kingfisher, and 4 species of so-called green kingfishers of the genus *Chloroceryle* of Mexico and C. and S. America. For other names and ranges, see Eisenmann (1955) and Blake, E. R., (1953), and for especially interesting details of the entire family, see Austin (1961), Gilliard (1958) and Fry (1980a, 1980b).

All of the fishing kingfishers dig burrows for nesting, usually in banks along creeks or rivers; they dig them with their bills, then push out the dirt from the burrow with their feet. In kingfishers, the male and female usually incubate the eggs and brood and feed the young about equally; however, Alexander Skutch found that in the Amazon kingfisher, *Chloroceryle amazona*, and in the green kingfisher, *C. americana*, the female alone incubates at night.

Gross (1965a) reported three records of albinism, apparently in the belted kingfisher, but gave no details.

Kingfishers are protected by federal law, but to sustain an injured or ill belted kingfisher until it can be turned over to an appropriate wildlife official, offer it small fishes; the tropical kingfishers feed on a wide variety of animals, such as large insects, lizards, and fishes (Walker, 1942).

Belted kingfisher, *Megaceryle alcyon* (meg-ah-SER-ih-lee AL-sih-on); genus name: Lat., from Gr. *megas*, large, and *kerylos*, a *halkyon*, or in Lat., *halycon* (HAL-sih-on), a kingfisher; species name: for Alcyone, or Halcyone, of Gr. mythology, daughter of Aeolus, god of the winds, who, with her husband, Ceyx, was transformed into a kingfisher. (Color ill., page 572.) Ranges over most of U.S. and Canada to Alaska, only kingfisher north of Tex. and Ariz.; 11–14½ in. long; striking appearance, usually seen near water; when perched, long heavy bill and large blue-gray head, with conspicuous crest, contrasting with small body, short tail, and tiny feet, make it appear top-heavy; sexes similar but female one of few N. American birds more colorful than male; both are blue-gray above with white collar and broad band of blue-gray across breast; both have ragged double crest; are white below, but female also chestnut band across belly and rufous flanks; winters over much of its nesting range in U.S. and s. Canada; lives wherever there is water, whether along seacoast or along brooks, creeks, ponds, lakes, or mountain streams; usually solitary except in nesting season, and within territory has regularly used perches, usually on dead branch of tree over water or stake or pier along coast (Bent, 1940), from which it watches for prey in water; in flight as it follows course of stream, flying well below treetops along banks, utters loud, rattling call, *rickety, crick, crick, crick,* which has been likened to sound of watchman's or policeman's rattle; sometimes dives below surface of water to escape attacks of peregrine falcon, Cooper's and sharp-shinned hawks; may roost at night on dead limb of tree along stream (Eckelberry,

1953) or in evergreens in forest near water (Bent, 1940).

Feeding Habits: Eats mainly small fishes (*see* discussion of fishes caught under Fishes and Birds); may dive from perch obliquely into water to seize fish in its powerful bill, or hover in air, 20–40 ft. above water, then make straight or spiral dive and disappear below surface for several seconds or often only shallow dive with head below surface; after seizing fish, rises and returns to perch, where it beats fish on limb, then tosses it into air and swallows it headfirst (Bent, 1940); catches and eats in same way large tadpoles of bullfrog (Terres, 1968b); also eats crabs, crayfishes, mussels, lizards, frogs, toads, newts, small snakes and turtles, grasshoppers, butterflies, moths, beetles, and other insects, young birds, mice, and even berries; along seacoast known to eat clams and oysters; has been found with its bill held fast in shell of live oyster and caught in same way by freshwater mussel; it disgorges pellets of fishbones and scales and other indigestible parts of food.

Nest: Horizontal or slightly upslanting burrow dug by pair in sand, clay, or gravel bank of creek, river, lake, pond, gravel or sand pit, railroad cut, may be far from water, about 3–4 in. in diameter, unlined, usually 3–7 ft. long, rarely to 15 ft., may require from 3 days to 3 weeks to dig depending on type of soil; nest chamber at end of burrow about 6 by 10 in., often lined with clean white fish bones and scales from ejected pellets of present and previous occupants (Bent, 1940); sometimes nests in top of hollow stump or in cavity in tree.

Eggs: Apr.–July; 5–8, usually 6–7, white.
Incubation: 23–24 days (Nice, 1954); age when young leave nest not definitely known but at least 23 days or more.
Other Names: Halcyon; lazy-bird.
Flight Speed: Timed in Calif., 36 m.p.h. (McLean, 1930); in N.J., 45 m.p.h. aided by following wind (Terres, 1968a).
Weights: In fall, coastal N.J. (14), 127–175 gr. (Murray and Jehl, 1964), or about 4½–6 oz.
Range: Nests from c. Alaska, s. Yuk., sw. Mack., c. Alta, east to c. Labrador and Newfoundland, south to s. Calif., s. N.M., east to s. Fla.; winters scattered over much of breeding range, generally from n. U.S. south to Baja Calif., into Mexico, C. America, West Indies, and Bermuda.

Green kingfisher, *Chloroceryle americana* (cloh-row-SER-ih-lee ah-mer-ih-CANE-ah); genus name: Lat., from Gr. *chloros*, green, and *kerylos*, a *halkyon*, or in Lat., *halcyon*, a kingfisher; species name: Lat., of America. (Color ill., page 572.) Mexican, C. and S. American species; a rare straggler in fall and winter into the Santa Cruz drainage and San Pedro Valley of Ariz. (Phillips *et al.,* 1964); in Tex., an "uncommon *resident,* Brownsville north to Kerrville, San Marcos, and along the Rio Grande to the Pecos R." (Peterson, 1963); 7–8 in. long; small for a kingfisher, not much larger than a big sparrow; without head crest; bill like pickax; above, *dark glossy green;* wings spotted and barred with white; white collar and white belly; male has broad *chestnut or rufous* *band across chest;* similar female has double band of green spots across breast; prefers to live along shaded, clear rivers and shaded brooks and quiet backwaters, where it perches on roots over water or on boulders in stream or along shore, watching for prey and jerking tail up and down; travels in swift buzzy flight low over streams, uttering *cheep* note; also a sharp, rattling twitter, more shrill and different from loud, harsh rattle of belted kingfisher; alarm note is *tick tick tick* (Bent, 1940).

Feeding Habits: Plunges from low perch into water for small minnows, rarely hovers over water.

Nest: Digs horizontal burrow in bank of stream, distinguished from burrow of other kingfishers by its small entrance, about 2–3 in. in diameter, burrow about 2–3 ft. deep, usually well hidden and near top of bank under roots of trailing plants.

Eggs: Tex., Apr.–June; Mexico, Mar.–June; 3–6, commonly 5, white (Bent, 1940).

Incubation: 19–21 days; young leave nest 22–26 days after hatching (Gilliard, 1958).

Other Name: Texas kingfisher.

Range: See above.

Ringed kingfisher, *Megaceryle torquata* (meg-ah-SER-ih-lee tore-QUAY-tah); genus name: *see* Belted kingfisher; species name: from Lat. *torquatus,* collared (Coues, 1882). (Color ill., page 572.) Mexican, C. and S. American species; also in West Indies; ranges north to s. Tex.; 15–16½ in. long; largest kingfisher in W. Hemisphere; casual or rare visitor in Rio Grande Valley but from early winter 1966 to spring 1970 seen there with increasing frequency until McGrew (1971) discovered on Apr. 8, 1970, a pair carrying minnows into a burrow near Rio Grande, 2 mi. below Falcon Dam, apparently first reported nesting of the species in U.S.; much larger than belted kingfisher, bill quite large; male blue above, hind neck with conspicuous white collar; throat white; *breast and belly rufous;* undertail coverts (crissum) white; tail narrowly barred with white; female similar to male but with broad blue band across chest (Blake, E. R., 1953); in Mexico and C. America, prefers living near murky waters of densely shaded stagnant pools and lagoons, and prefers larger and more open streams than those sometimes inhabited by smaller kingfishers; has regular routes it flies up and down streams with lookout perches every few hundred yards; in flight utters a single loud measured *kleck* or *cla-ack,* a note varied to suit its reactions; when danger threatens, rapid *kleck* becomes harsh rattle (Bent, 1940).

Feeding Habits: Plunges into water to catch both large and small fishes in its powerful bill; also catches and eats frogs and small water reptiles.

Nest: Usually digs burrow in vertical bank, sometimes long distance from water. McGrew (1971) found nest burrow 200 ft. away from Rio Grande at head of small arroyo; entrance, 9 in. high, 7 in. across top, 4½ in. wide at bottom, was 4 ft. below top of bank; also often digs burrow along riverbanks, burrows 5–8 ft. deep.

KINGFISHER FAMILY
Members of the kingfisher family build horizontal burrows for nesting, usually in a riverbank. The belted kingfisher, digging with its bill and feet, may take up to 3 weeks to excavate its 3–7 foot long burrow.

Eggs: Mar.–May; 3–6, commonly 4–5.
Incubation: Period of not reported; young fly 34–35 days after hatching (Bent, 1940).
Other Names: Great rufous-bellied kingfisher,
Weights: 10¼ oz.
Range: See above.

Texas kingfisher. *See* Green kingfisher.

KINGLET
See in Warbler—Old World Warbler Family.

KING OF BIRDS
See Eagle, golden, in Hawk Family.

KIRTLAND
JARED P(OTTER) (1793–1877). Of Cleveland, Ohio, founder of Cleveland Medical College; Cleveland Academy of Natural Sciences (see Gruson, 1972); was a physician, teacher, horticulturist, naturalist identified with the zoology, especially the fishes, of Ohio (Palmer, 1928). In 1852, his friend Spencer F. Baird named a warbler for Kirtland from a specimen of the bird presented to him by Kirtland which had been collected on the shore of Lake Erie, near Kirtland's farm (Mayfield, 1960).

KISKADEE
See Flycatcher, Kiskadee, in Flycatcher—Tyrant Flycatcher Family.

KITE
See in Hawk Family.

KITTIWAKE
See in Gull Family.

KITTLITZ
FRIEDRICH HEINRICH (1779–1874). German soldier who became an explorer-naturalist (Gruson, 1972); accompanied a Russian expedition to Kamchatka (1826–29) (Wynne, 1969). In 1828 (Jan. 1829), Nicholas Aylward Vigors, British zoologist, in the *Zoological Journal*, gave a murrelet new to science the species name of *brevirostre* (now *brevirostris*), but with the English name of Kittlitz's murrelet.

KIWI
(KEE-wih). *See* Eggs and Egg-laying; Flightless Birds; Language; Smell.

KLEPTOPARASITISM
Term of ornithologists for the forceful taking of food by one species of bird from another. For examples, *see* Feeding and Food-Getting under Behavior; *also* Parasite.

KNEE
See Feet and Legs.

KNIFE-BILL
See Black skimmer in Skimmer Family.

KNOT
See in Sandpiper Family.

KNOTTY
See Dovekie in Auk Family.

KOILIN LINING
Term for the lining of the muscular stomach or gizzard of birds. The koilin lining can be shed, or molted, in many—perhaps most—species of birds (Farner, 1960).

KOPROPORPHYRIN
See Colors of Feathers.

KOW-KOW
A common name of the black-billed and yellow-billed cuckoos, imitative of their calls.

KREEKER
See Sandpiper, pectoral, in Sandpiper Family.

KRONISM
or CRONISM. European term for swallowing of some of the young, usually weak or dead, by parent birds; has been reported for white stork, kestrel, and red-backed shrike in Europe, and is suspected in other European birds. All birds average more eggs than the average number of young fledged (raised to flying stage) and, according to Schüz (1957), swallowing of some of young has the effect of regulating the populations of certain species. Siegenthaler (1953) reported that during periods of bad weather, when mice or other foods scarce, and especially in years of low mouse populations (*see* Cycle), the European tawny owl, *Strix aluco*, and the barn owl, *Tyto alba*, will eat their young, selecting first the smallest or weakest. The name for the act is from the ancient Gr. myth about Kronus (Cronus), son of Uranus, who ate his own children (Schüz, 1957).

In N. America, Ohmart (1973) reported that if the food supply of the roadrunner, *Geococcyx californianus*, diminishes during the nesting period, the adults sometimes eat their youngest nestlings, thereby increasing the chances of survival of the rest of the brood.

In large colonies of gulls, in which the first-hatched chick is usually 24 hours older than the second- and third-hatched, the older one because of its larger size and hunger gets most of the food brought by parents; the two siblings, underfed, may be eaten by the parents (Fisher and Lockley, 1954); however, if food plentiful, second and third chicks hatched may soon reach growth of first and survive. *See* Cannibalism; Fratricide.

KUMLIEN
THURE LUDWIG THEODOR. *See* Gull, Kumlien's, in Gull Family.

IBIS FAMILY

Glossy ibis
This Old World bird crossed the Atlantic Ocean from Africa to South America in the 19th century and quickly expanded its range northward. Glossy ibises first nested in the United States in the 1880s; today they range as far north as Maine and the Great Lakes. Like their close relatives, the storks, ibises fly with head and neck extended and feet trailing behind. With their sickle-shaped bills, they probe for the occupants of fiddler crab and crayfish holes. They also catch snakes, including the feared cottonmouth.

Glossy ibis

White ibis

One of the most spectacular sights of the Florida Everglades is the evening flight of the white ibis, when flocks totaling thousands upon thousands of birds pour into their mangrove roost after feeding all day in distant marshes. But even a single white ibis is breathtaking: snow-white plumage, black wing tips, bright-red face and bill, and, in breeding season, crimson legs as well. White ibises nest in colonies on tangled mangrove islands; 3 to 4 eggs are laid on a platform of sticks. The young hatch in 3 weeks and make their first flights when 5 weeks old. White ibises play a vital role in Everglades ecology. They eat great quantities of crayfish that otherwise would decimate fish populations; and their droppings enrich the water around ibis colonies, increasing plankton growth that is the foundation of the marsh food chain.

White ibis

White ibis

White ibis, chick

White ibis, immature

White-faced ibis
An inhabitant of both freshwater and coastal marshes in the West and Southwest, the white-faced ibis can be told from the glossy ibis only in the breeding season, when it sports a narrow border of white feathers around its bare facial skin.

Roseate spoonbill
The largest member of the ibis family in North America, with a wingspread of more than 4 feet, the roseate spoonbill is at once beautiful and grotesque. However, the bill that spoils esthetic perfection is incredible in more ways than appearance. When feeding, a spoonbill rhythmically sweeps its bill—6 inches long and 2 inches wide—along the shallow margins of a mangrove pool. Armed with sensitive nerve endings, the bill snaps shut when it touches living prey—small fish, mollusks, crabs, insects—which the bird swallows with a toss of its head.

JACANA FAMILY

Jacana
Extraordinary toes that are nearly 4 inches long enable this unusual shorebird to walk atop the floating vegetation of tropical marshes, gleaning insects, snails, and seeds. A resident of Central America, the jacana is an occasional visitor to southern Texas.

Roseate spoonbill

White-faced ibis

Jacana

KINGFISHER FAMILY

Belted kingfisher
More colorful than her mate, the female belted kingfisher is identified by a band of chestnut across the belly and rufous flanks. The only native kingfisher north of our borderlands with Mexico, the belted kingfisher nests in a burrow dug several feet deep into a dirt bank. Fish, frogs, crayfish, and aquatic insects are caught on headlong dives into water that may be only a few inches deep.

Green kingfisher
Hardly larger than a sparrow, this Central and South American kingfisher perches on roots and rocks along shaded tropical streams, watching for small minnows.

Ringed kingfisher
The largest kingfisher in the New World, this tropical species was first reported nesting along the Rio Grande in 1970. Murky waters of stagnant pools and lagoons are its preferred fishing places.

LARK FAMILY

Horned lark
A striking facial pattern, including 2 tufts of black feathers (the "horns"), identify the horned larks that swirl over windswept fields and plains in winter, often in the company of snow buntings and Lapland longspurs. Scurrying over hard-crusted snow, sometimes in enormous flocks, they glean weed seeds and waste grain.

Skylark
An Old World bird justly famed for its aerial courtship song, the skylark was introduced on Vancouver Island, British Columbia, around 1902. Now well established in one farming region, with a population of about 1,000, the skylark has gone on to colonize some small, grassy islands in Puget Sound. But further expansion of its range in the Pacific Northwest appears to be blocked by dense, inhospitable rain forests.

LIMPKIN FAMILY

Limpkin
A relative of cranes and rails, the limpkin is the sole survivor of an ancient line of swamp-dwelling birds whose fossil remains reach back 54 million years. Skulking about the Everglades or Okefenokee Swamp in search of freshwater snails, the limpkin moves with a peculiar halting gait (a "limp"). Its call is a frightening scream that shatters the nighttime calm of wetlands from Georgia to Argentina.

Belted kingfisher, immature male and female

Green kingfisher

Ringed kingfisher, female

Horned lark

Skylark

Limpkin

LOON FAMILY

Arctic loon

A bird of the tundra and boreal forests, from Alaska to Hudson Bay, the Arctic loon spends its winter along the Pacific coast as far south as the Gulf of California. The legs of loons are set so far back on their bodies that walking on land is quite difficult; indeed, the name "loon" is believed to have come from a Scandinavian word, "lom," meaning "clumsy" or "lame." But loons are powerful swimmers. Sleek and torpedo-shaped, propelled by their webbed feet, they use only their wings underwater for maneuvering in pursuit of fish, which are seized in the daggerlike bill.

Common loon

Summer in the northern lake country would not be complete without the wails and wild laughter of common loons. But these are birds of the wilderness with little tolerance for human intruders, and they are being driven from many of their historic haunts by second-home development and careless boaters who roar too close to nesting places. Both loon parents share incubation duties and care of the chicks. Baby loons are immediately fed whole food—small fishes, crustaceans, and bits of plants. By the age of 2 weeks they are skilled at swimming and diving.

Red-throated loon

The smallest loon is distinguished by a slender, upturned bill that separates it from the common and arctic loons in their pale winter plumages. The nest of the red-throated loon may be either a heap of mud and aquatic plants at the edge of a pond or simply a damp depression on bare ground. Males often build copulating platforms some distance from their nests.

Yellow-billed loon

More numerous in Eurasia than North America, the largest of all loons is a bird of the high Arctic. In both summer and winter plumage it is similar to the slightly smaller common loon, except for its ivory-yellow bill. Loons are among the very few birds with solid rather than air-filled bones. They are able to sink beneath the surface, leaving scarcely a ripple, by expelling air from their bodies and feathers.

Arctic loon

Red-throated loon, winter

Red-throated loon

Yellow-billed loon

Common loon

Common loon, winter

MOCKINGBIRD FAMILY

Gray catbird
A familiar and fearless dooryard bird, the gray catbird is named for its mewing call; but it also mimics the voices of many other birds and has a rambling, much-varied mating song of its own. Two to 6 young are raised on a diet of insects and berries in a nest built in garden shrubs or dense thickets.

Mockingbird
Famed as a mimic, the mockingbird can imitate the songs of other birds so expertly than even electronic analysis cannot tell the copy from the original. On warm moonlit nights, a mockingbird may sing for hours on end, pouring forth the songs of as many as 36 different birds — plus the sounds of frogs, insects, dogs, barnyard hens, even a tinkling piano.

Bendire's thrasher
While most thrashers of the Southwest desert escape danger by scurrying over the ground and fly only when hard-pressed, Bendire's thrasher readily takes to the air. The male is an accomplished vocalist, its song a clear, sweet warble.

Brown thrasher
Though it is a talented mimic, the brown thrasher's repertoire is not nearly as large and varied as those of the mockingbird and catbird. Also unlike its extroverted relatives, the brown thrasher is a shy and secretive bird, an inhabitant of briar patches, dense thickets, fencerows, and second-growth woodlands.

California thrasher
A denizen of the chaparral and mountain foothills, this western thrasher, with its long sickle-shaped bill, is found only in California and Baja California.

Curve-billed thrasher
A desert resident from Arizona to Texas, the curve-billed thrasher often builds its nest of twigs in the fork of a cholla cactus, undeterred by thousands of thickly woven thorns.

Le Conte's thrasher
The hottest, most barren deserts are this thrasher's haunts. It forages for insects during the cool hours of dawn and dusk, retiring to shade during the middle of the day.

Long-billed thrasher
A Mexican bird that regularly nests in south Texas, this species resembles the well-known brown thrasher of the East. It is abundant in mesquite-cactus country and riverside forests of ebony and palms.

Sage thrasher
Western sagebrush plains are the home of this small thrasher. Thrushlike in appearance, it scurries over the ground like a robin, feasting on a wide variety of insect life, from grasshoppers to wasps.

Gray catbird

Mockingbird

California thrasher

Bendire's thrasher

Brown thrasher

Curve-billed thrasher

Long-billed thrasher

Sage thrasher

Le Conte's thrasher

NIGHTJAR FAMILY

Chuck-will's-widow
The loud, whistled call of the largest nightjar in North America is one of the most familiar sounds of a summer night across the rural South. A South Carolina ornithologist counted 834 consecutive calls by one bird, with a pause of 2½ seconds between each announcement of its name. The female lays 2 eggs in the forest litter and is alone responsible for rearing the young.

Common nighthawk
Equally at home in town or country, the common nighthawk frequently nests on flat, graveled rooftops, swooping low over the streets at dusk as it sweeps insects into its gaping mouth. The fare of the common nighthawk ranges from huge moths to tiny flies; scientists recently discovered that many nightjars swallow stones to help them grind up hard-shelled beetles.

Lesser nighthawk
While the common nighthawk is noisy on the wing, sounding a nasal "peent" every 2 or 3 seconds, its smaller cousin is comparatively quiet while hunting low over the arid pastures and brushlands of the Southwest. Its call is described as a soft, toadlike trill.

Pauraque
A Central and South American bird that also nests in Texas, the pauraque is virtually invisible in daylight as it rests in the litter of twigs and leaves. Its name is a native interpretation of its cry, a slurred "pur-wheeer."

Poor-will
The smallest nightjar, a resident of open lands throughout the West, the poor-will is the only bird in the world known to hibernate. When long cold spells in the desert decimate the insect populations on which it feeds, the poor-will retreats to a rocky niche and sleeps, lowering its body temperature to that of its environment.

Whip-poor-will
Often heard by night, the whip-poor-will is seldom seen by day even by experienced woodsmen because of its cryptic coloration. Perched on a favored singing post—a stone wall, fence, or low branch—it calls its name once every second; the record number of consecutive calls is 1,088, counted many years ago by the great naturalist John Burroughs.

Chuck-will's-widow

Common nighthawk

Lesser nighthawk

Chuck-will's-widow, chicks

Pauraque

Poor-will

Common nighthawk

Whip-poor-will

Lesser nighthawk

NUTHATCH FAMILY

Brown-headed nuthatch
A resident of southern woodlands, the brown-headed nuthatch is the only North American bird reported to use a tool in feeding. It has been observed uncovering insects by flaking off tree bark with another piece of bark held in its bill. Long toes and sharp claws enable nuthatches to forage head-downward on tree trunks, probing crevices for insect life. Brown-headed nuthatches are often seen hanging from terminal clusters of pine needles.

Pygmy nuthatch
Our smallest nuthatch, about 4 inches long, the pygmy nuthatch is a resident of mountain pinelands in the West. Digging their own cavity in a dead tree or rotting stump or recycling an old woodpecker hole, a pair of pygmy nuthatches will raise 5 to 9 young. In fall and winter, pygmy nuthatches drift through the treetops in large and noisy flocks, often in the company of chickadees and titmice. At night, groups of as many as 100 birds will roost in a single cavity.

Red-breasted nuthatch
The seeds of conifers, rather than insects, are the primary food of this bird of northern spruce and fir forests; thus occasional failures of the seed crop send large numbers of red-breasted nuthatches migrating southward in fall and winter. Nesting pairs smear pine pitch about the entrance to their cavity, apparently to discourage predators.

Pygmy nuthatch

Pygmy nuthatch

Red-breasted nuthatch

Red-breasted nuthatch

Brown-headed nuthatch

White-breasted nuthatch

L

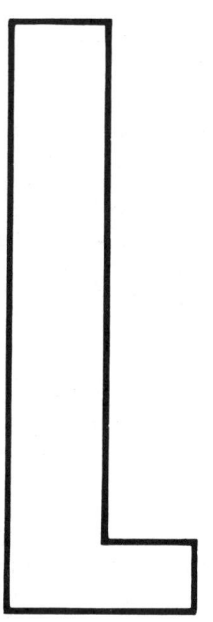

White-breasted nuthatch
A familiar visitor to bird feeders, our largest nuthatch is found from coast to coast wherever suitable habitat is available — deciduous woodlands in the East, coniferous or mixed forests in the West, farm woodlots, rural towns, and large parks. A pair of white-breasted nuthatches remain together year round, occupying a feeding territory of 25 to 50 acres.

LABRADOR TWISTER
See Woodcock, American, in Sandpiper Family.

LA BREA TAR PITS
Name for ancient pools of crude petroleum at Hancock Park, Los Angeles, Calif., in which birds and other animals have been trapped and have died enmeshed by the sticky tar. At Rancho La Brea, the collection of fossils from the asphalt deposits is one of the greatest yet discovered by paleontologists and geologists (Stock, 1961). Closest approach in age, nature of preservation, and in kinds of material preserved has been found in two additional brea occurrences in Calif. — at Carpinteria, Santa Barbara County, and at McKittrick, in Kern County. Students of fossil evidence are convinced that the Rancho La Brea assemblage dates from late in Pleistocene times, a period in geological history about 2 million years ago. *See* Geological Time Scale.

Up to the time of the report by Howard (1962b), more than 85,000 bird fossils, representing a minimum of 5,845 individuals and 133 species, had been recognized from La Brea. So abundant are the skeletal remains in the asphalt that they can be recognized and reassembled as mounted skeletons, many of which are displayed at the Los Angeles County Museum.

Rainwater accumulating on the surface of the tar pools in this dry land attracted animals that came there to drink; when these became enmeshed in the tar below the surface water, their dead or dying bodies attracted the larger flesh-eaters, which in turn became victims. According to Miller (1937), waterfowl have been seen to descend to their destruction by alighting on the pools at twilight. *See* Accidents. Stock (1961) lists the following birds, both extinct fossil birds and species of those now living today, from the La Brea tar pits—grebes, storks, egrets, herons, ibises, roseate spoonbills, swans, geese, ducks, hawks, eagles, falcons, and vultures. Within the group of raptors, a giant extinct condorlike bird, *Teratornis merriami*, was discovered and first described from Rancho La Brea, though its bones were also uncovered from other Pleistocene deposits in Carpinteria and McKittrick and in Fla. and Mexico.

Teratornis (literally "monster bird") is one of the most striking large birds ever discovered and was even larger than the present-day California condor and the Andean condor of S. America. It had a wingspread of at least 12 ft. and weighed possibly 50 lbs. According to Miller (1937), who discovered and described the extinct bird, which he named in honor of Dr. John C. Merriam, University of California paleontologist, its big wing bones exceeded in length and diameter the largest bones of a 6-ft. man. Its feet, however, were no more predatory than those of a turkey and it is probable that it was a scavenger that lived on dead animals. *See* Fossil Birds.

Golden eagles, which persisted from Pleistocene times to our present-day fauna, were found more abundantly at La Brea than any other bird. According to Stock (1961), there are more than 800 individuals of this bird represented in the Los Angeles County Museum col-

lection. Less numerous are remains of bald eagles recovered from the tar pits.

Quail, and an extinct fowl-like bird resembling a turkey, cranes, ploverlike birds, pigeons, doves, the roadrunner, owls of species still living, some of our present-day woodpeckers, and no less than 36 kinds of passerines, or songbirds, have been recovered from the tar pits—from larks, jays, crows, ravens, magpies, and thrashers to towhees and sparrows. An extinct species of towhee has been discovered and described from the tar pits; also an extinct blackbird (Stock, 1961).

LACHRYMAL (LAK-rih-mal) GLANDS
See Harderian Glands.

LADY-OF-THE-WATERS
See Heron, Louisiana, in Heron Family; so named by John James Audubon because of its elegance and grace.

LAMELLAR (lah-MEL-er) CORPUSCLES
Composed of small, thin plates or layers. *See* Herbst's corpuscles under Feather.

LAMELLATE
Term for the condition, for example, of a duck's bill and of a flamingo's, which have numerous lamellae, or tiny transverse, toothlike ridges just inside the tomium, or cutting edge, of the bill. These comblike teeth, or serrations, on the inside edges of both the upper and lower mandible, serve the bird as a sieve in its feeding. When the bird's mouth is closed, the tiny teeth form a strainer. As the bird feeds with its bill in water, it frequently presses its tongue against the roof of its mouth, which forces the water out the sides of its bill. The comblike teeth (lamellae) prevent the escape of the solid food particles, which are kept within the bird's mouth for swallowing. *See* Swallowing. *See also* Duck Family; Anseriformes; Flamingo Family.

LAMMERGEYER
or LAMMERGEIR. *See* Altitude of Bird Flight; Digestion; Flight.

LAND BIRD
Term for a general grouping (not a classification) of N. American birds that live largely or entirely on land. They include members of the following families: American Vulture Family; Hawk Family; Osprey Family; Falcon Family; Curassow Family; Grouse Family; Pheasant Family; Turkey Family; Pigeon Family; Parrot Family; Cuckoo Family; Barn Owl Family; Typical-Owl Family; Nightjar Family; Swift Family; Hummingbird Family; Trogon Family; Kingfisher Family; Woodpecker Family; and the 29 families of songbirds in N. America in the order Passeriformes, from Cotinga Family to Finch Family. *See* these families listed under Classification.

LAND-RAIL
See crakes in Rail Family.

LANGUAGE
Few groups of animals have as elaborate a system of communication as do birds. Communica-

LANGUAGE
The male herring gull makes its presence known to a female by a trumpeting "long call," which also serves to repel other males from its established territory.

tion is the primary function of language, and to that extent human language and bird song are comparable. A bird's vocal repertoire may include a dozen, even 20 or more, calls and songs, each serving a function in communicating with others of its kind, other species of birds, and even predators. A blue jay that utters an alarm call usually warns other birds besides its own kind, for many songbirds and even mammals such as deer pay heed to jays' cries. "The means of expression of birds are inherited and with very few exceptions, cannot be changed. Animal language is more like our laughing and crying than our speech" (Heinroth and Heinroth, 1958).

For example, a robin's song during mating season seems to be a warning in "bird language" to other robins to keep out of singing bird's territory. *See* Songs and Singing. If song is not heeded and strange robin enters singing bird's territory, it may stop singing and crouch in threatening attitude before actually flying or running at strange bird to drive it away. *See* Territory. In some of the courtship performances of avocets, they make specific head movements with which they communicate with others in flock. Through this sign language, it is believed, avocets are able to perform large group movements in which up to dozen circle about in almost perfect cadence in a courtship dance prior to selecting a mate (Gilliard, 1958). Thus the gestures and positions of a bird's head and body may be a language that others of its kind understand. *See* Water-Dance, and Murre and Puffin in Auk Family; *see also* Waterfowl and in Crane Family.

When a bird is caught by snake, hawk, or other predatory animal, or even when held by human being, it usually calls loudly in distress when first seized; its cries may attract attention of many kinds of birds, which often assemble, then mob or attack snake, hawk, or other "enemy." *See also* Alarm Calls. Occasionally, parent birds may be so distressed that they will attack a human being who has caught and is holding in the hands a squealing young bird. Blue jays, goshawks, great horned and screech owls, mockingbirds, catbirds, peregrine falcons, terns, and others can be very aggressive in defense of their young. *See* Young and Their Care.

Many young birds, when first on the wing, utter a cry that parent birds heed and which seems to stimulate parents to hunt for food and to feed the young; special calls uttered by adult yellow warblers and by least flycatchers stimulate the feeding response in the nestlings (Collias, 1960). Young songbirds, when parent birds are in sight, usually accompany their "food calls" with trembling or shivering of the wings, which seems to stimulate parents further in feeding of the young. Food calls of young birds, when hidden in trees, grass, or shrubbery, seem also to be *location calls* whereby parents can find the young when they return to them with food.

Call notes of birds serve many purposes and are different from a bird's song (*see* Songs and Singing). "A bird's call note, in contrast to its song, is a brief sound with a relatively simple acoustic structure" (Thorpe, 1956a). In songbirds "it is in general of one or two syllables

and practically never more than 4 or 5 notes" (Thorpe, 1964a). Bobwhite quail have a special call to gather together mated pairs or members of the covey after they have been separated; as do crows to assemble the flock (see Chamberlain and Cornwell, 1971). Adults and young of game birds and shorebirds have special calls that keep the brood of young together or unite them after they have been scattered. Birds in migration use special call notes rarely heard at any other time, which are thought to keep them in contact with each other and may even be reassuring to them. *See* Migration.

According to Willoughby and Cade (1962), many birds have calls or notes uttered in a special social context—the American kestrel has three; the domestic fowls, or chickens, have six classes of adult auditory signals (Collias, 1960); the Canada goose, eight; and passerines, or songbirds, may have up to a dozen or more different calls (Thorpe, 1961).

Songs and some calls help to prevent interbreeding among closely related species. *See* Sympatric Species. For example, the barn and cliff swallows, which may breed on or in the same barn, have calls so distinctive that they apparently aid in species recognition and keep these two separate and distinct (Samuel, 1971).

Some birds are clever imitators. Although mimicry of sounds made by other animals may not be a language, both songbirds and parrots can do it. Mockingbirds, for example, weave call notes and songs of other birds into their own songs, and parrots can whistle and imitate words spoken by man, and crows are also good mimics. See Chamberlain and Cornwell (1971) for an interesting theory of the function of mimicking ability. Birds are the only animals, other than man, that can make sounds they were not born to make (Heinroth and Heinroth, 1958). *See* Mimicry (vocal).

Sounds birds make to communicate with each other are not always made with their voices. The flightless kiwi, national emblem of New Zealand, stamps its feet when annoyed, storks and some herons rattle their bills, and woodpeckers drum with their bills on hollow limbs to announce their territories to other woodpeckers; drumming also attracts the opposite sex during courtship (both sexes drum). Wing feathers of some kinds of ducks make a specific whistling which is recognized by others of their own kind. The tail and wing feathers of some birds are used by them in flight to make special sounds during the breeding season. The nighthawk, during his courtship, dives downward toward his mate, producing a booming sound as he turns upward in the dive and the wind rushes through his wing primaries (Bent, 1940).

The common snipe, when flying about in the spring dusk over its marshland home, produces weird, quavering sounds called "bleating," or "drumming." See Hall (1960); *see also* Courtship Flight under Flight. Ruffed grouse beat the air with their wings in drumming performances that make a throbbing sound like thunder. *See* in Grouse Family; *see also* Drumming; see Emlen (1960) for an interesting discussion of communication between animals by sounds.

LAPPET
(LAP-et). *See* Wattle.

LAPWING
See in Plover Family.

LARDER
Term for place (thorn or twig on bush or tree, or barb of barbed-wire fence) on which shrikes have impaled small animals to be eaten at once, a few days later, or as much as a week or so later. Is close to storage, but storage in its true form means gathering together a considerable quantity of food for future use without at the time partaking of it extensively. *See* Food and Feeding Habits. "The object of the American shrikes' habit of impaling, then, is not truly storage" (Miller, A. H., 1950). *See* Shrike Family; Crow Family.

LARID
(LAR-id). A shortened term for a member of the Gull Family.

LARIDAE
See Gull Family.

LARK FAMILY
Alaudidae (ah-LAW-dih-dee); from Lat. *alauda*, lark. 75 species, small songbirds predominantly an Old World group, across Eurasia from tundra southward to Africa and Madagascar, Australia; no member of family on an oceanic island; includes in N. America only 2 species: the native, circumpolar horned lark throughout much of N. America to s. Mexico, of which an isolated group has established itself in the highland savannas of Colombia in S. America, and the European skylark, most famous of the Lark Family, introduced by man and established in s. Vancouver Is., B.C., and introduced in 1880s near Flatbush and Flatlands section of Brooklyn, N.Y. With rapid development of open land, disappeared from Brooklyn by 1913 (Bull, 1964).

Larks are ground-dwelling, most live in open bare lands—deserts, beaches, grasslands, plowed ground, and along edges of rivers (they are distantly related to swallows and pipits); they walk rather than hop; the hind claw is usually long and straight; the wings long and pointed; sexes outwardly alike or nearly so; are often gregarious but not colonial, and many sing elaborate and beautiful songs when flying about over their nesting territories. The skylark, the "blithe spirit" of the poet Shelley's verse, nests in the Old World from near the Arctic Circle across Eurasia, from the British Isles to the Kamchatka Pen. in Siberia, south to India and n. Africa. Besides in N. America, the skylark has been introduced and established in New Zealand and in the Hawaiian Is. For other details see Austin (1961) and Meinertzhagen (1964b).

Members of the Lark Family are protected by law (*see* Legal Protection) and may not be kept in captivity without a permit; however, ill or injured birds may be kept alive until able to fend for themselves by offering them mockingbird food, mealworms, yolk of boiled eggs, meat, fruit, lettuce (Walker, 1942).

Lark, common. Another name for meadowlarks in Troupial Family.

Lark, desert horned. *See* Lark, horned.

Lark, field. Another name for meadowlarks in Troupial Family.

Lark, horned, *Eremophila alpestris* (er-ee-MOE-phil-ah al-PES-tris); genus name: Lat., desert-loving; species name: Lat., of the Alps (Coues, 1882). (Color ill., page 573.) Arctic coasts of N. Hemisphere south to n. Africa; in N. America, Alaska, and Canada to Mexico and n. Ga.; 7–8 in. long; wingspread 12¼–14 in.; brown-backed ground bird; male has black forehead, with black whisker mark down sides of face; black collar below pale throat; face yellow to white; "horns" (feather tufts) on head black, but not always noticeable; tail mostly black; underparts white; walks (does not hop); female and immatures similar to male but duller colors (Peterson, 1961); do not have black on crown; claw on hind toe very long, nearly straight (the "larkspur"); flight undulating, folds wings tightly to body after each beat; seen overhead in flight, black tail with white corners contrasts with pale body; some winter in nesting range; others migrate to winter in s. or se. U.S.; winters in small or enormous flocks on open barren plains, deserts, fields, golf courses, airports, sand dunes along coasts, flat, open brackish meadows; sometimes lone birds or in company with snow buntings or Lapland longspurs; most of horned larks that nest in Alaska and Canada have left wintering grounds in U.S. by end of Apr.; "millions" fly about over plowed fields of Man. on way to nesting places, often while snow is still deep; among others that nest on their wintering grounds in U.S., male has established territory by Feb. and Mar. (Pickwell, 1942) on both cultivated and unbroken land wherever wide areas of bare soil; sings from clod or any other slight elevation on ground and from air; flight song is begun silently on climb into sky from 270 to more than 800 ft., where he circles singing *pit-wit, wee-pit, pit-wee, wee-pit;* closes song with headlong drop to earth with wings closed; most common call note is *zeet.*

Feeding Habits: Walks or runs over ground in foraging: eats mostly weed seeds; waste grain in stubble fields; picks at grass stalks, never alighting on them as do snow buntings and longspurs; in summer eats caterpillars, ants, ichneumon flies (wasps), grasshoppers, leafhoppers, also spiders, small mollusks; in winter often feeds in freshly manured fields.
Nest: Built by female in open on bare ground in slight hollow often dug by female or in natural hollow, near clod of earth or dried horse or cattle droppings; shallow cup of fine grasses sometimes lined with feathers, plant down, hairs.
Eggs: Feb.–July; 2–5, commonly 4, gray-white or green-white, finely speckled with browns.
Incubation: By female, 11 days (Pickwell, 1942; Verbeek, 1967); young fly at 9–12 days; one brood at high altitudes and latitudes (Verbeek, 1967); two and possibly more at lower ones (Du Bois, 1935).

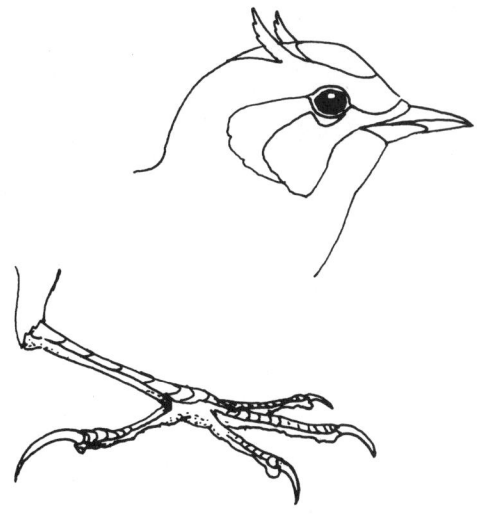

LARK FAMILY

LARK FAMILY

In its courtship flight, the male horned lark climbs silently to considerable heights—often 800 feet—where it begins its high-pitched, tinkling flight song as it circles. At the end of the song, it will drop headlong to earth with wings closed until almost the last second.

Other Names: Life bird; northern horned lark; prairie bird; prairie horned lark; road chippie; road lark; road trotter; shore lark; spring bird; wheat bird; winter horned lark.

Flight Speed: Timed in Calif., 32–54 m.p.h. (McLean, 1930); 23–28 m.p.h. (Wetmore, 1916); 28 m.p.h. (Tyler, 1933).

Host to Cowbirds: Infrequent (Friedmann, 1963).

Weights: Adult males, Mont., summer (15), 32.3 gr., or about $1\frac{1}{8}$ oz.; adult females (7), 30.6 gr. (Verbeek, 1967); 25–40 gr. (Trost, 1972).

Range: In N. America, nests from Alaska and Canada's Arctic coast, south to Baja Calif., s. Mexico, Tex., sw. La., n. Miss., n. Ga., and N.C.; moves southward in fall or winter from northern part of range.

Lark, Northern horned. *See* Lark, horned.

Lark, Prairie horned. *See* Lark, horned.

Lark, road. *See* Lark, horned.

Lark, shore. *See* Lark, horned.

Lark, snow. Another name for the snow bunting in Finch Family.

Meadowlark. Not a lark, name of a bird in the Troupial Family.

Skylark, *Alauda arvensis* (ah-LAW-dah are-VEN-sis); genus name: Lat., lark; species name: from Lat. *arvum,* field. (Color ill., page 573.) Native of Eurasia, Africa, resident in N. America on Vancouver Is., B.C., where about 100 released on Saanich Pen. in 1902 or 1903; well established there by 1937, with increased population of 219, mostly in farm fields; about 1,000 estimated on Saanich Pen. by Mar. 1962 (Weisbrod and Stevens, 1974); first *recent* report in U.S. (see Phillips, 1928, and Bull, 1964, for history of earlier N.Y. "colony") was in state of Wash. (San Juan Is.) in 1961 (Bruce, 1961); first recent nesting in continental U.S. (with three young) discovered San Juan Is., May 17, 1970, by Wahl and Wilson (1971), who estimated 12 pairs of skylarks in area at that time; in Mar. 1972, Weisbrod and Stevens (1974) saw 27 males displaying over an open field on San Juan Is., and counted 63 there in a census of Aug. 1973; 7–7½ in. long; sexes outwardly alike; slender bill, upperparts brown, heavily streaked; has small head crest, which it raises frequently when excited; underparts buff-white; *breast streaked;* buffy eye stripe; white in outer tail feathers; ground-dwelling bird, lives in open country of broad fields, extensive cropland, meadows, marshy flats, sandy coasts, barren heaths; male in courtship display runs around female with raised crest and tail and drooping wings; in courtship song-flight, he rises higher and higher in air until mere speck in sky singing trills and cadenzas; performance unparalleled by any other bird (Jourdain, 1942); also utters liquid, bubbling *chirrup* at intervals during low, undulating flight.

Feeding Habits: Of vegetable food (about half of diet) eats mostly weed seeds, some waste grain; also insects, spiders, earthworms, slugs, millipedes, among animal food.

Nest: In meadow grass or in crop field; a mere hollow in ground lined with roots, grasses, horsehair.

Eggs: Apr.–July (Jourdain, 1942); 3–4, gray-white, thickly spotted with olive or brown.

Incubation: By female, 11–12 days; young leave nest about 9–10 days after hatching but may not fly until about 21 days old (Jourdain, 1942). See also details in Sprot (1937).

Other Names: European skylark; lark; skylark.

Age: One (banded) reported from Czechoslovakia, lived to 8 years, 9 months (Clapp, 1976).

Weights: 30–45 gr. (Meinertzhagen, 1964b), or about 1–1 ⅔ oz.

Range: See above.

Skylark, European. *See* Skylark.

Skylark, Missouri. Another name for Sprague's pipit in Pipit Family.

Skylark, prairie. Another name for Sprague's pipit in Pipit Family.

LARYNX

See Voice and Sound-making.

LAWRENCE

GEORGE NEWBOLD (1806–95). Born and died in New York City; one of founders of American Ornithologists' Union and authority in his time on birds of tropical America. With his friend John Cassin, he assisted Spencer F. Baird in authorship of the famous Vol. IX of the *Reports of Exploration and Surveys for a Railroad Route from the Mississippi River to the Pacific Ocean* (1858) and wrote *Catalogue of Birds Observed in New York . . .* (1866). In 1850 Cassin named for him the Lawrence's goldfinch (Palmer *et al.*, 1954). See also Gruson (1972).

LAWRENCE

NEWBOLD T(ROTTER) (1855–1928). Born in New York City; for whom Harold Herrick named the Lawrence's warbler, later discovered not to be a true species but a hybrid. Lawrence was a nephew of George Newbold Lawrence; he was an amateur ornithologist and published a few papers about birds (Crosby, 1930).

LAWYER

See Avocet, American, and Stilt, black-necked, in Avocet Family and Double-crested cormorant in Cormorant Family.

LAZY-BIRD

See Cowbird, brown-headed, in Troupial Family and Belted kingfisher in Kingfisher Family.

LEACH

WILLIAM ELFORD (1790–1836). Zoologist at the British Museum, London. In 1820, C. J. Temminck, Dutch ornithologist, named a petrel, *Procellaria leachii*, in his honor. It was discovered later that a previous species name, *leucorhoa*, (now called *Oceanodrama leucorhoa*), published in 1817, had priority; however, the English name still honors Leach. Leach studied medicine in London and Edinburgh, then went to the British Museum in 1813, where he remained to become a renowned authority on crustaceans; he also published "copiously on fishes, mammals, insects, and much else" (Murphy, 1962). See *Dictionary of National Biography* (1950, Vol. XI); see also Gruson (1972).

LEAD POISONING

Death of waterfowl—ducks, geese, and swans —from lead poisoning has been known in N. America since it was noted in ducks at Stephenson Lake, Tex., as early as 1874. In 1901 George Bird Grinnell cited symptoms in ducks and whistling swans at Currituck Sound, N.C., and in 1908, J. H. Bowles reported lead poisoning of mallards at Puget Sound, Wash. W. L. McAtee in the same year wrote of it in canvasbacks at Lake Surprise, Tex.

Other early records include several whistling swans from Back Bay, Va. (1915), and many mallards and pintails in the Bear R. marshes of Utah (Wetmore, 1919a), scaup and Canada geese from Mich., and an adult trumpeter swan and six cygnets that died from lead poisoning in B.C. in 1925, and, more recently, 13 trumpeter swans affected by lead poisoning found by Dr. Ian McT. Cowan in Feb. 1943 on Vancouver Is., B.C. (Bellrose, 1959).

Contrary to popular belief, lead shot or pellets in the flesh of waterfowl wounded by hunters does not cause lead poisoning and may not kill the birds unless the shot has damaged vital organs or tissues. Some ducks have a remarkable ability to survive flesh wounds and even broken bones (Terres, 1946a), but lead poisoning is deadly if waterfowl have *swallowed* lead pellets. The pellets come to rest in the gizzard (*see* Gizzard), where they remain as grit and are gradually worn down by the abrasive action of sand, gravel, and other debris.

Some of the lead compounds are then absorbed by the bloodstream of the bird through its intestinal walls, and apparently damage the liver and kidneys. The compounds appear to be directly harmful to the muscles of the digestive tract, thus seriously impairing digestion and the assimilation of food by birds (Jordan and Bellrose, 1951).

Wetmore (1919a), explaining results of some of his pioneering experiments with feeding lead shot to captive ducks, wrote: "It was found that six pellets of No. 6 shot constituted an amount of lead that was always fatal. Two or three . . . were sufficient to cause death in several [ducks] and as the number of shot [in the gizzards of mallards] was increased the resistance of individual birds decreased. In one experiment, two mallards were each given one No. 6 shot. One died 9 days later while the other was able to throw off the effects of the lead. . . ."

In examining wild ducks that had died of lead poisoning, Wetmore discovered that the usual number of shot in the stomach of a single bird that had been feeding in waters over which hunters had been shooting was 15–40; the largest number was 76, in the gizzard of a mallard shot near the place at which the Bear R. empties into Great Salt Lake in Utah. However,

lead pellets may not always be present in the gizzard of a duck at the time that it dies of lead poisoning. J. S. Jordan (cited by Bellrose, 1959) found in controlled experiments with captive mallards that 21% of those fed from one to four No. 6 shot had none in their gizzards at the time of their deaths. Apparently in these ducks the lead had passed out of their digestive tracts, but at such late stages of the illness that they did not recover. In tests with mallards, those that did not void the shot, but carried it in their gizzards for an average of 23 days, died.

According to Bellrose (1964b), the number of ingested shot that can kill waterfowl varies among individuals—only one shot kills some birds but several shots may not affect others. Among wild adult drake mallards trapped in c. Ill. and e. Colo., dosed individually with No. 6 shot, banded (*see* Banding), then released, of those fed only one shot, 12% died; of those fed two shots, 44% died; of those fed six shots, 66% died. However, individual variation in the effect of lead toxemia on waterfowl apparently depends on the amount and kind of food the poisoned bird eats; those that eat more are strikingly less susceptible to death by lead poisoning than those that do not. Passing of food through the digestive tract apparently eliminates many of the soluble lead compounds from the bird's body.

SYMPTOMS. Most people who see ducks, geese, or swans dying from late stages of lead poisoning are deeply moved by it. In the beginning, the appetite of the poisoned bird falls off or it may stop eating because its gizzard is partly paralyzed. It begins to lose weight and then develops diarrhea, emitting greenish droppings that stain its vent. During its second or third week of illness, the bird becomes weak and tires easily; during the third or fourth week, these symptoms increase. Then the keel bone, or sternum, of the emaciated duck begins to show prominently, and it carries its wings up, and level with its back—the "roof-shaped" position. It may weakly try to fly or to dive below the surface of the water to escape when approached by a man or predatory animal, or try to hide behind bushes or other available cover.

At this stage, in some waterfowl, a combined drooping of its chest and wings, and the abnormally high position in which it holds its tail, give it a rocking motion as it moves about. Now it commonly rests its neck on its back, and often falls and has difficulty rising (Jordan and Bellrose, 1951). Death for it may then be merciful, whether from a predator or from a man, when it is beyond recovery.

Examination of lead-poisoned birds shows striking emaciation at the time of death, when up to 40–50% of its original weight may have been lost. The large flight muscles of its breast are reduced to remnants of their former size; the liver and kidneys show wasting; and the enlarged gall bladder in some ducks may be five times its normal weight. According to Jordan and Bellrose (1951), such ducks do not have lead content in their remaining skin and flesh, therefore would not poison people that might want to eat them; however, they are so emaciated that they have little food value.

AVAILABILITY OF LEAD PELLETS. According to Bellrose (1964b), the average hunter fires 5–30 shotgun shells for every duck he bags; therefore as many as 7,500 pellets for every duck killed may be in waters where hunters have been shooting, as these are usually places where the birds feed. An estimated 6,000 tons of lead shot, fired by hunters, falls into marshes each autumn in the U.S. (Harris, V. T., 1972). On muddy bottoms of ponds, lakes, and bays, the lead pellets may sink out of reach of waterfowl, but on bottoms of sand and gravel, lead shot available to feeding waterfowl may be up to 120,000 an acre. On bottoms of deep peat and the muck of marshes and pond bottoms, however, available shot may be only about 3,500 an acre. The lead pellets, which resemble the seeds of pondweeds, a favored food of mallards and pintails, for example, are most apt to be eaten by waterfowl from late autumn through the winter.

MORTALITY. Waterfowl die from lead poisoning every year, but mortality varies—in one place a few to a dozen or no birds may die; in another year, perhaps up to 10,000. In Jan. 1948, 110,000 mallards died in a spectacular case of lead poisoning near Grafton, Ill. Greatest mortality has been in the Mississippi Flyway (*see* Waterfowl), especially in La., Ill., Mo., Ind., and Ark. Heaviest losses have been of mallards, pintails, and Canada geese. Whistling swans have sometimes been reported dying in large numbers from lead poisoning at Back Bay, Va., and Currituck Sound and Lake Mattamuskeet, N.C., and in marshes of the Great Lakes in Ohio, Mich., and Wisc., and Bear R., Utah. Almost all species of waterfowl have been reported, at some time, to have died of lead poisoning, which causes an annual loss estimated by Bellrose (1964b) at about 2–3 % of the waterfowl population.

SPECIES MOST AND LEAST AFFECTED. Mortality is most severe among mallards in the Mississippi Flyway and may be up to 4% of the population yearly. There are also large losses of pintails, but deaths from lead poisoning are relatively low among blue-winged teal, greenwinged teal, shovelers, and wood ducks because few individuals of these species swallow lead shot. According to Bellrose (1964b), lead poisoning is even less significant in American wigeons and gadwalls, which ingest few shot because they prefer soft plant foods to hard seeds or grain.

Redheads, ring-necked ducks, canvasbacks, and lesser scaups have the highest rate of shot ingestion of all species because they feed on the bottom, digging for seeds and tubers of aquatic plants. Although Canada and snow geese usually eat only a few shot, a great many of them die of lead poisoning; however, some individuals eat a large number of pellets. A lead-poisoned Canada goose had eaten 110, but this could not compare with a trumpeter swan in B.C. which had eaten 451.

Lead poisoning has been noted rarely in other birds. In N.M. a dead scaled quail was found with 13 lead pellets in its gizzard; among wild pheasants, reports of it are few. Stoddard (1931) wrote that a single pellet in the gizzard of a bobwhite quail up to 41 days of age could cause its death; Westemeier (1966) reported a juvenile female bobwhite that had died from eating four lead shots.

According to Bellrose (1964b), a way to reduce the deaths of waterfowl from lead poisoning is for hunters to use shot other than lead. In experiments, massive doses of *iron* shot pellets fed to mallards had no harmful effects on them. After considerable experimenting, a sporting arms and ammunition company developed a spherical pellet of an iron alloy that has little or no effect on modern gun barrels; however, the iron shot at a range of more than 45 yds. was less effective than lead shot. But lead persists for long periods in water or on the ground and the accumulation has reached the point where its effect produces an annual loss of ducks averaging close to the total number produced each year in N.D. and S.D. "If lead shot continues to be scattered in waterfowl marshes across the country it is inevitable that losses from lead poisoning will increase" (Bellrose, 1964b). *See also* Poisons; Botulism; Diseases. As of 1979, the problem was still unresolved, but there is continual pressure on the U.S. government to require hunters to use the softer iron shot, especially in regions where concentrations of lead shot have caused unusually large losses of waterfowl.

LEAF BATHING
See Bathing.

LEARNING
See Behavior.

LEATHER-BACK
Another name for the ruddy duck because its feathers said to be impervious to hunter's gunshots. *See* in Duck Family.

Le CONTE
(lee-KONT), JOHN L(AWRENCE), M.D. (1825–83). Eminent entomologist, born New York City, son of Maj. John Eatton Le Conte, a naturalist (*Appleton's Cyclopedia of American Biography*, 1887). Audubon named a sparrow for John L. Le Conte (it was collected [shot] by John G. Bell May 24, 1843, while with Audubon on the upper Missouri R.), *Emberiza Le Conteii*. It is now Le Conte's sparrow, *Ammospiza leconteii* (see *The Auk*, Apr. 1973). Of the naming of "Le Conte's Sharp-tailed Bunting," as he called it, Audubon wrote: "after my young friend Doctor Le Conte, son of Major Le Conte." In 1851, George Newbold Lawrence named for John Lawrence Le Conte a thrasher, *Toxostoma lecontei*, from one or more of these birds collected presumably by Le Conte in 1851 in Calif. while exploring the Colorado R.

LEECHES
See Parasite.

LEGAL PROTECTION
On Aug. 16, 1916, representatives of the governments of Great Britain, in Canada, and the U.S. signed an international agreement, the Migratory Bird Treaty, to protect birds that migrate between Canada and the U.S. The treaty needed enabling legislation to make it enforceable; on July 3, 1918, President Woodrow Wilson signed the Migratory Bird Treaty Act, and the two governments had the power to establish a closed season, or no killing at any time of migratory insectivorous birds (mostly songbirds) and other migratory non-game birds; the act prohibits the sale, purchase, taking, or possession of any wild migratory birds, their parts (feathers, for example), nests, or eggs, and prohibits the interstate transportation of wild migratory birds taken contrary to law. It also empowers the federal government to regulate the hunting season for migratory game birds, bag limits, how these birds may be taken—for example, in 1979, it included certain ducks, geese, and swans, the sandhill crane, and certain doves (*see* in Pigeon Family), and two of the shorebirds (the woodcock and common snipe)—and their possession, transportation, and importation. It also governs the taking of wild migratory game birds for their propagation or for scientific and educational purposes, and provides for exceptions for the control of those birds causing damage to agricultural or other interests. *See* Control. The close (or closed) season is between Mar. 10 and Sept. 1. Most violations of the Migratory Bird Treaty Act are called misdemeanors, or "petty offenses," and anyone convicted of an offense under the act is subject to a heavy fine or a prison term or both. See Swift and Lawrence (1966).

On Feb. 7, 1936, the U.S. and Mexico entered into a similar agreement—the Convention for the Protection of Migratory Birds and Game Mammals, and these two treaties, between the U.S. and Great Britain (represented by Canada), and the U.S. and Mexico, extended migratory bird protection to all of N. America. Later laws broadened the federal role in wildlife protection of birds—especially the amended Migratory Bird Treaty Act of June 20, 1936, and the Bald Eagle Act of June 8, 1940, amended Oct. 24, 1962, to provide protection for the golden eagle (Swift and Lawrence, 1966); also the Endangered Species Preservation Act of 1966, the Endangered Species Conservation Act of 1969, and the Endangered Species Act of 1973, amended in 1977. See discussion of these by the Environmental Law Institute (1977).

With the signing of the convention with Mexico, and its later amendments of Mar. 10, 1972 (see discussion of these by Anonymous, 1972c), extra protection, especially from wanton shooting, was extended to 32 additional families of birds. Of particular significance was the inclusion of 6 families that encompass all birds of prey—the eagles, hawks, kites, falcons, owls, ospreys, and vultures. It also extended protection within the U.S. and Mexico to the following families: Albatross; Anhinga; Cormorant; Crow; Flamingo; Frigatebird; Ibis; Jacana; Kingfisher; Limpkin; Pelican; Skimmer; Stork; Trogon; and Tropic-bird. Thus, with those birds listed as protected in the U.S. Fish and Wildlife Service publication *Birds Protected by Federal Law* (Wildlife Leaflet No. 494, Nov. 1970), practically all families of N. American birds are legally protected from being taken year-round. Some exceptions are waterfowl and upland game birds such as grouse, pheasants, certain doves, etc., and the two shorebirds mentioned above, on which there is a specified hunting season for a certain period decided upon by the federal and state governments, and the introduced house sparrow and starling, which are not protected at any time. Other birds, such as blackbirds, cowbirds, and others that, because of their large winter flocks concentrated in certain areas, may become an occasional nuisance, may be subject to control by killing (*see* Control) through special permits under justified circumstances. Others that may be an occasional nuisance are crows and magpies (Crow Family) and horned owls, which at certain times and places may require some control. Permits are also issued by federal and state governments for the use of certain predatory birds in falconry. General falconry requirements under the Migratory Bird Treaty Act were promulgated Jan. 10, 1976, 41, *Federal Register* 2237. For a general discussion, details, and court suits, fines, etc., relative to the Migratory Bird Treaty Act, what it is, and does, violations, etc., see report of the Environmental Institute (1977). See also a review of bird protection laws by Wallace (1963) and an early history by Pearson (1933). See also the reports of the American Ornithologists' Union (1975a; 1975b).

Violations of the law protecting wild birds—by anyone who pursues, hunts, shoots, or shoots at, wounds, kills, traps, captures, collects, or poisons them, or harasses them in any way such as destroying their nests and eggs—should be reported to the local State Conservation officer, or the nearest U.S. Game Management Agent (federal warden). Anyone finding an injured American robin or other bird protected by the Migratory Bird Treaty Act, and wishing to care for it until it is well, may get temporary legal possession of it by writing the nearest U.S. Fish and Wildlife Service office and requesting a permit (Swift and Lawrence, 1966). Most young birds, however, that appear to be abandoned usually have parents nearby and should be left alone. See discussion of this in Terres (1977). *See also* Care and Feeding of Abandoned or Injured Wild Birds.

LEGS
See Feet and Legs.

LEK
A word probably from the Swedish *leka,* to play; means to gather, or assemble, a gathering. The term *lek* in ornithology was first applied to a small "court," or ground area, defended by the male ruff of Eurasia during its breeding season (*see* Ruff in Sandpiper Family). Hjorth (1970) describes the lek as a traditional, collective display ground composed of grouped "display territories," each of which is defended by a different male. Males gather on these leks to display in the breeding season; females visit leks for copulation with males. See Shepard (1975). *See* Arena Bird.

LESSON
RENÉ PRIMIVÈRE (1794–1849). Naturalist, and naval apothecary on French corvette *Coquille;* sailed from Toulon, Aug. 11, 1821, to Pacific, returned to Toulon, Mar. 31, 1825; in 1826 Lesson published the first new descriptions of birds collected on the trip, thenceforth an enthusiastic ornithologist who lost no opportunity to describe new species. For some time hummingbirds were his favorites; in 1830 he gave the blue-throated hummingbird the species name *clemenciae* for his wife, Clémence, from the type specimen collected in Mexico. See Stresemann (1975); Wynne (1969).

LETTUCE-BIRD
See Goldfinch, American, in Finch Family. Name from habit of eating seeds of lettuce.

LEUCINO
See Albinism.

LEUCISM
See Abnormal Colors under Colors of Feathers.

LEUCOCYTES
See Circulatory System.

LEUCOCYTOZOON
See Internal Parasites under Diseases.

LEUCOSTICTE
(lew-coe-STICK-tee). One of common names of the rosy finches (*see* in Finch Family); it is also their genus name. *See* Genus.

LEVEE WALKER
Local name in La. for the little blue heron, from its habit of hunting for crayfishes along levees of rice fields.

LEWIS
MERIWETHER (1774–1809). Born Charlottesville, Va., of distinguished family, captain in regular army, and for several years secretary to Thomas Jefferson, President of the U.S. Jefferson, in 1803, recommended Lewis to Congress to command an exploring expedition to find an overland route to the Pacific O. On the expedition, called the Lewis and Clark expedition, on July 20, 1805, near the present site of Helena, Mont., Capt. Lewis saw a strange woodpecker, "black as a crow." In May 1806, members of the expedition collected several of these black woodpeckers near Kamiah, Idaho; later Alexander Wilson examined them and in Vol. III of his *American Ornithology* gave the bird the English name Lewis's woodpecker (Bock, 1970).

L'HERMINIER
FÉLIX-LOUIS (1779–1833). French naturalist who lived on Guadaloupe Is., West Indies, 1798–1829 (Wynne 1969), in exile from France (Gruson, 1972); also his son Dr. Ferd. J. L'Herminier lived on Guadaloupe; Lesson, French zoologist, gave the species name *lherminieri* to a shearwater in honor of either the father or son, or both, but did not identify which in *Revue Zoologique,* Vol. II, No. 3, 1839.

LICE
The so-called bird lice, biting lice, or feather lice of the order Mallophaga (mal-LOFF-ah-gah) are the most common external parasites of birds and the ones frequently seen by ornithologists in handling live or dead birds (Herman, 1955). The Mallophaga belong to an order of wingless insects that are parasitic externally on birds, and on many mammals, but not on

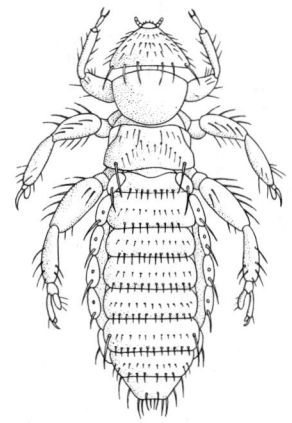

LICE
Mallophaga, tiny bird lice, are the most common external parasites on birds. Obligatory parasites, they live their entire lives deep in the plumage of their host.

man—in handling birds, one need not fear that the bird lice will transfer themselves to one's own skin or hair. They are tiny—from those just under a mm. long that infest some game birds to the 10 mm. long kinds that infest some hawks. They can be distinguished from other insects by the large, broad head and flattened appearance, and when an infested bird is held in the hand, they may be seen crawling rapidly over the bird's body. They are photonegative (will move away from light) and have a positive reaction to the smell and warmth of their bird hosts; they keep well within the plumage. They are *obligatory* parasites (*see* Parasite) and spend their complete life cycles on their hosts. If their bird hosts die, they die with them unless they can transfer quickly to another bird host of the same species.

Mallophaga feed on fragments of feathers, tissue fluids and flakes of a bird's skin, which they bite off with their strong mandibles. In feeding upon the feathers of birds, they generally confine themselves to the down feathers or to the downy part of the larger feathers. *See* Feather. Some Mallophaga may live entirely on blood and serum of birds or may add this to their main diet of feathers. One of the chicken lice, *Menacanthus stramineus*, lives on a mixed diet of feathers and blood. It uses its mandibles to puncture the young feathers in quill (pinfeather) and sucks blood from the central pulp supplying the growing feather. *See* How Feathers Grow under Feather.

Members of the genus *Piagetiella* live attached to the inner walls of the throat pouches of pelicans and cormorants, where it is believed their diet consists of blood and serum and possibly epidermal debris from the walls of the pouch. Another species spends part of its life cycle inside the shafts of the flight feathers of curlews; the nymphs of another live on the liquid secretions of the eyes of swifts (Rothschild and Clay, 1957).

The number of lice (Mallophaga) on birds varies considerably from one bird to another, even of the same bird species. According to Rothschild and Clay, a curlew from Ireland, in excellent condition of body and plumage, had 1,803 lice; another from Suffolk, England, 1,047; and a rook (*see* introduction to Crow Family) had about 300. The world's record for number of lice in the body plumage of a single bird seems to be that of an African cormorant, *Phalacrocorax nigrogularis*, which had more than 7,000. These numbers were unusually high. In small songbirds, each may have no lice or from one to ten; more than twenty is uncommon. Young birds tend to have more lice than adults; sick birds more than healthy ones.

A bird may be heavily infested with lice without apparently being harmed, but when the numbers are abnormally heavy on sick, captive, or young birds, the effect on the host bird may be serious. Weakened birds apparently are unable to keep their lice in check by preening. *See* Preening. Chickens heavily infested with the biting lice lose weight and their egg production goes down, and some may suffer anemia (Turner, 1971). According to Malcolmson (1960), there are more than 2,600 recorded species of living Mallophaga, of which 800 species have been discovered on some 500 species of birds.

See also lists of bird lice and the orders of birds that are host to them, also methods of collecting lice from birds, in Turner (1971).

The bird lice themselves may be hosts to other, smaller animals. Rothschild and Clay (1957) reported that mites and their eggs are sometimes found attached to bird lice and that the mites seem relatively harmless to them. Mallophaga, in turn, are known to attach themselves to hippoboscid flies, and thus be carried to birds—for example, to mourning doves in Tex. (Couch, 1962). *See* Phoresy; Hippoboscid Flies.

Bathing by birds in water and taking dust baths (*see* Bathing) and their subsequent preening help to rid them of parasites. That dust is effective in helping rid birds of their lice is suggested by the fact that lice have been found in the dust of dust baths habitually used by chickens. The phenomenon of "anting" may be another way by which a bird gets rid of its lice and other parasites of its skin. *See* Anting.

With a captive bird, a safe and quick-acting insecticidal dust such as pyrethrum, sifted through its feathers, will cause the lice to crawl to the edge of the bird's feathers and drop off their host; however, care must be taken not to get the insecticide in the bird's eyes (Turner, 1971); 1–2% Malathion powder is more effective and less toxic.

LICHTENSTEIN

M. HEINRICH, or HINRICH (1780–1857). Director of Zoology, Berlin Museum, 1815–51 (see Gebhardt, 1964), whom Johann Wagler in 1829 honored by giving the English name Lichtenstein's oriole to an oriole he named and described as *Icterus gularis*. Wagler, a German systematist, was appointed professor of zoology at the University of Munich in 1826; he visited the Berlin Museum in 1828 at the time Lichtenstein was Director of Zoology there (Stresemann, 1975). *See* Wagler.

LIFE EXPECTANCY

Term for the number of years that a species of bird may be expected to live in the wild. It differs from longevity, which usually means the natural or *potential* life span of a bird if it is not killed by accidents or diseases.

In contrast, the life expectancy of a bird is based upon the actual records of how long the species has lived in the wild before it was killed (such records are based upon banding returns —*see* Banding). Life expectancy is much shorter than a bird's longevity, or potential length of life, because of the hazards to birds in the wild. The mortality of young birds in their first years may be up to 75% and may be at the rate of 45% a year (*see* Age). It varies as to species of birds and may vary geographically. Generally, small birds tend to have shorter life expectancies than large ones. The life expectancy of the American robin, for example, has been estimated, from banded birds that were recovered after they were killed, at about 1 year, 2 months; of a wild mallard duck, 1½ years; of a herring gull, about 2½ years; of grouse and quail about 1½ years. See Wing (1956); Pettingill (1972). See Lack (1943a; 1943b) for the life expectancies of some British birds.

LONGEVITY

This is the term for the inherited duration of a bird's life, or its *potential* life span, as indicated often by captive birds which have died of old age rather than from accidents, predators, diseases, and so on. *See* some of the greatest ages reached by birds under Age. The *potential* life span usually attained by birds in nature is indicated by banding records. These show that large birds usually live longer than small birds. *See* some of these under Age; *see also* in the biography of each bird under the heading Age. Terres (1977) compiled banding records of some ages of birds, mostly songbirds.

LIFE HISTORY STUDY

See suggested reference under Ornithology.

LIFE LIST

Term among birders for the listed species of birds each has seen during years or a lifetime of birding. *See* especially the 600 Club under Birder; also article by Emerson (1940); Peterson (1948).

LIFE ZONE

See discussion of under Distribution.

LIGHT

(effects of on birds). Light has a profound influence on the daily and yearly rhythms of birds —it affects their anatomy, physiology, behavior, and distribution (Welty, 1962). Nearly all activities of birds and other animals are related in some way to the influence of the sun.

DAILY RHYTHMS. The beginning of daylight brings on the definite awakening times of birds, which vary with different species (robins are among the earliest to awaken; blue jays and crows are relatively late risers); determines the beginning of morning song and its duration (*see* Songs and Singing), and the times of cessation of song in the evening, and times of roosting (*see* Roosting). The rhythm of diurnal birds is inverted in those relatively few nocturnal N. American birds, such as some of the owls and the crepuscular members of the Nightjar Family (whip-poor-wills, for example), which are active between dusk and dawn.

A full eclipse of the sun with its gloom can suddenly disturb a bird's daily activities and can cause some birds to cease singing, others to start their evening songs and calls, and some even go to roost though it may be midday (Wing, 1956). For some interesting details of the effects of total solar eclipses on birds, see Kellogg and Hutchinson (1964); Du Mont (1970); Baker (1971b); Elliott and Elliott (1974).

ANNUAL RHYTHMS—PHOTOPERIODISM. At middle and high latitudes of the North Temperate Zone, the most regular environmental factor, and hence the most reliable in its effect on the annual breeding of birds, is the seasonal change in the length of the day. In spring, the lengthening days bring on the gonadal development, especially of male birds, in which complete production of sperms is induced by the stimulation of increased light (Immelmann, 1971). *See* Physiological Preparation under Courtship; *also* Endocrine Glands.

In N. America, William Rowan, at the University of Alberta in Canada, made the first detailed experiments that demonstrated the effect of the daily photoperiod on birds. He confined dark-eyed (slate-colored) juncos and common crows in outdoor aviaries at below-zero temperatures in fall and winter but with artificial lighting in the cages that was gradually increased each day to simulate advancing spring. For comparison, in other outdoor cages he kept other juncos and crows (the controls) under the same conditions, without artificial lighting, and subject to the natural daily declining light of fall and winter.

The birds exposed to the increasing daily light (photoperiod) when later dissected had gonads that had enlarged to the spring maximum. Gonads of the controls, already quite small when the birds were trapped in fall, had continued to diminish in size until they reached the winter minimum in Nov. See details in Rowan (1931); see also Bissonnette (1937; 1939) for similar experiments with starlings and blue jays. For other tests with caged birds and the effects of light (photoperiodism) and other stimuli on them, see the summary by Wallace (1963, pp. 266–68).

Control of annual events in the lives of birds by photoperiodism is widespread but is not universal. It operates mostly in birds that breed in the Temperate Zones. Since many of these species live where there are marked seasonal changes in climate, photoperiodism helps them by inducing certain of their activities only during the appropriate seasons. It also synchronizes events among individuals of the population (Wolfson, 1959). *See* Eggs and Egg-laying; Nests and Nesting. According to Immelmann (1971), photoperiodism has been demonstrated in about 60 species of birds of the North Temperate Zone, of different orders and families. For other effects of light, *see* Migration; Molts and Molting.

Besides light, other factors in the environment combine with the urge of birds to breed. For example, warming temperatures in spring and early summer stimulate the growth of plants which give nesting cover, and the abundant production of seeds, fruits, insects and other animal life on which the young birds are fed. See examples by Moreau (1964a) of the synchronization of broods of birds with emerging insects and other environmental influences.

LIGHTNING AND BIRDS
See Weather.

LIGHT PHASE
Term in ornithology for a pale-colored (sometimes normal for the species) bird. The term is used in contradistinction to birds of the same species that are excessively dark in color. *See* Abnormal Colors under Colors of Feathers; *also* Color Phase.

LILY-TROTTER
See Jacana Family.

LIMBERNECK
Name for a part of the paralytic symptoms in birds suffering from a bacterial intoxicant called botulism. *See* Botulism. The term "places undue emphasis on a symptom that is by no means constant and, when it is observed, is a part of a generalized paralysis. Paralysis of the legs and wings is almost always apparent before the neck muscles are obviously affected. 'Limberneck' is a symptom of severe cases of botulism but, in . . . milder intoxications, the affected birds may be able to hold up their heads throughout the course of the disease" (Jensen, 1962).

LIMPKIN FAMILY
Aramidae (ah-RAM-ih-dee); from *Aramus*, a word of uncertain derivation and meaning (Coues, 1882). A New World family of 1 species; lives mostly in marshes, swamps; about 26 in. long; only member of its family and a lone survivor of an ancient line of long-legged birds, a group whose fossil remains go back to Eocene deposits of 54 million years ago (Austin, 1961); is in order Gruiformes and related to the cranes and rails; long, slightly downcurved bill is twice as long as head; long legs and toes, claws sharp; feet not webbed but is efficient swimmer. Sexes outwardly alike. See other details of family in Austin (1961); Gilliard (1958); Palmer (1964).

Skulks jerkily, with tail twitching, along edges of marshes, swamps, often along established paths; lifts feet high as it walks, somewhat hunched like a rail; frequently snaps head up to look around, often probes bill into mud or water to catch mussels and snails either by sight or by feeling with sensitive bill; sometimes perches in tops of tallest trees to rest or look around; when persecuted by hunters, may be most active by dusk and at night; where no reason to fear man, is very tame and active by day.

Before they were protected by law and sanctuaries, limpkins, because they are palatable and almost foolishly tame, had been hunted almost to extinction in southern swamps by the early 1900s (Bent, 1926a); now are again numerous enough to be seen by day in places in Fla. such as Okefenokee Swamp, around Lake Okeechobee, Wakulla Springs, and Everglades National Park.

Albinism not reported in limpkins, according to Gross (1965a).

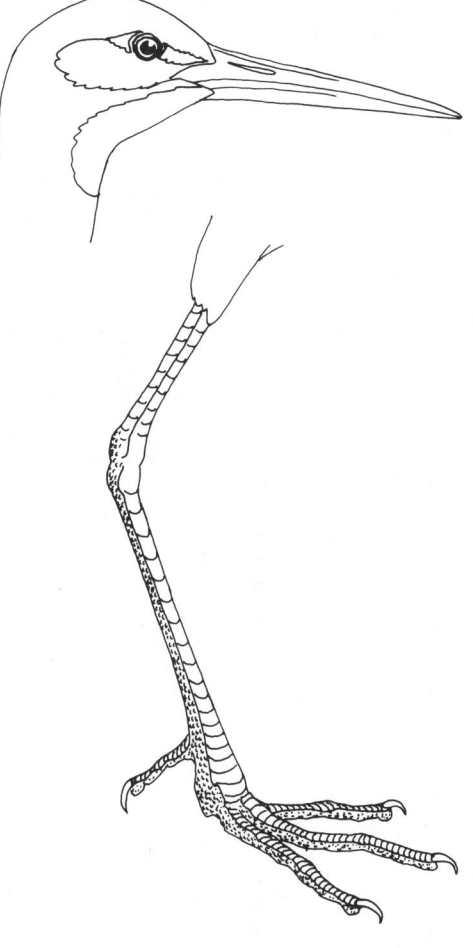

LIMPKIN FAMILY

Limpkin, *Aramus guarauna* (ARE-ah-mus gwah-ROU-nah); genus name: of unknown origin; species name: Brazilian name of the bird; *limpkin,* from the bird's peculiar halting gait. (Color ill., page 573.) Largely nonmigratory, living from s. Ga., Fla., and Mexico south through Cuba and C. America to Argentina; 23–28 in. long; wingspread 42 in.; long-billed, long-legged, brown feathers have sheen of metallic green; is about size of similar-appearing American bittern, but streaks and *spots of white on back, head, and neck* are distinguishing, also much longer *dark* legs and longer neck; has cranelike flick or jerk of wings in flight; especially noted for its loud, wailing screams, *kur-r-ee-ow, kur-r-ee-ow, kur-r-ee-ow, k-row, k-row,* which resemble cries of lost child; may be heard for more than half mile (Hall, 1950); uttered much at night or on cloudy days; lives in freshwater marshes of saw grass, bulrushes, clumps of myrtle with open water chan-

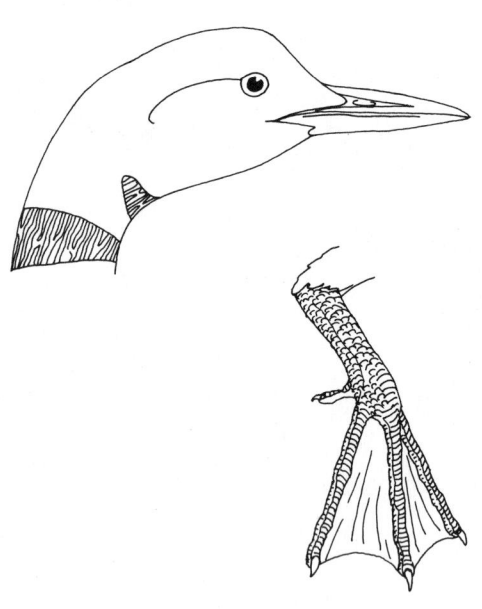

LOON FAMILY

nels, or along marshy riverbanks at edges of swamps, where it feeds in shallows or on mud flats; in flight, rises from marsh with neck fully extended, legs dangling, flies short distance; when drops to ground, cries out long and loud (Bent, 1926a).

Feeding Habits:: Freshwater snails, especially of genus *Pomacea*, also freshwater mussels, some lizards, frogs, insects, worms, crayfishes. See Snyder and Snyder (1969) for details of how it opens and eats snails and mussels from shell.

Nest: Builds platform of dried rushes just above water in saw grass or loose mass of leaves, in vines (5–8 ft. up) growing over shrubs along streams, or in bushes or trees along deeper streams (3–17 ft. up).

Eggs: Jan.–Aug., but in Fla. usually Mar.–Apr.; 4–8, buff, spotted or blotched with grays and browns.

Incubation: By both sexes, but period of unreported; young leave nest the day they are hatched.

Other Names: Carau; clucking hen; courlan; crippled bird (from its gait); crying bird; Indian pullet (assumed poultry of Indians); mourning widow; screamer; speckled curlew.

Weights: In Fla., adults (31), 0.9–1.27 kg. (Nesbitt *et al.*, 1976), or 2–2¾ lbs.

Range: Resident from se. Ga., through peninsular Fla. to Cuba, Isle of Pines, and other West Indian is., from Mexico south to Argentina; casual in S.C.

LINCOLN
THOMAS (1812–33). Born Dennysville, Me., for whom Audubon in 1834, in Vol. II of his *Ornithological Biography,* named the Lincoln's sparrow. When 21-year-old Lincoln accompanied Audubon on his Labrador expedition in the summer of 1833, the bird Lincoln collected, which was named for him, was the only one new to science obtained by Audubon on that trip (Palmer, 1928). See also Gruson (1972).

LINCOLN INDEX
Name for an equation, or formula, to determine populations of birds or other animals. A sample population of a bird species, for example, is captured, marked for later identification, and then released. Later, a second sample is captured in the same place or area. The ratio of marked to unmarked birds gives the researcher an estimate of the total population. See details in Lincoln (1930). *See also* Banding; Populations.

LINNAEUS
CARL (1707–78). Famous Swedish botanist of Uppsala who stimulated the study of animals and plants and their classification with the publication of 10th ed. (1758) of his *Systema Naturae.* In it, for the first time, he used throughout his binomial, or two-name, system of Latin names for classifying birds and other animals. He was professor of medicine and botany at the University of Uppsala from 1741 to his death in 1778; he influenced ornithology, as he did all natural sciences, not in his descriptions of individual birds (he was not an ornithologist) so much as in his simple and clear method of nam-

ing and classifying birds. See Allen, E. G. (1951). He described and named 133 species of American birds (McAtee, 1957b), among them the strictly N. American turkey vulture, bald eagle, kestrel, or sparrow hawk, screech owl, blue jay, northern (Baltimore) oriole, pileated woodpecker, and others. See latest A.O.U. *Check-list* for names of American birds described by Linnaeus, and for definitive biography of the man, see Blunt (1971).

LINNET
See Finch, house, and Finch, purple, in Finch Family.

LIPOCHROMES
See Carotenoids.

LITTLE BLACK-BREAST
See Dunlin in Sandpiper Family.

LITTLE DUKELET
See Screech owl in Owl—Typical Owl Family.

LITTLE SNOWY
See Egret, snowy, in Heron Family.

LITTLE STRIKER
See Tern, least, in Gull Family. Name alludes to small size of this tern and its habit of striking water in diving for fishes.

LIVER
A bilobed (two-lobed) organ of which the right lobe is usually larger than the left. Its role in digestion of birds is primarily in production of bile (*see* Digestion). In its non-digestive functions it stores extra lipids and glycogen (fats and sugars), which are non-digestive (Farner, 1960), and serves in intermediary metabolism, in synthesis of proteins and glycogen, and in forming uric acid.

According to Magnan (1910), the liver is relatively smallest in the carnivores (flesh-eating birds) and in the graminivores (grass-eating birds), largest in birds that eat fishes and insects. Magnan reported (1912) that ducks fed on a diet of fishes had much larger livers than those fed on grain or meat. Some birds have a gall bladder for storage of bile, but many do not. *See* discussion under Gall Bladder.

LIVE TRAPS
Term for any kind of trap which captures a bird or other animal alive and unharmed—usually wire-covered "cage traps" or wooden box traps. *See* Banding.

LIVING BIRD, THE
A publication. *See* Ornithological Periodicals.

LIZARD BIRD
One of the common names of the roadrunner in Cuckoo Family, which is fond of lizards. *See also* Reptiles and Birds.

LIZARDS AND BIRDS
See Reptiles and Birds.

LOAFING BAR
Term of game biologists for an area—a sandbar, a log in the water, or an artificial raft or

platform on the water—where a male duck and his mate can find isolation and freedom from being harassed or molested by other drakes. It is mainly a trysting place; the hen usually nests elsewhere, perhaps a mile or more away; daily, or more often during the egg-laying period and into the incubation period, the hen visits the male at his loafing bar (Wallace, 1955). See also Addy and MacNamara (1948) and Uhlig (1963). *See also* Waterfowl.

LOBATE WEBBING

Term for the lobed feet of grebes, the toes of which, instead of being connected by leathery skin as in ducks and other waterfowl, have each toe fringed with stiff, horny flaps. Only three other bird families in the world, besides grebes, have lobate webbing of the feet—the phalaropes, the coots, and the finfoots, or sungrebes, of C. and S. America, tropical Africa, and tropical se. Asia and Sumatra (Austin, 1961). *See* Gruiformes; *also* Grebe Family; Feet and Legs; Podicipediformes.

LOCATION CALLS

See Language.

LOCOMOTION

See Climbing Birds; Running Birds; Hopping and Walking; Swimming and Diving; *also* Flight.

LOGCOCK

Rural name in e. U.S. for the ivory-billed and pileated woodpeckers. *See also* Woodcock in Sandpiper Family.

LOGGERHEAD

See Loggerhead shrike in Shrike Family.

LONG JOHN

Another name for the great blue heron in allusion to its thinness or scrawny appearance. *See* in Heron Family.

LONGSHANKS

See Stilt, black-necked, in Avocet Family.

LONGSPUR

See in Finch Family.

LONG WHITE

Name given the great egret by plume hunters. *See* in Heron Family.

LOOK-UP

Local name of the American bittern because of habit of standing still with bill pointed upward. *See* in Heron Family.

LOOMERY

British name for a colony of murres.

LOON FAMILY

Gaviidae (gay-VEE-ih-dee); from Lat., sea smew; *loon* is thought to have come from an old Scandinavian name, *lom*, meaning a lame or a clumsy person, in reference to the loon's clumsiness on land (McAtee, 1959); see, however, Gruson (1972) for different interpretation. Loons are foot-propelled diving birds; 4 species of both n. Eurasia and n. N. America, of which

all 4 nest in N. America; were once thought to be related to the grebes but show no relationship to any living order of birds (Austin, 1961); Sibley (1960) suggested they may be allied to the order Charadriiformes; earliest fossils of loons go back to the Paleocene about 65 million years ago; they are large; 23–36½ in. long; largest is the yellow-billed; smallest, red-throated loon; sleek bodies wider than high for stability on the surface of both fresh and salt water; in Europe called "divers"; among most proficient at diving of all diving birds; dive to depths of up to 240 ft. below surface, but Austin (1961) suggests that tales of their remaining underwater for more than 5 minutes, and of swimming a half mile while submerged, should be regarded with suspicion; their principal food is fishes, which they chase in shallow water and grasp with bill; seldom stay under for more than a minute. *See* Swimming and Diving; Fishes and Birds.

In loons, the sexes are outwardly alike but females are usually smaller than males; are thick-necked with daggerlike, pointed bills and relatively small, pointed wings; a well-developed but short tail, which has 16–20 feathers (in grebes the tail feathers are loose, and hairlike); the three front toes are webbed (in grebes they are *lobed* and separated from each other except at base); loons have 14–15 neck vertebrae (grebes 17–21); the plumage of adult loons is hard and compact but feathers of head and neck are soft and velvety (in grebes, the feathers all over are "furry" or hairy); newly hatched grebes are conspicuously striped; newly hatched loons are never striped; loons usually nest on land, are single-brooded, lay two dark, *spotted* eggs, which they do not cover when they leave the nest; grebes build nests that float on water, lay pale, *unspotted* eggs, which they cover with damp plant debris on leaving the nest; grebes eat their own feathers and some feed them to their chicks, but feathers may never be found in a loon's stomach (Sutton, 1967b); loons copulate on land (grebes on the nest) and at least two species of loons build copulating platforms ashore (Palmer, 1962).

Loons and grebes have flattened tarsi, and legs set so far back on the body that walking is extraordinarily difficult and awkward (the leg muscles, unlike those of any other birds, are a part of their streamlined body mass—see Storer, 1960a); on land, loons can scarcely hold their bodies erect and shuffle along a few clumsy steps at a time, but on water they are powerful swimmers, and underwater, unlike members of the Auk Family, propel themselves by their feet alone and use their wings only for balancing or turning underwater; many bones of the body are solid rather than filled with air spaces (pneumatized); their specific gravity is near that of water; they can increase it sufficiently, by expelling air from their bodies and from within their feathers, so that they can sink slowly and quietly below the surface, leaving scarcely a ripple; like other diving birds, they undergo changes in the respiratory and circulatory physiology which allow them to remain underwater for fairly long periods (normally about 1 min.); they have large amounts of myoglobin in their muscles (*see* Flight Muscles

under Flight), a respiratory pigment that permits loons to store relatively larger amounts of oxygen for underwater use; other changes include a reduced heart rate and a relatively high tolerance of many organs for continued operation with a reduced supply of oxygen (see Jones and Johansen, 1972).

Loons (except for the red-throated loon) cannot fly from land, and from water need a long running start before they are airborne, but once aloft are swift, powerful fliers with speeds of 60 m.p.h. or more; in flight, they thrust the neck forward and down, which gives them a humpbacked appearance; they hold feet backward beyond the tail, together, sole to sole; all are migratory, move north and south especially along seacoasts, some in flocks, especially the arctic loon along Pacific coast.

On northern lakes where they nest in summer, loons utter long-drawn, wailing cries and screams at night which are blood-curdling to those people who have never heard them before; to others these cries are one of the wild musical sounds associated with the northern wilderness; the wild demoniac "laughter" of loons has given rise to the expression "crazy as a loon."

Both parents share incubating of eggs and caring for young; incubation is about 28 days; young first fly about 56 days after hatching; small loon chicks are sometimes brooded by parents, mostly after the last egg hatches; the chicks of loons climb up on parent from the rear, a habit that has survival value, as the loon chick, because of its down feathers, is easily soaked (Palmer, 1962) and might perish from exposure if wet.

In summer, loons live on lakes, ponds, slow-flowing rivers; in winter, they are essentially marine and frequent coastal waters; are mostly solitary, usually seen singly or in pairs; some are killed or disabled by oil discharged from tankers at sea. To care for an ill or injured loon, follow same care and feeding suggested in introduction to Grebe Family.

Albinism is apparently rare; Gross (1965a) reported 5 individuals of 2 species.

Arctic loon, *Gavia arctica* (GAY-vih-ah ARK-tih-kah); genus name: *see* family introduction; species name: Lat., northern, of the Arctic. (Color ill., page 574.) In summer, around the world in Arctic tundra, absent in Greenland; in N. America, from s. Alaska to Hudson Bay; winters along Pacific coast, rare on Atlantic coast; 23–29 in. long; wingspread 43–50 in.; resembles larger common loon while in breeding plumage but is *light gray* on crown and back of neck; has long white vertical stripes on sides of *black* throat glossed with purple or green; black bill is slender and *straight;* eyes (irises) ruby red; in winter, upperparts blackish brown; underparts white; can be distinguished from common loon by smaller size, smaller slender bill, and head and neck often paler than blackish back; and from similar winter-plumaged red-throated loon by straight bill (lower mandible of red-throated *angles upward*); immature similar to adults but back feathers edged broadly with gray, giving a somewhat scaly appearance; usually seen singly, in pairs, or in small groups, often migrates in small

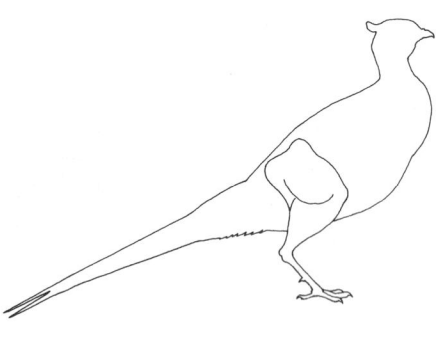

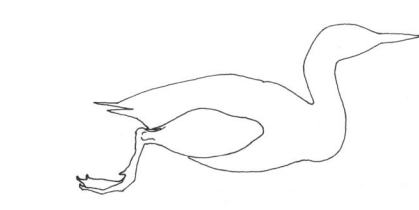

LOON FAMILY
The loon's legs and webbed feet, which are well suited to diving and swimming, are placed very far back on its trunk, and the leg muscles are part of its streamlined body mass. Unlike the pheasant, which has strong legs and clawed feet adapted to ground living, the loon walks on land with great difficulty.

flocks; is highly migratory although some merely move to coastal waters near breeding range; winters on salt water mainly along Pacific coast; in breeding season utters sounds more varied than those of common loon—a guttural *kwuk-kwuk-kwuk-kwuk* often in flight, a rapid *qua-qua-qua* like quack of duck; various growls and croaks, a plaintive *ah-hah-wee* (Sutton, 1932), also shrieks, squeals, and yelps. See references by Dunker (1974, 1975) and Sjölander (1978) for more data on the natural history of the arctic loon.

Feeding Habits: Eats small fishes such as shiners, small herrings, also crustaceans, mollusks, and aquatic insects.
Nest: Solitary nester; usually prefers larger and deeper freshwater lakes than red-throated loon; flat tundra to mountainous, treeless or forested country, from near coast to far inland, near water's edge, ashore, or on islet; nest varies from mere scrape or depression to a mound of earth and plants, also floating nests.
Eggs: June–July; 1–2, green-olive to dark brown, with some black spots or blotches.
Incubation: By both sexes, 28–30 days; both parents attend young, which follow adults to salt water at end of summer; young first fly about 60 days after hatching.
Other Names: Arctic diver; black-throated diver; black-throated loon; Eurasian loon (British Isles); Pacific loon; green-throated loon.
Age: One, banded Rossiten, Germany, lived for 18 years (Austin, 1961).
Flight Speed: Ten flying over McConnell R., Northwest Territories, Aug. 1968, timed at ground speed of 36.6–49.5 m.p.h. (Davis, R. A., 1971).
Hybrids: Gray (1958) reported a "presumed" hybrid between arctic loon and common loon.
Weights: Male, immature, collected Mo., Oct. 1969, 4 lbs. 15 oz. (Easterla and Lawhon, 1971); to 5¾ lbs. (Palmer, 1962); a male about 6 lbs., two females 5 lbs. and 5 lbs. 8 oz. (Manning *et al.*, 1956).
Range: Nests around world in Arctic tundra in Eurasia and in N. America (but absent from Greenland), s. Alaska, Yuk., Mack., and s. Hudson Bay; winters on open waters from Arctic coasts and se. Alaska along Pacific coast to s. Baja Calif., nw. Mexico, strays to Atlantic coast rarely or uncommonly, Que., N.H., and Long Is., N.Y., and N.J. at Shark R. Inlet (Bull, 1964); very rare fall and winter visitor to Ariz. (Phillips *et al.*, 1964); sometimes on freshwater lakes in migration; accidental in Utah, Colo., Iowa, and one collected in Mo., fall 1969.

Big loon. *See* Common loon.

Black-throated loon. *See* Arctic loon.

Common loon, *Gavia immer* (GAY-vih-ah IM-mer); genus name: *see* family introduction; species name: variant of an English word, *ember*, related to Swedish *immer* and *emmer*, gray or blackened ashes of a fire, apparently relating to dark plumage of this loon (see Coble, 1954; Gruson, 1972); note, however, Lat. *immergo*, to immerse, and *immersus*, submerged (see Jaeger, 1955). (Color ills., page 575.) Nests in Iceland, and Greenland, and

throughout lake country of n. U.S. and Canada; large; 28–36 in. long; wingspread to 58 in.; heavy-headed, stout, short neck; long-bodied, swims low in water with neck curved, has straight robust bill; in summer, adults, along with outwardly similar yellow-billed loon, are only loons with head all-black (no gray) and a white necklace around black throat; common loon's *black* bill distinguishes it from yellow-billed; eyes brown-ruby; in summer, head and neck glossy black; back is checkered black and white; white underparts; in winter, head, neck, and upperparts dark gray or dark brown; cheeks, throat, and underparts white; adult has fine white spots in front and above eyes that appear as *white eye-ring*; immature in first winter has back feathers broadly edged with gray as in arctic and yellow-billed loons; winters along Pacific coast, on Great Lakes, and Atlantic and Gulf coasts (some winter on inland lakes and streams or remain north as far as unfrozen waters and winter's food supply of fish); usually sleeps on water but sometimes comes ashore to sleep; migrates singly or in small groups from 2 to 15; mostly by day; spring migration northward usually in Apr.–May, when seen off coasts or flying overland to nesting territories, where arrival is timed to breakup of ice on freshwater lakes; fall return begins Sept. and into Nov.; to become airborne, must run across surface of water with wings beating for 20 yds. up to a quarter mile before taking flight (Palmer, 1962); thus sometimes trapped by quick freezing of ponds, from which unable to gain flight and are shot or starve; in fall have dropped to deck of ship or to water because of ice-coated wings while in flight; breeds on freshwater lakes both large and small in open or forested country but water must be deep enough for escape-diving from enemies and large enough from which to take flight and clear surrounding trees; territories may range from entire lakes of more than 100 acres to bays of 15–20 acres; Vermeer (1973), in study of breeding common loons on 19 lakes in w. Alta., found all preferred to nest on lakes with many islands, and where a minimum chance of disturbance by people in summer camps or in motorboats, which cause adults to desert nest and eggs fail to hatch; in this way, loons indicated wilderness quality of fishing lakes; on breeding grounds utters wide variety of calls but of four basic types (Palmer, 1962): *tremolo*, the most familiar call and often referred to as loon's laughter; the *yodel* of infinite variations, repeated, rising and undulating, usually heard at dusk or during night and early morning (according to Rummel and Goetzinger, 1975, yodel is uttered with crouch posture in territorial defense); the *wail*, or long call; and *talking* calls of simple, often one-syllabled notes that appear to be conversational, but usually almost silent in other seasons; calls can be imitated by human voice or on a small wind instrument, the ocarina (Bent, 1919), to lure loons near (*see also* Tolling). See Sjölander and Agren (1972) for information on reproductive behavior.

Feeding Habits: Dives from surface usually with forward thrust of body; underwater chases and catches in bill such freshwater fishes as suckers, minnows, pike perch, sunfishes, crappies, gizzard shad, smelt, trout, bass, pike, bullheads, etc., and in salt water, rock cod, flounders, sea trout, herring, etc. (see Palmer, 1962), and in turn, may be eaten by large fishes (*see* Fishes and Birds); also eats crayfishes, shrimps, crabs, amphipods, snails, leeches, frogs, salamanders, and aquatic insects; some loons dive to depths of 200 ft. (Schorger, 1947); may remain under 8½–60 seconds and under stress (pursued by enemy) up to 3 min. (Palmer, 1962).

Nest: On islands if available, if not, in sheltered places in coves and on promontories or headlands, as close to water as possible, on bare soil or in depression; built of matted grasses, rushes, twigs, some on floating bog or on muskrat houses; same nest site used, presumably by same pair, year after year (believed to mate for life—see Sjölander and Agren, 1972); Vermeer (1973) reported that 25 of 26 nests in w. Alta. were on islands, 1 on mainland; 22 on wooded islands; 3 on islands without trees; most nests on water's edge, none more than 4 ft. from a lake.

Eggs: Usually in mid-May to latter half of June; 1–3, usually 2, frequently 1, olive-green to dark brown, usually with small, scattered dark brown spots.

Incubation: By both sexes, in turn, about 29 days (Olson and Marshall, 1952); both parents help raise chicks; adults do not feed young by regurgitation; even 1-day-old chick fed small whole fishes, crustaceans, bits of plants; small young sometimes ride on parents' backs; 10–13 days after hatching, are skilled at swimming and diving; estimated that first flights are 70–77 days after hatching.

Other Names: Big loon; black-billed loon; call-up-a-storm (*see* Folklore); ember-goose; great northern diver (British Isles); greenhead; guinea duck; imber diver; ring-necked loon; walloon.

Age: One, banded Lake Huron, Ont., found dead at Beach Haven, N.J., when 7½ years old.

Flight Speed: Timed in Que., ground speed of 53 m.p.h.; air speed, 62 m.p.h. (Preston, 1951); in N.C., chased by airplane 80–100 m.p.h. (Pittman, 1953).

Hybrids: See under Arctic loon.

Weights: Adult males average heavier than females but weights greatly overlap; usually 6½–8½ lbs.

Range: Nests from Iceland, Greenland, and across Canada to Alaska, also n. U.S. in Me., N.H., Mich., and N.D.; casually in N.Y., Pa., n. Ohio, n. Ind., n. Ill., n. Iowa, nw. Mont., Calif.; winters along Atlantic coast from Me. to lower Fla. keys, on Great Lakes, and along Pacific coast from s. Alaska south to Baja Calif., and Gulf coast from Tex. to Fla. and on inland lakes and streams.

Eurasian loon. *See* Arctic loon.

Little loon. *See* Red-throated loon.

Pegging-awl loon. *See* Red-throated loon. Bill likened to awl formerly used by shoemakers.

Pepper-shinned loon. *See* Red-throated loon. Name refers to speckling of legs.

Red-throated loon, *Gavia stellata* (GAY-vih-ah stel-AY-tah); genus name: *see* family introduction; species name: Lat., starred, in reference to fine white speckling on back of this species in its winter plumage. (Color ills., page 574.) Most widely distributed loon; lives in Eurasia and in N. America, nests in Alaska, Greenland, and Canada; winters along Atlantic and Pacific coasts; smallest loon; 24–27 in. long; wingspread 42–45 in.; distinguished by its *upturned* slender bill; in breeding plumage has gray head (red on throat or fore neck) and plain gray back (backs of other loons show conspicuous black and white); in winter, uptilted bill separates it from common and arctic loons; bill is smaller and much slenderer than that of yellow-billed loon, in which bill also slightly upturned; in winter, adults and immatures paler than other loons with gray back finely speckled with white; singles, pairs, loose groups, usually seen on salt water outside of breeding season; off Cape May, N.J., a favorite feeding place in winter, up to 175 may concentrate, and in spring migration, up to 500; in Calif., seen more often on inshore ocean places and enclosed bays than arctic loon (Palmer, 1962); migrates by day or night, high-flying, swift rapid wingbeats direct and sustained with long neck pointed ahead, white breasts glistening in sunlight; main routes follow coast of Atlantic and Pacific; on Atlantic coast peak flights off New England in spring, in Apr., when 1,000 seen in day; arrive northern nesting grounds in late Apr. and May; common migrant off Calif. and Wash., Apr.–June; return in fall off Atlantic coast mainly in Oct., fly singly, about 1–2 mi. offshore; in interior, a rarity in fall except on Great Lakes; off Calif. shores by Sept.–Oct.; can leap up from water directly into flight (other loons require a running start) and is the only species of loon that can take off directly from land; on nesting grounds is noisy; at other times calls infrequently; in flight, a rapid, guttural *kwuk-kwuk-kwuk* similar to that of arctic loon, also henlike clucks and cacklings, deep groans, growls, and a hideous, far-carrying *gayorworrk* uttered for minute or more on end throughout summer, etc. (Palmer, 1962); prolonged wails or shrieks, a loud *kark.*

Feeding Habits: Dives reported to 29 ft. deep; has been caught in fish nets 70 ft. below surface of large lakes in Northwest Territories, Canada; maximum duration underwater timed at 90 seconds; catches fish by grasping it with bill; eats mostly fishes; in salt water, sculpins, capelin, codfishes, gunnel, sand launces; in fresh water, brook trout and sticklebacks; also eats shrimps, leeches, snails, aquatic insects and some aquatic plants (see in Palmer, 1962).

Nest: Usually a solitary nester, sometimes associated in loose colonies (male may build copulating platform some distance from nest), nest varies from eggs laid in damp depression on bare ground to large mound of mud and wet plants on edges of lakes or ponds usually smaller and shallower than those used by arctic loon, both near coast and on tundra far inland, on bank or on hummock in water.

Eggs: June–July; 1–3, usually 2, olive-green to dark brown.

Incubation: By both sexes, in turn, 27–29 (?) days; age when young first fly unknown, but probably about 60 days after hatching (Palmer, 1962).

Other Names: Cape drake; cape race; cape racer; cobble; little loon; pegging-owl loon; pepper-shinned loon; rain-goose; red-throated diver (British Isles); scape-grace; sprat loon.

Age: One, banded at Göteborg, Sweden, recovered 23 years later (Austin, 1961).

Flight Speed: Two timed flying low over McConnell R., Northwest Territories, Aug. 1968, at 47.1 and 48.8 m.p.h. (Davis, 1971).

Weights: Males average heavier than females, 3 lbs. 9 oz. to 4 lbs. 5 oz.; females 3 lbs. 8 oz. to 4 lbs. (Palmer, 1962).

Range: Nests around world on tundra from Iceland to Scotland and Scandinavia east across n. Siberia to Kamchatka; in N. America, from Greenland and n. Alaska south to coast of B.C.; east to James Bay, Anticosti Is., and Newfoundland, reported in summer south to Calif., n. Mich., and Md.; winters from southern edge of nesting range south along Pacific coast to n. Mexico; on Great Lakes (casually), and from Me. south to s. Fla. and along Gulf coast; casual in migration in Idaho, Mont., Colo., and Mississippi Valley south to Ark., in e. Tex. and W.Va.

Sprat loon. *See* Red-throated loon. Name from feeding on small kind of herring called sprat.

Yellow-billed loon, *Gavia adamsii* (GAY-vih-ah AD-am-sih-eye); genus name: *see* family introduction; species name: in honor of Edward Adams, English surgeon-naturalist, who served on 19th-century voyage to Arctic in search of Sir John Franklin during which this species discovered (see details of Adams in Gruson, 1972). (Color ill., page 574.) Nests in Eurasia; in N. America, above tree line along Arctic coasts of Alaska and Arctic Canada east to Melville Pen.; largest loon; 30–36½ in. long; wingspread to 55 in.; outwardly similar in all seasons to common loon but has large *yellowish or ivory-white, upturned* bill (upper mandible straight, but lower one angles slightly upward); voice and calls resemble those of common loon but generally more silent (Peterson, 1961); utters wild, ringing laugh like common loon but harsher, and a loud, drawn-out wail and raucous, hilarious call in evening and into night; yodels like common loon; in flight utters an evenly pitched *ha-ha-ha-ha-ha-ha-ha* (see details in Palmer, 1962); N. American population of this primarily Eurasian bird appears not very large; mostly a bird of Arctic; from relatively restricted wintering range on bays, inlets, open ocean off coast of B.C. and se. Alaska, migrates along coast and around Alaska Pen. to breeding range of freshwater lakes, rivers, shallow ponds of tundra, which it reaches May–June; overland route to breeding range east and northeast of Great Slave Lake; in fall migration in Sept. returns along same coastal route; one of best-known birds in legends and folklore of Eskimos, known as weather prophet, etc.; can be decoyed by waving a cloth and shouting.

Feeding Habits: On salt water eats mostly fishes; dives for rock cod, sculpin, tomcod; also mollusks, crustaceans, marine worms, etc.

Nest: Solitary nester at lakes, large ponds, occasionally large rivers; on shores close to water, on islands or hummocks in water; nest varies from one with little or no material to sizable flattened heap, often of mud.

Eggs: June–July; 2, yellow-olive to brown, spotted or blotched with dark brown.

Incubation: Period of and age when young first fly unknown.

Other Names: White-billed diver (British Isles); white-billed northern diver.

Weights: In Nov. 1968, Jehl (1970) collected a 7¼-lb. immature female just north of Coronada Is., Baja Calif.; Manning *et al.* (1956) reported one of 10½ lbs.; another, 11¼ lbs.; also a female about 14 lbs. and a male about 12½ lbs.

Range: In Eurasia, nests from Murmansk coast, possibly from n. Finland and Novaya Zemlya, east through n. Siberia; in Alaska, north of tree limit, from Cape Prince of Wales south to Salmon R., Alaska, Mack. R. delta, and w. Keewatin; winters in se. Alaska, rarely to Vancouver Is., B.C., a casual winter visitor along Calif. coast, mostly seen Bodega Bay, Sonoma County, to Monterey Bay (Small, 1974); accidental in Greenland, Long Is., N.Y., and Colo. south to Baja Calif.

LORD-AND-LADY

See Duck, harlequin, in Duck Family. Name for the pair or for the species, from handsome plumage of male.

LORE

Term for a small area on each side of a bird's face, between its eyes and the base of the upper part of its bill. *See* Topography.

LOTUS-BIRD

See Jacana Family.

LOUSE COMB

See Feather Comb

LOWER AUSTRAL ZONE

One of the six *life zones* of N. America, each of which is characterized by its plant life and by certain birds and other animals. Life zones are still relied upon by some authorities in mapping, locally, the ecological distribution of N. American birds. The Lower Austral is transcontinental, but its eastern humid division (from the Atlantic coast west to the 100th meridian) is called the *Austroriparian,* the western humid division, the *Lower Sonoran.* See some details in Chapman (1930) about the extent of these subdivisions and of characteristic birds, also in Bailey (1902). For details and comparisons of the Lower Austral Zone with the major biotic communities listed under Distribution, see Pettingill, (1970). *See* discussion of life zones and biomes under Distribution.

LOW-GROUND-STEPHEN

See Towhee, rufous-sided, in Finch Family.

LUNG

See Respiratory System.

LURE DISPLAY

See Distraction Display.

LYMPH

See Circulatory System.

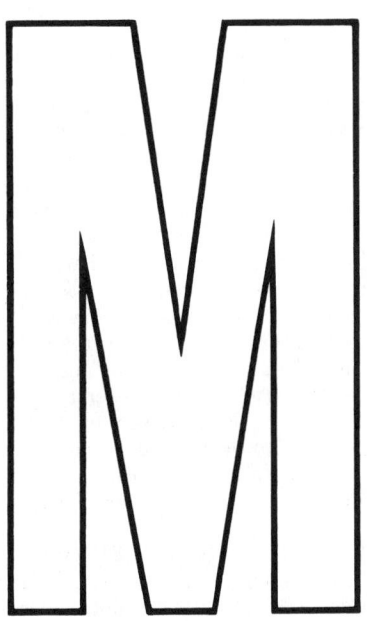

M

MacDOUGALL
PATRICK, M.D. (1770–1817). Of Glasgow, Scotland, referred to also as M'Dougall or McDougall, for whom Col. G. Montagu, British ornithologist, named the roseate tern, *Sterna dougallii,* in his Supplement to *Montagu's Ornithological Dictionary* (1813). In naming the tern, Montagu wrote: "To Dr. M'Dougall of Glasgow, the amateurs of Science are indebted for this valuable discovery, several of which [terns] were shot in the Western Highlands of Scotland." See Wynne (1969); Gruson (1972).

MacGILLIVRAY
WILLIAM (1796–1852). Scottish ornithologist who wrote much of the technical information about birds for Audubon's *Ornithological Biography,* published originally in five volumes (1831–39). Audubon met MacGillivray in Edinburgh in 1830 and hired MacGillivray's services to "revise and correct" Audubon's manuscript "at two guineas per sheet of sixteen pages" (Herrick, 1917). Audubon named MacGillivray's warbler for him—*see* discussion in biography of this bird in Warbler—American Wood Warbler Family. MacGillivray produced a number of books—his largest and most important a five-volume *History of British Birds;* he was also a lecturer and professor (1841–52) in Marischal College and University, Aberdeen (Herrick, 1917). See also Palmer (1928) and Audubon, M. R. (1960).

MACKEREL-GOOSE
See phalaropes in Phalarope Family.

MACROCLIMATE
The climate of a region or other large area. In zoology, the prefix *macro-* (MACK-row) means unusually large. *See* Microclimate.

MAGAZINES
See Ornithological Periodicals.

MAGPIE
See in Crow Family.

MAINE AUDUBON NEWS
See Ornithological Periodicals.

MAIZE THIEF
See Grackle, common, in Troupial Family.

MALAR (MAY-ler) **STRIPE**
or MALAR PATCH. Marking on cheek of a bird, especially the yellow-shafted (common) flicker, the males of which have a black "mustache" on the sides of the face. *See* Flicker, yellow-shafted, in Woodpecker Family. *Malar* is from Lat. *mala,* the cheek. The malar stripes of the male flicker are useful to him in sex recognition during courtship and mating. *See* How Birds Recognize Their Own Species and Sex under Courtship. *See also* Behavior; Allopatric Species.

MALARIA
See Avian Malaria.

MALLARD
See in Duck Family.

MALAR STRIPE
The black-feathered "mustache" of this male common (yellow-shafted) flicker is the only visual difference between the sexes.

MALLEE FOWL
See Megapode.

MALLEMUCK
MOLLEMAUK or MOLLYMOKE. According to Allen, E. G. (1951), these names were used indiscriminately by fishermen for several birds in the order Procellariiformes, especially for fulmars and the smaller albatrosses. *See* Procellariiformes; *also* Northern fulmar in Shearwater Family.

Murphy (1936) wrote: "Mollymauk, according to a learned commentator, is a sailors' corruption of an English word which was corrupted from a German word corrupted in turn from the Dutch! It was originally a name of the Arctic (northern) fulmar . . . today it is applied by mariners of nearly all nations to the smaller albatrosses of the southern oceans. As I heard the word on the whaling brig 'Daisy' in the Roaring Forties, it would have been rendered 'Mollymoke.'"

See especially the White-capped and Yellow-nosed albatrosses in Albatross Family.

MALLOPHAGA
See Lice.

MALPIGHIAN (mal-PIG-ih-an) CELLS
A remarkable life-giving restorative layer of germinative cells called the *Malpighian layer.* They are in the deeper portion of the epidermis (the outer layer of the skin), and from it are derived the more superficial, or outer, layers of the skin, together with such modifications or outgrowths of the skin as feathers, hairs, and nails. The Malpighian layer was named in honor of Marcello Malpighi (1628–94), who first discovered and made known its significance (Walter and Sayles, 1949). *See* Skin.

MAMMALS AND BIRDS
Birds, especially hawks and owls, prey heavily on mammals, in particular the abundant and widespread native rats and mice (Cricetidae), such as the field mice, or voles *(Microtus)* and deer mice in the order Rodentia. This order also includes other families of the smaller American mammals eaten by predatory birds—the tree and ground squirrels, pocket gophers, kangaroo rats and pocket mice, the jumping mice, and the introduced Old World house mouse and Norway rat. (Rabbits and hares are in the order Lagomorpha.) Native mice and rats (Cricetidae) made up 57.63% of mammals eaten by birds, and all mammals were 23.65% of the vertebrates identified in the stomachs of 80,000 N. American birds examined by the federal government (McAtee, 1932b).

Hawks, owls, gulls, ibises, storks, cranes, herons, ravens, crows, magpies, jays, and other birds are quickly attracted to large concentrations of field mice (the so-called mouse plagues) and flock to them to gorge on these animals, thus helping to suppress their outbreaks. Piper (1909) reported a plague outbreak of mountain, or montane, voles *(Microtus)* in the lower Humboldt Valley of Nev. in 1906 in which these mice were an estimated 8,000–12,000 per acre (see also Piper's report of 1908).

According to McAtee's 1932 report, meadow mice were eaten by 44 species of birds; deer mice by 35 species; house mice by 23 species; 5 species had preyed on muskrats, a larger member of the rodent group; 11 species had preyed on pocket gophers, which, like moles (order Insectivora), spend most of their lives underground. Vernon Bailey, former Chief Field Naturalist, U.S. Biological Survey, cited 9 species of hawks and 6 of owls that destroy pocket gophers; and A.K. Fisher, 17 species of hawks and owls that feed on rabbits; 8 on jackrabbits. In McAtee's 1932 report, the abundant and easily available rabbits and hares (order Lagomorpha) were about 10½% of the mammals eaten by birds. For the species of hawks, owls, and eagles that prey on these animals, *see* biographies of these birds in Hawk Family and Owl Family.

Members of the Squirrel Family (order Rodentia), which include both the tree and ground squirrels, made up about 5½% of the mammalian food (McAtee, 1932b) eaten by birds, and these included such diverse members of the family as the spermophiles, prairie dogs, chipmunks, ground hogs, the gray, red, and fox squirrels, etc.—all eaten by the larger hawks and owls.

The tiny shrews and moles (order Insectivora) were 8.7% of the mammalian food of birds; 27 species had fed on the widespread short-tailed shrews *(Blarina)* and 23 species had eaten *Sorex* shrews; five individuals of one species of *Sorex* were in the stomach of a great gray owl (McAtee, 1932b).

Bats (order Chiroptera), the only mammals with true flight, which fly about at dusk and at night, are also preyed upon by birds. McAtee (1932b) reported bats in the stomachs of 6 bird species, and for many years, park naturalists at Carlsbad Caverns, N.M., have watched Cooper's, sharp-shinned, Swainson's, redtailed, and ferruginous hawks, marsh hawks, American kestrels, and great horned owls attack and capture bats in flight as they poured out of the caverns in the evening to begin their nightly feeding. Peregrine falcons at Ney and Bracken caves, Tex., catch and feed on bats there and are very efficient about it, according to Baker (1962).

In Okla. observers saw several Mississippi kites at 500 ft. up in the air, chasing free-tailed bats as the bats returned to a roosting cave (Brown and Amadon, 1968). Huey (1926) in marshes near San Diego, Calif., found pellets (*see* Pellet) cast up by short-eared owls that held the skulls of western red bats and of a small pipistrellid bat. Allen, G.M., (1939) cited long-eared owls in Ill. that had eaten hoary bats and a species of evening bat *(Nycticeius).* He believed that the barn owl, from the number of bat remains in its pellets, may eat more bats than any other owl.

Black vultures, en masse, attack and kill skunks and opossums and eat them, and the golden eagle occasionally attacks and kills foxes, young deer, and young pronghorns. A golden eagle in B.C., in Apr. 1956, caught on the ground a young black bear cub that weighed about 10 lbs. It carried it 100 ft. into the air, then dropped it to its death on the rocks, after which the eagle descended to feed on it. Great horned owls frequently kill and eat skunks, also muskrats, woodchucks, wild house cats, and occasionally even porcupines.

MAMMALS THAT PREY ON BIRDS. Many mammals are fond of birds—opossums, bobcats, domestic cats, dogs, foxes, coyotes, raccoons, badgers, weasels, minks, and skunks—all kill and eat birds when they can catch them and many, including some of the squirrels, also eat birds' eggs. See especially Pettingill (1976) for red squirrel, chipmunk, and weasel predation on birds. De Weese and Pillmore (1972) cited a black bear that had climbed an aspen tree in Colo., had ripped open the nesting cavity of a common (red-shafted) flicker, and had eaten the young; another observer reported black bears climbing to the nests of goshawks to eat eggs or young. See other accounts under Eggs and Egg-laying; *also* Food and Feeding Habits.

MANAGEMENT (OF BIRDS)
See Songbird and Game-Bird Management; Census; Control; and Economic Ornithology.

MANDIBLE
The lower half of a bird's bill; equivalent to the lower jaw in a human being; used in the plural (mandibles) to indicate both the upper and lower halves of the bill. The upper half of the bill is called the *maxilla. See* Bill.

MAN-O'-WAR-BIRD
See Frigatebird Family.

MANTLE
Name in ornithology for the plumage of the back of a bird and the wing coverts on the top of its wings, especially applied to hawks and gulls; specifically the feathers of the back and the folded wings. *See* Feather; Topography.

MANUS
(MAY-nus). The "hand" part of the wing—the carpometacarpus bone and the digital phalanges which bear the primaries (flight feathers) and the alula. *See* Alula; Primary Feather; Flight.

MARABOU
(MAR-ah-boo). A stork; *see* Size.

MARBLE-BELLY
See Goose, white-fronted, in Duck Family.

MARBLED
Marked irregularly with spots, speckles, blotches, or streaks; usually in reference to the plumage of a bird. *See* Colors of Feathers.

MARBLEHEADER
See Fulmar, northern, in Shearwater Family.

MARINE BIRD
See Seabird; *also* Distribution.

MARIONETTE
See Bufflehead in Duck Family.

MARKET HUNTING
Term for hunting and killing wild birds to supply their flesh for the market. A number of species of N. American birds were either shot

to extinction in the late 19th century, largely by market hunters, or brought to the edge of extinction, or brought so low in numbers that it took up to half a century of strict protection by law and sanctuaries to bring some of them back. For stories of some, *see* Eskimo curlew in Sandpiper Family; Wood duck in Duck Family; Passenger pigeon in Pigeon Family. *See also* Feather Trade for references to extreme killing of birds for the millinery trade.

MARKING
See Banding.

MARLIN
See Godwit, Hudsonian, and Godwit, marbled, in Sandpiper Family.

MARLINSPIKE
Another name for the jaegers (*see* in Skua Family) and for tropicbirds (*see* Tropicbird Family); for reason for name, *see* Bosun Bird.

MARSH BIRD
General term for a bird that lives in or around marshes (treeless wet tracts of grasses, sedges, cattails, and other herbaceous wetland plants) and swamps (wet, soft, low, water-saturated land, dominated by trees and shrubs). American ornithologists, according to Bent (1926a), call, collectively, members of the following families marsh birds: Heron Family; Stork Family; Ibis Family; Flamingo Family; Crane Family; Limpkin Family; and Rail Family. This is a general *wet habitat* grouping of place where the birds nest or live, not a classification (*see* Classification) and includes many unrelated species of birds. *See also* Land Bird; Water Bird; Waterfowl; Shorebird.

MARSH HARRIER
See Hawk, marsh, in Hawk Family.

MARSH HEN
Local name for rails, gallinules, and coots in Rail Family; also for the American bittern in Heron Family.

MARSH QUAIL
See Meadowlark, eastern, in Troupial Family.

MARTIN
See in Swallow Family.

MASSACHUSETTS AUDUBON
See Periodicals.

MASSÉNA
ANNA DE BELLE. *See* Anna, Duchess of Rivoli.

MAST
Collective term of biologists for acorns, chestnuts, hazelnuts, hickory nuts, beechnuts, etc., and for the seeds of pines, firs, and other "needle" evergreen trees. *See* Food and Feeding Habits.

MATE-FEEDING
See Courtship Feeding.

MATE RELATIONSHIPS
See Sexual Relationships.

MATING
A vague, general term in popular use for the pairing, or selection of mates, by birds; also, often used to suggest the act of copulating, or the "mating act." According to Davis (1955), the term may mean pairing, copulation, or even courtship. *See* Copulation and Copulatory Organs; *also* Courtship.

MATING SYSTEMS
See Sexual Relationships.

MAURI
ERNESTO (1791–1836). Distinguished Italian botanist, director of the Botanical Gardens of Rome, honored in 1838 by Charles Lucien Bonaparte in the name *Heteropoda mauri* for the western sandpiper; however, his scientific name did not follow a certain rule, or rules, of zoological nomenclature (Palmer, 1931). In 1856, Jean Louis Cabanis, German ornithologist at the Berlin Museum and a founder and first editor of *Journal für Ornithologie*, named the bird *Ereunetes mauri* (now *Calidris mauri*)—see American Ornithologists' Union (1973). According to Gruson (1972), Mauri was a collaborator of Bonaparte's, especially in botanical matters, in producing the impressive *Iconografia della Fauna Italica*.

MAXILLA
See Mandible.

MAXIMILIAN
ALEXANDER PHILLIP. Prince of Wied-Neuwied. *See* Wied.

MAY-BIRD
See Bobolink in Troupial Family; also Great crested flycatcher in Flycatcher—Tyrant Flycatcher Family.

MAYNARD
CHARLES (JOHNSON) (1845–1929). Mass. naturalist, traveler, commercial collector of birds, and a prolific writer who published most of his books privately (see Batchelder, 1937). In 1887 Robert Ridgway named Maynard's cuckoo for him, which later proved to be not a distinct species but a Fla. subspecies of the mangrove cuckoo. A subspecies, *Vireo griseus maynardi*, the white-eyed vireo of Key West, Fla., also was named for him.

McCOWN
JOHN P(ORTER) (1815–79). Born Tenn., captain in U.S. Army, who did much collecting of birds while on military service in w. Tex. in middle of 19th century. In 1851 George Newbold Lawrence named for him McCown's longspur from two specimens of the bird sent to Lawrence that Capt. McCown had collected (shot) "on the high prairies of western Texas." See also Gruson (1972); Wynne (1969).

McGREGOR
RICHARD CRITTENDEN (1871–1936). Of Sydney, Australia, went to Calif. in 1880s, was graduated from Stanford University in 1898; a

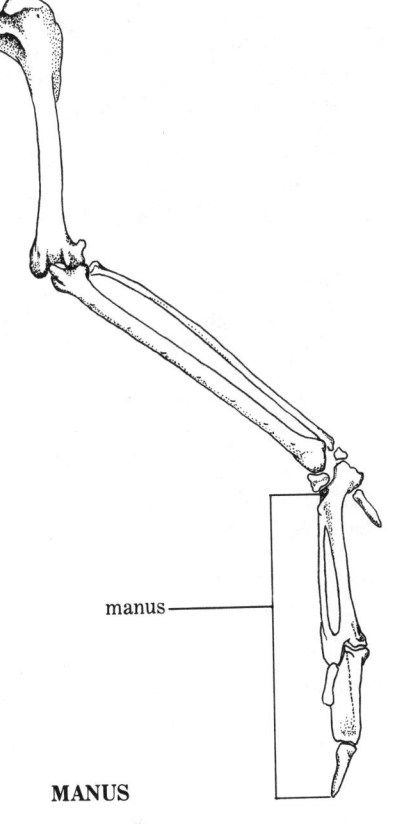

manus

MANUS

fellow of the American Ornithologists' Union; member of Cooper Ornithological Society; in 1920 published *Index to the Genera of Birds of the World* (Palmer, 1928); in 1897 A. W. Anthony, Calif. ornithologist, named for him the McGregor's house finch, which was later (1973) determined not to be a distinct species but a subspecies of the house finch.

McKAY

C(HARLES) L(ESLIE) (?–1883). U.S. Signal Corps observer at Bristol Bay, Alaska, collected birds there for the U.S. National Museum while stationed at Fort Alexander from spring 1881 until his death by drowning Apr. 19, 1883. Robert Ridgway, who named McKay's bunting for him, wrote (1884) that the vernacular (English) name of the bird was in memory of one "who sacrificed his life on the prosecution of natural history investigations in Alaska and in whose collections the species was first noticed." See also Gabrielson and Lincoln (1959).

MEADOW HEN

Local name for rails, gallinules, and coots in Rail Family; also for the American bittern in Heron Family.

MEADOWLARK

See in Troupial Family.

MEASUREMENTS

See Dimensions; Weight; Size.

MEAT HAWK

See Jay, gray, in Crow Family.

MEATUS

See external auditory canals under Ears and Hearing.

MEDALS

Following are some of the American awards (medals and plaques, or scrolls) for services to ornithology, to the literature of ornithology, or to conservation.

ARTHUR A. ALLEN MEDAL. Established at Cornell Laboratory of Ornithology, Ithaca, N.Y., in 1966 to honor Arthur A. Allen (*see* Allen, Arthur Augustus), in recognition of his services in widening popular interest in ornithology. The medal is awarded annually to someone who has either contributed distinguished service to ornithology or helped through popular or scientific writing to foster understanding and appreciation of birds. Recipients are chosen by five members of a committee of professional ornithologists selected by the Laboratory of Ornithology.

BREWSTER MEDAL. Awarded at its annual meeting (if a suitable recipient has been agreed upon) by the American Ornithologists' Union. In 1919, shortly after the death of William Brewster, a pioneer American ornithologist (*see* Brewster, William), his friends raised a memorial fund in his honor. This money was invested in Liberty bonds and the income used for the Brewster Memorial Medal (usually called the Brewster Medal), awarded every

year (for any work published in the previous six to ten calendar years) to the author-ornithologist who, in the judgment of the council of the A.O.U., had published the most important work relating in whole or in part to birds of the W. Hemisphere (*The Auk,* Apr. 1972). This geographical limit is no longer in effect.

ELLIOTT COUES AWARD. Originated in 1972 by a committee of the American Ornithologists' Union as an honorary certificate or plaque, as the council of the A.O.U. may designate, "to be awarded when merited to a contribution (publication) that has had an important impact on the study of birds within the W. Hemisphere but which (recipient and publication) has not received the Brewster Award" (*The Auk,* Apr. 1972).

THE JOHN BURROUGHS MEDAL. Awarded each year (if a suitable recipient can be found) at its annual Apr. meeting by the John Burroughs Memorial Association, Inc., at the American Museum of Natural History, New York City. The medal is for distinguished nature writing in a published book which combines literary quality with accuracy, based on observations in nature, and the conclusions of the author. A panel of judges, members of the John Burroughs Memorial Association, makes the choice of the eligible book and its author. (*See* Burroughs, John.)

AUDUBON MEDAL. In May 1946, at a meeting of the board of directors of the National Audubon Society, it was proposed that the society sponsor a medal for distinguished individual service to conservation. The medal was to be awarded annually in any year that the board agreed upon a deserving recipient. At a later meeting in 1946, the board agreed upon these principles and subsequently engaged the noted sculptor Paul Manship to design the medal. The Audubon Medal is awarded at the annual dinner of the National Audubon Society.

DANIEL GIRAUD ELLIOTT MEDAL. The medal and an honorarium are awarded annually (sometimes to an ornithologist) by the National Academy of Sciences for the most meritorious work in zoology or in paleontology published during the year. (*See* Elliott, Daniel Giraud.)

LEIDY MEDAL. A bronze medal and honorarium awarded every three years to a worthy recipient by the Academy of Natural Sciences of Philadelphia, Pa. It is conferred as a reward for the best publication or work accomplished in exploration, discovery, or research, and the recipients are chosen by a committee selected by the academy. Some ornithologists have received the medal. The endowment for it was made by the Leidy family in memory of Joseph Leidy, distinguished biologist, and president of the Academy of Natural Sciences (1882–91).

MEGAPODE

(MEG-ah-pode or MEG-ah-pod). These are the brush turkeys, scrub fowl, mallee fowl, mound-builders, thermometer birds, incubator birds, and megapodes, as they are variously called, all members of the family Megapodiidae. They are

large-footed gallinaceous birds, resembling domestic fowls and pheasants, and live in Australia, New Guinea, Malaya, and the Micronesian islands east to Samos and north to the Philippines (Gilliard, 1958).

There are no megapodes in N. America, but their method of incubating their eggs is so striking that it is included here for comparison with that of other birds. Their closest relatives are the New World guans (including the chachalaca) and curassows and the Old World chickens and pheasants. *See* Galliformes. They are the only group of birds known that do not incubate the eggs by sitting on them; rather, the eggs are hatched by the natural heat from piles of trash, leaves, limbs, and debris scratched into a heap, in which the females lay their eggs. These are the incubators, which hatch the eggs from warmth captured from the sun and from underground volcanism. The period of incubation for the eggs of one of the megapodes, the scrub fowl, *Megapodius freyciner,* is usually 49 days, the longest-known in birds (Gilliard, 1958). *See also* Incubation.

Before the female lays her eggs in the mound, the males of mallee fowl regularly test the temperature of the fermenting pile of debris by probing the mound with the bill. If the first high fermentation makes the mound too hot, the male cools it by digging into the top and turning over the mixture. When the temperature is declining, the male then permits the female to lay her eggs in the mound. Throughout the incubation period of the eggs, the male tends the mound, testing it with his bill, and exercising some control over its temperature. The bird is believed to test the temperature, not with its bill, but with its tongue (Frith, 1964).

When the megapode chick finally emerges from its dark, warm prison, its feathers are free of their waxy sheathing, and the plumage is so well developed that it can, if necessary, leap into the air and fly. It is fully able to take care of itself from the time it hatches. *See* Young and Their Care.

MELANIN

See Colors of Feathers.

MELANISM

See Abnormal Colors under Colors of Feathers.

MELEAGRIDIDAE

See Turkey Family.

MERGANSER

See in Duck Family.

MERLIN

See in Falcon Family.

MESOZOIC

(mess-oh-ZO-ik). Term for one of the great eras in geological history. According to Simpson *et al.* (1957), it was the Age of Reptiles and included the first and the last of dinosaurs and the first mammals and birds; it lasted from about 225 million to about 65 million years ago and included the Cretaceous, Jurassic, and Triassic periods. For details of these periods, *see* Geological Time Scale.

MESQUITE

(mess-KEET). An extensive *postclimax* plant association of mesquite (*see* discussion of it under Subclimax Community), a spiny, deep-rooted desert tree or shrub that grows over wide areas of sw. Tex. and s. N.M. Some of its typical nesting birds are the golden-fronted woodpecker and the black-crested titmouse. Seeds, or beans, of mesquite are much eaten by Gambel's quail; *see* in Pheasant Family.

METABOLISM

Term for "the sum total of chemical activities in a living organism which provide energy for heat, movement, irritability, growth, repair, energy storage, and reproduction" (Welty, 1975). The foods of birds (*see* Food and Feeding Habits) must first be broken down by digestion and then through metabolism changed back into substances that the bird's body can use to provide it with heat and energy. Birds in general have a higher metabolic rate than mammals, that is, the speed with which energy can be produced—a higher body temperature, faster heart rate, and faster rate of respiration. High, or rapid, metabolism is indicated in a bird by its body temperature of about 101–112°F. compared with man's usual, or normal, 98.6°. *See* Temperature.

High metabolism gives a bird quick energy for daily flights or for migration, for growth, for reproduction, for repair and the molting of its feathers, and for warmth to survive winter cold (*see* Cold and Birds); but it demands that a bird, especially a small one, keep "stoking" its fires with food—with carbohydrates, fats, and proteins. It must eat rapidly, often, and much, and, as a rule, foods rich in potential energy—seeds, nectar, fruits, fishes, insects, and rodents—and its body must make efficient use of the food with relatively little waste.

The metabolic rate, or rate at which food is burned in producing heat and energy, is relatively greater in small than in large animals because of the greater surface area in smaller animals (which is involved in heat loss) relative to their body mass (which is involved in heat production). See Kendeigh (1969; 1970) for discussion. Each bird species has its own "standard metabolic rate" which varies with the activity of the bird. It is faster in smaller birds than in larger ones, but smaller birds generally have more feathers per unit of body weight than larger ones, which helps with heat retention (Hutt and Ball, 1938). *See* Number of Contour Feathers on a Bird under Feather. For discussions of how metabolic rate is calculated, see Welty (1962); Rand (1967). For standard metabolic rates of 60 species of birds, see Table II in King and Farner (1961).

Hummingbirds, smallest of birds, with relatively the highest intake of food of any vertebrate animal in the world, and the highest output of energy per unit of body weight, must feed almost continuously all day to keep up their high rate of metabolism for their bodily energy needs. Hummingbirds, and shrews, the smallest of mammals, have apparently evolved into the smallest theoretically possible of the warm-blooded animals and if any smaller might not be able to eat food fast enough to keep from starving to death (Pearson, 1953). *See*, however, Torpidity.

Even the size of a bird's heart is correlated with its metabolism. Most birds are strong fliers or much on the wing, and shorebirds, kingfishers, swallows, warblers, vireos, and hummingbirds, for example, have relatively larger hearts than the limited fliers such as turkeys and quail (Wallace, 1963). *See* Heart; *also* Flight.

The "secret" of the warm-bloodedness (homoiothermism), or the relatively constant and high body temperatures of most birds, which makes them virtually independent of the temperature of their environment, and their subsequent high metabolism, began with the evolution of a four-chambered heart. As in mammals, including man, a bird's blood supply has double circulation. The two right chambers of a bird's heart receive used deoxygenated blood from the body and pump it to the lungs for renewal of oxygen and release of carbon dioxide. *See* especially under Circulatory System. The two left chambers receive and pump the freshened blood, with its supply of oxygen, throughout the body, where its load of oxygen can combine with the products of food in the chemical process of metabolism, thus supplying the bird with energy and high body temperatures.

Land vertebrates other than birds and mammals—reptiles and amphibians—are "cold-blooded" (poikilothermous) and their distribution in the world depends much on the temperature of their environment. Their aerated (freshened) blood and used blood are mixed together, and therefore not capable of supplying a high enough level of oxidation to maintain high body temperatures—they "are slaves to the environment in which they find themselves" (Walter and Sayles, 1949).

Birds, with their high body temperatures and a protective, or insulating, coat of feathers (*see* Feather), have penetrated the coldest regions of the earth; even the smaller ones can survive the winter if they have sufficient available food. See interesting studies of how some small birds survive in the North by Brooks (1968) and by Mugaas and Templeton (1970). For detailed, technical discussions of metabolism in birds, see Whittow (1965), Hazelwood (1972), Calder and King (1974), and Paynter (1974).

METACARPAL

In the "hand" (*see* Manus) of each wing of a bird, there are three separate metacarpal bones. The first and fifth metacarpals of the typical quadruped hand were lost in birds through evolution; the third and fourth are united at their ends and form the hand, or manus, which bears the primary wing feathers; the second is fused with the base of the third but has some movement of its own; it bears the alula. *See* Flight; *also* Alula; Bipedalism; Origin of Birds and of Bird Flight in Fossil Birds.

METATARSAL

(bones). *See* Tarsus.

METATARSUS

See Tarsus.

METER

The fundamental unit of length in the metric system, often used by ornithologists in their studies and reports. One meter (m.) equals 39.37 inches; one square meter equals approximately 1,550 square inches, or about 10.76 square feet.

METERICK

Another name for the black-legged kittiwake; from call note. *See* in Gull Family.

MICROCLIMATE

The climate of small areas (microhabitats) where animals live (nest or sleep, for example); Odum (1953) has called attention to the dramatic differences in living conditions in these local climates, compared with general climate, or macroclimate.

In Alaskan studies, during a period of winter cold, air temperatures above the snow were −60–70° F.; 2 ft. below the snow, at ground level, the temperature was 80° higher, or less cold. Thus, above the snow, the caribou, arctic fox, and arctic hare, adapted to the extreme cold, can survive; 2 ft. below them, mice or voles of the genus *Microtus*, with thin hair and not adapted to extreme cold, can also survive because they live in a relatively "warm" microclimate of the same region.

Most birds, owing to their body covering of feathers and high body temperatures, can tolerate extreme cold (*see* Cold and Birds) and a wide range of habitats in which to live or to dwell in temporarily. *See* Habitat Choices of Birds under Distribution; *also* Habitat. However, birds build their nests and rear their young in microclimates. As Wing (1956) has pointed out, changes in slopes and exposures of the ground can influence the choices of birds for a nest site. Along a river, cliff swallows may avoid building their mud nests on the hot, exposed rocks of a sunny area, but will occupy the cool, shaded rocks around the bend. In a study of 12 species of N. American warblers nesting in a mixed conifer and deciduous forest of N.Y., Kendeigh (1945a) found that each selected ecologically separate places in the forest to nest. Apparently differences in the plant life in different parts of the forest influenced their choices; also, their individual, and possibly "species," preferences for moisture or dryness, sunshine or shade. *See* Ecological Niche. Wing (1956) wrote that some birds prefer the low light intensities of shade; others the high light intensities of treetops or of the open. Even available perches may play a part in the choice of a bird for its nest site. *See* Nests and Nesting.

Some of the external parasites of birds live in a microclimate that is exclusively the body of the "host bird" to which they are attached. Bird lice, or feather lice (*see* Lice), pass their entire life cycles on birds and are so closely linked to them that their own distribution closely parallels that of the bird species which are their hosts. The bird, not the external world, is their habitat (Rothschild and Clay, 1957).

Some of the bird fleas spend the larval parts of their lives in the nests of certain birds which they parasitize, and are limited in where they can live by the microclimate that exists in each type of nest. *See* Fleas; Parasite.

MICROHABITAT
See Microclimate.

MIDDENDORFF
ALEXANDER VON (1815–94). German scientist who did much exploring in Russia, traveled to Siberia and c. Asia (Gruson, 1972). In 1853, he described and named for science the grasshopper warbler, whose English name, Middendorff's grasshopper warbler, honors him. See Wynne (1969) for references. Middendorff also first suggested (1855) that birds were capable of detecting the magnetic poles. *See* How Do Birds Find Their Way? under Migration.

MIGRANT
A bird that migrates—that is, makes regular trips to and from a nesting or wintering area. It does not include those species that may wander in the non-breeding season without a definite goal. A migrant is also a term for a bird that passes through a particular area—it does not nest there or live there during the non-breeding season; it is seen there only during its migration. The preferred term here (locally) for such a bird is *transient*. *See* Where Do Birds Live? under Distribution. *See also* Migration.

MIGRANT, THE
A publication. *See* Ornithological Periodicals.

MIGRATION
Term derived from the Latin *migrare*, to go from one place to another. Migration is a regular movement and, as used here, refers to the spring movements of birds from their wintering to their summering or nesting places, and the fall movements from their nesting grounds to their wintering places. In N. America, migrating birds generally move from south to north and from north to south, although there are some birds that arrive at their northern nesting grounds or southern wintering places by first migrating over regular routes obliquely or even laterally for considerable distances before arriving at their destinations.

WHY BIRDS MIGRATE. A number of explanations have been given for the migrations of birds. Among them are the greater availability of food and longer days in which to gather food for nestlings. These factors enhance the chances of survival for the brood.

PHYSIOLOGY OF MIGRATION. Although migratory behavior is inherited (in those N. American species that migrate, such as warblers, most hummingbirds, flycatchers, swallows, etc.), birds do not migrate without the proper physiological stimulus. After the breeding season, in late summer, usually after the molting time of birds, and just before they migrate, the metabolism of these birds undergoes profound changes. Apparently owing to the action of the hormones prolactin and corticosterone, released at different times of the day by the pituitary gland and adrenal glands (see Meier, 1973; Meier and Davis, 1967), migratory birds begin to accumulate large amounts of fat just under the skin. For example, the migratory blackpoll warbler, which normally weighs about 11–12 gr., may weigh 20–23 gr. or more at the time of its fall migration—enough fat reserves for it to fly nonstop over the Atlantic for about 85 hours to the mainland of S. America (Williams and Williams, 1978). Experiments by Lasiewski (1963) suggest that a male ruby-throated hummingbird weighing about 4½ gr., of which 2 gr. is fat, could fly nonstop for 26 hours. At an average speed of 40 km. an hour, in 26 hours, it could travel 1,040 km.—far enough to span the Gulf of Mexico. *See* the actual migration of the ruby-throated hummingbird under Hummingbird Family.

These accumulations of fat in the bodies of migratory birds provide energy (*see* Metabolism) for the long migration flights. Meier (1973) discovered that, in caged migratory birds, it is the time-spaced interaction of two hormones—prolactin of the pituitary gland and corticosterone—that apparently controls the fat buildup and causes the noticeable premigratory restlessness, called by German ornithologists *Zugunruhe*. These hormones are regulated in their action by the daily photoperiod, or amount of light during a day length a bird is subjected to, at least in some birds. See Meier (1973).

Cold weather also stimulates birds in this physiological state to start migrating. A migratory flight may exhaust some migrants, which may arrive emaciated at their various stopping places (staging points) along the migration way. There the birds eat increased amounts of food (hyperphagia) and have a special ability to replenish their fat reserves in preparation for the next flight. These changes in physiology are unique to migrants—sedentary birds such as quail, pheasants, and others that do not migrate show much smaller increases after the breeding season, when a bird's weight is usually at its lowest. They do not have the same ability to replenish their reserves and do not show the unusual metabolic cycle of migrants (Dorst, 1974).

When spring migration starts, the increased action of the pituitary brings an added stimulus in the enlarging gonads of the migratory birds for the breeding cycle ahead. The pituitary controls both the sexual and migratory cycles simultaneously, but the control of the migratory urge depends on the action of several endocrine glands (Dorst, 1974). See especially a review of this subject by Berthold (1975).

THEORIES OF THE ORIGIN OF MIGRATION. One of the theories is that the ancestors of presently migratory birds had, at one time in the geological past, their original homes in their present wintering range (south of their present nesting ranges); that in spring, they gradually left the southern wintering grounds as the weather moderated in the North, where they began to breed and raise their families. When severe weather of fall and winter, with its lack of food, came, they retreated southward from the nesting range to their original homes to winter, thus beginning the migratory habit.

Others have speculated that the original homes of birds now migratory were in their present northern breeding areas, which were warmer in past geological times. With the changes of climate and environment in the North, brought on by the advancing and retreating glaciers during the great Quaternary "Ice Age," some birds were gradually forced to migrate southward to survive, and those that did not perished (Dorst, 1962). Thus the migratory habit may have been formed. However, studies of present migration routes of birds, and knowledge of the geological changes in the country where these migration routes lead, indicate that some birds are still following the direction taken by ancient and long since altered Tertiary watercourses, before the more recent Ice Ages of the Pleistocene Epoch (Howard, 1962b). Dorst (1962; 1974) suggests that although migration in birds preceded the Quaternary glaciers, the glaciers must have had a powerful influence on the migratory patterns of birds in Europe and N. America, and were responsible for much of the geography of avian migrations today. These and other theories that have been proposed are all suggestive of what *may* have happened (Wetmore, 1926; Thomson, 1926), but it is almost certain that the migratory habit is older than the last glacial epochs and was developed as a need in times when the climate was very different from what it is today (Marshall, 1961a).

Migratory patterns of birds today are not fixed. Undoubtedly Pleistocene glaciers influenced migration routes in the past, but other influences—climatic, ecological, or environmental—are also working to cause some birds to lengthen or shorten their migration routes, to change their directions, and, in some, to gradually eliminate them altogether. *See* Distribution.

BIRDS THAT DO NOT MIGRATE. Berger (1961) reported that of 215 species of birds that nest in Mich. less than 20 are wholly nonmigratory there. These are: several species of grouse, the greater prairie chicken, bobwhite quail, several species of owls, pileated, red-bellied, and downy woodpeckers, tufted titmouse, white-breasted nuthatch, Carolina wren, and cardinal. Everywhere in the U.S. the house sparrow is sedentary (many starlings are sedentary but some migrate); also the ring-necked pheasant, adult mockingbirds (the young may migrate), and wren-tit are resident, and Townsend's solitaire in winter scarcely moves out of its nesting range. Year-round residents of the Arctic and northern part of the Temperate Zone are: willow ptarmigan, snowy owl, northern three-toed woodpecker, raven, gray jay, red-breasted nuthatch, boreal chickadee, and snow bunting. *See*, however, periodic migrations of some under Irruption.

BIRDS THAT MIGRATE. Apparently as an adaptation to their long flights, all migrants have relatively longer and more pointed wings than closely related nonmigrants, and weigh relatively less. Usually, the more severe the climate, the more species migrate; in Canada, more migrate than in the U.S., and fewer still in Mexico. At least two thirds of those species breeding in n. U.S. migrate south to winter (Emlen, 1975a). Some that winter in n. U.S. travel only a few hundred miles southward from their northern nesting grounds—for example, some American goldfinches, tree sparrows, Lapland longspurs, dark-eyed (slate-colored) juncos, and meadowlarks. House wrens, some American robins, the eastern bluebird, some hermit thrushes, the yellow-rumped (myrtle) warbler, the eastern fox sparrow, some vesper and chipping sparrows, the pine warbler and some tree swallows, some orange-crowned warblers, the yellow-throated warbler (a southern species), and others, spend the winter in the southern states. (For details of the wintering range of these birds, *see* in their biographies.)

Many of those that nest in Canada and in n. U.S. pass southward each fall to winter throughout parts of the Northeast south to areas along the Gulf of Mexico. They include, besides those listed above, white-throated and some white-crowned sparrows (the related golden-crowned of the West winters along the Pacific coast and in the Southwest), the yellow-rumped (myrtle) warbler, and some black-and-white warblers, brown creepers, golden-crowned kinglets, eastern phoebes, and hordes of grackles, red-winged blackbirds, brown-headed cowbirds, and other smaller birds, also various species of ducks, the whooping crane (Tex.) and some greater sandhill cranes (n. Fla.), and the American woodcock and common snipe. The sw. U.S., especially Calif. with its mild climate, is a wintering ground for many migrants. (Again, *see* details of wintering range in biography of each.)

More than 100 species of birds that summer in the U.S. leave our country to winter in the West Indies or in C. and S. America (Lincoln, 1950c). A few of these migrants—gray catbird and northern (Baltimore) oriole, for example—sometimes winter in Canada or in ne. U.S. near feeding stations that offer suitable food (see in Terres, 1977). *See also* the biography of each of these birds.

The main wintering area of many N. American species, however, is in Mexico and in C. America to Panama. Nowhere in America, or in any other part of the world, according to Dorst (1962), is there such an extraordinary concentration of winter residents. In C. America, especially, during the N. American winter, Dorst suggests that "every biological zone . . . literally swarms with North American migrants." However, in Tramer's studies (1974) in tropical Mexico, during the winter dry seasons, N. American birds there were a rather small proportion of the birdlife, and Karr (1976) reported that wintering migrants in the American tropics tend to occupy cut-over or disturbed tracts, and forest edges, rather than the primary rain forest.

SOME LONG-DISTANCE MIGRANTS. Comparatively few N. American land-bird migrants pass beyond the S. American tropics. However, some winter in Brazil south of the Equator—nighthawks, barn swallows, cliff swallows, some of the thrushes, and vireos. Bobolinks travel about 5,000 mi. from their summer homes in s. Canada and n. U.S. to s. Brazil and n. Argentina. Some individual nighthawks and barn swallows travel still farther and, of all N. American land birds, have probably the longest migration routes in their travels from their summer homes in Yuk. and Alaska south to

MIGRATION
At the beginning of the autumn migration of the American golden plover, the birds gather in Labrador, then fly to the coast of Brazil and on to the Argentine pampas where they winter. Returning to the Arctic tundra by another route, they fly over Central America and the Mississippi valley. A western subspecies, the Pacific golden plover, winters in Southeast Asia, Australia, and the South Pacific.

breeding range

winter range

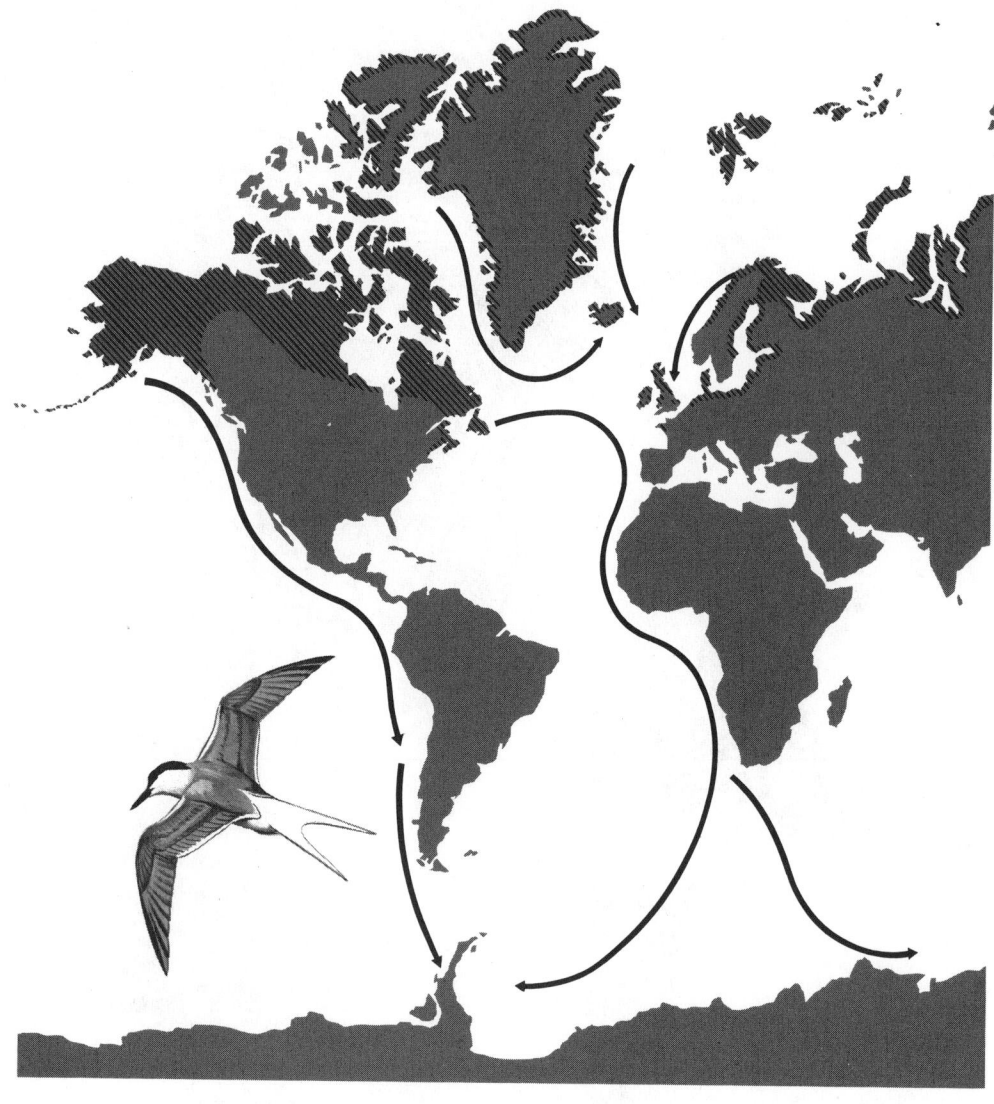

migration route of the Arctic tern

 breeding range

MIGRATION
*In the autumn, the Arctic tern migrates from
its nesting sites in northern Canada, Alaska,
and Greenland to Antarctica, where it spends a
"second summer." Its most extreme range —
from eastern Canada, across the Atlantic,
down the western coast of Europe and Africa —
is a round-trip of more than 22,000 miles.*

Argentina, 7,000 mi. away. The cliff swallow,
Swainson's thrush, yellow-billed cuckoo, and
Swainson's hawk are regular migrants south to
n. Argentina (Wetmore, 1926), and the annual
round trip of Swainson's hawk may be 11,000–
17,000 mi., probably the longest regular migration of any N. American member of the Hawk
Family.

The arctic tern (a seabird) makes one of the
longest and most spectacular of all migration
journeys, one of the most striking in the avian
world (see Austin, 1928; Storr, 1958). In N.
America it nests from Greenland and islands in
the Arctic, Alaska, and Canada to Mass., and
migrates from the Arctic to the Antarctic.
Those that nest in e. Canada, for example, start
their autumn journey by crossing the Atlantic
to Europe, then fly southward along the west
coasts of Europe and Africa and reach wintering range off s. Africa and southward to the
Antarctic Circle, an annual round trip reported
at 22,000–25,000 mi. See some banding returns
from this tern and other details in Dorst (1962);
see also in the biography of this bird in Gull
Family.

Many shorebirds (*see* Shorebird) are long-distance migrants; some go to the West Indies and
C. America to spend the northern winter, others deep into S. America, to lakeshores of the
high Andean plateaus and along both coasts of
S. America. Some of the surfbirds that winter
along 12,000 mi. of the Pacific coast—from
Alaska to the Straits of Magellan—travel
about 24,000 mi. a year in their migrations. The
white-rumped sandpiper migrates from
the Canadian Arctic to Tierra del Fuego and
the Falklands Is. in the S. Hemisphere, about
8,000–9,000 mi. each way each year; the Baird's
sandpiper annually travels from its Arctic nesting grounds to s. S. America (Patagonia) and
back; the red knot from Arctic Canada to the
Straits of Magellan and back, a round trip
of about 19,000 mi. each year. See also long
migration of pectoral sandpiper in Houston
(1965).

But of all N. American shorebird migrations,
that of the American golden plover has been
publicized as one of the most interesting, as it
travels in an enormous loop over the New
World. After nesting in the tundras of Alaska
and n. Canada, these plovers assemble in Labrador, then take off over 2,400 mi. of ocean to
the Brazilian coast, then onward through s.
Brazil and Uruguay to spend the northern winter on the Argentine pampas. On their return
northward in spring, they travel a different
course, over nw. S. America and C. America to
the Gulf of Mexico, then up the Mississippi Valley to their tundra breeding grounds, some
8,000 mi. north of their wintering quarters.
Their entire route is a giant ellipse with a major
north-south axis of 8,000 mi., an east-west axis
of 2,000 mi. *See also* the remarkable long-distance migration of the Pacific golden plover
under Plover Family. For migrations of ducks,
geese, and swans, *see* Waterfowl.

NIGHT MIGRANTS. Larger birds that live
secretively by day (rails and woodcock, for example) and most small insect-eating birds migrate by night—cuckoos, tyrant flycatchers,
nuthatches, creepers, wrens, most thrushes,

kinglets, vireos, wood warblers, tanagers, orioles, and the majority of sparrows. Many of the small nocturnal migrants, while feeding by day, may also move slowly along during part of their migrations.

DAY MIGRANTS. Small birds of strong flight, such as swifts, swallows, and hummingbirds, which can feed on the wing, usually migrate by day, although swifts and hummingbirds migrate also at night; hawks, eagles, cranes, storks, pelicans, and vultures migrate by day, herons by day and night, and gulls probably both by day and by night (Able, 1978). Some of our native doves and pigeons, crows, jays, and the smaller pipits, waxwings, shrikes, and most blackbirds migrate by day; nighthawks and the eastern kingbird by day and by night; the American robin may be both a day and a night migrant; the horned lark, eastern bluebird, pine grosbeak, and snow bunting migrate by day.

OTHER DAY AND NIGHT MIGRANTS. Loons, grebes, ducks, geese, swans, shorebirds, auks, and murres migrate both by day and by night.

Brewster (1886) credited the time of migration as correlated with the manner that a bird gets its food, its disposition, and its strength of flight. Bold, restless, strong-winged birds which migrate by day have greater security from winged enemies and can feed as they travel. Most small birds, including passerines, or songbirds, feed and rest by day and migrate at night, when they are not vulnerable to the attacks of hawks, gulls, and other enemies.

BEHAVIOR OF NOCTURNAL MIGRANTS. Lowery and Newman (1955), by focusing telescopes on the full moon (called "moon-watching"), and Lack (1959), by using radar, reported that birds start their night migrations soon after dark and that their numbers are greatest between 10 P.M. and 1 A.M., with the maximum numbers of birds observed between 11 P.M. and midnight. Then comes a gradual dwindling in numbers to virtually none at dawn, when the birds descend to earth to feed and rest.

Lowery and Newman believed that herons, geese, and shorebirds migrate in close formation at night but that almost all small birds fly alone and are more or less distributed over large parts of the sky. (Bellrose, 1971, reported small nocturnal migrants flying singly and in groups, or loose aggregations.) They also believed from their observations that nocturnal migrants generally fly with the wind, whereas low-flying day migrants often fly into the wind. See also Lowery (1951b) and especially Bellrose (1967). See a broad review of the subject by Balcomb (1977), whose study revealed that most passerines migrate singly at night and randomly spread, but with some "clumping" regularly.

During their night flights, migrants utter sharp and often melodious peeping and piping calls that differ in some species from their daytime calls; these are reputed to keep the individuals in touch with each other. Some species utter their loudest and most frequent calls just before dawn. See interesting discussion of subject by Tyler (1916); Ball (1952).

HEIGHTS OF BIRDS IN MIGRATION. Apparently little was known of the heights at which N. American birds fly in night migration until 1960 and 1961 (Terres, 1968a; 1975). In earlier studies in England, Lack (1959), using radar, found that common passerines migrate mainly below 5,000 ft. but tend to fly higher in spring than in autumn, and higher at night than by day. He occasionally recorded what he thought were small passerines flying at 14,000 ft. and up to 21,000 ft. above sea level. See also Gauthreaux (1972).

In the fall and spring of 1960 and 1961, Nisbet (1963) at Cape Cod, Mass., used radar that permitted observations of birds in night migration at various heights, except those flying very low, within 600 ft. of the ground. Within 3 or 4 hours after sunset, birds were most frequently flying between 1,500 and 2,500 ft. above sea level; most were flying below 5,000 ft. but on May 18, 1961, Nisbet's radar tracked many birds flying over the Cape between 6,000 ft. and 9,000 ft. with some up to 15,000 ft. A few nights later, his radar picked up bird echoes at 19,000 ft.

On several nights in Sept. 1961, Nisbet got strong bird echoes that were between 8,000 ft. and 15,000 ft. high and some at 20,000 ft., most frequently after midnight and just before and after sunrise. The high-flying birds were speeding at about 46–80 m.p.h. and moving southeastward out to sea. From their speed and great height, Nisbet thought they were possibly black-bellied plovers, semipalmated sandpipers, and certain other shorebirds that are known to migrate through the Cape region in fall and spring.

In general, radar studies have suggested that nocturnal migration is much heavier (includes many more birds) than diurnal migration; that most nocturnal migrants fly between 2,000 and 3,000 ft. above sea level, and even lower for passerines (Able, 1970), and that night migration is heaviest when the sky is clear (Berger, 1961). See also Blokpoel and Burton (1975). However, radar studies by Bellrose (1966) and airplane flights (Bellrose, 1971) showed almost as many migrants flying under overcast skies as under clear skies, and that many nocturnal migrants fly only 500–1,000 ft. above the ground. *See* Altitude of Bird Flight for high-altitude records.

SOME EFFECTS OF WEATHER. When a bird is internally (physiologically) prepared for migration, weather is one of the external influences that can cause it to migrate. In the fall, a large cool mass of air (high-pressure area), as it moves southward from the Canadian Arctic, can trigger birds into migratory flight. The cool air mass brings relatively low or falling temperatures, winds moving in the direction of the migration of birds, and clear skies. However, if the leading edge (cold front) of the high-pressure area in which birds are migrating meets warmer air (a *low-pressure* area), clouds, rain, hail, snow, or fog may be formed. Fog, especially, causes birds to descend to the ground and migration usually stops; however, any of these that suddenly closes in on birds in their night flights can cause disaster. *See* especially accounts under Accidents; *also* Waterfowl and Weather. See also in Terres (1956a).

In e. U.S., in spring, a warm, moist mass of air (low-pressure area with its higher or rising temperatures), moving up from the Gulf of Mexico or the Caribbean, with winds out of the south, can start a wave of migrating birds to move northward from the American tropics or from s. U.S. See Gauthreaux (1971). A southward-moving cold front meeting such a warm air mass that is carrying birds northward in spring often stops migration immediately or within 24 hours (Dennis, 1954). With the return of south winds and rising temperatures, the birds will again start northward. See especially Bagg *et al.* (1950); Raynor (1956). Although birds will sometimes fly through rain showers, sleet or a steady rain will ground them altogether. See, however, Cochran *et al.* (1967). Most migrants fly below clouds, sometimes above (Bellrose, 1967), and sometimes through clouds (Bellrose and Graber, 1963; Griffin, 1972; 1973).

Wind direction affects migration—head winds slow a bird's ground speed; tail winds increase it, and birds can apparently use the wind in several ways to their advantage (Bellrose, 1967; 1971). High winds, however, exceeding 50 km. an hour (about 31 m.p.h.), coming from any direction, can prevent small birds from migrating (Dinnendahl, 1954), and strong crosswinds can cause them to drift sidewise for considerable distances and may be disastrous to small land birds carried out to sea. See, however, Bellrose (1967).

Some authorities believe that wind direction may also bring about "reversed," or "retreat," migrations. These are local movements of migrating birds in which they turn and travel in the opposite direction. There have been many observations, both in fall and in spring (more commonly in fall), of reversed migration, especially in Europe. Lack and Lack (1953) noted common chaffinches (a passerine, or songbird), in autumn in France, flying east-northeast instead of southward when a wind from the south brought with it masses of fairly warm air. Similar reversed migrations have also been reported in Europe for starlings, common chaffinches, lark pipits, and some thrushes (Dorst, 1962).

Northbound migrants at Lake Erie and along the New England coast have been reported in spring to occasionally turn about and fly southward when they meet sudden cold fronts. See Lewis (1939); for observations in fall, see Baird and Nisbet (1959).

Some birds, especially in the high western mountains of N. America, make altitudinal ("vertical") migrations instead of north-south. In late fall or early winter, jays, chickadees, nuthatches, kinglets, and juncos that live high in the mountains in summer do not make long north-south migrations but merely descend to lower levels and milder weather of the lower slopes and valleys, then go back in spring to nest in the higher parts of the mountains. Mountain quail which nest to 10,000 ft. or more in the c. Calif. mountains, in late fall and early winter leave that region of deep snow and migrate on foot downward to below 5,000 ft. altitude; in spring they return again on foot to the higher elevations to nest.

Some birds also move northward after the

breeding season in what has been called post-breeding, or "vagrant," wandering—the young and adults especially of herons, also gulls, terns, barn owls, and the southern bald eagle, which nests in Fla. See special discussion in Ch. 7 of Van Tyne and Berger (1959); and in Berger (1961); Wallace (1963). *See also* Dispersal.

SPEED OF TRAVEL. The daily rate of migration by birds varies considerably. For example, the American robin, a slow but steady migrant, in spring, like the Canada goose, follows the 38° isotherm, moving northward at an average of about 38 mi. a day during that part of its migration in a 3,000-mi. trip from Iowa to Alaska. Some species of birds travel as slowly but at varying speeds in different parts of the migration route. For example, the blackpoll warbler, moving up from S. America, along part of its spring migration route from the Gulf of Mexico to Minn. averages about 30–35 mi. a day. Then it speeds up and travels at more than 200 mi. a day until it reaches its northernmost nesting grounds in n. Canada and nw. Alaska. See Lincoln (1950c); Cooke (1915a).

Stresemann (1955) reported that, in Europe, birds in general migrate faster in spring than in fall and, in some songbirds, the trip northward, when under the nesting urge, may take only half the time required for the trip in fall to reach their wintering grounds. According to Dorst (1962), an average migratory flight of the smaller songbirds (passerines) is 90–200 mi. but some migrants may average only 65 mi. a day. Waterfowl and shorebirds fly much farther—usually 500–1,000 mi. in a flight; occasionally 2,000 mi. (Bellrose, 1978). Nocturnal migrants usually do not fly night after night in migration but stop at the end of each night's flight to rest and feed.

In e. Pa., Middleton (1939) reported that migrating small birds—warblers, thrushes, towhees, wrens, and fox sparrows—stayed over at his banding station from 4½ to 7 or 8 days before moving on. However, Cochran *et al.* (1967) discovered that of three species of radio-tagged thrushes (which in their night flights flew at 23–35 m.p.h.), some were capable of migrating on two successive nights with only one day between to rest and feed. Graber (1965) reported a gray-cheeked thrush that flew, in one migratory night flight, 400 mi. during 8 hours, without rest, at an average speed of 50 m.p.h., aided by a strong tail wind. See also Nisbet (1963).

SOME SPEEDSTERS AND LONG-DISTANCE MIGRANTS. Some birds travel long distances in a remarkably short time. A shorebird, a lesser yellowlegs, banded at North Eastham, Cape Cod, Mass., on Aug. 28, 1935, was killed 6 days later, 1,900 mi. away, on Martinique, West Indies. It had traveled an average daily distance of more than 316 mi. Another shorebird, a ruddy turnstone, banded Aug. 23, 1965, on St. George Is., Pribilofs, Alaska, was collected (shot) 3½ days later on French Frigate Shoals in the Hawaiian Is. It had traveled 649 mi. a day and at an average speed of 27 m.p.h.

Dorst (1962) cited a peregrine falcon bearing the mark of King Henry IV, King of France, that escaped from Fontainebleau and was recovered later in Malta, 1,350 mi. away. It had traveled at an average speed of about 56 m.p.h. for 24 hours. A peregrine banded as a nestling in Northwest Territories, Canada, July 29, 1965, was shot in Jan. 1966 in the province of Chaco, Argentina, 9,000 mi. away, which set a long-distance record for migration of this species (Kuyt, 1967). See also Mueller and Berger (1959). *See also* speed of travel of some waterfowl under Waterfowl; Duck Family; of some shorebirds under Plover Family; Sandpiper Family. *See also* Speed of Flight under Flight, and records under Homing.

ROUTES OF TRAVEL. Banding of birds has proved that many individuals migrate back and forth to the same wintering area and the same breeding area, which are often thousands of kilometers apart. *See* Return to Nest Sites and Wintering Places under Banding. It has been difficult, if not impossible, however, to prove that the same bird uses *exactly the same* migration route each fall and spring. The moon-watching observations reported by Lowery (1951b) and Lowery and Newman (1955) suggest that many species of birds in their nocturnal migrations spread out over a broad front in N. America, although a few have regular, narrow lanes of travel—for example, Ross' goose, savannah sparrow (Ipswich race), and Harris' sparrow. See Ross' goose in Linduska and Nelson (1964) and accounts of the sparrows in Lincoln (1950c).

According to Lincoln, migration routes may vary from a narrow path that adheres to some geographical feature, such as a seacoast or river valley, to a broad area over the continent. From thousands of banding records of recovered birds, Lincoln described some of the main migration routes used especially by waterfowl, and by smaller birds as well, which he called "flyways." He described each of these as "a vast geographic region with extensive breeding grounds [at the northern end] and wintering grounds [at the southern end] connected with each other by a complicated system of migration routes" (Lincoln, 1950c). The flyway concept is a useful descriptive concept only for waterfowl and some shorebirds; see also observations of waterfowl migration by Bellrose (1966). *See* discussion of flyways under Waterfowl; also by Dorst (1962) and in Linduska and Nelson (1964).

Most birds are believed to use the same routes in their northward and southward migrations; however, a few travel a different route in spring from that in fall. For example, the Connecticut warbler and a western subspecies of the palm warbler, which commonly travel through New England in fall, travel up the Mississippi Flyway in spring (Wallace, 1963). The American golden plover travels in a giant loop, moving southward over one route in fall, northward over another in spring.

HOW DO BIRDS FIND THEIR WAY? *Orientation* (taking up a direction) and *navigation* (the ability to maintain a direction independently of landmarks) by migrating birds have been great ornithological mysteries since man first began to study birds scientifically. The ancients explained it simply—that Providence guides birds in their long flights, therefore it was no mystery at all.

Although biologists have studied migratory behavior for decades, most of the current knowledge of how birds find their way has been gained only since the late 1940s and early 1950s, when Gustav Kramer, German ornithologist at the Max Planck Institute for Biology at Wilhelmshaven, gave the first experimental evidence that the sun provides migratory birds with directional cues (Emlen, 1975b).

ORIENTATION BY THE SUN. Early investigators (Schneider, 1906; Ruppell, 1944) suggested that migrating birds might use the sun as a guide, but it was Gustav Kramer who offered the first experimental evidence of its importance to migrating birds. His captive European starlings showed a spontaneous pre-migratory restlessness when they were placed outdoors in a cage and oriented in the proper migratory direction in spring *as long as they could see the sun.* However, under overcast skies, their orientation declined.

These experiments and others (see in Emlen, 1975a) showed that starlings oriented in a consistent migratory direction, compensating for movement of the sun. In later training experiments with starlings, homing pigeons, and western meadowlarks, Kramer and his associates were able to calculate that these birds did adjust their orientation correctly in allowing for the sun's apparent passage through the sky. For such an accomplishment, it was believed that daytime migrants and homing birds, using simple sun compass for orientation, may also use an internal time sense ("biological clock") to correct their courses to compensate for the movement of the sun across the sky (Emlen, 1975b). See Emlen (1975a, pp. 155–62) for a detailed discussion of the theory of internal biological clocks in birds and their use in navigation. See also in Matthews (1968).

Waterfowl (several species of ducks) also use the sun compass for a guide in orientation (see Bellrose, 1958; 1963), and even European songbirds that are chiefly nocturnal migrants—red backed shrike and barred warbler, also the N. American white-throated sparrow (Able and Dillon, 1977)—have been shown through experimentation to possess a sun compass that can compensate for time.

ORIENTATION BY THE STARS. Franz Sauer, a German ornithologist of the University of Freiburg, after earlier experiments in the 1950s with orientation of birds by the stars, later extended this work (see Sauer, 1957) by testing three migratory European songbirds—blackcaps, garden warblers, and lesser whitethroats. He reported that while in outdoor cages under autumn skies, they oriented in the proper southerly direction of migrants at that time of year. While the brighter stars were visible, the birds maintained their migratory direction, but if the stars were blotted out by a cloud overcast, they circled randomly in their cages or stopped their actions altogether. Later, when Sauer tested two blackcaps in spring, they also selected the appropriate migratory direction for that season—north-northeast. For a fine, well-illustrated article of methods and equipment used to test the orientation of birds by the stars, see Emlen (1975b); see also Emlen (1975a, pp. 162–76).

In other tests, nocturnal orientation by the stars, with the direction appropriate to the season, has been confirmed for white-crowned sparrows (Mewaldt and Rose, 1960; Mewaldt *et al.*, 1964), bobolinks, yellow-billed and black-billed cuckoos (Hamilton, 1962a; 1966), and the rose-breasted grosbeak and indigo bunting (Emlen, 1967a; 1967b). It has also been confirmed in Russia (Shumakov, 1965) with eleven small songbird migrants.

Hamilton (1962b) found that his hand-reared blue-winged teal ducklings oriented correctly by using either the sun or the stars for clues.

INFLUENCE OF THE MOON. According to Matthews (1968), some European investigators did not believe that the moon was essential to birds in migration and thought that it might, in fact, lessen the accuracy of the birds' orientation. Matthews (1963), after his experiments with free-flying mallards released on clear nights with a half to a full moon, reported that they oriented more poorly than under stars alone. He thought the glare of the moon hid part of the star pattern and concluded that birds do not use the moon as a substitute for the daytime sun compass. At present, there is no evidence that the moon plays any role in migratory orientation.

USE OF LANDMARKS AS GUIDES. Possibly the most obvious cues suspected of aiding birds in migration are the features of the earth. Many that migrate by day are apparently influenced by their recognition of the topography of the land beneath them, and may reach their destinations by simple piloting based upon familiar landmarks. Some small birds follow coastlines and avoid flights over large bodies of water, although many fly across them directly; others, such as waterfowl, may at times follow river valleys and are guided by large rivers, lakes, and ponds important to them as stopovers along the migration route. Hawks, eagles, and other large birds that migrate by day concentrate especially in fall along certain mountain ridges, gliding along almost effortlessly on the strong updrafts of air. See Ch. 5 in Terres (1968a; 1975).

According to radar studies by Bellrose (1964a; 1967), small nocturnal migrants, and even waterfowl which also fly at night, do not appear in their night migrations to be influenced by the courses of large rivers such as the Missouri, Mississippi, Ohio, and Illinois, but continue along predetermined directions quite different from the courses of the river valleys. There is growing evidence from radar studies that nocturnal migrants—waterfowl and shorebirds as well as songbirds—largely ignore the most obvious landscape features beneath them (Emlen, 1975a).

Birds can depend on the stars for orientation on clear nights, and, according to Bellrose (1967), when stars are obscured, or landscape features are wanting, they may use the structure of wind turbulence for orientation. They may also correct their line of flight for wind drift, even under cloudy skies, and select nights for migration and altitudes of flight that have winds blowing in the direction of their destinations, and at speeds favorable to their flight. (Migrating waterfowl and shorebirds select winds of high speed; small birds, winds of lower speed.)

Apparently learned landmarks become important to pigeons only when near their final destination. In tracing homing pigeons by airplane, investigators in e. Mass. noted that it was not until the pigeons came within sight of a tall building in the Boston area that they turned and flew directly to the home loft. In plotting the track location where the pigeons made their final correction of their sun orientation toward home, the investigators concluded that the pigeons were not guided by landmarks until they were within 15–20 km. (9–12 mi.) of the home loft. See these and other experiments discussed in detail by Emlen (1975a).

THE EARTH'S MAGNETIC FIELD. It was A. von Middendorff (1855), German scientist, followed by others, who first suggested that birds were capable of detecting the earth's magnetic field, and it has been debated now for more than 100 years whether birds can use geomagnetism to guide them in their migratory flights (Keeton, 1971). The first experimental report, suggesting that tiny magnets, attached to the wings of homing pigeons, disrupted their receptivity to the earth's magnetic field, and thus their orientation, was that of Yeagley (1947). His ideas were immediately challenged, on theoretical grounds, by a half dozen authorities, and Yeagley's later experiments, and those of others, all failed to substantiate Yeagley's 1947 report. It was not until the 1960s that some positive evidence of the response of birds to magnetism, from new experimental techniques, stimulated further discussions of magnetic orientation. See reviews by Keeton (1972); Emlen (1975a).

Working with pigeons, which use the sun as a compass in homing, William T. Keeton (1969), at Cornell University, discovered that under totally overcast skies, in the absence of the visible sun to orient them, pigeons could still take up an initial bearing toward the home loft. This suggested to Keeton that they were using some other cue, or cues, in their orientation.

Later, in an attempt to discover if his homing pigeons might respond to the earth's magnetic field, Keeton experimented with two groups of pigeons. In one group, he attached miniature *non*-magnetic brass bars, glued to their backs; in the other, miniature magnets that potentially could disrupt effects upon them of the earth's magnetic field. When released some distance away from the home site, under a total cloud overcast, in five of seven tests birds wearing the non-magnetic brass bars oriented toward the home loft. The others, wearing the magnets, scattered at random (for details, see Keeton, 1971; 1972). According to Emlen (1975a), these results provided some of the clearest evidence, up to the time, of a magnetic effect upon bird orientation.

Walcott and Green (1974) also made tests on homing pigeons, using a miniature pair of coils that produced a magnetic field around the head of each bird. When the pigeons were released

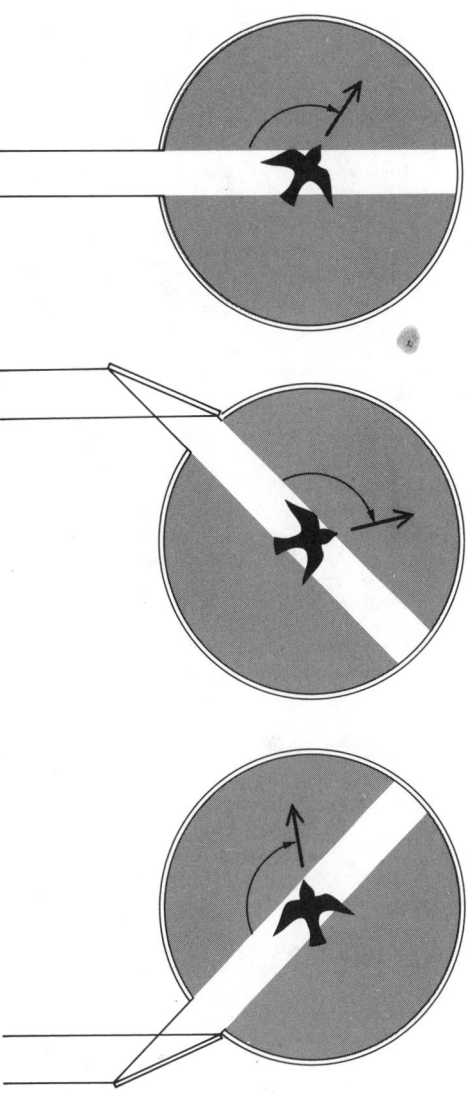

MIGRATION
Experiments have demonstrated that some birds orient themselves in migration by the position of the sun. A bird in a windowed, circular cage flutters in the direction it would take in spring or fall in relation to the direction of the sunlight. When mirrors are used to deflect the true angle of the sun, the bird will alter its direction accordingly, fluttering in the same relative position to its perception of the sun's rays.

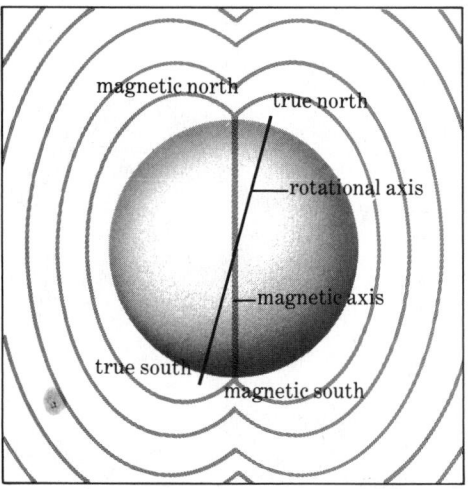

MIGRATION

The earth, like a giant magnet, is surrounded by a magnetic field of influence with poles located 11.5° from the true geographic poles. Although the evidence is still being debated, experiments have indicated that birds respond to the earth's magnetic field and may use this to supplement their other navigational clues, especially when the sky is overcast.

on a sunny day, some distance from the home site, they returned to the home loft, but when released under overcast skies, their orientation was disrupted.

Other studies have shown that the earth's magnetism influences the orientation of migratory birds. William Southern (1969; 1971; 1972) got indirect evidence that geomagnetism affects the orientation of young ring-billed gulls, and the work of Merkel, Fromme, and Wiltschko in Frankfurt, Germany, suggested that European robins *(Erithacus rubecula)* can use the earth's magnetic field to determine their migratory direction. The Wiltschkos extended their investigations to include three European warblers *(Sylvia communis; S. cantillans;* and *S. borin)* and reported that these species showed magnetically directed migratory restlessness.

Later, at the invitation of Emlen and his co-workers at Cornell, the Wiltschkos came there to collaborate for a year in studies of the effects of magnetism on the orientation of other migratory birds. Using indigo buntings, a N. American species, the investigators demonstrated, under rigorously controlled experiments, that caged buntings, ready to migrate, will orient their movements to the dominant magnetic field, either to the earth's natural one or to an artificial field of the same strength. See Lancaster and Johnson (1976); and see also Lancaster and Johnson (1975) for a preliminary report by William Cochran on the positive response of Swainson's thrushes to the earth's magnetic field.

In summarizing his chapter on orientation and navigation by birds, Emlen (1975a) emphasized that a migratory bird has many potential sources, or cues, that may guide its migratory flight, from topography of the land, through meteorological, to the sun, stars, the earth's magnetism, and others. Bird navigation is very complex; birds do not depend on any single clue or sensory system, and seem to depend on various cues. Preliminary findings suggest that birds may even prefer one cue or navigational aid over another, and despite years of work "we still have a long way to go . . . the sum total of our knowledge today is still insufficient to explain how an individual might find its way over the thousands of kilometers between its breeding territory and its overwintering destination." See also review of bird navigation, and its possible evolutionary development, in Bellrose (1972).

MIGRATIONAL HOMING
See Waterfowl.

MIGRATORY BIRD TREATY ACT
See Legal Protection.

MILLIMETER
One thousandth of a meter, or 0.03937 inch. Measurements of birds in scientific papers, reports, journals, and books are usually given in millimeters (mm.)—the total length of the bird, length of closed wing, of extended wings, etc. *See* details in Dimensions. There are about 25 millimeters to an inch. Measurements of birds in popular books and articles are usually given in inches and feet.

MIMICRY
(of form and color). *See* Colors of Feathers; *also* Behavioral Mimicry under Behavior.

MIMICRY
Although some songbirds inherit the ability to sing the song of their species without listening to others of their kind, others must listen and imitate their parents and other conspecifics in order to develop a normal song. Still others listen and imitate other species. This imitative ability is called *vocal mimicry*. Vocal copying in birds is proverbial and there is much evidence that some songbirds learn part, or even all, of their territorial songs from fellow members of their species (Nottebohm, 1975; *see* Songs and Singing). However, some birds also appropriate parts of the songs and calls of other species. The function served by a mockingbird appropriating into its own repertoire the songs, or parts of songs, of robins, blue jays, and many others is difficult to perceive. According to Thorpe (1956b), some element of play involved when a bird practices "mimicry" of other birds' songs. However, such complex songs (for example, a mockingbird's) may play a vital role in developing an individually distinctive song that may also convey information about the age of the singer and its success in achieving such age. Some theorize that mimicking may be simply an outlet for a bird's surplus "drive" or "urge" to sing. See also theories reviewed by Armstrong (1963), Thorpe and North (1965), and Dobkin (1979).

Mockingbirds are by far the most famed for vocal mimicry among N. American birds. Many, perhaps most, are remarkable mimics. According to Townsend (1924), one imitated 55 other species of birds in an hour, and one reported by Chapman (1930) near Chester, S.C., imitated the songs of 32 species within 10 minutes. Another, whose voice was recorded by the Laboratory of Ornithology at Cornell University, uttered the songs of at least 30 species. Charles L. Whittle (1922) wrote that a mockingbird which lived in Arnold Arboretum, in Boston, became famous for its mimicry of the songs of 39 species of birds, the call notes of 50, and the notes of a tree frog and crickets. Forbush (1925–29) reported mockingbirds whose mimicry included the cry of an eagle, crowing of a rooster, cackling of a hen, caw of a crow, cooing of a mourning dove, barking of a dog, squeaking of a wheelbarrow, the postman's whistle, and the plaintive peeping calls of young chickens and turkeys.

In Calif., Miller (1938) reported that mockingbirds there imitated the songs or calls of shrikes, the acorn woodpecker, Brewer's blackbird, Bullock's (northern) oriole, killdeer, California (scrub) jay, California quail, sparrow hawk (American kestrel), black phoebe, burrowing owl, and a tree frog *(Hyla).*

Near Wichita, Kans., in the summer of 1923, Frank F. Gander (1929) heard a mockingbird imitate all the songs and calls of the birds in that area. However, its outstanding accomplishment was a perfect vocal imitation of the long, rattling, drumming sounds of a red-headed woodpecker that hammered with its bill on a metal projection on the roof of a house.

The gray catbird, like the mockingbird, has a

remarkable talent for mimicking the calls and songs of other birds, and other sounds that it hears. Individuals give perfect imitations of birds in their area—the harsh cry of a great crested flycatcher, squawk of a hen, cry of a lost chicken, the call of a whip-poor-will, and, according to Townsend (1905), the songs or calls of some 40 species—the blue jay, bobwhite quail, common flicker, American robin, barn swallow, American goldfinch, rose-breasted grosbeak, veery, wood thrush, red-eyed, yellow-throated, and solitary vireos, brown thrasher, greater yellowlegs, and many others. Aretas A. Saunders also reported its imitations of these and other birds and has heard the catbird imitate the tree frog, *Hyla versicolor*. Its range of imitations seems almost limitless, including the spitting of a cat (Gross in Bent, 1948). Interestingly, one of its common calls, a mewing note, not imitative, has given it its name.

The catbird even includes double (vocal and visual) mimicry in its imitations: it has been known not only to learn the song of the bobolink but to utter the song while on the wing (flight song) and descending toward the earth with its wings in a slow jerky motion just as the bobolink does. A catbird was also seen to swoop down one July day and fly across the Ipswich R. in Mass. with a perfect imitation of both a kingfisher's flight and its rattling call.

OTHER NORTH AMERICAN MIMICS. The brown thrasher, although not as famed a mimic as its relatives the mockingbird and catbird, does occasionally imitate the songs or calls of the mockingbird, common flicker, cardinal, tufted titmouse, crested flycatcher, yellow-breasted chat, and wood thrush (McAtee, 1940a). Saunders (in Bent, 1948) heard brown thrasher imitations of songs of the eastern phoebe, American robin, white-eyed vireo, red-winged blackbird, northern (Baltimore) oriole, vesper sparrow, and field sparrow. See also Hancock (1964). Beals taught a brown thrasher to speak words and phrases (see in Terres, 1958).

Blue jays give a perfect rendition of the plaintive *kee-you, kee-you* call of the red-shouldered hawk, but there is some disagreement about whether this is true mimicry (see Gross in Bent, 1946). Charles O. Handley credits two blue jays in Va. with mimicking the cry of the *red-tailed* hawk in Mar. 1927. A captive young blue jay owned by Charles J. Maynard (1928) imitated perfectly the song of a male robin, and in a short time learned to imitate Maynard's whistled renditions of the calls of bobwhite and of the whip-poor-will. See also the experiences of Ramsay (1972) with hand-raised blue jays; not only was he able to teach them the "wolf whistle" but they learned to give an exact imitation of the warning calls of common crows, *as heard at a distance.* Frank M. Chapman recorded in his journal of Dec. 6, 1886, at Gainesville, Fla., that the blue jays of that area were better mimics than the northern subspecies and cited one that uttered such an exact imitation of a sparrow hawk's (American kestrel) *killy, killy* cry that it frightened a passing killdeer.

Crows also are mimics—imitating the whine of a dog, cry of a child, squawk of a hen, and crowing of a young rooster—and in captivity imitate simple spoken words and human laughter. *See also* Language.

The Carolina wren has been reported to utter songs that resemble the rattling call of the belted kingfisher, the call of a common flicker, and songs of the pine warbler, rufous-sided towhee, red-winged blackbird, eastern meadowlark, northern (Baltimore) oriole, eastern bluebird, gray catbird, white-eyed vireo, scarlet tanager, and song sparrow, an ability that has given it one of its names—"mocking wren" (Bent, 1948); the Bewick's wren has also been cited as a mimic. See, however, Hartshorne (1973).

Both males and females of the northern shrike sing and mimic the calls and notes of other birds, and the red-eyed vireo has imitated the notes of the olive-sided flycatcher, great crested flycatcher, and eastern bluebird. See also Benton (1952). The white-eyed vireo also has a reputation as a mimic (Bent, 1950).

The introduced European starling is an extraordinary mimic; Allard (1939) reported one (captive) in Apr. 1938 which had learned to imitate a common flicker's call and then to reproduce the flicker's tattoo by drumming with its bill, as the flicker does, on top of its nest box. This was another example of double mimicry; it was also a remarkable feat for the starling, as it has no instinct to drum as a woodpecker has. Not all starlings are mimics, but some have imitated the calls of the bobwhite quail, killdeer, common flicker, and song notes of eastern phoebes and eastern wood pewees, distant cawing of a crow, and notes of the black-capped chickadee, eastern bluebird, ruby-crowned kinglet, northern yellowthroat, house sparrow, eastern meadowlark, northern (Baltimore) oriole, grackle, brown-headed cowbird, and American goldfinch. Others report its mimicry of the notes, songs, and calls of a long list of songbirds, woodpeckers, gulls, hawks, rails, guinea fowl, and others, thus rivaling the mockingbird, whose song it also imitates.

Starlings in England are reported to imitate almost any sound and in captivity can be taught to whistle tunes and even to articulate words (Bent, 1950). In late spring of 1951, a starling in the English garden of S. H. Chalke (1952) imitated a telephone ringing so well that it deceived Mrs. Chalke into coming in from her garden to pick up the receiver.

"TALKING" BIRDS. Among the "talking" birds, the parrots and their close relatives (family Psittacidae) and the Asian mynas (*Acridotheres*), which are passerines, are excellent mimics. An Amazon parrot reported by Lashley (1913) could enunciate from 50 to 100 distinct words. One African gray parrot, a species which is an especially good mimic, usually needed much practice for good imitation, nevertheless could suddenly repeat a word perfectly, without practice, a week or two after hearing it (Baldwin, 1914). A German scientist wrote of a budgerigar that, with a few days teaching, could learn phrases of three or four words, and was also trained to count up to ten (Thorpe, 1956b). "Sparkie," a budgerigar owned by Mrs. Mattie Williams of Bournemouth, England, could speak about 550 words and recite several complete nursery rhymes (Fisher and Peterson, 1964).

The mynas are famous for their mimicry, both in the wild and in captivity (Armstrong, 1963), and their special fame, especially in China, is their ability to imitate human speech with great accuracy. A trained Indian Hill myna, kept in London in 1664, not only "talked" but could neigh or whinny like a horse; another sang "All the nice girls love a sailor" and uttered "wolf whistles."

The National Zoological Gardens, Washington, D.C., depends on appropriations from Congress for its maintenance. In the 1930s, during Franklin Delano Roosevelt's first term in office, a myna bird at the zoo was taught by its keeper to say: "How about the appropriation?" President Roosevelt heard about the bird and its famous phrase, but when he visited the zoo and stood before its cage, it would not utter a word! (Terres, 1936–1970)

Thorpe (1959) reported that the Indian Hill myna surpasses parrots in the accuracy of its mimicry, and uses its voice resonators to reproduce vowel sounds at which parrots are much less expert. See spectrographs of mynas' sounds compared with human speech in Greenewalt (1968).

Heinroth and Heinroth (1958), Lanyon and Tavolga (1960), Thorpe (1961), and others believe there is no satisfactory evidence that wild parrots ever mimic sounds in their natural environment. But recent work has indicated that parrots may use this ability to mimic each other, thus strengthening the pair and group bonds between them. *See* The Pair Bond under Courtship. In captivity, once mimicry of speech is awakened, it can be so strong that if one speaks or whistles to some species of caged parrots, they approach, ruffle the ear coverts, and listen closely; sometimes they practice these sounds afterward. Mowrer (1950) found that the best way to get a bird to talk is to feed it by hand, and as the food is offered, to utter the word one wishes the bird to learn.

Apparently parrots and budgerigars learn to imitate human speech because in close company with people, and away from their kind, they become socially attached (perhaps affectionately) to their human keepers (Mowrer, 1950). They soon learn that by uttering sounds they draw closer attention from the owner, and that they have a more intimate association with the human keeper as he teaches them words and phrases. Parrots, for example, will talk more when the owner is out of the room or just after he has left, apparently in an attempt to bring him back (Thorpe, 1961).

From time immemorial S. Americans tamed parrots and taught them to talk. Alexander von Humboldt, while exploring S. America, heard a parrot speak a dead language—all the people of the tribe in which it had been reared had been exterminated (Armstrong, 1963). Pliny and other ancient Romans referred to talking parrots.

Parrots and their relatives are the only birds, other than songbirds, that can learn, and produce, vocal imitations. Voice imitation is highly developed in many songbirds. Besides the Old World mynas and the starling, for example, and N. American species that are excellent mimics, such as the mockingbird, gray catbird, etc. (*see* above; accomplished C. and S. American mimics are few, according to Armstrong, 1963), many European species are good mimics. The marsh warbler (*Acrocephalus palustris*) and European jay (*Garrulus glandarius*) are outstanding, and the sedge warbler (*Acrocephalus schoenobaenus*), redstart (*Phoenicurus phoenicurus*) and red-backed shrike (*Lanius collurio*) are also accomplished mimics (see Armstrong, 1963).

Tinbergen (1958) cites a remarkable example of mimicry by captive European jays he was studying in a camp for his students in Holland. Tinbergen often awakened his students at 6 or 7 A.M. by whistling reveille and tapping each tent with a stick. His captive jays began to give wonderfully exact renditions of his whistled reveille. One morning, when the jays began to perform at 4 A.M., the students awakened, dressed hurriedly, and came sleepily out of their tents before they discovered that the jays had fooled them.

Tretzel (1967) noted European blackbirds uttering a strange whistle he had never heard from them before. After a considerable search of the neighborhood, he came upon the source —a man who had been calling his cat for years by whistling to it.

In 18th-century Europe, bird fanciers commonly taught their pet birds to whistle tunes they played for them by means of the bird flageolet; Mozart bought a starling that had been taught to sing, published his notations of the song, and may have used the melody (Armstrong, 1963).

The birds of paradise and bowerbirds of New Guinea and Australia are good mimics, and Marshall (1950) listed some 50 species of Australian birds that mimic. The lyrebird, related to the crows, mimics not only the calls of other birds, such as owls and the kingfisher called kookaburra, or laughing jackass, but the voices of people, the rustling sounds of parrots' wings, and automobile horns. Marshall (1954) wrote that the Australian spotted bowerbird imitates the crying of cats, barking of dogs, wood-chopping, and many other sounds. Its imitations of the calls of a certain eagle are so precise that it has caused a hen and her chicks to run for shelter (Welty, 1962).

MIMIDAE
See Mockingbird Family.

MINISTER
See Gull, great black-backed, and Gull, glaucous, in Gull Family.

MIOCENE PERIOD
See Geological Time Scale.

MIRROR
Term once used for a brightly colored area on the wings of birds, especially ducks. *See* Speculum.

MISSISSIPPI FLYWAY
See Waterfowl.

MISTLETOE BIRD
An Australian bird, *Dicaeum hirundinaceum;* one of the flower-peckers, a group of small to medium-sized, tree-dwelling songbirds of tropical Asia and the Australian Region (*see* Distribution) that are fond of mistletoe berries. Heumann (1926) kept mistletoe birds in captivity and discovered that they are so sensitive to cold that they went into a kind of torpor when exposed to cool weather, during which they gripped their perches so tightly that they could be removed only by force. *See* Torpidity. He also discovered how the mistletoe is "planted" or regenerated by these and other birds; during digestion of the berries, which they swallow whole, a very sticky substance forms around the seed, which when passed by the bird holds the seed fast to the branch or twig on which it is dropped; it dries instantly and a new mistletoe plant grows from that part of the branch. Littlejohns (1950), from his Australian studies, concluded that mistletoe spread from tree to tree by birds is not a menace to the plants on which it grows; also, that the mistletoe bird is almost entirely responsible for the distribution of mistletoe in Australia.

Sutton (1951a) found that most of the cedar waxwings he collected in Tex. and in other parts of the South had partly digested mistletoe berries in their intestinal tracts; in Mexico, the beautiful little stub-tailed "tanagers," known as euphonias, are gluttonous eaters of mistletoe berries of the genus *Phoradendron;* also, the gray silky flycatchers, *Ptilogonys cinereus*, gorged themselves on these berries.

On the deserts of sw. U.S., Gila woodpeckers eat mistletoe berries, and phainopeplas eat mainly the berries of a mistletoe, *Phoradendron californicum*, which is parasitic on the widely distributed mesquite, a large spiny desert shrub, *Prosopis chilensis*. Van Dersal (1938) lists—besides phainopeplas—mockingbirds, sage thrashers, robins, and bluebirds as depending almost wholly on mistletoe berries for food; they are also eaten by Gambel's quail and some of the flycatchers. *See* Commensalism for a related discussion; *see also* Food and Feeding Habits; Feeding Habits in the bird biographies.

MIST NET
See Banding.

MITES
See Ectoparasite.

MOA
See Flightless Birds.

MOANING BIRD
See Shearwater, wedge-tailed, in Shearwater Family.

MOBBING
Term used in ornithology for the massing together of birds, often of different species, and their attack upon or general aggression against a common enemy. *See* discussion of it in Self-protective Behavior under Behavior; *see* examples under Nests and Nesting.

MOCK FEEDING
In some species of birds, mated pairs go through the motions of feeding each other, though no food is passed between them. It is a behavior pattern that resembles courtship feeding (Berger, 1961). *See* Courtship Feeding.

MOCKINGBIRD FAMILY
Mimidae (MY-mih-dee or MIM-ih-dee); from Lat. *mimus*, mimic, or imitator. 31 species, all in W. Hemisphere, from s. Canada through C. America and West Indies to S. America (Van Tyne and Berger, 1976); 11 species reported in N. America (1, the Bahama mockingbird, a West Indian species, has reached Fla.); about 8–12 in. long; songbirds (*see* Passeriformes), all are fine singers and many mimic the calls or songs of other birds; family includes mockingbirds, catbirds, and thrashers; they are most closely related to thrushes and are called by some authorities mockingthrushes to show their close relationship (Lapham, 1979). Their habits are thrushlike—they build bulky, cuplike nests in bushes or on ground; members of the family are more slender than thrushes and have longer tails and rictal bristles. Their wings are relatively short and rounded with 10 primary feathers; legs are rather long and sexes outwardly alike. All are active, aggressive, and inquisitive, most live near ground, eat insects, seeds, berries; very rarely seen in flocks; are usually solitary or in pairs. Some are migratory, especially those that nest in Canada and northern and middle latitudes of U.S., others are resident, or year-round, in one area.

Most famous member of family is the mockingbird, symbolic of the South, and a skilled mimic—*see* Mimicry; has imitated songs or calls of 32 species of birds within 10 minutes, also notes of frog, cricket, piano, and squeak of wheelbarrow; is state bird of five southern states (*see* State Bird); a strong defender of its territory both in summer and in winter (dives repeatedly at dogs, cats, or people near its nest or young); repeatedly chases other birds from feeding stations and from pyracantha, holly, and other bushes with berries over which assumes proprietary rights.

The small gray catbird, one of much-loved dooryard birds in America, is famed for its tameness and quiet ways, but can be vigorous in defense of nest and young (see Slack, 1976); noted for its catlike mewing call; has pleasing song and mimics calls or songs of other birds but not so skillfully or accurately as does mockingbird.

Thrashers, most of which are brown above, white below, with streaked breasts, are large members of Mockingbird Family with noticeably long tails, long legs adapted to running over ground, and short, rounded wings (not strong fliers); have long, downcurved, strong bills, with which they dig in ground for food; 17 species of which all 10 in genus *Toxostoma* live in U.S. and Mexico. Eight live within U.S., best-known of which is the brown thrasher of e. and c. U.S.; like other members of family, it sometimes lives in dooryard shrubbery; largest number (7 species) live in West. The 12-inch-long California thrasher is largest member of Mockingbird Family; like sage thrasher, crissal thrasher, and Le Conte's of dry, arid Southwest, feeds mostly on ground.

Albinism has been reported by Gross (1965a) for 73 individuals of 4 species in family; according to Sprunt (1948), it is not rare in mockingbirds.

Members of family are protected by law, but to sustain injured or crippled bird until its release, offer it mockingbird food, fruit, hard-boiled eggs, mealworms, and other insects; also ground raw meat, chopped lettuce or other greens, bread crumbs. See also details in Terres (1968c).

Catbird, gray, *Dumetella carolinensis* (due-meh-TELL-ah cah-row-lin-EN-sis); genus name: from Lat., dim. of *dumetem*, thicket, a little thicket (dweller); species name: Lat, of Carolina; common name: from nasal catlike mewing call. (Color ill., page 576.) Common over most of U.S. except Pacific coast and Southwest; 8–9¼ in. long; wingspread 11–12 in.; no other bird is plain slate gray with reddish undertail coverts; has distinctive black cap and black tail; migrates north abundantly, largely at night, many strike tall buildings, TV towers, especially in fall migration; lives in low dense thickets, tangles of vines, small bushy trees often on border of marshes, streams, roadsides (many killed by auto traffic), and edge of forests; also in hedges and shrubs of gardens; males arrive on nesting grounds few days before females, immediately begin singing from top of thicket or in bush, tail depressed, body low to perch, sweet varied phrases, pauses, mixed with occasional harsh notes: *eweet, twit-twit-twit, cherooeekoo, tereet, erokeet,* occasionally calls in grating chatter, *kak-kak-kak,* a *mew* or soft mellow *chuck,* often sings at night, also a low, barely audible "whisper song" in autumn; imitates calls of jays, quail, hawks, whip-poor-will, many songbirds, squawk of hen, peep of chick and of tree frog, kingfisher's rattle (Gross, 1948a); often remarkably fearless and tamable (see "Smoky the Catbird," in Terres, 1958).

Feeding Habits: Almost half of food is insects, largely crickets, grasshoppers, beetles, especially Japanese beetles and June beetles, cankerworms and other smooth caterpillars; hairy ones of gypsy and brown-tail moth; also ants, aphids, treehoppers, cicadas, sawflies, termites, large moths such as cecropia, prometheus, and sphinx; also dragonflies, millipedes, centipedes, spiders, rarely small trout, also many kinds of wild and cultivated grapes, berries, and at feeding stations takes cheese, bread, raisins, currants, peanuts, milk, cream, corn flakes, boiled potatoes, soda crackers.

Nest: Often built in garden shrubs—deutzia, lilacs, mock orange, near porch or shed—in Osage orange hedges, in coniferous trees, in thickets near creeks, swamps; usually 3–10 ft. above ground; ragged mass of sticks, weed stems, grasses, leaves, twigs, cup lined with pine needles, rootlets, fine shreds of bark, horsehair (Gross, 1948a).

Eggs: May–Aug.; 2–6 usually 4, glossy, dark greenish-blue.

Incubation: 12–15 days; young leave nest when 10–15 days old; adults often raise two broods in one season (Nickell, 1965c).

Other Names: Black mockingbird (in South); black-capped thrush; cat flycatcher; chicken bird; slate-colored mockingbird.

Age: Ten, banded Nashville, Tenn., lived at least 4 years; one, Minn., to 7 years; one at Demarest, N.J., 10 years old.

Albinism: Relatively common (Gross, 1965a).

Flight Speed: Timed in New England, 16 m.p.h. (White, 1929).

Host to Cowbirds: Infrequent; cowbird generally unsuccessful because catbird usually throws cowbird's eggs out of its nest (Friedmann, 1963). See, however, Woodward (1976).

Weights: In Mich. (10), 31.2–39 gr. (Becker and Stack, 1944); along N.J. coast, fall (591), 23.2–45.3 gr. (Murray and Jehl, 1964), or ¾–1½ oz.

Range: Nests from s. B.C., c. Alta., c. Sask., s. Man., w. Ont., n. Wisc., s. Que., N.B., and Nova Scotia, south through n. and e. Wash. and e. Ore. to n.-c. Utah, e.-c. Ariz., n.-c. N.M., w. Okla., Tex., c. La., c. Miss., c. Ala., and s. Ga., rarely s. Fla. and Bermuda; winters from se. Tex., n. La., se. Ark., c. Ala., c. Ga., c. S.C., e. N.C., se. Va. (casually farther north to Long Is., N.Y., south through e. Mexico to Panama, and West Indies; casual in winter to S.D., se. Mo., s. Mich., s. Ont., Pa., N.Y., Vt., s. Me.; has wandered to Calif., Nev., and w. Tex.

Mockingbird, *Mimus polyglottos* (MY-mus or MIM-us pol-ih-GLOT-os); genus name: *see* family introduction; species name: Lat., from Gr., meaning many-tongued. (Color ill., page 576.) Lives across country from e. U.S. to Calif.; one of most widely known and popular songbirds in America; discovered almost 250 years ago by Mark Catesby, Englishman and "founder of American ornithology" (Allen, E. G., 1951), who called it the "Mock-Bird of Carolina"; bird famed as mimic and for rapturous singing on moonlit nights among magnolias and moss-covered live oaks of South; robin-sized, but slimmer; 9–11 in. long; wingspread 13–15 in.; sexes alike; medium gray above, gray-white below; long-tailed with white wing patches and white outer tail feathers conspicuous in flight; usually lives as year-round resident in trees, shrubbery of suburban or country gardens; edges of open woods, pastures, rail-fence corners, farm hedges; in West, in isolated shrub patches or trees of prairie, ranch-house orchards, fig-bordered vineyards; in Southwest, in sage, prickly pear cactus, and chollas, or long-jointed cactuses, and up to 5,000 ft. elevation (Bent, 1948); males have "dance" in which they confront each other at border of territory, rapidly hopping sideways like bantams sparring for opening; male sings by day or night, strongly musical song with almost endless variations from perch in bush, tree, or on chimney or in flight; repeats each phrase several times before starting next one; has "whisper song," infinitely soft and tender; especially noted for mimicry of sounds so expertly copied that an electronic analysis cannot detect difference from original; besides 39 species songs and 50 call notes, has imitated cackling of hen, barking of dog, postman's whistle, and even notes of piano (Forbush, 1925–29); call notes are harsh, grating *chair* and *tchack.*

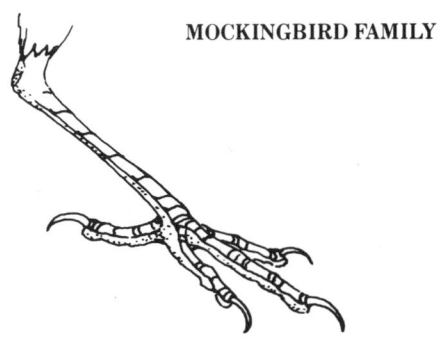

MOCKINGBIRD FAMILY

Feeding Habits: Grasshoppers and beetles large part of diet; has habit of raising wings archangel-like, supposedly to flush insect prey (*see* Wings); weevils, ants, caterpillars, also spiders, crayfishes, sow bugs, and snails; lizards, small snakes. Wild fruit about 43% of diet: holly, smilax, elderberry, pokeberry, blackberry, mulberry, grapes, red cedar, black alder, bayberries, berries of poison ivy, fruit of prickly pear cactus, also comes to feeding stations for suet, bread, raisins.

Nest: Built by both sexes, 1–50 ft. above ground, usually 3–10 ft., in fork or on branch of small bushes, vines, cactus; trees such as red cedar, spruce, arborvitae, pine, boxwood; built of compact outer layer of twigs, dry leaves, plant stems, fiber, paper, sheep wool, cotton, string, cloth, lined with grasses, rootlets.

Eggs: Mar.–Aug.; 3–6, usually 4–5, shades of blue or green, marked heavily with browns.

Incubation: By female, 12–12½ days; young leave nest when 10–12 days old (Laskey, 1962); two or three broods a season.

Other Names: Mimic thrush; mock bird; mocker; mocking thrush.

Age: One, banded Calif., recaptured alive when 9 years old; another, reported in Calif. by Michener (1951), 12 years old; another more than 10; Laskey (1962) hand-raised nestling male, lived to 15 years, 4 months.

Albinism: Not rare, from pure white to those with few white feathers in wings and tail; total (complete) albino reported S.C., 1940 (Sprunt, 1948).

Flight Speed: Timed in Tex., 22 m.p.h. (Sooter, 1947).

Host to Cowbirds: Infrequent; a few records to brown-headed cowbird and is rare host to bronzed cowbird (Friedmann, 1963).

Weights: In fall, coastal N.J. (5), 45.1–60.9 gr. (Murray and Jehl, 1964), or 1½–2 oz.

Range: Resident, has extended its range much farther north in recent years; now common resident in many states where once was rare visitor; nests s. Ore. east to n. Utah, Wyo., Newfoundland, and Nova Scotia; south to s. Baja Calif., s. Mexico, and West Indies; introduced and established in Hawaii.

Mockingbird, Bahama, *Mimus gundlachii* (MY-mus or MIM-us gund-LOCK-ih-eye); genus name: *see* family introduction; species name: given in 1855 by Dr. Jean Cabanis, German zoologist, for Dr. Juan C. Gundlach (1811–96), German naturalist, who settled in Cuba and for nearly 50 years was a recognized authority on Cuban birds. West Indian species; first N. American record and first one seen outside of West Indies was one seen and described in detail on East Key, Dry Tortugas, Fla., May 3, 1973 (Kale, 1973); 13 in. long; "larger than the (northern) mockingbird; upperparts brown-gray, indistinctly streaked with dusky on head and back; *very little white on wing and tail;* underparts whitish streaked with dusky posteriorly" (Bond, 1961). According to Bond, the song is not so melodious and is less variable than that of the northern mockingbird, *Mimus polyglottos;* the notes are more abrupt; it does not mimic the songs or calls of other birds. On the Bahama islands and cays off n. Cuba, and in s. Jamaica, it lives in semiarid scrub country

and about settlements; lives virtually through the Bahamas but not reported from Grand Bahama and Great Abaco; not present on Bimini and Cat Cays; nest like that of other mockingbirds of its genus; eggs cream-white or pink-white, spotted.

Other Names: Mockingbird (Bahamas); Spanish mockingbird; Spanish nightingale; Spanish thrasher.

Mockingbird, brown. *See* Thrasher, brown.

Mockingbird, French. Another name for the loggerhead shrike.

Mockingbird, mountain. *See* Thrasher, sage.

Mockingbird, sage. *See* Thrasher, sage.

Mockingbird, sandy. *See* Thrasher, brown.

Mockingbird, Spanish. *See* Mockingbird, Bahama.

Mockingbird, Yellow. Another name for the yellow-breasted chat, a wood warbler.

Thrasher, Bendire's, *Toxostoma bendirei* (tox-OSS-toh-mah ben-DIE-reh-eye); genus name: Lat., from Gr. *toxon*, bow, and *stema*, mouth (bill); species name: given in 1873 by Elliott Coues for Charles E. Bendire, Maj., U.S. Army, who collected the bird at Tucson, Ariz. (Hume, 1942). (Color ill., page 577.) Lives in deserts of sw. U.S.; 9–11 in. long; olive-brown above; smoke gray below with faint but distinct streaked, triangular spots pointing upward on breast and flanks; long tail; *eyes clear yellow* without orange tint as in curve-billed thrasher; *bill short*, lower mandible almost straight; often cocks tail wrenlike over back when running on ground; one of several kinds of pale, clay-colored thrashers that live in southwestern deserts, is limited to Calif., Ariz., and rarely N.M., lives in open country, farmlands, and valleys, especially where open ground meets tall dense bushes or cholla cacti (Phillips *et al.,* 1964); also up to 4,000 or even 6,500 ft. elevation in mountains (Bent, 1948); is pronounced migrant by late Aug. from n. Ariz., returns to Tucson area by Jan.; male is fine singer equal to brown thrasher and song suggestive of mockingbird, a clear, flowing, sweet, continuous warble "with double quality as though bird were singing two songs at once" (Phillips *et al.,* 1964).

Feeding Habits: No comprehensive study but evidently lives largely on beetles, caterpillars, and other insects it finds while foraging on ground.

Nest: Built 2–12 ft. above ground, in cactuses, tesota, *Lycium,* catclaw, and mesquite, average height 3–5 ft. up; not as bulky as other thrashers' nests, of twigs, lined with grass, weeds, rootlets, wool, cotton, pieces of cloth, horsehair, thread.

Eggs: Feb.–Aug.; 3–4, pale gray-green to green-white, with pale brown spots.

Incubation: Period of and age when young first fly unknown.

Host to Cowbirds: Only one record (Friedmann, 1963) to brown-headed cowbird in Ariz.

Range: Nests from se. Calif. to s. Nev., s. Utah, and nw. Ariz. south to sw. N.M. and into Mexico. Phillips (1968a) believed that Bendire's thrasher and the rufous-winged sparrow, both collected by Bendire in 1872, were "the last two really distinct species of United States birds to be discovered."

Thrasher, brown, *Toxostoma rufum* (tox-OSS-toh-mah ROOF-um); genus name: *see* Thrasher, Bendire's; species name: from Lat. *rufus*, red, or rufous. (Color ill., page 577.) Well-known, popular bird, e. N. America, from s. Canada to Gulf, from Atlantic coast to base of Rocky Mtns.; state bird of Ga.; 10½–12 in. long; wingspread 12½–14 in.; reddish brown above; pale buff to white below, heavily streaked underparts; bill blackish, rather long, slightly downcurved; long, rounded tail; wings short with two white bars; eyes of adults deep yellow; immatures, gray to yellowish; arrives New England late Apr., rather shy, lives in dry thickets of wooded, farming country, brushy pastures, second-growth woods, fencerows, brier patches, roadsides, sometimes in shrubbery of gardens; male sings from top or tree or tall bush, head high, long tail drooping, series of short, rapid, musical phrases (like mockingbird but wilder), usually in pairs; to give tempo, has been rendered by one listener as like telephone conversation: *Hello, hello, yes, yes, who is this? who is this? I should say, I should say, how's that? how's that?;* also sings low, warbled "whisper songs" in spring and fall; call note a loud *smack!* Mimics calls or songs of other birds—flicker, cardinal, titmouse, chat, wood thrush, etc.—but not as frequently as gray catbird and mockingbird (Bent, 1948); however, for remarkable mimicking ability, see "A Brown Thrasher Talks His Way to Fame," in Terres (1958).

Feeding Habits: Most of time on or near ground, forages among fallen leaves under trees, shrubs, seldom scratches with feet but uses bill to dig and to toss leaves aside; sometimes leaps into air to catch flying insect; walks, runs, and hops; eats June beetles and grubs, Japanese beetles, rose beetles, cotton-boll weevil, curculios, wireworms, tent caterpillars, gypsy moth caterpillars, grasshoppers, crickets, cankerworms, army worms, cutworms, leafhoppers, treehoppers, cicadas; also sow bugs, lizards, snakes, salamanders, tree frogs; blackberries, blueberries, holly berries, elderberries, pokeberries, raspberries, hackberries, and others; figs, acorns, waste corn and wheat. See also in Terres (1968c).

Nest: Sometimes on ground, especially in New England and parts of Midwest; usually low in smilax, lilac, forsythia, gooseberry bush, privet, Osage orange hedge, thorn apple, honey locust, wild plum, etc., or in brush piles; usually 1–10 ft. up, sometimes to 15 ft., in small apple, orange, or other trees; nest large, often of several "baskets" or layers of twigs, dead leaves, paper, thin bark, grasses, cup lined with rootlets.

Eggs: Mar.–July; 3–6, usually 4–5, pale blue, blue-white, or white, finely spotted with browns.

Incubation: By both sexes, 12–14 days; young first fly at 9–13 days old; adults often vigorous in defending young, fly at head of intruder; often two broods in one season (Bent, 1948).

Other Names: Brown thrush; brown mockingbird; fox-colored thrush; ground thrush; mavis; red mavis; red thrush; sandy mockingbird; song thrush; thrasher.

Age: At Nashville, Tenn., one 8 years; in N.C., banded one, still alive at 9 years, 8 months, old; another wild banded bird, recaptured and released when 12 years, 10 months, old (Kennard, 1975).

Albinism: One partial albino—grayish white but without pink eyes—Collingswood, N.J., at bird feeder, 1949.

Flight Speed: Timed at 19 and 22 m.p.h. (Wood, 1933).

Host to Cowbirds: Is largest passerine (songbird) victimized, except for those few "accidental" victims of brown-headed cowbird; 31 records (Friedmann, 1963).

Weights: Coastal N.J., in fall (78), 51.9–75.4 gr. (Murray and Jehl, 1964), or 1¾–2¾ oz.; in Mich. (16), 65.1–82.3 gr. (Becker and Stack, 1944), or about 2⅓–3 oz.

Range: Nests from se. Alta. across s. Canada to sw. Que. and sw. Me., and east of Rocky Mtns. to n. Tex., Gulf Coast, and s. Fla., migratory in northern part of nesting range; winters from e. Okla. east to N.C., s. Md., south to s. Fla., irregularly farther north in winter, has wandered to Calif., Ore., and other western states.

Thrasher, California, *Toxostoma redivivum* (tox-OSS-toh-mah red-ih-VIE-vum); genus name: *see* Thrasher, Bendire's; species name: Lat., revived (rediscovered). (Color ill., page 576.) In U.S., lives only in Calif., where common; 11–13 in. long; dark brown-olive above; underparts unstreaked, pale cinnamon belly and undertail coverts; long, downward-curved bill, sickle-shaped (Peterson, 1961); eyes brown with light streak above, tail long (Le Conte's thrasher is much paler); lives from western slopes of Sierra Nevada and higher mountains of s. Calif. to the Pacific, most abundant along bases of mountains and up to altitude of 5,000 ft. (Woods, 1948a); avoids forests, favors dense, chaparral-covered slopes and stream borders; also foothill towns with mixed brush and short trees; lives mostly on ground, swift runner with tail tilted up; in air has awkward jerky flight, with drooping head and tail; very tame about dwellings, often associates with brown towhee and wren-tit; male, despite favored ground, rises to sing from top of bush or tree, rich, low, leisurely phrases, each uttered once or twice, not several times as does mockingbird (female also sings), interspersed with utterances of red-tailed hawk, flicker, house finch, quail, goldfinch, black-headed grosbeak, Bullock's oriole, and other birds, also frog, postman's whistle, and even the short howl of coyote (Woods, 1948a).

Feeding Habits: Rakes fallen leaves away with bill, beneath bushes, also digs, pick-fashion, with bill into soil, eats crickets, beetles, grubs, ants, wasps, bees, caterpillars, cocoons, and moths, also spiders, seeds of berries, hazelnuts, weed seeds, figs, grapes, and cactus fruits; comes to bird feeders for crumbs and table scraps; bathes in birdbath.

Nest: Built by both sexes, usually within few feet of ground, well inside large bush or small tree; large, loose cup of twigs, lined with rootlets, plant fibers, grasses.

Eggs: Dec.–June, but height of season is Mar.–May; 2–4, commonly 3, pale blue or blue-green, spotted or flecked with pale browns.

Incubation: By both sexes, 14 days; young leave nest when 12–14 days old; fed for some time after by male, often while female incubating second set of eggs.

Other Name: Sonoma thrasher (subspecies).

Age: Two, banded Calif., found dead when each at least 5 years old.

Range: Resident from n. Calif. to n. Baja Calif.

Thrasher, crissal, *Toxostoma dorsale* (tox-OSS-toh-mah dors-AIL-ee); genus name: *see* Thrasher, Bendire's; species name: from Lat. *dorsalis,* of the back, but allusion unclear; crissal, from Lat., *crissalis,* in reference to the crissal area (crissum) of reddish undertail coverts. Deserts of sw. U.S.; 10½–12½ in. long; distinguished from curve-billed thrasher by its unspotted breast and rustier, reddish undertail coverts; olive brown above; smoke gray below; bill greatly decurved; eyes straw-colored; very secretive; in Ariz. common resident; rarely comes out of home in dense mesquite of lowlands or chaparral of mountains up to around 6,000 ft. elevation (Phillips *et al.,* 1964); one has only fleeting glimpse of bird as it darts away into or under brushy thickets of fertile irrigated valleys or canyons, hillsides, about ranches; seldom ventures out onto desert; moves quickly about with long graceful strides beneath dense cover; male, when may feel safe from observation, works way agilely up through thorny tree or bush to perch at tip, where he pours out song of remarkable sweetness (Bent, 1948). While hidden much of time, at dawn and dusk crissal thrashers utter churring call, *toit-toit,* which reveals true abundance (Phillips *et al.,* 1964); another call is *pichoory, pichoory.*

Feeding Habits: Very little known; observed to eat wild berries, wild grapes, also insects at all seasons; sometimes small lizards.

Nest: Saddled on branch of willow close to trunk or, usually, in fork of mesquite, sometimes in sagebrush, *Atriplex,* greasewood, wild currant, commonly 2½–8 ft. above ground; bowl-shaped, of fine withered grasses, stems of plants, shredded inner bark, all neatly felted into compact nest.

Eggs: Feb.–July; 2–4, commonly 3, blue or green like robin's or catbird's eggs.

Incubation: By both sexes, 14 days; young leave nest when 11–12 days old.

Other Name: Red-vented thrasher.

Range: Resident, from se. Calif. to s. Nev., sw. Utah, to w.-c. Tex., ne. Baja Calif., south to c. Mexico.

Crissal thrasher

MOCKINGBIRD FAMILY

Thrasher, curve-billed, *Toxostoma curvirostre* (tox-OSS-toh-mah cur-vih-ROS-trih); genus name: *see* Thrasher, Bendire's; species name: from Lat. *curvus*, curved, and *rostrum*, beak. (Color ill., page 577.) Deserts of sw. U.S.; 9–11½ in. long; gray-brown above, buffy below, faintly spotted breast distinguishes it from plain-breasted Le Conte's and crissal thrashers; orange-red eyes; longer downcurved bill than that of similar yellow-eyed Bendire's thrasher; is the only one of the four gray and brown western thrashers with markedly downcurved bills—others are California, crissal, and Le Conte's—which ranges east of 100th meridian; in Ariz. common in sparse brush of arid plains mostly below 3,000 ft. elevation; in open growth of small mesquites, greasewood, creosote bushes, interspersed with cactuses of varied forms and colors; also in s. Tex., in chaparral, prickly pear cactuses; sometimes lives about ranch houses, where may become very tame; in movements, behaves like brown thrasher, runs rapidly or hops lightly over ground, skims swiftly from one low bush to another; male perched on topmost branch of cholla sings loud, clear carol; also utters low trills and wrenlike chatterings.

Feeding Habits: Digs vigorously into ground with curved bill; eats insects, seeds of cactus, berries and other fruits; fond of water, comes to birdbaths or dripping faucets about houses or at open water holes.
Nest: Usually in fork of cholla cactuses bristling with thorns, sometimes in yucca, in mistletoe of mesquite and cottonwood, 2½–10 ft. above ground; built of coarse, loosely laid, fine thorny twigs, lined with fine grasses, rootlets, feathers, some horsehair.
Eggs: Mar.–Aug., but height of season is Apr.–May; 2–4, usually 3, often 4, blue-green to green-blue, speckled with browns.
Incubation: By both sexes, about 13 days; young leave nest when 14–18 days old (Bent, 1948).
Other Name: Palmer's thrasher.
Age: One, banded Ariz., when retrapped and released at place of banding, was at least 3 years old.
Host to Cowbirds: Apparently rare, only one record, to brown-headed cowbird in Tex. (Friedmann, 1963).
Range: Resident from nw. Ariz. to s. Tex. and south to s. Mexico.

Thrasher, desert. *See* Thrasher, Le Conte's.

Thrasher, Le Conte's, *Toxostoma lecontei* (tox-OSS-toh-mah leh-KON-teh-eye); genus name: *see* Thrasher, Bendire's; species name: given in 1851 by George N. Lawrence for John L. Le Conte, Philadelphia medical doctor and eminent entomologist (Palmer, 1928). (Color ill., page 577.) Uncommon, local, in deserts of sw. U.S.; 10–11 in. long; another of the curve-billed thrashers, very pale throughout, upperparts light gray-brown except dusky or black tail; underparts immaculate pale buffy white; underside of tail yellowish buff; bill black, slender, and downcurved; eyes brown (much paler bird than crissal thrasher; distinguished by unmarked breast from curve-billed thrasher with spotted breast); lives mainly in lowest, most barren, and hottest desert plains of sw. and w. Ariz. and se. Calif.; in Calif., in dense growth of saltbush (*Atriplex*) that remains in San Joaquin Valley; in Ariz., in open creosote bush deserts (Phillips *et al.*, 1964); one of least approachable of all birds; in driving across desert one may see long, slim, dull-colored bird running swiftly, with black tail cocked upward, dodging out of sight in low bushes; in desert in spring, male sings, from low bush, loud, rich, sweet song in early morning, tail hanging down, head thrown back, long curved bill open; sings again in evening coolness, sometimes into starry desert night (Bent, 1948); common call is a low, whistled *hew-eep.*

Feeding Habits: Scarcely known; one stomach held remains of small katydid and some ants.
Nest: Built by both sexes, prefers densest, most thickly branched cholla cactuses (*Opuntia*), also in sagebrush, paloverde, mesquite, saltbushes, thorny ocotillo, and ironweed trees; bulky nest of large mass of thorny twigs and sticks, inside of cup lined with plant down, leaves.
Eggs: Feb.–June; 2–4, usually 3, green-blue or light blue-green, finely spotted with pale brown.
Incubation: By both sexes; period of and age when young leave nest unknown.
Other Name: Desert thrasher.
Host to Cowbirds: One record, to bronzed cowbird (Friedmann, 1963).
Range: Resident but also some withdrawal in Ariz. southward in fall from northern parts of range; from c. Calif. to sw. Utah, south in w. and sw. Ariz., south to Baja Calif. and nw. Mexico.

Thrasher, long-billed, *Toxostoma longirostre* (tox-OSS-toh-mah lonj-ih-ROS-trih); genus name: *see* Thrasher, Bendire's; species name: from Lat. *longus*, long, and *rostrum*, beak. (Color ill., page 577.) Mexican thrasher that enters U.S. in s. Tex.; once thought to be a subspecies or race of brown thrasher, which it resembles; 10–12 in. long; upperparts darker and less reddish than upperparts of brown thrasher; has grayer sides of head and neck; *black* spots, or streaks, on breast, bill black, longer and more downcurved than brown thrasher's; abundant in mesquite and cactus chaparral and even commoner in dense forests of mesquite, ebony, palms, and dense undergrowth along resacas or stagnant watercourses in s. Tex. (Bent, 1948). The northern subspecies, or race, of this Mexican bird that enters Tex. was named *sennetti*, for George B. Sennett (1840–1900), extensive collector and student of birds of Tex. (Palmer, 1954). Male's song and behavior very much like brown thrasher's; call notes higher-pitched and sharper.

Feeding Habits: Eats mostly insects, spiders, centipedes, occasionally small frog, hackberries.
Nest: In thorny prickly pear, yucca, mesquite bush, in heart of tree or plant, 4–8 ft. above ground; of thorny twigs lined with grasses and straws.
Eggs: Apr.–June; 2–5, usually 4, blue-green or green-white, finely dotted with cinnamon.
Incubation: Period of and age when young leave nest unknown.
Other Name: Sennett's thrasher.
Flight Speed: Timed in Tex., 23 m.p.h. (Sooter, 1947).
Host to Cowbirds: Only one record of host to brown-headed cowbird (Friedmann, 1963); three of host to bronzed cowbird.
Range: Resident from s.-c. Tex. south to e.-c. Mexico.

Thrasher, Palmer's. *See* Thrasher, curve-billed.

Thrasher, red-vented. *See* Thrasher, crissal.

Thrasher, sage, *Oreoscoptes montanus* (oh-reh-oh-SKOP-teez mon-TAN-us); genus name: Lat., from Gr. *oros, oreos*, mountain, and *skoptes*, mocker; old common name was *mountain mockingbird;* species name: Lat., pertaining to mountains; but both misnomers because it is not a mockingbird or a bird of mountains. (Color ill., page 577.) W. Canada and w. and sw. U.S.; 8–9 in. long; brown-gray upperparts; short, straight, slender bill; heavily streaked breast; one short, one long, white wing bar; spots on outer tail feathers; eyes yellow, tail relatively short; smaller than robin and most thrushlike in appearance of all thrashers; small size, short tail, and striped breast distinguish it from other western thrashers; lives on sagebrush plains and limited almost entirely to semi-dry regions where grows sea of pale gray-green sage, *Artemisia tridentata;* though confined mainly to valleys and mesas, ranges in many places into foothills where sage gives way to junipers and mahogany woods up to 4,000–6,000 ft. elevation; withdraws southward in fall from northern parts of summer range; on nesting range, usually shy and difficult to approach; in early morning, male mounts to top of tall sage, pours out song equal to mockingbird's in sweetness, a warbling filled with tenderness (Bent, 1948); also sings in flight; utters alarm note of *chuck, chuck,* like that of blackbird.

Feeding Habits: Runs about over ground like robin, eats great numbers of grasshoppers, Mormon "crickets," alfalfa weevils, beetles, beet leafhoppers, caterpillars, ants, bees, wasps, also spiders; after nesting season visits ranches in summer and fall, where tame as it searches for berries and grapes in gardens, also likes wild currants, gooseberries, serviceberries.
Nest: Sometimes on ground but usually in low bushes, especially sage, also in greasewood, rabbit brush, from a few inches to several feet above ground; sometimes in higher thorny bushes; of coarse twigs, plant stems, shreds of sage leaves and bark, lined with fine rootlets, hairs, fur.
Eggs: Apr.–July; 4–7, commonly 4–5, deep blue or green-blue, boldly spotted with shades of brown.
Incubation: Period of and age of young when first fly unknown.

Other Names: Mountain mockingbird; sage mockingbird.
Flight Speed: Timed in w. U.S., 22–29 m.p.h. (Cottam *et al.,* 1942b).
Host to Cowbirds: One record, Utah (Friedmann, 1963).
Range: Nests from s.-c. B.C. southeast to n. and se. Wyo., and southward, east of Coast Ranges, to s.-c. Calif., west to Utah, south to n.-c. N.M., east to nw. Tex. and w. Okla.; also in sw. Sask.; winters south to Baja Calif. and n. Mexico.

Thrasher, Sennett's. *See* Thrasher, long-billed.

MOCK NEST
See Dummy Nest.

MOLLUSKS AND BIRDS
Practically all kinds of birds eat mollusks, despite the hard protective shells of many (McAtee, 1932b). Mollusks, most kinds of which live in water, include the familiar mussels, cockles, oysters, clams, chitons, tooth shells, periwinkles, abalones, conchs, whelks, snails, and limpets—all with an outer shell—and the soft-bodied slugs, cuttlefishes, squids, and octopuses (Parker and Haswell, 1928).

Ducks, geese, and swans eat mollusks—a single scaup duck examined by the U.S. Biological Survey, now the Fish and Wildlife Service, had 74 freshwater snails in its stomach (Henderson, 1933). The American flamingo apparently lives entirely on small mollusks (Allen, 1956a), and limpkins, rails, ibises, egrets, gulls, terns, grebes, coots, the red-throated loon, and black-necked stilt eat snails and other mollusks; phalaropes, knots, curlews, plovers, and other shorebirds also eat them (Henderson, 1933).

Seabirds—murrelets, auks, puffins, guillemots, and petrels—feed on mollusks, and albatrosses, shearwaters, and penguins eat cephalopod mollusks, among them the soft-bodied marine squids and cuttlefishes (Murphy, 1936); the internal calcareous plate in the cuttlefish is given cage birds as a source of lime salts (Buchsbaum, 1938).

The oystercatcher *(Haematopus),* which gets its name from its predilection for shellfish, has a powerful, laterally flattened bill that it uses to pry limpets and other mollusks from their places of attachment to rocks and other surfaces (Bent, 1929).

MOLLUSKS THAT DROWN BIRDS. The oystercatcher does not always catch mollusks with impunity. Baldwin (1946) reported an American oystercatcher that was the victim of a clam. In June 1939, on the Cape Romain National Wildlife Refuge, S.C., Baldwin found a dead adult on the beach with its bill still in the grip of a hard-shelled clam. The oystercatcher had presumably been probing the sand at low tide when the clam, just under the wet surface, closed its shell on the tip of the bird's bill, so securely that when the tide rose, the bird drowned. In England, Ginn (1973) reported a European oystercatcher that had been trapped and had died in the same way.

From a Long Is., N.Y., salt marsh, Post (1973) reported a young common tern that had drowned after a littleneck clam, *Venus mercenaria,* had closed its shell on the bird's bill, and he sighted a green heron flying over the marsh with a medium-sized clam attached to the toes of one foot. Earlier (1967) Post saw an American bittern in flight with one leg weighted down in the grip of a large mussel.

De Groot (1929) reported in Calif. clapper rails that had died after mussels had closed their shells on the feet and bills of these birds; kingfishers have also been caught in a similar way by mussels, presumably as the kingfishers plunged below the surface of the water. Cottam (1939) reported a common eider found dead with a blue mussel clamped on its tongue. *See also* Accidents.

The octopus, another mollusk, may also be a threat to birds. Hindwood (1964) reported that a small octopus in the waters off Tasmania had caught a crested tern and had wrapped its tentacles around the bird; another killed a crested tern on waters about 70 mi. north of Sydney, Australia, and an octopus caught a little penguin, *Euduptula minor,* at the Spit, Sydney Harbor. The birds were either resting on the water or feeding below it when attacked. *See* similar examples under Fishes and Birds.

OTHER BIRDS THAT EAT MOLLUSKS. Gulls, ravens, and crows eat the contents of hard-shelled mollusks along ocean beaches and have an interesting way of opening them. Alighting on the shore, they pick up in the bill a clam or mussel exposed by the lowered tide. Then they fly aloft over rocks, a hard road, moored boats, or a beach and drop the mollusk, thus usually cracking it open, after which they descend to pick out the meat from the broken shell. *See also* Egg-eating and Food and Feeding Habits.

Some birds eat snails, which belong to a group of mollusks called gastropods. The rare and vanishing Everglade kite, locally called snail hawk, apparently lives exclusively on the apple, green, or moon, snail, *Pomacea (Ampullaria) paludosa,* and the limpkin is reported to make this freshwater snail about 70% of its food (Cottam, 1936). Harper (1936) showed that the distribution of the limpkin in the South follows closely the distribution of the *Pomacea* snail, on which it feeds so frequently.

Besides waterfowl, the Everglade kite, and marsh birds, many land birds eat snails. Thrushes like them, and Terres (1962a), after watching a wood thrush break up a land snail on the hard surface of a woodland path, and eat part of it, saw the thrush dab a remaining piece among its feathers ("ant" with it—*see* Anting) before swallowing it. The European song thrush, *Turdus philomelos,* opens the shells of snails by hammering them on stones it uses as "anvils" (Hartley, 1964).

Aquatic snails have been found attached to the feathers of a white-faced glossy ibis (Roscoe, 1955), and Ramsden (1914) collected (shot) several migrating male bobolinks at Guantánamo, Cuba, in Apr. 1913, which had live snails among their feathers. The snails were *Succinea riisei,* "known from the islands of St. Croix and Porto Rico, but not from Cuba," thus demonstrating how snails might

MOLLUSKS AND BIRDS
One of the most specialized feeders, the rare Everglade kite lives exclusively on the green snail of the southern freshwater marshes. Holding the snail in its foot, the kite extracts the mollusk's soft body from the shell with its hooked bill and may swallow it whole.

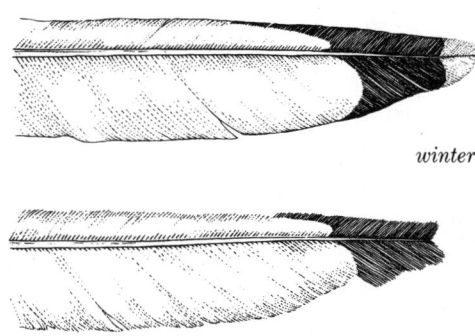

winter

summer

MOLTS AND MOLTING

Dark (melanin-bearing) feathers have been found to resist wear better than white ones, as shown by the condition of a gull's flight feather newly molted in winter and worn in early summer. The wing tips of many flying birds are black, which is advantageous because they get the most wear.

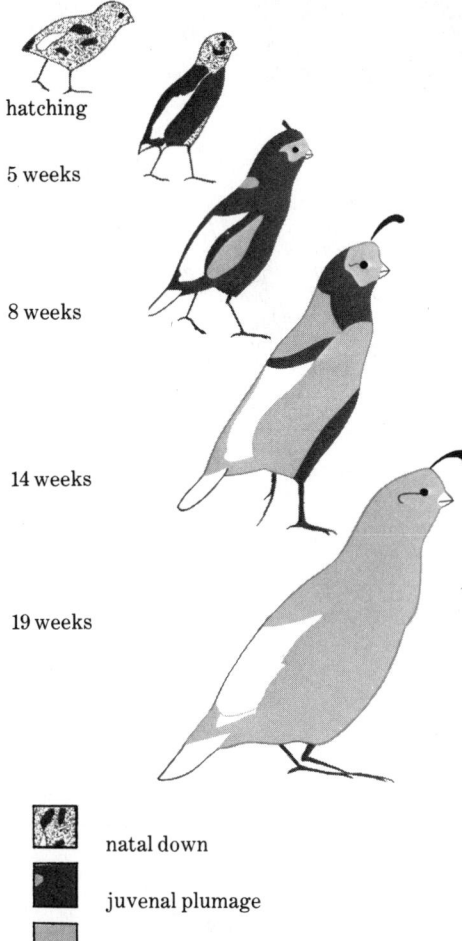

hatching

5 weeks

8 weeks

14 weeks

19 weeks

natal down

juvenal plumage

first basic (first winter) plumage

MOLTS AND MOLTING

The quail chick is down-covered at hatching but replaces its natal down with juvenal plumage within the first couple of weeks. After the first prebasic (postjuvenal) molt, beginning at about 7 weeks, the quail begins to grow its first basic (first winter) plumage. In its second spring after hatching, the young quail will molt into a first alternate (first nuptial) plumage, and after its second prebasic (first postnuptial) molt, it will have its adult plumage.

be distributed by birds. *See also* Phoresy; Lice; Hippoboscid Flies.

Other songbirds, such as starlings, thrashers, and mockingbirds, eat small mollusks. In Colo., large flocks of waxwings (unidentified as to species) were seen eating small aquatic snails at the edges of watercress swamps (Henderson, 1933). Carter (1961) made a remarkable observation in Fla. of a boat-tailed grackle diving underwater to catch a snail.

MOLLYMAUK
See Mallemuck.

MOLLYMOKE
See Mallemuck.

MOLTS AND MOLTING

The periodic replacement of feathers; the shedding of old feathers and the growth of new ones. All adult birds (and some others) molt at least once a year, many twice, a few three times, very rarely four times. Typically, all feathers are renewed in one of these periods—the *prebasic* (*postnuptial*) molt, generally occurring after breeding, at least in birds of north Temperate Zone. In the other periods of molting, only part of the feathering may be renewed, commonly on head and body, so that the wings and tail are retained from the preceding feather generation or plumage. The bird then is wearing feathers from two generations; together they comprise the total feathering. There are many variations. For example, in eagles and vultures, only part of the large wing feathers are renewed in one prebasic molt, the rest being retained until the next prebasic molt; possibly some are not renewed until yet another molting period. This is an adaptation for maintaining effective flying ability throughout the period of molting.

TIMING OF THE MOLT. Feathers make up 4–12% of a bird's body weight (Pettingill, 1972); therefore molting takes a lot of a bird's energy to replace them. For migratory N. American birds, the complete prebasic molt is adaptively timed, coming when food is still plentiful but after the energy demands of the breeding season are over and before the energy demands of migration have begun (Amadon, 1966a). The molt recurs about every 12 months in most Temperate Zone birds (Palmer, 1972).

FEATHER WEAR. Although feathers seem fragile, they are quite tough and resilient; however, the tips of a bird's feathers do gradually wear away or break off because of their often abrasive contact with the environment. Wing and tail feathers are especially worn away when they contact the ground, coarse grasses, or tree branches in taking off and alighting. Feathers may be worn away by flying through trees and shrubs while the bird is feeding itself or its young, or from entering and leaving its nest in tree or shrub or a nesting hole or burrow. Since a full-grown feather is a dead structure and cannot grow further, it must be replaced at molting time by a new one (*see* How Feathers Grow under Feather); however, if a complete feather is lost between molts, a new one begins at once to replace it. A change in the

brilliance or pattern of a bird's plumage may be brought about by a wearing away or breaking off of the tips of the feathers. The male house sparrow acquires its black bib of the breeding season through a gradual wearing-away of gray feathers in winter which hide it. Male bobolinks acquire their attractive black-and-white breeding plumage by a wearing-away of the yellowish tips of feathers that hide the black.

FUNCTION OF MOLTS. The main function of the prebasic molt is therefore to renew worn and faded plumage; it is a general, overall molt and usually is complete (Harrison, J. M., 1964a); that is, involves most feathers.

A good many species have a *prealternate* (formerly called *prenuptial*) molt during late winter or spring, usually a partial one. In egrets the breeding plumage involves only the growth of the long, flowing plumes used in courtship, sex recognition, and so on; otherwise the plumage is the same as in the non-breeding plumage. The plumes are shed when the breeding season is over.

In a few birds, the brighter spring plumage of the male, which functions in his courtship, territorial defense, etc., is revealed because of a wearing away or abrasion of the edges of the feathers (starling and snow bunting, for example) that grew in during the prebasic molt of the previous summer, or through a prealternate molt in spring (Palmer, 1972). The prealternate molt usually tends to make the males more prominent than the females (*see* Colors of Feathers), except in the phalaropes, for example, and a few other birds in which the females wear the brighter plumage. *See* polyandry under Sexual Relationships.

PATTERN OF THE MOLT. Within the same species the sequence or progression of the molt tends to be relatively the same; in many birds the body feathers are molted progressively in "waves," beginning on the head, face, and throat, and extending backward toward the tail. There is usually a symmetrical loss of feathers from both sides of the body, which balances feather loss, so that the bird still functions.

Most birds molt wing and tail feathers, so critical for flight, symmetrically and one or two pairs at a time. As a result of the gradual balanced loss of the flight feathers, most birds are able to fly at all times, although they are secretive and less active during the late-summer molt. Exceptions to the above are many aquatic or water birds—loons, grebes, anhingas, flamingos, ducks, geese, swans, most cranes and rails, and many in the auk family—which lose all their flight feathers at about the same time. This renders them flightless until the new wing feathers grow enough to allow them to fly (Berger, 1961). For a discussion of recent molt terminology, see Palmer (1972).

In some groups of birds, notably most male ducks, the full adult plumage at the end of the breeding season is replaced by a dull *basic* plumage (formerly called *eclipse* plumage), in which, for about 2 months, the males resemble the females. The basic plumage is then replaced by a fresh adult plumage which the male duck wears until the end of the breeding season of the following year. *See* Eclipse Plumage; *see also* introduction to Duck Family.

TWO OR MORE MOLTS A YEAR. This situation is very common in birds, as implied above under Molts and Molting. All the feathering is renewed during one of these molts (prebasic) and a lesser amount, typically head, body, and often tail feathers, in the other molt (prealternate). The latter molt usually produces the display feathering. Some New World sparrows and wrens that live in coarse grass have complete molts twice a year involving both their flight feathers and their body feathers (see Payne, 1972). A few species of ptarmigans in the arctic and alpine regions of the N. Hemisphere have three sets of feathers—a summer brown plumage, one mixed with brown and white in fall (and in spring), and white plumage in winter—all function to help conceal the bird against its seasonal background. *See* Seasonal Dimorphism; *also* Frightmolt.

WHAT INDUCES THE MOLT? Both inner and outer (environmental) stimuli are involved in bringing about the molt. Changes in the length of the day (influence of light) are important as influencing the action of the endocrine glands—especially the pituitary and thyroid glands (see details and discussion by Dorst, 1974, and by Assenmacher, 1958). Wolfson (1961) suggests that the *hypothalamus* (group of cell bodies or "centers" in the brain), connected with the pituitary gland, is probably involved. Pettingill (1972) states that the molt is, in part, governed by hormones, especially the sex hormones, and thus the timing of the complete prebasic molt may be connected with the stages of the reproductive cycle (*see* role of the thyroid under Endocrine Glands) and the beginning of the molt may depend on whether or not the bird bred successfully. Those birds that fail to breed in any given nesting season usually start molting early. According to Salomonsen (1938), there is evidence that temperature may be critical in determining the time of molt in the rock ptarmigan.

MONGREL
See Sandpiper, stilt, in Sandpiper Family.

MONK
See Parakeet, monk, in Parrot Family.

MONOCULAR VISION
See Eyes and Eyesight.

MONOGAMOUS
Having but one partner, mate, spouse; mating with but one of the opposite sex. Most species of birds are said to be monogamous; however, *see* details under Courtship; Sexual Relationships.

MONOPHAGOUS
(moe-NOFF-ah-gus). Term for a bird limited in its feeding to a single type of food; apparently this habit among animals is rare in nature. The Everglade kite is an example of it. *See* in Hawk Family. *See also* Euryphagous; Stenophagous; Food and Feeding Habits.

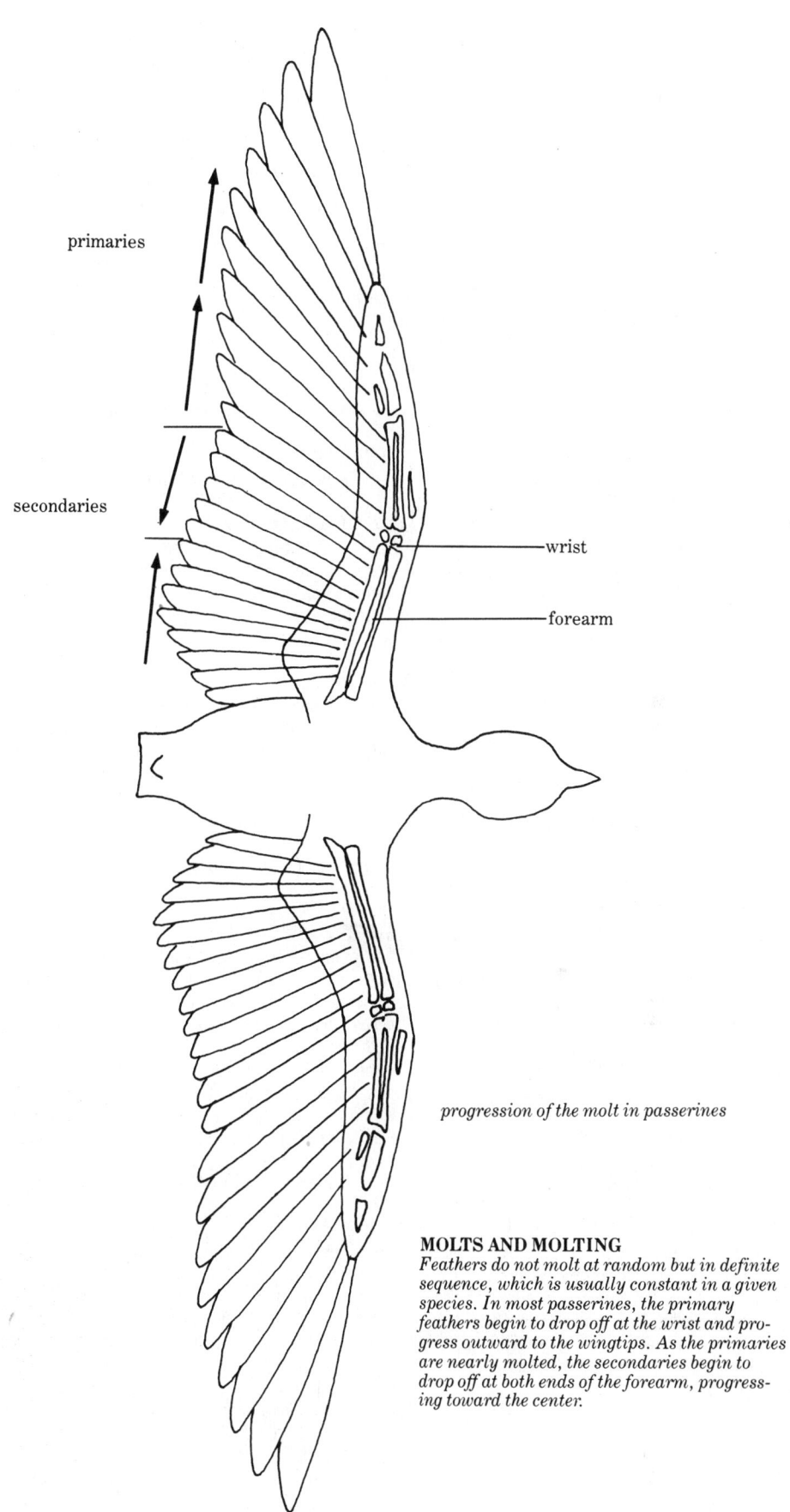

primaries

secondaries

wrist

forearm

progression of the molt in passerines

MOLTS AND MOLTING
Feathers do not molt at random but in definite sequence, which is usually constant in a given species. In most passerines, the primary feathers begin to drop off at the wrist and progress outward to the wingtips. As the primaries are nearly molted, the secondaries begin to drop off at both ends of the forearm, progressing toward the center.

MONOPHYLETIC (mon-ohfie-LET-ik) DESCENT

Term for the "one line of descent" origin of birds. According to Mayr (1942), it means "descendants of a single interbreeding group of populations, in other words, descendants of a single species."

It is believed that all birds are descended from a single parental form; however, because the earliest-known fossil birds were both those that could fly (*Archaeopteryx* and *Ichthyornis*) and those that were flightless (*Hesperornis* and *Diatryma,* for example), some paleontologists took different views. Some authors, notably Percy R. Lowe (1933; 1939), believed that birds had a diphyletic origin, that they are not from one, but from two lines of descent: (1) a line of ancestry from which our present-day penguins, ostriches, and other flightless species of birds are descended; and (2) another from which present-day flying birds are descended. Simpson's study (1946) of fossil penguins has established for most scientists that penguins were descended from flying ancestors, and Wetmore (1951a) concludes from studies of a fossil ostrichlike bird, *Eleuthornis,* that flightless groups of modern birds have come from ancestors that could fly. Today avian paleontologists believe that all birds evolved from a single ancestral stem, possibly one close to *Archaeopteryx. See* Origin of Birds and of Bird Flight under Fossil Birds; Geological Time Scale; Phylogenetic Relationship.

MONOTYPE

(MON-oh-type). The only representative of its group, as a single species of bird constituting the entire genus under which it is classified. *See* Genus. *Monotypic species* are those which do not have more than one recognizable race or subspecies; they consist of only a single subspecies (Mayr *et al.,* 1953). Examples are the osprey, gray catbird, ruby-throated hummingbird, chimney swift, Lewis' woodpecker, piñon jay, and bobolink. Most birds are *polytypic:* they vary and become subspecies, or "varieties," in different parts of the range of the species as a whole, owing to the influence of the different habitats, climate, or other causes (e.g., genes). *See* Subspecies. According to Mayr (1951), about 60–80% of temperate-zone birds are polytypic; in New Guinea, about 80% of all species are polytypic.

MONUMENTS TO BIRDS

Several have been erected to N. American birds, one (a plaque) commemorating the extinct passenger pigeon (*see* in Pigeon Family) in Wyalusing State Park, Wisc. Another, the Gull Monument in Salt Lake City, Utah, commemorates the California gull for its services during the great Mormon cricket plague of 1848. *See* account under Economic Ornithology. A third, the world's first monument to a songbird, the Kirtland's warbler, was unveiled at Mio, Mich., in the heartland of the limited nesting range of this species, on July 27, 1963. The dedicatory ceremony, featuring an address by Roger Tory Peterson, artist and ornithologist, was conducted during the fourth annual Great Lakes Forestry exposition in Mio. The 4-ft.-high stone monument of the Kirtland's warbler, erected on the lawn of the Oscoda County Courthouse in Mio, was sculptured by Leo Nelson of Kalkaska, Mich. A bronze plaque on the statue states that Mio, the place of dedication, is the main area of the nesting range of the Kirtland's, one of the rarest warblers in N. America. See issues of the *Bay City Times,* June 1, 1963, and July 29, 1963. *See also* Rare and Threatened Species.

MOON-WATCHING

See Behavior of Nocturnal Migrants under Migration.

MOOSE BIRD

One of common names for the gray jay (*see* in Crow Family) from habit of perching on moose; *see also* relationship under Whiskey Jack.

MORPH

See discussion of under Color Phase.

MORPHOLOGY

(more-FOL-oh-jih). The science of form or shape; term used in ornithology to cover all external characters of birds, including coloration; the term now includes also the study of internal characters, or anatomy. *See* Anatomy.

The classification of birds (*see* Classification) is based chiefly on their morphology (including that of species known only from fossils); the problem is to distinguish true resemblances, indicating a common descent in evolution, from superficial or functional resemblances due to parallel evolution (in unrelated groups), or convergent evolution (similar adaptations, also in unrelated groups). *See* discussion of this under Convergent Evolution and Phylogenetic Relationship.

MORTALITY

See some discussion of under Age; *also* Nesting Success and Failure under Nests and Nesting. For detailed discussions of the death rates (mathematics of) and causes in various groups and species of birds, see especially Lack (1954; 1964a; 1966), and the technical discussion on mortality by von Haartman (1971). For a popular account, see in Pettingill (1972). For some causes of mortality, *see* under Accidents; Diseases; Migration; Parasite; Predation; Weather; and in the biographies of each bird.

It is difficult to determine natural death in birds because so few are found at the time of their dying. Anecdotal evidence supplied by a few observers shows that birds apparently do die naturally—that is, without being killed by hawk, owl, or other predator—and apparently while in full flight or in some other normal activity. Whether death came suddenly in following examples, because of heart attack as in man or as a result of some wasting infection(*see* especially Avian Tuberculosis), is not known because the birds were not preserved for pathological examination. Most ornithologists agree that observing the natural end of a bird's life is rare.

According to Huey (1924), he had been observing birds for 17 years before seeing one die of other than external causes. At 6:30 A.M. on Apr. 4, 1924, as he sat quietly skinning birds (*see* Bird Skins) on his porch in San Diego, he heard the loud chipping notes of an Audubon's warbler which sounded like it was in distress; after searching a nearby thicket, he was surprised to see a female Audubon's warbler climbing and fluttering upward on the vertical stem of a rosebush. The bird continued to mount, chipping loudly, rose into the air, circled until about 10 ft. above the ground then suddenly closed its wings and fell dead. Huey examined the bird carefully, and found no external injuries; after skinning it, he found no apparent disorder or infection in its internal organs; he concluded that it had died a natural death.

Henry M. Stevenson (1941) cited Huey's unusual observation and reported a similar experience with a fox sparrow. He had flushed the sparrow from unusually close range in an apple orchard on Long Is., N.Y. It perched on a limb of a large tree, with every appearance of good health, but a few seconds later, it dropped into the grass under the tree, head foremost. Stevenson found it lying on the turf, trembling; it died a few seconds later. He could find no external parasites on the bird; he reported that freezing or starvation was unlikely at the time, as the ground was bare of snow and food was available. Stevenson concluded that aside from these two records (Huey's and his own) he could find no records of a bird's death from causes presumed natural.

In January 1951, Capt. Joseph Tilton, superintendent of Phipps Estate, Island Beach, N.J., watched a herring gull soaring above the beach; it suddenly folded its wings and fell to the sand. When Tilton picked it up, the gull was dead, possibly from a heart attack or "other natural cause" (Terres, 1936–1970).

MOSQUITOES AND BIRDS.

See Mosquitoes and Birds under Insects and Birds.

MOTACILLIDAE

See Pipit Family.

MOTHER CAREY'S CHICKENS

Name of seafaring men for the storm-petrels (*see* in Storm-petrel Family). The name Mother Carey (or Cary) has been anglicized by sailors from *Mater cara,* said to be an epithet of the Virgin Mary, who was regarded as a protector of sailors. Storm-petrels were thought by superstitious people to be "soul birds." Fishermen in Brittany say that skippers who treat their crews badly are condemned forever to flutter over the seas as storm-petrels. Others say that these birds are the souls of drowned sailors seeking the prayers of the living, or devil birds flitting over the corpses of the lost (Armstrong, 1958).

In fact, they are small, harmless seabirds that belong to all oceans and all zones (Murphy, 1936). *See also* Birds as Weather Prophets under Folklore.

MOTMOT FAMILY

See Coraciiformes.

MOUNT

In museum parlance, to prepare a bird skin (*see* Bird Skins) or skeleton and set it up in a natural position. *See* Collections. In falconry, a falcon is said to *mount* as it ascends higher and higher in the air; also to "ring up" (Wood and Fyffe, 1943). *See* Falconry.

MOUNTAIN ACCENTOR

See in Hedge Sparrow Family.

MOUSE HAWK

Any of the large, soaring N. American hawks of the genus *Buteo*. They are the red-tailed hawk, red-shouldered hawk, Swainson's hawk, rough-legged hawk, and ferruginous hawk. A smaller one of this group is the broad-winged hawk. Almost anywhere in the U.S., a large hawk sitting on a conspicuous perch (usually a dead tree), or soaring about in large circles in the sky, is likely to be a "mouse hawk," or a *Buteo*. The term "mouse hawk" comes from the general preference of these hawks for mice, as shown by studies of their food habits. They have broad, fanned-out tails in flight, and broad wings, the undersides of which show a dark marking at the "wrist" of the wing as they soar overhead. *See* Food and Feeding Habits; *also* Flight Patterns.

MOUTH

or BUCCAL CAVITY. The internal area from the bill to the pharynx of a bird, including the tongue (*see* Tongue) and a hard palate (roof of mouth), which becomes continuous with the soft roof of the pharynx at the rear of the mouth. In rear of the palate there is usually an elongate, or long, depression that corresponds to the shape of the bird's tongue (Farner, 1960). See details of palate in Bellairs (1964a).

Most birds do not have a soft palate; in fact, its absence in most birds and beaklike hardness are among peculiarities of the bird mouth (Coues, 1884); pigeons have a softer mouth condition, however, that enables them to swallow successive gulps of water without lifting the head as most birds do (Pettingill, 1956). *See* drinking under Swallowing.

The palate and the roof of the pharynx in birds usually have tiny backward-pointing protuberances (Farner, 1960); the soft floor of the mouth is the mucous membrane and skin between the jaws, with muscles. In some birds (pelicans, for example), the floor of the mouth is a large pouch capable of enormous dilation (Coues, 1884).

In seed-eating birds, the soft parts of mouth are well supplied with relatively small mucous glands that moisten dry food just before the bird swallows. In aquatic birds, mucous glands in the mouth are usually scanty, and pelicans have none. Many birds, especially shorebirds, moisten their food in water before swallowing it. *See* discussion under Swallowing.

The gray-crowned rosy finches have a pair of food-carrying pouches in the mouth that enable them to carry extra food to young (Miller, 1941), and the pine grosbeak has mouth pouches that are almost identical to those in the gray-crowned rosy finch (French, 1954). *See* Young and Their Care; *also* Crop.

The distribution and number of taste buds in the mouths of birds vary greatly—generally they are most numerous in the soft part of the palate and may be beneath the tongue and scattered in places about the *salivary glands;* however, one investigator was unable to find taste buds in the domestic chicken (Farner, 1960), although free nerve endings exist there. *See* details under Taste.

Salivary glands are poorly developed in most birds, are usually in the pharynx in those that have them; are abundant, however, in seed-eaters, in which they even exude a starch-digesting enzyme. Primary function of salivary glands and saliva is to provide moisture and lubrication for food (Farner, 1960). Antony (1920) has written extensively of salivary glands in their adaptations in birds to their various kinds of foods—in general, birds that eat relatively slippery foods (for example, herons, which eat frogs or fishes) have poorly developed salivary glands; ducks and geese, whose usual food has little lubrication, have fully developed salivary glands, as do seed-eating, insect-eating, and many omnivorous species that eat a wide variety of foods.

In woodpeckers, there is a large distinctive salivary gland of two sections whose ducts open beneath the tongue. The rearmost one produces an extremely sticky fluid that characteristically coats the tongues of woodpeckers (Farner, 1960) and makes insects get stuck there (J. G. Harrison, 1964b). The alkaline secretions of the unusually large salivary glands of the yellow-shafted (common) flicker are thought to neutralize the formic acid of the ants that it eats so frequently.

Bock (1961) discovered in the gray jay (and in other jays of the same genus) a pair of woodpecker-sized, mucous-secreting mandibular glands. The glands are unique in the Corvidae (Crow Family) and are probably unique in passerines, or songbirds. Sticky mucus from these glands apparently coats the tongue of the gray jay and makes it adherent while probing into crevices for insects and under scales of cones for seeds during winter when other foods are scarce. *See* discussion under Tongue. Bock believes these mouth glands are probably a basic feeding adaptation and a critical innovation that has permitted a new feeding development in the gray jay and its invasion into a new ecological niche. Further research has shown that this secretion is used by gray jays to make food particles stick together which they attach to twigs as food stores. *See* Ecological Niche.

Some swifts have probably the most remarkable salivary glands of any birds in the world. Many, including the N. American chimney swift, use the sticky secretions from their salivary glands to glue their nests together and to attach them inside chimneys, hollow trees, or on walls of caves. Some of the swiftlets of the genus *Collicalia* in the East Indies build nests entirely of saliva from their greatly enlarged salivary glands, which are used in the Orient to make "bird's nest soup." The glands enlarge in the breeding season, just as the testes do, then decrease to usual size after the nesting season is over.

According to Rand (1955), the gluelike material as it comes from the mouth of a swiftlet resembles a saturated solution of gum arabic. It is quite viscid and if a strand drawn out of a swiftlet's mouth is rotated on a rod, one can wind up a thread of saliva until the salivary glands of the bird are emptied. The material dries quickly and is the substance of which the nest is made. *See* in Swift Family.

According to Stresemann (1927–34), the European house martin, *Delichon urbica*, a white-bellied, green-backed swallow resembling the N. American tree swallow, builds its nest of mud mixed with saliva, and its salivary glands are twice as large in nest-building time as later in summer. This is of special interest to scientists, as it suggests possible convergent evolution (*see* Convergent Evolution) between swifts and swallows. Antony (1920) noted the increase in size of these glands in the house martin during the breeding season.

MUD DUCK

See Coot, American, in Rail Family.

MUD HEN

Local name for rails, gallinules, and coots in Rail Family; also for the American bittern in Heron Family.

MUDLARK

See Meadowlark, eastern, in Troupial Family.

MUD-PEEP

See Sandpiper, least, in Sandpiper Family.

MURRE

See in Auk Family.

MURRELET

See in Auk Family.

MURRELET, THE

A publication. *See* Ornithological Periodicals.

MUSCICAPIDAE

See Flycatcher—Old World Flycatcher Family.

MUSCOVY

(MUS-koh-vih). A duck native from Mexico to Brazil. The name is thought to be a corruption of "musk duck"; *see*, however, under Domestication and in Duck Family.

MUSCULAR SYSTEM

Muscles are bundles or sheets of muscle cells called muscle fibers. They are held together and surrounded by *fascia* (FASH-ih-ah; pl.: *fasciae*—FASH-ih-ee), which are sheets of connective tissue. According to Berger (1961), about 175 different muscles, most of which are paired, have been described in birds.

There are three muscle types: (1) *Skeletal* (striated muscle), so named because at least one end attaches to one or more bones of the skeleton. They are under the conscious control of the bird in the movements of its wings, legs, etc., and therefore are called *voluntary muscles*. These contract, and move the bones to which they are attached, but only when nerve impulses controlled by the bird direct them to do so. (2) *Smooth muscle fibers*, which are long spindle-shaped cells containing a single nucleus. Because they are under the control of the autonomic nervous system, which controls

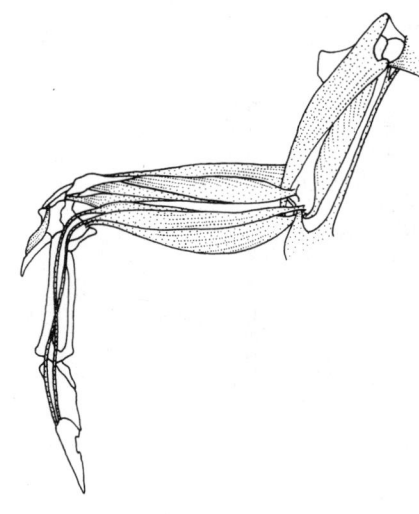

ventral view of pigeon's wing muscles.

MUSCULAR SYSTEM
During flight, while a bird's wing is being raised and lowered by the supracoracoideus and pectoralis muscles, other muscles in the wing itself act to flex or extend the joints of the wing, to tilt the wing forward or backward, or to change the position of the alula and other flight feathers.

such actions as circulation or digestion, they are called *involuntary muscles.* An example of them is the skin muscles that attach to all the contour feather follicles; the smooth muscles are so attached to these that on proper stimulation of the nervous system, the bird can raise or depress its feathers or move them laterally (Welty, 1962). *See* Feather Muscles under Feather. (3) *Cardiac* (heart) *muscle* is similar to skeletal muscle in that both have striations, but cardiac muscle, which has its own inner rhythmicity, can contract, thus keeping the heart beating, without stimulation of the nervous system (Berger, 1961).

"A muscle can only pull; it cannot push" (Berger, 1961). For each pair or group of muscles that produces a certain movement—for example, bending or drawing in the wing by contracting the muscles—another pair or group of muscles on the other side of the bones can produce the opposite movement when the bird extends or straightens its wing.

According to Berger (1961), the different muscles of birds have been grouped for convenience of study as follows: "muscles of the skull and jaws; orbit and ear; tongue, trachea, and syrinx; upper limb (wing); lower limb (leg); vertebral column; and body wall." Four of these muscle groups have been used in the classification of birds—syrinx, jaws, and the two limbs. *See* Classification. For a detailed illustrated chapter on the muscles of birds, see especially Berger (1960) and the volume by George and Berger (1966); see also general discussions by Welty (1962; 1975); Wallace (1963); Pettingill (1972); Dorst (1974).

MUSKEG
Of Algonquian N. American Indian origin; Crees called it *maskek;* Ojibways, *mashkig;* usually defined as a sphagnum bog with tussocks of sedges or other acid-tolerant plants; a bog is a low and wet small marsh which lacks drainage; however, Hanson and Smith (1950), in their waterfowl studies in Arctic Canada, describe five distinct types of muskeg, as follows, with photographs to illustrate them: (1) well-timbered muskeg, (2) open muskeg, (3) lakeland muskeg, (4) pothole muskeg, and (5) "smallpox" (pocked) muskeg.

MUSSELS AND BIRDS
See Mollusks and Birds.

MUTATION
Changes in the genetic material that are the basis for variations in population of organisms, and thus the cause of new hereditary types. Genes are immensely complex protein molecules. A mutation, or change, in a gene causes changes in those characters of a bird's offspring controlled by that gene. Such results of a mutation may be very evident—for example, albinism (*see* Albinism)—or may be hidden and subtle, but, perhaps even more important, some are lethal. See Dobzhansky (1961); also Kalmus and Crump (1948); Cain (1964).

Although mutations are unpredictable, the same gene tends to occasionally produce the same mutation (albinism again being an example). Also, some agents—for example, X rays—will increase the frequency of mutation. Each species contains a reservoir of previous mutations (within its genes), and within the fertilized egg (*see* Fertilization) these can recombine in endless ways with those of the partners, producing different results in subsequent generations. Thus there is a pool of variability upon which the environment acts to select individuals and characteristics best suited to survive in a given set of environmental conditions. *See* Species; Subspecies.

MUTTONBIRD
See Shearwater, short-tailed, in Shearwater Family.

MUTUAL PREENING
Also called *allopreening. See* discussion under Preening.

MYCOSIS
(my-KOH-sis). Any disease caused by an infestation by a fungus. *See* fungus diseases under Diseases.

MYNA
or MYNAH. *See* in Starling Family; also Mimicry (vocal).

MYOGLOBIN
(my-oh-GLOW-bin). Molecular equivalent in the muscles to the hemoglobin in the blood. It is the respiratory pigment of the corpuscles of all vertebrate animals. *See* Vertebrate. Physiologically, myoglobin acts to store oxygen (Millikan, 1939) and to facilitate diffusion of oxygen between blood and muscle cells (Prosser and Brown, 1962). *See* discussion of its function in Flight Muscles under Flight.

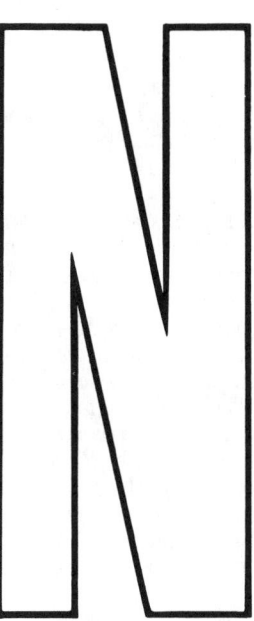

N

NAIL

or UNGUIS. Term for the horny tip on the upper mandible (maxilla) of ducks, geese, and swans. *See* Bill.

NAME CHANGES

See discussion under Names and Naming.

NAMES AND NAMING

The scientific names of birds and of other animals are given them by scientists (professional taxonomists) in compliance with approved standards that go back to the publication in 1758 of the 10th ed. of Carl Linnaeus' *Systema Naturae. See* Linnaeus. The first International Zoological Congress met in Paris in 1889; at the third meeting in 1895, an International Commission on Zoological Nomenclature (*see* Nomenclature) was appointed and still functions in classifying and interpreting rules and procedures for naming animals.

The naming of birds and other animals is a highly technical procedure, but, briefly, the rules are that a genus name can be used only once within the animal kingdom. For example, if the genus name for the marsh hawk, *Circus* (Lat. for a kind of hawk, and from its circling in the air) has been applied first to the bird, as it has been in this example, then a new genus of spiders, insects, salamanders, or some other group of animals cannot later be given the same genus name.

The same species name, however, may be used repeatedly for birds of different genera (for example, *passerina,* for sparrowlike, has been given to the chipping sparrow, *Spizella passerina;* also to the ground dove, *Columbina passerina*) but may not be used twice within the same genus. Using the same species name in closely allied genera of birds is not advisable because if the two genera are subsequently combined, one of the bird species will need to be renamed. Because of the law of priority (the earliest publication of a scientific name is the one that stands) the species name cannot be changed if the name was correctly applied (procedurally) to the bird in the first place (Wallace, 1955). *See* an interesting example of the change of the scientific name of the Franklin's gull, but not of its common name, in biography of Franklin's gull (*see also* Ross' gull) in Gull Family. See also discussion in Ch. 11, "The Principle of Priority," in Mayr *et al.,* 1953; *see also* Binomial Nomenclature.

In the U.S., a Committee on Classification and Nomenclature of the American Ornithologists' Union—a special committee of experts on the taxonomy of birds—passes judgment on the names, both scientific and common, for N. American birds (see, for example, American Ornithologists' Union, 1973). It periodically publishes the A.O.U. *Check-list of North American Birds,* a volume that lists orders, families, species, and subspecies of birds, in the sequence of their relationships, north of Mexico—for example, in its 1957 (5th) ed. (*see* North America, for its defined limits); however, the forthcoming 6th ed. will include Mexico and parts of Middle, or Central, America. The volume also gives the ranges, or distribution, of each species and subspecies of bird, with details of their nesting and wintering ranges.

nail

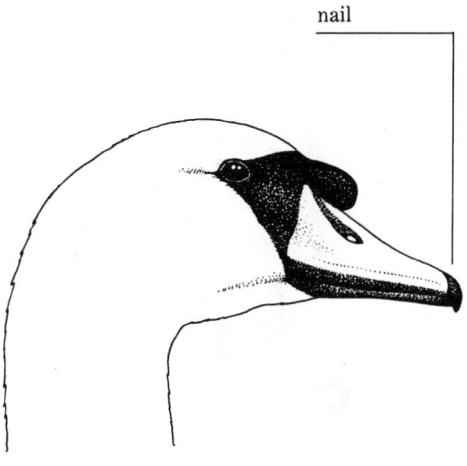

NAIL
The hard, horny nail on the soft upper mandible of the mute swan enables it to pull up aquatic plants, which are its main diet and nest-building material.

Semipalmated plover

NATAL DOWN

Most bird books, popular and scientific, and writers in ornithology follow it for spelling, for classification, and for authoritative common and scientific names.

COMMON NAMES OF BIRDS. Local or regional bird names have usually been given to birds by settlers and farmers, and by native tribes, though many of the common names were given to birds by the early ornithologists and others who studied them scientifically. Some names of birds were derived from folklore about them. *See* Folklore. For example, nightjars in Europe (similar to the American nighthawk) were called goatsuckers because many European country people thought that these birds sucked milk from their goats. This belief goes back to Aristotle. The nightjar (so called because of its loud, rapid churring calls at night) often sweeps low in its flight over grazing herds of goats, but instead of seeking milk from them, it is catching insects that are stirred up by the grazing animals. *See* other examples under Autolycism.

Other common, or vernacular, names were given to birds because of the fancied name or word that they utter. To many people, the call of the rufous-sided towhee (also called che-wink) is distinctly *To-whee!* or *Che-wink!;* the bobwhite quail whistles *Bob-WHITE!;* and the killdeer, chickadee, dickcissel, phoebe, whip-poor-will, and other birds call out a fancied word or phrase that has given them their common names. *See* Songs and Singing. Many common names of birds commemorate their discoverers—the persons who first collected (shot, trapped, or netted) the birds; others for the taxonomists who scientifically described and named them; and so on (see Mayr *et al.,* 1953, and Skutch, 1950a).

SCIENTIFIC NAMES OF BIRDS. The early ornithologists of the Old World named the birds with long descriptive Latin sentences until Carl Linnaeus originated his simplified system of giving each animal and plant two names only— a genus name and a species name. The names are Latin, or taken from Greek or other languages with Latinized endings. No matter how many common or local names a bird may have, it has only one scientific name, by which it can be recognized anywhere in the world. *See* Binomial Nomenclature.

Because many species of birds have geographical races, called subspecies, many of them have three parts to their scientific names —the genus name, the species name, and subspecies name. *See* Classification; *also* Genus; Species; Subspecies.

CHOICE OF A GENUS NAME. In naming a genus of birds (or of other animals), zoologists usually decide on one or more distinctive features, either morphological (form) or biological (life), of the new genus of birds to be named, then select several Greek words or combine forms which represent or describe these characteristics. They may also choose a mythological or heroic name, a proper name used by the ancients, the name of some person in ornithology, or zoology generally, whom they wish to commemorate (and even a loved one—*see* Zenaida dove and

Grace's warbler, for example), the name of a ship (possibly one used on an expedition during which the new genus of birds was discovered), and so on. The genus name is a single word, and is customarily a Latin word of Greek origin (Mayr *et al.,* 1953).

CHOICE OF A SPECIES AND A SUBSPECIES NAME. In choosing a name for a species of bird, taxonomists may use a Latin adjective, a noun, or substantive, a participle, or a compound word; or they may use a descriptive name, a geographical name, an ecological one, or a patronymic, in which a bird is named for a person. The same rules apply to a choice of a subspecies name; however, it must be coordinate with the species name (Mayr *et al.,* 1953). In choosing and using these names properly, whether they are adjectives, nouns, participles, compound words, and so on, zoologists are guided by certain simple rules of Latin grammar.

BIRDS NAMED FOR PEOPLE. These are usually given to honor those who have done outstanding work in ornithology. Often a bird previously unknown to science is named for the man who collected it. For example, Townsend's solitaire, *Myadestes townsendi* (*see* in Thrush Family), was collected by John K. Townsend near Astoria, Ore., in the 1830s. He sent it, as he had done with a number of birds new to science that were unnamed, to John James Audubon, who named this particular species *townsendi,* to honor the man who had collected it (Coues, 1882).

When a scientist gives a bird a specific, or species, name (in this case *townsendi*) to honor some person, the rule for naming it is as follows: in forming the scientific name, the person's surname (here, Townsend) is considered the stem of a Latin noun, even though the name may have a true Latin form. The ending in the masculine singular is *-i* (thus *townsendi*— TOWN-send-eye) and the name is written in lowercase according to the rules established by the American Ornithologists' Union in 1885. The masculine plural ending is *-orum,* as in *Icterus parisorum,* an oriole named by Charles Lucien Bonaparte for the Paris brothers, whose labors in collecting birds in Mexico have been commemorated in the scientific name of this bird, commonly called Scott's oriole.

In the feminine singular, names end in *-ae*— for example, *Dendroica graciae,* Grace's warbler—and in the feminine plural, in *-arum.* Scientists call these patronymic names and ordinarily "they are considered as memorials to, or as recognition for, the efforts of individual scientists" (Mayr *et al.,* 1953).

COMMON NAMES THAT HONOR PEOPLE. In the A.O.U. *Check-list of North American Birds* (5th ed., 1957), about 98 of the approximately 796 species listed (*see* discussion in Recent Period under Geological Time Scale) have *common* names that commemorate people. Some of the familiar ones are Anna's hummingbird, Audubon's warbler, Baird's sandpiper, Bullock's oriole, Clark's nutcracker, Forster's tern, Lewis' woodpecker, Say's flycatcher, and Steller's jay. In most of these, the personal name appears in both the scientific and the common name; in others, the personal name is still preserved in the common name, but the scientific name may have been changed because a prior name had been given the bird by an earlier scientist. *See,* for example, Franklin's gull in Gull Family. Palmer (1928) reported that the names of Lewis and Clark, Bullock, Say, and Steller were associated with early explorations from the northwest coast of N. America to Mexico, and that it is fitting that such field workers who endured the hardships of exploration in the early days should have their names associated with some of the most conspicuous N. American birds; while such men were not primarily ornithologists, they encouraged others and collected specimens of the birds named for them in the course of their work.

BIRDS NAMED FOR STATES. At least 12 birds have been named (common name) for states of the U.S. They are: Arizona woodpecker, California gull, California quail, California thrasher, Carolina chickadee (named for S.C.), Connecticut warbler, Kentucky warbler, Louisiana heron, Louisiana waterthrush, Mississippi kite, Oregon junco, and Tennessee warbler. *See also* State Bird; National Bird.

NAPE
The back part of the neck. In a bird, the nape is the part of the hind neck just below the occiput, or back part of the head. *See* Topography.

NARIS
(NAY-ris; pl.: *nares*—NAY-reez). *See* Nostrils.

NASAL CAVITIES
See Nostrils.

NASAL GLAND
See Nostrils.

NATAL DOWN
First coat of feathers worn by a bird (*see* Feather). A young bird may have natal down upon hatching or it may develop it later. *See* discussion under Altricial. The downy first coat of feathers usually lasts for a short time—up to several weeks in some species, for example hawks and owls—but may be worn for a year by the young of the king penguin, *Aptenodytes patagonicus,* but in this case there are two coats of down, one following the other. Other birds also have at least two successive coats of down; in some—peregrine falcon and vultures, for example—three coats of down appear in early life. *See* related discussion under Metabolism. The natal down is lost completely when it is pushed out by the incoming feathers of the juvenal plumage during the postnatal (prejuvenal) molt. *See* Nestling; Fledgling; Molts and Molting.

In many downy young birds, especially of precocious species such as the young of plovers, which may leave the nest almost immediately after hatching, the down is so patterned and colored that it simulates the young bird's background and is of protective value. *See* Colors of Feathers; Young and Their Care.

Some birds—woodpeckers, kingfishers, swifts, and hummingbirds—are hatched com-

pletely naked and usually go directly into the juvenal plumage without an apparent downy state. Baby ducks, chickens, quail, pheasants, and other gallinaceous birds are examples of those hatched with a complete covering of down. A few birds, for example the megapodes (*see* Megapode), pass through the downy stage within the egg itself. When they hatch they are already molted into the juvenal plumage and are able to fly.

NATIONAL AUDUBON SOCIETY
Named for John James Audubon, painter of birds and 19th-century naturalist; founded on Jan. 30, 1905, in New York City as the National Association of Audubon Societies for the Protection of Wild Birds and Other Animals, Inc., with the name later changed to the National Audubon Society. It is one of the largest nonprofit conservation organizations in the world, with many branches and affiliates, and a national and international membership open to anyone interested in supporting its work. The society publishes *Audubon* (originally *Bird-Lore* and then *Audubon Magazine*) and *American Birds* (formerly called *Audubon Field Notes*) (*see* Ornithological Periodicals), regular news releases, and the *Audubon Leader,* a special newsletter guide to conservation issues and problems. Home office is at 950 Third Avenue, New York, N.Y. 10022. For a concise history of the Audubon Society, see Buchheister and Graham (1973); for a history of *Audubon* magazine, see Peterson (1973).

NATIONAL BIRD
The bald eagle, of the Great Seal of the United States, was officially adopted as our national emblem by act of Congress, June 20, 1782. According to Morris (1960), professor of history, Columbia University, the story of choosing the national emblem began on July 4, 1776. On that day the Declaration of Independence had just been adopted, and Congress chose Benjamin Franklin, John Adams, and Thomas Jefferson as a committee to pick a seal.

The final design was by William Barton, a private citizen of Philadelphia, who combined some skill in drawing with a knowledge of heraldry, was and modified by Charles Thomson, a Philadelphian, and Secretary of Congress. They made the bald eagle the central figure on the seal, with a bundle of arrows, emblematic of war power, clutched in its left foot, and in the right, an olive branch.

Benjamin Franklin did not like the choice of the bald eagle as the national symbol; he thought it "a bird of bad moral character . . . too lazy to fish for himself," often robbing the "fishing-hawk" (osprey) of its prey. He preferred the wild turkey, also a native American, which, even though "vain and silly," was a bird of great courage. See the spirited defense of the bald eagle as our national symbol by the American zoologist and scholar Francis Hobart Herrick, and the history of its choice, in Evans (1966).

The bald eagle was given special protection by Congress on June 8, 1940, when Congress passed the Protection of the Bald Eagle Act. *See* Legal Protection; *also* State Birds.

Green-winged teal

Ruffed grouse

NATAL DOWN
The natal down of ground-nesting birds such as grouse, ducks, and plovers is protectively patterned, enabling these nidifugous ("nest-fleeing") chicks to blend into their respective habitats.

NECTAR AND BIRDS
Hummingbirds are highly adapted to nectar—feeding with long bills and grooved tongues designed for reaching into flowers. The hovering flight of hummingbirds is another adaptation for this mode of life.

NATURAL DEATH.
See under Mortality.

NATURAL HISTORY
A publication. *See* Ornithological Periodicals.

NATURALIZED BIRDS
See Introduced Birds.

NATURAL REGIONS
See Faunal Regions.

NATURAL SELECTION
The process whereby those individual birds (also other animals, and plants) that are most fit, or best suited to their habitat or ecological niche through competition for food, space, shelter, mates, etc., are "selected"—that is, they survive and pass on to their descendants their superior qualities. Those that are unfit, or less fit, perish without issue or with fewer offspring. The result of natural selection is *evolution*, and it is the key process in evolution as set forth by Darwin (see biography of Darwin by Gray, 1961), and now accepted by biologists generally. See especially discussion by Dodson (1961). Natural selection brings about, of course, only an average result. Some unfit individuals will get by; some superior ones will succumb or fail to leave offspring. The net effect is change with time in the direction of greater fitness and increased adaptation to the environment in the broadest sense, whether the environment is stable or changing.

NAVIGATION
See How Do Birds Find Their Way? under Migration; *see also* Echolocation; Homing.

NEARCTIC REGION
A faunal region (*see* Faunal Regions) considered by some zoogeographers to include all of N. America north of the tropics. It does not coincide along its complex southern boundaries with N. America as delineated by the A.O.U. *Check-list* (1957). *See* North America. Nearctic birds include about 650 species of some 65 families that nest in the region, and only 1 family, the wren-tits (Chamaeidae), is endemic (Pettingill, 1972).

About 41 of the 65 families are widely distributed (Darlington, 1957) and include grebes, loons, pelicans (local), hawks and New World vultures, herons, ducks, quails, and grouse, turkeys (almost exclusively Nearctic), cuckoos, cranes, rails, plovers and sandpipers, gulls, pigeons, owls, goatsuckers, kingfishers, swifts, hummingbirds, woodpeckers, tyrant flycatchers, larks, swallows, thrushes and mockingbirds, wrens, pipits, shrikes, waxwings, creepers, nuthatches, titmice and chickadees, vireos, wood warblers, tanagers, cardinals, and finches, troupials (orioles, blackbirds, etc.), and crows and jays.

Ten additional families enter the southern edge of the Nearctic Region from the tropics, and reach to or near the southern edge of the U.S.—ibises, the woodstork, a flamingo, a cracid (the chachalaca), the limpkin, a jacana, parrots, a trogon, a motmot (to n. Mexico), and a cotinga (the rose-throated becard).

Nearctic birds are a mixture of Old World

Palaearctic birds (*see* Palaearctic Region) and tropical American groups. Northward the Nearctic Region includes Newfoundland, the Arctic Archipelago, and Greenland. Southward the Nearctic faunal forms a complex transition with the Neotropical (*see* Neotropical Region); the boundary is usually set in s. Mexico where the cooler Mexican highlands meet the tropical lowlands (Darlington, 1957). *See* Distribution. See especially detailed discussion of the Nearctic by Mayr (1964b).

NEBOUX
ADOLPHE SIMON. Little known; for whom Alphonse Milne-Edwards, French zoologist, named in 1882 the blue-footed booby, *Sula nebouxii*. Was surgeon major on the French frigate *Vénus*. The ship sailed from Brest, France, Dec. 29, 1836, on a voyage around the world. Along the "Pacific coast of America," either off Calif., Baja Calif., or west coast of Mexico, the expedition in 1837 collected a specimen, or specimens, of the booby which honors Neboux's name. See Palmer (1928); American Ornithologists' Union (1957).

NEBRASKA BIRD REVIEW, THE
See Ornithological Periodicals.

NECTAR AND BIRDS
According to Meeuse (1961), about 2,000 species of the approximately 8,650 species of birds in the world, and of some 50 families, visit flowers more or less regularly; about two thirds of these are specialists in their feeding, relying on energy-giving nectar for a considerable part of their food (besides nectar, some also eat pollen, insects, and spiders from flowers).

In N. C., and S. America, hummingbirds (*see* Hummingbird Family) are great eaters of nectar; in the Hawaiian Is., the Hawaiian honeycreepers (Drepaniidae); in Australia and New Guinea, such birds as honey eaters and brush-tongued parrots (*see* discussion of how tongue is used in nectar-gathering under Tongue); in Africa, sunbirds, sugarbirds, white-eyes, and bulbuls; some of the weavers (Ploceidae), Old World orioles (Oriolidae), shrikes, Old World warblers, and mousebirds (Coliidae) have been watched taking nectar from flowers (Melville, 1964).

In C. America, among the honeycreepers (family Coerebidae), a family of small songbirds restricted to tropical America, the long-billed, blue honeycreeper, now called red-legged honeycreeper, *Cyanerpes cyaneus*—see details in De Schauensee (1970)—probes flowers for nectar, and the favorite occupation of the brisk, little bananaquits, *Coereba flaveola*, is probing the hearts of nectar-bearing flowers of many kinds; they even visit the flaring yellow trumpets (longer than themselves) of the cultivated *Allamanda* to pierce with their bills the flower corollas at their bases for nectar; unable to hover like hummingbirds, they cling beside the blossoms in every conceivable position; another member of the family, the slaty flower-piercer, *Diglossa baritula*, of Guatemala, has a highly specialized bill for feeding; with its sharply hooked upper mandible and awl-like lower mandible, it pierces the bases of tubular flowers to extract nectar (Skutch, 1954). *See* Honeycreeper Family.

In N. America, besides hummingbirds, which have especially adapted flight, relatively long bills, and tongues for nectar-feeding, many birds, not so adapted—such as the common (red-shafted) flicker, Scott's oriole, hooded oriole (see observations of Leck, 1974), spotted-breasted oriole, house finch, western tanager, phainopepla, bushtit, verdin, and mockingbird —also have been seen drinking nectar from the open cups of some flowers (Pickens, 1929b); Cassin's finches, purple finches, and evening grosbeaks have been seen biting off flowers of cherries, blueberries, and maples, then squeezing base of flower with bill to get nectar (Gullion, 1950). One of the most important and dramatic relationships between flowers and birds, however, is that of hummingbirds and their specially adapted flowers. For discussion, *see* Pollination; *also* Symbiosis. For a comparable habit, *see* Sap-feeding.

NEMATODE

(NEM-ah-toad); from Gr. *nema, nematos,* a thread, and *ode,* like; "a thing like" (Jaeger, 1955). Name for any one of cylindrical, smooth-skinned worms of the class Nematoda, which do not show rings on their surfaces as earthworms and leeches do. They are generally called roundworms, threadworms, or hairworms. Some of them are parasitic in man and in other animals. Many nematodes are not parasitic and live in the soil, in the sea, in fresh water, or any place that provides them with sufficient moisture (Lapage, 1963).

Their thin bodies are pointed at both ends, and many of the tiny white nematode worms appear like animated bits of sewing thread as they thrash about when dug up in garden soil or in aquatic debris, which may teem with millions of them in a single spadeful. Of the 55 species known in man, only about a dozen are common parasites, and some of these are harmless, but others cause serious diseases such as hookworm, trichinosis, and ascariasis. See accounts of these and others in Buchsbaum (1938) and Lapage (1963).

Wehr (1971) treated 21 genera (or groups) of roundworms of about 25 species that parasitize birds. Of these, the gapeworm, *Syngamus trachea,* attaches itself to the inside walls of the trachea and less frequently to the bronchi (*see* Respiratory System) of chickens, turkeys, peafowl, and pheasants and has caused great losses of pen-raised pheasants in the U.S. and elsewhere.

The embryonated eggs or larvae of the gapeworm are picked up by pheasants, for example, in their food or water or they get them from natural foods such as earthworms and other invertebrates which also eat the eggs and larvae of *Syngamus trachea.* Young birds are most seriously affected; the rapidly growing gapeworms obstruct the trachea, or windpipe, and cause the infected birds to suffocate and die. Affected birds gape with opened bill and make short whistling sounds and jerk their heads as though to free themselves from some obstruction in the throat. After a week or so, parasitized birds begin to refuse food, cease moving, and then squat with drooping wings;

heavily parasitized birds are extremely emaciated, breathe with difficulty, and usually die. Thiabendazole, administered in the food of captive birds, is effective against gapeworms, but such control is not practical for wild birds (Wehr, 1971).

Another nematode, the crop worm, *Capillaria contorta,* occurs in domestic ducks, chickens, turkeys, and pigeons, and is known in the wild in bobwhite quail, ring-necked pheasants, wild ducks, the dovekie, black guillemot, ringed plover, gull-billed tern, some gulls, the Eurasian ruff, avocet, and lapwing, some hawks, grouse, crows, the starling, and others (see list in Wehr, 1971). Susceptible hosts become infected by swallowing the infective eggs when feeding, or by eating earthworms and other invertebrates that have ingested the eggs with their food. The worms mature in the host birds, which become droopy, weak, and emaciated. They move slowly when disturbed, with an unsteady gait, and occasionally fall back on their hock joints and assume a penguinlike position. Others extend and retract their heads and necks as though trying to swallow an obstruction in the throat; heavily infected quail squat with their legs folded under their bodies (Wehr, 1971).

From late Dec. 1973 into late Feb. and Mar. 1974, the Massachusetts Audubon Society received reports of hundreds of blue jays dying in the wild from the crop worm, *Capillaria contorta,* embedded in the crop lining of the jays, with thousands of others infected—from e. Mass. westward across Conn. and into s. N.H. (Center for Short-lived Phenomena, 1975). Autopsies performed on the blue jays by Dr. George Faddoul, University of Massachusetts, indicated infection by the crop worm, *Capillaria contorta,* which was confirmed by Dr. Elizabeth Boyd, parasitologist at Mt. Holyoke College, South Hadley, Mass.

The crop worms so irritated the esophagus of the jays that they could not swallow and consequently starved to death, or the worms blocked the trachea, making it impossible for the birds to breathe. According to Boyd (1974), some of the crop worms in seven of the blue jays she examined were in the floor of the mouth at the base of the tongue, some beneath the tongue, others in the forward end of the windpipe, and some in the roof of the mouth. The worms averaged 25 per jay, in contrast with only 3 per bird in a previous study by Boyd. The crop worm, *Capillaria contorta,* has been reported from 39 species of birds in 5 orders (Wehr, 1971). Wehr reported that captive birds may be treated with methyridine, which is highly effective in removing crop worms from infected quail.

Nematodes of other species live in the air sacs of birds, especially hawks; some live in the caecum and sometimes in the small intestines of partridges, grouse, quail, and pheasants, and one of these causes the disease in quail called blackhead. *See* Blackhead. Some are common parasites of fish-eating birds, and one, the spiral stomach worm, *Dispharynx nausata,* lives in the glandular stomach (proventriculus) of many songbirds and game birds. It is one of the most destructive parasites

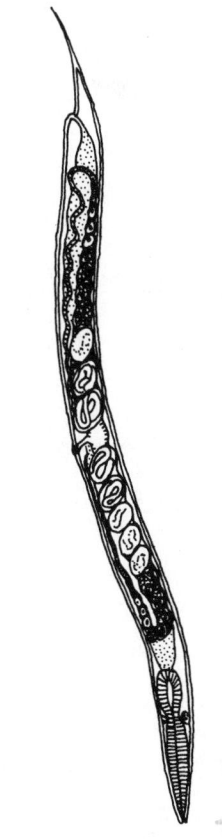

Strongyloides skercolalis

NEMATODE

About 25 species of nematodes—thin-bodied, smooth-skinned worms—parasitize birds. Some occur with fatal results in the bird's trachea, crop, esophagus, and stomach.

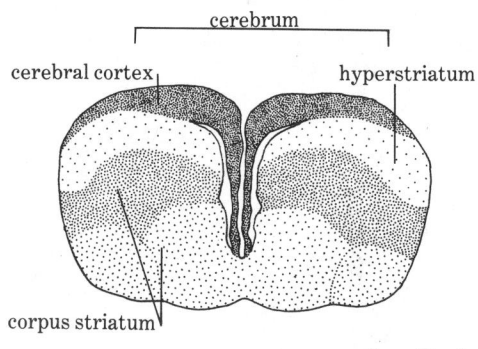

cerebrum

cerebral cortex
hyperstriatum

corpus striatum

cross-section of brain

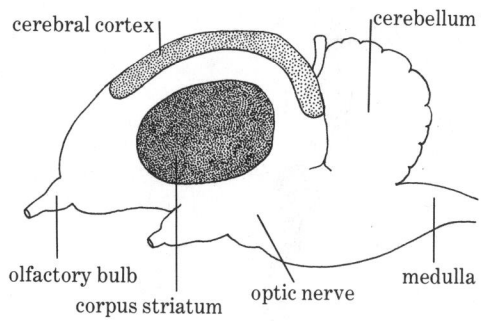

cerebral cortex
cerebellum

olfactory bulb
medulla

corpus striatum
optic nerve

sagittal section of cerebral hemisphere

NERVOUS SYSTEM

The smooth and rudimentary cerebral cortex encases the two hemispheres of the cerebrum and is the center of conscious motor control. The corpus striatum is the dominant coordination center of the brain, the site of controls for instinctive behavior and sensory perception. The hyperstriatum, which appears to be sensitive to hormones, is unique to birds, and its function has not been definitively established. The large cerebellum indicates excellent coordination and balance.

of ruffed grouse, and can kill pigeons (Wehr, 1971). *See* Heterakiasis; Parasite; Diseases.

NEORNITHES

(nee-OR-nih-theez). The true birds, a subclass of class Aves, which include all recent N. American birds as listed in the A.O.U. *Checklist of North American Birds* (1957). The Neornithes also include the New World toothed fossil birds. *See* Ichthyornis; Hesperornis; *also* Classification; Fossil Birds.

NEOTROPICAL REGION

Its usual designation is tropical America, the non-tropical parts of S. America, the West Indies, and other islands near S. America, which is the real home of the Neotropical fauna. The Neotropical Region extends from the northern edge of the tropical rain forest in Mexico south to Cape Horn. It is the richest avifauna in number of species in the world. See Mayr (1964c); *see* in Distribution.

NERVOUS SYSTEM

Along with the endocrine system (*see* Endocrine Glands), coordinates the bird into a whole animal that acts as a unit. According to Rand (1967), the two systems are closely related in their "cooperative sending of messages through the bird body, but work in different ways. The messages sent as electrochemical impulses along the neurons—nerve cells and their fibers—may be likened to telephone calls that produce instant action; messages sent by the endocrine system are carried by hormones in the blood and may be likened to messages by letter; they promote gradual changes—growth, metabolism, sexual and seasonal changes." *See* Endocrine Glands; *also* Instinct.

The nervous system receives and interprets "messages" from inside and outside the body; "is composed of conducting elements—neurons and supporting elements—neuroglia and ependyma. A neuron is a nerve cell made up of a cell body with its processes (nerve fibers) that conduct an impulse either toward (via the dendrite) or away from (via the axon) the cell body and its endings. Typically, each neuron has multiple dendrites but a single axon. A "nerve" is a collection of many nerve fibers, both dendrites and axons, held together and surrounded by a connective-tissue sheath. The brain and spinal cord make up the *central nervous system;* cranial and spinal nerves with their associated ganglia (groups of nerve cell bodies outside the central nervous system) make up the *peripheral nervous system*" (Van Tyne and Berger, 1976). *See* Brain.

THE CENTRAL NERVOUS SYSTEM. Within the cerebral hemispheres of the bird's brain there is a massive development during the bird's embryonic life of specialized groups of nerve cells—the corpus striatum in the basal (bottom) part, and the hyperstriatum on the dorsal, or top, side (Portmann and Stingelin, 1961).

Knowledge of the functions of parts of hemispheres of the bird's brain has been discovered by "extirpation" studies on pigeons conducted since the beginning of the 19th century. Experiments showed, by removal of different parts of the brain, that parts of the corpus striatum control eating, drinking, eye movements, vocal utterances, conditioned responses, the ability to learn, to form pairs at courting time, to copulate, build nests, incubate eggs, and care for the young. However, "sensory and motor activities of pigeons can continue, even in the absence of the hemispheres. Such pigeons can fly, run, peck, and avoid obstacles—vision therefore remains intact" (Portmann and Stingelin, 1961).

The cerebral cortex (outside skin) lacks the direct motor pathway to the spinal cord, and as a result it is likely that birds have less conscious control of their body motions than mammals do. The corpora striata and cerebral hemispheres, for all their size and importance, do not completely dominate body activities, and in this, the bird's brain, with its functions of the different regions, resembles the brain mechanisms of fishes and amphibians (Welty, 1962). In the evolution of the bird brain, however, those of superior intelligence, such as crows and parrots, have larger cerebral hemispheres than the more primitive grebes, fowls, plovers, and ostriches, for example.

The *spinal cord* of birds has the structure and position typical of vertebrate animals as a whole. As in all vertebrates, the spinal cord has paired (left and right side) spinal nerves, each with two roots: one, a dorsal pair of sensory nerves with spinal ganglia that receive sensory messages from the body; the other a ventral pair of motor nerves without ganglia that send movement messages throughout the body (Portmann and Stingelin, 1961).

THE PERIPHERAL NERVOUS SYSTEM. According to Van Tyne and Berger (1959), the peripheral nervous system consists of the eleven cranial nerves from the brain, a varied number of spinal nerves, and the autonomic nervous system, which American neuroanatomists consider to be entirely a general visceral efferent, or internal message, system that is composed of motor fibers which distribute messages to glands and to smooth muscle of the viscera and blood vessels. All of these perform involuntary actions—those not consciously controlled.

NEST BOXES

See Bird-attracting.

NESTLING

Term for a young bird from time of its hatching until its normal departure from the nest—that is, without human or other disturbance (Palmer, 1962). "Nestling" is usually applied to a young bird that remains in the nest for some time. Passerines, or songbirds, for example, have much longer periods of time as nestlings than do the downy young (chicks) of game birds, most of which leave the nest soon after hatching (*see* discussion of these *precocial* chicks under Altricial). When hatched, passerines are naked except for a scant growth of filmy down on the upper part of the body. This is the *natal down* (Dwight, 1900), or the *neossoptiles* (*see* Feather), which are quickly succeeded by the *juvenal,* or nestling, plumage. This is sufficiently grown in most passerines so that, in about 8–14 days after hatching, the young bird can fly or flutter from the nest. At this time its tail feathers are only about half grown and the wing feathers barely long enough to permit it to make short, uncertain flights (Chapman, 1930).

An *immature* is, in general, a young bird during its first year of life, before it has acquired its adult plumage. However, some birds, such as gulls, may require several years to acquire their adult plumage; during this time, in their various immature plumages, they are called subadults. *See* Subadult.

According to Wood (1946), a *juvenile* is a young bird that is out of the nest and able to care for itself but has not completed its post-juvenal molt. *See* reference under Molts and Molting to two different systems for the names of the sequences of birds' molts; *see also* Fledgling; Sexual Maturity; Bursa of Fabricius.

NEST PARASITISM
Term for habit of some birds of using the nests of others in which to lay their eggs and raise their young. *See* examples in Re-use of Old Nests under Nests and Nesting. *See* other types of parasitism at birds' nests under Brood Parasitism; Obligate Parasite; Protocalliphora.

NESTS AND NESTING
A bird's nest—its home, where it raises its family—is usually thought of as the familiar bowl-like structure of a robin, built of grasses, twigs, rootlets, mosses, and mud, or the big stick nest of a heron or a red-tailed hawk or an eagle; however, it may not be built of materials at all —it may be simply a spot or place in the bird's chosen environment (*see* Habitat; *also* Habitat Choices of Birds under Distribution) which is usually near its food supply.

Dovekies and murres lay their eggs, without any nest materials, on the bare rocks of sea cliffs (*see* Eggs and Egg-laying); oystercatchers, in shallow, unlined depressions they dig with their feet in sandy beaches; nighthawks and killdeers, on bare ground, farm pastures, or on the flat roofs of buildings; vultures, in logs or on the floors of abandoned buildings or, like whip-poor-wills, on the leafy floor of the forest; woodpeckers, in the bottoms of nesting holes they dig with their bills, usually in the dead or dying branches and trunks of trees; kingfishers and bank swallows, in burrows they dig in sandy banks, using their bills and feet. (For specific information about the nesting habits of each, *see* under each bird's biography).

The earliest birds probably had the simplest and most primitive nest-making habits, first laying their eggs on the ground or on rock ledges and in cavities without any nest materials, later building simple structures of sticks or reeds or themselves excavating holes for their nests. The most highly evolved or specialized birds of today—the passerines, or songbirds— build complex nests, but hummingbirds, which are not classified in the songbird group (*see* Classification), also build nests of exquisite artistry.

PROTECTION OF NESTS. A bird's nest, usually inconspicuous, often hidden and camouflaged by its materials and its location, helps to hide the parent bird incubating the eggs (*see* Incubation) or sheltering the helpless young (and the eggs or young in the parents' absence) from predators. *See* Mammals and Birds. The nest also helps protect the eggs or young from exposure to storms, prolonged cold, or excessive heat, which also might destroy them. For altricial birds, whose young hatch in a relatively helpless state, the nest is the protective nursery in which the young share warmth and food brought to them by the parents; a place where they begin to develop their learned and instinctive responses to their world, and achieve their growth to the time when they can flutter or fly away from the nest. *See* Young and Their Care; *also* Dispersal.

Protection of nests and their contents may ordinarily be assured by their inaccessibility on rock faces of cliffs or on islands; by being built at the tips of slender twigs or branches out of sight or out of reach of predators, or in holes in trees or in burrows in the ground; or by the strength and size of the parent birds or simply by their aggressiveness. Hummingbirds drive away birds many times their size, and kingbirds and martins are noted for their attacks on the larger grackles, crows, hawks, and other big birds that occasionally fly over the smaller birds' territories.

Birds that nest in colonies on sandy beaches may rout their enemies by mobbing them. *See* Self-Protective Behavior under Behavior. At Machias Seal Is., Me., nesting arctic terns chased crows threatening their eggs, and terns nesting in n. Europe attacked and drowned an invading hooded crow by massing about it and driving it into the water (Hawksley, 1957). At Churchill, Man., oldsquaws (diving ducks) nest close to arctic terns, apparently a deliberate choice for protection because the arctic terns attack and drive away egg-eating gulls, jaegers, and ravens (Evans, 1970). See also Langham (1974). The Russian zoologist I. B. Chernyarskii, working on Wrangell Is., Siberia, in 1964, reported (1967) that the arctic fox was the chief predator of the snow goose, especially in years when the lemming population was low (*see* Cycle). The snowy owl is a fierce opponent of the arctic fox, successful in repelling it, and small colonies of snow geese, black brant, and common eiders nested around the owl's nest sites.

Some small or medium-sized birds find protection in the lower parts of the nests of large predatory birds. American kestrels and western kingbirds sometimes nest in the stick nests of the golden eagle on cliffs; common grackles and house sparrows, in the nests of ospreys, where they not only get some protection from the hawk but get scraps of its left-over food. Kelso (1929) reported that a pair of house sparrows built a nest in the lower part of a great horned owl's nest in Colo. Apparently the large predatory birds do not molest the smaller birds, either because they are too small and elusive for them to catch, or because they are not their ordinary prey.

Usually ospreys and other birds choose a firm foundation on which to build their nests, but an osprey at Portsmouth, N.H., chose a nest site near the sea that subjected the bird to a strange situation. It built on an old windmill from which the floats had blown off. When the wind blew and the rudder turned, the sitting bird on her nest swung round and round in the breeze.

In the Old World and New World tropics, to gain protection from predators, many small birds build their nests near those of wasps. In Australia, the black-throated warbler, *Gerygone palpebrosa* (family Sylviidae), is called the hornet-nest bird because it frequently nests close to the nests of hornets (Chisholm, 1952). Pettingill (1942) described the interesting relationships between tropical American ants, which nested in a bull-horn acacia, and kiskadee and social flycatchers nesting in the same bush. Up to 8 or 10 nests of the S. American cacique, *Cassicus cela,* may be clustered about a wasp's nest (Welty, 1975). Apparently in most, if not all, of these associations, it is the birds that choose to nest close to the stinging insects. The wasps ignore the birds but attack people and predatory animals that come too close. See also Hindwood (1959).

TYPES OF NESTS. Nests range from the *scrape* —a shallow cup or saucer scratched by the adult bird in the ground or in leaves—to the *platform nests* built in the tops of trees (hawks, herons) or on shallow water (grebes and coots, for example), and the *cup nests*, the most common type, built by songbirds (the American robin and common grackle, for example). Some of these cup nests are built of mud (for example, by barn swallows and phoebes) and plastered by the birds to the sheltered vertical surface of a barn or cliff wall. These cup nests are called *adherent nests*. Chimney swifts glue with saliva their shallow cup nests of sticks to the inside walls of a chimney or hollow tree. Vireos build their *pensile* cup nests hanging from the fork of a tree branch; orioles weave baglike nests that they suspend from the tips of branches (*pendulous nests*). See other examples in Pettingill (1972).

SIZES OF NESTS. The sizes of birds' nests usually vary with the size of the builder, although some small birds build relatively huge individual nests. A small S. American bird, called the firewood gatherer, *Anumbius annumbi*, of the Argentine, makes its nest 2 ft. deep and 1 ft. across of big sticks obliquely resting in the branches of a tree (Marchant, 1964a). Hummingbirds make the smallest nests—the ruby-throated builds one about an inch deep and about an inch across and may saddle it on a branch no more than an inch or less thick.

Apparently eagles and storks build the largest individual nests; the white stork of Europe and Asia, *Ciconia ciconia* (the fabled stork of Europe that children are told brings babies), is protected because of the belief that its presence brings good luck. *See* Folklore. It usually builds its nest on rooftops, and the nest may be 6 ft. deep and 5 ft. across and weigh more than a ton (Gilliard, 1958).

The largest nests on record in N. America have been built by the bald eagle. One, at Vermilion, Ohio, occupied by eagles for 35 years, was estimated to weigh about two tons when it crashed to the ground (Herrick, 1934). A bald eagle's nest in a tree near St. Petersburg, Fla., was possibly the largest N. American tree nest

oriole's nest

NESTS AND NESTING
Pendulous nests, such as those built by orioles, are woven together and hang from the tips of branches.

yellow warbler's nest

The well-made cup nest of the yellow warbler is fastened to upright branches in a bush or tree.

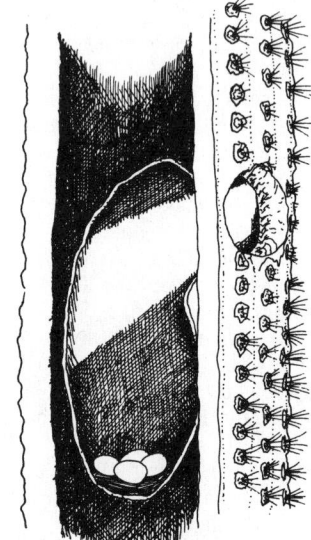

gila woodpecker's nest

The gila woodpecker commonly places its cavity nest high up in the giant saguaro cactus. If the woodpecker does not return to the same site the next year, the cavity may be appropriated by another desert bird such as a screech owl or a kestrel.

ever known. It was 20 ft. deep and 9½ ft. across (Broley, 1947).

The largest birds' nests in the world are built by the megapodes (*see* Megapode) of the Australian Region, which scratch up mounds of debris sometimes to a height of 15 ft.; one on record had a diameter of 50 ft.; however, these are usually 5–7 ft. high and about 20 ft. in diameter. The largest mounds are the product of many generations of birds and are very durable (Gilliard, 1958).

RE-USE OF OLD NESTS. Eagles and some hawks return to the same nest year after year and, instead of building a new one, may add fresh sticks to the rim, building a new rampart around the center, which is much downtrodden from the previous year's use. Some of these tree nests have been continuously occupied by eagles or by hawks for many years. (Brown noddies—*see* in Gull Family—sometimes reuse the same nest year after year.)

In New England an osprey nest in a dead locust tree was occupied every year for 44 years by a pair of these birds; two others for 41 years; another for 45 years (Bent, 1937). Some of the nesting ledges favored in e. N. America by peregrine falcons were used for 50 years or more and one for at least 80; an eyrie in the British Isles still used by peregrines in the 1940s had been occupied each year by a pair since Elizabethan times (Peterson, 1948). *See* Return to Nest Sites and Wintering Places under Banding.

Some birds take over nests built by others; most often practiced by birds of prey but other birds do it too. The great horned owl does not build a nest but appropriates the old nests of hawks, crows, or squirrels (Austing and Holt, 1966). In Fla., great horned owls have preempted the nests of bald eagles, and one shared a bald eagle's nest, with both incubating their eggs within a few feet of each other. *See* Nest-sharing. Nests built by hawks may have a succession of owners. One near Saybrook, Conn., built by a Cooper's hawk in a tall chestnut tree, was occupied the next year by a pair of great horned owls; the following year by red-tailed hawks; the next year by barred owls (Bent, 1938).

Passerines, or the so-called perching birds, or songbirds, usually build a new nest for each set of eggs, but some songbirds will use their own nests again. In n. N. America, wheatears, redpolls, snow buntings, and possibly Lapland longspurs generally re-use old nests, merely returning to them each year, which evidently saves them nest-building time in the short Arctic summer (Wynne-Edwards, 1952). Even one of the shorebirds, which usually nest on the ground, the solitary sandpiper, lays its eggs in the old nests of American robins, common grackles, cedar waxwings, Brewer's blackbirds, kingbirds, and gray jays.

American robins, which often return to the same yard or garden each spring, build durable nests with mud linings, which they sometimes use again. One that built atop an old gray catbird's nest in a honeysuckle bush in Mich. used it to raise three broods in one season (Nickell, 1957); however, American robins usually build a new nest for each set of eggs. Mourning

doves occasionally lay their eggs in parts of the stick nests of herons (Nickell, 1954).

McClure (1944), in an Iowa study of songbirds' nests that survive over winter, discovered that, of 489 nests built by 9 species, those that survived best were built by American robins, Baltimore (northern) orioles, and mourning doves. Wood (1951) reported a nest of a mourning dove in a white pine tree near Harrisburg, Pa., which doves used every nesting season for at least 9 years before it fell to the ground. Barn swallows have a strong tendency to use the old foundation of the previous year's nest, rather than build a new one. Those birds that build no nest but lay their eggs in the nests of other birds are brood-parasitic. *See* Brood Parasitism; *also* Dump Nests.

WHERE SOME BIRDS USUALLY NEST. Within any outdoor area that one might choose in which to study the nests of birds, provided it is large enough to include several kinds of habitats, it will be obvious that it is the plant communities within the area that are the prime factors limiting, or determining, the distribution of nesting birds (Beecher, 1942). For example, different kinds of birds, many of them not even closely related, nest on the ground in fields, pastures, and prairies because of the grasses and other herbaceous plants there that provide them with certain nesting materials, certain protective cover, certain places for their nests, and certain kinds of food suited to them and their young, and to which they may have become adapted from ancient times; others, for the same reasons, are limited to wet marshes and open water; others to woodlands; others to swamps, or to brushy hillsides, and so on. *See* some details of choices under Habitat.

SELECTING THE NEST SITE. Once the pair bond is established and copulation has begun (*see* The Pair Bond under Courtship), the female, which in many birds selects the nest site, may begin building the nest. The nest itself, either simple or complex, seems to be determined by the inherited aptitude of the builder, the materials it uses, the site it chooses, and possibly its ability to imitate the design of nests built by birds of its own kind. *See also* factors that govern a choice under Microclimate. Several observers have noted that some young robins, for example, building their first nests, do not always build a typical robin nest on the first try, but apparently many birds become more skilled at it with experience. See Tinbergen (1951b, p. 139). Hormones exert a profound effect on bird behavior; prolactin is responsible for broodiness and possibly for nest building, according to Höhn (1961), and estrogen stimulates nest building (Lehrman, 1959). *See* discussion of hormones under Endocrine Glands.

While selecting the nest site, the bird often goes through the motions of building the nest. A female American robin may for several days try out a nesting place in a crotch of a tree that interests her, crouching and slowly spinning around in it as she does in nest making.

Millicent Ficken (1963), in her studies of the nesting of the American redstart, a small warbler, watched both the female and the male try out sites. The female then approached a site the male had been testing and sat in the crotch, turning round and round as he had. "However," wrote Mrs. Ficken, "no female built in a crotch that a male had thus 'directed' her to . . . the ultimate site is determined solely by the female."

Sometimes it is the male that selects the initial nest site. The males of some hole-nesting migratory birds, such as the house wren and prothonotary warbler, which arrive on the breeding grounds ahead of the females in spring, may select not only one but several nesting places. The males of both these species may build several partly completed "dummy nests" (see Dummy Nest) within their established territories, in natural cavities in trees or stumps, in abandoned woodpecker holes, or in birdhouses, but the final choice of one of these as the active nest is usually made by the female, which then completes the nest herself or may build a new one.

Among birds in which the pairs remain together through most of the nesting season (see Courtship; Behavior), there are a number of categories in which either of the sexes takes a dominant, equal, or supporting role in building a nest or excavating the site (see Collias, 1964). (1) Both sexes build the nest: (a) with male and female sharing about equally in nest building: example, kingfishers, woodpeckers, bank swallows, and waxwings; and (b) the male builds dummy nests from which the female may select the one to complete and to use: example, many wrens. (2) The female builds but the male brings the materials: example, mourning dove and ground dove. (3) The female builds without help from the male: example, hummingbirds, red-eyed vireo, ovenbird. (4) The female builds but both sexes gather the materials: example, common raven and American robin. (5) The male builds but the female provides the materials.(6) The male alone builds the nest: example, some shrikes, weaverbirds, bobwhite quail (usually), and phainopepla (the male builds most of the nest). (7) No nest is built: example, tropic-birds, most shorebirds, skimmers, auks, nighthawks,whip-poor-will, chuck-will's-widow, and poor-will.

In most orders of birds, there are some that build primitive nests that are little more than a platform of twigs or sticks; for example, cormorants, anhinga, frigatebird, herons, bitterns, egrets, storks, some accipiter hawks, many pigeons and doves; also by songbirds, or passerines, but by a very few; for example, the rose-breasted grosbeak. Songbirds usually build the most complex nests, often above the ground in trees or shrubs. These are the cuplike nests, lashed with strong plant fibers, in an upright crotch, or in a fork of a branch, suspended from the tip of a branch, or simply saddled on a limb with the weight of the nest holding it in place. Progressively, these range from the coarse but sturdy, mud-lined nest of the American robin, typical of the nests of thrushes, to the exquisitely built nests of some of the vireos and flycatchers, the hummingbirds, the blue-gray gnatcatcher, and the American goldfinch. Some of the most elaborate nests of all N. American birds are the pendulous nests, woven of plant fibers, of the orioles, which reach their highest perfection in those of their C. and S. Ameri-

barn swallow's nest

NESTS AND NESTING

Adherent nests are attached to vertical surfaces such as the inside of a chimney or a hollow tree by means of mud plaster or, in some species, saliva.

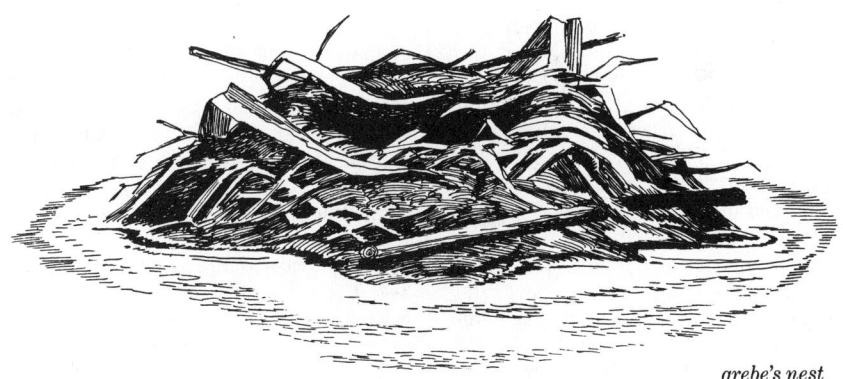

grebe's nest

Grebes, coots, and some other waterbirds build floating platform nests of marsh reeds and mud that are anchored to and often concealed by water plants.

puffin's burrow

Many birds such as kingfishers, puffins, petrels, and bank swallows nest in burrows, which they either dig themselves or take over from former occupants.

can relatives—the caciques, oropendolas, and troupials. *See* Troupial Family.

DESERTION OF NEST BUILDING. Some birds may suddenly stop building their nests at the onset of cold weather, or desert the nest after being frightened during its construction (Marshall, 1961a). Indigo buntings, cardinals, bobwhite quail, and many other birds may desert if disturbed in the slightest while building, or their nest-building cycle is temporarily halted if the nest is destroyed. Later the birds usually build in a different place, as most of them will persist until a nest is completed, eggs laid, and one or more broods raised, depending on whether they are single- or multiple-brooded. *See* Brooding; *also* Eggs and Egg-laying.

HOW A ROBIN REBUILDS HER NEST. At Port Sanilac, Mich., a woman watched at close range, through a window, a female robin rebuild her nest on a ledge over the woman's front door. She saw it replaster with mud the inside of the foundation of the previous year's nest, then bring soft dead grasses from the lawn and drop them in the cup of the nest. Then the bird hopped inside and squatted, with the ends of the grasses sticking up all around her, lowered her tail over the edge of the nest, and threw her weight forward against her breast. Then she began to kick a tattoo against the sides and bottom of the nest with her feet, alternately resting, turning a little, and tucking the grasses into the nest with her bill.

HOW LONG DOES IT TAKE TO BUILD A NEST? Using its bill and feet as its principal "hands," how long does it take a bird to build a nest? This may depend on the size of the bird, whether it nests in the tropics, the Temperate Zone, or the Arctic (birds in the Arctic, with shorter summers, have less time to build a nest and raise a family than those in the tropics), how elaborate the nest, materials used, how far the bird or birds must travel to get materials, and whether the nest is the first of the season or a later one.

Frank M. Chapman (1929) reported that it took 3–4 weeks for a female Wagler's oropendola in a nesting colony in a tree in the Panama Canal Zone to build its elaborately woven, 3-ft.-long, pouchlike nest. Pettingill (1942) reported that it took 24 days for a pair of kiskadee flycatchers in Mexico to build their nest, and Wing (1956) compared a tropical black-throated oriole that took 3–4 weeks to build its nest in Tamaulipas with a northern (Baltimore) oriole in the U.S. which required 10–12 days.

A golden eagle, flying to its cliff or tree nest site with large sticks or pieces of brush in its bill that it has broken off trees or shrubs (Bent, 1937), may require 2 months to build its nest (Welty, 1962), but thereafter the nest may be used by the eagles, with some repairs, during their entire lifetime. *See* Age, and ages given under each bird biography.

Most of the small passerines, or songbirds, build their nests in a few days, usually in less than a week, if it is the first nest of the season. They may build later nests more quickly or more slowly. Eastern bluebirds may build a nest in 4–5 days, sometimes within 2 days, or as much as 12 days (Hartshorne, 1962); cardinal, in 3, 4, and 9 days for three individual nests (Bent *et al.*, 1968); gray catbird, in about 5–6 days (Bent, 1948); American robin, in 6–20 days (Bent, 1949); northern (Baltimore) oriole, one nest completed in 4½ days; other authorities give 5–8 days; another 15 days (Bent, 1958); red-winged blackbird, usually 6 days (Allen, 1914); rufous-sided towhee, one record of 5 days (Bent *et al.*, 1968); American goldfinch, average of 13 days for nests built during the first two weeks of July, but only 5.6 days for nests built in the last two weeks of Aug. (Stokes, 1950). The red-eyed vireo can build its nest in about 5 days (Bent, 1950); cedar waxwing, average of 5.6 days (Putnam, 1949); prothonotary warbler, 3.3 days (average of 54 nests) (Walkinshaw, 1953); mockingbird, some built in 2 days, record of one built in 1 day (Bent, 1948); field sparrow, early nests 3–7 days, usually 4–5 days; later nests built in 2–3 days (Walkinshaw, 1968a); dipper, 15 days (Welty, 1962); downy woodpecker, 5–8 days to dig fall roosting holes (*see* Roosting), later enlarged for spring nesting (Kilham, 1962b).

HOW MUCH MATERIAL TO MAKE A NEST? Most birds fly to the nest site with the materials clasped in the bill, but some of the hawks (accipiters) carry them in their feet. A great amount of material and many trips back and forth to carry it may go into the building of a nest. Barn swallows may make more than 1,200 trips to carry mud to one nest, and the long-tailed tit of Europe and the British Isles may carry, by actual count, 2,457 feathers to its nest. Wing (1956) found a nest of the black-throated oriole, *Icterus gularis*, in Mexico, with 3,387 separate pieces of grass and plant fibers, many of them 3–4 ft. long, and the nest of a rose-throated becard with 1,844 pieces of leaves, twigs, grasses, and fibers, some 18–41 in. long. Terres (1964a) counted 1,282 items in a house sparrow's nest near Chapel Hill, N.C. These were mostly grasses and some strips of grapevine bark, but included part of an envelope postmarked "New York 17" and a piece of a letter bearing the typed words "difficult struggle," candy wrappers, cigarette filters, cellophane, Kleenex, cotton and cotton thread, twine, and 28 feathers of blue jays, cardinals, and gray catbirds.

SOME TYPICAL MATERIALS IN BIRDS' NESTS. The cup of the nest built by many songbirds, resting upon a foundation nest of twigs, is interwoven grasses, weed stems, or rootlets, lined with finer grasses, strips of bark, dead leaves, pine needles, mosses, animal hairs, feathers, or plant down, which they find in or around the nest site. Most ducks, geese, swans, gulls, and terns do not carry materials but merely reach out with their bills to gather it while sitting in the nesting place.

Certain songbirds use mud or leaf mold to hold the nest together—for example, American robins and wood thrushes—and American robins may fly a quarter of a mile away to get mud if none is close by (Howell, 1942); cliff swallows build their nests entirely of mud. Some of the swifts and hummingbirds secrete large amounts of sticky saliva from glands in the mouth to cement together twigs, grasses, feathers, clay, plant down, and other nest materials. The chimney swift uses its saliva to glue its small nest of sticks to the inside wall of tree cavities or of chimneys. *See* Mouth. Many birds weave a piece of paper into the wall of the nest; others use, typically, pieces or strips of bark in the lining (vireos, nuthatches); and others (eastern bluebirds) may build their nests entirely of pine needles, or of weed stems, or of grasses, or a combination of these, depending on whatever may be most available.

More than 30 species of birds, especially the hole-nesting crested flycatcher and tufted titmouse, use pieces of cast-off snakeskin in their nests, but will use cellophane or other shiny materials as a substitute. During an infestation on Staten Island, N.Y., of seventeen-year cicadas, a crested flycatcher lined its nest plentifully with the cast-off skins of those emerging insects. A naturalist in W.Va. noted an onion skin in the nest of a crested flycatcher, and during years of study, identified the sloughed skins of black snakes, black racers, water snakes, green snakes, and milk snakes in the nests of this bird.

Some birds line their nests plentifully with the hairs of mammals. Of 794 nests in the Museum of Vertebrate Zoology at Berkeley, Calif., 622, or 78%, contained hair of various mammals (Riney, 1951). Early in this century, the chipping sparrow was called hair-bird because it so frequently lined its nests with the hair of horses. A crested flycatcher at Boonton, N.J., used the long black hairs of a dead skunk lying in the woods with which to entirely line its nest; in Fla., a loggerhead shrike built its nest almost entirely of hairs from a dead cow nearby. Tufted titmice make considerable use of animal hairs to line their nests, plucking them from the backs of live opossums, woodchucks, and squirrels, and have even pulled hairs from the heads of people sitting quietly in the garden where the birds were building their nests.

In the Arctic (Baffin Is.), rock ptarmigan hens in spring molt from their white winter plumage to the brown feathers of summer. *See* Seasonal Dimorphism; Molts and Molting; *also* Feather. Redpolls, snow buntings, and longspurs take advantage of this and use the white ptarmigan feathers to line their nests. *See* Commensalism.

Purple martins have the habit of lining their nests with green leaves, alighting in willow trees to pluck off the leaves. P. A. Taverner, Canadian ornithologist, noted the martins in his colony gathering fresh green leaves from adjacent treetops, then taking them into the nesting compartments of the bird box. He assumed the leaves were needed to supply moisture for the eggs, as the birds were incubating at the time. *See* Eggs and Egg-laying; Incubation.

SOME MAN-MADE MATERIALS USED BY BIRDS. Some birds are so adaptable that with scarcity of their usual nest materials they will use all sorts of the material products of man. A warbling vireo's nest discovered in Calif. by E. A. Stoner was built almost entirely of Kleenex; Enoch Peterson, a Minn. farmer, found a brown thrasher's nest with a five-dollar bill woven into the cup; in Tex., a white-necked raven's urge to built its nest was so strong that, in the absence of sticks and other natural materials, it built the nest completely of barbed wire; in Fresno County, Calif., a pair of canyon wrens built an 8-in.-high nest on the beam of an office building entirely of office supplies—paper clips, straight pins, safety pins, rubber bands, thumbtacks, rawhide shoelaces, a darning needle, paper fasteners, insulated wire, matches, toothpicks, and other materials, for a total of 1,791 countable items. The nest with all its hardware weighed 2½ lbs. See uses of colored yarn by birds in Williams (1934); see also remarkable account in biography of Double-crested cormorant in Cormorant Family.

ADAPTABILITY OF BIRDS—NESTS IN UNUSUAL PLACES. On treeless islands, birds that ordinarily nest in trees may nest on the ground (osprey, mourning dove, American robin), and herring gulls may sometimes nest in trees, presumably for the safety of their nests. The killdeer sometimes lays its eggs among small stones of flat roofs; also a large colony of least terns and six common terns has been reported nesting on the roof of a department store at Pompano Beach, Fla. (Wass, 1974). For additional records of killdeers nesting on roofs, see in its biography in Plover Family. Red-tailed hawks occasionally nest on crossarms of towers of high-tension power lines, and barn owls, besides nesting in cupolas and attics of buildings, and in silos and barns, have nested below ground in a dry well for several years near Shafter, Calif. (McClure, 1962); in an open field, chimney swifts nested inside a well, 4 ft. below the ground (Sprunt, 1954a); an ash-throated flycatcher at Colton, Calif., nested in a crevice in a steam shovel which was digging dirt and moving forward as much as 200 ft. in a day; the flycatcher brought off its young successfully.

Wild ducks, turkeys, swallows, and shorebirds have built nests and reared young within a few feet of railroad tracks where trains frequently thundered by; horned larks on the ground of busy airports; tree swallows and prothonotary warblers on ferryboats traveling daily across rivers; and a barn swallow on a narrow-gauge, slow-moving train carrying freight and passengers in B.C., Canada. See also Adaptations to Mankind.

NESTING SUCCESS AND FAILURE. Margaret M. Nice (1957) made a statistical study of the nesting of altricial birds (see Altricial) and discovered that the hole-nesting birds (titmice, tree swallows, bluebirds, etc.) were distinctly more successful: an average of 66% of birds fledged from the nest compared with 49% for birds that built open nests on or above ground (for example, mourning doves, yellow warblers, red-winged blackbirds, etc.). The open-nesting birds, however, tend to raise more broods each season than the hole-nesting birds, which might tend to compensate by the end of the nesting year for the higher losses of the open-nesting birds. See Eggs and Egg-laying; also Egg-eating.

Hickey (1955) found that gallinaceous birds (pheasants, quail, partridges, grouse, prairie chickens, and ptarmigans), which build open nests on the ground, had a nesting success comparable with that of the open-nesting songbirds. In a statistical analysis of about 5,600 nests, he found the average success was about 45%.

HOW LONG IS THE BREEDING, OR NESTING, SEASON? In many Temperate Zone birds, the breeding season is adapted to nest-site and food availability; the pairs can breed only when the environment changes sufficiently in spring to give them their traditional nesting cover (Marshall, 1961a). See Habitat; Microclimate; also Habitat Choices of Birds under Distribution, and Types of Behavior under Behavior. Other birds are less dependent on new leaves or grasses for cover—for example, the common crow, American robin, and mourning dove, and the woodcock and killdeer; however, early nests of crows, robins, and mourning doves are often in evergreen trees. Early nests of meadowlarks are usually built in fields in dead mats of old grasses before the new green growth has begun; also red-winged blackbirds build their early nests in the dead standing stalks of the previous year's cattails (Beecher, 1942).

The breeding and nesting season of most N. American birds is in spring and summer and is usually timed so that the young are reared during a period of abundant food (see discussions by Davis, 1933, and Lack, 1950; also by Ohmart, 1973); it is earlier for some meat-eaters, such as the great horned owl; later for birds that eat insects and seeds; however, as Berger (1961) points out, in s. Mich., one might find active nests of birds in each month from Feb. to Oct., but no one species is known to breed throughout that period. The nesting season begins there with the great horned owl, which is often incubating its eggs while snow is still on the ground; for most N. American songbirds, it usually begins in Apr. and May and ends in July, Aug., and Sept., with the nesting of goldfinches and cedar waxwings, and extends into Oct. with the prolonged nesting of some mourning doves. Apparently, barn owls in the U.S. may nest at any time of the year, for nestlings have been banded in every month of the year (Stewart, 1952). See Banding.

In Fla., the southern bald eagle lays eggs from early Nov. to early Feb. (Broley, 1947), and the boat-tailed grackle, which usually has its nesting period in Fla. in spring, also nested for the second time near Orlando in Nov. of 1956, 1959, and 1960, the first fall nesting records ever reported for grackles (Selander and Nicholson, 1962). In 1960, Orians reported the second nesting of tricolored blackbirds in the Sacramento Valley of Calif. in Oct. and Nov. 1959. However, most birds in c. and n. U.S. reach the height of their nesting in May and June; some may reach peak nesting earlier farther south, and later farther north.

For accounts of small animal life that dwells in the nests of birds, see Inquilines; Microclimate; Protocalliphora. For further information about nests and nesting, see Young and Their Care.

NEST SANITATION
See Young and Their Care.

NEST-SHARING
Occasionally, females of the same species will share a nest and incubate their eggs together and care for the young after they are hatched. See also Eggs and Egg-laying. Forbush (1925–29) reported two song sparrows that built their nests about 30 ft. apart on the bank of the Merrimack R. in ne. Mass.—one about 6 ft. above the ordinary summer level of the water, the other about 12 ft. above it. After the nests were built the female of the lower nest deserted and joined with the female in the upper nest. They laid a total of nine eggs between them. The two sparrows took turns incubating the eggs, and after the young had hatched, the two pairs of adult sparrows fed the young and brought them off safely. Meanwhile, the lower, deserted nest was submerged after a heavy rainstorm by the rising waters of the river, which would have drowned any young that might have been in the lower nest. Forbush also reported two pairs of tree swallows attending the same nest.

In the summer of 1961, two female wood ducks incubated their eggs together inside a nest box put up for wood ducks near Addison, Vt. One of the females had herself hatched the summer before only one third of a mile away. The nest box she shared with the other wood duck held thirteen eggs, which were presumed to be the laying of both females (Fuller and Bolen, 1963). Sometimes both females covered the eggs at the same time, as the box was big enough for them both. When the ducklings hatched, while one female covered them on the nest, the other swam about on the water below and apparently called for the young ducks to leave the nest box and jump to the water, as is customary with this species. Frank Bellrose (1943) reported two female wood ducks laying eggs in the same nest and incubating side by side; he also reported that two canaries often lay and incubate in the same nest; sometimes, in Utah, two female long-billed curlews may share the same nest, and a willet and a long-billed curlew laid eggs in the same nest and both guarded it.

In the summer of 1967, at Topeka, Kans., Rice (1969) reported that a partially albino female cardinal shared a nest with a normally colored female and both incubated the five eggs that apparently were the product of both birds and fertilized by the one male.

After the young hatched, the two females and the male fed them. Sometimes the albino passed food to the normal female while she was on the nest brooding or hovering the nestlings, at which the normal female turned and fed the young cardinals beneath her. Rice commented that shared nesting is relatively uncommon among birds, and for normally monogamous (having one mate), strongly territorial birds such as the cardinal, it must be rare.

Even more remarkable was the nest, reported by Bailey and Niedrach (1936), of an American robin in Denver, Colo., shared by a house finch, an entirely different species. The female finch, smaller than the robin, laid six eggs in the robin's nest, and later the adult pair of house finches were seen feeding the half-

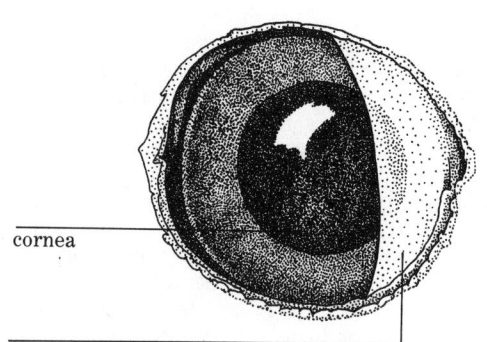

cornea

nictitating membrane

NICTITATING MEMBRANE
Most birds blink regularly by drawing the thin, transparent nictitating membrane across the eyeball, thereby cleaning and moistening the cornea. This "third eyelid" especially protects the eyes from drying air currents when the bird is in flight.

grown robins and two of their own small, newly hatched young. The house finches and the adult robins all fed the mixed brood, but eventually the young house finches were smothered by the larger young robins. After the loss of their own young, the finches kept on feeding the young robins even after they had left the nest. *See* also account of bald eagle and horned owl sharing a nest under Nests and Nesting. For other details of shared nesting, *see* Helpers among Birds.

NEWCASTLE DISEASE
See Diseases.

NEW JERSEY AUDUBON
See Ornithological Periodicals.

NEW WORLD
See Western Hemisphere under Hemispheres.

NIAGARA FALLS SWAN TRAP
See Swan, whistling, in Duck Family.

NICHE
(pron. as in *rich*). *See* Ecological Niche.

NICTITATING MEMBRANE
Name for a third lid, a thin transparent (or opaque in owls) membrane that lies under the bird's eyelids. *See* Eyelid. When not used, it is curled up in the inner, or nasal, corner of the bird's eye but can be quickly drawn horizontally or obliquely across the eyeballs to clean and moisten them without shutting out the light. It is of great importance to a bird in flight exposed to a stream of air which could quickly dry the cornea. "There are many ornithologists who believe that the nictitans is held over the eye most or all of the time that a bird is in the air—the forerunner of the motorist's goggles" (Walls, 1942). Most birds blink occasionally, but most of them do so, regularly, only with the nictitating membrane.

Some aquatic diving birds, such as ducks, loons, and members of the Auk Family, have a clear, lenslike window in the nictitating membrane. This bends light rays and helps adjust the bird's vision for seeing underwater. See details in Tansley (1964).

NIDICOLE
Term often applied to the young usually of altricial birds (*see* Altricial) that remain for some days or weeks in the nest. The term means "nest dweller," and examples are the young of pelicans, pigeons, parrots, hawks, swifts, hummingbirds, owls, kingfishers, cuckoos, woodpeckers, and passerine birds. The term is also used for the fauna of birds' nests, other than the birds themselves. *See* Inquiline; Parasite. *Nidifugous* (nih-DIF-you-gus) is a term for birds whose young leave the nest shortly after hatching. A more restricted term than *precocial*, which refers also to the condition of the young—densely covered with down and with the eyes opened on hatching. *See* Altricial; Nidicole.

NIDIFICATION
(nid-ih-fih-KA-shon). Nest building. *See* Nests and Nesting.

NIGHTHAWK
See in Nightjar Family; also another name for the Black-tailed shearwater in Shearwater Family.

NIGHT HERON
See in Heron Family.

NIGHTINGALE
A thrush of Europe. Also another name for the N. American hermit thrush and veery in Thrush Family. *See also* White-throated sparrow in Finch Family.

NIGHTJAR FAMILY
Caprimulgidae (cap-rih-MULL-jih-dee); from Lat. *caper*, goat, and *mulgeo*, to milk, to suck (Jaeger, 1955), from legend that members of the family, also called goatsuckers, sucked milk from goats in the night; *nightjar*, from loud distinctive cries of these birds—the churring or jarring note of the European nightjar is the origin of the English family name. 67 species almost worldwide, not in New Zealand and on most of the oceanic islands (Van Tyne and Berger, 1976); some are migratory, 7 species in N. America; crepuscular to nocturnal; medium size; 7–13 in. long; not songbirds, but somewhat owl-like; nearest relatives may be owls; not usually predatory, mostly insect-eaters; have long, pointed wings, very small, weak feet; tail rather long; flight is easy and usually silent; they often perch lengthwise on branches, not usually crosswise as most birds do, and also spend much time on ground; a group remarkable for the flat head, small bill but wide, gaping mouth, large dark eyes, and soft, penciled plumage; many have long rictal bristles about the mouth; legs very short and tarsus feathered in some species; toes and claws small but middle toe is long with pectinated claw, called the feather comb (*see* Feather Comb). For other details about this group and its relatives, *see* Caprimulgiformes.

All are basically brown or gray, and plumage is cryptic (concealing); many are mottled, barred, or streaked with black, dark gray, and brown; some with white throat or white areas on wings and tail; loose fluffy plumage is very soft; lay eggs directly on ground (no nesting materials); color of sexes is normally somewhat different; both (or female only) incubate the eggs and both care for the young (Junge, 1964b); calls are purring, rasping, or whistled; Jenkinson and Mengel (1970) discovered that many members of the family regularly swallow stones, apparently to help them digest hardshelled beetles, which are a large part of the diets of many (*see* Gizzard), and individuals of at least one N. American species—the poor-will —hibernate (*see* Torpidity).

All members of the family are protected by law and a permit is required to keep them in captivity; however, an ill or injured bird may be sustained until it can fend for itself by offering it mealworms, moths, beetles, mockingbird food, and ground meat rolled into small balls (Walker, 1942).

Chuck-will's-widow, *Caprimulgus carolinensis* (cap-rih-MUL-gus cah-row-lin-EN-sis); genus name: *see* family introduction; species name: Lat., of Carolina; *chuck-will's-widow,* from its call. (Color ills., pages 578, 579.) Common in summer in woods of se. U.S.; largest N. American member of family; 11–13 in. long; wingspread 24½–25½ in.; brown and gray, resembles whip-poor-will but larger, and buffier (Peterson, 1947); the whip-poor-will has white crescent at lower edge of black throat; chuck-will's-widow has buffy line at edge of brownish-red throat; and has very few white feathers compared with whip-poor-will; call is different (see below); distinguished from nighthawk by lack of white in wings; female chuck-will's-widow is tan or dark buff where male is white; lives in rural South of farm fields interspersed with pine and oak woods; active at night feeding and calling; often perches on roads at night; eyes shine from reflected light (*see* Eyeshine); usually perches on tree limb lengthwise, also perches crosswise on small branches (Sprunt, 1940); during day crouches on leaf litter in woods, on log, or sometimes in natural tree cavity or in hollow log, where it dozes; when flushed, flies silently with mothlike flight; its call is loud whistle—an emphatic, four-syllabled song with accent on third syllable—*chuck-will's-WID-ow;* Sprunt (1940) counted 834 consecutive calls with pauses of 2½ seconds between each on warm June night (see also Harper, 1938); male usually sings most at dusk and on nights of half moon or brighter (also sometimes during day), from "song posts" above ground on tree branches and fence posts throughout his territory; also utters a growl, *cluck* or *chuck,* in flight and an infrequent wing-clapping (see details in Mengel and Jenkinson, 1971, and Mengel and Sharpe, 1972).

Feeding Habits: At night flies along edges of woods and fields, catches beetles, moths, and other insects in 2-in.-wide opened mouth, with supposed aid of rictal bristles at corners of mouth (*see,* however, Bristle under Feather); also catches and swallows whole, small birds.
Nest: None; lays eggs on dead dry leaves of forest floor.
Eggs: Fla., Mar.–June; elsewhere, Apr.–June; 2, glossy, pink-cream or buff, blotched, marbled, and spotted with brown, lavender, gray (for discussion of egg-carrying by chuck-will's-widow, see in Sprunt, 1940, and *see* Eggs and Egg-laying).
Incubation: By female, 20 days or more (Hoyt, 1953); 17 days after hatching, young can fly 50–150 ft.; are cared for by female; single-brooded (see Rohwer, 1971).
Other Names: Chick-a-willa; chip-fell-out-of-a-oak; chuck; Dutch whip-poor-will (all sonic); mosquito hawk; nightjar.
Range: Nests from Long Is., N.Y., at Oak Beach, May 24, 1975, first nesting for N.Y. (Kane and Buckley, 1975), and from s. N.J. south to Fla. and Gulf coast and c. Tex., from e. Kans., Mo., s. Ill., s. Ind., to s. Ohio; one reported dead in Conn., June 1969; winters from Gulf coast through e. Mexico and C. America to Colombia and throughout Bahamas and Greater Antilles; rarely north to e. N.C.

Nighthawk, Booming. *See* Nighthawk, common.

Nighthawk, common, *Chordeiles minor* (core-DIE-leez MY-nor); genus name: from Gr. *chorde,* a stringed musical instrument, and *deile,* afternoon or evening, in allusion to crepuscular habits of this bird with its frequent, loud piercing calls (see also in Gruson, 1972); species name: Lat., smaller, lesser, appropriate at one time when this species was classified in genus *Caprimulgus* with the larger whip-poor-will and much larger chuck-will's-widow, but now in genus *Chordeiles* is larger than the other N. American member of its genus—the lesser nighthawk—therefore species name no longer appropriate; *nighthawk,* probably because of bird's resemblance to smaller hawks when seen in flight (Gross, 1940); *common,* because it summers over towns, cities, suburbs, open plains, and mountains of most of N. America, from n. Canada south into Mexico. (Color ills., pages 578, 579.) 8½–10 in. long; wingspread about 21–24 in.; sexes similar, gray or gray-brown; especially distinguished during its darting flight, with regular or quick erratic beats of its long slender, pointed, blackish wings, flying low or high in air over treetops and houses, woodlands, and fields in late afternoon, early morning, at dusk or during the night and on dull days, uttering a nasal *beer!* or *peent* call; has broad white bar across wings, and male has white bar across the slightly forked tail, and a white throat; female also has white bar across wings but *lacks white band across tail,* and has *buffy* instead of white throat; at bottom of male's courtship dive, wings make loud *woof* or muffled boom, *sw-r, r-r-r-oonk,* the last part accented and resonant as rush through air vibrates his primaries (see courtship in Gross, 1940); when not in flight, nighthawk often seen perched on rail fences and posts with closed wings extending beyond tip of its tail, which distinguishes it from other members of family; nighthawks also lack rictal bristles about the mouth; in fall migration, at times seen in flocks of up to 1,000.

Feeding Habits: Sweeps insects out of air at any time of day or night into capacious mouth, largely while in flight, either high in air or close to ground, at least 50 different kinds from large moths and beetles to tiniest flies and mosquitoes; one stomach of nighthawk in Me. held 2,175 ants; another, in Mass., more than 500 mosquitoes; also eats enormous quantities of beetles, plant lice, grasshoppers, locusts, horseflies, stable flies, etc. (see list in McAtee, 1933a; Gross, 1940); also drinks water while in flight by skimming surface of lakes, streams, with bill.
Nest: Usually solitary, no nest; eggs laid on spot chosen by female on open barren rocks or bare gravelly soil of pastures, beaches, especially favors burned-over tracts left by forest fires, and graveled and tarred roofs of cities and towns; old fields, also on ground in vineyards, corn and potato fields, and even gardens; sometimes atop stump or fence rail up to 8 ft. above ground.
Eggs: Calif., Mar.–July; Fla. and Tex., Apr.–July; Northeast and Midwest, May–July; 2, cream-white to pale olive-buff or greenish, speckled with browns, grays.

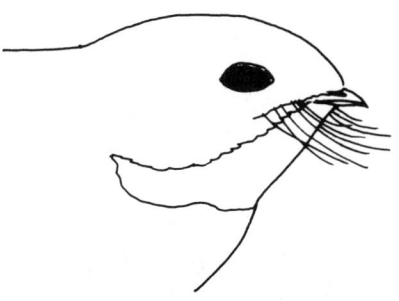

NIGHTJAR FAMILY

Incubation: Mostly by female, 19–20 days; young first fly about 21 days after hatching (Gross, 1940); male feeds incubating female and helps feed young; eggs and young often moved by adult within territory if temperature at nest site high; adults practice "gular flutter" for evaporative cooling of body to help withstand heat (Sutherland, 1963); *see* Heat and Birds.

Other Names: Booming nighthawk (Tex.); bull-bat; burnt-land bird; mosquito hawk; moth hunter; pisk; pork-and-beans; will-o'-the-wisp.

Flight Speed: Timed in Tex., 20–35 m.p.h. (Sooter, 1947); in Kans., 12–22 m.p.h. (Wood, 1923).

Weights: In summer, near Washington, D.C., one male, 69.3 gr.; one female, 67.9 gr. (Wetmore, 1936); three, w. U.S., averaged 80 gr. (Hughes, 1970), or about 2¾ oz.; one coastal N.J., fall, 81 gr. (Murray and Jehl, 1964), or about 2¾ oz.

Range: Nests from s. Yuk., w. Mack., n. Sask., n. Man., n. Ont., and Que. and Newfoundland south to s. Calif., c. Nev., nw., c., and se. Ariz., ne. Sonora, and n.-c. Mexico, to Bahamas, Jamaica, and Puerto Rico; winters from n. S. America to c. Argentina.

Nighthawk, lesser, *Chordeiles acutipennis* (core-DIE-leez ah-cute-ih-PEN-is); genus name: *see* Nighthawk, common; species name: from Lat. *acutus*, pointed, and *penna*, wing, in reference to the pointed wings of this species; *lesser* because smaller than common nighthawk. (Color ills., pages 578, 579.) Summers from c. Calif. in sw. U.S. to s. Tex.; 8–9 in. long; smaller and browner than common nighthawk, and white wing bar of male (buffy in female) is nearer tip of wing (Peterson, 1961); (immature has no wing bar); flies low, seldom high, does not dive as does common nighthawk; also, is bird of lowlands in Southwest, where common nighthawk is in mountains; identifiable by very different calls; instead of *peent* or *beer!* note of common nighthawk, utters a low *chuck chuck* and a soft, toadlike trill (trilling nighthawk is one of its common names); lives in open arid country of dry fields, lowlands, and areas of scattered scrubby growth; is also one of members of family that can become torpid with lack of food and onset of cool weather; Austin (1970) induced torpor in a male in Nev. by withholding food for 36 hours, then putting it in a refrigerator.

Feeding Habits: Eats many kinds of insects caught in mouth, usually in low flight near ground; is abroad in numbers in morning, feeding until about 11 A.M., thus more diurnal than others in family; also feeds around bright city lights far into night (Phillips *et al.*, 1964); after dark also feeds in open on ground (Bent, 1940); favored foods are beetles, moths, grasshoppers, winged ants.

Nest: Eggs laid on bare spot in open on sandy or gravelly ground, sometimes at base of a bush, on dry barren tablelands, sides of canyons, crests of rocky hills; in Brownsville, s. Tex., on flat roofs of adobe houses.

Eggs: Apr.–July; 2, pale gray to pale cream or pink-white, minutely peppered with dots of tan, gray, lilac.

Incubation: By female, 18–19 days; male helps feed young (is by regurgitation); age when young first fly unknown but probably about 21 days after hatching.

Other Names: Texas nighthawk; trilling nighthawk.

Weights: A male caught in May in Nev., 58 gr., or about 2 oz.

Range: Nests from c. Calif., s. Nev., sw. Utah, w. and c. Ariz., s. N.M., w. and s. Tex., south to n. Chile, Brazil; winters from s. Baja Calif. and nw. Mexico southward.

Nighthawk, Texas. *See* Nighthawk, lesser.

Nighthawk, trilling. *See* Nighthawk, lesser.

Nighthawk, western. *See* Nighthawk, common.

Nightjar, buff-collared, *Caprimulgus ridgwayi* (cap-rih-MUL-gus RIDG-way-eye); genus name: *see* family introduction; species name: given in 1897 by E. W. Nelson for Robert Ridgway, then Curator of Birds, National Museum, Washington, D.C. Mexican species reported in se. Ariz., where one collected in Guadalupe Canyon; according to Phillips *et al.* (1964), believed to breed there and in adjacent N.M.; lives in brush-covered hills and rocky slopes; 8½–9 in. long; similar to whip-poor-will but has buffy or tawny collar on hind neck (Peterson, 1961); and different voice, an unbirdlike, staccato, insectlike *cuk-cuk-cuk-cuk-cuk-cuk-cuk-cukacheeee*, resembling stridulations of a katydid (Davis, 1972).

Other Names: Cookacheea; preste-me-tucuchillo (from its call); Ridgway's cookacheea; Ridgway's whip-poor-will.

Range: W. Mexico, Guatemala, Honduras; reported in se. Ariz.

Pauraque, *Nyctidromus albicollis* (nick-TID-roh-mus al-bih-COL-is); genus name: from Gr. *nyx, nyktos*, night, and *dromos*, running, "night runner," in allusion to its activity at night; species name: from Lat. *albus*, white, and *collum*, neck, in reference to conspicuous crescent of white feathers around throat; *pauraque* (por-OCK-ee or poo-RAH-kay), native Mexican name imitative of one of its cries. (Color ill., page 579.) One of best-known of Mexican nightjars, also C. and S. American species, that in N. America reaches s. Tex., where resident; 10–12 in. long; differs from whip-poor-will and chuck-will's-widow by white band across each wing (Peterson, 1961); white band nearer wing tips than in similar nighthawk; also has long, *rounded* tail, not forked or with white bar across tail as in common nighthawk; utters peculiar whistle, long-drawn *ko, whe-e-e-e-e-ew*, raised to high pitch at end (Bent, 1940); Blake, E.R. (1953), wrote that in Mexican lowlands it utters soft, distinctive, much-repeated *who are you?;* most frequently heard at dusk and into night, call also interpreted as hoarse whistled *pur-we-eeeeeer*; lives in woodlands, open chaparral, or brush; winters in dense thickets along rivers, and in Tex. also seen along coastal prairie; likely to be flushed from

Buff-collared nightjar

NIGHTJAR FAMILY

forest paths or seen at night along roadsides; frequently flies low along road in front of car for 100 yds. or more and can be seen feeding on insects in beams of car headlights.

Feeding Habits: Sometimes perches on low dead limb or top of bush to watch for flying insects; in flight, catches many beetles, moths, also bugs, butterflies, wasps, bees.

Nest: Lays eggs on low level ground (no nest materials) in open brushland, near rivers or up arroyos.

Eggs: Mex. and Tex., Mar.–June; 2, salmon to pink-buff, usually more or less evenly marked with small blotches, spots, or dots of pale buff or cinnamon.

Incubation: In turn, by both sexes; period of and age when young first fly unknown.

Other Name: Merrill's pauraque.

Range: Permanent resident in Tex., mainly north along lower Rio Grande to Starr County; on coastal plain to Rockport, Beeville, Tex. (Peterson, 1963), and south from Sinaloa, Mexico, into C. America to e. Peru, Bolivia, Paraguay, ne. Argentina; also on Tres Marías, Mujeres, and Cozumel Is., Mexico.

Poor-will, *Phalaenoptilus nuttallii* (fal-ee-NOP-til-us nut-ALL-ih-eye); genus name: from Gr. *phalaina*, moth, and *ptilon*, feather, "moth-feathered," in reference to the soft, mothlike texture of the plumage; species name: given by John James Audubon in 1844 in honor of Thomas Nuttall, English immigrant, who, in America, became a distinguished 19th-century botanist and ornithologist; *poor-will*, from bird's cry. (Color ill., page 579.) Lives in w. U.S. from s. Canada and Calif. east to Neb., south to Ariz., Tex.; is western counterpart of the whip-poor-will of e. U.S.; in N. America, the least migratory member of its family, and, at present, only bird known to go into hibernation, although some other species in family and in other families of birds become torpid as means of fasting; sexes similar; 7–8 in. long; according to Peterson (1963), appears like a very small short-tailed whip-poor-will but generally grayer; has *rounded* wings; the outer tail feathers of male are black, broadly tipped with white; those of female only narrowly tipped with white; throat and sides of face black; white necklace around throat; lives in arid, stony hills and up slopes of mountains to 8,000–10,000 ft.; in open areas in mixed chaparral-grassland in n. Calif.; in sparse brushland of hot desert, also on open prairies, and in pinyon-juniper country; at dusk, into night, and at dawn, utters loud, harsh, whistled cry, at distance this is a melancholy, cadenced *poor-will* or *poor-jill*; when bird is near, one hears a three-part *poor-will-low, poor-will-ee*, or *poor-will-uck*; in flight, a *cluck* note.

Feeding Habits: Rests on ground amid shrubbery or tall weeds during day but at night hunts on or near ground; flits about silently like large moth; at night eyes shine pink from reflected light, especially noticed when perched on highways; eats insects, mostly night-flying moths, beetles, chinch bugs, also grasshoppers and locusts; many insects picked up from ground or by leaping from ground into air for them.

Nest: A bare scrape in ground, or eggs may be laid on hard gravelly ground or even on a flat rock, often partly shaded by bush or near bunch of weeds or tuft of grass.

Eggs: Calif., Mar.–Aug.; Tex., Apr.–June; Colo., May–July; 2, white or pale cream to pink, unmarked.

Incubation: By both sexes; period of and age when young first fly unknown.

Other Names: Common poor-will; dusky poor-will; Nuttall's poor-will.

Weights: One caught in Pocatello, Idaho, Sept. 1967, 59.1 gr. (Ligon, 1970b), or about 2 oz.; two adults, Calif., 51.4 and 44.8 gr., or about 1¾ oz. and 1½ oz. (Marshall, 1955).

Range: Nests from s.-c. B.C., se. Mont., nw. S.D., Neb., and sw. Iowa south on Pacific coast from c. Calif. to s. Baja Calif., and through e. Kans. and c. Tex. to c. Mexico; winters from c. Calif., s. Ariz., and s. Tex. southward; reported hibernating in Calif. and N.M.

Poor-will, common. *See* Poor-will.

Poor-will, dusky. *See* Poor-will.

Poor-will, Nuttall's. *See* Poor-will.

Whip-poor-will, *Caprimulgus vociferus* (cap-rih-MUL-gus voh-SIFF-er-us); genus name: *see* family introduction; species name: Lat., clamorous, noisy, in reference to loud repeated calls of this species; *whip-poor-will*, from its calls. (Color ill., page 579.) In summer, east of Great Plains from s. Canada to Tex. and se. U.S.; also in Southwest and occasionally s. Calif.; 9–10 in. long; wingspread 16–19½ in.; if flushed by day, flies away like large brown moth and showing *rounded* wings in which no white, but male shows large white patches in tail which flash in flight (Peterson, 1961); are also flashed by male in a display when hovering above ground (see Bruce, 1973); female in flight appears largely brown; she lacks broad white outer ends of tail feathers of male and her throat is buff instead of white; perched on ground or lengthwise on branch of tree, tips of folded wings of whip-poor-will do *not* come to end of tail; wings are broad and short compared with those of nighthawk and are moved in easy sweep with none of jerkiness of flight of nighthawk (Bent, 1940), common in rural country, where it favors ungrazed farm woodlots and woodlands throughout range, also in densely wooded mountains and canyons of Southwest; some are very tame and allow close observation in dusk or dark if one sits quietly near its "singing posts" on low branch, stone wall, or on ground; eyes shine red with reflected light on or along roadside, where often takes dust baths; from spring to late summer utters loud, whistled, rapidly reiterated *whip-poor-will, whip-poor-will*, mostly from dusk until about 9.30 P.M., then from 2 A.M. until dawn; heard close by, song sounds like *cuck-rhip-oor-ree*; about one call per second; 50–100 repetitions common; record number of consecutive calls was 1,088, reported by John Burroughs; almost equal number counted by Cleaves (1945), who rendered call *purple-RIB, purple-RIB.*

Feeding Habits: Flies about in open after dark, usually near ground; with opened mouth catches and eats flying insects: large moths such as cecropia, luna, and polyphemus, smaller noctuids; also moths of tent caterpillar and of tussock moth; also beetles, grasshoppers, caterpillars, crickets, mosquitoes, etc. (see McAtee, 1933a; Bent, 1940).

Nest: Eggs laid on open floor of woods such as mixed oak, beech, pine, often near edge where clear of dense undergrowth.

Eggs: Usually May–July; in Southwest, into Aug.; 2, white or cream-white, with spots or small blotches of gray overlaid with small dots of brown; some unmarked.

Incubation: Apparently by female only, 19–20 days; young first fly about 20 days after hatching.

Other Names: Eastern whip-poor-will; Stephens's whip-poor-will.

Age: One, banded Powdermill Nature Reserve, Rector, Pa., caught in same area and released when 3 years, 11 months, old (Kennard, 1975).

Weights: In Conn., in summer, an immature female, 51.7 gr. (Wetherbee, 1934), or about 1¾ oz.; in Mich. (17), 46.3–68.6 gr., or about 1½–2½ oz.

Range: Nests from c. Sask. east to s. Que., n. Me., and Nova Scotia south (east of Great Plains) to ne. Tex., n. La., n. Miss., c. Ala., n. Ga., nw. S.C., e.-c. N.C., and e. Va., and in mountains of se. and c. Ariz., s. N.M.; also a rare and local summer visitor to Riverside and San Diego counties, Calif. (Small, 1974); winters from nw. Mexico, s. Tex., Gulf coast, and S.C. to Costa Rica.

Whip-poor-will, eastern. *See* Whip-poor-will.

Whip-poor-will, Ridgway's. *See* Nightjar, buff-collared.

NIGHT-WALKER

See Ovenbird in Warbler—American Wood Warbler Family.

NOCTURNAL

Active at night. Some birds—certain owls, the nighthawks, and whip-poor-wills, for example —are habitually active at night and are called nocturnal birds. At one time, a section of the raptorial birds—the owls—was called Nocturnae (nok-TER-nee), contrasted with other birds of prey, active in daylight, which were called Diurnae. Many birds that are active only during the day most of the year migrate at night. *See* Migration.

NODDY

See in Gull Family; also a common name for the northern fulmar in Shearwater Family.

NOMENCLATURE

(NO-men-clay-tyour, or -chure). A system of names; the term is derived from Lat. *nomen*, a name, and *calare*, to call. Literally, nomenclature means to call by name; it is the "language" of zoology and the rules of nomenclature are its grammar. These include the vernacular, or common, names by which native and country peoples of all nations identified birds, mam-

The fulmar has a pair of tubelike, horny structures of the upper mandible that lead to the nostrils. All members of the shearwater family—as well as albatrosses and storm-petrels, which also have these specialized nostrils—are known as tubenoses.

cere

In the prairie falcon, as in all birds of prey, the nostrils open into a fleshy area, the cere, at the base of the upper mandible.

NOSTRILS

operculum

In members of the pigeon family, the nostrils are imperforate and each nostril is protected and nearly covered by a swollen layer of skin, called the operculum.

The turkey vulture, believed to have a keen sense of smell, has an incomplete nasal septum, which is thus called perforate.

mals, fishes, insects, frogs, and so on. These common names were often inadequate because the same name was frequently applied to different kinds of animals in different regions or countries. A universal nomenclature of scientific names was needed and was finally evolved with the system of Carl Linnaeus. *See* Linnaeus; Binomial Nomenclature; Names and Naming. *See also* Taxonomy.

NOMINATE SUBSPECIES

or NOMINATE RACE. When a species such as the red-winged blackbird was divided by taxonomists into several subspecies (*see* Subspecies), the subspecies that contained the population from the locality from which the first red-winged blackbird was described became the *nominate subspecies.* According to Mayr *et al.* (1953), Carl Linnaeus in 1766 described and named for science the first red-winged blackbird (*Agelaius phoeniceus)* from Mark Catesby's drawing (*see* Catesby) and description of the red-winged blackbird from South Carolina. South Carolina was fixed then as the red-winged blackbird's *type locality* (*see* Type Locality). When the red-winged blackbird was divided by taxonomists into a dozen or more subspecies, mainly in the U.S. and Canada, based on this bird's differences in different parts of N. America, the subspecies that occupies most of eastern N. America (including S.C.) became the nominate subspecies, namely, *Agelaius phoeniceus phoeniceus.* This species as a whole is *Agelaius phoeniceus*, but the nominate subspecies is recognized in print by repetition of the species name, in this example, *phoeniceus*. See the names of subspecies of the red-winged blackbird and their ranges in the latest edition of the *A.O.U. Check-List of North American Birds;* see there also other examples of nominate subspecies. *See* Names and Naming; Classification. Not all species of birds, however, become subspecies: *see* Monotype.

NONMIGRATORY

Ornithological term for a bird that does not migrate—for example, many game birds, and the cardinal and Carolina wren among songbirds. *See* Migration.

NONOBLIGATE PARASITE

See Obligate Parasite.

NONPAREIL

(non-pah-REL). Literally, "without equal"; one of the names of the painted bunting, in reference to the male's brilliant and diversified colors. *See* in Finch Family.

NORTH AMERICA

Mentioned frequently in accounts of N. American birds; has been geographically defined by the American Ornithologists' Union (see A.O.U. *Check-list*, 1957) as all of the continental U.S., Alaska, Canada, Baja Calif., and the islands of Greenland and Bermuda. This does not exactly coincide with the N. American faunal region—the Nearctic—as defined by some zoogeographers. *See* Nearctic Region; Faunal Regions; *also* Hemispheres.

NORTH AMERICAN ELEMENT

See Distribution.

NORTH ATLANTIC OCEAN

Watson (1966) has shown that the N. Atlantic is all of the Atlantic O. north of a line eastward from off the coast of Ga. and S.C. through Bermuda and on to the Canary Is. off the west coast of Africa, or above 33° N. Lat. *See* birds of the N. Atlantic under Seabird.

NORTHERN HEMISPHERE

See Hemispheres.

NOSTRILS

In birds, external openings in the upper part of the bill which allow them to breathe without opening the mouth. The nostrils are, in most birds, the beginning of the air passages of the breathing system (*see* Respiratory System), just as in man. They are called the *external nares* (NAY-reez) and they vary in shape in different groups of birds from round to oval or they may be mere slits, or closed completely. In most birds they open in the upper mandible (*see* Bill) between the beginning of the bird's bill at its face and part way out toward the tip. The nostrils are specialized in some birds—in nighthawks and their relatives they are long, soft, flexible tubes, and in the marine albatrosses, shearwaters, fulmars, storm-petrels, and diving petrels they are double horny tubes on top of the bill. In kiwis (New Zealand birds), the nostrils are, uniquely, at the tip of the bill, where they apparently function in helping the kiwis to smell their underground prey of earthworms. *See* discussion of the ability of birds to smell under Smell.

The nostrils (external nares) of some birds such as crows, ravens, and grouse are protected by feathers or by bristles, which may serve these birds also as organs of touch (*see* Touch; *also* Bristle under Feather); the nostrils of hawks and falcons are surrounded by a soft membrane *(cere);* and in pigeons and doves, each nostril is protected or partly covered by a swollen *opercula*, a cover of skin which leaves only a narrow slit for the passage of air.

The external nares (nostrils) are often cited by taxonomists as a character in the classification, or grouping, of certain birds; in most, the nostrils are open *(pervious)*, but according to Pettingill (1972), in adult gannets, frigatebirds, cormorants, and anhingas, the nostrils are absent, or completely closed by bone *(impervious)*, and presumably these birds must breathe through the mouth. However, gannets and cormorants, for example, have a permanently open slit at the gape (corners of the mouth) which permits them to breathe without opening the jaws (Dorst, 1974). This slit is protected by a horny lid that apparently closes when a gannet or cormorant dives, and it may remain closed as long as the bird is underwater; it has been considered an adaptation especially of gannets in their diving headfirst into water from a great height (see Macdonald, 1960).

The external nares open into the *nasal cavities* just inside the bird's upper mandible. In many birds, the nasal cavities are separated, or divided, longitudinally by a complete bony nasal septum. When a bird's septum is complete, it is called *imperforate,* but in cranes, American vultures, and rails, for example, which have a central opening in the septum, it is called *perforate* (Van Tyne and Berger, 1959).

Inside the nasal cavities, extending from each outer wall, are three thin, scroll-like *conchae* (that is, shaped like a shell)—a large front and middle one, and a small rear one in which the bird's olfactory nerve originates (Salt and Zeuthen, 1960). The conchae may be covered with a mucous-secreting membrane; the mucous traps dust; the membrane warms the breathed-in air (Pettingill, 1972); the conchae modify and sample the respiratory air (Lasiewski, 1972). The nasal cavities enter into the mouth through the internal or posterior nares, and the passage of air from a bird's mouth to its lungs begins in the glottis (*see* Glottis; *also* Respiratory System).

ANOTHER USE OF THE NOSTRILS. For years ornithologists wondered how seabirds of many kinds could drink salt water all their lives and survive. These birds, and man, must limit the concentration of salt in their blood and body fluids to about 1%—less than a third of the salt concentration in sea water (Schmidt-Nielsen, 1959). If a man drinks sea water, the salt only intensifies his thirst and he must excrete the excess salt through his kidneys, which requires additional water drawn from the fluids in his body, which causes dehydration. It was known that the kidneys of birds were far less efficient in getting rid of excess salt than those of man, and that too much salt would kill chickens and pigeons. Yet thick-billed murres, which were fully adapted to life on the sea, had been drinking salt water all their lives, and petrels and shearwaters were apparently such obligatory drinkers of salt water that they would die of thirst without it, though plenty of fresh water was available (Coles, 1925).

Comparative anatomists knew that all birds had in their heads paired structures called lateral nasal, or supraorbital, glands in a depression of the skull near the eye-socket area that varied in size, shape, and location, but they did not know their function (Schmidt-Nielsen, 1959).

In 1957–58, Knut Schmidt-Nielsen and his coworkers in the U.S. discovered that the double-crested cormorant and the Humboldt's, or Peruvian, penguin could excrete from their lateral nasal glands a fluid with a remarkably high concentration of salt—higher even than that of sea water. It appears that the lateral nasal glands, called more appropriately by Schmidt-Nielsen and Fange (1958) salt glands, are larger and better developed in all seabirds than in land birds, especially in albatrosses, pelicans, gulls, terns, cormorants, gannets, eider ducks, geese, coots and rails (Carpenter and Stafford, 1970), which at times, or regularly, take in large amounts of salt in their food or drinking water. Functional salt glands have not been discovered in passerines (songbirds) despite investigations of some of those more likely to have them, but are known in numerous birds in thirteen orders (*see* Order), in which they are functional. See in Shoemaker (1972).

The function of the salt glands is to get rid of excess salt in a bird's body, thus preventing dehydration. Petrels forcibly shoot out the salty fluid from their tubular nostrils, but in other seabirds it dribbles out of the external and internal nares. Internally, the excess salt is picked up by the blood and transferred to the salt gland, then the duct of each gland conveys the concentrated salt solution to the nasal cavities, from which it flows through the external nares (nostrils) and to the tip of the bill. In adult cormorants and gannets, in which the external nares are closed, the fluid trickles from the internal nares in the roof of the mouth and then flows to the tip of the bill.

In one of Schmidt-Nielsen's experiments, 10 minutes after 5 gr. of sodium chloride (salt) had been given to a Humboldt's penguin, a clear colorless liquid containing the excess salt started to drip from the tip of its bill (Schmidt-Nielsen and Sladen, 1958), which the bird shook away vigorously in the characteristic head-shaking movement so common among most seabirds. Two thirds of the salt fed to this bird was eliminated through its nose; the kidneys proved only one tenth as efficient as the salt gland during the same period of time of the experiment. According to Schmidt-Nielsen (1959), unlike the bird's kidneys, which secrete continuously, though at a varying rate, the salt gland functions only intermittently in response to the need to eliminate salt. The salt gland's activity depends on the concentration of salt in the blood, and apparently nerves in the brain or ganglia in the salt glands stimulate the gland to respond; it is also influenced by hormones from the adrenal glands (Assenmacher, 1973). See experiments with ducks in Schmidt-Nielsen and Kim (1964).

NOTORNIS
See Gruiformes.

NOVICE
(NOV-iss). Term applied by some biologists to a female wild duck that returns her first summer to the area where she herself was hatched, in order to nest, and is "lacking previous nesting experience" (Fuller and Bolen, 1963). *See* Abmigration.

NUCHAL
(NYOU-kal). Pertaining to the back of the neck, or the nape (nucha). *See* Nape; Topography.

NUISANCE BIRDS
See discussion under Control.

NUMBERS OF BIRDS
See Census. For total number of birds in world, and for most numerous species, or kinds, of birds, *see* Populations. For number of species in N. America, *see* Species.

NUN
Name for a female scaup, from her dark plumage and white face. *See* in Duck Family.

NUPTIAL
In ornithology, pertaining to the breeding season of birds—for example, nuptial (breeding) plumage. *See* Courtship; Molts and Molting.

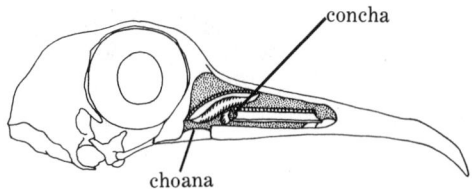

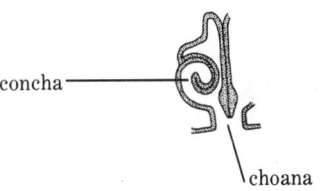

cross-section of a nasal cavity

NOSTRILS
The outer walls of the nasal passage have three scroll-like extensions, the conchae, which are covered by a mucous-secreting membrane that filters and warms inhaled air. The smallest, posterior concha is the site of the olfactory receptors. The nasal passages open into the roof of the mouth through a slit, the choana.

COMMON NUTHATCH FAMILY

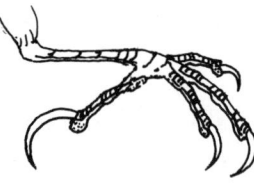

NUPTIAL FEEDING
See Courtship Feeding.

NUTCRACKER
See in Crow Family.

NUTHATCH—COMMON NUTHATCH FAMILY

Sittidae (SIT-ih-dee); from Gr. *sitte*, used by Aristotle for a bird that pecks at the bark of trees, probably the nuthatch (Macleod, 1954); *nuthatch*, from hacking open with bill seeds and nuts by several Old World species, a habit sometimes seen in American nuthatches *(hatch is a corruption of hack)*. 22 species of small, tree-dwelling songbirds (*see* Passeriformes) that live in forested regions around northern parts of world—N. America and Eurasia (Van Tyne and Berger, 1976); 4 species in N. America; like their nearest relatives, the titmice, are most represented in Old World, where they may have originated; are the only tree-trunk foraging birds that regularly feed moving head downward (when John Kieran, American naturalist, first saw picture of N. American white-breasted nuthatch descending a fence post in this way, he could not believe it—see Kieran, 1952, p. 13). From this angle, descending nuthatches may find food in bark crevices overlooked by "up the trunk" foraging tree creepers and small woodpeckers (Tyler, 1948a). Nuthatches are short (3½–7 in. long) and stocky; sexes outwardly alike, or nearly so; gray-blue above, white below; bills thin, straight, and sharp-pointed, nostrils somewhat covered with stiff feathers; wings long, pointed, each with 10 primary feathers; legs short, strong, long toes have sharp claws that enable them to cling to vertical tree bark; use feet to hold them in place; descend trees in short, jerky hops, or move along underside of branches in same way with back to ground; fly up and down (undulating) in flight, like woodpeckers. Most are not migratory but in some years of food shortages in North, great irruptions of red-breasted nuthatches southward (*see* Irruption). Nuthatch Family unknown south of Mexico; largest N. American species is white-breasted nuthatch; smallest, pygmy nuthatch, which lives in West; brown-headed, in se. U.S., is possibly first N. American bird reported to use a "tool" in feeding (see Morse, 1968). Most American nuthatches come to feeding stations; individuals often tame when hungry and can be lured to fly to one's hands for halved peanuts or other food (see in Terres, 1968; 1977); some will nest in birdhouses built for them. All members of Common Nuthatch Family are protected by law and not to be kept captive, but to sustain an injured or ill one until able to fend for itself, offer same foods recommended under Titmouse Family.

Black-eared nuthatch. *See* Pygmy nuthatch.

Brown-headed nuthatch, *Sitta pusilla* (SIT-ah pew-SIL-ah); genus name: *see* family introduction; species name: from Lat. *pusillus*, very small. (Color ill., page 581.) Se. U.S.; 4–5 in. long; wingspread about 7¾ in.; sexes outwardly alike; blue-gray above except for buffy brown cap and nape; a spot of white in brown of nape where it meets back; white below (a paler form, or subspecies, of extensive open pinelands of Fla. has grayish crown); brown-headed nuthatches, when not in pairs in nesting season, travel in family groups of small flocks, sometimes with woodpeckers, kinglets, pine warblers, titmice (Bent, 1948); especially favor open pine woods, clearings, and burned-over tracts, also mixed forests of pines and hardwoods and small cypress swamps in such woods, also in woods of residential areas; while flock moves about in trees feeding, utter nasal notes, reedier and harsher than other nuthatches—a liquid conversational *pit, pit,* chirps, and kissing notes, and a *dee-dee-dee* call like chickadee; in breeding season, utters song-like *pri-u, de-u, de-u.*

Feeding Habits: Forages over branches, twigs at ends of branches, often hangs head downward from cluster of pine needles, creeps either up or down trunks, fence posts, utility poles, buildings, for beetles, bugs, roaches, caterpillars, moths, ants, scale insects, pine seeds, and spiders. Remarkable discovery by Morse (1968) that this nuthatch sometimes uses a tool in feeding: holds piece of bark in bill to flake off another piece of bark to uncover insects.

Nest: Pair dig cavity in tree, stub, fire-blackened stump, utility pole, post, 2–50 ft. above ground, usually less than 10 ft. (sometimes nest in bird box); fill cavity with dried grasses, weed stems, strips of bark, leafy part of pine seeds, chips of wood, wool, cotton, corn husks, feathers.

Eggs: Mar.–July; 3–9, usually 5–6, white, dotted, spotted, or blotched with browns.

Incubation: By both sexes, about 14 days; young leave nest about 18 days after hatching.

Other Name: Gray-headed nuthatch.

Age: One, banded Chapel Hill, N.C., caught in same area when 4 years, 5 months, old (Kennard, 1975).

Weights: N.C. (21), averaged 10.8 gr. (Teulings and Teulings, 1971), or less than ½ oz.

Range: Resident from se. Okla., c. Ark., La., Miss., Ala., n. Ga., sw. N.C., s. Va., s. Md., and s. Del., south to e. Tex., Gulf coast, Fla., and Grand Bahama Is.; casual north to N.J.; accidental Mo., Iowa, and N.Y.

Canada nuthatch. *See* Red-breasted nuthatch.

Florida nuthatch. *See* White-breasted nuthatch.

Gray-headed nuthatch. *See* Brown-headed nuthatch.

Inyo nuthatch. *See* White-breasted nuthatch.

Nevada nuthatch. *See* Pygmy nuthatch.

Pygmy nuthatch, *Sitta pygmaea* (SIT-ah pig-ME-ah); genus name: *see* family introduction; species name: from Lat. *pygmaeus*, pygmy. (Color ills., page 580.) Rocky Mtns. to Pacific coast, smallest of N. American nuthatches; 3¾–4½ in. long; western counterpart of the brown-headed nuthatch, which it resembles in plumage and habits; sexes outwardly alike; *has gray-brown cap* which extends down to eyes (red-breasted and white-breasted nuthatches have *black caps* and white line over eyes); blue-gray black, white underparts and outer tail feathers; pygmy lives especially in ponderosa pines up to 10,000 ft. elevation in Rockies; also in pinyons, junipers in Ariz. and in ponderosa and other pines of Pacific coast; except in nesting season, when in pairs, travels in small family flocks which increase to large numbers by fall and winter; drift noisily through tops of pines, calling incessantly to one another, *ti-di, ti-di, ti-di,* or soft *kit, kit, kit;* twitter constantly, resembling flocks of bushtits that travel in similar disconnected way but low in shrubbery, often travel with other small birds—yellow-rumped (Audubon's) warbler—plain titmouse, mountain chickadee, roost in groups at night in cavities of trees, one report of 100 in one cavity (Bailey and Niedrach, 1965), also in bird box.

Feeding Habits: Searches by short hops over branches, outermost twigs, and pine cones, also up and down tree trunks to catch with bill wasps, ants, spittle insects (of pine needles), beetles, moths and caterpillars, grasshoppers, spiders, and pine seeds.

Nest: Pair dig with bill small circular hole and cavity, usually near top of dead pine or on underside of branch or in upright post, also in woodpecker hole; 8–60 ft. up, lined with pine-cone scales, plant down, leaves, fur, feathers.

Eggs: Apr.–June; 4–9, usually 6–8, peppered or spotted with red-browns.

Incubation: Mostly by female, 15½–16 days; young leave nest 22 days after hatching (Norris, 1958).

Other Names: Black-eared nuthatch; Nevada nuthatch; pine nuthatch; white-naped nuthatch.

Age: One, banded at South Rim, Grand Canyon, at least 5 years old when retrapped same place; another, banded Idyllwild, Calif., caught (and released) in same area when 7 years, 3 months, old (Kennard, 1975).

Range: Resident from mountainous areas s. B.C., east to n. Idaho, w. Mont., e. Wyo., sw. S.D., south to n. Baja Calif., Ariz., N.M., and south in highlands to s.-c. and e.-c. Mexico.

Red-breasted nuthatch, *Sitta canadensis* (SIT-ah can-ah-DEN-sis); genus name: *see* family introduction; species name: Lat., of Canada. (Color ills., page 581.) E. and w. U.S. and Canada, north to Alaska; 4½–4¾ in. long; wingspread 8–8½ in.; blue-gray above, buffy or red-brown below; black cap, white stripe above eyes, black line through eyes; female similar but has blackish blue cap; usually a resident of forests of balsam fir and spruce of the North, also in fir forests of Pacific coast, but recently is extending its range southward to e. N.Y. and Pa., nesting in Norway spruces and other ornamental conifers (Buckley *et al.,* 1975); an irregular migrant southward, sometimes in great numbers when seed crops of spruce, pine, and other conifers of the northern environment fail (see also details in Bagg, 1970); moves over bark of trees very rapidly or winds about small twigs and needles of conifers at ends of branches; darts out into air for flying insects, travels in small companies at end of summer; one of commonest notes is *it, it, it* or *hit,* and others (see Tyler, 1948b); also a high-pitched nasal *ank, ank, ank,* and song like a high-pitched penny trumpet, *wa-wa-wa-wa-wa.*

Feeding Habits: Very fond of seeds of pines, spruces, firs, and other conifers; deftly pries open cone scales with bill and extracts seeds, takes some insects—beetles, wasps, and caterpillars, insect eggs, crane flies, moths of spruce budworm; comes to feeding stations for chopped kernels of walnuts, pecans, suet, sunflower seeds; will take food from hands (see details in Terres, 1968; 1977); usually wedges food into bark crevices with bill (does not hold with feet as chickadees do), then breaks off in pieces to swallow; also picks up seeds from ground, sometimes feeds in stands of giant ragweed (Tyler, 1948b).

Nest: Usually digs cavity in tree stub or branch of dead tree—pine, cottonwood, and others; 5–100 ft. up, usually about 15 ft. above ground; also uses deserted woodpecker holes, and will nest in bird boxes. Habitually smears pitch of coniferous trees with bill around entrance to nest cavity, whether hardwood or coniferous tree or bird box (see de Kiriline, 1952); nest inside built of grasses, rootlets, mosses, shredded bark, plant fibers.

Eggs: Apr.–June; 4–7, usually 5–6, peppered and spotted with browns.

Incubation: By both sexes, 12 days; young leave nest 18–21 days after hatching (Tyler, 1948b).

Other Names: Canada nuthatch; devil-down-head; red-bellied nuthatch; topsy-turvy-bird.

Age: A male, banded Mt. Desert, Me., caught and released in same area when 7 years, 6 months, old (Kennard, 1975).

Host to Cowbirds: Rare, one record (Friedmann, 1963).

Weights: Coastal N.J., in fall (312), 8–12.7 gr. (Murray and Jehl, 1964), or about ⅓–¼ oz.

Range: Resident from se. Alaska to s. Yukon, sw. Mack., c. Sask., s. Man., James Bay, w. and n. Ont., s. and e. Que., Newfoundland, and south to s. Calif., se. Ariz., w.-c. and se. Colo., Wyo., sw. S.D., Mont., se. Man., c. Minn., Wisc., n. Mich., s. Ont., through the Appalachian Mts., to e. Tenn., w. N.C., also s. N.Y., w. Conn., and Mass.; in 1973 and 1975, nested near Brookhaven Laboratory, Upton, Long Is., N.Y., also at Dingmans Falls, Pa., etc. (Buckley *et al.,* 1975); winters irregularly south to s. Ariz., s. N.M., Tex., and n. Fla. to Gulf coast. For true story of family of these birds, see "Irrepressible Nuthatch," in Terres (1958).

Slender-billed nuthatch. *See* White-breasted nuthatch.

White-breasted nuthatch, *Sitta carolinensis* (SIT-ah cah-row-lin-EN-sis); genus name: *see* family introduction; species name: Lat., of Carolina. (Color ill., page 582.) E. and w. U.S.; largest of N. American nuthatches; 5–6 in. long; wingspread 9¼–11½ in.; sexes much alike; blue-gray above with *black cap and nape,* clear white below, sides of face and neck white, flanks tawny; white patches in each side

White-breasted nuthatch

Brown-headed nuthatch

COMMON NUTHATCH FAMILY

White-breasted nuthatches work their way down a tree trunk finding grubs and insects in bark crevices that other tree foragers, working upward, would miss. Brown-headed nuthatches feed on insects and pine seeds among the clusters of pine needles at the ends of branches.

of tail; spends most of life in large trees of forests, farm woodlots, country towns, and parks; hops over bark of trunks and main branches, usually moving head downward toward ground; sometimes hops about on ground under trees in search of nuts, insects; one study has shown that resident pairs remain together in limited feeding territory of 25–50 acres throughout the year; small family groups break up in fall; each member of pair often alone in winter woods but within calling distance of each other; roost alone (except in very cold weather) in hole in tree; when feeding sometimes joined by chickadees, creepers, and downy woodpeckers feeding in same tree; do not usually migrate, but some migration reported in New York City (Bull, 1964) and in Md. between Sept. 15 and Nov. 10 (see discussion in Heintzelman and MacClay, 1971); individuals quite tame, can be lured to one's hands for food, or even to one's lips for halved peanut, sunflower seed, piece of walnut kernel; very agile, can catch falling nut in midair, run down a swaying rope, or hang upside down swinging from tiny branch; sings every month in year, most frequently in late winter and spring, whistled song a series of 6–8 notes, each with slightly rising inflection, *wee-wee-wee-wee-wee-wee*, a nasal call note, *yank, yank, yank, yank* (see details in Tyler, 1948b).

Feeding Habits: In fall and winter eats mostly beechnuts, acorns, hickory nuts, sunflower seeds, corn; in spring and summer, bugs, ants, flies, grasshoppers, moths, cankerworms, caterpillars of gypsy moth, forest and tent caterpillars, weevils, wood-borers, tree hoppers, aphids, scale insects; comes to feeding stations for suet, wild bird seed mixture (see details in Terres, 1968c).

Nest: Often high up in large tree, in natural cavity, woodpecker's hole, or knothole, in oak, elm, maple, apple tree, usually 15–50 ft. up, also in bird boxes; nest materials in cavity are shreds of inner bark, rabbit's fur, wool, cow hair, feathers; sometimes plucks hairs from gray squirrels (Tyler, 1948b).

Eggs: Mar.–June; 5–10, commonly 8, white, heavily marked with browns, reds, purple, gray.

Incubation: By both sexes, 12 days; young first fly about 14 days after hatching.

Other Names: Carolina nuthatch; common nuthatch; devil-down-head; Florida nuthatch; Inyo nuthatch; Rocky Mountain nuthatch; sapsucker; slender-billed nuthatch; topsy-turvy-bird; tree mouse; yank.

Age: One, banded Conn., 8 years old when recaptured; one, banded N.Y., 9 years old when retrapped; another, banded Longmont, Colo., caught again when it was 9 years, 9 months, old (Kennard, 1975).

Host to Cowbirds: Rare (Friedmann, 1963); only five records.

Weights: Coastal N.J., one in fall, 18 gr. (Murray and Jehl, 1964), or about ¾ oz.; in Mich. (12), 19.6–22.9 gr. (Becker and Stack, 1944).

Range: Resident from s. B.C., se. Alta., nw. and c. Mont., s. Man., s. Ont., s. Que., n. Me., n.-c. N.B., Prince Edward Is., Cape Breton Is., and c. Nova Scotia, south to s. Baja Calif., s. Mexico; absent from most of Great Plains of U.S.

White-naped nuthatch. *See* Pygmy nuthatch.

NUTTALL

THOMAS (1786–1859). Born in England, came to U.S. in 1808; a noted botanical explorer and ornithologist, for whom William Gambel named the Nuttall's woodpecker; Audubon, the poorwill and yellow-billed magpie; and in whose honor Ridgway established the genus name *Nuttallornis* for the olive-sided flycatcher; also, the Nuttall Ornithological Club of Cambridge, Mass., was named in his honor. Nuttall was professor of natural history and curator of the botanical gardens at Harvard; he was the author of *Manual of Ornithology of the United States and Canada* (1833–34) and in 1834, with John K. Townsend, crossed the Rocky Mtns. to Ore. and Calif. (Herrick, 1917). He returned to England in 1842 and died there. See also Palmer (1928); Gruson (1972).

NUTTING

C(HARLES) C(LEVELAND) (1858–1927). Zoologist, long-time professor of zoology at the University of Iowa, and collector of zoological specimens for museums (Ewan, 1950), for whom Ridgway (in Nutting, 1882) named a flycatcher from collections of birds made by Nutting in Costa Rica.

OBERHOLSER

HARRY CHURCH (1870–1963). Born Brooklyn, N.Y.; from 1895 to 1941, a professional biologist of the Division of Economic Ornithology, later called the Bureau of Biological Survey, then the U.S. Fish and Wildlife Service. His name is commemorated in the species name of the dusky flycatcher, *Empidonax oberholseri*, and in a subspecies of the curve-billed thrasher. "During 46 years of government service, Oberholser functioned primarily as an expert in the identification of birds" (Aldrich, 1968); he was known in the ornithological profession as a "splitter," with an extraordinary ability to detect slight morphological differences between geographical populations of birds. He published more than 900 papers on ornithology, and a book, *Bird Life of Louisiana* (1938), and wrote *The Bird Life of Texas* (published posthumously in 1974 by the University of Texas Press). See Aldrich (1968) for other details.

OBLIGATE PARASITE

Term in biology for an animal or plant that is limited to the single life condition of being a parasite (*see* Parasite; see also in Ch. 6, Rothschild and Clay, 1957, a discussion of the evolution of parasitism and of parasites). Hanson, Herbert C., (1962) defines an obligate parasite as one that cannot attain complete development independent of its host. Among N. American birds, cowbirds are *obligate parasites* because they require other birds to hatch their eggs and rear their young. *See* discussion under Brood Parasitism, and about cowbirds in Troupial Family.

Nonobligate parasites among birds are those that occasionally, or even regularly, lay their eggs in the nests of other birds either of their own kind or of other species; however, normally they incubate their own eggs and raise their own young; they are not completely dependent on other birds to raise their young as cowbirds are. This semi-parasitic habit of the nonobligate parasite may be a step in evolution toward becoming an obligate parasite (Berger, 1961).

Some examples of birds that are nonobligate parasites are the black-billed and yellow-billed cuckoos, eared and pied-billed grebes, Virginia rail, roadrunner, brown thrasher, starling, house sparrow, and house finch. The habit even exists among some N. American sparrows. In June 1965, Wiens (1971) in Wisc. found a nest of a pair of Savannah sparrows in a field with a full clutch (five) of their eggs and two of a grasshopper sparrow. Late in July he returned to find the adult Savannah sparrows feeding in their nest one of their own young, which had hatched, and one young grasshopper sparrow. The habit, by which one kind of bird is victimized in this way and raises the young of another species, is more likely to succeed when the food of young and adults are similar. *See* other examples under Foster Parents.

Several members of the Pheasant Family occasionally, or even frequently, lay their eggs in the nests of other species; for example, California quail lay their eggs in the nests of other birds, including that of the ground-nesting, or close-to-the-ground-nesting, rufous-sided (western spotted form) towhee. Samuel A. Grimes, a Fla. ornithologist, found a nest of an eastern meadowlark with four eggs of the meadowlark and two of a bobwhite. Alexander Bain discovered four bobwhite eggs in a ring-necked pheasant's nest, and this pheasant's eggs have been found in the nests of wild ducks; ring-necked pheasants also lay their eggs in each other's nests (Berger, 1961). *See also* Dump Nest.

In the spring of 1956, an observer near Beaverton, Ore., found eight eggs of a ring-necked pheasant in a nest of a ruffed grouse. The nest also held eleven eggs of the grouse, which the observer discovered after he had flushed the grouse from her nest (Kebbe, 1958).

According to Berger (1961), who has summarized the subject of nonobligate parasites among birds, the Duck Family has the largest number of nonobligate parasites, and some of these lay their eggs in other birds' nests so frequently as to be called semi-parasitic species. Weller (1959b) reported 21 different species of ducks whose eggs have been found in nests other than their own, and some of these ducks laid their eggs in the nest of a bird of their own species.

The redhead, *Aythya americana*, and the ruddy duck, *Oxyura jamaicensis*, whose attachment to their own nests and eggs is weaker than in other ducks, had this habit more than other ducks studied; also, they desert their young at an earlier age. *See* in Duck Family; *see also* Young and Their Care; Nests and Nesting.

OBLITERATIVE SHADING

See Colors of Feathers.

OCCIPUT

(OK-sih-put). The back part of the head or skull. In a bird it is the part between the crown and nape. *See* Topography.

OCEANIA

(OH-she-an-ih-ah or OH-she-AY-nih-ah), or O-CEANICA (OH-she-an-ih-kah). Name for scattered island groups in s. and c. Pacific O.—Micronesia, Melanesia, and Polynesia; also considered by some to include Australia, New Zealand, and the Malay Archipelago.

OCEANIC BIRD

See Seabird.

OCELLATED

(OS-eh-late-ed); from Lat. *ocellatus*, from *ocellus*, a little eye. Having ocelli; like an eye or ocellus, as the ocellated spots in the tail feathers of the ocellated turkey of Mexico and parts of C. America; also in the tail feathers of the peacock.

OCREATE

(OCK-ree-ate). Booted, as the tarsus of some birds. *See* Tarsus; Feet and Legs.

OCTOPUS AND BIRDS

See Mollusks and Birds.

ODONTOGNATHAE
(oh-don-TOG-nah-thee [*th* as in *thin*]). A super-order of extinct New World toothed birds (see Wetmore, 1956). *See* Hesperornis; Ichthyornis; Fossil Birds; *also* Classification.

OILBIRD
A tropical American bird of the Nightjar Family; *see* Echolocation; Caprimulgiformes; Smell; it is also another name for the northern fulmar in Shearwater Family.

OIL GLAND
See Skin Glands.

OLD INJUN
See Oldsquaw in Duck Family.

OLDSQUAW
See in Duck Family.

OLD WIFE
See Oldsquaw in Duck Family.

OLD WORLD
See Hemispheres.

OLD WORLD ELEMENT
See Distribution.

OLD WORLD FLYCATCHER FAMILY
See under Flycatcher.

OLD WORLD WARBLER FAMILY
See under Warbler.

OLFACTION
See Smell.

OLIGOCENE PERIOD
See Geological Time Scale.

OMENS
See Augury; Auspices; Folklore.

OMNIVOROUS
(om-NIV-oh-rus). Term applied to a bird or any other animal that eats both animal and plant food. It is synonymous in its use in ornithology with *euryphagous*. *See* Euryphagous; *also* Stenophagous. *See* Carnivorous; Insectivorous; Food and Feeding Habits. *See also* Feeding Habits in the biography of each bird.

ONTOGENY
(on-TODGE-e-nih). The life history of an individual bird or other animal and its development, in contradistinction to phylogeny or the evolution of an order, family, or species. *See* Phylogeny.

OOLOGY
(oh-OL-oh-jih). The scientific study of the eggs of birds—of the shapes, sizes, colors, numbers in a clutch, and so on. *See* Clutch; Collections; Eggs and Egg-laying. Dr. Adolphus Heermann, a pioneering field ornithologist in Calif., for whom the Heermann's gull was named, was the first ornithologist credited with using the term *oology* in American ornithology.

OPERCULUM
See Nostrils; *also* Topography.

OPPORTUNISM
See Commensalism.

ORAL CAVITY
See Mouth.

ORBIT
The cavity in the bird skull that houses each eye; eye socket; sometimes used to mean the eye itself. The *orbital ring* is a circular marking surrounding the eye, which Coues (1884) called the *orbital* or *circumorbital region*—a small space forming a ring around the eye. *See* Eyes and Eyesight; Skeleton.

ORDER
One of the higher collective categories in the classification of birds. An order includes one or more families (*see* Family) and is a category below class and above family. Along with classes and phyla of animals, it has proved one of the most stable categories for grouping birds of broad structural likenesses, in that bird members of an order have recognizable basic structural patterns of the skeleton and other parts of the anatomy (*see* Morphology), which were established early in the history of evolution. *See* Evolution; Origin of Birds and of Bird Flight under Fossil Birds. *See* especially the discussion of how birds are classified according to their relationships under Phylogenetic Relationship.

The bird members of an order are widely distributed throughout the world (Mayr *et al.*, 1953). *See* Distribution. The scientific names of all orders of birds (there are 20 in N. America) end in *-iformes*, by which the name of an order can be recognized. *See* the orders of N. American birds listed under Classification. *See* each order listed alphabetically here in the text, with details about each order itself (and the bird families that compose each), under their various names—for example, Anseriformes; Apodiformes; Caprimulgiformes; Charadriiformes; and so on.

For some of the major characters that distinguish or set apart the orders and families of N. American birds, see in Pettingill (1970); for additional characters that distinguish them, refer to Brodkorb (1968). For characters that distinguish all of the bird families of the world, refer to Ch. 13 in Van Tyne and Berger (1959). Pettingill (1972) has listed the names of 33 orders of birds, living and extinct, of the world, of which 27 are still living. See also Storer (1960b).

ORDERS OF NORTH AMERICAN BIRDS
See list of orders and families of N. American birds under Classification.

ORGAN OF CORTI
The receptive part of the cochlea of the inner ear of birds; collectively, "the basilar membrane, accessory supporting cells, nerve fibers, and the tectorial membrane," all within the cochlea itself. "It is the displacement of the basilar membrane, and consequent deformation of its hair cells, that is the immediate cause of excitation of cochlear nerve fibers," which results in the sensation of hearing (Pumphrey, 1961a). *See* How a Bird Hears under Ears and Hearing.

Sturkie (1954) reports that the number of these hair cells in the organ of Corti in birds averages about 1,200 according to one authority; about 3,000 according to another. There are considerably more in man, who has a reported 24,000.

ORIENTAL REGION
See Distribution; Faunal Regions.

ORIENTATION
See How Do Birds Find Their Way? under Migration; *also* Homing; Echolocation.

ORIGIN OF BIRDS AND OF BIRD FLIGHT.
See under Fossil Birds.

ORIOLE
See in Troupial Family.

ORIOLE FAMILY
Oriolidae; a family of some 28 or 34 brightly colored species of Old World birds. They are essentially tropical and subtropical; range widely throughout Africa, s. Asia, and East Indies to New Guinea and e. Australia (Austin, 1961; Moreau, 1964b); are not related to birds called "orioles" in N. America. They have 10 primary (wing) feathers—American orioles have 9—and, anatomically, they are allied to starlings, crows, and jays; the American orioles are closely related to tanagers. The word "oriole," from Lat. *aureolus* (golden, or yellow), was given originally to the brilliant golden oriole, *Oriolus oriolus*, which nests widely throughout Europe and w. Asia (Austin, 1961). For American orioles, *see* in Troupial Family.

ORIOLE, THE
A publication. *See* Ornithological Periodicals.

ORNITHOCOPROPHILOUS
An ecologist coined this term—from *ornithocopros*, bird dung, or guano—to express a certain relationship between bird dung and a plant. According to Rand (1955), this relationship is as follows: On the Arctic barrens of N. America, a bright yellow or red lichen, known to scientists as *Xantheria* or *Xanthoria*, grows on boulders there. Snowy owls, hawks, gyrfalcons, and other birds use these rocks as lookout perches. When their droppings (excreta) fall on the rocks, they provide a nutrient layer necessary for the growth of the lichens. It is believed that these lichens are carried from place to place by the birds, which carry the soredia (propagating part) of the lichens on their feet. It is in recognition of this close relationship between birds and plant that the term "ornithocoprophilous" was proposed. See also Tuck's interesting account (1961), and Ratcliffe (1969). *See also* Guano.

ORNITHOLOGICAL PERIODICALS
Following are some journal and serial publications available that publish material about

birds helpful to beginning and advanced birders and others. Most are published in the U.S. and Canada; included in the list are a few foreign publications for those interested in birds outside of N. America. Some may be referred to in the local library or in the library of the nearest natural history museum. They can usually be obtained by subscription or through membership in the organizations that publish them.

American Birds, incorporating *Audubon Field Notes*, about the distribution, migration, nesting, and numbers of N. American birds. Six issues a year, including the Christmas Bird Count, published by National Audubon Society, 950 Third Ave., New York, N.Y. 10022.

Audubon, official publication of the National Audubon Society, six issues a year. See address above.

Auk, The, quarterly journal, official publication of the American Ornithologists' Union. Permanent address: National Museum of Natural History, The Smithsonian Institution, Washington, D.C. 20560.

Bird-Banding, quarterly publication of the Northeastern Bird-Banding Association. Treasurer: Robert H. Shaw, 631 Main St., Concord, Mass. 01742.

Birding, a monthly published by the American Birding Association, 1616 Lavaca, Austin, Tex., 78701.

Bird News Survey, quarterly publication. Jon E. Rickert, Avian Publications, Inc., P.O. Box 310, Elizabethtown, Ky. 42701.

Cassinia, a bird annual of the Delaware Valley Ornithological Club, Academy of Natural Sciences, 19th and the Parkway, Philadelphia, Pa., 19103.

Chat, The, published quarterly by the Carolina Bird Club, which includes coverage of birds in N.C. and S.C. Address: Shuford Memorial Sanctuary, P.O. Box 1220, Tryon, N.C. 28782.

Condor, The, journal of the Cooper Ornithological Society, published quarterly. Treasurer as of 1979: Jane R. Durham, P.O. Box 520, Tempe, Ariz. 85281. Office of Publication: Dept. of Zoology, University of California, Los Angeles, Calif. 90024.

Ecology, official publication of the Ecological Society of America, published quarterly by Duke University Press, Box 6697 College Station, Durham, N.C. 27702.

Elapaio, The, published monthly by the Hawaii Audubon Society, P.O. Box 22832, Honolulu, Hawaii 96822.

Florida Naturalist, The, published quarterly by the Florida Audubon Society, P.O. Drawer 7, Maitland, Fla. 32751.

Guide to the Literature of the Zoological Sciences, by Roger C. Smith, published by Burgess Publishing Co., 426 S. Sixth St., Minneapolis, Minn. 55415. Not a periodical but one of best general directories of scientific libraries and catalogue of guides to their contents.

Indiana Audubon Quarterly, The, published by the Indiana Audubon Society, Inc. Membership Chairman: Dick D. Heller, Jr., 141 S. 2nd, Decatur, Indiana 46733.

Iowa Bird Life, published quarterly by the Iowa Ornithologists' Union, 235 McClellan Blvd., Davenport, Iowa 52803.

Jack Pine Warbler, The, quarterly publication of the Michigan Audubon Society. Permanent address: 7000 North Westnedge, Kalamazoo, Mich. 49007.

Journal of Wildlife Management, The, quarterly, official publication of the Wildlife Society, Suite 611, 7101 Wisconsin Ave., N.W., Washington, D.C. 20014.

Kentucky Warbler, The, published quarterly by the Kentucky Ornithological Society, Mrs. F. W. Stamm, 9101 Spokane Way, Louisville, Ky. 40222.

Kingbird, The, published quarterly by the Federation of New York Bird Clubs, Inc., Cornell Laboratory of Ornithology, 159 Sapsucker Woods Rd., Ithaca, N.Y. 14850.

Linnaean Society News-Letter, The, published monthly by the Linnaean Society of New York, also *Proceedings* and *Transactions* (published irregularly), American Museum of Natural History, Central Park West at 79th St., New York, N.Y. 10024.

Living Bird, The, annual published by the Laboratory of Ornithology, 159 Sapsucker Woods Rd., Ithaca, N.Y. 14850.

Maine Quarterly Audubon, published quarterly by the Maine Audubon Society, Gilsland Farm, 118 Old Route One, Falmouth, Me. 04105.

Maryland Birdlife, published quarterly by the Maryland Ornithological Society, Inc., Cylburn Mansion, 4915 Greenspring Ave., Baltimore, Md. 21209.

Massachusetts Audubon, published 10 times a year by the Massachusetts Audubon Society, Lincoln, Mass. 01773.

Migrant, The, published quarterly by the Tennessee Ornithological Society, Ray Jordan, Dept. of Biology, Tennessee Technological University, Cookeville, Tenn. 38501.

Natural History, published ten times a year by the American Museum of Natural History, Central Park West at 79th St., New York, N.Y. 10024.

Nebraska Bird Review, The, published quarterly by the Nebraska Ornithologists' Union, University of Nebraska State Museum, Lincoln, Neb. 68588.

New Jersey Audubon, published quarterly by the New Jersey Audubon Society, Ewing Ave., Franklin Lakes, N.J. 07417.

Oriole, The, published quarterly by the Georgia Ornithological Society, John M. Swiderski, P.O. Box 38214, Atlanta, Ga. 30334.

Pacific Discovery, published six times a year by the California Academy of Sciences. Editorial Offices: Golden Gate Park, San Francisco, Calif. 94118.

Passenger Pigeon, The, published quarterly by the Wisconsin Society for Ornithology, Inc., Alex F. Kailing, W. 330 N. 8275 West Shore Drive, Hartland, Wisc. 52309.

Raven, The, published quarterly by the Virginia Society of Ornithology, Bill Williams, 157 West Queens Drive, Williamsburg, Va. 23185.

South Dakota Bird Notes, published quarterly by the South Dakota Ornithologists' Union, Nelda Holden, Route 4, Box 68, Brookings, S.D. 57006.

Western Birds, Journal of the California Field Ornithologists, published quarterly by Western Field Ornithologists, 376 Greenwood Beach Rd., Tiburon, Calif. 94920.

Wildlife Review, abstracts, many about birds, of scientific papers originally published in scientific journals. Issued for the information of cooperators of the U.S. Fish and Wildlife Service, Colorado State University, Fort Collins, Colo. 80523.

Wilson Bulletin, The, quarterly journal of the Wilson Ornithological Society. Address: c/o The Museum of Zoology, University of Michigan, Ann Arbor, Mich. 48104.

CANADA

Blue Jay, The, published quarterly by the Saskatchewan Natural History Society, Regina, Box 1784, Sask., Canada S7K 351.

Canadian Field-Naturalist, The, published quarterly by the Ottawa Field-Naturalists' Club, Ottawa, Box 3264, Postal Station C., Ont., Canada K1Y 4J5.

Canadian Journal of Zoology, published by the National Research Council of Canada, Ottawa, Ont., Canada K1A OR6.

MEXICO

Revista de la Sociedad Mexicana de Historia Natural, Apartado Postal 1079, Mexico, D.F. Mexico.

ENGLAND

Bird Study, British Trust for Ornithology, published quarterly. Editorial Office: Beech Grove, Tring, Hertfordshire, HP23 5NR England.

British Birds, published monthly by Mamillan Journal, Ltd., 4 Little Essex St., London, WC2R 3LF, England.

Bulletin of the British Ornithologists' Club, published monthly. Mrs. D. Bradley, 53 Osterley Rd., Islesworth, Middlesex, England.

Ibis, The, journal of the British Ornithologists' Union, published quarterly by the British Ornithologists' Union, c/o Zoological Society of London, Regent's Park, London NW1 4RY, England.

AUSTRALIA

Emu, The, journal of the Royal Australasian Ornithologists' Union. Permanent address: 119 Dryburgh St., N. Melbourne, Vic. 3051, Australia.

For a list of ornithological periodicals, worldwide, see Pettingill (1970).

ORNITHOLOGIST

(or-nih-THOL-oh-jist). One who is versed in ornithology or makes a special study of birds. The term is usually applied to those who are systematic and scientific in their studies. *See also* Birder; Ornithology.

ORNITHOLOGY

The scientific study of birds. Researches into the problems of ornithology have been listed by Thomson (1964k) under five main categories, as follows: (1) *General zoological studies* of the form and function of a bird—anatomy, physiology, and embryology—all of which are broadly fundamental to ornithological knowledge, or an understanding of the bird as an animal. (2) *Systematics*, which uses the methods of taxonomy (*see* Taxonomy) and includes paleontology in the classification studies of birds (*see* Classification), which proceeds into studies of evolution and genetics. (3) The study of the *distribution* and *ecology* of birds leads into studies of

OSPREY FAMILY

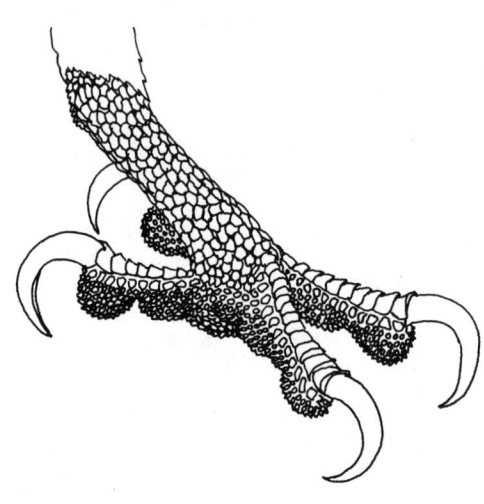

food and feeding habits, migration, and populations. (4) *Ethology*, or studies of birds' habits and psychological studies of their behavior. (5) *Applied ornithology*, which includes studies of the economic and aesthetic relations of birds to man, domestication of birds, the management of birds in the environment, and the conservation of birds.

Apparently a good general history of American ornithology and ornithologists is yet to be written, but many historical facts are in *Fifty Years' Progress of American Ornithology, 1883-1933*, published by the American Ornithologists' Union (1933), and a chapter by Ernst Mayr in Erwin Stresemann's *Ornithology: from Aristotle to the present*, published in 1975. Some of the history of American ornithology is in the biographies or obituaries of American ornithologists—see, for example, *Biographies of Members of the American Ornithologists' Union (1884-1954)*, by T. S. Palmer and others, edited by Paul H. Oehser, The Lord Baltimore Press (1954). See also obituaries periodically published in past issues of *The Auk*, official publication of the American Ornithologists' Union, titled "In Memoriam." For lists of periodicals that publish studies in ornithology, *see* Ornithological Periodicals.

ORNITHOMANCY

(OR-nih-tho-MAN-sih). Divination from observance of the flights of birds. *See* Augury; Auspice.

ORNITHOPHILOUS

Term applied to plants whose pollination is accomplished by birds. *See* Pollination; *also* Nectar and Birds.

ORNITHOSIS

(or-nih-THO-sis). *See* newer name, Chlamydiosis.

ORNITHOTIC PNEUMONIA

See Chlamydiosis.

OROPENDOLA

See in introduction to Troupial Family.

ORTOLAN

(OR-toe-lan); from a Fr. word meaning a gardener. A common name for the ortolan bunting, *Emberiza hortulana*, of Europe, so called because it frequents the hedges of gardens; in America, name applied to the bobolink and to the Carolina rail (sora) by some hunters and restaurateurs (Coues, 1884). *See* Bobolink in Troupial Family and Sora in Rail Family.

ORTSTREUE

See Return to Nest Sites and Wintering Places under Banding.

OSCINES

(OS-ih-neez); New Lat., from Lat. *oscen*, pl.: *oscines*, a singing bird, especially in auspices (*see* Auspices); a divining bird. The Oscines are equivalent to the birds in the suborder Passeres, order Passeriformes. *See* Passeres. They are songbirds "characterized by having several distinct pairs of intrinsic muscles of the syrinx [*see* Voice and Sound-making] inserted into the ends of the upper bronchial half-rings, constituting a complex and effective musical apparatus" (*Century Dictionary and Cyclopedia*).

Although the Oscines are commonly referred to as "songbirds," many of them do not sing. *See* Language; Songs and Singing.

OSPREY FAMILY

Pandionidae (pan-die-ON-ih-dee); for Pandion, in Gr. legend, King of Athens, father of Philomena and Procne. 1 species; one of most widely distributed birds in the world; lives in Europe, Asia, south to Spain, n. Africa, s. China, the East Indies and Australia, and on some of the sw. Pacific islands; also in W. Hemisphere (Van Tyne and Berger, 1976) but, within defined limits of N. America, does not breed south of Baja Calif.; northern populations migrate to warmer climates in winter; feeds almost exclusively on fishes (*see* Fishes and Birds), therefore lives along seacoasts, bays, and large unfrozen rivers and lakes of the continents; is a hawk in the order Falconiformes, but has been following its own evolution for long time (Brown and Amadon, 1968) and is in family by itself, ranked between Hawk Family and Falcon Family (A.O.U. *Check-list*, 1957); differs from all other diurnal birds of prey—eagles, hawks, kites, falcons, for example—in certain parts of its internal structure, and outwardly in its long, strong claws, curved about one third of a circle, and completely round (not concave and grooved beneath), in equal length of its toes (not unequal as in other raptors), and in the heavy, peculiarly scaled (reticulated) tarsus (shank) and short, dense feathering of the thighs (Friedmann, 1950). The lower surface, or pads, of the toes are covered with spicules, which help it hold slippery fishes; also, it is the only hawk that has outer toe reversible as in owls; this enables it to grasp its prey with two toes in front, two in back. Its plumage is compact, which helps blunt its impact and reduces wetting when it plunges into the water (Brown and Amadon, 1968).

Ospreys are protected by law, but to sustain an ill or injured one, offer it fresh whole fish until it is strong enough to fend for itself and release in wild. For notes on captive ospreys, see Abbott (1911).

Osprey, *Pandion haliaetus* (pan-DIE-on hal-ih-ay-EE-tus); genus name: *see* family introduction; species name: Lat., sea eagle. (Color ills., pages 647, 648.) In summer along lakes, rivers, seacoasts of U.S., Canada, Alaska; local, uncommon, or widely scattered over most of range; even in migration usually follows water of interior river valleys, seashore; 21–24½-in. long; wingspread 54–72 in.; almost eagle size; females larger than males; sexes outwardly alike; adults very dark brown above with purplish gloss; clear white below; breast somewhat spotted or streaked with brown; head largely white like bald eagle, but broad black mark through cheeks, sides of neck; bill and claws black; eyes yellow to brown; cere pale blue; legs and feet green-white; overhead, distinguished by white underparts, narrow wings, black patch at sharp bend, or "wrist," of wings; tail fairly long, narrowly barred; flies with slow powerful wingbeats alternated with glide; immatures like adults but upperparts flecked with white; underparts buffy; usual call is melodious whistle, *chewk-chewk-chewk* or *cheap-cheap-cheap;* migrates north in spring from general wintering grounds, S. America, Mexico, s. U.S.; begins in Feb., arrives n. U.S. Mar.–Apr.; in Canada, Alaska, Apr. into May (Bent, 1937); has become rare as nesting bird in some parts of U.S., especially in North and East, where unsuccessful reproduction believed result of chemical pollution of waters and fishes on which osprey preys, but see Ames and Mersereau (1964) and Peterson (1969) for evidence of catastrophic decline and factors causing it in population of osprey from N.J. north to Me., and in Mich. (Postupalsky, 1969; 1971); failure to show population decline in migration at Hawk Mountain, Pa., discussed by Spofford (1969) and Taylor (1972); decline also attributed to man's encroachment on osprey's estuaries and seacoast nesting habitat, and shooting of ospreys (Kenyon, 1947; Dunstan, 1970), especially in migration (Henny and Wight, 1969); Chesapeake Bay population, Talbot County, Md., most successful in East; population thriving or holding its own in Fla. and in parts of West; first American osprey sanctuary established in 1969 on Crane Prairie Osprey Management Area in Deschutes National Forest, Ore., where largest colony of nesting ospreys (48 active nests in 1969) in Pacific Northwest (Roberts, 1970); for a Calif. report, see Kahl and Garber (1972) and for coastal Carolinas, Henny and Noltemeier (1975); for continental surveys and status of osprey, see Dunstan (1970) and Henny and Ogden (1970). To help ospreys with nesting platforms, see illustrated article in Pettingill and Lancaster (1970). (In the feather, or millinery, trade, egret plumes were often called "osprey plumes," but ospreys have no plumes; apparently the feathers were never sought in the trade; also, plumage of osprey has peculiar oily odor that permeates its feathers, and even its eggshells, for many years—Wetmore, 1937a.)

Feeding Habits: Spends much time near water perched on dead snag of tree or on rocks; flies out occasionally over fresh or salt water to hunt; flies about 30–100 ft. above surface; when sights fish, hovers with wings beating, legs trailing under body, sometimes plunges into water from straight flight; in dive, feet and head project ahead with wings held above back, tail spread, may strike water with tremendous splash; sometimes disappears below surface with only wing tips showing. Rises from water with fish gripped in both feet, pauses in midair to shake water from plumage, and to arrange fish with head pointed forward, which reduces its resistance to air, flies with it to habitual perch to eat or to nest to feed young. Reported to carry fish up to 4 lbs. or more (Bent, 1937). *See* Weight-Carrying Capacity. If bald eagle soaring overhead sees osprey make catch, it dives upon osprey and forces it to drop the fish, which eagle often catches in its talons before fish strikes water. Osprey eats almost exclusively fishes—alewives, herring, bluefish, blowfish, bonito, bowfin, carp, catfish, eels, flounders, flying fishes, goldfish, horned pout, menhaden, mullet, perch, pickerel, pike,

salmon, shad, squeteague, suckers, and many others; also occasionally catches and eats small rodents and small birds (see in Wiley and Lohrer, 1973). Bent (1937) cites amusing experience of W. B. Savary, who watched an osprey catch and lose in succession four blowfish, or swellfish, *Spheroides maculatus,* one of the spiny-rayed saltwater fishes of the Atlantic; the fish escaped by inflating themselves until hawk's talons lost their hold and fish dropped back into water. Osprey also known to catch snakes, frogs, storm-petrels, sandpipers, ducks, possibly at times when fishes not available. See Bent (1937) and especially Tait *et al.* (1972).

Nesting: Either in colonies or singly, in standing trees, living, partially dead, or dead, usually not far from water or over water, on top of duck blinds, channel markers, roots of upturned trees, on cartwheel on pole put up by people to attract ospreys, on platforms built for them in marshes, nests on top of chimneys of houses, on school buildings, utility poles (some power companies protect their lines from nests but help ospreys—see Anonymous, 1955a); tops of windmills, on rocks, rock pinnacles in West, and even on ground high up on beach and on islands (Bent, 1937); nests built up each year by pair, occupancy of nests may be for decades, built of sticks, seaweeds, bones, driftwood, cornstalks, other trash from marshes, beaches, nest may weigh up to half a ton (Abbott, 1911); adults snap off dead branches of trees with feet while in flight or carry to nest from ground.

Eggs: Fla., Dec.–Apr.; Baja Calif., Mexico, Jan.–Apr.; in temperate parts of U.S., Canada, Apr.–June; 2–4, usually 3, handsomest of all hawks' eggs (Bent, 1937); white to pink or cinnamon, heavily blotched and spotted with dark browns.

Incubation: Begins with first egg laid, and usually by female in N. America, although Garber and Koplin (1972) reported both sexes incubating in Calif.; female does not catch fish herself during her incubation but depends on male to feed her; incubation period, 35–38 days in Europe; 32–33 days in America (Brown and Amadon, 1968); 38–43 days in Calif. (Garber and Koplin, 1972); 28–33 days (Bent, 1937; Ames, 1964); young make first flights 51–59 days (usually 52–53 days) after hatching; 48–59 days, and young, after first flight, fly back to nest although awkwardly (Stotts and Henny, 1975); banding shows that some young ospreys return to natal area when 2 years old, or in 3rd year; do not breed until 3 years old (Henny and Wight, 1969; Postupalsky, 1971); adults fierce in defense of nest, often attack, and may even strike, intruder climbing nest tree.

Other Names: American osprey; fish eagle; fish hawk; fishing eagle; sea hawk.

Accidents: Occasionally lock talons in salmon or sturgeon too large to bring to surface and are drowned (*see* Fishes and Birds); may strike water too hard and break wing (*see* Swimming and Diving); nest tree sometimes struck by lightning and young and female injured or killed (Abbott, 1911).

Age: One, banded Gardiners Is., N.Y., in 1914, found dead at same place in 1935 when 21 years old. Gillespie (1960) reported, of 457 banded as nestlings, N.J. and Del., oldest one recovered

OSPREY FAMILY
Rising from the water with its slippery prey gripped in both feet, the osprey carries a fish with its head pointed forward, making flight easier by reducing the resistance to air.

was 18 years; one banded N. Cedar Branch, Del., found dead (possibly shot) along Herring Creek, Del., when 32 years old (Kennard, 1975). *Flight Speed:* Timed in migration in Pa., 20–80 m.p.h. (Broun and Goodwin, 1943); in w. U.S., 25–27 m.p.h. (Cottam *et al.,* 1942b). *Weights:* Males (10), 2 lbs. 10 oz. to 3 lbs. 8½ oz.; females (14), 2 lbs. 12 oz. to 4 lbs. 3¾ oz. (Brown and Amadon, 1968). *Range:* In N. America, nw. Alaska, c. Yukon, s. Mack., n. Man., to Newfoundland, south locally to Baja Calif., Mexico, Gulf coast, and Fla.; winters from s. Calif., s. Tex., La., s. Miss., s. Ala., c. Fla., Bahamas, south to Peru and Brazil; also known on every continent except Antarctica.

OSTEOLOGY

(OS-tee-OL-oh-jih). The scientific study of the bones of birds *and* other vertebrate animals. *See* Bones; Skeleton Anatomy.

OSTRICH

See Crop; Eggs and Egg-laying; Flightless Birds; Weight; Size; Running Birds.

OTOLITH

(OH-toe-lith). A calcareous (bonelike) concretion in the internal ear of a vertebrate animal. For a discussion of them in birds, *see* Ears and Hearing. In fishes, otoliths are often called "ear stones." *See* Pellet; Fishes and Birds.

OUZEL

(OO-zl). *See* Dipper Family.

OVARY

The female sexual gland in which the eggs are produced. *See* discussion of under Fertilization. *See also* Endocrine Glands; Eggs and Egg-laying.

OVENBIRD

See in Warbler—American Wood Warbler Family.

OVENBIRD FAMILY

Furnariidae. Group of Mexican, C. and S. American birds, not related to N. American ovenbird, which is in American Wood Warbler Family. Members of Ovenbird Family are primitive songbirds, named for their nests of clay, shaped like old-fashioned Dutch ovens. For details, see Van Tyne and Berger (1959); Austin (1961).

OVIDUCT

(OH-vih-duct). A tube or duct which serves for the passage of the eggs of a female bird from the vicinity of the ovary to the urodeum. *See* Eggs and Egg-laying.

OVIPAROUS

(oh-VIP-ah-rus). Term applied to a bird or any other animal that lays eggs from which the young are hatched, in contrast to *viviparous* (vie-VIP-ah-rus) animals, whose young are born alive from the body of the female. All birds are oviparous; most mammals are viviparous. *See* Eggs and Egg-laying.

OVIPOSITING

(oh-vih-POS-ih-ting). Laying eggs; the act of laying eggs.

OVULATION

(OH-view-LAY-shun). When a mature egg, protruding from the ovary of a female bird, bursts its covering of ovarian tissue and enters the body cavity of the bird, ovulation is said to have taken place (Berger, 1961). *See* Eggs and Egg-laying.

OWL—BARN OWL FAMILY

Tytonidae (tie-TON-ih-dee); from Gr. *tyto,* owl. Includes 11 species of barn owls and their allies worldwide except in extreme northern parts of world, in New Zealand and some islands of Malaysia (Van Tyne and Berger, 1976); introduced in Hawaii; in N. America, only 1 species, lives over wide area of warmer parts of U.S.; rare in northern tier states north of 40° N. Lat.; increases in abundance southward, especially numerous in s. Calif. (Bent, 1938).

Barn owls are closely related to the typical owls—the great horned, barred, etc. (*see* Owl—Typical Owl Family, which follows). However, the barn owls are different in having a facial disc of feathers *triangular,* or *heart-shaped,* not round; a short, square to emarginate tail (typical owls usually have rounded, rarely square, tails), long legs, and inner edge of claw of middle toe pectinated (Pettingill, 1970), or with a serrated edge.

Barn owls are not usually migratory, but some make southward flights in fall and in winter, especially young of the year, and northward in spring (see Stewart, 1952; Henny, 1969); Stone (1937) cited two banded barn owls in s. N.J. that indicated extensive southward migration; when flying overhead, at night, utters harsh, whistling gasp, *eeee SEek!* Bird of open country rather than woods, flies lightly and silently, mothlike flight, not swiftly; hunts over fields and meadows, woods, roads, and clearings, about barns, granaries, and buildings in towns and cities; like all owls, has leading edge of first primary (wing) feather with saw-tooth edge; Raspet (1960) offered hypothesis that this behaves in same way as twisted wire swung through air, which reduces vortex noise emitted by the flow of air over the wings; thus can fly silently; sometimes during nesting season, hunts at twilight or on cloudy days but usually at night; seldom seen by humans in dark; however, by making squeaking notes at night where owls likely to hunt, one can sometimes lure it to fly overhead or perch nearby.

Barn owls can see by day but eyes adapted to night; spend daylight hours roosting and sleeping in old buildings, caves, burrows, or in hollows of trees or thick foliage such as that of pines and cedars; often sleeps so soundly that not easily aroused until darkness comes. In s. Calif., where barn owls resident all year, in winter up to 50 found roosting together in grove of live oaks (Bailey, 1902). In Ariz. has been found roosting in old mines, wells, large cottonwoods and willows, rows of palm trees in towns, and in stacks of baled hay (Phillips *et al.,* 1964). Its dark eyes, relatively small for an owl, are directed forward (binocular sight); it is solitary except when nesting or occasionally on south-

OSPREY FAMILY

Osprey

This large, fish-eating bird constructs a bulky nest of sticks, usually in a dead tree along the shore of a lake or near saltwater. Such nests, and the birds that built them, used to be a familiar sight along waterways in North America, but high levels of pesticides, seeping into the water from croplands and absorbed by the fish, have seriously depleted the North American population. Recently the pesticide levels have been reduced, and there are now signs that the osprey may be staging a partial comeback.

Osprey

OWL—BARN OWL FAMILY

Barn owl

Originally nesting in hollow trees and caves, the adaptable barn owl now breeds in buildings as well; for many years a pair raised young in the bell tower of the Smithsonian Institution, where ornithologists kept track of their success from year to year. These beneficial birds begin incubating as soon as the first egg is laid, and this results in a brood of young of different ages and sizes. When food is scarce, the smaller nestlings are the first to starve. By concentrating the available food on the older and stronger young, a pair of barn owls increases its chances of producing at least a few healthy offspring every year.

Osprey

Barn owl, nestlings

Barn owl

OWL—TYPICAL OWL FAMILY

Barred owl
This familiar bird of wooded swamps is well known for its loud hooting call, heard not only at night but also on days when it is overcast. Barred owls usually nest in hollow trees, but when these are scarce they raise their young in abandoned nests of other birds or even in holes in the ground.

Boreal owl
Boreal owls are secretive birds of the coniferous forests of Alaska, Canada, and Eurasia, remaining concealed in dense spruces and firs during the day and hunting for mice at night. Occasionally a bird is spotted in the northern United States during the winter, but these birds are so difficult to find that we know little of their migrations.

Burrowing owl
In the days when teeming prairie dog "towns" covered large areas of the western plains, burrowing owls were abundant, nesting in the abandoned burrows of these ground-dwelling rodents. Where no rodent burrow is available, these long-legged, diurnal owls can dig one of their own, and they are still found in small numbers from southern Canada to Tierra del Fuego, with isolated populations in Florida and the West Indies.

Elf owl
This sparrow-sized owl feeds on large insects, mice, and lizards, and nests in woodpecker holes from southern Texas and California to central Mexico. These entirely nocturnal birds can be hard to find, but thousands of birders have paid their respects to a pair that obligingly nests every year in a telephone pole in Madera Canyon, just outside Tucson, Arizona.

Barred owl

Boreal owl

Elf owl

Burrowing owl

Burrowing owl

Ferruginous owl
This small tropical owl reaches the northern limit of its range along the Mexican border, where its soft, monotonous call can be heard both day and night coming from dense thickets along rivers.

Flammulated owl
The flammulated owl is a small western relative of the screech owl. Unlike its more widespread relative, it does not have 2 color phases; all flammulated owls are gray. It inhabits coniferous forests from British Columbia to central Mexico.

Great gray owl
The great gray owl is usually considered a very rare winter visitor to the northern United States from the cool coniferous forests of Canada and Alaska. But in the winter of 1978−1979 an unprecedented invasion took place, and several hundred birds were seen. In many states from New England to the Great Lakes, more great gray owls were seen in a single season than had been recorded in all years previous. Most of these birds were seen for only a day or two, but others remained in the same place for several weeks and attracted large crowds of birders.

Great horned owl
The deep, muffled hooting of this, the largest of our "eared" owls, can be heard as much as a mile away on still moonlit nights. The great horned owl inhabits forested and desert areas throughout the Western Hemisphere, preying on a variety of birds and mammals. Apparently indifferent to the strong odor, it even feeds on skunks.

Great horned owl

Great horned owl, chick

Ferruginous owl

Flammulated owl

Great gray owl

Hawk owl
The hawk owl preys on small rodents and birds, pursuing them during the day in the spruce and fir forests of Alaska and Canada. In its actions it resembles a kestrel, coursing along close to the ground and swooping upward just before it lands on a branch, then bobbing its tail as if trying to keep its balance.

Long-eared owl
This medium-sized owl, named for its conspicuous ear tufts, nests throughout the forested regions of North America and in the Old World. It is a secretive bird, and most birders have seen it only during the winter, when it gathers in groups of a dozen or more to roost in groves of pines or spruces. Active only at night, it hunts for rodents in fields and marshes near its roost.

Pygmy owl
A mountain-inhabiting relative of the ferruginous owl, this sparrow-sized bird often hunts during the day. Although it is usually shy and inconspicuous, it is relatively easy to find during the spring, when males spend much time uttering an almost continuous series of short, hollow whistles, all on one pitch. By carefully tracing the sound to its source, one can find the bird perched in the concealment of a dense conifer.

Saw-whet owl
One of the most nocturnal of our owls, the saw-whet spends the day roosting in dense thickets, often within a few feet of the ground. At such times it is amazingly tame, and there are many records of roosting birds being picked up and handled. At dusk, the birds become active and alert and begin their night-long hunt for mice and other small mammals.

Long-eared owl

Hawk owl

Long-eared owl

Pygmy owl

Saw-whet owl

Screech owl

This is probably the commonest owl in North America, living in a variety of habitats and even nesting on the outskirts of cities and in residential areas. The two color phases—gray and red—were misunderstood by early naturalists. Until well into the 19th century, the red-phased birds were thought to be females or young. But red and gray individuals appear in the same brood, and the difference is not dependent on sex or age.

Short-eared owl

Although the short-eared owl is often said to be diurnal, it usually begins to hunt in late afternoon, spending most of the day resting quietly on the ground in grasslands or marshy areas. In its open-country habitat, it nests on the ground as well, placing its 5 to 7 chalky white eggs in a shallow nest of grass or rushes concealed under a bush or in a stand of tall weeds.

Screech owl, red phase

Screech owl, gray phase

Screech owl, immatures

Short-eared owl

Short-eared owl

Snowy owl

Roughly every 4 years, this imposing white owl from the Arctic tundra appears in large numbers in southern Canada and the northern United States. These invasions coincide with population declines in its favorite prey, the tundra-inhabiting rodents known as lemmings. While the snowy owl is with us, it hunts during the day in open fields and salt marshes, and often visits garbage dumps to feed on rats.

Spotted owl

The spotted owl is a western relative of the barred owl and like it has a distinctive barking call. It is an inhabitant of mountain forests from British Columbia to central California, and from Colorado to beyond the Mexican border. It is sensitive to human disturbance and seems to suffer from competition with the larger great horned owl.

Whiskered owl

This small, retiring owl of mountain oak forests in southeastern Arizona is named for the long bristles at the base of its bill. It is otherwise very similar to the screech owl and is best distinguished by the soft, rhythmic hooting of the males, who begin calling soon after they arrive from the wintering grounds in Mexico.

Spotted owl

Snowy owl

Snowy owl

Spotted owl

Whiskered owl

OYSTERCATCHER FAMILY

American oystercatcher

This boldly patterned shorebird feeds on mussels and other mollusks, prying them open with its long, laterally compressed bill. In recent years it has been extending its breeding range northward along the Atlantic coast, and it now nests on Long Island and in Massachusetts. Here, in early summer, one can find breeding pairs accompanied by their pale gray, long-legged chicks. When an intruder approaches such a family too closely, the adults fly off; the young bird remains behind, flattened on the ground, often hiding its head beneath a tuft of marsh grass like the proverbial ostrich.

American oystercatcher

Black oystercatcher

American oystercatcher

Black oystercatcher

Black oystercatcher
The black oystercatcher nests on wave-lashed rocky shores from the Aleutian Islands south to Baja California. Along this coastline it is nowhere abundant, being absent from many apparently suitable places. Its feeding is timed by the tides; at low tide it preys on mollusks and barnacles, and at high tide when its feeding areas are covered it rests quietly among the dark rocks, where it is often difficult to see.

ward flights in fall or winter when flocks of dozen or. more may associate in favored roosts (Bent, 1938).

Barn owls believed to remain mated as long as each member of pair lives before taking another mate; of all owls, the one most closely associated with man (Austin, 1961). It was the barn owl on which Payne (1962) experimented and discovered that, in complete darkness, it locates its prey by hearing.

Barn owl's long legs feathered to toes. Besides outer and inner anatomical differences that set barn owls apart from typical owls, after molting, its tail feathers are renewed from center of tail outward; in other owls, from outer tail feathers inward (Gilliard, 1958).

Owls are protected by law (*see* Legal Protection), but to help a crippled, starving, or sick owl (if unable to place with a zoo, wildlife sanctuary, or animal care society), put it, if possible, in large wire cage or old poultry house. There it will be free to move about; to give comfort and sleeping place, attach a box on wall (with perch at entrance) into which owl can retire in daytime to roost; if it cannot fly, put box on floor or ground; on floor of box put sawdust or wood chips.

Do not put together owls of different species and sizes—the larger owls may kill and eat smaller ones. Owls of same species, if kept in clean, adequate quarters, may mate. See Crandall (1917) for details. Put branches of trees or old stumps in pen for perches. Barn owls have been bred successfully in captivity in the British Isles; reported as early as 1867; in Cambridge, in 1892 a pair in confinement raised eight young (see Prestwich, 1955; Maestrelli, 1973).

In feeding (once a day for adult owls, several times a day for young ones), offer a freshly killed small chicken, whole with feathers on, a pigeon, house sparrows, or mice, especially for small owls, and at dusk, an owl's natural feeding time. Remove left-over food from enclosure after owl has fed. If natural foods not available, offer, temporarily, lean fresh beef, liver, or other meat but must be free of fat. Most of time, offer animals with fur or feathers on, as these especially needed by owls for proper forming of pellets, later cast up. See Snediger (1963) for details. Supply also a shallow pan, at least 24 in. in diameter and not more than 2–3 in. deep, filled with fresh water for drinking and bathing by owl each night. For surgical care of broken wings and other injuries, see Mutchler (1972; 1973).

Barn owl, *Tyto alba pratincola* (TIE-toe AL-bah pray-TIN-koh-lah or pray-tin-KOH-lah); genus name: *see* family introduction; species name: Lat., white; subspecies name: from Lat. *pratum*, meadow, and *incola*, inhabitant; *barn owl*, from nesting in barn lofts. (Color ills., page 649.) Besides in N. America, lives in Eurasia and Africa; 14–20 in. long; wingspread 43–47 in. (Sprunt, 1954a); light-colored, whitish below, rusty buff above, speckled with black, face white and *heart-shaped* (the strange, monkeylike face arouses great interest and fear in some people); *no ear tufts*, relatively slim owl, wings long, pointed, fold beyond tail; has long, feathered legs, claws very long and

BARN OWL FAMILY

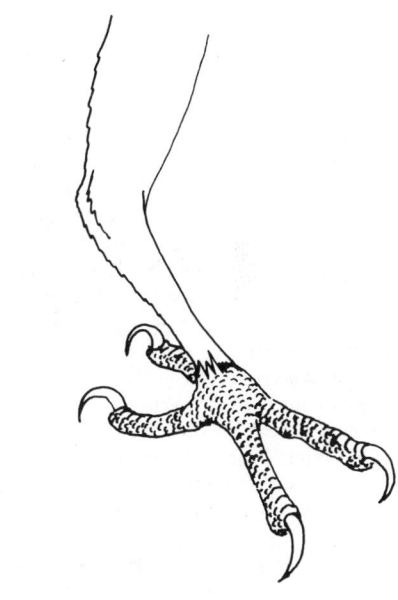

sharp; large round head; small dark eyes; seen from below, this owl appears white. Golden brown of upperparts varies, but generally slightly darker in female; sexes very much alike, females slightly larger; while perched has curious habit of lowering head and swaying it from side to side. Typical calls are long-drawn screams and loud raspy hiss, *sss-ksch*; also utters chuckling notes, one of which is like a snore.

Feeding Habits: Eats mostly mice, moles, shrews, cotton rats, barn rats, gophers, ground squirrels, cottontails and jackrabbits, occasionally bats, muskrats, skunks; a small part of its food is birds: pigeons, petrels, jays, green herons, sparrows, red-winged blackbirds, grackles, starlings, soras, meadowlarks, towhees, flickers, bluebirds, swallows, clapper rails (Bent, 1938). See also ffrench (1967). The barn owl itself is occasionally killed and eaten by great horned owls, and an occasional one struck down by a prairie falcon.

Nest: Any secluded place such as a cave, barn, tree cavity, bird box, belfry; in Ariz. nests in mines, holes in banks (Phillips *et al.,* 1964); builds no nest; in Md. nests in duck blinds offshore.

Eggs: 3–11, usually 5–7, white or buff-white, unmarked; Feb.–Oct., with most nesting Mar.–July in the Northeast; in Southeast, Mar.–Dec.; in Calif., nesting season is mid-Jan. to early June (Stewart, 1952; Bent, 1938).

Incubation: By female, 32–34 days (Nice, 1954); young fly when 52–56 days old; male helps feed and guard young; on being fed, young utter hissing note like escaping steam.

Other Names: American barn owl; church owl; golden owl; monkey-faced owl; rat owl; steeple owl; stone owl; white owl; in England called white-breasted barn owl.

Accidents: Some killed by traffic when flying low across highways at night; many illegally shot, and those that linger too far north in severe winters die from intense cold and lack of food (Bent, 1938). Sprunt (1932) saw a barn owl alight on a ship 12–15 mi. off N.C. coast in Nov. 1931, apparently carried to sea by offshore wind.

Age: A European barn owl, banded in Helgoland, was recovered almost 15 years later (Austin, 1961); an American barn owl, banded in Calif. as a nestling, lived 10 years, 4 months; when found dead it had a full-grown jay clutched in its talons (Cooke, 1937b). In U.S., oldest barn owl in wild lived to 11 years, 6 months, 4 days; was banded Escondido, Calif.; caught near place of banding in Oct. 1946 when still alive but died soon thereafter; another, reported from Holland, 17 years, 10 months, old (Clapp, 1976).

Weights: Females 510–680 gm.; males about 570 gm. (Forbush, 1925–29).

Range: Look for it during day roosting in evergreen trees, sycamores, cottonwoods, or eucalyptus, or in belfries or towers of old buildings even in cities; flies about at night over fields looking for prey; nests in W. Hemisphere from sw. B.C., N.D., to s. Minn., s. Wisc., s. Mich., extreme s. Ont., s. Que., and Mass. south through U.S. to Baja Calif., Mexico, south through C. America, West Indies, to Tierra del Fuego; ranges casually north to s. Sask., s. Man., n. Minn., s. Ont., n. Vt., s. Me., and Nova Scotia; also lives in Eurasia, Africa, the Orient, and Australia (see details, A.O.U. *Check-list,* 1957).

OWL—TYPICAL OWL FAMILY

Strigidae (STRIJ-ih-dee). Lat. from Gr. *strix,* an owl; a night bird (Jaeger, 1955). All owls, except the barn and bay owls, belong to the Strigidae; about 140 species live almost everywhere in world except on some oceanic islands and in Antarctica (Van Tyne and Berger, 1976); 17 species in N. America; most are not migratory, at least not regularly; the N. American elf owl is smallest owl in the world; in N. America the great horned owl and snowy owl are the most powerful; the gray owl is, dimensionally, the largest; the snowy owl, the heaviest; the screech owl, noted not only for its wide distribution (in N. America) but for its two color phases. Gross (1965a) reported nine individual examples of albinism among five species in the family.

Sight and hearing of owls is extraordinarily keen; the eyes (*see* Eyes and Eyesight) are relatively very large; eyeball of 2-ft.-long snowy owl is almost as large as a man's; owls can see in daytime—the short-eared, barred, and snowy owls often hunt by day; the pygmy and hawk owls, regularly, but most owls are crepuscular or nocturnal. The opaque nictitating membrane, or third eyelid, through adaptation, is well developed to protect the highly sensitive retina of owls' eyes from the bright light of day.

Ears of owls are more remarkable than the eyes; they are openings in sides of the head surrounded by deep, soft feathers which the owl can spread to make a funnel to each ear opening. In some owls this opening is very large and is protected by a movable flap of skin which may serve to focus sounds from below when it is perched, listening for movements of its prey. In many owls the two ear openings are unlike; one is larger and of different shape from the other, and this asymmetry extends even to the form of the owl's skull (Beebe, 1906). These differences in the ears help the owl, as in triangulation, to detect exactly from where, in direction and distance, a sound has come.

Facial discs of owls are believed to function acoustically by collecting and focusing sound waves as do the parabolic reflectors of technicians who record bird songs and calls; the facial discs probably aid owls in detecting their prey by sounds. See Payne (1962).

Owls' feathers are long and soft; gray, white, brown, brown-black, or chestnut; streaked and barred; many species have earlike tufts of feathers above the eyes or on top of the head. Tarsus is completely covered with feathers and, in some owls, the toes, at least slightly. Four toes on each foot; the outer toe of each is reversible, so that owl may perch either with two toes forward, two back (usual), or with three forward, one back, as in perching songbirds. Bill is strong, short, and hooked with a cere at base. Large eyes are directed forward; head large, neck short; sexes appear alike or nearly so in color, but female usually larger than male, except in burrowing owl, in which males are slightly heavier and have slightly longer wings.

Owls can fly silently owing to serrations on front edge of first primary feather of wings (*see* discussion in introduction to Barn Owl Family). Owls strike their prey on the ground or out of the air, grasping the bird, mammal, snake, insect, or other prey in their powerful feet and sharp talons; usually bring prey back to perch to eat it. Like hawks and eagles, they use their feet and talons in defense rather than the bill.

Through analysis of their coughed-up (regurgitated) pellets, scientists, studying their food habits, have discovered the presence of small mammals in places previously unsuspected. Charles and Myrtle Broley of Delta, Ont., one winter collected the pellets of snowy owls from strawstack roosts of the owls on a prairie; a skull in one pellet was that of the small, rare least weasel.

Eggs of owls are usually incubated by the female; in some species by both male and female. Baby owls when hatched are covered with white down and, unlike hawks and eagles, are hatched with their eyes closed (Voous, 1964a); according to Ligon (1968), owls have one brood a year.

Owls are protected by law, but in an emergency, to help a sick or injured bird, offer same food as to hawks and to barn owls; if in outdoor cage provide box in a corner of cage in which owl may sleep during the day. Small owls such as screech and saw-whet eat insects, besides live mice, also young rats and other small rodents. *See* Barn Owl Family for other details.

Enemies of owls are mostly men who shoot and trap them either out of prejudice or in the mistaken belief that they are economically harmful to game animals. Some of the larger owls occasionally catch and eat smaller ones. *See* in biographies that follow.

Acadian owl. *See* Saw-whet owl.

Arctic owl. *See* Snowy owl.

Arctic saw-whet owl. *See* Boreal owl.

Barn owl. *See* in Owl—Barn Owl Family.

Barred owl, *Strix varia* (STRIKS VAY-rih-ah); genus name: Lat., screech owl, from Gr. *strizo,* to screech (Macleod, 1954); species name: Lat., variegated (in plumage). (Color ill., page 650.) East of prairie states; one of commonest owls of deep woods, especially abundant in Fla. (in Far West, where not found, its counterpart is the spotted owl); 17–24 in. long; wingspread 40–50 in.; large, gray-brown, barred and spotted with buff, dark brown, and white; without "ear" tufts; puffy round head, large *brown* eyes (all other typical owls of e. U.S. have yellow eyes); eyesight especially keen, even in full daylight may fly about when disturbed; although usually nocturnal, hunts sometimes on cloudy days but mostly at dawn and dusk; hearing sharp, comes from 50 yds. away in response to squeaking or mouselike sounds made to attract small birds; is barred crosswise on breast, but lengthwise streaking on belly; back spotted with white; flight buoyant and noiseless, flaps and glides skillfully through or around branches of forest trees, suddenly slides upward to alight; noisy in most seasons, calls sometimes in day, but usually at night; antiphonal hootings of pair more emphatic and slightly higher-pitched than "moan" of great horned owl; usual call is series of eight accented hoots ending in *oo-aw*, with downward pitch at end; sometimes rendered phonetically as *Who cooks for you? who cooks for you-all!* Responds to its imitated calls.

Feeding Habits: Eats mostly mice of many species, also chipmunks, red and gray foxes, and flying squirrels, minks, opossums, weasels, rabbits, shrews, bats, doves, grouse, quail, small owls, purple gallinules, flickers, kingfishers, crows, jays, cardinals, and other birds; frogs, crayfishes, lizards, small snakes, snails, salamanders, fiddler crabs (Fla.), is said to wade into water to catch fishes, also eats flesh of terrapins, grasshoppers, crickets, large beetles, spiders; however, gentle in comparison with great horned owl; has weaker claws and talons. Uses same nest site for many years.

Nest: In tree cavity but often in abandoned nest of hawk, crow, or squirrel; in Fla., favorite nesting sites are in cavities or broken-off tops of trees in hammocks of dense mixed cabbage palmettos and live oaks, usually near extensive marshes, sloughs, and ponds; one Fla. record on ground (Robertson, 1959).

Eggs: N. U.S., Feb.–May; Fla., Jan.–Mar.; Tex., Feb–June; 2–3, rarely 4, white.

Incubation: Possibly by both adult owls, but mostly by female, about 28 days; young do not fly until about 42 days after hatching (Bent, 1938).

Other Names: Black-eyed owl; bottom owl; crazy owl; hoot owl; laughing owl; old-folks owl; rain owl; round-headed owl (from lack of ear tufts); swamp owl; wood owl.

Accidents: Some struck at dusk or dawn by cars along highways; in N.J., one sealed by ice in its nesting hole; has been caught by feet on hooks when striking at fishing lures cast into air (Higgins, 1971).

Age: One lived for 8 years, 5 months, in National Zoo, Washington, D.C., but was adult when caught (Mann, 1934); Stott (1948) reported one that lived in a Calif. zoo for 23 years; one banded wild one lived to 8 years, 8 months (Kennard, 1975).

Albinism: Apparently rare, "a fine specimen" (albino) in collections of Museum of Natural History, Niagara Falls, N.Y. (Deane, 1876).

Weights: Males average 630 gm.; females average 800 gm. (Earhart and Johnson, 1970).

Range: Resident in deep, deciduous, swampy woods, generally east of Rockies, from Nova Scotia, Newfoundland, s. Que., across s. Canada to Sask., B.C., n. Alta., south to Gulf coast of Fla. and Tex.; recent record of nest in e. Wash.; many move south from northernmost part of range in winter; also resident through mountains and highlands of Mexico and into C. America.

Big cat owl. *See* Great horned owl.

Billy owl. A pet name, term of affection. *See* Burrowing owl.

Black-eyed owl. *See* Barred owl.

Bog owl. *See* Short-eared owl.

Boreal owl, *Aegolius funereus* (ee-JOLE-ih-us few-NEE-ree-us); genus name: from Gr. *aigolios*, a kind of owl; species name: Lat., funereal, applicable to an owl when regarded as a bird of ill omen, or with reference to its dismal cry as if "wailing the dead" (Coues, 1882); *boreal* alludes to its northern range in coniferous forests around the world. (Color ill., page 651.) Appears, rarely, irregularly, in n. U.S. in winter; formerly called Richardson's owl; 8½–12 in. long; small tame owl with relatively large head; is near size of screech owl but lacks ear tufts of screech owl; can be distinguished from its close relative, the smaller saw-whet owl, by its facial discs, which are edged with black, and yellowish bill (saw-whet's is black); boreal owl has many small white spots on its crown, nape, and back; courtship song is like the slow, tolling of a soft but high-pitched bell, *ting, ting, ting, ting,* rising and falling (Seton, 1911), or slow liquid notes like the sound of water dropping slowly from a height; its cry at night is a single melancholy note repeated at interval of a minute or two; sometimes takes up quarters, apparently for shelter from bitter cold, in abandoned igloos in Arctic and in barns in midwinter in Me.; a true "night owl," during day in n. Alaska remains in thick foliage of bushes or trees; has often been caught alive by hand because of its virtual fearlessness of man; because Eskimos thought its ease of capture was from bad vision in daylight, they called it "the blind one."

Feeding Habits: Mostly mice and insects, with some small birds.

Nest: In tree cavity, deserted woodpecker holes, especially those of the pileated woodpecker.

Eggs: Apr. into June; 3–10, usually 4–6, pure white.

Incubation: 27–28 days by female only; age of young when first fly not certain but estimated at about 28–33 days after hatching.

Other Names: Arctic saw-whet owl; Richardson's owl; sparrow owl; in Europe, Tengmalm's owl.

Age: One banded boreal owl reported from Germany lived to 15 years, 11 months (Clapp, 1976).

Weights: Males average 100 gm.; females average 140 gm. (Earhart and Johnson, 1970). A female, quite fat (collected with her nest and four eggs June 1963 in Central Brooks Range, Alaska), weighed 194 gr., or about 6 oz. (Campbell, J. M., 1969).

Range: Lives in coniferous forests of North; in N. America, nests from n. Alaska, n. Yuk., Mack., c. Sask., n. Man., n. Ont., Que., Labrador, and probably Newfoundland, south to n. B.C., c. Alta., s. Man., w. Ont., N.B. (Grand Manan Is.); winters in part throughout nesting range, but spreads southward to s. B.C., n. Mont., N.D., s. Minn., s. Mich., Ont., s. Que., and to Mass.; casual to s. Ore., Idaho, Colo., Neb., Ill., Pa., N.Y. (one picked up dead at Cedar Beach, Long Is., N.Y., Jan. 15, 1975, was southernmost record for state and fourth for

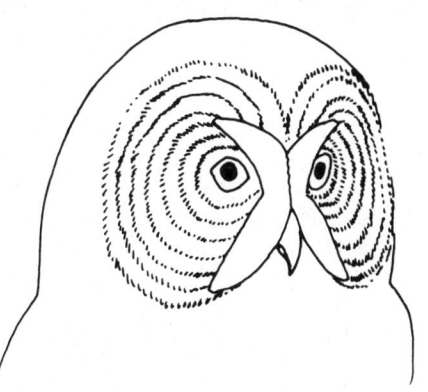

TYPICAL OWL FAMILY

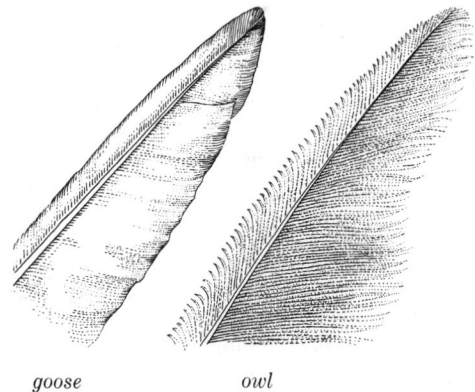

goose   *owl*

TYPICAL OWL FAMILY
Most owls have a soft, saw-toothed leading edge on their first primary (flight) feathers. This reduces the vortex noise of the air passing over the wings and allows owls to fly silently.

New York City region—Buckley and Kane, 1975); also to Conn. and R.I.; nests in mountain forests of Eurasia (see in A.O.U. *Check-list*, 1957).

Bottom owl. *See* Barred owl.

Burrowing owl, *Athene cunicularia* (ah-THEEN-ee cue-nik-you-LAH-rih-ah); genus name: from Greek goddess of wisdom, Pallas Athene, to whom the owl was a sacred bird; species name: Lat., miner, burrower. (Color ills., page 651.) In w. U.S. and Fla.; 9–11 in. long; wingspread 20–24 in.; small, brown ground owl, short tail, long-legged, often seen in daytime standing on prairies, deserts, barren treeless country; frequently bobs up and down on long legs; also perches on fence posts; on western plains usually lives in prairie-dog towns (see below); in Fla., a permanent resident of prairies and around airports; migratory only in northern part of range (Robbins *et al.*, 1966); commonest call when alarmed is a tremulous chattering; at night, utters high mournful cry, *coo-coo-roo* or *co-hoo*, like call of a dove or roadrunner but higher pitched (see Martin, 1973b); when moon is bright, calls come from near and far in "billy" country; occasionally seen at twilight hovering about 20 ft. above ground, evidently hunting; often startled from roadside in evening and flies off; in Fla., not only perches on fence posts but on utility wires; flight is low and undulating (see studies by Coulombe, 1971; Thomsen, 1971).

Feeding Habits: Eats mostly insects and rodents—grasshoppers, moths, beetles, crickets, caterpillars, dragonflies, many caught by the owl in flight; hunts mostly in early evening and throughout night, more rarely by day; eats mice, rats, ground squirrels, young prairie dogs, rabbits, gophers, chipmunks, shrews, and bats; also, occasionally, small birds: horned larks, meadowlarks, vireos, sparrows; also lizards, frogs, toads, snakes, salamanders, fishes, scorpions, centipedes, myriapods, and crayfishes (Bent, 1938; Errington and Bennett, 1935; Fautin, 1946); has curious habit of following a moving dog or horse, apparently to catch any acceptable prey stirred up by it. Burrowing owl–prairie dog–rattlesnake association, or living in same burrow congenially at same time, is folklore. See Coues' explanation in Bent (1938).

Nest: Often in colonies in West, in abandoned burrows of prairie dogs or ground squirrels or of woodchucks, foxes, badgers, armadillos; in Fla., also in burrows of gopher tortoise; owl enlarges and modifies nest burrow by digging with feet; nest sometimes lined with dried cattle or horse droppings beginning at entrance; when not disturbed, uses same burrow year after year.

Eggs: Mar.–July; 6–11, usually 7–9, white, but soiled by earth in burrow.

Incubation: By both sexes, about 28 days; age at which young first fly unknown; distress call of young perfectly mimics rattling of prairie rattlesnake (Martin, 1973b); has been bred in aviaries in England and in London Zoo, also in Czechoslovakia (Prestwich, 1955).

Other Names: Billy owl; ground owl; "howdy" owl; long-legged owl; prairie dog owl; prairie owl.

Accidents: Nesting burrows may be invaded by cats, snakes, which eat young and eggs; many killed at night by traffic when swooping low over highways; also from rodent-poisoning campaigns (Bent, 1938).

Age: One banded wild bird lived to 8 years, 8 months (Kennard, 1975). Captive taken in Calif. as nestling was still alive at age 11.

Albinism: Rare, one reported near Fort Worth, Tex., almost all-white, a partial albino (Sutton, 1912).

Flight Speed: Timed in cruising and foraging flights at 12 m.p.h. (Cottam *et al.*, 1942b).

Weights: Males average 160 gm.; females average 150 gm. (Earhart and Johnson, 1970).

Range: Only in W. Hemisphere; largely resident (see, however, Butts, 1976); western form nests on plains and open areas from s. B.C., s. Alta., Sask., and s.-c. Man. south through e. Wash., Ore., Rogue River valley of Ore., and Calif., including Farallon Is. and Channel Is., also Baja Calif., including coastal islands and Guadalupe Is., east to eastern border of Great Plains in Minn., nw. Iowa, c. Kans., Okla., c. Tex., and La. south through Mexico to C. and S. America; migratory north of Ore. and n. Kans. (see Bremckle, 1936); some winter over much of breeding range except in n. Great Basin and Great Plains region; migrates to s. La., s. Miss., and w. Fla. and south through s. Mexico, West Indies, and w. C. America to w. Panama; accidental in Ind., Mich., s. Ont., N.H., Mass., N.Y., and Va. The Fla. form, or subspecies, is resident on prairies of c. and s. Fla. and Keys (Sprunt, 1954a); accidental in Ala., S.C., N.C., and Va. (see review of these records in Sykes, 1974b); also in Cuba.

Canadian owl. *See* Hawk owl.

Cat owl. Name from resemblance, because of round head, "ear" tufts, and eyes, to a cat. *See* Great horned owl, Long-eared owl, and Screech owl.

Church owl. *See* Barn owl in Owl—Barn Owl Family.

Crazy owl. Name from wild, eerie calls. *See* Barred owl.

Day owl. *See* Hawk owl.

Death owl. Its calls thought a bad omen. *See* Screech owl.

Deer owl. Calls at feeding time of deer (Okefenokee Swamp). *See* Barred owl.

Eagle owl. From large size and ferocity. *See* Great horned owl.

Elf owl, *Micrathene whitneyi* (mick-rah-THEE [*th* as in *thin*] -nee WHIT-ney-eye); genus name: from Gr. *mikros*, small, and the Greek goddess of wisdom, Pallas Athene, to whom the owl was a sacred bird; species name: for Prof. J. D. Whitney, Director, Geological Survey of Calif., in late 19th century (Coues,

1882). (Color ill., page 651.) *Smallest owl in the world;* most abundant owl in Ariz. (Phillips *et al.*, 1964); lives only in W. Hemisphere; sparrow size; 5–6 in. long; wingspread about 15 in.; without ear tufts; *short tail* distinguishes it from pygmy owl and ferruginous owl; "eyebrows" white; underparts ochreceous, gray, and white; yellow eyes and round head separate it from flammulated owl; good place to see it from spring into summer is at dusk in saguaro deserts at entrance of holes of saguaro cactus; also lives in wooded canyons and from low desert in Ariz. to 7,000 ft. in forests of mountains of extreme Southwest; nocturnal, at nightfall one can hear its whistled calls as these birds emerge from hiding places; for its small size has extraordinarily loud voice—"chucklings" and "yips" are like sounds of a puppy dog, attributed to duets of male and female (Ligon, 1968a); males respond to tape-recorded playbacks of their songs.

Feeding Habits: Insects caught on the wing (with feet) or on the ground; sometimes hovers for insects at tree foliage, flowers, or over ground or darts out from perch into air like flycatcher to catch beetles; eats sphinx and noctuid moths, grasshoppers, crickets; takes scorpions, removes or crushes sting before eating (Ligon, 1968a), occasionally takes lizards, small snakes (Bent, 1938).

Nest: Is entirely dependent on woodpecker holes for nesting; uses little or no nesting materials; male arrives on nesting grounds before female; locates one or more nesting cavities before her arrival; sings from cavity to entice female; she responds and enters prospective nesting hole (Ligon, 1968). Though noted as nesting in cavities largely excavated by gila and gilded flickers in giant cactus, or saguaro, also occupies holes dug by acorn, Arizona, gilded, and golden-fronted woodpeckers in mesquites, streamside sycamores or walnuts, and dead pine trees elsewhere in its range; females roost in nesting cavities during day from 2 weeks before eggs laid to time young are 3 weeks old; both sexes roost, other than at nesting time, in dense foliage of trees and bushes in desert and oak zone.

Eggs: Early May to early June; 1–5, usually 2–3, sometimes 4, white, unmarked.

Incubation: By female, 24 days; young capable of first flights 28–33 days after hatching; male feeds female from time of pair formation and at nesting hole until young are half grown; female passes food from male to young; one brood a season as in all typical owls (Ligon, 1968a).

Other Name: Whitney's owl.

Age: A pair of captives in National Zoo, Washington, D.C., at least 7 years old in Oct. 1971, when still alive and healthy (Iliff, 1971); a pair sent National Zoo, in 1964 from Arizona–Sonora Desert Museum, Tucson, bred in captivity in spring 1967 and raised one young which continued to live in aviary with the parent owls —apparently first record of breeding of this owl in captivity; were fed on freshly killed mice and entirely on large crickets when adults were feeding (and caring for young) (Muller, 1970).

Weights: Adults, 35–55 gr. (Ligon, 1968a), or about 1¼–1¾ oz.

Range: Nests in extremely hot, dry areas in se. Calif. (sporadically) and now known there only from a few oases in the northern Colorado Desert (Small, 1974); widely in s. and c. Ariz., in N.M., southwestern part of state in a zone 50–75 mi. wide adjacent to Ariz. line, and from Mexican border north into Gila River valley; first record for Nev., a pair nesting at Fort Mohave, July 1975 (Kingery, 1975); in Tex., in Big Bend region, basin of Chisos Mtns., and Brewster County in extreme s. Tex., in Hidalgo County, where presently common, and especially in Benson State Park, where rediscovered after lapse of 70 years, reported in 1963 (Ligon, 1968a); south to Revilla Gigedo Is. (off west coast of Mexico), s. Baja Calif., and n. Mexico; migrates in fall and winters in the Río de las Balsas basin (Ligon, 1968a); see also Phillips *et al.* (1964); resident in lower Rio Grande Valley of Tex., Mexico, and Baja Calif.

Ermine owl. *See* Snowy owl.

Ferruginous owl, *Glaucidium brasilianum* (glaw-SID-ih-um brah-sil-ih-AY-num); genus name: Lat., from Gr. *glaux,* dim.: *glaukidion,* a kind of owl, so-called from its glaring eyes; species name: Lat., of Brazil, type locality where first specimen (or specimens) known to science collected; *ferruginous* (fer-OO-jin-us), from rust color. (Color ill., page 653.) Small, uncommon owl in N. America; in most of range is extremely abundant; *rusty* relative of the northern pygmy owl; sw. U.S.; 6½–7 in. long; a small "earless" owl, similar to northern pygmy but distinguished from it by its plain *rusty* back, not spotted as in northern pygmy (Robbins *et al.,* 1966); characteristically jerks or flips its tail; longer tail than elf owl; lives in wooded river bottoms and saguaro deserts near Mexican border; in Ariz., generally sparse resident at northern limits of its range in Ariz., where it lives chiefly in mesquites and cottonwoods along streams; also found in mesquites in saguaro desert; the similar northern pygmy owl lives mostly in mountains and wooded or forested parts of e. Ariz. (Phillips *et al.,* 1966); is active by day, especially dawn and late afternoon, but more active at night. Song is series of evenly spaced whistled notes, *puk-puk-puk . . . ,* sometimes 50–60 notes in series; most frequently heard at dawn, dusk, and moonrise; often flips tail slightly with each note.

Feeding Habits: Hunts from perch; lizards, crickets, and other large insects are most commonly taken prey, but also eats scorpions, caterpillars, and small birds and mammals; is remarkably strong and courageous for small size.

Nest: In hollows of trees, and in deserted woodpecker holes in saguaros, mesquite, and cottonwood trees; used year after year, no nesting materials.

Eggs: Tex., late Mar. to late May; Mexico, Mar. to early June; 3–4, occasionally 5; white, laid in bottom of cavity.

Incubation: 28 days, by female; male feeds sitting female and both feed nestlings; young fly at 27–30 days after hatching (Scherzinger, 1977).

Other Name: Ferruginous pygmy owl.

Weights: Males average 62 gm.; females average 75 gm. (Earhart and Johnson, 1970).

Range: Largely tropical, resident from s. Ariz., also from lower Rio Grande Valley, Tex., south in lowlands of Mexico; abundant in C. and S. America; ranges to Straits of Magellan.

Ferruginous pygmy owl. *See* Ferruginous owl.

Flammulated owl, *Otus flammeolus* (OH-tus flah-ME-oh-lus); genus name: Lat., horned owl; species name: dim. of Lat. *flammeus,* flame-colored, or "small, flaming-red." (Color ill., page 653.) Rare and local western owl with short ear tufts; 6–7 in. long, even smaller than pygmy owl (Robbins *et al.,* 1966); lives in ponderosa pine forests from Rocky Mtns. westward; largely nocturnal; smaller than screech owl and, like screech owl, has both a gray and a rusty phase, or form; facial disc of flammulated redder than rest of head; only *small* N. American owl with dark eyes (Peterson, 1961); screech owl has yellow eyes; ear tufts of flammulated and its tawny or gray color inconspicuous; sings often and persistently, primarily on moonlit nights—*boo-BOOT*—the second syllable accentuated and louder than first (Bent, 1938), or a single mellow hoot; double-noted call from a distance resembles a single note. Usually perched in upper parts of tree close to trunk (Ligon, 1961, says rarely one may be seen in thick foliage or on ground beneath some concealing shrub); responds to imitation of its song and thus may be drawn closer to observer, even to perch on low exposed branch.

Feeding Habits: In ponderosa pine forests, in Ariz. also in oak forests, feeds on moths captured with feet in flight about trees, and beetles and spiders caught at tips of branches at end of swift flight; also, grasshoppers, crickets, caterpillars, ants, scorpions, and an occasional small bird or mammal.

Nest: A few wooden chips and feathers in bottom of abandoned flicker or other woodpecker nesting hole in dead pines, aspens, in high mountains of N.M. to 8,000 ft. (Ligon, 1961).

Eggs: Colo., early May to late June; Ariz., N.M., May 18–June 11 (Bent, 1938); 3–4, sometimes only 2, white.

Incubation: Period of and age when young first fly unknown.

Other Name: Flammulated screech owl.

Weights: Males average 54 gm.; females average 57 gm. (Earhart and Johnson, 1970).

Range: Nests in mountains west of Great Plains from s. B.C., Idaho, n. Colo., south through mountains to s. Calif., Ariz., N.M., w. Tex.; Mexico and to Guatemala; winters mainly south of U.S., rarely in s. Calif. (San Bernardino Mtns.); accidental in La.; see also Balda *et al.* (1975).

Flat-faced owl. *See* Short-eared owl.

Gnome owl. *See* Pygmy owl.

Golden owl. *See* Barn owl in Owl—Barn Owl Family.

Gray owl. *See* Great gray owl.

Great gray owl, *Strix nebulosa* (STRIKS neb-you-LOH-sah); genus name: *see* Barred owl; species name: Lat., dark, clouded, in sense here of plumage color. (Color ill., page 653.) 24–33 in. long; wingspread 54–60 in.; *dimensionally,* possibly largest N. American owl but weight exceeded by great horned owl and snowy owl (Bent, 1938); rare and local in n. and c. Sierra Nevada and Rockies at high elevations in pine and spruce forests, common only in timbered regions of Far North; large size and round head *without ear tufts,* prominent gray concentric circles on facial disc; *small* yellow eyes, gray underparts striped; dark chin spot, long tail; call is loud resonant *hoo-hoo-hooo,* also single hoots, also tremulous vibrating notes; sometimes fearless, can be caught in hands or approached closely in thick woods; hunts by day in Far North; irruptive flights far south of northern range owing to food shortages; in winter 1970–71, largest invasion into e. Canada since unprecedented one of winter 1965–66 (Goodwin and Rosche, 1971a); another large flight into e. Canada and U.S. in winter of 1978–79.

Feeding Habits: Eats mice, rats, shrews, moles, gophers, rabbits, hares, red squirrels, crows, and, occasionally, small birds (Bent, 1938; Earhart and Johnson, 1970).

Nest: In spruce and pine forests, frequently near swamps or clearings; usually in old hawk or eagle nests, but a few records of eggs laid and young raised on top of stumps; one record of nest on ground; does not build nest, but will deepen it.

Eggs: Alta., Mar. 23 to mid-May; Alaska and Arctic Canada, mid-May into July; 2–5, usually 2–3, white.

Incubation: About 30 days, by female; in n. Sweden, Wahlstedt (1969) watched three pairs, discovered that male hunted over rather small, open parts of muskeg, near nest, and *mostly* at night but occasionally by day; male provided most of nestlings' food; when nestlings small, gave food to female at nest, which then fed young; later, when nestlings older, male fed them directly. Female brooded young; when brooding ceased, she mostly watched over nest; young left nest 21–28 days after hatching and began climbing about in nest tree; they used nest at night for roosting and in daytime for a refuge when alarmed.

Other Names: Gray owl; spectral owl; spruce owl.

Weights: Males average 940 gm.; females average 1,300 gm. (Earhart and Johnson, 1970).

Range: Lives around northern parts of world; in N. America, from tree limit nests in boreal forests from c. Alaska, n. Yuk., n. Mack., n. Man., and n. Ont., south in mountains to c. and n. Sierra Nevada in Calif. (now most frequently seen in Canadian Zone forests along borders of meadows in Yosemite National Park); also in n. Idaho, w. Mont., Wyo., east of the mountains to Alta., Man., to n. Minn., and Ont.; also seen in summer in s. Que.; winters in breeding range and south and east irregularly to n. Calif., s. Mont., s. Minn., Wisc., Mich., N.Y. (Long Is. and Adirondacks), very rarely to Mass. and Conn.

(Bull, 1964). Two great gray owls banded Jan. 18, 1947, near Toronto, Canada, first of their kind ever banded in history of governmental banding work (Lambert, 1947).

Great horned owl, *Bubo virginianus* (BEW-boh ver-jin-ih-AY-nus); genus name: Lat., owl; "eagle owl" of Pliny; species name: Lat., of Virginia, type locality where first specimen (or specimens) known to science collected. (Color ills., page 652.) Widespread over U.S. and Canada, from wooded wilderness to city parks and suburbs; one of largest and most powerful of all N. American owls; related to eagle owl of Eurasia; largest N. American owl with ear tufts; 18–25 in. long; wingspread, 36–60 in. (Sprunt, 1954a); sexes outwardly alike but female larger; in general, body brown, spotted with darker brown, white throat feathers contrast with dark *cross-barred* underparts (similar long-eared owl is more boldly streaked and *lengthwise* of body on underparts); plumage variable, regionally, from very pale Arctic subspecies to dark one of Pacific Northwest, paler in se. U.S. and Southwest; call is variable, but usually deep, soft, resonant, six-noted hoot—*whoo! whoo-whoo-whoo! whoo! whoo!*—of great carrying power; young when on wing following parents utter blood-curdling screams (hunger cries); adults lean forward when hooting, vibrate the white throat feathers and lift their short tails; respond to imitation of their cries; is migratory in n. Canada and southward movement in fall and winter of some from far northern range; roosts during day in thick tops of evergreen trees, close to trunk, ear tufts erect, or in tops of trees to which leaves cling through winter; is often discovered on roost by noisy flocks of crows or jays and pursued by string of birds that "mob" it in flight.

Feeding Habits: Mainly nocturnal but hunts both by day and by night in woods, mountains, marshes, dunes, and in open desert (Bent, 1938; Phillips *et al.,* 1964); hearing extremely acute. Flies silently, swoops and catches prey in powerful feet and talons, animals from smallest shrews weighing fraction of ounce to large hares and rabbits, gray, red, flying, and fox squirrels, in daytime will fly at and strike leaf nests of squirrels to flush them into open; eats chipmunks, wood rats, Norway rats, mice, muskrats, minks, weasels, skunks (owl's body feathers and nest often smell strongly of skunk), ground squirrels, pocket gophers, woodchucks, opossums, and even attacks porcupines (Bent, 1938; Parkes, 1950); also large snakes, domestic cats, and bats. Cottontail rabbits are prominent food, and in heavy forests of Sask., main prey is the cyclic snowshoe hare (Houston, 1975); record of this owl's captures often seen in snow; also kills and eats grebes, wild ducks, Canada geese, swans, bitterns, small herons, coots, gallinules, rails, phalaropes, pheasants, grouse, domestic turkeys, chickens, guinea fowl, mourning doves, marsh, Cooper's, red-tailed, and red-shouldered hawks; barn, barred, long-eared, and screech owls; flickers and other woodpeckers, jays, crows (taken off night roosts), blackbirds, meadowlarks, snow buntings, juncos, sparrows, mockingbirds, robins, and even descends into house chimney to catch swifts (Anonymous, 1953); also eats frogs, eels, dace, goldfish, bullheads, perch, crayfishes, crickets, beetles, grasshoppers, katydids, and scorpions. See Bent (1938); Errington (1932); and Errington *et al.* (1940) for details. Uses regular feeding roost near nest site, to which it brings prey to be torn up and eaten—usually an old unoccupied nest, hollow stump, fallen log—where bones, hair, and feathers of victims and pellets of the owl collect (Austing and Holt, 1966).

Nest: Usually uses nest of red-tailed hawk, bald eagle, heron, or crow, or occasionally an old leaf nest of squirrel, 15–70 ft. up, also in rocky caves of cliffs, in hollows of trees, and even on ground (see Truslow, 1966); some may accept artificial nest platforms built for them in trees (Scott, 1970). Pairs hoot much during winter or spring courtship; most individuals do not breed until 2 years old (Weller, 1965).

Eggs: Laid as early as Jan. and Feb. as far north as New England and N.Y. (Bent, 1938); in Ariz., nest in spring and fledge young in June (Phillips *et al.,* 1964); 1–6 eggs, usually 2–3, white.

Incubation: By both sexes, 26–30 days (Bent, 1938); possibly 34–35 days (Kendeigh, 1952b); in closely related eagle owl, 34–36 days; young first fly 63–70 days after hatching; adults feed young on ground after they leave nest before able to fly; some pairs fiercely defend young, may strike intruder; have attacked men wearing fur caps presumably mistaking furry cap for prey. A pair of great horned owls in captivity in England produced and raised to maturity three young in 1859 (Prestwich, 1955).

Other Names: Big hoot owl; cat owl; chicken owl; eagle owl; hoot owl; horned owl; king owl; Virginia horned owl.

Accidents: Some killed by automobile traffic when flying across roads at night; also from entanglement in string or wire, some electrocuted, some fly into objects, such as barbed-wire fences, and become impaled; some starve (Stewart, 1969), some die of diseases, possibly viral (Terres, 1940).

Age: Widmann (1907) had captive male that lived to 29 years; Holland (1926b) had female that laid eggs more than 19 years; one banded in Iowa in wild lived to 13–14 years before it was shot near place of banding (Stewart, 1969). Stewart reported that of 374 great horned owls in U.S. (most banded as juveniles), shooting by hunters and others killed 52%; he concluded from evidence that about 322 of 374 may have been shot, or 86%.

Albinism: Apparently rare; a partial albino young one reported in N.Y., May 1950 (Spofford, 1952).

Flight Speed: Timed in w. U.S., 40 m.p.h. (Cottam *et al.,* 1942b).

Hybrids: Has been crossbred in captivity with Eurasian eagle owl, *Bubo bubo* (Gray, 1958).

Weights: Adults range from 680 to 2,503 gm. (Earhart and Johnson, 1970).

Range: Resident all year widely over U.S. and Canada; from dense wilderness forests to suburban woodlands and city parks and along coasts, through most of N. America from limit of trees in Arctic south through C. and S. America to Straits of Magellan (not in West Indies).

Great white owl. *See* Snowy owl.

Ground owl. *See* Burrowing owl.

Hawk owl, *Surnia ulula* (SUR-nih-ah YOU-lew-lah); genus name: established by Dumeril in 1806 but etymology unknown (Jaeger, 1955); species name: Lat., imitative of this bird's call; name of Pliny for the screech owl (Coues, 1882); *hawk owl,* because its appearance when perched, its flight, and its habits resemble those of some of the smaller hawks. (Color ill., page 654.) Medium-sized tame, "earless," day-flying owl of muskegs of n. Canada and around northern regions of the world; an irregular invasion of species from Far North into s. Canada, n. U.S., New England; 14½–17½ in. long; wingspread 33 in. (Hoffman, 1927); a blackish-brown owl on upperparts, no ear tufts; face whitish, heavily bordered with black "sideburns"; underparts *cross-barred,* which also distinguishes it from smaller saw-whet and boreal owls; tail is *long, rounded, falconlike,* broadly barred; a day-hunting owl, perches in open in treetops; raises tail and slowly lowers it; flight is hawklike, straight and rapid on short, pointed wings; usually flies low; alternates flapping and gliding; also hovers like kestrel, or sparrow hawk; is tame, with seeming utter lack of fear; has been approached by observers and caught in hands (Bent, 1938); utters rolling, trilling whistle; in summer in North, lives about half-open woods, parklands, and spruce-tamarack bogs.

Feeding Habits: Flies after and catches with its feet and talons mice, lemmings, young snowshoe hares, ground squirrels, weasels, ptarmigans, ruffed grouse, small birds; also grasshoppers and other insects; in Alta., has been seen following farmers loading haycocks on wagons, at which hawk owl pounced on mice uncovered.

Nest: Often in hollow tops of dead spruces, birches, natural tree hollows, abandoned woodpecker holes, also in deserted nests of crows and birds of prey; apparently uses no nesting materials when nesting inside hollows or tops of dead trees (Bent, 1938).

Eggs: Alaska and Arctic Canada, late Apr. to mid-June; Alta., Apr. 1–June 4; 3–7, usually 5–6, sometimes 9 or more, pure white, glossy.

Incubation: Mainly by female, about 28 days; age when young first fly unknown.

Other Names: American hawk owl; Canadian owl; day owl, Hudsonian owl.

Weights: Males (2 collected in Alaska, June 1963), 317 gr. and 346 gr., or about 10–11 oz.; a female, 418 gr., or about 15 oz.—these birds collected in Central Brooks Range at nest with four young in hollow top of cottonwood tree; apparently northernmost record of hawk owl in Alaska at 67° 35′ N. Lat., 152° 12′ W. Long. (Campbell, J. M., 1969).

Range: In N. America, nests from n. Alaska, Yuk., nw. and c. Mack., n. Sask., n. Man., n. Que., Labrador, and Newfoundland, south to n. B.C., c. Alta., e.-c. Sask., n. Mich., c. Ont., s. Que., and N.B.; casual in summer to Idaho and Mont.; winters south to s. Canada and n. U.S., casual visitor in winter to Wash., nw. Mont., ne. N.D., Neb., Iowa, Wisc., Ill., s. Mich., n. Ohio,

Pa., N.Y., Conn., and N.J. During large invasion of 1918–19, reached Dakotas by mid-Oct., peak of invasion in Minn. and Ont., no fewer than 10 seen inside city limits of Toronto; in spring 1963, nest of hawk owl discovered at Ramsayville, Ont., two nests in Wisc., 18 hawk owls seen in Minn. (see issues of *Audubon Field Notes*, Vol. 17, for details); also nests in forests of Eurasia. See A.O.U. *Check-list*, 1957.

Hoot owl. *See* Barred owl and Great horned owl.

Horned owl. *See* Great horned owl.

"Howdy" owl. Name from bobbing movements suggestive of greeting. *See* Burrowing owl.

King owl. In allusion to large size. *See* Great horned owl.

Laughing owl. From its calls resembling wild laughter. *See* Barred owl.

Little cat owl. *See* Screech owl.

Little gray owl. *See* Screech owl.

Long-eared owl, *Asio otus* (AH-sih-oh OH-tus); genus name: Lat., Pliny's name for long-eared owl (Macleod, 1954); species name: Lat., a kind of owl with long "ear" feathers. (Color ills., page 654.) In both Old and New World; widely distributed over the U.S. and wooded parts of Canada; also lives in tree belts along streams of western plains and even in desert oases; medium-sized with ear tufts and *slimmest* of all N. American owls; locally common in either broad-leaved or coniferous woods; 13–16 in. long; wingspread 36–42 in.; gray or brown-gray; eyes bright yellow; might be confused with great horned owl but breast is streaked up and down, not cross-barred as in great horned; also, the long blackish ear tufts, inner edges light gray, are more near center of head than horned owl's; lacks white throat of horned; has long slim body with long wings and tail; in flight, flattens ear tufts against head; flight light and buoyant, mothlike; more strictly nocturnal than other N. American owls except elf and saw-whet owls; most of day, roosts in dense groves of cedars, pines, vine-covered trees and thickets, palms in desert oases; one of most secretive of owls; when disturbed on roost by day, raises ear tufts high, compresses feathers close to body, making it resemble upright piece of bark or stub of tree limb, thus easily overlooked. *See* Freezing. Hunts over open ground mainly at dusk, early morning, or on moonlit nights; utters soft, musical hoots, *quoo-quoo-quoo,* and single quavering hoots, also shrieks, whistles, and groans when excited (see Bent, 1938).

Feeding Habits: Hunts almost exclusively at night; main food: meadow mice, deer mice, house mice, pine mice; also Norway rats, shrews, moles, bats, squirrels, chipmunks, pocket gophers, and young rabbits; rarely kills large birds—a few records of eating quail,

ruffed grouse, and occasionally takes blue jays, starlings, red-winged blackbirds, meadowlarks, horned larks, cardinals, towhees, juncos, goldfinches, warblers, kinglets, thrushes, bluebirds, scarlet tanager, and brown thrasher; also eats beetles and other insects, frogs, and an occasional small snake (Bent, 1938; Rusling, 1951; Armstrong, W. H., 1958).

Nest: In e. N. America, in old nests of squirrels, and of crows in pines 10–40 ft. above ground; in West, in old nests of ferruginous hawks and magpies or in old nests of herons, ravens, or crows along streams, sometimes in cavity of old stump; occasionally on ground when tree nests scarce.

Eggs: Early Mar. to late May; 3–10, usually 4–5, white, oval and glossy.

Incubation: About 26–28 days (Nice, 1954); young leave nest about 23–26 days after hatching, but not able to fly until about 34 days old (Armstrong, W. H., 1958). Parent birds boldly defend young; with weird piercing screams and anguished cries, try to lure away intruder by "crippled-bird act"; rarely one of parents will attack and strike an intruder with its talons.

Other Names: American long-eared owl; cat owl; lesser horned owl; Wilson's owl.

Age: a banded long-eared owl in Germany lived to 27 years, 9 months (Clapp, 1976).

Weights: Males average 245 gm.; females average 280 gm. (Earhart and Johnson, 1970).

Range: Nests in N. America from s. Mack., c. B.C., s. Man., to w. and s. Ont., s. Que., N.B., and Nova Scotia, south in e., c., and w. U.S. to s. Calif., w. Baja Calif., s. Ariz., N.M., w. Tex., n. Okla., Ark., and Va.; in fall, some migration southward from northern parts of range; returns north in spring; winters from s. and e. Canada to n. Baja Calif., and into Mexico, and from n. U.S. south to s. Tex., La., Ala., Fla., and Bermuda Is.; accidental in s. Alaska and Cuba; also lives in Europe and Asia (see A.O.U. *Check-list*, 1957).

Long-legged owl. *See* Burrowing owl.

Marsh owl. *See* Short-eared owl.

Monkey-faced owl. *See* Barn Owl in Owl—Barn Owl Family.

Mottled owl. *See* Screech owl.

Old-folks owl. *See* Barred owl.

Prairie dog owl. *See* Burrowing owl.

Prairie owl. *See* Burrowing owl and Short-eared owl.

Pygmy owl, *Glaucidium gnoma* (glaw-SID-ih-um NO-mah); genus name: *see* Ferruginous owl; species name: Lat., from Gr. *gnome,* a mark, sign, opinion, to know (Jaeger, 1955); myths about the owl relate to Minerva (Pallas Athena, or Athene), goddess of wisdom; according to Coues (1882), *gnoma* is an apt name for an owl, as "it combines a reputation for wisdom with certain superstitions connected with the gnome-like or goblin-like quality of its knowingness." (Color ill., page 655.) The small pygmy owl lives in either coniferous or decidu-

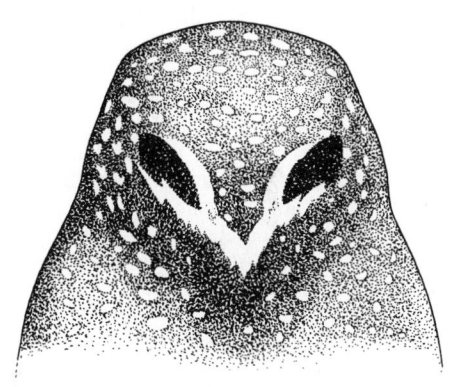

TYPICAL OWL FAMILY
The pygmy owl of the southwest has false eye spots on the back of its head, thought to deceive predators.

ous forests of w. U.S., and in dry regions, in wooded canyons; it hunts by day or by night (see Gashwiler, 1960) but is mainly nocturnal; is about size of a bluebird; in N. America only the elf owl is smaller; 7–7½ in. long; wingspread about 15 in.; is a tame little owl; *without ear tufts;* is rust-brown or gray-brown; no other small owl has *black streaks on its flanks;* eyes bright yellow; the *long tail* is barred with white; when perched its tail projects beyond its folded wing tips and is usually cocked at an angle. Utters single clear whistle from hiding place in tall yellow, or ponderosa, pine (Ligon, 1961) or from top of limber pine or dead lodgepole pine; repeats whistle at intervals of one second or more; also has cooing dovelike notes; calls both by day and on moonlit nights; in Ariz. most of its songs are two notes; imitating this owl's whistle not only attracts the owl but draws small birds that come to mob it as an enemy. Its flight, from perch to perch, with quick wing beats, and just above the ground, is like a shrike's; is active early in morning and late afternoon; likes pine forests of mountains; has a ferocity and strength out of proportion to its small size; beware of thrusting bare hand into its nesting hole (Phillips *et al.,* 1964).

Feeding Habits: Main foods are mice and large insects such as grasshoppers, crickets, beetles, an occasional butterfly, also ground squirrels (sometimes twice its own bulk), and gophers and chipmunks; sometimes eats sparrows, robins, juncos, pine siskins, purple finches, towhees, kinglets, small woodpeckers, vireos, warblers, and marsh wrens, also small snakes and lizards.

Nest: Uses abandoned holes drilled by woodpeckers from size of hairy woodpecker to flicker and acorn woodpecker; also nests in natural tree cavities; usually no lining.

Eggs: Calif., April 24–June 28; Ariz., May 19–June 14; eggs laid on bare bottom of hole, usually 3–4, sometimes 2, 5, 6, or even 7, pure white.

Incubation: By female only (Bent, 1938); about 28 days; young hatch May, June, and early July; are fed by both parents while in nest about 28 days.

Weights: Males average 62 gm.; females average 73 gm. (Earhart and Johnson, 1970).

Other Name: Gnome owl.

Range: Resident all year from se. Alaska, through B.C., w. Alta., south through Wash. and Ore., through Calif. and in mountains of s. Calif. and Cape District of Baja Calif.; also in mountains of Great Basin and Rockies from n. Idaho and w. Mont. through Wyo., Utah, and w. and c. Colo. to Ariz., N.M., and highlands of Mexico and Guatemala.

Rain owl. *See* Barred owl.

Rat owl. From its fondness for rats. *See* Barn owl in Owl—Barn Owl Family.

Red owl. *See* Screech owl.

Richardson's owl. Once thought to be a new species, the Richardson's owl was named and described in 1838 by Charles Lucien Bonaparte for Sir John Richardson, Scottish naturalist,

from a specimen of this little owl collected (shot) at Bangor, Me. It was later discovered that it was not a new species but a subspecies of the previously described and named boreal owl. *See* Boreal owl.

Round-headed owl. From its lack of ear tufts. *See* Barred owl.

Saw-whet owl, *Aegolius acadicus* (ee-JOLE-ih-us ah-KADE-ih-cus); genus name: *see* Boreal owl; species name: Lat., of Acadia, or Nova Scotia, the type locality where the first specimen, or specimens, collected from which the bird was given its scientific species name; *saw-whet,* from some of its calls which closely resemble sounds made by a man filing (whetting), or sharpening, a large mill saw (Bent, 1938). (Color ill., page 655.) Smallest owl of e. U.S., a nocturnal bird of dense woods, seems to prefer coniferous to deciduous woods, often in low swamps; also in Great Smoky Mtns.; sexes outwardly alike, but female usually larger; 7–8½ in. long; wingspread 17–20 in.; upperparts rich dark brown with some white spots; the white underparts streaked and dappled with light chestnut-brown; the only tiny owl *without ear tufts* to be seen east of Rocky Mtns. and north of Tex.; smaller than screech owl; in West, range overlaps that of flammulated owl, which has dark eyes and *ear tufts,* and the round-headed pygmy owl, which is slender and *long-tailed;* yellow-eyed, round-headed saw-whet is similar to closely related boreal owl, but saw-whet lacks black edging on its facial discs, and has a *black,* not yellow, bill; also, top of saw-whet's head is *streaked with white,* not spotted as in boreal owl; has more white on breast than boreal owl; immature saw-whets in first summer are almost evenly rich dark brown with a *conspicuous white, V-shaped patch from base of bill up and over eyes;* a marked character of saw-whet is its tameness; some of the fully grown adults may be stalked in their daytime roosts and caught with the hands; although dull and sleepy by day, at dusk becomes active, animated; is seldom seen in high treetops and during day may doze in hole in tree or on its perch not far above ground in thickets of pine, hemlocks, rhododendrons; some roost all winter under cover of Japanese honeysuckle vines (Bent, 1938). Flight is rapid and like that of woodcock, when hunting at dusk or at night, seems to float on noiseless wings along edges of open parks or meadows; drops on mice and insects in grass. Its song, unlike that of the barred and screech owls, is seldom heard at night except for a few weeks during the courtship period; the saw-filing song reaches its height in Mar. and ends by May 1 (Bent, 1938); the famous rasping, saw-filing notes are uttered in threes—*skreigh-aw, skreigh-aw, skreigh-aw*—also described as *t-sch-whet-t!*—also a single whistled note like the *whew!* of a veery, and some bell-like or metallic sounds. By imitating the soft, scraping whistle, or saw-filing notes at night, may be lured to fly by overhead or to come within reach of one's hands. See, however, Schaeffer (1973).

Feeding Habits: Usual food is insects; feeds rarely on mice, especially woodland species,

small rats, young of flying squirrels and red squirrels, chipmunks, shrews, bats, occasionally sparrows, juncos, and warblers. John K. Terres (1936–70) recovered pellets of a saw-whet owl roosting in holly thicket in Central Park, New York, in Nov. that held fur and bones of young Norway rat; Catling (1971) reported 4 saw-whet owls of 35 caught and banded in spring migration at Toronto that held a decapitated hermit thrush and winter wrens in their talons; in fall, pellets held remains of kinglets, wrens, and sparrows.

Nest: In abandoned woodpecker holes, 14–60 ft. above ground, often those of flicker in woods and swamps, also in natural tree cavity; also will nest in flicker-size nesting box built for it and attached to large tree at edge of grove (see Terres, 1968c). In Ore. has nested in boxes put up for wood ducks (Anonymous, 1959b).

Eggs: Late Mar. into July (see Bent, 1938); 4–7, usually 5–6, white.

Incubation: Almost entirely by female, 26–28 days; young first fly 27–34 days after hatching (Terrill, 1931).

Other Names: Acadian owl; Kirtland's owl; saw-filer; sparrow owl; whetsaw; white-fronted owl.

Accidents: Some fly into cars along highways at night (Terres, 1962b); some caught in storms while crossing large bodies of water and drowned (see Saunders, 1907).

Age: One in captivity for 4 years, still alive (Matheson, 1969); of two captive females, one lived for 17 years, the other for 17½ years, and both were in adult plumage when acquired (Schumacher, 1964).

Weights: Banded in Wisc. (213), adults averaged 91.2 gr.; immatures 88.5 gr. (Mueller and Berger, 1967), or about 3 oz.; in Mich., Oct.–Nov. (10), 85.1–113.6 gr. (Walkinshaw, 1965a).

Range: Nests from s. Alaska, c. B.C., c. Alta., e. Sask., s. Man., n. Ont., c. and e. Que., and Nova Scotia, south in e. U.S. to Md., W.Va., and in Great Smoky Mountains National Park (Stupka, 1963), and to c. Ohio, Mo., Okla., and south in w. U.S. to s. Calif. (mountains of San Diego County) and in highlands of Mexico to Veracruz; winters through and south of breeding range to southwestern deserts of Calif. and Ariz. and to La., S.C., Ga., Fla., casual in Bermuda and Newfoundland; fall migration a general withdrawal southward (Bent, 1938); at Toronto, Catling (1971) reported northward spring migrant saw-whets arriving and then departing for farther north between Mar. 24 and late Apr.; height in mid-May. See also Forbes and Warner (1974).

Screech owl, *Otus asio* (OH-tus AH-sih-oh); genus name: Lat., horned owl; species name: *see* Long-eared owl. (Color ills., page 656.) Lives from extreme s. Canada throughout U.S.; has two color phases—red and gray; 7–10 in. long; wingspread 18–24 in.; the smallest owl with ear tufts in e. U.S.; common about villages, small woodlots, and old orchards, in wooded canyons and along wooded streams in West, and in giant cactus country of Southwest; one of most strictly nocturnal of N. American owls; red, intermediate and gray phases (bright rust brown, brown, or all-gray) are in e. U.S.; west of Rockies, is generally gray, but see Phillips *et al.* (1964) for discussion of exception and Bent (1938)—for example, the large dark race of screech owl of Puget Sound that has a red phase. *See* Color Phase. Call is not screech but a soft, mournful whinny, a tremulous whistle that in eastern screech owl rises, then falls down the scale; heard most often in spring and fall; call has aroused great suspicion and fear among country people; in western screech owls, the whistled notes are different—a series of monotonous, *evenly pitched* notes that start slowly, then cadence increases until whinny at end (Phillips *et al.*, 1964); both eastern and western screech owls come readily at night to easily imitated calls; also to squeaking notes; roosts during day in hollow trees, where often sits at entrance facing bright sunlight (can see in brightest daylight); in dark corners of old buildings, or huddled close to trunks of densely foliaged trees; usually quiet, gentle bird; can be lifted from roosting hole or nest without resistance; other than ominous bill-snapping, seldom uses needlelike claws; makes good pet (but protected and illegal to keep), likes to be stroked or to have head scratched, drinks water freely, is fond of bathing; in wild, has bathed at night in backyard birdbaths.

Feeding Habits: Hunts soon after dusk, flies over meadows, treetops; catches largely mice, shrews, and insects; rarely, young wood rats, Norway rats, kangaroo rats, gophers, pocket mice, grasshopper mice, moles, flying squirrels, chipmunks, occasional bat; crayfishes; snakes, lizards, frogs, toads, salamanders, fishes (horned pouts, trout, whitefish); snails, scorpions, spiders, centipedes, millipedes, earthworms. Also, many feed extensively on insects: beetles, cutworms, caterpillars, grasshoppers, crickets, ants, cicadas, hellgrammites (Bent, 1938); while in flight, with feet snatches June beetles from twigs or leaves of trees; others in midair with beak (Sutton, 1929); also cecropia moths; reported to have killed domestic pigeons, quail, ruffed grouse, American woodcock, sparrow hawk, or kestrel, other screech owls, downy woodpecker, eastern kingbird, eastern phoebe, eastern wood pewee, horned lark, blue jay, Steller's jay, starling, blackbirds, northern (Baltimore) oriole, American goldfinch, dark-eyed (slate-colored) junco, canary (flew down chimney into home and attacked and killed canary in cage), indigo bunting, house sparrow, and many other small birds.

Nest: On bottom of natural cavity in trees, usually no nesting materials, also in hollow stumps, abandoned nesting holes mostly of common flicker in sycamores, elms, dead pines, oaks, saguaros and mesquites in deserts, and in many other trees, some in trees along streams of West; also in woodpecker holes in utility poles along railroads, in flicker-size nest boxes (Terres, 1968c).

Eggs: Feb.–July over its enormous range; usually 4–5, sometimes 2–8, white, oval or round.

Incubation: Largely or entirely by female, but male may roost in the nesting hollow during day while female is incubating; 26 days (Sherman, 1911); male usually provides food for female while she incubates; both feed young,

which first fly about 28 days after hatching; adults may dive at or even strike human intruders near nest.

Other Names: Gray owl; little cat owl; little dukelet; little gray owl; little horned owl; mottled owl; red owl; scritch owl; shivering owl; squinch owl; whickering owl; whinnerying owl.

Accidents: Some caught in traps set on poles for large hawks and owls; killed on highways by traffic at night when alighting on road to catch insects; one caught by neck in tree crotch in Cooke County, Ill., died of starvation (Hodges, 1950); many electrocuted, along with other birds, by electric fences on farms in N.C. (see Stewart 1973).

Age: A banded wild screech owl at Pasadena, Calif., lived to be 13 years old (Sumner, 1940).

Weights: Considerable variation in N. America; males 88–178 gm.; females 92–220 gm. (Earhart and Johnson, 1970).

Range: Resident over most of nesting range except in northern parts, from which some withdraw southward in winter; nests from se. Alaska, s. B.C., s. Man., s. Ont., s. Que., and Me. south throughout U.S. (is never far from trees) to Fla., Baja Calif., and Mexico.

Scritch owl. *See* Screech owl.

Shivering owl. From tremulous call. *See* Screech owl.

Short-eared owl. *Asio flammeus* (AH-sih-oh FLAH-me-us); genus name: *see* Long-eared owl; species name: Lat., flaming, fiery; named in 1763 by Erik Pontoppidan, Danish naturalist, from a specimen, or specimens, of this owl from Sweden, apparently in reference to its plumage; however, this owl in N. America varies considerably in color over its extensive range—from tawny to buff on upperparts including head and chest. (Color ills., page 657.) A ground owl that lives on every continent except Australia (Townsend, 1938); on grasslands, tundra, marshes, and dunes; hunts by day and night; 13–17 in. long; wingspread 38–44 in.; tawny brown; large, buff-colored patches on upper sides of wings show in flight; dark patches on undersides of bend of wings similar to those of rough-legged hawk; small ear tufts difficult to see; appears big-headed and neckless in buoyant mothlike flight; quarters fields and marshes, often drops straight down with wings upheld and pounces on mouse; sometimes sits on fence posts to watch ground for prey; loud clapping of one's hands while crossing marsh or field may flush it from ground; roosts on ground, often in large colonies; in winter, in n. U.S., sometimes roosts in evergreen groves near marsh (Terres and Jameson, 1943); has spectacular courtship flight (Townsend, 1938); maintains winter territories and gives loud *eeee-yerp* during territorial defense (Clark, 1975); in migration is silent but on nesting grounds utters high-pitched rasping *wak, wak, wak*, like barking of small dog, or *toot-toot-toot-toot-toot*, rapidly, 15–20 times; also sawing or filing notes and a whistlelike squeal. Like most owls, both adults and young snap bills and hiss; short-eared is one of owls most frequently seen by man; assembles and hunts in large numbers over prairies, marshes, and fields

where mice abundant; hunts in afternoon but more frequently at dusk, at dawn, and at night; often chases crows, marsh hawks, and great blue heron, aggressively if in nesting season or possibly in play at other times.

Feeding Habits: When hunting, circles and glides close to ground like marsh hawk; sometimes alights on ground to watch for rodents, which are main food, especially meadow mice (*Microtus*), also occasionally eats white-footed, pine, and house mice, shrews, cotton rats, rabbits, pocket gophers, and bats; is especially abundant predator in n. Alaska, when lemming populations high (Maher, 1970). Also eats many insects; eats large numbers of grasshoppers, June beetles, cutworms, also takes small birds—meadowlarks, Savannah, sharp-tailed, and other "field" sparrows—and has preyed on nesting terns; also black rail and sora.

Nest: On ground, sometimes in small colonies, generally in slight depression, sparsely lined with grasses and weed stalks, and a few feathers, in open field or marsh, often at base of clump of tall weeds or grasses; sometimes returns to exactly same nesting spot following year (Urner, 1923).

Eggs: In prairie states of c. and n. U.S., Mar. into mid-June; Alaska and Arctic Canada, June; usually 4–7, but up to 9 and even 14 reported; white; according to Lack (1968), many lay up to 9 eggs during a plague year of meadow voles when prey numbers are high, though only half that number in years when voles not at peak of abundance. According to Urner (1923), short-eared owls sometimes remove their eggs or helpless young to escape unusually high tides, and if eggs destroyed, probably lay a second set.

Incubation: By female, about 21 days (Townsend, 1938) but may be 23 days; young fly about 31–36 days after hatching; remain in vicinity of nest for about 42 days; adults will perform "crippled-bird act" to lead away intruder, also will attack and even go into part of its courtship flight in its excitement.

Other Names: Bog owl; flat-faced owl; marsh owl; prairie owl.

Accidents and Age: One reported to National Audubon Society in New York City in 1950s that had flown into TV aerial on house near Long Is. marsh and was impaled by wing; could no longer fly, lived in captivity 10 years; a banded short-eared owl reported from Holland lived to 12 years, 9 months (Clapp, 1976).

Albinism: A partial albino, entire plumage suffused with white, killed at Portland, Conn., Apr. 1883 (Sage, 1883).

Flight Speed: Timed in w. U.S., 15–26 m.p.h. (Cottam *et al.*, 1942b).

Weights: Female usually, but not always, larger than male; males average 315 gm.; females average 380 gm. (Earhart and Johnson, 1970).

Range: In N. America, resident from n. Alaska, n. Mack., Keewatin, se. Baffin Is., Labrador, and Newfoundland, south to s. Calif.; however, according to Small (1974), primarily a non-breeder in s. Calif. and seen in saltwater marshes, freshwater marshes, tall grass meadows, and agricultural lands at almost any time of year, but most commonly late Aug.–mid-

Apr.; also nests in Nev., Utah, ne. Colo., Kans., Mo., s. Ill., n. Ind., s. Ohio, N.Y., N.J., and Va. (tidewater areas); winters occasionally almost throughout breeding range but some migration to Tex., Gulf coast, and Fla., from parts of nesting range when snow covers fields and rodent food; also lives in n. Europe and Asia, some islands in Pacific, Hawaii; also Hispaniola and Puerto Rico; Galápagos Is., and into S. America to Tierra del Fuego and Falkland Is.

Skunk owl. From habit of eating skunks. *See* Great horned owl.

Snake owl. From its hissing sounds. *See* Barn owl in Owl—Barn Owl Family.

Snowy owl, *Nyctea scandiaca* (NIK-tee-ah skan-DIE-ah-kah or skan-dih-AY-kah); genus name: from Gr. *nykteros,* nocturnal; species name: Lat., of Scandinavia, from which (Lapland) the type specimen came (*see* Type Specimen). (Color ills., pages 658, 659.) Circumpolar throughout Arctic regions of Old and New worlds; large white owl, without eartufts; active by day; one of largest, the most powerful and heaviest of N. American owls; 20–27 in. long; wingspread 54–66 in.; white owl with some dark barring; no other white bird so heavily built; large rounded head, yellow eyes; immatures more heavily barred and go farther south in fall and in winter (Robbins *et al.,* 1966); adult female more heavily barred than adult male (Bent, 1938); in Far North lives on tundra, where perches on ground; during its periodic heavy invasions of s. Canada and U.S., when lemmings scarce in Arctic, often seen around marshes, meadows, seacoasts, lakes, rivers; perches on ground, posts, utility poles, haystacks, dunes, on ice near water, roofs of buildings, seldom in trees; watches alertly, turning head from side to side to scan surroundings; usually shy and wild, does not allow approach closer than 200–300 ft. (Bent, 1938); has broad, rounded wings; flight is strong and direct, with long smooth downward strokes of wings but upward strokes jerky; often sails for some distance; calls with deep, hoarse, raven-like croak, a shrill whistle, and a loud, hollow, barking growl; hooting is its territorial "song" uttered from ground; in May, in Arctic, hoots at all times of day, frequently heard from 2 mi. away (Taylor, P. S., 1973); male has courtship flight (aerial display), and he displays to female on ground (see illustrations of these displays in Taylor, P. S., 1973).

Feeding Habits: In Alaska, is especially associated as predator on mouse and lemming populations, its main foods (Maher, 1970); also takes ptarmigans, grebes, small gulls, murres, puffins, razorbills, dovekies, ducks, young geese, coots, sandpipers, crows, and, where waters unfrozen, wades in and catches in its taloned feet fishes and small marine animals; when these scarce, owls move to more southern places where they subsist on whatever they can find; catches and eats hares, rabbits, ground squirrels, rats, weasels, moles and shrews, and, when hard-pressed for food, attacks fur-bearing animals caught in traps; also scavenges on dead animals; on its nesting grounds in Arctic,

has been known to kill young peregrine on eyrie, but may, in turn, be killed by the adult peregrines.

Nest: On ground, a mere hollow, scooped out of earth by the adult owls, on summit of hillocks or other rises of land, usually on highest and driest part of tundra; sometimes on gravel bank, rocky ledge or cliff, the hollow lined with a little moss and a few feathers. Most northerly and probably first nest of this species ever found was in Grinnell Land, Ellesmere Is., Northwest Territories, at 82° 40′ N. Lat., June 20, 1876 (Bent, 1938).

Eggs: N. Canada, May 25–June 30; Arctic Alaska, June; 5–7, or 8; sometimes 3–4 and up to 13; more eggs laid when lemming populations high and food supply abundant; if lemmings scarce, the owls may not even attempt to nest (see Gross, 1947a; Lack, 1966; Wynne-Edwards, 1962); eggs creamy white, more elongated than most eggs of owls.

Incubation: By female, begins incubating with laying of first egg, thus a considerable size difference between first-hatched and last-hatched young; period of incubation, 32–33 days per egg (Parmalee *et al.,* 1967); young leave nest about 16 days after hatching, scatter over nearby tundra, where male feeds them; when all have left nest, both parents attend the brood; first flights of young 43–57 days after hatching; adults will use "crippled-bird act" to lead intruder away; male actively defends his mate, the eggs, nest, and young against enemies, even against wolves and arctic foxes; adults will swoop low and strike at human intruder near the nest (Sutton, 1932). Snowy owl has bred and raised young in captivity in England; first success reported in 1875 (see Prestwich, 1955).

Other Names: Arctic owl; ermine owl; great white owl; harfang; wapachthu; white owl.

Age: One, banded in wild in 1960, lived to 9 years, 5 months (Hilton, 1976); another, to 14 years in a zoo in Calif. (Stott, 1948).

Flight Speed: Timed Long Is., N.Y., 50 m.p.h. (Teale, 1965).

Weights: Males average 1,650 gm.; females average 1,960 gm. (Earhart and Johnson, 1970).

Range: Nests north of limit of trees on Arctic tundra and barren grounds; in N. America, from islands of Bering Sea, the Yukon Delta, Melville Is., and n. Greenland south to c. Mack., c. Keewatin, and n. Ungava; winters from Arctic coast south to the southern Canadian provinces and irregularly to Calif., Nev., Utah, Colo., Okla., Mo., Ind., Neb., Tex., N.C., S.C., Ala., La., and Ga., also in Bermuda; during irregular big winter flights south of nesting range, some may wander far at sea; have alighted on ships 200–500 mi. off Atlantic coast; many shot while in s. Canada and U.S. and never return northward; others do in early spring. See details in Gross (1946b; 1947a) and Bent (1938); also A.O.U. *Check-list* (1957).

Sparrow owl. Local common name for the boreal owl and the saw-whet owl, either from their small, sparrow size or from their occasional eating of sparrows and other small birds.

Spectral owl. *See* Great gray owl.

Spotted owl, *Strix occidentalis* (STRIKS ock-sih-den-TAIL-iss); genus name: *see* Barred owl; species name: Lat., western. (Color ills., pages 658, 659.) A rare resident of woods in canyons or in deep coniferous forests of West and Southwest—on Threatened Wildlife List (see Office of Endangered Species, 1973); medium-sized, dark brown owl; 16½–19 in. long; wingspread about 45 in.; nocturnal; roosts by day in shaded rocky gorges or in dense-foliaged trees in canyons; seldom seen because of retiring habits during day; is the western counterpart of the eastern barred owl, but more spotted with white, less barred on its rounded head and on back; has dark eyes, no ear tufts as in the yellow-eyed great horned owl; one of its calls, similar to eastern barred owl's, is series of deep notes uttered shortly after dusk, like barking dog, from wildest mountain canyons or from deep forests—*whoo-whoo-hoo-hoo*—with full-throated explosive effect of a baying hound (female's notes much higher-pitched than male's). This call is easily imitated and owl responds at night and may come close; also gives a low musical whistled *whee-ee;* by making squeaking notes one may attract this owl on a dark day or at night.

Feeding Habits: Catches in its talons, at dusk or at night, wood rats, white-footed and deer mice; also preys on the red tree mouse, *Phenacomys longicaudus,* which lives mostly in coniferous trees of the humid coastal belt of Calif. and Ore., also bats and, occasionally, small birds; also pygmy owls, screech owls, moths, crickets, and large beetles (Marshall, 1942).

Nest: In cavities in cliffs of wooded canyons, or in old ravens' nests on cliffs, or in old hawks' nests in canyon trees; sometimes on bare floor of caves or washouts of clay bank or on bare ground at base of large rock; also in cavities in trees (Bent, 1938); up to 6,700 ft. altitude in San Mateo Mtns. of N.M. (Ligon, 1961); rare in Ariz. but reported from every life zone (Phillips *et al.,* 1964).

Eggs: Calif., Mar. 1–May 10; Ariz. and N.M., early to mid-Apr.; 2–3, usually 2, very rarely 4 (Bent, 1938); white, oval, laid on bare floor of cave or tree cavity, usually only a few feathers or debris around eggs.

Incubation: Period of and age when young first fly unknown. Adults are gentle and tame, do not strike intruder at nest in defense of their young; may alight near intruder but make no threats. See Ligon (1926).

Weights: Males average 580 gm.; females average 640 gm. (Earhart and Johnson, 1970).

Range: Resident of Pacific coast region from forests of the Cascades and Sierra Nevada westward in sw. B.C., Wash., Ore., and Calif.; s. Rocky Mtns. from c. Colo. south through e. Ariz., N.M., and w. Tex. into w. Mexico.

Spotted screech owl. *See* Whiskered owl.

Spruce owl. *See* Great gray owl.

Squinch owl. Name is corruption of "screech." *See* Screech owl.

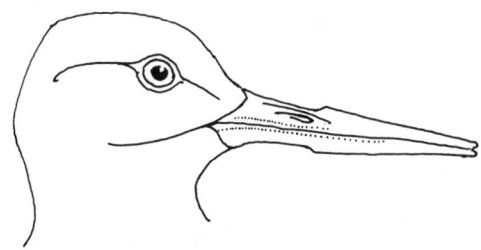

Steeple owl. *See* Barn owl in Owl—Barn Owl Family.

Stone owl. *See* Barn owl in Owl—Barn Owl Family.

Swamp owl. *See* Barred owl.

Tengmalm's owl. *See* Boreal owl.

Whinnerying owl. From its call like whinnying of a horse. *See* Screech owl.

Whiskered owl, *Otus trichopsis* (OH-tus try-COPE-sis); genus name: Lat., horned owl; species name: Lat., from Gr. words meaning hair and countenance, "hairy-faced" (Coues, 1882). (Color ill., page 659.) Small, common, nocturnal owl of wooded mountain canyons of the Southwest, in oak, oak-pine, and sycamores; 6½–8 in. long; has ear tufts, is gray, and strikingly resembles the closely related screech owl (gray phase); their ranges overlap; whiskered owl has longer "whiskers" (bristles on front of its face) than screech owl; has large white spots on its scapulars, and coarser black spots on its underparts, all this distinguishable only when in the hand; however, can be easily identified at night by its voice (Peterson, 1961), which is not difficult, because males often answer imitation of their calls, a rapidly uttered series of three to four notes or more—*boot-boot-boot-boot*—the cadence slowing at end; both sexes utter *choo-you-coo-coo* notes when greatly disturbed, also click bills (for an interpretation of its "songs" or vocalizations, see Martin, D. J., 1974). Marshall (see in Pough, 1957) wrote that song of the female is higher-pitched than *boot-boot* notes of male and that the male may become so incensed by imitated notes of his song within his territory that he sometimes struts along the ground toward his human imitator and allows himself to be picked up; roosts by day close to trunk on tree branches of oaks, junipers, sycamores.

Feeding Habits: Catches prey in talons by short flights among tree branches or to ground; catches moths, mantises, grasshoppers, larvae of large beetles, centipedes, spiders.
Nest: In natural cavities of oaks and sycamores or in flicker holes in wooded canyons.
Eggs: May; 3–4, white.
Incubation: Period of and age at which young first fly apparently not known.
Other Name: Spotted screech owl.
Weights: Males average 85 gm.; females average 92 gm. (Earhart and Johnson, 1970).
Range: Resident in mountains from se. Ariz. and sw. N.M. south to El Salvador and Honduras.

White-fronted owl. *See* Saw-whet owl.

White owl. *See* Barn owl in Owl—Barn-Owl Family and Snowy owl.

Whitney's owl. *See* Elf owl.

Wood owl. *See* Barred owl.

OWLET-FROGMOUTH FAMILY
See Caprimulgiformes.

OX-EYE
See Black-bellied plover in Plover Family; *also* Least sandpiper and Semipalmated sandpiper in Sandpiper Family.

OYSTERCATCHER FAMILY
Haematopodidae (he-mah-toe-POD-ih-dee); Lat., from Gr. *haimatopous*, blood foot, brightly colored feet. Large and spectacular shorebirds; 15–21 in. long; 6 species (Van Tyne and Berger, 1976)—the European, or Eurasian, oystercatcher of the Old World, the sooty oystercatcher of Australia, the Magellanic oystercatcher, *Haematopus leucopodus*, of the coasts of Chile and Argentina, the blackish oystercatcher, *Haematopus ater*, of Peru, Argentina, and Uruguay (Meyer de Schauensee, 1970), and 2 species of N. America, the black and the American oystercatchers. Oystercatchers, in Europe often called sea-pies, are mostly birds of the seashores along the temperate and tropical coasts of the world; all are largely black and white or pure black, with sturdy pink feet and legs, feet with three toes, slightly webbed, and no hind toe (hallux); have relatively long, pointed wings, short tail; most distinguishing feature is the long sturdy red bill, more than twice as long as the bird's head, laterally compressed, shaped almost like the double-edged knife of oystermen, with a chisel-like tip with which oystercatcher pries shellfishes from shoreside rocks or from place of attachment underwater; bivalves carried ashore to beach or rocks with slender chisel-shaped bill inserted between the two shells, the strong abductor muscle that closes the shell is severed; food includes mussels, clams, chitons, limpits, barnacles, oysters, also probes with bill in mud and sand for crabs, marine worms, and other invertebrates. Oystercatchers often wade, belly-deep, in water to search for prey; can swim well; on ground, usually walk but can run rapidly; flight is rapid and direct with somewhat shallow beats of wings; are noisy and restless, sometimes by night as well as by day; outside of nesting season may gather in flocks of thousands in certain favored places along seacoasts; in N. America, especially in winter along coast of Bulls Is., S.C., in Cape Romain National Wildlife Refuge; some oystercatchers are migratory.

Gross in his summary (1965a) reports one record of albinism in one species, which he does not identify.

Oystercatchers are protected by law, but to sustain an ill or injured one until it is able to fend for itself, offer it small pieces of fish, worms, bread crumbs, and green, leafy vegetables.

American oystercatcher, *Haematopus palliatus* (he-MAT-oh-pus pal-ih-AY-tus); genus name: *see* family introduction; species name: Lat., cloaked, in allusion to black head, neck, breast and dark back—appears to be wearing a cloak. (Color ills., pages 660, 661.) Uncommon or rare through most of U.S., seen along Atlantic coast usually from Long Is., N.Y. (recently, Mass.), and N.J. south, and Pa-

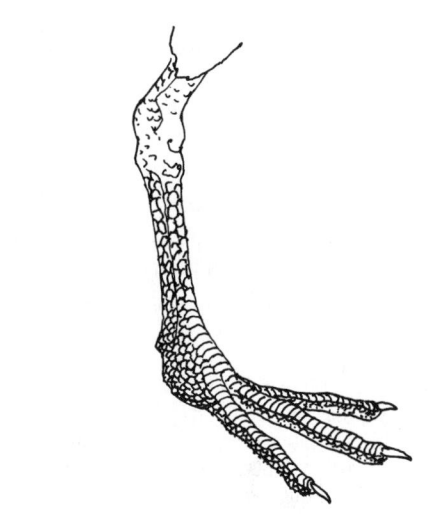

OYSTERCATCHER FAMILY

OYSTERCATCHER FAMILY
The oystercatcher's bill is long, laterally compressed, and shaped rather like an oysterman's double-edged knife. Its chisel-like tip enables the oystercatcher to poke into the half-open shells of bivalves underwater or to pry shellfish off rocks at low tide.

cific coast of Baja Calif.; 17–21 in. long, of which bill 2¾–4 in. long; wingspread 30–36 in. —largest of the oystercatchers; sexes outwardly alike but female larger; black head and neck, back brownish, white patches in wings, shows long white wing stripe in flight; white underparts; large red bill (bill brown in immatures), contrasting white and dark plumage is distinguishing; eyes yellow; end of tail dark brown; upper part of tail white; legs and feet pink; usually seen along shore in very small flocks apart from other shorebirds; shy and wary, one usually gets only fleeting glimpse of this bird as it flies away over hot shimmering sands of U.S. beaches; once seen regularly along n. Atlantic coast north to Nova Scotia and Labrador in time of Audubon, later uncommon north of Va. capes but recently more common; never hunted as much as other shorebirds but some hunting took toll over years; is mainly year-round resident over present range except newer, northern part; a strong swift flier, utters loud cries on its breeding grounds, *wheep, wheep, wheeop*, also a creaking note, *crik, crik, crik*, when it takes flight.

Feeding Habits: Eats mostly oysters, clams, and other bivalves, also small sea urchins, starfish, crabs, marine worms. See details in Tomkins (1947) and Bent (1929).

Nest: A hollow in sand of dry flat beaches, well above high-water mark, without lining and on little mounds of sand, from which incubating bird has lookout for approaching intruders (Bent, 1929).

Eggs: Carolinas and Ga., Apr.–May; 2–4, usually 2–3, green-brown or buff, marked with dark brown spots or blotches.

Incubation: By male and female, in turn, 27 days (Palmer, 1967); both parents feed young; carry pieces of oysters in throat and drop them near chicks; bill of young not sufficiently developed to get oysters for themselves until at least 60 days after hatching, but they eat other food; probably first fly about 35 days after hatching (Palmer, 1967).

Other Names: Bank bird; brown-backed oystercatcher; Frazar's oystercatcher; sea crow.

Accidents: Some caught by bill by clam and held so firmly that oystercatcher drowns with rising tide (*see* Mollusks and Birds).

Age: One, banded Long Is., N.Y., trapped near same place and released when 10 years old (Kennard, 1975).

Weights: 495–625 gr. or 1 lb. 1 oz.–1 lb. 6 oz. (10 specimens).

Range: Along Atlantic coast from Mass., where nesting along coast since 1967 or 1968 (Finch, 1975), R.I. in 1977 (Lapham, 1979), also Long Is., N.Y., where breeding since 1957 (Bull, 1964), and s. N.J., south through West Indies to e.-c. Argentina; mainly resident from Fla. to Tex. on Gulf coast to e. Mexico; along Pacific coast from Baja Calif. south to n. Chile; in winter, seldom seen north of N.C.; straggles occasionally north to N.B., and on Pacific coast to Calif.

Black oystercatcher, *Haematopus bachmani* (he-MAT-oh-pus BACK-man-eye); genus name: *see* family introduction; species name: given in 1838 by John James Audubon for his friend the Rev. John Bachman of Charleston, S.C. (Color ills., pages 660, 662.) Resident along Pacific coast; a large all-black or all-brownish bird with bright red bill, pink legs and feet; immatures are browner and have dusky bill, orange at base; often seen on rocky ledges along outer beach, where pries off shellfish exposed by retreating tides; is larger than black turnstones, which often frequent same rocks (Hoffman, 1927); 16½–18½ in. long; moves sedately with slow, jerky movements; when startled calls sharply, *whick, whick*, or when flying, a soft *phee-ah*.

Feeding Habits: Much like those of American oystercatcher; eats mussels, marine worms, but feeds more on limpets of surf-hammered rocks where these shellfish plentiful.

Nest: Hollow in gravel of beach above tide line or in hollow of rocky islet or reef.

Eggs: May–June; 1–4, usually 2–3, buffy, spotted with dark brown.

Incubation: By both sexes, in turn, 26–27 days, parents alternate attending brood; chicks can run well 3 days after hatching, catch insects at 5 days, at 30 days after hatching they can fly and remove limpets and mussels with bill (see in Webster, 1941).

Other Name: Redbill.

Hybrids: In Baja Calif., where range of black oystercatcher overlaps that of the Frazar's (American) oystercatcher, there is some interbreeding between the two species, according to Pough (1957).

Weights: 513–849 gr. or 1 lb. 2 oz.–1 lb. 14 oz. (4 specimens).

Range: Resident along coast from Kiska Is., Aleutians, Alaska, south to Baja Calif.; casual in winter on Pribilof Is. and Yukon, does not migrate; flocks in winter seldom wander more than 30 mi. from nesting place (Palmer, 1967).

Eurasian oystercatcher. *See* European oystercatcher.

European oystercatcher, *Haematopus ostralegus* (he-MAT-oh-pus os-TRAL-eh-gus); genus name: *see* family introduction; species name: Lat., from Gr. *ostreon*, oyster, and Lat. *lego*, to collect, or gather (Jaeger, 1955). A Eurasian species that has strayed to s. Greenland; 16–17 in. long, of which *red-orange* bill 2¾–3½ in. long; eyes crimson; black head, breast, and upperparts contrast with pure-white underparts; has white stripe on wings and white tail with broad black terminal band; sturdy pink legs; lives along coastal shores and estuaries and now adapting in Britain and in Europe to cultivated land.

Feeding Habits: Tinbergen and Norton-Griffiths (1964) watched adults walk about in water 3–4 in. deep and put head under to catch mussels; they also carried marine worms to young and an occasional crab—crabs were first demolished with bill by adults, then fed in pieces to young; some mussels had already been taken out of shell and were fed to young without any further preparation; crabs dug from sand were killed by throwing them on their backs and then stabbing bill into underparts and breaking up into pieces; Heppleston (1971) wrote: "After a mussel (underwater with shell open) has been stabbed, the bird inserts its bill . . . and severs the adductor muscles without damaging the shell."

Other Names: Eurasian oystercatcher; oyster-plover; pied oystercatcher; sea-pie.

Age: One 34 years old banded at Vogelwarte, Helgoland (Nice, 1962b) and one 36 years old (Nice, 1966a).

Weights: To about 1 lb. 8 oz. (Palmer, 1967).

Range: Nests mainly on seacoasts of Iceland, British Isles, Europe, s. Africa, e.-c. Asia, and Australian Region; winters over most of nesting range; casual·in s. Greenland.

Frazar's oystercatcher. A Pacific coast (Baja Calif.) race or subspecies, *Haematopus palliatus frazari*, of the American oystercatcher (*see* American oystercatcher); originally named as a distinct species, *Haematopus frazari*, by William Brewster in 1888 in honor of M. Abbott Frazar, a veteran collector of birds.

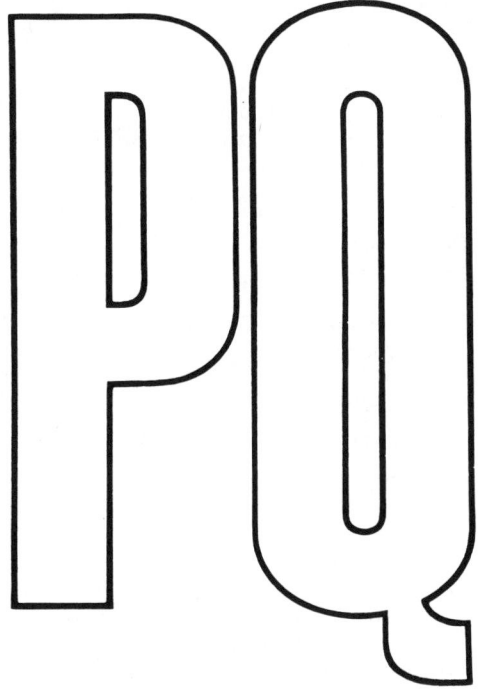

PACIFIC DISCOVERY
A publication. *See* Ornithological Periodicals.

PACIFIC FLYWAY
See Waterfowl.

PAINTED-SNIPE
See Shorebird.

PAIR BOND
See Courtship; Sexual Relationships.

PAISANO
One of common names of the roadrunner in Cuckoo Family.

PALAEARCTIC REGION
A faunal region (*see* Faunal Regions); one of six in the world; "it comprises the whole of Europe, Africa north of the Sahara, and Asia north of the Himalayas. The Palaearctic Region is so called because it includes the part of the Old World that lay under Arctic conditions during the Quaternary Glaciation, which terminated some 10,000 years ago" (Meinertzhagen, 1964c). *See* Geological Time Scale.

The boundaries of the Palaearctic are clearly defined on the west, north, and east by the Atlantic, Arctic, and Pacific oceans, which separate it from the Nearctic (N. American) Region (*see* Nearctic Region). A land bridge once extended across the Bering Straits, joining the land and the birdlife in the Palaearctic Region with that of the Nearctic Region; so many families of birds live in both of these regions and nowhere else in the world that some authorities prefer to group the Palaearctic and Nearctic regions into one, the Holarctic (*see* some of its typical birds under Holarctic Region). According to Pettingill (1970), there are 750 species of birds of 69 families in the Palaearctic Region. See Meinertzhagen (1964c) for a detailed discussion of the Palaearctic Region, its features, boundaries, and birdlife.

PALATE
See discussion of the bird palate under Mouth; for a long detailed account, see in Bellairs (1964a).

PALEOCENE PERIOD
See Geological Time Scale.

PALEONTOLOGY
or PALAEONTOLOGY. The scientific study of the fossilized remains of birds and other animals and plants. *See* Fossil Birds; Geological Time Scale.

PALE RING-NECK
See Plover, piping, in Plover Family.

PALMATE
(PAL-mate). Having the shape of the hand; resembling a hand with the fingers spread; webbed. In birds, having the three front toes fully webbed, as in ducks. *See* Feet and Legs.

PAMPRODACTYL
(pam-pro-DAK-til). *See* Feet and Legs.

PAN AMERICAN ELEMENT
See Distribution.

PANBOREAL (pan-BOE-ree-al) **ELEMENT**
See Distribution.

PANCREAS
(PAN-kree-ass). In birds, a thin, lobulated gland which lies just inside the curve, or the U-shaped loop, of the duodenum. The duodenum is the first part of the small intestine. *See* duodenum under Intestine. From 1 to 3 pancreatic ducts pass from the right side of the pancreas into the right side of the duodenal loop of the small intestine. Through these ducts, important digestive ferments or enzymes (amylase, trypsin, and lipase) are secreted by the pancreas into the small intestine, also a buffering solution which neutralizes the stomach acid. These are functions of the exocrine part of the gland.

The pancreas is both an endocrine and an exocrine gland. As an endocrine gland its internal islets of Langerhans secrete two hormones —glucagon and insulin, which enter the blood and regulate metabolism (Ziswiler and Farner, 1972; Assenmacher, 1973). *See* Digestion; Endocrine Glands.

PANDIONIDAE
See Osprey Family.

PANTROPICAL ELEMENT
See Distribution.

PAPILLA
(pl.: *papillae*). A papilla in the skin of a bird (*see* Skin) is a highly specialized unit composed of a relatively large core of dermis (underlayer of skin), covered by a thin layer of epidermis (outer layer). All parts of the adult contour feather of a bird—the shaft, barbs, and barbules—arise from the epidermal component of the papilla as a result of its contact relationship with the underlying mesodermal component. Neither of these alone is capable of producing a feather (Rawles, 1960). The papilla is necessary for the formation of a feather; if it is removed experimentally, no feather develops afterward from the operated follicle. *See* Feather.

PARAKEET
See in Parrot Family.

PARALLEL EVOLUTION
See Convergent Evolution.

PARASITE
A plant or animal that lives on, in, or with some other living organism (called its host) and that lives at the host's expense, the parasite getting food, shelter, or some other advantage from its host.

Some animal parasites—fleas and lice, for example—that cannot attain complete development independent of their hosts are called *obligate parasites* (*see* Obligate Parasite); others —ticks, for example—that live most of the time on their hosts but also live independent of them at necessary times in their life cycles are *facultative parasites;* mosquitoes and blackflies, which visit their hosts occasionally for food (blood), are called *temporary parasites.* Some parasites, such as fleas and lice, that live *outside* of the host's body are called *ectoparasites;* others, such as intestinal worms, bacteria, viruses, and certain fungi, that live *inside* the host's body are called *endoparasites.*

An ordinary "normal" bird in relatively good health can, or often does, support a large number of parasites. As a defense against ectoparasites, birds have developed preening, dust bathing, blinking, and, in certain species, "anting" to such a degree that they generally keep them under control. However, according to Rothschild and Clay (1957), at times when feather lice and mites heavily infest a bird's plumage, they may completely destroy its feathers; certain flies can devour the superficial layers of a bird's skin and its waxy feather exudations; mites and tongue worms invade the nasal cavities, bronchial tubes, air sacs, and lungs to feed on their secretions. Fleas, lice, fly larvae, mosquitoes, midges, bugs (Hemiptera), leeches, and ticks suck the bird's blood from the outside. Inside, protozoans such as the malaria-producing plasmodia (there may be millions in a chicken dying of infection with *Plasmodium gallinaceum*) destroy the red blood cells (*see* Avian Malaria); others, such as trypanosomes, are flagellate protozoans in the blood, bone marrow, and lymph vessels of birds; other flagellates swarm in the bird's crop, throat, and mouth, and species of *Trichomonas* may invade virtually every organ of a bird's body. *See* trichomoniasis under Diseases.

Various kinds of worms—tapeworms, flukes, roundworms, spiny-headed worms, and leeches—also may be found in almost every organ of the body (some leeches may fix themselves inside the vent, and some inside the throat pouches of pelicans). Not only is there a large number of species of parasites that can attack birds but some, besides the plasmodia, may inhabit an individual bird in great numbers—more than 10,000 roundworms (*see* Nematode) have been reported from the intestine of a single grouse; more than 1,000 feather lice from the plumage of a single curlew (Rothschild and Clay, 1957).

Rand (1959) points out that a single city pigeon, flying or walking about, is not really alone but can have a whole community of parasites that live in or on it. It is a living house that may be inhabited by at least 71 or more different kinds of plants and animals—2 species of ticks, 8 of mites, 1 fly, 1 bug (Hemiptera), 6 lice, 9 roundworms, 18 tapeworms, 3 flukes, 8 protozoans (Stabler, 1974, listed a dozen or more kinds of protozoans one might find in a pigeon), 2 fungi, 9 bacteria, and 4 viruses. Sometimes relationships between birds may even be determined by their insect parasites. *See* discussion under Classification.

BIRDS AS PARASITES. Birds themselves may have parasitic roles in relation to other species of birds. One of these is called *brood parasitism,* in which females of some species lay their eggs in the nests of other species of birds, which then hatch the eggs and raise the young as though they were their own. The European cuckoo (*see* in Cuckoo Family), the honey guides of Africa (*see* Piciformes), and the N. American cowbirds (*see* in Troupial Family) are well-known examples of this parasitic relationship (*see* Brood Parasitism) and are called obligate parasites because they do not raise their own progeny and are completely dependent on other species of birds to do so. Many species, apart from cuckoos, honey guides and cowbirds, practice brood parasitism to a lesser degree—ducks and some of the N. American cuckoos, for example. These usually raise their own young but sometimes lay their eggs in the nests of other kinds of birds—they are called *nonobligate* parasites. *See* discussion under Obligate Parasite; *also* Dump Nest; Nests and Nesting.

In another close association between birds or between birds and other animals, one kind may gain some benefit from the other. If the benefited one (may gain additional food, for example) causes neither harm nor benefit to the other, the association is called *commensalism* (*see* Commensalism); if in their association *both* kinds of birds (or a bird and another animal) are benefited from the association, it is called *symbiosis* (*see* Symbiosis). If, however, a bird in its close association with another causes direct or indirect harm to it (*see* effects of brood parasitism, for example, on Kirtland's warbler in biography of this species under Warbler—American Wood Warbler Family), then the association is called *parasitism.*

In another parasitic association between birds, a habit called *kleptoparasitism,* skuas, jaegers, frigatebirds, eagles, and gulls regularly rob smaller birds of their prey. *See* examples in Feeding and Food-getting under Behavior. Although birds do parasitize others in these ways, they are far more subject to parasitism by the smaller parasites that live upon them or inside them.

Many biologists see in a parasite a form of predatory animal, which, instead of killing and devouring its prey whole, does so by eating it little by little. According to Elton (1936), while the carnivore destroys its prey and eats it at once, the parasite levies a daily toll from its victim—the carnivore lives upon capital; the parasite on income. Parasitism is usually a chronic condition and not always spectacular by causing direct mass mortality, but it may render the host bird more susceptible to predation, malnutrition, extremes of weather, and other stresses (Trainer, 1974). *See* Predation.

For a discussion of the parasites of birds and of parasitism in general, see in Baer (1952); Rothschild and Clay (1957); Benbrook (1959); Cameron (1961); Southern (1964); Biester and Schwarte (1965); Garnham (1966); Van Nostrand (1968); Beer (1970); Part III, "Parasitic Infections," in Davis *et al.* (1971); Noble and Noble (1971); Levine (1973). For a discussion of the external parasites on N. American birds and methods of collecting them, see Peters (1930); Turner (1971); see also Peters (1936); Fox (1940); Hubbard (1947); Boyd (1951), for other lists of ectoparasites of some N. American birds. *See also* Fleas; Hippoboscid Flies; Lice; Ectoparasite.

PARASITIC BIRD
See Birds as Parasites under Parasite; *also* Brood Parasitism.

PARASITIC INSECTS
(of birds). *See* Fleas; Hippoboscid Flies; Lice; Protocalliphora. *See also* Ectoparasite; Parasite; Diseases.

PARASITISM
See Parasite

PARATHYROID GLAND
See Endocrine Glands.

PARAUQUE
See Pauraque in Nightjar Family.

PARENTAL CARE
See Young and Their Care.

PARIS BROTHERS
Two brothers, dealers in natural history materials and living in Paris, France, in 1837, for whom Charles Lucien Bonaparte, in the *Proceedings* of the Zoological Society of London, Vol. V, 1837, gave the species name *parisorum* to a handsome oriole (Scott's oriole) from a specimen from Mexico, where the Paris brothers had done considerable collecting (Palmer, 1928). In 1854, Lt. (later Gen.) D. N. Couch, U.S. Army, named an oriole from ne. Mexico *Icterus scotti* in honor of Gen. Winfield Scott, who had commanded the American forces in the Mexican War. This proved to be the same species, *parisorum,* previously named by Bonaparte; however, Scott's name is retained in the common, or English, name of the bird. *See* discussion of the law of priority under Names and Naming.

PARROT FAMILY
Psittacidae (sih-TAS-ih-dee); from Lat. *psittacus,* parrot. Only 2 species of wild parrots, both native to the W. Hemisphere, have occurred in the U.S.—the thick-billed parrot, a rare visitor from Mexico, and the now extinct Carolina parakeet, which, before the coming of Europeans, ranged through N. American deciduous forests from s. Va. south through Fla. and westward to edge of the river valley forests of e. Tex., Okla., Kans., and Neb. (Greenway, 1958). The Carolina parakeet is gone and the thick-billed parrot, which formerly came into Ariz. and N.M., is now rare even in its home forests of Mexican Sierra Madre. Other foreign species in Parrot Family—for example, the budgerigar, canary-winged parakeet, and monk parakeet—are cage birds that have been introduced into the wild in the U.S.

There are 315 species of parrots in the world (Van Tyne and Berger, 1976), and their center of dispersion in the New World is the Amazon Basin; in the Old World, the Australian Region (Dorst, 1964); all are typically forest birds and eat nuts, seeds, fruits, and berries; some eat insects and nectar; thick bills and fleshy tongues enable some to crack and eat large, hard-shelled nuts, which they eat holding in one foot. The feet are zygodactyl. *See* Feet and Legs. When not nesting, parrots are social and travel in screaming and squawking flocks;

many sleep in holes in trees; sexes usually outwardly alike; most do not migrate.

Parrots, macaws, cockatoos, and others have been kept as pets since ancient times, by both civilized and primitive people. At one time, members of the Parrot Family were excluded from importation into the U.S. because they are hosts to "parrot fever" (*see* Chlamydiosis) and can transmit the disease to people. With the discovery of specific antibiotics for treatment of the disease, the ban was lifted, which resulted in enormous numbers of members of the Parrot Family being imported into the U.S. (see, for example, in Banks, 1970a).

Of all animals, parrots (along with mynas) are best at imitating human speech but don't understand a word of what they say and learn to "talk" only in captivity (Austin, 1961). They use one foot as a hand in eating, and, individually, are right- or left-handed (Friedmann and Davis, 1938). In climbing they use the bill as a third "hand." Some parrots live to 50–100 years or more.

Parakeets are small, slender parrots with long, graduated tails—for example, the budgerigar, or grass parakeet, of c. Australia, possibly the most popular of all cage birds. The extinct Carolina parakeet was not closely related to the Old World parakeets but to a group of somewhat small, tropical New World parrots called conures. The Carolina parakeet was the only parrot native to the U.S.; it never nested south of this country, according to Chapman (1930), and was the most northern in its range of any parrot in the world. In s. Fla., budgerigars and other parakeets have escaped from captivity, or been released (also in the New York City region and s. Calif.), and are now established in the wild as breeding species. Albinism is apparently rare in the Parrot Family; Gross (1965a) listed only one record and in only one species. Albino parrots lacking melanin appear yellow from the carotenoid pigments. *See also* discussion of parrots under Psittaciformes.

Budgerigar, *Melopsittacus undulatus* (mel-oh-SIT-ah-cus un-dul-AY-tus); genus name: Lat., from Gr. *melos*, song, and Lat. *psittacus*, a parrot, or "song parrot"; species name: Lat., wavy, full of waves, perhaps alluding to the bird's undulating flight or to marks in plumage; according to Lorenz (1937), *budgerigar* is a corruption of *betcherrygah*, native Australian for "good parrot." (Color ill., page 695.) Original home in Australia; now established in wild in s. Fla.; budgerigars were introduced into Great Britain at time of Crystal Palace Exhibition in Hyde Park, London, in 1851, and thereafter became favorite cage birds; 6–7½ in. long, with long, graduated tail; the wild budgerigar is grass green with bright yellow on head and a blue tail. Outer sexual differences are limited to color of cere, legs, and feet; adult males have rich blue cere, bluish legs and feet; adult females have pale brown to dark brown cere, pinkish legs and feet. As adults get older, iris color of eyes changes from dark brown to white (Brockway, 1964). Budgerigar is probably most widely domesticated of the parrots; has been extensively bred for cage-bird market with different plumage colors.

Feeding Habits: In wild, feeds almost entirely on the ground; takes seeds from tall grasses; food is never held in foot; flocks scattered throughout dry grasslands of c. and w. Australia, colonial throughout year, nomadic; appears each summer near water holes and rivers bordered by eucalyptus trees with suitable nest holes (Brereton, 1963).
Eggs: May lay throughout year, usually 4–7, and especially after heavy but characteristically sporadic rain in native land (Brockway, 1964); no nest, eggs laid in natural cavity or in nest box.
Incubation: By female, about 18 days; male feeds female at nest (Brereton, 1963); young hatch naked; both sexes feed young; eyes open about 11th day after hatching; fully feathered when about 21 days old; young first fly about 30–36 days after hatching (Brockway, 1964).
Other Names: Budgie; grass parakeet; shell parakeet.
Hybrids: Has crossbred (and produced hybrids) with lovebirds *(Agapornis)* and with Bourke's grass parakeet (Gray, 1958).
Weights: Six averaged 39 gr. (Hughes, 1970), or about 1½ oz.

Parakeet, canary-winged, *Brotogeris versicolurus* (broh-TODGE-er-is ver-sih-COL-oor-us); genus name: Lat., with human voice; species name: Lat., of various colors, variegated (Prestwich, 1963). S. American parakeet introduced and well established in the Miami area, Fla., where first free-flying birds noted in late 1960s; by 1973, at least 15 nests and at least 2,000 birds seen (see details in Owre, 1973); introduced in ne. U.S.; flocks of up to 50 reported at feeding stations on Long Is., N.Y., and in e. Conn. (Bull, 1973); in s. Calif., where also escaped or released from captivity, by 1973 free-flying birds common locally on Palos Verdes Pen. and some nesting (see Hardy, 1973); about 8–9 in. long; adults, sexes alike, generally dull green, darker on back and scapulars; tail long and pointed; has yellow wing patches that show conspicuously especially in flight; outer wing bluish-green; remaining remiges (flight feathers) whitish to green; coverts yellow and green; bill horn-colored to yellowish; iris dark brown, legs gray-pink; in immature, less white and more greenish in wings (Forshaw, 1973); in flight or when perched, utters rapid, repeated shrill, metallic note; when feeding, utters high-pitched chatter. In S. America, common permanent resident of most types of wooded country to highest part of tropical zone, also in parklands, usually in flocks of 8–10 and up to 50; occasionally in flocks of hundreds; flies swiftly and directly; in flight can be identified from below.

Feeding Habits: Eats seeds, fruits, berries, blossoms; in Calif. seen eating fruit of avocado trees, primrose, and rusty-leaf figs, also buds of orange trees.
Nest: In S. America, in hollow limb or in hole in tree or in arboreal termites' mound; in s. Calif., in dead fronds of palm trees; in w. Brazil, hunts for nesting sites in June; in ne. Peru, nests in July.
Eggs: In captivity, 5, pure white.

PARROT FAMILY

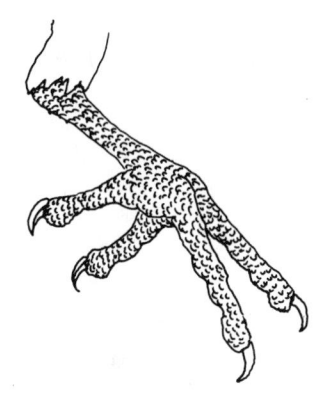

nasofrontal hinge

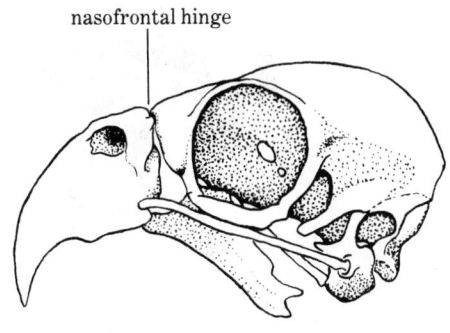

PARROT FAMILY
The upper mandible of the parrot has a well-developed hinge connecting it to the base of the skull which gives it leverage and mobility and enables the parrot to use the bill in climbing and when cracking large, hard-shelled nuts.

Canary-winged parakeet

PARROT FAMILY

Carolina parakeet

Incubation: By female, about 26 days; young leave nest 56 days after hatching (Forshaw, 1973).
Weights: Males, wild-caught in Fla. (17), 62.4–80.8 gr. (Fisk, 1977), or about 2¼–2¾ oz.; females (10), 60.8–74.3 gr.
Range: French Guiana, the Amazon Basin in n. Brazil, se. Columbia, and e. Ecuador south to n. Argentina, Paraguay, se. Brazil; introduced into U.S. (see above), the Lima area, c. Peru, and into Puerto Rico (Forshaw, 1973).

Parakeet, Carolina, *Conuropsis carolinensis* (con-your-OP-sis cah-row-lin-EN-sis); genus name: from Gr. *konos*, cone, *oura*, tail, and *opsis* or *opseos*, appearance, "having the appearance of"; a name coined in 1891 by Count Adelardo Salvidori, Italian ornithologist, while working in the British Museum of Natural History, to indicate the similarity of the Carolina parakeet to the members of the parrot genus *Conurus* (now *Aratinga*)—for example, the tropical American orange-fronted parakeet, seen in wild around Miami, Fla.; species name: Lat., of Carolina. Native N. American parrot; *extinct;* average size was about 12½ in. long, with long, pointed tail; sexes outwardly alike; a green parrot with a yellow head and cheeks rich orange to around bill, some yellow and dark blue on wings; bill large, pale yellow, cere feathered; immatures, duller; lived in deciduous forests and edges in e. U.S. west to wooded river bottoms of plains; was highly gregarious, traveled in flocks when not nesting; roosted together, hanging by bill and claws, tail downward, while sleeping inside hollow trees; as many as 30 sleeping in hollow of large sycamore; flight was rapid and undulating, with much yelling and screeching; when resting or feeding, uttered querulous chattering, conversational notes (Chapman, 1930); was in demand as cage bird, trapped by professional bird-catchers, and shot in great numbers by hunters because brilliant plumage in demand for millinery trade; shot in greatest numbers by landowners because of parakeets' habit of flocking to apple orchards and tearing fruit apart to get at seeds, and because of habit of eating corn and other grain crops. See details in Greenway (1958).

Feeding Habits: Seeds, especially of cockleburs, thistles, cypress, maple, elm, sycamore, pine, and wild and cultivated fruit.
Nest: In bottom of natural cavity of tree.
Eggs: Fla., Apr.; 2, white.
Incubation: About 19–20 days (Reilly, 1968); was bred successfully in captivity in Cincinnati Zoological Gardens, where last captive died in Sept. 1914 (Greenway, 1958). In wild, Frank M. Chapman saw a group of 13 in Fla. in Apr. 1904. Although some later reports of Carolina parakeets, the Florida flocks may have been the last survivors.
Other Names: Carolina paroquet; kelinkey; parrot; wild parrot.
Age: One lived in National Zoo, Washington, D.C., to age 15 years, 7 months.
Range: Formerly lived from s. Va. along Atlantic seaboard south through Fla., west to edge of river valley forests of e. Tex., Okla., Kans., and Neb. to about 40° N. Lat.; sometimes wandered north to Md., e. Pa., N.Y., Great Lakes, and to Wisc. and Colo. (Greenway, 1958).

Parakeet, grass. *See* Budgerigar.

Parakeet, gray-breasted. *See* Parakeet, monk.

Parakeet, gray-headed. *See* Parakeet, monk.

Parakeet, monk, *Myiopsitta monachus* (my-oh-SIT-ah MON-ah-cuss); genus name: Lat., from Gr. *myia*, a fly, and Lat. *psitta*, from Gr. *psittakos*, a parrot; species name: Lat., from Gr. *monachos*, a monk; name apparently in reference to gray feathers covering head and neck, suggesting a monk's hood. (Color ill., page 697.) S. American parrot escaped from captivity or deliberately released in U.S.; by 1972–73, apparently established in wild in ne. U.S. and in s. Fla., breeding in Miami area since 1969 or earlier (Owre, 1973) and in New York City area (Bull, 1971, 1973), though not reported more recently; about 11½ in. long, of which blue-green tail is 5½ in. long; about size of a mourning dove or slightly smaller; more slender, and, like dove, has long, pointed tail; sexes outwardly alike; usually a bright green or green-gray on back; tail green and blue; upper belly lemon yellow to olive-yellow, rest of underparts bright green; wings mostly blue, soft Quaker gray over head and breast; bill rosy flesh color; feet dark; has been brought into U.S. by thousands as cage birds (12,000 in 1968—see Banks, 1970a); tractable and intelligent; in captivity has become a favorite cage bird, easy to care for, can be taught to mimic human speech but voice said to have unpleasant sound (Trimm, 1972); reported to be one of worst pests about agricultural crops in its native Argentina, where reported most damaging of all parrots—eats crop-grown sunflower seeds, corn, sorghum, millet, also fruits including citrus; has predilection for sunflower seeds and corn; control methods used against monk parakeet in S. America not successful, escaped birds in England also destructive to gardens and orchards (see details in Bump, 1971); first reported in New York City area (w. Long Is., n. N.J., and New York City parks) from about 1967 into 1970 with increasing frequency; imported shipments noted frequently at Kennedy International Airport, N.Y., rumored that a crate of these parrots was dropped there one day in unloading and that the birds escaped (not known how many) and were soon reported widely in metropolitan area; in Northeast during its period of early expansion, reported as single birds or a pair, also in groups of 6–8, and one flock of 25 at New Brunswick, N.J.; does not migrate (Bump, 1971); travels in groups or loose flocks; flies swiftly, usually within 30 ft. of ground, wingbeats are rapid; in winter in U.S. comes to bird feeders, where up to eight seen at single feeder (Bull, 1974); see also Bull and Ricciuti (1974); prefers sunflower seeds, also eats mixed bird seeds, cracked corn, pine seeds, which it extracts with bill from cones; suet, acorns, seeds of grasses, apples, cherries, grapes, raisins, currants; is aggressive and drives other birds from feeders. See Freeland (1973).

Feeding Habits: In S. America eats seeds of thistles, wild berries, large amounts of legumes, and large insects, besides ripening maize and fruit; travels considerable distances, often in large flocks, to food sources.

Nest: In native S. America, is large, bulky, built of dry twigs in topmost branches of trees, preferably thorny ones; nest in a single chamber occupied by only one pair not uncommon, but the enormous communal nests occupied by many pairs, each with its own chamber, are conspicuous (Forshaw, 1973); uses nests both for roosting and for raising of the young; up to a dozen pairs, and up to 20 compartments reported; is unique among members of Parrot Family in building nests in branches of trees, to which it adds sticks year after year until a huge colonial structure (Friedmann, 1927); most others in family nest inside hole in tree; also may be one of few parrots that nest communally; young ones in nests in se. Bolivia at beginning of Dec., eggs taken from nest in Matto Grosso, Brazil, at end of Nov.; may rear two broods a season in S. America (Forshaw, 1973). Escaped birds in U.S. build round or domed stick nests in summer, fall, or winter about 3 ft. in diameter, some against tree trunk or at ends of branches; one at Valley Stream, N.Y., about 35–40 ft. up in spruce tree; one built atop a transformer box on a utility pole; another, in Central Park, inside the broken glass globe of spotlight that illuminates obelisk called Cleopatra's Needle; others on Long Is. built on rain gutters of houses—all nests had entrance or exit holes in side of nest near bottom or top; each was occupied by two pairs of monk parakeets (Bull, 1971).

Eggs: 5–9, white; in S. America laid in Nov.; in U.S. not enough records as of 1971–72 to be precise, but in summer (Bull, 1971). See Freeland (1973).

Incubation: 31 days (Caccamise and Alexandro, 1976).

Other Names: Gray-breasted parrot; gray-headed parakeet; green monk parakeet; monk; Quaker parakeet.

Weights: One from University of Miami collections, sex undetermined, 140 gr. (Fisk, 1977), or about 5 oz.

Range: Resident in s. S. America, from Bolivia, Paraguay, s. Brazil, Uruguay, and Argentina south to province of Río Negro (de Schauensee, 1970); in U.S. reported from Long Is., N.Y., and New Brunswick, N.J., seven building colonial nests on Long Is., Oct. 31, 1970; flock of 25 seen at New Brunswick, N.J., where may have nested summer 1970 (Boyajiian, 1971a); adult seen feeding a young one in Conn., spring 1971 (Boyajiian 1971b); several reported to have survived in mild winter 1970–71 in Pleasantville, N.J., and built several large nests for roosting (Scott and Cutler, 1971); winter 1971–72 gradually expanding range and seen on Christmas Bird Count that winter at Cape May, N.J.; in e. Mass., single birds seen south of Boston, July–Oct. 1972, a pair building nest at Braintree, Mass., Nov. 1972 (Finch, 1973), a pair built nest in Norway spruce at Schenectady, N.Y., June 1972 (Boyajiian, 1973); first appearance near Elmira, N.Y., mid-July, 1972; one built nest under eaves of building at Waterloo, N.Y., fall 1972; reached Pittsburgh, Pa., summer 1972, where

raised three young; also appeared just north of Columbus, Ohio, where two seen for first time in midwestern prairie region (Kleen and Bush, 1973); monk parakeets reached southern plains, Sept. 1972, when pair seen building nest in large tree at Norman, Okla., also at Tulsa (Williams, 1973); a pair sighted about 20 mi. north of Tamiami Trail in s. Fla. in May 1972 (Kale, 1972); pair nested to Key Biscayne (Ogden, 1972); appeared at Asheville, N.C., late summer 1972; one at bird feeder, Meadville, Pa. (Hall, 1973). In the Seventy-ninth Audubon Christmas Bird Count of 1978 (see *American Birds*, July 1979 issue) the highest count for the monk parakeet was 7 in Ft. Lauderdale, Fla.; a total of 6 were seen in Brooklyn, N.Y., but no more were reported in N.Y. state. For other accounts of parrots and other exotics introduced into Fla., see Robertson (1971); Stevenson (1971); Owre (1973).

Parakeet, orange-fronted, *Aratinga canicularis.* (ah-rah-TING-gah cah-NICK-you-lar-iss); genus name: Lat., colored like an Ara (macaw); species name: Lat., pertaining to the Dog Star (Sirius), the brightest star in the night sky, hence the center of attraction (Prestwich, 1963). (Color ill., page 696.) Called half-moon in pet trade; lives from Sinaloa, w. Mexico, south to nw. Costa Rica; by 1972, caged birds, either released or escaped pets, were scattered in wild about Miami, Fla., also seen 50 mi. north at Delray Beach, feeding on conelike fruits of casuarina (Ogden, 1972); one seen south of Las Cruces, N. M., July 24, 1971; 9–10 in. long; green above with blue on crown, yellow bare patch around eyes and *bright orange-colored patch on forehead;* much blue on wings and on long, pointed tail; throat and breast pale olive brown; other underparts pale green; utters raucous screech, *can-can-can* or *ca-ca-ca* (Peterson and Chalif, 1973); abundant in native habitat which is edges of woods and in scrubby open places; roosts in trees bordering rivers and streams in Guatemala (Land, 1970); during day feeds in large noisy flocks.

Feeding Habits: Eats especially wild figs, also seeds, nuts, berries, blossoms and possibly insects.

Nest: In holes; in native habitat usually in a termite's nest (termitarium) and usually an occupied one.

Eggs: Throughout range lays eggs in most months of the year; 1–5, usually 3–5.

Incubation: By female, usually 30 days to hatch first egg (lays an egg every other day); young fly about 42 days after hatching.

Other Name: Orange-fronted conure.

Weights: In Fla., one captive, 58.3 gr., one male in wild, 68 gr., or about 2 oz. and 2⅓ oz.; from Nicaragua, two males, 82 and 95.6 gr., or 2⅞ oz.–3⅓ oz.; two females, 80 and 82 gr., or about 2⅞ oz. (Fisk, 1977).

Parakeet, Quaker. *See* Parakeet, monk.

Parakeet, ring-necked. *See* Parakeet, rose-ringed.

Parakeet, rose-ringed, *Psittacula krameri.* (sit-TACK-you-lah KRAM-er-eye [or

KRAY-mer-eye]); genus name: Lat., from *psittacus,* parrot, with diminutive suffix, hence, a smaller parrot; species name: for G. H. Kramer, a naturalist whose principal work was *Elenchus Vegetabilium et Animalium per Austriam inferiorum observatorum,* etc. (Prestwich, 1963). (Color ill., page 697.) Called ring-necked parakeet in pet trade; an Asiatic and African species; caged birds have escaped from captivity or been released in s. U.S.; pair at Hampton, Va., apparently nested in Mar. 1972 (Scott and Cutler, 1972); also formerly nesting in Los Angeles, Calif. (see Hardy, 1964); in Fla., first reported in wild in 1968, seen repeatedly in July 1972 in n. Miami in flock of 25–30 (Ogden, 1972); nesting in suburban Dade County, adults often in company of immatures visit bird feeding stations (Owre, 1973); 15–16¾ in. long; adult male mostly yellow-green, a narrow black line from top of bill (cere) to each eye; iris pale yellow, upper mandible dark red, black toward tip; lower mandible black, with dark red markings near base; *black chin and stripes on lower cheek;* narrow rose-pink collar encircles back of neck; nape somewhat suffused with blue; central feathers of long, pointed tail bluish tipped with yellow-green; adult female resembles male but lacks black on chin or cheeks, lacks rose-pink collar, nape not suffused with blue, shorter central tail feathers than in male; immatures resemble female with short central tail feathers, bill coral pink with pale tip; iris gray-white (Forshaw, 1973); call is a loud screeching *kee-ak . . . kee-ak,* uttered while in flight or at rest.

Feeding Habits: Eats seeds, berries, fruits, blossoms, and nectar; is a serious pest in orchards, coffee plantations, and croplands in native lands.

Nest: In Africa, always high up in hollow of limb or in hole in tree; in India, may be in cavity under a roof of house or hole in wall.

Eggs: 2–6, usually 3–4, laid in layer of debris or decayed wood dust in bottom of cavity.

Incubation: 22–24 days; young leave nest 42–49 days after hatching (Forshaw, 1973).

Other Name: Ring-necked parakeet.

Weights: One adult male, University of Miami collections, 120 gr., or about 4½ oz.; one immature male, about 4⅔ oz.; an adult female, 139.2 gr., or 4⅞ oz. (Fisk, 1977).

Parakeet, shell. *See* Budgerigar.

Parrot, Cuban. Local name and misnomer for the smooth-billed ani in Cuckoo Family.

Parrot, gray-breasted. *See* Parakeet, monk.

Parrot, thick-billed, *Rhynchopsitta pachyrhyncha* (ring-koh-SIT-ah pack-ih-RING-kah); genus name: Lat., from Gr. *rhynchos,* beak, and *psitta,* shortened form of *psittakos,* parrot; species name: from Gr. *pachys,* thick, and *rhynchos,* beak. (Color ill., page 696.) Mexican species at one time seen in Ariz. and N.M.; 15–16½ in. long, chunky, dull olive-green parrot with long, pointed tail; heavy black bill and red forehead; red at bend of wings and on lower thighs; small patch of yellow or gray on un-

swallow

warbler

sparrow

creeper

crow

PASSERIFORMES

derwing coverts is conspicuous (Blake, E. R., 1953). Flight rapid, wingbeats shallow; flock glides much from one feeding place in pine forest to another; calls of flock earsplitting; can be heard for a half mile; flocks have habit of following anyone traveling through their home forests and keeping up such uproar that it drives off or alerts wild animals naturalist may be seeking.

Feeding Habits: Opens pine cones with strong bill and eats seeds. Said not to be sought as pet because it bites savagely, also is difficult to rear in captivity (Vincent, 1966).

Nest: No records for U.S., but in tree cavity, often in nesting burrow 6–7 in. in diameter dug in tall dead pine by nearly extinct imperial woodpecker, *Campephilus imperialis,* which is limited to highest and remotest parts of the Sierra Madre, Mexico.

Eggs: 1–2, white.

Incubation: Period of and age when young first fly not known.

Range: Now rare, lives in pine forests of Sierra Madre of Mexico; formerly ranged in flocks, mainly in winter, across Rio Grande into mountains of Ariz. and N.M., where flock might stay for weeks; last reliably reported in U.S. in Ariz. in 1922 and 1936; last major flight, 1917–18 (Phillips *et al.,* 1964); maintenance of some of its original forest in Mexico necessary for its continued existence. *See* Rare and Threatened Species.

PARROT FEVER
See Psittacosis.

PARROT-TOED
See Pigeon-Toed.

PARTHENOGENESIS
(par-theh-no-JEN-eh-sis). *See* Fertilization.

PARTRIDGE
See in Pheasant Family; *see also* Grouse, ruffed, in Grouse Family.

PARULA (PARR-you-la) **BLUE**
A color, blue in hue, of low saturation and medium brilliance. The northern *parula warbler* is a small grayish-blue bird of the Warbler—American Wood Warbler Family.

PARULID
(PARR-you-lid). A popular collective name for any bird of the Warbler—American Wood Warbler Family.

PARULIDAE
See Warbler—American Wood Warbler Family.

PASSENGER PIGEON
See in Pigeon Family; *also* Extinct Birds of North America.

PASSENGER PIGEON, THE
A publication. *See* Ornithological Periodicals.

PASSERES
(PASS-er-eez); New Lat. plural noun of Lat. *passer,* a sparrow, a *suborder* within the large order Passeriformes; includes about 4,000 species throughout the world. All the passerines found in N. America, except the tyrant flycatchers and cotingas, belong to the suborder Passeres. The Passeres are also known as the Oscines. *See* Oscines. All other suborders in the order Passeriformes are called, collectively, the Suboscines. *See* Classification. Van Tyne and Berger (1959) say that Passeres is the older name for the order Passeriformes. *See* Passeriformes.

PASSERIFORMES
(pass-er-ih-FOR-meez); from Lat., *passer,* a sparrow, and *forma,* form; sparrow-shaped (Coble, 1954). The passerines, or "perching" birds, make up the largest order (*see* Order) of birds in the world—59 families and about 5,100 species of the world's 8,650 species, or about three fifths of all living birds (Storer, 1971b). Numerically, they are the dominant land birds on all continents; they range in size from the largest passeriform—the 22–26-in.-long raven, with a wingspread of more than 4 ft.—to the small, 4–6-in.-long kinglets, warblers, and sparrows.

In N. America, the order Passeriformes includes 29 families (*see* list under Classification) —from the tropical cotingas through the tyrant flycatchers, larks, swallows, crows, titmice, nuthatches, creepers, wrens, thrushes, and thrashers to the pipits, waxwings, shrikes, starlings, vireos, finches, buntings, and many others.

The Passeriformes are believed to be the highest, or evolutionarily most advanced, birds of all—the most adaptive and intelligent—for example, members of the Crow Family. Many of the oscines of the passerine birds are noted for their singing (*see* Voice and Sound-making; Songs and Singing), especially the wrens, thrashers, and thrushes. They all have in common a foot with three toes directed forward and one backward, with all on same level and easily movable, and adapted to gripping a perch—a slender branch, and, in small birds, even a twig, reed, or grass stem. Also, the muscles and tendons of the legs are so arranged that if the bird has a tendency to fall backward, they tighten its grip on the perch (Thomson, 1964l). *See* discussion of this under Feet and Legs. In the Passeriformes, the toes are never webbed, even in the few passerines that have become semiaquatic in their habits (*see,* for example, under Dipper Family; *also* Swimming and Diving).

The primary wing feathers, or flight feathers (*see* Flight; Topography), are either 9 or 10 in number, and the tail usually has 12 feathers; also, the spermatozoa have a form characteristic of this group (Thomson, 1964l). *See* Fertilization.

For a discussion of how birds are grouped according to their relationships, *see* Classification; Morphology; Phylogenetic Relationship; *also* Check-list; Check-list Order.

PASSERINES
(PASS-er-ins or PASS-er-ines). Birds belonging to the order Passeriformes. *See* Passeriformes.

PASTEURELLOSIS
(pas-ter-e-LOW-sis). *See* Avian Cholera; Diseases.

PASTURE-BIRD
See Killdeer and Plover, American golden, in Plover Family; *also* Sandpiper, upland, in Sandpiper Family.

PATE
A local name for the ivory-billed woodpecker, from one of its call notes.

PATRONYMIC (pat-row-NIM-ik) NAMES
Term of scientists for the scientific names of birds and other animals named for people (Mayr *et al.*, 1953). *See* Names and Naming.

PAURAQUE
See in Nightjar Family.

PEA-BIRD
See Oriole, Baltimore (northern), in Troupial Family.

PEABODY-BIRD
See Sparrow, white-throated, in Finch Family.

PEACOCK
See Domestication.

PEAFOWL
See Domestication; *also* Pheasant Family.

PECK ORDER
See Social Order among Birds under Behavior; *also* Dominance.

PECTEN
See Eyes and Eyesight.

PECTINATE
Term for the toothlike projections on the claw of the middle toes of whip-poor-wills, nighthawks, and certain other birds. *See* Feather Comb.

PECTORAL GIRDLE
See Skeleton.

PEDIUNKER
See Shearwater, black-tailed, in Shearwater Family.

PEEP
Local name for some of the small look-alike shorebirds, a group that includes the smallest N. American sandpipers: the sparrow-sized least, Baird's, semipalmated, western, and white-rumped sandpipers (Peterson, 1947); occasionally applied also to the smaller plovers; name apparently derived from some of their calls and from their small sizes, likened to small downy chicks of domestic hen, also called peeps (McAtee, 1955a; 1956a). *See also* Bull-peep.

PEET-WEET
A common name for the solitary and spotted sandpipers, from call note.

PEGGY-WHITETHROAT
See Warbler, willow, in Warbler—Old World Warbler Family.

PELAGIC
(pe-LAJ-ik). Term for birds that are of the ocean—for example, petrels, shearwaters, fulmars, and other birds that frequent the high seas and are rarely seen from land.

PELECANIDAE
See Pelican Family.

PELECANIFORMES
(pel-eh-can-ih-FOR-meez); from Lat. *pelecanus*, a pelican, and *forma*, form; pelican-shaped (Coble, 1954). An order (*see* Order) of 55 species of wide-ranging, temperate- and tropical-zone water birds that includes within 6 families the tropic-birds, pelicans, boobies, gannets, cormorants (also called shags), anhingas (also called darters), and frigatebirds (also called man-o'-war-birds). Members of the Pelecaniformes are the only birds that share in common a *totipalmate* foot—that is, all four toes on each foot, including the hind one, or hallux, are united by a web of skin (Wallace, 1961d). *See* discussion under Feet and Legs.

The Pelecaniformes are an ancient group, dating from remains of a cormorantlike bird discovered in deposits of the Cretaceous Period at least 100 million years old. *See* Archaeopteryx for discussion of most ancient bird; *see also* Geological Time Scale. The 6 families of the Pelecaniformes are all represented in N. America. *See* list of the families under Classification.

All of these birds have short legs and big wings, all are fliers, and most of them swim well but walk poorly. *See* Swimming and Diving. All have long bills, longer than or about as long as the head, and all, except the tropic-birds, have small nostrils, which sometimes lack an external opening. *See* discussion of this under Nostrils. Members of the Pelecaniformes usually have a gular pouch, often unfeathered (of bare skin), which reaches its greatest development in the pelicans. *See* Gular Pouch; Heat and Birds. For a discussion of how birds are grouped according to their relationships, *see* Classification; Morphology; Phylogenetic Relationship. *See also* Check-list Order.

PELICAN FAMILY
Pelecanidae (pel-ih-KAY-nih-dee); from Lat. *pelecanus*, from Gr. *pelekon* or *pelekan*, a pelican. 6 species in the world (Van Tyne and Berger, 1976); 4 in Old World, 2 species native to N. America—the brown pelican of our southeastern and western seacoasts and the white pelican mainly of inland lakes. All pelicans have an enormous pouched bill, crested head, and grossly proportioned, short-legged, large body; more like a caricature of a bird than a real one; celebrated in Dixon Lanier Merritt's famous limerick that begins: "A wonderful bird is a pelican, His bill will hold more than his belican" (Austin, 1961).

Pelicans are among the largest living birds—water birds 4–6 ft. long, with wingspreads 6½–9 ft.; weigh 10–17 lbs.; are the largest of the Pelecaniformes, an order of birds that includes their relatives the tropic-birds, cormorants, anhingas, frigatebird, gannets, and boobies.

tropicbird

frigatebird

anhinga

gannet

cormorant

pelican

PELECANIFORMES

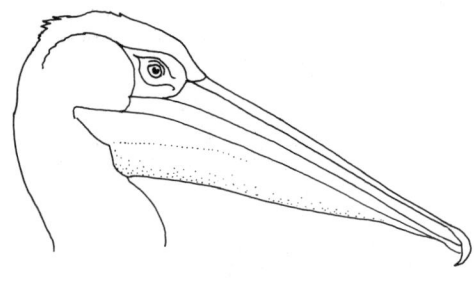

PELICAN FAMILY

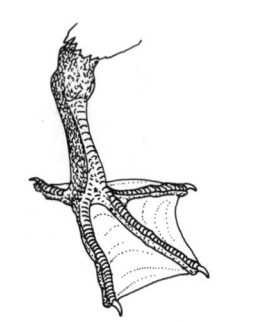

The enormous naked skin pouch suspended from the lower half of the pelican's long, straight bill, hooked at the tip, *does* hold more than its stomach; according to Austin (1961), in the white pelican, by two or three times, or about 3 gallons of water that the pelican might scoop up with the fish it has caught. Momentarily it holds the fish in its distensible pouch long enough to squeeze out the water from the corners of its mouth before swallowing its catch. Fish are never carried in the pouch, but in the gullet, or esophagus. The pouch, besides acting as a dip net, serves pelicans in hot weather; when roosting in the sun, they will open the bill and pulsate the pouch for cooling. See Bartholomew *et al.* (1968).

Pelicans are highly social and gregarious—they live in flocks, with young and adults of both sexes together through much of the year. They are not graceful on land, but waddle about with a stately, dignified air; on water, they float high with great buoyancy (their system of internal air sacs is remarkably developed, not only in their bones but also just under the skin). They are strong swimmers, driving themselves with strokes of their fully webbed feet—young ones just able to fly can swim at 3 m.p.h. (Palmer, 1962).

To become airborne, without wind to help the takeoff, they must run over the water, beating their big wings and pounding the surface with both feet in unison (Palmer, 1962). Once in the air they are splendid fliers, rivaling eagles in their graceful flight as they soar about on their great expanse of wings, sometimes rising to tremendous heights in the deep blue sky. See Bent (1922); Terres (1975).

In level flight, pelicans fly in groups, with their heads held back on their shoulders, the bill resting on the folded neck; they fly with great solemnity and dignity, with slow, powerful beats of their wings, about one or two each second (Palmer, 1962). Like cormorants or geese, they may fly in a V, but usually in regular lines or in single file.

Pelicans eat almost entirely fishes (white pelicans occasionally a few salamanders and crayfishes). The two N. American pelicans differ in their methods of fishing. The brown pelican is a plunge diver and fishes almost exclusively over salt water. Seldom uttering a sound and barely skimming the waves when bucking a head wind, on sighting a fish from the air they dive steeply, sometimes from 60–70 ft. high. Sometimes they submerge completely with a great splash, or only partly, depending on height of the dive. Air sacs under the skin cushion the impact and bring them up again like corks, always facing into the wind, ready for takeoff. See brown pelican's method of diving and then catching fish underwater in Schreiber et al. (1975)

The white pelican, living in summer on inland lakes of the West with a few on the coast of Tex., does not dive for its food, and it also practices cooperative fishing. Individually, a bird sighting a fish from the air lands with a splash, its feet extended forward, then plunges its head under and scoops up the fish. In group fishing, four or five white pelicans swim abreast, gliding quietly in a semicircle facing shore. With a great commotion of flapping wings and splashing, they drive fishes ahead into shallow water, where they easily catch them. There is a record of a group of white pelicans that fed and kept alive a blind one in the colony. *See* Helpers among Birds.

Adult pelicans are usually silent, sometimes utter piglike grunts; young have low, whining grunt or piercing scream (Palmer, 1962); young brown pelicans utter a snakelike hiss (Lowery, 1960).

Birds as large as pelicans require much food; the daily amount for an adult is about 4 lbs. See Schreiber (1976). Fortunately, pelicans eat "rough" fishes not usually considered commercially valuable—in fresh waters, carp, chubs, shiners, catfishes, etc.; in salt waters, menhaden, silversides, mullet, etc. Pelicans have been proved not to be competitive with commercial or sport fisherman. See references to food-habits studies of pelicans in Palmer (1962).

Brown pelican, *Pelecanus occidentalis* (pel-ee-KAY-nus ock-sih-den-TAY-liss); genus name: Lat., pelican; species name: Lat., western. (Color ills., pages 698, 699.) Smallest member of Pelican Family; state bird of La.; strictly coastal, lives locally on salt water of Pacific, Atlantic, and Gulf coasts, rarely seen inland, sometimes carried north along Atlantic coast to Nova Scotia, also inland, by hurricanes; 42–54 in. long; wingspread 6½–7½ ft. (Palmer, 1962); dark, bulky, distinguished from larger white pelican by the invariable brown upperparts and habit of diving for fish from air; adult: sexes outwardly similar, males average slightly larger; head white, pale yellow wash on crown; bill grayish; back, rump, and tail streaked with gray and dark brown; breast and belly blackish brown; eyes pale yellow; legs and *feet* black; immatures: brown-gray neck; gray-brown back; white underparts. By 1962, once flourishing population of 50,000 breeding brown pelicans in La. had vanished, and sharp decline in Tex. coast colonies to a few pairs (see Laycock, 1969, and Lowery, 1974, for details), attributable to hard pesticides, DDT and dieldrin, both widely found in the marine food chain. Reports from Calif., where brown pelican seemed doomed to extinction, were documented spring 1969 by Dr. Robert W. Risebrough on visits to Anacapa Is., where 2,000 birds in breeding colonies of previous years reduced to about 600 adult birds; no longer successfuly nesting because of eggshell thinning (result of DDT) and resulting breakage in nests of eggs and no young raised; only 5 young raised in Calif. in 1969; see, however, Anderson *et al.* (1975). See also Jehl (1973b) for effects of insecticides on brown pelican decline in nw. Baja Calif. Brown pelican preys only on marine fishes, which in coastal waters of s. Calif. more contaminated with chlorinated hydrocarbons than are most freshwater fishes in the state. See excellent review by Anderson and Anderson (1976). In May 1968, L. E. Williams, Jr., of Fla. Game and Freshwater Commission, made first annual count of brown pelicans along Atlantic coast and around Fla. Keys and west coast of Fla.; estimated about 20,000 brown pelicans left in Fla. (as of 1978, this population stable); however, even in S.C. and Fla., where brown pelican colonies appeared healthy, thickness of their eggshells had been reduced 7–18% compared with eggs laid before 1947; thinness of shells results of ingested chlorinated hydrocarbon pesticides in fish food (Laycock, 1969). On Threatened Species List (Office of Endangered Species, 1973). See proposed study of decline by Anonymous (1975a); see also Anonymous (1978).

Feeding Habits: Dives from air for menhaden (90–95% of food of many colonies from S.C. to Tex.), also pigfish, pinfish, herring, sheepshead, silversides, mullet, grass and top minnows, also some crustaceans, usually prawns (Palmer, 1962).

Nest: In colonies in trees, bushes, or on ground; if nest in trees, is reeds, grasses, straw heaped on mound of sticks interwoven into supporting branches; if on ground may be a shallow scrape lined with a few feathers and rim of soil and debris built up 4–10 in. above ground or large mound of soil and debris with cavity in top.

Eggs: Laying time variable; 2–3, usually 3, chalky white, soon soiled with guano. In most of U.S., peak of laying in Mar.–Apr. (Palmer, 1962); at Pelican Island National Wildlife Refuge, Indian R., Fla., eggs and chicks of various ages may be found in nests through about 11 months of year (Laycock, 1969).

Incubation: About 28–30 days, but not certainly known (Palmer, 1962); young walk out of nests on ground about 35 days after hatching but do not leave nests in top of mangroves (Fla.) until about 63 days after hatching and able to fly; young fly 71–88 days after hatching but average is 74–76 days (Schreiber, 1976).

Other Names: American brown pelican; common pelican.

Age: Record of one, banded as fledgling on Merritt Is., Fla., found dead along Indian R. with fish's fin stuck in throat when 6 years, 3 months, old (Cooke, 1937b); one, banded Brevard, Fla., lived to 31 years, 5 months (Kennard, 1975); a captive lived in National Zoo, Washington, D.C., to 29 years, 5 months.

Flight Speed: Timed in Fla., 26 m.p.h. (Longstreet, 1930); in Calif., 14–22 m.p.h. (Smith, 1924); reported to 35 m.p.h. (Palmer, 1962).

Hybrids: Brown pelican × white pelican was in National Zoo, Washington, D.C., in 1937 (Gray, 1958).

Weights: To at least 8 lbs. (Palmer, 1962).

Range: Nests along Atlantic coast from N.C. south to Fla., and on Gulf coasts of Ala., La., and Tex., south to Cuba, Bahamas, West Indies, Trinidad, and ranges casually along northern coast of S. America to mouth of Amazon (Watson, 1966); also nests along Pacific coast on islands and coastal lagoons from c. Calif. to s.-c. Chile, and on Galápagos Is., wanders north after nesting season to Vancouver Is., B.C.; northernmost Calif. breeding station a small colony at Bird Is., Point Lobos Reserve, Monterey County; accidental in Colo., Wyo., the Dakotas, Neb., Iowa, Wisc., Ill., Ind., Tenn., Conn., R.I., Mass., N.Y. (Long Is.), N.J., N.H., and Nova Scotia.

White pelican, *Pelecanus erythrorhynchos* (pel-eh-KAY-nus er-ith-roh-RING-koss); genus name: *see* Brown pelican; species name: from Gr. *erythros,* red, and *rhynchos,* beak. (Color ills., pages 700, 701.) 50–70 in. long; wingspread 8–9½ ft.; adult: very large white bird with black wing tips and enormous orange or salmon-colored bill; bare skin about bill is blue-gray; eyes orange-yellow; legs and feet orange-red; sexes appear alike; immatures: essentially dusky with streaked dark crown; in later development of feathering, mostly white with black wing tips; flies with head drawn back, bill resting on breast (color pattern like gannet, snow goose, whooping crane, and wood stork, but these fly with neck *extended*). From late winter until after eggs are laid, vertical horny plates adorn top of bills of white pelicans.

Feeding Habits: Eats almost entirely fishes of little commercial value: carp, chubs, shiners, perch, catfish, suckers, bass, sticklebacks, and jackfish; also some salamanders and crayfishes. See Palmer (1962); often gathers in groups for cooperative fishing. See especially account of Cottam *et al.* (1942a).

Nest: On islands in brackish and freshwater lakes; more rarely on floating islands of marsh plants; in colonies from a few to several hundred pairs; nest may be from no materials at all on level ground to slight depression or considerable mounds of dirt and debris, with rim, usually 24–36 in. across, 15–20 in. high.

Eggs: Early Apr. through early June; 1–6, usually 2, but 1 not uncommon; dull white.

Incubation: By both sexes, in turn; period unknown according to Palmer (1962); 36 days (Reilly, 1968); in feeding, young put bills into throats of parents to eat partly predigested fish; leave nest about 21–28 days after hatching and gather in groups called pods; on hot days, young flutter gular pouches for body-cooling or temperature control (see Bartholomew *et al.,* 1953); age at first flight about 60 days.

Age: One, banded Yellowstone National Park, shot in Mont. 8 years later; one, banded in wild, Arrowwood National Wildlife Refuge, N.D., shot in Minn. when 16 years, 1 month, old (Kennard, 1975); a captive in National Zoo, Washington, D.C., lived to 34 years, 4 months.

Other Names: Rough-billed pelican; American white pelican.

Hybrids: See in biography of brown pelican.

Weights: Usually 10–17 lbs. but reportedly to 30 lbs. (Palmer, 1962).

Range: Nests on isolated islands in lakes of inland N. America, formerly from B.C. and Prairies Provinces of Canada to s. Calif., w.-c. Nev., n. Utah, c. Colo., n. Minn., and n. Iowa, south to Tex., Ariz., Ark., Kans., Neb., and coasts of Fla. and La., now with main breeding area in Prairie Provinces and in scattered colonies in e. Wash., s. and n. Calif., w. Nev., s. Idaho, n. Utah, Mont., Wyo., the Dakotas, w. Minn., and coastal Tex. (Reilly, 1968); largest nesting colony in N. America is at Chase Lake National Wildlife Refuge, N.D., where in 1973 about 8,000 pairs bred (Strait and Sloan, 1975); migrates almost entirely inland; *winters* in c. Calif. and along Pacific coast to Guatemala, along shores of Gulf of Mexico (common along coastal La.—Lowery, 1960), and Ala. (Imhof, 1962) and throughout most of Fla., has been reported from ne. Ont., s. Que., N.B., Nova Scotia, and all states east of Mississippi R. except N.H., Vt., and Del. (A.O.U. *Check-list,* 1957); population below that of pre-settlement times; individual colonies fluctuate owing to human persecution, especially by fishermen, who believe that pelicans eat game fishes despite evidence to contrary; shooting is largest single known cause of mortality; white pelican has been protected since Migratory Bird Treaty (1972); some shot every year when mistaken for snow geese (Strait and Sloan, 1975); also imperiled by insecticides but at present (1969) not as much as brown pelican; however, recently discovered that eggshells of white pelican are much thinner and said to be significant (Laycock, 1969); see also Bocker (1972). In 1979, on National Audubon Society's Blue List (see Arbib, 1979); a major decline at least in Calif. owing to drainage of lakes where white pelicans formerly nested; estimated (1979) that about 15 colonies of white pelicans left in world, with total of 34,000 birds. See Remsen (1979).

PELLET

A bolus (mass) of undigested parts of a bird's food, usually consisting of fur, feathers, bones, bills, claws, and teeth of small mammals and birds eaten by birds of prey. It may also consist of the hard exoskeleton of insects and crustaceans and of indigestible parts of plants. A hawk or an owl usually regurgitates the pellet, or "casting" as falconers call it, often with retching or vomiting motions, and then leans forward to drop the pellet out of its mouth. The habit, best known in the eagles, hawks, and owls, is also widespread in birds worldwide and in at least 60 species of British birds (Knight, 1964).

The pellets of hawks and owls are usually gray or brown, and may be spherical, oval, oblong, or plug-shaped. They vary from about an inch or two long in a large bird of prey to about a half inch in a small songbird. An analysis of the contents of sufficient pellets throughout the year may give accurate information about the seasonal food habits of a bird of prey and without the necessity of killing the bird, as would be the case for stomach analyses (Craighead and Craighead, 1956). *See* Economic Ornithology; Food and Feeding Habits.

Places to find pellets are at the regular roosts or nesting sites of hawks and owls—under coniferous trees, in marsh or field grasses (marsh hawk and short-eared owl), at ground nesting burrows (burrowing owl), at the bases of cliffs, and in church belfries, barn lofts, and silos (barn owls). When looking for a source of the often difficult-to-see pellets, Hamerstrom (1939b) advises one to look first for the white spotting of the excreta (urates) of hawks and owls on cliff faces, on the leaf litter under trees, or on the rocks or ground as a clue to their roosting or nesting places.

Before dissecting them for analysis, pellets may first be soaked in a dish of warm water and then the food remains separated in a tray or dish. These may be examined for identification under a magnifying hand lens or a low-power microscope (Knight, 1964). For statistical methods in the identification and appraisal of food items in hawk and owl pellets, see Craighead and Craighead (1956).

FUNCTION OF PELLET-FORMING. Besides allowing a bird to get rid of indigestible parts of its food, pellet formation seems necessary for the health of a bird of prey. In captivity these birds are never so well and active as when their raw meat diet is varied regularly with a freshly killed mouse, sparrow, chicken, or pigeon. The indigestible bones, feathers, and fur of these animals when regurgitated seem to produce a scouring action on the throat and gullet of a bird of prey that is necessary for its well-being. Beebe (1965) reported the death of a bird that was fed on meat alone. *See* care and feeding of captive birds of prey in the introduction to Hawk Family.

HOW PELLETS ARE FORMED. Smith and Richmond (1972), in experimental studies of a captive barn owl, suggested that pellets are formed in the gizzard, *within 6 hours after a meal,* by muscular action in the gizzard during digestion. At some stage after digestion is completed, the freshly formed pellet passes out of the gizzard (the muscular stomach) into the proventriculus (glandular stomach), where it remains until the bird receives the proper stimulus for its egestion. Many captive owls, including the barn owl, can be induced to disgorge a pellet if they see a live mouse or other prey. Apparently it is necessary for a raptor to cast a pellet before it eats its next meal. Grimm and Whitehouse (1963) found that it took about 10 hours for a pellet to form in the stomach of a great horned owl and the bird disgorged it about 16 hours after a meal. In England, Chitty (1938) reported that great horned owls regurgitated pellets 12 hours after feeding; barn owls, 9–11 hours.

Pellets are formed and cast by some raptors at an early age. Young great horned owls, fed whole mice or parts of furry or feathery prey, regurgitate appreciable castings when about 1 week old; young red-tailed hawks when about 3 weeks old (Hamerstrom, 1970).

SOME SURPRISING ITEMS IN PELLETS. Penelope Weigel had a screech owl house pet (see "Geoffrey," in Terres, 1958) that once cast a pellet that contained a straight pin, and a tame little owl, *Athene noctua,* of Europe, produced a pellet of hard insect parts well protected by numerous rubber bands the bird found in the shed where it was temporarily kept (Knight, 1964).

Bird-banders have reported, somewhat rarely, pellets of wild screech owls that contained the aluminum bands of small birds they had caught and eaten—tufted titmouse, black-capped chickadee, and American goldfinch. One long-eared owl pellet picked up under an owl roost in Dec. 1964 near Wayland, Mass., held an aluminum band placed on the leg of a blue jay banded only 2½ mi. away in July 1964. On June 22, 1966, Gary L. Hickman found a casting of a golden eagle under its nest near Burns, Ore., that had a bird band in the pellet. The band had been placed about 4 months before on the leg of a male American wigeon at Salton Sea National Wildlife Refuge in s. Calif. almost 1,000 mi. away!

OTHER SPECIES OF BIRDS AND PELLETS. Besides eagles, hawks, and owls, pellet-forming is known among grebes, herons and bitterns, cormorants, king and clapper rails, gulls and terns, shorebirds, kingfishers, crows, jays, and the raven, dipper, starling, wagtails, shrikes, thrushes, flycatchers, warblers, swallows and swifts, and possibly all insect-eating birds eject pellets of the hard chitinous parts of their prey (Tucker, 1944; Rea, 1973b). In Ariz., Rea discovered pellets in the stomachs of turkey vultures, a fact apparently never before reported in the American Vulture Family.

Pellets are cast up by most shorebirds—those which grind their food with grit they ingest along with the food (Tuck, 1972). Pellets disgorged by the common snipe were composed of chitin, mollusk fragments, grit, plant fibers, seeds, and sawdust; they were about 10 mm. long and were usually cast about 5–6 hours after the birds fed. Pellets are also regurgitated by the lesser yellowlegs about 8 hours after feeding, and by the killdeer, least sandpiper, and western sandpiper (Proctor, 1968).

Martini (1964) collected pellets of Caspian terns at breeding colonies near San Diego Bay, Calif., and by the differing otoliths, or "ear stones," in the fishes they had eaten, was able to identify 14 species of the terns' prey. *See* related articles under Digestion; Gizzard.

PELVIC GIRDLE
See Skeleton.

PEN
An old English sporting term for the female swan.

PENGUIN
See mention under Procellariiformes; *see also* under Auk Family and discussion of ancestry of penguins under Monophyletic Descent; *see also* Flightless Birds.

PENIS
See Copulation and Copulatory Organs; *also* Fertilization; Sex Determination.

PERCHING BIRDS
See Passeriformes.

PEREGRINE
See Falcon, peregrine, in Falcon Family.

PERFORATE
See Nostrils.

PERIODICALS
See Ornithological Periodicals.

PERIODISM
A tendency for changes to recur in populations of birds and other animals. The recurrence (rise or fall) may be inexact and at irregular intervals of time, or it may be quite precise and regular, when is called a cycle. *See* Cycle; *also* Populations.

PERMANENT RESIDENT
See Where Do Birds Live? under Distribution.

PERMIAN PERIOD
See Geological Time Scale.

PERMITS
(for scientific collecting of birds). *See* Collections; Legal Protection.

PERVIOUS
Taxonomists, in their studies of the parts of birds that help in their classification, often cite the condition of the external openings of the nasal cavities, or nostrils. Usually they are open, or pervious, but there are exceptions. *See* discussion under Nostrils. *See also* Impervious.

PEST BIRDS
See Control; Economic Ornithology.

PET BIRDS
See Age; Care and Feeding of Abandoned or Injured Wild Birds.

PETE BIRD
See Titmouse, tufted, in Titmouse Family.

PETREL
Seabirds belonging to the family of Shearwaters (Procellariidae) and the order of tubenosed swimmers (Procellariiformes). About 53 species in this family, of which about 20 are found in N. American waters. *See* Storm-petrel Family for account of origin of term *petrel; also see* Shearwater Family for species accounts.

PEWEE
See in Flycatcher—Tyrant Flycatcher Family.

PEWIT
See Lapwing in Plover Family; *also* Pewee in Flycatcher—Tyrant Flycatcher Family.

PHAETHONTIDAE
See Tropicbird Family.

PHAINOPEPLA
See in Flycatcher—Silky Flycatcher Family.

PHALACROCORACIDAE
See Cormorant Family.

PHALAROPE FAMILY
Phalaropodidae (fal-ay-row-POD-ih-dee); from Gr. *phalaris,* coot, and *pous,* foot, "cootfooted," in reference to the lobed, semipalmated toes. 3 species in world; small; 7½–10 in. long; dainty, most aquatic of all shorebirds (*see* Shorebird); belong to order Charadriiformes; two species—the red and northern phalaropes—nest in the Arctic and subarctic tundra, respectively, in both the Old and New worlds; the third, Wilson's phalarope, nests around freshwater sloughs and potholes of the central plains of N. America; phalaropes are migratory; they have moderate-size to long bills (slightly longer than the head); the wings are long and pointed; the tail moderately long and graduated at end; the "leg" (shank) is rather long, with toes lobed; phalaropes swim well and are at home on both land and water; two—the red and northern phalaropes—are the only truly oceanic shorebirds; no larger than a robin;

spend much of the year on the ocean; have salt glands, as in the truly pelagic birds (*see* function of salt glands under Nostrils), and dense breast and belly feathers and a layer of down which provides a raft of trapped air on which they float high and corklike on water; they rest and sleep while afloat; as they swim jerkily about, bobbing their heads back and forth, they dab with bill to pick up small crustaceans from ocean, known as "brit"; also tiny fishes, jellyfishes, and other animals of the marine plankton; they also drop the head below the surface in a search underwater for food; sometimes they rotate on surface, like a spinning top, dabbing at surface with the bill as they turn (Wilson's phalarope, the inland species, has been seen spinning at 60 revolutions a minute, spearing water with the bill at each turn); in shallow water, the spinning, or "pirouetting," is thought to stir up food lodged on bottom; in deep cold pools of Greenland it is believed to activate mosquito larvae when they are inert in the water and invisible (see Tinbergen, 1935); are notably tame near the nest; flight is swift.

In the phalaropes, the role of the sexes is reversed; females are larger and more highly colored than the males, and take the initiative in courtship. Sometimes males alone build the nests, in which female lays the eggs, then she may leave the nesting grounds and the male incubates the eggs and rears the young. Shortly before his incubation begins, the male sheds the feathers from his abdomen and the bare skin thickens and becomes engorged with blood in two "brood patches," which male applies to the eggs to keep them warm and later to the young. The female does not produce brood patches.

In a group of Wilson's phalaropes on the nesting grounds, a female courting a male will keep close to him, following him wherever he swims. If another female approaches, she lowers her head and swims toward the intruder. When a few feet away, she flies at the intruding female, with her neck extended, legs dangling, which usually drives away the intruder; actual fights are rare; thus a male phalarope becomes accustomed to the company of a particular female, to which he later directs his sexual advances; males show little aggression at any time (Höhn, 1969). When a female northern phalarope indicates her readiness for mating, she utters a low note, then crouches on the water; the male rises like a miniature helicopter, hovers above female, then descends to her back and presses her partway underwater as they copulate (Bent, 1927).

In tests, Höhn (1969) and his colleagues discovered that in birds in which males are dominant (mallards, domestic fowl, red-winged blackbirds, for example), the amount of testosterone, the male hormone, was five to ten times greater in the testis of the male than in the ovary of the female; in phalaropes, there was about as much testosterone in the ovary of the female as in the testis of the male, and sometimes more; conclusion: the brilliant plumage of the female phalarope is due to high production of an androgen (male hormone) in her ovary and is probably responsible for her aggressive behavior.

Albinism is apparently rare among phala-

ropes; Gross (1965a) noted only one record for an individual of one species but did not identify it.

To feed an ill or injured phalarope: Leffler (1966) was successful in keeping a wing-injured northern phalarope in good health for 13 days before releasing it by keeping it in a protective enclosure (washtub partly filled with fresh water, with an anchored wooden platform for resting and feeding); he found that it preferred and quickly ate freshly killed or live adult flies, maggots, small butterflies, and moths placed on surface of water, and food such as chopped raw meat, boiled egg yolk, and cottage cheese placed on wooden platform or on water.

Flat-billed phalarope. *See* Red phalarope.

Gray phalarope. *See* Red phalarope.

PHALAROPE FAMILY

Northern phalarope, *Phalaropus lobatus* (fal-AY-row-pus low-BAY-tus); genus name: Lat., from Gr. *phalaris,* coot, and *pous,* foot; species name: Lat., lobed. (Color ills., pages 702, 703.) In summer around northern regions of the world; nesting range extends much farther south than that of red phalarope; 6½–8 in. long; wingspread 13½–14½ in.; smallest, most abundant, and most widely distributed phalarope (Bent, 1927); in nesting season, females gray on upperparts with some rufous red on sides of neck, throat white; males similar but browner; in winter, both have gray upperparts, white below, black line through eyes; have lobed toes, straight needlelike black bill almost 1 in. long; dark legs and feet; in all seasons a white bar down dark wing, no white on rump; in flight, resemble sanderlings but have darker back; white wing stripe is shorter than sanderling's, flies with deeper wing stroke (Peterson, 1947); is more slender-billed and black line through eyes is distinguishing; call is faint, plaintive *pe-et* or *wit-wit* (Bent, 1927); in migration may be seen on any waters but scarce inland east of north-south line from Man. to Ariz.; winters at sea; on ocean in winter swims with buoyancy of gull, upends like duck, pecks at water like a hen; when ashore, runs around like a sandpiper; in spring migration along both Atlantic and Pacific coasts and from Mexico to Canada, from late Mar. into May; some arrive on nesting areas by May, others in early June; by July adults begin to appear on salt water, assemble in flocks; one of noted concentration places in May and early Aug. is mouth of Bay of Fundy, where assemble in tens of thousands to hundreds of thousands. Some males may have more than one mate (promiscuous) or female may be polygamous, sequentially mating with more than one male (Raner, 1972). Both sexes may take turns shaping a nest scrape in ground, and both line it with grasses or each may make one or several nests separately, after which female selects one in which to lay her eggs and leads male to it (Palmer, 1967).

Feeding Habits: Often spin, toplike, on water while feeding on plankton, insects, mosquito larvae, brine shrimp; on fresh water, food is largely tiny insect larvae (mosquitoes, midges), some tiny crustaceans, mollusks, etc.; eat animal plankton.

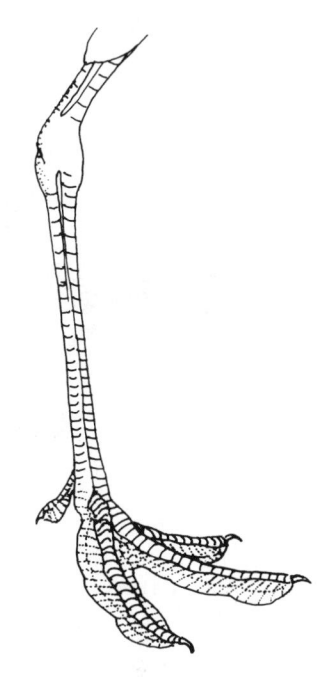

Wilson's phalarope

female

male

PHALAROPE FAMILY
The colorful female phalarope takes the initiative in courtship and aggressively drives off rival females. Here, the male and female Wilson's phalarope remain motionless for a few seconds in a characteristic display after copulation.

Nest: Domed cup of grass in moist tundra.
Eggs: May (?)–June; 4, olive, blotched or rarely dotted with dark browns.
Incubation: By male (Palmer, 1967); 22½ days (Jehl and Hussell, 1966); male tends brood; female usually departs after male starts incubating; chicks fly when less than 21 days old (Palmer, 1967).
Other Names: Bank-bird; gale-bird; hyperborean phalarope; mackerel-goose; red-necked phalarope; sea-goose; sea-snipe; web-footed peep; whale-bird; white bank-bird.
Accidents: Killed at sea by gales; oil from ships may be hazard (Palmer, 1967).
Weights: 1–1¾ oz. (Palmer, 1967).
Range: Circumboreal, nests on more southerly tundra, mainland, and various islands and open places within forest zone; winters at sea, abundant off Peru, part of w. Africa, in Indian O., in S. China Sea, many wander about on water almost anywhere; in N. America nests from w. and n. Alaska, east to Greenland, south to s. Alaska, Aleutian Is., s. Yukon, east to Labrador (coast); migrates abundantly along Pacific and Atlantic coasts, often offshore and inland in West from B.C. and Alta., south to n. Ariz., rarely interior of East; winters in S. Hemisphere.

Red phalarope, *Phalaropus fulicarius* (fal-AY-row-pus few-lick-AY-rih-us); genus name: *see* Northern phalarope; species name: from Lat. *fulica,* coot, "coot-like." (Color ills., pages 702, 703.) Circumpolar, nests farther north (mainly above Arctic Circle), migrates farther south, is more maritime than the other phalaropes; coastal stragglers may appear anywhere; 8–9 in. long; wingspread 14–16 in.; in breeding plumage, *the red underparts,* which may appear black at some distance, and the *white face* are distinctive; male has similar color pattern but duller; in fall and winter, both sexes blue-gray above and white underparts with black eyeline characteristic of phalaropes; in this plumage, according to Peterson (1947), is similar to northern phalarope, but is slightly larger and paler, no stripes on back; has shorter, slightly broader, yellow bill with black tip; utters low, musical *clink, clink,* like sound of tapping together of two small bars of steel, a clear whistle, and sometime a *creak* note (Bent, 1927); in summer lives on tundra flats with pools in Far North, also along river flats; swims purposefully, spins on water as though pivoting, pecks at surface; in May or June arrival on nesting grounds, female selects territory and "advertises" for male in displays like those of northern phalarope, including rearing up of pairs on water; on land, male may run to female and crouch in contact with her breast (Palmer, 1967); a high count of red phalaropes in fall 1972 was 20,000 4 mi. off Brier Is., Nova Scotia (Finch, 1973).

Feeding Habits: In nesting season, feeds on mosquitos, crane flies, and other common Arctic aquatic invertebrates; at sea eats larval fishes, small jellyfishes, crustaceans.
Nest: Semi-colonial; depression in dry or moist tundra, not far from sea, on coastal islands, well concealed, domed with grasses, runway through grasses leading to nest; sometimes lined by male with grasses or other plants.
Eggs: June–July; 4, gray-buff to olive brown, blotched or spotted with chestnut and black; the polyandrous females (*see* Sexual Relationships) may lay more than one clutch of eggs in a season with different mates (Mayfield, 1978).
Incubation: By male, 19 days; chicks first fly when about 18 days old (Parmelee *et al.,* 1967).
Other Names: Bank-bird; brown bank-bird; flat-billed phalarope; gray bank-bird; gray phalarope (in British Isles); gulf bird; mackerel-goose; red-footed tringa; sea-goose; sea-snipe.
Accidents: Sometimes strike lighthouses and other tall structures when migrating (Bull, 1964; Stoddard and Norris, 1967).
Weights: 1½–2¼ oz. (Palmer, 1967).
Range: In N. America, nests on parts of mainland and islands of Arctic Circle, south to upper west coast of Hudson Bay and across Canada to w. and n. Alaska; also nests on Eurasian mainland and various islands; migrates well offshore down both seacoasts; sometimes (rarely) blown inland by storms; winters in Pacific at sea off Aleutian Is., Baja Calif., south locally to c. Chile; in Atlantic, apparently off Argentina (Palmer, 1967).

Red-necked phalarope. *See* Northern phalarope.

Wilson's phalarope, *Phalaropus tricolor* (fal-AY-row-pus TRY-color); genus name: *see* Northern phalarope; species name: Lat., in reference to three colors of this bird: white, black, brown-red; common name: in honor of Alexander Wilson, early American ornithologist. (Color ills., pages 702, 703.) Largest and most land-dwelling of the phalaropes, only one limited to New World; a freshwater bird; summers in interior grasslands of n. Great Plains of s. Canada and n. U.S.; 8½–9½ in. long; wingspread 14½–16 in.; both sexes have toes with narrow, lateral membranes (not lobes); female much larger and more brightly colored in breeding plumage with pale gray crown, back, wings, and tail; broad black streak through eyes down neck blending into cinnamon; in flight, this dark-winged phalarope shows no white stripe in wings; has white rump, thin black bill longer than in other phalaropes; in fall and winter, both sexes gray above, white below, with white streak above each eye; utters a nasal grunt or subdued quack; prolonged migration, sometimes flocks linger at favored feeding places; in spring, leaves S. America from late Mar. into May; many reach U.S. Apr. through May and s. Canada usually by May 1; on nesting grounds several females may chase a male; a female, after attaching herself to a male, defends him against approaches of other females, defends vicinity of male, not a specific area; no evidence of territorial behavior or supposed polyandry, according to Höhn (1967).

Feeding Habits: Is more land-based than other phalaropes; gets most of food while walking about on muddy shores or while wading in shallow water, often probing bottom with head submerged; however, also whirls about on water dabbing at surface with bill forward or backward, with or against whirling motion of its body; eats mostly larvae of mosquitoes and of crane flies, also eats predacious diving beetles; those feeding on salt flats of Great Basin sometimes gorge on alkali flies and brine shrimps, and seeds of various aquatic plants (Wetmore, 1925); in May 1971, Siegfried and Batt (1972) watched Wilson's phalaropes on flooded meadow near Delta, Man., associate closely with shoveler ducks; as ducks fed, they stirred up small aquatic animals, which phalaropes quickly seized in their bills; those attending ducks picked up prey at rate three times that of a phalarope feeding alone (*see* Commensalism).

Nest: Semi-colonial nester, about margins of quiet shallow waters, ponds, sloughs, ashore or on islets, well-concealed grass-lined hollow in grass or marsh; according to Höhn (1967), female takes part in making, or may even be sole maker, of nest scrapes; some evidence, however, that male may do some nest building.

Eggs: May–June; 3–4, usually 4, buffy, heavily overlaid with dark brown dots, blotches.

Incubation: By male, whose incubation patches develop during his nest building; 20 days; female nearby much excited if nest approached by an intruder; male tends brood (Palmer, 1967); Höhn (1967) reported that females leave nesting grounds in early June as soon as males begin to incubate.

Other Name: Summer phalarope.

Host to Cowbird: Two records, Bear River National Wildlife Refuge, June 1938, of two phalarope nests 25 yds. apart, concealed in damp salt grass of lower marshes, each held four phalarope eggs, two of brown-headed cowbird; nests later flooded, all eggs destroyed (Friedmann, 1963); one nest, Moosehorn, Man., June 1970, held four phalarope eggs, one of brown-headed cowbird (Hatch, 1971).

Weights: 1½–3 oz. (Palmer, 1967); males (100) averaged 50.17 gr., or about 1¾ oz.; females (53) averaged 68.09 gr., or about 2½ oz. (Höhn, 1967).

Range: Nests from sw. Canada (B.C.) east across s.-c. Canada to Que. and N.B. south to s.-c. Calif., ne. Colo., n. Ind., N.Y., and Mass; winters chiefly in s. S.A., and Falkland Is., and has wintered from s. Tex. southward; some migration along Atlantic coast but most migrants travel north and south over interior prairies west of Mississippi R.; migrates to coast in Calif. in fall.

PHALAROPODIDAE
See Phalarope Family.

PHARYNX
Name for the cavity of the throat just behind the buccal cavity, or mouth. The pharynx leads to the esophagus (*see* Esophagus) and into the trachea, or windpipe. *See also* Digestion; Mouth; Respiratory System; Swallowing.

PHASE
See Color Phase.

PHASIANID
(fay-sih-AN-id). Shortened name for any member of the Pheasant Family (Phasianidae).

PHASIANIDAE
See Pheasant Family.

PHEASANT
See in Pheasant Family; *see also* Grouse, ruffed, in Grouse Family.

PHEASANT FAMILY
Phasianidae (fay-sih-AN-ih-dee); Lat., from Gr. *phasianos*, the Phasian bird (*see* origin of name in biography of ring-necked pheasant). About 174 species, natural range is worldwide except in polar regions and in Oceania (Van Tyne and Berger, 1976); predominantly an Old World family and includes the New World quails (only members of Pheasant Family native to W. Hemisphere), the Old World quails, partridges, pheasants, spur fowls, francolins, peafowls, etc. (see in Delacour, 1964), and the red jungle fowl, ancestor of the domestic fowl, or chicken; the members of the Pheasant Family are related to six other families of fowl-like birds—grouse, turkeys, etc.; sizes range from 5 to 92 in. long; from the tiny 5–6-in.-long painted quail, *Excalfactoria chinensis*, of se. Asia and Australia, to the 72–84 in. (including the long tail) great argus pheasant, *Argusianus argus*, of the jungles of Indochina and the Malay Pen., remarkable for its chain of eye spots down center of its long and wide secondary wing feathers and from these spots, named for Argus of Gr. mythology, who had a hundred eyes, to the very large, 80–92-in.-long common peafowl, *Pavo cristatus*, of India and Ceylon; some of the most strikingly colored and impressive birds in the family are the peafowl, with their elegant trains of feathers, which are the long upper tail coverts, supported by the coarse ordinary-appearing feathers of the true tail; most of the smaller quails and partridges in the family are drab or dull-colored, but the pheasants include some of the most beautiful birds in the world whose colors rival those of American hummingbirds and the birds of paradise of New Guinea and Australia. For brilliant color illustrations of pheasants, see especially in Beebe (1936); Delacour (1977); Austin (1961).

In N. America, total of 9 species in family: 6 native American quails, and 3 introduced species from Old World and now established in U.S.—two partridges, one pheasant (*see* Domestication); all members of family are chickenlike, with stout bills, similar to bills of grouse, and long, strong legs with four-toed, clawed feet, which, like bill, are adapted to scratching in ground for food; differ from members of Grouse Family in having the tarsus, or shank, bare of feathers; nostrils mostly exposed or bare of feathers; no member of Pheasant Family has inflatable "air sacs" as do some in Grouse Family, but many of them do have combs, wattles, and naked areas of bare skin about eyes, and some, on rear of tarsus, have spurs, used with remarkable skill by domestic fowls, turkeys, pheasants, and peafowl in their battles for dominance—the spurs of peafowl are long and sharp and occasionally used so vigorously in fights that both contestants may be killed (Beebe, 1906). According to Austin (1961), chickens kept by primitive people for cockfighting may have been responsible for

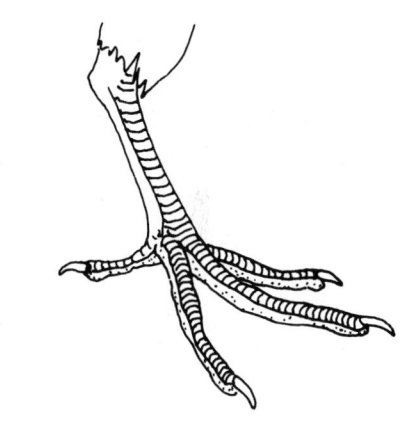

PHEASANT FAMILY

early distribution and domestication of these birds.

Pheasants are large with very long, pointed tails; quails and partridges are smaller with short, rounded tails (see other general characters of family under Galliformes); wings are short, rounded, curved, usually fit close to body; flight is swift but cannot be sustained for long (see Flight Muscles under Flight) except by some of the Old World migratory quails (Delacour, 1964); in most (except quails and partridges) sexes are outwardly *unlike*, and males are much larger and much more highly colored than females; also, nearly all pheasants and peafowl are polygamous, the eared pheasant and blood pheasant apparently being exceptional in this regard.

The afterfeathers on the contour feathers of members of the family are large, a character shared by members of the Grouse Family. *See* Afterfeather.

The New World quails (bobwhite, for example), classified in the subfamily Odontophorinae, are small to medium-sized, usually under 12 in. long and seldom larger than a bantam hen; they lack the spurs of the pheasants but the cutting edge of the lower mandible is slightly serrated, or toothed (inconspicuous in some); all are monogamous (see Sexual Relationships) and the male usually remains with the female during nesting season to help her rear the young (Johnsgard, 1973); about 33 species are distributed between s. Canada and extreme ne. Argentina; some live in forests, others on brushy plains and deserts or on open farmlands as does the popular bobwhite.

The New World quails are not migratory; some Old World quails of the genus *Coturnix* are; Old World quails, partridges, etc. (subfamily Perdicinae), of about 95 species (Austin, 1961); are usually plain-colored birds, small to medium in size; are stouter and with deeper build than the New World quails. The monogamous chukar and gray partridges, introduced successfully into U.S., are larger than the American quails and they differ from them in lacking the toothed cutting edge on the lower mandible; also, some species in the subfamily have blunt spurs on the rear of the tarsus; the Perdicinae are widespread over most of Africa, Eurasia, and the Australia and Malay Archipelago regions (Austin, 1961).

Gross (1965a) reported albinism in 99 individuals of 8 species (including introduced ones) in N. American members of the Pheasant Family. Hybridization also fairly common in Pheasant Family, being reported for 5 of native N. American quails.

For care and feeding of ill, injured, or healthy captives, see especially the section "The Care of Pheasants in Captivity" in Beebe (1936); also in Delacour (1977).

Bobwhite, or Bobwhite quail, *Colinus virginianus* (koh-LINE-us ver-jin-ih-AY-nus); genus name: Lat. form of Sp. and Fr. *colin*, a quail, from Nahuatl Indian *zolin*, for American quail; species name: Lat., of Virginia; *bobwhite*, from male's song or call; *quail*, from Old Fr. *quaille*, Old Scottish *quailzie* (Newton, 1893–96), from calls of Eurasian migratory quail, *Coturnix coturnix*. (Color ills., pages 704,

705.) The bobwhite is resident over virtually entire e. U.S. and e. Canada from s. Ont., s. Me., south to Gulf of Mexico and west to se. Wyo., also in Southwest and introduced in parts of West; lives on farms with hedges, woods, crop fields, old pastures, in roadside hedges and brushy fencerows on farms and across prairies; in wooded river valleys, in open pine woods but avoids deep forest, in brushy canyons and hillsides of Southwest, on dry grasslands with scattered mesquite and cactus; 9½–10½ in. long; wingspread 14–16 in.; sexes outwardly similar; in general, over most of U.S., a small, red-brown chickenlike bird, smaller than ruffed grouse, with short brown to black bill; male has conspicuous white stripe over eyes and a white throat (in female, eye stripe and throat buffy); may be confused with smaller meadowlark of open fields, which, however, *shows white outer tail feathers in flight;* introduced gray partridge has no white or pale buff about head and has uniformly *gray* chest; in spring and summer, male bobwhite, from perch on rail fences, orchard tree, or from ground, utters challenge call to other males, a distinctive whistled *bob-WHITE!* or *bob-bob-WHITE!* with rising inflection on *white!;* also an odd caterwauling like cat at all seasons; the pairs in summer and scattered members of fall and winter coveys also utter a poignant assembly call, *ka-loi-kee? ka-loi-kee?*, that brings them back together; both sexes utter many conversational notes (see Stoddard, 1931; Bent, 1932); *see also* Language; when flushed, rises swiftly with loud whirring of rapidly beating wings but to no great height, then scales away with wings sharply downcurved; tail dark, not chestnut or red-brown as in the gray partridge; immature in first year can be distinguished in hand from adults by two outer primary (wing) feathers which are more pointed than other primaries (see in Johnsgard, 1973); is gregarious most of year; in late summer and early fall, families with their young join together in coveys (flocks) of up to 30 birds, which at roosting time, just before dark, assemble into groups of about 10–15 birds, which roost near each other on ground, each group in a circle with heads pointed outward, tails pointed to sky, bodies packed closely together, which conserves body heat of sleeping birds, especially valuable in winter in northern parts of range; covey headquarters usually in a thicket, thorny tangle, weedy fence corner, or wood's edge, with covey often sleeping in grass under open sky; if undisturbed may return there to roost each night for 2 weeks or more; in roosting circle, if one detects danger, instantly warns others and all rise with loud roar of wings, often disconcerting to hunter, whether a fox or a man; members of covey scatter in all directions and reassemble next morning; in summer, before female starts incubation, adult pairs roost side by side on ground, facing same direction, some may roost in vines or in densely leaved tree, on lower rail of weedy fence, or on top of log in woods, often in poultry house, barn, or stable; in fall during poultry shortages, may travel on foot in short migrations to new food supply but not migratory; is rapid and tireless runner; also wanders restlessly in fall, disperses into cities and to town and country gardens and other

unexpected places, but not in "crazy" fall flights of ruffed grouse; in spring (Apr. into May) coveys begin to break up into pairs; some pairing within the coveys, where fierce fighting between males; male confronts female in courtship displays with spread wings and tips dragging ground, tail spread, and bowing before female and turning head to show white markings, walks or advances toward her in short rushes; if both members of pair live into following year, same pair may be together again. Johnsgard (1973) reported an estimated 35 million bobwhites were shot by hunters during the open season of 1970; Edminster (1954) stated that most of harvest in 1950s was in 17 states from Va. to Iowa, and south to Tex., was legal game in 30 states but protected in others where considered too attractive to be hunted.

Feeding Habits: About an hour after sunrise, pair or covey may start on foot toward weed patch, stubble field, berry patch, etc., where the birds eat for an hour or two, then retire to some sheltered spot for midday rest; return again to feeding place about two hours before sunset; basic food is seeds of grasses, wild and cultivated legumes such as lespedezas, cowpeas, soybeans, mesquite, peanuts, and tick trefoil, also partridgeberry, and seeds of pines, sweet gum, ash, and especially acorns, also grains—corn, sorghum, wheat, rye, buckwheat—and wild fruit such as raspberries, blackberries, strawberries, bayberries, wax myrtle, hackberry, grapes, plums, rose hips, dogwood berries, pokeberries, persimmons, and many more; in spring, eats succulent leaves of clovers and other tender green plants; in summer, about 30% of food is animal matter (Johnsgard, 1973), soft-bodied grasshoppers and flies, also bugs and some spiders; comes regularly to feeding stations in backyards and gardens where mixtures of wild bird seeds and grain are spread on ground for the birds. Nice (1910) found that a captive bobwhite ate 568 mosquitoes in 2 hours, another 5,000 plant lice (aphids) in a day, another 1,000 grasshoppers and 532 other insects in a day, also 600–30,000 weed seeds each day; is also a great destroyer of potato beetles. See details of food habits and economic value of food habits in Bent (1932); Forbush (1925–29); see also Stoddard (1931); *also* Economic Ornithology.

Nest: In shallow depression in ground; may be dug by either sex and lined and arched over with grasses with small opening in side; well concealed along weed-grown fencerows, brushy corners of old fields, in woods under piles of brush, at edges of woods, thickets, swamps, in fields of hay, grain, alfalfa, at base of tree in orchard, at woody or grassy edges of golf courses (Bent, 1932); if first nest destroyed, pair may build second, third, or even fourth nest if these destroyed, or until brood is raised (Stoddard, 1931).

Eggs: Tex., Mar.–Aug.; Fla., Apr.–July; elsewhere, usually Apr.–Sept.; 7–30, more than 18 laid by two or more hens in same nest, usually 14–16 eggs by one female, white or cream-white.

Incubation: By both sexes, 23–24 days; young leave nest soon after hatching; attended by both parents, which use "crippled-bird act" to lure away enemies from young; young can fly when less than 14 days old; start to feed as covey before 21 days old; at 49 days after hatching, roost in characteristic circle of adults and can make considerable flights (Edminster, 1954).

Other Names: Colin; common bobwhite; partridge; Virginia partridge.

Accidents: Adults sometimes killed by mowing machine while sitting on nest; in suburbs, killed by striking picture windows; sometimes drown in fall wandering by falling into water while flying across rivers; Mullan and Applegate (1969) reported covey of 20 bobwhites that drowned in large reservoir in Ark. while trying to fly across it in dense early-morning fog.

Age: One reported (Stoddard, 1931) in captivity, 7 years old, and other captives up to 8 or 10 years; one shot in Mo., 7 years old; one lived National Zoo, Washington, D.C., 8 years, 7 months.

Albinism: Stoddard (1931) cited some records of pure albino bobwhites of a cream tint, and one report of a pure-white covey near Pavo, Ga., and an even rarer reddish (erythristic) color phase (*see* Color Phase) of several bobwhites in Tenn. (see also Gross, 1965a).

Flight Speed: Timed in Tex., 28 m.p.h. (Sooter, 1947); in S.C., 48 m.p.h. (Anonymous, 1924); 49 m.p.h. (Huntington, 1934); in Ga., 28–38 m.p.h. (Stoddard,1931).

Hybrids: Bobwhite × scaled quail; bobwhite × California quail (Gray, 1958).

Weights: According to Hamilton (1957), who cites other authorities, bobwhites are lighter in s. U.S., heavier in n. U.S., weighing from average of 5.7 oz. in Fla. to heaviest, slightly more than 7 oz., in Wisc., thus following, or bearing out, Bergmann's Rule (*see* Bergmann's Rule); heaviest male on record was Wisc. bird of 8⅞ oz. killed in 1934; also an 8½-oz. hen from same area in 1941 (Martin and Nelson, 1952).

Range: Resident from s. Ont., s. Me., west to s. Minn., s. S.D., se. Wyo. south to Gulf coast and e. Mexico to Guatemala, also introduced and established in e. Ore., e. Wash., w. Idaho, and a discrete population in s. Ariz. and Mexican state of Sonora, where largely extirpated (Johnsgard, 1973), also in Cuba and on Isle of Pines.

Bobwhite, masked, *Colinus virginianus ridgwayi.* (koh-LINE-us ver-jin-ih-AY-nus ridg-WAY-eye); genus and species names: *see* Bobwhite; subspecies name: Lat., of Ridgway, so named by William Brewster in 1885 for Robert Ridgway, Curator of Birds, U.S. National Museum, Washington, D.C. A geographic race of the bobwhite, originally widespread in nw. Mexico and a narrow strip in s. Ariz. 40–50 mi. north of the Mexican border (see Bent, 1932); by early 1900s, native populations were gone from Ariz., one of first birds to be extirpated in U.S.; grazed out of existence by arrival of great herds of cattle which destroyed native tall grass essential to its survival, and droughts that came later; before 1890, common on tall grass plains from Baboquívari Mtns. in Ariz. to upper Santa Cruz Valley, was state's most famous bird (Phillips *et al.*, 1964; Ligon, 1952); about 10 in. long; famed for its handsome color pattern; no crest, male with throat and face

black; above, brown, black, and pale buff; underparts rich chestnut-brown to brick red; female and immature with no solid black or chestnut, throat white to pale buff, underparts buffy, barred with black; in 1967, U.S. Fish and Wildlife Service began studies of masked bobwhites in Mexico to determine its status and feasibility of raising some in captivity for release in s. Ariz.; from wild masked bobwhites captured in Mexico in 1968, 1969, raised sufficient young at Patuxent Wildlife Research Center, Laurel, Md., to release 160 in s. Ariz. in 1970 and 250 in 1971, of which some survivors seen into Nov. 1971 (Anonymous, 1974a); only about 1,000 left in world in last part of its range in c. Sonora, Mexico (Office of Endangered Species, 1973). See what is known of life history in Bent (1932).

Chukar, *Alectoris chukar* (ah-LEK-tore-iss choo-KAR); genus name: from Gr. *alektor,* a cock; species name: from Hindustani *cakor,* from Sanskrit *cakora,* a partridge; also *chukar* from its calls. (Color ills., pages 704, 705.) Introduced from Eurasia and established as game bird in w. U.S.; according to Watson (1962), all stock of the chukar partridge existing in wild in U.S. is referable to *Alectoris chukar,* whose native range is Asia Minor and s. Asia, not to the rock partridge, *Alectoris graeca* (GREEK-ah) of Greece, listed in A.O.U. *Check-list* (1957); according to Watson (1962), besides a number of minor differences in plumage, *A. graeca* differs greatly from *A. chukar* in voice; males of *A. graeca* utter a series of clear, ringing whistles; *A. chukar* only clucking or cackling sounds; the chukar has been introduced into at least 42 states of U.S. and 6 Canadian provinces but in only one province in w. Canada and in 10 states of West have these introduced birds become successfully established, with introductions beginning there in 1930s (Johnsgard, 1973); chukars are 13–15½ in. long; sexes outwardly identical, but males somewhat larger than females and with slight spurs on legs; a plump, chickenlike bird, somewhat larger than gray partridge, smaller than ruffed grouse; bill reddish; upperparts generally sandy or brown-gray, has white or buffy cheeks and a prominent black line that extends across forehead through eyes, then down sides of neck and across upper breast like a necklace; *chest gray,* other underparts, and flanks, buffy; *flanks have conspicuous vertical chestnut bars;* outer tail feathers chestnut-brown or rufous; feet and legs reddish; lives generally west of Rocky Mtns. on dry sagebrush-grasslands and deserts, on rocky, brushy, or grassy slopes, brushy creek bottoms, and in arid mountains and rugged canyons, from sea level in Death Valley of Calif. to 12,000 ft. in White Mtns. of e. Calif. and sw. Nev.; in most of its range in U.S. summers are hot and short, winters moderately cold and long; snow on higher mountains may cause some chukars to move down into valleys below snow line—several major losses of chukars reported when snow 6–8 in. persisted for several weeks, covering its food supply, but can stand winter temperatures to −30° F. (Christensen, 1970); from fall until spring, moves about in coveys of 5–40 birds or more, with average about 20; roost on ground on talus slopes in protected rocky niches and in

Masked bobwhite

PHEASANT FAMILY

caves on rocky faces of cliffs, sometimes under shrubs or low trees; have been seen roosting in circle similar to habit of bobwhite; converse (contact notes) among themselves almost constantly when active; like bobwhite, has a "rally" or assembly call to regroup scattered members of covey, a series of slowly repeated then rapid *chuck* notes that sound like *per-chuck* or *chuckara*, also utters a shrill *whitoo!* of alarm from ground or when flushed or held in hand; from Feb. through Mar. coveys disband gradually as pairing begins; is basically monogamous, but some males may pair with two females (see details, also of chukar's courtship, in Johnsgard, 1973); is swift afoot and prefers to escape by running; according to Johnsgard, in 1947, Nev. was first state to open a hunting season on chukars, followed in later years by Wash., Idaho, Calif., Wyo., Ore., Utah, Mont., and Colo., the main states in which most chukars are harvested (also in B.C., Canada), with a total of about 5½ million killed by hunters to and through 1967.

Feeding Habits: Forages much during midmorning and into afternoon, moving widely in search of seeds and leaves, especially of downy chess, or cheatgrass, and seeds of Russian thistle, filaree, fiddleneck, and other weeds, also kernels of wheat, crowns and seeds of bunchgrass, leaves of alfalfa, clover, and sweet clover, seeds of black locust trees, fruits of serviceberry (*Amelanchier*); in spring, eats leaves of dandelion, fringe cup, shepherd's purse, and other weeds (see Johnsgard, 1973), and some insects, especially grasshoppers; apparently not aggressive toward other birds; at water holes seen drinking amicably with ring-necked pheasants, gray partridges, and California quail; in summer, during hot dry season, chukars make daily trips to their watering places, often starting in late afternoon and loitering around water for an hour or more; toward evening, disperse to nearby foothills or brushy sides of canyons.

Nest: Built on ground beside shrub, rock, or clump of grass, among rocks or brushy cover, a shallow depression lined with dried grasses and feathers.

Eggs: Late Apr. into May; 10–20, usually 14–16, yellow-white, spotted or speckled with brown.

Incubation: Usually by female, 24 days; some authorities say male not only may help raise brood but may take over incubation of first clutch of eggs while female lays second, others that only one set of eggs usually laid (although may renest if first broken up) and that males desert females early in their incubation to join other males, which spend summer in groups of dozen or more (see Edminster, 1954; Johnsgard, 1973); chicks can fly some 30–60 ft. when 14 days old; are about full-grown when 84 days old; families join in large groups in late summer.

Other Names: Chuckar; chuckor; Indian hill partridge.

Running Speed: Timed in N.D., 12 m.p.h., and in Mo., 18 m.p.h., by Cottam *et al.* (1942b).

Weights: Males 21–26 oz.; females 16–19 oz. (Christensen, 1970).

Range: Present range (Johnsgard, 1973) in N. America, from s. interior B.C. southward through Wash., Ore., and Calif. to northern Baja Calif.; eastward in Great Basin through Nev., Idaho, Utah, w. Colo., and Mont., with small populations in Ariz., N.M., w. S.D., and s. Alta.

Partridge. Misnomer for ruffed grouse in Grouse Family; also one of common names of the bobwhite. *See* introduction to Pheasant Family for some of physical differences between the New World quails, such as the bobwhite, and the Old World partridges. Name *partridge* is from Middle Eng. *partriche* or *pertriche* (*see also* Partridge, gray).

Partridge, birch. Another name for the ruffed grouse in Grouse Family.

Partridge, bohemian. *See* Partridge, gray.

Partridge, California. *See* Quail, California.

Partridge, English. *See* Partridge, gray.

Partridge, European. *See* Partridge, gray.

Partridge, gray, *Perdix perdix* (PER-dicks); genus and species names: Lat., partridge, from Gr. *perdix*, a partridge; the word probably imitative of the whir of the wings of this species in flight (see Gruson, 1972, for other details). (Color ill., page 706.) Native of Eurasia; in late 19th and early 20th centuries, first introduced into N. America (see Phillips, 1928), now widely established as game bird in separated populations across s. Canada and n. U.S., from N.Y. west to Ore.; 12–13 in. long; wingspread 18–22 in.; sexes outwardly similar; plump with short, rounded wings and tail; appears in flight a gray-brown bird without bright markings but shows *rusty outer tail feathers* as does chukar; however, larger chukar has *conspicuous white throat;* bobwhite is smaller and shows dark gray tail in flight; face and throat of gray partridge is orange-brown and has chestnut patch in center of breast; bill, legs, and feet gray; immatures have yellow legs and feet (see in Bent, 1932; Johnsgard, 1973); likes cool, moderately dry climate; is resident on gently rolling hayfields and grain fields, and pastures; also on grasslands; highest populations are on northern plains; in Wash. lives up to at least 5,000 ft. elevation on open grassy ridges; likes brushy canyons and brushy stream bottoms of West, and irrigated agricultural lands; in late summer and early fall, two or more families of about 10 birds each may form a single covey of up to 30 birds, but usually about 12–15 in covey, which may decline in numbers during winter; coveys are sedentary and seldom range over more than quarter of a mile; even in winter in bitter cold and stormy weather, prefer open grain stubble, cornfields or hayfields, and open grasslands; when flushed, covey takes off in single noisy burst of flight with wing-whirring and calls of *keep, keep,* and males cackling; frequently fly to a knoll or ridge and drop out of sight; in flight stay together, unlike members of covey of bobwhites, which, when flushed, usually scatter; during winter, often roost in circle on ground (see method under Bobwhite) or may plunge into snowdrift to spend night; McCabe and Hawkins (1946) recognize six different calls of gray partridge—when excited they utter *kuta-kut-kut-kut;* another is "rusty gate" *keee-UCK!* crowing of unmated males, etc.; in Feb.–Mar., much fighting between cocks in coveys when pairing begins, at which time coveys begin to break up (see courtship in Johnsgard, 1973); an estimated average of about 650,000 gray partridges shot in U.S. by hunters each year, according to Johnsgard.

Feeding Habits: Chief foods are seeds of cultivated grains such as oats, wheat, barley, and corn, also seeds of weeds and grasses—lamb's-quarters, crabgrass, foxtail grasses, smartweeds (*Polygonum*), prickly lettuce, and many others; also, especially in winter, leaves of clover, alfalfa, bluegrass, wheat, dandelion, wild mustard, etc.; eats some insects in hayfields and grain fields, such as grasshoppers, caterpillars of butterflies and moths, also ants, ground beetles, and others; gets most of water needs from dew; requires grit for grinding food (just as do other members of Pheasant Family), which it often gets from gravel roads.

Nest: Female builds nest (while male stands guard) by first scratching out hollow about 2½ in. deep, 6–8 in. wide; lines it with weed stems, dead grasses, and a fine inner layer of soft leaves, grasses, and feathers; is commonly in wild grass or in hayfields or grain fields within 24–50 ft. of edge of field or along fencerows or roadsides (Edminster, 1954).

Eggs: May–Aug. (Edminster, 1954); 5–20 or more, usually 15–17 for first nesting of season; slightly less for second nesting (Johnsgard, 1973); olive; 20 or more often represents laying of more than one gray partridge hen in same nest; ring-necked pheasant also known to lay eggs in nest of gray partridge; *see* Dump Nest; Obligate Parasite.

Incubation: Mostly by female, 24½–25 days (Johnsgard, 1973); both parents at nest when chicks hatch; lead them away as soon as chicks are dry; if family alarmed by intruder, both adults practice "crippled-bird act"; one brood a year, if first nests destroyed, will renest; chicks first fly about 14 days after hatching.

Other Names: Bohemian partridge; English partridge; European partridge; Hun; Hungarian partridge.

Accidents: Many killed in hayfields each year by mowing machines; adults frequently fly against utility poles and wires, especially in winter, also strike barbed-wire and electric fences; many killed by automobiles along highways.

Albinism: Not specifically reported as such but McCabe (1970) has noted a rare pale or dilute color aberration; *see* Abnormal Colors under Colors of Feathers.

Hybrids: Gray (1958) reported crossbreeding and hybrids, apparently in captivity, of gray partridge with chickens, or domestic fowl, with silver and ring-necked pheasants and others, including European grouse.

Flight Speed: Timed in England, 25–35 m.p.h. (Roberts, B. B., 1932), and 53 m.p.h. (Portal, 1922).

Running Speed: Timed in Ore., 9 m.p.h. (Cottam *et al.*, 1942b).

Weights: Slightly less than 1 lb.; males average 14 oz., with a large male in N.D. of 16 oz.; females average about 13½ oz., with one large hen of 14⅓ oz. (Martin and Nelson, 1952); 12–15 oz. (Edminster, 1954).

Range: Native to Europe and Asia; introductions from there into N. America, probably from several different geographical races; in N. America, is resident in three major regions: in Far West, in n. Calif., n. Nev., Ore., Wash., Utah, Idaho, and s. B.C., Canada; in Great Plains, from and including Canadian provinces of Alta., Sask., Man., south to Mont., Wyo., N.D., S.D., w. Minn., and nw. Iowa; in Great Lakes area, in e. Wisc., e. Ind., w. Ohio, s. Ont., and n. N.Y.; there are also established populations in e. Canada on Prince Edward Is., s. N.B., and Nova Scotia (Johnsgard, 1973).

Partridge, Hungarian. *See* Partridge, gray.

Partridge, Indian hill. *See* Partridge, chukar.

Partridge, mountain. *See* Quail, mountain.

Partridge, rock, Common name of *Alectoris graeca,* the species introduced in early years in U.S. from Europe, which has since disappeared (see Johnsgard, 1973) and has been displaced by introduction of the chukar partridge, *Alectoris chukar.* For details see Watson (1962). *See* Partridge, chukar.

Partridge, swamp. *See* Grouse, spruce, in Grouse Family.

Partridge, Virginia. *See* Bobwhite.

Pheasant, China or Chinese, *See* Pheasant, ring-necked.

Pheasant, English. *See* Pheasant, ring-necked.

Pheasant, Mexican. Local name in Tex. for the chachalaca in Curassow Family.

Pheasant, ring-necked, *Phasianus colchicus* (fay-sih-AY-nus COL-kih-kus); genus name: from Gr. *phasianos,* of the river Phasis of the ancients in the country along the east coast of the Black Sea (Phasis now called the Rion, flows from the Caucasus to the Black Sea); species name: Lat. for Colchis (Kolchis), in Gr. mythology a province and city at the eastern end of the Black Sea on the river Phasis, from which the Greek Argonauts were said to have brought home the original pheasant stock to their own country; *ring-necked,* from the typical white ring, or collar, around the neck of the wild pheasant now dominant in N. America; *pheasant,* from Middle Eng. *fesant, fesaunt,* from Old Fr. *faisant* and Fr. and Sp. *faisan,* all from the original Gr. *phasianornis,* the bird of Phasis, or Phasian bird (see account in Austin, 1961). (Color ills., pages 706, 707.) See history of early introductions into U.S. beginning in Calif. in 1857, and releases of large numbers in Ore. in 1880s, in Austin (1961); Bent (1932); McAtee (1945); Palmer (1928). State bird of S.D.; now well established and a game bird in parts of s. Canada and across n. U.S. from New England west to Ore. and Calif.; sexes outwardly different, but both have stout, yellowish, chickenlike bill, short, rounded wings; adult male is large gamecocklike bird; 30–36 in. long, including long, folded, streaming and tapering, pointed tail, which may be fully 21 in. long; wingspread about 32 in.; head and neck iridescent green-blue or purple, separated from rest of body by conspicuous white collar; has bright patch of bare red skin on cheeks and about eyes, forming red wattles below eyes; iridescent feathers along sides of head are long and form an erectile double crest; can raise ear feathers (auriculars) on sides of head, perhaps to aid in hearing (*see* Ears and Hearing); tarsus (*see* Tarsus) short and strong with small spur, lacking in female; upperparts of body rich bronze and brown-red with brown, black, white markings; mottled brown hen, without white neck ring and bright colors of male, is 21–25 in. long, including pointed, yellow-brown tail of about 11–12 in.; ring-necks live mostly on cultivated farmland amid crops of corn, wheat, oats, barley, and hay, grasses and legumes (see Labiskey *et al.,* 1964), with hedges used by pheasants for cover and travel lanes; they roost in trees or on ground in weedy ditches, marshes, small cattail swales, weed-grown fence corners, brush heaps, brier patches, and in small farm woodlots; is swift flier, when flushed, male rises with loud metallic whir of wings and in flight utters loud, hoarse croaks, *cuck-et, cuck-et,* suggestive of clucks of old domestic hen; females utter a querulous *queep, queep, queep* of alarm; male, where hunted, instead of flying may run swiftly away under thick cover of grass or weeds; while running carries tail cocked up at 45° angle, can also fly almost silently; if hemmed in by trees or buildings, can shoot almost straight upward (Bent, 1932); is usually sedentary and ranges over no more than about 1–2 mi.; is fond of dust bathing (*see* under Bathing) in cornfields, bare spots in pastures, along dirt roads, and on entrance mounds of woodchuck burrows, in which ring-necks sometimes find shelter from storms in winter or escape into from pursuit of a hawk; in fall, families join with others and form flocks of up to 30–40; up to 400 noted in a flock in fall in Ohio; flocks break up and scatter in spring; hen at all seasons more gregarious than males; males are polygamous (*see* Sexual Relationships); in spring courtship, beginning in Feb. and Mar., male struts before female with raised feathers of the ear tufts on sides of head, bare skin about eyes engorged and brilliant red (see other details of courtship in Bent, 1932; McAtee, 1945); to attract females and announce territory, male, out in open, crows a bantamlike *KOCK-cack!* followed by loud clapping of wings; within his crowing area of a few acres, usually within part of open field and adjacent woods, hedge, or patch of brush, etc., which he uses for escape cover, male fights intruding males; fights last until one runs away or is completely exhausted and beaten; young males said to crow when only 7–8 weeks old (Bent, 1932); successfully established male, within his defended territory, copulates with two, three, or even four or more hens, which establish nest

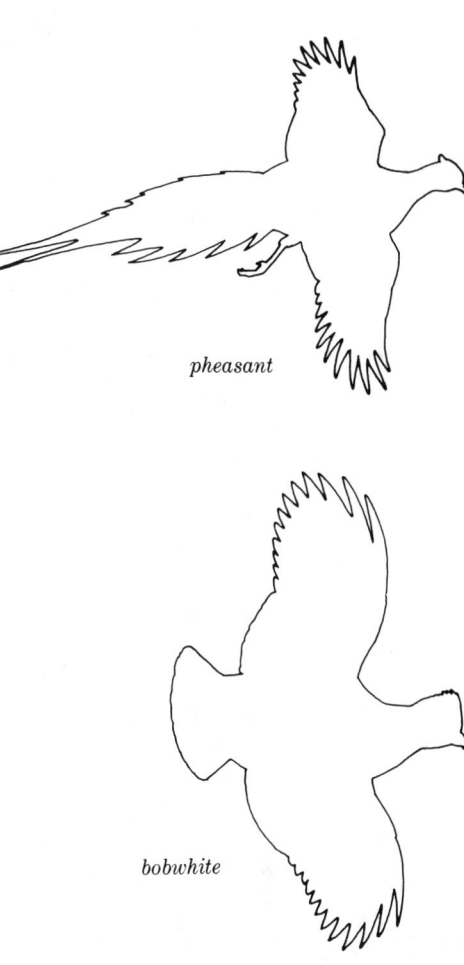

pheasant

bobwhite

PHEASANT FAMILY
In flight, the pheasant shows distinctively long, streaming tail feathers. The smaller, stouter bobwhite quail has a short, rounded tail and flies with wings downcurved.

sites within the male's crowing area. Edminster (1954) reported that in years of highest populations of pheasants in U.S., hunters kill 16–18 million, two thirds of which are killed in n. Great Plains.

Feeding Habits: Leave roost about daybreak and begin feeding about an hour after sunrise; eat mostly plant foods, largely waste corn, wheat, barley, oats, buckwheat, also weed seeds, especially ragweed, burdocks, etc., from cultivated and old fields, also eat acorns, pine seeds, and wild berries; eat green plant foods in spring, and cutworms, grasshoppers, crickets, potato beetles, caterpillars of gypsy and browntail moths, tent caterpillars, etc., also mice and snails; will come to feeding stations for corn or small grains spread on ground (*see also* discussion of use of grit under Calcium).

Nest: Usually on ground in a natural depression or a shallow one scratched out by female, and lined with bits of grasses or weeds; site is in fields of grass or grain, in brushy pastures, alongside hedges, roadsides, and ditches, sometimes in groups of 2–8 nests, each of these may be in crowing area of a single male (Leedy and Hicks in McAtee, 1945).

Eggs: Apr. into July–Aug.; 5–23, usually 10–12, dark green-buff or rich brown-olive; large clutches usually laid by two hens in same nest; hens also lay in nests of mallard, blue-winged teal, gray partridge, bobwhite, domestic hen and turkey, ruffed grouse and blue grouse, and woodcock (*see* Dump Nest; Obligate Parasite).

Incubation: Usually by female, 23–25 days, occasionally by cock; each season, one brood (Edminster, 1954); after hatching, chicks usually attended by female alone; when chicks about 35–42 days old, male may be with brood and hen to protect them—male in s. Pa. intimidated and drove away a red fox near hen and her nest and eggs (Ludwig, 1971); female often uses "crippled-bird act" to lure away predator or may fly noisily away while chicks scatter and hide; female hovers chicks during cold weather, in storms, and at night; helps them to find food (they feed themselves); chicks able to fly 4–5 ft. when only 7 days old.

Other Names: Chinese pheasant; English pheasant; ring-neck.

Accidents: Females sitting on nests in hayfields or grassy roadsides may be killed or have legs and feet cut off by mowing machines (one male survived with both feet cut off and was in good health when shot by a hunter (see "Everyday Hazards in the Lives of Birds" in Terres, 1960b); many killed by cars while crossing high-speed highways, others along railroad tracks by trains; others killed by flying against utility poles and wires, and farm fences; many die from diseases or parasites (*see* Nematode; Deformities).

Age: Life span in wild remarkably short; many young hatched in spring do not live beyond Oct. 1; average life span of males about 10 months; of females about 20 months; maximum age in wild about 8 years (Leedy and Hicks, in McAtee, 1945); one lived in National Zoo, Washington, D.C., for 6½ years.

Flight Speed: Timed in England, 27–38 m.p.h. (Anonymous, 1887); and 60 m.p.h. (Portal, 1922).

Hybrids: According to Gray (1958), in captivity has been crossbred and has produced hybrids with many other species of pheasants, also with grouse, domestic chicken, turkey, guinea fowl, capercaillie, etc.

Weights: Males average 2.7 lb.; females 2.1 lb.; large male in Valentine Refuge, Neb., of 4 lb.; a female, 3.2 lb. (Martin and Nelson, 1952).

Range: In N. America, resident from s. B.C. south through Wash., Ore., w. and s. Idaho, to lowlands of Calif., Utah, except in mountains and in desert; in Nev. and from s.-c. Alta., Sask., s. Man., Minn., Wisc., s. Mich., s. Ont., N.Y., s. Que., s. Vt., N.H., s.-c. Me., N.B., locally in Nova Scotia, south to n. Ariz., N.M., n. Tex., n.w. Okla., Kans., n. Mo., s. Ill., Ind., Ohio, and Pa., northern edge of Del., Md., and W.Va., also se. Ariz. and n. Baja Calif.; a population of 500–600 at Pea Island National Wildlife Refuge, N.C., said to have propagated from flock released there some years ago at Buxton, N.C., apparently the *only* successful introduction of ring-necked pheasants in the southern Atlantic coastal region (Teulings, 1973); native range in Asia from land between Black and Caspian seas, east to Manchuria, se. Siberia, Korea, s. China, Japan, and Formosa.

Quail, Arizona. *See* Quail, Gambel's.

Quail, black. *See* Quail, Montezuma.

Quail, blue. *See* Quail, scaled.

Quail, bobwhite. *See* Bobwhite.

Quail, California, *Lophortyx californicus* (low-FOR-ticks or lof-OR-ticks cal-ih-FOR-nih-cus); genus name: from Gr. *lophotos*, crested, and *ortyx*, quail; "crested quail"; species name: Lat., of California. (Color ill., page 708.) Originally native and resident along Pacific coast from s. Ore. to n. Baja Calif.; introduced into other parts of West—Nev., Idaho, Utah, Wash., etc.; state bird of Calif.; 9½–11 in. long; small, plump, gray chickenlike bird with a short black plume tilted forward from top of dark brown head; male has white stripe over eyes and across forehead and a black throat with a necklacelike border line of white (female lacks this black-and-white pattern of head and neck but otherwise resembles male); breast blue-gray; belly finely scaled (similar male Gambel's quail has black patch on plain buff belly) with broad white streaks on brown-gray flanks; upperparts of body gray to brown-gray; in s. Calif., a common dooryard bird; widespread in state but replaced in eastern parts of Colorado and Mojave deserts by the Gambel's quail; lives in coastal scrub, in broken chaparral, edges of woods, on farms, ranches, parks, estates, in foothills and valleys where low trees or tall shrubs have openings of weeds and grass with supply of water near by, such as streams, springs, irrigation ditches; is strongly gregarious, in fall gathers in coveys composed of families with adults; coveys well organized, with a sentinel watching from perch in a tree when covey is feeding (Bent, 1932); winter coveys vary from 10 to 200 in each (Edminster, 1954); roost at dusk in dense growth of trees or shrubs (not on ground as does bobwhite), about

15–25 ft. up, may all be in one tree or in several; when alarmed on ground, jumps into air in quick burst of flight, but not all at once as does covey of bobwhites, and each bird flies away in different direction; on alighting, runs at great speed; has an assembly call for regrouping members of scattered covey, sounds somewhat like that of bobwhite, a *ca-LOY-o, oh-HI-oh, ca-RO-ho,* or *key-CAR-go;* within winter coveys, males begin fighting each other in late Feb., then unobtrusively pair off with females, with coveys disbanded by late Apr.; male defends his mate against courting of other males but does not defend a nesting territory; the pairs are monogamous; pairs roost together, side by side on branch of tree; as a game bird has been hunted and killed in enormous numbers in Calif., in early years by market hunters (see details in Edminster, 1954), later by sportsmen.

Feeding Habits: Very regular, feeds about an hour or two after sunrise and an hour or two before sunset; travels in flocks at all times except in nesting season; will come to same good feeding place day after day; in hunting food, often travels long distances afoot; will not fly unless forced to; at one time came to watering places such as springs in enormous numbers but more recently in flocks of 50–60 (Bent, 1932); during day congregates near drinking places or rests in shade of trees or bushes; is mostly vegetarian; in winter eats leaves or other parts of chickweed, filaree, tips of grasses and buds in spring; also eats some insects—ants, beetles, bugs, caterpillars, grasshoppers, flies; also spiders and snails; during rest of year eats largely seeds of clovers, lupines, vetch, grasses, weeds, grains, acorns, and wild berries, grapes; also picks up grit to grind seeds (*see* Gizzard).

Nest: A slight hollow in ground, lined with grasses or leaves, may be well hidden under a bush, hedge, brush pile, beside log or rock, in thick clump of grass or weeds in orchard or vineyard or clump of cactus, even in cranny in rock; nest is often near a house or in a garden or beside a much-traveled road or path; sometimes builds nest in fork of tree branch and in vine-covered trellis to 10 ft. above ground (Bent, 1932).

Eggs: Calif., Jan.–Oct.; Wash. and B.C., May–July; usually 12–16 (more than 20 in same nest probably laid by two hens), cream-buff to ivory-yellow, well covered, or irregularly marked, with large blotches or minute dots of brown-gray; the hens sometimes lay their eggs in nests of the yellow-breasted chat and the roadrunner or sometimes drop eggs anywhere (*see* Dump Nest), and in nest of the rufous-sided towhee on ground and in nest 4 ft. above ground.

Incubation: Usually by female, alone, about 21–23 days; at hatching, chicks attended by both parents, with chicks hiding in thick underbrush; can fly short distance 10 days after hatching and at 14 days fly well but prefer to run to escape; are brooded on ground by adults for 28 days after hatching until they begin to roost in trees with parents (Edminster, 1954).

Other Names: California partridge; Catalina quail; helmet quail; top-knot quail; valley quail.

Accidents: Adults frequently killed by flying against fences, moving vehicles; some accidentally drown while drinking in stock watering tanks; others by poisons spread on ground for rodent control.

Age: One lived in National Zoo, Washington, D.C., for 9 years, 7 months; one, banded Berkeley, Calif., shot when 4 years, 9 months, old (Kennard, 1975); two males reached more than 6 years old in the wild (Leopold, 1977).

Flight Speed: Timed in Calif., 39, 51 m.p.h. and 38–58 m.p.h. (McLean, 1930).

Running Speed: Timed in Calif., 12 m.p.h. (Hunt, 1920).

Hybrids: Hybridizes occasionally with Gambel's quail where ranges overlap in s. Calif.; Gray (1958) also lists wild-taken hybrids of California quail × bobwhite, California quail × scaled quail, California quail × mountain quail.

Weights: Males average about 6¼ oz.; females slightly less; heaviest each, for both sexes, 7⅓ oz. (Martin and Nelson, 1952); along coastal Calif., adults (652) averaged 189.5 gr., or about 6¾ oz; the weights of 4 California subspecies increase toward the north (Leopold, 1977).

Range: Resident from s. Ore. and w. Nev. south to northern tip of Baja Calif.; introduced into s. B.C., Wash., Idaho, n. Ore., and Utah. See range map in Johnsgard (1973), and Leopold (1977).

Quail, Catalina. *See* Quail, California.

Quail, cotton-top. *See* Quail, scaled.

Quail, coturnix, Common name for a group of Old World quails of the genus *Coturnix,* of which the migratory quail, *Coturnix coturnix,* of Eurasia, is a small, mottled brownish bird, considerably smaller than the native N. American bobwhite. Because of the relative ease of breeding this species in captivity, numerous attempts were made to introduce it as a game bird into the U.S., but it did not become established. See other details in Austin (1961) and names and ranges of other *Coturnix* in Delacour (1964); Orcutt and Orcutt (1976).

Quail, desert. *See* Quail, Gambel's.

Quail, fool. Hunters' name for the Montezuma quail (formerly called the harlequin quail), from its habit of lying close when approached, and often running away rather than flying (Bent, 1932). *See* Quail, Montezuma.

Quail, Gambel's, *Lophortyx gambelii* (low-FOR-ticks gam-BELL-ih-eye); genus name; *see* Quail, California; species name: given by Thomas Nuttall in 1843 in honor of his protégé, William Gambel, an early field collector of birds in s. Calif. (Color ill., page 709.) Gambel's quail is resident of arid sw. U.S. and nw. Mexico; is generally limited to desert regions, which are usually avoided by the similar California quail; 9½–11 in. long; resembles California quail with its forward-tilted black plume, or crest, ending in a comma or teardrop shape, but male has *black patch in middle of pale belly,* which also lacks scaled appearance; crown more russet than that of California quail; female also lacks scaly belly pattern of California quail; male

Gambel's also has *black* forehead, not white as in California quail, and flanks of both sexes of Gambel's distinctly more rich red-brown (Johnsgard, 1973); lives in desert thickets, usually near water, with center of abundance in s. Ariz., where it lives in low river valleys with dense thickets of mesquite *(Acacia glandulosa),* which offer some shade, or in thickets of willows along streams and in dense forests of mesquite, hackberries, and other thorny trees and shrubs; usually requires permanent water of streams and water holes; especially fond of low tangled brush along creeks and close-growing chaparral of hills and mountain ravines. For other details of habitat, see Gullion (1960). Families join together in fall to form coveys of 12–24 or up to 40–50; very large groups usually associated at drinking places; in early morning, covey drops from roosting place in shrubs and low trees and travels afoot to nearby drinking place, then feeds for several hours if weather pleasant (Edminster, 1954); when foraging or moving, members of covey utter low chuckles or grunt like young pigs—*quoit, oit, woet;* also a "location" call uttered by a lone bird separated visually from its mate or from covey—a four-noted *chi-CA-go-go;* pairing is in late winter within coveys, which dissolve by Mar.; according to Edminster (1954), is most hunted game bird in Ariz. and parts of se. Calif., s. Nev., and sw. N.M.

Feeding Habits: Eats mostly same kinds of seeds and green plants as California quail; legumes are most important, with mesquite most used (seeds or beans), also grasses and grains as source of seeds and greens, eats fruits of cactuses: cholla, prickly pear, and barrel (see foods in Edminster, 1954).

Nest: A hollow scraped in ground at base of tall grass, mesquite bush, sage or other shrub, lined with grasses, sticks, feathers; occasionally hens lay eggs and incubate them in old nest of roadrunner; sometimes lay eggs in nests of thrashers and cactus wrens (Bent, 1932).

Eggs: Ariz., Mar.–Sept.; Calif., Mar.–June; 9–14, usually 10–12, occasionally to 20 (product of two hens); dull white to buff or pink-buff, irregularly blotched, spotted, or dotted with purples, browns.

Incubation: By female alone (male usually on guard on perch in tree or bush nearby), 21–23 days (will re-nest if first attempts broken up); when chicks hatch, family leaves nest site, not to return; as chicks move, are led by male with female at rear; one brood a season (Gorsuch, 1934).

Other Names: Arizona quail; desert quail; Gambel's valley quail.

Accidents: Some killed by flying against utility wires and moving vehicles; a few from flying into spines of cactuses; some drown while drinking from stock watering tanks on rangelands.

Age: One banded wild bird recaptured and released when 6 years, 5 months, old (Kennard, 1975).

Flight Speed: Timed in Calif., 41 m.p.h. (McLean, 1930).

Running Speed: Timed in Ariz., 14 m.p.h. (Cottam *et al.,* 1942b); in Calif., 15.5 m.p.h. (McLean, 1930).

Hybrids: See California quail.

Weights: Males average 6 oz.; heaviest, a male from Ariz., 7⅓ oz.; females average 5¾ oz.; heaviest, one from Ariz., 6⅞ oz. (Martin and Nelson, 1952).

Range: Resident from s. Nev., s. Utah, and w. Colo. south to ne. Baja Calif., and c. Sonora, nw. Chihuahua in Mexico, and in w. Tex.

Quail, harlequin. *See* Quail, Montezuma.

Quail, marsh. Another name for the eastern meadowlark in Troupial Family.

Quail, Massena. Local name in Tex. for the Montezuma (harlequin) quail.

Quail, Mearns' harlequin. *See* Quail, Montezuma.

Quail, Mexican. *See* Quail, scaled.

Quail, Montezuma, *Cyrtonyx montezumae* (SER-toe-nicks mon-teh-ZOO-me); genus name: from Gr. *kyrtos,* arched, curved, and *onyx,* nail, talon, or claw; in reference to the long, curved claws of this species which enable it to move with ease over the roughest, rockiest places; species name: Lat. form of Montezuma, last Aztec emperor of Mexico; named in Montezuma's honor in 1830 by N. A. Vigors, British zoologist. (Color ill., page 708.) U.S. and Mex.; 8–9½ in. long; sexes very different; male has beautiful facial pattern of black or blue-black and white (clownlike face) with soft tan crest extending back over neck (crest not always erected); blackish underparts with sides and flanks spotted with white, cinnamon, or brown; female, brown with less distinctive facial pattern; in w. Tex., a rare, local resident, lives in grassy oak canyons and on wooded mountain slopes with bunchgrass; in Ariz., ranges up sides of rocky ravines and into mountains up to 9,000 ft. in summer; moves about in pairs or in families, never far from oaks and pines; if alarmed, squats and sits motionless until almost stepped on, when rises in swift, direct flight; utters a soft quavering cry suggestive of screech owl's.

Feeding Habits: Scratches in ground for bulbs of chufa, or nut grass, and for other underground bulbs of plants, also eats acorns and seeds of legumes, grasses, pinyon pine, fruits of junipers, and insects such as beetles and caterpillars.

Nest: Female, sometimes helped by male, digs slight hollow in grassy ground, lines hollow with grasses; roofs over with grass.

Eggs: Apr.–Sept.; 6–14, usually 10–12, white.

Incubation: By both sexes (Bent, 1932), about 25–26 days (Johnsgard, 1973); chicks cared for by both parents; age at first flight unknown.

Other Names: Black quail; crazy quail; fool hen; fool quail; harlequin quail; Massena quail; Mearns' harlequin quail; Mearns' quail.

Weights: Males average 195 gr., females 176 gr. (Johnsgard, 1973).

Range: Resident from c. Ariz., c. N.M., to w. Tex., and south in Mexico to Oaxaca (Johnsgard, 1973).

Quail, mountain, *Oreortyx pictus* (or-ree-OR-ticks PICK-tus); genus name: from Gr. *oreos*, a mountain, and Lat. *ortyx*, a quail; species name: Lat., painted, of various colors. (Color ill., page 711.) Largest and handsomest of the native N. American quail; w. U.S., Nev. and Idaho west to Wash. and Calif.; 10½–11½ in. long; gray-brown quail of mountains, distinguished from California quail by a long straight head plume; chestnut sides have broad white stripes; female similar but with slightly duller colors and a shorter plume; lives in dense brush of mountains and edges of coniferous forests, around edges of mountain meadows, and in open forests and logged or burned-over forests; during nesting season lives at 1,500–2,000 ft. elevation up to 9,500 or 10,000 ft. (Johnsgard, 1973); in late summer and early fall, moves downward from mountains on foot, sometimes a distance of 20–40 mi., but sometimes will fly across canyons; coveys are small, 3–20 birds in each; are cautious, remain in dense cover when disturbed; are swift runners and usually escape by running away under dense cover even on steepest slopes; coveys roost on ground or in low bushes; sometimes several thousand may gather in summer at a large spring to drink; in Calif., mating begins in Mar. or early Apr. with pairing within coveys; unmated males utter a clear whistle from prominent stump, rock, etc.—*quee-ark, kyork,* or *queerk*—that may be heard up to mile away, other calls are a rapid, sweet *took-took-took-took-took* resembling "singing" of a domestic hen.

Feeding Habits: In spring and summer, eats mostly leaves, buds, and flowers of clovers, lupines, and other legumes, and underground bulbs of plants, also some grasshoppers, beetles, ants; and rest of year, eats seeds of sumac, grasses, hawthorn, pines, sweet clover, thistles, ragweeds, also fruits of hackberry, serviceberry, grapes, manzanitas, elder, etc., and acorns and seeds of pines (Johnsgard, 1973).
Nest: Usually well concealed, a slight depression scratched out in ground at base of bush, log, rock, or among ferns, tufts of grass, under shrubs, fallen branch of pine, at base of large tree; lined with a few dry leaves, pine needles, grasses (Bent, 1932); nests are often near paths or roads and always near water (Johnsgard, 1973).
Eggs: Mar.–June; 6–15, usually 9–10, cream to red-buff, unspotted.
Incubation: By female, sometimes by male, 24–25 days; one brood; young fly about 14 days after hatching.
Other Names: Mountain partridge; painted quail; plumed partridge; plumed quail.
Running Speed: Timed in Calif., 12 m.p.h. (Hunt, 1920).
Hybrids: See California quail.
Weights: Average for both males and females, 8¼ oz.; one male in Calif. reported at 10¼ oz. (Martin and Nelson, 1952).
Range: Resident of Coast Ranges from s. Vancouver Is., B.C., south to n. Baja Calif., and in Sierra Nevada and other ranges of Calif. and e. Nev.; introduced and established in se. Wash., e. Ore., w. Idaho, and c. Nev.; introduced but apparently unsuccessful in w. Colo.

Quail, painted. *See* Quail, mountain.

Quail, plumed. *See* Quail, Mountain.

Quail, scaled, *Callipepla squamata* (cal-ih-PEP-lah skway-MAY-tah); genus name: from Gr. *kallos*, beautiful, and *peplos*, a ceremonial robe; "beautifully adorned," in reference to this bird's plumage; species name: Lat., scaly, for scaled appearance of feathers. (Color ill., page 710.) Mexican species that reaches northern limit of its natural range in s. Colo.; 10–12 in. long; gray-backed, scaled below, has prominent bushy crest with "cotton" top; white-topped crest often visible from some distance and general gray coloration of this bird distinguish it from other quails of arid country where it lives; however, young are quite rufous; lives as resident on the elevated, high plateau country that extends north from Mexico into s. Ariz., N.M., and w. Tex.; much of it dry and barren except for scattered creosote bushes, dwarf sagebrush, stunted mesquite, and various cactuses and yuccas; shuns timbered country, lives on mesas between the mountain ranges and at mouths of canyons where underground streams supply some moisture; seldom flies but prefers to run from one to another of dense patches of thorny shrubs; is most abundant among weeds, grasses of dry washes and river valleys; makes daily trips to supply of water; becomes tame around farms and ranches with water available; numbers fluctuate widely and is adversely affected either by drought or by heavy rains (Pough, 1951); in winter, gathers in fairly large flocks of up to 100 or more birds; but coveys consist of 7–150 birds, with average of about 30 in winter, and ranging over 24 to about 84 acres; breakup of winter coveys begins from about Mar. 1 to Apr. 15; best-known call is the "location" call in which members of a pair or of a covey, separated, give a nasal, long-drawn whistle sounding like *pe-COS* or *pey-COS;* unmated males utter a single, slightly nasal whistle, *whock* or *kwook* (see in Johnsgard, 1973, and Anderson, 1978).

Feeding Habits: Eats many insects, also seeds of plants such as elbowbrush *(Forestiera),* catclaw *(Acacia),* mesquite and hackberry, also seeds of weeds such as Russian thistle, pigweed, sunflowers, ragweeds. See details in Kelso (1937); Johnsgard (1973).
Nest: In slight hollow scraped out by female, lined with dry grasses and a few feathers; built at base of tuft of grass or under low bush, sometimes in hayfield or grain field.
Eggs: Tex. and Mexico, Mar.–June; Ariz. and N.M., Apr.–Sept.; 9–16, usually 12–14, dull white to cream-white, some thickly speckled with small spots or dots of light brown.
Incubation: By female, sometimes by male, 22–23 days.
Other Names: Blue quail; cotton-top; cotton-top quail; Mexican quail; scaled partridge; topknot quail.
Hybrids: See Quail, California.
Weights: Average of both sexes about 6⅞ oz.; one heavy Okla. male, 8¼ oz. (Martin and Nelson, 1952).

PARROT FAMILY

Budgerigar
This Australian parakeet, a popular cage bird, now has a place on the list of North American birds because it has become established as a free-living species in southern Florida, where it is most numerous in the region around St. Petersburg. Unlike many such introduced species, it is flourishing and extending its range, and there are fears that it may become a pest in agricultural areas.

Budgerigar

Monk parakeet
During the 1960s and 1970s monk parakeets escaped from captivity and began nesting in the wild in parts of eastern North America. For a time, it appeared that this bird might become numerous enough to begin ravaging crops, as it does in its native Argentina, but for unknown reasons the species has failed to take hold and will probably soon disappear.

Orange-fronted parakeet
Native to open woodlands and light forests along rivers in southern Mexico and Central America, the orange-fronted parakeet has established itself in the warmer parts of Florida and southern California. In the United States, these birds are usually seen in small flocks feeding on seeds, berries, and flowers.

Rose-ringed parakeet
Originally a bird of light woodlands in the Old World tropics, the rose-ringed parakeet long ago adapted to the presence of man and now nests in large numbers in agricultural areas and even in cities in Africa and in parts of southern Asia. Thus, it is hardly surprising that the birds succeeded when they were accidentally introduced into the warmer parts of the United States. They have nested successfully in Florida, Virginia, and California and may soon become as well entrenched as the budgerigar.

Thick-billed parrot
This Mexican parrot feeds on pine seeds, which it extracts from the cones with its stout bill. It formerly appeared in great flocks in southern Arizona when the cone crop in its native mountains failed. The last time this happened was in the winter of 1917–18, when large numbers arrived to feed on the seeds of ponderosa pines. Although a few were seen as late as 1936, there will probably never be such an invasion of the species again, because much of the pine forest in northern Mexico has been cleared, and the normal range of these parrots is now far from our borders.

Thick-billed parrot

Orange-fronted parakeet

Monk parakeet

Rose-ringed parakeet

PELICAN FAMILY

Brown pelican

The brown pelican is the only exclusively marine member of the pelican family, and the only one that regularly dives for its food. Although it nests on the Atlantic coast from North Carolina to Venezuela, and on the Pacific from southern California to Chile, its numbers are steadily decreasing. Pesticides in water running off farmlands have caused the eggs to become thin-shelled and fragile, and this has resulted in the failure of whole colonies.

Brown pelican

Brown pelican

Brown pelican

Brown pelican

Brown pelican

White pelican
One of the most magnificent water birds of North America, the white pelican nests in colonies on inland lakes from British Columbia and Saskatchewan south to California and east to Minnesota. Pelicans often engage in cooperative fishing; a long line of swimming birds gradually surrounds a school of fish and then gathers into a closely knit bunch, scooping the fish out of the water with their pouches.

White pelican

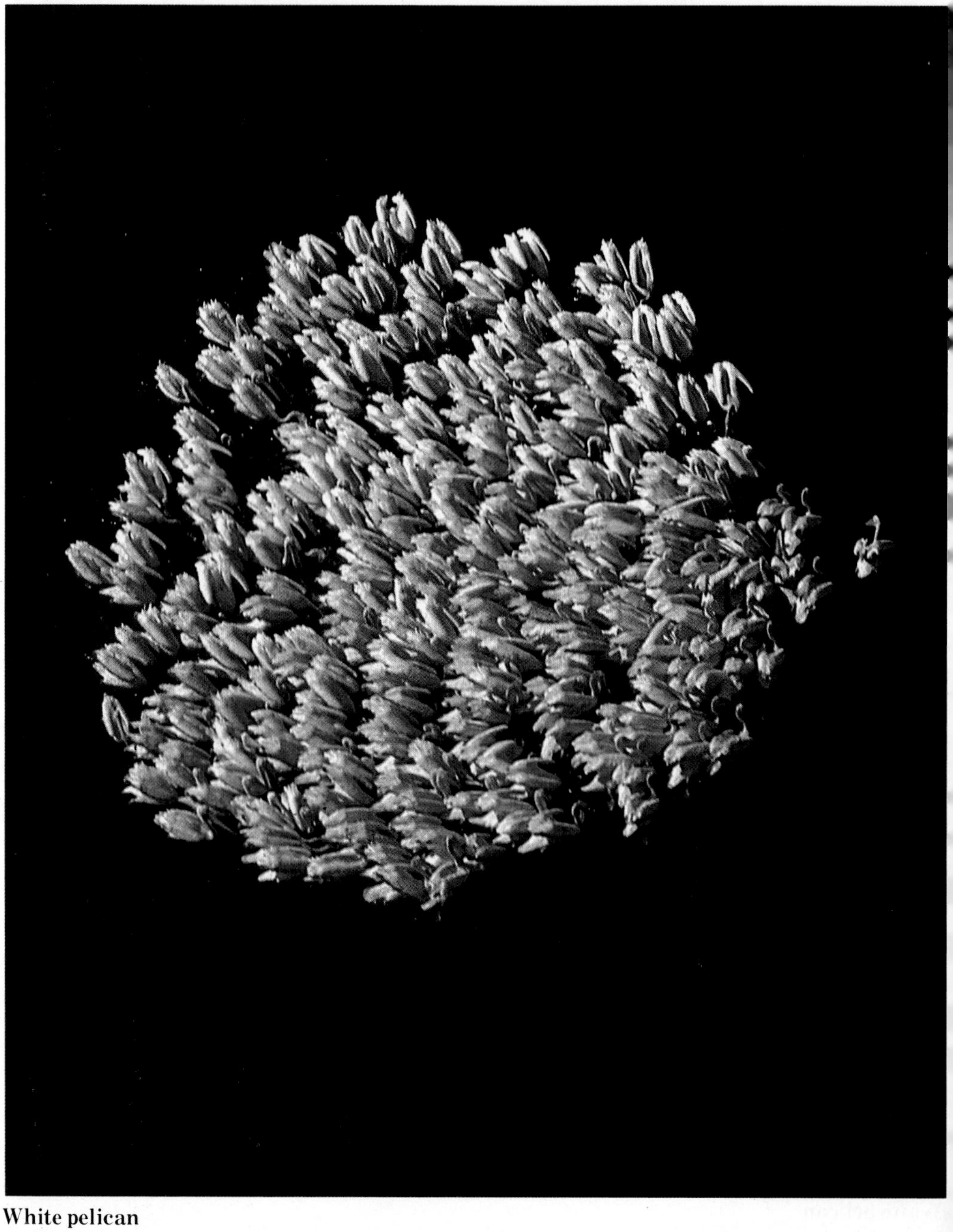

White pelican

White pelican

White pelican

White pelican

PHALAROPE FAMILY

Northern phalarope

Phalaropes are unusual among birds in that the females are more brightly colored than the males, which incubate the eggs and care for the young. At the end of the breeding season, northern phalaropes leave their breeding grounds in the Arctic tundra and spend the winter on the oceans of the Southern Hemisphere, where they feed on swimming crustaceans and other planktonic organisms.

Red phalarope

The red phalarope is the most marine of the 3 members of its family, spending the bulk of the year at sea feeding in immense flocks on jellyfish, crustaceans, and small fish. These flocks sometimes gather around pods of whales, eagerly consuming scraps of food left by the great sea mammals.

Wilson's phalarope

This elegant shorebird nests on marshes in the interior of western North America and winters on the plains and pampas of southern South America. Like the red and northern phalaropes, its sex roles are reversed and it is a capable swimmer. Unlike the other two species, however, the Wilson's phalarope does not feed at sea and is often seen sprinting about on a mudflat like a typical sandpiper.

Northern phalarope

Red phalarope

Wilson's phalarope

Northern phalarope, immature

Northern phalarope, female

Red phalarope, winter

Red phalarope, female

Wilson's phalarope, fall

Wilson's phalarope, female

PHEASANT FAMILY

Bobwhite

This familiar game bird, an inhabitant of meadows, pastures, and brushy fencerows, lays a clutch of as many as a dozen eggs and is usually abundant where conditions are favorable. But bobwhites are sensitive to severe winter weather; whole populations may be wiped out by hard freezes accompanied by heavy snows.

Chukar

The chukar is a stocky partridge introduced into North America from the arid rocky deserts of India and Turkey. In its new home in the western United States, it favors dry rocky hillsides, especially where there is a good growth of cheatgrass, whose seeds and leaves are a major part of its diet.

Bobwhite, male and female

Chukar

Bobwhite, chick

Chukar

Gray partridge
*Like the chukar, the gray partridge
is an introduced species. It has been
most successful in the farmlands of the
Midwest, where conditions resemble those
of its native Europe. Even in areas where
little natural cover remains, it manages
to maintain itself, no doubt in part
because it produces as many as 20 eggs
in a single clutch.*

Ring-necked pheasant
*Another introduced game bird, the
familiar ring-neck was first established in
Oregon in the 1880s. It must have found
its new home to its liking, for a mere
decade later 50,000 birds were reported
to have been shot in a single day. Since
then it has become one of the most widely
distributed and popular birds among
sportsmen, not only in the Great Plains,
where thousands are shot annually, but in
the more built-up parts of the Northeast.*

Gray partridge

Ring-necked pheasant, nestlings and eggs

Ring-necked pheasant, female

Ring-necked pheasant

California quail

The California quail, its curiously curled topknot made famous by Walt Disney, is a resident of agricultural areas and rangeland along the Pacific coast, where it feeds on the seeds of clover, lupine, and other herbs. At the end of the breeding season, family groups gather into large coveys. Where not molested, they often enter suburban areas and may be seen feeding unconcernedly on lawns.

Gambel's quail

The cheerful 3-noted call of the male Gambel's quail is not only a characteristic sound of the southwestern deserts: in the soundtracks of Western movies, it may now be heard from coast to coast.

Montezuma quail

The handsome Montezuma quail is found in pine-oak forest in the desert mountain ranges of Arizona, New Mexico, and Texas, and in much of Mexico. It is most numerous where there is an abundance of small lilies and grasses, whose bulbs are an important part of its winter diet. When startled, these stocky game birds usually crouch low and scurry away like small mammals, rather than flying off abruptly as other quails do.

Mountain quail

While the young of most American quails eat many insects, those of the mountain quail have the same diet as the adults, consuming berries, buds, and weed seeds in forest clearings in the mountains along the Pacific coast from Vancouver Island to northern Baja California.

Scaled quail

The "cotton-top," as it is known to hunters, is an inhabitant of the brushy deserts of the Southwest. Winter coveys, numbering as many as 150 birds, begin to break up in early spring, when males go off to establish nesting territories. The breeding success of this species is closely tuned to the amount of rainfall; in very dry years the birds may not nest at all.

California quail

Scaled quail

Montezuma quail

Mountain quail

Gambel's quail

PIGEON FAMILY

Ground dove
The ground dove is well named, for it not only feeds on the ground, but nests there as well, concealing its 2 white eggs in a flimsy nest of twigs and grass under a bush or in a clump of grass. It is a shy and inconspicuous bird, locally distributed in the southern part of the United States.

Inca dove
To the early settlers in the Southwest crossing the desert in search of water, the melancholy, monotonous call of the Inca dove sounded like the words "no hope," endlessly and ominously repeated. Today this slender, long-tailed dove is a common resident of gardens and suburban areas, cactus-covered slopes, and mesquite thickets.

Key West quail dove
This bird was named by Audubon, who found it at Key West in the early 19th century. However, it is only a casual visitor to southern Florida from the West Indies, where it feeds on the ground in woodland clearings and along roads.

Mourning dove
Although it lays only 2 eggs in a clutch, the mourning dove raises many broods in a season and has been found nesting in every month of the year in many parts of the United States. It is our most abundant and widespread dove, a protected "songbird" in some states and an esteemed game bird in others.

Ringed turtle dove
A popular cagebird descended from an African species, the ringed turtle dove has established itself as a free-living bird in downtown Los Angeles.

Mourning dove

Ground dove

Inca dove

Key West quail dove

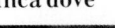

Ringed turtle dove

Rock dove
The wild rock dove nests on cliffs in Eurasia and North Africa. Its semi-domesticated descendant, the so-called pigeon, has found buildings sufficiently like the ancestral habitat to have become one of the most abundant birds in our cities. Their numbers are much greater than they would be if they were not fed by well-meaning citizens.

Spotted dove
The spotted dove is native to Southeast Asia, and has been introduced in southern California, where it is more widespread than the ringed turtle dove. It is a bird of gardens and residential areas in its new home.

White-fronted dove
A tropical species that reaches the northern limit of its range along the Rio Grande, the white-fronted dove is usually found alone or in pairs, feeding quietly on the ground in open woodlands and riverside thickets.

White-winged dove
One of our more gregarious doves, the white-wing nests in colonies, often very large, and like many fruit-eating birds feeds in flocks. It is a popular game bird in the deserts of the Southwest.

Band-tailed pigeon
Primarily a bird of coniferous forests, the band-tailed pigeon visits oak forests in the fall to feed heavily on acorns. Unlike most members of its family, it lays only 1 egg in a clutch, instead of the usual 2.

White-crowned pigeon
This handsome West Indian pigeon is a summer visitor to southern Florida, where it nests in colonies in mangrove swamps on wooded keys. Travelers on the highway to Key West often see flocks flying overhead moving from one feeding area to another.

Rock dove

Spotted dove

White-fronted dove

Band-tailed pigeon

White-winged dove

White-crowned pigeon

White-crowned pigeon

PIPIT FAMILY

Meadow pipit
This Eurasian pipit is an accidental visitor to North America. In the Old World it breeds in open fields and on dunes, and winters in flocks in marshes and moist grasslands.

Red-throated pipit
Nearly every fall in recent years, a few of these attractive Eurasian pipits have been found in open country in southern California. Evidently a single flock has established regular wintering grounds in the Western Hemisphere.

Water pipit
On its breeding grounds in Arctic and alpine tundra in North America and Eurasia, the water pipit has a spectacular display flight. After flying straight into the air as high as 150 or 200 feet, it flutters back down again, singing excitedly. In summer it feeds mainly on insects, while in winter, when it is common in much of North America, it is a seed eater.

Yellow wagtail
Yellow wagtails often gather for the night in large communal roosts, scattering over the surrounding countryside to feed during the day. In North America it is found only in Alaska and the northern Yukon, but it also nests throughout Eurasia.

Water pipit

Red-throated pipit

Water pipit, eggs

Meadow pipit

Yellow wagtail

PLOVER FAMILY

Killdeer
This familiar plover is common in agricultural areas and open country generally. It raises 1 or 2 broods a year, placing its 4 eggs on the ground in a shallow depression. The young leave the nest soon after hatching, and run about with the adults in search of small insects. If a predator appears, the adults engage in a display known as "injury feigning," leading the intruder away from the helpless chicks.

Lapwing
In December 1927, during a severe cold spell in Europe, large flocks of lapwings were caught in a storm and carried far out over the Atlantic. Hundreds of birds were blown all the way to the east coast of North America, where they arrived in an exhausted and starved condition in Newfoundland, Nova Scotia, New Brunswick, and Maine. Many of them were killed for food, and others died of starvation or froze to death; it is unlikely that any survived more than a few days.

American golden plover
This striking shorebird is a champion long-distance migrant, nesting in the Arctic and spending the winter on the pampas of Argentina and on islands in the South Pacific. In the fall, large flocks fly nonstop from southeastern Canada to northern South America, but a few appear along the Atlantic coast of the United States. In the spring, the bulk of the population travels northward over the Great Plains.

Black-bellied plover
The black-bellied plover is one of our wariest shorebirds. When a mixed flock of sandpipers and plovers is feeding on a beach or at a pool in a marsh, the black-bellies are often the first to spot an intruder, raising their heads and uttering a soft alarm note that causes the whole flock to take wing.

Killdeer

Killdeer, eggs

Killdeer, chick

Killdeer

American golden plover, winter

Black-bellied plover, winter

American golden plover

Black-bellied plover

Lapwing

Mountain plover

Most plovers, when an intruder approaches their nest, slip quietly off the eggs, run a short distance, and then spring noisily into the air, so that the exact location of the nest remains a secret. The mountain plover, a dull-colored bird of the short-grass plains, waits until the last minute and "explodes" into the air. This was probably a useful adaptation in the days when bisons roamed the plains, as it prevented these ponderous animals from stepping on the eggs.

Piping plover

Named for its melodious call-note, the piping plover is a bird of sandy beaches, both on the Great Lakes and along the Atlantic coast from Newfoundland to the Carolinas. So well does the bird's pale color match its background that even when one hears a piping plover calling close by, it is often impossible to spot it unless it moves or takes to the air.

Ringed plover

The ringed plover is a Eurasian shorebird that now breeds on Ellesmere and Baffin islands and elsewhere in the American Arctic. These birds reveal their Old World origins in the fall, when they migrate back to their ancestral wintering grounds in southern Eurasia and Africa.

Mountain plover

Piping plover

Ringed plover

Semipalmated plover
Semipalmated plovers, so named because of the partial webbing between their toes, are common migrants on American beaches and lakeshores. As in many plovers and sandpipers, many nonbreeding birds remain in the United States, far south of the Arctic nesting grounds, during the summer.

Snowy plover
This small plover is found in much of the Western Hemisphere and across Eurasia, where its pale coloration provides effective camouflage on the bright sandy beaches and sun-bleached salt flats that are the species' preferred habitat. The North American population nests along the Gulf coast and on salt plains in the interior of the western United States. In this stark habitat the birds can find food all year and so do not perform the long migrations of other plovers.

Wilson's plover
The large bill of Wilson's plover is probably an adaptation for eating fiddler crabs, an important food item. These birds nest in loose colonies on sandy beaches from New Jersey to Venezuela and from Mexico to Peru.

Wilson's plover

Semipalmated plover

Snowy plover

Snowy plover

RAIL FAMILY

American coot
Coots are stocky members of the rail family that have lobed toes and are adapted for swimming rather than for sneaking through marsh vegetation as most of our rails do. They feed by tipping, like mallards, or by diving for succulent marsh plants, snails, and small crustaceans. At times they leave the water and graze in meadows like geese.

Common gallinule
The common gallinule inhabits North and South America, Eurasia, and Africa, and is represented in Australia by an allied species. Like most other rails, it is a bird of marshlands, but it is equally at home on small ponds and in adjacent meadows. Up to a dozen eggs are laid in a nest concealed in marsh vegetation; the young leave the nest soon after hatching and move about with the adults, feeding on a variety of small animals and seeds.

Purple gallinule
This strikingly colored bird of our southeastern swamps uses its long toes to walk on the surface of lily pads, an adaptation that enables it to make use of a habitat accessible to few other birds. It eats a variety of food items, both animal and vegetable, and has even been seen climbing in bushes and small trees, grasping fruit in its feet and eating it like a parrot.

American coot

Common gallinule

American coot

Purple gallinule

Black rail

Almost as little known as the yellow rail, the black rail nests in salt marshes on the Atlantic and Pacific coasts and in grassy marshes in the Midwest. Although seldom seen, these skulking marsh birds reveal their presence by the piping call of the males, which may be heard for as much as a mile on a still spring night.

Clapper rail

The clapper rail, named for its rattling call, is a dull-colored bird of salt marshes, most often seen when it flushes from the dense Spartina grass, flies clumsily for a few yards, its legs dangling and its head held awkwardly above the level of its body, and then drops back out of sight. Although the clapper rail disappears when salt marshes are drained, it is still a familiar bird on the Atlantic coast from Connecticut southward and in southern California.

King rail

The richly colored king rail is a freshwater relative of the clapper rail. In a few places, where freshwater marshes adjoin coastal salt meadows, the two birds interbreed, prompting some authorities to consider them a single species.

Virginia rail

This retiring marsh bird nests throughout the warmer parts of North America, laying as many as a dozen eggs in a well-woven nest of cattail leaves or rushes attached to surrounding marsh plants. From time to time one may see an adult skulking through the reeds, accompanied by a brood of tiny all-black chicks.

Yellow rail

So secretive is this small inhabitant of grassy marshes that its call notes are still poorly known. More than once in the history of ornithology in North America some unfamiliar call, given by a rail hidden in a marsh, has been attributed to the yellow rail, only to prove on closer approach to have been uttered by a Virginia rail or sora.

Yellow rail

Clapper rail

King rail

Black rail

Virginia rail, chick

Virginia rail, eggs

Virginia rail

Sora

Sora

Soras nest in freshwater marshes from the interior of Canada southward throughout all but the southeastern part of the United States. They are common during migration and abundant on the wintering grounds along the Gulf coast, in the Southwest, and in Mexico and Central America. Although often hard to see, like other rails, they may at times be surprisingly tame, walking about in full view and approaching an observer who imitates their piping calls.

Range: Permanent resident from s. Ariz., n. N.M., e. Colo., and sw. Kans., w. Okla., south to c. Mexico; successfully introduced into c. Wash. and e. Nev. (Johnsgard, 1973).

Quail, sea. *See* Turnstone, ruddy, in Sandpiper Family.

Quail, snow. *See* Ptarmigan, white-tailed, in Grouse Family.

Quail, top-knot. *See* Quail, California, and Quail, scaled.

Quail, valley. *See* Quail, California.

Quail, white. *See* Ptarmigan, white-tailed, in Grouse Family.

PHOEBE
See in Flycatcher—Tyrant Flycatcher Family.

PHOENICOPTERIDAE
See Flamingo Family.

PHORESY
(FOR-ee-sih); from Gr. *phoresis*, being borne, or carried. A form of behavior, especially of certain parasitic insects which attach themselves to birds and other animals that are not host animals but serve as carriers to other parasitic insects, for example, and are thus carried to new hosts. *See* Hippoboscid Flies; *also* Lice; Parasite.

PHOTOGRAPHY
See Birder.

PHOTOPERIODISM
See Light.

PHYLOGENETIC (fie-low-jee-NET-ik)
RELATIONSHIP
Term of taxonomists in reference to the racial descent (or ascent) of birds, or their ancestral relationships. In classifying birds (*see* Classification), scientists of today usually rank them phylogenetically—from the most primitive, or "lowest," to the "highest," or the most recent. *See* Check-list Order.

Animals were once classified in groups, for convenience, based on many different considerations of their so-called similarities; once, upon their similar modes of life. According to Mayr *et al.* (1953), Pliny, for example, grouped apart those animals whose way of life was either on land, in water, or in the air; others grouped flying mammals (bats) with flying birds; the whales (mammals) with fishes; and all long-bodied invertebrate (*see* invertebrate under Vertebrate) animals simply as "worms."

Many of the early naturalists of the Linnaean period (*see* Linnaeus) grouped animals according to their similar adaptive structures (*see* Convergent Evolution)—that is, those birds (often unrelated) that had in common webbed feet or long legs and lived in or around water; the hawks of our present-day Falconiformes with the owls of the order Strigiformes because both had in common hooked bills, taloned feet, and carnivorous feeding habits. *See* Analogous.

Aristotle (*see* Classification) was the first to recognize that the most practical way to classify animals was to group them according to their anatomy (*see* Anatomy) or their closeness of form (*see* Morphology) and structure, without regard for function. Such a system has the advantage of being based on the total of many similarities and differences and therefore is more effective in grouping animals according to their natural affinities (Mayr *et al.*, 1953). See, however, Thomson (1964b).

The theory of evolution (*see* Evolution) brought further agreement on the naturalness of grouping animals in a system in which their similarity of form usually was shown to be the result of similarities of relationships (*see* Homologous under Analogous). Further, according to Mayr *et al.* (1953), "the more closely two animals are related, the more morphological characters they will usually have in common."

Although modern zoological classification of animals, including birds, is based upon phylogeny, classification and phylogeny are not always identical. Phylogeny is the actual evolutionary history of animals (Van Tyne and Berger, 1959); classification, by orders, families, genera, subspecies, is an artificial arrangement (*see* discussion under Classification), or man's attempt, through interpretation of available information about extinct and living birds, to reconstruct their phylogeny. *See* Monophyletic Descent.

PHYSIOLOGY
The science of bodily function. The study of the functions of organs, tissues, and other parts of the body. *See* examples of physiology in Metabolism; Temperature; Circulatory System; Brain; Nervous System; Endocrine Glands; Respiratory System; Fertilization; Urogenital System; Eggs and Egg-Laying; Eyes and Eyesight; Ears and Hearing; Smell; Taste; Touch. For reference see Darling and Darling (1962); Sturkie (1954; 1965).

PICID
(PIE-sid). Shortened name for any member of the Woodpecker Family (Picidae).

PICIDAE
See Woodpecker Family.

PICIFORMES
(PIS-ih-for-meez); from Lat. *picus*, a woodpecker, and *forma*, form; woodpeckerlike (Coble, 1954). An order or group of birds (*see* Order) of 375 species (Van Tyne and Berger, 1959), distinguished by their zygodactylous feet, which also distinguish the unrelated trogons, parrots, and cuckoos. *See* Feet and Legs; *also* Convergent Evolution.

The outer of the three front toes in most Piciformes is reversed, which gives the birds two toes forward and two behind. Woodpeckers, for example, in the Piciformes, are distinguished from songbirds (order Passeriformes) by their zygodactyl, or yoke-toed, feet. Only 1 family of the Piciformes—the Woodpecker Family—has representatives in N. America. See Woodpecker Family. All the Piciformes are predominantly tree dwellers.

woodpecker

PICIFORMES

There are 6 families in the Piciformes (Austin, 1961; Gilliard, 1958): the tropical American forest-dwelling jacamars (family Galbulidae) and puffbirds (family Bucconidae); the barbets (Capitonidae), which live in the tropical forests of both the New and the Old World; the brightly colored C. and S. American toucans (Ramphastidae), with their large colorful bills; the honey guides (Indicatoridae) of Africa, s. Asia, and Malaysia; and the woodpeckers, wrynecks, and piculets (Picidae). The wrynecks are small, 6-in.-long, drably colored birds of Eurasia, Africa, and Japan, named for their habit of twisting their necks in odd contortions (*see* discussion of them under Tongue); the piculets resemble the woodpeckers, but are smaller with a short tail, most species are in the tropical forests of America, but three species in se. Asia, one species in Africa.

The toucans and barbets are largely fruit-eaters; the jacamars and puffbirds eat flying insects; the woodpeckers drill in the bark of either living or dead trees for insects, and the sapsuckers (Woodpecker Family) also eat sap. *See* Woodpecker Family and discussion under Commensalism.

The honey guides are said to be unique among birds in eating beeswax (see Cerophagy), and the greater African honey guide has such a passion for it that native hunters through the ages have learned to follow the bird as it leads them to the wild hive—a practice for which it has been named.

In the more primitive parts of Africa, natives revere and protect these birds that guide them to the bees' stores of wild honey (Gilliard, 1958). *See* under Autolycism. The honey guides are one of the five bird families of the world that practice brood parasitism. *See* Brood Parasitism; see also details about this family in Friedmann (1955).

PICKET-TAIL
See Pintail in Duck Family.

PICULET
See Piciformes.

PIGEON FAMILY
Columbidae (coh-LUM-bih-dee); from Lat. *columba*, a dove or pigeon; *pigeon* (PIDGE-un), from Old Fr. *pijon*, Ital. *piccione* and *pipione*, a young piping or chirping bird, from *pipire*, to pipe or peep, imitative of the piping cries of nestling birds; *dove*, from Dutch *duyve*, Danish *due*, Icelandic *dufa*, became, in Middle Eng., *dove*, a name generally applied in the family to the smaller species with pointed tails; *pigeon*, for the larger species with square or rounded tails (Austin, 1961); however, there is no technical distinction between doves and pigeons and there are no strict rules of usage—the names are often used interchangeably; however, the preferred common names in the bird biographies that follow are in general well established. About 295 species in the world except in north and south polar regions and on some oceanic islands; small to medium (6–33 in. long); largest is 33-in. crowned pigeon, *Goura cristata*, of New Guinea; among smallest is the 6-in. N. American common ground dove; 17 species reported on N. American continent, including the extinct passenger pigeon and the introduced rock dove, or common domestic pigeon, the ringed turtle dove, and the spotted dove; family thought to be related to the extinct flightless dodo (*see* Columbiformes); all are plump with broad shoulders, rather short necks, small heads, and short, slender, rounded bills, which, in most, thicken toward hard tip and thinner in middle with waxy-appearing cere at base of upper mandible, in which slitlike nostrils open; most members of the family are sleek with soft, thick plumage of many colors; many have barred or "scaled" feather patterns and most have some metallic or iridescent, glossy feathers (there is no seasonal change in plumage color, and in most species sexes are outwardly alike, except female colors are duller); unless iridescent, plumage has dry, powdery appearance which may be correlated with lack of an oil gland in some species; the strong-shafted feathers are so loosely attached to the skin that the feathers drop out very easily, perhaps as protection against being caught in grasp of hawks or other predators; wings are pointed and short (in ground-dwelling species) to long, with 11 primary (flight) feathers, of which 10 are functional (Sutton, 1967b); they are strong fliers and the common pigeon is among swiftest of birds (*see* Speed of Flight under Flight); many are migratory or partly so; the tail, with 12–20 rectrices, may be medium or long, pointed or square; legs mostly short, sturdy feet have four toes; walk with mincing gait and bobbing head; utter coos, hisses, grunts, and whistles; may live from scrub deserts to woodlands; some are gregarious, others solitary (Reilly, 1968); males court by strutting before females with feathers raised or spread and some include a loud, wing-clapping display; when hatched, young are sparsely downy, eyes not open; thrust bills into parents' mouths to eat regurgitated food; for first few days, young, which are virtually helpless throughout fledgling life, are fed pigeon milk by both adults (*see* Crop); all in family have unusual habit among birds of immersing bill and sucking up water as a horse drinks. *See* Swallowing.

According to Gross (1965a), there are N. American records of albinism reported in only five individuals of two species; albinism apparently very rare in wild pigeons and doves.

To sustain an injured or ill bird until it can fend for itself, besides water, offer it grain, small amounts of greens (lettuce and vegetable tops), fruit, and grit to help it grind its food. *See* Gizzard. Very young mourning doves, a day or two old and fallen out of nest or abandoned by adults, had probably been on a diet of pigeon milk fed them by adults; to these, offer cooked oatmeal, Cream of Wheat, Wheatena, or Pablum, cooled after cooking. *See* Care and Feeding of Abandoned or Injured Wild Birds. See also Hollander (1966).

Members of the Pigeon Family protected from hunting in U.S. are the tiny Inca and common ground doves, and the larger and, relatively, rare red-billed pigeon and the white-tipped (white-fronted) dove (Cottam and Trefethen, 1968).

Dove, Carolina. *See* Dove, mourning.

Dove, Chinese spotted. *See* Dove, spotted.

Dove, ground, *Columbina passerina* (col-um-BINE-ah pass-er-EYE-nah); genus name: Lat., dim. of *columba*, a dove; a little dove; species name: Lat., sparrow, in allusion to small size; *ground dove* because spends most of time on ground. (Color ill., page 710.) Resident of s. and sw. U.S. into Mexico; small; 6–7 in. long; about sparrow size; male has short black tail and rounded wings which show red-brown patches on outer part when it takes flight; much on ground; some dark brown spots on brown back and wings, pink-brown below, dusky bill tipped with red or orange-red; legs and feet pink or yellow; females and young similar but much paler, grayer, and not so strongly spotted; one of most familiar dooryard birds in Fla., where may be seen walking briskly on short legs with graceful nodding of head, about houses, gardens, on quiet streets, very tame, allows close approach, usually does not fly until almost stepped upon; fond of sandy, cultivated lands, dirt roads, old weed-grown fields, cotton fields, pea patches, orange groves, open pine woods, on beaches, overgrazed pastures; common in summer in better-watered valleys of s. and c. Ariz.; sometimes perches on fence, branch of tree, or roof of building, from which male utters mournful *coo-oo*, rising at end, and repeated, with rest periods, for hours (Bent, 1932).

Feeding Habits: As it walks about, picks up seeds of weeds and grasses and waste grain in fields, also eats many insects especially in spring and summer, and small wild berries.
Nest: Often in slight depression on ground with little or no nest materials, on beach, on floor of woods, or in cultivated fields, also builds a slight nest of twigs or plant fibers in low bush, vine, on low stump, top of fence, or sometimes on branch of small or large tree, but nest usually about 1–21 ft. above ground, sometimes in deserted nest of cardinal; may pair for life; same pair may use same nest for second or even third brood (Bent, 1932).
Eggs: From Fla. to S.C., Feb.–Oct.; Tex., Mar.–Oct.; Ariz., May–Oct.; 2–3, usually 2, white.
Incubation: By both sexes, 12–14 days; young remain in nest until ready to fly; age at first flight unknown.
Other Names: Ground dove; little dove; moaning dove; tobacco bird; tobacco dove (from frequenting tobacco fields); walking dove (in contrast to free-flying mourning dove).
Age: A banded wild female was 6 years old when retrapped and released (Kennard, 1975).
Flight Speed: Timed in Tex., 26–32 m.p.h. (Sooter, 1947).
Host to Cowbirds: Rarely, only two records, to brown-headed cowbird, both from Brownsville, Tex., and an "accidental" victim to bronzed cowbird—one record in s. Ariz. (Friedmann, 1963).
Range: Resident from s. Calif. south through Baja Calif. into Mexico, and c. Ariz., s. N.M., to s. Tex., Gulf coast to Fla., Ga., S.C., and Bermuda south to Costa Rica, Bahamas, Greater and Lesser Antilles, and other islands in Caribbean, and south from Mexico to El Salvador, Belize, and from Colombia and Venezuela to Ecuador and Brazil; has strayed north to c. Calif., Iowa, Pa., N.J., and N.Y. (Reilly, 1968).

Dove, domestic ring. *See* Dove, ringed turtle.

Dove, Inca, *Scardafella inca* (skar-dah-FEL-lah IN-kah); genus name: Ital., for scaly appearance of feathers owing to color pattern (Coues, 1882); species name: given in 1847 by René Primivère Lesson, French naturalist and traveler, for the Inca Empire or its ruling chief. (Color ill., page 711.) Very small ground dove, resident of sw. U.S., Mexico, and into C. America; 7½–8 in. long; gray-buff of upperparts and whitish underparts have scaled appearance; like similar ground dove, in flight shows rufous-red on outer part of wings but differs in having long, square-ended tail, which sometimes appears pointed; has *white* outer tail feathers that show in flight; wings sometimes make twittering sound in flight; lives in fields and pastures of the arid Southwest, often seen feeding on bare, open ground or under scattered bushes or cactuses, but usually regarded as a "town" or "city" dove; feeds on lawns, in gardens, chicken yards, parks, and wherever water, so necessary to members of Pigeon Family, not far away; very tame dooryard bird that comes to birdbaths (Ligon, 1961); often perches on fences, clotheslines, and branches of trees; utters monotonous, mournful, two-noted *coe-coo*, or plaintive *whoo-oo-whoo* rapidly repeated over and over, with quality like sound made by blowing across open end of a bottle, also a conversational *cut-cut-ca-doo-ca-doo;* in summer, usually seen singly or in pairs, but in fall and winter, gathers in flocks up to 50, and roosts closely together in small groups in rows, sometimes with several perched atop others for warmth.

Feeding Habits: Walks about on ground picking up seeds of weeds and wheat and other small waste grains, some feed with poultry in yards.
Nest: Usually built on horizontal fork or flattened branch of tree or bush 4–25 ft. above ground, sometimes on beam of open shed, in hanging fern baskets; nest is small, compact shallow saucer or almost flat frail structure, 2–5 in. across, built of twigs, weed stems, dried grasses, rootlets, mosses, dead leaves, and feathers; sometimes uses old nests of mourning dove, mockingbird.
Eggs: Ariz., Jan.–Nov.; Tex., Apr.–Aug.; 2, white.
Incubation: About 14 days; young first fly about 14 days after hatching; has longest breeding season of any bird in Ariz., where four to five broods raised, at least in warm winters (Phillips *et al.*, 1964).
Other Names: Long-tailed dove; scaled dove; scaly dove.
Age: A female in wild, banded as nestling, trapped and released when 5 years, 10 months, old (Kennard, 1975).
Flight Speed: Timed in Tex., 28 m.p.h. (Sooter, 1947).

PIGEON FAMILY

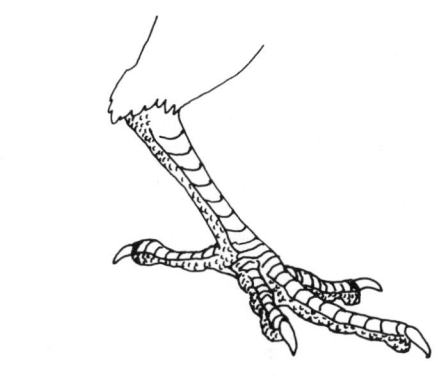

Weights: About 40 gr. (MacMillen and Trost, 1966), or about 1¼ oz.

Range: Resident in s. Ariz., N.M., s. Tex., south through coastal lowlands on both coasts of Mexico, south to nw. Costa Rica and Nicaragua; extending range northward in sw. U.S.; Cunningham (1966) reported that the Inca dove is known to have bred at Key West, Fla.

Dove, lace-necked. *See* Dove, spotted.

Dove, little. *See* Dove, ground.

Dove, moaning. *See* Dove, mourning, and Dove, ground.

Dove, mourning, *Zenaida macroura* (zen-AY-ih-dah mah-CROO-rah); genus name: applied by Charles Lucien Bonaparte, French zoologist, in 1838, in honor of his wife, Princess Zénaide Charlotte Julie Bonaparte, to a genus of doves that includes the Zenaida dove, white-winged dove, and, more recently, the mourning dove (see American Ornithologists' Union, 1973); species name: from Gr. *makros*, long, and *oura*, tail; *mourning*, from inferred sadness of the bird's call. (Color ill., page 710.) Has been classified as a game bird by federal government and 31 states; protected from hunting in 17 states (see list by Ruos, 1974); has widest distribution of any N. American game bird; only one to nest in all 48 conterminous states of U.S.; may be seen in summer from Alaska south into Mexico; 11–13 in. long; wingspread 17–19 in.; the long, narrow, pointed tail, bordered with large white spots, is 5½–7 in. long; female smaller than male and colors duller; a gray-brown dove with small head, bill small, slender and black; has long, rather pointed wings (its long, pointed tail gives it a streamlined shape distinctive at long distance); at close range shows small black spot on each side of face that distinguished it from the similar larger but now extinct passenger pigeon; also has a few black spots on scapulars and wing coverts; at all seasons the commonest native dove about suburbs and in farm country; flies swiftly and strongly like small hawk but with musical whistling of wings; highly adaptive, lives from farm fields, hedges, and open woods to windbreaks of Great Plains and arid semidesert mesquite of West and in mountains of Southwest up to 13,000 ft. (Ligon, 1961), but prefers farms or other open lands with scattered trees, shrubs, and open fields; usually seen in pairs in summer; some winter in n. U.S. but most south of line from s. Calif. east to Neb., N.J.; arrive, some already paired, in n. U.S. and s. Canada in Mar.–Apr.; start southward in fall, generally in mid-Sept., in small groups of a few to 20; mostly migrate by day and migration usually completed by early Dec.; in spring, male selects nesting territory and defends it by flying at and pecking other males; also by territorial cooing (songs) uttered from dawn to dusk early in spring, delivered from prominent perches in his territory on poles, wires, dead tree limbs, TV aerials, house ridges —a mournful, low-pitched, soft *oo-ah! cooo-cooo-coo,* the first phrase slurred upward, then the three coos that follow usually all at same

pitch as first *oo;* female sometimes answers weakly, almost inaudibly; Brackbill (1970a), after eight years of studies of banded mourning doves, concluded that they mate for life; total population in U.S. and Canada, fall of 1974, estimated by U.S. Fish and Wildlife Service at about 400 million (Banks, 1974); Crissey (1958) estimated annual kill by hunters at about 30 million (see also Peters, 1961).

Feeding Habits: During winter lives in small to large flocks where food plentiful and good roosting and protective cover in trees nearby; sometimes roosts on ground at night in winter (*see* Toughness of a Bird's Feet under Feet and Legs; *also* Cold and Birds); feeds mostly on ground in harvested crop fields, along railroad rights-of-way, roadsides; is almost wholly a seed-eater (about 98% of diet); eats enormous numbers of weed seeds in fields and waste places at all seasons; a stomach of one held 7,500 seeds of yellow wood sorrel *(Oxalis);* another, 6,400 seeds of foxtail grasses *(Setaria);* besides seeds of grasses eats waste grain—wheat, corn, rye, oats, barley, buckwheat, millet—peanuts, cowpeas, lespedezas, and seeds of pines, doveweed *(Croton),* and pokeberry; also some insects, snails (Tyler, 1932; Edminster, 1954), and picks up grit from gravel roads or sea beaches to help grind seeds in diet (*see* Gizzard); may fly long distances daily, especially in arid parts of West, for water.

Nest: Male brings twigs to female at nest site, mostly in crotch, or on branch, of tree, usually 5–25 ft. up and even to 80 ft. above ground; female arranges sticks in loose platform, also low in vines, tops of rock or rail fences, on stumps, and often, where trees are scarce, on ground; on roof gutters of houses, in chimney corners, on top of arbors in gardens, on top of nests of cardinals, American robins, blue jays, brown thrashers, mockingbirds, grackles, house sparrows, and occasionally in parts of stick nests of herons; in especially favored trees such as pines, Norway spruces, osage orange, may nest in colonies with ten or more nests in one tree (see details in Tyler, 1932; Edminster, 1954).

Eggs: N. U.S., Apr.–Aug.; Tex., Feb.–Sept.; Calif., Jan.–Dec.; 1–4, usually 2, pure white.

Incubation: By both sexes; male by day; female by night; 14–15 days; young brooded and fed by both adults; young fly directly from nest, usually about 14–15 days after hatching (see also Ludden, 1979); may return to it for roosting for first two or three nights; within a week after leaving nest, are on their own (Edminster, 1954); a pair may raise 2–5 broods in a nesting season; usually more broods raised each year in South because of climate that provides longer nesting season; may nest there in every month of the year.

Other Names: Carolina dove; moaning dove; turtle dove (not for turtles of U.S. but from Lat. *turtur,* species name of turtle dove of Europe —McAtee, 1954–55); wild dove; wood dove.

Accidents: In Fla., Stoddard and Norris (1967) reported 69 mourning doves killed striking TV tower during 11-year period; many also killed by striking utility wires.

Age: During their first year, large losses of young mourning doves from shooting and

other causes (about 70% of juveniles die within first year, and annual adult mortality is about 55%—Kiel, 1959); however, some live to 2, 3, and 5 years in wild; one, banded in Ohio, was shot in Mexico when 7 years old; one, banded at Cape Cod, Mass., lived to 10 years in wild; one in captivity still alive and healthy at 17 years old (Weber, 1972); another, a female raised from fledgling at Visalia, Calif., still alive when 17 years old; a male companion lived to 15 years.

Albinism: One almost all-white, mated with normally colored one in Ont., Canada (Armstrong and Noakes, 1977).

Flight Speed: Timed in Calif., 30–36 m.p.h. (Tyler, 1932) and 40–41 m.p.h. (Cooke, 1937a); in Ont., one timed June 1951 at 55 m.p.h. (Bastin, 1952).

Host to Cowbirds: Very uncommon, six records of host to brown-headed cowbird, of which three doubtful (Friedmann, 1963); three nest records of host to bronzed cowbird near Corpus Christi, Tex. (Friedmann, 1971).

Weights: Males (164) averaged 4.6 oz. with maximum, in an especially large male in Wisc., of 6 oz.; females (80) averaged 4.4 oz., a large female in Ohio weighed 5.5 oz. (Martin and Nelson, 1952).

Range: Nests from se. Alaska, s. B.C., Alta., Sask., Man., to s. Ont., s. Que., Me., and s. N.B. south to s. Baja Calif., through Mexico to w. Panama, Greater Antilles, Bahamas; winters from s. Canada and northern border states of U.S. but mainly from n. Calif., s. Nev., c. Ariz., c. Colo., Neb., and Iowa, Ill., Ind., s. Mich., Pa., and N.J. south into Mexico, w. Panama, Cuba.

Dove, prairie. *See* Gull, Franklin's, in Gull Family.

Dove, rain. Another name for the black-billed and yellow-billed cuckoos in Cuckoo Family.

Dove, ring. *See* Dove, ringed turtle.

Dove, ringed turtle, *Streptopelia risoria** (strep-toe-PEEL-ih-ah rye-SORE-ih-ah); genus name: Lat., from Gr. *streptos*, twisted, bent, and *peleia*, a dove (Jaeger, 1955); according to Gruson (1972), allusion may be to a pattern of colored patches on sides of neck of some species in this genus; species name: from Lat. *risor*, a laugher, one who mocks; Gruson suggests this may be an allusion to this dove's call; *ringed* refers to thin black band around back and sides of neck. (Color ill., page 711.) A domesticated dove throughout almost entire world; native origin unknown; introduced and established around Los Angeles, Calif.; reported in Fla.; 12–14 in. long; averages slightly larger than the mourning dove and much paler; distinguished by its sandy plumage and narrow black ring on hind neck; slimmer than rock dove, or common pigeon, and lacks that bird's white rump; also has moderately long, *rounded* tail with white in corners; call is cooing *hoo-hrrooo* (Robbins *et al.,*1966); common cage bird, an established resident population in

*See, however, Parkes (1975).

parks of urban center of Los Angeles since late 1920s—Pershing Square, grounds of Central Library, and in trees along Olvera Street; may number several hundred birds; population apparently stable, some seen in surrounding suburbs and even in rural places outside Los Angeles, where they occasionally visit bird feeding stations; breeding season through spring and summer, also possibly at other times (Hardy, 1973); Sprunt (1954a) reported one collected (shot) in Dade County, Fla., about 1923 or 1924, none reported again until Oct. 1951, when hunter shooting doves west of Hialeah killed one that was apparently a wild bird; in Mar. 1953, S. A. Grimes discovered three pairs of ringed turtle doves nesting along streets of St. Petersburg, Fla.; a nest discovered Jamaica Bay Wildlife Refuge, New York City, Aug. 26, 1970, near place where several had been liberated (Boyajiian, 1971a).

Feeding Habits: Eats mostly seeds picked up on ground, also eats berries, takes bread offered by people, and other foods.
Nest: Crudely built of sticks, usually in tree, bush, on building.
Eggs: 2, white.
Other Name: Domestic ring dove.

Dove, rock, *Columba livia* (col-UM-bah LIE-vih-ah); genus name: Lat., a dove or pigeon; species name: Lat., blue, blue-gray, or lead-colored (Jaeger, 1955), in allusion to its largely bluish plumage; *rock*, in reference to its preferred nesting habitat, in wild, on rocky places. (Color ill., page 712.) Eurasian species, domesticated and introduced around world (*see* brief history and uses in wartime under Domestication; *also* Homing); first introduced into N. America apparently by the French at Port Royal, Nova Scotia, in 1606; Virginia, about 1621 or 1622; Mass., about 1642 (Schorger, 1952b; see also Levi, 1957, for general information and descriptions of races and forms of the pigeon); 13–14 in. long; color pattern variable and sexes of many forms outwardly alike, but male somewhat larger with thicker neck; the feral, or wild, rock dove is generally blue-gray with a white rump; has iridescent feathers on head and neck that reflect green, bronze, and purple; two broad black bars across each wing, and a broad, dark band across end of tail; others in city or country flocks may be pure white; others, a mixture of white and gray without white rump; is not migratory; one of swiftest of birds in flight; though tame in city and town parks, where some feed from hands of people, retains timidity of wild bird and rises with clapping or slapping of wings at quick motion or sudden noise like backfire of car or truck; male, from ground or on other surfaces, utters frequent and sustained cooing, variously described as *coo-a-roo, coo-roo-cooo,* or *cock-a-war*, during which male may turn completely about as if dancing (Naether, 1939), but see courtship behavior interpreted, for example, in Fabricius and Jansson (1963).

Feeding Habits: In harvested grain fields, high on sea beaches, on lawns, waste places, eats grain, seeds of weeds, grasses, and clovers; also grasses and tender roots of, also takes a few berries, eats bread crumbs and pieces of table garbage; in cities, drinks from fountains, park ponds; some will alight on water to drink and can fly up easily from surface.
Nest: Flimsy platform of sticks, twigs, grasses, on building ledges, rafters or beams inside barns, and in natural environment on sea cliffs and in caves.
Eggs: Laid in every month of year but usually Mar.–June and Aug.–Nov., at least in New England; 1–2, usually 2, white.
Incubation: 17–19 days; young first fly 35–37 days after hatching (Bannerman, 1959); several broods each year.
Other Names: Blue rock; carrier pigeon; domestic pigeon; homing pigeon; pigeon; street pigeon.
Age: Cock pigeons live longer than hens (Levi, 1957); some to 16 years or more (Palmer, 1949); oldest recorded age was homing pigeon, Kaiser, a red-checkered cock, captured in 1918 from Germans in World War I, brought to U.S., housed in U.S. Army Signal Corps lofts at Fort Monmouth, N.J., where reported to have died Oct. 1949 at age 32 years, 8 months, but there has been some dispute as to validity of his age records (Levi, 1957). One banded wild rock dove reported from Great Britain, 6 years, 2 months, old (Clapp, 1976).
Flight Speed: Timed in Britain and in France, 28–82 m.p.h. (Riviere, 1922); 82–94.3 m.p.h. (Meinertzhagen, 1955).
Hybrids: In captivity, rock dove has crossbred with band-tailed pigeon and mourning dove, also with many Old World doves and pigeons (see Gray, 1958).
Weights: One, 286 gr. (Hughes, 1970), or about 10 oz.; may weigh up to about 1 lb. (Palmer, 1949).
Range: In native range is resident from Faeros Is., Norway, Russia, w. Siberia, Manchuria, and n. China, south through British Isles and w. Europe to Madeira, the Canary Is., Azores, Gold Coast of Africa, n. Sahara, Egypt, through Mideast to India, Ceylon, and Burma; now established from introduced domestic stock in larger cities of most of the world, and on Hawaiian Is., also in N.,C., and S. America, and parts of the West Indies.

The rock dove was apparently the first bird to be domesticated, about 4500 B.C. according to Zeuner (1963). In the beginning it was raised for its meat; later for its message-carrying ability. The ancient Romans were said to have used the rock dove to carry back to Rome news of Caesar's conquest of Gaul, and Napoleon's defeat at Waterloo reached England by carrier pigeon 4 days in advance of the news carried there by horse and ship (Terres, 1947b). Some homing pigeons have been trained to return to their home lofts from a few hundred up to a thousand miles away by taking them gradually farther and farther from the home loft and then releasing them.

Apparently homing pigeons (rock doves) are guided to the home loft by use of the sun as a compass for getting their proper home direction, then by using an internal time sense to correct their courses to compensate for the movement of the sun across the sky. See discussion by Matthews (1968). At Cornell University, working with homing pigeons, Dr. William T. Keeton (1969) discovered that there are several, perhaps many, alternative guidance systems used by these birds. For example, he found that under totally overcast skies, in the absence of the visible sun to orient them, the pigeons could still take an initial bearing toward the home loft. In later experiments, Keeton found that on cloudy days, with the sun obscured, his test pigeons could reach the home loft apparently by using the earth's magnetic field. See details and conclusions in Keeton (1971; 1972). *See* Migration.

Dove, sea. Another name for the dovekie in Auk Family.

Dove, singing. *See* Dove, white-winged.

Dove, Sonoran. *See* Dove, white-winged.

Dove, spotted, *Streptopelia chinensis* (strep-toe-PEEL-ih-ah chin-EN-sis); genus name: *see* Dove, ringed turtle; species name: Lat., of China. (Color ill., page 712.) Asiatic species, apparently introduced intentionally in Los Angeles; first wild ones (free birds) reported there in 1917; was common in much of Los Angeles basin by 1923; by 1933 had reached Santa Barbara, Pasadena, Alhambra; present population and range appear stable; common to abundant resident in coastal s. Calif.; ranges from Santa Barbara to San Diego and inland to the Salton Sea (Hardy, 1973); 12–13 in. long; gray-brown above, paler below, distinguished by its *band of black and white spots on back of neck* ("lace-necked"), and long, *rounded black tail with prominent white corners;* immatures lack spotted collar but may be distinguished from mourning dove by *rounded* tail; has black bill, legs and feet dark pink, claws black (Reilly, 1968); utters a vigorous *whóok-cu-coóoooo,* given more rapidly than call by mourning dove (Cogswell in Pough, 1957); not migratory, lives in residential areas of cities, towns, suburbs, and in parks, woods along rivers, requires large trees in habitat, especially eucalyptus (Hardy, 1973).

Nest: Platform of small sticks 8–40 ft. up in tree.
Eggs: Mar. and at least through May (Hardy, 1973); 2, white.
Other Names: Chinese dove; Chinese spotted dove; lace-necked dove.
Age: One, banded, reported from se. Asia, 6 years, 4 months, old (Clapp, 1976).
Range: From China to India, Ceylon, Burma, Indochina, to Malay Pen., Borneo; introduced in Calif.

Dove, tobacco. *See* Dove, ground.

Dove, turtle. *See* Dove, mourning, and Dove, ringed turtle.

Dove, white-fronted, *Leptotila verreauxi* (lep-TOE-til-ah ver-ROW-eye); genus name: from Gr. *leptos*, thin, slender, and *ptilon*, feather; "slender-feathered"; according to Gruson (1972), refers to narrow outer primary, which is attenuated (tapers gradually to a point); species name: given in 1855 by Charles Lucien Bonaparte, French zoologist, for Jules

Pierre Verreaux, French explorer and collector in natural history; *white-tipped*, for white-tipped feathers in tail. (Color ill., page 712.) Mexican, C. and S. American species that reaches N. America in lower Rio Grande Valley of Tex., where it is resident; 11–12 in. long; a large ground-dwelling dove, distinguished from others by its white belly, white undertail coverts, and white forehead and throat, and *white-tipped corners of its rounded tail;* breast gray, lacks white in wings characteristic of similar white-winged and Zenaida doves; its wings are uniformly brown above; in flight, shows bright chestnut underwing linings (Robbins *et al.,* 1966); bill black; feet and legs purple-red; irises pale yellow to orange-red (Reilly, 1968); utters soft, deep-toned *oo-whooooooo* (Peterson and Chalif, 1973); lives in dry woods, second growth, riparian thickets; solitary and retiring, walks beneath dense shrubbery in search of berries and seeds; if startled, may swiftly walk away through underbrush, but if flushed, will fly up with wings whistling like those of a woodcock (Pough, 1951).

Feeding Habits: Eats from ground or from low branches, seeds of hackberry, elm, ebony, anaqua, mesquite, prickly pear cactus, also seeds of grasses, some corn, sorghum, and a few crickets.

Nest: A platform of sticks and fibers, usually 5–12 ft. up on branch of small tree, in fork of bush, or in tangle of vines; sometimes on ground (Bent, 1932). See also Skutch (1964a).

Eggs: Tex., Mar.–July; 2, cream-buff.

Other Name: Wood pigeon.

Weights: 145–205 gr. (Leopold, 1959), or about 5–7 oz.

Range: From s. Tex. and in Mexico from c. Sonora south through tropical lowlands through C. and S. America to n. Argentina, Uruguay, and s. Brazil, including islands off n. coast of S. America.

Dove, white-tipped. *See* Dove, white-fronted.

Dove, white-winged, *Zenaida asiatica* (zen-AY-ih-dah   ay-zhih-AT-ih-kah); genus name: *see* Dove, mourning; species name: Lat., of Asia; species name given this bird by Carl Linnaeus, Swedish scientist, in belief that its native home was in East Indies (Asia); however, is limited in its native range to New World (see details in Cottam and Trefethen, 1968); *white-winged*, from considerable amount of white in wings. (Color ill., page 713.) Largely a tropical American species but with large summer population in U.S. mostly in West and Southwest; introduced in s. Fla.; 11–12½ in. long; sexes alike, although males slightly larger and more highly colored than females; distinguished by a broad white band across each wing (when perched shows white border along margins of folded wings); in flight, besides white in wings, shows large white corners in rounded tail; body brown above; crown and back of neck purple or red-purple; sides of neck reflect green-gold; a small black mark below and behind each orange-red eye; eyes surrounded by bare patch of blue skin (mourning dove's eyes are brown with no surrounding bare skin); tail with black band edging white corners; bill dark blue horn color; legs and feet red; starts in flight with loud clapping of wings like domestic pigeon; flight is more direct and less zigzagging than that of mourning dove, also tail shorter, not pointed; immatures much grayer than adults, neck brown without iridescent gloss; primary flight feathers have whitish tips; eyes brown to yellow-brown; legs and feet brown or red-brown; gregarious, whitewings feed together in large flocks especially after nesting season and use nesting trees and shrubs for roosting, from which they may fly 25 mi. or more for food and water; in Tex. and Ariz., drink from stock tanks, windmill troughs, reservoirs, irrigation canals, streams; MacMillen and Trost (1966), in studies of water economy and salt balance in whitewing, observed in desert of Ariz. it may rely on fruits of saguaro cactus as important source of water; in spring, from fields and woods of wintering grounds in C. America and s. Mexico, the migratory breeding population that nests in northern part of whitewing range travels 1,000 mi. or more north, many along east and west coasts of Mexico, to nesting grounds in U.S. in flocks of a few to 50; at times, 3,000–4,000 visible in flight; arrive on nesting grounds in southern border states, from Tex. west to Ariz., from late Mar. in-to May; most return southward in Sept. and Oct. over same migration routes; in Tex., total spring breeding population in 1967 about 667,000; in Ariz., in 1963, about 1,540,000 (for population counts and discussion of history in U.S., see Cottam and Trefethen, 1968).

Feeding Habits: Eats primarily seeds of wild sunflowers, doveweed, leatherweed, and others; also, acorns and other mast, and fruit; before native Tex. woodlands and brush were cleared for agriculture, lived on fruits and seeds of native trees and shrubs and on seeds of wild weeds, legumes, and grasses; with expansion of agriculture, whitewings readily accepted sorghums and other grains planted as crops, and flock to these fields, where they feed on ground or cling to heads of sorghum to eat its seeds; in desert, eats fruits and seeds of saguaro, organ-pipe, and other cactuses; also seeds of desert willow, ocotillo, nightshade, century plants, agave, and grasses; is especially fond of seeds of doveweed, and in years of abundant doveweed crops in pastures in Tex., may move to them in flights of 300,000 to 1 million birds (Cottam and Trefethen, 1968).

Nest: Some in colonies; others scattered; in lower Rio Grande Valley, Tex., forced to shift, with removal of native brushlands, to citrus groves; others nest in remaining native brushlands, and many in trees and ornamental shrubs in cities and suburbs; in s. Ariz., prefers to nest in mesquite, oak woods, and salt cedar, or tamarisk, the most heavily used with density of well over 200 nests per acre along Gila R. west of Phoenix (Cottam and Trefethen, 1968); also nests in trees of desert, in large shrubs, crotches of saguaro, in tangled vines, and in cholla cactus; male selects nesting territory and sings (coos) to advertise it, a low-pitched, flutelike *who-cooks-for-you,* like soft notes of a barred owl, monotonously repeated (Bent, 1932); female selects the limb, crotch, or clump of thorns that will be base for nest, usually in trees with dense foliage that will shade nest; builds nest of twigs (138 counted in one nest) brought to her by male; about 2–4 days to build early in nesting season; some pairs use old nest of previous season; others dismantle their old nests and use the twigs to build new one; some build nest atop old nests of thrashers, mockingbirds, flycatchers, orioles, and chachalacas.

Eggs: Tex., late Mar.–July; Ariz., Apr.–Aug.; normally 2, occasionally 1, or 3–4; dull cream-white to cream-buff, usually one or two broods.

Incubation: By both sexes; female from mid-afternoon through the night; male throughout day; usually 13–14 days; young leave nest 13–16 days after hatching; at 15 days usually able to fly well for short distance; as soon as young safely fledged, adults may begin nesting for second brood (Cottam and Tefethen, 1968).

Other Names: Cactus pigeon; singing dove; Sonoran dove; white-wing.

Age: Oldest whitewing known in wild, banded at Komatke Thicket near Phoenix, Ariz., shot during its 15th year near Colima, Mexico; in captivity one 17 years old still alive and in good health (Weber, 1972); all-time record, a pet kept by woman in Phoenix, Ariz., died in 1959 when at least 25 years old (Cottam and Trefethen, 1968).

Host to Cowbirds: A single record, to bronzed cowbird, in Sonora, Mexico, May 1931 (Friedmann, 1963).

Weights: About 140 gr. (MacMillen and Trost, 1966), or about 5 oz.; 4½–7 oz. (Cottam and Trefethen, 1968).

Range: Nests from s. Nev., se. Calif., c. Ariz., s. N.M., and lower Rio Grande Valley, Tex., south to Cape region of Baja Calif., and through Mexico and C. America to w. Panama and in West Indies and sw. S. America; winters on breeding range except lesser numbers in northern parts; has wandered to Vancouver Is., B.C., Wash., Colo. Ont., Me., N.Y., La., Miss., Ala., Fla., Ga., and Puerto Rico; captives released in 1959 at Homestead, Fla., were nesting there and by 1968 had increased in numbers to at least 200 coming to one feeding station (see Fisk, 1968; Ogden, 1970).

Dove, wild. *See* Dove, mourning.

Dove, wood. *See* Dove, mourning.

Dove, Zenaida, *Zenaida aurita* (zen-AY-ih-dah aw-RYE-tah); genus name: *see* Dove, mourning; species name: Lat., with ears; having large ears (Jaeger, 1960); name may refer to the auricular area or ear coverts of this dove, which are set off by a conspicuous black or dark violet-blue streak below, and, in some, above the auriculars. Mostly a West Indian species that, according to Bent (1932), bred at one time on islands near Indian Key, Fla., but since then seen only a few times in Fla.; on Apr. 24, 1903, several seen on Indian Key; and records on Fla. mainland, on Feb. 11, 1918, at Pass-a-Grille; Nov. 13, 1948, between Coot Bay and Flamingo, and Oct. 21, 1954, on Chassahowitzka National Wildlife Refuge, Hernando County; 10–11 in. long; resembles mourning dove, mainly gray-brown or fawn color above; head brown-cinnamon; hind neck usually distinctly gray; sides of neck iridescent purple-violet; a conspicuous black spot or streak below and, sometimes, above the ear coverts; wings black-spotted, and *with broad white stripe along back edge of inner "half" of wing which shows in flight;* also, *unlike* mourning dove, has somewhat square tail tipped with pearl gray (white-winged dove has diagonal white patch on wings, and corners of its tail are white; white-fronted dove has *no white in wings*).

Range: West Indies, Yucatán Pen. and Cozumel Is., Mexico; formerly to Fla. Keys, now accidental there.

Ground-dove, ruddy, *Columbina talpacoti* (col-um-BINE-ah tal-pah-KOH-tih); genus name: *see* Dove, ground. Small, 6–7-in.-long Mexican, C. and S. American dove; a male photographed in a tree Jan. 28, 1971, by W. A. Shifflett on the North Trail of Santa Ana National Wildlife Refuge, Alamo, Tex., was the first authenticated record for the species in the U.S.; the bird remained on the Refuge for 7 weeks; last reported Mar. 17, 1971; only previous report for the species in U.S. was a male seen near Harlingen, Tex., Dec. 1950 to Jan. 1951, but was listed as hypothetical (doubtful because of lack of satisfactory proof) in the A.O.U. *Check-list,* 1957. The species is widespread in tropical America to n. Argentina and ranges regularly north to s. Tamaulipas, Mexico (Shifflett, 1975b). Male is reddish above with a *pale blue-gray crown* and dark spots on wings; has clear pale reddish underparts, black outer tail feathers and a dark or dusky bill (similar common ground dove, *red on wings only,* has a *scaled or spotted throat and breast* and a *pink- or reddish-tipped bill*); female ruddy ground-dove mainly gray-brown with pale brown-gray underparts *without breast spots* of common ground dove (Blake, E. R., 1953); also lacks reddish color of male ruddy but has rufous in wings; according to Peterson and Chalif (1973), call is a *whoop* or *per-woop,* uttered 2–24 times.
Other Name: Talpacoti dove.

Pigeon, band-tailed, *Columba fasciata* (col-UM-bah fass-ih-AY-tah); genus name: *see* Dove, rock; species name: Lat., banded, alludes to conspicuous dark band across midpart of tail. (Color ill., page 713.) Summers in Far West; winters in sw. U.S. and tropical America; 14–15½ in. long; heavily built, resembles rock dove but larger and with dark blue-gray upperparts *without white rump;* besides dark band across mid-tail, has broad gray band, especially notable in flight, across tip of fanlike tail; at close range, adult has white band across hind neck; *yellow bill with dark tip; yellow feet;* red-lidded eyes are yellow; lives in woods and in mountains with tendency to alight in trees; frequents water holes and salt licks in large flocks; with protection, has recovered from former decimation, almost to extinction, by hunting in Pacific coast states (Bent, 1932); in spring, from wintering grounds in sw. U.S., Mexican tableland, and C. America, population that nests in northern and western part of the breeding range migrates in flocks that arrive Mar.–May

in Pacific coast states north to Wash. and B.C.; also, an interior population, nesting mostly in Ariz., N.M., Colo., and Utah, arrives there generally Apr.–May (Braun *et al.,* 1975); all return southward late Aug.–Oct. (Bent, 1932); flocks are fond of perching for long periods in tops of tall trees, not noticeable in leafy trees in summer but in leafless sycamores in winter, flocks very conspicuous (Cogswell in Pough, 1957); flight is strong and direct, very swift, like that of rock dove; at nesting time, flocks break up into pairs; from conspicuous perch in treetop, male frequently utters a deep, mellow, owl-like *whoo-whoo-hoo* or a two-syllabled *whoo-uh!* (Bent, 1932); according to Skutch (1964a), of all C. American pigeons, the band-tailed seems most in need of protection there, not only because its large conspicuous flocks are vulnerable to shooting, but because it lives in highlands there where human population is densest and it is an easy prey for hunters on mountain slopes, even into the nesting season.

Feeding Habits: Main food is nuts and berries; in summer, besides grasshoppers and other insects, eats wild grapes, elderberries, chokecherries, coffee berries, wild cherries, mulberries, blueberries, juniper berries, cascara, dogwood, salmon, salal, and manzanita berries, which they pick from shrubs by climbing about branches with fluttering wings, or pick up fallen berries from ground; also fond of wild peas, pine seeds, waste oats, barley, and corn; eats hazelnuts and especially fond of acorns, mainly of live, golden, and black oaks, which they eat in fall and winter and pluck from trees or ground and swallow whole, also eats some insects.
Nest: Frail platform of sticks or twigs, 6–8 in. across, 8–40 ft. or more from ground (sometimes on ground), built on branches of fir trees, or on fork of twigs in fir trees, black and golden oaks, Douglas spruce, or in alders or other shrubs; in Guatemala, Skutch (1964a) found nest on mountain, 20 ft. up on branch of pine tree at 9,000 ft. above sea level; usually nests in scattered pairs, but in Ariz. a colony reported of up to 35 pairs nesting among live oaks at head of short, wooded canyon (Bent, 1932).
Eggs: Wash., Ore., May–July; Calif., Mar.–Sept.; Ariz., N.M., Apr.–Oct.; 1–2, usually 1, white.
Incubation: By both sexes, about 18–20 days; young leave nest about 30 days after hatching (see Bent, 1932; Neff, 1947; MacGregor and Smith, 1955).
Other Names: White-collared pigeon; wild pigeon.
Age: A male, banded at Sedalia, Colo., trapped at Evergreen, Colo., and released, was 6 years old (Kennard, 1975).
Hybrids: See Rock dove.
Weights: 280–350 gr. (Leopold, 1959), or about 9⅞–12 oz.
Range: Nests from sw. B.C. east to mountains in Utah, n.-c. Colo., south through Wash., Ore., and Calif., mostly in mountains to Sierra San Pedro Mártir in n. Baja Calif. and through Sierra Madre of Mexico to mountains of c. Guatemala; winters from Sacramento Valley of Calif. south, most numerously in oak region of s. Calif. and in c. Ariz. and N.M. south, casually

north to B.C. and to Nev. and Idaho; has strayed to Okla. and N.D.; one at bird feeder on Sugarloaf Key, Fla., Sept. 1973; another at a feeder at Nashville, Tenn., Apr. 1974, first record for state. For a study of the habitats, hunting, and protection of the interior populations in Colo., Utah, N.M., and Ariz., see Braun *et al.* (1975).

Pigeon, cactus. *See* Dove, white-winged.

Pigeon, cape. Another name for the cape petrel in Shearwater Family.

Pigeon, carrier. *See* Dove, rock.

Pigeon, common. *See* Dove, rock.

Pigeon, domestic. *See* Dove, rock.

Pigeon, homing. *See* Dove, rock.

Pigeon, passenger, *Ectopistes migratorius* (ek-to-PIS-teez my-grah-TOE-rih-us); genus name: from Gr. *ektopizo,* to move from a place; *ektopistikos,* migratory (Jaeger, 1955); species name: Lat., migratory; common name *passenger,* in old sense of a "passer-through" or "passerby," a wayfarer, or traveler, in allusion to the wide wanderings of enormous flocks of these birds in search of food or in their irregular migrations in spring and fall (see Schorger, 1955). *Extinct;* formerly ranged over e. N. America from Canada south to the Gulf coast and west to Mont. and w. Tex.; was longest member of family in N. America—15–17 in. —including the graceful 8–9-in.-long pointed tail of 12 tapering feathers; wingspread 23–25 in.; had small slate-blue head; black bill, slender, short; eyes scarlet; iridescent feathers on sides and back of neck glowed a rich metallic gold, violet, or red-purple; back slate-gray tinged with gray-brown and olive brown; lower back and rump slate-blue; wings long and pointed, with some small black spots (checkers) on brownish-gray scapulars and bluish wing coverts; underparts of body, from throat to belly, rich russet or wine red; belly white, undertail coverts white; dark tail had white outer margin; legs and feet crimson red; female outwardly similar to male but smaller and colors duller (see details in Forbush, 1925–29; Schorger, 1955); passenger pigeon resembled mourning dove· but was much larger, more blue, and adult male had much more richly colored breast; also, both sexes had a *blue rump;* neither sex had the black spot on side of neck as in mourning dove; the spectacular numbers of the passenger pigeon were so great that Schorger (1955) believed that no other species of bird, to best of his knowledge, ever approached its numbers; Alexander Wilson in 1808 (Schorger, 1955) made first known attempt to estimate its numbers in a 1-mi.-wide spring flight in Ky. that passed him for 4 hours and stretched as far as his eyes could see, in tier upon tier of closely flying birds that darkened the sun and numbered about 2¼ billion birds; Audubon estimated another Ky. flight at more than 1 billion; and in Ont., Canada, W. Ross King reported in 1866 that at one time he had watched a May flight move northward

Rock dove

PIGEON FAMILY

A mincing, head-bobbing walk is typical of all pigeons.

Passenger pigeon

Red-billed pigeon

from the U.S. that was at least 300 mi. long, 1 mi. wide, and continued for 14 hours; it contained, by Schorger's estimate, 3 billion, 717 million birds; Schorger (1955) believed that the population of the passenger pigeon at time of discovery of N. America was 3–5 billion and that it formed 25–40% of the total bird population of what is now the U.S.; the land over which these birds roamed was almost a billion acres of forests (most of it later to become productive farmlands) that produced vast quantities of beechnuts, acorns, and other favored passenger pigeon foods (it preferred beech-oak-maple forests) and provided support for its nests which sometimes numbered up to 100 or more in a single tree (Wilson, 1808–14); perhaps as impressive as the densely populated nesting colonies were the immense numbers that, in fall and winter, roosted nightly in a specific woodland or swamp, flew about over the countryside by day to feed, and returned in enormous flocks to the roost at night; when masses of them settled in the trees, often in groups that settled atop one another, the weight of their numbers broke off trees 2 ft. in diameter and large limbs that, crashing to the ground, killed hundreds of pigeons, and left the forest as though swept by a tornado (Audubon, 1870); as late as 1871, 136 million passenger pigeons concentrated in a colonial nesting area of 850 sq. mi. in Wisc.; however, by 1870, it had ceased to nest in large groups except in the states surrounding the Great Lakes; the gradual decline had begun in ne. U.S. in 1851, and ended in all states with the last nest in the wild of a passenger pigeon reported in a Great Lakes state in 1894 (see details in Greenway, 1958); according to Greenway, the last record of a living passenger pigeon in the wild was one shot at Babcock, Wisc., in 1899; Schorger (1955) believed the last was one shot at Sargents, Pike County, Ohio, Mar. 24, 1900; the passenger pigeon declined swiftly from 1871 to 1880; in 1874, at one nesting colony in Mich. alone, 25,000 pigeons were killed daily for the market for 28 days by professional netters, or about 700,000 a month (Schorger, 1955); it was this kind of destruction, besides cutting off the forests for agriculture, that doomed the species; in Wisc. in 1947, a plaque was erected to the memory of the last wild passenger pigeon shot in that state (*see* Monuments to Birds); some had been bred in captivity but in a very small way, and the last living one, a captive in the Cincinnati Zoological Garden, named Martha (for Martha Washington), died there Sept. 1, 1914; she was sent to the U.S. National Museum, Washington, D.C., where she was exhibited in mounted form—she had lived to age 29 years; in spring, passenger pigeons had arrived in the forests of n. U.S. and in Canada in Mar. through April to breed; the male, in courting the female, instead of pirouetting before her and bowing as many other courting pigeons do, merely sidled up to her on a branch and pressed very close to her; the cooing of thousands of males in the colony during the courting period was a strange bell-like sound, along with loud croaking, chattering, and clucking noises; the passenger pigeon was a species whose existence seemed to depend on close association in large numbers with others of its kind; once the enormous colonies had been reduced, with remnants separated and scattered in small flocks, these seemed unable to reproduce in sufficient numbers to survive. See details in Schorger (1955).

Feeding Habits: In morning, the immense flocks of the passenger pigeon left their roosts in swift flight, going for food; from fall to spring, in the woods, they plucked from branches or from ground, with bill (they did not scratch in ground for food), beechnuts, acorns, and chestnuts, their principal food, uttering while they fed a babble of squeaking and twittering sounds; in summer, they ate wild berries—Juneberries, fruits of dogwoods, cherries, raspberries, elderberries, blueberries, currants, pokeberries, wild grapes, strawberries, and others; also caterpillars, grasshoppers, grubs, and earthworms, especially at nesting time; they frequented natural salt licks for salt, especially when feeding their young, and also ate seeds of maples and elms, grains such as rye, wheat, and buckwheat, and, sometimes, freshly planted corn, but in view of their abundance damage by passenger pigeons to agricultural crops was relatively small (Schorger, 1955).

Nest: Built in trees in vast colonies in wooded valleys, hills, also on islands; nest colonies varied in size from 20 acres or less to thousands of acres, some 40 mi. long; one 3 mi. wide by 10 mi. long was typical, but one in Wisc. in 1871 was largest ever reported—L-shaped, 100 mi. long and 3–10 miles wide (Schorger, 1955); also nested in single dispersed pairs and in loose groups of a dozen pairs or more; male brought female sticks and straws; she built nest on branch of tree in about 3 days; nest usually of small twigs only, saucer-shaped, about 6–7 in. across and about 2½ in. high, some so loosely built that eggs could be seen from ground, but mostly a compact nest and so interwoven with branches that, ordinarily, winds and storms could not dislodge them, nest usually built on limb near trunk but many were close together along limbs in rows or in bunches, 5–60 ft. but more often 12–25 ft. above ground, with 24–100 or even 300 or more nests in a tree (Schorger, 1955).

Eggs: Apr.–July; 1, pure white, glossy; in captivity, laid only 1 egg, according to Craig (1913) and Whitman (1919); in wild, occasionally 2 eggs in a nest but apparently laid by two females (Schorger, 1955).

Incubation: By both sexes, 12–14 days; both adults fed young, which put their bills in mouths of parents to eat regurgitated food (*see* Young and Their Care); young remained in nest 13–15 days, after which adults in colony abandoned them en masse; 3–4 days after their abandonment, while living on their body fat, young could fly well; apparently only one nesting by a pair each year.

Other Names: Blue-headed pigeon; blue meteor; blue pigeon; pigeon; red-breasted pigeon; wild pigeon; wood pigeon.

Accidents: When two columns of passenger pigeons, moving toward each other at same level, came together, many collided and stunned birds fell to ground.

Albinism: Apparently rare; a white one killed at Chilton, Wisc., Sept. 29, 1875; some records of partial albinos (see Schorger, 1955).

Flight Speed: Estimated by early observers at 40–90 or even 100 m.p.h., but Schorger suggests that its normal, or cruising, speed was about 60 m.p.h. and at most might have reached 70 m.p.h. if pursued and pressed by a falcon.

Hybrids: Has been crossbred in captivity with the ringed turtle dove, but only male hybrids were produced and these were sterile (see details in Schorger, 1955).

Weights: 9–12 oz.

Range: Before permanent settlement of N. America, nested east of Rockies from c. Mont., N.D., s. Man., Minn., Wisc., Mich., c. Ont., s. Que., N.B., and Nova Scotia south to e. Kans., Okla., Miss., and Ga.; wintered from Ark., Mo., Tenn., and N.C. south to Tex., La., Miss., Ala., and c. Fla.; occasionally north to Ind., Pa., and Conn.; strayed to Wash., Idaho, Nev., Wyo., and to B.C. and other parts of n. Canada to Baffin Bay; wandered to Bermuda, Cuba, Valley of Mexico; reports of in Scotland and in France in mid-19th century were probably escaped captives.

Pigeon, prairie. Another name for Franklin's gull in Gull Family, American golden plover in Plover Family, upland sandpiper and Eskimo curlew in Sandpiper Family.

Pigeon, red-billed, *Columba flavirostris* (col-UM-bah flay-vih-ROS-tris); genus name: *see* Dove, rock; species name: from Lat. *flavus,* yellow, and *rostrum,* beak; yellow-beaked; refers to bill, which is red but tipped with yellow. Mexican and C. American species that reaches U.S. in heavily wooded bottomlands of lower Rio Grande Valley of Tex., where uncommon resident, rare in midwinter (Robbins *et al.,* 1966); upriver to Falcon Dam and near coast to Norias (Peterson, 1961); 13–14 in. long; wingspread 24¾ in.; in Tex., according to Peterson, distinguished from all other pigeons there by its uniformly dark appearance (similar dark rock dove, or domestic pigeon, usually has white rump and is not often seen perched in trees); Skutch (1964a) describes the red-billed pigeon as strikingly beautiful in full sunlight; has deep maroon foreparts and deep purple-red on front part of surface of upper wings which contrasts with blue-gray of rump, tail, belly, and rest of wings; red bill, yellow-tipped; eyes orange or reddish; eyelids bright red; feet and legs red; in Tex., frequents river thickets of ebony, huisache, mesquite, and hackberry; flies swiftly, strongly, directly like domestic pigeon, often seen perched singly, in pairs, or rarely in large groups in trees; outside of nesting season flocks of 20–50 move about country in search of food; pairing may begin in Feb., song of male is loud, far-carrying *woooo, c'c'coo, c'c'coo, c'c'coo* (Skutch, 1964a); in tropics usually a bird of mature forests; in northern part of range lives in lowlands (Mexico) and in more or less arid country below 3,500 ft. Hunted in Mexico for sport and sometimes for meat but flavor at times unsavory (Bent, 1932).

Feeding Habits: Shy, usually feeds high in crowns of trees on berries and other fruits, also

acorns; not often seen on ground but in Tex. has learned to visit stubble fields to eat waste grain along with other pigeons; in Mexico, sometimes seen near houses and gardens with rock doves; fond of water, visits water holes and sandbars in streams to drink and bathe.

Nest: Solitary, frail structure of small twigs sometimes lined with fine stems and grasses, about 8 in. across and 2 in. deep, on horizontal branch of large tree or small sapling, in clump of small branches or in tree concealed by tangle of vines or brush.

Eggs: Tex. and Mexico, Mar.–Aug.; 1, rarely 2, pure white, slightly glossy.

Incubation: By both sexes; period of and age when young leave nest probably about same as that of band-tailed pigeon; raises several broods a season (Bent, 1932).

Range: Resident from s. Tex., south to Nicaragua.

Pigeon, red-necked. *See* Pigeon, scaly-naped.

Pigeon, scaly-naped, *Columba squamosa* (col-UM-bah skway-MOE-sah); genus name: *see* Dove, rock; species name: Lat., scaly, from *squama,* scale; refers to colors of feathers on hind neck (nape) of this bird that produce scaly appearance. Resident of Antilles, West Indies, has strayed twice to Key West, Fla. (see records under "Scaled" pigeon in Sprunt, 1954a); about 15 in. long; larger than white-crowned pigeon; has dark crown; basal part of bill red, tip gray; head, fore neck, and chest red-purple; hind neck metallic chestnut and purple with scaly appearance; rest of plumage slate gray; bare skin about eyes of male red; about eyes of female yellow; utters a protracted *cru-crú-crucucoo,* not so guttural as notes of white-crowned pigeon (Bond, 1961); largely arboreal, eats fruits, berries, grain, snails; gregarious, roosts in flocks, swift in flight (Bent, 1932).

Other Name: Red-necked pigeon.
Range: See above.

Pigeon, sea. Another name for harlequin duck in Duck Family, black tern and Bonaparte's gull in Gull Family, and black guillemot in Auk Family.

Pigeon, storm. Another name for the white-bellied storm-petrel. *See* Storm-petrel Family.

Pigeon, white-collared. *See* Pigeon, band-tailed.

Pigeon, white-crowned, *Columba leucocephala* (col-UM-bah lew-koh-SEFF-ah-lah); genus name: *see* Dove, rock; species name: from Gr. *leukos,* white, and *kephale,* head (Jaeger, 1955). (Color ills., page 713.) Resident almost throughout West Indies, except in s. Lesser Antilles and on other islands in Caribbean, and on Fla. Keys; about 14–15 in. long; completely dark pigeon (mostly slate gray) except for shining white crown from forehead to nape; at distance, in flight, appears a very large, very dark pigeon; bill yellow, with bright red base, eyes and orbital patch white; female crown duller white; in immatures, smoky gray;

PIPIT FAMILY

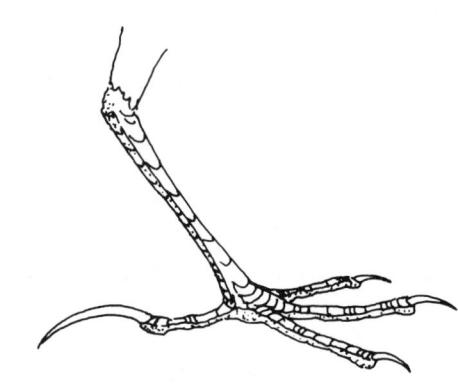

common in its range on Fla. Keys, where only other doves usually mourning and common ground dove; may be easily seen by motorists traveling Overseas Highway to Key West, sometimes perches at close range along road or flies singly or in groups across highway; Sprunt (1954a) counted up to 66 while traveling from Tavernier, Key Largo, Fla., to Key West, where this species seen along city streets (Audubon painted his illustration of this bird at Key West); 94 counted at Coot Bay, Fla., during Christmas Bird Count, Dec. 30, 1973; 74 counted Key Largo, Fla., during Christmas Bird Count, Dec. 27, 1978; generally gregarious, nests and roosts in large concentrations, thoroughly at home in thick foliage of trees; utters owl-like tremulous *wof, wof, woo, co-woo*, wild and very swift flier, often moves about country in large flocks for food (Bent, 1932).

Feeding Habits: Usually lives in trees and shrubbery, where it eats fruits of berry-producing plants, also eats seeds and some insects, seldom visits ground.
Nest: In colonies, at one time in vast numbers, usually on small islands or cays and among coastal mangroves; nest compactly built of twigs, lined with fibrous roots and grasses, from a few feet to many feet above ground, on top of cactus, bush, or on limbs of mangroves and in tops of palm trees (Bent, 1932).
Eggs: May–Dec.; 1–2, white, glossy.
Range: See above.

Pigeon, wild. *See* Pigeon, band-tailed; Dove, mourning; and Pigeon, passenger.

Pigeon, wood. *See* Dove, white-fronted.

Quail-dove, Key West, *Geotrygon chrysia* (jee-oh-TRY-gon CRIS-ih-ah); genus name: from Gr. *ge, ga,* or *gaia,* the earth, and *trygon,* a dove; "ground" dove; species name: Lat., from Gr. *chrysion,* a piece of gold (Jaeger, 1955); *Key West* refers to Key West, Fla., where John James Audubon first saw this species; *quail-dove,* from habit of living much on ground as quail do. (Color ill., page 711.) A tropical ground dove, nonmigratory but apparently a rare straggler to Fla. Keys, flies over water, possibly from Cuba or other islands of West Indies in its native range, where considered rare on most islands by Bond (1961); for remarks about N. American status, see Bent (1932); Sprunt (1954a); Pough (1951); 10–11½ in. long; mainly rufous or chestnut above, but *crown, hind neck, and back glossed with iridescent green and purple* (*see* Quail-dove, ruddy) and a *white streak below each eye;* eye irises red; red bill is black-tipped; legs and feet flesh-colored; resident in lowland tropical woodlands, most numerous in rather dry parts of Hispaniola, utters a mournful, expiring groan, or a protracted booming, like syllables *whoe-whoe-oh-oh-oh;* note is like that of ruddy quail-dove (Bond, 1961).

Feeding Habits: Walks about on ground under dense tangles of scrubby growth of dry hills and in open low moist woods to pick up and eat fallen fruits, seeds, small snails; bathes and drinks at secluded, shaded pools.
Nest: Either a loose collection of leaves on ground or a slight platform of sticks low or high in tree on large or small branches or atop parasitic creepers (Bent, 1932).
Eggs: Feb.–July; 2, cream-buff.
Incubation: Period of and age when young first fly apparently not known.
Weights: About 4–5 oz.
Range: Resident in Bahamas, Cuba, Isle of Pines, Hispaniola and adjacent islands, and sw. Puerto Rico.

Quail-dove, ruddy, *Geotrygon montana* (jee-oh-TRY-gon mon-TAN-a); genus name: *see* Quail-dove, Key West; species name: Lat., of the mountains, but somewhat of a misnomer because it lives mostly in tropical American lowlands. A nonmigratory ground-dwelling dove of Mexico, C. and S. America, and the West Indies; has strayed to Key West, Fla.; 8–10 in. long; male slightly larger than female, completely reddish but somewhat purple-brown on back and pinkish underparts (Peterson and Chalif, 1973), and with buffy streak below each eye (*see* Key West quail-dove); female somewhat similar but mainly dark olive brown above, paler below (Bond, 1961); lives in dense growths of jungle in humid forests and in coffee and cacao plantations; utters a low humming, and a prolonged booming note, sounding like a fog-buoy (Bond, 1961). Feeding and nesting habits similar to those of the Key West quail-dove; eggs buff-colored; incubation period of 11 days, unusually short, and young leave nest only 10 days after hatching (Skutch, 1976). See also Skutch (1949b).

Weights: 110–145 gr. (Leopold, 1959), or about 3⅞–5 oz.
Range: Resident in tropical lowlands in Mexico from s. Sonora and Tamaulipas south through C. America to Bolivia, Paraguay, and Brazil; also in Greater Antilles, Grenada, and Trinidad; accidental at Key West, Fla.

PIGEON'S MILK
See Crop; Endocrine Glands; Pigeon Family.

PIGEON-TOED
(also PARROT-TOED). An expression for one who walks with the toes turned inward, one foot swinging over the other, as a pigeon or parrot walks.

PILL-WILL
or PILL-WILL-WILLET. Name from bird's call. *See* Willet in Sandpiper Family.

PINE KNOT
See Dovekie in Auk Family.

PINFEATHER
A newly growing feather not yet unfolded; a feather just emerging from the skin of a bird and still enclosed for most of its length in a horny sheath which is later cast off. *See* Feather.

PINION

Term for the outer (distal) part of a bird's wing —the "hand" part and its bones that bear the flight feathers (see Flight); additionally, term for a single flight feather, or wing quill; also, the flight feathers (primaries), collectively, of a wing.

To temporarily prevent waterfowl or other birds, kept for breeding, or propagation, from flying out of sanctuaries or aviaries, the flight feathers of *one* wing may be cut off (called clipping), which renders the bird incapable of flight until the next molt (see Molts and Molting), when new flight feathers grow and the bird can fly again. To render waterfowl permanently flightless, the hand part, including the bones that bear the flight feathers, may be cut from one wing. This is called "pinioning" and is the practice of those who wish to keep waterfowl on a pond or in an open enclosure for an indefinite time, but a pinioned bird can never fly again. See details of pinioning and of keeping waterfowl in captivity in McAtee (1930).

PINK-EYED DIVER

See Horned grebe in Grebe Family.

PINTAIL

See in Duck Family.

PINYON-JUNIPER WOODLAND

One of the nine biomes (see Biome) in N. America north of Mexico used in mapping the ecological distribution of birds. See Major Biotic Communities (biomes) under Distribution. The Pinyon-Juniper Woodland is composed of two species of pinyon pines and several of junipers or cedar *(Juniperus)* with yuccas often prevalent; the biome is on hills and mountain slopes above deserts or grasslands and below the coniferous forest, mostly in the Great Basin (see Great Basin) and the Colorado R. region in Colo., Utah, Nev., Ariz., N.M., and the east side of the Sierra Nevada–Cascade Mtns. in Calif.; typical birds are the gray flycatcher, pinyon jay, plain titmouse, bushtit, and Bewick's wren (Pettingill, 1970; 1972).

PIPIT FAMILY

Motacillidae (moe-tah-SILL-ih-dee); from Lat. *motacilla*, wagtail (from habit of many in family of pumping tail up and down). 54 species worldwide, except on some Pacific islands (Van Tyne and Berger, 1976; Voous, 1964b); 8 species reported in N. America, including the meadow pipit, which nests in e. Greenland; small, sparrow-sized (5–8¾ in.), long-clawed birds, most are ground-dwelling, most have the hind claw long and spurlike but not usually as long as that of larks; all have nine functional primary feathers (they are "nine-primaried" songbirds—see Passeriformes); family includes both the pipits and the wagtails—slender birds, walk or run rapidly; have slender, pointed bills, live mostly on insects and in open country—moors of Old World, prairies of N. America, Arctic tundra, or along banks of brooks, lakes, and rivers, from shores of water upward into highest mountain ranges (Voous, 1964b); pipits and wagtails perhaps most widely distributed in Africa and Eurasia; pipits get name from their twittering voices and wag-

tails because they almost continuously wag their long tails up and down; most have the outer tail feathers white, which show when bird is in flight; they fly strongly, often with exaggerated undulations in wagtails; they call much in flight; most are migratory; in their structure and behavior, members of family are thought to be related to or to have affinities with Old World warblers and Old World thrushes; they have habits like larks and outwardly may resemble them, thus they are often called titlarks and field larks. For a detailed discussion of Old World wagtails and pipits, see Austin (1961); Voous (1964b).

Wagtails are mainly birds of the Old World; only 2 species nest in N. America—the white wagtail in Alaska and Greenland; the yellow wagtail in w. Alaska; the gray wagtail is a visitor to the Aleutian Is. Wagtails migrate from Alaska in winter back to the Old World, retracing their flight westward to Siberia, then southward (Austin, 1961).

Among pipits, the water, or rock, pipit is noted as one of the most widespread members of the family; the Sprague's pipit of N. American prairies is famed for its spectacular courtship flight; 4 species of pipits presently nest, or have nested, in N. America.

Pipits and wagtails are protected by law and may not be kept in captivity without a permit; however, to sustain an injured or ill one until it is able to fend for itself, offer it mealworms or any other insects available; also ground meat and soft well-ripened fruit and small amount of bread crumbs. Because they are rarely kept in captivity, no well-proved diet is known for them (Walker, 1942).

Gross (1965a) listed nine records of albinism in three species in the Pipit Family but did not name the species.

Pipit, American. *See* Pipit, water.

Pipit, meadow, *Anthus pratensis* (AN-thus [*th* as in *thin*] prah-TEN-sis); genus name: Lat., from Gr. *anthos*, a kind of bird; Macleod (1954) reported that according to Gr. legend, Anthus, a youth killed by his father's horses, was then changed into a bird; species name: from Lat. *pratum*, a meadow (Coues, 1882). (Color ill., page 715.) Common bird in Europe, nests occasionally in N. America on e. coast of Greenland; 5¾ in. long; olive brown above, whitish below with some yellow on breast; streaked above and below; outer tail feathers white; smaller and more boldly marked than the water pipit, which also nests in N. America (Tucker, 1950a). In nesting season, lives in grasslands, heaths, sand dunes, often in hill country; flushes with shrill call notes; flies in jerky flight before dropping to ground again.

Range: Nests in Greenland (occasionally), Iceland, and east across Europe and Russia; winters in parts of nesting range and southward.

Pipit, Pechora (peh-CORE-ah), *Anthus gustavi* (AN-thus GUS-tav-eye); genus name: *see* Pipit, meadow; species name: given in 1863 in honor of Gustave Schlegel (1840–1903), Dutch professor of natural history and director of Leyden Museum (see in Gruson, 1972); *Pe-*

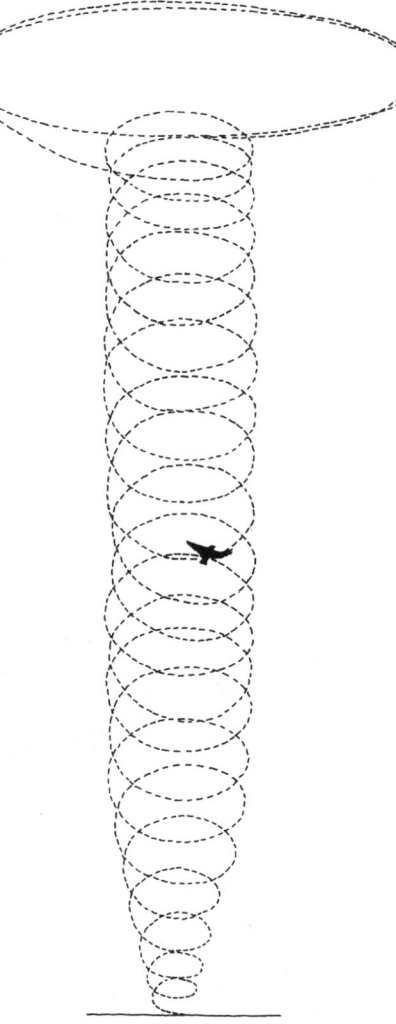

PIPIT FAMILY
In the courtship flight of the Sprague's pipit, the male spirals upward as high as 500 feet and circles with spread tail, uttering clear, sweet musical notes. Then the pipit closes its wings and plunges to earth silently, spreading its wings only just before alighting.

Sprague's pipit

PIPIT FAMILY

White wagtail

chora, for valley of the Pechora R. in ne. Russia, where it nests. First N. American record on St. Lawrence Is., Alaska, reported in 1938; second N. American record, one reported at Gambell, Alaska, June 16, 1975 (Gibson and Byrd, 1975); 5¾ in. long; slightly smaller than the water pipit, but plumage generally paler, spots on throat, breast, and flanks bolder and blacker than in water pipit; outer tail feathers buffy instead of white.

Range: See above.

Pipit, red-throated, *Anthus cervinus* (ANthus sir-VINE-us); genus name: *see* Pipit, meadow; species name: Lat., staglike, or tawny color, in allusion to rusty-colored face and throat of this species in summer. (Color ill., page 714.) Mainly a Siberian tundra species during summer; bred once at Wales, Alaska (1931); 62 counted at Cape Mt. Wales, Alaska, June 22–28, 1972, and one nest with 6 eggs (Gibson and Byrd, 1972); also records of its occurrence on St. Lawrence Is. (1931), and St. Michael Is., Alaska (1867); accidental (one record) in Baja Calif., Jan. 1883; accidental in Calif. with records of up to 15 near Imperial Beach, San Diego County, Oct. 12–27, 1964; up to 10 there Oct. 9–29, 1966, and again near Imperial Beach, Oct. 22–Nov. 4, 1967; one at Farallon Is. collected Nov. 3, 1968 (Small, 1974); 5¾ in. long; resembles water pipit, also meadow pipit, but in summer, male has pale rust or pink over throat and face (female usually less so); upperparts warm brown with bold black streakings on back, rump, and upper tail coverts (these parts practically unstreaked in meadow pipit); distinctive call note one of best means of identifying it; quite different from shrill notes of other pipits, it is a comparatively full, musical *chup;* nest built of dry grasses on moist tundra, often in recess in side of hummock, sometimes sheltered by dwarf birch, willow, etc. See Tucker (1950c) for other life history details.

Range: Nests on tundra of n. Europe and n. Siberia, nests rarely in Alaska; winters south to India, Iran, s. Sahara; accidental in Baja Calif., also Calif.

Pipit, rock. *See* Pipit, water.

Pipit, Sprague's, *Anthus spragueii* (ANthus SPRAIG-ih-eye); genus name: *see* Pipit, meadow; species name: given by John James Audubon in honor of Isaac Sprague, artist and botanical illustrator, who accompanied Audubon on his Missouri R. expedition of 1843. The bird, the first of its kind known to science, was collected by John G. Bell and Edward Harris, who fired together and shot the bird (McDermott, 1951); lives over interior grasslands of N. America from s. Canada south to Tex. and s. Mexico; 6¼–7 in. long; sexes outwardly alike; pale, sparrowlike, buffy underparts conspicuously streaked, not solidly dark or gray back as in similar water pipit; has white outer tail feathers as does the vesper sparrow, often associated with it, but pipit is slender, with sharp-pointed, warblerlike bill; vesper sparrow is stockier with short conical bill; Sprague's pipit migrates northward usually in Apr.; difficult to see on plains and prairies, as it remains hidden in grasses, and when flushed, takes off in long, bounding, erratic flight to drop quickly into cover again; more often heard than seen; male in summer spends most of day in sky, almost out of sight in courtship or territorial flight; spirals upward, climbing to 300–500 ft., then circles with spread tail, uttering clear, sweet musical notes resembling tiny sleigh bells or the sound of a light chain falling in coil to the ground; after singing and flying about, male closes wings and plunges earthward, spreading his wings only just before alighting on ground; sometimes female flies up from her nest to meet him, from this habit nests have been found (Bent, 1950).

Feeding Habits: In summer eats grasshoppers, crickets, beetles, etc., and weed seeds; in migration, and in winter, flocks often seen in weed-grown fields.

Nest: Built in hollow in ground or in tuft of grasses, cup of woven dried grasses, about 3 in. across.

Eggs: May–June; 3–6, usually 4–5, gray-white, thickly blotched with purple-brown.

Incubation: By female, period of unreported; young leave nest about 10–11 days after hatching (Bent, 1950).

Other Names: Missouri skylark; prairie skylark; titlark.

Flight Speed: Timed in w. U.S., 28 m.p.h. (Cottam *et al.*, 1942b).

Host to Cowbirds: One record from sw. Sask., May 1932: 3 eggs of pipit, 2 of brown-headed cowbird (Friedmann, 1963).

Range: Nests from n. Alta., c. Sask., and c. Man. south to Mont., N.D., and nw. Minn.; winters from s. Ariz., Tex., s. La., and nw. Miss. south to s. Mexico; casual visitor to Mich., S.C., Ga., Fla. (Bent, 1950).

Pipit, water, *Anthus spinoletta* (AN-thus spin-oh-LET-tah); genus name: *see* Pipit, meadow; species name: used mistakenly for *spipoletta*, dim. of Ital. *spipola*, or titlark (Macleod, 1954). (Color ills., pages 714, 715.) The water pipit summers in N. America on the treeless tundra or on mountaintops in the Arctic-Alpine zone, from barren coast of Labrador across the Arctic tundra to n. Alaska, w. coast of Greenland, and far to the south in the Rocky Mtns., from Wyo. and Colo. to Calif. and N.M.; 6–7 in. long; wingspread 10–11 in.; sexes outwardly alike; plain gray-brown above, *buffy below* with streaking; white outer tail feathers like vesper sparrow's but habit of sometimes bobbing tail up and down or swinging it, with body motion, from side to side, and nodding head like a dove while *walking* or running on ground; slender body, and thin, pointed bill, distinguish it from sparrows and longspurs; seen mostly on ground in open places, often winters on plains and lowlands, below mountain nesting grounds, in enormous flocks south into Mexico; much of spring migration northward is west of Alleghenies (Bent, 1950); flocks of 15–500 in Mar. and early Apr. in freshly plowed fields, newly grown wheat, pastures, mud flats of wet fields; most are on northern nesting grounds either on the Arctic tundra or on higher mountains above limit of trees by Apr.

and May; Verbeek (1970) studied nesting of water pipit on alpine tundra of Beartooth Plateau, Wyo., at 9,600 ft., and discovered habitat must be snow-free early in season, and have features such as tussocks (tufts of grass or sedge), tilted rocks of slopes, and boulder-strewn fields; according to Bent (1950), male in courtship flight or song flight, while flying almost vertically 50–150 ft. in air, sings tinkling weak notes (generally paired): *che-wee, che-whee, che-whee, chee-wee;* sings also, in migration, from ground or tree; call note is *wit-wit* or *tsip, tsip-it,* sounds to some listeners like *pip-it.*

Feeding Habits: Walks about daintily and plucks insects and seeds from ground, grasses, weeds; eats weevils, bugs, grasshoppers, crickets, aphids, ground beetles, caterpillars, plant bugs, ants, also spiders and mites and small mollusks and crustaceans; gets food also on bare rocky ground or open mud flats, on drifted sea wrack along coasts, and on salt or brackish marshes; about whaling stations in n. Ungava, where white whales left to rot, feeds on maggots of carcasses; also wades into shallow pools of tidal flats for aquatic worms and insects (Bent, 1950).

Nest: Built on ground in shelter of rock, bank, side of mossy hummock, or at foot of tussock, often only of dried grasses and twigs, but Verbeek (1970) found 16 nests that contained horsehair, 1 porcupine hair; some were shallow scrapes with no nest materials; some were built atop old nests of previous years; apparently only female builds nest, in about 4 days.

Eggs: June–July; 3–7, usually 4–5, often 6, gray-white, thickly blotched with browns.

Incubation: By female (males have no brood patches); average period, 14 days, 10 hours; when young leave nest 14–15 days after hatching, can fly short distances.

Other Names: American pipit; rock pipit; titlark; wagtail.

Age: One, banded, reported from Great Britain, 8 years, 10 months, old (Clapp, 1976).

Weights: Adults: males (10) averaged 21.8 gr.; females (10), 20.6 gr. (Verbeek, 1970), or about ¾ oz.

Range: Nests from Alaska (100 mi. south of Point Barrow), Aleutians, n. Yuk., n. Canada, w. Greenland, south in western mountains to Ore., Idaho, Utah, Calif. (first nesting record, a nest with 4 young on Aug. 1, 1975, at 10,500 ft., near Saddlebag Lake, Mono County—Stallcup and Winter, 1975), Ariz. (above timber in San Francisco and White Mtns.), and n. N.M., and across Canada south to s.w. Yuk., n. B.C., s. Mack., n. Man., n. Ont., n. Que., along coast of Labrador to Gaspé Pen. and Newfoundland and on mountains in Me.,; also nests in n. and se. Europe, Siberia, Kamchatka Pen., etc.; winters along ice-free coasts of N. America and in continental interior, from s. B.C., Ore., and Nev., s. Utah south to Baja Calif., w. Mexico to Tex., Ark., Tenn., W.Va., se. Pa., s. N.J., rarely Long Is., N.Y., and along Atlantic coast from Md. south, and to Gulf coast, Fla., and to Guatemala.

Wagtail, gray, *Motacilla cinerea* (MOE-tah-sill-ah sin-ER-ih-ah); genus name: Lat., wagtail, from habit of pumping tail up and down; species name: Lat., ash-colored, in reference to gray back. Eurasian species reported twice in Alaska to 1962: one collected (shot) June 4, 1961, on Amchitka Is., Aleutians, was first N. American record; a second collected on St. Paul Is., Alaska, Oct. 13, 1962 (see details in Jones and Gibson, 1975); about 7 in. long; according to Peterson *et al.* (1954), has blue-gray upperparts, breast brilliant yellow in summer, has buffy breast in winter; in any season is identifiable from other yellow-breasted wagtails by its very long black tail with white outer tail feathers. Is mostly a bird of streams, where it flits about over boulders, often close to rushing waters, or wades in shallows to catch insects (Gilliard, 1958).

Wagtail, white or pied, *Motacilla alba* (MOE-tah-sill-ah AL-bah); genus name: *see* Wagtail, gray; species name: Lat., white. Widespread Eurasian species that has nested locally in w. Alaska and Greenland (Robbins *et al.,* 1966); 6–7 in. long; small, slim, long-tailed; adult male is black, gray, and white (pied); with black cap, black bib, white underparts, white face, gray back (a black-backed race in Aleutian Is.), white patch in wings, black tail with white outer tail feathers; in female, gray in plumage is duller (Tucker, 1950d); immature distinguished by black necklace across pure-white breast, white underparts; spends much time on ground, where walks and runs actively, constantly moving tail up and down and bobbing head like a dove; flight strongly undulating, is succession of long curves with wings closed briefly, calls much in flight, *tschizzik* and *tzi-wirrup,* sometimes perches on buildings, fences, occasionally trees; prefers open country near water; wades in shallows of ponds, lakes, streams, also may live on cultivated land and about farm buildings; in Arctic, mostly coastal; male sings lively warbling twitter; in courtship, chases female in erratic flight; when she pauses, male postures before her, head high, bill pointed up, displaying glossy black throat (Tucker, 1950d).

Feeding Habits: Walks about on ground along coastal wrack line (high-water mark) or wades in water to forage for insects, snails.

Nest: Built by female (attended by male) in cavity in rocks, cliffs, steep banks, roots of trees, or in crevices in buildings, walls, inside sheds, under bridges, commonly from few feet to 9–10 ft. above ground, sometimes under clod in plowed field or among dune grasses.

Eggs: Apr.–July; 4–8, usually 5–7, gray or blue-white, freckled with gray or brown (Tucker, 1950d).

Incubation: Mostly by female, 12–14 days; young leave nest 14–15 days after hatching.

Range: Nests over much of Europe and Asia, from Iceland and British Isles, east to e. Siberia, south to Portugal and Syria; in N. America, has been reported in Greenland, ne. Que., Attu Is., Aleutians, Alaska, mouth of Yukon R. (nesting pairs with young and with eggs in Alaska—see Gibson, 1968), and La Paz, Baja Calif.; winters in s. Europe, Asia, and Africa.

Wagtail, yellow, *Motacilla flava* (MOE-tah-sill-ah FLAH-vah); genus name: *see* Wagtail, gray; species name: Lat., yellow. (Color ill., page 715.) Eurasian species established in Alaska; 6–7 in. long; male has olive-green back and face, white stripe over eyes; white throat, yellow underparts; long legs and long tail, which has white outer feathers; female similar but duller and browner above, paler below; immature is darker gray above, white below, with white streak over eyes; necklace of dark feathers around throat; flies with long, swinging, undulating flight, like woodpecker; walks about on ground with tail pumping up and down, head nodding; summers in arctic willow and dwarf alder thickets on tundra and along Alaskan coast from Point Barrow south to Kotzebue Sound and to mouth of Nushagak R. on Bering seacoast; probably on islands in Bering Sea (Bent, 1950); male in courtship of female rises in jerky flight from bank or from bushes, uttering jingling notes, then descends and glides away to alight in bush or on knoll; call note is frequent, weak *pe-weet.*

Feeding Habits: Not much known of in Alaska, but probably similar to the species' habits in Europe and Asia, where largely insects—beetles, flies, aquatic insects—small worms, and snails (Bent, 1950); also seen eating salmonberries in Alaska and around camps eating bread crumbs.

Nest: On ground under edge of tussock, or under slightly overhanging bank, under bunch of grass or under roots of willow along river, on grassy knoll; about 5 in. across, of grasses, plant stems, leaves, rootlets, mosses, lined with hair of reindeer, mouse, mosses, and few feathers.

Eggs: June–July (?); 4–7, commonly 5–6, variable colors, described as dark olive-buff to green-white, marked with spots of buff, gray, light brown, and red-brown (Bent, 1950).

Incubation: About 10–13 days; young leave nest 15–18 days after hatching; sometimes two broods a year (Turner, 1886).

Age: One, banded, reported from Great Britain, 6 years, 11 months, old (Clapp, 1976).

Range: Great Britain east to n. Siberia and w. Alaska, south in winter to S. Africa.

PIRACY AMONG BIRDS

See Behavior; Autolycism.

PITUITARY GLAND

See Endocrine Glands.

PLACE NAMES FOR BIRDS

See article by Ristow (1966); *see also* State Birds.

PLANKTON

Collective term for the mostly microscopic plants (phytoplankton) and animals (zooplankton) that make up the vast drifting ocean life—the so-called pastures of the seas—upon which all other marine (and freshwater) life depends. Phytoplankton—especially the dominant diatoms and dinoflagellates—is almost everywhere in the seas and is fed upon by the tiny zooplankton (animals), which, in turn, are eaten by millions of seabirds (and other animals).

PLOVER FAMILY

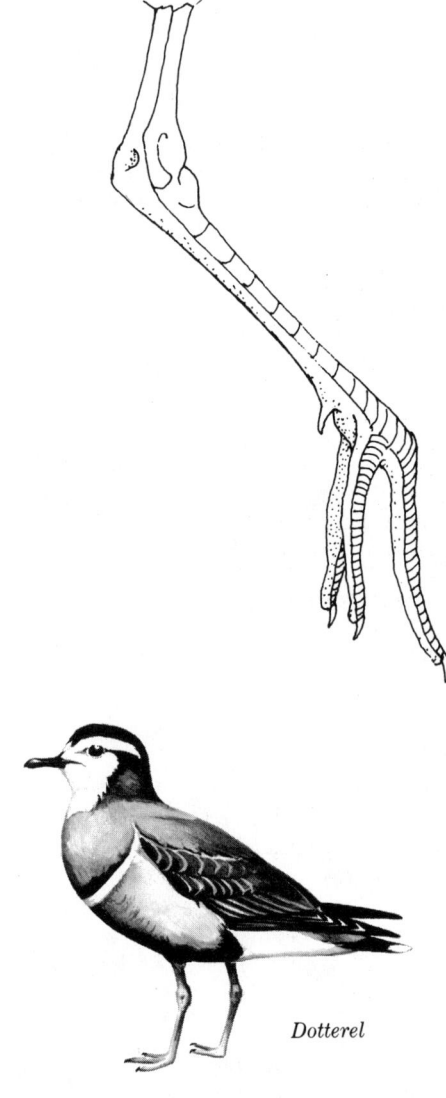

Dotterel

PLOVER FAMILY

Some of the marine zooplankton upon which seabirds feed are tiny copepods, amphipods, ostracods, shrimplike euphausids also called euphasian shrimps or "krill," pteropods, and tiny jellyfishes, and larval gastropods, oysters, cephalopods, and pelagic tunicates. *See* in Albatross Family; Auk Family; Phalarope Family; Shearwater Family; and Storm-petrel Family; *also* Food and Feeding Habits; Seabird. For a discussion of seabirds in relation to their foods, see Ashmole (1971), Lockley (1973), Watson (1975), Odum (1971), and Smith (1974).

PLANTAIN-EATER
See Cuculiformes.

PLANT COMMUNITY
See Climax Community; Subclimax Community; *also* Biotic Communities (Biomes) and Life Zones under Distribution.

PLANTING FOR BIRDS
See Bird-attracting.

PLASMA
See Circulatory System.

PLASMODIUM
See Internal Parasites under Diseases; Avian Malaria; Parasite.

PLAY BEHAVIOR
See Behavior.

PLAY NEST
See Dummy Nest; Nests and Nesting.

PLEISTOCENE PERIOD
See Geological Time Scale.

PLIOCENE PERIOD
See Geological Time Scale.

PLOCEIDAE
See Weaverbird Family.

PLOVER FAMILY
Charadriidae (car-ah-DRY-ih-dee); Lat., from Gr. *charadrios;* according to Gruson (1972), name was used by Aristotle in reference to "an inconspicuous waterbird that nests in ravines." 63 species worldwide (Van Tyne and Berger, 1976); 13 species in N. America, of which the dotterel, lapwing, Eurasian and Oriental plovers are visitors; small to medium-sized shorebirds (6–15½ in. long), compactly built, thick-necked; usually distinguished from other shorebirds by their pigeonlike bills (slightly swollen near tip) and bill always shorter than the round, dovelike head; eyes are relatively large; family includes the so-called true plovers and the lapwings—typical plovers are small with long, tapered wings, many have at least one conspicuous breast band; lapwings, of which Africa has largest number of species (there are 3 in W. Hemisphere in S. America), are medium to large, noisy plovers with broad, *rounded* wings; some have a crest, facial wattles, and wing spurs (see details in Austin, 1961; Hall, 1960); all in family fly strongly, run swiftly, and can swim, most are migratory and often active by night as well as by day; live along coastal beaches, lakes, streams, ponds, in fields, plains, and prairies, may travel in flocks of thousands; sexes alike or nearly so; some are brightly colored and many have striking patterns of brown, olive, gray, black, and white that show conspicuously in flight; however, on open ground their colors, owing to their visually disruptive pattern, make them difficult to see against rocks, pebbles, and broken ground colors. Legs are of various lengths, and feet of most lack a functional hind toe; have no more than basal webbing between the toes; tails short to medium long; some species utter melodious whistles; others, shrill cries; in most, both parents incubate the eggs and care for the young; at least two species—the dotterel and mountain plover—are known to be polyandrous (*see* Sexual Relationships).

The name *plover* (from Fr. *pluvier*, Old Fr. *plovier*) apparently had its origin in Lat. *pluvia*, rain, with which these birds were associated in ancient European folklore; however, they are neither more active nor more vocal during a rain than at other times; *lapwing* refers not to a crossing, or lapping, of the wings during flight, but to an odd, irregular lag in the wingbeats (Austin, 1961).

All plovers use the distraction display (*see* Distraction Display) to lead intruders, whether dogs, foxes, or men, away from the eggs or young; the display is especially well developed in the killdeer. The eggs of plovers have a broken color pattern (cryptic) that makes them very difficult for man or predatory bird to see against sandy or pebbly ground (*see* Cryptic, or Concealing, Colors under Colors of Feathers; *also* Eggs and Egg-laying); plover chicks leave the nest soon after hatching (or as soon as their down is dry) under the protection of the parents.

Albinism seems rare in N. American members of the Plover Family; Gross (1965a) could report only four individuals showing albinism, in two species.

To care for an injured or ill plover until it can be freed, offer it fishes, meat, grain, some chopped greens, bonemeal, crab-meat scraps or shrimp, all ground up, as mouths of these birds are rather small; they especially like mealworms.

Dotterel, *Eudromias morinellus* (you-DROW-mih-as more-ih-NELL-us); genus name: Lat., from Gr. *eudromias,* a good runner; species name: Lat., dim. of Gr. *moros,* foolish; *dotterel,* dim. of *dolt;* so called by wild fowlers of Great Britain because of bird's alleged stupidity in mimicking the motions of the fowler, a story discounted by Newton (1893–96) as silly. An inland Eurasian shorebird that has visited Alaska in summer—St. Lawrence Is., King Is., Cape Prince of Wales—has bred at least once at Point Barrow (Palmer, 1967); sexes outwardly alike; 8–9 in. long, with gray breast showing a faint to conspicuous white band across lower breast; upperparts brownish; gray axillars; appearance of an undersized American golden plover with short, thin bill, broad white stripe over each eye which continues across nape, white cheeks, chin, and throat.

Feeding Habits: Eats mostly insects, though it takes some annelid worms, snails, and seeds from pastures, grasslands, fields, and marshes (Jourdain, 1929a).

Nest: In Europe, eggs usually laid in a natural depression in ground on plateaus or slopes of mountains below highest tops, lined with lichens or leaves.

Eggs: British Isles, late May to mid-July; 2–4, usually 3, yellow-olive to red-brown, spotted with dark brown (Jourdain, 1929a).

Incubation: Sexes almost indistinguishable in field but from those collected (shot) from nest while covering the eggs, male usually incubates; in Finland and in Sweden, example of polyandry in this species discovered when larger female laid two clutches of eggs, each incubated by a different male (Bannerman, 1961). Male incubates, but females help at some nests (Pulliainen, 1970).

Range: Nests locally in mountains of Europe, Asia; casual in w. Alaska; winters south to N. Africa; has wandered to w. Wash. and Calif.; a male collected in Bermuda, Sept. 1958.

Dotterel, ringed. *See* Plover, ringed.

Killdeer, *Charadrius vociferus* (cah-RAD-rih-us voh-SIFF-er-us); genus name: according to Coues (1882), from a Gr. word meaning some kind of bird supposed to be a plover, and the watery places inhabited by such birds; species name: Lat., vociferous, vocal, in reference to voice; *killdeer*, a phonetic imitation of its loud cry. (Color ills., page 716.) Possibly the most widely distributed and best known of all N. American shorebirds; unlike most, lives in meadows, pastures, dry uplands, often many miles from water; in summer, lives over s. and c. Canada, and most of U.S. to Pacific coast; in winter, over much of southern half of U.S.; 9–11 in. long; wingspread 19–21 in.; sexes outwardly alike and about same size; in general color pattern resembles semipalmated plover but is larger; white below but distinguished by *two* black bands across chest (chick has only one); gray-brown above; *lower back, rump, and upper tail coverts bright rufous or orange;* slim black bill; legs and feet flesh- or straw-colored; has long, rounded tail with black band near end, tipped with white; white stripe along wings; seldom seen in large flocks but sometimes to 50; usually flies about singly in wavering erratic manner; in flight, utters noisy *kill-dee, kill-deer,* or *kill-deeah;* often heard at night, also a plaintive *deeah,* slurred upward at end, when disturbed by intruder, and a long, trilled *trrrrrrrrrr* when young are threatened or when killdeers are fighting or displaying (Townsend, 1929a); migrates by day or by night but migration not as noticeable as that of most shorebirds because killdeer often nests where it winters; males have greater tendency to return to same mates and same breeding sites than do females (Lennington and Mace, 1975); is one of earliest migrant shorebirds in spring; from wintering range in parts of s., e., and w. U.S. arrives in northern states, Canada, Feb.–Apr.

Feeding Habits: Alternately runs, then stands still as though to look or listen, then dabs sud-

denly with bill at ground; about 98% of food is insects gleaned from fields, riverbanks, irrigated lands, and even from lawns; eats mostly beetles, cotton-boll weevils, grasshoppers, caterpillars, ants, bugs, caddis flies, dragonflies; also eats centipedes, spiders, ticks, oyster worms, earthworms, snails, crabs, crayfishes, some weed seeds; often follows farmer plowing fields to feed on grubs of June beetles exposed in fresh furrows; sometimes feeds in shallow water but leaves water to defecate on dry land as do certain other shorebirds (Brackbill, 1970c).

Nest: In open, usually a slight depression in ground, lined with pebbles, grasses, weed stalks, in pastures, grazed meadows, cultivated fields, also on bare gravelly ground of roads, in driveways, on golf courses, spaces between ties of railroad tracks, and even on sloping graveled or tarred roofs of buildings 50 ft. above ground, from which chicks may reach ground by leaping off roof and fluttering to ground (see Wass, 1974); Mitchell (1954), in review of nesting of killdeers on roofs at Lincoln, Neb., Ontario, Calif., Los Angeles County Museum Building, etc., reported pair nesting on roof in Buffalo, N.Y.; all five young (chicks follow parents but find own food), unable to get over parapet of roof to tumble to ground, died of starvation; Wass (1974) recommends that, with killdeers nesting on roofs with parapet, concerned birders might catch young and carry them to ground; adults protect eggs and young by flying into faces of grazing livestock or lure away intruding foxes, dogs, man, etc., by "crippled-bird act." *See* Distraction Display; Young and Their Care.

Eggs: Tex. and Calif., Mar.–July; in latitude of Pa., Apr.–July; 3–5, usually 4, gray-buff, spotted, blotched, or scrawled with brown, black.

Incubation: 24 days; both parents attend brood; young first fly about 25 days after hatching; some killdeers raise two broods.

Other Names: Chattering plover; field plover; killdee; killdeer plover; noisy plover; pasture-bird.

Accidents: Some killed at night in migration by striking tall TV towers and cables (Stoddard and Norris, 1967).

Age: One, banded Long Is., N.Y., lived to 6 years; another, banded at Costa Mesa, Calif., found dead when 6 years, 6 months, old.

Flight Speed: Timed in Calif., 28, 35, and 55 m.p.h. (McLean, 1930); in w. U.S., 25 m.p.h., and running speed of 5 m.p.h. (Cottam *et al.*, 1942b).

Host to Cowbirds: Accidental, one record in Tex., killdeer is an inappropriate host (Friedmann, 1963).

Weights: Three, w. U.S., averaged 88 gr. (Hughes, 1970), or about 3 oz.; about 3–3¼ oz. (Forbush, 1925–29).

Range: Nests from nw. B.C., n. Alta., s. Mack., ne. Man., n. Ont., s. Que., Me., and N.B., south to s. Baja Calif., s.-c. Mexico, s. Tex., east along Gulf coast of U.S. to c. Fla., Bahamas, and Greater Antilles, and from coast of n. Peru to n. Chile ranges to n. Alaska; winters from s. B.C., Ore., n. Utah, Colo., Okla., to Ohio Valley and se. N.Y., south to Colombia, Peru, Chile, and Venezuela.

Lapwing, *Vanellus vanellus* (vay-NELL-us); Lat., dim. of *vannus,* a fan (Coues, 1884); a little fan, in reference to its winnowing wings (Sprunt and Chamberlain, 1949). (Color ill., page 717.) A Eurasian dark-backed plover, casual along ne. coast of N. America; 12–13 in. long; greenish-black and white; wings, broad and rounded, slow wingbeats; wing linings pure white; a bird of plowed fields, croplands, and pastures but prefers wetter places, including mud flats, flooded fields; according to Pough (1951), occupies niche in Old World similar to that of killdeer in N. America; up to 1927 only 7 records for N. American continent, but on night of Dec. 18–19, 1927, a large flight numbering thousands (Bent, 1929) left n. England and Scotland for their wintering grounds in Ireland; apparently, owing to strong winds and dense fog, were carried beyond destination to Labrador, Newfoundland, and Nova Scotia, where large numbers died from cold and all disappeared. For comparable transoceanic flight, *see* Fieldfare in Thrush Family. See history of other flights in Bagg (1967).

Feeding Habits: Largely earthworms, mollusks, including slugs and snails (*see* Mollusks and Birds), beetles, flies, caterpillars, spiders, weed seeds, and grain.

Nest: Male forms a little group of hollows or scrapes, almost always on slightly raised ground, and dug by male during his courtship ritual; scrapes are usually in a pasture, crop field, or wet meadow; one of these is chosen by female in which to lay her eggs; scrape is lined with grasses.

Eggs: England, usually Mar. and Apr. to late June; 4, rarely 5, pale brown, blotched with black.

Incubation: By both sexes, 24–25 days, sometimes to 27 or 28 days; young are precocial, swim readily; one brood each year.

Other Names: Green plover; pewit (from cry).

Age: One (banded) reported from Norway was 12 years, 6 months, old (Holgersen, 1957); another, from Holland, 19 years, 11 months (Clapp, 1976).

Range: Nests in British Isles, n. Europe, and Asia; casual in Greenland; has wandered to Baffin Is., Labrador, e. Que., Newfoundland, Nova Scotia, N.B., Me., R.I., N.Y. (Long Is.), N.J., N.C., S.C., the Bahamas, Barbados; winters in flocks in Ireland, Scotland, s. Europe, and China south to n. Africa, n. India, and Japan.

Plover, American golden, *Pluvialis dominica* (ploo-vih-AIL-iss dom-IN-ih-cah); genus name: Lat., pertaining to rain; species name: Lat., of Santo Domingo, early name of the island of Hispaniola, West Indies, where type specimen of this plover was collected (*see* Type Specimen). (Color ills., page 717.) Summers on tundra and coasts of Alaska, Arctic islands and mainland of Canada; 9–11 in. long; wingspread to 18–22½ in.; sexes outwardly alike and in size; in spring (when practically unknown west of Rockies and a straggler along Atlantic coast) is seen mostly in freshly plowed fields, burned-over areas, pastures, prairies, and on mud flats of c. U.S.; is dark above with golden spots; black below to tail; has dark rump and tail (black-bellied plover has white rump and tail); no white wing stripe as in black-bellied; axillars ("armpit" feathers seen in flight) are *gray* (they are black in black-bellied plover; white in Eurasian golden plover); a broad white stripe from over eyes and forehead extends down sides of neck; in fall, when mostly migrates far off Atlantic coast and across Pacific O., unless blown landward by strong winds, immatures and winter-plumage adults are brown overall, darker above than below, and without distinctive markings of black and white; can be distinguished from sandpipers by stocky plover build, short, stout bill; also habit of holding wings above its back after alighting; often bobs its head; call is *quee, quee-dle,* or *coodle,* unlike plaintive whistled *toor-ah-lee* of black-billed plover; flight is very swift and strong; migrating spring flocks sweep along over prairies in compact and ever-changing formations (once an abundant bird, almost wiped out by market gunners to end of 19th century, now coming back—see Bent, 1929; Forbush, 1912; Hall, 1960); one of champion long-distance migrants; from S. American winter home arrives U.S. in Mar.–Apr.; arrives nesting grounds, often in large flocks, in Arctic Canada and Alaska in May and June (Palmer, 1967); in fall most of population returns often in flocks to wintering grounds by flying southeast to coast of Labrador and Nova Scotia, some to Mass., then travel southward directly over Atlantic O. to S. American mainland, and to wintering grounds (*see* details of this remarkable annual elliptic flight under Migration); migrates by day or by night; on transoceanic migrations sometimes seen resting on ocean (Lincoln, 1950c). *See* migration route of western form, or subspecies, of the American golden plover under Pacific golden plover.

Feeding Habits: On plains, prairies, plowed lands, open sand or mud flats, eats mostly insects, largely grasshoppers and crickets, also grubs of beetles, caterpillars, cutworms, wireworms, on shores and open flats, some small mollusks and crustaceans; in n. Ungava in fall, before long migration, fills crop with crowberries (Bent, 1929).
Nest: A depression in tundra about 4 in. across, lined with mosses, dead leaves, lichens, grass.
Eggs: May–June (Palmer, 1967); 3–4, usually 4, cinnamon to light buff or cream, boldly and profusely marked with spots, blotches of black, brown; eggs difficult to see against tundra.
Incubation: By male during day, by female at night (Palmer, 1967), 26 days, 4 hours (Parmelee *et al.,* 1967); age when young first fly about 22–24 days.
Other Names: Black-breast; brass-back; bullhead; common plover; field-bird; field plover; frost-bird; golden-back; greenback; greenhead; green plover; hawk's eye; lesser golden plover; muddy-belly; muddy-breast; pale-belly; pale-breast; pasture-bird; prairie-bird; prairie pigeon; spotted plover; squealer; three-toed plover; three-toes; toad-head; trout-bird; whistling plover.
Flight Speed: Timed in Ill., 60 m.p.h. (Martin, 1916); in Iowa, a flock of 30 flew 70 m.p.h. (Youngworth, 1936). *See* Speed under Flight.

Weights: 4–6 oz. (Palmer, 1967).
Range: Nests from Arctic coast of Alaska (from Point Barrow eastward), n. Yuk., n. Mack., Banks Is., n. Victoria Is., Melville Is., and n. Devon Is., south to w.-c. and s.-c. Alaska (Nunivak Is. and Mt. McKinley), sw. Yuk., c. Mack., ne. Man. (Churchill), Southampton Is., and s. Baffin Is.; in migration, fall 1972, possibly more reports of this species along coasts of N.J., Del., Md., Va., than any other fall on record (Scott and Cutler, 1973); winters from Bolivia, Paraguay, and s. Brazil south to e.-c. Argentina, and Uruguay; casual in winter, coastal La., Miss. *See* range of western form of American golden plover under Pacific golden plover. See other life history details in Allen, A.A. (1939).

Plover, barnyard. Another name for the solitary sandpiper in Sandpiper Family.

Plover, black-bellied, *Pluvialis squatarola* (ploo-vih-AIL-iss squah-TAR-oh-lah); genus name: *see* Plover, American golden; species name: New Lat., from Ital. (Venetian) *squatarola,* the gray, or "grey," plover, name in Old World for the cosmopolitan black-bellied plover. (Color ills., page 717.) Largest American plover; summers in Arctic Alaska and Canada, seen especially in spring migration on both coasts and up Mississippi Valley; 11–13½ in. long; wingspread 22–25 in.; males average larger, more strikingly black; females duller; in spring breeding plumage, black face, black breast, and belly, upperparts pale gray spotted with black, white stripe over eyes and forehead extends down sides of neck (the similar but slightly smaller American golden plover has much *browner* back—see Plover, American golden, for differences); tail coverts snowy white; and has black axillars ("armpit" feathers), which distinguish it in all plumages (Bent, 1929); immatures and adults in winter plumage are grayish; distinguished from other shorebirds by stocky build, short, stout bill and black axillars; from northern parts of its winter range in s. U.S. starts northward on way to Arctic breeding grounds in Apr. in general movement across continent; is abundant migrant in spring up Mississippi Valley and through c. Canada, and up Atlantic coast to N.J., Long Is., N.Y., and Mass., in May moves north along nw. Pacific coast; from skies, rich wild, plaintive whistled *pee-oo-ee* or *toor-ah-lee, toor-ah-leee* announces arrival of migrating flocks as they descend to beaches, salt marshes, or inland lake shores, mud flats; wildness and wariness, and habit of traveling in smaller flocks than the American golden plover, saved it from destruction wreaked on golden plovers by market hunters of 19th century (see in Hall, 1960).

Feeding Habits: Along seacoasts feed on broad tidal sand and mud flats or in salt marshes, where they eat marine worms and insects, small mollusks, crabs and other crustaceans; inland around shores of lakes, in freshly plowed fields, wet meadows, pastures, devour grasshoppers, cutworms, beetles and their grubs, earthworms, and some seeds and berries.

Nest: A scratched-out hollow in tundra moss about 6 in. across and lined with dried grasses, mosses, lichens.
Eggs: May–June; usually 4, gray, green, whitish, or brown, spotted and scrawled with dark brown and black over entire egg; spotting not confined to one end of egg.
Incubation: By both sexes, 27 days; both attend chicks; age when young first fly 23 days (Hussell and Page, 1976).
Other Names: Black-breast; beetle-head; bottle-head; bullhead; chuckly-head; gray plover; gump; hollow-head; May cock; mud plover; owlhead; ox-eye; pilot; Swiss plover; whistling plover.
Flight Speed: Timed in Fla., 24 m.p.h. (Longstreet, 1930); 45 and 50 m.p.h. (McNeil, 1969; 1970).
Weights: 6–10½ oz. (Forbush, 1925–29).
Range: Nests in tundra from n. Russia across n. Siberia, to n. Alaska and Mack., probably east to Devon, Banks, Baffin, Southampton Is.; winters in Old World from British Isles, s. Europe, nw. India, s. China, s. Japan, south to Africa, Australia, New Zealand, Solomon Is.; in New World from sw. B.C. along Pacific coast, Calif. to Mexico, Chile, Galápagos Is., and along Atlantic coast from N.J. (rarely Mass.) south through West Indies to Argentina.

Plover, black-heart. Another name for the dunlin in Sandpiper Family.

Plover, chattering. *See* Killdeer.

Plover, chicken. Another name for the ruddy turnstone in Sandpiper Family.

Plover, Cuban snowy. *See* Plover, snowy.

Plover, Eurasian golden, *Pluvialis apricaria* (ploo-vih-AIL-us ap-rih-CAY-rih-ah); genus name: *see* Plover, American golden; species name: from Lat. *apricus,* sunny (Jaeger, 1955), applied here to golden color of the bird. Seen regularly in migration to s. Greenland, also occurs in Newfoundland; 11 in. long; wingspread to 22 in.; quite similar in size and appearance to American golden plover; distinguished in any plumage by dark upperparts richly spotted with gold, but differs from American golden plover in having *white* axillars (armpit feathers).

Other Name: Greater golden plover.
Weights: To 7 oz. (Palmer, 1967).
Range: Nests in Iceland, the Faeroes, n. Europe, and nw. Asia; winters in Europe and Africa, Baluchistan, and nw. India; in N. America, regular migrant to s. Greenland and in Newfoundland, where a few appear in late May on flats of Stephenville Crossing (Palmer, 1967).

Plover, field. *See* Killdeer and Plover, American golden; also another name for the upland sandpiper in Sandpiper Family.

Plover, golden. *See* Plover, American golden.

Plover, grass. Another name for the upland sandpiper in Sandpiper Family.

Plover, greater golden. *See* Plover, Eurasian golden.

Plover, green. *See* Lapwing; *also* Plover, American golden.

Plover, grey. *See* Plover, black-bellied.

Plover, lesser golden. *See* Plover, American golden.

Plover, marsh. Another name for the pectoral sandpiper in Sandpiper Family.

Plover, Mongolian, *Charadrius mongolus* (cah-RAD-rih-us mon-GO-lus); genus name: *see* Killdeer; species name: Lat., of Mongolia. Asiatic species that reaches w. Alaska; resembles dotterel but smaller; 7½ in. long; sexes outwardly similar, also in size; sandy above, white below; distinguished by band of chestnut across breast and nape (narrower and duskier in winter); bill and legs black; has white forehead and bib, black forecrown; ordinary call is mellow *kruit-kruit;* active like semipalmated sandpiper (Palmer, 1967).

Nest: Slight hollow in ground, lined with dried leaves, stems, seeds; in Alaska on Commander Is., nest not far from high-water line.
Eggs: Alaska, early June; 2–3, cinnamon-buff to olive-buff, evenly spotted with dark browns, black; like those of semipalmated sandpiper but larger.
Incubation: Shared, in turn, by both sexes; period of and age when young first fly unknown.
Other Names: Lesser sand plover; sand plover; short-billed sand plover.
Range: Resident (?) in Alaska in summer on dry alpine and tundra country in Commander Is., and dunes and coasts; in winter along coastal mud flats; nests in Asia, se. Siberia, nw. India, Tibet, Mongolia, e. Siberia, Komandorskie Is.; winters from s. Asia and Philippines to n. Australia; has also been reported in Alaska from Nunivak Is. and Cape Prince of Wales.

Plover, mountain, *Charadrius montanus* (cah-RAD-rih-us mon-TAN-us); genus name: *see* Killdeer; species name: Lat., of mountains, but not an especially appropriate name, because it is mainly a bird of the high plains and semi-desert regions of the West. (Color ill., page 718.) One of few shorebirds that live mainly away from water in dry regions; sexes similar in appearance and size; 8–9 in. long; wingspread about 17½–19½ in.; almost as large as killdeer, has brown back but no rings across its sandy-buff breast; during breeding season, has black forecrown with white forehead and white stripe over eyes; loses white face pattern in fall but can be distinguished by its thin white wing stripe that shows in flight and black tail band with white border; also, white wing linings show strikingly in flight; a fast runner, does not often fly, but if disturbed, takes off and flies low, briefly, with alternate

flapping and soaring, with wings downcurved; on re-alighting, either may run a few steps, then seem to stand on tiptoe as though to get better view of intruder, or may crouch on ground, when, owing to its protective coloration, may become virtually invisible; utters a low, pleasing, sometimes harsh and shrill, variable whistle; outside of breeding season, may be in flocks of fifteen to several hundreds feeding over alkaline flats, plowed ground, sprouting grain fields, grazed pastures; from wintering range in Far West and Southwest, generally arrives on nesting range in Wyo., Mont., Colo., mid-Mar.–mid-May (Bent, 1929).

Feeding Habits: In summer, on dry short-grass prairie of low scattered bunchgrass, miles from water, or in sandy, scattered sagebrush and cactus country, eats mostly, if not entirely, insects—grasshoppers, crickets, beetles, flies.
Nest: A slight depression on bare open ground on bare rolling dry prairie or plains, sometimes with slight lining of fine rootlets and dried grasses; adults protect nest and eggs by flying up into faces of moving cattle, or lure other intruders away with "crippled-bird act" (see details in Walker, 1955). *See also* Killdeer.
Eggs: May; 2–4, usually 3, olive, spotted and scrawled with black.
Incubation: 29 days; young can fly at least several hundred feet 33–34 days after hatching (Graul, 1975); after laying her first set of eggs, incubated by the male of the pair, female lays· a second set, which *she* incubates; some females remain with their original mates; others switch to other males prior to laying their second clutch of eggs; some males copulate with more than one female (Graul, 1973). *See* discussion of polygyny and polyandry under Sexual Relationships.
Other Names: Prairie plover; upland plover.
Range: Nests on high plains, plateau, formerly from n. Mont. to ne. N.D., south through e. Wyo., w. Neb., Colo., and w. Kans. to c. and se. N.M., w. Tex., w. Okla., but according to Graul (1973) range now more restricted, with small populations still breeding only in parts of Mont., Wyo., Okla., and N.M., with main breeding area ("present stronghold of the species") in ne. Colo.; winters from c. Calif., w. and s. Ariz., c. and coastal Tex. south to s. Baja Calif., and in c. Mexico; casual in s. Alta., s. Sask., Utah, and se. Neb.; accidental in Fla. and Mass.

Plover, noisy. *See* Killdeer.

Plover, Oriental, *Charadrius veredus* (cah-RAD-rih-us VER-eh-dus); genus name: *see* Killdeer; species name: Lat., "a horse for pursuit," apparently alluding to swiftness of running of plover. Asiatic species, one caught in Greenland, date not reported; 7½ in. long; sexes outwardly similar; upper parts gray-sandy, underparts white with broad, sharply delineated breast band; head white except crown, nape, and line from eyes back; legs and feet yellow; axillars ("armpit" feathers) *brown* (Palmer, 1967).

Plover, Pacific golden, *Pluvialis dominica fulva* (ploo-vih-AIL-us doh-MIN-ih-cah FULL-

Mongolian plover

PLOVER FAMILY

Pacific golden plover

vah); genus and species names: see Plover, American golden; subspecies name: Lat., tawny. Also called the lesser golden plover; a smaller, more brightly colored subspecies, or form, of the American golden plover; it nests from Arctic coast and tundra of Siberia east to Alaska (Cape Prince of Wales) and in w. Alaska along coasts of Norton Sound and the Bering Sea to Nunivak and Nelson Is.; it winters in se. Asia and throughout Oceania in c. and s. Pacific (A.O.U. *Check-list*, 1957); its migrations appear to be entirely across the Pacific (Bent, 1929); its wintering range is some 10,000 mi. wide, and about 8,800 mi. south of its Arctic breeding grounds (see details in Cooke, 1911). *See* Migration. It is casual in migration on the Pacific coast of N. America, reported from B.C., Alta., Wash., Ore., Calif., and inland at Lake Chatcolet, Idaho, also on Atlantic coast, one record at Scarborough, Me. (A.O.U. *Check-list*, 1957). *See* Plover, American golden, for range of the eastern form and habits of the golden plover as a species.

Plover, piping, *Charadrius melodus* (cah-RAD-rih-us mel-OH-dus); genus name: see Killdeer; species name: Lat., melodious, pleasantly singing (Jaeger, 1955). (Color ill., page 718.) Small whitish plover, summers along sandy beaches of Atlantic coast, south shores of Great Lakes, west to Neb., and across s. Canada; 6–7 in. long; wingspread 14–15¼ in.; sexes similar in appearance and size; like a semipalmated plover but much paler; upperparts sandy, match dry sand of beach (back of similar semipalmated is darker (Peterson, 1947); much white on head with narrow black band above forehead that reaches from eye to eye; white underparts have black, usually incomplete or very narrow ring around neck; orange-yellow legs; black-tipped yellow bill, which is black in winter; in winter may be without dark neck ring and dark band above forehead; flight is wilder than that of pale gray sanderling, which flies steadily ahead; piping plover twists and turns more; as it flies over sandy beaches utters clear, melodious whistle, *peep peep peep-lo,* or simply a two-noted *peep-lo!* when running over sand, so protectively colored that when it crouches it seems to disappear; seen usually singly or in small flocks; from wintering grounds in s. U.S., start northward in Mar. and on nesting grounds in n. U.S. and s. Canada by Apr. and May.

Feeding Habits: Very deliberate in feeding, runs short distance, then pauses and stares at sand, head tilted somewhat to one side, then picks up something; resembles habit of robin of running over lawns; eats marine worms, fly larvae, beetles, crustaceans, mollusks, and other small marine animals and their eggs (Tyler, 1929a).

Nest: Slight hollow in sand, sometimes lined with shells, pebbles, or driftwood, usually on sand bordering lake or ocean and well above high-water mark of upper beach or recent sand fill where no plants growing.

Eggs: Apr.–May; 3–4, usually 4, gray to pale sand color, sparingly dotted, spotted with purple, black; almost invisible on sand.

Incubation: 27 days; both parents attend young, which fly about 30–35 days after hatching; no evidence of two broods but pair will re-nest if first clutch is lost (Palmer, 1967).

Other Names: Beach bird; beach plover; belted piping plover; clam-bird; mourning bird; pale ring-neck; ring-neck; sand plover; western piping plover.

Age: Twelve banded on Long Is., N.Y., reached ages of 8–11 years; six lived to be at least 9 years old; three to at least 11 years (Wilcox, 1959). Another, retrapped June 5, 1961, at same place where banded, was almost 14 years old (Wilcox, 1962).

Weights: 1½–2¼ oz. (Palmer, 1967).

Range: Nests locally across Canada from c. Alta., s. Sask., s. Man., n. Mich., s. Ont., north shore Gulf of St. Lawrence, Prince Edward Is., to Magdalens and sw. Newfoundland, south to se. S.D., c. Neb., south shores on Lakes Michigan and Erie, and along Atlantic coast to Va.; winters south along coast from S.C. to Fla. and west along Gulf coast to Tex., rarely to Bahamas and Greater Antilles; has strayed to Wyo. and Colo.

Plover, prairie. *See* Plover, mountain; also another name for the upland sandpiper in Sandpiper Family.

Plover, red-legged. Another name for the ruddy turnstone in Sandpiper Family.

Plover, ringed, *Charadrius hiaticula* (cah-RAD-rih-us high-ay-TICK-you-lah); genus name: see Killdeer; species name: according to Macleod (1954), may mean "cleft bird," or "cleft dweller"; if so, a misnomer. (Color ill., page 719.) Eurasian species, in N. America, in summer, in Greenland, Ellesmere and Baffin Is., Canada, casual in Alaska—one adult with chicks collected St. Lawrence Is., Alaska (Palmer, 1967); for other more recent records see Kessel and Gibson (1978); generally indistinguishable from the semipalmated plover, with which it is, by some ornithologists, considered conspecific; however, is larger, has wider breast band, no distinct webbing between toes (Palmer, 1967); 7½ in. long; wingspread to 15 in.; brown above, white below with much white on head; a single, complete dark band across breast; legs and feet orange-yellow; bill somewhat orange with dark tip; in winter, breast band is brownish; utters clear, low-pitched whistle from ground as much as from the air; outside of nesting season, in large flocks (Jourdain, 1929b).

Feeding Habits: Eats aquatic insects, worms, mollusks, crustaceans, also seeds of *Polygonum,* etc.

Nest: Depression in sand of beach, above high-water mark on seashore; sometimes lined with fragments of shells, small stones, driftwood, rabbits' droppings; some ringed plovers lay eggs on bare pebbles of beach, some in British Isles nest in grain fields several miles from sea (Jourdain, 1929b).

Eggs: Ne. Greenland, mid-June–mid-July; 3–4, usually 4, buffy, spotted sparingly with browns or black.

Incubation: By both sexes, which relieve one another at short intervals (Jourdain, 1929b); 23 days; young first fly about 24 days after hatching; one brood a year at northern limits of nesting range; possibly three broods, rarely, at southern limits of nesting range (Palmer, 1967).

Weights: 1⅓–2¼ oz.

Range: Nests from n. Siberia to Chukotski Pen., south to n. Russia through c. Siberia, east to Bering Sea, Ellesmere and Baffin Is., Greenland, Iceland, British Isles, n. Europe south to Portugal, Spain, Sardinia, Italy, Sicily; winters from British Isles, Mediterranean region, Asia Minor, China, south to s. Africa, nw. India; New World population in ne. Canada migrates eastward through Greenland to w. Europe; a wanderer reached Barbados (Palmer, 1967).

Plover, ring-necked. *See* Plover, semipalmated.

Plover, rock. Another name for the surfbird, turnstones, and the pectoral sandpiper in Sandpiper Family.

Plover, sand. *See* Plover, piping, and Plover, Mongolian.

Plover, semipalmated, *Charadrius semipalmatus* (cah-RAD-rih-us sem-ih-pal-MAY-tus); genus name: see Killdeer; species name: from Lat. *semi,* half, and *palma,* hand, in reference to the partly webbed front toes and smaller web between middle and inner toe (it has no hind toe, or hallux). (Color ill., page 720.) Nests along coasts of Canada from Nova Scotia north to Arctic and west to B.C.; migrates along Atlantic and Pacific coasts and interior of U.S. and Canada; small shorebird to about 6½–8 in. long; wingspread to 14–15¼ in. (Palmer, 1967); sexes outwardly similar; dark brown above, white below with single dark breast band; legs yellow or orange; bill sometimes orange tipped with black and all-black in winter; in fall, breast band is gray-brown; immatures have all-black bill and pale yellow legs; usually a common bird of beaches and mud flats of seacoast, lakeshores, and rivers during spring and fall migrations; in flight shows faint white line on dark wings; migrates by day or by night; as flocks fly northward, they utter common call note, a clear, plaintive, two-noted whistle, *chee-wee, chur-wee,* or *tyoo-eep,* second note higher; daytime flocks, often compact, seen to twist and turn as though animated by signal from a member of flock (*see* Unity of the Flock in Flight under Flight); flocks often cluster at sunset on mud bar or above high-water mark on beach to sleep; tuck bills into feathers of back or sink head between shoulders as they roost for night; from winter range along coasts of s. U.S. and S. America, arrives in most of U.S. by Apr.–May and on most of Canadian nesting grounds by late May into early June.

Feeding Habits: Feed in plover fashion by running about on beach with heads up, then dabbing suddenly at ground, unlike sanderlings and other sandpipers that move along, close together, with heads down, probing the sand; associates most often with semipalmated and least sandpipers; on seacoast, frequents outer beaches, mud flats of creeks and tidal pools, and ponds in salt marshes; inland, visits similar places along shores of lakes and rivers, also freshly plowed fields for food; along seacoast, eats marine worms, small mollusks, small crustaceans, eggs of marine animals and insects, including larvae of the salt-marsh mosquito, *Aedes sollicitans;* inland eats great numbers of grasshoppers, including Rocky Mountain locusts (Townsend, 1929b), also earthworms.

Nest: Loosely colonial, a depression in sand or gravel of beach which bird may scoop out, or in moss or lichens above high-water mark, sometimes lined with bits of shells or grasses (see account in Sutton and Parmelee, 1955).

Eggs: June; 3–4, usually 4, buffy, boldly spotted, streaked, blotched with blacks or browns.

Incubation: By both sexes, 23–25 days (Jehl and Hussell, 1966); young leave nest and run after parents almost as soon as hatched; age when young first fly unknown but possibly 21 days after hatching (Palmer, 1967).

Other Names: Beach bird; red-eye; ring-neck; ring-necked plover; ring plover; semipalmated ring plover.

Accidents: Some killed in night migration when striking lighthouses.

Flight Speed: Timed in Fla., 32 m.p.h. (Longstreet, 1930); 30 and 35 m.p.h. (McNeil, 1969; 1970).

Weights: Coastal N.J., in fall (11), 32.2–69.1 gr. (Murray and Jehl, 1964), or about 1–2½ oz.; Manomet, Mass., in summer (17), 40–66 gr. (Fisk, 1971b), or about 1½–2⅓ oz.

Range: Nests from Alaska (rarely and locally, Nunivak Is., Hooper Bay, Colville Delta), n. Mack., Victoria Is., s. Somerset Is., Melville Pen., s. Baffin Is., and n. Labrador coast, south to Alaska Pen., Queen Charlotte Is., nw. B.C., s. Mack., coasts of Hudson Bay, north shore of Gulf of St. Lawrence, Newfoundland, Magdalen Is., Cape Sable Is., s. Nova Scotia; some non-breeding birds in summer along coast south to Calif., Panama, and Fla.; winters on Pacific coast from c. Calif. to c. Sonora and coast of Gulf of Mexico; along Atlantic coast from S.C. (rarely, N.J.) south into Mexico along both Atlantic and Pacific coasts, and through West Indies to Patagonia.

Plover, snowy, *Charadrius alexandrinus* (cah-RAD-rih-us alex-an-DRY-nus); genus name: *see* Killdeer; species name: Lat. name for Alexandria, Egypt, from which came the specimen of the bird on which Linnaeus based his scientific description. (Color ills., page 721.) Lives in widely separated places on continents and islands around the world; two subspecies in N. America live over different ranges: an eastern form, called the Cuban snowy plover, *Charadrius alexandrinus tenuirostris* (ten-you-ih-ROS-triss) (Lat., slender-billed), along Gulf coast from w. Fla. to Tex.; and a western form, the western snowy plover, *Charadrius alexandrinus nivosus* (niv-OH-sus) (Lat., snowy, in allusion to color), lives along Pacific coast and inland in w. U.S. to Tex.; one of smallest of plovers; 6–7 in. long, wingspread 13½ in.; slightly smaller than piping and semipalmated plovers and whiter even than the piping plover;

has *thin black bill,* longer than that of the piping plover, and black mark behind each eye and over forecrown; dusky, slate-gray, or green-black legs and feet (the semipalmated and piping plovers have yellow or orange legs); is extremely white; instead of black ring around neck, has simply a black slash mark on each side of lower throat; in winter, when bills of most piping and semipalmated plovers are also black, the dusky legs will identify snowy plover (see details in Peterson, 1963; Robbins *et al.,* 1966); is resident over most of its range, except n. Pacific coast, from which withdraws somewhat in winter; it favors the broad expanses of dry sand above the wash of the tides on ocean beaches; in interior N. America, favors shores of salt or alkaline lakes; outside of nesting season, when flocking, flocks travel either in closely massed formation or in open formation over beaches; flight may be direct or zigzag course; both in flight and on ground, chunky appearance helps distinguish them from small sandpipers; are quite tame and allow close approach, when, instead of flying, they may run ahead with long strides over beach; are usually quiet but at times utter low musical whistle, *pe-e-et* (Bent, 1929).

Feeding Habits: Forages mainly on wet sand of beaches and at surf line; like sanderling runs rapidly up and down beach following advance and retreat of waves; sometimes forages in compact groups, eating small crustaceans, marine worms, and other minute animals; inland, on muddy shores of ponds, lakes, eats insects such as beetles and flies.

Nest: Occasionally in loose colonies, sometimes male (?) scrapes out several nesting hollows (see discussion of this in Hall, 1960), and female lines one, in which she lays her eggs, with small pieces of shells; nesting hollows are on broad, open beach or on salt flats (in Fla. reported on periphery of least tern colonies).

Eggs: Apr.–May, sometimes into July (Calif.); usually 3, sometimes 2, buff-sandy, spotted, scrawled with black, gray.

Incubation: By both sexes, 24 days; both parents attend young and use distraction display to lead away intruders; apparently only one brood a year (Palmer, 1967).

Other Names: Kentish plover (in British Isles); snowy ringed plover; Western snowy plover.

Flight Speed: Timed in w. U.S., 30 m.p.h. (Cottam *et al.,* 1942b).

Weights: One, 37 gr. (Hughes, 1970), or about 1⅓ oz.; to 2 oz. (Palmer, 1967).

Range: In N. America, nests on Pacific coast from s. Wash., Ore., Calif., south to s. Baja Calif., also in Oreg., w. Nev., Utah, e. Colo., s. N.M., sw. Kans., nw. Okla., n.-c. and s. Tex., s. La., and w. Fla., south locally in West Indies (Bahamas and Greater Antilles) and coasts of Peru and Chile; winters on coast and adjacent islands from n. Ore. to s. Baja Calif., along Gulf of Calif., into Mexico; also coast of Gulf of Mexico from s. Tex. east to Miss., occasionally La., and from w.-c. Fla. and Bahamas through Greater Antilles to Virgin Is., south to coast of Yucatán and n. Venezuela; casual in Wyo. and Neb., accidental in Wisc. and s. Ont.; in Old World nests from s. England and s. Scan-

dinavia, s. Russia, se. Siberia to Komandorskie Is. and Japan; south in Europe and Mediterranean to s. Africa, Madagascar, Ceylon, Australia, and Tasmania.

Plover, snowy ringed. *See* Plover, snowy.

Plover, thick-billed. *See* Plover, Wilson's.

Plover, three-toed. *See* Plover, American golden.

Plover, upland. *See* Plover, mountain; also another name for the upland sandpiper in Sandpiper Family.

Plover, whistling. *See* Plover, black-bellied.

Plover, Wilson's, *Charadrius wilsonia* (cah-RAD-rih-us will-SON-ih-ah); genus name: *see* Killdeer; species name: given by George Ord, Philadelphia ornithologist, for his friend Alexander Wilson, who in May 1813 collected (shot) at Cape May, N.J., the type specimen on which Ord based his scientific description of the bird (*see* Type Specimen; Names and Naming). (Color ill., page 720.) Uncommon, rather local, summers along Atlantic coast from N.J. to Fla., Gulf coast to Tex., and Pacific coast of Baja Calif.; 7–8 in. long; wingspread 14–16 in.; sexes similar in size; plumage of female less contrasting; noticeably larger plover than semipalmated, which it resembles somewhat, and the piping and snowy plovers; has longer and broader eye stripe than semipalmated, and wider breast band, but can be distinguished from it by its long, heavy, entirely black bill; some males show brown on nape and sides of head; feet are dull pink; according to Tomkins (1944), Wilson's plover is a bird that prefers to run away from danger rather than fly from it; lives on open beach at mouths of rivers, edges of dunes; migrates early, Feb.–Mar., and short distance because it winters just south (in s. U.S.) of its breeding range; flocks of 20–30 may form after nesting season; flight is swift as flocks perform aerial evolutions low over beach or water; call note of anxiety from ground is a sharply whistled *wheet* or *whip;* in flight its whistled musical calls suggest those of the piping plover, but not so loud or rich in tone (Bent, 1929).

Feeding Habits: Eats fiddler and various small land crabs, shrimps, crayfishes, marine worms, mollusks, beetles, larvae of aquatic diving beetles, flies, spiders (Bent, 1929; Hall, 1960).

Nest: Sometimes in loose colonies, more often single, scattered, scraped hollow in sand, sometimes near nesting colonies of least tern; scrape-making is part of courtship performance of male, in which he scrapes, or appears to scrape, a hollow and invites female to settle there for her nest site (see Tomkins, 1944); female, after she has accepted, or established a nest hollow, on approach of human intruder may run about settling on sand in different places, pretending to scrape a new nest hollow, apparently to distract intruder away from true nest site; both adults, when eggs are in nest hollow, or before young chicks they attend have become independent, will practice injury-feigning, much like killdeer, to lead fox, dog, or man away.

Eggs: Apr.–July (in Tex., Sept.); most records in U.S. early May into June; 2–4, usually 3, buffy, usually thickly and evenly covered with small spots, irregular blotches, scrawls of black and browns.

Incubation: Shared, in turn, by both sexes, 24–25 days; age when young first fly unknown; one brood a year (Palmer, 1967).

Other Names: Belding's plover; thick-billed plover.

Weights: To 2¼ oz. (Palmer, 1967).

Range: On Pacific coast, the subspecies called Belding's plover is resident and nests locally from c. Baja Calif. and Sonora (Mexico) to Peru; once at San Diego, Calif.; nests on Atlantic coast, the eastern form, or subspecies, from s. N.J. to s. Fla., and along Gulf coast from w. Fla. to s. Tex., south in Caribbean area to Venezuela, Guyana, and through West Indies; in fall (Oct.) 1972, two seen on Cape Sable Is., Nova Scotia (Finch, 1973); winters on Atlantic coast south of S.C. to and from Gulf coasts of Tex., La., and Fla., south through West Indies to e.-c. Brazil.

PLOWSHARE BONE
See Pygostyle; *also* pygostyle under Skeleton.

PLUMAGE
Collectively, the feathers on a bird; the feather is the unit of the plumage. *See* Feather.

PLUMAGE TRADE
See Feather Trade.

PLUME
See Crest.

PLUME BIRD
Name of plume hunters for egrets and herons sought at one time for their nuptial plumes (*see* Heron Family) in the feather, or millinery, trade; specifically, little plume bird for snowy egret, big plume bird for common egret.

PLUMULES
Down feathers. *See* Feather.

POACHER
One of common names of American wigeon, from its habit of "stealing" parts of floating water plants uprooted by canvasbacks, scaups, coots, and mute swans. *See* Autolycism; *also* in Duck Family.

POCHARD
(POH-cherd). Johnsgard (1968), an American authority on waterfowl, considers 16 species of ducks, widely distributed around the world, and collectively called "pochards," to be a group of closely related species. These include, in N. America, the European pochard and the tufted duck—both visitors to our continental waters—the canvasback, redhead, ring-necked duck, and the greater and lesser scaups. All are grouped in a larger general category called "diving ducks." *See* discussion of diving ducks and of Baer's pochard in Duck Family.

POCKET-BIRD
See Scarlet tanager in Tanager Family.

PODICIPEDIDAE
See Grebe Family.

PODICIPEDIFORMES
(pod-ih-sih-ped-ih-FOR-meez); name derives from the Lat. *podex, podicis,* rump, and *pes, pedis,* foot, referring to the placement of the legs extremely far back on the body, and the Lat. *forma,* form. Austin (1961) states that Podicipediformes means "the rump-foots," in reference to their feet being so far to the rear of their bodies. It is an order of birds that includes only the Grebe Family, Podicipedidae, a group of foot-propelled, swimming and diving birds (they do not dive as deeply as loons, to which they are unrelated). *See* Swimming and Diving.

Like loons, grebes have short wings; grebes have tails that are rudimentary (loons have stiff tail feathers, or rectrices); and the toes of grebes are lobed (those of loons are palmate, or webbed). *See* Feet and Legs; *also* loons in Gaviiformes and Loon Family.

According to Peters (1979), there are about 20 species of grebes worldwide, except in the Arctic and Antarctic regions and on some oceanic islands. In 1974 a new species, *Podiceps gallardoi,* was discovered and described in Argentina. Thirteen species are in the W. Hemisphere, one of which, the giant pied-billed grebe, or Atitlán grebe, *Podilymbus gigas,* of Lake Atitlán, a mile above sea level in Guatemala, is rare (Vincent, 1966); another, the short-winged grebe, *Centropelma micropterum,* which lives on Lake Titicaca, 3,800 m. (12,500 ft.) above sea level in the Bolivian and Peruvian Andes, is flightless (Simmons, 1964b); *See* Flightless Birds. Three other species endemic to S. America and found largely in the Temperate Zone—the silver grebe, *Podiceps occipitalis,* the white-tufted grebe, *Rollandia rolland,* and the very large great grebe, *Podiceps major.*

For an account of the 6 N. American species, *see* Grebe Family; for a discussion of how birds are grouped, *see* Classification.

POISONS
Those of natural origin in the environment are apparently an ever-present threat to birds. One striking example is botulism, from which millions of waterfowl have succumbed (*see* Botulism). In 1902, Dr. Edgar A. Mearns, a surgeon of the U.S. Army, while stationed at Ft. Yellowstone in Wyo., noted mortality of birds and mammals there caused by a heavy gas, presumably carbon monoxide, which settled in certain depressions and in caves. The gas caused the deaths of all small birds or mammals that entered the caves; in the course of a few months, Mearns found the remains of 16 species of birds, including magpies, Townsend's solitaires, juncos, pine siskins, vireos, finches, and others (Mearns, 1903).

Waterfowl can die from eating certain species of blue-green algae, especially the alga *Nodularia spumigena,* which has been thought to cause diarrhea, vomiting, ataxia (inability to coordinate muscular movements),

grebe

PODICIPEDIFORMES

and eventually death (see Deem and Thorp, 1939, on toxic algae in Colo.); it also causes significant mortality in waterfowl in Canada (Trainer, 1974).

In Jan. 1970, 1,000 wild ducks died near Muleshoe National Wildlife Refuge in n. Tex.; they had been eating castor beans from the castor-oil plant, *Ricinus communis*, a stout, shrublike, ornamental herb introduced into N. America from the tropics. The plant has spread in the wild; the poisonous substance in the leaves and seeds is ricin, a phytotoxalbumin (Hardin, 1961). In tests of the poisonous effects of these beans on waterfowl, investigators of the U.S. Fish and Wildlife Service fed a male mallard two castor beans; it died within an hour after eating the first one; both a male and a female given four castor beans died within 48 hours (Harris, V. T., 1972).

The fungus *Aspergillus flavus* (or *oryzae*, see in Christensen, 1951) produces aflatoxin in moldy peanuts and in other seeds and grains, which has caused numerous deaths among domestic ducks and turkeys but has not been reported from wild birds (Hartung, 1971). *See*, however, Aspergillosis.

Phytotoxins are poisonous substances derived from any part of certain plants, including their roots, stems, leaves, flowers, and seeds (Schwarte, 1959). Some fruits and seeds containing phytotoxins are poisonous to both wild and domestic birds. For example, rattlebox, rattleweed, or *Crotalaria*, especially *Crotolaria spectabilis*, introduced from the tropics, grows wild in fields and roadsides of the se. U.S. The seeds of this plant contain a toxic alkaloid highly poisonous to chickens, quail, and doves (Thomas, 1934; see also Nestler and Bailey, 1941). Seeds of *Crotalaria spectabilis* are, however, apparently unpalatable to birds (*see* Taste) and ordinarily birds do not select them as food (Schwarte, 1959); according to McAtee (quoted p. 270 in Leopold, 1933), "Animals either possess a degree of immunity to poisonous foods, or ordinarily take them in quantities too small to do damage [to them] when mixed with a mass of non-poisonous things [foods]. . . ."

According to Trainer (1974), many toxins of plants are produced under specific conditions (dry periods) and at certain times of the year (fall); therefore many of the poisonous plants are not a threat at all times to birds.

Quail have eaten large amounts of the seeds of poison hemlock, *Conium maculatum*, without showing poisonous effects, but the meat of such quail has proved highly poisonous to dogs (Hartung, 1971). Forbush (1925–29) reported that ruffed grouse that were shot in the winter after they had been eating the leaves of laurel, *Kalmia latifolia*, caused well-known symptoms of poisoning in those persons who had eaten them. The poison, to which the grouse are apparently immune, is caused by acetylandromedo, or andromedotoxin (an-DROM-eedoh-TOX-in), which is probably the toxin in the various heath plants. See Hardin (1961) for a discussion of some of the plants poisonous to animals, the symptoms of poisoning, and its treatment.

MacGregor (1956) reported that some American goldfinches died after eating the seeds of almond, *Prunus amygdalis;* this plant was introduced into N. America from w. Asia (Bailey and Bailey, 1947). The deaths of the goldfinches were apparently caused by cyanide released by hydrolysis of amygdalis, a cyanogenic glucoside (Hartung, 1971).

Miller (1932) reported that 25 cedar waxwings were found dead in Feb. under an ornamental date palm, *Phoenix dactylifera*, in a Los Angeles garden. The next day, 17 were found either dead or fluttering on the ground, gasping for breath. The waxwings had been eating the flesh of the date palm fruits, and many had sticky fluids from the fermented fruit running out of their mouths. According to Miller, fermentation changes in the tannins and sugars, normal for these fruits, could easily have produced toxic alcohols or other complex organic compounds which could cause acute poisoning in the waxwings.

Birds have been noted poisoned by the juicy red fruits of Tatarian honeysuckle, *Lonicera tatarica*, an ornamental shrub introduced from s. Russia, but deaths of birds from eating them are apparently unusual. Grinnell (1926) reported "inebriated" robins that had been feeding in the summer of 1925 on the berries of Tatarian honeysuckle at Billings, Mont.; several times four or five robins lay on the ground, their wings awry, "much as chickens lie on dry soil to dust themselves. The robins were so stupified, or dulled by the fruit that one man picked three robins from the bushes and held them in his hands." Intoxication of the birds is from saponin in the fruit, a substance that is an irritant to the gastrointestinal tract, and has the effect of an anesthetic and muscle poison. Saponin can paralyze the greater nerve centers, and sufficiently large doses of it can kill by cardiac paralysis (Rand, 1955).

After a sudden late-spring snowstorm in 1940, Terres (1960b) reported that some robins near Utica, N.Y., after eating decayed frozen apples on a tree in an old orchard, were fluttering about drunkenly on the ground. See also accounts by Baynes (1915) of drunkenness of robins from eating fermented apples; also in Bent (1949).

At times, a robin's drunkenness can cause its death. Early in Jan. 1955, people on Anna Maria Is. off Fla., in the Gulf of Mexico, saw hundreds of robins that were intoxicated from eating the fermented fruits of the Chinaberry tree, *Melia azedarach*, widespread in se. U.S. and introduced from Asia.

One observer wrote that the unfortunate robins "teetered on telephone wires and tree branches, fluttered about feebly on the ground, or stretched out motionless. Many flew into passing automobiles and were killed. The highway was strewn with their dead bodies. After a day or two the remaining intoxicated birds sobered up and flew away" (Terres, 1960b). The poisonous agent in Chinaberry fruit is possibly an alkaloid, with narcotic effects, that attacks the entire central nervous system (Hardin, 1961).

A doctor of Toronto, Canada, reported that robins got intoxicated by gorging themselves on the red berries of mountain ash *(Sorbus)* in his garden. They then drank water from the birdbath, after which many of them flew wildly about and into the windows of the house (Phillips, 1959).

Cedar waxwings in Mass. have been reported intoxicated from gorging on chokecherries (Forbush, 1925–29), and mockingbirds in Fla. after eating fruits of a nightshade, *Solanum seaforthianum* (Sprunt, 1948). Even the yellow-bellied sapsucker, which drills holes in the bark of trees from which to drink the sap, may get intoxicated from the fermented sap and fall from the tree to the ground (see details in Terres, 1960b); *see also* Commensalism.

On June 1, 1968, a flock of 20 Canada geese flew in a V at an estimated height of 600 ft. over Calgary, Alta. Suddenly six of them, from all parts of the flock, plummeted from the sky and struck the ground. When all the geese were examined by the Veterinary Services Laboratory, it was discovered that all had multiple fractures, massive internal hemorrhages, and ruptured internal organs from striking the ground. None had shotgun wounds; all had oats in their gizzards (with only traces of DDT and its compounds), but all had a relatively high gizzard content of strychnine.

A farmer near Calgary, after hearing of the incident, admitted that he had placed grain bait (mixed with strychnine to kill gophers) on the ground close to the gopher burrows; the following day, he found two dead geese and one unable to fly. The investigators concluded that, although the geese had been killed by their fall, the strychnine poisoning which had caused them to have convulsions in the air was responsible for their deaths (Howell and Wishart, 1969).

Strychnine, put in the carcasses of dead animals on rangelands of the West to especially poison coyotes, also "1080" (sodium fluoroacetate), an extremely deadly poison, and cyanicides spread on the land in grain baits to attract and destroy rodents, have caused the deaths of hundreds of thousands of birds and mammals (not intended to be victims) after they fed on the poisoned carcasses or on the poisoned grain (Anonymous, 1971b).

Although the poisoning has been stoutly defended by stockmen, it has been vigorously attacked by some journalists (see Olsen, 1971) and by environmentalists and biologists who recognize that predation is a healthful and natural process in wild animal populations and should not be eliminated (*see* Predation) and that biological controls of rodents through good land management (controlled grazing, for example) are necessary to bring harmony in places in the West where poisoning and hunting of predators "seems to be the rule." See discussion of this complex problem in Allen, D. (1954, pp. 264–66). For specific examples of poisoning of bald and golden eagles by ranchers, see Anonymous (1971a; 1971d). For a technical discussion of poisons in the environment, and manufactured chemical poisons such as DDT and "1080" spread on the land for control of insects, rodents, etc., see Schwarte (1959) and Hartung (1971). *See* Lead Poisoning.

POKE

Local name for some of the herons and bitterns; shortened name for shitepoke. *See* in Heron Family; *also* Shitepoke.

POLITICIAN
Local name for the white-eyed vireo, not for frequent songs and calls but for putting pieces of newspaper into its nest (Torrey, 1885).

POLLEN AND BIRDS
See Nectar and Birds; *also* Pollination.

POLLEX
The thumb, or first digit, of the hand part of the wing. *See* Alula.

POLLINATION
The transfer of pollen from stamens of flowers to pistils in fertilizing the flower ovary, which usually results in subsequent growth of fruit or seeds by plants. Pollination is accomplished by many birds that visit flowers for energy-giving nectar. *See* Nectar and Birds; see also Meeuse (1961) for methods of pollination by wind, insects, bats, and birds.

Of all N. American birds that visit flowers, none has a more interesting relationship with them than hummingbirds. At times, birdwatchers have noted an unusual yellow or golden color on a hummingbird's face, bill, crown, chin, or throat, which became dusted with pollen from flower *stamens* as the hovering bird probed deep with its bill into the hearts of flowers for nectar. After leaving the flower and visiting the next one, some of the pollen on its bill, crown, or face may brush off on the *pistil* of the next flower, thus accomplishing cross-pollination.

The tubular or trumpet-shaped flowers that hummingbirds normally visit (called "hummingbird flowers") usually, by their structure —closed lips with no landing place for a bee, or long, narrow throat, for example—exclude bees, but not bills of hummingbirds; also, the nectaries, or glands that secrete nectar in hummingbird flowers, are usually deep within the flower or in long flower spurs. These are within reach of the slender, pointed bills and extensible tongues of the hummingbirds, but out of reach of the smaller, short-tongued bees (bees have easy access to the more open, cuplike or flattened inflorescences, called "bee flowers"). For a list of flowers that are especially attractive to hummingbirds, see in Terres (1968c).

According to Grant and Grant (1968), hummingbird flowers may have evolved (changed over enormous periods of time) from certain bee-pollinated flowers through exposure to repeated visits of hummingbirds; the length and shape of bills and tongues of hummingbirds are thought to have become adapted slowly to the slow-changing structure (under the influence of hummingbirds) of the flowers; in other words, hummingbirds and their flowers have become *co-adapted* in a more efficient relationship— the hummingbirds profit from an abundance of nectar food, with no competition from bees for it, and the flowers, by becoming specialized to "using" hummingbirds as pollinators, are no longer dependent in a highly competitive flower world on the services of bees as pollinators. See Grant and Grant (1968) for details of this relationship.

Hummingbirds are strongly attracted to red, and most of the hummingbird flowers are red; the ruby-throated hummingbird is so enamored of red that it has been known to hover in front of a man wearing a red necktie, around the head of a woman wearing a red ribbon in her hair, and before the red, sunburned noses of people; a broad-tailed hummingbird at Bingham, Utah, feeding at a patch of purple beeweeds, *Cleome serrulata,* flew up to a traffic light and twice poked its bill against the red light, as though trying to feed, but was not attracted to the green or amber lights. Hummingbirds do visit flowers of other colors, however—orange, pink, yellow, blue, purple, and, in the West, the large green flowers of a tobacco plant, *Nicotiana paniculata,* also certain white ones that offer them nectar and small insects and spiders that are inside the flower. *See* food habits of N. American hummingbirds in Hummingbird Family.

Apparently hummingbirds become conditioned to certain colors of hummingbird flowers (they apparently have a poor sense of smell— *see* Smell) that reward them with food. They distinguish between colors (*see* Eyes and Eyesight); in studies of Mexican hummingbirds, Wagner (1946) discovered that, at a given time and place, they came to his differently colored experimental feeding vials and usually chose the vial that was colored like their preferred flower, then in bloom. See Wagner's report (1946) and those of Grant (1966) and Grant and Grant (1968) for details; also Pickens (1929a; 1929b), and especially those of Lyerly *et al.* (1950) and Miller and Miller (1971). *See also* Symbiosis.

POLLUTION
See discussion of effects of insecticides on some birds in biographies of peregrine falcon and prairie falcon in Falcon Family; osprey in Osprey Family; bald eagle, goshawk, Cooper's hawk, marsh hawk, red-shouldered hawk, red-tailed hawk, and sharp-shinned hawk in Hawk Family; and brown pelican in Pelican Family; *also* Poisons; Lead Poisoning. See article "Perils and Poisons" in Fisher and Peterson (1964); Carson (1962); Graham (1970); Schwarte (1959); Hartung (1961); and Ratcliffe (1963).

POLYANDRY
See Sexual Relationships.

POLYCHROMATISM
See Color Phase.

POLYGAMOUS
Having more than one mate. Some species of birds are polygamous. *See* details under Courtship and especially polygyny and polyandry under Sexual Relationships.

POLYGYNY
See Sexual Relationships.

POLYMORPHISM
See Color Phase.

POLYTYPIC SPECIES
See Monotype.

POMPADOUR COTINGA
See introduction to Cotinga Family.

POND GUINEA
See Bittern, American, in Heron Family.

POND HEN
See Coot, American, and gallinules in Rail Family.

POND SHELDRAKE
See Merganser, common, in Duck Family.

POOR JOE
See Long John.

POOR-WILL
See in Nightjar Family.

POPE
See Bunting, painted, in Finch Family.

POPULATIONS
May refer to the total number of individuals in a certain area or to the total population of a species throughout its entire range. Fisher (1951), a British ornithologist, estimated there are more than 100 billion individual wild birds in the world, which is more than 25 times the present human population. The Wilson's stormpetrel, *Oceanites oceanicus,* a seabird, is probably the most numerous wild bird in the world, and the starling and the house sparrow may be the most abundant wild land birds (Fisher, 1951).

The total population of breeding wild land birds in the U.S. is estimated at not less than 5 billion and may be nearer 6 billion at the beginning of summer, or about 2½–3 birds per acre (Peterson, 1948). Peterson's estimate was based on the breeding-bird censuses of the National Audubon Society, in which counts of singing males on their territories were used as an index to the number of pairs per acre. *See* Census. Leonard Wing, using a more complicated method than Peterson, estimated a summer population of 5.6 billion birds in the U.S. and a winter population of about 3.75 billion. McAtee (1931) estimated there are about 2.6 billion breeding land birds in the U.S.

According to Peterson (1948), the commonest breeding bird, at that time (and possibly at present), in the deciduous forests of e. U.S. was the red-eyed vireo, and he thought the horned lark might be the most numerous breeding bird of the prairies. No present-day land-bird population, however, approaches that of the extinct passenger pigeon, estimated at 3 billion individuals at the time of the discovery of America.

Other abundant species today in the U.S. are the song sparrow, chipping sparrow, myrtle (yellow-rumped) warbler, American robin, mockingbird, red-winged blackbird, meadowlark, and cowbird (Dorst, 1974). Pettingill in 1966 believed that the red-winged blackbird may be the most abundant wild *native* land bird in N. America; von Haartman (1971), on the authority of federal biologists who have studied winter concentrations of blackbirds and starlings in the U.S., estimates their winter populations at 500 million, of which the starling, red-winged blackbird, and common grackle may number 100 million each. *See* their flocking numbers under Control.

All of these, however, are estimates. It is difficult if not impossible to get an accurate count of the total population of a widespread species of land bird, unless the population is concentrated within a limited area, either permanently or at a certain time of the year, thus permitting an accurate count. Some examples in which accurate counts were made of the remaining population are the rare California condor (see, however, Ricklefs, 1978), whooping crane, and Kirtland's warbler. *See* Vulture—American Vulture Family; Crane Family; Warbler—American Wood Warbler Family. *See* population estimates of ducks, geese, and swans under Waterfowl.

According to Fisher and Peterson (1964), about 44 species of birds in the world have had their population estimated with some certainty, and 14 of these were seabirds. The northern fulmar, northern gannet, greater shearwater, and Atlantic puffin are examples of seabirds whose populations have been censused world-wide. See details in Fisher and Lockley (1954). For a discussion of *population dynamics*—methods of calculating populations, factors affecting either population growth or decline, population structure, dynamic equilibrium, mortality, regulation of populations, etc.—see Lack (1954; 1964a); von Haartman (1971); Dorst (1974); Pettingill (1972).

PORK-AND-BEANS

In Me., name for the common nighthawk, in allusion to a common call often rendered *peent!* *See* Nightjar Family.

POST-BREEDING MIGRATION

See in Some Effects of Weather under Migration.

POSTCLIMAX

See Subclimax Community.

POST-DRIVER

See Stake-driver.

POSTNATAL WANDERING

See Dispersal.

POTATO-BUG BIRD

See Grosbeak, rose-breasted, in Finch Family.

POTOO FAMILY

See Caprimulgiformes.

POUCHES

See Mouth.

POWDER DOWN

See Feather.

POX

See Avian Pox.

PRAIRIE BIRD

See Lark, horned, in Lark Family.

PRAIRIE CHICKEN

See in Grouse Family.

PREACHER

Another name for the wood stork, from its black-and-white color and solemn demeanor (McAtee, 1955a).

PREACHER BIRD

See Red-eyed vireo in Vireo Family.

PRECOCIAL

See Altricial.

PREDATION

The act of one species of bird, or other animal, killing and eating an individual of another animal species. Among birds, it is especially notable in the hawks and owls, whose food habits have been much studied. Most hawks and owls prey mainly on rats, mice, birds, and other vertebrate animals (*see* Pellet; Food and Feeding Habits); however, predatory birds themselves are also victims of predation. Welty (1962) cited a study in England in which, of 24 nests and eggs of the short-eared owl, only 5 survived to hatch young, and only 2 raised young to fledging, because of predation by foxes and crows on the owl eggs or young. Welty suggested that predation in this case may have been especially severe because it came when meadow mice, ordinarily abundant in the area and a main food of foxes, were scarce.

Predation is far from being the sole reason for a decline in a bird population. It is one of the most complex of all biological phenomena to study because of its relation with other huge and varying factors that may help reduce a bird population, locally or regionally. Some of these pressures of the environment are weather (drought and extreme cold), diseases and parasites, an insecure habitat, and the population density (pairs per acre, or hectare) of the species itself (Dorst, 1974), which often affects the intensity of predation. All of these influences may make a bird or other animal, ordinarily secure in its environment, available to its enemies (Allen, D., 1954).

Usually, predator and prey are in equilibrium, but fluctuate as one or the other becomes more or less numerous. The predator, it should be noted, often spends much more time searching and attempting to catch prey than many smaller insectivorous and granivorous birds spend feeding. And in some predators, such as the short-eared owl, a 20% success rate in catching voles is probably normal. A European study showed that of 688 attacks on birds by hawks, only 7.6% of the attacks were successful in capturing prey.

It has been shown by investigators that predation is actually of benefit to a bird population as a whole. Those birds most easily caught by predators are more often the sick or old—a surplus in the population that has been doomed to die anyway. Eliminating the more easily caught sick, malformed, or weak reduces the number of those which may spread diseases and parasites. Predators also feed much on young birds, the surplus of which is also destined to disappear (Dorst, 1974).

To see the *necessity of predation* in helping limit wild bird populations to the *carrying capacity* of the environment, one need only refer to calculations by mathematicians of the theoretical increase a bird might attain if unchecked by nature. A single pair of American robins, though they raised only 2 broods of 4 young each year, along with their reproducing descendants, over 10 years *could produce about 19 million robins* (Dorst, 1974). The enormous overpopulation of the species as a whole from such an increase would be intolerable to the environment and to those landowners that would be subjected to the depredations of robins on fruit and other crops that would result. *See* Economic Ornithology. Of course, as Dorst points out, this does not happen because of environmental resistance (predation, for one example) to the robin's reproductive potential. For related articles, *see* Accipiter; Balance of Nature; Diseases; Egg-eating; Parasite; Bounty. For many examples of effects of predation on birds and on other animals, see "Predation" in Welty (1962). See also, Allen, D. (1954); Elton (1936); Errington (1946; 1967); and the dynamics of predation in Craighead and Craighead (1956; 1966). All of these publications have excellent bibliographies on the subject.

PREDATORS

Among birds, the so-called true predators are mostly in the Falcon Family, Hawk Family, Osprey Family (eats mostly fishes), and Owl families (Barn Owl and Typical Owl). However, some vultures, jaegers, fulmars, and gulls, also ravens, crows, magpies, and jays, eat the eggs or young of birds, and shrikes, and even the chuck-will's-widow and Wied's crested flycatcher, occasionally catch and eat small birds. *See* Feeding Habits in the biographies of these birds. *See* Predation; *also* Food and Feeding Habits; Egg-eating; Eggs and Egg-laying.

PREEN GLAND

See oil gland under Skin Glands.

PREENING

The basic and most important single act that a bird performs in the care of its feathers (Simmons, 1964a). A bird preens its plumage by grasping with its bill a feather at the base, usually one at a time, and nibbling along the feather toward the tip to remove oil, dirt, and ectoparasites (*see* Parasite), which it may occasionally swallow. Or it may simply draw the feather through its partly clamped bill in one movement to smooth the feather barbs (*see* Feather) and remove dirt from them so that they will lock together. Its preening movements also work into the feathers fresh oil from the oil gland at the base of its tail. Preening often follows bathing. *See* discussion of the oil gland, or preen gland, and how a bird uses it, under Skin Glands.

A bird may spend much time at preening while perched on the limb of a tree; at the edge of a body of water; or on a rock or some place on the ground where it has an unobstructed view around it in case of a surprise attack by a hawk or other predator. During its preening, a bird fluffs out its body feathers so as to get at them more easily; it bends its head and twists its neck in reaching the more inaccessible places, and it preens its head by scratching it or rubbing it against other parts of its body.

PREENING

Birds preen in order to clean their feathers, remove parasites, and smooth the feather barbs so they will lock together. Preening also distributes oil from the oil gland at the base of the tail.

albatross

shearwater

storm-petrel

PROCELLARIIFORMES

MUTUAL PREENING, ALLOPREENING, OR RECIPROCAL PREENING. Some birds help to preen each other's heads, and usually this reciprocal preening is by birds that are paired and when closely associated at the nest site. According to Simmons (1964a), sometimes it is only the dominant bird of the two that does the preening. Mutual preening is not known in most groups of birds, but is done by parrots, pigeons, herons, and, among songbirds, certain crows and others listed by Harrison (1965) in some 40 families, and in addition by falconets, weaver finches, crested caracaras, *Polyborus plancus*, and in barn owls in the London Zoo. Nice (1962a) reported that "social preening" (mutual preening) is practiced by albatrosses, petrels, cormorants, penguins, herons, tree ducks, parrots, bobwhite quail, anis, pigeons, and the bearded tit, bullfinch, some weaver finches, and others. Nice herself observed it in her captive young Virginia rails and soras 15–17 days after hatching, also in king rails at Trailside Museum. At Brookside Zoo she watched a European spoonbill vigorously preening a crested screamer which had its eyes closed, apparently enjoying the experience.

Tuck (1961) reported mutual preening in the wild between a pair of common murres, and Fitzpatrick (1975) watched and photographed two barred owls in Corkscrew Swamp, Fla., that were "allopreening." Each alternately picked with the bill about the facial feathers of the other as they sat on a tree branch within a foot of each other. Each owl stretched its neck in order to offer parts of its head for preening by the other.

Interspecific (between different species) preening is not common in most birds, except cowbirds, according to Payne (1969). Friedmann (1963) cites remarkable examples of his captive brown-headed and bronzed cowbirds approaching other birds in the aviary and inviting them to preen the head and neck. They did this by bowing the head to the other bird and ruffling the feathers of the neck, where much of the preening takes place. This display evoked preening from captive red-winged blackbirds, meadowlarks, house sparrows, and captive budgerigars, but common and great-tailed grackles and Inca and mourning doves did not respond. Mutual preening is not common, however, between cowbirds themselves, according to Friedmann. Two investigators in New York City noted cases in which house sparrows, invited to preen by cowbirds, hopped up on their backs to preen them more effectively.

Payne (1969) reported a captive giant cowbird, *Psomoculax orzivorus*, at the Fort Worth, Tex., zoo that frequently offered its head to people and solicited preening. Many responded by scratching the cowbird's head, and whenever they stopped, the cowbird displayed again to invite more preening. See also Selander and LaRue (1961). Anyone who has had a parrot may have had a similar experience, with the parrot inching along the perch in its cage and then bowing its head when at the cage bars in an invitation to scratch its head. Nice (1962a) said that all of her captive birds liked "being stroked by us."

FUNCTIONS OF MUTUAL PREENING. Mutual preening is always concentrated on the head and upper neck, which a bird cannot reach with its own bill. Goodwin (1956) suggested that in pigeons "mutual caressing" serves both the removal of ectoparasites or other foreign material from the mate's head and a sublimation of aggressive impulses between the birds (the mated pair) and maintenance of the pair bond. See also Fitzpatrick (1975). For related articles, *see* Head-scratching; Bathing.

PRIMARY FEATHER

One of the flight feathers attached to the manus, or the "hand" part of the wing. *See* Flight Feather; Topography; *also* Flight.

PRION

(PRY -on). Name for any one of the small group of 5 species of pearl-gray seabirds, about 1 ft. long, of the cold Antarctic seas. They are in the Shearwater Family and do not come north into N. American waters but fly about the Antarctic seas in large flocks. Murphy (1936) called them whale-birds; they were once in the genus *Prion* but more recently have been put in the genus *Pachyptila.* See Bourne (1964) for details; also Murphy (1936). *See* Shearwater Family.

PROCELLARIIDAE

See Shearwater Family.

PROCELLARIIFORMES

(pro-sell-ah-rye-ih-FOR-meez); from Lat. *procella*, a storm, pertaining to storms, and *forma*, shape; petrel- or fulmar-shaped (Coble, 1954). An order of seabirds called the tube-nosed swimmers in reference to their nostrils and pelagic lives; they have a peculiar, musky smell, possibly from the oil secreted in their stomachs which they spit out in self-defense and are thought also to use in preening. *See* Preening.

The order (a total of 93 species in 4 families in the world) includes albatrosses (Albatross Family), shearwaters and petrels (Shearwater Family), and storm-petrels (Storm-petrel Family) in N. American waters (*see* discussion under Seabird), and, elsewhere in the world, the Diving-petrel Family (Van Tyne and Berger, 1976). See details in Austin (1961). All are similar in having a hooked, deeply grooved bill with nostrils enclosed in one or two tubes on the bill; the wings long and narrow; the feet palmate (webbed—*see* Feet and Legs); and the hallux (hind toe) rudimentary or absent. They have thick plumage that is predominantly black and gray (Pettingill, 1956).

Through the distinctive tubular nostrils by which birds of this order are known, excess salt is excreted (*see* Nostrils for further discussion). The Procellariiformes are most closely related to penguins (order Sphenisciformes), and both are ancient groups.

PROGRESSION

See Climbing Birds; Hopping and Walking; Running Birds; Swimming and Diving. *See also* Flight.

PROMISCUOUS BEHAVIOR
See Sexual Relationships.

PROTECTION
See Legal Protection; *also* Banding; Sanctuary.

PROTECTIVE COLORATION
See Uses of Colors under Colors of Feathers; *also* Eggs and Egg-laying.

PROTECTIVE USES (BY BIRDS) OF OTHER ANIMALS
See Nests and Nesting; Commensalism; Autolycism.

PROTOCALLIPHORA
(pro-toe-cal-LIFF-oh-rah). Genus name for a group of bluebottle flies whose blood-sucking larvae, or grubs, are parasitic on nestling birds, especially on young of bluebirds, tree swallows, and others that raise the young in darkness of holes or cavities, also on young of those that build nests of mud, such as swallows. *See also* Screwworm. The bluebottle fly larvae are typically nocturnal and feed intermittently on the blood of the nestling birds; the larval and pupal stages of the fly are lived in the bird nest (Boyd, 1951). Deaths of fledglings from heavy infestations of the bluebottle fly larvae have been frequently reported (Kenaga, 1961). See also studies by Plath (1919); Mason (1944).

Sabrosky and Bennett (1956) recognized 21 N. American species of *Protocalliphora*. One of the common ones in nest boxes occupied by bluebirds and tree swallows (*see* Bird-attracting) is *Protocalliphora splendida*. The larvae of this species have also been found in nests of house wrens, barn swallows, American robins, starlings, and others (Mason, 1944) and in nests of house sparrows, flickers, and in mud nests of cliff swallows (Kenaga, 1961).

According to Lindquist (1962), a material known as Co-ral, which is recommended for use on poultry as a 0.5% spray to control lice and mites, is considered quite safe in direct application to poultry and, according to Lindquist, this concentration in a bird's nest is very likely to destroy *Protocalliphora* larvae. The pupae of the *Protocalliphora* are sometimes parasitized heavily by small parasitic wasps which are significant in natural control of populations of these bluebottle flies. See a method of protecting and encouraging parasitic wasps in birds' nests in Petrak (1969); Ch. 11 in Terres (1968c; 1977); see other details of parasitic wasps and their effects discussed by Mason (1944); *see* other insect parasites of birds under Fleas; Hippoboscid Flies; Lice. *See also* Parasite; Ectoparasite.

PROTOZOANS
See Diseases; *also* Parasite.

PROVENTRICULUS
(proh-ven-TRIK-you-lus). The glandular stomach of birds. *See* Digestion.

PROXIMAL
Nearest, or nearer, the trunk or midline of a bird. It is the opposite of distal, or terminal. *See* Distal.

PRUNELLIDAE
See Hedge Sparrow Family.

PSEUDO-MASCULINITY
See Endocrine Glands.

PSEUDOSUCHIA
See Origin of Birds and of Bird Flight in Fossil Birds.

PSILOPAEDIC
See Altricial.

PSITTACIDAE
See Parrot Family.

PSITTACIFORMES
(SIT-ah-sih-FOR-meez); from Lat. *psittacus*, parrot, and Lat. *forma*, form, parrotlike. An order of birds that resemble each other in structure (*see* Order); includes 1 family—the Parrot Family—of 315 species in the world (Van Tyne and Berger, 1959). Only 2 species occurred in the U.S. One, the thick-billed parrot, extended its range into the U.S. from tropical America. The Carolina parakeet was a Temperate Zone parrot that ranged widely in the U.S. *See* discussion under Parrot Family.

According to Dorst (1964), almost no other order of birds is more set apart from others by their distinctive appearance and structure than the Psittaciformes. All have a large head, short neck, and downcurved, hooked bill, with a bulging cere (*see* Bill; Nostrils) that is sometimes feathered at its base. All parrots have strong, grasping feet, and their legs are short; toes are zygodactylous (two in front, two in back); tarsi covered with numerous small scales. *See* Feet and Legs.

The sexes are usually colored alike and the body plumage may be solid green, red, yellow, occasionally very dark, or white with patches of brilliant blues, yellows, and reds on the wings, head, or tail. Members of the order have strong, rather rounded wings and can fly swiftly over long distances; however, the owl parrot or kakapo (*Strigops habroptilus*) of New Zealand is flightless. *See* Flightless Birds. The name parakeet is generally given only to the smaller species with long, pointed tails. *See also* Classification; Morphology; Phylogenetic Relationship.

PSITTACOSIS
"Parrot fever," a disease so named because it was once thought to be transmitted to man only by such cage birds as parrots, parakeets, cockatoos, cockatiels, macaws, and other members of the Parrot Family. *See* Chlamydiosis (new name for the disease). *See* parrotlike birds under Psittaciformes; *see also* Diseases.

PTARMIGAN
See in Grouse Family.

PTERYLAE
Feather tracts. *See* Feather.

PTERYLOGRAPHY
(ter-ih-LOG-rah-fih). Study of the arrangement or delineation of feathers in definite areas of growth on a bird's skin. *See* Feather.

parrot

PSITTACIFORMES

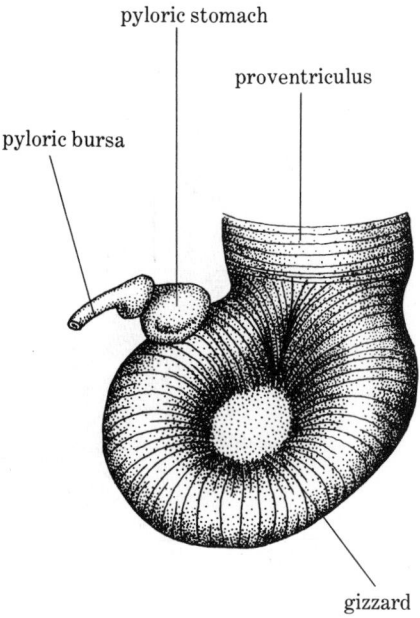

pyloric stomach

proventriculus

pyloric bursa

gizzard

PYLORIC STOMACH
In the stomach of some birds such as cormorants, anhingas, and herons, there is a third chamber, the pyloric stomach, located between the gizzard and the small intestine. Although its function has not been established, it may serve as a filter in those birds that take in much water with their food.

PTERYLOSIS
(ter-ih-LO-sis). The arrangement of feathers in definite areas or tracts on a bird's skin. *See* Feather.

PTILOPAEDIC
See Altricial.

PUBLICATIONS
See Ornithological Periodicals.

PUFFBIRD
See Piciformes.

PUFFIN
See in Auk Family.

PULL-DOO
See Coot, American, in Rail Family.

PUMPER
See Thunder Pumper.

PUMP HANDLE
Local name for American bittern (*see* in Heron Family), from its habit of standing still with bill pointed upward. *See* Freezing.

PYGOSTYLE
(PIE-go-stile). Term for the caudal (tail) end bone of the vetebral column, consisting of several vertebrae that have fused in the embryonic bird to form the terminal bone (Pettingill, 1972). This bone, shaped much like a plowshare, is the base of attachment for the rectrices, or stiff feathers of the tail, used by a bird in flight. *See* Skeleton; *also* Tail.

PYLORIC STOMACH
A separate or partially separated chamber in the alimentary tract between the gizzard and small intestine (Farner, 1960). It is also called the *pyloric orifice* and is guarded by the pyloric valve (Worden, 1964a). It exists in a number of groups of birds—in some cormorants, anhingas, herons, storks, grebes, in many shorebirds, in some ducks, geese, hawks, and cuckoos. It is possible that origins and functions of these "pyloric stomachs" differ in different groups of birds; it appears to be associated with intake of food with much water content (Swenander, 1902) or with fish intake, but neither theory explains it in hawks, geese, or cuckoos (Ziswiler and Farner, 1972).

According to Wetmore (1920), the pyloric stomach in grebes regularly contains feathers, which may function as a filter. For details, *see* discussion under Gizzard. *See also* Pellet. Among the anhingas, or darters, the mucous membrane of the pyloric stomach has long, hairlike processes which appear to function as a filter (Garrod, 1876; 1878). *See* Digestion.

PYRRHULOXIA
See in Finch Family.

QUA-BIRD
See night herons in Heron Family.

QUAIL
See in Pheasant Family.

QUAIL DISEASE
See Diseases.

QUAIL-DOVE
See in Pigeon Family.

QUAILY
See Sandpiper, upland, in Sandpiper Family.

QUANDY
See Oldsquaw in Duck Family.

QUAWK
See night herons in Heron Family; name from their cries.

QUETZAL
See under Trogon Family.

QUILL
See Calamus.

QUINDAR
or QUINDER. *See* Goldeneye, American, and scaups in Duck Family.

QUIT
Name applied to a number of small birds in the English-speaking West Indies. *See,* for example, Bananaquit in Honeycreeper Family.

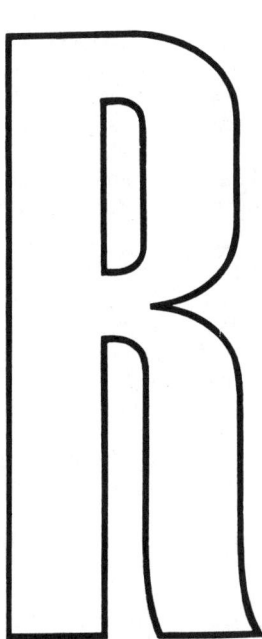

RACE

A subspecies. *See* Subspecies; Nominate Subspecies.

RACHIS

(RAY-kis), or RHACHIS. The central shaft of a feather; the part between the feather vanes. *See* Calamus; *also* Feather.

RACING PIGEON

See Homing; Domestication; *also* Rock dove in Pigeon Family.

RADAR

(detection of birds). *See* Migration.

RADIOTELEMETRY

See radio-tagged thrushes in Speed of Travel under Migration.

RAFT DUCK

See Duck, raft, in Duck Family.

RAILBIRD

See Sora in Rail Family.

RAIL FAMILY

Rallidae (RAL-ih-dee); from New Lat. *rallus*, and Fr. *râle*, rail. Worldwide except in polar regions; 132 species (Van Tyne and Berger, 1976); small, ground-dwelling, usually marsh or water birds; 5½–20 in. long; most are dark or of soft cryptic grays, browns, and other colors; some have a colored horny shield on forehead; body narrow; wings rounded; tail short; legs stout, toes long; sexes outwardly alike or nearly so (Van Tyne and Berger, 1959); 13 species in N. America (9 native, 4 foreign visitors); includes the coots, crakes, gallinules, rails, and the sora; their closest N. American relatives are the cranes and the limpkin (*see* Gruiformes). Some members of family, especially coots and gallinules, which resemble chickens in form, often called marsh hens, mud hens, or water hens. All rails can swim and dive, but coots even more adapted to water, are just as aquatic as ducks and can dive and swim very well with aid of lobe-webbed feet, similar to feet of grebes; some have been timed underwater as long as 16 seconds and may feed 25 ft. below the surface (Gilliard, 1958). Coots, like gallinules, spend much time on open water and, except in breeding season, are quite gregarious, in winter in South often gather in flocks of thousands on both fresh and brackish waters.

Although relatively weak-flying birds, many in Rail Family migrate long distances over water or land; and most, especially the rails, are largely solitary, secretive, and heard (at twilight and at night) more often than seen; their narrow bodies are an adaptation to their habit of running through thick marsh grasses or weeds; all have flexible wings with clawlike appendage at the tip of the manus (bend of wing) that helps them climb about in dense-growing marsh plants (Nice, 1962a); colors of plumage of brown, gray, or reddish, some striped, make them difficult to see against marsh background; legs are strong; toes long, which helps them walk over mud and grasses; rails are either long-billed as in Virginia, king, clapper, and water rails, or short-billed as in sora and the

RAIL FAMILY

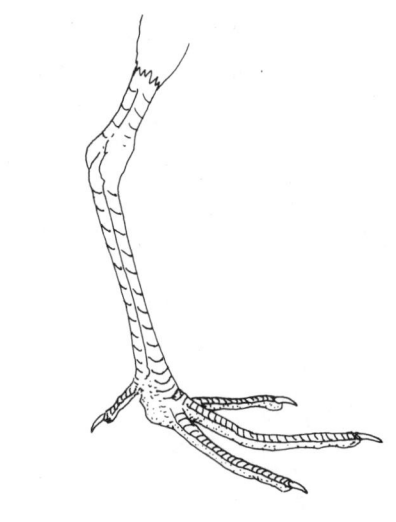

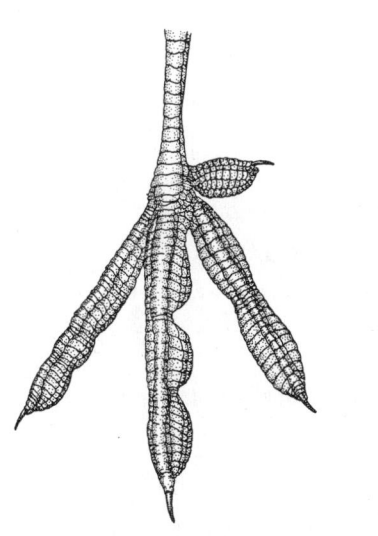

RAIL FAMILY
The feet of the coot are highly adapted to its aquatic environment. The feet are lobed, like those of the grebe, rather than webbed. The lobes, attached along the length of the toes, flare out on the back stroke, providing propulsion, and lie back on the forward stroke.

yellow and black rails; in Europe the short-billed rails are called crakes (Austin, 1961).

Gallinules (from Lat. *gallinula*, chicken, dim. of *gallina*, hen) are anatomically, in structure, between coots and rails; most have a frontal shield on the forehead more developed than that of coots and in some species it is brightly colored; they have long, webless toes that enable them to walk about over the water on floating plants such as lily pads. Like the coots, when swimming, they pump their heads back and forth. They nest in clumps of grass over water; are very inquisitive and often climb stalks of rushes or other water plants to peer from their hiding places at boats that pass along the waterways. When walking they lower the head and raise the short tail over the back, showing the white undertail feathers (Gilliard, 1958). Like the N. American rails and coots, gallinules are migratory; most members of the Rail Family in N. America are game birds (except three western subspecies of the clapper rail, facing extinction, and the yellow rail and the blackrail) may be hunted during open season. *See* Rare and Threatened Species. For general accounts of worldwide members of family, see Austin (1961); Gilliard (1958); Junge (1964c).

To sustain an ill or injured rail, coot, or gallinule until it can fend for itself, keep it in enclosure to protect it from cats, dogs, or other predatory animals and offer it *finely cut or ground* mixture of meat and fish with small amount of grain, plenty of finely chopped greens (leafy parts of plants), and bread crumbs; keep fresh water available and, if a coot or gallinule, provide a small pond (Walker, 1942).

Coot, American, *Fulica americana* (FEW-lih-kah ah-mer-ih-CANE-ah); genus name: Lat., coot; species name: Lat., of America. (Color ills., pages 722, 723.) In summer in N. America from s. Canada south to s. Baja Calif., Gulf states, and s. Fla. on shallows of freshwater lakes, ponds, and waterways of marshes; 13–16 in. long; wingspread 23–28 in.; slate gray, duck-like; short *white bill* (similar gallinules have red bill) and white patch under short tail; eyes red; legs and feet somewhat green; immatures, lighter color, have brown eyes, gray bill; like gallinules, coot pumps head back and forth when swimming, dives from surface like duck, and inclined to flock more than gallinules; usually in more open water of bays, lakes, where associates with ducks; in takeoff from water runs splashing across water for some distance, beating wings vigorously to become airborne, usually flies near water or 10–15 ft. above; in flight, white border shows on rear edge of wings; coots usually abundant in winter from Calif. to Fla., north to Va., on suitable lakes, ponds, bayous, marshes, marshy rivers; coots winter in large flocks, begin to return to more northern nesting grounds in Mar., when sometimes suffer severe mortality, hundreds die of starvation if they arrive too early in spring and open waters suddenly refreeze (Fredrickson, 1969); pairs display before each other on water in courtship or male chases female across surface of water (Bent, 1926a); pairs call *kuk-kuk-kuk-kuk* or *coo-coo-coo-coo* by day or night or utter loud cackles, whistles, croaks, grunts,

and babbling sounds with much splashing about in water; on land walk about actively with back hunched, suggestive of guinea fowl.

Feeding Habits: In feeding may tip up like a duck in shallows, with head below surface, or dives expertly in water 10–25 ft. deep for leaves, fronds, seeds, and roots of aquatic plants such as potamogetons, water milfoil, bur reed, also fond of chara, or muskgrasses (algae); sometimes eats wild celery uprooted by canvasbacks and other ducks (see review of this habit of coots by Anderson, 1974); eats small fishes, tadpoles, snails, worms, water bugs and other aquatic insects; sometimes flocks feed far from water, clipping off with bill grasses of meadows or sprouting grain; sometimes eats eggs of other marsh birds (*see* Egg-eating).

Nest: Built by both sexes, about 14 in. across, of stems of marsh plants on foundation of same materials, floats on water attached firmly to reeds or other standing plants; partly, or well, concealed in bulrushes or cattails of marsh, or at edge.

Eggs: Calif., Apr.–Aug.; elsewhere, Apr.–July; 6–22, most often 8–12, pink to dark buff, evenly spotted or dotted with browns (Bent, 1926a).

Incubation: By both sexes, 23–24 days (Nice, 1954); downy chicks black with red or orange about head, neck, and shoulders; red bill with black tip; soon after hatching and drying, swim well, follow parents to be fed; parents eat egg-shells or carry them from nest and drop into water; at night male does most brooding of chicks (and eggs) (Fredrickson, 1970; see also Gullion, 1954); chicks first fly probably about 49–56 days after hatching, according to Skutch (1976), 75 days.

Other Names: Baldface; blue hen; blue peter; crow-bill; crow-duck; flusterer; hen-bill; ivory-billed coot; meadow hen; moor-head; mud coot; mud duck; mud hen; pelick; pond crow; pull-doo; sea-crow; spatterer; shuffler; water hen.

Age: One lived in National Zoo, Washington, D.C., for 11 years, 9 months; one banded wild bird lived to 9 years, 6 months (Kennard, 1975).

Albinism: One partial albino—all-white feathers but with dark eyes—reported in La., fall 1958.

Hybrids: American coot × common gallinule —a presumed natural hybrid banded in 1936 (McIlhenny, 1937).

Weights: In Calif., in winter, females weighed 13½ oz. to 1 lb. 7 oz.; males 1 lb. 4 oz. to 1 lb. 13 oz. (Fredrickson, 1969); two females killed in fall at TV tower in Kans., 13½ oz. and 1 lb. ¾ oz. (Tordoff and Mengel, 1956).

Range: Nests from B.C., s. Mack., east through s. Canada to N.B., south to s. Baja Calif., along Gulf coast to s. Fla., south into C. America, Cuba, West Indies, also in Andes from Colombia to Ecuador; winters from s. B.C. south to Ariz., east to Tex, Ohio R. valley, and from Md. south; has wandered to Alaska, n. Ont., Labrador, Newfoundland, Greenland.

Coot, chicken-foot. *See* Gallinule, common.

Coot, European, *Fulica atra* (FEW-lih-kah AY-trah); genus name: *see* Coot, American; species name: Lat., black. European and Asiatic

bird, not reported in U.S. but has wandered to Greenland, Labrador, and Newfoundland in N. America; 15 in. long; about same size as American coot; a stout, slaty-black water bird with glossy jet-black head; conspicuous white frontal shield and bill; has *slate-gray undertail coverts instead of white*, as in American coot.

Age: Banded birds reported 5–9 years old in Switzerland; like ducks, many shot or might show greater age in wild; speed in migration, 160 mi. traveled a day (Nice, 1937a).

Hybrids: A presumed hybrid European coot × moorhen (*Gallinula chloropus*) reported by Gray (1958).

Coot, pied-wing. Another name for the white-winged scoter in Duck Family.

Coot, quill-tail. Another name for the ruddy duck in Duck Family.

Coot, sea. Name for scoters and eiders in Duck Family.

Crake, Carolina. *See* Sora.

Crake, corn. *Crex crex* (CRECKS); genus and species names: New Lat., from Gr. *krex*, a sort of long-legged bird; *corn*, from its habit of nesting in fields of grain (called corn in England); *crake*, from its rasping call, *crek*, *creak*, or *crake*. A short-billed, large brownish rail of Europe and Asia that has wandered to Baffin Is. and Maritime Provinces of Canada and to New England south to Md. and to Bermuda; 9–10 in. long; wingspread 17–18 in.; usually seen in upland hayfields and other crop fields, distinguished by short bill, red-brown wings, large size; buff-yellow above; light below, and white-barred, brown-red flanks; a strong flier, migrates long distances each year; may be lured near by running thumbnail briskly over points of teeth of comb to produce sounds like its call notes (Bent, 1926a). *See* Sounds That Attract Birds.

Feeding Habits: Usually eats insects, snails, slugs, earthworms, occasionally grain and other seeds.

Other Name: Land rail.

Range: Nests in Europe, Asia; winters in Africa, Madagascar, and Arabia.

Crake, spotted, *Porzana porzana* (por-ZANE-ah); genus and species names: from New Lat. *porzana*, from Ital. *porzana*, crake. Europe and Asia; has wandered to Greenland; 9 in. long; short, yellow bill, reddish at base; upperparts dark olive brown *streaked and spotted with white;* breast gray, speckled with white; short, dark brown wings; legs greenish.

Crake, yellow. *See* Rail, yellow.

Gallinule, American. *See* Gallinule, common.

Gallinule, common, *Gallinula chloropus* (gal-IN-you-lah CLO-roh-pus); genus name: Lat. *gallinula*, chicken, pullet, dim. of *galina* or *gallina*, hen; species name: from Gr. *chloros*, green, and *pous*, foot. (Color ill., page

722.) Almost worldwide, on all continents except Australia and Antarctica; in summer in marshes from c. Calif. to Ariz. and Tex. north to Neb., Minn., south throughout c. and e. U.S.; not in desert regions; slate-gray chickenlike bird; 12–15 in. long; wingspread 20–23 in.; with conspicuous *chickenlike red bill with yellow tip;* and *red* forehead (frontal shield); legs and feet yellow-green; pumps head back and forth when swimming; *white line along sides of adults;* white undertail coverts *divided by gray in middle* (similar, more southern purple gallinule has greenish back, pale blue frontal shield, undertail coverts all-white); lives in freshwater marshes of cattails, bulrushes, willows, with pools, ditches of open water 3–4 ft. deep and shallows 6–12 in. deep; not necessarily in a large marsh, may be in small patch of cattails at edge of lake or river, may be near large city or town, not shy, often seen in open and may allow close approach; long toes of unwebbed feet enable it to walk lightly and gracefully over lily pads; travels or climbs through densest reeds and rushes with ease, often swims with foreparts down, hindquarters raised, showing conspicuous white undertail coverts; often dives to feed or to escape enemies; rarely flies but when forced to, flutters away barely skimming water, half running, half flying along surface, then suddenly drops into marsh again, but when flying from pond to pond, flight is strong and direct, fairly swift, head extended, legs back to rear, acting as steering rudder; utters calls so varied that difficult to describe; male courting female calls harsh *ticket-ticket-ticket;* pairs give loud, henlike squeaks, clucks, screams, and a single explosive froglike *kup;* from wintering places in s. U.S. arrive on northern parts of breeding range usually Apr. into early May (Bent, 1926a).

Feeding Habits: Sometimes feeds on land, walking about, jerking tail as it picks up food, or from surface of water as it walks about on floating plants; it swims and dives mostly for seeds, grass, rootlets, soft parts of water plants; also eats snails, grasshoppers and other insects (Bent, 1926a).

Nest: Sometimes in small colonies, mass of dead stems of cattails, bulrushes, or other water plants, usually over water, may be partly floating, anchored or wedged into stems of bushes, about 13–20 in. in diameter but usually smaller than nests of coots (Fredrickson, 1971) with wide shallow cup in center for eggs, nest usually near open water, may also be in reed bed or on tussock at edge of cattail bed; nest usually 4–6 in. above water, with sloping runway of rushes, reeds to water, used by adults to reach or leave nest; pairs also build other nestlike platforms on which to brood young.

Eggs: Usually May–July; 4–17, commonly 7–12 (Fredrickson, 1971), cinnamon to olive-buff, spotted or dotted with browns.

Incubation: By both sexes, 18–21 days (Reilly, 1968); 21 days (Bent, 1926a); at hatching, downy chicks are black, with black-tipped red bill, skin at base of bill bright red, white-tipped curly hairs on chin and throat; adults eat eggshells after hatching of chicks, which are brooded by parents, then fed soon after hatch-

ing, mostly nymphs of dragonflies and mayflies (Fredrickson, 1971); age when first fly not reported but strong and active at 42–49 days old (Bent, 1926a).

Other Names: American gallinule; blue peter; blue rail; chicken-foot coot; Florida gallinule; moorhen; sedge peter; red-billed mud hen; water chicken; water hen.

Age: In wild, banded bird to 5½ years; another caught and released when 6 years, 3 months, old (Kennard, 1975).

Hybrids: See under American coot.

Weights: About 14 oz., male larger than female (Forbush, 1925–29).

Range: Nests from British Isles and n. Europe, n. Russia, s. Siberia, and Japan south to s. Africa, Madagascar, s. India to Philippines, Marianas Is., and Hawaii; in N. America from c. Calif. and c. Ariz. south into Mexico, and from Colo., Neb., S.D., c. Minn., s. Wisc., Mich., s. Ont., and s. Que. south to s. Fla. and to Mexico, Peru, n. Argentina, se. Brazil, West Indies, Bermuda, Galápagos Is.; winters in U.S. from c. Calif. to s. Ariz. south into c. Mexico, and along Gulf coast of U.S. and north to e. N.C.

Gallinule, Florida. *See* Gallinule, common.

Gallinule, purple, *Porphyrula martinica* (por-fih-ROOL-ah mar-TIN-ih-cah); genus name: dim. of *Porphyria,* genus name of the Old World purple gallinule, or swamp hen, from Gr. *porphyros,* red, brown, russet, also purple (Jaeger, 1955); species name: of the island of Martinique (Coues, 1882). (Color ill., page 723.) In U.S., mostly a resident year-round in southeastern coastal lowlands from e. Tex., sw. La., east to Fla. and north to S.C. and up large river courses to Tenn.; in summer to Del., where nesting and raising young in summer 1975 (Buckley *et al.,* 1975); usually favors great swamps or marshes with pickerelweed; is about size and shape of common gallinule, but far less common; no white side stripe on body; 12–14 in. long; wingspread about 22 in.; one of handsomest of all water birds, possibly second only to wood duck; adults: head, neck, and underparts deep rich purple; back dark green; bill bright red with yellow tip; forehead, or frontal shield, *light blue;* legs and feet bright green-yellow; all-white undertail coverts; immatures: dark gray above, pale gray and white below, bill and frontal shield pale gray; nods, bows, and twitches tail, showing flashes of white in undertail coverts; walks gracefully, its long toes supporting it as it treads lightly on lily pads, also wades, and when crossing deep open water, usually swims, pumping head back and forth, or may fly in labored slow, rail-like flight, with long yellow legs dangling just above water; also alights easily in bushes and climbs gracefully about in branches over water; noisy, gives henlike cackle in flight, *kek, kek, kek* (Bent, 1926a); not shy, and where protected, as in Everglades National Park, Fla., becomes tame enough to take peanuts from hands or lips of visitors.

Feeding Habits: In fall visits rice fields, where it bends stalks to reach seeds; generally eats grain and seeds from spatterdock, water lettuce; also frogs, small snails, aquatic insects,

worms, and sometimes eggs and young of boat-tailed grackle and other small marsh birds (McIlhenny, 1936).

Nest: A platform 8–10 in. or more across, built of sedges, grasses, rushes, cattails, pickerelweed, like a shallow basket, suspended among and woven into surrounding marsh plants, from 1 ft. to 3 or even 5 ft. above deep water of marsh, in islandlike patches of dense, living water plants; sometimes built in low branches of willow thickets growing in shallow water; builds several dummy nests nearby.

Eggs: Apr.–July; 5–10, usually 6–8, pink-buff, spotted with browns (Bent, 1926a).

Incubation: Period of and age when young leave nest unreported; downy young are glossy black, with many white, hairlike feathers on head and throat; yellow bill, black-tipped.

Other Names: Blue peter; marsh hen.

Weights: Probably about same as that of common gallinule (female 7½ oz.)

Range: In U.S. nests along coast of La., in Tenn., s. Miss., s. Ala., S.C., Ga., and Fla., north to Del. (*see* above), south through West Indies, and from Nayarit, Mexico, to Peru, and south from s. Tex. to Uruguay and n. Argentina; winters from Gulf coast south; has wandered to se. Canada, Bermuda (Reilly, 1968).

Rail, black, *Laterallus jamaicensis* (lat-eh-RAL-us jah-may-ih-SEN-sis); genus name: Lat., meaning a distinguished rail (Sprunt, 1954a); species name: of the island of Jamaica, where first discovered in 1760 (Bent, 1926a). (Color ill., page 725.) Wide gap in range in U.S.; in summer, c. Calif., n. Baja Calif., and Neb. south to Okla., east to Mass., south to Fla.; smallest of rails, about size of sparrow; 5–6 in. long; wingspread 10½–11½ in.; extremely difficult to find, rarely seen, but apparently locally common, and heard calling at night; usually seen as small, black, mouselike bird darting through sedges or grasses of its preferred salt-marsh home, but also along inland tidal creeks and marshes; black with black bill; red eyes; *black back speckled with white* (all young rails are glossy black and are sometimes reported as black rails by beginners); along seacoast, lives above and in back of beaches along edges of sandy *Salicornia* flats and in salt-hay meadows; rarely flushes, flight is weak fluttering with legs dangling, soon drops back into cover; usually silent but *male* black rail in breeding season utters series of metallic *kik* or *kuk* notes (see Bollinger and Bowes, 1973), described as *kic-kic-kerr* and *kick-ee-doo,* usually given at night from 1–2 hours after sunset to 1–2 hours before sunrise (Reynard, 1974); female calls *croo-croo-croo-o-a,* resembling first notes of yellow-billed cuckoo's call, or *who-who-who-whooo,* all in one pitch and lasting no more than a second (Reynard, 1974); another call sounds like *did-ee-dunk* (Bent, 1926a).

Feeding Habits: Little known but reported as insects, seeds of aquatic plants, and isopods—small marine crustaceans.

Nest: In or along edge of marsh, usually completely hidden in thick clump of marsh grass or at base of *Salicornia;* a loose cup of soft grasses, with green grasses arched over it so that hidden from above; sometimes on damp

ground but usually on mat of previous year's dead grasses (Pough, 1951; Bent, 1926a).
Eggs: N.J., May–Aug.; 4–13, usually 6–8, buff-white, dotted with browns.
Other Name: Little black rail.
Weights: 2–2¾ oz.
Range: Nests from c. Calif. to nw. Baja Calif., Colo., Neb., Kans., Ind., Ohio, s. N.Y., Conn., se. Mass., south to Okla., Mo., Ohio R. valley, W.Va., w. and c. Fla., south to Cuba, West Indies, and Peru to c. Chile; winters coastal Calif., s. La., s. Ga. south (Reilly, 1968).

Rail, blue. *See* Gallinule, common.

Rail, Carolina. *See* Sora.

Rail, chicken-billed. *See* Sora.

Rail, clapper, *Rallus longirostris* (RAL-us lonj-ih-ROS-tris); genus name: Lat., from Fr. *râle,* rail; species name: from Lat. *longus,* long, and *rostrum,* beak; *clapper,* from its clattering, cackling calls which resemble sound of old-fashioned clappers. (Color ill., page 724.) Usually a salt-marsh rail; nests along both coasts, w.-c. Calif. south to Peru (also along lower Colorado R. north of Yuma, where a form, or subspecies, the Yuma clapper rail, *yumanensis,* is only clapper rail to nest in freshwater marshes: about 500–1,000 birds left —*see* Rare and Threatened Species, and for details on major concentration places and chosen habitat of Yuma rail, see Tomlinson and Todd [1973]); along Gulf coast; and along Atlantic coast from Conn. south; 14–16½ in. long; wingspread 19–21 in.; a fairly abundant, henlike, gray or gray-brown rail with barred flanks; *gray cheeks;* short neck, long thin bill, slightly downcurved; very short, up-cocked tail, white below; body deep in profile as in other rails, laterally compressed; immature, similar to adults but darker above, soiled white below; harsh, loud clatter of this rail is one of familiar sounds of salt marshes, a *kek, kek, kek* or *cha, cha, cha;* noisiest at dusk, on moonlit nights, or just before a storm, but any sudden loud sound may startle them into a chorus which resembles cries of guinea fowl; sometimes swims; flies low with legs dangling; migrates at night; when walking, bobs the head and twitches tail.

Feeding Habits: Feeds mostly at low tide on mud flats, along banks of creeks in marsh; eats fiddler and other crabs, crayfishes, mollusks, worms, and other marine animals; also small fishes, aquatic insects, amphibians.
Nest: Built on highest, driest places in marshes, in small clumps of coarse green marsh grasses, 18–24 in. tall, nest 8–12 in. above mud; well cupped, 7–10 in. across, of dry sedges, grasses, some nests arched over with interlocked green sedges, but some in sight in short grass, nests usually with a well-defined runway in grass leading to them (Bent, 1926a).
Eggs: Calif., Mar.–July; Va., Apr.–July; N.J., N.Y., May–June; 6–14, usually 9–12, yellow-buff to green-buff, irregularly blotched or spotted with browns, usually darker and more heavily marked than eggs of king rail.
Incubation: 21–23 days (Nice, 1954); downy chicks are uniformly black; are independent of

parents 35–42 days after hatching; fly 63–70 days after hatching (Adams and Quay, 1958). See also Kozicky and Schmidt (1949).
Other Names: Common clapper; light-footed rail; marsh clapper; meadow hen; mud hen; salt-water marsh hen; sedge hen; Yuma clapper rail.
Albinism: One shot in Alameda marsh, Calif., in 1896, a partial albino with mottled white feathers over body that made it appear gray (McGregor, 1900).
Hybrids: Occasionally crossbreeds with king rail where their nesting ranges overlap; noted especially in Del., Va., and other places (see details in Meanley, 1969). See also discussion of close relationships of the clapper and king rails in Mayr and Short (1970).
Weights: 8–14 oz., females smaller than males (Forbush, 1925–29); adult males (13), 300–350 gr., or about 10½–12⅓ oz.; adult females (6), about 275 gr., or about 9⅔ oz. (Meanley, 1969).
Range: Along coast of Calif. from San Francisco region south to Baja Calif., to S. America, and from Conn. south to Mexico; also in lower Colo. R. valley.

Rail, common. *See* Sora.

Rail, great red-breasted. *See* Rail, king.

Rail, king, *Rallus elegans* (RAL-us EL-ee-ganz); genus name: *see* Rail, clapper; species name: Lat., elegant; *king,* for its large size and bright coloration. (Color ill., page 724.) Largest of N. American rails; lives in freshwater marshes in most of e. N. America; in summer, from Atlantic coast west to Great Plains and from Gulf of Mexico to s. Canada; most abundant in fresh and brackish tidal marshes of Atlantic and Gulf coastal plains (Meanley, 1969); 15–19 in. long; wingspread 21–25 in.; larger than clapper rail, its close relative, and considered by Mayr and Short (1970) and other authorities to be a freshwater race, or form, of the salt-marsh clapper rail; males generally larger and heavier than females; browner than grayish clapper rail, and with stronger barring on flanks; has bright red-brown breast; long, slender, slightly downcurved brown-tipped, yellow bill; king rail is twice size of the similar reddish Virginia rail, which has *gray* cheeks; migratory throughout most of its range; migrates at night mainly through Mississippi Valley and along Atlantic coast; on summer nesting grounds lives in great variety of habitats, from coastal saltwater and brackish marshes to shrublike swamps and even in upland fields near marshes; distribution coincides closely with that of muskrat, which creates openings in marsh and feeding and drinking places for it (Meanley, 1969); advertises its nesting territory to other rails with calls, *jupe-jupe-jupe-jupe* or *cheup-cheup-cheup,* sometimes *gelp-gelp-gelp,* also utters *chuck-chuck* calls resembling sound of teamster clucking to his horses, for which Ill. farmers named it stage driver; also calls *kik-kik-kik-kik* or *bup-bup-bup-bup* and *tuk-tuk-tuk,* and many other calls (see Meanley, 1969); during courtship period, male feeds female by holding in bill a crayfish or fiddler crab, which she takes from him (*see* Courtship Feeding); banded males and females have re-

turned to their same nesting territories in consecutive years.

Feeding Habits: Walks about, feeding mostly in water about 2–3 in. deep or on mud flats exposed at low tide; sometimes feeds in roadside ditches, immersing entire head and neck in water; much more varied in foods eaten than clapper rail; favors crustaceans—crayfishes, fiddler and other crabs—also small fishes, frogs, grasshoppers, crickets, weevils, beetles, seeds of weeds and aquatic plants, during winter eats large amounts of rice, wheat, oats, also takes wild berries; regurgitates in pellets the indigestible parts of food (*see* Pellet).
Nest: Male selects site, is more active than female in building nest, usually in shallow-water part of marsh or in rice fields, roadside ditches, low bushes, sometimes in oat or wheat field; a round, elevated platform about 10–14 in. across, with shallow depression for eggs, nest 6–8 in. above water in tussock of grass or sedge or between clumps, with cone-shaped or round canopy of standing plants pulled over nest to conceal it from above; built of dry, dead grasses, cattails, sedges, or rushes gathered near nest site, with grassy ramp from ground or water to nest (Meanley, 1969).
Eggs: Fla., Jan.–July; elsewhere, usually Mar.–June; 6–15, commonly 8–11, pale buff, sparingly and irregularly spotted with browns.
Incubation: In turn, by both sexes, 21–23 days; incubating bird may vigorously defend eggs by flying at intruder or feign injury and try to lead intruder away (*see* Distraction Display); day-old chick is black with greenish gloss, has vestigial claw on each wing; young make first short flights about 63 days after hatching (Meanley, 1969).
Other Names: Freshwater marsh hen; great red-breasted rail; marsh hen; meadow hen; mud hen; stage driver.
Accidents: Strikes TV towers, beacons, tall city buildings, lighthouses when migrating at night; on wintering marshes, seeks escape in muskrat burrows, gets caught in steel traps; often killed by cars when crossing highways, an increasing hazard where roads built through or near marshes; in flight, strikes utility wires and dies and gets impaled on barbed-wire fences.
Hybrids: See under Clapper rail.
Weights: 10–18 oz., females smaller than males (Forbush, 1925–29); adult males (9), 366–490 gr., or about 12¾–18 oz.; adult females (9), 253–325 gr., or about 9–11½ oz. (Meanley, 1969).
Range: Nests from se. N.D., Iowa, c. Minn., s. Wisc., c. Mich., s. Ont., N.Y. (Buffalo, Ithaca, Long Is.), Conn., Mass., south along Atlantic coast to s. Fla. and Gulf coast region to s. Tex., also in Mexico, Cuba, Isle of Pines, where resident; winters from northern part of range south along Atlantic coast from New York City and the tidewater country of Delaware Valley to se. Ga. and Fla. Everglades; in Mississippi Valley from Ark. rice belt, se. Mo., and Gulf coast marshes to Tex. and lower Rio Grande Valley; has wandered in winter to Okla., Mich., Ont., Me., Kans., Long Is., N.Y., and Md. south.

Rail, land. *See* Crake, corn.

Rail, light-footed. *See* Rail, clapper.

Rail, little red-breasted. *See* Rail, Virginia.

Rail, long-billed. *See* Rail, Virginia.

Rail, Sora. *See* Sora.

Rail, Virginia, *Rallus limicola* (RAL-us lie-MIK-oh-lah); genus name: *see* Rail, clapper; species name: Lat., mud dweller. (Color ills., page 725.) Summers in freshwater marshes from s. Canada south throughout U.S.; common, but seldom seen; 8½–10½ in. long; wingspread 13–14½ in.; a rust-colored rail with *long, slender,* slightly downcurved reddish bill; length distinguishes it from short-billed sora; has black barring on flanks; resembles king rail but smaller and has *gray cheeks,* dark red eyes; immature but grown young, in late summer and into winter, appear almost black; like other rails, difficult to flush, prefers to run swiftly through marsh when pursued; swims, can cling to grass or rush stems and climb bushes; flight is weak, short, fluttering, with long legs dangling, reddish forepart of wings conspicuous; flies low at night in migration but with power and speed, singly, and in direct course over rivers or low level land (Townsend, 1926); from marshes, courtship call in spring is metallic *kid-ick, kid-ick,* like click of telegraph key (Townsend, 1926), or *tic-tic-tic-McGreer* and *kik, kik, ki-queea* (Reynard, 1974), the so-called kicker song, sometimes repeated often by day and by night (for many years ornithologists were not sure of identity of the singer; Brewster, 1901, though not sure, attributed it to the black rail; Ames, 1902, and Kellogg *et al.,* 1959, to the yellow rail, and Kellogg, 1962b, to the black rail; however, proof that it is song of the Virginia rail was provided by Reynard and Harty, 1968, and by Bollinger and Bowes, 1973); the Virginia rail also utters *cut-ah, cut-ah* and ducklike *wak-wak-wak,* dropping in key and in volume; also piglike grunts and other odd calls which some listeners attribute to frogs and other creatures of the marsh; best way to observe this rail is to sit quietly and motionless at edge of marsh.

Feeding Habits: Probes mud with bill for earthworms and larval insects; also eats snails, slugs, small fishes, caterpillars, beetles, occasionally seeds of grasses (Townsend, 1926). Horak (1970), in studies in n. Iowa marshes, verified some of these food habits and noted, besides, large amounts of duckweed *(Lemna)* and some seeds of sedges and smartweeds, also crayfishes, but most of its food (62%) was insects.

Nest: Usually well concealed in freshwater marsh or near fresh water, occasionally in upper, drier parts of salt marshes, sometimes over water; rather loosely woven cup of coarse grasses, sedges, reeds, parts of cattails, sometimes 7–8 in. high and 8 in. across, fastened within clump of plants or on a tussock from a few inches to a foot above mud or water.

Eggs: Calif., Wash., Apr.–June; central, middle Atlantic, and northern states, May–June or

July; 5–12, buff, sparingly and irregularly spotted with browns, gray.

Incubation: About 20 days (Walkinshaw, 1957a); downy black chicks have yellow bill with black band around middle; age when young first fly unknown.

Other Names: Freshwater marsh hen; little red-breasted rail; long-billed rail; small mud hen.

Weights: In Mich. (1), 69.9 gr. (Becker and Stack, 1944), or slightly less than 3 oz.; in Conn. (2), 68 gr. (Wetherbee, 1934); in Kans., in fall, killed in night migration at TV tower: males (3), 73.7, 83.2, and 90.5 gr., or 2¾–3 oz., female (1), 67.3 gr. (Tordoff and Mengel, 1956).

Range: Nests from B.C., Alta., Mont., Sask., Man., Minn., Wisc., Mich., s. Ont., Que., N.B., and Nova Scotia, south to nw. Baja Calif., through C. America to e. and s. S. America; winters locally from s. B.C. south to Baja Calif., rarely in c. and s. Tex., s. La., s. Miss., s. Ala., more commonly near Atlantic coast from N.C. south to Ga., c. Fla., Mexico to Guatemala; irregularly in winter from Mont., Utah, Colo., Ark., Ill., Mich., Ohio, s. Ont., Mass., N.Y., N.J., Md., Va.

Rail, water, *Rallus aquaticus* (RAL-us ah-QUAY-tih-cus); genus name: *see* Rail, clapper; species name: Lat., living in or near water. European and Asiatic rail; the resident form that lives in Iceland has strayed to Greenland; has long red bill; resembles Virginia rail but adult has slate-gray breast.

Rail, yellow, *Coturnicops noveboracensis* (coe-TURE-nih-cops no-veh-boh-rah-SEN-sis); genus name: from Lat. *coturnix,* quail, and Gr., *ops,* appearance; species name: Lat., of, or pertaining to, New York. (Color ill., page 724.) Widely scattered from Nova Scotia to Calif.; in summer, generally east of Rockies from s. and w. Canada to N.B., and across n. U.S.; very small, extremely shy, sparrow size; 6–7½ in. long; wingspread 10–13 in.; short-billed, yellow-brown with dark stripes on back; *the only rail with a white patch on each wing, conspicuous in flight only;* if flushed, flutters into air for a few yards, then drops back into grass or other ground cover, but prefers to run to escape, so averse to flight that trained dogs can run them down and catch them (see account in Griscom, 1949); rarely appears in open; in fall and in winter, lives in high margins of saltwater marshes, savannas, grain fields, and hayfields, and even among garden crops, but in nesting season prefers shallow freshwater marshes and wet meadows where grasses not so tall and dense as in cattail marshes, preferred by other rails; utters clicking notes, a long-continued series of *tick-tick, tick-tick-tick,* or *tick-tick-tick, tick-tick* (in groups of two and three); heard in May in Del., and in Mar. and Apr. in Fla. (Reynard, 1974); *see* controversy over this bird's song in biography of Virginia rail; from wintering range in s. U.S., arrives generally on northern nesting range Mar.–Apr.

Feeding Habits: Only food reported: small snails, insects, seeds, grasses, clover leaves.

Nest: Often built on wisp of dead grasses of previous year or on grass tussock; a woven cup

RAIL FAMILY
The rail's narrow body, strong toes, and flexible wings are adaptations to its life in densely growing marsh grasses and weeds.

of fine grasses about 4 in. across, 2 in. deep, a little above water of marsh or meadow, with wisps of grass screening nest from above.

Eggs: N. U.S., May–June; 7–10, warm yellow-buff, usually speckled or densely spotted at large end with red-brown.

Incubation: Period of and age when young first fly unknown; downy young are black, slightly green gloss on top of head, and tinged brown on back.

Other Names: Little yellow rail; yellow crake.

Range: The relatively few nesting records are scattered, but breeds locally, in general, east of Rocky Mtns. in Canada and the U.S. (one nesting record in e.-c. Calif., but see Small, 1974), from Mack., Man., Ont., Que., N.B., and Me., south to Calif., Ariz., La., Miss., Ala., and Fla.; migrates and winters from Ore. to s. Calif. and along Gulf coast from Tex. east to Fla.; casual in Wash. One killed by a cat, Mar. 26, 1955, at Neavitt, Md., was first record for state in 25 years (Potter and Murray, 1955).

Rail, Yuma clapper. *See* Rail, clapper.

Sora, *Porzana carolina* (por-ZANE-ah car-oh-LINE-ah); genus name: *see* Crake, spotted; species name: Lat., of Carolina; *sora* thought to have been derived from an Indian name for the bird. (Color ill., page 726.) One of commonest and most abundant of N. American rails; in summer lives from c. Canada south to Baja Calif. and sw. U.S., and to Okla., Ohio, W.Va.; small, plump, gray-brown; 8–10 in. long; wingspread 12–14½ in.; distinguished by *short, yellow,* chickenlike bill; adults have black patch on face and throat; back and wings spotted with black and buff; below, irregular barring of thin white lines on gray; the buff-brown immature lacks black face and throat markings but, like adult, has white undertail coverts, which show when cocked in alarm; nests in dense growth of cattails, reeds, in almost any small freshwater marsh, bog, or bit of marsh along river or pond, even at edges of cities, also along borders of prairie sloughs or in wet, grassy meadows; usually arrives on nesting grounds Apr.–May; its spring song coming from marsh is plaintive *er-we,* with rising inflection, suggestive of rallying call of bobwhite or piping of spring peeper; also utters a pleasing whinny, a series of rapid, short bell-like whistles descending the scale and leveling off at end (Bent, 1926a); also will utter a sharp *keek* of alarm if one throws stick into habitat; can be seen best by sitting silent and motionless at edge of marsh or opening, where one of soras may come to feed; steps daintily over mud, picking up bits of food with short bill, flirting short tail up and down; toes are so long its body easily supported on mud or on lily pads or floating reeds; if alarmed, runs to cover with body narrowed and slips out of sight through spaces between reeds; swims across narrow lanes of water; has been seen to run nimbly along bottom of brook a foot deep, clinging to aquatic plants and traveling underwater downstream for some 15 ft. to other side (Bent, 1926a); a strong flier in migration, has one of longest migration routes of any member of family, probably little less than 3,000 mi. each way, fall and spring (Bent, 1926a); easily crosses Caribbean Sea (Lincoln, 1950c) to winter throughout West Indies; regularly visits Bermuda.

Feeding Habits: In spring and summer, eats many small mollusks and aquatic insects of marshes, but also discovered, from summer food habits in n. Iowa (Horak, 1970), that its diet is 73% (by volume) seeds, largely of smartweed (*Polygonum*), sedges, and foxtail grasses, and the leaves of duckweed (*Lemna*); is especially fond of seeds of wild rice; in late summer and fall, soras assemble with families in enormous numbers along banks of sluggish streams and freshwater marshes, where wild rice grows, until driven farther south by first sharp frost, when they suddenly disappear.

Nest: A small, loosely built basket of dead leaves of cattails, dry grasses, or reeds, about 6 in. in diameter, attached to standing stems of marsh plants, a few inches above water, usually well hidden among reeds, cattails, or grasses; are generally over deeper water and better built than nests of Virginia rail.

Eggs: Calif., Utah, Nev., Apr.–June; elsewhere, usually May–July; 6–18, commonly 10–12, rich buff, irregularly spotted with browns, grays.

Incubation: 18–20 days (Walkinshaw, 1957a); 19–20 days (Nice, 1962a); age when young first fly unknown; downy young are glossy black; chin feathers stiff, curled, bright orange; yellow bill is reddish at base.

Other Names: Carolina crake; Carolina rail; chicken-bill; chicken-billed rail; common rail; little American water hen; meadow chicken; mud hen; ortolan; railbird; sora rail.

Weights: In autumn migration, coastal N.J. (1), 61.4 gr., or about 2¼ oz. (Murray and Jehl, 1964); killed in fall 1954, Kans. TV tower: males (4), 68.7–89.9 gr., or 2½ to slightly more than 3 oz.; females (fat to very fat) (3), 62.6, 63.2, and 63.5 gr., or about 2 oz. (Tordoff and Mengel, 1956); 3–4 oz. (Forbush, 1925–29).

Range: Nests from B.C., Mack., Sask., n. Man., n. Ont., c. and s. Que., N.B., and Prince Edward Is. south to nw. Baja Calif., Nev., Ariz., s. N.M., Colo., Okla., Mo., Ill., Ind., c. Ohio, W.Va., and Pa.; winters from Calif., c. Ariz., s. Tex., to s. La., s. Miss., s. S.C., and Fla. south through Mexico, C. America, and West Indies to Peru, Venezuela, Trinidad, and Guyana; sometimes remains in winter north to n. U.S.

RAIN BATHING
See Bathing.

RAIN BIRD
Local name for the black-billed and yellow-billed cuckoos for their habit of often calling frequently just before a rainstorm. *See* Folklore.

RAIN-GOOSE
One of common names of the red-throated loon. *See* Folklore.

RALLIDAE
See Rail Family.

RANGE AND RANGE EXPANSION
See Ranges of Birds under Distribution. *See also* Range in the biography of each bird; *also* Dispersal.

RAPTOR
See Bird of Prey.

RARE AND THREATENED SPECIES
The species (and subspecies) of birds listed here are those of N. America as defined geographically by the American Ornithologists' Union (1957) and followed throughout this book. It is all of the continental U.S., Alaska, Canada, Baja Calif., and the islands of Greenland and Bermuda. The following list of birds is from *Threatened Wildlife of the United States,* Resource Publication 114, Mar. 1973, U.S. Department of the Interior, Bureau of Sport Fisheries and Wildlife, Washington, D.C. (Office of Endangered Species, 1973) and from the updated *List of Endangered and Threatened Wildlife and Plants* (U.S. Department of the Interior, 1979). For the status of each and the range of the various threatened subspecies, one must refer to these publications; however, the general range of each of the species as a whole is discussed in the biographies of each bird in the text. E = Endangered; T = Threatened.

E Eastern brown pelican, *Pelecanus occidentalis carolinensis* (Pelican Family)

E California brown pelican, *Pelecanus occidentalis californicus* (Pelican Family)

E Florida great white heron, *Ardea herodias* (a color form of the great blue heron) (Heron Family)

E Aleutian Canada goose, *Branta canadensis leucopareia* (Duck Family)

E Mexican duck, *Anas diazi* (Duck Family)

E California condor, *Gymnogyps californianus* (American Vulture Family)

E Florida Everglade kite, *Rostrhamus sociabilis plumbeus* (Hawk Family)

E* Bald eagle, *Haliaeetus leucocephalus* (Hawk Family)

E American peregrine falcon, *Falco peregrinus anatum* (Falcon Family)

E Arctic peregrine falcon, *Falco peregrinus tundrius* (Falcon Family)

E Attwater's greater prairie chicken, *Tympanuchus cupido attwateri* (Grouse Family)

E Lesser prairie chicken, *Tympanuchus pallidicinctus* (Grouse Family)

E Masked bobwhite, *Colinus virginianus ridgwayi* (Pheasant Family)

E Whooping crane, *Grus americana* (Crane Family)

E Mississippi sandhill crane, *Grus canadensis pulla* (Crane Family)

E California clapper rail, *Rallus longirostris obsoletus* (Rail Family)

E Light-footed clapper rail, *Rallus longirostris levipes* (Rail Family)

E Yuma clapper rail, *Rallus longirostris yumanensis* (Rail Family)

E Eskimo curlew, *Numenius borealis* (Sandpiper Family)

E California least tern, *Sterna albifrons browni* (Gull Family)

E Red-cockaded woodpecker, *Dendrocopos borealis* (Woodpecker Family)

E Ivory-billed woodpecker, *Campephilus principalis* (Woodpecker Family)

E Bachman's warbler, *Vermivora bachmanii* (American Wood Warbler Family)

E Kirtland's warbler, *Dendroica kirtlandii* (American Wood Warbler Family)

E Ipswich sparrow, *Passerculus sandwichensis princeps* (Finch Family)

E Dusky seaside sparrow, *Ammospiza maritima nigrescens* (Finch Family)

E Cape Sable seaside sparrow, *Ammospiza maritima mirabilis* (Finch Family)

*Not endangered in Alaska; T in Wash., Oreg., Minn., Wisc., and Mich.; E in all other states.

Following are some additions to the list in 1979, according to the Federal Register:

E   Short-tailed albatross, *Diomedea albatrus* (Albatross Family)
E   Bermuda petrel (cahow), *Pterodroma cahow* (Shearwater Family)
E   Greenland white-tailed eagle, *Haliaeetus albicilla greenlandicus* (Hawk Family)
E   Thick-billed parrot, *Rhynchopsitta pachyrhyncha* (Parrot Family)
E   San Clemente loggerhead shrike, *Lanius ludovicianus mearnsi* (Shrike Family)
T   San Clemente sage sparrow, *Amphispiza belli clementeae* (Finch Family)
E   Santa Barbara song sparrow, *Melospiza melodia graminea* (Finch Family)

For a general article on threatened species, see Aldrich (1966). *See also* Blue List.

RARE BIRD ALERT
Telephone service whereby one can make a call and, from a taped message, receive information about the latest rare birds seen in an area. As of 1980, these telephone "alert services," also called Dial-a-Bird, were in Ala., Ariz., Calif., Colo., Conn., Del., Ga., Ill., Kans., Me., Md., Mass., Mich., Minn., Neb., N.J., N.Y., Ohio, Pa., Tex., Vt., Wash., D.C., and B.C., Nova Scotia, and Ont. in Canada, but for more recent information see Drennan (1980). For an article and listing of cities and states with telephone numbers to dial, see Drennan (1975; 1980) and Rickert (1978).

RATITE
(RAT-ite). *See* Carinate; *also* Flightless Birds.

RAT RUN
Term of some bird behaviorists for a type of behavior characteristic of certain shorebirds. *See* Distraction Display. *See also* Shorebird; Behavior.

RAVEN
See in Crow Family.

RAVEN, THE
A publication. *See* Ornithological Periodicals.

RAZORBILL
See in Auk Family.

RECENT PERIOD
See Geological Time Scale.

RECIPROCAL PREENING
See Mutual Preening under Preening.

RECOGNITION SIGNALS
See Courtship; *also* Language; Behavior.

RECORDINGS
The recording of bird sounds began as a novelty in 1889, when the first recording of bird song in history was made by Dr. Ludwig Koch in Germany. Using a machine brought to him by his father from a Leipzig Fair, he recorded the sound of a bird singing in a cage. In 1902, he made the first recording of a wild bird singing under natural conditions in the open air (Strutt, 1954).

The first recording of bird song in America was made by Sylvester D. Judd, a biologist of the U.S. Biological Survey, Washington, D.C., who recorded with a Gramophone and trumpet speaker the songs of Rustler, his pet brown thrasher. In 1898, he played the record before the annual meeting of the American Ornithologists' Union (Judd, 1899).

In America, it was not until 1932 that technical developments in sound-receiving equipment at Cornell University made it practical to collect sounds in nature, especially the singing of wild birds. These recorded songs aided students of birds to learn the songs, both in the laboratory and in the field, and to enjoy the songs in playbacks of the records. They also enabled ornithologists to analyze and compare bird songs for their frequencies, temporal patterns, and intensity. See details of the development of recording and equipment and its history in Kellogg (1962a).

In the spring of 1932, Albert R. Brand, at Cornell University, with Peter Keane, published privately the first phonograph record of wild bird songs made at the university. It was a 12-in. 78-r.p.m. disc of two sides with the recorded songs of 21 species of birds, titled *Bird Songs from Nature*. In 1934, Brand published his first album, *Songs of Wild Birds* (New York: Thomas Nelson and Sons). It contained two double-faced discs with recordings of 35 species of birds; in 1936, he published a sequel, *More Songs of of Wild Birds* (same publisher), an album of three records with songs of 43 additional species.

After Brand's death in 1940, the Cornell Laboratory of Ornithology produced an album of six 10-in. 78-r.p.m. records titled *American Bird Songs*. The Cornell workers continued disc recording until 1949, when they changed to magnetic tape recordings with semi-portable equipment for field use. By 1979, members of the laboratory and co-workers had collected sounds of more than 3,200 species of birds from many parts of the world.

According to Stein (1962), with advances in sound recorders and the use of audiospectrographs to make spectrograms (which record vocalizations visually, giving a picture of the sound in graphic form, with pitch represented on one axis, time on the other, and with the sound portrayed with a degree of detail that the human ear cannot detect), it became possible to collect samples of birds' songs and calls and on the spectrogram to analyze and compare them with others. (Studying bird sounds by means of spectrograms is comparable to studying structural characters, such as feathers, under a microscope—Borror, 1975b.) The spectrogram shows the vocalizations as characteristic of each species of bird, in the same way that color patterns and form and structure are characteristic of each species, and thus can help the student to determine bird relationships. The graphs are like a bird's signature, and in some cases the individual differences among the songs of males of the same species can be detected. The individual males can be recognized by their songs upon their return to the nesting territory each spring (Beck, 1971). For an example of a study, based on sonograms, of a particular species of bird, see Borror (1967).

From the study of bird songs and calls (vocalizations) on recordings and from spectrograms, ornithologists are getting considerable information that increases their understanding of communication among birds (Pettingill, 1972). *See* Courtship; Language; Songs and Singing. For details of the making and practical use of spectrograms (audiospectrograms), see especially Borror (1960a); Stein (1958); see also Marler (1969). For information on recording equipment and its uses, see Gulledge (1976), and on recording of birds' voices, see Margoschis (1977).

RECTRICES
(reck-TRY-seez; sing.: *rectrix*). The main tail feathers. *See* Flight; Feather; Tail.

RECURVED
See Bill.

RECURVIROSTRIDAE
See Avocet Family.

RED-BACK
See Dunlin in Sandpiper Family.

REDBILL
See Black oystercatcher in Oystercatcher Family; *also* Tern, royal, and Tern, Caspian, in Gull Family.

REDBIRD
See Cardinal in Finch Family; *also* Scarlet tanager and Summer tanager in Tanager Family.

REDBREAST
See Robin, American, and Bluebird, Eastern, in Thrush Family; *also* Knot, red, in Sandpiper Family.

RED-HAMMER
See Flicker, red-shafted (common), in Woodpecker Family.

REDHEAD
See Redhead in Duck Family; *also* Woodpecker, red-headed, in Woodpecker Family.

REDLEG
See Duck, black, in Duck Family.

REDPOLL
See in Finch Family.

REDSHANK
See in Sandpiper Family; also another name for the common tern and royal tern in Gull Family.

REDSTART
See in Warbler—American Wood Warbler Family.

RED-TAIL
See Hawk, red-tailed, in Hawk Family.

REDWING
Shortened name for the red-winged blackbird in Troupial Family, but also a common name of a thrush of Europe. *See* reference to one in N. America in Thrush Family.

REED-BIRD

See Bobolink in Troupial Family.

REEVE

See Ruff in Sandpiper Family.

REFLECTION-FIGHTING

See Window-fighting under Territory.

REFUGE

See Wildlife Refuge; *also* Sanctuary.

REGURGITATION

Term for the casting up of incompletely digested food or other items from the stomach or crop of a bird (*see* Digestion; Pellet). Certain adult birds feed their young by regurgitating food that they partially predigest before feeding it to them. *See* Young and Their Care; *also* Crop. Such *emesis* (vomiting) is very easy for birds and is a means of self-defense—in vultures and fulmars, for example. Fish-eating birds such as herons, gulls, and petrels habitually vomit when wounded or molested.

All tubenoses (albatrosses, petrels, fulmars, storm-petrels, and diving petrels—*see* Tubenose) vomit upon being disturbed, but the fulmar seems to have been most successful in turning the habit to its own defense. When an enemy approaches a fulmar on its nest, the fulmar spits forth oil up to 2-3 ft. at the intruder. The young fulmar can spit oil while still in the egg—through the pipped shell—and it spits at its parents for a few days after hatching, until it has learned to recognize its parents as friends (Fisher and Lockley, 1954). Bird enemies of the fulmar are apparently intimidated by the oil sprayed at them, which is extremely foul-smelling and is probably residues, partly digested, from the stomach. It varies in its composition but can contain excess fat and vitamin A. *See also* Seabird.

Fisher (Fisher and Lockley, 1954) believes that the tubular nostrils of tubenoses are an anatomical adaptation for preening since tubular nostrils (*see* Nostrils) are present only in birds which produce stomach oil, and there is a discharge of oil from their nostrils when they are preening. *See* Preening; *also* Petrel.

RELEASER

See Sign Stimuli, or Releasers, under Behavior.

REMIGES

(REM-ih-jeez; sing.: *remex*). The wing feathers, either primaries or secondaries. *See* Feather.

REPRODUCTION ISOLATION

Term for the inability or aversion of species of birds to interbreed with other species. *See* discussion under Species; *also* Sibling Species and Sympatric Species for examples of reproductive isolation.

REPRODUCTIVE LIFE

Some long-lived birds continue to lay eggs and to produce young each year to a great age—albatrosses, gulls, geese, owls, boobies, and others. *See* details under Eggs and Egg-laying and in biography of each bird species. Even small birds may have a relatively long reproductive life. For example, a banded eastern phoebe near Culver, Ind., paired and raised young annually for at least nine summers and was mated and caring for young when last reported upon. Nine years exceeds by far the average length of life of most small birds, in the wild, and it appears that most birds are capable of reproduction throughout their lives. *See* Age; Longevity.

REPRODUCTIVE SYSTEM

See Fertilization; *also* Endocrine Glands.

REPTILES AND BIRDS

Various kinds of reptiles have defenses against any animal that would try to eat them. Snakes have intimidating actions of rearing and striking, hissing, inflating, and exuding offensive-smelling fluids from their anal glands; some bite and inject poisonous venom. Many lizards discard their tails easily to elude the grasp of enemies, and horned toads, besides their protective coloration, have prominent spines on the back of the head. Turtles have hard shells, and jaws and claws they may use in defense, and several species give off a strong musky odor. Yet the report of McAtee (1932b) on the stomach contents of 80,000 N. American birds showed that birds ate reptiles quite in proportion to their abundance and availability as food. (For exact identification, scientific names of reptiles follow Conant, 1958, and Stebbins, 1966).

SNAKES. Twenty-six species of birds had fed on snakes, according to the McAtee report. Crows, hawks, and owls were the most significant snake predators. Unexpectedly, the Carolina wren had eaten small snakes, and the red-shouldered and broad-winged hawks had eaten the "superlatively cryptic" (protectively colored) smooth green snake, *Opheodrys aestivus;* 5 species of hawks and the common crow had eaten the swift-running racer snakes *(Coluber),* and the red-tailed and Swainson's hawks had eaten the ominously bluffing and hissing hog-nosed snakes; and several species of birds had eaten garter snakes *(Thamnophis)* and water snakes *(Natrix),* which in self-defense can copiously exude a foul-smelling fluid from the anal glands. The red-shouldered hawk had eaten king snakes *(Lampropeltis),* which are powerful constrictors. A great blue heron had swallowed a banded water snake, *Natrix sipedon fasciata,* about 25 in. long. The only poisonous snake reported from McAtee's study was a rattlesnake, in the stomach of a great horned owl.

According to Klauber (1956), owls in general do not prey as much on snakes as hawks do; however, the great horned owl and even the 7½-in.-long pygmy owl and the burrowing and screech owls eat small snakes. Besides the Carolina wren, other small songbirds eat the smaller snakes, possibly because they are earthworm size. Robins frequently kill small snakes, especially garter snakes. One killed a 13-in.-long garter snake by pecking it, picked it up in its bill, and flew to its nest, where it tried to feed it to its young. Friedmann (1929) reported a robin that tried to feed a small garter snake to a young cowbird in its nest. In Sept. 1964, an observer watched a bluebird trying to swallow a small snake about 8 in. long, and 6 years later watched a brown thrasher kill and eat a 12-in.-long milk snake *(Lampropeltis).* Terres (1960b) reported a yellow-breasted chat about 7 in. long on Long Is., N.Y., that tried to swallow a 10-in.-long brown snake, *Storeria dekayi,* but it choked to death on the reptile.

Some snakes spend much of their lives underground, where they are safe from bird predators. However, Ditmars (1933) made a remarkable observation of some small scarlet snakes, *Cemophora coccinea,* of se. U.S. When forced out of their burrows by a heavy rain, they were killed by loggerhead shrikes, which impaled their partly eaten bodies on twigs.

Besides McAtee's scientific report, Guthrie (1932) assembled from the published literature up to that time a list of some 50 species of N. American birds that eat snakes. He also included some of the Old World snake-eating eagles, and the long-legged secretary-bird of Africa, famed as a snake killer which eats cobras up to 4 ft. or more long (Gilliard, 1958). The habit of eating snakes is widespread among birds, and whole groups make snakes part of their food, from albatrosses (which eat poisonous sea snakes) and frigatebirds, anhingas, and cormorants, to mallard ducks, ibises, wood storks, most herons, egrets, and bitterns, cranes, rails, domestic chickens, wild turkeys, vultures, kites, hawks, eagles, owls, the roadrunner, magpies, crows, jays, ravens, and shrikes.

Sandhill cranes, great blue herons, and American bitterns eat snakes, and American kestrels and red-tailed hawks regularly catch and eat garter snakes. The glossy ibis in Fla. eats many snakes (95% of them are water snakes, *Natrix*), and the red-shouldered hawk in Fla. is almost exclusively a snake-eater. A clapper rail in a salt marsh near Buzzards Bay, Mass., was seen tearing flesh with its bill from a water snake, *Natrix sipedon,* it had just killed, and in May 1974, a wild Rio Grande turkey in Brooks County, Tex., was seen pecking to death a 55-in.-long bull snake, *Pituophis melanoleucus sayi,* that weighed 11 lb.; another severely beat a 3-ft.-long rattlesnake with its wings (Beason and Pattee, 1975).

Wild turkeys in s. Tex. are great destroyers of rattlesnakes, and the flocks sometimes "gang up" on a rattlesnake to kill it (Schorger, 1966). Wild turkeys also kill and eat the poisonous cottonmouth moccasin, *Agkistrodon contortrix,* and the non-poisonous king snakes (Lewis, 1973). In Ohio, an observer watched a herring gull swallow part of a 3-ft.-long water snake, then fly away with part of it dangling from its mouth.

Ruffed grouse in N.Y., Mich., and Minn. eat garter snakes, and in Wisc., red-bellied snakes; domestic hens in Iowa and Ind. eat the smooth green snake, and one caught and swallowed a 12-in.-long Dekay's, or brown, snake; in Tex. another killed and swallowed a foot-long rattlesnake. Most observers agree that birds swallow small snakes entire, but the larger hawks and owls tear them up and eat them in pieces.

BIRDS AND POISONOUS SNAKES. Klauber (1956) reported that both bald and golden eagles in the West catch and kill rattlesnakes and carry them to the nest to feed their young. Western red-tailed hawks often kill their prey by carrying a still living rattlesnake high in the air, then dropping it on the rocks below.

Fitch *et al.* (1946), in a study of the feeding habits of red-tailed hawks in Calif., reported that the adults not only caught and killed many large Pacific gopher snakes, *Pituophis melanoleucus catenifer,* but also killed some western rattlesnakes, *Crotalus viridus,* all of which they carried to the nest and fed to their young. Jensen (1926) watched a red-tailed hawk near Sante Fe, N.M., attack a rattlesnake, which it killed only after a considerable struggle. Some of the western red-tailed hawks have apparently adapted to handling poisonous snakes with safety by decapitating them on capture.

Johnson (1964), in w. Pima County, Ariz., saw a red-tailed hawk perched on a branch of a mesquite, clutching in its talons the writhing body of a freshly killed snake. It was a 3-ft.-long black-tailed rattlesnake, *Crotalus molossus.* In Apr. 1970, two observers in N.M. watched a loggerhead shrike carrying in its bill a 16-in.-long desert massasauga rattlesnake, *Sistrurus catenatus,* that weighed about 1½ lbs. This was apparently the first record of a shrike killing a poisonous snake (Chapman and Casto, 1972). Interestingly, in Me., Frank T. Noble reported a loggerhead shrike that met its match when it tried to catch an 18-in.-long garter snake. The snake wound itself around the shrike's neck and had almost strangled the bird when Noble intervened. Samuel Grimes (1936), in Fla., saw a desperate struggle between a 46-in.-long black snake and a great horned owl. The owl had attacked the snake, but the snake had wrapped its black coils around the owl's neck and would have killed the exhausted bird had not Grimes ended the combat by collecting both the owl and the snake.

POISONOUS SNAKES KILLING HAWKS. Although red-tailed hawks kill poisonous snakes, the hawks themselves may be killed in the struggle. One large female red-tailed hawk in a field near Lincoln, Neb., reported by Hunter (1898) had been bitten twice by a small prairie rattlesnake she had caught. She was so weak she could not fly, and when Hunter returned the next day, both the hawk and the snake were dead.

In Dec. 1948, the *West Virginia Conservationist* reported that in Pocahontas County a red-tailed hawk had been found dead by a squirrel hunter with fang marks and blood on its neck. It was lying beside the bodies of two copperhead snakes it had killed. Reconstructing the drama, a conservation officer believed that, after killing one of the snakes, the hawk, while killing the other, was bitten by it just before it died.

SNAKES PREYING ON ADULT BIRDS. During the summer, when they are active, snakes prey consistently on birds. Birds, even the adults, especially those that nest on the ground, are vulnerable to many kinds of snakes. Bendire (1892) cited a large rattlesnake killed in Tex. that had swallowed five adult bobwhite quail at a meal; another had swallowed four bobwhites and a scaled quail. On May 27, 1967, along a beach in Onslow County, N.C., Grant (1970) collected a canebrake rattlesnake, *Crotalus horridus atricaudatus,* 4 ft. 2 in. long and about 6 in. in girth, that had in its stomach remains of a clapper rail and a small rodent.

Birds that live much on the water are preyed upon by snakes. On Aug. 12, 1941, Mal Jacobson (1947) saw a considerable commotion on the water of a small lake near Port Jervis, N.Y. Rowing to the spot, he found a hooded merganser with a 3½-ft.-long water snake entwined about its neck. Even though Jacobson forcibly removed the snake from the merganser, the bird, breathing heavily, soon died. In Surinam, in Dec. 1965, Haverschmidt (1970c) saw on the surface of a shallow lagoon the body of a large anaconda. The snake had its coils wrapped about an adult wattled jacana, *Jacana jacana.* Haverschmidt approached it quickly. He kicked the body of the snake several times, at which it vanished with a tremendous splashing of water. The jacana, apparently dizzy, walked unsteadily a few feet, then flew off seemingly unharmed.

PREYING ON EGGS AND YOUNG. Some snakes are excellent climbers—for example, the so-called pilot, or mountain, black snake, now called the black rat snake, *Elaphe obsoleta obsoleta;* the black racer, *Coluber constrictor;* the gopher snakes; the whip snake, *Mastocophis flagellum;* and the eastern milk snake, *Lampropeltis doliata triangulum.* All of these snakes climb trees and low bushes to birds' nests to eat the eggs and young. Edgar R. Harlan, director of the Iowa Natural History Society, once told Guthrie (1932) that he shot a pilot black snake while it was investigating a flicker's nesting hole 60 ft. above the ground. Nolan (1959) reported a male pileated woodpecker that apparently killed a black rat snake by striking it 50 or 60 times with its powerful bill while the snake was dangling from the woodpecker's nest hole 20 ft. above the ground. This is in contrast to a female flicker reported by Jackson (1970) that perched passively nearby while a black rat snake in her nesting hole swallowed her entire brood of young.

Black rat snakes, gray rat snakes, and bull snakes often climb to wood duck nests in cavities of trees or in nest boxes, and eat the duck eggs. Some of these snakes will swim long distances. In La., they have been found in wood duck nests in hollow trees, in standing water, more than a mile from land (Hester and Dermid, 1973). Gopher snakes and whip snakes prey on cactus wren nestlings (Austin and Tomoff, 1972); eastern milk snakes on eggs of the chipping sparrow and phoebe (Shelley, 1938); and milk snakes, rattlesnakes, and blue racers eat fledglings or eggs of field sparrows. Amelia Laskey reported in 1946 that black snake predation on bluebirds nesting in her bird boxes at Nashville, Tenn., was a serious problem, with eggs or young taken by snakes from 23–40% of nests each year. See also records by Pettingill (1976); *see also* Egg-eating.

The stories that snakes can "charm" birds, or put them under a hypnotic spell, are myths, according to Oliver, J. A. (1955). William Brewster, a respected ornithologist and close observer, once described a strange condition of a veery, perhaps brought on by fright, as a milk snake lay coiled about its nest after swallowing two of the veery's young. He wrote (1936) that the veery was in such a weak and seemingly "semi-conscious condition" that he almost caught it in his hands before the bird flew away. Cardinals, brown thrashers, blue jays, mockingbirds, and others will scream and circle excitedly over a snake, and brown thrashers and especially catbirds will sometimes viciously peck a snake near their nests.

Reports cited by Teale (1951) that mockingbirds in w. U.S. blind rattlesnakes by striking their eyes with the bill, and by Gilliard (1958) that, similarly, hummingbirds blind snakes, need further confirmation (Oliver, J. A., 1955).

ALLIGATORS AND BIRDS. The American alligator, *Alligator mississippiensis,* largest reptile in N. America, if widespread, might be a formidable predator on water birds. However, it is limited to the great river swamps, lakes, bayous, and marshes of Fla., the Gulf coast, and the lower Atlantic coastal plain. Schorger (1966) reported that an 11-ft. alligator killed in Tex. had in its stomach the remains of a partly digested wild turkey, but there seem to be few stomach records of birds eaten by alligators. Young cattle egrets (and probably the young of herons and egrets in colonies in Fla.) that fall from the nest to the floor of swamps are eaten quickly by alligators (Jenni, 1969). Audubon reported that if a duck or heron comes within reach of an alligator, it will strike it with its tail and then swallow it. Oliver, J. A. (1955) wrote that at the Bronx Zoo, New York City, alligators there in their outdoor enclosures have been seen stealthily stalking and catching wild starlings. Ditmars (1949) reported that large alligators eat waterfowl regularly and one can easily swallow a duck entire. They approach their prey from below the water and snatch them from the surface.

A few birds eat young alligators. Audubon reported that anhingas eat them, as do wood storks.

LIZARDS AND BIRDS. According to the report by McAtee (1932b), 45 species of N. American birds eat lizards, including such small songbirds as the Carolina wren and white-eyed vireo. Most frequent feeders on lizards are the roadrunner, jays, crows, shrikes, and Carolina wren; also wild turkeys, which eat many, including the horned toad (a lizard). See Schorger (1966) and Lewis (1973). Clay-colored robins occasionally eat small lizards, and the scrub jay, white-necked raven, and yellow-billed cuckoo eat them. The common grackle eats both snakes and lizards.

Red-tailed hawks studied by Fitch *et al.* (1946) in Calif. brought many lizards to their nests to feed the young hawks—especially whip-tailed lizards, *Cnemodophoros tesselatus,* and the western fence lizard, *Sceloporus occidentalis,* also Gilbert's skink, *Eumeces gilberti.*

At least 24 species of N. American birds eat

the green anole, or Carolina anole, *Anolis carolinensis*, a lizard of se. U.S. Stomach contents of a swallow-tailed kite contained seven it had eaten at one meal. The gray hawk of sw. U.S. is also fond of lizards, and Rohwer and Woolfenden (1968) reported that two gull-billed terns near Gulfport, Fla., had eaten anoles, which they picked up as they foraged over the brushy habitat of the area.

TURTLES AND BIRDS. In commenting on only 91 records of the remains of turtles in the stomachs of 80,000 N. American birds, McAtee (1932b) wrote that, from these relatively few records, "our birds can hardly assume the role of predators upon turtles except with the small young of these animals."

Bent (1937) reported turtles in the nests of bald eagles in Fla. Wible and Parkes (1955) found in pellets (*see* Pellet) of barn owls collected by them under the roosting tree of a pair in Everglades National Park, hard bits of the shells of the Florida box turtle, *Terrapene carolina bauri*. The turtles eaten had been about 2 in. long and were estimated to be about 6 months to 1 year old. Later the authors watched one of the barn owls drop down in daylight to the edge of a road and pick up a very small box turtle, which it carried to a perch in a tree. There it held the turtle against the limb with one foot, with the turtle belly up, and fed on it. After it ate, it dropped the shell, which was cleaned out neatly of all flesh. The Florida jay and the wood stork eat small turtles, and according to Audubon, the anhinga eats small terrapins.

On Organobo Beach, French Guiana, flocks of black vultures have been seen attacking and eating hatchling leatherback turtles as they emerged from their sandy nests (Mrosovsky, 1971), and an adult king rail at Buckeye Lake, Ohio, was seen to dig up and eat eggs of a painted turtle, *Chrysemys picta*.

The snapping turtle, *Chelydra serpentina*, may eat many birds, especially water birds. Coulter (1957), in a study of predation by snapping turtles in Me., found that of 171 snapping turtles collected in marshes, 157 had eaten birds. Forty-two turtle stomachs gave evidence of 52 birds eaten—25 ducks, 11 grebes, 3 rails, 13 unidentified. Most were young birds up to 6 weeks old—black duck, ring-necked duck, goldeneye, wood duck, and blue-winged teal—but three were adult birds. A 31-lb. snapping turtle had remains of five birds in its stomach—one ring-necked duck, one goldeneye, three pied-billed grebes. A 24-lb. turtle had eaten two black ducks, one unidentified surface-feeding duck, and one grebe. Surface-feeding ducks (more vulnerable) were taken twice as frequently by snapping turtles as diving ducks, although both groups were equally plentiful and available to the turtles. See also Pitman (1962a).

RESCUE
(of birds). *See* Cold and Birds.

RESIDENT
See Where Do Birds Live? under Distribution.

RESPIRATORY SYSTEM
Respiration is the act, or process, of breathing. When a bird inhales it takes air (by inspiration) into the lungs, where the oxygen of the air is picked up by the blood (*see* Circulatory System) and carried to the cells of the body. The cells use oxygen in the "burning" (oxidation) of digested food (*see* Digestion), a chemical reaction that releases energy (fuel) for the bird's daily needs, and in maintaining its high body temperature (*see* Temperature; *also* Metabolism). Carbon dioxide, one of the waste products of metabolism, carried by the blood to the lungs, is released from the body and expelled (by expiration) into the outer air when the bird exhales.

THE COURSE OF AIR IN BREATHING. When a bird inhales, it takes air through its nostrils and into the nasal cavities (*see* Nostrils), thence into the mouth and pharynx and through the glottis, a slitlike opening surrounded by the larynx. The larynx has no vocal cords as in man and other mammals. It is a valvular structure that opens and closes the glottis during breathing and aids in preventing the intake of foreign materials, such as swallowed food, into the bird's lower respiratory tract. The breathed-in air then moves through the glottis down through the trachea, or windpipe, and passes through the syrinx (*see* Voice and Sound-making). From the syrinx, air passes through the paired bronchi and into the lungs, and from the lungs through a series of air sacs peculiar to birds, but also known in some lizards and snakes and in some of the larger active insects (Lasiewski, 1972).

THE TRACHEA. The round flexible trachea, which allows a bird free movement of its neck, consists of a series of mostly cartilaginous rings which hold it open, permitting the passage of air in the bird's breathing. In most birds, the trachea follows a straight course from the glottis down to the bronchi—two tubes at the end of the trachea that join to and penetrate into the lungs. In some birds the trachea is looped, as in some chachalacas, the painted snipes, the trumpeter swan, and the whooping crane, in which it might act as a resonating chamber for the voice; in male ducks the trachea ends in a bony enlargement, the bulla, which functions in the male's sound production (*see* Bulla; *also* Voice and Sound-making).

THE LUNGS. Birds have a respiratory system that is the most efficient known among all vertebrate animals. The lungs are the center of a bird's breathing apparatus, with an intricate network of ramifying and intercommunicating air passages. The two bright red lungs, in the upper part of the thorax, are flattened and firmly attached against the ribs on either side of the backbone. They are small, highly vascularized (containing numerous blood vessels), and relatively inexpansible, with their lower sides covered with connective tissue in which are inserted several small weak muscles (Welty, 1962).

A bird's lungs are small relative to its body volume—in a mallard duck, about 2% compared with about 5% in man—however, a bird's air sacs are about 20% of its body volume (Mac-

donald, 1964) and about 80% of the total volume of its respiratory system (Lasiewski, 1972).

The two primary bronchi which lead into the lungs and course through them divide and decrease in size until they become a series of secondary bronchi. These, in turn, lead into numerous, minute parallel tubes, the *parabronchi* (or tertiary bronchi)—about 300–500 in each lung of a chicken and at least 1,800–2,000 or more in each lung of birds of strong flight such as ducks and pigeons (Lasiewski, 1972). The thin walls of the tiny parabronchi have openings with hundreds of tiny branching, intercommunicating "air capillaries" closely surrounded by an abundant network of blood capillaries, which, together, accomplish the exchange of oxygen and carbon dioxide between the lungs and the blood (Welty, 1962).

THE AIR SACS. Large, thin-walled, resembling soap bubbles, the bladderlike air sacs extend from the bronchial system of the lungs to different parts of the bird's body. They may number 6–14 in most birds, but 8–9 is typical; they have few blood vessels and play no direct part in oxygen and carbon dioxide exchange in the body, but do function in air exchange, although not directly. Typically there are four pairs and one unpaired air sac, the interclavicular, between the clavicles (see details in Lasiewski, 1972, and a discussion of air sacs in passerines, or songbirds, in Kloek and Casler, 1972).

Air sacs contribute to the necessary comfort and functioning of a bird; air coursing through them and the lungs provides more complete inner ventilation than needed for a bird's flying; this extra ventilation helps regulate a bird's body heat. Thus, without the sweat glands of man, the bird is able to reduce its body heat by internal radiation and vaporization, which serves the function of perspiring. See Heat and Birds. The air sacs send other branches, or diverticula, into nearly every part of the skeleton of some birds; the bones most frequently pneumatized are the humerus (upper "arm"), femur (upper legbone), ribs, and vertebrae (Van Tyne and Berger, 1959). Most large birds such as albatrosses and eagles have highly pneumatized bones, which suggests that flight and light weight of bones are in some way related (Bellairs and Jenkins, 1960). See Bones; *also* Skeleton.

Air sacs give buoyancy to many water birds, but in some diving birds such as loons, grebes, and anhingas, in which buoyancy would be an obstacle to their remaining underwater and swimming about in search of fishes and other prey, the air sacs and pneumaticity of the bones are reduced or minimal. See Bellairs and Jenkins (1960); *see* discussion under Swimming and Diving.

Air sacs just under the skin of the gannet and brown pelican seem to cushion the impact of these birds when they strike the water forcibly in diving for fishes. Others, such as the male frigatebird and the male prairie chicken, during their courtship displays inflate their colorful neck bladders through the diverticula of the cervical air sacs, and the male prairie chicken uses his inflated neck bladders as resonators for his booming courtship sounds.

BREATHING RATES AND CONTROL OF BREATHING. Birds are easily disturbed, which affects their breathing rates (Calder, 1968), but most flying birds, even at rest, breathe more rapidly than does a man or other mammal. Birds of little flight, however, such as chickens and domestic turkeys, while at rest take 16–18 breaths a minute, about the same as man. Among the smaller birds, the rate varies—45 breaths per minute in a cardinal to more than 80 in the smaller house wren. The rate at which a bird breathes varies with the species of bird, its age, sex, size, activity, the temperature surrounding it, the time of day, and other factors. Usually, the smaller the bird, the faster it breathes (Welty, 1962)

Odum (1943) found that the breathing rate of the black-capped chickadee sleeping at night ranged from 65 breaths a minute at a low air temperature of 52° F. to 95 a minute at a high air temperature of 90° F.—the higher breathing rate was correlated with the chickadee's need to lose heat, or to cool off, at the 90° temperature. *See* Heat and Birds. According to Welty (1962), Odum found that the breathing rate of a resting house sparrow was 50 times a minute, but increased to 102 times a minute when the sparrow was held quietly in the hand, then to 212 times a minute when it was released and allowed to fly about in a room. Just as in man, the breathing rate of a bird increases with vigorous exercise, and rapid breathing supplies more oxygen to meet the bird's metabolic demands of flight. *See* Heat and Birds; *also* Metabolism.

By contrast, a torpid, hibernating poor-will in Calif. showed no measurable breathing (*see* Torpidity), and the minimum breathing rate of torpid nestlings of the European swift, during their fasting periods (*see* Fasting), was about 8 times a minute but rose to a maximum of 90 breaths a minute when coming out of torpidity (Koskimies, 1950).

According to Pettingill (1972), because a bird's lungs are close to its rib cage, with its wings beating in flight and flexing the ribs, it would appear that a bird's breathing would be synchronized with each wingbeat. This is true of pigeons and crows—pigeons *exhale* with each downbeat of the wings; crows *inhale* with each downbeat (Salt and Zeuthen, 1960)—but this synchronization is not found in all birds. Investigators tested certain others by enclosing each bird's bill in a rubber balloon before allowing it to fly. They discovered that some birds in flight breathe irregularly—a western gull that beat its wings 242 times a minute, breathed 81 times; a lesser scaup duck that averaged 645 wingbeats a minute, breathed only 140 times; and a red-tailed hawk beat its wings 13 times without taking a breath. See details in Berger *et al.* (1970a; 1970b).

Apparently the breathing rates of birds are controlled, just as in mammals, by a nerve center in the medulla oblongata (back part) of the brain, with a special panting center in the forward-top region of the midbrain (interbrain). Although panting (*see* Heat and Birds) is ordinarily controlled by the panting nerve center, according to Sturkie (1965), its function could be taken over by the true respiratory center in the medulla. Experiments with birds showed

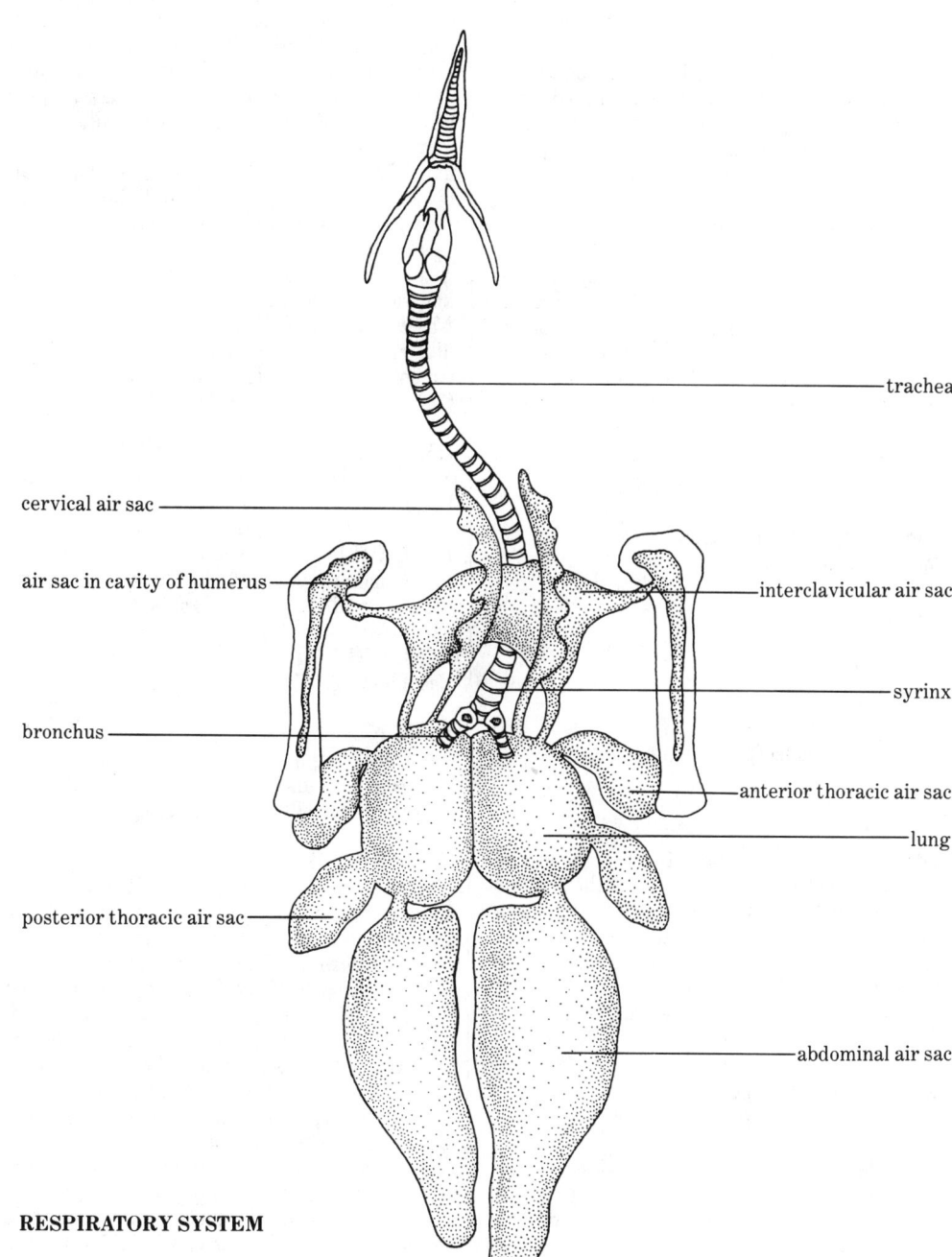

trachea

cervical air sac

air sac in cavity of humerus

interclavicular air sac

bronchus

syrinx

anterior thoracic air sac

lung

posterior thoracic air sac

abdominal air sac

RESPIRATORY SYSTEM

that either (or both) the respiratory center or the panting center in the brain regulates the bird's breathing rates by responding to changes in the temperature of blood flowing to the bird's head, to the pH value of its blood (measure of its acidity or alkalinity), and to carbon monoxide inhaled. Emotional disturbances in a bird, caused by sudden noises, also increase its breathing rate (Sturkie, 1965).

Apparently there are chemical receptors in the lungs that also are sensitive to the percentage of carbon dioxide inhaled by birds, which act either to increase or to decrease their breathing rates (Lasiewski, 1972). Besides the authorities already cited, see a detailed technical discussion of respiration by Macdonald (1964) and respiratory rates of other species of birds in Calder (1968); Blake (1958); Dorst (1974).

RETICULATE
(ree-TICK-you-late). *See* Tarsus.

RETRIEVING OF EGGS
See Eggs and Egg-laying.

RETURN
(to nest sites and wintering places). *See* Banding.

REVERSED MIGRATION
See in Some Effects of Weather under Migration.

REVIEWS
(of the ornithological literature). Most of the ornithological journals and many of the popular and semi-scientific natural history magazines publish a section in each issue that is devoted to reviews of current papers, articles, and books about birds and other animals. For a list of some of these journals and magazines, *see* Ornithological Periodicals.

RHAMPHOTHECA
(ram-foh-THEE-kah [*th* as in *thin*]). Hornlike covering of the bill (*see* Bill); a sheath that, like the outermost layers of a bird's skin, is composed of more or less keratinized layers; in most birds it is hard and hornlike, in others, such as waterfowl, sandpipers, plovers, and pigeons, the bill covering is softer and more leathery. *See* Cere; *also* Nostrils.

RHEA
See Flightless Birds; Running Birds.

RICEBIRD
See Bobolink in Troupial Family.

RICKETS
See oil gland under Skin Glands.

RICTAL BRISTLE
See Bristle under Feather.

RICTUS
The softer, more fleshy part of a bird's bill toward the back of the mouth. *See* Bill; Commissure; Gape.

RIDGWAY
ROBERT (1850–1929). Born Mount Carmel, Ill., a founder and past president of the American Ornithologists' Union, and for more than 50 years Curator of Birds in the U.S. National Museum, Washington, D.C. He is commemorated in the species name of the buff-collared nightjar, *Caprimulgus ridgwayi*, once called Ridgway's whip-poor-will; also in the scientific names of several subspecies of N. American birds. According to Stone (in Palmer *et al.*, 1954), Ridgway was the author of two "classics" in the literature of American ornithology, *A Manual of North American Birds* (1887) and the monumental series of volumes *Birds of North and Middle America* (1901–19). For an illustrated biography of Ridgway with a bibliography of his published writings, see Harris (1928); see also Oberholser (1933).

RIEFFER
See Hummingbird, Rieffer's, in Hummingbird Family.

RING-BILL
See Duck, ring-necked, in Duck Family and Gull, ring-billed, in Gull Family.

RINGING
See Banding.

RING-NECK
See Duck, ring-necked, in Duck Family; Pheasant, ring-necked, in Pheasant Family; Plover, ring-necked, in Plover Family.

RING-SPECIES
Term to express the concept that a species (*see* Species) may divide into a graded series of geographic races (subspecies) in which the extreme *end populations* of the series *later come into contact* because of the range expansion of the species and do not interbreed. Gradual or continuous changes in the color, size, etc., of the populations of wide-ranging species such as the song sparrow (*see* Subspecies; Cline) illustrate the sensitivity with which adjoining populations respond to slight differences in climate. These changes may eventually become so great over the entire wide range of a species that both of the end populations, or end subspecies, in the chainlike series become so different that they are *reproductively isolated* from each other and do not interbreed. These end populations act like separate species, but cannot be considered as good species in view of the interbreeding of other adjoining populations of the "ring." The development of their isolating mechanisms that prevent interbreeding (*see* Species), according to Mayr (1963), has been achieved because of retardation of the gene flow through a very long chain of populations. This kind of "speciation by distance" (Mayr, 1942) has evolved in the cosmopolitan herring gull, for example, in which chains of gradually differing subspecies of the herring gull form a ring in the N. Hemisphere (see map illustration in Mayr, 1963). In this classic case, it is theorized that the herring gull group (*Larus argentatus*) became separated in several isolated areas of Europe, Asia, and N. America during the Pleistocene (*see* Geological Time Scale).

The American isolate group evolved into the Iceland gull, *Larus glaucoides*, and when its range was invaded by the herring gull during the retreat of the glaciers, the Iceland gull did not hybridize with the herring gull owing to habitat differences between the two. In Europe and in Asia, the westernmost of a chain of the Eurasian populations of the herring gull evolved into the lesser black-backed gull, *Larus fuscus*, and the herring gull spread across N. America to meet it in Europe. The two now live in overlapping ranges (*see* Sympatric Species) without significant interbreeding. Other cases of circular overlap have been described for the great tit (*Parus major*), greenish warbler (*Phylloscopus trochiloides*), skylark (*Alauda arvensis*), ringed plover (*Charadrius hiaticula*), white-collared kingfisher (*Halcyon chloris*), and others. *See* Hybrid; *also* biographies of the herring gull, Iceland gull, and lesser black-backed gull in Gull Family. See details of other ring-species in Mayr (1963).

RIVER DUCK
See surface-feeding ducks discussed in introduction to Duck Family.

RIVOLI
VICTOR MASSÉNA, DUC DI (1798–1863). Son of André Masséna, field marshal of France and Prince d'Essling, for whom Lesson named the Rivoli's hummingbird, *Ornismyia rivolii*, the bird now known as *Eugenes fulgens*, the name given it by Swainson in 1827, two years earlier (Palmer, 1928). The Duke of Rivoli was one of the subscribers to Audubon's *Birds of America* and at 30 was "entirely devoted to natural history" (Audubon, M. R., 1960).

ROAD-BIRD
See Sparrow, lark, in Finch Family.

ROADRUNNER
See in Cuckoo Family.

ROAD TROTTER
See Lark, horned, in Lark Family.

ROBIN
See in Thrush Family.

ROC
(pron. like "rock"; also spelled *rukh*). A fabled bird of Arabia so large that it was said to carry off elephants to feed its young; the story is in the *Arabian Nights* of Sinbad the Sailor. In later times the home of the monster bird was placed in Madagascar, and may have been handed down by early men on the island who possibly linked the legendary roc with the huge, flightless elephant birds, *Aepyornis*, the largest of which were estimated to have weighed up to 1,000 lbs. Remains, including eggs, of elephant birds have been found on Madagascar from the Pleistocene (*see* Geological Time Scale) up to geologically recent times. *See* Eggs and Egg-laying; *see also* discussion under Flightless Birds.

ROCK-BIRD
See Turnstone, ruddy, in Sandpiper Family.

ROCKWEED BIRD
See Sandpiper, purple, in Sandpiper Family.

RODENT RUN
See Distraction Display.

ROLLER FAMILY
See Coraciiformes.

ROOK
See in introduction to Crow Family.

ROOKERY
Term in British Isles primarily for nesting colony of rooks, *Corvus frugilegus*, elsewhere to colonies of other gregarious nesting birds such as penguins; in U.S., term applied usually to nesting colonies of herons or crows; sometimes used interchangeably with *roost. See* Roost.

ROOST
Term for place where flocks of blackbirds, starlings, grackles, robins, and other species sleep together in trees, shrubbery, or reeds and other upright grasses in marshes. *See* Roosting; *also* Control.

ROOSTING
Defined by Cullen (1964) as the sleeping of a bird and its resting, even though awake, but does not apply to the occasional brief naps of a few minutes taken by birds between active periods. Most biologists agree that roosting is literally resting or sleeping on the roost, wherever that may be.

WHERE DO BIRDS ROOST? In general, birds roost in the same habitat, or types of places, where they nest—catbirds, cardinals, mockingbirds, thrashers, etc., in trees, thickets, vines, or a dense bush; owls, doves, blue jays, crows, and many smaller birds such as sparrows, warblers and grosbeaks, in leafy trees, often in evergreens; eagles, the larger falcons, ravens, and some of the larger owls and hawks roost in trees or on cliffs; hole-nesting birds such as woodpeckers, American kestrels, screech owls, and certain smaller owls and bluebirds roost in cavities of trees and utility poles, and in birdhouses or special roosting boxes built for them; chickadees in nesting holes they dig for themselves and in bird boxes. Some of these birds use the same roosting place night after night unless disturbed by man or a predator. Brown creepers sleep in crevices of tree bark or occasionally cling vertically, head up, to the outside of buildings under roof gables. Swifts roost in large chimneys, and flocks of swallows in migration, in reeds or bulrushes of marshes; purple martins, blackbirds, grackles, and robins, in trees.

During summer, a member of a pair of nesting birds may sleep, or roost, on the nest, especially while incubating eggs or brooding young. Downy, hairy, and red-cockaded woodpeckers excavate special roosting cavities, and some wrens build special nests for sleeping. They also roost in old open nests of American robins and other birds, and in holes in trees, stumps,

in buildings, birdhouses, and even in abandoned paper nests of hornets, and in folds of clothing (Carolina wren). See many details in "Where Do Birds Sleep?" in Terres (1960b). See also in the biography of each species.

Shorebirds, pelicans, ducks, geese, swans, gulls, skimmers, and terns often sleep on the sand of islands where protected from raccoons, cats, dogs, foxes, weasels, and skunks, and by day they sleep on open beaches as they wait for the tide that often determines food availability for them. However, some find their food largely by touch with the bill immersed in water or mud and can feed also at night.

In winter, the ruffed grouse dives into a snowbank to roost, and the European swift, *Apus apus*, sleeps on the wing while soaring about at night (Weitnauer, 1956).

Many oceanic birds—albatrosses and petrels, for example—can sleep on water, but the magnificent frigatebird cannot, because its plumage is not waterproof; it roosts in great numbers atop trees, mangroves, and shrubs on islands and the mainland. Gulls, terns, ducks, and pelicans may sleep floating on the water but at their peril. *See* Fishes and Birds.

BIRDS THAT ROOST ON THE GROUND. Bobwhite quail and the chukar and gray partridge roost in a tight circle on the ground, with their bodies pressed close together and their heads turned outward (*see* details under Pheasant Family). Horned larks in the Mojave Desert and at Warner Springs, San Diego County, Calif., with their bills, dig roosting holes in the ground in which to rest at night (Trost, 1972); marsh hawks (harriers) roost on the ground, frequently at the same spot night after night, and often roost in groups of 2–3 and up to 30, usually in broom sedge (*Andropogon*) fields of se. U.S. (Stoddard, 1931). Each bird roosts in a beaten-down spot in the grass, the place well lined with droppings and pellets. *See* Pellet.

Short-eared owls, besides roosting in evergreen trees, also roost on the ground. Weller *et al.* (1955) reported a dozen or more short-eared owls roosting with some marsh hawks in fields of c. Mo. in Feb. 1952. The owls roosted near the marsh hawks in a dense growth of grasses about a foot tall, and commonly were in tufts of grass.

SLEEPING POSTURES. These vary but birds usually sleep with the head and neck on the back and the bill buried in the shoulder feathers, or scapulars, not with the head under the wing. In this position the neck muscles may be relaxed and the bird's eyes protected from the cold (Kendeigh, 1934). A few species—pigeons, mourning doves, some plovers, storks, and grebes, for example—sleep with the head settled down into the shoulders and the bill pointed straight ahead. *See* in biographies of these birds; *also* Cullen (1964).

In sleeping, or roosting, on the ground, most birds squat and rest on the feet and belly—ducks, for example—but songbirds stand or sit down on a branch around which the feet are "locked" to the perch. *See* flexor tendons under Feet and Legs. Whip-poor-wills may roost on top of a branch by squatting on it lengthwise, not across as in most birds; woodpeckers cling

range map of the Iceland gull

range map of the herring gull

 winter range

 breeding range

RING-SPECIES
The Iceland gull and the herring gull, two members of a ring of closely related gulls found around the northern hemisphere, are now separated by both habitat and geography and do not interbreed.

to a vertical surface (*see* Climbing Birds), usually inside their roosting or nesting holes in trees. Many parrots sleep in holes in trees, clinging to the vertical surface with bill and claws; some hang upside down, clinging to a perch or branch as they sleep. Waterfowl and seabirds usually sleep floating on water with the head and bill turned back and tucked under the scapulars (Pettingill, 1972).

HOW SOUNDLY DO BIRDS SLEEP? In Europe, experiments were conducted (Bergman, 1950) with caged European robins, the lesser whitethroat (a European warbler), and the fieldfare (a thrush) to test intensity of their sleep. The tests showed that their sleep was deepest from one half to three hours after going to sleep, and during migration time was relatively light after the nightly period of migratory restlessness called *Zugunruhe* (*see* Migration). General conclusions from the experiments: birds that are very active in daytime sleep deeply, but if irregularly active, they sleep irregularly.

ROSS
BERNARD ROGAN (1827–74). Chief Factor of the Hudson's Bay Company, whom Cassin honored in 1861 by naming for him the small goose sent to Cassin by Ross from Great Slave Lake, Canada. Ross was a correspondent with the Smithsonian Institution in Washington, D.C., to which he contributed a considerable number of bird specimens. He was born Londonderry, Ireland; died at Toronto, Canada (Palmer, 1928).

ROSS
SIR JAMES CLARK (1800–62). British explorer and Arctic navigator, for whom Ross' gull was named; accompanied William Edward Parry, English explorer of the Arctic, on four expeditions there between 1819 and 1827; later Ross led an expedition (1848–49) to find and rescue Sir John Franklin, who was lost and died in the Arctic in search of the North Pole and the Northwest Passage. See *Encyclopaedia Britannica* for other details; for the interesting history of the naming of Ross' gull, *see* its biography in Gull Family.

ROSTRUM
Technical name for the bill, or beak, of a bird.

ROUGH-LEG
See Hawk, rough-legged, in Hawk Family.

ROUNDWORMS
See Nematode; *also* Parasite.

ROUP
See trichomoniasis under Diseases.

RUBYTHROAT
See in Thrush Family; *also* Hummingbird, ruby-throated, in Hummingbird Family.

RUFF
See in Sandpiper Family.

RUMP GLAND
See oil gland under Skin Glands.

RUMP POST
See Pygostyle.

RUNNING BIRDS
The South African ostrich, largest living bird in the world (*see* Size), is also quite possibly the swiftest running bird. Bannerman (1964a) noted that a frightened Masai ostrich, running in the African bush, was seen to catch up to and shoot ahead of a hartebeest going at a full gallop, and that when a month old the chicks can run at 35 m.p.h. Adult ostriches have been credited with speeds of 50–60 m.p.h., with 25 ft. taken at each stride (Wallace, 1963); however, Bernard Grzimek (1970), who has driven behind them in an automobile, wrote that they can maintain a speed of 30 m.p.h. for 15 or even 30 minutes without signs of fatigue, and are said to attain up to 44 m.p.h. with strides of 12 ft., which is possibly a more accurate report of their maximum speed. All of the large running birds of the world—including the emu and cassowaries of the Australian Region and S. American rheas—are flightless (*see* Flightless Birds) and depend on their speed afoot to escape enemies. Bustards, large ground-dwelling birds of the grassy plains of the Old World, although able to fly strongly, usually depend on running to escape enemies.

Among wild N. American birds, none are flightless, but some of those that can fly depend on running either to catch their prey or to escape by keeping under cover. The wild turkey often depends more on its legs than its wings, whether moving from one feeding place in woods and fields to another or running away when disturbed. Its running ability made a strong impression on some early colonists, one of whom wrote: "He hath the use of his long legs so ready, that he can runne as fast as a Dogge, and fly was well as a Goose."

In 1831, a visitor to s. Tex., riding horseback, chased some wild turkeys which he reported could run more swiftly than wolves and almost as rapidly as horses. Henry Davis (1949) watched a fox chase a flock of wild turkeys which outran the fox for 50 or 60 yards before they flew. Mosby and Handley (1943) timed an unfrightened hen turkey running at 12 m.p.h., and according to McLaurin (1957), the Fla. wild turkey can run 15–18 m.p.h. and can reach 30 m.p.h. in short spurts. In N.C., Amundson (1957) reported that a wild turkey can run at 30 m.p.h. but that its average is 15 m.p.h. Brandt (1951) in Ariz. timed the running speed of a wild turkey from his car at 19 m.p.h.

The strides of a wild turkey gobbler chased by a dog are about 3½–4 ft. long; the normal strides of an unfrightened bird are 2–3 ft. long (Schorger, 1966).

The roadrunner of sw. U.S. can run with astonishing speed and agility when chasing lizards, which it often feeds upon. See Reptiles and Birds. Cottam *et al.* (1942b), in an automobile, timed two that ran at 12 and 15 m.p.h. respectively in soft sand and on an upgrade; roadrunners are so swift and agile that they can outmaneuver hounds and outrun human pursuers (Bent, 1940). (An average man, not an athlete, can run 9 yards a second, or about 18 m.p.h.)

Cottam *et al.* also timed ring-necked pheasants at speeds of 8, 10, 12, 15, and 21 m.p.h. in Ore., Mont., and N.D., and a chukar (partridge) in N.D. at 12 m.p.h., another at 18 m.p.h. in Mo.

Other running birds have been timed—California quail at 12 m.p.h.; Gambel's quail in Ariz. at 14 m.p.h. and in Calif. at 15½ m.p.h.; mountain quail at 12 m.p.h.; and a gray, or Hungarian, partridge at 9 m.p.h. *See* running speeds and flight speeds and their documentation in the biography of each species. *See also* Hopping and Walking.

RUPTIVE PATTERN
See Colors of Feathers.

RYNCHOPIDAE
See Skimmer Family.

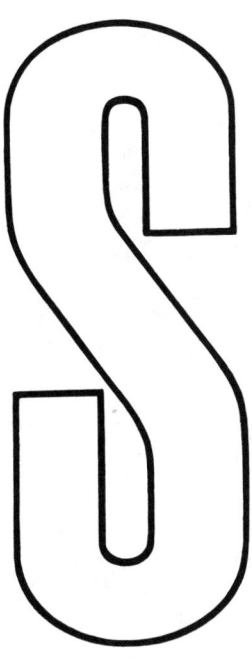

SABINE

(SAB-in), SIR EDWARD (1788–1883). Eminent British astronomer and physicist; his older brother, Joseph (1770–1837), named in his honor the Sabine's gull. Sir Edward and his brother accompanied Ross and Parry on their expedition to the Arctic in 1819–20 (Palmer, 1928), with Sir Edward as astronomer; the gull named in his honor was obtained from the Sabine Is., near Melville Bay, w. coast of Greenland.

SABINE

JOSEPH (1770–1837). Elder brother of Sir Edward Sabine. He not only described and named Sabine's gull for his brother but named another bird, the black-billed magpie of N. America, which he called *Corvus Hudsonius;* however, Carl Linnaeus had already named the European and Asiatic species of this bird *Corvus pica,* in his 10th ed. of *Systema Naturae,* published in 1758; therefore Sabine's specific name was given to the N. American subspecies now known as *Pica pica hudsonia.* In 1829, David Douglas named in Joseph Sabine's honor a N. American ruffed grouse, *Tetrao Sabini,* now regarded as a subspecies, *Bonasa umbellus sabini* (A.O.U. *Check-list,* 1957).

SADDLEBACK

In allusion to black mantle. *See* Gull, great black-backed, in Gull Family.

SAGEBRUSH

One of the nine biomes (*see* Biome) in N. America north of Mexico used in mapping the ecological distribution of birds. *See* Major Biotic Communities (biomes) under Distribution. It is a community (*see* biotic community under Ecosystem) above the lower deserts and valley floors of the Great Basin plateau (*see* Great Basin) between the Rocky Mtns. and the Sierra Nevada–Cascades; plants that compose it are the densely foliaged sagebrush, shad scale, rabbit brush, greasewood, and other woody plants 2–5 ft. high; typical birds are the sage grouse, sage thrasher, sage sparrow, and Brewer's sparrow (Pettingill, 1970; 1972).

SAGE HEN

See Grouse, sage, in Grouse Family.

SALAMANDERS AND BIRDS

See Amphibians and Birds.

SALIVARY GLANDS

See Mouth.

SALMONELLOSIS

(sal-moh-neh-LOW-sis). A disease caused by bacteria of the genus *Salmonella;* it is also called paratyphoid infection, bacillary white diarrhea, and fowl typhoid. All bacteria in the genus are considered to be potential pathogens for man and other animals; however, some members of the *Salmonella* differ widely in their host adaptations and in the signs and symptoms in the host. Salmonellosis usually occurs as an intestinal infection which may result in enteritis (inflammation of the intestines), diarrhea, and terminates in septicemia. According to Steele and Galton (1971), the reported incidence of *Salmonella* infections in the general wild bird population is extremely low; therefore wild birds are not a great threat as a natural reservoir and sources of infection for man and/or his domestic animals.

Macdonald and Cornelius (1959) noted outbreaks of salmonellosis from the bacterium *Salmonella typhimurium* during three months of winter in the south of England and reported that house sparrows and greenfinches apparently carry the infection. In Switzerland, Bouvier (1968) reported that he had known of previous infections by the bacterium *Salmonella typhimurium* only in pigeons, but in the bitterly cold winter of 1967–68, near Lausanne, he observed 3 cases of salmonellosis in house sparrows, *Passer domesticus,* 14 in the greenfinch, *Chloris chloris,* 1 in a grasshopper warbler, *Locustella naevia,* 6 in the brambling, *Fringilla montifringilla,* and 3 in the bullfinch, *Pyrrhula.* He speculated that the disease was transmitted from infected to uninfected birds when large groups of them assembled to feed.

The discovery of the incidence of *Salmonella* infections in birds in Switzerland in 1968 was paralleled earlier in the U.S. by a report of Faddoul *et al.* (1966) of 12 birds infected by *Salmonella typhimurium* in Mass. and R.I. Most were brown-headed cowbirds, with some house sparrows, white-throated sparrows, and herring gulls also infected.

As long as birds are not subjected to stress from crowding—for example, when feeding close together—little harm results, but when food for them is scattered on the ground and attracts large numbers, hundreds may die of the *Salmonella* infection. As the ground may become heavily contaminated by the droppings of infected birds, seeds should be placed in feeders above the ground.

In Marion County, Fla., from 1971 through Dec. 1973, birds died from salmonellosis at the feeding station of Mrs. Howard Pearl near Salt Springs. The incidence, reported by Nesbitt and White (1974), involved infected blue jays, tufted titmice, brown thrashers, house sparrows, red-winged blackbirds, common grackles, cardinals, chipping sparrows, white-throated sparrows, and ground doves. The heaviest mortality of birds was in late winter and early spring, and many of them had subcutaneous lesions (morbid changes in diseased parts) in the pectoral (breast) region. Cultures taken from the birds with lesions were positive for *Salmonella typhimurium.*

By Mar. 10, 1974, all those species of birds that had been infected earlier at Mrs. Pearl's feeders were devoid of any lesions and were otherwise in good condition, and cultures from them were negative for *Salmonella;* it was thought that the decline of the infection among the remaining birds had resulted from the die-off of infected birds. For prevention, it was recommended that all those who feed birds regularly should avoid feeding them on the ground, which can be contaminated with *Salmonella* bacteria, and should occasionally clean and thoroughly disinfect the above-ground feeders. *See* Bird-attracting; *also* Diseases. For a detailed account of *Salmonella* infections and the numerous ways they are

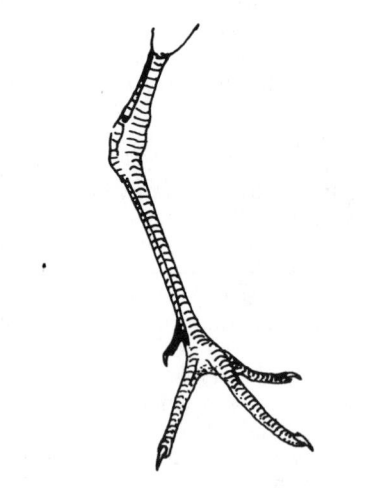

SANDPIPER FAMILY

transmitted to man, see Williams and Hobbs (1975).

SALT GLAND
See function of under Nostrils.

SANCTUARY
An inviolate refuge where all forms of wildlife are offered protection. A sanctuary may be as small as a city or country garden (where birds and other animals are protected from disturbance and harm and often are provided with supplementary food and water) or it may be a few acres of land and water, of farm size, or up to thousands of acres in size. An example of a large sanctuary is the Paul J. Rainey Wildlife Sanctuary of 26,000 acres in La., owned and administered by the National Audubon Society. In open country, outside of cities, it is usually necessary not only to post sanctuaries against hunting but, on large ones, to hire full-time wardens to patrol the areas.

According to a preliminary inventory published by the Wilderness Society of Washington, D.C., in 1950–51, there were 691 nature sanctuaries in the U.S. and Canada, totaling more than a million square miles. (Today there are many more but *see* the more recent references listed in Bird Finding under Birder). Many of the sanctuaries on this list give partial, not full, protection to wildlife (Kendeigh *et al.*, 1950–51). *See* Hawk Mountain Sanctuary; *also* Wildlife Refuge.

SANDERLING
See in Sandpiper Family.

SANDGROUSE
See Columbiformes for classification; *see also* Swallowing; *also* Bringing Water to the Young under Young and Their Care.

SANDPIPER FAMILY
Scolopacidae (skol-oh-PASS-ih-dee); Lat., from Gr. *skolopax*, word used by Aristotle for "woodcock," i.e., "woodcock" family, formed from Gr. *skolops, skolopos,* in reference to anything pointed (Jaeger, 1955), apparently in allusion to long, pointed bill of woodcock. 82 species worldwide (Van Tyne and Berger, 1976); includes such usually ground-dwelling wading birds (shorebirds) as the curlews, dowitchers, the dunlin, godwits, knot, sanderling, sandpipers, snipes, willet, woodcock, yellowlegs; most nest in N. Hemisphere at high latitudes; however, a few kinds of snipe nest in S. America, Africa, and New Zealand (Austin, 1961); their closest relatives are jacanas and painted snipes; *see* other relatives under Charadriiformes; Shorebirds; they differ from plovers in their general lack of bold colors and all have a short, elevated hallux (hind toe), which is lacking, however, in the sanderling; they have slenderer, more tapered bodies, longer, slenderer bills, either straight or curved, and relatively longer legs than plovers; they are gregarious and live much in flocks outside of breeding season; most migrate by day or night; they range from the sparrow-sized 5–6-in.-long least sandpiper (smallest) to the hen-sized 26-in.-long long-billed curlew (largest member of family); in 1973, 51 species listed for N. America, with reclassification of the surfbird and two species of turnstones transferred from the Plover Family to the Sandpiper Family (see American Ornithologists' Union, 1973), and an additional three species, all visitors from the Old World, reported in N. America between 1957 and 1973—the greenshank, spotted redshank, and great snipe; one species, the N. American Eskimo curlew, is virtually extinct. Of the 51 species, 36 nest in N. America, 15 are visitors from the Old World. Of the many species in the family formerly hunted, some almost to extinction, only the common snipe and the American woodcock are still legal game.

Many birds in Sandpiper Family frequent open country near water, and most species, except those that migrate through interior U.S. and Canada, travel in spring and fall along Pacific and Atlantic coasts, where many feed in flocks in daytime on beaches or in tidal marshes; many species are active at dusk; some, besides those that nest on tundra, or along shores of streams, ponds, lakes, or in upland fields, remain birds of marshes (pectoral sandpiper) or even woodlands (woodcock) throughout much of the year; many of larger members of family (for example, curlews and godwits) can walk or run rapidly; most can swim and dive underwater when necessary; some leave water to defecate.

Most members of family are brown or gray above, pale or white below; they are cryptically or protectively colored by seasonal change of plumage adapted to environment of summer and winter—in some, from black and chestnut of breeding plumage to paler winter plumage (the sexes are outwardly similar except in the ruff); in most species, the females are larger than the males; they have short tails, appropriate to wading birds; however, the bills range from long, slender, and *downcurved* in the curlews, and long and *upturned* in the godwits, to the straight, slender bills of the snipe and snipelike dowitcher, and the long, slender bill of the woodcock with its mobile tip.

Many species, like falcons, have long, "high-speed" pointed wings adapted to rapid flight; although many members of the family are noted for their long migratory flights, not all make such long journeys as the Hudsonian and bar-tailed godwits, the Eskimo and bristle-thighed curlews; for example, the woodcock, which is the only bird in the family with rounded rather than pointed wing tips (Sheldon, 1971), makes relatively short migrations. Many species in fall and winter travel either in flocks all of one kind or in mixed flocks, and when flushed, fly in close formation, rising, wheeling, and alighting with remarkable unity (see Unity of the Flock under Flight).

Most species have various elaborate courtship displays of wing-tilting and calling with flights over tundra; the young are precocial (see Altricial); although guided and guarded by parents most find their own food from the hour they hatch from the large eggs. Many adults have distraction displays that lure men or predatory animals away from eggs or young (see Distraction Display; Young and Their Care), and some members of the family are long-lived: a Eurasian curlew lived to 31½ years; two black-tailed godwits to 12 and 17 years respectively; a dunlin to 14½ years. Apparently albinism is not rare, as Gross (1965a) listed 39 records of it in 17 species in the Sandpiper Family. For feeding of captives see especially Serventy *et al.* (1962).

Curlew, black. Another name for the glossy ibis and white-faced ibis in Ibis Family; so called because they have a black silhouette at a distance and downcurved bill as in curlews.

Curlew, bristle-thighed, *Numenius tahitiensis* (new-MEAN-ih-us tah-hit-ih-EN-sis); genus name: Lat., from Gr. *noumenios*, of the new moon; curve of bill likened to new crescent moon; species name: Lat., of the island of Tahiti, where, in 1769, type specimen collected (*see* Type Specimen); *bristle-thighed*, from elongated barbless shafts of flank feathers; *curlew*, from Fr. *courlis, courlieu*, originally applied to two Old World species of curlews in imitation of their cries (Newton 1893–96). (Color ill., page 791.) Rare nesting bird in w. Alaska, only known nesting place in world for this species; 17½–19½ in. long, including 3¼-in.-long downcurved bill; wingspread 32–34½ in.; about same size and appearance as whimbrel, which also has long, downcurved bill, but bristle-thighed in summer more pink about neck and breast and has *bright rusty tail* that contrasts with somber brown back; call is long-drawn whistled *wheeu-whu*, similar to call of black-bellied plover; one of last N. American species of birds whose nest and eggs remained undiscovered well into 20th century; in 1948 discovered by expedition led by Arthur A. Allen to remote area on Arctic tundra of w. Alaska; 50 mi. inland from mouth of Yukon R. and 20 mi. north of Mountain Village, at lake nearby, Henry Kyllingstad, Alaskan schoolteacher and naturalist, and David A. Allen discovered first nest, eggs, and downy young ever reported by man, thus ending a 179-year mystery. See Allen A. A. (1951a) and Pettingill (1965). A male shot May 31, 1969, on northwest coast of Vancouver Is., B.C., was first N. American record outside of Alaska; it was 1,500 mi. south of Alaskan breeding area (Richardson, 1970).

Feeding Habits: Eats berries and probably insects, mollusks, and crustaceans; has unusual habit for a shorebird of eating the eggs of other birds— of albatrosses, frigatebirds, terns, boobies, and other seabirds (Hall, 1960).
Nest: The two known nests were moss-lined depressions in tundra lichens of Alaskan barrens.
Eggs: May; 4, brown-green or buff, with dark brown spots.
Incubation: Period of and age when young first fly unknown.
Weights: ¾–1 lb. (Palmer, 1967).
Range: Nests certainly in w. Alaska near mouth of Yukon R., reported in summer from Kobuk R. to Kenai Pen., wanders in summer to Seward Pen.; in Aug. when young are well grown, bristle-thighs gather along west coast of Alaska, fatten up on berries, and migrate directly over Pacific 4,800 km. (3,000 mi.) in spectacular flight comparable to that of golden plover (Hall, 1960; Pettingill, 1965); live most of

year on islands of c. and sw. Pacific, return to Alaska in May (Palmer, 1967); winters mostly in c. and e. Polynesia from Hawaii to Marshall Is., south to Fiji, Tonga, Samoa, Marquesas, and Tuamotu Is.; has wandered to Marianas and Caroline Is.; accidental in Japan (A.O.U. *Check-list*, 1957).

Curlew, brown. Another name for the white ibis, so called because the immatures, or birds of the year, are brown and, with downcurved bill, resemble curlews.

Curlew, common. *See* Curlew, Eurasian.

Curlew, Eskimo, *Numenius borealis* (new-MEAN-ih-us boh-reh-AY-lis); genus name: *see* Curlew, bristle-thighed; species name: Lat., northern. An upland shorebird, was most northern in its nesting of any N. American curlew, formerly on treeless tundra near shores of Arctic O. in nw. Canada and Alaska; smallest N. American curlew; in 1973, very close to extinction; one reported in Mass. in 1970, two in 1972 (*see* below); 12–14 in. long, including 2–2½-in.-long bill; wingspread 26–30 in.; closely resembles Hudsonian curlew (now called whimbrel); adults: sexes outwardly alike, general color warm buff or pale cinnamon-brown, much streaked and obscured with dusky or brown-black above; throat white to pale buff, upper breast streaked with dark brown; feathers of breast and flanks marked like line of V's, tail barred brown-black as in whimbrel; single very light stripe over each dark brown eye, dark line through eyes; may be distinguished from whimbrel by its paler underparts, dark finely streaked crown, usually with no median stripe, smaller size, unbarred primary (outer wing) feathers; also identifiable by shorter, only *slightly* downcurved, mostly black, slender bill, dark green legs (not bluish as in whimbrel), and *cinnamon-buff* of undersurface of wings (Forbush, 1925–29; 1912); utters soft, melodious whistle *tee! tee! tee!;* formerly a fabulously abundant bird, was reported in southern migration to have visited Newfoundland in millions that darkened the sky; Audubon off Labrador coast in July 1883 saw dense flocks that reminded him of vast numbers of passenger pigeons; another observer along Labrador coast in 1860 described flock a mile long and nearly as wide; the distant notes of these curlews resembled wind whistling through a ship's rigging, or a vast jingling of sleigh bells; in prairie states, numbers of Eskimo curlews in northward migration so resembled tremendous flights of passenger pigeons that they were called prairie pigeons; a single flock alighting in Neb. was said to have covered 40–50 acres of ground; from Arctic tundra nesting grounds, in Aug., migrated southeast to Labrador and Newfoundland, fattened there on crowberries, *Empetrum nigrum*, blueberries, and snails, then flew south over Atlantic O. for wintering grounds in grasslands of S. America, from s. Brazil south to pampas of s. Argentina and Chile; easterly storms or West Indian hurricanes sometimes drove them to New England coast; flocks came down over dunes and settled on sandy capes like brown windblown leaves or thronged salt meadows, brackish pools, and

Eskimo curlew

SANDPIPER FAMILY

tidal basins by thousands (Forbush, 1925–29; Hall, 1960); few went south over the interior U.S. (Greenway, 1958). In spring, they migrated north through western interior of S. America to Ecuador, then over water to Costa Rica, overland in C. America to s. Mexico, thence across w. Gulf of Mexico, usually arriving in s. Tex. in Mar.–Apr.; then north through western part of Mississippi R. drainage and eastern Prairie Provinces of Canada to reach tundra of n. Mack., some veering west to Alaska to reach breeding grounds in late May to early June (Palmer, 1967). The Eskimo curlew, considered a table delicacy, took the place of the already slaughtered passenger pigeon in the marketplace; its lack of suspicion and fear and its habit of traveling in great flocks made it extremely vulnerable to hunters; it was shot in its spring migration in the West often by the wagonloads; market hunters followed the curlews in their migration from state to state; on Atlantic coast in autumn, similar destruction, with record of 7,000 shot in one day on Nantucket Is., Mass. (Vincent, 1966); South Americans hunted them on the winter range; from 1870 to 1880, beginning of decline; between 1886 and 1892, no longer seen in numbers on Labrador coast; last one shot in New England, a lone one in Mass., Sept. 3, 1913; last one shot in U.S. of which there is record, one killed Apr. 17, 1915, 10 mi. south of Norwalk, Neb. (Forbush, 1925–29); last one shot in S. America, in Argentina, Jan. 11, 1925 (Greenway, 1958). Weston and Williams (1965) summarized 11 records of Eskimo curlews from 1932 to 1963: one reported shot in Labrador, Aug. 29, 1932; four reported a week later at Montauk, Long Is., N.Y.; two, Galveston Is., Tex., Apr. 29, 1945; one, Cape Romain Refuge, north of Charleston, S.C., June 1946; one, near Rockport, Tex., Apr. 17, 1950; one seen at Folly Is., near Charleston, S.C., July 15, 1956; one, Galveston Is., Mar. 22, 1959; one, Cape May, N.J., Sept. 20, 1959; one, Galveston Is., Apr. 3, 1960; three or four, Galveston Is., late Mar. to early Apr. 1962; one, south of Rockport, Tex., Apr. 11, 1963 (at same place where one seen Apr. 27, 1950). Besides these records, Nichols (1948) reported one seen by an experienced observer at Cedarhurst, Long Is., N.Y., Sept. 7, 1947; Peterson (1963) reported one seen Galveston Is., Apr. 5–26, 1959; one was collected (shot) Barbados, West Indies, fall of 1963—specimen in Philadelphia Academy of Natural Sciences. Even more recently, Finch (1971b) cited one identified by two highly skilled observers at Plymouth, Mass., Aug. 29, 1970; two reported together at Martha's Vineyard, Mass., Aug. 6–7, 1972 (Daniels, 1972). See also status in Greenway (1958); Vincent (1966); and Office of Endangered Species (1973).

Feeding Habits: Eats grasshoppers and their eggs, grubs and cutworms in plowed fields, berries and small snails (Bent, 1929).
Nest: On tundra, a mere depression in ground, lined with a few dead leaves or wisps of hay.
Eggs: June; 3–4, usually 4, dark green, brownish green, to blue, blotched with browns.
Incubation: Period of and age when young first fly unknown.

Other Names: Doe-bird; dough-bird (owing to fatness); fute; little curlew; prairie pigeon.
Weights: To about 1 lb., when fat.

Curlew, Eurasian, *Numenius arquata* (new-MEAN-ih-iss are-QUAY-tah); genus name: *see* Curlew, bristle-thighed; species name: Lat., bent, or bowed, in reference to bill. Has reached N. America, casual in Greenland; one shot on Long Is., N.Y., in 1853; 19–25 in. long, including 4–5-in.-long downcurved bill; the largest European wading bird, or shorebird; has buffy, streaked plumage but no head striping; has *white rump.*

Other Names: Common curlew; European curlew; jack curlew; large curlew (in Russia).
Age: One, banded as chick in Sweden, July 4, 1926, shot "in perfect condition and full vigour" at Norfolk, England, 31½ years later, Jan. 25, 1958 (Kuhk, 1960).
Hybrids: Eurasian curlew × slender-billed curlew, *Numenius tenuirostris,* of Europe—presumed hybrids have been reported (Gray, 1958).
Weights: 23–29 oz. (Palmer, 1967).
Range: Nests in northern parts of Europe and w. Asia, in c. and w. Europe south to British Isles, east to c. China; winters south to s. Africa, Madagascar, Philippines (Dement'ev *et al.,* 1969).

Curlew, European. *See* Curlew, Eurasian.

Curlew, hen. *See* Curlew, long-billed.

Curlew, Hudsonian. *See* Whimbrel.

Curlew, Jack. *See* Curlew, Eurasian; *also* Whimbrel.

Curlew, little. *See* Curlew, Eskimo.

Curlew, long-billed, *Numenius americanus* (new-MEAN-ih-us ah-mer-ih-CANE-us); genus name: *see* Curlew, bristle-thighed; species name: Lat., of America. (Color ill., page 792.) Western bird, s. Canada to Tex., once nested throughout grasslands of West, east to prairies of s. Wisc. and Ill., but disappeared from many places with plowing of plains and prairies for agriculture up to 1930s, which extirpated them from vast region, also decimated in fall by hunters along Atlantic coast (see in Forbush, 1912); largest bird in Sandpiper Family; formerly reported to appear each year in fall along eastern seaboard from N.B. to Fla., now virtually unknown north of S.C., where it still appears regularly (Sprunt and Chamberlain, 1949); however, three reported after hurricane on coast of N.C., Aug. 14, 1953 (Bull, 1964), and one on Long Is., N.Y., on July 4, 1975, there until July 30 (Buckley *et al.,* 1975); 21–26 in. long, including downcurved bill, 4¼–8¾ in. long, depending on sex of bird; see Forbush (1925–29); Palmer (1967); wingspread 36–40 in.; females average much larger; sexes outwardly alike; long-billed is notably larger than the whimbrel and with longer bill; does not have dark line through brown eyes or prominent stripes on top of head as in whimbrel; is more buffy or cinnamon below, has *bright*

pink-cinnamon on undersurfaces of wings which shows in flight; call is loud, plaintive *cur-lee!* or *cur-lew!* with rising inflection; except on nesting grounds is very wary; at cry of warning flock takes off; flight is strong and steady; in migration, often fly high in wedge-shaped flocks; walks gracefully and swiftly on land and can swim if necessary (Bent, 1929); roost on ground along coast on small sandy islands offshore, on prairies, at edges of ponds; from wintering grounds, Calif. to Guatemala, returns north in Mar.–Apr.

Feeding Habits: When migrating frequents shores of lakes, rivers, salt marshes of seacoast, and sandy beaches, where catches crayfishes, small crabs, snails, toads, and at times eats berries on prairies; eats especially grasshoppers, beetles, caterpillars; on nesting and on wintering grounds is upland feeder; in summer, far out on open prairies, feeds in grassy hollows or edges of prairie sloughs or ponds. See Palmer (1967); Stenzel *et al.* (1976).
Nest: In moist meadows or dry prairies, in slight hollow in open grassland, usually thinly lined with grasses or weeds; both sexes inconspicuous as they sit on nest with necks stretched out on ground; pairs may nest within sight of each other if habitat favorable; rarely, two females share same nest, each laying her set of eggs; one record of a willet and a long-billed curlew laying eggs in same nest and guarded by both birds (Bent, 1929).
Eggs: Apr.–May; 4, white to buff or deep olive, evenly spotted with dark brown.
Incubation: By both sexes; one record, Colo., 27 days, 14 hours (Graul, 1971); young at hatching have straight bill no longer than head.
Other Names: Big curlew; hen curlew; old hen curlew; sabre-bill; sickle-bill; sickle-billed curlew; smoker; Spanish curlew.
Flight Speed: Timed in w. U.S., 35–50 m.p.h. (Cottam *et al.,* 1942b); 35 m.p.h. (Jones, 1927).
Running Speed: Timed in Utah, 8–10 m.p.h. (Cottam *et al.,* 1942b).
Weights: 1 lb. 12 oz. to 2 lbs. (Forbush, 1925–29).
Range: Nests from s. B.C., Alta., Sask., Man., south to Utah, N.M., and Tex., formerly in Kans., Iowa, Minn., Wisc., and Ill.; winters from Calif., w. Nev., Ariz. (formerly), Tex., and La., south to Baja Calif. and Guatemala; sparingly along Atlantic coast from S.C. and Fla.; has wandered to Fort Simpson, Mack., and to Ont.

Curlew, pied-wing. *See* Willet.

Curlew, pigmy. *See* Sandpiper, curlew.

Curlew, pink. Another name for the roseate spoonbill.

Curlew, red. *See* Godwit, marbled.

Curlew, short-billed. *See* Whimbrel.

Curlew, sickle-billed. *See* Curlew, long-billed.

Curlew, Spanish. Another name for the white ibis; *see also* Curlew, long-billed, and Willet.

Curlew, speckled. Local name in Fla. for the limpkin.

Curlew, stone. Name for immature white ibis; *see also* Willet.

Curlew, straight-billed. See godwits.

Curlew, white. Another name for the white ibis.

Curlew, white-winged. See Willet.

Dowitcher, Eastern. See Dowitcher, short-billed.

Dowitcher, long-billed, *Limnodromus scolopaceus* (lim-NOD-roh-mus skol-oh-PASS-ee-us); genus name: Lat., from Gr. *limnodromos*, marsh runner; species name: Lat., from Gr. *skolopax*, snipe (*see* introduction to Sandpiper Family); *dowitcher* (DOW-itch-er), of Iroquoian Indian origin; common name for these snipelike shorebirds with characters intermediate between the true snipes (common snipe, for example) and the sandpipers. (Color ill., page 792.) Summers in Alaska, Canada, n. Russia; seen in migration mainly in w. U.S. and along Atlantic coast mainly in fall; 11–12½ in. long, including 2⅛–3-in.-long bill; wingspread 18–20 in.; sexes outwardly similar but females average larger; chunky, medium-sized shorebirds with long straight bills, in fall or winter plumage grayish all over; according to Pitelka (1950), long-billed in spring breeding plumage is more completely salmon below than the similar short-billed dowitcher, with dense spotting only on throat and upper breast; more *barring* of breast and belly and less spotted along flanks; long-billed is slightly larger than short-billed, with longer bill and longer legs; call is a single *keek* (short-billed utters *tu-tu-tu* note); long-billed's nesting range is separate (allopatric) and northwest of main nesting grounds of short-billed; 90% of long-billed dowitchers during migration prefer freshwater habitats; short-bills, given opportunity, usually feed on marine flats (Clement, 1960); according to Peterson (1963), dowitchers in any plumage are distinguished by snipelike bills; they feed on open mud flats; the true snipes (common snipe, for example) feed on *marginal* mud or in very shallow water, seldom venturing far from shelter of weeds or sedges; long-bill arrives on nesting grounds Apr.–May.

Feeding Habits: Prefers shallow fresh water and soft mud bars at grassy margins of marshes, where flocks probe mud with long bills, often immersing head entirely in water; most of food is insects, largely larvae of flies, midges, crane flies, soldier flies, dance flies, snipe flies, horseflies, brine flies, flower flies; also water beetles, and other aquatic insects; mollusks, crustaceans, marine worms, and spiders, also considerable plant food—seeds of bulrushes, pondweeds, widgeon grass, smartweeds, grasses, sedges, etc. (see Sperry, 1940).

Nest: In sedges and grasses with scattered low shrubs, trees, usually near shallow fresh water, in a depression in marsh in tuft of grass or moss, lined with leaves.
Eggs: May–June; 4, brown to olive, usually brown, marked with brown and gray (Bent, 1927).
Incubation: In beginning female and male, then by male only, apparently 20 days (Palmer, 1967); age when young first fly unknown.
Other Names: Greater gray-back; greater long-beak; red-bellied snipe; red-breasted snipe; western dowitcher.
Flight Speed: 43 m.p.h. (McLean, 1930).
Weights: Two averaged 130 gr. (Hughes, 1970), or about 4½ oz.; 4–5½ oz. (Forbush, 1925–29); to 4½ oz. (Palmer, 1967).
Range: In N. America, nests in Alaska on St. Lawrence Is. and on mainland coast from Bristol Bay north to Point Barrow and east along Arctic lowlands; in Canada, in Mack., at Anderson R. and Franklin Bay, also in n. Siberia; Siberian birds migrate to N. America across sea, so that winter range is largely from c. Calif. south to Guatemala; one may see long-bills across interior of U.S. and on Atlantic coast mostly south of N.Y., and in fall some birds, adults and young, reach the East Coast and are found as far south as Fla. and into the Caribbean; may remain in summer on their winter range; winter from c. Calif., w. Nev., s. Ariz., s. N.M., w.-c. Tex., Gulf coast, and Fla. south to Guatemala.

Dowitcher, short-billed, *Limnodromus griseus* (lim-NOD-roh-mus GRIS-e-us); genus name: *see* Dowitcher, long-billed; species name: Lat., gray, grizzled, general color in winter plumage. (Color ill., page 792.) Summers in muskeg of n. Canada to s. Alaska; seen in migration and in winter entirely across continent; short-billed is more commonly associated with salt water; long-billed more commonly with fresh water; sexes outwardly similar; females average larger, 10½–12 in.; chunky, with short greenish legs, long, straight bill; in spring breeding plumage, body dark above but paler than back of long-billed dowitcher; breast white to cinnamon-red; white rump patch extending up back in all plumages; in winter, gray all over (*see* Dowitcher, long-billed, which it very closely resembles, for comparison); in general, slightly smaller, shorter-billed, shorter-legged than long-billed, but longer-winged (Palmer, 1967); can be distinguished from long-billed by its call, *tu-tu-tu* or *pheu-pheu-pheu*, softer than similar call of greater yellowlegs; one of earliest fall migrants along New England coast (early July); on mud flats jabs long bill methodically up and down; similar common snipe feeds at *edge* of mud flats and has *dark*, not a white, rump; in spring, short-billed mainly migrates north through interior U.S. and Canada, arrives breeding grounds May–June; flies swiftly, sometimes at considerable heights.

Feeding Habits: Insects are greatest part of food and same foods as listed for long-billed dowitcher; also, along coast eats eggs of king, or horseshoe, crabs (*Limulus*) (see Sperry, 1940).
Nest: Edge of tundra, or in muskeg country (bogs within boreal forest), hollow in moss or

Long-billed dowitcher (winter)

Short-billed dowitcher (winter)

SANDPIPER FAMILY

clump of grass, lined with twigs, leaves, grasses.

Eggs: June; 4, buff-green or brown, with small brown flecks and splotches (Bent, 1927).

Incubation: By both sexes; one nest, 21 days (Jehl and Hussell, 1966); age when young first fly unknown; reported that only male takes care of brood.

Other Names: Brown-back; brown snipe; driver; eastern dowitcher; gray-back; gray snipe; red-breasted snipe; robin snipe; sea pigeon.

Weights: Autumn migration, coastal N.J. (1), 70.1 gr. (Murray and Jehl, 1964), or about 2½ oz.; summer, Manomet, Mass. (4), 104.5, 116.8, 131, and 136 gr. (Fisk, 1971b), or about 3¾–4¾ oz.; 3½–5 oz. (Forbush, 1925–29).

Range: Nests on coast of s. Alaska and from s. Mack., s. Keewatin, to n. Alta., n. Sask., and n. Man., n. Ont., and n. Que.; winters along Pacific coast from c. Calif., w. Nev., s. Ariz., s. N.M., w.-c. Tex., Gulf coast; along Atlantic coast from S.C. to West Indies, nw. Peru, and Brazil; casual in Bermuda, Greenland, and Europe (Reilly, 1968; A.O.U. *Check-list*, 1957).

Dowitcher, western. *See* Dowitcher, long-billed.

Dunlin, *Calidris alpina* (cal-ID-ris al-PIE-nah); genus name: Lat., from Gr. *kalidris*, a speckled water bird; species name: Lat., alpine, in reference to breeding habitat, which includes alpine mountaintops; common name (DUN-lin): shortened form of *dunling*, or a small dun-colored (brown) bird (Gruson, 1972). (Color ill., page 793.) Summers in n. Russia, Arctic Canada, Alaska, e. Greenland, and Europe; small sandpiper; 6¾–8 in. long, including 1–2-in.-long bill; wingspread 14½–15¾ in.; in N. America winters along Pacific and Atlantic coasts; sexes outwardly similar, females average larger; stout, short-necked, with relatively long, blackish bill, *slightly drooping (bent) at tip*, heavy at base; in fall and winter, gray above (browner than sanderling), white below; in spring and summer, back reddish brown, marked with black, and white below, has black patch on belly; rump dark in all seasons; in flight, fairly clear-cut, narrow white stripe shows along middle of wing; according to Peterson (1963), call is nasal, grating *cheezp* or *treezp*; starts gradual migration northward in Mar.–Apr. along Atlantic and Pacific coasts, arrives nesting grounds May to early June (Palmer, 1967); flocks perform remarkable synchronized movements in air (*see* Unity of the Flock in Flight under Flight); in migration often travels in such large flocks that from distance appear like swarms of insects (Bent, 1927).

Feeding Habits: At times dashes about on mud flats or muddy edges of pools or on beaches to probe with bill into ground for sand fleas and other crustaceans, marine worms, mollusks, insects; (occasionally gathers where fish are cleaned to catch flies and other insects attracted to offal); on wet tundra eats mostly larvae of flies, mosquitoes.

Nest: Of grasses, leaves, in a hummock or other dry site on wet, grass, or sedge tundra.

Eggs: May–June; 4, green to olive-buff, spotted with grays, rich red-browns.

Incubation: In turn, by both sexes, 21–22 days; young first fly about 25 days after hatching (Holmes, 1966); 20½–23 days; young first fly 18–22 days after hatching (Norton, 1972b); see also Dement'ev *et al.* (1969).

Other Names: Black-bellied sandpiper; black-breast; blackcrop; black-heart plover; brant-bird; crooked-bill snipe; fall snipe; lead-bird; little black-breast; ox-bird; red-back; red-backed dunlin; red-backed sandpiper; simpleton; stib; winter snipe.

Age: Average life expectancy in Finland study 3.5 years, but lived to 5.3 years on average (Soikkilii, 1970b); in Sweden, a banded dunlin reported still alive when at least 14 years, 6 months, old (Alnås, 1969).

Flight Speed: Timed in migration in Calif. from airplane at 45–110 m.p.h. (McCabe, 1942).

Weights: In Sweden, smaller race, or subspecies, averaged about 44–45 gr. (Mascher, 1966), or about 1½ oz.; in Alaska, summer 1964, Yarbrough (1970) found that 45 dunlins ranged from 47 to 72 gr., or about 1½–2½ oz.; 1½–3 oz. (Forbush, 1925–29).

Range: In N. America, nests on tundra and along Arctic coasts of e. Greenland, Southampton Is., nw. and s. coast of Hudson Bay, Somerset Is., Alaska, n. Mack.; in Old World, in n. Europe, Arctic coasts of Siberia; winters coastally from se. Alaska to Baja Calif., and from Mass. to s. Fla. and Gulf coast to Tex.; in Old World from s. Europe, s. Asia, south to n. Africa, Cape Verde Is.

Godwit, American black-tailed. *See* Godwit, Hudsonian.

Godwit, bar-tailed, *Limosa lapponica* (lie-MOH-sah lap-PON-ih-cah); genus name: from Lat. *limus*, muddy, in reference to its often favored habitat; species name: Lat., of Lapland; common name (GOD-wit): from Old World and origin uncertain; Gruson (1972) suggests it may have originated in Old Eng. phrase *god wicht*, or "good creature," possibly referring to its former position as delicacy on Old World menus of 15th and 16th centuries. (Color ill., page 793.) Eurasian bird that also nests in w. and n. Alaska; has wandered down Pacific and Atlantic coasts of N. America; large shorebird; like most other godwits, has long, slightly *upturned* bill, which distinguishes godwits from similar-appearing curlews, which have downcurved bills; 14–15 in. long, including 3–4-in.-long bill; wingspread to about 28 in.; sexes outwardly different; females average larger; male in spring and summer, underparts, from tail to head, a solid rich red-chestnut; female much paler, only slightly chestnut or pinkish underparts and has streaked breast; in both, *in any plumage*, rump is dull white and *tail has narrow bars of gray or black* (lacks head stripes of similar whimbrel); in winter, both sexes gray above, white below; in flight, *pulls neck back on shoulders*, feet project only *slightly* beyond tail, and utters harsh *kirrick* or *terrek, terrek*; outside of nesting season may be seen along coasts on beaches or on mud flats; wades in water in intertidal zone; flocks of 25–200 birds reported to arrive on Alaskan nesting grounds

(St. Michael Is., for example) in mid- to late May; males in courtship flight utter continuous loud, ringing *ku-wew, ku-wew, ku-wew*; frequent open grassy country; those nesting in Alaska have apparently extended range of the species from Eurasian mainland and most apparently return to Siberia across Bering Strait before their long migration to winter on islands of sw. Pacific (Clement, 1960).

Feeding Habits: On mud flats and sandbars, wades out into water probing deeply with bill to its full length for marine worms, crustaceans, mollusks.

Nest: Usually on wet, mossy, or hummocky tundra, also on drier slopes, generally not far from pools or ponds; may be hollow depression in lichens and mosses, sometimes built of grasses, concealed in clump of grass.

Eggs: May; 4, green or brown, with scattered markings of brown (Bent, 1927).

Incubation: By both sexes, period of unknown but possibly 21 days (Palmer, 1967); age when young first fly unknown.

Other Name: Pacific godwit.

Weights: 7–16 oz. (Palmer, 1967).

Range: Nests in Arctic Eurasia, w. and n. Alaska—tundra from Kuskokwim to Colville river deltas; migrates up and down Aleutian Is., accidental in fall in Mass., Long Is., N.Y., N.J., and B.C., Canada (A.O.U. *Check-list*, 1957); first record for Calif., July 1968, a female in "worn winter plumage," was also only second record on Pacific coast south of Alaskan breeding grounds (Gerstenberg and Harris, 1970); one wintered Port Canaveral, Fla., Oct. 1969 to Mar. 1970 (Bagg, 1971); winters along coast from British Isles, North, Baltic, and Black seas, Arabia, nw. India, se. China, and Philippine Is., south to Gambia and Somaliland, Australia, Tasmania, New Zealand, also Oceania from Hawaii to Gilbert, Samoa, and Tonga Is.

Godwit, black-tailed, *Limosa limosa* (lie-MOH-sah); genus and species names: *see* Godwit, bar-tailed. Eurasian species that has strayed to Greenland, Alaska, Mass., and N.J.; sexes similar in color pattern but females average larger; 16–17 in. long, including 3¾–4¾-in.-long bill; wingspread to more than 30 in.; similar to bar-tailed godwit, but in summer, chestnut is only on head and chest; underparts, rear half, white (*see* Godwit, bar-tailed). Peterson *et al.* (1954) distinguish it from bar-tailed by its *longer, straight bill*, longer legs; black band across white tail, and white wing bar; has white underwing linings (in Hudsonian godwit, wing linings are sooty, axillars, or armpit [wingpit] feathers, are black—Robbins *et al.*, 1966).

Age: In Europe, records of two (banded) that reached ages of 12 and 17 years.

Weights: 8–13 oz. (Palmer, 1967).

Range: Nests from Kamchatka west across c. Eurasia and in British Isles to Iceland, where breeding range increasing (Palmer, 1967); migratory, most Icelandic birds winter in Great Britain, others in Mediterranean countries, s. Asia, and Philippines to e.-c. Africa, Borneo, Australia, and Tasmania; has wandered to Greenland; on May 20, 1954, a female at Placentia Bay, Newfoundland; a casual spring migrant in Aleutian Is. and Bering Sea Is. (Kessel and Gibson, 1978); first record for continental U.S., one photographed on wet hilltop pasture at Dartmouth, Bristol County, Mass., on Apr. 23, 1967 (Baird, 1968b); one Brigantine National Wildlife Refuge, N.J., May–Aug. 1971 (Scott and Cutler, 1971).

Godwit, great. *See* Godwit, marbled.

Godwit, Hudsonian, *Limosa haemastica* (lie-MOH-sah he-MAS-tih-kah); genus name: *see* Godwit, bar-tailed; species name: Lat., from Gr. *haimastikos*, blood color, in reference to ruddy underparts of this species. (Color ill., page 793.) Summers in n. and c. Canada, w. Alaska; in U.S. rare; native only to W. Hemisphere; closely related to black-tailed godwit; has long, straight or partly upturned bill; 14–16¾ in. long, including 3-in.-long bill; wingspread to about 27 in.; sexes outwardly similar but female slightly larger, with greater amount of white flecking throughout plumage; underparts rich chestnut, barred with black from throat throughout below; brown back; white upper tail coverts; *base of black tail broadly banded with white* and *white wing stripe* distinguish it; in flight, underwing linings show dusky, and axillars (armpit [wingpit] feathers) are black (black-tailed godwit has *white* underwing linings); legs and feet dark slate blue; in fall has gray back and white breast but white upper tail coverts and black tail with narrow white tip are distinctive; call is *ta-it! toe-wit!* or *god-wit!* Hagar (1966) reported it a common breeding bird in c. and nw. subarctic Canada, conspicuous large flocks at end of summer on west shores of Hudson Bay and James Bay migration; uncommon in settled parts of Canada and U.S. during its travels to and from wintering range in Argentina (Patagonia to Tierra del Fuego); late Aug. peak departure from end of James Bay, 3,000–4,000 may move by in flocks of 70–350; the long black lines in undulating flight can be distinguished from pattern of any other shorebird (Bent, 1927); along upper Atlantic coast very few records of more than 100 in a flock; south of N.J., 10 together in fall is unusual; only from Argentina and Chile is it reported in numbers comparable to those at James Bay; apparently flocks go to sea north of New England coast; in southward flight over ocean pass to west of Bermuda, follow general line southward of e. Lesser Antilles, and reach S. American coast somewhere between mouths of Orinoco and Amazon rivers; distance there from James Bay involves great arc of 2,000–3,000 mi.; about month later, juveniles, at only about 10 weeks old, without adult guidance, leave from North in very impressive flight in which they presumably follow adult route; they do not stop in large numbers along New England coast (Hagar, 1966); most in spring usually reach coast of Tex. in Apr.; from Tex. and La. move northward through Mississippi Valley to c. Canada and Mackenzie Valley, most to Arctic coast; are on nesting grounds by May–June; silent in migration, noisy on nesting grounds (Bent, 1927).

Feeding Habits: Except in nesting season, seen along sandy beaches, mud flats, and shallows of fresh, brackish, and salt water; while feeding probe rapidly in mud with long bills, which they sometimes immerse to their eyes; often wade and feed in water so deep head completely under while feeding; swims easily across ponds from one sandy ridge to another; sometimes walks with neck closely drawn into body; eats marine worms, mollusks, crustaceans; on nesting grounds takes many insects, including flies and mosquitoes.

Nest: In wet bogs and marshes of North in open expanse within forest edge, also on nearby moist tundra not far from water; according to Hagar (1966), nest is typically a saucer-shaped depression about 5 in. across, in or under edge of a dwarf birch on top of a hummock in marsh, sometimes under small willow bushes, etc.; often with little lining except a few dead leaves.

Eggs: June; usually 4, dark olive green or green-brown, sparingly spotted with obscure browns.

Incubation: Female by day, male by night, 22–23 days; chicks leave nest about 24 hours after hatching; can run rapidly and swim when about 48 hours old and can catch their own insect food; are guarded, especially by male; young are fully feathered and near adult size 30 days after hatching (Hagar, 1966).

Other Names: American black-tailed godwit; black-tail; brant-bird; field marlin; goose-bird; red-breasted godwit; ring-tailed marlin; spot-rump; straight-billed curlew; white-rump.

Flight Speed: 45 m.p.h. (Cadieux, 1970).

Weights: About 11 oz. (Pough, 1951); a male (very fat) collected in Oaxaca, Mexico, May 1961, 241 gr., or about 8½ oz.; another male, same locality, 181.9 gr. (Binford, 1970), or about 6½ oz.; 9–13 oz. (Forbush, 1925–29).

Range: Nests locally along Arctic coast and tundra from nw. Mack. to ne. Man., on Akimiski Is. in James Bay, in Alaska, recently at Cook Inlet (Palmer, 1967); winters n. Argentina, n. Chile, Paraguay, and s. Brazil, Uruguay, to Tierra del Fuego and Falkland Is.; casual n. and w. Alaska, B.C., Idaho, Nev., Calif., and Bermuda; wanders to New Zealand; in fall migration, south along Atlantic seaboard to N.J., Va. (see Scott and Cutler, 1973).

Godwit, marbled, *Limosa fedoa* (lie-MOH-sah FED-oh-ah); genus name: *see* Godwit, bar-tailed; species name: Lat. version of an old and now unknown Eng. name; *marbled,* for its mottled plumage. (Color ill., page 793.) In summer, in s. Canada, w. U.S., rare in East (Robbins *et al.*, 1966); appears as spring and fall migrant along Pacific coast; occasionally a few seen in fall along Atlantic coast; next to long-billed curlew and oystercatchers, is largest of N. American shorebirds (Bent, 1927); 16–20 in. long, including 3–5½-in.-long bill; wingspread to 32 in. (Palmer, 1967); sexes outwardly similar, females average larger; very long, straight or perceptibly recurved *(upturned)* flesh-colored bill, dusky at tip; appears as a long-legged *buff-brown* bird, mottled above, finely barred below; blackish wings have red-brown on outer tips; underwing linings and axillars (armpit feathers) cinnamon-rufous; no white-banded tail as in Hudsonian and black-tailed godwits, nor a white rump as in bar-tailed godwit; tail is

Hudsonian godwit (winter)

SANDPIPER FAMILY

dark buff, barred with black; legs bluish; usually stands with bill pointing down, not horizontally as in whimbrel and willet; flight is strong, swift, with head drawn in somewhat, bill pointed straight ahead, feet stretched out behind beyond tail; when flying considerable distances, flocks fly in long lines with irregular, changing front; has various calls, common one is *terWHIT, terWHIT* or *godWIT, godWIT;* on nesting grounds flies to meet intruder, calls *eradica-radica-radica;* though it nests on grassy meadows of interior N. America, in migration seems to prefer seacoasts—sandy beaches, mud flats, margins of ponds—less frequent along shores of large lakes; during middle of 19th century, migrated in fall almost due east to Atlantic coast of New England; others still migrate westward in fall to Pacific coast and south, in interior, to Gulf coast; was once abundant migrant along Atlantic coast from New England south, but immense flocks that once passed along shores in fall and spring between Mass. and Fla. gradually disappeared until only a few stragglers ever seen; was once a game bird much slaughtered by hunters; apparently excessive shooting extirpated them from many of their former haunts (Bent, 1927); this species and the long-billed curlew, in their rapid decline, showed evidence of their relentless persecution, more than any other shorebirds (Forbush, 1912).

Feeding Habits: Probes with upturned bill in mud and tidal flats for mollusks, crustaceans, and worms, all of which it works skillfully up the long bill and into its mouth (Bent, 1927); on prairies and meadows, devours grasshoppers and insects of many other kinds; also tubers and seeds of pondweeds, sedges, and muskgrass (Sprunt and Chamberlain, 1949).

Nest: On grassy prairies often in plain sight, not far from water; uses a hollow in grass to which extra material seldom added.

Eggs: May–June; usually 4, green-brown, olive brown, sparsely spotted and blotched with browns.

Incubation: Period of and age when young first fly unknown.

Other Names: Badger-bird; brant-bird; brown marlin; doe-bird; dough-bird; great godwit; great marbled godwit; marlin; red curlew; red marlin; spike-bill; spike-billed curlew; straight-billed curlew.

Weights: About 12 oz. (Pough, 1951); 9½–18 oz. (Palmer, 1967); one about 13½ oz. (Hughes, 1970).

Range: Nests from Alaska (possibly), c. Alta., s. Sask., s. Man., south to c. Mont., c. N.D., ne. S.D., w.-c. Minn., formerly to c. Neb., c. Iowa, s. Wisc., birds not nesting seen in summer south to Mex., Calif., and S.C., formerly to Fla.; winters on coast from c. Calif., se. Tex., c. S.C., Ga., and Fla. south mainly along coasts to Guatemala, Belize, rarely to Ecuador, n. Peru, and Chile (A.O.U. *Check-list,* 1957); rare to uncommon but a regular fall migrant in N.Y. coastal areas, occasionally more numerous; very rare in spring; became a regular fall migrant in N.Y. area in early 1930s, also seen regularly along coast of N.J. and Va. (see *Audubon Field Notes* and *American Birds*

for recent records); is casual to B.C., Ore., and Nova Scotia.

Godwit, red-breasted. *See* Godwit, Hudsonian.

Godwit, tell-tale. *See* Yellowlegs, greater.

Greenshank, *Tringa nebularia* (TRING-gah neb-you-LAY-rih-ah); genus name: from Gr. *tryngas,* used by Aristotle for a white-rumped water bird (Macleod, 1954); species name: from Lat. *nebulosus,* dark, clouded, in allusion to plumage. Eurasian species seen on Pribilof Is., and w. Aleutian Is., Alaska; one, found dead on Buldir Is., Alaska, June 5, 1975, was third N. American record, according to Gibson and Byrd (1975); several seen since (see Kessel and Gibson, 1978); also one allegedly sighted at Onondaga Lake, N.Y. (Palmer, 1967); about 12 in. long, including 2-in.-long bill; shaped, and proportionately, like lesser yellowlegs, but larger, and long, straight bill has slight upswing as in greater yellowlegs; also has greenish legs, white lower back, rump, and upper tail coverts. See monograph by Nethersole-Thompson and Nethersole-Thompson (1979).

Range: Nests from Britain across n. Eurasia; migrates to s. Europe, s. Asia, Africa, New Zealand, Tasmania; has wandered to Argentina, and allegedly to Chile; Audubon's report of three collected May 1832 near Cape Sable, Fla., not considered satisfactory or acceptable (Palmer, 1967).

Jacksnipe. *See* Jacksnipe, European; *also* Snipe, common.

Jacksnipe, European, *Lymnocryptes minimus* (lim-no-CRIP-teez MIN-ih-mus); genus name: Lat., from Gr. *limne,* marsh, and *krypto,* hide, "marsh hider" (Gruson, 1972); species name: Lat., smallest; *jacksnipe,* small snipe (is smallest one). Eurasian species that has strayed to N. America; three records: in Labrador, late Dec.; in Calif., Butte County, late Nov.; St. Paul Is. (Pribilofs), Alaska, in spring (Palmer, 1967); 7½ in. long; sexes outwardly alike; resembles common snipe but *smaller, with relatively much shorter bill,* and *no white* in *wedge-shaped* brownish tail; tail feathers and outer secondaries pointed; usually solitary; rises silently with less zigzagging and slower flight than common snipe (Peterson *et al.,* 1954); its aerial territorial display flight is called "cantering"; the distinctive sound made during its steep dives, as air rushes through its tail feathers, has been likened to "clopping" of horse's hooves on hard, dry ground (Tuck, 1972); this display and sound similar to that of common snipe except that it is rather staccato, with no tremolo effect. Lives in open grassy marshes, swamps, bogs, wet meadows; occasionally in salt marshes and along shores.

Feeding Habits: Eats earthworms, insects and insect larvae, and mollusks; some vegetable (plant) matter (Witherby *et al.,* 1938–41).

Other Name: Half snipe (British Isles), in allusion to small size (McAtee, 1923).

Weights: To 3 oz. (Palmer, 1967); average of 328 collected (shot) in Orkney was 63.4 gr. (Tuck, 1972), or about 2¼ oz.

Range: Nests south of tundra in Siberia, n. Europe; winters from c. Europe, Near East, and India south to c. Africa, Ceylon, Formosa; accidental in Alaska, Calif., Labrador.

Knot. *See* Knot, red.

Knot, American. *See* Knot, red.

Knot, Eastern Asiatic. *See* Knot, great.

Knot, great, *Calidris tenuirostris* (cal-ID-ris ten-you-ih-ROS-tris); genus name: *see* Dunlin; species name: from Lat. *tenuis,* slender, and *rostrum,* bill (Jaeger, 1955); *great* refers to large size relative to other knots. An Asiatic, Old World, little-known species that has visited Cape Prince of Wales, Alaska, where an adult male was shot (collected) May 28, 1922; a few seen since on w. and c. Aleutian Is.; about 11½ in. long; larger than the red knot, which it resembles, but lacks rufous coloring and has black, white-spotted breast band and whitish underparts; has relatively short legs as in all sandpipers (Palmer, 1967).

Other Names: Eastern Asiatic knot; eastern knot.

Range: Nests in Siberia; winters Malay Archipelago, Molucca Is., Australia, India, Burma (Dement'ev *et al.,* 1969).

Knot, red, *Calidris canutus* (cal-ID-ris kay-NEW-tus); genus name: *see* Dunlin; species name: given by Linnaeus for Danish King Canute, or Knut, who was known for trying to hold back the tide, thus the name. (Color ills., page 795.) In N. America, summers mostly in Arctic Canada, some in Alaska, also in Old World; in N. America, main migration in fall along Atlantic coast, not as common on Pacific coast; largest of N. American beach sandpipers; 9½–10 in. long; wingspread to 20 in.; sexes outwardly similar, female larger; stocky, short-legged shorebird; compared with snipelike dowitchers, has *short bill,* and its white rump does not extend as a white streak up back (Robbins *et al.,* 1966); in spring, *robin red* head, neck, breast, and underparts (no other short-billed shorebird has red breast); back, like crown, mottled buff and black; in fall, a washed-out gray with white underparts; green-yellow legs; knot may be distinguished in fall and winter from similar sanderling by its larger size and, in flight, its *pale rump and tail;* knots fly swiftly in closely massed flocks, twisting and turning in unison, alternately showing, as they turn, first their gray backs, then their red breasts; flight calls are a single croaking, or honking *knut,* also *tlu tlu,* and a mellow *wah-quoit;* males on Arctic nesting grounds call *poor-me* (Parmelee and MacDonald, 1960); in migration feed mainly on sandy or stony beaches, in compact bunches, sometimes on tidal flats and in salt marshes; one of great long-distance migrants among N. American birds; from nesting places on Arctic Ellesmere Is., in fall some go south to Straits of Magellan (Forbush, 1912), a round trip each year of some

19,000 mi.; arrive on coasts of s. U.S. in late Apr., early May, abundant in spring on peninsular Fla., many migrate inland through Canadian provinces, but most go north along Atlantic coast, arrive on breeding grounds May–June (Palmer, 1967); at one time, one of most abundant of all shorebirds in N. America, but slaughtered in both spring and fall by market hunters in late 19th century (Forbush, 1912).

Feeding Habits: Sometimes feeds in muddy places, where probes with bill for food, but more often seen on beaches; eats mostly mollusks—snails, periwinkles, pelecypods *(Donax),* gem shells—eggs of horseshoe, or king, crab, some small fishes, marine worms, seeds of widgeon grass, bogbean, goosefoot, eelgrass, etc.; many insects—flies, including soldier flies, brine flies, midges, horseflies, dance flies, crane flies, some beetles, etc. (Sperry, 1940).

Nest: On drier, higher, and rocky tundra, from which adults fly to waters of fresh or marine shores to feed; nest in hollow of clumps of lichens among rocks and scant plant life of ridges and hills; first nest and eggs discovered by members of Admiral Peary's expedition to North Pole, on June 27, 1909, on Ellesmere Is.

Eggs: June–July; usually 4, buff-olive, spotted, scrawled, blotched with browns.

Incubation: Both sexes incubate; one nest 21.5–22.4 days (Nettleship, 1968); young first fly about 18 days after hatching (Parmelee and MacDonald, 1960).

Other Names: American knot; ash-colored sandpiper; beach robin; blue plover; buffbreast; buff-breasted plover; Canute's sandpiper; freckled sandpiper; gray-back; horsefoot snipe; knot; maybird; redbreast; red-breasted plover; red-breasted sandpiper; red sandpiper; robin breast; robin snipe; silver-back; silver plover; wahquoit; white-bellied snipe.

Age: One, banded Ellesmere Is., when nestling, found dead when 6 years, 2 months, old on St. Kilda Is., Scotland (Kennard, 1975); a juvenile banded in Lines, England, was found dead when 11 years old on its breeding grounds at Ellesmere Is.; an adult banded in Norfolk, England, in Aug. 1968 was killed 5 years later by a gyrfalcon on Ellesmere Is. (Morrison, 1975); a captive in London Zoo died when at least 13 years old (Olney, 1972).

Flight Speed: Timed in Fla., 38 m.p.h. (Longstreet, 1930).

Weights: Summer, at Manomet Bird Observatory, Mass. (4), 114.1, 160.6, 209.5, and 217.8 gr. (Fisk, 1971b), or about 4–7¾ oz.; 4–6½ oz. (Forbush, 1925–29); adult males in summer (13), average 125.5 gr.; females (9), 147.9 gr. (Parmelee and MacDonald, 1960).

Range: Nests occasionally in nw. Alaska (Point Barrow) and on nearby Cooper Is.; in Canada, from High Arctic islands (Ellesmere, Baffin) to Victoria Is., n. Melville Pen., Southampton Is., and in Greenland; in Old World, in Iceland, Spitsbergen, Taimyr Pen., Middendorff Bay, Siberia, etc. (Palmer, 1967); in W. Hemisphere, winters along coasts from s. Calif. and Mass. (rarely) south (casually along s. Atlantic coast) but most winter in temperate latitudes of S. America; in Old World, winters from British Isles, n. Europe, and s. Asia south to Africa, Australia, and New Zealand. Banding records and returns from knots reported by Morrison (1975) confirm that most or all of the knots breeding on Ellesmere and Baffin Is. winter in Britain, Ireland, and Holland, and that Iceland is an essential stopover for knots migrating from Europe to their breeding grounds in the Canadian High Arctic.

Redshank, *Tringa totanus* (TRING-gah TOTE-ah-nus); genus name: *see* Greenshank; species name: New Lat., from Ital. *totano,* redshank. Eurasian species; has strayed to e. Greenland; also reported Halifax County, Nova Scotia, Jan. 1960; and sighted Rockport, Tex., Apr. 1962 (Palmer, 1967); about 11 in. long; sexes outwardly similar; intermediate in size between greater and lesser yellowlegs; bill in slight upswing as in greater yellowlegs; has *reddish* black-tipped bill; orange-red legs; white back and rump, dark wings with white band on rear edges that shows in flight; black-and-white-barred tail; black and gray above; streaked below.

Other Name: Teuke.
Weights: 3½–5½ oz.
Range: Nests both inland and along coasts in open grasslands or heath in Iceland, Britain, much of Europe, Asia Minor, across c. Asia into e. China; winters in Iceland in fair numbers, Britain, continental Europe, Africa, s. Asia, and islands south, including Borneo, Sumatra. See life history in Bent (1927).

Redshank, spotted, *Tringa erythropus* (TRING-gah er-ITH-roh-pus); genus name: *see* Greenshank; species name: Gr., red-footed. Six seen on St. Paul Is., Pribilofs, Alaska, in 1961, of which two collected in Sept., first definite record of this species for N. America (see Kessel and Gibson, 1978, for other Alaskan records); single birds reportedly seen May 23, 1955, at Pea Is., N.C., and May 30, 1955, at Tiverton, R.I. (Clement in Hall, 1960); July 30, 1960, at Tinicum, Pa., and Apr. 16–17, 1962, near Rockport, Tex., one shot at Barbados, 1965 (Palmer, 1967); on mud flats near New Haven, Conn., Nov. 15, 1969, a female in winter plumage feeding with several greater yellowlegs, which it resembled, was collected (shot); appeared slimmer than greater yellowlegs and did not bob; fed by running forward and swinging bill from side to side, and when it flew, pale rear edge of wings and white V on lower back were apparent; call note a mellow, distinct *chirrip* (Finch and Proctor, 1972), or *tchuit* (Peterson *et al.,* 1954), who describe it as about 12 in. long; in summer is sooty-black plumage, speckled above; has white rump, barred tail; dark red legs in summer, orange-colored in winter. According to Palmer (1967), sexes outwardly similar—"a sort of black-feathered yellowlegs with very dark legs describes it briefly."

Weights: To 5¾ oz.
Range: Nests in swamps and other wet places, also occasionally in drier places of open forests from n. Scandinavia east to e. Siberia, across temperate Eurasia; winters from Mediterranean and Black seas and s. Asia south through Africa.

Ruff, *Philomachus pugnax* (fil-OM-ah-kus PUG-nax); genus name: Lat., from Gr. *philomachos,* warlike; species name: Lat., pugnacious; both names in reference to aggressiveness of males in courtship; *ruff,* for remarkable frill of long feathers that grow from male's neck just before breeding season. (Color ills., page 794.) Eurasian species, straggler to N. America, rare, but becoming regular spring and fall transient especially along Atlantic coast, Canada to N.C., also reported inland; rare in n. Alaska, Aleutian Is., and Bering Sea Is. (Kessel and Gibson, 1978); 9–12½ in. long (females so much smaller than males and so different in plumage during breeding season that she is known in Europe as the *reeve;* however, the species is called *ruff*); adults when seen in N. America usually associated with either greater or lesser yellowlegs, but in size in between the two, also shorter-legged, and has shorter and heavier straight bill, yellowish at base (Hall, 1960); legs dull yellow to olive green, never the brilliant yellow of the yellowlegs; adults in winter, brown-gray above, whitish below, with pale brown on breast and sides; immatures browner above (Peterson, 1947); in flight, tail has striking pattern of broad black stripe down center with an oval-shaped white patch on each side of tail; is usually a silent bird but when flushed may utter low *tu-whit;* in breeding plumage, male has extraordinary erectile ruff and a pair of erectile owl-like ear tufts on sides of his head; no two of these showy feather ruffs are alike; they may be black, brown, white, buff, barred, or a speckled mixture with purple iridescence; few other birds and no other shorebirds have such variations in courtship dress or such an extraordinarily different courtship (*see* Arena Bird); males lose ruff by molt after breeding season, when sexes appear more alike; prefers mud shores of lakes, ponds, marshes, wet meadows, but in N. America reported mostly along coast about salt marshes and banks of narrow, winding channels (Pough, 1951).

Feeding Habits: Moves about rather slowly; probes mud for food, seldom walks into water; eats mostly aquatic insects, especially beetles, also flies, some worms, crustaceans, mollusks, and freshwater algae, weed seeds, and some grain (Jourdain, 1929c).

Nest: In North, in Eurasia, on tundra; in southern parts of range, in marshland; a grass-lined depression in meadow, marsh, or clump of grass.

Eggs: Europe, May and June; 4, pale green, gray or buff, boldly spotted with browns.

Range: Nests from Britain across Eurasia within forested and agricultural areas; migrates to s. Asia and most of Africa; straggler in N. America to Alaska, Greenland, Maritime Provinces of e. Canada; along Atlantic coast, Me. to N.C.; inland, Ont. to Ohio, Ind., Iowa, Mo., also to Calif. and to West Indies (especially Barbados), Trinidad; 30 reports of this species in e. N. America in 1963; recently recorded breeding in Alaska (Gibson, 1977).

Sanderling, *Calidris alba* (cal-ID-ris AL-bah); genus name: *see* Dunlin; species name: Lat., white, in reference to winter plumage; *sanderling*, from Icelandic *sanderla*, suggesting its sandy habitat. (Color ills., page 795.) Summers in Siberia and Canadian Arctic; in fall and spring, common migrant east of Rocky Mtns. throughout interior and especially along Atlantic, Pacific, and Gulf coasts, where preeminently the sandpiper of the sea beach; 7–8¾ in. long, wingspread to 15 in.; sexes outwardly similar in winter plumage, but females average larger; closely resembles semipalmated sandpiper but larger; plump, sleek; on sand flats or outer beaches, chasing retreating edge of waves; in breeding plumage, male generally more brightly colored than female; red-gold or rusty on head, back, breast; chunky and short-necked; in winter, whitest of all sandpipers, when matches sand; sometimes called whitey; has white forehead, pale gray above, white below; dark shoulders; in all plumages, in flight, shows conspicuous flashing white wing stripe and black wrist; legs black; bill black, rather straight, short and stout, about as long as its head (Forbush, 1925–29); call note is soft, distinctive *kip* or *ket, ket, ket;* differs from others in family by lack of hind toe; often stands for long time on one leg, as do all waders; may be seen in small or large flocks, or solitarily; defends winter feeding territory; when feeding one may frequently fluff its feathers until it appears humpbacked and aggressively chase another until it takes wing; when resting, usually at high tide, up to 100 or more may gather close together on higher beach (Stone, 1937); one of cosmopolitan globe-trotters; few species equal its worldwide wanderings; nests in Arctic of both hemispheres, migrates through all continents and many islands to southernmost limits of S. America and Africa, and even to Australia (Bent, 1927) and New Zealand; some make annual spring flight from c. Chile to ne. Greenland, about 8,000 mi. (Matthiessen, 1973); spring migration starts in Mar., main flight northward through much of U.S. in May, a few linger into June (Bent, 1927); arrive on nesting grounds late May and early June; both sexes arrive together in small flocks on inland nesting grounds.

Feeding Habits: On Arctic nesting islands, eats flies and their larvae and other insects; on wet beaches of coasts, probes vigorously with partly opened bill, making series of small holes in straight or curving lines to catch minute crustaceans (beach "fleas," hippa crabs, shrimps, etc.), also eats small mollusks (mussels, for example), marine worms (Bent, 1927); sometimes, at low tide, may visit sandbars and flats of bays near inlets and rocks covered with seaweeds; inland, where usually less common, seen mostly along beaches of lakes, river bars (Pough, 1951).

Nest: In High Arctic (in Greenland to 84° N. Lat.) nests on dry, often stony tundra or on well-drained ridges; a slight depression or shallow cup dug by pair and lined with mosses or willow leaves, at edge or in tuft of low plants.

Eggs: June–July; female selects one of several nest scrapes or hollows in which to lay; usually 4 eggs, sometimes 3, dull green-olive or olive brown, sparsely spotted with browns, black (Parmelee, 1970); may lay 2 clutches, male incubating one, female the other (Parmelee and Payne, 1973).

Incubation: 24–31 days; one of pair deserts nest at time incubation begins; adult that incubates leads chicks from nest when they are 1 day old; are capable of sustained flight 17 days after hatching.

Other Names: Beach bird; beach plover; bull peep; ruddy plover; surf snipe; white snipe; whitey.

Flight Speed: Timed in Fla., 41 m.p.h. (Longstreet, 1930).

Weights: Summer, Manomet, Mass. (23), 41.9–90 gr. (Fisk, 1971b), or about 1½–3 oz.; 2–3⅛ oz. (Palmer, 1967).

Range: Better-known nesting grounds include n. and ne. Greenland south to Scoresby Sound and Spitsbergen; extent of breeding range in Soviet Union little known, although reported nesting in Taimyr Pen., Severnaya Zemlya, etc.; a rare nester along Arctic coast of Alaska; breeding range in Canada still ill-defined, practically absent from Baffin Is.; a major breeding ground is Prince of Wales Is., also Banks Is., possibly Melville Is., etc.; winters coastally from s. B.C., Gulf coast of U.S., Mass., south to s. S. America; in Old World, from British Isles, Mediterranean, Caspian Sea, n. India, Burma, China, and Marianas, Marshall, and Hawaiian Is., south to s. Africa, Madagascar, s. India, Ceylon, Indonesia, Australia, etc.

Sandpiper, Aleutian. *See* Sandpiper, rock.

Sandpiper, American green. *See* Sandpiper, solitary.

Sandpiper, Baird's, *Calidris bairdii* (cal-ID-ris BAIRD-ih-eye); genus name: *see* Dunlin; species name: given by Elliott Coues in 1861 for Spencer F. Baird, 19th-century American zoologist, writer, scholar. (Color ill., page 797.) Summers in Siberia and Arctic N. America; migration east of Rockies to Mississippi R., mostly over Great Plains; juveniles rare but regular fall migrant along both Atlantic and Pacific coasts; in spring, north through interior N. America; small; to 7–7½ in. long; wingspread 15–16½ in.; sexes outwardly alike; larger and paler than western and semipalmated sandpipers; head and breast *buffy*, finely streaked, back has dark "scaly" appearance; dark bill, straight; blackish legs; *rump dark*, underparts white; when perched, the *long wings extend well beyond the tail;* body held more horizontally than most peeps (Robbins *et al.*, 1966); wing stripe indistinct; often mingles with other sandpipers; is one of most difficult to identify (Palmer, 1967); see also details in Bent (1927); rather tame, call note is *kreep* uttered in flight; one of long-distance migrants, from Arctic to s. S. America (Patagonia) and return each year; begins leaving winter range in S. America in Mar., passes through U.S. and Canada in Apr. to early May; arrives Arctic breeding grounds in May (Palmer, 1967); in migration often with flocks of other small sandpipers but leaves

them upon alighting and feeds by itself (Pough, 1951); moves about over soft mud or through shallow water in quick successive runs of 8–10 ft., frequently stops to pick up small bits of food; does not often probe with bill in mud or in water (Bent, 1927); in fall, when migrating along coast, favors feeding in rotting kelp of upper beach (Palmer, 1967); often seen along edges of coastal ponds in back of beach and on places in marsh grass where cover thin or cut over; inland, feeds along shores of lakes, reservoirs, irrigated or wet fields, sometimes seen at lakes high in mountains (10,000–12,000 ft. elevation) of Chile and in Colo. (Forbush, 1925–29).

Feeding Habits: On northern nesting grounds eats amphipods, algae, beetles, weevils, regularly eats larvae of mosquitoes and crane flies; also eats grasshoppers and other insects (Preble and McAtee, 1923).

Nest: Shallow depression on dry tundra, usually amid scant, low, matted plants or among lichen-covered rocks or in tuft of tussock (Palmer, 1967).

Eggs: June; 4, pink to olive-buff, dotted and blotched with rich dark browns.

Incubation: By both sexes, in turn (Norton, 1972a), 19½–21½ days; young first fly 16–20 days after hatching (Norton, 1972b).

Other Name: Grass-bird.

Weights: 1¼–2¼ oz. (Palmer, 1967).

Range: Nests along coast in ne. Siberia, on Chukotski Pen. and nearby islands; in N. America, on St. Lawrence Is., and Arctic mainland of Alaska east to some parts of Canadian mainland (Yukon, n. Mack., n. Keewatin) but mostly on islands to north and east—Victoria, Melville, and Ellesmere—and nw. Greenland, south, in w. Alaska to Cape Romanzof; n. Mack., King William Is. and sw. Baffin Is.; winters in S. America in high Andes from e. Ecuador south to Chile, and from sw. Bolivia to s. Argentina; has strayed to Galápagos Is., Falkland Is., England, and s. Africa, Australia.

Sandpiper, Bartramian, or Bartram's. *See* Sandpiper, upland.

Sandpiper, black-bellied. *See* Dunlin.

Sandpiper, Bonaparte's. *See* Sandpiper, white-rumped.

Sandpiper, buff-breasted, *Tryngites subruficollis* (trin-JIGH-teez sub-roof-ih-COL-lis); genus name; Lat., from Gr. *trynga*, a sandpiper (Coble, 1954), and *ites*, like (Jaeger, 1955); species name: from Lat. *subrufus*, somewhat reddish, and *collum*, neck. (Color ill., page 796.) Summers n. Alaska, n. Canada; 7½–8¾ in. long; wingspread to 16½ in.; sexes outwardly similar, but *males average larger; distinguished from all other sandpipers by all-buff underparts including throat and undertail coverts;* short bill, round head, long neck, upright posture give it appearance of a plover; also prefers dry, upland fields, pastures, burned-over grasslands and prairies over shores; bill dark, has white eye-ring, dark feathers of back edged with buff, pale yellowish legs; underwing linings flash silver-white in flight; is tame; stands still (freezes) to avoid detection, prefers to run rather than fly when disturbed; when flushed, twists and turns like a snipe, utters low *pr-r-r-reet*; is gregarious, during migration in small flocks or joins flocks of other shorebirds, such as golden plovers and the ploverlike upland sandpipers; in migration seen on grassy hillsides near seacoast, sometimes near water, and even on beach; also on short grass of golf courses, airports, prairies, a rare fall migrant along Atlantic coast; migrates largely overland and at night but crosses Gulf of Mexico; in spring, apparently leaves wintering grounds in S. America in mid-Mar., seen regularly in U.S., especially along Gulf coast of Rockport, Tex., by Apr. 15, migration largely over Great Plains in May, arrives near Edmonton, Alta., by mid-May; at northern limit of nesting range by mid-June (Palmer, 1967); decades ago was (compared with present numbers) abundant, but tameness and density of flocks made it vulnerable to slaughter by market hunters; once thought on way to extinction (see Forbush, 1912; Clement, 1960).

Feeding Habits: Eats mostly insects—beetles and their larvae, also larvae and pupae of flies —eats some spiders, also seeds of aquatic plants (Bent, 1929).
Nest: A shallow cavity in dry, mossy or grassy tundra.
Eggs: June; 4, white to buff or olive, spotted, blotched with browns.
Incubation: Sutton (1967a) reported the male is polygynous and incubation is entirely by female; period of incubation and age when young first fly unknown (Palmer, 1967).
Other Name: Hill grass-bird.
Weights: About 2–3 oz. (Palmer, 1967).
Range: Nests in n. Alaska, n. Yuk., n. Mack., Melville Is., Bathurst Is., south to King William Is.; winters in c. Argentina; migrates through w. interior Canada and in U.S. east of Rocky Mtns.; in fall, in small numbers, east to Ont., e. Que., south to New England, south and along Gulf coast to w. Fla.; casual in e. Siberia, Kurile Is., Honshu, B.C., Wash., Calif., Neb., Newfoundland, West Indies, and Venezuela (Palmer, 1967).

Sandpiper, Canute's. *See* Knot, red.

Sandpiper, curlew, *Calidris ferruginea* (cal-ID-ris fer-oo-JIN-ee-ah); genus name: *see* Dunlin; species name: Lat., rusty red, in reference to summer plumage; *curlew* alludes to downcurving, curlewlike bill. (Color ill., page 797.) Asiatic species; rare visitor to N. America but in summer 1962 nested for first time in W. Hemisphere at Barrow, Alaska (Palmer, 1967); considered rare breeder in n. Alaska (Kessel and Gibson, 1978); about 7½ in. long; wingspread 14½–16½ in.; male much brighter than female; bill somewhat longer than its head and slightly downcurved; in fall and winter, plumage is similar to dunlin's, but bill is more slender and downcurved through its length (dunlin's at tip); has an *all-white rump* and less spotting on breast than dunlin, also has longer legs; summer plumage, bright red-brown on head, neck, breast, and belly; utters soft, musical *chirrup* in flight; alarm call is *wick-wick-wick*; in winter, individuals or small groups

seen along coasts on mud flats, also on sand beaches; associates mostly with dunlins, occasionally with knots; most N. American records are coastal but may appear almost anywhere (Palmer, 1967); seen along Atlantic coast from N.B., Me., Mass., to Long Is., N.Y. (where seen regularly in spring but rarer in fall), and N.J.

Feeding Habits: Active, erratic feeder, often wades belly deep in water; on northern nesting grounds, main food is insects, especially beetles, also flies and their larvae; eats leeches, worms; in migration, small coastal crustaceans, minute mollusks, and some vegetable matter (Jourdain, 1927).
Nest: A hollow in dry slope or on ridge above wet tundra, in reindeer "moss," lined with mosses, lichens, occasionally willow leaves.
Eggs: June–July; usually 4, yellow to pale yellow-white or green-white, spotted with black or browns.
Incubation: Holmes and Pitelka (1964) found that only female incubates; period of incubation about 21 days; age when young first fly unknown (Jourdain, 1927). In June 1962, small population nested for first time in N. America, in Alaska, about 5 mi. east of Barrow; possibly 12 birds present on area 10 mi. square, five males were defending territories; three were associated with, and soliciting, females; nests of two pairs found in June, one with three eggs; eventually all eggs in two nests disappeared, apparently eaten by wandering non-breeding parasitic and long-tailed jaegers (Holmes and Pitelka, 1964); nesting area was flat coastal tundra—a mosaic of wet, marshy lowlands with drier ridges and dotted with small lakes and ponds. Gibson and Byrd (1972) reported the second N. American breeding record: seven nests at Barrow, July 7–14, 1972, of which two, and possibly six, nests fledged young.
Other Name: Pigmy curlew (British Isles).
Weights: 1¾–2¼ oz. (Forbush, 1925–29); to 3½ oz. (Palmer, 1967).
Range: Nests in n. Siberia from mouth of Yenisei R. east to delta of the Kolyma and to Cape Bolshaya Baranov; then a gap of 750 mi. to nearest Alaskan mainland (Holmes and Pitelka, 1964); winters from British Isles, Mediterranean region, s. Asia and Philippines, south to s. Africa, Madagascar, Ceylon, Australia, Tasmania, and New Zealand; besides recent Alaska nesting records (1962 and 1972—*see* details above) an earlier record of a male at Barrow in breeding plumage, June 6, 1883, and a second, east of Barrow, an adult female, June 25, 1956; in Canada, a male collected Queen Charlotte Is., B.C., June 31, 1936 (Holmes and Pitelka, 1964); others reported (A.O.U. *Check-list,* 1957) from B.C., Ont., and N.B., Me., Mass., Conn., N.Y. (Long Is.), N.J., Tex. (Galveston Is.), La. (Cameron), and West Indies. One banded night of Sept. 1–2, 1969, at Zeebrugge, Belgium, was shot morning of Sept. 16, 1969, at Barbados, West Indies, in a salt marsh; it had crossed southwest over Atlantic O. 7,000 km. (4,350 mi.) in a maximum of 340 hours (Kuyken and Burggraeve, 1971).

Sandpiper, gray-rumped. *See* Tattler, Polynesian.

Curlew sandpiper

SANDPIPER FAMILY

Sandpiper, least, *Calidris minutilla* (cal-ID-ris min-you-TIL-ah); genus name: *see* Dunlin; species name: Lat., very small; *least*, for its small size. (Color ill., page 797.) Smallest of N. American sandpipers; summers in Alaska, Canada; migrates through interior U.S. and along Atlantic and Pacific coasts; 5¾–6¼ in. long; wingspread 11–12 in.; sexes outwardly similar; brown-gray above; resembles slightly larger semipalmated sandpiper, but browner, dark bill more slender, neck and sides of breast fairly dark and usually more streaked than in other sandpipers; also, least has *paler legs*—dusky green, green-yellow, or yellow-green—never black or blackish as in semipalmated; belly and undertail coverts white; along coast, more frequent on bay flats, muddy margins of brackish ponds or creeks, and in wet short grass of salt marshes than semipalmated; also on sandy or gravelly ocean or bay beaches more often in spring than in fall; inland, frequents mud bars and beaches of rivers, shores of lakes and ponds, rain pools; is tame and, if observer stands quietly, may run about close by; outside of nesting season, travels in small or large flocks, also mingles with semipalmated sandpipers, plovers, and other shorebirds; when flushed, zigzags in flight like a common snipe or pectoral sandpiper; shows white wing stripe, calls *wheet, wheet, wheet,* whinnies, also utters a grating *kreep,* the *ee* sound is diagnostic (Bent, 1927); migrates at night; in spring, most travel through U.S. in late Apr. and early May; arrive nesting grounds May–June (Palmer, 1967).

Feeding Habits: In marshes, preferred feeding grounds, frequents short grass, open sloughs, mud holes, where snaps up mosquitoes, grasshoppers, and other insects or probes for insect larvae in mud and shallow water; observed to pick up small crustaceans, especially beach "fleas" (*see* Crustaceans and Birds), along coastal beaches; probably worms and small mollusks, the same fare as that of other small sandpipers.

Nest: A grass- or leaf-lined cup, usually in grass or moss hummock in open marsh or in sedge or sphagnum bog of subarctic forest just south of treeless tundra, sometimes on dry ridges of bog or in brushy upland close to a pond, tidal water, or seacoast (Bent, 1927).

Eggs: June; 4, buffy, dotted, blotched with dark browns.

Incubation: Mostly by male, 19½–21½ days (Jehl and Hussell, 1966); age when young first fly unknown.

Other Names: American stint; little sand-peep; mud-peep; ox-eye; peep; sand-peep; Wilson's stint.

Age: One, banded Great Bend, Kans., found dead same area when 7 years, 2 months, old (Kennard, 1975).

Flight Speed: Timed in Calif., 45 and 55 m.p.h. (McCabe, 1942).

Weights: In fall migration, coastal N.J. (6), 18.4–32.3 gr. (Murray and Jehl, 1964), or about ⅔–1 oz.; summer, at Manomet, Mass. (2), 19.4 and 21.5 gr. (Fisk, 1971b), or about ¾ oz.; summer, in Alaska (58), 19–29.5 gr. (Yarbrough, 1970), or about ¾–1 oz.; Irving (1960) found migrating males in Alaska 23–33 gr.

Range: Nests mostly in subarctic from vicinity of tree line, from w.-c. Alaska and Aleutians in broad belt extending from low Arctic tundra into sedge bogs of the muskeg (Hall, 1960), across Ungava east of Hudson Bay, south to margins of James Bay in Ont., and east across Que. to Newfoundland and Sable Is. off Nova Scotia and on Anticosti and Magdalen Is. in Gulf of St. Lawrence (Palmer, 1967); one record for Mass.; winters from coastal Ore., Calif., to s. Nev., w. and c. Ariz., s. Utah, N.M., c. Tex., along Gulf coast, and north on Atlantic coast to N.C., south through Mexico, C. America, and West Indies to Galápagos Is., c. Peru, and c. Brazil (A.O.U. *Check-list,* 1957).

Sandpiper, long-legged. *See* Sandpiper, stilt.

Sandpiper, pectoral, *Calidris melanotos* (cal-ID-ris mel-an-OH-toes); genus name: *see* Dunlin; species name: Lat., from Gr. *melas,* black, and *noton,* back; *pectoral* (pertaining to breast), for the male's two sacs beneath skin of neck and breast, one on each side, that male inflates during his courtship of female, which produces low, hollow, liquid, booming sounds—*too-u, too-u, too-u* (Bent, 1927; see also in Pitelka, 1959). (Color ill., page 797.) Summers in Siberia, Alaska, Arctic Canada, migrates mostly through U.S. interior but seen, although uncommon, in spring and fall along Atlantic and Pacific coasts; sexes outwardly alike but male significantly larger; 8–9 in. long; wingspread 15–16 in.; crown, dark brown, white stripe over each eye; rust-brown back is streaked with black and with lines of white; brown breast streaking *ends sharply at white underparts;* erect posture, short bill, green-yellow legs are distinctive; similarly colored least sandpiper is much smaller; similar sharp-tailed sandpiper, of Pacific coast of U.S., in fall has buffy or browner breast than pectoral; in migration along coast, frequents grassy marshes, salt meadows, and pools on wet fields rather than exposed mud flats; may be seen on cut-over meadows after rainstorms and at rain pools on golf courses (Bull, 1964); resembles common snipe; often flushes close at hand with startling harsh cry and dashes away in zigzag course (does not show a white stripe in wings), may fly only short distance, then pitch back into grass; one of its common names, grass snipe, is accurate; commonly flies in flocks of 20–40 (Palmer, 1967) but more often flushed singly; utters reedy, short, sharp notes, *krick, krick,* and creaky *kerr, kerr* or *prrrp, prrrp;* notes like western sandpiper; begins leaving S. American wintering grounds in late Feb.; Apr. or May time of greatest passage through U.S. and Canada; arrives breeding grounds in May and early June; is long-distance migrant.

Feeding Habits: On nesting range eats mostly flies, some beetles, and other insects; many amphipods, some mites, spiders, seeds of grasses, lupine, violets (Preble and McAtee, 1923); also crickets, worms, and, in fall, grasshoppers, fiddler crabs, but food is chiefly insects from grassy habitat (Bent, 1927).

Nest: Usually built on upland rolling tundra or on dry grasslands of tidal flats; a well-built cup of grasses and leaves, usually hidden under bunch of grass or in depression in ground, sometimes in grasses near border of small pool or along banks of gullies and streams.

Eggs: June; 4, white to pale buff-olive, splotched with dark browns.

Incubation: By female alone, 21–23 days; female also raises young, which first fly about 21 days after hatching (Pitelka, 1959); 19–20½ days; young first fly 18–22 days after hatching (Norton, 1972b); males often leave tundra before eggs hatch; Pitelka (1959) suggests this behavior is evolutionary step toward "lek" behavior of ruff. *See* Arena Bird; see Hamilton, 1959.

Other Names: Brown-back; brownie; fat-bird; grass-snipe; hay-bird; kreeker; marsh plover; meadow snipe; short-neck; squat snipe; squatter; triddler.

Weights: Two in w. U.S. averaged 85 gr. (Hughes, 1970), or about 3 oz.; 2–3¼ oz. (Palmer, 1967).

Range: Nests on Siberian mainland tundra; in N. America along w. and n. coasts of Alaska, nw. Mack., Victoria Is., on various islands to Southampton Is., south to e.-c. Mack., s. Keewatin, and south shore of Hudson Bay; winters abundantly in southern part of S. America (Palmer, 1967).

Sandpiper, Pribilof. *See* Sandpiper, rock.

Sandpiper, purple, *Calidris maritima* (cal-ID-ris mar-IT-ih-mah); genus name: *see* Dunlin; species name: from Lat. *marinus,* maritime, of the sea (Coues, 1882); *purple,* from purplish iridescence sometimes seen on shoulder feathers (Hall, 1960). (Color ill., page 797.) Summers in Arctic Canada, Europe, and Asia; in fall and winter, mainly along Atlantic coast; 8–9½ in. long; wingspread 14–15½ in.; sexes similar, but females average larger; stocky, dark sandpiper (darkest species on Atlantic coast) with darkly mottled brown-gray or purple-gray back and breast, breast streaked in breeding season, unstreaked in winter; white belly; thin bill, *yellow at base;* has white eye-ring and white eye-stripe in breeding plumage, a small white spot in front of eye in winter plumage; legs short, *yellow;* outside of nesting season, is restricted by its feeding habits to rocky coasts, islets, and rock jetties; *winters farther north along Atlantic coast than any other shorebird*—from Newfoundland and New England south to Md. (Forbush, 1925–29) and occasionally to Ga., casual inland; one of tamest of shorebirds, a common winter visitor, has increased markedly and extended its range with building of rock breakwaters along coast; rarely seen on beach unless rocky places nearby (Bull, 1964) but occasionally feeds among sea wrack of upper beach; flight of individual purple sandpiper suggests that of spotted sandpiper; flock, often closely bunched, wheels and turns in unison, showing alternately dark backs and white bellies; can swim, often alights on floating seaweed on water's surface; rather sedentary, flocks can be found feeding and resting in certain favored rocky places at edge of surf all winter, and year after year; when about to take flight, flock utters swallowlike twitterings, a low *weet-wit* or *twit;* start to move northward toward breeding grounds in Mar., but some linger much later into late May.

Feeding Habits: Walks about on coastal rocky promontories, ledges, reefs, moves surefootedly over wet, slippery rocks, flipping over seaweeds or probing into them; pulls crustaceans out of rock crevices or snaps up in bill tiny mollusks at edge of crashing wave (Palmer, 1967); in Europe, known to turn over stones to catch and eat small shrimps, and amphipod crustaceans such as beach "fleas," or sand hoppers (*see* Crustaceans and Birds), young crabs, insects, such as beetles, larvae of flies, also eats small mollusks, algae, grasses, mosses (Bent, 1927); on nesting grounds, early arrivals pick through cracks in ice of lakes, later eat midge larvae (Palmer, 1967).
Nest: Pairs breed on moist or dry tundra among lichens or low heath plants, seldom far from coast; nesting pairs widely scattered (Palmer, 1967); nest is grass-lined hollow on ground.
Eggs: May–June; 4, greenish, spotted and blotched with sepia and lines of black or dark brown.
Incubation: Largely by male but both sexes have incubation patches; incubation period estimated at 21 days; young probably fly about 21 days after hatching (Palmer, 1967).
Other Names: Rock-bird; rock plover; rock sandpiper; rock snipe; rockweed bird; winter rock-bird; winter snipe.
Weights: 2–3 oz. (Palmer, 1967).
Range: Nests in e. Arctic Canada south to islands in e. Hudson Bay, also in Greenland, Iceland, Arctic Europe and Asia; winters in N. America from southern part of breeding range south on Atlantic coast to Fla.; casual inland as far as Midwest (Ohio, Ind., Ill., Mich., Wisc., s. Ont., Man.).

Sandpiper, red-backed. *See* Dunlin.

Sandpiper, red-breasted. *See* Knot, red.

Sandpiper, red-necked. *See* Sandpiper, rufous-necked.

Sandpiper, rock, *Calidris ptilocnemis* (cal-ID-ris til-ock-NEE-mis); genus name: *see* Dunlin; species name: Lat., from Gr. *ptilon*, feather, and *knemis*, greave, or boot, in allusion to crus (drumstick) (Coues, 1882), being feathered down to the heel. (Color ill., page 799.) Summers in Asia and Alaska, in winter along Pacific coast; 8–9 in. long; sexes outwardly alike, but females average larger; in form, and especially in winter plumage, resembles purple sandpiper; it is slate gray with white eye-ring, white eye-stripe, and white belly; white wing stripe (does not have a broad white band across its tail as does its associates on rocks, the black turnstone and surfbird); difficult to distinguish from purple sandpiper (Peterson, 1961); in spring plumage, upperparts darker than purple sandpiper's with much rusty intermixed and with large gray patch in center of breast; call is loud, clear whistle, much repeated, like call of flicker; in late summer and fall, most of those that have bred on Chukchi Pen. in e. Asia apparently

cross water to Alaska and move southward to winter along Pacific coast of N. America; return northward and arrive on breeding grounds in May (Palmer, 1967).

Feeding Habits: Prefers rocky shores, where it eats crustaceans, small mollusks, insects, worms, some algae, seeds, berries.
Nest: From close to sea, above beaches on tundra, to hills or mountaintops; a depression in mosses and lichens.
Eggs: May–June; 4, olive, spotted with browns.
Incubation: By both sexes, about 20 days; age when young first fly unknown.
Other Name: Aleutian sandpiper; Pribilof sandpiper.
Range: Nests in extreme e. Asia and on Komandorskie, Sakhalin, and Kurile Is., and in U.S. territory on islands in Bering Sea, on mainland of parts of w. Alaska, the Aleutians, western end of Alaska Pen., and on Shumagin Is.; winters in Asia, mainly on Kurile and Komandorskie Is., and in N. America, from Aleutians and mainland of Alaska south along Pacific coast to n. Calif., rarely c. Calif.

Sandpiper, rufous-necked, *Calidris ruficollis* (cal-ID-ris rue-fih-COL-lis); genus name: *see* Dunlin; species name: Lat., from *rufus*, rusty, and *collum*, neck. Asiatic species; in summer, reaches Alaska; about 6 in. long; size of least sandpiper but distinguished from it in spring by its *rufous head, throat, and neck*, black bill and *black* legs; in winter, strikingly like semipalmated sandpiper, but with small bill as in least sandpiper (Peterson, 1961); when flushed, call is *pit-pit-pit* (Pough, 1957); several nesting records in Alaska since discovery at Cape Prince of Wales in 1933 of first N. American nest (Hall, 1960); see account of in Bailey (1943); leaves wintering range in s. Asia in Mar.–Apr.; arrives on Alaskan nesting grounds in May; outside of nesting season, seen on mud flats both tidal and inland, frequently along beaches (Palmer, 1967).

Feeding Habits: Eats insects, worms, crustaceans, mollusks.
Nest: A cavity along stream bed, in tundra moss or in grass; usually in tussock or in patch of plants, built of dry plants (Palmer, 1967).
Eggs: June; 4, yellow, dotted with rufous-cinnamon at larger end.
Incubation: By both sexes; period of and age when young first fly unknown.
Other Names: Eastern little stint; red-necked sandpiper; red-necked stint; rufous-necked stint.
Weights: Both sexes (88), 17.0–27.5 gr.
Range: Nests in Siberia in e. Taimyr Pen., Tiksi Bay area, n. and se. coasts of Chukotski Pen.; rarely in n. Alaska; has been seen at Nome, and on St. Paul Is. in Pribilofs; one photographed July 1962 at Ashtabula, Ohio; winters from s.-c. China, Formosa, Philippines, and on mainland and islands south to Tasmania, a few to New Zealand (Palmer, 1967).

Sandpiper, Schinz's. *See* Sandpiper, white-rumped.

Sandpiper, semipalmated, *Calidris pusillus* (cal-ID-ris pu-SILL-us); genus name: *see*

Rufous-necked sandpiper (winter)

SANDPIPER FAMILY

Dunlin; species name: Lat., petty, very small; *semipalmated* refers to webbing between front toes. (Color ill., page 799.) Summers on tundra Alaska and Canada, migrates in fall and spring mainly east of Rockies through interior U.S. and Canada and along Atlantic coast, casual on Pacific coast; in N. America, possibly the most abundant of all shorebirds (Robbins *et al.*, 1966); 5½–7 in. long; wingspread 11–13 in.; sexes outwardly alike, but females average larger; light line over each eye; gray above; white below; has sturdier bill than similar least sandpiper, is grayer above with less streaking on breast; usually has dusky legs, not yellowish as in least sandpiper; differs from similar western sandpiper in having shorter, slimmer bill; immatures have unstreaked, faintly buffy or smoky breasts; large flocks whirl through air, settle on mud, then spread out to feed; on beaches run about just above wave line or on mud flats at low tide and along edges of marsh creeks, visit pools on salt-hay meadows; inland, frequent muddy shores of lakes, rivers; in flight, flocks twist and turn with military precision, showing alternately light breasts, dark backs; in flight utters loud *cherk;* when flushed, a short *ki-i-ip* (Townsend, 1927); at high tide, together with least sandpipers, sanderlings, and semipalmated plovers, flocks often stand huddled on sand facing the wind; sleep standing on one or both legs with bill tucked into feathers of back; some may even hop away on one leg, making it difficult to distinguish them from crippled, one-legged birds; leaves winter range about Apr.; passes through U.S. middle two weeks of May; arrives breeding grounds at end of May into June (Palmer, 1967); see Harrington and Morrison (1979) for migration; abundant, about 75,000 seen May 24, 1964, at Kitts Hummock, Del.

Feeding Habits: With head down, runs along snatching at food with bill here and there but occasionally probes sand, not so deeply or as systematically as sanderling; bulk of food is aquatic insects—beetles, especially water scavengers, also bugs such as back swimmers, many fly pupae, also small mollusks (*Littorina*), worms, crustaceans such as amphipods (beach "fleas," for example).
Nest: Leaf- or grass-lined depression in grass hummock or on knoll of low, wet tundra, often near small lakes or on grassy coastal dunes of North (Townsend, 1927).
Eggs: June; usually 4, yellow to buff or olive, spotted with cinnamon, hazel, or chestnut (Palmer, 1967).
Incubation: By both sexes, in turn (Norton, 1972a), 18–21½ days; young first fly 14–19 days after hatching (Norton, 1972b).
Other Names: Black-legged peep; little peep; peep; sand ox-eye; sand-peep.
Age: One, banded South Amboy, N.J., trapped and released same area when 7 years, 2 months, old (Kennard, 1975).
Flight Speed: Timed in Fla., 32 m.p.h. (Longstreet, 1930); 40, 50, 50 m.p.h. (McNeil, 1969; 1970).
Weights: Fall migration, coastal N.J. (102), 19.8–41.3 gr. (Murray and Jehl, 1964), or ¾–1½ oz.

Range: Nests on tundra from Arctic coast of n. Alaska, n. Yuk., nw. Mack., Victoria Is., King William Is., Boothia Pen., c. Baffin Is., and n. Labrador, south to sw. Alaska, ne. Mack., se. Keewatin, ne. Man. (Churchill), locally along s. coast of Hudson Bay and n. Que., non-breeding birds reported in summer south to Gulf of Mexico and Panama; winters from S.C. on Atlantic coast and Gulf coast south through e. Mexico and West Indies to Peru, n. Chile, Paraguay, s. Brazil.

Sandpiper, sharp-tailed, *Calidris acuminata* (cal-ID-ris ack-you-min-AY-tah); genus name: *see* Dunlin; species name: Lat., pointed, or sharpened, in allusion to tail. (Color ill., page 798.) Siberian species that occurs as fall migrant along Pacific coast from Alaska to s. Calif.; 8¼–9¼ in. long; wingspread to 17 in.; appearance like pectoral sandpiper, but ruddier in winter plumage; in fall, immature has buffy breast and narrowly streaked or spotted on sides of breast only; does not have heavy bib-like streaking of pectoral or its sharp contrast between dark breast and white belly; habits apparently are like those of pectoral sandpiper, with which it often associates when migrating; in U.S., usually seen in small flocks of 10–50 or single birds may be flushed from grassy flats of saltwater marshes; in flight utters soft, metallic *pleep, pleep* (Bent, 1927).

Feeding Habits: Eats insects—beetles, flies—also crustaceans, and mollusks.
Nest: On wet tundra of Siberia where grassy expanses with patches of scrub willows or birch (see Palmer, 1967, for details).
Other Name: Siberian pectoral sandpiper.
Weights: About 2½ oz.
Range: Nests in Siberia east possibly to Chukotski Pen.; migrates overland along coasts to winter from southern mainland of e. Asia to New Guinea, New Caledonia, and Tonga to Australia, Tasmania, and New Zealand; in N. America, occurs rarely along Pacific coast from Alaska south to Wash. and Calif., rare south of B.C.; a female collected (shot) near Homestead, Fla., Oct. 1, 1967, was first report of this species in N. America away from Pacific coast (Ogden, 1968).

Sandpiper, solitary, *Tringa solitaria* (TRING-gah sol-ih-TAY-rih-ah); genus name: *see* Greenshank; species name: Lat., alone, solitary; common name: because usually seen alone; however, also in pairs or in small groups of 3–4 and, on occasion, more. (Color ill., page 799.) One of "tattlers" (*see* Tattler); nests in Alaska, Canada, and one record for U.S., July 11, 1973, on Mississippi R., Verdon, Minn. (Harrison, 1979); migrates through w. and interior U.S. and Canada, and along Atlantic coast; 7½–9 in. long; wingspread 15–17 in.; sexes outwardly alike; dark-backed sandpiper, white below; somewhat larger than similar spotted sandpiper, but upperparts much darker and *spangled* with white, including wings (no white stripe in wings); has white eye-ring; *conspicuous white sides of tail are barred horizontally with black;* in flight, *dark rump* of solitary distinguishes it from stilt sandpiper and yellowlegs, which have white rumps; call is like

that of spotted sandpiper but shriller and usually a three-syllabled *peet-weet-weet!* (Bent, 1929); starts north from wintering grounds in Mar., through U.S. in Apr. and into May, when arrives on breeding grounds; prefers fresh water; usually seen in migration about shores of woods streams, pools, in swamps, and along lake and river shores, but along coast seen about secluded shores of bays, rarely on mud flats or in salt marshes; frequently bobs head and body like spotted sandpiper, but more deliberately, more of a bow than a tip-up (Bent, 1929); flight is light, airy, often zigzag, and swallowlike; upon alighting, lifts wings high above back before folding them; wades in shallow water, swims readily, can dive to escape predatory birds; usually tame and unsuspicious of people.

Feeding Habits: Walks about small stagnant pools fringed with weeds, grass, and along miry tidewater ditches in marshes, also in pools in meadows and savannas, snatching up in bill dragonfly nymphs, water scavenger beetles, water boatmen, grasshoppers, caterpillars, also spiders, worms, small crustaceans, and small frogs; also probes for food in water and in mud with bill; while walking through water, shakes or trembles forward foot to stir up aquatic insects from bottom (Bent, 1929).
Nest: In muskeg country of North, perches readily in trees; female lays her eggs in nests about muskeg and woodland pools, using old nests of rusty blackbird, American robin, common grackle, cedar waxwing, Bohemian waxwing, eastern kingbird, gray jay; nests that range from 3½ to about 36 ft. above ground, to which solitary sandpiper may add some nest materials of its own; usually in nests in coniferous trees, some in deciduous trees; it is not known if solitary sandpiper ever pre-empts active nests of other species, but it occasionally adopts freshly built ones.
Eggs: May–June; 4, green or cream-buff, spotted and blotched with chocolate, violet (Palmer, 1967).
Incubation: Female has incubation patch but period of and age when young first fly unknown (Palmer, 1967); no one seems to have seen the young sandpipers leave the tree nests; young are precocial and apparently must leave nest soon after hatching; possibly jump to ground, as mossy muskeg is soft (Clement, 1960).
Other Names: American green sandpiper; American wood sandpiper; barnyard plover; black snipe; green sandpiper; peet-weet; solitary tattler; wood sandpiper; wood tattler.
Weights: In fall, coastal N.J. (1), 37.8 gr. (Murray and Jehl, 1964), or about 1⅓ oz.; 1¾ oz. (Forbush, 1925–29).
Range: Nests throughout Canadian spruce forest, from c. Alaska, n. Mack., n. Man., n. Ont., c. Que., c. Labrador, south to e.-c. B.C., s. Alta., c. Sask., s. Man., c. Ont., c. Que., s.-c. Labrador, south in summer to n. U.S.; one nesting record in U.S. in Verdon, Minn.; winters from Baja Calif. (rarely), Gulf coast, se. Ga., Fla., and West Indies (rarely) south to se. Argentina.

Sandpiper, spoon-billed, *Eurynorhynchus pygmeus* (you-rih-no-RING-kus pig-ME-us); genus name: Lat., from Gr. *euryno*, to widen, and *rhynchos*, beak; species name: Lat., a dwarf, in reference to its small size. A rare Asian visitor to Alaska (nests in extreme e. Siberia); two collected from a flock near Wainwright, Alaska, Aug. 1914; a female seen June 2, 1977, Buldir Is. (Kessel and Gibson, 1978); suspected that it may breed in general area of Wainwright Inlet (Palmer, 1967); about 6 in. long; a small sandpiper with spoon-shaped bill (at tip) which may be difficult to see; outwardly similar in spring plumage to rufous-necked sandpiper but smaller and with all-white underparts; has rust-colored head and breast; dark streaks on upper breast and flanks, but in winter has only trace of rusty and is gray above, white below, with black legs, feet, and bill; during courtship flights on nesting grounds utters high-pitched, cicadalike buzzing trill, *zee-e-e, zee-e-e, zee-e-e.* For details of life, see Bent (1927).

Weights: About 1 oz.
Range: Nests along north shore of Chukotski Pen., ne. Siberia; winters in e. Assam, Burma, and se. China; casual in nw. Alaska; recent record from Wash. (Harrington-Tweit *et. al.*, 1978).

Sandpiper, spotted, *Actitis macularia* (ack-TIE-tis mack-you-LAY-rih-ah); genus name: Lat., from Gr. *aktitis*, a shore dweller; species name: Lat., spotted. (Color ills., pages 798, 799.) Possibly best-known shorebird in America; lives along shores of fresh waters in interior N. America, from coast to coast, from edge of sea to shores of mountain lakes; common to abundant; in summer, from northern limit of trees in N. America south into s. U.S.; small; 7–8 in. long; wingspread 13–14 in.; sexes outwardly similar, but adult females average slightly larger, with more spotting than males; definitely spotted below; in breeding plumage, breast has large round spots, dark brown and black; in winter plumage adults and immatures lack the spots; generally gray-brown above, white below; white spot often shows above bend of each wing; wings with white stripe; seen along shores of lakes, ponds, streams, characteristically holds body tilted forward, head low, bobs its tail up and down almost constantly, from which often called teeter-tail; flutters from shore out over water with wings stiffly downcurved and vibrating like taut wire; wingbeats shallow; utters sharp, clear, whistled *peet-weet!* with accent on first note; sometimes in courtship, song prolonged to *weet, weet, weet, weet, weet;* usually seen alone or in pairs or small groups (compare with solitary sandpiper); walks over rocks near water or up and down logs; both adults and young can swim; adults can dive from surface or from air to escape hawks (see Kelso, 1926); can perch on twigs in treetops and on thin utility wires; roosts at night on stumps, logs, rocks; on wintering grounds, roosts in loose flocks in mangroves and even on boat docks, also on mud flats (Gochfeld, 1971); migrates at night; moves from wintering places northward through Apr. into June (Palmer, 1967).

Feeding Habits: Along seacoast, searches for food both on beach and on muddy shores of creeks and inlets; often wades into water; inland, feeds along margins of sandy ponds, sluggish meadow streams, mountain torrents; in farm country, goes into meadows, fields, gardens; easily catches flying insects out of air; stalks, and snaps up in bill, flies from ground; eats many grasshoppers, crickets, cutworms, cabbage worms, army worms, beetles, grubs, and other insects of cultivated land; also catches young fishes, including trout fry, from shallows of streams; also eats small crustaceans (Tyler, 1929b).

Nest: In saucer-shaped hollow or depression on ground, often hidden in grass, from sea level to 14,000 ft. altitude; may be lined with grasses, weeds, is sometimes a deep cup of grasses or mosses in North; on sandy knolls of islands, in thick rank sedges, sometimes under a bush or log or ledge of rocks, often not far above water where driftwood accumulates or may be sparsely distributed over hills and pastures far from water, even under steep bank of roadside; sometimes nests in colonies; Hays (1972), in her study of a breeding population of spotted sandpipers on Great Neck Is., N.Y., discovered that most females were not only more aggressive than males, holding territories and displaying to males, but were polyandrous (had more than one mate)—see Sexual Relationships—although a few females were monogamous, or mated with only one male; males did most of incubating of eggs and cared for the young (for other examples of this breeding behavior and its significance, see Oring and Knudson, 1972).
Eggs: May–July; commonly 4, brown-, green-, or pink-buff, evenly spotted with brown.
Incubation: 20–21 days (Palmer, 1967), mostly by male; young, as soon as they hatch, run over the ground teetering tail in manner of adults; chicks can swim and dive to escape danger but rely more on suddenly lying motionless on ground, where extremely difficult to see (Tyler, 1929b); males attend chicks and lead them away from nest soon after hatching; young fly 13–16 days later (Palmer, 1967); when chick threatened, one adult reported to fly off with one young clasped between thighs (Merrill, 1898). This behavior doubted by some authorities but *see* discussion Birds That Carry Their Young under Young and Their Care.
Other Names: Gutter snipe; peep; peet-weet; river snipe; sand lark; sand peep; sand snipe; seesaw; teeterer; teeter peep; teeter-tail; tilt-up; tip-up.
Accidents: Some killed or crippled by flying into utility wires; reported caught by toes and held fast by mussel; has been killed in fall migration at TV tower (Stoddard and Norris, 1967).
Age: One, banded Boxford, Mass., July 1, 1923, found dead under telephone wires at Babson Park, Needham, Mass., July 25, 1927, when 4 years old; Hays (1972) cited one banded male 6 years old, two 5 years; three 4 years; one, banded Modesto, Calif., trapped and released same area when 8 years, 5 months, old (Kennard, 1975).
Flight Speed: Timed in w. U.S., 21–30 m.p.h. (Cottam *et al.*, 1942b); in Mich., 25 m.p.h. (Schnell, 1965).
Host to Cowbirds: One record, an accidental, or freak case—at Edmonton, Alta., Robert Turner found one egg of brown-headed cowbird in nest of this sandpiper (Friedmann, 1966); another nest held four eggs of spotted sandpiper, one of brown-headed cowbird, on island in Lake Manitoba, June 1970 (Hatch, 1971).
Weights: In fall migration, coastal N.J. (1), 28 gr. (Murray and Jehl, 1964), or about 1 oz.; w. U.S. (2), average 41 gr. (Hughes, 1970), or about 1½ oz.; 1½–2 oz. (Forbush, 1925–29).
Range: Nests from nw. Alaska, n. Yuk., n. Mack., to Labrador south to mountains of s. Calif., s. Nev., c. Ariz., n. N.M., c. Tex., c. Miss., n. Ala., w. N.C., Va., and e. Md.; winters from sw. B.C., w. Wash., sw. Ariz., s. N.M., s. Tex., Gulf coast, w. Fla., and coastal N.C. south through C. America and West Indies to n. Chile, c. Bolivia, and s. Brazil.

Sandpiper, stilt, *Micropalama himantopus* (my-crow-PAL-ah-mah high-MAN-toh-pus); genus name: Lat., from Gr. *mikros*, small, and *palame*, web, in reference to basal webbing between toes; species name: from Gr. *himanto*, thong, or strap, and *pous*, foot, in reference to long, leatherlike legs; *stilt*; with long legs. (Color ill., page 799.) Summers on tundra above northern limit of trees in w. Alaska, Canada; migrates north and south mainly between Mississippi R. and Rocky Mtns. in U.S.; rare in East in spring; in fall, an uncommon to common migrant along Atlantic coast; 7½–9 in. long; wingspread 15½–17 in.; sexes outwardly similar, but females average slightly larger; has somewhat long, slender, blackish bill, straight or *slightly downcurved* toward tip; long *green-yellow* legs; front toes webbed at base; in spring, has *rusty cheeks* and heavily *cross-barred underparts;* in fall, gray above, white below with faint breast markings (no cross-barring); and has clear white rump, wings without white stripe; resembles lesser yellowlegs, with which it often associates, but smaller; has *greenish*, not bright, yellow legs (in past called bastard yellowlegs and mongrel; however, Jehl, 1973a, believes it is most closely allied to the curlew sandpiper); in fall also resembles dowitchers: feeds with them, wades belly deep as they do, and often uses same rapid up-and-down movement of bill and head; however, whiter below, has shorter bill, longer legs (Peterson, 1947); flies in dense flocks, common flight call is much like whistled *whu* of lesser yellowlegs, with which it often associates, but lower-pitched and hoarser (Bent, 1927); rather unwary; once common along New England coast, where shot as a game bird, became scarce and irregular in New England early in 19th century (Forbush, 1912), seems to be increasing; in migration and at wintering places prefers sheltered, shallow, even stagnant inland and coastal pools, also muddy edges of channels in marshes, either fresh or brackish, and shallow coves of ponds and lakes; much less frequent at edges of broad open water or on beaches (Palmer, 1967); in spring, moves north through U.S. from Mar. into May, usually arrives on nesting grounds late May and early June; however, some remain on wintering range through the summer (Palmer, 1967).

Feeding Habits: Gathers in compact flocks to feed, bodies almost touching; often plunges head underwater to feed on bottom; eats worms, fly and mosquito larvae, small mollusks, seeds, roots, leaves of aquatic plants.

Nest: On tundra near marshes or shallow ponds or on higher, much drier slopes (see details in Jehl, 1973a); nest is dug about 4–5 in. across and an inch or so deep, and shaped by bird rotating its breast against soft terrain; no lining, mostly atop small hummocks of sedge or low, well-drained gravel ridges, usually fully exposed; male takes lead in nest-scraping but female determines which scrape will be used as nest; old pairs tend to re-use nest scrape of previous year (Jehl, 1973a).

Eggs: June; usually 4, pale green to olive green, heavily dotted with dark brown.

Incubation: Both sexes have incubation patches and incubate in turn, apparently male by day, female at night; period of 19½–21 days; chicks leave nest as soon as last one hatched dries; adults very protective of chicks, may make direct threat display toward human intruder; male remains with chicks until about 14 days old, when he deserts them; at that time, chicks very inconspicuous, fully independent, and can swim well; fly about 17–18 days after hatching (Jehl, 1973a).

Other Names: Bastard yellowlegs; frost snipe; long-legged sandpiper; mongrel.

Weights: On summer nest-range in Man., Canada, adult males (24), 48–60.8 gr., or about 1¾–2⅛ oz.; adult females (15), 52–68 gr., or about 1¾–2½ oz. (Jehl, 1973a); to 4 oz. when very fat (Palmer, 1967).

Range: Nests across N. America in tundra, from ne. Alaska to James Bay, and probably in n. Ont. south to continuous forest; winters from extreme s. U.S. (rarely) and south through C. America and S. America to Uruguay and c. Argentina (Palmer, 1967).

Sandpiper, upland, *Bartramia longicauda* (bar-TRAM-ih-ah lonj-ih-CAW-dah); genus name: in 1813 Alexander Wilson named this bird *Tringa bartramia,* for his friend William Bartram, an early American naturalist; however, the species name given by Wilson, *bartramia,* was later discarded because Dr. J. M. Bechstein (1757–1822), German forester and namer of birds, in 1812 had already published the prior species name of *longicauda* for this bird; in 1831, Lesson established a new genus name for it, *Bartramia,* thus perpetuating Wilson's wish to honor Bartram; species name: from Lat. *longus,* long, and *caudum,* tail. (Color ill., page 801.) The upland sandpiper, formerly called upland plover, is an inland and upland shorebird; in summer, in grassy country locally from Alaska south to Colo., Okla., and Va.; uncommon; 11–12½ in. long; wingspread 17–20 in.; sexes outwardly alike, about same size; larger than killdeer of comparable environments; brown, streaked plumage with no conspicuous marks, has small dovelike head, long neck, short, black-tipped yellow bill with long (for a shorebird) wedge-shaped tail bordered with white and finely barred with black; has conspicuous dark rump; eyes brown; legs green-yellow; unlike most other sandpipers, seldom seen near water; lives in hayfields,

meadows, rolling or hilly pastures of e. U.S., and on prairies of Midwest, where known as field plover, prairie dove, and affectionately, quaily, from one of its calls; on nesting grounds often flies slowly 15–20 ft. above ground, vibrating its wings and uttering liquid rolling trills or flutelike notes; if flushed from nest, utters *quitty-quit-it* or *quip-ip-ip* notes, flies close to ground with short rapid beats of downcurved wings, suggesting flight of a spotted sandpiper; often alights on fences, utility poles, rocks, or stumps to watch intruder; after alighting, for a few seconds holds wings high above back before folding them; on ground, movements are ploverlike; runs swiftly, then stops suddenly; in courtship flight, sings on spread wings as it circles high in sky, a melodious whistle that may carry almost a mile; first few notes like water gurgling from bottle, then a loud *whip-whee-ee-you,* somewhat like long-drawn, whistled cry of a hawk (Bent, 1929); in migration flight, usually in evening or at night at great height, flies swiftly and strongly (Bent, 1929); usually from one to four seen, rarely in large numbers in East; formerly enormously abundant in spring migration on prairies of Midwest and in e. U.S. as woodlands were cut off for farmland, then came great destruction by market hunters of upland sandpipers, beginning about 1880, when supply of passenger pigeons slaughtered by hunters for market began to decline (see Forbush, 1912, for details); has never regained its former numbers but showing signs of again adapting to nesting in open croplands, alfalfa fields, and even seen on airports in migration, along with killdeers and horned larks; leaves wintering grounds on S. American pampas in mid-Feb., reaches coast of Tex. and La. early in Mar.; main migration then directly north between Mississippi R. and Rockies; arrives on nesting grounds over most of U.S. and Canada in Apr. and May; on arrival on Gulf coast of La., reported to have commonly 20–30 snails of genus *Physa* under their wings, which they had transported from elsewhere—snails that "have a propensity for clinging to the feathers among which they are placed" (McAtee, 1914).

Feeding Habits: Almost half of food is grasshoppers, crickets, and weevils such as cotton-boll weevil, clover-leaf and clover-root weevils, also eats cowpea curculios, billbugs, leaf beetles, wireworms, click beetles, white grubs of May beetles, cutworms, army worms, cotton worms, sawfly larvae, crane-fly larvae, moths, ants, flies, centipedes, millipedes, spiders, snails, and earthworms; also eats waste grain, and seeds of foxtail grass, sandspurs, buttonweeds, etc. (Bent, 1929).

Nest: A grass-lined depression in ground, about 3 in. deep, among rank grasses, along sloughs of prairie, or in clearings of spruce-muskeg in North, less often in drier places (Palmer, 1967).

Eggs: May–June; usually 4, cream to pink-buff, speckled or spotted with red-brown.

Incubation: 21–24 days, by both sexes in turn; 22–27 days (Higgins and Kirsch, 1975); young first fly about 30–31 days after hatching.

Other Names: Bartramian sandpiper; Bartram's sandpiper (plover); field plover; grass

plover; highland plover; hill bird; papebotte; pasture-bird; pasture plover; prairie pigeon; prairie plover; prairie snipe; quaily; uplander; upland plover.

Age: One, banded, reported 5 years old.

Host to Cowbirds: Accidental (Friedmann, 1963); a single record, nest in Minn. contained four eggs of upland sandpiper, one of brown-headed cowbird.

Weights: W. U.S. (1), 141 gr. (Hughes, 1970), or about 5 oz.; 6–7 oz. (Forbush, 1925–29).

Range: Nests locally from s. Alaska, sw. Yuk., s. Mack., c. Sask., s. Man., c. Minn., s. Ont., c. Wisc., c. Mich., s. Que., c. Me., south to e. Wash., ne. Ore., Idaho, s. Mont., n. Utah, se. Wyo., c. Colo., N.D., nw. Okla., n.-c. Tex., c. Mo., s. Ill., s. Ind., s. Ohio, c. Tenn., n. and e. W.Va., c. Va., and Md., formerly farther south; winters from s. Brazil to s.-c. Argentina, occasionally to Chile.

Sandpiper, western, *Calidris mauri* (cal-ID-ris MOW-rye); genus name: *see* Dunlin; species name: given in 1838 by Charles Bonaparte for his friend Ernesto Mauri (see details in Palmer, 1931). (Color ills., page 800.) Larger than semipalmated sandpiper and is its western counterpart; sexes outwardly alike, females average slightly larger; 6–7 in. long; wingspread 12–14 in.; almost identical with semipalmated sandpiper, but *bill longer* (at least as long as head), *heavier at base,* and slightly downcurved (drooping) at tip; usually carries bill pointed more downward, even in flight (Palmer, 1967); in breeding plumage of spring, rustier on back and crown than semipalmated and more heavily streaked on breast, in fall with rust color in scapulars (Bent, 1927); many are quite pale-headed (Peterson, 1947); legs *black* (similar least sandpiper has green-yellow legs); in flight utters plaintive *cheerp, cher-eep,* or *kreep;* migrates mainly along Pacific coast, a few through interior, and common along Atlantic coast from Mass. south; spring migration, almost entirely coastal, usually third week of Apr. into June; some arrive Alaskan breeding grounds in late May.

Feeding Habits: About same as semipalmated sandpiper, but sometimes feeds with head immersed; on wettest mud snatches up invertebrates before buried from sight.

Nest: Sometimes in loose colonies, with one to two pairs on an acre (Holmes, 1972, 1973) in slight depression on ground, lined with grasses, leaves, on moist to dry tundra and mossy slopes of mountains, nest sometimes arched over by sedges, grasses, low heath plants.

Eggs: May; usually 4, cream to light brown, spotted and blotched with red-browns.

Incubation: By both sexes, 18–19 days; age when young first fly unknown (Palmer, 1967).

Flight Speed: Timed in Calif., 44 and 52 m.p.h. (McLean, 1930).

Weights: In fall migration, coastal N.J. (15), 19.4–33.1 gr. (Murray and Jehl, 1964), or about ¾–1 oz.; ⅘–1½ oz. (Palmer, 1967).

Range: Nests, as far as known, only on coasts of w. and n. Alaska from Nunivak Is. and Kashunuk R. to Seward Pen., and to Point Barrow; in summer, some non-breeders may remain south to Calif., Gulf coast of U.S., and to Panama; winters from coast of s. Alaska (rarely), and to Calif., also along Gulf coast and along Atlantic coast from N.C. (rarely from N.J.), south in Mexico along both coasts to Colombia, Ecuador, Peru, Venezuela, and in West Indies.

Sandpiper, white-rumped, *Calidris fuscicollis* (cal-ID-ris fuss-ih-COL-lis); genus name: *see* Dunlin; species name: from Lat. *fuscus*, brown, dark, and *collum*, neck. (Color ill., page 801.) Summers in Alaska and Arctic Canada; sexes outwardly alike; about 6½–8 in. long; wingspread 14–16½ in. (Forbush, 1925–29); bill straight, somewhat tapering; small streaked sandpiper; white rump stands out in flight (Peterson, 1947) and set off by very dark tail; only other short-legged sandpiper with white rump is rather rare curlew sandpiper, which is larger, has longer bill; white-rumped also has finely and sharply streaked head and breast; in spring, back appears striped and wings, when perched, extend well beyond tail; also in spring, crown and scapulars of white-rumped somewhat pink-buff; in fall, gray above (grayer than other small peeps), white below; larger than least or semipalmated; usually silent but utters short, sharp, finchlike note in flight, *tzeep*, *tzip*, or squeaky *jeet*; on nesting grounds, male in his courtship flights makes odd *quo-ick, quo-ick, quo-ick* sound, and a "typewriter-carriage" buzz (Sutton, 1932); migrates in spring north through interior plains and Prairie Provinces of N. America; in fall, south through interior but on broader front, east to n. Atlantic coast; a regular but never abundant migrant on coast of Mass.; starts north from S. American wintering grounds in early Mar., does not reach U.S. until May; arrives nesting grounds early June; one of long-distance migrants, from Canadian Arctic to Tierra del Fuego and Falkland Is. in S. Hemisphere, almost 8,000 mi. each way (Clement, 1960); like some other sandpipers, the white-rumped fly many thousands of miles (about 9,000 one way) during migration (*see* Migration); outside nesting season, seen in small groups to large flocks; in migration, feeds at low tide and prefers shallow, grassy pools, wet meadows, marshes, also mud flats, sandbars, beaches; during high tide, when flats covered, mixes with vast flocks of other shorebirds resting, sleeping, preening on upper beaches.

Feeding Habits: Often immerses entire head in water when feeding, also probes with bill in mud for food; eats marine worms *(Nereis)* that prey on oysters; also grasshoppers, clover-root curculio, snails, weed seeds (Bent, 1927).
Nest: A slight cup in grass or moss of tundra, often near water to quite distant from it on elevated dry ridges (Palmer, 1967).
Eggs: June; 4, buff-olive or pale green, heavily spotted and speckled with dark browns.
Incubation: By female; 22 days; young first fly 16–17 days after hatching. According to Sutton (1970), males are polygynous and the skin of the fore neck of courting males is thickened, flaccid, and highly vascularized in breeding season, though less so than that of pectoral sandpiper. Females nesting, when intruded upon,

scuttle through grass uttering mouselike squeaks as they shake all over, feigning injury.
Other Names: Bonaparte's sandpiper; bull peep; sand-bird; Schinz's sandpiper.
Age: One, banded Great Bend, Kans., killed when 5 years old (Kennard, 1975).
Flight Speed: Timed at 45 and 50 m.p.h. (McNeil, 1969, 1970).
Weights: 1¼–1¾ oz.
Range: Nests along coast of n. Alaska, n. Yuk., and on various islands, also on mainland of Canadian Arctic east to Baffin Is.; winters east of Andes in S. America from Paraguay to southwestern parts of Tierra del Fuego and Falkland Is.

Sandpiper, wood, *Tringa glareola* (TRING-gah glah-REE-oh-lah); genus name: *see* Greenshank; species name: Lat., dim. of *glarea*, gravel, apparently meaning "little gravel bird" (Macleod, 1954); *wood*, apparently from habit, like that of related N. American solitary sandpiper, of nesting within forested regions in tree nests of other birds, although it also nests on ground on tundra (see Jourdain, 1929d). Eurasian bird that has appeared occasionally in Alaska: on Sanak Is., Amchitka, Pribilofs; first breeding record for N. America, three downy chicks on Amchitka, July 2, 1969 (see details in White *et al.*, 1974); wanders to Hawaii, and has been reported from Barbados, West Indies (Palmer, 1967); 7½–8 in. long; wingspread to about 16 in.; in summer, dark brown above, peppered with white; head, neck, and breast streaked; has white eye stripe (very similar N. American solitary sandpiper has white eye-*ring*). See details in Peterson *et al.* (1954).

Weights: To 2½ oz. (Palmer, 1967).
Range: Nests on somewhat open ground near water in northern forested region and on tundra in northern half of Eurasia; winters from s. Asia, s. Europe, to s. Africa, Ceylon, Indonesia, to Australia; accidental in Alaska.

Snipe, black. *See* Sandpiper, solitary.

Snipe, bog. *See* Snipe, common.

Snipe, common, *Capella gallinago* (cap-ELL-ah gal-ih-NAY-go); genus name: dim. of Lat. *caper*, goat, or "little goat"; a she-goat (Jaeger, 1955); possibly in allusion to its goat-like bleating sounds during territorial flights (*see* below); species name: from Lat. *gallina*, a hen (Jaeger, 1955); together, genus and species names mean, literally, a "goatlike chicken" (Tuck, 1972). (Color ill., page 803.) Cosmopolitan; lives in both Old World and New World; in N. America, hunted in fall as a game bird; in summer nests in marshes and bogs from Alaska to N.J.; only snipe native to N. America; sexes outwardly similar, but females average heavier and with longer bill; 10½–11½ in. long; wingspread 17½–20 in.; closely related to woodcock and about same size, but less stocky, more streaked, and with longer bill; 14–16 tail feathers with rounded ends (Tuck, 1972); is generally brown with distinctly striped (lengthwise), not barred (across), head and back; is much more streaked than similar dowitchers; has long, straight, slender bill about 2½–2¾ in.

Wood sandpiper

SANDPIPER FAMILY

SANDPIPER FAMILY
The common snipe performs a territorial flight over its breeding and nesting grounds by diving through the air with tail feathers spread. Air causes the two distended outer tail feathers to vibrate, producing a hollow whistling sound that can be heard for a half mile.

long (eyes brown and somewhat like woodcock's, are set far back in head; can see both forward and in back); tail orange with black bars and white tip; streaked breast and barred flanks, whitish belly; takes off in rapid *zigzag* flight uttering harsh, nasal alarm note, *scaip*, as it rises from wet pastures and meadows, boggy edges of marshes and small streams; prefers wetter places than does woodcock (Tuck, 1972); in migration sometimes feeds in brackish and salt marshes; in territorial flights over nesting area (also, at times, even in migration and on wintering grounds) male spreads outer tail feathers in dives which produce weird *woo-woo-woo-woo* sounds (*see* Territorial Flight below); around nest utters loud, protesting, often repeated, whistled *wheat, wheat, wheat, wheat* or *whuck, whuck, whuck, whuck* (Bent, 1927); nesting pairs sometimes perch in trees or on fences and scold intruder (Rand, 1966); can swim and dive; uses both feet and wings underwater (*see* Swimming and Diving) to escape from enemies; is largely crepuscular in feeding, and groups, or flocks, fly high in close formation in fall; migration is mostly by night; start flying just before dusk and keep in touch in flight with low *scaip* notes; in spring, some migration northward from wintering grounds in Feb. and Mar.; many males are on their breeding ranges by Apr. and into May (Tuck, 1972); formerly extremely abundant in N. America, especially on wintering grounds in s. U.S., where slaughtered in late 19th century by market hunters: in La., one hunter during 20 years (1867–87) killed 69,087 snipe, or about 3,500 each winter; possibly more snipe have been killed in N. America than any other game bird (Bent, 1927; see also in Forbush, 1912), but days of slaughter are over, though still hunted each fall, with bag limit; many conservationists do not believe snipe (no longer abundant, common locally) should be a game species (Hall, 1960); see, however, Ch. 14 in Tuck (1972) for full discussion of influences on N. American snipe population.

Feeding Habits: Usually walks with bill directed slightly downward and gets most of food by plunging bill straight down into soft earth or mud; bill is rather soft and pliable but tip rather hard; searches for food underground with bill that is highly sensitive to touch; can raise an¹ curve upper mandible to seize earthworms and crane-fly larvae and pull them out of ground (Tuck, 1972); works food up length of bill with spines at base of tongue and backward-projecting serrations of inside of upper mandible until food passes into gullet (Rand, 1966); insects are about 50% of food, eats especially larvae of crane flies, midges, soldier flies, horseflies, flower flies, houseflies, mosquitoes, beetles, especially predacious diving beetles, water scavenger beetles, also water bugs; catches flying dragonflies and damselflies; eats crickets, locusts, larval Dobson flies, caterpillars, mayfly nymphs, crustaceans such as water fleas *(Daphnia)*, beach "fleas" *(Talitridae)*, crayfishes, fiddler crabs, mollusks (freshwater snails), earthworms; leeches, salamanders, frogs, lizards, spiders, centipedes, seeds of sedges, grasses, grit, etc. (Sperry,

1940); casts up in pellets indigestible parts of food; also drinks large amounts of water daily (Tuck, 1972).

Nest: Female selects nest site; makes several scrapes on ground, sometimes 4–5 before selecting one; site is usually fairly dry place even if surroundings wet, as in grassy meadows with alders, wet pastures, in high grass near sloughs, on hummocks of sedges in bogs, edges of tamarack-spruce swamps, muskegs, on mounds of sphagnum moss in willow swamps, or in dry places among dwarf birches; female crouches and turns in scrape to mold mosses and grasses to cup shape, adds grass or sedge lining.

Eggs: N. America, Apr.–July; usually 4, dark olive buff or pale olive, with spots, scrawls, and blotches of brown.

Incubation: By female, usually 18–20 days (Tuck, 1972); soon after hatching, when chicks are dry, both parents lead them from nest; attend chicks and brood them; each may care for part of the brood but tendency of female is to care for more chicks than male; adults flutter about like wounded birds if fox, man, or other enemy appears (*see* Distraction Display); chicks take food directly from parent's bill during first week after hatching or may pick up from ground where dropped in front of chick by adult; chick probes ground for food, and 10 days after hatching is probably self-sustaining; by that time, chick's bill may be half length of bill of adult (see Tuck, 1972, for other details); chicks fly some at 14–18 days old but sustained flight not until about 20 days old.

Territorial Flight: The bleating, winnowing, or whinnying of the common snipe is primarily a sexual display over the home, or nesting, range to warn other males against intruding into established male's territory, but is also directed toward female mate on ground, later toward the nest (Tuck, 1972); it is most frequent when bird is flying at 300–360 ft. above ground and may be performed by either sex during early part of breeding season or occasionally by both at once; sound reverberating over home bog or swamp can carry for half a mile; is produced by air vibrating the two outer tail feathers (one on each side of tail!), which are spread laterally; by diving, bird gains necessary speed (about 24–52 m.p.h.) to make outer tail feathers vibrate (Tuck, 1972); maximum bleating period over home nesting range is during twilight of either morning or evening; on clear moonlit nights at height of breeding season (Apr.–May) will bleat all through night; bleating may be suppressed by strong wind and rain, and in dense fog, performing snipe may drop immediately from sky to ground; also ceases to bleat at any unusual and loud sound—backfiring of a truck, whistle of train, for example—although snipe may stay in air and resume bleating when sound ceases.

Other Names: Alewife bird; American snipe; bleater (British Isles); bog snipe; English snipe; gutter snipe; jacksnipe; marsh snipe; meadow snipe; shad bird; shad spirit; Wilson's snipe.

Albinism: One pure-white one shot in a Toronto marsh, May 1884; only dark shades were a few dusky touches on scapulars, flanks, subterminal tail band; legs and bill yellow-flesh color (Seton, 1885); another, a partial albino, shot in Oct. 1894 in Nova Scotia (Piers, 1898); a melanistic one reported by Van Tyne (1945).

Age: About 1,000 banded in N. America (1924–58); of those recovered, most were on wintering grounds; oldest was 6 years.

Flight Speed: Up to 100 km. an hour (Tuck, 1972), or about 62 m.p.h.

Hybrids: In Europe, common snipe × great snipe, a possible natural hybrid reported in 19th century (Gray, 1958).

Weights: 3¼–6¼ oz. (Palmer, 1967).

Range: In N. America, nests from subarctic Alaska (just south of tundra) east across Canada to Labrador, south locally in Calif., Ariz., Colo., Neb., Iowa, n. Ill., Mich., Ohio, Pa., and N.J.; in W. Hemisphere, usually winters from southern part of breeding range south to Oreg., Utah, Colo., east through Neb. to w. Ky., n. Ala., Ga., Va., south to Colombia and Venezuela in S. America (Palmer, 1967); although a few winter near warm open springs north to Alaska and Newfoundland, most go far south of breeding range, especially in Gulf states in rice fields, sugarcane, wet pastures; in Old World nests south of tundra in Eurasia, including Iceland and Great Britain; winters in s.-c. Africa, s. India, Ceylon, c. Indonesia, Philippines, and Japan.

Snipe, crooked-bill. *See* Dunlin.

Snipe, double. *See* Snipe, great.

Snipe, English. *See* Snipe, common.

Snipe, jack-, European. See Jacksnipe, European.

Snipe, great, *Gallinago media* (gal-ih-NAY-go ME-dih-ah); genus name: from Lat. *gallina,* a hen; species name: Lat., medius, in the middle (in size). A migratory Eurasian species; one reported in Canada (Sperry, 1940), also one photographed in color at Cape May Point, N.J., Sept. 7, 1963; about 11 in. long, including bill about 2½ in. long; closely resembles the common snipe, but somewhat larger and heavier; bill much stouter at base and appears "heavy"; flanks more boldly or strikingly barred with black (it is distinguished on ground by its dark, more barred appearance); wing coverts have conspicuous white tips and the three outer tail feathers on each side of tail are white except for 2–3 dark bars (Palmer, 1967); normally has 16 tail feathers but occasionally 14–18; unlike common snipe, great snipe rises rather slowly and quietly when flushed, does not give the rasping *scaip* call of common snipe; also flies directly, not erratically, and usually low over ground (Tuck, 1972); on breeding grounds, male assembles with other males after sunset in an exposed arena, or "lek," and there copulates with any receptive female.

Feeding Habits: Eats largely earthworms and larvae of insects, especially crane flies; also small snails, slugs, some beetles, and caddis-fly larvae (Sperry, 1940).

Other Names: Double snipe (larger than jacksnipe); solitary snipe.

Hybrids: See under Common snipe.

Weights: In spring, 140–170 gr., or about 5–6 oz.; in fall, 153–225 gr., or about 5½–8 oz. (Tuck, 1972).

Range: Nests in forest and forest steppes of Europe and w. Siberia; eastern boundary of breeding range is Yenisei R.; also nests in Poland, n. Germany, Denmark, Finland, Sweden; winters most abundantly in se. and s. Africa, but also common in winter in Kenya and Tanganyika; also in small numbers in Sierra Leone and Nigeria (Tuck, 1972); accidental in Canada, N.J.

Snipe, half. *See* Jacksnipe, European.

Snipe, Irish. Another name for the American avocet in Avocet Family.

Snipe, jack-. *See* Jacksnipe, European; *also* Snipe, common.

Snipe, meadow. *See* Snipe, common, and Sandpiper, pectoral.

Snipe, red-bellied. *See* Dowitcher, long-billed.

Snipe, red-billed. Another name for the American oystercatcher in the Oystercatcher Family.

Snipe, red-breasted. *See* Dowitcher, short-billed.

Snipe, river. *See* Sandpiper, spotted.

Snipe, robin. *See* Knot, red, and Dowitcher, short-billed.

Snipe, rock. *See* Sandpiper, purple, and Tattler, wandering; *also* Surfbird.

Snipe, stone. *See* Yellowlegs, greater, and Yellowlegs, lesser.

Snipe, surf. *See* Sanderling.

Snipe, white. *See* Sanderling.

Snipe, Wilson's. *See* Snipe, common.

Snipe, wood. *See* Woodcock, American.

Stint, Eastern little. *See* Sandpiper, rufous-necked.

Stint, long-toed, *Calidris subminuta* (cal-ID-ris sub-min-YOU-tah); genus name: *see* Dunlin; species name: Lat., very small; *stint* is common name in British Isles for any of the smaller sandpipers. Asiatic species; one reported at Otter Is. (Pribilofs), June 1885, now considered rare migrant at Aleutian Is. and Bering Strait area (Kessel and Gibson, 1978); 6¼ in. long; resembles least sandpiper, which may be its closest relative; difficult to distinguish in field from rufous-necked sandpiper, but in hand can be told from all other peeps, or stints, by its longer toes, especially the middle and hind toes (Palmer, 1967).

Range: Nests within forest zone of w. Siberia, also on Bering, Komandorskie, Sakhalin, and Kurile Is.; winters e. India, Ceylon, coast of se. Asia, etc. (Palmer, 1967).

Stint, rufous-necked. *See* Sandpiper, rufous-necked.

Stint, Wilson's. *See* Sandpiper, least.

Surfbird, *Aphriza virgata* (ah-FREE-zah ver-GAY-tah); genus name: from Gr. *aphros,* froth, sea foam, meaning "to live, or I live, in sea foam"; species name: Lat., twiggy, made of twigs, and streaked (Jaeger, 1955), in allusion to heavily streaked back and breast in summer plumage; *surfbird,* because it feeds at surf line when on coast, unmindful of flying spray. (Color ills., page 802.) Nests in mountains of Alaska; in fall, winter, and into spring along rocky Pacific coast; 9–9½ in. long; wingspread to 20 in.; sexes outwardly similar; stocky; in winter, head, breast, and upperparts dark gray; short black bill *has yellow at base of lower mandible;* legs and *feet yellow;* surfbird might be mistaken at distance on coastal rocks for slightly smaller black turnstones, but in flight does not blossom suddenly into striking pattern of black and white; instead shows broad white stripe on wings and a *conspicuous white rump and tail with black triangle at tip,* and no white down middle of back as in black turnstone; also much less noisy but occasionally utters a plaintive *ke-week* or *kee-ah-wee;* wandering tattler of same habitat has dark rump and is without wing stripe; surfbird leaves extreme southern part of wintering range in S. America in early Mar.; arrives on Alaskan nesting grounds in May and June; because it winters along 12,000 mi. of Pacific coast—from Alaska to c. Chile; nesting grounds of this species remained a mystery well into the 20th century until O. J. Murie discovered a pair with a downy young one on a mountain slope above timberline in Mt. McKinley Park, c. Alaska, on July 13, 1921; on May 28, 1926, when George M. Wright almost stepped on a nest and eggs of a surfbird on a barren rocky ridge, 1,000 ft. above timberline in Mt. McKinley district, he became "the first white man, of which we have any record, to lay eyes on the nest and eggs of this . . . bird" (Dixon, 1927c).

Feeding Habits: In nesting season, runs rapidly about over mountain rocks, where picks up insects, which make up almost entire food: flies, beetles, caterpillars, wasps, bees, ants; also harvestmen (daddy longlegs), snails, seeds; at other seasons, when on rocky or stony shores, eats soft parts of barnacles and other crustaceans, and small mollusks (Bent, 1929).

Nest: In small depression of bare dry rock on ridge, lined with a few lichens and moss or dried bits of leaves.

Eggs: May–June; 4, buff, spotted with dark red-browns.

Incubation: Probably by both sexes (Jehl, 1968b); period of and age when young first fly unknown; both parents seen with brood (Palmer, 1967); like mountain plover, when either a man or a mountain sheep steps near nest, the incubating bird suddenly "explodes" from the nest directly into the man's or the sheep's face, causing intruder to recoil and step away from nest and momentarily threatened eggs. *See* Distraction Display.

Other Names: Plover-billed turnstone; rock plover; rock snipe.

Weights: 5–6½ oz. (Palmer, 1967).

Range: Nests high in mountains of s.-c. Alaska; has occurred in summer in w. Yuk. and in spring along coast of Tex.; winters from se. Alaska along Pacific coast south to Chile, casual to Straits of Magellan (Blake, 1977).

Tattler, Alaskan. *See* Tattler, wandering.

Tattler, Eurasian. *See* Tattler, Polynesian.

Tattler, gray-rumped. *See* Tattler, Polynesian.

Tattler, long-legged. *See* Yellowlegs, greater, and Yellowlegs, lesser.

Tattler, Polynesian, *Heteroscelus brevipes* (heh-teh-ROSS-keh-lus BREV-ih-peez); genus name: from Gr. *heteros*, other, different, and *skelos*, leg, alludes to legs of this species different from those of other sandpipers, in reference to the peculiar scutellation of the tarsus (the tarsus is scutellated instead of reticulated at the back—Bent, 1929)(*see* Tarsus); species name: from Lat. *brevis*, short, and *pes*, foot. Asiatic species that has wandered to St. Paul Is. (Pribilofs) and St. Lawrence Is., and northern Alaska; about 10 in. long; sexes outwardly alike, but females average larger; similar in appearance to slightly larger wandering tattler; however, differs from wandering tattler in being paler, shorter-legged, and rump barred with white; also has clear white belly and white undertail coverts in all plumages, whereas these parts in wandering tattler are barred in the breeding plumage; utters irregular "screech" different from call of wandering tattler (Bent, 1929).

Feeding Habits: Feeds very close to sea on rocky shores, probably eats food similar to that of wandering tattler.

Nest: Two nests known in alpine environment: one on ground, one bird laid its eggs in thrush nest in tree.

Eggs: 4.

Other Names: Eurasian tattler; gray-rumped sandpiper; gray-rumped tattler.

Weights: 2½–4¾ oz.

Range: Probably nests in mountains of e. Siberia (see details in Dement'ev *et al.*, 1969); winters from Malay Pen. and Philippines south to Indonesia and Australia.

Tattler, wandering, *Heteroscelus incana* (heh-teh-ROSS-keh-lus in-CANE-ah); genus name: *see* Tattler, Polynesian; species name: Lat., gray; *wandering*, from its famed habit of wandering. (Color ills., page 803.) In summer, in nw. Canada and in Alaska; winters along Pacific coast of N. America and south to Equator; has wandered to Japan, Australia, and New Zealand; 10–10½ in. long; sexes outwardly much alike, but females average larger; somewhat larger and heavier bird than the Polyne-

sian tattler; in winter, very dark, solid gray above; medium gray to white below; has white line over each eye; legs yellow; can be distinguished in flight from three other associates on rocky Pacific shores—black turnstone, surfbird, and spotted sandpiper—by lack of black-and-white pattern (back and wings dark, unmarked); if approached too closely, utters loud, piercing *deedle-deedle-dee* like lesser yellowlegs or *weet, weet, weet* similar to spotted sandpiper's call; flies short distance, then alights on rocks and sometimes bobs and teeters head and body somewhat like spotted sandpiper; also utters a clear, flutelike, quavering *tew, tew, tew,* somewhat like call of greater yellowlegs; blackish bill is longer than that of spotted sandpiper, and underparts, from breast to tail, *heavily barred* during nesting season; can swim but toes not webbed; does not associate closely with other shorebirds and quite noisy in groups of own kind—nesting habits were unknown until early in 20th century; adults with young had been seen in different parts of interior Alaska, its probable breeding grounds; however, first nest and eggs not discovered until summer of 1912, when found on a gravel bar of small stream in Yuk. about 25 mi. south of Arctic O. (Bent, 1929); 10 years later, in summer 1922, a second nest and eggs were discovered at 4,000 ft. elevation in Mt. McKinley National Park (see Murie, 1924); it was later determined to be a common nesting bird in the park, where it lives about seepage meadows and glacial streams above timberline (Hall, 1960); migrates northward from wintering places, Mar. into May, along Pacific coast and from Hawaiian Is.

Feeding Habits: On nesting grounds feeds along gravelly and rocky beds of mountain streams, at edges or wades in shallows, and submerges bill or entire head in search of caddis-fly larvae; also eats crane flies, beetles, amphipods, and mollusks; in migration and in winter, usually alone or two or three together, along rocky shores, eats mollusks, marine worms, etc. (Bent, 1929).

Nest: In hollow in rocky or gravelly place on ground in dry bed of mountain stream, a slight to firm structure of rootlets, twigs, and leaves.

Eggs: May–June; 4, shades of green, heavily spotted or blotched with browns.

Incubation: By both sexes; 23–25 days; both parents tend brood; chicks can swim well; age when young first fly unreported (Palmer, 1967).

Other Names: Alaskan tattler; rock snipe.

Weights: One, Pacific coast, 146 gr. (Hughes, 1970), or about 5 oz.

Range: Nests in mountains above timberline in Alaska from Mt. McKinley National Park south to Prince William Sound (Seaman, 1959, reported discovery of this species nesting in summers of 1956, 1957, 1958, in new area of Alaska on treeless tundra along Eagle Creek, ne. of Fairbanks); it also nests in nw. B.C. and Yuk.; also in the Anadyr range of ne. Siberia; winters along Pacific coast (one reported Salton Sea, Calif., Aug. 12, 1971, was fourth record for this inland locality—McCaskie, 1971) and islands from s. Calif. (rarely from Ore. and Wash.) south to Galápagos Is., Colombia, Ecuador, also from Hawaiian Is. to the Marianas and Philippines south to Fiji Is., Samoa, Society Is.,

and the Tuamotu Archipelago; migrates mostly over water.

Turnstone, black, *Arenaria melanocephala* (are-eh-NAY-rih-ah mel-ah-no-SEFF-ah-lah); genus name: Lat., pertaining to a sandy place (habitat); species name: from Gr. *melas*, black, and *kephale*, head; *turnstone*, from well-known habit of these birds and ruddy turnstone of turning over, with short, stout bill, stones, shells, clods of earth, seaweed, and other objects in their search for food (Bent, 1929). (Color ill., page 803.) Nests in Alaska and winters along Pacific coast south to Mexico; is commoner on Pacific coast than ruddy turnstone; about 9 in. long; sexes outwardly similar; a plump, dark shorebird, dark upperparts and breast but with white belly; in spring, has white round spot in front of eyes; bill black, legs dusky; in flight, shows striking black-and-white (pied) pattern; is a characteristic winter bird of Pacific coast on barnacle-covered reefs and rocky shores; as common on outlying islands and ledges as on mainland, seldom seen feeding on sands as do ruddy turnstones (Bent, 1929); occasionally seen on muddy shores of bays; on nesting grounds utters fine *peet-weet-weet* similar to call of spotted sandpiper; feeding groups utter subdued chatter; voice or call is like that of ruddy turnstone but higher-pitched, very noisy on nesting grounds, where scolds intruder; starts northward migration along Calif. coast early in Apr.; much of flight is over ocean; arrives Alaskan nesting grounds usually in May.

Feeding Habits: Lives at water's edge along coast, where picks up barnacles, slugs, small mollusks, crustaceans from wet rocks or crevices, also with bill turns over seaweeds for small marine animals; also known to eat berries (Bent, 1929).

Nest: Adults hollow out a depression in dead, flat grass near edge of lowland brackish pond near shore, add little or no lining.

Eggs: May; 4, olive-yellow, spotted or blotched with browns.

Incubation: Apparently by both sexes, as both have incubation patches; 21 days, age when young first fly unreported.

Other Name: Rock plover.

Weights: One, Pacific coast, 118 gr. (Hughes, 1970), or about 4 oz.

Range: Nests on coast and on nearby islands in Alaska from Seward Pen. to Sitka district; on Kodiak Is., and has been reported (not nesting) on St. Lawrence Is.; reported in summer from B.C. to n. Baja Calif.; winters from se. Alaska along coast south to Baja Calif., in c. Sonora, Mexico; also seen in summer throughout most of wintering range; has wandered inland to Watson Lake, Yuk.; the Atlin region and Nulki Lake, B.C.; Washington County, Ore.; Salton Sea and Needles, Calif.; also in Mont.

Turnstone, ruddy, *Arenaria interpres* (are-eh-NAY-rih-ah in-TER-pres); genus name: *see* Turnstone, black; species name: an interpreter, explainer, go-between (Jaeger, 1955); Gruson (1972) suggests this is in reference to its alarm cry, which warns other birds of danger. (Color ill., page 803.) Nests in Arctic Canada, Greenland, n. Alaska, also in n. Europe, n. Siberia; in N. America, winters along Pacific, Atlantic, and Gulf coasts of U.S.; 7¾–9¼ in. long; wingspread to 17½ in.; sexes outwardly similar, but some females larger; a chunky, squat, orange-legged, ploverlike bird; in breeding plumage with harlequin color pattern of bold black, white, and rust-red markings that show strikingly in flight; bill dark, short, pointed, slightly upturned at tip; in fall, immatures and adults are subdued in color but have recognizable brown breast bib pattern, rest of underparts white; in migration, travel in large flocks and quite high, but feed usually in small numbers, often singly, among mixed flocks of other shorebirds along stony, rocky, or sandy beaches; fly strongly, swiftly, and usually directly; flight note is a three-syllable *ket-ah-kek* or *kit-it-it* and a single sharp *kewk*, also a rarer, ploverlike whistled *kee-oo;* migrates northward mostly in May along Atlantic coast, in Great Lakes region and along Pacific coast; rare in Mississippi Valley and rest of interior U.S.; arrives on breeding grounds early in June.

Feeding Habits: Besides using bill to lift stones and other objects in search of food, sometimes roots like a pig in windrows of seaweed and other rubbish cast up on rocks or beach, where it catches and eats sand "fleas" (amphipods), worms, insects and their larvae; digs holes with bill (or by scratching) in wet sand to turn up eggs of horseshoe crabs, also small black snails and other mollusks; feeds on white grubs of flesh flies from carcasses of slain seals in North (see Lancaster and Johnson, 1973; also Thompson, 1973); eats soft parts of barnacles, chases and eats small fiddler crabs along muddy banks of tidal creeks; sometimes resorts to marshes to eat grasshoppers; also eats berries; eats eggs of sooty terns on Laysan Is. (Bent, 1929) and Dry Tortugas (Parkes *et al.,* 1971) and those of common terns in L.I., N.Y.; on Fla. Keys gleans crumbs from picnic tables and ground or eats chunks of bread on beaches; has even taken bread from a person's hand (Palmer, 1967).

Nest: A depression in tundra beside rock, clump of plants, or in niche, lined with some fragments of dry plants.

Eggs: Usually in June; 4, green-olive, heavily marked with black spots.

Incubation: By both sexes, 21½–22 days (Ellesmere Is.); both adults feed brood; young fly 24–26 days after hatching (Palmer, 1967).

Other Names: Bishop plover; brant-bird; beadbird; calico bird; calico jacket; checkered snipe; chicken; chicken plover; chuckatuck (from call); common turnstone; creddock (from call); horsefoot snipe; jinny; king-crab bird; red-legged plover; red-legs; rock-bird; rock plover; sand runner; sea dotterel; sea quail; sparked-back; stone-pecker; streaked-back.

Accidents: Individuals sometimes fly into utility wires and break wings.

Age: One, banded in Norway, 9½ years old (Holgersen, 1957); one, banded, recaptured, and released near Tokyo, Japan, was at least 9 years old (Thompson, 1973); one died in London Zoo at least 13 years old (Olney, 1972).

Flight Speed: Timed in Fla., 27 m.p.h. (Longstreet, 1930); in N.C., 33 m.p.h. (Cooke, 1937a); 35 and 40 m.p.h. (McNeil, 1969; 1970); a remarkable record of one banded St. George Is., Pribilofs, that flew to French Frigate Shoals, Hawaiian chain, 2,272 mi. in 3½ days, or calculated flight of 649 miles a day (Lancaster and Johnson, 1973); great concentrations, in fall migration, on St. Paul and St. George Is. in Pribilofs before moving on to wintering grounds in c. and sw. Pacific O. (see maps of route in Thompson, 1973).

Weights: In fall, coastal N.J. (1), 107 gr. (Murray and Jehl, 1964), or about 3¾ oz.; in summer, Manomet, Mass. (2), 100.4 and 124 gr. (Fisk, 1971b), or about 3½ oz. and 4⅓ oz.; to 4½ oz. (Palmer, 1967); in fall, on Pribilofs, 85–195 gr. (Thompson, 1973).

Range: Nests on continents and islands of Arctic, northwestern limits in Greenland (about 84° N. Lat.), from Bristol Bay, Alaska, St. Lawrence Is., and Yukon delta, and in Canadian Arctic to Southampton Is., and in Europe and Asia, e. coast of Scandinavia and e. Siberia on shores of Anadyr Gulf; winters mainly on coasts and islands in N. America, from Calif. south to Galápagos Is. and Chile, and along Atlantic coast from N.J. south to Fla. and along Gulf coast, south to s. Argentina, casual to Tierra del Fuego; in Old World from Britain, Mediterranean, and coasts of w. Asia and Hawaii south to s. Africa, s. India, Indonesia, Australia, New Zealand, and Oceania. See also wintering grounds from banding returns of Max Thompson in Lancaster and Johnson (1973); see also Thompson (1973).

Whimbrel, *Numenius phaeopus* (new-MEAN-ih-us FEE-oh-pus); genus name: *see* Curlew, bristle-thighed; species name: from Gr. *phaios,* gray, and *pous,* foot, gray-foot; *whimbrel,* so named in England from uttered note which sounded like *whim,* to which the suffix added for diminutive (see Newton, 1893–96). (Color ill., page 804.) Circumpolar, nests in Eurasia and in Alaska and Canada; in migration fairly common along Pacific and Atlantic coasts; rare migrant in interior U.S.; 15½–18¾ in. long, including 3–4-in.-long bill; wingspread 31–33 in.; sexes outwardly alike, but females slightly larger; a medium-sized curlew (for comparison with other curlews, *see* Curlew, Eskimo), the whimbrel is noticeably smaller than the long-billed curlew, with shorter bill; also has dark line through eyes and a distinctly striped black-and-white crown; has paler underparts and back is grayer; in flight, like ducks and geese, fly high in migration in V-shaped flocks or in long irregular lines with long bills extended, legs trailing behind, each calls to companions in long, rolling tremolo notes, *krek, krek, krek, krek, kew, kew, kew, kew, whi, whi, whi, whi,* or the long-drawn curlew cry, *kur-leeou! kur-leeou!* (see Bent, 1929; Peterson, 1947; Hall, 1960); whimbrel was not slaughtered as much for market in 19th century as Eskimo curlew; in fall mostly over water off Atlantic coast; also was wild and wary and difficult for hunters to stalk (see in Bent, 1929) but not so wary now; in migration along seacoasts, commonly seen in its stopovers on land feeding on tidal flats at low water; at high tide retires sometimes to wide salt marshes to feed and rest; sometimes frequents beach grass near sandy shores, especially feeds around estuaries and tidal creeks, also inland in flooded fields, edges of shallow lakes, river bars; roosts in flocks on islands in marshes or on sandbars; migrates northward along Pacific coast in Mar.; reaches Alaska about mid-May; migrates in Mar. from Fla. along Atlantic coast; reaches Mass. by mid-May.

Feeding Habits: On beaches and sand flats picks up in bill insects, worms, spiders, small mollusks, and crustaceans, often probes for sand "fleas" (amphipods) in wet sand, and on mud flats catches fiddler crabs; also eats crowberries in Arctic and other wild berries.

Nest: A saucer-shaped depression in top of a low hummock of mosses or grasses on tundra.

Eggs: Usually June–July; 3–5, commonly 4, olive, spotted with browns, lavender.

Incubation: 22–23½ days (Jehl and Hussell, 1966), by both sexes; young first fly about 30 days after hatching (Palmer, 1967).

Other Names: American whimbrel; blue-legs; crooked-bill marlin; foolish curlew; Hudsonian curlew; jack; jack curlew; short-billed curlew; striped-head.

Age: Female (adult), banded Ft. Churchill, Man., recaptured there when at least 11 years old.

Flight Speed: Timed in Fla., 34 m.p.h. (Longstreet, 1930).

Weights: To about 1¼ lbs. (Palmer, 1967).

Range: In New World, nests from w. and n. Alaska east along Arctic coast to nw. Mack., south to Mt. McKinley National Park, sw. Yuk., and along western side of Hudson Bay to nw. James Bay; non-breeding birds in summer on coasts of Calif., and N.J. south to S.C.; winters locally on Pacific coast from c. Calif. south to Galápagos Is. and s. Chile, rarely on coasts of Tex., La., S.C.; also winters on Caribbean coast of Colombia and Venezuela to Brazil and s. Argentina; in Old World, nests from Iceland, Faeroes, n. Scandinavia, n. Russia, nw. Siberia inland to ne. Siberia and locally in Scotland; winters from British Isles, Mediterranean region, s. Philippines, Marianas Is., south to s. Africa, Madagascar, Mascarene Is., Ceylon, to Australia, New Zealand, Fiji, and Caroline Is.

Willet, *Catoptrophorus semipalmatus* (cat-op-TROW-for-us sem-ih-pal-MAY-tus); genus name: from Gr. *katoptron,* mirror, and *phoros,* bearing, in reference to striking white pattern in wings; species name: Lat., half-webbed, in reference to toes; *willet,* from its cry. (Color ill., page 805.) Nests along Atlantic coast and interior Great Plains of w. U.S. and in c. Prairie Provinces of Canada; 14–16¼ in. long, including 2–2¾-in.-long bill; wingspread 24–31 in.; sexes outwardly similar, but females larger; gray above, white below; lightly barred on flanks; at rest, appears uniformly gray, but in flight *flashing black-and-white wings and white tail* are distinctive; heavy bluish bill, somewhat compressed laterally; legs bluish (similar greater yellowlegs has yellow legs); flight strong and direct, occasionally sets wings and scales downward; in nesting territory, often hovers on quivering wings; not especially

Willet (winter)

SANDPIPER FAMILY

shy and very noisy at nesting time; often perches on bushes, trees, fences, posts, and buildings to watch intruder and to scold with loud cries (is one of the "tattlers"); mated pair call *kuk, kuk, kuk, wek, wek, wek,* or *kip, kip, kip,* occasionally utter melodic whistled *pill-will-will* or *pill-will-willet* and *pill-o-will-o-willet;* bobs head when walking and, when standing, more moderately and less frequently than yellowlegs; a habitual wader, often to belly; swims readily; when migrating above ocean probably alights occasionally on water (Bent, 1929); male in ceremony at nest bows low before female before exchanging places with her on nest (see Vogt, 1938, for discussion of courtship and ceremonial flashing of white in wings); as result of market hunting in late 19th and early 20th century, willet almost disappeared north of Va. along Atlantic coast (Forbush, 1912); within recent years have made comeback, in some places into former range; with protection and unmolested nesting have increased and have spread into new territory; in June 1966, three pairs nested on salt-marsh island near Jones Beach, N.Y., for first records of breeding in N.Y. (Davis, 1968a); pair nested in York County, Me., summer 1971, for first nesting of this species in New England in about a century (Finch, 1971c); willets that nest north of their wintering range start moving north along Atlantic coast in Mar., reach Mass. by May; inland nesting population of interior of Ore., Idaho, and Canada usually move north through Mississippi Valley and interior valleys of Calif. in Apr.; most are on nesting grounds by May 1 (Bent, 1929); in fall, some of this western population moves west or southwest to Pacific coast, some east or southeast to Atlantic coast and winter along s. Atlantic and Gulf coasts with willets of eastern population; willets that nest in Nova Scotia apparently migrate largely over Atlantic O. to West Indies (Bent, 1929).

Feeding Habits: Feeds in salt and brackish marshes or on saline flats; on broad mud flats or sand flats in the bayous, bays, and estuaries on coast; also along muddy banks of creeks and ditches or about pond holes in salt marshes; common on rocky shores on West Coast; rises with loud outcry if disturbed; probes with bill or snatches food from ground—aquatic insects, marine worms, small crabs such as fiddlers and hippa crabs, small mollusks, and small fishes; also eats some grasses, tender shoots, seeds, and even cultivated rice (Bent, 1929); see also Stenzel *et al.* (1976).

Nest: Semi-colonial; along seacoasts prefers nesting on sandy offshore islands with tall, thick grasses, and on upper coastal beaches and along edges of dunes, under shrubs in brushy land near inland edges of salt marshes, or on banks of ditches and other high dry places in marsh; in w. U.S., nests on open prairies, sometimes far from water; or in short marsh grass, on alkali flats near water runways or on grassy dikes, some on flooded mountain meadows; on ground and varies from eggs laid in slight depression to deep hollows in sand, hidden in grass, to thick cup of weeds and grasses on open sand far from grass or bushes (Bent, 1929).

Eggs: Apr.–May; 4, olive, boldly spotted, blotched with browns.
Incubation: By female, possibly by male at night (Palmer, 1967), 22 days; age when young first fly unknown; *see also* Birds That Carry Their Young under Young and Their Care).
Other Names: Bill-willie; duck snipe; eastern willet; humility; pied-wing curlew; pill-willet; pill-will-willet; semipalmated snipe; Spanish plover; stone curlew; western willet; white-winged curlew; will-willet.
Albinism: A partial albino (nearly white, with traces of normal color pattern on back and wings; bill flesh color at base, dark at tip) reported May 1956 at Mecox, Long Is., N.Y., was accompanied by two normally colored willets; a completely white-plumaged male, mated with a normally plumaged female, was photographed in marsh near Brigantine, N.J., June 29, 1970 (Anonymous, 1970d); a partial albino chick at Fortesque, N.J., June 29, 1930 (Stone, 1937).
Flight Speed: Timed in Fla., 27 m.p.h. (Longstreet, 1930); in w. U.S., 35–40 m.p.h., and small flocks (3–12 birds) at 45–47 m.p.h. (Cottam *et al.,* 1942b).
Weights: One, Pacific coast, 270 gr. (Hughes, 1970), or about 9½ oz.; 7–16 oz. (Forbush, 1925–29); 6¼–12 oz. (Palmer, 1967).
Range: Nests from e. Ore., Idaho, c. Alta., c. Sask., s. Man., south to ne. Calif., Nev., n. Utah, n. Colo., and e. S.D.; Nova Scotia, south locally along Atlantic and Gulf coasts (recently in Me. and Long Is., N.Y.) and from N.J. to Fla., s. Tex., and locally in West Indies to St. Croix Is., and in Tamaulipas, Mexico; winters along coast from n. Calif. to Gulf of Mexico, and from Carolinas along n. coast of S. America, rarely to Brazil and Peru.

Woodcock, American, *Philohela minor* (fil-OH-he-lah MY-nor); genus name: from Gr. *philos,* loving, and *helos, helios,* marsh, or swamp, in reference to its habitat; species name: Lat., smaller, lesser, compared with larger European woodcock; *woodcock,* from habitat. (Color ill., page 804.) A shorebird that "has forsaken its ancestral haunts of mud flats and marshes for the uplands" (Sheldon, 1971); migratory game bird hunted in fall in all states east of Mississippi R., also in Minn., Mo., Kans., Okla., Tex., La., and Ark., estimated about 1 million killed each year by hunters, mostly in ne. U.S. (Anonymous, 1970e; see also in Sheldon, 1971; Clark, 1972); nests over almost entire e. N. America, from s. Canada south to Fla., and from Atlantic O. to line running approximately north-south from Minn. to e. Tex.; however, most of nesting is in northern part of range in n. U.S., in young forests with some scattered openings and on poorly drained land (Sheldon, 1971); 10½–11½ in. long; wingspread to 18 in.; sexes outwardly similar, but females average larger; chunky, with short neck, short legs, very long, tapered, flesh-colored bill (about 2¾ in. long in female; 2½ in. in male); squatted on ground, has dead-leaf pattern of variegated browns, black, gray above, and rusty below, very difficult to see; tail quite short; large head across rear of crown has three wide dark bands, separated by narrow rufous bands; large dark eyes set far back and high in head; broad, rounded wings (the three outer primaries of each are stiffened and modified with narrow vanes which produce twittering whistle when bird is startled into vigorous flight); seldom seen by day, is usually flushed from almost underfoot in wet swamp or thicket; flutters up through trees in weak, irregular or zigzag flight; when clear of obstacles, flies more swiftly and directly (Bent, 1927); is crepuscular; active mostly from dusk to dark, toward dawn, on moonlit nights, and somewhat on cloudy days; lives where soil is moist and can find earthworms in damp woods or in alder thickets with nearby clearings; in rich bottomlands, scrubby hollows overgrown with willows, maples, sumacs, along banks of meandering streams or spring-fed boggy runs, edges of dry second-growth woods mixed with birches; very rarely in old mature forest; in spring, summer, and fall, at dusk flies or walks from woods or brush cover out into open fields or clearings (Krohn, 1971), either to feed or for male to perform spectacular courtship flight to advertise his presence to females (Sheldon, 1971); male begins his flights even on wintering grounds in La. in late Jan., continues them on "singing sites" or "breeding fields" (each male may be strongly attached to his specific field) on nesting range throughout spring and summer; leaps from ground, rises in widening circles on whistling wings to about 300 ft.; hovers momentarily as he pours out song—a series of liquid chirps—then drops, still chirping, in series of sideslips, upswoops, like falling leaf as he zigzags to ground; after alighting, utters intermittent, nasal *peent* similar to note of nighthawk; when he alights, walks stiff-legged to female waiting on ground and they copulate (Sheldon, 1971); males are believed to be polygynous (Pettingill, 1936; Norris *et al.*, 1940); or at least promiscuous (Sheldon, 1971); one of earliest migrants, woodcock starts north in spring from wintering grounds in se. U.S.—Fla. to e. Tex.—in Jan.–Feb.; probably spends 4–6 weeks on northward journey, following a zone in which ground has recently thawed and main food (earthworms) is thus available; migrates in heavy flights in Mar.–Apr., when most arrive on northern breeding grounds (Sheldon, 1971); in fall seen moving at treetop level at dusk and into night in loose groups or small flocks of 4–10 or 30–50 birds—sometimes several hundreds to thousands in one flock; in migration some may appear in such unexpected places as city parks, yards, gardens, orchards, and even on lawns.

Feeding Habits: Feeds mostly at dusk, early morning, sometimes during day; may plunge bill, which has upper mandible flexible, to full length into soil to probe with highly sensitive mobile tip, with which it apparently *feels* for earthworms (*see,* however, Smell); can open tip of bill below surface to seize its prey (*see* comparable bill and feeding method in biography of common snipe); is voracious feeder known to eat its weight or more in earthworms within 24 hours (Bent, 1927; Sheldon, 1971); its presence revealed by its numerous borings, often close together, in ground; reported to stamp foot on earth with quick sharp blows, apparently to stir earthworm into movement before plunging bill

into ground; Sperry (1940) discovered that 90% of American woodcock's food is animal life, of which 75% is earthworms (*see* Earthworms and Birds); during dry spells turns over leaves with bill and picks up slugs, sow bugs, insects and their larvae; known to eat grasshoppers and to pick up ants from ground or rocks; also eats larvae of crane flies, snipe flies, horseflies, and long-legged flies that live in moist ground; eats cutworms, crickets, locusts, millipedes, centipedes, spiders, occasionally salamanders, frogs, small land snails, and seeds of sedges, violets, alder, blackberries, and weed and grass seeds (Sperry, 1940); captive woodcocks frequently drink water and appear to suck it up in bill (Sheldon, 1971). For instructions in care and feeding of captive woodcocks, see Stickel *et al.* (1965); also Wallace (1972).

Nest: A mere hollow or cuplike depression in ground, lined with dead leaves and a few twigs around rim; usually within 100–150 yds. of a male's occupied "singing field" (Sheldon, 1971); may be in open rocky hollow near swampy ravine, but usually in alder and swamp woods, brushy corners of pastures, or in underbrush or tall weeds along edges of woods; nest is often at foot of small tree or bush or beside log or stump or under fallen brush; usually many dead leaves around nest on which bird depends for its background concealment (*see* Cryptic, or Concealing, Colors under Colors of Feathers).

Eggs: Jan.–Feb. in extreme southern part of range; elsewhere, usually laid Mar.–May; usually 4, buffy or cinnamon, somewhat evenly spotted with browns, grays, purple; remarkably large for small bird; each about size and weight of egg of much larger ruffed grouse; one woodcock reported to move her eggs on disturbance to new location 8 ft. away (see Bent, 1927). *See* discussion of egg moving under Eggs and Egg-laying.

Incubation: By female, 20–21 days (Bent, 1927); may incubate so closely when eggs near hatching that she can be stroked on nest; when flushed from nest while chicks hatching or recently hatched, flies off with tail depressed, legs dangling, alights nearby to feign injury on ground until she leads intruder about 100 yds. away, when she flies up into air, circles, and returns to her brood; Sheldon (1971) reports care is by female, and young that may be weak when first hatched are brooded by her for first day or two, after which she may lead chicks about 100 yds. away from nest; if young too feeble to run from presence of human intruder, female reported to fly off with young, one at a time, clasped between her legs or thighs, to place of safety; see detailed accounts in Bent (1927) and others by reliable observers, such as Grinnell (1922); Schorger (1929); Preble (1927); also Sheldon's discussion of it (1971); some believe action is accidental (Reilly, 1968); young first fly 14 days after hatching; when almost full-grown, at 28 days, can fly strongly (Pettingill, 1936); Sheldon (1971) suggests that young, after they have resorbed egg yolk during first few days after hatching, feed themselves by probing for worms just as adults do (see Brown, 1954) and that most broods break up and each young goes its separate way about 42–56 days after hatching; apparently only one brood a year, although if first nest broken up

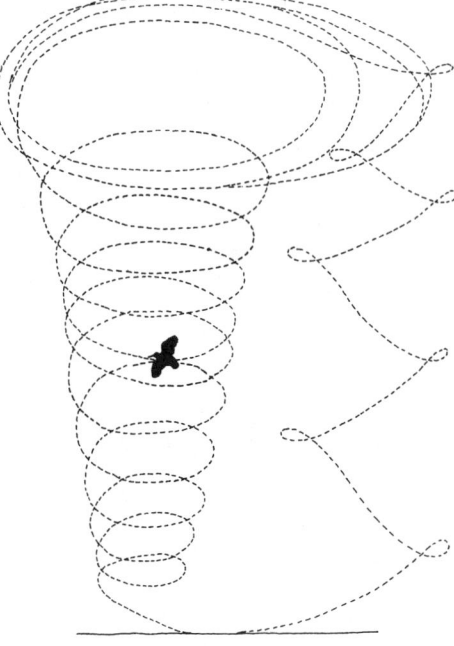

SANDPIPER FAMILY
The woodcock begins his courtship flight by leaping from the ground and ascending in a widening spiral to about 300 feet, where he circles while singing and then begins his descent, zigzagging like a falling leaf.

will re-nest; both sexes breed in their first spring on breeding grounds when 10–12 months old (Sheldon, 1971).

Other Names: Becasse (bay-CASS—local, in La., from Fr. *bécassine,* a snipe); big-eyes; big-headed snipe; big mud snipe; blind snipe; bog-bird; bog-borer; bogsucker; hookum-pake; Labrador twister; night partridge; night peck; pewee; siphon snipe; timber-doodle; whistler; whistling snipe; wood hen; wood snipe.

Accidents: In night migration, flying low, killed striking utility wires, lighthouses, TV towers, buildings, and other structures; also struck by automobiles when birds fly low across highway; thousands perish on wintering grounds, and in migration, in some years during long spells of cold and freezing weather when unable to find food; also threatened on breeding and wintering grounds by hydrocarbon pesticides sprayed for insect control (see details in Sheldon, 1971).

Age: Record of one banded American woodcock that lived to be 8 years old (Wilcox, 1959); Sheldon (1971) reported three males still alive at 5 years old, one 6 years, another 7 years; adult females, on average, live longer than males but not subjected to as many hazards (see in Sheldon, 1971); a banded female found dead on highway at Rocky Mt., N.C., when 8 years, 6 months, old (Kennard, 1975).

Flight Speed: Timed in New England, 5 m.p.h. (White, 1933); 13 m.p.h. (Wood, 1933); in Tex., 35 m.p.h. (Baker and Newman, 1942).

Weights: Females are consistently heavier than males—males average 6.2 oz., with heaviest 7.2 oz.; females average 7.7 oz., heaviest to 9.8 oz. (Martin and Nelson, 1952); see also Sheldon (1971) for details of weights.

Range: Nests from se. Man., w. and c. Ont., s. Que., n. N.B., Prince Edward Is., Nova Scotia, and s. Newfoundland west to c. Minn., c. Iowa, w.-c. Mo., Ark., e. Tex. (rarely), and south to La., Miss., s.-c. Ala., Ga., c. Fla. (sparingly); winters mainly in se. Ark., La., and sw. Miss., in lesser numbers from e. Okla., s. Mo., sw. Tenn., n. Miss., n. Ala., w. S.C., w.-c. N.C., se. and w. Va., south to e. Tex., and se. La., and s. Miss., s. Ala., and s. Fla., rarely north to c. Mo. and s. Ill., s. Ind., s. Ohio, w. W.Va., and to N.J., occasionally in more northern parts of nesting range; has strayed to Colo., Mont., and Bermuda.

Woodcock, European or Eurasian, *Scolopax rusticola* (SKOL-oh-pax rus-TIH-co-lah); genus name: *see* family introduction; species name: incorrect spelling of Lat. *rusticula,* country, rural, "little countryman" (Coues, 1884). Straggler to N. America; reported from Greenland; St. John's, Newfoundland; Chambly, Que.; Shrewsbury, N.J.; Chester and Northampton counties, Pa.; Newport, R.I.; Geauga County, Ohio; Loudoun County, Va.; and Bear Swamp, Autauga County, Ala.; 13½ in. long; sexes similar in outward appearance and size; *larger than American woodcock* (weighs about twice as much), closely resembles it, but underparts of European bird are *narrowly barred* with brown on pale buff background and vermiculated with dusky brown (Sheldon, 1971); also, the American bird has more distinctive longitudinal stripes down its back; outer primaries of European bird not narrow as in American woodcock; has similar bill, similar foods and feeding habits (Bent, 1927).

Weights: Of 653, average of 12 oz.; some to 18 oz. (Sheldon, 1971).

Range: Nests in n. British Isles and from northern limit of forests in n. Norway, n. Sweden, n. Finland, n. Russia, the Urals, and across s.-c. Siberia to Sakhalin and south, also in Azores, Madeira, and Canary Is.; winters from British Isles south to nw. Africa, s. Asia, and Philippines (rarely), also in Azores, Madeira, and Canary Is.

Yellowlegs, bastard. *See* Sandpiper, stilt.

Yellowlegs, greater, *Tringa melanoleuca* (TRING-gah mel-an-oh-LEW-kah); genus name: *see* Greenshank; species name: from Gr. *melas,* black, and *leukos,* white, refers to black and white in its plumage; *greater,* because larger than lesser yellowlegs. (Color ill., page 806.) In summer, common on muskeg in Alaska, Canada; trim, long-legged; 12½–15 in., including 2–2⅓-in.-long bill; wingspread 23–26 in.; sexes outwardly similar, but female slightly larger; alert, wary, very noisy on disturbance; tall sandpiper with long, slightly upturned bill; long, slender neck; long, bright yellow legs; back dark gray-brown (browner than similar willet) and speckled or streaked with white; underparts white; breast and flanks speckled in spring, almost white in fall and winter; in flight, *white rump and tail;* flies swiftly, sometimes at great height, identified by long legs extending beyond tail and frequent calls, may descend in response to whistled imitation of its cry; distinguished from similar lesser yellowlegs by larger size, longer, stouter, slightly upturned bill, and loud, clear, usually 3–5-noted whistle, *few, few, few* or *whew, whew, whew,* the characteristic whistle in spring and fall (lesser yellowlegs utters single *cu* or *cu,cu,* occasionally *cu,cu,cu,* flatter and less ringing than call of greater yellowlegs); in spring, greater also calls in rolling *too-whee, too-whee* or *whee-oodle, whee-oodle* (see Nichols, 1920, and Bent, 1927, for various interpretations of its calls); wilder, and less gregarious than lesser yellowlegs; when walking sometimes bobs whole body up and down; toes webbed at base, may wade in water to belly but usually prefers shallow water; in migration along coasts seen at margins of small pools in salt marshes, also on tidal mud flats, occasionally on ocean beach; inland, along creeks and river bars, occasionally in pastures, flooded golf courses (Palmer, 1967); migrates in spring from wintering grounds by day or night, usually in small flocks, along both Atlantic and Pacific coasts and interior U.S.; begins in Mar., reaches n. U.S. in Apr. and through May or into June; most are on breeding grounds in May.

Feeding Habits: Does not probe with bill, but pecks or dabs at water to pick up food; also, while walking through water, swings bill from side to side, skimming it; sometimes "plows" surface of water with lower mandible, pushing straight ahead (Dusi, 1968), or runs about rapidly as it chases and catches in bill small killi-

SANDPIPER FAMILY

Bristle-thighed curlew
This large curlew, whose Alaskan breeding grounds were unknown until a nest was found in 1948, spends the winter on islands in the mid-Pacific. Here a major food source is the eggs of terns, albatrosses, and other seabirds. The curlews often break the eggs by carrying them aloft in their bills and dropping them on hard sand.

Bristle-thighed curlew

Long-billed curlew
The long-billed curlew breeds on dry prairies and meadows in western North America and winters from the southern United States to Guatemala. It was much more abundant in the early 19th century, before it began to suffer the effects of habitat destruction and heavy hunting.

Long-billed dowitcher
The two dowitchers differ slightly in color pattern and length of bill, and have different calls. These differences are not always evident in the field, and many birds must be identified as merely "dowitchers." The long-billed dowitcher is somewhat more partial to freshwater habitats and migrates southward later in the season, after most short-billed dowitchers have reached their wintering grounds.

Short-billed dowitcher
This large, snipelike sandpiper uses its long bill for probing in mud flats. When probing, a dowitcher uses a very rapid up-and-down motion that liquefies the mud and enables the bird to seize worms, insect larvae, and small crustaceans.

Dunlin
Unlike most of our other small sandpipers, the dunlin winters in North America, where it is especially common along the coast. Many young shorebirds migrate south while still in their juvenile plumage, but young dunlins, whose breasts are covered with round black spots like those of a wood thrush, have their first molt while still in the Arctic; so few bird-watchers ever see this distinctive plumage.

Bar-tailed godwit
This elegant shorebird nests in Eurasia and northern Alaska and winters in the Old World. Very rarely a bird appears on the Atlantic coast. It feeds both by picking from the surface of the mud and probing. When probing, it inserts its bill and then swings it rapidly from side to side, rather than using the up-and-down "sewing machine" method of the dowitchers.

Hudsonian godwit
Each fall, large numbers of Hudsonian godwits gather at the south end of Hudson Bay and then apparently fly nonstop to South America. For this reason, they are seldom seen in any number in the United States. In recent years, however, more and more have been turning up along the Atlantic coast. The presence of these birds probably indicates a change in migration routes rather than an increase in the overall number of the species.

Marbled godwit
These duck-sized shorebirds are quite social, usually feeding in flocks and nesting in loose colonies on prairies in the interior of North America. Although often rather silent, the birds are very noisy on the breeding grounds. This species was more common and widespread in the 19th century.

Long-billed curlew

Long-billed dowitcher

Short-billed dowitcher

Marbled godwit

Marbled godwit

Bar-tailed godwit, summer and winter

Hudsonian godwit

Dunlin

Red knot

Red knots are birds of sandy beaches and mud flats. They fly in dense flocks and do not spread out after landing to feed. This habit made them an easy mark in the days when shorebirds were shot for game, and the species had become scarce by the end of the 19th century. Given protection, they have again become numerous. On the breeding grounds, young birds tend to concentrate in good feeding areas, broods tended by their parents joining together.

Ruff

The ruff, whose female is called a reeve, is primarily an Old World species, once considered accidental in the Western Hemisphere. But it is now reported with such regularity that some suspect it has begun nesting somewhere in North America. In the breeding season, males acquire boldly colored plumes on the head and neck, and display in groups to which the reeves come to mate.

Sanderling

A common bird on broad, sandy beaches, the sanderling is noted for its habit of sprinting down the sand in pursuit of retreating waves and snatching up small crustaceans and other animals before they have a chance to burrow into the sand. Sanderlings nest in the Arctic and winter on beaches all over the world. It has been said that no beach in the world is without its sanderlings.

Ruff

Ruff, female (reeve)

Ruff

Red knot

Red knot, winter

Sanderling, eggs

Sanderling

Sanderling, autumn

Baird's sandpiper

Baird's sandpiper nests on coastal tundra in Greenland, Canada, Alaska, and eastern Siberia, and winters in the Andes and the cooler parts of southern South America. Most birds migrate south along the Rocky Mountains, bypassing the wetlands where other shorebirds congregate. When feeding, these birds pick small items from the surface of the ground or mud and do not normally probe with their bills.

Buff-breasted sandpiper

The buff-breasted sandpiper is much less common than formerly, and in many parts of North America it is considered a rarity. Its tameness and its habit of traveling in tight flocks made it especially vulnerable to hunting. When feeding on migration, it often associates with lesser golden plovers.

Curlew sandpiper

The curlew sandpiper, so named because of its curved bill, is a Siberian bird that winters in the southern part of the Old World, but a few individuals turn up each year in North America. In its rich chestnut breeding plumage, the curlew sandpiper is unmistakable, but in its dull-gray winter plumage it can be difficult to distinguish from the dunlin, with which it often associates. As soon as it flies, however, its pure white rump singles it out from the dark-rumped dunlins.

Least sandpiper

The smallest of our sandpipers, this species is a bird of quiet grassy pools in marshes, where it often feeds with other shorebirds. It obtains food both by picking small animals from the surface of the mud and by probing. When feeding, least sandpipers scatter out to find food singly, but when danger threatens they fly up in unison and quickly gather in a tight flock.

Pectoral sandpiper

During the breeding season, male pectoral sandpipers have 2 saclike structures under the streaked feathers of the neck and breast. When the birds engage in courtship displays, these sacs are inflated, lifting the breast feathers to form what has been described as a "prehensile balloon." Throughout the year pectoral sandpipers feed in wet meadows and grassy marshes; they were known to early gunners as "grass snipe."

Purple sandpiper

This stocky, rather tame sandpiper nests in the tundra and winters on rocky coasts of the North Atlantic, searching for small animals beneath the seaweed. Most purple sandpipers depart for the breeding grounds early in the spring, but a few, probably first-year birds too young to nest, remain on our east coast all summer.

Buff-breasted sandpiper

Baird's sandpiper

Curlew sandpiper, winter

Pectoral sandpiper

Purple sandpiper

Least sandpiper

Least sandpiper, juvenile

Rock sandpiper

The Pacific counterpart of the purple sandpiper, this species also feeds on seaweed-covered rocks. Some authorities believe the two birds should be considered forms of a single, rather variable species. They look more alike during the winter, when their gray-brown plumage matches the color of the rocks, than during the breeding season, when the rock sandpiper, with a black patch on its breast, looks more like a dunlin.

Semipalmated sandpiper

A grayer and slightly larger bird than the least sandpiper, this species seems less partial to freshwater than its smaller relative. Semipalmated sandpipers are abundant on the Atlantic coast during migration, but most birds spend the winter farther south. It feeds both by picking items from the surface of the mud and by probing shallowly.

Sharp-tailed sandpiper

The sharp-tailed sandpiper is a very rare fall migrant on the Pacific coast from Alaska to California, on its way to its wintering grounds in the Southern Hemisphere. For reasons not understood, most of the birds that turn up in North America are immatures.

Solitary sandpiper

The first nest of this abundant North American sandpiper was discovered in 1903, built in an old robin's nest in a larch in Alberta. Many books published prior to 1903, and even some afterward, contain descriptions of nests and eggs that actually pertain to the spotted sandpiper. Although as its name implies it usually forages singly, during migration it is possible to see many birds together at some particularly favorable feeding area.

Spotted sandpiper

Spotted sandpipers are rather solitary birds, feeding singly or in pairs, but never in flocks, along the margins of ponds and streams throughout most of North America. They nest both along waterways and in grassy or brushy places well away from water. Males do most of the incubating of the eggs and caring for the young, and there is some evidence that females have more than one mate. Spotted sandpipers are easily identified in the breeding season by their spotted underparts, and at all times of the year by their habit of "teetering"—rhythmically bobbing their tails up and down—and by their distinctive, stiff-winged flight.

Stilt sandpiper

The stilt sandpiper prefers grassy marshes and the margins of ponds, where it often associates with yellowlegs and dowitchers. Some early hunters believed it to be a hybrid between these two species. Foraging on mud, it obtains food by probing, picking items from the surface, and by swinging its bill from side to side through the water.

Sharp-tailed sandpiper

Spotted sandpiper, winter

Rock sandpiper

Solitary sandpiper

Semipalmated sandpiper

Stilt sandpiper

Spotted sandpiper

Upland sandpiper

Upland sandpipers nest in grassy clearings, meadows, and pastures in Canada and the northern United States. Although the species must have increased its range when the forest was cleared, much of this open country has reverted to woodland in recent decades, and the upland sandpiper is becoming scarce in many parts of its breeding range. Unlike many of its relatives, it often perches on fence posts, telephone poles, and even in trees.

Western sandpiper

This species is a longer-billed, western relative of the semipalmated sandpiper. The two birds are easily distinguished when they are in breeding plumage but nearly impossible to tell apart during the winter. For years it was assumed that birds spending the winter on the east coast of the United States were semipalmated sandpipers, but careful examination of museum specimens has recently shown that these birds are all westerns and that the semipalmated sandpiper withdraws almost entirely from North America in the winter.

White-rumped sandpiper

In both spring and fall, most rumped-white sandpipers migrate through the interior of North America, but small numbers appear along the coast. At all seasons, it is easily identified in flight by its white rump, a feature not shared by any of the other small sandpipers with which it associates. It often travels in large flocks, especially on migration in the Great Plains. It feeds both by probing and by picking food from the surface.

Western sandpiper

Western sandpiper, winter

Upland sandpiper

White-rumped sandpiper

Common snipe
The common snipe is a bird of bogs and marshes that usually sits quietly until an intruder is nearby, then flushes suddenly and rushes off in zigzag flight, uttering a grating call. Males have a territorial display in which they engage in a prolonged flight with much swooping and diving, the tail feathers fanned and vibrating to produce a hollow "winnowing" sound.

Surfbird
The name surfbird fits this species well during most of the year, for on migration and in the winter it spends its time on wave-lashed rocks along the Pacific coast, feeding primarily on small mussels. It nests in rocky places above timberline in the mountains of Alaska, where it feeds on insects.

Wandering tattler
In flight the wandering tattler holds its wings stiffly, like a spotted sandpiper. It nests along gravelly mountain streams in Alaska and British Columbia, where it feeds on insect larvae. In winter it feeds on rocks along the coast as far south as Peru and on islands in the tropical Pacific.

Black turnstone
The black turnstone is a darker relative of the ruddy turnstone, nesting along the coast of Alaska south of the breeding range of its more brightly colored and widespread cousin. In their habits, the two species are much the same, but the black turnstone shows more of a tendency to feed on rocks, where it is found with surfbirds and rock sandpipers.

Ruddy turnstone
This handsome adaptable bird was named for one of its many methods of feeding, flipping pebbles over to search for small crustaceans. It also digs holes in the sand, sometimes very deep, cracks open mussels and other animals clinging to rocks, steals scraps from picnics, breaks open the eggs of terns and other birds, pulls bits of meat from racks of drying fish, and catches flies that have gathered at decaying seaweed or carcasses on the beach.

Surfbird

Surfbird, winter

ack turnstone

Wandering tattler

mmon snipe

Wandering tattler, winter

uddy turnstone

Whimbrel
Our commonest curlew, the whimbrel escaped the destruction suffered by the Eskimo and long-billed curlews at the hands of early gunners, probably because the species migrates chiefly over water. Its nesting habitat in Canada and Alaska has not been disturbed, unlike the prairies where the long-billed curlew nests.

Willet
This large sandpiper is easily identified by its loud, rolling call and by its flashing white wing patches, which are conspicuous not only when the bird flies but also during displays. Willets are social birds, nesting in loose colonies that are easy to locate because of the constant loud calling of the adults. If a predator such as a marsh hawk approaches a colony, several pairs may fly up to mob it.

American woodcock
Woodcocks spend the day resting quietly in wooded areas, coming out at dusk to probe in soft mud for earthworms. The tip of the bird's upper mandible is flexible, so that it can seize worms several inches down in the mud. In dry weather, when the ground is hard, these birds can obtain food by turning over leaves in search of insects, sow bugs, and spiders.

Lesser yellowlegs
A smaller and more delicate bird than the greater yellowlegs, this species tends to feed in quieter parts of the marshes and more often travels in flocks. It feeds by picking food off the surface of the mud and does not swing its bill from side to side like its larger relative.

American woodcock

Whimbrel

Willet

Lesser yellowlegs

Greater yellowlegs

Greater yellowlegs
This tall, common sandpiper is very wary, and at the approach of an intruder it is often the first species to sound the alarm, uttering a loud ringing cry that brings other shorebirds into the air as well. It usually feeds on mud flats, but despite the length of its bill it does not probe; instead it picks small animals from the surface or swings its bill from side to side through shallow water.

fishes and top minnows; besides fishes, also eats aquatic and other insects and their larvae, snails, crabs, worms, tadpoles, berries.
Nest: In muskeg country of scattered trees with wet clearings, ponds, or at edge of tundra or on dry ridge; nests hard to find; on ground in slight depression in mosses of hummock, usually near water.
Eggs: May–June; usually 4, buff, irregularly spotted and blotched with dark browns, grays.
Incubation: Probably by both sexes, 23 days (Reilly, 1968); age when young first fly about 18–20 days.
Other Names: Big cucu (from call); big tell-tale; big yellow-legged plover; big yellow-legs; cucu; greater tattler; greater tell-tale; greater yellow-shanks; horse yellowlegs; long-legged tattler; stone-bird; stone snipe; tell-tale godwit; winter yellowlegs; yellow-shins; yelper.
Flight Speed: 40, 45, and 45 m.p.h. (McNeil, 1969; 1970).
Weights: W. U.S. (2), average 212 gr. (Hughes, 1970), or about 7½ oz.; 5–10 oz., usually 6–8 oz. (Forbush, 1925–29).
Range: Nests from Cooke Inlet, Alaska, c. Alta., c. B.C., and northern parts of Prairie Provinces east to n.-c. Que., Labrador, Newfoundland; many non-breeders remain along our coasts in summer; winters from sw. B.C., Oreg., c. Calif., s. Nev., sw. Ariz., c. N.M., c. Tex., s. La., s. Miss., s. Ala., S.C. (lowlands), now regularly from Long Is., N.Y., rarely Mass., south through Mexico, C. America, and West Indies to extreme s. S. America.

Yellowlegs, horse. *See* Yellowlegs, greater.

Yellowlegs, lesser, *Tringa flavipes* (TRING-gah FLAY-vih-peez); genus name: *see* Greenshank; species name: from Lat. *flavus,* yellow, and *pes,* foot. (Color ill., page 805.) In summer, Alaska and across Canada; one of tattlers; like greater yellowlegs, very noisy on nesting grounds at approach of intruder; 9½–11 in. long, including 1¼–1½-in.-long bill; wingspread 19½–21½ in.; sexes outwardly alike, but females larger; is almost identical to greater yellowlegs, but about a third smaller, more delicate, also bill is finer, shorter, and *straight* (not slightly upturned as in greater); slimmer-bodied with long lemon-yellow legs that are shorter than greater's; whistled call note is distinctive from greater yellowlegs' call, a single *cu,* or *cu-cu,* uttered when it is in flight or when flushed, is flatter and weaker than loud, more prolonged call of greater yellowlegs (see Nichols, 1920, and Bent, 1927, for details); more apt to be seen in large flocks than is greater yellowlegs; is much less shy, although usually watchful and wary, at times surprisingly tame (Bent, 1927); in migration seen about coastal ponds and pools in salt marshes, inland on mud flats and on wet short-grass marshes with ponds, and at rain pools in wet fields; total population may exceed that of greater yellowlegs and often more numerous at favored places (Palmer, 1967); in spring, migrating north from Patagonia, arrives Fla. late Mar.; moves up both coasts Apr.–May but in far greater numbers

up western side of Mississippi Valley; rare but regular in spring along Atlantic coast to Long Is., N.Y. (Bull, 1964); arrives nesting grounds in Canada Apr.–May.
Feeding Habits: Similar to those of greater yellowlegs but does not swing bill from side to side in water when feeding; not a prober, snatches food with bill; eats small fishes but mainly insects, especially aquatics such as water boatmen, diving beetles, dragonfly nymphs, etc., also land beetles, grasshoppers, ants, flies, small crustaceans, bloodworms, spiders, etc. (Bent, 1927).
Nest: To edge of tundra in more open muskeg of Canadian spruce forest, prefers grassy marshes and bogs between the patches of black spruce, nests in drier places than greater yellowlegs (but often in its company), in natural clearings or burned-over areas of forest with scattered stumps, fallen tree trunks; nest a depression in ground on slope or ridge sometimes quite far from water (Bent, 1927).
Eggs: Usually mid-May to late June; usually 4, buff, more gray or more yellow than eggs of greater yellowlegs, spotted or blotched with dark browns.
Incubation: By both sexes (Bent, 1927), 22–23 days; age at first flight about 18–20 days after hatching.
Other Names: Common yellowlegs; lesser long-legged tattler; lesser tell-tale; lesser yellow-shanks; little stone-bird; little stone snipe; little tell-tale; little yelper; small cucu; summer yellowlegs; yellow-legged plover.
Flight Speed: 40 and 45 m.p.h. (McNeil, 1969, 1970).
Weights: In fall, coastal N.J. (1), 81.7 gr. (Murray and Jehl, 1964), or about 3 oz.; 2¾–4½ oz. (Palmer, 1967).
Range: Nests in n.-c. Alaska from Kotzebue Sound and c. interior, also in n. Yuk., nw. Mack., s. Keewatin, ne. Man. (Churchill), extreme n. Ont., nw. Que. (Ungava Pen.), south into e.-c. B.C., c. Alta., c. Sask., s. Man., n. Ont., w.-c. Que.; non-breeders in summer, casually south to Argentina; a few winter in s. U.S. (Tex., La., Fla., and S.C.), very rarely north to Long Is., N.Y., south through C. America and West Indies to Chile and Argentina; has strayed to Greenland, Europe; one caught at sea 600 mi. northwest of Hawaii (Palmer, 1967).

Yellowlegs, summer. *See* Yellowlegs, lesser.

Yellowlegs, winter. *See* Yellowlegs, greater.

SAND RUNNER
See Turnstone, ruddy, in Sandpiper Family.

SANITARY HABITS
The parents of many kinds of birds remove excreta of their young from the nest (*see* Young and Their Care); some birds wash their food before eating it (*see* Swallowing); and shorebirds and herons have been reported leaving their feeding areas in water and going ashore to defecate. See details in Brackbill (1970c); Recher and Recher (1972).

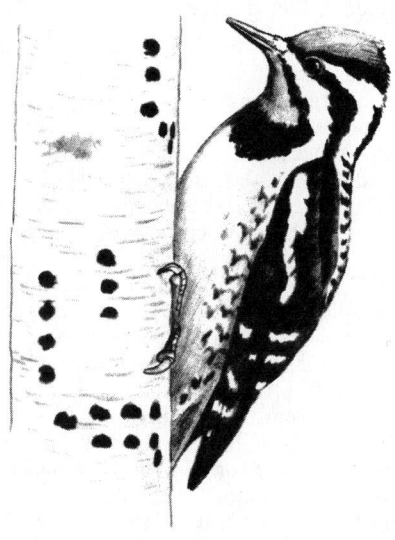

SAP-FEEDING
The yellow-bellied sapsucker drills small holes, called "sap wells," into the bark of a tree. Clinging to the trunk, it feeds with its long, bristly tongue on the oozing sap and insects trapped in it.

SAP-FEEDING

A habit reported for at least 32 or more species of N. American birds, especially of Woodpecker Family, of which the sapsuckers (Williamson's and yellow-bellied) and the downy woodpecker drill their own sap "wells" or holes in bark of trees, then cling to trunk or limb to feed with tongue (*see* Tongue) as sap exudes from hole in bark. *See* their food habits in Woodpecker Family.

Red-bellied, red-headed, hairy, and northern three-toed woodpeckers apparently do not drill their own sap wells but visit those dug by sapsuckers, as do Anna's hummingbird, the broad-tailed, ruby-throated, and rufous hummingbirds, also white-breasted and red-breasted nuthatches, ruby-crowned kinglets, Audubon's (yellow-rumped) warbler, black-throated blue, black-throated green, Cape May, myrtle (yellow-rumped), and pine warblers, northern waterthrush and painted redstart; pine siskin, American goldfinch, Oregon (dark-eyed) junco, and white-crowned sparrow (Foster and Tate, 1966); and cardinal; also evening grosbeaks, Bohemian and cedar waxwings, which drink sap from broken twigs or injured bark of trees. Besides eating sap, many of these birds also eat insects attracted to, and drowned in, the fluid in the holes made by sapsuckers. *See* Commensalism. Some birds get intoxicated from the sap. *See* Poisons.

In n. U.S., little sap flows in winter (although sapsuckers eat some sap in winter), but in spring, with warming temperatures, water and sweet sap with its stored nutrients from roots and stems rise in phloem (a thin layer just under outer bark of tree or shrub) at time when farmers harvest maple sap and migrating sapsuckers return north. The sap contains nutrients used by the plants for growth and maintenance, and sap-feeding is a way of tapping this source of nutrition. In their own way, these birds are using a food source, also used by aphids on a much smaller scale, which live on the sap of leaves.

During spring period of upward flow of sap, sapsuckers often make holes in single rows around trunk or branches, most commonly in trees that leaf and flower first—aspens, maples, elms, also red pines and hemlocks; later birches, which in North become main source of sap for them during summer (Foster and Tate, 1966).

Sapsuckers are known to bore feeding holes in at least 258 kinds of trees, shrubs, and vines in U.S. (McAtee, 1926), some of which may cause weakening or death of trees or blemishes in those grown for lumber; the work of yellow-bellied sapsuckers on trees varies with season and, on the Atlantic coast, is spread over territory 3,000 mi. long or more; during migrations, north or south, when birds scattered or on move, little harm done, but on northern nesting grounds and in winter quarters in southern states, yellow-bellied sapsucker is often a "problem bird" to forester or lumber industry; however, according to Dale and Krefting (1966), it would cost more to "control" the bird than its losses caused to lumber industry; also, it has some value as destroyer of the damaging larch sawfly. *See*, however, Economic Ornithology; *also* Sapsucker, yellow-bellied, in Woodpecker Family.

Sapsuckers offer also a food supply to other birds which may not eat sap. Many insects are attracted to the exuding sweet fluid and come to feed on it—butterflies, moths, click beetles, hornets, fruit flies and other flies. Some of these may gather at sap wells or form cloud in air around them which attracts insect-eating crested and least flycatchers, eastern phoebe, American robin, warbling vireo, and some of the wood warblers. *See* Food and Feeding Habits. *See also* nectar-feeding under Pollination.

SAPSUCKER
See in Woodpecker Family.

SAWBILL
See mergansers in Duck Family.

SAW-FILER
See Saw-whet owl in Owl—Typical Owl Family.

SAY
THOMAS (1787–1834). Born Philadelphia, Pa.; brilliant entomologist who accompanied Maj. Stephen H. Long's expedition to the Rocky Mtns. (1819–20), and prepared the report on birds (Palmer, 1928). His name is commemorated in the English and scientific names of Say's phoebe, *Sayornis saya*, and a genus name of the phoebes *(Sayornis)*. The Say's phoebe was named for him by Bonaparte in 1825. See also Ewan (1950); Wynne (1969); Gruson (1972).

SCANSORIAL
Of climbing, or suited to climbing. *See* Climbing Birds.

SCAPE-GRACE
See Loon, red-throated, in Loon Family. Name from Cape Race, Newfoundland, where often seen.

SCAPULARS
A group of prominent feathers arising from a bird's shoulders. *See* Topography.

SCAUP
See in Duck Family.

SCAVENGERS
Birds that help in sanitation of the environment; they help eliminate sewage wastes, garbage, and dead animal life on N. American waters and in fields, forests, meadows, on beaches, etc. In N. America, avian scavengers include albatrosses, shearwaters, petrels, the brown pelican, frigatebird, vultures, the California condor, eagles, some hawks, the caracara, jaegers, the skua, gulls, the snowy owl, the raven, crows, magpies, Clark's nutcracker, jays, the house sparrow, and the domestic pigeon. See details about these birds in Stager (1966); *see also* in biography of each.

SCHIZOCHROISM
See Colors of Feathers.

SCISSORBILL

See Black skimmer in Skimmer Family.

SCLATER

P(HILIP) L(UTLEY) (1829–1913). Born Hampshire, England; British ornithologist, world-renowned zoogeographer, and author of *The Geographic Distribution of the Members of the Class Aves* (1851). He was editor of *The Ibis* and a fellow of the Royal Society, also secretary of the Zoological Society of London (1859–1903). Sclater visited the U.S. in 1856 and both the U.S. and Canada in 1884. In 1897, Otto Kleinschmidt, German ornithologist, named a chickadee from s. Mexico *Parus sclateri* (the Mexican chickadee) in his honor. See also Gruson (1972) and especially Stresemann (1975); see also Wynne (1969) for references.

SCLEROTIC RING

See under Skull in Skeleton.

SCOGGIN

Local name especially in the Carolinas for a heron or bittern; possibly traceable to name of John Scoggin, court fool to Edward VI of England; applied to herons because of their often ungainly or comic appearance (McAtee, 1955c; 1959).

SCOLDENORE

See Oldsquaw in Duck Family.

SCOLDER

See Oldsquaw in Duck Family; so named for its garrulity.

SCOLOPACIDAE

See Sandpiper Family.

SCOTER

See in Duck Family.

SCOTT

WINFIELD (Scott's oriole). *See* Paris Brothers.

SCRATCHING

(with feet). *See* methods of under Double Scratch; *see also* Head-scratching.

SCREAMER FAMILY

See Anseriformes.

SCREWWORM

Name sometimes given the larva, or grub ("worm"), of the bluebottle flies—*Protocalliphora avium, P. splendida,* and others—which lay their eggs on nestling birds; when eggs of the flies hatch, the grub begins feeding by sucking blood of the nestling (*see* Protocalliphora). According to Essig (1942), however, *screwworm* is name for the larva of a related group of parasitic flies of which the most important in N. and S. America is the screwworm *Callitroga (americana) hominivorax,* which lays its eggs in open sores of man and domestic and wild animals; the grubs on hatching feed on living flesh and cause severe myiasis, which may result in death (Lapage, 1963).

SCRUB DESERT

One of the nine biomes (*see* Biome) in N. America north of Mexico used in mapping the ecological distribution of birds. *See* Major Biotic Communities (biomes) under Distribution. The Scrub Desert is composed of widely spaced plants 3–6 ft. high—creosote bush, mesquite, paloverde, catclaw, ironwood, ocotillo, agaves, cactuses, and yuccas, with, occasionally, grasses (see Pettingill, 1970, for scientific names of the plants)—which grow on lowlands and valley floors from w. Tex. west to sw. Calif.; its typical birds are Gambel's quail, the roadrunner, elf owl, lesser nighthawk, Costa's hummingbird, gilded flicker, Gila woodpecker, vermilion flycatcher, verdin, cactus wren, Bendire's, Le Conte's, and the crissal thrashers, black-tailed gnatcatcher, and phainopepla (Pettingill, 1970; 1972).

SCUTELLATE

(skew-TELL-late). *See* Tarsus.

SCUTELLUM

(Lat., a little shield). Scutella are horny scales arranged in definite vertical series up and down a bird's tarsus and along its toes. The scutella are apt to be somewhat imbricated, or arranged like shingles, the lower edge of one overlapping the upper edge of the next. Many birds have these; they are most often in the front of the tarsus—the part of the bird's foot corresponding to our instep—and are almost always on the tops of the toes; they are also on the sides or back of the legs of some birds (Coues, 1884). *See* Tarsus.

SEABIRD

General term applied by some ornithologists—for example, Alexander (1928); Fisher and Lockley (1954)—to any bird that spends much of its life on or over salt water. The term therefore applies to many water birds—boobies, tropic-birds, gannets, frigatebirds, loons, cormorants, pelicans, certain ducks, gulls, terns, etc. *See* Water Bird.

Seabird, or possibly *oceanic bird,* applies especially to albatrosses, shearwaters, petrels, and storm-petrels, or those seen much over the oceans. They live far from land most of the year, except at breeding time, when they return to their nesting places on oceanic islands or along seacoasts. These are the most abundant and characteristic birds of the ocean, and among them, the Wilson's storm-petrel has been called the most abundant bird in the world. *See* Populations; *see also* Storm-petrel Family. Shearwaters are also enormously abundant. *See* Shearwater Family; Procellariiformes. See Bourne (1964).

Fisher and Lockley (1954) list mid-oceanic birds in the N. Atlantic as the British storm-petrel, Leach's storm-petrel, the fulmar, and many auks—the dovekie, puffins, razorbill, and guillemots, or murres—all of which often wander over the ocean; also the skua, shearwaters, jaegers, and the black-legged kittiwake. (Watson, 1966, has defined the N. Atlantic as all of the Atlantic O. north of a line from the coast of Ga. or S.C. east through Bermuda and on to the Canary Is. off the west coast of Africa, or above 33° N. Lat.) See Wynne-Edwards (1964).

Gulls, cormorants, gannets, and pelicans are mainly coastal—although herring gulls occasionally join the kittiwakes following ships out of sight of land, also lesser black-backed gulls. Flocks of red and northern phalaropes in spring and autumn are often seen far from land in the N. Atlantic. See Ashmole (1971).

In the temperate N. Pacific, according to Alexander (1928), the open ocean species are the black-footed albatross, Laysan albatross (more southern), and the very rare short-tailed albatross. See Palmer (1962) for its status, and Vincent (1966). See Tramontano (1970) and Sanger (1970) for seabirds of the N. Pacific, and Bartonek and Gibson (1972) for some discussion of oceanic birds off the west coast of the Alaska Pen. See also Peterson (1961) for a list of seabirds off the west coast of N. America under "Accidental and Marginal Species."

SEA-CROW

Another name for the razorbill in Auk Family, American coot in Rail Family, and American oystercatcher in Oystercatcher Family.

SEA-DOG

See Black skimmer in Skimmer Family. Name from its repeated call which resembles dog's barking.

SEA DUCK

See in Duck Family.

SEA-GOOSE

See phalaropes in Phalarope Family.

SEA GULL

See Gull, herring, in Gull Family.

SEA HEN

Name of fishermen for a sizable bird seen at sea; *see* Skua and jaegers in Skua Family.

SEA HORSE

See Fulmar, northern, in Shearwater Family.

SEA MOUSE

See Duck, harlequin, in Duck Family. Name from its squeaking notes.

SEA PARROT

See Puffin, common, in Auk Family.

SEA-PIE

See in Oystercatcher Family.

SEA-SNIPE

See phalaropes in Phalarope Family.

SEASONAL DIMORPHISM

See Colors of Feathers.

SECONDARY FEATHER

One of the flight feathers attached to the ulna (forearm), nearer the bird's body than the primary feathers. *See* Topography.

SECONDARY SEXUAL CHARACTERS

See Endocrine Glands; Sex Determination; *also* Sexual Dimorphism.

male

female

SEX DETERMINATION

The sex of Brewer's blackbirds can be determined by plumage and eye color. The male has yellow irises and glossy purple-black head plumage; the female is brown-eyed and its plumage is dull brown.

SECRETARY-BIRD

See Falconiformes; Reptiles and Birds.

SEDENTARY

Nonmigratory; a resident. *See* Where Do Birds Live? under Distribution.

SEDGE HEN

See Rail, clapper, in Rail Family.

SEEDEATER

See in Finch Family.

SEED-SNIPE

See Shorebird.

SEESAW

See Sandpiper, spotted, in Sandpiper Family.

SEE-SEE

See Bananaquit in Honeycreeper Family.

SEMICIRCULAR CANALS

Three semicircular canals within the ear of a bird (*see* Ears and Hearing) serve as its gravity-balancing organ. Within the semicircular canals, a fluid called *endolymph* helps a bird to maintain its equilibrium.

A bird or any other animal must maintain both a static and a dynamic equilibrium with its environment. To keep its "sense of balance," uprightness, or "even keel" involves within a bird the complex coordination of impulses beginning in the semicircular canals, in which the fluid (endolymph) in shifting about stimulates hair cells in both right and left inner ears (Wing, 1956; Van Tyne and Berger, 1959).

According to Van Tyne and Berger, through the initial stimulus, and the subsequent association with motor neurons, the bird can compensate for the movements of its body, head, neck, eyes, etc., whenever necessary. This is essentially an unconscious or reflex adjustment while the bird is in motion. According to Beecher (1951), various birds—wood storks, pelicans, herons, spoonbills, and ducks—either at rest or in flight, hold their heads in a position (by raising or depressing the bill) whereby the external semicircular canal is horizontal. Though the bird may twist and turn its body in flight, it holds its head in this position. See also in Matthews (1968).

SEMISPECIES

See Hybrid.

SENSE ORGANS

See Ears and Hearing; Eyes and Eyesight; Smell; Taste; Touch. *See also* Migration.

SERRATE

(SIR-rate). *See* Tarsus.

SET

(of eggs). *See* Clutch.

SEWICK

Another name for the least flycatcher in Flycatcher—Tyrant Flycatcher Family.

SEX DETERMINATION

(identification). Some birds in which the sexes are colored alike and about equal in size, and especially the newly hatched young, may be "sexed" in the hand by examining the cloaca for the presence or absence of a penis (phallus) in those groups of birds that have one. *See* Copulation and Copulatory Organs. According to Witschi (1961), all ancestral male birds probably had a penis-like copulatory organ; however, in birds of today only a few have retained it. Among N. American birds, the males of swans, ducks, and geese develop a phallus and a vestige of it remains in herons and flamingos and in domestic chickens, turkeys, and pheasants (Pettingill, 1956).

In the early fetal stages of the duck, a genital tubercle appears in both sexes in the ventral (top) circumference of the bird's cloaca (*see* Cloaca); it remains rudimentary in females but in males grows to a considerable size even before hatching. Witschi states that in most birds the phallus persists as only a very small vestige, or disappears altogether.

In the domestic chick, a small genital tubercle forms in the embryo (*see* Embryo and Its Development) about the twelfth day of its incubation. In female chicks it usually disappears by hatching time, but the rudiment persists in males, or cockerels, and may even enlarge to some extent. This makes it possible for poultrymen to determine the sex of chicks upon hatching with an accuracy of 95–100% (Witschi, 1961). For the sex ratio of birds at hatching, *see* Hatching. *See also* Bursa of Fabricius.

In some other birds in which the sexes are alike, or very close in outward appearance, males may be told from females by eye color. The female starling, for example, may be distinguished from the similar male by a yellow ring along the outer edge of the irises (irides) of the eyes. It is usually conspicuous in females more than 6 weeks old, but is absent in males (Kessel, 1951). In Brewer's blackbird, the breeding male has a pale yellow iris; the female, a brown one (Walls, 1942). *See also* Colors of Eyes under Eyes and Eyesight; *also* Sexual Dimorphism.

The male yellow-breasted chat, during the breeding season, usually has a solid-black bill, or has small light stripes or dots on the lower mandible; also, the inside of his mouth is jet black early in the breeding season—a secondary sexual character that begins to fade to the flesh color of the inside of the mouth of the female toward the end of the breeding season (Dennis, 1958). *See* discussion of seasonal change in bill color under Endocrine Glands.

Margaret M. Nice has pointed out that during the nesting season the sexes of some birds that are outwardly alike may be distinguished by examining them for the *incubation patch* (*see* Incubation), a method often used by bird-banders who trap or catch the birds on the nest.

Only the *females* of titmice, chickadees, and wrens, for example, in which the sexes outwardly look alike, have the incubation patch. This test does not work for woodpeckers, however, in which both sexes incubate and both have the patch, but male and female woodpeckers usually have outer differences in plumage markings that distinguish them in the field. For determining the sexes of eagles, owls, and herons, by analyzing the plasma steroid hormones, see Dieter (1973).

WHAT DETERMINES THE SEX OF A BIRD? According to Domm (1955), the sex of a bird, which is genetically determined, is not fixed. *See* Sexual Reversal under Endocrine Glands. It is influenced by sex hormones in the embryo which determine whether the bird will be a male or female—sex cords proliferate in the early embryo which, if the bird is to be a male, become sperm-forming tubules; if a female, an ovary. Male hormones stimulate the growth of the male sexual structures in the embryo and inhibit growth of those of the female; female hormones stimulate the development of female sexual structures and inhibit the development of male organs. *See* other details of sexual differentiation and when it begins under Embryo and Its Development. See also Cain (1964b).

SEXES
(relative sizes of). *See* Sexual Dimorphism.

SEX RATIO
See Hatching.

SEX RECOGNITION
(between birds). *See* Courtship.

SEXUAL CHARACTERS
The specific physical and physiological differences between male and female. The primary sexual characters are the testis of the male and ovary of the female (Thomson, 1964n). *See* Eggs and Egg-laying; Fertilization. Secondary sexual characters—apart from those of reproduction—are notably in the colors of the plumage, voice, size, and behavior. *See* Endocrine Glands; Sexual Dimorphism.

SEXUAL DIMORPHISM
Term for the differences in structure, size, and appearance between males and females of a species or subspecies at an equal age and during the same season (Thomson, 1964n). Many birds, probably more than any other vertebrate animals, show pronounced outward differences between adult males and females of the same species, although at hatching both usually look the same. Soon the sexes, as they grow, begin to differ in size, plumage, colors, and development or lack of development of combs and spurs, and later, when adult, in songs (voice) and breeding behavior. *See* Embryo and Its Development; Courtship; Courtship Feeding; Territory. *See also* Songs and Singing.

The primary characters that distinguish males from females are the testes of the male and the ovary of the female. External characters that distinguish males from females are called *secondary* (or accessory) *sexual characters*. It is usually the male that has the greatest number of secondary sexual characters—brighter-colored feathers, bright patches of skin, the development of large combs and spurs in domestic fowl, and spurs in pheasants and peafowl, largely due to the influence of sex hormones. *See* Endocrine Glands. Females of many species are duller or protectively colored.

See Colors of Feathers. In a few species, the female is more brightly colored in those practicing polyandry (*see* Sexual Relationships)—for example, in the phalaropes and in the Old World painted snipe and button-quails.

DIFFERENCES IN COLORS BETWEEN SEXES—PERMANENT AND SEASONAL. In some species the color differences may be permanent—for example, in pheasants and in ducks, except for those ducks in which for short periods in summer the males (drakes) are in eclipse (basic) plumage, which resembles the plumage of the female. *See* Eclipse Plumage. In some birds the males have bright plumage during the breeding season only—for example, bobolink, scarlet tanager, American goldfinch, indigo bunting, lark bunting, longspurs—and in winter have a plumage very similar to that of the female, which is accomplished through a postnuptial (prebasic) molt after the breeding season. *See* Molts and Molting. Some males are more colorful than females throughout the year: hummingbirds, woodpeckers, vermilion flycatcher, American redstart, orchard oriole, summer tanager, cardinal, pyrrhuloxia, blue grosbeak, rose-breasted grosbeak, rufous-sided towhee, painted bunting. *See also* discussion of sexual reversal under Endocrine Glands, and sex aberrations under Hermaphrodite; Gynandromorph. Even the colors of the eyes of males and females may be different during the breeding season. *See* Sex Determination.

USES OF SECONDARY SEXUAL CHARACTERS. The brightly colored parts of a bird's plumage—on the head, wings, rump, and tail, for example—are used by birds in their displays as social signals with others of their own species, in courtship, as warnings, recognition, etc. *See* Colors of Feathers. Most of the bright colors and other secondary sexual characters function as releasers of social reactions, and possibly all striking color designs and bizarre structural parts, such as elongated plumes (herons, for example), inflatable pouches (sage grouse and prairie chicken), and colorful combs and wattles and other parts of naked skin of some species, have an exclusive use in some instinctive act that represents a releasing ceremony (Lorenz, 1937). *See* Breeding Behavior under Behavior, and Courtship Rituals under Courtship.

It is advantageous to the perpetuation of a species (*see* Species) to have plumage colors and displays so specific that only a male and female of its own kind respond to the other's "sign stimuli." *See* Language. This assumes the evolution of "innate perceptory patterns" in the females which ensures their response to a male of their own species.

SEXUAL DIFFERENCES IN SIZE. Sexual dimorphism in birds is not only a matter of differences in colors between males and females of many kinds, but is sometimes one of marked differences in size. In most species of birds, the males are larger than the females. In those species in which the males are larger and more brightly colored than the females, the males, in courtship, are usually the aggressive sex. Their larger size is presumed to be for the reason that they compete for mates and larger in-

male

female

SEXUAL DIMORPHISM
The male oldsquaw is a boldly patterned piebald duck with a very long, slender tail. The female is duller and more protectively colored and lacks the long tail. These secondary sexual characteristics are largely due to the influence of hormones. The male oldsquaw is the only duck that has two distinct, bright seasonal plumages and an eclipse plumage.

dividuals have an advantage (Amadon, 1977). In birds of prey, however—eagles, hawks, and owls—the female is usually larger than the male, as she is in the somewhat predatory skua and frigatebird. In a few species in which the females are the aggressive sex in courtship—in phalaropes, for example—the females are larger and more brightly colored than the males (Amadon, 1959).

There has been considerable speculation among ornithologists as to the origin and significance of sexual dimorphism in size of birds and what advantages it may have. Some—for example, Storer, R. W. (1952; 1966) and Selander (1966)—suggest that, in predatory birds, the difference in sizes permits, between the pair, the killing and eating of a wider range of prey —the capability of the larger female to kill larger prey; of the smaller male to handle smaller prey. Those species that are most rapacious and kill the largest prey relative to their own size show the greatest differences in size between males and females—for example, among the larger falcons and some small accipiters and some small owls (Amadon, 1975).

Earhart and Johnson (1970) studied sexual dimorphism and food habits of 18 species of N. American owls. In most of these the females range up to 28% larger by weight than males and took larger food, which suggested to them that the evolution of the size differences in the two sexes of this group is closely related to their food habits.

Amadon (1975), after a critical review of these and other hypotheses offered by various investigators, suggested that sexual dimorphism in sizes is correlated with mating behavior. "Raptors have become unusually aggressive birds, presumably because they hunt and kill active prey at some risk of injury to themselves. Furthermore the male, as in birds in general, may be expected to be the more aggressive sex, at least at the time of mating and pair formation. Armed as he is with formidable beak and talons, he would pose a threat to the physical well-being of the female during pair formation, which in birds involves aggression by the male during its earlier stages. To offset this, [natural] selection would favor greater physical prowess in the female, and hence that sex has become the larger one, especially in the most aggressive species." See also Cade (1960) and reviews of the subject by Reynolds (1972) and Selander (1972).

SEXUAL MATURITY

Most songbirds, many ducks, pigeons and doves, and the smaller owls and most gallinaceous birds—for example, pheasants, grouse, and quail—usually reach sexual maturity and breed within 9 months to 1 year after hatching, or sometime in the spring or summer following their birth. See some interesting exceptions under Fertilization. The males of some pheasants, however, and males of the eastern wild turkey may not breed until 2 years old. According to Leopold (1944), females of the eastern wild turkey, *Meleagris gallopavo silvestris*, breed freely when 1 year old, but males in their first year, according to Schorger (1966), are usually dominated by the older gobblers and psychologically prevented from copulating

with the hens (*see* Turkey Family; *also* Copulation and Copulatory Organs). Males and females of Merriam's turkey, a subspecies, *merriami* (*see* Subspecies), do not usually breed until 2 years old (Ligon, 1946), but domestic turkeys, males and females, mate when 1 year old.

Many gulls, shorebirds, geese, small hawks, crows, and swifts usually breed for the first time at 2 years; cormorants, boobies, and larger gulls when 3 or more years old; storks and swans when 4–5; larger eagles at 4, 5, or 6 years; male ostriches when 4 years old, females when 3½ (Welty, 1962). Albatrosses do not breed until they are 7–9 years old, and sooty terns when 4–8 years old, and some, not until 10 years old (Harrington, 1974). *See* Age, and ages given under biography of each species. *See* especially Bursa of Fabricius; *also* Courtship; Eggs and Egg-laying; Nests and Nesting.

SEXUAL MOSAICS
See Gynandromorph.

SEXUAL RELATIONSHIPS
Among birds, the relationships in which pairs come together in producing and raising young vary in duration depending on the length and strength of the pair bond (attachment) established between members of the pairs. This may vary considerably in different species and even between individuals of the same species—some mated pairs may remain together for life, or at least for the life of one member of the pair, for several years, for only one year, etc. *See* The Pair Bond under Courtship.

The pair bond which holds pairs together may be personal recognition of mates for each other or possibly something like human affection or it may be a powerful attachment of each member of the pair to its territory to which each returns year after year (*see* Territory); however, many species, including black-capped chickadees and American goldfinches, become paired before they establish nesting territories (Welty, 1962).

The commonest sexual relationship among birds is monogamous, in which a pair remain together through at least one nesting season; among small monogamous birds, however, some may pair with the same mates the following year or for several successive years; others, such as house wrens, bank swallows, and other hole-nesting birds, may remain together for only one brood; and the pairing of hummingbirds may be so brief (a few hours) that it is often called a promiscuous relationship—in which a female, after building her nest, copulates with the first male of her kind she meets, then lays her eggs; afterward she rears the young usually without any help from the male; meanwhile the male meets and copulates with other females. See details in Wagner (1954); *see also* discussion under Hummingbird Family; Species; Hybrid. Sexual promiscuity, in which sexes come together only to copulate, exists also in the ruff, prairie chicken, sage grouse, manakins, and other groups, listed by Welty (1962). Tuck (1972) describes the great snipe, *Gallinago media*, of Eurasia as promiscuous, with males assembling in a "lek," where they

copulate with any receptive female. See Arena Bird.

Polygamy among birds is well known—it may be *polygyny*, in which one male is mated to several females, or *polyandry*, in which a female is mated to more than one male. Polygyny is commonest, and occurs regularly, in particular, among gallinaceous birds (*see* account under Arena Bird), such as pheasants and peacocks, and among songbirds—for example, in red-winged blackbirds, bobolinks (Martin, S.G., 1973), dickcissels (Zimmerman, 1966), and house wrens. Usually, in polygyny, a male copulates with several females, then, in separate nests, each female incubates her eggs with no assistance in incubation from the male. Sutton (1967a), from some of his earlier Arctic studies, was convinced of polygyny in the buff-breasted, pectoral, and white-rumped sandpipers; it is also known occasionally even among such usually monogamous birds as hawks, swans, doves, flycatchers, sparrows, titmice, thrushes, warblers, and noted twice in the purple martin (Brown, 1975). See various types of mating associations in songbirds (passerines) listed in Verner and Willson (1969).

Polyandry is relatively rare or uncommon; however, Oring and Knudson (1972) believe it is more common than previously supposed. It is known usually among birds in which the role of the sexes in their family lives is reversed—the females are larger, usually have brighter plumage (*see* Sexual Dimorphism), solicit the males, and defend a common territory with the males, which are smaller and drabber. The males build the nest, incubate the eggs, and care for the young. It is known (see discussion of it in Lack, 1968, and Orians, 1969) or postulated, for example, among rheas, tinamous, jacanas (*see* Jacana Family), painted-snipe (*see* Shorebird, and details in Austin, 1961), also in button-quail (*see* Gruiformes), infrequently in the dotterel (Plover Family), and the spotted sandpiper (Sandpiper Family). See details in Hays (1972) and in Oring and Knudson (1972). See also details of polyandry in general in Armstrong (1964c).

Sex role reversal may occur in birds that have not evolved polyandry; therefore it cannot be assumed that certain birds are polyandrous simply on the basis of sex role reversal, until studied carefully. For example, although members of the Phalarope Family, in which sex role is reversed, have been considered to be polyandrous, Höhn (1965, 1967) and Johns (1969) suggested that Wilson's phalarope is probably monogamous but might be promiscuous; also, Höhn (1967) believed that no real evidence of polyandry existed in the other species—the red and the northern phalaropes; however, Raner (1972) in Sweden found polyandry in an individually color-banded population of the northern phalarope. See also Mayfield (1978), who reported a low incidence of polyandry in red phalaropes.

True polyandry, as defined by Jenni and Collier (1972) in their Costa Rican studies of the American jacana, *Jacana spinosa*, is one female mated simultaneously, or having simultaneous pair bonds, with more than one male. This can be proved only with observations of individually marked birds; Jenni and Collier color-banded their jacanas to distinguish them on a breeding pond. During 4 years, the wild jacanas studied by them had a total breeding population of 15 females and 34 males, or an average of slightly more than 2 males per female. Each female had a large territory on the water plants of the pond's surface that included the smaller territories of from 1 to 4 of the smaller males. Each female not only defended her territory against females of her kind, but helped her males drive away other intruding jacanas.

In 1964, 4 territorial males on the pond were all mated with the same female; she solicited copulation from them and afterward laid clutches of 4 eggs each in the nests of at least 2 of her mates with which she had copulated successfully—in the sense that fertilized eggs and broods resulted. In handling the jacanas, the investigators noted that only the males had the incubation patches (see Incubation) and each did all of the incubating of eggs in the nest that each had built.

After hatching of the chicks, each male brooded his family (see Brooding) and kept company with the chicks (they apparently fed themselves, as male was not seen to feed them) and defended them until they were about 4 weeks old and able to care for themselves; they are able to fly about 35 days after hatching; at this time, adult males that had cared for them were again copulating with females, which laid eggs in the nests of the males for successive broods (Jenni and Collier, 1972).

Birds have sexual aberrations, but breeding within a family group (inbreeding), for example, is rare in most species in the wild owing in part to dispersal (see Dispersal) of the young after the nesting season (see also Fall Shuffle) and intolerance of adults toward the grown young. Even though some young songbirds of the previous year may return to the home site of the adults the following spring (see Return to Nest Sites and Wintering Places under Banding), inbreeding is so rare that Nice (1937b), despite all the banding of birds in America in previous years, could summarize only three undoubted cases of inbreeding: a brother-and-sister mating of a pair of downy woodpeckers, and one in a pair of song sparrows, and a record in Germany of a father-and-daughter mating in barn (Clobes') swallows, *Hirundo rustica;* besides these, Welty (1962) cites banding records of father-and-daughter mating in the dark-eyed (slate-colored) junco, *Junco hyemalis,* and mother-and-son matings in both barn and tree swallows, *Iridoprocne bicolor;* sister-and-brother matings in the wild mallard and dark-eyed (slate-colored) junco. See Inbreeding. Certain birds raised by people have formed pair bonds with their keepers and have courted them as though they were of their own kind. See Lorenz (1952).

Homosexual pairs have been noted among captives when birds of the same or even of different species were compelled to live together in a limited space—swans and ducks on a pond, for example. Owing to sexual drives, two males or two females of the same or related species may pair and attempt to mount each other and copulate. *See* Copulation and Copulatory Organs. These homosexual pairs may remain together permanently even though a heterosex-

ual partner is introduced on the pond for breeding (Katz, 1937).

According to Armstrong (1942), "homosexual" behavior has been reported in snakes, lizards, and apes; among birds, captive black-crowned night herons have formed into unisexual pairs—for example, if a male entered an unpaired male's territory and adopted a subservient attitude, he might become the other's partner. In many species of birds, if a male does not react to another male with masculine behavior, especially among birds that show little outward differences in sexes, he is treated as a female (see, for example, the ruffed grouse in How Birds Recognize Their Own Species and Sex under Courtship).

Homosexual behavior in the wild has been noted in avocets, the ruff, and sage grouse; also in the rock dove, or domestic pigeon, by Brackbill (1941), who watched two feral males take turns mounting and treading each other. Rea (1973a) cited a male house sparrow that mounted and copulated repeatedly with a male brown-headed cowbird. Canada geese, which are normally monogamous, often form unisexual pairs of either males or females. Starkey (1972) reported a pairing (in a captive population of the giant Canada goose, *Branta canadensis maxima,* kept in a county park in Minn.) of a male giant Canada goose and a male snow goose, *Chen caerulescens.* In their relationship, the much larger goose assumed the "female" role, followed the smaller, more aggressive snow goose about, and roosted close to him at night; however, the pair were never seen to attempt copulation or to build a nest. Recently, homosexual pairings among females in colonies of wild ring-billed, California, and western gulls have been documented (Conover et al., 1979). In these species a small percentage of the females form homosexual pairings and usually produce double-sized clutches of 4–6 eggs in single nests. Although in the western gull most of these eggs have been found to be infertile, a fairly high proportion of such clutches in ring-billed and California gulls have proven to be fertile, and presumably are the result of earlier heterosexual or promiscuous matings. The adaptive significance of this surprising discovery remains to be determined. *See* Courtship; Fertilization; Nests and Nesting; Eggs and Egg-laying; Hatching; Young and Their Care.

SEXUAL REVERSAL
See Endocrine Glands.

SEXUAL SELECTION
See Sexual Dimorphism.

SHAD BIRD
or SHAD SPIRIT. Names for the common snipe in Mass. because spring appearance of bird coincides with appearance of spawning shad (McAtee, 1955c).

SHADOW-BOXING
See Window-fighting under Territory.

SHAG
Name often applied to cormorants; in N. America along N. Atlantic coast it is another name for the double-crested and great cormorants

(Townsend, 1922a); also, in British Isles, shag is the common name of the cormorant, *Phalacrocorax aristotelis* (Peterson et al., 1954); however, shag not used in general for N. American species. *See* Cormorant Family.

SHANK
Straight part of a bird's foot immediately above its toes. *See* Tarsus; Feet and Legs.

SHARP-SHIN
See Hawk, sharp-shinned, in Hawk Family.

SHEARWATER
One of the common names of the black skimmer in Skimmer Family, not to be confused with true members of Shearwater Family.

SHEARWATER FAMILY
Procellariidae (pro-sell-ah-RYE-ih-dee), from Lat. *procella,* a storm, pertaining to storms. Some 53 species of mostly migratory offshore seabirds (see Seabird); about 11–36 in. long; live over oceans of world (Van Tyne and Berger, 1976); 19 species in N. American waters; are related to albatrosses (see other relatives under Procellariiformes); are commonly called "tubenoses" because of their unusual nostrils (see Nostrils); family includes in N. America, besides 12 species of shearwaters, from which family gets its name, the northern fulmar (actually a large petrel), the related Cape petrel, or Cape pigeon, very rare in N. American waters, and 5 species of gadfly petrels of the genus *Pterodroma.* Apparently the gadfly petrels got their name from Lat. *Oestralata,* the former genus name of the black-capped petrel and other gadfly petrels, from Gr. *oistrelatos,* goaded on, as by a gadfly (Jaeger, 1955), or by a goad, as cattle are; thus *gadfly* petrels apparently in reference to the mysterious impulse which seems to drive these wide-ranging birds over the ocean waves (Coues, 1882). The smaller storm-petrels are in the Storm-petrel Family.

All in Shearwater Family have bills short and heavy to rather long and slender, and hooked at the tip. The two tubular nostrils are enclosed in a horny tube on the culmen, or "ridgetop," of the bill.

Some birds of the family (prions) have filtering plates, or lamellae, of the bill that apparently help them gather food from the water; the legs are short to medium long; the feet webbed (palmate); the tail short; wings usually long, narrow, pointed; flight is rapid and gliding, usually close above surface of water; pick food from surface in passing flight or may dive or swim about on surface to feed; all completely marine in feeding, alone or in groups, on fishes, squids, crustaceans, offal of fishes and whales; sexes outwardly alike, usually come ashore only for breeding, nest in colonies in burrows or rock crevices (a few large species on open ground), sometimes on headlands, cliffs, or mountain slopes of mainland or on small remote islands in ocean; all females lay one white egg; both parents incubate eggs and care for the young.

On land members of family do not stand upright on their toes as songbirds, for example, do, but rest their weight on both the toes and

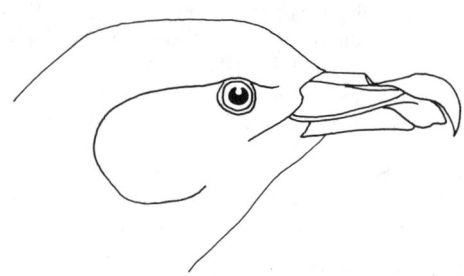

SHEARWATER FAMILY

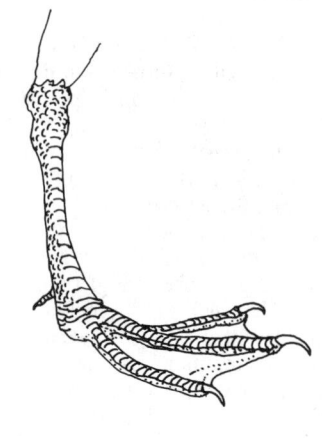

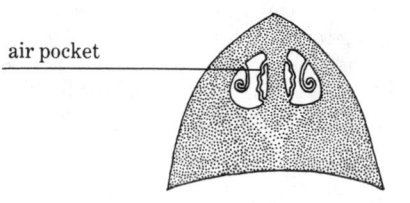

air pocket

cross-section of nasal passage

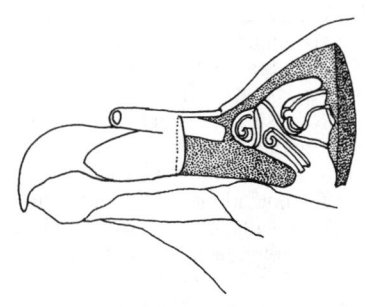

SHEARWATER FAMILY
Small pockets occur in the middle chamber of the nasal passages of the fulmar and other dynamic soarers, and these may function as a sensory organ, opening and closing in response to the pressures of the varying velocities of ocean air currents.

lower legs; the somewhat crouching posture on land gives appearance of being weak-legged.

All members of the Procellariidae Family regurgitate an unpleasant musky oil that seems to be a residue of their food. The oil gives the petrels, and their nesting sites, an unpleasantly strong odor. Rich in vitamins, the oil resembles that of the oil gland, and is regurgitated by adults when alarmed, when preening, and when feeding chicks.

The northern fulmar lives in N. American waters and around northern waters of world; it is a large, gull-like seabird, actually a large petrel (Fisher, 1952); there are enormous numbers of these birds; the Dutch whalers called them *mallemugge*—same name they had for teeming midges of the polar grasslands; Charles Darwin thought them most numerous birds in the world, but see Fisher and Lockley (1954).

The gadfly petrels superficially resemble shearwaters, but their wings are broader, the tail usually *longer and wedge-shaped*, especially in the smaller species. The short black bill is strongly hooked, heavily grooved, and has prominent tubular nostrils; they flap and glide like shearwaters but swoop more erratically in great arcs and hold their wings *noticeably* bent at the wrists, not extended stiffly as do shearwaters; also, they fly higher, often rising above horizon of the ocean. They feed almost exclusively on squids and occasionally on crustaceans they reach down and take with bill from surface while in flight; they seldom alight on water and do not dive (Watson, 1966).

Shearwaters got their name from skimming low over the ocean and sailing on long, pointed wings low in troughs between the waves and seeming to shear the water with their wing tips. Sometimes on a windy day, one may sail with wings fixed in gliding position for a mile and a half, often only inches over the water, in its searches for food. Shearwaters do not usually follow ships, are generally silent at sea, except when quarreling over food with high-pitched screams; at nesting time, utter cackling notes or weird sobbing, wailing, or cooing notes.

Shearwaters are either all-dark or dark with white underparts; they are heavy-bodied and have long, narrow wings, usually short, rounded tails, and a long, slender bill, sharply hooked at tip, with paired horny tubes along ridge (culmen) of bill. Shearwaters fly with alternate bursts of wing flaps and long glides; they bank low over surface to snatch from surface (some alight on water) in bill small fishes and squids or by shallow dives below water; they often stay with schools of fishes that swim near surface; six species are widely distributed throughout the tropical, or S., Atlantic O. (Watson, 1966).

Most shearwaters raise their families on islands or islets in oceans of the S. Hemisphere; they are among the world's greatest avian travelers (*see* Migration) and make long migrations in spring, summer, and fall into the N. Hemisphere, sometimes in great flocks (see account by Austin, 1961); about a dozen species have been seen (some regularly each year) off either the Atlantic or Pacific coast of N. America. John Ray (1627–1705), English naturalist, gave

the shearwaters the generic name *Puffinus* in the mistaken idea that they were puffins (Newton, 1893–96). *See* puffins in Auk Family.

Prions, small petrels that breed in the Antarctic and feed directly on the smaller zooplankton of the oceans, do not come north into the N. Hemisphere.

Albinism was reported by Gross (1965a) in 7 individuals of 3 species, but he did not identify them.

Fulmar, northern, *Fulmarus glacialis* (FOOL-mah-rus glay-sih-ALE-iss); genus name: Lat. form of Icelandic *fulmar*, sea smew; species name: Lat., icy, in reference to its northern environment; *fulmar* means "foul gull" (it is not a gull), one of its oldest names (Fisher, 1952), from rank odor of the musky oil it discharges from its stomach in defense when handled or disturbed by an enemy. (Color ill., page 839.) Off Atlantic and Pacific coasts of U.S., mostly in winter; 17–20 in. long; wingspread to 42 in.; stocky seabird with large, round head, dark brown eyes; short, massive, yellow bill hooked at tip, with *high, prominent nasal tubes* which distinguish it from gulls; in *light phase,* generally with white head and white underparts, gray back, wings, and tail (*see* Color Phase)—these pale birds appear superficially gull-like; in *dark phase,* entire plumage almost uniformly medium gray, in which it is superficially like sooty shearwater, but short, thick neck of fulmar, dumpy body, short, rounded tail distinguish it (Fisher, 1952); its feet are webbed as in gulls and ducks; it is nearest in appearance to an albatross of any bird that flies in N. Atlantic (*see* definition of N. Atlantic under Seabird); usually seen on high seas beyond range of most gulls; is magnificent flier, or glider, like sailplane, even in strongest gale; holds somewhat blunt-appearing wings straight and stiff, with alternate flaps and glides, usually flies very fast in long arcs up and down over waves, tail very flexible in flight, tilted up on either side.

Feeding Habits: Single birds wander widely at sea; large numbers gather where food of fishes, mollusks, crustaceans, etc., is abundant around reefs and edges of currents (see Palmer, 1962); follow fishing vessels, very bold when flying close to ships, sometimes within reach of people aboard. Feeding flocks are noisy, uttering hoarse "whirring" cackles, or grunts when quarreling over food; float or swim on surface while eating; reported as diving to 6 ft. below surface; "fly" underwater with half-spread wings; drink seawater; swallow water by suction (Fisher, 1952), like pigeon, not by taking sip and tilting head back as in many birds. In calmest weather can take off from flat ground by springing into air; only young or ill adults get stranded on land.

Nest: In colonies from a few pairs up to 200,000 —some 100,000 on Baffin Is., Canada (Palmer, 1962); before reaching breeding age, fulmars probably do not come to land until 3–4 years old; first breed when 7–9 years old (Fisher, 1952); nest usually in hollow on cliff or among moist herbage (on castle walls in Britain); also on small islands.

Eggs: May–July (Bent, 1922); 1, white, sometimes stained with red spots.

Incubation: By both sexes, about 55 days; young leave nest site and may fly down to sea from cliff 46–51 days after hatching; one brood a year; young and adults defend themselves or nest area by spitting up foul-smelling stomach oil. At Orkney Is., Scotland, a white-tailed eagle that had apparently attacked young fulmars on a nesting ledge was later found flapping and struggling on the water, unable to fly because oil spat out by young fulmars had caused its plumage to become water-soaked (see Dennis, 1970; Sweenen, 1974). Major predator has been man killing fulmars for flesh and feathers (Palmer, 1962); have been caught on baited hooks by fishermen, whalers, and explorers; also at nest may be killed by arctic weasels; occasionally attacked by bald eagle in Aleutian Is., by white-tailed eagle in Iceland, and by peregrine in Britain, and possibly by gyrfalcons on Baffin Is.; glaucous and herring gulls are serious predators on eggs of fulmar; jaegers and the skua occasionally attack fulmars in flight and try to force them to disgorge food.

Other Names: Fulmar petrel; John down; mallemuck; mallemugge; marbleheader; molly hawk; mollymoke; noddy; oil-bird; sea horse; white hagdon.

Age: Two birds banded in 1950 still breeding in 1974. Adults first breed at 6–12 years of age; thus, these two birds probably about 34 years old (Cramp, 1977).

Albinism: A few white ones, evidently pure albinos, reported from N. Atlantic; one pure albino reported from Pacific (Palmer, 1962).

Flight Speed: Estimated at 40–50 m.p.h. when gliding over wake of ship.

Weights: 1½–2½ lb.

Range: In N. America, nests on isles, or islets, rocky cliffs along coasts of Aleutians, Alaskan Pen., e. Franklin District of Canada to Greenland; also in n. Europe; offshore in winter from Labrador to New England and Pacific coast south to Baja Calif.; casual to Lake Ontario, Que., coastal Conn. and Va.; south of Newfoundland Grand Banks, ranges uncommonly to N.C. (Lee and Booth, 1979), and recent records off N.J. and Md.

Petrel, ashy. Ashy storm-petrel is its proper name; it is in Storm-petrel Family.

Petrel, Bermuda, *Pterodroma cahow* (ter-OD-roh-mah kah-HOO or kah-HOW); genus name: from Gr. *pteron*, wing, and *dromos*, a running, a running course (Jaeger, 1955); species name: onomatopoetic name from the bird's strange wild cry apparently heard only in Oct. and Nov. (Greenway, 1958). *Very rare*, nearing extinction (*see* Rare and Threatened Species); one of gadfly petrels; in Bermudas in nesting season, Nov.–May; sexes outwardly alike; about 15 in. long; wingspread about 36 in.; is similar to black-capped petrel, its closest relative, brown above, white below, but black-capped is larger, darker, and has heavier bill. Its cap is darker than that of black-capped and has a dark, not a white, rump; it is possibly a subspecies of a group that includes the black-capped petrel and others (Palmer, 1962); Bermuda petrel, which has upperparts more or less

uniform, could be mistaken for common shearwater but has short bill, white face and underparts, and especially white on underwings (similar South Trinidade petrel has dark underwings); Bermuda petrel's white forehead distinguishes it from the greater and Audubon's shearwaters (Greenway, 1958); was for a long time thought to be extinct, but rediscovered by Beebe in 1935; see also Murphy and Mowbray (1951), and especially Greenway (1958); still under 100 left, according to Vincent (1966). See report of Zimmerman, D. R. (1973).

Feeding Habits: Eats largely squids taken at surface of water (Watson, 1966; but see Zimmerman, D. R., 1973); is nocturnal, at least when nesting.

Nest: In burrow or holes in rocks.

Eggs: Jan. 1–10 (Palmer, 1962); 1, chalky white.

Incubation: 51–54 days, by both sexes; young fly about 90–100 days after hatching.

Other Names: Cahow; cowhaw; cowkoe (in imitation of its cry).

Range: Now limited in breeding season to small islets near se. coast of Bermuda; range at other times unknown.

Petrel, black. Black storm-petrel is its proper name; it is in Storm-petrel Family.

Petrel, black-capped, *Pterodroma hasitata* (ter-OD-roh-mah hass-ih-TAY-tah); genus name: *see* Petrel, Bermuda; species name: Lat., correctly *haesitatus*, made fast, or stuck fast, the describer of the bird in doubt, therefore *hesitating* to name it (Coues, 1882). One of the gadfly petrels, once very rare, now considered a recovered species (Vincent, 1966); some ornithologists believe that this "capped" petrel is a subspecies of a group that includes the Bermuda petrel and others; see Palmer (1962) for discussion; 14–18 in. long; wingspread 35–40 in. (Watson, 1966); heavy-bodied bird; ash-gray back, wings, and tail; *forehead white;* black cap and white collar; underwings white with black border; *white rump very conspicuous in flight* distinguishes it from greater shearwater (Greenway, 1958), and white face distinguishes it from most shearwaters; in dark phase (*see* Color Phase), is sooty-colored except for white upper tail coverts; bill and feet dark; legs pinkish; calls at night around breeding islands are mournful, owl-like.

Feeding Habits: Eats largely squids taken in bill from surface of water (Watson, 1966).

Nest: Breeds on steep cliffs of the Massif de la Selle, Haiti; locally common in 1963, no fewer than 4,000 at time, but could again be threatened by introduced mongoose and other problems (see Greenway, 1958; Vincent, 1966); nests in burrows, probably 1,500 ft. above sea level, possibly in sandy burrows or in rock crevices.

Eggs and Incubation: Probably like that of Bermuda petrel.

Other Names: Diablotin (die-yah-BLOW-tan), or "little devil," so called by blacks of West Indies on hearing its cries at night; also blue mountain duck; dry-land booby; West Indian petrel.

Range: Nests (now or formerly) in mountains of Jamaica, Guadeloupe, Dominica, Hispaniola (see Wingate, 1964); ranges over Atlantic O.

Bermuda petrel

SHEARWATER FAMILY

from off e. Brazil north to latitude of Fla.; regular but uncommon at least to N.C.; noted after tropical hurricanes north to Ont., N.H., Conn., N.Y. (Long Is.), Ohio, Ky., Va., Fla.; on Sept. 11, 1964, one found dead at base of a 673-ft. television tower in Leon County, Fla., about 20 mi. north of Tallahassee (Stoddard and Norris, 1967).

Petrel, black-tailed. *See* Shearwater, black-tailed.

Petrel, blue-footed. *See* Petrel, Cook's.

Petrel, Cape, *Daption capense* (DAP-tee-on cah-PEN-see); genus name: from Gr. *daptein,* to devour, apparently in reference to its eating habits; however, Murphy (1972) claims that *Daption* is an invented "nonsense" word, an anagram of the Sp. adjective *pintado;* species name: Lat., of the Cape of Good Hope. Not a gadfly petrel but one more closely related to the fulmar; accidental in N. American waters; 15–16 in. long; wingspread, 32–37 in. (Watson, 1966); all-black head; has boldly "pied," or checkered, back; two large and many small white patches on each wing; white tail with black across tip; underparts white; flaps more and glides less than most petrels, and usually close to water; follows ships readily; the most familiar seabird of Antarctic waters; in flocks or singly, notably unwary, passing, or sitting on water, close to ships (Palmer, 1962).

Feeding Habits: Dives well and may, in flight, take food from surface, also foot-paddles on surface, eats fishes, squids, marine crustaceans, blood, fat, and flesh of whales at Antarctic whaling stations; also ships' garbage.
Nest: On seaside cliff in niches and hollows on islands in Antarctic.
Other Names: Cape pigeon; pigeon petrel; pintado (pied or painted) petrel.
Weights: About ¾–1 lb. (Palmer, 1962).
Range: Nests on islands in Antarctic; regularly ranges north to s. Brazil and Africa in Falkland and Benguela currents and to Tristan da Cunha (Watson, 1966); records in N. America probably not valid (McCaskie *et al.,* 1970).

Petrel, Cook's, *Pterodroma cookii* (ter-OD-roh-mah COOK-ih-eye); genus name: *see* Petrel, Bermuda; species name: for Captain James Cook (1728–79), English explorer of New Zealand and circumnavigator of world. A gadfly petrel that ranges north to Pacific coast off Baja Calif. (regularly) and Calif. (rarely); small; about 10½ in. long; a long-winged, long-tailed petrel; gray upperparts, white face and white underparts; bill black, long, slender, grooved and hooked, with short, raised nasal tubes; similar to scaled petrel in appearance but no gray band on belly.

Feeding Habits: Little known but possibly squids (Palmer, 1962) and small fishes.
Other Name: Blue-footed petrel.
Range: The nominate subspecies, *cookii,* nests in New Zealand and may winter in n. Pacific; ranges over s. and se. Pacific, off coast of Peru and north to Aleutians; reported once near Adak Is., and seen off coast of Baja Calif.

Petrel, Coues'. Ashy storm-petrel is its proper name; it is in Storm-petrel Family.

Petrel, fork-tailed. Fork-tailed storm-petrel is its proper name; it is in Storm-petrel Family.

Petrel, frigate. Another name for the white-faced storm-petrel in Storm-petrel Family.

Petrel, fulmar. *See* Fulmar, northern.

Petrel, Guadalupe Island. Guadalupe storm-petrel is its proper name; it is in Storm-petrel Family.

Petrel, Harcourt's. Harcourt's storm-petrel is its proper name; it is in Storm-petrel Family.

Petrel, Leach's. Leach's storm-petrel is its proper name; it is in Storm-petrel Family.

Petrel, least. Least storm-petrel is its proper name; it is in Storm-petrel Family.

Petrel, Madeiran. Another name for Harcourt's storm-petrel in Storm-petrel Family.

Petrel, mottled. *See* Petrel, scaled.

Petrel, Peale's. *See* Petrel, scaled.

Petrel, pigeon. *See* Petrel, Cape.

Petrel, pintado. *See* Petrel, Cape.

Petrel, scaled, *Pterodroma inexpectata* (ter-OD-roh-mah in-ex-peck-TAY-tah); genus name: *see* Petrel, Bermuda; species name: Lat., unexpected, might well apply to its vagrant wanderings and unexpected appearances. A medium-sized gadfly petrel; 14 in. long; wingspread 27 in.; sexes outwardly similar; rather heavily built with contrasting gray and white mottled markings; grayish above with dark gray abdomen and *prominent black bar across ulnar part of underwing* (Watson, 1975; Warham *et al.,* 1977); tail short, rounded; black bill heavy, grooved and hooked (Palmer, 1962); in fresh plumage, back is lightly scaled with white; rapid flight in great arcs; does not follow ships, silent at sea.

Feeding Habits: Small squids and fishes.
Nest: Pair digs burrow in cliffs, tussock grassland, in rock crevices, caves, etc., about 30–36 in. deep.
Eggs: Most laid Dec. 15–22 (Warham *et al.,* 1977); 1, white.
Incubation: About 50½ days, by both sexes about equally, each incubates in periods of 12–14 days; young fly about 90–105 days after hatching (Warham *et al.,* 1977).
Other Names: Mottled petrel; Peale's petrel.
Weights: Average of 88–100 live birds in New Zealand, 316 gr., or about ¾ lbs.
Range: At present known to breed only on islands in Foveaux Strait and off Stewart Is., s. New Zealand, and on Snares Is., Nov.–Apr. (Watson, 1975); common May to Oct.; resident of northern and eastern parts of n. Pacific O.; in migration reaches s. Alaska and Aleutian waters; records (mostly Feb.–Aug.) for B.C.,

Wash., Ore., Calif., and N.Y. (Ainley and Manolis, 1979).

Petrel, South Trinidade, *Pterodroma arminjoniana* (ter-OD-roh-mah are-min-john-ih-AY-nah); genus name: *see* Petrel, Bermuda; species name: for Capt. Vittorio Arminjon, commander of first Italian naval vessel to sail around the world; on this trip, scientific members of party collected at South Trinidade Is., Brazil, the bird later described in 1868. A gadfly petrel rare in N. American waters in N. Atlantic; about 15 in. long; wingspread 38–40 in.; three color phases: either all dark brownish gray; dark brownish gray above and mottled white below; or intermediate—light-phase birds which have white flecking on face and indistinct band across upper breast; underwings show pale flash in dark birds, white flash in light phase; bill shorter and weaker than in other gadfly petrels (Watson, 1966); rather long-tailed.

Albinism: Some have shown traces—one white-headed bird and one prevailingly white over back (Palmer, 1962).
Range: Nests on Trinidad and Martin Vas islands off coast of Brazil, and islands east of Madagascar in Old World; individuals have crossed Equator and ranged north in Atlantic O. during storms; one on N. American continent, Aug. 1933, when hurricane blew it to village of Caroline Center near Ithaca, N.Y.

Petrel, stormy. Storm-petrel is its proper name; it is in Storm-petrel Family.

Petrel, wedge-rumped. Galápagos storm-petrel is its proper name; it is in Storm-petrel Family.

Petrel, white-rumped. Leach's storm-petrel is its proper name; it is in Storm-petrel Family.

Petrel, Wilson's. Wilson's storm-petrel is its proper name; it is in Storm-petrel Family.

Shearwater, allied. *See* Shearwater, little.

Shearwater, Audubon's, *Puffinus lherminieri* (PUFF-in-us ler-min-EER-eye); genus name: Lat. form of *puffin,* the genus name incorrectly applied because of mistaken idea that these birds were puffins; species name: given by Lesson in 1839, either for Dr. Félix-Louis l'Herminier, French naturalist, or for his son Dr. Ferdinand J.; common name: for John James Audubon. (Color ill., page 840.) Casual along Atlantic and Gulf coasts; 12 in. long; wingspread 27 in.; black above, white below; very small, black-capped shearwater, resembling color pattern of greater shearwater but does not have white in tail; wings beat much faster than those of other shearwaters.

Feeding Habits: Probably small fishes and squids; spends much time on water; does not follow ships, dives freely.
Nest: In colonies on small islands, sometimes in rock crevices or under thick plant cover.
Eggs: March; 1, white (Palmer, 1962).
Incubation: About 51 days, by both sexes; first flight of young about 72 days after hatch-

ing; first breed when 8 years old (Harris, M. P., 1972).

Other Names: Dusky shearwater; pimlico (in Bermuda and Antilles).

Age: Adult (banded) reported by Harris, M. P. (1972) at least 11 years old.

Weights: A lone male collected Sept. 1961 on Pacific, 113.9 gr., or about 4¾ oz.; two other males, 133.1 and 147.3 gr. (Binford, 1970).

Range: Oceanic in Atlantic, Pacific, and Indian oceans; nests on small islands of Caribbean, Lesser Antilles, Bahamas, and Bermuda; ranges north to N.C.; casual to Mass. and to Tex. coastal areas. The nominate subspecies, *lherminieri,* nests on Bermuda but rare there; only two or three breeding pairs in 1956 and 1959 (Palmer, 1962). Occurs off Atlantic coast largely after breeding season, seen annually by ornithologists off coast of Fla. from 1958 to 1966 in July, Aug., Sept., follows Gulf Stream north, more than 100 reported off N.C. coast following a storm in July; reported off coast of Va. and about 120 mi. southeast of New England coast from ships at sea; most records of dead or dying birds along Atlantic coast and inland result of hurricanes in Aug. and Sept.; away from coast, all reports were near Gulf Stream (Post, 1967); however, sometimes abundant off N.C. from Apr. to Nov. (Lee and Booth, 1979).

Shearwater, black-vented. *See* Shearwater, Manx.

Shearwater, Buller's. *See* Shearwater, New Zealand.

Shearwater, Cape Verde. *See* Shearwater, Cory's.

Shearwater, cinereous. *See* Shearwater, Cory's.

Shearwater, common. *See* Shearwater, Manx.

Shearwater, common Atlantic. *See* Shearwater, greater.

Shearwater, Cooper's. *See* Shearwater, pink-footed.

Shearwater, Cory's, *Puffinus diomedea* (PUFF-in-us die-oh-me-DEE-ah); genus name: *see* Shearwater, Audubon's; species name: same as genus name of albatrosses, possibly because of this bird's albatrosslike flight; common name: for Charles B. Cory, American naturalist. (Color ill., page 841.) In summer and fall off Atlantic coast; 16–18 in. long; wingspread to 44 in.; upperparts uniformly gray-brown; merge into white underparts; throat, sides, and underwings white; undertail coverts white; large, thick yellow-brown or pink-yellow bill; bird resembles greater shearwater in general, but greater shearwater has *black* bill; Cory's is a large, rather lightly built, long-winged shearwater; its flight differs from other N. Atlantic shearwaters, is much more free, with slower wingbeats, buoyant, and albatrosslike.

Feeding Habits: Eats large squids and crustaceans taken at night from surface of ocean, to a lesser extent follows schools of fishes such as mackerel to feed on young fishes driven in toward shore.

Nest: Usually no nest materials, in burrow or rock crevice.

Eggs: Early May to June; 1, white.

Incubation: Period of and age when young first fly unknown.

Other Names: Cape Verde shearwater; cinereous shearwater; Mediterranean shearwater; North Atlantic shearwater.

Albinism: Several reported from Cape Verde Is., partial albinos, and a "perfect albino" reported in 1898.

Range: In N. Atlantic, nests in Azores, Madeira, and Canary Is., also on Cape Verde Is., Apr.–July; ranges off N. American coast from Newfoundland to S.C. in late summer; is common to abundant visitor in late summer and fall off Long Is., N.Y.; rare in winter. *See also* Seabird.

Shearwater, Coues'. *See* Shearwater, pink-footed.

Shearwater, dark-bodied. *See* Shearwater, sooty.

Shearwater, dusky. *See* Shearwater, Audubon's.

Shearwater, flesh-footed, *Puffinus carneipes* (PUFF-in-us car-NEE-ih-peez); genus name: *see* Shearwater, Audubon's; species name: from Lat. *carneus,* of flesh, and *pes,* foot; pale-footed. (Color ill., page 840.) A rare visitor off Pacific coast of N. America, usually in July and Aug.; mainly an offshore rather than a pelagic species; large; 19–20 in. long; sexes outwardly similar; solid, heavily built, with short, rounded tail; larger than similar and abundant sooty shearwater; has two color phases—a uniformly dark brown one and another with dark grayish brown above and gray or white below (Palmer, 1962)—with dark-tipped, thick, massive, straw-colored bill, and short, raised tubular nostrils, flesh-colored legs and feet (the sooty shearwater, similar to the flesh-footed shearwater, has all black bill and *whitish* wing linings, those of flesh-footed shearwater are dark); has flutter-and-glide flight of the diving shearwaters—several successive wingbeats, then a glide low over water.

Feeding Habits: Eats fishes and squids; has acquired habit of diving for bait on fishing lines (Palmer, 1962).

Nest: Digs burrow or clears out old one in bare or vegetated earth; tunnels about 4½ ft. long, have nest chamber at end.

Eggs: Most laid first week in Dec.; 1, white.

Incubation: Period of unknown; young first fly about 89–95 days after hatching.

Other Name: Pale-footed shearwater.

Weights: To 1¼ lb.

Range: Nests on islands off Australia and New Zealand; wanders to n. Pacific and along U.S. coast south to Calif. (no records for S. America valid).

Shearwater, gray-backed. *See* Shearwater, New Zealand.

Shearwater, great. *See* Shearwater, greater.

Shearwater, greater, *Puffinus gravis* (PUFF-in-us GRAVE-iss); genus name: *see* Shearwater, Audubon's; species name: Lat., heavy. (Color ill., page 841.) In spring and summer, migrates along Atlantic coast; 18–20 in. long; wingspread 40–48 in.; large, heavily built; dark-billed brown-and-white shearwater; has clearly defined dark cap, back, and tail; undersurfaces of wings white with brown margins; pale collar, pale band across rump; white underparts; in flight holds wings stiff and straight; tail short and rounded; typical flutter-and-glide flight; seldom appears high above waves (Palmer, 1962).

Feeding Habits: Follows and catches surface-feeding fishes, also squids, crustaceans, and small fishes such as sand launces; dives under surface for fishes and rises back into air to swallow catch; also eats offal from fishing boats and whale feces.

Nest: Colonial nester; uses some grass for nest in bottom of burrow.

Eggs: Usual average laying around Nov. 11 (Palmer, 1962); 1, white.

Incubation: About 55 days; chick tended by both parents; first flights about 84 days after hatching (Palmer, 1962); young fledge in Apr. and May. See Watson (1971).

Other Names: Cinereous puffin; common Atlantic shearwater; great shearwater; hag; hagdon; haglet; wandering shearwater.

Weights: About 1½–2 lb.

Range: Population estimated at five million pairs nests in the S. Atlantic on islands of the Tristan da Cunha group, Gough Is., and a single record from the Falkland Is. (Watson, 1975); migrates north in spring and summer over w. Atlantic off Fla. coast north to Grand Banks, Newfoundland; sometimes thousands found dead on beaches after hurricanes.

Shearwater, great gray. *See* Shearwater, black-tailed.

Shearwater, little, *Puffinus assimilis* (PUFF-in-us as-SIM-ih-lis); genus name: *see* Shearwater, Audubon's; species name: Lat., like. Rare in N. America, reported twice off Atlantic coast (A.O.U. *Check-list,* 1957); 10 in. long; smallest shearwater, smaller than similar Audubon's shearwater, but with mostly white instead of dark undertail coverts, more white on sides of neck and head; legs and feet bluish (Palmer, 1962).

Feeding Habits: Appears very small and short-winged in flight, with flutter-and-glide type of the diving shearwaters, but wings seem almost to whir as it hurtles through air like a small auk. Swims and dives freely, usually seen alone; feeds on fishes and squids.

Nest: In colonies on turfy and rocky remote islands, offshore islets, and mainland cliffs in Pacific and Atlantic.

Eggs: 1, white.

Incubation: 52–58 days, by both sexes (Palmer, 1962).

Other Name: Allied shearwater.

Range: Nests in Atlantic on Tristan da Cunha, Gough Is., Canary Is., Salvages, Madeira, and Azores; accidental off S.C. and Nova Scotia.

Shearwater, Manx, *Puffinus puffinus* (PUFF-in-us); genus and species names: *see* Shearwater, Audubon's; common name: for Isle of Man but has not nested there since about 1800 (Austin, 1961). (Color ill., page 841.) Nests mostly on small islands off Europe and Baja Calif.; off e. U.S. coast, essentially an off-shore bird; off w. coast, rarely found more than 10 mi. from coast or from islands; the one species of shearwater most likely to be seen from shore in west; crosses Atlantic from Britain to Grand Banks, Newfoundland; a medium-sized shearwater with slender dark bill; in flight long, slender wings held straight or slightly bent; glides on rigid wings for long periods with occasional few rapid wingbeats; 12½–15 in. long; wingspread about 33 in. (Watson, 1966); adults, sexes outwardly alike; northern subspecies very nearly black above and white below, underparts flash as birds turn about over the waves in flight (Palmer, 1962); similar to Audubon's shearwater but larger and with shorter tail; in Atlantic, *long white undertail coverts;* in Pacific forms, *undertail coverts are blackish or sooty,* common off Pacific coast, where formerly called black-vented shearwater; this is a white-breasted shearwater, similar to pink-footed shearwater, but smaller, blacker above (Peterson, 1961); seen along Atlantic coast during early and middle 19th century, but unrecorded regularly until about 1950 (see Post, 1967); now a regular visitor off Atlantic coast, and first nesting record on N. American continent on Penikese Is., Mass., June 6, 1973 (see account of Bierregaard *et al.*, 1975, and photographs in *American Birds,* Feb. 1974, pp. 115, 135); adults migrate northward off Bermuda in substantial numbers between early Feb. and early Apr. on way to Europe to nest (Post, 1967); young non-breeders apparently move northward during late May and early June, following same pattern as flocks of sooty shearwaters; non-breeding Manx shearwaters disperse westward, possibly summer on or near Grand Banks, Newfoundland, and move inshore off New England coast, as do greater shearwaters, during July, Aug., and Sept. (Post, 1967); small flocks seen off St. John's, Newfoundland, in Aug. 1966; one banded at Skokholm Is., Wales, Aug. 29, 1968, found dead June 23, 1970, on Cape Sable Is., Nova Scotia (Finch, 1970).

Feeding Habits: Excellent swimmer and diver, known to dive into water with partly opened wings; eats small fishes (herring, pilchard, anchovies, sardines), crustaceans, and squids, for which it sometimes swims underwater for short distances, aided by its wings.
Nest: Usually in colonies, some in vast numbers, mainly on turf of islands, seldom on continental coasts (Palmer, 1962); both sexes dig new burrow to 6 ft. deep, or refashion old one, sometimes burrow is in rocky soil, is lined with green or dried plants; same pair may return to same burrow in succeeding years; around nesting colony, adults may be active only at night.

Eggs: Mostly Apr.–May; 1, white, is about 15% of female's weight.
Incubation: By both sexes, in turn, 51 days (Harris, 1966); one of pair may incubate without relief for 5 days (Palmer, 1962) while other adult may wander, in feeding, 500–600 mi. away from nest burrow; in about 60 days, after chick has shed most of its down, and is well feathered, is deserted by both parents; thereafter, for 11–15 days, chick remains in burrow ("starving period"), coming to surface at night to exercise its wings, finally climbs to some elevated spot outside of burrow and launches into breeze for first flight at about 70–75 days after hatching. See details in Palmer (1962).
Age: To 12 years (Lockley, 1942).
Other Names: Common shearwater; black-vented shearwater (in Pacific).
Homing Ability: One carried by plane from its nesting place on Skokholm Is. off Wales to Boston, Mass., released, returned to nesting burrow on Skokholm, 3,200 statute mi. across Atlantic, in 12½ days (Mazzeo, 1953).
Weights: 14–17 oz. (Lockley, 1942).
Range: Nests on small islands off Iceland, British Isles, and Canaries, Azores, Madeira (formerly on Bermuda), also on islands off west coast of Baja Calif., and on N. American mainland (see above); a regular visitor off Atlantic coast; wanders to S. America, Mediterranean countries, western Europe, and common (the Pacific forms, or subspecies) along Pacific coast to Calif.

Shearwater, Mediterranean. See Shearwater, Cory's.

Shearwater, New Zealand, *Puffinus bulleri* (PUFF-in-us BULL-eh-rye); genus name: *see* Shearwater, Audubon's; species name: for Sir Walter Lawry Buller, noted 19th-century ornithologist and lawyer of New Zealand (see in Oliver, 1955). (Color ill., page 841.) In N. American waters a rather rare, white-bellied shearwater that reaches Pacific coast regularly; 15–18 in. long; sooty black on crown, back of neck, on lesser wing coverts and tail; the dark bar crossing top of wings and lower back shows in flight as a broad, dark M or W; has brilliant white underwing, gray back and gray greater wing coverts, undertail coverts edged with gray (Alexander, 1928); long tail is *wedge-shaped;* at close range, shows *yellow* feet.

Feeding Habits: Eats squids and crustaceans.
Nest: In burrow, sometimes shares burrow with a large lizard, the tuatara (too-ah-TAH-rah).
Eggs: About end of Oct.; 1, white (Palmer, 1962).
Other Names: Buller's shearwater; gray-backed shearwater.
Weights: About 15 oz. to about 1 lb.
Range: Nests in large colonies on islets around North Is., New Zealand; ranges east to coast of Chile, and regularly in late summer to fall off coast of Monterey, Calif., to Ore. (mouth of Columbia R.), Wash. (Gray's Harbor), and B.C.

Shearwater, North Atlantic. See Shearwater, Cory's.

Shearwater, pale-footed. See Shearwater, flesh-footed.

Shearwater, pink-footed, *Puffinus creatopus* (PUFF-in-us cree-AT-oh-pus); genus name: *see* Shearwater, Audubon's; species name: from Gr. *kreas, kreatos,* flesh, and *pous,* foot, in reference to the pink or flesh-colored feet. (Color ill., page 841.) This white-bellied shearwater "frequently associates with the dark-bodied abundant sooty shearwater" off Pacific coast of N. America from spring into fall (Peterson, 1961); 19–20 in. long; gray-brown above; white below (often mottled); has thick, straight, light yellow bill with dark tip; pinkish legs and feet; is larger than the white-bellied Manx shearwater and larger than the dark-bodied sooty tern. Palmer (1962) considers the pink-footed shearwater not a full species but a subspecies, or form, *Puffinus carneipes creatopus,* of the flesh-footed shearwater with similar food habits.

Feeding Habits: Eats small crustaceans and fishes such as pilchards; breeding habits same as flesh-footed shearwater.
Other Names: Cooper's shearwater; Coues' shearwater; red-footed shearwater.
Range: Nests on islands off coast of Chile; ranges from spring into fall off Pacific coast of N. America, from Baja Calif. to Ore., rarely to B.C. and se. Alaska.

Shearwater, short-tailed, *Puffinus tenuirostris* (PUFF-in-us ten-you-ih-ROS-tris); genus name: *see* Shearwater, Audubon's; species name: from Lat. *tenuis,* thin, and *rostrum,* beak. (Color ill., page 841.) Ranges to Pacific coast of N. America; 13–16 in. long; wingspread about 36–39 in.; a dark, entirely sooty-brown shearwater resembling the closely related sooty shearwater, but smaller with short, straight, dark bill; very short, rounded tail; usually darker wing linings, and some with white on throat; separable from the flesh-footed shearwater by its smaller size, dark bill and legs; from wedge-tailed shearwater by dark legs, short, rounded (fan-shaped) tail (Palmer, 1962); faster flight.

Feeding Habits: Fishes taken from surface or by diving for them.
Nest: In colonies, in burrows.
Eggs: Nov.; 1, white.
Incubation: 52–55 days.
Other Names: Muttonbird; slender-billed shearwater; whalebird (in Alaska).
Age: Serventy (1970) reported five breeding in Bass Strait, Tasmania, recaptured 22 years after banding as adults that were at least 30 years old.
Albinism: Apparently very rare.
Weights: 1–1¼ lb.
Range: Nests on coastal islands of S. Australia, Victoria, and Tasmania, including Bass Strait; ranges off N. American coast from Baja Calif. to Alaska, Oct.–Jan., especially numerous Nov.–Dec.; makes enormous figure-eight, clockwise, transequatorial flight in Pacific, apparently correlated with prevailing winds (Palmer, 1962). Murphy (1936) cites an observer of a flight of these shearwaters in Bass Strait of 150 million birds. This is the famous "mut-

tonbird" of Australia and Tasmania of which the young are taken for food, with the down, oil, and fat as by-products. See account especially in Murphy (1936, Vol. II, p. 675) and in Palmer (1962) under "Slender-billed shearwater."

Shearwater, slender-billed. *See* Shearwater, short-tailed.

Shearwater, sooty, *Puffinus griseus* (PUFF-in-us GRIS-ee-us); genus name: *see* Shearwater, Audubon's; species name: Lat., grizzly, gray, in reference to gray-brown or brown-gray plumage. (Color ill., page 840.) The most far-ranging of the "cool current" shearwaters; ranges in Atlantic, Pacific, and Antarctic oceans, in N. America off Atlantic and Pacific coasts, Sept. (Reilly, 1968); a dark, gull-like seabird; 19–20 in. long; wingspread to 43 in.; with slender, dark bill; "narrow wings with *pale undersurfaces* held straight and rigid as it glides and tilts over waves" (Peterson, 1961); has short, thick neck, short, rounded tail; most common shearwater, in migration often in large flocks of millions; in N. Atlantic, unlikely to be confused with very many species; dark-phase fulmars are more stocky and have a pale "watermark" on wings (see details in Palmer, 1962); dark jaegers have white at base of primary (wing) feathers (*see* comparisons with flesh-footed and short-tailed shearwaters along Pacific coast in biographies of those species).

Feeding Habits: Eats small fishes (capelin, sand launce, and anchovies), squids, and crustaceans, for which it may dive and swim underwater; also extremely fond of oily fish livers and often appears suddenly when chopped liver or fish oil is thrown overboard from ships at sea (Pough, 1951).
Nest: In colonies, in burrows on islands.
Eggs: Usually latter half of Nov.; 1, white.
Incubation: About 56 days; chicks occupy burrow about 3 months, begin first flights at about 100 days or more after hatching (Palmer, 1962).
Other Names: Black hag, black hagdon (by Newfoundland fishermen); dark-bodied shearwater.
Albinism: A number of partial albinos reported; white most often on head and neck, although whole body may be pied (Palmer, 1962).
Weights: About 1½ lb.
Range: Nests Nov.–Mar. on islands and islets off s. S. America, New Zealand, and se. Australia; ranges northward into N. Hemisphere: *along Atlantic coast* in May and June, but usually from July to late Sept., to Canada, Labrador, and s. Greenland waters, then migrates eastward out to sea in late summer to e. Atlantic (Bull, 1964); *off Pacific coast*, migrates in vast flocks north and south, feeding so close to land that sometimes millions are seen from shore.

Shearwater, Townsend's, *Puffinus auricularis* (PUFF-in-us aw-rick-you-LAY-rus); genus name: *see* Shearwater, Audubon's; species name: Lat., from *auris*, ear, in reference to dark color of cap which extends over "ear" part of bird's head; common name: for Charles H. Townsend, American ornithologist, who de-

scribed it from Clarion Is., Mexico, in 1890. Sometimes considered a subspecies of the Manx shearwater; smaller than the Manx; about 12–15 in. long; has slightly darker upperparts, and markings on breast sometimes more prominent.

Habits: Probably very similar to those of the Manx shearwater; egg-laying starts in Feb., maybe earlier.
Weights: Average about 330 gr., or about ¾ lb. (Jehl, unpubl.).
Range: Nests on Revilla Gigedo Is. off west coast of Mexico and ranges north to Baja Calif.

Shearwater, wandering. *See* Shearwater, greater.

Shearwater, wedge-tailed, *Puffinus pacificus* (PUFF-in-us pah-SIF-ih-cus); genus name: *see* Shearwater, Audubon's; species name: Lat., in reference to Pacific O., where it mainly lives. (Color ill., page 841.) 17–19 in. long; in dark phase an all-brown shearwater with long, wedge-shaped tail; pinkish or grayish bill; yellowish feet; in light phase, underparts and wing linings are whitish.

Feeding Habits: Squids are principal food.
Nest: In burrow, which it digs.
Eggs: 1, white.
Other Name: Moaning bird.
Range: A bird of tropical seas; nests on islands off New Zealand and Australia and in the Pacific and Indian oceans; on smaller islands of Hawaii and one of the Revilla Gigedo Is. off w. coast of Mexico; ranges north to s. Baja Calif. coast in warmer waters.

SHELDRAKE
SHELL-DRAKE, or SHELLDRAKE. *See* Shelduck, Canvasback, and mergansers in Duck Family.

SHELDUCK
or SHELD-DUCK. *See* in Duck Family.

SHIELD
See Frontal Shield.

SHITEPOKE
One of local common names for the green heron, from its habit of excreting when frightened and in flight. *See also* Chalk-line; Poke.

SHIVERING
(function of). *See* Cold and Birds.

SHOREBIRD
Name in America for any one of a large group of similar or related birds of 203 species in 12 families worldwide (Van Tyne and Berger, 1959); their nearest relatives are gulls and terns. *See* Charadriiformes. They are classified in a suborder, Charadrii (A.O.U. *Check-list*, 1957). *See* Classification.

Those strictly called shorebirds in N. America include: the tropical American jacana, one species of thick-knee, the oystercatchers, plovers (including the killdeer and dotterel), surfbird, turnstones, woodcock and snipe, curlews, whimbrel, sandpipers, tattlers, willet, yellow-

legs, knot, dunlin, dowitchers, godwits, sanderling, avocet, stilt, and phalaropes.

Seventy-five species in 7 families of shorebirds had been reported to the time of species accounts by Palmer (1967). *See* biographies of each N. American shorebird in Avocet Family (2 species); Jacana Family (2 species); Oystercatcher Family (3 species); Phalarope Family (3 species); Plover Family (13 species); Sandpiper Family (51 species); and Thick-knee Family (1 species).

Most shorebirds (called waders in Great Britain) are long-legged, graceful, and wild, and most live along the margins (shores) of the continent that are under water much of the time and become mud flats or sandy shores only at low tide. About half their lives are lived on sandy shores; about half in swift flight or living on marshy meadows, some in upland grassy fields. For abilities of some in water, *see* in their biographies; *see also* Swimming and Diving; *also* Smell.

Most shorebirds migrate long distances (*see* Migration); some from their nesting places in the Far North to the southern part of S. America. See details in Wetmore (1926); Matthiessen (1967; 1973). In spring, late summer, and fall, shorebirds throng our oceanic beaches, often near our coastal resorts, in their travels to and from their nesting and wintering grounds. There are also tropical shorebirds that live in C. and S. America—the double-striped thick-knees, one of which has reached N. America (*see* Thick-knee Family); the painted-snipe (family Rostratulidae); also oystercatchers, plovers, sandpipers, stilts, avocets, seed-snipe (family Thinocoridae), and sheathbills (family Chionididae). See details of these in Hall (1960); Austin (1961); Pitman (1964c). For care and feeding of captive shorebirds, see Serventy *et al.* (1962).

SHORT-NECK
See Sandpiper, pectoral, in Sandpiper Family.

SHORT WHITE
Name given snowy egret by plume hunters.

SHOT-POUCH
Another name for the ruddy duck, from its reputation among hunters of being hard to kill.

SHOVELER
or SHOVELLER. *See* Shoveler, northern, in Duck Family.

SHRIKE FAMILY
Laniidae (lane-EYE-ih-dee); from Lat. *lanius*, butcher; *shrike* is cognate with *shriek*, in reference to the shrill calls of these birds (Olivier, 1964). 74 species in world (Van Tyne and Berger, 1976); predominantly an Old World group with center of development and abundance in tropical Africa (Austin, 1961); 25 species of "true shrikes," the only truly predatory songbirds, in that they consistently prey on vertebrate animals, comparable in their killing role to hawks and owls; most are widespread throughout Africa and Eurasia, with only 2 species in N. America—the northern shrike, which lives around the northern regions of the world, and the smaller loggerhead shrike, wide-

SHRIKE FAMILY

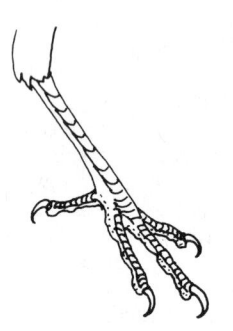

spread across s. Canada and the U.S., south into Mexico, the only shrike that lives wholly within the W. Hemisphere; there are none in C. and S. America (Austin, 1961).

Despite habit of killing small birds and small rodents, snakes, and lizards, insects are most favored when available—for example, grasshoppers, dragonflies, locusts, bumblebees, and crickets, which, if shrikes do not eat at once, they hang up on thorns or sharp twigs in trees and bushes or on barbs of wire fences as a "larder"—thus, the name butcher.

Throughout most of year, except when nesting, shrikes are solitary; live in open places, where often perch conspicuously on top of tree or on branch, or on fences or utility wires along highways, from which have good view and swoop down to ground to catch prey or dart out in flight to catch insect out of air; launch out from perch by dropping low and then, in undulating flight like woodpecker, sweep low over ground, then suddenly upward at last moment to alight in tree or on wire. American shrikes (adults) are patterned gray, black, and white; look superficially like chunky mockingbirds (the loggerhead in s. U.S. is often called French mockingbird), but have thick, large heads and bills, and black band through and behind eyes.

When hunting mice, shrikes sometimes hover momentarily over prey before dropping to it; have toothlike structure on cutting edge of upper mandible, and corresponding notch on lower half of bill, strikingly like that of falcons. According to Cade (1967), these tomial "teeth" play a part in the shrikes' mechanism of killing prey; a highly specific kind of bill structure that has independently evolved in shrikes (songbirds) and falcons.

The shrike not only hunts from vantage point of perch above ground but moves actively on ground by hopping or through branches of trees in apparent attempt to flush birds from their perches, but birds are safe if they remain in dense cover, where shrike is usually unsuccessful; if they fly out, shrike pursues and either strikes victim to ground with blow from bill or seizes bird in air with its strong feet, armed with sharp claws, and bears bird to earth (does not have talons as in hawks and owls). On ground, the northern shrike, for example, kills prey with a series of sharp bites with its strong, hooked bill which sever neck vertebrae of the victim. The loggerhead shrike kills prey in same way; to kill a mouse on the ground, shrike harasses it, jumping about it until it sees opening, then seizes mouse by neck with bill; does not use feet to catch mouse, which might bite shrike's feet.

Shrikes catch small insects in bill and eat them in one gulp while in air or on perch, but hold larger insects such as grasshoppers in foot while reaching down to tear off pieces as kestrels do. When the northern shrike kills a large insect, small bird or rodent, it shows an urge to impale it by carrying prey to suitable spike or to hang it in fork of branch; carries smaller animals less than 20 gr. (about ¾ oz.) from point of capture to impaling place, in bill, but larger quarry of more than an ounce, picks up in bill, then just as it launches into air, transfers prey to its feet. After arriving at tree, bush, or barbed-wire fence, works quarry onto suitable thorn, pointed twig, etc., with head of victim *up*, body hanging suspended, or wedges it into fork of branch. If hungry, feeds at once, beginning with head of victim, eating progressively toward lower part.

Cade (1967) did not find northern shrikes insatiable killers as often reported; they did not take prey in excess of their needs, and many small animals impaled for "storage" did not go to waste; with few exceptions they ate them. Now and then a carcass might hang for week or more but eventually was eaten. Chapman and Casto (1972) reported loggerhead shrikes in Tex. visiting frogs they had impaled on barbed-wire fence up to 8 months after capture, when they still pecked at mummified remains. Shrikes show remarkable sense of location, or memory—did not forget where they hung their quarry. See Cade (1967) for account of northern shrikes' habits and of hunting with them as with a falcon.

Shrikes hunt only by day (are diurnal predators) and have remarkable eyesight, comparable to that of hawks, eagles, and falcons. Thielke (1956) reported that northern shrike can recognize mouse running on ground 80 m. away (about 240 ft.), and reacts to one of its own kind about 1,250 ft. away; Cade (1967) has seen wild northern shrikes fly directly from treetop perch more than 600 ft. to a trap on ground baited with a live, active mouse; and fly from 3,000 ft. away to attack caged shrike or trained free-flying one. One of Cade's shrikes could sight flying bumblebee at least 300 ft. away, fly after it, and pluck bee out of air in bill. *See* Food and Feeding Habits.

Northern shrike, if hungry, gulps small mouse or bird almost whole, then later disgorges pellets of fur, feathers, and other indigestible parts (Bent, 1950). *See* Digestion; Pellet. Will come to a feeding station to eat suet or raw hamburger.

Although shrikes utter harsh, rattling or rasping cries, both males and females of northern shrike sing a pleasing though hoarse warble, and mimic calls of other birds. The loggerhead shrike is also credited with liquid flutelike singing (Sprunt, 1950).

N. American shrikes are migratory; the northern shrike irregularly in periodic invasions from the North. See Bent (1950) and Cade (1967) for other details of life habits. Shrikes are protected by law and may not be kept in captivity without a permit (*see* Legal Protection); however, to care for an ill or injured one, offer it mealworms or any other insects available. Shrikes will eat almost any kind of raw meat, dead birds, or mice (mice seem to be preferred to other foods), mockingbird food, boiled eggs, lettuce, and bread. *See also* Rare and Threatened Species.

Albinism must be very rare, as Gross (1965a) reported only one record for one individual, but species not identified by Gross.

Loggerhead shrike, *Lanius ludovicianus* (LANE-ih-us lewd-oh-VICK-ih-ANE-us); genus name: Lat., butcher; species name: Lat., in reference to Louisiana Territory, the type locality of the species. (Color ill., page 843.) Lives in s. Canada and most of U.S.; 8–10 in. long; wingspread 12½–13 in.; gray above, white below, black "mask" through eyes; black wings with white patch; large head, slim black tail with white outer tail feathers; slightly smaller than robin; paler gray than mockingbird. Prefers open country, thinly wooded or scrubby land with clearings, meadows, pastures, old orchards and thickets along roads, and hedges, especially Osage orange hedges in some parts of range (Bent, 1950); known only from W. Hemisphere.

Feeding Habits: Because of wide range in U.S., takes great variety of foods; mice and birds make up 28% of food through most of year, but in winter may be 76% of food; eats mice in all seasons, which in winter make up half its food; small birds taken are: warblers, sparrows, mockingbirds, bluebirds, swallows, and other passerines, or songbirds; are no more than 15% of its food in Calif., where insects more available through the year (Miller, A. H., 1950); about 68% of food is insects in summer, mostly grasshoppers and crickets, also beetles, ants, wasps, snails, spiders; prefers thorny trees, shrubs, or barbed wire on which to impale all kinds of animal food: small birds, crayfishes, frogs, mice, small fishes, and in one larder (a bush) near High Point, N.C., no less than 15 small snakes (Pearson, 1936; *see also* Reptiles and Birds), ticks, grasshoppers, and other prey. The mockingbird sometimes takes advantage of the larders of the loggerhead (*see* Commensalism); the loggerhead will defend its nesting territory in summer and feeding territory in winter with aggressive wing-fluttering display. See details in Smith (1973).

Nest: In Fla., S.C., and Ga., early nesting begins Feb.; either female or both sexes build nest (Sprunt, 1950; Miller, 1931), bulky, cup-shaped, of twigs lined with rootlets, grasses, string, feathers, deer hairs, in bush or tree, 8–15 ft. above ground (Sprunt, 1950).

Eggs: Calif., Fla., Feb.–July; Ariz., Mar.–June; Tex., Mar.–June; elsewhere in U.S., s. Canada, Apr.–July; 4–7, dull white to light gray or buff, spotted.

Incubation: By both sexes, 10–12 days (Sprunt, 1950); by female alone, 16 days (Miller, 1931); young leave nest about 20 days after hatching (Miller, A. H., 1950); two broods a season; impaling instinct appears in young when 30–40 days old; young independent of parents 36 days after hatching (Miller, 1931).

Other Names: Butcher bird; French mockingbird; migrant shrike; Nelson's shrike; nine-killer; southern butcher bird; southern loggerhead shrike; white-rumped shrike; also cotton-picker, from habit of using cotton in nest (Sprunt, 1950).

Accidents: Often killed by automobiles early in morning on highways, where shrikes often attracted to insects killed by cars at night.

Age: Of two banded at Carmangay, Alta., one killed just 6 months later at the Grove, Tex.; the other at Granger, Tex., about 1 year, 6 months, after it had been banded; another shot when 6 years, 1 month old (Kennard, 1975).

Albinism: Two all-white young with black eyes fed by normally colored adult, reported Hampton, S.C., summer 1971 (Anderson, 1971).

Flight Speed: Timed in w. U.S., 22 m.p.h. (Cottam *et al.*, 1942b); in Tex., 39 m.p.h. (Sooter, 1947).

Weights: Adult males, Calif. (24), 40–54.5 gr., or 1½–2 oz.; adult females (6), 40–47.4 gr., or 1¼–1¾ oz. (Miller, 1931); in autumn migration, coastal N.J. (1), 47.4 gr., or 1¾ oz. (Murray and Jehl, 1964).

Range: Nests from s. interior of B.C., s. Man., c. Alta., and c. Sask., s. Ont., s. Que., s.-c. Me., and sw. N.B. south through Great Basin, in Calif., to Baja Calif., Mexico, the Gulf coast and s. Fla.; winters from southern half of breeding range south to Gulf coast and s. Fla., and Mexico.

Migrant shrike. *See* Loggerhead shrike.

Nelson's shrike. *See* Loggerhead shrike.

Northern shrike, *Lanius excubitor* (LANE-ih-us ex-CUBE-ih-tore); genus name: *see* Loggerhead shrike; species name: Lat., a watchman, or sentinel (Coues, 1882); literally, the "watchful butcher"; Linnaeus, in naming the bird, suggested that its cries on sighting a hawk might be a warning to small birds; also called great grey shrike in Great Britain. (Color ill., page 842.) A panboreal bird nesting across northern part of N. America and throughout much of Eurasia (Cade, 1967). According to Peterson (1947), a gray, robin-sized bird in northern states in winter sitting in tip-top of a tree in open country is likely to be a northern shrike; 9–10¾ in. long; wingspread 13½–16½ in.; gray above, white below, black mask through eyes, *finely barred breast;* lower half of bill (lower mandible) usually pale-colored (similar and slightly smaller loggerhead shrike has solid-black bill, and its black mask meets over the bill; northern shrike's does not) (Peterson, 1947); wings black with white; heavy, hooked bill; females and young are duller or slightly olive or brown with markings similar to male; lives in broad belt of coniferous forest, or "taiga," that stretches across Canada and Alaska, but this shrike strongly prefers not dense forest but edges, and open country of willow brush in Alaska (Cade, 1967), and brush-bordered swamps and bogs; utters a call, *shek-shek,* and a grating *jaaeg* (Peterson, 1961), and sings in caws and scraping notes, with short liquid trills and whistles in series like that of a thrasher; also mimics notes of brown thrasher and blue jay and mew of catbird (Bent, 1950).

Feeding Habits: In its territory, perches, exposed, on tops of trees to watch for prey below, or looks upward for attacks from above by hawks; although ordinarily rather wary, in pursuit of bird prey is fierce as a goshawk, even attacking birds larger than itself such as blue jays; eats grasshoppers and crickets, about 24% of spring-to-fall diet of some shrikes; also caterpillars, cutworms, beetles, ants, wasps, bumblebees, flies, spiders; especially fond of meadow mice (voles), also eats lemmings, white-footed mice, red-backed mice, gophers, many small birds—chickadees, snow buntings, longspurs, crossbills, redpolls, pine grosbeaks, horned larks, woodpeckers, goldfinches, kinglets, field sparrows, fox sparrows, Savannah

sparrows, house sparrows, white-crowned sparrows, thrushes, Old World warblers, siskins, starlings, cardinals, American robins, blue jays, sandpipers, mourning doves (Bent, 1950; Cade, 1967); also snakes, lizards, frogs; in winter, may come to feeding stations to eat suet or hamburger.

Nest: Bulky, loose twig structure built in spruces, willows, or bushes, 5–20 ft. above ground.

Eggs: May–June; 2–9, usually 4–6, gray-white or green-white, heavily spotted with brown, lavender, etc.; fledged young (Alaska) per successful nest, 5–6 (Cade, 1967).

Incubation: Period of unknown; young leave nest 20 days after hatching, are still fed by parents for another 10 days, when young apparently can fly.

Other Names: Butcher bird; great grey shrike; great northern shrike; nine-killer; northern butcher bird; northwestern shrike; winter butcher bird; winter shrike.

Age: One, banded Switzerland, lived to about 12 years (Nice, 1966a); an adult, banded Harwich, Mass., found dead at Clarenceville, Que., 1 year, 6 months, later.

Flight Speed: Timed in Wash., 32–45 m.p.h. (Rathbun, 1934); in Calif., 28 m.p.h. (Wetmore, 1916).

Weights: One first-year male, Calif., 67.5 gr. (Miller, 1931), or about 2½ oz.; one in Mich., Nov., 57.5 gr., or about 2 oz. (Becker and Stack, 1944); Cade (1967) cites a 75-gr. juvenile male (about 2¾ oz.) and a 70-gr. adult female (2½ oz.).

Range: In N. America, nests from n. Alaska, c. Yuk., nw. Mack., n. Man., n. Ont., n. Que., and c. Labrador south to s. Alaska, nw. B.C., n. Alta., and c. Sask.; winters from southern parts of breeding range south to n. Calif., c. Nev., c. Ariz., s. N.M., s. Kans., c. Mo., s.-c. Ill., Ind., c. Ohio, Pa., Md., D.C., n. Va.; casual to n. Tex., Ark., n.-c. Ky., N.C., and Bermuda; in Europe and Asia, from Scandinavia, n. Russia, n. Siberia, south to n. Africa, Arabia, India, n. China, and n. Japan; also reaches British Isles in winter (Olivier, 1964).

White-rumped shrike. *See* Loggerhead shrike.

SIBLING SPECIES

also called CRYPTIC SPECIES and DUAL SPECIES. Two or more strikingly similar species of birds—similar at all times of the year—that may be almost indistinguishable from each other. They may be regarded as belonging to one species until a more satisfactory analysis of them clears up the mistake of supposing them to be one species. They are sympatric (live together on areas or ranges that coincide or overlap—*see* Sympatric Species) and do not interbreed; they are reproductively isolated. They are not very common among birds and usually are dull-colored (Mayr, 1942).

One well-known example includes the European tree creeper (*Certhia familiaris*, called the brown creeper in N. America) and the short-toed tree creeper (*Certhia brachydactyla*). Populations of both species were treated as the European tree creeper until about 1830, when C. L. Brehm discovered that there were two

Willow flycatcher

Alder flycatcher

SIBLING SPECIES

In 1973, Traill's flycatcher was officially divided into two separate species: the willow flycatcher and the alder flycatcher. Research has established that these remarkably similar sibling species do not interbreed where they occur together, and their ecology, songs, and nests differ recognizably.

species of tree creepers in Europe, virtually indistinguishable in the field.

Certhia brachydactyla, has a more curved, slightly longer bill but shorter claws. According to Mayr (1942), ornithologists for almost 70 years after Brehm's discovery refused to admit that *brachydactyla,* the short-toed tree creeper, was any more than a subspecies (*see* Subspecies) of *familiaris*—they could not believe that two birds so similar in appearance could be two different species. Brehm's conclusions, according to Griscom (1945), have been thoroughly tested; the two birds often live in the same areas in Europe but do not interbreed.

A recent and parallel example of a N. American sibling species was the Traill's flycatcher (Phillips *et al.,* 1966), which for years was treated as one species; however, based on the researches of Stein (1963) and the conclusions of Eisenmann (1970), Mayr and Short (1970), and others, the American Ornithologists' Union (1973) classified it as two species—the alder flycatcher and the willow flycatcher.

Stein (1963) in his studies found that the two remarkably alike flycatchers build recognizably different nests, sing different songs, and apparently do not interbreed on their common nesting grounds in both N.Y. and B.C. One of the criteria for determining a species is its reproductive isolation—it does not or cannot interbreed with birds in nature other than with its own kind. *See* discussion of what constitutes a species under Species.

Two Mexican nightingale-thrushes—*Catharus occidentalis* and *Catharus frantzii*—are so strikingly similar in outward appearance that their status as separate species was only recently established (Raitt and Hardy, 1970).

SICKLE-BILL
See Curlew, long-billed, in Sandpiper Family.

SILKY FLYCATCHER FAMILY
Ptilogonatidae (til-oh-go-NAT-ih-dee); according to Gruson (1972), this is the conventionalized form of Gr. *ptilogony,* meaning an angled or tapered feather in allusion to the tapered central tail feathers of this bird. Small to medium-sized songbirds; 7¼–9¾ in. long; 4 species in world, all in W. Hemisphere, live in dry brushy country—Mexico to c. Panama; only 1, phainopepla, reaches U.S. (in Southwest); they resemble their relatives the waxwings; have soft, silky plumage, prominent crests, eat fruit, but also eat insects, which they catch like flycatchers by darting out into air from tree or shrub perch; resemble flycatchers, have long slender tails and conspicuous rictal bristles (Austin, 1961).

When not nesting, travel in small flocks; often sit on perches in full view of observer, crest raised; have shorter wings and longer tails than waxwings, but bill is short and rather broad; the wanderings of the silky flycatchers are strongly influenced by presence or absence of berries; mistletoe berries are a favorite food; sexes outwardly unlike; albinism apparently unknown; not reported by Gross (1965a).

To sustain an ill or injured one in captivity, offer it mealworms and any other insects available; also mockingbird food, hard-boiled eggs, and ground meat; make water available.

Phainopepla, *Phainopepla nitens* (fay-no-PEP-lah NIGH-tenz); genus name: Lat., from Gr. words meaning shining robe; species name: Lat., shining, in allusion to silky, shiny plumage. (Color ills., pages 842, 843.) Calif. and Utah south into Mexico; 7–7¾ in. long; male is slim, glossy, uniformly dark, with tall head crest, red eyes, long tail, white patches in wings, show in flight; female and immature, gray with even paler gray patch on wings, but lack yellow band at end of tail as in similar-appearing cedar waxwing; flight is flitting, zigzag, wings held high, almost like butterfly; first discovered in U.S. in 1852 by Col. George A. McCall, Inspector General, U.S. Army, while on tour of duty in Calif.; phainopepla lives mostly in trees or shrubs along watercourses in "mesquite country" because one of main foods is berries of mistletoe parasitic on mesquite; large populations winter in the Sonoran desert of Calif. and Ariz. In Calif., breeding occurs in this desert in Mar. and Apr. Phainopeplas then migrate in Apr. and May into the chaparral and riparian communities of wetter areas of Calif., such as the Pacific slope. Here, a second breeding occurs in June and July. Phainopeplas perch on topmost twigs of trees and shrubs; males especially make sallies into air (flycatcher fashion) to catch insects; occasionally hover before bunch of berries or cling to them while they eat; frequently utter liquid *quirt* or *lerp;* song is sweet gargling of rich blackbird quality, often sung by male in flight (Woods, 1950).

Feeding Habits: Eats mistletoe berries and the scarlet berries of buckthorn (*Rhamnus*) along watercourses, also those of juniper, elder, and, in settled places, pepper tree (*Schinus*); also eats flower petals of guava (*Feijoa*), and many insects.

Nest: Built almost exclusively by male, in mesquites, cottonwoods, hackberries, willows, sycamores, oaks, orange trees, etc., 4–50 ft. above ground, saddled in crotch of tree or in small fork concealed in foliage, sometimes in dense clump of mistletoe; of small twigs, plant fibers, held together by spider's silk, interior lined with bits of wool, hair, down.

Eggs: Feb.–July; 2–4, usually 2–3, gray-white, spotted with browns, scrawled with black.

Incubation: 14–16 days; young leave nest permanently when about 19 days old; are fed crushed berries and tiny insects (Woods, 1950); one, two, or three broods a season.

Other Names: Black flycatcher; black-crested flycatcher; shining crested flycatcher; shining fly-snapper; silky flycatcher.

Host to Cowbirds: Rare (Friedmann, 1963), only two records, one near Tucson, Ariz., the other near Alhambra, s. Calif.

Range: C. Calif., s. Nev., s. Utah, sw. N.M., and w. Tex. south to s. Baja Calif. and c. Mexico; population in northern part of range moves southward in winter; accidental at Nantucket Is., Mass., e. Canada, R.I. (Block Is.).

SILVER TERNLET
See Tern, least, in Gull Family.

SILVER TONGUE
See Sparrow, song, in Finch Family.

SIMPLETON
See Dunlin in Sandpiper Family.

SINGING
See Songs and Singing; *also* Voice and Sound-making.

SINGING GROUND
Term of biologists for the "singing site," or "breeding field," of the American woodcock and of other similarly displaying birds.

SISKIN
See in Finch Family.

SITE TENACITY
Term for the attachment of birds or succeeding generations of the same species of bird to their nesting site. *See* especially Re-use of Old Nests under Nests and Nesting, and Return to Nest Sites and Wintering Places under Banding.

SITTIDAE
See Nuthatch—Common Nuthatch Family.

SIX HUNDRED CLUB
See Birder.

SIZE
General sizes of birds are measured in at least two ways—by dimensions and by weight. Dimensions include, primarily, length of bird, from tip of bill to end of tail, and its wingspread. *See* details under Dimensions. Weight also gives an idea of the size, or bulk, of a bird compared with others. *See* in biographies of each bird, when known, its approximate length, wingspread (of large birds), and weight.

A suggested descriptive classification, or grouping, of birds, based on their *approximate* relative lengths, would be:

Small birds (up to and including 6 in. long). Some examples: N. American hummingbirds, swifts, elf owl, chickadees, titmice, bushtits, kinglets, nuthatches, creepers, most wrens, gnatcatchers, vireos, most warblers, downy woodpecker (6 in.), most swallows, the small flycatchers—least, Acadian, alder, vermilion, willow, yellow-bellied—buntings, and many N. American sparrows.

Medium birds (from more than 6 to less than 10 in.). Some examples: catbird (9 in.), cardinal, most thrushes, bluebirds, tanagers, martins, grosbeaks, towhees, finches, starling (8½ in.), some woodpeckers—hairy, red-bellied, red-headed—waxwings, pipits, shrikes, orioles, cowbird, red-winged blackbird, whip-poor-will, poor-will, saw-whet owl, pygmy owl, burrowing owl, and many sparrows, including the English, or house, sparrow (about 6¼ in.).

Large birds (from 10 in. up). Some examples: American robin (10 in.), screech owl (10 in.), mockingbird (about 10½ in.), most pigeons and doves, jays, anis, belted kingfisher (13 in.), grackles, cuckoos, flickers (13 in.), most thrashers, and up to the larger coots (about 15 in.), loons, crows, magpies, ravens, pileated woodpecker (17 in.), many owls—barn owl (18 in.), barred owl, great horned owl (18–25 in.), and snowy owl—eagles, hawks, pheasants, grouse, turkey, ducks, geese, swans, pelicans, and many other water birds, and the condors and vultures.

SMALLEST BIRD. The bee hummingbird, *Mellisuga helenae*, of Cuba, 2¼ in. long from tip of bill to tip of tail, wingspread of 4 in., is recognized as the smallest bird in the world. Fisher and Peterson (1964) calculated, on the basis of the bee hummingbird's weight, that it would require 100,000 of them—probably more of them than there are in the world—to sit on a scale and balance the weight of an ostrich. *See* Weight.

Smallest bird in U.S. is the calliope hummingbird of the West; male is about 2¾ in. long, female slightly larger, about 3 in. Average weight of calliope hummingbird is only about 3 gr. (about ⅒ oz.) or less—about half the weight of an Anna's hummingbird of Calif., of a kinglet, or of a bushtit, each a very small bird (Grinnell and Storer, 1924). Based on available measurements, published in N. American books, especially Wetmore (1964), Reilly (1968), and Forbush (1925-29), the golden-crowned kinglet is the smallest songbird, or perching bird, in N. America (hummingbirds are not songbirds—*see* Hummingbird Family); it is 3¼-4¼ in. long; next-smallest are the black-tailed gnatcatcher and bushtits (3¾-4¼ in. long—Blake, E. R., 1953), ruby-crowned kinglet and lesser goldfinch (3¾-4¼ in. long); other small birds include the verdin (*see* in Titmouse Family) and the marsh wren and winter wren (*see* in Wren Family)—4-4½ in. long. (Individual sizes of birds vary; it is possible that some might be larger or smaller than sizes reported: precision in measuring depends on the one making measurements.) *See* Dimensions for instructions in measuring birds.

LARGEST BIRD. Heaviest and tallest of all living birds is the African ostrich, with weight of male to 345 lbs. and up to 8-9 ft. tall (Bannerman, 1964a). *See* Running Birds.

The tallest native N. American birds appear to be the whooping crane at about 5 ft. (Bent, 1926a) and the California condor, which, when standing with wings raised, may be more than 5 ft. (see Atkinson, 1972); also, the American flamingo, which wanders from tropics to s. U.S., is almost 5 ft. tall, according to Palmer (1962). Other tall birds include the long-legged wood stork, cranes, and herons.

Largest wingspread of any living seabird (*see* Albatross Family) is that of the wandering albatross at reported maximum of 11 ft. 4 in. (Murphy, 1936); largest wingspread of any land bird may be that of the marabou stork of Africa, which Fisher and Peterson (1964) suggest may reach 12 ft. Largest flying bird known was *Teratornis incredibilis*, with an estimated wingspread of 16–17 ft. *See* Fossil Birds.

Largest wingspread of any N. American bird is that of California condor at maximum

SILKY FLYCATCHER FAMILY

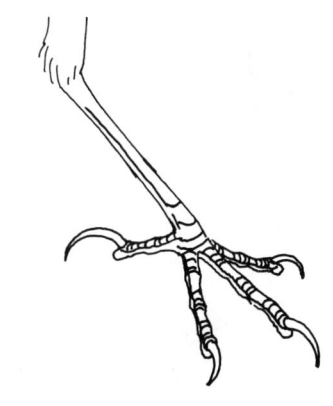

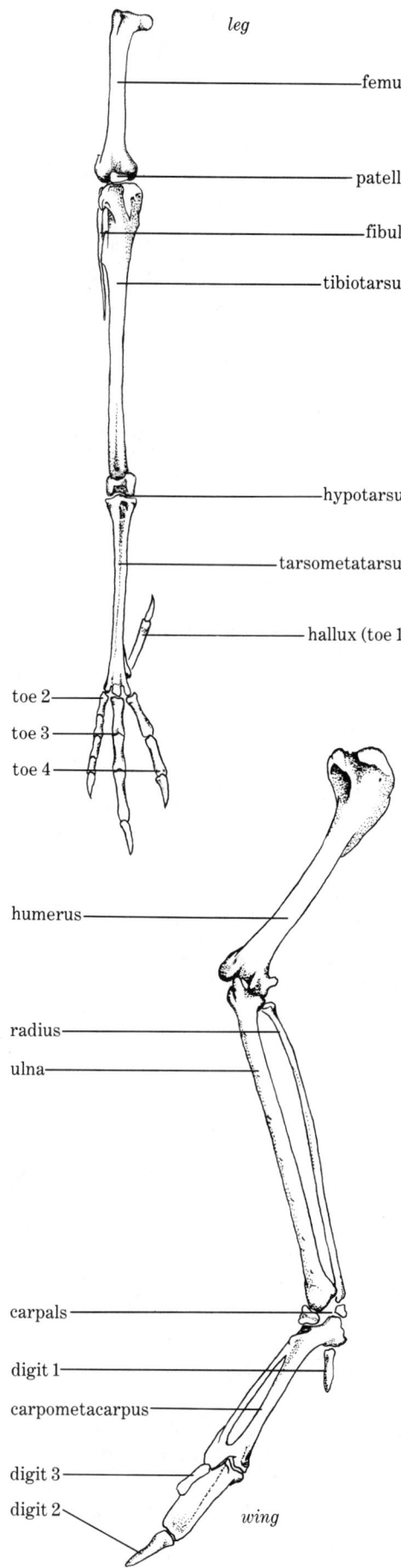

leg

femur

patella

fibula

tibiotarsus

hypotarsus

tarsometatarsus

hallux (toe 1)

toe 2

toe 3

toe 4

humerus

radius

ulna

carpals

digit 1

carpometacarpus

digit 3

digit 2

wing

SKELETON

of 9 ft. 7 in. (Koford, 1953). The Andean condor, *Vultur gryphus,* has a wingspread to 10 ft. 6 in. Brown and Amadon (1968) believe that the California and Andean condors, based on a combination of their wingspreads and weights of 20-25 lbs. each, are the largest flying birds in the world (for largest eagles, *see* under Hawk Family). The white pelican has second-largest wingspread, 8–9½ ft., of any N. American bird; also, the trumpeter swan has next-largest span with up to 8 ft. 2 in. (Banko, 1960). *See* under Duck Family; *see also* wingspreads of all large N. American birds in biography of each. *See* discussion of giant birds of the past in Fossil Birds.

There is a minimum size beyond which birds could not exist. Hummingbirds have evolved into the smallest possible for warm-blooded animals. They have relatively the highest intake of food of any vertebrate animal in the world (*see* Vertebrate) and must feed almost continuously to keep up their high rate of metabolism for warmth and for energy for flight. *See* discussion under Metabolism. A smaller bird, or one less than 2 in. long, with a necessarily higher metabolism and greater food requirements, would probably need more fuel than it would have time enough to get, even in the tropics, where food is abundant (Fisher and Peterson, 1964).

The maximum size of a flying bird is limited because it must be comparatively light in weight, especially in relation to the strength of the muscles that move its wings (*see* Flight). Because of the physical limitations of muscle and bone strength and the relationship of wing surface to body weight, there are upper limits to a bird's size beyond which it could not fly, and the heavier the bird, the faster it must fly to stay aloft.

This is markedly different from aircraft; the size of a plane can be increased as the power of the motors (the mechanical muscles) is increased (Colbert, 1955).

Sir D'Arcy Thompson (1942), eminent British scientist, made a theoretical calculation (using the linear dimensions of a house sparrow, which weighs about 1 oz., and an ostrich, which is flightless, of 250 lbs.) that proved that if an ostrich could fly, it would have to do so at a minimal speed of 100 m.p.h. to stay aloft.

According to Storer (1960a), the larger albatrosses, storks, pelicans, swans, condors, turkeys, and the bustards of the Old World "must represent the largest size to which flying birds can evolve."

The average minimal speed of birds in order to remain aloft is reported to be about 16½ ft. per second, or about 11 m.p.h. (Stillson, 1954). *See* Speed of Flight under Flight; *also* the flight speed, when known, reported in the biography of each bird.

See Metabolism; Weight. For other facts about size, *see* Sexual Dimorphism.

SIZZLE-BRITCHES
Local name in Mass. for the American goldeneye, in allusion to its speed or to the whistling of its wings in flight.

SKAIT-BIRD
See Jaeger, parasitic, in Skua Family.

SKELETON
The skeleton, or skeletal system, the supporting framework of the entire bird, is composed of hard calcareous bones and tough, springy cartilaginous bones. The bones provide the attachment places for the muscles and so play an indispensable part in any of the bird's movements. *See* Muscular System. The bony skeleton also protects the bird's vital parts, such as the heart and brain (Bellairs, 1964b).

The skeleton of a bird, specialized for strength and lightness, has evolved striking adaptations for flight, walking, and running. With its lightness and rigidity, owing to the slender, hollow, air-filled bones (*see* Respiratory System), and the strength by fusion of different bones, it has achieved reduction in the number of its parts (Van Tyne and Berger, 1959) and thus has simplified the moving parts. Each section of the skeleton has a particular specialization, and the main divisions usually considered separately are: the skull; vertebral column and ribs (with the pelvic girdle); sternum (breastbone); the pectoral girdle; and bones of the wings and legs (Bellairs, 1964b).

SKULL. The skull is light and in general is made up of a rounded brain case, roof of mouth, jaws, and palate. The brain case has large eye sockets, or "orbits," in the skull, and around the eyes thin overlying bony plates called the *sclerotic ring,* which protect and strengthen the eyeball (see Darling and Darling, 1962). The bill, or beak (in modern birds, without teeth), is distinctive and is an extension of the bony jaws. The bill is used by a bird as one might use a pair of forceps, in grasping food or picking it up, picking up nest materials, and in preening (Rand, 1967). *See* Bill. The external nostrils in most birds are usually near the base of the bill (Bellairs, 1964b), but *see* Nostrils.

The attachment of the upper half of the bill (upper mandible) to the skull roof in most birds is quite flexible and the bird is able to move it slightly, thus increasing its gape. This condition is called *cranial kinesis* and is generally recognized as characteristic of most living birds. See Beecher (1962); Bock (1964). The upper jaw in parrots is especially flexible because of a well-developed hinge between the bill and skull. The skeleton of the tongue (hyoid apparatus) is a series of bony or cartilaginous segments (Bellairs, 1964b). (*See* ill., page 1014.)

VERTEBRAL COLUMN AND RIBS. The neck of a bird (upper part of the vertebral column) has been likened by Rand (1967) to an arm that moves the bill about. The neck is very long in some birds—swans, cranes, herons, flamingos, for example—and its flexibility derives from the large number of cervical, or neck, vertebrae, also to the odd shape of the articulating (connecting) surfaces of the vertebrae, which allows a bird great movement in lowering or raising its neck or moving it from side to side.

Man has only 7 neck vertebrae, but some birds (common pigeon, for example) have 14; swans, 25; geese, 19; ducks, with shorter necks,

16 or 17; and hummingbirds, surprisingly, 14 or 15 (Allen, 1925).

The forepart (thoracic region) of the skeleton of the bird's body, like that of man, has a backbone, ribs, and a breastbone (sternum). The thoracic vertebrae, below the neck vertebrae, bearing the complete ribs, have little movement, and the last thoracic vertebrae fuse with 10–23 vertebrae (Berger, 1961) below it, which form the *synsacrum*. The two hip bones articulate (connect) with the pelvis, or *pelvic girdle*. The pelvic girdle is composed of three bones—*ilium, ischium* (IS-kih-um), and *pubis*—fused with the synsacrum. These form a supporting arch, so that the weight of the bird body, when borne by the legs, is broadly distributed along the backbone.

Following the synsacrum are 4–9 movable tail, or *caudal*, vertebrae, ending in the *pygostyle*, the terminal bone of the vertebral column. The pygostyle carries the tail feathers, and the movable caudal vertebrae in front of it provide the flexibility for movement of the tail feathers so important in flight (Bellairs, 1964b; Darling and Darling, 1962).

STERNUM, OR BREASTBONE. Evolution of the breast muscles (pectorals) that drive the wings of a bird was paralleled by an increase in the size of the sternum in all modern flying birds. It is a somewhat flattened, platelike bone that protects the chest and part of the belly of a bird against physical blows. It has a deep keel *(carina)* that strengthens the sternum and gives extra space for the attachment of the flight muscles. *See* Flight Muscles under Flight. The flightless ratite birds—ostrich, rhea, cassowary, emu, and kiwi—have a flat, unkeeled sternum.

PECTORAL GIRDLE. The pectoral girdle, an arch of bones including the *scapulae, coracoids,* and *clavicles*, gives support to the wings of a bird. It is a tripod of strong bones, among them the heaviest bones in the bird's body—the two upright coracoids with their bases resting on the sternum. The sternum is connected to the rigid backbone by the ribs, strong, flexible struts which, together with the thoracic vertebrae above them and the sternum below, form a bony cage that surrounds and protects the heart and lungs.

Attached to and suspended in front of the two coracoid bones is the *furcula*, or "wishbone." Its two bones are the *clavicles*—one on the right, one on the left—pointing downward and forward from their point of attachment at the tops of the coracoid bones. They are the equivalent of the collarbones of man. The angle, or spread, of these two clavicles is generally widest in birds of strong flight, with each clavicle serving as a strut to brace the wings apart. According to Bellairs (1964b), it is believed that a bird cannot fly if one side of the furcula (a clavicle) is broken.

The scapulae (sing.: scapula), or shoulder blades, from their point of attachment at the top rear of the coracoid bones, point backward above the ribs and parallel to the backbone.

WINGS. At the top of each coracoid, at the point of attachment of the scapulae (shoulder

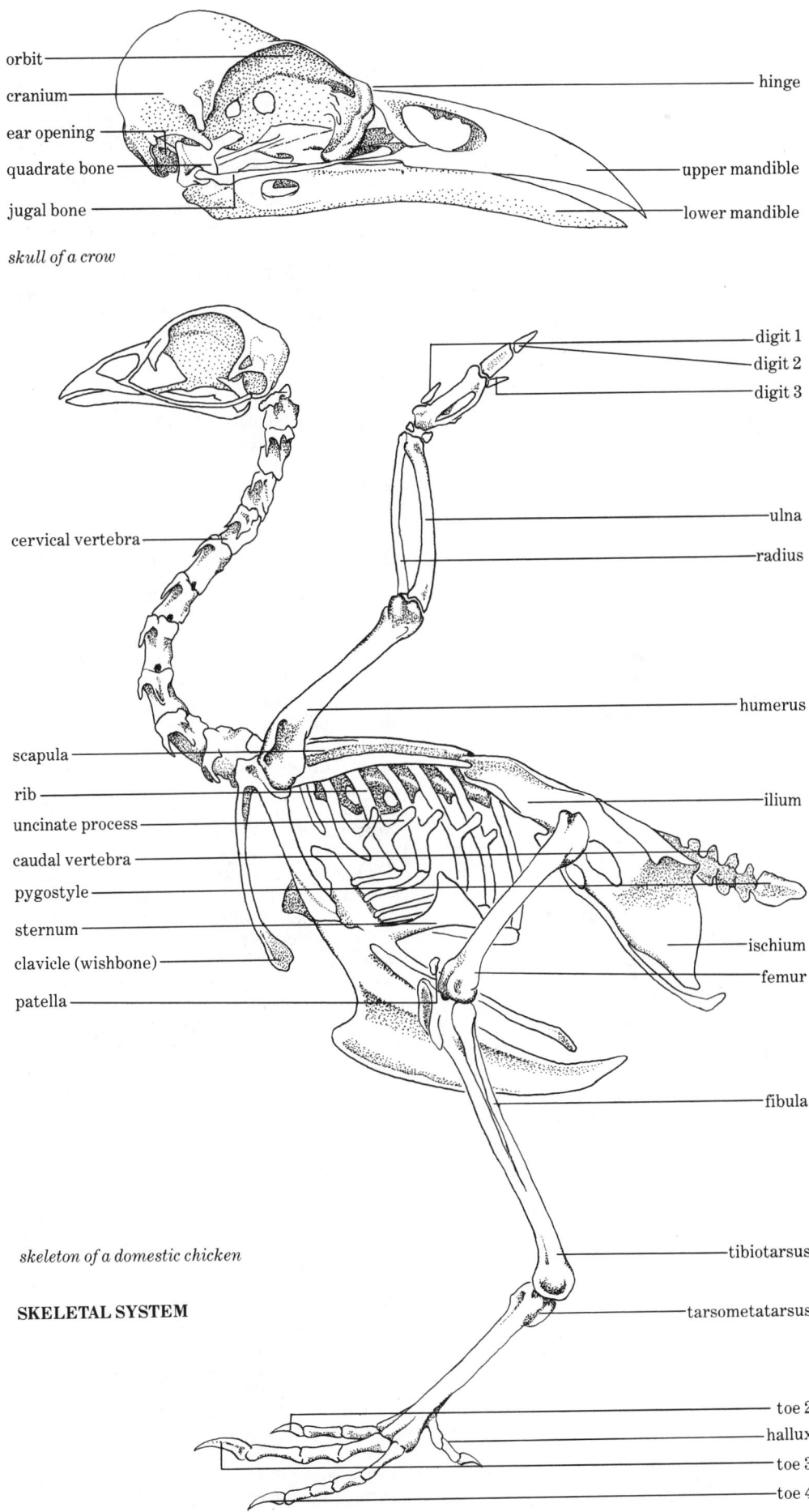

skull of a crow

- orbit
- cranium
- ear opening
- quadrate bone
- jugal bone
- hinge
- upper mandible
- lower mandible

skeleton of a domestic chicken

SKELETAL SYSTEM

- digit 1
- digit 2
- digit 3
- ulna
- radius
- humerus
- ilium
- ischium
- femur
- fibula
- tibiotarsus
- tarsometatarsus
- toe 2
- hallux
- toe 3
- toe 4
- cervical vertebra
- scapula
- rib
- uncinate process
- caudal vertebra
- pygostyle
- sternum
- clavicle (wishbone)
- patella

blades), is a socket called the *glenoid cavity.* The basal part of the wing bone, called the *humerus,* fits into, and articulates with, this cavity. The humerus is comparable to that section of a man's arm between the shoulders and elbow. The next section outward, or downward, in the wing of a bird, and comparable to a man's forearm, is composed of two bones, the *radius* and *ulna.* The ulna, the heavier of the two forearm bones, bears the secondary flight feathers. The next section of the wing outward, called the "wrist," along with the reduced "fingers" of the "hand" part of the wing, bears the primary flight feathers and the feathers of the *alula. See* Alula. For a discussion of the hind limbs of a bird, *see* Feet and Legs. *See* related articles Bones; Feather; and illustrated Topography.

SKIMMER FAMILY

SKIMMER FAMILY

Rynchopidae (ring-KOP-ih-dee); Lat., from Gr., referring to bill, or beak, and face. Only 3 species in world; coastal water birds not closely related to terns and gulls as once believed (see Sears *et al.,* 1976); 14½–20 in. long; the black skimmer of N. and S. America is largest; the similar but smaller African skimmer, *Rynchops flavirostris,* lives along both coasts and large rivers of tropical Africa, and the Indian skimmer, *Rynchops albicollis,* ranges along larger rivers of India, Burma, and southeast Asia (Van Tyne and Berger, 1959); all three species have long bills, the knifelike mandibles compressed to thin blades, lower one longer than the upper, long, pointed wings, short, forked tails, and legs very short; sexes outwardly alike, but female smaller; general plumage pattern black to brown above, white below; skimmers are only birds with lower part of bill markedly longer than upper, and have specific method of fishing; they skim low over the water with longer lower half of bill shallowly cutting the water; when bill strikes small crustacean or fish, the skimmer clamps down the upper part of bill tightly; as the upper mandible closes on its prey, the skimmer moves its head backward and downward (see Zusi, 1962, for details), then, without changing its steady flight, drags bill from water and swallows its prey, then lowers bill to water to continue its fishing in flight; besides skimming water, they often skim sand near nest with bill, a habit for which some Latin Americans call it *rayador,* or "one who draws lines."

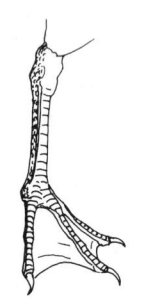

To feed an ill or injured skimmer until it can be released, offer it live minnows in shallow water (not over 3 in. deep) in which it can wade and pick up fishes by direct forward movement of head and bill; if minnow thrown to it on hard surface, it will be compelled to turn its head sidewise to pick it up; it may also eat fresh meat. The captive should have plenty of water for bathing and swimming and some shore space for resting and roosting.

Black skimmer, *Rynchops niger* (RING-kops NYE-jer); genus name: from Gr., referring to beak and face; species name: Lat., black. (Color ills., pages 844, 845.) Ranging in summer in U.S. along Atlantic coast from Mass. south to Fla. and along Gulf coast to Tex.; first reported on Salton Sea, Calif., 1968; five nests,

summer 1972, first breeding record for Calif. and w. U.S. (McCaskie, 1972); crow size, slender build; 16–20 in. long; wingspread 42–50 in.; adult, black above, including cap, but with white forehead; all-white below; remarkable scissorlike bill, red with black tip; legs and feet bright red; toes slightly webbed but skimmer rarely tries to swim; does not dive; at rest on beach, wings reach well beyond the short, forked tail (outer primary is longest); eyes dark brown with vertical pupil which may be narrowed to slit to protect eyes of skimmer from glare of sun off water and white sand (Wetmore, 1919b); during feeding flights over water, because skimmer must keep body close to surface, beats wings shallowly above horizontal plane of body, and not with full downward stroke; however, is swift and graceful in flight, gregarious at all seasons; like shorebirds, when flying in flock, movements are synchronous, whole flock twisting, turning, wheeling, rising or falling in perfect unison (*see* Unity of the Flock in Flight under Flight); from wintering grounds about shallow bays, estuaries, and creeks, from Gulf coast south along both coasts of S. America, arrives on U.S. nesting grounds of low sandy islands and beaches of Atlantic coast in Apr. and May; when group flies to meet intruder on nesting grounds, utters in chorus nasal barking notes, *kak, kak, kak* or *yap, yap, yap* or *kuk, kuk, kuk,* also pair utters soft notes, *kow, kow* or *keow, keow,* suggestive of certain gull notes (Bent, 1921); roost by day in dense flocks on sandbars or beaches, all standing with heads pointing in one direction.

Feeding Habits: Feeds mostly in early evening and at night when waters usually calm and small fishes and crustaceans are near surface of water.

Nest: In colonies, usually of no more than 100–200 pairs, generally by themselves but often close to nesting colonies of gulls and terns; eggs laid in hollow about 1–2 in. deep, 4–5 in. across, scraped out of sand by skimmers, above high-water mark on upper beach; eggs and young often destroyed by dogs and unseeing people walking or running on mainland beaches; presence of people has driven some colonies to nesting on lower sandy coastal islands subjected to flooding, but spoil banks piled along coastal waterways from dredging have provided new nesting places.

Eggs: May–July; 1–5, usually 4–5, blue-white or cream-white, heavily marked with browns, lilac, gray.

Incubation: By female; period of and age when young first fly unknown; one brood a year; buff-colored downy young when first hatched difficult to see lying flat on sand; young also hide by kicking sand into air, which falls on back of young bird in depression it has dug (Hays and Donaldson, 1970); at first young eat food regurgitated on ground in front of chick by parent; is later fed small fishes which adult brings carried crosswise in bill; upper and lower halves of bill of young are of same length at hatching; lower mandible does not start to grow longer than upper until young almost full-grown and ready to fly (Bent, 1921).

Other Names: Cut-water; knifebill; scissorbill; sea-dog; shearwater; storm gull.

Accidents: Sometimes blown by hurricanes far north of range along Atlantic coast (Forbush, 1925–29).

Age: Of two banded as fledglings at Brant Beach, N.J., one caught on fishhook 8 years later at Ocean City, N.J., and released; the other was injured by airplane at St. Petersburg, Fla., 6 years after banding; it revived after being struck and flew away; another, banded on Long Is., N.Y., retrapped there and released when 12 years old (Kennard, 1975).

Flight Speed: Timed in Fla., 18 m.p.h. (Longstreet, 1930); a flock of twelve at 30 m.p.h. (Cottam *et al.*, 1942b).

Range: Nests locally along Atlantic and Gulf coasts from Mass. to Yucatan, on Pacific coast from nw. Mexico south to Ecuador (casually in Calif.), on the Caribbean and Atlantic coasts, and the larger rivers of n. and e. S. America to n. Argentina; winters from northern shores of Gulf of Mexico, e. Fla., w. Mexico, to Argentina and Chile.

SKIN

The skin, or integument, is the protective and containing covering of the body of a bird. One is seldom aware of it because most of the bird's skin is covered by feathers. Like all other vertebrate animals, birds have skin of two layers—the outer *epidermis* and the underlying *dermis*. A bird's skin, compared with that of other vertebrates, is quite thin, and extremely so in owls and members of the Nightjar Family.

The epidermis, or "outer" skin, is made up of layers of flattened epithelial cells renewed from the basal Malpighian layer. These epithelial cells can produce large amounts of keratin (*see* Keratin), of which the claws and scales of birds are made, and the special structures such as feathers, the horny sheathing of the bill, and the covering of legs and feet. Bare parts about the head in some birds have outgrowths of the skin, such as the combs of chickens and the wattles of turkeys and other birds. See interesting details in Pettingill (1972); Lucas and Stettenheim (1972).

The underlying layer (dermis) is relatively thick and has muscles, blood vessels, and nerves. This layer nourishes the overlying epidermis. It also helps to contain, or regulate, heat loss by a bird. The blood vessels give the bare skin the capability of changing color, or flushing, as in the head or neck skin of a turkey when it is emotionally aroused. *See* Caruncle. The bottom layer of the dermis often has much stored fat, valuable to a bird for shock absorption, heat insulation, and as stored food which it may draw upon during migration or in forced fasting. *See* Migration; Fasting.

Using the smooth muscles in the dermis, which are connected with the feather follicles (*see* Feather), a bird fluffs its feathers to keep warm on a cold day or presses them close to its body to help lose heat on a hot day. Or it may use the skin muscles to spread certain feathers in its flight or in its courtship and other displays. *See* Courtship Rituals under Courtship. Birds do not have sweat glands in the skin and must cool off in other ways. *See* Heat and Birds. *See also* the related article Bird Skins.

For an extraordinary treatise on the bird skin and its structures, see Lucas and Stettenheim (1972).

SKIN GLANDS

According to Stettenheim (1972), birds have three types of skin glands: (1) oil gland (the uropygial, or preen, gland); (2) outer ear glands, and (3) anal glands. Birds do not perspire, and skin glands corresponding to the sweat glands in man are not known in birds.

OIL GLAND. The oil gland is just above the base of the tail in those birds that have one (and most of them do) and its secretions are used by birds in preening their feathers. *See* Preening.

Writing of the oil glands of birds, Coues (1884) reported that "it is a two-lobed or rather heart-shaped gland . . . at the root of the tail, and hence sometimes called the uropygial . . . or rump gland. . . . It is composed of numerous slender tubes or follicles which secrete the greasy fluid, the ducts of which, uniting successively in larger tubes, finally open by one or more pores, commonly upon a nipple-like elevation."

When preening, many birds rub the bill and head on the preen gland orifice, thus gathering the oily substance, which, in ducks, contains much fatty acid, some fat, and wax. The preening bird then rubs the oily secretion over its body and wing feathers, or the scales of its feet (Stettenheim, 1972). *See* related account under Head-scratching.

Elder (1954) experimented to determine the function of the oil gland (relatively large in aquatic birds) in ducks and came to a number of conclusions about it. He found that the secretion maintains the water-repellent quality of a bird's feathers, either directly or by preserving the physical structure of the feathers. Without the secretion, feathers lose much of their function in a bird's flight and in the heat retention of its body. *See* Feathers; Cold and Birds. Elder thought it probable that birds from which the oil gland had been removed could not survive in the wild. In his experiments, the plumage of birds from which the oil gland had been removed degenerated more in waterfowl than in domestic chickens; more in chickens than in pigeons. The secretion from the oil gland also helps a bird maintain the surface structure and gloss of its bill; without it the bill becomes dry and shows some sloughing of the surface.

Apparently all ducks do not need the uropygial gland as an absolute requirement for waterproofing the plumage. In Europe, Fabricius (1959) experimented with the tufted duck, *Aythya fuligula.* He found that young ducklings from which the oil gland had been removed had plumage as water-repellent as those with oil glands; apparently large amounts of air distributed in the feathers were responsible for their waterproofing. Individual studies by Rutschke (1960) suggest that the oil gland is only indirectly involved in the waterproofing of a bird's feathers, which depends primarily on feather structure. Wallace (1963) pointed out that a duck's closely imbricated feathers are structurally waterproof, but when its feathers are matted from an oil slick, trapped air in the plumage is lost—the duck

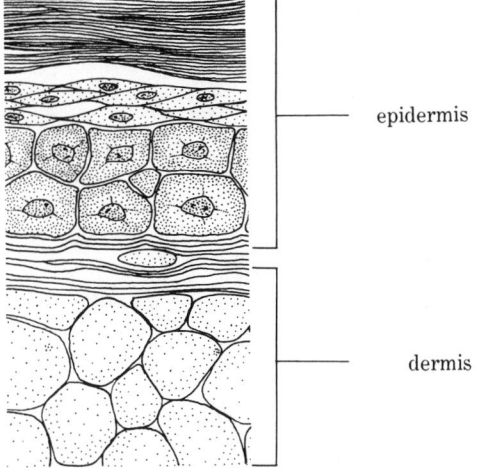

epidermis

dermis

SKIN
The epidermis, the outer layer of skin, consists of layers of flattened epithelial cells, which produce keratin, the protein that composes feathers, scales, beaks, and claws. The underlying dermis is penetrated by nerves, blood vessels, which regulate heat loss, and smooth muscle, which controls the movement of feathers.

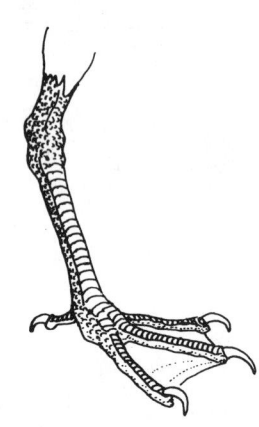

SKUA FAMILY

loses its buoyancy and cannot stay afloat. Ordinarily, most waterfowl, after submerging, pop to the surface and the little water they carry with them instantly rolls off.

Both cormorants and anhingas have an oil gland, but their wettable plumage, while swimming underwater in pursuit of fishes, can become so sodden that they must come out of the water and crawl up on a perch to dry. Obviously, having preen glands "is not the whole secret of the resistance of plumage to water" (McAtee and Stoddard, 1945). See also Casler (1973).

Some ornithologists have pointed out that the exact functions of the oil gland are still not definitely known; in fact, some birds have no oil gland—the ostrich, emu, cassowaries, bustards, frogmouths, some parrots, some pigeons, and some woodpeckers (Van Tyne and Berger, 1959).

In most nightjars, whip-poor-wills, and nighthawks and in some pigeons it exists but hardly functionally. The occurrence and non-occurrence of this gland in closely related birds is said to make its use difficult to interpret; however, it may have different uses in different birds (Rawles, 1960).

The oil gland is double in some birds (two-lobed); single in others. Typically each lobe contains a central cavity that collects the oily secretion and discharges it through a duct that usually opens into a nipplelike process at the surface of the skin.

Studies by a Chinese investigator (Hou, 1929) support the belief that the oil gland secretion contains a precursor of vitamin D (Stettenheim, 1972) and helps to prevent rickets in some birds. The vitamin forms when the oil distributed in the feathers is activated by the sun's rays, and is then absorbed through the skin or by the bird's swallowing feather particles during its preening. Removal of the oil gland does not cause rickets in house sparrows and starlings, which may get their vitamin D in a different way, or it may demonstrate that the threshold of vitamin D deficiency is quite different in various species (Friedmann, 1935).

OUTER EAR GLANDS. Some authors consider that, besides the oil gland of the tail, there are additional wax-producing glands of the bird's skin. For example, Lucas and Stettenheim (1972) described a row of shallow glands in the wall of the external, or outer, ear canals of domestic fowl whose structure was described by a German author in 1942. The ear glands secrete a wax but the glands differ greatly from the uropygial gland.

ANAL GLANDS. According to Stettenheim (1972), birds of most orders (*see* Order) have glands in the skin around the anal opening and along the anal canal. These differ from the cloacal glands and are outside the cloacal chambers. The anal glands secrete a mucus whose function is unknown; however, in Japanese quail *(Coturnix)* the secretion seems to be associated with "the mechanics of internal fertilization" (Stettenheim, 1972).

SKIPJACK
Another name for Wilson's storm-petrel in Storm-petrel Family.

SKUA (SKEW-ah) FAMILY
Stercorariidae (ster-koh-ray-rih-EYE-dee); from Lat. *stercorarius*, pertaining to dung, scavenger. 4–6 species in world; 17–24 in. long; largely oceanic, piratical birds of both northern and southern oceans that resemble their close relatives the gulls but differ in having a hawk-like fleshy "cere" across base of the upper mandible through which the nostrils open.

Skuas are larger and darker than jaegers, showing a broad white wing patch. The great skua has representatives in both hemispheres and is the only bird in the world to nest in both the Arctic and the Antarctic (Austin, 1961); the 3 species of the family called jaegers (YAY-ger)—a name taken from the German word for hunter, which was originally applied to wild huntsmen along the Rhine who were plunderers and robbers—are smaller than true skuas, are more falconlike, with long, pointed wings. The bill is strongly hooked at the tip, legs are short and strong, toes webbed, with sharply curved claws. All three—the long-tailed, parasitic, and pomarine jaegers—are northern species that nest around the world in the Arctic tundra. All three have elongated central tail feathers that extend 2–8 in. or more beyond the other tail feathers; the parasitic and pomarine jaegers (Maher, 1974) have two color phases: one gray-white, the other dark sooty brown. Sexes are outwardly alike; female slightly larger. Albinism is apparently rare; Gross (1965a) reported three records but did not identify the species.

Jaegers are the most numerous birds of prey in the Arctic and there, and over the oceans, have the same roles that hawks, falcons, and vultures have on land. Although they may feed on dead fish and seabirds, they live largely by chasing smaller seabirds, and forcing them to disgorge fishes they have eaten (gulls and terns are principal victims); on their nesting grounds they live largely on lemmings and other rodents, also carrion and small birds.

Jaegers are strong, fast fliers and in winter wander over the seas, associating with terns, shearwaters, and other seabirds; winter mainly in oceans of S. Hemisphere, to Chile, Argentina, New Zealand. All show a flash of white near tips of wings.

In captivity, feed ill or injured member of the family small pieces of meat, mice, small rats, fishes; should have a pool in which to bathe.

Jaeger, arctic. *See* Jaeger, long-tailed.

Jaeger, Buffon's. *See* Jaeger, long-tailed.

Jaeger, long-tailed, *Stercorarius longicaudus* (ster-koh-RAY-rih-us lonj-ih-CAW-dus); genus name: *see* family introduction; species name: from Lat. *longus*, long, and *cauda*, tail. (Color ill., page 846.) Is longest-tailed (the central tail feathers) but smallest-bodied and slimmest of all jaegers; circumpolar breeding range; in summer on tundra, islands, and marine coasts of entire Arctic O.; in N. America, coasts of w. and n. Alaska; n. Canada; also in n.

Eurasia (see Maher, 1974); its N. American range is practically coextensive with that of its main avian prey, the Lapland longspur (Godfrey, 1966); migrates at sea to winter in oceans of S. Hemisphere off Peru and in c. Pacific, but exact wintering grounds unclear (Watson, 1966). 20–23 in. long; wingspread 30 in.; light gray-brown above with distinct black cap; resembles parasitic jaeger closely in general color pattern except for underparts; white of throat and yellow of cheeks extends around back of neck, making a more complete collar than in parasitic jaeger; immatures have only stubs of central tail feathers (in adults these may be 8–10 in. but usually 3–6 in. long); less white on wings than in other jaegers; long-tailed also has *blue-gray* legs; parasitic has black. Arrives Arctic nesting grounds in May; flight is buoyant and graceful, courses like swallow or tern over grassy borders of tundra ponds in search of food, or perches on mossy hummocks to rest; is so dependent on lemmings for food that in summers of lemming scarcity (every 3–4 years) may move on to breed or summer elsewhere; utters shrill *pheu-pheu-pheu-pheo* while in flight, when quarreling, or chasing each other, also a rattling *kr-r-r, kr-r-r, kri, kri-kri-kri.*

Feeding Habits: The least inclined of the jaegers to harry gulls, terns, and other seabirds; on tundra often hovers above lemmings and mice before dropping to ground; seizes prey in bill, also catches and eats butterflies, flies, and other insects, and fishes, eats eggs and young from nests of other birds, picks up dead crustaceans, worms, and other carrion; during late summer may feed largely on crowberries *(Empetrum nigrum)* and other berries before migrating to S. Hemisphere over route that has long been a mystery; departs from Arctic in what appears to be family groups (Bent, 1921).
Nest: A depression on a knoll or ridge of open tundra, sometimes on dry rolling uplands, where it scrapes a few bits of dry grass, leaves, or pieces of moss together in slight hollow, sometimes among rocks; adults very bold in defense of nest, swoop down at human intruder or fly straight at his face; may even land on humans; attacks arctic foxes near nest.
Eggs: June–July; 1–3, usually 2, olive or brown, irregularly spotted or blotched with browns.
Incubation: By both parents, 23 days; young first fly about 21 days after hatching. See Drury (1960); Maher (1974). To lead intruders away from nest, adults will feign injury, thrashing around on ground as though in great suffering (Bent, 1921).
Other Names: Arctic jaeger; Buffon's jaeger; gull-teaser; long-tailed skua (British Isles); whip-tail.
Weights: An immature female (very fat) collected (shot) on open ocean off Puerto Angel, w. coast of Mexico, Apr. 1964, 298 gr. (Binford, 1970), or about 10½ oz; adult females (2), Banks Is., Canada, 10½ and 12½ oz. (Manning *et al.,* 1956); adult males (5), Ellesmere Is., about 8½–11 oz.; adult females (8), about 8½–13 oz. (Parmelee and MacDonald, 1960).
Range: Nests in N. America from w. Alaska, n. Yukon, Mack., Banks Is., Melville Is., Ellesmere Is., and n. Greenland south to Southamp-

ton Is., and n. Que.; winters offshore in Atlantic O. from 40° N. Lat. to 50° S. Lat., and in Pacific off S. America from 10° S. Lat. to 50° S. Lat.

Jaeger, parasitic, *Stercorarius parasiticus* (ster-koh-RAY-rih-us par-ah-SIT-ih-cus); genus name: *see* family introduction; species name: from habit of living on food caught by other birds. (Color ill., page 846.) Possibly most numerous member of family, but see Maher (1974); Eurasia; in summer, in N. America, nests on marine coasts of Arctic O. and on Arctic tundra; in fall migration largely over oceans but often seen along N. American coasts, rarely in inland waters; the most coastal of the jaegers in winter and migration; frequently seen chasing terns; this is jaeger that joins migrating arctic terns to pirate from them on their long ocean journeys; 15–21 in. long; wingspread about 36 in.; adult distinguished from larger, heavier pomarine jaeger by short, flat, *pointed* central tail feathers; two color phases with intermediates, light and dark: dark phase, adults are medium dusky brown above, with darker cap, but light gray-brown below and on cheeks (Reilly, 1968); in light phase, dark above, with cap, but white abdomen and white throat, a gray chest band, and pale yellow cheeks; immatures are brown above, with mottled white on wings, throat, underparts, lack the pair of central tail feathers; at Fair Isle Bird Observatory, Scotland, Kenneth Williamson found color phases of arctic skua (parasitic jaeger) could be divided into dark, intermediate, and pale (white-bellied) types; there they got most of their food by chasing the abundant kittiwakes and forcing them to disgorge small fishes; according to Williamson, parasitic jaegers do not breed until 3–5 years old; in spring moves northward along both Atlantic and Pacific coasts; arrives off Fla. coast Apr.–May; on Arctic nesting grounds May–June (Bent, 1921).

Feeding Habits: On breeding grounds on Arctic tundra, feeds on lemmings (see Maher, 1970), shrews, and mice, also catches and eats longspurs, redpolls, and other small birds, which it swallows whole with feathers on; also their eggs and young and those of eiders and gulls, besides causing terns to drop fishes or disgorge contents of gullet; eats fishes and shellfishes cast up on beaches; eats crowberries.
Nest: In colonies, a simple depression in ground.
Eggs: N. Canada, Alaska, June–July; usually 2, indistinguishable from those of long-tailed jaeger.
Incubation: By both sexes; 24–28 days; usually 25–26 days; young first fly when about 28–35 days old, but variable (Witherby *et al.,* 1938–41).
Other Names: Arctic hawk gull; arctic skua; black-toed gull; boatswain; dung hunter; gull-chaser; jiddy hawk; man-o'-war; marlinespike; Richardson's jaeger; skait-bird; teaser; whip-tail.
Age: A female arctic skua (parasitic jaeger) lived on the Isle of Foula, Shetland Is., as a free but tame bird for 23 years; it came to the house of a man to be fed daily. Another tamed one lived on Hermanness, came to a warden of the

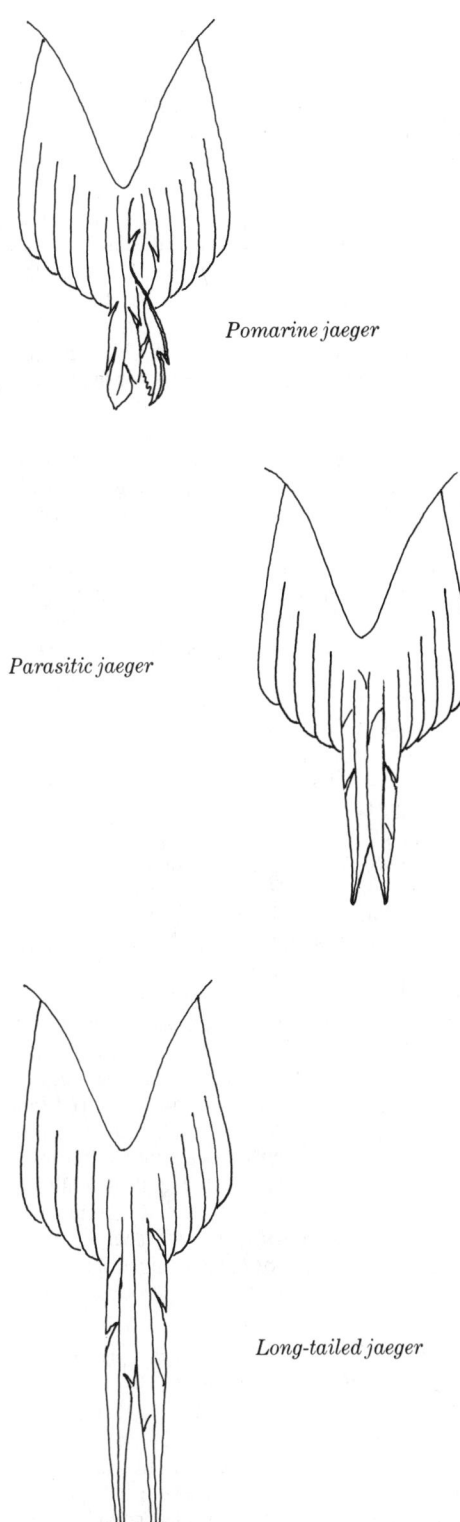

Pomarine jaeger

Parasitic jaeger

Long-tailed jaeger

SKUA FAMILY
The three smaller members of the skua family that are known as jaegers—oceanic, piratical birds of the northern seas—have elongated central tail feathers.

island to be fed, returned to the island regularly for more than 30 years (Oldham, 1933).
Weights: Adult female (1), Banks Is., Canada, 1 lb. 2¼ oz. (Manning *et al.*, 1956); adult females (4), Victoria Is., Canada, averaged 1 lb. 13 oz.; adult males (6), about 1 lb. 8 oz. (Parmelee *et al.*, 1967).
Range: In N. America nests from n. Alaska, N.W.T., Banks Is., Greenland, n. Ellesmere Is., south to Alaska Pen., Aleutian Is., Kodiak Is., s. Mack., Man., Southampton Is., Baffin Is., Ont., n. Que., and n. Labrador; winters from Fla. and from s. Calif., south to Chile and Argentina and waters off w. Africa south to Cape of Good Hope (Watson, 1966).

Jaeger, pomarine, *Stercorarius pomarinus* (ster-koh-RAY-rih-us pom-ah-RINE-us); genus name: *see* family introduction; species name: Lat., from Gr. *poma*, lid, and *rhis, rhinos*, nose; having the nostrils somewhat roofed over by the horny plate forming the ridge of the bill—that is, *pomarine* (POH-mahrine, rhymes with *fine*). (Color ill., page 847.) Largest of the jaegers, almost size of herring gull; nests on islands and coasts of entire Arctic O.; 20–23 in. long; wingspread 48 in.; biggest and most powerful of the three jaegers, has proportionately the stoutest bill and most white in wings; adults similar (female larger), have two stubby, elongated central tail feathers that are twisted, with webs vertical, appear spatulate like blade of an oar, giving tail a heavy, awkward appearance from distance; there are two color phases, light and dark; common lightphase birds have a black cap, yellow-white cheeks and collar, and white throat and underparts, with a distinct band across upper breast; rarer dark phase is all dark sooty-gray with almost black cap, and a white wing flash in the primaries; young birds lack the elongated tail feathers and are either all dark brown or are mottled and barred with tan above, with brown below (Watson, 1966); usual call is a sharp *which-yew*, also a squeaky whistle, occasional squealing note, *week-week*; off coasts of N. America in northward spring migration Apr.–May; arrives Arctic nesting grounds May–June.

Feeding Habits: On tundra depends on lemmings and voles for sufficient food for successful breeding in n. Alaska (Maher, 1970); when hunting flies above tundra at 15–25 ft.; when lemming sighted, alights and grabs it in bill; the feet never used for this purpose; after ground thaws, digs lemmings out of peat soil with bill; also catches and eats phalaropes, sandpipers, ptarmigans, small birds and their eggs, carrion such as dead caribou and seals; later, when they go to sea for winter, in Aug.–Sept., fly among feeding terns, gulls, shearwaters, which they rob of their food catches (Bent, 1921); also follow fishing boats for offal thrown overboard; in tropics may take live fishes from surface over a feeding school of tuna; alights on surface to eat galley refuse from ships; most important indicator to fishermen for locating schools of tuna in tropical waters (Watson, 1966); few jaegers and other interesting pelagic seabirds ever seen from shore; one must visit offshore fishing banks (Pough, 1951).

Nest: A slight depression formed on dry hillock above tundra.
Eggs: Alaska, June; 2–3, shades of brown to green, sparingly spotted with browns, grays.
Incubation: 27–28 days; young first fly about 35–42 days after hatching.
Other Names: Gull-chaser; gull hunter; jaeger gull; jiddy hawk; marlinespike; pomarine skua (British Isles); pomatorhine skua; whip-tail.
Weights: Females collected in n. Alaska averaged 745 gr., or about 1 lb. 10¼ oz.; males averaged 648 grams, or about 1 lb. 6⅞ oz. (Maher, 1970); adult males (2), Banks Is., Canada, 1 lb. 6 oz. and 2 lb. 6 oz. (Manning *et al.*, 1956).
Range: In Eurasia and in N. America; nests from w. Alaska, Banks Is., Melville Is., Somerset Is., Southampton Is., and Baffin Is., n. Que., to w.-c. Greenland; winters at sea regularly from Cape Hatteras south to Caribbean and w. Africa with stragglers (specimen records) to Venezuela and Guyana; sight records for Uruguay and Argentina, however, main wintering areas in Atlantic, as far as known, lie in upwelling fish-rich waters off West Africa from Cape Vert, Senegal, to Gulf of Guinea; in Pacific, from s. Calif. to Humboldt Current off Peru; extreme southern records in W. Hemisphere are on Antarctic Pen. (Escalante, 1972).

Jaeger, Richardson's. *See* Jaeger, parasitic.

Skua, *Catharacta skua* (kath-are-ACK-tah SKEW-ah); genus name: from Lat. *cathar*, from Gr. *katharos*, pure, *kathartes*, purifier, cleanser, in reference to this bird's frequent scavenging; species name: from common name, given it by inhabitants of the Faeroes, Danish islands in Atlantic O. north of British Isles, so named probably in imitation of its cry. (Color ill., page 847.) Does not nest in N. America but ranges off Atlantic coast; 20–22 in. long; wingspread about 59 in.; wings wider, more rounded than those of jaegers; near size of herring gull but chunkier; dark brown, rusty above, white at bases of wing primaries; at distance, appears like dark, short-tailed herring gull; massive-appearing in flight; leisurely but powerful wingbeats which speed up and are audible from nearby when it is chasing other seabirds (Watson, 1966).

Feeding Habits: At sea plunders mainly fishes from gannets, gulls, terns, shearwaters; when pursued bird drops or disgorges prey, skua darts down and usually snatches it out of air before it strikes water; kills and eats ducks, gulls (Meinertzhagen, 1959); at sea follows ships and often alights on water to eat galley scraps while swimming; on nesting grounds preys upon both young and mature seabirds and small mammals, and eats carrion (Wynne-Edwards, in Thomson, 1964).
Nest: In colonies, a shallow depression on higher ground, on rocky slopes, or at base of cliffs.
Eggs: Iceland, May–June; 1–3, usually 2, yellow to green or brown, blotched, spotted with browns, purple.
Incubation: By both sexes, 26–29 days (Fisher and Lockley, 1954); young fly 60 days after

hatching but stay around nest 3–4 weeks longer; monogamous, but polygamy reported on Signy Is. (Burton, 1968).
Other Names: Bonxie; great skua; sea hawk; sea hen; skua gull.
Weights: About 2½ lb. (Pough, 1951); and possibly 3 lb. or more.
Range: Nests in Iceland in N. Hemisphere, also in the Faeroes, Shetland, and Orkney Is. (the only bird to breed in both the Arctic and Antarctic—different populations, however, see Watson [1975]); outside the nesting season ranges widely over N. Atlantic, off Canadian Maritime Provinces and New England; winters mainly offshore in e. Atlantic, sparingly off N. American coast to Newfoundland, very rarely off Mass.; at eastern end of Long Is., N.Y., four occurrences: two picked up dead in 19th century; two sighted, both at Montauk Point, Nov. and Dec. 1937 (Bull, 1964).

Skua, arctic. *See* Jaeger, parasitic.

Skua, great. *See* Skua.

Skua, long-tailed. *See* Jaeger, long-tailed.

Skua, pomarine. *See* Jaeger, pomarine.

Skua, pomatorhine. *See* Jaeger, pomarine.

SKULL
See Skeleton.

SKUNK BIRD
See Bobolink in Troupial Family.

SKUNK-HEAD
See Scoter, surf, in Duck Family.

SKY-GAZER
Local name for the American bittern, from its habit of standing still with bill pointed upward. *See* Freezing.

SKYLARK
See in Lark Family; also a misnomer for Sprague's pipit in Pipit Family.

SLEEP
See Roosting.

SLEEPING NEST
See Dummy Nest; *also* Nests and Nesting.

SLEEPY BROTHER
Another name for the ruddy duck, because it is often lethargic.

SMELL
Olfaction, or the sense of smell, is possibly the oldest of all animal senses. It began with the evolution of nostrils and specialized chemical receptors among early fishlike vertebrates in the ancient seas of the world, before the land animals had arrived (Simpson *et al.*, 1957). *See* Evolution; Geological Time Scale. Later, when air-breathing animals evolved, they retained the sense of smell; however, because olfaction, by its nature, is subjective, it is especially difficult to measure in birds (Stager, 1964) and many other animals.

Because of the complexity of the problem of whether or not birds can smell, it has been debated for more than a century (Van Tyne and Berger, 1959). Scientists have made relatively few controlled experiments of olfaction in birds (Sturkie, 1954) and many of these were either contradictory or inconclusive (Duncan, 1964a).

For example, Strong (1911) put ringed turtle doves, *Streptopelia risoria*, in a labyrinth in which they could go to one of four separate chambers: three were empty, the fourth contained food along with the odor under test. Strong tried to train the doves to go into the chamber containing food. He finally decided from their behavior that of various odorous substances he used, their sense of smell was sometimes stimulated by oil of bergamot, but his results were not conclusive.

Walter (1943) got completely negative results in his test of pigeons for sense of smell, and two investigators in America, in separate series of conditioning experiments with pigeons to test their olfactory sense, got conflicting results (Duncan, 1964a). Bang (1960) wrote: "It seems curious that the large olfactory organs of certain species [of birds] have so often been pointed out by anatomists, yet most olfactory studies have been done on feebly equipped birds such as pigeons and have tended to keep alive in textbooks the idea that the chemical sense [of smell] in birds is minimal or lacking."

Bobwhite quail learned to associate the odor of coumarin with food—it was repellent to them—and to discriminate what was thought to be their own species odor transferred to their feeding trays after they had touched them. The experiments indicated a relatively well-developed sense of smell in bobwhites (Hamrum, 1953; Frings and Boyd, 1952).

Studies of the olfactory lobes in the brain of birds show they vary considerably in size—they are larger in ducks than in passerines, or songbirds. There is only one olfactory lobe in the house sparrow; two in the crow (Van Tyne and Berger, 1959). The olfactory lobes of some birds are so large that they lend credence to field observations suggesting that certain birds have a good sense of smell.

Field experiments with some of the nocturnal, flightless kiwis of New Zealand strongly suggested that they smell the underground earthworms on which they feed (*see also* experiment with American robins in introduction to Thrush Family); another experimenter could get no such response (Allen, 1925). The olfactory lobes of kiwis are large and comparable in structure with those of mammals (Van Tyne and Berger, 1959), many of which are noted for their keen sense of smell. According to Sturkie (1954), kiwis, which have weak eyesight, are believed to have a good sense of smell, and Portmann (1950b) stated that they must rely on olfaction to survive.

The olfactory lobe of the brain is well developed in emus and in geese, and in shearwaters and other petrels. Bang (1960) called attention to the large and heavily innervated nasal organs of the turkey vulture, oilbird, and black-footed and Laysan albatrosses. She suggested that the morphological and behavioral evidence —behavior long known in albatrosses and petrels—indicates a well-developed olfactory

sense in these species. Murphy (1936) reported that in the Antarctic the behavior of albatrosses, skuas, and petrels strongly suggested that these seabirds can smell meat, blood, and hot fat or oil on the sea; Grubb's studies (1973) suggested that young Leach's petrels, seeking nesting places, may use the sense of smell to help them locate musky-smelling burrows in ground under the forest canopy.

In a study of the size of the olfactory bulb in 108 species of birds, Bang and Cobb (1968) concluded from their survey that—besides the kiwis, turkey vulture, and tube-nosed marine birds, in which olfaction is apparently of primary importance—most water birds, marsh dwellers, and waders (shorebirds), and possibly echolocating species, have a useful olfactory sense, and that in the other species studied, it may be relatively unimportant.

Some birds, when holding food in the mouth, apparently can test its odor very quickly. Stresemann (1927–34) noted that some falcons and owls, which usually eat fresh meat, will immediately toss aside tainted meat after holding it in the bill for only a moment.

Kenneth E. Stager (1964), of the Los Angeles County Museum, traced the remarkably long and often heated controversy over whether or not the American turkey vulture can detect food by its sense of smell. The debate had continued for 138 years before it was resolved. It began after the crude experiment of Audubon (1826) and ended with Stager's own carefully controlled experiments and anatomical research on the olfactory sense of vultures.

Audubon firmly believed that vultures lacked a sense of smell and that they relied solely on sight to locate from the air the carcasses of their dead prey; however, he appeared to have experimented with the N. American black vulture, according to Stager, and not the turkey vulture.

In spite of Audubon's findings, most American observers—Bent (1937), F. M. Chapman in 1889 (see Austin, 1967), Dickey and van Rossem (1938), Forbush (1925–29), Gosse (1847), Grinnell (1933), Hopkins (1888), Howell (1932), and many others—were convinced by the behavior of turkey vultures in the wild that they detected their food by a sense of smell.

Stager began his field experiments in 1935. For 25 years he picked up dead animals and hid them in bushes and hollow trees, and he noted that in every one of his experiments the vultures, in low-altitude hunting flights of 100–200 ft. above the ground, approached the hidden bait with the wind blowing to them from the hidden carcasses. These and other field tests suggested to Stager that one of the vulture's senses other than sight aided it in finding carrion.

To make more exact tests, Stager developed a special method. He hid the carcasses inside a unit and used a blower and an electric fan to waft the odors of the dead animals from the ground into the sky. He gathered from the countryside dead animals of the kinds the vultures were accustomed to eating—deer, bobcats, and other native animals. To prevent the day-flying vultures from seeing them, he put them into the unit at night.

From the large numbers of turkey vultures

he found gathered around the unit on the following days, Stager got what he considered conclusive proof that the turkey vulture does find its food, first, by its odor. *See also* discussion under Vulture. In similar tests with aegypiine (Old World) vultures in India, Stager found that they depended solely on *sight* to locate their prey.

Among five different genera of vultures of the New World that Stager studied anatomically, the turkey vulture (*Cathartes*) had the largest olfactory lobes, also the largest nares (nostrils). *See* Nostrils. The king vulture (*Sarcoramphus*) of tropical America, whose habits are little known, had the second-largest olfactory lobes. In the N. American black vulture (*Coragyps*), the California condor (*Gymnogyps*), and the S. American condor (*Vultur*), Stager could find no evidence, in either their behavior or their anatomy, that olfaction plays more than a minor role, if any, in their food-getting. They depend on their eyesight to find dead animals, and often watch the hunting flights of turkey vultures, then descend to the ground to drive them from their prey. *See* discussion of "stealing" under Behavior; *see also* Autolycism; Commensalism.

Duncan (1964a) concludes that birds apparently have adequate olfactory organs, but that in some species the sense of smell is poorly developed and plays little or no part in their lives; that further experiments with other species, using a wider range of olfactory stimuli, must be made before definite conclusions can be reached about the sense of smell of birds. For a review of the sense of smell in birds, see Wenzel (1973). *See also* Taste; Touch.

SMEW
See in Duck Family.

SMITH
GIDEON B. (1793–1867). Physician of Baltimore, Md., and friend and correspondent of John James Audubon (Audubon, M. R., 1960); see also Gruson (1972). Audubon named a longspur for Smith which was later found to have been previously named by William Swainson in Swainson and Richardson's *Fauna Boreali-Americana;* however, the English name, Smith's longspur, has been retained.

SMOKE BATHING
Some birds, in the process of "anting," in which they place ants among their feathers (it is suggested that this helps in feather care and discourages feather parasites—*see* discussion under Anting), also bathe in smoke, steam, or even expose themselves to the heat of flames in what is thought to be a part of their feather care. See Whitaker (1957); *see also* Preening.

Chisholm (1959) cites a remarkable record of a tame magpie in Great Britain that regularly picked up ants, flew with them in its bill to its owner's shoulders, but before dabbing the ants among its feathers, dipped the ants in the hot ashes of the man's pipe. Another tame magpie in England pounced on discarded, still-burning cigarette butts and applied the burning, smoking end—never the unlit end—to its feathers in what was thought to be a part of its feather care. Perhaps a related action of birds is the regular habit of many of exposing themselves to great heat in taking sun baths. *See* Bathing; *also* Heat and Birds.

Chisholm reports further that red-browed finches "smoke-bathed in the smoke of a brush fire," and a tame black-backed magpie often perched above a boiler house with its wings outstretched over the escaping steam.

A boy in Australia reported to Chisholm (1959) that at a county cricket match in New South Wales, on a very hot day, he saw a spectator throw away a cigarette butt, and when a spotted-sided finch flew away with it, the breeze fanned the lighted end of the cigarette. When she reached her grassy nest, it took fire, then burning fragments fell to the dry grass below the tree and thereby "a brush fire was started."

Edwin Way Teale (1965) reported that in the Rio Grande region of s. Tex. the green jay has been seen anointing its plumage with smoke from smoldering logs.

SNAILS AND BIRDS
See Mollusks and Birds.

SNAKEBIRD
See in Anhinga Family.

SNAKE DISPLAY
Term of ethologists, or those who study animal behavior, for a type of behavioral mimicry of snakes by hole-nesting birds. *See* Behavioral Mimicry under Behavior.

SNAKE KILLER
One of the common names of the roadrunner, for its fondness for eating snakes. *See* Reptiles and Birds.

SNAKE RIVER BIRDS OF PREY NATURAL AREA
Official name of the 26,555-acre refuge set aside by the Bureau of Land Management, U.S. Department of the Interior, along a 30-mi. stretch of the Snake R. in sw. Idaho. The refuge, to protect the high concentration of birds of prey nesting in the canyon, was set aside as a unique and exceptional sanctuary especially for the golden eagle and prairie falcon and other persecuted birds of prey that visit, or live in, the canyon.

On Aug. 24, 1971, Rogers C. B. Morton, Secretary of the Interior, dedicated the natural area in official ceremonies on the brink of Snake River Canyon near Swan Falls, Idaho. The land within the refuge, about 30 mi. south of Boise, is not to be sold or leased under the public land and general mining laws, and no recreational development permitted that will interfere with the residence of the birds.

At least 100 eyries of the golden eagle were estimated to be in sw. Idaho in 1970; in spring 1970 and spring 1971, Kochert (1972) made intensive searches for golden eagles in the refuge area and counted 11 pairs; according to Meiners (1970), 49 pairs of the increasingly rare prairie falcons were sighted in the canyon.

In 1970–71, Kochert (1972) studied golden eagle populations along 150 linear mi. of the Snake R. that included the Snake River Birds of Prey Natural Area.

Density of the known breeding pairs of golden eagles in the largest area of Kochert's study ranged from one pair per 35.5 sq. mi. in 1970 to one pair per 25.4 sq. mi. in 1971. (Dixon, 1937, in a 30-year study of the golden eagle in Calif., found that each pair ranged over 19–59 sq. mi., or an average of about 36 sq. mi. for each pair.)

According to Kochert, the density of pairs of golden eagles in his principal study area along the Snake R. in 1971—one pair per 25.4 sq. mi. —compared favorably with the densities of nesting golden eagles in Scotland, where, according to Brown (1966), densities of this eagle may approach maximum for the species. Densities in Scotland ranged from one pair per 15.7 sq. mi. in the Northeast Highlands (Watson, 1957) to one pair per 27.9 sq. mi. (Brown and Watson, 1964). In Snake River Canyon, Kochert found one pair of golden eagles nesting for each 3 mi. of river; in Mont., McGahan (1968) noted that pairs nested about 1–10 mi. apart.

Kochert found that the population of the Snake R. golden eagles was stable, and reproductively healthy, but may be threatened in the future if large tracts of land adjacent to the Snake R. on which the eagles find their prey animals goes into agricultural production; the eagles may become increasingly subject to disturbance by people; and may be threatened by possible increases of farm chemicals on the land. This could adversely affect the golden eagle population density and breeding success. Later, the Snake River Birds of Prey Study Area, an area twice the size of the Natural Area, was established around the Natural Area. This was to protect the feeding range of the golden eagles until it could be determined how much land should be kept out of agriculture to give the birds full protection. See discussion by Anonymous (1980). *See* status of eagles elsewhere in N. America under Hawk Family.

The Snake River Birds of Prey Natural Area is managed from the Boise District Office, Bureau of Land Management, 230 Collins Road, Boise, Idaho 83702. The address for the management of the whole preserved area is Deer Flat National Wildlife Refuge, Box 448, Nampa, Idaho 83651.

SNAKES AND BIRDS
See Reptiles and Birds.

SNAKESKIN BIRD
Another name for the great crested flycatcher.

SNIPE
See in Sandpiper Family.

SNOOD
See in description of turkey in Turkey Family.

SNOWBIRD
See Junco, slate-colored (dark-eyed), and Bunting, snow, in Finch Family.

SNOWFLAKE
See Bunting, McKay's, and Bunting, snow, in Finch Family.

SNOWSHOES
See Feet and Legs.

SOARING
See Flight.

SOCIAL BIRDS
See Flocks and Flocking.

SOCIAL HIERARCHY
See Social Order among Birds under Behavior; *also* Dominance.

SOCIAL PARASITISM
See Brood Parasitism.

SOCIAL PREENING
See Mutual Preening under Preening.

SOFT-BILLED BIRD
Term for one that eats insects and fruit—for example, warblers, orioles, and thrushes. *See* Hard-billed Bird.

SOLITAIRE
(sol-ih-TARE). *See* Solitaire, Townsend's, in Thrush Family; *see* Old World solitaires under Columbiformes.

SONGBIRD AND GAME-BIRD MANAGEMENT
Term for the encouragement of birds by managing or creating the environments that benefit them. (In the control or suppression of "pest birds," environments might be made unsuitable in order to discourage the presence of certain kinds—*see* Control.) The usual result of *positive* methods of management is an increase in the bird population (in total numbers and often in number of species), possibly up to the capacity of the birds themselves to increase and the limitations of the habitats and of the food supply to support them. *See* Carrying Capacity; *see*, however, Mortality; Accidents; Diseases; Predation—all of which drain the bird population.

The best-managed environments for songbirds (or game birds) provide food, shelter, nesting places, and water in proper proportion and relationship; these management measures can increase songbird populations from an average of 1 pair per acre in e. U.S. to about 10–12 pairs per acre. Some remarkable results have been accomplished with bird-attracting methods (*see* Bird-attracting); for example, at Golden Gate Park, San Francisco, with 404 pairs to 40 acres; at Olney, Ill., 70 pairs to 8 acres; and at Chevy Chase, Md., 224 pairs to 23 acres. See examples in Kalmbach and McAtee (1930); also McAtee (1940b). Increasing the bird population by putting up nest boxes for insect-eating birds can help in suppression of destructive insects in forests and gardens. See especially Dowden and Mitchell (1966). *See also* Economic Ornithology; Bird-attracting; and Census.

SONGBIRDS
See Passeriformes; Songs and Singing; *see also* especially fine songsters in Finch Family; Tanager Family; Thrush Family; Troupial Family; Wren Family.

SONGS AND SINGING

The songs and singing of birds interest many people—ornithologists because of the function of singing in communication between wild birds, and the role that singing plays in their behavior; both ornithologists and birders (*see* Birder), because in knowing birds' songs (and calls) they can identify birds even though the birds themselves may be hidden from view; and these people and many others, because of the beauty or simple appropriateness of a wild bird's song and its power to add to the loveliness and interest of the natural world.

BIRD SONG AND ITS FUNCTION. Most passerines have sounds that advertise territoriality and availability as a mate. Usually delivered during a restricted period of the year, these primary songs are often complex, with elaborate patterns of notes grouped into phrases. In this way they are usually differentiated from calls. The primary song is what we commonly hear in spring and summer, and its functions are associated with the major activities at that time of year: courtship and territoriality. Only the male usually sings the primary song (*see* Females that Sing), which is under hormonal control. The male, through his song, advertises his presence in a chosen territory to potential and actual intruders and attracts a mate (Nice, 1943; Thorpe, 1964b; Borror, 1975a; Thielke, 1976). *See* Courtship; Territory. In most songbirds, the primary song is typically a male *secondary sexual character* (Lanyon, 1960). *See* Sexual Dimorphism. Each passerine sings a song characteristic for that species. See Thorpe (1961); Armstrong (1963); Jellis (1977).

THE "TRUE" SONGBIRDS. Although song is primarily a characteristic of most passerine birds (the "songbirds"), some that are not songbirds have pleasing whistled or other vocal sounds that are functional as songs. Some of these are the bobwhite quail, mourning dove, and upland sandpiper (Van Tyne and Berger, 1959). However, this article is concerned with those birds in which songs are best developed, which in N. America belong to the suborder Passeres (*see* Passeres).

Besides their primary song, or songs, the songbirds also have a *subsong*—a random subdued warbling of longer duration than the primary song. The subsong has some of the bird's recognizable call notes interspersed among the warbling notes but is typically without any phrases suggestive of the definitive primary song characteristic of the species. In captive birds, the subsong first may appear in young birds, with the juvenile call notes incorporated into the random warbling, during the first month after the bird has fledged; however, its first appearance varies among species and even among individuals of the same species (Lanyon, 1960). See some examples in Nice (1943, p. 141).

According to Lanyon, the next change in the singing of the young male songbird is the addition of some notes that are suggestive of the primary song of the adult males of its kind. With these added to the call notes interspersed with the random warbling, its subsong now becomes more variable. In this form the subsong in young birds of many species seems to be a rehearsal or practice for the full song to come later. This "rehearsal" song becomes established by the first autumn. Finally, the transition from rehearsal song to primary song is accompanied by the dropping out of its random warbling and call notes, with a simplification of the total song which comes during the bird's first winter and early spring. The primary song motifs—a sequence of notes in a definite pattern, repeated in some songs—once incorporated into a bird's repertoire at the end of its first spring, are usually remarkably stereotyped and seemingly are fixed for life. Some birds, such as many wood warblers, often have secondary songs, as complex as primary songs, and often alternated with them.

According to Lanyon, adult birds in spring go through a similar pattern of singing, from *muted song* to primary song, as they pass from the sexually quiescent period of winter to the reproductive cycle of spring and summer. Muted song may be like subsong or simply an abbreviated soft form of primary song. Some young female songsters also develop a subsong similar to that of the male, but they do not develop the rehearsal song or the primary song; as adults they may continue to sing the subsong occasionally.

Besides the practical functions of song for a bird, and its use as "a normal outlet of excess energy in many birds" (Nice, 1943), Thorpe (1956a) has pointed out that "the possibility of birds singing for pleasure is by no means ruled out." For a discussion of this, see Armstrong (1963). Birds can hear the sounds made by their own kind and at least some of the sounds made by other species. Hearing range varies considerably among different species. *See* ranges of hearing of some under Ears and Hearing; see also Armstrong (1963).

"WHISPER" SONG, OR "MUTED" SONG. This is a "very quiet, inward rendering of the primary song, with or without slight variations or additions and with an audibility limited to no more than about 20 yards" (Nicholson, 1929). It is the quietest form of song (or subsong) of a songbird (Armstrong, 1963). Amelia R. Laskey at Nashville, Tenn., reported that an old female mockingbird sang frequently "a lovely whisper song" in Oct. A number of songbirds, while sitting on the nest and incubating the eggs or brooding the young, will sing soft whisper songs which seem to suggest contentment—American goldfinch, warbling vireo, a male catbird, rose-breasted and black-headed grosbeaks, and a brown thrasher (Armstrong, 1963). Adults, when slightly alarmed, in rain, and at other times, also sing the whisper song, or muted song, in place of primary song. Usually the whisper song is sung from concealment in trees, shrubbery, or other cover, and may be sung by both the males and some females. Whisper songs are also credited to the gray jay, scrub jay, and evening grosbeak.

DUETTING AND ANTIPHONAL SINGING. These are terms for the remarkable singing in unison of pairs, mainly of certain tropical birds in C. and S. America, Australasia, and Africa in which the female and male sing either the same songs *together*, different songs, or different

Blue-winged warbler

Henslow's sparrow

Vesper sparrow

SONGS AND SINGING
Different species of songbirds may have different habitual perches from which they sing. The blue-winged warbler sings from an exposed perch at the top of a tree; Henslow's sparrow may cling to the stalk of a tall weed; the vesper sparrow often utters its melodious song from the ground.

parts of the same song *alternately;* they may be so exactly timed that the total song sounds as though uttered by one bird (Pettingill, 1970). See also discussion in Van Tyne and Berger (1959) and Jellis (1977). *See also,* below, Females That Sing.

THE SONG PERCH. Some songbirds occasionally sing from the ground (American robin and indigo bunting, for example, and the vesper sparrow of the open fields), but most sing from a perch above the ground. For the horned lark it may be a large boulder or even a clod of earth or a fence post; the savannah and Henslow's sparrows may sing while clinging to a tall weed; the indigo bunting often sings from the top of a bush or from the branch of a tall tree. The blue-winged and golden-winged warblers sing from an exposed perch high in a bush or tree (Berger, 1961). Thrushes, mockingbirds, and thrashers also sing their primary, or advertising, songs from favorite perches in trees in different parts of their territories, either within or close to cover where they are reasonably protected from attacks by hawks or other predatory birds.

FLIGHT SONGS. Many birds that nest in open fields, such as the skylark, horned lark, and Sprague's pipit, sing while in flight over their territories; they may soar or flutter to 800 ft. above the ground while singing; the bobolink, Lapland longspur, snow bunting, and upland sandpiper also sing in flight. See details in Berger (1961); *see also* Courtship and Territorial Flight under Flight.

WHEN DO BIRDS SING? One may hear some early bird songs in late winter (white-breasted nuthatch and pine warbler, for example, in eastern forests), but singing increases rapidly from early spring to about midsummer and is at its height for N. American birds during the courting and nesting seasons. Some songbirds that tend to defend their territories throughout the year—mockingbirds, wrentits, and the cactus wren, for example—sing during the winter, but not as frequently as early in the nesting period (Berger, 1961; Borror, 1975a). Chickadees, tufted titmice, and cardinals often sing on clear cold days in Jan. and Feb. Some birds sing in migration—wood warblers, Swainson's thrushes, fox sparrow, and white-throated and white-crowned sparrows.

Singing virtually ends in Temperate Zone birds after the nesting season and especially during the postnuptial molt (*see* Molts and Molting), but some birds sing during a brief period in late summer and early fall, after the molt is over (Borror, 1975a). Frequently this is the soft "whisper," or muted, song.

DAILY SONG CYCLE. Songbirds sing much in early morning, with singing usually diminishing by midday, but increasing in late afternoon. According to Berger (1961), midday slackening of song is often correlated with high heat, and birds sing less or shift to muted songs when it is windy or if the day is humid, but may sing on cloudy days and during a light rain. Countersinging may occur at any time a territorial owner hears an adjacent male sing. The red-eyed vireo sings more or less continuously throughout the day regardless of weather and not only in the nesting season but at other times, and sometimes at night. *See* in biography of this bird in Vireo Family. Thrushes are noted for singing songs at dusk, and many songbirds that sing by day also sing at night—for example, black-billed and yellow-billed cuckoos, marsh wrens, mockingbird, ovenbird, yellow-breasted chat, and the field, Henslow's, and grasshopper sparrows (Berger, 1961).

NUMBER OF SONGS IN A DAY. A few American ornithologists have counted the number of songs sung by an individual wild bird during the day, with the "singing day" lasting from just before or after sunrise to late afternoon or just before sunset. Nice (1943), in Ohio, based on counts of the songs of the song sparrows she was studying, estimated that one, in full song, sings about 1,500 songs a day; however, on one May day, a male wild song sparrow, 8–9 years old, sang 2,305 songs. She also reported a black-throated green warbler that sang 1,680 songs in 7 hours and estimated that on a typical day of 16 hours he would have sung more than 3,000 songs.

In Mich., on June 21, 1956, Harold Mayfield (see in Berger, 1961) watched a pair of Kirtland's warblers the day before the first egg in the nest hatched. On that day, the male sang 2,212 songs between 4:57 a.m. (his first song of the day) and 7:56 p.m. (last song, which he sang about half an hour before sunset). The world's record for number of songs given in a day is apparently that of a red-eyed vireo which sang 22,197 songs (de Kiriline, 1954).

DURATION (LENGTH OF TIME) OF A SONG. According to Hartshorne (1958), the primary song of most of the songbirds is given for less than 4 seconds, and the longest "fixed (primary) bird song" he knew was that of the winter wren of 8–10 seconds. W. H. Thorpe reported that the song of the European chaffinch, a songbird, lasts about 2½ seconds with pauses of 10–20 seconds between songs. A. A. Saunders, in Bent (1968), reported that the rose-breasted grosbeak's song varies from 2 to 6.8 seconds and that the songs of the male cardinal vary from 1.8 to 4.2 seconds. Some birds, such as brown thrashers and mockingbirds, may sing an essentially unbroken series of song phrases for several minutes.

FEMALES THAT SING. Singing by female songbirds is less common among N. American birds than among those in other parts of the world. Female song sparrows occasionally sing before the nesting season begins, and female mockingbirds sing to defend their wintering territories. During the nesting season the female mockingbird and females of several other species may sing songs almost as elaborate as those of the male—female catbird, gray-cheeked thrush, Baltimore (northern) oriole, cardinal, pine grosbeak, house finch, and female rose-breasted and black-headed grosbeaks (Nice, 1943; Armstrong, 1963).

Some N. American females—Carolina wren, gray-cheeked thrush, and cardinal—with their mates, practice *duetting* or *antiphonal singing* (Nice, 1943; Berger, 1961). In some of these species in which the female sings as well as the male, apparently her singing is part of the courtship, helps in maintaining the pair bond with her mate, and possibly assists him in territorial or other quarrels with members of their species (Armstrong, 1963).

WHEN DO YOUNG BIRDS START TO SING? The first singing of young songbirds is generally an indefinite warbling and may begin when some are still in the nest. Nice (1943) reported that four of her hand-raised song sparrows uttered their first warbling subsongs 13–20 days after hatching, and two song sparrows had developed their adult primary songs by their first winter when they were 159 and 192 days old.

George M. Sutton reported that his young captive Henslow's sparrows sang "little whisper songs" (subsongs) 11 days after leaving the nest (20 days after hatching). According to Wallace (1949), young Bicknell's (gray-cheeked) thrushes started to sing 15–25 days after hatching, and other investigators reported that young California thrashers began their first subsongs at 19–30 days and young curve-billed thrashers at 20 days.

Amelia R. Laskey, in Tenn., had two hand-raised female cardinals that sang their first warbling subsongs (completely *unlike* the songs of the adults) 3–4 weeks (21–28 days) after hatching; male mockingbirds, at 24–28 days, and a female at 73 days after hatching. She also reported young American robins' first subsong at about 21 days.

Berger (1961) heard the first singing of one of his hand-reared Kirtland's warblers at about 38 days after hatching, when it uttered a low, hoarse warble resembling the song of a purple finch.

ARE SONGS INHERITED OR ARE THEY LEARNED? Little has been known up to recent times about song-learning in N. American birds, but evidence gathered by European investigators suggests that the call notes and songs are completely hereditary in some songbirds and are modifiable in others. In the European whitethroat, *Sylvia communis*, individuals isolated all their lives still uttered the songs or calls of their kind in precisely the same situation in which the wild whitethroats do (Armstrong, 1963). In the blackbird, *Turdus merula*, of Europe the pure juvenile song (subsong) is innate, but the adult song is partly learned and only after hearing other blackbirds sing.

The songs of the skylark and the linnet, *Carduelis cannabina*, are almost entirely learned, and the European robin and the chaffinch must learn their songs to some extent (Thorpe, 1956b). Lanyon (1957) discovered from his studies of the N. American meadowlarks that their call notes are inherited, or if learned, learned during the nestling period, but the primary adult songs mostly were learned from other meadowlarks. In learning songs, birds must have the ability to imitate, which in some species is extraordinary. *See* Mimicry.

HOW BIRDS PRODUCE VOCAL SOUNDS. Birds lack vocal cords, and their voice box, the syrinx, is in the lower part of the windpipe. The syrinx is a resonating chamber associated with elastic vibrating membranes, and the whole is controlled by specialized muscles. By changing the air pressure from its lungs, a bird can vary the intensity of volume of its voice, also its pitch. *See* details under Voice and Sound-making. See also Greenewalt (1968). That the mouth plays only a minor role in singing is suggested by observations of birds singing with the bill closed and singing while carrying a billful of food.

Usually the birds with the most syringeal muscles have the greatest potential for producing different songs and calls, and most songbirds have at least 4 pairs of syringeal muscles (Hartshorne, 1973). Such versatile sound-producers as the crow and starling, not regarded as good singers, but good mimics, and the catbird, a fine singer, have pairs of syringeal muscles.

FINEST NORTH AMERICAN SONGSTERS. Hartshorne (1973) prepared a subjective list of the better singers among birds of the world based upon such criteria as (1) his personal observations, (2) information from regional bird books, (3) study of bird-song recordings (*see* Recordings), and (4) reading in the ornithological journals. He listed, as best among native N. American birds, 18 singers within the 48 contiguous states of the U.S., as follows: Bewick's wren, Carolina wren, winter wren, mockingbird, sage thrasher, brown thrasher, crissal thrasher, Townsend's solitaire, hermit thrush, wood thrush, eastern meadowlark, western meadowlark, bobolink, cardinal, pyrrhuloxia, and lark sparrow, Bachman's sparrow, and song sparrow. Hartshorne cited other songbirds as "much better than mediocre singers"—the rose-breasted grosbeak, black-headed grosbeak, fox sparrow, white-throated sparrow, lark bunting, eastern purple finch, house finch, pine grosbeak, Swainson's thrush, veery, gray catbird, Bendire's thrasher, long-billed thrasher, curve-billed thrasher, solitary vireo, cañon wren, and "perhaps the long-billed marsh wren." Other ornithologists might not be in complete disagreement but would have their own favorites. Dr. Arthur A. Allen (1963) composed a list of his 10 favorites in order of their excellence, as follows: hermit thrush, wood thrush, veery, mockingbird, brown thrasher, white-throated sparrow, fox sparrow, American robin, song sparrow, and rock wren.

SONOGRAM
See spectrogram under Recordings.

SORA
See in Rail Family.

SOUND-MAKING
See Alarm Notes; Bulla; Drumming; Echolocation; Language; Songs and Singing; Voice and Sound-making; and wing noises in Courtship and Territorial Flight under Flight; *see also* Recordings.

SOUND RECORDING
See Recordings.

SOUNDS THAT ATTRACT BIRDS
These include whistled imitations of their songs and calls, and kissing sounds made by sucking on the palm or back of one's hands, a skill known among professional and amateur ornithologists as "squeaking." Squeaking is especially effective in drawing near to the observer small birds that he wants to see more clearly, and imitations of the calls of owls are especially successful in getting responses from barred, great horned, screech, and saw-whet owls. Even some hawks, such as the Cooper's and sharp-shinned, respond to squeaking sounds (apparently because the fine squeaks resemble those of mice or birds), especially if one is hidden under the downsweeping branches of a tree or in the dense cover of undergrowth. For details, see Terres (1968b; 1977). *See also* Bird-attracting.

SOUTH AMERICAN ELEMENT
See Distribution.

SOUTH DAKOTA BIRD NOTES
See Ornithological Periodicals.

SOUTHEASTERN PINE WOODLAND
An extensive *subclimax* (*see* Subclimax Community) on the coastal plain of se. U.S.; it is composed of open pine forests (*see* discussion of it in biography of red-cockaded woodpecker), and some of its typical nesting birds are the red-cockaded woodpecker (a threatened species), the brown-headed nuthatch, and Bachman's sparrow.

SOUTH-SOUTH-SOUTHERLY
Another name for the oldsquaw, a phonetic rendition of its calls.

SOUTHWESTERN OAK WOODLAND
One of nine biomes (*see* Biome) in N. America north of Mexico used in mapping the ecological distribution of birds. *See* Major Biotic Communities (biomes) under Distribution. The Southwestern Oak Woodland is in sw. U.S., mainly in Utah, Nev., Calif., N.M., Ariz., and parts of Colo. and Ore. It is usually on hills and mountain slopes; is a partly open woodland of oaks 20–50 ft. tall with spaces between trees covered with grasses and shrubs. Typical birds of this biome are: Nuttall's and Arizona woodpeckers, bridled titmouse, Hutton's vireo, Virginia's warbler, and black-throated gray warbler (Pettingill, 1970).

SPARROW
See in Finch Family and in Weaverbird Family.

SPARROW WAR
A once popular term for a spirited debate over the merits and demerits—economic and aesthetic—of the house (English) sparrow, introduced into the U.S. in the winter of 1850–51. The debate lasted long and was fiercely fought by American ornithologists and others, and reached its height in Mass. during the winter of 1877–78. See details in Batchelder (1937), and *see* biography of the house sparrow in Weaverbird Family.

SPECIATION
See Species.

SPECIES
(sing.: SPEE-shiz; pl.: SPEE-sheez). In ornithology, as in other branches of biology, the species is important because it is, apart from the individual, the most basic category into which living things are divided. A species is an interbreeding, or potentially interbreeding, group of birds or other animals or plants that does not in nature interbreed significantly (enough to break down species identity) with any other group (Mayr *et al.*, 1953).

A species is a "kind" of bird. A robin, a bluebird, a wood thrush, a blue jay, and a cardinal are each a member of a separate, easily recognizable species. Some species may look very much alike and still will not interbreed. For example, there are five species of small, brownish thrushes in e. N. America—wood thrush, hermit thrush, Swainson's thrush, gray-cheeked thrush, and veery—some of which breed and nest within the same woodland. These are, outwardly, strikingly similar birds, yet no intermediate or hybrid between them has ever been seen. Once two species are reproductively isolated, they are separated henceforth, because there is no turning back or reversal of the evolutionary process.

WHAT KEEPS SPECIES SEPARATED? Perhaps one of the most interesting observations of field naturalists, corroborated by the detailed scientific studies of ethologists, or those who study animal behavior, is that birds mate with their own species successfully (produce a continuing line of descendants) because of the specific behavior of the opposite sex. Signs and signals that pass between the two potential partners must be right for each species; the males of every species have specific courtships, or displays, to which, usually, only the females of the same species are receptive. *See* discussion of this under Behavior; Courtship; Sexual Dimorphism.

According to Mayr (1963), these behavioral barriers to random mating constitute the largest and most important class of the isolating mechanisms in birds. Because each of any two species has its own special patterns of courtship, interbreeding is prevented just as effectively as if the two species, now living side by side, were thousands of miles apart.

This species reaction of males and females toward each other is often loosely referred to as "species recognition." *See* Courtship; Language. Songs, calls, and other acoustic signals are also precise and specific, and may be even more effective than visual signals for recognition between potential mates (Mayr, 1963).

Besides the barrier between species posed by incompatible courtship behavior, their psychological and physiological readiness for mating may not occur at the same period during the breeding season, or they may never meet because each is adapted specifically to separate habitats, even though living in the same environment. According to Mayr, habitat selection by species is a very effective isolating mechanism. See Smith, N.G. (1966) about four species of arctic gulls; see, however, Selander (1971).

If the potential mates of different species should meet, even if they bridge their differences in courtship rituals and copulate, the male might not transfer sperms to the female. There are other barriers to producing fertile young. If each of the two different species managed to copulate and the male transferred sperms (*see* Fertilization), the resulting egg, or eggs, might not hatch because the male's sperms did not fertilize the female's ova, or the ova were fertilized but the zygotes died; also, even if the egg, or eggs, hatch, the hybrids may not be fertile (hybrid sterility) or might not be very fit (hybrid inferiority), and potential reproduction by the hybrids ends or is minimized. Some species do cross and produce hybrids, but this is comparatively rare among wild birds that have definite pair bonds and engagement periods (Mayr, 1942). *See* The Pair Bond under Courtship; *also* Hybrid.

HOW DO SPECIES BEGIN? THE SPECIATION PROCESS. Speciation is a term for the evolutionary process whereby a population of birds or other organisms that were formerly of one species have been split into two species. There has been much discussion among scientists about whether speciation is sudden or gradual. Some of the early students of evolution believed that new species might normally rise as individual "sports"—mutants—by a process they called "saltation" (jumping). A mutant, or a different bird, may be hatched within the population of a single species, but a lone mutant rarely leads to a new species (Simpson *et al.*, 1957).

Biologists have returned to Darwin's belief that speciation is usually gradual. For example, a lone population of birds may have become isolated from the mainland by colonizing an island. *See* Hawaiian Honeycreeper Family. Or a population of a bird species, formerly one, or with a common ancestor, may have in time become geographically separated from other populations of its kind by changes in climate, glaciation, changes in sea level, by vegetational barriers that are incompatible to them (*see* discussion of this under Hybrid), by rising mountains, or other physical changes in the earth's surface. *See* Distribution; Allopatric Species.

Separation may lead to gradual differences in courtship behavior, choice of habitat, and so on. During the period of isolation, the population becomes genetically changed, which may lead to reproductive isolation from its former relatives and adaptation to a different habitat. By then, the isolated population may have become a different species and can reinvade the range of the parental population (Mayr, 1951) without hybridizing with it. *See* Sympatric Species; Ring-Species.

HOW LONG FOR A SPECIES TO FORM? According to Mayr (1963), there is nothing about speciation that is so little known as its rate—we shall probably never have accurate general information about it. However, Mayr (1951) wrote that there are a few accurate timings. R. E. Moreau, for example, from his studies of races, or subspecies, of larks associated with the alluvial soils of the Nile delta, concluded that 5,000 years is not far from the minimum time required for the development of these subspecies, which still were not entirely isolated from the surrounding races of larks at the time of Moreau's studies. "There is valid evidence that some of the endemic races of Scandinavian birds developed within the last 10,000 to 15,000 years" (Mayr, 1963). According to Selander (1971), the shortest estimated time for speciation in birds is 10,000–18,000 years; Moreau (1966) believed that full species can evolve in a few thousand years (others think the process may be even more rapid), and patterns of geographic variation in characters of color and size have evolved in house sparrows in N. and S. America (since the species was introduced from Europe in the mid- and late 1800s) to the extent that taxonomists might distinguish conventional subspecies (Johnston and Selander, 1964; 1971).

WHAT ABOUT DISCOVERIES OF NEW SPECIES? There were 796 species of N. American birds officially recognized by the American Ornithologists' Union in its *Check-list* of 1957, of which 87 were of casual occurrence and 12 had been introduced by man (Wetmore, 1959). Except for those casual species that may arrive in N. America, or those deliberately or accidentally introduced, this figure is likely to remain fairly constant, except for the re-evaluation of species already known. Mayr (1946b) estimated that there were probably less than 100 undiscovered species of birds left in the world (an estimate now considered too low); about 8,600 known species of birds worldwide; and about 28,500 subspecies—new subspecies were being described at the rate of about 200 a year. *See* Subspecies.

The discovery of a new species, however, is a different matter, and becomes less and less likely as the bird fauna becomes better and better known. This is suggested by the fact, disclosed by Mayr (1942), that less than 200 species had been described in the world during the previous 25 years, with the last N. American species, the Colima warbler, discovered in 1889; however, another is the Dickey jay, *Cyanocorax dickeyi*, a striking species, discovered in nw. Mexico in the 1930s. Although Arthur H. Howell reported in 1919, in Fla., a bird he termed a new species—the Cape Sable seaside sparrow, which he discovered in 1918—Mayr *et al.* (1953) and the A.O.U. committee (1973) consider it a subspecies, or race, of the common seaside sparrow, *Ammospiza maritima*. *See* in Finch Family.

More recently, however, in previously unexplored and isolated areas outside of N. America but within the W. Hemisphere, a surprising number of new species have been discovered, many from S. America, especially from Peru, and even an owl classified in a new genus (new genera are much rarer discoveries than new species). See issues of *The Condor, The Wilson Bulletin,* and *The Auk* for descriptions and names of some of these birds.

In 1972, the Elfin Woods warbler, *Dendroica angelae*, a new species, was named and described from the Elfin Woodland in Puerto Rico, a country whose bird life has been much studied. It was discovered by Cameron B. Kepler and Kenneth C. Parkes (1972), who gave it the species name *angelae* in honor of Kepler's wife. Apparently the reason that the Elfin Woods warbler had long been overlooked was the fact that it strikingly resembles the black and white warbler, *Mniotilta varia*, a common N. American migrant and winter resident seen in Elfin Woodland, and utters sounds like those made by the bananaquit, *Coereba flaveola*, a common bird in the same woods. *See* Warbler, black and white, in Warbler—American Wood Warbler Family; Bananaquit in Honeycreeper Family; *also* Birds Named for People under Names and Naming.

SPECIES LISTING
See methods of under Check-list.

SPECIES RECOGNITION
(between birds). *See* Courtship.

SPECKLE-BELLY
See Gadwall and Goose, white-fronted, in Duck Family.

SPECKLE-CHEEK
See Woodpecker, ladder-backed, in Woodpecker Family.

SPECTROGRAM
See Recordings.

SPECULUM
(SPECK-you-lum—in Roman antiquity, a mirror, especially a metal mirror). Name applied in ornithology to a small patch of usually metallic-colored, or iridescent, feathers, especially in ducks, showing in the secondary feathers of each wing and contrasting with the differently colored feathers surrounding it; it is present in most of the surface-feeding, or dabbling, ducks (*see* in Duck Family); also in some of the diving ducks—for example, the eiders and harlequin duck (Brooks, 1937). Males of most species of ducks that have a speculum use it frequently in a ritualized courtship display called "preening behind the wing" that exposes the speculum and its colors to the female (see details in Johnsgard, 1965; 1968). *See also* brief discussion of some of the waterfowl displays under Waterfowl; *also* general information in Duck Family.

SPEED OF BIRDS
See Flight; Running Birds; Swimming and Diving.

SPHENICIFORMES
(sfee-nis-ih-FOR-meez). An order (*see* Order) that includes the penguins. *See* brief discussion of penguins in introduction to Auk Family; *also* Monophyletic Descent.

SPIDERS AND BIRDS
Birds are fond of spiders as food; stomach records of birds studied by the U.S. Biological Survey, now the U.S. Fish and Wildlife Service, showed more than 10,000 records of spiders in the stomachs of more than 300 species of N. American birds. The quantities of spiders eaten by individual birds may be astonishing—81 had

each eaten 10–49; 28 had eaten 50–99; 15 had eaten 100–200; and one bird had more than 300 in its stomach. A house, or English, sparrow had eaten 420 spiders; an eastern meadowlark, 425; a grackle, 621; a starling, 631; and a crow, 722. A Say's phoebe at one meal had eaten 25; a greater yellowlegs, 33; a wood duck, 46; a Louisiana heron, 58; a starling, 187; and a hairy woodpecker, 300.

Many of the spiders were the common orb weavers of backyards, gardens, and woodland borders; others were the crab spiders so often seen on flowers; others were jumping spiders, and the big formidable lycosids, or wolf spiders, some of whose bodies are up to an inch long and which are often seen running about the ground in forests and open fields. Some birds also ate the cocoons, or egg cases, of spiders; however, in bulk, the proportion of spiders in a bird's total diet did not run high—up to 6–8% in some of the thrushes and small flycatchers.

Birds ate spiders or fed them to their young, despite the fact that some of the larger spiders have venom sufficient to kill birds if the birds are bitten by them. Birds usually disable or kill spiders by a quick jab of the bill, or pick up a spider and crush it between the mandibles. Apparently, only in the tropics are there spiders large enough to attack and kill birds. Among the wandering, or hunting, spiders, the tropical tarantulas are veritable giants, up to 3 in. long. Armed with long, strong fangs, they are able to kill and feed on frogs, toads, and lizards, and are able to subdue and eat small rattlesnakes. Some of the S. American tree-dwelling tarantulas, or mygales, are known to kill small birds, for which they are called "bird spiders." For a discussion of how spiders feed, see Gertsch (1949).

It is doubtful, however, that any N. American spiders would habitually attack and kill birds, although hummingbirds, sparrows, goldfinches, kinglets, bushtits, and other small birds have been accidentally caught in the strong meshes of some of the American orb-weaving spiders. See Accidents. Spiders are arachnids (ah-RAK-nids), not insects, from which they differ in one general way: spiders have eight walking, or functioning, legs; insects have six. Some 30,000 spiders have been named in the world up to 1968; about 3,000 are known from Europe; about 650 species are known from N.Y. and the New England states. See Food and Feeding Habits; also Arthropod.

SPIKE-BILL

See Godwit, marbled, in Sandpiper Family.

SPIKE-TAIL

See Pintail in Duck Family.

SPINY-HEADED WORMS

See Parasite.

SPIRIT BIRD

Local name for certain birds that disappear ("miraculously") very quickly beneath water when frightened or fired upon, such as certain ducks (bufflehead and ruddy duck), grebes, the anhinga, and the common loon.

SPOONBILL

See Spoonbill, roseate, and Spoonbill, white, in Ibis Family; is also a common name for the shoveler in Duck Family and for the spoon-billed sandpiper in Sandpiper Family.

SPRAGUE

ISAAC (1811–95). Born Hingham, Mass.; botanical artist; with Edward Harris, John G. Bell, and Lewis Squires, accompanied Audubon on his Missouri R. expedition of 1843. Audubon, in his *Birds of America* (octavo ed., Vol. VII, 1844), named a bird for Sprague which Sprague collected June 19, 1843, near Ft. Union, w. N.D. Audubon called it *Alauda spragueii*, "Sprague's Missouri Lark," now known as *Anthus spragueii*, Sprague's pipit. In 1834, Sprague came into possession of Nuttall's *Manual of Ornithology of the United States and Canada*, became interested in birds, and spent 10 years studying and drawing them. In 1840, Audubon visited a friend in Hingham, met Sprague, and was much impressed with his drawings. This led Audubon to take Sprague on the Missouri R. expedition to assist him in making drawings and sketches. For nearly half a century, Sprague was the most skillful botanical draftsman in America, illustrating Gray's *Text-book of Botany* and many large and important botanical works of the time (Anonymous, 1895).

SPRIG

also SPRIG-TAIL. Common names for the pintail in Duck Family, in reference to the long tail of the male.

SPUR

See discussion of spurs under Feet and Legs; *see also* in introduction to Pheasant Family.

SQUAB

Term for a young pigeon or young dove.

SQUATTER

Another name for the pectoral sandpiper, from its habit of squatting on the ground.

SQUAW

See Oldsquaw in Duck Family.

SQUEALER

Common name for the American golden plover; also the fulvous tree duck, harlequin duck, and wood duck.

STAGE DRIVER

See Rail, king, in Rail Family.

STAKE-DRIVER

Local name for the American bittern, from its guttural sounds which from a distance resemble the thud of someone pounding a stake into the ground.

STAMPS

(depicting birds). See Duck Stamps; see also Stanley (1966); Bengston (1968).

STARLING FAMILY

Sturnidae (STIR-nih-dee); from Lat. *sturnus*, starling. 111 species in world (Van Tyne and Berger, 1976); 3 species introduced into N. America; medium to large songbirds (7–17 in. long); entirely Old World, are in the order Passeriformes, are primarily tropical although several species reach Europe, China, Japan; group is well represented in East Indies and India (Amadon, 1964b), every continent except S. America; family includes the mynas: the hill myna, *Gracula religiosa*, commonly called grackle in India, a large, glossy black starling, one of best talking birds in the world (Austin, 1961) and introduced into Fla.; the crested myna, *Acridotheres cristatellus*, of s. Asia, introduced into N. America (Pacific Northwest) and into almost as many parts of the world as has been the European starling, *Sturnus vulgaris*, which was introduced into U.S. in late 19th century; although ancestry of the family is uncertain, Austin (1961) suggests that starlings may have risen from some primitive thrushlike progenitors; are possibly related to other Old World songbirds such as the Oriolidae or to the weaverbirds (Amadon, 1956).

The name starling, which means "little star," is from spangled appearance of the European starling, now so common in America, in its fresh fall plumage; the buff-colored, starry spots wear off gradually during the winter, leaving bird a shining glossy black by spring. *See* Feather Wear under Molts and Molting.

Starlings are spirited, active birds, generally dark-colored, chunky, with black metallic sheen; strong legs and bills; most of them walk with a waddle, tails usually short and square, wings of many are pointed, with 10 primary feathers in each wing; flight is strong, direct; are highly social birds, many are migratory, usually travel in winter in flocks sometimes of enormous size; gather in spectacular roosts at night; are noisy and chatter almost continually in flight and on roost (Austin, 1961); none has well-developed song but may utter variety of pleasing whistles (Amadon, 1956); most eat insects, fruit, etc. (omnivorous); many prefer open country and shun deep woods or forests, as does the common, or European, starling, which is adaptable and aggressive; was first introduced successfully in Central Park, New York, when 60 imported and released in 1890, 40 more in 1891 (Chapman, 1925); started to breed immediately, first nest in N. America found under eaves of American Museum of Natural History, next to Central Park, in summer 1890; by 1952 had extended its range throughout entire U.S. except s. Fla., and throughout s. Canada (Kessel, 1953); by Feb. 4, 1959, 69 years after introduction into New York, reported first time at San Diego, Calif., most southwestern county in U.S. (Stott, 1959) —had previously been reported in n. Calif. in 1942 (Bent, 1950).

Crested myna, or Chinese starling, was introduced into N. America at Vancouver, B.C., about 1897; climate seemed not to have favored increase in its abundance or extension of its range; population appeared to have reached thousands in Vancouver area about 1925, 1927,

STARLING FAMILY

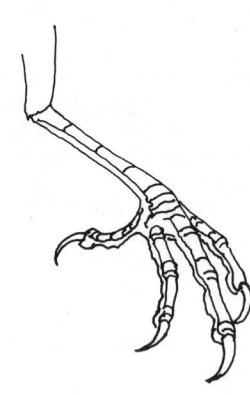

thereafter no increase during following few years (Scheffer and Cottam, 1935); according to Godfrey (1966) declining in past 35 years. See Amadon (1956; 1964b) for technical discussions of Starling Family.

Myna, crested, *Acridotheres cristatellus* (ah-krid-oh-THEE-[th as in *thin*]-reez cris-tah-TELL-us); genus name: from Gr. *akridos*, locust, and *therao*, to hunt after, in reference to its insect-chasing habits; species name: Lat., dim. of *cristatus*, crested (Jaeger, 1955), for short bushy crest on forehead of this species; *myna*, from Hindu *maina*, name for these birds. Asiatic species introduced at Vancouver Is., B.C.; resident in and near Vancouver City; sexes outwardly alike; 10½ in. long (about robin size); short, chunky, almost wholly glossy black except patch of white on each wing which shows in flight; square tail has white tips on outer tail feathers; has short, ragged crest; eyes, legs, bill, and feet yellow; has somewhat labored straightaway flight; usually walks on ground instead of hopping; bird of open country, gleans fields and follows plowman for insects turned up; sometimes rides back of cattle as perch in search for insects; roosts in winter in flocks on buildings or in trees; utters starlinglike chattering notes and rolling trill; in native China, noted as good talking cage bird and a mimic of calls of wild native birds (Scheffer and Cottam, 1935).

Feeding Habits: Omnivorous but is partial to fruits and to foods about garbage dumps and manure piles; eats many kinds of wild and cultivated berries, small amounts of grain, many insects, also eggs and young of small birds; is competitive especially with flickers for nesting holes (see details in Bent, 1950).

Nest: Built in cavity in tree, woodpecker hole, crevices in buildings, bird boxes; nest consists of weeds, grasses, foil, cellophane, candy and gum wrappings, feathers, shed skins of snakes, rubber bands, rootlets.

Eggs: Vancouver area, Apr.–June; 4–7, usually 4–5, green-blue, glossy.

Incubation: At least 15 days; young leave nest about 27 days after hatching.

Other Names: Chinese crested myna; Chinese starling. See other details in Mackay and Hughes (1963).

Range: Resident in and around Vancouver City, B.C., local on s. Vancouver Is., casual in w. Wash., nw. Ore. (Peterson, 1961); native of se. Asia, also introduced in Philippine Is. and Japan.

Myna, hill, *Gracula religiosa* (GRACK-you-lah ree-lij-ih-OH-sah); genus name: from Lat. *graculus* or *gracculus*, grackle, jackdaw, jay bird (Levine *et al.*, 1967); species name: Lat., pious, devout, religious. Asiatic species, one of best of all talking cage birds; released, or escaped, from captivity in Fla.; locally in pairs or in small groups along a narrow coastal strip from Homestead, Fla. (where a pair nested in a woodpecker hole in top of a dead royal palm Mar.–May 1972), north at least to Boynton Beach, Palm Beach County (Kale, 1972). About 12–15 in. long; glossy black and purplish iridescent; small white patch on wings, a large

SHEARWATER FAMILY

Northern fulmar
These stocky relatives of the shearwaters are inveterate ship followers and often swarm around commercial fishing fleets, feeding on scraps and refuse. The great increase in commercial fishing in the North Atlantic in this century has caused a similar increase in the number of fulmars. Fulmars come in several color phases, ranging from "normal" birds, largely white with pale gray back and wings, to individuals that are uniformly dark gray.

Northern fulmar, dark phase

Audubon's shearwater
Recently, an increasing number of bird-watchers have been traveling to sea in search of rare seabirds. One of the discoveries made is that Audubon's shearwater is seen off the Atlantic coast as far north as Long Island. These birds have followed the warm waters of the Gulf Stream north from their nesting grounds in the Caribbean and on Bermuda.

Cory's shearwater
This large, dull-colored shearwater nests on islands in the eastern Atlantic and the Mediterranean, and visits the east coast of North America after the breeding season.

Flesh-footed shearwater
At the end of the breeding season, in late May, flesh-footed shearwaters that have nested in New Zealand leave their colonies and move north toward Japan, on the first leg of a great circular migration that brings them to the Pacific coast of North America in mid-summer.

Greater shearwater
Five million pairs of greater shearwaters nest on islands of the Tristan da Cunha group in the middle of the South Atlantic. At the end of the breeding season, in late April, they move northward, arriving off the east coast of North America in May and generally departing in October.

Manx shearwater
Previously known as an occasional visitor to the western Atlantic, presumably from nesting colonies in the British Isles or Iceland, in 1973 a pair of Manx shearwaters was found nesting on Penikese Island in Massachusetts.

New Zealand shearwater
The New Zealand shearwater nests on a few islands off the coast of North Island, New Zealand, and is a non-breeding visitor to the Pacific coast of North America in the fall.

Pink-footed shearwater
The pink-footed shearwater may be seen off the Pacific coast of North America at any time of year but is most numerous during the summer.

Short-tailed shearwater
Like the flesh-footed shearwater, this species performs a circular migration around the Pacific Ocean, arriving off the coast of North America in the fall and staying until mid-winter.

Sooty shearwater
The most familiar and widespread of our shearwaters, the sooty is a common summer visitor to both coasts. It usually feeds out of sight off land, but in a stiff onshore breeze one can often see many birds flying just beyond the surf.

Wedge-tailed shearwater
The wedge-tailed shearwater nests on islands in the western Pacific and is only a very rare visitor to the Pacific coast of North America.

Flesh-footed shearwater

Audubon's shearwater

Sooty shearwater

Wedge-tailed shearwater

Short-tailed shearwater

New Zealand shearwater

Cory's shearwater

Pink-footed shearwater

Manx shearwater

Greater shearwater

SHRIKE FAMILY

Loggerhead shrike
This is a smaller and more southerly species than the northern shrike. It is a bird of open country, and in areas like New England, where meadows and fields are reverting to woodland, it is much less common now than it was 50 years ago.

Northern shrike
Shrikes are predatory songbirds, catching insects, small birds, and rodents, which they impale on thorns or barbed wire and then tear apart with their strongly hooked bills. The northern shrike is one of two species occurring in North America; it nests in Alaska and Canada and is an uncommon winter visitor to the northern United States.

SILKY FLYCATCHER FAMILY

Phainopepla
After nesting in early spring in the deserts of the Southwest, many phainopeplas disappear. It has recently been found that these birds, which roam about in search of fruit, move westward over the Coast Ranges in California and raise a second brood. No other North American bird is known to nest in two different regions in the same season.

Northern shrike

Phainopepla, female

Phainopepla

Loggerhead shrike

SKIMMER FAMILY

Black skimmer
The black skimmer feeds by flying with its elongated lower mandible slicing through the water, snapping up small fish that cross its path. When not feeding, it rests on sandy beaches, where its catlike vertical pupils, unique among birds, enable it to tolerate the glaring sunlight.

Black skimmer

Black skimmer, chick

Black skimmer

Black skimmer

SKUA FAMILY

Long-tailed jaeger
Since it breeds farther north than the other two jaegers and spends much of the year far out at sea, the long-tailed jaeger is the least known member of this family. It nests in small colonies, each pair incubating two eggs placed in a shallow, grass-lined depression in the tundra.

Parasitic jaeger
Jaegers are powerful, predatory relatives of gulls, with strongly hooked bills. During the summer on the Arctic tundra, they prey on small rodents, nestling birds, and eggs, and at other seasons they chase other seabirds, such as gulls and terns, forcing them to drop food they are carrying. Parasitic jaegers have two color phases—the "typical" light-breasted bird and an all-dark form.

Pomarine jaeger
The largest of the jaegers, the pomarine not only chases gulls and terns but the two smaller jaegers as well. Jaegers spend the winter on the ocean and are seldom seen in inland areas, but there is evidence that many reach their Arctic nesting grounds by migrating overland at high altitudes. A passing storm front may force these migrants down, accounting for their occasional appearance on lakes or rivers hundreds of miles from the coast.

Skua
The Skua is an over-sized relative of the jaegers that nests on the tundra and spends the rest of the year at sea, preying on small seabirds, stealing food from larger ones, and feeding on fishes and refuse. Skuas breed in both the Arctic and the Antarctic; information obtained in the last few years strongly suggests that the northern populations are a different species from the southern ones and indeed that there may be two distinct species in the Antarctic.

Long-tailed jaeger

Parasitic jaeger

Skua

STARLING FAMILY

Starling

Like the house sparrow, the starling was introduced from Europe in the 19th century. But it did not spread as fast and only reached parts of the west coast within the last few decades. Starlings are well adapted to life in towns and cities, which offer an abundance of food and nesting sites and a relative absence of predators. Nesting pairs raise several broods a year. After they have fledged, the dull-colored young starlings leave the cities to forage in the surrounding countryside in ever-increasing flocks, to be joined finally by the adults when the nesting season comes to a close.

STORK FAMILY

Wood stork

Although they were formerly more widespread, North America's wood storks now nest only in Florida swamps, where two or three thousand pairs breed in less than 20 colonies. Nesting success in these colonies depends on the water level; when there is a severe drought the species may not nest at all. In such years wood storks sometimes wander far from Florida, turning up in New England or California.

Starling, winter

Starling

Wood stork

Wood stork

Wood stork, immature

STORM-PETREL FAMILY

Ashy storm-petrel
The ashy storm-petrel nests only off the coast of California, where most breed on a single island group, the Farallons. It is usually seen at sea feeding alone or in small groups and is reported by some observers to follow ships. Little is known of its migratory movements or winter range; it is apparently absent off California in winter and early spring.

Black storm-petrel
After the nesting season, black storm-petrels wander northward from their Mexican colonies as far as Marin County, California, departing again in October to spend the winter at sea far to the south. This species is a ship follower and feeds on a wide variety of small marine animals.

Fork-tailed storm-petrel
This gregarious storm-petrel is sometimes seen in flocks numbering several hundred, gathered at some favorable feeding area. It often alights on the water to feed and does not follow ships. It is confined to the North Pacific, but has a much larger breeding range than most of our other Pacific storm-petrels, nesting from Alaska south to northern California in the east, and to the islands north of Japan in the west.

Leach's storm-petrel
The only storm-petrel that breeds in both the North Atlantic and the North Pacific, this species is most abundant at higher latitudes, but its breeding range extends farther south along coasts where there is an upwelling of cold water. It nests in colonies on offshore islands, coming to land only at night to avoid gulls and other predators. The weird nocturnal cries of hundreds of Leach's storm-petrels coming ashore on some nesting island have terrified stranded mariners.

Least storm-petrel
Our smallest storm-petrel, this poorly known species nests on islands off northwestern Mexico and has been seen at sea from northern California to Ecuador. It is easily identified not only by its small size—it is scarcely larger than a warbler—but by its wedge-shaped tail.

Wilson's storm-petrel
Wilson's storm-petrel is said by some to be the most abundant bird in the world. It nests in immense colonies on islands in the cold seas of the Southern Hemisphere and visits us during the southern winter. It is very common in the North Atlantic between May and September, outnumbering Leach's storm-petrel except at higher latitudes. It is an inveterate ship follower, and so it is seen more readily than Leach's, which does not follow ships. It often enters the mouth of a bay, especially during severe weather.

Least storm-petrel

Leach's storm-petrel

shy storm-petrel

ork-tailed storm-petrel

Black storm-petrel

Wilson's storm-petrel

SWALLOW FAMILY

Purple martin
Our largest swallow, the purple martin originally nested in colonies in tall dead trees full of woodpecker holes but now usually nests in multi-dwelling martin houses. In 1903, a severe cold spell with heavy rains eliminated the flying insects they feed on and purple martins were virtually wiped out in New England.

Bank swallow
By nesting in large colonies in steep sand banks, bank swallows not only take full advantage of a relatively scarce nesting habitat but also increase their chances of finding enough food for their young. An adult that has found few flying insects on previous trips will follow other foraging birds the next time it sets out in search of food; the odds are good that these birds will lead it to a more productive area.

Barn swallow
Barn swallows must be much more numerous now than they were in primeval North America, when they nested only on cliffs and on sheltered ledges along streams. Today, with rare exceptions, they build nests in garages and barns.

Cliff swallow
The cliff swallow, which until eastern North America was settled had been more or less confined as a breeding bird to cliffs and escarpments in mountainous country, were quick to switch from cliffs to barns, and became much more common than they had been. Now, after decades of unsuccessful competition with house sparrows, they have lost ground in all this territory.

Rough-winged swallow
Unlike the bank swallow, which it closely resembles, the rough-winged swallow usually nests in isolated pairs, digging a tunnel in a steep bank along a stream or building a flimsy nest in a culvert or pipe.

Tree swallow
Like the other members of its family, the hole-nesting tree swallow feeds on flying insects during most of the year. However, in the winter it feeds on the fruit of the bayberry, which sustains the birds during cold weather and enables them to spend the winter as far north as Long Island.

Violet-green swallow
This is the common breeding swallow of mountain forests in the West, where it usually nests in a tall dead snag that towers over the surrounding trees. It also nests in suburban areas, building its nest in a birdhouse or on a sheltered porch.

SWIFT FAMILY

Black swift
Like other nestling swifts, the single young of the black swift can survive periods of bad weather when its parents can find no food by becoming torpid.

Rough-winged swallow

Violet-green swallow

Purple martin

Bank swallow

Cliff swallow

ree swallow

Black swift

arn swallow

Chimney swift

Chimney swift
Tropical relatives of the chimney swift nest in hollow trees. The North American birds long ago abandoned this ancient breeding site, and now nest almost exclusively in chimneys, where they are free from predators and their only enemy is toxic fumes.

starlinglike bird (called a grackle in India) with yellow wattles on head; travels through forests in small noisy flocks, eats mostly fruit; notes of wild hill mynas from low hoarse chuckles to low ringing whistles. In captivity their vocal imitations of human speech excel those of parrots (Austin, 1961).

Other Name: Indian hill myna.
Weights: Two in wild at Homestead, Fla., caught and weighed, were 125 and 129.4 gr. (Fisk, 1977), or about 4½ oz.

Starling, *Sturnus vulgaris* (STIR-nus vul-GAY-ris); genus name: Lat., starling; species name: Lat., common. (Color ills., page 848.) Eurasian species, introduced into N. America late 19th century, now resident most of U.S., s. Canada to se. Alaska; sexes outwardly alike; 7½–8½ in. long; wingspread about 15½ in.; dark, chunky, distinguished from other black birds and cowbird by its short tail; longer, pointed, slender bill; walks with short jerky steps over lawns, grassy fields, pastures; in spring, black, glossed with purple and green, and with a *yellow* bill; bill dark in winter and dark plumage speckled; female can be distinguished close up by yellow ring along outer edge of irises of eyes (Kessel, 1951), lacking in male; immature, gray-brown with white on throat, chin; from late summer into winter, forages by day in open country, returns in small groups late afternoon in straight direct flight to roost; sometimes gathers in enormous numbers in marshes, groves of trees, often with blackbirds, cowbirds, grackles, American robins; later, when leaves drop in cold weather, roost by themselves on city buildings, viaducts, about cities, towns; attempts by many methods to break up roosts (see details in Kalmbach, 1937) not permanently effective, nor by noises, including broadcast of starlings' alarm squeal (see Boudreau, 1968; Anderson, 1969). Starling is permanent resident within breeding range in N. America; however, some individuals migrate, in N. America as in Europe, from mid-Feb. to early Mar. in spring; from late Sept. and Oct. through Nov. in fall (Kessel, 1953; see also Davis, G. J., 1970); over its nesting range, starling is very competitive with flicker and great crested flycatcher for nesting holes, also bluebird (see methods of reducing competition in Terres, 1968c); in spring sit in groups in treetops uttering chorus of squeaks, chatters, creaks, chirps, interspersed with a rising whistle, *pheeeWW!,* likened to human "wolf whistle," during which often imitates calls or songs of bobwhite, killdeer, flicker, phoebe, wood pewee, distant cawing of crow, etc. (Bent, 1950), even barking of dog and mewing of cat (*see* Mockingbird Family; Mimicry); aerial maneuvers of flocks of starlings, wheeling, twisting, turning in perfect precision, with no apparent leader (*see* under Flight), now in loose formation, then in tight ball to frustrate attacking hawk, are remarkable. *See* Behavior.

Feeding Habits: Forages much on ground for food, about half is insects; is considered highly beneficial (*see* Economic Ornithology), is most effective enemy of clover weevil in America, also destroys cutworms and Japanese beetles (Bent, 1950); in e. Tex. eats even more insects,

winter

summer

STARLING FAMILY
In fall and winter, the plumage of the starling is speckled with white or light tan spots and its bill is grayish. In spring, the lighter tips of the feathers wear away, leaving the plumage glossy black, and the bill of the male becomes distinctly yellow.

largely grasshoppers and beetles (Russell, 1971); also takes ants, bees, wasps, eats millipedes, spiders, earthworms, land snails, beach "fleas," salamanders, garbage, cultivated cherries and holly berries, and considerable wild fruit; also weed seeds and grain.

Nest: Built in natural cavity in tree, woodpecker hole, building crevice, bird box; of grasses, straw, twigs, debris (has bred and raised young in captivity—see Miller, 1969).

Eggs: Early Apr. to July; 2–8, usually 4–6, white, pale blue, or green-white.

Incubation: By both sexes, commonly 12 days; first flight of young from nest usually 21 days after hatching and 4–5 days later are independent of parents (Kessel, 1957); two, sometimes three, broods a season.

Other Names: Church-martin; common starling; English starling; European starling.

Age: Banding records, N.Y., Ohio, Pa., from 5 years to 16 years, when still alive; one lived to 9 years, 1 month, in National Zoo, Washington, D.C.; one, banded Islip, N.Y., trapped and released in same area when 11 years, 9 months old (Kennard, 1975); one lived in wild to 16 years in Europe (Anonymous, 1935); one to 20 years reported from Belgium (Clapp, 1976).

Albinism: One out of four in nest in N.H. was total, or pure, albino: milk-colored feathers, pink eyes, white legs and feet; one partial albino with body white, head, wings, tail normal color, at Washington, D.C., white feathers lacked barbules and gave bird fluffy appearance (Davis, 1936).

Flight Speed: Timed in New England, 18 m.p.h. (White, 1929); 28, 35 m.p.h. (Wood, 1933); in N.Y., 55 m.p.h. with no wind blowing (Jameson, 1942).

Host to Cowbirds: Extremely rare, only two records, Beltsville, Md., and Amboy, Ill.

Weights: Series of live starlings in Conn., 64.3–88 gr. (Wetherbee, 1934), or about 2¼–3 oz.; 2½–3½ oz. (Forbush, 1925–29).

Range: Resident in N. America, se. Alaska, c. Sask., across s. Canada to Newfoundland, south throughout most of U.S. to s. Mexico.

Starling, Chinese. *See* Myna, crested.

Starling, common. *See* Starling.

Starling, English. *See* Starling.

Starling, European. *See* Starling.

Starling, red-shouldered. Another name for the red-winged blackbird in Troupial Family.

STATE BIRD
Chosen by state legislatures, state commissions, governor's proclamation, unofficially, by popular vote, or by schoolchildren in each of the 50 states of the United States and the District of Columbia; they are: *Alabama:* yellow-shafted (common) flicker; *Alaska:* willow ptarmigan; *Arizona:* cactus wren; *Arkansas:* mockingbird; *California:* California quail; *Colorado:* lark bunting; *Connecticut:* American robin; *Delaware:* blue hen chicken; *District of Columbia:* wood thrush; *Florida:* mockingbird; *Georgia:* brown thrasher; *Ha-*

waii: nene, or Hawaiian goose; *Idaho:* mountain bluebird; *Illinois:* cardinal; *Indiana:* cardinal; *Iowa:* American goldfinch; *Kansas:* western meadowlark; *Kentucky:* cardinal; *Louisiana:* brown pelican; *Maine:* black-capped chickadee; *Maryland:* Baltimore (northern) oriole; *Massachusetts:* black-capped chickadee; *Michigan:* American robin; *Minnesota:* common loon; *Mississippi:* mockingbird; *Missouri:* eastern bluebird; *Montana:* western meadowlark; *Nebraska:* western meadowlark; *Nevada:* mountain bluebird; *New Hampshire:* purple finch; *New Jersey:* American goldfinch; *New Mexico:* roadrunner; *New York:* eastern bluebird; *North Carolina:* cardinal; *North Dakota:* western meadowlark; *Ohio:* cardinal; *Oklahoma:* scissor-tailed flycatcher; *Oregon:* western meadowlark; *Pennsylvania:* ruffed grouse; *Rhode Island:* Rhode Island Red (chicken); *South Carolina:* Carolina wren; *South Dakota:* ring-necked pheasant; *Tennessee:* mockingbird; *Texas:* mockingbird; *Utah:* California gull; *Vermont:* hermit thrush; *Virginia:* cardinal; *Washington:* willow goldfinch (a western subspecies of the American goldfinch); *West Virginia:* cardinal; *Wisconsin:* American robin; *Wyoming:* western meadowlark. For details of dates of adoption, etc., see list by National Audubon Society, Public Relations Department, 950 Third Avenue, New York, New York 10022. See also Briggs (1966); *also* National Bird; Names and Naming.

STELLER
GEORG WILHELM (1709–46). Born Windsheim, Germany; noted zoologist and traveler; in St. Petersburg, while attached to Russian Academy of Science, joined Vitus Bering's Arctic expedition on the *St. Peter,* on which Steller was listed as ship's surgeon and mineralogist; sailed from Avatcha Bay on Kamchatka's eastern shore June 4, 1741; arrived at Alaska mainland, July 16, and then Bering Is., where Bering and some of his men died from hardships and scurvy. Steller is said to have been the first European to set foot in Alaska (Sutton and Sutton, 1956), where he collected birds, including the jay given the English name Steller's crow by John Latham and the scientific species name *stelleri* by Gmelin, and observed the sea eagle that bears his name. In 1769, Peter Simon Pallas, eminent German zoologist and traveler, who explored in Russia and Siberia, named the eider duck obtained in Kamchatka Steller's eider, with the species name *stelleri*. Steller was the only naturalist ever to see the now extinct spectacled cormorant alive. After returning to Kamchatka in 1742, Steller died at Tyumen, Siberia, while traveling overland to St. Petersburg (Sutton and Sutton, 1956). See also Palmer (1928); Wynne (1969); Gruson (1972).

STENOPHAGOUS
(sten-OFF-ah-gus). Term for birds that are limited in their feeding to a restricted diet. Hummingbirds, with their long bills and brushy-tipped or tubular tongues (*see* Tongue), are restricted to nectar and insects as food; the long, sensitive bills of snipes and woodcocks are adapted to probing the soft earth for

worms and other invertebrates (*see* Vertebrate), which limits them to those kinds of food. *See* Earthworms and Birds. A bird such as the Everglade kite that is even more limited, to *one* kind of food only, is said to be *monophagous. See* Monophagous. Although hummingbirds, and snipes and woodcocks, for example, avoid competition from other birds by eating a special kind or class of food, they may pay a heavy price if that food is eliminated or much reduced in nature.

From 1931 to 1933, a blight killed more than 90% of the eelgrass, *Zostera marina,* in waters along the Atlantic coast of N. America. Eelgrass is a staple food of the brant, *Branta bernicla.* With the eelgrass gone, an estimated 80% of the brant population along the Atlantic coast disappeared. Partial recovery of the eelgrass from the blight and the adaptiveness of some of the brant in learning to eat an abundant alga called sea lettuce and other available water plants, also in grazing on upland fields, apparently saved them (Addy, 1964). *See* in Duck Family; *also* Eelgrass.

As Welty (1962) has pointed out, a species with broad food habits (euryphagous), such as the roadrunner of sw. U.S., might never be subjected to such a fate. The roadrunner eats snakes, scorpions, centipedes, mice, rats, small birds, lizards, and such a variety of other available foods of its environment that it would have no difficulty if the supply of one or several kinds of its foods should fail. *See also* Foods and Feeding Habits; Euryphagous.

STERCORARIIDAE
See Skua Family.

STERNUM
or BREASTBONE. *See* Skeleton.

STIB
See Dunlin in Sandpiper Family.

STIFF-TAIL
Another name for the ruddy duck.

STILT
See in Avocet Family.

STINT
Common name, especially in Great Britain, for some of the small sandpipers.

STOCK
Term, apparently more often used among breeders of livestock and of cultivated plants than in ornithology, for a "strain," race, or group of related individuals in a breed or species. *See* Subspecies; *also* Species.

STOMACH
See Digestion.

STOMACH OIL
Foul-smelling liquid regurgitated by some seabirds in self-defense. *See* under Procellariiformes; Albatross Family; Storm-petrel Family; Fulmar, northern, in Shearwater Family; *also* Regurgitation.

STONE-CURLEW
See under Thick-knee Family.

STOOL PIGEON
Term for a captive passenger pigeon (*see* in Pigeon Family) that was used to lure wild flocks of these birds to the ground, where they were caught in nets by trappers who then killed and removed the pigeons from under the net. The "stool," or lure, pigeon was a trained live one attached firmly to a "stool," or small padded platform, at the end of a handle that was attached to a stake in the ground. See details in Schorger (1955).

STORAGE
(of food). *See* Food and Feeding Habits.

STORK FAMILY
Ciconiidae (sick-oh-NYE-ih-dee); from Lat. *ciconia*, stork. Includes the storks and jabirus, of which there are collectively 17 species in the tropical and temperate parts of the world (Van Tyne and Berger, 1959), 1 reaches N. American region in se. U.S.; most members of family are in tropical Africa (including Madagascar) and Eurasia, except northern part, and 2 in Australia; family is predominantly Old World; 3 species in the W. Hemisphere: the maguari stork, *Euxenura galeata*, ranging from the Guianas to Argentina; the jabiru, *Jabiru mycteria*, largest stork in the New World, which ranges from s. Mexico to Argentina; and the American wood stork, formerly called wood ibis, resident from Fla. to s. S. America.

One of best known of all is the white stork, *Ciconia ciconia*, of Europe and Asia, "whose legendary role in human obstetrics is one of the happier and most persistent . . . myths in our cultural history" (Austin, 1961).

Storks are large to very large (30–60 in. long) and stand 2–4 ft. tall (*see* Size); sexes alike, have very long legs; long, stout, pointed bills; in some species bill is straight, in others decurved (downcurved) or recurved (bent upward); are heavily built with long, broad wings and short tails; in some, the face (in others, entire head and neck) is bare of feathers; most are gregarious; they fly strongly and soar with long legs extended behind, with their *necks fully extended* ahead, not tucked back on shoulders as in herons; their nearest relatives are members of the Ibis Family, Heron Family, and Flamingo Family, but storks differ from birds in these groups mainly by lacking powder-down feathers and the serrated middle toenail and in having short toes, partly webbed at base; also, they do not have muscles in the syrinx, or voice box; they are almost voiceless except for low grunts or hisses, but they loudly rattle and snap their bills; some give remarkable dancing displays before each other; most nest in trees, often at great heights, some on cliffs; the white stork, possibly a former cliff nester, now nests wholly on rooftops in Europe; storks are long-lived; banded white stork, killed when it flew into electric power line in Rhodesia, was 17 years, 4 months, old; another lived to 19 years, 2 months (Harwin, 1971); Kahl (1963) discovered that the American wood stork lowers its body temperature by urinating on its legs (*see* Urohidrosis; Heat and Birds);

albinism is apparently unreported (Gross, 1965a). To feed ill or injured stork, offer it fish, meat, ground bread, finely chopped green plants and vegetables; will take its food from ground or from solid floor of enclosure (Walker, 1942). See Austin (1961) and Gilliard (1958) for general accounts of Stork Family; see also interesting details in Kahl (1963; 1964; 1971a; 1971b).

Jabiru, *Jabiru mycteria* (JAB-ih-roo mick-TEE-rih-ah); genus name: Amazonian Indian name for the bird; species name: Lat., from Gr. *mykter*, nose or snout. Mexican, C. and S. American species that has reached s. Tex.; 48–57 in. long; one of largest of flying birds; a very large all-white stork with an extremely large, black bill, *straight or slightly upturned* (the white wood stork, *with black in wings and tail*, has a slightly downcurved bill); jabiru has black, featherless head and neck with a broad red or orange band of skin separating its white-feathered body from the bare black skin of its head and upper neck; lives on savannas with scattered trees and marshes (Peterson and Chalif, 1973); a rare resident in lowlands of Mexico in s. Veracruz and Chiapas (Blake, E.R., 1953); also to Campeche and Quintana Roo. One sighted on King Ranch, Kleberg County, Tex., on Aug. 11, 1971, remained in vicinity of Escondido Lake, 7 mi. southwest of Kingsville, until last seen, Sept. 9, 1971. A previous record of a jabiru in U.S. was claimed in 1867, when one reported collected near Austin, Tex., but this record considered unsatisfactory (see on Hypothetical List, A.O.U. *Check-list*, 1957). The 1971 report is first acceptable record for the species in the wild in N. America; the bird was photographed and positively identified by Clarence Cottam (Haucke and Kiel, 1973).

Stork, American wood. *See* Stork, wood.

Stork, wood, *Mycteria americana* (mick-TEE-rih-ah ah-mer-ih-CANE-ah); genus name: Lat., from Gr. *mykter*, nose or snout; species name: Lat., of America. (Color ill., page 849.) The only native N. American stork, formerly called wood ibis; now resident and limited to peninsular Fla., and according to authorities, a steadily declining species; once nested Nov.–Apr. along Atlantic and Gulf coasts from S.C. to Tex.; 35–45 in. long; wingspread about 65 in.; about 3½ ft. tall; sexes outwardly alike, but male larger; naked skin of head and neck *black*; dark, stout bill, somewhat downcurved; wood stork is distinguished from similar white ibis in flight by black tail feathers and whole rear part of outstretched wings black, clear to white body; unlike herons, flies with neck extended, long stiltlike legs, held straight back, are black; feet pink; flock flaps and soars alternately and in unison high over trees of cypress swamps, sometimes mounts in circles to tremendous height, then suddenly dashes downward or soars away out of sight; wary, difficult to stalk, usually silent but adults at nest hiss, young are noisy; according to Rafferty (1969), in early 1900s, about 150,000 wood storks in Fla.; in mid-1930s, some 30,000 nested in Corkscrew Swamp, now a National Audubon Society sanctuary; another 50,000 about heads of Shark and

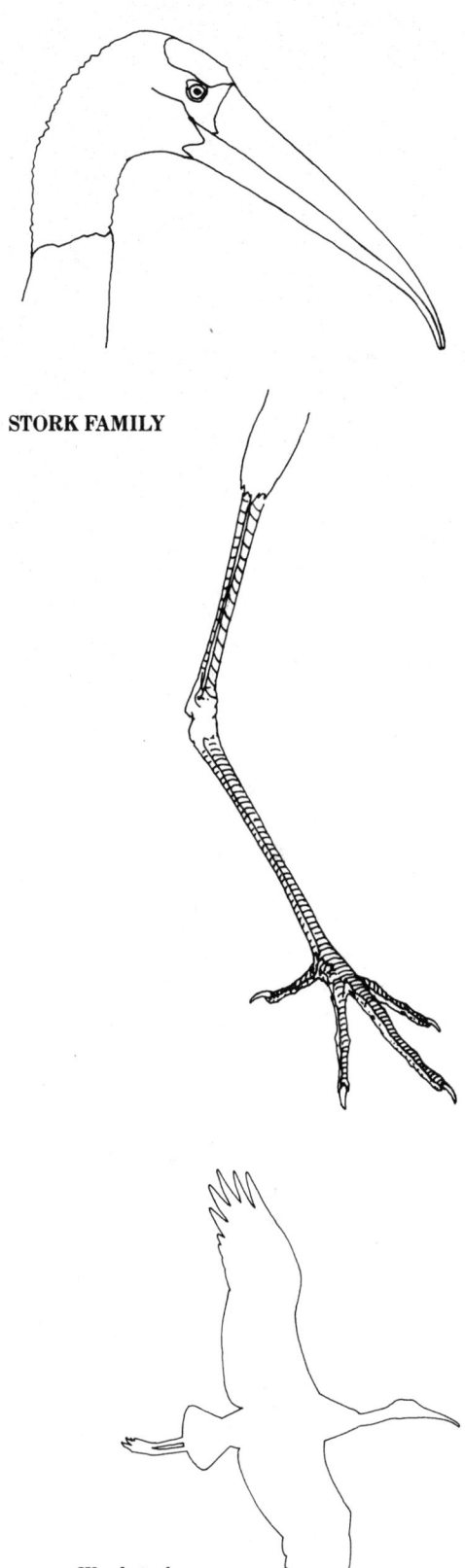

STORK FAMILY

Wood stork

STORK FAMILY
Like ibises and cranes, storks fly with neck extended, long legs trailing. They are heavily built, broad-winged birds with stout bills.

STORM-PETREL FAMILY

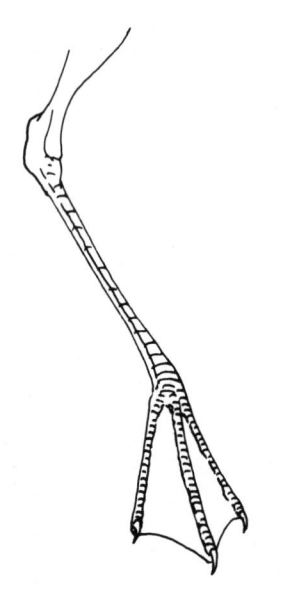

Lane R. in what is now Everglades National Park; other smaller Fla. colonies brought total to about 100,000 (Sprunt and Kahl, 1960); since then a steady decline owing to lumbering of big cypress in swamps (main nesting sites), drainage, and lowering of water table in Fla., droughts, and drying up of feeding areas. By 1957, stork population reached new low of no more than 8,000–10,000 breeding pairs (Allen, 1965b); in Fla. Everglades, only 2,000 individual birds left in 1973; authorities of Everglades National Park believed wood stork might be gone from there by 1980, considered it one of most endangered N. American species; in Corkscrew Swamp Sanctuary, under protection of National Audubon Society, in 1971 no more than 4,500 breeding birds but a good nesting season with 3,000 nestlings, one of most productive years since 1967 (Line, 1971). During late summer, along Atlantic and Gulf coasts, when waters are higher and fish food widely dispersed, wood storks scatter throughout the Southeast; in early winter, at beginning of dry season, they return to s. Fla. nesting sites and start to court and breed. Females may begin to lay eggs earlier or later in certain years, depending on when the rains end and water levels start to fall. As marshes dry, fish populations become highly concentrated in shrinking waters and make increased, and more available, food supply; it is increase in available food that triggers the wood stork's reproductive cycle; in winters following inadequate rain, when relatively few fishes are produced, the storks do not assemble at their nesting areas and may fail to breed (Kahl, 1971a).

Feeding Habits: Walks about in shallows or up to belly in freshwater ponds, marshes, sloughs, often two to four together with egrets and herons, groping with bill in often muddy waters, swallowing any living thing partly opened bill touches; main food is "rough" fishes of no interest to sportsmen, also frogs, tadpoles, snakes, young alligators, and other aquatic animals, including insects.

Nest: Built by pair, with male carrying materials to female at nest; in colonies from 20–30 pairs to thousands; nest is flimsy platform of sticks, usually in swamp in giant cypress trees 75–80 ft. up or more; sometimes 12–20 nests in one tree, also in mangroves a few feet above water.

Eggs: Fla., Nov.–Apr.; 3–4, dull white.

Incubation: By both sexes in turn, 28–32 days; young, unless disturbed, stay in nest 50–55 days after hatching before first flights (Sprunt and Kahl, 1960); parents feed about 50 lb. of fishes to each young during its life in nest; hundreds or thousands of young in nest colony can be heard long way off; utter loud grunts, squeals, bellows, coughs, wheezes, bleats (Sutton, 1924); an injured captive female (adult) ate about 2 lb. of fish (mullet) a day.

Other Names: American jabiru; American wood stork; flinthead; gannet; gourdhead; hammerhead; ironhead; preacher; Spanish buzzard.

Age: One lived in National Zoo, Washington, D.C., 6 years, 8 months.

Weights: Captive adult female weighed 6 lb.; males weigh 10 lb. or more (Allen, 1965b).

Range: Fla. (formerly, Tex., La., S.C., Ga.) and coastal areas of Mexico, C. and S. America to Argentina; wanders to former nesting range, s. Calif., Ariz., w. Tenn., casually northward.

STORM-PETREL FAMILY

Hydrobatidae (high-drow-BAT-ih-dee); Lat., from Gr. *hydor, hydros,* water, and *batein,* to tread. 22 species that range over oceans of the world (Van Tyne and Berger, 1976); 12 species (1 extinct) reported in N. American waters; are in the order Procellariiformes; smallest of seabirds (5¼–10 in. long), from sparrow to robin size; known to seamen as Mother Carey's chickens. *See* Folklore. They are related to the members of the Shearwater Family, and live all of their lives at sea (except when nesting); many follow ships for animal fats or oils thrown overboard; any small black birds with white rump patches and fluttering near water far out at sea are storm-petrels. Sometimes rove singly, more often in scattered flocks; their sudden appearance during windy weather seemed to sailors to presage a storm; thus their name storm-petrels.

All are more or less dark with white on rump or underparts; have slender, hooked bills in which nostrils open in a single tube atop bill; legs are slender, usually long in proportion to size of bird; toes webbed; tail either square or forked; wings long, flight erratic, fluttery, languid, depending on species; when feeding, hover close to surface with wings spread; some patter their feet on the water as they snatch up in bill small fishes, crustaceans, other marine animals, or oil from wounded whales or seals. From habit of "walking" on water, name of petrel was given to these birds—petrel, a diminutive (little Peter)—after St. Peter, who, according to Scriptures (Matthew 14:29), walked upon the water with Jesus' help.

Sexes are outwardly alike; some nest in colonies of thousands in burrows or rock crevices, usually on marine islands or islets; most species migratory; banding has shown that older breeding birds are first to return home in spring and that pairs return to same nest burrow year after year; probably mate for life (Fisher and Lockley, 1954). Each female usually lays single, oval, white egg in a burrow which is dug 2–3 ft. deep in soft soil by both members of pair (only male in Leach's storm-petrel).

Incubation about 5½–7 weeks (Austin, 1961); while nesting, storm-petrels, visiting burrows at night, fill air with twittering cries; spend day at sea. About nesting grounds, storm-petrels utter chirping, squealing, cooing notes; discharge oil in self-defense from mouth and nostrils when handled or otherwise disturbed. *See* Regurgitation. Both parents feed young by regurgitation—first, a clear, musky stomach oil; later, when young are older, partly digested shrimps or squids.

Cats, introduced as pets on islands where storm-petrels nest, attack and kill them in their burrows, and apparently storm-petrels have some enemies at sea—large fishes or marine animals may occasionally snatch them from surface of water and peregrine falcons prey widely on storm-petrels even in midocean (Craddock and Carlson, 1970).

Petrel, Bermuda. One of petrels in the Shearwater Family; also called cahow; *see* Shearwater Family for account of species.

Petrel, black-capped. One of petrels in the Shearwater Family; *see* Shearwater Family for species account.

Petrel, cape. One of petrels in the Shearwater Family; also called cape pigeon; *see* Shearwater Family for account of species.

Petrel, common fork-tailed. *See* Stormpetrel, Leach's.

Petrel, Cook's. One of petrels in the Shearwater Family; *see* Shearwater Family for species account.

Petrel, Coues'. *See* Storm-petrel, ashy.

Petrel, frigate. *See* Storm-petrel, whitefaced.

Petrel, Madeiran. *See* Storm-petrel, Harcourt's.

Petrel, scaled. One of the petrels in the Shearwater Family; *see* Shearwater Family for species account.

Petrel, Trinidad. Another name for the South Trinidade petrel in the Shearwater Family; *see* Shearwater Family for species account.

Petrel, wedge-rumped. *See* Storm-petrel, Galápagos.

Petrel, wedge-tailed. *See* Storm-petrel, least.

Petrel, white-rumped. *See* Storm-petrel, Leach's.

Storm-petrel, *Hydrobates pelagicus* (highdrow-BAY-teez peh-LAJ-ih-cus); genus name: Lat., from Gr. *hydor, hydros,* water, and *batein,* to tread; species name: Lat., pertaining to the sea. N. Atlantic O.; accidental (one record) in N. American waters; 6 in. long; tiny, sooty black with white upper tail coverts; can be distinguished from other similar petrels by smaller size and by small white patch on underside of wings; tail almost square; feet and legs (black) do *not extend in flight beyond tail.*

Feeding Habits: Small fishes, crustaceans, mollusks, habitually follows ships in Atlantic for wastes thrown on water.
Nest: No materials; eggs laid in burrows dug by pair, or in holes or cavities of cliffs, among loose stones or boulders.
Eggs: May–July; 1, often finely marked with brown.
Incubation: By both sexes, about 35 days (Bent, 1922); age at which young first fly unknown.
Other Names: British storm-petrel; Mother Carey's chicken; stormy petrel.
Range: European side of Atlantic O. and Mediterranean Sea; in winter south to Red Sea and w. coast of Africa; apparently first capture of

live bird and definite record in N. America was at Sable Is., Aug. 10, 1970 (McNeil and Burton, 1971).

Storm-petrel, ashy, *Oceanodroma homochroa* (oh-see-ah-NED-roh-mah hom-MOK-roah); genus name: from Gr. words meaning ocean and running; species name: Gr., of one color. (Color ill., page 851.) Summers along Calif. coast; 8 in. long; smallest of the all-black, fork-tailed storm-petrels; adult: entire body black-gray, darkest on crown, ashy gray on underside of wings and on head and neck not visible at distance; flight is more fluttery than that of larger black storm-petrel; sexes alike outwardly and in size.

Feeding Habits: Little known, assumed to be fishes, small shellfishes, and algae; in s. Calif., chief food is larvae of spiny lobster *(Panulirus).*
Nest: In rock cavities and burrows, in colonies.
Eggs: On Farallon Is., May–Aug.; 1, white, often spotted at larger end. Coulter and Risebrough (1973) discovered some thinning of eggshells in 1969 on Farallon Is.; thinning attributed to chlorinated hydrocarbon pesticides in Calif. coastal and marine ecosystem—*see* Pollution.
Incubation: By both sexes in turn; period of unknown.
Other Names: Ashy petrel; Coues' petrel.
Migration: Nothing known about migration; it is gone from nesting islands from Dec. to Apr., but not known where (Palmer, 1962).
Range: At sea from n. Calif., Point Reyes, south to c. Baja Calif.; nests on Farallon and on Channel Is. of Calif.; a few on Los Coronados, Mexico.

Storm-petrel, black, *Oceanodroma melania* (oh-see-ah-NED-roh-mah meh-LAN-ihah); genus name: *see* Storm-petrel, ashy; species name: Lat., blackness (Coble, 1954). (Color ill., page 851.) Pacific coast; 9 in. long; most common of all fork-tailed black storm-petrels of Calif. coast; distinguished by larger size, more graceful, or languid, flight.

Feeding Habits: Eats larvae of spiny lobster and possibly plankton, small fishes, but little else known of its relation to oceanic environment (Pough, 1957); follows ships.
Nest: In rock crevice or abandoned burrows of other birds.
Eggs: In Baja Calif., late May to early Sept.; 1, white.
Other Name: Black petrel.
Range: Nests May–Sept. on islands off coast of Baja Calif. (Los Coronados and others) and in Gulf of Calif.; winters from Mexico to Ecuador, n. Peru.

Storm-petrel, British. *See* Storm-petrel.

Storm-petrel, fork-tailed, *Oceanodroma furcata* (oh-see-ah-NED-roh-mah fur-KAYtah); genus name: *see* Storm-petrel, ashy; species name: Lat., forked, furcate. (Color ill., page 851.) Pacific coast; 8–9 in. long; wingspread to 18 in.; pale gray above; almost white below, especially chin and undertail coverts; distinctly

Ashy storm-petrel

STORM-PETREL FAMILY

Black storm-petrel

forked tail; wing linings and area around eyes dark.

Feeding Habits: Small fishes and crustaceans.
Nest: In burrows on islands or in deep holes in rocks and on grassy slopes up to a mile or more inland, in dense colonies (Pough, 1957).
Eggs: Alaska, Ore., June–July; 1, white, with ring of dark spots around larger end.
Other Name: Fork-tailed petrel.
Range: In N. America, from Bering Sea to s. Calif. (rarely); nests on Aleutian Is., and from Alexander Archipelago, Alaska, to n. Calif.

Storm-petrel, Galápagos, *Oceanodroma tethys* (oh-see-ah-NED-roh-mah TEE-this [*th* as in *thin*]); genus name: *see* Storm-petrel, ashy; species name: from Gr. Tethys, a sea goddess, sister of Saturn and wife of Oceanus (Jaeger, 1955). Recent record, Calif.; about 6½ in. long; sooty black, slightly darker than larger Leach's storm-petrel; triangular white area on rump; slightly forked tail.

Feeding Habits: Unknown.
Nest: In rock crevices and cavities in honeycombed rocks.
Eggs: June (probably height of nesting season —Murphy, 1936); 1, white.
Other Name: Wedge-rumped petrel.
Weights: A female of smaller Peruvian subspecies, *kelsalli*, weighing only 12 gr., or about ½ oz., found alive in backyard in Carmel, Calif., ¼ mi. from ocean, Jan. 1969, during period of intense stormy weather; died same day found (Yadon, 1970).
Range: Nests on Galápagos Is., and along coast of Peru.

Storm-petrel, Guadalupe, *Oceanodroma macrodactyla* (oh-see-ah-NED-roh-mah mack-row-DAK-tih-lah); genus name: *see* Storm-petrel, ashy; species name: from Gr. *makros*, long, and *daktylos*, digit, a finger or a toe (middle toe of this species very long). Probably *extinct;* not one seen since 1911 (Greenway, 1958); was about 8 in. long; forked tail; blackish above and brown below; domestic cats brought to island, preying on colony, at least partly responsible for its disappearance.

Feeding Habits: Probably small fishes, crustaceans.
Nest: In burrows among pines and oaks, 2,500 ft. above sea.
Eggs: Mar.–May; 1, white, with wreath of spots around larger end.
Other Name: Guadalupe Island petrel.
Range: Formerly nested on Guadalupe Is. off coast of n. Baja Calif.

Storm-petrel, Harcourt's, *Oceanodroma castro* (oh-see-ah-NED-roh-mah CASS-troh); genus name: *see* Storm-petrel, ashy; species name: from Sp. meaning "ruin of old fortified place"; common name: Harcourt, English traveler and writer, first saw this species on Desertas Is. in Madeira, where it was known as the roque (rook) de Castro (Gruson, 1972). Accidental inland, rare in e. U.S. and along coast; about 7 in. long; brown to black; slightly forked tail; white patch on rump (Alexander, 1928).

Other Names: Harcourt's petrel; Hawaiian storm-petrel; Madeiran petrel.
Age: A banded adult reported by Harris, M. P. (1972) at least 11 years old.
Range: A bird of tropical oceans; nests in Atlantic from Azores to Ascension Is., on Hawaiian and Galápagos Is.; accidental off Atlantic coast of U.S.; a few storm-borne records in Ont., Pa., D.C., Ind., and Mo.

Storm-petrel, Hawaiian. *See* Storm-petrel, Harcourt's.

Storm-petrel, Leach's, *Oceanodroma leucorhoa* (oh-see-ah-NED-roh-mah lew-CORE-oh-ah); genus name: *see* Storm-petrel, ashy; species name: Lat., from Gr. *leukos*, white, and *orrhos*, rump (Coble, 1954); common name: for William Elford Leach, early-19th-century British zoologist (Murphy, 1962); see details in Gruson (1972). (Color ill., page 850.) 7½–9 in. long; wingspread to 19 in.; forked tail, black-brown with lighter bar on upper part of wings and conspicuous *white rump;* interrupted in most Pacific coast birds by vertical dark stripe; some west coast birds are all dark (*fide,* J. R. Jehl, Jr.); "in flight bounds about erratically above water, much like butterfly or nighthawk" (Peterson, 1947).

Feeding Habits: Fishes, crustaceans, small squids, ships' refuse, but not a ship follower.
Nest: In colonies, in burrows in ground; male digs burrow; nocturnal at nesting time.
Eggs: May–June (Palmer, 1962); 1, white.
Incubation: 41–42 days (Gross, 1947b); chicks hatch with eyes closed, open 15 days after hatching; young in one nest left burrow 75 days after hatching; some make first flights 63–70 days after hatching, when go to sea. See also Wilbur (1969).
Other Names: Common fork-tailed petrel; kerry chicken; Leach's fork-tailed petrel; Leach's petrel; Mother Carey's chicken; white-rumped petrel.
Age: Gross (1947b) reported 27 banded when adults on islands off coast N.B., Canada, and Me., recaptured 6 years after banding: 14 at least 9 years old; 2, 11 years; 2, 12 years after banding as adults, were at least 13 years old; another, banded Kent Is., Me., caught in its nest burrow when 24 years old (Kennard, 1975).
Weights: 1¾–2¾ oz. (Palmer, 1962).
Range: Abundant and wide-ranging over N. Hemisphere; nests in Aleutians and Alaska south on islands to s. Calif. (Prince Is.) and to c. Baja Calif. islands (San Benito, Guadalupe); in Atlantic on Islands from s. Labrador south to Newfoundland, Me., and Mass.; a few records of birds carried inland on storms in Vt., Ohio, D.C., S.C., and Fla.; in winter ranges into S. Hemisphere in Atlantic and in Pacific at least to Peru (*fide,* J. R. Jehl, Jr.).

Storm-petrel, least, *Halocyptena microsoma* (hal-oh-sip-TEE-nah mike-row-SOH-mah); genus name: Lat., from Gr. words meaning salt sea and winged; species name: Lat., from Gr. meaning small (Coues, 1882). (Color ill., page 850.) Pacific coast; smallest petrel, 5½–6 in. long; dark with wedge-shaped tail, not

forked; found either singly or in flocks at sea; appears uniformly dark; flight low over water, erratic, swift.

Feeding Habits: Eats zooplankton (minute, floating animal life in fresh and salt water).
Nest: In colonies, nest unlined, in crevices in ledges or among loose stones; "sings" while hidden in nesting burrow (Palmer, 1962).
Eggs: July; 1, white.
Incubation: Period of and age when young first fly unknown.
Other Names: Least petrel; wedge-tailed petrel.
Range: Nests off w. coast of Baja Calif. and on islands in n. Gulf of Calif., ranges from off San Diego coast north to Humboldt County (De Sante and Remsen, 1973); south in Pacific O. from Mexico to Ecuador.

Storm-petrel, long-legged. *See* Storm-petrel, Wilson's.

Storm-petrel, white-bellied, *Fregetta grallaria* (freh-GET-tah grah-LAR-ee-ah); genus name: Lat., from Ital. *fregata*, or Eng. frigate, man-of-war vessel; little frigate; species name: Lat., from *grallitores*, or long legs (Coues, 1882). Very rare in N. America, one record, Fla.; 7½–8½ in. long; wingspread to 19 in.; square-tailed, very long legs and short, webbed toes; mainly dark above with white rump and belly; a dark phase breeds on Lord Howe Is. in sw. Pacific.

Feeding Habits: Little known but stomachs of four adults had remains of cephalopods.
Other Name: Storm pigeon (Tristan da Cunha Is.).
Weight: Slightly more than 2 oz. (Palmer, 1962).
Range: Nests in s. and sw. Pacific and in Dec.–Feb. at Tristan da Cunha Is. group in s. Atlantic; ranges over southern oceans north to tropics; Fla. record was seven caught with hook and line from boat at anchor at St. Marks (Palmer, 1962).

Storm-petrel, white-faced, *Pelagodroma marina* (pel-ag-OD-ro-mah ma-RYE-nah); genus name: from Gr. *pelagos*, sea, and *dromos*, running; species name: Lat., of the sea. Atlantic coast; rare in N. American waters; 7½–8 in. long; wingspread 17 in.; small, light gray (gray cap and back) but strikingly black on wings and tail (Palmer, 1962); tail almost square; white underparts and white underwings; white line over eyes and black mask; in flight, long legs with webs of black feet mainly yellow, trail behind tail (Watson, 1966); a pied storm-petrel about size of Leach's (Palmer, 1962); white-faced can be recognized at long range by its erratic flight.

Feeding Habits: Pelagic; eats surface plankton, also small squids, larvae of barnacles, sea fleas, and prawns; does not follow ships closely.
Nest: In colonies in burrows on oceanic islands.
Eggs: S. Atlantic, Oct.–Nov.; Cape Verde Is., Feb. (Palmer, 1962); 1, white, with wreath of dark dots around larger end.
Incubation: 55–56 days, by both sexes in turn; young first fly 52–67 days after hatching.

Other Name: Frigate petrel.
Flight Speed: One timed off coast of Del., 8–15 knots (about 9–17 m.p.h.).
Weights: 1½–2 oz.
Range: Temperate and subtropical waters in the N. and S. Atlantic, the s. Indian O., and on islands off Australia and New Zealand (Watson, 1975); 14 sightings in N. Atlantic, between 1890 and 1967, mostly far at sea; closest one 30 mi. north of Cape Cod, Mass., in Oct.; three records, Aug.–Sept., 125–150 mi. east of N.J.; two at Oregon Inlet, N.C., Oct. 1971, just after hurricane; one seen and photographed Aug. 26, 1972, 22 mi. east of Rehoboth Beach, Del. (see Barnhill and Du Mont, 1973).

Storm-petrel, Wilson's, *Oceanites oceanicus* (oh-see-ah-NIGH-teez oh-see-AN-ih-cus); genus name: from Lat. Oceanitis, daughter of Oceanus, sea deity; species name: from Lat. *Oceanus,* ocean, pertaining to the ocean (Coble, 1954); common name: for Alexander Wilson. (Color ill., page 851.) Usually seen off Atlantic coast of N. America, May–Sept.; and casually to Calif. in Pacific; thought by some ornithologists to be the most abundant bird in the world (Fisher, 1940); along with the greater and sooty shearwaters and several other pelagic species, it is one of the breeding birds of the S. Hemisphere that summers in north temperate and Arctic waters; resembles the larger Leach's petrel, but wings shorter, more rounded; is 7 in. long; wingspread 15–16½ in.; sexes outwardly similar; sooty brown or black; conspicuous white rump patch; bill black; in flight, long, spindly black legs extend the yellow-webbed feet beyond the short, square tail; flight is graceful, swallowlike, drops to surface to patter over waves; in N. American waters north to Labrador, scattered single birds and in small groups but sometimes several hundred assemble at food sources, such as fishing vessels (Palmer, 1962); far commoner off N. American shores than Leach's petrel (Peterson, 1947); most numerous in Gulf Stream, a favored habitat; moves inward to fishing banks and coastal waters; sometimes seen in New York City harbor; rarely seen from beaches except after storms (Bull, 1964); believed to be the storm-petrel first called Mother Carey's chicken by sailors.

Feeding Habits: In Antarctica, eats mainly plankton (euphausids), small fishes, squids; in N. Atlantic, plankton, and commonly follows ships and fishing boats to pick up scraps (Palmer, 1962).
Nest: In colonies on islands off tip of S. America and in Antarctic O.; preferably in burrows but usually in crevices under rocks; banded individuals have returned to same burrow in successive years.
Eggs: Dec.–Jan.; 1, white, usually with fine wreath of dark dots around larger end.
Incubation: 39–48 days, average of 43 days (Roberts, 1940); chick fed by parents; eyes closed until 8–11 days old (Palmer, 1962).
Other Names: Common stormy petrel; long-legged storm-petrel; Mother Carey's chicken; skipjack; Wilson's petrel.
Weights: About 1¼ oz.

Range: Nests in vast numbers on Antarctic continent and all islands of South Shetland, South Orkney, South Georgia, Falkland, Tierra del Fuego, and Kerguelen; disperses across Equator in Atlantic, Indian, and Pacific O.; north in Atlantic O. to Labrador, in Pacific, casually to Calif.

Stormy-petrel, common. *See* Storm-petrel, Wilson's.

STORMS
See Weather.

STRIGIDAE
See Owl—Typical Owl Family.

STRIGIFORMES
(stridg-ih-FOR-meez); from Lat. *strix, strigidis,* screech owl, which, according to Coble (1954), was believed in ancient times to suck the blood of young children (*see* Folklore), and Lat. *forma,* form. An order, or grouping, of birds that resemble each other fundamentally in structure (*see* Order); includes 2 families—the Barn Owl Family and the Typical Owl Family. *See* under Owl. There are about 134 species of owls worldwide (Van Tyne and Berger, 1959).

All owls have in common soft plumage, large heads, and large eyes that look forward and are surrounded by a facial disc of feathers. *See* Eyes and Eyesight. The bill is usually short, hooked, and not especially strong; it is partly hidden by the facial-disc feathers, which meet between the eyes. The nostrils (*see* Nostrils) are in the soft cere of the bill; the feet are strong, the claws sharply hooked; the toes zygodactylous, with the fourth toe reversible (Pettingill, 1970).

Owls are the night-hunting counterparts of the day-hunting birds of prey (*see* Falconiformes), although not all owls hunt only by night. According to Voous (1964a), owls show a convergent development (*see* Convergent Evolution) with the Falconiformes, but differ from them structurally—for example, in not having a crop (*see* Crop) and in having a long caecum, with club-shaped ends. *See* Caecum.

However, the similarities of owls and the diurnal birds of prey (hawks, falcons, eagles) may indeed indicate that these groups are each other's closest relatives, in which case the differences represent evolutionary change that has occurred since the separation of these two lineages from a common stock. On the basis of plumage similarity, another candidate for nearest relatives of owls is the order of birds that includes the nighthawks and nightjars (Caprimulgiformes). For a discussion of how birds are grouped according to their relationships, *see* Classification; Morphology; Phylogenetic Relationship. *See also* Check-list; Check-list Order.

STRIKER
Another name for the common tern, least tern, and royal tern in Gull Family; also the Cooper's hawk in Hawk Family.

STRUTHIONIDAE
Family to which ostriches belong. *See* Flightless Birds; Running Birds.

Wilson's storm-petrel

STORM-PETREL FAMILY
A storm-petrel plucks small fish, crustaceans, and plankton from the water as it hovers, its feet pattering lightly over the surface as if it were walking on water.

barn owl

STRIGIFORMES

typical owl

STRUTTING GROUND
See Dancing Ground.

STURNIDAE
See Starling Family.

SUBADULT
Term of ornithologists for a young bird of a species that requires more than one year to mature. *See* discussion under Fertilization. Most small birds acquire their adult plumage and breed in the spring following the summer in which they were hatched. Albatrosses, eagles, gulls, shearwaters, and certain other large birds are exceptions, and some of these may require 3 years or more to gain their adult plumage. *See* discussion under Nestling. *See also* Molts and Molting.

SUBCLIMAX COMMUNITY
Frequently the climatic climax (*see* Climax Community), or final state of plant succession, of a region is not achieved in some of its parts. These areas, called subclimax, may be arrested for a long time. This next-to-last succession to the climatic climax is often the consequence of repeated burning, cutting, grazing, flooding, or other causes. An example of the subclimax is the pine forests of se. U.S. in which the subclimax pines are able to survive the recurring fires of the region which exclude the hardwood trees that would eventually become the climax forest of the region. For a full discussion of the maintenance of this subclimax for its forest products, see in Thompson (1971). *See* brief account of this subclimax and some of its associated birds under Southeastern Pine Woodland.

Another plant association, called a *postclimax*, that has its distinctive birdlife is the so-called *mesquite*. Mesquite, a thorny desert tree or shrub, may invade and spread almost solidly over the climax dry grasslands of the desert plains of the Southwest as a result of overgrazing of the grassland (Weaver and Clements, 1938). *See* brief discussion of this community and some of its associated birds under Mesquite.

SUBFAMILY
An extra division, or category, in the classification of birds. The subfamily is below a family and above a genus. All subfamily scientific names end in *-inae*. *See* Classification.

SUBORDER
An extra division, or category, in the classification of birds. It is next below an order and above a family. It may be equivalent to a superfamily (*see* Superfamily) or designate a category between the superfamily and the order. *See* Classification.

SUBOSCINES
(sub-OS-ih-neez). *See* Passeres.

SUBSPECIES
If a species of bird lives widely over geographical areas of different environments—from warm to cold or from arid to humid climates, for example—it is likely that its populations, from one geographical area to the next, will respond to the influences of the different climates or environmental factors by subtle changes, noticeable in their outer characters. *See* discussion of these changes, some of them dramatic, in the song sparrow under Cline. As a result of environmental selection, the changes may be in the color of the bird—it may have become gradually darker (in humid climates) or paler (in dry, cool climates), or its body or bill may be slightly larger or smaller over the species' broad range. Some of these changes are roughly correlated with changes in the geographical areas in which the various populations of the species live. *See* discussion of some of these predictable changes under Cline.

In some widely distributed species, however, the changes in the outer characters of the populations, instead of being gradual, may appear abrupt when they have been separated for ages by a mountain range, desert, broad expanse of grassland, great forest, or large body of water. See "Geographic Variation" in Selander (1971). When such isolated populations become noticeably and consistently distinct, and yet are believed not to be species (because they still interbreed where they meet, or for other reasons), they are often formally named as *subspecies*. All subspecies are potentially new species if they continue to diverge.

A subspecies may be defined, then, as "a geographical population of a species that shares a variable combination of characteristics and is able to interbreed with other populations of the species when they meet. Subspecies are separated only geographically, not reproductively" (Pettingill, 1972).

Subspecies are indicated in print by a third scientific name, or *trinomial* (*see* Trinomial Nomenclature). For example, the giant Canada goose, a subspecies of the Canada goose, is listed as *Branta canadensis maxima*. *Branta* is the genus name, *canadensis* is the species name; *maxima* is the subspecies name. *See* in Duck Family; *see also* discussion under Names and Naming.

The American Ornithologists' Union (1957), in the 5th ed. of their *Check-list*, recognized (and outlined the ranges of) about 900 subspecies among the 796 species recorded in N. America up to that time. Besides the song sparrow, which has an unusual number of 31 subspecies, species of birds such as the American robin, blue jay, winter wren, and others have subspecies. A species such as the ruby-throated hummingbird has no subspecies and is said to be *monotypic*. *See* other examples under Monotype. If a species is represented by two or more subspecies, it is called *polytypic*. *See also* under Monotype. *See also* discussion of subspecies under Classification, and for discussions of both species and subspecies, see Amadon (1966b); Cain (1964a); Mayr *et al.* (1953); Mayr (1959); Van Tyne and Berger (1976); Thomson (1964o); see especially "The Subspecies" in Selander (1971).

SUBSTITUTE ACTIVITY
See Displacement Activity.

SUBSTRATE
Term for the earth (ground, vegetation, or snow) on which birds spend much of their time when not flying. The feet and legs of birds are adapted to the type of substrate on which they spend much time. *See* Adaptations of the Feet under Feet and Legs. Water is frequently a substrate for many water birds and their adaptations to water are obvious and well known—webbed feet, powerful leg muscles, large uropygial glands (preen gland), and dense waterproof plumage. *See also* Swimming and Diving; Adaptive Characters; Hopping and Walking.

SUGAR BIRD
See Bananaquit in Honeycreeper Family.

SULIDAE
See Booby Family.

SUMMER RESIDENT
See Where Do Birds Live? under Distribution.

SUN BATHING
See Bathing.

SUN-GREBE
See Gruiformes; *also* Rail Family.

SUPERFAMILY
A category in classification above the family (that is, more inclusive) and below the suborder. All scientific superfamily names end in *-oidea*. *See* Classification.

SUPERORDER
A rank or division of birds in their classification that is below the class (Aves) and above an order. *See* Classification.

SUPERSPECIES
Term of ornithologists for two or more species, or kinds, of birds, separated geographically, and very similar in form, habits, and breeding, so closely related that if they were brought together in nature, if the geographical barriers between them were broken down, they would probably interbreed and produce fertile, and continuing, offspring, proving thereby that they were one species. A few examples are the barred owl of e. N. America and the spotted owl of w. N. America; three species of gannets around the world; the N. American marsh hawk, with representatives on every continent; the N. American red-tailed hawk; and the common buzzard of Europe (Amadon, 1966b). For discussions of other designated superspecies, see Mayr and Short (1970); Short (1971).

SUPRAORBITAL GLAND
See salt gland under Nostrils.

SURFACE-FEEDING DUCK
See under Duck Family.

SURFBIRD
See in Sandpiper Family.

SWAINSON
WILLIAM (1789–1855). Born Liverpool, England; an experienced and versatile English naturalist and a prolific writer and illustrator in zoology, whose name is commemorated in the Swainson's hawk, named for him by Bonaparte in 1838; the Swainson's warbler, named for him in 1834 by his friend Audubon; and in the English name of Swainson's thrush. From childhood he had a passion for all kinds of animals which drove him to collect and to draw them. In 1816, the year he became a member of the Linnaean Society, he traveled to Brazil and after two years returned to England with large zoological collections, including 760 bird skins—some species were new to science. In 1820 he became a member of the Royal Society; he practiced lithography so that he could illustrate his own books (he published many). See especially in Stresemann (1975); also Palmer (1928); Herrick (1917). Swainson's most important published contribution to N. American birds was in *Fauna Boreali-Americana*, a four-volume work in which he and William Kirby assisted Sir John Richardson; it was published in London (1829–37). Swainson named and described more than 20 species of N. American birds. See American Ornithologists' Union (1957).

SWALLOW FAMILY
Hirundinidae (hir-un-DINE-ih-dee); from Lat. *hirundo*, swallow; *swallow*, from Old Norse *svala*, and Anglo-Saxon *swalwe*, which became Middle Eng. *swalowe*. 79 species (Van Tyne and Berger, 1976), worldwide except in polar regions, New Zealand, and some oceanic islands; small songbirds (*see* Passeriformes), often mistaken for swifts but not related to them; includes both swallows and martins; 11 species in N. America; although not on wing as much as swifts, swallows and martins probably spend more time in daytime flight than any other passerine (songbird). Some outward differences between swallows and swifts: swallows have 12 feathers in tail, swifts 10; swallows have facial bristles, swifts do not; swallows are not as fast as swifts, usually fly lower (Austin, 1961), more erratically in flocks of small groups; when feeding, dive almost brushing ground, grass tops, or heads of men and cattle.

Swallows and martins are especially adapted to aerial life and show no close ties to any other bird group. They are slender, sleek, the plumage glossy or iridescent; usually dark above; have long, pointed wings with 9 primary feathers up to twice as long as longest secondary wing feathers; in darting flight, hold tiny but wide-gaping mouths fully open to scoop hundreds of flying insects out of air; legs short, feet small and weak, unlike swifts, which alight and cling usually to vertical rock wall or inside chimney, swallows perch readily on wires, tops of sticks, rooftops, all favorite resting places because they do not normally perch in leafy parts of trees (flocks in fall roost in marshes at night, cling to stems of reeds, grasses, etc.). On ground, when gathering mud or other nesting materials, walk with shuffling gait short distances, apparently with great difficulty (Austin, 1961).

In N. America, swallows and martins are widely beloved because of their insect-eating habits (see Beal, 1918), cheerful, twittering notes while perched or in flight, tameness in nesting on, in, or about man's dwelling places, and because for ages their appearance has been a sign of spring. Their dates of arrival, however, may vary as much as 2 weeks from spring to spring because northward movement is governed largely by weather's influence on available insect food; they migrate by day, feeding as they go; northward advance, as illustrated by barn swallow, which closely follows isotherm of 48° F. (Austin, 1961), generally follows temperature warming. A few individuals, popularly called "scouts," may arrive ahead of main flocks and consequently suffer from lack of food or cold of late spring freeze.

The charming legend that the swallows (cliff swallows) return each spring to their nesting places on walls and arches of the San Juan Capistrano Mission in s. Calif. on Mar. 19 each year is not quite accurate; the swallows do return faithfully each spring, but date of return may vary according to weather as with return of swallows elsewhere (Austin, 1961). According to Hochbaum (1955), an authority at the Mission claims the swallows first took residence there in 1776.

N. American swallows are among earliest migrants in fall; gather in large flocks, often in thousands, after nesting is over in summer, assemble by day often on utility wires near marshes, roost at night among the reeds; this custom, with subsequent disappearance of birds on their migration southward, gave rise to belief in medieval Europe that swallows hibernated in mud of marsh ooze; some birds do hibernate or go into torpor during night or in cool weather, but this has never been proved for swallows. *See* Torpidity.

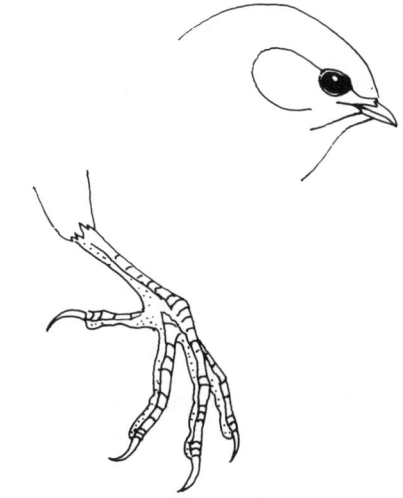

SWALLOW FAMILY

Martin, bank. *See* Swallow, bank.

Martin, bee. Another name for the kingbird in the Flycatcher—Tyrant Flycatcher Family.

Martin, black. *See* Martin, purple.

Martin, Cuban, *Progne cryptoleuca* (PROG-nee crip-toh-LEW-cah); genus name: Lat., from Gr. Prokne, daughter of Pandion and fabled to have been changed into a swallow; species name: from Gr. *kryptos*, hidden, and *leukos*, white, referring to concealed white on lower abdomen. Rare and accidental visitor to Fla., three records (A.O.U. *Check-list*, 1957); about 7½ in. long; adult male strikingly like purple martin, except that feathers of lower belly have concealed bands of white (Bent, 1942); considered by some taxonomists to be not a full species but a subspecies, or race, of the purple martin.
Range: Nests in Cuba and on neighboring Isle of Pines; casual in s. Fla.

Martin, field. Another name for the kingbird in the Flycatcher—Tyrant Flycatcher Family.

Martin, gourd. Another name for the purple martin, from its habit of nesting in gourds, especially in the South.

Martin, gray-breasted, *Progne chalybea* (PROG-nee kah-LIB-ee-ah); genus name: *see* Martin, Cuban; species name: Lat., from Gr. *chalybeios,* steel-colored (Jaeger, 1955), in reference to blue-purple (steely) color of back of male. Mexican, C. and S. American species that has wandered casually in summer to the Rio Grande Valley, Tex.; about 7 in. long; size of purple martin; both sexes much like a female purple martin, with sides of head, throat, breast, and sides gray-brown, becoming white on belly and crissum; male, glossy blue-purple above, appears black at distance; female and immature similar to male but upperparts basically brownish, somewhat glossed with purple (Blake, E.R., 1953). Apparently does not nest in U.S. (see Bent, 1942, for life history), but about cities and towns in C. America, has adapted to nesting under the eaves of tall buildings; also has learned to nest in bird boxes. Austin (1961) once saw a pair of gray-breasted martins in British Guiana that nested in a bird box attached to the taffrail of a small river steamer; the adults reared brood after brood as the boat made its weekly trips up and down the river. *See* Nests and Nesting.
Other Name: White-bellied martin.

Martin, gully. *See* Swallow, rough-winged.

Martin, house. *See* Martin, purple.

Martin, little. *See* Swallow, tree.

Martin, purple, *Progne subis* (PROG-nee-SUE-biss); genus name: *see* Martin, Cuban; species name: Lat., name applied by Pliny, Roman naturalist, to a bird that breaks eagles' eggs (Coues, 1882). (Color ill., page 852.) In summer, locally, s. Canada south to Mexico, Atlantic to Pacific coast; largest N. American swallow; 7¼–8½ in. long; wingspread 15½–16¾ in.; male not purple but *uniformly blue-black throughout;* appears black at distance; tail moderately forked; female and immature, *gray to white below,* upperparts mixed blue and gray; apparently never lived in great forests of early America, likes open grassy river valleys, shores of lakes, meadows about ponds and coastal marshes; also in glades of pine forests and cut-over woods in Fla. (Sprunt, 1942b), in parts of Ariz., depends on saguaro forests for nesting holes (Phillips *et al.,* 1964); its absence, like that of cliff swallow, from apparently suitable environment over its wide range still puzzles ornithologists; originally nested, and still does in parts of Fla., for example, in natural cavities or in woodpecker holes in trees, or in e. and w. U.S. in cavities in cliffs or among loose rocks (see Banks and Orr, 1965); however, has adapted to "martin houses" (see survey by Jackson and Tate, 1974) put up on poles or compartments on sides of buildings in towns, villages; was originally enticed by N. American Indians to nest in gourds or calabashes they put up for them, which is still practiced by people especially in South (Sprunt, 1942b); martins appear in U.S. migrating northward from late

Jan. through Apr.; males usually arrive ahead of females at nesting place, utter loud rich chirruping; usually nests in colonies, darts about with rapid flapping of wings, soaring, turning, often flies about calling at night; pair may select nesting place from one-room nest box on post to apartment-house box on pole 15–20 ft. up, with 20–30 or even 200 rooms (see Terres, 1968c, for examples of fidelity of return, specifications for martin houses, gourds, and sources, etc.); on July 17, 1947, John Heaventhal, Hurffville, N.J., reported 270 pairs in his 379-room martin house, largest colony in state at time; occasionally, colonies over entire regions periodically decimated by cold, prolonged spring and summer rains, and starvation resulting from lack of flying insects, chief food of martins (Forbush, 1925–29; see also Finlay, 1976); this is in contrast to late in season (Aug.) when insects more abundant, more varied, and larger, at time when martins at peak numbers, beginning their molt, putting on fat, and starting migration (Johnston, 1967).

Feeding Habits: Most of insect food caught in air; some while walking on ground: largely ants, wasps, beetles, grasshoppers, stink bugs, treehoppers, dragonflies (a favorite), some caterpillars, moths, butterflies, mosquitoes (see debate about role of martins in mosquito control by Sprunt, 1942b; Kale, 1968; Pettingill and Lancaster, 1968), horseflies, robber flies, etc.; also spiders; in drinking and bathing in flight, martins skim surface of ponds and rivers with bill, dipping hind part of body, usually early morning and late afternoon; are very fond of bits of eggshells (hens' eggs) scattered on ground for them (Sprunt, 1942b); apparently for needed calcium.
Nest: In colonies; both sexes carry grasses, leaves, twigs, feathers, mud, rags, paper, string, shreds of bark, even crayfish legs, into martin house compartments; occasionally pile rim of dirt at front of nest apparently to keep eggs from rolling out; sometimes carry green leaves into nest box. See also homing experiments (return to nest) in Southern (1968). According to Allen and Nice (1952), the male defends a room in the martin house; the female chooses room, thereby acquires a mate.
Eggs: Mar.–July; 3–8, usually 4–5, white.
Incubation: By female, 15–16 days (male guards nest during her absences); young leave nest 28 days after hatching or later (Allen and Nice, 1952); according to Finlay (1971), incubation 16–18 days; young fly 26–31 days after hatching; one brood each year (Reilly, 1968); in Aug.–Sept., after young can fly, martins abandon nest boxes and range country during day, gather to roost at night in enormous flocks in shade trees of towns or even in cities; sometimes in mixed flocks with starlings, grackles.
Other Names: Black martin; gourd martin; house martin; western martin.
Age: Of eight banded birds, one lived to 4 years, two to 5 years, one to 6 years; four were more than 7 years old when retrapped where first banded; one in Ohio to 8 years old.
Albinism: A total, or complete, albino young with pink eyes raised by parents in martin house, Norfolk, Va. (Lincoln, 1958).

Flight Speed: Timed in Mich., about 17–22½ m.p.h. (Schnell, 1965); maximum range to 41 m.p.h.
Host to Cowbirds: One record, Detroit, Mich., but adult martins threw eggs out of martin house (Friedmann, 1963).
Weights: Two males killed by cold in Mar. in N.C., 45.3 and 44.9 gr., or about 1¾ oz.
Range: Nests west of Cascade Range and Sierra Nevada from sw. B.C. south to Baja Calif., Sonora, and Arizona; east of Rocky Mtns. from ne. B.C., c. Alta., east through n. Minn., n. Wisc., s. Ont., to c. Nova Scotia, south to the Gulf coast and s. Fla.; winters in S. America.

Martin, sand. *See* Swallow, bank.

Martin, western. *See* Martin, purple.

Martin, white-bellied. *See* Martin, gray-breasted.

Swallow, Bahama, *Callichelidon cyaneoviridis* (kal-ih-KEL-ih-don sigh-AN-eh-oh-VER-ih-dis); genus name: from Gr. *kalos,* beautiful, and *chelidon,* swallow; species name: Lat., from Gr. *kyanos,* blue, and *viridis,* green, blue-green, in reference to color of upperparts of this bird. Resident of Bahama Is., reported twice in Fla.; 6 in. long; similar to tree swallow but tail deeply forked; male, velvety green crown and back; steel blue on wings; white underparts; female duller, smaller; a wanderer among the islands; disappears at certain times, movements possibly influenced by abundance or lack of insect food (Bent, 1942); sometimes seen among flocks of tree swallows in winter (Bond, 1961).
Other Names: Golondrina; summer swallow.

Swallow, bank, *Riparia riparia* (rih-PAY-rih-ah); genus and species names: from Lat. *riparius,* frequenting riverbanks. (Color ill., page 852.) Eurasia and N. America; in summer, Alaska to Calif. and s. U.S.; smallest N. American swallow; 4¾–5½ in. long; wingspread 10–11 in.; sexes alike; brown back with white underparts; *brown band across white breast* just below throat; tail slightly forked; twists and turns in erratic, zigzag flight; summers wherever available nesting places in sand or gravel banks, exposed and kept steep by cutting of stream or wave action of lake, bay, or ocean; also steep sides of gravel pits, railroad and highway embankments cut by man; migrates northward in spring in flocks, up river valleys and coasts, mostly in Apr.; after arriving at colony nesting bank, sleeps in previous year's nesting holes or quickly begins to dig new ones (Forbush, 1925–29); some fighting to settle territorial claims to burrows, which sometimes are less than a foot apart; the swallows often dart about carrying and dropping white feather—play or part of courtship; utter twittering notes, also a gritty *speed-zeet, speed-zeet;* nesting burrows usually near top of vertical bank, are dug straight into bank or slightly upward, by both sexes, alternately working at hole; in beginning, cling to face of bank and dig with bill, once inside, kick dirt backward out of hole with feet; dig holes about

1 in. high, 2 in. wide; burrows range from 16 in. to 4–5 ft. long, usually about 28–36 in. (Gross, 1942a).

Feeding Habits: Eats mostly flying insects caught in flight: termites, ants (winged forms), treehoppers, leafhoppers, aphids, beetles, mosquitoes, houseflies, crane flies, some dragonflies, moths, caterpillars, etc. (Gross, 1942a).

Nest: Built by both sexes at end of burrow; flimsy, built of dry grasses, straws, weed stems, rootlets, pine needles, bits of wool, horsehair, feathers.

Eggs: Apr.–July; 4–8, usually 4–5, white.

Incubation: By both sexes, alternately, 14–16 days (Stoner, 1936); young fly when 18–22 days old (Gross, 1942a).

Other Names: Bank martin; sand martin; sand swallow.

Age: Of 3,519 banded and recovered in Iowa and N.Y., not one more than 4 years old; one caught in burrow near same place where banded (Stoner and Stoner, 1937) was 6 years old; another 7 years when recaught; MacBriar (1970) reported one in Wisc. 8 years old.

Flight Speed: Timed in Mich., 13–31 m.p.h. (Schnell, 1965).

Host to Cowbirds: One record, in Ill. (Friedmann, 1963).

Weights: 13–16 gr. (Stoner, 1936), or about ½ oz.; females (average), 14.8 gr.; males, 13.7 gr.

Range: Nests from tree limit in Eurasia and in N. America from n.-c. Alaska, s. Yukon, nw. and s.-c. Mack., n. Ont., s. Que., s. Labrador, sw. Newfoundland, south to s. Alaska, B.C., mainly east of coast ranges to s. Calif., w. Nev., n. Utah, Colo., Okla., Tex., Ark., n. Ala., c. W.Va., and e. Va.; casually to S.C.; winters in C. America.

Swallow, barn, *Hirundo rustica* (hir-UN-doh RUS-tih-kah); genus name: Lat., swallow; species name: Lat., rustic, rural; known in Europe simply as swallow; *barn* swallow in N. America from habit of nesting in barns. (Color ill., page 853.) Europe and Asia; in N. America, Alaska and Canada to Mexico, Atlantic to Pacific; one of best-loved American birds because summer dooryard companion of country people from time of first colonists; our only swallow with deeply forked tail; also only one with white spots in tail; 5¾–7¾ in. long; wingspread 12½–13½ in.; male, metallic blue-black above with red-brown forehead; rich red-brown breast, paler below; females, usually duller colors but not always; from winter range in S. America, migrates by day, northward mostly in Apr.; arrives s. Canada late in month, Alaska by May (Bent, 1942); from nesting colony in barn or rock cave, male chases female in long courtship flights over fields or water, utters constant twitter, *kvik-kvik*, *wit-wit*; in pair formation has courtship notes distinct from those of cliff swallow, which often nests in same barn; this helps keep the two from interbreeding (Samuel, 1971). *See* Language; Species.

Feeding Habits: Catches flying insects in air, in light, swift, tireless flights over fields, meadows, marshes, ponds; follows farmer plowing fields or mowing grass to catch insects stirred up; eats grasshoppers, crickets, dragonflies,

treehoppers, leafhoppers, beetles, codling moths, etc. (Bent, 1942); drinks and bathes by skimming water.

Nest: In colonies, sometimes singly, in farm outbuildings, eaves of old houses, under bridges, boat docks over water, rock caves, crevices in cliffs along lakes or ocean, holes or natural cavities in cutbanks, sometimes even on slow-moving trains or boats (Bent, 1942); both sexes build nest; may take 1–2 weeks (Herroelen, 1957–59); cup of mud or clay pellets mixed with straws, dried grasses, lined with white poultry feathers, horsehair, plastered against horizontal or vertical surface; solitary pair in building or even up to 30 pairs; 5–18 pairs in barns in Mass. (Davis and Davis, 1936).

Eggs: Alaska, June–July; elsewhere in U.S., usually Apr.–July; usually 4–5, white, spotted, speckled with browns.

Incubation: 13–17 days; young fly 18–23 days after hatching (Davis, 1937); young, after leaving nest, may return to it to roost for several nights; family remain together 11 days after young leave nest (Smith, 1937a); usually two broods a year in warm or temperate parts of range (Reilly, 1968).

Other Names: American barn swallow; barn-loft swallow; European swallow; fork-tailed swallow.

Accidents: One killed on golf course, struck by golf ball; one, banded as nestling, found dead stuck on asphalt roof in Fla.; while migrating low over water, sometimes struck by waves and drowned at sea; killed when overtaken by sudden cold weather.

Age: Of two banded N.D., each lived to more than 6 years; one, banded Mass., caught again and released when 7 years old; one, banded State College, Pa., trapped and released in Vt. when 8 years, 3 months, old (Kennard, 1975); a European barn swallow lived to 16 years old (Thomson and Leech, 1952).

Albinism: A pure-white one, but eyes, feet, bill dark, reported near Stone Dam, N.Y., summer 1956, was harassed by other barn swallows.

Flight Speed: Timed in Mich., 17–33 m.p.h. (Schnell, 1965); in Calif., 42–46 m.p.h. (McLean, 1930).

Host to Cowbirds: Infrequent; six records (Friedmann, 1963), one, Mich. (Nickell, 1964a).

Hybrids: Gray (1958) reported cross of barn swallow and cliff swallow; also, one reported by Axtell (1945).

Weights: In fall, coastal N.J. (7), 17–19.8 gr. (Murray and Jehl, 1964), or about ¾ oz.

Range: Nests n.-c. Alaska, sw. Mack., c. Sask., s. Man. east to Newfoundland and w. Greenland and south through U.S. into c. Mexico; winters from Panama south to s. S. America; some individual barn swallows may have longest migration routes of any N. American land birds—from Yuk. and Alaska in summer south in winter to Argentina, 7,000 mi. away (Lincoln, 1950c).

Swallow, blue-backed. *See* Swallow, tree.

Swallow, bridge. *See* Swallow, rough-winged.

Swallow, cave, *Petrochelidon fulva* (pet-row-KEL-ih-don FULL-vah); genus name: Lat.,

Cave swallow

SWALLOW FAMILY

from Gr. *petros*, stone, or *petra*, rock, in allusion to places where nests often built, and *chelidon*, swallow; species name: Lat., tawny, or reddish yellow, in reference to chestnut forehead, throat, and sides of neck. Very local, in spring and summer around Carlsbad Caverns National Park, N.M., to s.-c. Tex.; 5–6 in. long; similar to cliff swallow but *dark chestnut* forehead (Blake, E.R., 1953), instead of buff-yellow; nests in colonies in limestone caves and sinkholes or under overhanging cliffs, but noted in 1973 to have extended its range in c. Tex. and nesting in large numbers in culverts with barn swallows, also in culverts with its near relative the cliff swallow (see Martin, R.F., 1974).

Nest: A mud cup plastered to rock wall or inside of concrete culvert, made of mud pellets gathered by these birds from edges of springs, desert streams.
Eggs: 2–5, usually 4, white with fine spots of brown; two broods each year.
Other Names: Buff-throated swallow; Coahuila cliff swallow; Cuban cliff swallow.
Range: Nests from se. N.M. and s.-c. Tex. to s. Mexico and West Indies; accidental in Fla.

Swallow, chimney. Another name for the chimney swift in Swift Family.

Swallow, cliff, *Petrochelidon pyrrhonota* (pet-row-KEL-ih-don pih-row-NO-tah); genus name: *see* Swallow, cave; species name: Lat., red-backed, in allusion to rump. (Color ill., page 852.) In summer, locally, Alaska, Canada, south to Mexico, Pacific to Atlantic coasts; 5–6 in. long; wingspread 12–12¼ in.; sexes similar; forehead dull white to buff; crown, back, wings, tail *blue-black;* rump *rusty* or buffy; back streaked with white; throat and face brownred; sides and flanks gray or gray-brown; belly white; almost *square tail;* immature similar to adults but duller colors; summers in open country similar to that of barn swallow; as land cleared by settlers for pastures, crop fields, and buildings, more insects and shelter available for cliff swallows, they apparently expanded across country from primitive cliff dwelling sites to close association with man; like purple martin, its distribution today puzzling, abundant some regions, in others, in apparently similar country, may be absent or rare; like purple martin, periodically decimated by prolonged spring or summer rains; decreases may also be caused by some landowners who want to rid their buildings of cliff swallows' mud nests; others attract and build up their colonies. See in Terres (1968c) remarkably successful experiment of Wisc. barn owner in building colony from a few to more than 2,000 pairs. From winter home in S. America, arrives Calif. in Mar.; reaches U.S. generally in Apr.; Alaska in May; aerial courtship accompanied by rapid twittering, chattering; song is an unmusical creak, rather than twitter.

Feeding Habits: Eat insects, especially beetles, such harmful kinds as cotton-boll weevil, also bugs such as chinch bugs, flying ants, wasps, grasshoppers, dragonflies, corn rootworms, mosquitoes, occasionally spiders, fruit of junipers (Gross, 1942b).

Nest: In colonies, each nest built by pair, usually retort-shaped (like flask or bottle), of mud or clay pellets, with a narrow entrance on side, either a protruding neck of 5–6 in. or no neck at all; may also be open cup like barn swallow's nest, inside lined with a few grasses and feathers; built close together against vertical surface under eaves of houses, churches, banks, stores, or barns from mud gathered by each pair and carried in mouth in flight to nest site; sometimes *inside* of sheds or barns on rafters, under bridges and in culverts; original sites, still used, are walls of bluffs, canyons, deep gorges in mountains (rosy finches roost in them in winter)—*see* account in Finch Family; also plastered to trunks and under branches of large pine trees (Calif.); 5 days or up to 10–14 to build each nest; colonies may number from few to 800, 1,000, or more on barn, face of cliff or face of large dam; some colonies have thousands of birds.
Eggs: Apr.–Aug.; 3–6, usually 4–5, white, cream-white, pink-white, some dotted, spotted with browns.
Incubation: By both parents, 12–14 days; 15–16 days(?); young fly when 23 days old; according to Gross (1942b), two broods each year.
Other Names: Barn swallow; crescent swallow; eave swallow; jug swallow; moon-fronted swallow; mud swallow; Republican swallow.
Age: Of two banded Long Is., N.Y., one retrapped same place and released when at least 5 years old; another retrapped same barn when 4 years old.
Flight Speed: Timed in Mich., 9–23 m.p.h. (Schnell, 1965); in w. U.S., 29 m.p.h. (Cottam *et al.*, 1942b).
Host to Cowbirds: Rare; seven records, Pa.; one in Ill. (Friedmann, 1963).
Hybrids: A presumed hybrid of cliff swallow and tree swallow reported by Gray (1958); *see also* under Barn swallow.
Range: Nests from c. Alaska, c. Yuk., w. Mack., c. Sask., s. Man., c. Ont. and s. Que., N.B., and Nova Scotia, south to c. Mexico, w.-c. Tex., c. Mo., w. Ky., w.-c. Tenn., n. Ala., and w. N.C.; winters in S. America.

Swallow, crescent. *See* Swallow, cliff.

Swallow, eave. *See* Swallow, cliff, and Swallow, tree.

Swallow, fork-tailed. *See* Swallow, barn.

Swallow, jug. *See* Swallow, cliff.

Swallow, mud. *See* Swallow, cliff.

Swallow, republican. *See* Swallow, cliff.

Swallow, rough-winged, *Stelgidopteryx ruficollis* (stel-jih-DOP-teh-ricks rue-fih-COL-is); genus name: from Gr. *stelgidos*, scraper, and *pteryx*, wing (Jaeger, 1955), "scraperwinged," in reference to the recurved hooks along outer primary of each wing feather; thus: *rough-winged;* species name: from Lat. *rufus*, reddish, and *collum*, neck (Jaeger, 1955). (Color ill., page 852.) S. Canada throughout U.S. to S. America; 5–5¾ in. long; wingspread 11½–12¼ in.; sexes outwardly similar; larger

than similar bank swallow; brown above; white below but with *dusky brown or gray throat and upper breast* (no clearly defined band across breast as in bank swallow); tail slightly forked; in adults, outer primary (9th) wing feather has small hooks along edge, whose function is thought to be unknown, however, Lunk (1962) believes serrations on outer primary, by producing shrill quickly repeated whistle in flight, plays a part in their pairings; from winter home in s. U.S., Mexico, arrives in most of U.S. in Mar. and Apr.; usually solitary or mixed with flocks of other swallows; pairs usually solitary, although several may nest in holes in favored gravel pit; lives almost anywhere, even in mountains which contain steep banks of sand, clay, or gravel; male in courtship flight, chasing female, spreads long white undertail coverts until conspicuous along sides of tail; flight is strong, direct, with less abrupt turns than bank swallow (Dingle, 1942); usually a silent bird but sometimes utters squeaky *quiz-z-zeep.*

Feeding Habits: Courses low over ground or water to catch in mouth flies, wasps, bees, winged ants, beetles, dragonflies, etc.
Nest: In burrow sometimes dug, using feet, by pair themselves; dig burrow from 9 in. to about 28 in. or even 6 ft. long, depending on soil, in stream banks, gravel pits; uses old burrows of bank swallows, kingfishers, ground squirrels, also holes in masonry walls, sides of buildings, quarries, caves, in drainpipes, sewer pipes, etc.; nest material in burrow, or hole, loose grasses, rootlets, bark chips, leaves. See interesting experiment in Homing.
Eggs: Apr.–July; 4–8, usually 6–7, white.
Incubation: By female, 12 or 16 days (Dingle, 1942); 16 days (Lunk, 1962); young leave nest when about 19–21 days old; one brood each year. Blake, C.H. (1953) reported a banded male that nested in same burrow for 5 years, but with different mate each year.
Other Names: Bridge swallow; gully martin; rough-wing.
Accidents: In June 1949, in Mass., one killed when two collided in flight over small pond.
Weights: In summer, Manomet, Mass. (24), 12.1–18.1 gr. (Fisk, 1971b), or about ½–⅔ oz.
Range: Nests from B.C., s. Alta., sw. Sask., se. Man., w. and s. Ont., sw. Que., c. Vt., and N.H., south to Argentina, Atlantic to Pacific in U.S.; winters from s. U.S. southward.

Swallow, sand. *See* Swallow, bank.

Swallow, sea. Another name for terns in Gull Family.

Swallow, stump. *See* Swallow, tree.

Swallow, tree, *Iridoprocne bicolor* (ih-rih-do-PROCK-nee BYE-color); genus name: Lat., from Gr. *iris, iridos*, iris, bright color, and Prokne, mythical daughter of Pandion who was changed to a swallow; species name: Lat., of two colors. (Color ill., page 853.) Summers Alaska and Canada to Calif., Va.; wherever open water with marsh or wet meadow; 5–6¼ in. long; wingspread 12–13¼ in.; sexes similar; steely blue-black or green-black above; pure white below (similar western violet-green swallow has white rump patches); somewhat resembles purple martin in flight because of triangular shape of wings (Tyler, 1942d); generally winters from s. U.S. south; migrates in large flocks by day; earliest of swallows to move north (Feb.–Mar. in most of U.S.); in cold weather can rely on berries and some seeds if insects scarce; flocks roost in bushes or reeds of marshes at night; usually nest in isolated pairs but often in loose colonies; nesting holes often scarce and will accept man-made nest boxes put up for it in open fields; male courts female in flight pursuit of aerial gyrations; common note is rapidly repeated *silip*; sometimes sings, a sweet, liquid chatter flying about over pond and even at night, also from perches near nest; some males may have two mates at same time; usually different mate each year.

Feeding Habits: In flight courses over meadows, ponds, rivers, veers from side to side, quickly doubles back to snatch from air flying beetles, ants, flies, also takes some bees, wasps, grasshoppers; sometimes alights on beach or marshy shore to feed on minute insects and tiny beach "fleas"—a crustacean—also eats water boatmen, spiders, seeds of bulrushes, sedges, smartweed, and fruits of bayberry.

Nest: Built by female, sometimes with help of male, of grasses and straws, lined with chicken feathers (prefers white ones); in natural tree cavity, abandoned woodpecker hole, bird box, cavity in eaves or cornices of old farm buildings, rural mailbox. See experiments in attracting tree swallows in Terres (1968c).

Eggs: Apr.–June; 4–6, white.

Incubation: 13–16 days; young fly about 16–24 days after hatching (Tyler, 1942d).

Other Names: Blue-backed swallow; eave swallow; stump swallow; white-bellied swallow; white-breasted swallow.

Age: Of six banded in New England, five retrapped when 6 years old, one 7 years old; one, banded Princeton, Mass., lived to at least 9 years (Kennard, 1975).

Albinism: A "complete" albino reported in *EBBA News* (1966).

Flight Speed: Timed in Mich., 5–19 m.p.h. (Schnell, 1965); in New England, 24 m.p.h. (White, 1933); 25 m.p.h. (Wood, 1933).

Host to Cowbirds: Rare, several records in Wisc. (Friedmann, 1963).

Hybrids: See under Cliff swallow.

Weights: In fall, coastal N.J. (28), 16.4–22.2 gr. (Murray and Jehl, 1964), or about ½–¾ oz.

Range: Nests n.-c. Alaska, sw. Yuk., w.-c. and s. Mack., n. Alta., n. Sask., east to Newfoundland, south to se. Alaska, along Pacific coast to s. Calif., w.-c. Nev., e.-c. Oreg., se. Wash., Idaho, w.-c. Utah, w. Colo., se. Wyo., s. N.D., e. S.D., e. Neb., ne. Kans., s.-c. Mo., nw. Tenn., s. Ill., s.-c. Ind., c. Ohio, n. W.Va., Va., c. Md., ne. Pa., e. N.Y., n. Conn., R.I., and Mass.; casually farther south to Ark., La., Miss., and N.J.; winters from s. Calif., sw. Ariz., Mexico, Gulf coast, se. Va., and occasionally e. Mass. and L.I., N.Y., south to C. America and Cuba.

Swallow, violet-green, *Tachycineta thalassina* (tak-ih-sin-EE-tah thal-AS-ih-nah);

genus name: from Gr. *tachys*, swift, and *kinetos*, to move (Jaeger, 1955), "swift-moving" (in flight); species name: Lat., sea green, refers to green of back and wings; *violet-green*, from purple-green gloss of upperparts. (Color ill., page 852.) Widespread west of Great Plains; Alaska to Mexico; small; 5–5½ in. long; sexes outwardly similar; dark upperparts glossed with green and purple, pure white below; distinguished from similar tree swallow by *white patches on sides of rump that almost meet over tail;* also white of throat extends well up sides of neck and over eyes; in summer, common at low altitudes about towns, villages of Alaska, B.C., and at Seattle, Wash., also in clearings of woods where dead trees for nesting, especially near lakes, streams; from low altitudes to high in mountains of Calif., Colo., Ariz., N.M., shows preference for nesting in mountains in southern part of range (Bent, 1942); wintering flocks from C. America, Mexico, and s. Calif. migrate northward early (Feb.–Apr.); like tree swallow, with which often associates, sometimes nests in loose colonies where standing dead trees offer nest sites; male sings courtship songs in flight in dark before sunrise, repeating over and over *tsip tseet tsip;* ordinary note is rapid twitter.

Feeding Habits: Apparently entirely insects taken in flight: leafhoppers, leaf bugs, flies, ants, wasps, bees, beetles, moths, etc.; sweeps about in loose flocks or in small groups low over open fields, surfaces of small ponds, up and down canyon streams; circles at great height when insects flying high; perches in long rows on utility wires.

Nest: Built of weed stems, grasses, feathers (may take feathers from one's fingers), sometimes in colony of up to 20 pairs in holes of single dead pine, in deserted woodpecker holes, natural cavities in trees, rocks, crevices of rocky cliffs, bird boxes (see Narver, 1970, for account of this habit in Alaska); for 16 consecutive years at Seattle, Wash., bird box occupied by different pairs.

Eggs: May–July; 4–7, usually 4–5, white.

Incubation: 13–14 days; young leave nest 10 days after hatching but return for several days (Gabrielson and Lincoln, 1959); one brood (Bent, 1942).

Albinism: A pure-white one with pink eyes reported Sequoia National Park, Calif., Aug. 1954.

Flight Speed: Timed in w. U.S., 28 m.p.h. (Cottam *et al.*, 1942b).

Range: Nests from Yukon R. valley through s. Alaska, w. and s. B.C., sw. Alta., Mont., sw. S.D., and nw. Neb., south to s. Baja Calif., w. Mexico, and through Colo., N. Mex., and w. Tex.; winters south to C. America.

Swallow, white-bellied or white-breasted. *See* Swallow, tree.

SWALLOWING

Birds pick up food with the bill and food is mixed in the mouth with saliva (*see* Mouth), then swallowed. In general, food is propelled by the bird to the back of the pharynx (rear

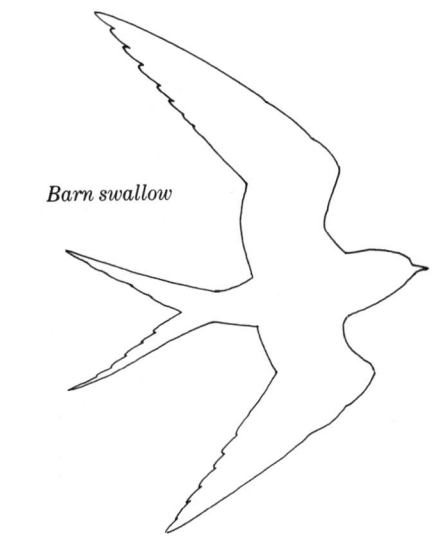

Barn swallow

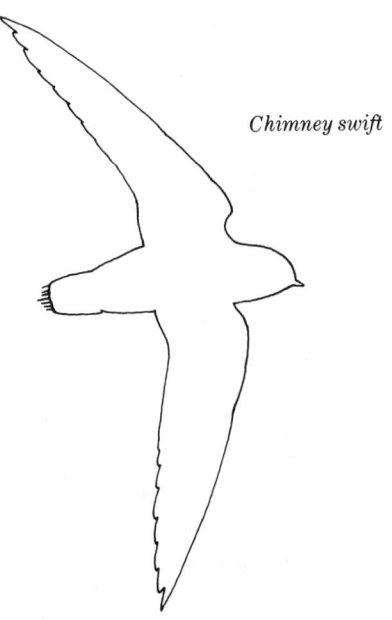

Chimney swift

SWALLOW FAMILY

In flight, swallows are often mistaken for swifts. Many swallows have forked tails, and while this is also true of some swifts, most have short, stiff tails, sometimes spine-tipped. Swifts have stream-lined bodies and long, slender wings that curve backward, and they fly with rapid, shallow wingbeats and short glides. Swallows fly quite low, often diving for insects very close to the ground.

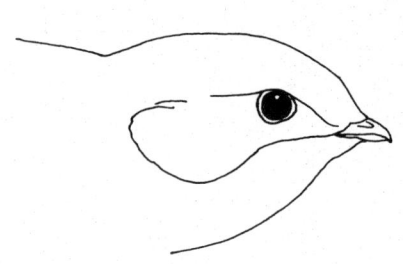

SWIFT FAMILY

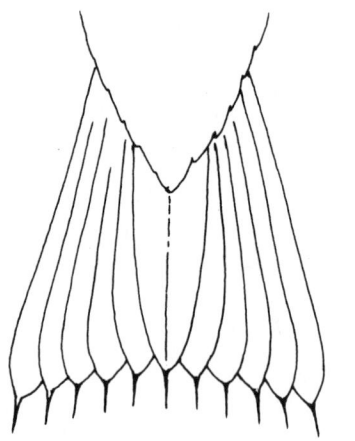

of mouth) by raising the head and/or a quick forward thrust of the head. A reflex simultaneously closes the glottis, thus preventing food, or water, from going down the trachea, or windpipe, which leads to the lungs. Once food is out of the mouth and pharyngeal cavity and into the esophagus, rhythmic contractions (peristalsis) apparently begin in response to the presence (pressure) of food and move it along to the glandular stomach. *See* Respiratory System. *See* Care and Feeding of Abandoned or Injured Wild Birds; *also* Digestion.

Occasionally birds try to swallow prey that is too large for them. On Long Is., N.Y., a 7-in.-long yellow-breasted chat tried to swallow a 10-in.-long DeKay's, or brown, snake, got it partway down, then choked to death (Terres, 1960b). *See* Reptiles and Birds. Munro (1936), while studying ring-billed gulls on an island in a lake in Alta., Canada, found five of these gulls dead, each with the paired feet of a ground squirrel protruding from its mouth; others regularly swallowed smaller ground squirrels without difficulty. *See* Esophagus for some large foods that birds swallow. *See also* Accidents; Food and Feeding Habits.

Drinking by a bird is somewhat different in method; a bird dips its bill into water, holds water in its mouth, then tips its head up at a sharp angle, at which the water flows down the bird's throat (Farner, 1960). Some birds, after dipping the bill into water and holding it there, drink somewhat like a horse, making pumping or sucking motions in the throat—these are pigeons and doves; also at least one species of estrildine finch, *Poephila gouldiae*, of n. Australia, and fulmars (*see* in Shearwater Family).

Sandgrouse, although resembling grouse in general shape, color, and choice of habitat, are, according to Gilliard (1958), an evolutionary offshoot of the stock that produced pigeons. *See* Columbiformes. Recent evidence, however, suggests that sandgrouse are not related to the doves and pigeons, but to the Charadriiformes, an order of birds that includes the shorebirds. *See* Charadriiformes. After studies of two species of sandgrouse in the Kalahari Gemsbok Park of South Africa, Maclean (1967) proposed that sandgrouse (presently in the family Pteroclididae) be included in the order Charadriiformes instead of in Columbiformes (see, however, Stegmann, 1969). He also discovered that the sandgrouse he studied swallowed water like most birds do, by lifting the head, and not sucking it up as previously reported.

Many birds occasionally *wet their food* before eating it—some gulls, for example (see Bent, 1921)—this may aid swallowing besides cleaning it of mud or sand. Evenden (1943) watched a pair of dippers (*see* Dipper Family) in the mountains of w. Ore. wash or wet insects and grubs before feeding them to their young. They held the food crosswise in the bill and twisted the head rapidly from side to side in water to wash and wet the food before carrying it to the nest.

In Egypt, a cattle egret, after catching a large beetle, walked to water and immersed the insect three times before swallowing it. In Great Britain, after an observation in Holland in 1946 of curlew sandpipers wetting food,

came a host of records: a whimbrel wetting crabs; a snipe, earthworms; godwits wetting food—in curlews it was reported to be normal—and dunlins, greenshanks, redshanks, ringed plovers, and oystercatchers, all reported washing or wetting their food as a possible aid to swallowing it. Apparently the practice may be normal among shorebirds—the sandpipers, snipes, plovers, and their relatives (Rand, 1955). *See* Shorebird.

SWALLOWS OF CAPISTRANO
See introduction to Swallow Family.

SWAMP
See definition under Marsh Bird.

SWAMP ANGEL
See Thrush, hermit, and Thrush, wood, in Thrush Family.

SWAMP BIRD
See general definition under Marsh Bird.

SWAN
See in Duck Family.

SWAN SONG
For many years, the legend of the song of the dying swan was regarded as a myth (*see* Folklore), but Delacour (1954) thought it might be based on truth, in that a swan, when shot, exhaling air from its long trachea, or windpipe (*see* Voice and Sound-making), can make a prolonged musical note. Elliott (1898), a very reliable observer, wrote that a whistling swan shot from a considerable height over Currituck Sound, N.C., by a member of his hunting party, at once began its "song" as it fell, which continued until it struck the water almost half a mile away. Elliott knew every note a whistling swan ordinarily utters, but this one from the stricken bird was a sound he had never heard before—it was "the song of the dying swan."

Hochbaum (1955), a scientist and specialist in studies of waterfowl, wrote that the "departure song" of the whistling swan is one of the most beautiful utterances of waterfowl—a melodious, soft, muted series of notes that always precedes its takeoff into the air, and that this "is probably the swan song of legend, for when a swan is shot and falls crippled to the water, it utters this call as it tries in vain to rejoin its fellows in the sky." *See* biographies of swans in Duck Family.

SWAN UPPING
See Swan, mute, under Duck Family.

SWEAT GLANDS
Birds do not have them, but are able to lose some of their body heat by vaporization of the moisture from the skin; however, birds are pre-eminently "panting animals" and their evaporative cooling comes mostly from the moist membranes lining the respiratory tract (Sturkie, 1965). *See* Respiratory System; Heat and Birds.

SWIFT FAMILY
Apodidae (ah-POD-ih-dee); Lat., from Gr. *apous, apodos*, without feet. Swifts have feet,

but legs so small and weak that if swift alights on ground, may have difficulty taking off (Lack, 1964b); capable of swiftest flight among small birds; about 80 species, worldwide (Van Tyne and Berger, 1976), except in polar regions and some oceanic islands; 4 species regularly in N. America and 3 stragglers from Asia; not songbirds, or perching birds, but classified with hummingbirds (*see* Apodiformes); superficially resemble swallows, which are songbirds (see some differences in introduction to Swallow Family); have streamlined bodies, sparrow size to small, slender hawk size; sexes outwardly alike; bill short, tiny, slightly downcurved; mouth wide, gape (mouth opening) extends back under eyes; long, pointed wings curve backward like scimitars, adapted to high-speed flight (have "high-speed wings" like falcons, sandpipers, swallows); have 10 long primary feathers, tail has 10 feathers; in some species, tail is short, stiff, with needlelike spiny tips; in others, deeply forked (Gilliard, 1958); swifts have strong claws adapted to clinging to rock walls, chimneys, and other vertical surfaces; colors are usually plain grays or solid browns; some with patches of white or pale gray.

Swifts are gregarious (social); live largely on insects they catch in air (Alpine swift of s. Europe may carry 600 in ball in throat while feeding young—see Arni-Willi, 1959); probably spend more hours in flight than any other land birds; long-held belief that some European swifts, *Apus apus*, ascend to considerable heights in sky to spend night on wing (Lack, 1956) confirmed by Swiss observer (Weitnauer, 1956) from aircraft; swifts are so adapted to aerial life that all food-gathering, courting, drinking, bathing, gathering of nest materials, and even copulation (also at nest) accomplished while flying.

The 3½-oz. adult Alpine swift, *Apus melba*, of mountains of s. Europe and Himalayas, while flying at 37–62 m.p.h. catches insects in opened mouth (Arni-Willi, 1959); often flies at 80 m.p.h. when feeding (Meinertzhagen, 1955); in India, speeds of 172 and 218 m.p.h. said to have been attained by needle-tailed swifts (Stuart-Baker, 1922; Collins and Brooke, 1976). See, however, Wallace (1963, p. 118).

A European swift is estimated to fly at least 560 mi. a day during nesting season (Hess, 1951); a banded American chimney swift that lived for 9 years was estimated, during its lifetime, to have flown 1,350,000 mi., including round trips each year between U.S. (its summer home) and S. America, where it winters (Wing, 1956).

Typical flight of swift is series of rapid shallow wingbeats followed by short glides; wingbeats so fast, hard to follow; was once believed that N. American chimney swift and European swift each beat their wings alternately in flight —"an optical illusion," according to Lack (1956) —until Westover (1932) showed by slow-motion photography that chimney swift beats its wings in unison; this verified stroboscopically by Savile (1950); however, when chimney swift turns sharply in flight, it beats one wing more strongly than the other. Wings of swifts have short massive bones, compared with slender bones of swallows' wings; rigidity of swifts' wings makes flight seem jerky or "flickering"

compared with swallows' fluid wingbeats (Savile, 1950).

Most swifts glue their nest materials together with saliva from their large salivary glands, unusually large in nesting season; one group of Far East swiftlets builds nests entirely of saliva (*see* discussion under Mouth).

Some swifts become torpid during periods of cool weather when flying insects unavailable—for example, the N. American white-throated swift and the common swift, *Apus apus*, of Europe (Lack, 1964b).

Swifts are long-lived: one pair of Alpine swifts used same nest site for 11 years, and a male for 17 years, was found dead at the nest in 18th year (Arni-Willi, 1959); a European swift, *Apus apus*, banded in Sweden, was retrapped when 17 years old.

Swifts are protected by law (*see* Legal Protection) and may not be kept in captivity without a permit; however, to help an injured or sick bird, offer it mealworms, canned dog food, ground meat, mockingbird food, rolled into small balls (Walker, 1942); also flies, beetles, and other insects.

Black swift, *Cypseloides niger* (sip-seh-LOY-deez NYE-jer); genus name: Lat., from Gr. *kypselos*, swift, and *eidos*, likeness, like or pertaining to swifts; species name: Lat., black (Coble, 1954). (Color ill., page 853.) In N. America, summers from Alaska to s. Calif., and in much of Rocky Mtn. region (Bent, 1940); rare or uncommon, largest of N. American swifts, not often seen because flies high over western mountains and in canyons; sexes alike; 7–7½ in. long; wingspread 15 in.; is nearly solid black, somewhat silvery on forehead and under wings; has narrower, longer wings than similar male purple martin; wings curved but without bend at "wrists" as in martin and other swallows; slightly forked tail, fanned wide sometimes when bird in flight; was unreported in N. America until 1857; first N. American nest discovered on Calif. sea cliff in June 1901 (Bent, 1940); lives where rocky cliffs available for somewhat specialized nest site; but with superb powers of flight often ranges far away from nesting area; as summer storm approaches, like European swift, comes from wide area to flock at edge of clouds, follows cloud for hundreds of miles to feed in warm insect-laden air mass; from this habit often called cloud swift; on clear days may ascend until invisible at height of several thousand feet; while circling and gliding, holds wings downward below body (anhedral position —see illustration in Jack, 1953), which increases ability to make quick turns; usually silent but in nesting area pairs utter high-pitched chattering *plik-plik-plik-plik*.

Feeding Habits: Feeds entirely on wing, eats caddis flies, mayflies, crane flies, flesh flies, midges, also beetles, termites, flying ants, aphids, ants, bees, wasps, spiders. Glick (1939), sampling air from aircraft, found abundance of flies, aphids, etc., also spiders up to great heights in air.

Nest: In small colonies, on sea cliff, ledge, or in deep dark crevice of moist mountain canyons, near or behind waterfalls; round shallow or

SWIFT FAMILY

During migration, a flock of swifts will gather at a chimney at sunset and circle, sometimes for nearly an hour, until the birds closest to the opening begin to drop into the shaft to roost; the rest of the flock follows in a thin stream.

deep cup of mud, mosses, algae on ledge under overhanging rock or in cave.

Eggs: June–July; 1, white.

Incubation: Period of and age when young first fly unknown; young can and do go long periods without food; young fed partly digested insects by parents.

Weights: 43–47 gr. (Collins, C. T., unpubl.).

Range: Nests from se. Alaska, B.C., s. Alta., w. Wash., Mont., south to Rocky Mtn. states of Colo., N.M., Nev., and to s. Calif., south to Costa Rica and West Indies; winter range not precisely known, but tropical America.

Chimney swift, *Chaetura pelagica* (kee-TOO-rah peh-LADGE-ih-kah); genus name: Lat., from Gr. *chaite,* stiff hair, bristle, or spine, and *oura,* tail; spine-tailed; species name: Lat., from Gr. *pelagios,* of the sea (Coble, 1954), but see discussion by Gruson (1972). (Color ill., page 854.) Usually only swift east of Missouri and Mississippi R.; summers from s. Canada, Dakotas, to Atlantic, south to Tex. and Fla.; sexes outwardly alike; 4½–5½ in. long; wingspread 12–12¾ in.; entirely sooty gray, short-bodied; long, narrow, curved wings, almost always seen flying; wing strokes jerky, hurried, batlike; appears like flying cigar, has short, spine-tipped tail (helps prop swift when clinging to vertical surface); in summer seen in continual rapid daylight flight over open country, towns, woods; sails and circles on set wings, then with flickering wingbeats shoots like arrow through air, uttering sharp chippering notes; often flies in threes (two males chasing a female—Fischer, 1958); moves north, often in loose flocks, through U.S. usually in Apr.–May; when migrating flock goes to roost, choose large capacious chimney or airshaft, assemble in air and circle above it during hour before sunset, all flying in same direction, around and around, when lowest birds start dropping into opening, followed by others, appears like column of smoke going back into chimney (Fischer, 1958); inside, swifts cling with sharp nails to sooty walls in rows and clusters, overlapping like shingles on a roof; larger flocks in fall; Groskin (1945) watched 10,000 enter large chimney in Pa. in Sept., all inside within 37 minutes; many return to same barns or chimneys to nest; courtship is rapid flight of pair or small groups with loud twittering; sometimes fly at night when feeding young (Tyler, 1940a).

Feeding Habits: Eats beetles, flies, ants, termites, bugs, caught in flight, also spiders. *See* discussion of availability of insects in air under Black swift.

Nest: Site is generally dark, sheltered place, primitive site, hollow trees, now commonly in chimneys, barns, silos; a shallow bracketlike cup glued against wall or on joists, rafters, inside buildings; sometimes in open well, cistern; built of twigs broken off by feet of swift while in flight, cemented together and attached, for example, to inside wall of chimney with glutinous saliva of swift (*see* discussion under Mouth); sometimes nest together in large numbers, as in air shafts, Kent State University, Ohio, but usually one pair in smaller house chimney, several feet from top, 2–22 ft. down;

late-spring or early-summer chills and subsequent fires built in fireplace or starting of automatic furnace may dump young swifts into fireplace or living room.

Eggs: May–July; 2–7, usually 4–5, white.

Incubation: By both sexes, 19–21 days; young first fly when 30 days old (Fischer, 1958); young regularly return to nest after first flight.

Other Names: Chimney-bird; chimney swallow; chimney sweep.

Accidents: One struck by lightning found badly burned at Quincy, Ill. Large group killed by carbon monoxide gas while roosting in chimney of large store.

Age: Few live beyond 4 years; one 9, one 11 at Nashville, Tenn.; Dexter (1960) retrapped banded bird when it was at least 13 years old; another reported by Kennard (1975) when it was 14 years old.

Flight Speed: Timed in Mich., 15–21 m.p.h. (Schnell, 1965).

Weights: 1,893 birds, 16.1–33.5 gr., average 22.8 gr. (Coffey, 1958).

Range: Nests from se. Sask. east to Nova Scotia, south to se. Tex., Gulf coast states, c. Fla.; winters upper Amazon Basin, S. America; casual in N.D., Mont., N.M., and Utah.

Common swift, *Apus apus* (AY-pus); genus and species name: from Gr. *apous,* without feet; *see* family introduction. Eurasian swift of n. Eurasia, Africa, n. India, ne. China, straggler on St. Paul Is., Pribilof Is., Alaska; 6–7 in. long (about twice size of chimney swift); dark above, paler below with white throat, long wings, short, moderately forked tail. See Lack (1956) for life history.

Vaux's swift, *Chaetura vauxi* (kee-TOO-rah VAUKS-eye); genus name: *see* Chimney swift; species name: for 19th-century Philadelphia naturalist, William Sansom Vaux. Smallest N. American swift; western counterpart of chimney swift but with paler underparts; 4–4½ in. long; wingspread 11½ in.; sexes alike; appears and acts like chimney swift; summers from Alaska south to c. Calif., east to Mont., through most of range less numerous than chimney swift of e. U.S.; more or less common around Seattle, Wash., where arrives in late Apr.; comparatively recent nesting in chimneys, still a wilderness bird; a common nesting place is hollow of tall dead stub of redwood or other tree and inside burned-out stumps, but as forests disappear, expected to adapt more and more to nesting in chimneys; flies about, darting erratic batlike flight; likes to feed over lakes and rivers that provide openings in forest; in fall migration, often roosts in very large flock within tall hollow tree or chimney; flock whirls down and enters like long black rope (Bent, 1940); in flight utters rapid, faint twitter, *chip-chip-chip-cheweet-cheweet,* usually only during courtship.

Feeding Habits: Catches flying insects in air, usually high above trees, sometimes close to ground on dull, damp days.

Nest: Small, usually built within 20 in. to 6 ft. up from bottom of cavity; saucer-shaped, of twigs or spruce and pine needles glued to inside wall of hollow tree or chimney.

Vaux's swift

SWIFT FAMILY

White-throated swift

Eggs: May–July; 3–6, commonly 4–6, white.
Incubation: Probably about 19 days; young first fly when 20–21 days old.
Weights: About 17 gr., or about ⅔ oz.
Range: Locally, from se. Alaska, ne. B.C. and w. Mont., south to c. Calif., also to C. America; winters casually from c. Calif., s. La., south, regularly from Mexico to Panama.

White-rumped swift, *Apus pacificus* (AY-pus pah-SIF-ih-cus); genus name: *see* Common swift; species name: Lat., of the Pacific. E. Asiatic species that has strayed once to St. George Is., Alaska; 6½–7½ in. long; dark swift distinguished by its white rump, well-forked tail, barred underparts (Lack, 1956). See Jourdain (1940) for life history.

White-throated needle-tailed swift,
Hirundapus caudacutus (hear-UN-da-puscow-da-COO-tus). First record for N. America on May 21, 1974, when swift was collected on Shemya Is., Aleutian Is. Normally breeds in temperate Asia, n. China and Japan; other races nest in Himalayas, Malaysian Pen., Sumatra, Java, and Taiwan.

White-throated swift, *Aeronautes saxatalis* (ay-err-oh-NAW-teez sacks-AT-ih-lis); genus name: Lat., from Gr. *aer*, air, and *nautes*, sailor; species name: Lat., pertaining to a rock; sometimes called rock swift. Summers in mountains of Far West, s. Canada to Tex.; 6–7 in. long; sexes similar; generally sooty black with white throat and *broad white streak* down center of breast to belly, *white patches along sides at rear* (similar violet-green swallow is *all-white below*); tail slightly forked; distinguished from other swifts by its boldly black-and-white pattern; summers on coastal cliffs, in steep mountain canyons, rugged foothills, ranges over adjacent valleys in West; one of fastest-flying swifts and possibly fastest-flying N. American bird; has been seen escaping from stoop of peregrine falcon at speeds estimated at more than 200 m.p.h. (Cogswell, 1957c); arrives on nesting range Mar.–May; courtship entirely on wing, copulation in air with bodies together, pinwheeling downward through air; also in nesting crevices; flight is dashing at tremendous speed, darts, swoops, changes direction in flash; call note a shrill, laughing *he he he he* when two or three coursing together; also shrill twitter; nests in rocky cliffs of seacoasts, on rocky islands, and in mountains to 10,000–13,000 ft.

Feeding Habits: In flight, catches flies, beetles, bees, wasps, winged ants, bugs, leafhoppers, squash bugs.
Nest: In cracks, crevices on rocky, high, often inaccessible cliff faces, extremely difficult to reach by predators or man; sometimes flimsy or well-rounded cup of feathers, grasses, cemented together with swift's saliva, glued to wall, usually well back in crevice; some have nested in cracks of walls of buildings, particularly in the old mission at San Juan Capistrano, Calif.; some swifts have been found dormant in Jan. in Calif. within rock crevices (Hanna, 1917); see also Bartholomew *et al.* (1957) and *see* under Torpidity.

Eggs: May–June; 3–6, commonly 4–5, white.
Incubation: Period of and age when young first fly unknown.
Weights: 26–36 gr., about 1¼ oz. (Collins, C. T., unpubl.).
Range: Nests from s. B.C., s. Alta., to Mont., nw. S.D., nw. Neb., se. Wyo., e. Colo., N.M., w. Tex., west to s. Calif., c. Ariz., and southward to C. America. Overwinters in south part of breeding range and in C. America.

SWIMMING AND DIVING

All birds float, even such land birds as blue jays and American robins, because of the buoyancy of the air held in their feathers, air sacs associated with the lungs (*see* Respiratory System), and air-filled bones. They are not webfooted, densely plumaged, heavy swimming birds, however, and if carried onto water by storms or otherwise undergo accidental immersion, and their feathers become sodden, they may drown (for an exception, *see* Dipper Family). All aquatic birds swim, but not all can dive and swim skillfully and deeply below the surface. Some of the truly aquatic N. American birds that dive and swim well underwater are: loons, grebes, cormorants, anhingas, and members of the Auk Family, and many ducks—the oldsquaw, harlequin, eiders, scoters, ruddies, and mergansers, for example. These swimming and diving birds have become adapted to living in or on the water much of the time; they have webbed feet, powerful leg muscles, large oil (uropygial) glands, and dense, air-filled plumage. *See* discussions under Skin Glands; Preening.

THE SWIMMER'S FOOT. Many unrelated birds that can swim—the petrels, gulls, auks, members of the Duck Family (ducks, geese, and swans), for example—have webbed feet that serve them as paddles. Two types of the webbed swimming foot are the *palmate* foot, as in loons, petrels, gulls, auks, and ducks, in which three toes are joined together by webs, and the *totipalmate* foot, as in cormorants, gannets, pelicans, and their relatives (*see* Pelecaniformes), in which the four toes are joined by webs—the so-called "perfect" swimming foot (Boyd, 1964). A third kind is the *lobed* foot, as in coots, grebes, and phalaropes, in which each toe, along its edges, has independent webs. *See* Feet and Legs.

HOW BIRDS SWIM. In swimming on the surface, a bird such as a duck or goose moves its feet alternately, as in walking. When it pushes a foot backward against the water to drive the bird ahead, its toes and webs are fully spread and the strong muscles of its leg drive it forward. When the bird brings the foot forward its webs and toes are folded together so that the leg can move with almost no resistance against the water. Grebes, with their lobed feet, differ in turning the foot 90° and bringing the foot more or less sideways on one stroke. The only surface-swimming bird that is known to go about it differently on occasion is the mute swan, and then only when it is threatening another swan or other intruder in its territory (Heinroth and Heinroth, 1958). In its excitement or anger it paddles vigorously with both feet at the same time, causing water to "boil," or foam up, against its breast.

SWIMMING UNDERWATER. Most birds that dive from the surface of the water to feed below use one of two methods of propelling themselves underwater: either by swimming with the paddling feet or by "flying" underwater, using both wings, with the feet trailing behind. Cormorants, anhingas, loons, and grebes, in their foot-propelled dives, use their feet synchronously while underwater, although alternately when swimming on the surface (Townsend, 1909) (cormorants and anhingas may also use their wings); most diving ducks swim underwater with their feet, and hold their wings tightly against the body (Welty, 1962), with the exception of some wing motion by eiders and the white-winged scoter (Boyd, 1964). See, however, A. Brooks (1945) for interesting details. According to Heinroth and Heinroth (1958), most diving ducks, also loons and grebes, while swimming underwater, keep their wings folded in the oily flank feathers that form a pocket on each side of the body (called a "feather pocket"), in which the wings are kept dry and ready for instant flight upon reaching the surface (Welty, 1962).

Mallards and swans, which dive only occasionally, do so with the wings partly extended (Boyd, 1964), but members of the Auk Family—auklets, dovekies, murres, puffins, and diving petrels—are able and highly specialized divers that use their short, stubby wings to "fly" underwater and steer usually with their feet. Their wings, still useful for flying through the air, are less adapted to underwater flight than the penguins' flippers, which have lost the power of aerial flight. *See* Auk Family. The dipper, or water ouzel, of mountain streams of w. N. America, also uses its wings to "fly" underwater. The members of the small Dipper Family are the only truly aquatic songbirds known. *See* Dipper Family.

DEPTH OF DIVES. Most birds usually dive from the surface by arching slightly out of water, then nosing downward (ducks, for example), but often the heavier, deep-diving birds simply settle or sink down in the water. To do so, they bring their specific gravity (relative density) close to that of water. Some diving birds such as loons and grebes have relatively solid rather than lighter, more hollow bones of typical flying birds. This makes them less buoyant and, like cormorants and anhingas, they make themselves even less so by expelling air from their air sacs, also by depressing the body plumage, thus forcing out air normally trapped in the feathers. See Casler (1973). While underwater they obtain oxygen from oxyhemoglobin in the blood and oxymoglobin in the muscles, two respiratory pigments of which diving birds have greater amounts (Schorger, 1947; Storer, 1960a).

Apparently, some diving birds can go under to remarkable depths. The common loon has been taken in commercial fishermen's nets 180 and 200 ft. below the surface (Roberts, T.S., 1932); the oldsquaw, a diving duck, has been caught frequently in the Great Lakes in gill nets set 90–162 ft. below the surface, and elsewhere at 180 ft. deep, and in incredible numbers (Schorger, 1947). *See also* records of birds under Auk Family.

HOW LONG DO BIRDS STAY SUBMERGED? According to Schorger (1947), Dr. Stresemann, a noted German ornithologist, thought that dives of birds feeding below the surface seldom last more than 90 seconds; the longest dive noted by Schorger of an oldsquaw was 70 seconds; however, according to Jourdain (1913), a wounded loon was still alive after 15 minutes underwater, and other loons have remained below for 8–10 minutes. See interesting review by Kooyman *et al.* (1971).

Douglas D. Dow (1964) timed "feeding" dives of seven kinds of water birds near Vancouver, B.C., in fall and early winter: horned grebe, 29–40 seconds; pelagic cormorant, 24–60 seconds; common goldeneye, about 25–41 seconds; oldsquaw, about 48–67 seconds; surf scoter, 33–65 seconds; red-breasted merganser, about 42–47 seconds; and American coot, 2–12 seconds. Heintzelman and Newberry (1963) timed a pied-billed grebe's dives at 6 or 8 to about 16 seconds; a ruddy duck, 17.4–21.8 seconds.

THE "PLUNGE" DIVERS. Tropic-birds feed by plunging from 50 ft. or more above the surface into the sea, but are rather poor swimmers and divers; the gannet, like its relatives the boobies, in its fishing is a spectacular plunge diver; it streaks headlong into the sea and hits with tremendous impact that carries it deep below the surface. One was reported to have struck a board about 6 ft. below the surface with such force that the impact drove its bill firmly into the wood and broke its neck (Lane, 1954). The gannets and boobies have special adaptations to prevent damage from diving—an especially strong skull and a system of air sacs just below the skin that, like those of the brown pelican, also a plunge diver, are believed to be primarily shock-absorbing (Boyd, 1964). Many terns plunge-dive for their food but do not go far below the surface. Kingfishers and the osprey (land birds) also plunge-dive from considerable heights. After sighting a fish, the osprey folds its wings and plunges toward the water, but breaks its dive just before striking the surface, reaches below with its feet and talons, and sometimes, although not always, submerges completely. Kingfishers, however, dive headfirst into water for small fishes from a perch or from a hovering place in the air in shallow dives but do not regularly swim (Boyd, 1964). *See* Kingfisher Family.

SOME OTHER BIRDS THAT SWIM AND DIVE. Nearly all of the rails swim well, but only gallinules and coots (in Rail Family) are primarily aquatic birds. Among shorebirds, phalaropes have lobed toes adapted to swimming; avocets and stilts swim well, and the greater yellowlegs swims easily for some distance on water. The spotted sandpiper can dive and remain underwater if attacked by a hawk, as reported by Kelso (1926). *See also* Jacana Family.

LAND BIRDS THAT SWIM OR ALIGHT ON WATER. Great blue herons alight on the water and may rest on the surface for a while before rising into the air again (Grasett, 1926; Longley, 1960); an observer in n. Greece saw a night heron alight on a lake for about 10 seconds, pick up something from the surface in its bill, then easily take off; also, a little bittern alighted on a lake, then sprang up from the surface and flew off (Squire, 1965). J. K. Potter reported in *Bird Lore* (1936) an immature black-crowned night heron that he watched swimming and searching for food on a pond covered with duckweed. Heard (1960) saw a covey of bobwhites swim ashore after alighting on a lake in Okla.; *see*, however, another account of covey that drowned in biography of bobwhite in Pheasant Family.

In an aerial encounter between two bald eagles fighting over a cormorant in the Pacific O. off B.C., one of the eagles dropped the cormorant. It immediately swooped to the surface of the water to retrieve its prey but could not fly into the air with it. It then towed the cormorant for about 150 yds. across the water to a rocky islet, where it dried its plumage, then flew with its prey about 3 mi. to shore (Campbell, R.W., 1969). Bent (1937) reported an even more spectacular event in which a bald eagle in Fla., after catching a double-crested cormorant, was lying flat on the water with its wings spread wide, apparently too exhausted to fly. It was joined by two other eagles; the three of them then took turns towing the cormorant to shore, where they immediately began to feast on it. *See also* Dragging, or Towing, Food under Food and Feeding Habits.

SYLVIIDAE
See Old World Warbler Family under Warbler.

SYMBIOSIS
(sim-bih-OH-sis). Term for a relationship between two different species of animals (or plants) that live in a close association from which they both receive mutual benefit. According to Rothschild and Clay (1957), a bird that may justifiably be considered a symbiotic partner of man is the barn owl. It regularly nests and roosts in church steeples, silos, sheds, and barns, and in return for such man-provided available shelter, renders valuable economic services to man by destroying large numbers of rats, mice, and other rodents often especially harmful to farm crops. *See* Economic Ornithology; *see* biography of barn owl in Owl—Barn Owl Family.

Another casual but frequent symbiotic relationship is that between starlings and domestic sheep and cows in Europe, in which starlings, feeding on insects stirred up by the feet of the grazing animals, reportedly alight occasionally on the backs of the sheep and cows to pick off and eat disease-carrying ectoparasites (*see* Parasite). Magpies, jackdaws, and rooks not infrequently perch on the backs of sheep to pick off ectoparasites and to pluck out fly larvae that live just below the sheep's skin (Rothschild and Clay, 1957).

Red phalaropes frequently attend surface-shoaling large fishes and whales to gain food when removing troublesome ectoparasites from the backs of these marine animals. A similar symbiotic relationship may exist between the Egyptian plover, or crocodile bird, *Pluvianus aegyptius*, and the spur-winged plover, *Vanellus spinosus*, and crocodiles. Each of these birds is said, at times, to enter the opened mouths of basking crocodiles to pluck leeches from their gums. The subject, however, is controversial because many experienced observers of these birds have not noted the habit. Meinertzhagen (1959) gives his own reports, however, including apparently authoritative accounts by others, of seeing both of these birds, in separate incidents, enter a crocodile's mouth to pick its teeth, with the crocodile opening its mouth at the appearance of the birds "as though the crocodile expected and invited the birds. . . . It has also been suggested that the spur-winged plover serves to warn crocodiles of danger, while the bird profits from the partnership by feeding on insects at the basking ground, in addition to removing parasites and debris from the crocodile's mouth" (Meinertzhagen, 1959).

In N., C., and S. America, hummingbirds have a true symbiotic relationship with certain flowering plants. With their long, slender bills they gather nectar and insects from flowers and in doing so pick up pollen on the feathers of the breast and head and on the bill, which they carry from flower to flower, thus effecting cross-pollination. *See* Pollination.

Birds that eat fruit, such as catbirds, mockingbirds, starlings, robins, and waxwings, for example, have a symbiotic relationship with berry-producing trees, shrubs, and vines. The birds are attracted to the often colorful fruit, eat the pulp, and either regurgitate or excrete the seeds. After falling on the ground, the seeds often sprout and grow into a new plant. In this way, the birds "repay" the plants for the benefit of their fruit and the plants achieve dispersal and continued propagation. *See also* Autolycism; Commensalism; Parasite, for other interesting relationships of birds with other animals or with plants of the environment.

SYMPATRIC (sim-PAT-rick) **SPECIES**
Term for birds (or other animals) whose ranges of distribution are over much the same area, yet the two remain specifically distinct. *See* Species; related discussion under Allopatric Species. *See also* Sibling Species.

SYNDACTYL
(sin-DAK-til). *See* Feet and Legs; for examples of birds with syndactylous feet, *see* Coraciiformes.

SYNSACRUM
(sin-SAY-crum). A solidly fused series of vertebrae in the pelvic (hip) region of a bird. The last thoracic (rib-bearing) vertebra and the sacral and caudal vertebrae form the rigid, girderlike synsacrum. *See* Skeleton.

SYRINX
(SIR-ingks). The "voice box" of a bird. *See* Voice and Sound-making; Songs and Singing.

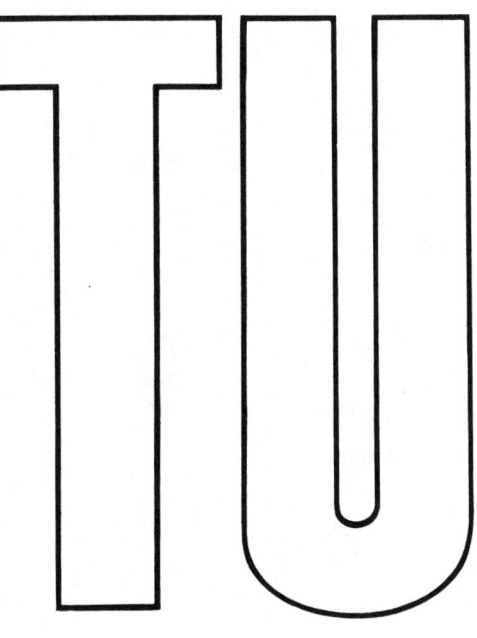

TAIGA

(TIE-gah). Russian word for the coniferous forest land of vast parts of the North Temperate Zone; the taiga is just south of the Arctic tundra (*see* Tundra) and is also called the *Transcontinental Coniferous Forest* (Pettingill, 1970). In N. America it extends in general across c. and s. Canada, paralleling the Arctic tundra on the north. *See* Major Biotic Communities under Distribution. The taiga is in general dense forests of pines, spruces, hemlocks, firs, white cedars *(Thuja)*, and Douglas fir *(Pseudotsuga)*. Some typical birds of the taiga are: the goshawk, spruce grouse, hawk owl, the three-toed woodpeckers, gray jay, redbreasted nuthatch, winter wren, hermit thrush, the kinglets, many American wood warblers, pine grosbeak, crossbills, juncos, and the white-throated sparrow. See Pettingill (1970) for more detailed lists.

TAIL

When ornithologists refer to the tail of a bird, they usually mean the conspicuous feathers of the tail (quills) so important to a bird in flight. A bird uses its tail feathers, especially when spread in flight, to supplement the lifting surfaces of its wings, as a rudder to steer to left and right, as an "elevator" when raising and lowering the tail, and as a brake when depressed to slow its forward speed (Pettingill, 1970).

Some birds with efficient tails (crows, ravens, peregrine falcons, for example) can loop the loop, fly upside down, or do backward somersaults somewhat like a tumbler pigeon (Beebe, 1906; 1965). Some birds with short tails and small wings, such as ducks, cannot make sharp turns in the air as can the longer-tailed and broader-winged soaring hawks. *See* Flight.

The tail feathers, or "steering feathers," are called collectively the *rectrices* (sing.: *rectrix*), and the fusing of the bones of the tail into a pygostyle (*see* Pygostyle; *also* Skeleton) has resulted in drawing together the paired tail feathers into a fan shape (Beebe, 1965). The separate tail feathers are identified, or referred to, by a numbering system, counting outward from the right and left members of the central pair. They are numbered 1 to 6 on each side of the center of the tail. Most commonly there are 12 rectrices in the passerines, or songbirds. In a few others among N. American birds there are a total of 8 tail feathers (anis), and in some birds (most hummingbirds, swifts, and cuckoos) 10; 16 in grouse; 18 in the ring-necked pheasant; 24 in the American white pelican (see Van Tyne and Berger, 1959).

Among N. American birds, tails range in length from the rudimentary tails in grebes and the short, stubby tails of wrens to the long, handsome tails of the scissor-tailed flycatcher, the swallow-tailed kite, the magpies, and the introduced ring-necked pheasant. A tail is said to be *long* when it is longer than the bird's body; *short* when it is shorter than the body length. Above and below the true tail feathers are the *upper* and *lower* tail coverts, which grow from the skin above and below the true tail feathers and conceal their bases. *See* Topography.

In addition to using the true tail feathers in

graduated (Black-billed cuckoo)

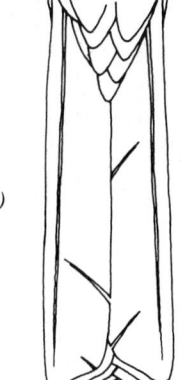

square (Sharp-shinned hawk)

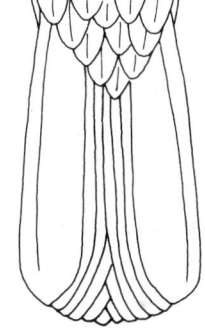

rounded (Common crow)

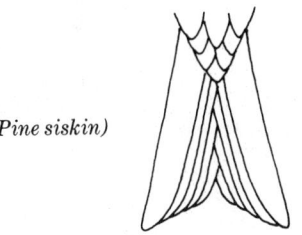

emarginate (Pine siskin)

TAIL

The shape of the tail is determined by the relative length of the flight feathers of the tail, or rectrices, and is a useful structural character in field identification. A tail is graduated if the rectrices become longer toward the center; in a rounded tail this progression is slight. A square tail has a straight tip formed by rectrices that are all approximately the same length, and an emarginate tail is formed by feathers that are progressively longer from the center out.

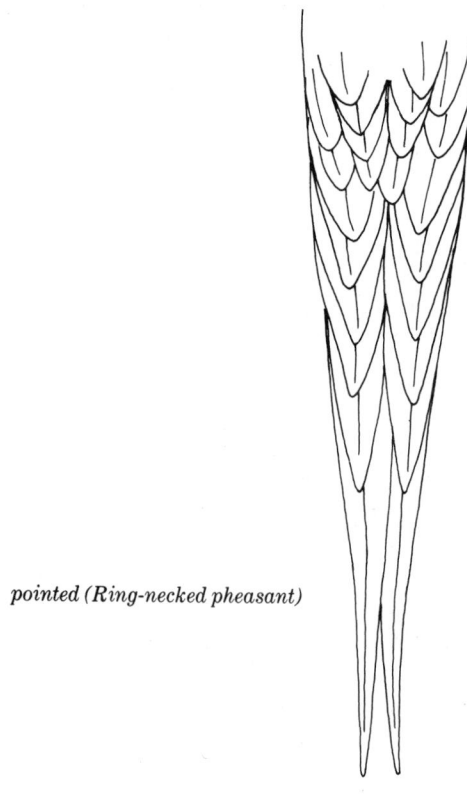

pointed (Ring-necked pheasant)

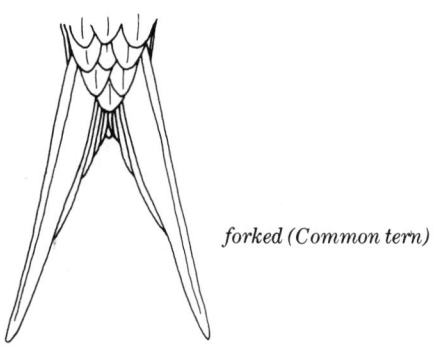

forked (Common tern)

TAIL
A pointed or acute tail is one in which the rectrices in the center are distinctly longer than those on the outside. The tail is forked if the outer rectrices are very much longer than those in the center.

flight, four groups of New World birds—the tropical woodhewers and the N. American creeper, woodpeckers, and some swifts—use their tails as a prop, or support, when clinging to, or moving up, the vertical surfaces of trees, walls, etc. *See* Climbing Birds. These birds may be said to sit on their tails, but they also use them as a rudder for steering in flight.

If the tail is of any considerable size, whether it has ornamental plumes as in the peacocks, or not, it often plays a large part in the displays of birds, especially in courtship, when it is often raised or sometimes depressed. It is partly spread in the courtship of the ring-necked pheasant; it is raised and widely fanned especially by the wild turkey.

Many birds move the tail when excited. Wrens, whose tails are turned up and often carried very high over the back, often twitch and jerk the tail with every passing mood (Beebe, 1906; 1965). The least flycatcher jerks its tail with its every uttered *che-bec!* note, and some birds that live along streams, ponds, or other waterways bob the tail up and down almost constantly (spotted sandpiper, solitary sandpiper) or bob the body and move the tail up and down (northern waterthrush), and some pipits and wagtails wag the tail or bob it up and down. Many birds raise the tail in defecating, which helps prevent soiling of the undertail coverts; both the females and males usually deflect the tail laterally during copulation.

"TALKING" BIRDS
See Mimicry; *also* in introduction to Parrot Family; Starling Family.

TALON
See Claws under Feet and Legs.

TAMENESS
Most adult wild N. American birds, like those in other parts of the world, usually fear people and, as Lack (1953) wrote, "avoid mankind, usually with too good cause." Their normal reaction to the approach of a person is to hide, fly, or become wary and ready for flight (*see* Escape Distance), just as they do at the sight of their natural enemies. Young birds (song sparrows, for example) are conditioned in the nest by the behavior of their parents to what to fear and what not to fear; others acquire it from the parents soon after they leave the nest (*see* discussion of this under Fear). However, there are some remarkable exceptions to fear behavior shown by N. American birds.

According to Thorpe (1956b), just as wildness of behavior may be inherited in certain species and populations of birds, so may tameness be genetic. There are all gradations in birds of fear and of tameness, between species, and even within a species, and between local populations of a species. At times, often for reasons unknown, individual birds show extraordinary fearlessness of man.

As pointed out by Rand (1955), some American robins, so tame in our gardens, in wilderness areas may be very wild and will fly away apparently in great fear while the human intruder is still far distant. On the other hand, Henry Kyllingstad, while banding birds in northern forests, picked up fearless but wild

kinglets from the branches of spruce trees as one might pluck wild fruit. The kinglets did not recognize him as an enemy, or at least as something to fear.

The most striking and characteristic trait of the Canada (gray) jay of the northern forests is its tameness or boldness, which matches that of the smaller chickadees. Around wilderness camps, it will enter tents and cabins or perch on the bow of a canoe within a couple of feet of the human paddler, and in its curiosity will often fly to within a few feet of a stranger in the woods to scrutinize him close up, and then will follow him to see what he will do (Bent, 1946). Pine grosbeaks, pine siskins, and crossbills of the north woods in winter are so tame that one can approach them and almost catch them in one's hands (Bent, Part I, 1968). Burleigh (1930), reporting an invasion (*see* Irruption) of Bohemian waxwings from northern forests onto the campus of the University of Washington, wrote that about 800 of these birds were so tame that one could walk up to within a foot of them; one alighted on Burleigh's shoulders, another on his head.

The following accounts by reliable witnesses show that other adult wild birds, at certain times and under certain circumstances, are extraordinarily fearless of people. In the spring of 1943, a six-year-old girl walked from her garden into her home at Louisville, Ky., trailed by a golden-crowned kinglet. It hopped along the ground, followed the girl into the house, and then flew to her shoulders. The kinglet showed an unusually strong attachment to the child and even a marked possessiveness. The child's mother took the tiny bird to Harry B. Lovell of Louisville, who banded it. It showed no fear of Lovell or of his family, and he released the banded kinglet in his garden to allow it to continue its apparently interrupted northward migration to its nesting grounds. As a species, the golden-crowned kinglet is a tame or fearless (of man) bird.

R. P. Sharples (1908) related a remarkable experience with the unexplainable tameness of a great crested flycatcher, usually a wary bird. In the Pa. mountains, he saw the flycatcher moving about restlessly in the trees overhead. He called to it, and it suddenly flew near him and perched on a low branch. Sharples approached the bird cautiously and it allowed him to reach out and gently smooth its feathers. In Nova Scotia one chilly, rainy day in 1915, Harrison F. Lewis walked up to a black-capped chickadee feeding in an alder bush. When it paid no attention to him, Lewis moved closer, then reached out a hand and gently caught the bird. It struggled violently to get away, and when Lewis released it, it flew away in strong sustained flight as though in the best of condition (Bent, 1946).

Thorpe (1956b) points out that inborn fear of man is relatively recent in the evolution of bird behavior, that birds may now have a general inherited wariness, and he raises the question of how this wariness of man is so readily overcome by some birds in some situations but not by others.

In certain regions where most of them are very shy and wild, individual ruffed grouse, either male or female, have developed attachments to or a decided interest in one or more people with no sign of fear of them. Many grouse are belligerent, especially during the courting and nesting season, which may account for some individual fearless behavior. Carleton D. Howe (1904) told of a hen grouse which developed a strong attachment to a farmer and even let herself be handled by other people; the relationship lasted about 2 years. When the farmer called to the hen grouse, she flew out of the woods and came to sit on his knees, then flew to his shoulders, then to the ground, repeating this half a dozen times and clucking all the while.

Howard Cleaves (1920) knew of a belligerent male ruffed grouse that came out of the woods to fight a farmer's tractor. Apparently attracted by the noise of the machine, he would approach until the farmer stopped the tractor for fear of running over the bird. When the man got off the machine, the grouse, with his ruffs raised and his head lowered, would dart toward the man's feet like a bantam rooster and peck at his trousers. When he walked away, the grouse ran after him and struck at him with his wings and bill; if he extended his hand the bird would peck it, yet he would let himself be picked up and would perch on the man's hands, wrists, or shoulders.

There are numerous other accounts of these remarkably individual, or abnormal, grouse. They usually live in some restricted area where they can be called by a human voice, or whistle, and come to the sound of a moving vehicle, a woodsman's chopping, or a stick rustled by someone in the leaves. They follow people about like pet dogs, can be coaxed to eat from one's hands, and eventually allow themselves to be picked up (Bent, 1932).

Robert W. Nero, a Canadian ornithologist, in Apr. 1969 reported a belligerent male sharp-tailed grouse that, from his territory in the grassy center strip of a four-lane highway near Winnipeg, was dashing at automobiles as they passed. Sometimes he ran alongside a car briefly, then returned to his original place as though satisfied that he had driven off his imaginary rival. Similarly, a greater prairie chicken at Hibbings Airport, Minn., each morning in the spring of 1955 and 1956, from his territory on the airstrip, challenged incoming planes. He was finally killed when one of the aircraft struck him.

Some individual owls, and certain owls as a species, may be unusually tame. Screech owls are ordinarily somewhat wary, but in Mass., William Brewster, on his farm along the Concord R., one day walked up to a red-phase screech owl roosting in a clump of oak sprouts without frightening it away. Reaching out a hand, he gently stroked the owl's soft-feathered feet and then its back. The small boreal owl of the North and the saw-whet owl, as species, are extraordinarily tame and may be approached and caught in the hands. In the U.S., bird-banders seek out the saw-whet owl on its winter roosts, usually low in evergreens. After cautiously approaching them, they pick some of these little owls off their roosts and then band them. In the wilder parts of the U.S. and Canada, where the saw-whet owls have little contact with people, at night, and apparently out of

curiosity, they will sometimes enter tents of campers (Taylor and Shaw, 1927). The great gray owl and hawk owl of the North are so fearless of human intruders that some can be approached closely enough to be caught with the hands.

Some of the smaller songbirds, besides golden-crowned kinglets cited above, have shown astonishing tameness. In 1924, a girl, while attending the National Girl Scout Camp at Briarcliff Manor, N.Y., had a remarkable experience with a pair of house wrens. She was living in a tent by herself and the wrens were building a nest inside a hollow formed by the rolled-up sides of the tent. The wrens were so tame that they hopped about on the floor almost oblivious of the girl's presence. Early one morning she was awakened by something tugging at her hair. It was the pair of wrens on her pillow, trying to pull out some of her long hair for nesting material.

Years ago, Dr. MacGailliard of Granite City, Iowa, found a ruby-throated hummingbird on the street during a cold rain in Oct. He rescued the bird and kept it in his office, where he fed it for about 10 days on sugar water. When it got hungry, it uttered a mouselike squeak. If the doctor did not immediately feed it, the bird flew to him at his desk and fluttered about his face or alighted on his hands and darted out its tongue as it did when feeding at flowers. It especially enjoyed being stroked, and when the doctor ran a hand gently over its head, back, and wings, it sat perfectly still. When the cool spell was over, the doctor took the bird outside and gave it freedom to continue its migratory journey.

The fearlessness of birds while sitting on the nest, incubating their eggs or brooding their young, has been especially noted in vireos and other small birds. Bradford Torrey (1889) wrote of a solitary vireo that allowed him to stroke her while she sat on her nest. Then he fed her from his fingers aphids from his rosebushes. Sharples (1908) also reported a female wood thrush that, while sitting on her nest, gradually allowed him to stroke her and finally ate bread from his hands. This fearlessness has been attributed to the strong attachment a bird has for her eggs when they are close to hatching or for her hatched young. Thorpe (1956b) states that it is well known that birds may be very tame at one period of their life cycles and extremely wild in others. He cites tight-sitting birds that could be lifted off their eggs without taking fright, but directly such birds have left their eggs they are wild again, which suggested to Thorpe that in these experiences "it is suppression of timidity rather than tameness." In another example, Lewis O. Shelley (1935a), a New England bird-bander, wrote that a female song sparrow, nesting in a rosebush in his yard, allowed him "to stroke her crown gently," after which he carefully pushed her off the nest to band her four youngsters.

HAND-TAMING OF WILD BIRDS. Of all ways by which fear of man may be broken down in wild birds, feeding seems to be the most effective. *See* methods of under Bird-attracting. Even cranes, among the wariest and wildest of all N.

American birds, have been conditioned to man's presence by feeding and protecting them. A pair of exceptionally tame wild sandhill cranes nested for 13 years in a small marsh about 1,000 yds. from the home of W. E. Browne (1937) at Grandin, Putnam County, Fla. During the nesting season they came in turns to his back door for food, and at the time were the only reported wild N. American cranes to become so tame. See, however, "My Greater Sandhill Cranes" and "A Whooping Crane Named Bill" in Terres (1958).

It is not difficult to get a wild bird to come to one's hands for food. Although Terres (1936–70) in Central Park, New York, in winter had black-capped chickadees and a white-breasted nuthatch come to his hands for food, success will be more assured if one is feeding birds regularly at a special place such as a backyard or garden, and especially while feeding them in winter, when birds are hungrier. There are a few simple rules for success in attracting songbirds to your hands to feed: 1. Do not try to hand-tame a bird until you have birds accustomed to coming to your feeders. 2. Be sure your feeders are empty before you try. 3. If you have tried in mild weather without success, try early in the morning of a cold, storm-threatening day, or after a snowfall or ice storm, when birds are very hungry. 4. If you have been feeding birds at a window-shelf feeder, open the window and put some food in your palm (or on your gloved hand if it is a cold day), rest your hand, palm up, on the feeder, and hold your hand very still. If you want to try at your open feeder, stand by it, and keep perfectly motionless as you hold out food in one hand, resting it for steadiness on top of your feeding tray. 5. Offer a few crumbled pieces of walnut kernels in your outstretched palm (most songbirds are very fond of them) or a few sunflower seeds. 6. If a bird flies to your open palm to pick up the food in your hand, do not stare into its eyes, as this may frighten it. Keep motionless and, above all, do not make any quick movements with your hands. 7. Never, never try to catch a bird after it alights on your hand. Whether or not you catch it and release it, you will break its trust in you and you may never get that bird to come to your hands again. See other details in "Hand-feeding, or Hand-taming" in Terres (1977).

Some wild birds that have fed from people's hands in fall and in winter are: chickadees, crossbills, purple finch, flickers, goldfinches, evening and pine grosbeaks, blue jay, gray jay, juncos, ruby-crowned kinglet, mockingbird, red-breasted and white-breasted nuthatches, redpolls, pine siskin, tree sparrow, white-crowned and white-throated sparrows, tufted titmouse, pine warbler, downy, hairy, and red-bellied woodpeckers, Carolina wren. Some birds that have taken food from people's hands in summer, usually to carry it to the nest to feed the young, are: bluebird, indigo bunting, gray catbird, American robin, chipping sparrow, summer tanager, wood thrush, red-eyed and solitary vireos. Hummingbirds have come to small vials held in people's hands to drink sugar water. See also details in Terres (1977).

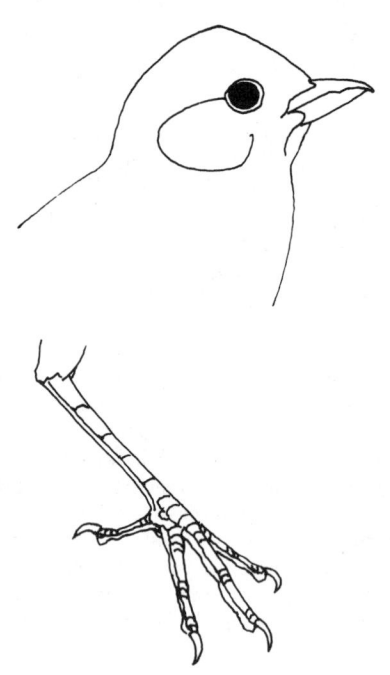

TANAGER FAMILY

TANAGER FAMILY

Thraupidae (THRAW-pih-dee); Lat., from Gr. *thraupis*, a kind of finch; *tanager* is from language of Tupi Indians of Amazon region, who called these brightly colored tree-dwelling birds *tangaras; tanager* is the anglicized version used since 19th century (Austin, 1961; Skutch, 1964b). Family of 236 species limited to W. Hemisphere, from northern limit of trees in N. America south to n. Chile and n. Argentina, and in C. America and West Indies (Van Tyne and Berger, 1959); very small to medium-sized or large songbirds (3½–12 in. long); tanagers are among the most brilliantly colored and varied birds; tanagers are usually monogamous, and many appear to remain in pairs all year (Skutch, 1954); of entire family, only 5 species reach N. America, and another (blue-gray tanager) was introduced locally in s. Fla.; members of family have 9 primary (wing) feathers; Tanager Family called "nine-primaried" songbirds; outer (10th) primary is minute, and usually concealed (Storer, 1969); tanagers have rictal bristles around mouth or bill, which distinguishes them from members of Troupial Family—orioles, etc.—many of which are also brightly colored, but not from cardinal finches, to which they appear more closely allied—they differ from N. American sparrows mainly in their fruit- and nectar-eating habits (Austin, 1961); most are poor or weak singers and many have no song at all; however, some have beautiful voices, including the tropical rose-breasted thrush-tanager, *Rhodinocichla rosea* (Gilliard, 1958), and the red-crowned ant-tanager, *Habia rubica*, and gray-headed tanager, *Eucometis penicillata*, and the N. American scarlet and summer tanagers (Skutch, 1954); besides birds called tanagers, the group includes the euphonias, chlorophonias, the striking black-and-white magpie tanager, *Cissopis leveriana*, and others. See descriptions, sizes, and ranges of these birds in De Schauensee (1970). See Gilliard (1958), Austin (1961), and Skutch (1954) for reviews and summaries of the Tanager Family, its closest relatives, and habits of individual members.

Tanagers are protected by law and may not be kept in captivity without a permit, but to sustain an ill or injured bird until it is able to care for itself, offer it soft ripe bananas and oranges, mockingbird food, mealworms and other insects, boiled eggs, and lettuce.

Blue-gray tanager, *Thraupis virens* (*episcopus* of some authorities) (THRAW-pus VIR-enz); genus name: *see* family introduction; species name: Lat., being green. (Color ill., page 887.) One of most widespread and familiar tanagers of tropical America; apparently some escaped (a popular cage bird) and became established in wild in s. Fla.; two pairs first reported (Arnold, 1961) to have been in Hollywood, Fla., beginning June 1960 and nesting there in 1961, 1962 (Paulson and Stevenson, 1962); reported increasing in s. Fla. in summer 1972; two adults and a fledged juvenile seen at a bird feeder in n. Miami; a pair seen north of Hollywood at Dania, Fla. (Ogden, 1972); sexes outwardly similar but female colors duller; about 7 in. long; body light blue-gray, paler underparts, bright sky blue on wings and tail; both sexes sing a slight but pleasant song somewhat like American redstart's; remain paired throughout year; active and restless birds of treetops, shade trees about houses, ornamental trees of city parks; in tropical America in coffee plantations, pastures with scattered trees, and open groves (Skutch, 1954); at Hollywood, Fla., around 1900 block of Thomas St., Arnold (1961) reported these tanagers easy to find, as they utter rather unmusical calls by which members of pair keep in touch with each other; they also utter a high rapid whistle, slightly up and down scale, and a *t-ee-nk* when hiding from human observer; name in Spanish is *azulejo;* have habit of traveling in small bands, roost in groups in dense foliage.

Feeding Habits: Eat variety of soft fruits, hunt small animal life among leaves, under branches of trees, shrubs; catch insects in air; come to bird feeders even if on ground; at feeders male may offer pieces of banana to mate; at Hollywood, Fla., are attracted to fruit of sapodilla tree.

Nesting: Built by both sexes, a cuplike structure from ground level to 100 ft. up; also in open sheds, and uses abandoned nests of other birds; one pair nested in large pine at Hollywood about Sept. 1 (Stevenson, 1973).

Eggs: S. America, begins early Dec.; Panama Canal Zone, Jan.; Caribbean, Feb.; Costa Rica, Mar.–July (Skutch, 1954); in Trinidad reported all year round; 2–3.

Incubation: By female only, 13–14 days, male feeds her on nest; young fed by both parents; young, unless disturbed, do not leave nest until 17–20 days after hatching, when they can fly well; in Costa Rica, at least two broods a season (Skutch, 1954).

Age: An adult banded in Panama Canal Zone, Nov. 1963, found dead 9 years, 6 months, later less than a kilometer from where banded (Loftin, 1975).

Range: Resident in C. and S. America.

Canada tanager. *See* Scarlet tanager.

Cooper's tanager. *See* Summer tanager.

Hepatic tanager, *Piranga flava* (pie-RANG-gah FLAH-vah); genus name: apparently S. American name for a bird; species name: Lat., yellow; *hepatic,* from liver-red color of male. (Color ill., page 888.) S. and C. American and Mexican species, in summer in U.S. in Ariz., N. M., and Tex.; 7–8 in. long; male is wholly dark orange-red (can be distinguished from uniformly red male summer tanager by his dark cheek patch); *both sexes* of hepatic tanager during nesting season have dark or black bills—summer tanager has yellow-brown bill (Blake, E.R., 1953); female, olive above, yellowish below; in summer, usually arrives Apr.–May in sw. U.S.; common in dense oaks, pines, large pinyons throughout most of Ariz., except northern and northwestern part, where local (Phillips *et al.,* 1964); in summer in N.M. most common in southern part, nests in higher forested places up to about 7,000 ft. in Black Range (similar summer tanager likely to be seen in the lower valleys and along watercourses—Ligon, 1961); in Tex. nests in Chisos, Davis, and Guadalupe Mtns. (Peterson, 1960); first reported in U.S. in 1854 in San Francisco Mtns., Ariz., by pioneering American naturalist Dr. S. W. Woodhouse; male sings loud, clear song from tall trees—a warble strikingly like that of black-headed grosbeak, but less varied (summer tanager's song is much like robin's); call note is low *chuck, chuck,* several times repeated (Bent, 1958); suggests call of hermit thrush.

Feeding Habits: Moves slowly about high in pines, oaks, sycamores, looking for insects; sometimes flies out into air to catch them in bill; in late summer, eats wild grapes, wild cherries.
Nest: Built high in fork, often near end of horizontal limb, of pines, sycamores, etc., about 15–50 ft. above ground; saucer-shaped, of grasses, weed stems, flower stalks and blossoms, lined with finer grasses.
Eggs: May–July; 3–5, usually 4.
Incubation: Period of and age when young first fly unknown.
Host to Cowbirds: Several records, to bronzed cowbird (Friedmann, 1963).
Range: Nests from n. Ariz., n. N.M., w.-c. and s. Tex., recently in se. Calif., s. Nev., south to Brazil, Argentina; mostly summer resident in U.S., retreats south of Mexican border in winter, although some winter in se. Ariz.

Louisiana tanager. *See* Western tanager.

Rose tanager. *See* Summer tanager.

Scarlet tanager, *Piranga olivacea* (pie-RANG-gah ol-ih-VAY-see-ah); genus name: *see* Hepatic tanager; species name: Lat., olive (color). (Color ills., pages 888, 889.) Summers in e. U.S. and s. Canada, west to N.D., Neb., Okla.; 6½–7½ in. long; wingspread 11–12 in.; male, bright scarlet *with black wings and black tail* (no other N. American bird has male's color combination); female, immature, and winter male, dull green above, straw-yellow below, with dark wings and tail; female distinguished from female summer tanager by yellow-green plumage (female summer tanager is orange-yellow) and by smaller, darker bill (Robbins *et al.,* 1966); from winter home in S. America, arrives in most of U.S. through Apr.; in n. U.S. and s. Canada by early to mid-May; summers in dense deciduous woods of oak, tulip tree, hickory, ash, etc., sometimes mixed with hemlock, pine, also in wooded parks and large shade trees of suburban residential areas; male usually arrives several days ahead of female; on arrival, he takes up territory in tall trees of woods; as defense of territory against other males, sings frequently from treetops a short, buzzy caroling song; sounds like phrase *querit, queer, queery, querit, queer,* even rhythm with hoarse burr in voice, robinlike in form; along with call note, *CHIP-churr* or *CHICK-burr,* warns rivals; when female arrives she is attracted to singing of male; male courts her by hopping about on low perches in woods near ground, spreading wings, and displaying scarlet back to female overhead—when his jet-black wings are folded normally, they almost obscure his scarlet back (Prescott, 1965).

Feeding Habits: Eats insects while foraging in treetops, in shrubs, or on ground: aphids, nut weevils, wood borers, leaf beetles, cicadas, scale insects, dragonflies, ants, termites, caterpillars of gypsy moth, parasitic wasps, bees, etc. (Tyler, 1958b); also slugs, snails, worms, spiders, millipedes; comes to bird feeders for bread, doughnut crumbs, and peanut butter and cornmeal mixture; eats mulberries, Juneberries, huckleberries, and other wild fruit.
Nest: Usually built by female in 1–2 days or up to 7 days, shallow, saucer-shaped, usually well out on limb of large oak, ash, beech, tamarack, hemlock, maple, etc.; loosely built of twigs, rootlets, coarse grass, weed stems, lined with finer grasses or pine needles; 4–75 ft. above ground; while gathering, or flying about with, nest materials, female sometimes sings short, hurried songs (Prescott, 1965).
Eggs: May–Aug.; 3–5, usually 4, pale blue or pale green, minutely speckled or boldly spotted with browns.
Incubation: By female, 13–14 days (Tyler, 1958b); young leave nest about 9–11 days after hatching (Prescott, 1965) or up to 15 days reported by Kohler (1915).
Other Names: Black-winged redbird; Canada tanager; firebird; pocket-bird; scarlet sparrow.
Accidents: Sometimes killed by storms in night migration—Lowery (1945) found 27 dead at Baton Rouge, La., Apr. 21, 1933, apparently killed by thunder- and hailstorm previous night.
Albinism: A female collected at Germantown, Pa., in company with normally colored scarlet tanagers (Stone, 1888).
Age: One at least 9 years old—a male, adult when banded Norristown, Pa., Sept. 1948, found dead near Boonton, N.J., Aug. 1956 (Middleton, 1958); male with broken wing at Washington Crossing, Pa., June 1954, kept as pet, still alive 10½ years later (Prescott, 1965).
Host to Cowbirds: Most commonly parasitized species of Tanager Family in N. America, by brown-headed cowbird; still is not among chief hosts of cowbird—about 50 records (Friedmann, 1963).
Hybrids: Cockrum (1952) reported a scarlet tanager × western tanager and a scarlet tanager × summer tanager, as did Mengel (1963) in Ky.; Gray (1958) summarizes some of these and gives other records.
Weights: In fall, coastal N.J. (21), 21.5–42.5 gr. (Murray and Jehl, 1964), or ¾–1½ oz.; in summer, Conn. female (1), 28.9 gr. (Wetherbee, 1934), or about 1 oz.
Range: Nests from c. Neb., e. N.D., se. Man., w.-c. Ont., ne. Minn., n. Mich., s. Ont., s. Que., N.B., s.-c. and c. Me., south to se. and n.-c. Okla., c. Ark., w.-c. Tenn., nw. and c. Ala., n. Ga., nw. S.C., w. and c. N.C., c. and w. Va., and Md.; winters in S. America; accidental in Alaska, B.C., Sask., Calif., Ariz., Colo., Wyo., and Bermuda.

Stripe-headed tanager, *Spindalis zena* (spin-DAY-liss ZEE-nah); genus name: from Gr. *spinos,* a linnet, or "siskin," in reference to its finchlike appearance, and *dalos,* a firebrand, or shining brightness; species name: given by Linnaeus, of uncertain meaning. West Indian species now established in Fla.; 6–8 in. long;

exceedingly variable in color and in size (Blake, E. R., 1953); variation is geographic, with different islands having very distinct subspecies; male mainly identifiable by the striking two white stripes on each side of his black head, has sparrowlike bill, a yellow throat patch; collar and chest rufous; breast yellow; wings and tail marked with black and white (Peterson and Chalif, 1973); female, a plain olive-brown, finchlike bird, with some of male's wing pattern (see other details in Blake, E.R., 1953; Bond, 1961); seldom-heard song is a prolonged, weak warble; call, a drawn-out *seep* (Bond, 1961); lives in forests and in shrubbery; most numerous in hills and mountains on larger islands of native home.

Feeding Habits: Eats insects and small fruits, including berries.
Nest: A loosely built and often remarkably small cup of plant materials in a tree or bush.
Eggs: 2–3, spotted or marbled.
Other Names: Black-backed spindalis (Miller *et al.,* 1957); cashew bird; mark-head; orange bird (Bond, 1961).
Range: Mainly Bahamas, Greater Antilles; in Mexico, only on Cozumel Is. off coast of Quintana Roo, Yucatán Pen. One of earliest records in Fla. was male seen several times May 12–20, 1961, at Marathon, Fla., showed no signs of having been a captive (Stevenson, 1961); a male seen at Key Biscayne, Miami, May 1962; singing males near Tavernier, Dec. 1962; one collected Upper Key Largo, Fla., June 17, 1963, was *first specimen record* for U.S. (Stevenson, 1963); by spring 1973, apparently nesting on Hypoluxo Is., near Lantana, in Palm Beach County, Fla.; for continuing Fla. records, see "Florida Region" in *Audubon Field Notes,* 1966, 1967, 1968, and in *American Birds,* 1972 and 1973 issues.

Summer tanager, *Piranga rubra* (pie-RANG-gah RUBE-rah); genus name: *see* Hepatic tanager; species name: from Lat. *ruber,* red. (Color ill., page 889.) E. and c. U.S. (Atlantic coast to prairies) and Tex. to N.M. and se. Calif.; the southern representative in U.S. of Tanager Family; 7–7¾ in. long; wingspread, 11¼–12 in.; male is *overall bright rose-red throughout year;* unlike cardinal, or redbird, has no crest; female, olive above; *orange-yellow below,* not yellow-green as in female scarlet tanager, also wings not dusky or blackish; summer tanager has longer bill, yellowish in breeding season, lighter than in scarlet tanager; female is color of female orioles in e. U.S. but lacks their white wing bars; from winter home in Mexico, C. and S. America, early arrivals in U.S. reach Fla. before end of Mar. but main northward migration in U.S. is Apr. to early May; summers in dry open woods, in stands of oaks, pines, hickories in Southeast; in willows and cottonwoods at low elevations along streams and in canyons in Southwest; male sings rich musical song; resembles song of scarlet tanager but not buzzy or harsh; louder, better sustained, like that of robin, but more hurried; often utters descending call note, *chicky-tucky-tuck* or *pih-tuck;* deliberate in movements, rather solitary, usually in concealing foliage of woodland trees.

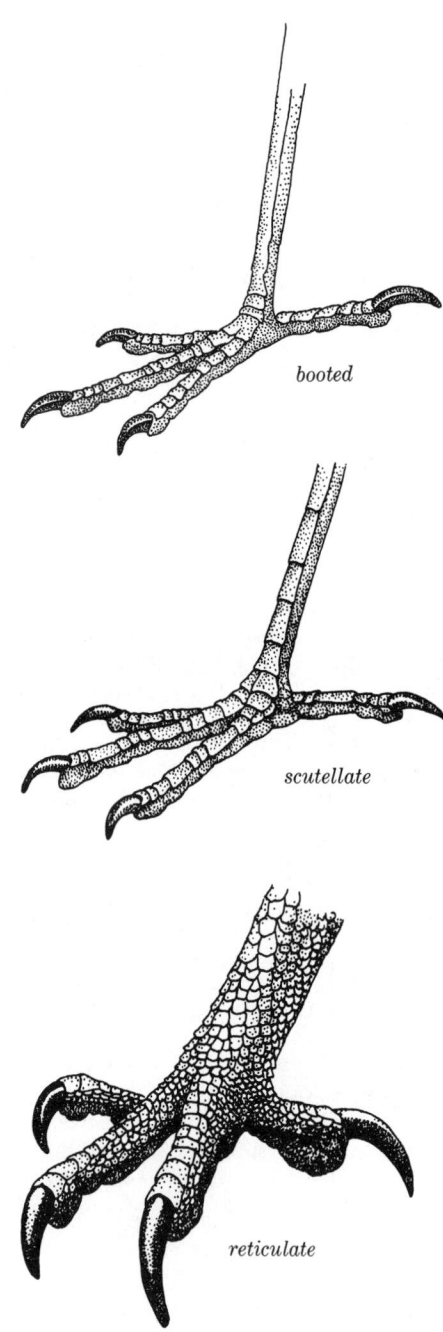

TARSUS

The tarsi of the robin are booted (smooth); in the starling they are scutellate (shingled); and in the bald eagle they are reticulate (plated).

booted

scutellate

reticulate

Feeding Habits: Not thoroughly studied but noted as avid eater of bees and wasps (Bent, 1958); about apiaries, noted catching bees out of air, also fond of soft white grubs in nests of wasps, especially those of *Polistes,* or ring wasps, which suspend open comb nests under eaves of porches, sheds, barns, etc. (*see* Insects and Birds); also eats round-headed wood borers, click beetles (adults of wireworms), bumble flower beetles, weevils, bark beetles, periodical cicadas (McAtee, 1933a); caterpillars of tomato sphinx moth, dragonflies; also spiders and small fruits—blackberries and whortleberries; in gardens may become very tame; at Chapel Hill, N.C., male came to people's hands in same garden for several years for peanut butter and cornmeal mixture.

Nest: Built well out on horizontal limb of dogwood, oak, pine, 10–35 ft. above ground; loosely built shallow cup of weed stems, leaves, bark, grasses, lined with fine grasses (Bent, 1958).

Eggs: Mar.–Aug., mostly May–June; 3–5, usually 4, pale blue or pale green, speckled, spotted, or blotched with browns, grays.

Incubation: 12 (?) days; age when young leave nest unreported.

Other Names: Bee bird; calico warbler; Cooper's tanager (southwestern subspecies); crimson tanager; redbird; rose tanager; smooth-headed redbird; summer redbird.

Age: One, banded Hillsborough, N.C., caught and released when 5 years, 11 months, old (Kennard, 1975).

Host to Cowbirds: Uncommon, 18 records of host to brown-headed cowbird, 2 records of host to bronzed cowbird (Friedmann, 1963).

Hybrids: See under Scarlet tanager.

Weights: Average of 45, N.C., 31 gr. (Teulings and Teulings, 1971), or slightly more than 1 oz.

Range: Nests from se. Calif., s. Nev., c. Ariz., c. N.M., c. Tex., c. Okla., se. Neb., s. Iowa, c. Ill., c. Ind., c. Ohio, W.Va., Md., and Del. south to s. Fla., Gulf coast, and n. Mexico; winters from s. Baja Calif. and c. Mexico to s.-c. Peru, w. Bolivia, w.-c. Brazil; has wandered north to Ont., N.B., Nova Scotia, Me., N.Y., Mich., Minn.

Western tanager, *Piranga ludoviciana* (pie-RANG-gah lewd-oh-vick-ih-ANE-ah); genus name: *see* Hepatic tanager; species name: Lat., refers to Louisiana Territory; named Louisiana tanager by Alexander Wilson for bird discovered by Lewis and Clark in western part of then broad Louisiana Territory; now known only as rare spring migrant or winter visitor in state of La. (Bent, 1958). (Color ill., page 888.) Summers from se. Alaska south to s. Calif., in sw. U.S.; one of most colorful birds of Rocky Mtn. region; 6¼–7½ in. long; wingspread 11–12 in.; male in summer has red head and face, body yellow, back, wings, and tail black (red fades in fall); has two white bars on each wing; female dull greenish above, yellow below; female and young have the white wing bars which distinguish them from other N. American tanagers; female has shorter, stouter, paler bill than female northern (Bullock's) oriole, with which she might be confused; from wintering grounds in Mexico and C. America, arrives in U.S. through Apr. and May; summers generally in mature forests of Douglas fir, pine, spruce, and aspen, in mountains up to 10,000 ft.; male sings song very similar to that of scarlet tanager; described as robinlike, but hoarser, lower in pitch, with suggestion of wildness and freedom in it (Bent, 1958); call note is *pit-ic* or *prit-titic,* sometimes followed by lower *chert-it.*

Feeding Habits: Eats many wasps and ants, nut weevils, wood borers, caterpillars, cicadas, scale insects, click beetles, grasshoppers, termites, bull pine sawflies (McAtee, 1933a); elderberries, cherries, hawthorn apples, and other fruit; comes to dried fruit or halved freshly cut oranges in bird feeders; also takes bread and cake, and will bathe in birdbath.

Nest: On outer ends of limbs of pines, firs, tamarack, oaks, aspens, 10–65 ft. above ground; loosely built of twigs, rootlets, grasses, mosses, lined with hair and plant down.

Eggs: May–July; 3–5, often 3, pale blue, irregularly spotted or blotched with browns.

Incubation: By female, 13 days; both adults feed young; age when young leave nest unreported.

Other Name: Louisiana tanager.

Age: Of three banded Calif., each retrapped at same place when 3 years old; male picked up under a tree at Tacoma, Wash., after violent storm in June 1948, lived for 15 years, 4 months, in captivity.

Host to Cowbirds: Only about four records, two in B.C., one in Alta., one in Mont., to brown-headed cowbird (Friedmann, 1963).

Hybrids: See under Scarlet tanager.

Range: Nests from s. Alaska to c. Sask., south to n. Baja Calif., s. Nev., sw. Utah, c. and se. Ariz., sw. N.M., and w. Tex., east to w. S.D., nw. Neb., and c. Colo., with 1 record in Wisc.; has wandered east to Que., Mo., Me., Mass., Conn., R.I., Miss.; in New York City area at least 12 records (mostly Oct.–Jan.), including Long Is., N.J., eating berries of Russian olive *(Elaeagnus)* (Bull, 1964); usually winters from s. Baja Calif., n.-c. Mexico, to Costa Rica; casually north to Calif., se. Ariz., and s. Tex.

TAPEWORMS
See Cestodes; *also* Parasite.

TARSAL SHEATH
The horny, unfeathered skin, or investment, on the tarsus, or "shank," of a bird, just above its toes. See Tarsus.

TARSOMETATARSUS
See Tarsus; Feet and Legs.

TARSUS
(also called TARSOMETATARSUS and METATARSUS by some authorities). The straight part of a bird's *foot* immediately above its toes—the part of the foot that bears the toes; it corresponds to the arch of the human foot. The tarsus consists of three metatarsal bones which, through evolution, have become consolidated, or fused, with the lower tarsal bones into one. Among recent birds (*see* Geological Time Scale), the three metatarsal bones are partly distinguishable in penguins, but in all birds, except ostriches, the original distinction is indicated by the three ridges on the leg lead-

ing to three prongs, or stumps, at the lower end of the bone where they form articulate surfaces for the three front toes (Coues, 1884).

The tarsus is commonly called the shank, and, like the toes themselves, it is usually covered with a scalelike skin, called the *podotheca*, or tarsal sheath, which extends to the tips of the toes. *See* Feet and Legs.

The tarsus has different characters in certain birds and these may be used in their classification; in some species—grouse, for example, and many owls—the tarsus is partly or wholly feathered, but in most birds it is bare (Van Tyne and Berger, 1959). The bare skin of the tarsus is a horny covering, or investment (*see* Skin), and in different birds this investment may be broken up in various patterns by which different birds or groups of birds may be recognized. These are: *scutellate*, in which the horny skin is cut up into overlapping scales that are like the shingles on a roof—for example, in the tarsus of a grosbeak, finch, sparrow, and bunting; it is called *reticulate* in a plover, pelican, and stilt, for example, in which the skin is cut up by polygonal plates; it is *serrate* in a grebe, in which the skin of the tarsus has serrations on the rear edge; it is *scutellate-reticulate* in a pigeon, in which the investment of the tarsus is *scutellate* in front, *reticulate* in back; it is *booted*, or *ocreate*, in a thrush such as the robin, in which the skin of the tarsus is continuously smooth without scales or plates; it is *scutellate-booted* in the catbird, in which the skin of the tarsus is *scutellate* in front, *booted* in back; *spurred* when the rear part of the tarsus has skin that is modified to form a spur, as in the ring-necked pheasant and domestic rooster. *See* Spurs under Feet and Legs; *also* in introduction to Pheasant Family.

TASTE

Many birds bolt their food quickly and because of lack of teeth, bony jaws, and chewing ability (*see* Digestion) do not keep food in the mouth as man and other toothed mammals do. A striking feature of a bird's mouth (*see* Mouth) is its small number of "taste buds"—ovoid clusters of chemical sensory receptors that are mostly in the soft area at the base of a bird's tongue (Duncan, 1964b), although parrots with a fleshy tongue have them on the tongue itself (Walter and Sayles, 1949). *See* Tongue.

A rabbit has about 17,000 taste buds in its mouth; a man about 9,000; there are 27–59 in the mouth of a domestic pigeon; 8 in a day-old domestic chick; and 24 in a 3-month-old cockerel (Duncan, 1964b). *See* Chicken.

WHAT IS THE SENSE OF TASTE? Taste is the sense by which certain qualities—acid, bitter, sweet, salt—of bodies or of substances are distinguished. The chemical stimulus of taste is brought about by contact of the chemoreceptors (taste buds) in the mouth with substances in solution—liquids are tasted; gases are smelled (Walter and Sayles, 1949). *See* Smell.

Tastes, as distinguished in everyday life, are not the result of simple chemical stimulation alone but in part are tactile (*see* Touch), thermal (sensitive to heat and cold), and olfactory (*see* Smell), each of which is detected by separate receptor systems (Duncan, 1964b). Accord-

ing to Duncan, the relatively small number of taste buds in birds has suggested that in general their sense of taste is rudimentary. If the taste buds in a bird's mouth are stimulated by food, the "tastes" are carried to the brain by nerve impulses along the ninth cranial nerve, the glossopharyngeal.

In "taste" experiments with chickens, Duncan (1964b) reported that they responded positively when their tongues were rinsed with distilled water, salt, glycerine, quinine, and acetic acid solutions, but did not respond to sucrose and saccharine solutions. Pigeons responded to all of these, except quinine, and 50% responded positively to saccharine.

Results from many experiments with pigeons and chickens suggest that they both have an apparently well-developed sense of taste, and they markedly rejected a surprising variety of substances. Duncan concluded from the tests and from others that these birds are able to detect at least some substances that taste salt, sour, and bitter, but that, in general, the sense of taste may play only a little part in the bird's selection of food.

According to Lorus and Margery Milne (1962), some parrots, with about 400 taste buds, have more than any other birds; most species of birds are said to have 30–70 taste buds (Van Tyne and Berger, 1976); however, they seem able to use their lesser number—fewer than in many mammals, including man—in evaluating their foods. In tests with tame pigeons, the Milnes discovered that these birds can detect that starch is different from protein. They reported that after the protein-rich embryo (the "eye") had been cut out of kernels of corn, the pigeons refused to eat them, and pointed out that man, even with his 9,000 taste buds, cannot distinguish between starch and protein in a kernel of corn.

After four years of backyard feeding experiments with 43 species of wild, free-ranging N. American songbirds, giving them a wide choice of natural foods, Davison (1967) concluded that they first, quite definitely, sampled the foods offered them before eating. From a long series of experiments he concluded that the birds selected their food chiefly on the basis of taste, and that color, shape, and texture were not significant under the conditions of his experiments. Size was a factor only when the seed or fruit was too large to be swallowed. *See* Bird-attracting.

Rand (1955) experimented with the taste and learning of young curve-billed thrashers which he raised, feeding them by hand. He first fed them white of hard-boiled egg cut into small squares, which the thrashers liked. Then he soaked some of the squares of boiled egg white in formalin, which, to Rand, tasted bad. The birds ate some of the squares from the food dish, but then, for a week after the experiment, refused to eat any offered them. Rand wrote: "They had quickly learned to avoid the ill-tasting food."

Rand also raised a barred owl from nestling to adult and sometimes fed it frogs, which it seemed to like. One day he offered it a toad, which it seized in its bill, then spat out, presumably because it disliked the poisonous secretions from the toad's paratoid glands, which

are on the back of the toad's neck and exude a fluid when the toad is bitten or squeezed roughly. The milky secretion causes nausea and muscular paralysis in many animals that try to eat toads (Noble, 1931); however, many birds feed on toads in nature and apparently with impunity. *See* Amphibians and Birds.

Rand's pet barred owl not only refused to accept toads after that, but also refused frogs, which apparently to the owl had the appearance of toads. It had learned its lesson in one distasteful experiment. *See* Trial-and-Error Learning under Behavior; *also* Food and Feeding Habits, and Feeding Habits under biography of each bird.

Research in the last two decades has shown that many birds do react to a variety of taste stimuli, but it has not shown how the degree of taste sensitivity they possess affects their selection of food or their feeding behavior. See Wenzel (1973) for a review of taste in birds.

TATTLER

Common name for the wandering tattler and the Polynesian, or Eurasian, tattler, both of which are wary of human intruders and utter loud cries if disturbed; other shorebirds (*see* Shorebird) that have been called tattlers are the greater yellowlegs (greater tattler or greater tell-tale), the lesser yellowlegs (lesser tell-tale), and the willet (tell-tale). The yellowlegs are especially noisy when disturbed. In the days before their protection, when all shorebirds were legal game, the yellowlegs were a great annoyance to hunters. Of these birds, Bent (1927) wrote: "The names, telltale and tattler, have long been applied to both the yellowlegs and deservedly so, for their noisy, talkative habits are their best known traits. They are always on the alert and ever vigilant to warn their less observant or more trusting companions by their loud, insistent cries of alarm that some danger is approaching. Every sportsman knows this trait and tries to avoid arousing this alarm when other more desirable game is likely to be frightened away. And many a yellow-legs has been shot by an angry gunner as a reward for his exasperating loquacity."

Coues (1884) wrote of the willet, or "semipalmated tattler," as a large, stout tattler, "a noisy, restless, and wary bird of marshes . . . too plentiful for the convenience of gunners as its shrill reiterated cries, incessant when its breeding places are invaded, alarm the whole neighborhood."

Although the solitary sandpiper has been called wood tattler in the past, it is usually a quiet, summer inhabitant of N. American woods and swamps, is tame and unsuspicious, allowing itself to be closely approached without flying, but if put to flight, utters sharp cries much like those of the spotted sandpiper. *See* the biographies of all of these "tattlers" in Sandpiper Family.

TAXONOMY

(TACKS-on-oh-mih), or SYSTEMATICS. The science of classification of birds and other animals and plants. In ornithology it may be divided into: (1) classification, or the *sorting* of birds into orders, families, genera, species, and subspecies (*see* Classification); (2) naming, or nomenclature (see Nomenclature); and (3) describing (see Described). Earlier taxonomists (those who practice taxonomy) concerned themselves largely with studying the relationships of birds by analyzing and comparing the feathers, or plumage, and studying a bird's anatomy, or internal form. In addition to these studies, taxonomists, in classifying a bird today, consider also its physiology, place where it lives, its parasites, its foods, its courtship and other patterns of behavior, and its general geographic distribution, also its relationship in the wild with other populations of birds. See Ch. 17 in Dorst (1974).

According to Mayr et al. (1953), "The taxonomist in his practical work selects from the hundreds of taxonomic characters those that are most significant as being diagnostic or as indicating relationship. The ability to select these significant characters distinguishes the superior taxonomist."

The word taxonomy is from Greek words meaning arrangement and law, and was proposed by A. P. de Candolle in 1813 for the theory of classification of plants. See also Curator; Collections; Bird Skins.

TEACHER-BIRD
See Ovenbird in Warbler—American Wood Warbler Family.

TEAL
See in Duck Family.

TEAR GLANDS
See Harderian Glands.

TEETER-TAIL
See Sandpiper, spotted, in Sandpiper Family.

TELEOPTILES
(tel-ee-OP-tils). Mature feathers, but specifically the feathers of an adult bird. They are "adult type" feathers; the feathers or down which succeed the neossoptiles (Van Tyne and Berger, 1959). See neossoptiles under Feather.

TELEVISION TOWERS
Cause of enormous destruction of birds, especially in fall migration (see details under Accidents; see also in Terres, 1956a; Vosburgh, 1966).

TEMPERATURE
The body temperature of birds and of man is the result of oxidation—metabolism, or burning of "fuel" (see Metabolism)—and is regulated in the body by circulation of the blood, much as the temperature of a building is regulated by the hot-water pipes of the building's heating plant; such regulation is necessary because of unequal production of heat-energy by different tissues, or parts, of the body (Walter and Sayles, 1949). The normal body temperature of man is 98.6° F. (37° C.); small birds have higher temperatures than large birds; in many species of birds it may range from a low in more primitive ones—grebes and pelicans, for example—of about 103° F. to about 109° F. in the evolutionarily more developed perching birds, or songbirds—cardinal and song sparrow, for example (Wetmore, 1921). Neumann

et al. (1968) cite body temperatures of 401 species of birds in 24 orders from throughout the world. The temperatures ranged from a low of 34.0° C. (93.2° F.) in the lesser nighthawk to 44.6° C. (112.3° F.) in the song sparrow. Although considerable overlap occurs, the passerines tested (142 species) had the highest body temperatures as a group.

Apparently, for a bird a body temperature of 113° F. is the lethal limit; it may die at this temperature. However, Baldwin and Kendeigh (1932) experimentally induced a body temperature of 116.3° F. in a house wren before it died, and a low of 75° F. body temperature in another, which was later revived; however, about 90° F. body temperature is about the lowest most birds can endure before they will die.

Unlike man, in whom a rise or fall of body temperature by 1–2° may cause trouble (Walter and Sayles, 1949), birds may have a large variation in daily body temperature without effect on the bird's health. A daily variation of 10.6° F. has been reported for the American robin; 10° F. in the song sparrow (Wing, 1956). Changes in a bird's body temperature vary with its activities—rising with exercise or a rapid rise in the temperature of its environment and falling to normal when the bird is at rest. Normal diel (daily) temperature of a diurnal bird (active by day) rises to maximum by noon or late afternoon, after which it drops gradually during the night.

In nocturnal birds—kiwis, owls, nighthawks, whip-poor-wills, etc.—the daily cycle of temperature rise and fall is reversed; it is highest at night, lowest during the day. See also Torpidity. Also, a bird's body temperature rises with digestion of its food (full stomach), and falls when it is hungry (empty stomach); the fluctuating range may be 8–10° F.; changes vary more in small birds than in large ones (Simpson and Galbraith, 1905).

Birds, like man, are "warm-blooded" (see Homoiothermous) and are able to maintain the body and brain at a nearly constant temperature (Hutchinson, 1964a), but are very sensitive to fluctuations in the outdoor temperatures of their environments. By various means—physiological and behavioral—they adjust their body temperatures to the outside temperature variations (Udvardy, 1951).

A temperature control center is in the thalamus or hypothalamus of a bird's brain (see Brain) and it responds to temperature receptors in the bird's skin; to inner temperatures of its body; and to hormones. The center controls, either directly by nerve impulses (see Nervous System) or indirectly through endocrine secretions (see Endocrine Glands), the reactions of the bird to temperature changes: it controls or directs the raising, or fluffing out, of a bird's feathers and shivering in response to cold (see Cold and Birds; Respiratory System) and, in response to heat, the increase of a bird's respiration (breathing) rate and panting (see Heat and Birds), which prevents overheating by cooling (lowering) the body temperature through water evaporation (Udvardy, 1951). See also Rodbard (1953) for interesting details. For discussions of temperature regulation and energy metabolism in birds, see King and Farner

(1961), Dawson and Hudson (1970), Calder (1974), and Calder and King (1974).

Newly hatched altricial birds (see Altricial), such as the young of robins, bluebirds, and many others that are helpless and usually naked at hatching, are essentially "cold-blooded," or without the high temperature control of the adult. Therefore they must be covered much, or "brooded," by a parent bird until chick's temperature regulation has developed to that of the adult. See details of this under Young and Their Care.

TERATORNIS
(ter-ah-TOR-nis); literally, "monster bird." See La Brea Tar Pits; Fossil Birds.

TERN
See in Gull Family.

TERRITORY
Almost all species of birds establish at some time, and defend aggressively against rivals (usually individuals of their own kind), an area called a territory. According to Tinbergen (1964), territories, and classification of the birds that occupy them, vary. The territories may be large or small, may be owned by males or females, pairs or families, or even by large groups; the territory may be defended at various times of the year—in the nesting season, or only during part of it—or a territory may be defended the whole year round. "The very essence of territory," wrote Nice (1933b), "is its exclusiveness; if it is not defended it is not a territory."

The territory is a part of the bird's habitat and may be from little more than a nest and its immediate surroundings (see below) to the many square miles of open country of the territory of a pair of golden eagles. Within it the eagles court, build the nest, feed and raise their young. Some types of territory may be defended because of a single or most obviously important need, such as food—for example, a winter feeding territory patrolled and defended by a mockingbird or the stored food cache defended by a red-headed woodpecker; it may be a summer feeding territory (patch of flowers or a hummingbird feeder containing sugar water) watched over and defended by a hummingbird; or a selected roosting place (cavity or hole in a tree) defended by a woodpecker. See Roosting.

The object defended may also be a bird's mate, its young, a covey (quail, for example), or a singing, or lookout, perch within the territory (Hinde, 1956). See Songs and Singing.

Nearly all birds have a territory of some kind during the breeding season. Some breeding birds defend an area they use for mating only, a mating station away from the nesting place and feeding areas—for example, the prairie chicken, sage grouse, and sharp-tailed grouse (see discussion under Arena Bird). Other birds defend an area they use only for a mating and nesting territory—for example, grebes, and some of the songbirds that are social, or live in flocks most of the year—goldfinches, and blackbirds, especially the red-winged blackbird, which feeds amicably with others of its kind on a neutral feeding ground not far from the nest, but at or near the nest vigorously attacks and chases away any other intruding redwing (Pettingill, 1972).

One of the most restricted in size of all territories is the *mating and nesting territory* of the colonially nesting pelicans, cormorants, murres, herons, gulls, and terns. They feed on neutral ground away from the nest and their defended territories are limited to the nest itself, where the pairs mate, attend the nest, incubate the eggs, and feed the young, usually without touching their neighbors.

The most widespread territorial system, and the one most familiar to most people, is that of many woodpeckers and most songbirds—for example, the mockingbird, wood warblers, vireos, thrushes, horned lark, song sparrow, snow bunting, and many others, which have an all-inclusive territory. During the breeding season, all their activities take place there—courtship, pairing, mating, food-seeking, and raising the young.

According to Nice (1941b), the theory of territory in bird life is that pairs are spaced through the pugnacity of the male toward other males of his kind, that his songs and displays of his plumage and other signals are a warning to other males to keep away, and an invitation to the female to stay in the territory and pair with him; that males (and some females) fight primarily for territory and not for mates; that the owner of a territory is dominant there and has a psychological advantage over the intruding males and is virtually invincible in his territory. Finally, birds which fail to gain a territory form a reserve supply on the territorial fringes. If the owners of a territory are killed by predators, diseases, or other causes, these reserves move into the territory to replace them.

To test this hypothesis, one spring biologists of the U.S. Fish and Wildlife Service conducted an experiment in a spruce-fir forest in Me. They shot as many as possible of the pairs of warblers, vireos, and other songbirds that occupied the territories in the tract. As suspected, almost immediately other males and females moved in from adjacent areas and established themselves in the same places that members of their kind had previously occupied. The experiment proved that a "floating population" of birds was waiting for a suitable habitat in which to nest. See Pettingill's discussion of this experiment (1970, p. 313).

The reason for the spacing of birds in their territories is still debated. Some ornithologists believe that it is to ensure an adequate food supply for the young; prevention of undue increase of the species; protection of the pair from despotism and interference in their nesting and family lives from others of their kind, thus allowing each pair in the territory an orderly sequence of their nesting cycle (Nice, 1941b). Others believe that familiarity with a territory permits the pair more efficient foraging, reduction of fear in familiar surroundings, and earlier nesting. Attachment to the nesting site, to which many birds return year after year, also gives opportunity for re-mating of the same members of the pair, without cost of time in establishing the pair bond with new mates. *See* The Pair Bond under Courtship; *also* Return to Nest Sites and Wintering Places under Banding.

FIGHTING. By patrolling its territory and singing its territorial songs (*see* Songs and Singing), and by using various kinds of threat displays, a bird can usually keep away, or drive off, an intruding rival. But when singing and threat displays are not effective, the defending bird will fight his or her rival. In these battles, usually little damage is inflicted by either combatant on the other; however, there are reports of savage physical contests in which one or both birds have been killed.

Fighting is usually between individuals of the same species, and males against males, females against females. In aerial battles over feeding territories, a hummingbird attacking its rival darts at it with the threatening pointed bill aimed straight ahead, thrusting, feinting, and retreating, but never actually striking with the bill. When territorial fighting occurs in birds, the opponents often strike out with claws, and sometimes tumble to the ground, locked together. Cassin's auklets, which nest close together in colonies, when digging a nest burrow sometimes pause to fight with a neighbor. The fighting birds stand face to face, then leap at each other like birds in a cockfight. Tuck (1961) told of vicious fights between female thick-billed murres in their nesting colonies. Some fights lasted an hour or more, with the battling contestants first on the nesting ledge, then on the water below. In many of these the fighting murres died "from having their bills twisted or torn off" by a rival.

Amadon (1964a) cited an extraordinary record of two golden eagles in Scotland that were found dead, side by side, after battling with each other in defense of their overlapping territories. Gray (1871) told of a savage aerial battle between two male gray sea eagles in w. Scotland. Upon reaching the ground, one of the eagles was so badly injured that it could not fly.

Male willow ptarmigans fight fiercely on their spring strutting grounds, and in many battles between adversaries, feathers are plucked and the blood flows. According to Sprunt (1954a), male painted buntings of se. U.S. fight viciously over territory and their battles sometimes end only after one of them is blinded or wounded. Sprunt wrote: "Sometimes a fighting pair can be picked up in one's hands . . . [so intent are they in their fighting] and some of them have their heads denuded of feathers and bleed profusely."

In the spring of 1953, at Baldwin, Long Is., N.Y., a reliable witness reported an unusually savage territorial fight between two male American robins. After a desperate battle in flight and then on a lawn, one of the birds fell over and died from the stabbing of the other's bill, which penetrated its brain. Cottrille (1950), one Mar. day in Mich., watched two male prairie horned larks in a prolonged aerial and ground fight over territory on a snow-covered field. One finally fell over and died from blows on its skull struck by the bill of its rival.

Sometimes excitement in fighting can kill birds when the blood pressure rises beyond a margin of safety. Dilger (1955) reported a male cardinal, exhausted by repeated territorial bat-

Red-winged blackbird

Yellow-headed blackbird

TERRITORY
Confronted with a male rival, both of these related blackbirds are aggressive defenders of their territory: the red-winged spreads its tail and wings to display its bright epaulets; the yellow-headed exposes more of its yellow throat and breast.

Territorial Sizes in Some North American Birds

Species	Locality	Size (acres or sq. mi.) for each pair	Authority
bunting, snow	Greenland	0.5—7.0 acres	Tinbergen (1939)
chickadee, black-capped	N.Y.	8.4—17.1 acres	Odum (1941)
eagle, bald	Fla.	2—3 sq. mi.	Howell (1949)
eagle, golden	Calif.	19—59 sq. mi.	Dixon (1937)
eagle, golden	Utah	25.4—35.5 sq. mi.	Kochert (1972)
flycatcher, least	Mich.	0.37—0.50 acres	MacQueen (1950)
hawk, red-tailed	Calif.	320 acres (ave.)	Fitch *et al.* (1946)
longspur, chestnut-collared	Sask.	1—2 acres	Fairfield (1968)
meadowlark, eastern and western	Wisc.	3—15 acres	Lanyon (1957)
mockingbird	Calif.	0.1—1.5 acres	Michener and Michener (1935)
ovenbird	Mich.	0.5—4.5 acres	Hann (1953)
robin, American	Wisc.	0.11—0.6 acres	Young (1951)
sapsucker, yellow-bellied	Ont.	5.1—5.4 acres	Lawrence (1967)
sparrow, song	Ohio	0.5—1.5 acres	Nice (1937a)
vireo, red-eyed	Ont.	1.4—2.1 acres	Lawrence (1953)
warbler, prothonotary	Mich.	1.9—6.38 acres	Walkinshaw (1953)
woodpecker, downy	Ont.	5—8 acres	Lawrence (1967)
woodpecker, hairy	Ont.	6—8 acres	Lawrence (1967)
wren, house	Ohio	0.25—3.6 acres	Kendeigh (1941)

tles with another male, that died but showed no outer effects of the fight. An internal examination of the bird showed that a rupture in the heart ventricle had caused its death, probably due to high blood pressure brought on in the heat of fighting.

Despite these and other reports of desperate fighting between birds, most territorial disputes between them are settled by bluff, or threat displays, rather than by physical contact (Berger, 1961).

WINDOW-FIGHTING, SHADOW-BOXING, OR REFLECTION-FIGHTING. Many birds during the breeding season, especially American robins, cardinals, and other songbirds that nest in and around backyards and gardens, fight the supposed rival they see in their own images reflected from a window or other reflective surface. At Sullivan, Ind., C. Russell Mason in May 1939 photographed an American robin that for three consecutive days fought its reflection from the hub cap of a car. Its bout with its image generally lasted 15–20 minutes at a time. One day, the robin battered itself so badly that blood was visible on the hub cap and on the concrete curb by which the car was parked.

George M. Sutton described a female cardinal that he watched in mid-Apr. 1946 fight her reflection from a basement window near Ithaca, N.Y. He cited a similar experience of a woman in Greenville, Tenn., who watched a female cardinal attacking her reflection from a window. The belligerent female was accompanied by a male which "behaved as a bystander and never became sufficiently interested to join in the attack. . . ." In Calif., John McB. Robertson watched both the male and the female of a pair of bushtits fight their reflections in a window about 100 ft. away from their nest, and a male brown towhee at the Museum of Vertebrate Zoology, Berkeley, Calif., came each day for 64 days (May 1 to July 4, 1932) to fight his image reflected from a window. He and his mate had a nest nearby and his act was a territorial defense. On Sept. 23, he appeared again and fought his image "for some weeks" (Dickey, 1916). Dr. Frank M. Chapman once determined the boundaries of a male cardinal's territory by using a mirror. The bird ceased fighting its reflection only when the mirror was set down about 110 ft. away from its nest.

John Burroughs (1894) was an early reporter of window-fighting. A pair of bluebirds had a nest in a birdhouse attached to the wall of his farm outhouse, which had a window on one of its sides. "At almost any hour of the day," wrote Burroughs, "from spring to early summer, the male bird could be seen fluttering and pecking against this window. . . . The bird saw its image in the mirror of the glass and was making war, he supposed, upon a rival."

SIZES AND SHAPES OF TERRITORIES. According to Pettingill (1970), many variables control the size of a bird's territory: the larger the bird, the larger its territory; the greater the population (density), the smaller is each bird's territory within a given tract. Some individual birds or pairs are more aggressive than others, and these demand and maintain a larger territory. The size of the territory also depends on the amount of habitat available (*see* Habitat) and whether it is of good quality (optimal) or poor (marginal) and whether the food supply within the territory is limited or abundant. Territories of N. American birds range in size from that of the golden eagle, reported by Dixon (1937) as averaging 36 sq. mi., to those of the American robin and mockingbird, little more than an acre or less. Territories of some birds shrink in size as the breeding season progresses, and some males that may arrive early on the nesting grounds (McCown's longspur, for example) claim large territories, which later they must decrease in size as other males arrive (Welty, 1962). See also discussion by Wallace (1963).

Some species—house wren and field sparrow, for example—show a similar dwindling of territorial size from population pressure of new arrivals. In certain years of high populations, house wrens, when squeezed into smaller territories, destroy the nest, eggs, and young of other house wrens and even of other species, such as bluebirds and house sparrows, nesting within their territories (Kendeigh, 1941). *See also* Egg-eating.

In those birds that nest in wide-open places —for example, the chestnut-collared longspur of the northern prairies, and the red-tailed hawk on the western plains, where the environment is fairly uniform—the territories are almost circular (Harris, 1944; Fitch *et al.*, 1946). In other environments, in which the plant types and other environmental features are less regular (woods, combined with fields, hedges, etc.), the size and shape of a bird's territory will vary with the surroundings and perhaps its needs. Also, it is usually governed by adjacent territories of others of its kind. In a study of territories of the Abert's and brown towhees near Tucson, Ariz., Joe T. Marshall depicted the outlines of their various territories as oblong, oval, pear-shaped, and almost square (see in Berger, 1961). Lanyon (1957) discovered that territories of meadowlarks go through changes in size and shape throughout the breeding season.

TERTIAL
See Tertiary Feather.

TERTIARY
Name frequently used for five geological periods—Pliocene, Miocene, Oligocene, Eocene, and Paleocene—a convenient collective title for designating all of the geological periods dating back to 65 million years ago and preceding the ice ages of the Pleistocene period. *See* these periods and some of their fossil birds and other animals under Geological Time Scale.

TERTIARY FEATHER
or TERTIAL. In descriptive ornithology, any one of the three secondary feathers that grow rearmost, or the last three wing feathers closest to the bird's body. *See* Topography. In certain species of birds these are much modified and are quite different from the rest of the secondary feathers (Pettingill, 1956).

Of the tertiary feathers, Van Tyne and Berger (1976) agree that these inner secondary feathers are often differently colored and shaped in certain birds, and "behave differently" in the molt (*see* Molts and Molting), but

if one tries to count them separately from the other secondaries, it is confusing when comparing them with those of birds in which the secondary feathers do not differ in form, color, or structure. They state: "Modern students of pterylosis [*see* Pterylosis] have usually advocated the practice advocated here and have termed 'secondaries' all feathers attached to the ulna." *See* Wing.

A. Landsborough Thomson (1964q) suggests that the term *Tertiary*, or *tertial*, be treated as obsolete.

TESTIS
(pl.: *testes*). Male gonad. *See* Fertilization.

TESTOSTERONE
(tes-TOS-teh-rone). A male sex hormone. *See* Endocrine Glands.

TETRAONIDAE
See Grouse Family.

TEUKE
See Redshank in Sandpiper Family.

TEXAN BIRD OF PARADISE
See Flycatcher, scissor-tailed, in Flycatcher—Tyrant Flycatcher Family.

THAYER
JOHN ELIOT (1862–1933). Born Boston, Mass.; a distinguished ornithologist and patron of science, for whom W. S. Brooks in 1915 named a gull from Ellesmere Is., Canada, *Larus thayeri*, or Thayer's gull. *See* history of this gull's changed status under Thayer's gull in Gull Family. Thayer, at his home in Lancaster, Mass., established the Thayer Museum, containing one of the largest private collections of birds in the U.S. at that time, and a valuable ornithological library (Palmer, 1928). He left his ornithological collections to Harvard (Batchelder, 1937).

THERMOREGULATION
See Temperature; *also* Cold and Birds; Heat and Birds.

THICK-KNEE FAMILY
Burhinidae (bue-RIN-ih-dee); Lat., from Gr. *burhinus*, ox-nosed. 9 species in world, grouped with shorebirds in the order Charadriiformes; live in temperate and tropical Europe, Africa, Asia, Australia, and tropical America—Mexico to nw. Brazil; s. Peru, Hispaniola (Van Tyne and Berger, 1959); 2 species in W. Hemisphere—the South American thickknee, *Burhinus superciliaris*, of sandy, brushy deserts of Peru and Ecuador, and the double-striped, or two-striped, thick-knee, *Burhinus bistriatus*, which has reached N. America; members of family are called thick-knees because of large "knee" joints—actually these are the heels, or intertarsal joints (*see* Feet and Legs); in Europe the one member of family there is called stone-curlew, because it frequents stony or pebbly open ground; also stoneplover; their closest relatives are other shorebirds and they outwardly resemble plovers; sexes are outwardly similar, but female slightly smaller; 14–20 in. long; are dull gray-

Double-striped thick-knee

THICK-KNEE FAMILY

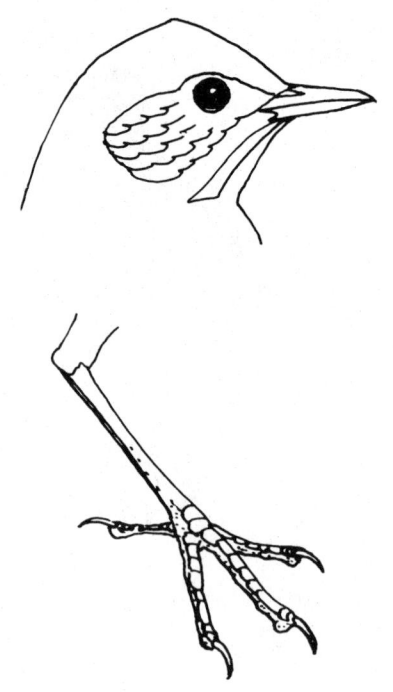

THRUSH FAMILY

brown, streaked and barred; chin and throat white; have short, ploverlike bill; large, broad head, very large eyes, wings medium size to long and pointed, in some species wings are short and rounded; tail has 12 feathers, slightly graduated; yellow or green legs rather long; the three toes partly webbed and like so many running birds, such as ostriches and bustards, for example, have in their evolution lost the hind toe, or hallux; they run swiftly with head lowered, neck indrawn; crouch to ground to avoid detection; can fly strongly but usually short flights; when alighting, open wings wide before folding them; some in northern part of range are migratory; live on open stony or sandy ground, some along beaches; eat insects, especially grasshoppers, crickets, beetles, also worms, mollusks, crustaceans, frogs, lizards, mice, seeds; usually feed at night; very wary, motionless by day, crouch down on feet in shade of a bush, when rarely seen; usually travel in pairs and in small groups; call to each other with whistles, or wailing, mournful owl-like cries, especially noisy at night; usually lay 2 eggs (Lack, 1968); white to buff and heavily spattered with grays or browns, laid directly on ground, usually in shallow unlined depression; adults known to move eggs to new location when threatened (*see* Eggs and Egg-Laying); eggs incubated by female, usually assisted by male, about 27 days; downy brown young attended by both parents; chicks may spend some time in nest or leave within a day.

To sustain an ill or injured member of family, feed it mixture of ground or finely chopped fish or meat, seeds, bread, green plants, and mealworms. For other details of family, especially in Old World, see in Austin (1961); Gilliard (1958); Pitman (1964c).

American thick-knee. *See* Double-striped thick-knee.

Double-striped thick-knee, *Burhinus bistriatus* (bue-RYE-nus bye-strih-AY-tus); genus name: Lat., from Gr. *bous*, ox, and *rhis, rhinos*, nose, named from an incorrect illustration showing a very broad bill; species name: Lat., double- or two-striped, in reference to marks on head. Mexican, C. and S. American species that has reached Tex., where a female collected (shot) in Kleberg County, Dec. 5, 1961 (Palmer, 1967); 17-20 in. long; sexes similar; large buffy head has broad white stripe over and around eyes which runs in streak down back and sides of neck; bill thick, short, dark, about 2 in. long; eyes and eyelids yellow; crown and hind neck dusky, especially on sides; neck largely buffy, finely streaked with brown; breast gray-buff, finely streaked; belly white; upperparts dusky brown; white graduated tail tipped with black; sudden bobbing of head and body downward is characteristic habit; lives in more or less dry open country with scattered brush and trees; is fairly numerous in some places, crepuscular and nocturnal, usually crouches on ground or runs to escape but may flush by day, when flies swiftly; utters chattering notes; is typically shy, but if caught when young and kept as pet, as in S. America and Panama, where semi-domesticated, becomes fearless and acts as would a noisy watchdog at night.

Other Names: American thick-knee; Mexican thick-knee; two-striped thick-knee.
Range: Mexico (Oaxaca, Chiapas, Veracruz, Tobasco), part of C. America south into Costa Rica, Hispaniola, and large areas of S. America.

Mexican thick-knee. *See* Double-striped thick-knee.

Two-striped thick-knee. *See* Double-striped thick-knee.

THISTLE-BIRD
Another name for the American goldfinch and European goldfinch, from their habit of using thistles for food (seeds) and for nesting materials (thistledown).

THRASHER
also THRUSHER. Both words derived from, and a variant (corruption) of, the English word "thrush" (see details in Newton, 1893–96). See thrashers in Mockingbird Family.

THRAUPIDAE
See Tanager Family.

THREAD FEATHER
See filoplumes under Feather.

THREADWORM
See Nematode.

THREATENED SPECIES
See Rare and Threatened Species.

THRESKIORNITHIDAE
See Ibis Family.

THROAT-CUT
See Grosbeak, rose-breasted, in Finch Family.

THRUSH FAMILY
Turdidae (TUR-dih-dee); from Lat. *turdus*, thrush. 306 species in world (Van Tyne and Berger, 1976); almost worldwide, none in Antarctica, or on some oceanic islands; 19 species reported in N. America; 4½–13 in. long; songbirds; family includes some of finest singers of all birds—for example, hermit thrush of N. America and nightingale and song thrush of Europe. Others, such as strictly W. Hemisphere bluebirds and American robin, are loved for their tameness or as symbols of spring; closest relatives of Thrush Family are Old World warblers and flycatchers (Austin, 1961) and thrashers, wrens, and dippers (Reilly, 1968); eat mostly insects and fruit, have 10 primary feathers in each wing, and tarsus is unscaled, or "booted," and have perching foot. Other foreign, famed members of Thrush Family include European blackbird (male resembles an all-black American robin), one of the "four and twenty blackbirds baked in a pie" of old nursery rhyme; mistle thrush, so named because of its fondness for mistletoe berries; fieldfare; also, redwing, *Turdus musicus*, of which an individual seen Jamaica Bay Refuge, Feb. 1959, was first continental record in N. America (Bull, 1964).

In N. America, bluebirds are among best-known and most beloved of birds; are only members of family to nest regularly in cavities or in birdhouses; eastern bluebird is decimated periodically on southern wintering range by ice and cold (*see* Bluebird Trail); American robin, known over virtually entire N. American continent, is noted for dawn singing in Apr. and May, one of most thrilling of all bird choruses, sweeps northward with advance of spring (Tyler, 1949); grass-lined mud nest built almost anywhere; famous for blue color of eggs, fondness for eating earthworms, which sometimes forced to share with starlings, brown thrashers, house sparrows, which snatch worm away as robin pulls it from ground; robin *sees* worm in its burrow; does not hear it, according to experiments of Heppner (1965); robin also famed for roosting in flocks on nesting grounds in late summer and for enormous gatherings in winter in South; is highly susceptible to DDT poisoning (see Mehner and Wallace, 1959); and sometimes gets intoxicated from fermented fruit. *See* Poisons.

The European robin, also called robin redbreast, is smaller than the American robin and similar in form, color, and behavior, not to American robin, but to eastern bluebird; has been introduced in America but never became established (see Terres, 1960a).

Five species of N. American thrushes—gray-cheeked, hermit, Swainson's, wood thrush (which has become a dooryard bird), and veery—are unusually fine singers; some of these, outwardly very similar, nest in same woodlands together but do not interbreed; good examples of reproductive isolation or maintenance of species distinction. *See* discussion under Species; Sibling Species.

Solitaires, of which Townsend's solitaire is only one in N. America, are mostly tropical American thrushes, from Mexico and West Indies south into S. America; outstanding singers with flutelike songs.

All members of Thrush Family are protected by law, but to care for injured or ill bird, offer grapes, cherries, mockingbird food, boiled eggs, mealworms, ground meat, chopped greens, and small pieces of bread (Walker, 1942). *See* Care and Feeding of Abandoned or Injured Wild Birds; also in Terres (1968c; 1977).

Bluebird, eastern, *Sialia sialis* (sigh-AY-lih-ah SIGH-al-iss); genus and species names: Lat., from Gr. *sialis*, a kind of bird (Jaeger, 1955). (Color ill., page 891.) Summers from Atlantic coast over e. N. America west to Rocky Mtns. and s. Canada; state bird of Mo. and N.Y.; on Blue List (Arbib, 1971; 1972), its future of concern to conservationists; 6½–7½ in. long; wingspread 11½–13¼ in.; male in breeding plumage bright blue above; breast, sides, and flanks reddish brown, rest of underparts white; eyes dark brown; female paler and duller than male; immatures grayish, have breast speckled; back white-spotted; bluebird has hunched appearance when perched; lives in open country, farms, cut-over woods, gardens, parks, fields, hedges, orchards, roadsides, where perched much on utility wires and fences; has serious competition for nesting holes from starlings and house sparrows; many remain on nesting grounds in winter; others not far south; to many people, return tells end of winter (Bent, 1949); call in flight or perched is short *chir-wi*, same notes warbled softly, tremulously by male have been rendered *tru-a-lly, tru-a-lly!*

Feeding Habits: Eats mostly insects, often flutters from fence, wire, or low tree to ground to catch grasshoppers, crickets, katydids, beetles, which are greatest part of diet; also eats spiders, millipedes and centipedes, sow bugs, snails, earthworms, few lizards, tree frogs; eats blackberries, bayberries, fruit of honeysuckles, Virginia creeper, red cedar, wild grapes, pokeberries, sumac seeds; can be attracted to windowsill with mealworms; to feeders with peanut butter and cornmeal mixture. See in Terres (1968c; 1977).

Nest: Built mostly by female in natural tree cavity, old woodpecker holes, holes in stumps, rail fences, bird boxes, 3–20 ft. above ground; of dried grasses, pine needles, weed stems, fine twigs, lined with finer grasses, hairs, feathers. See Hartshorne (1962).

Eggs: Mar.–July; 3–7, usually 4–5, pale blue, sometimes white.

Incubation: Mostly by female, 13–16 days; young leave nest 15–20 days after hatching; average of 18.8 days (Pinkowski, 1975); usually two broods; in fall and winter may gather in flocks of hundred or more (Bent, 1949).

Other Names: American bluebird; azure bluebird; bluebird; blue redbreast; blue robin; common bluebird; Wilson's bluebird.

Accidents: Deadly trap is chimney stacks of tobacco barns in South (see Partin, 1958); one had both wings broken in hailstorm, Sioux City, Iowa (Lincoln, 1931).

Age: At Nashville, Tenn., banded birds reported to 4 and 5 years old; one, banded Round Oak, Ga., lived to 6 years, 6 months.

Albinism: Gross (1965a) reported 21 records; one bird with "yellowish light cast" through which normal plumage pattern seen (Deane, 1876).

Flight Speed: Timed in New England, 17 m.p.h. (Wood, 1933).

Host to Cowbirds: Infrequent, but possibly most victimized of all hole-nesting songbirds; about 30 records (Friedmann, 1963).

Hybrids: An eastern bluebird × western bluebird produced three young, one of which was reared (Gray, 1958); Lane (1968b) collected a male hybrid of eastern bluebird and mountain bluebird from a nest box in sw. Man., Canada.

Weights: In Conn., Apr., adult males (10), 27.6–31.6 gr.; females (10), 27.3–34 gr. (Wetherbee, 1934), or about 1–1¼ oz.

Range: Nests from s. Sask. east across s. Canada to Nova Scotia, south to s. Fla. and south from eastern foothills of Rocky Mtns. from Mont., Wyo., Colo., and Dakotas to se. Ariz., Tex., and Nicaragua, Bermuda; winters in middle parts of e. N. America (casually farther north), south into Mexico, Gulf coast, and s. Fla.

Bluebird, mountain, *Sialia currucoides* (sigh-AY-lih-ah cure-you-COY-deez); genus name: *see* Bluebird, eastern; species name: from Lat. *carruca*, carriage (old name of warblers) and Gr. *eidos*, appearance, resemblance. (Color ills., page 891.) W. N. America, mostly in mountains; eastern slope of Cascades and Sierras to Great Plains; state bird Idaho and Nev.; on blue list (see Arbib, 1971; 1972; 1974), its future of concern to conservationists; 6½–7¾ in. long; male in breeding plumage all turquoise blue, paler blue below, distinguished from western bluebird by its blue underparts; belly white; female dull brown with blue on rump (Peterson, 1961); immatures resemble female; lives from just below timberline at 10,000–12,000 ft. in meadows or clearings down to foothills, on pine ridges, groves of aspen and cottonwood in open coniferous forests, and about ranch buildings (Bent, 1949). Male sings clear, short warble, higher-pitched than that of eastern bluebird; suggests caroling of robin.

Feeding Habits: Throughout most of year lives on insects; darts from boulder in meadow or from low branch of tree to catch flying insects or hovers, then drops to ground; takes many beetles, weevils, also ants, bees, wasps, cicadas, assassin bugs, caterpillars, grasshoppers, crickets; also currants, grapes, elderberries, mistletoe, hackberries, etc.

Nest: Built in cavities same as eastern bluebird, also in cavities about buildings, sometimes in old nest of cliff swallow; of weed stems, rootlets, grasses, outer bark of sagebrush (Bent, 1949).

Eggs: Apr.–July; 4–8, commonly 5–6, pale blue, rarely white.

Incubation: 14 days; age when young first fly unknown.

Other Names: Arctic bluebird; Rocky Mountain bluebird.

Age: One, banded at Denver, Colo., still alive at 4 years.

Hybrids: See under Eastern bluebird.

Flight Speed: Timed in w. U.S., 18 m.p.h. (Cottam *et al.*, 1942b).

Host to Cowbirds: One record, Alta., Canada (Friedmann, 1963).

Range: Nests from c. Alaska, s. Yuk., east to sw. Man., and south in mountains to nw. and s.-c. Calif., c. and se. Nev., n. Ariz., s. N.M., w. Okla., Colo., w. Neb., S.D., and ne. N.D.; winters from s. B.C., w. Mont., south to n. Baja Calif., Mexico, s. Tex.; extending to Pacific coast and offshore islands and to w. Kan., w. Okla., and w. Tex.

Bluebird, western, *Sialia mexicana* (sigh-AY-lih-ah meks-ih-CANE-ah); genus name: *see* Bluebird, eastern; species name: Lat., of Mexico. (Color ill., page 890.) W. N. America, Pacific and Rocky Mtn. states; on Blue List (Arbib, 1971; 1972), its future of concern to conservationists; 6–7½ in. long; male in breeding plumage like eastern bluebird, but has *blue throat* and *rusty upper back*; female and immature browner above than eastern bluebird female and immature, with grayer throat; lives in open, parklike woodlands with scattered coniferous or hardwood trees of mountains, and in oak forests of foothills, also about farms, orchards, and woods clearings (see especially interesting story in Gander, 1960); in Mar. small flocks break up into pairs; male sings—tempo much like robin's song—*f-few, f-few, f-few,* also in spring a double note, *pa-wee*, resembling goldfinch's call (Bent, 1949); gathers in large flocks in fall in foothills and mountains.

Feeding Habits: Often darts into air from high perch to catch insects in flight or from low perch, flutters to ground; eats largely insects, mostly grasshoppers, caterpillars, and beetles, also ants, spiders, earthworms, snails, sow bugs; blackberries, raspberries, elderberries, mistletoe berries, fruits of palm (Bent, 1949).
Nest: Built in natural cavities of oaks, yellow pines, in abandoned nest holes of woodpeckers; inner lining of fine grasses surrounded by loose network of twigs and weed stems; attracted to bird boxes about homes, which competes for with violet-green swallow and house wren.
Eggs: Apr.–May; 3–8, commonly 4–6, pale blue.
Incubation: Period of and age when young first fly unknown.
Other Names: California bluebird; chestnut-backed bluebird; Mexican bluebird.
Albinism: Three, incomplete, all-white feathers but dark eyes, Los Alamos, N.M.
Host to Cowbirds: Very rarely.
Hybrids: See under Bluebird, eastern.
Range: Resident from s. B.C. and c. Mont. south in mountains to n. Baja Calif. and Mexico.

Bluethroat, *Luscinia svecica* (lew-SIN-ih-ah SWEE-sih-cah); genus name: Lat., nightingale, an Old World long-legged thrush related to nightingale; species name: Lat. for Swedish (Gruson, 1972); country from which first described by Linnaeus in 1758. (Color ill., page 891.) In N. America only in Alaska; 5½–6 in. long; male in breeding plumage brown-backed with buffy or white eye stripe, and brilliant blue throat with chestnut patch in center; white underparts; female and immature have pale throat bordered with black; best field mark in all plumages is bright rufous at base of tail, shows in flight; lives in thickets near water in Arctic willows and scrub birches; skulks close to ground, behaves like wren; male sings at all hours of Arctic summer from perches atop bush or tree, also while in flight; like nightingale, has loud, sweet remarkably varied song; includes metallic *ting, ting, ting,* compared to note struck on metal triangle.

Feeding Habits: Eats mostly insects—beetles and flies and their larvae, some aquatic insects; also earthworms, small snails, some seeds and berries.
Nest: Built in thickets on ground in small hollow or in clump of grass near edge of lake; of string, leaves, twigs, rootlets, strips of inner bark, mosses, plant down, lined with cattle or reindeer hair.
Eggs: Alaska, June–July; 4–7, often 6, green, with dots of brown.
Incubation: By female, about 14 days; young leave nest at 14 days old (Tucker, 1949).
Other Name: Red-spotted bluethroat.
Range: Nests on coast of n. Alaska from Wales to Point Barrow; in Siberia, Russia, n. Europe; winters in Africa, Iran, and nw. India.

Fieldfare, *Turdus pilaris* (TUR-dus pill-AY-ris); genus name: Lat., a thrush; species name: from Lat. *pilus,* hair (see in Gruson, 1972). In N. America, small population of this Old World thrush lives in Greenland; 10 in. long; robinlike, with gray head and rump, chestnut back, white below, with rufous spotted breast; lives in open forests of n. Europe and Asia; previous nearest record to U.S. in N. America was dead one from Jens Munk Is., Foxe Basin, Canada; in June 1968, one found dead in Alaska (Soikkili, 1970a); a wild one seen at Larchmont, N.Y., Feb. 1973, shy and wary (Boyajiian, 1973); only a few Greenland records before January 1937, when large flock, migrating from sw. Norway southwesterly across North Sea toward British Isles, were caught in strong gale and carried across N. Atlantic to Jan Mayen Is. and ne. coast of Greenland (Salomonsen, 1951). Following accidental invasion of Greenland first nest of fieldfare found along sw. coast; by 1949 was commonly nesting there. *See* Egret, cattle, in Heron Family for another example of bird added to N. American avifauna without help of man.

Feeding Habits: Largely insects, also slugs and small land snails, earthworms, spiders, berries of hawthorn, holly, rowan, yew, juniper, fallen apples, grain, seeds; in winter, moves about in Greenland in flocks of up to 30 birds.
Nest: In Greenland, builds robinlike nest of straw with hard inner layer of mud, both on ground and low in willows and birches (Salomonsen, 1951).
Eggs: Apr.–June; 3–8, usually 5–6, gray-green or pale blue-green, freckled with reddish brown.
Incubation: 13–14 days, by female; both sexes feed young, which leave nest when about 14 days old (Tucker, 1949).
Weights: Male found dead Point Barrow, Alaska, June 1968, 83 gr. (Soikkili, 1970a), or 3 oz.
Range: Nests in n. Europe, Siberia, s. Greenland; winters in Greenland and from British Isles, c. Europe, Siberia, south.

Redwing, *Turdus iliacus* (TUR-dus eye-lih-AY-cus); genus name: *see* Fieldfare; species name: Lat., pertaining to flanks (marked); 8¼ in. long; Eurasian thrush, reported from e. Greenland and from N.Y. (Bull, 1964); a little larger than wood thrush, but with *streaked* breast; all brown above; distinguished from any other American or European thrush by conspicuous pale eye stripe and chestnut-red flanks (Tucker, 1949).
Other Name: Red-winged thrush.

Robin, American, *Turdus migratorius* (TUR-dus my-grah-TOE-rih-us); genus name: *see* Fieldfare; species name: from Lat. *migrator,* wanderer, wandering. (Color ill., page 893.) Largest N. American thrush, in summer over most of N. America; state bird of Conn., Mich., Wisc.; 9–11 in. long; wingspread 14¾–16½ in.; male in breeding plumage gray above but variable; head, wings, tail almost black, outer tail feathers tipped with white; breast from light brown to rich dark brick red, usually darker in male; female duller and paler; immature has speckled breast; lives from tree limit in sparsely wooded barrens and up to 12,000 ft. in mountains of West, along forest borders, hedges, orchards, cut-over woods, in gardens,

TANAGER FAMILY

Blue-gray tanager
At the end of the breeding season family groups of blue-gray tanagers, native to tropical America and introduced in Miami, Florida, gather in small flocks and search for fruit-bearing trees.

blue-gray tanager

Hepatic tanager
Tanagers are birds of the American tropics, and only a few species have succeeded in establishing themselves in the temperate forests of North America. The hepatic tanager is a bird of the pine-oak forests of the Southwest, where it feeds on fruit and insects.

Scarlet tanager
Once the nesting season is over, the male scarlet tanager loses its brilliant red plumage and acquires a coat of olive green. During most of the year it resembles the female, except for its black wings and tail.

Summer tanager
The all-red summer tanager is the common member of its family in the southeastern United States, where it inhabits dry deciduous woods or mixed stands of broad-leafed trees and pines. It places its nest on a horizontal limb, usually in an oak tree. As with other tanagers, only the female builds the nest and incubates the eggs.

Western tanager
Like most tanagers, this bird of western coniferous forests feeds mainly on fruit during most of the year but eats insects during the nesting season. Despite its different coloration, the western tanager is very closely related to the scarlet tanager of the East; the two species occasionally hybridize.

Hepatic tanager

Western tanager

Scarlet tanager, winter

ummer tanager

carlet tanager

THRUSH FAMILY

Eastern bluebird
A bird of open country and woodland edge, the eastern bluebird must have benefited from forest clearing by the early settlers. However, when the house sparrow arrived and began competing for nest sites, bluebird numbers dropped. The species has increased again where communities have established "bluebird trails"—long lines of birdhouses attached to fence posts—in the farmlands of eastern North America.

Mountain bluebird
Compared to the eastern and western bluebirds, the all-blue mountain bluebird has longer wings and is more a bird of the air, often hovering over the ground like a tern over water and then dropping down to seize a grasshopper or beetle.

Western bluebird
This species is a close relative of the eastern bluebird, differing mainly in having a blue rather than reddish throat. Both species nest in tree cavities and in birdhouses.

Bluethroat
A Siberian thrush that has established itself in northwestern Alaska, the bluethroat nests in shrubby tundra. Each fall, the birds return to their ancestral wintering grounds in the Old World tropics.

Western bluebird

Bluethroat

Mountain bluebird, female

Mountain bluebird

Eastern bluebird

American robin
The American robin, formerly a forest bird, has successfully adapted to the habitat offered by suburban areas—wide lawns for feeding and tall trees for nesting—and has become one of the most abundant and familiar American birds.

Townsend's solitaire
Townsend's solitaire is a plain-colored, elusive thrush of western coniferous forests. It is the northernmost member of a group of slender thrushes found in mountain forests southward to Bolivia. It nests on or near the ground, and its nest has a characteristic "apron" of grass and pine needles hanging from the front, the function of which is unknown.

Gray-cheeked thrush
Of all our spotted thrushes, the gray-cheek nests the farthest north. It favors the cold coniferous forests of Canada and isolated mountaintops in New York and New England, and even travels across the Bering Strait to breed in Siberia.

Hermit thrush
Thought by many to have the most beautiful song of any North American bird, the hermit thrush is easily distinguished from the other spotted thrushes by its reddish brown tail. While the other spotted thrushes migrate far to the south for the winter, often as far as South America, the hermit thrush regularly winters in the northern states. Here it is usually a solitary bird, feeding quietly on berries and other small fruits.

Swainson's thrush
Large numbers of Swainson's thrushes pass through the United States each spring on the way to their nesting grounds in Canada. This thrush sings frequently during migration, not only in the United States but in the tropics, where it adds its reedy, spiraling song to the chorus of tropical antbirds, toucans, and tanagers.

Gray-cheeked thrush

Swainson's thrush

merican robin

ownsend's solitaire

Hermit thrush

Varied thrush

The handsome varied thrush spends most of its time feeding on the ground in the humid coniferous forests along the Pacific coast, but males ascend into the tops of tall trees, and utter their evocative song while concealed in the foliage.

Wood thrush

The wood thrush is the largest of our spotted thrushes, and the only one that regularly nests around houses. Although it is famous for its beautiful song, the fullest song is heard only during a few weeks early in the nesting season, when territories are being established. Later, when the young are being fed, it sings but briefly in the early morning and at dusk, and its song is not as inspiring.

Veery

The ground-nesting veery is a frequent host of the brown-headed cowbird, and raises the young cowbirds often at the expense of its own nestlings. The fact that the veery has not evolved a behavioral adaptation that protects it from cowbirds may mean that there were originally no cowbirds in the breeding range of the veery, and that the two species came together only after the settlers had cleared much of the forest in eastern North America.

Wheatear

The wheatear, easily distinguished by its white rump and tail patches, is a common bird in open country in the Old World whose breeding range extends to Greenland, parts of Arctic Canada, and Alaska. In the fall, wheatears nesting in North America migrate back to the Old World and are only very rarely found in southern Canada or the United States.

Wood thrush

Varied thrush

Wheatear

Veery

TITMOUSE FAMILY

Bushtit
During much of the year, bushtits are highly social birds, traveling in small flocks that consist of a mated pair and their most recent brood of young. In the spring, the young birds leave the territory of their parents and set up territories of their own.

Black-capped chickadee
Each fall, many black-capped chickadees leave the woodlands where they have nested and appear in suburban areas, where they are usually the most numerous and familiar visitors to feeders. Bands of chickadees, often accompanied by nuthatches, downy woodpeckers, and brown creepers, are quite regular in their movements, often arriving at a particular bird feeder at roughly the same time every day.

Boreal chickadee
Periodically, mass movements of black-capped chickadees occur in the eastern United States. Among the millions of black-caps that pour through in the fall, there are nearly always a small number of boreal chickadees, coming south from their breeding grounds in the spruce-fir forests of Canada.

Carolina chickadee
The Carolina chickadee is a species of the southeastern United States whose range extends north to central New Jersey, Ohio, and Illinois. The region to the north is inhabited by the very similar black-capped chickadee, but in most places the ranges of the two species are separated by a no-man's-land where neither occurs. In most respects, the habits of both species are the same.

Carolina chickadee

Black-capped chickadee

Bushtit

Boreal chickadee

Chestnut-backed chickadee

Each major forested area in North America has its own chickadee. This richly colored species is the chickadee of the humid coniferous forests along the Pacific coast. Although each pair of chickadees defends a territory, the territories of several pairs may be small and close together, forming a loose colony.

Mountain chickadee

The mountain chickadee, easily recognized by its white eyebrow, inhabits the mountainous parts of the West from southern British Columbia to Baja California and western Texas. In the fall, some birds wander down the slopes, where they enter the range of the black-capped chickadee.

Black-crested titmouse

This species is a permanent resident of river-bottom woodlands and suburban areas from Oklahoma and Texas to central Mexico. Along the northern border of its range, where it inhabits the same woodlands as the tufted titmouse, the two birds are now known to hybridize freely, and for this reason they are both placed in a single species.

Bridled titmouse

The bridled titmouse is a Mexican species that barely crosses the United States border, nesting in the dry oak woodlands of southeastern Arizona and New Mexico. Like most other members of the titmouse family, it nests in cavities in trees or in birdhouses.

Plain titmouse

This dull-colored bird is the common titmouse in the juniper thickets and oak woodlands of the western United States. It nests in old woodpecker holes or in crevices in buildings, laying 5 to 8 spotted eggs that are incubated by the female alone.

Tufted titmouse

Although chickadees gather in flocks and roam widely in search of food during the winter, tufted titmice are usually sedentary, remaining paired for life and staying near their nesting place throughout the year.

Verdin

A bird of the southwestern deserts, the verdin is a cavity nester, like other members of the titmouse family, but instead of adopting a cavity in a tree or birdhouse, or excavating one of their own, these birds build a firm, well-insulated ball of thorny twigs with an entrance in the side. In the dry desert climate, such nests may last for years, creating the impression that verdins are far more numerous than they actually are.

Bridled titmouse

Tufted titmouse

Black-crested titmouse

Plain titmouse

ountain chickadee

Chestnut-backed chickadee

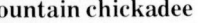

erdin

TROGON FAMILY

Coppery-tailed trogon

Trogons are brightly colored, retiring birds found mainly in tropical regions. Of the many species that occur in Central America, one, the coppery-tailed, has nested for years in a few wooded canyons in southeastern Arizona. Even here they are difficult birds to find, and their presence is usually revealed by their loud, cooing call.

TROPICBIRD FAMILY

Red-billed tropicbird

Tropicbirds, as their name implies, are birds of tropical seas, nesting on small islands and feeding on the ocean. They catch fishes and squid by diving from the air. Once caught, a fish is swallowed immediately; tropicbirds are never seen carrying food as terns do. Red-billed tropicbirds nest on islands off Baja California and in the West Indies, and wander occasionally northward. Most records of the species in the United States are from the Pacific coast.

White-tailed tropicbird

The white-tailed tropicbird ranges farther north in the West Indies than the red-billed, nesting regularly in the Bahamas. As a result, this is the species most likely to be seen along the Atlantic coast of North America. Unlike the red-billed, this species is known to be partially migratory; the birds of the Bahamas move southward after the breeding season and probably spend the winter in the Lesser Antilles or off the coast of South America.

Coppery-tailed trogon

White-tailed tropicbird

Red-billed tropicbird

TROUPIAL FAMILY

Brewer's blackbird
A bird of farmlands and brushy country in the west, the Brewer's blackbird breeds in loose colonies of up to two dozen pairs, building its nest in thick vegetation, in crevices in cliffs, or on the ground. After the breeding season these birds feed in a wider variety of habitats, readily entering suburban areas.

Red-winged blackbird
A marsh with nesting red-wings is a noisy place in spring and early summer, as the males sing and display at rivals. Male red-wings are sometimes polygamous, maintaining a large territory in which 2 or even 3 females nest. Shortly after the young have fledged, the birds depart, leaving the marsh in relative peace and quiet until the following year.

Rusty blackbird
Unlike the related Brewer's blackbird, this bird of swamps and marshes in the northern coniferous forest is not colonial; each pair defends a large territory around its nest, which is a bulky cup of grass and twigs placed in a spruce or fir. In migration rusty blackbirds generally keep to themselves and do not travel with flocks of red-wings or grackles.

Tricolored blackbird
The tricolored blackbird is the most intensely social member of its family in North America. Some California marshes contain colonies of as many as 200,000 nesting pairs.

Yellow-headed blackbird
This species nests in colonies of up to 30 pairs in marshes in the western part of North America. The song of the male is like that of the red-winged blackbird, but harsher and more nasal. In the fall some yellow-headed blackbirds wander widely and turn up with flocks of red-wings far from their normal range.

Red-winged blackbird

Red-winged blackbird, female

Brewer's blackbird

Rusty blackbird

Tricolored blackbird

Yellow-headed blackbird

Bobolink

During the summer months, the bobolink is a handsomely plumaged songbird of northern meadows and farmlands, well known for its cheerful song and its habit of catching harmful insects to feed its young. During the rest of the year, in drab winter plumage, it travels in large flocks through the farmlands of southern South America, eating valuable grain.

Bronzed cowbird

Like its relative the brown-headed cowbird, this is a brood parasite that lays its eggs in the nests of other songbirds. Cowbirds often associate with cattle, catching insects stirred up by the grazing cows and searching their hides for ticks.

Brown-headed cowbird

Like the European cuckoos, cowbirds lay their eggs in the nests of other songbirds and their young are raised by unwitting foster parents. The association between the brown-headed cowbird and its victims is an ancient one, and many of the host species have evolved ways of combating cowbird parasitism. The yellow warbler often places a new nest lining over a cowbird egg, even burying eggs of its own, and it has a special alarm note heard only when a cowbird appears near its nest.

Boat-tailed grackle

The boat-tailed grackle nests in colonies in swamps and salt marshes from New Jersey south to Florida, and along the Gulf coast to Louisiana and eastern Texas. Here its range overlaps that of its close ally, the great-tailed grackle. Although many members of the blackbird family are polygamous, there is evidence that the boat-tail is merely promiscuous.

Common grackle

One of the most abundant birds east of the Rockies, the common grackle has adapted well to suburban areas and agricultural land, nesting in small colonies in evergreens and feeding on lawns, in barnyards, and at garbage dumps.

Great-tailed grackle

So similar is the great-tailed grackle to the boat-tailed grackle that the two were until recently thought to be a single species. However, it is now known that they nest within sight of each other without interbreeding.

Eastern meadowlark

The eastern meadowlark is another species that has benefited from the colonization of North America by Europeans. The clearing of the forests of eastern North America added thousands of square miles to its breeding range.

Western meadowlark

The two species of meadowlarks are so similar in appearance that their songs are the best way to distinguish them. Where their ranges have come together as a result of forest clearing, the eastern and western meadowlarks may nest in the same field and occasionally interbreed.

Western meadowlark

Eastern meadowlark

oat-tailed grackle

Common grackle

rown-headed cowbird

Bronzed cowbird

obolink

Great-tailed grackle

Black-headed oriole
Although not as rare as Lichtenstein's oriole, the other large oriole nesting along the Rio Grande, the black-headed oriole is a shy bird, usually keeping out of sight in the dense thickets along the river. As a result it is the least known of our orioles.

Hooded oriole
The delicate hooded oriole is a common bird around farms and towns and in woods along rivers from southern Texas west to California. It is one of the most frequent victims of the bronzed cowbird, whose young take so much food intended for the nestling orioles that the latter sometimes starve to death.

Lichtenstein's oriole
Our largest oriole, Lichtenstein's is a tropical species that reaches its northern limit in the Rio Grande valley in Texas, where it is rare. Its nest is a woven, hanging basket, like that of other orioles, and is placed in full view at the end of a leafless branch.

Lichtenstein's oriole

Black-headed oriole

Hooded oriole, female

Hooded oriole

Northern (Baltimore) oriole

The eastern counterpart of Bullock's oriole, the Baltimore is one of the most familiar songbirds between the eastern seaboard and the Great Plains. It prefers to nest among the outer hanging branches of elms and willows.

Northern (Bullock's) oriole

Until the late 19th century, the breeding ranges of the 2 forms of the northern oriole were separated by the Great Plains, with the Bullock's oriole nesting in the western part of the continent and the Baltimore oriole in the east. Since they had strikingly different color patterns, the two were considered distinct species. Then, as a result of habitat disturbance by man, the two birds came together and began to interbreed. At present, because of this hybridization, these birds are placed in a single, rather variable species.

Orchard oriole

The orchard oriole is smaller than the northern oriole, the only other oriole found in most of eastern North America. It nests in shade trees, especially along rivers and on the shores of ponds and lakes. In the Deep South, where it is more common than the northern oriole, it also nests in city parks and suburban areas.

Scott's oriole

The commonest oriole in the southwestern deserts, Scott's oriole usually conceals its nest along the dried leaves of a yucca plant. It feeds on insects during the breeding season and mainly on fruit and nectar during the rest of the year.

Spotted-breasted oriole

Native to Central America, the handsome spotted-breasted oriole became established in Miami, Florida, in 1949, and is now a common resident in suburbs as far north as Fort Lauderdale and Homestead. Like many introduced birds, it is most successful in disturbed habitats rather than in natural areas, where there may be other, better adapted species.

Northern (Baltimore) oriole

Northern (Bullock's) oriole

cott's oriole

rchard oriole

potted-breasted oriole

Scott's oriole, female

Orchard oriole, female

TURKEY FAMILY

Turkey

An abundant game bird in colonial times, the wild turkey was all but exterminated in most of its range as a result of habitat destruction and because it was shot for food. Now, through the efforts of conservation agencies, turkeys are again numerous in many states and are being re-established in others.

Turkey

Turkey, chick

Turkey

Turkey, female

VIREO FAMILY

Bell's vireo
Bell's vireo usually nests within 3 feet of the ground in dense thickets from the Mississippi valley to the Pacific coast. It is a frequent victim of the brown-headed cowbird, but readily abandons a nest when a cowbird egg has been laid in it.

Black-whiskered vireo
The black-whiskered vireo is a West Indian bird that just reaches the United States, nesting in mangroves and dense scrub along the coast of southern Florida. It spends the winter in northern South America.

Philadelphia vireo
The Philadelphia vireo, so named because the first specimen was collected near that city in the 1840s, is a bird of coniferous and mixed forest in northern New England and southern Canada. Because of its drab color and its close resemblance to the red-eyed vireo, it is often overlooked and is the least known of the eastern vireos.

Red-eyed vireo
The red-eyed vireo is one of the most abundant birds in North American deciduous forests, where it sings almost continuously from dawn to dusk, uttering its short warbling phrases even while swallowing an insect or incubating its eggs. The nest is a neat cup suspended from a slender forked branch. Just how numerous these birds are becomes evident after the leaves have fallen; a walk through the woods in late autumn reveals many vireo nests concealed during the breeding season.

Black-whiskered vireo

Philadelphia vireo

ed-eyed vireo

ell's vireo

Solitary vireo
This species nests in coniferous and mixed forest in much of North America. In most parts of its range, it has an olive-green back and yellowish sides, but birds that nest in the Rockies are very gray—different enough to look like a separate species.

Warbling vireo
A drowsy, warbling song, issuing from a tall shade tree along a river or at the edge of a pond, is usually the best indication that a warbling vireo is present. The dull-colored bird is often difficult to see as it picks its way deliberately through the foliage high overhead, searching for insects.

White-eyed vireo
The thicket-inhabiting white-eyed vireo breeds as far north as central New England and Nebraska. Its song is a fast, explosive jumble of notes, unlike the methodical phrases of most other vireos.

Yellow-throated vireo
The most brightly colored of our vireos, this species is a bird of rich deciduous forest. Its song is a series of short phrases, like that of other vireos but more musical.

Yellow-throated vireo

Solitary vireo

Warbling vireo, nestlings

Warbling vireo

White-eyed vireo

VULTURE—
AMERICAN VULTURE
FAMILY

California condor
The California condor has been declining in numbers since before Columbus, and now it nests only in the mountains of Los Padres National Forest, near Santa Barbara. In 1980, only 2 pairs attempted to nest in the wild, and it now appears that breeding in captivity offers the only hope of saving this ancient bird from extinction.

Black vulture
The black vulture is a stockier, shorter-winged bird than the turkey vulture and is most common in the southeastern United States. Like its more widespread relative, it feeds chiefly on carrion, which it locates by sight, but it supplements its diet with small birds and mammals when it can catch them.

Black vulture

Black vulture, chick

California condor

Black vulture

Turkey vulture

Turkey vulture

A carrion feeder, the turkey vulture locates its food both by sight and, recent experiments have shown, with its sense of smell, which is unusually keen for a bird. Although it can only hop about clumsily when on the ground, in the air it is one of our most graceful birds, soaring for long periods of time with an occasional flap of its long wings.

parks of cities, country, and suburbs; enormous flocks once slaughtered in southern states; starts north in Feb., follows closely average daily temperature of 37° F. (Tyler, 1949); small flocks of wild wary males arrive in northern states in Mar.; males begin singing in Apr. with arrival of females, a familiar caroling, *cheer-up, cheer, cheer, cheer-up;* males now fight each other and their own reflected images in windows, shiny parts of automobiles.

Feeding Habits: Runs over lawns, golf courses, meadows, in search of earthworms (Heppner, 1965, after series of experiments, concluded that the robin, as many observers always believed, does not find worms in their burrows by sound, but by sight), also eats insects, such as beetles, weevils, grasshoppers, cicadas, ants, termites, cutworms, and other caterpillars, butterflies; also much fruit, bayberries, grapes, Juneberries, mistletoe berries, pokeberries, chinaberries, etc. (Tyler, 1949); comes to feeding stations for bread (see in Terres, 1968c; 1977).

Nest: Built from ground to treetops, usually where sheltered from rain and saddled on firm support, early ones in fork or crotch of protective evergreen; later ones in maples, elms, and other deciduous trees, usually 5–20 ft. above ground, sometimes on rail fences, roof gutters, porch gables, fire escapes (see others in Tyler, 1949), a neat deep cup of mud and grasses, lined with fine grasses (Reilly, 1968).

Eggs: Apr.–July; 3–6, usually 4, unmarked pastel blue ("robin's egg blue" has become accepted color standard).

Incubation: Almost entirely by female, 12–14 days, one record of a 7-day incubation (Taft, 1970); young first fly when 14–16 days old; usually two broods, sometimes three each year.

Other Names: Canada robin; common robin; migratory thrush; northern robin; redbreast; robin redbreast; San Lucas robin; southern robin; western robin.

Accidents: One returned to same yard two summers with twig projecting from back (Terres, 1960b); bird-bander, Amsterdam, N.Y., caught one in live trap that had large thorn stuck in throat.

Age: One banded wild bird lived to 11 years, 8 months (Kennard, 1975); captive at Tarrytown, N.Y., lived for 17 years; another, at Redmond, Ore., alive and healthy at 17.

Albinism: Common; pure-white one with pink eyes at Amsterdam, N.Y., rescued from cat, lived 5 years as pet; melanistic ones also reported (Tyler, 1949).

Flight Speed: Timed in w. U.S., 25 m.p.h. (Cottam *et al.*, 1942b); in New England, 20–32 m.p.h. (White, 1927); 36 m.p.h. (Aymar, 1935).

Host to Cowbirds: Uncommon.

Hybrids: Gray (1958) reported crossbreeding of American robin with song thrush of Europe in captivity.

Weights: In fall, coastal N.J. (49), 64.8–84.2 gr. (Murray and Jehl, 1964), or 2⅓–3 oz.

Range: Nests from limit of trees in n. N. America south to s. Calif., Gulf coast, s. Ga., and s. Mexico; winters regularly from s. Canada and n. U.S. south to Baja Calif., Gulf coast, s. Fla., to Guatemala; casually farther north.

THRUSH FAMILY

Robins in their juvenal plumage can be distinguished from mature robins by their speckled breasts.

Rufous-backed robin

THRUSH FAMILY

Clay-colored robin

Robin, beach. Another name for the red knot in Sandpiper Family.

Robin, clay-colored, *Turdus grayi* (TUR-dus GRAY-eye); genus name: *see* Fieldfare; species name: given in 1837 by Charles Lucien Bonaparte, who dedicated it to G. R. Gray, "a young ornithologist," who in 1831 was a zoological assistant in the British Museum and who later published many zoological works. Mexican, C. and S. American species that has strayed to s. Tex.; 9–9½ in. long; sexes outwardly similar; resembles American robin in appearance and in habits, but back of adult is gray-brown or olive brown; *throat pale buff,* is lightly streaked; below is virtually an even tawny or cinnamon-buff (clay color), whereas American robin has ruddy breast, white belly; bill is dull green-yellow; immature clay-colored robin is similar to adults but a darker and richer brown above (less olive); wing coverts have buff spots (Blake, E. R., 1953)—see illustrations in Peterson and Chalif, 1973; common about villages and cultivated country; in s. Mexico and in all of C. America, except in high mountains, has relation to man like that of American robin; lives close to human habitations; one of most generally known and best-loved tropical American songsters; song similar to American robin's but "sweeter" (Skutch, 1960); call note is *meoo* or *meow,* often repeated (Peterson and Chalif, 1973).

Feeding Habits: Like some other thrushes, forages much on ground but in secluded spots; eats worms, slugs, caterpillars, insect pupae, occasional lizard, very fond of wild figs, wary of man but comes to feeding stations for bananas, plantains; at home from wettest parts of Caribbean coast and more arid places of interior, in orchards, irrigated plantations, ranges to 4,000 ft. in Mexico and to at least 5,000–8,000 ft. in C. America.

Nest: Bulky, built in dense cover of tree or small bush; usually 5–12 ft. from ground, in dooryards, plantations, shady pastures, hedges (Skutch, 1960); "a replica of American robin's, even to mud-layer" (Dickey and van Rossem, 1938).

Eggs: Late Mar. into June; 2–4, pale blue, gray-blue or blue-green.

Incubation: About 12 days (Skutch, 1960).

Other Names: Gray's robin; Tamaulipas thrush.

Age: An adult, banded Sept. 1964 in Panama Canal Zone, found dead 9 years, 7 months, later, not far from place where banded (Loftin, 1975).

Weights: About 74 gr. (Smithe, 1966), or about 2⅔ oz.

Range: E. and sw. Mexico, from c. Tamaulipas and Nuevo León south and through C. America to n. Colombia; sighted at Brownsville, s. Tex., Mar. 10–17, 1940; at Mission, Tex., May 14–19, 1959 (records cited in Peterson, 1961, Appendix I); reported in Santa Ana Refuge, s. Tex., Dec. 28, 1969 (Webster, 1970); a singing male in Anzalduas area, Rio Grande Delta, Tex., June 14–28, 1972 (Webster, 1972); another in Santa Ana Refuge, June 19, 1973 (Webster, 1973); first one collected in U.S. shot Feb. 1973 in open loblolly pine woods near Huntsville, Walker County, Tex. (Moldenhauer, 1974).

Robin, golden. Another name for the northern (Baltimore) oriole in Troupial Family.

Robin, Gray's. *See* Robin, clay-colored.

Robin, ground. Another name for the rufous-sided towhee in Finch Family.

Robin, rufous-backed, *Turdus rufopalliatus* (TUR-dus RUE-foh-pal-lih-AY-tus); genus name: *see* Fieldfare; species name: from Lat. *rufo,* dyed or colored red, and *palliatus,* wearing a cloak *(pallium),* in reference to the *rufous wash on the back* of this species. A native of Mexico, has strayed to s. Ariz. and sw. Tex.; 9–9½ in. long; sexes outwardly similar; superficially resembles American robin, but underparts paler, cinnamon, has white throat conspicuously streaked; *rufous back* is distinctive; bill yellow; female slightly paler and duller colors than male; immature is buff-streaked above; underparts boldly spotted with black; throat immaculate white; bill dusky (Blake, E.R., 1953); its calls weaker than American robin's, but song is clear with robinlike phrases but more liquid; a casual straggler from Mex., one near Nogales, s. Ariz., Dec. 16–18, 1960, was in company of American robins; a native of deciduous tropical woods and in lowlands, foothills, and highland valleys along Pacific slope of Mexico.

Feeding Habits: Is fruit-eater and lives in fruiting tops of forest trees, in dense shrubbery of parks and gardens (the conspicuous American robin, with gray back, prefers higher altitudes and pines—Peterson and Chalif, 1973).

Range: W. Mexico from s. Sonora to Oaxaca; Tres Marías Is. off Pacific coast. In N. America, one also reported at Tucson, Ariz., Dec. 29, 1965; records of this species continue to increase, with reports of one seen at Big Bend National Park, Tex., in Oct. and Nov. 1966; another (banded) was at Carefree, near Phoenix, Ariz., Nov. 14, 1966, to Mar. 14, 1967; another (unbanded) seen in Phoenix, Apr. 17, 1967 (Snider, 1967); for other Ariz. records, see Snider (1970, 1971a–c), and for Tex. records, Webster (1973); see also continuing issues of *American Birds* for other reports.

Robin, San Lucas. *See* Robin, American.

Robin, swamp. *See* Thrush, hermit, and Thrush, Swainson's; also another name for the rufous-sided towhee in Finch Family.

Rubythroat, Siberian, *Luscinia calliope* (lew-SIN-ih-ah cal-EYE-oh-pee); genus name: *see* Bluethroat; species name: Lat., pleasant-voiced, Calliope, one of the Muses. Asiatic bird, has wandered in June to Aleutian Is., Alaska, possibly crossed Bering Sea from Kamchatka or from e. Russia; 6 in. long; olive brown, gray breast; slender, thrushlike bill; rather large sturdy legs; male has bright *scarlet throat* bordered with black; white eye stripe, white mustachial mark downward from corners of mouth; female has *white throat*, buffy eye stripe; at distance resembles its thrush relative, the bluethroat (*see* Bluethroat); exquisite songster; lives in hillsides or lowlands covered with brush, sings from tops of bushes or lower limbs of small trees. For other life history details, see Bent (1949).

Other Name: Kamchatka nightingale. Ruby-throat is also another name for the ruby-throated hummingbird.

Solitaire, Townsend's, *Myadestes townsendi* (my-ah-DESS-teez TOWN-send-eye); genus name: Lat., from Gr. *myia*, fly, and *edestes*, eater; species name: given in 1838 by John James Audubon for John K. Townsend, young Philadelphia ornithologist, who collected (shot) the first one known to science along Columbia R. (see Stone, 1903). (Color ill., page 893.) W. N. America; 8–9½ in. long; sexes alike; slender gray bird with white eye-ring; white outer tail feathers, and buffy wing patches that show in flight; acts like flycatcher, darting out into air for insects; sings like a thrush; immature has buffy wing patch but spotted above and below; lives during summer or throughout year in mountains up to 12,000 ft., in lower canyons in winter; favors open forests of pine and fir on gentle to steep rocky slopes, and wide canyons with scattered, stunted cedars; usually solitary, quiet, often seen singly or in pairs or family groups; in fall large numbers may gather at spring of fresh water; runs gracefully like robin; in flight flaps wings slowly and flies irregular course (Bent, 1949); male sings in spring and in winter, glorious prolonged warbled rapid notes, from tree perch, sweet, clear, and loud; somewhat like song of purple finch; also has exquisite flight song.

Feeding Habits: Eats caterpillars and beetles, some ants, termites, bees, wasps, bugs, also spiders and earthworms; much fruit—berries of cedar, mistletoe, madrona, rose, poison ivy, wild cherries, and others; also pine seeds.
Nest: On or sunken in ground, partly concealed at base of pine or fir, under overhanging bank along mountain trail; of sticks, twigs, grasses, pine and fir needles, rootlets, on platform of bits of bark, weed stalks, grass stems.
Eggs: May–Aug.; 3–5, usually 4, dull white, pale blue, pale pink, spotted with browns.
Incubation: Period of and age when young first fly unknown.
Other Names: Fly-catching thrush; Townsend's fly-catching thrush.
Flight Speed: Timed at 20 m.p.h. (Cottam et al., 1942b).
Range: Nests from e.c. Alaska, s. Yuk., s. Mack., Alta., sw. S. D., south in mountains to s. Calif., ne. Ariz., n. N.M., nw. Mexico; in winter withdraws somewhat from northern part of summer range and to lower altitudes, s. B.C., and w. Neb., south to Baja Calif. and Mexico (Reilly, 1968).

Thrush, Alice's. *See* Thrush, gray-cheeked.

Thrush, Bicknell's. *See* Thrush, gray-cheeked.

Thrush, brown. Another name for the brown thrasher in Mockingbird Family.

Thrush, eye-browed, *Turdus obscurus* (TUR-dus ob-SKEW-rus); genus name: *see* Fieldfare; species name: Lat., dark, inconspicuous. Asiatic species accidental in N. America and Aleutian Is. (Amchitka); a male collected at Amchitka, May 27, 1956, was first N. American record; one seen Oct. 19, 1957, at Amchitka; one collected at Amchitka, in 1961, and May 26, 1969; one seen Amchitka, June 10, 1969 (Jones and Gibson, 1975); and a male collected (shot) at Barrow, Alaska, June 16, 1971, was first record for the Alaskan North Slope (Gibson and MacDonald, 1971); 7½ in. long; according to Peterson *et al.* (1954), male is distinguished by gray upper breast and orange-buff sides; *white stripe above eyes*, and a white patch between eye and chin; female outwardly similar but duller colors; in Kamchatka, lives mainly in birch forests with undergrowth, and in mixed forests on banks of reservoirs; and in spruces and larches (Dement'ev *et al.*, 1968; see also Vaurie, 1959).

Feeding Habits: Not known.
Nest: Built in trees, 3–15 ft. above ground, usually in heavy fork; a cup of grasses, rootlets, bark, small twigs, sometimes lined with soil and bits of grass.
Eggs: Usually June; 5–6, sometimes 4, in color greatly resemble those of fieldfare.
Incubation: Period of and age when young first fly unknown (Dement'ev *et al.,* 1968).
Other Names: Gray-headed thrush; olive-colored thrush (in Russia).
Range: Nests in Siberia; winters in Formosa, Philippines, Malay Pen., Sumatra, Borneo, and Palau Is.; strays to c. Europe, west to Belgium, France, Italy; straggler to Komandorskie Is. and Alaska.

Thrush, golden-crowned. Another name for the ovenbird in Warbler—American Wood Warbler Family.

Thrush, gray-cheeked, *Catharus minimus* (CATH-ah-rus MIN-ih-mus); genus name: Lat., from Gr. *katharos*, pure, here referring to purity of song; species name: Lat., least, or smallest. (Color ill., page 892.) In summer most northern of all N. American thrushes south to n. U.S.; 6¼–8 in. long; wingspread 10½–13½ in.; sexes outwardly alike; olive or gray-olive above; pale below with lightly spotted breast; *cheeks gray;* not a distinct eye-ring as in Swainson's thrush; no rufous tail as in hermit thrush; differs in short song (which rises at end) from veery's rich, descending "spiral"; is champion migrant of all small N. American thrushes; from Peru, southern part of wintering range, north to Alaska; in spring migration over e. U.S., from Atlantic coast to Mississippi Valley, sparingly farther west; when migrating, almost anywhere: woods, roadside shrubbery, parks, gardens of cities and villages; lives in summer in damp Canadian woods or forests of spruce and tamarack to barrens of Arctic land, in dwarf willows and alders in n. Alaska and crosses Bering Strait to nest in ne. Siberia, where has extended range from N. America

(Bent, 1949). Like other thrushes, gray-cheeked is usually shy; male sings from top of bush or small tree; reedlike notes, *whee-wheeoo-titi-whee,* the ending slurred quickly upward.

Feeding Habits: Eats largely beetles, weevils, ants, caterpillars, cicadas, also spiders, crayfishes, sow bugs, and earthworms; blackberries, raspberries, wild cherries, grapes, etc. (Bent, 1949).
Nest: Ground level to 20 ft. up, in willows, alders, spruces, usually 6 ft. above ground; of dried grasses, some mud, sedges, strips of fine bark, mosses, decayed leaves with little or no lining.
Eggs: June–July; 3–6, usually 4, light green-blue to pale blue, faintly marked with browns.
Incubation: 13–14 days (one nest 12 days, Jehl and Hussell, 1966); young first fly at 11–13 days old (Wallace, 1949).
Other Names: Alice's thrush; Bicknell's thrush (Bent, 1949).
Weights: In fall, coastal N.J. (32), 23.9–35.3 gr. (Murray and Jehl, 1964), or 1–1¼ oz.
Range: ne. Siberia, n. Alaska, n. Mack., n. Man., east to Newfoundland, south to sw. Alaska, n. B.C., c. Sask., se. N.Y. and nw. Mass.; winters from Nicaragua and West Indies to n. S. America (Reilly, 1968).

Thrush, gray-headed. *See* Thrush, eye-browed.

Thrush, hermit, *Catharus guttatus* (CATH-ah-rus gut-AY-tus); genus name: *see* Thrush, gray-cheeked; species name: Lat., spotted, speckled. (Color ill., page 893.) Widespread in summer, northern states, Canada, and Alaska; known for exquisite song; state bird of Vt.; 6½–7¾ in. long; sexes outwardly alike; olive brown or russet brown above; slender bill; spotted white breast; *rufous on rump and tail* conspicuous in flight; habit of slightly raising and lowering tail especially after alighting, accompanied by *chuck* note peculiar to hermit; some males sing in winter in South; also in northern states while in migration, at dawn and sunset from thick shrubbery or woods; opens with clear flutelike note, followed by ethereal, bell-like tones, ascending and descending in no fixed order, rising until reach dizzying vocal heights and notes fade away in silvery tinkle; in summer lives in many habitats: in North in spruce woods, sphagnum bogs, hardwoods and coniferous forests, dry pine woods, rocky pastures, in Ariz. in thickly wooded canyons, in Calif. and Nev. up to 8,000–10,000 ft., in spruce and fir forests of Rocky Mtns. to 12,000 ft. (Bent, 1949).

Feeding Habits: Eats insects mostly from ground, largely beetles, and ants, also caterpillars, some bugs, grasshoppers and crickets, also spiders, sow bugs, snails, earthworms, sometimes feeds salamanders to young; also eats much fruit, especially in fall and winter: pokeberries, blueberries, serviceberries, grapes, elderberries, mistletoe berries, raspberries.
Nest: Usually built on ground in natural depression under small fir or hemlock, edge of woods road, edges of pastures, sometimes in small tree 2–5 ft. above ground, sometimes on

rafter of building in mountains; of twigs, strips of bark fiber, dried grasses, ferns, mosses, lined with pine needles, plant fibers, rootlets.
Eggs: May–August; 3–6, usually 3–4, plain green-blue or pale blue, sometimes spotted with brown.
Incubation: 12 days; young first fly at 12 days old (Gross, 1949a).
Other Names: American nightingale; rufous-tailed thrush; solitary thrush; swamp angel; swamp robin.
Age: One banded in Calif. retrapped and released when past 7 years old.
Albinism: Not frequent, only two reported to Gross (1949a); partial albino at Portland, Conn., total albino shot, Stamford, Conn.
Host to Cowbirds: Rather uncommon (Friedmann, 1963).
Weights: In Mich. (44), 23.8–35.3 gr. (Becker and Stack, 1944), or about 1–1¼ oz.
Range: Nests from c. Alaska, s. Yuk., sw. Mack., nw. Sask., east across Canada to Newfoundland, south to mountains of s. Calif., n. N.M., and c. Wisc., ne. Ohio, east to w. Md., s. N.Y., Conn., and Mass.; winters from sw. B.C. south to s. Ariz. and s. Baja Calif., in east from Conn. south to Tex., Gulf coast, s. Fla., to Guatemala.

Thrush, olive-backed. *See* Thrush, Swainson's.

Thrush, red. Another name for the brown thrasher in Mockingbird Family.

Thrush, rufous-tailed. *See* Thrush, hermit.

Thrush, russet-backed. *See* Thrush, Swainson's.

Thrush, solitary. *See* Thrush, hermit.

Thrush, song. *See* Thrush, wood; also another name for the brown thrasher in Mockingbird Family.

Thrush, Swainson's. *Catharus ustulatus* (CATH-ah-rus yewst-you-LAY-tus); genus name: *see* Thrush, gray-cheeked; species name: from Lat. *ustulare,* to singe; singed (color); common name: for William Swainson, early-19th-century English ornithologist. (Color ill., page 892.) Summers in coniferous forests of n. U.S., Canada, and Alaska; 6½–7¾ in. long; sexes outwardly alike; buff-brown above; light below, breast spotted; *buffy eye-ring, buffy cheeks and breast* distinguish it from similar gray-cheeked thrush; migrates at night, when plaintive calls sound like piping of spring peepers in dark; moves northward Apr. into June, by day often with wood warblers in trees of woods, orchards, parks, feeding on insects of opening foliage; sings much, song spirals upward, like *whip-poor-will-a-will-e-zee-zee-zee,* going up high and fine at end (Bent, 1949); call note, *whoit,* like drop of water in barrel; on nesting grounds in Alaska, with others, sings ringing choruses almost continuously at night as well as by day; in summer lives in spruce, fir, and balsam forests of n. New England and across Canada, sometimes in deciduous growth; west of Sierras, in willow thickets of

lowlands along shaded streams; in Rocky Mtns. of Colo. 6,000–9,000 ft.
Feeding Habits: Eats beetles of all kinds, weevils, ants, wild bees, wasps, caterpillars, spruce bud moth, mosquitoes, crane flies, treehoppers, cicadas, also spiders, millipedes, snails, sow bugs, earthworms; domestic and wild cherries, blackberries, raspberries, seeds of twinberry, elderberry.
Nest: Built 2–20 ft. above ground, in some places in willows, more often on horizontal branch, usually close to trunk of small coniferous, sometimes deciduous, tree or bush; of twigs, fine sedges, leaves, ferns, plant fibers, strips of cedar bark, lichens, and especially mosses, cup lined with dead leaves, lichens, rootlets.
Eggs: Calif., Apr.–July; height of laying, May–June; 3–5, usually 3–4, pale blue, evenly spotted with pale brown.
Incubation: By female, 11–14 days; young leave nest when 10–14 days old (Gabrielson and Lincoln, 1959).
Other Names: Alma's thrush; olive-backed thrush; russet-backed thrush; swamp robin.
Accidents: Often killed at night in migration when striking TV towers, tall buildings.
Age: Two, banded, both retrapped and released when slightly past 3 years old.
Host to Cowbirds: Very seldom, less than a dozen records (Friedmann, 1963).
Weights: In fall, coastal N.J. (138), 22.9–37.3 gr. (Murray and Jehl, 1964), or ¾–1⅓ oz.; in Mich. (23), 24.6–39.4 gr. (Becker and Stack, 1944).
Range: Nests from c. Alaska, n. Yuk., Mack., to n. Man., east across Canada to s. Labrador and Newfoundland, south to Alaska Pen., s. Alaska, s. Calif., Colo., n. Great Lakes region, east to se. N.Y., Vt., and Me., south in Appalachians to W.Va.; winters from s. Mexico to Argentina.

Thrush, Tamaulipas. *See* Robin, clay-colored.

Thrush, tawny. *See* Veery.

Thrush, varied, *Ixoreus naevius* (icks-OH-reh-us NEE-vih-us); genus name: Lat., from Gr. *ixos,* mistletoe (likes mistletoe berries), and *oreos,* mountain; species name: Lat., spotted, varied. (Color ill., page 894.) Along Pacific coast N. America; in actions, form, similar to robin; 9–10 in. long; male in breeding plumage blackish gray above; orange stripe over eyes and orange in wings distinguish it from robin; belly and tips of outer tail feathers white; female has paler breast bands, paler underparts, immature has incomplete breast band often speckled orange, underparts speckled dusky; summers in moist woodlands of Northwest, from summit of Cascades to shores of Pacific and along heavily forested humid coastal belt north throughout B.C. to Alaska; favors dense stands of firs dripping with moisture and especially about mountain lakes; some movement in spring from lowlands to higher altitudes; forages on ground, keeps among shady retreats among mosses and rocks; male sings rich, melancholy long quavering whistle, a pause, then another succession of

vibratory notes, sometimes high, then low, fading away at end.
Feeding Habits: Often ground feeder, eats beetles, ants, bees, wasps, bugs, flies, caterpillars, grasshoppers, crickets, some spiders, myriapods, snails, sow bugs, earthworms; also acorns, weed seeds, snowberries, juniper berries, blackberries, raspberries, berries of madrone, buckthorn, poison oak, pepperberries.
Nest: Built on horizontal branch, usually of small fir, spruce, hemlock, vine maple, willow, or in crotch, 10–15 ft. above ground; of twigs, dead leaves, green mosses, sometimes mud, strips rotten wood, bark, cup lined with soft leaves, dry grasses.
Eggs: Apr.–July; 2–5, usually 3–4, pale blue, sparingly dotted with browns.
Incubation: By female, about 14 days (Bent, 1949); age when young first fly unknown.
Other Names: Alaska robin; northern varied thrush; Oregon robin; Pacific varied thrush.
Accidents: One, Berkeley, Calif., had acorn impaled on its bill, weak and unable to fly, was freed of acorn and released (Nichols, 1940).
Range: Nests from n.-c. Alaska, c. Yuk., nw. Mack., south to nw. Calif., n. Idaho, and nw. Mont.; winters from s. B.C. and n. Idaho south to s. Calif. (Reilly, 1968); casual visitor to major parts of Nev., Utah, Wyo., and Colo., especially constant in winter; wanders eastward across s. Canada from Sask. to sw. Que., Minn., Wisc., n. N.Y., New England, Long Is. and Staten Is., N.Y., and N.J. See Keith (1968) for full details.

Thrush, willow. *See* Veery.

Thrush, Wilson's. *See* Veery.

Thrush, wood, *Hylocichla mustelina* (high-low-SICK-lah mus-teh-LIN-ah); genus name: from Gr. *hyle,* wood, and *kickle,* thrush; species name: Lat., pertaining to weasel (color). (Color ill., page 894.) Largely e. U.S., official bird of D.C.; 7½–8½ in. long; wingspread 13–14 in.; sexes alike; heavy-bodied, brown above; *russet head;* white underparts boldly marked on breast, sides, and flanks *with large round or oval black spots*—not streaked as in long-tailed, yellow-eyed brown thrasher, and has large *dark* eyes and *shorter* tail; summers in low, cool, damp deciduous forests, also on wooded slopes in New England to 2,000 ft.; often near streams; has adapted to living in city and country gardens and parks (Weaver, 1949); males first appear in Mar.–Apr. in s. U.S., move north, when arrive on chosen nesting territories begin singing; early in season from tops of tallest trees, later only about 15 ft. above ground and from ground, logs, edge of nest; loud, sweet, liquid song with bell-like notes, repeated *ee-oh-lee, ee-oh-lay,* calm, unhurried, peaceful; call note a sharp *pit, pit, pit* or liquid *quirt!;* when alarmed adults and young raise feathers of head like crest.

Feeding Habits: Catches insects from tree foliage but mostly on or near ground: beetles, ants, caterpillars, moths, grasshoppers, flies, bugs; also, spiders, myriapods, sow bugs, snails, earthworms (Terres, 1962a, watched wood thrush "anting" with snail); also eats berries of spicebush, dogwood, Virginia creeper, blackberries, elderberries, pokeberries, mulberries, etc. (Martin *et al.*, 1951).

Nest: Much like that of robin but distinguished by dead leaves and mosses, also lined with rootlets, not grasses as in robin's nest, 6–50 ft. up (usually 6–12 ft.) in crotch or saddled on branch of shrub, sapling, or large tree, often with piece of paper or white cloth conspicuously incorporated.

Eggs: Apr.–July; 2–5, usually 3–4, immaculate pale blue or blue-green.

Incubation: By female, 13–14 days; young leave nest when 12–13 days old (Weaver, 1949); two broods each year.

Other Names: Bellbird; song thrush; swamp angel; swamp robin; wood robin.

Age: One, N.J., retrapped where banded when 6 years, 10 months, old; one, banded Radnor, Pa., found dead, Phila., Pa., when 8 years, 10 months, old (Kennard, 1975).

Albinism: One, pure white with pink eyes (total albino), reported Winston-Salem, N.C., Sept. 1916; H. Brackbill, in Md., banded a partial albino female.

Host to Cowbirds: Frequent, more than 75 records (Friedmann, 1963).

Weights: In fall, coastal N.J. (8), 42.7–52 gr. (Murray and Jehl, 1964), or 1½–1¾ oz.; one female, spring, Washington, D.C., 60.4 gr., or about 2¼ oz.; adult male, killed Kans. TV tower in fall, 54.2 gr. (Tordoff and Mengel, 1956).

Range: Nests from se. S.D., c. Minn., c. Wisc., n. Mich., s. Ont., s. Que., n. Vt., c. N.H., and sw. Me., south to se. Tex. and Gulf coast east to n. Fla., casually north to s. N.B. and w. to sw. N.D.; winters from s. Tex., Mexico to Panama; casually north to c. Tex. and Fla.; casual in Colo. and Bahama Is. (Reilly, 1968).

Veery, *Catharus fuscescens* (CATH-ah-rus fuss-KESS-enz); genus name: *see* Thrush, gray-cheeked; species name; Lat., from *fuscus,* dusky. (Color ill., page 895.) West to Rocky Mtns. and across s. Canada; 6½–7¾ in. long; sexes outwardly alike; evenly tawny above; *faintly* spotted buffy breast, least spotted of all N. American brown thrushes; white below; in spring, travels north from S. America, sometimes arrives in migration, arrives U.S. in Apr., still common in migration mid-May; on northern nesting grounds by late Apr., early May, summers in various habitats: likes deciduous woods with dense undergrowth, or hemlock woods and ravines, bushy burnt-over woods, willow and alder swamps, sometimes in dry oak and pine woods, and wooded lowlands along streams and lakes; male often sings from favorite tree perch, especially appealing when heard as darkness falls in hemlock grove or wooded ravine: a series of four or five downward-spiraling phrases, *whree-u, whree-u, whree-u, whree-u;* calls with soft whistled *phew!*

Feeding Habits: Often forages on forest floor, hopping along, turns over leaves with bill; also feeds much in trees; eats click beetles, wood borers, leaf chafers, June bugs, sawfly larvae, ants, cutworms, caterpillars of gypsy moth, also eats many spiders, some sow bugs, snails, earthworms; half of food is wild fruit: Juneberries, strawberries, blackberries, wild cherries,

grapes, elderberries, dogwood berries, etc. (Bent, 1949).

Nest: Usually on or near ground, bulky, at base of shrub, in clump of weeds, in shrub or low tree; if ground wet, first builds thick foundation of dead leaves, adds weed stems, grasses, strips of bark, lined with dried grasses.

Eggs: May–June; 3–5, usually 4, pale blue, usually unmarked.

Incubation: 11–12 days; young leave nest when 10 days old (Bent, 1949).

Other Names: Nightingale; tawny thrush; willow thrush; Wilson's thrush.

Age: Two, banded, at least 3 years old when retrapped; one, banded Island Beach, N.J., killed when 9 years, 11 months, old (Kennard, 1975).

Host to Cowbirds: Fairly common but frequency varies in different parts of veery's range (Friedmann, 1963).

Weights: In fall, coastal N.J. (57), 24.1–38.9 gr. (Murray and Jehl, 1964), or 1–1½ oz.

Range: Nests across s. Canada from e. B.C. to c. Newfoundland, south through Rocky Mtns. to ne. Ariz., ne. S.D., s.-c. Minn., east to s. Wisc., southern edge Great Lakes region, and south in Appalachians from N.J. to n. Ga.; winters from C. America to Brazil.

Waterthrush. Name for two warblers in Warbler—American Wood Warbler Family.

Wheatear, *Oenanthe oenanthe* (ee-NAN-thee [*th* as in *thin*]); genus and species names: from Gr. *oine,* vine, and *anthos,* blossom, Aristotle's name for the bird, perhaps so called because it appeared in Greece at time of flowering of the vines (Macleod, 1954); according to Austin (1961), *wheatear* has nothing to do with wheat or ear, "but is a euphemism for the Anglo-Saxon, 'white arse,' in reference to its distinctive white rump." (Color ill., page 895.) Small Old World thrush that long ago arrived from Europe in Greenland in N. America (apparently before the Ice Age) and in Alaska more recently from its home in Eurasia across Bering Strait (Bent, 1949); comparable to bluebird (but smaller) in shape, flight, feeding habits, but coloring very different; 5½–6¼ in. long; male in breeding plumage clear gray above with black mark through each eye bordered above with white; white underparts and sandy buff on breast; outstanding field marks are *white rump and tail* and inverted black T mark on tail, also black wings. One form, the so-called Greenland wheatear, individuals of which reported mainly in U.S. in fall and winter, south along Atlantic coast to Long Is., N.Y., and N.J., is remarkable for migration; a transatlantic migrant, it apparently follows ancestral route by which it invaded Greenland; from its winter range in w. Africa passes through England mainly in May or in Apr., crosses N. Atlantic to Greenland, thence to n. Que. and Labrador; return trip is mostly in Sept.–Oct. (Bent, 1949); the Alaskan bird (*see* above) migrates to e. Asia; lives on bare hillsides, dunes, stony barrens; utters mostly scolding *chack-chack;* male sings on nesting grounds a short, modulated warble from perch on clod or stone, often in flight in which he rises to great height then glides to earth.

Feeding Habits: Insects, centipedes, spiders, also, in Alaska, seeds, bulblets of plants, fruit.

Nest: A cavity in or under rocks, heaps of stones, in rabbit burrows, a loosely built cup of grasses, mosses, lined with finer grasses, rootlets, hair, feathers, wool, plant down.

Eggs: Apr.–June; 3–8, usually 5–6; pale blue, some with red-brown specklings.

Incubation: Mostly by female, 14 days; young leave nest about 15 days after hatching.

Other Names: European wheatear; Greenland wheatear; northern wheatear.

Age: One (banded) reported from Great Britain, 7 years old (Clapp, 1976).

Weights: A female collected (shot) in summer, w. Hudson Bay, 36.8 gr. (Lein and Maher, 1970), or about 1⅓ oz.; another adult female, collected Ellesmere Is., Canada, 27.6 gr., or about 1 oz.; and two males, 29.1 and 29.8 gr. (Parmelee and MacDonald, 1960).

Range: Nests from n. Asia to n. Alaska and to s. Alaska, n. Yuk., and Mack., and from Europe to Iceland; Greenland south to Baffin Is., Canada, w. Hudson Bay, Northwest Territories, n. Que., and s. Labrador; winters from Pribilof Is. and Nunivak Is., Alaska, to India, and in tropical Africa; increasingly reported along Atlantic coast from N.B. south to N.Y. and N.J., also in Bermuda and Cuba.

THUNDER BIRD

Legendary bird of N. American Indians of huge size that Indians believed caused thunder when it flapped its wings. In European folklore, the common snipe is called the thunder bird, and is believed to cause thunderstorms (Tuck, 1972).

THUNDER PUMPER

Local name for the American bittern, from its hollow "pumping" sounds uttered from marsh.

THYMUS (THIGH-mus) **GLAND**

Elongated, runs along undersurface of a bird's neck; it is larger in juvenile birds, decreases in size at maturity, then re-enlarges following bird's first, and possibly later, sexual cycles. It is considered to be an endocrine gland (*see* Endocrine Glands), but its hormonal function still remains to be demonstrated (Höhn, 1961). *See* discussion under Bursa of Fabricius.

TIBIOTARSUS

A bone in the legs of birds; the "drumstick." *See* Feet and Legs; *also* Skeleton.

TICK BIRD

See anis in Cuckoo Family.

TICKS

See Ectoparasite.

TIDBITTING

See Courtship Feeding.

TIP-UP

Another name for the solitary sandpiper, spotted sandpiper, and greater yellowlegs in Sandpiper Family.

TIT

Shortened name for some members of the Titmouse family, such as tufted tit, bridled tit, and

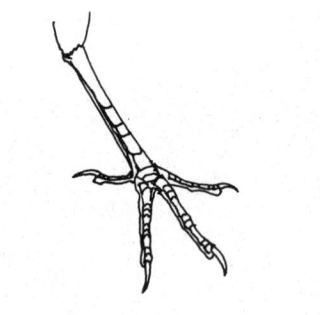

TITMOUSE FAMILY

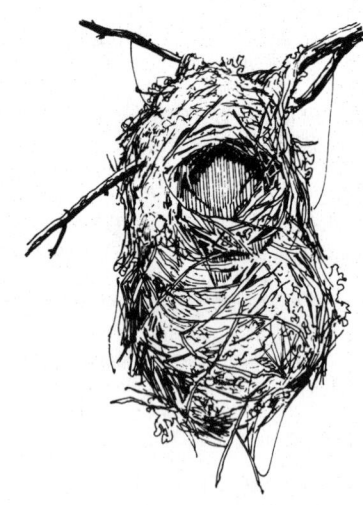

The bushtit's nest is a gourd-shaped pocket made with twigs, mosses, and plant matter and is suspended from a bush or tree.

bushtit; also by extension to such small birds as the unrelated wrentit.

TITLARK

Popular name applied in Great Britain to species of pipits, especially to the meadow pipit, and in N. America, by Audubon, to the Sprague's pipit—a misnomer, as pipits are not related to larks and are in a different family. *See* Lark Family; Pipit Family.

TITMOUSE FAMILY

Paridae (PAY-rih-dee); from Lat. *parus*, a titmouse; *titmouse* comes from Old Icelandic *titr*, meaning something small; *mouse* is a corruption of *mase*, Anglo-Saxon for a kind of bird (Macleod, 1954). 65 species in both Old and New World (Van Tyne and Berger, 1959); songbirds, or perching birds, most of them less than 6 in. long; friendly, curious, relatively tame in presence of man, many in family can be lured to feed from one's hands; includes in N. America 13 species—the bushtits, chickadees, titmice, and the verdin; many in family will nest in bird boxes built for them. Sexes usually outwardly alike; all have soft, thick plumage, mostly grays and browns; all have short, stout, pointed bills; nostrils partly covered with bristles; small but strong legs and feet; rounded wings, each with 10 primary feathers, with outermost, or first, one only half length of second.

Titmice show affinities in behavior, structure, and distribution with crows and jays but are considered closely related to nuthatches, and possibly are of Old World origin; very hardy black-capped chickadee, for example, can usually withstand bitter winter cold; greatest development of family is in N. Hemisphere; in New World, range south to Guatemalan highlands; are most adaptable and teachable of the small birds (see Austin, 1961, and especially Thorpe, 1956b).

Most are migratory but some merely withdraw southward (for example, chickadees in certain years); after nesting season, titmice (chickadees and tufted titmouse, for example) roam woods in small family groups; loose bands in midwinter may join with nuthatches, creepers, kinglets, and woodpeckers; all feeding over limbs and trunks of trees; at bird feeders, chickadees and tufted titmouse are fond of suet, peanut butter and cornmeal mixture; sunflower seeds; tufted titmouse stores sunflower seeds in bark crevices and in ground (Laskey, 1957).

About 45 species are grouped together in a subfamily (Parinae) whose members are mostly cavity nesters; it includes, for example, the N. American black-capped chickadee, and among most studied of all birds, the Eurasian great tit and blue tit (Snow, 1964c); also the closely related sultan tit of the e. Himalayas, largest (8 in. long) in Titmouse Family (tufted titmouse is largest of family in N. America); in another subfamily (Aegithalinae) ornithologists have grouped 8 tiny titmice with long tails —typical is the long-tailed tit of Eurasia; it also includes probably smallest member of the family—the pygmy tit of Java, barely 3 in. long; N. American members of this group are the socia-

ble little bushtits of w. U.S. and the Mexican highlands; a third subfamily (Remizinae), called penduline tits, includes the N. American verdin of chaparral country of w. U.S.

All members of the Titmouse Family are protected by law, but to sustain an injured or ill bird, offer it mockingbird food, fruit, boiled eggs, ground meat, mealworms and other insects, some greens, and bread crumbs, also commercial bird seed mixture and sunflower seeds. See in Terres (1968c; 1977).

Bushtit, *Psaltriparus minimus* (sal-TRIP-ah-rus MIN-ih-mus); genus name: Lat., from Gr. *psaltris*, player of the lute or zither, and Lat. *parus*, titmouse; species name: Lat., least. (Color ill., page 897.) Smallest of N. American Titmouse Family and one of the smallest N. American birds; Pacific coast and deserts and mountains of West; 3¾–4½ in. long; all males and newly hatched young have dark eyes, adult females have light cream-colored eyes (Phillips *et al.*, 1964); tiny, long-tailed, gray-brown, with very short bill; no prominent marks in plumage; drift through live oaks and shrubby thickets in loose flocks of from half a dozen to 20, 30, or 50 birds, except in nesting season, uttering high-pitched twittering, *tsit-tsit-tsit* as they feed (have no song); are sociable, friendly toward each other and toward people, behave like chickadees and travel in company of other small birds in winter, such as kinglets, wrens, chickadees; are usually resident, or year-round, in deciduous and live oaks of Pacific and up to 6,000–8,000 ft. in Rocky Mtns., pinyon and juniper woods, chaparral, brushy streamsides, and in trees and shrubs of residential districts; flocks in winter sometimes roost in eucalyptus trees in Calif.; often visit birdbaths in gardens; pairs begin to separate from flocks in Jan. and Feb. and begin courtship (Bent, 1946).

Feeding Habits: Glean insects and spiders from foliage as they flit about actively in trees and bushes; make short, weak, undulating flights; eat many aphids, treehoppers, leafhoppers, and scale insects; also beetles, wasps, ants, caterpillars, and pupae of codling moth; also some fruit.

Nest: Gourd-shaped, hanging pocket, 7–10 in. or more long, usually suspended in plain sight from trees, saplings, or bushes, 6–25 ft. up, sometimes concealed among lichens; built of twigs, mosses, rootlets, lichens, oak leaves and flowers, bound with spider's silk; hole usually left in one side near top, below it a horizontal passage leads to inside bowl, where eggs laid (Bent, 1946); 34–50 days to complete.

Eggs: Apr.–July; 5–13, commonly 5–7, white.

Incubation: By both sexes, 12 days; young leave nest 14–15 days after hatching.

Other Names: Black-eared bushtit; black-tailed bushtit; coast bushtit; common bushtit; lead-colored bushtit; Lloyd's bushtit.

Host to Cowbirds: Rarely, nine records, in Calif. and B.C. (Friedman, 1963; Smith and Atkin, 1979).

Range: Lives year-round in coastal ranges from sw. B.C. south to s. Baja Calif., in interior from s. and se. Oreg., sw. Idaho, n.-c. Utah, w. Colo., w. Okla., and c. Tex., south into Mexico and to Guatemala.

Bushtit, black-eared. Once considered a distinct species, *Psaltriparus melanotis* (A.O.U. *Check-list*, 1957); has been described by the American Ornithologists' Union (1973) as a black-eared "morph"—variation—or an example of polymorphism in the bushtit, *Psaltriparus minimus*, and now considered one of its subspecies, *Psaltriparus minimus lloydi*. See detailed discussion of the black-eared trait —a broad black mask of color through the eyes of some bushtits—and other variations in their colors in Phillips *et al.* (1964).

Bushtit, black-tailed. *See* Bushtit.

Bushtit, common. *See* Bushtit.

Bushtit, lead-colored. *See* Bushtit.

Chickadee, Acadian. *See* Chickadee, boreal.

Chickadee, black-capped, *Parus atricapillus* (PAY-rus ay-trih-cap-ILL-us); genus name: Lat., titmouse; species name: from Lat. *ater, atri*, black, and *capillus*, hair (crown). (Color ill., page 896.) Across middle and n. N. America; state bird of Me. and Mass.; 4¾–5¾ in. long; wingspread 7½–8½ in.; sexes alike; light gray above, including long tail; white below; feet and claws strong; bill short; *black cap, black bib*, and *white cheeks*, which stand out distinctly when seen some distance away; in winter, sides and flanks deep brownish buff (Forbush, 1925–29); call note, *chicka-dee-dee-dee*, from which got its name, good identifying character; although resident in most parts of range, some migration, even across water, from northern regions (Bent, 1946), and in some years large irruptions (see details in Bagg, 1969; 1970); usually prefers mixed hardwood-coniferous forests; also woodland groves and trees, shrubbery or residential places; some individuals very tame, allow close approach and may flutter to one's hands for walnut kernels (see Terres, 1977); flight slow, flitting, but remarkably quick-moving at pine cones, twigs, now upright, now hanging with back toward ground; when two or more together, chatter much; also utters clear, sweet whistle, throughout winter, when traveling in flocks and in spring and summer; an even note followed by descending notes, *spring, com-ing* or *hear, hear-me* is so-called "phoebe" whistle; responds over and over to imitated notes.

Feeding Habits: Besides foraging over twigs, branches, peeps under bark scales and in crannies for caterpillars, insect eggs, codling moths and larvae; spiders, also beetles, bugs, ants, sawflies, aphids, scale insects, millipedes, snails, small amphibians; also seeds of conifers, bayberries, and other wild fruit (Bent, 1946); also comes to feeding stations for doughnuts, peanut butter and cornmeal mixture, sunflower seeds.
Nest: Dug by pair in rotted birch or pine branch or stub, usually 1–10 ft. up, also nests in abandoned woodpecker holes, knotholes, or in bird box; female carries inside plant fibers, hairs, wool, mosses, feathers, insect cocoons for nest.

Eggs: Apr.–July; 5–10, usually 6–8, white, dotted with brown.
Incubation: By both parents, 11–13 days; young leave when 14–18 days old (Odum, 1941–42); if disturbed, incubating bird in hole utters explosive hiss, like that of snake (Forbush, 1925–29).
Other Names: Black-capped tit; black-capped titmouse; common chickadee; long-tailed chickadee; Oregon chickadee; Yukon chickadee.
Accidents: Sometimes stuck in burrs of burdocks; one caught by wing tips in needles of cedar released by discoverer.
Age: Löf (1967), in Conn., reported 17 banded ones reached 6 years; seven, 7 years; three, 8 years; one, 9 years; one, 10 years, 10 months; another, banded Bedford, N.H., caught and released in same area when 12 years, 5 months, old (Kennard, 1975).
Albinism: Rare; partial albinos (white tail feathers), Va. and Mass.; another, N.Y., crown, chin, and throat *white* instead of black; melanistic one, Ithaca, N.Y., 1933, crown, throat, chin, and *cheeks* black, appeared black-hooded (Anonymous, 1959b).
Host to Cowbirds: Rarely, only four records.
Hybrids: Black-capped × Carolina chickadee; black-capped × mountain chickadee (Gray, 1958); see Brewer (1963) and Rising (1968) for details of chickadee hybridizing.
Weights: In Mich. (19), 9.2–11.8 gr. (Becker and Stack, 1944), or about ⅓ oz.
Range: Resident from c. Alaska, s. Yuk., c. Sask., to Newfoundland, south to nw. Calif., ne. Nev., c. Utah, n. N.M., ne Okla., c. Mo., s.-c. Ill., c. Ind., s. Ohio, W.Va., e. Tenn., w. N.C., w. Md., Pa., and n. N.J.

Chickadee, boreal, *Parus hudsonicus* (PAY-rus hud-SOAN-ih-cuss); genus name: *see* Chickadee, black-capped; species name: Lat., Hudsonian. (Color ill., page 897.) In vast coniferous forests of North to limit of trees; 5–5½ in. long; appears like black-capped chickadee but is only chickadee with *brown* cap, back, and sides; utters call like black-capped, but hoarser, more drawling, *chick-a-deer-deer* or *chick-chee-day-day;* has short, warbled song; tame in presence of man; lives in northern spruce, balsam, and dense pine forests, also near white cedar and hemlock swamps, seen in birches, streamside willows; on forested northern coastal islands; less active and less noisy than black-capped; travel in flocks among themselves; sometimes accompanied by golden-crowned kinglets but less likely to join winter parties of black-capped and other small birds.

Feeding Habits: Often feeds high up in balsam firs, works among cones to extract seeds, hops and flits about restlessly; eats, from tree twigs and branches, caterpillars, moths, beetles, insect pupae and eggs, and seeds of gray birch; comes to feeding stations in winter.
Nest: In natural cavities or abandoned woodpecker holes, or dug by pair (mostly by female) in rotten tree stub, 1–10 ft. above ground; female alone builds nest inside (McLaren, 1975); may fill cavity with dry or green mosses, lichens, fine strips of inner bark of cedars, down from ferns, lined with deer hairs, rabbit fur (Bent, 1946).

Bushtit

TITMOUSE FAMILY

Eggs: June; 4–9, usually 6–7, white, dotted with browns.
Incubation: By female (fed on nest or outside nest hole by male), 11–16 days, most eggs hatch at 15 days; both parents feed young, which fly at 18 days after hatching (McLaren, 1975).
Other Names: Acadian chickadee; brown-capped chickadee; Hudsonian chickadee.
Age: Male banded when adult at Greenville, Tenn., retrapped same place when at least 7 years old.
Range: From tree limit in n. Alaska and Canada to n. U.S.; irregular south in winter, Iowa, Ohio, Md., N.Y., N.J.

Chickadee, brown-capped. *See* Chickadee, boreal.

Chickadee, Carolina, *Parus carolinensis* (PAY-rus cah-row-lin-EN-sis); genus name: *see* Chickadee, black-capped; species name: Lat., of Carolina. (Color ill., page 896.) Year-round in se. U.S.; small; 4¼–4¾ in. long; closely resembles in appearance black-capped chickadee, but smaller and with narrow gray edging on wing feathers, a smaller black bib, shorter tail; usually can be identified by location, as range is south of that of black-capped; some overlap in mountains of N.C., for example, and in winter; call note, *chick-a-dee-dee-dee-dee*, higher-pitched and more rapid than that of black-capped; clear whistled song has four notes instead of two or three of black-capped; uttered in two pairs, first note followed by one of lower pitch, as *sufee-subee* (Dingle, 1946; Brewer, 1961); confined to woods more than black-capped and more sedentary, not only lives in great swamp areas of coastal plains of Southeast but ranges in Blue Ridge Mtns. to 5,000 ft. elevation; is also resident in trees, shrubbery of residential places; may begin nesting in early Feb.; pairs remain mated long time; Nice (1933a) reported pair continuously together for three winters and two summers; except in nesting season, travel in flocks, in fall invariably with tufted titmice, yellow-throated and pine warblers, brown-headed nuthatches, and downy woodpeckers.
Feeding Habits: Almost half of annual food is moths and caterpillars, also eats stink bugs, shield bugs, leafhoppers, treehoppers, aphids, scale insects, ants, bees, wasps, beetles, cockroaches, katydids, also spiders, and seeds of mulberry, redbud, pine, ragweed; come to bird feeders for suet, doughnuts, etc.
Nest: In natural cavity or one excavated by pair, 1–20 ft. up, usually 5–6 ft., or in abandoned woodpecker holes, iron pipes used to support clotheslines and small bridges, in birdhouses; in cavity builds thick foundation of mosses, strips of bark, grasses, down of ferns, feathers, the cup well padded with milkweed down or thistledown, hair of rabbits, cattle, deer, and mice.
Eggs: Mar.–May; 3–8, commonly 6, white, dotted with browns.
Incubation: By both sexes, 11 days; age when young first fly unknown (Dingle, 1946); incubating bird, if disturbed, utters hiss from inside cavity, strikingly like that of copperhead snake.

Other Names: Florida chickadee; plumbeous chickadee; Texan chickadee.
Age: One, banded at Elmer, N.J., caught in same area and released when 10 years, 11 months, old.
Host to Cowbirds: Rarely; only two records (Friedmann, 1963).
Hybrids: See under Chickadee, black-capped.
Weights: A male banded in Ohio, between fall and spring varied from 10½ to 12 gr. (Nice, 1933a), averaged less than ½ oz.; in fall, coastal N.J. (3), 9.6–10.4 gr. (Murray and Jehl, 1964), or about ⅓ oz.; in summer, Kans., females (2), 10.5 and 11.5 gr.; male (1), 11 gr. (Rising, 1965a).
Range: Resident from se. Kan., sw. and e.-c. Mo., c. Ill., c. Ind., c. Ohio, sw. and se. Pa., and south to e.-c. Tex., Gulf coast, and c. Fla.

Chickadee, chestnut-backed, *Parus rufescens* (PAY-rus roof-ESS-enz); genus name: *see* Chickadee, black-capped; species name: from Lat. *rufescere*, to become reddish. (Color ill., page 899.) Pacific coast; 4½–5 in. long; sexes outwardly alike; resembles black-capped chickadee, but has *bright chestnut back, rump, and sides, and dusky brown cap;* lives in dark, coastal, humid coniferous forests along narrow range from Sitka district of s. Alaska southward to south of Monterey Bay, Calif., also in broad-leaved woods along streams or in residential areas, and in redwoods and in large groves of eucalyptus trees of Calif., favors heavy, dark forests of firs, spruces, pines, dense cedar, tamarack, and hemlock woods; fearless, sociable, curious like other chickadees; often travels in flocks of 4 up to 20, loosely associated with mountain chickadees, brown creepers, golden-crowned kinglets, red-breasted nuthatches, song sparrows, dark-eyed (Oregon) juncos; swings from upon dried seed heads and flower clusters of shrubs; utters conversational notes like *kissadee* and *tseek-adee-dee,* "song" like chipping sparrow's; mounts to limb of fir, sings *chick, chick, chick, chick, chick, chick* (Bent, 1946), but no whistled song as in other chickadees.
Feeding Habits: Gleans over trunks of trees, usually high up, but may descend to big crumbling logs of forest floor, flits about tangled branches of salal, elderberry, birches, dogwoods, alders, to catch caterpillars, leafhoppers, treehoppers, scale insects, wasps, beetles, also spiders, some fruit pulp, seeds of conifers; comes to feeding stations for baby chick scratch feed.
Nest: In natural cavity or pair digs own in dead fir, also in knothole of oak, post, or woodpecker hole, usually 1–20 ft. up, sometimes to 80 ft., sometimes in loose colonies; inside builds foundation of green mosses, cotton, hairs of animals, small feathers, sometimes of screech owl.
Eggs: Mar.–June; 5–9, commonly 6–7, white, dotted with red-brown.
Incubation: Period of and age when young first fly unknown.
Other Names: Barlow's chickadee; California chickadee; Nicasio chickadee.
Range: Resident along coasts and coastal islands from s.-c. Alaska to s.-c. Calif., inland along coast ranges to se. Wash., n. Idaho, and nw. Mont.

Chickadee, gray-headed, *Parus cinctus* (PAY-rus SINK-tus); genus name: *see* Chickadee, black-capped; species name: Lat., girdled. Most northern of all chickadees; an Old World species that has crossed Bering Strait from Siberia to become established in Alaska; 5½ in. long; larger and paler than boreal chickadee, and does not have brown sides but pale buff; similar to black-capped chickadee, but has *gray* cap; lives in scattered stands of spruces, willows, and birches along rivers at northern limits of boreal forest; usually the only chickadee to be seen in its northern environment.
Feeding Habits: Voraciously feeds on adult and immature insects and insect eggs, also seeds of conifers and berries in winter; and scraps of food around settlements; has been seen eating fat of frozen caribou carcass when temperature −20° F. Characteristic call is *dee-deer, chee-ee,* or *pee-vee.*
Nest: Usually in abandoned woodpecker hole or pairs chip out with bill a cavity or nest in natural cavities of trees, stumps; build soft bed of mosses, rabbit and lemming fur inside cavity.
Eggs: June–July (?); 7–9, white, finely dotted with browns.
Incubation: Period of and age when young first fly unknown.
Other Names: Alaska chickadee; Siberian chickadee.
Range: In N. America, in n. Alaska, n. Yuk., and nw. Mack.; in Old World, in n. Europe and n. Asia.

Chickadee, Hudsonian. *See* Chickadee, boreal.

Chickadee, long-tailed. *See* Chickadee, black-capped.

Chickadee, Mexican, *Parus sclateri* (PAY-rus SKLAY-teh-rye); genus name: *see* Chickadee, black-capped; species name: for P. L. Sclater, British ornithologist and a founder of the British Ornithologists' Union (Palmer *et al.,* 1954). In U.S. only in Ariz. and N.M.; 5 in. long; sexes alike; similar to black-capped chickadee but has large black bib and gray flanks; only chickadee within its limited range in U.S.; lives as common resident in pine and spruce-fir forests in Chiricahua Mtns. of Ariz. and Animas Mtns. of N.M. (Phillips *et al.,* 1964); in summer, up to 7,000–8,000 ft. elevation; outside of breeding season, can be seen at lower altitudes in flocks in pine-oak woods and groves or Arizona cypress; a common call note is *kabree, kabree, kabree, kabree* or *dzay-dzee.*
Feeding Habits: No information but probably eats insects and seeds as do other chickadees.
Nest: In cavity of dead willow stub, tree trunk or branch; nest is of rabbits' fur and wool.
Eggs: Apr.–May; 5–8, usually 6, white, dotted with reddish brown.
Incubation: Period of and age when young first fly unknown.
Other Name: Sclater's chickadee.
Range: Resident from se. Ariz. and sw. N.M. south through highlands to s.-c. Mexico.

Chickadee, mountain, *Parus gambeli* (PAY-rus GAM-bell-eye); genus name: *see* Chickadee, black-capped; species name: given by Robert Ridgway for William Gambel, mid-19th-century pioneering Calif. ornithologist. (Color ill., page 899.) Mountains of West; 5–5¾ in. long; resembles black-capped chickadee, but only chickadee with white stripe over eyes; grayer than black-capped, with brown-gray sides; lives in nesting season throughout forests of lodgepole pine, spruces, firs, hemlocks, yellow pines, junipers of inner coast ranges, the Sierra Nevadas, and the Rocky Mtns., and in the San Bernardino Mtns. of s. Calif., up to 10,000 ft. elevation or more; after nesting season flocks in fall and winter often range down to blue and valley oaks and in foothills and valleys in cottonwoods and willows along streams, often associate in their foraging in oaks, cedars, pines with migrating warblers and vireos; call is *chick-a-dee-a-dee-a-dee*, not *chick-a-dee-dee* of black-capped, also sweet whistled call of three or four notes, *fee-bee-bay* or *fee-bee, fee-bee,* last notes coming down scale like nursery song "Three Blind Mice" (Bent, 1946).

Feeding Habits: Little published data but probably like those of other chickadees; comes to feeding stations for baby chick scratch feed and sunflower seeds.
Nest: In natural cavity or one dug by pair in rotted stump, tree, from few inches above ground to 80 ft. up, usually 6–15 ft., in woodpecker hole, sometimes in bird box; built of soft plant materials, lined with rabbit and squirrel fur, hairs of cattle.
Eggs: Apr.–July; 6–12, usually 8–9, white, unspotted or spotted with browns.
Incubation: 14 days (Bent, 1946); age when young leave nest about 20 days but no detailed studies.
Other Names: Bailey's chickadee; Grinnell's chickadee; Inyo chickadee; short-tailed chickadee.
Age: One banded wild one caught and released when 7 years, 9 months, old (Kennard, 1975).
Hybrids: Mountain × black-capped chickadee (Gray, 1958).
Range: Resident in mountains from se. Alaska, B.C., and sw. Alta. south to n. Baja Calif., c. and se. Ariz., se. and c. N.M., and sw. Tex.

Chickadee, plumbeous. *See* Chickadee, Carolina.

Chickadee, short-tailed. *See* Chickadee, mountain.

Chickadee, Siberian. *See* Chickadee, gray-headed.

Titmouse, black-capped. *See* Chickadee, black-capped.

Titmouse, black-crested, *Parus bicolor atricristatus* (PAY-rus BIE-color ay-trih-kris-TAY-tus); genus name: *see* Chickadee, black-capped; species name: Lat., two-colored; subspecies name: from Lat. *ater, atri,* black, and *cristatus,* crested. (Color ill., page 898.) Now considered a subspecies of the tufted titmouse, *Parus bicolor;* Mexican bird in U.S. in Tex. and Okla.; 5½–6 in. long; gray upperparts, whitish below, rusty flanks; long *jet-black* pointed *crest* of male, usually erect, and *dark crest* of female, distinguish them from tufted titmouse; is Mexican counterpart, in behavior, of tufted titmouse (Blake, E. R. 1953); lives in groves of deciduous trees, heavy timber, shade trees of towns and in woodlands along creeks, and in scrub oaks and cedars of hillsides; common wherever trees grow; noisy, active, friendly, during nesting season in pairs, but later in family groups and in winter in loose companies about towns; calls *peter, peter, peter,* like tufted titmouse but shorter; also series of monotonous whistles, *hew, hew, hew, hew, hew, hew,* also rasping, scolding notes.

Feeding Habits: Insects and their eggs, spiders, berries, and some soft-shelled nuts (pecans, which they crack open with bills) and acorns.
Nest: In natural cavity of tree, stump, 3–20 ft. up, or in telephone poles, fence posts, woodpecker holes, bird boxes; built of mass of cow hair, rabbit fur, green lichens, mosses, cedar bark, feathers, grasses, wool, rootlets, hemp, tissue paper, onion skins, shed snakeskins, etc.
Eggs: Mar.–Apr.; 4–7, usually 5–7, white, spotted with red-brown.
Incubation: Period of and age when young leave nest unknown.
Other Name: Sennett's titmouse.
Host to Cowbirds: Rare, only two records (Friedmann, 1963).
Hybrids: According to Dixon (1955), crossbreeds with tufted titmouse in narrow zone where ranges of the two overlap in Tex.
Range: Resident from c. Tex. south to e.-c. Mexico.

Titmouse, bridled, *Parus wollweberi* (PAY-rus woll-WEB-er-eye); genus name: *see* Chickadee, black-capped; species name: given in 1850 by Charles Lucien Bonaparte for Wollweber, a 19th-century traveler and collector of birds in Mexico; *bridled,* from black-and-white markings on its head, which suggest outline of a horse's bridle. (Color ill., page 898.) Mexican species that reaches northern limits of its range in sw. N.M. and s. Ariz.; 4½–5 in. long; sexes outwardly alike; small, light gray, has sharply pointed crest, black-and-white "bridled" face; most attractive of all crested titmice; similar mountain chickadee has no crest; lives in oak-covered foothills of Huachuca Mtns., where abundant, up to 5,000–6,000 ft. elevation; nests occasionally to 7,000 ft.; except in nesting season, roams in small flocks; prefers evergreen oaks; in winter may wander down from mountains to wooded valleys and streams; like other titmice, after nesting season travels in family groups and small flocks in fall (Bent, 1946); at human imitation of hoots of pygmy owl, quickly sounds alarm notes, which bring other small birds into view; call is harsh, squealing *chick-a-dee-dee-dee,* and high-pitched, quickly repeated two-note *fee-bee* whistle.

Feeding Habits: Spends much time in oak groves, foraging over branches and in crevices of bark for insects, their eggs and larvae.

Gray-headed chickadee

Mexican chickadee

TITMOUSE FAMILY

Nest: In natural cavities of trees, stumps, 4–28 ft. above ground, lined with down of cottonwoods, dried grasses, leaves, cotton, downy coverings of leaf buds, flowers, catkins, lichens, rabbit fur, cocoons of insects or of spiders.

Eggs: Mar.–May; 5–7, white.

Incubation: Period of and age when young leave nest unknown.

Other Name: Wollweber's titmouse.

Range: Resident from c. and se. Ariz. and sw. N.M. south to s. Mexico.

Titmouse, crested. *See* Titmouse, tufted.

Titmouse, gray. *See* Titmouse, plain.

Titmouse, plain, *Parus inornatus* (PAY-rus in-or-NAY-tus); genus name: *see* Chickadee, black-capped; species name: Lat., unadorned (plain). (Color ill., page 898.) The common plain gray titmouse of West; western counterpart of eastern tufted titmouse; 5–5½ in. long; gray or gray-brown above, pale gray or whitish below, with jaunty crest appears like miniature jay; lives on oak-clad sunny slopes and foothills or in pinyons and junipers where food and shelter are year-round; from Rocky Mtns. to Pacific coast, and from Ore. to Baja Calif., also in urban residential areas where trees available; pairs have tendency to remain mated for at least 2 years; forages over bark prying into crevices with bill, often clings upside down from twig or branch and hammers food, never gathers in large flocks, highly inquisitive; spring song is clear whistled *witt-y, witt-y, witt-y;* common note is *tsick-a-dee-dee* or *tsick-a-dear;* often roosts in cavities in trees, sometimes in pines.

Feeding Habits: From limbs, twigs, or off ground, takes many insects: bugs, black scales, leafhoppers, aphids, beetles, weevils, caterpillars, grasshoppers, ants, leaf galls; also weed seeds, pinyon nuts, acorns, oats, cherries (Bent, 1946); also comes to bird-feeding trays.

Nest: Selected by female (Dixon, 1949), in natural cavities in trunks, limbs of trees, sometimes pair dig cavity in rotten wood of living tree; also nests in poles or woodpecker holes, 3–35 ft. up, also use cavities for roosting places (absence of may limit population), nests in bird boxes; nest built of mosses, grasses, weed stems, fibers, lined with feathers, cow hair, rabbit fur; defend territories, 3–12 acres during nesting season.

Eggs: Mar.–July; 3–9, commonly 6–8, white, sometimes faintly dotted with reddish brown.

Incubation: By female (she has brood patch, male does not); male feeds her at nest; incubation is 14–16 days; young leave nest when about 16–21 days old by climbing up to cavity opening, and when not able to fly more than a few feet (Dixon, 1949).

Other Names: Gray titmouse; Oregon titmouse; San Diego titmouse.

Age: Two, banded Calif., retrapped same place when 5 years old; Price (1936) reported one, banded while nesting in bird box, recaptured same place when 7 years old.

Weights: About 13.7 gr. (Dixon, 1949), or about ½ oz.

Range: Resident from s. Ore., Nev., se. Idaho, sw. Wyo., s.-c. Colo., south to Baja Calif., c. and se. Ariz., c. N.M., w. Tex.

Titmouse, tufted, *Parus bicolor* (PAY-rus BIE-color); genus name: *see* Chickadee, black-capped; species name: *see* Titmouse, black-crested. (Color ill., page 898.) Common mainly east of Great Plains in woodlands of se. U.S.; small, yet largest N. American member of Titmouse Family; 6–6½ in. long; wingspread 9¼–10¾ in.; sexes alike; gray above, white below; *flanks rusty brown; prominent, pointed crest;* relatively large dark eyes; lives in deciduous woodlands, prefers those of swamps and river bottoms; has adapted to residential woods, shade trees of villages, city parks; active, vivacious, flits about foliage of trees, often hangs head downward while inspecting twigs, leaves, or clings to trunk or branches, searching in bark crevices for insect food, wanders about in winter in small flocks; tame, comes near at sounds of human voices, intelligent, quick to learn (Bent, 1946); takes food from one's hands (see Terres, 1977), quickly stores sunflower seeds in bark crevices or in ground; responds to "squeaking" (see example in Terres, 1968c), imitations of its calls bring it near with remarkable boldness; loud whistled call of 4–8 phrases given any month of year, commonly translated as *peto, peto, peto* or *peter, peter, peter,* both sexes sing, but females much less than males (Brackbill, 1970d); also commonly utter harsh, peevish *day-day-day* (Bent, 1946); male dominant over female, pairs may form at any season, separate from winter flocks by Feb., mated until death or disappearance of one of pair, one pair remained together 3 years, 4 months (Brackbill, 1970d); males feed females in courtship.

Feeding Habits: Eats especially caterpillars, also opens cocoons of moths, also eats beetles, ants, many wasps, and especially sawfly larvae, bees, bugs, treehoppers, scales, cockroach eggs, a few snails, some spiders; blackberries, blueberries, elderberries, serviceberries, mulberries, wild cherries, seeds of sumac, tulip trees, alder, poison ivy, bayberry, and acorns, chinquapins, beechnuts—holds nuts under feet on branch and opens with rapid blows of bill; comes to feeding stations for suet, bread, etc. (see in Terres, 1968c).

Nest: In natural cavities of trees, 3–90 ft. up, in abandoned woodpecker holes, bird boxes, hollow metal pipes, fence posts; nest of wool, mosses, cotton, leaves, fibrous bark, hair, pieces of shed snakeskin—will pluck hairs from live woodchucks, squirrels, opossums, and from human beings seated quietly near nest site.

Eggs: Mar.–May; 5–8, commonly 5–6, white or cream-white, speckled with browns.

Incubation: By female, 13–14 days (Laskey, 1957; Brackbill, 1970d); young climb out of cavity when 17–18 days old; both parents feed young; sometimes two broods a season; young of first brood sometimes help care for second brood.

Other Names: Crested titmouse; crested tomtit; pete bird; tufted chickadee; tufted tit.

Age: One nested each year in bird box in Pa. backyard, last caught by bander when 7 years, 4 months, old (Middleton, 1949); possibly same bird caught again by Middleton and released when it was 12 years old (Kennard, 1975).

Host to Cowbirds: Uncommon, only a few records (Friedmann, 1963).

Hybrids: Two from crossbreeding of tufted titmouse and black-capped chickadee cited by Cockrum (1952); *see also* under Black-crested titmouse.

Weights: In Ohio (35), 20.3–25.3 gr. Nice (1933a), or about ¾–1 oz.; in Tenn. (14), average 20.5 gr. (Laskey, 1957); in Mar., in Pa. (9), average 22.6 gr. (Condee, 1970).

Range: Resident from se. Neb., c. and e. Iowa, se. Minn., s. Wisc., s. Mich., s. Ont., n. Ohio, nw. Pa., c. N.Y., and New England south to se. Tex., Gulf coast, and c. Fla.; has been spreading north in large numbers.

Verdin, *Auriparus flaviceps* (aw-RIP-ay-rus FLAY-vih-seps); genus name: from Lat. *aurum,* gold, and *parus,* titmouse; species name: from Lat. *flavus,* tawny, and *caput,* head; *verdin* (VUR-din): from Fr., meaning yellowhammer. (Color ill., page 899.) No crest as in titmice; deserts of sw. U.S.; 4–4½ in. long; tiny, brown-gray above, paler below, head and throat of male largely bright yellow (female duller); feathers at bend of wings bright reddish chestnut, but not conspicuous unless wings opened; immatures have no yellow on head, no chestnut on wings; similar bushtits have longer tails; common, lives in mesquite, hackberry, hawthorn, catclaw, screw bean, paloverde, chollas, and other scattered stiff-twigged thorny trees or shrubs; shares environment with cactus wrens, crissal and curve-billed thrashers, and horned toads of desert (Bent, 1946); moves and behaves like related chickadees, flits about in bushes searching for food, often clings and hangs head downward at ends of twigs; shy in nesting season, when remains hidden in thickets, in winter shows little fear of human observers; roams desert in pairs or small family groups; remarkable voice has great depth and carrying power for small bird, utters loud whistled song, *tswee, tswee, tswee, tsweet!,* common call is rapid *tsit, tsit, tsit* and chickadeelike *tsee-tu-tu* when hunting.

Feeding Habits: Searches among terminal twigs, buds, and under leaves for insects, their larvae and eggs; also eats some wild fruit and berries, from which probably gets sufficient moisture for needs, as sometimes nests 10 mi. from water.

Nest: Oval or ball-shaped mass, up to 8 in. in diameter, of thorny twigs, from few hundred twigs to two thousand, and often exposed near end of low limb, or in crotch of bush or tree, 2–20 ft. above ground; lined with leaves, grasses, feathers, plant down, spider's silk; verdins also build roosting, or winter, nests (Bent, 1946).

Eggs: Mar.–June; 3–6, usually 4–5, blue-white or green-white, sparingly dotted with reddish brown.

Incubation: 10 (?) days; young leave nest when about 21 days old; return to nest at night to sleep.

Other Names: Bushtit; eastern verdin; goldtit.
Host to Cowbirds: Rarely, a few records (Friedmann, 1963).
Range: Resident from se. Calif., s. Nev., sw. Utah, w. and s. Ariz., s. N.M., Tex. south to s. Baja Calif. and c. Mexico.

TOADS AND BIRDS
See Amphibians and Birds.

TOBACCO BIRD
See Dove, ground, in Pigeon Family.

TODY FAMILY
See Coraciiformes.

TOE
See Feet and Legs.

TOLMIE
WILLIAM FRASER (1812–86). Born Inverness, Scotland; educated at Glasgow; a medical officer with the Hudson's Bay Company in Canada beginning in 1832. John K. Townsend met Dr. Tolmie at Ft. Vancouver, Wash., in 1836, and in 1839, in his *Narrative of a Journey Across the Rocky Mountains,* Townsend named the Tolmie's warbler (now called MacGillivray's) *Oporornis tolmiei* in his honor. Tolmie became Chief Factor of the Hudson's Bay Company in 1856; retired in 1860; died at Victoria, B.C. (Palmer, 1928).

TOMIAL TOOTH
Term for toothlike projection on each side of the cutting edge (tomium) of the upper half of the bill (upper mandible) in falcons and shrikes. *See* Falcon Family; Shrike Family; *also* Bill.

TOMTIT
or TOMMYTIT. Another name for the tufted titmouse.

TONGUE
Because the tongue in most birds is often adapted, either in part or collectively, by its shape, sensitivity, mobility, size, texture, and extensibility, to helping each bird get the kinds of food it eats, it is enormously varied. It may be used by certain birds to identify food by taste (*see* Taste); by others through touch—the long-billed herons, ibises, sandpipers, and snipe (Gardner, 1925), and possibly woodpeckers, finches, and parrots, whose tongues are thick with tactile corpuscles (Welty, 1962) (*see* Touch); in grazing swans and geese, it may be a powerful tearing structure to help the bill bite off weeds and grasses (Coues, 1884).

In some fish-eating birds, such as mergansers and penguins, that have well-developed tongues (kingfishers and many other fish-eating birds do not), backward-pointing projections of the tongue's surface may hold the slippery prey; in woodpeckers, the pointed extensible tip is often used as a spear or probe; in ducks, the serrated edges as a sieve; in hummingbirds and sunbirds, as a troughlike tube; in sap-sucking woodpeckers, as a brush to draw in sap by capillary attraction; in hawks and vultures, the rough surface may be used as a rasp; in parrots and sparrows, as a finger (Gardner, 1925).

A parrot can manipulate a nut, a sparrow a seed, by turning it about with the tongue; the mobility of a parrot's tongue may help it to mimic human speech. Birds such as crossbills and goldfinches use their tongues to extract kernels from seeds they crack with the bill (Gardner, 1925), and megapodes (brush turkeys and mallee fowl) are thought to use the tongue to test the temperatures of their nesting mounds (Frith, 1964). *See* discussion under Megapode.

The muscular tongue is attached rearward in the floor of the mouth, and it may be thick and horny, especially toward the tip. In general, its shape conforms to that of the bill and the muscles that move it are attached to the paired hyoid bones which give the tongue its support and mobility (Harrison, J.G., 1964b).

Tongues range in size from a nodule, or "a mere toothpick of flesh" (Gardner, 1925), in cormorants, gannets, pelicans, and anhingas—all of which are fish-eaters (*see* Fishes and Birds) and must be able to swallow a large fish whole and quickly (*see* Esophagus)—to the large thick, fleshy tongue of the flamingos. The American flamingo eats small mollusks (*see* Mollusks and Birds) and actually uses its large tongue to help it gather the most minute foods (Allen, 1956a).

BIRDS WITH THE LONGEST TONGUES. Most woodpeckers, especially the ant-eating flickers, have unusually long-reaching tongues, aided by extensible hyoid bones, which, rearward, divide into two slender bony and muscular "horns" (Bellairs and Jenkin, 1960) that curve backward around the base of the skull, then upward and over the forehead and attach in or near the nostrils. This remarkable adaptation allows woodpeckers with their barbed-tip tongues, coated with saliva, to reach deep into cracks and crevices of bark and into the galleries of ants and burrows of wood-boring beetle larvae and other insects on which they feed.

The muscular and bony arrangement by which the woodpecker's tongue is protruded and withdrawn was described by R. Waller in England in 1716 and by others before him, and was very thoroughly studied by Leiber (1907). *See* under Woodpecker Family.

When the long hyoid processes of woodpeckers are withdrawn and not in use, they are said to be compressed like the folds of a concertina (Hess, 1951). The hyoid bone of many is about two and one half times as long as the upper mandible (maxilla); in the green woodpecker, *Picus viridus,* of Europe, it is four times the length of the upper half of the bill; in the small wryneck, *Jynx torquilla,* a bird of Eurasia, n. Africa, and Japan, related to the woodpeckers, it is five times the length of the upper mandible (Hess, 1951). *See* Mandible; Bill.

Roberts (1939) found the wryneck's tongue and hyoid processes to be nearly two thirds the length of the bird's body, excluding the tail, and believed it to have, relatively, the longest-known tongue of any bird in the world.

Other woodpeckers, such as the N. American hairy and downy woodpeckers and the white-headed woodpecker of the Far West (*see* under Woodpecker Family), have shorter tongues than the ground-feeding flickers, but they have

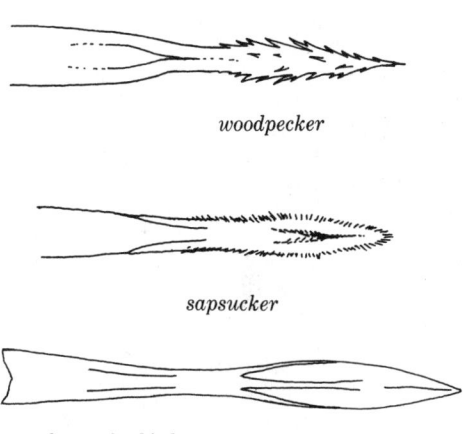

TOMIAL TOOTH
In the peregrine falcon, as in most falcons, the bill is conspicuously toothed.

TONGUE
Woodpeckers and hummingbirds have long, extensible tongues that enable them to exploit less accessible food sources. The woodpecker's tongue has barbs and a spearlike tip with which it extracts insects and grubs from holes and crevices. The sapsucker's tongue has brushy hairs that take up sap by capillary action. Hummingbirds, most of which have forked tongues, roll the sides into troughs, where insects and nectar are trapped when the tongue is inserted into the corolla of a flower.

more barbs on the tips, which aid them in extracting grubs of beetles and other insects from their burrows (Gardner, 1925).

In sapsuckers (a woodpecker) the extensibility of the tongue is reduced to a minimum in the group, and instead of a barbed tip, the tongue has a fine brush of hairs that serve it by capillarity to draw in sap of trees on which these birds often feed. *See* Commensalism.

Lories and lorikeets, members of the Parrot Family that are numerous in the Australian Region (*see* Australian Region), have brush-tipped tongues that aid them in gathering nectar and insects from flowers (Gilliard, 1958).

TONGUES OF HUMMINGBIRDS. Hummingbirds and certain other nectar-eaters—sunbirds, honeyeaters, and various honeycreepers—have long, usually forked and extensible tongues, the sides of which they often roll into trough-like tubes for gathering nectar (Wallace, 1963). Hummingbirds and sunbirds have the long, bifid tongue folded over to form two tubes, or grooves, the ends of which are frayed, or fringed. When they work the tongue in and out of flowers at great speed, nectar, and insects entangled in the fringed tip, are forced into the tubes (Harrison, J.G., 1964b).

For years it was believed that hummingbirds had hollow tongues and used them as "soda straws" to suck up nectar from flowers. To dispel these and other misunderstandings, Weymouth *et al.* (1964), studied anatomically in the laboratory the tongues of Allen's, Rivoli's, ruby-throated, rufous, and Costa's hummingbirds. They concluded that the hummingbird's tongue does not and cannot serve as a "soda straw," or sucking organ—it is not hollow—and that the troughlike tubes of the *forked* parts of the tongue probably take up nectar by capillary action, not by suction.

In feeding, when the hummingbird retracts the tongue into its mouth, it then swallows the nectar in a normal way (*see* Swallowing).

Hummingbirds and honeyeaters also have the long hyoid processes that encircle the skull, as in woodpeckers, which allows the great extensibility of the tongue (Welty, 1962).

TONGUES OF SOME OTHER BIRDS. Flesh-eaters—vultures, hawks, and owls—have a comparatively simple tongue (Lucas, 1895), and most passerines, or songbirds, apparently have a tongue that reaches out little more than the length of the bill. Although it can be seen to move when the bird sings, it does not play any part in singing (Harrison, J. G., 1964b). *See* Songs and Singing. It may, however, have adaptations such as backward-pointing papillae that aid it in swallowing food.

Titmice and nuthatches have tiny forklike projections at the tip of the tongue that help them collect small insects and spider's eggs from the crevices of tree bark (Gardner, 1925).

A TYPICAL SONGBIRD'S TONGUE. The tongue of the American robin (a thrush) is rather thin and horny and slightly curled. It is somewhat thickened at the base, or hind part, is slightly split at the tip, and at the rear has a row of fleshy, backwardly directed spines. Except for these spines, whose function seems to be to direct food toward the gullet (*see* Esophagus), the robin's tongue shows no adaptations to any particular kinds of foods. It may be called, according to Lucas (1895), the typical pattern of the tongue of thrushes, warblers, and a great host of N. American birds. It is a type that has endless variations, or patterns, in the amount of its curvature, number of posterior (rear) points, and extent of fraying, or "feathering," of the tip.

Among the so-called "talking" birds—parrots, parakeets, crows, canaries, and the brown thrasher, for example—it is apparently not known whether the tongue is used by these birds in producing sounds that imitate human speech—just how it is done is still a mystery (Thorpe, 1964a). The advice to split the tongue of a pet crow (which already has a slightly split tongue) to help it to talk is an old wives' tale, and even if it could be done, would inflict cruelty on the bird, without aiding its ability, if not stifling it altogether. *See* Folklore; *also* Mimicry; Parrot Family; Starling Family.

TONGUE WORMS
See Parasite.

TOOL-USING
According to Thorpe (1956b), the use of tools by birds or by other animals is the manipulation of objects that serve as an extension of the body of the animal itself. It has been reported in nature for relatively few and unrelated species: the black-breasted buzzard kite and the Egyptian vulture (*see* Egg-eating); the long-tailed tailorbird, which uses spider's silk as thread; the satin bowerbird, which uses fibrous material held in its bill as a brush to paint the sticks of its bower; and the Galápagos woodpecker-finch, which uses long cactus spines as an extension of its short, stout bill to poke into crevices for spiders or insects—when they try to escape it drops the cactus spine and seizes them in its bill (Lack, 1947).

More recently, Morse (1968) reported what appears to be the first example of tool-using by a N. American bird. In forests of w. Tangipahoa Parish, La., in the fall and winter of 1963–64, he watched brown-headed nuthatches, in their food-hunting, first pry off with the bill a small scale of bark from a pine tree. Then each used its bark scale as an extension of its bill to remove another bark scale from a tree to get at insects and spiders that hide under the pine bark. Occasionally each of the nuthatches carried its bark-scale tool in the bill and flew short distances to another pine tree to repeat the process there.

Meyerriecks (1972) watched a double-crested cormorant use one of its own molted feathers, which it picked up in its bill from the ground, to reach back and get oil from its preen gland (*see* Preening) on the feather. It then repeatedly applied the molted feather, presumably with the oil on it, to the feathers of its right wing.

The green heron has been observed to stir the water with a piece of bread in its bill, then strike at fish coming to nibble on the bread.

In another example of "tool-using" by a N. American bird, Jones and Kamil (1973) reported that an adult blue jay, which they had raised in their laboratory, was seen one day to rip a piece of paper from the floor of its cage. Then it thrust the extended piece of paper back and forth between the wires of the next cage to rake food pellets from the adjacent cage close enough to reach them with its bill. The authors knew of no previous reports of "tool use" in the wild by blue jays. On different occasions, they offered the blue jay a piece of straw, a paper clip, and a tie for a plastic bag, all of which it used as a tool to sweep the food pellets in the adjacent cage close enough to eat them. *See also* Curiosity and Memory under Behavior; *also* Birds That Store Food under Food and Feeding Habits.

TOOTHED BIRDS
See Hesperornis; Ichthyornis—both believed from fossil evidence to be the last birds that had teeth. *See also Archaeopteryx* under Origin of Birds and of Bird Flight in Fossil Birds.

TOPOGRAPHY
The "map" of a bird. For precision and accuracy when describing the outer observable parts of birds, ornithologists refer commonly to distinct areas of the body and certain distinguishing features of the bill, wings, tail, and toes. For example, in describing certain body regions, perhaps to describe areas that have certain colors, they refer to the nape (back of neck), lore, chin, jugulum, and so on; feathers that belong to certain groups are identified, for example, as scapulars, primaries, rectrices, and so on; parts of the bill are the upper mandible and lower mandible; the foot is divided into two parts, the tarsus and the toes (the leg—thigh, crus, or "drumstick," and knee—is concealed by feathers). *See* Feet and Legs; Skeleton.

TOPSY-TURVY-BIRD
Another name for the red-breasted nuthatch and white-breasted nuthatch.

TORCH-BIRD
Another name for the Blackburnian warbler.

TORPIDITY
A state of inactivity that is brought about by certain physiological changes—greatly lowered heart rate, breathing rate, and metabolism, and a greatly reduced response to external stimulation. A few hummingbirds and the poorwill enter a state of torpor, the former for short periods of several hours at night, the latter for weeks at a time in response to an inadequate supply of insects (Dawson and Hudson, 1970; Calder and King, 1974).

For centuries men believed that, in winter, swallows and other birds hibernated in the mud, or flew to the moon, but on Dec. 29, 1946, Prof. Edmund C. Jaeger of Riverside College, Calif., began studies of the first scientifically documented record of a bird in hibernation (Jaeger, 1948), although a previous observation of a poor-will by Lyman Belding (1890), and one by Culbertson (1946) of a poor-will half buried beneath a pine branch in below-freezing weather near Fresno, Calif., had strongly suggested the condition.

With two students, Jaeger was walking through a narrow, high-walled canyon in the

Chuckawalla Mtns. of se. Calif. when they saw a poor-will, *Phalaenoptilus nuttallii*, resting snugly in a small hollow crypt in the face of the rock wall. Jaeger touched the bird and later picked it up. He found its feet and eyelids cold to the touch, and even shouted to awaken it, without rousing it from its deep sleep, or torpor. He returned the bird to its place in the rock wall.

During Jaeger's later observations, the poor-will slept for about 88 winter days, and even though the air temperature around the bird varied considerably, Jaeger found that the bird's internal temperature, determined with a rectal thermometer, varied only from 64.4° to 67° F., compared with the normal internal temperature of 106° F. in an active poor-will. Jaeger could detect no heartbeat or breathing in the bird and it lost weight slowly and continuously during its hibernation period. In late Feb., when the poor-will returned to normal, he estimated that it had taken the bird about a week to come out of its lethargy (Jaeger, 1949). Jaeger reported that the Hopi Indians of this region apparently knew of the poor-will's hibernating habit, for they called it *holchko*, or "the sleeping one."

A number of other hibernating poor-wills have been discovered since Jaeger's record, but especially interesting was one found hibernating on a porch at San Bernardino, Calif., on Dec. 27 during the Christmas Bird Count of 1959; another, at Carlsbad Caverns National Park by a Christmas Bird Count group on Dec. 26, 1961, who had the thrill of examining the sleeping bird in the hand. *See* Christmas Bird Count.

After Jaeger's discovery, Howell and Bartholomew (1959) experimented with captive poor-wills and discovered that when they subjected the birds to temperatures ranging from 35.6° to 66° F., the poor-wills became torpid, and that 10 gr. (less than ½ oz.) of stored fat in a poor-will would sustain it in hibernation for 100 days if the temperature remained at 50° F. Marshall's experiments (1955) showed that torpidity in poor-wills was not caused directly by cold, but when denied food, and after losing 20% of their weight, they became torpid.

Although most adult birds (*see* Young and Their Care) maintain a high body temperature at all times (*see* Cold and Birds; Metabolism), a few species, though unable to hibernate like the poor-will, can become torpid temporarily, especially certain insect-eating birds; this permits them to survive short periods of cool or cold weather when food may be unavailable. *See* Fasting.

A state of torpor has been induced in widely unrelated birds: owls, nighthawks, hummingbirds, swifts, colies, swallows, and titmice. Reduced body temperature, but not deep torpor, has been reported for the smooth-billed ani, greater roadrunner, and turkey vulture (Calder and King, 1974). Heath (1962) found that the body temperature of a captive turkey vulture decreased during the night, and he suggested that this was a distinct advantage to a carrion feeder such as a vulture, which does not always find food during the day.

In 1964, Lasiewski and Dawson reported experimental hypothermia (below-normal body

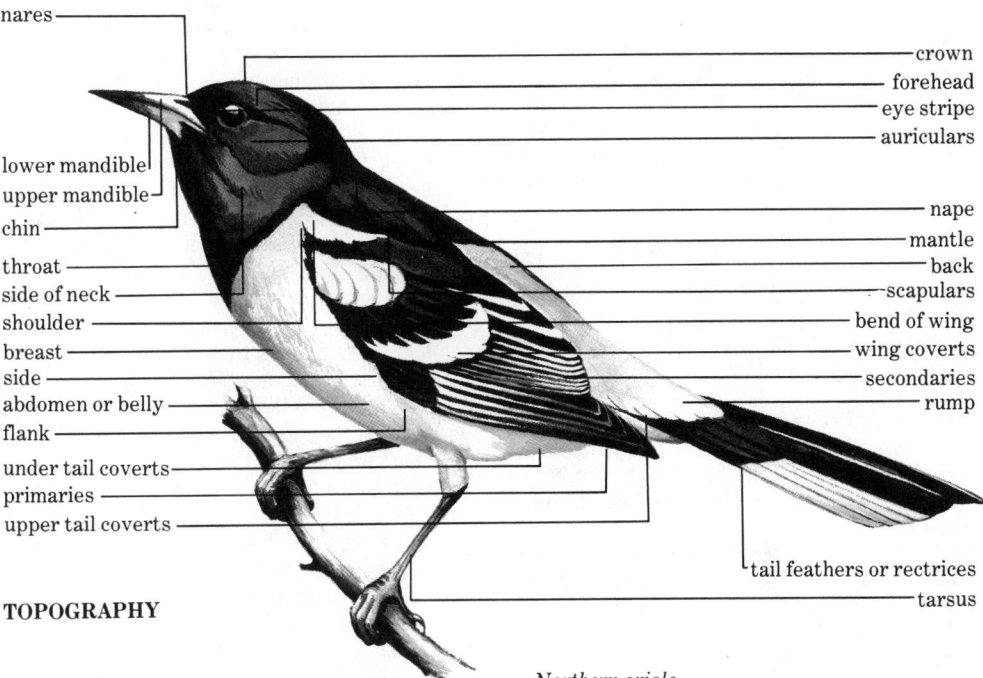

TOPOGRAPHY

Northern oriole

nares — crown — forehead — eye stripe — auriculars — lower mandible — upper mandible — chin — nape — mantle — back — scapulars — bend of wing — wing coverts — secondaries — rump — throat — side of neck — shoulder — breast — side — abdomen or belly — flank — under tail coverts — primaries — upper tail coverts — tail feathers or rectrices — tarsus temperature) in the common nighthawk upon losses in the experimental birds of 28–34% of their initial weight; in Europe, Peiponen (1965) reported below-normal body temperatures and torpidity in the common nightjar, *Caprimulgus europaeus;* Dawson and Fisher (1969) reported on the spotted nightjar, *Eurostopodus guttatus;* and MacMillen and Trost (1967) recorded nighttime lowering of body temperature in the Inca dove as a possible emergency measure in this bird in response to restricted food and/or water. See also Ivacic and Labisky (1973).

Hummingbirds have been known to become torpid since Alexander Wilson, "father of American ornithology," described in 1810 the recovery of a ruby-throated hummingbird from torpidity that lasted half a day. John Gould, British artist and illustrator, in his 19th-century monograph on the hummingbirds published in 1861, reported that two species of S. American hummingbirds in his laboratory became torpid at 63–70° F. and sat on their perches, heads drawn into their shoulders, and "showed . . . no spark of life; they could be moved about and laid on a table like so many dried skins."

Oliver L. Pearson (1950), after studying N. American Allen's and Anna's hummingbirds, reported that at night they became torpid—their body temperature dropped to within a few degrees of an environmental temperature of 70° F. Because of their high metabolic rate (*see* Metabolism), limited energy reserves, and inability to feed at night, such small birds would apparently starve to death before morning unless they could minimize their energy losses. To overcome this handicap, hummingbirds go into a deathlike torpor—their body temperature is lowered, breathing reduced, and metabolic rate lowered. The condition resembles the hibernation of the poor-will, except that it is usually maintained only until daylight, when flower nectar or insect food again becomes available.

Most N. American hummingbirds are migratory and can escape severe and prolonged cold and lack of food in winter; apparently some, if not all, poor-wills do not migrate and can hibernate (prolonged torpor) to survive the winter.

Pearson (1960) reported that female hummingbirds, while sitting on the nest incubating eggs or brooding nestlings, do not go into a torpor at night, thus maintaining the temperature of the eggs and nestlings. Insulation of the nest itself helps retain warmth and the young hummingbirds do not become torpid until after they leave the nest (Matthews, 1964b). See Anna's and Calliope hummingbirds in Hummingbird Family.

Pearson also pointed out that there is a considerable saving of food calories (potential energy) for a hummingbird each 24 hours by becoming torpid at night, but according to Lasiewski (1963), experimenting with 67 individuals of 5 species—Costa's, Anna's, Allen's, rufous, and calliope—hummingbirds do not become torpid every night, and torpidity is probably an emergency measure for a hummingbird when its energy reserves are low. Also, temporary hypothermia (below-normal body temperature) in hummingbirds has been seen in the field as well as in the laboratory, but

it is difficult to judge its incidence under natural conditions; presumably, hummingbirds are unable to survive torpor at below-freezing temperatures; they must fly to warmer regions or find shelter, such as in caves, as reported by Pearson (1953) in S. American hummingbirds in high mountains where the temperatures may drop to freezing at night.

Active hummingbirds, however, have been seen flying about at below freezing—rubythroated hummingbirds in late-spring cold of 22–28° F. in Canada during the last two weeks of May 1936, and a female rubythroat in a N.C. garden was seen daily from Dec. 3, 1963, to Jan. 3, 1964, during which time temperatures dropped to below freezing on 28 nights and below 20° F. on 7 consecutive nights. The bird appeared to depend almost wholly on sugarwater syrup put out for it each day in a hummingbird feeder; its nightly roost could not be discovered. See Bird-attracting. Fla. and s. Ala. are usually the northern part of the rubythroated hummingbird's winter range.

In a later study, Weymouth *et al.* (1964), a team of investigators that included Lasiewski, found that hummingbirds, especially the Rivoli's, have a well-developed crop that rises as an outpocketing of the wall of the esophagus; hummingbirds in the laboratory used their crops to store insects and/or sugar solution. The investigators concluded—in view of Lasiewski's previous discovery (1963) that hummingbirds do not necessarily go into a torpor each night—that the stored food in the crop has importance in sustaining hummingbirds overnight just as it has in evening grosbeaks and other finches in the winter in the North, which fill their crops with seeds late in the day or just before going to sleep. See Cold and Birds; Crop.

Even the young of certain birds that become torpid gain from this ability. Nestlings of the European swift, *Apus apus,* become torpid when cool or rainy weather prevents the parents from getting enough food for them (Koskimies, 1948; Lack and Lack, 1951). The young swifts can go for days without food—a period of fasting that would kill nestlings of most birds. See Fasting. While unfed, the swifts lose weight steadily as their metabolism draws on the fat and body tissues and they may even recover after losing up to 50% of their weight.

WHAT BRINGS ON TORPIDITY? According to Bartholomew *et al.* (1957), the physiological factors controlling torpor in birds and mammals remain unknown, but there is "sufficient descriptive data" to suggest that torpor is not the same in all species. In contrast to many hibernating mammals, birds enter torpidity rapidly and uninterruptedly. In swifts and hummingbirds, low environmental temperature is not necessary for them to go into and to maintain torpidity. Although neurological data are lacking, the abruptness of the lowering of the body temperature in poor-wills and other birds suggests that the central nervous system may control the start of the hypothermia in both swifts and hummingbirds. *See* discussion under Temperature. *See also* Respiratory System; Nervous System.

TOTIPALMATE
All four toes connected by webbing. See Feet and Legs.

TOUCAN
(too-KON). See Piciformes.

TOUCH
The most universal of all the senses, touch has its receptors in the nerve endings in the skin of man and many other animals; it is the great *confirmatory sense*, bearing supplementary witness to the major sense of *sight* (Walter and Sayles, 1949). See Eyes and Eyesight.

The sense of touch is believed to be highly developed in birds although little is known of it except "from field observations, from analogy to it in man, and from histological evidence"— studies of the microscopic structure of the tactile nerve endings in the skin (Duncan, 1964c).

Birds notice the slightest touch on their feathers. They have in the skin, at the bases of the feathers and elsewhere, and especially at bases of wing and tail feathers, tactile nerve endings which respond to a touch on the feather tips (Beebe, 1906). Some birds also have whiskers, or rictal bristles, about the mouth, which are thought to function in touch, but evidence for it is lacking (Duncan, 1964c). See discussion in Bristle under Feather.

Grandry's corpuscles, a name for a group of nerve endings that appear to be receptors of touch, and known only in birds, are in the tongue and palate of many species (Portmann, 1961). In s. Fla., Kahl (1964), in 7 years of seasonal studies of the breeding and feeding habits of the wood stork (*see* Stork), discovered that it gets its prey largely by tacto-location— "swallowing anything that touches its partly opened bill as it walks through shallow muddy water." See Food and Feeding Habits.

Beebe (1906) was impressed with the remarkable "delicacy of the tactile sense . . . in those long-billed birds which seek their food in the muddy bottom of shallow water, detecting by means of their sensitive bills the presence of worms and snails—aided little or not at all by eyesight."

Allen (1925) remarked about semipalmated sandpipers probing the wet beach sands with their sensitive bills in feeding, and Bent (1927) wrote of the long bill of the woodcock as being well supplied with sensitive nerves. Beebe (1906) thought the upper mandible of the woodcock's bill was probably unique in its sensitivity and *mobility*, in that the bird, after plunging its bill into the damp soil of swamps in search of earthworms, could curve the outer third of the upper mandible in such a way as to feel about and to seize the worm it was seeking. See in Sandpiper Family; *also* Earthworms and Birds.

Herbst's corpuscles, a name for a special group of nerve endings that were formerly believed to be receptors of touch, are known only in birds, and are especially abundant in the tips of the tongues of woodpeckers (*see* Tongue; *also* Drumming) and on the upper surface of the bills of snipe (Portmann, 1961). They are also in the tips of the bills of many unrelated birds—for example, the kiwis (*Apteryx*) of New Zealand, ducks, flamingos, swallows, and parrots (Van Tyne and Berger, 1959), and especially along the margins of the bills of sandpipers and ducks. According to Portmann (1961), "the older interpretation that they are touch receptors has been rejected. They have recently been considered *vibration receptors.*"

Bent (1939) cites a discussion by several field observers of how woodpeckers find the grubs of wood-boring beetles hidden in the trunks of trees. One observer brought up the subject of touch receptors. Some watchers thought that woodpeckers listen for the grubs as they actively crunch wood inside their burrows; others that the woodpeckers smell the borers, which give off a strong odor (*see* Smell). Another, watching a hairy woodpecker, *Dendrocopus villosus*, noted that it strikes its bill into the wood, then holds the point of its mandible for a moment in the dent it has made. From this action, the observer suggested that the bird detects vibrations produced by the insect, which are conveyed through the bill and skull to the brain, the view held by most ornithologists today. See discussion by Roberts, T. S. (1932); Bent (1939); Davis (1965); Ramp (1965). This discussion is reminiscent of the long-time debate on whether the American robin sees or hears the earthworm in its burrow. *See* introduction to Thrush Family.

Herbst's corpuscles are not only in the bill and mouth but also in the cloaca of birds, in their tibias, or legs, forearms, and skin, especially at the bases of the wing and tail and other contour feathers (*see* Feather), such as bristles, and in the oil gland (Schildmacher, 1931). *See* oil gland under Skin Glands and under Preening; *also* Head-scratching.

"The considerable number of Herbst's corpuscles that have been discovered between the tibia and fibula of the leg bones (*see* Skeleton) of several species of birds are especially interesting in their function. Experimental work with the bullfinch, *Pyrrhula pyrrhula*, of the Old World, which occasionally wanders eastward to Alaska, suggests that Herbst's corpuscles in its legs detect vibrations—these birds are remarkably sensitive to shaking of their perches" (Duncan, 1964c).

Schwartzkopff (1949) dispelled a long-standing mystery about birds when he discovered that the extraordinary and well-authenticated sensitivity of birds to distant explosions is probably due not to the hearing of birds, as had been believed, but to the excitation of groups of Herbst's corpuscles in their legs from vibrations transmitted through the ground. *See* discussion under Ears and Hearing.

Later, Schwartzkopff (1955b) demonstrated that the Herbst's corpuscles of birds are independent of their hearing. See discussion of touch in birds by Schwartzkopff (1973).

TOURACO
(too-rah-KOH). *See* Cuculiformes.

TOWHEE
See in Finch Family.

TOWNSEND
CHARLES H(ASKINS) (1859–1944). Born Parnassus, Pa.; member of American Ornithologists' Union; described for science the shearwater that bears his name; also described several species of birds new to science from the Calif. coast and adjacent islands (Palmer, 1928); see American Ornithologists' Union (1957). Townsend worked for the U.S. Fish Commission under Spencer F. Baird, and from 1897 to 1902 was chief of the Division of Fisheries; from 1902 to 1937 he was director of the New York Aquarium. See Palmer *et al.* (1954).

TOWNSEND
JOHN K(IRK) (1809–51). Born Philadelphia, Pa., of a highly intellectual family; for whom Audubon named, in 1839, the Townsend's solitaire from one collected by Townsend along the Columbia R. near Astoria, Ore.; his name is also commemorated in the Townsend's warbler and in a subspecies of the dark-eyed junco, rock ptarmigan, fox sparrow, and snow bunting. According to Palmer (1928), he was a "brilliant young ornithologist who lived in advance of his time and was best known for his 'Narrative of a Journey Across the Rocky Mountains'" (1839). Townsend, of Quaker ancestry, was educated at Westtown Boarding School in Chester County, Pa., the famous Quaker institution attended by Thomas Say, John Cassin, Edward Drinker Cope, and others who became prominent in science. In 1834, when 25 years old, Townsend accompanied Thomas Nuttall on a trip across the continent, stayed in the West for 3½ years, and collected bird specimens whenever possible—material that was the basis for many new species described by Audubon, John Bachman, and John Cassin. Townsend had been elected a member of the Academy of Natural Sciences in Philadelphia in 1833; in 1837, he was made a curator; in 1842, he was hired by the National Institute of Washington, D.C., to obtain and mount birds for their exhibits. In 1845, Townsend returned to Philadelphia, where, after a time, he fell ill, apparently from the effects of powdered arsenic with which he had cured so many bird skins; he died Feb. 6, 1851 (Stone, 1903).

TOXICATION
(of birds). *See* Poisons; Lead Poisoning.

TRACHEA
(TRAY-kee-ah). *See* Respiratory System; *also* Mouth; Swallowing; Voice and Sound-making.

TRAILL
THOMAS STEWART, M.D. (1781–1862). Born at Kirkwall, Orkney, Scotland; naturalist and a founder of the Royal Institution of Liverpool; appointed professor of medical jurisprudence at the University of Edinburgh in 1832; later edited the 8th ed. of the *Encyclopaedia Britannica*. When Audubon visited Liverpool in 1826, Traill assisted him in a search for subscribers to *The Birds of America*. In appreciation, Audubon named a N. American flycatcher, new to science, in his honor. See Herrick (1917); Palmer (1928); Audubon, M. R. (1960).

TRAMP
See House sparrow in Weaverbird Family.

TORPIDITY
In a torpid state—lowered body temperature, heartbeat, and respiration—certain birds are able to conserve energy when food is unavailable, as may happen during an unseasonable cold spell. Prolonged torpidity, which occurs in poor-wills, is known as dormancy.

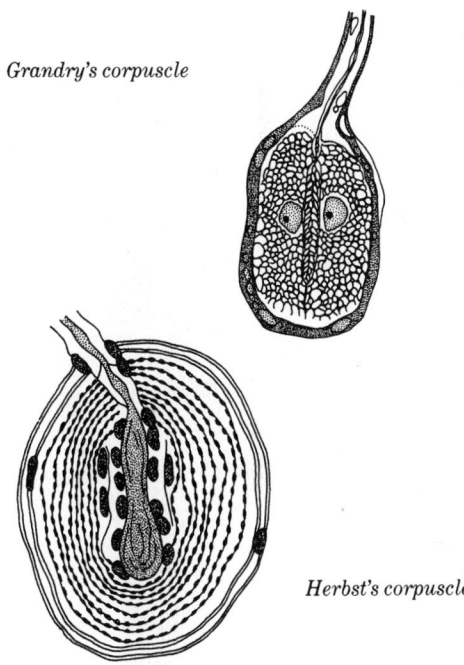

Grandry's corpuscle

Herbst's corpuscle

TOUCH
Two kinds of tactile nerve endings are located in the dermis of the skin. Grandry's corpuscles can be found in the tongue and buccal cavities of many species that locate their prey by touch. Herbst's corpuscles, believed to be vibration receptors, have been found in the tibia of several birds and in the tongues of woodpeckers that may locate insects by vibration. Numerous Herbst's corpuscles in feather follicles may perform a pressure-sensitive function in flight.

TROGON FAMILY

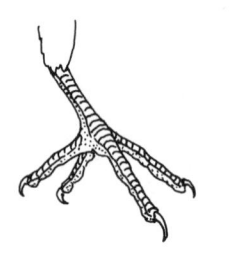

trogon

TROGONIFORMES

TRANSIENT

A bird that moves in and out of a region within any season of the year. *See* Where Do Birds Live? under Distribution; *also* Migration.

TRANSITION ZONE

One of the six *life zones* of N. America, each of which is characterized by its plant life and certain birds and other animals. Life zones are still relied upon by some authorities in mapping, locally, the ecological distribution of N. American birds; the system has advantages and disadvantages. The Transition Zone is transcontinental; the name for its eastern humid division is Alleghanian; its western arid and western humid divisions are called Arid Transition and Humid Transition. For other details and comparisons of the Transition Zone with the Major Biotic Communities listed under Distribution, see Pettingill (1970); see also in Bailey (1902). *See* discussion of life zones and biomes under Distribution.

TRAP

See cage traps under Banding; *see* deathtraps under Accidents.

TREECREEPER

See Sibling Species. Also the name in England for the brown creeper.

TREE DUCK

See whistling-ducks in Duck Family.

TREE-GIRDLER

See Sapsucker, yellow-bellied, in Woodpecker Family.

TREE MOUSE

Another name for the white-breasted nuthatch.

TREE SPARROW

See in Finch Family; Weaverbird Family.

TRIASSIC PERIOD

See Geological Time Scale.

TRICHOMONIASIS

See Diseases; Parasite.

TRICOLOR

Another name for the red-headed woodpecker, from its three striking colors.

TRICOLORED REDWING

See Blackbird, tricolored, in Troupial Family.

TRIDACTYL

See Feet and Legs.

TRINOMIAL (or TRINOMINAL) NOMENCLATURE

See Binomial Nomenclature. In naming birds, a third scientific name (the trinomial) is used, along with the genus name and species name (the binomial), to designate a geographic variety of the species of bird, or to indicate that it is a race, or subspecies. *See* Subspecies; Names and Naming.

TRITURATION

(TRIT-you-ray-shun). The grinding of food (hard-shelled seeds, nuts, insects); the digestive action of a bird's gizzard. *See* Gizzard; Digestion.

TROCHILIDAE

See Hummingbird Family.

TROCHILIFORMES

See introduction to Hummingbird Family.

TROGON FAMILY

Trogonidae (troh-GON-ih-dee); from Gr. *trogon*, gnawer (Coble, 1954), possibly from the serrated edge of the bill in some species. 35–40 species of pantropical forest birds; sexes differ, males with breast of pink, red, orange, or yellow, and, in most species, brilliant metallic green back, tail coverts, and central tail feathers. Only 1 species nests in U.S., the coppery-tailed trogon of s. Ariz., regarded as a subspecies of the elegant trogon (*Trogon elegans*) of C. America. All trogons inhabit forests, woodlands, or second growth; in American tropics also live in coffee plantations (Eisenmann, 1964). Possibly their closest allies are the kingfishers (family Alcedinidae). See Sibley and Ahlquist (1972). Of the 24 species of trogons in the New World (Edwards, 1974), the resplendent quetzal (ket-SAL) is considered by many one of the most beautiful birds in W. Hemisphere; it has 14-in.-long body and 24-in. tail plumes; was regarded as sacred by Aztecs and Mayas, and is national bird of Guatemala; although now protected, was once hunted for millinery trade; even today seen only locally in humid mountain forests of Mexico and C. America where once abundant (Blake, E. R., 1953; LaBastille *et al.*, 1972).

Coppery-tailed trogon, *Trogon elegans* (TROH-gon EL-ee-ganz); genus name: *see* family introduction; species name: Lat., elegant. (Color ill., page 900.) 11–12 in. long; male has head, upper breast, and back dark, glossy green or golden bronze; underparts bright rose-red, with white band across breast; short, thick yellow bill; long tail with black terminal band; female similar, but head and upperparts brown with much less red below and small white patch behind each eye; usually solitary or in pairs; in summer, lives mostly in sycamores of lower canyons of Huachuca Mtns. and in recent years in the Santa Rita and Chiricahua Mtns. of s. Ariz. (Phillips *et al.*, 1964); also roams among surrounding live oaks and pines; both males and females utter loud hoarse series of *co-ah* notes, from which its Mexican name of *coa*, and a turkeylike *cowm-cowm-cowm-cowm* or *cory, cory, cory;* perches erectly on branch of tree with tail hanging straight down; when calling, throws back head with heavy bill pointed almost straight up (Bent, 1940); flight is slow and undulating.

Feeding Habits: Flies upward from perch to hover before leaves and to pick off in bill insects or fruit: eats more insects than other foods, grasshoppers, mantids, bugs, leaf beetles, caterpillars and moths, sawfly larvae; also grapes, cherries, and other fruit.

Nest: Built inside natural cavities of large streamside trees such as sycamores, or in deserted woodpecker holes, 12–40 ft. above the ground; of hay, straw, trash, mosses, wool, feathers, thistledown.

Eggs: Mar.–June; 3–4, white.

Incubation: Period of and age when young first fly unknown.

Other Name: Elegant trogon.

Range: Nests from s. Ariz. and n. Mexico south to nw. Costa Rica; winters from n. Mexico south, wanders to lower Rio Grande Valley, Tex.

Eared trogon, *Euptilotis neoxenus* (youptil-OH-tis neo-ZEE-nus); common name derived from elongated ear tufts projecting back behind the eyes; female similar but head and upper breast brownish instead of green and without ear tufts; occurs in the mts. of nw. Mex., where it inhabits the pine and pine-oak forests from 1,830 (6,000 ft.) to 3,280 m. (10,000 ft.); considered rare within its range; upperparts of male metallic green, lower breast and abdomen bright red, tail feathers broadly tipped with white below and lacking bars and vermiculations.

First U.S. record in Oct. 1977 from Cave Creek Canyon in se. Ariz. (Zimmerman, 1978).

TROGONIFORMES

(troh-gon-ih-FOR-meez); from Gr. *trogon,* gnawer, and Latin *forma,* form. An order of birds that are among the most beautiful (*see* Order); includes 1 family—the Trogon Family with 35–40 species inhabiting tropical regions of world. Only 1 species, the coppery-tailed (elegant) trogon, nests in the U.S.; another 23 species live in the forests of Mexico, West Indies, C. America, and through much of S. America. 3 species live in Africa and 11 species in tropical Asia. Closest relatives may be the kingfishers (family Alcedinidae). Trogons have large eyes adapted to the dim light of the forests where they feed on insects and other arthropods and on fruit; bill is short, wide at base, with several "teeth" on upper mandible (*see* Bill); wings are short, rounded, with 10 primaries; tail is long, broad, graduated (*see* Tail), with 12 rectrices (tail feathers); legs and feet small and weak; toes unique in having 2 (toes I and II) turned backward (heterodactylous condition). In most trogons, sexes differ; females usually bright below, but duller above and on head and with the metallic sheen absent or greatly reduced. *See* Trogon Family; Sexual Dimorphism.

TROOP FOWL

See scaups in Duck Family.

TROPICBIRD FAMILY

Phaethontidae (fay-eh-THON-tih-dee); after Phaethon, son of Helios, the sun god, who in Gr. mythology drove his father's fiery sun chariot across the skies; named apparently in allusion to the sunny tropical home of these birds. 3 species of white pigeon-sized seabirds; live over or around warm parts of Atlantic, Pacific, and Indian oceans; no other members in family; they are related to pelicans, boobies, gannets, etc. (*see* Pelecaniformes), but are far more seagoing. Aptly named; however, all three have

been seen over N. America waters; on long, pointed wings they fly rapidly, directly, over ocean, resembling flashingly white pigeons, but with two long, streaming white central tail feathers as long as or longer than bird's body (Van Tyne and Berger, 1976). The two central tail feathers, extending far beyond tail proper, were thought by sailors to resemble the marlinespike carried by boatswains, therefore they called them marlinespike and bosun (BOH-sun) birds; another view held that name came from shrill piping whistle of larger tropicbirds, which sounds like piping of boatswain's whistle.

When tropicbirds sight prey of small fishes and squids, they hover over water, then dive with half-closed wings, sometimes spiraling downward before plunging like gannets below surface (*see* Swimming and Diving). Catch their prey in long, slightly downcurved bill and, on surfacing, float lightly on water, head held high, tail angled jauntily upward. Tropicbirds are not followers of ships, but on sighting one may approach it and circle it with loud screams, then suddenly fly away and disappear over the waves. They may be numerous about the common nesting cliffs, where 6–12 birds are often seen together, flying in noisy courtship flights, but at sea they are often solitary or fly, silently, in pairs; usually fly about 50–100 ft. above water, and from nesting places on oceanic and offshore islands, often make daily flights of 60–80 mi. out to sea and are sometimes seen hundreds of miles from land; are migratory or wanderers (Van Tyne and Berger, 1959). *See* Seabird.

Remarkably graceful in flight, tropicbirds are clumsy on ledges and cliffs where they nest, somewhat colonially. Their relatively small legs are so far back on body that they must crawl on belly when moving about (compare with northern fulmar, also a seabird); the four toes, fully webbed, help in paddling and in digging a shallow nest scrape; on steep cliffs where they nest, usually can take off by leaning over edge, without walking or leaping into air. Stonehouse (1964) reported incubation period as from 41 days in smaller species to 44–45 days in larger ones; incubation period of white-tailed, smallest of the tropicbirds, in following account, is 28 days (Palmer, 1962; Austin, 1961), considerably at variance with that of Stonehouse's report.

Red-billed tropicbird, *Phaethon aethereus* (FAY-eh-thon ee-THEE-[*th* as in *thin*]-rih-us); genus name: *see* family introduction; species name: Lat., heavenly. (Color ill., page 901.) One of the largest of the tropicbirds, occasionally seen along Pacific coast; 18–20 in. long; if the two elongated white central tail feathers ("streamers") are included, 36–42 in. long; wingspread about 40–42 in.; flies with rapid, pigeonlike, steady wingbeats; generally silky white, with variable black barring on back; a slender bird, slightly smaller than the California gull; has black wing tips; dark band from in front of eyes runs to back of head; pointed, slightly downcurved *crimson bill;* sexes appear alike; immatures have orange or yellow bill; legs gray, feet black; this species has

TROPICBIRD FAMILY

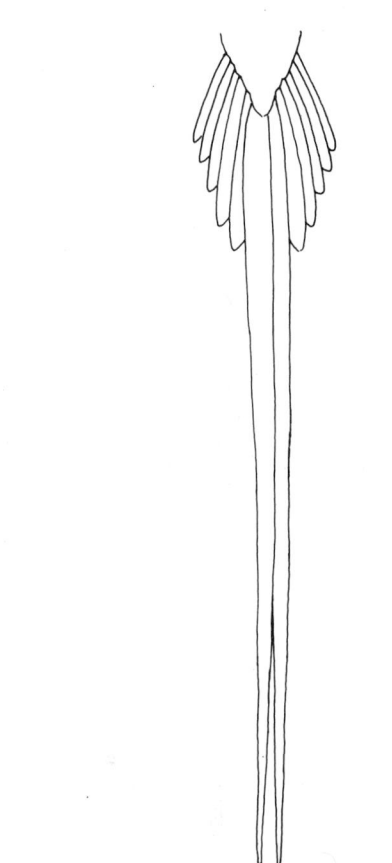

Red-tailed tropicbird

TROPICBIRD FAMILY

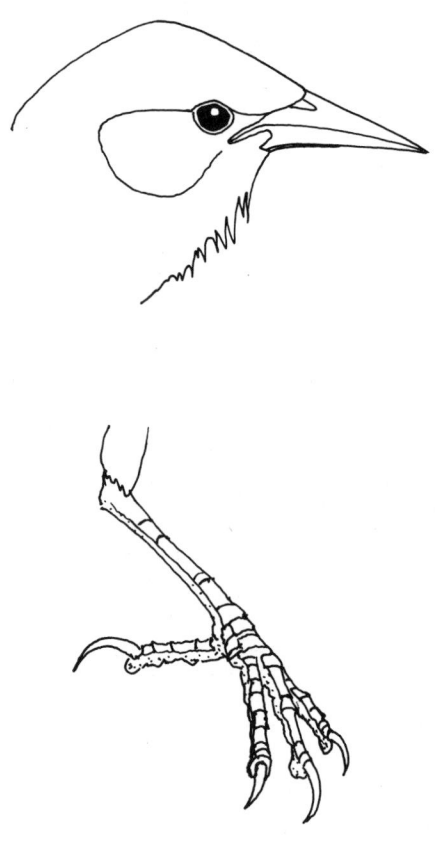

TROUPIAL FAMILY

broadened flange on middle claw, lacking in other tropicbirds (Palmer, 1962).

Feeding Habits: Eats fishes and squids, never dives from surface for prey but from air; catches it in bill sideways and swallows prey either underwater or on surface; never flies with fish in bill (Palmer, 1962).
Nest: No materials, but in burrow or in cavity of cliff.
Eggs: Laying season variable, Jan.–July or all through year (see Palmer, 1962, for details); 1, whitish buff or red-brown, spotted or blotched.
Incubation: According to Stonehouse (1964), 44–45 days, by both sexes alternately; young leave nest as fully fledged juveniles some 3–4 months after hatching.
Other Names: Bosun bird; marlinespike.
Age: One, banded as adult on Midway Is. in Pacific, at least 10 years old when recaptured (Clapp and Sibley, 1966).
Range: Nests in Pacific from Gulf of Calif. and the Revilla Gigedo Is. south to the Galápagos and islands near coast of Ecuador; in S. Atlantic, from ne. Panama and coast of Venezuela to Lesser Antilles in Caribbean; nesting in S. Atlantic from late Jan. into Mar.; ranges casually, after nesting season, north to Newfoundland Banks and in s. Calif. waters; has strayed to Wash. on Pacific coast and inland to Ariz.

Red-tailed tropicbird, *Phaethon rubricauda* (FAY-eh-thon rube-rih-CAUD-ah); genus name: *see* family introduction; species name: from Lat. *ruber,* red, and *cauda,* tail; the two long central tail feathers in this species are *bright red.* One of largest of all tropicbirds, reported off Pacific coast of N. America; 18–36 in. long; plumage silky white in beginning of breeding season with rosy tinge; broad black crescent in front of and behind eyes; black flanks and wing bar.

Feeding Habits: Fishes and squids, principally.
Nest: No materials, on bare rock in crevice of cliff.
Eggs: 1, yellowish or reddish, splotched.
Other Names: Bosun bird; marlinespike.
Age: One banded wild one reported to 9 years old (Kennard, 1975).
Range: Tropical waters of Indian and Pacific oceans to w. Hawaiian Is.; ranges casually to waters off Baja Calif.

White-tailed tropicbird, *Phaethon lepturus* (FAY-eh-thon lep-TYOU-rus; genus name: *see* family introduction; species name: Lat., from Gr. *leptos,* thin, and *oura,* tail (Jaeger, 1955) in reference to long, thin central tail feathers ("streamers"). (Color ill., page 901.) A straggler in N. Atlantic off N. America and rare along Calif. coast; smallest tropicbird; 15–16 in. long; if the two long white central tail feathers are included, 28–32 in. long; wingspread to about 36 in.; adult has white back; black stripe on wings and outer primaries to scapulars; back is not barred as in red-billed tropicbird, and bill is *orange;* sexes outwardly similar, about same size; legs gray, feet black; immature irregularly barred above, has yellow bill and lacks long central tail feathers; utters in flight a shrill, piping *keek* or *keck-keck-keck;*

remarkable record of a lone adult male along coast of Calif. that tried to copulate with radar-controlled model gliders (see Hetrick and McCaskie, 1965); nearest nesting place to Calif., in Hawaiian Is., and on Midway Is.

Feeding Habits: Small fishes, squids, crabs, obtained by diving from heights of 50–100 ft. or more above water.
Nest: No nest materials, eggs laid on bare rock or on soil in crevices, holes, caves, at edge of ledge of cliff, under grass or shrubbery; best-known population is on Bermuda, where tropicbirds are now protected and population is high (Palmer, 1962), although recently declining with real estate development in nesting areas.
Eggs: Bermuda, Mar. and June; 1, pinkish, speckled.
Incubation: About 28 days (Palmer, 1962; Austin, 1961), but about 41 days according to Stonehouse (1964); first flight of chick about 62 days after hatching.
Other Names: Bosun bird; marlinespike; yellow-billed tropic-bird.
Weights: To about 1 lb.
Range: Oceanic, in Atlantic nests on Bahamas, Bermudas, and islands in Caribbean, and south to Ascension Is., also in e. Atlantic and Indian O. to c. and w. Pacific; first record in e. Pacific, one seen May 24–June 23, 1964, at Newport Bay, Orange County, Calif. (Small, 1974); ranges casually along Gulf coast to Fla., N.C., S.C., and accidentally from Long Is., N.Y., to Mass. and waters off Nova Scotia.

Yellow-billed tropicbird. *See* White-tailed tropicbird.

TROUPIAL FAMILY
Icteridae (ick-TER-ih-dee); from Gr. *ikteros,* jaundice, name given to a yellow-green bird; *troupial* (TROOP-ih-al), from habit of gathering in a large flock, or troupe. Family only in W. Hemisphere, or New World; 91 species of songbirds (Van Tyne and Berger, 1976); 22 species in N. America, including the introduced spotted-breasted oriole, and more recent arrivals, the black-vented and scarlet-headed orioles; members of family have 9 primary (wing) feathers; most closely related to tanagers, weaverbirds, and finches; some members of Troupial Family are the well-known N. American blackbirds, grackles, orioles, meadowlarks, cowbirds, and the bobolink; others, the less well-known troupials, oropendolas, and caciques (kah-SEEKS) of the American tropics; Troupial Family is remarkably diverse group in colors, size (6½–21 in. long), and habits (Blake, E. R., 1964); some with plumage a uniform black often with brilliant metallic gloss (blackbirds and grackles), others with striking combinations of black and brown, chestnut, buff, orange, crimson, or yellow (orioles, blackbirds, bobolink, and meadowlarks); sexes usually unlike in appearance; males usually more highly colored; many migratory but tropical species are not (Blake, E. R., 1964).

Of the family, some of best-known in N. America are the often polygamous male red-winged blackbird with his brilliant scarlet-and-yellow shoulder patches, gurgling spring song, and enormous numbers—some ornithologists believe redwing is most numerous land bird in N. America; the bright, yellow-breasted eastern and western meadowlarks of open plains and fields, whose songs have meant spring to country people for generations; the dashing male bobolink with his bubbling flight song; the cowbirds with their remarkable evolution of social parasitism; and the American orioles with their glorious colors and songs, whose nest building is one of the most complex of any N. American birds. Outstanding singers in the Troupial Family are the tropical American yellow-rumped cacique, *Cacicus cela*, the spotted-breasted oriole, *Icterus pectoralis*, and the melodious blackbird, *Dives dives*. For other interesting details about the family, see Blake, E. R. (1964); Austin (1961); Gilliard (1958).

Cowbird is name for small to medium-sized blackbirds that have remarkable habit of laying their eggs in nests of other birds, thus getting foster parents to raise their young. According to Friedmann (1929), the parasitic habits of cowbirds may have originated when they lost their drive to defend territory; see, however, review of Friedmann's theory and other theories by Hamilton and Orians (1965).

Three of the five species of cowbirds that have the parasitic habit live in S. America; two within the U.S., one of which reaches Canada; they are the only N. American birds that are completely dependent on other birds to raise their young; they are *obligatory* nest parasites. *See* Obligate Parasite.

The brown-headed cowbird, *Molothrus ater*, lives over an enormously wide area of U.S. and parts of Canada; the bronzed cowbird, *Molothrus aeneus*, enters U.S. only in relatively small part of Southwest. Cowbirds got their name from associating with cows (originally with bison of Great Plains, where called buffalo birds by trail herders and cowboys); walk with waddling motion over ranges and pastures of country and lawns of suburban areas; according to Friedmann (1971), the brown-headed cowbird has been reported to lay its eggs in nests of 214 species; most frequently victimized are birds smaller than cowbird or near its size which build open nests in trees, bushes, or on ground; hole-nesting birds, such as woodpeckers, bluebirds, chickadees, etc., are not often victimized (Friedmann, 1963).

Female within her breeding territory watches in advance while a small bird builds its nest; Mayfield (1960), in studies of Kirtland's warbler in Mich., reported that female cowbird visits Kirtland's warbler's nest in dim light before sunrise, usually while female Kirtland's is away from nest and has not begun to incubate her own clutch of eggs. Cowbird enters nest roughly and hastily, lays her egg, returns later to remove egg or eggs of her host; jabs into nest and flies away with pierced egg in her bill; when short distance away, stops to eat contents and sometimes the shell (see discussion of this by Hann, 1941).

Cowbird can discriminate between her host's eggs and her own and takes away only eggs of her host; host bird often deserts nest if cowbird lays in it before she is ready to lay her own eggs (Hann, 1953); most frequent deserters are yellow-breasted chat and cardinal (Friedmann,

1963). About half of host species incubate the brown-speckled white egg of the cowbird along with their own and raise nestling as if it were their own; often the larger cowbird nestling crowds out or throws smaller nestlings from nest of host bird; on the other hand, some host species (gray catbird and American robin, for example) throw out eggs of cowbird from their nests; some bury cowbird egg as well as own by building new nest bottom over old, then lay new clutch of eggs. Each cowbird not always raised at expense of host's entire brood; Nice (1939) found each cowbird was raised at expense of one song sparrow of brood.

In late summer, fledged cowbirds join flocks of their own kind. For full details, see Friedmann's publications; also Bent (1958); Byers (1950); Berger (1955); Mayfield (1960); Nice (1937b; 1939; 1949); Walkinshaw (1949b); Young (1963).

Most members of the Troupial Family are protected by law and a permit is required to keep them in captivity (*see* Legal Protection); however, to sustain an injured or ill bird until it can be freed to fend for itself, offer it seeds, bread, fruit (halved oranges and grapes), greens, mealworms and other insects, and ground meat.

Blackbird, Brewer's, *Euphagus cyanocephalus* (YOU-fah-gus sigh-an-oh-SEFF-ah-lus); genus name: Lat., from Gr. *euphagein*, to eat well; species name: from Gr. *kyanos*, blue, and *kephale*, head; common name: for Dr. Thomas M. Brewer, Boston physician and ornithologist (Palmer, 1928). (Color ill., page 903.) Mostly in w. N. America; 8–10 in. long; adult male black with pale yellow eyes; appears all-black at distance; head and neck show *purplish* gloss, body shows *greenish* reflections in good light; female medium gray above, lighter gray below; has *brown* eyes; similar female rusty blackbird has pale yellow eyes; often seen in large, conspicuous flocks, sometimes with redwings in open country, about farms and pastures, irrigated places, freshly plowed soil, in towns, city parks, golf courses, lawns (Williams, 1958); also lives in mountain wildernesses and along lonely Pacific coast beaches; utters hoarse call note, *check!*; also squeaks, trills, whistled notes; roosts in flocks in groves of trees and in marshes, has extended range eastward as nesting bird to Ont., e. Minn., Wisc., and Ill.

Feeding Habits: Walks about on ground with short forward jerks of head; eats grasshoppers, crickets, forest tent caterpillars, cankerworms, termites, weevils, aphids, and others; follows farmer or rancher plowing to eat insects turned up; eats waste grains, weed seeds, fruit (Williams, 1958).

Nest: Built in loose colonies of 3–20 pairs or more, but not in such dense ones as those of yellow-headed blackbirds; nests on ground in hayfields and up to 10,000 ft. elevation in mountain meadows in Colo., also in marshes and in bushes and trees along streams, lakes, also in windbreak hedges of ranches; nest of twigs, pine needles, grasses, some with matrix of mud or dried cow dung, cup lined with rootlets, horsehair.

Eggs: Mar.–July; 3–7, commonly, 5–6, pale gray or pale green-gray, spotted and blotched with gray-brown, browns.

Incubation: By female, 12–14 days; males may be polygynous, male guards nest or nests; young fly about 13–14 days after hatching; sometimes two broods (Williams, 1958). A captive pair in Berlin Zoo hatched and raised three young in spring 1972. See Grummt, 1972.

Other Name: Glossy blackbird.

Age: One, Escondido, Calif., 5 years, 10 months, old.

Albinism: Partial noted in 40% of flock of 500 in Wash. (Edson, 1928).

Flight Speed: In w. U.S., 28–29 m.p.h. (Cottam *et al.*, 1942b); in Wash., 27–38 m.p.h. (Rathbun, 1934).

Host to Cowbirds: Frequent in s. Canada, Alta. to Sask., in Colo., Minn., and Calif.

Range: Nests B.C. east to s. Man., n. Minn., w. Ont., and n. Wisc., south to n. Baja Calif., s.-c. and e.-c. Calif., s. Nev., sw. and c. Utah, c. Ariz., w. and s.-c. N.M., n. Tex., Okla., n. Iowa, s. Wisc., ne. Ill., nw. Ind., and sw. Mich.; winters from sw. B.C., n. Wash., c. Alta., e.-c. Mont., c. Okla., Kans., Ark., sw. Tenn., ne. Miss., Ala., Ga., w. N.C., and w. S.C., south to s. Baja Calif., c. Mexico, Gulf coast, casually east to w. Fla.

Blackbird, China-eyed. See Grackle, common.

Blackbird, crow. See Grackle, common.

Blackbird, glossy. See Blackbird, Brewer's.

Blackbird, marsh. See Blackbird, red-winged.

Blackbird, parrot. Another name for the smooth-billed ani in Cuckoo Family.

Blackbird, red-shouldered. See Blackbird, red-winged.

Blackbird, red-winged, *Agelaius phoeniceus* (ah-jeh-LAY-us fee-NIH-seh-us); genus name: Lat., from Gr. *agelaios*, belonging to or of a flock; species name: Lat., purple-red, deep red. (Color ills., page 902.) Marshes from Atlantic to Pacific; 7–9½ in. long; wingspread 12–14½ in.; male after second year glossy black except for red shoulder patch, or "epaulet," with lower border of yellow (sometimes red concealed and only yellow border shows), when a year old is similar to female but less streaked and with some red on epaulets; female brown above, heavily streaked below; light streak over each eye; sharp-pointed bill; redwing lives in marshes and sloughs or where bushes and small trees grow in and around ponds, lakes, sluggish streams; ranges into adjacent upland fields, orchards, woods; except in nesting season, travels in enormous flocks with cowbirds and grackles; one winter roost in Dismal Swamp, Va., held estimated 15 million birds; one of earliest spring migrants from wintering places in s. U.S., flocks of males usually arrive in n. U.S. in Feb. and Mar. ahead of females (see Allen, 1914); feeds during day in open farm country, is in breeding marshes early morning and late afternoon, where males stake out territories a few days before arrival of females (Williams, 1958); male spends much time in tops of bushes or clinging to old cattail stalks in marsh, singing liquid, gurgling *konk-la-reeee* or *o-ka-leeee*, common call is *chack*, also utters plaintive whistled alarm note; very aggressive defending territory, attacks crows, ravens, magpies, hawks, ospreys flying near, sometimes rides back of crow pecking with fury; with surplus of females, some males polygynous (see Nero, 1956).

Feeding Habits: On ground, walks deliberately or runs or hops when trying to keep up with feeding flock; in late summer and fall, thousands mix with grackles, cowbirds, starlings, feed in open fields on weed seeds and waste grain; year-round food about 73% vegetable matter, 27% animal: eats mayflies, caddis flies, moths, beetles, caterpillars of gypsy moth, forest tent caterpillars, geometrid moth caterpillars, cankerworms, grubs in plowed fields, grasshoppers, spiders, myriapods, mollusks, snails; also blackberries, blueberries, and other fruit; eats bread and bird seed mixtures in backyard feeders.

Nest: In cattails, rushes, bushes, trees, sometimes over water, in alfalfa and other plants of upland fields, even on ground, in dense grass, clover; loosely woven cup of dried cattail leaves, sedges, fastened to stalks or twigs with plant fibers, cup lined with fine grasses, rushes.
Eggs: Mar.–July; 3–5, usually 4, pale blue-green, spotted or with zigzag lines of black, browns, purple.
Incubation: By female, 11–12 days, one record of 10 days (Allen, 1914); young, blind and naked at hatching, ready to leave nest when 10 days old, climb about in cattails before can fly, if falls into water can swim but often caught by water snakes, bullfrogs, snapping turtles; two broods a season.
Other Names: Marsh blackbird; red-shouldered blackbird; red-shouldered starling; red-wing; red-winged oriole; red-wing starling; swamp blackbird.
Accidents: In Scott County, Iowa, May 1937, one strangled when it slipped from perch and caught by neck in crotch of tree.
Age: Two alive 9 years after banding; male shot and killed 14 years after banding (Fankhauser, 1967); a male, banded Branchport, N.Y., found dead in N.C. when 14 years, 5 months, old (Kennard, 1975); two 8-year-old males returned to same breeding colony, Madison, Wisc., 1955 (Nero, 1956).
Albinism: Partial albinism frequent over entire range.
Flight Speed: Timed in Mich., 17–23 m.p.h. (flapping) (Schnell, 1965); 28 m.p.h. (Aymar, 1935).
Host to Cowbirds: Fairly common locally to brown-headed cowbird but rarely in nesting colony of redwings in cattail marshes (see Friedmann, 1963); four records of host to bronzed cowbird.
Weights: May–Aug., near State College, Pa., males (73), 62–65 gr., or about 2½ oz.; females (28), 37–43 gr., or about 1¼–1½ oz. (Benner, 1967).
Range: Nests s. Yuk. across Canada to Nova Scotia, south to Baja Calif., Costa Rica, w.

Cuba, and n. Bahamas; in winter withdraws from northern part of nesting range; winters over much of U.S., especially in s. U.S.

Blackbird, rusty, *Euphagus carolinus* (YOU-fah-gus cah-row-LIN-us); genus name: *see* Blackbird, Brewer's; species name: Lat., of Carolina; *rusty*, from brown edges of new feathers in fall. (Color ill., page 903.) Summers mostly in Canada, migrant and wintering in U.S.; 8½–9¾ in. long; wingspread 13–15 in.; male in spring entirely black with dull *greenish* gloss on head; shaped like robin; eyes almost white, or straw-colored; female slate-colored; resembles female Brewer's blackbird, but grayer and with yellow eyes instead of dark; in spring migrates northward from South in noisy, chuckling, squealing, whistling flocks that sometimes travel in enormous numbers, follow plowman in fields, flocks blacken stubble of grain fields; pass by in clouds overhead or gather to sing in leafless treetops of roadsides or swamp woods; arrives n. U.S. about time spring peepers calling (Feb.–Apr.); flocks break up into pairs on breeding grounds of wet swamp woods with alders and shallow pools in n. U.S. and Canada; male sings high, squeaky *tolalee—eek; tolalee—eek* from treetops; calls *kick* or *chuck*, not so loud as redwing's *chack* call note.

Feeding Habits: Walks along wet shores of woods pools or wades in shallows; about 50% of year-round food is animal life; eats aquatic beetles, weevils, caterpillars, grasshoppers, ants, bugs, dragonflies, caddis flies, mayflies, crustaceans, snails, salamanders, small fishes; also weed seeds and grain, especially corn, also dogwood berries, buffalo berries, hackberries.
Nest: Built not in colonies as other blackbirds do; in dense clumps of conifers or in shrubs over water, 2–20 ft. up, bulky, outer frame of twigs, lichens, dried grasses, with cup or bowl of hardened mudlike material lined with rootlets, fine green grasses.
Eggs: May–June; 4–5, pale blue-green, blotched with browns and grays.
Incubation: By females, 14 days; young fly when about 13–14 days old (Bent, 1958).
Other Names: Rusty crow; rusty grackle; rusty oriole; thrush blackbird.
Age: One, banded Ind., killed Tenn. when 5 years, 8 months, old; another banded one lived to 8 years, 7 months, old (Kennard, 1975).
Flight Speed: 19–23 m.p.h. (Wood, 1933).
Host to Cowbirds: Rarely, two records from Alta., Canada.
Range: Nests n. Alaska, n. Yuk., nw. and c. Mack., to Newfoundland, south to c. Alaska, c. B.C., se. Alta., c. Sask., c. Man., s. Ont., ne. N.Y., n. Vt., n. N.H., c. Me., s. N.B. and Nova Scotia; winters east of Rocky Mtns. from southern edge of breeding range south to se. Tex., the Gulf coast, and n. Fla.

Blackbird, saltwater. *See* Grackle, boat-tailed.

Blackbird, skunk. *See* Bobolink.

Blackbird, thrush. *See* Blackbird, rusty.

Blackbird, tricolored, *Agelaius tricolor* (ah-jeh-LAY-us TRY-color); genus name: *see* Blackbird, red-winged; species name: Lat., three-colored. (Color ill., page 903.) Calif. and Ore.; 7–9½ in. long; male black, like red-winged blackbird except has much darker red "epaulet" or shoulder patch than redwing, bordered by *white* instead of yellow; female like female redwing but darker, lower part of breast and lower back sooty, which obscures streaking; lives in nesting colonies of enormous numbers in great interior valleys of Calif., north into Ore., one of most highly gregarious of N. American birds; lives in open valleys and foothills, rarely at high altitudes, in streamside timber, alfalfa and rice fields, tules and cattails in marshes and edges of reservoirs, one such roosting place in Calif. marsh of 30–40 acres once attracted almost half million birds (Bent, 1958), today total population declining because of drainage of marshes; gregarious at all times, not only roosts in marshes or trees and forages in grain fields in flocks but nests in colonies of thousands with every day of nesting and egg-laying beginning in concert; each male may hold territory of only 6 sq. ft., in which he sings and which he defends against other males, in one 60-acre marsh an estimated 200,000 nests (Bent, 1958); polygamous males may have several females nesting within their small territories, with nests touching each other; male sings songs that resembles redwing's but lacks its liquid quality, an *oh-kee-quay-a* with braying quality, common call note is nasal *kape*.

Feeding Habits: About 80% animal life; in summer, mostly beetles, caterpillars, spiders caught in grass or in alfalfa; in fall and winter, weed seeds, grain.
Nest: In colonies, usually in marshes, but also in willow and blackberry thickets and on ground in clumps of nettles; a basket of coarse grasses, sedges, with matrix of macerated leaves with some mud, in marsh lashed within group of upright cattail stems (Bent, 1958).
Eggs: Apr.–June; 3–4, pale blue-green, with fine, dark lines or spots.
Incubation: By female, about 11 days; young fed by both parents; leave nest when about 13 days old; two broods each year.
Other Names: Tricolored oriole; tricolored redwing.
Age: Of two banded, Calif., one lived to 4 years, 10 months; another to 6 years; one, banded Shafter, Calif., trapped in same general area and released when 12 years, 10 months, old (Kennard, 1975).
Flight Speed: Timed in Calif., 46–52 m.p.h. (flapping) with wind (McLean, 1930).
Range: Nests from s. Ore. (east of Cascades) to nw. Baja Calif.; winters within range in Calif.

Blackbird, white-winged. *See* Bobolink; also another name for the lark bunting in Finch Family.

Blackbird, yellow-headed, *Xanthocephalus xanthocephalus* (zan-tho-SEFF-ah-lus); genus and species names: Lat., from Gr. *xanthos*, yellow, and *kephale*, head. (Color ill., page 903.) Marshes of w. N. America, Canada to s. U.S.; 8–11 in. long; head, neck, and upper breast bright yellow; body sooty black; small areas of white in black wings show in flight; females smaller, browner, with clear yellow throat, no white in wings; summers in small to large colonies in marshes or sloughs from prairies to Pacific slope, where tall tules (bulrushes), reeds, cattails, grow in water 3–4 ft. deep; in Rocky Mtns. of Colo., from plains to about 5,000 ft. elevation in foothills; flocks of males precede females north in spring (Bent, 1958); male selects territory in marsh, defends against other males, sometimes fights severely with rivals; drives away and excludes red-winged blackbirds from certain parts of marsh; yellow-headed nests only if plant habitat is over standing water (Miller, R. S., 1968); male sings cacophonous series of high-pitched liquid and clacking notes, *klee klee klee ko-kow-w-w*, the last a drawn-out buzz or squeal; call note is low, hoarse *ka-ack;* adults quick to attack hawks, crows, and has severely attacked bittern visiting marsh; male may strike human intruders when young are in nest.

Feeding Habits: Spends much time walking about in mud close to water, also in fields, eats beetles, alfalfa weevils, caterpillars, grasshoppers, Mormon "crickets," army worms, ants, wasps, dragonflies, spiders, snails; eats oats, corn, seeds of barnyard and panic grasses, ragweed, smartweed, pigweed.

Nest: In colonies, but nests not as close together as those of tricolored blackbird; is built by female, deep, basketlike, of water-soaked dead grasses, reeds, cattails, woven and wound around reed stems, bulrushes, flags, partly canopied at top, forms tight nest when dry, from few inches to several feet above water, sometimes in willows.

Eggs: Apr.–June; 3–5, commonly 4, pale gray to pale green, evenly splotched or speckled with browns, grays.

Incubation: By female, 12–13 days; young leave nest when 9–12 days old, remain in dense plants of marsh until able to fly at about 21 days old (Bent, 1958).

Other Name: Copperhead.

Age: One, banded S.D., killed by cat in N.D. when 8 years old; male, banded Houghton, S.C., caught and released at Hoven, S.D., when 9 years old (Kennard, 1975); one in Philadelphia Zoo, lived for 18 years, was still alive in July 1928.

Albinism: Reported.

Flight Speed: Single birds, 20–29 m.p.h.; flock of 75, 30–35 m.p.h. (Cottam *et al.,* 1942b).

Host to Cowbirds: Occasional, 11 records to brown-headed cowbird (Friedmann, 1963).

Range: Nests from w. Oreg., c. Wash., c. B.C., ne. Alta., ne. Sask., e. and se. Man., n. Minn., n.-c. Wisc., ne. Ill., nw. Ohio, south to s. Calif., ne. Baja Calif., se. and sw. Utah, c. and e.-c. Ariz., s. N.M., n. Tex., nw. Okla., s. Kans., nw. Ark., sw. and ne. Mo., c. Ill., and nw. Ind.; winters n. to c. Calif., c. Ariz., s. N.M., c. and sw. Tex. and s. La., south to s. Baja Calif. and s. Mexico; wanders north of breeding range and to Atlantic coast, has reached Nova Scotia and s. Fla.

Bobolink, *Dolichonyx oryzivorus* (doll-ih-KOH-nix aw-rih-ZIV-oh-rus); genus name: Lat., from Gr. *dolichos*, long, and *onux*, claw; species name: Lat., rice-eating (Coues, 1882). (Color ill., page 905.) In summer, northern states and s. Canada, Atlantic to Pacific; 6–8 in. long; wingspread 10¼–12½ in.; bill short, conical, like sparrow's; male in breeding plumage, black head, wings, tail, and underparts; rump white, and broad white streak from lower back to bend of wings; nape buffy yellow; tail feathers stiff and pointed like woodpecker's; female yellow-brown, broad streak of brown over eyes, dusky-brown streaks on back, rump, and sides; male in fall and winter plumage resembles female in her summer coat, but is larger, darker; immatures resemble female, but yellower below; migrates northward from wintering grounds in s. Brazil and n. Argentina, in longest migration of any in family; 5,000 mi. to green summer meadows of n. U.S. and s. Canada, where males, which arrive few days or week ahead of females, sing bubbling, tinkling, joyous songs as they flutter about in air over grass or grain field territory; song difficult to render phonetically but one of best from poem "Robert of Lincoln," by William Cullen Bryant: "Bob-o'-link, bob-o'-link, spink, spank, spink," and another by an early American ornithologist: "Tom Noodle, Tom Noodle, you owe me, you owe me, ten shillings and sixpence"; a call note is metallic *pink*, often heard in migration; spring flood northward is through Atlantic states, mainly east of Alleghenies; reaches northern nesting grounds late Apr., early May; when females arrive, besides courtship flights of chasing female, male courts on ground, with head down, partly opens wings, gurgles, lifts buffy nape feathers, drags spread tail on ground like pigeon. Males strongly polygynous, according to Martin, S. G. (1973).

Feeding Habits: In summer, eats beetles, alfalfa weevils, caterpillars, grasshoppers, seeds of barnyard grass, panic grass, smartweed, ragweed, some grain, but in southward migration flocks sometimes destructive to rice and other unharvested grain crops; on southward flyway that took them through great rice fields in S.C. in 19th and early 20th century, descended in millions on crop, causing immense losses to planters, who called them ricebirds; were killed by thousands to protect crop and sold in markets of Philadelphia, New York, and Boston as reed-birds; in Jamaica still called butter-birds. Rice culture has declined along its main migration route; species is protected by law, but has never come back to former numbers.

Nest: Built by female on ground in slight depression she scrapes or selects in tall grass, alfalfa, clover, weeds, sometimes in old rut made by farm machinery; skillfully hidden in densest growth of field, flimsy, of coarse grass and weed stems, lined with finer grasses.

Eggs: May–July; 4–7, usually 5–6, pale gray to pale brown, irregularly blotched with browns, purple, lavender.

Incubation: By female, 13 days; young fly when about 10–14 days old; male helps feed and care for young; one brood a year.

Other Names: American ortolan; Bob-Lincoln; butter-bird; May-bird; meadow-bird; meadow-wink; reed-bird; ricebird; skunk blackbird; skunk-head blackbird; white-winged blackbird.

Accidents: Many nests and eggs destroyed by landowners in early summer cutting of hayfields and grain fields.

Age: Martin, S. G. (1973) reported 8 banded bobolinks, some 4 and 5 years old, one, 6 years old.

Albinism: "White one" reported by Deane (1876).

Host to Cowbirds: Infrequently over most of bobolink's range but commonly in Iowa (Friedmann, 1963).

Weights: In autumn migration, coastal N.J. (10), 20.4–34.5 gr., or ¾–1¼ oz; in Ill., birds averaged 46.2 gr. (Graber and Graber, 1962), or 1¾ oz.; in Pa., 1½–1⅞ oz. (Forbush, 1925–29).

Range: Nests in southern parts of the s. Canadian Provinces from B.C. to Nova Scotia, southward to ne. Calif., c. Nev., n. Utah, c. Colo., c. Neb., ne. Kans., n. Mo., c. Ill., s.-c. Ind., sw. and e.-c. Ohio, n. W.Va., w. Md., c. N.J., occasionally in Ariz. and N.M.; may be seen in migration along Mississippi R. and Atlantic seaboard; casual in Bermuda; accidental in Labrador, se. Que., and n. Ont.; winters in c. S. America.

Cowbird, bronzed, *Molothrus aeneus* (moll-OTH-rus EE-nee-us); genus name: Lat., a vagabond; species name: Lat., of brass or bronze. (Color ill., page 905.) Mostly in Tex. and sw. U.S. south through C. America; 6½–8¾ in. long; male entirely black with green-bronze metallic gloss, sometimes more blue-black on wings; *red eyes* show at close range (brown-headed cowbird has brown eyes); slightly larger and much longer-billed than brown-headed; more like Brewer's blackbird, with which it often associates in fields, but distinguished by red eyes (Brewer's has yellow eyes) and its shorter, stouter bill; female slightly paler than male and both sexes have erectile ruff on back of neck in breeding season, but female's smaller; in C. America, often in flocks in fields with giant cowbirds, *Psomocolax oryzivorus,* great-tailed grackles, *Cassidix mexicanus,* and melodious blackbirds, *Dives dives,* where they turn stones with bill to find edible matter (Bent, 1958). Song is lower-pitched and wheezier than that of brown-headed cowbird.

Feeding Habits: Associates considerably with cattle, snatching up insects disturbed by grazing animals; also alights on backs of horned cattle and mules in C. America to pluck ticks and other insects from skin of animals; prefers open fields and pastures; eats, besides insects, primarily grain and seeds of grasses (Bent, 1958).

Nest: None; lays eggs in nests of 52 species of birds—largely orioles, blackbirds, and finches; is more selective, or restricted, in its choice of hosts than the brown-headed cowbird (Friedmann, 1963).

Eggs: Usually 1 laid in each host nest; largest number ever found in one nest, an orchard oriole's, was 4; occasionally two females lay in same host nest; eggs are light blue-green, without markings; much more glossy than eggs of other cowbirds.

Incubation: 12–13 days; incubation by host (Friedmann, 1929).

Other Names: Glossy cowbird; red-eye; red-eyed cowbird.

Age: Probably about same as that of brown-headed cowbird.

Range: From C. America west into s.-c. Tex., sw. N.M., c. and s. Ariz., w. Chihuahua and Yucatán, Mexico, south to w. Panama; winters throughout breeding range and only partially (to a degree) migratory in lower Rio Grande Valley; small proportion of population moves farther south for winter; accidental in se. Calif.; in Fla., first one collected (shot) there, in Gainesville, Nov. 1968; a previous record (photographs) at Sarasota, 1962 (Matteson, 1970).

Cowbird, brown-headed, *Molothrus ater* (moll-OTH-rus AY-ter); genus name: *see* Cowbird, bronzed; species name: Lat., black. (Color ill., page 905.) Throughout most of U.S. and s. Canada; 6–8 in. long; wingspread 11¾–13¾ in.; male black with *coffee-brown* head, short, conical, sparrowlike bill; female same but uniformly gray; cowbird has longer tail than starling (which also has *pointed* bill), and differs from red-winged blackbird, Brewer's blackbird, and grackles by heavier bill, uptilted tail, slighter build; song is bubbly *glug-glug-glee;* call is *chuck;* flight note is a high whistle.

Feeding Habits: Eats many insects—grasshoppers appear to be its favorite animal food; also eats beetles, caterpillars, alfalfa weevils, cotton weevils, bugs, flies, wasps, ants; occasionally spiders and snails; eats more plant food than animal—corn, wheat, oats, buckwheat, seeds of ragweed, dandelion, barnyard grass, panic grasses; also small amount of fruit —some blackberries, huckleberries, cedar berries, wild cherries, and wild grapes (Bent, 1958).

Nest: None; female lays white eggs speckled with brown in nests of other birds, usually 1 per nest; Payne (1965) offers evidence that each female lays 10–12 eggs each nesting season.

Incubation: 11–12 days; incubation by host (Nice, 1954).

Other Names: Brown-headed blackbird; brown-headed oriole; buffalo bird; cow blackbird; cow bunting; cow-pen bird; cuckold; lazybird.

Age: One, banded in Tex., shot when 7 years, 9 months, old; one lived in National Zoo, Washington, D.C., for 8 years, 5 months; a female, banded Syracuse, N.Y., trapped and released at Salisbury, N.Y., when 13 years, 10 months, old (Kennard, 1975).

Albinism: 28 records (Gross, 1965a); partial albinism locally frequent.

Flight Speed: Timed in Mich., 13–27 m.p.h. (Schnell, 1965).

Weights: In Mich. (41), 34.3–53.9 gr. (Becker and Stack, 1944), or 1–1¾ oz.; coastal N.J. (4), 38.1–44.3 gr. (Murray and Jehl, 1964), or 1⅓ –1½ oz.; 1½–1¾ oz. (Forbush, 1925–29); female smaller than male.

Range: Nests from c. and ne. B.C., s.-c. Mack., across s. Canada to s. Nova Scotia, south throughout U.S. to n. Baja Calif. and into Mexico, and to La., s. Miss., and S.C.; winters from c. Okla., c. Mo., s. Mich., s. Ont., N.Y., and Conn., west and south across country to w. and s. Calif., se. Ariz., s. N.M., ne. Tex., se. La., south to s. Baja Calif., Mexico, Gulf coast, and s. Fla.; rarely north to n. Me.; casual in Bermuda.

Cowbird, red-eyed. *See* Cowbird, bronzed.

Grackle, boat-tailed, *Quiscalus major* (KWIS-kah-lus MAY-jer); genus name: from New Lat., *quiscala,* quail; species name: Lat., greater, larger; *boat-tailed* refers to long tail creased in flight like keel of a boat; *grackle,* from Lat. *graculus,* a daw, or jackdaw. (Color ill., page 905.) E. and se. U.S., Atlantic and Gulf coasts; male about 16–17 in. long; wingspread about 21–23½ in.; tail 6¼–7¼ in. long (keel shape of tail distinguishes this bird from fish crow); adult male, glossy purple upperparts less extensive than in male of similar great-tailed grackle; purple more toward rear of neck, back, humerals, abdomen, but flanks more conspicuously green-blue, and head and neck appear much larger than that of great-tailed grackle (Selander and Giller, 1961); eye color of boat-tailed variable: iris is yellow to tan, and usually brown to gray-brown, never intensely yellow as in great-tailed grackle (the brown-eyed form of boat-tailed lives from se. Fla. west along Gulf coast through Miss. and La. to se. Tex; the yellow-eyed form, along s. Atlantic coast from s. N.J. to Ga., winters from Va. south to Fla.—see details in Selander and Giller, 1961); female boat-tailed, 12–13 in. long; wingspread about 18 in.; dark brown above, buffy below; eyes brown or *dull* yellow; boat-tailed lives mostly along coast in tidal saltwater marshes and barrier and sea islands; seldom seen more than 20 mi. inland except in peninsular Fla., where, besides living along both coasts, is scattered across state where many ponds, streams; also lives about farmlands and in towns and cities such as Charleston, S.C., nests primarily in coastal marshes in Miss. and in La.; travels in small flocks (except in nesting season), often with other blackbirds; roosts with them at night in groves of trees; male in spring courtship perches in trees, on utility poles, on ground, or on shrubs about marshes; spreads tail, wings, bobs, bows, showing off glossy plumage before females; utters guttural, rasping clicks, chips, churs, kwees, a loud clear "wolf whistle," and a peculiar rolling, guttural rattle (Sprunt, 1958) quite different from "song" of great-tailed grackle, and by which female boat-tailed apparently distinguishes (and mates with) her kind (Selander and Giller, 1961); males are *polygynous* and where range overlaps that of great-tailed grackle, as between Houston, Tex., and Lake Charles, La., the two outwardly similar species do not interbreed (see details in Selander and Giller, 1961).

Feeding Habits: In feeding, walks about on ground with tail held high, both in dry fields and, especially, on mud flats in summer, where it often wades into water to catch with black bill small fishes, shrimps, crabs, frogs, snails, even the large green (*Pomacea*) snail, a favorite food in Fla. Everglades (Snyder and Snyder, 1969); also aquatic insects, spiders, crayfishes, which it often snatches from mouths of glossy ibises; also kills and eats small birds and especially nestlings of red-winged blackbird and, along with fish crows and black vultures, eats eggs and newly hatched young of herons and ibises, also eats freshwater mussels; perches on cattle in Fla. and snaps insects from their backs; also eats caterpillars, grasshoppers, beetles, grubs in plowed fields; also grain (largely corn and some rice).

Nest: In Fla., in loose colonies in saw grass, cattails, bulrushes, in wax myrtle and other bushes over or near water or in live oaks, 3–12 ft. up or to 50 ft. in trees; in Tex., often in enormous numbers in heron colonies, sometimes in herons' stick nests; also abundant nester in many towns and cities along Atlantic coast; in Charleston, nests always near water in wax myrtle, palmettos, pines, or up to 80 ft. high in live oaks; in Va., in cedars and pines; nest built by female, in marshes, bulky, of coarse, partly decayed rushes, mud, cattails, marsh grasses (Sprunt, 1958), in trees, usually of twigs and weed stalks in foundation into which incorporates Spanish moss, string, rags, paper, feathers, often uses mud or cow dung as "cement" for foundation material.

Eggs: Mar.–June; 3–5, light blue to blue-gray, marked with brown, gray, purple, or black.

Incubation: By female, 13–14 days; young fly about 20–23 days after hatching.

Other Names: Crow blackbird; daw; jackdaw; saltwater blackbird.

Age: One, banded Gulfport, Fla., shot when 12 years, 9 months, old near St. Petersburg (Kennard, 1975).

Albinism: Occasional; one shot in S.C., 1944, body white, wings and tail black.

Flight Speed: Timed in Tex., 27–39 m.p.h. (Sooter, 1947); 28 m.p.h. (Aymar, 1935).

Range: Nests along Atlantic coast from s. N.J. south to Fla., Ga., and e. Tex.; mainly resident from se. Tex., s. La., s. Miss., s. Ala., and Fla., south to Fla. Keys; Atlantic coast population winters from Va. south to Fla.

Grackle, bronzed. *See* Grackle, common.

Grackle, common, *Quiscalus quiscula* (KWIS-kah-lus KWIS-cue-lah); genus and species names: *see* Grackle, boat-tailed; *grackle* originated in Europe, where applied to members of Starling Family of Old World, originally applied in N. America to grackles of the genus *Quiscalus* (Newton, 1893–96). (Color ill., page 905.) In summer lives over most of N. America east of Rocky Mtns.; 11–13½ in. long; wingspread 17–18½ in.; all-black, glossy; in New England and West, subspecies shows bronze reflections from back; east of Alleghenies, purple; in Southeast, greenish; all adults have yellow eyes; long, sharp-pointed black bills; long, wedge-shaped tails, held in flight like V or keel of boat; female smaller, duller; young are brown with brown eyes; lives over farmlands, orchards, swamps, seen much on lawns and in evergreen trees in cities, parks, suburbs; highly gregarious at all times; in nesting season, those not incubating eggs roost together at night; large noisy roost of thousands, with starlings, redwings, cowbirds, robins, sometimes in cities or suburban shade trees; flies in level flight, not undulating as red-winged blackbirds do; most winter not far south of nesting range; flocks arrive in n. U.S., western states, and Canada middle of Mar. to early Apr.; in Fla., where permanent resident, begins nesting in Mar., in swamps, pine woods, palmetto hammocks, orange groves; male puffs out plumage and displays before females, sometimes on ground, raises shoulder feathers in ruff, drops wings, utters harsh, squeaky song, *koguba-leek*, that has been likened to squeaking of rusty-hinged gate; common call is loud *chack*.

Feeding Habits: On ground walks with slow dignified gait or occasionally runs and leaps high after insect; also forages in shrubs and trees, probes ground for earthworms, snatches them from feeding robins; eats boll weevils, beetles—Japanese, June, and rose beetles—follows plow for grubs, eats grasshoppers, army worms, caterpillars of sphinx moth in tobacco fields, periodical cicadas, ants, flies, some spiders, cocoons, and eggs, also myriapods, snakes and lizards; wades belly deep in streams, ponds, for crayfishes, minnows (see Darden, 1974), goldfishes, small frogs, salamanders; chases and catches mice on ground, bats in the air; eats eggs and young of smaller birds; kills adults, especially house sparrows; eats acorns, chestnuts, weed seeds, grain, especially corn, wild and cultivated fruit.

Nest: Singly or in colonies up to dozens of pairs in tall ornamental evergreen trees of country lanes or city parks, also in elms, maples, etc., cedars of hillside pastures, in cattail marshes, in holes of trees or stumps, in willow swamps, low shrubs about lakes and ponds, sometimes in old buildings and in lower parts of ospreys' nests; bulky but compact mass of twigs, weed stalks, grasses, seaweeds, sometimes with foundation of mud, lined with dried grasses, feathers, paper, strings, rags.

Eggs: Mar.–June; 4–7, commonly 5–6, pale green or light brown, blotched or streaked with lines, dashes of brown, lavender.

Incubation: About 14 days (13 days, 4 hours, according to Maxwell and Putnam, 1972); incubation period 13–14 days; young fly about 14–16 days after hatching (Graber and Graber, 1977); young fly when 18–20 days old (Gross, 1958a).

Other Names: Blackbird; bronzed grackle; China-eyed blackbird; crow blackbird; Florida grackle; keel-tailed grackle; maize thief; New England jackdaw; purple grackle; purple jackdaw; white-eyed jackdaw.

Age: One banded Paoli, Pa., found dead Upper Darby, Pa., when 14 years old; one, banded Whiting, N.J., trapped and released at E. New Brunswick, N.J., when 16 years, 1 month, old (Kennard, 1975); one, banded S. D., Aug. 1924, recovered Minn., Oct. 1940, when at least 17 years old (Gross, 1958a).

Albinism: Frequent but largely partial; 23 records (Gross, 1965a).

Flight Speed: Timed in N.H., 27–30 m.p.h. (White, 1927); 20–28 m.p.h. (Wood, 1933).

Host to Cowbirds: Rare, only six records (Friedmann, 1963).

Weights: In Mich. (143), 83.5–137 gr. (Becker and Stack, 1944), or 3–5 oz.; in winter, in Conn. (1), 152.5 gr., or about 5⅓ oz. (Wetherbee,

1934); in Canada (204), males, 105–140 gr.; females, 95–104 gr. (Snyder, 1937).

Range: Nests from ne. B.C., s. Mack., east to Nova Scotia (in Canada into boreal forest, especially in Northwest, where reaches Great Slave Lake—Godfrey, 1966), but sparsely populated there, main range east of 100° W. Long. and south of 48° N. Lat. (Erskine, 1971b); nests east of Rockies south to c. Colo., sw. Kans., c. and s.-c. Tex., the Gulf coast, and s. Fla., migratory in northern part of range; winters casually north to the Great Lakes region; winters commonly in se. U.S.; has been reported occasionally from west of the Rocky Mtns. (Reilly, 1968).

Grackle, Florida. *See* Grackle, common.

Grackle, great-tailed, *Quiscalus mexicanus* (KWIS-kah-lus meks-ih-CANE-us); genus name: *see* Grackle, boat-tailed; species name: Lat., of Mexico. (Color ill., page 905.) In summer, Ariz. east to Tex.; meets nesting range of similar boat-tailed grackle in Tex. and La.; about same size as or larger than boat-tailed grackle; adult male, glossy purple or violet extends backward from head and breast over much of abdomen and flanks and to mid-back and humeral coverts, grades to green-blue on rear part of flanks, abdomen, back; overall, more uniformly colored than boat-tailed and more purplish; eyes: *irises almost invariably intense yellow* (Selander and Giller, 1961); adult female, smaller than male; metallic sheen less conspicuous; irises yellow; great-tailed in N. America lives over open ground with standing water (not in forests) and never far from ocean or lakes, ponds, streams; in desert or prairie, confined to watercourses or to irrigated land where trees available.

Feeding Habits: Apparently same as boat-tailed grackle.

Nest: In Rio Grande Valley and on Gulf coastal plain of s. Tex., nesting colonies are most common in mesquite, also regularly in huisache (*Acacia*), hackberry (*Celtis*), prickly ash, oaks, cottonwood, prickly-pear cactus, willows, and even in tall grass, also in canebrakes bordering lagoons and in rushes in salt marshes on Gulf coast; rarely nests in freshwater marshes as at Welder Wildlife Refuge near Sinton, Tex., where large breeding colony in 1959 at edge of shallow lake; nests in marshes only where trees not available; nesting colonies in trees on prairie or in towns or about farm and ranch houses; in cedar elms (*Ulmus*) and live oaks, may also nest on utility poles or other man-made structures. Males *polygynous* as in boat-tailed grackle, and in breeding zone of sympatry with boat-tailed, nests in mixed breeding colonies, the two species not interbreeding; males hold mutually exclusive territories and solicit mating in females, which select males of their own kind based on their courtship displays and "song," part of song of male great-tailed is loud, piercing *cha-we* note or *may-ree, may-ree!* and high falsetto squeal, *quee-ee, quee-ee,* much like flicker's *week-it, week-it* call; nest built by female from 2 ft. above water in marshes to about 50 ft. (usually 5–15 ft.) up in tall

live oaks; usually not distinguishable from nest of boat-tailed grackle.

Eggs: Mar.–June; 3–4, bluish, average darker than eggs of boat-tailed, slightly longer, appear less rounded, markings more numerous and pronounced at small end of egg.

Incubation: By female, 13–14 days.

Other Names: Crow blackbird; daw; jackdaw.

Range: Nests, and possibly resident, from s. and se. Ariz., n.-c. and c. N.M., and w., s.-c., and e.-c. Tex., south through Mexico and C. America to nw. Peru and Caribbean coast of Colombia; occasional in winter east of breeding range along Gulf coast to Avery Is., La.

Grackle, purple. *See* Grackle, common.

Meadowlark, eastern, *Sturnella magna* (stir-NEL-ah MAG-nah); genus name: dim. of Lat. *sturnus,* starling; species name: Lat., great, large (Coues, 1882). (Color ill., page 904.) Lives in Southwest and eastward from prairie country of Midwest and Canada to Atlantic coast; 8½–11 in. long; wingspread 13½–17 in.; adults, sexes similar, streaked brown above with yellow breast marked by broad black V; white outer tail feathers show both when on ground and in flight, resembles quail in alternate quick flaps and sailing on set wings; perches much on fence posts, utility poles or wires along grassy fields; many winter in New England and other northern nesting range; others, in spring, migrate north at night and by day from wintering range in middle and southern states; males usually arrive in n. U.S. and s. Canada in early Apr. (Gross, 1958b); two weeks later, when females arrive, resident male in established territory of about 7 acres now sings more; plaintive whistled song, *tee-you, tee-air,* or *spring-o'-the-year;* from poles, fence posts, trees, or on ground; also gives flight song, somewhat like that of bobolink, and utters harsh, chattering alarm note, all proclaiming territory; polygynous male may have more than one mate.

Feeding Habits: Walks about on ground like a quail, in grassy or weed-grown fields, and roadsides; about 74% of food is animal: beetles, bugs, grasshoppers, crickets, cutworms, caterpillars, scale insects, weevils, ants, wasps, spiders, sometimes eats dead traffic-killed birds (Terres, 1956b); also eats grain (flocks in spring migration sometimes eat sprouting corn) and weed seeds.

Nest: On ground in depression 1–3 in. deep or in hoofprint of cattle or horses (Roseberry and Klimstra, 1970), in meadows, pastures, corn, wheat, alfalfa, and clover fields, weedy orchards, grass islands in plowed fields, edges of marsh; of dried grasses, plant stems, lined with grasses, lespedezas, pine needles, horsehair, often domed with grass, entrance on side, built against dense clump of grass or weeds. See Roseberry and Klimstra (1970) for details.

Eggs: Apr.–Aug.; 3–7, commonly 5, usually white, suffused with pink, spotted and speckled with browns, lavender.

Incubation: By female, 13–14 days (Nice, 1954); usually two broods; female sitting in nest often responds to flight song of male with low, sweet, chuckling notes; may turn eggs five times in hour (*see* Eggs and Egg-Laying); both parents feed young, which leave nest when 11–12 days old (Gross, 1958b); families gather in small flocks in fall.

Other Names: Arizona meadowlark; common lark; common meadowlark; crescent stare; field lark; marsh quail; medlar; medlark; mudlark; Rio Grande meadowlark; southern meadowlark.

Accidents: One electrocuted by electric fence in Ill. (Tate, 1962).

Albinism: Several reported, all partial albinos; a melanistic one collected (shot) in N.J. (Townsend, 1883).

Age: One, banded June 1926, Ridley Park, Pa., shot Feb. 1935, Beaufort, N.C., when about 10 years old (Anonymous, 1935).

Flight Speed: Timed in Tex., 25 m.p.h. (Sooter, 1947).

Host to Cowbirds: Uncommon, but somewhat frequent in Ill. (Friedmann, 1963).

Hybrids: Hybridizes with western meadowlark (Gray, 1958), but Lanyon (1957), from detailed study of overlapping ranges of the two species from Okla. northward into s. Ont., could find no clear evidence of wild hybrids but suggests it may occur. In overlapping ranges of two species in Wisc., they appeared to be reproductively isolated, largely through differences in behavior, a barrier to random mating.

Range: Nests from nw. and c. Ariz. and s. N.M., north to sw. S.D., n. Minn., n. Wisc., n. Mich., se. Ont., sw. and s.-c. Que. and c. Nova Scotia, and south to n. S. America; winters short distance south of northern edge of breeding range, common in winter only south of Ohio R. Valley and coastal Md. (Reilly, 1968).

Meadowlark, western, *Sturnella neglecta* (stir-NEL-ah nee-GLEK-tah); genus name: *see* Meadowlark, eastern; species name: Lat., neglected (overlooked), so named by John James Audubon because it was overlooked by Lewis and Clark expedition. (Color ill., page 904.) State bird of Kans., Mont., Neb., N.D., Ore., and Wyo.; western counterpart of eastern meadowlark; lives from eastern border of plains and prairies to Pacific; from s. Canada to Mexico; 8–11 in. long; sexes similar; like eastern meadowlark but paler; can be distinguished in field with certainty from eastern by its very different song—flutelike, gurgling, doublenoted, has "the flutelike quality of the wood thrush with the rich melody of the Baltimore oriole" (Bent, 1958); summers on prairies and grassy plains, and in valleys; ranges into mountain parks and foothills in Wash. up to 5,600 ft.; in Calif., from sea level to 7,000 ft.; in Utah, up to 8,000 ft.; in mountains of Ariz. and Colo., to 10,000 and 12,000 ft.; male behaves like eastern meadowlark in defending his territory by singing from tall weeds, posts, and trees and while in flight (see Bent, 1958, for details).

Feeding Habits: Walks about on ground like eastern relative, sometimes seen about streets and grassy lanes of villages; in spring and summer, pairs may forage together; in fall and winter, in flocks of 10–75; animal food about 65–70% of diet: beetles, alfalfa weevils, cutworms, wireworms, caterpillars, Mormon "crickets" and their eggs, grasshoppers, crane flies, spid-

ers, sow bugs, a few snails, etc.; also eats oats, wheat, barley, some corn, some weed seeds (Bent, 1958); seen eating an egg of a horned lark at lark's nest; also eats flesh of other birds killed on highway (Creighton and Potter, 1974).

Nest and Eggs: Like those of eastern meadowlark; however, female usually builds her nest on dry ground rather than on wet or damp ground preferred by her eastern relative. See details in Bent (1958); also Lanyon (1962).

Albinism: A complete albino, June 1942, mounted as specimen, University Museum, Lincoln, Neb. (McClure, 1943); at Cheyenne, Wyo., pure-white one flushed three times on sheep ranch in Sept. 1956; many partial albinos reported (Gross, 1965a).

Flight Speed: Timed in Kans., 20 m.p.h. (Wood, 1933); in Calif., 40 m.p.h. (Tyler, 1933).

Host to Cowbirds: Uncommon, 24 records (Friedmann, 1963).

Hybrids: See under Eastern meadowlark.

Weights: One alive, wounded Jan. 1971 by sparrow hawk in Colo., 87.5 gr. (Wolhuter, 1971), or about 3 oz.

Range: Nests from c. B.C., c. Alta., east to s. Ont., n. Mich., nw. Ohio, south to Baja Calif., Mexico, c. Tex. and La.; some withdrawal southward in fall from northern parts of range.

Oriole, Alta Mira. *See* Oriole, Lichtenstein's.

Oriole, Audubon's. *See* Oriole, blackheaded.

Oriole, Baltimore (northern), *Icterus galbula galbula* (ICK-teh-rus GAL-bew-lah); genus name: Lat., from Gr. *ikteros*, jaundice; name given to small yellow bird by ancients, the sight of which cured jaundiced persons, at which the bird died, according to Gr. belief; species and subspecies names: Lat., a small yellow bird; common name: from its colors, which resemble those chosen by Sir George Calvert, an early colonizer of Md., 1st Baron of Baltimore, for his livery or coat of arms (Coues, 1882). (Color ill., page 908.) State bird of Md.; for years considered a distinct species, but American Ornithologists' Union (1973) classified it as a subspecies of the northern oriole; Baltimore oriole summers in c. and s. Canada, e. U.S., west to plains and prairies, where it often interbreeds with its western counterpart, the Bullock's oriole; 7–8 in. long; wingspread 11¼–12¼ in.; male bright orange and black with one narrow white wing bar; black head, neck, upper breast, wings, tail; orange-yellow underparts, rump, and outer tail feathers (its all-black head distinguishes it from similar male Bullock's oriole); female and young, olive above; yellow below and on rump, sometimes with black about head, neck, and back; each dusky wing has *two* white wing bars; female similar to female Bullock's but much more yellow-orange below, not so white on belly (Peterson, 1947); migrating northward from winter home in Mexico and S. America, travels through se. U.S. in Mar.–Apr., arrives n. U.S. and Canada, Apr.–May; male precedes female by a few days, settles in his territory among flowering orchards, newly leaved tall shade trees of country roads, towns, edges of woods near streams; in

courtship displays before female, bows, spreads tail, raises wings and shows bright colors; song is loud, clear, flutelike, varied whistle, easy to imitate but difficult to describe; alarm is long, rolling chatter.

Feeding Habits: Gleans trees and shrubbery especially for caterpillars, including the hairy or spiny kinds—fall webworms, tussock caterpillars, tent caterpillars, those of gypsy and brown-tail moths, also beetles, ants, bugs, grasshoppers, scale insects, aphids, nut weevils, sawfly larvae, wood borers, and a host of others (see Tyler, 1958a, for details); also eats garden peas, wild cherries, Juneberries, blackberries, grapes, and other fruit, probes flowers for nectar, also comes to feeding stations for suet and peanut butter mixture; from 1949 through 1968, many individuals wintered increasingly in e. U.S. (Atlantic states) and Canada because of food supply in yards and gardens (Erickson, 1969); also eats halved oranges nailed to feeders and sugar water in summer from hummingbird feeders. See Terres (1977).

Nest: Gray, swinging pouch, 5–6 in. deep, suspended by its rim from drooping branch of maple, elm, poplar, orchard tree, or conifer; woven by female of plant fibers, hairs, string (cloth when available) and lined inside with wool, hair, fine grasses; nest usually 25–30 ft. up, rarely 6 ft. or up to 90 ft. above ground (Tyler, 1958a); orioles will accept short pieces of colored yarn put out for their use (see in Terres, 1968c).

Eggs: May–June; 4–6, commonly 4, gray-white or pale blue-white, streaked, blotched, with irregularly shaped lines.

Incubation: 12–14 days; young fly about 12–14 days after hatching.

Other Names: Baltimore-bird; English robin; firebird; fire-hang-bird; golden oriole; hammock-bird; hang-bird; hang-nest; pea-bird.

Accidents: Many caught around neck and strangled by horsehair or string used in nest building; one electrocuted May 1948, campus of Kent State University, Ohio, when perched on electric wire. *See* Electrocution.

Age: An adult, banded Fargo, N.D., retrapped and released at same place when 7 years old (Kennard, 1975); a pet at Riverhead, N.Y., picked up as fledgling when fell out of nest, June 1956, alive and well in June 1970 when 14 years old.

Flight Speed: Timed in New England, 26 m.p.h. (White, 1927).

Host to Cowbirds: Infrequent, only 13 records (Friedmann, 1963).

Hybrids: Baltimore oriole × Bullock's oriole— first hybrid reported in 1906 in Sask., where ranges of two meet. Interbreeds extensively with Bullock's oriole in w. Okla. and w. Neb.; *see* discussion in Hybrid; see also Gray (1958).

Weights: In fall, coastal N.J. (235), 25–47.2 gr. (Murray and Jehl, 1964), or about 1–1¾ oz.

Range: Nests from c. Alta. east across s. Canada to c. Me., c. N.B., Nova Scotia, from n. Mich. south to w.-c. Okla., ne. Tex., se. La., s. Miss., n. Ala., n.-c. Ga., w. S.C. and w. N.C., c. Va., n. Md., and Del.; sometimes winters in se. Canada and e. U.S. but usually from s. Mexico to n. S. America.

Oriole, black-headed, *Icterus graduacauda* (ICK-teh-rus grad-you-ah-CAW-dah); genus name: *see* Oriole, Baltimore; species name: from Lat. *gradus*, step, and *caudum*, tail; gradual tail or graduated tail. (Color ill., page 906.) Mexican species that ranges north into Tex., 8–9¼ in. long; male, bright lemon yellow with *green-yellow* back; black head, upper breast, wings, and tail; female similar; lives in dense woods, thickets of mesquite, ebony, huisache, and other heavy undergrowth along stagnant watercourses of lower Rio Grande and in thicketed banks of streams, ponds, forest openings; inconspicuous, quiet, usually in pairs that stay hidden; pair together all year, seem closely attached; flight is low and rapid, male sings sweet, low, haunting song, like boy learning to whistle, not often heard (Bent, 1958).

Feeding Habits: Pairs forage close to ground for insects, hackberries.
Nest: Semipensile, about 3 in. deep, often in dense mesquite trees, or bushes, 6–14 ft. above ground, firmly attached by contracted rim at top, and by sides, to small branches and twigs; built of dry woven grasses.
Eggs: Apr.–June; 3–5, pale blue or gray-white, slightly flecked with markings and hairlines of brown, purple.
Incubation: Period of and age when young first fly unknown.
Other Name: Audubon's oriole.
Host to Cowbirds: Frequent victim of its relative the bronzed cowbird and one old record of host to brown-headed cowbird (Friedmann, 1963).
Range: Resident, nests from s. Tex. (occasionally wanders north to c. Tex.) south into Mexico and to nw. Guatemala.

Oriole, black-throated. *See* Oriole, Lichtenstein's.

Oriole, black-vented, *Icterus wagleri* (ICK-teh-rus WAG-ler-eye); genus name: *see* Oriole, Baltimore; species name: given in 1857 by P. L. Sclater, British ornithologist, for J. G. Wagler, professor of zoology (1827–32) at Munich University; *black-vented,* for black undertail coverts covering "vent," or cloaca. Mexican species first reported in U.S. when a male seen near Big Bend National Park, Tex., Sept. 19, 1968; one on Oct. 22, 1968, at same locality (Snider, 1969); 7½–9 in. long; sexes outwardly similar; black hood, black wings and tail, and *black crissum* (undertail feathers); orange breast, rump, and belly; resembles Scott's oriole but has no white bar on wings (see Peterson and Chalif, 1973; Sutton, 1951b; Blake, E. R., 1953); lives in second-growth woods, scrub, and edges of woods in native Mexico and C. America.

Other Name: Wagler's oriole.
Range: Lives in n. Mexico (except Tamaulipas) in highlands south to Nicaragua, in Guatemala from elevation 3,000–6,000 ft. (Griscom, 1932).

Oriole, brown. *See* Oriole, orchard.

Oriole, Bullock's (northern), *Icterus galbula bullockii* (ICK-teh-rus GAL-bew-lah bull-OCK-ih-eye); genus and species names: *see* Oriole, Baltimore; subspecies name: given in 1827 by William Swainson, British ornithologist, from a bird collected near Mexico City by William Bullock, English traveler and proprietor of Bullock's Museum in London. (Color ill., page 908.) W. U.S., Great Plains to Pacific slope; for years considered a distinct species, but not so classified by the American Ornithologists' Union (1973), which considers it a western subspecies of the northern oriole; it is the commonest oriole over most of West and counterpart of the Baltimore oriole; 7–8½ in. long; male fiery orange, has *black crown* and *orange cheeks* (not a completely black head as in Baltimore oriole), large white patch on each dark wing; female olive above, buffy white below; yellow on tail, two white wing bars; young similar but young males have black throats like adults; summers in cottonwoods, willows, sycamores that line streams and irrigation ditches of open country, prairies, farmlands and up into lower mountain canyons, trees about ranches, and in semiarid mesquite groves in Ariz.; male's whistled song similar to that of Baltimore oriole but not so variable, both sexes chatter much; devoted pair vigorously defend nest, eggs, and young against magpies and other egg-eating birds; often nests close to western kingbird in Ariz., to scissor-tailed flycatcher in Tex.

Feeding Habits: About 80% animal matter; feeds heavily on caterpillars, especially of codling moth, beetles, acorn weevils, cotton-boll weevils, alfalfa weevils, ants, black olive scales, leafhoppers, treehoppers, aphids, also grasshoppers, catches alfalfa butterflies in air; most of vegetal food is fruit: cherries, apricots, figs, persimmons, blackberries, hawthorn berries, raspberries, elderberries; drinks nectar from flowers.
Nest: Oval-shaped woven bag, 6 in. deep, attached by rim or sides to ascending twigs out on branches of cottonwood, birch, willow, sycamore, juniper, or in bunch of mistletoe, 6–15 ft. above ground, sometimes to 50 ft.; built of fibers and bark of plants and lined with horsehair, plant down, wool, fine mosses.
Eggs: Apr.–June; 3–6, commonly 4–5, pale gray or pale blue, peppered or spotted and scribbled with lines of gray, brown, or black.
Incubation: By female, about 14 days; young fly about 14 days after hatching.
Flight Speed: Timed in Wash., 28–32 m.p.h. (Rathbun, 1934).
Host to Cowbirds: Frequent victim to bronzed cowbird in Tex., rare to brown-headed cowbird.
Hybrids: See under Baltimore oriole.
Range: Nests from s. B.C., s. Alta., sw. Sask., Mont., sw. N.D., and c. S.D., south to n. Baja Calif., Mexico, w. Okla., c. Tex.; winters from c. and s. Mexico to Costa Rica, casually north to c. Calif., s. Tex., and s. La.

Oriole, flame-headed. *See* Oriole, scarlet-headed.

Oriole, hooded, *Icterus cucullatus* (ICK-teh-rus cue-cue-LAY-tus); genus name: *see* Oriole, Baltimore; species name: Lat., hooded. (Color ill., page 907.) Sw. U.S.; 7–7¾ in. long;

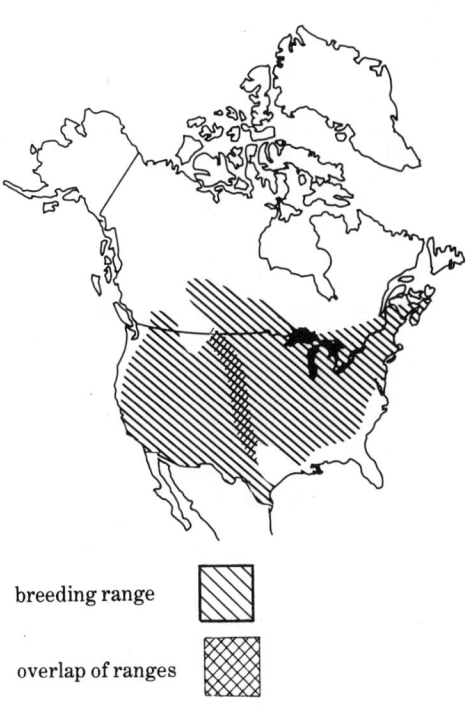

breeding range

overlap of ranges

TROUPIAL FAMILY
The eastern Baltimore oriole and the western Bullock's oriole, once thought to be separate species, are now classified as subspecies of the northern oriole. Despite differences in appearance, the two subspecies interbreed freely where their ranges overlap in the Great Plains.

male, *orange crown and back* of neck, *black throat and breast* and *all-black, graduated tail;* female, olive green above, yellow below, with dark gray wings, two white wing bars; immatures resemble female, young males have black throat (they nest in this plumage—Phillips *et al.*, 1964); summers in thickets and woods of semiarid country, and about ranches and towns, lives in cottonwoods, sycamores, along streams, common in palm trees in s. Calif., also in walnut, cypress, gum, and others; arrives in Mar. in Calif., Tex., in Apr. in Ariz., from wintering along Mexican border and southward; male courts female by chasing and exaggerated bows and posturings on limbs of trees; chatters much like Bullock's oriole, in song utters warbled throaty whistles, interspersed with chatter; seldom alights on ground, restless, often shy, haunts dense foliage of tall trees and low shrubbery in search for food; climbs through foliage, sometimes hangs upside down like chickadee in search for caterpillars.

Feeding Habits: Insects; also spends much time probing blossoms of agaves, aloes, hibiscus, lilies, and other tubular flowers for insects and nectar; like Bullock's oriole, comes to feeding stations in yards and gardens in Calif. for sugar-water mixture, bread, cake, fresh and dried fruit.

Nest: Female builds thin-walled woven cuplike nest sewn with fibers to palmetto leaves, yuccas, in bunch of Spanish moss, or in clump of mistletoe (Bent, 1958); suspended from branch of sycamore, mesquite, hackberry, occasionally under eaves of house (Phillips *et al.*, 1964); lined with dried grasses, mosses, horsehair, wool, feathers, 6–45 ft. above ground (Bent, 1958).

Eggs: Apr.–Aug.; 3–5, usually 4, white, pale yellow or pale blue, blotched and spotted with browns, purples, grays.

Incubation: By female, 12–14 days; young leave nest about 14 days after hatching (Bent, 1958); sometimes two or three broods each year (Phillips *et al.*, 1964).

Other Names: Sennett's oriole; palm-leaf oriole (in s. Calif., from habit of nesting in the native Washington fan palms).

Age: A male, banded Pt. Loma, Calif., found dead at San Diego when 6 years old (Kennard, 1975).

Host to Cowbirds: One of chief victims of bronzed cowbird; a few records for brownheaded cowbird (Friedmann, 1963).

Range: Nests in c. Calif., s. Nev., south to s. Baja Calif., c. and se. Ariz., s. N.M., w. and s. Tex., south to s. Mexico, Baja Calif., Belize; winters mainly in Mexico.

Oriole, Lichtenstein's, *Icterus gularis* (ICK-teh-rus gew-LAY-rus); genus name: *see* Oriole, Baltimore; species name: Lat., pertaining to the gula, the throat; common name: for M. H. C. Lichtenstein, Director of Zoology, Museum of Berlin (1815–51). (Color ill., page 906.) Mexican and C. American bird that ranges north into s. Tex., where rare and irregular; 8¼–10 in. long; like a large hooded oriole, but distinguished from it by bright *yellow* or *orange* wing bar in upper part of wings; sexes

alike; young are greenish on back, pale yellow below, less black on throat than adults; lives in treetops of heavy forest, in trees along fields and streams, in scattered groves in pastures; male sings quick, repeated two or three notes in clear tone of Baltimore (northern) oriole, call is soft, flutelike note (Bent, 1958).

Feeding Habits: Searches leaves of trees for caterpillars, eats ants and other insects, also spiders, figs, berries, and other fruit.

Nest: Round, pendant, about 2 ft. long, usually conspicuous, built high in leafless trees, sometimes suspended from utility wire; of tough grasses and other plant fibers; about 18 days to build (Sutton and Pettingill, 1943).

Eggs: Apr.(?)–May; 3–4, white, spotted and scrawled with browns.

Incubation: Period of and age when young first fly unknown.

Other Names: Alta Mira oriole; black-throated oriole.

Host to Cowbirds: Frequent, to bronzed cowbird in lowlands of El Salvador, also in Tamaulipas, Mexico, and around San Antonio, Tex. (Friedmann, 1966).

Range: Resident, Rio Grande Valley, Tex., south into Mexico and C. America.

Oriole, northern, *Icterus galbula.* General common and scientific names (see American Ornithologists' Union, 1973) for the species representing two closely related subspecies of orioles—*see* Oriole, Baltimore, and Oriole, Bullock's. Each of these on most official lists before 1973 had been considered a distinct species, until closer studies of their relationships indicated that each was a geographic representative of a single species.

Oriole, orchard, *Icterus spurius* (ICK-teh-rus SPEW-rih-us); genus name: *see* Oriole, Baltimore; species name: Lat., false, from former common name "bastard Baltimore oriole," thus an undeserved or inappropriate scientific name (Coues, 1882). (Color ills., page 909.) C. and e. U.S.; 6–7¼ in. long; wingspread 9¼–10¼ in.; adult male in breeding plumage, only N. American oriole that is *reddish*, or rich dark *chestnut*, but with black head, neck, breast, back, wings (with single white wing bar), and tail; female and young, olive green above, dull yellow below; wings dusky with *two* white wing bars; immature male has black chin and throat; orchard oriole summers in rural country, in old orchards, shade trees along village streets, in prairies in timber along streams, in trees about farms, ranches, in nurseries, common about plantation homes in South, sometimes near ponds, marshes; migrates in spring northward from Mexico, S. America; arrives s. U.S. Mar.–Apr.; moves up Mississippi Valley, where more numerous than in Atlantic states; reaches n. U.S. early May (Bent, 1958); restless, usually hidden in foliage but not especially shy; male sings from trees as he hops from twig to twig; during courtship has flight song high over treetops; song, unlike Baltimore oriole's, has robinlike quality, usually ends in down-slurred note; rhythm suggested by *"Look here, what cheer, what cheer, whip yo, what cheer, wee-yo"* (Bent, 1958).

Feeding Habits: Searches trees, shrubs for insects—about 90% of food—eats mayflies, beetles, ants, grasshoppers, crickets, aphids, caterpillars, including cabbage "worms," cankerworms, also eats boll weevils, spiders, cherries, raspberries, strawberries, grapes, figs, mulberries.

Nest: Sometimes in loose colonies (114 nests on 7 acres in La.), also nests singly, often nests near eastern kingbird; nest is open pouch, beautifully woven cup about as wide as deep; suspended from forked end of tree branch or in bush, sometimes in bunch of Spanish moss, 6–20 ft. up; of woven grasses, thin-walled, inside bottom thickly wadded with plant down.

Eggs: Apr.–July; 3–7, usually 4–5, pale blue to pale gray, blotched, spotted, or scrawled with browns, purples, grays.

Incubation: By female, 12–14 days; young fly when 11–14 days old (Dennis, 1948); male helps feed young.

Other Names: Basket-bird; bastard Baltimore; brown oriole; orchard hang-nest; orchard starling.

Age: One, banded N. Little Rock, Ark., retrapped and released at same place when at least 7 years old.

Host to Cowbirds: Fairly frequent, to brownheaded cowbird; frequent victim of bronzed cowbird in lower Rio Grande Valley (Friedmann, 1963).

Weights: One, coastal N.J., 20.9 gr., or about ¾ oz.

Range: Nests from s. Man., c. and se. Minn., c. Wisc., s. Mich., s. Ont., n.-c. Pa., e.-c. N.Y., c. and ne. Mass., south through N.D., ne. Colo., n.-c. and w. Tex., to Mexico, along Gulf coast and n. Fla.; winters from s. Mexico to n. S. America; accidental in Calif.

Oriole, scarlet-headed, *Icterus pustulatus* (ICK-ter-us pus-tue-LAY-tus); species name: *see* Oriole, Baltimore; species name: Lat., blistered; from blistered appearance (black spots on back). Native of w. Mexico; winter visitor to Ariz., four records for San Diego County, Calif., May–Oct., one in Los Angeles County, Jan. 1966 (Small, 1974); one of most brilliantly colored orioles seen in N. America (Bent, 1958); 7½–8 in. long; adult male superficially resembles hooded oriole, but deeper color around head—orange-red—has narrower black throat patch; *back streaked with black and orange,* not solid black as in hooded (Phillips *et al.*, 1964); adult female similar to male, but much duller colors, gray or olive back streaked as in male (Blake, E. R., 1953); no records of nesting in N. America (see habits in Bent, 1958).

Other Names: Flame-headed oriole; western streak-backed oriole.

Oriole, Scott's, *Icterus parisorum* (ICK-ter-us par-eye-SO-rum); genus name: *see* Oriole, Baltimore; species name: given in 1838 by Charles Lucien Bonaparte, French ornithologist, for the Paris brothers, who did considerable pioneer collecting of birds in Mexico; common name: for Gen. Winfield Scott, who served in the Mexican War (Jaeger, 1950). (Color ill., page 909.) Mexico and semi-desert of sw. U.S.; 7¼–8¼ in. long; adult male, black and deep *lemon yellow;* has solidly black head, throat, upper breast, and back; rump yellow; black wings with one white wing bar; black tail with yellow outer tail feathers (patterned like tail of American redstart); female olive green above with *streaked back;* dingy green-yellow below, two white wing bars; best field mark is dusky cheek; old females sometimes have black throat (Phillips *et al.,* 1964); first-year males like female, and may have indistinctly marked or speckled black throat, but in some entire head is black; summers mostly north of Mexican border, between mountains and desert, in pinyon-juniper belt of foothills, desert slopes of mountains, or more elevated semiarid plains; males arrive on nesting range in Southwest before end of Mar. or during first half of Apr.; about a week before females (Bent, 1958); feeding in tops of trees, males sing incessantly throughout day (females sometimes sing softly near nest), male's song rich, varied whistled notes, resembles that of western meadowlark.

Feeding Habits: Eats grasshoppers, small beetles, caterpillars, butterflies, berries, fruits of cactus; probes flowers of aloes, cactuses, and other plants for nectar and insects.
Nest: Cup-shaped, about 3 in. deep, 4 in. wide, often sewn to down-slanting dead leaves of yucca where they join plant; 4–20 ft. above ground; also in Joshua trees; in sycamores 18 ft. up, in oaks, pines, junipers; nest is thin-walled, of fibers of yucca leaves, grasses, and lined with grasses, cotton batting, horsehair.
Eggs: Apr.–June; 2–4, usually 3, pale blue, blotched, streaked, spotted with black, brown, gray.
Incubation: By female, about 14 days; young leave nest when about 14 days old.
Host to Cowbirds: Rare host to bronzed cowbird, one record (Friedmann, 1963).
Range: Nests from Nev., Utah, n.-c. Ariz., n.-c. N.M., w. Tex., south through se. Calif. to s. Baja Calif. and south into Mexico; winters n. Baja Calif., casually sw. Calif., south into Mexico.

Oriole, Sennett's. *See* Oriole, hooded.

Oriole, spotted-breasted, *Icterus pectoralis* (ICK-teh-rus peck-toh-RAL-iss); genus name: *see* Oriole, Baltimore; species name: Lat., pertaining to the breast, on or worn on, in reference to heavy black spots on sides of breast. (Color ill., page 909.) Mexican and C. American species now around Miami, Fla.; 8–8½ in. long; adults orange with black throat, wings, center of back, tail; *black spots on sides of breast, much white in wings;* immature, similar, but duller-colored and without spots; lives in open woods, country and gardens where tall trees present; in Miami introduced, first one seen Aug. 1949 at Coconut Grove, but not positively identified until one killed by a cat in spring 1952 in Miami area (Sprunt, 1954a); nesting there and becoming common (see details in Brookfield and Griswold, 1956, and for later account of its continued spread in Fla., see Owre, 1973); male sings loud, liquid whistled notes; a noted singer.

Feeding Habits: No definitive studies of, but known to be largely a fruit and nectar feeder;

clips off hibiscus blossoms with bill to get nectar.
Nest: Pouch-shaped, woven of grasses and plant fibers, cradled in branch of tree; in its native tropics often builds in yuccas.
Eggs: Fla., Apr.; 2–4, or 3–5, pale blue, marked with dark colors; young hatched in Fla. in early May and young also hatched in July (Sprunt, 1954a); two broods a year.
Incubation: Period of and age when young first fly unknown.
Age: One, banded Homestead, Fla., caught and released in same area when 7 years, 4 months, old (Kennard, 1975).
Host to Cowbirds: Frequent to bronzed cowbird in lowlands of El Salvador (Friedmann, 1963).
Range: Resident s. Mexico to Costa Rica; and at Miami, Fla.

Oriole, streak-backed. *See* Oriole, scarlet-headed.

Oriole, Wagler's. *See* Oriole, black-vented.

TRUDEAU
JAMES DE BERTZ (or DE BERTY) (1817–87). Of French descent, born on a plantation near New Orleans, La.; a physician whom Audubon met while in La.; Trudeau's name is commemorated in a S. American tern named for him by Audubon in 1838 from a single one, the type specimen of this species, obtained by Trudeau at Great Egg Harbor, N.J. According to Gruson (1972), Trudeau had a peripatetic career in medicine in various cities in Europe and in the U.S. and for 15 years practiced medicine in New York City. During the Civil War he served as a brigadier general in the Confederate Army; he was wounded at Shiloh, taken prisoner in 1864; after the war he settled in New Orleans. See also Palmer (1928).

TRYPANOSOMES
See Parasite.

TUBENOSE
Term of some ornithologists for the Tubinares —albatrosses, petrels, fulmars, storm-petrels, and diving petrels—which have paired tubes along the ridge of the bill. Through these the birds breathe air that is carried back to their nostrils and then to the lungs; hence the name tubenoses, or properly Tubinares. *See* Regurgitation; Nostrils.

TUBERCULOSIS
See Avian Tuberculosis.

TUBINARES
(tube-ih-NARE-eez). *See* Tubenose.

TUMORS
According to Sanger (1971), tumors (neoplasms), both malignant and benign, may originate in any part of a bird's body. Tumors often form on the wings and many that form there are of the malignant, sarcomatus (fleshy) type. They may be single or multiple, and metastasis (me-TAS-tah-sis)—a secondary growth of the malignant tumor—frequently occurs; the most common metastatic site is the lungs. Most of

the records of tumors in birds come from zoo statistics or reports from animal hospitals or diagnostic laboratories, where hundreds or even thousands of birds have been examined through many decades.

Zoo records show that animals other than birds have tumors twice as often as do birds, and it has been suggested that birds may be more resistant to tumor development than other animals, with the exception of the shell parakeet (*see* Budgerigar in Parrot Family) and the domestic chicken. Sanger suggests, however, that wild birds may suffer more from tumors than is realized, but they die in out-of-the-way places and are never recovered for examination. See a discussion of tumors, or skin growths, noted on wild birds caught for banding by Michener and Michener (1936).

By far the highest incidence of tumors among all birds, excluding domestic chickens, is in captive shell parakeets, in which tumors are more frequent than in any other animals, including man. In one report, 24.2% of all deaths in 866 parakeets were caused by neoplasia, or tumors (Sanger, 1971). In the U.S., pituitary tumors were the most common type in parakeets; in Great Britain, they were most frequent in the thoracic and abdominal viscera.

Tumors in birds may or may not respond to treatment, and Sanger suggests that, when feasible, radiation or surgical removal may be started, although recurring tumors following removal are common in the malignant ones. Some avian tumors have been transplanted experimentally from one bird to another and in parakeets they can be induced by carcinogenic agents. An extensive number of references to tumors in wild birds are in Halloran (1955); also, tumors are discussed at length in Biester and Schwarte (1959; 1965). *See also* Diseases.

TUNDRA
(TOON-drah [*oo* as in *foot*]). Russian, of Lappic origin; name for the level or undulating, frozen or half-frozen treeless plains of the northern Arctic regions of N. America and the Old World; one of nine biomes (*see* Biome) in N. America north of Mexico used in mapping the ecological distribution of birds. See Major Biotic Communities (biomes) under Distribution.

The N. American *arctic tundra* lies just north of the coniferous taiga (*see* Taiga); it extends from n. Alaska across n. Canada to the coast of Greenland, south along coasts of Hudson Bay and through most of Labrador and to Newfoundland; only the gyrfalcon, snowy owl, common raven, and willow and rock ptarmigans are permanent bird residents of this land; in summer, besides waterfowl and shorebirds, some characteristic ones include the red-throated loon, whistling swan, black brant, white-fronted and snow geese, oldsquaw, king eider, jaegers, glaucous and Sabine's gulls, horned lark, water pipit, longspurs, and snow buntings (Pettingill, 1972).

The *alpine tundra* is above timberline with open meadows and rugged rocky ground in high mountains from Alaska south to Calif. and N.M.; some of its birds are the water pipit, white-tailed ptarmigan, and rosy finch. *See* other communities (biomes) listed under Distri-

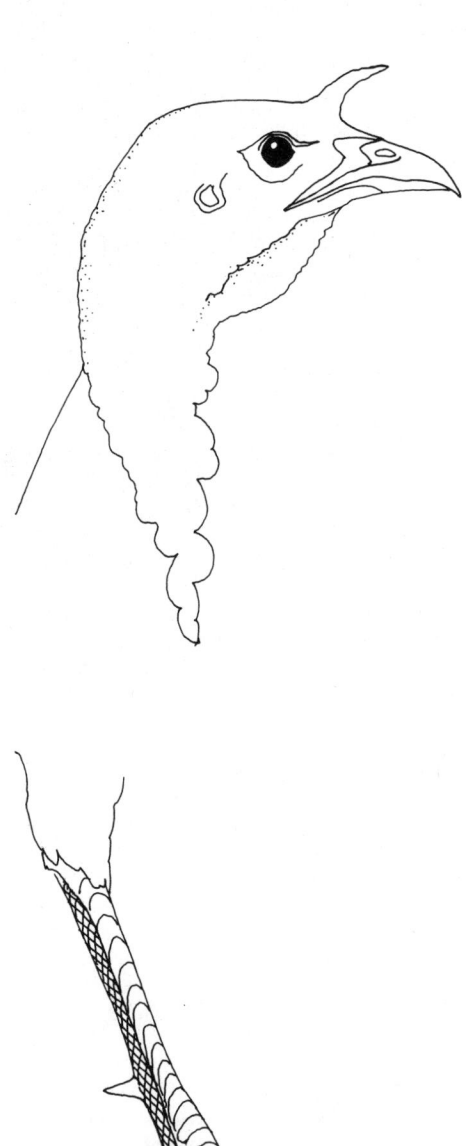

TURKEY FAMILY

bution, and analyses of them by Kendeigh (1954) and Amadon (1966b).

TUNDRA–CONIFEROUS FOREST ECOTONE

Term for an ecotone (*see* Ecotone), or transitional area, between the *arctic tundra* (*see* Tundra) and the *Coniferous Forest* biomes; this area, loosely called "timberline" in the Arctic, is a land of low tundra shrubs and stands of stunted conifers; some of the breeding birds are the gray-cheeked thrush, northern shrike, blackpoll warbler, common redpoll, tree sparrow, and Harris' sparrow; none of these birds is characteristic of either the open uninterrupted tundra on the one side or of the deep spruce forest on the other (Taverner and Sutton, 1934). *See* Tundra; Coniferous Forest. According to Pettingill (1970), the Tundra-Coniferous Forest Ecotone corresponds in its plants and birdlife to the Hudsonian Life Zone. *See* Hudsonian Zone. See Pettingill (1970; 1972) for other details of other biotic communities within those Major Biotic Communities (biomes) listed herein under Distribution; also for his discussion of ecotones and of seral (developing) communities within the biomes.

TURACO

or TOURACO. *See* Cuculiformes.

TURKEY FAMILY

Meleagrididae (mel-ee-ag-RID-i-dee); named by Linnaeus (1758) from domesticated wild turkey of Mexico carried to Europe early in 16th century, from Lat. *meleagris*, ancient Roman name for the guineafowl, a bird which early European writers often confused with the turkey—both had come to most of Europe via the Turkish Empire; both imports were called "turkey" (Aldrich, 1965). Nearest relatives of turkeys are pheasants of Asia and guinea fowls of Africa; turkeys, along with pheasants, quail, grouse, etc., belong to a large group (order) of fowl-like upland game birds (Galliformes); turkeys are native only to W. Hemisphere, only 2 species—the more numerous and more widely distributed wild turkey, *Meleagris gallopavo*, of N. America and mountains and northeastern coastal plains of Mexico, and the less common ocellated turkey, *Agriocharis ocellata*, of the subtropical lowlands of Mexico, Belize, and Guatemala.

Turkeys are large and powerful (36–48 in. long, and may stand 3–4 ft. tall when alert); have bare, red or blue heads and necks, with caruncles; necks are long; wings and tail broad and rounded; legs long; shank spurred; feet large; body feathers broad and square-ended (Aldrich, 1967); feathers dark metallic brown, barred with black; live much on ground in wooded country; travel in flocks, often prefer to run along ground under cover to escape enemies but can fly swiftly and powerfully for short distances; usually roost in flocks in trees; polygamous males noted for loud gobbling, which, during breeding season, attracts hens; males of wild turkey, *Meleagris gallopavo*, usually have tuftlike beard hanging from chest, as do some females (see Mosby and Handley, 1943).

According to Schorger (1966), in pre-Colum-

bian times, when the wild turkey, *Meleagris gallopavo*, numbered an estimated 10 million in the U.S., it was domesticated by Indians, especially in Mexico and sw. U.S. It was taken from Mexico to Europe by Spanish conquistadores early in 16th century; English settlers brought the domesticated turkey back to America. *See* brief history of turkey and guineafowl under Domestication.

All turkeys in temperate N. America, including the domestic turkey, are of one species, *Meleagris gallopavo*, of which, in the wild, there are six recognizably different geographic races, or subspecies (Aldrich, 1967), that have become markedly different in appearance in response to the influence of the different environments in which they live. These are: the eastern turkey, *Meleagris gallopavo silvestris* (meaning "forest" turkey), of e. U.S., distinguished by dark chestnut upper tail coverts and buffy tips of its tail feathers; the Florida turkey, *M. g. osceola*, of peninsular Fla. (named for Osceola the famous Seminole Indian chief), which differs in being smaller than the eastern turkey and smallest of all turkey subspecies (see Aldrich, 1967, and Schorger, 1964, for other differences in each race); the Rio Grande turkey, *M. g. intermedia* (indicating the intermediate appearance of it in relation to other races), with glossy black rump and upper tail coverts buff to cinnamon, which lives in arid brush country of Tex. and ne. Mexico; the South Mexican turkey, *M. g. gallopavo*, the nominate race of the species, so called because the first to be named, and the race that was domesticated and introduced into Europe, now limited in the wild to the southern part of Michoacán, a Mexican state along the Pacific coast (Schorger, 1964); feathers of rump and upper tail coverts tipped with buff or white, and rectrices (tail feathers) tipped with white (the white-tipped tail persists in the domestic turkey but the whitish rump has disappeared in most—Schorger, 1966); Gould's turkey, *M. g. mexicana* (meaning Mexican turkey), resident in the Sierra Madre of nw. Mexico; and Merriam's turkey, *M. g. merriami* (named for C. Hart Merriam, first chief of the U.S. Biological Survey, now the Fish and Wildlife Service), the turkey of the Rocky Mtns.

The N. American wild turkey can be distinguished from the similar bronze domestic turkey not only by its inherent wildness but by its more slender, comparatively streamlined body, lighter build, longer neck and legs, and smaller, flatter head (the eastern wild turkey also by its brown or buff-tipped tail). See Aldrich (1967) for other differences.

The turkey was once so common in America and so well thought of that it was considered a choice for our national emblem, along with the bald eagle. See Benjamin Franklin's remarks about the wild turkey and bald eagle in Evans (1966); *see* National Bird. The wild turkey was also Plate No. 1 painted by John James Audubon in *The Birds of America*.

Following settlement of N. America by Europeans, wild turkeys disappeared from large parts of their original range, especially in the northern and northeastern parts of the U.S., because of relentless hunting of them for food and elimination of much of their forest habitat;

however, although not as abundant as in former times, wild turkeys are more widely distributed in U.S. today than in early part of 20th century because of reintroductions and improvement of its habitat (see Aldrich, 1967; Bent, 1932; Edminster, 1954; Hewitt, 1967; Lewis, 1973; Mosby and Handley, 1943; and Schorger, 1966, for interesting details of history of the wild turkey, its hunting, management, and status in N. America).

In 1965, according to figures in Aldrich (1967), in 26 states that allowed hunting of turkeys, up to 95,000 were reported killed in that year; the estimated total population of wild turkeys in 35 states in which wild turkeys had been reported was about 750,000. States with 50,000 or more wild turkeys were Ala., Fla., Miss., Okla., Pa., and Tex. Henry S. Mosby, a longtime authority on wild turkeys, estimated that, in 1970 (based on a compilation of wild turkey censuses in 30 states), there were 1¼ million wild turkeys in the U.S. (Lewis, 1973).

Turkey, *Meleagris gallopavo* (mel-e-AY-gris gal-low-PAY-voe); genus name: Lat., a guineafowl, from Meleager (mel-e-AY-jer), in Gr. mythology the hero of the Calydonian boar hunt; species name: from Lat. *gallus,* a cock, and *pavo,* a peafowl, meaning chickenlike peafowl, inappropriate and reminiscent of early confusion of the turkey with *meleagris,* Roman name of the guineafowl (Aldrich, 1967). (Color ills., 910, 911.) The largest N. American upland game bird; present natural range, in open woods with clearings, from e. U.S. west to Colo., Ariz., south in Mexico; 36–48 in. long; wingspread 4–5 ft.; males larger than females, which may average 10 in. shorter; a fleshy snood, or "leader," projects from forehead above bill; naked head and upper neck red to blue, purple, and white, covered with warty excrescences; eyes brown; body plumage generally brilliant metallic bronze with gold, green, and red reflections, barred with black, dark wings barred with white; female paler and buffier; tail medium long and broad; beard hangs from midbreast, may reach 10–12 in. long in old males, usually short in females that have beard; long, strong legs, reddish to gray or even silvery in older birds; males have spur on each leg, curves upward in older birds and may be 1¼ in. long, used in fighting but rarely inflict injury (Schorger, 1966); turkeys are permanent residents within range, essentially birds of wooded country, live from forests and plains of northern states to swamps of Southeast, semiarid mountains of Southwest, Edwards Plateau and ranchlands of Tex., to low moist, hot coastal plains and mountains of Mexico; wintering flocks of Rio Grande turkeys may be up to 500 in Okla. and Tex., but in eastern turkey seldom exceed 40–50; ordinarily, sexes in separate flocks in winter; in spring, most of breeding by older dominant gobblers, whose gobbling attracts sexually ready hens to wooded clearings or other open places, where gobbler's famous strutting display (see details in Lewis, 1973) usually precedes copulation with prostrate hen; courtship and breeding begins in late Feb. or Mar. in s. U.S., in early Apr. in North; ends usually by May or mid-June;

males may gobble in any season, but in early spring any loud noise may stimulate gobbling —an airplane roaring overhead, hooting of an owl, slamming of car door, sound of radio, etc. (see account in Terres, 1969); on still day, gobble may be heard mile away; gobbling season triggered by increasing day length and warming temperature; old gobblers have deep bass gobble; young ones, high-pitched, hoarse; in spring, gobblers especially attracted to imitation of gobble (see methods of calling turkeys in Lewis, 1973, and Schorger, 1966); male has a breast sponge that functions as reservoir of energy when he is occupied with breeding; in late summer, turkeys take dust baths in oval-shaped depressions of woods roads; besides gobble of male, turkeys utter several basic calls: assembly, *cluck* or *cut;* alarm of *putt* or *pert;* contact call, or communicatory yelp, *keouk-keouk-keouk;* etc. (Lewis, 1973).

Feeding Habits: Forage mostly on ground; two main feeding periods are first few hours after leaving tree roost at dawn, and last few hours before sunset and return to tree roost; flock may feed sparingly any time of day as they travel; scratch in ground or leaf litter for seeds, nuts, acorns, which are staple food; eat fruits of junipers, dogwoods, grapes, etc., corn and other grains; seeds of pines, grasses; in winter, early spring, when other foods scarce, eat fresh green blades of grass and buds of trees; in winter, with much snow, may fast up to week; in summer, eat many grasshoppers and other insects; also eat some frogs, salamanders, toads, lizards, snakes, fiddler crabs, etc. (see details of general and regional food habits in Hewitt, 1967); a large gobbler may eat a pound of food at a meal (*see* How Much Will a Bird Eat? under Food and Feeding Habits); powerful gizzard can crush hardest foods (*see* Gizzard).

Nest: Leaf-lined scrape or natural depression in ground near woods road or opening, at edges of alfalfa and other fields, in thickets of greenbrier, under branches of fallen trees.

Eggs: Feb.–July (Bent, 1932); 8–20, usually 10–12, white to cream or buff, sometimes blotched or spotted with brown, red; laid directly on leaves or ground over period of 15–18 days; size, 2 by 2½ in.

Incubation: By female, 27–28 days; may attack intruder at nest; 24–28 hours after chicks first pip eggs, hen leads them from nest; poults cannot fly until about 2 weeks after hatching, then able to fly short distances to low perches; hen broods them during flightless period (Lewis, 1973).

Other Names: American turkey; common wild turkey; wild turkey; wood turkey.

Age: Banded Rio Grande female turkeys reported 6 and 9 years old; gobbler to almost 14 years; turkeys 9 years or older probably rare (Lewis, 1973); Mosby and Handley (1943) reported gobblers 7 and 12 years old; one, reported in W.Va., lived to 12 years, 6 months, old (Kennard, 1975); Florida turkeys to 7, 8, and 9 years (Powell, 1963).

Albinism: Apparently rare, according to Mosby and Handley (1943); a white one seen in 1811 near Ft. Osage on Missouri R.; a "pure" albino with pink eyes shot in W.Va., 1908; me-

lanistic turkeys reported from N.C. and Mexico.

Flight Speed: Timed in Tex., 32–42 m.p.h. (Glover, 1947); 55 m.p.h. (Kanoy, 1936).

Hybrids: Schorger (1966) summarized records of crossbreeding and resulting hybrids: in wild, between a turkey and a grouse in Europe; in captivity, between turkey and pheasant; turkey and chicken; turkey and capercaillie; turkey and guinea fowl; turkey and peafowl; and turkey and ocellated turkey (*Agriocharis*).

Weights: Martin and Nelson (1952) reported average weight of males as 16 lb. 5 oz., and a "giant" gobbler in Mich. of 23 lb. 13 oz.; females averaged 9 lb. 5 oz., and a very large one in Va. reported at 12 lb. 5 oz. See other weights reported in Mosby and Handley (1943); Lewis (1973).

Range: According to Aldrich (1967), both natural and introduced populations resident from s. Vt., se. Mass., south to s. Fla., west to se. Ariz., s.-c. Calif., in e.-c. Utah, parts of Ore., Wash., Wyo., Mont., east to N.D., Wisc., Mich., south through parts of Neb., Kans., to Tex. and Gulf states and south in mountains of e. and w. Mexico; also introduced, locally, in Hawaii; the domestic turkey has been introduced throughout civilized world.

Water turkey. Another name for the anhinga in Anhinga Family.

TURNSTONE
See in Sandpiper Family.

TURTLES AND BIRDS
See Reptiles and Birds.

TYPE LOCALITY
The place where a type specimen was collected. *See* Type Specimen.

TYPE SPECIES
Term for the species selected which represents the genus of a bird species. The type species of a genus is known as the type genus. Theoretically it is that species of a genus defining the character of that genus. If the genus contained only one species when proposed, that species is the type species.

TYPE SPECIMEN
The specimen, or individual bird, on which the original scientific description of a species or subspecies was based. *See* Species; Subspecies.

TYPHOID
See Salmonellosis.

TYPICAL OWL FAMILY
(Strigidae). *See* under Owl.

TYRANNIDAE
See Flycatcher—Tyrant Flycatcher Family.

TYRANNULET
Another name for the beardless flycatcher.

TYRANT FLYCATCHER FAMILY
See under Flycatcher.

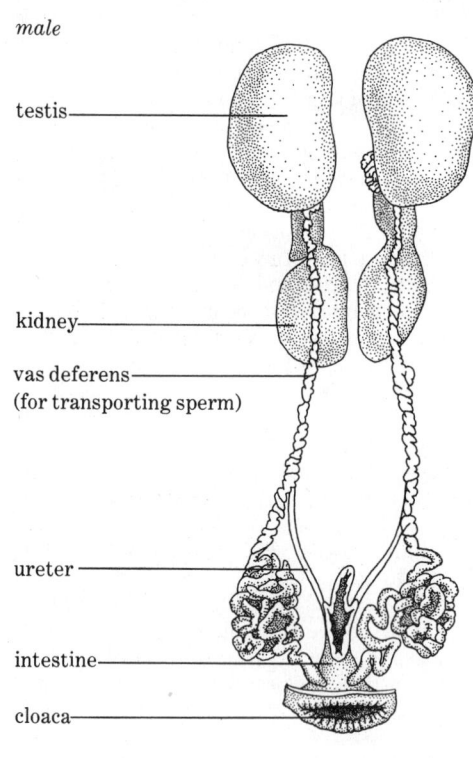

male

testis

kidney

vas deferens
(for transporting sperm)

ureter

intestine

cloaca

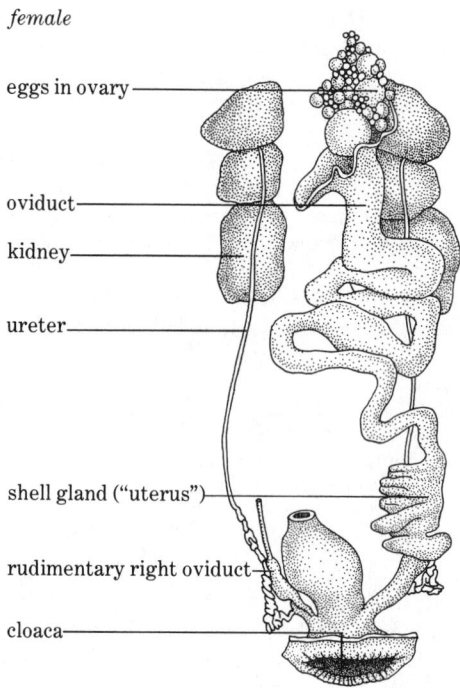

female

eggs in ovary

oviduct

kidney

ureter

shell gland ("uterus")

rudimentary right oviduct

cloaca

UROGENITAL SYSTEM

TYTONIDAE
See Owl—Barn Owl Family.

UMBRELLA BIRD
See Cotinga Family.

UNANALYZED ELEMENT
See Distribution.

UNGUIS
(UNG-gwis). A claw or nail. Specific term for the nail at the tip of the upper mandible of ducks, geese, and swans. *See* Nail; *also* Bill.

UPPER AUSTRAL ZONE
One of the six *life zones* of N. America, each of which is characterized by its plant life and by certain birds and other animals. Life zones are still relied upon by some authorities in mapping, locally, the ecological distribution of N. American birds. The eastern humid division of the Upper Austral Zone is called the *Carolinian;* the western arid division is the *Upper Sonoran.* For other details and comparisons of the Upper Austral Zone with the Major Biotic Communities listed under Distribution, see Pettingill (1970); see also in Bailey (1902). *See* discussion of life zones and biomes under Distribution.

URINARY SYSTEM
See Urogenital System.

URODEUM
(you-row-DEE-um). *See* Cloaca.

UROGENITAL SYSTEM
Includes both the *urinary system* (organs by which birds produce and excrete urine) and the reproductive system (organs by which birds produce sperm and eggs). Although each has completely separate functions, the systems are usually considered together because they are closely associated physically in the body of the bird.

The urinary system, also called *excretory system*, includes the two kidneys and the two ureters. The kidneys are elongated and, in most birds, divided into three major lobes, each of which has numerous lobules (Shoemaker, 1972). The kidneys lie imbedded in a concavity of the backbone formed by the fusion of the pelvic bones and the synsacrum (Wallace, 1963). *See* synsacrum under Skeleton. Besides extracting certain wastes and impurities from the blood, especially the elimination of the end products of protein metabolism, the kidneys maintain a healthful balance of salts in the fluids of the body. And, when necessary, they remove or conserve water and maintain its balance in the body fluids. The two ureters, one from each kidney, carry the usually cream-colored urine with its wastes to the cloaca, where it mixes with the feces (waste matter from digestion) and is voided in a semi-solid state. *See* urine passed with feces under Digestion. There is no bladder in birds, except in the ostrich.

The *reproductive system* of male and female birds includes the primary sex organs, the *gonads.* In the male these are the two *testes*, which produce the male germ cells (spermatozoa, or "sperms"). The testes are oval or elliptical and are in the body cavity at the front end of each kidney; the secondary sex organs of the male are the *vas deferentia* (singular, *vas deferens*) and in some birds a *cloacal penis.* The female gonads *(ovaries)* produce the *ova* (singular, *ovum*), the eggs or female reproductive cells. The secondary sex organs of the female are the *oviducts. See* details of the reproductive process under Fertilization and under Eggs and Egg-Laying.

UROHIDROSIS
(you-row-high-DROH-sis); from *uro*, denoting urine, and *hidrosis*, to sweat; excretion of sweat, or perspiration. Name proposed by Kahl (1963), who discovered that, besides black vultures, most species of storks, including the American wood stork, wet their legs with their urine during times of excessive heat, and that this has functional similarity to sweating in its cooling effect. According to Kahl (1971b), urohidrosis has been noted also in the great cormorant, *Phalacrocorax carbo. See* Heat and Birds; *also* Stork Family; Vulture—American Vulture Family. *See* related discussions under Temperature; Cold and Birds.

UROPYGIAL GLAND
The preen, or oil, gland just above the base of the tail feathers in most birds. It is on the bird's back near the end of the spine. The *uropygium* —New Lat., from Gr. words meaning the end of the os sacrum (*orrhos*) and the rump (*pyge*)—is the fleshy and bony prominence at the rear end of the bird's body which supports the tail feathers. *See* account under Skin Glands. *See also* Tail.

USES OF BIRDS
(by man). *See*, for example, Domestication; Eider Down; Falconry; Feather Trade. *See also* introduction to Cormorant Family. For reading about uses of birds by man, see Seminar IX in Pettingill (1972); Ch. 13 in Wallace (1963); and especially Peterson (1966). See also Herman (1966); Shaklee (1966); Collins (1966).

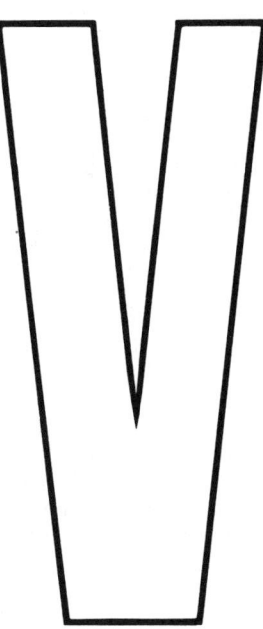

VAGINA
See function of under Eggs and Egg-Laying.

VAGRANT
Term for a bird that has wandered outside its normal migration range; also a term for those resident birds that migrate irregularly because of food shortages or for other reasons. *See* Irruption; Migration.

VALLISNIERI
(sometimes spelled VALLISNERI), ANTONIO (1661–1730). Born Trasilico, Italy; died at Padua; Italian naturalist, professor of medicine, University of Padua, in whose honor Linnaeus named the plant genus *Vallisneria*. Wild celery, tape grass, or eelgrass as it is called *(Vallisneria americana)*, is a favorite food of the canvasback (duck). In reference to its fondness for wild celery, Alexander Wilson used the genus name of this plant for the canvasback duck but misspelled it *valisineria* (Palmer, 1928). *See* Canvasback in Duck Family.

VALUE OF BIRDS
See Economic Ornithology; Uses of Birds.

VANED FEATHER
One of the contour feathers that covers a bird's body and gives it its form, including the flight feathers of the wings and tail. *See* Feather; Flight.

VANISHING SPECIES
See Rare and Threatened Species.

VARIETY
In the classification of birds (*see* Classification), a term originally applied to a subspecies of bird; used also for a domesticated breed. *See* Domestication; *also* Form; Subspecies.

VASCULAR SYSTEM
See Circulatory System.

VAS DEFERENS
(pl.: *vas deferentia*). *See* Fertilization.

VAUX
(VAWKS), WILLIAM SANSOM (1811–82). Born Philadelphia, Pa.; a friend of John K. Townsend, who in 1839 named for him a swift, new to science, that Townsend discovered in the Far West along the Columbia R. (Palmer, 1928). According to Gruson (1972), Vaux was vice-president of the Philadelphia Academy of Natural Sciences, to which he donated his collections in mineralogy and archaeology with an endowment to maintain them.

VEERY
See in Thrush Family.

VEINS
See Circulatory System.

VENT
Term for the opening of the cloaca, or anus. *See* Cloaca.

VENTRAL
Pertaining to the belly or undersurface of a bird's body. *See* Dorsal.

VENTRICULUS
Technical name for the gizzard.

VERDIN
See in Titmouse Family.

VERNACULAR NAME
The common or popular (often local) name of a bird. *See* Names and Naming. *See also* in biography of each bird.

VERREAUX
(ver-ROE), JULES PIERRE (1807–73). French explorer and collector in natural history, in whose honor Charles Lucien Bonaparte in 1855 gave the white-fronted (formerly called white-tipped) dove the species name *verreauxi*. In the 1850s, in Paris, Jules and his younger brother Edouard (1810–68) directed the most important shop in the world (established in 1838) dealing in natural history specimens. Jules, a tireless collector, traveled with his brother to many parts of the world to collect exotic specimens (Stresemann, 1975). See other details also in Gruson (1972).

VERTEBRATE
(vir-tee-BRATE). Term for any animal (of the so-called higher or more complex animals, such as mammals, including man, birds, reptiles, amphibians, and fishes) that has a backbone or vertebral column. *See* Aves.
   Invertebrates, which make up about 95% of all animal species, do not have a backbone; they usually have colorless blood, and many have an outer "skeleton," or protective armor on the outside of the body, called an exoskeleton—for example, the lobsters, crabs, crayfishes, scorpions, many insects, and centipedes. The invertebrates not only are the most numerous of all animal species but have great variation in their body structures—from the one-celled soft-bodied protozoa to hydras, jellyfishes, corals, and sea anemones, flatworms, the parasitic flukes and tapeworms, the round unsegmented worms, rotifers, oysters and clams, earthworms, snails, starfishes, and sea urchins and the enormous phylum Arthropoda, or joint-legged animals. *See* Arthropod. This is the largest division of the animal kingdom with its crabs, lobsters, spiders, ticks, millipedes, centipedes, insects, etc.; it represents about three fourths of all known animal species (Buchsbaum, 1938). Invertebrates are a basic food for many N. American birds. *See* Food and Feeding Habits; Economic Ornithology. *See* especially other details under Crustaceans and Birds; Earthworms and Birds; Insects and Birds; Mollusks and Birds; Spiders and Birds.

VERTICAL MIGRATION
See Some Effects of Weather under Migration.

VESTIBULE
A central chamber in the internal ear of a bird. *See* Ears and Hearing.

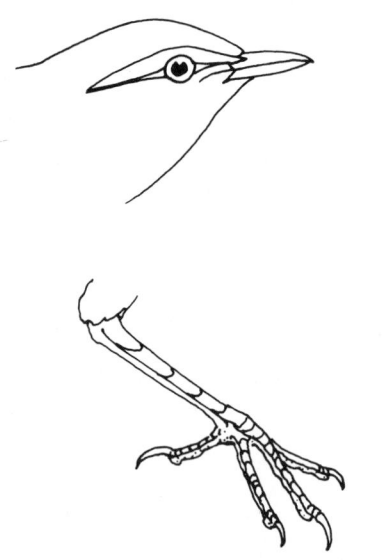

VIREO FAMILY

VIREO FAMILY

The nest of a vireo is a cup of woven plant fiber and twigs, usually built in the fork of a branch sometimes quite low on a tree and near a source of water.

VIBRATION RECEPTORS
See Touch.

VIBRISSA
See Bristle under Feather; *see also* Touch.

VIREO FAMILY
Vireonidae (vih-ree-ON-ih-dee); from Lat. *vireo* (VIH-ree-oh), a kind of bird; according to some authorities, the green finch; *virere*, to be green. Only in W. Hemisphere, Canada to Argentina and in West Indies, 38 species (Van Tyne and Berger, 1976); 12 reported in N. America; small songbirds, 4–7 in. long; believed by most authorities to be most nearly related to the American wood warblers and Hawaiian honeycreepers; by others, to the tropical American tanagers and honeycreepers (Reilly, 1968); plain olive green or gray above, white to yellow below, sexes outwardly similar or nearly so with no seasonal changes in plumage (Bond, 1964); in all, the nostrils and part of the forehead are partly covered with bristlelike feathers; bill usually short, rather straight, somewhat flattened at base, slightly hooked at tip with small notch; wings have 10 primary feathers in each, but outermost one is rudimentary, or little developed (Pettingill, 1970); as a group, the vireos seem to have originated in the New World tropics (Gilliard, 1958), where most winter; in spring some migrate north into N. America to breed; some are tree dwellers, some seldom descend below upper branches of tall trees, others live in dense shrubbery including mangroves of tropical coasts; they eat mostly insects and berries. Albinism is apparently very rare, at least in N. American vireos; Gross (1965a) listed only a single albino (species not named) among 1,847 albinistic N. American birds; Phillips (1966) added two more.

Vireos are protected by law and may not be kept in captivity without a permit; however, to sustain an ill or injured one until it is well enough to release, feed it mealworms and other insects, also ground meat, fruit, and mockingbird food.

Arizona vireo. *See* Bell's vireo.

Bell's vireo, *Vireo bellii* (VIH-ree-oh BELL-ih-eye); genus name: *see* family introduction; species name: given by John James Audubon in 1844 for John G. Bell, taxidermist who accompanied Audubon on his Missouri R. expedition of 1843. (Color ill., page 913.) W. U.S. and n. Mexico; 4¼–5 in. long; wingspread 7–8 in.; western counterpart of white-eyed vireo, with which sometimes associates, but eyes of Bell's vireo dark; one of most nondescript of all vireos, small, greenish-backed, white below with yellowish flanks, pale bill, distinguished from warbling vireo by narrow, barely discernible eye-ring and two faint white bars on each wing; the somewhat flattened vireo bill with hook at tip distinguishes it from a kinglet; summers in Southwest and in prairie country, Tex. north to Wisc.; lives along rivers in moist thickets of wild plum, hazel, alders, haws, willows, cottonwoods, and, in Tex., in mesquite, woods margins, tangled brush, hedges, etc. (Bent, 1950); from winter home in Baja Calif. and interior Mexico, arrives nesting range in U.S. from

late Mar. through Apr.; timid, but when nesting quite tame, seldom more than 6 ft. above ground, active, restless, flits about in bushes and difficult to see; male sings from bush not far from nest; he sometimes sings while on nest; low husky phrases, like *cheedle cheedle chee?*, then seems to answer questioning phrase with *cheedle cheedle chew!*, also utters harsh scolding note as bird moves about foraging for food in bush or tree (Peterson, 1947).

Feeding Habits: About 99% insects; no other vireo known to eat so many large, bulky insects such as grasshoppers; also eats beetles of many kinds, some bees, wasps, ants, also spiders and a few snails, and wild fruit.
Nest: Built in fork of slender branch of tree, shrub; hung 1–10 ft. up, but commonly 2–3 ft. above ground, often near water; outside made of soft, gray strips of plants, leaf fragments, small pieces of bark, lined with fine grasses, plant down, horsehair; about 2½–3 in. in diameter.
Eggs: Apr.–July; 3–5, commonly 4, white, with few fine dots of brown or black, sometimes immaculate.
Incubation: By both parents, 14 days; young leave nest 10½–12 days after hatching.
Other Names: Arizona vireo; Bell's greenlet; least vireo; Texas vireo.
Host to Cowbirds: Frequently, about 82 records, but these considered only fraction of real parasitization by brown-headed cowbird.
Weights: In fall, coastal N.J. (1), 10.2 gr. (Murray and Jehl, 1964), or about ⅓ oz.
Range: Nests from Central Valley of Calif., s. Nev., c. Ariz., w. Tex., e. Colo., c. Neb., se. S.D., Iowa, sw. Wisc., and ne. Ill., south to n. Baja Calif., c. Mexico, s. Tex., and nw. La.; winters from s. Baja Calif., n. Mexico, s. Tex., and s. La. (one record) south to Nicaragua; strays east to N.H., Long Is., N.Y., and N.J. (Bull, 1964); casual in migration to Ala. (Imhof, 1962). See also Barlow's study (1962).

Bermuda vireo. *See* White-eyed vireo.

Black-capped vireo, *Vireo atricapilla* (VIH-ree-oh ay-trih-cap-ILL-ah); genus name: *see* family introduction; species name: Lat. black hair(ed); *capillus*, hair of head (Coues, 1882). Summers in s.-c. U.S.; 4¼–4¾ in. long; male only N. American vireo with jet-black head combined with white "spectacles" formed by eye-ring and white patch between eyes and bill; back, shoulders, and rump light green-gray; underparts white with yellowish flanks; each wing has two yellowish bars; eyes red; female similar but slaty gray where male is black; lives in low, brushy dry country, in deep ravines with strong salt stream running at bottom, in scrub oak ridges, in cedars, chaparral brush on steep rocky slopes of mountains; unlike other vireos, is very active, usually difficult to see, stays under cover, may be discovered by singing of male, persistent, musical warble, often hurried, phrased as loud, emphatic *there now, wait-a-bit* or *come here, right-now-quick*, resembles song of white-eyed vireo; sings from arrival on nesting grounds in U.S. in Mar. until mid-Aug.; male has habit of Bell's vireo of singing while on nest; female also sings, softer, less noticeable.

Feeding Habits: Need comprehensive study; however, eats small beetles, some spiders, small fleshy fruits; feeds low among dwarf oaks and other thickets, searching for insects and their eggs (Bent, 1950).
Nest: Suspended from fork of slender twigs of oak, dogwood, wild plum, etc., 2–15 ft. above ground, usually 3–8 ft.; small cup with walls thickly felted with fine strips, cedar bark, leaves, coarse grasses, catkins, spiders' cocoons.
Eggs: Apr.–July; 3–5, usually 4, white.
Incubation: By both sexes, 14–17 days; young leave nest about 10–12 days after hatching. See details in Graber (1961).
Other Name: Black-capped greenlet.
Host to Cowbirds: Infrequent or fairly uncommon host to brown-headed cowbird, 11 known records (Friedmann, 1963); however, according to Friedmann (1966), considerably more records as result of study by Graber (1961); since then clearing of brush in Tex. has resulted in increase of cowbird population there and subsequent parasitism.
Range: Nests from s.-c. Kans. south through c. Okla., to w. and c. Tex. and n. Mexico; winters in c. Mexico; has wandered to Neb.

Black-whiskered vireo, *Vireo altiloquus* (VIH-ree-oh al-tih-LOW-qus); genus name: *see* family introduction; species name: from Lat. words meaning high, and I speak (Coues, 1882). (Color ill., page 912.) West Indies and, in summer, s. Fla.; about 6½ in. long; olive green above, white below washed on sides with yellow-green, white stripe over red eyes; is almost exact counterpart of red-eyed vireo but has black streak (malar stripe), or "whisker," along sides of throat; more easily recognized by variable songs of 2–4, usually 3, notes, resembling such phrases as *whip-tom-KELLY!* and *sweet-John! John-to-whit!* or *cheap-John-stir-up!;* songs similar to those of red-eyed vireo; in Fla., lives mostly in mangroves along coasts and along Fla. Keys; according to Sprunt (1954a), is not shy and moves deliberately about in trees much like red-eyed vireo; difficult to see owing to wet dense mangrove habitat but sometimes moves to upland, also can be seen from Overseas Highway; arrives Key West, Dry Tortugas, and mainland Fla. in Apr.

Feeding Habits: Eats caterpillars, earwigs, beetles, wasps, assassin bugs, flies, mosquitoes, also spiders, barberries, seeds of ragweed, etc. (Bent, 1950).
Nest: Cup of woven plant fibers suspended from fork of slender twigs of tree or shrub, about 5–15 feet above ground or water.
Eggs: Fla., May–June; 2–3, white, with minute dots of brown.
Incubation: Period of and age when young leave nest unreported.
Range: Nests s. Fla. through Antilles; winters mainly in S. America. See also Duncan (1976).

Blue-headed vireo. *See* Solitary vireo.

Brotherly-love vireo. *See* Philadelphia vireo.

Cassin's vireo. *See* Solitary vireo.

Gray vireo, *Vireo vicinior* (VIH-ree-oh vih-SIN-ih-or); genus name: *see* family introduction; species name: from Lat. *vicinus,* neighboring, related; in allusion to close resemblance of the species to others (Coues, 1882). Southwest; Great Basin area; 5–5¾ in. long, wingspread 8¾ in.; gray-backed, white below; has narrow white eye-ring and lores and only one faint wing bar, not two as in Bell's vireo; also only vireo to have habit of flicking its tail like a gnatcatcher; choice of dry brush of arid mountains and mesas is distinctive (Bell's prefers shrubbery along streams); also, song one of best of all vireos (Bent, 1950), given rather steadily by male in syllables with different inflections, *chu-wee, chu-wee, che-weet, chee, che-churr-weet;* when alarmed, scolds like wren, or gives low harsh *churr* or *schray;* from wintering places in Baja Calif., and Sonora and Durango, Mexico, arrives in Calif. late Mar., in Ariz. and Tex. usually in Apr. (Bent, 1950).

Feeding Habits: Hops about, jerkily, wrenlike, in bushes, flicking drooping tail; usually hidden in favored chaparral, also in pinyons, junipers, and sagebrush or in mesquite, "a dry-slope forager" in niche not occupied by other vireos (Bent, 1950); ranges 1–12 ft. above ground, rarely higher; no detailed studies of food but takes insects such as beetles, caterpillars, small moths, bugs, treehoppers, tree crickets, dobsonflies, cicadas, and grasshoppers.
Nest: Similar to nests of other vireos and hung from twigs or fork of tree or bush; woven cup of plant fibers and bits of leaves, spider's silk and cocoons, usually 2–8 ft. above ground.
Eggs: Apr.–July; 3–5, commonly 4, white (pink when fresh), spotted with black, browns.
Incubation: Period of and age when young leave nest unreported.
Albinism: Phillips (1966) reported one partial albino, an adult male, from Ariz.
Host to Cowbirds: Frequent, to brown-headed cowbird; several records especially in Calif. (Friedmann, 1963).
Range: Nests from s.-c. Calif., s. Nev., sw. Utah, nw. Ariz., and sw. N.M., south to n. Baja Calif. and c. Ariz., locally to N.M., Okla., and w. Tex.; winters in s. Sonora and s. Baja Calif.

Hutton's vireo, *Vireo huttoni* (VIH-ree-oh HUT-ton-eye); genus name: *see* family introduction; species name: given in 1851 by John Cassin, Philadelphia ornithologist, for William Hutton, a field collector of birds, about whom little is known (Palmer, 1928); Hutton was at Monterey, Calif., from May 1847 to Nov. 1848, where he obtained the vireo which bears his name. Lives from B.C. south through Calif. west of Sierras, and in sw. U.S.; 4½–4¾ in. long; dull olive to gray-olive above; dull buffy olive below; has two broad white bars in each wing, a whitish eye-ring broken by dark spot over eyes, and a large white spot between eyes and bill; sits more upright than similar-appearing *Empidonax* flycatchers; resembles female ruby-crowned kinglet, but larger, has stouter *pale* bill and feet; movements slower; seldom

Black-capped-vireo

Gray vireo

Hutton's vireo

VIREO FAMILY

VIREO FAMILY
A red-eyed vireo crouches with tail fanned in an aggressive display before a rival male.

flicks wings; very tame; has simple song, a distinctive, hoarse, rising *tchee-ree* or *ser-ree* or *chu-wee* or *chu-ween*, repeated in paired notes, the second note either lower or higher than the first, sometimes repeated in a continuous series for 781 times in 11 minutes (Bent, 1950); call is low *whit, whit* or *kip, kip, kip;* through most of its range prefers to be in live and golden (evergreen) oaks; also in mountain canyons in sycamores, maples, and in tall chaparral; in willows along streams; in humid forests of Pacific states in understory of broad-leaved trees and shrubs of Douglas fir and redwood forests.

Feeding Habits: In relatively few stomachs examined, spring to fall, mostly insects, a few spiders, some seeds of berries, also plant galls.
Nest: Almost fearless in attachment to nest, suspended by rim from horizontal or slanting branch at forked twigs of live oak, bay, willow, pine, Douglas fir, or bush; round deep cup of lichens 7–35 ft. up, well out at end of branch.
Eggs: Feb.–June; 3–5, usually 4, white, sparingly dotted with browns.
Incubation: By female, about 14 days; young leave nest about 14 days after hatching (Van Fleet, 1919).
Other Name: Stephens' vireo.
Host to Cowbirds: Seldom reported—8 records: 6 in Calif., 1 in Tex., 1 in N.M. (Friedmann, 1963).
Range: Resident, sw. B.C., w. Wash., and w. Ore. south to nw. Baja Calif., and from c. Ariz., extreme sw. N.M., and w. Tex., south to highlands of s.-c. Guatemala; partly migratory in Ariz.

Key West vireo. *See* White-eyed vireo.

Least vireo. *See* Bell's vireo.

Mountain vireo. *See* Solitary vireo.

Philadelphia vireo, *Vireo philadelphicus* (VIH-ree-oh phil-ah-DEL-fih-cus); genus name: *see* family introduction; species name: Lat., of the city of Philadelphia; named and described by John Cassin in 1851 from one collected (shot) Sept. 1842 in woods near Philadelphia, Pa. (Color ill., page 912.) Summers in n. U.S. and s. Canada; known through most of eastern half of U.S. as migrant; 4½–5 in. long; wingspread 8–9 in.; resembles both the warbling vireo and the red-eyed vireo, but has yellowish wash across breast; according to Peterson (1947), the only N. American vireo that has combination of *no bars on wings,* and *yellowish underparts;* gray-green or olive green above, with somewhat indistinct stripe over eyes; stout bill and chubby build distinguish it from needle-billed, slender warblers (Tennessee, for example); is tame and slow in movements in migration, when prefers low or medium levels of trees, shrubs (Bent, 1950); from winter home in C. America, n. S. America, moves north through U.S., from Mississippi Valley east, usually in May, along with waves of late-migrating warblers; generally not common or abundant anywhere, easily overlooked, as it sings very little while migrating; on nesting grounds, male

sings songs that closely resemble those of red-eyed vireo, but generally pitched higher, phrases weaker, and slower; summers in edges of woods, in young growth of old clearings, burned-over tracts, and in willows and alders along streams, lakes, ponds; feeds both in shrubbery and in treetops of moist places (Pough, 1949).

Feeding Habits: Moves about very actively, often hangs upside down, chickadeelike, from cluster of leaves when picking off insects with bill, but many taken while it flutters before a bunch of leaves; most of food is insects: caterpillars, moths and butterflies, beetles, wasps, bees, ants, ichneumon flies, flies, bugs; also spiders and some fruit—bayberries, rose hips, wild grapes.
Nest: Deep, neat woven cup hung in horizontal fork of slender branch of aspen, willow, alder, maple, 10–40 ft. above ground; built of birch bark, lichens, grasses, plant down, bound to twig or branch by insect webbing, spider's silk.
Eggs: June–July; 3–5, usually 4, white, with dark brown spots, specks.
Incubation: By both sexes, about 14 days; age when young leave nest unknown (Bent, 1950).
Other Names: Brotherly-love vireo; Philadelphia greenlet.
Host to Cowbirds: Rarely reported; only 2 records: 1 in Alta., 1 in Ont., to brown-headed cowbird.
Weights: In fall, coastal N.J. (53), 8.9–15.2 gr. (Murray and Jehl, 1964), or ⅓–½ oz.; in fall, in Kans., killed at TV tower, adult males (2), 12.1 and 15.9 gr.; adult females (2), 12 and 15.2 gr., all moderately to very fat (Tordoff and Mengel, 1956).
Range: Nests from ne. B.C. and c. Alta. east across s. Canada to c. Que., sw. Newfoundland, south to c. N.D., s. Ont., s. Que., n. N.H., c. Me., and N.B., rarely in mountains of ne. N.Y.; winters from c. Guatemala to Panama, nw. Colombia; casual in Mont.

Plumbeous vireo. *See* Solitary vireo.

Red-eyed vireo, *Vireo olivaceus* (VIH-ree-oh ol-ih-VAY-see-us); genus name: *see* family introduction; species name: Lat., olive-colored; green obscured with neutral tint (Coues, 1882). (Color ill., page 913.) Summers across Canada and almost entire U.S. except Southwest; once considered one of three most abundant birds of the deciduous forests of e. N. America but recently showing some decline (*see* discussion under Census); 5½–6½ in. long; wingspread 9¾–10¾ in.; olive to greenish upperparts, white underparts, and without wing bars, has gray cap; white stripe over ruby-red eyes, black stripe through eyes (similar, but grayer, warbling vireo, also without wing bars, does not have head distinctly striped); from winter home in S. America moves north through e. U.S. from Mar. into May; summers wherever woodlands with undergrowth of slender saplings, or in wooded clearings, borders of burns, open woods of all kinds, along brook or bog openings in virgin forest, in prairie groves, in residential areas wherever orchards, parks, gardens, street trees; male in courtship of female or when feeding young may sway back and forth in front of bird he is facing (Tyler, 1950b); is famed singer; no other N. American bird sings so persistently through hottest days of summer; sings while feeding; some characteristic phrases of a song are *cherry-o-wit, cheree, sissy-a-wit, tee-oo;* according to Wright (1936), sings short, preacherlike phrases, *you-see-it— you-know-it—do you hear me? do you believe it?;* possibly record for singing most frequently by a N. American bird established by a red-eyed vireo that sang 22,197 songs during 10-hour summer day (de Kiriline, 1954); also sings sometimes at night; alarm note, nasal *tschay!*

Feeding Habits: Forages in trees, eats mostly insects: largely caterpillars and moths, is also effective enemy of gypsy and brown-tail moths, fall webworms, and takes beetles, wasps, bees, ants, bugs, flies, walking sticks, cicadas, spittle insects, treehoppers, scale insects, etc. (McAtee, 1926); likes blackberries, elderberries, fruits of spicebush, dogwood, Virginia creeper, sassafras, and magnolia trees in South (Tyler, 1950b).

Nest: Dainty, thin-walled cup, built in fork of horizontal twig near end of branch of shrub, or low branch of tree, 2–60 ft. above ground (usually 5–10 ft. up); of fine grasses, rootlets, bits of birch bark, strips of grapevine bark, paper from wasps' nests, bound together with webbing of tent caterpillar, spider's silk, decorated outside with bits of lichens.

Eggs: May–Aug.; 3–5, usually 4, white, sparingly dotted with blacks and browns.

Incubation: By female (Lawrence, 1953), 11–14 days; young leave nest 10–12 days after hatching.

Other Names: Little hang-nest; the preacher; preacher bird; red-eye; red-eyed greenlet.

Age: One, banded Powdermill Nature Reserve, Rector, Pa., trapped and released in same area when 10 years old (Kennard, 1975).

Host to Cowbirds: One of commonest hosts to brown-headed cowbird; no species is victimized more either in total number of records or in percentage of its nests parasitized; more than 875 records (Friedmann, 1963).

Weights: In fall, coastal N.J. (667), 12.3–25.7 gr. (Murray and Jehl, 1964), or about ½–1 oz.

Range: Nests from sw. and ne. B.C., sw. Mack., ne. Alta., c. Sask., c. Man., n. Ont., c. Que., Prince Edward Is., and Nova Scotia, south, east of Coast Ranges, to n. Ore., n. Idaho, sw. and c. Mont., through Wyo., e. Colo., Kans., and w. Okla., to c. Tex., Gulf coast, and c. Fla.; winters in Amazon Basin of S. America; migrates through West Indies and C. America; has strayed to Calif., Ariz., Utah.

Rio Grande vireo. *See* White-eyed vireo.

Solitary vireo, *Vireo solitarius* (VIH-ree-oh sol-ih-TAY-rih-us); genus name: *see* family introduction; species name: Lat., alone, solitary. (Color ill., page 914.) Summers across Canada, Great Lakes states, and New England, south in mountains to Ga.; Rocky Mtn. states to Pacific coast; 5–6 in. long; wingspread 8¼–9¾ in.; dark olive green above, with *blue-gray head* conspicuous; white eye-ring; white below, has two white bars in each wing; usually yellowish

feathers along flanks; in e. U.S., first vireo to appear in spring (Forbush, 1925–29); from winter home in Nicaragua, Mexico, and s. U.S., moves northward in prolonged migration, Mar.–May, to reach nesting grounds, usually arrives northern states in Apr. in vanguard of host of small warblers and other migrants, usually at least a week ahead of other vireos (Bent, 1950); lives in coniferous or mixed coniferous-deciduous woods about openings where undergrowth in which to build nest; ranges up to 6,000 ft. in Appalachians, and to 9,000 ft. in wooded canyons in Chiricahuas of Ariz.; male courting female fluffs out yellow flank feathers conspicuously, then bobs and bows to her; follows female singing low songs; male's song is higher-pitched than red-eyed vireo's, sweeter, clearer, phrases of 2–6 notes delivered more slowly with pauses, may burst into rich warble of 15–20 notes; remarkably tame and fearless, incubating bird may allow itself to be stroked or lifted up while on nest, and may even accept food from one's fingers (Bent, 1950); but rather a solitary recluse of woods, often hidden in treetops; call notes are harsh, nasal *see-a* and *see-weep.*

Feeding Habits: Forages deliberately in treetops while feeding, getting most of insect food from twigs and foliage, sometimes flies up into air to catch passing insect; eats large amounts of caterpillars and moths; bugs, especially stink bugs (Pentatomidae), beetles, bees, wasps, ants, stone flies, dragonflies, grasshoppers, crickets, etc., some spiders, and some fruit: wild grapes, dogwood and viburnum berries, etc. (Chapin, 1925).

Nest: A deep cup built in fork of twigs of horizontal branch, generally about halfway up, or at middle of, a small conifer, sometimes in a small bush or a deciduous tree, 4–30 ft. above ground, usually 4–12 ft. up.

Eggs: Apr.–July; 3–5, usually 4, white to creamwhite, sparingly dotted with browns, black.

Incubation: By both sexes, 11–12 (?) days; age when young leave nest unreported.

Other Names: Blue-headed vireo; blue-headed greenlet; Cassin's vireo; mountain vireo; plumbeous vireo.

Albinism: A partially albinistic female reported from s. Ariz. (Phillips, 1966).

Host to Cowbirds: Fairly frequent host to brown-headed cowbird, but less commonly than white-eyed and yellow-throated vireos, much less common victim than either Bell's or red-eyed vireo; one record of host to bronzed cowbird in Ariz. (Friedmann, 1963).

Weights: In fall, coastal N.J. (17), 12.3–16.1 gr. (Murray and Jehl, 1964), or ½–⅔ oz.; in Kans., killed in fall at TV tower, adult males (9), 16.6–19.5 gr.; adult females (7), 15–21.6 gr., moderately to very fat (Tordoff and Mengel, 1956), or up to ¾ oz.

Range: Nests from c. B.C., sw. Mack., c. Sask., c. Man., n. Ont., s. Que., Newfoundland, Nova Scotia, south to s. Baja Calif., Guatemala, and El Salvador; winters from Ariz., s. Tex., and s. S.C., south to s. Baja Calif., Nicaragua, and Cuba.

Stephens' vireo. *See* Hutton's vireo.

Texas vireo. *See* Bell's vireo.

Warbling vireo, *Vireo gilvus* (VIH-ree-oh JIL-vus); genus name: *see* family introduction; species name: Lat., pale yellow. (Color ills., page 915.) Summers over most of U.S. and across c. and s. Canada; 5–6 in. long; wingspread 8½–9¼ in.; grayest and palest of the N. American vireos; no wing bars, no distinctive head markings such as eye-ring, but head does have indistinct stripe over eyes; has whitish breast sometimes with yellowish wash; from shape of bill and slow movements distinguished as a vireo; from winter home in Mexico and C. America, spreads out through Apr. and May over vast nesting range in U.S.; summers in isolated trees of open country; open woods; and in elms, alders, sycamores, silver maples along streams, lakes; in orchards and shade trees of towns, villages, roadsides, and hedges; in broad-leaved trees of mountain canyons of West; tree-filled gulches of foothill mesas; groves of aspens and cottonwoods; and in prairie groves; a treetop bird, male sings hour after hour, filling days with charming simple melody, matching summer calm of country from spring through hottest days of July and Aug. and into Sept.; unlike abrupt, broken, short phrases of other vireos, song is long, flowing warble, rhythm like slowly pronounced phrase, *brigadier, brig-adier, brigate;* male often sings while on nest; call is harsh, tense snarl, *quee,* with rising inflection, and a ticking, katydidlike note.

Feeding Habits: Eats caterpillars, eggs of moths and butterflies, aphids, beetles, grasshoppers, ants, bugs, scale insects, flies, dragonflies, etc., also some spiders and some berries.

Nest: Typical vireo cup, suspended from fork of slender twigs at end of branch, usually much higher in trees than nests of other vireos; 30–60 ft. up in elm, linden, pecan, sycamore, oak, maple, also much lower, in alders, coffeeberry bushes (in Calif.), spirea, chokecherry, apple tree, 4–15 feet up (Bent, 1950).

Eggs: Apr.–July; 3–5, usually 4, white, with few scattered dots of browns, black.

Incubation: By both sexes, about 12–14 days; young leave nest about 12–14 days after hatching (Bent, 1950).

Other Names: Eastern warbling vireo; warbling greenlet; western warbling vireo.

Age: One, banded Point Reyes Observatory, Calif., as adult, June 1966, recaptured there, May 8, 1976, when at least 9 years, 11 months, old (Peasley and Sorrie, 1976); up to time, greatest age reported for any vireo.

Host to Cowbirds: Frequent host to brownheaded cowbird; 64 records (Friedmann, 1963).

Weights: In fall, coastal N.J. (4), 13.4–16.3 gr. (Murray and Jehl, 1964), or ½–⅔ oz.; in Kans., killed in fall at TV tower, adult males (12), average 15 gr., fat; immature males (8), average 16.64 gr.; adult females (5), 13.7–18 gr., fat to very fat (Tordoff and Mengel, 1956).

Range: Nests from B.C., s. Mack., c. Sask., s. Man., w. Ont., n. Minn., n. Mich., s. Ont., s. Que., s. Me., se. N.B., and c. Nova Scotia, south to Baja Calif., n. Mexico, c. Tex., s. La., n. Ala.,

w. N.C., and se. Va.; winters from c. Mexico to Guatemala and El Salvador.

White-eyed vireo, *Vireo griseus* (VIH-ree-oh GRIS-ee-us); genus name: *see* family introduction; species name: Lat., gray, grizzly. (Color ill., page 915.) Summers over most of e. U.S. west to prairies and north to e. Canada; 4½–5½ in. long; wingspread 7½–8½ in.; small, olive-green bird of thickets; white below; has yellow "spectacles" and white throat; *white eyes;* two white bars in each wing; yellow flanks; from wintering range in s. U.S., Mexico, West Indies, C. America, moves northward through nesting range in U.S. from Mar. to early May; summers in blackberry, greenbrier thickets on low swampy or moist ground, also old fields where growth of maple and elm saplings or shrub growth of wild plum, witch hazel, dogwoods, willows, also brushlands high in Appalachians; male courts female by fluffing feathers, spreading tail, utters snarling *yip, yip, yaah;* each male has several individual songs, he sings one over and over, then changes to another (Bent, 1950); has unvireo-like song, phonetic sounds are common in song and stand out, one is sharp *chick! ticha wheeyo chick!,* another, *chick-ah-per-weeoo-chick,* in South *quick, take me to the railroad, quick!,* in Bermuda *gingerbeer-quick!,* in Ill. *chick'ty-beaver-lim'ber, stick;* call is mewing note and short *tick;* is fairly good mimic; imitates parts of songs or notes of gray catbird, American robin, song sparrow, house wren, and many others (Bent, 1950).

Feeding Habits: Seldom seen far from ground, hunts through thickets for insects, spiders, snails, small lizards (anole), small fruits; in spring and fall eats berries of dogwood, wax myrtle, wild grapes, etc.
Nest: Deep cup or like inverted cone in shape, suspended from fork of twigs at end of horizontal branch of sapling or shrub near opening in woods, about 1–8 ft. above ground; woven of inner bark, grasses, soft plant fibers and down, rootlets, bound together with spider's silk, lined with fine grasses, decorated on outside with mosses, lichens, bits of paper and of wasps' nests.
Eggs: Mar.–July; 3–5, usually 4, white, dotted with dark brown, black.
Incubation: By both sexes, 12–15 days; age when young leave nest unreported (Bent, 1950); apparently one brood raised in North, two in South.
Other Names: Basket-bird; Bermuda vireo; hanging bird; Key West vireo; politician; Rio Grande vireo; white-eyed greenlet.
Age: One, banded Homestead, Fla., trapped and released in same area when 5 years, 11 months, old (Kennard, 1975).
Host to Cowbirds: Fairly frequent host to brown-headed cowbird; 57 records (Friedmann, 1963).
Weights: In N.C. (16), average 11.9 gr. (Teulings and Teulings, 1971), or less than ½ oz.; in fall, coastal N.J. (12), 10.7–12.4 gr. (Murray and Jehl, 1964); near Washington, D.C., males (4), 12–14.8 gr. (Wetmore, 1936), or about ½ oz.
Range: Nests from e. Neb., s. Ind., Iowa, s. Wisc., and N.Y., and first Canadian nesting re-

cord at Rondeau, Ont., summer 1971 (Gauthreaux, 1971a), south to ne. Mexico, Gulf coast, s. Fla., and Bermuda; winters from s. Tex., Gulf coast, s. La., and S.C. south to Guatemala, Honduras, Cuba.

Yellow-green vireo, *Vireo flavoviridis* (VIH-ree-oh flay-voh-VIH-rih-dis); genus name: *see* family introduction; species name: from Lat. *flavus,* yellow, and *viridis,* green. Resident of C. America, counterpart of N. American red-eyed vireo; rare summer resident in extreme s. Tex. (Peterson, 1963); 6¼–6¾ in. long; similar to red-eyed vireo; has red eyes and similar but less distinct head stripes; distinguished from red-eyed, however, by bright yellow sides and yellow undertail coverts (red-eyed has white undertail coverts); common resident and widespread on Pacific slope and central highlands of both Costa Rica and Guatemala, in open forests, orchards, hedges, roadside trees, coffee plantations (Skutch, 1950b); in Tex. in summer, in wooded resacas (dried-up watercourses) and in shade trees, edges of forest, brushy pastures; song is like red-eyed vireo's but more abrupt.

Feeding Habits: Insects and spiders, also eats mistletoe berries and some seeds.
Nest: Suspended cup, like that of other vireos, fastened with spider's silk to horizontal fork of outer slender branch of tree or shrub, 5½–40 ft. above ground (usually not over 10 ft.) or water.
Eggs: Mar.–June; 2–4, usually 3, white, finely speckled with browns.
Incubation: 13–14 days (Skutch, 1976); young leave nest when barely able to fly, 12–14 days after hatching.
Host to Cowbirds: Only one record (Friedmann, 1963), near Mazatlán, Sinaloa, Mexico, to brown-headed cowbird; one in Guatemala to bronzed cowbird (Skutch, 1950b).
Range: Nests from Tex. and n. Mexico south to e. Guatemala and w. Costa Rica; winters in S. America; single records in Que. and Calif.

Yellow-throated vireo, *Vireo flavifrons* (VIH-ree-oh FLAY-vih-frons); genus name: *see* family introduction; species name: from Lat. *flavus,* yellow, and *frons,* forehead. (Color ill., page 914.) Summers over e. U.S. and e. Canada, west to prairies; 5–6 in. long; wingspread 9½–10 in.; olive green above; yellow eye-ring, like spectacles, bright yellow underparts; white belly; two white bars in each wing, and gray rump are distinguishing marks; from winter home in Mexico, C. America, and n. S. America, travels in Mar. and Apr. to nesting grounds in U.S.; generally uncommon over its range, has disappeared from parts of its nesting range in New England (Aldrich and Robbins, 1970); summers in tops of tall trees of groves and open woods of oaks, maples, etc., along streams, lakes, and roadsides, and in shade trees of towns, villages; also in orchards; avoids dense undergrowth and coniferous forest; male sings long, continued, halting songs of short, husky, low-pitched, 2–3 note phrases of rising and falling inflection (like questions and answers), separated by longer pauses than in red-eyed and solitary vireos, *de-ar-ie, come here*

Yellow-green vireo

VIREO FAMILY

with concluding phrase *three-eight*, louder, more reedlike, but individuals sometimes sing song pattern of solitary vireo (Bent, 1950).

Feeding Habits: Forages in leafy tops of trees, eats mostly insects: eggs and caterpillars of moths and butterflies, also adult moths, stink bugs, assassin bugs, scale insects, aphids, leafhoppers, beetles, sawflies, grasshoppers, crickets, dragonflies, cicadas, mosquitoes, midges; also sassafras berries, wild grapes.
Nest: Very handsome, thick-walled, deep cup, 3 in. in diameter, suspended from fork of twigs of horizontal branch of beech, elm, oak, hickory, tulip tree, honey locust, or other hardwood, sometimes in orchard tree, rarely in conifer, 3–60 ft. above ground; outside of cup covered with green and gray lichens and mosses, held in place by masses of spider's silk, inside of cup lined with fine grasses or pine needles.
Eggs: Apr.–July; 3–5, usually 4, white to cream or pink-white, strongly spotted especially at large end with browns, lavender.
Incubation: By both sexes, about 15 days; young leave nest about 15 days after hatching.
Other Name: Yellow-throated greenlet.
Age: One, banded Willow Springs, Ill., trapped and released in same area when 5 years, 11 months, old (Kennard, 1975).
Host to Cowbirds: Frequent, about 100 records (Friedman, 1963).
Weights: In N.C. (5), average 17.9 gr. (Teulings and Teulings, 1971), or about ⅔ oz.; in spring, Washington, D.C., male (1), 16.6 gr. (Wetmore, 1936).
Range: Nests from s. Man., n.-c. Minn., c. Wisc., c. Mich., s. Ont., s. Que., n. N.H., locally in sw. Me., south through e. N.D. to c. and e. Tex., Gulf coast, and c. Fla.; winters from Mexico south to Panama; casually to nw. S. America; rarely in s. Tex. (Harlingen and Rockport) and West Indies.

VIREONIDAE
See Vireo Family.

VIRUS
(Lat., a slimy liquid, or poison). Name for an infectious agent, the poison or contagium of a disease, or a pathogenic microorganism present in the juices of, for example, a bird or another animal that has an infectious disease and from, or by, which the disease is passed on to another animal. The term is now used as the equivalent of a filterable virus, which, after it has passed through a porcelain filter (a filter so fine that all bacteria are removed), still has the ability to infect susceptible animals. A virus is not in itself a living thing in the same sense that bacteria are (*see* Bacterium); but it can cause infectious diseases. *See* Diseases.

Viruses are made up, essentially, of a protein outer coat enclosing a core of nucleic acid; it is the same sort of chemical molecule as that which makes up the hereditary genes; the virus, however, cannot make its own enzymes and proteins. It cannot independently transform raw materials with nutrients to carry out complex chemical processes of life as can the cells of bacteria, plants, and animals (Long, 1966). Viruses are absolute parasites, and can multiply only by raiding a living cell, commandeering its chemical machinery, and forcing it to serve the virus's needs; in this way the virus can multiply.

Viruses cannot be seen with an ordinary microscope, but an electron microscope will reveal their different shapes—some appear like fluffy balls of cotton; others, not all of which cause human diseases, are hexagonal; some are rod-shaped; others are many-sided. It is possible that humans (and possibly other animals) live with viruses that do them no detectable harm (Long, 1966). *See* Virus Diseases under Diseases, and a detailed discussion of viruses by Lauffer (1961).

VISION
(keenness of). For examples, *see* introduction to Shrike Family. *See also* Eyes and Eyesight.

VISUAL ACUITY
Sharpness of vision in respect to the ability to distinguish fine details. The visual acuity of birds, especially of larger birds, is often said to be sharper than that of human beings, but scientists claim that the available evidence tends to support the belief that the acuity of birds is in the same order as that of men, but that the *rate of assimilation of detail in the physical field* is very much higher in birds. The vision of birds as a whole is no sharper but adjusts a great deal faster than that of men. It is conceded that large hawks, eagles, and vultures may exceed man in optical acuity by a factor of 2 or 3, but not by much more (Pumphrey, 1961b). *See* Eyes and Eyesight.

VISUAL PURPLE
See rhodopsin under Eyes and Eyesight.

VITELLINE MEMBRANE
See Embryo and Its Development.

VIVIPAROUS
See Oviparous.

VOCALIZATIONS
(songs and calls). *See* Alarm Notes; Songs and Singing; Voice and Sound-making.

VOICE AND SOUND-MAKING
The human voice box (larynx), and that of other mammals, is in the upper part of the trachea (windpipe) and is activated when its vocal cords are moved by an exhaled breath. Birds also have a larynx at the upper extremity of the windpipe, but it lacks vocal cords and is thought to have little or no part in producing voice sounds (Hill, 1964). Its function in birds is primarily as a valve to regulate the flow of air between the pharynx and trachea. *See* Respiratory System.

A bird's voice box is the syrinx (SIR-ingks), in the *lower* part of the windpipe at the point where it divides into two bronchi, each of which passes directly to the corresponding left and right lung. Of all animals, only birds have a syrinx, and its position and weight distribution lower in the body, near the lungs rather than the throat, help the aerodynamic balance of a bird. *See* Flight.

The boxlike, membranous or bony syrinx typical of most birds is a resonating chamber as-

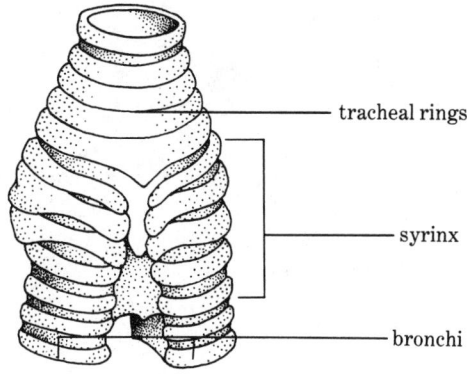

dorsal view

— tracheal rings

— syrinx

— bronchi

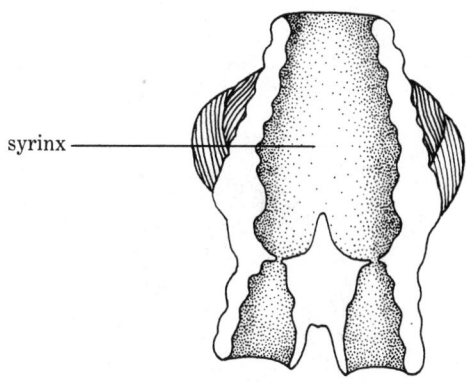

syrinx —

longitudinal section

VOICE AND SOUND-MAKING
The voices of birds are produced in the syrinx, an organ unique to birds, located at the lower end of the windpipe where it branches into the two bronchi.

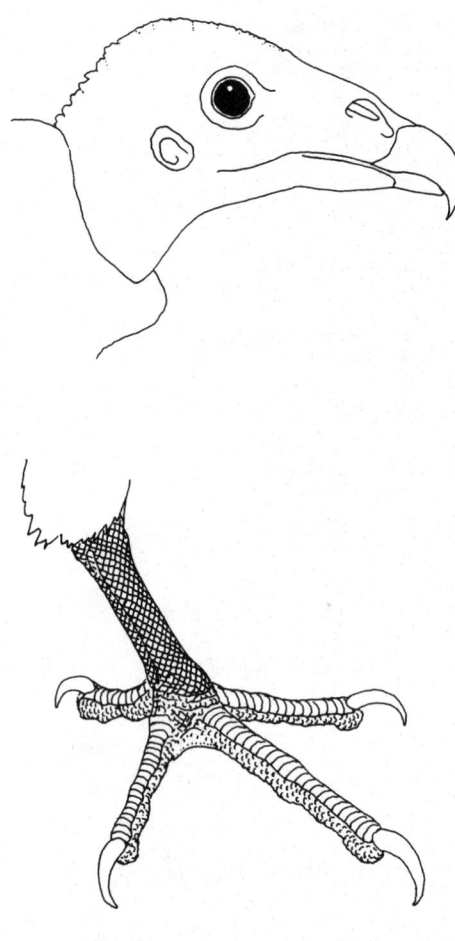

AMERICAN VULTURE FAMILY

sociated with elastic vibrating membranes, the whole of which is controlled by specialized muscles (Hill, 1964). These muscles, the so-called intrinsic muscles of the trachea and syrinx (Berger, 1960), are capable of alternating the tension and position of the membranes and thus of changing the pitch (frequency) of a bird's voice much as greater or lesser tension on a violin string can change its pitch. By changing the air pressure from its lungs, a bird can vary the intensity of volume of its voice, also its pitch. Most birds make their voice sounds by expelling air from the lungs.

Usually, those birds with the most *syringeal muscles* have the greatest potential for producing different complex songs or calls. *See* Songs and Singing. Pigeons have a single pair of syringeal muscles, most songbirds have 5–9 pairs, and versatile vocalists such as the crow, catbird, and starling have 7–9 pairs (Miskimen, 1951); however, the superb lyrebird, *Menura novaehollandiae*, of Australia, a fine songster, has a primitive syrinx with only 3 pairs. See Gilliard (1958). Turkey vultures have no syrinx or the structures associated with it (Miskimen, 1957), and storks and ostrichlike birds have no functioning syringeal muscles. Such birds are usually called "voiceless," but they can grunt, hiss, or make booming sounds.

The paired air sacs (cervicals) in the necks of certain game birds, such as the prairie chicken and sharp-tailed grouse, act as resonating chambers when the males utter their tooting, booming courtship calls in spring. *See* Air Sacs under Respiratory System; *also* Dancing Ground. The booming sounds of prairie chickens are so penetrating that on a still day they can be heard a mile away (Edminster, 1954) and over water up to 2 mi. away (Stoddard, 1922). *See* under Grouse Family.

The volume (loudness) of a bird's voice seems to depend more on resonance than on pressure of air from the lungs, and the trachea seems to act like a resonating pipe. In some birds, the longer and wider it is, the deeper the bird's voice; the shorter and narrower, the higher the bird's voice. Stresemann (1927–34) cited experiments with domestic chickens that tended to confirm this length-to-pitch voice relationship, but there are doubts (Greenewalt, 1968) that long windpipes amplify or modify a bird's voice; see, however, Delacour and Amadon (1973).

Trumpeter swans and whooping cranes, birds of two entirely different families, have enormously long windpipes that are thought by some ornithologists to give their voices their deep, trombonelike sounds. Through parallel evolution (*see* Convergent Evolution), each has developed an extraordinarily long trachea, part of which is coiled within the keel of the breastbone. Dr. Elliott Coues (1874) measured the windpipe of a whooping crane and found it to be 58 in. long, quite as long as the bird itself; about 2 ft. of the trachea was "coiled away in the breastbone." This is the trumpet, according to Bent (1926a), through which the bird produces its loud, sonorous notes, from which it is named —sounds that are said to be audible at a distance of 3 mi.

Johnsgard (1971) concluded that in the Anatidae (Duck Family) the trachea, or windpipe, modifies the sound produced by the syrinx by acting as a resonator of the open tube (i.e., trumpet). Some male ducks have an enlargement (bulla) at the base of the windpipe that is apparently responsible for the differences in sounds uttered by males compared with those by females. *See* Bulla. Chachalacas also utter loud sounds. *See* in Curassow Family.

SOUNDS OTHER THAN VOICE. Some birds stamp their feet when angry (the kiwi of New Zealand); others make sounds with their feathers by wing action (ruffed grouse drum, for example—*see* Drumming) or by diving through the air (nighthawk—*see* Courtship Flight under Flight; also the common snipe and the woodcock—*see* under Sandpiper Family); by hammering or tapping with their bills (woodpeckers—*see* Drumming); by snapping, or clapping, the mandibles together (storks, herons, owls, and roadrunner). The common goldeneye duck makes such a noticeable sound with its wings in flight that one of its given common names is whistler; the wings of the mourning dove whistle while it is flying. Some birds— grouse and quail, for example—produce a thunderous roar or loud whirring of the wings when startled into flight—a sound which may disconcert a stalking fox so much as to cause it to miss its prey, or a hunter to miss his shot. At other times grouse and quail can fly soundlessly. For a related discussion, *see* Frightmolt; *see also* Courtship; Songs and Singing. For more details on bird sound, see Thielcke (1976) and Jellis (1977).

VOMITING
See Regurgitation.

VOODOO BIRD
See Ani, smooth-billed, in Cuckoo Family.

VULTURE—AMERICAN VULTURE FAMILY
Cathartidae (kath-ARE-tih-dee); from Gr. *kathartes*, cleanser, hence scavenger (Coble, 1954). Family limited to W. Hemisphere, or New World; large birds, 25–44 in. long; includes 7 species—the Andean condor, California condor, king vulture, yellow-headed vulture, greater yellow-headed vulture, turkey vulture, and black vulture (Brown and Amadon, 1968). Representatives of the family range from s. Canada to Tierra del Fuego and the Falkland Is.; only 4 species in N. America. The Andean, or South American, condor, *Vultur gryphus*, is the most famous and is largest bird of prey in the world, with wingspread of about 10 ft. (*see* discussion under Size); it ranges through w. S. America from Venezuela and Colombia to Tierra del Fuego and Patagonia.

The California condor, one of rarest of all N. American birds, still holds out in Calif. mountains; the king vulture, *Sarcoramphus papa*, third-largest in family, ranges from Mexico to Paraguay, Bolivia, and n. Argentina, but west of the Andes, only south to Ecuador; the N. American turkey vulture, *Cathartes aura*, is the most widespread in family, ranging from N. America throughout S. America; and the very similar yellow-headed vulture, *Cathartes burrovianus*, is limited to the northern three quarters of S. America; the greater yellow-headed vulture, *Cathartes melambrotus*, to n. S. America; and in N. America the black vulture, *Coragyps atratus*, is only slightly less widespread than the turkey vulture (Marchant, 1964b).

Although similar in appearance and habits to the Old World vultures, profound internal differences separate the American Vulture Family from them (Friedmann, 1950). Some outward differences between American vultures and hawks, eagles, and falcons, all of which are classified in the same order (Falconiformes), include the following: In vultures and condors, the whole head, and in some the neck also, is naked of feathers, although covered with short down in the young; the skin of the head, usually rough, is black, red, yellow, or orange in different species; in some, plumage commences abruptly on the lower neck in the form of a more or less conspicuous ruff into which the head may be drawn by flexing the neck (condors, for example); eyes are prominent, and not shaded by bony shield as in eagles, hawks, and falcons; the nostrils are oval and perforate, and, like those of hawks and falcons, open in a soft cere; the bill is medium to very thick, rounded, and hooked, and the feet weakly raptorial, with claws strong but not so sharp or adapted to seizing and killing or holding prey as those of eagles, hawks, and falcons. The neck is short; wings very long and broad, with 11 primaries; tail rounded or even, has 12–14 quill feathers (rectrices); sexes outwardly alike or nearly so; sounds they utter are soft croaks, grunts, hisses. Young are naked at hatching, acquire down; parents feed young by regurgitation.

American vultures are powerful and graceful fliers, probably the most perfect example of static soaring flight (*see* under Flight); noted for keen eyesight; much of time, when not at rest, spent soaring in air watching ground below for carrion, on which they feed. At other times may sit on treetop or cliff with fully outstretched, motionless wings.

A. Raspet (1950), a biophysicist, by using a sailplane to follow turkey vultures in their flight, discovered that the turkey vulture has a slightly greater buoyancy in the air than the black vulture; he suggested that this difference may account for the turkey vulture's ability to range much farther north than the aerodynamically heavier black vulture.

Stager (1964) apparently settled a long controversy by showing, through experiments over 25 years, that turkey vultures, unlike the California condor and black vulture (which find their prey by sight), use their well-developed sense of smell to find their prey, although they are aided, or also find their prey, by sight.

Both the black vulture and the turkey vulture perform a useful sanitation service in cleaning up dead animals about dumps and along highways, where animals struck by cars offer them an often dependable food supply. Livestock owners, however, accuse the black and turkey vultures of carrying on their bills and feet the bacteria of anthrax, a destructive livestock disease, and the virus of hog cholera, but vultures seldom come into contact with livestock; also, it has been found, according to

Howell (1932), that the virus of hog cholera is destroyed by passing through a vulture's digestive system. See also accounts of anthrax in Stein and Van Ness (1956), and of hog cholera in Torrey (1956).

Kahl (1963) noted that when black vultures are subjected to high temperatures, they will wet their legs with their urine as a means of cooling, or lowering, their body temperatures. Hatch, D.E. (1970) made the same discovery in experiments with captive turkey vultures.

Members of the Vulture Family usually live solitarily, although some gather in large roosts; they do not build nests but lay their eggs on the ground or on floors of caves, cliffs, abandoned buildings, and in hollows of stumps, standing trees, and in hollow logs. Most are not migratory, but in N. America black and turkey vultures migrate south of summer range in fall. Members of the family are long-lived, some to 50 years in zoos; fossil fragments in some 8 fossil genera in N. America show that oldest go back some 65 million years to the Paleocene (Brodkorb, 1971).

In captivity, feed ill or injured vulture large pieces of fresh meat, which can be on the bone (apparently they eat well-decayed carcasses in the wild because of their inability to cut into the body of a large dead animal); also offer dead rabbits, chickens, or carcasses of traffic-killed animals picked up on highways; vultures will drink water freely from any kind of receptacle; young ones will gorge themselves with food; Roddy (1888) had a young turkey vulture that swallowed in a single meal a house, or milk, snake 3½ ft. long, and digested it entirely in 1½ hours. Parent vultures feed their young for a considerable time by regurgitating predigested food from their stomachs into the bill; the young insert their bills into the mouth of the parent and drink the soupy food much as a fowl drinks water.

All members of American Vulture Family are now protected by federal law, since signing of Migratory Bird Convention with Mexico, Mar. 10, 1972; the amendment also gives U.S. government authority to arrest individuals caught taking any endangered species, including the California condor, also protected from killing or capture by Calif. state law; California condor included in U.S. Bureau of Sport Fisheries and Wildlife 1966 list of rare and endangered species. See, however, later report by Ricklefs (1978) and *see* under Rare and Threatened Species.

The California condor was depicted on an 8-cent stamp issued in 1971 in one of the wildlife conservation series of the U.S. Postal Service.

Condor, California, *Gymnogyps californianus* (JIM-no-jips kal-ih-for-nih-ANE-us); genus name: Lat., from Gr. *gymnos*, naked, in reference to head, naked of feathers, and *gyps*, vulture; species name: Lat., of California; *condor* (KON-der or KON-door), from Sp. *cóndor*, and Quechua Indian name in S. America probably applied to the Andean condor. (Color ill., page 917.) The last of estimated 20–30 California condors (Ricklefs, 1978) survive in U-shaped area about 200 mi. long of rugged canyons, gorges, and forested mountains of s.

Calif., from Fresno south to Fillmore; huge birds, 43–55 in. long; wingspread 8 ft. 2 in. to 9 ft. 6 in.; largest wingspread of any N. American land bird; is living fossil whose numbers reached peak in Pleistocene of million years or more ago (Koford, 1953); formerly ranged in 1800s from B.C., Canada, and from Columbia R. in Ore. south to Baja Calif., and (from fossil remains in caves) in prehistoric times, to Nev. and across s. U.S. from Calif. and N.M. to Tex. and Fla.; sexes outwardly alike, but males slightly larger; huge dark birds twice size of turkey vulture; adult: most of plumage black but pure white on lower surface of forepart of wings; bare skin of head yellow to orange or pink; a purple-red patch on lower side of neck; eyes red, bill white, legs pink; walks with slouching gait, leaves footprints in sand 5–7 in. across from claw to claw (Koford, 1953); immatures at various ages appear like enormous dark vultures; bare gray head and neck; underwings mottled with brown and white; tail in flight notably pointed, not rounded as in adult; requires 5–7 years for immature to become fully adult and reach breeding age; gradually acquires red or orange head and neck and other characters of adult; magnificent in flight, in permanent home in Calif. mountains leaps into air from favored tree roosts on slopes above nesting ledges, or from cliffs, on breeze blowing up canyons, or flaps into flight and rises in spirals on heated air (thermals) or in wind, with great wings extended sideward in straight line, wing tips only slightly uptilted and head extended, turns in circles much larger than those of turkey vulture, which appears headless in flight by comparison (similar golden eagle overhead appears to have long neck); in oncoming glide condor often mistaken for an aircraft; in soaring and gliding, wings whistle musically in rush of air through spread, fingerlike primaries as condor glides or flaps over crests of ridges and slopes of chaparral and coniferous forests; over high ridges and peaks near roosting areas on trees or cliffs, one seldom sees condor soaring more than 500 ft. above ground, over lower hills may rise to 3,000 ft. (Koford, 1953), but sometimes rises to 15,000 ft. (Bent, 1937); most of known nest sites all within Calif., protected within U.S. Forest Service Los Padres National Forest in two sanctuaries, the 53,000-acre Sespe Condor Sanctuary, Ventura County, and the 1,200-acre Sisquoc Condor Sanctuary, Santa Barbara County. See Borneman (1970; 1971; 1972), also Malette *et al.* (1970), Wilbur *et al.* (1972), and Wilbur (1976) for details and results of annual condor surveys begun in 1965, and review of history of condor conservation program; see also Hilton (1971c). According to Miller *et al.* (1965) and Borneman (1972), greatest threat to condors is shooting; secondary poisoning of condors from feeding on dead coyotes poisoned in control work; and loss of cattle ranches (where condors feed on dead livestock) to housing and other changes in land use. See also in Ricklefs (1978). For protection, condors need especially freedom from human disturbance at roosts, nest sites, and at dead animals on which they feed, which they may desert if frightened away. When not nesting, spend most of time roosting or foraging for food; spend at least 15 hours out of 24 at roost

(5 P.M. to 8 A.M.), often more; utter hisses, grunts, growling notes, hiccups or coughs; during day spend much time sunning and preening on perch, especially in morning before taking off to feed.

Feeding Habits: No record of California condor ever attacking a living animal (Koford, 1953); in gliding or soaring over countryside watches, keen-eyed, for large or small dead animals lying in open, or watches other condors, ravens, turkey vultures circling over carrion, to which it descends and eats in any state of decay —beef cattle (especially dead calves), with sheep, deer, ground squirrels, and horses, are 95% of its food—also eats dead coyotes, rabbits, bobcats, domestic dogs, and even dead grizzly bear. Dr. Adolphus Heermann, pioneering ornithologist in Calif., in citing great muscular power of California condor, told of four that grasped in their bills carcass of a young, 100-lb. grizzly, which they dragged about 200 yds. (Bent, 1937); may travel from roost 12 to 25 or 35 mi. each day to feeding place, stands on dead animal or alongside it and pulls flesh away with its bill; each condor eats about 2–3 lb. of meat a day when food available; can survive for several days without feeding; Koford (1953) in his studies did not find any condors that had gorged themselves so much that they could not take off; in getting under way from flat ground, condors hop and run for about 40 ft. until wingbeats lift them into the air.

Nest: Not known whether condors mate for life, but some pairs occupy same nest sites over many years and pairs seen at all seasons (Koford, 1953); nest site is floor in a cavity (pothole, cave, or cleft) in a cliff among boulders, no nesting materials; four or five nest sites have been found within distance of half a mile; one rare site was a cavelike hollow in a Calif. big tree (*Sequoia gigantea*).

Eggs: Feb. 10–May 25; single egg laid on sand or in detritus on cave floor, sometimes 30 ft. from entrance; blue-white or green-white; average size of 46 condor eggs, 110 by 67 mm. (about 4½ in. long by 2¾ in. in girth) with capacity of 250 cc.; possibly largest California condor egg known was 5⅜ in. long (131 mm.). One fresh egg weighed 10½ oz., contents alone weighed 8¾ oz., the shell held 9 fluid oz. of water. Although female California condor lays one egg in wild every other year only, owing to care of young into its second year, a condor acquired as young bird by the National Zoo, Washington, D.C., in 1903, laid one egg each year in Mar. or Apr. from 1919 on, until it was at least 32 years old (Koford, 1953). *See* Reproductive Life; Age.

Incubation: By both sexes in turn, period of not definitely known but at least 42 days (Koford, 1953); possibly more than 50 days; chick is brooded first few weeks of life as constantly as eggs, and by both sexes; fed once in morning and once in afternoon; later is fed only once a day; may walk from nest site about 150 days (5 months) after hatching but another 60 days before it can fly about quarter of a mile; in spring after hatching, when about 10–12 months old, can fly well enough to search for food but still may be fed by parents into summer of its second year. Total reproductive life of pair to pro-

duce one chick, about 18 months (Amadon, 1964a).

Other Name: California vulture.

Accidents: So large and clumsy, some break wing or leg when gliding and striking objects near ground or in alighting; one drowned in water tank on Calif. ranch; two killed by hailstones (Rett, 1938); one killed in flight May 24, 1965, when collided with high-tension power line in Fresno, Calif. (Anonymous, 1965a).

Age: In 1939, Koford saw three condors at the National Zoo, Washington, D.C., that had arrived there as young of year (in 1901, 1903); one was 38 years old, two were 36 years old; the last-surviving one of the three lived to age 45 years. Koford thought life span of 40 years may never be reached in the wild. "Topatopa," young condor abandoned by parents in Topatopa Mtns., Ventura County, Feb. 1967, picked up emaciated, has been kept in Los Angeles Zoo; at time, apparently only captive California condor in world (Borneman, 1972); Finley (1910) raised young pet condor, which he gave to Bronx Zoo, New York; on visit there two years later, was greeted by condor with remarkable show of affection.

Flight Speed: In normal soaring or gliding, about 35–40 m.p.h. (Koford, 1953).

Weights: 18–31 lb. (Brown and Amadon, 1968); 21½–23 lb.; others, 27, 29, 31 lb. (Koford, 1953).

Range: Now limited to s. Calif., formerly from B.C. (see Wilbur, 1973) through Ore. to Nev., into Utah and Ariz. (see Phillips *et al.*, 1964, for sight records principally in 1880s in Utah and Ariz.), formerly nested in Tex., 1,500–3,000 years ago, and occurred in Baja Calif. until about 1930s (see Koford, 1953, for details), but no breeding records in historical times; not more than two dozen condors at a time there; news report of "colony" there in San Pedro Mártir Mtns. in spring 1971 proved to be one condor and four feathers (Borneman, 1971).

Vulture, black, *Coragyps atratus* (CORE-ah-jips ah-TRAY-tus); genus name: Lat., from Gr. *korax*, raven, and *gyps*, vulture; species name: Lat., black; *vulture*, from Lat. *vultur*, from *vello*, to pluck, or to tear, in reference to its feeding (Macleod, 1954). (Color ills., pages 916, 917.) Common over most of its range in N. America; in se. and c. U.S., ranges west across s. U.S. to s. Ariz.; 23–27 in. long; wingspread 54–60 in. (4½–5 ft.); big bird, overall black; sexes outwardly alike; both adults and young have bare skin of head and neck black, wrinkled; eyes brown; in flight, distinguished by short, square tail, which scarcely reaches past hind edge of relatively short wide wings (turkey vulture has longer, narrower tail), and by its large white patch on undersurface at base of wing primaries; flies with several rapid flaps, then a short glide; quick, labored flight in comparison with slow wingbeats of turkey vulture; while longer-tailed turkey vulture soars in majestic circles, riding a thermal upward, black vulture on same up-currents may be forced to flap wings from time to time (see details in Townsend, 1937, and technical discussion of flight of black vulture in Newman, 1958); young turkey vultures also have black heads and are sometimes mistaken for black vultures; black vulture resident over most of range but

in fall migrates southward from northern parts of range; also, a marked spring migration northward (Townsend, 1937); along seacoast generally outnumbers turkey vultures, which are usually more numerous inland; in competition between black and turkey vultures for food, more aggressive black vulture usually drives turkey vulture from animal carcass; black vulture males court female with several walking about her on ground, strutting with wings partly spread, rapid bobbing of heads; usually silent, but hisses, grunts, and utters low barking notes when fighting over food; is somewhat social, often soars in flocks, roosts in flocks, sometimes with turkey vultures, often perches with wings spread wide in sun; unlike turkey vulture, seeks food by sight and usually soars higher when hunting (Stager, 1964).

Feeding Habits: Congregates about city dumps, sewers, slaughterhouses for food, mostly carrion, and along highways for traffic-killed animals; also kills and eats baby herons in their nesting colonies, domestic ducks, newborn calves, baby lambs, skunks, opossums, and young turtles (Mrosovsky, 1971). Also eats eggs, and at times ripe and rotten fruit and vegetables.

Nest: Usually no nest materials; eggs laid in hollow bases of trees or stumps, seldom more than 10–15 ft. above ground, on floor of shallow caves, on floor of old abandoned farm buildings, on ledge of cliff, on ground under dense thicket, in holes under rocks, in hollow log, and, in American tropics, in crannies of tall city buildings.

Eggs: Tex., Fla., and N.C., Jan.–July; 1–3, usually 2, usually pale gray-green or pale blue-white, dull white, blotched or spotted with browns.

Incubation: By both parents, 32–39 days (Brown and Amadon, 1968); 39–41 days (Nice, 1954); young can fly some at about 63–70 days after hatching, but usually do not leave nest until 70 days old. Stewart (1974) watched pair on floor of old building in Va.; each adult worked central and inner toe of each foot beneath each egg to bring the two eggs side by side under the body before settling on eggs to incubate; period was 38 days; young first flew from floor of building to open window 80 days after hatching; flew away from nest area on 91st day after hatching.

Other Names: Black buzzard; black scavenger; carrion crow; Jim Crow; John Crow.

Age: One lived in National Zoo, Washington, D.C., 21 years, 1 month; one wild bird banded at Avery Is., La., was caught in trap at Lutcher, La., when 16 years, 6 months, old (Kennard, 1975); Prestwich (1955) reported that at Amsterdam Zoo in 1907 some captive black vultures had bred successfully; also, Crandall (in Prestwich) wrote that in 1920 a pair of black vultures at Bronx Zoo, New York, had bred; female hatched the two eggs but raised only one young to maturity.

Hybrids: In 1937, in National Zoo, a presumed natural hybrid of a black vulture × turkey vulture.

Weights: 4½–6 lb. (Forbush, 1925–29); 4 lb. 8 oz. (Pough, 1951).

Range: Resident in tropical and warm temperate parts, from s. Ariz., n. Mexico, w. Tex., e. Okla., se. Kans. (formerly), Mo., s. Ill., s. Ind., s. Ohio, e. W.Va., Md., and District of Columbia, south through Mexico to southern S. America; casual in N.D., S.D., Ohio, Ont., N.Y., Mass., Que., Me., N.B., Nova Scotia, and Baja Calif.

Vulture, California. *See* Condor, California.

Vulture, king, *Sarcoramphus papa* (sar-koh-RAM-fus PAH-pah); genus name: Gr., flesh-beaked, referring to wrinkled fleshy caruncle on bill; species name: Lat., bishop, or pope (Gruson, 1972), perhaps in reference to large impressive size and black-and-white plumage; *king*, because of heavy bill and because other vultures give way before it at carcasses. Mexican, C. and S. American species, straggled formerly to St. Johns River, Fla.; accidental in Ariz. (Reilly, 1968); 28–32 in. long; wingspread 6½ ft. (Blake, E. R., 1953); sexes outwardly similar; adults mainly cream-white on shoulders, underparts and back, tinged with pink; wing feathers, rump, and tail black; bare skin of head and upper neck is orange, red, and blue; cere with conspicuous wrinkled caruncle; eyes white; dusky ruff of feathers on lower neck; immature mainly sooty brown; underparts usually with more or less white; a magnificent large white-and-black vulture, especially abundant in lowlands of s. Mexico, where large flocks likely to be attracted to decaying carcasses of animals; resident of forests or semi-forests, also in C. America and S. America.

Feeding Habits: From one to ten may be seen soaring above jungle in search of carrion of all kinds: dead tapirs, cattle, etc.; also reported to kill live reptiles, calves, etc.; bill more powerful than that of any other American vulture.
Nest: Although fairly common bird, its breeding cycle in wild has never been fully described; on Feb. 27, 1965, Smith, N. G. (1970) found in Panama a king vulture in a rotten tree stump incubating a single, cream-white, unmarked egg on floor of stump not far above ground in dense, wet second-growth woods; egg was about 3⅔ in. long and 2½ in. in girth; on July 6, 1966, Smith was shown another egg on forest floor near base of small spiny palm, lying in nest scrape in leaves.
Incubation: In captivity, period of 56 and 58 days respectively in 1960 and 1961 at Catskill Game Farm, N.Y.; a young one, successfully reared there in 1960, was reported in 1967 to have lost its last remaining juvenile feathers (Prestwich, 1968).
Age: One lived in captivity in Calif. for 24 years (Stott, 1948).
Weights: (5), about 6¾–8¼ lb. (Brown and Amadon, 1968).
Range: See above.

Vulture, turkey, *Cathartes aura* (kath-ARE-teez OW-rah); genus name: *see* family introduction; species name: Latinized name from a S. American or Mexican name (Coues, 1882); according to Coble (1954), from Lat. *aurum*, gold; common name: from red skin of head and dark body feathers resembling turkey. (Color

ill., page 918.) Lives over most of U.S. in summer, s. Canada southward; 26–32 in. long; wingspread 68–72 in.; big, black or blackish brown; sexes similar in size, outwardly alike; adults: bare skin of head and neck dull red to purple-red with some sparse bristles; eyes gray-brown; legs pale, fleshy white; in flight overhead, pale silvery lining of rear part of wings contrasts with dark coverts of forepart of wings; small red naked head (black in immature bird) and long slim tail while gliding or soaring, with long upswept wings held in flattened V as it sways and tilts in flight, are characteristic; usual hunting flights about 200 ft. above ground or just above tops of woods and over fields as it searches for prey by sight and smell (Stager, 1964); also soars to tremendous height; in migration to 4,000–5,000 ft. as it moves northward; in mild winters may remain throughout much of summer breeding range; usually arrives on nesting range in n. U.S. and s. Canada Feb.–Apr.; lives over open plains, desert, forest, jungle; pairing is often preceded by group "dance" in which numbers gather on ground in open area, where each hops (with wings trailing) toward its neighbor, which in turn hops toward a third vulture (see Loftin and Tyson, 1965); on ground is awkward, hops clumsily with hitch sideways, has ungainly walk; to get into air from ground leans forward, stumbles a few steps, hops, gives quick push with legs, and, visibly straining, flops wings until at last gets under way; usually silent but over coveted animal carcass group may push, flop, hiss, and fight in bloodless way, occasionally grunt or utter raucous growl suggesting a note of some of larger herons (Tyler, 1937); at night, groups of a few or up to 70 or more may roost in trees, from which they leave, often late in morning, when warm air rises in thermals, upon which they soar over countryside. See details in "Adventures with Vultures," in Terres (1968a).

Feeding Habits: Eats almost entirely carrion, fresh to putrid; from single vulture to many gather quickly after death of animals, from alligators to traffic-killed raccoons, opossums, pigs, skunks, snakes, turtles, small birds; occasionally kills and eats newly born pigs and young herons and ibises in nest but small birds show no fear of turkey vulture; even known to eat grasshoppers, fish, dead tadpoles, and, when pressed for food, pumpkins (Tyler, 1937).
Nest: No materials; eggs laid on bare floor of caves, rocks of cliffs, on rotted wood inside hollow logs, hollow trees, or in hollow stumps, on ground inside dense shrubbery, often in swamp, sometimes under floor or on bare floors of abandoned buildings in woods; both parents may roost inside dark nest cavity after eggs are laid; adult may feign death if caught in hands at nest or regurgitate foul-smelling food.
Eggs: Mar.–June; s. U.S., Feb.–June; 1–3, usually 2, dull white to cream-white, spotted, blotched, splashed with brown; some unmarked.
Incubation: By both sexes, 38–41 days (Brown and Amadon, 1968); adults feed young by regurgitation; young make good pets and

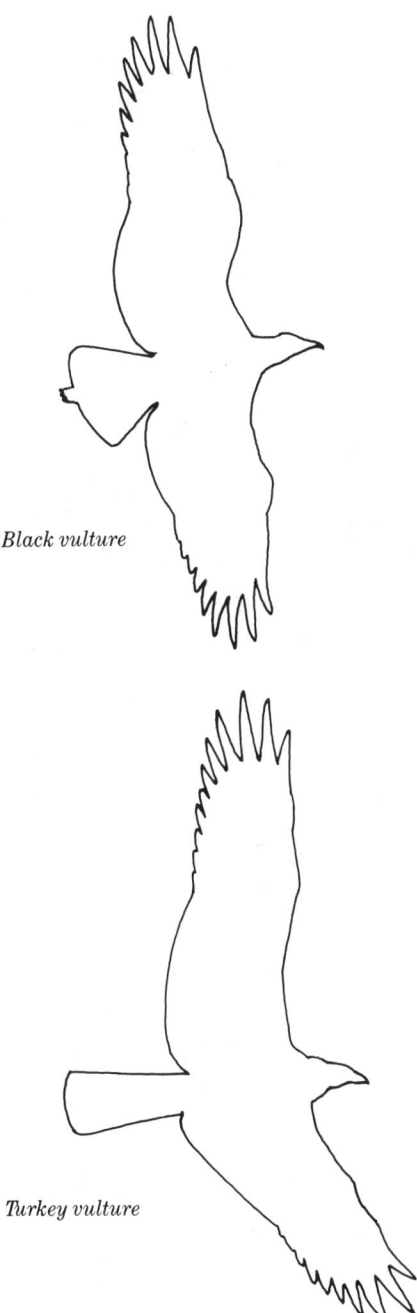

Black vulture

Turkey vulture

AMERICAN VULTURE FAMILY
In flight, the black vulture may be distinguished from the turkey vulture by its short, square tail and the light patches near the tips of its short, wide wings. It flies with rapid flaps and brief glides. The turkey vulture has a longer, slimmer tail, shorter neck, and longer wings, which it holds in a shallow V. It soars in wide circles, tilting from side to side, and sustains itself with only occasional slow flaps of its wings.

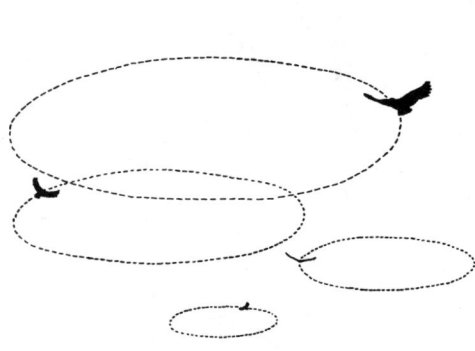

AMERICAN VULTURE FAMILY

American vultures are among the most accomplished of static soarers, using thermal updrafts to maintain altitude while circling in search of carrion. When one bird discovers food and descends, the other circling vultures see the descent and converge on the carcass.

follow one about like dog, are fond of being handled; fly when 70–80 days old.

Other Names: Buzzard; carrion crow; John Crow; red-necked buzzard; turkey buzzard.

Accidents: Sometimes dropped from exposed tree roost by late-winter freezing rain; Nagy (1972a) at Hawk Mt., Pa., found 7 of 30 had fallen from roost during night to snow-covered ground, with wings and backs so encased with ice, they could not fly.

Age: One lived in National Zoo, Washington, D.C., 20 years, 9 months.

Flight Speed: Timed in Mo., 21 m.p.h. (Anonymous, 1905); 15 m.p.h. (Wood, 1933); in Fla., gliding, 20 m.p.h. (Teale, 1951); migrating, 34 m.p.h. (Broun and Goodwin, 1943).

Hybrids: See under Black vulture.

Weights: Hatch, D.E. (1970) reported that of wild vultures shot in Mo., Sept.–Oct., in late afternoon with crops full, one adult male weighed 2,180 gr. (about 4 lb. 12 oz.); an adult female, 2,347 gr. (about 5 lb. 2 oz.); of three shot from roost at dawn in early Oct., one adult female weighed 1,990 gr. (about 4 lb. 6 oz.); an adult male, 2,079 gr. (about 4 lb. 9 oz.); and a juvenile, 2,387 gr. (about 5 lb. 4 oz.); weights of five captives, 1–2 years old, ranged from 1,530 gr. (about 3 lb. 6 oz.) to 2,590 gr. (about 5 lb. 10 oz.).

Range: Resident, except in northern parts of range, from which migrates in fall, from s. Canada to s. S. America, also in Bahamas and West Indies; in winter, generally withdraws south from east-west line, n. Calif. to Md., in winter only occasionally seen farther north.

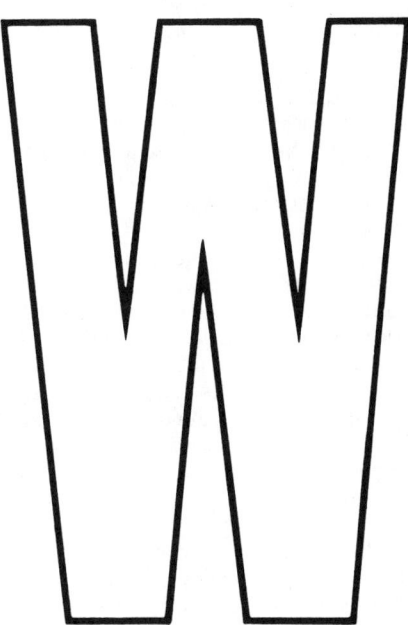

WADER

In British ornithological usage, synonymous with the American term *shorebird.* *See* Shorebird.

WADING BIRDS

Term for those water birds that usually do not swim or dive for their prey but wade in shallow edges of lakes, ponds, creeks, and other waters for food not available on shore. These are the flamingos, herons, egrets, spoonbills, ibises, cranes, stilts, avocets, curlews, and godwits, for example, which have, proportionately, very long legs adapted to wading. They also have short tails, and long necks and bills (the bill is highly specialized in the flamingos), used in probing under the water or in making long swift strikes (herons, for example) to seize fishes, frogs, aquatic insects, crustaceans, and other prey. *See* Food and Feeding Habits; *also* Bill.

WAGLER

J(OHANN) G(EORG) (1800–32). Born Nuremberg, Germany; for whom P. L. Sclater, British ornithologist, in 1857 named a Mexican oriole, new to science, *Icterus wagleri,* or Wagler's oriole, now called black-vented oriole. Wagler was the son of an eminent lawyer and studied natural history at Erlangen from 1818 to 1820. He was a systematist and on May 15, 1826, was appointed professor extraordinary of zoology in the newly founded University of Munich and director of the zoological museum there. In 1827 Wagler published his *Systema Avium;* he visited the Berlin Museum in the autumn of 1828, and published his monograph on parrots in 1832; died Aug. 23, 1832, after he was hit by a stray shot while hunting (Stresemann, 1975); see also Palmer (1928); Wynne (1969). *See also* Lichtenstein.

WAGTAIL

See in Pipit Family.

WAHQUOIT

See Knot, red, in Sandpiper Family.

WAKE-UP

and WICK-UP. Another name for flickers. *See* in Woodpecker Family.

WALKING

See Hopping and Walking.

WALL CREEPER

See under Altitude of Bird Flight.

WALLOON

and WARLOON. Local names in N.C. for the common loon; McAtee (1954–55) suggests these are sonic, imitative of one of the bird's cries.

WAMP

Another name for the common eider; in Duck Family; from an Indian name meaning white.

WAMP'S COUSIN

Another name for the king eider.

WARBLER—AMERICAN WOOD WARBLER FAMILY

Parulidae (par-you-LIE-dee); from Lat. *parula* (diminutive form of *parus,* titmouse). About 109 species, all in New World (some authorities include the Honeycreeper Family); 56 species in N. America; gray, olive, or green; many brilliantly patterned with bright yellow, red, orange, blue, or black and white; underparts may be plain, streaked or striped; often called "butterflies" of bird world; includes, besides N. American birds called warblers, the ground-chat, yellow-breasted chat, ovenbird, redstarts, waterthrushes, and yellowthroats.

American wood warblers live from Alaska to Labrador and south through N. and Central America, the West Indies, to n. Argentina; most N. American species are migratory; most live in woodlands or low swampy places; of the 56 species listed for N. America, 54 breed, or nest, in America north of Mexico—the fantailed warbler has appeared casually in Baja Calif., the Bahama yellowthroat in Fla.; one of the great and exciting annual features of N. American bird life is migrating waves of wood warblers in spring and fall which fill country, town, and city woodlands, thickets, and hedges; migrating at night past large city buildings, tall television towers in country, thousands are killed by striking these structures.

In number of species it is second largest family of N. American *songbirds,* exceeded only by Finch Family; one mark of wood warblers is the 9 primary flight feathers in the wings, a feature shared, for example, by their relatives, some of the honeycreepers (the unrelated Old World Warblers have 10 primaries); the N. American wood warblers are also thought to be related to the finches, vireos, tanagers, and Hawaiian honeycreepers. The short bill is slender, sharp-pointed; in some, bill rather broad and flattened —members of the latter group (redstarts, for example) catch insects in flight; legs are slender, toes long and slender, have the perching foot of all songbirds, or perching birds. *See* Passeriformes; Feet and Legs.

Wood warblers very active, flit about in leaves of trees, in thickets or on ground; most eat largely insects but some add berries and grapes; some eat sap from trees (*see* Commensalism).

Largest N. American wood warbler is yellow-breasted chat; Kirtland's warbler has the most limited breeding range of any continental N. American bird; nests only in area 60 by 80 mi. in c. Mich., and only in dense stands of pines 3–18 ft. tall (Parkes, 1964). *See* Monuments to Birds. Bachman's warbler is rarest in family and is rarest of all N. American songbirds (Peterson, 1947; Vincent, 1966); two—blue-winged warbler and golden-winged warbler—regularly hybridize where their breeding ranges overlap and produce the famous hybrids— Brewster's and Lawrence's warblers; one, the black-and-white warbler, has become so specialized in its feeding habits that it creeps over the trunks and limbs of trees like the brown creeper.

Redstarts, common name for two species— the American and the painted redstart—are flycatcherlike in their habit of aerial sallies to catch insects (they have little in common with

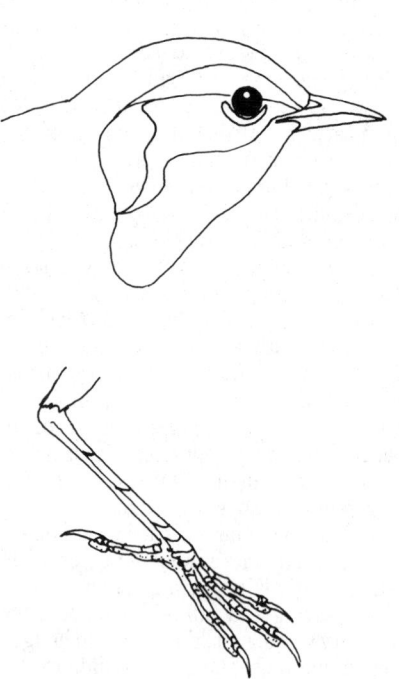

AMERICAN WOOD WARBLER FAMILY

Tropical parula

AMERICAN WOOD WARBLER FAMILY

Old World birds called redstarts, except an outer resemblance); marked characters are the relatively wide flat bills and rictal bristles (*see* under Feather). Besides our two N. American redstarts, in W. Hemisphere there are about 10 species of tropical American redstarts of the genus *Myioborus*, which, like the painted redstart, differ from the American redstart in that males and females are equally bright in color (Parkes, 1964).

Most N. American wood warblers build their nests in trees, shrubs, or vines; the ovenbird, waterthrushes, and yellowthroats, however, nest on the ground, and two, the prothonotary warbler and Lucy's warbler, nest in natural holes in trees or in stumps; another, the northern parula, nests in the South in hanging bunches of Spanish moss *(Tillandsia)*, in the North in old-man's-beard *(Usnea)*, a lichen that superficially resembles the Spanish moss of the South. Most warblers roost in places typical of where they nest, and most give elaborate displays of injury-feigning to lead intruders away from the nest (*see* Distraction Display).

Gross (1965a) reported albinism in 31 individuals of 11 species of wood warblers but did not name them. Many warblers are the most victimized of all birds by the parasitic cowbird. *See* cowbirds, in Troupial Family; *also* Brood-Parasitism.

If trying to save an ill or injured wood warbler until it can fend for itself (all members of the family are protected by law), offer it mealworms, small insects, ground meat, canned dog food (beef base), and well-ripened fruit such as grapes (take off skin and cut in halves), or orange sections. *See* Care and Feeding of Abandoned or Injured Wild Birds.

Chat, long-tailed. *See* Chat, yellow-breasted.

Chat, yellow-breasted, *Icteria virens* (ick-TER-ih-ah or ick-TEE-rih-ah VER-enz); genus name: from Gr. *ikteros*, jaundice, hence yellowness, refers here to yellow of throat and breast; species name: Lat., becoming green, verdant (Jaeger, 1955), referring to olive green back of this species; *chat*, from the bird's notes (chatter, prattle). (Color ill., page 983.) One of most aberrant of all N. American wood warblers; only species in its genus, stout-bodied, long-tailed, behaves and sounds more like member of Mockingbird Family than a wood warbler (Parkes, 1964); in summer, across s. Canada and n. U.S., south to Fla. and Baja Calif.; 6½–7½ in. long; wingspread 9–10 in.; has white "spectacles" and bright yellow throat and breast; olive green above; bill large, heavy, curved, *no white in wings or in long tail;* male slightly brighter yellow about face, but bill usually solid black with small light stripes or dots on lower mandible during breeding season; its song a medley of strange sounds, some musical, some harsh, resembling catcalls, whistles, and various bird notes such as soft *caws* (there is some disagreement as to whether it is a mimic); often sings at night, and voice is lowest-pitched of any in American Wood Warbler Family (Bent, 1953); is secretive and elusive; usually stays under cover in dense thickets but at times, when it sings, may fly from one bush

to another, legs dangling, wings flopping awkwardly.

Feeding Habits: Eats largely insects—grasshoppers, beetles, bugs, ants, weevils, bees, wasps, moths, mayflies, tent caterpillars, currant "worms"; also fond of blackberries, raspberries, strawberries, elderberries, wild grapes.

Nest: Cup-shaped, built of dead leaves, coarse straws, grapevine bark, lined with grasses, fine plant stems, leaves; built in small bushes, vines, briers, about 2–8 ft. above ground (Bent, 1953), occasionally on ground; according to Dennis (1958), sometimes nests in groups or "colonies" but territories separate.

Eggs: Ariz., late Apr. to Aug. 1; Calif., early May to mid-July; Ga., early May to June; Tex., Apr.–June; Pa., mid-May to late June (Bent, 1953); 3–6, usually 5, white or light cream speckled with rust or violet.

Incubation: 11–12 days; young first fly about 8–11 days after hatching (Petrides, 1938).

Other Names: Chat; common chat; long-tailed chat; polyglot chat; yellow chat; yellow mockingbird.

Age: One, banded Nashville, Tenn., still alive when 5 years old; another, banded Pt. Pleasant, W.Va., trapped and released at Marietta, Ohio, when 8 years, 11 months, old (Kennard, 1975).

Host to Cowbirds: Frequent to brown-headed cowbird and locally; in some places one of its chief victims, in others only occasionally; about 180 records across s. Canada south to Mexico; also 2 records in which victimized by bronzed cowbird—Brownsville and Refugio, Tex. (Friedmann, 1963).

Weights: In New England, Md., and Va., averages of 24.5 and 27.1 gr., or about 1 oz. (Dennis, 1958); in N.C. (26), average 27.6 gr. (Teulings and Teulings, 1971); in fall, coastal N.J. (103), 19.4–33.4 gr. (Murray and Jehl, 1964), or ¾–1 oz.

Range: Lives about edges of woods or in dense thickets and brambles in low wet places near streams, pond edges, or swamps, and in shrubby old pastures across s. Canada from s. B.C. into s. Minn., s. Wisc., s. Mich., s. Ont., c. N.Y., s. Vt., and s. N.H., south to Fla. and Gulf coast and n. Fla., s.-c. Baja Calif., and Mexico; winters from s. Baja Calif., c. Mexico, s. Tex., and Yucatán, south to w. Panama.

Ground-chat. *See* Yellowthroat, gray-crowned.

Ground-chat, Mexican. *See* Yellowthroat, gray-crowned.

Ground-chat, Ralph's. *See* Yellowthroat, gray-crowned.

Ground-chat, Rio Grande. *See* Yellowthroat, gray-crowned.

Ovenbird, *Seiurus aurocapillus* (sigh-YOU-rus aw-roh-kah-PILL-us); genus name: Lat., from Gr. *seio*, to shake, to move to and fro, and *oura*, tail; in reference to the vibratory motions of tail when walking (one of its common names is wood wagtail); species name: from Lat. *aurum*, gold, and *capillus*, hair (crown); in reference to pale orange patch on crown; *oven-bird*, from unusual nest; shape resembles tiny Dutch oven. (Color ill., page 984.) In summer, across Canada from ne. B.C. to Newfoundland, south to Colo., Okla., and n. Ga.; 5½–6½ in. long; wingspread about 9–10 in.; sexes alike; olive brown above; throat, sides, and breast streaked black; white below; brownish-orange stripe over center of head extending from bill to nape is black-edged; brown eyes have white eye-ring; legs and feet pale *pink;* usually seen walking over forest floor; lives in mature woods without heavy undergrowth; song a loud ringing chant in rising crescendo, *teacher, teacher, teacher, TEACHER!*, given from low branch; also sings different and lovely flight song in late afternoon, at dusk, or at night.

Feeding Habits: Walks on floor of woods turning over leaves with bill searching for snails, slugs, earthworms, weevils, beetles, moths, caterpillars, aphids, crickets, ants, and spiders; also eats a few seeds and fruit such as mulberries.

Nest: In slight depression of open forest floor, female builds arched, ovenlike nest, near trail or woods road, of dead grasses, leaves, weed stems, rootlets, mosses, and hair, with opening in front; dead-leaf roof sheds rain and conceals nest (Gross, 1953b).

Eggs: May–July; 3–6, usually 4–5, white, speckled with brown or gray. Eggs much subjected to predation by snakes (*see* Reptiles and Birds), red squirrels, weasels, skunks; female will perform crippled-bird act when flushed from nest (*see* Distraction Display).

Incubation: By female alone, 11–14 days (Hann, 1937); young hatch with eyes closed, open by 5th day, follow parents from nest at 8 days old; first flights when 8–11 days old.

Other Names: Golden-crowned accentor; golden-crowned thrush; golden-crowned wagtail; nightingale; night-walker; teacher-bird; wood wagtail.

Accidents: Of 59,032 warblers of 37 species reported killed in previous 20 years (Taylor, W. K., 1972) during autumn migration at tall structures and at ceilometer beams in e. Canada and the U.S., 11,236 (19%) were ovenbirds.

Age: Of 38 adults banded in Mich., oldest retrapped and released when 7 years old; two others, banded elsewhere, were recaptured when 7 years old; one, banded, was recaptured in N.J. when at least 8 years old (Kenny and Leck, 1972).

Host to Cowbirds: Very frequent; more than 280 records to brown-headed cowbird (Friedmann, 1963).

Weights: In fall, coastal N.J. (61), 14.8–26.3 gr. (Murray and Jehl, 1964), or about ½–1 oz.

Range: Nests from ne. B.C., s.-c. Mack., c. Sask., eastward to Newfoundland and ne. U.S., south to s. Alta., e. Colo. se. Okla., n. Ark., n. Ala., and n. Ga.; winters from ne. Mexico, Gulf coast, s. Ga., and s. S.C. south to nw. S. America and Lesser Antilles (A.O.U. *Check-List*, 1957).

Parula, northern, *Parula americana* (PAR-you-lah ah-mer-ih-CANE-ah); genus name: from Lat. *parula*, dim. of *parus*, titmouse; little titmouse; species name: Lat., of America. (Color ill., page 984.) E. N. America,

especially common in swamps of Southeast; one of tiniest warblers; 4¼–4¾ in. long; wingspread 7–7¾ in.; male in spring, gray-blue above with yellow-green patch on back; belly white; two conspicuous white wing bars; dark band across yellow throat; female and immatures like male but duller; breast band indistinct or lacking; while migrating frequents almost any kinds of trees, with preference for deciduous, in highest tops with mixed groups of warblers, often in trees of roadsides, parks, orchards, and gardens, but on nesting grounds lives usually in humid woodlands near ponds, lakes, swamps, and in North most often where trees hung with old-man's-beard (*Usnea*), a long, gray-green lichen; in South where trees draped with Spanish moss (*Tillandsia*); also at times where neither grows; more sedate and deliberate in movements than most treetop warblers, often fearless and easily approached. Male sings throughout migration and on nesting grounds into late July; a high-pitched buzzy trill, rising in pitch to explosive ending: *zeeeeeeee-yip!;* also buzzy series ending in *zh-zh-zh-zheeee!*

Feeding Habits: Creeps along branches and hops from twig to twig, often hangs head downward under cluster of leaves, chickadee-like, sometimes clings to tree trunk like nuthatch, searching for small beetles, fall and spring cankerworms, small hairy tent caterpillars and those of gypsy moth; ants, bees, wasps, fly larvae, scale insects, and many spiders.

Nest: Usually in hollowed-out bunches of hanging *Usnea* lichen or Spanish moss, in either deciduous tree or conifer; usually scantily lined with finely shredded moss, fine grasses, plant down, a few hairs, or built in hanging cluster of twigs of hemlocks or spruces.

Eggs: Apr. (in South) to July; 3–7, usually 4–5, white or cream-white, speckled and spotted with browns.

Incubation: 12–14 days; age when young first fly unknown (Bent, 1953; Graber and Graber, 1951).

Other Names: Blue yellowback; blue yellow-backed warbler; finch creeper; southern parula warbler.

Age: One, banded in Me., reported still alive at age 4 years (Patterson, 1971); a male, banded Marshfield, Vt., trapped and released in same area when 4 years, 3 months, old (Kennard, 1975).

Host to Cowbirds: Uncommon or rare; only 12 records (Friedmann, 1963).

Hybrids: Two reported near Martinsburg, W.Va.—northern parula × yellow-throated warbler (hybrid called Sutton's warbler or Potomac warbler); and presumed natural hybrids of northern parula × American redstart (Gray, 1958).

Weights: In N.C. (8), average 8.4 gr. (Teulings and Teulings, 1971), or about ⅓ oz.; in fall, coastal N.J. (28), 6.3–11.8 gr. (Murray and Jehl, 1964).

Range: Nests from se. Man. east to n. Me., n. N.B., Nova Scotia, south to e. Tex., Gulf coast, and nw. and c. Fla.; winters from Fla., Bahamas, south to Barbados Is. and from c. Mexico to Nicaragua.

Parula, tropical, *Parula pitiayumi* (PAR-you-lah pit-ih-YOU-mih); genus name: *see* Parula, northern; species name: based on an Indian name for the bird. Small tropical American warbler that ranges into U.S. only in s. Tex.; appears much like closely related northern parula but without dark breast band, and usually more extensive yellow underparts; 4–4¾ in. long; adult male, blue-gray above with patch of olive green in center of back; *cheeks black, no white in eyelids;* throat, breast, and forepart of belly rich tawny yellow fading to white on belly and under tail; two white wing bars, sometimes one; female duller; lives in low dry woodlands or in semi-dry cultivated valleys with scattered trees (Skutch, 1957b); in s. Tex., passes summer in thick woods near edges of lagoons where there is Spanish moss; at one time fairly common around Brownsville, especially near dry old river beds where trees, mostly small mesquites, are draped with an "air plant" (*Tillandsia*), or Spanish moss; male sings bright, rapid song from trees and thickets, resembles song of yellow warbler, but more complex, accelerated at end almost to trill (Skutch, 1957b), almost identical with that of northern parula warbler.

Feeding Habits: Largely insects, but diet little known.

Nest: 8–40 ft. up; a hollow formed in mass of air plants (epiphytes) such as Spanish moss, and small orchids, 8 ft. or more above ground; nest built within of green moss, shreds of inner bark of palmetto, fine grasses, rootlets, cattle hairs, lined with plant down and a few feathers.

Eggs: Tex., Apr.–May; 3–4 (2 in tropics), white to cream-white, speckled with browns, usually wreathed at large end.

Incubation: Period of and age when young first fly unknown.

Other Name: Olive-backed warbler; Sennett's warbler; Sennett's olive-backed warbler.

Range: Nests from s. Tex. and n. Mexico south through C. America to Peru, n. Argentina, and Uruguay.

Redstart, American, *Setophaga ruticilla* (see-TOFF-ah-gah root-ih-SILL-ah); genus name: from Gr. *ses, setos*, moth, and *phagein*, to eat; species name: from Lat. *rutillus*, red, and New Lat. *cilla*, tail; *cilla* is "a spurious suffix" according to Macleod (1954), "a misapprehension dating back to the fourteenth century"; *cauda* is Lat. for tail (Jaeger, 1955); redstart is a corruption of the Old Ger. *rothstert*, meaning "red tail" (Gruson, 1972); the common English name *redstart* was originally applied in Great Britain to the redstart, *Phoenicurus phoenicurus*, and *redstart* applied later to the N. American redstart, which was thought to resemble the European bird (see Newton, 1893–96); called in Cuba and other places in Latin America *Candelita*, "little torch." (Color ill., page 984.) In summer from s. Alaska, western Canada across Canada, n. U.S. to eastern U.S.; 4½–5¾ in. long; male is glossy black with white belly, with patches of orange on wings, sides, and tail; in female, gray and yellow replace black-and-orange pattern of male; bill, legs, and feet black, bill has rictal bristles about mouth; female and immatures in

Bachman's warbler

AMERICAN WOOD WARBLER FAMILY

fall are light gray above; immatures have yellow as in female; males do not acquire adult plumage until their second year; one of most animated of all warblers; characteristically droops wings, fans tail, and leaps into air to catch insects; woodland bird, thought to be one of most common warblers nesting in N. America; utters thin, sibilant songs—one is *tseet, tseet, tseet.*

Feeding Habits: Eats mostly forest tree insects; flea beetles, leaf beetles, round-headed wood borers, caterpillars of brown-tail and gypsy moths, cankerworms, also spittle insects, moths, treehoppers, leafhoppers, scale insects, plant lice (aphids), also spiders, daddy longlegs, wasps, crane flies, lantern flies, also eats fruit of barberry, Juneberries, seeds of magnolia trees.

Nest: Built by female, in upright crotch, usually of deciduous tree or shrub, 4–70 ft. above ground (commonly 10–20 ft.), of plant down, fibers of bark, rootlets, grasses, outside ornamented with lichens, bits of birch bark, bound with spider's silk, sometimes lined with feathers of tanagers, indigo bunting, or wood thrush; sometimes uses old or deserted new nests of vireos (Bent, 1953).

Eggs: May–July; 2–5, usually 4, white to cream-gray or green-white, speckled and spotted with grays, browns.

Incubation: 12 days; young first fly 8–9 days after hatching.

Other Names: Common redstart; fire-tail; redstart flycatcher; redstart warbler; yellow-tailed warbler.

Age: A female, banded when immature in July 1949 at Groton, Mass., killed by cat a mile away, June 1954, when about 5 years old; one, banded Me., still alive at 4 years, 2 months (Patterson, 1971); a female, banded at Stow, Ohio, trapped and released in same area when 4 years, 11 months, old (Kennard, 1975).

Albinism: A partial albino, bill pink, forepart of head white, with white spots over rest of head and throat, etc., at Norristown, Pa. (Middleton, 1936).

Host to Cowbirds: One of commonest victims of brown-headed cowbird; at least 200 records across Canada and in Midwest and e. U.S. (Friedmann, 1963).

Hybrids: Presumed natural hybrids of American redstart × northern parula (warbler). See Gray (1958).

Weights: In fall, coastal N.J. (358), 5.5–11.3 gr. (Murray and Jehl, 1964), or about ⅓ oz.

Range: Nests from se. Alaska to Newfoundland, south to e. Ore., n. Utah, n. Colo., se. Okla., s. La., c. Ala., and c. Ga.; winters from s. Baja Calif., c. Mexico, and West Indies south into n. S. America.

Redstart, common. *See* Redstart, American.

Redstart, painted, *Myioborus pictus* (my-yoh-BORE-us PICK-tus); genus name: from Gr. *myia,* a fly, and *borus,* greedy; species name: Lat., painted, variegated. (Color ill., page 985.) In summer, in mountain canyons of Southwest; a Mexican and C. American species; 5–5¾ in. long; scarlet breast and belly, head and upperparts black, with white patches in wings and tail; eyes brown; bill, legs, and feet black; sexes alike; actions strikingly like its relative the American redstart; droops wings, fans tail as it climbs about sides of trunks or over stumps, logs in well-watered canyons of desert home 5,000–7,000 ft. up; lives among oaks, sycamores, ashes, maples, cedars, and pines; male's song is clear, ringing *weecher, weecher, weecher,* call note is like peep of a young chicken (Bent, 1953).

Feeding Habits: Darts out from perch to catch insects in air; apparently wholly insectivorous from observations.

Nest: Built on ground under small boulder or bank, under clump of grass, or under roots of tree or shrub; made of coarse bark, fibers of weed stalks, lined with animal hairs and grasses.

Eggs: Apr.–July; 3–4, usually 4, cream-white, delicately dotted with browns.

Incubation: 13–14 days (Griscom *et al.,* 1957).

Range: Nests from nw. and n.-c. Ariz., sw. N. M., w. Tex., south through mountains to Guatemala, El Salvador, and n. Nicaragua; casually north in summer to sw. Utah and nw. N.M.; winters from n. Mexico southward; casually north to s. Calif. and s. Ariz.; accidental in Canada (Speirs, 1972) and in Mass., La., and N.Y.

Warbler, Arctic. Name for a bird in the Warbler—Old World Warbler Family.

Warbler, Audubon's (yellow-rumped), *Dendroica coronata auduboni* (den-DROY-cah coh-row-NAY-tah aw-dew-BON-eye); genus name: Lat., from Gr. *dendron,* tree, and *oikein,* to dwell (Coble, 1954); species name: Lat., crowned; subspecies name: formerly *Dendroica auduboni;* subspecies name: given for John James Audubon by John K. Townsend, Philadelphia ornithologist, in 1837; considered by American Ornithologists' Union (1973) not to be a distinct species, *Dendroica auduboni,* but a subspecies of a species with general name of yellow-rumped warbler. (Color ill., page 997.) It is a western subspecies, counterpart of the subspecies of e. U.S., the myrtle warbler; 5–5½ in. long; wingspread 8¾–9 in.; adult male in breeding plumage, upperparts blue-gray, streaked with black; crown patch and rump bright yellow as in eastern myrtle warbler; however, wings have *broad* white patch (myrtle has two narrow white wing bars), breast black as in myrtle warbler, also with yellow on sides but has yellow throat (myrtle has white throat); adult female similar but duller; in winter, adults brownish-streaked and white-breasted but still have identifiable yellow rump patch. Nesting range in summer does not extend as far north as myrtle warbler but higher up (to 12,000 ft. in Colo. Rockies) and farther south (into c. Mexico); in winter, may move to lowlands from high mountains and spend winter almost as far north as in summer (Bent, 1953); hardy, abundant, active, these small birds fly out from trees, bushes, or tall groves and are even on Pacific coast beaches; on warm days fly straight up from bush or tree to catch insect in air; utters sharp, metallic *tsip* note;

song of male, often given from tops of pines or firs, begins *tsit, tsit, tsit*, followed by energetic trill at lower pitch (Hoffmann, 1927).

Feeding Habits: Ants, wasps, houseflies, crane flies, gnats (many caught on wing), scale insects, plant lice (aphids), beetles, caterpillars, etc., also spiders and some berries and seeds—will come to feeding trays for raisins (Bent, 1953). *See* Bird-Attracting.
Nest: Usually built on horizontal limb, sometimes in crotch of Douglas fir, hemlock, spruce, balsam, ponderosa pine, willow, aspen, oak, rosebush, 3–50 ft. above ground; of twigs, weed stems, bark strips, rootlets, the cup lined with feathers of grouse, bluebirds, jays, and others.
Eggs: Apr.–July; 3–5, almost always 4, gray or cream-white, spotted with grays or browns.
Incubation: 12–13 days, both parents feed young; age when young first fly unknown (Bent, 1953).
Other Names: Black-fronted warbler; western yellow-rumped warbler.
Host to Cowbirds: Only 4 records (Friedmann, 1963); 2 in B.C., 1 in Calif., 1 in Mont.
Hybrids: Crosses at times in wild with myrtle warbler (Gray, 1958) where ranges overlap. See Hubbard (1969; 1970).
Range: Nests c. B.C. to se. Mont., w. S.D., south in mountains to s. Calif., n. Baja Calif., s. Ariz., s. N.M., and c. Mexico; winters along Pacific coast from sw. B.C., c. Wash., c. Nev., sw. Utah, c. N.M., and s. Tex. south to Costa Rica; accidental in Neb., Ill., Pa., Conn., and Mass.

Warbler, autumnal. *See* Warbler, bay-breasted; *also* Warbler, blackpoll.

Warbler, azure. *See* Warbler, cerulean.

Warbler, Bachman's, *Vermivora bachmanii* (ver-MIV-oh-rah back-MAN-ih-eye); genus name: from Lat. *vermis*, worm, and *vorare*, to devour; species name: given by John James Audubon in 1833 for his friend the Rev. John Bachman, who discovered the species in a swamp near Charleston, S.C. Very rare southern warbler; according to Peterson (1947), the rarest songbird in N. America; on the rare and endangered list (see United States Department of the Interior, 1979); believed by Stevenson (1972b) to be on verge of extinction; 4¼–4½ in. long; brown-olive above, yellow below; yellow forehead and face, with black crown, black bib; yellow eye-ring, no white in tail; like hooded warbler of same environments (swampy woods), but smaller and does not have complete black hood or white spots in tail as does hooded warbler (Robbins *et al.*, 1966); female has blue-gray cap and nape, and a yellow forehead, a distinct yellow eye-ring, no black bib; immature males have smaller, partly obscured black throat patch; song is thin, wiry, like that of a listless northern parula (Bent, 1953), call note is a low, hissing *zee-ee-eep*.

Feeding Habits: Little known but apparently insects—takes caterpillars and ants (Sprunt, 1957a).
Nest: Built in bushes, blackberry vines or canes, on swamp palmetto leaf, in densest watery swamps, 2–5 ft. above ground; a cup of

stalks of weeds, grasses, skeletonized leaves, mosses, lined with black fibers of *Ramalina* lichen.
Eggs: Mar.–June; 3–4, pure white, glossy, rarely spotted with brown.
Incubation: Period of and age when young first fly unknown.
Status: So rare that in present breeding or wintering distribution, only an occasional non-breeding bird reported; it is protected by federal law and not even scientific collecting of it is permitted; possible reason for rarity is drainage and cutting off of river-bottom forests where it lived (Committee on Rare and Endangered Wildlife Species, 1966). See also Vincent (1966), and for interesting history, see Bent (1953); Sprunt (1957a).
Range: Nests in heavily wooded swamps and bottomlands, extremely local; now, or formerly, in se. Mo., ne. Ark., s.-c. Ky., c. Ala., and se. S.C.; has been seen in nesting season also in Va. and in N.C. and south to La., Miss., and s. Ala.; in migration keeps to tallest trees along swampy rivers; winters in Cuba and Isle of Pines; rarely north to s. Miss. and s. Ga. (Okefenokee Swamp); transient in Fla. Keys and Bahamas.

Warbler, bay-breasted, *Dendroica castanea* (den-DROY-kah cas-TAY-nee-ah); genus name: *see* Warbler, Audubon's (yellow-rumped); species name: Lat., a chestnut, in allusion to the bay, or chestnut, color of this species (Coues, 1882). (Color ill., page 985.) Summers in northern coniferous forests; one of larger warblers; 5–6 in. long; wingspread 8¼–9¼ in.; *crown chestnut, chin, throat, sides chestnut;* upperparts gray with black streaking, *patch on side of neck buffy,* two white wing bars; outer tail feathers spotted with white; rest of underparts buffy or whitish; eyes brown; legs light brown; female duller; immatures in fall olive green above, buffy white below; sometimes chestnut tinge on sides; male sings high-pitched, thin sibilant notes; similar in quality to that of Blackburnian, blackpoll, black-and-white, and Cape May warblers (see Bent, 1953, for details); moves deliberately about around small northern forest openings, feeding at all heights, passing from branch to branch by hops or short flights.

Feeding Habits: At times very active in trees, especially at mid-level, searches each leaf and flower, sometimes flits about terminal twigs, also "flycatches" in air, eats beetles, flies, moths, cankerworms, green spanworms, leaf-hoppers, grasshoppers, sometimes eats berries of Virginia creeper and mulberries (Oberholser, 1957).
Nest: Loosely built, of coarse dried grass stalks, twigs, roots, mosses, lichens, bark strips, lined with bark strips and hairs of northern hare; built on horizontal branch of spruce, hemlock, birch, or other tree, and even in shrub, usually 5–20 ft. or to 50 ft. above ground.
Eggs: May–July; 3–7, usually 4–5, white, blue-white, green-white, or pale gray, spotted or blotched with brown or lilac.
Incubation: By female, 12–13 days; young first fly 11–12 days after hatching (Mendall, 1937).

Other Names: Autumnal warbler; bay-breast; little chocolate-breast titmouse.
Host to Cowbirds: Only 2 records, both from Kamouraska, Que., one July 1951, another June 1952; protected from cowbird parasitism because breeding range and environment mostly different from that of brown-headed cowbird (Friedmann, 1963). *See* cowbirds in Troupial Family.
Hybrids: A cross between a bay-breasted warbler and a blackpoll warbler reported (Gray, 1958).
Weights: In fall, coastal N.J. (14), 9.3–13.4 gr. (Murray and Jehl, 1964), or ⅓–½ oz.; in Kans., adult male (1), 19.2 gr., or about ¾ oz.; adult female (1), 11.7 gr. (Tordoff and Mengel, 1956).
Range: Nests in evergreen or mixed evergreen-hardwood forests, from c. Man., n. Ont., c. Que., N.B., and c. Nova Scotia south to s. Man., ne. Minn., n. Wisc., s. Ont., s. Que., ne. N.Y., c. Vt., N.H., and s. Me.; winters from c. Panama to n. Colombia, w. Venezuela; reported in summer in ne. B.C., sw. Mack., n. and c. Alta., and se. Sask., and n. Mich.; accidental in Greenland and Bermuda.

Warbler, Birch. *See* Warbler, Nashville.

Warbler, black-and-white, *Mniotilta varia* (nye-oh-TILL-tah VAY-rih-ah); genus name: from Gr. *mnion*, moss, and *tillein*, to pull out; species name: Lat., variegated, refers to varied markings of plumage. (Color ill., page 985.) Common in deciduous woods in summer from s.-c. Canada south through prairie states to Tex., east to n. La. and Atlantic coast and north to Newfoundland; 4½–5½ in. long; wingspread 8¼–9 in.; striped lengthwise with black and white; sides streaked, belly white, conspicuous white stripe over and under each eye; slender bill, unlike other warblers, is slightly curved; *creeps* along branches and trunks of trees; female like male but has duller white underparts; as male moves over branches in mature or second-growth deciduous and mixed deciduous-coniferous forests, sings a thin, wiry *weesee, weesee, weesee, weesee, weesee;* call note is *chip!*, like that of blackpoll.

Feeding Habits: In searches over trunks and larger limbs of trees, eats caterpillars of gypsy moth, ants, moths, flies, bugs, click beetles, round-headed wood borers, leaf beetles, weevils, leafhoppers, plant lice, etc., also many spiders and daddy long legs (Tyler, 1953a).
Nest: Usually on ground against shrub or tree, in cavities at top of stumps, in depression at base of stump, rock, or log; of dry leaves, coarse grass, strips of inner bark, pine needles, and rootlets; cup lined with finer grasses, horsehair, or even fine copper wire when available.
Eggs: Apr.–June; 4–5, usually 5, white or cream-white, finely speckled with browns.
Incubation: About 10–12 days; young leave nest 8–12 days after hatching.
Other Names: Black-and-white creeper; black-and-white creeping warbler; blue-and-white striped or pied creeper; creeping warbler; striped warbler; varied creeping warbler; whitepoll warbler.

Age: One reported by Anderson and Maxfield (1967) at least 6 years old; one female, banded near Hillsboro, N.C., Sept. 1957, killed Philadelphia, Pa., Sept. 1968, by flying into window, when at least 11 years old (Blake and Cadbury, 1969).

Host to Cowbirds: Somewhat uncommonly; only 38 records (Friedmann, 1963), distributed Alta. to Ont., and Que. southward to Mass., R.I., Conn., N.Y., Pa., Ohio, Ill., Mich., Miss., Iowa, Kans., and S.C.

Weights: In fall, coastal N.J. (247), 7.9–14.9 gr. (Murray and Jehl, 1964), or ¼–½ oz.; in Kans., adult male killed at TV tower, 12.5 gr.; adult females (2), 10 gr. each (Tordoff and Mengel, 1956).

Range: Nests from ne. B.C. across c. and s. Canada to Newfoundland, south to c. Tex., se. La., n. Miss., c. Ala., c. Ga., c. S.C., and se. N.C.; winters from s. Baja Calif., Mexico, s. Tex., and c. Fla. to n. S. America and the Bahamas.

Warbler, black-and-yellow. *See* Warbler, magnolia.

Warbler, Blackburnian, *Dendroica fusca* (den-DROY-kah FUSS-kah); genus name: *see* Warbler, Audubon's (yellow-rumped); species name: Lat., dark, dusky; in 1788 named *Motacilla blackburniae* by Johann Gmelin for Anna Blackburne, 18th-century English botanist; later *blackburniae* was discarded because of a prior specific name, *fusca*, given the bird by P. L. S. Müller, Dutch professor at Erlangen, Germany, in his *Natursystem* (1776). (Color ill., page 985.) In summer mostly s.-c. and se. Canada, ne. U.S., south in mountains of e. U.S. to Ga.; 4¼ in. long; wingspread 7½–8½ in.; male in breeding plumage has black-and-white upperparts, *brilliant orange* about head, on throat and upper breast; black back is white-streaked; black wings with white patches; sides streaked with black; belly buff-white; legs and feet black; female duller and with white wing *bars* instead of patches; immatures have pale yellow face, indistinctly streaked on sides; is a treetop warbler in summer in both deciduous and coniferous northern forests or in mixed (both), especially with large spruces, firs, hemlocks, or pines; in spring on nesting grounds, likes to perch on highest tip of spruce or dead chestnut with fiery breast gleaming in sunlight, singing thin, wiry song (see Peterson, 1961, for phonetic rendition of two songs).

Feeding Habits: Eats beetles, small caterpillars, ants, crane flies; hops from limb to limb of tall trees looking over leaves and twigs, occasionally darts out and catches insects in the air (Bent, 1953); will also eat berries.

Nest: On horizontal branch of spruce, pine, hemlock, cedar, well out from trunk, 5–80 ft. up; built of fine twigs, plant down, *Usnea* lichens, is deeply cupped and lined with rootlets, bark strips, hair.

Eggs: May–July; 4–5, usually 4, white or pale green-white, spotted and blotched with browns.

Incubation: About 11–12 days (Harrison, 1975).

Other Names: Fire-brand; hemlock warbler; orange-throated warbler; torch bird.

Host to Cowbirds: Very uncommon; about 10 records, host to brown-headed cowbird in Ont., Mich., Minn., N.Y.; John James Audubon was first to report this warbler as cowbird victim, 84 ft. above ground in tree of lower Hudson Valley, N.Y., and was "altitude record" for egg of a cowbird (Friedmann, 1963). *See* cowbirds in Troupial Family.

Weights: In fall, coastal N.J. (6), 7.3–10.3 gr. (Murray and Jehl, 1964), or about ⅓ oz.

Range: Nests from Alta. and s.-c. Sask. across s. Canada to n. Nova Scotia, south to c. Minn., c. Wisc., c. Mich., s. Ont., ne. Ohio, c. and w. Pa., se. N.Y., Mass., and south in Appalachians to e. Tenn., w. N.C., n.-c. Ga., nw. S.C.; winters from Guatemala to Venezuela and c. Peru; accidental in w. Mont., N.M., and Bermuda.

Warbler, black-fronted. *See* Warbler, Audubon's (yellow-rumped).

Warbler, black-headed. *See* Warbler, hooded.

Warbler, black-masked. *See* Yellowthroat, common.

Warbler, blackpoll, *Dendroica striata* (den-DROY-kah stry-AY-tah); genus name: *see* Warbler, Audubon's (yellow-rumped); species name: Lat., striped, refers to black stripes on back, rump, and flanks. (Color ill., page 985.) One of most abundant N. American warblers; in summer nests from Alaska across Canada and ne. U.S.; 5–5¾ in. long; wingspread 8–9¾ in.; male in spring, a striped smoky-gray warbler with *solid-black cap;* has white cheeks, and white throat, which distinguish it from black-and-white warbler and similar black-throated gray warbler (Robbins *et al.,* 1966); upperparts gray, streaked with black; two white wing bars; white markings on outer tail feathers; underparts white, sides streaked with black; females less heavily streaked, without black crown patch; an abundant and late migrant in spring in Atlantic states; late in May and June in Northeast, when most warblers have moved north, blackpoll moves through newly leafed forests, also trees of parks and gardens; one of common songs is high, thin, wiry *tsit, tsit, tsit, tsit,* rising slowly louder toward middle, then falling softer at end (Gross, 1953a).

Feeding Habits: Eats aphids, scale insects, and others that infest trees, gleans leaves and twigs, sometimes darts out into air to snap up in bill a passing fly, also eats many beetles, gnats, mosquitoes, cankerworms, sawflies, wasps, ants, termites; also takes spiders and their eggs, and pokeberries.

Nest: In dwarfed firs, spruces of northern part of coniferous forest, somewhat bulky, well concealed against trunk of spruces or on branches; built of twigs, sprays of spruce, pieces of bark, dried grasses, weeds, bits of moss, lichens, lined with rootlets, hair, feathers of gulls, ducks, ptarmigan, grouse, 2–12 ft. above ground (Gross, 1953a).

Eggs: June–July; 3–5, usually 4–5, white, cream-buff, or pale green, speckled with brown and lavender.

Incubation: At least 11 days; eyes open when 5 days old; both adults feed young, which fly 11–12 days after hatching.

Other Names: Autumnal warbler; blackpoll; black-polled warbler.

Accidents: Some killed by storms in migration; formerly great destruction while migrating at night through striking lighthouses, now many killed by striking tall buildings and TV towers.

Albinism: Apparently not rare (Gross, 1953a); one in collections at Philadelphia Academy of Natural Sciences with "entire plumage suffused with white" (Townsend, 1883).

Hybrids: Has occasionally crossbred with bay-breasted warbler and Cape May warbler (Gray, 1958); one extraordinary hybrid between blackpoll and northern waterthrush (Short and Robbins, 1967).

Weights: In fall, coastal N.J. (143), 8.5–22.1 gr. (Murray and Jehl, 1964), or ⅓–¾ oz.; in summer, Alaska (42), 11–15.5 gr. (Yarbrough, 1970). See migration and weight losses in Nisbet *et al.* (1963); Nisbet (1970).

Range: Nests from n.-c. Alaska and n. Yuk. south to B.C. and across s. and c. Canada to Newfoundland, south to Me., nw. Mass., and e. N.Y.; winters from c. Equador, c. Colombia, and n. Venezuela south to Peru, Chile, and Brazil; migrates through West Indies.

Warbler, black-throated blue, *Dendroica caerulescens* (den-DROY-kah see-roo-LES-enz); genus name: *see* Warbler, Audubon's (yellow-rumped); species name: from Lat. *caeruleus,* blue; turning blue, in reference to blue-gray back of male. (Color ill., page 986.) Nests across se. Canada and n. U.S., south in Appalachians to ne. Ga.; 4½–5½ in. long; wingspread 7–8 in.; male in breeding plumage, upperparts blue, sides of face and body black, square white patch on wings is diagnostic; underparts white; bill dark; eyes brown; legs and feet dark; female has olive-green upperparts, also white wing patch, which may be very small or partly concealed; a white streak over eyes; underparts buffy; one of commonest migrants in e. U.S.; in trees of parks and gardens in spring en route to summer home in northern coniferous and mixed deciduous forests with dense undergrowth; in Appalachians, in evergreen or deciduous undergrowth; one of typical songs floating up from rhododendron thickets is three or four slowly drawled notes, the last commonly slurred up—*zee-zee-zee-ee* or *I am la-zy.*

Feeding Habits: Eats moths, tent caterpillars, flies, beetles, aphids, also seeds and fruits.

Nest: Built close to ground in dense undergrowth in fork of rhododendrons, laurel, yews, small firs, hemlocks, spruces, raspberry and blueberry bushes, 1–4 ft. above ground; of strips of birch bark, straws, ferns, dry leaves, lined with black rootlets, horsehair, skunk fur, mosses, and even porcupine quills.

Eggs: May–July; 3–5, usually 4, white or cream-white, speckled or blotched with browns, grays.

Incubation: By female; adults extraordinarily fearless of persons at nest when pair feeding young; incubation 12 days, female broods young, both parents feed them; first fly 10 days after hatching.

Other Names: Black-throat; blue flycatcher.
Host to Cowbirds: Very infrequent; only 10 records, distributed in Ont., Que., R.I., and N.Y. (Friedmann, 1963).
Weights: In fall, coastal N.J. (88), 7.5–13 gr. (Murray and Jehl, 1964), or about ¼–½ oz.; in Kans., killed in autumn at TV tower, immature males (2), 13.8 and 14.1 gr., excessively fat; immature female (1), 11.4 gr., fat (Tordoff and Mengel, 1956); in fall migration, in Fla., adult males (93), 9.6–14 gr.; adult females (94), 9.6–13.8 gr. (Taylor, W.K., 1973).
Range: Nests from c. Sask. across s. Canada, south to c. Minn., n. Mich., s. Ont., n. Conn., and in Appalachians south to ne. Ga.; winters from Gulf coast south to Greater Antilles, Virgin Is., Bahamas, and Bermuda; has strayed to Calif. and S. America.

Warbler, black-throated gray, *Dendroica nigrescens* (den-DROY-kah nih-GRES-enz); genus name: *see* Warbler, Audubon's (yellow-rumped); species name: Lat., blackening, in reference to dark or dusky parts of plumage. (Color ill., page 986.) W. N. America; 4½–5 in. long; male in breeding plumage has black head, chin, and throat, horizontal white line above eyes and below cheeks; upperparts blue-gray; underparts white with black-streaked sides; two white wing bars; tiny spot of bright yellow in front of dark eyes; females similar, but have white throat and tend to be gray where male is black; in North lives about openings in fir forests, and through most of range favors dry deciduous or coniferous scrub on slopes such as oaks, pinyons, junipers, and manzanitas (Bent, 1953); sings lazy, drawling *wee-zy, wee-zy, wee-zy, wee-zy-weet.*

Feeding Habits: Forages among leaves of trees and bushes for insects, especially fond of oakworms and other green caterpillars; no detailed study made of its diet.
Nest: In northern parts of range (Wash.) builds in fir trees 7–50 ft. up on branch; nest of plant fibers, dry grasses, weed stalks, lined with feathers and hairs of horses, cows, and rabbits, mosses, stems of flowers; also built in crotch of manzanita bushes, and golden oak saplings farther south usually 3–10 ft. up (Calif.).
Eggs: May–July; 3–5, usually 4, white, cream-white, speckled, spotted with browns.
Incubation: Period of and age when young first fly unknown.
Host to Cowbirds: Only 3 records, all victimized by brown-headed cowbird, in s. Ariz., San Bernardino County, Calif., and Oakley, Cassia County, Idaho (Friedmann, 1963), but this warbler studied so little that relationship with cowbirds is poorly documented.
Range: Nests from sw. B.C., w. Wash., c. Ore., sw. Idaho, n. Utah, sw. Wyo., nw. and c. Colo., south in mountains to n. Baja Calif., Ariz., and e. and s. N.M.; winters from coastal and s. Calif., s. Ariz., south to s. Baja Calif. and s. Mexico; accidental in several eastern states.

Warbler, black-throated green, *Dendroica virens* (den-DROY-kah VIR-enz); genus name: *see* Warbler, Audubon's (yellow-rumped); species name: Lat., becoming green. (Color ill., page 986.) In summer, across s. Can-
ada and n. U.S. and south in Appalachians; 4¼–5½ in. long; wingspread 7–8 in.; male in breeding plumage is bright yellowish and olive green above, sometimes spotted or streaked with black; *sides of face and sides of throat bright yellow*—no other eastern warbler has cheeks this color (Robbins *et al.*, 1966); male has *black throat;* flanks and sides streaked with black, rest of underparts white; two white wing bars; female similar but duller, with no black on throat; likes open woods and northern coniferous forests with large pines, hemlocks, and spruces, and larches in bogs, also second-growth hardwoods, and old cedar-grown pastures, but prefers woods; also rather common in pine barrens in Me., jack pines in Mich. (Bent, 1953); a persistent singer, has dreamy, attractive lisping or buzzing songs with series of *zree* notes; one song likened to *trees, trees, murmuring trees;* remains hidden in trees when singing and difficult to see.

Feeding Habits: Eats beetles, flies, moths, foliage-eating caterpillars such as tent caterpillars, also cankerworms, leaf rollers, and berries of poison ivy (Bent, 1953).
Nest: In crotch usually of small or large evergreen or in hardwood tree, on horizontal branch, 8 in. to 80 ft. above ground, a neat cup of twigs, grasses, strips of inner bark, mosses, lichens, spider's silk, lined with mammal hairs and birds' feathers.
Eggs: May–July; 4–5, usually 4, gray-white or cream-white, speckled, spotted, or blotched with browns, purple.
Incubation: Mostly by female, 12 days; young leave nest 8–10 days after hatching; both parents feed and care for young (Bent, 1953). See also Pitelka (1940) and Nice (1939) for interesting details.
Other Names: Evergreen warbler; green black-throat; green black-throated flycatcher.
Age: A male reported by Patterson (1971), banded in Me., still alive at 6 years old; another, banded when immature at Overbrook, Pa., Oct. 1934, was shot by an Indian at Tetela, Oaxaca, Mexico, Apr. 1936 (Lincoln, 1936b).
Host to Cowbirds: Very infrequently reported; only 15 records to brown-headed cowbird (Friedmann, 1963).
Weights: In fall, coastal N.J. (21), 6.5–11.5 gr. (Murray and Jehl, 1964), or about ⅓ oz.
Range: Nests from s.-c. Mack., n.-c. Sask., n.-c. Man., east to Newfoundland and s. Nova Scotia, south to c. Alta., s. Man., e-c. Minn., c. Wisc., c. Mich., e. and se. Ohio, Pa., and n. N.J., south in Appalachians to n. Ala. and n. Ga.; winters from s. Tex. and s. Fla. south through e. Mexico to Panama and Greater Antilles; has strayed to Bermuda, Colo., Calif., where casual in spring, very rare in fall (see Small, 1974), also to Ariz., where a rare fall and spring migrant (Phillips *et al.*, 1964), Labrador, Greenland, and Germany; common in migration in e. N. America.

Warbler, blue. *See* Warbler, cerulean.

Warbler, blue-winged, *Vermivora pinus* (ver-MIV-oh-rah PIE-nus); genus name: *see* Warbler, Bachman's; species name: from Lat. word meaning pine tree (Coues, 1882); name is
misnomer because it is not associated with pines (Bent, 1953). (Color ill., page 987.) 4½–5 in. long; wingspread 6¾–7½ in.; eastern warbler; male in breeding plumage has bright yellow head, breast, and underparts (unstreaked); upperparts bright olive green; *narrow black line through eyes;* blue-gray wings with two white wing bars also distinctive; eyes dark brown; legs and feet dark bluish; female duller, less yellow on crown; immatures, olive green with wings like adults; uncommon, in summer lives in old brushy pastures, weed-grown fence-rows, sometimes in deep swamp woods, edges of woods, and in clearings, and near borders of streams; unobtrusive, quiet and deliberate movements like vireo, stays fairly close to ground, but male sings from treetop perch, drowsy insectlike *sw-e-e-e-e ze-e-e-e-e* (Bent, 1953), likened to spoken syllables *bee-buzz, bee-buzz,* first note usually higher in pitch.

Feeding Habits: Eats small beetles, ants, caterpillars, spiders.
Nest: Close to or on ground, cone-shaped, of dead leaves and grasses, fragments of bark, cup lined with bark of wild grapevine, horsehair, or fine grasses, built in upright stems of blackberry, weeds, grasses, also under bushes on ground and between exposed roots of stump.
Eggs: May–July; 4–7, usually 5–6, white, finely speckled with browns, grays.
Incubation: About 10–12 days; young leave nest when 10–11 days old.
Other Names: Blue-winged swamp warbler; blue-winged yellow warbler.
Age: One, banded Ramsay, N.J., at least 5 years old when retrapped (Dater, 1967); another, banded Ashtabula, Ohio, trapped and released in same area when 5 years, 11 months, old (Kennard, 1975).
Host to Cowbirds: Fairly frequent; 35 records distributed in Ala., Conn., Ind., Iowa, Md., Mich., Minn., Mo., N.J., N.Y., Ohio, Pa., and Va. (Friedmann, 1963).
Hybrids: Interbreeds with golden-winged warbler, a close relative, and produces Brewster's warbler, sometimes followed in second generation by Lawrence's warbler, another hybrid; also crossbreeds with Kentucky warbler, which produced famous Cincinnati warbler (see "Hypothetical List" in A.O.U. *Check-list*, 1957), and with mourning warbler (McCamey, 1950; Cockrum, 1952).
Weights: In fall, coastal N.J. (4), 8.3–11 gr. (Murray and Jehl, 1964), or about ⅓ oz.
Range: Nests from e.-c. Neb., c. Iowa, se. Minn., s. Wisc., s. Mich., n. Ohio, nw. Pa., w. and se. N.Y., se. Mass., south to Md., Del., n. Va., and N.C., and nw. Ark., e.-c. Mo., s. Ill., c. Tenn., and n. Ala; winters from s. Mexico to Nicaragua, rarely to n. Colombia; seen occasionally west to Calif., Cuba, and Bahamas.

Warbler, blue-winged yellow. *See* Warbler, blue-winged.

Warbler, blue-winged yellow-backed. *See* Parula, northern.

Warbler, Brewster's, *Vermivora leucobronchialis* (ver-MIV-oh-rah lew-koh-BRON-

Colima warbler

Brewster's warbler

AMERICAN WOOD WARBLER FAMILY

kih-ale-iss); genus name: *see* Warbler, Bachman's; species name: Lat., white-throated; common name: for William Brewster, who described it as a new species in 1874 from a bird he collected (shot) in 1870 at Newtonville, Mass. It was later determined to be a hybrid between the blue-winged warbler and the golden-winged warbler. The blue-winged and golden-winged often interbreed wherever their nesting ranges overlap.

Brewster's warbler, the hybrid, is similar in size to the parent warblers—about 4–5 in. long—and a typical Brewster's is marked very much like a blue-winged warbler but with *whitish underparts* instead of the solid-yellow underparts of the blue-winged. There is considerable variation in the hybrid Brewster's warblers—some have yellow wing bars like the parent golden-winged warbler instead of white wing bars as in the blue-winged, but the thin black mark through the eyes is the same as in the blue-winged. With the largely whitish underparts, sometimes tinged with yellow, these are the distinctive, or diagnostic, characters of the Brewster's warbler (Peterson, 1947). It may sing songs like either of its parents, and it mates, not with other Brewster's warblers, but with one of its parent forms.

Range: According to the A.O.U. *Check-list* of 1895, numerous Brewster's warblers had been collected by ornithologists up to that time in s. New England, the lower Hudson Valley of N.Y., in N.J., Va., and Mich. The breeding range coincides with the northern part of the range of the blue-winged warbler, but its center of distribution or abundance is in the lower part of the Connecticut R. valley and Hudson R. valley, where there is heavy interbreeding of blue-winged and golden-winged warblers. This crossbreeding produces not only the Brewster's warbler but also the much rarer, recessive hybrid the Lawrence's warbler. *See* Warbler, Lawrence's.

T. D. Carter, in reviewing his 6 years of watching a male Brewster's warbler he banded about 40 mi. northwest of New York City in Passaic County, N.J., reported that in five of its six nesting seasons it was mated to a female golden-winged warbler. In an area there called the Wyanokie Plateau, largely woodland, there are clearings, swamps, and second-growth woods—ideal country for the nesting of blue-winged and golden-winged warblers. Both are common nesting birds there, and, according to Carter, the Brewster's and Lawrence's hybrid offspring would be expected.

In migration, Brewster's warblers have been seen from La. and se. Okla. northward to Wisc. and Mass. (Broun, 1957). It has been collected (shot for scientific study) in winter in Costa Rica and Venezuela, which suggests that its wintering range may be similar to that of the golden-winged warbler (Eisenmann, 1957).

Feeding Habits: Probably like those of the blue-winged and golden-winged warblers, which are largely insect-eaters.

Warbler, Calaveras. *See* Warbler, Nashville.

Warbler, calico. Another name for the summer tanager in Tanager Family.

Warbler, Canada, *Wilsonia canadensis* (will-SO-nih-ah can-ah-DEN-sis); genus name: for Alexander Wilson, "father of American ornithology"; species name: Lat., of Canada. (Color ill., page 987.) Nests in s.-c. Canada, ne. U.S., south in Appalachians to Ga.; 5–5¾ in. long; upperparts slate gray; *bright yellow below, with black necklace on breast;* ring of yellow around eyes runs forward to bill (the "spectacles"); eyes brown; feet and legs pale yellow-brown; female and immature like male, but necklace sometimes barely discernible. Lives in luxuriant undergrowth of mature, mixed hardwoods, preferably near streams and swamps, also in deciduous second growth; very active, darting out of shrubbery in "flycatching" flights to snap insects with click of bill, also gleans them from leaves and twigs. Not especially shy or timid; male sings through much of summer, rich, animated, varied warble.

Feeding Habits: Eats beetles, mosquitoes, flies, moths, smooth caterpillars such as cankerworms.

Nest: On or near ground, usually moist place, sometimes over water, in mossy hummock, on moss-covered log or stump, in cavity in bank, in upturned roots of tree; formless, built of leaves, shreds of bark, dry grasses, weed stalks, lined with plant fibers, rootlets of ferns, horsehair.

Eggs: May–June; 3–5, usually 4, white or cream-white, speckled, spotted, or blotched with browns, purples.

Incubation: Period of and age when young first fly unknown (Bent, 1953).

Other Names: Canada flycatcher; Canadian flycatching warbler; necklace warbler; speckled Canada warbler; spotted Canadian warbler.

Age: One at least 6 years old (Anderson and Maxfield, 1967); a female, banded Candor, N.Y., found dead at Cleveland Heights, Ohio, when 7 years, 11 months, old (Kennard, 1975).

Host to Cowbirds: Regular, but infrequent; reported in Sask., Ont., N.B., N.Y., Mich., Minn., and Ind. (Friedmann, 1963).

Weights: In fall, coastal N.J. (48), 7.3–13 gr. (Murray and Jehl, 1964), or about ¼–½ oz.

Range: Nests from n.-c. Alta. across s. Canada, to s. Que., south to s. Man., c. Minn., n. Wisc., c. Mich., and n. Ohio, south through Appalachians to e. Tenn., n.w. Ga., w. N.C., w. Va., w. Md., e.-c. Pa., n. N.J., se. N.Y., Conn., R.I., Mass., Me., N.B.; n. and w. S. America; has wandered to Greenland, Alaska, and St. Croix and Guadalupe in West Indies.

Warbler, Cape May, *Dendroica tigrina* (den-DROY-kah tig-RYE-nah); genus name: *see* Warbler, Audubon's (yellow-rumped); species name: from Lat. *tigrinus,* striped (like tiger, *tigris*); common name: for Cape May, N.J., where the first one scientifically described was collected (shot) in maple swamp, May 1811 (Wilson, 1808–14). (Color ill., page 987.) 5–5½ in. long; wingspread 7½–8½ in.; male in breeding plumage, yellow underparts heavily streaked with black; yellow rump; black cap; *chestnut patch on cheeks;* upperparts olive green striped with black; large white wing patch; bill black; eyes brown; legs and feet dark; female, color pattern similar to male but duller; no chestnut on cheeks; little white in wings; immature like female but duller. Once considered rare, now seen more frequently as hurried migrant through e. U.S. and Mississippi Valley; passes through hardwood and coniferous woods and trees, shrubs of parks, towns; on northern nesting grounds, prefers open, park-like mature stands of spruces and firs; male feeding in top of tall fir sometimes sings faint, listless *zee-zee-zee-zee,* unhurried monotone, suggests notes of black-and-white warbler.

Feeding Habits: Darts into air, or may search among fir needles or in thickets; eats beetles, crickets, dragonflies, small moths, caterpillars, spruce budworms, flies, ants, wasps, small bees, daddy longlegs, and spiders, also punctures grapes with bill for juice; takes sap from holes drilled in bark by sapsuckers.
Nest: Round or cuplike, on branch of spruce or fir, near top, 30–60 ft above ground.
Eggs: June; usually 6–7, rarely 4–9, cream-white, richly spotted with browns, grays.
Incubation: Period of and age when young first fly unknown.
Host to Cowbirds: Only 1 record (Friedmann, 1963).
Hybrids: Reported crosses of Cape May with blackpoll warbler, Townsend's warbler, and hermit warbler (Gray, 1958).
Weights: About ¼–½ oz.; in fall migration, in Fla., adult males (24), 10.2–15.2 gr., or about ⅓–½ oz.; adult females (20), 10–14.2 gr. (Taylor, W. K., 1973).
Range: Nests from n. B.C. across Canada to s. Que., south to ne. N.D., Minn., n. Wisc., n. Mich., s. Ont., ne. N.Y., s. Me., c. Vt., s. N.B., and c. Nova Scotia; winters in s. Mexico and in West Indies; accidental in Calif., Ariz., and, in winter, in W.Va.

Warbler, cerulean, *Dendroica cerulea* (den-DROY-cah see-RULE-ee-ah); genus name: *see* Warbler, Audubon's (yellow-rumped); species name: Lat., blue, azure (Coues, 1882). (Color ill., page 987.) Mostly in East and Midwest; male is only blue-backed, white-throated warbler (Robbins *et al.,* 1966); 4–5 in. long; wingspread 7¼–8¼ in.; male in breeding plumage, light blue-gray above; white underparts; blue-black band across chest; flanks streaked with black; two white wing bars; bill black; eyes dark brown; feet and legs dusky; female, and immatures in fall, duller, without breast band; yellow-white stripe over eyes; migrates north mostly in Mississippi Valley, mainly in summer west of Alleghenies, east of Great Plains, but local; lives in open hardwoods either upland or along streams, difficult to see, stays mostly in tops of tallest deciduous trees; male perches and sings from daybreak to dark in nesting season; two different songs; common one, rising in pitch at end, is *wee wee wee wee, bzzz* (Bent, 1953).

Feeding Habits: Catches flying insects or picks from leaves, while keeping out of sight; warily flies from tree to tree; like other warblers, eats mainly insects, but diet little studied.
Nest: Usually built in tall elm, oak, maple, basswood, tulip tree, 15–90 ft. above ground, well

out on branch, often over forest opening; woven of fine strips of bark, weed stalks, grasses, decorated outside with mosses, lichens, spider's silk; cup very shallow, lined with mosses, hairs.
Eggs: May–July; 3–5, usually 4, gray-, cream-, green-white, speckled, spotted, or blotched with browns.
Incubation: 12–13 days, by female (Harrison, 1975).
Other Names: Azure warbler; blue warbler.
Host to Cowbirds: Uncommonly reported; according to Friedmann (1963), because (like Cape May warbler) nests high in trees, where nests rarely discovered, but enough records (12) to establish cerulean warbler as uncommon victim of brown-headed cowbird; reported from Ont., Mich., Ind., N.Y., Pa., and Va.
Range: Nests from se. Neb., n. Iowa, se. Minn., s. Wisc., s. Mich., s. Ont., to e. Pa., se. N.Y., n. N.J., south to ne. Tex., se. La., c. Ala., c. N.C., c. Va., s. Md., and Del.; winters in n. S. America south to Bolivia; has strayed to Colo., Man., Calif., and Baja Calif., N.D., Conn., Mass., R.I., N.H.

Warbler, chestnut-sided, *Dendroica pensylvanica* (den-DROY-kah pen-sill-VAY-nih-kah); genus name: *see* Warbler, Audubon's (yellow-rumped); species name: Lat., of Pennsylvania, or "Penn's Woods." (Color ill., page 987.) Considered a rare bird in early 19th century—Audubon saw it only once—later, as woodlands of e. and middle U.S. cut off and chestnut-sided's favorite second-growth woodlands multiplied, it increased until one of commonest warblers, especially in northern half of U.S. east of Great Plains (Bent, 1953); 4½–5¼ in. long; *only warbler that is all-white below, except for its broad stripe of chestnut on sides, at all seasons;* male in breeding plumage and female have combined yellow–green crown and chestnut sides; upperparts light olive with black streakings; two pale yellow-white wing bars; eyes dark brown; legs and feet slate blue; females generally duller; immatures uniform olive green above, white below, no chestnut sides or trace only; in spring, main eastern migration route is north along or near Alleghenies and the Mississippi Valley; is sprightly, active in cut-over woods, thickets, and bushes along country roads; male, tail high, wings drooping, chases insects or rises to top of bush to sing territorial song—loud musical phrases, rhythm often expressed in human phrases: *I wish, I wish, I wish to see Miss Beecher!* and *sweet, sweet, sweet, I'll switch you!*

Feeding Habits: Forages between ground and tops of small trees; "flycatches" or flutters before leaves or gleans foliage of shrubs or low plants; eats cankerworms, caterpillars of gypsy moth, small moths, small grasshoppers, spiders, also eats a few seeds or berries.
Nest: Built in shrub or sapling 1–4 ft. up from ground in fork of blackberry, hardhack, hazel, azalea, viburnum, huckleberry bushes; of fine strips of cedars and grapevines, shredded weed stems, plant down and fibers; cup lined with fine grasses, horse and cow hairs.

Eggs: May–July; 3–5, usually 4, white, cream-white, or green-white, speckled, spotted, or blotched with browns, purple.
Incubation: By female, 12–13 days; young first fly at 10–12 days old, when leave nest (Bent, 1953).
Other Names: Bloody-side warbler; golden-crowned flycatcher; Quebec warbler; yellow-crowned warbler.
Age: One, banded Manchester, N.H., trapped and released in same area when 5 years, 1 month, old (Kennard, 1975).
Host to Cowbirds: Frequent; more than 75 records, distributed over Sask., Ont., and Que., Me., Mass., Conn., N.Y., N.J., Pa., Md., Ohio, Mich., Minn., Iowa, and Neb.
Weights: In fall, coastal N.J. (14), 8–11.5 gr., or about ⅓ oz.
Range: Nests from e.-c. Sask. across s. Canada to N.B. and Nova Scotia, south to n.-c. N.D., e. Neb., se. Minn., s. Wisc., s. Mich., n. Ohio, c. and w. Md., se. Pa., c. N.J., N.Y., Mass., and Me., and south in mountains to Ga., also nw. S.C.; formerly in Iowa, Mo., and Ind., winters from s. Nicaragua to Panama; has strayed to Calif., Wyo., Colo., Okla., Alta., Bermuda, Greenland; first record state of Wash., June 1960 (Marshall, 1970).

Warbler, Cincinnati. A hybrid. The first one known to science was shot near Cincinnati and described in 1880 as a new species (Langdon, 1880), but was apparently a hybrid between a blue-winged warbler and a Kentucky warbler (Ridgway, 1880). A second one was collected (shot) in sw. Mich. on May 28, 1948 (Tyler, 1953b).

Warbler, Colima, *Vermivora crissalis* (ver-MIV-oh-rah kris-ALE-iss); genus name: *see* Warbler, Bachman's; species name: Lat., pertaining to the tail, and the crissum, or brightly colored undertail coverts; common name: for state of Colima (coe-LEE-mah), sw. Mexico, where type specimen collected. A Mexican species first reported nesting in U.S. in 1932 in Chisos Mtns., sw. Tex.; one of least-known of all N. American warblers, but common in summer, according to Van Tyne (1957), in Boot Spring Valley, Chisos Mtns., among young maples and deciduous oaks; 4½–5 in. long; male has chestnut cap, gray-brown to olive-brown upperparts, pale, smoke-gray breast, with very little yellow (closely related similar Virginia's warbler has gray upperparts, yellowish breast); Colima also has brighter yellow crissum and more intense yellow rump; female similar to male with no yellow on breast; in Chisos lives at altitude of 6,000–7,500 ft.; in stunted oaks, maples, pines of slopes and canyons; moves about rather deliberately, like vireo; not shy; call note is sharp *psit!;* male sings a long trill somewhat like pine warbler or chipping sparrow from bushes and small trees or from 20-ft. treetop (Van Tyne, 1957).

Feeding Habits: Insects, but no detailed studies of.
Nest: Hidden by leaves, on ground between rocks on bank of dry stream bed or on edge of talus slope; of loosely woven grasses, dry

leaves, mosses, strips of cedar bark, lined with fur or hair.

Eggs: May; 4, cream-white, wreathed at larger end with browns.

Incubation: Period of and age when young first fly unknown.

Range: Nests in Chisos Mtns., Tex., south in Sierra Madre Occidental, ne. Mexico; winters in s. Mexico but precise limits of range still not known.

Warbler, Connecticut, *Oporornis agilis* (op-or-OR-nis AH-jih-liss); genus name: Lat., from Gr. *opora,* autumnal, and *ornis,* bird; species name: Lat., active, nimble, busy; common name: Alexander Wilson discovered this warbler in Conn. in 1812 and named it for the state, although it is only a visitor there in fall migration. (Color ill., page 989.) Not much known about it for 70 years after its discovery (in 1883, E. T. Seton found in Man. Canada, first nest known to ornithologists); 5¼–6 in. long; olive green above; pale yellow below; gray hood (head, throat, upper breast) is sharply defined where gray breast meets yellow underparts; has *white* eye-ring (buffy in immature); female and immature like male but duller, hood faint; in migration seen in thickets of low wet woods or wet meadows; in summer, lives in spruce-tamarack bogs in n. U.S. and e. Canada; in w. Canada, where more numerous, lives on dry ridges or in poplar and aspen woods; a shy elusive bird on nesting grounds, remains hidden from observer but male's frequent, loud singing locates bird; one song phrased *beecher, beecher, beecher, beecher,* like song of ovenbird but no rise in sound or pitch; another, *whip-pity, whip-pity, whip,* with emphasis on last syllable, is like song of yellowthroat; call is sharp metallic *peek* or *plink,* different from that of other warblers (Bent, 1953).

Feeding Habits: Feeds on or near ground; *walks* along branches picking up insects and spiders from cracks or crevices in bark.

Nest: On ground, sunk in mound of moss in bog or beside bunch of dry grass or weeds near poplar woods; built of grasses, bark strips, lined with plant fibers or hair.

Eggs: June; 3–5, cream-white, speckled and blotched with black, brown, and lilac; no wreath at larger end as in eggs of other warblers.

Incubation: Period of and age when young first fly unknown.

Other Names: Bog black-throat; swamp warbler; tamarack warbler.

Weights: In fall, coastal N.J. (29), 10.9–20.3 gr. (Murray and Jehl, 1964), or ⅓–¾ oz.

Range: Nests across Canada from B.C. to n. Ont. and nw. Que., south to n. Minn., n. Wisc., n. Mich., and c. Ont.; winters in Mexico and nw. S. America; has wandered to Utah and Ariz.

Warbler, crape. *See* Warbler, mourning.

Warbler, creeping. *See* Warbler, black-and-white.

Warbler, desert. *See* Warbler, Lucy's.

Warbler, dusky. *See* Warbler, orange-crowned.

Warbler, evergreen. *See* Warbler, black-throated green.

Warbler, fan-tailed, *Euthlypis lachrymosa* (YOUTH-lip-iss lack-rih-MOE-sah); genus name: from Gr. word meaning an agreeable finch; species name: Lat., tearful (Skutch, 1957a); sad, lamentable (Levine *et al.,* 1967). Mexican and C. American species reported only once in N. America (Baja Calif., 1925); 5½–6 in. long; head largely black with yellow; crown spot and a conspicuous white spot on each eyelid and between eye and bill; upperparts dark grayish olive, no markings on dark wings but conspicuous white tips on outer feathers of broad tail; underparts yellow, very bright on throat, breast tawny; female like male, sometimes paler; walks like ovenbird and waterthrushes over rocks and fallen logs of tropical forest floor in small parties seeking insects; sometimes follows swarms of army ants; constantly fans and contracts tail feathers; songs of male rich, long, and varied; nothing known of nesting habits.

Range: Locally common in Mexico (except extreme north) and along Pacific slope of C. America to Nicaragua (Skutch, 1957a).

Warbler, golden. *See* Warbler, prothonotary, and Warbler, yellow.

Warbler, golden-cheeked, *Dendroica chrysoparia* (den-DROY-kah kris-op-AY-rih-ah); genus name: *see* Warbler, Audubon's (yellow-rumped); species name: from Gr. *chrysos,* gold, and *pareia,* cheek; "golden-cheeked." 4½–5 in. long; rare over general range; once common in limited, narrow nesting range in Tex., becoming rare because of habitat destruction and cowbird parasitism; upperparts of male in breeding plumage deep black from crown to tail; *golden cheeks, margined with black,* and a black eye streak (similar black-throated green warbler does not have black cap and has olive-green upperparts); underparts white, except black throat; two white wing bars; upperparts of female golden-cheeked streaked, not solid black; female similar to male but back dark green, throat white; not a bird of tall-tree forest but summers in growth of mountain cedar (juniper), Spanish, black, and live oaks 10–20 ft. high, especially in cedar "brakes" and associated brush on dry upper slopes and ridges of Edwards Plateau in s.-c. Tex.; female shy and seldom noted on nesting range, but male conspicuous, very active, continually flying from tree to tree when feeding; on clear days, from dawn to dusk, sings short, hurried *tweeah, tweeah, twee-sy,* and a slower *tweeah, easeh, eachy*—quality of voice resembling song of black-throated green warbler (Bent, 1953); golden-cheeked threatened by brush removal and cutting of old cedars, replaced by grass for grazing; in 1964, estimated *total* population 15,000 (Vincent, 1966). *See* Rare and Threatened Species.

Feeding Habits: Insects, but no detailed studies.

Nest: Usually in upright fork of older, mature Ashe cedars, 6–20 ft. above ground; built of shredded cedar bark, grasses, rootlets, spider's silk, cup lined with hairs and feathers, especially of quail and cardinal.

Eggs: Apr.–June; 3–5, usually 4, white or cream-white, speckled and spotted with browns and grays.

Incubation: Period of and age when young first fly unknown.

Host to Cowbirds: 9 records in Tex., to brown-headed cowbird, 6 from Comal County, 3 from Kerr County.

Range: Nests in several counties of s.-c. Tex., in Edwards Plateau region; winters in C. America.

Warbler, golden-crowned. *See* Warbler, myrtle (yellow-rumped).

Warbler, golden-winged, *Vermivora chrysoptera* (ver-MIV-oh-rah kris-OP-ter-ah); genus name: *see* Warbler, Bachman's; species name: from Gr. *chrysos,* gold, and *pteron,* wing. (Color ill., page 989.) An uncommon warbler of e. U.S.; 5–5¼ in. long; only warbler that has combination of black throat and yellow patch in wings; pearl gray above, white below; has black patch through eyes; resembles black-capped chickadee but has yellow crown; female like male, but eye patch and throat gray; on nesting range lives along brier-grown edges and in openings of swampy deciduous woodlands, or in old pastures and hillsides overgrown with dense scrubby thickets; in Allegheny Mtns., lives in high dry chestnut sprout and scrub pine lands; male sings generally from high branch bare of leaves; throws head back, points bill to sky, but song is buzzy, insectlike; one is *beee-bz-bz-bz.*

Feeding Habits: Sprightly when feeding, swings upside down from twigs like chickadee, from treetops to lower shrubs, looking under leaves for small green or brown caterpillars ("measuring worms") that eat leaves of forest, fruit, and shade trees, also takes spiders.

Nest: Bulky, generally on or near ground, supported by stalks of goldenrod, meadow rue, or at base of shrub or tree, or hidden deep in clump of grass; built of dried grasses, strips of grapevine bark, the cup lined with shredded bark or a few hairs.

Eggs: May–June; 4–7, usually 4–5, white or cream-white, speckled or blotched with browns.

Incubation: Reported about 10 days; young first fly at 10 days old.

Other Names: Blue golden-winged warbler; golden-winged flycatcher; golden-winged swamp warbler.

Age: A male, banded Powdermill Nature Reserve, Rector, Pa., trapped and released in same area when 6 years, 11 months, old (Kennard, 1975).

Host to Cowbirds: Occasional; 17 records, distributed through Mass., N.Y., N.J., Pa., Mich., and Wisc., to brown-headed cowbird; where golden-winged abundant, is regular victim.

Hybrids: Interbreeds with blue-winged warbler where their nesting ranges overlap. *See* Warbler, Brewster's, and Warbler, Lawrence's; Hybrid.

Range: Nests from se. Man., e.-c. Minn., n.-c. Wisc., n. Mich., s. Ont., c. N.Y., s. Conn., e. Mass., south to se. Iowa, n. Ill., n. Ind., s. Ohio,

e. Tenn., n. Ga., nw. S.C., W.Va., n.-c. Md., and se. Pa.; winters in C. America and n. S. America; has wandered to Me., N.H., and Vt.

Warbler, Grace's, *Dendroica graciae* (den-DROY-kah GRACE-ih-ee); genus name: *see* Warbler, Audubon's (yellow-rumped); species and common names: given in 1865 by Spencer F. Baird for then 18-year-old Grace Darling Coues, sister of Dr. Elliott Coues, surgeon-naturalist, U.S. Army, Ft. Whipple, Ariz., from bird Coues shot in 1864 (Palmer, 1928). *See* Names and Naming. Grace's is a small warbler; lives in mountains of Southwest; closely related to yellow-throated warbler of se. U.S.; 4½–5 in. long; light gray above; streak of yellow over each dark eye; brilliant yellow throat and breast; white belly; two white wing bars; female duller; active, restless warbler; in summer spends most of time in towering tops of yellow pines, sometimes in hemlocks and firs, only occasionally near ground in oak thickets, 6,000–8,000 ft. up in mountains of Ariz., Colo., and N.M.; when feeding passes along branches of coniferous trees or darts into air to catch passing insect or flutters about clusters of needles or cones, searching for small insects; sometimes shares pine tops with Audubon's and olive warblers; male sings from trees, rapid notes like chipping sparrow, *tsip, tsip, tsip, tsip, tsip* (Bent, 1953).

Feeding Habits: Insects, but no detailed studies made.
Nest: Of few known, on limb of pine or fir, 20–60 ft. up; built of plant fibers and down, wool, and caterpillar's webbing, cup lined with horsehair and feathers.
Eggs: May–June; 3–4, usually 3, white or cream-white, speckled and spotted with browns, wreathed at larger end.
Incubation: Period of and age when young first fly unknown.
Other Names: Grace warbler; northern Grace's warbler.
Host to Cowbirds: Rarely reported host to brown-headed cowbird; 3 records—2 in Ariz., 1 in N.M.
Range: Nests from s. Utah and s. Colo. south in mountains through Ariz., N.M., and Tex., to n. Nicaragua; first Calif. record, a female collected (shot) near Imperial Beach, San Diego County, Sept. 8, 1968 (Craig, 1970); winters in Mexico and C. America.

Warbler, Hemlock. *See* Warbler, blackburnian.

Warbler, hermit, *Dendroica occidentalis* (den-DROY-kah ock-sih-den-TAY-lis); genus name: *see* Warbler, Audubon's (yellow-rumped); species name: Lat., western. (Color ill., page 989.) Bird of western coniferous forests; 4½–5 in. long; male in breeding plumage has *clear unmarked yellow head,* mottled dark gray nape; chin and throat black; gray upperparts streaked with black; white belly, sides streaked; two white wing bars; white outer tail feathers; female, and immatures in fall, similar but no solid black throat; entirely yellow face of female and of immature distinguishes them from Townsend's warbler; in

summer lives in forests of pine, spruce, and Douglas fir from Wash. southward to s. Sierra Nevadas in Calif., up to 7,600 ft.; is not a recluse, as common name implies, but spends most of time in tallest trees, 100–200 ft. above ground, where difficult to see; moves about feeding in densely needled branches, sometimes feeds in oaks and shrubbery closer to ground; often associates with Audubon's warbler; male sings from highest trees, rapid energetic song, first three or four notes lisping, followed by others that end in rising note, *zweeo-zweeo-zwee-zwee-zwee-zweek* (Bent, 1953); call is sharp *tsik;* can be lured to eye level by imitating call of saw-whet owl.

Feeding Habits: Flits along branches of conifers from trunk out, sometimes hangs from twigs like chickadees; eats beetles, caterpillars, small flying insects, spiders.
Nest: Saddled on limb of pine or fir, usually well out from trunk, 2–50 ft. above ground, usually 20–40 ft.; built of plant down and fibers, dead fir twigs, lichens, weed stems, lined with bark strips, plant down, horsehair, hairs of squirrels, birds' feathers.
Eggs: May–June; 3–5, commonly 4, dull white, heavily spotted with browns, reds, and lavender, wreathed at large end; "handsomest of all warblers' eggs" (Bent, 1953).
Incubation: Period of and age when young first fly unknown.
Host to Cowbirds: Only a single record, near Nevada City, Calif., June 1942.
Hybrids: Several records of hermit warbler × Townsend's warbler reported from Wash. and Ore., where ranges overlap (Jewett, 1944); usually nests at higher elevations in mountains of Wash. and Ore. than Townsend's, which accounts for only occasional hybridization (Stein, 1962).
Range: Nests from sw. Wash. through Coast Ranges and Sierra Nevadas to nw. and c. Calif.; winters from s.-c. Mexico to Nicaragua; rarely in coastal Calif.; has wandered to Minn., Conn., Tex., and Colo.

Warbler, hooded, *Wilsonia citrina* (will-SO-nih-ah sit-RYE-nah); genus name: *see* Warbler, Canada; species name: Lat., lemon-colored. (Color ill., page 989.) E. U.S.; 5–5¾ in. long; wingspread about 8–8¼ in.; male in breeding plumage has black hood completely surrounding bright yellow forehead and face; upperparts olive green; underparts bright yellow; no distinctive markings on body or wings but large white spots in tail; female and immature similar to male but duller and without black hood; in summer lives almost entirely within eastern half of U.S. in North, in moist forests of mixed beech, maple, basswood, hickory, oak, and some hemlock in ravines with heavy undergrowth; in Southeast, in cypress-gum swamps; a lively woodland bird that moves about in forest thickets seldom more than 15 ft. above ground; shows great curiosity if one sits down quietly in woods; approaches with sharp *cheep* or *chip* notes; frequently fans tail in and out showing white spots; although spends most of life low in forest understory, male often rises to treetops to perch motionless, making forest ring with loud two-note

Grace's warbler

AMERICAN WOOD WARBLER FAMILY

phrases; one song, rhythmically, seems to say *weeta-weeta-wee-TEE-oh* sometimes with several additional notes, all uttered quickly.

Feeding Habits: Expert "flycatcher," sometimes rises in air to snap with bill insects out of air; eats beetles, bugs, moths and their caterpillars, flies, ants, wasps, grasshoppers, aphids, caddis flies, and spiders (Bent, 1953).
Nest: Built in fork of beech, oak, or other sapling, or in holly, sweet pepperbush, buttonbush, laurel, alders, from 10 in. to 5 ft. up or rarely to 18 ft. in tree; made of dead leaves, plant fibers and down, bound with spider's silk, cup lined with fine grass, horsehair.
Eggs: Apr.–June; 3–5, commonly 3, creamwhite, spotted, blotched, usually at large end, with browns.
Incubation: 12 days; young leave nest at 8–9 days old (Bent, 1953).
Other Names: Black-headed warbler; hooded flycatching warbler; hooded titmouse; mitered warbler.
Age: One, banded Wyanokee, N.J., lived to 4 years, 11 months (Kennard, 1975).
Host to Cowbirds: Uncommon to frequent, local; 32 records distributed in Conn., N.Y., N.J., Pa., Md., Va., Ga., Ala., Ind., Ill., and Mich.
Weights: In N.C. (46), average 10.7 gr. (Teulings and Teulings, 1971), or less than ½ oz.; in fall, coastal N.J. (3), 8–10.1 gr., or about ⅓ oz.
Range: Nests from se. Neb., c. Iowa, n. Ill., s. Mich., s. Ont., nw. Pa., to c. and se. N.Y., s. Conn., and R.I., south to se. Tex., Gulf coast, and n. Fla.; winters from e.-c. Mexico to Panama.

Warbler, jack-pine. *See* Warbler, Kirtland's.

Warbler, Kentucky, *Oporornis formosus* (op-or-OR-niss for-MOE-sus); genus name: *see* Warbler, Connecticut; species name: Lat., comely, beautiful; common name: Alexander Wilson discovered this warbler and in 1811 named it for the state in which he found it. (Color ill., page 989.) Locally common in summer over most of southeastern part of U.S., especially Mississippi Valley; 5–5¾ in. long; male in breeding plumage, olive green above, bright yellow below, with *black forehead, and black "sideburns" down sides of throat; yellow streak over and around dark eyes* reaches to bill; no distinctive markings (such as white) in wings or tail; female duller, less black about head and throat; immature like adults but black much obscured; lives in thickets of damp, heavily shaded deciduous woods, bottomlands near creeks and rivers, ravines in upland woods, and borders of swamps; spends most of time on ground; walks gracefully over woods floor and, like waterthrushes and ovenbird, bobs its tail up and down; female very shy and elusive, often leaves nest before discovery; nests difficult to find; in nesting season, male a persistent singer from low branches or from ground as he constantly moves about; song likened to phrase *tur-dle, tur-dle, tur-dle, tur-dle,* much like song of Carolina wren, also *churry-churry-churry;* alarm note, series of rapid *chips;* also has flight song given at dusk.

Feeding Habits: Walks rapidly over ground, bill overturning leaves, peeps under sticks, into crevices, leaps up to snatch insect or spider from overhanging leaf or branch; eats moths, caterpillars, aphids, grubs, etc. (Bent, 1953).
Nest: On ground at foot of tree, bush, under fallen branch, or just off wet earth in fork of shrub, fern, or weed; bulky open cup of leaves, weed stems, grasses, strips of grapevine, lined with rootlets and hair of cows or horses.
Eggs: May–June; 3–6, usually 4–5, white or cream-white, speckled, spotted, and blotched with browns.
Incubation: 12 days; young leave nest 10 days after hatching.
Other Name: Kentucky wagtail.
Host to Cowbirds: Locally common victim of brown-headed cowbird; about 150 records ranging from Del., Pa., Ohio, Ind., Ill., and Mich. to Iowa, Kans., Okla., and Ky.
Hybrids: The Cincinnati warbler, once thought to be a full species, was later considered to be a cross between a Kentucky warbler and a blue-winged warbler (Ridgway, 1880); *see also* under Warbler, blue-winged.
Weights: In N.C. (12), average 14 gr. (Teulings and Teulings, 1971), or ½ oz.
Range: Nests from se. Neb., c. Iowa, sw. Wisc., ne. Ill., c. Ind., c. and e. Ohio, s. Pa., n. N.J., se. N.Y., and sw. Conn., south to S.C., c. Ga., nw. Fla., west to se. Tex.; winters from s. Mexico to n. S. America; has wandered to n. N.Y., Mass., Vt., Mich., s. Ont., s. Que., and Nova Scotia, and west to Calif.: one at Point Loma, San Diego County, June 4, 1968; one on Farallon Is., June 2, 1969; one on Farallon Is., July 1972 (Small, 1974).

Warbler, Kirtland's, *Dendroica kirtlandii* (den-DROY-kah kirt-LAND-ih-eye); genus name: *see* Warbler, Audubon's (yellow-rumped); species name: given by Spencer F. Baird in 1852 for Jared P. Kirtland, physician and naturalist of Cleveland, Ohio. (Color ill., page 989.) One of rarest warblers, unusual in that nesting range limited entirely to relatively small area in c. Mich., and first songbird in world to have monument erected to it (*see* Monuments to Birds); 5¾ in. long; male in breeding plumage, blue-gray above with black streaks; yellow below with some black spots on sides and sometimes on breast; broken white eye-ring and black lores; female similar but duller, without black lores or "mask"; bobs tail up and down; lives on lower peninsula of Mich. only in predominantly young jack pines, *Pinus banksiana,* 5–12 ft. tall, which spring up after forest fires; when pines grow to 18 ft. high and shade out shrubby ground cover, Kirtland's warblers no longer use them (Van Tyne, 1953); is on endangered species list, with estimated less than 1,000 left; U.S. Forest Service has established Kirtland's Warbler Management area on 4,000 acres of Huron National Forest, where controlled burning and other methods maintain or produce habitat; birds also strictly protected by state and federal laws. In census of June 1971, total count of singing males only 201, a 60% decline in 10 years (Mayfield, 1972); see also Walkinshaw (1972), but Mayfield (1973) reported reason for optimism about future of the Kirtland's was control of brown-headed

cowbirds (*see* Brood Parasitism), which heavily parasitize the Kirtland's warbler; by end of summer 1975, about 1,200 Kirtland's warblers reported owing to control of cowbird (Anonymous, 1975c); in June 1973, count of 216 singing males; male sings so constantly all day through nesting season that easily found in thick cover; difficult to describe song because of changes and unfinished ones but resembles songs of northern waterthrush and house wren.

Feeding Habits: Sometimes feeds on ground, sometimes in tops of pines or in short scrub oaks; eats small moths, spanworms (inchworms), caterpillars, horseflies, deerflies, grasshoppers, crickets, also centipedes and exuding pitch from pines.
Nest: On ground, well concealed under arching plants and near base of jack pine; built entirely of dead grasses and other plant fibers, lined with grasses, mosses, or deer hairs.
Eggs: May–June; 4–5, cream-white or pink-white, speckled, spotted, and blotched with browns. Males and females sometimes remarkably tame—may eat from fingers (Van Tyne, 1953).
Incubation: 14–15 days, male feeds incubating female; young leave nest when 12–13 days old.
Other Names: Jack-pine bird; jack-pine warbler.
Age: Oldest-known lived to at least 9 years old; a female to at least 8 years (Berger and Radabaugh, 1968); average age of 2 years (Mayfield, 1960).
Host to Cowbirds: Frequent; perhaps only species of bird whose survival is threatened by brood parasitism of cowbird. See Mayfield (1960) for details; also Friedmann (1963).
Weights: Apparently first one ever caught and banded *in migration,* a male, in May 1959, at Point Pelee National Park, Ont., Canada, 15.6 gr. (Woodford, 1959), or about ½ oz.
Range: Nests only in c. Mich.; winters in Bahamas; recently solitary singing males reported in Minn. and in Canada.

Warbler, Lawrence's. Once thought to be a separate species—*Vermivora lawrencei* (ver-MIV-oh-rah LAW-rence-eye); genus name: *see* Warbler, Bachman's; species name: for Newbold Trotter Lawrence—but later discovered to be a hybrid (a recessive type) from the crossbreeding of the blue-winged and golden-winged warblers.

Harold H. Herrick, an insurance executive of Long Is., N.Y., and amateur ornithologist, collected (shot) in the 1870s a warbler unknown to him along the Passaic R. near Chatham, N.J. In the 1874 *Proceedings of the Academy of Natural Sciences* (Philadelphia) he described it as a new species and named it Lawrence's warbler in honor of Newbold Trotter Lawrence, a former classmate, also an amateur ornithologist of the New York City area, and nephew of George N. Lawrence (Crosby, 1930).

From the time of the discovery of the Lawrence's warbler there were ornithologists (William Brewster especially) who considered the Lawrence's and the Brewster's warblers to be hybrids of the blue-winged and golden-winged warblers. It was not until the 1910 ed. of the

A.O.U. *Check-list*, however, that they were no longer recognized officially as species and were dropped from the *Check-list*.

Lawrence's warbler has the general size (about 4–5 in. long) and body coloration and markings of the blue-winged warbler, usually with yellow underparts and white wing bars, but with the *black facial markings* and *black bib* of the golden-winged. According to Peterson (1947), the Lawrence's warbler is "the only yellow-bellied warbler with *both* a black bib and a black ear patch"—the rare Bachman's warbler of the southern river swamps has a yellow belly and black bib but no black ear patch.

Lawrence's warbler may sing songs like both its parents and it usually associates with them. So far it has been found mated only to a blue-winged warbler, with no record of ever pairing with another Lawrence's warbler (Broun, 1957).

Range: It has been identified in Ohio, e. Pa., n. N.J., se. N.Y., Conn., and more recently in Fla. It can be expected especially where the nesting ranges of the blue-winged and golden-winged warblers overlap, and possibly along their migration routes or on their wintering ranges.

Feeding Habits: Probably like those of the parent species, which eat mostly insects.

Warbler, Lucy's, *Vermivora luciae* (ver-MIV-oh-rah LEW-sih-ee); genus name: *see* Warbler, Bachman's; species and common names: Dr. James G. Cooper, prominent 19th-century Calif. ornithologist, discovered this warbler in 1861 and named it for Lucy Hunter Baird, then 13-year-old daughter of Spencer F. Baird, later secretary of the Smithsonian Institution (Palmer, 1954). (Color ill., page 988.) Only wood warbler that nests in hot desert of Southwest (Monson, 1957a); very small; 4 in. long; sexes alike; gray above, white below, with red-brown patch in crown; only N. American warbler with reddish rump; has white eye-ring; very active, might be confused with a gnatcatcher or immature verdin; lives among larger mesquites, especially along watercourses and in willows along rivers such as the San Pedro, Santa Cruz, Gila, and Colorado in Ariz.; in se. Ariz., also lives in foothills; nesting range extends along Virgin R. valley into sw. Utah, along bottom of Grand Canyon and into San Juan drainage in se. Utah; also along Rio Grande in N.M. (Monson, 1957a). In Ariz., males, along with yellow warblers, are earliest warblers (that do not winter there) to appear in spring; by late Mar., sing loudly from tops of mesquites and cottonwoods (Phillips *et al.*, 1964); song is like that of yellow warbler; has been represented as succession of double notes, *whee-tee, whee-tee, whee-tee, whee-tee, wheet.*

Feeding Habits: Mostly insects it catches in foliage and flowers of mesquites and other desert trees and shrubs.

Nest: In natural cavities, under loose bark, in abandoned woodpecker holes and deserted verdins' nests; female does building; small compact nest of bark, weeds, mesquite leaf stems, cup lined with fine bark, horse and cow hair and rabbit fur.

Eggs: Apr.–June; 3–7, usually 4–5, white or cream-white, finely speckled with browns, usually concentrated at larger end; female very shy about nest, may desert if disturbed.
Incubation: Period of and age when young leave nest unknown.
Other Name: Desert warbler.
Host to Cowbirds: Frequent, locally, to brown-headed cowbird; records from Ariz., Calif., and Hudspeth County, Tex.
Range: Nests from s. Nev., s. Utah, sw. Colo., and nw. N.M., west to Calif. and Nev. banks of Colorado R., probably Imperial Valley, Calif., east to Rio Grande between Socorro, N.M., and El Paso, Tex.; south to n. Sonora and ne. Baja Calif.; winters in Mexico (Monson, 1957a).

Warbler, lutescent, *See* Warbler, orange-crowned.

Warbler, MacGillivray's, *Oporornis tolmiei* (op-or-OR-niss toll-MIH-eye); genus name: *see* Warbler, Connecticut; species name: given in 1839 by John K. Townsend, Philadelphia ornithologist, for Dr. William Fraser Tolmie, Scottish medical officer of the Hudson's Bay Company; later, John James Audubon, not knowing of previous name by Townsend, named it for William MacGillivray, Scottish ornithologist; both men are commemorated in the bird's scientific and common names (Palmer, 1928). (Color ill., page 991.) Western counterpart of mourning warbler; 4¾–5½ in. long; male in breeding plumage, olive upperparts, yellow below; gray hood; black lores; two white spots above and below eyes (mourning warbler has no eye spots, also has blacker chest); female MacGillivray's similar to male but hood and throat paler; immatures have either a broken or complete white eye-ring. Lives locally over large part of w. N. America, including Rocky Mtns.; prefers cut-over or fire-swept areas of second-growth woodland, dead and fallen trees, brushy areas near low moist ground; brushy dry hillsides not far from water, thicketed draws and canyons; dense willows along stream bottoms; is timid, and elusive, skulks close to ground but can be coaxed out of hiding by squeaking (*see* Sounds That Attract Birds); in breeding season, male bolder, often sings, alternating between thickets and treetop perch, throws back head and puts much effort into liquid song; double notes likened to *swee-eet, swee-eet, swee-eet, peachy, peachy, peachy* (Bent, 1953).

Feeding Habits: Forages close to ground in densest thickets, catches and eats click beetles, flea beetles, caterpillars, and other insects, but no comprehensive study of food has been made.
Nest: Between upright stems of fir saplings, scrub oaks, alders, or in *Spiraea*, salal, chokecherry, and other bushes, 2–5 ft. above ground, in dense, moist places or amid tall weeds and ferns; loosely built of weed stalks, straws, dried grasses, cup lined with grasses, rootlets, few horsehairs.
Eggs: May–July; 3–6, usually 4, white or cream-white, speckled, spotted, or blotched with browns.

Lawrence's warbler

AMERICAN WOOD WARBLER FAMILY

Incubation: 11 days (Griscom *et al.*, 1957); young leave nest when 8–9 days old (Bent, 1953).

Other Names: Northern MacGillivray's warbler; Tolmie's warbler.

Host to Cowbirds: Regularly but not very frequently; 9 records distributed in B.C., Calif., Colo., Wash., and Ore.

Hybrids: Some hybridizing, MacGillivray's warbler × mourning warbler where ranges of two meet in s. Alta., Canada. See details in Cox (1973).

Range: Nests from s. Alaska, sw. Yukon, ne. B.C., c. Alta., to sw. Sask., south to c. Calif., c. Ariz., c. N.M.; winters s. Baja Calif. and n. Mexico to Panama.

Warbler, magnolia, *Dendroica magnolia* (den-DROY-kah mag-NO-lih-ah); genus name: *see* Warbler, Audubon's (yellow-rumped); species name: given by Alexander Wilson for the magnolia trees among which he saw these warblers migrating about the year 1810 near Ft. Adams, Miss. (see Wilson 1828–29). (Color ill., page 990.) Ranges over great areas of e. and c. U.S. to reach nesting grounds in coniferous forests in n. U.S. and Canada; one of handsomest N. American warblers; 4½–5 in. long; male in breeding plumage, upperparts black to gray; underparts and rump yellow; breast and flanks streaked with black; white wing patch; white line over each eye; broad white band in tail; black facial mask; female like male but colors less brilliant; in fall adults and immatures have distinct narrow gray breast band; in migration, prefers lower parts of forest and thickets along edges of woods, sometimes seen in gardens, orchards, but on nesting grounds prefers hemlocks, low dense thickets of spruces and balsam firs, clearings, and swamp and pond borders where small trees grow; active and sprightly, flits about trees or bushes, wings drooping, tail spread, showing black-and-white markings, not especially shy, male sings series of rich notes; William Brewster, Mass. ornithologist, suggested rhythmic swing of song by phrases *she knew she was right, yes, she knew she was right* and *pretty, pretty, Rachel.*

Feeding Habits: Gleans bark of conifers for pest insects—weevils, leaf beetles, click beetles, leafhoppers, aphids, scale insects, sawfly larvae, ants, flies, caterpillars, moths, also spiders and daddy longlegs.

Nest: Built usually on horizontal branches or against trunks of coniferous trees, 1–35 ft. above ground, usually less than 15 ft.; of loose twigs, coarse grasses, lined with black rootlets.

Eggs: May–June; 3–5, usually 4, white to cream-white or green-white, speckled, spotted, or blotched with browns, wreathed or solid at larger end.

Incubation: 11–13 days; young leave nest 8–10 days after hatching.

Other Names: Black-and-yellow warbler; blue-headed yellow-rumped warbler; spotted warbler.

Age: One, banded in Me., still alive at 6 years old; another at 7 years (Patterson, 1971); a male, banded Mt. Desert Is., Me., trapped and released in same area when 6 years, 11 months, old (Kennard, 1975).

Host to Cowbirds: Seldom reported, probably infrequent; only 17 records (Friedmann, 1963).

Weights: In fall, coastal N.J. (63), 5.8–9.3 gr. (Murray and Jehl, 1964), or about ⅓ oz.; in Mich. (3), 9–11.7 gr. (Becker and Stack, 1944).

Range: In Canada, nests from s.-c. and sw. Mack., south to c. B.C., east through Prairie Provinces to n. and s. Ont., c. and e., Que., and sw. Newfoundland, south to ne. Minn., c. Wisc., c. Mich., and s. Ont., rarely to ne. Ohio, c. W.Va., w. Va., c. and nw. Pa. nw. N.J., and Mass.; winters from s.-c. Mexico and Yucatán through C. America to Panama and West Indies, casual in Fla., Miss., Va.; reported in Calif., a very rare spring and fall migrant along coast and at desert oases (Small, 1974); casual migrant in Ariz. (Phillips *et al.*, 1964).

Warbler, Middendorff's grasshopper. Name for a bird in the Warbler—Old World Warbler Family.

Warbler, mitered. *See* Warbler, hooded.

Warbler, mourning, *Oporornis philadelphia* (op-or-OR-nis fill-ah-DEL-fih-ah); genus name: *see* Warbler, Connecticut; species name: Alexander Wilson discovered this warbler on borders of a marsh within a few miles of Philadelphia and in 1810 named the bird for that city; *mourning warbler,* so named by Wilson because of black markings on its breast which suggested one in mourning. (Color ill., page 990.) Eastern counterpart of MacGillivray's warbler; 5–5¾ in. long; male in breeding plumage has gray hood with black breast (similar Connecticut warbler has gray hood but also has white eye-ring); olive green above; yellow below; female like male but has pale gray on throat; on its northern nesting grounds prefers old woods clearings, extensive brushy cut-over woods, or lowland thickets of raspberry and blackberry tangles, nettles and jewelweed; very secretive, pairs skulk from one tangle to another; respond with scolding notes to imitated screech owl's call; males often rise from tops of bushes or small trees to sing *chirry, chirry, chorry, chorry,* with falling notes.

Feeding Habits: Eats insects and spiders, but no detailed studies made.

Nest: Bulky, on or near ground, often at base of weed stems in briers or in bunch of ferns or goldenrod, tussock of grass, or even in bush 2 ft. above ground; built of dead coarse grasses, weed stalks, leaves, lined with grasses and a few horsehairs.

Eggs: May–July; 3–5, usually 4, white or cream-white, speckled with browns.

Incubation: About 12 days; young leave nest when 7–9 days old (Cox, 1960).

Other Names: Black-throated ground warbler; crape warbler; mourning ground warbler; Philadelphia warbler.

Host to Cowbirds: Fairly frequent locally by brown-headed cowbird, but in general uncommon.

Hybrids: A presumed hybrid of mourning warbler × blue-winged warbler (Gray, 1958). *See also* under MacGillivray's warbler.

Weights: In fall, coastal N.J. (14), 9.7–13.2 gr. (Murray and Jehl, 1964), or about ⅓–½ oz.; in

Mich., adult males (7), 11.1–14.5 gr. (McCamey, 1950).

Range: Nests from c. Alta. across Canada to Newfoundland, south to ne. N.D., e.-c. Minn., c. Wisc., n.e. Ill., s. Mich., n. Ohio, ne. Pa., se. N.Y., Mass., c. N.H., s. Me., and c. N.S., south in higher Appalachians to e. W.Va. and nw. Va.; winters from Nicaragua to n. S. America.

Warbler, myrtle (yellow-rumped), *Dendroica coronata* (den-DROY-kah koh-row-NAY-tah); genus name: *see* Warbler, Audubon's (yellow-rumped); species name: Lat., crowned; *myrtle,* from its fondness for berries of eastern wax myrtle, *Myrica cerifera,* and northern bayberries. (Color ill., page 997.) Second to yellow warbler as one of best-known of all American warblers; most numerous of all in e. U.S.—an estimated 24,000 flew by an observer one Mar. day along coastal S.C. between 9 A.M. and 1 P.M.; has one of most extensive nesting ranges of all American warblers (Bent, 1953); it is the nominate subspecies of the species now called the yellow-rumped warbler, *Dendroica coronata* (see Warbler, yellow-rumped); 5–6 inches long; adult male in spring has upperparts blue-gray, streaked with black; black chest; two white wing bars; yellow patch on crown, rump, and sides of breast; underparts white; *white throat* distinguishes it from its counterpart, the western Audubon's warbler; winter adults and immatures, brown above, white below; can be identified in any plumage by yellow rump and sharp call note, *check!;* one of first migrant warblers north in spring, moves in waves, males preceding females; drift through leafless tops of trees, brushy places, gardens, hedges, along coastal beaches; males sing weak juncolike trill; on northern nesting grounds lives in coniferous woods but prefers more open stands and edges of forest clearings; also in spruce-tamarack bogs.

Feeding Habits: Often very tame when hopping close by, feeding on ground or flitting about bushes, bark of trees, or fluttering in air; eats beetles, weevils, wood borers, scale insects, sawfly larvae, aphids, flies, mosquitoes, gnats, also spiders, and is one of few warblers that can live for long time on fruit of bayberry, dogwoods, cedar, Virginia creeper, poison ivy, palmetto berries; drinks juice of broken fallen oranges, also drinks sap from trees, eats seeds of grasses, sunflower, and goldenrod; suet, doughnuts, and peanut butter mixture (Terres (1968c; 1977).

Nest: Generally on horizontal branch of spruce, pine, or cedar tree, 5–50 ft. above ground, usually about 15 ft. up, close to trunk; built of fine coniferous twigs, rootlets, grasses interwoven with horsehair, occasionally moose hairs, cup lined with fine hairs and feathers.

Eggs: May–June; 3–5, commonly 4–5, cream-white, speckled, blotched with browns.

Incubation: Entirely by female, 12–13 days; young leave nest 12–14 days after hatching.

Other Names: Golden-crowned flycatcher; golden-crowned warbler; myrtle-bird; yellow-rump.

Age: One, banded Huntington, Long Is., N.Y., killed at Dunbar, S.C., when at least 6½ years old; at Thomasville, Ga., and elsewhere, banded ones showed tendency to return there to winter in same place; one at least 5 years old had made four round trips to and from northern breeding grounds.

Host to Cowbirds: Commonly in s. Canada but seldom common elsewhere; reported Alta. east to Que., Me., Mich., and Wisc.

Weights: In fall, coastal N.J. (28), 10–18.8 gr. (Murray and Jehl, 1964), or about ⅓–¾ oz.

Range: Nests from n. Alaska south to n. B.C., s. Alta., across Canada to Labrador and Newfoundland, south to n. Minn., n. Mich., c. Ont., ne. N.Y., Mass., and Me.; winters from nw. Ore. south to n. Baja Calif., and Kans., southern Great Lakes region, and s. New England south to Panama.

Warbler, Nashville, *Vermivora ruficapilla* (ver-MIV-oh-rah rue-fih-cap-ILL-ah); genus name: *see* Warbler, Bachman's; species name: from Lat. *rufus*, reddish, and *capillus*, hair (crown); common name: discovered in 1808 near Nashville, Tenn., by Alexander Wilson, who saw it in migration there and named it for that city. (Color ill., page 990.) Ranges in spring and summer widely over e.-c. N. America, and in Sierras of West, where called Calaveras warbler; small; 4½–5 in. long; only N. American warbler with combined blue-gray head, white eye-ring, bright yellow throat, and *no* wing bars (Robbins *et al.,* 1966); adult male in spring, upperparts olive green; barely discernible chestnut crown; underparts yellow, *unstreaked;* females duller and may lack chestnut crown; immatures like females and always lack chestnut crown; migrating north in spring, seen more in middle story of open deciduous woods, often in flocks of mixed species of warblers, also in thickets along edges of woods, cut-over or burned woods, and in orchards, gardens, shade trees; in northern part of range, nests in bogs with some tamarack and spruce; in southern part, e. U.S., nests in second-growth aspen, white birch, widespread in wake of lumbering; in West, frequents chaparral of both slopes of Sierra Nevada and in belts of yellow, Jeffrey, and sugar pines and up into red fir zone, also on slopes among black oaks and maples (Bent, 1953); male sings from perch in tree, one common song is *see-bit, see-bit, see-bit,* followed by rolling twitter lower in key than first part.

Feeding Habits: Forages from ground to tree-top but mainly low in trees and thickets at edge of forest; eats tent caterpillars, and those of brown-tail and gypsy moths, leafhoppers, aphids, flies, grasshoppers.

Nest: On ground at base of bush, small oak, spruce, fir, birch saplings, stump, clump of grass, or sunk in haircap moss; built of mosses, stems of ferns, pine needles, rabbit fur, lined with rootlets, fine grasses, pine needles, and hairs of deer or moose.

Eggs: May–Aug.; 4–5, white or cream-white, speckled with browns.

Incubation: 11–12 days; young first fly about 11 days after hatching (Lawrence, 1948).

Other Names: Birch warbler; Calaveras warbler; Nashville swamp warbler; red-crowned warbler.

Host to Cowbirds: Uncommon to rare; only 16 records (Friedmann, 1963).

Weights: In fall, coastal N.J. (35), 6.1–9.3 gr. (Murray and Jehl, 1964), or about ⅓ oz.

Range: Nests from s. B.C., s. Sask., to Nova Scotia, south to c. Calif., n. Utah, s. Minn., n. Ill., s. Mich., n. Ohio, n.e. W.Va., and Pa., south to w. Md.; winters from Mexico, s. Tex., and s. Fla. south to Guatemala.

Warbler, necklace. See Warbler, Canada.

Warbler, olive, *Peucedramus taeniatus* (pew-SED-rah-mus tee-nih-AY-tus); genus name: from Gr. *peuke,* pine, and *dramein,* to run; "a runner in pines"; species name: from Lat. *taenia,* headband, apparently refers to black mask through eyes (Gruson, 1972). (Color ill., page 991.) C. American and Mexican warbler that ranges north into U.S. in c. Ariz. and N.M.; 4½–5 in. long; adult male, head, throat, upper breast orange-brown, with black mask through eyes; upperparts, lower hind neck, and extreme upper back yellowish olive-green; back, rump, and upper tail coverts mouse gray; wings blackish with two broad white wing bars; white outer feathers in forked tail; belly dull white; female similar, but head and chest much paler, mask faint, has unstreaked yellowish breast; in U.S. nests in open forests of pine and fir on or near summits of Chiricahua and Huachuca Mtns. at 8,500–12,000 ft. elevation; some winter there, associate with nuthatches, creepers, and western bluebirds; arrive on nesting grounds in early Apr.; male sings from branches of pine trees; melodious whistled notes, one song resembles *peto, peto, peto* song of tufted titmouse.

Feeding Habits: Largely apparently insects; creeps when feeding over limbs of pines like pine warbler.

Nest: On tree limb usually out near end of branch, sometimes hidden by pine needles or cluster of mistletoe, 30–70 ft. up in pine or fir; compact, cup-shaped, built of rootlets, flower stems of *Spiraea,* hulls of pine buds, plant down, inside cup lined with plant down and rootlets.

Eggs: May–July; 3–4, gray-white or blue-white, spotted with grays, olive, browns.

Incubation: Period of and age when young first fly unknown.

Other Name: Northern olive warbler.

Range: Nests from c. and se. Ariz., and sw. N.M., south into Mexico and through mountains to Nicaragua.

Warbler, olive-backed. *See* Parula, tropical.

Warbler, orange-crowned, *Vermivora celata* (ver-MIV-oh-rah see-LAH-tah); genus name: *see* Warbler, Bachman's; species name: Lat., concealed (reference to orange crown). (Color ill., page 991.) Common in West, rare in East except along Gulf coast in winter (Robbins *et al.,* 1966); 4½–5½ in. long; plain, dusky olive green above, brown-orange patch on crown usually concealed; underparts greenish-yellow, *faintly streaked* (similar Nashville has clear yellowish underparts with no streaking); no

Olive warbler

AMERICAN WOOD WARBLER FAMILY

white wing bars or other distinctive markings; sexes alike; immatures like adults in fall but no visible orange crown patch. Main migration route of eastern subspecies is Mississippi Valley; northwestward in spring, southeastward in fall; migration of western races apparently north and south in Rocky Mtns. and Pacific states; lives in dense thickets both in migration and on nesting grounds; in Alaska and Canada dwells in dwarf trees or thickets along streamsides and in open woodlands with thick understory; in Ore. up to 6,000 ft. elevation; in Pacific states likes thickets of aspen, poplar, yellow pine in meadows of subalpine parks, chaparral hillsides, and brushy open woods (Bent, 1953); where eastern form winters in Fla. and along Gulf coast, likes live oaks, magnolias, myrtle thickets, brushy edges of fields on nesting grounds, male restless, lively, moves about in topmost twigs of trees singing loud *chip-e*, *chip-e*, *chip-e*, *chip-e*, like chipping sparrow.

Feeding Habits: In Calif., eats mostly leaf bugs, leafhoppers, scale insects, aphids, caterpillars, flies, also spiders; flits about through oaks feeding at tips of boughs, leaves, tree blossoms; eastern form eats berries in winter and peanut butter, suet, and doughnuts at bird-feeding stations.

Nest: Usually on ground at base of bush, in side of bank, edge of woods path near swamp, or in forest opening, sometimes up 2–4 ft. or more in bush; built of coarse grasses, strips of bark, leaves, plant down, cup lined with fine grasses, deer or porcupine hairs, and feathers.

Eggs: Apr.–July; 3–6, usually 4–5, white, spotted with dark reds and browns.

Incubation: Period of and age when young first fly unknown.

Other Names: Dusky orange-crowned warbler; eastern orange-crowned warbler; lutescent orange-crowned warbler; orange-crown; Rocky Mountain orange-crowned warbler.

Age: One, banded Manor, Calif., trapped and released again in same area when 6 years old (Kennard, 1975).

Host to Cowbirds: Only 1 record, Vancouver Is., B.C.

Weights: In Kans., in fall, killed at TV tower, adult males (9), 7.7–10.9 gr.; adult females (5), 8.3–10.3 gr. (Tordoff and Mengel, 1956), or about ¼–⅓ oz.

Range: Nests from c. Alaska, n.w. and c. Mack., n. Man., east to n. Ont., nw. Que., south to n.w. Baja Calif., se. Ariz., w. Tex., se. Sask., s. Man., w. and c. Ont., and islands off sw. Calif.; winters from n. Calif., s. Nev., c. Ariz., s. Tex., the Gulf coast, and S.C. south to s. Baja Calif., s. Fla., and Guatemala.

Warbler, orange-throated. *See* Warbler, blackburnian.

Warbler, palm, *Dendroica palmarum* (den-DROY-kah palm-AY-rum); genus name: *see* Warbler, Audubon's (yellow-rumped); species name: from Lat. *palma*, of palms; misnamed because seldom seen among palms, although frequents low-growing saw palmetto on Fla. wintering range. (Color ill., page 992.) Lives in summer in sphagnum bogs (muskeg) of n. U.S. and Canada; 4½–5½ in. long; sexes similar;

adults in spring have chestnut cap, yellow streak over eyes; olive brown above with narrow dark streaking and rump yellow-green; underparts yellow or white tinged with yellow; breast and sides finely streaked with chestnut; spends most of time on ground; constantly wags (raises and lowers) tail; two forms, or races, with slight differences—eastern and western—migrating north in spring spread out over nesting grounds east and west of longitude of Hudson Bay; eastern race, called yellow palm warbler, moves up Atlantic coast to n. New England and e. Canada; western race, called western palm warbler, up Mississippi Valley to main nesting grounds in c. Canada (Tyler, 1953c); early migrant in New England (Apr.) with hermit thrush and ruby-crowned kinglet, ahead of myrtle and black-and-white warblers; forages on ground over burned-over grasslands or flits in shrubbery of country roadsides; western race in Mississippi Valley, along fences or borders of fields, both sometimes in towns and gardens; males sing in migration and in sphagnum bogs of nesting grounds; rises to tree to sing buzzy trill, *tsee*, *tsee*, *tsee*, *tsee*, like song of chipping sparrow or junco.

Feeding Habits: Forages on ground (also beaches in migration) and from twigs and cones of conifers on nesting grounds; catches in bill celery leaf tier and other beetles, mosquitoes, flies, gnats, ants, aphids, grasshoppers, small green caterpillars and cotton "worms," also eats bayberries, raspberries.

Nest: In open tamarack-spruce bog or on barrens, on ground in hummock of moss or lichens, at base of small spruce, fir, birch; sometimes 6–24 in. up in crotch of small conifer; built of bark and stalks of dead weeds, dried grasses, lined with finer grasses, rootlets, feathers.

Eggs: May–June; 4–5; white or cream-white, spotted, speckled, blotched with browns, usually wreathed at large end.

Incubation: About 12 days; young first fly about 12 days after hatching.

Other Names: Redpoll warbler; tip-up warbler; wag-tail warbler; western palm warbler; yellow palm warbler; yellow redpoll warbler; yellow tip-up warbler.

Age: One, banded Homosassa Springs, Fla., recaptured there and released when 5 years, 10 months old; one, banded Sanibel, Fla., trapped and released in same area when 6 years, 7 months, old (Kennard, 1975).

Host to Cowbirds: Rare; only 7 records (Friedmann, 1963).

Weights: In fall, coastal N.J. (66), 7.9–13.4 gr. (Murray and Jehl, 1964), or about ⅓–½ oz.

Range: Nests from n. B.C. east to s. Newfoundland, south to n. Minn., c. Mich., and Me.; winters from La., Miss., Tenn., N.C., south to Yucatán Pen., Mexico, Bermuda, West Indies, and n. Honduras; some visit southern gardens in winter, a few stay north to New England.

Warbler, parula. *See* Parula, northern, and Parula, tropical.

Warbler, pileolated. *See* Warbler, Wilson's.

Warbler, pine, *Dendroica pinus* (den-DROY-kah PIE-nus); genus name: *see* Warbler, Audubon's (yellow-rumped); species name: Lat., pine, from its habitat (Color ill., page 993.) E. N. America; in nesting season and on wintering range, usually in open groves of pine; 5–5¾ in. long; adult male in spring, olive green above, unstreaked, with greenish rump; yellow line over each eye; bright yellow-green breast, usually with obscure dusky streaks; white undertail coverts; white patches at ends of two outer tail feathers; female duller with less yellow on breast; both adults more brown in fall; immatures plain, often with no trace of yellow; is one of few N. American warblers whose winter range includes much of nesting range; most migration is within northernmost part of range; one of earliest spring warblers in New England; in migration quite as much in deciduous trees as in pines, visits orchards, lowland thickets (Bent, 1953); male sings in summer and in winter, simple, sweet liquid trill, like chipping sparrow but more musical and slower; usually tame and approachable; quite deliberately creeps while foraging over trunks and branches; lively at times, flies for some distance from one tree to another or may flutter out into air for passing insect.

Feeding Habits: Eats beetles, cotton-boll weevil, moths and their caterpillars, grasshoppers, bugs, aphids, scale insects, flies, also spiders; and when insects or arachnids not available, eats seeds of sumacs, pines, grasses, berries of dogwood, poison ivy, Virginia creeper, wild grapes; will come to feeding stations for peanut butter and cornmeal mixture. See formula in Terres (1977).

Nest: Usually in pines, sometimes red cedar, 8–80 ft. above ground, saddled on branch or in cluster of needles at end of branch, over road or path; built of weed stems, strips of bark, pine needles and twigs, bound with caterpillar's or spider's silk, cup lined with plant down, hair, bristles, or feathers.

Eggs: Mar. (in South) to June; 3–5, usually 4, white, gray-white, greenish white, speckled with browns.

Incubation: Period of and age when young first fly unknown.

Other Names: Pine creeper; pine-creeping warbler.

Age: One, banded East Wareham, Mass., caught again at same station when "at least 5 years old"; another, banded at same station, retrapped there when it was 7 years old.

Host to Cowbirds: Seldom; only 10 records (Friedmann, 1963).

Weights: In N.C. (172), average 14.1 gr. (Teulings and Teulings, 1971), or ½ oz.

Range: Nests from s. Man. to s. Que. and c. Me., south to se. Tex., the Gulf coast, Fla., Dry Tortugas, south to Hispaniola; winters in southern half of breeding range, Ark., Tenn., S.C., southward.

Warbler, Potomac. A hybrid. The so-called Potomac or Sutton's warbler, of which a male and a female were shot about 18 mi. apart south of Martinsburg, W.Va. (see Brooks, M., 1945), is believed by Mayr (1963) and others to be a hybrid between the northern parula (rare in that area) and a yellow-throated warbler. Mayr believes that pairing of the two species was facilitated by their similar nesting behavior.

Warbler, prairie, *Dendroica discolor* (den-DROY-Rah DISS-color); genus name: *see* Warbler, Audubon's (yellow-rumped); species name: Lat., of different colors. (Color ill., page 992.) Does not live on western prairies but winters on flat grassy lands among scattered trees in South, called prairies; nests in young stands of pines, scrub oak pine barrens, deciduous saplings in cut-over woods, e. U.S.; 4¼-5¼ in. long; wingspread 6¼-7¼ in.; male in spring, olive green above with inconspicuous chestnut marks on back; bright yellow below; sides striped with black; yellow sides of face have black streak through eyes and below eyes; two pale yellow wing bars; white patches on outer tail feathers; female like male but duller; immatures without wing bars; from winter home in West Indies and Fla. starts north in early Mar.; has grown more abundant with increase of cut-over forest, abandoned farms and old pastures, but distribution spotty and numbers vary from year to year; male sings from top of tree, series of distinctly separated notes gradually rising in pitch, or chromatic scale—*zee, zee, zee, zee, zee, zeet!*; song period lasts from arrival on nesting grounds into July (Bent, 1953).

Feeding Habits: No comprehensive study made, but mostly insects and spiders; active chasing prey, twitches tail from side to side as it flits about bushes; catches flies on wing, takes insects from tops of shrubs by hovering.
Nest: Concealed in bushes 2-3 ft. above ground, sometimes in clump of fern, juniper, blackberry, laurel, or in saplings of oak, cedar, sweet gum, poplar, maple, holly bush, or wax myrtle, or 10-15 ft. up on limbs of coastal pines, 6-10 ft. up in mangroves; built of plant down, shreds of bark, straws, dry leaves, bound with spider's silk, cup lined with hairs and feathers.
Eggs: Apr. (in South) to June; 3-5, usually 4, white, cream-white, or green-white, spotted or speckled with browns.
Incubation: 12-14 days; young leave nest about 8-10 days after hatching.
Age: A male, banded at Kingston, R.I., lived to 10 years, 3 months (Kennard, 1975).
Host to Cowbirds: Frequent; about 35 records (Friedmann, 1963).
Weights: In N.C. (8), average 8 gr. (Teulings, 1971), or about ⅓ oz.; in fall, coastal N.J. (45), 6-10.7 gr. (Murray and Jehl, 1964).
Range: Nests from se. S.D., Iowa, s. Wisc., n. Mich., s. Ont., se. N.Y., s. Vt., and s. N.H. south to c. Okla., s. La., n. Miss., s. Ala., c. Ga., Fla., and the Fla. Keys; winters on islands off se. Mexico and c. America, and from c. Fla. south through West Indies to Nicaragua.

Warbler, prothonotary, *Protonotaria citrea* (pro-tow-no-TAY'-rih-ah SIGH-tree-ah); genus name: from Low Lat. *protonotarius,* in Roman Catholic Church, a papal notary who wears yellow hood; species name: Lat., lemon color. (Color ill., page 993) E. N. America west to Great Plains, in wooded swamps and streamsides; 5¼-5½ in. long; male in breeding plu-

mage, entire head, neck, breast, and belly deep yellow; back olive green; wings blue-gray, no white wing bars, but white under tail; female similar but duller; immatures resemble female; lives in damp and swampy river bottoms with standing pools of water, low-lying woods frequently flooded, willow-lined riverbanks and sluggish streams; male arrives on nesting grounds ahead of female, selects territory and nesting site before pairing with female (*see* discussion under Nests and Nesting); male sings persistently and energetically from time of arrival on territory, a ringing *peet, tsweet, tsweet, tsweet, tsweet* (from distance sounds like call of solitary sandpiper), also flight song ending in warble.

Feeding Habits: Hops about on floating driftwood or over inclining, half-submerged logs peeping into crevices to catch with bill beetles or spiders, clings to trunks like nuthatch; eats also mayflies, caterpillars, larvae of aquatic insects and some seeds; no detailed studies made of diet (Bent, 1953).
Nest: Only warbler in e. U.S. that nests in natural tree cavity; also in boxes of bluebird size put up for it along streams of habitat (*see* Bird Attracting); usually in rotted hollow of dead stub over water or near it, 3-32 ft. up, usually 5-10 ft.; also uses abandoned holes of woodpeckers or chickadees; dummy nests built by male but functional nest completed by female; made of mosses, grasses, dry leaves, twigs, cavity for eggs is rounded, cup-shaped hollow, lined with fine roots, feathers.
Eggs: Apr. (in South) to June; 3-8, usually 4-6, rich cream color or pink, spotted with browns, grays.
Incubation: 12-14 days; young first fly about 11 days after hatching.
Other Names: Golden warbler; golden swamp warbler; willow warbler.
Age: A male, banded in Calhoun County, Mich., trapped and released in same area when 5 years, 11 months, old (Kennard, 1975).
Host to Cowbirds: Surprisingly frequent; no less than 54 records; unusual host because brown-headed cowbird not known to often parasitize nests of birds in holes in trees (Friedmann, 1963).
Weights: In N.C. (4), average 14.4 gr. (Teulings and Teulings, 1971), or about ½ oz.; in fall, coastal N.J. (1), 17.8 gr. (Murray and Jehl, 1964), or about ⅔ oz.
Range: Nests from e.-c. Minn., s.-c. Wisc., s. Mich., s. Ont., c. N.Y. and N.J., south through e. Neb., e. Kans., c. Okla., e. Tex., to Gulf coast and c. Fla.; winters from s. Mexico and Yucatán Pen. south to n. S. America; occasionally north to N.H., Me., N.B., west to Wyo., Ariz., and Calif.

Warbler, red-faced, *Cardellina rubrifrons* (car-dell-INE-ah RUBE-rih-fronz); genus name: from Lat. *carduelis,* goldfinch, little finch; species name: from Lat. *ruber,* red, and *frons,* forehead. (Color ill., page 993.) Mexican and C. American warbler locally common in summer high in mountain forests of Ariz. and N.M.; 5-5¼ in. long; sexes alike; scarlet or carmine-red face, throat, breast, and sides of neck; crown and sides of head back of eyes black;

white patch on back of neck; upperparts medium gray with white rump; belly white; sides washed with gray; in summer lives in U.S. in southwestern mountain canyons at 6,500-9,000 ft. elevation, where sloping sides of canyons covered with ponderosa pine, Engelmann spruce, and Douglas fir; but also lives in aspen and oak thickets (Monson, 1957b); arrives early Apr. on mountain nesting grounds, often with other migrating warblers; is small and quick; male sings clear whistled notes, rendered *a tink, a tink, tsee, tsee, tswee, tsweep;* more ringing and bell-like than song of Grace's warbler, which often associates with it in yellow pines, and quite like song of yellow warbler.

Feeding Habits: Forages on outer parts of conifers with constant small jerks of tail; darts into air to snatch prey; apparently eats mostly insects, but food habits unknown.
Nest: Always on ground, in small scratched-out depression, usually concealed beneath or beside sheltering rock, log, wildflower, tuft of grass, trunk of tree or oak sprout, among fallen leaves; built of dry leaves, fir needles, plant stems, strips of bark, cup lined with grasses, plant fibers, horse or cow hairs.
Eggs: May-June; 3-4, white, finely speckled with browns.
Incubation: Period of and age when young first fly unknown.
Range: Nests in high mountains of c. and se. Ariz. and sw. N.M., west of the Rio Grande, south to c. Mexico; winters from Mexico to Guatemala, but limits of winter range uncertain (Monson, 1957b).

Warbler, redpoll. *See* Warbler, palm.

Warbler, Sennett's. *See* Parula, tropical.

Warbler, Socorro, *Parula graysoni* (for A. J. Grayson). Not considered a valid or full species by American Ornithologists' Union (1973), but a subspecies, or race, *Parula pitiayumi graysoni,* of the olive-backed warbler, now called the tropical parula warbler. Its range is Socorro Is., one of the Revilla Gigedo group of Mexico, about 250 mi. southwest of southern tip of Baja Calif.; it also ranges to Cape Region of Baja Calif. *See* its habits under Parula, tropical.

Warbler, striped. *See* Warbler, black-and-white.

Warbler, summer. *See* Warbler, yellow.

Warbler, Sutton's. *See* Warbler, Potomac.

Warbler, Swainson's, *Limnothlypis swainsonii* (lim-no-THLIP-iss swain-SON-ih-eye); genus name: Gr., marsh finch; species name: bird discovered by the Rev. John Bachman in S.C. in 1832 and described and named by Audubon for his friend William Swainson, brilliant English ornithologist of early 19th century. (Color ill., page 993.) Uncommon warbler of se. U.S. and considered a "lost" species (until rediscovered) for more than 40 years (Dingle, 1953); 5-6½ in. long; sexes outwardly alike; brown and olive above, with tawny cap; conspicuous white stripe over each eye; bill long and sharply pointed; dingy white underparts; no wing bars; difficult to see this obscure brown bird *walking* gracefully about in gloom of thickets or flitting close to ground; lives in two completely different habitats: in coastal country Ga., Fla., S.C., in depressions of low open pineland where brook and sluggish interconnecting channels are margined with dense growth of cane; in southern highlands of Tenn., N.C., Va., and W.Va., at 2,000–3,000 ft. elevation, in tangles of rhododendron, laurel, hemlock, and holly. Male is first to arrive on nesting grounds, usually early Apr.; sings from perch with bill pointed straight to sky or while on ground of established territory, loud, rich song; phrases like *whee, whee, whee, whip-poor-will;* resemble from distance songs of hooded warbler and Louisiana waterthrush.

Feeding Habits: Little known and from few birds only; small green caterpillars of aquatic plants, ants, bees, and spiders (Dingle, 1953).
Nest: Built entirely by female, bulky, in fork or between stems of bushes, canes, mass of vines, briers, 2–10 ft. above ground; of leaves of oak, gum, holly, maple, tupelo, cane, lined with pine needles, fibers of Spanish moss *(Tillandsia),* rootlets, grass, horsehair.
Eggs: May–July; 3–5, usually 3, white, rarely speckled with browns; female is close sitter, one can touch her on nest (Dingle, 1953).
Incubation: By female, about 14–15 days; young leave nest about 12 days after hatching (Sprunt and Denton, 1957).
Host to Cowbirds: Possibly very local and rare; 6 records, host to brown-headed cowbird; most of breeding range of Swainson's outside range of this cowbird (Friedmann, 1963).
Age: A male, banded Whaleyville, Md., recaptured same place at estimated minimum age of 5 years, 11 months (Weske, 1976).
Weights: Apparently first one reported in N.J., caught and banded Linwood, 13.7 gr. (Savell, 1968), or about ½ oz. See also Meanley (1971b).
Range: Nests, locally, ne. Okla., se. Mo., s. Ill., sw. Ind., s. Ohio, W.Va., s. Va., se. Md., south to e. Tex., the Gulf coast, n. Fla.; winters from Yucatán Pen., Mexico, south to Belize and West Indies; casual west to Neb., and Colo., Bahamas, Vera Cruz., has strayed to N.J.

Warbler, swamp. Another name for Connecticut, prothonotary, and Tennessee warblers.

Warbler, sycamore. *See* Warbler, yellow-throated.

Warbler, Tennessee, *Vermivora peregrina* (ver-MIV-oh-rah per-reh-GRIN-ah); genus name: *see* Warbler, Bachman's; species name: Lat., wandering, alien, from foreign parts; common name: Alexander Wilson discovered this warbler in migration on banks of Cumberland R., Tenn., and named it for that state. (Color ill., page 993.) Main nesting range is Canada; 4–5 in. long; male in breeding plumage bright olive green above with gray head, *conspicuous white stripe over eyes;* gray-white below, with no streaking; female similar but some olive green on crown; underparts slightly yellowish;

immatures greenish above, dingy yellow below, yellowish line over eyes. *Main* migration route north seems to be from Mexico to Tex. to Mississippi Valley, then spreads widely to reach nesting grounds; in some places floods treetops of both upland and lowland woods, also tall trees of lakeshores, streams, farms; in summer, lives about openings of northern woodlands, edges of dense spruce forests, cleared balsam-tamarack bogs, or grassy places of open aspens and pines. Male moves about restlessly in trees, sings over and over short, loud notes, like chippering of chimney swift, *wi-chip, wi-chip, wi-chip, wi-chip, chip, chip, chip, chip, chip* (Bent, 1953).

Feeding Habits: Forages over terminal twigs, leaves of trees, or hangs suspended like titmouse; gleans dense patches of weeds; eats small beetles, weevils, grasshoppers, leafhoppers, scale insects, aphids, small leaf-eating caterpillars, and spiders; also punctures wild and domestic grapes for juice; eats seeds of sumac, berries of poison ivy; comes to feeding stations for ripe bananas, suet, peanut butter mixture.
Nest: Built in hollow of sphagnum moss in bog, or on higher level ground or hillside, in thickets or in open at base of bush or in grass; built of dried grasses, some moss, lined with fine grasses, rootlets, and sometimes hairs of porcupine or moose.
Eggs: June–July; 4–7, commonly 6, white or cream-white, spotted or speckled with browns.
Incubation: Probably 11–12 days (Harrison, 1975).
Other Names: Swamp warbler; Tennessee swamp warbler.
Age: One, banded Little Falls, Minn., trapped and released in same area when 4 years, 11 months old (Kennard, 1975).
Albinism: Only one record (a partial albino) among 2,000 examined among bird collections of American museums and among birds killed in migration at TV towers (Raveling and Warner, 1965).
Host to Cowbirds: Uncommon or rare; 3 records (Friedmann, 1963).
Weights: In fall, coastal N.J. (15), 7.5–9.8 gr. (Murray and Jehl, 1964), or about ⅓ oz.; in Kans., killed in migration in fall at TV tower, adult male (1), very fat, 10.9 gr.; immature male (1), very fat, 12.9 gr.; adult females (2), fat, 9.1 and 12.5 gr. (Tordoff and Mengel, 1956).
Range: Nests from s. Yuk., c. Mack., n. Man., east to c. Labrador, Newfoundland, south to s.-c. B.C., nw. Mont., c. Alta., c. Sask., s. Man., n. Minn., n. Wisc., n. Mich., s.-c. Ont., ne. N.Y., s. Vt., c. N.H., s. Me., s. N.B., Nova Scotia; winters from s. Mexico to n. S. America; one record (very rare) at feeding station in Jan. 1955 in New York City (Terres, 1960b).

Warbler, Tolmie's. *See* Warbler, MacGillivray's.

Warbler, Townsend's, *Dendroica townsendi* (den-DROY-kah TOWN-send-eye); genus name: *see* Warbler, Audubon's (yellow-rumped); species name: for John K. Townsend (Palmer, 1928; see also Stone, 1903). (Color ill., page 994.) Western counterpart of the eastern

black-throated green warbler; lives in summer in tall treetops of coniferous forest of Pacific Northwest; 4½–5 in. long; male in breeding plumage, upperparts olive green streaked with black; distinguished by black and yellow striped head (black cheek patch); black throat; yellow breast striped on sides with black; two white wing bars; white in outer tail feathers; female and immature with throat mostly yellow instead of black; both have black and yellow facial markings; spring migration apparently northward from Mexico; singing flocks go through live oak trees, often in low deciduous growth, feeding as they go; many arrive on nesting grounds in Pacific Northwest in Apr. and May (Bent, 1953); in summer fond of treetops in coniferous forests, spend most of time in tops of tallest spruces and firs; at height of nesting season, male sings in all weathers— *weazy weazy weazy weazy tweea,* notes rising in spirals, similar to song of black-throated gray warbler of more open and younger forests.

Feeding Habits: In Calif., individuals (Oct.– Jan.) eat great numbers of weevils, bugs, leafhoppers, scale insects, caterpillars, some spiders, also at feeding stations in winter, eat cheese, marshmallows, peanut butter mixture (Bent, 1953).
Nest: Of few ever found, in spruces or firs saddled on limb, 9–15 ft. above ground, but may nest much higher, as nests difficult to discover in trees 100 ft. tall or more; bulky, compact, and shallow; of plant fibers, strips of inner bark, grasses, lichens, cocoons of spiders, lined with hairs and feathers.
Eggs: May–June, 3–5, white, speckled with browns.
Incubation: Period of and age when young first fly unknown.
Hybrids: Several, Townsend's warbler × hermit warbler in Wash. and Ore. where ranges overlap (Jewett, 1944). See especially Stein (1962).
Range: Nests from s. Alaska and s. Yuk. south along coast and islands to nw. Wash., east to c. and se. Wash., n. Idaho, c. and ne. Ore., nw. and s.-c. Mont., and nw. Wyo.; winters from w.-c. and s. Calif. to Nicaragua; casually in interior to s. Ariz.; has straggled east to Prospect Park, N.Y. City, Pa., Kans., Tex., and Miss.

Warbler, Virginia's, *Vermivora virginiae* (ver-MIV-oh-rah ver-GIN-ih-ee); genus name: *see* Warbler, Bachman's; species name: for Virginia Anderson, wife of Dr. William W. Anderson, an assistant surgeon, U.S. Army, who in 1858 discovered the bird in N.M. (Palmer, 1928). (Color ill., page 995.) Small warbler of mountains of Southwest; 4¼–4½ in. long; male in breeding plumage, all-gray above with chestnut crown; *rump and undertail coverts bright yellow-olive green* distinguish it from very similar Lucy's warbler; has conspicuous white eye-ring; no white wing bars or tail patches; breast and usually throat lemon yellow; sides gray, rest of underparts dull white; female duller; immatures resemble female but browner above; moves north in spring from winter home in Mexico, sometimes in willows along streams before arrival in summer home in foothills of Rocky Mtns., from Ariz. and N.M. north to Nev., Utah, and Colo.; nests mainly 6,000–9,000 ft. elevation in ravines or sides of steep, rocky mountain slopes covered with dense scrub oaks, mountain mahogany, or in sagebrush, plum thickets, and cottonwoods and willows close to mountain creeks, where males sing while foraging in tall birches, or perched on dead stub, a sprightly *che-we, che-we, che-we, che-we, che-a, che-a, che* (Bent, 1953).

Feeding Habits: No scientific studies made; shy and elusive, this warbler seen foraging on ground in thick brush and flying into air to catch insects; both parents seen carrying foliage-devouring caterpillars to young.
Nest: On ground, sunken in dead leaves or loose soil at base of bush or tuft of grass under mountain mahogany, oaks, chokecherry; built of mosses, lichens, strips of bark, grasses, rootlets, lined with same and hair.
Eggs: May–June; 3–5, usually 4, white, finely speckled with browns.
Incubation: Period of and age when young first fly unknown.
Host to Cowbirds: Single record near Daniels Park, Colo., July 1949 (Friedmann, 1963).
Range: Nests from c. Nev., se. Idaho, ne. Utah, n. Colo., south to se. Calif., s. Nev., c. and se. Ariz., and n.-c. N.M.; winters in Mexico.

Warbler, wagtail. See Warbler, palm; *also* Ovenbird; Waterthrush, Louisiana; and Waterthrush, northern.

Warbler, western palm. *See* Warbler, palm.

Warbler, whitepoll. *See* Warbler, black-and-white.

Warbler, willow. *See* Warbler, prothonotary; *also* Warbler, willow, in Warbler—Old World Warbler Family.

Warbler, Wilson's, *Wilsonia pusilla* (will-SO-nih-ah pew-SILL-ah); genus name: *see* Warbler, Canada; species name: Lat., very small; common name and genus name: for Alexander Wilson (*see* discussion under Canada warbler), who apparently saw only a few migrating in N.J. and Del. (Color ill., page 994.) In w. U.S. has enormous north-south nesting range, from Alaska to N.M.; fairly common in e. U.S. in migration; small yellow "flycatching" warbler; 4½–5 in. long; wingspread 6¾–7 in.; male in breeding plumage, olive green above, bright yellow below, head with *round, glossy black cap* (not always observable); no streaking, no wing bars or tail spots, golden with yellow stripe above black eyes; females sometimes show trace of black cap, immatures do not; migrating, appears as sunny flash of gold in swamp thickets and roadside shrubbery; also in well-grown woodlands, city parks, and gardens; nesting grounds is to limit of trees in Arctic, where it lives in thickets and second-growth saplings of clearings, or in spruce-tamarack, balsam fir, and sphagnum bogs, or in alders and birches near streams and ponds; as he flits about restlessly, male sings bright, hur-ried, rolling twitter, drooping in pitch at end, *t'le, t'le, t'le, t'le, chee-chee-chee* (Forbush, 1925–29).

Feeding Habits: Usually stays within 10 ft. of ground; while feeding, lively, jerks tail as it gleans leaves of bushes especially near water, darts into air frequently to catch flying insects. No comprehensive study of diet yet made.
Nest: On ground, sometimes rather closely associated in loose colonies; bulky, sunken in moss or sedges, sometimes at base of alders; built of mosses, dead leaves, fine weed stalks, grasses, lined with finger grasses; female is close sitter, but after flushed from nest, soon returns even though intruder standing near (Bent, 1953).
Eggs: Apr. (Calif.) to June–July (Alaska); 4–6, commonly 5, white or cream-white, finely speckled with browns.
Incubation: 10–11 days; young leave nest when 10–11 days old (Bent, 1953); 11–13 days; young leave nest 8–10 days after hatching (Stewart, R.M., 1973).
Other Names: Golden pileolated warbler; green black-capped warbler; northern pileolated warbler; pileolated warbler; Wilson's black-cap; Wilson's black-capped flycatching warbler; Wilson's pileolated warbler.
Host to Cowbirds: Seldom reported but locally may be common host to brown-headed cowbird; 14 records (Friedmann, 1963).
Weights: In fall, coastal N.J. (20), 6.1–8.3 gr. (Murray and Jehl, 1964), or about ¼ oz.
Range: Nests from n. Alaska, n. Yuk., to n.e. Man., east to s. Labrador, Newfoundland, south to s. Calif., c. Nev., n. Utah, n. N.M., c. Sask., s. Man., n. Minn., s. Ont., n. Vt., c. Me., and Nova Scotia; winters from s. Baja Calif. to Mexico, s. Tex., to Panama.

Warbler, worm-eating, *Helmitheros vermivorus* (hell-mih-THEE[*th* as in *thin*]-roze ver-MIV-oh-rus); genus name: from Gr. words meaning worm-hunter; species name: from Lat. *vermis*, worm, and *vorare*, to devour, worm-eating. (Color ill., page 994.) In e. U.S., except northernmost part east of prairies, rarely eats earthworms (Bent, 1953), but does eat spanworms (smooth caterpillars); in summer lives over much of central part of U.S. and rather uncommon (Robbins *et al.*, 1966); 5–5½ in. long; sexes outwardly alike; dark olive; buff colored head has dark stripes; olive green above, unmarked buff-white below (similar ovenbird has spotted breast); walks on floor of wooded hillsides, ravines; migrates northward from Mexico and West Indies, reaches Tex. and Fla., first week of Apr.; north through Mississippi Valley and states east of Alleghenies, arrives nesting grounds by May; seldom seen away from woods; male sings while perched 10–20 ft. above ground or from ground; droops tail and wings, fluffs out body feathers, throws back head, and utters a bubbling trill, *che-e-e-e-e-e*, similar to song of chipping sparrow but richer; also gives varied and musical flight song as he flies through woods; walks slowly with tail held high.

Feeding Habits: Largely insectivorous; eats small grasshoppers, walkingsticks, weevils, beetles, sawfly larvae, spanworms, and spiders.

Nest: On ground, well hidden in drift of dead leaves on woods floor, prefers steep wooded hillsides, steep shaded banks, ravines, built under bushes or against sapling; of dead leaves, interior lined with flower stems of hair-cap mosses, stems of maple seeds, and horsehair.
Eggs: May–June; 3–6, usually 4–5, white, speckled with browns.
Incubation: By female, 13 days; young leave nest 10 days after hatching; female with young in nest does crippled-bird act (*see* Distraction Display); one dashed at man near nest and scratched at his legs (Bent, 1953).
Other Names: Worm-eater; worm-eating swamp warbler.
Host to Cowbirds: Uncommon; 37 records, but in some places incidence of cowbird parasitism high.
Weights: In fall, coastal N.J. (1), 12.7 gr. (Murray and Jehl, 1964), or about ½ oz.
Range: Nests from ne. Kans. to n. Ill., east to c. Pa., c. and se. N.Y., s. Conn., w. Mass., south to ne. Tex., c. Ark., s.-c. La., w. Tenn., n. Ala., n. Ga., n.w. S.C., and ne. N.C.; winters from s. Mexico and West Indies to Panama; rarely to n. Fla.; casual to Neb., Wisc., Ont., Vt., and Bermuda.

Warbler, yellow, *Dendroica petechia* (den-DROY-kah peh-TEE-chih-ah); genus name: *see* Warbler, Audubon's (yellow-rumped); species name: according to Gruson (1972), Lat. for "red spots on the skin," alluding to chestnut streaks on sides and breast. (Color ills., page 995.) Has greatest range of all wood warblers, nests from Atlantic to Pacific and from Barren Grounds in Canada to Mexico and the Gulf states; well-known symbol of spring and summer; lights gardens and country thickets with brilliant flash of color; 4½–5¼ in. long; only bird that appears *all*-yellow from distance; male in breeding plumage, underparts and sides of head bright yellow; forehead and front of crown orange-yellow, sometimes tinged with reddish brown; rest of upperparts olive green; sides and breast streaked with chestnut, seen only at close range; has yellow spots in tail; female and immatures similar to male but duller, more greenish above, paler yellow; lack streaking. In summer lives in shrubbery of yards and gardens, favors edges of small streams and ponds bordered by willows, alders, elderberry; brush-grown fences, hedges, and roadside thickets; cut-over woods grown up to wild raspberry and blueberry; in Far North, prairies, and mountains of West, wherever patches of trees or shrubs grow; males increase singing from territories they establish soon after arrival on nesting grounds; bright, rapid musical *wee wee wee witita weet* or *sweet sweet sweet* (Bent, 1953), with goldfinchlike ending.

Feeding Habits: Eats or feeds young many caterpillars destructive to foliage of trees and shrubs: cankerworms and other "measuring worms," gypsy moth and brown-tail moth larvae; bark beetles, borers, weevils, small moths, aphids, grasshoppers, and spiders.
Nest: Built mostly by female, attended closely by male as she works; usually tame, allows close observation; nest built in upright fork or

crotch of bush, sapling, large tree, from 2 ft. up (usually 6–8 ft. above ground but in streamside cottonwoods and shade trees up to 40–60 ft.); a well-formed cup of interwoven plant down, fibers, fine grasses, bits of wool, fur, lichens, mosses, bound with spider's silk or tent caterpillar's webbing, lined with plant down, hairs, cotton.

Eggs: Apr.–July; 3–6, usually 4–5, gray-, green-, or blue-white, glossy, spotted or blotched with browns, olive, gray, wreathed around large end; when cowbird lays egg or eggs in nest, female may build roof over eggs, including her own, and lay new set.

Incubation: 11 days; young leave nest at 9–12 days old.

Other Names: Blue-eyed yellow warbler; golden warbler; summer warbler; summer yellowbird; wild canary; yellowbird; yellow poll; yellow titmouse.

Age: One, banded Nashville, Tenn., recaptured when 5 years old; two, banded as adults, retrapped in Mass. and Mich. when at least 7 years old (Nice, 1935d).

Host to Cowbirds: One of most frequent of all bird hosts; more than 1,000 records, from almost every province in Canada and state in U.S. (Friedmann, 1963); exception: where yellow warblers nest near colonies of red-winged blackbirds, redwings drive away cowbirds.

Weights: In fall, coastal N.J., 6.9–13.7 gr. (Murray and Jehl, 1964), or about ⅓ oz.

Range: Nests from n.c. Alaska east to Newfoundland and south to Alaskan Peninsula, s. Baja Calif., n. S. America, Galápagos Is., Antilles Is., Bahama Is., and Fla. keys; winters from s. Baja Calif., c. Mexico, to Bahamas, south to Peru and Brazil.

Warbler, yellow-crowned. *See* Warbler, chestnut-sided.

Warbler, yellow palm. *See* Warbler, Palm.

Warbler, yellow-rumped, *Dendroica coronata.* General common and scientific names (see American Ornithologists' Union, 1973) for the species representing a group of closely related warblers characterized by a yellow rump and other similarities. For biographies of the two N. American subspecies of the Yellow-rumped warbler, *see* Warbler, Audubon's (yellow-rumped) and Warbler, Myrtle (yellow-rumped). Each of these on most official lists before 1973 had been considered a distinct species, but closer studies of their relationships and frequent crossbreeding indicated that they were geographic representatives of one species, not two.

Warbler, yellow-throated gray. *See* Warbler, yellow-throated.

Warbler, yellow-throated, *Dendroica dominica* (den-DROY-kah dom-IN-ih-kah); genus name: *see* Warbler, Audubon's (yellow-rumped); species name: Lat., of Santo Domingo, early name of island of Hispaniola in West Indies, where type specimen of this warbler was collected. (Color ill., page 997.) A handsome warbler of the Southeast and Mississippi Valley; 4¾–5¾ in. long; male in breeding plu-

mage blue-gray above; rich yellow throat and breast; black-and-white head with white patch on sides of neck; white belly; white stripe over eyes; two white wing bars; sides striped with black; females slightly duller, have less black about head; in fall, immatures and adults washed with brown above; some live year-round in southern part of nesting range; others migrate north from their winter quarters in C. America and West Indies; along s. Atlantic coastal plain, dwells in ancient live oaks draped with Spanish moss (*Tillandsia*), typical of old plantation home grounds of South; others in southern pine forests and cypress swamps; a western race, or subspecies, called the sycamore warbler, summers in Mississippi Valley north to Wisc.; lives much in bottomland sycamores along streams, also about orchards, shade trees, and lawns of towns of valleys; male from trees sings loud, ringing song like that of waterthrush or indigo bunting.

Feeding Habits: Besides slowly inching over trunks and branches in search of food, is skillful "flycatcher"; eats beetles, moths and their caterpillars, grasshoppers, crickets, houseflies, mosquitoes, ants, scale insects, aphids, spiders; comes to feeding stations for bread crumbs (Sprunt, 1953).

Nest: Where no Spanish moss usually builds nest on limbs of sycamore, pine, or cypress, 10–120 ft. above ground; in Southeast, usually builds in clump of Spanish moss near end of limb of tree or in shrub; of fine grasses, weed stems, plant down, and caterpillar's silk, cup lined with plant down and feathers (Sprunt, 1953).

Eggs: Apr.–June; 4–5, usually 4, dull green-white or gray-white, blotched and speckled with lavender, gray, wine red.

Incubation: Probably 12–13 days (Harrison, 1975); two broods in Southeast.

Other Names: Eastern yellow-throated warbler; Dominican yellowthroat; sycamore yellow-throated warbler; yellow-throated creeper; yellow-throated gray warbler.

Accidents: Sometimes adults entangled and die in golden webs of Carolina silk spider, spun in trees of cypress lagoons of Southeast.

Host to Cowbirds: A single record, Okla. (Friedmann, 1963).

Hybrids: Two, near Martinsburg, W.Va.—yellow-throated warbler × northern parula warbler, hybrid called Potomac or Sutton's warbler.

Range: Nests from c. Okla., c. Mo., s. Ill., c. Ind., s. Ohio, sw. W.Va., c. Va., e. Md., s. Del. and c. N.J., south to e. Tex., Gulf coast, s.-c. Fla., and n. Bahamas, seen casually farther north; winters from s. Tex. and s. S.C., c. Ga., n. Fla., south to C. America and West Indies.

Waterthrush, Louisiana, *Seiurus motacilla* (sigh-YOU-rus moh-tah-SILL-ah); genus name: *see* Ovenbird; species name: from Lat. words meaning water wagtail; *Louisiana*, because seen in that state by early ornithologists. (Color ill., page 996.) E. U.S.; a ground-walking "wagtail warbler" closely related to the ovenbird; though not a thrush, resembles one and shows fondness for living near water; habit of constantly bobbing head and foreparts of body

up and down (teetering) with springing motion of legs, like spotted sandpiper, and raising and lowering tail as it walks over ground, are good identifying characteristics of waterthrushes; 5¾–6¼ in. long; sexes alike; plain olive gray or olive brown above; crown slightly darker; conspicuous broad *white* stripe over each eye; white *unstreaked* chin and throat; underparts white or buffy white; breast sides and flanks striped with olive (similar northern waterthrush has *buffy* eye stripe; striped throat; sulphur-yellow striped underparts); ovenbird, closely related to both waterthrushes, has an eye-ring and *no stripe* over eyes. Lives in summer near both sluggish and swift-flowing streams, but in northern part of range, where it overlaps that of northern waterthrush, prefers living near rapid-flowing water of hill or mountain streams; sometimes lives in bottomlands, borders of creeks, lagoons, and swamps with prothonotary warbler (Bent, 1953); walks or runs about (never hops) over stones and moss of stream margins, sometimes flies up into thickets that border stream; male chasing male out of territory sometimes pours out song in flight, but usually from tree or ground, wild, ringing, sweet notes, *pseur, pseur, per see ser* (Forbush, 1925–29).

Feeding Habits: Dragonflies, crane-fly larvae, beetles, bugs, ants, caterpillars, scale insects, small mollusks, killifishes, snails (Bent, 1953); minnows.

Nest: Most frequently along banks of streams or close to water, either in banks or under roots of tree; also in cavity of upturned roots of fallen trees just above or near water or in niche in rock wall of ravine; built of dead leaves, mosses, rootlets, twigs, nest hollow lined with finer rootlets, stems of ferns, grasses, deer hair.

Eggs: Apr.–June; 4–6, usually 5, white or cream-white, speckled, spotted, or blotched with browns and grays.

Incubation: 12–14 days; young leave nest at 9–10 days old.

Other Names: Large-billed waterthrush; southern waterthrush; wagtail; wagtail warbler; water wagtail.

Age: A male, banded Powdermill Nature Reserve, Rector, Pa., trapped and released in same area when 3 years, 11 months, old (Kennard, 1975).

Host to Cowbirds: Rather frequent, much more so than northern waterthrush (Friedmann, 1963).

Weights: In N.C. (11), average 22.4 gr. (Teulings and Teulings, 1971), or about ¾ oz.

Range: Nests from e. Neb., n.c. Iowa, c. Minn., s. Mich., s. Ont., c. N.Y., c. Vt., sw. N.H., and R.I., south to e. Okla., e. Tex., c. La., s. Miss., s. Ala., sw. and c. Ga., and c. and ne. N.C.; winters from c. Mexico to West Indies and nw. S. America; casually to Md.; occasionally in Calif., Me.

Waterthrush, northern, *Seiurus noveboracensis* (sigh-YOU-rus no-veh-bore-ah-SEN-sis); genus name: *see* Ovenbird; species name: Lat., of or pertaining to New York. (Color ill., page 996.) Summers n. U.S., Canada, and Alaska; like Louisiana waterthrush but smaller bill, *buffy* stripe over eyes, and *streaked* throat; 5–6½ in. long; sexes outwardly alike; olive brown above; whitish to sulphur yellow below; throat, upper breast, and sides heavily streaked; in spring migration from wintering in West Indies, n. S. America, traveling up Atlantic coast states or Mississippi Valley, appears in yards, gardens, walking about lawns or under shrubbery; more often in thickets along edges of swamps, ponds, or banks of streams, muddy shores of woodland pools; on nesting grounds in North, lives in shrub-grown bogs, near swamp pools or edges of northern lakes, less often near rushing streams favored by more southern Louisiana waterthrush; seems fond of walking down log of which lower end is in water; continually bobs body and moves tail up and down; male sings loud, sweet song even in migration, and in nesting territory, sometimes from top of small tree in swamp or while walking along limb of hemlock tree: *wheet wheet chip chip chip-u* or *twit twit twit—twee twee twee-chew chew chew.*

Feeding Habits: Eats water beetles, flea beetles, damselflies, weevils, caterpillars, moths, caseworms; hunting over ground, picks up in bill soggy leaves and throws aside to uncover, besides insects, slugs, mollusks, crustaceans; occasionally eats small minnows.

Nest: In small cavity in moss-covered stump over water, under overhanging bank of lakeshore, in upturned roots of fallen trees in swamps or along streams; built of green mosses, twigs, pine needles, strips of inner bark, and fine black rootlets, the inside lined with fine grasses and animal hairs.

Eggs: May–June; 3–6, usually 4–5, cream-white or buff-white, speckled, spotted, or blotched with browns, grays.

Incubation: Period of and age at which young first fly unknown.

Other Names: Aquatic thrush; aquatic wood wagtail; Grinnell's waterthrush; New York waterthrush; northern small-billed waterthrush; wagtail; wagtail warbler; water wagtail.

Age: One, banded Marshfield, Vt., trapped and released in same area when 6 years, 11 months, old (Kennard, 1975).

Host to Cowbirds: 20% of nests parasitized in s. Ont.; 15 records (Friedmann, 1963).

Hybrids: See extraordinary record of hybrid under Blackpoll warbler.

Weights: In fall, coastal N.J. (134), 13.1–24.6 gr. (Murray and Jehl, 1964), or about ½–¾ oz.

Range: Nests from n.-c. Alaska across Canada to c. Labrador, Newfoundland, south to B.C., n. Idaho, and w. Mont., east to n. Wisc., n. Mich., ne. Ohio, n. Pa., and Mass., south in c. Alleghenies to W.Va. and Md.; winters from s. Baja Calif., c. Mexico, and West Indies to n. S. America; accidental in France.

Yellowthroat, Bahama, *Geothlypis rostrata* (jee-OTH-lip-iss ros-TRAY-tah); genus name: from Gr. *ge*, the earth, and *thlypis*, a kind of finch (Jaeger, 1955), a "ground bird"; species name: Lat., beaked, hooked, in reference to bill. Native of West Indies; on Oct. 19, 1968, Paul W. Sykes, Jr., mist-netted (*see* Banding) an adult male at Loxahatchee National

Wildlife Refuge, Palm Beach County, Fla., in thicket of willows along a cypress strand on eastern edge of Fla. Everglades; first record for this West Indian bird in U.S. and on N. American continent; nearest home of this species to Fla. is Grand Bahama and Andros Is. (see Sykes, 1974a).

According to Bond (1961) Bahama yellowthroat is about 6 in. long, and closely resembles the common yellowthroat, *Geothlypis trichas*, but is decidedly larger with longer and heavier bill; males have more or less yellow on upper border of the black facial mask, is not as active as common yellowthroat; in native habitat, lives in shrubs and bracken; sings a loud *wi-chi-tu, wi-chi-tu, wi-chi-tu, wich*, very like songs of yellowthroats of se. U.S.; call note not so harsh as that of common yellowthroat.

Range: Grand Bahama and Abaco, also on many offshore cays (keys) and on Andros, New Providence, and Eleuthera Is. (Bond, 1961).

Yellowthroat, Belding's, *Geothlypis beldingi* (jee-OTH-lip-iss BELL-ding-eye); genus name: *see* Yellowthroat, Bahama; species name: discovered in s. Baja Calif. in 1882 by Lyman Belding, Calif. field ornithologist, and named for him by Robert Ridgway. Is larger and more richly colored with more extensive yellow on its underparts than common yellowthroat; like common yellowthroat in appearance, including black mask of male, but mask bordered behind by yellow instead of blue-white; lives in lowlands along marshy borders of rivers, canyons, in cattails and tule rushes.

Feeding Habits: Apparently insects, but no details of.

Nest: At Comondú on east coast, in clumps of cattails 1½–4½ ft. above ground or water, resemble some song sparrow nests; built outwardly of dry leaves of cattails, thinly lined with fine plant fibers and a few horsehairs, or made of dry tule (rush) strips, tied to living tule stalks, lined with palm fiber.

Eggs: Mar.–May; 2–4, more often 3, white or cream-white, sparingly speckled with browns and grays, usually at large end.

Other Names: Belding's peninsular yellowthroat; peninsular yellowthroat.

Range: Resident (year-round) in c. and s. Baja Calif.

Yellowthroat, common, *Geothlypis trichas* (jee-OTH-lip-iss TRY-kas); genus name: *see* Yellowthroat, Bahama; species name: some kind of thrush (Jaeger, 1955), inappropriate here applied to a warbler. (Color ill., page 998.) One of most abundant of all warblers, nests in Alaska and across Canada and U.S. from Atlantic to Pacific; in West, south to Mexico; 4½–5¾ in. long; olive green above; male has black facial mask (retained all year), bordered above and behind by band of blue-white; chin, throat, breast, undertail coverts pale yellow; belly white; female similar but lacks mask; prefers wild lands, especially low near ground in briers, damp brushy places, tangled rank weeds and grasses along country roads, by streamsides, margins of swamps, woods, and among cattails, bulrushes, sedges in freshwater and salt-water marshes; male may breed with more than

one female (*see* Sexual Relationships); he scolds intruder with chirps, chattering notes—*chack!*—darts about wrenlike, disappears in dense cover, reappears to scold again, occasionally rises to sing in thicket in full view, loud, clear *witchity, witchity, witchity, witchity* or *witch-a-wee-o, witch-a-wee-o.*

Feeding Habits: No detailed studies, but observed catching and eating small grasshoppers, dragonflies, damselflies, mayflies, beetles, grubs, cankerworms and other caterpillars, moths, butterflies, flies, ants, aphids, leafhoppers, leaf rollers, and spiders gleaned from leaves of shrubbery or in grasses and weeds.

Nest: Large, bulky, frequently on, or few inches above, ground, attached in tussocks of grass, reeds, briers, sometimes in green plants such as skunk cabbage; sometimes in tall weed stalks, cattails, or shrubs up to 3 ft. above ground; of dead grasses, sedges, weed stems, dead leaves, grapevine bark, dead ferns, lined with fine grasses, bark fibers, hairs.

Eggs: Apr.–July; white or cream-white, speckled mostly at large end with browns, black, gray.

Incubation: By female, 12 days; young usually leave nest 8 days after hatching (Stewart, 1953).

Other Names: Black-masked ground warbler; Florida yellowthroat; ground warbler; Maryland yellowthroat; northern yellowthroat; olive-colored yellow-throated wren; western yellowthroat.

Age: At Nashville, Tenn., two banded yellowthroats were at least 5 years old, three were 6 years; a female was trapped and released near Nashville when 7 years old (Kennard, 1975).

Host to Cowbirds: One of common victims of brown-headed cowbird; more than 270 records; occasionally yellowthroat will bury cowbird eggs under new nest lining (*see* cowbirds in Troupial Family; Brood-Parasitism).

Weights: In fall, coastal N.J. (348), 7.3–13.6 gr. (Murray and Jehl, 1964), or about ¼–½ oz.

Range: Nests from se. Alaska, s. Yuk., across Canada to sw. Newfoundland, south to n. Baja Calif., s.-c. Mexico, Gulf coast, and s. Fla.; winters from n. Calif., s. Ariz., s. Tex., Gulf coast, and s.c. Panama and West Indies.

Yellowthroat, gray-crowned, *Geothlypis poliocephala* (jee-OTH-lip-iss pol-ih-oh-SEFF-ih-lah); genus name: *see* Yellowthroat, Bahama; species name: Lat., from Gr. *polios*, hoary, gray, and *kephale*, head; "gray-headed." 5–5½ in. long; tropical American warbler related to the common yellowthroat; in U.S. has reached s. Tex.; olive green above, crown and hind neck grayish; yellow throat and a white or yellowish patch on each eyelid, vireolike bill rather thick, downcurved, underparts canary yellow fading to white on abdomen; in male, lores are black (*see* Lore; Topography); sings with low-pitched, pleasing warble; female resembles male but duller and smaller amounts of black on lores; some individuals have no black; long conspicuous legs are pale flesh color; tail almost as long as body.

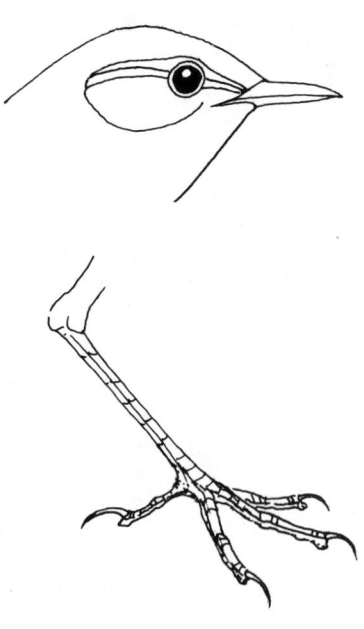

OLD WORLD WARBLER FAMILY

Feeding Habits: Probably largely insects but eats some berries; lives in grassy places diversified by scattered low trees and bushes.
Nest: Built of coarse grasses surrounding finer grasses and lined with horsehair; open cup near ground often in clump of grass.
Eggs: Apr.–May; 2–4, white or creamy, speckled with brown mostly at larger end.
Incubation: Period of and age when young first fly unknown.
Other Names: Ground-chat; Mexican ground-chat; Ralph's ground-chat; Rio Grande ground-chat; thick-billed yellowthroat.
Range: At one time reached N. America in s. Tex. (see Peterson, 1963) but rare in recent years; lives through Mexico and in C. America to Panama.

Yellowthroat, peninsular. *See* Yellowthroat, Belding's.

Yellowthroat, thick-billed. *See* Yellowthroat, gray-crowned.

WARBLER—OLD WORLD WARBLER FAMILY

Sylviidae (sill-VIE-ih-dee); from Scopoli's name *Sylvia,* "the woodland (bird)," from Lat. *sylva,* "a wood" (Macleod, 1954), given to a genus of Old World warblers of this family. Small, active, insect-eating birds in order Passeriformes. 398 species, mostly Old World, includes the American gnatcatchers and kinglets; not related to American wood warblers; are related to Old World flycatchers and thrushes (family Muscicapidae); gnatcatcher is common name for 8 species of genus *Polioptila* that live from S. and C. America north, with one, the blue-gray gnatcatcher, reaching n. U.S.; all are small, slender, with long, thin, pointed bills, soft gray feathers, some with white in tail feathers and black markings on head; blue-gray gnatcatcher is typical of group, and, along with others, has been likened to a tiny mockingbird (Austin, 1961).

Gnatcatchers seem always to be pumping their long tails up and down or jerking them from side to side as they forage through the outer leaves of trees in their hunt for insects; their songs are varied, high-pitched trills and warbles; they also mimic the songs of other birds.

Kinglets are active and unsuspicious; among smallest of N. American birds (*see* under Size); they move actively through leaves of deciduous trees and needles of conifers in search of insects and their eggs and larvae. They pay little attention to human observers close by; in winter, they travel in small scattered groups or within mixed flocks of chickadees, creepers, and woodpeckers in northern woods. Sometimes they eat small seeds, apparently when insects are scarce; call note of golden-crowned kinglet is thin, high *zee-zee,* so fine that some people may not hear it; the ruby-crowned kinglet, however, has a loud, bubbling, sweet song (Austin, 1961).

Only 3 of the Old World warblers—small, largely Asiatic, African, and European species —have reached N. America: the arctic warbler, Middendorff's grasshopper warbler, and willow warbler (A.O.U. *Check-list,* 1957).

WARBLER— AMERICAN WOOD WARBLER FAMILY

Yellow-breasted chat
Secretive and elusive, the largest wood warbler acts and sounds more like a member of the mockingbird clan. Indeed, there is disagreement in scientific circles as to whether it properly belongs in the warbler family. The chat's song is described as a medley of strange sounds —some musical, some harsh—resembling catcalls, whistles, and a variety of bird notes. Like the mockingbird, it often sings at night. Dense thickets are the habitat of the yellow-breasted chat, which nests across the United States and into Central America.

Yellow-breasted chat

Ovenbird
Perhaps the best known of all warbler songs is the ringing "teacher, teacher, teacher, teacher" of the ovenbird, a species named for the oven-shaped nest that it builds on the forest floor.

Northern parula
Especially common in the swamps of the Southeast, this tiny warbler nests in hanging bunches of Spanish moss or, in northern forests, in the lichen known as old-man's beard.

American redstart
One of our most abundant warblers, the American redstart has the distinctive habit of drooping its wings, fanning its orange-flecked tail, and leaping into the air in pursuit of insects.

Painted redstart
Found in the mountain canyons of the Southwest, this handsome Central American warbler behaves much like its eastern namesake, darting out from its perch to snare flying insects.

Bay-breasted warbler
A bird of northern coniferous forests, the bay-breasted warbler builds its nest of grass, twigs, roots, lichen, moss, and bark strips as high as 50 feet in a spruce or hemlock.

Black-and-white warbler
Creeping over tree trunks and limbs like a nuthatch, the black-and-white warbler hunts ants, caterpillars, moths, flies, beetles, and woodborers. Four or 5 young are raised in a nest built on the ground against a stump, rock, or log.

Blackburnian warbler
Brilliant orange markings on the head and throat identify this inhabitant of the treetops, one of the hardest warblers for bird-watchers to locate. In breeding season, the male will sing from the highest tip of a spruce tree, and its nest may be built 80 feet from the ground.

Blackpoll warbler
This summer resident of Canada's boreal forests is famous for its migration feats. In fall, southbound blackpoll warblers head out to sea over the New England coast. From there, they fly nonstop 2,300 miles to the tropical forests of South America. Their flight over the Atlantic and Caribbean takes 86 hours; to gain favorable winds, they fly as high as 21,000 feet. Perhaps half of those that set out on their long journey never reach land.

Ovenbird

Northern parula, male and nestling

American redstart

Blackburnian warbler

Painted redstart

ay-breasted warbler

Black-and-white warbler

ay-breasted warbler, female

Blackpoll warbler

Black-throated blue warbler
A common migrant in the East, this tame visitor to gardens and parks is one of the first warblers that a bird-watcher learns to identify.

Black-throated gray warbler
Regularly found in dry western scrubland, this drab-colored species blends well with the gray-green foliage of junipers. It feeds extensively on oak worms and other, green caterpillars.

Black-throated green warbler
Another abundant migrant on its way to northern nesting grounds, the black-throated green warbler has a persistent and easily recognized song—a lisping "zee-zee-zee-zoo-zee."

Blue-winged warbler
An uncommon inhabitant of overgrown pastures, thickets, and the woodland edge, the blue-winged warbler often interbreeds with the closely related golden-winged warbler.

Canada warbler
Damp, mossy places on or near the ground are the preferred nesting sites of this favorite of warbler-watchers. Quickly identified by its black necklace, the Canada warbler forages in the forest's understory, flitting from bush to bush in pursuit of flying insects.

Cape May warbler
Chestnut cheek patches identify this bird of northern spruce forests. The species is named for Cape May, New Jersey—an ornithological hot spot during migration periods—where the first specimen was collected in 1811.

Cerulean warbler
Though fairly common in deciduous river-bottom forests, the cerulean warbler is difficult to find because it feeds and nests in the tops of the tallest trees. Its nest, a shallow cup decorated with spider's silk, lichens, and mosses, is usually situated far out on a slender branch.

Chestnut-sided warbler
A bird of thickets and second-growth woodlands, the chestnut-sided warbler was an uncommon species before the virgin forests of the Midwest and Northeast were leveled, creating vast areas of new habitat. Its nest is usually found within 4 feet of the ground in a shrub, sapling, or bramble.

Black-throated blue warbler

Black-throated gray warbler

Black-throated green warbler

Blue-winged warbler

Cerulean warbler

ape May warbler

anada warbler

Chestnut-sided warbler

Connecticut warbler
Though it passes through Connecticut only on its fall migration, this shy, seldom-seen warbler bears the name of the state where it was first collected in 1812 by the pioneer ornithologist Alexander Wilson. It nests in spruce-tamarack bogs from south-central Canada to northern Michigan.

Golden-winged warbler
When feeding on small forest caterpillars, the golden-winged warbler often swings upside down from twigs like a chickadee. Its song, like that of the closely related blue-winged warbler, is an insectlike buzz.

Hermit warbler
The canopy of great coastal forests, from Washington to California, is the haunt of the hermit warbler. Though uniquely marked with a golden head and black bib, it is rarely seen—for it feeds in the tops of Douglas firs, redwoods, and pines 100 to 200 feet tall.

Hooded warbler
Skilled at catching flying insects, the hooded warbler is a common breeding bird in eastern deciduous forests with dense undergrowth and cool, shaded ravines. Its nest is a cup of dead leaves and plant fibers, bound with spider webs and wedged in the fork of a sapling.

Kentucky warbler
A bird of damp, dark deciduous forests across the East, the Kentucky warbler spends much of its life on the ground, turning over leaves and probing under sticks in search of insect life.

Kirtland's warbler
An endangered species, its breeding population reduced to a few hundred birds by shrinking habitat and heavy cowbird parasitism, Kirtland's warbler nests in only a few counties of Michigan's lower peninsula. Its survival is tied to an abundance of young jack pines, a tree that germinates only when its cones are opened and their seeds scattered by the intense heat of a forest fire. Successful cowbird control and prescribed burning to create new habitats apparently have stemmed the decline of this world-famous songbird.

Lucy's warbler
The only warbler to breed in the hot deserts of the Southwest, and one of the few to nest in tree cavities, Lucy's warbler is found in riverside mesquites and cottonwoods. Its song, similar to that of the well-known yellow warbler, is commonly heard by rafters on the Colorado River deep within the Grand Canyon.

Lucy's warbler

ermit warbler

Golden-winged warbler

irtland's warbler

Hooded warbler, male and female

onnecticut warbler

Kentucky warbler, male and female

MacGillivray's warbler
Found over much of the West, from southeastern Alaska to New Mexico, this species was named by John James Audubon in honor of a Scottish ornithologist, William MacGillivray. It haunts dense thickets, where it forages near the ground for beetles and caterpillars.

Magnolia warbler
Alexander Wilson named this attractive bird for the flowering trees where he collected the first specimen, in Mississippi, about 1810. Especially numerous on migration, the magnolia warbler has the distinctive habit of fanning its tail to display a broad white band and yellow rump.

Mourning warbler
To Wilson, the black patch on the breast of this bird suggested a person wearing crepe in mourning. Skulking about thickets overgrown with brambles, nettles, and jewelweed, the mourning warbler builds a bulky nest of dead grass, weeds, and leaves in a clump of ferns or goldenrod.

Nashville warbler
Discovered near that Tennessee city by Wilson in 1808, the Nashville warbler has 2 widely separated breeding populations in the East and West. A bird of second-growth woodlands and overgrown farmland, its population exploded after the clearing of virgin forests for lumber and agriculture.

Olive warbler
A Central American species, the olive warbler ranges north into Arizona and New Mexico, where it nests in open and fir forests above an elevation of 8,000 feet.

Orange-crowned warbler
"Nondescript" is the best word for this warbler, a common bird in the West but fairly rare in the East. The brownish-orange patch on its crown is seldom seen unless the bird is alarmed or courting.

Mourning warbler

Magnolia warbler

Nashville warbler

range-crowned warbler

Olive warbler, female

MacGillivray's warbler

Palm warbler
A tail-wagging inhabitant of northern bogs, the palm warbler builds its nest on a hummock of sphagnum moss at the foot of a small spruce or tamarack. Wintering in the South, it is often seen in groves of saw palmettos.

Pine warbler
Aptly named, this plain-colored warbler spends summer and winter in open groves of pine trees and is one of the few North American warblers whose wintering range includes much of its breeding range. Pine warbler nests are concealed in clusters of needles, often near the tip of a branch.

Prairie warbler
This is a bird not of the prairies but of pine-oak scrublands and abandoned farms across the eastern United States. In south Florida, it is found in mangrove swamps. Twitching its tail from side to side, a prairie warbler will chase insects through the bushes, on occasion hovering over the top of a shrub to snatch its prey.

Prothonotary warbler
The scientific and common name of this denizen of river-bottom swamps and flooded woods was suggested by the protonotarius, a papal official in the Roman Catholic Church who wears a yellow hood. This is the only warbler in the eastern United States to nest in tree cavities.

Red-faced warbler
This strikingly colored warbler from Central America is locally common during the nesting season in the mountain forests of New Mexico and Arizona. It nests on the ground, scratching out a depression next to a log, rock, or tree seedling.

Swainson's warbler
Named by Audubon for his friend William Swainson, a brilliant English ornithologist of the early 19th century, this is an uncommon and little-known bird of the southeastern states. Dull-colored, shy, and sedentary, it frequents both lowland swamps and canebrakes and mountainside tangles of rhododendron and laurel.

Tennessee warbler
Alexander Wilson once again is responsible for a misleading name, having discovered this species in 1811 on the banks of the Cumberland River in Tennessee. It is found there only on migration, for the Tennessee warbler nests in open woodlands across Canada.

Palm warbler

Prairie warbler

Prothonotary warbler

Red-faced warbler

Tennessee warbler

Swainson's warbler

Pine warbler

Townsend's warbler
A western counterpart of the black-throated green warbler, this species summers in the towering coniferous forests of the Northwest from Alaska to Wyoming, foraging in the treetops for weevils, leafhoppers, scale insects, and caterpillars.

Virginia's warbler
This small warbler of the mountains of the Southwest is found in pinyon-juniper brushland and chaparral between 6,000 and 9,000 feet. Virginia's warbler, named for the wife of an army surgeon who discovered the species, winters in Mexico.

Wilson's warbler
A round, glossy black cap marks the male Wilson's warbler, a species that nests in northern forests from Alaska to Newfoundland and New England and, in the West, ranges as far south as New Mexico. On migration, it appears as a sunny flash of gold in roadside shrubs or swamp thickets, refueling on insects gleaned from leaves or caught in midair forays.

Worm-eating warbler
Resembling a sparrow in size, color, and behavior, the worm-eating warbler hunts not earthworms, as one might surmise from its name, but moth caterpillars, especially spanworms. It is a bird of the deciduous forest floor, where it walks about with tail cocked high, searching the leaf litter for food.

Yellow warbler
Our best-known warbler has a greater range than any other member of its family, nesting from ocean to ocean and from the barren grounds of Canada to Mexico. Its favored nesting places are small streams and ponds bordered by willows and alders; its nest, built by the female, is a tightly woven cup of plant down, fine grass, bits of wool and fur, and lichens, bound with tent caterpillar webbing and spider's silk. Yellow warblers feed on a host of insects that are destructive to shrubs and shade trees.

Worm-eating warbler

Wilson's warbler

Townsend's warbler

Virginia's warbler

Yellow warbler, female

Yellow warbler

Yellow-rumped warbler

Until recently, the myrtle warbler and Audubon's warbler were considered 2 distinct species. However, the birds are similar in appearance except for the color of their throats (white in the myrtle warbler, yellow in Audubon's), and where their ranges overlap, they readily interbreed. Thus taxonomists ruled they were only geographic races of one species, newly named the yellow-rumped warbler. In the East, it is the most abundant of all migrating warblers; 24,000 passed by an observer on the South Carolina coast in a 5-hour period.

Yellow-throated warbler

This handsome bird of the South frequents live oaks draped with Spanish moss, cypress swamps, riverside sycamores, and pine forests. Like the black-and-white warbler, it will creep over trunks and branches in quest of food.

Louisiana waterthrush

Thrushlike in appearance, with a fondness for living near water, these unusual warblers forage over the ground, bobbing up and down like spotted sandpipers. The Louisiana waterthrush, the less common of the 2 waterthrushes, nests from Minnesota to New England, and south to Texas and Georgia. It frequents fast-running streams and river swamps, hiding its nest close to water in a bank, under tree roots, or in a rock niche.

Northern waterthrush

Boglands and lakeshores across the North from Alaska to Labrador are the haunt of the northern waterthrush. In addition to insect life, it regularly eats slugs, mollusks, and crustaceans uncovered by tossing aside soggy leaves, as well as small minnows. An early migrant, the northern waterthrush begins its southward movement by mid-July.

Louisiana waterthrush

Northern waterthrush

ellow-rumped (Audubon's) warbler

ellow-rumped (Myrtle) warbler

llow-throated warbler

Common yellowthroat

Common yellowthroat

Marshy places across the continent are the habitat of this abundant warbler, whose well-known song is a loud, ringing "witchity, witchity, witchity." The yellowthroat's nest is a mass of grasses, sedges, bark, and ferns, often attached to reeds, cattails, or even skunk cabbages. Male yellowthroats perform an aerial display during the breeding season.

Old World warblers are quite different from the wood warblers of the New World. Most of them are fine singers (wood warblers have weak, lisping voices); have softer, more fluffy plumage; and have 10 functional primaries, or flight feathers (the American wood warblers have 9) (Van Tyne and Berger, 1959). They are generally small, about 3½–6 in. long; are green, brown, or pale gray, with fine or slender pointed bills; and in most there are no outward differences between males and females. They move about in trees, shrubs, low scrub, and some of them in reeds and in grass, where they search for small insects, spiders, and berries (Voous, 1964c). The Old World warblers are songbirds or perching birds.

The arctic warbler, the only Old World warbler that nests in N. America, is unusually interesting in that it is a species of the forests of the Far North that is spreading around the world and has reached Alaska and n. Scandinavia in the expansion of its range from its original home in Asia.

Apparently the arctic warbler crossed Bering Strait from Siberia to eventually nest in Alaska after glacial times, and late in each summer recrosses Bering Strait to e. Asia before migrating south to its wintering grounds in tropical se. Asia, Indonesia, and the Philippines (Tucker, 1949).

Strikingly similar is the migratory route of those N. American gray-cheeked thrushes that nest in ne. Siberia and return across Bering Strait, then travel across our continent to e. N. America before migrating southward to the American tropics.

According to Reilly (1968), the arctic warbler apparently arrives in Alaska in June and departs sometime between Aug. and early Nov. Its song, generally delivered from trees or from shrubby growth, is a few clicking *tzick* notes followed by a high-pitched trill of *si-zi-zi* notes, a fairly regular alternation of monotonous song phrases (Tucker, 1949) lasting about 3 seconds. Its call note is a husky *tssp!* or a metallic *chit!* Reilly (1968) reported the arctic warbler as now "very rare in Alaska." Gross (1965a) noted 6 records of albinism in 1 species of the Old World Warbler Family but did not name the species.

Members of the family are protected by law, but to care for an injured, ill, or crippled bird, offer mealworms or any insects available, and ground raw meat; also, try soft well-ripened fruit such as grapes, and a small amount of bread crumbs (Walker, 1942).

Gnatcatcher, black-capped, *Polioptila nigriceps* (pol-ih-OP-tih-lah NIG-rih-seps); genus name: from Gr. *polios,* hoary, or gray, and *ptilon,* feather; species name: Lat., black-capped. Native of Mexico, has reached Ariz.; 4½ in. long; breeding male is black-capped (without white lores or white eye stripe) and has no white eye-ring as in blue-gray gnatcatcher; in winter, male has no black cap, head is same color as the back, and no white eyebrow stripe; back and rump blue-gray; wings brown-slate, the wing tertials edged with whitish; considered by some ornithologists to be a race, or subspecies, of the white-lored gnatcatcher, *Polioptila albiloris;* males of black-capped in

Black-capped gnatcatcher

OLD WORLD WARBLER FAMILY

summer closely resemble male white-lored gnatcatchers (for details see Blake, E. R., 1953; Peterson and Chalif, 1973).

Other Name: Black-headed gnatcatcher.
Range: From w. Mexico south to Nayarit, or possibly Jalisco; first nesting record of this native Mexican species in U.S. was summer of 1971; near Nature Conservancy Bird Sanctuary, Patagonia, Ariz., the adults of a pair and their three young were collected (shot) on June 22 by student of University of Arizona (Carr, 1971); see details also in Phillips *et al.* (1973).

Gnatcatcher, black-headed. *See* Gnatcatcher, black-capped.

Gnatcatcher, black-tailed, *Polioptila melanura* (pol-ih-OP-tih-lah mel-an-OO-rah); genus name: *see* Gnatcatcher, black-capped; species name: Lat., from Gr. *melanos*, black, and *oura*, tail, "black-tailed." (Color ill., page 1,031.) 3¾–4¼ in. long; black-tailed is fairly common in desert scrub growth, washes, and ravines (Robbins *et al.*, 1966) of sw. U.S., n. Mexico; male in breeding season is blue-gray, resembling blue-gray gnatcatcher, but has *glossy black cap* assumed in Feb., has white eye-ring and black bill; is white below and long tail has white *only* on outer web and tip; tail appears largely black; utters whining, querulous mewing note, thin and plaintive; male often utters short, harsh notes.

Feeding Habits: Searches along branches and twigs of shrubs; sometimes hovers like kinglet to pick off insect from leaf; about 98% of food is insects: beetles, wasps, ants, bugs, caterpillars, small moths, flies, and grasshoppers; also eats small amounts of seeds, some spiders.
Nest: Small, deep cup of hemplike fibers, leaves of sage, plant down, spider's silk, built in bushes 2–3 ft. above ground.
Eggs: Ariz., about mid-Apr.–mid-July; Calif., about mid-Mar.–mid-June; 3–5, usually 4, green or pale blue, spotted with browns.
Incubation: By both sexes, about 14–15 days (Woods, 1949); young leave nest about 9–10 days after hatching.
Other Names: California gnatcatcher; plumbeous gnatcatcher.
Host to Cowbirds: Occasional (Friedmann, 1963); only 13 records in Calif., Baja Calif., and Ariz., but assumed by Friedmann to be more commonly victimized than records show.
Range: Lives year-round in mesquite thickets in desert country of Southwest and Rio Grande Valley; from s. Calif., s. Nev., c. Ariz., s. N.M., and sw. Tex. into Mexico and Baja Calif.

Gnatcatcher, blue-gray, *Polioptila caerulea* (pol-ih-OP-tih-lah see-RUE-lee-ah); genus name: *see* Gnatcatcher, black-capped; species name: Lat., blue. (Color ill., page 1,032.) In summer, across U.S. from Calif. to n. N.J., south to Baja Calif. and Gulf coast; 4–5 in. long; wingspread 5¾–6½ in.; blue-gray above, white below, with long, largely black tail with white outer tail feathers; white eye-ring; male in spring has a black forehead stripe and black stripe over eyes; appears like tiny mockingbird; tail often cocked straight up like wren's tail, sings low, warbling ditty, opening with *zee-u*

zee-u; call a distinctive, thin, banjolike twang; common, fidgety, slender and frail bird of treetops of moist forests; also oak woods, chaparral, and open pinyon and juniper country.

Feeding Habits: Intensely active, searches over leaves, flowers, buds, and twigs for insects or "flycatches" them by flitting from tree branches out into air; eats beetles, flies, ants, gnats, and insect eggs and larvae; also spiders (Weston, 1949). See especially Root (1967).
Nest: On horizontal branch, sometimes in vertical crotch of tree, from a few feet to 70 ft. above ground, but usually less than 25 ft. up; a handsome, lichen-covered, cuplike nest of plant fibers lined with bark strips, feathers, hair, and fine grasses, often anchored to a 2-in.-thick branch by spider's silk.
Eggs: Calif., early Apr.–mid-July; S.C. and Tex., mid-Apr.–mid-May; 3–6, usually 4–5, pale blue, usually spotted with red-brown, some immaculate.
Incubation: By both sexes in turn, about 13 days; young first fly about 10–12 days after hatching; both parents feed and brood young (Weston, 1949).
Other Names: Chay-chay; common gnatcatcher; little blue-gray wren; small blue-gray flycatcher; sylvan flycatcher.
Age: An adult female, banded at Powdermill Nature Reserve, Rector, Pa., May 9, 1969, was killed by boy with slingshot at Llano Grande, Jalisco, Mexico, Nov. 1, 1970, when at least 2½–3 years or more old; this was first recovery of a banded blue-gray gnatcatcher south of U.S. and only the third recovery of banded blue-gray gnatcatchers ever reported (Parkes and Clench, 1972).
Host to Cowbirds: Fairly common (Friedmann, 1963); 39 records.
Weights: In fall, coastal N.J. (3), 5.7–7.2 gr. (Murray and Jehl, 1964), or about ¼ oz.; in summer, in Kans., males (3), 6.4–6.9 gr. (Rising, 1965a).
Range: Nests from S.D., c. Nev., s. Utah, Ore., c. Minn., s. Wisc., s. Mich., s. Ont., Ohio, w. N.Y., n. N.J., se. N.Y. (Long Is.), and Conn., south to s. Baja Calif., Guatemala, Gulf coast, c. Fla., and Bahamas; winters s. U.S. from Va. along Atlantic coast south into Mexico, Cuba, and C. America.

Gnatcatcher, plumbeous. *See* Gnatcatcher, black-tailed.

Kinglet, golden-crowned, *Regulus satrapa* (REG-you-lus SAT-rah-pah); genus name: Lat., dim. of *rex*, a king; a kinglet; species name: Lat., from Gr. *satrapes*, a ruler; one wearing a golden crown (Jaeger, 1955). (Color ill., page 1033.) 3¼–4¼ in. long; wingspread 6½–7 in.; short-tailed, olive green above, pale below, smaller than warblers, has conspicuous orange crown patch (yellow in female) bordered with yellow and black; bill black; eyes brown, two whitish wing bars; unlike warblers, has habit of nervously flicking wings when hopping from twig to twig; utters three-note lisping call; song seldom heard except on northern breeding grounds, opens with series of fine notes, similar to call, ends with louder, harsh, staccato notes that descend in pitch; rendered

phonetically: *zee-zee-zee-zee-zee, why do you shilly-shally?* (Bent, 1949); astonishingly fearless of people, comes into open cabins, allows itself to be stroked at times and even picked up.

Feeding Habits: Food is almost entirely insects and their eggs (bark beetles, scale insects), and especially plant lice (aphids); in winter socializes and feeds with flocks of chickadees and with brown creepers and downy woodpeckers; drinks tree sap (*see* Commensalism).
Nest: Globular with entrance in top, attached to twigs, usually of evergreen, from 4 ft. up, usually 30–60 ft. above ground; only 3–4 in. across, 2¾–3¾ in. deep; built of mosses, lichens, lined with soft bark and rootlets and feathers.
Eggs: Apr.–July; 5–10, usually 8–9, white to cream, spotted or blotched with brown or gray; very tiny, each only about ½ in. long; nest so small eggs must be deposited in two layers (Bent, 1949).
Incubation: Period of unknown, but may be about 14–15 days as in the related European firecrest, *Regulus ignicapillus;* age when young first fly unknown.
Other Names: Fiery-crowned wren; flamecrest; gold-crest; golden-crested kinglet; golden-crowned wren.
Accidents: Sometimes gets entangled in burrs of burdock. See Accidents.
Hybrids: Golden-crowned kinglet × ruby-crowned kinglet (Gray, 1958).
Weights: In fall, coastal N.J. (2), 5.3 and 5.8 gr. (Murray and Jehl, 1964), or about ⅕ oz.
Range: Nests from s. Alaska, B.C., to Newfoundland, south in mountains to s. Calif., Ariz., N.M., from n. Man. east to Ont., s. Que., south to e. Tenn., N.C., c. Mass., and s. Me.; also in highlands of Mexico and in Guatemala; winters at least casually from se. Alaska, B.C., Alta., s. Minn., s. Wisc., Mich., s. Ont., N.Y., N.B., and Newfoundland south to s.-c. Tex., Gulf coast, and n. Fla.

Kinglet, ruby-crowned, *Regulus calendula* (REG-you-lus cal-EN-dyou-lah); genus name: *see* Kinglet, golden-crowned; species name: from Lat. *calendus*, glowing, in allusion to red crown patch of male. (Color ill., page 1,033.) Slightly smaller than smallest warbler; 3¾–4½ in. long; wingspread 6¾–7½ in.; olive above, whitish below, with large dark eyes and white eye-ring that gives it staring expression; male has red crown patch, usually concealed; is flashed when bird is excited; has two white wing bars; song is remarkably full and of great volume, a prolonged and varied warble; phonetic rendition has it *liberty, liberty, liberty;* sings both in spring and in fall; call notes are wrenlike *cack* and lisping *zhi-dit;* on breeding grounds in coniferous forests, seen singly or in small groups; associates in migration and on wintering grounds loosely with warblers, titmice, nuthatches, creepers, and golden-crowned kinglets in thickets, woods, hedges; winters farther south and nests farther north than golden-crowned; throughout most of U.S. seen only in migration.

Feeding Habits: Like golden-crowned, feeds at tips of branches, hovers at twigs, may search the ground among fallen leaves or on twigs of herbaceous plants, low oaks, trunks, limbs, and twigs and needles of pines for food, most of it bugs, wasps, ants, beetles, butterflies, moths, caterpillars, flies; drinks tree sap; eats spiders and pseudoscorpions; some fruit, especially elderberries, and some weed seeds, etc. (Bent, 1949).

Nest: Usually in spruce trees, sometimes in firs, pines, 2–100 ft. up; pensile, materials like those of golden-crowned kinglet.

Eggs: May–July; 5–11, usually 7–9, virtually indistinguishable from those of golden-crowned.

Incubation: Believed to be 12 days (Bent, 1949); young first fly about 12 days after hatching.

Other Names: Ruby-crown; ruby-crowned warbler; ruby-crowned wren.

Host to Cowbirds: Rare (Friedmann, 1963); only 6 records—3 in Que.; 1 each in Me., Alta., and Calif.

Hybrids: See Golden-crowned kinglet.

Weights: In fall, coastal N.J. (69), 4.5–7.5 gr. (Murray and Jehl, 1964), or about 1/6–1/4 oz.

Range: Nests from nw. Alaska, nw. Mack., n. Man., n. Ont., c. Que., s. Labrador, and Newfoundland south to Guadalupe Is. off Baja Calif., c. Ariz., c. N.M., n. Mich., s. Ont., n. N.Y., n. Me., and Nova Scotia; winters from se. B.C., c. Wash., e. Ore., and from Neb., s. Iowa, n. Ill., s. Ont., s. Ohio, W.Va., Md., and N.J., south to Baja Calif., Mexico, Guatemala, Gulf coast, and Fla.; has strayed to Greenland and Great Britain.

Warbler, Arctic, *Phylloscopus borealis* (fill-OS-koh-pus boh-reh-AY-lis); genus name: Lat., from Gr. *phyllon*, leaf, and *skopeo*, look at, to see, from habit of peering under leaves for insects; species name: Lat., northern. (Color ill., page 1,032.) In N. America, nests in Alaska; about 4¾ in. long; very active, vireolike in appearance; olive green above, white below washed with yellow; a yellow-white eye-stripe; bill blackish; a narrow white wing bar, legs pale yellow; song, a repeated *tchik*, followed by trill (Peterson *et al.*, 1954).

Feeding Habits: Eats mainly mosquitoes (the crops of some of these birds in Norway were crammed with them); also eats the larvae (caterpillars) of moths, ants, adult beetles, bugs, and other insects (Tucker, 1949).

Nest: Globe-shaped, or dome-shaped, with entrance on side, made of weed stems, grasses, and mosses, lined with finer grasses and sometimes with a few ptarmigan feathers; built on ground under bushes or in tall grasses of scrubby forests or willow growth or among birches or briers.

Eggs: July; 5–7, usually 6, white, often but not always spotted with red-brown.

Incubation: Period of unknown, but by female alone and only one brood raised each year (Tucker, 1949); age when young first fly unknown.

Other Names: Arctic willow warbler; Evermann's warbler; Kennicott's willow warbler.

Range: Nests in sparse patchy woods of Far North in deciduous, coniferous, and mixed growth; commonly along water courses

among willows and in birch forests; from limit of trees in n. Eurasia south to Great Britain, n. Italy, n. Russia, across Siberia to n. Mongolia, Korea, to s. Japan; nests in w. Alaska, from Koluk R. and w. Brooks Range to St. Michael, Nusagak, Aleknagik, upper Nome R., Katmai National Monument, and Mt. McKinley National Park; winters in Africa.

Warbler, Middendorff's grasshopper, *Locustella ochotensis* (low-cus-TEL-lah oak-oh-TEN-sis); genus name: Lat., dim. of *locusta*, locust, or grasshopper, possibly in allusion to insectlike song or calls; species name: from Gr. *ochos*, anything which bears, a wagon, and *tenon, tenontos*, a tendon, a tightly stretched bandage (Jaeger, 1955); application of name to bird obscure; however, see Gruson (1972); common name: in honor of Dr. A. v. Middendorff (1815–94), who traveled in Siberia on expedition in mid-19th century (Wynne, 1969); he described the warbler in 1853. Reported in Alaska (Nunivak Is.); about 5¼ in. long; rather similar to the arctic warbler but buffy brown above and very pale gray below.

Range: Nests in Asia; winters in Malay Archipelago.

Warbler, willow, *Phylloscopus trochilus* (fil-OS-koh-pus TROCK-ill-us); genus name: *see* Warbler, Arctic; species name: term originally applied by Herodotus to Egyptian species of plover, also by ancients to some small bird (Coues, 1882). 4¼ in. long (compares with smaller N. American songbirds); upperparts olive brown; underparts buffy white washed with yellow; legs usually light brown; a slim, dainty, vireolike bird; Peterson *et al.* (1954) call the willow warbler the most abundant summer visitor to northern half of Europe.

Other Names: Peggy-whitethroat; willow wren.

Age: One, banded Sweden, June 1925, recovered in France, Aug. 1930, when at least 5 years old (Nice, 1934b).

Range: Nests from n. Europe, n. Russia, and Siberia south through Europe and British Isles; winters in Africa. Accidental in Greenland.

Warbler, Arctic willow. *See* Warbler, Arctic.

Warbler, Kennicott's willow. *See* Warbler, Arctic.

WARM-BLOODED
See Homoiothermous; *also* Metabolism; Temperature.

WARNECOUTAI
or WARNECOOTAI. Another name for the king eider; from *ouarnicouti*, of Indian origin, meaning "head filled out full" (McAtee, 1956b).

WASHING FOOD
See Swallowing.

range map of the Arctic warbler

OLD WORLD WARBLER FAMILY
The Arctic warbler is one of a small number of essentially Eurasian birds whose ranges extend a short distance into northwestern North America. Most of these species spend the winter in the warmer parts of the Old World.

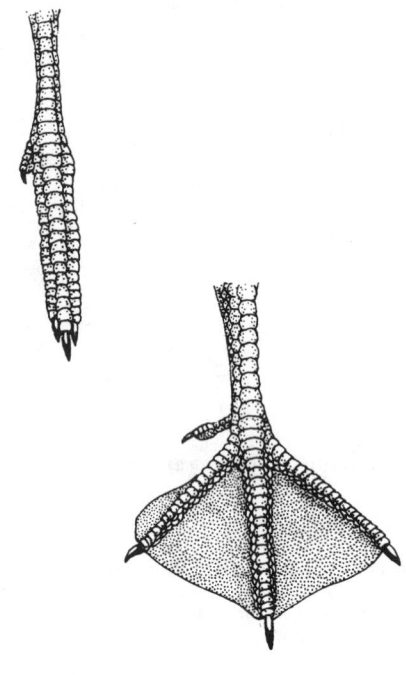

WATERFOWL
Ducks and other waterfowl have palmate feet well suited for swimming. To bring the foot forward through the water with the least resistance, the duck folds its toes and webs together. On the backstroke, its toes and webs are fully spread.

WASPS AND BIRDS
See Insects and Birds.

WATER-BELCHER
Local name for the American bittern, because of sounds it makes when it gulps air and forces it out of mouth under pressure. *See* Esophagus.

WATER BIRD
General term (not a classification; *see* Classification) for any bird that lives part of its life in or around water, especially the swimming, diving, and wading birds. *See* Swimming and Diving. It also might include the coastal and inland pelicans, anhingas, and cormorants, the coastal and offshore boobies, gannets, and frigatebirds, and all marsh birds (*see* Marsh Bird), the waterfowl (*see* Waterfowl), the shorebirds (*see* Shorebird), and most members of the Gull Family and the Auk Family. The true seabirds, or *oceanic birds*, are usually those that live most of their lives at sea. *See* Seabird.

WATER DANCE
A form of mutual and group display by alcids, members of the Auk Family. Murres, for example, gather in small groups and begin to skitter over water, feet touching the surface, in long curving lines, loops, and even figure eights, sometimes with great speed with help of wings but do not take flight; a dancing quality about these movements; the water dance may continue underwater. See Tuck (1961) for interesting details; *see also* in biography of pigeon guillemot in Auk Family.

WATERFOWL
Term applied, especially by American sportsmen and game biologists, to the ducks, geese, and swans—in Great Britain called wildfowl. *See* under Duck Family. The broader term *water bird* usually includes most or all of those birds that live in or around water.

Waterfowl are probably the most written about (in the scientific and popular wildlife literature) of any group of birds; their migrations and behavior (*see* Behavior; Migration) have been especially studied by biologists. Glover (1964) reported that of 11 million records of birds banded in N. America, 4 million were waterfowl, and slightly less than half of the 600,000 birds banded each year, as of the 1960s, also were waterfowl. About four fifths of the banded birds (about 40,000 a year) recovered, or those reported as shot, found dead, or caught alive and released, were waterfowl. See popular articles by Cant (1959) and by Terres (1964b).

Many N. American waterfowl migrate southward from their northern breeding grounds each fall to winter in many parts of the U.S.—in Calif., on interior lakes and reservoirs of middle America and of the Southeast and Southwest, along large river valleys, and along the Pacific, Atlantic, and Gulf coasts. Most ducks that migrate south of the U.S. winter in Mexico —26 species (see Saunders, 1964).

According to the U.S. Fish and Wildlife Service (Anonymous, 1975d), about 100 million ducks, geese, and swans migrated in the fall of 1975. Salt marshes, sloughs, creeks, and ponds nationwide were the wintering homes of more than 90 million ducks of 36 species, about 3–4 million geese of 7 species, and upward of 150,000 swans of 2 species.

The pintail, green-winged teal, and blue-winged teal have the longest migrations of any N. American waterfowl—both reach S. America. *See* migrations and wintering grounds of these and other species of waterfowl under Duck Family.

Large numbers of waterfowl regularly use certain migration routes between their nesting and wintering grounds (Lincoln, 1950c) and most waterfowl migration is at night (Bellrose, 1966); some waterfowl move along travel lanes that are like a narrow path close to a river valley or a north-south coastline in their daytime migrations; in other travel lanes, waterfowl spread out broadly, especially at night. See the observations of nocturnal waterfowl migration by Bellrose (1966). If one were to plot all major migration routes of several species of waterfowl on a single map, it would be a confusing crisscross pattern through much of Canada and the n. U.S., but as the waterfowl fly southward, they would tend to separate into groups in which they would fly along distinct travel routes (Lincoln, 1939). These have been labeled "flyways" by waterfowl biologists and are called, from east to west, the Atlantic, Mississippi, Central, and Pacific flyways. For the geographical location of these flyways and discussion of the kinds of waterfowl that use each, see details in Linduska and Nelson (1964), also Dorst (1962). See, however, different conclusions of Phillips (1951) and observations of waterfowl migration by Bellrose (1966).

While the flyway concept is important administratively for the management of waterfowl, the flyways cover too broad an area to describe adequately the routes taken by waterfowl in their migratory movements. Therefore, Bellrose (1976) developed the concept of *migration corridors* to explain the direction and distribution of such movements. Each year, the U.S. Fish and Wildlife Service conducts a Jan. survey of the waterfowl population on their wintering grounds. This is the time of year—after the hunting season is over and before the spring migration—when waterfowl populations are lowest. It is this survey, along with the success or failure of the waterfowl nesting season each summer, that helps the federal government determine the length of the hunting season each fall and the bag limit for various species. See, however, other details in Parker and Findlay (1964). *See* Bag Limit.

BEHAVIOR OF WATERFOWL IN MIGRATION.
Many waterfowl stay in their winter homes until spring (*see* time of spring and fall flights in biography of each species in Duck Family), then move north to nesting grounds. Ducks and geese may travel 40–60 m.p.h. in migration (*see* Speed of Flight under Flight). Some early migrants in spring are the bufflehead, the goldeneyes, mallards, and pintails (Glover, 1964).

Once migration begins, the late starters, such as the brant, snow geese, blue-winged teal, shoveler, gadwall, and ruddy duck, may travel rapidly enough to overtake the early ones. The speed of waterfowl migration depends upon the species. Arctic-bound birds in spring tend to leave the wintering grounds late and hurry northward. Most ducks migrate at night and continue their flight into the early morning, if necessary, to reach suitable habitat. Geese are prone to migrate both by day and by night.

Recoveries of banded waterfowl in fall have shown that they require about a month or more to travel about 1,000 mi. southward; however, some move much faster, as though in haste to reach the wintering grounds. For example, a black duck banded in Ont., Canada, was killed 12 days later in Mississippi, slightly more than 1,000 mi. from where it had been banded. Many blue-winged teal, banded on their prairie nesting grounds in U.S. and Canada, had traveled 2,000–3,000 mi. in 30 days, and an immature blue-winged teal flew 3,800 mi. from the Athabasca Delta in n. Man. to Maracaibo, Venezuela, in 30 days (Glover, 1964).

Ducks and geese tend to migrate over the same route year after year, and many ducks return in spring, repeatedly, to the same marsh where they were hatched. Waterfowl biologists call this *migrational homing (see also* Homing); the annual return of cliff swallows to Capistrano is a well-known example; and the tendency is strong in ducks. See Sowls (1955). A female shoveler banded in a Delta, Man., marsh returned to nest in the same meadow for 4 consecutive years; a ring-necked duck in Me. nested at the same site for 4 years, each time building a nest precisely on top of the old one (*see* Re-use of Old Nests under Nests and Nesting); and individual wood ducks often return to the same nesting boxes (Mendall and Nelson, 1964).

"Goldie," an albino gadwall, returned to the same nesting place in the Lower Souris National Wildlife Refuge in N.D. each year between 1947 and 1953. Migrational homing seems stronger in females, especially in ducks, which often pair on the wintering grounds. Even young hens that have never nested before return to the place in the wild where they were hatched and reared. Drakes, old and young, may be guided by the hens wherever the hens go (*see* Abmigration), thus establishing traditional homing patterns. Apparently some of these homing patterns are inherited; others are acquired by young birds through experience (see details in Hochbaum, 1955).

In fall, immature ducks are generally the first to start their migration southward from the breeding grounds, but the young of blue-winged teal and of pintails are exceptions. In these two species, the adult drakes start southward early in fall and precede the young toward the wintering grounds (Glover, 1964).

Probably all ducks, both old and young, at least once each fall join together in a mass migration southward over traditional routes (Hochbaum, 1955). These great flights begin from some northern marsh in late afternoon of a clear day under a fair-weather pattern, each kind traveling in a group of its own, the individuals stringing across the sky in an arc, or rarely in a sharp-pointed V. See account of these "grand passages" or "big flights" by Bellrose and Sieh (1960). By the following spring, all ducks, including juveniles, have had experience in traveling their routes of migration before they return to the breeding grounds. For color maps and a discussion of the migration routes of 16 species of N. American waterfowl, see Aldrich *et al.* (1949).

Waterfowl are highly social and whatever they do is done in pairs, in small groups, or in flocks. The companionship of waterfowl is functional—in feeding together, the small group or larger flock finds food more efficiently than can a lone individual; in loafing together, the alertness to danger of the many is more protective than that of a lone bird (*see* Flocks and Flocking).

Snow geese (and their blue color form, the blue goose), Canada geese, white-fronted geese, and brant tend to travel in flocks of their own kind that are composed of many families; in contrast, mallards and black ducks, which often pair in winter or in spring, travel as pairs in the flock when they fly northward together (Glover, 1964). In spring, as in fall, there are "waves" of waterfowl that start together toward the nesting grounds, and the timing of these flights is governed by the weather. A south wind and warming temperature usually marks the beginning of the heaviest spring migration (*see* effect of weather on migration under Migration). Masses of waterfowl move along their ancestral flyways, and even though these masses are composed of small flocks, all move together in the general direction of their breeding grounds.

In their migrations, waterfowl apparently use their observations of the sun and stars to help guide their direction of flight. See experiments with mallards by Bellrose (1958) and by Matthews (1961) and with blue-winged teal by Hamilton (1962b), who discovered that his hand-reared birds in a testing apparatus oriented correctly by using either the sun or the stars as clues; their orientation failed when the sun or stars were not visible. Johnsgard (1968) concluded, from these experiments, that the sensory abilities of these birds appear to provide them with a navigational method for long-range migrations, and for initial orientation when they are in an environment unfamiliar to them. *See also* discussion under Migration, and in Hochbaum (1955); Bellrose (1966).

Bad flying weather—fog, mist, or rain, and especially fog—will usually cause migrating waterfowl to come to the ground, especially if they are just starting their migration and a fog suddenly closes in; however, if caught under way in heavy snowstorms, they have been known to fly blindly against beacons and lighthouses, crashing into the structures even during the day. At McCreary, Man., a flight of redheads, canvasbacks, and scaups, meeting fog after dark on Apr. 28, 1955, dashed into buildings, trees, and wires and were killed; in Wisc., in Apr. 1954, migrating whistling swans, Canada geese, and ducks flew into torrential rains and hail. Later, 35 of the whistling swans were found dead, scattered over the countryside. They had broken necks, burst livers and hearts, and lung hemorrhages, caused by the hail and by the impact when they struck the ground (see comparable physical destruction of an enor-

WATERFOWL

In the head-up, tail-up display, a mallard drake draws its head and tail up and stretches its folded wings, exposing its iridescent blue wing patches, or speculums. Then, relaxing this posture, he turns his head toward the female. This display may be followed by another: stretched low over the water, the drake swims with a short burst of speed, then looks away from the female.

grunt-whistle display

WATERFOWL
In the grunt-whistle display—variations of which are common to all dabbling ducks—a male pintail rises out of the water with neck arched and shakes a billful of water in the direction of the female he is courting, giving a short, loud whistle call.

incitement display

WATERFOWL
If a rival drake intrudes upon the territory of newly paired pintails, the female may turn her head over her shoulder and utter guttural sounds, which will sometimes provoke her mate to attack the rival.

mous flight of Lapland longspurs in Roberts, T. S., 1932, and in Terres, 1948).

In all of these disasters, the waterfowl had probably started their flights in fair weather, and when they overtook the storms or fog, had tried to continue, with fatal results (Hochbaum, 1955). *See* similar disaster to Canada geese under Poisons; other accidents under Duck Family; and considerable mortality under Diseases; *see also* Weather.

PAIRING AND DISPLAYS. Waterfowl go through various ritualized displays, apparently inherited (Johnsgard, 1968), in their pair-forming, also before and after copulation, which help maintain the pair bond (*see* The Pair Bond under Courtship). Among geese and swans, pairs seem to keep their bond firm through the repeated performance of the *triumph ceremony* (usually each time a male has chased an intruder), in which both birds, while standing side by side, lift up the head and chin, shake their wings, and call loudly into each other's ears.

Among the dabbling ducks, in which in numerous species the males have elaborate plumage, no two species have exactly the same plumage or the same series of displays. Some males, however, give certain displays common to all dabblers—the so-called *head-up–tail-up*, one of the most spectacular, in which the drake, swimming rapidly about on the water, jerks up his head and tail and lifts his folded wings to display the speculum (*see* Speculum). The *grunt-whistle* is equally remarkable; in this the male scoops up water in his bill, draws the bill toward his breast, whistles loudly, throws an arc of water droplets aside toward the female he is courting, then rears up and shakes his head and tail.

Females perform an *incitement* display, the commonest female courtship pattern, by which she provokes her mate, or male consort, to attack an enemy or another pursuing or intruding male. The female mallard, for example, performs her inciting movement by turning her head back over her shoulder and uttering a peculiar nagging sound (Lorenz, 1971).

Female shelducks and sheldgeese of the tribe Tadornini, not native to N. America (see in Johnsgard, 1968), are extremely aggressive, and usually incite their mates to attack almost any living object. If her mate responds and then returns from the fight beaten, the seemingly implacable female often will promptly reject her mate and begin to court the victorious male, no matter what species he may be!

Other displays of males, especially in sea ducks—eiders, surf scoters, oldsquaw, and goldeneyes, for example—are so elaborate that they almost defy description. For details and illustrations, see in Johnsgard (1965; 1968).

Sounds play a highly important role in communication between waterfowl. A duck, for example, is aware of its companions by the sounds they make as well as by their movements and displays. The peeping of ducklings enables them to keep together in dense reeds or grasses, and their notes tell their position to their mother; in turn, they follow her low utterances as she moves ahead of them. Ducks and geese keep together in night migration by "con-

tact calls"; they also have special notes that identify the *situation* facing them—alarm calls, for example, or calls at the presence of food, or the "contentment calls" when they are loafing. A series of loud, descending quacks by mallards, called "decrescendo calls," is given only among undisturbed groups, and so on. *See* Language. The sounds uttered by waterfowl range from the wheezy "huffing" of the Muscovy duck (*see* in Duck Family) to the loud clarion calls of the trumpeter swan. *See* Voice and Sound-making.

Among dabbling ducks, there is much variation in their calls, but males of most species utter whistled notes, especially in pair formation with the females, and male wigeons have no calls other than whistles. *See* Bulla. Male cinnamon teal and shovelers utter nasal notes, and females of all dabbling ducks utter the quacking decrescendo calls. Females also utter other calls, especially during the courtship display (Johnsgard, 1968).

WATERFOWL AND THE ENVIRONMENT. Once there were about 127 million acres of wetlands, or waterfowl habitat, in the U.S., but by the 1950s drainage for farming, housing, and other land uses had reduced these to about 82 million acres (Briggs, 1964), and drainage since then has further reduced this acreage which is so absolutely essential to the lives and continuing populations of waterfowl.

The numbers of waterfowl vary from year to year and decade to decade, depending largely on the condition of the environment. Many biologists believe that the general trend of the waterfowl population is downward with the disappearance of wetland breeding places. As the present numbers of these birds must be accommodated on less and less habitat, the problem of diseases and parasites that may be transmitted from bird to bird takes on a new significance (Jensen and Williams, 1964). *See*, for example, Avian Tuberculosis.

As of 1975, total waterfowl habitat preserved by the U.S. Fish and Wildlife Service's National Wildlife Refuge System (*see* Wildlife Refuge), by state conservation agencies, by some 11,000 private waterfowl hunting clubs and by individual conservationists, by Ducks Unlimited of Canada, and by private conservation organizations such as the Nature Conservancy and the National Audubon Society, amounted to more than 22,900,000 acres in the U.S. and 1,800,000 acres in Canada. See details, with breakdown of total figures and annual losses of waterfowl habitat, in Anonymous (1975b). *See also* Duck Stamps.

WATER HEN
See Coot, American, and gallinules in Rail Family.

WATER OUZEL
(OO-zl). *See* under Dipper Family.

WATER REQUIREMENTS
All animals require water, which makes up a considerable part of the living animal's body. The protoplasm (semi-fluid of each cell body and its nucleus) of most animals is about 75% water (Berger, 1961), and much fluid not in pro-

toplasm bathes the cells or moves about through arteries, veins, lymphatics, etc. All animals (and plants) will die if their water supply is inadequate (Simpson *et al.*, 1957). Birds, and other terrestrial organisms, face two problems in maintaining an adequate water balance: the acquisition of water and the conservation of water (see Shoemaker, 1972).

AVAILABLE SOURCES OF WATER. In general, most birds depend on surface water for their needs. They drink from many sources—from pools, springs, water holes, streams, ditches, birdbaths, etc.—but some birds of the desert, where water is scarce or unavailable, depend on succulent plant foods for their moisture requirements and especially upon insects and other invertebrates that they eat. See Bartholomew and Cade (1956); Miller (1963); Moldenhauer and Wiens (1970).

LOSS AND CONSERVATION OF WATER. Birds and other terrestrial animals have the problem of controlling, or offsetting, losses of water that may be excreted in urine and in respiration (breathing). Birds, however, lose relatively very little water in excretion compared with most mammals because most of the water filtered through the kidneys is resorbed, leaving only the semi-solid uric acid salts voided in the bird's feces (Berger, 1961). They do lose water, through respiration (*see* Heat and Birds), and even though they do not have sweat glands, several studies by investigators have shown that pigeons, and especially birds living in dry habitats (deserts, for example), under the stress of heat may have considerable losses of moisture by evaporation through the skin. The Chinese painted quail, *Coturnix (Excalfactoria) chinensis*, of e. Asia and Australia, no larger than a sparrow, is one example, and Lasiewski (1972) cited five other small birds of dry habitats that proved, under investigation, to lose much moisture through the skin under heat stress.

The large intestine apparently plays an important role in conserving water. By a reverse peristalsis (rhythmic contractions of the wall of the alimentary canal), urine is passed from the cloaca into the large intestine, where it is concentrated following the extraction of water. The control for this water-saving mechanism is probably hormonal.

Seabirds, although living on or near a watery world, face the problem of taking in food that is much saltier than their own body fluids. To counteract this tendency, salt glands located on the skull above the eyes perform the important function of concentrating salt from the blood and excreting salt droplets through the nostrils or the mouth.

Among N. American birds, Smyth and Bartholomew (1966) have demonstrated that both the black-throated sparrow and the rock wren are able to dispense with drinking water if green plants or insects are available as food. Immelmann and Immelmann (1968) have demonstrated that African estrildid finches, though basically seed-eaters, may not drink water for weeks or months if they supplement their diet with insects.

Recent studies show that certain species of birds living in deserts are able to physiologically reduce their water losses (by lower metabolic rates, for example) sufficiently to live for long periods of time on a diet of dry seeds alone, without drinking water.

Examples are the budgerigar and zebra finch of Australia, and the cut-throat finch, Stark's finch, and the gray-backed finch-lark of Africa (Moldenhauer and Wiens, 1970). The N. American sparrows—black-throated and Brewer's—have this capability (Ohmart and Smith, 1971); the black-throated sparrow is the best-adjusted to desert life of any N. American seed-eater (Serventy, 1971). See also a review of adaptations of birds to desert life by Austin (1976); Brown (1968).

According to Serventy (1971), field naturalists have noted many species of birds in arid and desert areas which, though surface water is available, never appear to use it. He has also cited the publications of several observers in Africa who prepared lists of birds that never, or rarely, drink water. Some birds, such as pigeons and doves, that penetrate deserts and live mostly on dry seeds, depend on surface water and fly many miles each day to drink. See discussion by Berger (1961) and especially by Serventy (1971) of birds of dry habitats in Australia that fly regularly to water holes and other water sources; also, birds in the dry sw. U.S. at times are more attracted to water put out for them than to food (Terres, 1977).

WATERTHRUSH
See in Warbler—American Wood Warbler Family.

WATER WITCH
Another name for the horned grebe and pied-billed grebe in Grebe Family.

WATTLE
Naked, fleshy, usually brightly colored pendant skin that in one type, called a "throat wattle," or *dewlap*, hangs from the lower part of the bill of domestic chickens and also in all varieties of domestic turkeys and in the wild turkey, and in certain other members of the order Galliformes, also in the so-called African goose, a brown domestic breed of the Asiatic swan goose, *Anser cygnoides*. Almost without exception the dewlap wattles of the male chicken are larger than those of the female (Lucas and Stettenheim, 1972). *See also* Comb.

Wattles of another kind *(lappets),* which grow from the corners of the mouths of some birds, are naked, flaplike, fleshy extensions of the rictus (*see* Rictus). They are called, besides lappets, "rictal wattles," and are worn by the wattlebirds (family Callaeidae) of the primeval forests of New Zealand. The paired, fleshy rictal wattles at the corners of the mouths of the wattlebirds are usually yellow or orange-colored, except in the wattled crow, *Callaeus cinerea*, a large blue-gray, jaylike bird in the Wattlebird Family, in which they are blue-gray. Wattles are also worn by the wattled starling, *Creatophora cinerea*, of South Africa, which is a noted eater of locusts and is widely protected. The wattled starling is unusual in that the males, and occasionally some females, shed their head feathers and grow their conspicuous wattles during the nesting season. The function of combs, wattles, and lappets lies in display and recognition between sexes and may be subject to hormonal control. See Endocrine Glands. For discussion of the colorful wattles and other skin adornments of certain birds, see Austin (1961); Fleming (1964); Lucas and Stettenheim (1972); Pettingill (1972). *See also* Casque; Caruncle.

WAVEY
or WAVY. Common name for some of the wild geese of N. America. The name was derived from Indian words that relate to the calls of these birds; in Ojibway, *wewe;* in Cree, *whey-whey;* in Chinook, *wawa*. The name has been applied to all wild geese but perhaps most consistently to the white kinds (McAtee, 1957a). The snow geese have been called wavey, common wavey, and little wavey; the blue goose, black wavey and blue wavey to contrast it with the white wavey, or lesser snow goose; the Ross' goose has been called barking wavey from its vociferation, and the Canada goose, wild wavey. *See* in Duck Family.

WAX-EATING
See Cerophagy.

WAXWING FAMILY
Bombycillidae (bom-bih-SILL-ih-dee); from combined Lat. and Gr. word meaning silky-tailed (*see* Jaeger, 1955). Small songbirds (6¼–8¾ in. long) of 3 species in subarctic and temperate parts of N. Hemisphere; 2 species in N. America, of which cedar waxwing limited to W. Hemisphere; have soft, silky plumage of drab colors, somewhat short, thick bills, slightly hooked and notched, with broad gape, short legs, and 10 primary feathers in each wing; they apparently belong to a relict group of birds whose close relatives have vanished; appear related to Silky Flycatcher Family (see discussion by Arvey, 1951), but relationship to other birds is obscure; waxwings are soft, sleek, with prominent crests and smooth velvety plumage, mostly fawn to soft dark gray; sexes outwardly similar; name waxwing is for the bright red, drop-shaped, waxlike material that forms on tips of adults' secondary wing feathers and less so in tail feathers; function of waxy droplets, which are prolongation of feather shafts, is unknown (Austin, 1961).

Waxwings are mostly tree-dwelling, although often feed on ground, generally live in coniferous and birch forests of North, migrate and winter in flocks and remain close together even on nesting grounds; flight is graceful, strong, undulating, and fairly fast; are nomadic and are not strongly territorial (they defend no territory except nest); there are intervals of 3–7 years when large flocks of Bohemian waxwings move southward (see in Bent, 1950) from normal wintering range into places where they are seldom seen except in irruptive years; nomadism may be governed by available food; they eat many kinds of berries and small fruit, both wild and cultivated; in spring and summer eat insects, flower petals; are attracted to flowing sap; feed entirely insects to their young nestlings; eat much fruit and digest food very rapidly (Austin, 1961).

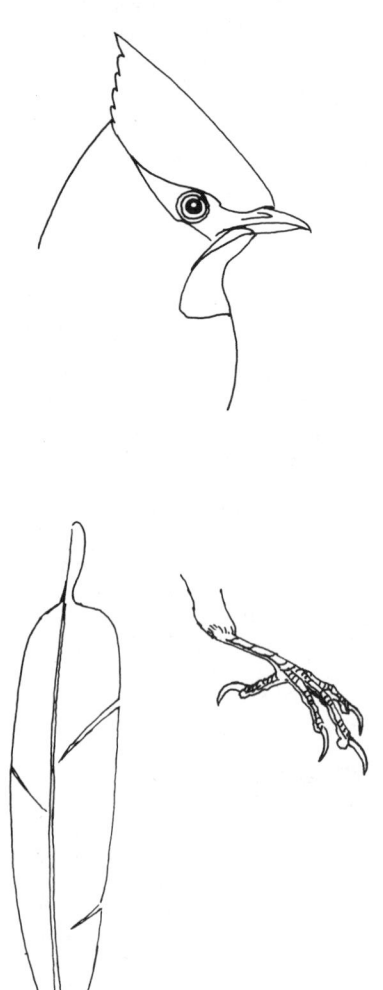

WAXWING FAMILY

Waxwings are protected by law and may not be kept in captivity without a permit but to sustain an ill or injured one until it can fend for itself, offer it the same foods suggested under Pipit Family.

Gross (1965a) lists 8 records of 2 species of albinistic waxwings but does not name the species.

Bohemian waxwing, *Bombycilla garrulus* (bom-bih-SILL-ah GAR-you-lus); genus name: *see* family introduction; species name: Lat., talkative, chattering, but named from its resemblance to the European jay, whose generic name is *Garrulus.* (Color ills., page 1,035.) Largest of waxwings; lives around northern parts of the world; in N. America, in summer, Alaska, w. Canada, and nw. U.S.; in fall and winter, may periodically invade U.S. over broad front when main food supply of berries in north fails; large invasions reported in relatively recent winters: 1958–59, 1961–62 (James, 1962), and one of greatest in history, 1968–69 (see Bagg, 1969; Plunkett, 1969); 7½–8¾ in. long; wingspread 13–14 in.; sexes outwardly alike; adults, soft warm gray including crest, grayer below, distinguished as waxwing by narrow black mask, long crest, and yellow margin at end of tail; differs, however, from similar cedar waxwing in having white marks on red- and yellow-bordered wings; *both adults and young* have cinnamon or chestnut undertail coverts; young similar to adults but more brown above and heavily streaked below; to most people, Bohemian waxwings are birds of mystery; in fall and winter may come and go like bands of gypsies; from vast coniferous forests of n. Canada, small groups or immense flocks may swoop down unexpectedly in winter in n. U.S. and more regularly in the Rocky Mtn. region; in flight flock keeps up incessant twittering; call is *zir-r-r-r,* buzzy note, or a low rough *scree.*

Feeding Habits: In summer on nesting grounds eats mostly insects and some berries; is expert at darting from perch and catching insects out of air, including swift dragonflies, but turns to fruit such as wild raspberries as they begin to ripen, also chokecherries, fruits of hawthorns, roses, and many others; apparently most important fruits are those of mountain ash and berries of cedars and junipers (see Bent, 1950); also likes sap of maple trees, frozen or rotted apples; will come to feeding stations for raisins, dried currants, minced prunes, and other kinds of dried fruit or berries, but take sunflower seeds rarely; very tame, may alight on one's shoulders or head.

Nest: Built in isolated spruce, tamarack, or pine tree in open muskeg, on horizontal limb well out from trunk, 4–50 ft. above ground; flat, built of twigs, grasses, lichens, lined with finer grasses, mosses, pine needles, etc. (Bent, 1950).

Eggs: May–July; usually 4–6, pale blue, much spotted and scrawled with black dots, lines.

Incubation: Period of in wild unreported, but 14 days in captivity; young leave nest about 13–15 days after hatching.

Other Names: Bohemian chatterer; northern chatterer; northern waxwing.

Host to Cowbirds: Rare; only one record (Friedmann, 1963), apparently because nesting range is largely outside that of brown-headed cowbird.

Range: From n. Scandinavia east to w. U.S.; in N. America, nests from w. Alaska, n. Yuk., n. Mack., and Man., south to s. Alta., nw. Mont., n. Idaho, c. Wash.; winters irregularly over broad front southward, depending on food supply, from Canada to s. Calif., Ariz., N.M., Tex., Ark., Ill., Tenn., Pa., New England, N.J., and Nova Scotia.

Cedar waxwing, *Bombycilla cedrorum* (bom-bih-SILL-ah see-DROH-rum); genus name: *see* family introduction; species name: Lat., of cedars. (Color ill., page 1,034.) In summer, from se. Alaska across Canada and in n. U.S.; winters across U.S. and south to Panama; often unpredictable movements; may visit almost any state at any time of year; 6½–8 in. long; wingspread 11–12¼ in.; sleek brown bird with long conspicuous crest, black mask; yellow band at end of tail; red waxy tips on secondaries of grayish wings; differs from Bohemian waxwing especially in having pale *yellow* belly and *white* undertail coverts, and lack of conspicuous white and yellow markings on wings; immatures are grayer, usually lack waxy appendages, and are streaked below; sexes similar, but according to Yunick (1970), black throat distinguishes males (about 91% reliable), brown throat, the females (with bird in hand); live in small companies or flocks through most of year; in winter, rove about in country or in gardens and parks of towns, suburbs, villages, eating berries of cedar trees and their favorites—berries of European mountain ash (rowan tree)—and fruit of *Pyracantha* (fire thorn), privet, palm berries, mulberries, etc.; feed close together in trees, may gorge until they can scarcely fly; sometimes get drunk on overripe fruit; occasionally drop to ground to drink from rain puddles or melted snow; utter high-pitched lisping sounds as they feed; migration not usually a regular north-south movement as with most N. American birds; may breed and nest at odd times in summer, usually late, but many nestings—in N.Y., for example—in June (Tyler, 1950a); have charming ritual in which pair or group of cedar waxwings may sit in a row on a limb and pass a cherry back and forth before one swallows it, or, in courtship, pair may pass flower petal or insect back and forth.

Feeding Habits: Besides fruit, eats sap from maple trees, flower petals of apple and pecan trees; eats many insects in summer, especially elm leaf beetles, weevils, carpenter ants, sawfly larvae, cicadas, scale insects, caterpillars, and especially fond of cankerworms; feeds very young nestlings insects, but within few days adds cherries or berries, which adults carry in throat to young (Tyler, 1950a).

Nest: In deciduous or coniferous tree or shrub, in orchard or shade trees or in open stands of scattered trees, or in swamps; in fork or on horizontal limb, 6–50 ft. above ground; sometimes nests built in colonies of up to dozen nests in one clump of pines; nest of twigs, dry grasses, weed stalks, mosses, lichens, pine needles, wool; adults sometimes take material from other birds' nests (kingbird); and so tame that in garden during nesting season will come to one's hands for short pieces of string and yarn and even known to pluck hairs from woman's head for nesting material (Terres, 1965); return to same nesting area not always predictable, seems to depend on abundance or lack of supply of berries or other fruit that forms major part of diet.

Eggs: June–Sept.; 3–6, usually 3–5, pale gray or blue-gray, marked with black spots or small dots.

Incubation: By female, 12–16 days (Crouch, 1936; Putnam, 1949); young leave nest about 14–18 days after hatching; usually one, sometimes two broods a season.

Other Names: Canada robin; cedar bird; cherry-bird; recellet; southern waxwing.

Age: Pet, crippled when nestling, lived for 7½ years at Tenafly, N.J.; another (Matteson, 1924) was still active and bright after living as captive more than 8 years. One wild one, banded at Powdermill Nature Reservoir, Rector, Pa., found dead in winter at Greenville, N.C., when 5 years, 7 months, old (Kennard, 1975).

Flight Speed: Timed in Mich., 21–29 m.p.h. (Schnell, 1965).

Host to Cowbirds: Seldom; about 22 records (Friedmann, 1963).

Weights: In fall, coastal N.J. (57), 22.9–37.2 gr. (Murray and Jehl, 1964), or about ¾–1⅓ oz.

Range: Nests from se. Alaska, n.-c. B.C., n. Alta., east across Canada to se. Que. and Newfoundland, south to Calif., n. Utah, Colo., Okla., c. Mo., s. Ill., s. Ind., c. Ky., Tenn., n. Ala., and n. Ga.; winters from s. B.C., nw. Wash., n. Idaho, ne. Ore., c. Calif., c. Ariz., n.-c. N.M., ne. Colo., s. Neb. c. Mo., s. Ill., s. Mich., s. Ont., and Mass., south to Gulf coast and c. Fla; irregularly to Panama; casually to Bermuda, West Indies, and n. S. America.

Northern waxwing. *See* Bohemian waxwing.

Southern waxwing. *See* Cedar waxwing.

WEARY WILLIE

Another name for the golden-crowned sparrow in Finch Family.

WEATHER

Birds, like all wildlife, are benefited and harmed by the effects of weather. They are helped in their migrations by wind and by the effects of cold or warm air masses that can trigger migration (*see* Migration); however, unusually powerful winds and storms during migration, or at any time, can kill birds. Extremes of cold and heavy rains or drought may have such devastating effects that they periodically cause local or regional declines in populations of birds. Whereas climate, working over a long time, influences the distribution of birds and the seasonal cycles of their lives, weather brings about day-to-day variations in the bird's environment (Lamb, 1964).

SOME EFFECTS OF WEATHER. Prolonged cold rains early in spring and in summer, even if lasting only a few days or a week, can be destructive to adult and nestling chimney swifts,

swallows, purple martins, wood warblers, and other birds that feed on insects and especially those birds that feed on flying insects which they catch in the air in flight. The birds may starve to death because of cold-delayed hatching of their insect food (*see* Insects and Birds) or because the cold numbs the insects to such an extent that they cannot fly or kills them outright (Chapman, 1930; Terres, 1956d). After an early-spring ice storm in 1940 near Quincy, Ill., Musselman (1941) estimated that 30–50% of the bluebirds of that region died (*see* an even more recent severe winter kill of bluebirds and other songbirds wintering in the South under Disaster Species).

In S.C. and La., periodic, unusual freezing cold, with snow- and ice-covered ground in Jan. and Feb., has caused enormous numbers of the American woodcock to die from starvation on the wintering grounds. See Sheldon (1971). In Mar. 1904, a wet snowstorm killed millions of Lapland longspurs during their northward migration in w. Iowa and Minn., where an estimated 750,000 lay dead on two ice-covered lakes alone. (See Roberts, T. E., 1932; Terres, 1960b.) During the cold month of May 1907, a tremendous destruction of warblers, called by ornithologists the Great Death, occurred in Wisc., Iowa, and Minn. Yet, despite these enormous losses, most of the birds returned to near normal numbers within a few years. See discussion by Lack (1954). *See also* Botulism; Diseases.

HAIL. Hailstorms are among the most destructive of all storms, even more so than tornadoes. Hailstorms kill thousands of wild birds, domestic livestock, and other animals and even men. Most dangerous hailstorms occur in June and July, in the afternoon, and more hail falls in the center of the N. American continent than along the coasts.

Rett (1938) found two of the rare California condors dead near the carcass of a horse after a hailstorm and the condition of their bodies suggested that hail had killed them. Two widespread hailstorms covering over 700 sq. mi. in Alta., Canada, in July 1953 killed an estimated 150,000 waterfowl—ducks and geese with their young—with terrible destruction of songbirds, hawks, owls, crows, grouse, coots, grebes; hailstorms in 1954 killed as many waterfowl in the same area (Smith, 1960). Hailstorms in Oct. and Nov. 1960 north of Elida, N.M., killed thousands of lesser sandhill cranes and many small birds (Merrill, 1961).

HURRICANES. The powerful winds of hurricanes often carry seabirds far outside their normal ranges. Most hurricanes in the U.S., with winds sometimes exceeding 100 m.p.h. sweeping up the Atlantic coast, originate between 10° and 20° N. Lat. in the Atlantic O. and usually occur in late Aug. and in Sept. Peterson (1948) gives a long account of hurricanes that have carried seabirds far north of their tropical homes. In Sept. 1876, one struck the West Indies and carried sooty terns from the Bahamas and Dry Tortugas of Fla. north to New England, a tropic-bird to N.Y., and a frigatebird to Nova Scotia; in Aug. 1893, another carried some black-capped petrels northward and

dropped them, dead, dying, or exhausted, in Va., N.Y., Mass., and Vt. One of the most destructive hurricanes on record in the U.S. struck New England on Sept. 21, 1938. Roaring northward from the tropics and increasing in power and violence, it carried with it, like swimmers in a strong current, yellow-billed (now called white-billed) tropic-birds, which nest in Bermuda, all the way to Vt., and Cory's and greater shearwaters, oceanic travelers which never voluntarily leave salt water, inland into Mass., and Vt. For the destructive effects of a tornado on birds, see McClure (1945).

ICE. Ice can down birds in flight when it forms on their wings and bodies, much as ice can down aircraft in unfavorable weather. During World War II, many common loons from a flock flying over the Atlantic O. fell to the deck of a U.S. destroyer, their wings encased in ice. At Quincy, Mass., W. G. Sheldon (see in Hochbaum, 1955) found hundreds of starlings helpless on the ground with their wing feathers heavily iced. (For an account of some of the effects of fog on birds, *see* Waterfowl.)

LIGHTNING. Records of birds killed by lightning are rare, although it may happen oftener than the few published reports suggest. John James Audubon saw two nighthawks struck down by lightning at Indian Key, Fla., during a tremendous thunderstorm. Alexander Sprunt, Jr. (1941), reported that in Apr. 1941, during a violent electrical storm on Wadmalaw Is., S.C., four double-crested cormorants fell out of a flock after a sharp flash of lightning. When picked up, their feathers were unmarked but all were dead.

John T. Zimmer of the American Museum of Natural History, while watching a large flock of migrating snow geese in the Midwest, saw a flash of lightning streak through the birds in the sky. More than 50 fell to the ground and were killed; one was badly mangled, and some, after autopsy, showed internal injuries from their impact with the ground. In Apr. 1939, 34 white pelicans of a flock of about 75 were struck by lightning during an electrical storm near Nelson, Neb., and fell to the ground. All were dead and some had their white feathers singed from the lightning bolt (Lincoln, 1941). Howell (1941) reported that a bald eagle incubating her eggs on a nest in a pine tree in Fla. was killed by lightning, and a female osprey while on her nest in a tall tree was killed when lightning struck the tree. *See also* Accidents; see Birds as Weather Prophets under Folklore.

WEAVERBIRD FAMILY

Ploceidae (ploh-SEE-ih-dee); from Gr. *plokeos*, a braider, or weaver, in reference to the nest-weaving habits of some members of the family. Old World family of about 260 species in Eurasia, Africa, Madagascar, Australia, New Caledonia, Tasmania, and the Fiji Is. (Reilly, 1968); according to Austin (1961), members of family have their greatest development in Africa and have been classified under four distinct groups: buffalo weavers, sparrow weavers, the typical weavers, and the widow weavers; named weavers because many members of

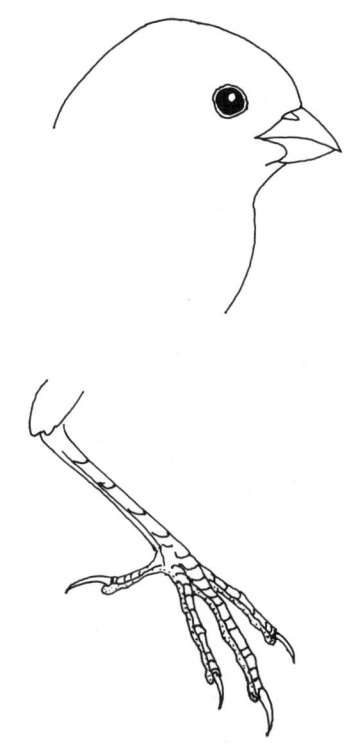

WEAVERBIRD FAMILY

family (in Africa and Asia) weave with their bills the most complex nests, and, relative to the size of the birds, the largest nests in the bird world (see Gilliard, 1958, for interesting details); in N. America, the family is represented by 2 introduced species—the house sparrow and European tree sparrow—neither of which is noted as a nest builder; both are classified in the group called by Austin sparrow weavers; in most weavers, bill is short, conical, and adapted to cracking seeds; weavers are songbirds, or perching birds (*see Passeriformes*), with 10 primary feathers in each wing and 12 rectrices (tail feathers); according to Austin, they show no close relationship to any other Old World bird family and resemble most closely members of the Finch Family; according to Reilly (1968), the weaverbirds are most closely related to the troupials, tanagers, and finches; only a few migrate; those introduced into America do not.

The European tree sparrow, first introduced into N. America Apr. 25, 1870, in Lafayette Park, St. Louis, Mo., when 12 released there, became established until similar but stronger and more aggressive house sparrow was introduced in St. Louis about 1875; it soon drove out the European tree sparrow, which spread to suburbs and rural areas; still lives within about 50–85-mi. radius of St. Louis and slowly expanding its range northward in c. Ill. and ne. Mo. (see details in Barlow, 1973); locally may be common; great numbers (up to 5,000 individuals) live within 30-mile radius of Jacksonville, Morgan County, Ill.; in day-long Christmas Bird Counts of National Audubon Society (1967–72 inclusive) European tree sparrows reported each year, especially at three places—Orchard Farm, Mo., near St. Louis; East St. Louis, Ill.; and Pere Marquette State Park, Ill. The Audubon Christmas Bird Count of 1978 reported a total of 62 counted in Mo.; 194 in Ill.

The house, or English, sparrow was first introduced in N. America in 1850 by Nicolas Pike, director of the Brooklyn Institute, who brought 8 pairs from England and released them in Brooklyn in spring of 1851, but they did not thrive. In 1852 Pike returned to England and shipped a large number to Brooklyn, of which most were released in Greenwood Cemetery, Brooklyn, in the spring of 1853. There they bred and multiplied. See Pike's account in Bent (1958); Phillips (1928); Kinkead (1978). During the following 20 years the house sparrow was also introduced throughout much of New England, parts of Canada, and into the Midwest, Utah, Tex., and Calif.; by 1940 range covered entire continental U.S. and far north into Canada (Kalmbach, 1940); its occupation of N. America was faster than that of the starling and virtually completed in 40 years (Wing, 1943) because much more widely introduced than starling (Bent, 1958); see details of its spread and present abundance in Robbins (1973).

Next to the American robin, albinism is reported in house sparrow more than in any other N. American bird (Gross, 1965a).

To sustain an ill or injured bird, offer it seeds, bread, fruit, greens, and mealworms and insects, also ground meat.

Domestic sparrow. *See* House sparrow.

English sparrow. *See* House sparrow.

Eurasian tree sparrow, *Passer montanus* (PASS-er mon-TAN-us); genus name: Lat., sparrow; species name: Lat., of or relating to a mountain. (Color ill., page 1,035.) Resident in Eurasia, Near East, and Middle East; introduced into Philippines, Australia, and N. America at St. Louis, Mo., in 1870 and 1879; since introduction, despite competition with house sparrow, possibly 25,000 individuals have become established over 8,500 sq. mi. in extreme e.-c. Mo. and w.-c. Ill. (see details in Barlow, 1973; also in Flieg, 1971); 6–6¾ in. long; sexes alike; distinguished from similar house sparrow by brown-red crown (not gray as in house sparrow), and black patch on side of white cheek (ear patch), but has black throat as in house sparrow; back smoke gray to brown; belly and sides white to pale gray; eyes brown; lives in farm country and in city parks around St. Louis, where resident; generally shy and retiring, yet less easily frightened than house sparrow; in places where both live, Eurasian tree sparrow seldom around buildings, but where no house sparrows, lives about buildings, homes (Horner, 1957); very gregarious, in flocks of 25–50, which may mix with house sparrows, but usually does not associate with other species; more likely to be seen in trees than house sparrow; common call note is a frequently repeated *chib, tchic* (Horner, 1957); song is medley of tinkling notes.

Feeding Habits: No thorough study yet made of in N. America; but visits grain fields to eat some wheat, oats, and corn; also eats many weed seeds, some insects (Bent, 1958).
Nest: Built in cavity of trees, old woodpecker hole, holes in cliffs, under eaves of houses, in box of size built for bluebird but with 1⅛-in.-diameter entrance hole (see bluebird box details in Terres, 1968c); attach box to large tree or under eaves of building (Horner, 1957); untidy nest is of grasses, hay, straw, feathers, rubbish.
Eggs: Late Apr. to early August; 2–7, usually 5, white or pale gray, dotted with browns.
Incubation: By both sexes, 12–14 days; young leave nest about 12–14 days after hatching; usually three broods a year, sometimes two, rarely four.
Age: One (banded) reported from Belgium, 10 years old (Clapp, 1976).
Hybrids: In Old World, Eurasian tree sparrow × house sparrow—"presumed natural hybrids" frequently reported (Gray, 1958).
Weights: In Old World (Poland), 22.5–22.7 gr., or about ¾ oz.; in U.S., in Ill., adults average 23.5 gr. (Barlow, 1973).
Range: British Isles, Scandinavia, west to Siberia, south to s. Europe, c. Near East, se. Asia; in U.S. introduced in e.-c. Mo. and w.-c. Ill.

European tree sparrow. *See* Eurasian tree sparrow.

House, or English, sparrow, *Passer domesticus* (PASS-er dom-ESS-tih-kus); genus name: *see* Eurasian tree sparrow; species name: from Lat., *domus*, house; "belonging to a household," in reference to its habit of living about homes. (Color ill., page 1,035.) Native through British Isles, most of Europe, Asia, Africa, etc.; introduced around world and in N. America at Brooklyn, N.Y., middle 19th century, now throughout most of U.S. and across c. and s. Canada (see Robbins, 1973, for details, and Phillips, 1928, for early introductions); 5½–6¼ in. long; wingspread 9½–10 in.; common city bird, more robust than native N. American sparrows of Finch Family; head large, bill heavy, conical; crown, rump, and tail grayish; male has back and wings buff-brown; underparts pale gray; *black bib;* cheeks pale gray, chestnut nape; female (often confused with some N. American sparrows and finches) has dingy, *unstreaked* breast, bold buff-colored line over each eye; noisy chirps and chatter distinguish it; has no black bib, light buff-brown above, dark streak through eyes; year-round resident in cities, towns, in streets, in, on, or around buildings in farmyards in country and even about homesteads in wilderness, always close to man (for history of its early effects on American crops and native birds, bounties to try to control it, etc., see Forbush, 1925–29); noisy, boisterous, gregarious, often aggressive toward other birds; intelligent, sometimes snatches worms or other food from under bill of American robin, starling (see examples of intelligence in Bent, 1958); although a songbird, has no identifiable song, but utters repeated *cheep, cheep;* but in captivity has learned to sing songs of canaries; has even been seen to play, according to Jaeger (1951)—some on roof of building at West Point, Neb., and at Riverside College, in Calif., dropped pebbles on sloping doors or pavement below, then listened for sounds as pebbles struck. *See* Play under Behavior. In courtship, group of males with wings drooped, almost scraping ground, circle female; fight each other viciously for her favor, tumbling about on ground; promiscuous male copulates frequently with female, up to 14 times in succession, while female flutters wings and utters soft *tee, tee, tee, tee, tee, tee;* roost in noisy flocks on branches of city trees or on ivy-covered walls of buildings, under eaves of houses.

Feeding Habits: In summer eats Japanese beetles, click beetles, leaf beetles, grasshoppers, crickets, caterpillars, aphids, moths, flies, also spiders and small fruits, succulent plants, eats seeds of crabgrass and other weeds into winter, along with oats, wheat, corn, and other waste grain and garbage; former abundance early in 20th century thought to have been result of vast food supply of seeds in horse droppings, with decline of horses number of sparrows declined.
Nest: A favorite place for nest is bird box, which they fill with grass, straw, chicken feathers, cotton, string, etc.—see nest items described and counted by Terres (1964a); in natural hollows of trees such as old apple trees, behind blinds, shutters of houses, on rafters of buildings, under eaves, or build an outside large dome-shaped nest of straw, grasses, etc., in trees, bushes, vines, with small openings in side leading to nest chamber.

Eggs: Reported for every month in year (Bent, 1958), but usually Apr.–Sept.; 3–7, commonly 5, white, pale blue, or pale green, marked with a few gray or brown dots.
Incubation: Mostly by female, 11–14 days (Weaver, 1943); young leave nest when 15–17 days old; adults feed very young insects, by regurgitation; two or three broods a year.
Other Names: Domestic sparrow; European house sparrow; gamin; hoodlum; tramp.
Albinism: Commonly reported (Gross, 1965a).
Age: Two wild house sparrows, banded at Kent, Ohio, caught again in trap half mile from where banded, were each 13 years, 4 months, old; male raised from fledgling, Albany, N.Y., lived to 12 years, 7 days; Flower (1938) reported three caged house sparrows in England that lived for 11½, 14, and 23 years.
Flight Speed: Timed in Mich., 5–39 m.p.h. (Schnell, 1965); in Tex., 20 m.p.h. (Sooter, 1947); 28–35 m.p.h. (Wood, 1933).
Host to Cowbirds: Very seldom (Friedmann, 1963); about 6 records.
Hybrids: See under Eurasian tree sparrow.
Weights: In fall, in Ohio (14), average 27 gr., or about 1 oz.; in winter (22), average 27.8 gr.; in summer (15), average 26.8 gr. (Kendeigh, 1934).
Range: Mainly resident British Isles west to Siberia, south to n. Africa, Middle East, se. Asia (Burma); in W. Hemisphere, in N. America, from c. Canada and throughout U.S. south into Mexico, to Fla. Keys, Bermuda, and West Indies; also in Chile, Argentina, Paraguay, Brazil, and the Falkland Is.

WEAVER FINCH

Name sometimes confused with the weaverbirds (*see* Weaverbird Family); according to Gilliard (1958), weaver finches are in the family Estrildidae, and include the Old World waxbills, grass finches, manakins, and Java sparrows, many of which are colorful and popular cage birds.

WEB-FOOTED PEEP

See Northern phalarope in Phalarope Family; *see also* Peep.

WEIGHT

Partly a function of size (*see* Size), weights may vary enormously between species of birds, ranging from about ⅒ oz. in some hummingbirds to about 345 lbs. recorded for a male ostrich.

Some nestling birds double their weight by one day after hatching, and the young of some swallows, pelicans, eagles, and others weigh more than their parents before leaving the nest. The rate of increase in the weights of young birds varies considerably with the species. Young songbirds may attain their full adult weight in about 10 days after hatching, whereas young emus may not have their full growth and weight until they are about 18 months old (Perrins, 1964).

The ratio of heart size to body weight in birds is much larger than in mammals. In many hummingbirds, for example, the heart is about 20% of the total weight of the bird, although it is more often about 10%. *See* Heart. In mammals

generally it is about 0.4–0.5% of the body weight (Simons, 1960).

Birds' weights can vary, geographically and seasonally; for example, kittiwakes, *Larus tridactylus*, from Britain weigh about 12.4 oz., whereas those from Arctic Russia weigh about 14.35 oz., following Bergmann's Rule that individual birds from more northern latitudes are larger and heavier than those from temperate zones (Perrins, 1964). Many migrant birds increase their weight considerably by storing energy as subcutaneous fat before migration (*see* Migration) and, in some species, before the molt (*see* Molts and Molting).

Birds can lose relatively much weight during stages of their migration flights. Nisbet *et al.* (1963) estimated that blackpoll warblers leaving Mass. on migration during Oct. 1962, averaging about 20.72 gr., on arriving in Bermuda 32 hours later would have lost about 3.43 gr. each, or about 16% of their weight. A ruddy turnstone, banded on St. George Is., Pribilofs, Aug. 23, 1965, weighed 174 gr. Three and one half days later, after a flight of 2,272 mi., it was recaptured on French Frigate Shoals, Hawaiian Is. It weighed 154.8 gr., having lost 19.2 gr, or about 11% of its weight. *See* reference to this under Migration.

Some small passerine birds lose as much as 12% of body weight in cold weather; generally they weigh the most in late afternoon and least in the morning. Most female birds gain weight early in the breeding season, partially owing to the weight of their unlaid eggs and increased size of their gonads. Adults of most species may lose weight during the breeding season, presumably because of the energy expended in rearing their young (Perrins, 1964).

In many species, average weights of males and females are similar, but either sex may be larger. In waterfowl and in many other birds, the males are generally heavier than the females, but in most hawks and many owls the females are significantly larger than the males. *See* Sexual Dimorphism.

HEAVIEST BIRD. The African ostrich, with weight of the male to 345 lbs., is the heaviest bird in the world. *See* Largest Bird. There has been some disagreement or indecision over which wild N. American bird is the heaviest, owing to the variations in their reported weights. If domesticated birds were included (*see* Domestication), the domestic turkey would be rated the heaviest American bird, with weights to 40 or even 60 lbs. The wild turkeys, according to authorities who have most studied the bird, of which the males, or gobblers, are much heavier than the hens, weigh no more than 20–25 lbs.; any that weigh more are thought to have a hereditary infusion of domestic turkey. *See* under Turkey Family.

Schorger (1966) reported weights of wild gobblers to 30 lbs. and records, or estimates, by American pioneers, of gobblers that were said to have weighed 50–60 lbs., but these reports are not considered reliable by today's authorities.

The trumpeter swan, largest in its size, or dimensions (*see* Dimensions), of all waterfowl and of all swans (wingspread of female, 6 ft.; of male, 8 ft. 2 in.—Banko, 1960), may have a legitimate title to the *heaviest N. American native wild bird*, with weights averaging 30 lbs., according to Delacour (1954); males, 21–38 lbs. (Kortright, 1943). (In N. America, the 2¾-in.-long calliope hummingbird, smallest bird in the U.S., weighs about ⅛ oz.)

The introduced mute swan (*see* in Duck Family) ordinarily weighs about 27 lbs. (Pough, 1951); 25–30 lbs., according to Kortright (1943). Another large and heavy N. American bird is the California condor; it weighs about 20 lbs., with records of 21½ and up to 23 lbs. (Koford, 1953).

Other large and heavy N. American birds: white pelican, 15–17 lbs. (Ligon, 1961), reported to 30 lbs. (Palmer 1962): bald eagle, 8–14 lbs. (Imler and Kalmbach, 1955): golden eagle, 8–13 lbs. (Brown and Amadon, 1968): sandhill crane, 8–12 lbs. (Walkinshaw, 1949a) and to 14 lbs. 4 oz. (Huey, 1959): whooping crane, 8–10 lbs. (Audubon, 1870): Canada goose (larger typical race), 8½–13 lbs. (Martin and Nelson, 1952) and the giant Canada goose, to 18 lbs. (Delacour, 1954) and even up to 22 lbs. (Martin and Nelson, 1952). *See* weights of birds, when known, given in biography of each.

WEIGHT-CARRYING CAPACITY
On a windless day in Calif., Laurence M. Huey (1962) watched a house finch carry in her bill a large piece of rag, weighing about 5 gr., to her nest. The average weight of this finch is about 20–21 gr. (about ¾ oz.); Huey estimated that the finch could therefore lift and carry away in flight about 23% of her own weight. Huey cited the experiments of Walker and Walker (1940) in testing the weight-carrying capacity of a male golden eagle and concluded, because the eagle could comfortably carry in flight about 2 lbs., that it could carry away about a fifth, or 21%, of its own weight.

During the spring of 1937, C. C. Sperry tested the weight-lifting ability of a wild golden eagle, caught near Fort Davis, Tex. He fastened weights to the feet of the 11-lb. bird and then released it. The eagle (presumably a female) could not fly from the ground with a 5¼-lb. weight attached to its feet (Arnold, 1954).

Cameron (1908), however, watched a golden eagle in Mont. carry away in its talons a 7 lb. jackrabbit, and Arnold (1954) believed that under exceptionally favorable circumstances, larger weights might be carried by golden eagles, although they may often have trouble getting off the ground with a full crop (estimated capacity of 1–2 lbs.), and in carrying a ground squirrel (larger ones weigh 1–2 lbs.) may take a circuitous aerial route back to the nest using the lifting power of the wind or rising air currents (thermals). *See* Flight.

Stephen (1950), in his field studies of golden eagles in Scotland, wrote that 10 or 11 lbs. had been suggested as the maximum weight that a golden eagle can carry aloft; however, he had never seen any animal "approaching ten pounds . . . carried to the eyrie."

The weight-carrying capacity of a bald eagle was tested by N. R. Casillo (1937). He anchored a 4-lb. dead pickerel to an underwater rock weighing less than 10 lbs., and the female eagle grasped in her talons the floating fish but was unable to lift it and the rock; she did succeed in dragging the fish and rock for about 20 ft. along the bottom but not out of the water. *See* Dragging or Towing Food under Food and Feeding Habits.

Apparently the small predatory loggerhead shrike has a remarkable ability to lift relatively heavy objects. Sprunt (1950) reported a loggerhead that carried, in its bill, from the ground to the top of a utility pole, a 16½-in.-long rough green snake. The snake weighed much more than the shrike. Apparently much is yet to be learned about the weight-carrying capacities of birds.

Bent (1937) watched individual ospreys carry in flight in their talons fishes weighing "at least four pounds," or about the weight of a large female osprey, and thought they might carry fishes up to 6 lbs.

Weydemeyer (1971a) reported watching a male calliope hummingbird fly down to a stunned female that had struck a window and had fallen to the ground. The male hovered for a moment, then grasped the bill of the motionless female and lifted her 3 ft. in the air before she slipped from his bill and fell to the ground. After repeatedly lifting the female to this height, he flew to a nearby shrub. Weydemeyer picked up the bird, warmed her in his hands, at which she flew away. The male had proved that he could lift at least his own weight.

Fairfield (1968) watched an adult female chestnut-collared longspur, weighing about 20 gr. (¾ oz.), fly from her nest with a dead 14-gr. nestling which she carried in her bill through the air for about 5 ft. before dropping it. *See* Sanitation under Young and Their Care.

Southern (1974a) saw American kestrels in n. Ill. twice carry adult Norway rats in their talons while in labored low flight over the ground. The weight of each rat compared with the weight of this small hawk showed that it was capable of carrying in flight almost, or perhaps, twice its own weight.

WESTERN BIRDS
Term for those birds that usually live west of the 100th meridian in the U.S., which is a mapped line that runs northward through c. Tex., w. Okla., w. Kans., c. Neb., S.D., and N.D. The line is an ecological one in that it runs approximately along the eastern edge of the semiarid Great Plains. It is where drier, short-grass plains of the West meet the more moist, tall-grass prairies to the east. See Pough (1949). It is the eastern limit of the range of most western birds except those few species that regularly roam eastward in autumn to the Atlantic coast. *See*, however, Barrier; Distribution; *also* Eastern Birds.

WESTERN DUCK SICKNESS
See Botulism; *also* Diseases.

WESTERN HEMISPHERE
Synonymous with the New World. *See* Hemispheres.

WHALE-BILLED STORK FAMILY
See Ciconiiformes.

WHALE-BIRD
See phalaropes in Phalarope Family; *also* Shearwater, slender-billed, in Shearwater Family; *also* Prion.

WHEATEAR
See in Thrush Family.

WHEEP
General local name in U.S. for the great crested flycatcher, from its call.

WHIMBREL
See in Sandpiper Family.

WHIP-POOR-WILL
See in Nightjar Family.

WHIP-POOR-WILL'S SHOES
See Folklore.

WHIP-TAIL
Another name for the jaegers in Skua Family, whose long central tail feathers move freely in flight (McAtee, 1957a).

WHISKEY JACK
or WHISKEY JOHN. In Canada, phonetic rendering of *wisk-i-djak* or *wisk-e-djan*, Cree Indian name for the spirit that speaks from the "moose bird" (gray jay) directing the Indian hunter to a moose (McAtee, 1957a); name was generally applied by woodsmen to the gray jay itself.

WHISTLER
Another name for the common goldeneye and West Indian tree duck in Duck Family and American woodcock in Sandpiper Family.

WHISTLE-WING
See Goldeneye, common, in Duck Family.

WHISTLING-DUCK
See whistling-ducks in Duck Family.

WHITEBACK
See Canvasback in Duck Family.

WHITE-BILL
See Junco, slate-colored (dark-eyed), in Finch Family.

WHITEBIRD
See Bunting, snow, in Finch Family.

WHITE-EYE
See Pochard, Baer's, in Duck Family.

WHITE HAGDON
See Fulmar, northern, in Shearwater Family.

WHITE RING-NECK
See Plover, piping, in Plover Family.

WHITETHROAT
See Sparrow, white-throated, in Finch Family.

WHITE-WING
See Scoter, white-winged, in Duck Family and Dove, white-winged, in Pigeon Family.

WHITEY
See Sanderling in Sandpiper Family.

WHITNEY
JOSIAH DWIGHT (1819–96). Born Northampton, Mass.; eminent geologist, state geologist, director of the Geological Survey of California (1860–74), and Sturgis Hooper professor of geology at Harvard from 1865 until his death. Dr. James G. Cooper, while collecting for the Geological Survey of California, which Whitney headed, got at Ft. Mohave, Ariz., on the Colorado R., on Apr. 26, 1861, a small owl (the elf owl) new to science. Dr. Cooper gave it the scientific species name *whitneyi* in honor of the director of the Survey (Palmer, 1928). See Gruson (1972) for other details of Whitney's career.

WHOOPER
See Sandhill crane and Whooping crane in Crane Family; *also* Swan, whooper, in Duck Family.

WIDE-AWAKE
See Tern, sooty, in Gull Family.

WIDGEON
(old spelling). *See* Wigeon, American, in Duck Family.

WIED
(German pron., VEED; American, WEED), ALEXANDER PHILLIP MAXIMILIAN, Prince of Wied-Neuwied (1782–1867). Noted German traveler and naturalist; in 1831 (in *Beiträge zur Naturgeschichte Brasiliens*, 1824–33) named a flycatcher as new to science from his collections in Brazil. Later, taxonomists discovered it was the species named earlier (1776) by P. L. S. Müller, Dutch professor of natural history in Erlangen, from a specimen of the bird from French Guiana. The bird's English name had been Wied's flycatcher; it is now known as Wied's crested flycatcher. Besides his explorations in Brazil (1815–17), Wied, or Maximilian, traveled up the Missouri R. in 1833; during this trip he discovered and described a subspecies of the turkey vulture near New Harmony, Ind., and the piñon jay, often known to earlier writers as Maximilian's jay, which Wied (Maximilian) collected at the junction of the Missouri and Yellowstone rivers in Mont. (Palmer, 1928). See also Gruson (1972).

WIED-NEUWIED
PRINCE OF. *See* Wied.

WILD AREA
A designation of the U.S. Forest Service, Department of Agriculture, for an area owned by the Service of less than 100,000 acres which is managed more for hunting, fishing, bird-watching, camping, hiking, and other public recreational values than for growing timber. It may be so designated by the Chief of the Forest Service. It is identical in purpose and management with a U.S. Forest Service *wilderness area*, which differs from a wild area in that it contains more than 100,000 acres and is established by the Secretary of Agriculture. *See* U.S. Department of Agriculture (1963). *See* Wilderness Act in Vol. 12, *The Audubon Nature En-*

cyclopedia (Philadelphia-New York: The Curtis Publishing Company, 1964).

WILD CELERY
Vallisneria americana. (*Vallisneria spiralis* of some biologists, but see Fassett, 1940; and Fernald, 1950.) A favorite food of waterfowl, especially of canvasbacks and other ducks. It is a common herbaceous aquatic plant that grows wholly submerged in shallow lakes, ponds, and rivers of e. U.S. and e. Canada; its stems, buried in the mud, send up long, flexible, ribbonlike leaves of light translucent green. The leaves are about ¼–¾ in. wide; the plant does not resemble cultivated celery, but the white root is said to resemble a small celery stalk (Wilson, 1828–29). Canvasbacks, for example, eat its underground roots, winter buds, leaves, and seeds. The natural range of wild celery is from c. Minn. through the Great Lakes region to Nova Scotia, and from e. Kans. to e. Tex. and east to the Atlantic coast. It grows best in firm but fertile bottoms in fresh water to depths of 3½–6½ ft. (McAtee, 1939). *See also* Eelgrass.

WILDERNESS AREA
See Wild Area.

WILDFOWL
See Waterfowl.

WILDLIFE
A term sometimes restricted by game biologists to game species (elk, deer, quail, wild turkeys, rabbits, gray squirrels, etc.); however, the term is used by ecologists to include all life in the wild, from invertebrates such as insects and crustaceans to higher forms such as songbirds, grizzly bears, and all plant life.

WILDLIFE MANAGEMENT
See brief discussion of under Economic Ornithology.

WILDLIFE REFUGE
Term usually of the federal government in reference to its *refuge system*, in which areas of land and water have been bought and set aside for the needed protection of certain wild birds and mammals. In refuge management, predacious birds and mammals have often been killed, or "controlled," and still are to a lesser extent on the theory of benefiting waterfowl and other game species; also songbirds and insectivorous birds. In contradistinction, a sanctuary is, in practice, as in name, an *inviolate* refuge where all wildlife gets protection. Also, hunting is not permitted in sanctuaries, whereas on certain wildlife refuges hunting may be allowed at times if the concentration of certain birds in the refuge—for example, ducks, geese, and blackbirds—is causing local damage to farm crops outside of the refuge area.

A leaflet of the U.S. Fish and Wildlife Service issued in 1953 has summarized the history of the refuges:

"A tiny island in Indian River on the east coast of Florida was the birthplace of the National Wildlife Refuge System. By executive order of Theodore Roosevelt in 1903, Pelican Island became our first refuge.... Many reser-

voir areas and bird-nesting rocks or islands and some larger areas were added in the next few years. Most of the great waterfowl areas were acquired and developed since 1935 after our waterfowl had dwindled alarmingly. These refuges are distributed along the four principal migration routes up and down the country—the Atlantic and Pacific Flyways along the coasts, and the Mississippi and Central Flyways through the interior."

Refuges not only protect large concentrations of geese, swans, and diving ducks, but also protect rare or threatened species of birds. On the Fla. Keys, the establishment of the Great White Heron Refuge and the Key West Refuge has conserved the great white heron, the roseate spoonbill, and the white-crowned pigeon. The rare whooping crane is protected in winter on the Aransas Refuge in Tex., and the Red Rock Lakes Refuge in sw. Mont. west of Yellowstone Park has been chiefly responsible for saving the trumpeter swan in the U.S. More than 100 of the refuges have full-time managers who can grant permission to enter the areas. Names and addresses of the refuge managers and regional directors and a list of the refuges may be had by writing the U.S. Fish and Wildlife Service, Washington, D.C.

As of 1975, the U.S. Fish and Wildlife Service administered, as part of its National Wildlife Refuge System, 276 waterfowl refuges and 68 migratory-bird refuges which include, together, 8,337,700 acres of land and water (Anonymous, 1975b). *See also* Waterfowl.

WILLET
See in Sandpiper Family.

WILLIAMSON
ROBERT STOCKTON (1824–82). Born New York City; graduated from West Point in 1848. Lt. Stockton was an accomplished army engineer; when only 32 years old he was assigned to head one of the Pacific Railroad exploratory expeditions to the Far West. While operating in n. Calif. and in Ore., Dr. Newberry, the surgeon of the expedition, collected a woodpecker which he thought new to science and named it in honor of his commanding officer, *Picus williamsonii*, or Williamson's woodpecker. *See* the interesting story of this bird in the biography of the Williamson's sapsucker in Woodpecker Family; *see also* Henshaw; *see also* Gruson (1972).

WILL-O'-THE-WISP
See Nighthawk, common, in Nightjar Family.

WILSON
ALEXANDER (1766–1813). Born Paisley, Scotland, emigrated to America; on July 14, 1794, landed Newcastle, Del. With a companion walked 35 miles to Philadelphia and on the way saw a red-headed woodpecker which he thought the most beautiful bird in the world (Allen, E. G., 1951). According to Coues (1884), Wilson had genius, and was a pioneer American ornithologist (he became a citizen June 9, 1804) who because of his accuracy as an observer, patience, hard work, and thoroughness in learning the living bird in its environment, be-

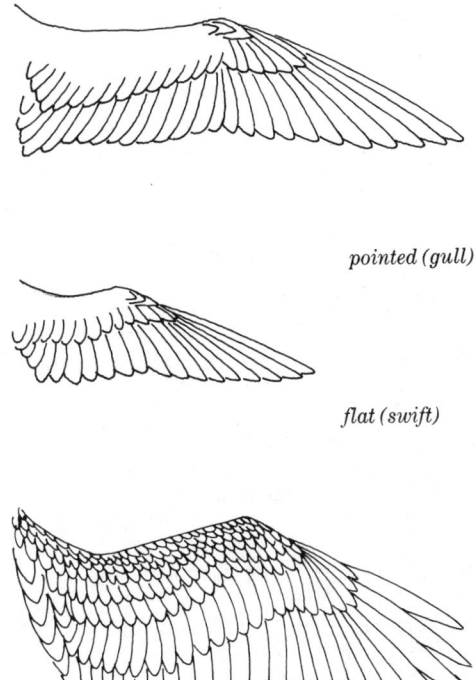

pointed (gull)

flat (swift)

round and concave (grouse)

WING
Different wing shapes are determined by the relative lengths of the primary feathers and by the curvature of the wing's undersurface. In pointed wings, such as those of gulls, the outermost primaries are longest; pointed wings are most suitable for long-distance flight over the ocean. Grouse have very concave, cupped wings, enabling them to take off rapidly and fly short distances quickly. Swifts have very flat wings, which give them maneuverability and quick flight.

came known as the "father of American ornithology."

At Philadelphia, he saw through to publication the first seven volumes of his *American Ornithology* (1808–13) before he died in his 48th year. The eighth and ninth volumes were completed in 1814 by his friend, editor, and biographer, George Ord. According to Allen, E. G. (1951), Wilson painted or drew 320 figures of American birds representing 262 species which he had observed on his travels by boat, horseback, and afoot in e. N. America. Encouraged in his drawing by the naturalist William Bartram, his sympathetic adviser, teacher, and friend, Wilson by 1806 had his purpose clearly fixed, to produce his illustrated *American Ornithology* (Herrick, 1917). Wilson's work was overshadowed by Audubon's, but his name is commemorated in Wilson's storm-petrel, Wilson's phalarope, Wilson's snipe, Wilson's plover, and Wilson's warbler, and in the genus name of several N. American wood warblers (Palmer, 1928). For a definitive biography of Wilson, see Cantwell (1961). *See also* Wilson Ornithological Society.

WILSON BULLETIN, THE
See Ornithological Periodicals; *also* Wilson Ornithological Society.

WILSON ORNITHOLOGICAL SOCIETY
A nonprofit educational membership organization founded in 1888 as The Wilson Ornithological Club, later Society, and named for Alexander Wilson, pioneer American ornithologist. The main purpose of the society is the advancement of the scientific study of birds and their habits, and the publication of articles, notes, reviews, etc., in its official journal, *The Wilson Bulletin* (see details under Ornithological Periodicals). The *Bulletin* is issued quarterly each year and its major aim is to publish original and important contributions to ornithological science.

The society, which meets annually, was organized originally as a chapter of the Agassiz Association, but became an independent group in 1902. Its first official publication was a small magazine called *The Curlew*, published in 1888 and 1889. After several changes in title during the next nine years, it became *The Wilson Bulletin*, as it is known today.

WINDHOVER
See Kestrel, American, in Falcon Family.

WINDOW-FIGHTING
See Territory.

WINDPIPE
See Trachea under Respiratory System.

WINGBEAT RATE
See Flight.

WING-CLAPPING
See Courtship.

WING-CLIPPING
See Pinion.

WING-FLASHING
See Wings; *see also* Food and Feeding Habits.

WING-LOADING
See Soaring Flight under Flight.

WING-QUIVERING
See Courtship Feeding; Wings; Young and Their Care.

WINGS
The main use of wings is for flight (*see* Flight), but they are also used solely for swimming by penguins and formerly by the extinct great auk (*see* Extinct Birds of North America). Some flying birds use their wings in diving and in swimming underwater—the members of the Auk Family, for example. Diving ducks such as scoters and oldsquaws use their wings probably for steering and legs as paddles when swimming underwater (Johnsgard, 1965). *See* Swimming and Diving. All flying birds use their wings for balancing, especially when perched on a swaying wire, branch, or other object or when buffeted by the wind while perching. Some birds—geese and swans, for example—use their powerful wings to strike an opponent (*see* Fighting under Territory) or even to flail human intruders that come near the nest (*see* Mute swan in Duck Family).

According to Harrison, J. G. (1964c), the spur-winged plover, *Vanellus* (or *Hoplopterus*) *spinosus*, which associates with crocodiles and lives in sw. Asia, the Mediterranean Region, and Africa, has a well-developed spur on each wing. It uses these wing spurs against an opponent while in flight, turning and striking with its spurs, which can inflict mortal injury on another bird.

Some male birds use their wings in courtship displays, spreading and vibrating them before the female. Many females, especially among small songbirds, spread their wings and quiver them before the male as part of the "begging" posture in which the female invites her mate to feed her (*see* Courtship Feeding). Some waterbirds (anhingas and cormorants, for example) spread their wings to dry them, others (vultures) to cool their body temperatures. *See* Heat and Birds.

Males of some birds use their wings while in courtship flights to make clapping sounds (short-eared owl) or booming (nighthawk) or throbbing sounds (common snipe). *See* Courtship and Territorial Flight under Flight. Some birds use their raised wings to intimidate others of their kind; some in injury-feigning (*see* Distraction Display); and some in certain kinds of food-getting (*see* Wing-flashing under Food and Feeding Habits).

WING SOUNDS
See Courtship and Territorial Flight under Flight; *also* Drumming.

WINGSPAN
See Wingspread.

WINGSPREAD
See, when known, in biography of each bird. *See* how taken under Dimensions.

WING-SPREADING
See Wings.

WING SPURS
See Wings.

WINTER CHIPPY
See Sparrow, tree, in Finch Family.

WINTER RESIDENT
See Where Do Birds Live? under Distribution.

WINTER SHELDRAKE
See Merganser, common, in Duck Family.

WIRE-TAIL
See Duck, ruddy, in Duck Family.

WISHBONE
See Furcula under Skeleton.

WOBBLE
See Auk, great, in Auk Family.

WOLLWEBER
An obscure 19th-century German naturalist and traveler about whom little is known. He collected birds in Mexico, and at Zacatecas got the first specimen, or specimens, of the bridled titmouse known to science. In 1850, Charles Lucien Bonaparte, who reported on his collections, gave the bird the scientific species name *wollweberi* in his honor. See also Gruson (1972).

WOODCHUCK
Another name for the whip-poor-will and the pileated woodpecker; woodland birds that utter a *chuck* note.

WOODCOCK
Rather general folk name for the large, strikingly impressive pileated and ivory-billed woodpeckers. *See also* woodcocks in Sandpiper Family.

WOODCREEPER
See Climbing Birds.

WOODHEWER
See Climbing Birds.

WOOD HOOPOE (HOO-poo) **FAMILY**
See Coraciiformes.

WOODPECKER FAMILY
Picidae (PIS-ih-dee); from Lat. *picus*, woodpecker. About 200 species worldwide, except in north and south polar regions beyond limit of trees and in New Guinea, New Zealand, Australia, and most of Oceania (Van Tyne and Berger, 1959); are not songbirds (Passeriformes), from which they may be distinguished especially by their zygodactylous feet (*see* below), but are in order Piciformes; 3½–23 in. long; from the tiny tropical piculets of Old and New World to the big imperial woodpecker; about 23 species reported in N. America; most are usually seen in pairs, or solitarily, because of their competition for similar food, and seldom seen in flocks; most are sedentary, and because their lives are centered on trunks and

branches of trees, are distinctive and easily recognizable.

Woodpeckers, while most frequently associated with wooded regions, are also common in savannas; they are an ancient group and, according to Austin (1961), the most primitive members of family are species of wrynecks in Old World that got their name from the way they twist their heads and necks in snakelike contortions when feeding.

The true woodpeckers (subfamily Picinae), to which all native N. American woodpeckers belong (see Steinbacher, 1964), have adapted to life on tree trunks and branches more successfully than any other birds (Austin, 1961); most live, heads up, tails down, perched on, or moving up, vertical surfaces of tree trunks; all (except three-toed woodpeckers) are four-toed, with two of the front toes (II and III) pointing forward, the fourth (outer) toe turned laterally at a right angle to the trunk, and the reduced hallux, or hind toe, pointing down the trunk or to the side (Spring, 1965). In the three-toed woodpeckers, the hallux (hind toe) is missing; usually two of the toes are pointed forward, and the outer one turned laterally at a right angle to the trunk; on horizontal surface of ground or limb of tree, the fourth toe of most woodpeckers is usually rotated backward, parallel to the hind toe, typical of the permanently zygodactylous foot of the ground-inhabiting woodpeckers such as the flicker (Spring, 1965).

The legs of woodpeckers are short, the toes long and strong, with sharp, curved nails, with which they cling to bark; they prop themselves upright with their strong, pointed tail feathers (rectrices) against surface of the tree; tail is usually round or wedge-shaped. According to Steinbacher (1964), the stiff central pair of tail feathers on which the woodpeckers depend to prop themselves when climbing, or at rest, usually are shed in the molt only *after* the new central pair have grown in to replace them—an adaptation that preserves the function of the tail at all times.

Plumage of woodpeckers may be black, white, yellow, red, brown; many are barred, spotted, or streaked either on back or on underparts; some are crested, and in most species the sexes differ mainly in head markings.

Woodpeckers have straight, hard, pointed bills which most use as a chisel to peck or hack into bark and wood of trees in feeding on insects or in excavating a hole in a tree or in a branch for nesting or as place to roost at night (*see* Roosting), or as a hammer to drum or tap during courtship (*see* Drumming; Language); the nostrils usually are covered with bristlelike feathers that apparently protect them from wood dust raised by the woodpecker's bill when drilling into a tree (Steinbacher, 1964).

Woodpeckers utter harsh calls and sharp ringing cries, and have an extensive vocabulary, including some songlike calls. Some use drumming as well as voice in proclaiming their territories (Winkler and Short, 1978). The woodpecker's thick-walled skull, the narrow space between the tough outer membrane of the brain and the brain itself, and the strong muscles of skull and bill, absorb the shock of pounding with the bill, which is driven by the powerful muscles of the bird's strong, wiry

WOODPECKER FAMILY

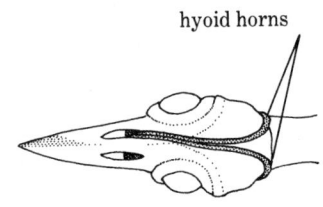

hyoid horns

hyoid horn

tongue

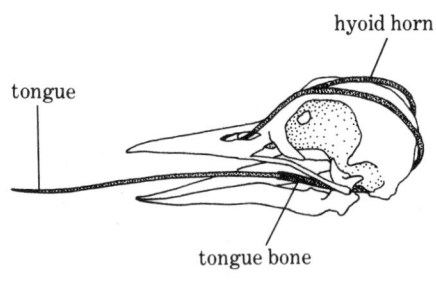

tongue bone

WOODPECKER FAMILY

To support the extension of their remarkably long tongues, woodpeckers have a hyoid apparatus consisting of a tongue bone that branches into 2 cartiliginous hyoid bones, or "horns." The horns curve upward along the skull, over the forehead, and attach inside the right nostril.

neck. Woodpeckers generally build their homes by excavating with the bill holes in limbs and trunks of trees. Lawrence (1967), in her studies of woodpeckers in Canada, noted that sapsuckers and hairy woodpeckers prefer live trees; flickers and downy woodpeckers prefer to drill their holes in dead trees and stubs; flickers sometimes nest in previously used holes; sapsuckers do so occasionally; most woodpeckers (about 77%) of the four species studied by Lawrence drilled their nesting holes facing south or east, perhaps to gain advantage of early-morning light and warmth of rising sun (see, however, Conner, 1975, for other data and conclusions). Woodpeckers tunnel downward 6–18 in. deep, with the excavation larger at bottom for the egg chamber, which is bare except for a few chips of wood on which the 2–8 dull white or glossy white eggs are laid; both sexes incubate, the male usually at night (Steinbacher, 1964); young at hatching are blind and naked, and in many species are very noisy when about to leave the nest (Sutton, 1967b). The smaller woodpeckers such as the downy are often tame in presence of people; the larger ones are usually shy.

Woodpeckers have extraordinarily long, extensible, wormlike tongues which they can protrude to astonishing lengths when seeking; they are highly mobile and can be extended because of the supporting "horns" of the hyoid bones, which curve around the back of the skull and attach in front of the skull or even to, or into, the nostrils (*see* details under Tongue). The hard barbed tip of the tongue is bordered with bristles; when coated with saliva, a woodpecker can use its sticky tongue for catching ants, or it can use it as a brush for licking sap of trees (sapsuckers), or as a lance to spear wood-boring insects; "the long tracheo-hyoid muscles retract the tongue" (Steinbacher, 1964).

Woodpeckers seem to depend on their hearing to detect insects such as the larvae of wood borers gnawing or moving within bark or in the wood of trees (Gilliard, 1958; Davis, 1965) and to pick up buzzing of hibernating insects such as cluster flies, *Pollenia rudis*, which hide in large groups under wooden shingles of houses. *See,* however, discussion in biography of hairy woodpecker. The adults of most woodpecker species eat wood-boring beetles (both larvae and adults), ants, aphids, flies, caterpillars, bugs, and other insects picked off trees or the ground, or caught in flight; others eat acorns, pine seeds, nuts, berries, and other fruit, some grain and sap, and some store food—the acorn, Lewis,' and red-headed woodpeckers, for example. *See* Birds That Store Food under Food and Feeding Habits. For an account of woodpeckers helping suppress a plague of bark beetles, see Olson (1953).

In feeding, some woodpeckers may start at base of trunk, probing in the crannies of bark for insects and spiders, and either move directly up the trunk or spiral around it (see Spring, 1965); or they explore larger limbs and sometimes cling with back to ground, tapping bill on underside of a horizontal branch; after reaching top of tree, swoop out in flight and drop to base of next tree and begin climb upward again; they have stout wings, rather

rounded; fly strongly but not swiftly, and usually not for long distances; are recognizable by their undulating flight—several wingbeats that carry them upward, then a swoop downward with wings closed briefly, then more wingbeats and another swoop (Austin, 1961). Many tropical, and some other, woodpeckers obtain most of their food without pecking into the tree surface (Short, 1978). Very few species are migratory, although some move irregularly southward in winter, or from higher mountains to lower valleys; they generally can remain where it is cold because their food supply of insect pupae and larvae is available under bark or in dead or rotted wood where it is out of reach of most birds. *See,* however, Commensalism. Some woodpeckers also come to bird feeders in winter and in summer for suet and other foods.

Flickers are medium to large woodpeckers that feed much on the ground, where they probe anthills with the bill and extended tongue for ants (a favorite food), also for other insects (Beal, 1895); flickers of N. America are represented by one species, the common flicker, two subspecies of which, the red-shafted and yellow-shafted flickers, are most widely distributed and best known; they are migratory; the gilded flicker of sw. U.S., another subspecies of the common flicker, is not migratory and is fairly common.

The ivory-billed woodpecker, largest N. American species, with a large crest, is near extinction (or may be extinct outside Cuba); the very similar but smaller pileated woodpecker is still fairly common, especially in se. U.S.; largest of all woodpeckers, and related to the ivory-bill, is the nearly extinct 23-in.-long imperial woodpecker, *Campephilus imperialis,* of Mexico, on which the rare thick-billed parrot depended almost entirely for its nesting holes. *See* similar dependence of bufflehead (in Duck Family) on flicker nesting holes in n. U.S. and Canada and discussion of the use of old woodpecker holes by other birds under Autolycism.

Sapsuckers eat sap that oozes from holes they drill in tender bark of trees; other birds, especially downy woodpeckers, warblers, and hummingbirds, which like the sap, also drink from these "wells"; *see also* intoxication of birds from sap-drinking under Poisons. Sapsuckers also eat insects attracted to the oozing sap. These birds are often accused of damaging fruit and ornamental trees with their drilling, but though these tiny holes may disfigure the bark, they do not cause permanent damage; in healthy trees the bark soon heals, and sapsuckers themselves are never numerous enough to be a problem (Austin, 1961; see also Lawrence, 1955; see, however, McAtee, 1926, and Bent, 1939, for discussion of sapsucker damage); pileated and red-headed woodpeckers have caused some damage to utility poles (see discussions by Dennis, 1963; 1964; Benton and Dickinson, 1966; Rumsey, 1970), and flickers and hairy woodpeckers to the wooden gables, corners, and siding of houses and other buildings (see discussion of this in Terres, 1968c; Lawrence, 1967).

Sapsuckers of w. U.S., especially the red-breasted, the red-naped, and the yellow-bellied of the East, which ranges west, have been the subject of controversy about their relationships. Some authorities—for example, Howell (1952); the authoritative A.O.U. *Check-list* (1957); Phillips *et al.* (1964); and Bent (1939)—have treated the yellow-bellied sapsucker, *Sphyrapicus varius*, as one species, with two subspecies called the red-breasted sapsucker and the red-naped sapsucker. Short (1969b) and Short and Morony (1970) treat the red-breasted and red-naped sapsuckers, not as forms, or subspecies, of the yellow-bellied sapsucker, but as separate, or distinct, species, *Sphyrapicus ruber* and *Sphyrapicus nuchalis*, respectively. Devillers (1970) gives details and comparisons of color and markings of the red-breasted, red-naped, and yellow-bellied sapsuckers; the ranges of these have been given in detail in Bent (1939).

Albinism has been reported in 48 individual woodpeckers of 10 species, thus ranking with the Hawk Family as the tenth in frequency of albinism reported for any family of N. American birds (Gross, 1965a).

All woodpeckers are protected by law and are rarely kept in captivity even in zoos (Walker, 1942); however, to help an injured or ill one until it can fend for itself, offer it mealworms, meat, suet, fruit, some bread, grain, yolk of hard-boiled egg, and mockingbird food; also make available fresh water daily; supply it with large cage for its protection and with short, upright, rough-barked limbs to which it may cling and perch vertically. For an absorbing account of woodpecker behavior, see Lawrence (1967); also Short (1971).

Flicker, common, *Colaptes auratus* (koh-LAP-teez oh-RAY-tus); genus name: Lat., from Gr. *kolapter*, a hammer, chisel, and *kolapto*, to peck with bill (Jaeger, 1955); species name: Lat., gilded, ornamented with gold, in reference to yellow linings of wings and tail; *flicker*, apparently from act of flicking: to strike lightly with a quick jerk (of bill); also, to flicker: to flutter or flap wings without flying; *auratus* is now the species name for all three similar N. American flickers—gilded, red-shafted, and yellow-shafted—all of which interbreed where their ranges meet, and produce hybrids so commonly that they are now considered races, or subspecies, and collectively represent what is now called the common flicker (American Ornithologists' Union, 1973). See also discussion by Phillips in Phillips *et al.* (1964), and Short (1965). *See* under, Flicker, gilded (common), Flicker, red-shafted (common), and Flicker, yellow-shafted (common).
Range: Nests from limit of trees, c. Alaska, nw. Mack., n. Man., James Bay, c. Que., s. Labrador, and Newfoundland, south to Baja Calif., s. Tex., Gulf coast, Fla. Keys, Nicaragua, Cuba, and Grand Cayman; winters from near northern limits of breeding range south.

Flicker, gilded (common), *Colaptes auratus mearnsi,* formerly *Colaptes chrysoides mearnsi* (koh-LAP-teez oh-RAY-tus MERNS-eye); genus and species names: *see* Flicker, common, subspecies name: given by Robert Ridgway in 1911 in honor of Dr. Edgar A. Mearns, U.S. Army surgeon and field naturalist; *gilded* refers to the golden appearance of undersides of wings and tail. (Color ill., page

1,037.) Once considered a distinct species, *Colaptes chrysoides* (A.O.U. *Check-list*, 1957), of which *mearnsi* was the only subspecies in the U.S., but determined by American Ornithologists' Union (1973), following Short (1965), to be a subspecies *(mearnsi)* of the common flicker, *Colaptes auratus;* 10–12 in. long; smaller than the other flickers; the small desert form, Mearns' gilded flicker of s. Ariz. and se. Calif., is confined mostly in breeding season to giant cactus region of the Southwest (Bent, 1939), where it digs its nesting and roosting holes 11–30 ft. above ground in the saguaro cactus far from water, and 5–25 ft. up in cottonwoods and willows along wooded banks of rivers and canals; distinguished from yellow-shafted flicker by its *brown crown*, gray face, and, in male, *red* malar stripe ("mustache"); is an almost exact duplicate outwardly of the red-shafted flicker except that undersides of its wings and tail are yellow or orange-yellow instead of scarlet-orange or salmon-red of the red-shafted flicker; hybrids with red-shafted flickers inhabit river valleys of Ariz. (Short, 1965); calls like those of other flickers but slightly higher-pitched.

Feeding Habits: Feeds much on ground; eats ants and various other insects, fruit of cactus and wild berries; very fond of watermelon slices placed on bird feeders (Bent, 1939).
Nest: See above.
Eggs: Ariz., Apr.–June; Baja Calif., Apr.–May; usually 3–5, white.
Incubation: Period of and age when young first fly unknown.
Other Names: Common flicker; Mearns' gilded flicker; wakeup, or wick-up, and yucker (from call notes).
Hybrids: Commonly interbreeds in wild: gilded flicker × red-shafted flicker where their ranges meet.
Weights: Two averaged 116 gr. (Hughes, 1970), or about 4 oz.
Range: See above.

Flicker, Mearns' gilded. *See* Flicker, gilded (common).

Flicker, northern. *See* Flicker, yellow-shafted (common).

Flicker, red-shafted (common), *Colaptes auratus cafer* (koh-LAP-teez oh-RAY-tus KAF-er); genus and species names: *see* Flicker, common; subspecies name: Latinized form of "Kaffir" (when Johann Gmelin, German systematist, named this bird as a distinct species in 1788, he mistook the origin of the type of this bird on which he based his name and description, assuming it came from the Cape of Good Hope, South Africa, hence Kaffir, "from the country of the Kaffirs," whereas it had come from the Bay of Good Hope, Nootka Sound, Vancouver Is., B.C.); *red-shafted*, for the red undersurfaces of the wings and tail. (Color ill., page 1,036.) Formerly considered a distinct species, *Colaptes cafer* (A.O.U. *Check-list*, 1957), but determined by American Ornithologists' Union (1973) to be a subspecies of the common flicker, *Colaptes auratus;* this subspecies and others of the red-shafted group range from

Alaska south through w. Canada and w. U.S. and Baja Calif.; 12½–14 in. long, about same size as yellow-shafted flicker, which it resembles closely and with which it interbreeds widely (see interesting details in Short, 1965); its back and wings are brown barred with black; black crescent across the upper breast with numerous round black spots on sides, lower breast, and belly; also like yellow-shafted in its undulating flight and the conspicuous white mark on its rump, but has *gray face* and *brown crown* with no red on back of head, and male has a *red* malar stripe ("mustache"), not black as in male yellow-shafted, and has *salmon-red* underlinings of wings and tail (not yellow as in yellow-shafted); like yellow-shafted flicker, one of its calls is a loud *wick, wick, wick, wick, wick*, also *klee-yer* (see under Flicker, yellow-shafted (common)); ranges widely through many kinds of open country, sparsely wooded regions and conifers with open ground below; is usually resident year-round from Rocky Mtns. to sea level on Pacific coast; a common bird near human dwellings, in towns and villages, agricultural lands, also lives in wilder foothills, canyons, and mountain slopes up to timberline (in Yellowstone National Park ranges up to 9,500 ft. elevation), but not on treeless plains or deserts; in parts of West most abundant about farms and cut-over woods, nests commonly near barnyards and pastures. Courtship like that of yellow-shafted flicker, also similar feeding habits and foods, nesting, number of eggs, etc. See details in Bent (1939).

Other Names: Common flicker; high-holder; high-hole; northwestern flicker; red-hammer; wake-up, or wick-up, and yucker (from call notes).
Age: One, banded Thorne Ecological Institute, Colo., caught and released in same area when 5 years, 7 months, old (Kennard, 1975).
Flight Speed: Timed in Calif., 43–44 m.p.h. (McLean, 1930); 25 m.p.h. (Wetmore, 1916); in w. U.S., 27–29 m.p.h. (Cottam *et al.*, 1942b); 27 m.p.h. (Gignoux, 1921).
Hybrids: Red-shafted interbreeds freely with yellow-shafted flicker in a vast hybrid zone from B.C. through Alta. and the Great Plains to Tex., and also with the gilded flicker in Ariz. (Short, 1965). *See* discussion under Hybrid. Every possible blending or mixing of the characters of the two has been discovered, and their interbreeding has been noted from the Great Plains westward to the Pacific coast and east to Pa. and New England. *See* in biography of gilded flicker.
Weights: Two averaged 125 gr. (Hughes, 1970), or about 4½ oz.
Range: See above.

Flicker, southern. *See* Flicker yellow-shafted (common).

Flicker, yellow-shafted (common), *Colaptes auratus auratus* (koh-LAP-teez oh-RAY-tus); genus and species names: *see* Flicker, common; *yellow-shafted*, for the yellow undersurfaces of the wings and tail. (Color ill., page 1,036.) State bird of Alabama; formerly considered a distinct species, *Colaptes* *auratus* (A.O.U. *Check-list*, 1957), but determined by American Ornithologists' Union (1973) to be a subspecies of the wide-ranging bird now called the common flicker, *Colaptes auratus;* the species includes, besides the yellow-shafted group and its subspecies, the red-shafted group and the gilded flickers, all of which interbreed where their ranges overlap (*see* discussion under Flicker, common; Flicker, gilded (common); and Flicker, red-shafted (common). The nominate subspecies *auratus auratus* (discussed here)—*see* Nominate subspecies —called the southern yellow-shafted flicker, along with the northern yellow-shafted flicker, *borealis,* and a geographically intermediate subspecies, *luteus,* constitute a group of the yellow-shafted that nests from the limit of trees in c. Alaska, nw. Mack., n. Man., c. Que., s. Labrador, and Newfoundland, south (east of the Rocky Mtns.) to n. Tex., Gulf coast, Fla. Keys, Cuba, and Grand Cayman (the yellow-shafted nests farther north than any other woodpecker except the northern three-toed woodpecker—Godfrey, 1966); one of most widely known of all woodpeckers (Bent, 1939); 12–14 in. long; wingspread about 18½–21 in.; its back and wings are brown, barred with black; black crescent across upper breast with numerous prominent round black spots on its sides, lower breast, and belly; both sexes have a red crescent on back of head not present in other flickers; male has *black* malar stripe ("mustache"), gray crown, brown face and throat, yellow underlinings of wings and tail (where breeding ranges of yellow-shafted and red-shafted approach in Great Plains, hybrids may have orange-yellow undersurfaces of wings, or one "mustache" on one side of face black, the other red, etc.); lives usually in open country; favors farms, orchards, scattered woodlots, also trees of village streets and in partly wooded parks of towns and cities (for example, in Central Park, New York City); in fall and in winter, many move southward from northern parts of range (others overwinter) and then more apt to wander in open woods, fields, and meadows or to seek shelter of coniferous woods and swamps; goes to roost before sundown in one of its roosting holes in trees, sometimes roosts inside unused chimneys; will drill holes in barns and in sides of houses or under eaves for winter roosts (see discussion of damage in Terres, 1968c); when it flies up from ground, white rump patch is conspicuous; in short ordinary flight bounds up and down, undulating; migrates during day, when flight is steady, strong, and fairly swift; travels above treetops in detached flocks often far apart; in spring, males arrive on range or nesting territory a few days ahead of females, some from early Feb. into early Apr. in n. U.S. (Bent, 1939); arrival is announced by its loud, challenging call from top of tall tree, a rapid *wick, wick, wick, wick* or *yuck, yuck, yuck, yuck,* and with loud drumming from resonant tree limbs, trunks, and utility poles, metal roof of house, etc.; the *wick, wick* call is similar in sound to pileated woodpecker's loud so-called location call (see courtship and "dances" in Bent, 1939; Kilham, 1959b; Lawrence, 1967); also commonly utters a *klee-yer* call, a long-distance cry from one member of family to another; fledglings use this call both in and out of nest to attract parents' attention; see numerous phonetic renditions of yellow-shafted's calls in Bent (1939); see also Short (1972) for behavior.

Feeding Habits: Feeds much on ground, hopping about on lawn or open place in woods and fields, probing for ants; about 75% of its food is animal, of which ants are 45% (Beal, 1911); eats more ants than any other N. American bird (see accounts in Bent, 1939); also eats beetles, wasps, grasshoppers, crickets, chinch bugs, wood lice, caterpillars, grubs, and various flying insects which it catches by darting out into air after them; about 25% of food is vegetable, mostly wild fruits and berries of dogwood, Virginia creeper, hackberries, blueberries, pokeberries, serviceberries, elderberries, wild plums, etc., also eats seeds of clovers, grasses, pigweeds, mullein, ragweed, poison ivy, and poison sumac; comes to bird feeders for suet, bread, peanut butter mixture, etc. (see in Terres, 1968c; 1977; Dennis, 1975); sometimes drinks water from birdbath and eats snow (Bent, 1939).

Nest: Male plays principal role in selecting the nest site; digs it with bill, alternating with female, often in stub or trunk of a dead tree above surrounding bushes; some dead stubs may have 25–30 old nesting holes (see nesting densities per acre in Dennis, 1969; Erskine, 1971b); also often nests in old nest hole of previous years; excavating new hole or refurbishing old one may require a week or two; eggs are laid on fresh chips at bottom of cavity; fresh chips at base of tree are clue to nest site; old apple trees of old orchards were once a favorite site, also chooses sycamore, oak, butternut, cherry, maple, elm, dead white pines, and other trees; also digs nest hole in utility poles and fence posts especially in open farming country or prairies where trees scarce; the usually round nest holes are 2–4 in. in diameter and 10–36 in. deep; may be 2–90 ft. above ground (in n. U.S. and Canada, the bufflehead [duck] depends almost entirely on old nesting holes of flickers and pileated woodpeckers for its nesting places); will also nest in "flicker nest boxes" put up for it in woods, backyards, or gardens (see size of nesting box and placement in Terres, 1968c); competition with aggressive starlings for flickers' nesting holes may be severe; in Colo. a decline of flickers since 1950 owing to increased competition from starlings (Bock and Smith, 1971).

Eggs: Fla., Mar.–July; middle Atlantic states, n. Nova Scotia, and Canada, usually Apr.–June; 5–10, white, laid on mat of wooden chips in bottom of nesting hole.

Incubation: By both sexes, always by male at night, 11–12 days; young fed by regurgitation, adult bill inserted into gape of young; young leave nest and fly 25–28 days after hatching (Sherman, 1910).

Other Names: Has at least 132 common names. Some are: Clape; gaffer woodpecker; golden-winged woodpecker; harry-wicket; heigh-ho; high-holder; high-hole; northern flicker; pigeon woodpecker; southern flicker; wake-up, walk-up, and wick-up (from the "hic-cup" call); wood pigeon; yarrup; yawker bird; yellow-hammer; yellow-shafted woodpecker.

Age: One, banded as nestling, Lakewood, Ohio, found dead in same place 5 years later; another, banded N.D., was killed in Okla. when 5 years, 8 months old; another (see Kennard, 1975) reached 12 years, 5 months.

Flight Speed: Timed in N.H., 20, 25 m.p.h. (White, 1927; 1929); 23 m.p.h. (Wood, 1933).

Albinism: Eighteen records of albinism in yellow-shafted flicker listed by Gross (1965a); two out of six young in a nest near Paris, Ohio, were cream-white, eyes pink, yellow only in shafts of tail feathers; one died in nest, the other had weak eyesight and tended to fly in circles; disappeared after a month, probably killed (Petry, 1908); one, melanistic, reported by Deane (1876).

Hybrids: See interbreeding under Flicker, gilded and Flicker, red-shafted.

Weights: 4–6 oz. (Forbush, 1925–29); two males killed in migration at TV tower in Kans., 126 and 139.4 gr. (Tordoff and Mengel, 1956); in fall, coastal N.J. (26), 112–153 gr. (Murray and Jehl, 1964), or about 4–5 oz.

Range: See above and under Flicker, common.

Sapsucker, common. *See* Sapsucker, yellow-bellied.

Sapsucker, Natalie's. *See* Sapsucker, Williamson's.

Sapsucker, northern red-breasted. *See* Sapsucker, red-breasted.

Sapsucker red-breasted (yellow-bellied), *Sphyrapicus varius ruber* (sfie-rah-PIE-kus VAY-rih-us RUBE-er); genus name: from Gr. *sphyra,* a hammer, or mallet, in reference to bill and its use, and Lat. *picus,* a woodpecker; species name: from Lat. variegated, in reference to various colors of plumage; subspecies name: Lat., red, in reference to red of the hood. A Pacific coastal race, or subspecies of the yellow-bellied sapsucker (*see* family introduction), but considered by Short (1969b), Short and Morony (1970) and Mayr and Short (1970) a distinct species, who so classify it because interbreeding with red-naped and yellow-breasted sapsuckers at places where their ranges meet is very limited. Adults of red-breasted sapsuckers are distinguished at first glance by the complete scarlet hood, which includes the head, nape, and breast (Devillers, 1970); one of the few woodpeckers in which sexes are alike; a similar woodpecker east of the Rocky Mtns. is the red-headed woodpecker, but the red-breasted sapsucker is distinguished from it by its long, narrow white wing stripe and its finely mottled back. Habitat, feeding and nesting habits, eggs, and incubation are similar to those of the red-naped and yellow-bellied sapsuckers.

Range: Nests from "se. Alaska, w. B.C., south in coastal belt to n. Calif. and through Cascades, Sierras, to high mountains in s. Calif.; winters in lowlands and along coast to Baja Calif., casual in Ariz." (Peterson, 1961). See details of zone of hybridization with other sapsuckers, range, and habitat in Devillers (1970).

Sapsucker, red-naped (yellow-bellied), *Sphyrapicus varius nuchalis* (sfie-rah-PIE-kus VAY-rih-us new-KAY-liss); genus and species names: *see* Sapsucker, red-breasted; subspecies name: Gr., pertaining to the nape, *nucha*, back of neck, which is red. (Color ill., page 1,036.) A western race, or subspecies of the yellow-bellied sapsucker (*see* family introduction); the red-naped is similar to the yellow-bellied sapsucker and the red-breasted sapsucker in size and appearance, but, according to Devillers (1970), can be distinguished from the yellow-bellied fairly easily: the nape of the red-naped is always more or less red but the throat is *entirely* red in males and mainly red in females (chin may be white); the red area covers the posterior (rear) part of the black malar ("mustache") stripe, thus interrupting it and actually coming into contact with the white of the cheek; the red also extends over the upper part of the breast patch, and often the auricular (ear) area is tinged with red; the white on the back is restricted to two definite broken white stripes converging posteriorly; these stripes are narrower than those of the yellow-bellied sapsucker and they are chainlike through interruption by black bars; the underparts are less strongly tinged with yellow than in the yellow-bellied (see Ridgway in Bent, 1939); lives in suitable places rather commonly throughout country between the Sierra Nevada and the Rocky Mtns.; favors, in summer, groves of large aspens near head of upper canyons high up in the mountains; very rare throughout w. Nev. but abundant in higher mountains of eastern part of that state; in nw. Mont., lives most abundantly and typically in mixed broad-leaved and coniferous woods along streams, where it nests regularly; ranges less commonly into virgin forests of fir, larch, yellow pine, and hemlocks in the valleys (see in Bent, 1939).

Feeding Habits: Like those of yellow-bellied sapsucker; also is charged with damaging peach and apple trees in same manner as yellow-bellied sapsucker; also drills holes in bark of many western trees for sap and the soft cambium layer, just under the bark, of various pines, spruces, hemlocks, firs, redwoods, cedars, cypresses, junipers, cottonwoods, aspens, willows, bayberry, walnuts, hop hornbeam, oaks, laurels, western dogwood, madrona, mesquite, ironwood, maples, etc. (McAtee, 1911b). *Nest:* Drills holes with bill mostly in live aspens, some in live larches, some in dead Engelmann spruces; entrance hole, round, about 1¼ in. in diameter, cavity about 8 in. deep, about 4 in. wide at bottom; up to 20 ft. above ground; completes digging of nest hole in 6–10 days (Bent, 1939). Eggs, incubation, like that of yellow-bellied sapsucker. Weydemeyer (1926), a careful and accurate observer, watched pair of red-naped sapsuckers gather sap from their borings in an aspen, an alder, and a willow, and carry sap in bill to nest to feed it to the young. *Range:* Nests in Rocky Mtn. region from s.-c. B.C. and sw. Alta. south on east slope of Cascade Mtns. to ne. Calif., also in the White Mtns. of e. Calif., in Nev., except in region of Lake Tahoe, c. Ariz., n. N.M., and extreme w. Tex.; winters from southern part of breeding range

south through c. and s. Calif., Baja Calif., most of Ariz., s. N.M., and nw. Mexico; casual in Kans., Neb., and Okla. See Devillers (1970) for areas of interbreeding with the yellow-bellied sapsucker; also hybridizes rarely with Williamson's sapsucker.

Sapsucker, red-throated. *See* Sapsucker, yellow-bellied.

Sapsucker, southern red-breasted. *See* Sapsucker, red-breasted.

Sapsucker, Williamson's, *Sphyrapicus thyroideus* (sfie-rah-PIE-kus thigh-ROY-dee-us); genus name: *see* Sapsucker, red-breasted; species name: from Gr. *thyreos*, a shield, and *eidos*, like, resembling; in allusion to dark shieldlike patch of feathers on breast of female; common name: on Aug. 23, 1855, a Dr. Newberry, surgeon to the Pacific Railroad Survey, collected (shot) a woodpecker which he thought new to science and named it *Picus williamsonii*, in honor of Lt. R. S. Williamson, his commanding officer; it was later discovered, however, that the female of this species had already been described by John Cassin in 1852, who had given it the specific name of *thyroideus*; because of the law of priority in dates of publication of scientific names of birds and other animals in zoology, Cassin's name *thyroideus* stands; however, the bird is still known by the common name of Williamson's sapsucker (Palmer, 1928). (Color ill., page 1,037.) *See* similar examples under Gull, Franklin's, and Gull, Ross' in Gull Family; *also* Names and Naming. A resident in mountains in B.C. and w. U.S.; uncommon; sexes outwardly so unlike that the male and female were each described originally as separate species; that they are same species was reported in 1875 by Henry W. Henshaw (see story in Bent, 1939); 9–9½ in. long; *male* has glossy green-black head, neck, back, breast, wings, and tail, with long white shoulder patch; also has two white facial stripes on dark face, and a narrow bright red patch on throat; yellow belly; in flight, male appears black and shows white rump and white shoulder patches; *female* has brown head; is "zebra-backed" (has bars of brown and white across back); black patch on her breast, larger than that of female yellow-bellied sapsucker; has barred sides, yellow belly, white rump; adults utter explosive, shrill *cheeer*, like scream of red-tailed hawk; a rolling *k-k-r-r-r-r-r*; also a weak, wheezy *whang* or *whether* (Bent, 1939); shy, suspicious of human intruder; movements when working up and down tree trunk are quick, active but secretive when disturbed; mostly confined to higher elevations in mountains among pines, in contrast to haunts of red-naped sapsucker at lower levels among deciduous trees.

Feeding Habits: Drills horizontal rows of tiny pits in bark of lodgepole pine, hemlock, red and white firs, Jeffrey pine, and aspen, from which it drinks sap and eats the cambium (a layer of soft green tissue just under the bark); also eats ants, which may make up 86% of its animal food (Bailey, 1928), and whitewood-boring larvae, moths of spruce budworm, etc.; in winter eats

Red-breasted sapsucker

WOODPECKER FAMILY

dormant adult insects or larvae in crevices of bark.

Nest: Within hole often dug in trunk or dead top of partly decayed pines, firs, aspens, 5–60 ft. above ground.

Eggs: May–June; 3–7, commonly 5–6, pure china white.

Incubation: By both sexes; 12–14 days; young fly from nesting hole about 28–35 days after hatching (Crockett and Hansley, 1977).

Other Names: Black-crowned sapsucker (male); brown-headed woodpecker (female); Natalie's sapsucker; Williamson's woodpecker.

Hybrids: Two adults, both crosses between Williamson's and the red-naped sapsucker, described by Short and Morony (1970); one, a female, from 6,000 ft. elevation in Huachuca Mtns. in 1929 in Ariz.; the other, a male, in 1891 in n. Chihuahua, Mexico; both resembled Williamson's sapsucker more than the red-naped.

Weights: Three averaged 43 gr. (Hughes, 1970), or about 1½ oz.

Range: Resident in mountains from s. B.C. south through c. and e. Wash., Ore., east to w. Mont., Wyo., Colo., to s. Calif., s. Nev., c. Ariz., and n. N.M.; winters at lower elevations and south to n. Baja Calif., nw. Mexico, and w. Tex.; casual in w. Calif. and Neb.

Sapsucker, Yankee. In s. U.S., name for the yellow-bellied sapsucker ("from the North").

Sapsucker, yellow-bellied, *Sphyrapicus varius* (sfie-rah-PIE-kus VAY-rih-us; genus and species names: *see* Sapsucker, red-breasted; (Color ill., page 1,037.) In summer, across n. U.S. and Canada to Alaska and Pacific coast; also in c. U.S. and Southwest, in East south to n. Ga. (the western red-breasted and red-naped sapsuckers are considered, by some authorities, to be forms, or subspecies, of the yellow-bellied sapsucker, but *see* opposing views cited in family introduction); 8–9 in. long; wingspread 14–16 in.; plumage shows variation between individuals, but in general adults have scarlet-red forehead, a long white stripe down each wing, and the back is cross-barred with black and white (male has patch of red on *both* forehead and throat); female has a white throat; both sexes have two white horizontal stripes across face, one originating at eyes, the other at bill, and both have a black bib across upper breast, straw-yellow underparts, and a white rump patch; black tail with white bars across central tail feathers; immatures are brown but distinguished by the long patch of white along the closed wing; utters low, snarling, nasal *mew*, a *che-err* of alarm, a *yew-ick, yew-ick* at nesting hole, and a low-toned *tuck* (Tyler, 1939b); a *kee-yew* on nesting grounds (see interpretations and illustrations of calls and of "aggressive-social" displays in Lawrence, 1967); all sapsucker calls have characteristic *mewling* quality reminiscent of cry of a cat; some of its cries resemble calls of the blue jay and others of the red-shouldered hawk; during courtship, when pairs chasing each other, utter notes like *hoih-hoih*, but when clinging upright to trunks of trees usually silent (Tyler, 1939b); both sexes drum on dry limbs, tin roofs, utility poles, etc.; drumming begins with short roll and ends with 5 or 6 disconnected taps—for example, *tap-tap-trrrrrrrr-tat-tat—tat;* they also communicate by slow tapping (*see* Tapping under Drumming); migrates, arrives nesting grounds in s. Canada, n. U.S., in Mar.–Apr.; sometimes when snow still on ground (males precede females by about a week).

Feeding Habits: Drills both horizontal and vertical, square or round holes about ¼ in. in diameter in trunks of at least 275 species of coniferous and deciduous trees (also in shrubs and in some vines) to get at soft inner bark (see McAtee, 1911b, and Tate, 1973, for details) and especially to lap up with long, brush-tipped tongue sap that fills the shallow holes, or "wells," which also attract insects, hummingbirds, other woodpeckers, warblers, flying squirrels, etc. (*see* Commensalism); sap important food in winter, spring, and summer as energy source (Bolles, 1891); feeds its young mixture of sap and insects; also eats ants, wasps, hornets (*see* Insects and Birds), mayflies, stone flies, moths of forest tent caterpillars, of spruce budworm, and beetles; eats scale insects, psyllids, and other bark and tree insects (Tate, 1973); also fruit and small berries; buds of aspen; in winter comes to gardens and backyards for suet, suet mixtures, doughnuts, grape jelly, and sugar water in hummingbird feeders (Dennis, 1975).

Nest: Both sexes involved in selection of nest site but male plays principal role; in North shows strong preference for nesting in live aspens, which have soft wood and core, also in dead aspen stubs, in dead birches, elms, butternut (see also in Kilham, 1962a; 1971); may start one of several nesting holes before deciding on final one; 10–45 feet up, nest hole dug by both sexes, entrance about 1¼–1½ in. in diameter, with male doing most of work; nest entrance most often faces south or east (Lawrence, 1967); averages about 14 in. deep (Tyler, 1939b).

Eggs: Apr. to well into June; 4–7, usually 5–6, white (Tyler, 1939b).

Incubation: By both sexes, by male at night; 12–14 days (?); young leave nest hole 25–29 days after hatching; both parents feed young with food carried in bill—direct feeding (Lawrence, 1967).

Other Names: Common sapsucker; red-throated sapsucker; sap-sipper; sup-sap; Yankee sapsucker (s. U.S.); yellow-bellied woodpecker.

Accidents: Adult female killed at Chapel Hill, N.C., Apr. 1965, when struck picture window; immature female, in Oct. 1952, in migration flew into side of building, New York City; also killed when striking TV towers in migration (Stoddard and Norris, 1967).

Age: One, banded Chapel Hill, N.C., caught in same area and released when 6 years, 8 months, old (Kennard, 1975); one, banded Pimisi Bay, Ont., lived to 6 years (Lawrence, 1967).

Hybrids: See under Red-bellied sapsucker and Red-naped sapsucker.

Weights: In fall, coastal N.J. (7), 40.5–50.1 gr. (Murray and Jehl, 1964), or 1¼–1¾ oz.; w. U.S. (2), average 46 gr. (Hughes, 1970).

Range: Nests from c. Mack., ne. B.C., c. Alta., n. Man., n. Ont., s. Que., s. Labrador, and Newfoundland south to s. Alta., S.D., Iowa, e. Mo., c. Ill., nw. Ind., n. Ohio, w. Pa., sw. N.Y., w. Mass., nw. Conn., and in mountains to nw. Ga.; winters from Mo., Ill., Ind., and the Ohio Valley, and s. N.J., rarely farther north, south through s. U.S. to Tex., Gulf coast, Fla., Mexico, C. America to w. Panama; also in West Indies; accidental in Wyo., e. Colo., sw. Greenland, and Bermuda; casual in Ariz.

Woodpecker, acorn, *Melanerpes formicivorus* (mel-an-ER-peez for-mih-SIV-oh-rus); genus name: from Gr. *melas, melanos,* black, refers to sooty black of head, neck, and breast, and *herpes,* a creeper (Jaeger, 1955); species name: from Lat. *forma,* an ant, and *voro,* to devour, in reference to its ant-eating habits; *acorn,* from its special fondness for acorns. (Color ill., page 1,036.) A resident in Far West, from Ore. south through Calif. to Ariz., N.M., to w.-c. Tex.; in Calif., one of commonest and most conspicuous birds throughout its range; closely related to the red-headed woodpecker; 8–9½ in. long; wingspread 17 in.; distinguished by its clownlike pattern of black, white, and red about head, and whitish eyes; has bright red cap from forehead to back of head; female like male, but has black crown (*see* Topography); has black back, a white rump, and small white patch on each wing which show in its undulating flight; when flying overhead, or facing observer, white abdomen and broad black chest band are distinctive; in spring, very noisy, talkative, utters harsh notes when calling to mates which sound like raucous notes of a parrot; frequently calls *ja-cob, ja-cob* or *whack-up, whack-up* or *kerack, kerack;* most social of all N. American woodpeckers, lives in closely-knit groups where food plentiful; sometimes up to six seen in same tree (Bent, 1939); lives year-round in groups of 2–15 birds of both sexes and all ages (MacRoberts and MacRoberts, 1976), in oak woods, also in coniferous forests where oaks are in occasional groves; requires available supply of acorns in environment and wood or bark into which it can drill its food-storage holes.

Feeding Habits: With bill digs holes in bark of oaks, chiefly live oaks, over immense areas, also in sycamores, yellow pines, utility poles, gables, cornices of wooden structures, in which to store the dried acorns (also eats green ones) on which it lives from fall into spring (one giant sycamore in Calif. reportedly had some 20,000 acorns in its huge trunk—Dawson, 1923); the drilled holes apparently not deep enough to harm trees (Ritter, 1938); acorn woodpecker also eats almonds, walnuts, and pecans; in Calif. in competition for food with Lewis' woodpeckers; during summer eats mostly insects, often taken on the wing—grasshoppers, ants, beetles, flies; also takes occasional fruit such as cherries, apples, figs, also green corn (Bent, 1939); a major food especially in June and July is tree sap from small holes it drills in branches of live oaks (MacRoberts, 1970), also from holes dug by sapsuckers (Bent, 1939).

Nest: Excavated by both sexes of pair, sometimes assisted by other adult members of the social group (*see* discussion under Helpers among Birds), in oak trees, both living and

dead, in sycamores, cottonwoods, large willow trees, sometimes in utility poles; circular entrance hole about 1⅗ in. in diameter, inside cavity 8–24 in. deep, 12–60 ft. above ground (Bent, 1939; MacRoberts and MacRoberts, 1976).
Eggs: Early Apr.–mid-June; second and third broods found Sept. and Oct. (Bent, 1939); 4–6, usually 4–5, white.
Incubation: About 14 (?) days; young first fly 30–32 days after hatching; immatures and other members of the social groups of acorn woodpeckers help to feed young.
Other Names: Ant-eating woodpecker; California woodpecker; Mearns' woodpecker.
Weights: Two averaged 63 gr. (Hughes, 1970), or about 2¼ oz.; 74.5 gr. (Bock, 1970), or about 2⅔ oz.
Range: Resident sw. Ore., in Calif. west of Sierra Nevadas, and Ariz., N.M., and w.-c. Tex. south through highlands to s. Baja Calif. and through C. America to Colombia, S. America.

Woodpecker, Alpine three-toed. *See* Woodpecker, northern three-toed.

Woodpecker, American three-toed. *See* Woodpecker, northern three-toed.

Woodpecker, Ant-eating. *See* Woodpecker, Acorn.

Woodpecker, Arctic three-toed. *See* Woodpecker, black-backed three-toed.

Woodpecker, Arizona, *Picoides arizonae* (pick-oh-EYE-deez ah-rih-ZONE-ee); genus name: from Lat. *picus,* a woodpecker, and Gr. *eidos,* appearance, resembling woodpeckers; species name: Lat., of Arizona, the type locality. (Color ill., page 1,037.) Mexican species that reaches N. America in se. Ariz. and sw. N.M., where a resident; closely related to, and often treated as, same species as the brown-barred, or Strickland's, woodpecker, *Picoides stricklandi,* of Mexico, and to the hairy woodpecker; 7–8 in. long; back is virtually a uniform sooty brown (unmarked); face striped with white; male has black crown with red patch on back of head (female has all-black crown); underparts boldly spotted and barred with black; some white bars in flight feathers; dark rump; immatures have some red in crown, less so in female than in male; fairly common resident in its limited range in U.S. on pine-oak mountain slopes at 4,000–7,000 ft. elevation, especially in mountains of se. Ariz., and on oak-juniper foothills; rare in winter in adjacent lowlands (see Phillips *et al.,* 1964; Ligon, 1961); climbs easily and rapidly over limbs and trunks of oaks and forages more on oaks than on any other trees (Davis, 1965); moves about in groups of 5–15, occasionally singly or in pairs (Bent, 1939); rather shy, "never noisy, never at rest"; utters sharp *spik* or *tseek,* also a hoarse whinny (Peterson, 1961).

Feeding Habits: Feeds mainly on insects and their larvae (see discussion by Davis, 1965, of how it finds wood-boring larvae or pupae by tapping with bill, then listening for sounds of disturbed larvae or pupae inside tree); also eats to some extent fruits and acorns; on alighting on trunk or limb of tree, immediately starts untiring search for insects; ascends tree rapidly in spirals, then, in undulating flight, moves to next tree.
Nest: Excavates with bill a cavity in dead stub or in dead branch of sycamore, walnut, oak, maple, or in dead stalk of mescal; 8–50 ft. up.
Eggs: Ariz., mid-April to mid-May; 3–4, white.
Incubation: By both sexes (Bent, 1939), but period of and age when young first fly unknown.

Other Name: Brown-backed woodpecker.

Woodpecker, black. *See* Woodpecker, pileated.

Woodpecker, black-backed. *See* Woodpecker, black-backed three-toed.

Woodpecker, black-backed three-toed, *Picoides arcticus* (pick-oh-EYE-deez ARK-tih-cus); genus name: *see* Woodpecker, Arizona; species name: Lat., Arctic, northern, in reference to its range; *three-toed* (tridactyl foot) refers to foot with hind toe (hallux) missing (Color ill., page 1,037.) A resident in Alaska, Canada, and n. U.S., southward in mountains; 8–10 in. long; wingspread 14–16 in.; bill about as long as head, stout, straight, very wide at base with black bristles covering nostrils; male has yellow crown; both sexes distinguished by soot-black and heavily barred flanks (similar northern three-toed woodpecker has a black-and-white-barred back, or simply white back); uncommon even in preferred habitat of coniferous forests, mostly in spruce, larch, fir, and cedar; signs of its presence indicated by large patches of bark scaled from dead conifers; tame and unsuspicious, allows close approach as it works noisily on a trunk of dead tree, often in logged or burned-over woods; some wander southward from breeding range each winter; in some years, large irruptive flights (*see* Irruption) into ne. U.S. (Van Tyne, 1926; Forbush, 1925–29); utters short, sharp *pik* or *kik,* and a *tschuck;* quite noisy on nesting grounds, drums on dry stubs in breeding season. For breeding and behavior, see Short (1974).

Feeding Habits: Flakes off bark of dead conifers to get at grubs (larvae) of destructive wood-boring beetles (about 75% of food—Beal, 1911); also eats weevils and other beetles, some ants and other insects, also spiders; eats wild fruits, acorns, nuts, some inner bark (cambium) of trees.
Nest: Excavated by both sexes, but mostly by male, a cavity in dead stubs or trunks of dead spruces, lodgepole pine, birches, etc., often near water; entrance hole about 1½–2 in. in diameter, with lower edge of entrance hole beveled by the pair which serves as "doorstep" into cavity, about 10 in. deep, usually 2–15 ft. above ground, some to 50–80 ft. up, and usually within opening in forest (Bent, 1939).
Eggs: Mid-May to mid-June; 2–6, usually 4, white.
Incubation: About 14 (?) days; age when young first fly unknown.
Other Names: Arctic three-toed woodpecker; black-backed woodpecker.
Range: Resident from c. Alaska, s. Mack., n. Man., n. Ont., n. Que., s. Labrador, and Newfoundland, south to the Cascades and Sierra Nevadas in Calif., where uncommon or rare, also to w. Nev., nw. Wyo., sw. S.D., n. Minn., ne. Wisc., n. Mich., se. Ont., n. N.Y., Vt., N.H., and n. Me.; casual in winter to Neb., Ill., Ind., Ohio, Pa., and c. N.Y., rarely south to Long Is., N.Y., and n. N.J. (Bull, 1964); one seen repeatedly at Hockessin, Del., Nov. 1–30, 1969, was second record for state (Scott and Cutler, 1970).

Woodpecker, Brewster's. *See* Woodpecker, Gila.

Woodpecker, brown-backed. *See* Woodpecker, Arizona.

Woodpecker, cactus. *See* Woodpecker, ladder-backed.

Woodpecker, California. *See* Woodpecker, acorn.

Woodpecker, crow. *See* Woodpecker, Lewis'.

Woodpecker, downy, *Picoides pubescens* (pick-oh-EYE-deez pew-BEE-senz); genus name: *see* Woodpecker, Arizona; species name: Lat., "with hairs of puberty; downy" (Jaeger, 1955); *downy,* for soft, downy appearance of plumage. (Color ill., page 1,037.) Resident from s. Alaska across Canada and in suitable places over most of U.S. to Gulf coast and Fla.; smallest woodpecker in U.S. and Canada; not closely related to the larger and outwardly similar hairy woodpecker, but to the ladder-backed woodpecker of w. U.S. (Mayr and Short, 1970); lives in broken, or in mixed-composition, forests in almost all wooded parts of N. America (rare in deserts), also in small woodlots, in willows, poplars, and other trees along rivers, in parks and in gardens and shade trees of cities, towns, villages, and in orchards; 6–7 in. long; wingspread about 11–12 in.; small black-and-white woodpecker with *white back;* it and hairy woodpecker are only ones in U.S. with plain white back without bars; *no white in rump* as in many other woodpeckers; downy is almost identical in plumage pattern to larger hairy woodpecker, with similar white spotting in wings, but differs in having *much smaller bill* and with black spots or bars in white of its outer tail feathers, which are clear white in hairy woodpecker; male downy, like male hairy woodpecker, also has small red patch on back of head (this is lacking in females of both species); from tree utters short, flat *peek,* not as wild and ringing as similar call of hairy woodpecker (Tyler, 1939a); its most penetrating call, uttered by both sexes, sounds like whinnying of a small horse or the sound of a steel chisel dropped and reverberating on cement paving—a handful of staccato *tschick, tschick, tshick* notes usually descending in pitch that may be heard quarter of a mile away; apparently effective in bringing the sexes together (Lawrence, 1967); both sexes drum (usually begin in Jan. and Feb. in e. U.S.); drumming on utility poles, etc., a long, unbroken roll, *trrrrrrrrrrrrrr,* which is a territorial pronouncement to other downy woodpeckers, and also functions to bring males and females together in courtship, sexual displays, and establishment, or renewal by past mates, of their pair bond (some downy woodpeckers may remain paired for 4 successive years) and subsequent breeding (Kilham, 1962b; 1974a; Lawrence, 1967). Either member of the pair may also try to attract the other to a potential nest site by drumming or tapping. In fall, both sexes dig fresh holes in dead stubs of trees for winter roosting place; 5–8 days to dig; Kilham (1962b) watched two females dig individual holes in an ash stub, where they roosted peacefully inside within a few feet of each other for several months but were quick to defend their individual roosting holes against invasion by others, and especially against larger hairy woodpecker, which sometimes enlarges downy's roosting hole to use for the night.

Feeding Habits: Clings to trunk or branch of tree to dig out beetle grub or to flake off bark to get at insect cocoon or batch of insect eggs; moves in quick, jerky hops, or descends a little way in downward hitches on trunk, may flit to outer twigs in search for food; quickly slips around branch or trunk to hide from human intruder or to escape attack of hawk; takes off for another tree in swift, undulating flight, usually silently but sometimes with rustling of wings; eats click beetles (the adults of wireworms), flat-headed wood borers, round-headed apple tree borers, pine and nut weevils, bark and spruce beetles, carpenter ants, gypsy and codling moths, tent caterpillars, bollworms, chinch bugs, woolly aphids and other plant lice, grasshoppers and their eggs, periodical cicadas, grubs of gall wasps, etc. (McAtee, 1933a); also eats spiders, snails, berries of poison ivy, mountain ash, Virginia creeper, dogwoods, strawberries, pokeberries, serviceberries, seeds of apples, of hornbeams, and of mullein; flower petals and buds; acorns, beechnuts, hazelnuts, some corn, and sap at "wells" of sapsuckers; comes to backyard feeding stations for suet, doughnuts, corn bread, cracked walnuts, peanut butter (see in Terres, 1968c); bathes in snow in winter; usually solitary (except nesting season) but individuals may accompany mixed flocks of chickadees, titmice, and other small birds in woods in winter.

Nest: Most often excavated in dead stubs of trees, both sexes share in digging; round entrance hole is 1¼ in. in diameter, drilled in tree 5–50 ft. above ground, rarely higher, generally in dead snag, sometimes in solid branch; inside of cavity is roughly gourd-shaped, depth of 8–12 in. (Tyler, 1939a); pair usually leave some chips in bottom of cavity on which female lays her eggs (will also nest in bird box designed for it—see in Terres, 1968c).

Eggs: Apr.–June; 3–7, usually 4–5, white.

Incubation: By both sexes, 12 days; adults feed young on insects directly from bill about every 2 or 3 minutes, and carry away fecal sacs; young appear at nest entrance hole about 14 days after hatching; ready to fly within 21–24 days after hatching; male occupies nest cavity at night (Kilham, 1962b); after leaving nest, young follow parents; separate from them and go their own ways when they learn to find food for themselves; one brood raised in North; possibly two broods in South.

Other Names: Batchelder's woodpecker; black-and-white driller; Gairdner's woodpecker; little guinea woodpecker; little sapsucker; Tommy woodpecker.

Accidents: In low flight across highways, often killed when struck by cars.

Age: Three, banded Nashville, Tenn., lived to 4, 5, and 6 years old; one, banded in Ill., retrapped at same place when it was 7 years, 8 months, old; another, 7 years old, reported from Wayland, Mich.; one, banded St. Paul, Minn., caught and released in same area when 10 years, 5 months, old (Kennard, 1975).

Hybrids: Three records of downy woodpecker × Nuttall's woodpecker. See details in Short (1971).

Weights: In fall, coastal N.J. (101), 21.4–31.6 gr. (Murray and Jehl, 1964), or about ¾–1 oz.; in Mich. (5), 26.2–28.9 gr. (Becker and Stack, 1944), or about 1 oz.

Range: Mostly resident from se. Alaska, sw. Mack., n. Alta., c. Sask., n. Man., James Bay, s. Que., and Newfoundland, south to s. Calif., c. Ariz., n. N.M., s.-c. Tex., Gulf coast, and Fla.; some migrate or withdraw to southward from northern part of range in fall and winter; others descend from higher mountains.

Woodpecker, Gairdner's. *See* Woodpecker, downy.

Woodpecker, Gila (HE-lah), *Melanerpes uropygialis* (mel-an-ER-peez you-row-PIDJ-ih-AY-liss); genus name: *see* Woodpecker, acorn; species name: from Gr. *oura*, tail, and *pyge*, rump, in allusion to black-and-white-barred rump and central tail feathers; *Gila*, for Gila R. in Ariz., where this bird was discovered. (Color ill., page 1,036.) Lives mostly in saguaro deserts, dry washes, river woods, and cottonwood groves, also in towns and cities, from se. Calif., sw. Nev., s. Ariz., and sw. N.M. south into Baja Calif. and c. Mexico; 8–10 in. long; male has *round red cap;* both sexes fawn-colored, with *back, wings, and tail banded or cross-striped with black and white* ("zebra-backed"—similarly marked flickers are *brown-backed*); in flight shows *white patch toward tip of each wing;* gray-brown head and underparts; female similar to male but lacks red crown patch; year-round resident, conspicuous, noisy, always much in evidence, center of abundance is great desert mesas of s. Ariz., where soil scantily covered with creosote bushes, low mesquites, occasional cholla or barrel cactus, and with scattered giant cactus, or saguaro; also common in river bottoms with heavier growth of mesquite, and in canyons of foothills among cottonwoods, willows, sycamores; ranges from near sea level in Colorado Valley up to 4,000 ft. or more in canyons and foothills (Bent, 1939); its many nesting cavities, especially in saguaro, provide living quarters for American kestrels, elf owls, ferruginous owls, screech owls, ash-throated and crested flycatchers, cactus wrens, Lucy's warblers, western martins, lizards, snakes, rats, and mice; utters sharp, shrill *pit* or *huit* repeated two or three times while in flight, and a rasping *churr.*

Feeding Habits: Eats mostly insects such as ants, beetles, grasshopper, grubs of gall in-sects (see especially Speich and Radke, 1975), and, in season, largely the sweet, figlike fruits of the saguaro, also eats white berries of mistletoe, and eggs of small birds; comes to feeding stations in yards or gardens for table scraps—eats meat, raw or cooked, and suet—and especially fond of slices of ripe watermelon, also eats grapes, and corn from ears (Bent, 1939).

Nest: A cavity, with entrance hole about 2 in. in diameter, 9–20 in. deep, excavated in branch or trunk of cottonwoods, willows, in mesquite trees, but most in saguaro, and usually about 15–25 ft. above ground; pair may use same nesting hole for more than one season unless it is appropriated by an owl; also digs fresh cavities after raising brood of young, used in following year (Bent, 1939).

Eggs: Early Apr. to late May; 3–5, usually 3–4, white.

Incubation: About 14 days, shared by both sexes; age when young first fly unknown, but young are fed and cared for by adults for long time after leaving nest; two or three broods a year (Phillips *et al.*, 1964).

Other Names: Banded woodpecker; Brewster's woodpecker; cardon woodpecker; saguaro woodpecker.

Albinism: One reported all summer of 1959 near Phoenix, Ariz., but no details of degree of albinism.

Weights: One, 68 gr. (Hughes, 1970), or about 2⅓ oz.

Hybrids: Interbreeds with golden-fronted to some extent in w. Mexico (Selander and Giller, 1963).

Range: See above.

Woodpecker, golden-fronted, *Melanerpes aurifrons* (mel-an-ER-peez AW-rih-frons); genus name: *see* Woodpecker, acorn; species name: from Lat. *aurum*, gold, and *frons*, forehead; "golden forehead," in allusion to yellow patch just above bill in adult male. (Color ill., page 1,036.) Closely related to red-bellied woodpecker but where its range meets and overlaps range of red-bellied by a few miles in Tex., does not interbreed with it (Mayr and Short, 1970); 8½–10½ in. long; wingspread about 15–18 in.; about same size as red-bellied, which it resembles, but male golden-fronted has separate patches of color on head—yellow about bill, red atop head, separated from the spot of gold or orange on hind neck by patch of buff or gray (the red-bellied male has entire crown and nape continuously red, female with red on nape); golden-fronted is "zebra-backed" like red-bellied, but golden-fronted has *all lower part of rump white* instead of barred as in red-bellied; female golden-fronted outwardly similar to male but has *no red in crown;* both sexes show white wing patch in flight; immature lacks patches of color on head; in general behavior and habits, golden-fronted is like red-bellied woodpecker; is noisy, utters rolling *cher-r-r-r, cher-r-r-r* similar to that of red-bellied, and a long series of flickerlike notes, *kek, kek* or *chek, chek* (Bent, 1939); lives in mostly drier country than red-bellied woodpecker, especially fond of mesquite forests, upland forests of mixed oaks, pecan groves, also in woods with large trees along river bottoms.

Feeding Habits: Eats mostly insects such as beetles, ants, grasshoppers, and acorns, Indian corn, various wild berries and fruits.

Nest: Both sexes excavate nesting cavity, about 6–10 days of work, in either live or dead trees, sometimes in dead stump or limb, also in utility poles, fence posts, cavity 12 in. deep, 3–25 ft. above ground, same cavity often used year after year.

Eggs: Tex., late Mar. to late July; 4–7, usually 4–5, white.

Incubation: By both sexes, about 14 (?) days; age when young first fly unknown.

Other Name: Golden-front.

Range: Resident from n.-c. Mexico, sw. Okla., and Tex. to n. Nicaragua and islands off coast of Yucatán and Bay Is. of Honduras.

Woodpecker, hairy, *Picoides villosus* (pick-oh-EYE-deez vil-OH-sus); genus name: *see* Woodpecker, Arizona; species name: Lat., hairy, shaggy, rough, in reference to appearance of plumage (Jaeger, 1955). (Color ill., page 1,037.) Resident in all types of forests throughout Canada and the U.S., south to c. America; its closest relatives include the Arizona woodpecker and the brown-barred woodpecker of Mexico; 8½–10½ in. long; wingspread 15–17½ in.; almost identical in plumage pattern to downy woodpecker; male has red patch on back of head, lacking in female; upperparts black and white; white below; dark back is striped and spotted with white; wings barred with rows of white spots, also a *broad white stripe down back* as in downy woodpecker but distinguished from it by larger size, *longer, heavier bill*, and *unmarked* white outer tail feathers; utters high, sharp, metallic *peek*, much louder than similar note of downy, and *hueet*, also a loud kingfisherlike rattle, slurring down the scale (see Bent, 1939, Lawrence, 1967 and Winkler and Short, 1978, for various call notes and interpretations of them); both sexes drum, accompanied by courtship ritual flights in which the wings are beaten against the flanks to produce a loud sound; females often drum as intensively as males in Nov. and Dec.; also drum Jan.–Apr.; the long, rolling tattoo is louder than that of downy woodpecker and not quite so long; hairy woodpeckers appear to be semipaired throughout the year (Kilham, 1960); are not regularly migratory (see, however, Bent, 1939); adult is highly sedentary, and when settled on a territorial range, tends to stay there for life (Lawrence, 1967); is much shyer than downy woodpecker but also more active and noisier, will usually not allow close approach of human intruder but dodges around trunk of tree to hide, or takes off in graceful, bounding flight; lives mostly in forests but in fall and in winter may move into open country of scattered woods, trees, and orchards, and into parks and shade trees of towns and villages; both sexes excavate roosting holes, and each may have several; young, especially, excavate such holes in fall.

Feeding Habits: Is expert climber, at home on trunk or undersides of branches, often strikes bill into wood or bark and holds it there; presumed to detect, by *feeling*, the vibrations, and locations, of wood-boring insects; however,

Roberts, T.S. (1932), Davis (1965), and Ramp (1965) suggest that this bird may detect the grubs by hearing them crunch on wood (*see* Ears and Hearing); more than 75% of food is insects, largest item is larvae of wood borers, such as those of round-headed wood borers (100 from stomach of one hairy woodpecker—see McAtee, 1926), which is first in abundance in its food, lesser pine borer, flat-headed wood borers (110 in one stomach), engraver and bark beetles, also spruce bark beetles, a threat to spruce forests, and white pine borers, etc.; wood-boring larvae 21–41% of food of hairy woodpecker and eaten every month of year; taps more loudly and more often than downy woodpecker; also eats click beetles, June beetles, stag beetles and ants, some spiders, and millipedes, also some wild fruit—raspberries, blackberries—and acorns, hazelnuts, beechnuts; eats sap at "wells" of sapsucker; comes to feeding stations for suet, sunflower seeds, meat scraps, cracked walnuts and pecans, peanut butter, cheese, apples, and bananas (see Terres, 1968c; Dennis, 1975).

Nest: Cavity excavated by both sexes, mostly in dead or dying branches of living trees such as maples, apple trees, aspens, beech, etc., sometimes in tops of dead trees; male plays principal part in selecting the nest site, and does most of digging (Lawrence, 1967); may take 7–21 days to complete (Bent, 1939); entrance hole 1½–2 in. in diameter, cavity 10–15 in. deep, 5–30 ft. or more above ground, with soft bed of fresh chips in bottom; will also nest in birdhouse designed for it (see Terres, 1968c).

Eggs: Over its wide N. American range, females lay from third week in Mar. into third week of June; 3–6, usually 4; white.

Incubation: By both sexes, male at night; about 14 days (Bent, 1939); young leave nest about 28–30 days after hatching (Lawrence, 1967); one brood raised in a nesting season but if nest robbed of eggs will lay second, or even third, set, sometimes in same nesting hole (Bent, 1939).

Other Names: Big guinea woodpecker; Cabanis' woodpecker; Chihuahua woodpecker; Harris' woodpecker; Harry; Modoc woodpecker; Newfoundland woodpecker; Queen Charlotte woodpecker; sapsucker; white-breasted woodpecker.

Age: One banded Pleasant Valley Sanctuary in Mass., seen there almost every winter for 11 years then disappeared (Wallace, 1963); one, banded Stillwater, N.J., caught in same area and released when 12 years, 10 months, old (Kennard, 1975), another in Minn. still alive at 14 years.

Flight Speed: Timed in Tex., 20 m.p.h. (Sooter, 1947).

Hybrids: Up to 1970, only one record of hybridization—hairy woodpecker × ladder-backed woodpecker (Mayr and Short, 1970).

Weights: One, Mich., 62.1 gr. (Becker and Stack, 1944), or about 2¼ oz.; female smaller (Forbush, 1925–29).

Range: resident from tree limit in Alaska, and Canada, south to n. Baja Calif., Gulf coast, and Fla., Bahama Is., through C. America to w. Panama.

Woodpecker, ivory-billed, *Campephilus principalis* (cam-PEE-fil-us or cam-PEF-ih-lus prin-sih-PAY-liss); genus name: from Gr. *kampe*, caterpillar, and *philos*, loving, in reference to its feeding on insect larvae; species name: Lat., first, original; *ivory-billed* for ivory-white color of bill. "Probably very close to extinction . . . only recent records are for se. Texas, southern Louisiana and central South Carolina. Considerable effort has failed to produce reliable records elsewhere in its range" (Office of Endangered Species, 1973); decline caused by lumbering of vast forests in s. U.S., including hardwood forests of river bottoms, and areas of dead and dying trees—these supply its chief food, the larvae of wood-boring beetles; illegal shooting also a factor; resident (nonmigratory); original range was in bottomlands and swampy forests of the Atlantic and Gulf coastal plain, from se. N.C. south to ne. Tex., and northward, in lower swamps of Mississippi Valley to s. Ill. and se. Okla. (Tanner, 1942); up to 1971, last pair reported were photographed (May 22) "somewhere in Louisiana"; pair had been seen in area for three years (Stewart, J., 1971); several pairs also reported previously (1967) in Big Thicket country of e. Tex. (Dennis, 1967); 20 in. long; largest woodpecker in N. America, somewhat less than second largest woodpecker in world, the 23-in.-long imperial woodpecker of Mexico; very large black-and-white woodpecker; male with bright red crest (female has black crest); *has large white wing patches evident when bird is perching; large bill is ivory-white* (similar pileated woodpecker has black bill); general shape is long and slender, accentuated by long neck and long, tapering, pointed tail; as it flies overhead in *level flight, whole rear edge of ivory-bill's wings are white;* utters sharp, plaintive, nuthatchlike, single note, *kent* or *pait,* like tooting of a child's toy trumpet, sometimes this note uttered in series, *kent, kent-kent, kent* (Tanner, 1942).

Feeding Habits: Larvae of wood-boring beetles that live between bark and wood of dying and newly dead trees are principal food, also some fruits and nuts.

Nest: Excavated by both sexes or by female alone (Allen and Kellogg, 1937), a cavity in almost any species of tree in its habitat, in large dead or partly living tree, entrance hole usually oval, about 5–7 in. high, 3–4 in. across, 15–70 ft. above ground.

Eggs: Jan.–May; 1–5, usually 1–3, white.

Incubation: By both sexes, about 20 days; both sexes feed and care for young; age when young first fly unknown.

Other Names: Caip; Indian hen; ivory-bill; kate; kent (from call notes); king of the woodpeckers; logcock; log-god; southern giant woodpecker; white-billed woodpecker; woodchuck; woodcock.

Weights: According to Tanner (1942), Mark Catesby reported weight as 20 oz., or about 1¼ lbs.; a male shot in Hernando County, Fla., in Jan. 1877, weighed 1 lb.

Range: Resident formerly in se. U.S. from ne. Tex., se. Okla., ne. Ark., se. Mo., se. Ill., s. Ind., and se. N.C. southward to the Brazos R. of Tex., Gulf coast, and s. Fla., also Cuba, where about a dozen apparently still persist. See Greenway (1958) for other details and location of specimens (skins) of this woodpecker in various museums of the world.

Woodpecker, ladder-backed, *Picoides scalaris* (pick-oh-EYE-deez skay-LAY-ris); genus name: *see* Woodpecker, Arizona; species name: Lat., pertaining to a ladder, in reference to ladderlike pattern of bars across its back, also origin of its common name. (Color ills., page 1,037.) Closely related to Nuttall's woodpecker and to downy woodpecker; ladder-backed lives mostly in West and Southwest; 6–7½ in. long; about size of downy woodpecker, which has *white* back, not barred; the ladder back is distinctive; black-and-white-striped face is duller, less white than similarly striped face of its relative, Nuttall's woodpecker, which, in Calif., lives west of the Sierras (Peterson, 1961); however, where ranges of these two meet and overlap in San Bernardino County, Calif., and in n. Baja Calif., there is some hybridizing between the two (see Short, 1971, for details); typical male ladder-backed has red cap and red nuchal patch with red on forehead streaked with black; black rump and tail, with outer tail feathers barred with white; female resembles male but has *black cap;* is distinguished from Gila and golden-fronted woodpeckers (which also have "ladder backs") by its dark rump and finely spotted sides and striped face; also no white patch in wings (Robbins *et al.,* 1966); utters single, high-pitched *tschick* or *peek,* resembling call of hairy woodpecker, and series of rapid, descending notes, *chee-dee-dee-dee-dee-dee,* like similar call of downy woodpecker; often calls as it flies, and drums in rapid bursts on dry limbs in spring (Bent, 1939); for courtship and calls, see Short (1971); resident in wooded canyons, cottonwood and prairie groves, riparian woods in desert, and in dense growth of cholla cactus, creosote bush, catclaw, and other low-growing plants on borders of deserts in which it feeds and rests; also in post oak woods, mesquite forests, brush-lined streams, hackberry shade trees in towns; also lives on lower slopes of mountains, rarely above 5,500 ft. (Bent, 1939).

Feeding Habits: Forages in small trees and shrubs and often feeds on ground; lives mainly on larvae of wood-boring beetles which it gleans from trunks and branches of trees; also eats larvae of codling moth and other caterpillars, including the cotton worm, also eats ants, weevils, and fruits of saguaro and other cactuses.

Nest: Digs cavity near top of giant cactus (saguaro) about 20 ft. above ground, also 2–30 ft. up in dead willows, entrance hole about 1½ in. in diameter, cavity 10 in. deep, sometimes in mesquite, hackberry, cottonwood, oak, walnut, or other tree or in stems of cactus, agave, and yucca trees, also in fence posts and utility poles.

Eggs: Usually mid-Apr. into July; 2–6, usually 4–5, white (Bent, 1939).

Incubation: By both sexes, about 13 days; age when young first fly unknown.

Other Names: Cactus woodpecker; Mexican woodpecker; speckle-cheek; Texas woodpecker.

Range: Resident in desert regions of sw. N. America, from se. Calif., s. Nev., sw. Utah, and s. Colo. south to Ariz. and s. N.M.; occupies virtually all of Baja Calif., and into mainland Mexico south to Honduras; within U.S. its habitat includes the Chihuahuan and Sonoran deserts; does not live above western fringes of desert in Calif. where Nuttall's woodpecker lives, but in absence of Nuttall's, ranges up to 6,000 ft. in Little San Bernardino and Argus Mtns. (Short, 1971).

Woodpecker, Lewis', *Melanerpes lewis* (mel-an-ER-peez); genus name: *see* Woodpecker, acorn; species name: for Meriwether Lewis, leader of Lewis and Clark exploratory expedition of 1803–06 across American continent; in May 1806, the Lewis and Clark party collected (shot) several "black woodpeckers" near Kamiah, Idaho; these were later examined by Alexander Wilson, who gave the bird the common name of "Lewis's woodpecker," in honor of Meriwether Lewis (Bock, 1970). (Color ill., page 1,039.) A western species, mainly Colo. west to Pacific and from s. B.C. south to nw. Mexico; is monotypic (has no subspecies); very widespread; locally common; 10½–11½ in. long; wingspread about 20–21 in.; adult is large, dark, with green-glossed black back; brown-red face patch; pale gray collar; *pink-red belly;* in flight looks more like a crow than a woodpecker (Bent, 1939); sexes outwardly almost identical, but male larger, especially in length of bill; female slightly less strikingly colored than male (Bock, 1970); during first few months brownish-backed immatures show little or no development of gray collar or red face and belly; drab gray below; Lewis' is especially similar in its ecology and behavior to red-headed woodpecker of e. U.S.; red-headed meets range of Lewis' in c. Mont., e. Wyo., Colo., and N.M.; no known hybrids between the two (Bock, 1970); Lewis' is most specialized of N. American woodpeckers in "flycatching" behavior and its unusually slow, almost soaring flight related to its aerial "flycatching" habits; breeding males utter a short, rather loud, harsh *churr, churr, churr,* sometimes up to eight times in succession, which serves to attract a mate and to proclaim its territory (drums very little), also utters "chatter calls" throughout the year, a rapidly descending series of short squeaks, especially during courtship displays (see in Bock, 1970); when disturbed, male utters alarmed *yick;* female, *yick-ick,* which helps distinguish sexes; pairs permanently mated, remain together year-round, may return to nest in same cavity year after year (Bock, 1970); summers in open ponderosa pine forests, the major breeding habitat; is widespread in mountains of West at altitudes of 2,000–9,000 ft. in Ariz. and Calif., also breeds in logged or burned-off coniferous forest, pinyon-juniper groves of mountains, also open cottonwood groves along streams near open meadows and marshlands; some migration, usually sporadic and irregular, withdraws from northern parts of range in nomadic flocks Aug. into Oct., at onset of cold weather, to nearest wintering habitat of oak woods or commercial nut orchards (see Bock, 1970; Hadow, 1973); in spring

Ivory-billed woodpecker

WOODPECKER FAMILY

moves back into breeding habitats in Apr.–May.

Feeding Habits: One of most aerial in feeding of all woodpeckers; during nesting season, from perches on tops of low stumps and fence posts to tops of tallest trees, scans air and then launches out in level, graceful glide to catch flying ants, beetles, flies, mayflies, etc., with bill; Bock (1970) saw a Lewis' woodpecker fly directly in steady, level crowlike flight to an insect 180 ft. away, snatch it out of air, and return to perch to eat it; sometimes remains in air flying about; Bent (1939) reported a pair flying about for 30 minutes with barn and cliff swallows over a meadow, catching insects; also scans ground from low perches or sides of trees, then drops to ground or into low bushes for grasshoppers, crickets, tent caterpillars, etc., also gleans insects from limbs and trunks of trees by probing into natural crevices and chipping off bark, but does not frequently hammer trees vigorously or dig into bark with bill in feeding as most other woodpeckers do; in fall migration, eats insects, also berries of mountain ash, currant, huckleberries, strawberries, chokecherries, juniper berries, wild grapes, also invades commercial apple and pear orchards and date crops in Ore., Calif., causing damage to fruit, and eats pomegranates and quinces in Ariz. (Bent, 1939); in winter, in absence of insects, lives in oak woods where acorn crop high, or in commercial orchards of almonds, walnuts, picks off and shells and stores acorns and cracks open nuts and stores the nutmeats in rough bark of oaks or in cracks in utility poles; in Calif., competes intensively for acorn crop with the related acorn woodpecker (*see* details of this storing habit in Food and Feeding Habits).

Nest: Male apparently does most of excavating of nesting cavity, mostly in dead stubs or trunks of dead trees, and in some live trees such as cottonwoods, sycamores, oaks, junipers, pines, many of which are decayed inside; entrance hole 2–3 in. in diameter, cavity 9–30 in. deep, 4–150 ft. above ground; some nest in cavity where no excavating required or use roosting hole for nesting, also uses old flicker nesting holes.

Eggs: Calif., Apr.–June; Colo., May–Aug.; Ore., May–June; 5–9, usually 6–7, white.

Incubation: Both sexes incubate and both develop brood patches (*see* Incubation); 12–13 days (Bailey and Niedrach, 1965); 13–14 days (Bock, 1970); male incubates eggs at night; young are fed insects, berries, and first fly 28–34 days after hatching; a few days before, begin to venture out on nesting stub, when often caught by American kestrels (Utah).

Other Names: Black woodpecker; crow woodpecker.

Weights: About 3¾ oz. (Bock, 1970).

Range: Nests from s. B.C. and Vancouver Is., w. Alta., Mont., and sw. S.D. south to s. Calif., c. Ariz., s. N.M., east to nw. Neb. and e. Colo.; winters from n. Ore., occasionally s. B.C., to n. Baja Calif., n. Sonora, Mexico, and s. Ariz., and from c. Colo. and s.-c. Neb. to s. N.M. and w. Tex.; has strayed to Sask., Man., Iowa, Kans., Okla., Ill., and R.I., where one collected (shot) Nov. 1928; one at bird feeder in Ossining, N.Y.,

Oct. 27–Nov. 6, 1954 (Bull, 1964); also, one seen Jan. 1, 1969, in Marinette County, Wisc., for first state record; one at bird feeder in West Newbury, Mass., June 2–4, 1969, for second state record; one seen at Windsor, Ont., Feb. 6–Mar. 10, 1973. See reports in *Audubon Field Notes* and in *American Birds.*

Woodpecker, northern three-toed, *Picoides tridactylus* (pick-oh-EYE-deez or pie-SOY-deez try-DACK-tih-lus); genus name: *see* Woodpecker, Arizona; species name: Lat., from Gr. *tridaktulos*, three-toed (Macleod, 1954). (Color ill., page 1,039.) Resident around northern parts of world, breeds farther north in N. America than the black-backed three-toed woodpecker; resident from tree limit in Alaska, w. and c. Canada, south in western mountains to sw. U.S.; locally common in western coniferous forests, rare in e. U.S. (Robbins *et al.*, 1966), where it lives in spruce and balsam fir forests of n. N.Y., Me., N.H. (Bent, 1939); sometimes appears irregularly south of summer range but less so than black-backed three-toed, and rarely as common as black-backed where the two occur together; 8–9½ in. long; wingspread about 13–15 in.; male, like male of similar black-backed three-toed woodpecker, has yellow cap lacking in the female, which has a black crown; this species distinguished from black-backed by its *black and white barring down middle of black back* (ladder-backed) or the back may be entirely white (the black-backed three-toed has a *solidly black back*); eastern birds sometimes very black with little trace of white on back (Short, 1974); both species have barred sides, which distinguishes the female northern three-toed from the similar-appearing female hairy woodpecker; immatures resemble adults but duller in color and with some yellow in crown, which disappears in female when adult; is normally silent, its weak notes like squealing of yellow-bellied sapsucker or squeak of a small mammal, also utters short *pik*, softer than note of black-backed three-toed woodpecker and a rattle somewhat like that of hairy woodpecker; drumming and tapping on trees less loud and penetrating than that of black-backed, downy, and hairy woodpeckers (Bent, 1939); is tame and unsuspicious and less active than most other woodpeckers, spends minutes at a time clinging to trunk of tree at one spot. See Short (1974) for comparison and interactions with black-backed three-toed woodpecker.

Feeding Habits: Almost identical to those of black-backed three-toed woodpecker; eats especially wood-boring insects such as wood-boring beetle larvae and adult beetles, also spiders, berries, and some cambium, or inner bark.

Nest: Excavated 5–50 ft. up in stumps or in trees of flooded swamp such as spruces, tamaracks, pines, balsam firs, white cedars, aspens, or in conifers of mountain slopes; entrance hole about 1¾ in. by 2 in. and about 10–15 in. deep (Bent, 1939).

Eggs: Mid-May–mid-June; 4, white.

Incubation: By both sexes, about 14 (?) days; age when young first fly unknown.

Other Names: Alaska three-toed woodpecker; Alpine three-toed woodpecker; American three-

toed woodpecker; ladder-back woodpecker; white-backed three-toed woodpecker.

Range: In N. America from limit of trees in Alaska, n. Yuk., n. and w. Mack., south through B.C. (including Vancouver Is.), Alta., and w. Sask. to mountains of s. Ore., n. Idaho, and nw. Mont., south in Rocky Mtns. to e. Nev., e. Ariz., and c. N.M. (accidental in Neb.); also resident in c. and e. Canada from n. Man., n. Ont., n. Que., n. Labrador, and Newfoundland south to n. Minn., c. Ont., n. N.Y. (Adirondacks), n. Vt., n. N.H., and n. Me.; casual in winter to s. Wisc., Mich., s. Ont., Long Is., N.Y., Mass.; in Pa., a female seen at Longwood Gardens, Apr. 3, 1974, and in Del., a female seen Apr. 7, 1974, at Delaware City (Scott and Cutler, 1974); in Old World, resident from tree limit in Eurasia south to Alps, mountains of c. Asia, s. Korea, and n. Japan (Reilly, 1968).

Woodpecker, Nuttall's, *Picoides nuttallii* (pick-oh-EYE-deez NUT-all-ih-eye); genus name: *see* Woodpecker, Arizona; species name: given in 1843 by William Gambel, 19th-century Calif. field ornithologist, for Thomas Nuttall, English-American botanist and ornithologist. (Color ill., page 1,039.) Resident from s. Ore. and n. Calif. south to nw. Baja Calif., common especially in live oaks and chaparral west of Sierras; closely related to ladder-backed and downy woodpeckers; 7–7½ in. long; similar to ladder-backed woodpecker but differs from it in having more contrasting black-and-white face (i.e., has *broad black ear coverts*), also male has *black cap*, or crown, and red nuchal patch (back of head and hind neck); Nuttall's also has shorter bill and *white* nasal bristles that contrast sharply with black crown; female similar to male but lacks red nuchal patch—see other details in Short (1971); ranges of Nuttall's and the more desert-dwelling ladder-backed are separate throughout most of Calif. except some overlapping (with some hybridizing) in Kern Basin, Kern County, and in Morongo Valley, San Bernardino County, also in n. Baja Calif. (Short, 1971); utters hoarse, ringing *prrip* or *pi-dit*, often lengthened to rattling *prrrrrrrt*, also utters a thin, sharp *quee-quee-quee-quee'p;* drums on resonant timber or on utility poles in spring; for courtship and territorial displays, see Short (1971); lives in Calif. foothills up to 6,000 ft. elevation in oak, live oak, chaparral, in canyons with sycamores, alders, bay trees growing at bottom along streams lined with live oaks (Bent, 1939); in c. and n. Calif., is almost confined to oak woods and especially to large live oaks in s. Calif. and n. Baja Calif., and along streams there lined with willow, cottonwood, and sycamore woodlands (Short, 1971).

Feeding Habits: Forages mostly on trunks and branches of oaks, also in sycamores and willows along streams, in dense groves of cottonwoods, in spring, eats cottonwood buds, also forages in dwarf willow thickets down to ground; creeps, nuthatchlike, diagonally over bark, probing in crevices or flaking off bark, infrequently tapping or drilling as it eats wood-boring insects and their larvae, insect eggs, ants, caterpillars, also eats some wild berries (Beal, 1911).

Nest: Excavated by both sexes in Feb. and Mar., female does much of work; entrance hole 1½ in. in diameter, 5 in. across inside, and 10–12 in. deep, 2½–60 ft. above ground, in willow, oak, alder, elder, cottonwood, sycamore (Bent, 1939), fence post.

Eggs: About third week in Mar. to mid-June; 3–6, commonly 4–5, white.

Incubation: By both sexes, about 14 (?) days; age when young first leave nest unknown.

Hybrids: Some hybridizing with downy and ladder-backed woodpeckers. See details in Short (1971).

Weights: (50), 28–47 gr., (Short, in press), or 1–1¾ oz.; males average slightly heavier than females.

Range: Resident from s. Ore. and Calif. west of Sierras and deserts, south to nw. Baja Calif.; accidental in Ariz. (Phoenix).

Woodpecker, pileated, *Dryocopus pileatus* (dry-OCK-oh-pus pie-leh-AY-tus); genus name: from Gr. *drys*, a tree, especially an oak (Jaeger, 1955), and *kopis*, cleaver; a "tree cleaver" or "wood cutter"; species name: Lat., capped, i.e., crested, in reference to its large crest; common name: pron. PIE-leh-ated or PIL-eh-ated. (Color ill., page 1,038.) Not closely allied to the ivory-billed woodpecker but to the lineated woodpecker, *Dryocopus lineatus*, of Mexico and S. America; resident (some wander in fall) in forests from w. Canada and nw. U.S. across n. U.S. and c. Canada to Nova Scotia, south through e. U.S. to e. Tex. and s. Fla.; in early 1900s, almost gone from many parts of N.Y. and s. New England, where once common, but started to reappear in 1920s with apparent adaptation to less primeval conditions (see accounts in Bent, 1939); in North lives in forests of mixed conifers and hardwoods, in balsam fir and white cedar swamps, on wooded ridges; in Rocky Mtns. prefers growths of larch, ponderosa pine, Douglas fir; in Ore., burned-over wooded tracts; in South, cypress swamps and heavily timbered bottomlands, edges of woodland meadows, margins of large and small streams (Bent, 1939) and lakes; 16–19½ in. long; wingspread 27–30 in.; large, black, crow-sized woodpecker; both sexes have red crest and when perched show *solidly black back* (ivory-billed when perched shows white on lower half of folded wings and two white stripes down back (*see* other comparisons in biography of ivory-billed); pileated has large *black* bill and male has scarlet "mustache" extending from base of bill rearward more than half the length of his head; in female, only rear half of crest is scarlet, and she has a *black streak* extending rearward from bill; flight is usually level (Hoyt, 1957), sometimes undulating as it bounds through air from tree to tree; white patches on *front half of wings* distinguish it in flight from either a crow or an ivory-billed woodpecker; calls are entirely different from those of ivory-billed; both sexes utter a flickerlike *yucka, yucka, yucka* (Bent, 1939); Kilham (1959a) reported a slow, irregular *cuk*, a location call to mate, and a loud "high call," *cuk, cuk, cuk, cuk, cuk, cuk,* higher-pitched in female, the main breeding note that expresses dominance in its area, also rendered *wick, wick, wick* or *bick, bick, bick* (this call, like flicker's

call, but louder, also given when it is flying to roosting hole); both sexes drum, females less than males, usually on resonant place on dead tree or on dead stub, a rolling tattoo lasting 3–5 seconds; drumming advertises territory and attracts a mate; pileated also drums when about to go to roost at night (Kilham, 1959a); pairs appear to occupy same territory year after year; see courtship displays in Hoyt (1957); Kilham (1959a); according to Hoyt, each member of pair digs and uses its own several individual roosting cavities within the territory and often not far from nesting cavity; each may alternate in using its own roosting cavities, but a male near Ithaca, N.Y., used same roosting hole most nights for six winters; enters roosting hole about 30 minutes before sunset; leaves it before sunrise; its roosting cavities often used by wood ducks for nesting and by flying squirrels.

Feeding Habits: Eats about 75% animal food; about 25% vegetal; in winter, eats especially carpenter ants and gets at colonies deep in hearts of forest trees by chiseling out with powerful bill chips of wood 3–6 in. across and holes in tree 6 in. square; also strips off bark of dead trees to reach species of wood-boring beetles; sometimes digs them from low stumps or rotten logs on or near ground, also digs into anthills on ground; eats acorns, beechnuts; in summer and fall, eats flies, mosquitoes, moths, ants, grubs, also wild grapes, seeds of sumac, fruits of Virginia creeper, sour gum, poison oak, poison ivy, and dogwoods, also wild cherries; comes to bird feeders for suet, pecan and walnut meats, also for mixture of ground pecans and melted suet (Hoyt, 1957). In captivity, Rumsey (1968) kept adult pileateds in an outdoor aviary where they soon learned to eat mealworms.

Nest: In hole excavated by both sexes (female does most of work) from late. Feb. into Mar. or later, may take 30 days to complete (Bent, 1939); cavity usually dug in dead tree in shaded place in woods or in dead branch of living tree, in beech, poplar, tulip tree, birches, oaks, hickories, maples, hemlocks, pines, ash, elms, basswood, cypress, sycamore, sweet gum, hackberry, or in live trunk of tall cottonwood, elm, or oak at edge of woods or in timber near stream or pond, usually in same woods or area where pair spend most of their time; usually a new hole dug for each year's brood, although same nesting cavity may be used for several years; nesting tree may be on side of mountain but more often in valleys or bottomlands; one of requirements of location may be nearness to water (Hoyt, 1957); in Md., Kilham (1959a) saw pileateds that roosted by the Potomac R. sometimes fly down to the water to drink just before entering their roosting holes for the night; nesting cavity 15–85 ft. above ground, often 28–35 ft. up; entrance hole usually triangular, 3½ in. across at top, about 4½ in. across bottom, drilled through bark, more frequently through bleached and bonelike surface of a stub from which bark long ago stripped away; inside of cavity about 8 in. across, 10–30 in. deep, with a few chips on bottom (Bent, 1939); sometimes causes damage to wooden utility poles by digging into them for ants or for nest-

ing place (*see* discussion in introduction to Woodpecker Family).

Eggs: Alta., Canada, early May to third week in June; Ark., early Apr. to mid-May; Fla., third week in Mar. to third week in May; elsewhere, usually Apr.–May; 3–8, usually 4, sometimes 3, white.

Incubation: By both sexes, more by male, which incubates part of day and at night; 18 days; young hatch naked with eyes closed, eyes open 8 days after hatching (Hoyt, 1957); male broods young overnight while female sleeps in roosting hole nearby; adults feed young (one brood each season) throughout nest life, and for some time after they leave nest, with regurgitated ants, beetles, caterpillars, and other insects by inserting long bill into throats of young; adults are vigorous in defense of eggs or young; one adult seen attacking a pilot black snake that had crawled into the nesting cavity (*see* Reptiles and Birds); another carried its eggs in its bill to new nesting site when top of nesting tree broke off in storm (*see* Birds That Carry Their Eggs under Eggs and Egg-Laying); family group stays together at least into Sept., or later in North; young when independent of adults may move 20 mi. away from place of hatching (Hoyt, 1957).

Other Names: Black woodpecker; carpenter bird; cock-of-the-woods; good-god; great black woodpecker; Indian hen; logcock; log-guard; Lord-God; woodchuck; woodcock; wood kate.

Age: One nestling, banded near Glenevis, Alta., shot and killed near there 9 years, 10 months, later; a 9-year-old male, banded at Ithaca, N.Y., killed by a car about 20 mi. from where banded (Hoyt, 1952); two others, banded near Ithaca, lived to 9 and 10 years old respectively; another in Minn. still alive at 13 years.

Weights: 10–16 oz. (Forbush, 1925–29).

Range: Resident, locally, of forests from c. and ne. B.C., south through Wash., w. Idaho, w. Mont., and Ore. to c. Calif. and Sierra Nevada Mtns., and from s. Mack., s. Man., n. Ont., c. Que., N.B., and Nova Scotia south to ne. B.C., w. Alta., e. Kans., Okla., c. Tex., Gulf coast, and s. Fla.

Woodpecker, red-bellied, *Melanerpes carolinus* (mel-an-ER-peez cah-row-LIN-us); genus name: *see* Woodpecker, acorn; species name: Lat., of Carolina (S.C.) from Catesby's illus. of this bird; so named by Carl Linnaeus in 1758; *red-bellied* refers to pink or reddish tinge on belly. (Color ill., page 1,039.) Closely related to the golden-fronted woodpecker, but where ranges of these species meet and overlap by a few miles in Tex., apparently no interbreeding between the two (Selander and Giller, 1959); resident (some wander irregularly in winter) in e. U.S., from northern north-central states south to Fla., west to e. Tex., se. Neb.; 9–10½ in. long; wingspread 15–18 in.; is "zebra-backed" and very similar to golden-fronted woodpecker, but male red-bellied has *entire crown and nape scarlet;* female has red nape (back of head and hind neck), not orange or yellow as in golden-fronted woodpecker; reddish tinge on belly difficult to see in field identification of red-bellied; is noisy, has many varied calls, softer, more scolding than flicker's higher-pitched calls; utters soft, querulous *chuf-chuf-chuf* or *churr-churr-churr*, and a slow *br-r-r-r-t* or *crer-r-r-r-r*, similar to call of *Hyla versicolor*, the gray tree frog (or tree "toad") of e. U.S. (see details of calls of red-bellied and illustrations of its threat displays in Kilham, 1961); both sexes call, drum (a pleasant rolling tattoo), and tap, males more so than females; drumming seems to serve as an assertion of territorial dominance, also associated at times with conflicts between individuals; males may stay on their breeding territories the year around (Kilham, 1961); lives in heavily timbered bottomlands, swamps, and wooded groves of hardwood and mixed conifers with large trees, in flat, low pine woods, in oak woods, and in elms along river and creek bottoms, in shade trees of towns; not especially shy, visits yards and gardens wherever trees and shrubs.

Feeding Habits: After undulating flight from tree to tree, hammers on trunks and limbs for larvae of wood-boring insects; also feeds much on ground, eats ants, beetles, grasshoppers, crickets, caterpillars, flies, also acorns, beech-nuts, pine seeds, juniper berries, mulberries, elderberries, blackberries, bayberries, straw-berries, etc., wild grapes, fruits of palmetto and sour gum, also cherries and apples, and in Fla. eats pulp and juice of oranges from those on tree or on ground; eats some corn (Bent, 1939); drinks sap from "wells" of yellow-bellied sap-sucker, rather rarely reported to carry away or eat eggs or young of other birds (Brackbill, 1969a; Conner, 1974); stores acorns, nuts, insects, and pulp of fruit; comes to feeding stations for suet, peanut butter, nuts, etc.

Nest: Both sexes assist in digging nesting cavity in old stumps, decayed tops of dead trees; digs in softer-wooded trees such as elms, cottonwood, basswood, maple, poplar, willows, sycamores, but partly decayed stub or limb seems preferred, in cabbage palm, hackberry, chinaberry, pecan, water elm, also drills nesting hole in wooden utility poles, fence posts; round entrance hole about 2 in. in diameter, cavity 10–12 in. deep, 5–70 ft. above ground but usually less than 40 ft.; sometimes uses same nesting cavity in succeeding nesting seasons; also nests in old cavities of other woodpeckers (Bent, 1939).

Eggs: Apr.–July; 3–8, usually 4–5, white.

Incubation: In turn, by both sexes, male incubates at night; female incubates slightly more than male; about 11½ days (Stickel, 1965); both parents brood young during first week of their nest life; young leave nest 24–26 days after hatching; young remain near nest site for about 2 days before leaving area to follow parents; about 42 days after leaving nest, young appear capable of caring for themselves (Stickel, 1965); probably one brood in North but in South two or three (Bent, 1939).

Other Names: Cham-chack; jam-jack; ram-shack; sham-shack (all imitative of one of red-bellied's call notes); zebra-back (from black-and-white-barred back); zebra bird; zebra woodpecker.

Age: An adult female, banded at Leetonia, Ohio, was last trapped there and released when she was 6½ years old; a male, banded at Hillsboro, N.C., caught in same area and released on Feb. 22, 1967, when 20 years, 8 months, old (Kennard, 1975); this was greatest known age at time of any wild N. American woodpecker.

Weights: In N.C. (52), average 72.5 gr. (Teulings and Teulings, 1971), or about 3 oz.

Range: Resident from se. Minn., s. Wisc., s. Ont., w. N.Y., Conn., and south through Iowa and e. Neb. to s. Tex., Gulf coast, and Fla. Keys; has strayed to Colo. and R.I.; prior to 1955, was a straggler in New York City area but since then has extended range into n. N.J., Long Is., and sw. Conn., and has nested in sw. N.J. (Delaware Valley), and at Princeton, N.J., for first time, in 1962 (Bull, 1964); nested for first time in Conn. Apr. 24, 1971, near Greenwich, Fairfield County (Boyajiian, 1971b).

Woodpecker, red-cockaded, *Picoides borealis* (pick-oh-EYE-deez boh-reh-AY-liss); genus name: *see* Woodpecker, Arizona; species name: Lat., northern, so named in 1807 by Louis Jean Pierre Viellot, French scientist, who in first decade of 19th century spent many months in s. U.S. and assumed, mistakenly, that the southern red-cockaded woodpecker ranged into n. U.S.; *red-cockaded*, so named by Alexander Wilson for the small tuft of red feathers (the cockade) on either side of male's black crown. (Color ill., page 1,041.) Uncommon and local resident in pine woods from e. Okla., s. Mo., e. Ky., Tenn., east to s. Md., south to e. Tex., Gulf coast, and s. Fla.; is on Threatened Wildlife List (see Office of Endangered Species, 1973); an estimated 3,000–10,000 left; has one of most limited habitats of all N. American woodpeckers (Ligon, 1971b); its scarcity owing to its almost complete dependence for nesting on old-age southern pines; most of these afflicted with fungus-caused disease, red heart, or red-ring rot, which attacks heartwood of the trees only (Affeltranger, 1971); old-age trees, usually incompatible with commercially managed pine forests, gradually being cut off; see, however, discussions of future by Lay and Russell (1970) and in Thompson (1971); red-cockaded considered by some authorities to be closely related to ladder-backed and Nuttall's woodpeckers, but Jackson (1971) suggests relationship to the hairy woodpecker; about 8½ in. long; has *black-and-white cross-barred back* ("zebra-backed"); *black* cap and nape (red-bellied woodpecker is zebra-backed but has a *red* cap and nape); red-cockaded has distinctive white cheeks, its most conspicuous field mark, separating it quickly from hairy and downy woodpeckers, which have black mark through white cheeks; the small bright red cockades on each side of black cap, lacking in female, difficult to see in field; lives in open pine woods of South; is noisy as it travels, often in groups, constantly calling back and forth or drumming on resonant wood of trees; utters harsh, discordant cries, almost exactly like those of its pineland associate the brown-headed nuthatch, and a *yank, yank*, resembling call of white-breasted nuthatch (Murphey, 1939); also a *sripp* or *shilp* (Peterson, 1963); its calls are very distinctive (Winkler and Short, 1978); male in summer begins excavating with bill a roosting cavity through sapwood and into heartwood of a pine within the colony (*see* below under Nest), most often on west or south side of trunk; may require a year or more to complete (Baker, 1971b); 4–70 ft. up, but usually 12–20 ft. above ground; later used as a nesting cavity by a (presumably) permanently mated pair (Beckett, 1971b); the roosting and nesting cavities may be used by generations of red-cockaded woodpeckers, some for 40–50 years if these old nesting trees are not destroyed (Beckett, 1971b); red-cockaded often lives in groups called clans, which may include 3 or even 5–7 adults active in nesting season with extra unmated birds, almost always young of the previous season, helping with young; in winter, up to 9 individuals seen in a group in S.C.

Feeding Habits: Eats many wood-boring insects and beetle larvae in trunks of pines as it spirals around trunk or climbs straight upward; in winter in La., feeds almost exclusively on trunks of pines (Morse, 1972), usually not close to ground; within its territory literally combs pine forest throughout year from trunks to outer branches and into crowns (Baker, 1971a); 86% of food is insects; beetle larvae about 16% (Beal, 1911; Beal et al., 1916); eats ants at all seasons, also moths, caterpillars, grasshoppers, crickets, bugs; spiders, centipedes, millipedes; berries of wax myrtle, magnolia, and black gum trees, poison ivy berries, blueberries, pokeberries, wild grapes, wild cherries, and pecans, hunts especially in ears of standing corn in fields next to pine forest for the corn earworm, *Heliothis zea*, which is a major food of red-cockaded for several weeks in summer; may eat up to 8,000 earworms per acre; a whole clan of up to 7 birds may feed together in a field (Baker, 1971a); Ligon (1968b) noted in Fla. that sexes fed in separate parts of pines, but this not noted by other observers (Morse, 1972); comes to feeding stations within its daily range to drink water and eat suet (Baker, 1971b).

Nest: Usually in roosting cavity with a few dried chips on bottom, in soft heartwood of mature living pine, mostly but not always in one infected by fungus-caused disease, red heart, in trees usually 65–110 years old (Beckett, 1971b); disease spores are spread by the wind (see Steirly, 1957; Affeltranger, 1971); entrance hole about 2 in. in diameter, nest cavity, gourd-shaped, about 8–12 in. deep or more (Murphey, 1939); in s. Va., nesting trees were usually in colonies, with three or four close by; there may be 6 active nests in trees on one third of an acre; some nest trees 25–75 ft. apart; in one colony, three active nests were in trees within a circle with 100-ft. radius (see Steirly, 1957; Murphey, 1939); colonies spaced about ½ mi. apart (Beckett, 1971b; Baker, 1971b); one nest cavity in Tex. used for 11 years; another for 20 years (Lay and Russell, 1970); when a nest tree broken off in a storm or killed by lightning, usually abandoned; red-cockaded woodpeckers dig, and keep open, conical pits 1 in. across in bark and sapwood of living trunk, around, above, and below nesting cavity; the exuding resin flows down trunk; according to Dennis (1971) and Jackson (1974), the sticky resin is disagreeable to predatory animals that touch it and is especially repellent to tree-climbing snakes; after years of flow, the resin-coated nest trees stand out like whitish columns distinguishing them from darker trunks of neighboring trees (see also Steirly, 1957).

Eggs: Fla., early Apr. to late May; S.C., late Apr. to late May; 2–5 eggs, usually 3–4, white (Murphey, 1939); but only 1 or 2 young raised by pairs without helpers, especially in second-growth pine forests (Ligon, 1970a; 1971b); only one brood raised in a nesting season.

Incubation: By both sexes, by male at night; 12–13 days; young leave nest 22–28 days after hatching (Beckett, 1971b); 26–29 days, and after fledging, young depend on adults for food for 150 days or longer (Ligon, 1970a).

Weights: Three males in S.C., Oct., 1⅞–2 oz. (Beckett, 1971a).

Range: Distribution of red-cockaded woodpecker is correlated with the distribution of mature longleaf, slash, loblolly, and shortleaf pines in South; and with distribution of forest fires, which maintain open, parklike habitat that red-cockaded prefers; and with proportion of land that is forested; has been most numerous in open pine woods of Fla., Ga., and S.C. (Jackson, 1971—*see* total range in beginning of this biography); has strayed to e. Pa. (near Philadelphia, in 1861), and N.J., where one collected at Hoboken prior to 1866 (Stone, 1937).

Woodpecker, red-headed, *Melanerpes erythrocephalus* (mel-an-ER-peez eh-rith-row-SEF-ah-lus); genus name: *see* Woodpecker, acorn; species name: Lat., from Gr. *erythros*, red, and *kephale*, head, refers to red head of this species. (Color ill., page 1,041.) Closely related to the western acorn woodpecker; uncommon over much of its range, lives mostly in open deciduous woods and in prairie country from central s. Canada east to Ont. and New England, south to N.M., Tex., Gulf coast, and s. Fla.; almost the ecological counterpart in e. U.S. of Lewis' woodpecker of w. U.S. in its choice of habitats and feeding habits (Bock *et al.*, 1971); was once (prior to 1890) a common bird in much of ne. U.S., but with advent of automobile (according to Bent, 1939, seems more often killed on highways within its range than other species of birds) and after the introduction of the European starling in 1890s, which competed with red-headed woodpecker for nest holes, was markedly reduced in numbers especially after 1900, with further losses in 1930s (Bull, 1964); still substantially reduced into early 1970s; 8½–9½ in. long; wingspread 16–18 in.; sexes outwardly alike; adult with *entire head*, also neck and upper breast, *bright red;* black upper back; large square of white on rear part of wings and on upper rump, especially noticeable in its flight; pure-white underparts; immatures have buffy-brown head and neck; also have large white wing patches; utters loud *queer, queer, queer* or *quee-o-quee-o-queer* and a henlike *ker-r-r-ruck, ker-ruck-ruck-ruck;* in summer, lives in open groves of large trees or those scattered in old fields and pastures, also likes cut-over forest "slashings" and lives about tree stubs in burned-over deciduous and pine tracts; also along river bottoms, frequently dwells in hearts of small cities and nests in utility poles of village streets, along rural roads and across prairies (Bent, 1939); irregular migrations southward from northern parts of range and local movements in

fall and winter prompted by scarcity or lack of acorns and beechnuts (Bent, 1939).

Feeding Habits: From perch on wooden posts, tops or sides of tall trees and utility poles, much like Lewis' woodpecker, darts out into air to catch flying insects, both in summer and in winter; apparently rarely drills into trees for insects (Bock *et al.*, 1971) although it does some drilling for grubs in dead wood; forages on ground and in shrubs for insects; animal food about 50% of diet, includes ants, wasps, and beetles and especially June beetles, weevils, predacious ground beetles (carabids), tiger beetles; also millipedes, centipedes, and spiders (Beal, 1895); also takes young or eggs of other birds—bluebirds, house sparrows, chickadees, titmice, etc.—and mice (Bent, 1939); vegetable food includes some corn, berries of dogwood, huckleberries, strawberries, etc., wild and cultivated cherries and grapes, acorns, beechnuts; stores food, especially acorns, beechnuts, corn, and even grasshoppers, wasps, and crickets (*see* Birds That Store Food under Food and Feeding Habits); takes sap from "wells" of sapsuckers; will come to bird feeders for suet, sunflower seeds, cracked corn, raisins, nuts, and bread.

Nest: Drills a cavity 8–24 in. deep usually in dead tops or stumps of oaks, ashes, maples, elms, sycamores, cottonwoods, willows, etc., about 5–80 ft. above ground, entrance hole 1¾ in. in diameter; sometimes in natural cavities, and on treeless prairies, under roofs of houses, in fence posts, utility poles, in hub of broken wheel, etc., also will nest in bird box built for it (see in Terres, 1968c); its nesting hole often taken over by starlings.

Eggs: Extreme dates, Apr. 20–Aug. 20; over most of range, early May into July; 4–7, commonly 5, white.

Incubation: By both sexes, about 14 (?) days; age when young first fly unknown; two broods in some parts of its range.

Other Names: Flag bird; half-a-shirt; jelly coat; patriotic bird; redhead; shirttail bird; tricolor; tricolored woodpecker; white-shirt.

Accidents: Many struck by traffic when flying down to road to pick up insects (Bent, 1939).

Age: One in Mich., found dead at Battle Creek, where it had been banded, was at least 10 years old.

Weights: In Mich. (5), 70.5–88 gr. (Becker and Stack, 1944), or about 2½–3 oz.; in fall, coastal N.J. (1), 66.4 gr. (Murray and Jehl, 1964), or 2⅓ oz.

Range: Resident from s. Sask., s. Man., east to sw. Ont., s. Que., N.Y., and s. N.H., south through c. Mont., e. Wyo., and c. Colo. to n. N.M., c. Tex., Gulf coast, and s. Fla.; has strayed to Alta., N.B., Nova Scotia, Utah, Ariz.; first *live* one in Calif. reported at Niland, Imperial Valley, July 17–Aug. 22, 1971 (Cardiff and Driscoll, 1972).

Woodpecker, three-toed. *See* Woodpecker, black-backed three-toed, and Woodpecker, northern three-toed.

Woodpecker, white-headed, *Picoides albolarvatus* (pick-oh-EYE-deez al-boh-lar-VAY-tus); genus name: *see* Woodpecker, Arizona;

species name: from Lat. *albus*, white, and *larvatus*, masked, apparently refers to white feathers that cover entire head, throat, and upper breast. (Color ills., pages 1,040, 1,041.) According to Mayr and Short (1970), is probably close relative of the N. American hairy woodpecker and the Mexican brown-barred woodpecker (*see* under Woodpecker, Arizona); resident from Wash. and Idaho south to s. Calif.; about 9 in. long; *only N. American woodpecker with a white head;* has black body with large white wing patch at base of primaries (flight feathers), conspicuous in flight; male has narrow red patch on back of head; immatures resemble adults and show more or less red on crown (Bent, 1939); sometimes drums on resonant wood; utters a sharp *chick* or *ick,* occasionally rapidly repeated, also a sharp rattling cry similar to ringing "dropped chisel" call of downy woodpecker; lives in pine and fir forests of mountains of West, at 4,000–9,000 ft. elevation during nesting season but may descend to lower levels in winter; closely identified with the ponderosa, or yellow, pine (Bent, 1939); flies in direct and rather slow flight, often alights on trunks or branches upside down or sidewise.

Feeding Habits: Forages on cones, branches, trunks, and bases of sequoias, sugar pines, and Douglas firs, both living and dead; pries or flakes off with slanting blows of bill successive scales and layers of bark to get at bark beetles, spiders, also eats ants, fly larvae, etc., sometimes darts out into air and catches passing insects; however, lives largely on seeds of ponderosa pines (Beal, 1911); frequently drinks water (Bent, 1939; Ligon, 1973).

Nest: Often digs nest cavity in standing dead pine stumps, sometimes drills several holes in same stump, entrance hole 1½–1¾ in. in diameter, cavity about 8–15 in. deep, 4–25 ft. above ground (Bent, 1939).

Eggs: Calif., Apr. 24–June 16; 3–7, commonly 4, often 5, white.

Incubation: Period of and age when young first fly unknown.

Other Names: Northern white-headed woodpecker; southern white-headed woodpecker.

Range: Resident from n.-c. Wash. and n. Idaho south to s. Calif. and w. Nev.; has strayed to s. B.C.

Woodpecker, willow. *See* Woodpecker, downy.

Woodpecker, zebra. *See* Woodpecker, red-bellied.

Wryneck, *Jynx torquilla* (JINGKS tore-QUILL-ah); genus name: from Gr. *iynx, iynges,* wryneck (Jaeger, 1955), used in charms, also perhaps from *iuzo,* to yell, with reference to its shrill call (Macleod, 1954); species name: Lat., dim. from *torqueo,* to twist, "little twister," in reference to snakelike way in which this bird twists its neck when captured (Macleod, 1954). Eurasian species, one record in N. America at Wales, Alaska, Sept. 8, 1945; about 6–7 in. long; soft feathers, rather weak bill; is in Woodpecker Family but appearance and posture like that of a passerine, or songbird; in its mottled and vermiculated plumage pattern of grays, browns, resembles a member of the Nightjar Family; upperparts and rather long, rounded tail are gray, brown, buff; underparts buff, checkered with brown; call is a nasal *kew, kew, kew* (Peterson *et al.*, 1954); wrynecks apparently have relatively longest tongues of any birds in world.

Range: Nests from England and n. Eurasia, sw. Siberia to nw. Africa, se. Europe, n. India, c. China, and Japan; winters south to c. Africa and s. Asia; has strayed once to Alaska (Reilly, 1968).

WOOD PEWEE

See in Flycatcher—Tyrant Flycatcher Family.

WOODSTAR

See in Hummingbird Family.

WOOD WARBLER

See Warbler—American Wood Warbler Family.

WORMS

See Earthworms and Birds; Food and Feeding Habits; *also* Nematode; Parasite.

WORTHEN

CHARLES K(IMBALL) (1850–1909). Born Warsaw, Ill.; a knowledgeable naturalist who collected and sold natural history specimens and became well known to museum curators in America. In 1884, Robert Ridgway named a sparrow, *Spizella wortheni*, Worthen's sparrow, in his honor, from the type specimen, a male collected by Charles H. Marsh at Silver City, N.M., and sent to Ridgway by Worthen, who, in Ridgway's words, "has . . . done much to develop the ornithology of New Mexico."

WOUNDED-BIRD ACT

See Distraction Display; *see also* under Plover Family; Young and Their Care.

WREN FAMILY

Troglodytidae (trog-low-DIT-ih-dee); from Gr. *troglodytes*, creeper into holes, a cave dweller. Small songbirds; 59 species in world (Van Tyne and Berger, 1976); all in W. Hemisphere, where family originated, and only one species has spread to Old World, the one called in N. America winter wren, in Europe simply wren, which in times long past extended its range from N. America into Eurasia (probably by way of Alaska) and established itself there and in n. Africa, largely in mountainous country (Armstrong, 1964d); closest relatives are dippers and mockingbirds (Austin, 1961); 10 species in N. America, greatest concentration of species in C. and S. America; however, only two species of wrens in West Indies—one, the well-known N. American house wren; the other, the Zapata wren, which may have most limited range of any American bird; lives only in one swamp in Cuba of less than 5 sq. mi. along south coast; discovered there in 1926 (see Bond, 1961; Vincent, 1966); recent (1979–80) searches have failed to reveal it (Hardy, 1977).

Most wrens are small, extremely quick, active, both sexes outwardly similar; have brown or brown-gray plumage, striped, streaked, or spotted with black, gray, white, or brown; have slender, sharp-pointed bills, usually slightly downcurved; short, rounded wings, flight rather weak, quick, direct, buzzy, usually carry tail cocked straight up; most live close to ground, scold much, are usually solitary except when paired at nesting time; most sing well and through most of year in some species, both sexes sing (see lp record of wren songs, Hardy, 1977); most are resident except some that migrate in fall from northern parts of range; male wrens great nest builders; usually build several nests in territory, up to half dozen; some wrens are polygamous (Austin, 1961); albinism apparently uncommon—Gross (1965a) reported only 6 individuals of 3 species; all wrens protected by law.

Baird's wren. *See* Bewick's wren.

Bewick's wren, *Thryomanes bewickii* (thry-oh-MANE-eez or thrih-OM-ah-neez bue-ICK-ih-eye); genus name: Lat., from Gr. *thryon*, a reed, and *manes*, cup, alludes to cuplike nest, built not in reeds, however, but usually in cavity; species name: given by John James Audubon for his friend Thomas Bewick, English artist and wood engraver. (Color ill., page 1,043.) Mostly in se. U.S., Midwest, and w. U.S.; not as common in East as house wren; 5–5½ in. long; wingspread 7–7¼ in.; slender shape; *unstreaked* brown back, unlike other wrens has *white underparts* and *long, rounded tail, tipped with white spots* that show when tail spread; white stripe over eyes; lives in open woodlands, upland thickets, fencerows, near houses, orchards, about farm buildings, in country towns, backyards, gardens, old pastures, cut-over woods, in cactus and mesquite, hill cedar brakes, thickets along creeks in n. Calif., in mountain canyons of Ariz., N.M., and Tex. at 4,000–6,000 ft. elevation, in chaparral-covered hills and in ravines and brushy slopes of Pacific coast; valleys and bottomlands; a familiar dooryard bird in most of its range; creeps and hops about under eaves of buildings, and along fences, popping in and out of every hole and crevice; tail carried high over back; male sings clear, bold variable song, head thrown back, long tail hanging down, one song resembling song sparrow's, rendered in syllables *chip, chip, chip, de-da-a, te-dee;* roosts on sides of buildings, in pines (Bent, 1948).

Feeding Habits: Forages much on ground, limbs of trees, leaves of bushes, picks up in bill mostly insects (about 97% of food); boll weevils, beetles, black olive scales, leaf bugs, stink bugs, leafhoppers, treehoppers, ants, wasps, caterpillars, moths, grasshoppers, also spiders. *Nest:* In almost any cavity; knotholes, natural cavities in trees, fence posts, mailboxes, old woodpecker holes, brush heaps, in tin cans, clothing hung in buildings, baskets, bird boxes, oil wells, cow skulls in pastures, crevices in stone, brick, or tile walls (Bent, 1948); nest materials of green mosses, sticks, dead leaves, cotton, hairs, wool, pieces of cast-off snakeskin, the inner cup lined with feathers. *Eggs:* Mar.–June; 4–11, usually 5–7, white, irregularly dotted, spotted with browns, purples, lavender, gray,

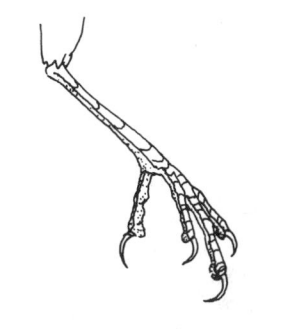

WREN FAMILY

Brown-throated wren

WREN FAMILY

Incubation: By female, 14 days; young leave nest about 14 days after hatching (Bent, 1948).
Other Names: Baird's wren; long-tailed wren, Nicasio wren; sooty wren; Texas wren; Vigors' wren.
Host to Cowbirds: Infrequent; to brown-headed cowbird, only 6 records; a single record of host to bronzed cowbird (Friedmann, 1963).
Range: Mostly resident from sw. B.C., c. Wash., Nev., s. Utah, sw. Wyo., c. Colo., se. Neb., s. Iowa, s. Wisc., s. Mich., s. Ont., Ohio, c. Pa., and Va., south to Guadalupe Is. and s. Baja Calif., c. Mexico, northern edges of Gulf states; winters at lower altitudes in mountainous parts of range, and south to Gulf coast and s. Fla.

Brown-throated wren, *Troglodytes brunneicollis* (trog-low-DIE-teez broon-ih-COL-lis); genus name: *see* family introduction; species name: from Lat. *brunneus*, brown, and *collum*, neck. (Color ill., page 1,042.) Mexican species that reaches U.S. only in Ariz.; close relative of house wren; 4½–5 in. long; rusty-brown upperparts, like house wren but has buffier line over eyes; rich cinnamon buff below; barred flanks (Blake, E.R., 1953); resident (Robbins *et al.*, 1966), first discovered in U.S. 1945; uncommon, nests in oak forests at 7,000–8,000 ft. elevation in Rincon, Santa Rita, Huachuca, and Chiricahua Mtns. in Ariz. and Mexico; song and habits much like those of house wren; many authorities consider the brown-throated wren to be a form, or subspecies, of the house wren. See discussion in Phillips *et al.* (1964) and in Wetmore *et al.* (1964).

Weights: 11 gr. (Pough, 1957), or about ⅓ oz.

Cactus wren, *Campylorhynchus brunneicapillus* (cam-pih-low-RING-kus broon-ih-CAP-ill-us); genus name: from Gr. words meaning curved beak; species name: from Lat. *brunneus*, brown, and *capillus*, hair, in reference to brown cap and back. (Color ill., page 1,042.) Lives in deserts of sw. U.S.; state bird of Ariz.; largest wren in U.S.; 7–8¾ in. long; rusty brown above with white markings; a conspicuous broad white stripe over each eye; underparts pale, breast *heavily spotted;* tail not usually cocked as in other wrens; outer tail feathers barred with black and white; in flight, widely fanned tail shows conspicuous white band (Woods, 1948b); lives over wide range from Tex. to Pacific and from Mexican border to Utah, Nev., but actually limited to regions where thorny shrubs and trees offer nesting sites; typical are sunny hillsides of mesas next to mountains and along gravelly watercourses; primarily in low country but up to 6,000 ft. elevation in N.M.; also in shade trees and about buildings in towns; male sings from prominent perch at top of tree, building, or pole, a series of grating syllables with deep throaty quality, *chuh-chuh-chuh-chuh;* each pair usually has several extra, or "dummy," nests for roosting; can run swiftly but usually flies if going considerable distance.

Feeding Habits: When searching for food approaches leaf or a movable object on ground, inserts bill under it and lifts up, then peers under for any creature hiding there; eats beetles, ants, wasps, grasshoppers, bugs, some spiders and occasional lizard and tree frog; also cactus fruit, elderberries, cascara berries, some seeds, sometimes visits bird feeders for bread, pieces of raw apple, fried potatoes (Terres, 1968c).
Nest: Shaped like a retort (bulb of glass with bent beak used in laboratories), conspicuous, built mostly in cholla cactus, catclaw, and other thorny bushes, tree yuccas, etc., even in cactus in yards, 2½–9 ft. up, occasionally in orange trees, sometimes in hollow cornice of building or in old woodpecker hole in tree, nest serves as home throughout year; built of coarse and fine plant fibers, and thickly lined with fur or feathers; entrance a long passageway from side, near top of nest; new nests built in spring and summer for raising broods; old nests kept in repair, serve as roosts (Woods, 1948b).
Eggs: Mar.–Aug.; 3–7, commonly 4–5, white to pink-white, finely dotted with browns.
Incubation: 16 days; young leave nest 19–23 days after hatching; sometimes three broods a year (Anderson and Anderson, 1957; 1959; 1960; 1961; 1962; 1963; 1965).
Other Names: Brown-headed cactus wren; Bryant's cactus wren; Coues' cactus wren.
Age: One, banded Tempe, Ariz., retrapped and released at same place when 4 years old.
Range: Resident from s. Calif. south to s. Baja Calif., s. Nev., sw. Utah, w. and s.-c. Ariz., s. N.M., and c. Tex. south to Mexico.

Cañon, or canyon, wren, *Catherpes mexicanus* (cath-ER-peez meks-ih-CANE-us); genus name: Lat., from Gr. *katherpein*, to creep down (Coble, 1954); species name: Lat., of Mexico, from which came the original specimen or specimens from which this species was named. (Color ill., page 1,043.) Bird of western U.S.; well named, as it prefers to live in steep, especially watered, canyons; 5½–5¾ in. long; wingspread 7½ in.; upperparts brown-red; its gleaming, clear white throat and breast and rich red-brown belly distinguish it from the grayish rock wren; lives in Grand Canyon and rocky slopes of other canyons, where it dodges in and out of cracks, crannies, and dark little caves—from eastern edge of Rocky Mtns. to Pacific slope and from B.C. south to Tex. and Mexico; has even adapted to living in business areas of towns and on old rock buildings in Tex.; sometimes about houses and barns; usually heard long before seen; male sings frequent outbursts of silvery whistles that echo from walls of canyons as he creeps mouselike among loose rocks and crevices; his liquid notes trip down the scale, *peupp, peupp, peupp, peupp,* each note slightly lower in pitch than the last (Bent, 1948).

Feeding Habits: Climbs over, under, and around rocks searching for insects and spiders, sometimes pairs come into open door of ranch houses and tamely hop about on floor; in Tex., Martin (1971) watched two of these wrens fly in and out of an abandoned cabin to feed on spiders stored in mud cells by a mud-dauber wasp.
Nest: Built under rocks, on shelves in caves, rocky ledges of cliffs, in holes, gully banks, stone walls, and sometimes in hollow stumps, logs, inside miners' cabins, ranch houses; first

builds foundation of small twigs, then mosses, spider's silk, bits of leaves, catkins, bud scales of trees, the cup lined with fur and feathers.

Eggs: Mar.–July; 4–7, usually 5–6, white, sparingly dotted with browns.

Incubation: Period of and age when young leave nest unknown.

Other Names: Dotted wren; white-throated wren.

Range: Resident from c. coastal Calif., s.-c. B.C. to sw. S.D., south to c. Tex., s. Baja Calif., and Mexico.

Carolina wren, *Thryothorus ludovicianus* (thry-OTH-oh-rus lewd-oh-VIS-ih-ANE-us); genus name: Lat., from Gr. *thryon*, a reed, and *thouros*, rushing, leaping, springing, possibly in allusion to its movements among rushes or reeds; species name: Lat., of Louisiana, the type locality, or place where the first specimen or specimens of this bird, at that time unknown to science, was collected (at New Orleans along Mississippi R.); common name: for Carolinas, where a common bird. (Color ill., page 1,043.) E. U.S., common in Southeast; state bird of S.C.; largest and reddest wren of e. N. America; 5¼–6 in. long; wingspread 6¾–7¾ in.; rich red-brown above; white chin, conspicuous white stripe over eyes; buff underparts; lives year-round in undergrowth near water, fallen tree-tops, brush heaps, rocky places in woods, often hidden but appears in response to squeaking notes; lives about shrubbery in yards or gardens but many prefer wilder woods, thickets, swamps, hammocks (Fla.), isolated trees and bushes on prairies, pine barrens of South; pairs sometimes together all winter, seldom still, dodge in and out of underbrush, woodpiles, jerking upturned tail, chattering; male occasionally stops to sing in all kinds of weather throughout year; many songs also imitations of songs of pine warbler, meadowlark, bluebird, and others (Bent, 1948); utters loud, rich whistled notes, rhythm in the syllables *tea-kettle, tea-kettle* or *sweet-heart, sweet-heart* or *which jailer, which jailer* suggests most characteristic song; reported roosting in cavities, old clothing, buildings; has extended range north to New England and s. Canada but sometimes dies in severe northern winters because not migratory.

Feeding Habits: Eats mostly arthropods—beetles, cotton-boll weevils, stink bugs, soldier bugs, leafhoppers, chinch bugs, also scale insects, caterpillars, moths, grasshoppers, crickets, cockroaches and eggs, crane flies, spiders and harvestmen, sow bugs, millipedes, snails, also lizards, tree frogs, and some berries and seeds; comes to bird feeders for food (see details in Terres, 1968c).

Nest: Built in cavity in tree, stump, or in open crotch of tree, among upturned roots of fallen tree, hole in bank, stone wall, old woodpecker holes, about buildings in small baskets, pails, open bags, rafters, pockets of old clothes, mailboxes, birdhouses, etc. (Bent, 1948); nest of grasses, weed stalks, inner bark, leaves, mosses, rootlets, feathers, pieces of molted snakeskin.

Eggs: Apr.–July; 4–8, usually 5–6, white, pale pink, spotted with browns.

Incubation: By female, about 14 days; young leave nest 13–14 days after hatching; two broods a year (Bent, 1948; Laskey, 1948; Nice and Thomas, 1948).

Other Names: Florida wren; great Carolina wren; Lomita wren; Louisiana wren; mocking wren.

Age: At Nashville, Tenn., banded ones recaptured when 4½–5 years old; an adult, banded Little Rock, Ark., lived at least 6 years.

Albinism: Partial albino reported in Md., banded Dec. 1959.

Host to Cowbirds: Uncommon; 5 records; Maslowski (1953) saw one egg of brown-headed cowbird with five of Carolina wren in nest wren had built in open glove compartment of old truck.

Weights: In fall, coastal N.J. (3), 14.2–19.7 gr. (Murray and Jehl, 1964), or about ½–¾ oz.; in summer, Washington, D.C., male (1), 21.1 gr. (Wetmore, 1936).

Range: Resident from se. Neb. east to s. Ont., se. Mass., and south to c. Tex., Gulf coast, s. Fla., and Mexico.; occasionally north to se. Minn., s. Wisc., e.-c. Mich., c. N.Y., Vt., s. N.H., and sw. Me.

Cattail wren. *See* Long-billed marsh wren.

Dotted wren. *See* Cañon wren.

Freshwater marsh wren. *See* Long-billed marsh wren.

Grass wren. *See* Short-billed marsh wren.

House wren, *Troglodytes aedon* (trog-low-DIE-teez ay-EE-don); genus name: *see* family introduction; species name: from Gr. Aedon, Queen of Thebes in Gr. mythology, who was changed by Zeus into a nightingale; so named in 1807 by Louis Jean Pierre Viellot, amateur French ornithologist, possibly alluding to a comparison of the house wren's song with that of the European nightingale's; "house" possibly because it will nest in holes or crevices in or about homes or because it readily nests in bird "houses" (boxes) provided for it. *See* Bird-Attracting. (Color ills., page 1,045.) Lives from Atlantic to Pacific coasts and from Canada south to Tierra del Fuego, Argentina, Trinidad, and Tobago; plainest wren, and the commonest one in e. U.S.; 4½–5¼ in. long; wingspread 6–7 in.; unstreaked, gray-brown; pale gray below; sharp bill, narrow blackish bars on wings and tail; indistinct light streak over eyes; resembles winter wren but larger; cocked tail longer, underparts paler; migratory; males arrive on nesting grounds in U.S. from Mar. into May, usually ahead of female; adults return almost invariably to territory where previously nested (Kendeigh, 1941); summers usually in low tract of deciduous woods, along edges of woods or in sunny openings, in residential places in yards, parks, and gardens; male advertises and defends territory of ¼–3½ acres by much singing; clear, loud, bubbling notes, the syllables *tsi-tsi-tsi-tsi-oodle-oodle-oodle* suggest its song, the pitch rising at beginning, falling at end (Gross, 1948b), also gives chattering, scolding notes; some males may have two mates at same time in nesting season but only a small percentage of them (Kendeigh, 1941; Brackbill, 1970b). With arrival of female, ardent courtship begins, female visits stick nests built by male before her arrival, finally chooses one and lines it for her eggs and future broods; the adults sometimes feed and care for young of other species (Gross, 1948b). When population of house wrens is highest and competition for territories keen, some males may puncture eggs or kill young of wrens and other songbirds in adjacent territories, which may be one of natural forms of population regulation.

Feeding Habits: Eats almost entirely insects —grasshoppers, crickets, beetles, caterpillars of gypsy moth and of cabbage white butterfly, ants, bees, wasps, flies, bugs, ticks, plant lice (aphids), etc.; also many spiders, some millipedes, snails.

Nest: Usually in cavity but extremely varied: in natural cavities or woodpecker holes in trees or stumps; in bird boxes, empty cow skulls hung up in pasture; abandoned paper nests of hornets, deserted nests of swallows and other birds, in fishing creel hung in shed, in watering pots, old hat, tin cans, teapots, in flower pots, old boots, shoes, nozzle of pump, in iron pipe railing, weather vane, holes in wall, in axle of automobile in use daily, etc.; nest has foundation of sticks and twigs, usually lined with feathers, hair, wool, spiders' cocoons, catkins. See McCabe (1965). For other odd nesting places and some odd nesting material, see Gross (1948b), also in Terres (1968c).

Eggs: Apr.–July; 5–9, commonly 6–8, white speckled with brown.

Incubation: 13–15 days; young leave nest 12–18 days after hatching; may die in nest when heavily infested with larvae (blood-sucking grubs) of a bluebottle fly (see Kibler, 1969); two, sometimes three, broods in a season.

Other Names: Apache wren; brown wren; common wren; Jenny wren; Parkman's wren; short-tailed wren; stump wren; western wren; wood wren.

Accidents: Two females successively occupying nest box in Neb., stung to death by wasps in box (Eigsti, 1950).

Age: Of 193 nestlings banded in Ohio, six lived to 5 years, two to 6 years; another wild banded bird lived to 7 years, 2 months (Kennard, 1975).

Albinism: A complete or total albino reported by James Bond in 1949; in July 1955, an albino was nesting with a normally colored male, Mankato, Minn.

Host to Cowbirds: Very infrequent; only 6 records (Friedmann, 1963).

Weights: In fall, coastal N.J. (5), 9.9–12 gr. (Murray and Jehl, 1964), or about ⅓–½ oz.; in summer, Washington, D.C., males (2), 11.5 and 13.3 gr. (Wetmore, 1936).

Range: In summer nests from s. B.C. across s. Canada to N.B., south to n. Baja Calif. and n. Ga.; winters from s. Calif. east across s. U.S. to Ga., Va., to s. Fla., along Gulf coast, and into Mexico; other subspecies, or forms, live throughout C. and S. America, Trinidad, and Tobago.

Jenny wren. *See* House wren.

Long-billed marsh wren, *Cistothorus palustris* (sis-TOTH-oh-rus pal-US-tris); genus name: from Gr. *kistos*, a flowering shrub, rock-rose, and *thouros*, rushing, running, leaping through; species name: Lat., marshy, in reference to its habitat. (Color ill., page 1,044.) Lives from Atlantic to Pacific coast and from Canada to Mexico, but limited to marsh habitat; 4½–5½ in. long; wingspread 5–7 in.; upperparts brown, cap black, long, slender bill; *black and white streaks on back*, combined with *conspicuous white stripe over each eye*, are good identifying characteristics to separate it from other wrens; underparts whitish; usually lives in cattail marsh or in bulrushes, reeds, tules, tall marsh grasses of tidal creeks, salt and brackish marshes and marshy borders of sluggish waters of coastal region and inland river valleys; migratory, in spring and summer, songs of male bubble up by day or often at night from marsh as he clings to rushes, cattails, flags, tail frequently slanted forward over back; sometimes rises straight up into air, sings while fluttering back into marsh, where usually hidden; song begins with scraping notes followed by trill, with gurgles, rattles, and ends abruptly in short, musical trill; sometimes nest in colonies, males often have more than one mate living in adjacent territories. *See* discussion under Sexual Relationships.

Feeding Habits: Eats aquatic insects—dragonflies, crane flies, mosquito larvae, caterpillars, snails; if disturbed by least bitterns or red-winged blackbirds also nesting in marsh, may eat or puncture their eggs (Bent, 1948).
Nest: Large, coconut-shaped, usually built about 1–3 ft. above water, almost entirely by female; she lashes stems of supporting cattails, bulrushes together, then weaves outer wall of strips of coarse water-soaked cattails, sedges, etc., with opening left in side for entrance, then weaves inside layer of grasses, rootlets, cattail; lines central cavity with finely shredded plants and feathers. Male often builds up to six or more dummy nests before and after arrival of female.
Eggs: Mar.–Aug.; 3–10, commonly 5–6, dull brown, evenly sprinkled with dots of brown.
Incubation: By female, 13–16 days; young fly 11–16 days after hatching (Verner, 1965).
Other Names: Alberta marsh wren; cattail wren; Louisiana marsh wren; Marian's marsh wren; marsh wren; prairie marsh wren; reed wren; saltwater marsh wren; tule wren; Wayne's marsh wren; western marsh wren; Worthington's marsh wren.
Weights: In fall, coastal N.J. (1), 15 gr., or about ½ oz.; in Kans., adult male (1), 10.8 gr.; adult female (1), 9.2 gr., both killed at TV tower while migrating at night (Tordoff and Mengel, 1956).
Range: Nests from c. B.C. across s. Canada to s. Me., e. N.B., south to n. Baja Calif, s.-c. Mexico, Gulf coast, and s. Fla.; generally resident and winters along both Atlantic and Pacific coasts, but in winter seldom seen north of Gulf coast in states between Rocky Mtns. and Appalachians (Reilly, 1968).

Long-tailed wren. *See* Bewick's wren.

Louisiana marsh wren. *See* Long-billed marsh wren.

Marsh wren. A proposed new name for the long-billed marsh wren. *See* Long-billed marsh wren.

Meadow wren. *See* Short-billed marsh wren.

Mocking wren. *See* Carolina wren; so called because of mimicry of songs of other birds.

Mouse wren. *See* Winter wren.

Prairie marsh wren. *See* Long-billed marsh wren.

Reed wren. *See* Long-billed marsh wren.

Rock wren, *Salpinctes obsoletus* (sal-PINK-teez ob-so-LEE-tus); genus name: from Gr. *salpinktes*, a trumpeter, apparently in allusion to this bird's loud songs; species name: Lat., indistinct, in reference to the generally dull plumage; *rock* refers to its rocky habitat. (Color ill., page 1,044.) Fairly common in rocky barrens of w. U.S., from western edge of Great Plains to Pacific; 5–6¼ in. long; wingspread about 9 in.; a pale wren, upperparts gray-brown; finely streaked white breast, white streak over each eye; has buffy rump and flanks; black band near end of frequently cocked tail; lives on dry, bare, windswept rocky surfaces in valleys, foothills, far from water, in talus slopes, piles of broken rocks, limestone quarries, rough cliffs of deeper canyons, on rock walls in towns, and, in summer, upward in Rockies to 8,000–10,000 ft.; seldom seen in watery canyons where cañon wren lives; dodges about among rocks, perches on stones to scold human intruder; sings sprightly song that echoes from canyon walls, *keree keree keree, chair chair chair, deedle deedle deedle, tur tur tur, keree keree trrrrrr,* suggests song of a mockingbird or brown thrasher (Bent, 1948).

Feeding Habits: Little reported, but apparently beetles and other insects, also spiders, all abundant about bare rocks; in Okla., earthworms and larval insects; in Utah, grasshoppers.
Nest: In gopher burrows, in steep banks of arroyos and gulches, in cavities and in small crevices under loose rocks, in holes in rocks, openings in stone reservoirs, adobe buildings; places stones near opening to nests, sometimes for 8–10 in. out from hidden nest built of grasses, rootlets, and weed stems, lined with fur, horsehair, feathers; one passageway of a hole in earth to nest was lined with 1,665 items, of which 492 were small granite stones, 769 bones of rabbits, fishes, birds, and nesting materials (Bent, 1948).
Eggs: Jan.–July; 4–10, commonly 5–6, white, dotted with browns.
Incubation: Period of and age when young leave nest unknown.
Other Name: Common rock wren.
Host to Cowbirds: 17 records, 16 in Kans., 1 in Colo. (Friedmann, 1963).
Range: Nests from s.-c. B.C. east to s. Sask., nw. N.D., s. S.D., c. Neb., w. Okla., c. Tex.,

WARBLER— OLD WORLD WARBLER FAMILY

Black-tailed gnatcatcher
The black-tailed gnatcatcher inhabits brushy washes and arroyos in the southwestern deserts, where it chases insects in the same active, nervous manner as the more widespread blue-gray gnatcatcher. In contrast to the blue-gray, it usually builds its nest within 3 or 4 feet of the ground.

Black-tailed gnatcatcher

Blue-gray gnatcatcher

The blue-gray gnatcatcher, which resembles a miniature mockingbird, feeds almost entirely on insects, which it pursues actively through the foliage of tall trees. Its nest, an exquisitely made cup of plant fibers and down decorated on the outside with bits of lichen, is built between 4 and 70 feet above the ground.

Golden-crowned kinglet

Golden-crowned kinglets nest in spruce and fir forests in the far north and on high mountains and are common winter birds in most of the United States and southern Canada. In winter they are social birds, moving in small flocks through pines and other evergreens, gleaning small hibernating insects from the foliage. Because of their small size and dull coloration, they are often difficult to see, but their presence is revealed by their call, a high-pitched, two-noted lisp.

Ruby-crowned kinglet

The ruby-crowned kinglet lacks the facial stripes of its small relative, the golden-crowned kinglet, and its "crown," a tuft of erectile red feathers on top of the head of the male, is only seen when the bird is excited. Ruby-crowns usually spend the winter in the southern United States and are rather scarce in the north at this season. They are also less partial to conifers and can just as easily be found in deciduous thickets.

Arctic warbler

The arctic warbler is the only North American member of a large group of Old World songbirds known as "leaf-warblers," more closely related to thrushes than to the American wood warblers. It is a summer visitor to western Alaska, where it nests on the ground in thickets of willow or birch.

Arctic warbler

Blue-gray gnatcatcher

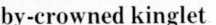
uby-crowned kinglet

Golden-crowned kinglet

WAXWING FAMILY

Bohemian waxwing
Bohemian waxwings are intensely social birds, with many of the same habits as the smaller cedar waxwings. They are found mainly in the cool evergreen forests of western Canada and Alaska, as well as in Eurasia, but occasionally flocks appear in the northern United States. Sometimes a bohemian waxwing becomes separated from a flock of its own species and takes up with a band of cedar waxwings; such stray individuals may travel as far south as the Gulf coast.

Cedar waxwing
Cedar waxwings are fruit eaters, and many of their habits are influenced by this fact. Flocks travel widely in search of fruiting shrubs or trees and often arrive suddenly in an area to exploit a crop of berries, disappearing again when the supply is exhausted. They nest late in the season, when a good supply of fruit assures sufficient food for their young, although like many fruit-eating birds they also eat insects during the breeding season to obtain additional protein.

WEAVERBIRD FAMILY

Eurasian tree sparrow
In April 1870, a few pairs of Eurasian tree sparrows, sent from Germany, were set free in a park in St. Louis. Since then the species has spread to nearby parts of Missouri and Illinois. It nests mainly in suburban areas and in the countryside around towns, leaving the urban habitat to the more aggressive house sparrow.

House sparrow
First introduced into North America from Europe in the 1850s, the house sparrow spread so rapidly that by the beginning of the 20th century it had occupied the entire United States, much of Canada, and a large portion of Mexico. It is also established in parts of South America, Africa, Australia, and New Zealand, and on many oceanic islands. It is now the most widespread free-living songbird in the world.

Cedar waxwing

Bohemian waxwing

Eurasian tree sparrow

Bohemian waxwing

House sparrow

WOODPECKER FAMILY

Common (gilded) flicker
*The gilded flicker is a permanent resident
in the deserts of the southwestern states. It
is somewhat isolated from the other forms
of the species.*

Common (red-shafted) flicker
*In most of the West, the breeding form of
the flicker is the red-shafted.*

Common (yellow-shafted) flicker
*The yellow-shafted flicker is found in
eastern North America, where it feeds both
in trees and on the ground.*

Williamson's sapsucker
*In most woodpeckers the sexes look alike
or nearly so, but they are so different in
Williamson's sapsucker that they were
once thought to be 2 species.*

Yellow-bellied sapsucker
*In its various forms, this is the most
widespread sapsucker. They drill small
holes in the bark of trees and feed on the
oozing sap and the insects attracted to it.*

Yellow-bellied (red-naped) sapsucker
*In the forests of the Rocky Mountains and
the smaller ranges in the Great Basin,
this is the representative of the more
widespread yellow-bellied sapsucker.*

Acorn woodpecker
*Acorn woodpeckers are gregarious birds,
often roosting in groups of up to a dozen
in a single tree cavity. They store acorns
in tree trunks and fence posts.*

Arizona woodpecker
*Although the Arizona woodpecker is a
typical bird of the oak forests of southern
Arizona and New Mexico, it usually nests
in some other species, such as the walnut.*

Black-backed three-toed woodpecker
*One of our most northerly woodpeckers,
this species occurs in the coniferous
forests of Alaska and Canada, and south
in the western mountains to California.*

Downy woodpecker
*This is the smallest member of its family
in most of North America.*

Gila woodpecker
*It often digs its nest cavities in tall
saguaro in its Southwest desert habitat.
These holes last for years.*

Golden-fronted woodpecker
*In river-bottom woodlands and mesquite
thickets from Oklahoma and Texas to
central Mexico, the golden-fronted
woodpecker is a common nesting bird.*

Hairy woodpecker
*This familiar bird is common from
Alaska to Panama, nesting in forests.*

Ladder-backed woodpecker
*The small size of this desert woodpecker
enables it to nest in places where the other
two woodpeckers in its habitat cannot.*

Common (Yellow-shafted) flicker

Common (Red-shafted) flicker

Yellow-bellied (Red-naped) sapsucker

Acorn woodpecker

Gila woodpecker

Golden-fronted woodpecker

Common (Gilded) flicker

Williamson's sapsucker

Yellow-bellied sapsucker

Arizona woodpecker

Black-backed three-toed woodpecker

Downy woodpecker

Hairy woodpecker

Ladder-backed woodpecker

Ladder-backed woodpecker, female

Lewis' woodpecker
Named for the explorer Meriwether Lewis, this large woodpecker inhabits open mountain forests and parkland in the western United States and adjacent parts of Canada. In addition to feeding in the usual manner of woodpeckers, it also catches insects on the wing like a flycatcher.

Northern three-toed woodpecker
Like the black-backed three-toed woodpecker, this species lives in bogs and burned-over areas in the cold Canadian taiga, but while the black-backed is confined to North America, the northern also breeds in Eurasia. It is a more sedentary bird than its relative, hardly ever wandering southward from its breeding grounds during the winter.

Nuttall's woodpecker
This relative of the ladder-backed woodpecker lives in wooded canyons and chaparral from southern Oregon to Baja California. It is an agile bird, often alighting on the underside of a branch and moving about with the ease of a nuthatch.

Pileated woodpecker
Except for the ivory-bill, which is probably extinct, the pileated is our largest woodpecker. It is a shy bird that became scarce when the forests were cleared, but it has increased again where fields have reverted to woodland. Even in mature forest it requires a large feeding territory, where it usually remains all year. In winter a favorite food is hibernating carpenter ants, which the birds dig out of dead stumps.

Red-bellied woodpecker
The red-bellied woodpecker is a common bird in forests in the southeastern United States. In places where it inhabits the same woodlands as the red-headed woodpecker, the preferred nesting sites of the two species differ, the red-headed nesting in dead limbs usually well above the canopy of foliage, the red-bellied in tree trunks beneath the canopy.

Pileated woodpecker

ed-bellied woodpecker

Northern three-toed woodpecker

Nuttall's woodpecker

Lewis' woodpecker

Red-cockaded woodpecker
The red-cockaded woodpecker nests in widely scattered, loose colonies in the pinelands of the southeastern states. Because of logging and other disturbances to its habitat, it is now decreasing throughout its range. The bird's "cockade," a tuft of red feathers on the side of its head, is usually covered by the black feathers of the crown and is seldom seen in the field.

Red-headed woodpecker
The red-headed woodpecker is a common bird in open forest and in fields with scattered trees, especially in the Midwest. Although rather shy, it is usually easy to see because it spends much time perched on the tips of dead branches, calling loudly.

White-headed woodpecker
Despite its bold pattern, the white-headed woodpecker can be very difficult to find, even where it is common in the mountain pine forests of the Far West. It is usually silent and manages to stay out of sight by slipping behind the trunk of a tree. When in plain view, the white head breaks up its outline and makes it all but invisible as long as it remains motionless.

White-headed woodpecker, male and immature female

Red-headed woodpecker

White-headed woodpecker, female

Red-headed woodpecker

Red-cockaded woodpecker

WREN FAMILY

Bewick's wren
Bewick's wren nests in most of the western United States and eastward to the Appalachians. Over this vast range, its song varies a great deal; in some areas, the song is almost indistinguishable from that of a song sparrow. Wherever Bewick's wren and the house wren occur together, the two compete for nesting sites, with Bewick's usually the loser. The absence of the species from the Atlantic seaboard may be due to competition with the house wren.

Brown-throated wren
The brown-throated wren is a Mexican bird that nests in a few mountain ranges in southern Arizona, where it skulks in the dense undergrowth of the trees. A secretive bird, it was unknown in the United States until 1945. Although it is currently listed as a distinct species, its status is uncertain; many authorities consider it no more than a local form of the house wren.

Cactus wren
The dry, churring song of the cactus wren is a characteristic sound in the deserts of the southwestern United States and northern Mexico. Our largest wren, it often builds its domed nest in a dense, heavily armed cholla cactus, where its eggs and young are nearly immune from predators. Cholla cacti have very sharp, barbed spines that penetrate human skin and even shoe leather at the slightest touch. How cactus wrens can hop around in one of these plants has never been satisfactorily explained.

Canyon wren
In brushy or wooded canyons from southern Canada to Mexico, a series of clear, silvery notes cascading down the scale and echoing off the rock walls is a sure sign that canyon wrens are present. The birds themselves are shy and often difficult to see as they move furtively through the underbrush in search of small insects, but the white breast can be conspicuous in dimly lit crevices and is an important part of the species' displays.

Carolina wren
The Carolina wren is our only member of a large group of tropical American wrens. It is a southern bird that seems to be very sensitive to cold weather. From time to time it gradually extends its range northward, colonizing parts of New England and southern Ontario, only to be exterminated in these newly won areas by the first hard winter.

Cactus wren

Brown-throated wren

Bewick's wren

Carolina wren

Canyon wren

House wren
Our most familiar and widespread wren, the house wren breeds from southern Canada southward into Mexico. Despite their size, house wrens are very aggressive and strongly territorial. Where populations are dense and competition for nesting sites is keen, as is often the case in residential areas with many birdhouses, the wrens enter their neighbors' nests and pierce the eggs. Pairs return year after year to the same site and raise 2 or 3 broods a season.

Long-billed marsh wren
Long-billed marsh wrens inhabit dense reedbeds and stands of cattails or bulrushes. There the males sing their trilling gurgling song, which has been likened to the sound of a sewing machine, and build many globular nests with an entrance in the side. Some males have more than one mate, each female occupying a small territory that is part of a larger one controlled by the male.

Rock wren
The rock wren prefers drier and more barren slopes than does its close ally the canyon wren. Its gray-brown color matches its habitat, and the birds are adept at creeping among the rocks, but singing males usually mount to the top of a boulder, where they are easy to see. The nest is carefully concealed in a crevice among the rocks, but its presence is often revealed by a curious path of small pebbles, leading up to the rim.

Short-billed marsh wren
This species might more aptly be called the "sedge wren," since it inhabits wet meadows and sedges at the upper borders of marshes, rather than true marshes with reeds and cattails. It is shy, and its distribution is patchy, so that it is probably the hardest of our wrens to find. Even in places where short-billed marsh wrens are known to breed, it is often difficult to find an occupied nest, because each male builds numerous dummy nests in its territory, only one of which will finally be chosen by the female.

Winter wren
In North America, where there are many species of wrens, the winter wren nests only in the coniferous forests of Canada and the northern United States; but in Eurasia, where no other wrens occur, it is much more widespread and is known simply as "the wren." These birds spend most of their time out of sight, creeping about in dense brush or among the roots of fallen trees, but when they are excited or curious, they often fly up to an exposed perch, bobbing nervously up and down and giving a sharp, 2-noted alarm call.

Rock wren

Short-billed marsh wren

Long-billed marsh wren

Winter wren

House wren

House wren, eggs

House wren, nestlings

Wrentit

WRENTIT FAMILY

Wrentit

Wrentits are birds of the brushy chaparral along the Pacific coast from Oregon to Baja California. Although their song is loud and easily recognized, and can be heard on the soundtracks of many movies made in southern California, the birds are very elusive, and one can spend hours in their dense habitat without even a glimpse. Wrentits are entirely sedentary; pairs remain mated for life and defend a single territory the year round.

south to s. Baja Calif. and through C. America to Costa Rica; winters from n. Calif. east to s. Utah, south to Ariz., N.M., s. Tex., and south, occasionally in nw. U.S. and B.C., Minn., Iowa, e. Kans., c. Okla., Ill., and Mich.

Saltwater marsh wren. *See* Long-billed marsh wren.

Sedge wren. A proposed new name for the short-billed marsh wren. *See* Short-billed marsh wren.

Semidi wren. *See* Winter wren.

Short-billed marsh wren, *Cistothorus platensis* (sis-TOTH-oh-rus plah-TEN-sis); genus name: *see* Long-billed marsh wren; species name: Lat., for Río de la Plata at Buenos Aires, Argentina, type locality, or where first specimen, or specimens, of this bird, previously unknown to science, collected. (Color ill., page 1,044.) E. U.S. and s. Canada but scarce and local; in sedge meadows; one of the smaller N. American songbirds; 4–4½ in. long; wingspread 5¼–6 in.; very small brown wren with short, slim bill, *streaked crown* and back; obscure buffy line over eyes; short, cocked tail; migratory; usually the wren of freshwater meadows where grasses and sedges grow with small scattered shrubs; little water or ground merely damp; sometimes, perhaps rarely, among cattails; also lives in sedge marshes among spruce flats, balsam-tamarack bogs at 1,500 ft. in w. Adirondacks of N.Y. (Terres, 1941), sometimes about margins of sphagnum bogs in Canada, higher parts of marshes above cattails in Mich., often only one or two pairs in a marsh, sometimes in colonies in favored marshes; usually hides, difficult to see; at times male perches, on small bush in or near marsh or top of sedge, to sing (sometimes at night) chattering trill, resembling sound of two sticks struck rapidly together: *chap—chap—chap-chap,chap, chap p-p-r-r-r.*

Feeding Habits: Eats bugs, weevils, beetles, moths, caterpillars, ants, grasshoppers, crickets, mosquitoes, also spiders.
Nest: Well-hidden ball of woven dry and green grasses and sedges, dry weed stems, with opening on side; lined with cattail down, catkins, fur, and feathers; built in sedges and grasses, close to ground, about 1–2 ft. above mud or shallow water; also builds "dummy" nests (*see* Dummy Nest) (Bent, 1948).
Eggs: May–July; 4–8, usually 6–7, white.
Incubation: By female, 12–14 days; young leave nest 12–14 days after hatching (Walkinshaw, 1935); two broods a season.
Other Names: Freshwater marsh wren; grass wren; meadow wren.
Weights: In Kans., killed at TV tower, three, rather fat, 8.1–8.2 gr. (Tordoff and Mengel, 1956), or about ⅓ oz.
Range: Nests from se. Sask., across s. Canada to s. Me., e. N.B. and from Me. south to Ark., W.Va., and Va., and from Mexico southward; winters from s. Tex., lower Mississippi Valley and Gulf coast, coastal Md., south to s. Fla. and Mexico.

Short-tailed wren. *See* House wren and Winter wren.

Sooty wren. *See* Bewick's wren.

Spruce wren. *See* Winter wren.

Stump wren. *See* House wren.

Tanaga wren. *See* Winter wren.

Tule wren. *See* Long-billed marsh wren.

Wayne's marsh wren. *See* Long-billed marsh wren.

White-throated wren. *See* Cañon wren.

Willow wren. An incorrect name for the willow warbler of the Warbler—Old World Warbler Family.

Winter wren, *Troglodytes troglodytes* (troglow-DIE-teez); genus and species names: *see* family introduction; *winter,* possibly from fact that a few hardy ones sometimes winter in n. U.S. and even in s. Ont., Canada; most, however, like other wrens, migrate southward in fall. (Color ill., page 1,044.) In summer, nests north to Alaska; also in Eurasia; one of smallest of N. American songbirds; 4–4½ in. long; wingspread 5½–6½ in.; smaller and darker than house wren; dark brown above and below with heavier, darker barring of tail, flanks, and under rear of body than house wren; also, its cocked tail usually much shorter; has habit of almost continuously bobbing its head; narrow brown stripe over eyes; summers in cool northern coniferous forests and swamps of n. U.S. and Canada with little sunshine and rotting stumps and fallen tree trunks thickly covered with mosses; also in mountain environment in s. Appalachians and treeless Aleutian Is. and the Pribilofs of Alaska; in dense spruce, fir, and redwood forests of Pacific coast and in Rockies; in Sierra Nevadas to 11,000 ft. (Bent, 1948); in spring migration drifts along from bush to bush, through gullies, creeps mouselike about woodpiles and brush heaps, edges of swamps, old stone walls; is on nesting grounds in s. Canada by early Apr.; male sings, from near ground, loud, rich, full song (also a soft whisper song), rising and falling, high-pitched notes in fine silver thread of music lasting about 7 seconds, contains 108–113 separate notes (Bent, 1948); call is sharp *tick* repeated, a sharp *chirr,* etc.; some are tame and come into summer camps for bread crumbs.

Feeding Habits: Eats almost entirely insects, in forests mostly bark beetles and weevils, round-headed wood borers, leaf beetles, aphids, lace bugs, moths of spruce budworm, ants, sawflies, caterpillars, also spiders; reported to eat berries of red cedar.
Nest: In cavity in upturned roots of fallen tree, under rotted stumps or roots, under stream banks, sometimes under curled bark of tree, in unoccupied log cabin; nest is bulky mass of twigs, mosses, grasses, rootlets, lined with hairs of deer, feathers of birds; male builds at least 1–4 "dummy" nests.

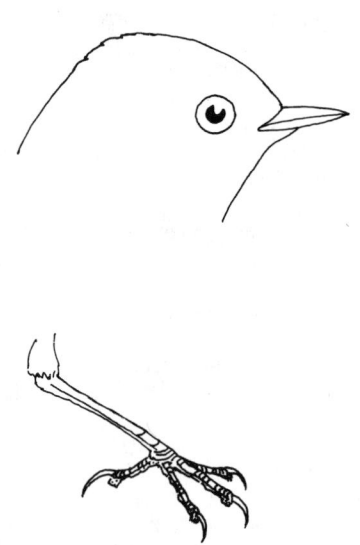

WRENTIT FAMILY

Eggs: Mar.–July; 4–7, commonly 5–6, white, dotted with browns.

Incubation: 14–16 days; young first fly about 19 days after hatching.

Other Names: Alaska wren; Aleutian wren; Kiska wren; Kodiak wren; mouse wren; Semidi wren; short-tailed wren; spruce wren; Stevenson's wren; Tanaga wren; Unalaska wren; western wren.

Accidents: Some find way into closed camp buildings in woods through small hole, die of starvation when unable to find way out; some may roost in a bird box (31 roosted in fall in bird box near Chacu, Wash.), and in winter in North find shelter in barns and other outbuildings.

Age: One, banded, reported from Holland, lived to 5 years, 9 months (Clapp, 1976).

Range: Nests from s. Alaska south to s.-c. Mack., c. Sask., east to Newfoundland, south to c. Calif., c. Idaho, Great Lakes region, to n. Ga.; winters largely in breeding range but at lower altitudes in mountains and from southern part of breeding range to s. Calif. Ariz., east to the Gulf coast and s. Fla.; also nests in n. Europe, Asia, south to Formosa, Korea, and s. Japan.

Wood wren. *See* House wren and Winter wren.

Worthington's marsh wren. *See* Long-billed marsh wren.

WRENTIT FAMILY

Chamaeidae (kah-ME-ih-dee); from Gr. *chamai,* on the ground, dwarf (Jaeger, 1955). Includes only 1 species and is the only family of birds that is solely in N. America; however, some authorities in classification of birds have placed the wrentit of America in the Babbler Family (Timaliidae) found mostly in Europe, Africa, Asia, and Australia (Van Tyne and Berger, 1976); they believe that the wrentit, isolated in the scrublands west of the Rocky Mtns., is the only member of the Babbler Family that long ago reached the New World. It shows no close affinities to any other of the American songbirds (Austin, 1961). *See* discussion under Head-Scratching.

To sustain an ill or injured wrentit, offer it grapes, cherries, mockingbird food, boiled eggs, mealworms, ground meat, chopped greens, and small pieces of bread (Walker, 1942).

Wrentit, *Chamaea fasciata* (kah-ME-ah fass-ih-AY-tah); genus name: *see* family introduction; species name: Lat., banded, or striped, apparently in reference either to the stripes, or streaks, on its breast, or as Coues (1882) suggests, to the indistinct bands across the tail feathers. (Color ill., page 1,-046.) 6–6½ in. long; sexes outwardly alike; gray-brown upperparts, streaked breast and lower parts are cinnamon brown; eyes white; long, rounded tail is cocked up at angle, hops rapidly from twig to twig like a wren; makes short, weak flights from bush to bush, tail pumping; not migratory; lives mostly in windswept brushland of Pacific coast in northern part of range, but in Calif. is everywhere west of Sierras, in extensive chaparral belt or in brushy margins of forests and streams, also in suburban gardens, parks; seldom seen, for rarely leaves dense bushes (Erickson, M. M., 1948); mated for life of either member of pair, sedentary, adults constantly together, spend most of lives on home territory of about 2½ acres of brushland; male sings, usually while hidden, throughout year, a series of loud, ringing whistles on same pitch and running together at end in trill, *pit-pit-pit-pit-tr-r-r-r-r-r;* female sings similar notes but without trill; both sexes utter notes *peeka, peeka, peeka;* besides foraging together, and preening each other's feathers, they roost together, leaning against each other on limb near crown of bush with feathers interlaced and inner legs drawn up, appearing as one ball of feathers (Erickson, M. M., 1948).

Feeding Habits: Hops about in shrubbery gleaning bark surfaces, rarely goes to ground, eats ants, wasps, beetles, caterpillars, bugs, flies, spiders, also elderberries, snowberries, toyon berries, etc.; will come to feeding stations for bread crumbs; in captivity eats bananas, cottage cheese, lettuce, etc.

Nest: Built by both sexes, in twigs of bush or small tree, 1–15 ft. up; compact cup of coarse bark, plant fibers, grasses, bound with spider's silk.

Eggs: 3–5, usually 4, pale green-blue.

Incubation: Mostly by female, 15–16 days; young leave nest 15–16 days after hatching.

Other Name: Gambel's wren-tit.

Age: Banded ones, Calif., 3–8½ years old; one, banded near Berkeley, at least 10 years old (Sumner, E. L., 1934).

Host to Cowbirds: Five records, Calif.

Range: From w. Ore. to n. Baja Calif.

WRIGHT

CHARLES (1811–85). Born Wethersfield, Conn.; self-taught botanist and a field collector of plants and some birds; collected extensively in sw. U.S., especially in N.M. and Ariz.; went to Tex. in 1837; his name is inseparably connected with the botany of Tex.; he collected plants there for Asa Gray for 8 years and remained in Tex. until 1852 (Geiser, 1948); he worked there through the Mexican War and on the Boundary Survey Commission of the U.S. as a botanist and surveyor; near El Paso he collected the bird which Spencer F. Baird in 1858 named in his honor, *Empidonax wrightii,* the gray flycatcher (Palmer, 1928).

WRYNECK

(RYE-neck). *See* in Woodpecker Family; *also* Piciformes; *see also* length of tongue under Tongue.

XANTHOCHROISM
See Colors of Feathers.

XANTUS
JOHN (1825–94). Born Csokonya, Hungary; for whom George Newbold Lawrence in 1860 named the Xantus' hummingbird, from a specimen collected by Xantus near Cape San Lucas, Baja Calif.; was one of the most energetic of the early collectors of birds in Calif. and Baja Calif. (Palmer, 1928). A murrelet Xantus named and described from one he got off the coast of Cape San Lucas also commemorates him in its English name, Xantus' murrelet. In 1850, Xantus came to the U.S.; he enlisted in the Army in 1855 as a hospital steward; while stationed at Ft. Riley, Kans. Terr., he became acquainted with Dr. William Alexander Hammond, the future Surgeon General, who got Xantus an appointment as an Acting Assistant Surgeon, U.S. Army. For a while Xantus assumed the name of Louis de Vesey, then L. X. de Vesey, then L. Xantus de Vesey; by 1859 he gave up his assumed name and signed his letters J. Xantus (Hume, 1942). It was in 1857–59, while serving at Ft. Tejon, Calif., that Xantus described a number of new species of birds, including Hammond's flycatcher, the spotted owl, and a vireo he named for John Cassin but later found to be a subspecies of the solitary vireo (see A.O.U. *Check-list*, 1957). For the details of this unusual man's life, see Hume (1942).

YELLOWBIRD
Another name for the American goldfinch in Finch Family and yellow warbler in Warbler—American Wood Warbler Family.

YELLOW-HAMMER
See Flicker, common (yellow-shafted), in Woodpecker Family.

YELLOWLEGS
See in Sandpiper Family.

YELLOW-NOSE
See Scoter, black, in Duck Family.

YELLOWSHANKS
See yellowlegs in Sandpiper Family.

YELLOWTHROAT
See in Warbler—American Wood Warbler Family.

YELPER
Another name for the American avocet and greater yellowlegs in Sandpiper Family, and a small race (cackling goose) of the Canada goose in Duck Family.

YOKE-TOED
See Zygodactyl.

YOLK
See Eggs and Egg-laying; Embryo and Its Development.

YOLK SAC
See Embryo and Its Development.

YOUNG AND THEIR CARE
Parents of young birds feed them and protect them from their time of hatching to their independence. In hatching, most young birds pip the eggs by using the egg tooth and hatching muscle and break out of the shell by struggling and kicking. *See* Hatching. The parents normally do not help but may lean attentively over the pipped eggs and pick gently at the shell or flick away tiny fragments. Young birds usually hatch in the morning, although some may be expected to hatch at any hour of the day or night (Skutch, 1952). Sometimes, even before the chicks hatch, the adult birds, in response to their peeps within the shell, may bring food to the nest and even offer it to the unhatched eggs.

Based on their development at the time of hatching, birds are said to be either *altricial* or *precocial* (*see* details under Altricial). At hatching, the helpless altricial young, incapable of leaving the nest and dependent on the parents for food, are called *nestlings;* the precocial young are called *chicks* or *downy young.* In general, although there are exceptions (for example, the ground-nesting sparrows, larks, etc.), most altricials are hatched in nests in trees or in shrubbery, and precocials in nests on the ground.

The young of the so-called precocial species (such as grebes, ducks, geese, rails, shorebirds, quail, pheasants, grouse, and chickens) are fully covered with down at hatching, with their eyes open, and are able to run about (or swim) shortly after hatching, some within an hour. The parents of most precocials usually leave the eggshells behind in the nest, and the young follow their parents away from the nest after hatching. Some precocials, while attended by their parents, immediately find their own food (for example, newly hatched ducks and shorebirds); others (young quail and young chickens) follow the parents, which show them food; others (grebes and rails) follow their parents and are fed by them (Nice, 1962a).

The young of most altricial species (for example, flycatchers, songbirds [Oscines], cuckoos, pigeons, kingfishers, woodpeckers, swifts, and hummingbirds) are helpless when hatched, their eyes are closed, and they have only a scant covering of hairlike down on the crown and back or may be naked; however, some of the so-called *semi-altricial* species (Nice, 1962a) are downy at hatching (for example, the young of herons, bitterns, ibises, vultures, hawks, owls, etc., of which the herons and hawks hatch with their eyes open; the owls with their eyes closed).

After the altricials hatch, the parent birds (except a few species, which leave the shells in the nest) either eat the eggshells or pick them up in the bill, fly off, and drop them some distance from the nest. This may prevent the betrayal of the nest location to a potential predator and possible injury to the nestlings from the shells' sharp edges (Armstrong, 1964b).

BROODING OF THE YOUNG. Adults *incubate* the eggs but *brood* the young by day or night and often in cool or rainy weather, and especially during the first few days after the young hatch. Birds that build open nests, such as the

American robin and wood thrush, usually brood nestlings of all ages during heavy rainstorms, and they may stand or crouch over them in the nest to shield them from the sun in hot weather (Berger, 1961). Mourning doves brood their young almost constantly and nearly to the time they leave the nest, and some penguins are such avid brooders that they may fight for the privilege of mothering the chicks (Welty, 1962). *See* other details under Brooding.

AGE WHEN SOME BIRDS' EYES OPEN. The eyes of nestling song sparrows are partly open 5 days after hatching and completely open at 6 days (Nice, 1943); the eyes of young horned larks open when 3½ days old (Verbeek, 1967); in the eastern bluebird, they begin to open at 4 days after hatching (Smith, 1937b); and in the short-eared owl, 8–12 days after hatching. A captive great horned owl opened its eyes and showed fear reactions at 8 days old (Nice, 1962a).

AGE OF ATTAINING TEMPERATURE CONTROL. Young of altricial species, such as American robins and other songbirds (passerines), which are not covered with down at hatching, are essentially "cold-blooded," in that their body temperatures may fluctuate with the changing temperature around them. This inability to control the body temperature by young birds is compensated for by the brooding and warming of them by the parents.

As they develop, young birds achieve temperature control, or "warm-bloodedness," a relatively uniform body temperature (called *homiothermy*), through an increase in their nervous and hormonal control as they grow, heat production from the food they eat (*see* Metabolism), and the growth of down or feathers that cover the bird's body and insulate it. Temperature control is fairly well developed in the ovenbird at 3½ days after hatching; in house wrens, at 6 days; in song sparrows, about 7 days after hatching; and is well established in chickadees at 9 days. In young phoebes and barn swallows, it is established at 9 or 10 days after hatching (Nice, 1943), and in chipping and field sparrows, when 7 days old (Dawson and Evans, 1957).

Temperature control in the downy young of precocial species, such as quail and chickens, starts earlier than in altricial species—and in some precocials such as the chicks of bobwhite quail, even before hatching (Welty, 1962). The female (hen) compensates for this by squatting and allowing the chicks to gather under the shelter of her wings and body on cool days or in rainy weather. The young of the killdeer, a precocial species, show a rapid increase in their temperature control for the first 10 days of their lives, when the adults still brood them, but do not attain a temperature control approaching that of the adults until 27 days after hatching (Berger, 1961).

OTHER "FIRSTS." The first preening attempts of young altricial birds (song sparrows and the American redstart, for example) begin at about 5 days after hatching before there are any feathers to preen, but preening is well established at 8 days in the song sparrow and at 11 days in the American redstart (Nice, 1943), just before, or about the time, these young birds can fly. *See* Preening. Young altricial birds do not begin to show crouching and "freezing" fear reactions to strange sounds or enemies at or near the nest until they are about ready to fly (*see* discussion of this under Fear). Captive song sparrows, 13, 14, and 17 days after hatching, dipped the bill into water and drank (Nice, 1943), which in the wild would be at a time when the young fledged sparrows were out of the nest and able to go to sources of water on their own.

FEEDING THE YOUNG. Most precocials (young ducks and quail, for example) soon after hatching usually follow one of the parents away from the nest and, instead of being fed, are led by the adults to a suitable place where they find food for themselves. However, the parents of *semi-precocial* downy young (terns and gulls, for example, which are able to walk but stay at the nest) bring food to the chicks in the nesting colony. On the other hand, the naked newly hatched nestlings of the altricial species (such as young thrushes and sparrows), with their eyes closed at hatching, are so weak they can barely hold up their heads. Yet, within a few minutes after hatching, a young robin or a wood thrush not only can lift up its head but can call (weakly) and "gape" with widely opened mouth in a begging display before either of its parents as they alight on the edge of the nest with food in the bill. *See* Directive Marks.

KINDS OF FOOD. Parent songbirds, whether they themselves prefer fruits and seeds (a vegetable diet), feed the young an animal diet rich in proteins—for example, insects and other small invertebrates. Adult house sparrows, which themselves eat about 96% vegetable matter (grain, seeds, etc.), feed their nestlings about 70% animal matter (Kalmbach, 1940), almost all of it insects, especially grasshoppers and beetles (Judd, 1901). Cardinals, which as adults prefer weed seeds, corn, wheat, and other grain, and wild fruit, feed their nestlings up to 95% insects—cicadas, grasshoppers, caterpillars, and beetles (McAtee, 1908). In Mich., Van Tyne (1951) reported an adult male cardinal that on the way to its nest to feed its young a billful of small green "worms" (caterpillars), stopped at a feeding tray, put down the caterpillars, ate a few sunflower seeds, and then picked up the caterpillars and flew on to its nest to feed them to its young. Many adult birds that feed mainly on insects also feed them to their young, and most adults, as the young grow older, feed them more and more the kinds of foods that the adults themselves eat. From hatching, fish-eating birds (such as pelicans, ospreys, and kingfishers) feed their young fishes; reptile-eating birds (many of the eagles, kites, and hawks) feed their young reptiles; and both seed-eating and fruit-eating birds give seeds and much fruit to their young. *See* Insects and Birds; Food and Feeding Habits.

BRINGING WATER TO THE YOUNG. Ordinarily, the food that most parents feed young birds in the nest contains all the moisture they need. However, great cormorants in hot weather carry water in the gular pouch and crop to the nest and pour a stream of water over the chicks and into their opened bills (Palmer, 1962), and parents of the common raven, both of which feed the young, carry water on hot days in the throat and bill and empty it into the throats of the young (Hauri, 1956; Goodwin, 1976).

One of the most remarkable examples of birds carrying water to the young is that of the Old World sandgrouse. These are superficially grouselike birds of the arid open country of e. and s. Eurasia and Africa, which stay together in flocks, usually fly relatively little, and spend all day on the ground feeding on seeds and vegetable shoots (Gilliard, 1958). They fly rapidly with their long pointed wings up to 50 mi. or more to and from special watering holes (Maclean, 1968). The chicks leave the nest soon after hatching and eat largely dry seeds. To provide moisture, until the young are able to fly with the flock, the male brings them water from long distances away from the nesting place. The male has specially modified abdominal feathers, which have a much greater capacity to hold water than the rest of his plumage; the male uses these to carry water to the chicks. In the morning, he flies to a water hole to drink and to soak up water in his belly feathers. On his return flight to the chicks, the male Namaqua sandgrouse, *Pteroctes namaqua*, of the Kalahari Desert, South Africa, may fly 15–20 mi. and lose some of the moisture to the dry desert air in flight, but retains enough for the needs of his chicks. On his arrival they come out of their hiding places under the sparse desert shrubs and crowd about him, behaving "like a litter of puppies," to strip the water from his wet feathers with their bills. The chicks cannot fly very well until they are about 6 weeks old, and probably do not fly to water holes to drink until they are about 2 months old. See details in Cade and Maclean (1967); Maclean (1968).

HOW THE ADULTS FEED THE YOUNG. Many adult birds (including cuckoos, woodpeckers, songbirds, and others) feed their nestlings directly from the bill. After the adults appropriately manipulate and crush the food in the bill, they thrust it deep into the nestling's throat; however, many adults swallow the food first, then regurgitate it at the nest. Cedar waxwings, for example, feed their young wild cherries, blueberries, and insects (mostly grasshoppers) and almost always regurgitate it, softened and partially digested, into the mouths of the young ones at the nest (Herrick, 1901). Regurgitation allows the adult to carry more food each time to the young and helps the young digest the food more easily.

All pigeons and doves regurgitate "pigeon's milk" for the young during its first few days of life, which the small squab, helpless and with eyes not open, gets by sticking its bill into the throats of the adult birds. *See* details of this and the production of crop milk under Crop. Seed-eating goldfinches, siskins, and crossbills feed softened and regurgitated seeds to their young, and some woodpeckers feed the young regurgitated food. Adult albatrosses and storm-petrels feed their young a regurgitated semi-liquid oily food (see Fisher and Lockley, 1954), and a young spoonbill or tube-nosed swimmer (albatross, shearwater, petrel, and relatives) nibbles at the adult's bill and then inserts its bill (crosswise) between the adult's mandibles as the latter opens it to regurgitate food for its chick. The American flamingo feeds its chick a regurgitated liquid, a drop at a time, into the young bird's opened bill in response to the newly hatched chick's head-bobbing and faint "puppylike barking" (Allen, 1956a). The female hummingbird, which raises the young, feeds them in the nest by thrusting her long, needlelike bill deep into their throats. Then she pumps regurgitated food—nectar, tiny insects, and spiders—into the young bird's gullet. *See* Regurgitation.

Herons, egrets, and bitterns also regurgitate food for their nestlings, at first a predigested liquid soup, later whole, or partly digested, fishes, frogs, etc. (see in Skutch, 1976). Most gulls regurgitate food on the ground in front of the chick, which then picks it up; storks onto the nest rim and the young help themselves. Adult pelicans open their huge mouths to let the young reach deep into the large gular pouch for the fishes and shrimps the adults have caught for them. A cormorant seems almost to swallow the head of a young one to allow it to take food from the gullet.

Predatory birds (eagles, hawks, and owls) carry food to the nest, and while holding the rabbit, rodent, snake, etc., under the feet, with the bill tear off pieces of a size the young can swallow and feed it to them. Later, when the young grow larger, after the adults deliver prey to the nest, the young seize it, tear off pieces, and feed themselves.

Some adult birds even feed young not their own or adopt other species, and the young of first broods of some birds often help to feed the second brood. *See* Helpers among Birds; Foster Parents. Also, many songbirds hatch the eggs of the cowbirds (social parasites) and raise the young as though they were their own. *See* Brood Parasitism.

HOW MUCH DO YOUNG BIRDS EAT? The amount of food brought to nestlings by the adults is astonishing to anyone seeing it for the first time. Allen (1961) cites an experiment with a young American robin which, on the day it was to leave the nest, was fed all the earthworms it could eat. It ate 14 ft. of earthworms on that day. Experiments in feeding young crows proved that they need at least half their own weight in food each day just to keep alive, and could eat up to their full weight in food each day.

Nestling passerines do not eat much at a time but their digestion is so rapid that their parents must feed them almost continuously, from early morning until evening. However, they do not require as much food when they are newly hatched as when they are ready to leave the nest. Lack (1954) reported that H. N. Kluijver, in his studies of the food of nestling starlings in Europe, found that each received from its parents up to 6/7 of its weight in food per day during the early part of its nestling period. Nestling belted kingfishers will eat 1–1¾ times their weight in fish daily (White, 1939). *See also*

YOUNG AND THEIR CARE
All members of the pigeon family regurgitate "pigeon milk" during the first few days of their nestlings' life. This nutritive fluid is secreted by the lining of the bird's crop.

A wood thrush feeds its young by thrusting crushed protein-rich food directly into the nestlings' gaping mouths. Like other songbirds, thrushes bring food to the nest throughout the day, but most actively in the morning.

the amounts of food eaten by adults under Food and Feeding Habits.

FREQUENCY OF FEEDING. Jones (1913) watched a pair of house wrens feeding their young for a period of 65 hours in which the adults visited the young with food 667 times (about once every 6 minutes); 560 visits by the male; 107 by the female. Perhaps a record number of feeding visits by an individual house wren in one day was at Macomb, Ill., by a lone male that had lost his mate (presumably killed). On June 26, when the nestlings were 12 days old, he visited the nest 1,217 times to feed the young, between 4:15 A.M. and 8:00 P.M., an average of one visit every 47 seconds.

According to Skutch (1976), the rate at which songbirds carry food in the bill to the nestlings varies enormously from species to species, but 4–12 meals fed per nestling per hour is the average feeding rate for a wide variety of small birds.

Adult songbirds feed their nestlings most actively early in the morning, when the young are hungriest after a night without food. When the nestlings are satisfied, the parent birds may relax somewhat and feed themselves. After the young have digested their early-morning meals, the parents begin to feed them again and may continue throughout the day. Sometimes the parents reach another peak of feeding of the young late in the day; some continue to feed the nestlings during a light shower, but may slow down their rate of feeding the young during a heavy downpour (Skutch, 1976).

Birds do not feed their young in rotation, as one might expect, but usually feed the hungriest one first. As a rule, the young with the highest raised opened mouth gets the meal, but when it is satisfied or does not swallow the food, the parent picks it out of the nestling's throat and may give it to the next one, and so on, until all have been fed. However, the smallest or weakest nestling may not get enough food, and if it does not, dies in the nest.

According to Allen (1961), some young hawks are fed by their parents about once an hour; hummingbirds about once every 20 minutes; and a pair of chickadees watched by Allen fed their young once every minute. A pair of rose-breasted grosbeaks fed their nestlings 426 times in 11 hours, or an average of 38 times an hour.

SANITATION—KEEPING THE NEST CLEAN. Parents of songbirds not only carry away the eggshells of newly hatched young but also dispose of their excrement. The feces when expelled by the nestlings are enclosed in a tough mucous membrane, called a fecal sac. It is small, whitish, and black-tipped, and most adult songbirds (and woodpeckers), when they visit the nest to feed the young, instinctively remove the fecal sacs and either eat them or carry them away as they leave the nest. Adult bluebirds usually eat the fecal sacs until about the 5th or 6th day of the nestling's life, when they begin to carry them away in the bill up to 20–50 yds. before dropping them while in flight.

Some bluebirds leave infertile eggs in the nest with the nestlings, but others carry them away; parent bluebirds, usually the female, will drag a dead nestling to the entrance hole of the nesting cavity, then fly off with it (Hartshorne, 1962). Lee (1970) watched a female purple martin carry a 10-day-old dead nestling in her bill 125 ft. from a compartment in a nest-box colony before dropping it.

In their zeal for keeping the nest clean of any foreign objects, as bird-banders know, the parents may seize the shiny bands on the legs of the newly banded nestlings and, in trying to rid the nest of them, throw out the young with the bands. Hervey Brackbill, a bird-bander, watched a red-eyed vireo whose nestlings he had just banded drag three of her young out of the nest; he put the young back in the nest, and by the next morning the female had gotten used to the bands and did not react to them. Parent song sparrows, horned larks, and, in England, a female chaffinch and a pair of European robins threw bands and young attached to the bands out of the nest.

Hawks and falcons will carry away eggshells and uneaten intestines and other parts of leftover prey from the nest in the early part of the nestling period of the young, and the young raptors themselves instinctively back up to the edge of the nest to defecate over the side.

LENGTH OF NESTLING PERIOD. According to Berger (1961), a bird is a nestling from the time it hatches until it leaves the nest (see Nestling); a fledgling, from the time it leaves the nest until it is independent of the parents' care. The nestling period in some birds is approximately the length of the incubation period: great crested flycatcher (12–18 days), horned lark (9–12 days), evening grosbeak (13–14 days). It may be shorter than the incubation period in others: dickcissel (7–9 days), field sparrow (7–8 days), song sparrow (10 days).

Some birds, especially hole nesters, have nestling periods longer than incubation periods: swifts, swallows, and woodpeckers; and the starling, which is incubated only about 12 days, is in the nest about 21 days and is independent of its parents 4 or 5 days later. However, many nestling songbirds leave the nest before they can fly—often they may be frightened out of the nest by the close approach of a human intruder—and hop about in bushes or trees, where they utter their "food calls," or location calls (see Language), and are fed and cared for by the parents for days or even weeks until they are finding their own food and gradually drift away. The purple martin has one of the longest nestling periods of any N. American passerine (songbird)—the young usually remain in the nest for 28 or up to 35 days (Berger, 1961).

To get some young birds that are ready for flight to leave the nest, the parents—exceptionally, according to Skutch (1976)—may withhold food from the young, and some parents may push or pull the young out of the nest. See discussion and examples in Skutch (1976) and in Welty (1975). Even when the parents do nothing to get the young to leave the nest, they seem to sense the imminence of the departure of the young by their increased restlessness. When a young one flies off for the first time, a parent may escort it in a "shielding" or protective flight, just above or below the flying young one, and fly with it until it reaches the safety of a perch in a tree or bush. See Skutch (1976). Few young birds, once they leave the nest, come back to it, with the exception of the young of certain woodpeckers, wrens, and swallows, which return to the nest to sleep, especially if the nest place is sheltered, as in a hole in a tree or a roofed-over (wren) nest.

DO YOUNG BIRDS "LEARN" TO FLY? To discover whether or not young birds need to learn to fly by exercising their wings before leaving the nest, a German scientist, J. Grohmann (1938), raised some young pigeons in narrow tubes that prevented them from moving their wings. At the same time he allowed another group of pigeons of the same age to be raised by the parents in a nest in the normal way; these young pigeons, as they grew, could exercise their wings by vigorously flapping them while they were still in the nest, as young hummingbirds, hawks, and eagles often do, an exercise called wing-fanning. When both groups of pigeons had developed to the age when their flying ability could be tested, Grohmann took the young birds and tossed them into the air. The young pigeons raised in the tubes flew away as strongly as those that had been unrestrained in the nest. Grohmann had proved that the behavior pattern of flight matures in a young bird at a steady rate, whether or not it can practice "flying" by fanning and exercising its wings. Apparently there are exceptions in the need for wing exercises among young birds. Young turkey vultures, confined in cages too small to permit wing motion, were unable to fly even when 3 months old (Welty, 1975).

Moreau (1940), in his studies of hornbills raised in captivity in roomy boxes, reported that they never exercised their wings but started to fly quite suddenly. In nature, they are raised in holes in trees in which there is no room for wing exercises. However, young birds must learn to alight, how to use the tail as a rudder, and how to use the wind in alighting and taking off, and must develop other skills in flying which they improve upon in nature by practice. See Hochbaum (1955).

DEFENSE OF THE YOUNG. Nestlings of altricial birds or the chicks of precocial species try to defend themselves against detection by enemies by crouching motionless in the nest or on the ground and remaining inconspicuous. Some parent birds vigorously defend their young, by threats or direct attacks against intruders, both man and predatory animals, or by attracting attention to themselves to allow the young to escape (see accounts under Distraction Display), and sometimes by moving the young to a safer place. See also Birds That Carry Their Eggs under Eggs and Egg-laying.

Blue jays, mockingbirds, brown thrashers, gray catbirds, bluebirds, and other birds will attack cats or dogs and even persons near the nest by dive-bombing them and may chase them away by the fury of their attacks. The parents of altricial nestlings defend them most vigorously just before the young leave the nest; the parents of precocial species, such as grouse, wild turkeys, ptarmigans, guineafowl, domestic fowl, etc., at the time the young hatch or shortly afterward.

Gulls can be vigorous in defense of their chicks. W. H. Behle had his hat knocked off several times by California gulls in a nesting colony, and a student, while banding some of these young gulls, was struck by an adult, receiving an 8-in. wound in his scalp. Arctic terns defend their nests with great vigor. T. Gilbert Pearson, onetime president of the National Association of Audubon Societies, was attacked by an adult arctic tern that pierced his scalp with its bill, and John Gillespie, while banding black skimmer chicks along the N.J. coast, was struck by an adult and suffered a bloody scalp wound.

Dixon (1927b) described how a male willow ptarmigan attacks mew gulls in the Canadian North when the gulls try to eat the eggs of the hen; and how a male guarding a female with her brood furiously attacked him when he tried to catch one of the chicks. It flew directly into his face, knocked his glasses to one side, and slapped his face with its beating wings. Dixon reported that a male willow ptarmigan attacked and routed a large grizzly bear that stumbled on the ptarmigan's nest.

Goshawks and peregrine falcons can be dangerous to anyone climbing to the nest, and have inflicted severe wounds and even knocked down persons standing near the nest tree or eyrie. Brown noddies (tropical terns) and sooty terns are fierce in defense of their young and will attack a human intruder, knock off his hat, and strike his bare head hard enough with the bill and feet to draw blood.

Incubating Virginia rails may be fearless in defending their nests; one leaped at the extended hand of observer Lawrence Walkinshaw and pecked it severely; another struck the lens of a camera set up near its nest; and parent king rails at hatching time have struck the human observer on the legs and chest.

BIRDS THAT CARRY THEIR YOUNG. Many birds have been reported carrying their young to protect them against threats to their safety. Still, except for young water birds riding the backs of their parents, this is a rare and irregular activity. Hopcraft (1968) reported that while he was in a boat approaching an African jacana with chicks in Kenya, the alarmed adult at first crouched and allowed the three chicks to run under its wings. When the parent stood up, it held its wings firmly to its sides, clasping its chicks, and walked away with them under the wings. Merrill (1898), on a small rocky islet, watched an adult spotted sandpiper circling about over him with a young one beneath its body, apparently clasped between the parent's legs. The chick's head was directed forward, the adult's legs were hanging down as it flew for about 60 yds., "heavily and silently," to alight on a large island nearby. A. T. Wayne (1910), an excellent and reliable observer, in May 1899 watched one of the adults of a pair of willets, when threatened by his presence, carry away four young. It took them, one at a time, held between its legs, and in transporting its chicks, it flew across three creeks to an island one quarter mile away.

Otto von Frisch (1966), while watching a nest of a Montagu's harrier, a European hawk similar to our American marsh hawk, saw a 3-day-old chick crawl away from its nest in the sun to shade nearby. Upon seeing the young one outside the nest, the mother rose from the nest, walked to the chick, and with her bill picked it up by its crown. Then she carried it back to the nest. Nice (1962a) reported that three species of rails—our native Virginia and clapper rails and the European water rail, *Rallus aquaticus*—have been seen carrying their young in the bill. A common gallinule that had nested in a bush about 6 ft. above water carried its young in its bill, two chicks, one at a time, to water where three other of its chicks were swimming with the other parent (Nice, 1962a). The European woodcock, most often cited there as a carrier of its chicks, transports them either in its bill, in its feet, or held between its legs and breast (von Frisch, 1966).

WATERFOWL CARRYING YOUNG. Whistling ducks, *Dencrocygna javanica*, in the Orient have been seen carrying their young in their feet, and Yocum (1952) cited accounts of Canada geese removing young one at a time in the bill from a high nest site to the ground; barnacle geese in Greenland were seen flying down from a high cliff nest site with their young carried in the bill. Ruddy sheldrakes have been observed carrying their young to water by tucking them between the neck and shoulder and volplaning down to the shoreline. Some swans (black, mute, and black-necked swans) and grebes carry their young on their backs while swimming during the first 2 weeks of the lives of the young, or even longer. See details of these in review by Johnsgard and Kear (1968). *See also* Waterfowl.

YUCKER
Another name for flickers in Woodpecker Family, from a common call note.

ZÉNAIDE
PRINCESS ZÉNAIDE CHARLOTTE JULIE BONAPARTE (1804–54). Eldest daughter of Joseph Bonaparte, King of Spain (1803–13), niece of Napoleon Bonaparte, cousin and wife of Charles Lucien Bonaparte, Prince of Musignano, who married her in Brussels, Belgium, June 29, 1822 (Palmer, 1928). This was shortly before she and her husband and her father came to America. They lived at Bordentown, N.J., and Philadelphia, Pa., until she and her husband went to Italy in 1828. See Charles Lucien's career and life in America in Palmer (1928) and Stresemann (1975). In 1825, while at the Philadelphia Academy of Natural Sciences, Charles Lucien Bonaparte gave the species name *zenaida* to a dove from s. Fla. in honor of his wife. The dove also bears the English name Zenaida's dove; *Zenaida* is the established scientific genus name for the Zenaida dove and more recently for the mourning dove. See American Ornithologists' Union (1957; 1973).

ZOOGEOGRAPHIC REGIONS
See Faunal Regions.

ZOOGEOGRAPHY
(zoe-oh-jee-OG-rah-fih). Term for the study or description of the distribution of birds and other animals in groupings that are characteristic of certain large regions of the world. *See* Faunal Regions. Zoogeography has been defined as the scientific study of the distribution of animals on the earth and the mutual influences of environment and animals upon each other (Allee and Schmidt, 1951). Studies in zoogeography are important to an understanding of the evolution of birds, their variations, paleontology, and so on. *See also* Biogeography; Distribution.

ZOONOSIS
(zoh-ON-oh-sis; pl.: *zoonoses*—zoh-ON-oh-seez). Term for a disease communicable from one animal to another and to man; the zoonoses include communicable or infectious diseases caused by viruses, bacteria, protozoa, and the larger parasitic worms. They may be spread by contaminated food, contaminated air, direct injection by the bite of a blood-sucking mosquito or fly, for example, or by direct penetration through the skin (Herman, 1966). *See* Diseases. Veterinary public health specialists report more than a hundred diseases of animals in the wild that can be transmitted to man. Most of the diseases that affect birds do not occur in man, however, either because man is not susceptible or, if he is, because opportunities for the transfer of the disease-causing organisms between birds and man do not normally occur (Herman, 1966). See especially Hull (1963).

ZOOPLANKTON
See Plankton.

ZUGUNRUHE
See Migration.

ZYGODACTYL
(zie-go-DAK-til). Yoke-toed. *See* Adaptations of the Feet under Feet and Legs. For examples of birds that are zygodactylous, *see* Cuculiformes; Piciformes; Psittaciformes; Strigiformes.

ZYGOTE
(ZIE-goat). The fertilized egg cell. The union of male and female gametes (sperm and ovum) is called fertilization; the resulting single cell is a zygote. *See* Fertilization.

Selected Reading List, Bibliography,
and Acknowledgments

SELECTED READING LIST

In the October 1971 issue of *American Birds* the editors asked seven leading ornithologists to provide their choices for a basic bird book library. From their selections, Robert Arbib of that journal drew up a thoughtful and valuable "Master List of Bird Books for North American Readers." In 1976 the master list was revised, and the editors of *American Bird* have kindly granted permission to reprint this latest edition here as a preface to my bibliography. The list has been reissued in a supplement entitled "On the Building of a Basic Ornithological Library, 1977," which also includes an annotated selection of regional bird books and the commentary of five of the seven authorities who have made additions to their original choices: Olin Sewell Pettingill, Jr., Kenneth C. Parkes, Thomas R. Howell, Dale Zimmerman, and Dean Amadon. The supplement is available from *American Birds,* 950 Third Avenue, New York, New York 10022.

J.K.T.

FIELD GUIDES

A selection of these must be a part of every basic library. Those listed here are the best of those devoted to North and Middle America, as well as those useful in identifying strays to this continent. Fine field guides to many other areas of the world are now available but do not rightfully belong in a North American master list. Field guides might well come at the end of the basic list, but since the first bird book in almost anyone's library is one of these, we start our list here.

Alexander, W. B. 1954. *Birds of the ocean.* Rev. ed. New York: G. P. Putnam's Sons. (Primitive, but no other field guide yet covers it.)

Bond, J. 1960. *Birds of the West Indies.* London: William Collins Sons & Co., Ltd.

ffrench, R., and O'Neill, J. P. 1976. *A guide to the birds of Trinidad and Tobago.* Rev. ed. Valley Forge, Pa.: Harrowood Books.

Fitter, R.; Heinzel, H.; Parslow, J. 1972. *Birds of Britain and Europe.* Philadelphia: J. B. Lippincott Company. (Includes North Africa and the Middle East. The most complete European guiide, useful mainly to Easterners.)

Harrison, H. H. 1975. *A field guide to birds' nests.* Boston: Houghton Mifflin Company. (Eastern birds.)

Pough, R. H. *Audubon guides:* 1946 *Eastern land birds,* 1951 *Water birds,* 1957 *Western birds.* New York: Doubleday & Co., Inc. (Eckelberry's plates illustrate many plumages not in other guides.)

Peterson, R. T. 1947. *A field guide to the birds.* Boston: Houghton Mifflin Company. (Completely new version due in 1980.)

———. 1960. *A field guide to the birds of Texas.* Boston: Houghton Mifflin Company. (Includes Hawaii.)

———. 1961. *A field guide to western birds.* Boston: Houghton Mifflin Company.

———, and Chalif, E. 1973. *A field guide to Mexican birds.* Boston: Houghton Mifflin Company. (Includes Belize, Guatemala, El Salvador.)

Pettingill, Jr., O.S. 1953. *A guide to bird-finding west of the Mississippi.* (Revision due in 1980.) 1977. *A guide to bird-finding east of the Mississippi.* 2nd ed. Boston: Houghton Mifflin Company.

Ridgely, R. S. 1976. *A guide to the birds of Panama.* Princeton, N.J.: Princeton University Press. (Useful north to Honduras.)

Robbins, C. S.; Bruun, B.; Zim, H. S. 1966. *Birds of North America.* New York: Golden Press.

Scott, Peter. 1957. *A coloured key to the wildfowl of the world.* New York: Charles Scribner's Sons. (Handy for those exotic zoo escapees.)

GENERAL ORNITHOLOGY TEXTBOOKS

Farner, D. S.; King, J. R.; and Parkes, K. C. 1974.

Avian biology. 5 volumes. New York: Academic Press, Inc.

Pettingill, Jr., O. S. 1970. *Ornithology in laboratory and field.* 4th ed. Minneapolis, Minn.: Burgess Publishing Co.

Van Tyne, J., and Berger, A. 1976. *The fundamentals of ornithology.* 2d ed. New York: John Wiley & Sons, Inc.

Wallace, G., and Mahan, H. D. 1975. *An introduction to ornithology.* 3rd ed. New York: The Macmillan Company.

Welty, J. C. 1975. *The life of birds.* 2nd ed. Philadelphia: W. B. Saunders Company.

MAJOR REFERENCES

Austin, Jr., O. L., and Singer, A. 1961. *Birds of the world, a survey.* New York: Golden Age Press.

Gilliard, E. T. 1958. *Living birds of the world.* New York: Doubleday & Co., Inc.

Peterson, R. T. 1977. *The birds.* Morristown, N.J.: Silver Burdett.

Thompson, A. L. 1964. *The new dictionary of birds.* New York: McGraw-Hill Book Company.

CHECKLISTS

American Ornithologists' Union. 1957. *The A.O.U. checklist of North American birds.* 5th ed. Baltimore: Lord Baltimore Press. (With supplements published in the *Auk.*)

Eisenmann, E. 1955. *The species of Middle American birds.* New York: Linnaean Society of New York.

Gruson, E. S., and Forster, R. A. 1976. *A checklist of the world's birds.* New York: Quadrangle Books.

IMPORTANT REGIONAL BOOKS

Bent, A. C. *et al.* 1919–1968. *Life histories of North American birds.* 23 volumes. New York: Peter Smith and Dover.

deSchauensee, R. M. 1971. *A guide to the birds of South America.* Waterford, Conn.: Livingston Publishing Company. (Now from Harrowood Books, Valley Forge, Pa.)

Godfrey, W. E. 1967. *The birds of Canada.* Ottawa: National Museum of Canada.

Palmer, R. S., ed. 1962, 1976. *Handbook of North American birds.* 3 volumes. New Haven, Conn.: Yale University Press.

Reilly, E. M. 1968. *The Audubon illustrated handbook of birds.* New York: Interbook, Inc.

Ridgway, R., and Friedmann, H. 1901–1950. *The birds of North and Middle America.* Washington, D.C.: Government Printing Office.

Witherby, H. F. *et al.* 1938–1941. *The handbook of British birds.* London: H. F. and G. Withby, Ltd.

In addition, every library should include one or more state, provincial or regional books, including that of the home area.

SPECIALIZED SUBJECTS

There are books on everything from avian energetics and radar ornithology to avian parasites and evolution; your choice depends on your special interests.

Armstrong, E. A. 1963. *A study of bird song.* London, New York: Oxford University Press.

Dorst, J. 1962. *The migration of birds.* Boston: Houghton Mifflin Company.

Griffin, D. R. 1974. *Bird migration.* New York: Dover Publications, Inc.

Matthews, G. V. T. 1968. *Bird navigation.* 3d ed. New York: Cambridge University Press.

Storer, J. H. 1948. *The flight of birds.* Bloomfield Hills, Mi.: Cranbrook Institute of Science Bulletin, 28.

Thorpe, W. H. 1961. *Bird-song.* New York: Cambridge University Press.

BEHAVIOR

Armstrong, E. A. 1942. *Bird display and behavior.* New York: Oxford University Press.

Lack, D. 1970. *The life of the robin.* Brooklyn Heights, N.Y.: Beekman Publishers.

Nice, M. M. 1937, 1943. *Studies in the life history of the song sparrow.* Parts 1 and 2. New York: Linnaean Society of New York.

Skutch, A. F. 1975. *Parent birds and their young.* Austin, Tex.: University of Texas Press.

Tinbergen, N. 1971. *The herring gull's world.* New York: Harper and Row.

CONSERVATION

The multitude of titles in this field makes it impossible to include a representative list here. The following are specifically concerned with problems of bird survival.

Greenway, Jr., J. C. 1967. *Extinct and vanishing birds of the world.* New York: Dover Publications, Inc.

Hickey, J. J., ed. 1969. *The peregrine falcon populations, their biology and decline.* Madison, Wisc.: University of Wisconsin Press.

Schorger, A. W. 1973. *The passenger pigeon.* Norman, Okla.: University of Oklahoma Press.

Vincent, J., ed. 1971 and sequels. *Red data book.* Morges, Switzerland: International Union for Conservation of Nature and Natural Resources.

BOOKS ON SPECIAL GROUPS OF BIRDS

More of these books are appearing each year. Here are three good ones, the last two classics.

Brown, L., and Amadon, D. 1968. *Eagles, hawks and falcons of the world.* 2 volumes. New York: McGraw-Hill Book Company.

Eckert, A. E., and Karalus, K. E. 1974. *The owls of North America.* New York: Doubleday & Co., Inc.

Murphy, R. C. 1936. *Oceanic birds of South America.* 2 volumes. New York: The Macmillan Company.

BOOKS WITH FINE ILLUSTRATIONS

Forshaw, J. M. 1974. *Parrots of the world.* New York: Doubleday & Co., Inc.

Greenwalt, C. H. 1960. *Hummingbirds.* New York: Doubleday & Co., Inc.

Jacques, F. L. 1973. *Artist of the wilderness world, Florence Page Jacques.* New York: Doubleday & Co., Inc.

Line, L. 1976. *The Audubon Society book of wild birds.* New York: Harry N. Abrams. (Bird photography as art.)

Marsham, F. G. ed. 1971. *Louis Agassiz Fuertes and the singular beauty of birds.* New York: Harper and Row.

Stout, G. D. *et al.* 1967. *The shorebirds of North America.* New York: Viking Press. (The best showcase in print of the art of Robert Verity Clem.)

Sutton, G. M. 1975. *Portraits of Mexican birds: Fifty selected paintings.* Norman, Okla.: University of Oklahoma Press.

BIRD WATCHING

Fisher, J. 1941, 1951. *Watching birds.* Hammondsworth, Eng.: Pelican Books. (A fine brief introduction.)

Hickey, J. J. 1975. *A guide to bird watching.* New York: Dover Publications, Inc.

GOOD READING

Many of the books in this list are good reading; the two books listed in this section are anthologies.

Krutch, J. W., and Eriksson, P., eds. 1962. *A treasury of bird lore.* New York: Doubleday & Co., Inc.

Peterson, R. T., ed. 1957. *The bird watcher's anthology.* New York: Harcourt, Brace & Co., Inc.

HISTORY

Stresemann, E. 1975. *Ornithology, from Aristotle to the present.* Cambridge, Mass.: Harvard University Press.

ATTRACTING BIRDS

McElroy, Jr., T. 1961. *The new handbook of attracting birds.* New York: Alfred A. Knopf, Inc.

Terres, J. K. 1968. *Songbirds in your garden.* New York: Thomas Y. Crowell Company, Inc.

In the years since the compilation of this list, several news books have been published that I feel deserve mention in the context of a basic bird library:

Bull, J., and Farrand, Jr., J. 1977. *The Audubon Society field guide to North American birds.* New York: Alfred A. Knopf, Inc.

Dennis, J. V. 1975. *A complete guide to bird feeding.* New York: Alfred A. Knopf, Inc.

Harrison, C. 1978. *A field guide to the nests, eggs and nestlings of North American birds.* London: William Collins Sons & Co., Ltd.

Pasquier, R. F. 1977. *An introduction to ornithology.* Boston: Houghton Mifflin Company.

Stokes, D. W. 1979. *A guide to the behavior of common birds.* Boston: Little Brown and Company.

BIBLIOGRAPHY

A

Abbott, C. G. 1911. *The home-life of the osprey.* London: H. F. Witherby & Co.

Abbott, III, D. J., and Finch, D. W. 1978. First variegated flycatcher *(Empidonomus varius)* record for the United States. *Amer. Birds* 32: 161–63.

Able, K. P. 1970. A radar study of the altitude of nocturnal passerine migration. *Bird-Banding* 41(4):282–90.

————. 1978. Personal communication.

Able, K. P., and Dillon, P. M. 1977. Sun compass orientation in a nocturnal migrant, the white-throated sparrow. *Condor* 79(3):393–95.

Abramson, I. J. 1976. The black hawk *(Buteogallus anthrocinus)* in South Florida. *Amer. Birds* 30(3):661–62.

Adams, B. 1970. First Harris's sparrow banded in New Jersey. *Bird-Banding* 41(2):133.

Adams, D. A., and Quay, T. L. 1958. Ecology of the clapper rail in southeastern North Carolina. *Jour. Wildlife Management* 22(2):149–56.

Addy, C. E. 1964. Atlantic flyway. In *Waterfowl tomorrow,* ed. J. P. Linduska and A. L. Nelson. Washington, D.C.: U.S. Dept. Inter., Fish and Wildlife Service.

Addy, C. E., and MacNamara, L. G. 1948. *Waterfowl management on small areas.* Washington, D.C.: Wildlife Management Inst.

Adolphson, D., and Jonkel, G. 1969. Raptor Populations Committee Report for 1968. *Raptor Research News* 3(3):43.

Affeltranger, C. 1971. The red heart disease of Southern Pines. In *The ecology and management of the red-cockaded woodpecker: Proceedings of a symposium at Okefenokee National Wildlife Refuge, Folkston, Ga.,* ed. R. L. Thompson. *May 26–27.* Tallahassee, Fla.: Tall Timbers Res. Station.

Ainley, D. G., and Manolis, B. 1979. Occurrence and distribution of the mottled petrel. *Western Birds* 10:113–23.

Ajello, L. 1967. Comparative ecology of respiratory mycotic disease agents. *Bacteriol. Rev.* 31(1):6–24.

————. 1968. The ecology and epidemiology of the deep mycoses: Transmission mechanisms. In *Ciba Foundation symposium on systemic mycoses,* ed. G. E. W. Wolstenholme and R. Porter. London: J. & A. Churchill, Ltd.

————. 1975. Personal communication.

Aldrich, E. C. 1945. Nesting of the Allen hummingbird. *Condor* 47:137–48.

Aldrich, J. W. 1965. The turkey. In *Water, prey, and game birds of North America,* ed. A. Wetmore *et al.* Washington, D.C.: Natl. Geographic Soc.

————. 1966. Before it is too late. In *Birds in our lives,* ed. A. Stefferud and A. L. Nelson. Washington, D.C.: U.S. Dept. Inter., Fish and Wildlife Service.

————. 1967. Chapters 1 and 2. *The wild turkey and its management,* ed. O. H. Hewitt. Washington, D.C.: Wildlife Soc.

————. 1968. In memoriam: Harry Church Oberholser. *Auk* 85:25–29.

————. 1972. A new subspecies of sandhill crane from Mississippi. *Proceedings of the Biological Society of Washington* 85(5):63–70.

————. 1979. Status of the Canadian sandhill crane. In *Proceedings of the 1978 Crane Workshop.* Pp. 139–48. Fort Collins, Colo.: Colorado State University Press.

Aldrich, J. W., and Baer, K. P. 1970. Status and speciation in the Mexican duck *(Anas diazi).* *Wilson Bull.* 82:63–73.

Aldrich, J. W., and Robbins, C. S. 1970. Changing abundance of migratory birds in North America. In *The avifauna of northern Latin America,* ed. H. K. and J. H. Buechner. Washington, D.C.: Smithsonian Press.

Aldrich, J. W. *et al.* 1949. *Migration of some*
North American waterfowl: A progress report and analysis of banding records. U.S. Dept. Inter., Fish and Wildlife Service, Spec. Sci. Rept.—Wildlife, no. 1.

Alexander, W. B. 1927. Snow buntings in the North Atlantic. *Auk* 44:253.

————. 1928. *Birds of the ocean.* New York: G. P. Putnam's Sons.

Ali, S. 1963. Recent studies of bird migration and bird ticks in India. *Proc. [XIIIth] Internatl. Ornith. Congress,* ed. C. G. Sibley 1:354–61. Ithaca, N.Y.: Amer. Ornith. Union.

Ali, S., and Ripley, S. D. 1971. *Handbook of the birds of India and Pakistan.* Vol. 6. London and New York: Oxford University Press.

Alison, R. M. 1973. Delayed nesting in oldsquaws. *Bird-Banding* 44:61–63.

————. 1975. *Breeding biology and behavior of the oldsquaw* (Clangula hyemalis). Amer. Ornith. Union, Monogr. no. 18.

Allard, H. A. 1934. Speed of the ruby-throated hummingbird's flight. *Auk* 51:84.

————. 1939. Vocal mimicry of starling and mockingbird. *Science* 90:370–71.

Allee, W. C. 1931. *Animal aggregations.* Chicago: University of Chicago Press.

————. 1938. *Co-operation among animals.* London: Sir Isaac Pitman and Sons, Ltd.

Allee, W. C., and Schmidt, K. P. 1951. *Ecological animal geography.* 2d ed. New York: John Wiley & Sons, Inc.

Allee, W. C. *et al.* 1949. *Principles of animal ecology.* Philadelphia: W. B. Saunders Co.

Allen, A. A. 1914. The red-winged blackbird: A study in the ecology of a cattail marsh. *Proc. Linnaean Soc. New York* 24–25:43–128.

————. 1930a. *The book of bird life.* 1st ed. New York: D. Van Nostrand Company.

————. 1930b. Ruby-throat. *Bird-Lore* 32(3):223–31.

————. 1937. Hunting with a microphone the voices of vanishing birds. *Natl. Geographic Magazine* 71(6):697–723.

————. 1939. *The golden plover and other birds.* Ithaca, N.Y.: Comstock Pub. Co., Inc.

————. 1951a. The curlew's secret. *Proc. [Xth] Internatl. Ornith. Congress,* p. 613. Uppsala, Sweden: Almquist and Wiksell.

————. 1951b. *Stalking birds with color camera,* ed. G. Grosvenor. Washington, D.C.: Natl. Geographic Soc.

————. 1961. *The book of bird life.* 2d ed. New York: D. Van Nostrand Company.

————. 1962. Cornell's laboratory of ornithology. *Living Bird,* 1st annual, pp. 7–36.

————. 1963. Personal communication.

Allen, A. A., and Kellogg, P. P. 1937. Recent observations of the ivory-billed woodpecker. *Auk* 54:164–84.

Allen, C. A. 1878. An albino Anna's hummingbird. *Nuttall Ornith. Club. Bull.* 3:192–93.

Allen, D. 1954. *Our wildlife legacy.* New York: Funk & Wagnalls Company.

Allen, E. G. 1951. The history of American ornithology before Audubon. *Trans. Amer. Philos. Soc.* 41(3):385–591.

Allen, G. M. 1925. *Birds and their attributes.* Francestown, N.H.: Marshall Jones Co.

————. 1939. *Bats.* Cambridge, Mass.: Harvard University Press.

Allen, J. A. 1896. Alleged changes in color in the feathers of birds without moulting. *Bull. Amer. Mus. Nat. Hist.* 8:13–44.

————. 1909. Biographical memoir of Elliott Coues 1842–1899. *Nat. Acad. Sci.* 6:395–446.

Allen, R. P. 1942. *The roseate spoonbill.* Nat. Audubon Soc. Res. Report no. 2.

————. 1952. *The whooping crane.* Nat. Audubon Soc. Res. Report no. 3. New York.

————. 1954. A report on the flamingo. *Audubon* 55(5):210–13, 224.

————. 1956b. *The flamingos: Their life history and survival.* Nat. Audubon Soc. Res. Report no. 5. New York.

———. 1956b. *A report of the whooping crane's nesting grounds.* Nat. Audubon Soc. Supplement to Res. Report no. 3. New York.

———. 1965a. Ibises and spoonbills. In *Water, prey, and game birds of North America,* ed. A. Wetmore et al. Washington, D.C.: Natl. Geographic Soc.

———. 1965b. The wood ibis. In *Water, prey, and game birds of North America,* ed. A. Wetmore et al. Washington, D.C.: Natl. Geographic Soc.

Allen, R. P., and Mangles, F. P. 1940. Studies of the nesting behavior of the black-crowned night heron. *Proc. Linnaean Soc. New York* 50–51:1–28.

Allen, R. P., and Nice, M. M. 1952. A study of the breeding biology of the purple martin *(Progne subis). Amer. Midland-Nat.* 47(3):606–65.

Allen, R. P., and Peterson, R. T. 1936. The hawk migrations at Cape May Point, New Jersey. *Auk* 53(4):393–404.

Allen, T. T. 1961. Notes on the breeding behavior of the anhinga. *Wilson Bull.* 73(2):115–25.

Alnås, I. 1969. The activities at Ottenby bird station 1963 and 1964. *Vår Fågelvärld* 28:9–17.

Amadon, D. 1943. Bird weights and egg weights. *Auk* 60:221–34.

———. 1944. *A preliminary life history study of the Florida jay, Cyanocitta c. coerulescens.* Amer. Mus. Novitates no. 1252. New York.

———. 1947. Ecology and the evolution of some Hawaiian birds. *Evolution* 1(1–2):63–68.

———. 1949. Comments on recent literature. *Wilson Bull.* 61(4):237–38.

———. 1950. The Hawaiian Honeycreepers *(Aves, Drepanididae). Bull. Amer. Mus. Nat. Hist.* 95:151–262.

———. 1956. *Remarks on the starlings, family sturnidae.* Amer. Mus. Novitates no. 1803. New York.

———. 1959. The significance of sexual differences in size among birds. *Proc. Amer. Philos. Soc.* 103(4).

———. 1962. Personal communication.

———. 1964a. Evolution of low reproductive rates in birds. *Evolution* 18:105–10.

———. 1964b. Starling. In *A new dictionary of birds,* ed. A. L. Thomson. New York: McGraw-Hill Book Company.

———. 1965. The hawks. In *Water, prey, and game birds of North America,* ed. A. Wetmore et al. Washington, D.C.: Natl. Geographic Soc.

———. 1966a. Avian plumages and molts. *Condor* 68:263–78.

———. 1966b. *Birds around the world: A geographical look at evolution and birds.* Garden City, N.Y.: Doubleday/Natural History Press.

———. 1970. Variation in the trachea of the cracidae (galliformes) in relation to their classification. *Nat. Hist. Bull. of the Siam Society* 23(3):239–48.

———. 1975. Why are female birds larger than males? *Raptor Research* 9(1–2):1–11.

———. 1977. Personal communication.

American Birding Association. 1975. *A. B. A. checklist: Birds of continental United States and Canada.* Austin, Tex.: American Birding Association.

American Ornithologists' Union. 1886a. *Bull. No. 2 of the Committee on Protection of Birds.* New York: Amer. Ornith. Union.

———. 1886b. *The code of nomenclature and check-list of North American birds.* New York: Amer. Ornith. Union.

———. 1895. *Check-list of North American birds.* 2d ed. New York: Amer. Ornith. Union.

———. 1910. *Check-list of North American Birds,* 3d ed. New York: Amer. Ornith. Union.

———. 1931. *Check-list of North American birds.* 4th ed. Lancaster, Pa.: Amer. Ornith. Union.

———. 1933. *Fifty years progress of American ornithology.* Lancaster, Pa.: Science Press.

———. 1945. Twentieth supplement to the American Ornithologists' Union check-list of North American birds. *Auk* 62(3):436–49.

———. 1957. *Check-list of North American birds.* 5th ed. Lancaster, Pa.: Amer. Ornith. Union.

———. 1973. Thirty-second supplement to the American Ornithologists' Union check-list of North American Birds. *Auk* 90(2):411–19.

———. 1975a. Report of the American Ornithologists' Union, Ad Hoc Committee on Scientific and Educational Use of Wild Birds. *Supplement to the Auk* 92(3):1A–27A

———. 1975b. Report of the American Ornithologists' Union Committee on Conservation 1974–1975. *Supplement to the Auk* 92(4):1B–16B.

———. 1976. Thirty-third supplement to the American Ornithologists' Union check-list of North American birds. *Auk* 93(4):875–79.

Ames, J. H. 1902. A solution to an ornithological mystery. *Auk* 19(1):94–95.

Ames, P. L. 1964. Notes on the breeding behavior of the Osprey. *Atlantic Nat.* 19:15–27.

Ames, P. L., and Mersereau, G. S. 1964. Some factors in the decline of the osprey. *Auk* 81: 174–85.

Ammann, G. A. 1937. Number of contour feathers in *Cygnus* and *Xanthocephalus. Auk* 54: 201–2.

———. 1957. *The prairie grouse of Michigan.* Michigan Dept. Cons. Lansing, Mich.

Amundson, R. 1957. The wild turkey. *Wildlife in North Carolina* 21(8):6–10.

Anderson, A. H. 1965. Notes in the behavior of the rufous-winged sparrow. *Condor* 67(2):188–90.

———. 1968. Arizona pyrrhuloxia. In *Life histories of North American cardinals, grosbeaks, buntings, towhees, finches, sparrows, and allies,* comp. A. C. Bent et al., ed. O. L. Austin, Jr. U.S. Natl. Mus. Bull. no. 237, pt. 1. Washington, D.C.

Anderson, A. H., and Anderson, A. 1957. Life history of the cactus wren. Part I. Winter and pre-nesting behavior. *Condor* 59:274–96.

———. 1959. Life history of the cactus wren. Part II. The beginning of nesting. *Condor* 61:186–205.

———. 1960. Life history of the cactus wren. Part III. The nesting cycle. *Condor* 62:351–69.

———. 1961. Life history of the cactus wren. Part IV. Development of nestlings. *Condor* 63:87–94.

———. 1962. Life history of the cactus wren. Part V. Fledgling to independence. *Condor* 64:199–212.

———. 1963. Life history of the cactus wren. Part VI. Competition and survival. *Condor* 65:29–43.

———. 1965. The cactus wrens on the Santa Rita Experimental Range, Arizona. *Condor* 67:344–51.

Anderson, B. W., and Daugherty, R. J. 1974. Characteristics and reproductive biology of grosbeaks *(Pheucticus)* in the hybrid zone in South Dakota. *Wilson Bull.* 86(1):1–11.

Anderson, B. W., and Timken, R. L. 1969. A hybrid lesser scaup × ring-necked duck. *Auk* 86(3):556–57.

Anderson, D. W., and Anderson, I. T. 1976. Distribution and status of brown pelicans in the California Current. *Amer. Birds* 30(1):3–12.

Anderson, D. W., and Hickey, J. J. 1970. Eggshell changes in certain North American birds, ed. K. H. Voous. *Proc. [XVth] Inter. Ornith. Congress,* pp. 514–40. Leiden, Netherlands: E. J. Brill.

Anderson, D. W.; Hickey, J. J.; Risebrough, R. W.; Hughes, D. F.; and Christensen, R. E. 1969. Significance of chlorinated hydrocarbon residues to breeding pelicans and cormorants. *Canadian Field-Nat.* 84:351–56.

Anderson, D. W.; Jehl, Jr., J. R.; Risebrough, R. W.; Woods, Jr., L. A.; Deweese, L. R.; and Edgecomb, W. G. 1975. Brown pelicans improved reproduction off the southern California coast. *Science* 190:805–8.

Anderson, K. S., and Maxfield, H. K. 1967. Warbler returns from southeastern Massachusetts. *Bird-Banding* 43(3):218–33.

Anderson, M. B. 1971 White birds outdraw golf at Hampton Club. *Chat* 35(3):88.

Anderson, M. G. 1974. American coots feeding in association with canvasbacks. *Wilson Bull.* 86(4):462–63.

Anderson, R. M. 1932. *Methods of collecting and preserving vertebrate animals.* Natl. Mus. Canada Biol. Series no. 18. Ottawa. 162 pp.

Anderson, S. H. 1970. Water balance of the Oregon junco. *Auk* 87(1):161–63.

Anderson, T. E. 1969. Identifying, evaluating, and controlling wildlife damage. In *Wildlife management techniques,* ed. R. H. Giles, Jr. Washington, D.C.: Wildlife Soc.

Anderson, W. L. 1978. Vocalizations of Scaled Quail. *Condor* 80 (1):49–63.

Andrle, R. F. 1969. "Thayer's" gull in the Niagara frontier region. *Auk* 86:106–9.

———. 1972. Another probable hybrid of *Larus marinus* and *L. argentatus. Auk* 89(3):669–70.

Andrle, R. F., and Rew, F. M. 1971. White-throated sparrow breeding in downtown Buffalo, New York. *Auk* 88(1):172–73.

Angell, T. 1969. A study of the ferruginous hawk: Adult and brood behavior. *Living Bird,* 8th annual, pp. 225–41.

———. 1978. *Ravens, crows, magpies and jays.* Seattle, Wash.: University of Washington Press.

Anonymous. 1836. A visit to Texas. 2d ed., New York.

———. 1887. Experiments to ascertain the velocity of flight of birds. *Field* [London] 69:242–43.

———. 1895. Obituary of Isaac Sprague. *Garden and Forest* 8 no. (370, March):130.

———. 1905. How fast do birds fly? *Field and Stream* 65:330.

———. 1924. How fast can a quail fly? *Outdoor Life* 53:151.

———. 1931. The speed of the sharp-tailed grouse. *Fins, Feathers, and Fur* 97:10.

———. 1935. Returns. *Bird-banding notes* 2(13): 214.

———. 1953. Report. *Pennsylvania Game News* 24(9):36.

———. 1954. Report. *Animal Kingdom* 57(1):31.

———. 1955a. Operation osprey. *Audubon* 57: 176–67.

———. 1955b. *Outdoor News Bulletin* (Wildlife Management Institute, Washington, D.C.), January.

———. 1959a. *Bird ailments and accidents: Their treatment and cure.* London: Cagebirds.

———. 1959b. *Wild birds.* Washington, D.C.: U.S. Bur. Customs.

———. 1960. *Bird-Banding: The hows and whys.* U.S. Dept. Inter., Fish and Wildlife Service, *Conservation Notes.* Cir. 79. Washington, D.C.

———. 1965a. Condor killed. *Audubon Leader's Conserv. Guide* 6(14), July 15.

———. 1965b. *National survey of fishing and hunting.* U.S. Dept. Inter., Fish and Wildlife Service Res. Publ. no. 27. Washington, D.C.

———. 1968a. Captive American eagle stirs curiosity at Albany. *New York Times,* March 31.

———. 1968b. Trumpeter swan no longer rare and endangered. *U.S. Dept. Inter., Fish and Wildlife Service News Release,* December 8.

———. 1970a. Audubon field notes discovery award. *Audubon Field Notes* 24(5):654.

———. 1970b. Fowl cholera in Maryland took toll. *Outdoor News Bulletin,* June.

———. 1970c. Fulvous ducks in Oregon. *Oregon State Game Commission Bull.,* June:2–4.

———. 1970d. What bird is that? *Audubon Field Notes* 24(6):back cover.

———. 1970e. Woodcock pesticide samples being taken in Maine. *U.S. Dept. Inter., Fish and Wildlife Service News Release,* October 8.

———. 1971a. A slaughtering of eagles (editorial report). *Audubon* 73(5):72–73.

———. 1971b. Poisoned bait for coyotes and prairie dogs is taking huge toll of other wildlife. *Audubon News Release*, September 7.

———. 1971c. Science refutes ranchers' claims: Eagles are not a serious threat to the sheep interests. *Audubon News Release*, September 7.

———. 1972a. Ornithologist breeds 3 more falcons in captivity. *New York Times*, May 4.

———. 1972b. Powerlines—eagle deathtraps. *Outdoor News Bulletin*, September.

———. 1972c. Protection provided for 32 additional families, birds in convention with Mexico. *U.S. Dept. Inter., Fish and Wildlife Service News Release*, April 23.

———. 1973a. Canvasback, redhead ducks to be aided by restrictive hunting regulations, etc. *U.S. Dept. Inter., Fish and Wildlife Service News Release*, September 27.

———. 1973b. Duck virus threatens North American waterfowl. *U.S. Dept. Inter., Fish and Wildlife Service News Release*, November 2.

———. 1973c. Reproductive failure in peregrine falcons increases. *U.S. Dept. Inter., Fish and Wildlife Service News Release*, November 1.

———. 1974a. Fish and Wildlife Service to release masked bobwhites in Mexico. *U.S. Dept. Inter., Fish and Wildlife Service News Release*, May 14.

———. 1974b. Gadwall expands range in eastern N.A. *Wildlife Management Inst., Outdoor News Bulletin*, February.

———. 1975a. Brown pelican decline puzzles experts. *U.S. Dept. Inter., Fish and Wildlife Service News Release*, September 30.

———. 1975b. Ducks need stamp of approval from non-hunting public. *U.S. Dept. Inter., Fish and Wildlife Service News Release*, October 17.

———. 1975c. Warbler stages a comeback. *Wildlife Management Inst., Outdoor News Bulletin*, October.

———. 1975d. Waterfowl migration begins. *U.S. Dept. Inter., Fish and Wildlife Service News Release*, October 20.

———. 1976. Acrylic painting of Ross' geese wins duck stamp contest. *U.S. Dept. Inter., Fish and Wildlife Service News Release*, November 17.

———. 1978. State reports. U.S. Dept. Inter., Fish and Wildlife Service, Endangered Species Technical Bulletin 3(2):5, 3(5):4. Washington, D.C.

———. 1979a. Analysis of mid-winter bald eagle survey reading results completed. *Eyas* 3(2):3.

———. 1979b. Death claims the great white bird. *U.S. Dept. Inter., Fish and Wildlife Service News Release*, April 2. Washington, D.C.

———. 1980a. Birds of prey area opposed. *Audubon Leader* 21(1, January 11).

———. 1980b. The ten most endangered species in North America. *U.S. Dept. Inter., Fish and Wildlife Service News Release*, January 27.

Antony, M. 1920. Über die Speicheldrüsen der Vögel. *Zool. Jahrb. Abt. Anat. u. Ontog. Tiere* 41:547–660.

Ap.Evans, H. 1960. *Falconry for you.* Newton Centre, Mass.: Charles T. Branford Co.

Arbib, R. 1971. Announcing—The blue list: An "early warning system" for birds. *Amer. Birds* 25(6):948–49.

———. 1972. The blue list for 1973. *Amer. Birds* 26(6):932–33.

———. 1973. The blue list for 1974. *Amer. Birds* 27(6)943–45.

———. 1974. The blue list for 1975. *Amer. Birds* 28(6):971–74.

———. 1979. The blue list for 1980. *Amer. Birds* 33(6):830–835.

Archibald, H. L. 1974. Directional differences in the sound intensity of ruffed grouse drumming. *Auk* 91(3):517–21.

Armstrong, E. A. 1942. *Bird display and behavior.* New York: Oxford University Press.

———. 1958. *The folklore of birds.* London: William Collins Sons & Co., Ltd.

———. 1963. *A study of bird song.* London: Oxford University Press.

———. 1964a. Folklore. In *A new dictionary of birds*, ed. A. L. Thomson. New York: McGraw-Hill Book Company.

———. 1964b. Parental care. In *A new dictionary of birds*, ed. A. L. Thomson. New York: McGraw-Hill Book Company.

———. 1964c. Polyandry. In *A new dictionary of birds*, ed. A. L. Thomson. New York: McGraw-Hill Book Company.

———. 1964d. Wren (1). In *A new dictionary of birds*, ed. A. L. Thomson. New York: McGraw-Hill Book Company.

Armstrong, E. R., and Noakes, D. L. G. 1977. Albino mourning dove sightings in Ontario. *Auk* 94:158.

Armstrong, H. G. 1952. *Principles and practice of aviation medicine.* Baltimore: The Williams & Wilkins Company.

Armstrong, W. H. 1958. *Nesting and food habits of the long-eared owl in Michigan.* Michigan State Univ. Biol. Series 1 (2).

Arni-Willi, H. 1959. Photographic studies of some less familiar birds. Alpine swift. (Text by Arni-Willi.) *Brit. Birds* 52 (June):221–25.

Arnold, I. Z. 1961. Blue-gray tanagers (*Thraupis virens*). *Florida Nat.* 34:44–45.

Arnold, L. W. 1954. *The golden eagle and its economic status.* U.S. Dept. Inter., Fish and Wildlife Service, Circ. 27. Washington, D.C.

Arthur, S. C. 1937. *Audubon, an intimate life of the American woodsman.* New Orleans: Harmanson.

Arvey, M. D. 1951. Phylogeny of the waxwings and allied birds. *Univ. Kansas Publ. Zool.* 3: 473–530.

Arvin, John; Arvin, Jimmy; Cottam, C.; and Unland, G. 1975. Mexican crow invades south Texas. *Auk* (2):387–90.

Ashby, W. R. 1961. Homeostasis. In *The encyclopedia of the biological sciences*, ed. P. Gray. New York: Reinhold Publishing Corporation.

Ashmole, N. P. 1971. Sea bird ecology and the marine environment. In *Avian biology*, ed. D. S. Farner, J. R. King, and and K. C. Parkes. Vol. 1. New York: Academic Press, Inc.

Ashmole, N. P. and Tovar H. 1968. Prolonged parental care in royal terns and other birds. *Auk* 85:90–100.

Assenmacher, I. 1958. La mue des oiseaux et son déterminisme endocrinen. *Alauda* 26:241–89.

———. 1973. The peripheral endocrine glands. In *Avian biology*, ed. D. S. Farner, J. R. King, and K. C. Parkes. Vol. 3, pp. 183–286. New York: Academic Press, Inc.

———. 1973. The peripheral endocrine glands. In *Avian biology*, ed. D. S. Farner J. R. King, and K. C. Parkes. Vol. 3. New York: Academic Press, Inc.

Atkinson, B. 1972. *This bright land.* Garden City, N.Y.: Doubleday/Natural History Press.

Audubon, J. J. 1826. Account of the habits of the turkey buzzard, *Vultor aura*, particularly with the view of exploding the opinion generally entertained of its extraordinary power of smelling. *Edinb. New Phil. J.* 2:172–84.

———. 1870. *Birds of America.* 8 vols. New York: Geo. R. Lockwood and Son.

Audubon, M. R. 1960. *Audubon and his journals*, Vols. 1 and 2. Reprint (paperback). New York: Dover Publications, Inc.

Austin, E. S. 1967. *Frank M. Chapman in Florida: His journals and letters.* Gainesville, Fla.: University of Florida Press.

Austin, G. T. 1970. Experimental hypothermia in a lesser nighthawk. *Auk* 87(2):372–74.

———. 1976. Behavioral adaptations of the verdin to the desert. *Auk* 93(2):245–62.

Austin, G. T., and Russell, S. M. 1972. Interspecific aggression of ash-throated flycatchers and Cassin's sparrows. *Condor* 74:481.

Austin, G. T., and Smith, E. L. 1974. Use of burrows by towhees and black-throated sparrows. *Auk* 91(1):167.

Austin, G. T., and Tomoff, C. S. 1972. Snake predation on cactus wren nestlings. *Condor* 74(4): 492.

Austin, Jr., O. L. 1928. Migration routes of the Arctic tern (*Sterna paradisaea brünnich*). *Bull. Northeastern Bird-Banding Assoc.* 4(4): 121–25.

———. 1961. *Birds of the world.* New York: Golden Press.

———. 1968a. Japanese hawfinch. In *Life histories of North American cardinals, grosbeaks, buntings, towhees, finches, sparrows, and allies*, comp. A. C. Bent *et al.*, ed. O. L. Austin, Jr. U.S. Natl. Mus. Bull. no. 237, pt. 1. Washington, D.C.

———. 1968b. Mexican (yellow-eyed) junco. In *Life histories of North American cardinals, grosbeaks, buntings, towhees, finches, sparrows, and allies*, comp. A. C. Bent *et al.*, ed. O. L. Austin, Jr. U.S. Natl. Mus. Bull. no. 237, pt. 2. Washington, D.C.

Austin, O. L., and Austin, Jr., O. L. 1931. Food poisoning in shore birds. *Auk* (2):195–97.

Austing, G. R. 1964. *The world of the red-tailed hawk.* Philadelphia: J. B. Lippincott Company.

———. 1967. Breeding project report. *Raptor Res. News* 1(1):10.

Austing, G. R., and Holt, Jr., J. B. 1966. *The world of the great horned owl.* Philadelphia: J. B. Lippincott Company.

Avery, M.; Spring, P. F.; and Cassel, J. F. 1976. The effects of a tall tower on nocturnal bird migration. *Auk* 93(2):281–91.

Axtell, H. H. 1945. The cliff swallow. In *Arbor day and bird day. Bull. to the Schools* 31(7):232–36. Albany: State Univ. of New York Press.

Aymar, G. C. 1935. *Bird flight.* Garden City, N.Y.: Garden City Pub. Co., Inc.

B

Babcock, E. B., and Clausen, R. E. 1927. *Genetics in relation to agriculture.* New York: McGraw-Hill Book Company.

Backus, G. J. 1959. Observations in the life history of the dipper in Montana. *Auk* 76(2):90–207.

Baepler, D. H. 1968. Lark sparrow. In *Life histories of North American cardinals, grosbeaks, buntings, towhees, finches, sparrows, and allies*, comp. A. C. Bent *et al.*, ed. O. L. Austin, Jr. U.S. Natl. Mus. Bull. no. 237, pt. 2. Washington, D.C.

Baer, J. G. 1952. *Ecology of animal parasites.* Urbana, Ill.: University of Illinois Press.

Baerg, W. J. 1944. Ticks and other parasites attacking northern cliff swallows. *Auk* 61(3):413–14.

Bagg, A. M. 1967. Factors affecting the occurrence of the Eurasian lapwing in eastern North America. *Living Bird*, 6th annual, pp. 87–121.

———. 1969. The changing seasons. *Audubon Field Notes* 23(1):4–12.

———. 1970. The eruptions of 1969 in the changing seasons. *Audubon Field Notes* 24(1):5.

———. 1971. The changing seasons. Fall migration. *Amer. Birds* 25(1):16.

Bagg, A. M.; Gunn, W. W. H.; Miller, D. S.; Nichols, J. T.; Smith, W.; and Wolfarth, F. P. 1950. Barometric pressure-patterns and spring bird migration. *Wilson Bull.* 62:5–19.

Bailey, A. M. 1933. The baikal teal from King Island, Alaska. *Auk* 50(1):97.

———. 1943. The birds of Cape Prince of Wales, Alaska. *Proc. Colorado Mus. Nat. Hist.* 18(1): 1–113.

———. 1945. On the trail of the roadrunner. *Audubon* 46(4):224–29.

———. 1948. *Birds of Arctic Alaska.* Colorado Mus. Nat. Hist. Popular Ser., no. 8. Denver.

Bailey, A. M., and Niedrach, R. J. 1933. The prairie falcon. *Amer. Forests* 39:356–58, 384.

_____. 1936. Community nesting of western robins and house finches. *Condor* 38:214.

_____. 1965. *The birds of Colorado*. 2 vols. Denver: Denver Mus. Nat. Hist.

Bailey, F. M. 1902. *Handbook of birds of the western United States*. Boston: Houghton Mifflin Company.

_____. 1919. Olive Thorne Miller. *Condor* 21:69–73.

_____. 1928. *Birds of New Mexico*. Albuquerque, N.M.: New Mex. Dept. of Game and Fish.

Bailey, L. H., and Bailey, E. Z. 1947. *Hortus Second*. New York: The Macmillan Company.

Bailey, R. E. 1952. The incubation patch of passerine birds. *Condor* 54:121–36.

Bailey, R. O., and Batt, B. D. J. 1974. Hierarchy of waterfowl feeding with whistling swans. *Auk* 91(3):488–93.

Bailey, R. W., and Rinell, K. T. 1967. Events in the turkey year. In *The wild turkey and its management*, ed. O. H. Hewitt. Washington, D.C.: Wildlife Soc.

Baird, J. 1963. Fulvous tree duck. *Audubon Field Notes* 17(1):6–8.

_____. 1964. The irruptive phenomenon. *Audubon Field Notes* 18(1):5–6.

_____. 1968a. Eastern Savannah sparrow. In *Life histories of North American cardinals, grosbeaks, buntings, towhees, finches, sparrows, and allies*, comp. A. C. Bent *et al.*, ed. O. L. Austin, Jr. U.S. Natl. Mus. Bull. no. 237, pt. 2. Washington, D.C.

_____. 1968b. A United States record of the black-tailed godwit. *Auk* 85:500–501.

Baird, J., and Nisbet, I. C. T. 1959. Observations of diurnal migration in the Narragansett Bay area of Rhode Island in fall 1958. *Bird-Banding* 30:171–81.

Baker, J. H. 1942. The director reports to you. *Audubon* 49:117–18.

_____. 1951. News of wildlife and conservation. *Audubon* 53:124–26.

_____. 1952. The president reports to you. *Audubon* 54:240.

Baker, J. K. 1962. The manner and efficiency of raptor depredations on bats. *Condor* 64(6):500–504.

Baker, R. H., and Newman, C. C. 1942. Speed of a woodcock. *Auk* 59(3):442.

Baker, W. W. 1971a. Observations of the food habits of the red-cockaded woodpecker. In *The ecology and management of the red-cockaded woodpecker: Proceedings of a symposium at Okefenokee National Wildlife Refuge, Folkston, Ga., May 26–27*, ed. R. L. Thompson. Tallahassee, Fla.: Tall Timbers Res. Station.

_____. 1971b. Progress report on life history studies of the red-cockaded woodpecker at Tall Timbers Research. In *The ecology and management of the red-cockaded woodpecker: Proceedings of a symposium at Okefenokee National Wildlife Refuge, Folkston, Ga., May 26–27*, ed. R. L. Thompson. Tallahassee, Fla.: Tall Timbers Res. Station.

Balch, L. G.; Bohlen, H. D.; and Rosenband, G. B. 1979. The Illinois Ross' gull. *Amer. Birds* 33:140–42.

Balcomb, R. 1977. The grouping of nocturnal passerine migrants. *Auk* 94(3):479–88.

Balda, R. P., and Bateman, G. C. 1971. Flocking and annual cycle of the piñon jay. *Condor* 73:287–302.

_____. 1973. Unusual mobbing behavior by incubating piñon jays. *Condor* 75:251–52.

Balda, R. P.; McKnight, B. C.; and Johnson, C. D. 1975. Flammulated owl migration in the southwestern United States. *Wilson Bull.* 87(4):520–33.

Balda, R. P.; Weisenberger, G.; and Strauss, M. 1970. White-crowned sparrow (*Zonotrichia leucophrys*) breeding in Arizona. *Auk* 87(4):809.

Baldwin, D. H.; Burger, G. V.; and Kortright, F. H. 1964. Cousins by the dozens. In *Waterfowl tomorrow*, ed. J. P. Linduska and A. L. Nelson.

Washington, D.C.: U.S. Dept. Inter., Fish and Wildlife Service.

Baldwin, J. M. 1914. Deferred imitation in West African gray parrots. *9th International Congr. Zool.*, pp. 536–37.

Baldwin, P. H. 1945. The Hawaiian goose: Its distribution and reduction in numbers. *Condor* 47(1):27–37.

_____. 1953. Annual cycle, environment and evolution in the Hawaiian honeycreepers. *Univ. Calif. Publ. Zool.* 52:285–398.

_____. 1968. Hoary redpoll. In *Life histories of North American cardinals, grosbeaks, buntings, towhees, finches, sparrows, and allies*, comp. A. C. Bent *et al.*, ed. O. L. Austin, Jr. U.S. Natl. Mus. Bull. no. 237, pt. 1. Washington, D.C.

Baldwin, S. P., and Kendeigh, S. C. 1932. Physiology of the temperature of birds. *Sci. Publ. Cleveland Mus. Nat. Hist.* 3:1–196.

_____. 1938. Variations in the weights of birds. *Auk* 55:416–67.

Baldwin, W. P. 1946. Clam catches oystercatcher. *Auk* 63(4):589.

Ball, S. C. 1952. *Fall migration on the Gaspé Peninsula*. Peabody Mus. Nat. Hist. Bull. no. 7. New Haven, Conn.: Yale University Press.

Bang, B. G. 1960. Anatomical evidence of olfactory function in some species of birds. *Nature* 188(4750):547–49.

Bang, B. G., and Cobb, S. 1968. The size of the olfactory bulb in 108 species of birds. *Auk* 85(1):55–61.

Banko, W. E. 1960. *The trumpeter swan*. N. Amer. Fauna no. 63. Washington, D.C.:U.S. Dept. Inter., Fish and Wildlife Service.

Banko, W. E., and Mackay, R. H. 1964. Our native swans. In *Waterfowl tomorrow*, ed. J. P. Linduska and A. L. Nelson. Washington, D.C.: U.S. Dept. Inter., Fish and Wildlife Service.

Banks, R. C. 1964. Geographic variation in the white-crowned sparrow, *Zonotrichia leucophrys*. *Univ. Calif. Publ. Zool.* 70:1–123.

_____. 1968a. Baird's junco. In *Life histories of North American cardinals, grosbeaks, buntings, towhees, finches, sparrows, and allies*, comp. A. C. Bent *et al.*, ed. O. L. Austin, Jr. U.S. Natl. Mus. Bull. no. 237, pt. 2. Washington, D.C.

_____. 1968b. Desert black-throated sparrow. In *Life histories of North American cardinals, grosbeaks, buntings, towhees, finches, sparrows, and allies*, comp. A. C. Bent *et al.*, ed. O. L. Austin, Jr. U.S. Natl. Mus. Bull. no. 237, pt. 2. Washington, D.C.

_____. 1970a. *Birds imported into the United States in 1968*. U.S. Dept. Inter., Fish and Wildlife Service, Spec. Sci. Rept.—Wildlife, no. 136. Washington, D.C.

_____. 1970b. Records of the brambling in North America. *Auk* 87(1):165–67.

_____. 1974. Personal communication.

_____. 1979. *Human-related mortality of birds in the United States*. U.S. Dept. Inter., Fish and Wildlife Service, Spec. Sci. Rept.—Wildlife, no. 215. Washington, D.C.

Banks, R. C., Clench, M. H., and Barlow, J. C. 1973. Bird collections in the United States and Canada. *Auk* 90(1):136–70.

Banks, R. C., and Johnson, N. K. 1961. A review of North American hybrid hummingbirds. *Condor* 63(1):3–27.

Banks, R. C., and Laybourne, R. C. 1968. The red-whiskered bulbul in Florida. *Auk* 85(1):141.

Banks, R. C., and Medina, D. R. 1963. An albinistic Anna's hummingbird. *Condor* 65(1):69–70.

Banks, R. C., and Orr, R. T. 1965. An unusual habit for purple martin. *Auk* 82(2):271–73.

Bannerman, D. A. 1959. *The birds of the British Isles*. Vol. 8. Edinburgh: Oliver & Boyd, Ltd. Pp. 349–60.

_____. 1961. *The birds of the British Isles*. Vol. 9. Edinburgh: Oliver & Boyd, Ltd.

_____. 1962. *The birds of the British Isles*. Vol.

11. London: Oliver & Boyd, Ltd. Pp. 310–22.

_____. 1964a. Ostrich. In *A new dictionary of birds*, ed. A. L. Thomson. New York: McGraw-Hill Book Company.

_____. 1964b. Secretary-bird. In *A new dictionary of birds*, ed. A. L. Thomson. New York: McGraw-Hill Book Company.

Baptista, L. F. 1973. Leaf-bathing in three species of emberizines. *Wilson Bull.* 85:346–47.

Barash, D. P. 1975. Evolutionary aspects of parental behavior: Distraction behavior of the alpine accentor. *Wilson Bull.* 87(3):367–73.

Barker, W. 1966. Tales once told. In *Birds in our lives*, ed. A. Stefferud and A. L. Nelson. Washington, D.C.: U.S. Dept. Inter., Fish and Wildlife Service.

Barlow, J. C. 1962. The natural history of the Bell vireo, *Vireo bellii* (Audubon). *Univ. Kans. Publ. Mus. Nat. Hist.* 12:241–96.

_____. 1973. Status of the North American population of the European tree sparrow. In *A symposium of the house sparrow* (Passer domesticus) *and European tree sparrow* (P. montanus) *in North America*. Amer. Ornith. Union, Monogr. no. 14.

Barlow, J. D.; Klaas, E. E.; and Lenz, J. L. 1963. Sunning of bank swallows and cliff swallows. *Condor* 65(5):438–40.

Barnes, I. 1955. Enemies in nature. *Atlantic Nat.* 11(2):55.

Barnhill III, M. Y., and DuMont, P. G. 1973. Observations of a white-faced storm petrel off Delaware. *Amer. Birds* 27:17.

Barrett, L. L. 1955. Blue jay attacks little brown bat. *Flicker* 27(4):175.

Barruel, P. 1954. *Birds of the world: Their life and habits*. New York: Oxford University Press.

Barrus, C. 1925. *The life and letters of John Burroughs*. 2 vols. Boston: Houghton Mifflin Company.

Barry, T. W. 1956. Observations of a nesting colony of American brant. *Auk* 73(2):193–202.

_____. 1962. Effect of late seasons on Atlantic brant reproduction. *Jour. Wildlife Management* 26(1):19–26.

_____. 1964. Brant, Ross' goose and emperor goose. In *Waterfowl tomorrow*, ed. J. P. Linduska and A. L. Nelson. Washington, D.C.: U.S. Dept. Inter., Fish and Wildlife Service.

Barth, E. K. 1955. Egg-laying, incubation and hatching of the common gull, *Larus canus*. *Ibis* 97:222–39.

Bartholomew, G. A. 1942. The fishing activities of double-crested cormorants in San Francisco Bay. *Condor* 44:13–21.

Bartholomew, G. A., and Cade, T. J. 1956. Water consumption of house finches. *Condor* 58:406.

_____. 1957. The body temperature of the American kestrel, *Falco sparverius*. *Wilson Bull.* 69(2):149–54.

Bartholomew, G. A., and Dawson, W. R. 1953. Respiratory water loss in some birds of the southwestern United States. *Physiol. Zool.* 26:162.

_____. 1954. Temperature regulation in young pelicans, herons, and gulls. *Ecology* 35:466.

Bartholomew, G. A.; Dawson, W. R.; and O'Neill, E. J. 1953. A field study of temperature regulation in young white pelicans, *Pelecanus erythrorhynchos*. *Ecology* 34:554–60.

Bartholomew, G. A.; Howell, T. R.; and Cade, T. J. 1957. Torpidity in the white-throated swift, Anna's hummingbird, and the poor-will. *Condor* 59:145–55.

Bartholomew, G. A.; Hudson, J. W.; and Howell, T. R. 1962. Body temperature, oxygen consumption, evaporative water loss, and heart rate in the poor-will. *Condor* 64:117–25.

Bartholomew, G. A.; Lasiewski, R. C.; and Crawford, Jr., E. C. 1968. Patterns of panting and gular flutter in cormorants, pelicans, owls, and doves. *Condor* 70(1):31–34.

Barton, Roger. 1955. *How to watch birds.* New York: McGraw-Hill Book Company.

Bartonek, J. C., and Gibson, D. D. 1972. Summer distribution of pelagic birds in Bristol Bay, Alaska. *Condor* 74:416–22.

Bartsch, Paul. 1968. *Mollusks.* New York: Dover Publications, Inc.

Bastin, E. W. 1952. Flight-speed of the mourning dove. *Wilson Bull.* 64(1):47.

Batchelder, C. F. 1937. *An account of the Nuttal Ornithological Club, 1873 to 1919.* Memoirs of the Nuttall Ornithological Club, vol. 8, pp. 1–109. Cambridge, Mass.

Bateman, G. C., and Balda, R. P. 1973. Growth, development, and food habits of young piñon jays. *Auk* 90:39–61.

Bates, M. 1950. *The nature of natural history.* New York: Charles Scribner's Sons.

———. 1960. *The forest and the sea.* New York: Random House, Inc.

———. 1961. *Man in nature. Foundations of modern biology.* New York: Prentice-Hall Publishing Co., Inc.

Bateson, P. P. G. 1961. Studies of less familiar birds: The little auk. *Brit. Birds,* 54:272–77.

Bateson, P. P. G., and Plowright, R. C., 1959. The breeding biology of the ivory gull in Spitsbergen. *Brit. Birds* 52(4):105–14.

Baumgarten, H. E. 1968. Lark Bunting. In *Life histories of North American cardinals, grosbeaks, buntings, towhees, finches, sparrows, and allies,* comp. A. C. Bent *et al.,* ed. O. L. Austin, Jr. U.S. Natl. Mus. Bull. no. 237, pt. 2. Washington, D.C.

Baumgartner, A. M. 1968a. Harris's sparrow. In *Life histories of North American cardinals, grosbeaks, buntings, towhees, finches, sparrows, and allies,* comp. A. C. Bent *et al.,* ed. O. L. Austin, Jr. U.S. Natl. Mus. Bull. no. 237, pt. 2. Washington, D.C.

———. 1968b. Tree sparrow. *In Life histories of North American cardinals, grosbeaks, buntings, towhees, finches, sparrows, and allies,* comp. A. C. Bent *et al.,* ed. O. L. Austin, Jr. U.S. Natl. Mus. Bull. no. 237, pt. 2. Washington, D.C.

Baynes, E. H. 1915. *Wild bird guests.* New York: E. P. Dutton.

Beal, F. E. L. 1895. *Preliminary report on the food of woodpeckers.* U.S. Dept. Agric. Bull. no. 7. Washington, D.C.

———. 1897. *Some common birds in their relation to agriculture.* U.S. Dept. Agric. Farmer's Bull. no. 30, pp. 13–17. Washington, D.C.

———. 1898. *Cuckoos and shrikes in their relation to agriculture.* U.S. Dept. Agric. Bull. no. 9. Washington, D.C.

———. 1911. *Food of the woodpeckers of the United States.* U.S. Dept. Agric., Bur. Biol. Surv. Bull. no. 37. Washington, D.C.

———. 1912. *Food of our more important flycatchers.* U.S. Dept. Agric., Bur. Biol. Surv. Bull. no. 44. Washington, D.C.

———. 1915. *Food of the robins and bluebirds of the United States.* U.S. Dept. Agric. Bull. no. 171. Washington, D.C.

———. 1918. *Food habits of the swallows, a family of native birds.* U.S. Dept. Agric. Bull. no. 619. Washington, D.C.

Beal, F. E. L.; McAtee, W. L.; and Kalmbach, E. R. 1916. *Common birds of southeastern United States in relation to agriculture.* U.S. Dept. Agric. Farmer's Bull. no. 755, pp. 34–35.

Beason, S. L., and Pattee, O. H. 1975. An encounter between a turkey and a bullsnake. *Wilson Bull.* 87(1):279–80.

Beaver, D. L., and Baldwin, P. H. 1975. Ecological overlap and the problem of competition and sympatry in the western and Hammond's flycatchers. *Condor* 77:1–13.

Beck, H. H. 1949. Status of the upland plover in Lancaster County, Pa. *Auk* 66:202–4.

Beck, R. 1971. *A study of wood thrush song.* Cornell Laboratory of Ornith., *Newsletter to Members,* no. 62. Ithaca, N.Y.

Becker, E. R. 1959. Protozoa. In *Diseases of poultry,* ed. H. E. Biester and L. H. Schwarte. Ames, Iowa: Iowa State University Press.

Becker, G. B., and Stack, J. W. 1944. Weights and temperatures of some Michigan birds. *Bird-Banding* 15(2):45–68.

Beckett, III., T. A. 1971a. Personal communication.

———. 1971b. A summary of red-cockaded woodpecker observations in South Carolina. In *The ecology and management of the red-cockaded woodpecker, Proceedings of a symposium at Okefenokee National Wildlife Refuge, Folkston, Ga., May 26–27,* ed. R. L. Thompson. Tallahassee, Fla.: Tall Timbers Res. Station.

Beckwith, S. L., and Hosford, H. J. 1957. A report on the seasonal food habits and life history notes of the Florida duck in the vicinity of Lake Okeechobee, Glades County, Florida. *Amer. Midland-Nat.* 57:461–73.

Bedard, J. 1969. Adaptive radiation in the alcids. *Ibis* 3:189–98.

Bedford, duke of. (Hastings, William Sackville R.) 1954. *Parrots and parrot-like birds.* Fond du Lac, Wis.: All Pets, Inc.

Beebe, F. L. 1960. The marine peregrines of the northwest Pacific coast. *Condor* 62:145–89.

———. 1967. Experiments in the husbandry of the peregrine. *Raptor Res. News* 1(4):61–86.

———. 1969. The known status of the peregrine falcon in British Columbia. In *Peregrine falcon populations: Their biology and decline,* ed. J. J. Hickey. Madison, Wis.: University of Wisconsin Press.

Beebe, W. 1906. *The bird: Its form and function.* New York: Henry Holt & Company, Inc.

———. 1935. Rediscovery of the Bermuda "cahow." *Bull. New York Zool. Soc.* 38:187–90.

———. 1936. *Pheasants: Their lives and homes.* Garden City, N.Y.: Doubleday, Doran & Company, Ltd.

———. 1965. *The bird: Its form and function.* New York: Dover Publications, Inc.

Beecher, C. E. 1900. Othniel Charles Marsh as an ornithologist. *Osprey* 4(5)74–76.

Beecher, W. J. 1942. *Nesting birds and the vegetation substrate.* Chicago: Chicago Ornith. Soc.

———. 1951. A possible navigation sense in the ear of birds. *Amer. Midland-Nat.* 46:374.

———. 1962. The bio-mechanics of the bird skull. *Bull. Chicago Acad. Sci.* 11:10–33.

Beer, C. G. 1964. Incubation. In *A new dictionary of birds,* ed. A. L. Thomson. New York: McGraw-Hill Book Company.

Beer, J., and Tydyman, W. 1942. The substitution of hard seeds for grit. *Jour. Wildlife Management* 6(1):70–82.

Beer, R. E. 1970. Ectoparasites of birds: A brief review. In *Ornithology in laboratory and field,* by O. S. Pettingill, Jr. Minneapolis: Burgess Publishing Co.

Behle, W. H. 1973. Clinal variations in white-throated swifts from Utah and the Rocky Mountain region. *Auk* 90(2):299–306.

Behle, W. H., and Goates, W. A. 1957. Breeding biology of the California gull. *Condor* 59:235–46.

Belding, Lyman. 1890. *Land birds of the Pacific district of California.* Calif. Acad. Sci. 2:1–274.

Belknap, J. B., Giraud, Jr., J. P. 1960 *Kingbird* 10(1):12

Bell, J. 1971. News from the department of ornithology at the New York Zoological Park. *Avicultural Magazine* 77(1):37–38.

Bellairs, A. d'A. 1964a. Palate. In *A new dictionary of birds,* ed. A. L. Thomson. New York: McGraw-Hill Book Company.

———. 1964b. Skeleton. In *A new dictionary of birds,* ed. A. L. Thomson. New York: McGraw-Hill Book Company.

Bellairs, A. d'A, and Jenkins, C. R. 1960. The skeleton of birds. In *Biology and comparative physiology of birds,* ed. A. J. Marshall. Vol. 1. New York: Academic Press, Inc.

Bellairs, R. 1960. Development of birds. In *Biology and comparative physiology of birds,* ed. A. J. Marshall. Vol. 1, chap. 5. New York: Academic Press, Inc.

Bellrose, Jr., F. C. 1943. Two wood ducks incubating in the same nesting box. *Auk* 60:446–47.

———. 1955. *Housing of wood ducks.* Illinois Nat. Hist. Surv., Circ. no. 45. Urbana.

———. 1958. Celestial orientation by wild mallards. *Bird-Banding* 29:75–90.

———. 1959. Lead poisoning as a mortality factor in waterfowl populations. *Illinois Nat. Hist. Surv., Bull.* no. 27, art. 3, pp. 235–88.

———. 1963. Orientation behavior of four species of waterfowl. *Auk* 80:257–89.

———. 1964a. Radar studies of waterfowl migration. *Trans.* [29th] *N. Amer. Wildlife and Nat. Res. Conf.,* pp. 128–43.

———. 1964b. Spent shot and lead poisoning. In *Waterfowl tomorrow,* ed. J. P. Linduska and A. L. Nelson. Washington, D.C.: U.S. Dept. Inter., Fish and Wildlife Service.

———. 1966. Orientation in waterfowl migration. In *Animal orientation and navigation. Proc. 27th Ann. Biol. Coloquium, May 6–7, 1966.* Corvallis, Oregon: Oregon State University Press.

———. 1967. Radar in orientation research. *Proc.* [XIVth] *Internatl. Ornith. Congress,* ed. D. W. Snow, pp. 281–309. Oxford: Blackwell Scientific Publications.

———. 1971. The distribution of nocturnal migrants in the air space. *Auk* 88(2):397–424.

———. 1972. Possible steps in the evolutionary development of bird navigation. In *Animal orientation and bird navigation.* National Aeronautics and Space Administration. NASA. SP-262:223–57.

———. 1976. *Ducks, geese and swans of North America.* Harrisburg, Pa.: Stackpole Books.

———. 1978. Personal communication.

Bellrose, Jr., F. C., and Graber, R. R. 1963. A radar study of the flight directions of nocturnal migrants. *Proc.* [XIIIth] *Internatl. Ornith. Congress,* pp. 362–389. Ithaca, N.Y.: American Ornithologists' Union.

Bellrose, Jr., F. C., and Sieh, J. G. 1960. Massed waterfowl flights in the Mississippi flyway, 1956 and 1957. *Wilson Bull.* 72(1):29–59.

Belopol'skii, L. O. 1957. *Ecology of sea colony birds of the Barents Sea.* Jerusalem: Israel Program for Scientific Translations.

Benbrook, E. A. 1959. External parasites of poultry. In *Diseases of poultry,* ed. H. E. Biester and L. H. Schwarte. 4th ed. Ames, Iowa: Iowa State University Press.

Bendire, C. E. 1892. *Life histories of North American birds.* U.S. Natl. Mus. Bull. no. 1 (vol. 1). Washington, D.C.

Bené, F. 1947. *The feeding and related behavior of hummingbirds: With special reference to the black-chin.* Boston: Charles T. Branford Co.

Bengston, B. 1968. Wildlife on Christmas seals. *Canadian Audubon,* November–December, pp. 134–37.

Benner, Fred J. 1967. Seasonal correlations of reserve energy of the red-winged blackbird. *Bird-Banding* 38(3):195–211.

Bennett, L. J. 1938. *The blue-winged teal.* Ames, Iowa: Collegiate Press, Inc., of Iowa State College.

Benoit, J. 1950. *Oiseau.* In Traité de zoologie, vol. 20, ed. P.-P. Grassé. Paris: Masson et Cie.

———. 1956. *Etats physiologiques et instinct de reproduction chez les oiseaux.* Fondation Singer. Polignace. 12–260. Paris: Masson et Cie.

Benson, D., and Bellrose, F. 1964. Eastern production areas. In *Waterfowl tomorrow,* ed. J. P. Linduska and A. L. Nelson. Washington, D.C.: U.S. Dept. Inter., Fish and Wildlife Service.

Bent, A. C. 1919. *Life histories of North American diving birds.* U.S. Natl. Mus. Bull. no. 107. Washington, D.C.

_____. 1921. *Life histories of North American gulls and terns.* U.S. Natl. Mus. Bull. no. 113. Washington, D.C.

_____. 1922. *Life histories of North American petrels and pelicans and their allies.* U.S. Natl. Mus. Bull. no. 121. Washington, D.C.

_____. 1923. *Life histories of North American wild fowl.* U.S. Natl. Mus. Bull. no. 126, pt. 1. Washington, D.C.

_____. 1925. *Life histories of North American wild fowl.* U.S. Natl. Mus. Bull. no. 130, pt. 2. Washington, D.C.

_____. 1926a. *Life histories of North American marsh birds.* U.S. Natl. Mus. Bull. no. 135. Washington, D.C.

_____. 1926b. Passerine birds eating trout fry. *Auk* 43:558.

_____. 1927. *Life histories of North American shore birds.* U.S. Natl. Mus. Bull. no. 142, pt. 1. Washington, D.C.

_____. 1929. *Life histories of North American shorebirds.* U.S. Natl. Mus. Bull. no. 146, pt. 2. Washington, D.C.

_____. 1932. *Life histories of North American gallinaceous birds.* U.S. Natl. Mus. Bull. no. 162. Washington, D.C.

_____. 1937. *Life histories of North American birds of prey.* U.S. Natl. Mus. Bull. no. 167, pt. 1. Washington, D.C.

_____. 1938. *Life histories of North American birds of prey.* U.S. Natl. Mus. Bull. no. 170, pt. 2. Washington, D.C.

_____. 1939. *Life histories of North American woodpeckers.* U.S. Natl. Mus. Bull. no. 174. Washington, D.C.

_____. 1940. *Life histories of North American cuckoos, goatsuckers, hummingbirds, and their allies.* U.S. Natl. Mus. Bull. no. 176. Washington, D.C.

_____. 1942. *Life histories of North American flycatchers, larks, swallows, and their allies.* U.S. Natl. Mus. Bull. no. 179. Washington, D.C.

_____. 1946. *Life histories of North American jays, crows, and titmice.* U.S. Natl. Mus. Bull. no. 191. Washington, D.C.

_____. 1948. *Life histories of North American nuthatches, wrens, thrashers, and their allies.* U.S. Natl. Mus. Bull. no. 195. Washington, D.C.

_____. 1949. *Life histories of North American thrushes, kinglets, and their allies.* U.S. Natl. Mus. Bull. no. 196. Washington, D.C.

_____. 1950. *Life histories of North American wagtails, shrikes, vireos, and their allies.* U.S. Natl. Mus. Bull. no. 197. Washington, D.C.

_____. 1953. *Life histories of North American wood warblers.* U.S. Natl. Mus. Bull. no. 203. Washington, D.C.

_____. 1958. *Life histories of North American blackbirds, orioles, tanagers, and their allies.* U.S. Natl. Mus. Bull. no. 211. Washington, D.C.

Bent, A. C. et al., comps. 1968. *Life histories of North American cardinals, grosbeaks, buntings, towhees, finches, sparrows, and their allies,* ed. O. L. Austin, Jr. U.S. Natl. Mus. Bull. no. 237, pts. 1–3. Washington, D.C.

Benton, A. H. 1952. Song mimicry of red-eyed vireo. *Kingbird* 2(2):343.

Benton, A. H., and Dickinson, L. E. 1966. Wires, poles, and birds. In *Birds in our lives,* ed. A. Stefferud and A. L. Nelson. Washington, D.C.: U.S. Dept. Inter., Fish and Wildlife Service.

Bequaert, J. C. 1922. The predaceous enemies of ants. *Bull. Amer. Mus. Nat. Hist.* 15(3):271–331.

_____. 1953. The hippoboscidae or louse-flies (*Diptera*) of mammals and birds. Part I. Structure, physiology and natural history. Reprinted from *Entomologica Americana* n.s., vol. 32 (February 20):1–209, and n.s., vol. 33 (May 26):211–442.

Berger, A. J. 1951. Ten consecutive nests of a song sparrow. *Wilson Bull.* 63:186–88.

_____. 1953a. Green frog catches young phoebe. *Bird-Banding* 24(2):67–68.

_____. 1953b. Three cases of twin embryos in passerine birds. *Condor* 55:157–58.

_____. 1955. Six-storied nest of a yellow warbler with eleven cowbird eggs. *Jack-Pine Warbler* 33:84.

_____. 1956. Two albinistic flycatchers at Ann Arbor, Michigan. *Auk* 73:137–38.

_____. 1960. The musculature. In *Biology and comparative physiology of birds,* ed. A. J. Marshall. Vol. 1. New York: Academic Press, Inc.

_____. 1961. *Bird study.* New York: John Wiley & Sons, Inc.

_____. 1968. Eastern vesper sparrow. In *Life histories of North American cardinals, grosbeaks, buntings, towhees, finches, sparrows, and their allies,* comp. A. C. Bent et al., ed. O. L. Austin, Jr. U.S. Natl. Mus. Bull. no. 237, pt. 2. Washington, D.C.

_____. 1972. *Hawaiian bird life.* Honolulu, Hawaii: University of Hawaii Press.

Berger, A. J., and Howard, D. V. 1968. Anophthalmia in the American robin. *Condor* 70(4): 386–87.

Berger, A. J., and Radabaugh, B. E. 1968. Returns of Kirtland's warblers to the breeding grounds. *Bird-Banding* 39(3):161–86.

Berger, M., and Hart, J. S. 1974. Physiology and energetics of flight. In *Avian biology,* ed. D. S. Farner, J. R. King, and K.C. Parkes. Vol. 4, pp. 416–78. New York: Academic Press, Inc.

Berger, M.; Hart, J. S.; and Roy, O. Z. 1970a. The co-ordination between respiration and wing beats in birds. *Zeit vergleich Physiol.* 66:190–200.

Berger, M.; Hart, J. S.; and Roy, O. Z. 1970b. Respiration, oxygen consumption, and heart rate in some birds during rest and flight. *Zeit vergleich Physiol.* 66:201–14.

Bergman, G. 1950. Experimentella undersökningar övaer sömndjupet hos olika smafagelsarter [Investigations on the depth of sleep in passerine birds]. *Ornis Fennica* 27(4):109–24.

Bergmann, A. 1847. Über die verhältnisse der Wärmeökonomie der Thiere zu ihrer Grösse. *Göttinger Studien,* pt. 1:595–708.

Bergstrom, E. A. 1952. Extreme old age in terns. *Bird-Banding* 23:72–73.

_____. 1956. Extreme old age in birds. *Bird-Banding* 27:128–29.

_____. 1958. Random notes on the blue jay. *Bird-Banding* 29(1):43–44.

Bergtold, W. H. 1907. The house finch from an office window. *Bird-Lore* 9(2):61–64.

_____. 1916a. Eyeshine in birds. *Auk* 33:81.

_____. 1916b. Pseudo-masculinity in birds. *Auk* 33(4):439.

Berry, R. B. 1970. Captive breeding behavior of American goshawk (Part 2). *Raptor Res. News* 4(1):18–31.

Berthold, P. 1967. On the adherent colors of birds: Rusty coloration by iron oxide in the bearded vulture and in other species. *Zool. Jahrb. Syst. Bd.* 93 S:507–95.

_____. 1975. Migration: control and metabolic physiology. In *Avian biology,* D. S. Farner, J. R. King, and K. C. Parkes. Vol. 5. New York: Academic Press, Inc.

Bierregaard, Jr., R. O.; David II, A. B.; and Baird, T. D. 1975. First northwestern Atlantic breeding record of the manx shearwater. *Auk* 92(1): 145–47.

Biester, H. E., and Schwarte, L. H., eds. 1959. *Diseases of poultry.* 4th ed. Ames, Iowa: Iowa State University Press.

_____. 1965. *Diseases of poultry.* 5th ed. Ames, Iowa: Iowa State University Press.

Binford, L. C. 1970. Audubon's shearwater, hudsonian godwit, and long-tailed jaeger in Oaxaca, Mexico. *Condor* 72:366.

Binford, L. C.; Elliott, B. G.; and Singer, S. W.

_____. 1975. Discovery of a nest and the downy young of the marbled murrelet. *Wilson Bull.* 87(3): 303–19.

Binford, L. C., and Remsen, Jr., J. V. 1974. Identification of the yellow-billed loon (*Gavia adamsii*). *Western Birds* 5:111–26.

Bishop, L. B. 1944. *Ornithological notes from Point Barrow, Alaska.* Zool. Ser. 29, no. 12. Chicago: Field Mus. Nat. Hist.

Bissonnette, T. H. 1937. Photoperiodicity in birds. *Wilson Bull.* 64:197–220.

_____. 1939. Sexual photoperiodicity in the blue jay (*Cyanocitta cristata*). *Wilson Bull.* 51:227–32.

_____. 1944. A four-winged cock pheasant. *Bird-Banding* 15:145–50.

Blackwelder, R. E., and Boyden, A. 1952. The nature of systematics. *Syst. Zool.* 1:26–33.

Blaine, G. 1936. *Falconry. The sportsman's library.* Vol. 15. London: Philip Allan & Co., Ltd.

Blake, C. H. 1947. Wing-flapping rates of birds. *Auk* 56: 619–20.

_____. 1950. Raised ear coverts. *Auk* 67:105–6.

_____. 1953. Notes on the rough-winged swallow. *Bird-Banding* 24(3):107–8.

_____. 1958. Respiration rates. *Bird-Banding* 29(1):38–40.

_____. 1962. Wing length of slate-colored junco. *Bird-Banding* 33(2):97–99.

_____. 1964. Observations on bird ticks. *Bird-Banding* 35(2):127.

_____. 1969. Notes on the indigo bunting. *Bird-Banding* 40(2):133–39.

Blake, C. H., and Cadbury, J. M. 1969. An old warbler. *Bird-Banding* 40(3):255.

Blake, E. R. 1953. *Birds of Mexico: A guide for field identification.* Chicago: University of Chicago Press.

_____. 1964. Oriole (2). In *A new dictionary of birds,* ed. A. L. Thomson. New York: McGraw-Hill Book Company.

_____. 1977. Manual of neotropical birds. Vol. 1. Chicago: University of Chicago Press.

Blokpoel, H., and Burton, J. 1975. Weather and height of nocturnal migration in east central Alberta: A radar study. *Bird-Banding* 46(4): 311–28.

Blunt, W. 1971. *The compleat naturalist: A life of Linnaeus.* New York: The Viking Press.

Boardman, R. 1972. Tower hazard. *Audubon Leader* 13 (September 15): 16.

Bock, C. E. 1970. *The ecology and behavior of the Lewis' woodpecker* (Asyndesmus lewis). Univ. California Publ. Zool. no. 92. Berkeley, Calif.: University of California Press.

Bock, C. E.; Hadow, H. H.; and Somers, P. 1971. Relations between Lewis' and red-headed woodpeckers in southeastern Colorado. *Wilson Bull.* 83(3):237–48.

Bock, C. E., and Smith, R. B. 1971. An analysis of Colorado Christmas counts. *Amer. Birds* 25(6): 945–47.

Bock, W. J. 1961. Salivary glands in the gray jays (*Perisoreus*). *Auk* 78(3):355–65.

_____. 1964. Kinetics of the avian skull. *Jour. Morph.* 114:1–42.

_____. 1965. Analysis of the avian passive perching mechanism. *Amer. Zool.* 5:251.

Bock, W. J.; Balda, R. P.; and Vander Wall, S. B. 1973. Morphology of sublingual pouch and tongue musculature in Clark's nutcracker. *Auk* 90:491–519.

Bock, W. J., and Wahlert, G. von. 1965. Adaptation and the form-function complex. *Evolution* 19:269–99.

Bocker, E. L. 1972. A survey of white pelican nesting colonies in 1971. *Amer. Birds* 26(1):24.

Boeker, E. L., and Ray, T. D. 1971. Golden eagle population studies in the Southwest. *Condor* 73(4):463–67.

Bogert, C. M. 1964. Amphibian. In *The Audubon nature encyclopedia,* ed. J. K. Terres, Vol. 1. Philadelphia: Curtis Publishing Company.

Böker, Hans. 1927. Die biologische Anatomie der

Flugarten der Vögel und ihre Phylogenie. *Jour. f. Ornith.* 75:304–71.

Bolander, Jr., L. P. 1932. A robin roost in Oakland, California. *Condor* 34:142–43.

Bolen, E. G. 1971. Some views on exotic waterfowl. *Wilson Bull.* 83:430–34.

Bolen, E. G., and Cottam, C. 1967. Wood duck nesting records from south Texas. *Southwestern Naturalist* 12:189–205.

Bolles, F. 1891. Yellow-bellied woodpeckers and their uninvited guests. *Auk* 9:109–19.

Bollinger, R. C., and Bowes, E. 1973. Another chapter in the "ornithological mystery story." *Amer. Birds* 27(4):741–42.

Bond, G. M. 1963. Geographic variation in the thrush (*Hylocichla ustulata*). *Proc. U.S. Natl. Mus.* 114 (3471):373–87.

Bond, J. 1961. *Birds of the West Indies.* Boston: Houghton Mifflin Company.

———. 1964. Vireo. In *A new dictionary of birds,* ed. A. L. Thomson. New York: McGraw-Hill Book Company.

———. 1968. Bahama black-faced grassquit. In *Life histories of North American cardinals, grosbeaks, buntings, towhees, finches, sparrows, and allies,* comp. A. C. Bent *et al.,* ed. O. L. Austin, Jr. U.S. Natl. Mus. Bull. no. 237, pt. 1. Washington, D.C.

Bond, R. M. 1936a. Live weights of certain hawks. *Condor* 38:178.

———. 1936b. Speed and eyesight of a pigeon hawk. *Condor* 38(2):85.

———. 1942. Development of young goshawks. *Wilson Bull.* 54:81–88.

———. 1943. Variation in western sparrow hawks. *Condor* 45:168–85.

Borchelt, P. L. 1972. Dustbathing in bobwhite quail (*Colinus virginianus*): A regulating model. Ph.D. dissertation, Michigan State University, East Lansing.

Bordner, D. L. 1958. Cardinal banded in Connecticut re-trapped in Pennsylvania. *Bird-Banding* 29(4):244.

Borelli, G. A. 1681. *De motu animalium.* Vol. 2. Rome.

Borneman, J. C. 1970. *California Condor News letter* no. 1. Ventura, Calif.: Natl. Audubon Soc.

———. 1971. *California Condor Newsletter* no. 2. Ventura, Calif.: Natl. Audubon Soc.

———. 1972. *California Condor Newsletter* no. 3. Ventura, Calif.: Natl. Audubon Soc.

Borror, D. J. 1960a. The analysis of animal sounds. In *Animal sounds and communication,* ed. W. E. Lanyon and W. N. Tavolga. Amer. Inst. Biol. Sci. Publ. no. 7. Washington, D. C.

———. 1960b. *Dictionary of word roots and combining forms.* Palo Alto, Calif.: N-P Publications.

———. 1967. Songs of the yellowthroat. *Living Bird,* 6th annual, pp. 141–61.

———. 1975a. Bird song. *Amer. Birds* 29(1):3–7.

———. 1975b. Personal communication.

Boudreau, G. N. 1968. Alarm sounds and responses of birds and their application in controlling problem species. *Living Bird,* 7th annual, pp. 27–46.

Bourliere, F. 1964. *The natural history of mammals.* 3d ed. New York: Alfred A. Knopf, Inc.

Bourne, W. R. P. 1964. Petrel. In *A new dictionary of birds,* ed. A. L. Thomson. New York: McGraw-Hill Book Company.

Bouvier, G. 1968. Salmonella in wild birds, especially small passerines in the region of Lausanne. *Nos Oiseaux* 29(320):293–95.

Bowen, V. T., and Nicholls, G. D. 1968. An egret observed on St. Paul's rocks, equatorial Atlantic. *Auk* 85(1):130–31.

Boyajiian, N. R. 1971a. Hudson–St. Lawrence region. *Amer. Birds* 25:32–33.

———. 1971b. Hudson–St. Lawrence region. *Amer. Birds* 25(4):713.

———. 1971c. Hudson–St. Lawrence region. *Amer. Birds* 25:841.

———. 1973. Hudson–St. Lawrence region. *Amer. Birds* 27:33, 594.

Boyd, E. M. 1951. The external parasites of birds: A review. *Wilson Bull.* 63(4):363–69.

———. 1974. Mortality of blue jays, *Cyanocitta cristata,* in eastern Massachusetts due to parasitism by the esophageal nematode, *Capillaria contorta. Bird News of Western Mass.* 14:2.

Boyd, H. J. 1964. Swimming and diving. In *A new dictionary of birds,* ed. A. L. Thomson. New York: McGraw-Hill Book Company.

Brackbill, H. 1941. Possible homosexual mating of the rock dove. *Auk* 58:581.

———. 1948. Anting by four species of birds. *Auk* 65(1):66–77.

———. 1953. Notes on the drumming of some woodpeckers. *Bird-Banding* 24(1):18

———. 1958. Nesting behavior of the wood thrush. *Wilson Bull.* 70:70–89.

———. 1969a. Red-bellied woodpeckers taking birds' eggs. *Bird-Banding* 40(4):323–24.

———. 1969b. White-breasted nuthatch bill abnormality corrected by wear. *Bird-Banding* 40(2):145.

———. 1970a. New light on the mourning dove. *Maryland Birdlife,* spring, pp. 8–11.

———. 1970b. A polygynous house wren. *Bird-Banding* 41(2):118–21.

———. 1970c. Shorebirds leaving water to defecate. *Auk* 87:160.

———. 1970d. Tufted titmouse breeding behavior. *Auk* 87(3):522–36.

Brand, A., and Kellogg, P. P. 1939. Auditory responses of starlings, English sparrows and domestic pigeons. *Wilson Bull.* 51:38–41.

Brandt, H. 1940. *Texas bird adventures in the Chisos Mountains and on the northern Great Plains.* Cleveland, Ohio: Bird Research Foundation.

———. 1951. *Arizona and its bird life.* Cleveland, Ohio: Bird Research Foundation.

Brasher, M. E. 1962. *Rex Brasher, painter of birds.* New York: Rowman and Littlefield, Inc.

Braun, C. E., and Blumberg, R. G. 1973. An albinistic blue grouse from Colorado. *Condor* 75:345–46.

Braun, C. E.; Brown, D. E.; Peterson, J. C.; and Zapatka, T. P. 1975. *Results of the Four-Corners cooperative band-tailed pigeon investigation.* U.S. Dept. Inter., Fish and Wildlife Serv., Res. Publ. no. 126. Washington, D.C.

Brauner, J. 1953. Observations on the behavior of a captive poor-will. *Condor* 55(2):68–74.

Bray, C. W., and Thurlow, W. R. 1942. Temporary deafness in birds. *Auk* 59:379–87.

Breckenridge, W. J. 1956. Measurements of the habitat niche of the least flycatcher. *Wilson Bull.* 68:47–51.

Breder, Jr., C. M. 1948. *Field book of marine fishes of the Atlantic coast.* New York and London: G. P. Putnam's Sons.

Bremckle, J. F. 1936. The migration of the western burrowing owl. *Bird-Banding* 7:166–68.

Brereton, J. L. G. 1963. The life cycles of three Australian parrots: Some comparative and population aspects. *Living Bird,* 2d annual, pp. 21–29.

Brett, J. 1976. Personal communication.

Brewer, R. 1961. Comparative notes on the life history of the Carolina chickadee. *Wilson Bull.* 73(4):348.

———. 1963. Ecological reproductive relationships of black-capped and Carolina chickadees. *Auk* 80(1):9–47.

Brewster, W. 1883. On an apparently new gull from eastern North America. *Bull. Nuttall Ornith. Club* 8(4):214–19.

———. 1886. Bird migration. Mem. Nuttall Ornith. Club, no. 1. Cambridge, Mass.

———. 1901. An ornithological mystery. *Auk* 18:321–28.

———. 1936. *October farm.* Cambridge, Mass.: Harvard University Press.

Briggs, F. P. 1964. Waterfowl in a changing continent. In *Waterfowl tomorrow,* ed. J. P. Linduska and A. L. Nelson. Washington, D.C.: U.S. Dept. Inter., Fish and Wildlife Service.

Briggs, S. A. 1966. Symbols of states. In *Birds in our lives,* ed. A. Stefferud and A. L. Nelson. Washington, D.C.: U.S. Dept. Inter., Fish and Wildlife Service.

Brimley, H. H. 1934. Unusual actions of a phoebe (*Sayornis phoebe*). *Auk* 51:237–38.

Brockway, B. F. 1964. Ethological studies of the budgerigar (*Melopsittacus undulatus*): Nonreproductive behavior. *Behavior* 22:3–4.

Brodkorb, P. 1935. A sparrow hawk gyandromorph. *Auk* 52(2):183–84.

———. 1949. The numbers of feathers in some birds. *Quart. Jour. Florida Acad. Sci.* 12(4):241–45.

———. 1960. How many species of birds have existed? *Bull. Florida State Mus.* 5(3):41–53.

———. 1963. Catalogue of fossil birds. Part I. *Bull. Florida State Mus.* 7:179–293.

———. 1964. Catalogue of fossil birds. Part II. *Bull. Florida State Mus.* 8:195–335.

———. 1968. Birds (Part 5). In *Vertebrates of the United States,* ed. W. F. Blair. New York: McGraw-Hill Book Company.

———. 1971. Origin and evolution of birds. In *Avian biology,* ed. D. S. Farner, J. R. King, and K. C. Parkes. Vol. 1. New York: Academic Press, Inc.

———. 1978. Catalogue of fossil birds, pt. 5. *Bull. Florida State Mus.* 23(3):1–228.

Broley, C. L. 1947. Migration and nesting of Florida bald eagles. *Wilson Bull.* 59(1):3–20.

———. 1950. The plight of the bald eagle. *Audubon* 60(4):162–71.

Brookfield, C. M., and Griswold, O. 1956. An exotic new oriole settles in Florida. *Natl. Geographic Magazine* 109:261–64.

Brooks, A. 1937. The swans, ducks, and geese. In *The book of birds,* ed. G. Grosvenor and A. Wetmore. Vol. 1. Washington, D.C.: Natl. Geographic Soc.

———. 1945. The underwater actions of diving ducks. *Auk* 62(4):517–23.

Brooks, E. W. 1971. Thirty-fifth breeding bird census. *Amer. Birds* 25(6):996.

Brooks, M. 1945. George Sutton and his warbler. *Audubon* 47(3):145–50.

Brooks, W. S. 1968. Comparative adaptations of the Alaskan redpolls to the Arctic environment. *Wilson Bull.* 80(3):253–80.

Broun, M. 1941. Gulls eating fruit of cabbage palmetto. *Auk* 58(4):579.

———. 1947. Golden eagle captures red-tailed hawk. *Auk* 64(2):312–18.

———. 1949. *Hawks aloft: The story of hawk mountain.* New York: Dodd, Mead & Company.

———. 1957. Brewster's warbler. In *The warblers of America,* ed. L. Griscom *et al.* New York: The Devin-Adair Co.

———. 1963. *Hawk migration and the weather.* Hawk Mt. Sanctuary Assoc. Leaflet. Kempton, Pa.

Broun, M., and Goodwin, B. V. 1943. Flight speeds of hawks and crows. *Auk* 60:486–92.

Brown, C. P. 1954. Notes on woodcock chicks raised in captivity. *Bird-Banding* 25(4):149–50.

Brown, C. R. 1975. Polygamy in the purple martin. *Auk* 92(3):602–4.

Brown, Jr., D. W. 1968. *Desert biology.* New York: Academic Press, Inc.

Brown, G. 1942. Some aspects of instinctive behaviour and display in birds. *Ibis* 84(6):133–35.

Brown, J. L. 1963. Social organization and behavior of the Mexican jay. *Condor* 65:126–53.

———. 1970. Cooperative breeding and altruistic behavior in the Mexican Jay, *Aphelocoma ultramarina. Jour. Animal Behaviour* 18:366–78.

———. 1972. Communal feeding of nestlings in the Mexican jay (*Aphelocoma ultramarina*): interflock comparisons. *Jour. Animal Behaviour* 20:395–403.

———. 1973. Behavior elicited by electrical stimulation of the brain of the Steller's jay. *Condor* 75:1–16.

Brown, L., and Amadon, D. 1968. *Eagles, hawks, and falcons of the world.* 2 vols. New York: McGraw-Hill Book Company.

Brown, L. H. 1958. The breeding biology of the greater flamingo, *Phoenicopterus ruber,* at lake Elmenteita, Kenya colony. *Ibis* 100:388–420.

———. 1964a. Falcon. In *A new dictionary of birds,* ed. A. L. Thomson. New York: McGraw-Hill Book Company.

———. 1964b. Flamingo. In *A new dictionary of birds,* ed. A. L. Thomson. New York: McGraw-Hill Book Company.

———. 1964c. Hawk. In *A new dictionary of birds,* ed. A. L. Thomson. New York: McGraw-Hill Book Company.

———. 1966. Observations on some Kenya eagles. *Ibis* 108:531–72.

———. 1970. Eagles. New York: Arco Publications.

Brown, L. H., and Watson, A. 1964. The golden eagle in relation to its food supply. *Ibis* 106(1):78–100.

Brown, W. H. 1971. Winter population trends in the red-shouldered hawk. *Amer. Birds* 25(5):813–17.

Brown, W. Y. 1976. Growth and fledging age of sooty tern chicks. *Auk* 93(1):179–83.

Brown, W. Y., and Robertson, W. J. 1975. Longevity of the brown noddy. *Bird-Banding* 46(3):250–51.

Browne, T. G. 1922. Some observations on the digestive system of the fowl. *Jour. Compar. Pathol. Therap.* 35:12–32.

Browne, W. E. 1937. A visit to "Many Wings." *Bird-Lore* 39:358–61.

Bruce, J. A. 1961. First record of European skylark on San Juan Island, Washington. *Condor* 63:418.

———. 1973. Tail-flashing display in the whippoor-will. *Auk* 90:682.

Brush, A. H. 1971. Feather-bird. In *Encyclopedia of science and technology.* New York: McGraw-Hill Book Company.

Buchheister, C. W. 1960. What about problem birds? *Audubon* 62:116–18.

Buchheister, C. W., and Graham, Jr., F. 1973. From the swamps back: A concise and candid history of the Audubon movement. *Audubon* 75:4–43.

Buchsbaum, R. 1938. *Animals without backbones.* Chicago: University of Chicago Press.

———. 1961. Invertebrates. In *The encyclopedia of biological sciences,* ed. P. Gray. New York: Reinhold Publishing Corporation.

Buchsbaum, R., and Buchsbaum, M. 1957. *Basic ecology.* Pittsburgh: The Boxwood Press.

Buckley, J. L., and Cottam, C. 1966. An ounce of prevention. In *Birds in our lives,* ed. A. Stefferud and A. L. Nelson. Washington, D.C.: U.S. Dept. Inter., Fish and Wildlife Service.

Buckley, P. A. 1969. Ross' goose in North Carolina: First Atlantic seaboard occurrence. *Auk* 86(3):551–52.

———. 1970. Brown booby, magnificent frigatebird and sabine's gull new to Virginia. *Audubon Field Notes* 24(5):651.

———. 1971. The changing seasons. *Amer. Birds* 25(3):541, 543, 544.

———. 1972. The changing seasons. *Amer. Birds* 26(3):568–70.

———. 1973. Plumage aberrancies. *Amer. Birds* 27(3):585.

Buckley, P. A., and Buckley, F. G. 1970. Color variation for soft parts and down of royal tern chicks. *Auk* 87(1):1–13.

Buckley, P. A., and Kane, R. 1975. Hudson–St. Lawrence region. *Amer. Birds* 29(3):670.

Buckley, P. A., Paxton, R. O., and Cutler, D. A. 1975. Hudson–Delaware region. *Amer. Birds* 29(5)951–53.

Buffon, G. L. L. de. 1771. *Histoire naturelle . . .*

avec la description du cabinet du roi 17:145. Paris.

Bull, J. 1958. The changing seasons. *Audubon Field Notes* 12:392.

———. 1964. *Birds of the New York area.* New York: Harper & Row, Publishers, Inc.

———. 1971. Monk parakeets in the New York City region. *Linnaean Soc. N.Y. Newsletter* 25(1):1–2.

———. 1973. Exotic birds in the New York City area. *Wilson Bull.* 85:501–5.

———. 1974. *Birds of New York State.* Garden City, N.Y.: Doubleday/Natural History Press.

Bull, J., and Ricciuti, E. R. 1974. Polly want an apple? *Audubon* 76(3):48–54.

Buller, R. J. 1964. Central flyway. In *Waterfowl tomorrow,* ed. J. P. Linduska and A. L. Nelson. Washington, D.C.: U.S. Dept. Inter., Fish and Wildlife Service.

Bulmer, W. 1970. First specimens of chestnut-collared longspur and little gull from Connecticut. *Wilson Bull.* 82(2):226–27.

Bump, G. 1971. *The South American monk, quaker, or gray-headed parakeet.* U.S. Dept. Inter., Wildlife Leaflet no. 496. Washington, D.C.

Bump, G.; Darrow, R. W.; Edminster, F. C.; and Crissey, W. F. 1947. *The ruffed grouse.* Life History, propagation and management. Albany, N.Y.: N.Y. State Cons. Dept.

Bump, G., and Robbins, C. S. 1966. The newcomers. In *Birds in our lives,* ed. A. Stefferud and A. L. Nelson. Washington, D.C.: U.S. Dept. Inter., Fish and Wildlife Service.

Burger, G. V. 1973. *Practical wildlife management.* New York: Winchester Press.

Burger, J. 1973. Competition between American coots and Franklin's gulls for nest sites and egg predation by the coots. *Wilson Bull.* 85(4):449–51.

Burget, M. L. 1957. *The wild turkey in Colorado.* Fed. Aid in Wildlife Restor., Project W-39-R. Washington, D.C.

Burkhart, R. L., and Page, L. A. 1971. Chlamydiosis (ornithosis-psittacosis). In *Infectious and parasitic diseases of wild birds,* ed. J. W. Davis, R. C. Anderson, L. Karstad, and D. O. Trainer. Ames, Iowa: Iowa State University Press.

Burleigh, T. D. 1930. Notes on the bird life of northwestern Washington. *Auk* 47(1):48–63.

———. 1958. *Georgia birds.* Norman, Okla.: University of Oklahoma Press.

Burroughs, J. 1871. *Wake-robin.* Boston: Houghton Mifflin Co. Riverside Press.

———. 1894. Riverby. In *The complete nature writings of John Burroughs.* Vol. 6. New York: William H. Wise & Co.

———. 1936. *Birds of America.* Vol. 3: 238. Garden City, N.Y.: Garden City Pub. Co., Inc.

Burton, M. 1954. *Animal courtship.* New York: Praeger Publishers, Inc.

Burton, R. W. 1968. Breeding biology of the brown skua, *Catharacta skua lombergi* (Matthews) at Signy island, South Orkney islands. *Brit. Antarct. Surv. Bull.* 15:9–28.

Butts, K. O. 1976. Burrowing owls wintering in the Oklahoma panhandle. *Auk* 93(3):510–16.

Butts, W. K. 1931. A study of the chickadee and white-breasted nuthatch by means of marked individuals. *Bird-Banding* 2:1–26.

Buturlin, S. A. 1906. The breeding grounds of the rosy gull. *Ibis* (8)6:131–39, 333–37, 661–66.

Byers, G. W. 1950. Black and white warbler's nest with eight cowbird eggs. *Wilson Bull.* 62:136–68.

C

Caccamise, D. F., and Alexandro, P. J. 1976. Growth rate in the monk parakeet. *Wilson Bull.* 88(3):495.

Cadbury, J. M. 1966. Twenty-three-year-old cormorant. *EBBA News* 29(1):18.

Cade, T. J. 1955. Experiments on winter territori-

ality of the American kestrel, *Falco sparverius. Wilson Bull.* 67(1):5–17.

———. 1960. Ecology of the peregrine and gyrfalcon populations in Alaska. *Univ. California Publ. Zool.* 63(3):151–290.

———. 1967. Ecological and behavorial aspects of predation by a northern shrike. *Living Bird,* 6th annual, pp. 43–86.

———. 1968. The gyrfalcon and falconry. *Living Bird,* 7th annual, pp. 237–40.

———. 1971. Survival of the peregrine falcon: Protection or management. *Raptor Res. News* 5(2, March–April):83–87.

———. 1973. Sun-bathing as a thermoregulatory aid in birds. *Condor* 75:106–8.

Cade, T. J., and Fyfe, R. 1970. The North American peregrine survey, 1970. *Canadian Field-Nat.* 84(3):231–45.

Cade, T. J.; Lincer, J. L.; White, C. M.; Roseneau, D. G.; and Schwartz, L. G. 1971. DDE residues and eggshell changes in Alaskan falcons and hawks. *Science* 172:955–57.

Cade, T. J., and Maclean, G. L. 1967. Transport of water by adult sandgrouse to their young. *Condor* 69(4):323–43.

Cade, T. J.; White, C. M.; and Haugh, J. R. 1967. Peregrines and pesticides in Alaska. *Raptor Res. News* 1(2):23–38.

Cadieux, F. 1970. *Capacité de vol et routes de migration automnale de certains oiseaux de rivage nord-américains (Charadriidae et scolopacidae).* Thèse de Maitrise ès Sciences (M.SC.), Université de Montréal.

Cadwalader, C. M. B. 1938. Greater yellowlegs swimming. *Auk* 55:275.

Cahalane, V. H. 1944. A nutcracker's search for buried food. *Auk* 61:643.

Cain, A. J. 1960. *Animal species and their evolution.* New York: Harper & Brothers.

———. 1964a. Evolution. In *A new dictionary of birds,* ed. A. L. Thomson. New York: McGraw-Hill Book Company.

———. 1964b. Genetics. In *A new dictionary of birds,* ed. A. L. Thomson. New York: McGraw-Hill Book Company.

Cain, B. W. 1973. Effect of temperature on energy requirements and northward distribution of the black-bellied tree duck. *Wilson Bull.* 85:308–17.

Calder, W. A. 1968. Respiratory and heart rates of birds at rest. *Condor* 70:358–65.

———. 1971. Temperature relationships and nesting of the calliope hummingbird. *Condor* 73(3):314–21.

———. 1974. Consequences of body size for avian energetics. In *Avian energetics,* ed. R. A. Paynter, Jr. Cambridge, Mass.: Nuttall Ornith. Pub. no. 15.

Calder, III, W. A. 1974. Consequences of body size for avian energetics. In *Avian energetics,* ed. R. A. Paynter, Jr. Cambridge, Mass.: Nuttall Ornith. Pub. no. 15.

Calder, W. A., and King, J. R. 1974. Thermal and caloric relations of birds. In *Avian biology,* ed. D. S. Farner, J. R. King, and K. C. Parkes. Vol. 4, pp. 259–413. New York: Academic Press, Inc.

Callison, C. H. 1975. New audubon bird preserve honors Sprunt. *Audubon* 77(2):124–25.

Cameron, E. S. 1907. The birds of Custer and Dawson counties, Montana. *Auk* 24:389–406.

———. 1908. Observations on the golden eagle in Montana. *Auk* 22:158–67.

Cameron, J. 1929. *The bureau of biological survey, its history, activities, and organization.* Baltimore: Johns Hopkins Press.

Cameron, T. W. M. 1961. Parasitism. In *The encyclopedia of the biological sciences,* ed. P. Gray. New York: Reinhold Publishing Corporation.

Campbell, J. M. 1969. The owls of Central Brooks Range, Alaska. *Auk* 86(3):565–68.

Campbell, L. W. 1946. A 16-year-old marsh hawk. *Auk* 63(1):88–89.

Campbell, R. W. 1968. Notes on twenty-year-old

glaucous-winged gull. *Bird-Banding* 39(3):226–27.

——. 1969. Bald eagle swimming in the ocean with prey. *Auk* 86(3):561.

Cant, G. 1959. When you see this, act. *Sports Illustrated*, October, pp. 80–92.

Cantwell, R. 1961. *Alexander Wilson: Naturalist and pioneer*. Philadelphia: J. B. Lippincott Company.

Capple, R. S. 1959. Albino cardinal in Kansas. *Audubon* 61(3):103

Cardiff, E. A., and Driscoll, A. T. 1972. Red-headed woodpecker in the Imperial Valley of California. *Calif. Birds* 3(1):23–24.

Carhart, A. H. 1954. Sagebrush is going! *Audubon* 56(5):200–204.

Carleton, A. R., and Owre, O. T. 1975. The red-whiskered bulbul in Florida: 1960–71. *Auk* 92(1):40–57.

Carleton, G. 1967. Hudson–St. Lawrence region. *Audubon Field Notes* 21(3):400.

Carothers, S. W.; Sharber, N. J.; and Foster, G. F. 1974. Scaly-leg (knemidokoptiasis) in a population of evening grosbeaks. *Wilson Bull.* 86(2):121–24.

Carpenter, F. H. 1883. Screech owl breeding in confinement. *Ornithologist and Oologist* 8:93–94.

Carpenter, R. E., and Stafford, M. A. 1970. The secretory rates and the chemical stimulus of secretion of the nasal salt glands in the Rallidae. *Condor* 72:316–24.

Carr, W. H. 1971. Another tragedy in Arizona. *Def. Wildlife News* 46(2, Summer):back cover.

Carson, R. 1962. *Silent spring*. Boston: Houghton Mifflin Company.

Carter, B. C. 1958. *The American goldeneye in central New Brunswick*. Canadian Wildlife Serv., Wildlife Management Bull., ser. 2, no. 9.

Carter, C. E. 1961. Unusual feeding habit of boat-tailed grackle. *Auk* 78(1):97.

Casillo, N. R. 1937. A few random notes on the bald eagle. *Nature Magazine* 30(3):171–72.

Casler, C. L. 1973. The air-sac systems of the anhinga and double-crested cormorant. *Auk* 90(2):324–40.

Catling, P. M. 1971. Spring migration of saw-whet owls of Toronto, Canada. *Bird-Banding* 42(2):110–14.

Center for Short-lived Phenomenon. 1975. *Massachusetts blue jay mortality*. 1974 Annual Report no. 55–56. 138 Mt. Auburn St., Cambridge, Mass.

Chalke, S. H. 1952. Starling imitating telephone bell. *Brit. Birds* 45(10):365.

Chamberlain, B. R. 1954. Safety factor in a hanging nest. *Chat* 18:48–50.

——. 1955. Regional reports: Southern coastal region. *Audubon Field Notes* 9(1):17.

——. 1957. Southern Atlantic coast region. *Audubon Field Notes* 11(4):334.

Chamberlain, D. R., and Cornwell, G. W. 1971. Selected vocalizations of the common crow. *Auk* 88(3):613–34.

Chamberlain, E. B. *et al.*, comps. and eds. 1972. *Waterfowl status report, 1972*. U.S. Dept. Inter., Spec. Sci. Rept.—Wildlife, no. 166. Washington, D.C.

Chandler, R., and Anderson, J. M. 1974. Notes on Everglade kite reproduction. *Amer. Birds* 28(4):856–58.

Chapin, E. A. 1925. *Food habits of the vireos*. U.S. Dept. Agric. Bull. no. 1355. Washington, D.C.

Chapin, J. P. 1922. The function of the oesophagus in the bittern's booming sound. *Auk* 39:196–202.

——. 1932. In memoriam: Waldron Dewitt Miller. *Auk* 49(1)1–8.

——. 1954. The calendar of Wideawake Fair. *Auk* 71:1–15.

——. 1958. The 1957 Christmas counts in Colorado. *Colorado Bird Notes* 5:29–31.

——. 1963. The touracos: An African bird family. *Living Bird*, 2d annual, pp. 57–67.

Chapman, B. R., and Casto, S. D. 1972. Additional vertebrate prey of the loggerhead shrike. *Wilson Bull.* 84:496–97.

Chapman, F. M. 1900. *Bird-life: A guide to the study of our common birds*. New York: D. Appleton & Company.

——. 1903. *Color key to North American birds*. Garden City, N.Y.: Doubleday, Page & Co.

——. 1905. A contribution to the life history of the American flamingo (*Phoenicopterus ruber*) with remarks upon specimens, *Bull. Amer. Mus. Nat. Hist.*, no. 21, pp. 53–77.

——. 1907. *The warblers of North America*. New York: D. Appleton & Company.

——. 1917. Daniel Giraud Elliott. *Auk* 34(1):1–10.

——. 1925. The European starling as an American citizen. *Natural History* 25:480–85.

——. 1929. *My tropical air castle*. New York: D. Appleton & Company.

——. 1930. *Handbook of birds of eastern North America*. New York: D. Appleton & Company.

——. 1933. *Autobiography of a bird-lover*. New York: D. Appleton–Century Company, Inc.

——. 1951. In memoriam: Albert Kenrick Fisher. *Auk* 68(2):210–13.

Chase, R. M. 1926. Crow alighting in the water. *Auk* 43(1):237.

Chattin, J. E. 1964. Pacific flyway. In *Waterfowl tomorrow*, ed. J. P. Linduska and A. L. Nelson. Washington, D.C.: U.S. Dept. Inter., Fish and Wildlife Service.

Chernyarskii, F. B. 1967. On the interrelationships of an Arctic fox and some species of tundra birds. *Zool. Zhurn.* 46(6):937–40.

Chettleburgh, M. R. 1952. Observations on the collection and burial of acorns by jays in Hainault Forest. *Brit. Birds* 45(10):359–64.

Childs, Jr., H. E. 1952. Hybrid between a shoveler and a blue-winged teal. *Condor* 54:67–68.

——. 1968. Anthony's brown towhee and San Francisco brown towhee. In *Life histories of North American cardinals, grosbeaks, buntings, towhees, finches, sparrows, and allies*, comp. A. C. Bent *et al.*, ed. O. L. Austin, Jr. U.S. Natl. Mus. Bull. no. 237, pt. 2. Washington, D.C.

Chisholm, A. H. 1952. Bird-insect nesting associates in Australia. *Ibis* 94:395–405.

——. 1959. The history of anting. *The Emu* 59:101–30.

Chitty, D. 1938. A laboratory study of pellet formation in short-eared owls, *Asio flammeus*. *Proc. Zool. Soc. London* 108 (ser. A): 267–87.

Choate, E. A. 1973. *The dictionary of bird names*. Boston: Gambit, Inc.

Choate, T. S. 1963. Habitat and population dynamics of white-tailed ptarmigan in Montana. *Jour. Wildlife Management* 27:684–99.

Christensen, C. M. 1951 *The molds and man: An introduction to the fungi*. Minneapolis: University of Minnesota Press.

Christensen, G. C. 1970. *The chukar partridge in Nevada*. Nevada Fish and Game, Biol. Bull. no. 1. Carson City.

Christy, Bayard H. 1942. Acadian flycatcher. In *Life histories of North American flycatchers, larks, swallows, and their allies*, by A. C. Bent. U.S. Natl. Mus. Bull. no. 179. Washington, D.C.

Chute, H. L. 1959. Diseases caused by fungi. In *Diseases of poultry*, ed. H. E. Biester and L. H. Schwarte. 4th ed. Ames, Iowa: Iowa State University Press.

Clapp, R. B. 1974. Albinism in the black noddy (*Anous tenuirostris*). *Condor* 76:464–65.

——. 1976. Review of longevity records by W. Rydzewski. *Bird-Banding* 47(3):279–81.

Clapp, R. B., and Hackman, C. D. 1969. Longevity record for a breeding great frigatebird. *Bird-Banding* 40(1):47.

Clapp, R. B., and Sibley, F. C. 1966. Longevity records of some central Pacific birds. *Bird-Banding* 37(3):193–97.

Clark, A. H. 1948. *Animals alive*. New York: D. Van Nostrand Company.

Clark, C. C.; Johnson, C. A.; and Cockaday, L. M. 1941. *This physical world*. New York: McGraw-Hill Book Company.

Clark, E. R. 1972. *Woodcock status report, 1971*. U.S. Dept. Inter., Fish and Wildlife Service, Rept.—Wildlife, no. 153. Washington, D.C.

Clark, G. A. 1961. Occurrence and timing of egg teeth in birds. *Wilson Bull.* 73:268–78.

Clark, Jr., G. A. 1969. Spread-wing postures in pelecaniformes, Ciconiiformes, and Falconiformes. *Auk* 86:136–39.

——. 1970. Apparent lack of the double-scratch in two species of *Spizella*. *Condor* 72:370.

——. 1975. Additional records of passerine terrestrial gaits. *Wilson Bull.* 87(3):384–89.

Clark, R. J. 1975. A field study of the short-eared owl, *Asio flammeus* Pontoppidan in North America. *Wildl. Monogr.* 47:1–67.

Clark, W. S. 1974. Second record of the Kestrel (*Falco tinnunculus*) for North America. *Auk* 92:172.

Clarke, C. H. D. 1938. Organisms of a malaria type in ruffed grouse, with a description of the schizogony of *Leucocytozoon bonasae*. *Jour. Wildlife Management* 2:146–49.

Cleaves, H. 1920. A partridge Don Quixote. *Bird-Lore* 22(6):329–34.

——. 1945. Whip-poor-will endurance. *Auk* 62:304–5.

Clement, R. C. 1960. An introduction to shorebirds. In *A gathering of shorebirds*, by H. M. Hall. New York: The Devin-Adair Co.

——. 1966. Mark what you leave. In *Birds in our lives*, ed. A. Stefferud and A. L. Nelson. Washington, D.C.: U.S. Dept. Inter., Fish and Wildlife Service.

——. 1968. Common redpoll. In *Life histories of North American cardinals, grosbeaks, buntings, towhees, finches, sparrows, and allies*, comp. A. C. Bent *et al.*, ed. O. L. Austin, Jr. U.S. Natl. Mus. Bull. no. 237, pt. 1. Washington, D.C.

Clements, F. E., and Shelford, V. E. 1939. *Bioecology*. New York: John Wiley & Sons, Inc.

Clench, M. H.; Banks, R. C.; and Barlow, J. C. 1976. Bird collections in the United States and Canada: Addenda and corrigenda. *Auk* 93(1):126–29.

Coatney, G. R., and Roundabush, R. L. 1949. A catalogue of the species of the genus *Plasmodium* and index of their hosts. In *Malariology*, ed. M. F. Boyd. Vol. 1. Philadelphia: W. B. Saunders Company.

Coble, M. F. 1954. *Introduction to ornithological nomenclature*. Los Angeles: American Book Institute.

Coburn, C. A. 1914. The behavior of the crow, *Corvus americanus*. *Jour. Animal Behaviour* 4:185–201.

Cochran, W. W., and Graber, R. R. 1958. Attraction of nocturnal migrants by lights on a television tower. *Wilson Bull.* 70:378–80.

Cochran, W. W.; Montgomery, G. G.; and Graber, R. R. 1967. Migrating flights of *Hylocichla* thrushes in spring: A radiotelemetry study. *Living Bird*, 6th annual, pp. 213–25.

Cockrum, E. L. 1952. A check list and bibliography of hybrid birds of North America north of Mexico. *Wilson Bull.* 64:140–59.

Coffey, L. C. 1958. Weights of some chimney swifts at Memphis. *Bird-Banding* 29:98–104.

Cogswell, H. C. 1957a. Allen's hummingbird. In *Audubon western guide*, ed. R. H. Pough. Garden City, N.Y.: Doubleday & Co., Inc.

——. 1957b. Anna's hummingbird. In *Audubon western bird uide*, ed. R. H. Pough. Garden City, N.Y.: Doubleday & Co., Inc.

——. 1957c. White-throated swift. In *Audubon western bird guide*, by R. H. Pough. Garden City, N.Y.: Doubleday & Co., Inc.

——. 1968. Ashy rufous-crowned sparrow. In *Life histories of North American cardinals*, *grosbeaks, buntings, towhees, finches, sparrows, and allies,* comp. A. C. Bent *et al.,* ed. O. L. Austin, Jr. U.S. Natl. Mus. Bull. no. 237, pt. 2. Washington. D.C.

Cohn, J. M. W. 1968. The convergent flight mechanisms of swifts (Apodi) and hummingbirds (Trochili) (Aves). Ph.D. thesis. Ann Arbor, Mich.: University of Michigan.

Coker, C. M. 1931. Hermit thrush feeding on salamanders. *Auk* 48(2):277.

Coker, R. E. 1954. *Streams, lakes, ponds.* Chapel Hill, N.C.: University of North Carolina Press.

Colbert, E. H. 1955. *Evolution of the vertebrates.* New York: John Wiley & Sons, Inc.

Colburn, P. W. 1966. Albino adventure nets rare Anna's. *Audubon* 68 (May):476–78.

Coldwell, C. 1972. Raven banding in Nova Scotia. *Bird-Banding* 43:288.

Cole, L. J.; Stoddard, H. L.; and Komarek, E. V. 1949. Red bobwhite: A report and a correction. *Auk* 66(1):28–35.

Coles, R. J. 1925. Sea-birds at Cape Lookout, North Carolina. *Auk* 42:123–24.

Coles, V. 1944. Nesting of the turkey vulture in Ohio caves. *Auk* 61:219–28.

Collias, N. E. 1960. An ecological and functional classification of animal sounds. In *Animal sounds and communication,* ed. W. E. Lanyon and W. N. Tavolga. Amer. Inst. Biol. Sci. Publ. no. 7, pp. 368–91.

———. 1962. Personal communication.

———. 1963. A spectograph analysis of and vocal repertoire of the African village weaverbird. *Condor* 65:517–27.

———. 1964. The evolution of nests and nest-building in birds. *Amer. Zool.* 4:175–90.

Collias, N. E., and Jahn, L. R. 1959. Social behavior and breeding success in Canada goose *(Branta canadensis)* confined under seminatural conditions. *Auk* 76(4):478–509.

Collias, N. E., and Taber, R. D. 1951. A field study of some grouping and dominance relations in ring-necked pheasants. *Condor* 53:265–75.

Collins, C. T. 1968. Notes on the biology of Chapman's swift, *Chaetura chapmani* (Aves: Apodidae). *Amer. Mus. Novitates* no. 2320. New York.

———. 1970. The black-crowned night heron as a predator of tern chicks. *Auk* 87:584–86.

———. 1976. A review of the lower Miocene swifts (Aves: Apodidae). In Collected papers in avian paleontology honoring the 90th birthday of Alexander Wetmore, ed. S. L. Olsen. *Paleobiology* 27:129–32.

Collins, C. T., and Brooke, R. K. 1976. A review of the swifts of the genus *Hirundapus* (Aves: Apodidae). *Los Angeles Co. Mus. Contrib. Sci.* 282:1–22.

Collins, H. B. 1966. Long, long ago. In *Birds in our lives,* ed. A. Stefferud and A. L. Nelson. Washington, D.C.: U.S. Dept. Inter., Fish and Wildlife Service.

Committee on Rare and Endangered Wildlife Species. 1966. *Rare and endangered fish and wildlife of the United States.* U.S. Dept. Inter., Fish and Wildlife Service, Res. Publ. no. 34. Washington, D.C.

Comstock, J. H. 1947. *An introduction to entomology.* 9th ed. Ithaca, N.Y.: Comstock Pub. Co., Inc.

Conant, R. 1958. *A field guide to reptiles and amphibians of eastern North America.* Boston: Houghton Mifflin Company.

Condee, R. W. 1970. The winter territories of tufted titmice. *Wilson Bull.* 82(2):177–83.

Conder, P. J. 1964. Avocet. In *A new dictionary of birds,* ed. A. L. Thomson. New York: McGraw-Hill Book Company.

Congreve, W. M., and Blair, H. M. S. 1968. Brambling. In *Life histories of North American cardinals, grosbeaks, buntings, towhees, finches, sparrows, and allies,* comp. A. C. Bent *et al.,* ed. O. L. Austin, Jr. U.S. Natl. Mus. Bull. no. 237, pt. 1. Washington, D.C.

Conner, R. N. 1974. Red-bellied woodpecker predation on nestling Carolina chickadees. *Auk* 91(4):836.

———. 1975. Orientation of entrances to woodpecker nest cavities. *Auk* 92(2):371–74.

Conover, M. R.; Miller, D. E.; and Hunt, Jr., G. L. 1979. Female-female pairs and other unusual reproductive associations in ring-billed and California gulls. *Auk* 96:6–9.

Conway, W. G. 1961. They show their age—Hummingbirds with wrinkles. *Animal Kingdom* 64(5):151–54.

———. 1962. Personal communication.

Cooch, F. G. 1951. Ecological aspects of the blue-snow goose complex. *Auk* 78:73–89.

———. 1961. Avian salt gland and botulism. In *Canadian Wildlife Service: Research progress report—1961.* Ottawa: Dept. National Affairs and National Resources.

———. 1964a. A preliminary study of the survival value of a functional salt gland in prairie anatidae. *Auk* 81:380–93.

———. 1964b. Snows and blues. In *Waterfowl tomorrow,* ed. J. P. Linduska and A. L. Nelson. Washington, D.C.: U.S. Dept. Inter., Fish and Wildlife Service.

Cook, R. S. 1971a. Haemoproteus. In *Infectious and parasitic diseases of wild birds,* ed. J. W. Davis, R. C. Anderson, L. Karstad, and D. O. Trainer. Ames, Iowa: Iowa State University Press.

———. 1971b. Leucocytozoon. In *Infectious and parasitic diseases of wild birds,* ed. J. W. Davis, R. C. Anderson, L. Karstad, and D. O. Trainer. Ames, Iowa: Iowa State University Press.

Cooke, F., and Cooch, F. G. 1968. The genetics of polymorphism in the goose, *Anser caerulescens. Evolution* 25:483–96.

Cooke, F., and Mirsky, P. J. 1972. A genetic analyses of lesser snow goose families. *Auk* 89:863–71.

Cooke, M. T. 1923. *Report in bird censuses in the United States, 1916 to 1920.* U.S. Dept. Agric. Bull. no. 1165. Washington, D.C.

———. 1937a. *Flight speed of birds.* U.S. Dept. Agric. Circ. no. 428. Washington, D.C.

———. 1937b. Some longevity records of wild birds. *Bird-Banding* 8(2):52–65.

———. 1937c. Some returns of banded birds. *Bird-Banding* 8(4):149.

———. 1942. Returns of banded birds: Some longevity records of wild birds. *Bird-Banding* 13(1):34–37.

———. 1945. Transoceanic recoveries of banded birds. *Bird-Banding* 16(4):123–29.

Cooke, W. W. 1911. Our greatest travelers. *Natl. Geographic Magazine* 22:346–65.

———. 1915a. *Bird migration.* U.S. Dept. Agric. Bull. no. 185. Washington, D.C.

———. 1915b. *Preliminary census of birds of the United States.* U.S. Dept. Agric. Bull. no. 187. Washington, D.C.

Coon, N. C., and Locke, L. N. 1968. Aspergillosus in a bald eagle *(Haliaecetus leucocephalus). Bull. Wildlife Disease Assoc.* 4:51.

Cornelius, L. W. 1969. Field notes in salmonella infection in green finches and house sparrows. *Bull. Wildlife Disease Assoc.* 5:142–43.

Cornwallis, R. C. 1964. Irruption. In *A new dictionary of birds,* ed. A. L. Thomson. New York: McGraw-Hill Book Company.

Cornwell, G., and Hochbaum, H. A. 1971. Collisions with wires—A source of anatid mortality. *Wilson Bull.* 83:305–6.

Cortopassi, A. J., and Mewaldt, R. L. 1965. The circumannual distribution of white-crowned sparrows. *Bird-Banding* 36(3):141–69.

Cory, C. B. 1888. The European kestrel in Massachusetts. *Auk* 5(1):110.

Cott, Hugh B. 1941. *Adaptive coloration in animals.* London: Methuen and Co., Ltd.

Cottam, C. 1936. Food of the limpkin. *Wilson Bull.* 48(1):11–13.

———. 1939. *Food habits of North American div-ing ducks.* U.S. Dept. Agric. Tech. Bull. no. 643. Washington, D.C.

———. 1966. A conservationist's view. In *Birds in our lives,* ed. A. Stefferud and A. L. Nelson. Washington, D.C.: U.S. Dept. Inter., Fish and Wildlife Service.

Cottam, C., and Addy, C. E. 1947. Present eelgrass condition and problems on the Atlantic coast of North America. *Trans.* [12th] *N. Amer. Wildlife Conf.,* pp. 387–98.

Cottam, C., and Munro, D. A. 1954. Eelgrass status and environmental relations. *Jour. Wildlife Management* 18:449–60.

Cottam, C., and Trefethen, J. B., eds. 1968. *Whitewings: The life history, status and management of the white-winged dove.* Princeton, N.J.: D. Van Nostrand Company.

Cottam, C., and Uhler, F. M. 1937. *Birds in relation to fishes.* U.S. Dept. Agric., Wildlife Res. and Management Leaflet no. BS-83. Washington, D.C.

Cottam, C.; Williams, C. S.; and Sooter, C. A. 1942a. Cooperative feeding of white pelicans. *Auk* 59(3):444–45.

———. 1942b. Flight and running speeds of birds. *Wilson Bull.* 54:121–31.

Cottrille, B. D. 1950. Death of a horned lark in territorial combat. *Wilson Bull.* 62(3):134–35.

Couch, A. B. 1962. Phoretic mallophagans from hippoboscids of mourning doves *(Zenaidura macroura). Jour. Parasitol.* 48(3):497.

Coues, E. 1874. *Birds of the Northwest: A handbook of ornithology.* Washington, D.C.: U.S. Gov. Printing Office.

———. 1882. *The Coues check list of North American birds.* 2d ed. Boston: Estes and Lauriat.

———. 1884. *Key to North American birds.* Boston: Estes and Lauriat.

———. 1903. *Key to North American birds.* 2 vols. Boston: Estes and Lauriat.

Coulombe, H. N. 1971. Behavior and population ecology of the burrowing owl in the Imperial Valley of California. *Condor* 73:162–76.

Coulson, J. C. 1966. The influence of pair-bond and age on the breeding biology of the kittiwake gull, *Rissa tridactyla. Jour. Animal Ecology* 35(2):269–77.

Coulson, J. C., and White, E. 1958. Observations on the breeding of the kittiwake. *Bird Study* 5(2):74–83.

Coulter, M. 1957. Predation of snapping turtles upon aquatic birds in Maine marshes. *Jour. Wildlife Management* 21:17–21.

Coulter, M. C., and Risebrough, R. W. 1973. Shell-thinning in eggs of the ashy petrel *(Oceanodroma homochroa)* from the Farallon Islands. *Condor* 75:254–55.

Courser, William D. 1971. Red-tailed hawk preys on cattle egrets. *Auk* 88(3):669–70.

Cox, G. W. 1960. A life history of the mourning warbler. *Wilson Bull.* 72(1):5–28.

———. 1973. Hybridization between mourning and MacGillivray's warblers. *Auk* 90:190–91.

Cox, H. R.; Jellison, W. L.; and Hughes, L. E. 1941. Isolation of western equine encephalomyelitis virus from a naturally infected prairie chicken. *Public Health Report* 56:1905.

Craddock, D. R., and Carlson, R. D. 1970. Peregrine falcon observed feeding far at sea. *Condor* 72(3):375–76.

Craig, A. M. 1970. Two California records of Grace's warbler. *Calif. Birds* 1(2):77–78.

Craig. W. 1913. Recollections of the passenger pigeon in captivity. *Bird Lore* 15:93–94.

———. 1943. *The song of the wood pewee,* Myiochanes virens Linnaeus: *A study of bird music.* New York State Mus. Sci. Serv. Bull. no. 334. Albany.

Craighead, F. C., and Craighead, J. J. 1939. *Hawks in the hand.* Boston: Houghton Mifflin Company.

———. 1956. *Hawks, owls and wildlife.* Harrisburg, Pa.: Stackpole Co.

Craighead, J. J., and Craighead, F. C. 1940. Nesting pigeon hawks. *Wilson Bull.* 52(4):241–48.

Craighead, J. J., and Craighead, Jr., F. C. 1966. Raptors. In *Birds in our lives*, ed. A. Stefferud and A. L. Nelson. Washington, D.C.: U.S. Dept. Inter., Fish and Wildlife Service.

Craighead, J. J.; Craighead, G. C.; and Craighead, D. 1967. Sharing the lives of golden eagles. *Natl. Geographic Magazine* 132:420–39.

Cramp, S., chief ed. 1977. *Handbook of the birds of Europe, the Middle East, and North Africa.* Vol. 1. London: Oxford University Press.

Crandall, L. S. 1917. *Pets: Their history and care.* New York: Henry Holt & Company, Inc.

Crawford, J. A., and Bolen, E. G. 1975. Spring lek activity of the lesser prairie chicken in west Texas. *Auk* 92(4):808–10.

Crawford, R. L. 1974. *Bird casualties at a Leon County, Florida TV tower: October 1966–September 1973.* Bull. Tall Timbers Res. Sta. no. 18. Tallahassee, Fla.

Creighton, P. D., and Potter, D. K. 1974. Nest predation and interference by western meadowlarks. *Auk* 91:177–78.

Creighton, W. S. 1950. *The ants of North America.* Bull. Mus. Compar. Zool. at Harvard College, vol. 104. Cambridge, Mass.

Crew, F. A. E. 1923. Studies in intersexuality II: Sex reversal in the fowl. *Proc. Royal Soc.* 95 (ser. B) 256–78.

Crissey, W. F. 1958. *Mourning dove newsletter.* U.S. Dept. Inter., Fish and Wildlife Service, Issue no. 13. Washington, D.C.

————. 1969. Prairie potholes from a continental viewpoint. Saskatoon Wetlands Seminar. *Canadian Wildlife Serv. Rept. Series* 6: 161–71.

Crockett, A. B., and Hansley, P. L. 1977. Coition, nesting, and postfledging behavior of Williamson's sapsucker in Colorado. *Living Bird,* 16th annual, pp. 7–19.

Crook, J. H. 1964. Dominance (2). In *A new dictionary of birds*, ed. A. L. Thomson. New York: McGraw-Hill Book Company.

Crosby, G. T. 1971. Home range characteristics of the red-cockaded woodpecker in north central Florida. In *The ecology and management of the red-cockaded woodpecker: Proceedings of a symposium at Okefenokee National Wildlife Refuge, Folkston, Ga., May 26–27,* ed. R. L. Thompson. Tallahassee, Fla.: Tall Timbers Res. Station.

————. 1972. Spread of the cattle egret in the Western Hemisphere. *Bird-Banding* 43:205–12.

Crosby, M. S. 1930. In memoriam: Newbold Trotter Lawrence. *Auk* 47(1):8.

Crossin, R. S., and Huber, L. H. 1970. Sooty tern egg predation by ruddy turnstone. *Condor* 72: 372–73.

Crouch, James E. 1936. Nesting habits of the cedar waxwing *(Bombycilla cedrorum). Auk* 53(1):1–8.

Crowell, Jr., J. B., and Nehls, H. B. 1971. Northern Pacific coast region. *Amer. Birds* 25(3):615.

Cruickshank, A. D. 1959. Fifty-ninth Christmas bird count. *Audubon Field Notes* 13:72–75.

————. 1961. Sixty-first Christmas bird count. *Audubon Field Notes* 15:84–89.

————. 1966. To see; to record. In *Birds in our lives*, ed. A. Stefferud and A. L. Nelson. Washington, D.C.: U.S. Dept. Inter., Fish and Wildlife Service.

————. 1967. Sixty-seventh Christmas bird count. *Audubon Field Notes* 21(2, April):12.

Cruickshank, A. D., and Cruickshank, H. G. 1958. *1,001 questions about birds.* New York: Dodd, Mead & Company.

Cruickshank, A. D. *et al.* 1957. *Hunting with the camera.* New York: Harper & Brothers.

Cruickshank, H. G., ed. 1957. *John and William Bartram's America.* American Naturalists Series. New York: The Devin-Adair Co.

Culbertson, A. E. 1946. Occurrence of poor-wills

in the Sierran foothills in winter. *Condor* 48(4):158–9.

Cullen, J. M. 1964. Roosting. In *A new dictionary of birds*, ed. A. L. Thomson. New York: McGraw-Hill Book Company.

Cunningham, C. H. 1959. Fowl pox. In *Diseases of poultry*, ed. H. E. Biester and L. H. Schwarte. 4th ed. Ames, Iowa: Iowa State University Press.

Cunningham, R. L. 1966. Florida region. *Audubon Field Notes* 20:412–16.

Curry-Lindahl, K. 1970. Spread-wing postures in Pelecaniformes and Ciconiiformes. *Auk* (2): 371–72.

Cuthbert, N. L. 1954. A nesting study of the black tern in Michigan. *Auk* 71(1):16–35.

Cutright, P. R. 1940. *The great naturalists explore South America.* New York: The Macmillan Company.

Cutting, P. M. 1972. A behavioral attitude of saw-whet and boreal owls. *Auk* 89(1): 194–96.

D

Dale, F. H. 1954. Influence of calcium on the distribution of the pheasant in North America. *Trans. [19th] N. Amer. Wildlife Conf.,* pp. 316–22.

Dale, F. H., and Krefting, L. W. 1966. Birds and forests. In *Birds in our lives*, ed. A. Stefferud and A. L. Nelson. Washington, D.C.: U.S. Dept. Inter., Fish and Wildlife Service.

Dall, W. H. 1915. *Spencer Fullerton Baird.* Philadelphia: J. B. Lippincott Company.

Dalke, P. D. 1938. Amount of grit taken by pheasants in southern Michigan. *Jour. Wildlife Management* 2(2):53–54.

Daniels, G. G. 1972. Possible sight record of Eskimo curlew on Martha's Vineyard, Mass. *Amer. Birds* 26:907–8.

Darden, T. 1974. Common grackles preying on fish. *Wilson Bull.* 86(1):85–86.

Darling, F. F. 1934. Speed of a golden eagle's flight. *Nature* [London] 134:325–26.

Darling, L., and Darling, L. 1962. *Bird.* Boston: Houghton Mifflin Company.

Darlington, Jr., P. J. 1957. *Zoogeography: The geographic distribution of animals.* New York: John Wiley & Sons, Inc.

Dater, E. 1967. Some old-age records. *EBBA News* 30(2, March–April):67.

Dau, C. P., and Gibson, D. D. 1974. Common rose finch, a first record for North America. *Auk* 91:185–86.

Davis, D. E. 1942. Number of eggs laid by herring gulls. *Auk* 59:549–54.

————. 1954. The breeding biology of Hammond's flycatcher. *Auk* 71(2):164–71.

————. 1955. Breeding biology of birds. In *Recent studies in avian biology*, ed. A. Wolfson. Urbana, Ill.: University of Illinois Press. Chap. 9, p. 266.

————. 1959. Observations on territorial behavior of least flycatchers. *Wilson Bull.* 71(1):73–85.

————. 1974. Emigration of northern shrikes, 1959–1970. *Auk* 91(4):821–25.

Davis, E. M. 1937. Observations on nesting barn swallows. *Bird-Banding* 8(2):66–73.

Davis, E. M., and Davis, W. M. 1936. Banding barn swallows. *Bird-Banding* 7:149–56.

Davis, G. J. 1970. Seasonal changes in flocking behavior of starlings as correlated with gonadal development. *Wilson Bull.* 82(4):391–99.

Davis, H. E. 1949. *The American wild turkey.* Georgetown, S.C.: Small-Arms Technical Publishing Company.

Davis, I. 1945. Rose-throated becard nesting in Cameron County, Texas. *Auk* 62(2):316–17.

Davis, I., and Webster, F. S. 1970. An intergeneric hybrid flycatcher *(Tyrannus × Muscivora). Condor* 72(1):37–42.

Davis, J. 1958. In memoriam: Walter Kenrick Fisher. *Auk* 75(2):130–33.

————. 1965. Natural history, variation, and distribution of the Strickland's woodpecker. *Auk* 82(4):537–90.

Davis, J.; Fisler, G. F.; and Davis, B. S. 1963. The breeding biology of the western flycatcher. *Condor* 65:337–82.

Davis, J. W.; Anderson, R. C.; Karstad, L.; and Trainer, D. O. 1971. *Infectious and parasitic diseases of wild birds.* Ames, Iowa: Iowa State University Press.

Davis, L. I. 1972. *A field guide to the birds of Mexico and Central America.* Austin, Texas: University of Texas Press.

Davis, M. 1936. A peculiar albinistic starling. *Auk* 53(4):449.

————. 1969. Siberian crane longevity. *Auk* 86(2):347.

Davis, R. A. 1971. Flight speed of Arctic and red-throated loons. *Auk* 88(1):169.

Davis, T. H. 1968a. Willet nesting on Long Island, New York. *Wilson Bull.* 80:330.

————. 1968b. Winter recoveries of snowy egrets banded on Long Island. *Bird-Banding* 39(4): 317.

Davis, W. B. 1933. The span of the nesting seasonal birds in Butte County, California, in relation to their food. *Condor* 35:151–54.

Davis, W. M. 1970. Inland records and first specimen of black-legged kittiwake from Mississippi. *Auk* 87(4):804.

————. 1971. A specimen of the little gull from northern Mississippi. *Auk* 88(2):437–38.

Davison, V. E. 1967. *Attracting birds from the prairies to the Atlantic.* New York: Thomas Y. Crowell Company, Inc.

Dawson, W. L. 1923. *The birds of California.* San Diego, Calif.: South Moulton Company.

Dawson, W. R. 1954. Temperature relation and water requirements of the brown and abert towhees, *Pipilo fuscus* and *Pipilo aberti. Univ. California Publ. Zool.* 59:81–124.

————. 1968. Abert's towhee. In *Life histories of North American cardinals, grosbeaks, buntings, towhees, finches, sparrows, and allies*, comp. A. C. Bent *et al.*, ed. O. L. Austin, Jr. U.S. Natl. Mus. Bull. no. 237, pt. 2. Washington, D.C.

Dawson, W. R., and Evans, F. C. 1957. Relation of growth and development to temperature regulation in nestling field and chipping sparrows. *Physio. Zool.* 30:315–27.

Dawson, W. R., and Fisher, C. D. 1969. Responses to temperature by the spotted nightjar *(Eurostopodus guttatus). Condor* 71:49–53.

Dawson, W. R., and Hudson, J. W. 1970. Birds. In *Comparative physiology of temperature regulation*, ed. G. C. Whittow. Vol. 1, pp. 223–310. New York: Academic Press, Inc.

Dawson, W. R., and Tordoff, H. B. 1959. Relation of oxygen consumption to temperature in the evening grosbeak. *Condor* 61(4):388–96.

Day, A. M. 1946. Personal communication.

Deane, R. 1876. Albinism and melanism among North American birds. *Bull. Nuttall Ornith. Club* 2(1):20–24.

————. 1878. Additional cases of albinism and melanism in North American birds. *Bull. Nuttall Ornith. Club* 3:27–30.

————. 1880. Additional cases of albinism and melanism in North American birds. *Bull. Nuttall Ornith. Club* 5(1):25–30.

de Beer, G. 1954. *Archaeopteryx lithographica.* London: British Museum (Natural History).

————. 1958. The Darwin-Wallace centenary. *Annual Rept. Smithsonian Inst.,* pp. 333–57.

Deck, R. S. 1945. The neighbors' children. *Nature Magazine* 38:241–42, 272.

Deem, A. W., and Thorp, Jr., F. 1939. Toxic algae in Colorado. *Jour. Am. Vet. Med. Assoc.* 95(752):542.

DeGraaf, R. M., and Thomas, J. W. 1974. A banquet for the birds. *Natural History* 83(1):40, 45.

De Groot, D. S. 1929. The California clapper rail:

Its nesting habits, enemies, and habitat. *Condor* 29(6):259–70.

de Kiriline, L. 1952. Red-breast makes a home. *Audubon* 54(1):16–21.

———. 1954. The voluble singer in the tree-tops. *Audubon* 56:109–11.

Delacour, J. 1951. *The pheasants of the world.* New York: Charles Scribner's Sons.

———. 1954. *The waterfowl of the world.* Vol. 1. London: Country Life Ltd.

———. 1956. The waterfowl of the world. Vol. 2. London: Country Life, Ltd.

———. 1959. *The waterfowl of the world.* Vol. 3. London: Country Life Ltd.

———. 1961a. Anseriformes. In *The encyclopedia of biological sciences,* ed. P. Gray. New York: Reinhold Publishing Corporation.

———. 1961b. Cage and aviary design. *Avicultural Magazine,* May–June.

———. 1961c. Galliformes. In *The encyclopedia of biological sciences,* ed. P. Gray. New York: Reinhold Publishing Corporation.

———. 1964. Pheasant. In *A new dictionary of birds,* ed. A. L. Thomson. New York: McGraw-Hill Book Company.

———. 1977. The pheasants of the world. 2d ed. Hindhead, Eng.: Saiga Publ. Co., Ltd.

Delacour, J., and Amadon, D. 1973. *Curassows and related birds.* New York: Amer. Mus. Nat. Hist.

Delacour, J., and Mayr, E. 1945. The family Anatidae. *Wilson Bull.* 57:3–55.

DeLaRonde, G. G., and Greichus, Y. A. 1972. Care and behavior of penned double-crested cormorants. *Auk* 89(3):644–50.

Delius, J. D., and Emmerton, J. 1978. Sensory mechanisms related to homing in pigeons. In *Animal migration, navigation and homing,* ed. K. Schmidt-Koenig and W. T. Keeton. Heidelberg: Springer-Verlag.

Dement'ev, G. P. et al. 1966. *Birds of the Soviet Union* (paperback ed.). Vol. 1. Washington, D.C.: Smithsonian Press.

———. 1968. *Birds of the Soviet Union* (paperback ed.). Vol. 6. Washington, D.C.: Smithsonian Press.

———. 1969. *Birds of the Soviet Union* (paperback ed.). Vol. 3. Washington, D.C.: Smithsonian Press.

———. 1970. *Birds of the Soviet Union* (paperback ed.). Vol. 5. Washington, D.C.: Smithsonian Press.

Dennis, J. V. 1948. Observations of the orchard oriole in the lower Mississippi delta. *Bird-Banding* 19:12–20.

———. 1950. Bird dominance at the feeding station. *Audubon* 52(6):394–400.

———. 1951. A sapsucker and its associates. *Bull. Mass. Audubon Soc.* 35(3):107–9.

———. 1954. Meteorological analysis of occurrence of grounded migrants at Smith Point, Texas, April 17–May 17, 1951. *Wilson Bull.* 66:102–11.

———. 1957. Food distributors in tree trunk and tree top. *Audubon* 59(1):36, 38–41.

———. 1958. Some aspects of and breeding ecology of the yellow-breasted chat. *Bird-Banding* 39(3):169–83.

———. 1963. Preventing bird damage. *Proc. Southeastern Wood Pole Conf., University of Florida, Gainesville,* pp. 89–93.

———. 1964. Woodpecker damage to utility poles: With special reference to the role of territory and resonance. *Bird-Banding* 35(4):225–53.

———. 1967. The ivory-bill flies still. *Audubon* 69:38–44.

———. 1969. The yellow-shafted flicker (*Colaptes auratus*) on Nantucket Island, Massachusetts. *Bird-Banding* 40(4):290–308.

———. 1971. Utilization of pine resin by the red-cockaded woodpecker and its effectiveness in protecting roosting and nest sites. In *The ecology and management of the red-cockaded woodpecker. Proceedings of a symposium at Okefenokee National Wildlife Refuge, Folkston, Ga., May 26–27,* ed. R. L. Thompson. Tallahassee, Fla.: Tall Timbers Res. Station.

———. 1975. *Complete guide to bird-feeding.* New York: Alfred A. Knopf, Inc.

Dennis, R. 1970. The oiling of large raptors by fulmars. *Scot. Birds* 6(4):198–99.

Dent, R. H. 1965. Breeding biology of the pigeon guillemot, *Cepphus columba. Ardea* 53(3–4):99–160.

De Sante, D., and Remsen, V. 1973. Middle Pacific coast region. *Amer. Birds* 27(1):113.

De Schauensee, R. M. 1970. *A guide to the birds of South America.* Wynnewood, Pa.: Livingston Publishing Company.

Devillers, P. 1970. Identification and distribution in California of the *Sphyrapicus varius* group of sapsuckers. *Calif. Birds* 1(2):47–76.

Devlin, J. C. 1971. Audubon Society poses a "mystery." *New York Times,* February 7.

Devlin, J. M. 1954. Effects of weather on nocturnal migration as seen from one observation point in Philadelphia. *Wilson Bull.* 66:93–101.

DeWeese, L. R., and Pillmore, R. E. 1972. Bird nests in an aspen tree robbed by black bears. *Condor* 74:488.

DeWolfe, B. B. 1968. Nuttall's and Gambel's white-crowned sparrow. In *Life history of North American cardinals, grosbeaks, buntings, towhees, finches, sparrows, and allies,* comp. A. C. Bent et al., ed. O. L. Austin, Jr. U.S. Natl. Mus. Bull. no. 237, pt. 3. Washington, D.C.

Dexter, R. W. 1953. Electrocution of a Baltimore oriole. *Bird-Banding* 24(3):109.

———. 1959. Two 13-year-old records for the house sparrow. *Bird-Banding* 30(3):182.

———. 1960. Analysis of chimney swift returns at Kent, Ohio, 1956–59. *Bird-Banding* 31(2):87–89.

Diamond, A. W. 1973. Notes on the breeding biology and behavior of the magnificent frigatebird. *Condor* 75:200–209.

Dice, L. R. 1943. *The biotic provinces of North America.* Ann Arbor, Mich.: Michigan University Press.

Dickerman, R. W. 1961. Hybrids among the fringillid genera, *Junco, Zonotrichia,* and *Melospiza. Auk* 78(4):627–32.

———. 1968. A hybrid grasshopper sparrow × Savannah sparrow. *Auk* 85(2):312–15.

Dickey, D. R. 1916. The shadow-boxing of Pipilo. *Condor* 18:93–99.

Dickey, D. R., and van Rossem, A. J. 1938. The birds of El Salvador. *Field Mus. Nat. Hist.* (*Zool. Ser.*) 23:1–609.

Dickinson, Jr., J. C. 1968. Rufous-sided towhee. In *Life histories of North American cardinals, grosbeaks, buntings, towhees, finches, sparrows, and allies,* comp. A. C. Bent et al., ed. O. L. Austin, Jr. U.S. Natl. Mus. Bull. no. 237, pt. 2. Washington, D.C.

Dieter, M. P. 1973. *Sex determination of eagles, owls, and herons by analyzing plasma steroid hormones.* U.S. Dept. Inter., Fish and Wildlife Service, Spec. Sci. Rept.—Wildlife, no. 167. Washington, D.C.

Dilger, W. C. 1955. Ruptured heart in the cardinal, *Richmondena cardinalis. Auk* 72:85.

———. 1956a. Adaptive modifications and ecological isolating mechanisms in the thrush genera, *Catharus* and *Hylocichla. Wilson Bull.,* September, pp. 171–99.

———. 1956b. Hostile behavior and reproductive isolating mechanisms in the avian genera *Catharus* and *Hylocichla. Auk* (3):313–53.

———. 1960. Agonistic and social behavior of captive redpolls. *Wilson Bull.* 72:115–32.

———. 1962. Methods and objectives of ethology. *Living Bird,* 1st annual, pp. 83–92.

Dillon, L. S. 1956. Wisconsin climate and life zones in North America. *Science* 123 (February 3):167–76.

Dingle, E. von S. 1942. Rough-winged swallow. In *Life histories of North American flycatchers, larks, swallows, and their allies,* by A. C. Bent. U.S. Natl. Mus. Bull. no. 179. Washington, D.C.

———. 1946. Carolina chickadee. In *Life histories of North American jays, crows, and titmice,* by A. C. Bent. U.S. Natl. Mus. Bull. no. 191. Washington, D.C.

———. 1953. Swainson's warbler. In *Life histories of North American wood warblers,* by A. C. Bent. U.S. Natl. Mus. Bull. no. 203. Washington, D.C.

Dinnendahl, L. 1954. Nachtlicher Zug und Windrichtung auf Helgoland. *Die Vogelwarte* 17:188–94.

Ditmars, R. L. 1933. *Reptiles of the world.* 2d ed. New York: The Macmillan Company.

———. 1949. *The reptiles of North America.* Rev. ed. Garden City, N.Y.: Doubleday & Co., Inc.

Dixon, J. S. 1927a. Black bear tries to gnaw into a woodpecker's nest. *Condor* 24(5):271.

———. 1927b. Contribution to the life history of the Alaska willow ptarmigans. *Condor* 29(5):213–23.

———. 1927c. The surf-bird's secret. *Condor* 29(1)3–16.

———. 1937. The golden eagle in San Diego County, California. *Condor* 39:49–56.

Dixon, K. L. 1949. Behavior of the plain titmouse. *Condor* 51:110–36.

———. 1955. An ecological analysis of the interbreeding of crested titmice in Texas. *Univ. California Publ. Zool.* 54:125–205.

Dobkin, D. S. 1979. Functional and evolutionary relationships of vocal copying phenomena in birds. *Z. f. Tierpsych.* 50:348–63

Dobzhansky, T. 1957. *Genetics and the origin of species.* New York: Columbia University Press.

———. 1961. Genetics. In *The encyclopedia of biological sciences,* ed. P. Gray. New York: Reinhold Publishing Corporation.

———. 1965. Dominance-subordination relationships in mountain chickadees. *Condor* 67(4):291–99.

Dock, Jr., G. 1948. What field glasses for birds? *Audubon* 50(5):316–18.

Dodson, E. O. 1961. Evolution. In *The encyclopedia of biological sciences,* ed. P. Gray. New York: Reinhold Publishing Corporation.

Domm, L. V. 1955. Recent advances in knowledge concerning the role of hormones in the sex differentiation of birds. In *Recent studies in avian biology,* ed. A. Wolfson. Urbana, Ill.: University of Illinois Press.

Donahue, J. M., and Olson, L. D. 1969. Survey of wild ducks and geese for *pasteurella. Bull. Wildlife Disease Assoc.* 5:201–5.

Dorst, J. 1962. *The migrations of birds.* Boston: Houghton Mifflin Company.

———. 1964. Parrots. In *A new dictionary of birds,* ed. A. L. Thomson. New York: McGraw-Hill Book Company.

———. 1974. *The life of birds.* Vols. 1 and 2. New York: Columbia University Press.

Douville, C. H., and Friley, Jr., C. E. 1957. Records of longevity of Canada geese. *Auk* 74(4):510.

Dow, D. D. 1964. Diving times of wintering water birds. *Auk* 81(4):556–58.

———. 1968. Dew bathing and related behavior of the cardinal. *Bird-Banding* 39(3):227–28.

Doward, E. F. 1962. Comparative biology of the white booby and brown booby, *Sula* spp., at Ascension. *Ibis* 102b:174–220.

Dowden, P. B., and Mitchell, R. T. 1966. Birds and bugs. In *Birds in our lives,* ed. A. Stefferud and A. L. Nelson. Washington, D.C.: U.S. Dept. Inter., Fish and Wildlife Service.

Downer, A. C. 1972. Longevity records of indigo buntings wintering in Jamaica. *Bird-Banding* 43:287.

Dreis, R. E., and Hendrickson, G. O. 1952. Wood

duck production from nest boxes and natural cavities in the Lake Odessa area, Iowa, in 1951. *Iowa Bird Life* 22:19–22.

Drennan, S. R. 1975. National directory of rare bird alerts. *Amer. Birds* 29(1):8–11.

Drennan, S. R. 1979. *The North American birder's library lifelist.* New York: Doubleday & Co., Inc.

———. 1980. National directory of rare bird alerts. *Amer. Birds.* In press.

Drent, R. 1975. Incubation. In *Avian biology,* ed. D. S. Farner, J. R. King, and K. C. Parkes. Vol. 5, pp. 333–420. New York: Academic Press, Inc.

Drent, R. H. 1965. Breeding biology of the pigeon guillemot, *Cepphus columba. Ardea* 53:99–160.

Drewien, R. C. 1973. Ecology of Rocky Mountain greater sandhill cranes. Ph.D. thesis. Moscow, Idaho: University of Idaho.

Drewien, R. C., and Kuyt, Ernie. 1979. Teaming up to help the whooper. *Natl. Geographic Magazine* 155(5):680–93.

Drinkwater, H. 1960. Personal communication.

Drury, Jr., W. H. 1960. Breeding activities of long-tailed jaeger, herring gull, and Arctic tern on Bylot Island, Northwest Territories, Canada. *Bird-Banding* 31:63–78.

———. 1966. Birds at airports. In *Birds in our lives,* ed. A. Stefferud and A. L. Nelson. Washington, D.C.: U.S. Dept. Inter., Fish and Wildlife Service.

Drury, Jr., W. H., and Kadlec, J. A. 1974. The current status of the herring gull population in the northeastern United States. *Bird-Banding* 45(4):297–306.

Dubinin, V. B. 1951. Feather mites (analgesoidea). Part I. Introduction to their study. Fauna U.S.S.R., *Arachnida* 6(5):1–363.

Du Bois, A. D. 1935. Nests of horned larks and longspurs on a mountain prairie. *Condor* 37:56–72.

———. 1956. A cowbird incident. *Auk* 73(2):286.

Du Bose, R. T. 1971. Quail bronchitis. In *Infectious and parasitic diseases of wild birds,* ed. J. W. Davis *et al.* Ames, Iowa: Iowa State University Press.

Du Erul, E. L. 1962. The general phenomenon of bipedalism. *Amer. Zool.* 2:205–8.

Duffy, D. 1971. Personal communication. (Unpublished data gathered by Amer. Mus. Nat. Hist.)

Duffy, E.; Creasey, O. N.; and Williamson, K. 1950. Distraction display of certain waders. *Ibis* 92:27–33.

Du Mont, P. G. 1970. Notes during sun eclipse at mouth of Chesapeake Bay. *Atlantic Nat.* 25(2):88–89.

———. 1973. Black-browed albatross sightings off the United States East Coast. *Amer. Birds* 27(4):739–40.

Duncan, C. J. 1964a. Smell. In *A new dictionary of birds,* ed. A. L. Thomson. New York: McGraw-Hill Book Company.

———. 1964b. Taste. In *A new dictionary of birds,* ed. A. L. Thomson. New York: McGraw-Hill Book Company.

———. 1964c. Touch. In *A new dictionary of birds,* ed. A. L. Thomson. New York: McGraw-Hill Book Company.

Duncan, R. A. 1976. The black-whiskered vireo: A summary of its status on the northern Gulf Coast. *Amer. Birds* 30(3):658–60.

Duncan, S. 1962. Wasp attack on a flicker. *Auk* 79(2):277.

Dunker, H. 1974. Habitat selection and territory size of the black-throated diver, *Gavia arctica* (L.), in south Norway. *Norwegian Jour. Zool.* 22:15–29.

Dunker, H. 1975. Sexual and aggressive display of the black-throated diver, *Gavia arctica* (L.). *Norwegian Jour. Zool.* 23:149–63.

Dunstan, T. 1970. Raptor Research Foundation continental osprey status survey—1969. *Raptor Res. News* 4:81–103.

Dusi, R. L. 1968. "Ploughing" for fish by the

greater yellowlegs. *Wilson Bull.* 80:491–92.

Duvall, A. J. 1961a. Personal communication. (Letter of July 5, 1961, from Chief, Bird-Banding Laboratory, U.S. Dept. Inter., Fish and Wildlife Service, Laurel, Md.)

———. 1961b. Personal communication. (Letter of December 29, 1961.)

———. 1966. Where do they go? In *Birds in our lives,* ed. A. Stefferud and A. L. Nelson. Washington, D.C.: U.S. Dept. Inter., Fish and Wildlife Service.

Dwight, J. 1900. *The sequence of plumages and moults of the passerine birds of New York.* New York Acad. of Science, vol. 13.

———. 1925. The gulls (Laridae) of the world. Their plumages, moults, variations, relationships, and distribution. *Bull. Amer. Mus. Nat. Hist.* 3, art. III. 63–401.

Dykstra, W. W. 1960. Nuisance bird control. *Audubon* 62:118–19.

———. 1966. To kill a bird. In *Birds in our lives,* ed. A. Stefferud and A. L. Nelson. Washington, D.C.: U.S. Dept. Inter., Fish and Wildlife Service.

Dzubin, A.; Miller, H. W.; and Schildman, G. V. 1964. White-fronts. In *Waterfowl tomorrow,* ed. J. P. Linduska and A. L. Nelson. Washington, D.C.: U.S. Dept. Inter., Fish and Wildlife Service.

E

Earhart, C. M., and Johnson, N. K. 1970. Size dimorphism and food habits of North American owls. *Condor* 72(3):251–64.

Easterla, D. A. 1970. First nesting colonies of the lark bunting in Missouri. *Wilson Bull.* 82(4):465–66.

Easterla, D. A., and Lawhon, F. 1971. First specimen of Arctic loon from Missouri. *Auk* 88(1):175.

Eaton, S. W. 1968. Northern slate-colored junco. In *Life histories of North American cardinals, grosbeaks, buntings, towhees, finches, sparrows, and allies,* comp. A. C. Bent *et al.,* ed. O. L. Austin, Jr. U.S. Natl. Mus. Bull. no. 237, pt. 2. Washington, D.C.

Eckelberry, D. R. 1953. Personal communication.

———. 1961. Personal communication.

Edeburn, R. M. 1964. Black-legged kittiwake in West Virginia. *Wilson Bull.* 76(3):294–95.

Edgerton, H. E.; Niedrach, R. J.; and Van Riper, W. 1951. Freezing the flight of hummingbirds. In *Stalking birds with color camera,* ed. G. Grosvenor. Washington, D.C.: Natl. Geographic Soc.

Edinger, Tilly. 1942. The pituitary body in giant animals fossils and living: A survey and a suggestion. *Quart. Rev. Biol.* 17:31–45.

Edminster, F. C. 1947. *The ruffed grouse: Its life story, ecology, and management.* New York: The Macmillan Company.

———. 1954. *American game birds of field and forest.* New York: Charles Scribner's Sons.

———. 1964. Farm ponds and waterfowl. In *Waterfowl tomorrow,* ed. J. P. Linduska and A. L. Nelson. Washington, D.C.: U.S. Dept. Inter., Fish and Wildlife Service.

Edson, J. M. 1928. An epidemic of albinism. *Auk* 45(3):377–78.

Edward, E. P. 1974. *A coded list of the birds of the world.* Sweet Briar, Va.: E. P. Edwards.

Edwards, E. P. 1943. Hearing ranges of four species of birds. *Auk* 60:239–41.

Eifert, V. 1962. *Men, birds, and adventure.* New York: Dodd, Mead & Company.

Eigsti, W. E. 1950. Wren death. *Nebraska Bird Rev.* 18(3):59–60.

Eiseley, L. 1961. *Darwin's century.* Garden City, N.Y.: Doubleday & Co., Inc.

Eisenmann, E. 1955. *The species of Middle American birds.* Trans. Linnaean Soc. New York no. 7.

———. 1957. Wood warblers in Panama. In *The*

warblers of America, ed. L. Griscom *et al.* New York: The Devin-Adair Co.

———. 1964. Trogon. In *A new dictionary of birds,* ed. A. L. Thomson. New York: McGraw-Hill Book Company.

———. 1970. *Review of "A distributional survey of the birds of Honduras," by Burt L. Monroe.* Amer. Ornith. Union, Monogr. no. 7. Ithaca, N. Y.

———. 1971. Range expansion and population increase in North and Middle America of the white-tailed kite *(Elanus leucurus). Amer. Birds* 25(3):529–36.

Eisner, E. 1960. The relationship of hormones to the reproductive behaviour of birds, referring especially to parental behaviour: A review. *Jour. Animal Behaviour* 8:155–79.

Elder, W. H. 1946. Age and sex criteria and weights of Canada geese. *Jour. Wildlife Management* 10:93–111.

———. 1954. The oil gland of birds. *Wilson Bull.* 66:6–31.

Elliott, D. G. 1898. *The wild fowl of the United States and British possessions, or the swans, geese, ducks, and mergansers of North America.* New York: Francis P. Harper.

———. 1901. In memoriam: Elliott Coues. *Auk* 23(1):5–7.

Elliott, J. A., and Elliott, G. H. 1974. Observations on bird singing during a solar eclipse. *Canadian Field-Nat.* 88:213–17.

Elliott, J. J. 1954. Bird notes. *Long Island Press,* July 6–18.

———. 1956. British goldfinch on Long Island. *Long Island Naturalist* 5:3–13.

———. 1962. Sharp-tailed and seaside sparrows on Long Island, New York. *Kingbird* 12:115–23.

———. 1968a. European goldfinch. In *Life histories of North American cardinals, grosbeaks, buntings, towhees, finches, sparrows, and allies,* comp. A. C. Bent *et al.,* ed. O. L. Austin, Jr. U.S. Natl. Mus. Bull. no. 237, pt. 1. Washington, D.C.

———. 1968b. Ipswich sparrow. In *Life histories of North American cardinals, grosbeaks, buntings, towhees, finches, sparrows, and allies,* comp. A. C. Bent *et al.,* ed. O. L. Austin, Jr. U.S. Natl. Mus. Bull. no. 237, pt. 2. Washington, D.C.

Elliott, J. J., and Arbib, Jr., R. S. 1953. Origin and status of the house finch in the eastern United States. *Auk* (1):31–37.

Ellis, H. R. 1948. Northward bound for godwits. *Audubon* 50:154–59.

Ellison, L. N. 1966–1968. *Game bird reports.* Vols. 7–9. Juneau, Alaska: Alaska Dept. of Fish and Game.

———. 1971a. Spruce grouse attacked by a northern shrike. *Wilson Bull.* 83(1):99–100.

———. 1971b. Territoriality in Alaskan spruce grouse. *Auk* 88:652–64.

———. 1973. Seasonal social organization and movements of spruce grouse. *Condor* 75:375–85.

Elton, C. S. 1936. *Animal ecology.* New York: The Macmillan Company.

———. 1958. *The ecology of invasions by animals and plants.* New York: John Wiley & Sons, Inc.

Ely, C. A. 1973. Returns of North American birds to their wintering grounds in southern Mexico. *Bird-Banding* 44(3):228–29.

Emerson, G. 1940. The lure of the list. *Bird-Lore* 42 (January–February): 37–39.

Emlen, Jr., J. T. 1952. Flocking behavior in birds. *Auk* 69:160–70.

———. 1955. The study of behavior in birds. In *Recent studies in avian biology,* ed. A. Wolfson. Urbana, Ill.: University of Illinois Press.

———. 1960. *Introduction to animal sounds and communication,* ed. W. E. Lanyon and W. N. Tavolga. Amer. Inst. Biol. Sci. Publ. Washington, D.C.

———. 1971. Population densities of birds

derived from transect counts. *Auk* 88(1):323–42.

———. 1973. Territorial aggression in wintering warblers at Bahama agave blossoms. *Wilson Bull.* 85:71–74.

Emlen, S. T. 1967a. Migratory orientation in the indigo bunting, *Passerina cyanea*. Part I: Evidence for use of celestial cues. Part II: Mechanism of celestial orientation. *Auk* 84:309–42, 463–89.

———. 1967b. Orientation of *zugunruhe* in the rose-breasted grosbeak, *Pheucticus ludovicianus*. *Condor* 69:203–5.

———. 1975a. Migration: Orientation and navigation. In *Avian biology*, ed. D. S. Farner, J. R. King, and K. C. Parkes. Vol. 5. New York: Academic Press, Inc.

———. 1975b. The stellar-orientation system of a migratory bird. *Scientific American* 233(2):102–11.

Emlen, S. T., and Ambrose III, H. W. 1970. Feeding interactions of snowy egrets and red-breasted mergansers. *Auk* 87:164–65.

Emlen, S. T., and Oring, L. W. 1977. Ecology, sexual selection, and the evolution of mating systems. *Science* 197:215–23.

Emlen, S. T.; Rising, J. D.; and Thompson, W. L. 1975. A behavioral and morphological study of sympatry in the indigo and lazuli buntings of the Great Plains. *Wilson Bull.* 87(2):145–79.

Encyclopedia Britannica. 1929. 14th ed. London and New York: Encyclopedia Britannica Company.

Enderson, J. H. 1964. A study of the prairie falcon in the central Rocky Mountain region. *Auk* 81:332–52.

———. 1969. Population trends among peregrine falcons in the Rocky Mountain region. In *Peregrine falcon population: Their biology and decline*, ed. J. J. Hickey. Madison, Wis.: University of Wisconsin Press.

———. 1971. An account of prairie falcons bred in captivity—1970. *Raptor Res. News* 5(1):44–47.

Eng, R. L. 1971. Two hybrid sage grouse × sharp-tailed grouse. *Condor* 73(4):491–93.

Environmental Law Institute. 1977. The evolution of national wildlife law. Washington, D.C.: U.S. Govt. Printing Office.

Erickson, C. J. 1973. Mate familiarity and the reproductive behavior of ringed turtle doves. *Auk* 90(4):780–95.

Erickson, J. E. 1969. Banding studies of wintering Baltimore orioles in North Carolina, 1963–66. *Bird-Banding* 40(3):181–98.

Erickson, M. M. 1948. Gambel's wren-tit. In *Life histories of North American nuthatches, wrens, thrashers, and their allies*, by A. C. Bent. U.S. Natl. Mus. Bull. no. 195. Washington, D.C.

———. 1968. Lazuli bunting. In *Life histories of North American cardinals, grosbeaks, buntings, towhees, finches, sparrows, and allies*, comp. A. C. Bent *et al.*, ed. O. L. Austin, Jr. U.S. Natl. Mus. Bull. no. 237, pt. 1. Washington, D.C.

Errington, P. L.; Hamerstrom, F.; and Hamerstrom, F. N. 1940. The great horned owl and its prey in the north central United States. *Iowa State Coll-Agri. and Mech. Arts Research Bull.* 277:758–850.

Errington, Jr., P. L. 1932. Studies in the behavior of the great horned owl. *Wilson Bull.* 44:212–20.

———. 1946. Predation and vertebrate populations. *Quart. Rev. Biol.* 21:144–77, 221–45.

———. 1948. An appreciation of Aldo Leopold. *Jour. Wildlife Management* (4, 12 October): 12(4):341–50.

Errington, Jr., P. L. 1964. Talon and fang. In *Waterfowl tomorrow*, ed. J. P. Linduska and A. L. Nelson. Washington, D.C.: U.S. Dept. Inter., Fish and Wildlife Service.

———. 1967. *Of predation and life.* Ames, Iowa: Iowa State University Press.

Errington, P. L., and Bennett, L. J. 1935. Food habits of burrowing owls in northwestern Iowa. *Wilson Bull.* 47:125–28.

Erskine, A. J. 1963. The black-headed gull (*Larus ridibundus*) in eastern North America. *Audubon Field Notes* 17(3):334–38.

———. 1971a. *Buffleheads.* Canadian Wildlife Serv., Monogr. Series no. 4. Ottawa.

———. 1971b. Some new perspectives on the breeding ecology of common grackles. *Wilson Bull.* 83(4):352–70.

Escalante, R. 1972. First pomarine jaeger specimen from Brazil. *Auk* 89:663–65.

Essig, E. O. 1942. *College entomology.* New York: The Macmillan Company.

Evans, R. M. 1970. Oldsquaws nesting in association with Arctic terns at Churchill, Man. *Wilson Bull.* 83(4):353–486.

Evans, T. 1966. The Nation's Symbol. In *Birds in our lives*, ed. A. Stefferud and A. L. Nelson. Washington, D.C.: U.S. Government Printing Office.

Evenden, Jr., F. G. 1943. Food-washing habit of the dipper. *Condor* 45(3):120.

Ewan, J. 1950. *Rocky mountain naturalists.* Denver: University of Denver Press.

Eyster, M. B. 1966. Why band birds? *Louisiana Conservationist*, January–February, pp. 17–18.

F

Fabricius, E. 1959. What makes plumage waterproof? *Report of the Wildfowl Trust* 10:105–13.

Fabricius, E., and Jansson, A. M. 1963. Laboratory observations on the reproductive behavior of the pigeon (*Columba livia*) during the pre-incubation phase of the breeding cycle. *Jour. Animal Behaviour* 11(4):534–47.

Faddoul, G. P.; Fellous, G. W.; and Baird, J. 1966. A survey of the incidence of salmonellae in wild birds. *Avian Diseases* 10:89–94.

Fairchild, H. L. 1887. *A history of the New York Academy of Sciences.* New York: Published by the author and New York Academy of Sciences.

Fairfield, G. M. 1968. Chestnut-collared longspur. In *Life histories of North American cardinals, grosbeaks, buntings, towhees, finches, sparrows, and allies*, comp. A. C. Bent *et al.*, ed. O. L. Austin, Jr. U.S. Natl. Mus. Bull. no. 237, pt. 3. Washington, D.C.

Fallis, A. M. 1945. Population trends and blood parasites of ruffed grouse in Ontario. *Jour. Wildlife Management* 9:203–6.

Fallis, A. M., and Trainer, Jr., D. O. 1964. Blood parasites. In *Waterfowl tomorrow*, ed. J. P. Linduska and A. L. Nelson. Washington, D.C.: U.S. Dept. Inter., Fish and Wildlife Service.

Fankhauser, D. P. 1967. Survival rates in red-winged blackbirds. *Bird-Banding* 38(2):139–42.

Farner, D. S. 1960. Digestion and the digestive system. In *Biology and comparative physiology of birds*, ed. A. J. Marshall. New York: Academic Press, Inc.

Fassett, N. C. 1940. *A manual of aquatic plants.* 1st ed. New York: McGraw-Hill Book Company.

Fautin, R. W. 1946. Biotic communities of the northern desert shrub biome in western Utah. *Ecol. Monogr.* 16:253–310.

Fay, L. D.; Kaufmann, O. W.; and Ryel, L. A. 1965. *Mass mortality of water-birds in Lake Michigan, 1963–64.* Univ. Michigan Mus. Zool. Mis. Publ. no. 13. Ann Arbor.

Feduccia, A. 1976. Osteological evidence for shorebird affinities of the flamingos. *Auk* 93:587–601.

———. 1978. *Presbyornis* and the evolution of ducks and flamingos. *Amer. Scientist* 66(3):298–304.

Feldman, W. H. 1938. *Avian tuberculosis infections.* Baltimore: The Williams & Wilkins Company.

———. 1959. Tuberculosis in poultry. In *Diseases of poultry*, ed. H. E. Biester and L. H. Schwarte. 4th ed. Ames, Iowa: Iowa State University Press.

Ferguson-Lees, I. J. 1957. Peregrine (*Falco peregrinus*). In The rarer birds of prey, their present status in the British Isles. *Brit. Birds* 50(4):149–55.

———. 1964. Treecreeper (1). In *A new dictionary of birds*, ed. A. L. Thomson. New York: McGraw-Hill Book Company.

Fernald, M. L. 1950. *Gray's manual of botany.* 8th (centennial) ed. New York: American Book Co.

Ferry, C. 1956. Note sur le determinisme du nombre des oeufs chez les laro-limicolae. *Alauda* 24(1):49–52.

ffrench, R. P. 1967. The dickcissel on its wintering grounds in Trinidad. *Living Bird*, 6th annual.

ffrench, R. P., and Haverschmidt, F. 1970. The scarlet ibis in Surinam and Trinidad. *Living Bird*, 9th annual, pp. 147–65.

Ficken, M. S. 1963. Courtship of the American redstart. *Auk* 80(3):307–17.

———. 1977. Avian play. *Auk* 94(3):573–82.

Ficken, M. S., and Ficken, R. W. 1968. Reproductive isolating mechanisms in the blue-winged warbler—golden-winged warbler complex. *Evolution* 22(1):166–79.

Ficken, R. W., and Dilger, W. C. 1961. Insect and food mixtures for insectivorous birds. *Avicultural Magazine* 67(2):46–55.

Fimreite, N.; Fyfe, R. W.; and Keith, J. A. 1970. Mercury contamination of Canadian seed eaters and their avian predators. *Canadian Field-Nat.* 84(3):269–76.

Finch, D. W. 1970. Northeast maritime region. The nesting season. *Audubon Field Notes* 24(5):661.

———. 1971a. Northeastern maritime region. *Amer. Birds* 25(4):705, 833.

———. 1971b. Northeastern maritime region (fall migration). *Amer. Birds* 25(1): 27, 29.

———. 1971c. Northeastern maritime region. The nesting season. *Amer. Birds* 25(5): 836.

———. 1973. Northeastern maritime region. *Amer. Birds* 27(1):26, 27.

———. 1975. Northeastern maritime region. *Amer. Birds* 29(3):747.

Finch, D. W., and Proctor, N. S. 1972. Spotted redshank in Connecticut. *Auk* 89:677.

Fink, L. C. 1958. Want to start a bird club? *Audubon* 60:20–23.

Finlay, J. C. 1971. Breeding biology of purple martins at the northern limit of their range. *Wilson Bull.* 83(3):255–69.

———. 1976. Some effects of weather on purple martin activity. *Auk* 93(2):231–44.

Finley, W. L. 1906. The barn owl and its economic value. *Condor* 8:83–88.

———. 1910. Life history of the California condor. Part IV. *Condor* 12:5–11.

Fischer, R. B. 1953. That big day. *Audubon* 55:114–17, 142.

———. 1958. *The breeding biology of the chimney swift*, Chaetura pelagica. New York State Mus. Sci. Serv. Bull. no. 368. Albany.

Fisher, A. K. 1920. In memoriam: Lyman Belding. *Auk* 37(1):33–45.

———. 1939. In memoriam: George Bird Grinnell. *Auk* 56(1):1–12.

Fisher, H. I. 1955. Avian anatomy, 1925–50, and some suggested problems. In *Recent studies in avian biology*, ed. A. Wolfson. Urbana, Ill.: University of Illinois Press.

———. 1958. The "hatching muscle" in the chick. *Auk* 75:391–99.

———. 1966. Airplane—albatross collisions on Midway atoll. *Condor* 68:229–42.

———. 1971. The Laysan albatross: Its incubation, hatching, and associated behaviors. *Living Bird*, 10th annual, pp. 19–78.

———. 1972. Sympatry of Laysan and black-footed albatrosses. *Auk* 89(2):381–402.

———. 1975. Longevity of the Laysan albatross,

Diomedea immutabilis. Bird-Banding 46(1): 1–6.

———. 1976. Some dynamics of a breeding colony of Laysan albatrosses. *Wilson Bull.* 88(1):121–42.

Fisher, J. 1940. *Watching birds.* Harmondsworth, England: Penguin Books.

———. 1951. *Watching birds.* Rev. ed. London: Penguin Books, Ltd. (Pelican Book).

———. 1952. *The fulmar.* London: William Collins Sons & Co., Ltd.

———. 1964. Extinct birds. In *A new dictionary of birds,* ed. A. L. Thomson. New York: McGraw-Hill Book Company.

———. 1966. *The shell bird book,* ed. E. Press and M. Joseph. London: George Rainbird, Ltd.

———. 1970. In *Wildlife crisis,* ed. Philip, Duke of Edinburgh, and J. Fisher. New York: Cowles Book Company, Inc.

Fisher, J., and Lockley, R. M. 1954. *Sea-birds.* Boston: Houghton Mifflin Company.

Fisher, J., and Peterson, R. T. 1964. *The world of birds.* Garden City, N.Y.: Doubleday & Co., Inc.

Fisher, J., and Vevers, H. G. 1943. The breeding distribution, history, and population of the North Atlantic gannet *(Sula bassana).* Part I. A history of gannet colonies and the census in 1939. *Jour. Animal Ecology* 12:173–213.

———. 1944. Part II. The changes in the world numbers of the gannet in a century. *Jour. Animal Ecology* 13:49–62.

Fisk, E. J. 1966. A happy newcomer in a fruitful land. *Florida Nat.* 39:10–11.

———. 1968. White-winged doves breeding in Florida. *Florida Nat.* 41:126.

———. 1971a. Increase of fall Traill's flycatchers in southern Florida. *Bird-Banding* 42(2):121.

———. 1971b. Personal communication. Letter of August 24.

———. 1971c. Personal communication. Letter of October 18.

———. 1974a. Second U.S. record of a Bahama woodstar. *Amer. Birds* 28(4):855.

———. 1974b. Wintering populations of painted buntings in southern Florida. *Bird-Banding* 45(4):353–59.

———. 1975. Least tern: Beleagured, opportunistic, and roof-nesting. *Amer. Birds* 29(1):15–16.

———. 1977. Personal communication.

Fiske, D. L. 1907. Confiding vireos. *Bird-Lore* 9(1):47.

Fitch, Jr., F. W. 1950. Life history and ecology of the scissor-tailed flycatcher. *Auk* 67:145–68.

Fitch, H. S. 1963. Observations on the Mississippi kite in southwestern Kansas. *Univ. Kansas Publ. Mus. Nat. Hist.* 12(11):503–19.

Fitch, H. S.; Swenson, F.; and Tillotson, D. 1946. Behavior and food habits of the red-tailed hawk. *Condor* 48(5):205–37.

Fitzpatrick, I. W. 1980. Foraging behavior of neotropical tyrant flycatchers. *Condor* 82:43–57.

Fitzpatrick, J. W. 1975. A record of allopreening in the barred owl. *Auk* 92(3):598–99.

Fleetwood, R. J. 1967. Observance and nesting of the hook-billed kite *(Chondrohierax uncinatus)* in Texas. *Auk* 84 (2):598–601.

———. 1973. Jaçana breeding in Brazoria County, Texas. *Auk* 90:422–23.

Fleming, C. A. 1964. Wattlebird. In *A new dictionary of birds,* ed. A. L. Thomson. New York: McGraw-Hill Book Company.

Fleming, J. 1822. *The philosophy of zoology or a general view of the structure, functions and classification of animals.* Vol. 2. Edinburgh and London: A. Constable & Co.

Fleming, J. H. 1908. The destruction of whistling swans *(Olor columbianus)* at Niagara Falls. *Auk* 25:306–9.

———. 1912. The Niagara swan trap. *Auk* 29: 445–48.

———. 1930. In memoriam: Jonathan Dwight. *Auk* 47(1):1–6.

Flieg, G. M. 1971. The European tree sparrow in the Western Hemisphere—Its range, distribu-

tion, life history. *The Audubon Bull., Ill. Aud. Soc., The* 157:2–10.

Flint, R. F. 1957. *Glacial and Pleistocene geology.* New York: John Wiley & Sons, Inc.

Flower, S. S. 1925. Contributions to our knowledge of the duration of life in vertebrate animals, IV. Birds. *Proc. Zool. Soc. London* 2:1365–1422.

———. 1938. Further notes on the duration of life in vertebrate animals, IV. Birds. *Proc. Zool. Soc. London,* ser. A108, pp. 195–235.

Fogarty, M. J., and Hetrick, W. M. 1973. Summer foods of cattle egrets in north-central Florida. *Auk* 90:268–80.

Forbes, J. E., and Warner, D. W. 1974. Behavior of a radio-tagged saw-whet owl. *Auk* 91(4):783–95.

Forbes, S. A. 1890. On the food relations of freshwater fishes. *Bull. of the Ill. State Lab. Nat. Hist.* 2:475–538.

Forbes, T. R. 1947. The crowing hen: Early observations on spontaneous sex reversal in birds. *Yale Jour. Biology and Medicine* 19:955–70.

Forbush, E. H. 1907. *Useful birds and their protection.* Boston: Mass. State Board of Agriculture.

———. 1912. *A history of game birds, wild-fowl and shore birds of Massachusetts and adjacent states.* Boston: Mass. State Board of Agriculture.

———. 1925–29. *Birds of Massachusetts and other New England states.* 3 vols. Boston: Mass. Dept. of Agriculture.

Ford, A., ed. 1969. *Audubon, by himself.* Garden City, New York: Amer. Mus. Nat. Hist./Natural History Press.

Ford, E. B. 1957. *Butterflies.* London: William Collins Sons & Co., Ltd. pp. 197–98.

Forshaw, J. M. 1973. *Parrots of the world.* Garden City, N. Y.: Doubleday & Co., Inc.

Foster, W. L., and Tate, Jr., J. 1966. The activities and coactions of animals at sapsucker trees. *Living Bird,* 5th annual, pp. 87–113.

Fox, D. L. 1944. Biochromes. *Science* 100:470–71.

———. 1953. *Animal biochromes and structural colors.* Cambridge: At the University Press.

Fox, I. 1940. *Fleas of the eastern United States.* Ames, Iowa: Iowa State College Press.

Foxall, R. 1979. Presumed hybrids of the herring gull and great black-backed gull. *Amer. Birds* 33:838.

Frankowiak, R. G. 1962. Mourning dove with three legs. *Auk* 79(2):278.

Franzreb, K. E., and Higgins, A. E. 1975. Possible bear predation on a yellow-bellied sapsucker nest. *Auk* 92(4):817.

Frazar, A. A. 1876. Intelligence of the crow. *Bull. Nuttall Ornith. Club* 1:76.

Frazier, F. P. 1952. Depigmentation of a robin. *Bird-Banding* 23:114.

Fredrickson, L. H. 1969. Mortality of coots during severe spring weather. *Wilson Bull.* 81(4):450–53.

———. 1970. Breeding biology of American coots in Iowa. *Wilson Bull.* 82:445–57.

———. 1971. Common gallinule breeding biology and development. *Auk* 88:914–19.

Freeland, D. B. 1973. Some food preferences and aggressive behavior by monk parakeets. *Wilson Bull.* 85:332–34.

French, C. E.; Lincinsky, S. A.; and Miller, D. R. 1957. Nutrient composition of earth-worms. *Jour. Wildlife Management* 21(3):348.

French, N. R. 1954. Notes on breeding activities and on gular sacs in the pine grosbeak. *Condor* 56:83–85.

———. 1959. Life history of the black rosy finch. *Auk* 76(2):159–80.

———. 1968. Black rosy finch. In *Life histories of North American cardinals, grosbeaks, buntings, towhees, finches, sparrows, and allies,* comp. A. C. Bent *et al.,* ed. O. L. Austin, Jr. U.S. Natl. Mus. Bull. no. 237, pt. 1. Washington, D.C.

Frick, G. F., and Stearns, R. P. 1961. *Mark Catesby: The colonial Audubon.* Urbana, Ill.: University of Illinois Press.

Friedmann, H. 1927. Notes on some Argentine birds. *Bull. Mus. Compar. Zool.* 68(4):177–78.

———. 1929. *The cowbirds: A study in the biology of social parasitism.* Springfield, Ill.: Charles C Thomas, Publisher.

———. 1935. Notes on the different threshold of reaction to vitamin D deficiency of the house sparrow and the chick. *Biol. Bull.* 69:71–74.

———. 1950. *The birds of North and Middle America.* U.S. Natl. Mus. Bull. no. 50. Washington, D.C.

———. 1955. *The honey guides.* U.S. Natl. Mus. Bull. no. 208. Washington, D.C.

———. 1963. *Host relations of the parasitic cowbirds.* U.S. Natl. Mus. Bull. no. 233. Washington, D.C.

———. 1966. *Additional data on the host relations of the parasitic cowbirds.* Smithsonian Misc. Coll. 149(11). Washington, D.C.

———. 1971. Further information on the host relations of the parasitic cowbirds. *Auk* 88(1) 239–55.

Friedmann, H., and Davis, M. 1938. Left-handedness in parrots. *Auk* 55(3):478–80.

Friend, M., and Trainer, D. O. 1969. Aspergillosis in captive herring gulls. *Bull. Wildlife Disease Assoc.* 5:271–75.

Fries, W. H. 1973. *The double elephant folio.* Chicago: The American Library Association.

Frings, H., and Boyd, W. A. 1952. Evidence for olfactory discrimination by the bobwhite. *Amer. Midland-Nat.* 48:181–84.

Frings, H., and Frings, M. 1959. The language of crows. *Scientific American* 201(11, November):119–31.

Frisch, O. V. 1959. Development of the young, breeding biology, and comparative ethology of waders. *Z. f. Tierpsych.* 16(5):545–83.

Frith, H. J. 1964. Megapode. In *A new dictionary of birds,* ed. A. L. Thomson. New York: McGraw-Hill Book Company.

Frohling, R. C. 1967. A partial albino laughing gull. *Bird-Banding* 38(3):235–36.

Fry, C. H. 1980a. The origin of Afrotropical kingfishers. *Ibis* 122:57–72.

Fry, C. H. 1980b. The evolutionary biology of kingfishers *(Alcedinidae). Living Bird* 18:113–60.

Fuertes, L. A. 1920. Falconry, the sport of kings. *Natl. Geographic Magazine* 38:429–60.

Fuller, R. W., and Bolen, E. 1963. Dual wood duck occupancy of a nesting box. *Wilson Bull.* 75(1):94–95.

Fyfe, R. W. 1969. The peregrine falcon in northern Canada. In *Peregrine falcon population: Their biology and decline,* ed. J. J. Hickey. Madison, Wis.: University of Wisconsin Press.

Fyfe, R. W.; Campbell, J.; Hayson, B.; and Hodson, K. 1969. Regional population declines and organo-chlorine insecticides in Canadian prairie falcons. *Canadian Field-Nat.* 83:191–200.

Fyfe, R. W.; Temple, S. A.; and Cade, T. J. 1976. The 1975 North American Peregrine Falcon Survey. *Canadian Field-Nat.* 90(3): 228–73.

G

Gabrielson, I. N. 1941. Baikal teal on St. Lawrence Island, Alaska. *Auk* 58(3):400.

———. 1951. *Wildlife management.* New York: The Macmillan Company.

———. 1968. McKay's bunting. In *Life histories of North American cardinals, grosbeaks, buntings, towhees, finches, sparrows, and allies,* comp. A. C. Bent *et al.,* ed. O. L. Austin, Jr. U.S. Natl. Mus. Bull. no. 237, pt. 3. Washington, D.C.

Gabrielson, I. N., and Lincoln, F. C. 1959. *The birds of Alaska.* Harrisburg, Pa.: Stackpole Co.

Gale, N. B. 1971. Tuberculosis. In *Infectious and parasitic diseases of wild birds,* ed. J. W. Davis *et al.* Ames, Iowa: Iowa State University Press.

Gambona, G. J. 1977. Predation on rufous hummingbird by Wied's flycatcher. *Auk* 94(1):157–58.

Gander, F. F. 1929. Notes on bird mimicry with special reference to the mockingbird. *Wilson Bull.* 36, n.s.147:93–95.

———. 1957. The brown towhee. *Audubon* 59:124–27.

———. 1958. The roadrunner. In *The Audubon book of true nature stories,* ed. J. K. Terres. New York: Thomas Y. Crowell Company, Inc.

———. 1960. Western bluebirds in my garden. *Audubon* 62:70–71.

Ganier, A. F. 1964. The alleged transportation of its eggs or young by the chuck-will's-widow. *Wilson Bull.* 76(1):19–27.

———. 1966. Some facts learned from nocturnal migration. *Migrant* 37:27–34.

Garber, D. P., and Koplin, J. R. 1972. Prolonged and bisexual incubation by California ospreys. *Condor* 74:201–2.

Gardner, L. L. 1925. The adaptive modifications and the taxonomic value of the tongue in birds. *Proc. U.S. Natl. Mus.* 67:2591.

———. 1927. On the tongues of birds. *Ibis,* ser. 12(3):185–96.

Garnham, P. C. C. 1966. *Malaria parasites and other haemosporidia.* Oxford, England: B. H. Blackwell, Ltd.

Garrod, A. H. 1876. Notes on the anatomy of *Plotus anhinga. Proc. Zool. Soc. London* 46:335–45.

———. 1878. Notes on the gizzard and other organs of *Carpophaga zatrans. Proc. Zool. Soc. London* 48:102–5.

Gart, J. 1975. Supplement: Bird-finding guides. *Amer. Birds* 29(5):1050–54.

Gashwiler, J. G. 1960. Hunting behavior of a pygmy owl. *Murrelet* 41:12–13.

Gates, J. M. 1962. Breeding behavior of the gadwall in northern Utah. *Wilson Bull.* 74:43–67.

Gause, G. F. 1934. *The struggle for existence.* Baltimore: The Williams & Wilkins Company.

Gauthier, J.; Bedard, J.; and Reed, A. 1976. Overland migration by common eiders of the St. Lawrence estuary. *Wilson Bull.* 88(2):333–43.

Gauthreaux, Jr., S. A. 1969. A portable ceilometer technique for studying low-level nocturnal migration. *Bird-Banding* 40(4):309–20.

———. 1971a. The changing seasons (nesting season). *Amer. Birds* 25(5):821, 828.

———. 1971b. A radar and direct visual study of passerine spring migration in southern Louisiana. *Auk* 88(2):343–65.

———. 1972. Behavioral responses of migrating birds to daylight and darkness: A radar and direct visual study. *Wilson Bull.* 84:136–48.

———. 1978. Personal communication.

Gauthreaux, Jr., S. A., and Shugart, H. H. 1970. The changing seasons. *Audubon Field Notes* 24(4):655.

Gavin, A. 1947. Birds of Perry River district, Northwest Territories. *Wilson Bull.* 59(4):195–203.

Gavrilov, V. 1972. How birds reduce heat loss. *Priroda* 1972 (10):110.

Gebhardt, L. 1964. *Die Ornithologen Mitteleuropas.* Giessen: Bruehl.

Geiser, S. W. 1948. *Naturalists of the frontier.* 2d ed. Dallas: Southern Methodist University Press.

George, J. C., and Berger, A. J. 1966. *Avian myology.* New York: Academic Press, Inc.

George, J. L. 1966. Farmers and birds. In *Birds in our lives,* ed. A. Stefferud and A. L. Nelson. Washington, D.C.: U.S. Dept. Inter., Fish and Wildlife Service.

Gershman, M.; Witter, J. F.; Spencer, Jr., H. E.; and Kalvaitis, A. 1964. Case report: Epizootic of fowl cholera in the common eider duck. *Jour. Wildlife Management* 28:587–89.

Gerstell, R. 1942. *The place of winter feeding in practical wildlife management.* Penna. Game Comm., Research Bull. no. 2. Harrisburg.

Gerstenberg, R. H., and Harris, Stanley W. 1970. A California specimen of the bar-tailed godwit. *Condor* 72(1):112.

Gertsch, W. J. 1949. *American spiders.* New York: D. Van Nostrand Company.

Gibb, J. 1947. Sun-bathing by birds. *Brit. Birds* 40(5):172–74.

———. 1958. Predation by tits and squirrels on the Eucosmid, *Ernarmonia conicolana* (Heyl). *Anim. Ecol.* 27:375–96.

———. 1960. Populations of tits and goldcrests and their food supply in pine plantations. *Ibis* 102:163–208.

Gibson, D. 1977. First North American nest and eggs of the ruff. *Western Birds* 18:25–26.

Gibson, D. D. 1968. Alaska region: Nesting season. *Audubon Field Notes* 22(5):637–38.

———. 1970. Alaska region. *Audubon Field Notes* 24(4):634.

———. 1971. Alaska region. *Amer. Birds* 25(1):92, (3):613.

Gibson, D. D., and Byrd, G. V. 1972. Alaska region. *Amer. Birds* 26:891, 892.

———. 1973. Alaska region. *Amer. Birds* 27(1):103.

———. 1975. Alaska region. *Amer. Birds* 29(5):1019, 1020.

Gibson, D. D., and MacDonald, S. O. 1971. Alaska region: Nesting season. *Amer. Birds* 25(4):786; (5):895.

Gibson, F. 1971. The breeding biology of the American avocet (*Recurvirostra americana*) in central Oregon. *Condor* 73(4):444–54.

Gignoux, C. 1921. Speed of flight of the red-shafted flicker. *Condor* 33:34.

Gill, F. B. 1980. Historical aspects of hybridization between blue-winged and golden-winged warblers. *Auk* 97:1–18.

Gill, G. 1946. Old age records of banded birds—Final list. *EBBA News* 9(3).

Gillespie, J. A. 1934. The homing instinct in the rough-winged swallow. *Bird-Banding* 5(1):43–44.

Gillespie, M. 1960. Long distance flyers—The ospreys. *EBBA News* 23:55–62.

Gilliard, E. T. 1958. *Living birds of the world.* Garden City, N.Y.: Doubleday & Co., Inc.

———. 1961. The bony treasure of Funk island. In *Discovery: Great moments in the lives of outstanding naturalists,* ed. J. K. Terres. Philadelphia: J. B. Lippincott Company.

———. 1962. On the breeding behavior of the cock-of-the-rock. *Bull. Amer. Mus. Nat. Hist.* 124, art. 2, pp. 31–68.

Gingerich, P. D. 1972. A new partial mandible of *Ichthyornis. Condor* 74:471–73.

Ginn, H. 1973. What a way to go. *Brit. Trust for Ornithology News* 48:7.

Glase, J. C. 1973. Ecology of social organization in the black-capped chickadee. *Living Bird,* 12th annual, pp. 235–67.

Glasier, P. 1964. *As the falcon her bells.* New York: E. P. Dutton.

Glick, P. A. 1939. *The distribution of insects, spiders, and mites in the air.* U.S. Dept. Agric. Tech. Bull. no. 673. Washington, D.C.

Glinski, R. L. 1976. Bird-watching etiquette: The need for a developing philosophy. *Amer. Birds* 30(3):655–57.

Glover, F. A. 1947. Flight speed of wild turkeys. *Auk* 64:623–24.

———. 1964. Tundra to tropics. In *Waterfowl tomorrow,* ed. J. P. Linduska and A. L. Nelson. Washington, D.C.: U.S. Dept. Inter., Fish and Wildlife Service.

Gochfeld, M. 1971. Notes on a nocturnal roost of spotted sandpipers in Trinidad, West Indies. *Auk* 88(1):167–68.

———. 1973. Confused nocturnal behavior of a flock of migrating yellow wagtails. *Condor* 75:252–53.

Godfrey, W. E. 1966. *The birds of Canada.* Natl. Mus. Canada, Bull. no. 203. Ottawa.

Goethe, F. 1937. Beobachtungen und Untersuchungen zur Biologie der Silbermöwe (*Larus a. argentatus*) auf der Vogelinsel Memertsand. *Jour. f. Ornith.* 85:1–119.

Goldby, F. 1964. Nervous system. In *A new dictionary of birds,* ed. by A. L. Thomson. New York: McGraw-Hill Book Company.

Goldstein, P. 1947. *Genetics is easy.* New York: Lantern Press, Inc.

Goodwin, C. E., and Rosche, R. C. 1971a. Ontario–western New York region. *Amer. Birds* 25(3):573.

———. 1971b. Ontario–western New York region (fall migration 1969). *Amer. Birds* 25(1):52.

Goodwin, D. 1948. Incubation habits of the golden pheasant. *Ibis* 90:280–84.

———. 1956. The significance of some behaviour patterns of pigeons. *Bird Study* 3:25–37.

———. 1976. *Crows of the world.* Ithaca, N.Y.: Comstock Pub. Associates.

Goodwin, G. G. 1935. Winged monarchs of the air. *Natural History* 36:51–61.

Goodwin, R. E. 1961. Charadriiformes. In *The encyclopedia of biological sciences,* ed. P. Gray. New York: Reinhold Publishing Corporation.

Gordon, K. 1928. An albino kingbird. *Auk* 45(1):101.

Gorsuch, D. M. 1934. *Life history of the Gambel quail in Arizona.* Univ. Arizona Biol. Sci. Bull. no. 2.

Gosse, P. H. 1847. *Birds of Jamaica.* London: John van Voorst.

Gould, P. J. 1961. Territorial relationships between cardinals and pyrrhuloxias. *Condor* 63:246–56.

Gower, C. 1936. The cause of blue color as found in the bluebird (*Sialia sialis*) and the blue jay (*Cyanocitta cristata*). *Auk* 53:178–85.

———. 1939. The use of the bursa of Fabricius as an indication of age in game birds. *Trans. [4th] N. Amer. Wildlife Conf.* pp. 426–30.

Graber, J. W. 1961. Distribution, habitat requirements, and life history of the black-capped vireo (*Vireo atricapilla*). *Ecol. Monogr.* 31:313–36.

———. 1968. Western Henslow's sparrow. In *Life histories of North American cardinals, grosbeaks, buntings, towhees, finches, sparrows, and allies,* comp. A. C. Bent *et al.,* ed. O. L. Austin, Jr. U.S. Natl. Mus. Bull. no. 237, pt. 2. Washington, D.C.

Graber, R. R. 1965. Night flight with a thrush. *Audubon* 67(6):368–74.

Graber, R. R., and Graber, J. W. 1951. Nesting of the parula warbler in Michigan. *Wilson Bull.* 63:75–83.

———. 1962. Weight characteristics of birds killed in nocturnal migration. *Wilson Bull.* 74:74–88.

———. 1965. Variation in avian brain weights with special reference to age. *Condor* 67(4):300–317.

———. 1977. Grackles nesting on interstates. *Cornell Laboratory of Ornithology Newsletter to Members,* no. 83 (Winter 1977):2.

Graham, Jr., F. 1970. *Since silent spring.* Boston: Houghton Mifflin Company.

———. 1971. *Man's dominion.* New York: M. Evans and Company; Philadelphia: J. B. Lippincott Company.

———. 1976. Blackbirds: A problem that won't fly away. *Audubon* 78(3):118–25.

Grandy IV, J. W. 1972. Digestion and passage of blue mussels eaten by black duck. *Auk* 89(1):189.

Grange, W. B. 1948. *Wisconsin grouse problems.* Report of Wisconsin Dept. of Conservation. Madison.

———. 1949. *The way to game abundance.* New York: Charles Scribner's Sons.

Grant, G. S. 1970. Rattlesnake predation on the clapper rail. *Chat* 34(1):20–21.

Grant, G. S., and Quay, T. L. 1970. Sex and age criteria in the slate-colored junco. *Bird-Banding* 41(4):274–78.

Grant, K. A. 1966. A hypothesis concerning the red coloration in California hummingbird flowers. *Amer. Nat.* 100:85–97.

Grant, K. A., and Grant, V. 1968. *Hummingbirds and their flowers*. New York: Columbia University Press.

Grasett, F. G. 1926. Great blue heron *(Ardea h. herodias)* alighting on water. *Auk* 43(3):367.

Graul, W. D. 1971. Observations of a long-billed curlew nest. *Auk* 88(1):182–84.

———. 1973. Adaptive aspects of the mountain plover social system. *Living Bird,* 12th annual, pp. 69–94.

———. 1975. Breeding biology of the mountain plover. *Wilson Bull.* 87(1):6–31.

Gray, A. P. 1958. *Bird hybrids*. Tech. Communication no. 13. London: Commonwealth Agricultural Bureaux.

———. 1964. Hybrid. In *A new dictionary of birds,* ed. A. L. Thomson. New York: McGraw-Hill Book Company.

Gray, P. 1961. Darwin, Charles (1809–1882). In *The encyclopedia of the biological sciences,* ed. P. Gray. New York: Reinhold Publishing Corporation.

Gray, R. 1871. *The birds of west Scotland, including the outer Hebrides, with occasional records of the occurrence of the rarer species throughout Scotland generally*. Glasgow, Scotland: Thomas Murray & Son.

Green, C. H. 1948. Gaddy's geese. *Nature Magazine* 41(9):457–60, 498.

Greenewalt, C. H. 1960. *Hummingbirds*. Garden City, N.Y.: Doubleday & Co., Inc.

———. 1968. *Bird song: Acoustics and physiology*. Washington, D.C.: Smithsonian Press.

Greenhalgh, M. 1965. Migrating swallows and meadow pipits drowning in sea. *Brit. Birds* 58(1):21–22.

Greenlaw, J. S. 1973. An erythristic specimen of the rufous-sided towhee. *Auk* 90(2):428–29.

Greenway, Jr., J. C. 1958. *Extinct and vanishing birds of the world*. Amer. Committee for Intern. Wildlife Protection, Spec. Pub. no. 13. New York.

Gregory, J. J. 1952. The jaws of the Cretaceous toothed birds, *Ichthyornis* and *Hesperornis*. *Condor* 54(1):73–78.

Gress, F.; Risebrough, R. W.; Anderson, D. W.; Kiff, L. F.; and Jehl, Jr., J. R. 1973. Reproductive failures of double-crested cormorants in southern California and Baja California. *Wilson Bull.* 85(2):197–208.

Gress, F.; Risebrough, R. W.; and Sibley, F. C. 1971. Shell thinning in eggs of the common murre, *Uria aalge,* from the Farallon Islands, California. *Condor* 73:368–69.

Griffin, D. R. 1940. Homing experiments with Leach's petrels. *Auk* 57(1):61–74.

———. 1958. *Listening in the dark: The acoustical orientation of bats and men*. New Haven, Conn.: Yale University Press.

———. 1969. The physiology and geophysics of bird navigation. *Quart. Rev. Biol.* 44:255–76.

———. 1972. *Nocturnal bird migration in opaque clouds*. NASA Spec. Publ. NASA SP-262, pp. 169–88. Washington, D.C.

———. 1973. Oriented bird migration in or between opaque cloud layers. *Proc. Amer. Philos. Soc.* 117:117–41.

Grimes, S. A. 1936. Great horned owl and common black snake in mortal combat. *Florida Nat.* 9:77–78.

———. 1953. *An album of southern birds*. Austin, Texas: University of Texas Press.

Grimm, R. J., and Whitehouse, W. M. 1963. Pellet formation of a great horned owl: A roentgenographic study. *Auk* 80(3):301–6.

Grinnell, G. B. 1901. *American duck shooting*. New York: Forest and Stream Publishing Company.

———. 1922. Woodcock carrying its young. *Auk* 39:563–64.

Grinnell, H. W. 1940. Joseph Grinnell, 1877–1939. *Condor* 40(1):3–34.

Grinnell, J. 1924. Geography and evolution. *Ecology* 5:225–29.

———. 1926. Doped robins. *Condor* 28:97.

———. 1932. Archibald Menzies, first collector of California birds. *Condor* 34:243–52.

———. 1933. The vulture's fairway. *Condor* 35(4):164–66.

Grinnell, J., and Storer, T. I. 1924. *Animal life in Yosemite*. Berkeley, Calif.: University of California Press.

Griscom, L. 1932. The distribution of bird-life in Guatemala. *Bull. Amer. Mus. Nat. Hist.* 64:1–439.

———. 1945. *Modern bird study*. Cambridge, Mass.: Harvard University Press.

———. 1949. *Birds of Concord*. Cambridge, Mass.: Harvard University Press.

Griscom, L., and Snyder, D. E. 1955. *The birds of Massachusetts*. Salem, Mass.: Peabody Museum.

Griscom, L., and Sprunt, Jr., A., eds. 1979. *The warblers of North America*.

Griscom, L. et al. 1957. *The warblers of America*. New York: The Devin-Adair Co.

Groebbels, F. 1932. *Der vogel. Erster Band: Atmungswelt und Nahrungswelt*. Berlin: Verlag von Gebrüder Borntraeger.

Groff, M. E. 1946. Purple grackles "anting" with walnut juice. *Auk* 63(2):246–47.

Grohmann, J. 1938. Modification oder Funktionsreifung? Ein Beitrag zur Klärung der wechselseitigen Beziehungen zwischen Instinkthandlung und Erfahrung. *Z. f. Tierpsych.* 2:132–44.

Groskin, H. 1945. Chimney swifts roosting at Ardmore, Pennsylvania. *Auk* 62:361–70.

———. 1947. Duck hawks breeding in the business center of Philadelphia, Pennsylvania. *Auk* 64(2):312–14.

———. 1950. Observations on anting by birds. *Auk* 67:201–9.

———. 1952. Observations of duck hawks nesting on man-made structures. *Auk* 69:246–53.

Gross, A. O. 1928. The heath hen. *Memo. Boston Soc. Nat. Hist.* 6(4):491–588.

———. 1932a. Greater prairie chicken. In *Life histories of north American gallinaceous birds,* by A. C. Bent. U.S. Natl. Mus. Bull. no. 162. Washington, D.C.

———. 1932b. Heath hen. In *Life histories of North American gallinaceous birds,* by A. C. Bent. U.S. Natl. Mus. Bull. no. 162. Washington, D.C.

———. 1933. History and progress of bird photography in America. In *Fifty years progress of American ornithology, 1883–1933*. Lancaster, Pa.: Amer. Ornith. Union.

———. 1937. Birds of the Bowdoin-Macmillan Arctic Expedition, 1934. *Auk* 54: 29–30.

———. 1940. Eastern nighthawk. In *Life histories of North American cuckoos, goatsuckers, hummingbirds, and their allies,* by A. C. Bent. U.S. Natl. Mus. Bull. no. 176. Washington, D.C.

———. 1942a. Bank swallow. In *Life histories of North American flycatchers, larks, swallows, and their allies,* by A. C. Bent. U.S. Natl. Mus. Bull. no. 179. Washington, D.C.

———. 1942b. Northern cliff swallow. In *Life histories of North American flycatchers, larks, swallows, and their allies,* by A. C. Bent. U.S. Natl. Mus. Bull. no. 179. Washington, D.C.

———. 1946a. Eastern crow. In *Life histories of North American jays, crows, and titmice,* by A. C. Bent. U.S. Natl. Mus. Bull. no. 191. Washington, D.C.

———. 1946b. Snowy owl invasions. *Massachusetts Audubon Society* 30(2):9–32.

———. 1947a. Cyclic invasions of the snowy owl and the migration of 1945–46. *Auk* 64:584–601.

———. 1947b. Recoveries of banded Leach's petrels. *Bird-Banding* 18(3):117–26.

———. 1948a. Catbird. In *Life histories of North American nuthatches, wrens, thrashers, and their allies,* by A. C. Bent. U.S. Natl. Mus. Bull. no. 195. Washington, D.C.

———. 1948b. Eastern house wren. In *Life histories of North American nuthatches, wrens, thrashers, and their allies,* by A. C. Bent. U.S. Natl. Mus. Bull. no. 195. Washington, D.C.

———. 1949a. Eastern hermit thrush. In *Life histories of North American thrushes, kinglets, and their allies,* by A. C. Bent. U.S. Natl. Mus. Bull. no. 196. Washington, D.C.

———. 1949b. Nesting of the Mexican jay in the Santa Rita Mountains, Arizona. *Condor* 51(6): 241–49.

———. 1953a. Black-polled warbler. In *Life histories of North American wood warblers,* by A. C. Bent. U.S. Natl. Mus. Bull. no. 203. Washington, D.C.

———. 1953b. Eastern ovenbird. In *Life histories of North American wood warblers,* by A. C. Bent. U.S. Natl. Mus. Bull. no. 203. Washington, D.C.

———. 1956. The recent reappearance of the dickcissed *(Spiza americana)* in eastern North America. *Auk* 73(1):66–70.

———. 1958a. Bronzed grackle. In *Life histories of North American blackbirds, orioles, tanagers, and allies,* by A. C. Bent. U.S. Natl. Mus. Bull. no. 211. Washington, D.C.

———. 1958b. Eastern meadowlark. In *Life histories of North American blackbirds, orioles, tanagers, and their allies,* by A. C. Bent. U.S. Natl. Mus. Bull. no. 211. Washington, D.C.

———. 1965a. The incidence of albinism in North American birds. *Bird-Banding* 36(2):67–71.

———. 1965b. Melanism in North American birds. *Bird-Banding* 36(4):240–42.

———. 1968. Dickcissel. In *Life histories of North American cardinals, grosbeaks, buntings, towhees, finches, sparrows, and allies,* comp. A. C. Bent et al., ed. O. L. Austin, Jr. U.S. Natl. Mus. Bull. no. 237, pt. 1. Washington, D.C.

Gross, W. A. O. 1935. The life history cycle of Leach's petrel on the outer sea islands of the Bay of Fundy. *Auk* 52:382–99.

Grossman, M. L., and Hamlet, J. H. 1964. *Birds of prey of the world*. New York: Clarkson N. Potter, Inc., Publishers.

Grosvenor, G., and Wetmore, A. 1937. *The book of birds*. Vols. 1 and 2. Washington, D.C.: Natl. Geographic Soc.

Grubb, Jr., T. C. 1973. Colony location by Leach's petrel. *Auk* 90:78–82.

Grummt, W. 1972. Breeding of Brewer's blackbird in the Berlin Zoo. *Avicultural Magazine* 78:153–54.

Gruson, E. S. 1972. *Words for birds*. New York: Quadrangle/The New York Times Book Co., Inc.

Grzimek, B. 1970. *Among the animals of Africa*. New York: Stein & Day Publishers.

Gudmundsson, F. 1964. Diver. In *The new dictionary of birds,* ed. A. L. Thomson. New York: McGraw-Hill Book Company.

Guhl, A. M. 1956. The social order of chickens. *Scientific American* 194(2):43–46.

Guiget, C. J. 1956. Enigma of the Pacific. *Audubon* 58:164–67.

Gulledge, J. L. 1975. Personal communication.

———. 1976. Recording bird sounds. *Living Bird,* 15th annual, pp. 183–203.

Gullion, G. W. 1950. Carpodacus finches feeding on nectar. *Auk* 67:398–99.

———. 1954. The reproductive cycle of American coots in California. *Auk* 71:366–412.

———. 1960. The ecology of Gambel's quail in Nevada and the arid Southwest. *Ecology* 41: 518–36.

———. 1966. The use of drumming behavior in ruffed grouse population studies. *Jour. Wildlife Management* 30(4):717–29.

Gullion, G. W., and Marshall, W. H. 1968. Survival of ruffed grouse in a northern forest. *Living Bird,* 7th annual, pp. 117–67.

Gurney, J. H. 1899. On the comparative ages to which birds live. *Ibis* 7(5):19–42.

Guthrie, J. E. 1932. Snakes, versus birds; birds versus snakes. *Wilson Bull.* 44(2):88–113.

H

Hadow, H. H. 1973. Winter ecology of migrant and resident Lewis' woodpeckers in southeastern Colorado. *Condor* 75(2):210–24.

Hagar, J. A. 1966. Nesting of the Hudsonian godwit at Churchill, Manitoba. *Living Bird,* 5th annual, pp. 5–43.

Hagen, Y. 1942. Totalgewichts-Studien bei Norwegischen Vogelarten. *Arch Naturgesch* 11:1–173.

Hagiwara, S.; Chicbibu, S.; and Simpson, W. 1968. Neuromuscular mechanisms of wing beat in hummingbirds. *Zeit vergleich Physiol.* 60(2):209–18.

Hailman, J. P. 1958. Behavior notes on the Ipswich sparrow. *Bird-Banding* 29(4):241–44.

———. 1960. A field study of the mockingbird's wing-flashing behavior and its association with foraging. *Wilson Bull.* 72(4):346–57.

———. 1969. How an instinct is learned. *Scientific American* 271:98–106.

———. 1973. Double-scratching and terrestrial locomotion in emberizines: Some complications. *Wilson Bull.* 85:348–50.

Hainsworth, F. R. and Wolf, L. L. 1972. Crop volume, nectar concentration, and hummingbird energetics. *Comp. Biochem. and Physiol.* 42A:359–66.

Hale, J. B., and Wendt, R. F. 1951. Amphibians and snakes as ruffed grouse food. *Wilson Bull.* 63(3):200–201.

Hall, F. A., and Harris, S. W. 1968. Blue-winged teal and shoveler in northwestern California. *Condor* 70(2):188.

Hall, G. A. 1973. Appalachian region. *Amer. Birds* 27:61.

Hall, G. H. 1970. Great moments in action: The story of the sun life falcons (reprint). *Canadian Field-Nat.* 84(3):213–30.

Hall, H. M. 1950. Wakulla limpkins. *Audubon* 52:308–14.

———. 1960. *A gathering of shorebirds.* New York: The Devin-Adair Co.

Halloran, P. O'C. 1955. A bibliography of references to diseases in wild mammals and birds. *Amer. Jour. Vet. Res.* 16 (pt. 2):306.

Hamel, G., and Turner, C. C. 1914. Flying.

Hamerstrom, F. H. 1942. Dominance in winter flocks of chickadees. *Wilson Bull.* 54:32–42.

———. 1962. Winter visitor from the far north. *Audubon* 64(1):12–15.

———. 1969a. Bumblefoot. *Raptor Res. News* 3(2):24.

———. 1969b. A harrier population study. In *Peregrine falcon populations: Their biology and decline,* ed. J. J. Hackey. Madison, Wis.: University of Wisconsin Press.

———. 1970. Care and feeding of young raptors. *Raptor Res. News* 4(3):75.

Hamerstrom, Jr., F. N. 1939a. A study of Wisconsin prairie chicken and sharp-tailed grouse. *Wilson Bull.* 51:105–20.

———. 1939b. What eats what? *Bird-Lore* 41(1):31–33.

———. 1963. Sharptail brood habitat in Wisconsin's northern pine barrens. *Jour. Wildlife Management* 27:793–802.

Hamerstrom, Jr., F. N., and Hamerstrom, F. H. 1951. Grouse of the Brushlands. *Wis. Cons. Bull.* 16(10):7–9.

———. 1964. Grouse. In *A new dictionary of birds,* ed. A. L. Thomson. New York: McGraw-Hill Book Company.

Hamilton, M. 1957. Weights of wild bobwhites in central Missouri. *Bird-Banding* 28(4):222–28.

Hamilton, R. B. 1975. *Comparative behavior of the American avocet and the black-necked stilt* (Recuvirostridae). Amer. Ornith. Union, Monogr.no.17.

Hamilton, Jr., W. J. 1939. American mammals. New York: McGraw-Hill Book Company.

———. 1942. Crows feeding on larval amphibians. *Auk* 59(3):446.

Hamilton, III, W. J. 1959. Aggressive behavior in migrant pectoral sandpipers. *Condor* 61:161–79.

———. 1962a. Bobolink migratory pathways and their experimental analysis under night skies. *Auk* 79:208–33.

———. 1962b. Celestial orientation in juvenal waterfowl. *Condor* 64:19–33.

———. 1966. Analysis of bird navigation experiments. In *Systems analyses in ecology,* ed. K. E. F. Watt. New York: Academic Press, Inc.

———. 1973. *Life's color code.* New York: McGraw-Hill Book Company.

Hamilton, III, W. J., and Orians, G. H. 1965. Evolution of brood parasitism in altricial birds. *Condor* (4):361–82.

Hamrum, C. L. 1953. Experiments on the senses of taste and smell in the bobwhite quail, *Colinus virginianus. Amer. Midland-Nat.* 49:872–77.

Hancock, J. 1964. Song and mimicry in the brown thrasher. *Kentucky Warbler* 40(2):23–27.

Hann, Harry W. 1937. Life history of the ovenbird in southern Michigan. *Wilson Bull.* 49:145–237.

———. 1941. The cowbird at the nest. *Wilson Bull.* 53:211–21.

———. 1953. *The biology of birds.* Ann Arbor, Mich.: Ullrich's Book Store.

Hanna, W. C. 1917. Further notes on the white-throated swifts of Slover Mountain. *Condor* 19:3–8.

Hannah-Alava, Aloha. 1960. Genetic mosaics. *Scientific American* 202(5):118–30.

Hansen, H. A., and Nelson, H. K. 1964. Honkers large and small. In *Waterfowl tomorrow,* ed. J. P. Linduska and A. L. Nelson. Washington, D.C.: U.S. Dept. Inter., Fish and Wildlife Service.

Hansen, H. L. 1966. Silvical characteristics of tree species and decay processes as related to cavity production. In *Wood duck management and research,* ed. L. R. Jahn *et al.* Washington, D.C.: Wildlife Management Inst.

Hanson, Harry C. 1962. *Characters of age, sex, and sexual maturity in Canada geese.* Illinois Nat. Hist. Surv., Biol. Notes no. 49. Urbana.

———. 1965. *The giant Canada goose.* Carbondale, Ill.: Illinois University Press.

Hanson, Harry C., and Smith, R. H. 1950. *Canada geese of the Mississippi flyway.* Bull. Illinois Nat. Hist. Surv., vol. 25, art. 3. Urbana.

Hanson, Herbert C. 1962. *Dictionary of ecology.* New York: Philosophical Library, Inc.

Hardin, J. W. 1961. *Poisonous plants of North Carolina.* Agric. Exper. Sta. Bull. no. 414. Raleigh, N.C.

Hardy, J. W. 1957. *The least tern in Mississippi.* Mich. State Univ. Biol. Series 1.

———. 1961. *Studies in behavior and phylogeny of certain New World jays (Garrulinae).* Univ. Kansas Sci. Bull. 42, no. 2.

———. 1963. Epigamic and reproductive behavior of the orange-fronted parakeet. *Condor* 65:169–99.

———. 1964. Ringed parakeets nesting in Los Angeles, California. *Condor* 66:445–47.

———. 1973. Several exotic birds in southern California. *Wilson Bull.* 84:506-12.

———. 1977. The wrens. 33⅓ rpm lp phonodisc. Published privately, 1615 N.W. 14th Ave., Gainesville, Fla. 32605.

Hare, C. E. 1939. *The language of sport.* London: Country Life Ltd.

Harper, F. 1936. The distribution of the limpkin and its staple food. *Oriole* 1(3):21–23.

———. 1938. The chuck-will's-widow in the Okefenokee region. *Oriole* 3:9–14.

Harper, F., ed. 1958. *The travels of William Bartram.* Naturalist's ed. New Haven, Conn.: Yale University Press.

Harper, J. A., and Labiskey, R. F. 1964. The influence of calcium on the distribution of pheasants in Illinois. *Jour. Wildlife Management* 28:722–31.

Harrell, B. E. 1969. Raptor Research Foundation Meeting. *Raptor Res. News* 3(2):33, 87.

Harrell, B. E., and Hunter, D. V. 1968. Captivity breeding committee. *Raptor Res. News* 2(3):55.

———. 1969. Breeding project information exchange. *Raptor Res. News* 3(2):19.

Harrington, B. A. 1974. Colony visitation behavior and breeding ages of sooty terns *(Sterna fuscata). Bird-Banding* 45(2):115–44.

Harrington, B. A., and Morrison, R. I. G. 1979. Semipalmated sandpiper migration in North America. *Studies Avian Biol.* 2:83–99.

Harrington, B. A.; Schreiber, R. W.; and Woolfenden, G. E. 1972. The distribution of male and female magnificent frigatebirds, *Fregata magnificens,* along the Gulf Coast of Florida. *Amer. Birds* 26:727–931.

Harrington-Tweit, B.; Mattocks, Jr., P. W.; and E. S. Hunn, E. S.; eds. 1978. The nesting season (Northern Pacific Coast region). *Amer. Birds* 32:1199–203.

Harriott, M. C. 1970. Breeding behavior of the anhinga. *Florida Nat.* 43(4):138–43.

Harris, H. 1928. Robert Ridgway. *Condor* 30(1):1–118.

Harris, M. P. 1966. Breeding biology of the manx shearwater, *Puffinus puffinus. Ibis* 108(1):17–33.

———. 1972. Bird-ringing in the Galapagos. *Not. Galapagos* 19–20:3–7.

Harris, R. D. 1944. The chestnut-collared longspur in Manitoba. *Wilson Bull.* 56:105–15.

Harris, V. T., comp. 1972. *Wildlife research: Problems, programs, progress.* U.S. Dept. Inter., Fish and Wildlife Service, Res. Publ. no. 104. Washington, D.C.

Harrison, C. J. O. 1961. Rain-bathing. *Avicultural Magazine* 67:90–92.

———. 1966. Alleged xanthochroism in bird plumages. *Bird-Banding* 37(2):121.

———. 1965. Allopreening as agonistic behaviour. *Behaviour* 24:161–209.

———. 1969. Further records of allopreening. *Avicultural Magazine* 75(3):97–99.

Harrison, H. H. 1975. *A field guide to birds' nests.* Boston: Houghton Mifflin Company.

Harrison, H. H. 1979. *A field guide to western birds' nests.* Boston: Houghton Mifflin Company.

Harrison, J. G. 1964a. Leg. In *A new dictionary of birds,* ed. A. L. Thomson. New York: McGraw-Hill Book Company.

———. 1964b. Tongue. In *A new dictionary of birds,* ed. A. L. Thomson. New York: McGraw-Hill Book Company.

———. 1964c. Wing. In *A new dictionary of birds,* ed. A. L. Thomson. New York: McGraw-Hill Book Company.

Harrison, J. M. 1964a. Moult. In *A new dictionary of birds,* ed. A. L. Thomson. New York: McGraw-Hill Book Company.

———. 1964b. Plumage: Abnormal and aberrant. In *A new dictionary of birds,* ed. A. L. Thomson. New York: McGraw-Hill Book Company.

Harrison, T. H. 1964. Omens, birds as. In *A new dictionary of birds,* ed. A. L. Thomson. New York: McGraw-Hill Book Company.

Harshfield, G. S. 1959. Fowl cholera. In *Diseases of poultry,* ed. H. E. Biester and L. H. Schwarte. 4th ed. Ames, Iowa: Iowa State University Press.

Hart, C. M.; Lee, O. S.; and Low, J. B. 1950. *The sharp-tailed grouse in Utah.* Utah State Dept. Fish and Game, Publ. no. 3.

Hartley, P. H. T. 1964. Feeding habits. In *A new*

dictionary of birds, ed. A. L. Thomson. New York: McGraw-Hill Book Company.

Hartman, F. A. 1954. Cardiac and pectoral muscles of trochilids. *Auk* 71:467–69.

———. 1955. Heart weight in birds. *Condor* 57:221–38.

Hartman, F. E. 1968. White-headed cardinal. *Bird-Banding* 39(1):57.

Hartshorne, C. 1958. Some biological principles applicable to song-behavior. *Wilson Bull.* 70:45–56.

———. 1973. *Born to sing: An interpretation and world survey of bird song.* Bloomington, Ind.: Indiana University Press.

Hartshorne, J. M. 1962. Behavior of the eastern bluebird at the nest. *Living Bird,* 1st annual, pp. 130–49.

Hartung, R. 1971. Effects of toxic substances. In *Infectious and parasitic diseases of wild birds,* ed. J. W. Davis, R. C. Anderson, L. Karstad, and D. O. Trainer. Ames, Iowa: Iowa State University Press.

Harwin, R. M. 1971. White stork: Longevity record. *Ostrich* 42(1):81.

Harwood, M. 1973. *A view from Hawk Mountain.* New York: Charles Scribner's Sons.

Hasbrouck, E. M. 1883. Evolution and dichromatism in the genus *Megascops. Amer. Nat.* 27:521–33, 638–49.

Hatch, D. E. 1970. Energy conserving and heat dissipating mechanisms of the turkey vulture. *Auk* 87(1):111–24.

Hatch, D. R. M. 1971. Brown-headed cowbird parasitism on spotted sandpiper and Wilson's phalarope. *Blue Jay* 29(1):17–18.

Hatch, J. J. 1970. Predation and piracy of gulls at a ternery in Maine. *Auk* 87(2):244–54.

———. 1974. Longevity record for arctic tern. *Bird-Banding* 45(3):269–70.

Hatler, D. H. 1974. Bald eagle preys upon Arctic loon. *Auk* 91(4):825–27.

Haucke, H. H., and Kiel, Jr., W. H. 1973. Jabiru in south Texas. *Auk* 90(3):675–76.

Hauri, R. 1956. Contributions on the biology of the raven (*Corvus corax*). *Der Ornithologische Beobachter* 53(2):28–35.

Hauser, D. C. 1957. Some observations on sunbathing in birds. *Wilson Bull.* 69:78–90.

———. 1973. Comparison of anting records from two localities in North Carolina. *Chat* 37:91–102.

Hausman, L. A. 1944. *The illustrated encyclopedia of American birds.* Garden City, N. Y.: Garden City Pub. Co., Inc.

Haverschmidt, F. 1970a. Notes on the snail kite in Surinam. *Auk* 87(3):580–84.

———. 1970b. Ruddy turnstones making use of yellow-crowned night herons for food-finding. *Wilson Bull.* 82: 99.

———. 1970c. Wattled jaçana caught by an anaconda. *Condor* 72(3):364.

Haviland, M. D. 1917. Notes on breeding habits of the dotterel on the Yenesei. *Brit. Birds* 2:6–11.

Hawkins, A. S. 1964. Mississippi flyway. In *Waterfowl tomorrow,* ed. J. P. Linduska and A. L. Nelson. Washington, D.C.: U.S. Dept. Inter., Fish and Wildlife Service.

Hawksley, O. 1957. Ecology of a breeding population of Arctic terns. *Bird-Banding* 28:57–92.

Hay, O. P. 1887. The red-headed woodpecker as a hoarder. *Auk* 4:193–96.

Hayes, Jr., S. P. 1929. Speed of flying hummingbird. *Auk* 46:116.

Hays, F. A. 1949. Sex influence on the embryonic death rate of chicks. *Science* 110:533.

Hays, H. 1972. Polandry in the spotted sandpiper. *Living Bird,* 11th annual, pp. 43–57.

———. 1975. Probable common × roseate tern hybrids. *Auk* 92(2):219–34.

Hays, H., and Donaldson, G. 1970. Sand-kicking camouflages young black skimmers. *Wilson Bull.* 82:100.

Hays, H., and Risebrough, R. W. 1972. Pollutant concentrations in abnormal young terns

from Long Island Sound. *Auk* 89(1):19–35.

Hayward, C. L. 1935. The breeding status and migration of the Caspian tern in Utah. *Condor* 37:140–44.

Hazelwood, R. L. 1972. The intermediary metabolism of birds. In *Avian biology,* ed. D. S. Farner, J. R. King, and K. C. Parkes. Vol. 2. New York: Academic Press, Inc.

Healy, W. M., and Thomas, J. W. 1973. Effects of dusting in plumage of Japanese quail. *Wilson Bull.* 85(4):442–48.

Heard, W. R. 1960. A record of swimming in bobwhites. *Wilson Bull.* 72(2):201.

Heath, J. E. 1962. Temperature fluctuations in the turkey vulture. *Condor* 64:234–35.

Hediger, H. 1950. *Wild animals in captivity.* London: Butterworth & Co., Ltd./Butterworth's Scientific Publications.

Heilmann, G. 1927. *The origin of birds.* New York: D. Appleton & Company.

Heinroth, O., and Heinroth, K. 1958. *The birds.* Ann Arbor, Mich.: University of Michigan Press.

Heintzelman, D. S. 1970. *The hawks of New Jersey.* New Jersey State Mus. Bull. no. 13. Trenton.

———. 1972. *A guide to northeastern hawk watching.* Published privately, 35 Church Street, Lambertville, N.J. 08530.

Heintzelman, D. S., and MacClay, R. 1971. An extraordinary autumn migration of white-breasted nuthatches. *Wilson Bull.* 83(2):129–31.

Heintzelman, D. S., and Newberry, C. J. 1963. Some waterfowl diving times. *Wilson Bull.* 76(3):291.

Helling, R. 1961. Mendel, Gregor Johann (1822–1884). In *The encyclopedia of biological sciences,* ed. P. Gray. New York: Reinhold Publishing Corporation.

Helminen, M. 1968. Eastern rustic bunting. In *Life histories of North American cardinals, grosbeaks, buntings, towhees, finches, sparrows, and allies,* comp. A. C. Bent *et al.,* ed. O. L. Austin, Jr. U.S. Natl. Mus. Bull. no. 237, pt. 3. Washington, D.C.

Helms, C. W., and Drury, Jr., W. H. 1960. Winter and migratory weight and fat: Field studies of some North American buntings. *Bird-Banding* 31(1):1–40.

Henderson, I. F., and Henderson, W. D. 1929. *A dictionary of scientific terms.* New York: D. Van Nostrand Company.

Henderson, J. 1933. *The practical value of birds.* New York: The Macmillan Company.

Henderson, S. D., and Holt, Jr., J. B. 1962. Banding screech owls and kestrels at nest boxes. *EBBA News* 25:93–104.

Henny, C. J. 1969. Geographic variation, mortality rates and production requirements of the barn owl (*Tyto alba ssp.*). *Bird-Banding* 40(4):277–90.

Henny, C. J.; Anderson, D. R.; and Pospahala, R. S. 1972. *Aerial surveys of waterfowl production in North America, 1955–71.* U.S. Dept. Inter., Fish and Wildlife Service, Spec. Sci. Rept.—Wildlife, no. 160. Washington, D.C.

Henny, C. J., and Noltemeier, A. P. 1975. Osprey nesting populations in the coastal Carolinas. *Amer. Birds* 29(6)1073–79.

Henny, C. J., and Ogden, J. C. 1970. Estimated status of osprey populations in the United States. *Jour. Wildlife Management* 34:214–17.

Henny, C. J., and Wight, H. M. 1969. An endangered osprey population: Estimates of mortality and production. *Auk* 86:188–98.

Henry, C. J. 1941. The season. In *Audubon,* September–October, p. 476.

Henshaw, H. W. 1885. Hybrid quail (*Lophortyx gambeli* × *L. californicus*). *Auk* II:247–47.

———. 1920. In memoriam: William Brewster. *Auk* 37(1):1–23.

Heppleston, P. B. 1971. Feeding techniques of the oystercatcher. *Bird Study* 18:15–20.

Heppner, F. H. 1965. Sensory mechanisms and environmental clues used by the American robin in locating earthworms. *Condor* 67(3):247–56.

———. 1974. Avian flight formations. *Bird-Banding* 45(2):160–69.

Herbert, A. D. 1970. Spatial disorientation in birds. *Wilson Bull.* 82(4):400–419.

Herbert, R. A., and Herbert, K. G. S. 1965. Behavior of peregrine falcons in the New York City region. *Auk* 82(1):62–94.

Herman, C. M. 1937. A case of superparasitism. *Bird-Banding* 8(3):127.

———. 1938. Occurrence of larval and nymphal stages of the rabbit tick, *Haemaphysalis leporis-palustris* on wild birds from Cape Cod. *Bull. Brooklyn Ent. Soc.,* June, pp. 133–34.

———. 1949. Coccidiosis in native California quail and problems of control. *Annals New York Acad. Sci.* 52:621–23.

———. 1955. Diseases of birds. In *Recent studies in avian biology,* ed. A. Wolfson. Urbana, Ill.: University of Illinois Press.

———. 1962. The role of birds in the epizootiology of eastern encephalitis. *Auk* 79(1):99–103.

———. 1966. Birds and our health. In *Birds in our lives,* ed. A. Stefferud and A. L. Nelson. Washington, D.C.: U.S. Dept. Inter., Fish and Wildlife Service.

Herman, C. M.; Chatkin, J. E.; and Saarni, R. W. 1943. Food habits and intensity of coccidian infection in native valley quail in California. *Jour. Parasitol.* 29:206.

Herrick, F. H. 1901. *The home life of wild birds.* New York: G. P. Putnam's Sons.

———. 1917. *Audubon the naturalist: A history of his life and time.* 2 vols. New York: D. Appleton & Company.

———. 1934. *The American eagle.* New York: D. Appleton-Century Company, Inc.

Herroelen, P. 1957–59. On the breeding biology of the barn swallow. *Le Gerfaut* 47(2):115–26; (4):265–78; 49(1):11–30.

Hess, E. H. 1964. Imprinting in birds. *Science* 146:1128–39.

———. 1973. *Imprinting.* Foreword by Konrad Lorenz. New York: Van Nostrand Reinhold Company.

Hess, G. 1951. *The bird: Its life and structure.* New York: Greenberg, Publisher.

Hesse, R.; Allee, W. C.; and Schmidt, K. P. 1951. *Ecological animal geography.* New York: John Wiley & Sons, Inc.

Hester, E. H., and Dermid, J. 1973. *The world of the wood duck,* ed. J. K. Terres. Philadelphia: J. B. Lippincott Company.

Hetrick, W., and McCaskie, G. 1965. Unusual behavior of a white-tailed tropic-bird in California. *Condor* 67(2):186–87.

Heumann, G. A. 1926. Mistle-toe birds as plant distributors. *Emu* 26 (pt. 2):110–11.

Hewitt, O. H., ed. 1967. *The wild turkey and its management.* Washington, D.C.: Wildlife Soc.

Hewitt, R. 1940. Bird malaria. *Amer. Jour. Hyg.* 30 (sec. C):49.

Hickey, J. J. 1942. Eastern populations of the duck hawk. *Auk* 59:176–204.

———. 1943. *A guide to bird watching.* New York: Oxford University Press.

———. 1955. Some American population research on gallinaceous birds. In *Recent studies in avian biology,* ed. A. Wolfson. Urbana, Ill.: University of Illinois Press.

Hickey, J. J., ed. 1969. *Peregrine falcon populations: Their biology and decline.* Madison, Wis.: University of Wisconsin Press.

Hickey, J. J., and Anderson, D. W. 1968. Chlorinated hydrocarbons and eggshell changes in raptorial and fish-eating birds. *Science* 162:271–73.

———. 1969. The peregrine falcon: Life history and population literature. In *Peregrine falcon population: Their biology and decline,* pp. 3–41, ed. J. J. Hickey. Madison, Wisc.: University of Wisconsin Press.

Hickman, G. L. 1971. Escape responses and swimming abilities of nestling golden eagles. *Auk* 88(2):427.

Hicks, L. E. 1934. Individual and sexual variations in the European starling. *Bird-Banding* 5:103–18.

Hicks, L. E., and Dalmbach, C. A. 1935. Sex ratios and weights in wintering crows. *Bird-Banding* 6(2):65–66.

Hicks, N. 1971. Upstate biology professor, "thinking like a bird," breeds the rare peregrine falcon in captivity. *New York Times*, June 10, p. 31.

Higgins, K. F., and Kirsch, L. M. 1975. Some aspects of the breeding biology of the upland sandpiper in North Dakota. *Wilson Bull.* 87(1):96–102.

Higgins, T. 1971. Whoo, whoo will get the bait? Largemouth bass or owls? *Charlotte Observer*, July.

Hill, N. P. 1968. Eastern sharp-tailed sparrow. In *Life histories of North American cardinals, grosbeaks, buntings, towhees, finches, sparrows, and allies*, comp. A. C. Bent *et al.*, ed. O. L. Austin, Jr. U.S. Natl. Mus. Bull. no. 237, pt. 2. Washington, D.C.

Hill, W. C. O. 1964. Syrinx. In *A new dictionary of birds*, ed. A. L. Thomson. New York: McGraw-Hill Book Company.

Hilton, J. R. 1970. 1969 Raptor protection survey. *Calif. Condor* 5(1):4–6.

———. 1971a. Raptor report. *Calif. Condor* 6(1):9.

———. 1971b. Southern California: A guide to Raptor finding. *Calif. Condor* 6(4):1–4.

———. 1971c. What fate for Gymnogyps? *Calif. Condor* 6(2):1–5.

———. 1976. *The Raptor report.* Pacific Palisades, Calif.: Soc. for Preserv. of Birds of Prey.

Hinde, R. A. 1955. A comparative study of the courtship of certain finches. *Ibis* 97:706, fn.

———. 1956. The biological significance of the territories of birds. *Ibis* 98:340–69.

———. 1961. Behavior. In *Biology and comparative physiology of birds*, ed. A. J. Marshall. New York: Academic Press, Inc.

———. 1964a. Display. In *A new dictionary of birds*, ed. A. L. Thomson. New York: McGraw-Hill Book Company.

———. 1964b. Pair formation. In *A new dictionary of birds*, ed. A. L. Thomson. New York: McGraw-Hill Book Company.

———. 1973. Behavior. In *Avian biology*, ed. D. S. Farner, J. R. King, and K. C. Parkes. Vol 5. New York: Academic Press, Inc.

Hinde, R. A., and Fisher, J. 1952. Further observations on the opening of milk bottles by birds. *Brit. Birds* 44:393–96.

Hindwood, K. A. 1959. The nesting of birds in the nests of social insects. *Emu* 59(1):1–36.

———. 1964. Birds caught by octopuses. *Emu* 64:69–70.

Hirth, D. H.; Hester, A. E.; and Freeley, F. 1969. Dispersal and flocking of marked young robins (*Turdus m. migratorius*) after fledging. *Bird-Banding* 40(3):208–15.

Hjorth, I. 1970. Reproductive behaviour in Tetraonidae with special reference to males. *Viltrevy* 7:183–596.

Hochbaum, H. A. 1942. Sex and age determination of waterfowl by cloacal examination. Trans. [7th] *N. Amer. Wildlife Conf.*, pp. 299–307.

———. 1944. *The canvasback on a prairie marsh.* Washington, D.C.: Amer. Wildlife Inst.

———. 1955. *Travels and traditions of waterfowl.* Minneapolis: University of Minnesota Press.

Hodges, J. 1950. Unusual accidents of birds. *Auk* 67(2):249–50.

Hoffmann, R. 1927. *Birds of the Pacific states.* Boston: Houghton Mifflin Company.

Hogan-Warburg, A. J. 1966. Social behavior of the ruff, *Philomachus pugnax* (L.). *Ardea* 54:109–229.

Höhn, E. O. 1961. Endocrine glands, thymus, and pineal body. In *Biology and comparative physiology of birds*, ed. A. J. Marshall. Vol. 2. New York: Academic Press, Inc.

———. 1965. *Die Wassertreter (Phalaropodidae).* Neue Brehm-Bücherei no. 349. Wittenberg, Lutherstadt: A. Ziemsen Verlag.

———. 1967. Observations on the breeding biology of Wilson's phalarope (*Steganopus tricolor*) in central Alberta. *Auk* 84:220–44.

———. 1969. The phalarope. *Scientific American* 220(6):104–9, 111.

Holcomb, L. C. 1969. Egg turning behavior of birds in response to color-marked eggs. *Bird-Banding* 40(2):105–13.

Holdom, M. W. 1952. White-crowned sparrow (*Zonotrichia leucophrys pugetensis*) and bantam hen. *Canadian Field-Nat.* 66: 68.

Holgersen, H. 1957. Bird-banding in Norway, 1956. *Sterna* 2(5):137–84.

———. 1959. Bird-banding in Norway, 1958. *Sterna* 3(7):269–313.

Holgersen, N. E. 1971. Black-necked stilt nesting in Delaware. *Wilson Bull.* 83(1):100.

Holland, H. M. 1926a. Making amends to the sparrows. *Bird-Lore* 28:266–67.

———. 1926b. Who would have thought it of Bubo? *Bird-Lore* 38:1–4.

Hollander, W. F. 1966. Pigeons and doves. In *Birds in our lives*, ed. A. Stefferud and A. L. Nelson. Washington, D.C.: U.S. Dept. Inter., Fish and Wildlife Service.

Hollander, W. F., and Levi, W. M. 1940. Twins and late embryonic monstrosities in pigeons. *Auk* 57(3):326–29.

Holmes, R. T. 1966. Breeding ecology and annual cycle adaptations of the red-backed sandpiper (*Calidris alpina*) in northern Alaska. *Condor* 68:3–46.

Holmes, R. T. 1972. Ecological factors influencing the breeding season schedule of western sandpipers (*Calidris mauri*) in subarctic Alaska. *Amer. Midl. Nat.* 87:472–91.

Holmes, R. T. 1973. Social behaviour of breeding western sandpipers (*Calidris mauri*). *Ibis* 115:107–23.

Holmes, R. T., and Pitelka, F. A. 1964. Breeding behavior and taxonomic relationships of the curlew sandpiper. *Auk* 81:362–79.

Hooper, R. G.; Crawford, H. S.; Chamberlain, D. R.; and Harlow, R. F. 1975. Nesting density of common ravens in the Ridge-Valley region of Virginia. *Amer. Birds* 29(5):931–35.

Hopcraft, J. B. D. 1968. Some notes on the chick-carrying behavior in the African jaçana. *Living Bird*, 7th annual, pp. 85–88.

Hopkins, C. L. 1888. Notes relative to the sense of smell in the turkey buzzard (*Cathartes aura*). *Auk* 5:248–51.

Hopkins, M. N. 1972. Cattle egret recoveries from south Georgia nesting colonies. *Bird-Banding* 43:220–21.

Horak, G. J. 1970. A comparative study of the foods of the Sora and Virginia rail. *Wilson Bull.* 82(2):206–13.

Horner, C. 1957. St. Louis's own bird: The European tree sparrow. *Nature Notes: The Journal of the Webster Groves Nature Study Society* 28(11):85–86; 29(2):12–14.

Höst, P. 1942. Effect of light on the moults and sequences of plumage in the willow ptarmigan. *Auk* 59(3):388.

Hostetter, D. R. 1934. Albinism in the phoebe (*Sayornis phoebe*). *Auk* 51(4):524.

Hou, H. C. 1929. Relation of the preen gland (*Glandula uropygialis*) of birds to rickets. *Chinese Jour. Physiol.* 3:171–82.

Houston, C. S. 1965. Siberian recovery of pectoral sandpiper. *Bird-Banding* 36(2):112–13.

———. 1967a. Recoveries of black-crowned night herons banded in Saskatchewan. *Blue Jay* 25(3):112–13.

———. 1967b. Recoveries of red-tailed hawks banded in Saskatchewan. *Blue Jay* 25(3):109–11.

———. 1968a. Recoveries of marsh hawks banded in Saskatchewan. *Blue Jay* 26(1):12–13.

———. 1968b. Recoveries of Swainson's hawks banded in Saskatchewan. *Blue Jay* 26(2):86–87.

———. 1971. Northern great plains region. *Amer. Birds* 25(4):759.

———. 1975. Reproductive performance of great horned owls in Saskatchewan. *Bird-Banding* 46(4):302–4.

Houston, C. S., and Tryphonas, L. 1969. Avian tuberculosis in a Swainson's thrush. *Bird-Banding* 40(2):146–47.

Howard, H. 1950. Fossil evidence of avian evolution. *Ibis* 92:1–21.

———. 1962a. A comparison of avian assemblages from individual pits at Rancho La Brea, California. *Los Angeles County Mus., Contrib. Sci.*, 58:1–24.

———. 1962b. *Fossil birds.* Science ser. no. 17, Palenthology no. 10. Los Angeles County Museum.

Howe, C. D. 1904. A tame ruffed grouse. *Bird-Lore* 6(3):81–85.

Howell, A. B. 1944. *Speed in animals.* Chicago: University of Chicago Press.

Howell, A. H. 1932. *Florida bird life.* New York: Coward-McCann, Inc.

Howell, J., and Wishart, W. 1969. Strychnine poisoning in Canada geese. *Bull. Wildlife Disease Assoc.* 5:119.

Howell, J. C. 1941. Bald eagle killed by lightning while incubating its eggs. *Wilson Bull.* 53:42–43.

———. 1942. Habits of the American robin. *Amer. Midland-Nat.* 28(3):529–603.

———. 1949. Comparison of 1935, 1940, and 1946 populations of nesting bald eagles in east-central Florida. *Auk* 66(1):84.

———. 1962. The 1961 status of some bald eagle nest sites in east-central Florida. *Auk* 79(4):716–18.

———. 1968. The 1966 status of 24 nest sites of the bald eagle (*Haliaeetus leucocephalus*) in east-central Florida. *Auk* 85:680–81.

Howell, T. R. 1952. Natural history and differentiation in the yellow-bellied sapsucker, *Sphyrapicus varius*. *Condor* 54:237–82.

Howell, T. R., and Bartholomew, G. A. 1959. Further experiments on torpidity in the poor-will. *Condor* 61(3):180–85.

———. 1962. Temperature regulation in the red-tailed tropic-bird and the red-footed booby. *Condor* 64:6.

Howell, T. R., and Dawson, W. R. 1954. Nest temperatures and attentiveness in the Anna's hummingbird. *Condor* 56:93–97.

Hoyt, S. F. 1952. An additional age record of a pileated woodpecker. *Bird-Banding* 23(1):29–30.

———. 1953. Incubation and nesting behavior of the chuck-will's-widow. *Wilson Bull.* 65:204–5.

———. 1957. The ecology of the pileated woodpecker. *Amer. Midland Nat.* 38(2):246–56.

Hubbard, C. A. 1947. *Fleas of western North America.* Ames, Iowa: Iowa State College Press.

Hubbard, J. P. 1969. The relationship and evolution of the *Dendroica coronata* complex. *Auk* 86(3):393–432.

———. 1970. Geographic variation in the *Dendroica coronata* complex. *Wilson Bull.* 82(4):355–69.

———. 1973a. Avian evolution in the aridlands of North America. *Living Bird*, 12th annual, pp. 155–96.

———. 1973b. Review of Pleistocene and recent environments of the central Great Plains. *Auk* 90(4):921–22.

Hubbard, J. P., and Niles, D. M. 1975. Two specimen records of the brown jay from southern Texas. *Auk* 92(4):797–98.

Hubbert, W. T.; McCullough, W. F.; and Schnurrenberger, P. R., eds. and comps. 1975. *Diseases transmitted from animals to man.* 6th ed. Springfield, Ill.: Charles C Thomas, Publisher.

Hubbs, C. L. 1968. Dispersal of cattle egret and little blue heron into northwestern Baja California, Mexico. *Condor* 70:92–93.

Huber, W. 1923. New Mexican duck. In *Life histories of North American wild fowl,* by A. C. Bent. U.S. Natl. Mus. Bull. no. 126, pt. 1. Washington, D.C.

Hudson, W. H. 1892. *The naturalist in La Plata.* London: Chapman and Hall, Ltd.

————. 1901. *Birds and man.* London: Longmans, Green and Company.

————. 1920. *Adventures among birds.* New York: E. P. Dutton.

Huey, L. M. 1924. The natural end of a bird's life. *Condor* 26(5):194–95.

————. 1926. Bat eaten by short-eared owl. *Auk* 43(1):96–97.

————. 1962. Comparison of the weight-lifting capacities of a house finch and a golden eagle. *Auk* 79(3):485.

Huey, W. S. 1959. Weight of sandhill cranes. *Auk* 76(1):96–97.

Huggins, R. A. 1941. Egg temperatures of wild birds under natural conditions. *Ecology* 32:148–57.

Hughes, M. R. 1970. Relative kidney size in nonpasserine birds with functional salt glands. *Condor* 72:164–68.

Hull, T. G. 1963. *Diseases transmitted from animals to man.* 5th ed. W. T. Hubbert *et al.* Springfield, Ill.: Charles C Thomas, Publisher.

Humboldt, A. von. 1850. *Views of nature: Or contemplations on the sublime phenomenon of creation; with scientific illustrations.* London: Henry G. Bohn.

Hume, E. E. 1942. *Ornithologists of the United States Army Medical Corps.* Baltimore: Johns Hopkins Press.

Humphrey, P. S. 1961. Passeriformes. In *The encyclopedia of biological sciences,* ed. P. Gray. New York: Reinhold Publishing Corporation.

————. 1965. Auks, murres, and puffins. In *Water, prey, and game birds of North America.* Washington, D.C.: Natl. Geographic Soc.

Humphrey, P. S.; and Clark, Jr., G. A. 1961. Pterylosis of the mallard duck. *Condor* 63:365–85.

Humphrey, P. S., and Parkes, K. C. 1959. An approach to the study of molts and molting. *Auk* 76(1):1–31.

Hunt, M. L. 1975. Least tern breeding range extension in Maine. *Auk* 92(1):143–45.

Hunt, R. 1920. How fast can a roadrunner run. *Condor* 22:186–87.

Hunter, B. T. 1964. *Gardening without poisons.* Boston: Houghton Mifflin Company.

Hunter, D. V., and Harrell, B. E. 1967a. Breeding projects. *Raptor Res. News* 1(3):40.

————. 1967b. An evaluation of raptors nesting in South Dakota. *Raptor Res. News* 1(1):11–12.

————. 1967c. Raptor populations. *Raptor Res. News* 1(3):47.

Hunter, J. S. 1898. Hawk killed by rattlesnake. *Osprey* 3:46.

Huntington, A. P. 1934. Speed of quail. *Natl. Sportsman* 72(8):42.

Huntington, C. E. 1952. Hybridization in the purple grackle *Quiscalus quiscula. Syst. Zool.* 1:149–70.

Hurrell, H. G. 1964. Dipper. In *A new dictionary of birds,* ed. A. L. Thomson. New York: McGraw-Hill Book Company.

Hussell, D. G., and Page, P. 1976. Observations on the breeding biology of black-bellied plovers on Devon Island, N.W.T., Canada. *Wilson Bull.* 88:632–53.

Hutchinson, J. C. D. 1954. Heat regulation in birds. In *Progress in the physiology of farm animals,* ed. J. Hammond. Vol. 1. London: Butter-worth & Co., Ltd./Butterworth's Scientific Publications.

————. 1964a. Heat regulation. In *A new dictionary of birds,* ed. A. L. Thomson. New York: McGraw-Hill Book Company.

————. 1964b. Metabolism. In *A new dictionary of birds,* ed. A. L. Thomson. New York: McGraw-Hill Book Company.

Hutt, F. B. 1949. *Genetics of the fowl.* New York: McGraw-Hill Book Company.

Hutt, F. B., and Ball, L. 1938. Number of feathers and body size in passerine birds. *Auk* 55:651–57.

Huxley, J. S. 1934. *Bird-watching and bird behaviour.* London: Chatto & Windus/Phoenix Library Edition.

————. 1942. *Evolution: The modern synthesis.* New York: Harper & Brothers.

————. 1953. *Evolution in action.* New York: Harper & Brothers.

————. 1955. Morphism in birds. *Proc.* [XIth] *Internatl. Ornith. Congress.* pp. 309–27. Basel and Stuttgart: Birkhauser Verlag.

————. 1964. Polymorphism. In *A new dictionary of birds,* ed. A. L. Thomson. New York: McGraw-Hill Book Company.

Hyndman, C. C., and Hyndman, A. S. 1972. The shell pigment of golden eagle eggs. *Condor* 74(2):200–201.

I

Ickes, R. A., and Ficken, M. S. 1970. An investigation of territorial behavior in the American redstart utilizing recorded songs. *Wilson Bull.* 82(2):167–76.

Iliff, W. J. 1971. Personal communication.

Imhof, T. A. 1962. *Alabama birds.* Birmingham, Ala.: University of Alabama Press.

Imler, R. H., and Kalmbach, E. R. 1955. *The bald eagle and its economic status.* U.S. Dept. Inter., Fish and Wildlife Service Circ. no. 30. Washington, D.C.

Immelmann, K. 1966. Ecology and behaviour of African and Australian grass finches. *Ostrich Suppl.* 6:371–79.

————. 1971. Ecological aspects of periodic reproduction. In *Avian biology,* ed. D. S. Farner, J. R. King, and K. C. Parkes. Vol. 1. New York: Academic Press, Inc.

Immelmann, K., and Immelmann, G. 1968. Zur Fortpflanzungsbiologie einige Vögel in der Namib. *Bonner Zoologische Beiträge* 19, 329–39.

Impekoven, M. 1973. The response of incubating laughing gulls (*Larus atricilla L.*) to calls of laughing gull chicks. *Behaviour* 46:94–113.

Ingersoll, E. 1923. *Birds in legend, fable, and folklore.* New York: Longmans, Green & Company.

Ingram, C. 1933. Cattle feeding on geese droppings. *Brit. Birds* 26(10):309–10.

————. 1959. The importance of juvenile cannibalism in the breeding biology of certain birds of prey. *Auk* 76(2):218–26.

Irving, L. 1960. *Birds of Anaktuvuk Pass, Kobuk, and Old Crow.* U. S. Natl. Mus. Bull. no. 217.

Irving, L., and Krog, J. 1956. Temperature during the development of birds in Arctic nests. *Physiol. Zool.* 29:195–205.

Ivacic, D. L., and Labisky, R. F. 1973. Metabolic responses of mourning doves to short-term food and temperature stresses in winter. *Wilson Bull.* 85(2):182–96.

Ivor, H. R. 1943. Further studies of anting by birds. *Auk* 60(1):51–55.

————. 1944a. Aye, she was Bonnie. *Nature Magazine* 37:473–76.

————. 1944b. Birds' fear of man. *Auk* 61:203–11.

J

Jack, A. 1953. *Feathered wings: A study of the flight of birds.* London: Methuen & Co., Ltd.

Jackson, J. A. 1970. Predation by a black rat snake on yellow-shafted flicker nestlings. *Wilson Bull.* 82(3):329–30.

————. 1971. The evolution, taxonomy, distribution, past populations and current status of the red-cockaded woodpecker. In *The ecology and management of the red-cockaded woodpecker: Proceedings of a symposium at Okefenokee National Wildlife Refuge, Folkston, Ga., May 26–29,* ed. R. L. Thompson. Tallahassee, Fla.: Tall Timbers Res. Station.

————. 1974. Gray rat snakes versus red-cockaded woodpeckers: Predator-prey adaptations. *Auk* 91(2):342–47.

————. 1976. Blackbirds, scare tactics, and irresponsible legislation. *Wilson Bull.* 88(1):159–60 (editorial).

Jackson, J. A., and Tate, Jr., J. 1974. An analysis of nest box use by purple martins, house sparrows, and starlings in eastern North America. *Wilson Bull.* 86(4):435–45.

Jackson, M. E. 1959. A hybrid between Barrow's and common goldeneye. *Auk* 76(1):92–93.

Jacobson, M. 1947. Hooded merganser and a watersnake. *Auk* 64(3):457–58.

Jaeger, E. C. 1948. Does the poor-will hibernate? *Condor* 50(1):45–46.

————. 1949. Further observations on the hibernation of the poor-will. *Condor* 51(3):105–9.

————. 1950. *Our desert neighbors.* Stanford, Calif.: Stanford University Press.

————. 1951. Pebble dropping of house sparrows. *Condor* 53(4):207.

————. 1955. *A source-book of biological names and terms.* 3d ed. Springfield, Ill.: Charles C Thomas, Publisher.

————. 1960. *The biologist's handbook of pronunciations.* Springfield, Ill.: Charles C Thomas, Publisher.

Jahn, L. R., and Moyle, J. B. 1964. Plants on parade. In *Waterfowl tomorrow,* ed. J. P. Linduska and A. L. Nelson. Washington, D.C.: U.S. Dept. Inter., Fish and Wildlife Service.

Jahn, L. R. *et al.,* eds. 1966. *Wood duck management and research: A symposium.* Washington, D.C.: Wildlife Management Inst.

James, J. 1958. The changing seasons. *Audubon Field Notes* 12(3):256.

————. 1959. The changing seasons. *Audubon Field Notes* 13:271.

————. 1960. The changing seasons. *Audubon Field Notes* 14(3):285.

————. 1962. The changing seasons. *Audubon Field Notes* 16(3):306–307.

James, F. C.; Cooch, F. G.; Ficken, M. S.; Knoder, C. E.; Lanyon, W. E.; and Springer, P. F. 1974. Career opportunities in ornithology. *Amer. Birds* 28(4):741–46.

James, P. 1956. Destruction of warblers on Padre Island, Texas, in May 1951. *Wilson Bull.* 68:224–27.

Jameson, E. W. 1942. Speed of a starling. *Auk* 59(3):442.

Jameson, W. 1958. *The wandering albatross.* London: Rupert Hart-Davis, Limited, Publishers.

Jarosz, J. A. 1960. Food habits of the wood duck. *Flicker* 32(2):61.

Jeffries, J. A. 1883. Notes on an hemophrodite bird. *Bull. Nuttall Ornith. Club* 8(1):17–21.

Jehl, Jr., J. R. 1968. The systematic position of the surfbird, *Aphriza virgata. Condor* 70:206–210.

Jehl, Jr., J. R. 1968a. The egg tooth in some Charadriiform birds. *Wilson Bull.* 80:328–30.

Jehl, Jr., J. R. 1968b. *Relationships in the Charadrii (shorebirds): a taxonomic study based on color patterns of the downy young.* Trans. San Diego Soc. Nat. Hist., Memoir 3.

————. 1970. A Mexican specimen of the yellow-billed loon. *Condor* 72:376.

————. 1973a. Breeding biology and systematic relationships of the stilt sandpiper. *Wilson Bull.* 85:115–47.

————. 1973b. Studies of a declining population

of brown pelicans in northwestern Baja California. *Condor* 75:69–79.

Jehl, Jr., J. R., and Hussell, D. T. 1966. Incubation periods of some subarctic birds. *Canadian Field-Nat.* 80(3):179–80.

Jellis, R. 1977. *Bird sounds and their meaning.* London: British Broadcasting Corp. 256 pp.

Jenkinson, M. A., and Mengel, R. M. 1970. Ingestion of stones by goatsuckers (*Caprimulgidae*). *Condor* 72:236–37.

Jenni, D. A. 1969. A study of the ecology of four species of herons during the breeding season at Lake Alice, Florida. *Ecol. Monogr.* 39:245–70.

———. 1974. Evolution of polyandry in birds. *Amer. Zool.* 14: 129–44.

Jenni, D. A., and Collier, G. 1972. Polyandry in the American jaçana (*Jacana spinosa*). *Auk* 89:743–65.

Jensen, J. K. 1926. Red-tailed hawk killing snakes. *Auk* 43(3):368–69.

Jensen, W. I. 1962. Personal communication.

Jensen, W. I., and Williams, C. S. 1964. Botulism and fowl cholera. In *Waterfowl tomorrow*, ed. J. P. Linduska and A. L. Nelson. Washington, D.C.: U.S. Dept. Inter., Fish and Wildlife Service, Government Printing Office.

Jespersen, P.; Jesperson, T.; and Vedel, A., eds. 1950. *Studies in bird migration, being the collected papers of H. Chri. C. Mortensen.* Copenhagen: Munksgaard.

Jewett, S. G. 1944. Hybridization of hermit and Townsend warblers. *Condor* 46(1):23–24.

Jobanek, G. A. 1976. An apparent longevity record for the black noddy. *N. Amer. Bird Bander* 1(2):71.

Johns, J. E. 1969. Field studies of Wilson's phalarope. *Auk* 86:666–70.

Johnsgard, P. A. 1965. *Handbook of waterfowl behavior.* Ithaca, N.Y.: Cornell University Press.

———. 1968. *Waterfowl: Their biology and natural history.* Lincoln, Neb.: University of Nebraska Press.

———. 1971. Observations on sound production in the Anatidae. *Wildfowl* 22:46–59.

———. 1973. *Grouse and quails of North America.* Lincoln, Nebr.: University of Nebraska Press.

———. 1975. *Waterfowl of North America.* Bloomington, Ind.: Indiana University Press.

———. 1978. *Ducks, geese, and swans of the world.* Lincoln, Nebr.: University of Nebraska Press.

Johnsgard, P. A., and Kear, J. 1968. A review of parental carrying of young by waterfowl. *Living Bird*, 7th annual, pp. 89–102.

Johnson, A. ed. 1928. *Dictionary of American biography.* New York: Charles Scribner's Sons.

Johnson, C. E. 1915. A four-winged wild duck. *Auk* 32(4):469–80.

Johnson, G. B. 1953. Bird photography goes modern. *Bull. Mass. Audubon Soc.* 37(8):327–31.

Johnson, H. N. 1960. Public health in relation to birds: Arthropod-borne viruses. *Trans.* [25th] *N. Amer. Wildlife Conf.*, pp. 121–33.

———. 1974. Personal communication.

Johnson, L. L. 1971. The migration, harvest, and importance of waterfowl at Barrow, Alaska. M.S. thesis, University of Alaska, Fairbanks.

Johnson, R. A. 1935. Additional dovekie weights. *Auk* 52:309.

———. 1941. Nesting behavior of the Atlantic murre. *Auk* 58:153–63.

Johnson, R. D. 1964. Red-tailed hawk preys on black-tailed rattlesnake. *Auk* 81(3):435.

Johnston, D. W. 1956. The annual reproductive cycle of the California gull. *Condor* 58:134–62, 206–21.

———. 1965. Longevity, mortality, and causes of death in the kestrel, *Falco tinnunculus*. *Bird-Banding* 36(2):120–21.

———. 1971a. Age and sex distribution in indigo buntings. *Bird-Banding* 41(2):113–18.

———. 1971b. Niche relationships among some deciduous forest flycatchers. *Auk* 88(4):796–804.

Johnston, D. W., and Downer, A. C. 1968. Migratory features of the indigo bunting in Jamaica and Florida. *Bird-Banding* 39(4):277–93.

Johnston, D. W., and Haines, T. P. 1957. Analysis of mass bird mortality in October 1954. *Auk* 74(4):447–58.

Johnston, R. F. 1967. Seasonal variation in the food of the purple martin *Progne subis* in Kansas. *Ibis* 109:8–13.

Johnston, R. F., and Selander, R. K. 1964. House sparrows: Rapid evolution of races in North America. *Science* 144:548–50.

———. 1971. Evolution in the house sparrow. II. Adaptive differentiation in North American populations. *Evolution* 25:1–28.

Jollie, M. T. 1961. Falconiformes. In *The encyclopedia of biological sciences*, ed. P. Gray. New York: Reinhold Publishing Corporation.

Jones, D. R., and Johansen, K. 1972. The blood vascular system of birds. In *Avian biology*, ed. D. S. Farner, J. R. King, and K. C. Parkes. Vol. 2. New York: Academic Press, Inc.

Jones, L. 1913. Some records of the feeding of nestlings. *Wilson Bull.* 25:67–71.

———. 1927. Highway mortality and speed of flight. *Wilson Bull.* 39:8–10.

Jones, R. D., and Gibson, D. D. 1975. Specimens of birds from Amchitka Island, Alaska. *Auk* 92(4):811.

Jones, T. B., and Kamil, A. C. 1973. Tool-making and tool-using in the northern blue jay. *Science* 180 (4090):1076–77.

Jonkel, G. M. 1977. Personal communication.

Jonkel, G. M., and Pettingill, Jr., O. S. 1974. Retraction of a longevity record for a 36-year-old herring gull. *Auk* 91:432.

Jordan, J. S. 1953. Effects of starvation on wild mallards. *Jour. Wildlife Management* 17:304–11.

Jordan, J. S., and Bellrose, F. C. 1951. *Lead poisoning in wild waterfowl.* Illinois Nat. Hist. Surv., Biol. Notes no. 26.

Jourdain, F. C. R. 1913. *The British bird book*, ed. F. B. Kirkman. London and Edinburgh: T. C. and E. C. Jack.

———. 1927. Curlew sandpiper. In *Life histories of North American shorebirds*, by A. C. Bent. U. S. Natl. Mus. Bull. no. 142, pt. 1. Washington, D.C.

———. 1929a. Dotterel. In *Life histories of North American shorebirds*, by A. C. Bent. U.S. Natl. Mus. Bull. no. 146, pt. 2. Washington, D.C.

———. 1929b. Ringed plover. In *Life histories of North American shorebirds*, by A. C. Bent. U.S. Natl. Mus. Bull. no. 146, pt. 2. Washington, D.C.

———. 1929c. Ruff. In *Life histories of North American shorebirds*, by A. C. Bent. U.S. Natl. Mus. Bull. no. 146, pt. 2. Washington, D.C.

———. 1929d. Wood sandpiper. In *Life histories of North American shorebirds*, by A. C. Bent. U.S. Natl. Mus. Bull. no. 146, pt. 2. Washington, D.C.

———. 1937. Gray sea eagle. In *Life histories of North American birds of prey*, by A. C. Bent. U.S. Natl. Mus. Bull. no. 167, pt. 1. Washington, D.C.

———. 1938. Kestrel. In *Life histories of North American birds of prey*, by A. C. Bent. U.S. Natl. Mus. Bull. no. 170, pt. 2. Washington, D.C.

———. 1939. Contributions to *The Handbook of British birds*. London: H. F. & G. Witherby, Inc.

———. 1940. White-rumped swift. In *Life histories of North American cuckoos, goatsuckers, hummingbirds, and their allies*, by A. C. Bent. U.S. Natl. Mus. Bull. no. 176. Washington, D.C.

———. 1942. Skylark. In *Life histories of North American larks, swallows, and their allies*, by A. C. Bent. U.S. Natl. Mus. Bull. no. 179. Washington, D.C.

Judd, S. D. 1899. Collecting a brown thrasher's song. *Bird-Lore* 1:25.

———. 1901. *The relation of sparrows to agriculture.* U.S. Dept. Agric., Bur. Biol. Surv. Bull. no. 15. Washington, D.C.

———. 1902. *Birds of a Maryland farm.* U.S. Dept. Agric., Bur. Biol. Surv. Bull. no. 17. Washington, D.C.

Juhn, M. 1957. "Frightmolt" in a male cardinal. *Wilson Bull.* 69(1):108.

Jull, M. A. 1927. Races of domestic fowl. *Natl. Geographic Magazine* 51:379–452.

———. 1930. Fowls of forest and stream tamed by man. *Natl. Geographic Magazine* 57:326–71.

Junge, G. C. A. 1964a. Crane. In *A new dictionary of birds*, ed. A. L. Thomson. New York: McGraw-Hill Book Company.

———. 1964c. Rail. In *A new dictionary of birds*, ed. A. L. Thomson. New York: McGraw-Hill Book Company.

———. 1964b. Nightjar. In *A new dictionary of birds*, ed. A. L. Thomson. New York: McGraw-Hill Book Company.

K

Kahl, J., and Garber, D. 1972. Feathered fishermen of Eagle Lake. *Calif. Condor* 7(2):1–2.

Kahl, Jr., M. P. 1963. Thermoregulation in the wood stork with special reference to the role of the legs. *Physiol. Zool.* 36:141–51.

———. 1964. Food ecology of the wood stork (*Mycteria americana*) in Florida. *Ecol. Monogr.* 34:97–117.

———. 1971a. The courtship of storks. *Natural History* 80(8) 36–44.

———. 1971b. Social behavior and taxonomic relationships of the storks. *Living Bird*, 10th annual, pp. 151–70.

Kale, II, H. W. 1968. The relationship of purple martins to mosquito control. *Auk* 85:654–61.

———. 1971. Florida region. *Amer. Birds* 25(4): 730.

———. 1972. Florida region. *Amer. Birds* 26(4): 752, 753.

———. 1973. Florida region. *Amer. Birds* 27(4): 763.

Kale, II, H. W., ed. 1977. The spring migration: Florida region. *Amer. Birds* 31:988–92.

Kale, II, H. W.; Seiple, G. W.; and Tomkins, I. R. 1965. The royal tern colony of Little Egg Island, Georgia. *Bird-Banding* 36(1):21–27.

Kalmbach, E. R. 1920. *The crow in its relation to agriculture.* U.S. Dept. Agric. Farmer's Bull. no. 1102. Washington, D.C.

———. 1927. *The magpie in relation to agriculture.* U.S. Dept. Agric. Tech. Bull. no. 24. Washington, D.C.

———. 1937. *Suggestions for combating starling roosts.* U.S. Dept. Agric., Wildlife Res. and Management Leaflet no. BS-81. Washington, D.C.

———. 1940. *Economic status of the English sparrow in the United States.* U.S. Dept. Agric. Tech. Bull. no. 711. Washington, D.C.

Kalmbach, E. R.; Imler, R. H.; and Arnold, L. W. 1964. *The American eagles and their economic status.* Washington, D.C.: U.S. Dept. Inter., Bur. of Sport Fish and Wildlife.

Kalmbach, E. R., and McAtee, W. L. 1930. *Homes for birds.* U.S. Dept. Agric. Farmer's Bull. no. 1456. Rev. ed. Washington, D.C.

Kalmus, H., and Crump, L. M. 1948. *Genetics.* Baltimore: Penguin Books, Inc. (Pelican Books, paperback).

Kane, R., and Buckley, 1975. Hudson–St. Lawrence region. *Amer. Birds* 29(3):672; (4):830.

Kanoy, W. C. 1936. How fast can a wild turkey fly? *Field and Stream* 40(11):86–87.

Karr, J. R. 1976. On the relative abundance of migrants from the north temperate zone in tropical habitats. *Wilson Bull.* 88:433–58.

Karstad, L. 1961. Reptiles as possible reservoir hosts for eastern encephalitis virus. *Trans.*

[26th] N. Amer. Wildlife and Nat. Res. Conf., pp. 181–202.

———. 1971a. Arboviruses. In Infectious and parasitic diseases of wild birds, ed. J. W. Davis et al. Ames, Iowa: Iowa State University Press.

———. 1971b. Pox. In Infectious and parasitic diseases of wild birds, ed. J. W. Davis et al. Ames, Iowa: Iowa State University Press.

Katz, D. 1937. Animals and men: Studies in comparative psychology. London: Longmans, Green & Company, Ltd.

Kaufmann, O. W., and Fay, L. D. 1964. Clostridium botulinum type E toxin in tissues of dead loons and gulls. Univ. Michigan Agric. Exper. Sta. Quarterly Bull. no. 47. Ann Arbor.

Kearton, C. 1931. The island of penguins. New York: Robert M. McBride & Company.

Kebbe, C. E. 1958. Deposition of pheasant eggs in ruffed grouse nest. Murrelet 39(1):10.

———. 1959. Nesting records of saw-whet owls in Oregon. Murrelet 40(2):21.

Keeton, W. T. 1969. Orientation by pigeons: Is the sun necessary? Science 165:922–28.

———. 1971. Magnets interfere with pigeon homing. Proc. Natl. Acad. Sci. 68(1):102–6.

———. 1972. Effects of magnets on pigeon homing. NASA Spec. Publ. NASA SP-262, pp. 579–94.

Keith, A. R. 1968. A summary of the extralimital records of the varied thrush, 1848 to 1966. Bird-Banding 39(4):245–76.

Keith, S. 1963. The "600 club": America's top-ranking birders. Audubon 65(6):376–77.

Kellogg, P. P. 1962a. Bird-sound studies at Cornell. Living Bird, 1st annual, pp. 37–48.

———. 1962b. Vocalization of the black rail (Laterallus jamaicensis) and yellow rail (Coturnicops noveboracensis). Auk 79:698–701.

Kellogg, P. P.; Allen, A. A.; and Peterson, R. T. 1959. A field guide to bird songs. Boston: Houghton Mifflin Company.

Kellogg, P. P., and Hutchinson, C. M. 1964. The solar eclipse and bird song. Living Bird, 3d annual, pp. 185–92.

Kelly, J. W. 1956. Prolonged incubation of an Anna's hummingbird. Condor 58(1):163.

———. 1968. Golden-crowned sparrow. In Life histories of North American cardinals, grosbeaks, buntings, towhees, finches, sparrows, and allies, comp. A. C. Bent et al., ed. O. L. Austin, Jr. U.S. Natl. Mus. Bull. no. 237, pt. 3. Washington, D.C.

Kelso, J. E. H. 1926. Diving and swimming activities displayed by Limicolae. Auk 43(1):92–93.

Kelso, L. 1929. The English sparrow and the western horned owl. Condor 31(3):128.

———. 1937. Food of the scaled quail. U.S. Dept. Agric., Wildlife Res. and Management Leaflet no. BS84. Washington, D.C.

Kelso, L., and Nice, M. M. 1963. A Russian contribution to anting and feather mites. Wilson Bull. 75(1):23–26.

Kemsies, E. 1968. Smith's longspur. In Life histories of North American cardinals, grosbeaks, buntings, towhees, finches, sparrows, and allies, comp. A. C. Bent et al., ed. O. L. Austin, Jr. U.S. Natl. Mus. Bull. no. 237, pt. 3. Washington, D.C.

Kenaga, E. E. 1961. Some insect parasites associated with the eastern bluebird in Michigan. Bird-Banding 31:91–94.

Kendeigh, S. C. 1934. The role of environment in the life of birds. Ecol. Monogr. 4:299–417.

———. 1941. Territorial and mating behavior of the house wren. Illinois Biol. Monogr. no. 18(3):1–120.

———. 1945a. Community selection by birds on the Helderberg Plateau. Auk 62:418–36.

———. 1945b. Resistance to hunger in birds. Jour. Wildlife Management 9:217–26.

———. 1952a. In memoriam: Lynds Jones. Auk 69(3):258–65.

———. 1952b. Parental care and its evolution in birds. Urbana, Ill.: University of Illinois Press.

———. 1954. History and evaluation of various concepts of plant and animal communities in North America. Ecology 35:152–71.

———. 1961. Animal ecology. Englewood Cliffs, N.J.: Prentice-Hall Publishing Co., Inc.

———. 1969. Tolerance of cold and Bergmann's rule. Auk 86(1):13–25.

———. 1970. Energy requirements for existence in relation to body size of bird. Condor 72(1):60–65.

Kendeigh, S. C. et al. 1950–51. Nature sanctuaries in the United States and Canada. Living Wilderness 15(35): 1–46.

Kenesson, F. W. 1914. The hummer and his shower-bath. Bird-Lore 16(3):186.

Kennard, J. H. 1975. Longevity records of North American birds. Bird-Banding 46(1):55–73.

Kennedy, R. J. 1969. Sun-bathing behaviour of birds. Brit. Birds 62:249–58.

Kenny, J., and Leck, C. F. 1972. Longevity record for an ovenbird. Bird-Banding 43:214.

Kenyon, K. W. 1942. Hunting strategy of pigeon hawks. Auk 59(3): 443–44.

———. 1947. Breeding populations of the osprey in lower California. Condor 49:152–58.

———. 1961. Birds of Amchitka Island, Alaska. Auk 78(3):305–26.

Kenyon, K. W., and Rice, D. W. 1958. Homing of Laysan albatrosses. Condor 60(1):3–6.

Kepler, C. B., and Parkes, K. C. 1972. A new species of warbler (Parulidae) from Puerto Rico. Auk 89(1):1–18.

Kessel, B. 1951. Criteria for sexing and aging European starlings (Sturnus vulgaris). Bird-Banding 22:16–23.

———. 1953. Distribution and migration of the European starling in North America. Condor 55:49–68.

———. 1957. A study of the breeding biology of the European starling (Sturnus vulgaris) in North America. Amer. Midland-Nat. 58(2):257–331.

———. 1976. Winter activity patterns of black-capped chickadees in interior Alaska. Wilson Bull. 88(1):36–61.

Kessel, B., and Gibson, D. D. 1978. Studies and distribution of Alaska birds. Cooper Ornith. Soc., Studies in Avian Biol., no. 1. Berkeley, Calif.

Kibbe, D. P. 1976. The blue list for 1977. Amer. Birds 30(6):1031–32.

Kibler, L. F. 1969. The establishment and maintenance of a bluebird nest-box project. Bird-Banding 40(2):114–29.

Kiel, Jr., W. H. 1959. Mourning dove—An international resource. Outdoor Calif. 20(1):4–5.

Kieran, J. 1952. Footnotes on nature. Garden City, N. Y.: Doubleday & Co., Inc.

Kilham, L. 1957. Egg-carrying by the whip-poor-will. Wilson Bull. 69(1):113.

———. 1958a. Pair formation, mutual tapping, and nest hole selection of red-bellied woodpecker. Auk 75(3):318–29.

———. 1958b. Sealed-in winter stores of red-headed woodpeckers. Wilson Bull. 70:107–13.

———. 1958c. Territorial behavior of wintering red-headed woodpeckers. Wilson Bull. 70:347–58.

———. 1959a. Behavior and methods of communication of pileated woodpeckers. Condor 61:377–87.

———. 1959b. Early reproductive behavior of flickers. Wilson Bull. 71:323–36.

———. 1959c. Mutual tapping of the red-headed woodpecker. Auk 76(2):236.

———. 1960. Courtship and territorial behavior of hairy woodpeckers. Auk 77:259–70.

———. 1961. Reproductive behavior of red-bellied woodpeckers. Wilson Bull. 73:237–54.

———. 1962a. Breeding behavior of the yellow-bellied sapsucker. Auk 79:31–43.

———. 1962b. Reproductive behavior of downy woodpeckers. Condor 64:126–33.

———. 1970. Breeding behavior of downy wood-

peckers. 1. Preference for paper birches and sexual differences. Auk 87(3):544–56.

———. 1971. Reproductive behavior of yellow-bellied sapsuckers. 1. Preference for nesting in fomes-infected aspens and nest hole interrelations with flying squirrels, raccoons, and other animals. Wilson Bull. 83(2):159–71.

———. 1974a. Copulating behavior of downy woodpeckers. Wilson Bull. 86(1):23–34.

———. 1974b. Loud vocalizations by pileated woodpeckers on approach to roosts or nest holes. Auk 91(3):634–36.

———. 1974c. Play in hairy, downy, and other woodpeckers. Wilson Bull. 86(1):35–42.

King, J. E., and Pyle, R. L. 1966. Some birds like fish. In Birds in our lives, ed. A. Stefferud and A. L. Nelson. Washington, D.C.: U.S. Dept. Inter., Fish and Wildlife Service.

King, J. R., and Farner, D. S. 1961. Energy metabolism, thermoregulation and body temperature. In Biology and comparative physiology of birds, ed. A. J. Marshall. Vol. 2. New York: Academic Press, Inc.

King, W. 1975. Half-million birds killed at army base in Kentucky. New York Times, February 21, p. 10.

Kingery, H. E. 1975. Mountain West. Amer. Birds 29(5):1012.

Kinkead, E. 1978. In numbers too great to count. New Yorker, May 22, "Profiles," pp. 40–88.

Kinne, R. 1962. The complete book of nature photography. New York: A. S. Barnes & Company, Incorporated.

Kinsey, E. C. 1935. Parental instincts in black phoebes. Condor 37(6):277–78.

Kirkman, F. B. 1937. Bird behaviour. A contribution based chiefly on a study of the black-headed gull. London: Thomas Nelson & Sons.

Kirmse, P. 1966. New wild bird hosts for pox viruses. Bull. Wildlife Disease Assoc. 2:30–33.

———. 1967. Pox in wild birds: An annotated bibliography. Wildlife Diseases, 49.

Kish, Frank. 1971. American golden eagle family at the Topeka Zoo. Zoo 7(3):1–5.

Kishchiuskii, A. A. 1968. On the biology of the short-billed and long-billed (Kittlitz's and marbled) murrelets. Ornitologiya 9:208–13.

Kissling, R. E. 1959. Equine encephalomyelitis virus in birds. In Diseases of poultry, ed. H. E. Biester and L. H. Schwarte. 4th ed. Ames, Iowa: Iowa State University Press.

Klauber, L. M. 1956. Rattlesnakes: Their habits, life histories and influences on mankind. Berkeley, Calif.: University of California Press.

Kleen, V. M., and Bush, L. 1973. Middlewestern prairie region. Amer. Birds 27:66, 623.

Kloek, G. P., and Casler, C. L. 1972. The lung and air sac system of the common grackle. Auk 89(4):817–25.

Klopfer, P. H. 1965. Imprinting: A reassessment. Science 147:302–3.

Kluyver, H. N. 1961. Food consumption in relation to habitat of breeding chickadees. Auk 78:532–50.

Knight, M. 1964. Pellet. In A new dictionary of birds, ed. A. L. Thomson. New York: McGraw-Hill Book Company.

Knight, R. L. 1948. Dictionary of genetics. Waltham, Mass.: Chronica Botanica Co.

Kobayashi, H., and Wada, M. 1973. Neuroendocrinology in birds. In Avian biology, ed. D. S. Farner, J. R. King, and K. C. Parkes. Vol. 3. New York: Academic Press, Inc.

Kocan, R. M. 1969. Various grains and liquid as potential vehicles of transmission for Trichomonas gallinae. Bull. Wildlife Disease Assoc. 5:148–49.

Kocan, R. M., and Herman, C. M. 1971. Trichomoniasis. In Infectious and parasitic diseases of wild birds, ed. J. W. Davis et al. Ames, Iowa: Iowa State University Press.

Kochert, M. N. 1972. Population status and chemical contamination in golden eagles in southwestern Idaho. M. S. thesis, University of Idaho, Boise.

Koehler, A. 1968. The breeding of some raptors in captivity. *Der Falkner* 18:28–33.

———. 1969. Captive breeding of some raptors. *Raptor Res. News* 3(1):3–18.

Koford, C. B. 1953. *The California condor.* Natl. Audubon Soc. Res. Report no. 4. New York.

Kohlar, K. 1966. Breeding of the cattle egret (*Bubulcus ibis*). *Avicultural Magazine* 72(2): 45–6.

Kohler, L. S. 1915. Home life of the scarlet tanager. *Oriole* 3:4–8.

Kooyman, G. L.; Drabek, C. M.; Elsner, R.; and Campbell, W. B. 1971. Diving behavior of the emperor penguin, *Aptenodytes forsteri. Auk* 88:775–95.

Kortright, F. H. 1943. *The ducks, geese and swans of North America.* Washington, D.C.: Amer. Wildlife Inst.

Koskimies, J. 1948. On temperature regulation and metabolism in the swift, *Micropus apus*, during fasting. *Experientia* 4:274–82.

———. 1950. *The life of the swift, Micropus apus (L.), in relation to the weather.* Annales Academiae Scientiarum Fennicae Series A, IV., Biologica no. 12.

———. 1957. Terns and gulls as features of habitat recognition for birds nesting in their colonies. *Ornis Fennica* 34(1)1–6.

Kozicky, E. L., and Schmidt, F. V. 1949. Nesting habits of the clapper rail in New Jersey. *Auk* 66:355–64.

Krantz, W. C.; Mulhern, B. M.; Bagley, G. E.; Sprunt IV, A.; Ligas, F. J.; Robertson, Jr., W. B. 1970. Organochlorine and heavy metal residues in bald eagle eggs. *Pesticides Monitor Jour.* 3(3):136–40.

Krause, H. 1968. McCown's longspur. In *Life histories of North American cardinals, grosbeaks, buntings, towhees, finches, sparrows, and allies*, comp. A. C. Bent *et al.*, ed. O. L. Austin, Jr. U.S. Natl. Mus. Bull. no. 237, pt. 3. Washington, D.C.

Kreithen, M. L., 1978. Sensory mechanisms for animal orientation. In *Animal migration, navigation, and homing*, ed. K. Schmidt-Koenig and W. T. Keeton. Heidelberg: Springer-Verlag.

Kreithen, M. L. and Quine, D. B. 1979. Infrasound detection by the homing pigeon. *Jour. Compar. Physiol.* A 129(1):1–4.

Krohn, W. B. 1971. Some patterns of woodcock activities on Maine summer fields. *Wilson Bull.* 83:396–407.

Kroodsma, R. L. 1975. Hybridization in buntings (*Passerina*) in North Dakota and eastern Montana. *Auk* 92(1):66–80.

Kuerzi, R. G. 1941. Life history studies of the tree swallow. *Proc. Linnaean Soc. New York* 52: 1–52.

Kuhk, R. 1960. Ein 31½ jähriger Grosser Brachvogel (*Numenius arquata*). *Die Vogelwarte* 20: 233.

Kuroda, N. 1942. *A bibliography of the duck tribe.* Tokyo: Herald Press.

Kushlan, J. A. 1973. White ibis nesting in the Florida Everglades. *Wilson Bull.* 85(2): 230–31.

Kuyken, E., and Burggraeve, G. 1971. A remarkable recovery of a curlew sandpiper (*Calidris ferruginea*) in the Lesser Antilles. *Gerfaut* 61(2):162–63.

Kuyt, E. 1967. Two banding returns for golden eagle and peregrine falcon. *Bird-Banding* 38(1):78–79.

Kuzyakin, A. P. 1963. On the biology of the long-billed (marbled) murrelet. *Ornitologiya* 6:315–20.

L

La Bastille, A.; Allen, D. G.; and Durrell, L. W. 1972. Behavior and feather structure of the quetzal. *Auk* 89:339–48.

Labiskey, R. F.; Harper, J. A.; and Greeley, F. 1964. *Influence of land use, calcium, and weather on the distribution and abundance of pheasants in Illinois.* Illinois Nat. Hist. Surv., Biol. Notes no. 51.

Lack, D. 1940a. Courtship feeding of birds. *Auk* 57:169–78.

———. 1940b. Pair formation in birds. *Condor* 42:269–86.

———. 1943a. The age of the blackbird. *Brit. Birds* 36:166–75.

———. 1943b. The age of some British birds. *Brit. Birds* 36:193–97, 214–21.

———. 1943c. Partial migration. *Brit. Birds* 36: 22.

———. 1947. *Darwin's finches.* Cambridge: At the University Press.

———. 1947–48. The significance of clutch size. *Ibis* 89:302–52; 90:25–45.

———. 1950. The breeding seasons of European birds. *Ibis* 92:288–316.

———. 1953. *The life of the robin.* London: Penguin Books, Inc. (Pelican Books, paperback).

———. 1954. *The natural regulation of animal numbers.* Oxford: Oxford University Press.

———. 1956. *Swifts in a tower.* London: Methuen & Company, Ltd.

———. 1959. Migration across the North Sea studied by radar. Part I. *Ibis* 101:209–34.

———. 1964a. Population dynamics. In *A new dictionary of birds*, ed. A. L. Thomson. New York: McGraw-Hill Book Company.

———. 1964b. Swift. In *A new dictionary of birds*, ed. A. L. Thomson. New York: McGraw-Hill Book Company.

———. 1966. *Population studies of birds.* London: Oxford University Press.

———. 1968. *Ecological adaptations for breeding in birds.* London: Methuen & Company, Ltd.

Lack, D., and Lack, E. 1951. The breeding biology of the swift, *Apus apus. Ibis* 93:501–46.

———. 1953. Visible migration through the Pyrenees: An autumn reconnaissance. *Ibis* 95:271–309.

Lake, F. B. 1958. Treatment of sick and wounded birds. *Bird Study* 5(2):66–74.

Lamb, H. H. 1964. Meteorology. In *A new dictionary of birds*, ed. A. L. Thomson. New York: McGraw-Hill Book Company.

Lambert, G. 1947. A new species is added to North America. *Bird-Banding* 18(3):129.

Lancaster, D. A. 1970. Breeding behavior of the cattle egret in Colombia. *Living Bird*, 9th annual, pp. 167–94.

Lancaster, D. A., and Johnson, J. R., eds. 1973. Turnstone migration in the Pacific. *Cornell Laboratory of Ornith. Newsletter* no. 70.

———. 1975. Orientation by Swainson's thrushes. *Cornell Laboratory of Ornith. Newsletter* no. 76, p. 6.

———. 1976. Birds navigate by magnetic field. *Cornell Laboratory of Ornith. Newsletter* no. 82, p. 5.

Land, H. C. 1970. *Birds of Guatemala.* Wynnewood, Pa.: Livingston Publishing Co.

Lane, F. W. 1954. *Nature parade.* New York: Sheridan House, Inc.

Lane, J. 1968a. Baird's sparrow. In *Life histories of North American cardinals, grosbeaks, buntings, towhees, finches, sparrows, and allies*, comp. A. C. Bent *et al.*, ed. O. L. Austin, Jr. U.S. Natl. Mus. Bull. no. 237, pt. 2. Washington, D.C.

———. 1968b. A hybrid eastern bluebird × mountain bluebird. *Auk* 85(4):684.

Lang, H. 1924. *Ampullarius* and *Rostrhamus* at Georgetown, British Guiana. *Nautilus* 37:73–77.

Langdon, F. W. 1880. *Helminthophaga cincinnatiensis. Jour. Cincinnati Soc. Nat. Hist.* 3(2): 119–20.

Langham, N. P. E. 1974. Comparative breeding biology of the Sandwich tern. *Auk* 91(2):255–77.

Lanyon, W. E. 1957. *The comparative biology of the meadowlarks (Sturnella) in Wisconsin.* Publ. Nuttall Ornith. Club no. 1. Cambridge, Mass.

———. 1958. The motivation of sun-bathing in birds. *Wilson Bull.* 70:280.

———. 1960. The ontogeny of vocalizations in birds. In *Animal sounds and communication*, ed. W. E. Lanyon and W. N. Tavolga. Amer. Inst. Biol. Sci. Publ. no. 7. Pp. 321–47. Washington, D.C.

———. 1961. Specific limits and distribution of ash-throated and Nutting flycatchers. *Condor* 63:421–49.

———. 1962. Specific limits and distribution of meadowlarks of the desert grassland. *Auk* 79: 183–207.

———. 1964. *Biology of birds.* Garden City, N.Y.: Doubleday/Natural History Press.

Lanyon, W. E., and Tavolga, W. N., eds. 1960. *Animal sounds and communication.* Amer. Inst. Biol. Sci. Publ. no. 7. Washington, D.C.

Lapage, G. 1963. *Animal parasites in man.* Rev. ed. New York: Dover Publications, Inc.

Lapham, H. 1979. Personal communication.

Lashley, K. S. 1913. Reproduction of inarticulate sounds in the parrot. *Jour. Animal Behaviour* 3:361–66.

Lasiewski, R. C. 1963. Oxygen consumption of torpid, resting, active, and flying hummingbirds. *Physiol. Zool.* 36:122–40.

———. 1969. Physiological responses to heat stress in the poor-will. *Amer. Jour. Physiol.* 217:1504–9.

———. 1972. Respiratory function in birds. In *Avian biology*, ed. D. S. Farner, J. R. King, and K. C. Parkes. Vol. 2. New York: Academic Press, Inc.

Lasiewski, R. C.; Bernstein, M. H.; and Ohmart, R. D. 1971. Cutaneous water loss in roadrunner and poor-will. *Condor* 73(4):470–72.

Lasiewski, R. C., and Calder, W. A. 1971. A preliminary allometric analysis of respiratory variables in resting birds. *Resp. Physiol.* 11: 152–66.

Lasiewski, R. C., and Dawson, W. R. 1964. Physiological responses to temperature in the common nighthawk. *Condor* 66:447–90.

Laskey, A. R. 1935. Bird-banding brevities. *Migrant* 6:10–11.

———. 1939. A study of nesting eastern bluebirds. *Bird-Banding* 10:23–32.

———. 1943a. The nesting of bluebirds banded as nestlings. *Bird-Banding* 14:39–43.

———. 1943b. Some age records for banded birds. *Migrant* 14(1):5–8.

———. 1948. Some nesting data on the Carolina wren at Nashville, Tennessee. *Bird-Banding* 19(3):101–21.

———. 1952. A case of avian tuberculosis in an immature avocet. *Condor* 54:316.

———. 1957. Some tufted titmouse life history. *Bird-Banding* 28:135–45.

———. 1958. Blue jays at Nashville, Tennessee, movements, nesting, age. *Bird-Banding* 29(4): 211–18.

———. 1962. Breeding biology of mockingbirds. *Auk* 79(4):598–606.

Latham, R. M. 1947. Differential ability of male and female game birds to withstand starvation and climatic extremes. *Jour. Wildlife Management* 11:139–49.

———. 1960. *Bounties are bunk.* Washington, D.C.: Natl. Wildlife Fed. Leaflet.

Lauffer, M. A. 1961. Viruses. In *The encyclopedia of the biological sciences*, ed. P. Gray. New York: Reinhold Publishing Corporation.

Lavers, N. 1974. Three more cases of white-crowned sparrow parasitized by brown-headed cowbirds. *Auk* 91(4):829–30.

Law, J. E. 1929. Another Lewis' woodpecker stores acorns. *Condor* 31:233.

Lawrence, G. N. 1851. Descriptions of new species; birds of the genera Toxostoma (Wagler), Tyrannula (Swainson), and Plectrophanes (Meyer). *Annals of the Lyceum of Natural History* 5:121–23.

Lawrence, L. de K. 1948. Comparative study of the nesting behavior of chestnut-sided and Nashville warblers. *Auk* 65:204–19.

————. 1949. The red crossbill at Pimisi Bay, Ontario. *Canadian Field-Nat.* 63:147–60.

————. 1953. Nesting life and behaviour of the red-eyed vireo. *Canadian Field-Nat.* 67:47–77.

————. 1955. Is the sapsucker destructive? *Nature Magazine* 48:487–88, 500.

————. 1958. Homing and life expectancy in the chaffinch (review). *Bird-Banding* 29(3):190.

————. 1965. Birds over America (review). *Bird-Banding* 36(3):209–10.

————. 1967. *A comparative life-history study of four species of woodpeckers.* Amer. Ornith. Union, Monogr. no. 5.

Lawson, R. 1930. The stoop of a hawk. *Bull. of Essex (Mass.) Ornith. Club* 12:79–80.

Lay, D. W.; McDaniel, E. M.; and Russell, D. N. 1971. Status of investigations of range and habitat requirements. In *The ecology and management of the red-cockaded woodpecker: Proceedings of a symposium at Okefenokee National Wildlife Refuge, Folkston, Ga. May 26–27,* ed. R. L. Thompson. Tallahassee, Fla.: Tall Timbers Res. Station.

Lay, D. W., and Russell, D. N. 1970. Notes on the red-cockaded woodpecker in Texas. *Auk* 87: 781–86.

Laybourne, R. C. 1967. Bilateral gynandrism in an evening grosbeak. *Auk* 84:267–72.

————. 1974. Collision between a vulture and an aircraft at an altitude of 37,000 feet. *Wilson Bull.* 86(4):461–62.

Laycock. G. 1969. Where have all the pelicans gone? *Audubon* 71(5):10–17.

————. 1971. *The alien animals.* Garden City, New York: Doubleday/Natural History Press.

————. 1973. Saving western eagles from traps and zaps. *Audubon* 75(5):133.

Leach, M., ed. 1949. *Dictionary of folklore, mythology, and legend.* New York: Funk & Wagnalls Company.

Leck, C. F. 1973. Dominance relationships in nectar-feeding birds at St. Croix. *Auk* 90: 431–32.

————. 1974. Further observations of nectar-feeding by orioles. *Auk* 91:162–63.

Lederer, R. J. 1972. The role of avian rictal bristles. *Wilson Bull.* 84:193–97.

Lee, D. S., and Booth, Jr., J. 1979. Seasonal distribution of offshore and pelagic birds in North Carolina waters. *Amer. Birds* 33:715–21.

Lee, R. D. 1955a. The biology of the Mexican chicken bug, Haematosiphon inodorus (Hemiptera: Cimicidae). *Pan-Pacific Entomologist* 31:47–61.

————. 1955b. New locality records and a new host record for Haematosiphon inodorus (Hemiptera: Cimicidae). *Pan-Pacific Entomologist* 31:137–38.

————. 1959. Some insect parasites of birds. *Audubon* 61:214–15, 224–25.

Lee, T. A. 1970. Some observations on the dispersal of fledgling purple martins from the nesting site. *Chat* 34:1–2.

Leedy, D. L. 1961. Some federal contributions to bird conservation during the period 1885–1960. *Auk* 78:167–75.

Leffingwell, W. B. 1890. *Wild fowl shooting.* Chicago: Rand McNally & Company.

Leffler, S. R. 1966. Observations on a captive northern phalarope. *Wilson Bull.* 78:124–25.

Legg, K., and Pitelka, F. A. 1956. Ecological overlap of Allen's and Anna's hummingbirds nest-

ing in Santa Cruz, California. *Condor* 58:393–405.

Lehrman, D. S. 1959. Hormonal responses to external stimuli in birds. *Ibis* 101:478–96.

Leiber, A. 1907. Vergleichende Anatomie der Spechtzunge. *Zoologica, Stuttgart* 20:1–79.

Leibovitz, L. 1969. Natural occurrence and experimental study of pox and Haemoproteus infections in a white swan. *Bull. Wildlife Disease Assoc.* 5:130–36.

————. 1971. Duck plague. In *Infectious and parasitic diseases of wild birds,* ed. J. W. Davis et al. Ames, Iowa: Iowa State University Press.

Lein, M. R., and Maher, W. J. 1970. First nesting of the wheatear in western Hudson Bay, Canada. *Auk* 87(1):171–72.

Leitch, W. G. 1964. Water. In *Waterfowl tomorrow,* ed. J. P. Linduska and A. L. Nelson. Washington D.C.: U.S. Dept. Inter., Fish and Wildlife Service.

Lemmon, R. S. 1953. Some recollections of Frank M. Chapman. *Audubon* 55(6):252–55.

Lennington, S., and Mace, T. 1975. Mate tenacity and nesting site tenacity in the killdeer. *Auk* 92(1):149–51.

Leopold, A. 1923. The "following" habit of hawks and owls. *Condor* 25:180.

————. 1933. *Game management.* New York: Charles Scribner's Sons.

Leopold, A. S. 1944. The nature of heritable wildness in turkeys. *Condor* 46:133–97.

————. 1959. *Wildlife of Mexico: The game birds and mammals.* Berkeley and Los Angeles: University of California Press.

————. 1977. *The California quail.* Berkeley, Calif.: University of California Press.

Leopold, F. 1966. Experiences with home-grown wood ducks. In *Wood duck management and research: A symposium,* ed. L. R. John et al. Washington, D.C.: Wildlife Management Inst.

Lesson, R. P., and De Lattre, A. 1839. *Rev. zoologique,* ser. 2(1), pp. 15–16.

Levi, W. M. 1957. *The pigeon.* Sumter, S.C.: Levi Publishing Company.

Levine, E. B.; Beach, G. B.; and Bocchetta, V. E. 1967. *Latin dictionary.* Chicago: Follett Publishing Company.

Levine, N. D. 1973. *Protozoan parasites of domestic animals and of man.* 2d ed. Minneapolis: Burgess Publishing Co.

Lewis, H. F. 1939. Reverse migration. *Auk* 56: 13–27.

Lewis, J. C. 1967. Physical characteristics and physiology. In *The wild turkey and its management.* Washington, D.C.: Wildlife Soc.

————. 1973. *The world of the wild turkey.* Philadelphia: J. B. Lippincott Company.

————. 1974. Ecology of the sandhill crane in the southeastern Central Flyway. Ph.D. thesis. Norman, Okla.: Oklahoma State University.

————. 1977. Sandhill crane (Grus canadensis). In *Management of migratory shore and upland game birds in North America,* ed. G. C. Sanderson. Pp. 5–43. Washington, D.C.: International Association Fish and Wildlife Agencies.

————. 1979. Molt of the remiges of Grus canadensis. In *Proceedings of the 1978 Crane Workshop.* Pp. 255–59. Fort Collins, Colo.: Colorado State University Press.

Ligon, J. D. 1968a. *The biology of the elf owl,* Micrathene whitneyi. Univ. Michigan Mus. Zool. Misc. Publ. no. 136. Ann Arbor.

————. 1968b. Sexual differences in foraging behavior in two species of Dendrocopos woodpeckers. *Auk* 85:203–15.

————. 1970a. Behavior and breeding biology of the red-cockaded woodpecker. *Auk* 87(2):255–78.

————. 1970b. Still more responses of the poorwill to low temperatures. *Condor* 72:496–98.

————. 1971a. Notes on the breeding of the sulphur-bellied flycatcher in Arizona. *Condor* 73(2):250–52.

————. 1971b. Some factors influencing the num-

bers of the red-cockaded woodpecker. In *The ecology and management of the red-cockaded woodpecker: Proceedings of a symposium at Okefenokee National Wildlife Refuge, Folkston, Ga., May 26–27.,* ed. R. L. Thompson. Tallahassee, Fla.: Tall Timbers Res. Station.

————. 1973. Foraging behavior of the white-headed woodpecker in Idaho. *Auk* 90(4):862–69.

Ligon, J. S. 1926. Habits of the spotted owl (Syrnium occidentale). *Auk* 43:421–29.

————. 1946. *History and management of Merriam's wild turkey.* Albuquerque, N.M.: New Mex. Dept. of Game and Fish.

————. 1952. The vanishing masked bobwhite. *Condor* 54:48–50.

————. 1961. *New Mexico birds and where to find them.* Albuquerque, N.M.: University of New Mexico Press.

Lincer, J. L.; Cade, T. J.; and Devine, J. M. 1970. Organochlorine residues in Alaskan peregrine falcons (Falco peregrinus Tunstall), rough-legged hawks (Buteo lagopus Pontoppidan) and their prey. *Canadian Field-Nat.* 84:255–63.

Lincer, J. L.; Clark, W.S.; and LeFrance, Jr., M. N. 1979. *Working bibliography of the bald eagle.* Natl. Wildlife Fed. Scientific and Tech. Series, no. 2. Washington, D.C.

Lincoln, F. C. 1916. The discovery of the nest and eggs of Leucosticte australis. *Auk* 33:41–42.

————. 1930. *Calculating waterfowl abundance on the basis of banding returns.* U.S. Dept. Agric. Circ. no. 118. Washington, D.C.

————. 1931. Some causes of mortality among birds. *Auk* 48:538–46.

————. 1933. Bird banding. In *Fifty years progress of American ornithology.* Lancaster, Pa.: Amer. Ornith. Union.

————. 1935. *The waterfowl flyways of North America.* U.S. Dept. Agric. Circ. no. 342. Washington, D.C.

————. 1936a. Returns of banded birds. *Bird-Banding* 7(3):121–28.

————. 1936b. Some inland bird recoveries from Mexico. *Bird-Banding* 7(4):170.

————. 1939. *The migration of American birds.* Garden City, N.Y.: Doubleday, Doran and Company, Inc.

————. 1941. Pelicans killed by lightning. *Auk* 58:91.

————. 1946. Personal communication.

————. 1947. *Manual for bird banders.* Washington, D.C.: U.S. Dept. Inter., Fish and Wildlife Service.

————. 1950a. The American brant—Living bird or museum piece? *Audubon* 52:282–87.

————. 1950b. *Birds protected by federal law.* U.S. Dept. Inter., Wildlife Leaflet no. 327.

————. 1950c. *Migration of birds.* U.S. Dept. Inter., Fish and Wildlife Service Circ. no. 16. Washington, D.C.

————. 1958. An albino purple martin. *Auk* 75(2):220–21.

————. 1979. *Migration of birds.* Rev. ed. U.S. Dept. Inter., Fish and Wildlife Service Circ. no. 16. Washington, D. C.

Lindquist, A. W. 1962. Personal communication.

Lindsey, A. A. 1946. The nesting of the New Mexican duck. *Auk* 63:483–92.

Linduska, J. P., and Nelson, A. L., eds. 1964. *Waterfowl tomorrow.* Washington, D.C.: U.S. Dept. Inter., Fish and Wildlife Service.

Line, L. D. 1971. The storks came back. *Audubon* 73(5):26–27.

Linnaeus, C. 1758. *Systema naturae.* 10th ed. Vol. 1.

Linsdale, J. M. 1937. *The natural history of magpies.* Pacific Coast Avifauna no. 25. Berkeley, Calif. Cooper Ornith. Club.

————. 1942. In memoriam: Joseph Grinnell. *Auk* 59:269–85.

————. 1946. American magpie. In *Life histories of North American jays, crows, and titmice,* by

A. C. Bent. U.S. Natl. Mus. Bull. no. 191. Washington, D.C.

———. 1949. Survival in birds banded at Hastings reservation. *Condor* 51:88–96.

———. 1968a. Green-backed goldfinch. In *Life histories of North American cardinals, grosbeaks, buntings, towhees, finches, sparrows, and allies,* comp. A.C. Bent *et al.,* ed. O. L. Austin, Jr. U.S. Natl. Mus. Bull. no. 237, pt. 1. Washington, D.C.

———. 1968b. Lawrence's goldfinch. In *Life histories of North American cardinals, grosbeaks, buntings, towhees, finches, sparrows, and allies,* comp. A. C. Bent *et al,* ed. O. L. Austin, Jr. U.S. Natl. Mus. Bull. no. 237, pt. 1. Washington, D.C.

Linsdale, J. M., and Sumner, Jr., E. L. 1937. Weights of spotted towhees. *Condor* 39(4):162–63.

Lissaman, P. B. S., and Schollenberger, C. A. 1970. Formation flight of birds. *Science* 168: 1003–5.

Littlefield, C. D. 1970a. Flightlessness in sandhill cranes. *Auk* 87:157.

———. 1970b. A marsh hawk roost in Texas. *Condor* 72:245.

Littlejohns, R. T. 1950. Further notes on the mistletoe bird and the mistletoe parasite. *Emu* 50(2):84–90.

Lloyd, H. 1937. Twenty-year-old ferruginous rough-legged hawk. *Canadian Field-Nat.* 51: 137.

Lockie, J. D., and Ratcliffe, D. A. 1964. Insecticides and Scottish golden eagles. *Brit. Birds* 57:89–102.

Lockley, R. M. 1942. *Shearwaters.* London: J. M. Dent & Sons, Ltd.

———. 1953. *Puffins.* New York: The Devin-Adair Co.

———. 1973. *Ocean wanderers: The migratory sea birds of the world.* Harrisburg; Pa.: Stackpole Books.

Lockley, R. M., and Russell, R. 1953. *Bird-ringing: The art of bird study by individual marking.* London: Crosby Lockwood & Son, Ltd.

Lockwood, M. E. 1922. Hummingbird and bass. *Bird-Lore* 24:94.

Löf, R. A. 1967. Ten years of banding black-capped chickadees. *EBBA News* 30(5):195–98.

Loftin, H. 1975. Recaptures and recoveries of banded native Panamanian birds. *Bird-Banding* 46(1):19–27.

Loftin, H., and Tyson, E. L. 1965. Stylized behavior in the turkey vulture's courtship dance. *Wilson Bull.* 77:193.

Lofts, B., and Murton, R. K. 1973. Reproduction in birds. In *Avian biology,* ed. D. S. Farner, J. R. King, and K. C. Parkes. Vol. 3, p. 8. New York: Academic Press, Inc.

Logan, S. 1951. Cardinal, *Richmondena cardinalis,* assists in feeding robins. *Auk* 68:516–17.

Lokemoen, J. T. 1967. Flight speed of the wood duck. *Wilson Bull.* 79:238–39.

Long, P. H. 1966. Infectious diseases. In *Better homes and gardens family medical guide.* New York: Meredith Press.

Longley, W. H. 1960. Comment on flight distance of the great blue heron. *Wilson Bull.* 72(3):289.

Longstreet, R. J. 1930. Notes on speed of flight of certain water birds. *Auk* 47:428–29.

Lorenz, K. 1935. Der Kumpan in der Umwelt des Vogels: Der Artgenosse als auslöseades Moment sozialer Verhalttungswiesen. *Jour. f. Ornith.* 83(2):10–213.

———. 1937. The companion in the bird's world. *Auk* 54:245–73.

———. 1952. *King Solomon's ring.* New York: Thomas Y. Crowell Company, Inc.

———. 1970a. Companions as factors in the bird's environment. In *Studies in animal and human behaviour.* Vol. 1. Cambridge, Mass.: Harvard University Press.

———. 1970b. A consideration of methods of identification of species–Specific instinctive behaviour patterns in birds. In *Studies in animal and human behaviour.* Vol. 1. Cambridge, Mass.: Harvard University Press.

———. 1971. Comparative studies of the motor patterns of anatinae. In *Studies in animal and human behaviour.* Vol. 2. Cambridge, Mass.: Harvard University Press.

Lovejoy, III, T. E. 1970. Personal communication.

Lowe, P. R. 1933. On the primitive characters of the penguins, and their bearing on the phylogeny of birds. *Proc. Zool. Soc. London,* pt. 2, pp. 483–538.

———. 1939. Some additional notes on Miocene penguins in relation to their origin and systematics. *Ibis* 81:281–96.

Lowery, Jr., G. H. 1938. Hummingbird in a pigeon hawk's stomach. *Auk* 55(2):280.

———. 1945. Trans-Gulf spring migration of birds and the coastal hiatus. *Wilson Bull.* 57: 92–121.

———. 1946. Evidence of trans-Gulf migration. *Auk* 63:175–211.

———. 1951a. Edward Avery McIlhenny. *Auk* 68:135.

———. 1951b. A quantitative study of the nocturnal migration of birds. *Univ. Kansas Publ. Mus. Nat. Hist.* 3(2):361–472.

———. 1960. *Louisiana birds.* 2d ed. Baton Rouge, La.: Louisiana State University Press.

———. 1974. *Louisiana birds.* 3d ed. Baton Rouge, La.: Louisiana State University Press.

Lowery, Jr., G. H., and Newman, R. J. 1955. Direct studies of nocturnal migration. In *Recent studies in avian biology,* ed. A. Wolfson. Urbana, Ill.: University of Illinois Press.

Lowther, J. K., and Falls, J. B. 1968. White-throated sparrow. In *Life histories of North American cardinals, grosbeaks, buntings, towhees, finches, sparrows, and allies,* comp. A. C. Bent *et al.,* ed. O. L. Austin, Jr. U.S. Natl. Mus. Bull. no. 237, pt. 3. Washington, D.C.

Lucas, A. M., and Stettenheim, P. R. 1972. *Avian anatomy: Integument.* Vol. 2. Washington, D.C.: U.S. Dept. Agric.

Lucas, F. A. 1895. The tongues of birds. *Report of U.S. Natl. Mus.,* pp. 1001–19.

———. 1929. *Animals of the past.* Amer. Mus. Nat. Hist. Handbook series no. 4. New York.

Ludden, D. M. 1979. An intensive study of parental behavior in the mourning dove. *Indiana Audubon Quarterly* 57 (4): 209–32.

Ludwig, J. 1971. Pheasant chases fox. *Wilson Bull.* 83(1):101.

Luft, U. C. 1965. Aviation physiology–The effects of altitude. In *Handbook of physiology, respiration.* ed. W. O. Fenn and H. Rahn. Vol. 1. Washington, D.C.: Amer. Physiol. Soc.

Lunk, W. A. 1962. *The rough-winged swallow,* Stelgidopteryx ruficollis: *A study based on its breeding biology.* Nuttall Ornith. Pub. no. 4. Cambridge, Mass.

Lyerly, S. B.; Riess, B. F.; and Ross, S. 1950. Color preference in the Mexican violet-eared hummingbird, *Calibri t. thalassinus* (Swainson). *Behaviour* 2:237–48.

Lynch, J. 1952. Operation eyebrow. *Audubon* 54(5):322–29.

Lynch, J. F., and Ames, P. L. 1970. A new hybrid hummingbird, *Archilochus alexandri* × *Selasphorus sasin. Condor* 72:209–12.

Lyon, W. I. 1922. Owl kidnaps young flickers. *Wilson Bull.* 34:230–31.

———. 1938. Albinistic herring gulls. *Bird-Banding* 9(2):102.

M

Mabbott, D. C. 1920. *Food habits of seven species of American shoal-water ducks.* U.S. Dept. Agric. Bull. no. 862. Washington, D.C.

MacArthur, R. H. 1958. Population ecology of some warblers of northeastern coniferous forests. *Ecology* (39):599–619.

———. 1959. On the breeding distribution pattern of North American migrant birds. *Auk* 76(3):318–25.

MacBriar, Jr., W. N. 1970. Eight-year-old bank swallow *(Riparia riparia). Bird-Banding* 41(2):-130.

Macdonald, J. D. 1960. Secondary external nares of the gannet. *Proc. Zool. Soc. London* 135:357–63.

———. 1964. Respiratory system. In *A new dictionary of birds,* ed. A. L. Thomson. New York: McGraw-Hill Book Company.

Macdonald, J. W., and Cornelius, L. W. 1959. Salmonellosis in wild birds. *Brit. Birds* 62:28–30.

MacDonald, S. D. 1968. The courtship and territorial behavior of Franklin's race of the spruce grouse. *Living Bird,* 7th annual, pp. 5–25.

———. 1970. The breeding behavior of the rock ptarmigan. *Living Bird,* 9th annual, pp. 195–238.

MacDonald, S. D., and Macpherson, A. H. 1960. *Breeding places of the Ivory gull in Canada.* Natl. Mus. Canada, Bull. no. 183, pp. 111–17.

MacFarlane, R. R. 1891. Notes on and list of birds and eggs collected in Arctic America, 1861–66. *Proc. U.S. Natl. Mus.* 14:413–46.

MacGregor, W. G. 1956. Cyanicide poisoning of songbirds by almonds. *Condor* 58(2):370.

MacGregor, W. G., and Smith, W. M. 1955. Nesting and production of the band-tailed pigeon in California. *Calif. Fish and Game* 41:315–26.

Macior, L. M. 1959. Predation by gray jays on the young of the hoary bat. *Flicker* 31(3):100.

Mackay, V. M., and Hughes, W. H. 1963. The crested mynah in British Columbia. *Canadian Field-Nat.* 77:154–61.

Maclean, G. L. 1967. The systematic position of the sand grouse. *Jour. f. Ornith.* 108(2):203–17.

———. 1968. Field studies of the sand grouse of the Kalahari Desert. *Living Bird,* 7th annual, pp. 209–35.

Macleod, R. D. 1954. *Key to the names of British birds.* London: Sir Isaac Pitman and Sons, Ltd.

MacMillen, R. E., and Trost, C. H. 1966. Water economy and salt balance in white-winged and Inca doves. *Auk* 83(3):441–56.

———. 1967. Nocturnal hypothermia in the Inca dove, *Scardafella inca. Comp. Biochem. and Phys.* 23:243–53.

MacQueen, P. M. 1950. Territory and song in the least flycatcher. *Wilson Bull.* 62:194–205.

MacRoberts, B. R., and MacRoberts, M. H. 1972. A most sociable bird. *Natural History* 81(10):44–51.

———. 1976. *Social organization and behavior of the acorn woodpecker in central coastal California.* Amer. Ornith. Union, Monogr. no. 21.

MacRoberts, M. H. 1970. Notes on the food habits and food defense of the acorn woodpecker. *Condor* 72:196–204.

———. 1975. Food storage and winter territory in red-headed woodpeckers in northwestern Louisiana. *Auk* 92(2):382–85.

Mader, W. J. 1975. Biology of the Harris' hawk in southern Arizona. *Living Bird,* 14th annual, pp. 59–85.

———. 1979. Breeding behavior of a polyandrous trio of Harris' hawks in southern Arizona. *Auk* 96 (4): 776–88.

Madson, J. 1964. The cornfielders. In *Waterfowl tomorrow,* ed. J. P. Linduska and A. L. Nelson. Washington D.C.: U.S. Dept. Inter., Fish and Wildlife Service.

Maestrelli, J. R. 1973. Propagation of barn owls in captivity. *Auk* 90:426–28.

Magnan, A. 1910. Sur une certaine loi de variation du foie et du pancréas chez les oiseaux. *Compt. rend.* 151:159–60.

———. 1912. Variations expérimentales du foie et des reins chez les canards en fonction du régime alimentaire. *Compt. rend.* 155:182–84.

Maher, W. J. 1970. The pomarine jaeger as a brown lemming predator in northern Alaska. *Wilson Bull.* 82(2):130–57.

———. 1974. *Ecology of pomarine, parasitic, and long-tailed jaegers in northern Alaska.* Pacific Coast Avifauna no. 37. Los Angeles.

Maier, Gertrude. 1956. The birds' Christmas tree. *Audubon* 58:288.

Mailliard, J. 1924. Autobiography of Joseph Mailliard. *Condor* 26:10–29.

———. 1931. Charles Andrew Allen. *Condor* 33:20–22.

Malcolmson, R. O. 1960. Mallophaga from birds of North America. *Wilson Bull.* 72:182–97.

Malette, R. D.; Sibley, F. C.; Carrier, W. D.; and Borneman, J. C. 1970. California condor surveys, 1969. *Calif. Fish and Game* 56:199–202.

Mann, W. M. 1934. *Wild animals in and out of the zoo.* Smithsonian Scient. Series 6. New York: Smithsonian Press.

Manning, T. H.; Höhn, E. O.; and Macpherson, A. H. 1956. *The birds of Banks Island.* Natl. Mus. Canada, Bull. no. 143. Ottawa.

Manuwal, D.; Mattocks, Jr., R. W.; and Richter, K. A. 1979. First Arctic tern colony in the contiguous western United States. *Amer. Birds* 33:144–45.

Manville, R. 1963. Altitude record for mallard. *Wilson Bull.* 75(1):92.

Manwell, R. D. 1962. The homing of cowbirds. *Auk* 79(4):649–54.

Marcham, F. G. 1963. Louis Fuertes revisited. *Living Bird,* 2d annual, pp. 83–92.

Marchant, S. 1964a. Nest. In *A new dictionary of birds,* ed. A. L. Thomson. New York: McGraw-Hill Book Company.

———. 1964b. Vulture (2). In *A new dictionary of birds,* ed. A. L. Thomson. New York: McGraw-Hill Book Company.

Margoschis, R. 1977. Recording natural history sounds. Barnett, Herts., England: Print and Press Service, Ltd.

Marion, W. R. 1974. Status of the plain chachalaca in south Texas. *Wilson Bull.* 86(3):200–205.

———. 1976. Plain chachalaca food habits in south Texas. *Auk* 93(2):376–79.

Marion, W. R., and Shamis, J. D. 1977. An annotated bibliography of bird marking techniques. *Bird-Banding* 48(1):42–61.

Marler, P. 1969. Tonal quality of bird sounds. In *Bird vocalizations: their relations to current problems in biology and psychology,* ed. R. A. Hinde. Cambridge: At the University Press. England.

Marples, G., and Marples, A. 1934. *Sea terns or sea swallows.* London: Country Life Ltd.

Marquardt, R. E. 1961. Albinism in the small white-cheeked geese. *Auk* 78:99–100.

Marsh, O. C. 1880. *Odontornithes: A monograph of the extinct toothed birds of North America.* Washington, D.C.: U.S. Govt. Printing Office.

Marshall, A. J. 1950. The function of vocal mimicry in birds. *Emu* 50:5–16.

———. 1954. *Bower-birds.* London: Oxford University Press.

———. 1961a. Breeding seasons and migration. In *Biology and comparative physiology of birds,* ed. A. J. Marshall. Vol. 2. New York: Academic Press, Inc.

———. 1961b. Reproduction. In *Biology and comparative physiology of birds,* ed. A. J. Marshall. Vol. 2. New York: Academic Press, Inc.

———. 1964. Endocrine system. In *A new dictionary of birds,* ed. A. L. Thomson. New York: McGraw-Hill Book Company.

Marshall, D. B. 1970. Chestnut-sided warbler in Washington, *Condor* 72:246.

Marshall, Jr., J. T. 1942. Food and habitat of the spotted owl. *Condor* 44:66–67.

———. 1955. Hibernation in captive goatsuckers. *Condor* 57:129–34.

———. 1957. Broad-tailed hummingbird. In *Audubon western bird guide,* by R. H. Pough. New York: Doubleday & Co., Inc.

———. 1963. Rainy nesting season in Arizona. *Proc [XIIIth] Internatl. Ornith. Congress* 2:

620–22, ed. C. G. Sibley. Ithaca, N.Y.: Amer. Ornith. Union.

Marshall, Jr., J. T., and Johnson, R. R. 1968. Canyon brown towhee. In *Life histories of North American cardinals, grosbeaks, buntings, towhees, finches, sparrows, and allies,* comp. A. C. Bent *et al.,* ed. O. L. Austin, Jr. U.S. Natl. Mus. Bull. no. 237, pt. 2. Washington, D.C.

Marti, C. D. 1973. Food consumption and pellet formation rates in four owl species. *Wilson Bull.* 85(2):178–81.

Martin, A. C.; Erickson, R. C.; and Steenis, J. H. 1957. *Improving duck marshes by weed control.* U.S. Dept. Inter., Fish and Wildlife Service Circ. no. 19. Washington, D.C.

Martin, A. C., and Nelson, A. L. 1952. Every ounce counts. *Sports Afield,* September, pp. 17–23.

Martin, A. C., and Uhler, F. M. 1939. *Food of game ducks in the United States and Canada.* U.S. Dept. Agric. Tech. Bull. no. 634. Washington, D.C.

Martin, A. C.; Zim, H. S.; and Nelson, A. L. 1951. *American wildlife and plants.* New York: McGraw-Hill Book Company.

Martin, A. G. 1963. *Hand-taming wild birds at the feeder.* Portland, Me.: The Bond Wheelwright Co.

Martin, D. J. 1973a. Selected aspects of burrowing owl ecology and behavior. *Condor* 75(4):446–56.

———. 1973b. A spectograph analysis of burrowing owl vocalizations. *Auk* 90:564–78.

———. 1974. Copulatory and vocal behavior by a pair of whiskered owls. *Auk* 91(3):619–24.

Martin, E. T. 1916. The speed of ducks. *Forest and Stream.* 86:1147–48.

Martin, R. F. 1971. The cañon wren *(Catherpes mexicanus)* raiding food storage of a tripoxylid wasp. *Auk* 88:677.

———. 1974. Syntopic culvert nesting of cave and barn swallows in Texas. *Auk* 91(4):776–82.

Martin, S. G. 1973. Longevity surprise: The bobolink. *Bird-Banding* 44:57–58.

Martini, E. 1964. Otolithen in Gewöllen der Raubseeschwalbe [Otoliths in pellets of Caspian terns]. *Bonner Zoologische Beiträge* 15:59–71.

Mascher, J. W. 1966. Weight variations in resting dunlins *(Caladris a. alpina)* on autumn migration in Sweden. *Bird-Banding* 37(1):1–34.

Maslowski, K. H. 1953. Naturalist afield. *Cincinnati Enquirer,* May 17.

Mason; E. A. 1944. Parasitism by Protocalliphora and management of cavity-nesting birds. *Jour. Wildlife Management* 8(3):232–47.

Matheson, C. 1969. A short note on the treatment of gas gangrene in the Queen Charlotte sawwhet owl, *Cryptoglaux acadica brooksi. Avicultural Magazine* 75(4):151.

Matheson, R. 1944. *Handbook of the mosquitoes of North America.* 2d ed. Ithaca, N.Y.: Comstock Publishing Co., Inc.

Matoltsy, A. G. 1962. Mechanism of keratinization. In *Fundamentals of keratinization,* ed. E. O. Butcher and R. F. Sognnaes. Amer. Assoc. Advanc. Sci. Publication no. 70, pp. 1–25. Washington, D.C.

Matray, P. F. 1974. Broad-winged hawk nesting and ecology. *Auk* 91(2):307–24.

Matteson, E. A. 1924. Dandy. *Bird-Lore* 26:169–70.

Matteson, R. E. 1970. Bronzed cowbird taken in Florida. *Auk* 87(3):88.

Matthew, W. D. 1939. *Climate and evolution.* New York: New York Acad. of Sci., Special Publications.

Matthews, G. V. T. 1955. *Bird navigation.* London: Cambridge University Press.

———. 1961 "Nonsense" orientation in the mallard *(Anas platyrhynchos)* and its relation to experiments in bird navigation. *Ibis* 103a:211–20.

———. 1963. The astronomical bases of "nonsense" orientation in the mallard. *Proc. [XIIIth] Internatl. Ornith. Congress,* pp. 415–

29, ed. C. G. Sibley. Ithaca, N.Y.: Amer. Ornith. Union.

———. 1968. *Bird navigation.* 2d ed. (paperback). Cambridge: At the University Press.

Matthews, L. H. 1964a. Albatross. In *A new dictionary of birds,* ed. A. L. Thomson. New York: McGraw-Hill Book Company.

———. 1964b. Torpidity. In *A new dictionary of birds,* ed. A. L. Thomson. New York: McGraw-Hill Book Company.

Matthiessen, P. 1959. *Wildlife in America.* New York: The Viking Press.

———. 1967. Chapter 6. In *The shorebirds of North America,* ed. and spons. G. D. Stout. New York: The Viking Press.

———. 1973. *The wind birds.* New York: The Viking Press.

Matthysse, J. G. 1972. External parasites. In *Diseases of poultry,* 6th ed, ed. M. S. Hofstad *et al.* Ames, Iowa: Iowa State University Press.

Maunder, J. E., and Threlfall, W. 1972. The breeding biology of the black-legged kittiwake in Newfoundland. *Auk* 89:789–816.

Maxwell, II, G. R., and Putnam, L. S. 1972. Incubation, care of young, and nest success of the common grackle *(Quiscalus quiscula)* in northern Ohio. *Auk* 89:349–59.

May, J. B. 1935. *The hawks of North America: Their field identification and feeding habits.* New York: Natl. Assoc. Audubon Societies.

Mayfield, H. F. 1960. *The Kirtland's warbler.* Cranbrook Inst. Sci. Bull. no. 40. Bloomfield Hills, Mich.

———. 1972. Third dicennial census of Kirtland's warbler. *Auk* 89(2):263–68.

———. 1973. Kirtland's warbler census, 1973. *Amer. Birds* 27(6):950–52.

———. 1978. Red phalaropes breeding on Bathurst island. *Living Bird,* 17th annual, pp. 7–39.

Maynard, C. J. 1928. *Vocal organs of talking birds and some other species.* West Newton, Mass.: Privately published by the author.

Mayr, E. 1937. The homing of birds. *Bird-Lore* 39(1):5–13.

———. 1942. *Systematics and the origin of species.* New York: Columbia University Press.

———. 1946a. History of North American bird fauna. *Wilson Bull.* 58:3–41.

———. 1946b. The number of species of birds. *Auk* 63:64–69.

———. 1951. *Speciation in birds: Progress Report on the years 1938–50.* Pro. [Xth] Internatl. Ornith. Congress. Pp. 91–131. Uppsala, Sweden: Almquist and Wiksells Boktryckeric AB.

———. 1956. Is the great white heron a good species? *Auk* 73:71–77.

———. 1959. Trends in avian systematics. *Ibis* 101:293–302.

———. 1963. *Animal species and evolution.* Cambridge, Mass.: Harvard University Press.

———. 1964a. Inferences concerning the Tertiary American bird faunas. *Proc. Natl. Acad. Sci.* 51(2):280–88.

———. 1964b. Nearctic region. In *A new dictionary of birds,* ed. A. L. Thomson. New York: McGraw-Hill Book Company.

———. 1964c. Neotropical region. In *A new dictionary of birds,* ed. A. L. Thomson. New York: McGraw-Hill Book Company.

———. 1975. Materials for a history of American ornithology. In *Ornithology: From Aristotle to the present,* by E. Stresemann. Cambridge, Mass.: Harvard University Press.

Mayr, E.; Linsley, E. G.; and Usinger, R. L. 1953. *Methods and principles of systematic zoology.* New York: McGraw-Hill Book Company.

Mayr, E., and Short, L. L. 1970. *Species taxa of North American Birds.* Publ. Nuttall Ornith. Club no. 9. Cambridge, Mass.

Mazzeo, R. 1953. Homing of the Manx shearwater. *Auk* 70(2):200–201.

McAtee, W. L. 1908. *Food habits of the grosbeaks.*

U.S. Dept. Agric., Bur. Biol. Surv. Bull. no. 32. Washington, D.C.

———. 1911a. *Our vanishing shorebirds*. U. S. Dept. Agric., Bur. Biol. Surv. Circ. no. 79. Washington, D.C.

———. 1911b. *Woodpeckers in relation to trees and wood products*. U.S. Dept. Agric., Bur. Biol. Surv. Bull. no. 39. Washington, D.C.

———. 1914. Birds transporting food supplies. *Auk* 31:404–5.

———. 1915. *Eleven important wild-duck foods*. U.S. Dept. Agric. Bull. no. 205. Washington, D.C.

———. 1917. The shedding of the stomach lining of birds, particularly as exemplified by the Anatidae. *Auk* 34(4):415–21.

———. 1918. *Food habits of mallard ducks*. U.S. Dept. Agric. Bull. no. 720. Washington, D.C.

———. 1920. The local suppression of agricultural pests by birds. *Annual Rept. Smithsonian Inst*, pp. 411–38.

———. 1922. Notes on the food habits of the shoveler or spoonbill duck *(Spatula clypeata)*. *Auk* 39(3):380–86.

———. 1923. *Local names of migratory game birds*. U.S. Dept. Agric. Misc. Circ. no. 13. Washington, D.C.

———. 1924. Do bird families have any permanency? *Condor* 26:193.

———. 1926. The relation of birds to woodlots in New York State. *Roosevelt Wildlife Bull*. 4(1): 8–152.

———. 1927. The birds at dinner. *Holland's Magazine* 46(6).

———. 1930. *Propogation of aquatic game birds*. U.S. Dept. Agric. Farmer's Bull. no. 1612.

———. 1931. *Local bird refuges*. U.S. Dept. Agric. Farmer's Bull. no. 1644.

———. 1932a. A discussion of inbreeding: A real symposium on this subject. *Modern Game Breeding and Hunting Club News* 2 (October).

———. 1932b. *Effectiveness in nature of the so-called protective adaptations in the animal kingdom, chiefly as illustrated by the food habits of nearctic birds*. Smithsonian Mis. Coll. no. 85(7). Washington, D.C.

———. 1933a. Bird allies of the farmer. Excerpt from hearing before the subcommittee of House Committee on Appropriations, etc. U.S. Dept. Agric., Bur. Biol. Surv. Washington, D.C.

———. 1933b. Economic ornithology. In *Fifty years' progress of American ornithology: 1883–1933*. Lancaster, Pa.: Amer. Ornith. Union.

———. 1939. *Wildfowl food plants: Their value, propagation and management*. Ames, Iowa: Collegiate Press, Inc., of Iowa State College.

———. 1940a. Mimicry by a brown thrasher. *Auk* 57:574.

———. 1940b. A venture in songbird management. *Jour. Wildlife Management* 4(1):85–96.

McAtee, W. L., ed. 1945. *The ring-necked pheasant and its management in North America*. Washington, D.C.: Amer. Wildlife Inst.

———. 1946. The economic status of flocking birds. *Condor* 48(1)29–31.

———. 1950a. Adoption of a human parent by bobwhite chicks. *Auk* 67(4):513.

———. 1950b. Birds do hibernate! *Audubon* 52(6):376–79.

———. 1952. Thomas Pennant. *Nature Magazine* 45:98, 108.

———. 1954–55. Carolina bird names. *Chat* 18 (3, 4); 19 (1).

———. 1955a. Folk names of Florida birds. *Florida Nat*. 28:35–37, 64, 83–87, 91.

———. 1955b. Folk names of Georgia birds. *Oriole* 20(1):1–14.

———. 1955c. Folk names of New England birds. *Bull. Mass. Audubon Soc*. 39:307–16, 375–79, 441–46.

———. 1956a. Folk names of Florida birds. *Florida Nat*. 29(1):25–28.

———. 1956b. Folk names of New England birds. *Bull. Mass. Audubon Soc*. 40:17–22, 79–84, 127–30, 253–56.

———. 1956c. In memoriam: Theodore Sherman Palmer. *Auk* 73(3):366–377.

———. 1957a. *Folk names of Canadian birds*. Natl. Mus. Canada, Biol. Ser. 51, Bull. no. 149. Ottawa.

———. 1957b. The North American birds of Linnaeus. *Jour. Soc. for Bibliog. Nat. Hist*. 3(5): 291–300.

———. 1959. American bird names: Two studies. Chapel Hill, N.C.: Privately published by author.

McAtee, W. L., and Piper, S. E. 1936. *Excluding birds from reservoirs and fish ponds*. U.S. Dept. Agric., Bur. Biol. Surv. Leaflet no. 120. Washington, D.C.

McAtee, W. L., and Stoddard, H. L. 1945. Wettable water birds. *Auk* 62:303–4.

McCabe, R. A. 1965. Nest construction of house wrens. *Condor* 67(3):229–34.

———. 1970. A fawn-colored gray partridge *(Perdix perdix)* from Wisconsin. *Auk* 87(2):375–76.

McCabe, R. A., and Deutsch, H. F. 1952. The relationship of certain birds as indicated by their egg-white proteins. *Auk* 69:1–18.

McCabe, R. A., and Hawkins, A. S. 1946. The Hungarian partridge in Wisconsin. *Amer. Midland-Nat*. 36:1–75.

McCabe, T. T. 1942. Types of shorebird flight. *Auk* 59:110–11.

McCamey, F. 1950. A puzzling warbler from Michigan. *Jack-Pine Warbler* 28:67–72.

McCann, L. J. 1939. Studies of grit requirements of certain upland game birds. *Jour. Wildlife Management* 3(1):31–41.

———. 1961. Grit as an ecological factor. *Amer. Midland-Nat*. 65(1):187–92.

McCaskie, G. 1970. Cape petrel off Monterey, California. *Calif. Birds* 1(1):39–40.

———. 1971. Southern Pacific coast region. *Amer. Birds* 25:906.

———. 1972. Southern Pacific coast region. *Amer. Birds* 26:906.

———; Devillers, A. M.; Craig, A. M.; Lyons, C. R.; Coughran, V. P.; and Craig, J. T. 1970. A checklist of the birds of California. *California Birds* 1:4–28.

McClure, H. E. 1943. Albino western meadowlark. *Auk* 60(1):98–99.

———. 1944. Nest survival over winter. *Auk* 61(3):384–89.

———. 1945. Effects of a tornado on birdlife. *Auk* 62:414–18.

———. 1962. Ten years and 10,000 birds. *Bird-Banding* 33(1):1–21, 69–84.

McDermott, J. F., ed. 1951. *Up the Missouri with Audubon: The journal of Edward Harris*. Norman, Okla.: University of Oklahoma Press.

McElroy, Jr. T. P. 1974. *The habitat guide to birding*. New York: Alfred A. Knopf, Inc.

McGahan, J. 1966. Ecology of the golden eagle. M.S. thesis, University of Montana, Missoula.

McGregor, R. 1900. A list of unrecorded albinos. *Condor* 2:86–88.

McGrew, Albert D. 1971. Nesting of the ringed kingfisher in the United States. *Auk* 88(3):665–66.

McIlhenny, E. A. 1936. Purple gallinules *(Ionornis martinica)* are predatory. *Auk* 53:327–28.

———. 1937. Results of 1936 bird banding operation at Avery Island, Louisiana, with special reference to sex ratios and hybrids. *Bird-Banding* 8(3):117–21.

———. 1940. Albinism in mockingbirds. *Jour. Heredity* 41:433–38.

McKinney, F. 1965. The spring behavior of wild Steller eiders. *Condor* 67(4):273–90.

McLaren, M. A. 1975. Breeding biology of the boreal chickadee. *Wilson Bull*. 87(3):344–54.

McLaurin, E. 1957. You gotta out-smart 'em. *Florida Wildlife* 11(7):20–23, 35.

McLean, D. D. 1930. The speed of flight of certain birds. *Gull* 12(3):1–2.

McNab, B. K. 1966. An analysis of the body temperatures of birds. *Condor* 68(1):47–55.

McNeil, R. 1969. La détermination du contenue lipidique et de la capacité de vol chez quelques espèces d'oiseau de rivage (Charadriidae et Scolopacidae). *Canadian Jour. Zool*. 47:525–36.

———. 1970. Hivernage et estivage d'oiseaux aquatiques nord-americains dans le nord-est du Venezuela (Mue accumulation de graisse, capacité de vol et routes de migration). *Oiseaux et R.F.O.* 40:185–302.

McNeil, R., and Burton, J. 1971. First authentic North American record of the British storm petrel. *Auk* 88(3):671–72.

McNulty, F. 1966. The thread remains thin. *New Yorker* (August):83.

Meade, G. M. 1942. Calcium chloride—A death lure for crossbills. *Auk* 59(3):439–40.

———. 1945. A study of bird "pox," or "foot disease." *Bird-Banding* 16(1):38.

Meaden, F. 1971. Keeping dippers. *Aviculture Magazine* 77(5):171–72.

Meanley, B. 1969. *Natural history of the king rail*. N. Amer. Fauna no. 67. Washington, D.C.: U.S. Dept. Inter., Fish and Wildlife Service.

———. 1971a. *Blackbirds and the southern rice crop*. U.S. Dept. Inter., Fish and Wildlife Service. Res. Publ. no. 100. Washington, D.C.

———. 1971b. *Natural history of the Swainson's warbler*. N. Amer. Fauna no. 69. Washington, D.C.: U.S. Dept. Inter., Fish and Wildlife Service.

Mearns, E. A. 1903. Feathers beside the Styx. *Condor* 5(2):36–38.

Meeuse, J. D. 1961. *The story of pollination*. New York: The Ronald Press Co.

Mehner, J. F., and Wallace, G. J. 1959. Robin populations and insecticides. *Atlantic Nat*. 14: 4–9.

Meier, A. H. 1973. Daily hormone rhythms in the white-throated sparrow. *Amer. Scientist* 61(2): 184–87.

Meier, A. H., and Davis, K. B. 1967. *Gen. Comp. Endocrinol*. 8:110–14.

Meiners, W. R. 1970. *Snake River birds of prey natural area*. U.S. Bur. Land Management Report. Boise, Idaho.

Meinertzhagen, R. 1920. Some preliminary remarks on the altitude of migratory flight. *Ibis* 62:920–36.

———. 1955. The speed and altitude of bird flight. *Ibis* 97:81–117.

———. 1959. *Pirates and predators: The piratical and predatory habits of birds*. London: Oliver & Boyd, Ltd.

———. 1964a. Grit. In *A new dictionary of birds*, ed. A. L. Thomson. New York: McGraw-Hill Book Company.

———. 1964b. Lark. In *A new dictionary of birds*, ed. A. L. Thomson. New York: McGraw-Hill Book Company.

———. 1964c. Palaearctic region. In *A new dictionary of birds*, ed. A. L. Thomson. New York: McGraw-Hill Book Company.

Melville, R. 1964. Pollinators and distributors. In *A new dictionary of birds*, ed. A. L. Thomson. New York: McGraw-Hill Book Company.

Mendall, H. L. 1937. Nesting of the bay-breasted warbler. *Auk* 54:429–39.

———. 1958. The ring-necked duck in the Northeast. *Univ. Maine Bull*. 60(16):317.

Mendall, H. L., and Nelson, H. K. 1964. Adventuresome waterfowl. In *Waterfowl tomorrow*, ed. J. P. Linduska and A. L. Nelson. Washington, D.C.: U.S. Dept. Inter., Fish and Wildlife Service.

Meng, H. 1959. Food habits of nesting Cooper's hawks and goshawks in New York and Pennsylvania. *Wilson Bull*. 71(2):169–74.

Mengel, R. M. 1963. A second probable hybrid between the scarlet and western tanagers. *Wilson Bull*. 75(2):201–3.

———. 1964. The probable history of species formation in some northern wood warblers (Parulidae). *Living Bird*, 3d annual, p. 943.

———. 1970. The North American central plains as an isolating agent in bird speciation. In *Pleistocene and recent environments of the central great plains*, ed. W. Dort, Jr., and J. K. Jones, Jr. Lawrence, Kans.: University of Kansas Press.

Mengel, R. M., and Jenkinson, M. A. 1971. Vocalizations of the chuck-will's-widow and some related behavior. *Living Bird*, 10th annual, pp. 171–84.

Mengel, R. M., and Sharpe, R. S. 1972. Wing-clapping in territorial and courtship behavior of the chuck-will's-widow and poor-will. *Auk* 89(2):440–44.

Meredith, R. L. 1934. The ancient and noble sport of falconry. *Sportsman*, June, pp. 46–48.

Merrell, Jr., T. R. 1970. A swimming bald eagle. *Wilson Bull.* 82(2):220.

Merriam, C. H. 1894. Laws of temperature control of the geographical distribution of terrestrial animals and plants. *Natl. Geographic Magazine* 6:229–38.

———. 1898. *Life zones and crop zones of the United States*. U.S. Dept. Agric., Bur. Biol. Surv. Bull. no. 10. Washington, D.C.

Merrill, G. W. 1961. Loss of 1,000 lesser sandhill cranes. *Auk* 78(4):641–42.

Merrill, J. C. 1898. Spotted sandpiper removing its young. *Auk* 15:52.

Merritt, J. H. 1951. Little orphan ani. *Audubon* 53(4):224–31.

Mester, H., and Prünte, W. 1957. Flight copulation of the swift (*Micropus apus*). *Ornithologische Mitteilungen* 9:226.

Mewaldt, L. R., and Farner, D. S. 1953. Notes on a roosting flock of gray-crowned rosy finches. *Bird-Banding* 24(4):141–43.

Mewaldt, L. R.; Morton, M. L.; and Brown, I. L. 1964. Orientation of migratory restlessness in *Zonotrichia*. *Condor* 66:377–417.

Mewaldt, L. R., and Rose, R. G. 1960. Orientation of migratory restlessness in the white-crowned sparrow. *Science* 131:105–6.

Meyer, K. E. 1959. Ornithosis. 4th ed. In *Diseases of poultry*, ed. A. E. Biester and L. H. Schwarte. Ames, Iowa: Iowa State University Press.

Meyerrriecks, A. J. 1957a. "Bunching" reactions of cedar waxwings to attacks of a Cooper's hawk. *Wilson Bull.* 69(2):184.

———. 1957b. Field observations pertaining to the systematic status of the great white heron in the Florida Keys. *Auk* 74(4):469–78.

———. 1959a. "Foot paddling" behavior in a semi-palmated sandpiper. *Wilson Bull.* 71(3):277.

———. 1959b. Foot-stirring feeding behavior in herons. *Wilson Bull.* 71:153–58.

———. 1960. *Comparative breeding behavior of four species of North American herons*. Publ. Nuttall Ornith. Club no. 2. Cambridge, Mass.

———. 1962. Personal communication.

———. 1971. Further observations in use of the feet by foraging herons. *Wilson Bull.* 83:435–38.

———. 1972. Tool-using by a double-crested cormorant. *Wilson Bull.* 84:482–83.

Michael, C. W., and Michael, E. 1922. An adventure with a pair of harlequin ducks. *Auk* 38(1):14–23.

Michael, E. D. 1970. Wing-flashing in a brown thrasher and catbird. *Wilson Bull.* 82(3):330–31.

Michener, H., and Michener, J. R. 1935. Mockingbirds, their territories, and individualities. *Condor* 37:97–140.

———. 1936. Abnormalities in birds. *Condor* 38:102–9.

Michener, J. R. 1951. Territorial behavior and age composition in a population of mockingbirds at a feeding station. *Condor* 53:276–83.

Middendorf, A. X. 1855. Die Isepipetsen Russlands; Grundlagen zur Erforschung der Zugzeiten und Zugrichtungen der Vogel Russlands. *Mem. Acad. Sci. St. Petersbourg* 8:1–143.

Middleton, R. J. 1936. Interesting albinos. *Auk* 53(1):101.

———. 1939. The length of stay of migratory birds in southeastern Pennsylvania. *Bird-Banding* 10:145–49.

———. 1949. Tufted titmouse nesting seven years. *Bird-Banding* 20:151–52.

———. 1958. Scarlet tanager nine years old. *Bird-Banding* 29(1):43.

———. 1974. Fifty-two years of banding blue jays at Norristown, Pennsylvania. *Bird-Banding* 45(3):206–9.

Miliotis, P., and Buckley, P. A. 1975. The Massachusetts Ross' Gull. *Amer. Birds* 29(3):643–46.

Millar, M. 1967. *The birds and the beasts were there*. New York: Random House, Inc.

Miller, A. H. 1931. Systematic revision and natural history of the American shrikes (*Lanius*). *Univ. California Publ. Zool.* 38:11–242.

———. 1941. The buccal food-carrying pouches of the rosy finch. *Condor* 43:72–73.

———. 1950. California shrike. In *Life histories of North American wagtails, shrikes, vireos, and their allies*, by A. C. Bent. U.S. Natl. Mus. Bull. no. 197. Washington, D.C.

———. 1951. An analysis of the distribution of the birds of California. *Univ. California Pub. Zool.* 50:531–643.

———. 1955. Concepts and problems of avian systematics in relation to evolutionary processes. In *Recent studies in avian biology*, ed. A. Wolfson. Urbana, Ill.: University of Illinois Press.

———. 1957. Migratory flight of *Zonotrichia* at 10,000 feet above ground level. *Condor* 59:209–10.

———. 1963. Desert adaptations in birds. *Proc. [XIIIth] Internatl. Ornith. Congress*, pp. 666–74, ed. C. G. Sibley. Ithaca, N.Y.: Amer. Ornith. Union.

———. 1968. Northern sage sparrow, California sage sparrow, and Bell's sage sparrow. In *Life histories of North American cardinals, grosbeaks, buntings, towhees, finches, sparrows, and allies*, comp. A. C. Bent et al., ed. O. L. Austin, Jr. U.S. Natl. Mus. Bull. no. 237, pt. 2. Washington, D.C.

Miller, A. H.; Friedmann, H.; Griscom, L.; and Moore, R. T. 1957. *Distributional check-list of the birds of Mexico. Part II*. Pacific Coast Avifauna no. 33. Berkeley, Calif.: Cooper Ornith. Soc.

Miller, A. H.; McMillan, I. I.; and McMillan, E. 1965. *The current status and welfare of the California condor*. Natl. Audubon Soc. Res. Report no. 6. New York.

Miller, L. H. 1932. Waxwings eating spoiled fruits. *Condor* 34(4):189.

———. 1937. Bird trapping before Adam. *So. Alum. Quart. Rev.*, February, pp. 8–12.

———. 1938. The singing of the mockingbird. *Condor* 40:216–19.

Miller, R. C. 1947. Joseph Mailliard, 1857–1945. *Auk* 64(2):300–302.

———. 1950. Oldest bird nest. *Pacific Discovery* 3(4):29–30.

Miller, R. L. 1969. Starlings bred in captivity. *Auk* 86(4):763–64.

Miller, R. S. 1968. Conditions of competition between redwings and yellow-headed blackbirds. *Jour. Animal Ecology* 37(1):43–62.

———. 1973. The brood size of cranes. *Wilson Bull.* 85(4):436–41.

Miller, R. S., and Miller, R. E. 1971. Feeding activity and color preference of ruby-throated hummingbird. *Condor* 73(3):309–13.

Miller, W. de W. 1905. A note on the food of the bronzed grackle. *Bird-Lore* 7(2):144.

Millet, C. 1866. *Zoological Record* 3:46.

Millikan, G. A. 1939. Muscle hemoglobin. *Physiol. Rev.* 19:503–23.

Milne, L. J., and Milne, M. 1952. *Famous naturalists*. New York: Dodd, Mead & Company.

———. 1961. *The balance of nature*. New York: Alfred A. Knopf, Inc.

———. 1962. *The senses of animals and men*. New York: Atheneum Publishers.

Miner, R. W. 1950. *Field book of seashore life*. New York: G. P. Putnam's Sons.

Miskimen, M. 1951. Sound production in passerine birds. *Auk* 68:493–504.

———. 1957. Absence of syrinx in the turkey vulture, *Cathartes aura*. *Auk* 74:104–5.

Mitchell, D. L. 1967. Partial albino white-throated sparrow. *EBBA News* 30(4):149.

Mitchell, G. A. 1968. A golden eagle nesting in the pine ridge. *Nebraska Bird Rev.* 36(2):33–35.

Mitchell, H. D. 1954. An unusual killdeer nesting. *Kingbird* 4(3):66–68.

Mitchell, P. C. 1911. On longevity and relative viability in mammals and birds; with a note on the theory of longevity. *Proc. Zool. Soc. London* 81:425–548.

Moisan, G. 1967. *The green-winged teal: Distribution, migration, and population dynamics*. Washington, D.C.: U.S. Dept. Inter., Fish and Wildlife Service.

Moldenhauer, R. R. 1974. First clay-colored robin collected in the United States. *Auk* 91(4):839–40.

Moldenhauer, R. R., and Bryan, K. B. 1970. An interesting recovery of a banded evening grosbeak during the 1968–69 winter incursion into east Texas. *Bird-Banding* 41(1):39.

Moldenhauer, R. R., and Wiens, J. A. 1970. The water economy of the sage sparrow, *Amphiza belli nevadensis*. *Condor* 72:265–75.

Mollhoff, W. J. 1976. Avian tuberculosis in a saw-whet owl. *Wilson Bull.* 88(3):505.

Monroe, Jr., B. L., and Plunkett, R. L. 1976. *The blackbird problem*. Nat. Audubon Soc. Leaflet. New York.

Monson, G. 1957a. Lucy's warbler. In *The warblers of America*, ed. L. Griscom and A. Sprunt, Jr. New York: The Devin-Adair Co.

———. 1957b. Red-faced warbler. In *The warblers of America*, ed. L. Griscom and A. Sprunt, Jr. New York: The Devin-Adair Co.

———. 1968. Botteri's sparrow. In *Life histories of North American cardinals, grosbeaks, buntings, towhees, finches, sparrows, and allies*, comp. A. C. Bent et al., ed. O. L. Austin, Jr. U.S. Natl. Mus. Bull. no. 237, pt. 2. Washington, D.C.

Moody, P. A. 1953. *Introduction to evolution*. New York: Harper & Brothers.

Moore, R. 1964. *Evolution*. New York: Time Inc. Life Nature Library.

Moreau, R. E. 1940. Hornbill studies. *Ibis* 4 (14th ser.):639–56.

———. 1964a. Breeding season. In *A new dictionary of birds*, ed. A. L. Thomson. New York: McGraw-Hill Book Company.

———. 1964b. Oriole (1). In *A new dictionary of birds*, ed. A. L. Thomson. New York: McGraw-Hill Book Company.

———. 1966. On estimates of the past numbers and of the average longevity of avian species. *Auk* 83:403–15.

Morris, G. S. 1902. Edward Harris. *Cassinia* 6:1–5. Philadelphia.

Morris, R. B. 1960. Is the eagle un-American? *New York Times Magazine*, February 14.

Morrison, R. I. G. 1975. Migration and morphometrics of European knot and turnstone on Ellesmere Island, Canada. *Bird-Banding* 46(4):290–301.

Morse, D. H. 1968. The use of tools by brown-headed nuthatches. *Wilson Bull.* 80(2):220–24.

———. 1972. Habitat utilization of the red-cockaded woodpecker during the winter. *Auk* 89(2):429–35.

———. 1978. Structure and foraging patterns of flocks of tits and associated species in English woodland during the winter. *Ibis* 120:298–312.

Morse, M. E. 1963. Another albinistic blue jay. *Auk* 80(3):374.

Mosby, H. S., and Handley, C. O. 1943. *The wild*

turkey in Virginia. Richmond, Va.: Commission of Game and Inland Fisheries.

Moseley, D. 1925. The accuracy of the pecking response of chicks. *Jour. Compar. Psychol.* 5: 75–97.

Mosher, J. A., and Henny, C. J. 1976. Thermal adaptiveness of plumage color in screech owls. *Auk* 93:614–19.

Mosquin, T. 1970. Preface to the reprint, "Great moments in action. The story of the sun life falcons." *Canadian Field-Nat.* 84(3):211.

Mowrer, O. H. 1950. The psychology of talking birds: A contribution to language and personality theory. In *Learning theory and personality dynamics,* ed. O. H. Mowrer. New York: The Ronald Press Co.

Moynihan, M. 1962. The organization and probable evolution of some mixed species flocks of neotropical birds. *Smithsonian Misc. Coll.* 143:1–140.

Mrosovsky, N. 1971. Black vulture attacks live turtle hatchings. *Auk* 88(3):672–73.

Mueller, C. D., and Hutt, F. B. 1941. Genetics of the fowl. 12 sex-linked, imperfect albinism. *Jour. Heredity* 32:71–80.

Mueller, H. C., and Berger, D. D. 1959. A second peregrine falcon banding returns from Uruguay. *Bird-Banding* 30(3):182–83.

———. 1961. Weather and fall migration of hawks at Cedar Grove, Wisconsin. *Wilson Bull.* 73(2):171–92.

———. 1967. Observations on migrating saw-whet owls. *Bird-Banding* 38(2):120–25.

———. 1970. Prey preferences in the sharp-shinned hawk: The role of sex experience, and motivation. *Auk* 87(3):452–57.

Mueller, H. C.; Berger, D. D.; and Allez, G. 1977a. Longevity record for the red-tailed hawk. *Bird-Banding* 48(2):169.

———. 1977b. The periodic invasions of goshawks. *Auk* 94:652–63.

Mugaas, J. N., and Templeton, J. L. 1970. Thermoregulation in the red-breasted nuthatch *(Sitta canadensis). Condor* 72(2):125–32.

Muir, J. 1894. The water ouzel. In *The mountains of California.* New York: Century Co.

Mulhern, B. M.; Reichel, W. L.; Locke, L. N.; Lamont, T. G.; Belisle, A.; Cromarte, E.; Bagley, G. E.; and Prouty, R. M. 1970. Organochlorine residues and autopsy data from bald eagles, 1966–68. *Pesticides Monitor Jour.* 4(3):141–44.

Mullan, J. W., and Applegate, R. L. 1969. The drowning of bobwhites in a large reservoir. *Wilson Bull.* 81(4):467.

Muller, K. A. 1970. Exhibiting and breeding elf owls, *Micrathene Whitneyi,* at Washington Zoo. *Internatl. Zoo Yearbook* [Zool. Soc. of London] 10:33–36.

Munro, J. A. 1936. A study of the ring-billed gull in Alberta, Canada. *Wilson Bull.* 48(3): 169–80.

———. 1941. Studies of waterfowl in British Columbia. Greater scaup duck, lesser scaup duck. *Canadian Jour. Res.* 19:113–38.

Munson, E. L. 1930. Timing the ducks. *Field and Stream* 35(5):18–20, 70–71.

Murdoch, J. 1885. Natural history of the report of the international polar expedition to Point Barrow, Alaska, Part 4. [*Birds,* pp. 104–28].

Murie, O. J. 1924. Nesting records of the wandering tattler and surf-bird in Alaska. *Auk* 41: 231–37.

———. 1929. Nesting of the snowy owl. *Condor* 31:3–12.

Murphey, E. E. 1939. Red-cockaded woodpecker. In *Life history of North American woodpeckers,* by A. C. Bent. U.S. Natl. Mus. Bull. no. 174. Washington, D.C.

Murphy, R. C. 1936. *Oceanic birds of South America.* New York: The Macmillan Company.

———. 1950. Frank Michler Chapman, 1864–1945. *Auk* 67:307–15.

———. 1956. John James Audubon: An evalua-

tion of the man and his work. *New York Historical Soc. Quart.,* October.

———. 1962. Personal communication.

———. 1965. Gannets and boobies. In *Water, prey, and game birds of North America,* ed. A. Wetmore. Washington, D.C.: Natl. Geographic Soc.

———. 1972. In Review of: Birds of the Antarctic and Subantarctic. *Wilson Bull.* 84(4):505.

Murphy, R. C., and Mowbray, L. S. 1951. New light on the cahow, *Pterodrama cahow. Auk* 68:266–80.

Murray, B. G. 1968. The relationships of sparrows in the genera *Ammodramus; Passerherbulus,* and *Ammospiza* with a description of a hybrid Le Conte's × sharp-tailed sparrow. *Auk* 85(4):586–93.

Murray, Jr., B. G., and Jehl, Jr., J. R. 1964. Weights of autumn migrants from coastal New Jersey. *Bird-Banding* 35(4):253–63.

Murray, J. J. 1933. An albino Canada goose. *Bird-Lore* 35(4):207.

Murton, R. K. 1971. Man and birds. New York: Taplinger Publ. Co.

Mussehl, T. W. 1960. Blue grouse production, movements, and populations in the Bridger Mountains, Montana. *Jour. Wildlife Management* 24:60–68.

Musselman, T. E. 1928. Foot disease of chipping sparrow. *Auk* 30:137–47.

———. 1935. Three years of eastern bluebird banding and study. *Bird-Banding* 6:117–25.

———. 1941. Bluebird mortality in 1940. *Auk* 58:409–10.

Mutchler, T. 1972. Surgical treatment, by pinning, of longbone fractures, in raptors. *Hawk Mt. Sanctuary Assoc., News Letter to Members,* no. 44.

———. 1973. Notes on the care of sick and injured birds. *Hawk Mt. Sanctuary Assoc., News Letter to Members,* no. 45, pp. 42–45.

Myrcha, A., and Pinowski, J. 1970. Weight body composition and caloric value of postjuvenal molting European tree sparrows. *Condor* 72:175–81.

N

Naether, C. A. 1939. *The book of the pigeon.* Philadelphia: David McKay Company.

Nagy, A. C. 1972a. 1971 Curator's report. *Hawk Mt. Sanctuary Assoc. News Letter* no. 44.

———. 1972b. *The sparrow hawk.* Hawk Mt. Sanctuary Assoc. Leaflet, no. 44.

Narver, David W. 1970. Birds of the Chignik River Drainage, Alaska. *Condor* 72(1):102–5.

Naumberg, E. M. B. 1930. *The birds of Matto Grosso, Brazil.* Bull. Amer. Mus. Nat. Hist. no. 60.

Neff, J. A. 1947. *Habits, food, and economic status of the band-tailed pigeon.* N. Amer. Fauna no. 58. Washington, D.C.: U.S. Dept. Inter., Fish and Wildlife Service.

Nelson, B. 1968. *Galapagos: Islands of birds.* New York: William Morrow and Co.

Nelson, E. W. 1897. Preliminary descriptions of new birds from Mexico and Guatemala in the collections of the United States Department of Agriculture. *Auk* 14(1):50–76.

———. 1932. Henry W. Henshaw—Naturalist: 1850–1930. *Auk* 49:399–427.

Nelson, H. K. 1952. Hybridization of Canada geese with blue geese in the wild. *Auk* 69(4): 425–28.

Nelson, J. B. 1965. The behaviour of the gannet. *Brit. Birds* 58(7):233–88; (8):313–36.

———. 1975. The breeding biology of frigatebirds—A comparative review. *Living Bird,* 14th annual, pp. 113–55.

Nelson, M. W. 1969. The status of the peregrine falcon in the Northwest. In *Peregrine falcon populations: Their biology and decline,* ed. J. J. Hickey. Madison, Wisc.: University of Wisconsin Press.

Nelson, R. C. 1970. An additional nesting record of the Lucifer hummingbird in the United States. *Southwestern Naturalist* 15:135–36.

Nelson, R. W. 1968. Nest-robbing by Cooper's hawks. *Auk* 85:696–97.

———. 1971. Captive breeding of peregrines: Suggestions from their behavior in the wild. *Raptor Res. News* 5(2):54–82.

———. 1972. The incubation period in Peale's falcons. *Raptor Research* 6(1):11–15.

Nero, R. W. 1954. Plumage aberrations of the redwing. *Auk* 71:137–55.

———. 1956. A behavior study of the red-winged blackbird. *Wilson Bull.* 68(1):5–37; (2):129–50.

———. 1961. The gentle art of bird watching. *Canadian Audubon* 23:168–73.

———. 1970. Sharp-tailed grouse gives aggressive display to automobile. *Wilson Bull.* 82(2): 221–72.

Nesbitt, S. A.; Gilbert, D. T.; and Barbour, D. B. 1976. Capturing and banding limpkins in Florida. *Bird-Banding* 47(2):164–65.

Nestler, R. B. 1946. The mechanical value of grit for bobwhite quail. *Jour. Wildlife Management* 10(2):137–42.

Nestler, R. B., and Bailey, W. W. 1941. The toxicity of *Crotolaria spectabilis* seeds to quail. *Jour. Wildlife Management* 5:309.

Nestler, R. B., and Nelson, A. L. 1945. Inbreeding among pen-reared quail. *Auk* 62:217–22.

Nethersole-Thompson, D., and Nethersole-Thompson, M. 1979. *Greenshanks.* Vermillion, S.D.: Buteo Books.

Nettleship, D. N. 1968. The incubation period of the knot. *Auk* 85:687.

———. 1976. Gannets in North America: Present numbers and recent population changes. *Wilson Bull.* 88(2):300–313.

New Columbia encyclopedia. 1975. New York: Columbia University Press.

Newman, B. G. 1958. Soaring and gliding flight of the black vulture. *Jour. Exper. Biol.* 35:280–85.

Newman, G. A. 1970. Cowbird parasitism and nesting success of lark sparrows in southern Oklahoma. *Wilson Bull.* 82(3):304–9.

Newman, J. D. 1968. Arizona black-chinned sparrow. In *Life histories of North American cardinals, grosbeaks, buntings, towhees, finches, sparrows, and allies,* comp. A. C. Bent *et al.,* ed. O. L. Austin, Jr. U.S. Natl. Mus. Bull. no. 237, pt. 2. Washington, D.C.

Newman, R. J. 1959. The changing seasons. *Audubon Field Notes* 13(1):4.

Newton, A. 1893–96. *A dictionary of birds.* London: Adam and Charles Black, Ltd.

Newton, I. 1967. The feeding ecology of the bullfinch, *Pyrrhula pyrrhula* in southern England. *Jour. Animal Ecology* 36:721–44.

Nice, M. M. 1910. Food of the bobwhite. *Jour. Econ. Ent.* 3(3):295–313.

———. 1933a. Robin and Carolina chickadees remating. *Bird-Banding* 9(3):157.

———. 1933b. The theory of territorialism and its development. In *Fifty years progress of American ornithology, 1883–1933.* Lancaster, Pa.: Amer. Ornith. Union.

———. 1933c. Winter range of tufted titmice. *Wilson Bull.* 45:87.

———. 1934a. Longevity. *Bird-Banding* 5(3):142.

———. 1934b. Swedish banding papers. *Bird-Banding* 5(1):49–50.

———. 1935a. Finnish banding. *Bird-Banding* 6(3):108.

———. 1935b. Longevity. *Bird-Banding* 6(1):38–42.

———. 1935c. Longevity. *Bird-Banding* 6(2):73.

———. 1935d. Longevity. *Bird-Banding* 6(3):109.

———. 1937a. Results of ringing coots in Switzerland. *Bird-Banding* 8(3):128.

———. 1937b. *Studies in the life history of the song sparrow, Part 1.* Trans. Linnaean Soc. New York, no. 4.

———. 1939. *The watcher at the nest.* New York: The Macmillan Company.

_____. 1941a. Observations on the behavior of a young cedar waxwing. *Condor* 43:58–64.

_____. 1941b. The role of territory in bird life. *Amer. Midland-Nat.* 26(3):441–87.

_____. 1943. *Studies in the life history of the song sparrow.* Part 2. Trans. Linnaean Soc. New York, no. 6.

_____. 1949. The laying rhythm of cowbirds. *Wilson Bull.* 61:231–34.

_____. 1954. Problems of incubation periods in North American birds. *Condor* 56(4):173–97.

_____. 1957. Nesting success in altricial birds. *Auk* 74(3):305–21.

_____. 1962a. *Development of behavior in precocial birds.* Trans. Linnaean Soc. New York, no. 8.

_____. 1962b. Oystercatcher 34 years old—The oldest ringed bird to date at the Vogelwarte Helgoland! *Bird-Banding* 33(4):205.

_____. 1966a. Greatest ages reached by ringed birds in Switzerland. *Bird-Banding* 37(2):128.

_____. 1966b. Territory defence in the oystercatcher. *Bird-Banding* 37(2):132.

_____. 1968. Mississippi song sparrow. In *Life histories of North American cardinals, grosbeaks, buntings, towhees, finches, sparrows, and allies,* comp. A. C. Bent *et al.,* ed. O. L. Austin, Jr. U.S. Natl. Mus. Bull. no. 237, pt. 3. Washington, D.C.

Nice, M. M., and Nice, C. 1950. The appetite of a black and white warbler. *Wilson Bull.* 62:94–95.

Nice, M. M., and Thomas, R. H. 1948. A nesting of the Carolina wren. *Wilson Bull.* 60:139–58.

Nichols, C. K. 1948. Fall migration—New York region. *Audubon Field Notes* 2(1):6.

Nichols, D. V. 1940. Varied thrush trapped by acorn. *Condor* 42(3):164.

Nichols, Jr., E. R., 1965. Albino tree swallow. *EBBA News* 28(5):241.

Nichols, J. T. 1920. Limicoline voices. *Auk* 37:519–40.

_____. 1931. Notes on the flocking of shore birds. *Auk* 48:181–85.

Nicholson, E. M. 1929. *How birds live.* 2d ed. London: Williams & Norgate, Ltd.

Nickell, W. P. 1951. Studies of habitats, territory and nests of the eastern goldfinch. *Auk* 68:447–70.

_____. 1954. Mourning doves nest in black-crowned night heron nests. *Wilson Bull.* 66:137.

_____. 1957. Robin uses same nest for three sets of eggs in one season. *Auk* 74(1):95.

_____. 1964a. Brown-headed cowbird fledged in barn swallow nest. *Wilson Bull.* 76(1):94.

_____. 1964b. The effects of probable frostbite on the feet of mourning doves wintering in southern Michigan. *Wilson Bull.* 76(1):94–75.

_____. 1964c. Two albino herring gulls found at Rogers City, Michigan. *Auk* 81(4):560.

_____. 1965a. Adaptive behavior under handicaps of several species of Michigan birds. *Wilson Bull.* 77(4):396–400.

_____. 1965b. Birds and insects feed at sapsucker trees. *Bird-Banding* 36(3):192–93.

_____. 1965c. Habitats, territory and nesting of the catbird. *Amer. Midland-Nat.* 73(2):433–78.

_____. 1966. The nesting of the black-crowned night heron and its associates. *Jack Pine Warbler* 44(3):130–39.

_____. 1968. Return of northern migrants to tropical winter quarters and banded birds recovered in the United States. *Bird-Banding* 39(2):107–16.

Nisbet, I. C. T. 1963. Measurements with radar of the height of nocturnal migration over Cape Cod, Massachusetts. *Bird-Banding* 34:57–67.

_____. 1970. Autumn migration of the blackpoll warbler: Evidence for long flight provided by Regional Survey. *Bird-Banding* 41(3):207–40.

_____. 1976. Early stages in postfledging dispersal of common terns. *Bird-Banding* 47(2):163–64.

Nisbet, I. C. T.; Drury, Jr., W. H.; and Baird, J. 1963. Weight-loss during migration: Part I: Deposition and consumption of fat by the blackpoll warbler *Dendroica striata. Bird-Banding* 34(3):107–38.

Noble, E. R., and Noble, G. A. 1971. *Parasitology.* 3d ed. Philadelphia: Lea and Febiger.

Noble, G. K. 1931. *The biology of the Amphibia.* New York: McGraw-Hill Book Company.

_____. 1936. Courtship and sexual selection of the flicker. *Auk* 53:269–82.

_____. 1939. The role of dominance in the social life of birds. *Auk* 56:263–73.

Noble, G. K., and Lehrman, D. S. 1940. Egg recognition by the laughing gull. *Auk* 57:22–43.

Nolan, Jr., V. 1959. Pileated woodpecker attacks pilot black snake at tree cavity. *Wilson Bull.* 71(4):381–82.

_____. 1968. Eastern song sparrow. In *Life histories of North American cardinals, grosbeaks, buntings, towhees, finches, sparrows, and allies,* comp. A. C. Bent *et al.,* ed. O. L. Austin, Jr. U.S. Natl. Mus. Bull. no. 237, pt. 3. Washington, D.C.

Nopcsa, F. 1907. Ideas on the origin of flight. *Proc. Zool. Soc. London,* pp. 223–36.

_____. 1923. On the origin of flight in birds. *Proc. Zool. Soc. London,* pp. 463–77.

Norris, J. P. 1884. Instruction for collecting birds' eggs. *Young Oologist* 1:19.

Norris, R. A. 1958. Comparative biosystematics. Life history of the nuthatches *Sitta pygmaea* and *Sitta pusilla. Univ. California Publ. Zool.* 56:119–300.

_____. 1968a. Green-tailed towhee. In *Life histories of North American cardinals, grosbeaks, buntings, towhees, finches, sparrows, and allies,* comp. A. C. Bent *et al.,* ed. O. L. Austin, Jr. U.S. Natl. Mus. Bull. no. 237, pt. 1. Washington, D.C.

_____. 1968b. Seaside sparrow: Western gulf coast subspecies. In *Life histories of North American cardinals, grosbeaks, buntings, towhees, finches, sparrows, and allies,* comp. A. C. Bent *et al.,* ed. O. L. Austin, Jr. U.S. Natl. Mus. Bull. no. 237, pt. 2. Washington, D.C.

Norris, R. T.; Beule, J. D.; and Studholme, A. F. 1940. Banding woodcocks on Pennsylvania singing grounds. *Jour. Wildlife Management* 4:8–14.

Norris-Elye, L. S. T. 1944. Leopard frogs devouring small birds. *Auk* 61:643–44.

_____. 1945. Heat insulation in the tarsi and toes of birds. *Auk* 62:455.

North, M. E. W. 1944. The use of animate perches by the carmine bee-eater (*Merops nubicus*) and other African species. *Ibis* 86:171–75.

Norton, A. H. 1942. In memoriam: Nathan Clifford Brown—1856–1941. *Auk* 59(4):471–76.

Norton, D. W. 1971. Homing by nesting semipalmated sandpipers displaced from Barrow, Alaska. *Bird-Banding* 42(4):295–97.

_____. 1972a. Incubation schedules of four species of Calidridine sandpipers at Barrow, Alaska. *Condor* 74(2):164–76.

_____. 1972b. Personal communication.

Nottebohm, F. 1975. Vocal behavior in birds. In *Avian biology,* ed. D. S. Farner, J. R. King, and K. C. Parkes. Vol. 5, pp. 287–332. New York: Academic Press, Inc.

Novy, F. O., and McGrew, A. D. 1974. Orange-breasted bunting in southern Texas. *Auk* 91:178–79.

Nuttall, T. 1834. *Manual of ornithology of the United States and Canada.* Vol. 2. Boston, Mass.: Hilliard, Gray & Co.

Nutting, C. C. 1882. On a collection of birds from the hacienda "La alma," Gulf of Nicyoa, Costa Rica (with critical notes by R. Ridgway). *Proc. U.S. Natl. Mus.* 5:382–409.

Nye, Jr., A. G. 1963. Personal communication.

_____. 1966. Falconry. In *Birds in our lives,* ed. A. Stefferud and A. L. Nelson. Washington, D.C.: U.S. Dept. Inter., Fish and Wildlife Service.

O

Oberholser, H. C. 1919. An albino black-chinned hummingbird. *Condor* 21:122.

_____. 1933. Robert Ridgway: A memorial appreciation. *Auk* 50(2):159–69.

_____. 1957. Bay-breasted warbler. In *The warblers of America,* ed. L. Griscom and A. Sprunt, Jr. New York: The Devin-Adair Co.

Oberlander, G. 1939. The history of a family of black phoebes. *Condor* 41:133–51.

Odum, E. P. 1941–42. Annual cycle of the black-capped chickadee. *Auk* 58:314–33, 518–35; 59:499–531.

_____. 1943. Some physiological variations in the black-capped chickadee. *Wilson Bull.* 55:178–91.

_____. 1945. The heart rate of small birds. *Science* 101:153–54.

_____. 1953. *Fundamentals of ecology.* Philadelphia: W. B. Saunders Company.

_____. 1971. *Fundamentals of ecology.* 2d ed. Philadelphia: W. B. Saunders Company.

Odum, E. P., and Burleigh, T. D. 1946. Southward invasion in Georgia. *Auk* 63(3):389–401.

Odum, E. P.; Connell, C. E.; and Stoddard, Sr., H. L. 1961. Flight energy and estimated flight ranges of some migrating birds. *Auk* 78(4):515–27.

Odum, E. P., and Johnston, D. W. 1951. The house wren breeding in Georgia. *Auk* 68(3):357–66.

Oehser, P. H. 1952. In memoriam: Florence Merriam Bailey. *Auk* 69(1):19–26.

Office of Endangered Species, comp. 1973. *Threatened wildlife of the United States.* U.S. Dept. Inter., Fish and Wildlife Service Res. Publ. no. 114. Washington, D.C.

Ogden, J. C. 1968. Sharp-tailed sandpiper collected in Florida. *Auk* 85:692.

_____. 1970. Florida region. *Amer. Birds* 24:673–77.

_____. 1972. Florida region. *Amer. Birds* 26:848.

_____. 1974. The short-tailed hawk in Florida. I. Migration, habitat, hunting techniques, and food habits. *Auk* 91:95–110.

Ohlendorf, H. M. 1974. Competitive relationships among kingbirds (*Tyrannus*) in Trans-Pecos Texas. *Wilson Bull.* 86:357–73.

_____. 1976. Comparative breeding ecology of phoebes in Trans-Pecos Texas. *Wilson Bull.* 88:255–71.

Ohmart, R. D. 1969. Physiological and ethological adaptations of the rufous-winged sparrow (*Aimophila carpalis*) to a desert environment. Ph.D. dissertation, University of Arizona, Tucson.

_____. 1973. Observations on the breeding adaptations of the roadrunner. *Condor* 75:140–49.

Ohmart, R. D., and Lasiewski, R. C. 1971. Roadrunners: Energy conservation by hypothermia and absorption of sunlight. *Science* 172:67–69.

Ohmart, R. D., and Smith, E. L. 1970. Use of sodium chloride solutions by Brewer's sparrow and tree sparrow. *Auk* 87(2):329–41.

_____. 1971. Water deprivation and use of sodium chloride solutions by vesper sparrows (*Pooecetes gramineus*). *Condor* 73:364–66.

Oldham, C. 1933. Duration of life of Arctic skua. *Brit. Birds* 5:139.

Olendorff, R. R. 1968. A contribution to the breeding behavior of the American kestrel in captivity. *Raptor Res. News* 2(4):77–92.

_____. 1971. *Falconiform reproduction; a review. Part 1. The pre-nestling period.* Raptor Research Report no. 1. Vermillion, S.D.: Raptor Research Foundation.

_____, ed. 1972. Reports: Breeding project information exchange. *Raptor Research* 6(1, Spring):16–41.

Oliver, J. A. 1955. *The natural history of North American amphibians and reptiles.* New York: D. Van Nostrand Company.

Oliver, W. R. B. 1955. *New Zealand birds.* 2d ed. Wellington, N.Z.: A. H. and A. W. Reed.

Olivier, G. G. 1964. Shrike. In *A new dictionary of birds*, ed. A. L. Thomson. New York: McGraw-Hill Book Company.

Olney, P. J. S. 1972. Notes from the London zoo. *Avicultural Magazine* 78:212.

Olsen, J. 1971. *Slaughter the animals, poison the earth*. New York: Simon & Schuster, Inc.

Olson, C. S., and Johnson, H. M. 1971. Great white heron captures and eats black-necked stilt. *Auk* 88:668.

Olson, H. 1953. Beetle rout in the Rockies. *Audubon* 55:30–32.

Olson, S. L. 1972. A whooping crane from the Pleistocene of north Florida. *Condor* 74:341.

Olson, S. T., and Marshall, W. H. 1952. *The common loon in Minnesota*. Minnesota Mus. Nat. Hist. Occ. Papers, no. 5.

O'Meara, D. C., and Witter, J. F. 1971. Aspergillosis. In *Infectious diseases and parasites of wild birds*, ed. J. W. Davis et al. Ames, Iowa: Iowa State University Press.

Orcutt, Jr., F. S., and Orcutt, A. B. 1976. Nesting and parental behavior in domestic common quail. *Auk* 93(1):135–41.

Orians, G. H. 1960. Autumnal breeding in the tricolored blackbird. *Auk* 77(4):379–98.

———. 1969. On the evolution of mating systems in birds and mammals. *Amer. Nat.* 103:589–603.

Orians, G. H., and Orians, B. 1956. Albino red-tailed hawk. *Passenger Pigeon* 18(1):30.

Oring, L. W. 1973. Solitary sandpiper early reproductive behavior. *Auk* 90:652–63.

Oring, L. W., and Knudson, M. L. 1972. Monogamy and polyandry in the spotted sandpiper. *Living Bird*, 11th annual, pp. 59–73.

Orr, H. D., and Sudia, T. W. 1960. Flight distance of the great blue heron. *Wilson Bull.* 77(2):198–99.

Orr, R. T. 1939. Observations on the nesting of the Allen's hummingbird. *Condor* 41:17–24.

———. 1968. Cassin's finch. In *Life histories of North American cardinals, grosbeaks, buntings, towhees, finches, sparrows, and allies*, comp. A. C. Bent *et al.*, ed. O. L. Austin, Jr. U.S. Natl. Mus. Bull. no. 237, pt. I. Washington, D.C.

Osborn, F. 1962. William Beebe: 1877–1962. *Animal Kingdom* 65(4):120–23.

Osborn, H. F. 1900. Reconsideration of the evidence for a common dinosaur-avian stem in the Permian. *Amer. Nat.* 34:777–99.

Ostrom, J. H. 1974. Archaeopteryx and the origin of bird flight. *Quart. Rev. Biol.* 49:27–47.

Owen, D. F. 1959. Mortality of the great blue heron as shown by banding recoveries. *Auk* 76:464–70.

Owen, H., and Owen, P. 1956. Tufted titmice plant sunflower seeds. *Kentucky Warbler* 32(4):62.

Owre, O. T. 1967. *Adaptations for locomotion and feeding in the Anhinga and the double-crested cormorant*. Amer. Ornith. Union Monogr. no. 6.

———. 1973. A consideration of the exotic avifauna of southeastern Florida. *Wilson Bull.* 85:491–500.

———. 1976. Bahama woodstar in Florida: First specimen for continental North America. *Auk* 93(4):837–38.

———. 1977. Personal communication.

Oxford Universal Dictionary. 3d ed. 1955. London: Oxford at the Clarendon Press.

P

Packard, Fred M. 1968. Brown-capped rosy finch. In *Life histories of North American cardinals, grosbeaks, buntings, towhees, finches, sparrows, and allies*, comp. A. C. Bent *et al.*, ed. O. L. Austin, Jr. U.S. Natl. Mus. Bull. no. 237, pt. I. Washington, D.C.

Page, L. A. 1966. Revision of the family Chlamydiaceae. *Internatl. Jour. Syst. Bacteriology* 16(2):223–52.

———. 1968. Proposal for the recognition of two species in the genus *Chlamydia* Jones, Rake, and Stearns, 1945. *Internatl. Jour. Syst. Bacteriology* 18(1):51–66.

Paine, R. T. 1968. Brewer's sparrow. In *Life histories of North American cardinals, grosbeaks, buntings, towhees, finches, sparrows, and allies*, comp. A. C. Bent *et al.*, ed. O. L. Austin, Jr. U.S. Natl. Mus. Bull. no. 237, pt. 2. Washington, D.C.

Palmer, E. L. 1949. *Fieldbook of natural history*. New York: McGraw-Hill Book Company.

Palmer, R. S. 1941. *A behavior study of the common tern*. Proc. Boston Soc. Nat. Hist. no. 42.

———. 1954. *The mammal guide*. New York: Doubleday & Co., Inc.

———. 1962. Ed. *Handbook of North American birds*. Vol. 1. Loons through flamingos. New Haven, Conn., and London: Yale University Press.

———. 1964. Limpkin. In *A new dictionary of birds*, ed. A. L. Thomson. New York: McGraw-Hill Book Company.

———. 1967. Species accounts. In *The shorebirds of North America*, ed. and spons. G. D. Stout, text by P. Matthiessen, paintings by R. V. Clem. New York: The Viking Press.

———. 1968. Pine siskin. In *Life histories of North American cardinals, grosbeaks, buntings, towhees, finches, sparrows, and allies*, comp. A. C. Bent *et al.*, ed. O. L. Austin, Jr. U.S. Natl. Mus. Bull. no. 237, pt. 1. Washington, D.C.

———. 1972. Patterns of molting. In *Avian biology*, ed. D. S. Farner, J. R. King, and K. C. Parkes. Vol. 2. New York: Academic Press, Inc.

———, ed. 1976. Handbook of North American birds. Vol. 2 (pt 1); New Haven, Conn., and London: Yale University Press.

Palmer, S. F., and Trainer, D. O. 1971. Newcastle disease. In *Infectious and parasitic diseases of wild birds*, ed. J. W. Davis et al. Ames, Iowa: Iowa State University Press.

Palmer, T. S. 1918. Costa's hummingbird—Its type locality, early history, and name. *Condor* 20:114–16.

———. 1928. Names of persons whose names appear in the nomenclature of California birds. *Condor* 30:261–307.

———. 1931. The scientific name of the western sandpiper—Who was Mauri? *Condor* 33:243–44.

Palmer, T. S., *et al.* 1954. *Biographies of members of the American Ornithologists' Union*. Washington, D. C.: Amer. Ornith. Union.

Paris, P. 1913. Recherches sur la glande uropygienne des oiseaux. *Arch. Zool. Exp. Gen.* 53:139–276.

Parker, L. A. 1966. The legal basis. In *Birds in our lives*, ed. A. Stefferud and A. L. Nelson. Washington, D.C.: U.S. Dept. Inter., Fish and Wildlife Service.

Parker, L. A., and Findlay, J. D. 1964. A letter to a hunter. In *Waterfowl tomorrow*, ed. J. P. Linduska and A. L. Nelson. Washington, D.C.: U.S. Dept. Inter., Fish and Wildlife Service.

Parker, T. J., and Haswell, W. A. 1928. *A textbook of zoology*. Vol. 2. London: Macmillan & Company Ltd.

Parkes, K. C. 1950. Great horned owl vs. porcupine. *Wilson Bull.* 62(4):213–14.

———. 1951. The genetics of the golden-winged × blue-winged warbler complex. *Wilson Bull.* 63:5–15.

———. 1963. The contribution of museum collections to knowledge of the living bird. *Living Bird*, 2d annual, pp. 121–30.

———. 1964. Warbler (2). In *A new dictionary of birds*, ed. A. L. Thomson. New York: McGraw-Hill Book Company.

———. 1966. Speculations on the origin of feathers. *Living Bird*, 5th annual, pp. 77–87.

———. 1975. Notes on taxonomy. In *Avian biology*, ed. D. S. Farner, J. R. King, and K. C. Parkes. Vol. 5. New York: Academic Press, Inc.

Parkes, K. C., and Clark, Jr., G. A. 1964. Additional records of avian egg teeth. *Wilson Bull.* 76(2):147–54.

Parkes, K. C., and Clench, M. H. 1972. Recovery of a Pennsylvania-banded blue gray gnatcatcher in western Mexico. *Condor* 74(2):222.

Parkes, K. C.; Poole, A.; and Lapham, H. 1971. The ruddy turnstone as an egg predator. *Wilson Bull.* 83:306–8.

Parmelee, D. F. 1959. The breeding behavior of the painted bunting in southern Oklahoma. *Bird-Banding* 30:1–18.

———. 1964. Survival in the painted bunting. *Living Bird*, 3d annual, pp. 5–7.

———. 1968. Snow bunting. In *Life histories of North American cardinals, grosbeaks, buntings, towhees, finches, sparrows, and allies*, comp. A. C. Bent *et al.*, ed. O. L. Austin, Jr. U.S. Natl. Mus. Bull. no. 237, pt. 3. Washington, D.C.

———. 1970. Breeding behavior of the sanderling in the Canadian high arctic. *Living Bird*, 9th annual, pp. 97–136.

Parmelee, D. F., and MacDonald, S. D. 1960. *The birds of west-central Ellesmere Island and adjacent areas*. Natl. Mus. Canada, Bull. no. 169. Ottawa.

Parmelee, D. F.; Stephens, H. A.; and Schmidt, R. H. 1967. *Birds of southeastern Victoria Island and adjacent small islands*. Natl. Mus. Canada, Bull. no. 222, Biol. Ser. 78. Ottawa.

Parmelee, D. F., and Payne, R. B. 1973. On multiple broods and the breeding strategy of arctic sanderlings. *Ibis* 115:218–26.

Partin, L. 1958. Oil burners and bluebirds. Reprinted in *Audubon* 60(2):82–84.

Pasquier, Roger F. 1977. *Watching birds, an introduction to ornithology*. New York: Houghton Mifflin Company.

Patterson, R. L. 1952. *The sage grouse in Wyoming*. Denver: Sage Books, Inc.

Patterson, R. W. 1971. Warbler returns at Somesville, Maine. *Bird-Banding* 42(2):99–102.

Paulson, D. R., and Stevenson, H. M. 1962. Florida region. *Audubon Field Notes* 16:402, 403.

Paxton, R. O. 1968. Wandering albatross in California. *Auk* 85:502–4.

Payne, R. B. 1965. Clutch size and number of eggs laid by brown-headed cowbird. *Condor* 67(1):44–60.

———. 1969. Giant cowbird solicits preening from man. *Auk* 86:751–52.

———. 1972. Mechanisms and control of molt. In *Avian biology*, ed. D. S. Farner, J. R. King, and K. C. Parker. Vol. 2. New York: Academic Press, Inc.

Payne, R. S. 1962. How the barn owl locates prey by hearing. *Living Bird*, 1st annual, pp. 150–59.

Paynter, Jr., R. A. 1963. North American herring gulls nesting on a building. *Wilson Bull.* 75:88.

———. ed. 1974. *Avian energetics*. Cambridge, Mass.: Nuttall Ornith. Pub. no. 15.

Pearson, O. P. 1950. The metabolism of hummingbirds. *Condor* 52:145–52.

———. 1953. Use of caves by hummingbirds. *Scientific American* 188:69–72.

———. 1954. The daily energy requirements of a wild Anna's hummingbird. *Condor* 56(6):317–22.

———. 1960. Torpidity in birds. *Bull. Mus. Compar. Zool.* 124:93–103.

———. 1961. Flight speed of some small birds. *Condor* 63:506–7.

Pearson, R. 1972. *The avian brain*. New York: Academic Press, Inc.

Pearson, T. G. 1919. Olive Thorne Miller. *Bird-Lore* 21:76.

———. 1930. In memoriam: Edward Howe Forbush. *Auk* 47:136–46.

———. 1933. Fifty years of bird protection in the United States. In *Fifty years' progress of Ameri-*

can ornithology: 1883–1933. Lancaster, Pa.:
Amer. Ornith. Union.

———. 1935. A herring gull of great age. Bird-
Lore 37(6):412–13.

———. ed. 1936. Birds of America. Garden City,
N.Y.: Garden City Pub. Co., Inc.

———. 1937a. Adventures in bird protection.
New York: D. Appleton-Century Company, Inc.

———. 1937b. The gulls and terns. In The book
of birds, ed. G. Grosvenor and A. Wetmore.
Vol. 1. Washington, D.C.: Natl. Geographic
Soc.

Peasley, S., and Sorrie, B. 1976. Point Reyes. Ob-
serv. Newsletter 39:7.

Peckham, M. C. 1972. Vices and miscellaneous
diseases. In Diseases of poultry, ed. M. S. Hofstad et al. 6th ed. Ames, Iowa: Iowa State University Press.

Peek, F. W.; Franks, E.; and Case, D. 1972. Recognition of nest, eggs, nest site, and young in female red-winged blackbirds. Wilson Bull. 84:
243–49.

Peeters, H. J., and Jameson, Jr., E. W. 1970.
American hawking: A general account of falconry in the New World. Davis, Calif.: Privately published by authors.

Peiponen, V. A. 1965. On hypothermia and torpidity in the nightjar (Caprimulgus europaeus).
Ann. Acad. Sci. Fenn. A-4:387.

Pelzi, H. W. 1971. Nest parasitism by red-
breasted mergansers in Wisconsin. Auk 88(1):-
184–85.

Pennycuick, C. J. 1975. Mechanics of flight. In
Avian Biology, ed. D. S. Farner, J. R. King, and
K. C. Parkes. Vol. 5, p. 44. New York: Academic
Press, Inc.

Perdeck, A. C., and Spreck, B. J. 1964. Ringver-
slag van het vogeltrekstation. Limosa 37(1–2):
96–186.

Perrins, C. M. 1964. Weight. In A new dictionary
of birds, ed. A. L. Thomson. New York:
McGraw-Hill Book Company.

Peters, H. S. 1930. Ectoparasites and bird-banding. Bird-Banding 1(2):51–60.

———. 1936. A list of external parasites from
birds of the eastern part of the United States.
Bird-Banding 7(1):9–27.

———. 1961. The past status and management of
the mourning dove. Trans. [26th] N. Amer.
Wildlife and Nat. Res. Conf., pp. 371–74.

Peters, J. L. 1931. Check-list of birds of the world.
Vol. 1. Cambridge, Mass.: Harvard University
Press.

———. 1933. Collections of birds in the United
States and Canada: Study Collections. In Fifty
years' progress of American ornithology: 1883–
1933. Lancaster, Pa.: Amer. Ornith. Union.

———. 1937. Check-list of birds of the world. Vol.
3. Cambridge, Mass.: Harvard University
Press.

Petersen, Jr., P. C. 1966. Middlewestern prairie
region. Audubon Field Notes 20(4):515.

Peterson, R. T. 1941. How many birds are there?
Audubon 43.

———. 1942. Life zones, biomes, or life forms?
Audubon 44:21–30.

———. 1947. A field guide to the birds. Boston:
Houghton Mifflin Company.

———. 1948. Birds over America. New York:
Dodd, Mead & Company.

———. 1949. How to know the birds: An introduction to bird recognition. New York: The New
American Library of World Literature (paperback).

———. 1955. The Christmas count. Audubon 57:-
52–53, 64–65.

———. 1960. A field guide to the birds of Texas.
Boston: Houghton Mifflin Company.

———. 1961. A field guide to western birds. Boston: Houghton Mifflin Company.

———. 1962. Personal communication.

———. 1963. A field guide to the birds of Texas
and adjacent states. Boston: Houghton Mifflin
Company.

———. 1966. What are birds for? In Birds in our
lives, ed. A. Stefferud and A. L. Nelson. Washington, D.C.: U.S. Dept. Inter., Fish and Wildlife Service.

———. 1968. The birds. New York: Time Inc./
Life Nature Library.

———. 1969. Population trends of ospreys in the
northeastern United States. In Peregrine populations: Their biology and decline, ed. J. J.
Hickey. Madison, Wisc.: University of Wisconsin Press.

———. 1973. The evolution of a magazine. Audubon 75:46–51.

Peterson, R. T., and Chalif, E. L. 1973. A field
guide to Mexican birds. Boston: Houghton
Mifflin Company.

Peterson, R. T.; Mountfort, G.; and Hollom, P. A.
D. 1954. A field guide to the birds of Britain and
Europe. Boston: Houghton Mifflin Company.

Peterson, R. T., and Watson, G. E. 1971. Franklin's gull and bridled tern in Chile. Auk 88(3):
670–71.

Petrak, M. L., ed. 1969. Diseases of cage and aviary birds. Philadelphia: Lea and Febiger.

Petrides, G. A. 1938. A life history study of the yel
low-breasted chat. Wilson Bull. 50(3):184–89.

———. 1942. A hummingbird feeding habit. Auk
59(3):444.

Petrides, G. A., and Bryant, C. R. 1951. An analy-
sis of the 1949–50 fowl cholera epizootic in
Texas Panhandle waterfowl. Trans. [16th] N.
Amer. Wildlife Conf., pp. 193–216.

Petrinovich, L., and Patterson, T. 1978. Cowbird
parasitism on the white-crowned sparrow. Auk
95:415–17.

Petrovic, C. A., and King, Jr., J. 1972. Common
eider and king rail from the Dry Tortugas,
Florida. Auk 89(3):660.

Petry, L. C. 1908. Albino flickers. Bird-Lore 10:
127.

Pettingill, Jr., O. S. 1936. The American woodcock Philohela minor (Gmelin). Mem. Boston
Soc. Nat. Hist. 9:169–391.

———. 1937. The New Hampshire hummingbirds. Bird-Lore 39:191–95.

———. 1938. Intelligent behavior of a clapper
rail. Auk 55(4):411–15.

———. 1942. The birds of a bull's horn acacia.
Wilson Bull. 54(1):89–96.

———. 1956. A laboratory and field manual of
ornithology. 3d ed. Minneapolis: Burgess Publishing Co.

———. 1959. King eiders mated with common
eiders in Iceland. Wilson Bull. 71(3):205–7.

———. 1962. Hawk migration around the Great
Lakes. Audubon 64(1):44–45, 49.

———. 1965. Woodcock, curlews, and sandpipers.
In Water, prey, and game birds of North Amer-
ica, ed. A. Wetmore. Washington, D.C.: Natl.
Geographic Soc.

———. 1967. An "ancient" herring gull. EBBA
News 30(4):180.

———. 1968. In memoriam: Arthur A. Allen.
Auk 85:192–202.

———. 1970. Ornithology in laboratory and field.
4th ed. Minneapolis: Burgess Publishing Co.

———. 1976. Observed acts of predation on birds
in northern lower Michigan. Living Bird, 15th
annual, pp. 33–41.

Pettingill, Jr., O. S., ed. 1972. Seminars in ornithology. Ithaca, N.Y.: Cornell Laboratory of Ornithology.

Pettingill, Jr., O. S., and Lancaster, D. A. 1968.
Cornell Laboratory of Ornith. Newsletter to
Members no. 48.

———. 1970. Help for nesting ospreys. Cornell
Laboratory of Ornith. Newsletter to Members
no. 55.

———. 1972. Captive falcons produce eggs and
young. Cornell Laboratory of Ornith. Newsletter to Members no. 65.

———. 1973a. An ancient bird being reconstructed. Cornell Laboratory of Ornith. Newsletter to Members no. 67.

———. 1973b. Factors influencing non-random
mating of the ruff. Cornell Laboratory of Ornith. Newsletter to Members no. 68.

Phelps, Jr., J. H. 1968. Oregon junco. In Life histories of North American cardinals, grosbeaks,
buntings, towhees, finches, sparrows, and allies,
comp. A. C. Bent et al., ed. O. L. Austin, Jr. U.S.
Natl. Mus. Bull. no. 237, pt. 2. Washington, D.C.

Philip, Duke of Edinburgh, and Fisher, J. 1970.
North American paradise. In Wildlife crisis.
New York: Cowles Book Company, Inc.

Phillips, A. J. 1959. Robins intoxicated by mountain ash fruits. Audubon 61:6.

Phillips, A. R. 1939. The type of Empidonax
wrightii Baird. Auk 56:311–12.

———. 1949. Nesting of the rose-breasted becard
in Arizona. Condor 51(3):137–39.

———. 1951. Complexities of migration: A review. Wilson Bull. 63(2):129–36.

———. 1966. Some unusual vireos. Bird-Banding
37(4):286–87.

———. 1968a. Rufous-winged sparrow. In Life
histories of North American cardinals, grosbeaks, buntings, towhees, finches, sparrows, and
allies, comp. A. C. Bent et al., ed. O. L. Austin,
Jr. U.S. Natl. Mus. Bull. no. 237, pt. 2. Washington, D.C.

———. 1968b. Rock rufous-crowned sparrow and
Scott's rufous-crowned sparrow. In Life histories of North American cardinals, grosbeaks,
buntings, towhees, finches, sparrows, and allies,
comp. A. C. Bent et al., ed. O. L. Austin, Jr. U.S.
Natl. Mus. Bull. no. 237, pt. 2. Washington,
D.C.

Phillips, A. R.; Howe, M. A.; and Lanyon, W. E.
1966. Identification of the flycatchers of eastern North America with special emphasis on
the genus Empidonax. Bird-Banding 37(3):
153–71.

Phillips, A. R., and Lanyon, W. 1970. Additional
notes on the flycatchers of eastern North
America. Bird-Banding 41(3):190–99.

Phillips, A. R.; Marshall, J.; and Monson, G. 1964.
The birds of Arizona. Tucson, Ariz.: University
of Arizona Press.

Phillips, A. R.; Speich, S.; and Harrison, W. 1973.
Black-capped gnatcatcher: A new breeding
bird for the United States; with a key to the
North American species of Polioptila. Auk 90:
257–62.

Phillips, C. L. 1887. Egg-laying extraordinary in
Colaptes auratus. Auk 4:346.

Phillips, J. C. 1915. Experimental studies of hybridization among ducks and pheasants. Jour.
Exper. Zool. 18:69–143.

———. 1922–26. The natural history of the ducks.
4 vols. Boston: Houghton Mifflin Company.

———. 1928. Wild birds introduced or transplanted in North America. U.S. Dept. Agric.
Tech. Bull. no. 61. Washington, D.C.

Piatt, J. 1973. Adventures in birding: Confessions
of a lister. New York: Alfred A. Knopf, Inc.

Pickens, A. L. 1929a. Bird pollination problems in
California. Condor 31(6):229–32.

———. 1929b. Hummingbird flower lists. Condor
31(5):221.

Pickwell, G. 1942. Prairie horned lark. In Life
histories of north American flycatchers, larks,
swallows, and their allies, by A. C. Bent. U.S.
Natl. Mus. Bull. no. 179. Washington, D.C.

Piers, H. 1898. Remarkable ornithological occurrence in Nova Scotia. Auk 15(2):195–96.

Pinchon, P. R., and Vaurie, C. 1961. The kestrel
(Falco tinnunculus) in the New World. Auk
78(1):92–93.

Pinkowski, B. C. 1975. Growth and development
of eastern bluebirds. Bird-Banding 46(4):273–
89.

Piper, S. L. 1908. Mouse plagues: Their control
and prevention. U.S. Dept. Agric. Yearbook, pp.
301–310.

———. 1909. The Nevada mouse plague of 1907–
08. U.S. Dept. Agric. Farmer's Bull. no. 352.
Washington, D.C.

Pitelka, F. A. 1940. Breeding behavior of the black-throated green warbler. *Wilson Bull.* 52: 3–18.

———. 1941. Distribution of birds in relation to major biotic communities. *Amer. Midland Nat.* 25:113–37.

———. 1942. Territoriality and related problems in North American hummingbirds. *Condor* 44(5):189–204.

———. 1950. Geographic variation and the species problems in the shorebird genus *Limnodromus. Univ. California Publ. Zool.* 50(1):1–108.

———. 1951a. Breeding seasons of hummingbirds near Santa Barbara, California. *Condor* 53:198–201.

———. 1951b. Ecologic overlap and interspecific strife in breeding populations of Anna's and Allen's hummingbirds. *Ecology* 32:641–61.

———. 1959. Number, breeding schedule, and territoriality in pectoral sandpipers of northern Alaska. *Condor* 61:233–64.

Pitman, C. R. S. 1958. Snake and lizard predators of birds. *Bull. Brit. Ornith. Club* 78 (pt. 1): 82–86; (pt. 2):99–104; (pt. 3):120–24.

———. 1961. Birds perching on hippopotamus. *Bull. Brit. Ornith. Club* 81(8):148.

———. 1962a. Bird predation by the American snapping turtle, *Chelydra serpentina. Bull. Brit. Ornith. Club* 82:95–96.

———. 1962b. More snakes and lizard predators of birds. *Bull. Brit. Ornith. Club* 82 (pt. 1): 33–40; (pt. 2):45–55.

———. 1962c. Waterfowl predation in Canada by the northern pike (or jackfish) *Esox lucius. Bull. Brit. Ornith. Club* 82:64–67.

———. 1964a. Eggs. In *A new dictionary of birds,* ed. A. L. Thomson. New York: McGraw-Hill Book Company.

———. 1964b. Jacana. In *A new dictionary of birds,* ed. A. L. Thomson. New York: McGraw-Hill Book Company.

———. 1964c. Thickknee. In *A new dictionary of birds,* ed. A. L. Thomson. New York: McGraw-Hill Book Company.

Pitt, F. 1933. How fast do birds fly? Some experiments in timing by train and by car. *Field* [London] 162:829.

Pittman, J. A. 1953. Direct observation of the flight speed of the common loon. *Wilson Bull.* 65:213.

Plath, O. E. 1919. A muscid larva of the San Francisco Bay region which sucks the blood of nestling birds. *Univ. California Publ. Zool.* 19: 191–200.

Platt, S. W. 1975. The Mexican chicken bug as a source of raptor mortality. *Wilson Bull.* 87(4): 557.

Plumb, W. J. 1965. Observations on the breeding biology of the razorbill. *Brit. Birds* 58:449–56.

Plunkett, R. 1969. The changing seasons. *Audubon Field Notes* 23(3):442–45.

Polunin, N. 1961. Tundra. In *The encyclopedia of the biological sciences,* ed. P. Gray. New York: Reinhold Publishing Corporation.

Pomeroy, D. E. 1962. Birds with abnormal bills. *Brit. Birds* 55:49–72.

Poole, E. L. 1938. Weights and wing areas in North American birds. *Auk* 55:511–17.

———. 1961–62. *Herbert H. Beck. Cassinia* 56: 19–20. Philadelphia.

Portal, C. F. A. 1922. The speed of birds. *Field* [London] 139:233–34.

Porter, J. P. 1904. A preliminary study of the psychology of the English sparrow. *Amer. Jour. Psychol.* 15:313–46.

———. 1906. Further study of the English sparrow and other birds. *Amer. Jour. Psychol.* 17: 248–71.

———. 1910. Intelligence and imitation in birds: A criterion of imitation. *Amer. Jour. Psychol.* 21:1–71.

Porter, R. D., and Wiemeyer, S. N. 1969. Dieldrin and DDT: Effects on sparrow hawk eggshells and reproduction. *Science* 165:199–200.

———. 1972. Reproductive pattern in captive American kestrels (sparrow hawks). *Condor* 74(1):46–53.

Portmann, A. 1950a. Le developpement postembryonnaire. In *Traité de zoologie,* ed. P. P. Grassé. Vol. 15, *Oiseaux.* Paris: Masson & Company.

———. 1950b. Les organes des sens. In *Traité de zoologie,* ed. P. P. Grassé. Vol. 15, *Oiseaux.* Paris: Masson & Company.

———. 1961. Sensory organs: Skin, taste, and olfaction. In *Biology and comparative physiology of birds,* ed. A. J. Marshall. Vol. 2. New York: Academic Press, Inc.

Portmann, A., and Stingelin, W. H. 1961. The central nervous system. In *Biology and comparative physiology of birds,* ed. A. J. Marshall. New York: Academic Press, Inc.

———. 1964. Development, embryonic. In *A new dictionary of birds,* ed. A. L. Thomson. New York: McGraw-Hill Book Company.

Post, P. 1967. Manx, Audubon's and little shearwaters in the northwestern north Atlantic. *Bird-Banding* 38:278–305.

Post, W. 1973. Some encounters between birds and pelecypods. *Bird-Banding* 44:65.

Postupalsky, S. 1969. The status of the osprey in Michigan in 1965. In *Peregrine populations: Their biology and decline,* ed. J. J. Hickey. Madison, Wisc.: University of Wisconsin Press.

———. 1970. White-tailed sea eagle breeding in captivity. *Raptor Res. News* 4(1):3.

———. 1971. Bald eagle and osprey study in Michigan and Ontario: A report of the 1969 and 1970 nesting season. *California Condor* 6(1):1–3.

Potter, E. F. 1970. Anting in wild birds, its frequency and probable purpose. *Auk* 87(4):692–713.

Potter, E. F., and Hauser, D. C. 1974. Relationship of anting and sunbathing to molting in wild birds. *Auk* 91(3):537–63.

Potter, J. K., and Murray, J. J. 1955. Middle Atlantic coastal region. *Audubon Field Notes* 9(4):323.

Pough, R. H. 1935. A glider highway. *Bird-Lore* 37:317–21.

———. 1949. *Audubon and bird guide.* Garden City, N.Y.: Doubleday & Co., Inc.

———. 1951. *Audubon water bird guide.* Garden City, N.Y.: Doubleday & Co., Inc.

———. 1957. *Audubon western bird guide.* Garden City, N.Y.: Doubleday & Co., Inc.

Poulsen, H. 1953. A study of incubation responses and some other behaviour patterns in birds. *Vidensk. Medd. fra Dansk/naturh. Foren.* 115: 1–131.

———. 1956. A study of anting behaviour in birds. *Dansk Ornithologisk Forenings Tidsskrift* 50:267–98.

Powell, J. A. 1963. Florida wild turkey movements and longevity as determined by band returns. *Proc. Annual Conf. Southeastern Assoc. Game and Fish Comm.* 17:16–19.

Powers, L. R. 1973. Record of robin feeding shrews to its nestlings. *Condor* 75(2):248.

Pratt, D. W. 1943. Red-shouldered hawk caught in mink trap. *Auk* 60:99.

Pratt, H. M. 1970. Breeding biology of great blue herons and common egrets in central California. *Condor* 72:407–16.

Pratt, H. S. 1951. *A manual of common invertebrate animals (exclusive of insects).* Philadelphia: The Blakiston Co.

Preble, E. A. 1927. The vanishing woodcock. *Nature Magazine* 9:235–40.

Preble, E. A., and McAtee, W. L. 1923. *A biological survey of the Pribilof Islands, Alaska. N. Amer. Fauna* no. 46. Washington, D.C.: U.S. Dept. Agric., Biological Survey.

Preble, N. A. 1957. The nesting habits of the yellow-billed cuckoo. *Amer. Midland Nat.* 57:474–82.

Prescott, K. W. 1965. *Studies in the life history of the scarlet tanager, Piranga olivacea.* New Jersey State Mus. Investig. no. 2. Trenton.

———. 1971a. A melanistic blue jay (*Cyanocitta cristata*). *Bird-Banding* 42(1):48.

———. 1971b. Recovery of foot-pox diseased red-winged blackbird. *Bird-Banding* 42(1):47–48.

Preston, F. W. 1951. Flight speed of common loon. *Wilson Bull.* 63(3):198.

Prestwich, A. A. 1955. *Records of birds of prey bred in captivity.* London: Published by the author.

———. 1963. *I name this parrot . . .* 2d ed. Edenbridge, Kent, England: Arthur A. Prestwich.

———. 1968. News and views. *Avicultural Magazine* 74:104.

———. 1969. The longevity of parrots. *Avicultural Magazine* 75(5):198.

Prevett, J. P., and MacInnes, C. D. 1973. Observations of wild hybrids between Canada geese and blue goose. *Condor* 75:124–25.

Prevett, J. P., and Prevett, L. S. 1973. Egg retrieval by blue geese. *Auk* 90(1):202–4.

Prévost, J. 1955. Observations ecologiques sur le manchot empereur (*Aptenodytes fosteri*). *Acta XI Congr. Internatl. Ornith. 1954,* pp. 248–51.

Price, J. B. 1936. The family relations of the Plain titmouse. *Condor* 38:23–28.

Proctor, V. W. 1968. Long-distance dispersal of seeds by retention in digestive tract of birds. *Science* 160(3825):321–2.

Prosser, C. L., and Brown, F. A. 1962. *Comparative animal physiology.* Philadelphia: W. B. Saunders Company.

Pulich, Sr., W. M., and Pulich, Jr., W. M. 1963. The nesting of the Lucifer hummingbird in the United States. *Auk* 80(3):370–71.

Pulliainen, E. 1970. On the breeding biology of the dotterel (*Charadrius morinellus*). *Ornis Fenn.* 47(2):69–73.

Pumphrey, R. J. 1948. The sense organs of birds. *Ibis* 90(2):185.

———. 1961a. Sensory organs: Hearing. In *Biology and comparative physiology of birds,* ed. A. G. Marshall. New York: Academic Press, Inc.

———. 1961b. Sensory organs: Vision. In *Biology and comparative physiology of birds,* ed. A. J. Marshall. New York: Academic Press, Inc.

———. 1964. Hearing and balance. In *A new dictionary of birds,* ed. A. L. Thomson. New York: McGraw-Hill Book Company.

Purrington, R. D. 1970. Nesting of the sooty tern in Louisiana. *Auk* 87(1):159–60.

Putnam, L. S. 1949. The life history of the cedar waxwing. *Wilson Bull.* 61:141–82.

Pyecraft, W. P. 1898. A contribution towards our knowledge of the morphology of owls. *Trans. Linnaean Soc. London* 7:223–75.

R

R, E. P. 1913. How fast do ducks fly? *Forest and Stream* 80:41.

Rafferty, J. C. 1969. Adverse environmental influences on Everglades National Park. *Florida Nat.* 42(3):111–14.

Raikow, R. J. 1973. Locomotor mechanisms in North American ducks. *Wilson Bull.* 85:295–307.

Raitt, R. J., and Hardy, J. W. 1970. Relationships between two partly sympatric species of thrushes (*Catharus*) in Mexico. *Auk* 87(1):20–57.

Ralph, C. J., and Mewaldt, L. R. 1976. Homing success in wintering sparrows. *Auk* 93(1):1–14.

Ramp, W. K. 1965. The auditory range of a hairy woodpecker. *Condor* 67(2):183–85.

Ramsden, C. T. 1914. The bobolink (*Delichonyx oryzivorus*) as a conveyor of Mollusca. *Auk* 31(2):250.

Ramsey, A. O. 1972. Mimesis in hand-reared blue jays. *Bird-Banding* 43:214–15.

Rand, A. L. 1941. The courtship of the roadrunner. *Auk* 58:57–59.

———. 1942. Larus kumlieni and its allies. *Canadian Field-Nat.* 56:124–26.

———. 1943. Bass eats yellowthroat, young stilts, young ducks. *Auk* 60:95.

———. 1955. *Stray feathers from a bird man's desk.* Garden City, N.Y.: Doubleday & Co., Inc.

———. 1959. Pity poor pigeon: Host to a community. *Chicago Nat. Hist. Mus. Bull.* 30(8): 6–7.

———. 1960. Family Laniidae. In *Check-list of birds of the world,* ed. E. Mayr and J. C. Greenway. Vol. 9. Cambridge, Mass.: Harvard University Press.

———. 1961. Some size gradients in North American birds. *Wilson Bull.* 73(1):46–56.

———. 1962. Personal communication.

———. 1965. Gulls and terns. In *Water, prey and game birds of North America,* ed. A. Wetmore. Washington, D.C.: Natl. Geographic Soc.

———. 1966. The snipe rediscovered. *Audubon.* 68(5):351–54.

———. 1967. *Ornithology: An introduction.* New York: W. W. Norton & Co., Inc. (Also in paperback, 1969, New York: Signet Books/New American Library.)

Raner, L. 1972. Förekommer polyandri hos smalnäbbad simsnäppa *(Phalaropus zeobatus)* och svartsnäppa *(Tringa erythropus)?* *Fauna och Flora* 67:135–38.

Rankin, N. 1957. Longevity of a white-fronted goose. *Brit. Birds* 50(4):164.

Rapp, Jr. W. F. 1944. The swallow-tailed kite in the northeastern states. *Bird-Banding* 15:156–60.

Raspet, A. 1950. Performance measurements of a soaring bird. *Aeronaut. Engin. Rev.* 9(12):1–4.

———. 1960. Biophysics of bird flight. *Annual Rept. Smithsonian Inst.,* pp. 191–200.

Ratcliffe, D. A. 1963. The status of the peregrine in Great Britain. *Bird Study* 10:56–90.

———. 1969. Traditional use of nesting sites, Chapter 36. In *Peregrine falcon populations: Their biology and decline,* ed. J. J. Hickey. Madison, Wis.: University of Wisconsin Press.

Rathbun, S. F. 1934. Notes on the speed of flight of birds. *Murrelet* 15:23–24.

Rau, P. 1941. Birds as enemies of Polistes wasps. *Canadian Entomologist* 73:196.

Raveling, D. G., and Warner, D. W. 1965. Plumages, molt and morphometry of Tennessee warblers. *Bird-Banding* 36(3):169–79.

Rawles, M. E. 1960. The integumentary system. In *Biology and comparative physiology of birds,* ed. A. J. Marshall. Vol. 1. New York: Academic Press, Inc.

Raynor, G. S. 1956. Meteorological variables and the northward movement of nocturnal land bird migrants. *Auk* 73:153–75.

———. 1970. An African recovery of a North American common tern. *Bird-Banding* 41(4): 310–11.

Rea, A. M. 1973a. Interordinal copulation on coastal Venezuela. *Wilson Bull.* 85:337–38.

———. 1973b. Turkey vultures casting pellets. *Auk* 90:209–10.

Reagan, C. L. 1955. Personal communication.

Reaumur, R. A. F. de. 1756. Sur la digestion des oiseaux. *Mem. Acad. Science, Paris for 1752,* pp. 266–307.

Recher, H. F., and Recher, J. A. 1972. Herons leaving water to defecate. *Auk* 89:896–97.

Redfield, J. A. 1973. Variations in weight of blue grouse *(Dendragapus obscurus).* *Condor* 75: 312–21.

Reed, A. 1968. Habitat and breeding ecology. In *The black duck, evaluation, management, and research: A symposium, Atlantic waterfowl council.* Chestertown, Md.

Reed, N. P. 1973. Atlantic brant population low. *U.S. Dept. Inter. News Release,* February 8.

Reichel, W. L., et al. 1969. Pesticide residues in eagles. *Pesticides Monitor Jour.* 3(3):142–44.

Reichert, R. J., and Reichert, E. 1951. Know your binocular. *Audubon* 53:45–50, 105–9.

Reilly, Jr., E. M. 1968. *The Audubon illustrated handbook of American birds.* New York: McGraw-Hill Book Company.

Reimann, E. J. 1938. Loggerhead shrikes and snakes. *Auk* 55:540.

Remsen, Jr., J. V., and Binford, L. C. 1975. Status of the yellow-billed loon *(Gavia adamsii)* in the western United States and Mexico. *Western Birds* 6:7–20.

Remsen, V. 1979. Species of special concern, California's imperiled birds. *The Western Tanager* 45 (8): 1–8.

Rett, E. Z. 1938. Hailstorm fatal to California condors. *Condor* 40:225.

Reynard, G. B. 1974. Some vocalizations of the black, yellow, and Virginia rails. *Auk* 91(4): 747–56.

Reynard, G. B., and Harty, S. T. 1968. Ornithological "mystery" song given by male Virginia rail. *Cassinia* 50:3–8. (1966–1967 issue published in November 1968, Academy of Natural Sciences, Philadelphia.)

Reynolds, R. T. 1972. Sexual dimorphism in accipiter hawks: A new hypothesis. *Condor* 74(2): 191–97.

Rice, D. W. 1954. Symbiotic feeding of snowy egrets with cattle. *Auk* 71:472–73.

Rice, D. W., and Kenyon, K. W. 1958. Birds of Kurile Atoll, Hawaii. *Condor* 60:188–90.

———. 1962a. Breeding cycles and behavior of laysan and black-footed albatrosses. *Auk* 79(4):517–67.

———. 1962b. Breeding distribution, history, and populations of north Pacific albatrosses. *Auk* 79(3):365–86.

Rice, O. O. 1969. Record of female cardinals sharing nest. *Wilson Bull.* 81(2):216.

Richards, G. L. 1971. The common crow, *Corvus brachyrhynchos,* in the Great Basin. *Condor* 73(1):116–18.

Richardson, F. 1942. Adaptive modifications for tree-trunk foraging in birds. *Univ. California Publ. Zool.* 46:317–68.

———. 1961. Breeding biology of the rhinocerus auklet. *Condor* 63(6):456–73.

———. 1970. A North American record of the bristle-thighed curlew outside Alaska. *Auk* 87(4):815.

Rickert, J. E. 1978. *A guide to North American bird clubs.* Elizabethtown, Ky.: Avian Publications, Inc.

Ricklefs, R. E., ed. 1978. Report of the advisory panel on the California condor. *Audubon Conserv. Rept.* no. 6. New York: Natl. Audubon Soc.

Ridgway, R. 1880. Note on Helminthophaga cincinnatiensis, Langdon. *Bull. Nuttall Ornith. Club* 5(4):237–8.

———. 1884. Description of a new snow bunting from Alaska. *Proc. U.S. Natl. Mus.* 7:68–70.

———. 1886. Preliminary descriptions of some new species of birds from southern Mexico in the collection of the Mexican Geographical and Exploring Commission. *Auk* 3(3):331–33.

———. 1891. The hummingbirds. *U.S. Natl. Mus. Report 1890,* pp. 253–383.

———. 1898. Description of a new species of hummingbird from Arizona. *Auk* 15:325–26.

Riney, T. 1951. Relationships between birds and deer. *Condor* 53:178–85.

Ripley, S. D. 1965. Swans and geese. In *Water, prey, and game birds of North America,* ed. A. Wetmore. Washington, D.C.: Natl. Geographic Soc.

———. 1977. Rails of the world: A monograph of the family Rallidae. Boston: David R. Godine.

Risebrough, R. W.; Florant, G. L.; and Berger, D. G. 1970. Organochlorine pollutants in peregrines and merlins migrating through Wisconsin. *Canadian Field-Nat.* 84:247–53.

Rising, J. D. 1965a. Distributional notes on birds from western Kansas. *Kansas Ornith. Soc. Bull.* 16(4):25–27.

———. 1965b. A summer specimen of the Wright flycatcher *(Empidonax oberholseri)* from western Kansas. *Kansas Ornith. Soc. Bull.* 16(4): 24–25.

———. 1968. A multivariate assessment of interbreeding between the chickadees *Parus atricapillus,* and *P. carolinsis. Syst. Zool.* 17: 160–69.

Ristow, W. W. 1966. A covey of names. In *Birds in our lives,* ed. by A. Stefferud and A. L. Nelson. Washington, D.C.: U.S. Dept. Inter., Fish and Wildlife Service.

Ritchie, J. 1932. Systematic "beating" by herons. *Brit. Birds* 25:228.

Ritter, C. B. 1910. Speed of birds and animals. *Amer. Field* 73:200.

Ritter, W. E. 1938. *The California woodpecker and I.* Berkeley, Calif.: University of California Press.

Riviere, B. B. 1922. Speed of the domestic pigeon. *Brit. Birds* 15:298.

Robbins, C. S. 1966a. Birds and aircraft on Midway Islands: 1959–63 investigations. Washington D.C.: U.S. Dept. Inter., Fish and Wildlife Service.

———. 1966b. The Christmas count. In *Birds in our lives,* ed. A. Stefferud and A. L. Nelson. Washington, D.C.: U.S. Dept. Inter., Fish and Wildlife Service.

———. 1973. Introduction, spread, and present abundance of the house sparrows in North America. In *A symposium of the house sparrow* (Passer domesticus) *and European tree sparrow* (P. montanus) *in North America,* Amer. Ornith. Union, Mongr. no. 14.

Robbins, C. S.; Bruun, B.; and Zim, H. 1966. *A guide to field identification. Birds of North America.* New York: Golden Press, Publishers.

Roberts, B. B. 1932. On the normal flight speed of birds. *Brit. Birds* 25:220–22.

———. 1934. Notes on the birds of central and southeast Iceland with special reference to food habits. *Ibis* 4:252.

———. 1940. The life cycle of Wilson's petrel, *Oceanites oceanicus* (Kuhl). Brit. Graham Land Exp. 1934–37. *Brit. Mus. Sci. Repts.* 1:141–94.

Roberts, H. B. 1970. Management of the American osprey on the Deschutes National Forest, Oregon. *Raptor Res. News* 4:168–77.

Roberts, N. L. 1955. A survey of the habit of nest appropriation. *Emu* 55(2):110–26; (3):173–84.

Roberts, T. S. 1932. *The birds of Minnesota.* Minneapolis: University of Minnesota Press.

Roberts, W. W. 1939. Bird with the longest tongue in the world. *Ostrich* 10(2):133–36.

Robertson, Jr., W. B. 1959. Barred owl nesting on the ground. *Auk* 76:227–30.

———. 1969. Transatlantic migration of juvenile sooty terns. *Nature* 222(5194):632–34.

———. 1970. Florida region (fall migration 1969). *Audubon Field Notes* 24(1):38.

———. 1971. Florida region. *Amer. Birds* 25(1): 45, 47.

———. 1972. Personal communication.

Robins, J. D. 1971. A study of Henslow's sparrows in Michigan. *Wilson Bull.* 83(1):39–48.

Robinson, H. W. 1938. Longevity of black-headed gull. *Auk* 55(2):278.

Robinson, W. L. 1968–69. *Population ecology of* Canachites canadensis *in northern Michigan. Natl. Sci. F'dation Rept.* Marquette, Mich.: Northern Michigan University Press.

———. 1969. Habitat selection by spruce grouse in northern Michigan. *Jour. Wildlife Management* 33:113–20.

Robinson, W. L., and Maxwell, D. E. 1968. Ecological study of the spruce grouse on the Yellow Dog Plains. *Jack-Pine Warbler* 46(3):74–83.

Rockwell, R. B. 1910. An albino magpie. *Condor* 12:45.

Rodbard, A. 1953. Warm-bloodedness. *Scientific Monthly* 77:137–42.

Roddy, H. J. 1888. Feeding habits of some young raptores. *Auk* 5:244–48.

Roest, A. I. 1957. Notes on the American sparrow hawk. *Auk* 74(1):1–19.

———. 1961. Interspecific relationships among birds. *Auk* 78:433–35.

Rogers, J. P., and Hansen, J. L. 1967. Second broods in the wood duck. *Bird-Banding* 38(3):234–35.

Rohwer, S. A. 1971. Molt and annual cycle of the chuck-will's-widow, *Caprimulgris carolinensis*. *Auk* 88(3):485–519.

Rohwer, S. A., and Woolfenden, G. E. 1968. The varied diet of the gull-billed tern includes a shrub-inhabiting lizard. *Wilson Bull.* 80:330–31.

Romanoff, A. L., and Romanoff, A. J. 1949. *The avian egg*. New York: John Wiley & Sons, Inc.

Romer, A. S. 1933. *Man and the vertebrate animals*. 2 vols. Chicago: University of Chicago Press.

———. 1945. *Vertebrate paleontology*. 2d ed. Chicago: University of Chicago Press.

———. 1956. *The vertebrate body*. Philadelphia: W. B. Saunders Company.

Root, O. M. 1968. Clay-colored sparrow. In *Life histories of North American cardinals, grosbeaks, buntings, towhees, sparrows, and allies*, comp. A. C. Bent *et al.*, ed. O. L. Austin, Jr. U.S. Natl. Mus. Bull. no. 237, pt. 2. Washington, D.C.

Root, R. B. 1967. The niche exploitation pattern of the blue-gray gnatcatcher. *Ecol. Monogr.* 37:317–50.

Rosche, R. C. 1973. Western New York and northwestern Pennsylvania. *Amer. Birds* 27:57, 58.

Roscoe, E. J. 1955. Aquatic snails found attached to feathers of the white-faced glossy ibis. *Wilson Bull.* 67(1):66.

Roseberry, J., and Klimstra, W. D. 1970. The nesting ecology and reproductive performance of the eastern meadowlark. *Wilson Bull.* 82(3):243–67.

Rosen, M. N. 1969. Species susceptibility to avian cholera. *Bull. Wildlife Disease Assoc.* 5:195–200.

———. 1971a. Avian cholera. In *Infectious and parasitic diseases of wild birds*, ed. J. W. Davis *et al.* Ames, Iowa: Iowa State University Press.

———. 1971b. Botulism. In *Infectious and parasitic diseases of wild birds*, ed. J. W. Davis *et al.* Ames, Iowa: Iowa State University Press.

Rosen, M. N., and Bischoff, A. I. 1949. The 1948–49 outbreak of fowl cholera in birds in the San Francisco Bay area and surrounding counties. *Calif. Fish and Game* 35:185–92.

———. 1950. The epidemiology of fowl cholera as it occurs in the wild. *Trans. [15th] N. Amer. Wildlife Conf.*, pp. 147–54.

Ross, J. T. 1969. Kestrel boxes. *Raptor Res. News* 3(1):2.

Ross, R. K. 1976. Notes on the behavior of captive great cormorants. *Wilson Bull.* 88(1):143–45.

Ross, S. 1970. Nest-building, incubation period, and fledging in the black-chinned hummingbird. *Wilson Bull.* 82(2):225.

Rothschild, M. 1965. *Remarks on the life-cycles of fleas (Siphonaptera)*. Congr. Parasitol. Rome.

Rothschild, M., and Clay, T. 1957. *Fleas, flukes, and cuckoos*. New York: The Macmillan Company.

Rothstein, S. I. 1973. The occurrence of unusually small eggs in three species of songbirds. *Wilson Bull.* 85:340–42.

———. 1974. Mechanism of avian egg recognition: Possible learned and innate factors. *Auk* 91(4):796–807.

Rowan, W. 1928. Bears and birds' eggs. *Condor* 30(4):246.

———. 1931. *The riddle of migration*. Baltimore: The Williams & Wilkins Company.

———. 1948. *The ten-year cycle*. Alberta: University of Alberta, Dept. Extension.

———. 1950. The coming peak of the ten-year cycle in Canada. *Trans. [15th] N. Amer. Wildlife Conf.*, pp. 379–83.

Rudd, R. L. 1964. *Pesticides and the living landscape*. Madison, Wis.: University of Wisconsin Press.

Rudy, C. 1967. Albino purple finch. *EBBA News* 30(1):6.

Rue III, L. L. 1973. *The world of the ruffed grouse*, ed. J. K. Terres. Philadelphia: J. B. Lippincott Company.

Rummel, L., and Goetzinger, C. 1975. The communication of intraspecific aggression in the common loon. *Auk* 92(2):333–46.

Rumsey, R. L. 1968. Capture and care of pileated and red-headed woodpeckers. *Bird-Banding* 39(4):313–16.

———. 1970. Woodpecker nest failures in creosoted utility poles. *Auk* 87(2):367–69.

Ruos, J. L. 1974. *Mourning dove status report, 1972*. U.S. Dept. Inter., Fish and Wildlife Service, Spec. Sci. Report—Wildlife, no. 176. Washington, D.C.

Ruppell, W. 1944. Versuche über Heimfinden ziehender Nebelkrähen nach Verfrachtung. *Jour. f. Ornith.* 92:106–33.

Rusk, M. S. 1959. A partially albino chickadee. *Kingbird* 9(1):25; (2):74.

Rusling, W. J. 1951. Food habits of New Jersey owls. *Proc. Linnaean Soc. New York* (1945–1950), pp. 58–62.

Russell, D. N. 1971. Food habits of the starling in eastern Texas. *Condor* 73(3):369–72.

Russell, Jr., H. N., and Woodbury, A. M. 1941. Nesting of the gray flycatcher. *Auk* 58:28–37.

Russell, R. J. 1941. *Climate and man: Yearbook of agriculture*. Washington, D.C.: U.S. Govt. Printing Office.

Russell, Jr., W. L. 1940. *Falconry. A handbook for hunters*. New York: Charles Scribner's Sons.

Rutschke, E. 1960. Untersuchungen über Wasserfestigkeit, und Struktur des Gefieders von Schwimmvögeln. *Zool. Jahrb. Abt. Syst.* 87:441–506.

Ryder, R. A. 1967. Distribution, migration and mortality of the white-faced ibis (*Plegadis chichi*) in North America. *Bird-Banding* 38(4):257–77.

Ryves, B. H. 1944. Nest-construction by birds. *Brit. Birds* 37:182–88, 207–9.

S

Sabine, W. S. 1959. The winter society of the Oregon junco: The flock. *Condor* 61:110–35.

Sabrosky, C. W., and Bennett, G. F. 1956. The utilization of morphological, ecological, and life history evidence in the classification of *Protocalliphora* (diptera: calliphoridae). *Proc. Tenth Internatl. Congr. Entomol.*

Sage, B. L. 1962. Albinism and melanism in birds. *Brit. Birds* 55(6):201–22.

———. 1971. A study of white-billed divers in arctic Alaska. *Brit. Birds* 64:519–28.

Sage, J. H. 1883. A partial albino short-eared owl. *Bull. Nuttall Ornith. Club* 8(3):183.

Salomonsen, F. 1931. On the geographic variation of the snow bunting, *Plectrophenax nivalis*. *Ibis* 1 (ser. 13):57–70.

———. 1938. Notes on the moults of the rock ptarmigan (*Lagopus mutus*). *Proc. [IXth] Internatl. Ornith. Congress*, pp. 295–310. Rouen, France.

———. 1950. *Grønlands fugle*. [*The birds of Greenland*]. Copenhagen: Ejnar Munksgaard.

———. 1951. The immigration and breeding of the fieldfare (*Turdus pilaris*) in Greenland. *Proc. [Xth] Internatl. Ornith. Congress*, pp. 515–26. Uppsala, Sweden: Almquist and Wiksells Boktryekerie AB.

Salt, G. W., and Zeuthen, E. 1960. The respiratory system. In *Biology and comparative physiology of birds*, ed. A. J. Marshall. Vol. 1. New York: Academic Press, Inc.

Samuel, D. C. 1971. Vocal repertoires of sympatric barn and cliff swallows. *Auk* 88(4):839–55.

Sanger, G. A. 1970. The seasonal distribution of some seabirds off Washington and Oregon with notes on their ecology and behavior. *Condor* 72(3):339–57.

———. 1973. A new northern record of Xantus' murrelet. *Condor* 75:253.

Sanger, M. B. 1967. *World of the great white heron*. New York: The Devin-Adair Company, Publishers.

Sanger, V. L. 1971. Tumors. In *Infectious and parasitic diseases of wild birds*, ed. J. W. Davis *et al.* Ames, Iowa: Iowa State University Press.

Sauer, C. O. 1952. *Agricultural origins and dispersals*. New York: American Geographic Society.

Sauer, E. G. F. 1957. Die Sternenorientierung nächtlich ziehender Grasmücken (*Sylvia atricapilla, borin und curruca*). *Z. f. Tierpsych.* 14:29–70.

———. 1963. Migration habits of gold plovers. *Proc. [XIIIth] Internatl. Ornith. Congress* 1:454–67. Ithaca, N.Y.: Amer. Ornith.

Saunders, A. A. 1936. *Ecology of the birds of Quaker Run Valley, Alleghany State Park, New York*. New York State Mus. Handbook no. 16. Albany.

———. 1937. Injury-feigning of a wood duck. *Auk* 54:202.

———. 1954. *The lives of wild birds*. Garden City, N.Y.: Doubleday & Co., Inc.

———. 1961. Piciformes. In *The encyclopedia of biological sciences*, ed. P. Gray. New York: Rheinhold Publishing Corporation.

Saunders, G. B. 1964. South of the border. In *Waterfowl tomorrow*, ed. J. P. Linduska and A. L. Nelson. Washington, D.C.: U.S. Dept. Inter., Fish and Wildlife Service.

Saunders, G. B., and Clark, E. 1962. Yellow-billed cuckoo in stomach of a tiger shark. *Auk* 79(1):118.

Saunders, W. E. 1907. A migration disaster in western Ontario. *Auk* 24:108–110.

Savell, W. E. 1968. Swainson's warbler banded at Linwood, N.J. *Bird-Banding* 39(3):230.

———. 1969. New evening grosbeak longevity record. *EBBA News* 32:220.

Savile, D. B. O. 1950. The flight mechanisms of swifts and hummingbirds. *Auk* 67(4):499–504.

———. 1957. Adaptive evolution of the avian wing. *Evolution* 11:212–24.

Schaeffer, F. S. 1973. Tactile bristles of saw-whet owl are sensitive to touch. *Bird-Banding* 44(2):125.

Schartz, R. L., and Zimmerman, J. L. 1971. The time and energy budget of the male dickcissel (*Spiza americana*). *Condor* 73:65–76.

Schaughency, C. B. 1975. Harris' hawk kills egret. *Raptor Research* 9(1–2):11.

Scheffer, T. H., and Cottam, C. 1935. *The crested myna, or Chinese starling, in the Pacific Northwest*. U.S. Dept. Agric. Tech. Bull. no. 647. Washington, D.C.

Scheidegger, S. 1960. Ornithosis. In *Proc. [XIIth] Internatl. Ornith. Congress* 2:649. Helsinki: Tilgmannin Kirzapaino.

Scheithauer, W. 1967. *Hummingbirds*. New York: Thomas Y. Crowell Company, Inc.

Scherer, W. F. 1963. The importance of birds in the ecology of arthropod-borne animal viruses. *Living Bird*, 2d annual, pp. 131–37.

Scherzinger, W. 1977. Small owls in aviaries. *Avicult. Mag.* 83:18–21.

Schildmacher, H. 1931. Untersuchungen über die Funktion der Herbstchen Köperchen. *Jour. f. Ornith.* 79:374–415.

Schmid, B. 1934. Wie Weit sieht der Falke? [How far does the falcon see?] *Deutsche Jagd.* no 32, pp. 635–36.

Schmid, F. C. 1963. Record longevity of a wild red-shouldered hawk. *Bird-Banding* 34(3):160.

Schmidt-Nielsen, K. 1959. Salt glands. *Scientific American* 200:109–16.

Schmidt-Nielsen, K., and Fange, R. 1958. The function of the salt gland in the brown pelican. *Auk* 75:282–89.

Schmidt-Nielsen, K.; Jorgensen, C. B.; and Osaki, H. 1958. Etrarenal salt excretion in birds. *Amer. Jour. Physio.* 193:101–7.

Schmidt-Nielsen, K., and Kim, Y. T. 1964. The effect of salt intake on the size and function of the salt gland of ducks. *Auk* 81:160–72.

Schmidt-Nielsen, K., and Sladen, W. J. L. 1958. Nasal salt secretion in the Humboldt penguin. *Nature* 181:1217–18.

Schneider, G. H. 1906. Die Orientierung der Brieftauben. *Z. Psychol. Physio. Sinnesorg* 40: 252–79.

Schnell, G. D. 1965. Recording the flight speed of birds by doppler radar. *Living Bird*, 4th annual, pp. 79–87.

———. 1974. Flight speeds and wingbeat frequencies of the magnificent frigatebird. *Auk* 91(3):564–70.

Schorger, A. W. 1929. Woodcock carrying young. *Auk* 46:232.

———. 1947. The deep diving of the loon and old-squaw and its mechanism. *Wilson Bull.* 59: 151–59.

———. 1952a. Ducks killed during a storm at Hot Springs, South Dakota. *Wilson Bull.* 64:113–14.

———. 1952b. Introduction of the domestic pigeon. *Auk* 69(4):462–63.

———. 1955. *The passenger pigeon.* Madison, Wis.: University of Wisconsin Press.

———. 1957. The beard of the wild turkey. *Auk* 74:441–46.

———. 1960. The crushing of *carya* nuts in the gizzard of the turkey. *Auk* 77:337–40.

———. 1964. Turkey. In *A new dictionary of birds*, ed. A. L. Thomson. New York: McGraw-Hill Book Company.

———. 1966. *The wild turkey: Its history and domestication.* Norman, Okla.: University of Oklahoma Press.

Schreiber, R. W. 1970. Breeding biology of western gulls *(Larus occidentalis)* on San Nicolas Island, California, 1968. *Condor* 72(2):133–40.

———. 1976. Growth and development of nestling brown pelicans. *Bird-Banding* 47(1):19–39.

Schreiber, R. W.; Woolfeuden, G. E.; and Curtsinger, W. E. 1975. Prey capture by the brown pelican. *Auk* 92(4):649–54.

Schrenkiesen, R. 1963. *Field book of fresh-water fishes.* New York: G. P. Putnam's Sons.

Schumacher, D. M. 1964. Ages of some captive wild birds. *Condor* 66(4):309.

Schüz, E. 1927. Beitrag zur Kenntnis der Puderbildung bei den Vögeln. *Jour. f. Ornith.* 75: 86–223.

———. 1957. Swallowing of own young ("kronism") by birds and its significance. *Die Vogelwarte* 19(1):1–15.

Schwarte, L. H. 1959. Poisons and toxins. In *Diseases of poultry*, ed. H. E. Biester and L. H. Schwarte. Ames, Iowa: Iowa State University Press.

Schwartz, C. W. 1945. *The ecology of the prairie chicken in Missouri.* Univ. Missouri Studies no. 20.

Schwartzkopff, J. 1949. Über Sitz und Leistung von Gehör und Vibrationssinn bei Vögeln. *Zeit vergleich Physiol.* 31:529–608.

———. 1955a. On the hearing of birds. *Auk* 72: 340–47.

———. 1955b. Schallsinnesorgane, ihre Funktion und biologische Bedeutung bei Vögeln. *Acta XI Congr. Internatl. Ornith. Basel, 1954*, pp. 189–208.

———. 1973. Mechanoreception. In *Avian biology*, ed. D. S. Farner, J. R. King, and K. C. Parkes. Vol. 3, pp. 417–79. New York: Academic Press, Inc.

Schweppenberg, Frh. Geyr von. 1951. Tameness in birds. *Jour. f. Ornith.* 93(1):32–34.

Schwilling, M. D. 1969. A specimen of black-legged kittiwake taken in Kansas. *Kansas Ornith. Soc. Bull.* 20:27.

Sclater, P. L. 1857. On a collection of birds made by Signor Matteo Botteri in the vicinity of Orizaba in southern Mexico. *Proc. Zool. Soc. London* (1857), pp. 210–15.

Scott, A. G. O'Carroll. 1964. Falconry. In *A new dictionary of birds*, ed. A. L. Thomson. New York: McGraw-Hill Book Company.

Scott, F. A. 1961. Christmas count totals for 1960. *Audubon Field Notes* 15:441–44.

Scott, F. R., and Cutler, D. A. 1962. Middle Atlantic coast region. *Audubon Field Notes* 16(1):18.

———. 1967. Middle Atlantic coast region. *Audubon Field Notes* 21(3):402.

———. 1968. Middle Atlantic coast region. *Audubon Field Notes* 22(1):19.

———. 1970. Middle Atlantic coast region. *Audubon Field Notes* 24:29, 669.

———. 1971. Middle Atlantic coast region. *Amer. Birds* 25:718, 841.

———. 1972. Middle Atlantic coast region. *Amer. Birds* 26:42, 586, 745, 842.

———. 1973. Middle Atlantic coast region. *Amer. Birds* 27:38, 598.

———. 1974. Middle Atlantic coast region. *Amer. Birds* 28(4):787.

Scott, J. W. 1942. Mating behavior of the sage grouse. *Auk* 59:472–98.

Scott, L. 1970. Great horned owls occupy artificial nesting site. *Blue Jay* 28(3):123.

Scott, O. K. 1958. Great Basin central Rocky Mountain region. *Audubon Field Notes* 12(3): 298.

Scott. P. 1964. Duck. In *A new dictionary of birds*, ed. A. L. Thomson. New York: McGraw-Hill Book Company.

———. 1972. *The swans.* London: Michael Joseph Ltd.

Scott, W. E. D. 1890. An account of the flamingos *(Phoenicopterus ruber)* observed in the vicinity of Cape Sable, Florida. *Auk* 7:221–26.

Sealy, S. G. 1969a. Apparent hybridization between snow bunting and McKay's bunting on St. Lawrence Island, Alaska. *Auk* 86(2):350–51.

———. 1969b. Color aberrations in some alcids on St. Lawrence Island, Alaska. *Wilson Bull.* 81(2):213–14.

———. 1970. Egg teeth and hatching methods in some alcids. *Wilson Bull.* 82:289–93.

———. 1975. Aspects of the breeding biology of the marbled murrelet in British Columbia. *Bird-Banding* 46(2):141–53.

Seaman, G. A. 1959. A new breeding record of the wandering tattler in Alaska. *Auk* 76:230–32.

Sears, H. F.; Moseley, L. J.; and Mueller; H. C. 1976. Behavioral evidence on skimmers' evolutionary relationships. *Auk* 93:100–104.

Seiple, G. W. 1953. *Avian botulism: Information on earlier research.* U.S. Dept. Inter., Fish and Wildlife Service, Spec. Sci. Rept.—Wildlife, no. 23. Washington, D.C.

Selander, R. K. 1959. Polymorphism in Mexican brown jays. *Auk* 76(4):385–417.

———. 1966. Sexual dimorphism and niche utilization in birds. *Condor* 68(2):113–51.

———. 1971. Systematics and speciation in birds. In *Avian biology*, ed. D. S. Farner, J. R. King, and K. C. Parkes. Vol. 1. New York: Academic Press, Inc.

———. 1972. Sexual selection and dimorphism in birds. In *Sexual selection and the descent of man 1871–1971*, ed. B. Campbell. Pp. 180–230. Chicago: Aldine Publishing Company.

Selander, R. K., and Giller, D. R. 1959. Interspecific relations of woodpeckers in Texas. *Wilson Bull.* 71:107–24.

———. 1961. Analysis of sympatry of great-tailed and boat-tailed grackles. *Condor* 63:29–86.

———. 1963. Species limits in the woodpecker genus *Centurus* (Aves). *Bull. Amer. Mus. Nat. Hist.* 124:213–74.

Selander, R. K., and Hunter, D. K. 1960. On the functions of wing-flashing in mockingbirds. *Wilson Bull.* 72(4):341–48.

Selander, R. K., and LaRue, Jr., C. J. 1961. Inter-

specific display of parasitic cowbirds. *Auk* 78(4):473–504.

Selander, R. K., and Nicholson, D. J. 1962. Autumnal breeding of boat-tailed grackles in Florida. *Condor* 64(2):81–91.

Selby, L. A. 1975. Histoplasmosis. In *Diseases transmitted from animals to man*, comp. and ed. W. T. Hubbert, W. F. McCulloch, and P. R. Shnurrenberger. Springfield, Ill.: Charles C Thomas, Publisher.

Selous, E. 1901. *Bird watching.* London: J. M. Dent & Sons.

Semple, J. B. 1937. Smooth-billed ani in Florida. *Auk* 54(4):391.

Serventy, D. L. 1939. Notes on cormorants. *Emu* 38:357–71.

———. 1958. An analysis of the pelagic bird faunas of the Indo-Pacific oceans. *Proc. Pacific Sci. Congr. (Eight)* 3:461–87.

———. 1960. Geographical distribution of living birds. In *Biology and comparative physiology of birds*, ed. A. J. Marshall. Vol. 1, p. 118. New York: Academic Press, Inc.

———. 1970. Longevity records and banding data on short-tailed (slender-billed) shearwaters. *Austral. Bird Bander* 8(3):61–62.

———. 1971. Biology of desert birds. In *Avian biology*, ed. D. S. Farner, J. R. King, and K. C. Parkes. Vol. 1. New York: Academic Press, Inc.

Serventy, D. L.; Farner, D. S.; Nichols, C. A.; and Stewart, N. E. 1962. Trapping and maintaining shorebirds in captivity. *Bird-Banding* 33(3): 123–30.

Seton, E. T. 1885. Interesting records from Toronto, Canada. *Auk* 2(4):334–37.

———. 1911. *The Arctic prairies.* New York: Charles Scribner's Sons.

———. 1920. Why do birds bathe? *Bird-Lore* 22: 334–35.

Sexton, O. J., and Marion, K. R. 1974. Probable predation by Swainson's hawks on swimming spadefoot toads. *Wilson Bull.* 86(2):167–68.

Shahan, M. S., and Schoening, H. W. 1956. Equine encephalomyelitis. In *Animal diseases: Yearbook of agriculture (1956)*. Washington, D.C.: U.S. Govt. Printing Office.

Shaklee, W. E. 1966. Birds kept for food. In *Birds in our lives*, ed. A. Stefferud and A. L. Nelson. Washington, D.C.: U.S. Dept. Inter., Fish and Wildlife Service.

Sharp, B. 1970. A population estimate of the dusky seaside sparrow. *Wilson Bull.* 82(2):158–66.

Sharp, D. L. 1921. *The seer of slabsides.* Boston: Houghton Mifflin Company.

Sharp, W. M., and McClure, E. 1945. The pheasant in the sandhill region of Nebraska. In *The ring-necked pheasant and its management in North America*, ed. W. L. McAtee. Washington, D.C.: Amer. Wildlife Inst.

Sharples, R. P. 1908. Trustful birds. *Bird-Lore* 10(2):80–81.

Shaub, B. M., and Shaub, M. S. 1956. The evening grosbeak survey. *Passenger Pigeon* 18(1):3–15.

Shaub, M. S. 1960. Unusual plumage variations of the eastern evening grosbeak. *Passenger Pigeon* 22(1):18–21.

———. 1963. Evening grosbeak winter incursions —1958–59, 1959–60, 1960–61. *Bird-Banding* 34(1):1–22.

Sheldon, H. 1922. Top speed of the road-runner. *Condor* 24:180.

Sheldon, W. G. 1971. *The book of the American woodcock.* Amherst, Mass.: University of Massachusetts Press.

Shelley, L. O. 1934. Two pairs of tree swallows mated during two successive seasons. *Bird-Banding* 5(2):91.

———. 1935a. Known history of eastern song sparrows F 121239 and 34-148621. *Bird-Banding* 6(4):137–38.

———. 1935b. A pair of downy woodpeckers mated during four consecutive years. *Bird-Banding* 6(4):135–36.

———. 1938. Milk snake vs. birds. *Auk* 55(3):548.

Shepard, J. M. 1975. Factors influencing female choice in the lek mating system of the ruff. *Living Bird,* 14th annual, pp. 87–111.

Sherman, A. R. 1910. At the sign of the northern flicker. *Wilson Bull.* 22:135–71.

———. 1911. Nest life of the screech owl. *Auk* 28:155–68.

———. 1913. The nest life of the sparrow hawk. *Auk* 30:406–18.

Sherrod, S. K.; White, C. M.; and Williamson, F. S. L. 1976. Biology of the bald eagle on Amchitka Island, Alaska. *Living Bird,* 15th annual, pp. 143–82.

Sherwood, G. A. 1960. The whistling swan in the West with particular reference to Great Salt Lake Valley, Utah. *Condor* 62:370–77.

Shetter, D. S. 1939. Note on the speed of flight of the prairie chicken. *Wilson Bull.* 51(1):46.

Shields, R. H., and Benham, E. L. 1968. Migratory behavior of whooping cranes. *Auk* 85:318.

Shifflett, W. A. 1975a. First photographic record of the brown jay in the U.S. *Auk* 92(4):797.

———. 1975b. Ruddy ground dove in south Texas. *Auk* 92(3):604.

Shoemaker, V. H. 1972. Osmoregulation and excretion in birds. In *Avian biology,* ed. D. S. Farner, J. R. King, and K. C. Parkes. Vol. 2. New York: Academic Press, Inc.

Short, Jr., L. L. 1963. Hybridization in the wood warblers *Vermivora pinus* and *V. chrysoptera. Proc [XIIIth] Internatl. Ornith. Congress,* pp. 147–60. Ithaca, N.Y.: Amer. Ornith. Union.

———. 1965. Hybridization of the flickers (*Colaptes*) of North America. *Bull. Amer. Mus. Nat. Hist.* 129:307–428.

———. 1969a. An apparently melanistic hairy woodpecker from New Mexico. *Bird-Banding* 40(2):145–46.

———. 1969b. Taxonomic aspects of avian hybridization. *Auk* 86:84–105.

———. 1970. Bird-listing and the field observer. *Calif. Birds* 1(4):143–55.

———. 1971. Systematics and behavior of some North American woodpeckers, genus *Picoides* (aves). *Bull. Amer. Mus. Nat. Hist.* 145 (article 1): 5–118.

———. 1972. Systematics and behavior of South American flickers (Aves, *Colaptes*). *Bull. Amer. Mus. Nat. Hist.* 149:1–110.

———. 1974. Habits and interactions of North American three-toed woodpeckers (*Picoides arcticus* and *Picoides tridactylus*). *American Mus. Novitates* 2547:1–42.

———. 1978. Sympatry in woodpeckers of lowland Malayan forest. *Biotropica* 10:122–33.

———. In press. *Woodpeckers of the world.*

Short, Jr., L. L., and Morony, Jr., J. J. 1970. A second-hybrid Williamson's × red-naped sapsucker and an evolutionary history of sapsuckers. *Condor* 72(3):310–15.

Short, Jr., L. L., and Phillips, A. R. 1966. More hybrid hummingbirds from the United States. *Auk* 83:253–65.

Short, Jr., L. L., and Robbins, C. S. 1967. An intergeneric hybrid wood warbler (*Seiurus* × *Dendroica*). *Auk* 84(4):534.

Short, Jr., L. L., and Simon, S. W. 1965. Additional hybrids of the slate-colored junco and the white-throated sparrow. *Condor* 67(4):438–41.

Shumakov, M. E. 1965. Preliminary results of the investigation of migrational orientation of passerine birds by the round-cage method (in Russian). In *"Bionica"* [Moscow], 1965, pp. 371–78.

Shuster, Jr., C. N. 1964. Horseshoe crab. In *Audubon nature encyclopedia,* ed. J. K. Terres. Vol. 5. New York and Philadelphia: Curtis Publishing Company.

Sibley, C. G. 1938. Hybrids of and with North American anatidae. *Proc. [Xth] Internatl. Ornith. Congress,* pp. 327–55. Rouen, France.

———. 1950. Species formation in the red-eyed towhees of Mexico. *Univ. California Publ. Zool.* 50:109–94.

———. 1954. Hybridization in the red-eyed towhees of Mexico. *Evolution* 8:252–90.

———. 1957. The evolutionary and taxonomic significance of sexual dimorphism and hybridization in birds. *Condor* 59:166–91.

———. 1960. The electrophoretic patterns of avian egg-white proteins as taxonomic characters. *Ibis* 102:215–84.

———. 1961. Hybridization and isolating mechanisms. In *Vertebrate speciation,* ed. W. F. Blair. Austin, Texas: University of Texas Press.

———. 1970. *A comparative study of the egg-white proteins of passerine birds.* Peabody Mus. Nat. Hist. Bull. no. 32. New Haven, Conn.: Yale University Press.

Sibley, C. G., and Alquist, J. E. 1972. *A comparative study of the egg-white proteins of non-passerine birds.* Peabody Mus. Nat. Hist. Bull. no. 39. New Haven, Conn.: Yale University Press.

———. 1973. The relationships of the hoatzin. *Auk* 90:1–13.

Sibley, C. G., and Pettingill, Jr., O. S. 1955. A hybrid longspur from Saskatchewan. *Auk* 72:423–25.

Sibley, C. G., and Short, Jr., L. L. 1959. Hybridization in the buntings (*Passerina*) in the Great Plains. *Auk* 76:443–63.

Sibley, C. G., and West, D. A. 1958. Hybridization in the red-eyed towhees of Mexico: The eastern plateau populations. *Condor* 60:85–104.

———. 1959. Hybridization in the rufous-sided towhees of the Great Plains. *Auk* 76:326–38.

Sick, H. 1964. Hoatzin. In *A new dictionary of birds,* ed. A. L. Thomson. New York: McGraw-Hill Book Company.

Sieber, H. 1932. Beobachtungen über die Biologie des Kranichs (*Megazornis grus grus*). *Beitr. Fortpflbiol. Vögel* 8:134–39, 176–80.

Siegenthaler, S. 1953. Observations on the tawny owl. *Der Ornithologische Beobachter* 53(1):10–2.

Siegfried, W. R. 1972. Ruddy ducks colliding with wires. *Wilson Bull.* 84:486–87.

Siegfried, W. R., and Batt, B. D. J. 1972. Wilson's phalaropes forming feeding association with shovelers. *Auk* 89:667–68.

Sillman, A. J. 1973. Avian vision. In *Avian Biology,* ed. D. S. Farner, J. R. King, and K. C. Parkes. Vol. 3. New York: Academic Press, Inc.

Simkiss, K. 1961. Calcium metabolism and avian reproduction. *Biol. Rev.* 36:321–67.

Simmons, K. E. L. 1955. The nature of the predator reactions of waders toward humans; with special reference to the role of the aggressive, escape, and brooding drives. *Behaviour* 8:130–73.

———. 1961. Problems of head-scratching in birds. *Ibis* 37:37–47.

———. 1964a. Feather maintenance. In *A new dictionary of birds,* ed. A. L. Thomson. New York: McGraw-Hill Book Company.

———. 1964b. Grebe. In *A new dictionary of birds,* ed. A. L. Thomson. New York: McGraw-Hill Book Company.

———. 1966. Anting and the problem of self-stimulation. *Jour. Zool.* 149:145–62.

Simons, J. R. 1960. The blood-vascular system. In *Biology and comparative physiology of birds,* ed. A. J. Marshall. Vol. 1. New York: Academic Press, Inc.

Simons, T. R. 1980. Discovery of a ground-nesting marbled murrelet. *Condor* 82:1–9.

Simpson, G. C. 1946. Fossil penguins. *Bull. Amer. Mus. Nat. Hist.* 87:1–99.

———. 1949. *The meaning of evolution.* New Haven, Conn.: Yale University Press.

———. 1961. *Principles of animal taxonomy.* New York: Columbia University Press.

Simpson, G. G.; Pittendreigh, C. S.; and Tiffany, L. H. 1957. *Life: An introduction to biology.* New York: Harcourt, Brace & Co., Inc.

Simpson, S., and Galbraith, J. J. 1905. An investi-

gation into the diurnal variation of the body temperature of nocturnal and other birds and a few mammals. *Jour. Physiol.* 33:225–38.

Sincock, J. L.; Smith, M. M.; and Lynch, J. J. 1964. Ducks in Dixie. In *Waterfowl tomorrow,* ed. J. P. Linduska and A. L. Nelson. Washington, D.C.: U.S. Dept. Inter., Fish and Wildlife Service.

Sitzeman, J.; Hubbard, J. P.; and Kaufman, K.; eds. 1976. The nesting season: southwest region. *Amer. Birds* 30:985–90.

Sjölander, S. 1978. Reproductive behavior of the black-throated diver *Gavia arctica. Ornis Scand.* 9:51–65.

———, and Agren, G. 1972. Reproductive behavior of the common loon. *Wilson Bull.* 84(3):296–308.

Skeel, M. 1976. Longevity record for the whimbrel. *Bird-Banding* 47(1):74.

Skinner, M. P. 1938. Prairie falcon. In *Life histories of North American birds of prey,* ed. A. C. Bent. U.S. Natl. Mus. Bull. no. 170, pt. 2. Washington, D.C.

Skinner, R. W. 1963. Albinism in a Canada goose. *Auk* 80(3):366.

Skutch, A. F. 1940a. Rieffer's hummingbird. In *Life histories of North American cuckoos, goatsuckers, hummingbirds, and their allies,* ed. A. C. Bent. U.S. Natl. Mus. Bull. no. 176. Washington, D.C.

———. 1940b. White-eared hummingbird. In *Life histories of North American cuckoos, goatsuckers, hummingbirds, and their allies,* ed. A. C. Bent. U.S. Natl. Mus. Bull. no. 176. Washington, D.C.

———. 1949a. Do tropical birds rear as many young as they can nourish? *Ibis* 91:430–55.

———. 1949b. Life history of the ruddy quail-dove. *Condor* 51:3–19.

———. 1950a. On the naming of birds. *Wilson Bull.* 62(2):95–99.

———. 1950b. Yellow-green vireo. In *Life histories of North American wagtails, shrikes, vireos, and their allies,* ed. A. C. Bent. U.S. Natl. Mus. Bull. no. 197. Washington, D.C.

———. 1951. Life history of longuemare's hermit. *Ibis* 93:180–95.

———. 1952. On the hour of laying and hatching of birds' eggs. *Ibis* 94:49–61.

———. 1954. *Life histories of Central American birds. Families Fringillidae, Thraupidae, Icteridae, Parulidae, and Coerebidae.* Pacific Coast Avifauna no. 31. Berkeley, Calif.: Cooper Ornith. Soc.

———. 1957a. Fan-tailed warbler. In *The warblers of America,* ed. L. Griscom and A. Sprunt, Jr. New York: The Devin-Adair Co.

———. 1957b. Olive-backed warbler. In *The warblers of America,* ed. L. Griscom and A. Sprunt, Jr. New York: The Devin-Adair Co.

———. 1960. *Life histories of Central American birds.* Vol. 2. Pacific Coast Avifauna no. 34. Berkeley, Calif.: Cooper Ornith. Soc.

———. 1961. Helpers among birds. *Condor* 63(3):198–99.

———. 1962. The constancy of incubation. *Wilson Bull.* 74(2):115–52.

———. 1964a. Life histories of Central American pigeons. *Wilson Bull.* 76(3):211–347.

———. 1964b. Tanager. In *A new dictionary of birds,* ed. A. L. Thomson. New York: McGraw-Hill Book Company.

———. 1973. *The life of the hummingbird.* New York: Crown Publishers, Inc.

———. 1976. *Parent birds and their young.* Austin, Texas, and London: University of Texas Press.

Slack, R. D. 1976. Nest-guarding behavior of male gray catbirds. *Auk* 93(2):135–41.

Sladen, W. J. L. 1953. The adele penguin. *Nature* 171:952–61.

———. 1955. Some aspects of the behaviour of the adele and chinstrap penguins. *Acta XI Congr. Internatl. Ornith.* 1954:241–47.

Slessers, M. 1970. Bathing behavior of land birds. *Auk* 87(1):91–99.

Small, A. 1974. *The birds of California.* New York: Winchester Press.

Smith, A. G. 1960. Hail, great destroyer of wildlife. *Audubon* 62(4):170–71, 189.

Smith, Mrs. C. L. 1963. Personal communication.

Smith, C. R. 1924. Speed of the brown pelican and speed of the roadrunner. *Gull* 6(9):3.

Smith, C. R., and Richmond, M. E. 1972. Factors influencing pellet egestion and gastric pH in the barn owl. *Wilson Bull.* 84(2):179–86.

Smith, D. G., and Holland, D. H. 1974. Mobbing red-winged blackbirds force American kestrel into water. *Auk* 91(4):843–44.

Smith, D. G., and Murphy, J. R. 1972. Unusual causes of raptor mortality. *Raptor Research* 6(1):4–5.

Smith, J. M. 1958. *The theory of evolution.* Paperback. Baltimore: Penguin Books.

Smith, K. G. 1978. Range extension of the blue jay into western North America. *Bird-Banding* 49(3):208–14.

Smith, N. G. 1966. *Evolution of some Arctic gulls (Larus): An experimental study of isolating mechanisms.* Amer. Ornith. Union, Monogr. no. 4. Washington, D.C.

———. 1970. Nesting of king vulture and black hawk-eagle in Panama. *Condor* 72:247–48.

Smith, R. L. 1966. *Ecology and field biology.* 1st ed. New York: Harper & Row, Publishers, Inc.

———. 1968. Grasshopper sparrow. In *Life histories of North American cardinals, grosbeaks, buntings, towhees, sparrows, and allies,* comp. A. C. Bent *et al.,* ed. O. L. Austin, Jr. U.S. Natl. Mus. Bull. no. 237, pt. 2. Washington, D.C.

Smith, S. M. 1970. Foot-trembling feeding behavior by a killdeer. *Condor* 72(2):245.

———. 1973. An aggressive display and related behavior in the loggerhead shrike. *Auk* 90:287–98.

———. 1976. Ecological aspects of dominance hierarchies in black-capped chickadees. *Auk* 93(1):95–107.

Smith, W. J. 1966. *Communication and relationships in the genus* Tyrannus. Cambridge, Mass.: Nuttall Ornith. Pub. no. 6.

———. 1967. Displays of the vermilion flycatcher *(Pyrocephalus rubinus). Condor* 69:601–05.

———. 1970. Courtship and territorial display in the vermilion flycatcher, *Pyrocephalus rubinus. Condor* 72:488–91.

Smith, W. P. 1934. Observations of the nesting habits of the black and white warbler. *Bird-Banding* 5(1):31–36.

———. 1937a. Further notes on the nesting of the barn swallow. *Auk* 54(1):65–69.

———. 1937b. Some bluebird observations. *Bird-Banding* 8:25–30.

———. 1942. Nesting habits of the eastern phoebe. *Auk* 59(3):410–17.

Smithe, F. B. 1966. *The birds of Tikal.* Garden City, N.Y.: Natural History Press.

Smyth, M., and Bartholomew, G. A. 1966. The water economy of the black-throated sparrow and the rock wren. *Condor* 68:447–58.

Smyth, T. 1925. Studies in the life history of the ruffed grouse. Ph.D. dissertation, Cornell University, Ithaca, N.Y.

Snedigar, R. 1963. *Our small native animals: Their habits and care.* New York: Dover Publications, Inc.

Snetsinger, R., and Bordner, D. 1966. Heavy tick population on birds at Island Beach State Park Bird-banding Station. *EBBA News* 29(4):159–60.

Snider, P. R. 1967. Further observations on ticks at Island Beach State Park Bird-banding Station. *EBBA News* 30(4):185–86.

———. 1967. Southwest region. *Audubon Field Notes* 21(1):65, 446, 529.

———. 1968. Southwest region. *Audubon Field Notes* 22(5):635.

———. 1969. Southwest region. *Audubon Field Notes* 23(1):90; (5):614, 682.

———. 1970. Southwest region. *Audubon Field Notes* 24(1):78, 527.

———. 1971a. Southwest region. *Amer. Birds* 25(3):610, 890.

———. 1971b. Southwest region (the nesting season). *Amer. Birds* 25(5): 891.

———. 1971c. Southwest region (spring migration). *Amer. Birds* 25(4):784.

Snoeyenbos, G. H. 1966. Tuberculosis in a ruffed grouse. *Bull. Wildlife Disease Assoc.* 2:9.

Snow, D. W. 1964a. Manakin. In *A new dictionary of birds,* ed. A. L. Thomson. New York: McGraw-Hill Book Company.

———. 1964b. Oilbird. In *A new dictionary of birds,* ed. A. L. Thomson. New York: McGraw-Hill Book Company.

———. 1964c. Tit. In *A new dictionary of birds,* ed. A. L. Thomson. New York: McGraw-Hill Book Company.

Snyder, L. L. 1937. Some measurements and observations from bronzed grackles. *Canadian Field-Nat.* 51:37–39.

———. 1941. In memoriam: James Henry Fleming. *Auk* 58(1):1–12.

———. 1957. *Arctic birds of Canada.* Toronto: University of Toronto Press.

Snyder, N. F. R. 1974. Breeding biology of swallow-tailed kites in Florida. *Living Bird,* 13th annual, pp. 73–97.

Snyder, N. F. R., and Snyder, H. A. 1969. A comparative study of mollusc predation by Limpkins, everglad kites, and boat-tailed grackles. *Living Bird,* 8th annual.

Soikkili, M. 1970a. First record of the fieldfare on American continent. *Condor* 72:480.

———. 1970b. Mortality and reproductive rates in a Finnish population of Dunlin, *Calidris alpina. Ornis Fenn.* 47(4):149–58.

Solman, V. E. F. 1973. Birds and aircraft. *Biol. Conservation* 5(2):79–86.

Sooter, C. 1947. Flight speeds of some south Texas birds. *Wilson Bull.* 59:174–75.

Soper, J. D. 1930. *The blue goose: An account of its breeding grounds, migration, eggs, nests, and general habits.* Ottawa. Dept. of the Inter., North West Territories and Yukon Branch.

Southern, H. N. 1964. Parasitism. In *A new dictionary of birds,* ed. A. L. Thomson. New York: McGraw-Hill Book Company.

Southern, W. E. 1963. Winter population, behavior, and seasonal dispersal of bald eagles in northwestern Illinois. *Wilson Bull.* 75(1):42–45.

———. 1967. Colony selection, longevity, and ring-billed gull populations: Preliminary discussion. *Bird-Banding* 38(1):52–60.

———. 1968. Experiments on the homing ability of purple martins. *Living Bird,* 7th annual, pp. 71–84.

———. 1969. Orientation behavior of ring-billed gull chicks and fledglings. *Condor* 71:418–25.

———. 1971. Gull orientation by magnetic cues: A hypothesis revisited. *Annals New York Acad. Sci.* 188:295–311.

———. 1972. Influence of disturbances in the earth's magnetic field on ring-billed gull orientation. *Condor* 74:102–5.

———. 1974a. American kestrel transports Norway rat. *Wilson Bull.* 86(3):285.

———. 1974b. Florida distribution of ring-billed gulls from the Great Lakes region. *Bird-Banding* 45(4):341–52.

Sowls, L. K. 1955. Prairie ducks. Washington, D.C.: Wildlife Management Inst.

Spallanzani, L. 1787. Opuscules de physique. *J. Senbier,* trans. Vol. 2. Paris.

Speich, S., and Manuwal, D. A. 1974. Gular pouch development and population structure of Cassin's auklet. *Auk* 91(2):291–306.

Speich, S., and Radke, W. J. 1975. Opportunistic feeding of the Gila woodpecker. *Wilson Bull.* 87(2):275–76.

Speich, S., and Speich, M. A. 1972. Floating and swimming in passerines. *Calif. Birds* 3(3):65–68.

Speirs, D. H. 1968. Eastern evening grosbeak. In *Life histories of North American cardinals, grosbeaks, buntings, towhees, finches, sparrows, and allies,* comp. A. C. Bent *et al.,* ed. O. L. Austin, Jr., U.S. Natl. Mus. Bull. no. 237, pt. 1. Washington, D.C.

Speirs, D. H., and Speirs, J. M. 1960. Ontario–Western New York region. *Audubon Field Notes* 14:305–6.

Speirs, J. M. 1945. Flight speeds of the oldsquaw. *Auk* 62:135–36.

———. 1972. First record of painted redstart *(Setophaga picta)* for Canada. *Auk* 89:898.

Speirs, J. M., and Speirs, D. H. 1968. Lincoln's sparrow. In *Life histories of North American cardinals, grosbeaks, buntings, towhees, finches, sparrows, and allies,* comp. A. C. Bent *et al.,* ed. O. L. Austin, Jr. U.S. Natl. Mus. Bull. no. 237, pt. 3. Washington, D.C.

Sperber, I. 1960. Excretion. In *Biology and comparative physiology of birds,* ed. A. J. Marshall. Vol. 1. New York: Academic Press, Inc.

Sperry, C. C. 1940. *Food habits of a group of shorebirds: Woodcock, snipe, knot, and dowitcher.* U.S. Dept. Agric., Bur. Biol. Surv. Wildlife Res. Bull. no. 1. Washington, D.C.

———. 1957. Golden eagle attacks decoy duck. *Wilson Bull.* 69(1):107.

Spiker, C. J. 1930. A starling killed by lightning. *Wilson Bull.* 42(4):289.

Spofford, S. H. 1970. Obituary (of E. G. Allen). *Auk* 87(1):210–11.

Spofford, W. R. 1952. A partial albino horned owl. *Kingbird* 2(4):84.

———. 1964. *The golden eagle in the trans-Pecos and Edwards Plateau of Texas. Audubon Conserv. Rept.* no. 1. New York: Nat. Audubon Soc.

———. 1969. Hawk mountain counts as population indices in northeastern North America. In *Peregrine falcon populations: Their biology and decline,* ed. J. J. Hickey. Madison, Wisc.: University of Wisconsin Press.

———. 1971. The breeding status of the golden eagle in the Appalachians. *Amer. Birds* 25(1):3–7.

Spring, L.W. 1971. A comparison of functional and morphological adaptations in the common murre *(Uria aalge)* and thick-billed murre *(Uria lomvia). Condor* 73:1–27.

———. 1965. Climbing and pecking adaptations in some North American woodpeckers. *Condor* 67(6):457–88.

Sprot, G. D. 1927. Notes on the courtship of the rufous hummingbird. *Condor* 29:71–72.

———. 1937. Notes on the introduced skylark in the Victoria district of Vancouver Island. *Condor* 39:24–30.

Sprunt, Jr., A. 1931. Total albinism in the mallard *(Anas platyrhynchos) Auk* 48(3):414.

———. 1932. The barn owl at sea. *Auk* 49:86.

———. 1940. Chuck-will's-widow. In *Life histories of North American cuckoos, goatsuckers, hummingbirds, and their allies,* ed. A. C. Bent. U.S. Natl. Mus. Bull. no. 176. Washington, D.C.

———. 1941. Cormorants killed by lightning. *Auk* 58:568.

———. 1942a. Gray kingbird. In *Life histories of North American flycatchers, larks, swallows, and their allies,* ed. A. C. Bent. U.S. Natl. Mus. Bull. no. 179. Washington, D.C.

———. 1942b. Purple martin. In *Life histories of North American flycatchers, larks, swallows, and their allies,* ed. A. C. Bent. U.S. Natl. Mus. Bull. no. 179. Washington, D.C.

———. 1946. Florida jay. In *Life histories of North American jays, crows, and titmice,* ed. A. C. Bent. U.S. Natl. Mus. Bull. no. 191. Washington, D.C.

———. 1948. Eastern mockingbird. In *Life histories of North American nuthatches, wrens, thrashers, and their allies,* ed. A. C. Bent. U.S. Natl. Mus. Bull. no. 195. Washington, D.C.

———. 1950. Loggerhead shrike. In *Life histories of North American wagtails, shrikes, vireos, and their allies,* ed. A. C. Bent. U.S. Natl. Mus. Bull. no. 197. Washington, D.C.

———. 1953. Eastern yellow-throated warbler. In *Life histories of North American wood warblers,* ed. A. C. Bent. U.S. Natl. Mus. Bull. no. 203. Washington, D.C.

———. 1954a. *Florida bird life.* New York: Coward-McCann, Inc., and Nat. Audubon Soc.

———. 1954b. A hybrid between a little blue heron and the snowy egret. *Auk* 71(3):314.

———. 1955a. *North American birds of prey.* New York: Harper & Brothers.

———. 1955b. The spread of the cattle egret. *Annual Rept. Smithsonian Inst.,* pp. 259–76.

———. 1957a. Bachman's warbler. In *The warblers of America.* New York: The Devin-Adair Co.

———. 1957b. Yellow warbler. In *The warblers of America.* New York: The Devin-Adair Co.

———. 1958. Eastern boat-tailed grackle. In *Life histories of North American blackbirds, orioles, tanagers, and allies,* ed. A. C. Bent. U.S. Natl. Mus. Bull. no. 211. Washington, D.C.

———. 1968a. Eastern painted bunting. In *Life histories of North American cardinals, grosbeaks, buntings, towhees, finches, sparrows, and allies,* comp. A. C. Bent *et al.,* ed. O. L. Austin, Jr. U.S. Natl. Mus. Bull. no. 237, pt. 1. Washington, D.C.

———. 1968b. MacGillivray's seaside sparrow. In *Life histories of North American cardinals, grosbeaks, buntings, towhees, finches, sparrows, and allies,* comp. A. C. Bent *et al.,* ed. O. L. Austin, Jr. U.S. Natl. Mus. Bull. no. 237, pt. 2. Washington, D.C.

Sprunt, Jr., A., and Chamberlain, E. B. 1949. *South Carolina bird life.* Columbia, S.C.: University of South Carolina Press.

Sprunt, Jr., A., and Denton, J. F. 1957. Swainson's warbler. In *The warblers of America,* ed. L. Griscom and A. Sprunt, Jr. New York: The Devin-Adair Co.

Sprunt IV, A. 1969. Status of the bald eagle. Mimeographed. New York: Natl. Audubon Soc.

Sprunt IV, A., and Cunningham, R. L. 1962. *Continental bald eagle project: Progress report no. 2.* New York: Natl. Audubon Soc.

Sprunt IV, A., and Kahl, M. P. 1960. Mysterious mycteria: Our American stork. *Audubon* 62:-206–9, 234, 252.

Sprunt IV, A., and Ligas, F. J. 1966. Audubon bald eagle studies (1960–1966). Mimeographed. Proc. 62nd Ann. Conv. Natl. Aud. Soc., Sacramento, Calif.

Sprunt IV, A.; Ogden, J. C.; and Robertson, Jr., W. B. 1969. Florida region. *Audubon Field Notes* 23(5):652.

Squire, J. E. 1965. Swimming of landbirds. *Brit. Birds* 58(7):297.

Stabler, R. M. 1951. A survey of Colorado band-tailed pigeons, mourning doves, and wild common pigeons for *Trichomonas gallinae. Jour. Parasitol.* 37:371.

———. 1965. Personal communication.

———. 1969. Personal communication.

———. 1974. Personal communication.

Stabler, R. M., and Herman, C. M. 1951. Upper digestive tract Trichomoniasis in the mourning dove and other birds. *Trans. [16th] N. Amer. Wildlife Conf.,* pp. 145–63.

Stabler, R. M., and Kitzmiller, N. J. 1967. Entryl in the treatment of Trichomoniasis in pigeons and hawks. *Jour. N. Amer. Falconer's Assoc.* 7:47.

Stabler, R. M., and Mellintin, R. W. 1953. Effects of 2-amino-5-nitro-thiazole (enheptin) and other drugs on *Trichomonas gallinae* infection in the domestic pigeon. *Jour. Parasitol.* 39(6):637–42.

Staebler, A. E. 1941. The number of feathers in the English sparrow. *Wilson Bull.* 53:126–27.

Stager, K. E. 1964. *The role of olfaction in food location by the turkey vulture* (Cathartes aura). Contr. in Science no. 81. Los Angeles County Museum.

———. 1966. Housekeepers. In *Birds in our lives,* ed. A. Stefferud and A. L. Nelson. Washington, D.C.: U.S. Dept. Inter., Fish and Wildlife Service.

Stallcup, R., and Greenberg, R. 1974. Middle Pacific Coast region. S. A. (special article). *Amer. Birds* 28(5):945.

Stallcup, R., and Winter, J. 1975. Middle Pacific Coast region. *Amer. Birds* 29(5):1028.

Stamm, D. D. 1963. Susceptibility of bird populations to eastern, western, and St. Louis encephalitis viruses. *Proc.[XIIIth] Internatl. Ornith. Congress,* p. 591. Ithaca, N.Y.: Amer. Ornith. Union.

Stanley, W. F. 1966. Birds on stamps. In *Birds in our lives,* ed. A. Stefferud. Washington, D.C.: U.S. Dept. Inter., Fish and Wildlife Service.

Starkey, E. E. 1972. A case of interspecific homosexuality in geese. *Auk* 89:456–57.

Stebbins, R. C. 1966. *A field guide to western reptiles and amphibians.* Boston: Houghton Mifflin Company.

Steele, J. H., and Galton, M. M. 1971. Salmonellosis. In *Infectious and parasitic diseases of wild birds,* ed. J. W. Davis et al. Ames, Iowa: Iowa State University Press.

Stegmann, B. K. 1969. Über die systematische Stellung der Tauben and Aughuhner [On the systematic position of pigeons and sandgrouse]. *Zool. Jahrb. Syst.* 96:1–51.

Stein, C. D., and Van Ness, G. B. 1956. Anthrax. In *Animal diseases: Yearbook of agriculture,* ed. A. Stefferud. Washington, D.C.: U.S. Dept. Agric.

Stein, R. C. 1958. *The behavioral, ecological and morphological characteristics of two populations of the alder flycatcher Empidonax traillii* (Audubon). N.Y. State Mus. and Sci. Serv. Bull. no. 371. Albany.

———. 1962. A comparative study of songs recorded from five closely related warblers. *Living Bird,* 1st annual, pp. 61–71.

———. 1963. Isolating mechanisms between populations of Traill's flycatchers. *Proc. Amer. Philos. Soc.* 107(1):21–50.

Steinbacher, J. 1936. Zur Frage der Geschlechtsreife von Kleinvögelin. *Beitr. Fortpflbiol. Vögel* 12:139–44.

———. 1964. Woodpecker. In *A new dictionary of birds,* ed. A. L. Thomson. New York: McGraw-Hill Book Company.

Steinmetzer, K. 1924. Die zeitlichen Verhältnisse beim Durchwandern von Futter durch den Magendarmkanal des Huhnes. *Arch. ges. Physio. Pflüger's* 206:500–505.

Steirly, C. C. 1957. Nesting ecology of the red-cockaded woodpecker in Virginia. *Atlantic Nat.* 12: 280–92.

Stenzel, L. E.; Huber, H. R.; and Page, G. W. 1976. Feeding behavior and diet of the long-billed curlew and willet. *Wilson Bull.* 88(2): 314–32.

Stephen, D. 1950. *Days with the golden eagle.* Glasgow: A. & J. Donaldson.

Stettenheim, P. 1972. The integument of birds. In *Avian biology,* ed. D. S. Farner, J. R. King, and K. C. Parkes. Vol. 2. New York: Academic Press, Inc.

———. 1973. The bristles of birds. *Living Bird,* 12th annual, pp. 201–34.

Stevens, A. O. 1936. The first descriptions of North American birds. *Wilson Bull.* 43:203–15.

Stevenson, H. M. 1941. Natural death of a fox sparrow. *Auk* 58(2):266.

———. 1961. Florida region. *Audubon Field Notes* 15(4):404.

———. 1963. Florida region. *Audubon Field Notes* 17(3):322, 398, 456.

———. 1964. Florida region. *Audubon Field Notes* 18:349.

———. 1969. Florida region. *Audubon Field Notes* 23(3):472.

———. 1971. Florida region. *Amer. Birds* 25:570.

———. 1972a. Florida region. *Amer. Birds* 26(3): 592, 595.

———. 1972b. The recent history of Bachman's warbler. *Wilson Bull.* 84(3):344–47.

———. 1973. Personal communication.

Stevenson, J. 1933. Experiments on the digestion of food by birds. *Wilson Bull.* 45:155–67.

Stevenson, J. O., and Meitzen, L. H. 1946. Behavior and feeding habits of Sennett's white-tailed hawk in Texas. *Wilson Bull.* 58:198–205.

Stewart, Jr., J. 1971. Central southern region. *Amer. Birds* 25(5):868.

Stewart, P. A. 1937. A preliminary history of bird weights. *Auk* 54:324–32.

———. 1952. Dispersal, breeding and longevity of barn owls in North America. *Auk* 69:227–45.

———. 1969. Movements, population fluctuations, and mortality among great horned owls. *Wilson Bull.* 81:155–62.

———. 1970. Weight changes and feeding behavior of a captive-reared bald eagle. *Bird-Banding* 41(2):103–10.

———. 1971. Wood ducks nesting in chimneys. *Auk* 88(2):425.

———. 1972. Mortality of purple martins from adverse weather. *Condor* 74:480.

———. 1973. Electrocution of birds by electric fence. *Wilson Bull.* 85(4):476–77.

———. 1974. A nesting of black vultures. *Auk* 91(3):595–600.

———. 1975. Cases of birds reducing or eliminating infestations of tobacco insects. *Wilson Bull.* 87(1):107–9.

Stewart, P. A., and Mackey, Jr., J. P. 1953. A pair of mourning doves occupies same nest two successive years. *Bird-Banding* 29(1):16.

Stewart, R. E. 1953. A life history study of the yellow-throat. *Wilson Bull.* 65(2):99–115.

Stewart, R. E.; Geis, A. D.; and Evans, C. D. 1958. Distribution of population and hunting kill of the canvasback. *Jour. Wildlife Management* 22:333–70.

Stewart, R. E., and Manning, J. H. 1958. Distribution and ecology of whistling swans in the Chesapeake Bay region. *Auk* 75:202–12.

Stewart, R. M. 1973. Breeding behavior and life history of the Wilson's warbler. *Wilson Bull.* 85:21–30.

Stickel, D. W. 1965. Territorial and breeding habits of red-bellied woodpeckers. *Amer. Midland-Nat.* 74:110–18.

Stickel, W. H.; Sheldon, W. G.; and Stickel, L. F. 1965. Care of captive woodcocks. *Jour. Wildlife Management* 29(1):161–72.

Stieglitz, W. O., and Thompson, R. L. 1967. *Status and life history of the Everglade kite in the United States.* U.S. Dept. Inter., Fish and Wildlife Service, Spec. Sci. Rept.—Wildlife, no. 109, Washington, D.C.

Stiles, F. G. 1971. On the field identification of California hummingbirds. *Calif. Birds* 2(2):41–54.

———. 1972. Age and sex determination in rufous and Allen hummingbirds. *Condor* 74:25–32.

Stillson, B. 1954. *Wings: Insects, birds, men.* Indianapolis: The Bobbs-Merrill Co., Inc.

Stimson, L. A. 1961. Cape sable sparrows ... fire and range extension. *Florida Nat.* 34(3):139–40.

———. 1962. Escaped red-whiskered bulbuls (Pycnonotus jocosus) increasing in Dade County. *Florida Nat.* 35(3):193.

———. 1968. Cape Sable sparrow. In *Life histories of North American cardinals, grosbeaks, buntings, towhees, finches, sparrows, and allies,* comp. A. C. Bent *et al.,* ed. O. L. Austin, Jr. U.S. Natl. Mus. Bull. no. 237, pt. 2. Washington, D.C.

Stobo, W. T., and McLaren, I. A. 1971. Late winter distribution of Ipswich sparrow. *Amer. Birds* 25(6):941–44.

Stock, C. 1961. *Rancho La Brea: A record of Pleis-*

tocene life in California. Los Angeles County Mus., Sci. Ser. no. 20.

Stoddard, Sr., H. L. 1922. Notes on birds from southern Wisconsin. *Wilson Bull.* 34(2):67–79.

———. 1931. *The bobwhite quail: Its habits, preservation and increase.* New York: Charles Scribner's Sons.

———. 1961. The hunting of the Cooper's hawk. In *Discovery: Great moments in the lives of naturalists,* ed. J. K. Terres. New York and Philadelphia: J. B. Lippincott Company.

———. 1962. *Bird casualties at a Leon County, Florida, TV tower, 1955–1961.* Tall Timbers Res. Sta., Bull. no. 1. Tallahassee, Fla.

Stoddard, H. L., and Norris, R. A. 1967. *Bird casualties at a Leon County, Florida TV tower: An eleven-year study.* Tall Timbers Res. Sta., Bull. no. 8. Tallahassee, Fla.

Stokes, A. W. 1950. Breeding behavior of the goldfinch. *Wilson Bull.* 62:107–27.

———. 1971. Parental and courtship feeding in red jungle fowl. *Auk* 88(1):21–29.

Stokes, A. W., and Williams, H. W. 1971. Courtship feeding in gallinaceous birds. *Auk* 88(3):543–59.

Stoll, Jr., R. J., and Davis, J. A. 1974. A longevity record for the Appalachian ruffed grouse. *Bird-Banding* 45(3):270–71.

Stone, W. 1888. An abnormal scarlet tanager. *Auk* 5:322.

———. 1901. John Cassin. *Cassinia* 5:1–7.

———. 1903. John Kirk Townsend. *Cassinia* 7:1–5.

———. 1907. Adolphus L. Heermann. *Cassinia* 9:1–6.

———. 1921. Notes and news. *Auk* 38(2):317–18.

———. 1928. Notes and news. *Auk* 45(3):417.

———. 1929. Obituaries. *Auk* 46:279–80.

———. 1937. *Bird studies at old Cape May.* 2 vols. Proc. Delaware Valley Ornith. Club. Philadelphia.

Stonehouse, B. 1952. Breeding behaviour of the emperor penguin. *Nature* 169:760.

———. 1964. Tropicbird. In *A new dictionary of birds,* ed. A. L. Thomson. New York: McGraw-Hill Book Company.

Stoner, D. 1936. Studies on the bank swallow (*Riparia riparia riparia*) (Linnaeus) in the Oneida Lake region. *Roosevelt Wildlife Annals* 4(2):126–233.

———. 1939. Eastern sparrow hawk feeding on big brown bat. *Auk* 56(4):474.

Stoner, D., and Stoner, L. C. 1937. A six-year-old bank swallow. *Bird-Banding* 8(4):175–76.

———. 1945. An example of bumblefoot in the great horned owl. *Auk* 62(3):405–8.

Stoner, E. A. 1937. Killdeer nest on roof of a building. *Condor* 39(3):127.

———. 1947. Anna's hummingbird at play. *Condor* 49:36.

———. 1969. Bird banding in California. *Calif. Fish and Game* 55(1):4–11.

Stong, C. L. 1960. *The amateur naturalist.* New York: Simon & Schuster, Inc.

Storer, J. H. 1948. *The flight of birds.* Cranbrook Inst. Sci. Bull. no. 28. Bloomfield Hills, Mich.

———. 1952. Bird aerodynamics. *Scientific American* 186:25–29.

Storer, R. W. 1952. Variation in the resident sharp-shinned hawks of Mexico. *Condor* 54:283–28.

———. 1955. Weight, wing area, and skeletal proportions in three accipiters. *Acta XI Congr. Internatl. Ornith.,* pp. 287–90. Helsinki, Finland: Tilgmannin Kirjapaino.

———. 1960a. Adaptive radiation in birds. In *Biology and comparative physiology of birds,* ed. A. J. Marshall. Vol. 1. New York: Academic Press, Inc.

———. 1960b. The classification of birds. In *Biology and comparative physiology of birds,* ed. A. J. Marshall. Vol. 1. New York: Academic Press, Inc.

———. 1964. Auk. In *A new dictionary of birds,* ed. A. L. Thomson. New York: McGraw-Hill Book Company.

———. 1965. The color phases of the western grebe. *Living Bird,* 4th annual, pp. 59–63.

———. 1966. Sexual dimorphism and food habits in three North American accipiters. *Auk* 83:423–36.

———. 1969. What is a tanager? *Living Bird,* 8th annual, pp. 127–36.

———. 1971a. Adaptive radiation in birds. In *Avian biology,* ed. D. S. Farner, J. R. King, and K. C. Parkes. Vol. 1, pp. 149–88. New York: Academic Press, Inc.

———. 1971b. Classification of birds. In *Avian biology,* ed. D. S. Farner, J. R. King, and K. C. Parkes. Vol. 3, pp. 109–82. New York: Academic Press, Inc.

———. 1976. The behavior and relationships of the least grebe. *Trans. San Diego Soc. Nat. Hist.* 18 (6):113–26.

Storer, R. W., Siegfried, W. R.; and Kinahan, J. 1975. Sunbathing in Grebes. *Living Bird,* 14th annual, pp. 45–56.

Storr, G. M. 1958. Migration routes of the Arctic tern. *Emu* 58:59–62.

Stott, Jr., K. 1948. Notes on the longevity of captive birds. *Auk* 65(3):402–5.

———. 1959. The starling arrives in San Diego, California. *Condor* 61(3):373.

Stotts, V. D., and Henny, C. J. 1975. The age at first flight of young American ospreys. *Wilson Bull.* 87(2):277–78.

Strait, L. E., and Sloan, N. F. 1975. Movements and mortality of juvenile white pelicans from North Dakota. *Wilson Bull.* 87(1):54–59.

Stresemann, E. 1927–1934. Sauropsida, Aves. In *Handbuch der Zoologie.* Berlin und Leipsig: W. de Gruyter and Co.

———. 1935. *Ornith. Monatsber.* 43(4):114–15.

———. 1955. Die Wanderungen des Waldlaubsängers (*Phylloscopus sibilatrix*). *Jour. f. Ornith.* 96:153–67.

———. 1975. *Ornithology: From Aristotle to the present.* Cambridge, Mass.: Harvard University Press.

Strong, R. M. 1911. On the olfactory organs and sense of smell in birds. *Jour. Morph.* 22:619.

Strutt, G. M. 1954. British birds before the microphone. *Audubon* 56:180–81, 189.

Stuart-Baker, E. C. 1922. Speed of Indian swifts. *Brit. Birds* 15:31.

———. 1942. The speed of birds. *Country Life,* March.

Stull, W. De M. 1968. Eastern and Canadian chipping sparrows. In *Life histories of North American cardinals, grosbeaks, buntings, towhees, finches, sparrows, and allies,* comp. A. C. Bent et al., ed. O. L. Austin, Jr. U.S. Natl. Mus. Bull. no. 237, pt. 2. Washington, D.C.

Stupka, A. 1963. *Notes on the birds of Great Smoky Mountains National Park.* Knoxville, Tenn.: University of Tennessee Press.

Sturkie, P. D. 1954. *Avian physiology.* 1st ed. Ithaca, N.Y.: Comstock Pub. Associates.

———. 1965. *Avian physiology.* 2d ed. Ithaca, N.Y.: Cornell University Press.

Sturkie, P. D., ed. 1976. *Avian physiology.* 3d ed. New York: Springer-Verlag.

Sumner, Sr., E. L. 1934. Wren-tit banded in 1925 again trapped. *Condor* 36(4):170.

Sumner, Jr., E. L. 1929. Comparative studies of the growth of young raptores. *Condor* 31(3):85–111.

———. 1935. A life history study of the California quail: With recommendations for conservation and management. *Calif. Fish and Game* 21 (3–4):167–256; 277–342.

———. 1940. Longevity in raptorial birds as indicated by banding records. *Condor* 42(1):39–40.

Sumner, F. G. 1933. Young sparrow hawks and a screech owl in the same nest. *Condor* 35:231–32.

Sutherland, C. A. 1963. Notes on the behavior of common nighthawks in Florida. *Living Bird,* 2d annual, pp. 31–39.

Sutton, A., and Sutton, M. 1956. The adventures of Steller. *Natural History* 65:485–91.

Sutton, G. M. 1912. An albinic burrowing owl. *Bird-Lore* 14(3):184.

———. 1924. A visit to a wood ibis colony. *Bird-Lore* 26:391–95.

———. 1928. Notes on a collection of hawks from Schuylkill County, Pennsylvania. *Wilson Bull.* 40:84–95.

———. 1929. Insect-catching tactics of the screech owl (*Otus asio*). *Auk* 46:545–56.

———. 1932. *The birds of Southampton Island.* Mem. Carnegie Mus. no. 12 (pt.2). Pittsburgh.

———. 1936. Food-capturing tactics of the least bittern. *Auk* 53(1):74–75.

———. 1940. Roadrunner. In *Life histories of North American cuckoos, goatsuckers, hummingbirds, and their allies,* ed. A. C. Bent. U.S. Natl. Mus. Bull. no. 176. Washington, D.C.

———. 1943. *Notes on the behavior of certain captive young fringillines.* University of Michigan, Occas. Pap. Mus. Zool. no. 474. Ann Arbor.

———. 1946. Wing-flashing in the mockingbird. *Wilson Bull.* 58:206–9.

———. 1951a. Dispersal of mistletoe by birds. *Wilson Bull.* 63(4):235.

———. 1951b. *Mexican birds—First impressions.* Norman, Okla.: University of Oklahoma Press.

———. 1965. Grouse, ptarmigan, and prairie chickens. In *Water, prey, and game birds of North America,* ed. A. Wetmore et al. Washington, D.C.: Natl. Geographic Soc.

———. 1967a. Behavior of the buff-breasted sandpiper at the nest. *Arctic* 20(1):3–7.

———. 1967b. *Oklahoma birds: Their ecology and distribution with comments on the avifauna of the southern Great Plains.* Norman, Okla.: University of Oklahoma Press.

———. 1968. Review: The shorebirds of North America. *Wilson Bull.* 80:500–503.

———. 1970. Jenny Lind's Island. *Audubon* 72:14–35.

———. 1974. Personal communication.

Sutton, G. M., and Parmelee, D. F. 1955. The breeding of the semipalmated plover on Baffin Island. *Bird-Banding* 26:137–96.

Sutton, G. M., and Pettingill, Jr., O. S. 1943. The Alta Mira oriole and its nest. *Condor* 45:125–32.

Sutton, G. M., and Semple, J. B. 1941. The egg of the marbled murrelet. *Auk* 58(4):580–81.

Sviridenko, P. A. 1968. Food storage by the nuthatch (*Sitta europaea*). *Vestnik Zoologii* 1968 (1):89–90.

Swainson, W., and Richardson, J. 1832. *The birds.* ed. J. Richardson Vol. 2. London: Fauna Boreali-Americana. J. Murray & Son.

Swan, L. W. 1970. Goose of the Himalayas. *Natural History* 70(10):68–75.

Swanberg, P. O. 1950. On the concept of the incubation period. *Vär Fägalvärld,* 9:63–80.

———. 1951. Food storage territory and song in the thick-billed nutcracker. *Proc. [Xth] Internatl. Ornith. Congress,* pp. 545–54. Stockholm, Sweden: Almquist and Wiksells Boktryckerie AB.

Swartz, L. G. 1967. Sea-cliff birds. In *Environment of the Cape Thompson region, Alaska,* ed. N. J. Wilimovsky and J. N. Wolfe. U.S. Dept. Commerce, Publ. PNE-481 Clearinghouse for Fed. Sci. and Technol. Inform. Natl. Bur. Stds. Springfield, Va.

———. 1968. The experimental production of foot infections in birds: Observations on causes and cures. *Raptor Res. News* 2(1):10–25.

Sweenen, C. 1974. Observations on the effects of the ejection of stomach oil by the fulmar, *Fulmar glacialis,* on other birds. *Ardea* 62(½):111–17.

Swenander, G. 1902. Studien über den Bau des Schlundes und des Magens der Vögel. *Kgl. Norske Videnskab. Selskabs, Skriffer.* 6:1–240.

Swift, E., and Lawrence, C. H. 1966. Laws that protect. In *Birds in our lives*, ed. A. Stefferud and A. L. Nelson. Washington, D.C. U.S. Dept. Inter., Fish and Wildlife Service.

Swinton, W. E. 1960. The origin of birds. In *Biology and comparative physiology of birds*, ed. A. J. Marshall. Vol. 1. New York: Academic Press, Inc.

———. 1965. *Fossil birds*. 2d ed. London: British Museum (Natural History).

Sykes, P. W. 1964. Fulmar taken in Virginia. *Auk* 81(3):437.

———. 1974a. First record of Bahama yellowthroat in the U.S. *Amer. Birds* 28(1):14–15.

———. 1974b. Florida burrowing owl collected in North Carolina. *Auk* 91(3):636–37.

Sykes, P. W., and Kale II, H. W. 1974. Everglade kite feeds on non-snail prey. *Auk* 91(4):818–20.

T

Taber, W. 1955a. In memoriam: Francis Henry Allen. *Auk* 72:179–83.

———. 1955b. In memoriam: Arthur Cleveland Bent. *Auk* 72(4):332–39.

———. 1958. In memoriam. Charles Foster Batchelder. *Auk* 75:14–25.

———. 1968. White-winged crossbill. In *Life histories of North American cardinals, grosbeaks, buntings, towhees, finches, sparrows, and allies*, comp. A. C. Bent *et al.*, ed. O. L. Austin, Jr. U.S. Natl. Mus. Bull. no. 237, pt. 1. Washington, D.C.

Taber, W., and Johnston, D. W. 1968. Indigo bunting. In *Life histories of North American cardinals, grosbeaks, buntings, towhees, finches, sparrows, and allies*, comp. A. C. Bent *et al.*, ed. O. L. Austin, Jr. U.S. Natl. Mus. Bull. no. 237, pt. 1. Washington, D.C.

Taft, J. E. 1970. Possible seven-day incubation period in the robin, *Turdus migratorius*. *Audubon Field Notes* 24(5):652.

Tait, W. W.; Johnson, H. M.; and Courser, W. D. 1972. Osprey carrying a small mammal. *Wilson Bull.* 84:341.

Tanner, J. T. 1942. *The ivory-billed woodpecker*. Natl. Audubon Soc. Res. Report no. 1. New York: Natl. Audubon Soc.

———. 1958. Juncos in the Great Smoky Mountains. *Migrant* 29(4):61–65.

Tansley, K. 1964. Vision. In *A new dictionary of birds*, ed. A. L. Thomson. New York: McGraw-Hill Book Company.

Tate, Jr., J. 1962. Meadowlark killed by electric fence. *Wilson Bull.* 74(2):184.

———. 1973. Methods and annual sequence of foraging by the sapsucker. *Auk* 90(4):840–56.

Taverner, P. A. 1931. An albino empidonax. *Auk* 48(4):603–4.

———. 1941. Breeding grounds of Ross's goose at last discovered. *Auk* 58(1):92.

———. 1947. *Birds of Canada*. Toronto: The Musson Book Company, Ltd.

Taverner, P. A., and Sutton, G. M. 1934. The birds of Churchill, Manitoba. *Annals Carnegie Mus.* 23:1–83.

Taylor, J. W. 1972. *Hawk Mt. Sanctuary Assoc. Twenty-ninth Annual Report, 1971–1972*. Kempton, Pa.

Taylor, P. S. 1973. Breeding behavior of the snowy owl. *Living Bird*, 12th annual, pp. 137–54.

Taylor, W. K. 1972. Analysis of ovenbirds killed in central Florida. *Bird-Banding* 43(1):15–19.

———. 1973. Black-throated blue and Cape May warblers killed in central Florida. *Bird-Banding* 44(4):258–66.

———. 1974. A new hybrid bunting (*Passerina cyanea* × *Passerina ciris*). *Auk* 91(3):485–87.

Taylor, W. K., and Hanson, H. 1970. Observations on the breeding and biology of the vermilion flycatcher. *Wilson Bull.* 82(3):315–19.

Taylor, W. P., and Shaw, W. T. 1927. *Mammals and birds of Mount Rainier National Park.* Washington, D.C.: U.S. Dept. Inter., Natl. Park Service.

Teager, C. W. 1967. Birds sun-bathing. *Brit. Birds* 60(9):361–63.

Teague, R. 1971. *Manual of wildlife conservation*. Washington, D.C.: Wildlife Soc.

Teale, E. W. 1951. *North with the spring*. New York: Dodd, Mead & Company.

———. 1965. *Wandering through winter*. New York: Dodd, Mead & Company.

Tee-Van, J. 1962. In memoriam: William Beebe, 1877–1962. *Explorers Jour.* 40(3):40–41.

Tekke, M. J. 1954. The ruff: feathered knight of the tourney. *Audubon* 56(5):216–17, 238.

Temple, S. A. 1972. Chlorinated hydrocarbon residues and reproductive success in eastern North American merlins. *Condor* 74:105–6.

Temple, S. A., ed. 1977. Endangered birds: Management techniques for preserving threatnd species. Madison, Wisc.: University of Wisconsin Press.

Terres, J. K. 1936–1970. Unpublished journals.

———. 1940. Great horned owls dying in the winter of 1939–40. *Auk* 57(4):571–72.

———. 1941. Short-billed marsh wren in the western Adirondacks. *Auk* 58(2):263–64.

———. 1946a. Birds have accidents, too! *Audubon* 48(2):27–31.

———. 1946b. Dynamite in DDT. *New Republic*, March 25, p. 415.

———. 1946c. Feathered death in the sky. *Coronet*, August.

———. 1947a. Big brother to the waterfowl. *Audubon* 49(3):150–58.

———. 1947b. Sir Galahad in feathers. *Blue Book*, June, pp. 94–97.

———. 1947c. These fishes eat birds. *True Magazine*, August, p. 81.

———. 1948. Bird of tragedy. *Audubon* 50(2):90–95.

———. 1949. Care and feeding of wild birds. *Audubon* 51:187–89.

———. 1952. A glance backward. *Audubon* 54:219, 270.

———. 1953. *Songbirds in your garden*. New York: Thomas Y. Crowell Company, Inc.

———. 1956a. Death in the night. *Audubon* 58(1):18–20.

———. 1956b. Eastern meadowlark (*Sturnella magna*) eating a traffic-killed bird. *Auk* 73(2):289–90.

———. 1956c. The meaning of wildlife inventories. *Audubon* 58(4):149, 151, 174.

———. 1956d. Scarlet tanagers in trouble. *Audubon* 58(4):162.

———. 1958. *The Audubon book of true nature stories*. New York: Thomas Y. Crowell Company, Inc.

———. 1960a. Strangers in our gardens. *Flower Grower*, June, pp. 52–53.

———. 1960b. *The wonders I see*. Philadelphia: J. B. Lippincott Company.

———. 1961. Available check-lists of birds—Canada and the United States. *Audubon* 63:44–7, 62, 64.

———. 1962a. Anting behavior of a wood thrush with a snail. *Wilson Bull.* 74(2):187.

———. 1962b. Saw-whet owl near Chapel Hill, North Carolina in spring. *Chat* 26(2):46.

———. 1963. Obituary: W. L. McAtee, 1883–1962. *Jour. Wildlife Management* 27(3):494–99.

———. 1964a. The anatomy of a nest. *Audubon* 66(6):356.

———. 1964b. On the trail of our wandering birds. *Audubon* 66:100–103.

———. 1965. The friendly ones (birds and people). *Flower Grower*, May, pp. 36–59.

———. 1967. Cattle egrets eating earthworms. *Chat* 31(3):73–74.

———. 1968a. *Flashing wings: The drama of bird flight*. Garden City, N.Y.: Doubleday & Co., Inc.

———. 1968b. Kingfishers eating bullfrog tadpoles. *Auk* 85(1):140.

———. 1968c. *Songbirds in your garden*. Rev. ed. New York: Thomas Y. Crowell Company, Inc.

———. 1969. *From Laurel Hill to Siler's Bog: The walking adventures of a naturalist*. New York: Alfred A. Knopf, Inc.

———. 1975. *How birds fly: Under the water and through the air*. Paperback reprint of *Flashing wings: The drama of bird flight*. New York: Hawthorn Books, Inc.

———. 1977. *Songbirds in your garden*. 3d ed. Soft cover. New York: Hawthorn Books, Inc.

Terres, J. K., ed. 1961b. *Discovery: Great moments in the lives of outstanding naturalists*. New York and Philadelphia: J. B. Lippincott Company.

Terres, J. K., and Jameson, Jr., E. W. 1943. Plague of mice as food for short-eared owls. *Wilson Bull.* 55(2):131.

Terrill, L. M. 1931. Nesting of the saw-whet owl in the Montreal district. *Auk* 48:169–74.

———. 1968. Eastern fox sparrow. In *Life histories of North American cardinals, grosbeaks, buntings, towhees, finches, sparrows, and allies*, comp. A. C. Bent *et al.*, ed. O. L. Austin, Jr. U.S. Natl. Mus. Bull. no. 237, pt. 3. Washington, D.C.

Tessen, D. D. 1975. Western Great Lakes region. *Amer. Birds* 29(5):976–77.

Teulings, R. P. 1972. Southern Atlantic Coast region. *Amer. Birds* 26:844–45.

———. 1973. Southern Atlantic Coast region. *Amer. Birds* 27:42.

Teulings, R. P., and Teulings, E. 1971. Personal communication.

Thatcher, D. M. 1968. Gray-headed junco. In *Life histories of North American cardinals, grosbeaks, buntings, towhees, finches, sparrows, and allies*, comp. A. C. Bent *et al.*, ed. O. L. Austin, Jr. U.S. Natl. Mus. Bull. no. 237, pt. 2. Washington, D.C.

Thayer, G. H. 1909. *Concealing-coloration in the animal kingdom*. New York: The Macmillan Company.

Thielke, G. 1956. The preying technique of the northern shrike and other predators. *Z. f. Tierpsych.* 13(3):272–77.

———. 1976. *Bird sounds*. Ann Arbor, Mi.: University of Michigan Press.

Thomas, D. G., and Dartnell, A. J. 1971. Moult of the red-necked stilt. *Emu* 71:49–53.

Thomas, E. F. 1934. The toxicity of certain species of Crotolaria seed for the chicken, quail, turkey, and dove. *Jour. Am. Vet. Med. Assoc.* 85:617.

Thomas, E. S. 1958. In memoriam: Lawrence Emerson Hicks. *Auk* 75(3):278–81.

Thomas, L. A., and Eklund, C. M. 1960. Overwintering of western equine encephalomyelitis virus in experimentally infected garter snakes and transmission by mosquitoes. *Proc. Soc. Exptl. Biol. and Med.* 105:52.

Thomas, L. A.; Ecklund, C. M.; and Rush, W. A. 1958. Susceptibility of garter snakes (*Thamnophis spp.*) to western equine encephalomyelitis. *Proc. Soc. Exptl. Biol. and Med.* 99:698–700.

Thomas, R. H. 1941. Ticks affecting birds' eyesight. *Auk* 58:590–91.

Thompson, D. Q., and Person, R. A. 1963. The eider pass at Point Barrow, Alaska. *Jour. Wildlife Management* 27:348–56.

Thompson, D. W. 1910. Historia animalium. *The works of Aristotle*. Vol. 4. London: Oxford University Press.

———. 1942. *On growth and form*. Vol. 1. 2d ed. New York: Cambridge University Press.

Thompson, M. 1973. Migratory patterns of ruddy turnstones in the central Pacific region. *Living Bird*, 12th annual, pp. 5–23.

Thompson, M. C. 1961. The flight speed of a red-breasted merganser. *Condor* 63(3):265.

Thompson, R. L., ed. 1971. *The ecology and management of the red-cockaded woodpecker: Proceedings of a symposium at Okefenokee National Wildlife Refuge, Folkston, Ga., May*

26–27. Tallahassee, Fla.: Tall Timbers Research Station.

Thompson, W. L. 1960. Agonistic behavior in the house finch. Part I: Annual cycle and display patterns. *Condor* 62:245–71; Part II: Factors in aggressiveness and sociability. *Condor* 62:378–402.

Thomsen, L. 1971. Behavior and ecology of burrowing owls in the Oakland municipal airport. *Condor* 73:177–92.

Thomson, A. L. 1926. *Problems of bird-migration.* Boston: Houghton Mifflin Company.

———. 1959. The subspecies concept. *Bird Study* 16(1):1–13.

———. 1964a. Accentors. In *A new dictionary of birds,* ed. A. L. Thomson. New York: McGraw-Hill Book Company.

———. 1964b. Classification. In *A new dictionary of birds,* ed. A. L. Thomson. New York: McGraw-Hill Book Company.

———. 1964c. Cuckoo. In *A new dictionary of birds,* ed. A. L. Thomson. New York: McGraw-Hill Book Company.

———. 1964d. Flightlessness. In *A new dictionary of birds,* ed. A. L. Thomson. New York: McGraw-Hill Book Company.

———. 1964e. Gannet. In *A new dictionary of birds,* ed. A. L. Thomson. New York: McGraw-Hill Book Company.

———. 1964f. Geological factors. In *A new dictionary of birds,* ed. A. L. Thomson. New York: McGraw-Hill Book Company.

———. 1964g. Gull. In *A new dictionary of birds,* ed. A. L. Thomson. New York: McGraw-Hill Book Company.

———. 1964h. Ibis. In *A new dictionary of birds,* ed. A. L. Thomson. New York: McGraw-Hill Book Company.

———. 1964i. Intestine: In *A new dictionary of birds,* ed. A. L. Thomson. New York: McGraw-Hill Book Company.

———. 1964j. Naris. In *A new dictionary of birds,* ed. A. L. Thomson. New York: McGraw-Hill Book Company.

———. 1964k. Ornithology. In *A new dictionary of birds,* ed. A. L. Thomson. New York: McGraw-Hill Book Company.

———. 1964l. Passeriformes. In *A new dictionary of birds,* ed. A. L. Thomson. New York: McGraw-Hill Book Company.

———. 1964m. Sandpiper. In *A new dictionary of birds,* ed. A. L. Thomson. New York: McGraw-Hill Book Company.

———. 1964n. Sexual dimorphism. In *A new dictionary of birds,* ed. A. L. Thomson. New York: McGraw-Hill Book Company.

———. 1964o. Species. In *A new dictionary of birds,* ed. A. L. Thomson. New York: McGraw-Hill Book Company.

———. 1964p. Stork. In *A new dictionary of birds,* ed. A. L. Thomson. New York: McGraw-Hill Book Company.

———. 1964q. Tertiary. In *A new dictionary of birds,* ed. A. L. Thomson. New York: McGraw-Hill Book Company.

———. 1964r. Young bird. In *A new dictionary of birds,* ed. A. L. Thomson. New York: McGraw-Hill Book Company.

Thomson, A. L., and Leach, E. P. 1952. Report on bird-ringing in 1951. *Brit. Birds* 45:265–77.

Thomson, H. W. 1914. The building of a robin's nest. *Bird-Lore* 16(5):360–61.

Thomson, J. A. 1923. *The biology of birds.* New York: The Macmillan Company.

Thomson, W. A. R. 1959. *The Macmillan medical encyclopedia.* New York: The Macmillan Company.

Thorensen, A. C. 1964. The breeding behavior of the Cassin auklet. *Condor* 66:456–76.

Thorpe, W. H. 1944. Some problems in animal learning. *Proc. Linnaean Soc. London* 156:70–83.

———. 1956a. The language of birds. *Scientific American* 195(4):128–38.

———. 1956b. *Learning and instinct in animals.* London: Methuen & Co., Ltd.

———. 1959. Talking birds and the mode of action of the vocal apparatus of birds. *Proc. Zool. Soc. London* 132:441–55.

———. 1961. *Bird song: The biology of vocal communication and expression in birds.* Cambridge: At the University Press.

———. 1964a. Mimicry, vocal. In *A new dictionary of birds,* ed. A. L. Thomson. New York: McGraw-Hill Book Company.

———. 1964b. Singing. In *A new dictionary of birds,* ed. A. L. Thomson. New York: McGraw-Hill Book Company.

Thorpe, W. H., and North, M. E. W. 1965. The lonely tunesmiths of nature-men and the birds. *Saturday Rev.* 68:85–87.

Thut, R. N. 1970. Feeding habits of the dipper in southwestern Washington. *Condor* 72:234–45.

Tickell, W. L. N. 1968. The biology of the great albatrosses, *Diomedea exulans* and *Diomedea epimophora. American Geophysical Union, Antarctic Res. Ser.* 12:1–55.

———. 1975. Breeding biology of the black-browed albatross, *Diomedea melanophris,* and the grey-headed albatross, *D. chrystostoma,* at Bird Island, South Georgia. *Ibis* 117:432–51.

Tinbergen, N. 1935. Field observations of east Greenland birds. 1. The behaviour of the red-necked phalarope *(Phalaropus lobatus)* in spring. *Ardea* 24:1–42.

———. 1936. Zur Soziologie der Silbermöwe *(Larus a argentatus). Beitr. Fortpflbiol. Vögel* 12:89–96.

———. 1939. *The behavior of the snow bunting in spring.* Trans. Linnaean Soc. New York, no. 5.

———. 1951a. Recent advances in the study of bird behaviour. *Proc. [Xth] Internatl. Ornith. Congress,* pp. 60–74. Uppsala, Sweden: Almquist and Wiksells Boktryckerie AB.

———. 1951b. *The study of instinct.* Oxford: Oxford University Press.

———. 1953a. *The herring gull's world: A story of the social behavior of birds.* London: Collins, Ltd.

———. 1953b. *Social behaviour in animals.* London: Methuen & Co., Ltd.

———. 1958. *Curious naturalists.* New York: Basic Books, Inc.

———. 1960. The evolution of behavior in gulls. *Scientific American* 213:118–30.

———. 1962. Foot-paddling in gulls. *Brit. Birds* 55(3):117–20.

———. 1964. Territory. In *A new dictionary of birds,* ed. A. L. Thomson. New York: McGraw-Hill Book Company.

Tinbergen, N., and Norton-Griffiths, M. 1964. Oystercatchers and mussels. *Brit. Birds* 57:64–70.

Titus, H. W. 1949. *The scientific feeding of chickens.* 2d ed. Danville, Ill.: The Interstate.

Tixier-Vidal, A., and Follett, B. K. 1973. The adenophypophysis. In *Avian Biology,* ed. D. S. Farner, J. R. King, and K. C. Parkes. Vol. 3, pp. 109–82. New York: Academic Press, Inc.

Todd, Jr., K. S., and Hammond, D. M. 1971. Coccidia. In *Infectious and parasitic diseases of wild birds,* ed. J. W. Davis *et al.* Ames, Iowa: Iowa State University Press.

Tomback, Diana F. 1978. Foraging strategies of Clark's nutcracker. *Living Bird* 16:123–62.

———. 1980. How nutcrackers find their seed stores. *Condor* 82 (1):10–19.

Tomkins, I. R. 1936. Partial albinism in two species of birds. *Oriole* 1(2):19.

———. 1944. Wilson's plover in its summer home. *Auk* 61:259–69.

———. 1947. The oyster-catcher of the Atlantic coast of North America and its relation to oysters. *Wilson Bull.* 59:204–8.

———. 1959. Life history notes on the least tern. *Wilson Bull.* 71:313–22.

———. 1963. A royal tern choked by a fish. *Wilson Bull.* 75(2):198.

Tomlinson, R. E.; Levy, S. H.; and Levy, J. J. 1973. New distributional records of breeding Mexican ducks. *Condor* 75:120–21.

Tomlinson, R. E., and Todd, R. L. 1973. Distribution of two western clapper rail races as determined by responses to taped calls. *Condor* 75:177–83.

Tordoff, H. B. 1954. Social organization and behavior in a flock of captive nonbreeding red crossbills. *Condor* 56:346–58.

———. 1961. Aves. In *The encyclopedia of biological sciences,* ed. P. Gray. New York: Reinhold Publishing Corporation.

Tordoff, H. B., and Mengel, R. M. 1956. Studies of birds killed in nocturnal migration. *Univ. Kansas Publ. Mus. Nat. Hist.* 10(1):1–44.

Torrey, B. 1885. *Birds in the bush.* Boston: Houghton Mifflin Company.

———. 1889. A woodland intimate. In *A rambler's lease.* Boston: Houghton Mifflin Company.

Torrey, J. P. 1956. Hog cholera. In *Animal diseases: The yearbook of agriculture.* Washington, D.C.: U.S. Dept. Agric.

Townsend, C. H. 1883. Some albinos in the museum of the Philadelphia Academy. *Bull. Nuttall Ornith. Club* 8(2):126.

———. 1908. Sea birds as homing pigeons. *Bird Lore* 10(3):123–24.

———. 1930. In memoriam: Frederick Augustus Lucas. *Auk* 48(2):147–58.

Townsend, C. W. 1905. *The birds of Essex County, Massachusetts.* Mem. Nuttall Ornith. Club, no. 3. Cambridge, Mass.

———. 1909. The use of the wings and feet of diving birds. *Auk* 24:234–48.

———. 1919. Great auk. In *Life histories of North American diving birds,* ed. A. C. Bent. U.S. Natl. Mus. Bull. no. 107. Washington, D.C.

———. 1922a. Cormorant. In *Life histories of North American petrels and pelicans and their allies,* ed. A. C. Bent. U.S. Natl. Mus. Bull. no. 121. Washington, D.C.

———. 1922b. Wilson's petrel. In *Life histories of North American petrels and pelicans and their allies,* ed. A. C. Bent. U.S. Natl. Mus. Bull. no. 121. Washington, D.C.

———. 1923. Red-breasted merganser. In *Life histories of North American wild fowl,* ed. A. C. Bent. U.S. Natl. Mus. Bull. no. 126. Washington, D.C.

———. 1924. Mimicry of voice in birds. *Auk* 41:541–52.

———. 1926. Virginia rail. In *Life histories of North American marsh birds,* ed. A. C. Bent. U.S. Natl. Mus. Bull. no. 135. Washington, D.C.

———. 1927. Semipalmated sandpiper. In *Life histories of North American shorebirds,* ed. A. C. Bent. U.S. Natl. Mus. Bull. no. 142. Washington, D.C.

———. 1929a. Killdeer. In *Life histories of North American shorebirds,* ed. A. C. Bent. U.S. Natl. Mus. Bull. no. 146, pt. 2. Washington, D.C.

———. 1929b. Semipalmated plover. In *Life histories of North American shorebirds,* ed. A. C. Bent. U.S. Natl. Mus. Bull. no. 146, pt. 2. Washington, D.C.

———. 1932. Hudsonian spruce grouse. In *Life histories of North American gallinaceous birds,* ed. A. C. Bent. U.S. Natl. Mus. Bull. no. 162. Washington, D.C.

———. 1937. Black vulture. In *Life histories of North American birds of prey,* ed. A. C. Bent. U.S. Natl. Mus. Bull. no. 167, pt. 1. Washington, D.C.

———. 1938. Short-eared owl. In *Life histories of North American birds of prey,* ed. A. C. Bent. U.S. Natl. Mus. Bull. no. 167, pt. 2. Washington, D.C.

Trainer, D. O. 1974. Personal communication.

Tramer, E. J. 1974. Proportions of wintering North American birds in disturbed and undisturbed dry tropical habitats. *Condor* 76:460–64.

Tramontano, J. P. 1970. Winter observations of the short-tailed albatross in the western Pacific Ocean. *Condor* 72(1):122.

Trauger, D. L. 1974. Eye color of female lesser scaup in relation to age. *Auk* 91(2):243–54.

Trauger, D. L.; Dzubin, A.; and Ryder, J. P. 1971. White geese intermediate between Ross' geese and lesser snow geese. *Auk* 88:856–75.

Trefethen, J. B. 1964. *Wildlife management and conservation*. Lexington, Mass: D. C. Heath & Co.

Tremaine, M. M. 1972. Communications. *Amer. Birds* 26:565–67.

Tretzel, E. 1967. Imitation and transposition of human whistles by blackbirds. *Jour. Tierpsych.* 24:137–61.

Trimble, S. 1975. *Non-game birds of the west: An annotated bibliography*. The ecology & life histories of seven orders. Technical Note U.S. Dept Inter., Bureau of Land Management. Washington, D.C.

Trimm, W. 1972. The monk parakeet. *Conservationist* 26(6):4–5.

Trost, C. H. 1972. Adaptation of horned larks (*Eremophila alpestris*) to hot environments. *Auk* 89(3):506–27.

———. 1968. Dusky seaside sparrow. In *Life histories of North American cardinals, grosbeaks, buntings, towhees, finches, sparrows, and allies*, comp. A. C. Bent *et al.*, ed. O. L. Austin, Jr. U.S. Natl. Mus. Bull. no. 237, pt. 2. Washington, D.C.

Trumbull, G. 1888. *Names and portraits of birds which interest gunners*. New York: Harper & Brothers.

Truslow, F. K. 1966. Ground-nesting great horned owl: A photographic study. *Living Bird*, 5th annual, pp. 177–86.

———. 1970. Businessman in the bush. *Natl. Geographic Magazine* 137:634–75.

Tuck, L. M. 1961. *The murres: Their distribution, populations, and biology*. Canadian Wildlife Serv. Rept. Series, no. 1. Ottawa.

———. 1972. *The snipes: a study of the genus Capella*. Canadian Wildlife Serv., Monogr. Series no. 5. Ottawa.

Tucker, B. W. 1943. Brood-patches and the physiology of incubation. *Brit. Birds* 37:22–28.

———. 1944. The ejection of pellets by passerine and other birds. *Brit. Birds* 38:50–52.

———. 1949. Kennicott's willow-warbler, red-spotted blue-throat, and fieldfare. In *Life histories of North American thrushes, kinglets, and their allies*, ed. A. C. Bent. U.S. Natl. Mus. Bull. no. 196. Washington, D.C.

———. 1950a. Meadow Pipit. In *Life histories of North American wagtails, shrikes, vireos, and their allies*, ed. A. C. Bent. U.S. Natl. Mus. Bull. no. 197. Washington, D.C.

———. 1950b. Mountain accentor. In *Life histories of North American wagtails, shrikes, vireos, and their allies*, ed. A. C. Bent. U.S. Natl. Mus. Bull. no. 197. Washington, D.C.

———. 1950c. Red-throated pipit. In *Life histories of North American wagtails, shrikes, vireos, and their allies*, ed. A. C. Bent. U.S. Natl. Mus. Bull. no. 197. Washington, D.C.

———. 1950d. White wagtail. In *Life histories of North American wagtails, shrikes, vireos, and their allies*, ed. A. C. Bent. U.S. Natl. Mus. Bull. no. 197. Washington, D.C.

Tucker, V. A. 1968. Respiratory physiology of house sparrows in relation to high altitude flight. *Jour. Exper. Biol.* 48:55–66.

Tucker, V. A., and Schmidt-Koenig, K. 1977. Flight speeds of birds in relation to energetics and wind directions. *Auk* 88:97–107.

Tulloch, R. J. 1968. Snowy owls breeding in Shetland in 1967. *Brit. Birds* 61(3):119–32.

Turček, F. J. 1958. On bird-banding in the U.S.S.R. *Bird-Banding* 29:111–12.

Turček, F. J., and Kelso, L. 1968. Ecological aspects of food transportation and storage in the Corvidae. In *Communications in behavioral biology, Part A*, ed. S. A. Weinstein. Vol. 1. New York: Academic Press.

Turner, B. C. 1959. Feeding behavior of choughs. *Brit. Birds* 52(10–11):388–90.

Turner, Jr., E. C. 1971. Fleas and lice. In *Infectious and parasitic diseases of wild birds*, ed. J. W. Davis *et al.* Ames, Iowa: Iowa State University Press.

Turner, E. R. A. 1964. Social feeding in birds. *Behaviour* 24:1–46.

Turner, L. M. 1886. *Contribution to the natural history of Alaska*. U.S. Signal Service, Arctic Series, Pub. no. 2.

Twomey, A. C. 1936. Climograph study of certain introduced and migratory birds. *Ecology* 17:122–32.

Tyler, C. 1964. Eggshell. In *A new dictionary of birds*, ed. A. L. Thomson. New York: McGraw-Hill Book Company.

Tyler, J. G. 1933. Items from an oologist's notebook. *Condor* 35:186–88.

Tyler, W. M. 1916. The call-notes of some nocturnal migrating birds. *Auk* 33:132–41.

———. 1929a. Piping plover. In *Life histories of North American shorebirds*, ed. A. C. Bent. U.S. Natl. Mus. Bull. no. 146, pt. 2. Washington, D.C.

———. 1929b. Spotted sandpiper. In *Life histories of North American shorebirds*, ed. A. C. Bent. U.S. Natl. Mus. Bull. no. 146, pt. 2. Washington, D.C.

———. 1932. Eastern mourning dove. In *Life histories of North American gallinaceous birds*, ed. A. C. Bent. U.S. Natl. Mus. Bull. no. 162. Washington, D.C.

———. 1937. Turkey vulture. In *Life histories of North American birds of prey*, ed. A. C. Bent. U.S. Natl. Mus. Bull. no. 167, pt. 1. Washington, D.C.

———. 1938. Eastern sparrow hawk. In *Life histories of North American birds of prey*, ed. A. C. Bent. U.S. Natl. Mus. Bull. no. 170, pt. 2. Washington, D.C.

———. 1939a. Northern downy woodpecker. In *Life histories of North American woodpeckers*, ed. A. C. Bent. U.S. Natl. Mus. Bull. no. 174. Washington, D.C.

———. 1939b. Yellow-bellied sapsucker. In *Life histories of North American woodpeckers*, ed. A. C. Bent. U.S. Natl. Mus. Bull. no. 174. Washington, D.C.

———. 1940a. Chimney swift. In *Life histories of North American cuckoos, goatsuckers, hummingbirds and their allies*, ed. A. C. Bent. U.S. Natl. Mus. Bull. no. 176. Washington, D.C.

———. 1940b. Ruby-throated hummingbird. In *Life histories of North American cuckoos, goatsuckers, hummingbirds, and their allies*, ed. A. C. Bent. U.S. Natl. Mus. Bull. no. 176. Washington, D.C.

———. 1942a. Eastern kingbird. In *Life histories of North American flycatchers, larks, swallows, and their allies*, ed. A. C. Bent. U.S. Natl. Mus. Bull. no. 179. Washington, D.C.

———. 1942b. Eastern phoebe. In *Life histories of North American flycatchers, larks, swallows, and their allies*, ed. A. C. Bent. U.S. Natl. Mus. Bull. no. 179. Washington, D.C.

———. 1942c. Eastern wood pewee. In *Life histories of North American flycatchers, larks, swallows, and their allies*, ed. A. C. Bent. U.S. Natl. Mus. Bull. no. 179. Washington, D.C.

———. 1942d. Tree swallow. In *Life histories of North American flycatchers, larks, swallows, and their allies*, ed. A. C. Bent. U.S. Natl. Mus. Bull. no. 179. Washington, D.C.

———. 1943. In memoriam: Glover Morrill Allen. *Auk* (2):163–68.

———. 1946. Northern blue jay. In *Life histories of North American jays, crows, and titmice*, ed. A. C. Bent. U.S. Natl. Mus. Bull. no. 191. Washington, D.C.

———. 1948a. Brown creeper. In *Life histories of North American nuthatches, wrens, thrashers, and their allies*, ed. A. C. Bent. U.S. Natl. Mus. Bull. no. 195. Washington, D.C.

———. 1948b. White-breasted and red-breasted nuthatch. In *Life histories of North American nuthatches, wrens, thrashers, and their allies*, ed. A. C. Bent. U.S. Natl. Mus. Bull. no. 195. Washington, D.C.

———. 1949. Eastern robin. In *Life histories of North American thrushes, kinglets, and their allies*, ed. A. C. Bent. U.S. Natl. Mus. Bull. no. 196. Washington, D.C.

———. 1950a. Cedar waxwing. In *Life histories of North American wagtails, shrikes, vireos, and their allies*, ed. A. C. Bent. U.S. Natl. Mus. Bull. no. 197. Washington, D.C.

———. 1950b. Red-eyed vireo. In *Life histories of North American wagtails, shrikes, vireos, and their allies*, ed. A. C. Bent. U.S. Natl. Mus. Bull. no. 197. Washington, D.C.

———. 1953a. Black and white warbler. In *Life histories of North American wood warblers*, ed. A. C. Bent. U.S. Natl. Mus. Bull. no. 203. Washington, D.C.

———. 1953b. General remarks on the family Parulidae. In *Life histories of North American wood warblers*, ed. A. C. Bent. U.S. Natl. Mus. Bull. no. 203. Washington, D.C.

———. 1953c. Yellow palm warbler. In *Life histories of North American wood warblers*, ed. A. C. Bent. U.S. Natl. Mus. Bull. no. 203. Washington, D.C.

———. 1958a. Baltimore oriole. In *Life histories of North American blackbirds, orioles, tanagers, and allies*, ed. A. C. Bent. U.S. Natl. Mus. Bull. no. 211. Washington, D.C.

———. 1958b. Scarlet tanager. In *Life histories of North American blackbirds, orioles, tanagers, and allies*, ed. A. C. Bent. U.S. Natl. Mus. Bull. no. 211. Washington, D.C.

———. 1968. Eastern American goldfinch. In *Life histories of North American cardinals, grosbeaks, buntings, towhees, finches, sparrows, and allies*, comp. A. C. Bent *et al.*, ed. O. L. Austin, Jr. U.S. Natl. Mus. Bull. no. 237, pt. 1. Washington, D.C.

U

Udall, S. L. 1970. Paradise in peril. In *Wildlife crisis*, by Philip, Duke of Edinburgh, and J. Fisher. New York: Cowles Book Co., Inc.

Udvardy, M. D. F. 1951. Heat resistance in birds. *Proc. [Xth] Internatl. Ornith. Congress*, pp. 595–99. Uppsala, Sweden: Almquist and Wiksells Boktryckerie AB.

———. 1953. Contributions to the knowledge of the body temperature of birds. *Zoologiska Bidrag* 30:25–42.

———. 1958. Ecological and distributional analysis of North American birds. *Condor* 60:50–66.

Uhlig, H. G. 1963. Use of Minnesota ponds and pits by waterfowl. *Wilson Bull.* 75(1):78–82.

United States Department of Agriculture. 1962. *Chickens on farms—1961–62*. Washington, D.C.: Statistical Reporting Serv.

United States Department of the Interior. 1953. Fish and Wildlife Service, Refuge Leaflet no. 1. Washington, D.C.

———. 1960. *Bird banding: The hows and whys*. Fish and Wildlife Service Circ. no. 79. Washington, D.C.

———. 1961a. *Bird banding manual*. Loose-leaf booklet issued June 30. Washington, D.C.: Fish and Wildlife Service.

———. 1961b. *Migratory bird regulations, 1961–1962*. Washington, D.C.: Fish and Wildlife Service.

———. 1973. *Threatened Wildlife of the United States*. Bureau of Sports Fisheries and Wildlife, Resource Publication no. 114. Washington, D.C.

———. 1979. *List of endangered and threatened wildlife and plants*. January 17, pt. 2. Washington, D.C.: Fish and Wildlife Service.

Urner, C. A. 1923. Notes on the short-eared owl. *Auk* 40:30–36.

Usinger, R. L. 1947. Native hosts of the Mexican chicken bug, *Haematosiphon inodorus* (Duges). *Pan-Pacific Entomologist* 23(3):140.

V

Vacin, V. J. 1970. Banded five-year-old ruby-throated hummingbird recaptured in Oklahoma. *Bull. Okla. Ornith. Soc.* 3(3):22–3.

Valentine, J. M., Jr. 1979. The Mississippi sandhill crane—a status update. In *Proceedings of the 1978 Crane Workshop*. Pp. 135–38: Fort Collins, Colo.: Colorado State University Press.

Van Camp, L. F., and Henny, C. J. 1975. *The screech owl: Its life history and population ecology in northern Ohio.* N. Amer. Fauna no. 71. U.S. Dept. Inter., Fish and Wildlife Service. Washington, D.C.:

Van Dersal, W. R. 1938. *Native woody plants of the United States: Their erosion control and wildlife values.* Washington, D.C.: U.S. Govt. Printing Office.

Van Fleet, C. C. 1919. A short paper on the Hutton vireo. *Condor* 21:162–65.

van Lawick-Goodall, J. 1969. Tool-using bird, the Egyptian vulture. *Natl. Geographic Magazine* 133(5):630–41.

Van Nostrand. 1968. *Van Nostrand's scientific encyclopedia.* 4th ed. Princeton, N.J.: D. Van Nostrand Company, Inc.

van Rhijn, J. G. 1973. Behavioural dimorphism in male ruffs, *Philomachus pugnax* (L.). *Behaviour* 47:153–229.

van Rossem, A. J. 1936. A red phase of the black-crowned night heron. *Auk* 53(3):322–23.

Van Tyne, J. 1926. An unusual flight of Arctic three-toed woodpeckers. *Auk* 43:469–74.

———. 1945. A melanistic specimen of Wilson's snipe. *Wilson Bull.* 57(1):75–76.

———. 1951. A cardinal's *(Richmondena cardinalis)* choice of food for adult and young. *Auk* 68:110.

———. 1952. Principles and practices in collecting and taxonomic work. *Auk* 69(1):27–33.

———. 1953. Kirtland's warbler. In *Life histories of North American wood warblers,* ed. A. C. Bent. U.S. Natl. Mus. Bull. no. 203. Washington, D.C.

———. 1957. Colima warbler. In *The warblers of America,* ed. L. Griscom and A. Sprunt, Jr. New York: The Devin-Adair Co.

Van Tyne, J., and Berger, A. J. 1959. *Fundamentals of ornithology.* New York: John Wiley & Sons, Inc.

———. 1976. *Fundamentals of ornithology.* New York: John Wiley & Sons, Inc.

Van Velzen, W. T. 1971a. Recoveries of royal terns banded in the Carolinas. *Chat* 35(3):64–66.

Van Velzen, W. T., ed. 1971b. Thirty-fifth breeding bird censuses. *Amer. Birds* 25(6):960–61.

Van Wormer, J. 1968. *The world of the Canada goose,* ed. J. K. Terres. New York and Philadelphia: J. B. Lippincott Company.

———. 1972. *The world of the swan,* ed. J. K. Terres. New York and Philadelphia: J. B. Lippincott Company.

Vaurie, C. 1959. *The birds of the Palearctic fauna. A systematic reference. Order Passeriformes.* London: H. F. & G. Witherby, Ltd.

———. 1964. Bunting. In *A new dictionary of birds,* ed. A. L. Thomson. New York: McGraw-Hill Book Company.

Verbeek, N. A. M. 1962. On dew bathing and drought in passerines. *Auk* 79(4):719.

———. 1967. Breeding biology and ecology of the horned lark in alpine tundra. *Wilson Bull.* 79(2):208–18.

———. 1970. Breeding ecology of the water pipit. *Auk* 87(3):425–51.

———. 1971. Hummingbirds feeding on sand. *Condor* 73(1):112–13.

———. 1975. Northern wintering of flycatchers and residency of black phoebes in California. *Auk* 92:737–49.

Verheyen, R. 1948. Aspects et evolution die comportement maternal chez les oiseaux. *Gerfaut* 38:21–33.

Vermeer, K. 1963. *The breeding ecology of the glaucous-winged gull on Mandarte Island, B.C.* Occas. Pap. Prov. Mus. B.C. no. 13.

———. 1973. Some aspects of the nesting requirements of common loons. *Wilson Bull.* 85(4):-429–35.

Verner, J. 1965. Breeding biology of the long-billed marsh wren. *Condor* 67:6–30.

Verner, J., and Willson, M. F. 1969. *Mating systems, sexual dimorphism, and the role of male North American birds in the nesting cycle.* Amer. Ornith. Union, Monogr. no. 9. Washington, D.C.

Verplanck, W. S. 1957. *A glossary of some terms used in the objective science of behavior.* Supplement to the Psychol. Rev., Amer. Psychol. Assoc., Inc., no. 64, pt. 2.

Vincent, J., comp. 1966. *Red data book.* Vol. 2. *Aves.* International Union for Conservation of Nature and Natural Resources; Survival Service Commission, 1110 Morges, Switzerland.

Visscher, J. P. 1943. Master bird mind: A biographical sketch of Francis Hobart Herrick. *Bird-Life* 39(1):42–51.

Vogt, W. 1938. Will and Kate. *Yale Review* 27:733–43.

———. 1970. The avifauna of a changing ecosystem. In *The avifauna of northern Latin America,* ed. H. K. and J. H. Buechner. Washington, D. C.: Smithsonian Press.

von Frish, O. 1966. Montagu harrier retrieves its young. *Z. f. Tierpsych.* 23(5):581–83.

von Haartman, L. 1971. Population dynamics. In *Avian biology,* ed. D. S. Farner, J. R. King, and K. C. Parkes. Vol. 1. New York: Academic Press, Inc.

Voous, K. H. 1964a. Owl. In *A new dictionary of birds,* ed. A. L. Thomson. New York: McGraw-Hill Book Company.

———. 1964b. Wagtail. In *A new dictionary of birds,* ed. A. L. Thomson. New York: McGraw-Hill Book Company.

———. 1964c. Warbler (1). In *A new dictionary of birds,* ed. A. L. Thomson. New York: McGraw-Hill Book Company.

Vosburgh, J. 1966. Deathtraps in the flyways. In *Birds in our lives,* ed. A. Stefferud and A. L. Nelson. Washington, D.C.: U.S. Dept. Inter., Fish and Wildlife Service.

Vuilleumier, F. 1975. Zoogeography. In *Avian biology,* ed. D. S. Farner, J. R. King, and K. C. Parkes. Vol. 5, pp. 421–96.

W

Wagner, H. O. 1946. Food and feeding habits of Mexican hummingbirds. *Wilson Bull.* 58(1):69–93.

———. 1954. Versuch einer Analyse der Kolibribalz. *Z. f. Tierpsych.* 11:182–212.

———. 1957. The molting periods of Mexican hummingbirds. *Auk* 74:251–57.

Wahl, T. E. 1970. A short-tailed albatross record for Washington State. *Calif. Birds* 1(3):113–14.

———, and Wilson, H. E. 1971. Nesting record of European skylark in Washington State. *Condor* 73(2):254.

Wahlstedt, J. 1969. Hunting, feeding, and vocalizations of the great gray owl. *Vår Fågelvarld* 28:89–101.

Walcott, C., and Green, R. P. 1974. Orientation of homing pigeons altered by a change in the direction of an applied magnetic field. *Science* 184:180–82.

Walker, E. P. 1942. Care of captive animals. *Annual Rept. (1941) Smithsonian Inst.* Washington, D.C.

Walker, L. W. 1955. The mountain plover. *Audubon* 57:210–12.

Walker, L. W., and Walker, M. 1940. Headlines on eagles. *Nature Magazine* 33:321–23.

Walker, M. V. 1967. Revival of interest in the toothed birds of Kansas. *Trans. Kansas Acad. Sci.* 70:60–66.

Walkinshaw, L. H. 1935. Studies of the short-billed marsh wren *(Cistothorus stellaris)* in Michigan. *Auk* 52:362–69.

———. 1941. The prothonotary warbler, a comparison of nesting conditions in Tennessee and in Michigan. *Wilson Bull.* 53:21–31.

———. 1949a. *The sandhill cranes.* Bloomfield Hills, Mich.: Cranbook Inst. Sci.

———. 1949b. Twenty-five eggs apparently laid by a cowbird. *Wilson Bull.* 61:82–85.

———. 1953. Life history of the prothonotary warbler. *Wilson Bull.* 65:152–68.

———. 1957a. Incubation period of the sora rail. *Auk* 74(4):496.

———. 1957b. Yellow-bellied flycatcher nesting in Michigan. *Auk* 74:293–304.

———. 1959. A chipping sparrow nest in which eight eggs were laid and seven young reared. *Auk* 76:101–2.

———. 1965a. Mist-netting saw-whet owls. *Bird-Banding* 36(2):116–18.

———. 1965b. One hundred thirty three Michigan sandhill crane nests. *Jack-Pine Warbler* 43(3):136–43.

———. 1966a. Studies of the Acadian flycatcher in Michigan. *Bird-Banding* 37(4):227–57.

———. 1966b. Summer observations of the least flycatcher in Michigan. *Jack-Pine Warbler* 44:151–68.

———. 1968a. Eastern field sparrow. In *Life histories of North American cardinals, grosbeaks, buntings, towhees, finches, sparrows, and allies,* comp. A. C. Bent *et al.,* ed. O. L. Austin, Jr. U.S. Natl. Mus. Bull. no. 237, pt. 2. Washington, D.C.

———. 1968b. Le Conte's sparrow. In *Life histories of North American cardinals grosbeaks, buntings, towhees, finches, sparrows, and allies,* comp. A.C. Bent *et al.,* ed. O. L. Austin, Jr. U.S. Natl. Mus. Bull. no. 237, pt. 2. Washington, D.C.

———. 1971. Additional notes on summer biology of Traill's flycatcher. *Bird-Banding* 42(4):275–78.

———. 1972. Kirtland's warbler—Endangered. *Amer. Birds* 26(1):3–9.

———. 1973. *Cranes of the world.* New York: Winchester Press.

Wallace, C. J. 1972. The care and exhibition of American woodcocks at the Cincinnati Zoological Society. *Avicultural Magazine* 78:64–65.

Wallace, G. J. 1948. *The barn owl in Michigan.* Mich. State Coll. Agri. Exp. Sta. Tech. Bull. no. 208.

———. 1949. Bicknell's thrush. In *Life histories of North American thrushes, kinglets, and their allies,* ed. A. C. Bent. U.S. Natl. Mus. Bull. no. 196. Washington, D.C.

———. 1955. *An introduction to ornithology.* 1st ed. New York: The Macmillan Company

———. 1956. A case of microphthalmia in the American robin. *Wilson Bull.* 68(2)151–52.

———. 1961a. Columbiformes. In *The encyclopedia of biological sciences,* ed. P. Gray. New York: Reinhold Publishing Corporation.

———. 1961b. Coraciiformes. In *The encyclopedia of biological sciences,* ed. P. Gray. New York: Reinhold Publishing Corporation.

———. 1961c. Cuculiformes. In *The encyclopedia of biological sciences,* ed. P. Gray. New York: Reinhold Publishing Corporation.

———. 1961d. Gruiformes. In *The encyclopedia of biological sciences,* ed. P. Gray. New York: Reinhold Publishing Corporation.

———. 1961e. Pelecaniformes. In *The encyclopedia of biological sciences,* ed. P. Gray. New York: Reinhold Publishing Corporation.

———. 1963. *An introduction to ornithology.* 2d ed. New York: The Macmillan Company.

Wallace, G. J.; Nickell, W. P.; and Bernard, R. F. 1961. *Bird mortality in the Dutch elm disease program in Michigan.* Cranbrook Inst. Sci. Bull. no. 41. Bloomfield Hills, Mich.

Waller, R. 1962. *Der wilde Falk ist mein Gesell.* [*The wild falcon is my companion.*] Verl. J. Neumann-Neudamm, Melsungen. W. Germany.

Walls, G. L. 1942. *The vertebrate eye and its adaptive radiation.* Cranbrook Inst. Sci. Bull. no. 19. Bloomfield Hills, Mich.

Walsberg, G. E. 1977. The ecology and energetics of contrasting social systems in *Phainopepla nitens* (Aves: Ptilogonatidae). *Univ. California Publ. Zool.,* no. 108.

Walter, H. E., and Sayles, L. P. 1949. *Biology of the vertebrates.* 3d ed. New York: The Macmillan Company.

Walters, J. 1956. Egg-retrieving and orientation at the nest site in Kentish and little ringed plover (*Charadrius alexandrinus* and *C. dubius*). *Limosa* 29(4):103–29.

Warburton, M. 1967. Three-legged birds at Island Beach. *EBBA News* 30(5):224.

Warga, K. 1954. Voranzeige über die Erforschung der Vogelwelt des Kisbalaton. *Aquila* 59, 62:55–58, 169–87.

Warham, J.; Bourne, W. R. P.; and Elliott, H. F. I. 1974. Albatross identification in the North Atlantic. *Amer. Birds* 28(3):585–603.

Warham, J.; Keeley, B. R.; and Wilson, G. J. 1977. Breeding of the mottled petrel. *Auk* 94(1):1–17.

Warne, F. L. 1926. Crows is crows. *Bird-Lore* 28:110–16.

Warren, B. H. 1888. *Introduction to: Birds of Pennsylvania.* Harrisburg, Pa.

Wass, M. L. 1974. Killdeer nesting on graveled roofs. *Amer. Birds* 28(6):983–84.

Watmough, W. 1948. *The cult of the budgerigar.* London: Cage Birds & Bird Fancy. Dorset House.

Watson, A. 1957. The breeding success of golden eagles in the northeast highlands. *Scottish Nat.* 69:153–69.

Watson, G. E. 1962. Three sibling species of *Alectoris* partridge. *Ibis* 104:353–67.

———. 1966. *Seabirds of the tropical Atlantic Ocean.* Washington, D.C.: Smithsonian Press.

———. 1971. Molting greater shearwaters (*Puffinus gravis*) off Terra del Fuego. *Auk* 88(2):440–42.

———. 1975. *Birds of the Antarctic and sub-Antarctic.* Washington, D.C.: American Geophysical Union.

Watson, J. B. 1908. The behaviour of noddy and sooty terns. *Papers from the Tortugas Laboratory of the Carnegie Institution of Wash.* 2:187.

Watson, J. B., and Lashley, K. S. 1915. *Homing and related activities of birds.* Papers from Dept. of Marine Zoology, Carnegie Institution, Pub. no. 211. Washington, D.C.

Wayne, A. T. 1910. *Birds of South Carolina.* Contrib. from the Charleston Museum, no. 1. Charleston, S.C.

Weaver, F. G. 1949. Wood thrush. In *Life histories of North American thrushes, kinglets, and their allies,* ed. A. C. Bent. U.S. Natl. Mus. Bull. no. 196. Washington, D.C.

Weaver, J. E., and Clements, F. E. 1938. *Plant ecology.* New York: McGraw-Hill Book Company.

Weaver, R. L. 1943. Reproduction in English sparrows. *Auk* 60:62–74.

Weber, H. M. 1972. Whitewings (review). *Def. Wildlife News* 37:325.

Weber, W. J. 1975. Notes on cattle egret breeding. *Auk* 92(1):111–17.

Webster, Jr., F. S. 1970. South Texas region. *Audubon Field Notes* 24(3)520.

———. 1972. South Texas region. *Amer. Birds* 26(5):877–88.

———. 1973. South Texas region. *Amer. Birds* 27(1):85; (5)892.

———. 1975. South Texas region. *Amer. Birds* 29(5):1005.

———. 1978. South Texas region. *Amer. Birds* 32(6):1183.

———. 1979. South Texas region. *Amer. Birds* 33(6):878

Webster, H. M. 1944. A survey of the prairie falcon in Colorado. *Auk* 61:609–16.

Webster, J. D. 1941. The breeding of the black oystercatcher. *Wilson Bull.* 53:141–56.

———. 1968. Worthen's sparrow. In *Life histories of North American cardinals, grosbeaks, buntings, towhees, finches, sparrows, and allies,* comp. A. C. Bent, *et al.,* ed. O. L. Austin, Jr. U.S. Natl. Mus. Bull. no. 237, pt. 2. Washington, D.C.

Webster, N. 1944. *Webster's new international dictionary of the English language.* 2d ed. Springfield, Mass.: G. & C. Merriam Company.

Webster's Geographical Dictionary: A Dictionary of Names of Places. 1949. Springfield, Mass: G. and C. Merriam Company.

Weed, C. M., and Dearborn, N. 1903. *Birds in their relations to man: A manual of economic ornithology for the United States and Canada.* Philadelphia: J. B. Lippincott Company.

Wehr, E. E. 1959. Cestodes of poultry. In *Diseases of poultry,* ed. H. E. Biester and L. H. Schwarte. Ames, Iowa: Iowa State University Press.

———. 1971. Nematodes. In *Infectious and parasitic diseases in wild birds,* ed. J. W. Davis *et al.* Ames, Iowa: Iowa State University Press.

Weidmann, U. 1964. Laying. In *A new dictionary of birds,* ed. A. L. Thomson. New York: McGraw-Hill Book Company.

Weisbrod, A. R., and Stevens, W. F. 1974. The skylark in Washington. *Auk* 91(4):832–35.

Weiser, C. S. 1933. Flying with a flock of swans. *Auk* 50:92–93.

Weitnauer, E. 1956. On the question of the nocturnal behavior of the swift. *Der Ornithologische Beobachter* 53(3):74–79.

Wellein, E. G., and Lumsden, H. G. 1964. Northern forests and tundra. In *Waterfowl tomorrow,* ed. J. P. Linduska and A. L. Nelson. Washington, D.C.: U.S. Dept. Inter., Fish and Wildlife Service.

Weller, M. W. 1958. Observations in the incubation behavior of the common nighthawk. *Auk* 75(1):48–59.

———. 1959a. Albinism in *Podiceps grisegena* and other grebes. *Auk* 76(4):520–21.

———. 1959b. Parasitic egg-laying in the redhead (*Aythya americana*) and other North American Anatidae. *Ecol. Monogr.* 29:333–65.

———. 1961. Breeding biology of the least bittern. *Wilson Bull.* 73(1):11–35.

———. 1965. Bursa regression, gonad cycle, and molt of the great horned owl. *Bird-Banding* 36(2):102–12.

Weller, M. W.; Adams, Jr., I. C.; and Rose, B. J. 1955. Winter roosts of marsh hawks and short-eared owls in central Missouri. *Wilson Bull.* 67(3):189–93.

Welty, J. C. 1962. *The life of birds.* Philadelphia: W. B. Saunders Co.

———. 1975. *The life of birds.* 2d ed. Philadelphia: W. B. Saunders Co.

Wenzel, B. M. 1973. Chemoreception. In *Avian biology,* ed. D. S. Farner, J. R. King, and K. C. Parkes. Vol. 3, pp. 389–415. New York: Academic Press, Inc.

Werner, H. W. 1971. Cape Sable sparrows rediscovered on Cape Sable. *Auk* 88(2):432.

Weske, J. S. 1976. Age record for Swainson's warbler. *Bird-Banding* 47(3):277.

West, D. A. 1962. Hybridization in grosbeaks (*Pheucticus*) of the Great Plains. *Auk* 79:399–424.

West, G. C. 1960. Seasonal variation in the energy balance of the tree sparrow in relation to migration. *Auk* 77:306–29.

Westemeier, R. L. 1966. Apparent lead poisoning in a wild bobwhite. *Wilson Bull.* 78(4):471–72.

Weston, F. M. 1934. A melanistic laughing gull at Pensacola, Florida. *Auk* 51(1):82.

———. 1949. Blue-gray gnatcatcher. In *Life histories of North American thrushes, kinglets, and their allies,* ed. A. C. Bent. U.S. Natl. Mus. Bull. no. 196. Washington, D.C.

———. 1968. Bachman's sparrow. In *Life histories of North American cardinals, grosbeaks, buntings, towhees, finches, sparrows, and allies,* comp. A. C. Bent *et al.,* ed. O. L. Austin, Jr. U.S. Natl. Mus. Bull. no. 237, pt. 2. Washington, D.C.

Weston, F. M., and Williams, E. A. 1965. Recent records of the Eskimo curlew. *Auk* 82(3):493–96.

Westover, M. F. 1932. The flight of swifts. *Bird-Lore* 34:253–54.

Wetherbee, D. K. 1958. Unilateral microphthalmia in *Quiscalus quiscula* and *Mimus polyglottos. Auk* 75(1):101–3.

———. 1968. Southern swamp sparrow. In *Life histories of North American cardinals, grosbeaks, buntings, towhees, finches, sparrows, and allies,* comp. A. C. Bent *et al.,* ed. O. L. Austin, Jr. U.S. Natl. Mus. Bull. no. 237, pt. 3. Washington, D.C.

Wetherbee, K. B. 1932. Two pairs of tree swallows mated during two successive seasons. *Bird-Banding* 3(2):72–73.

———. 1934. Some measurements and weights of live birds. *Bird-Banding* 5(2):55–64.

Wetmore, A. 1916. The speed of flight of certain birds. *Condor* 18:112–13.

———. 1919a. *Lead poisoning in waterfowl.* U.S. Dept. Agric. Bull. no. 793. Washington, D.C.

———. 1919b. A note on the eye of the black skimmer (*Rynchops nigra*). *Proc. Biol. Soc. Wash.* 32:195.

———. 1920. A peculiar feeding habit of grebes. *Condor* 22:18–20.

———. 1921. *A study of body temperature of birds.* Smithsonian Misc. Coll. 72:12.

———. 1923. *Canaries: Their care and management.* U.S. Dept. Agric. Farmer's Bull. no. 1327. Washington, D.C.

———. 1925. *Food of American phalaropes, avocets, and stilts.* U.S. Dept. Agric. Bull. no. 1359. Washington, D.C.

———. 1926. *The migrations of birds.* Cambridge, Mass.: Harvard University Press.

———. 1927. *Our migrant shorebirds in southern South America.* U.S. Dept. Agric. Tech. Bull. no. 26. Washington, D.C.

———. 1933. Fossil birds. In *Fifty years progress of American Ornithology, 1883–1933.* Lancaster, Pa.; Amer. Ornith. Union

———. 1936. The number of contour feathers in passeriform and related birds. *Auk* 53:159–69.

———. 1937a. Eagles, hawks, and vultures. In *The book of birds,* ed. G. Grosvenor and A. Wetmore. Vol. 1. Washington, D.C.: Natl. Geographic Soc.

———. 1937b. The turkeys, grouse, quail, and pigeons. In *The book of birds,* ed. G. Grosvenor and A. Wetmore. Vol. 1. Washington, D.C.: Natl. Geographic Soc.

———. 1951a. Recent additions to our knowledge of prehistoric birds, 1933–1949. *Proc. [Xth] Internatl. Ornith. Congress,* pp. 51–74. Uppsala, Sweden: Almquist and Wiksells Boktryekene AB.

———. 1951b. *A revised classification for the birds of the world.* Smithsonian Misc. Coll. 117(4). Washington, D.C.

———. 1955. Paleontology. In *Recent studies in avian biology,* ed. A. Wolfson. Urbana, Ill.: University of Illinois Press.

———. 1956. *A check-list of the fossil and prehistoric birds of North America and the West Indies.* Smithsonian Misc. Coll. 131(5). Washington, D.C.

———. 1959. *Birds of the Pleistocene of North*

America. Smithsonian Misc. Coll. 138(4):1–24. Washington, D.C.

Wetmore, A., *et al.* 1964. *Song and garden birds of North America.* Washington, D.C.: Natl. Geographic Soc.

———. 1965. *Water, prey, and game birds of North America.* Washington, D.C.: Natl. Geographic Soc.

Weydemeyer, W. 1926. Sapsuckers feeding sap to young. *Auk* 43(2):236.

———. 1971a. Injured Calliope hummingbird lifted by another. *Auk* 88(2):431.

———. 1971b. Nesting habits of the Oregon junco in Montana. *Wilson Bull.* 83(1):103.

Weymouth, R. D.; Lasiewski, R. C.; and Berger, A. J. 1964. The tongue apparatus in hummingbirds. *Acta. anat.* 58:252–70.

Wharton, W. P. 1931. Parasites in birds taken at Summerville, South Carolina. *Bird-Banding* 2:34–35.

Whitaker, L. M. 1957. Anting in birds. *Wilson Bull.* 69:195–262.

White, C. M. 1963. Botulism and myiasis as mortality factors in falcons. *Condor* 65:442–43.

———. 1969. Population trends in Utah raptors. In *Peregrine falcon populations: Their biology and decline,* ed. J. J. Hickey. Madison, Wis.: University of Wisconsin Press.

White, C. M., and Baird, W. M. 1977. First North American record of the Asian needle-tailed swift, *Hirundapus caudacutus. Auk* 94:389.

White, C. M., and Cade, T. J. 1971. Cliff-nesting raptors and ravens along the Coville River in Arctic Alaska. *Living Bird,* 10th annual, pp. 107–50.

White, C. M., and Roseneau, D. G. 1970. Observations on food, nesting, and winter populations of large North American falcons. *Condor* 72(1):113–14.

White, C. M., and Weeden, R. B. 1966. Hunting methods of gyrfalcons and behavior of their prey (ptarmigan). *Condor* 68(5):517–19.

White, C. M.; Williamson, F. L.; and Emison, W. B. 1974. *Tringa glareola*—A new breeding species for North America. *Auk* 91:175–76.

White, F. N., and Kinney, J. L. 1974. Avian incubation. *Science* 186:107–15.

White, H. C. 1939. Change in gastric digestion of kingfishers with development. *Amer. Nat.* 73: 188–90.

White, J. 1970. Breeding project information exchange. B.P.I.E. No. 13, No. 14. *Raptor Res. News* 4(2):42–46.

White, W. B. 1927. Birds and motor cars. *Auk* 44:265–66.

———. 1929. Birds and motor cars. *Auk* 46:399.

———. 1933. Birds and motor cars. *Auk* 50:236.

Whitman, C. O. 1919. *The behavior of pigeons. Posthumous works of Charles Otis Whitman,* ed. H. A. Carr. Vol. 3. Washington, D.C.: Carnegie Institution of Washington.

Whitney, Jr., N. R. 1968. White-winged junco. In *Life histories of North American cardinals, grosbeaks, buntings, towhees, finches, sparrows, and allies,* comp. A. C. Bent *et al.,* ed. O. L. Austin, Jr. U.S. Natl. Mus. Bull. no. 237, pt. 2. Washington, D.C.

Whitson, M. 1975. Courtship behavior of the greater roadrunner. *Living Bird,* 14th annual, pp. 215–55.

Whittle, C. L. 1922. Additional data regarding the famous Arnold Arboretum mockingbird. *Auk* 39:496–506.

Whittow, G. C. 1965. Energy metabolism. In *Avian physiology,* ed. P. D. Sturkie. Ithaca, N.Y.: Comstock Pub. Associates.

Wible, M., and Parkes, K. C. 1955. Barn owls feeding on box turtles. *Florida Nat.* 28(3):74–75.

Widmann, O. 1907. A preliminary catalogue of the birds of Missouri. *Trans. Acad. Sci. St. Louis* 17:1–288.

Wiens, J. A. 1971. "Egg-dumping" by the grasshopper sparrow in a savannah sparrow nest. *Auk* 88(1):185–86.

Wilbur, A. M. 1969. The breeding biology of Leach's petrel, *Oceanodroma leucorhoa. Auk* 86(3):433–42.

Wilbur, S. R. 1973. The California condor in the Pacific Northwest. *Auk* 90:196–98.

———. 1976. Status of the California condor, 1972–1975. *Amer. Birds* 30(4):789–90.

———. 1978. The California condor, 1966–76: A look at its past and future. Washington, D.C.: U.S. Dept. Inter., Fish and Wildlife Service, N. Amer. Fauna No. 72.

Wilbur, S. R.; Carrier, W. D.; Borneman, J. C.; and Malette, R. W. 1972. Distribution and numbers of the California condor, 1966–1971. *Amer. Birds* 26:819–23.

Wilcox, L. 1959. A twenty-year banding study of the piping plover. *Auk* 76(2):129–52.

———. 1962. Oldest known shorebird in North America. *EBBA News* 25:45–46.

Wilder, N. G.; Addy, C. E.; Bryant, J. E.; Kamman, J. F.; and Phelps, C. E. 1968. *The black duck, evaluation, management, and research.* Chestertown, Md.: Atlantic Waterfowl Council and Wildlife Management Institute.

Wiley, J. W., and Lohrer, F. E. 1973. Additional records of non-fish prey taken by ospreys. *Wilson Bull.* 85(4):468–70.

Wiley, R. H. 1971. Song groups in a singing assembly of little hermits. *Condor* 73:28–35.

———. 1974. Evolution of social organization and life history patterns among grouse (Aves: Tetraonidae). *Quart. Rev. Biol.* 49:201–227.

Williams, C. S., and Neff, J. A. 1966. Scaring makes a difference. In *Birds in our lives,* ed. A. Stefferud and A. L. Nelson. Washington, D.C.: U.S. Dept. Inter., Fish and Wildlife Service.

Williams, F. 1973. Southern great plains region. *Amer. Birds* 27:80.

Williams, F. C., and Le Sassier, A. L. 1968. Cassin's sparrow. In *Life histories of North American cardinals, grosbeaks, buntings, finches, towhees, sparrows, and allies,* comp. A. C. Bent *et al.,* ed. O. L. Austin, Jr. U.S. Natl. Mus. Bull. no. 237, pt. 2. Washington, D.C.

Williams, H. S. 1934. Nest building—New style. *Natural History* 34:431–46.

Williams, L. 1958. Brewer's blackbird. In *Life histories of North American blackbirds, orioles, tanagers, and allies,* ed. A. C. Bent. U.S. Natl. Mus. Bull. no. 211. Washington, D.C.

Williams, Jr., L. E., and Phillips, R. W. 1972. North Florida sandhill crane populations. *Auk* 89:541–48.

Williams, L. P., and Hobbs, B. C. 1975. Salmonellosis. In *Diseases transmitted by animal to man,* ed. W. T. Hubbert, W. F. McCulloch, and P. R. Schnurrenberger. 6th ed. Chapter 3. Springfield, Ill.: Charles C Thomas, Publisher.

Williams, O., and Wheat, P. 1971. Hybrid jays in Colorado. *Wilson Bull.* 83(4):343–46.

Williams, R. B. 1947. Infestation of raptorials by *Ornithodorus aquilae. Auk* 64:185–88.

Williams, T. C., and Williams, J. M. 1978. An oceanic mass migration of land birds. *Scientific American* 239 (4):166–76.

Williams, T. C.; Williams, J. M.; Teal, J. M.; and Kanwisher, J. W. 1974. Homing flights of herring gulls under low visibility conditions. *Bird-Banding* 45(2):106–14.

Williamson, F. S. L., and Peyton, L. J. 1963. Interbreeding of glaucous-winged and herring gulls in the Cook Inlet region of Alaska. *Condor* 65(1):24–28.

Williamson, K. 1959. Changes of mating within a colony of Arctic skuas. *Bird Study* 6(2):51–60.

Willis, E. O. 1963. Is the zone-tailed hawk a mimic of the turkey vulture? *Condor* 65:313–17.

Williston, S. W. 1879. Are birds derived from dinosaurs? *Kansas City Rev. Sci.* 3:457–60.

Willoughby, E. J. and Cade, T. J. 1964. Breeding behavior of the American kestrel. *Living Bird,* 3d annual, pp. 75–96.

Willson, M. F. 1971. Seed selection of some North American finches. *Condor* 73:415–29.

Wilson, A. 1808–1814. *American ornithology, or the natural history of the birds of the United States.* 9 vols. Philadelphia: Bradford and Inskeep.

———. 1828–1829. *American ornithology or the natural history of the birds of the United States* (text). 3 vols. New York: Collins and Co. Edition of George Ord.

Wilson, L. P. 1959. Chuck-will's-widow nestings. *Migrant* 30:53–54.

Wimsatt, W. A. 1940. Homing instinct and prolificacy in the duck hawk. *Auk* 57(1):107–9.

Wing, L. 1943. Spread of the starling and English sparrow. *Auk* 60:74–87.

———. 1956. *The natural history of birds.* New York: The Ronald Press Co.

Wingate, D. B. 1964. Discovery of breeding blackcapped petrels on Hispaniola. *Auk* 81:147–59.

Winkler, H., and Short, L. L. 1978. A comparative analysis of acoustical signals in pied woodpeckers. *Bull. Amer. Mus. Nat. Hist.* 160:1–110.

Winterbottom, J. M. 1949. Mixed bird parties in the tropics, with special reference to Northern Rhodesia. *Auk* 66:258–63.

Witherby, H. F.; Jourdain, F. C. R.; Ticehurst, N. F.; and Tucker, B. W. 1938–41. *The handbook of British birds.* Vols. 1–5. London: H. F. and G. Witherby, Ltd.

Witschi, E. 1935. Seasonal sex characters in birds and their hormone control. *Wilson Bull.* 47: 177–88.

———. 1956. *Development of vertebrates.* Philadelphia: W. B. Saunders Co.

———. 1961. Sex and secondary sexual characters. In *Biology and comparative physiology of birds,* ed. A. J. Marshall. New York: Academic Press, Inc.

Witzeman, J.; Hubbard, J. P.; and Kaufman, K. 1975. Southwest region. *Amer. Birds* 29(4):891.

Wolf, L. L. 1970. The impact of seasonal flowering on the biology of some tropical hummingbirds. *Condor* 72(1):1–14.

Wolfe, L. R. 1968. Varied bunting. In *Life histories of North American cardinals, grosbeaks, buntings, towhees, finches, sparrows, and allies,* comp. A. C. Bent *et al.,* ed. O. L. Austin, Jr. U.S. Natl. Mus. Bull. no. 237, pt. 1. Washington, D.C.

Wolford, J. W., and Boag, D. A. 1971. Food habits of black-crowned night heron. *Auk* 88:435–37.

Wolfson, A. 1959. The role of light and darkness in regulation of the spring migration and reproductive cycles in birds. In *Photoperiodism and related phenomena in plants and animals.* Amer. Assoc. Advanc. Sci., publication no. 55, pp. 679–716. Washington, D.C.

———. 1961. Photoperiodism, animal. In *The encyclopedia of biological sciences,* ed. P. Gray New York: Reinhold Publishing Corporation.

Wolhuter, B. R. 1968. Second report of great horned owl preying on short-eared owl. *Bird-Banding* 39(4):319.

———. 1971. Sparrow hawk predation and meadowlark. *Bird-Banding* 42(3):221.

Wood, C. A., and Fyfe, F. M., trans. 1943. *The art of falconry of Frederick II.* Stanford, Calif.: Stanford University Press.

Wood, H. B. 1923. The speed of flight in birds. *Bird-Lore* 25:121.

———. 1933. Flight speed of some birds. *Auk* 50: 452–53.

———. 1945. The history of bird banding. *Auk* 256–65.

———. 1946. Names of age groups of young birds. *Bird-Banding* 17(1):32.

———. 1951. Nine-year-old nest of mourning dove. *Bird-Banding* 22(3):126.

———. 1953. John Beck, the second American bird-bander. *Bird-Banding* 24(2):67.

Wood, M. 1938. Food and measurements of goshawks. *Auk* 55(1):123–24.

Wood, R., and Gelston, W. L. 1972. *Preliminary*

report: *The mute swans of Michigan's Grand Traverse Bay region.* State of Michigan. Dept. Nat. Res. Report no. 2683. Lansing.

Woodford, J. 1959. Migrant Kirtland's warbler mist-netted. *Bird-Banding* 30(4):234.

Woods, C. A. 1975. Banding and recapture of wintering warblers in Haiti. *Bird-Banding* 46(4):344–46.

Woods, R. S. 1932. Acquired food habits of some native birds. *Condor* 34:237–40.

———. 1940. Anna's hummingbird. In *Life histories of North American cuckoos, goatsuckers, hummingbirds, and their allies*, ed. A. C. Bent. U.S. Natl. Mus. Bull. no. 176. Washington, D.C.

———. 1948a. California thrasher. In *Life histories of North American nuthatches, wrens, thrashers, and their allies*, ed. A. C. Bent. U.S. Natl. Mus. Bull. no. 195. Washington, D.C.

———. 1948b. Northern cactus wren. In *Life histories of North American nuthatches, wrens, thrashers, and their allies*, ed. A. C. Bent. U.S. Natl. Mus. Bull. no. 195. Washington, D.C.

———. 1949. Black-tailed gnatcatcher. In *Life histories of North American thrushes, kinglets, and their allies*, ed. A. C. Bent. U.S. Natl. Mus. Bull. no. 196. Washington, D.C.

———. 1950. Phainopepla. In *Life histories of North American wagtails, shrikes, vireos, and their allies*, ed. A. C. Bent. U.S. Natl. Mus. Bull. no. 197. Washington, D.C.

———. 1968. House finch. In *Life histories of North American cardinals, grossbeaks, buntings, towhees, finches, sparrows, and allies*, comp. A. C. Bent *et al.*, ed. O. L. Austin, Jr. U.S. Natl. Mus. Bull. no. 237, pt. 1. Washington, D.C.

Woodward, J. C. 1976. Successful parasitism of the gray catbird by a brown-headed cowbird. *Wilson Bull.* 88(3):504–5.

Woolfenden, G. E. 1956. Comparative breeding behavior of *Ammospiza caudacuta* and *A. maritima*. *Univ. Kansas Publ. Mus. Nat. Hist.* 10(2):45–75.

———. 1958. Returns of salt-marsh sparrows *(Ammospiza sp)*. *Bird-Banding* 29(3):183.

———. 1968. Northern seaside sparrow. In *Life histories of North American cardinals, grosbeaks, buntings, towhees, finches, sparrows, and allies*, comp. A. C. Bent *et al.*, ed. O. L. Austin, Jr. U.S. Natl. Mus. Bull. no. 237, pt. 2. Washington, D.C.

———. 1973a. Florida region. *Amer. Birds* 27(3):606.

———. 1973b. Nesting and survival in a population of Florida scrub jays. *Living Bird*, 12th annual, pp. 25–49.

———. 1975. Florida scrub jay helpers at the nest. *Auk* 92(1):1–15.

Woolfenden, G. E., and Fitzpatrick, J. W. 1978. The inheritance of territory in group-breeding of birds. *BioScience* 28(2):104–8.

Woolfenden, G. E., and Meyerriecks, A. J. 1963. Caspian tern breeds in Florida. *Auk* 80(3):365–66.

Worden, A. N. 1964a. Alimentary system. In *A new dictionary of birds*, ed. A. L. Thomson. New York: McGraw-Hill Book Company.

———. 1964b. Nutrition. In *A new dictionary of birds*, ed. A. L. Thomson. New York: McGraw-Hill Book Company.

Worth, C. B. 1937. A problem and plan relative to the study of bird diseases. *Bird-Banding* 8:109–13.

———. 1942a. Ticks affecting birds' eyesight. *Auk* 59(4):576–77.

———. 1942b. What killed cock robin? *Audubon* 44:41–47.

———. 1956. A pox virus of the slate-colored junco. *Auk* 73(2):230–34.

Worth, C. B.; Hamparian, V.; and Rake, G. 1957. A serological survey of ornithosis in bird banders. *Bird-Banding* 28(2):92–97.

Wright, A. H. 1914. Early records of the wild turkey. *Auk* 31:334–58, 463–73.

Wright, B. S. 1954. *High tide and an east wind: The story of the black duck.* Washington, D.C.: Wildlife Management Inst.

Wright, M. O. 1936. *Birdcraft.* New York: The Macmillan Company.

Wright, P. L., and Wright, M. H. 1944. The reproductive cycle of the male red-winged blackbird. *Condor* 46:46–59.

Wright, R. E. 1973. Observations on the urban feeding habits of the roadrunner *(Geococcyx californianus)*. *Condor* 75:246.

Wynne, O. E. 1969. *Biographical key—names of birds of the world.* Fordingbridge, Hants, England. Published by the author.

Wynne-Edwards, V. C. 1952. Zoology of the Baird expedition (1950). I. The birds observed in central southeast Baffin Island. *Auk* 69(4):353–91.

———. 1962. *Animal dispersion in relation to social behaviour.* London: Oliver & Boyd, Ltd.

———. 1964. Oceanic Birds. In *A new dictionary of birds*, ed. A. L. Thomson. New York: McGraw-Hill Book Company.

Wystrach, V. P. 1974. A note on the naming of the Blackburnian warbler. *Jour. Soc. for Bibliog. Nat. Hist.* 7(1):89–91.

———. 1975. Ashton Blackburne's place in American ornithology. *Auk* 92(3):607–10.

Y

Yadon, V. L. 1970. *Oceanodroma tethys kelsalli*, new to North America. *Auk* 87(3):588.

Yarbrough, C. G. 1970. Summer lipid levels of some subarctic birds. *Auk* 87(1):100–110.

Yates, V. J., and Miller, L. T. 1966. The isolation of avian tuberculosis from a starling. *Bull. Wildlife Disease Assoc.* 2:84–85.

Yeagley, A. L. 1947. A preliminary study of a physical basis of bird navigation. *Jour. Appl. Phys.* 18:1035–63.

Yocum, C. F. 1952. Techniques used to increase nesting of Canada geese. *Jour. Wildlife Management* 16:425–28.

———. 1956. Man-made homes for Canada geese. *Audubon* 58(3):106–9.

Young, H. 1951. Territorial behavior in the eastern robin. *Proc. Linnaean Soc. New York* 62:1–37.

———. 1963. Breeding success of the cowbird. *Wilson Bull.* 75(2):115–22.

Youngworth, W. 1936. The cruising speed of the golden plover. *Wilson Bull.* 48(1):53.

Yunick, R. P. 1970. An examination of certain aging and sexing criteria for the cedar waxwing *(Bombycilla cedrorum)*. *Bird-Banding* 41(4):291–99.

Z

Zahn, W. 1933. Über den Geruchsinn einiger Vögel. *Zeit vergleich Physiol.* 19:785.

Zeuner, F. E. 1963. *History of domesticated animals.* London: Hutchinson & Co. (Publishers), Ltd.

Zeuthen, E. 1942. The ventilation of the respiratory tract in birds. *Kgl. Danske Videnskabernes Selskab, Bibliogiske Meddelelser*, 17:1–51.

Zimmer, J. T. 1951a. Birds and lightning. *Natural History* 60(3):143.

———. 1951b. Singed feathers and cold feet. *Natural History* 60:146.

Zimmerman, D. A. 1973. Range expansion of Anna's hummingbird. *Amer. Birds* 27:827–35.

———. 1978. Eared trogon—immigrant or visitor? *Amer. Birds* 32:135–39.

Zimmerman, D. R. 1973. No longer extinct. *New York Times Magazine*, December 7.

Zimmerman, J. L. 1966. Polygyny in the dickcissel. *Auk* 83:534–46.

———. 1971. The territory and its density dependent effect in *Spiza americana*. *Auk* 88(3):591–612.

Ziswiler, V., and Farner, D. S. 1972. Digestion and the digestive system. In *Avian Biology*, ed. D. S. Farner, J. R. King, and K. C. Parkes. Vol. 2. New York: Academic Press, Inc.

Zumberge, J. H. 1958. *Elements of geology.* New York: John Wiley & Sons, Inc.

Zusi, R. 1962. *Structural adaptations of the head and neck of the black skimmer, Rynchops nigra* L. Publ. Nuttall Ornith. Club no. 3. Cambridge, Mass.

Zwickel, F. C.; Brigham, J. H.; and Buss, I. O. 1966. Autumn weights of blue grouse in north-central Washington, 1954 to 1963. *Condor* 68:488–96.

PHOTOGRAPHIC ACKNOWLEDGMENTS

Some photographers have pictures under agency names as well as under their own. Copyrights for all photographs remain the property of the photographers.

David G. Ainley 841 top middle; 851 center left
Peter Alden 513 top left

Amwest
Charles Summers 199, 433 bottom left

Ardea Photographics, Ltd
J. A. Bailey 573 top right
Hans and Judy Beste 695
J. B. and S. Bottomley 425 bottom left
Geoffrey K. Brown 714 bottom, 715 top right, 719 top
Donald Burgess 1043 top
Kevin Carlson 717 bottom
Graeme Chapman 431 top
Hans D. Dossenbach 372
John S. Dunning 369 top right
M. D. England 436 top, 840 center, 887
Andre Fatras 432 bottom
Kenneth W. Fink 301 bottom, 415 bottom left, 426 center, 528 top, 574 center right, 574 bottom, 658 top, 696 top, 799 bottom right, 800 bottom, 839
Robert L. Fleming 715 bottom
John Gooders 697 bottom
A. Greensmith 840 bottom
Wallace Heaton 710 bottom
Edgar T. Jones 312 bottom, 318 top, 514 center, 985 bottom right
C. R. Knights 706 top
J. P. Lamb 794 center
Abe Lindam 794 top, 794 bottom
P. Morris 427 bottom left
S. Roberts 299 top left
B. L. Sage 310 bottom, 800 top
Robert T. Smith 1035 top right
Bruno Sundin 1032 top
Jack Swedborg 506 top
Valeria Taylor 840 top
A. D. Trounson and M. C. Clampett 793 center
Richard Vaughan 424 center, 795 top right, 797 top right, 841 bottom left, 841 center left, 891 top left
Alan Weaving 909 center left, 909 bottom left
Wardene Weisser vii middle, 309 bottom, 576 bottom, 577 bottom left, 578 bottom, 890, 900, 988

B. T. Ariskowicz 725 top right
John Arvin 653 top left
Ron Austing v middle, 297 center right, 297 bottom right, 578 top, 654–55 top, 656 bottom, 854, 904 bottom, 914 bottom, 989 top right, 997 bottom
David E. Baker 895 top right, 985 center right, 987 top right, 987 bottom left, 987 bottom right, 993 center left
Bob Barrett 121 top, 510 top right, 654 bottom right, 801 top, 852 top left, 916 top
Greg Beaumont 297 top right, 514 top, 533 bottom left, 704 top, 891 center left, 891 bottom left
Tom Blagden, Jr. 204 top, 214 bottom
Tupper Ansel Blake iv middle, 46 center, 574 center left, 662, 793 top right
Donald Bradburn 321 bottom, 432–33
Jim Brandenburg 126 bottom, 299 center left, 509 bottom left, 805 bottom right
Fred Bruemmer 45 top right, 47 top right, 47 center left, 47 center middle, 121 bottom right, 207 top, 207 bottom right, 421 bottom middle
G. Vernon Byrd 45 bottom right, 47 bottom right
S. R. Cannings 530 top, 656 top right, 1039 center left, 1043 bottom right
Robert P. Carr vi right, 131 bottom left, 297 center left, 319 center left, 320 top, 323 top, 578 center, 579 center left, 579 center right, 799 top right, 910–11, 1036 bottom right, 1044 center left, 1045 top
Patricia Caulfield 44 top, 50 top
Paul Chesley 52
Herbert Clarke 298 center, 302 bottom, 304 bottom, 312 center, 314 bottom, 315 bottom right, 318 center, 324 top, 325 top, 367 top left, 423 bottom left, 528 bottom, 532 top, 533 bottom right, 533 center right, 577 bottom right, 714 center, 841 top right, 841 center right, 851 top, 888 center, 893 bottom left, 897 top, 898 bottom, 899 top right, 899 bottom, 908 bottom, 913 bottom, 983, 985 top right, 991 bottom

Bruce Coleman, Inc.
Jen and Des Bartlett 133 bottom left, 206 top, 212 center left, 212 center right, 225 top right, 228 top, 229 bottom, 1037 top left
Tom Brakefield 507 top, 507 bottom right, 649 bottom
Henry Lloyd Bunker IV 648 top
Bob and Clara Calhoun 129 bottom right, 417 top right, 529 bottom left, 529 bottom right, 529 center, 531 bottom right, 702 top, 898 top left, 1037 center left, 1039 right
Brian J. Coates 697 top
Lois and George Cox 127 top right
Thase Daniel 125 bottom left
E. R. Degginger 521 bottom left
Larry R. Ditto 130 bottom left, 889 top, 903 bottom right
John S. Dunning 363 bottom right, 534, 572 center
Harry Engels 208 top
Kenneth W. Fink 127 bottom left, 128 top, 208 bottom, 220 top, 513 bottom right, 892 top, 1036 center right
Martin W. Grosnick, 124 center
John H. Hoffman 989 top left
S. Halvorsen 40 top
Ron Johns 212 bottom
Edgar T. Jones 129 bottom right, 216 top, 892 bottom, 994 center
Gary R. Jones 1035 bottom left
M. P. Kahl 420 bottom, 420 top, 436 center, 517 top right, 521 bottom right, 525 bottom left, 572 bottom, 699 top right, 721 bottom right
Wayne Lankinen 211 top, 304 center, 307 center right, 716 bottom
George D. Lepp 723 top
C. C. Lockwood 525 bottom right
Robert E. Pelham v right, 700 bottom
Leonard Lee Rue III 209 top left
John Shaw 1037 center right
M. F. Soper 42 bottom
Lynn M. Stone 414 bottom
Sullivan and Rogers ii, right, 132–33, 326, 902 bottom
J. D. Taylor 229 top
Joseph Van Wormer 221 top right, 210 top
Gary R. Zahm 202 top

Cornell Laboratory of Ornithology
Betty Darling Cottrille 985 center left, 989 center left, 991 center, 993 top right
John S. Dunning 912 top
Bill Dyer 322 bottom
Samuel A. Grimes 993 bottom left
Michael Hopiak 124 top left, 131 top, 307 bottom left, 313 bottom right, 315 top, 315 bottom left, 321 bottom, 367 bottom, 368–69, 370 bottom, 533 top right, 576 top, 804–05 top, 908 top, 984 top, 986 bottom, 996 bottom, 1033 top right, 1037 bottom left
F. G. Irvin 898 center right
W. A. Raff 531 bottom left
J. Weissinger 912 bottom

Betty Darling Cottrille 314 top, 323 bottom, 364 top, 366, 430 top, 533 top left, 573 top left, 909 top right, 984 bottom, 985 bottom left, 989 bottom left, 990 top, 990 center

Lois and George Cox 120 bottom, 360, 362, 529 top left
Allan D. Cruickshank 311 top, 371 bottom left
Helen Cruickshank 217 top, 310 top, 434 top, 436 bottom, 700 top, 701 top left, 701 top right, 805 bottom left, 806, 888 top, 903 top right, 904 top, 905 center right
Thase Daniel 124 top right, 130 top, 131 bottom right, 205 bottom left, 211 center left, 216 center, 225 top left, 228 bottom, 298 bottom, 303 top, 306 top right, 306 bottom, 365 top right, 411 top, 519 top, 520 bottom, 524 bottom left, 653 top right, 711 top left, 724 bottom, 793 top left, 891 right, 905 top left, 984 center, 993 bottom right, 996 top, 1039 top left, 1041 bottom center, 1041 bottom right
Kent and Donna Dannen v left, 302 top, 580 top, 915 top left
Harry N. Darrow iii left, 297 top left, 299 top right, 301 top, 418 top, 424 top, 427 top, 434–35, 509 center left, 513 center left, 661 top, 703 top left, 703 bottom left, 792 bottom, 793 bottom right, 801 bottom, 906 bottom
E. R. Degginger vii left, 220–21, 438, 570–71, 901 bottom, 918
Jack Dermid 579 top left, 705 top left, 723 bottom; 1038
Adrian J. Dignan 797 bottom right, 987 middle left
Larry R. Ditto 203 bottom right, 409 bottom right, 515 bottom, 567, 651 bottom, 703 bottom right, 704–05 bottom, 709 top, 713 top middle, 725 top middle, 725 bottom, 845 top, 905 bottom left
John S. Dunning 298 top
Harry Engels 203 top, 215 bottom left, 215 bottom right, 227 bottom, 297 bottom left, 407, 412–13, 419 top right, 523 bottom right, 701 bottom, 722 top, 1036 middle left, 1037 top middle
Kenneth W. Fink 843 top left
M. P. L. Fogden 802 bottom
Jeff Foott i right, 45 top left, 45 bottom left, 48 bottom, 49 bottom left, 119, 128 bottom, 224–25, 226, 426 bottom, 430–31, 504, 523 top, 698 top, 699 left, 902 top
P. J. Fournier 653 bottom
D. A. Gill 795 top left
W. D. Griffin 200 bottom, 201 top, 218–19, 224 top, 421 top, 422 bottom, 569 bottom right, 716 top, 844 bottom, 844 top, 1045 bottom left, 1045
Russell C. Hansen 428 top, 581 top right, 850 bottom, 853 top left
David Hatler 308 bottom
Jim Hawkings 219 bottom, 424 bottom
Dale R. Hester 429 top left, 797 bottom left
F. Eugene Hester 205 bottom right
G. James 715 top left, 897 bottom, 985 top left
Joseph R. Jehl, Jr. 41 top left, 53 top left, 313 center right, 802 top, 803 top right, 841 top left, 847 bottom left, 851 center right
Isidor Jeklin ii left, iii middle, 227 top, 300 bottom, 305 top, 362 bottom left, 510 top left, 853 bottom, 1036 top left; 1041 top
Peter J. Kaplan 713 top right
G. C. Kelley 51 top left, 51 top right, 306 top left, 318 bottom, 362–63, 364–65, 369 top middle, 408 bottom left, 408 bottom right, 425 bottom right, 427 bottom right, 570 bottom, 577 center left, 696 bottom, 718–19 bottom, 722 bottom, 792 bottom, 804 bottom, 848 top, 849 top right, 905 bottom right, 906–07, 907 bottom right, 1042 top
Michael Kleinbaum 310 center left, 435 top left, 659 bottom right
Fred L. Knapp 49 bottom right, 307 bottom right, 524–25 top, 575 top, 576 center, 917 bottom, 995 bottom left, 1034, 1037 center middle
Stephen J. Krasemann/D R K Photo 45 center left, 49 top, 130 bottom right, 205 top, 307 top left, 307 top right, 311 bottom left, 416 center, 503, 717 center left, 720 bottom, 842–43, 903 top left, 1036 bottom left
Tom and Pat Leeson 201 bottom, 410 bottom, 411 bottom left

Les Line 50–51

Tom D. Mangelsen 122 top, 122–23, 122 bottom, 123 bottom, 209 top right, 210 center, 212 top, 213 center, 214 top, 512 top, 574 top, 707 bottom, 716 center left

Joe McDonald 134, 654 bottom left, 797 center right

Leslie McKim 577 top right, 911 bottom right, 995 bottom right

Wyman P. Meinzer, Jr. 132 bottom, 517 top left

Anthony Mercieca 708 bottom right

Wendell Metzen 526, 569 bottom left, 573 bottom, 698 bottom, 849 bottom right

Peter Mickelson 206 center, 222 top

S. J. Miller 416 top

C. A. Morgan 133 bottom right, 216 bottom, 373 center, 417 top left, 421 bottom right, 437 bottom, 532 bottom, 651 top middle, 710 top, 899 top left

Alan G. Nelson 214 center left, 302 center, 311 center left, 412 top, 415 bottom right, 429 top right, 907 bottom left

Peter P. Ott 517 bottom

James F. Parnell 319 bottom left, 724 top

Feodor Pitcairn 374

Photo Researchers Inc./National Audubon Society Collection

Phillip Boyer 369 top left

Tom Branch 129 top

Robert Bright 650

John Bova 659 top right

W. V. Critch 987 center right

Allan D. Cruickshank 361 top right, 702 bottom

Kent and Donna Dannen 124 bottom, 127 bottom right

Townsend P. Dickinson 359

Harry Engels 413 top left

Robert J. Erwin 1035 top left

Kenneth W. Fink 214 center right

George Galicz 296 top

Patrick Grace 211 bottom, 423 bottom right

Gilbert Grant 202 center, 579 bottom right

B. Brower Hall 531 top left

J. A. Hancock 418–19

Russell C. Hansen 308 top

Robert W. Hernandez 40–41, 42, 425 top

David O. Hill 45 center right

John O. Hallery 522

George Holton 46 top

Jerry Hout 299 center right

Paul and Lois Johnsgard 200 center

M. P. Kahl 373 top, 516, 657 top, 660 top, 713 top left

Steven C. Kaufman 419 top left

George Keliman iv right

G. C. Kelley 299 bottom, 368 top

Karl W. Kenyon 41 top right, 43 top

Russ Kinne i left, 39, 126 top, 207 bottom right, 712 bottom

L. and D. Klein 579 top right

Stephen J. Krasemann iii right, 572 top, 581 top left, 709 bottom

Gary Ladd 659 left

Calvin Larsen vi middle, 213 bottom, 845 bottom, 894–95 bottom

George Laycock 43 bottom left

Robert Lee 531 top right

Eric Lindgren 42 center

Alexander Lowry 127 top left

Thomas W. Martin 909 bottom right, 992 top, 992 bottom, 997 center, 1033 top left

Karl and Steve Maslowski 310 center right, 658 bottom, 717 center right

Steve Maslowski 317 top left

Tom McHugh 512 bottom, 657 bottom

Anthony Mercieca 215 top right, 312 top, 363 bottom left, 724 center, 791, 909 top left, 991 top

Wendell Metzen 568–69

Charles Ott vi left, 217 bottom, 371 bottom right, 577 top left, 1044 top

O. S. Pettingill, Jr. 361 bottom right, 423 top

Noble Proctor 53 bottom, 121 bottom left

William Ray 1042 bottom

Y. J. Rey-Miller 125 bottom right

J. H. Robinson 44 bottom, 295

Len Rue, Jr. 708 top, 852 bottom right

Leonard Lee Rue III 53 top right, 202 bottom, 421 bottom left

Robert M. Schmitt 720–21

Gregory K. Scott 125, top

Phillipa Scott 206 bottom, 211 center right, 230

Stephen Spotte 795 bottom right

Sandy Sprunt 713 bottom, 901 top

Alvin E. Staffan 989 bottom right

Dan Sudia 994 top

Bill Curtis Unger i middle, 54

R. Van Nostrand 513 top right

Helen Williams 577 center right, 712 bottom

Bill Wilson 47 top left, 215 top left, 215 center, 319 top right, 841 bottom right, 795 center right

Jim Zipp 655 bottom right

C. Gable Ray 581 bottom, 705 top right, 852 center

Rielle Enterprises

Richard Wright 209 bottom, 911 bottom left

Richard D. Robinson 296 bottom, 411 bottom right, 518, 652 top, 652 bottom, 846–47

Manuel Rodriguez 510–11

Allen Rokach 127 center left

D. G. Roseneau 47 center right

Len Rue, Jr. 708 bottom left, 712 top

Leonard Lee Rue III 48–49, 204 bottom, 300 top, 304 top, 408–09, 417 bottom, 511 top, 531 center left, 582, 649 top, 706 bottom, 707 top, 717 top right, 898 center left, 910 bottom

B. L. Sage 437 top

C. W. Schwartz 414–15

Gregory K. Scott iv right

Perry D. Shankle 365 top left, 514 bottom, 651 top right

John Shaw 313 left, 579 bottom left, 716 center right, 896 bottom, 913 top, 1037 top right

E. Sian 798 top, 853 top right, 1040

Caulion Singletary 435 top right, 647

Perry D. Slocum 317 top right, 842 top, 852 bottom left

Arnold Small 305 bottom, 309 top right, 311 top right, 319 center, 324 center, 367 top right, 509 top right, 529 top right, 575 bottom, 580 bottom, 651 top left, 714 top, 792 center, 797 left, 797 center left, 803 center left, 852 top right, 893 bottom right, 903 bottom left, 915 top right, 986 middle, 990 bottom, 994 bottom, 1036 top right, 1037 bottom middle, 1037 bottom right, 1041 bottom left

Tom Stack & Associates

Tom Brakefield, 506 bottom, 513 center right

George H. Harrison 889 bottom

Keith H. Muraham 725 top left

A. Nelson 311 bottom right, 426 top, 702 center

G. Y. Ovan 711 top right

Dave Spier 905 center left

Charles Summers 324 bottom, 416 bottom, 417 top center

Peter Thomas 905 top right

Bruce M. Wellman 307 center left

Alvin E. Staffan 316–17, 320 bottom, 322 top, 371 top, 433 bottom left, 656 top left, 893 top, 896 top, 915 bottom, 989 center right, 998, 1032–33, 1035 bottom right, 1043 bottom left

Ian C. Tait 703 center left, 799 bottom left, 803 center right, 843 top right, 1044 center right, 1044 bottom, 1046

Phillip S. Taylor 410 top, 413 top right, 795 bottom left

Frank Todd 203 bottom left, 208 center, 210 bottom, 218 bottom, 221 top left, 571 bottom, 847 bottom right, 848 bottom, 850 top, 951 bottom, 916 bottom, 917 top

John Trott 303 Bottom, 325 bottom, 721 bottom left, 888 bottom, 894 top

Valan Naturefotos

Harold V. Green 798 bottom

Wayne Lankinen 422 center left, 422 center right, 703 top right, 793 bottom left, 799 center left, 803 bottom, 846 bottom

Brian Milne 509 bottom right

Mark Tomalty 422 top

Verda International, Inc.

M. P. Kahl 520–21 top, 527 top, 527 bottom, 568 bottom, 849 left

R. W. Schreiber 699 bottom right

Larry West 523 bottom left, 986 top, 993 top left

Burdette White 530 bottom

Jack Wilburn 313 top right, 717 top left, 1039 bottom left

Steven C. Wilson/ENTHEOS 428–29, 519 bottom, 660–61, 1031

Gus Wolfe 505 top, 505 bottom, 508

Richard A. Wood 222–23, 703 center right, 796, 799 top left, 803 top left, 895 top left

Woodfin Camp and Associates

Hope Alexander 46, 47 bottom left, 120 top

Richard Wright 223 top

Gary R. Zahm 123 top, 200 top, 213 top, 409 bottom left, 726

Fred Zeillemaker 43 bottom right

Dale and Marion Zimmerman 316 top, 319 bottom right, 361 left, 370 top, 373 bottom, 507 bottom left, 509 top left, 513 bottom left, 515 top, 655 bottom left, 718 top, 995 top, 997 top

Leonard Zorn 309 top left, 362 bottom right

ILLUSTRATION ACKNOWLEDGMENTS

Grateful acknowledgment is made to the following for permission to reprint from previously published material:

Harper & Row Publishers, Inc.: Three charts from *Songbirds in Your Garden* by John Terres, 1968, revised 1977. Reprinted by permission of Hawthorne Books/Harper & Row Publishers, Inc.

The National Audubon Society: "The Master List of Bird Books for North American Readers" from the October 1976 issue of *American Birds* (Vol. 30, No. 5). Copyright © 1978, The National Audubon Society. Reprinted by permission.

Acknowledgment is also made to the following for permission to use material as reference in the preparation of illustrations for this work:

Illustration on page 16 is inspired by a drawing in *Bird*, Houghton Mifflin Co., written, illustrated, and copyrighted by Lois and Louis Darling, 1962.

Illustrations on pages 21, 66 (belted kingfisher), 100 (rock ptarmigan), and 171 are derived from plates from *The Audubon Society Field Guide to North American Birds, Western Region*, by M. D. F. Udvardy, published by Alfred A. Knopf, Inc.

Illustration on page 35 is derived from *A Field Guide to Insects* by Donald Borror and Richard E. White. Published by Houghton Mifflin Company. Copyright © 1970 by Donald J. Borror and Richard E. White. Used by permission of the publisher.

Illustration on page 66 (ruby-throated hummingbird) is derived from a photograph by Ron Austing. Used by permission.

Illustration on page 66 (long-billed curlew) is derived from a photograph. Copyright © John Markham/Bruce Coleman, Inc.

Illustration on page 66 (roseate spoonbill) is derived from a photograph. Copyright © Joseph Van Wormer/Bruce Coleman, Inc.

Illustration on page 67 is derived from a photograph by Les Line, copyright © 1976. Published in *Audubon*, November 1976.

Illustrations on page 100 (rooster) and page 636 (fulmar) derived from J. Hanzák, *Pictoral Encyclopedia of Birds*, Artia, pages 142, 407.

Illustrations on pages 111, 155, 248, 468, 491, 873–74, 929, and 1012 (gull and swift wings) are derived from pages 4, 6, 78, 123, 145, 158, and 193 of *Seminars in Ornithology* produced by the Laboratory of Ornithology, Cornell University, in collaboration with Andrew J. Berger, Richard Brewer, William W. Cochran, Millicent S. Ficken, Herbert Krause, Douglas A. Lancaster, Kenneth C. Parkes, Olin Sewall Pettingill, Jr., D.

Jean Tate, and James Tate, Jr., and edited by Olin Sewall Pettingill, Jr. Copyright © 1972 by Cornell Laboratory of Ornithology.

Illustration on page 118 (California quail) is derived from *Game Birds of North America* by Leonard N. Hue. Used by permission of Harper & Row, Publishers, Inc.

Illustration on page 135 is derived from an illustration from *Biology and Comparative Physiology of Birds*, Vol. 1, by A. J. Marshall. Copyright © 1960 by Academic Press.

Illustrations on pages 177, 743, and 815 are derived from illustrations from *Audubon Water Bird Guide* by Richard H. Pough, illustrated by Donald E. Eckelberry. Copyright 1951 by Doubleday & Company, Inc. Used by permission of the publisher.

Illustrations on pages 178 and 185 are derived from illustrations by Arthur Singer from *Birds of the World*. Copyright © 1961 by Western Publishing Company. Used by permission.

Illustration on page 241 is derived from a photograph. Copyright © Kenneth W. Fink/Bruce Coleman, Inc.

Illustration on page 286 (didactyl foot) is derived from *Watching Birds* by Roger F. Pasquier, illustrated by Margaret LaFarge. Published by Houghton Mifflin Company. Copyright © 1977 by Roger F. Pasquier. Used by permission of the publisher.

Illustration on page 330 is derived from *Birds of the West Indies* by James Bond. Used by permission of Collins Publishers.

Illustrations on pages 343 and 548 are derived from *A Field Guide to Mexican Birds* by Roger Tory Peterson and Edward L. Chalif. Published by Houghton Mifflin Company. Copyright © 1973 by Roger Tory Peterson and Edward L. Chalif. Used by permission of the publisher.

Illustration on page 444 is derived from a photograph courtesy of the American Museum of Natural History.

Illustration on page 584 is derived from *The Herring Gull's World* by Niko Tinbergen. Used by permission of Collins Publishers.

Illustration on page 589 is derived from *The Hunters*. Copyright © Marshall Editions Limited 1978.

Illustration on page 617 is derived from an illustration in *The Life of Birds* by Joel Carl Welty. Copyright © 1975 by W. B. Saunders Company. Used by permission of Holt, Rinehart and Winston.

Illustration on page 623 of (green-winged teal) derived from *A Field Guide to Nests, Eggs and Nestlings of North American Birds* by Colin Harrison. Used by permission of Collins Publishers.

Illustration on page 678 derived from *Parrots of the World* by Joseph Forshaw, illustrated by William T. Cooper. Copyright © 1973 by Joseph M. Forshaw. Used by permission of Doubleday & Company, Inc.

Illustrations on pages 740 (dotterel), 784, 865, 870, 951 (gray vireo), and 975 are derived from illustrations by Arthur Singer from *Birds of North America*. Copyright © 1966 by Western Publishing Company, Inc. Used by permission.

Copyrights for all artwork remain the property of the artists:

Sy Barlowe 4, 15 top, 19, 21, 33, 37, 38, 56, 58, 59, 61, 64, 67, 96, 97, 99, 101, 103, 106, 110, 111, 113, 160, 167, 232, 270, 277, 378, 397 top, 402, 443, 489, 492 top and middle, 555, 556, 558, 584, 615, 624, 639, 645, 673 bottom, 734 top, 750, 808, 811, 833, 861.

Frances Anne Curtis 15 middle, 16, 73 top, 83 top, 85 top, 599, 677 bottom, 824, 825.

John Hamberger 8, 10, 13, 17, 23, 26, 36, 62 bottom, 65, 69, 73 bottom, 78, 105, 114, 115 top, 117, 136, 142, 143, 145, 149, 155, 156, 169, 235, 269, 272, 284 top, 288, 289, 346, 349, 353, 355 left, 381, 397 bottom, 403, 445, 449 top and bottom, 456, 464, 468, 475, 476, 482, 483, 494, 540, 551, 552, 561, 564, 565, 585, 591, 592, 594, 611, 617, 622, 623, 628, 629, 633, 638, 644, 663, 665 top and middle, 673 top, 677 top, 682, 685, 686, 687, 691, 729, 736, 740 top, 753 top, 757, 768, 784, 814 top, 820, 822, 823, 826, 828, 829, 838, 857, 858, 863, 867, 868 top and bottom, 873, 875, 876, 884, 924, 929, 934, 935 top, 936, 946, 950, 952, 956, 959, 962, 982, 1003, 1004, 1007, 1008, 1012, 1013, 1027, 1048, 1051.

George V. Kelvin 14, 15 bottom, 87, 162 bottom, 607, 608, 616 bottom.

Enid Kotschnig 6, 35, 60, 66, 85 bottom, 100 bottom, 102, 108, 118, 157 bottom, 171, 265 left, 268, 280, 336, 395, 404, 444, 536, 538 bottom, 589, 597, 616 top, 621, 636, 665 bottom, 810, 919.

Margaret LaFarge ii middle, 27, 62 top, 76, 79, 81, 91, 94, 98, 115 bottom, 135, 140, 152, 154, 157 top, 170, 245, 246, 254, 255, 259, 262, 266, 267, 271, 281, 282, 284 bottom, 285, 286, 287, 355 right, 357, 375, 376, 384, 442, 449 middle, 453 top, 457 top, 474, 491, 542, 586, 620, 625, 626, 632, 637, 669, 737, 752, 753 bottom, 763, 789, 814 bottom, 827, 868 center, 869, 878, 933, 948, 955, 960, 1002, 1014.

Paul Singer 12, 14, 18, 20, 24, 29, 30, 31, 83 bottom, 88, 90, 93, 100 top, 104, 109, 138, 147, 148, 153, 159, 162 top, 164, 174, 176, 177, 178, 180, 185, 186, 190, 191, 193, 198, 236, 239, 241, 248, 265 right, 276, 294, 329, 330, 339, 342, 343, 347, 380, 382, 390, 392, 398, 399, 405, 439, 441, 453 bottom, 455, 457 bottom, 463, 465, 479, 492 bottom, 501, 502, 538 top, 545, 548, 549, 554, 603, 604, 613, 634, 678, 680, 681, 689, 728, 734 middle and bottom, 738, 740 bottom, 742, 746, 751, 765, 769, 771, 773, 777, 779, 783, 788, 815, 855, 859, 861 bottom, 865, 870, 883, 920, 925, 927, 929, 931, 934, 935 bottom, 943, 951, 964, 968, 971, 973, 975, 999, 1001, 1017, 1022, 1028.